2017
ALMANAC

115TH CONGRESS
1ST SESSION

VOLUME LXXIII

CQ Roll Call
1625 Eye Street, NW
Washington, D.C. 20006

MIX
Paper from responsible sources
FSC® C008955
www.fsc.org

SUMMARY TABLE OF CONTENTS

APPENDICES

TABLE OF CONTENTS

CHAPTER 1 — 2017 OVERVIEW

CHAPTER 2 — APPROPRIATIONS

CHAPTER 3 — BANKING & FINANCIAL SERVICES

CHAPTER 4 — BUDGET

CHAPTER 5 — CONGRESSIONAL AFFAIRS & POLITICS

CHAPTER 6 — DEFENSE, INTELLIGENCE & VETERANS

CHAPTER 7 — ECONOMIC AFFAIRS

CHAPTER 8 — ENERGY & ENVIRONMENT

CHAPTER 9 — EXECUTIVE BRANCH

CHAPTER 10 — FOREIGN POLICY & TRADE

CHAPTER 11 — HEALTH & EDUCATION

CHAPTER 12 — HOMELAND SECURITY & IMMIGRATION

CHAPTER 13 — LEGAL AFFAIRS

CHAPTER 14 — REGULATORY POLICY

CHAPTER 15 — SCIENCE & TECHNOLOGY

CHAPTER 16 — TAXES

CHAPTER 17 — TRANSPORTATION & INFRASTRUCTURE

APPENDICES

Chapter 1

2017 OVERVIEW

Republicans Overhaul Taxes, Confirm Gorsuch, but Falter at Health Care Push

For Republicans controlling Congress, the start of the Trump presidency created some opportunities and constant challenges. Following their eight years of struggles with President Barack Obama, a Democrat, they welcomed the prospect of a presidential signature on legislation that they had been advocating in some cases for many years.

GOP leaders, in particular, quickly became mindful that they needed to avoid antagonizing the sometimes mercurial President Donald Trump, lest he overturn their strategies or the details. Given the few formal proposals that Trump sent to Congress, it could be challenging or risky for them to decipher and approve his intentions.

Probably their most dramatic failure came in July, when Majority Leader Mitch McConnell of Kentucky crafted with Senate Republicans a bare-bones fallback plan aimed at fulfilling their promise to repeal and replace the 2010 health care law known as the Affordable Care Act.

Instead, Sen. John McCain, who had been diagnosed with brain cancer and was the swing vote, walked to the front of the Senate chamber and flashed his thumb down. Later, the Arizona Republican said he opposed the measure partly because of how it was built: without hearings, consultation with Democrats or consideration of recommendations by governors.

"This is clearly a disappointing moment," McConnell responded, in obvious understatement, as he pulled the bill from the floor.

Despite their legislative dominance and extensive campaign promises, Trump and congressional Republicans scored few accomplishments during their first year. Those successes typically had little, if any, Democratic support. As the majority party, they rarely showed an imperative to reach beyond their own ranks. Broad policy changes that might have attracted bipartisan support, such as repair of the nation's infrastructure, showed no signs of life.

In the Senate, Republicans took advantage of long-standing parliamentary tools to circumvent the 60-vote requirement to shut down filibusters, especially on budget and tax proposals. Plus, they exploited some new procedural ploys that expedited the repeal of Obama-era regulations and imposed new restraints on debate of presidential nominations.

The Democratic-controlled Senate in 2013 had relaxed the chamber's hallowed traditions of extended debate to expedite the approval of President Barack Obama's nominees, to the dismay of Republicans. As McConnell warned at that time, those changes became a source of great regret and second-guessing among Democrats in 2017. From both parties, the parliamentary changes exemplified the continuing breakdown of the deliberative process in Congress.

Separate from its challenges of dealing with Trump and with legislation, Congress in 2017 confronted two unusual internal crises.

At a ballpark in suburban Washington, members of the Republican baseball team became the target of a shooting as they practiced for a charity game that annually is a rare show of bipartisanship. House Majority Whip Steve Scalise, R-La, was severely wounded. And multiple members in both parties were forced to address allegations of sexual harassment or other improper personal behavior. Several lawmakers were forced to quit or abandon plans for reelection.

FACING PRESIDENTIAL TURBULENCE

With their relatively narrow majorities and often diverse views in the Senate and House, congressional Republicans faced a persistent challenge. In his first year as president, Trump positioned himself at the center of attention on Capitol Hill. That's not unusual for new presidents. But Trump's background as a real-estate entrepreneur and his often-disruptive leadership style typically were an awkward fit.

Trump had spent little time in Washington. He had never held public office and had minimal experience or skill in federal policy issues prior to moving into the White House.

As president, Trump demonstrated scant interest in the minutiae of legislation or the inner workings of Congress — even on topics, such as taxes or immigration, which he set as his personal priorities. In his frequent partisan rallies across the nation, Trump focused more on the broad framework of his agenda rather than on guidance to Congress.

Outside of the White House, Trump talked up his successes in Congress, including the regulatory rollbacks and judicial confirmations, plus the sweeping tax cuts enacted in December that were the centerpiece of his legislative accomplishments. He voiced unhappiness over his setbacks — not least, his promised repeal of the 2010 health care law and his frequent campaign pledges to build a wall along the U.S.-Mexico border.

Trump rarely engaged in the legislative details nor was he explicit on his specific aspirations. Instead, he reinforced the chaotic approach that he exhibited during his victory in the 2016 presidential election.

Even with Trump's status as an unconventional newcomer, lawmakers — especially Republicans — looked to him to assert the conventional tasks as chief executive. With their control of Congress, that included setting the policy agenda and the tone for the majority party.

In seeking to collaborate with the often tumultuous White House and defer to the president's spotlight on the center stage, lawmakers discovered that it became easier said than done to respond. The constant turnover of senior aides to Trump, for example, made it difficult for congressional Republicans to find reliable contacts and decision-makers at the White House.

Amid that personnel churn, the customary period for a new president's greatest opportunities instead was filled with policy turmoil and political turbulence. Trump's honeymoon seemed to last less than 24 hours, as his aides were forced to defend their dubious claim that his inauguration had attracted record crowds.

Trump also invited foreign policy conflicts, as he did with his June 1 announcement that the United States would withdraw from the Paris climate agreement. That move was greeted with outcry from Democrats and environmentalists, some of whom had previously complained about the toothless nature of the accord.

Elsewhere overseas, the president in August threatened "fire and fury" after a news report cited a U.S. intelligence assessment that

North Korea had produced a miniaturized nuclear warhead that could be carried by missiles, expanding the range of the country's nuclear weapons arsenal.

Another source of the president's repeated rhetorical outbursts raised the specter of a constitutional showdown. On May 17, Deputy Attorney General Rod Rosenstein appointed Special Counsel Robert S. Mueller III to investigate alleged collusion between Trump's campaign and Russian officials.

The investigation would yield indictments and convictions – although none related to collusion with Russians – and it would still be going strong into 2018.

With these and other obstacles, it was no surprise that Trump made little progress on the legislative battlefield. While the inability to pass health care legislation was largely the result of a fractured Republican caucus on Capitol Hill, responsibility for other priorities that fell by the wayside lay squarely in the executive branch.

On Sept. 5, Attorney General Jeff Sessions announced the administration was ending the Deferred Action for Childhood Arrivals immigration program, known as DACA, created by President Barack Obama. Like the proposed ban on refugees and travelers from Muslim-majority countries, this campaign promise faced multiple legal hurdles and generated little help from Capitol Hill.

Trump gave lawmakers six months to find a solution for the so-called Dreamers protected from deportation under DACA, but efforts to have Congress deal with the issue went nowhere.

That was pretty much the fate of the president's plans to cut spending, as well.

Mick Mulvaney, director of the Office of Management and Budget, submitted a "skinny budget" in March that was a bare outline for spending, then presented a detailed budget proposal in May that Congress promptly ignored. By year's end, the government had gone through two shutdown scares and was still operating on a continuing resolution.

A budget resolution, agreed to in October, at least cleared the way for the administration's biggest win of 2017, the overhaul of the tax system. Rewriting the tax code was a GOP congressional priority from the start, although it took time to get going as lawmakers attempted to repeal Obamacare.

DEEPENING DYSFUNCTION

The congressional handling of major legislation – including taxes and health care – reinforced the legislative dysfunction that had grown pervasive for both parties in recent years. Major bills were handled with few committee hearings or open sessions for legislative drafting, and virtually no opportunity for amendments or votes in the House and Senate chambers.

The continued weakening of the committee process and other parliamentary deliberations was accompanied by the growing control of McConnell in the Senate and House Speaker Paul D. Ryan, R-Wis.

Democrats said it was ludicrous, for example, that Senate Republicans had not unveiled the legislative text of their health care alternative until hours before an extended series of votes was set to begin. "This process is an embarrassment. This is nuclear-grade bonkers," said Sen. Chris Murphy, D-Conn.

On the tax bill, which Congress took up and approved during the final two months of the year, the markups in the tax-writing House Ways and Means and Senate Finance committees were largely perfunctory sessions. Lawmakers rubber-stamped proposals that had

been assembled under the close supervision of party leaders. Republicans on each panel rebuffed by party-line votes all the amendments offered by Democrats.

In the House, the tax bill was considered under a closed rule with no amendments permitted, and it was not otherwise modified from the version as reported by Ways and Means. In the Senate, numerous Republicans agreed to vote for the bill with the promise of a McConnell package of modifications that addressed their specific concerns.

Not a single Democrat in the House or Senate voted for passage of the tax bill. The disgruntled Republicans voting against the bill included 13 House members who mostly had concerns about how the measure would impact their district and Sen. Bob Corker of Tennessee, who has already announced his retirement. Later, Corker reversed his position and voted for the final House-Senate deal.

Corker had to fend off accusations that his vote had been "bought off" by the inclusion of pass-through provisions that benefit wealthy real estate investors such as Trump and himself. The tax writers defended Corker, noting that the provisions had earlier been part of the House bill and were simply added as part of routine conference-committee negotiations.

Along with the confirmation in April of Neil Gorsuch to the Supreme Court, the passage of the tax bill left most Republicans satisfied that they — and Trump — had delivered results to their party supporters. At the end of 2017, those successes were sufficient to override concerns about the Trump-centered tumult.

A VERY DIFFERENT PRESIDENT

The November 2016 election of Donald Trump was a shock to the usual routines of politics and legislation of Capitol Hill. In his first year, the new president loomed large over the congressional agenda in ways that went beyond the customary change at the White House and the takeover by a new team.

Trump's unpredictable and impulsive style, combined with the natural growing pains of a new administration, caused more than the usual uncertainties in Congress. That resulted in a less robust legislative agenda, especially given the unified partisan control of the legislative and executive branches.

In his inaugural address, Trump echoed a familiar theme from his campaign: "We assembled here today are issuing a new decree to be heard in every city, and in every foreign capital and in every hall of power," he said. "From this day forward, a new vision will govern our land, from this day forward, it's going to be only America first! America first!"

Making the switch from rhetoric to governing was not always a straight or obvious course. During Trump's initial months as president, he moved from hard-liner-in-chief to vacillator-in-chief, a not unsurprising development given his vague, detail-free and often contradictory promises during the campaign.

His limited focus on policy details gave Congress added flexibility in crafting legislation, so long as lawmakers kept from raising presidential alarms or tweets. Meetings between Trump and lawmakers often abandoned the customary script and might require several days of cleanup to clarify or fix the initial reports.

Despite the inconsistent rhetoric and presidential pivots, a series of policy pronouncements made clear that what one analyst termed the "fundamental contradiction of being both a fire-breathing absolutist and a non-ideological dealmaker" was going to result in, more or less,

a standard array of conservative scenarios. But they weren't always successful.

HEALTH INSURANCE FIX

The 2010 health care law survived several repeal attempts and remained the law of the land. Republicans could not fulfill a promise to "repeal and replace" that they had made since the law was enacted. The fact that the goal eluded a Republican-led Congress working with a president of their party set the tone for much of 2017.

Despite their promises, Republicans never developed replacement legislation. They agreed on general principles but never put forth legislative text for examination. With Americans fearful they might lose their health care coverage, congressional leaders and Trump grew cautious in developing their replacement plan.

When House Republicans took up the far-reaching bill (HR 1628), the chamber endured some bumps in the road. House GOP leaders on March 24 abruptly canceled a scheduled vote in the face of rebellion from both their most conservative and more moderate Republicans.

During the next few weeks, the leaders modified the bill to accelerate the repeal and further limit the expansion of Medicaid. Conservatives continued to object that the changes were insufficient and that more steps were needed to reduce costs. On May 4, the bill passed on a 217-214 vote, following additional revisions that required a delicate balance to appeal to multiple GOP factions.

The Senate could not to come up with a companion measure. Even an attempt by the Senate to cancel the 2010 law with a "skinny" eight-page, scaled-back alternative, while delaying a replacement, came to a theatrical end in the early morning hours of July 28 when McCain voted "no."

In September, Senate Republicans fell short in a final attempt to salvage their initiative with more of a halfway measure that preserved key parts of the 2010 law. Conservatives objected, as Sen. Rand Paul, R-Ky., called the proposal "Obamacare lite." The last-ditch effort was abandoned, without votes.

CUTTING TAXES

The tax bill that passed at the end of the year was driven by GOP leaders and Rep. Kevin Brady of Texas and Sen. Orrin G. Hatch of Utah, the respective chairmen of the House and Senate tax-writing committees. Even though the measure was filled with cuts for individual and businesses, plus long-sought changes that were designed as taxpayer-friendly, making the choices getting to "yes" was not easy for Republicans and their longtime allies in key constituencies such as the real estate industry. The details were massive.

Trump celebrated the new law as "the biggest tax cut in the history of our nation." He and Republicans argued that it would significantly boost economic growth and create jobs, ensuring that U.S. corporations remain competitive internationally and that businesses and jobs stay in the United States.

Democrats derided the result as a "tax scam," saying it represented a massive giveaway to corporations and the wealthy, including the president, while providing relatively little for middle-class families and adding more than a trillion dollars to budget deficits over the next decade. Sen. Bernie Sanders, I-Vt., called it "a moral and economic obscenity."

The legislative effort was highly partisan. Republicans developed much of the legislation behind closed doors, and no House or Senate Democrats voted for the measure. It was considered under the budget reconciliation process, which prevented a filibuster in the Senate and allowed the tax bill to pass by simple majority vote.

The tax overhaul was a GOP congressional priority from the start of 2017, although it took months to get started while lawmakers spent much of the summer on health care. The final measure made the most significant changes to the tax code in decades.

The legislation cut rates across the board, nearly doubled the standard deduction and the child tax credit, and capped deductions for state income taxes. The tax bill also achieved one result that multiple versions of the attempted Obamacare repeal could not: It eliminated the penalty for not having health insurance coverage, beginning in 2019.

HIGH COURT CONFIRMATION

The Senate confirmed Judge Neil Gorsuch in April to the Supreme Court, filling a seat that had been vacant since the death of Antonin Scalia in February 2016. The 54-45 vote, with three Democrats joining 51 Republicans in voting to confirm, culminated a partisan showdown that began when Obama nominated Merrick Garland in 2016. Republicans benefited from the election-campaign dynamics.

If Garland had been confirmed, the ideological balance of the court would have turned leftward. Senate Republicans balked, refusing to hold a Judiciary Committee hearing on the nomination. It was a political gamble that paid off when Trump was elected president and Republicans narrowly retained the Senate, following a campaign in which Garland was rarely mentioned.

In confirming Trump's first pick to the high court, Republicans further weakened the Senate's cloture rules and eliminated the filibuster for Supreme Court nominees.

Democrats spent much of the two months following Gorsuch's nomination trying to decide whether they should take the unprecedented step to filibuster a Supreme Court nominee. They ultimately forced Republicans to deploy what's known as the nuclear option.

Democrats in 2013 had already nixed unlimited debate of lower court nominees, plus executive branch officials, meaning only a simple majority vote is needed for confirmation. They knew a filibuster of Gorsuch to replace a fellow conservative on the court might blow up in their faces should Republicans end the filibuster in response, clearing a path for a future nominee who might be replacing one of the court's reliably liberal justices. Despite the risk, Democratic Leader Charles E. Schumer of New York got on board with the strategy and urged others to join him.

McConnell, who said that ending the judicial filibuster would likely be one of the "most consequential decisions I've ever been involved in," vowed that the Senate would preserve the filibuster option for legislation.

REGULATORY ROLLBACK

The Republican majorities in the House and Senate used Trump's arrival at the White House for an unprecedented deployment of the Congressional Review Act to nullify regulations. The CRA allows lawmakers to reverse regulatory actions with simple majorities and guaranteed votes, as long as they do it within 60 legislative days of submission of the rule to Congress and the president signs the legislation.

Republicans saw the Clinton-era law (PL 104-121) as a tool to line up the legislative agenda with the new president's executive plans. Both chambers passed 15 resolutions of disapproval in 2017 and Trump signed all of them to rescind actions taken during the Obama admin-

istration. Many of the resolutions passed on virtually party-line votes, though several Senate Democrats supported a few of the measures.

The resolutions nullified a variety of regulatory actions including environmental, labor, education, and firearms rules. In one case, objections by three Senate Republicans scuttled an effort to repeal an Interior Department rule limiting methane venting and flaring from oil and gas operations on federal lands.

Congress had used the CRA to block a regulation only once before, in 2001. Obama had vetoed five efforts to do so by the Republican Congress.

On a more conventional legislative route, the House moved to severely weaken a centerpiece regulatory policy of the Obama administration – the 2010 Wall Street regulation law known as Dodd-Frank (PL 111-203), which was written in the aftermath of the 2008 financial crisis.

The House, on a nearly party-line vote, passed on June 8 the administration-supported bill (HR 10). The sweeping measure changed how the federal government regulates banks and Wall Street and rescinded the Labor Department's fiduciary rule, a requirement that broker-dealers put their clients' interest ahead of their own in giving retirement advice.

Senators on the Banking, Housing and Urban Affairs Committee spent much of the year seeking a bipartisan alternative.

SPENDING GRIDLOCK

On fiscal policy in 2017, Congress was badly behind in its budget process and beset by deeper policy differences than usual. This fiscal impasse was all the more extraordinary since one party controlled both Congress and the White House.

The list of hang-ups and grievances was long. For starters, Trump had submitted his budget unusually late, even by the dilatory standards of an administration's first year. Detailed budget documents were not sent to Capitol Hill until May 23, nearly four months beyond the statutory deadline of the "first Monday in February" outlined in the Congressional Budget Act of 1974.

The House and Senate Appropriations committees normally rely on detailed guidance from federal agencies and the Office of Management and Budget as their baseline for spending decisions.

Congressional leaders also were to blame, having stalled final decisions on fiscal 2017 appropriations bills after the 2016 elections changed the game to the GOP's advantage. It was the first week of May when the House and Senate finally finished an omnibus spending bill (HR 244) for a fiscal year that was by that time more than half completed.

Appropriators wrestled with immigration, including the fate of some 800,000 so-called Dreamers, who had come to the United States illegally as children and who Trump had threatened to deport. House Minority Leader Nancy Pelosi, D-Calif., said her caucus would withhold support for spending bills if Republicans didn't negotiate an extension of Obama's Deferred Action for Childhood Arrivals program to help the Dreamers.

Trump, for his part, demanded approval of his request to spend $1.57 billion for a wall along the U.S.-Mexico border. That money was denied in the fiscal 2017 omnibus bill and in a short-term continuing resolution in September.

INVESTIGATING THE ELECTION

Deputy Attorney General Rod Rosenstein on May 17 appointed Mueller, who served as FBI director from 2001 to 2013, as special

counsel to investigate potential violations by Trump's campaign during the 2016 election.

As the investigations, recriminations and political speculation about the fate of Rosenstein, Mueller and others grew, lawmakers got into the act by introducing measures designed to protect Mueller.

A bipartisan proposal (S 1741), by Sens. Thom Tillis, R-N.C., and Chris Coons, D-Del., was aimed at giving a special counsel who is fired the ability to challenge that dismissal in federal court. Another measure (S 1735), from Sens. Lindsey Graham, R-S.C., and Cory Booker, D-N.J., required a judge to sign off on removing a special counsel. McConnell dismissed the possibility of such a scenario or the need for legislation.

Rumblings about Russian interference arose prior to the 2016 election, including on Capitol Hill. Once the election was over, the investigation took on a more public face. On Jan. 5, Senate Armed Services Chairman McCain compared Moscow's effort to influence the outcome of the election to an "act of war." Within days, the Senate Intelligence Committee said it would investigate possible links between Russian operatives and the Trump campaign.

On the House side, Intelligence Chairman Devin Nunes, R-Calif., said in late February that he had seen no evidence that Trump or his advisers had illegally communicated with Russian officials during the transition but committed his panel to investigate. He temporarily stepped aside following ethics complaints from what he described as "several leftwing activist groups" about his handling of classified information. He returned to the post later in the year.

On March 2, Attorney General Jeff Sessions recused himself from all campaign-related investigations. As a senator from Alabama, Sessions had been a senior national security adviser to Trump's presidential campaign and was one of the first Cabinet choices announced after the election. In the wake of Sessions' recusal, Rosenstein was put in charge of the Russia investigation in late April.

SHOOTING AT BASEBALL PRACTICE

Scalise, the House's third-ranking Republican leader, and four others were seriously wounded in June when a gunman opened fire on an early morning practice of the Republican congressional baseball team.

The gunman, James T. Hodgkinson of Belleville, Ill., a volunteer on Sanders' 2016 presidential campaign, was shot and killed by a Capitol Police security detail. The officers were at Eugene Simpson Stadium Park in Alexandria, Va., only because Scalise was a member of the GOP leadership team.

Participants described a bloody scene, with lawmakers and staffers scrambling to help the wounded and move others to safety. "He had crawled into the outfield leaving a trail of blood and we started giving him some liquids. I put pressure on his wounds in the hip," said Rep. Mo Brooks, R-Ala., who helped administer first aid to Scalise.

Scalise's wounds were severe. He returned to work in the Capitol more than three months later, after multiple surgeries and a painful and extended rehabilitation.

The incident sparked debate about the safety of lawmakers amid a highly partisan and divisive time in politics. There was little doubt that had Scalise and his detail not been at the practice field, the outcome would have been much worse.

"He probably saved everybody else's life because if you don't have a leadership person there, there would have been no security there," said Sen. Rand Paul, R-Ky., who was at the practice. "Had they not been there, it would have been a massacre."

Some lawmakers in leadership positions have received full-time

protective details from the Capitol Police. Other lawmakers can hire personal security using their official accounts, known as Members' Representational Allowances, only on a case-by-case basis with approval of the House Sergeant at Arms. Changes were considered to enhance security for members when they were away from the Capitol complex.

CHARGES OF IMPROPER SEXUAL BEHAVIOR

The "Me Too" movement combatting sexual misconduct arrived on Capitol Hill late in the final three months of 2017. It had gained prominence across the nation, notably in the entertainment world and the news media.

Nine members of Congress were accused of sexual harassment or other improper behavior in separate incidents. Of the group, four lawmakers resigned by the end of 2017: Sen. Al Franken, D-Minn., and Reps. John Conyers, D-Mich., Trent Franks, R-Ariz., and Tim Murphy, R-Pa. Three House members resigned or retired the following year. The two others denied the charges and sought re-election in 2018.

Many of the incidents involving lawmakers took place long before "Me Too" became a movement, according to the victims who brought the complaints.

Growing anger over the culture of harassment and secrecy on Capitol Hill resulted in a drumbeat to revamp problematic policies that governed the congressional workplace. More than 30 measures to rein in harassment were filed in the waning days of 2017.

A key target of legislative action was the Congressional Accountability Act, which Congress enacted in 1995 and set workplace protections for its offices and establishing the Office of Compliance to enforce them. That existing process was lengthy, complicated and secretive.

In seeking a clampdown on harassment, the House speaker called for a comprehensive review. The House Administration Committee took the lead, as it organized hearings, roundtable discussions with staff and member listening sessions. During the hearings, Reps. Barbara Comstock, R-Va., and Jackie Speier, D-Calif., described their experiences as former House aides.

The House on Nov. 29 approved a resolution (H Res 630) by Comstock that required all House members and employees to complete an annual program of training in workplace rights and responsibilities. In December, the Administration Committee approved guidelines.

The Senate on Nov. 9 approved a resolution (S Res 330) by Sen. Amy Klobuchar, D-Minn., to require training for senators and aides. Nearly 1,500 former staffers signed a letter to congressional leadership, saying the existing procedures were "inadequate and need reform." ∎

Chapter 2

APPROPRIATIONS

Completion of Fiscal 2017 Omnibus Nearly Bumps Into Fiscal 2018 Rampup

Congress spent almost half the year completing work on spending bills to cover fiscal 2017, which had started Oct. 1, 2016, based on work the previous Congress had done in calendar year 2016. The rest of 2017 was spent advancing – but not completing – work for fiscal 2018. That work dragged on until March of 2018, setting up another year of divided attention.

In signing the final 2018 measure (HR 1625 – PL 115-141), President Donald Trump called it a "ridiculous situation" that he would not repeat. "I will never sign another bill like this again. I'm not going to do it again," he vowed.

During the 2017 calendar year, lawmakers from both chambers were slow to pivot from the fiscal 2017 omnibus appropriations bill signed into law on May 5 to fiscal 2018 spending measures that were supposed to be enacted by Oct. 1.

The congressional agenda was dominated by the health care bill that the House passed but the Senate dropped, and by news about President Donald Trump's firing of FBI Director James Comey and accompanying revelations about the investigations into Russian interference in the 2016 presidential election. The Senate also was consumed early in the year with confirming Trump's nominees to the Cabinet and the Supreme Court.

"I'm very concerned. This will be the latest start since I've been here," Rep. Harold Rogers of Kentucky, a former chairman of the Appropriations Committee who first came to Congress in 1981, said in mid-May. "We haven't received the president's budget yet and the Budget Committee is just now beginning to explore things, so there is no timetable."

Trump, in fact, did not send his fiscal 2018 budget request to Capitol Hill until May 23. It did not matter a great deal, though, because when House appropriators began marking up their bills, they mostly ignored the administration's spending levels.

To make up for the delay, which made the normal appropriations process impractical, House Republicans in late May were considering an ambitious plan to assemble and pass a 12-bill appropriations package ahead of the August recess – effectively an "instant omnibus."

The biggest problem, though, was that such a package would stand little chance in the Senate, where the votes of Democrats would be needed to pass it because appropriations bills are subject to filibusters. In a further complication, Congress needed to extend the federal debt limit so the government could continue to borrow.

By the end of 2017, the House had passed one "minibus" to cover national security programs for 2018 (HR 3219) and a catch-all omnibus bill covering all 12 of the traditional bills (HR 3354).

In early September, with little prospect of agreement on an omnibus appropriations bill for fiscal 2018 and time running out in the fiscal year, the House and Senate agreed on a continuing resolution until Dec. 8, which was packaged with a debt limit increase and emergency aid for areas of Texas devastated by Hurricane Harvey in late August. The measure (HR 601 – PL 115-56) passed the House, on Sept. 6 and the Senate on Sept. 7. The following day, the bill cleared and Trump signed it.

Another extension (PL 115-90) pushed deadlines until Dec. 22 in hopes of increasing the chances for a year-end breakthrough, but Congress left town that day after enacting a four-week extension (HR 1370 -- PL 115-96) to keep the government open into mid-January 2018. ■

Spending: Irregular Order

Congressional leaders dropped any pretense of finishing appropriations bills on time in 2017 as the arrival of the turbulent Trump administration and months-long debates over health care and taxes crowded out spending bills. The House managed to pass six of its 12 regular fiscal 2017 appropriations bills on time, but only one, Military Construction-VA, made it into law in calendar year 2016. The rest of fiscal 2017 spending was consolidated into an omnibus in May 2017.

Fiscal 2018 appropriations didn't even get that far. A series of continuing resolutions kept the government running into January.

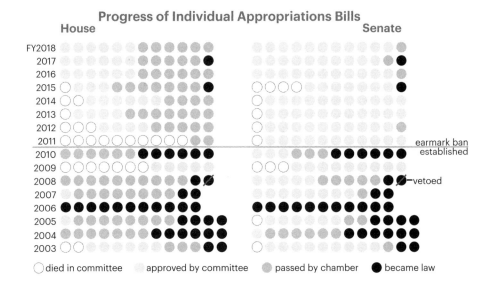

Progress of Individual Appropriations Bills

○ died in committee ● approved by committee ● passed by chamber ● became law

Late Spending Packages ...

For more than a decade, Congress has delivered its final spending measure well after the Oct. 1 deadline, almost always in a bill that bundles most or all of the titles.

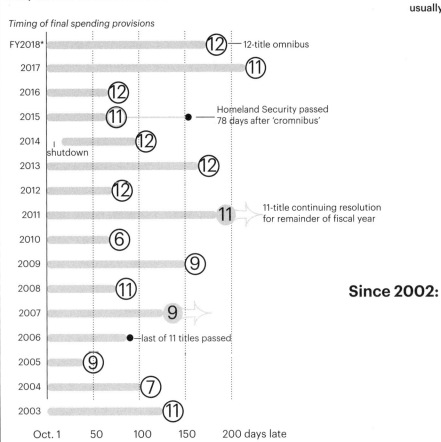

Timing of final spending provisions

... and Multiple Short Fixes

To keep the government operational while sorting out long-term funding, Congress passes short-term continuing resolutions. Further delays in the process usually mean more than one CR is needed.

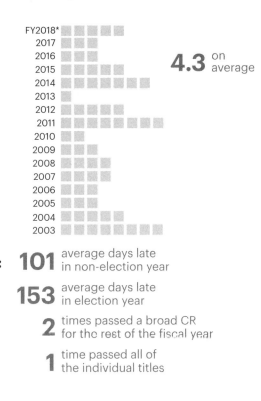

Continuing resolutions

4.3 on average

Since 2002:

101 average days late in non-election year

153 average days late in election year

2 times passed a broad CR for the rest of the fiscal year

1 time passed all of the individual titles

*The final omnibus was passed in 2018.
Source: Library of Congress, CQ appropriations coverage

By Randy Leonard

Congress Passes Fiscal 2017 Omnibus That Sidesteps Government Shutdown

Narrowly averting a government shutdown, Congress passed a $1.07 trillion omnibus appropriations bill (HR 244) on May 4 for fiscal 2017, which by then was more than halfway over. President Donald Trump signed it the following day, though he complained in a signing statement about dozens of sections of the bill, including restrictions on the transfer of detainees at Guantanamo Bay and a requirement that he notify Congress in advance of military actions in some cases.

Some Republicans also had been less than enthusiastic about the omnibus package. They longed for GOP policy priorities left out of the legislation, such as denying funds to "sanctuary cities" that don't cooperate with federal efforts to deport undocumented immigrants, and denying support to the women's health group Planned Parenthood.

"There's just not a decisive break that shows you who won the presidency, the House and the Senate," complained Rep. Dave Brat of Virginia, a member of the hard-line House Freedom Caucus.

Despite the periodic promises of party leaders to return to "regular order," in which each appropriations bill is negotiated and passed by both chambers and then signed into law by the start of the next fiscal year on Oct. 1, the budget process hasn't functioned effectively for decades. Congress hasn't completed appropriations work on time since the mid-1990s and relies instead catch-all omnibus packages interspersed with short-term funding patches, called continuing resolutions, to avoid government shutdowns.

Though versions of all 12 regular fiscal 2017 appropriations bills had been approved by House and Senate committees in 2016, and in some cases had been passed, only one bill had made it into law on time - the military construction-VA measure that was attached to a continuing resolution (HR 5325 - PL 114-223) that funneled emergency money to disaster relief and the fight against the mosquito-borne Zika virus. It was signed on Sept. 29, 2016. (2016 CQ Almanac, p. 2-32)

The omnibus passed in May also carried a fiscal 2017 intelligence authorization bill from the previous Congress (HR 6480) that included the establishment of a special executive branch group to counter perceived Russian assertiveness around the world.

HOUSE-SENATE NEGOTIATIONS

Appropriators had said for months they were itching to complete fiscal 2017 funding, but Republican leaders paused the work on appropriations with a mid-December 2016 CR that extended federal funding until April 28, 2017. That decision was meant to give the new Trump administration time to put its imprint on final fiscal 2017 spending.

But as negotiations resumed in February, appropriators and aides said it was more likely that the new administration would focus on the fiscal 2018 spending cycle and ask for supplemental spending for

BOX SCORE 2017 FISCAL YEAR

OMNIBUS APPROPRIATIONS

BILLS: HR 244 Fiscal 2017 omnibus appropriations.

LEGISLATIVE ACTION:

House concurred in Senate amendments to HR 244, with an amendment, 309-118 on May 3.

Senate concurred in House amendment to Senate amendments, 79-18, on May 4.

President signed HR 244 (PL 115-31) on May 5.

the Pentagon. By early March, the House was working on a fiscal 2017 defense appropriations bill and the outlook favored an omnibus measure that would incorporate the other 10 unfinished spending bills.

The defense appropriations bill revealed on March 2 gave the Pentagon a slight raise and directed billions of dollars toward weapons made in the states of senior congressional appropriators.

The legislation fell well within the budget control law's limits on overall defense spending, providing $577.9 billion, including $61.8 billion for overseas operations.

By comparison, both of the bills written by House and Senate appropriators in 2016 came in below $576 billion.

The new bill dropped a House-passed plan from 2016 that would have shortchanged war spending by more than $15 billion in order to use those funds for more weapons and other military programs favored by lawmakers.

"Unlike the Defense Appropriations bill passed by the House last June, this bill does not break statutory spending limits, nor does it create a shortfall in funding mid-year, which would have affected salaries and mission support for men and women serving bravely in harm's way," said Nita M. Lowey of New York, ranking Democrat on House Appropriations.

Adding in emergency defense funds included in the CR, the total Pentagon budget for fiscal 2017 rose to $583.7 billion, appropriators said - about 2 percent more than the fiscal 2016 level, which was not quite enough to keep pace with inflation.

The $583.7 billion figure did not include other security programs such as military construction and nuclear weapons projects run by the Energy Department.

"The rebuilding of our nation's military starts with this bill," said New Jersey Republican Rodney Frelinghuysen, the House Appropriations chairman, a reference to President Donald Trump's phrase for his planned defense buildup.

HOUSE ACTION

The House on March 8 voted 371 to 48 to pass the $577.9 billion defense bill (HR 1301).

The bill's adherence to the budget control law's spending caps (PL 112-25) helped minimize Democratic opposition to the measure. It included $61.8 billion for wartime spending, which is not limited by law. But House and Senate appropriators opted to scrap a House-passed plan opposed by Democrats to underfund the war accounts by $15 billion to make room in the Overseas Contingency Operations budget for base-budget items.

The ranking Democrat on Defense Appropriations, Peter J. Visclosky of Indiana, called the compromise measure a "product of

bipartisan negotiations."

"This is a good bill and I intend to support it," he said before the vote.

The total bill was $5.2 billion more than fiscal 2016 and $1.6 billion more than President Barack Obama requested in 2016. The CR included emergency defense funding, bringing total defense spending -- not including military construction-- for fiscal 2017 to $583.7 billion.

In terms of equipment, the defense bill provided $21.2 billion for 13 Navy ships, including an additional amphibious transport dock ship, an extra destroyer, one more Littoral Combat Ship and a down payment on an icebreaker ship for the Coast Guard.

The bill also set aside $8.2 billion for 74 F-35 fighter jets (11 more than requested) and $1.1 billion for 14 F/A-18E/F Super Hornet fighters (12 more than requested).

Appropriators rejected the Obama administration's proposed troop reductions. Instead, the bill provided funding for an additional 3,000 active-duty, Guard and reserve Army soldiers and 1,000 active-duty Marines.

ADMINISTRATION PROPOSALS

By the end of March, progress on individual appropriations measures ground to a halt amid broader plans by the administration and congressional leaders for an omnibus.

The Office of Management and Budget shared around proposals for $17.9 billion in specific spending cuts to offset higher proposed defense and border security spending in the remaining six months of fiscal 2017. The White House suggested, for instance, cutting Pell Grant funding by $1.3 billion; National Institutes of Health funding by $1.2 billion; and the Community Development Block Grant program by $1.5 billion, among billions of dollars in other reductions across federal agencies.

The Labor-HHS-Education Subcommittee took the biggest hit at $7.2 billion, while State-Foreign Operations was chopped by $2.8 billion. Defense and most of Homeland Security were not mentioned, though Trump earlier asked Congress for a $30 billion defense supplemental and $3 billion more for border security, both of which were part of the omnibus negotiations.

As an offset, Trump had asked Congress to cut $18 billion in nondefense spending but without offering any details at the time.

Cutting that much spending so far into a fiscal year would be problematic, said Oklahoma Republican Tom Cole, chairman of the Labor-HHS-Education Appropriations Subcommittee.

"No entering administration should be negotiating the budget for the year it's in, because they don't have the people there to do it," Cole said. "They just got an OMB director, they don't have a lot of their staff, they don't have their people in places in the Cabinet agencies in order to make intelligent decisions and even recommendations."

Sen. Lamar Alexander, R-Tenn., chairman of the Senate Energy-Water Appropriations Subcommittee, seemed to shake off the Trump fiscal 2017 request. "I think that's a little late," he said.

Though House Speaker Paul D. Ryan said in early April that congressional Republicans were working "hand in glove" with the Trump administration on a fiscal 2017 wrapup omnibus, the party appeared divided over whether the package would include $1.4 billion Trump wanted to start building the wall he had promised on the border with Mexico, or would include the $30 billion defense supplemental he had requested.

As budget talks continued over a two-week April recess, Mick Mulvaney, the South Carolina congressman Trump had put in charge of the Office and Management and Budget, warned his former colleagues not to ignore the new president.

"The president," Mulvaney said, "needs to see his priorities funded if he's going to be participating in signing these bills."

On April 24, with four days left before funding ran out and the government would have to shut down, Trump told a White House reception for conservative media outlets that he might sign an omnibus even if it left out construction money for the border wall. After that was reported, the next morning Trump tweeted, "Don't let the fake media tell you that I have changed my position on the WALL. It will get built and help stop drugs, human trafficking etc."

Republican negotiators soon sent Democrats a new proposal that left out money for the wall, but also omitted a provision Democrats wanted that would fund cost-sharing reduction subsidies extended in the 2010 health care law (PL 111-148, PL 111-152).

As the talks continued down the wire and both parties prepared a continuing resolution to buy more time if it was needed, a fresh problem arose with a shortfall in Medicaid funding that put Puerto Rico's neediest at risk of losing health care.

Some congressional action on Puerto Rico was necessary in 2017 because the island's Medicaid program was projected to exhaust the last of $6.4 billion in additional funds allocated for fiscal 2011 through 2019 as soon as the first quarter of fiscal 2018. Up to 900,000 U.S. citizens covered by Medicaid in Puerto Rico could have lost health coverage if the funding had run dry.

BUYING TIME; OMNIBUS TIME

Hours before the government would shut down April 28, the House passed a one-week continuing resolution (H J Res 99), 382-30, and sent it to the Senate. The measure extended funding through May 5.

Democrats said for weeks that they would not help Republicans pass a short-term spending bill if a final agreement on the fiscal 2017 omnibus was not close at hand, but Democratic Whip Steny H. Hoyer of Maryland announced that he would vote for the CR because an omnibus bill was imminent.

Frelinghuysen said the CR was necessary to allow lawmakers and their staffs to finish work on the omnibus and "prepare it for the floor."

"The continuing resolution is never anyone's first choice for funding the government," he said. "However, this is our best path forward." The Senate cleared the resolution and Trump signed it the same night.

House and Senate appropriators unveiled the text of their omnibus appropriations bill early on April 30. The more than $1 trillion package funneled extra money to the military but rejected many of President Donald Trump's other signature spending proposals.

The 1,665-page legislation (HR 244) comprises the 11 unfinished fiscal 2017 appropriations bills, providing fresh spending instructions for nearly every corner of the federal government. It provided an annualized total of $1.07 trillion in base spending for fiscal 2017, or $1.16 trillion including Overseas Contingency Operations funding for the military.

Democratic leaders touted the agreement as a victory, claiming to have blocked Republican policy provisions and stymied many of Trump's priorities, especially on border enforcement.

Republicans hailed the increases in defense spending and border security as highlights of the package. The $15 billion boost in supplemental spending for the Pentagon was about half the amount sought by Trump for a military buildup. It was designated for Overseas Contingency Operations spending, which didn't count against statutory caps.

Winners and Losers in Omnibus Bill

Democrats and Republicans both claimed victory in the fiscal 2017 omnibus, but a review showed there were clear winners and losers in the agreement:

WINNERS

Defense Advocates: The $1.07 trillion omnibus included $593 billion for defense — a $19.9 billion increase over fiscal 2016 and a significant victory for members of Congress who have urged more military spending and higher troop levels.

The military spending boost included $1.6 billion for 3,000 additional Army soldiers and 1,000 more Marines. Soldiers will also receive a 2.1 percent raise -the largest military pay raise in six years. The defense spending helped President Donald Trump partly deliver on his campaign promise to bolster the nation's military. Even though the bill didn't include the additional $30 billion he requested, it did give him $12.5 billion of that with the possibility of an additional $2.5 billion if the administration submits a counter-ISIS strategy to Congress.

Bipartisanship: Differences between the two parties on legislation, Trump's Cabinet nominees and the Senate's 60-vote threshold for Supreme Court nominees have all led to battle after battle.

The 11-bill omnibus was a chance for appropriators and party leaders to show that despite the bitterness caused by the 2016 presidential election, they could reach agreement on funding the government, even if the bill was seven months late.

Retired Coal Miners: Securing health care coverage for retired coal miners was a key agenda item for Democrats and Republicans, but the issue came to a head in December 2016 when Senate Democrats moved it to the forefront of negotiations on the second stopgap spending bill (PL 114-254). Working out funding for miners was a central sticking point throughout omnibus negotiations, which led to a $1 billion permanent fix.

Programs Trump Wanted Gone: Trump proposed killing off more than a dozen federal programs in his fiscal 2018 budget outline. Appropriators were not inclined to reduce or eliminate federal funding for any of those line items, including the Corporation for Public Broadcasting, the National Endowment for the Arts and the National Endowment for the Humanities.

Puerto Rico Medicaid Patients: Without the $295.9 million agreement to help bolster Puerto Rico's Medicaid program, an esti-

mated 900,000 people could have lost access to health coverage.

The territory's Medicaid program, which includes about 49 percent of its population, still needs legislative changes.

LOSERS

Social Conservative Agenda: The House Freedom Caucus spent most of its time in 2017 on the drive to repeal and replace the 2010 health care law (PL 111-148, PL 111-152) while appropriators were hashing out the omnibus' details. Freedom Caucus Chairman Mark Meadows, R-N.C., told reporters the group had been willing to "help" with the spending bill, but the lack of money to begin construction of a wall along the nation's Southern border, the absence of a provision blocking federal funds to sanctuary cities and no language prohibiting Planned Parenthood from receiving federal dollars frustrated the group. But with some Democrats willing to back the omnibus, Freedom Caucus votes weren't necessary.

Parity Between Defense and Nondefense: For years, Democrats have insisted that any increase in defense spending be matched by increases in nondefense discretionary spending, but that was not achieved in the omnibus. Republicans, who have loathed the parity requirement, were particularly happy.

Farmers: The omnibus did not include additional farm payments sought by cotton and dairy farmers who argued that the 2014 farm bill (PL 113-79) was inadequate given the industry's economic state. The omnibus required Agriculture Secretary Sonny Perdue to submit a report within 60 days detailing ways Congress and the administration might help cotton farmers. It also instructed Perdue to use administrative and budget tools to assist dairy farmers.

EPA Funding: When the Trump administration requested $33 billion more in fiscal 2017 for defense and border security, it also suggested Congress cut $18 billion from domestic discretionary programs to help offset some of that additional spending. Among the proposals were significant cuts in the EPA budget, including its Superfund remediation program, the Great Lakes Restoration initiative and research programs.

While the omnibus didn't include all of those cuts, it did reduce the EPA by $81.4 million — the lowest level of funding Congress has provided for the agency since fiscal 2009. The legislation also barred the EPA from regulating livestock emissions, and some forms of ammunition and fishing tackle which contain lead. ■

No funding was included for Trump's proposed wall on the Southern border or for a so-called deportation force, but the package provided another $1.5 billion for border security efforts, including new technology and repairing existing infrastructure.

The bill also contained $295.9 million to help shore up Puerto Rico's Medicaid fund and $1 billion to augment a health care and pension benefits fund for retired coal miners that was on the brink of extinction. Debate over the miners' pension fund nearly brought the government to a shutdown in December, but coal state lawmakers and party leaders were able to hash out a permanent solution in the omnibus.

The legislation also included:

• More than $8 billion in emergency and disaster relief funding to fight wildfires, flooding and other extreme weather events in states like North Carolina, California, Louisiana, West Virginia and more;

• $34 billion for the National Institutes of Health, a $2 billion or 6.2 percent increase from current levels;

• Restored year-round Pell Grants for low-income college students;

• $990 million in emergency famine relief, including $300 million for Food For Peace in South Sudan, Somalia, Yemen and Nigeria;

• $103 million to combat opioid abuse;

• $68 million to reimburse local law enforcement agencies for the costs of protecting Trump and his family, mainly in Manhattan. ■

Fiscal 2017 Omnibus in Depth: Details by Appropriations Title

Here are details on the 12 titles in the fiscal 2017 omnibus spending bill, as passed in May.

AGRICULTURE

Appropriators delivered a no-drama fiscal 2017 omnibus spending bill for the Department of Agriculture and the Food and Drug Administration.

The USDA and its programs would receive $20.9 billion in discretionary funding and $132.5 billion in mandatory funding in the bill. A large share of the mandatory money would go to the Supplemental Nutrition Assistance Program, or SNAP, which would receive $78.5 billion, a $2.4 billion decrease in funding from fiscal 2016.

The reduced sum reflected a decline in enrollment due to an improving economy and decisions by states to end extended food stamp benefits to single able-bodied adults without children under age 18. Mandatory spending on child nutrition programs, primarily the national school lunch and school breakfast programs, would reach $22.8 billion, which was $644 million above fiscal 2016 enacted levels.

The overall discretionary funding for USDA was $873 million below the enacted fiscal 2016 level.

Appropriators delivered a blow to cotton and dairy farmers who sought additional farm payments by arguing that the 2014 farm bill (PL 113-79) programs designed for them were inadequate as the farm economy entered a fourth year of lower prices and income.

Appropriators directed Agriculture Secretary Sonny Perdue to send them a report within 60 days of the fiscal 2017 spending bill's enactment identifying administrative options to help cotton farmers, along with legislative steps Congress could take to help cotton growers.

On dairy, Perdue was directed to use whatever administrative and budget tools he had to aid dairy farmers. In the past, the Agriculture department has bought cheese and other dairy products to reduce the amount of surplus dairy products in the market. The dairy industry has welcomed those purchases, but says farmers need a more sustained source of financial aid.

Appropriators preserved a $25 million increase in the Agriculture and Food Research Initiative, setting funding for the research program at $375 million.

Under the fiscal 2017 bill, research programs at USDA would receive $2.89 billion. The Agricultural Research Service would receive $1.2 billion.

ARS was directed to conduct a study on sodium or salt consumption by school-age children, apparently to determine if mandated reductions in federally funded school meals are scientifically justified.

The bill kept funding for rural water and waste water programs at $1.2 billion, the same level as fiscal 2016 enacted levels. There was a Buy American provision in the rural water and waste programs. It appeared to reflect the Trump administration's desire to use domestically produced sewer and water pipes as well as other equipment.

Appropriators provided $24 billion in loan authority for rural housing programs, including a $100 million increase for the direct loan program that provides credit to low-income rural borrowers to buy homes.

The Food and Drug Administration budget would take a modest cut for the remainder of fiscal 2017, decreasing spending by about $25 million compared to the fiscal 2016 levels, under the congressional spending deal. That would give the agency almost $4.7 billion total for this fiscal year.

Most of that cut in the omnibus spending bill was attributable to a decrease in the money the FDA collects from the drug and medical device industries, which would drop by about $65 million, from $1.96 billion to $1.89 billion. That amount was negotiated in advance and spread out over a five-year period, so the decrease was not a surprise.

Discretionary funding for FDA was increased by about $39 million for the overall fiscal year, for a total of almost $2.8 billion. Most of the increase was authorized by 2016's "21st Century Cures" law, with $30 million of the $39 million already included in the stopgap spending bill (PL 114-254) that passed in December 2016.

The accompanying committee report said that most of the cuts would be absorbed by administrative savings and that the FDA should continue with "all projects, activities, laboratories, and programs" included in fiscal 2016.

The spending bill continued to prohibit the agency from accepting any drug or device applications that involve the use of human embryos for the purpose of genetic modification, a prohibition that had been in the fiscal 2016 omnibus appropriations bill (PL 114-113).

The measure would continue to block the FDA from prohibiting the use of partially hydrogenated oils, also known as trans fats, in food. The Obama administration had sought to ban the use of trans fats by having the FDA consider them "unsafe" starting in 2013.

The bill also would prohibit the sale of genetically engineered salmon until the FDA finalized labeling guidelines for the food. The first altered salmon was approved by the FDA in 2015 but the sale of the fish, dubbed "Frankenfish" by critics, had been blocked through spending bill riders ever since.

The bill was otherwise free of controversial policy language. The original House bill included an amendment that would have had a big impact on how the FDA regulates the e-cigarette industry, but that appeared to be one of the policy riders that could not overcome Democratic objections.

COMMERCE-JUSTICE-SCIENCE

The Commerce-Justice-Science appropriations title increased funds for federal law enforcement and space exploration.

The $56.5 billion for the C-J-S portion of the bill remained relatively flat overall, a 1.4 percent increase over the $55.7 billion enacted level for fiscal 2016. The omnibus deal (HR 244) would fund the Justice and Commerce departments, NASA and scientific research, among other functions in the C-J-S title.

The section generally avoided controversial policy riders, including those on gun rights that have been a perennial source for partisan skirmishes. The bill kept current law by excluding new Republican policy riders on firearm sales and imports, as well as a Democratic measure to block firearm sales to people on terror watch lists.

Congress Rescues Miners' Health Care

Retired coal miners and their spouses at risk of losing their health care coverage can rest easier: The fiscal 2017 omnibus spending bill includes a provision that bails out the crippled fund that provides the coverage by extending unrelated customs fees.

The appropriations in the omnibus bill included a $1 billion infusion to the health care program, ensuring its solvency as it teetered on the edge of failure for some 20,000 retired coal miners and their dependents.

To pay for the measure, lawmakers extended custom user fees on goods and people entering the country — including merchandising processing fees — set to expire in September 2025, by three and half months.

The customs user fees had been the basis for a bill by Sen. Joe Manchin III, D-W.Va., which had earlier moved out of the Finance Committee on an 18-8 vote.

The issue brought the government to the brink of a partial shutdown in December 2016, when coal-state senators, led by Manchin, refused to grant-timing consents for a continuing resolution that included a four month extension for the health care, instead of the permanent fix they wanted.

"For years I have been working side-by-side with the United Mine Workers of America and West Virginia coal miners to keep the promise we made that these patriotic workers would never go without the healthcare they earned," Manchin said in a statement. "Today, I am thrilled to announce that Congress finally agreed to pass a permanent healthcare solution in honor of their hard work and dedication to this great nation."

The measure also extends eligibility for the health care to retired miners affected by coal company bankruptcies in 2012 and 2015, in which the bankruptcy plans dropped the health coverage. That measure was backed by Majority Leader Mitch McConnell, R-Ky., who introduced his own bill (S 176) that addressed the health care problem.

"Protecting these miners and their families from losing their health care has been a top priority of mine," McConnell said.

PENSION STILL LOOMS

Not included in the spending bill, however, was any funding to bolster the retired miners' pension program — likely a future battle for any must-pass legislation. Like the health care fund, the pension fund is closing in on depletion and coal state lawmakers have promised as tough a fight for those benefits as they did for the health care.

"President Truman recognized the vital role our coal miners played in our country's success and he believed their hard work earned them guaranteed health and pension benefits," Manchin said of Truman's 1946 decision to use federal dollars to support the funds and to end a crippling coal strike. "This agreement has always been a sacred bond between worker and country, and I am more determined than ever to fulfill our whole obligation and secure retired miners pension benefits as well."

Rep. David B. McKinley, R-W.Va., who led the push on the House side for a permanent fix, also vowed to "continue the fight to protect coal miner pensions."

Conservatives in Congress have balked at the proposal for fear of the precedent it could set in bailing out other struggling industries' pension problems.

Senate Finance Chairman Orrin G. Hatch, R-Utah, said he was supportive of the health care extension, but he could not get behind the pension fix, mainly due to the high cost. ■

Appropriators used the C-J-S bill to put a new focus on the Justice Department's role in immigration enforcement. For example, the spending bill directed DOJ to require all local law enforcement agencies applying for certain grant programs to certify that they were in compliance with federal immigration laws.

That fits closely with the Trump administration's executive order to stop grants from going to "sanctuary" jurisdictions that don't cooperate with federal enforcement of immigration laws. So did another provision directing the Bureau of Prisons to offer immigration officials — and not states or municipalities — the first opportunity to take into custody prisoners who have a hold on them for deportation.

The Executive Office for Immigration Review for the first time was to be funded as a separate account and would receive $20 million more to pay for 10 new immigration judges and support staff. Senate Republicans pointed out that the bill also urged the Justice Department to "reduce the extensive backlog of pending immigration cases" which cause months of delays and frustrate the country's immigration enforcement.

And the spending bill encouraged the Justice Department to speed up the hiring process for additional immigration judges that are already funded — the fiscal 2016 omnibus (PL 114-113) added $76 million for 55 additional immigration judges.

The Justice Department, which receives the largest chunk of the C-J-S funding, would get $28.9 billion in fiscal 2017. That was a decrease of $142 million, or less than 1 percent, from the $29.1 billion enacted level for fiscal 2016.

That includes $323 million for a new FBI headquarters building, as well as increases of $61 million to boost cybersecurity and $79 million to combat online sexual predators.

The Commerce Department would receive $9.2 billion, an increase of $9 million. That funding included an increase of $100 million over the fiscal 2016 enacted level for the Census Bureau to prepare for the 2020 Census, an effort that for years has been the target of cuts by appropriators.

The omnibus raised funding for the Economic Development Administration, one of the agencies Trump had called for eliminating in his fiscal 2018 budget blueprint, released before the omnibus, to $276 million — a $15 million increase from enacted levels. Within the EDA funding is $30 million in grants to be shipped to troubled coal-mining communities.

Another agency Trump was seeking to eliminate in 2018 was the Minority Business Development Agency, which he called "duplicative"

Spending Package Keeps Ban On Political Money Disclosure

The fiscal 2017 omnibus appropriations bill had mixed returns for proponents of strict campaign finance laws. Lawmakers did not load on many new riders targeting political money rules, but they kept in place existing ones.

The Securities and Exchange Commission, for instance, was still prohibited from issuing new rules requiring more disclosures of the political money that public companies spend. The omnibus also prohibited the IRS from finalizing guidance clarifying its standards for permitted political activities by nonprofit organizations.

"We obviously oppose those riders, but it's pretty hard to get riders out that were already in," said Fred Wertheimer, president of Democracy 21, a campaign finance proponent.

The omnibus also contained a prohibition on funding to require that companies bidding for federal contracts disclose their campaign contributions.

"Overall, the Democrats were successful at keeping the omnibus funding bill from being hijacked by inappropriate policy additions, keeping out over 160 proposed poison pill riders," said Lisa Gilbert, vice president of legislative affairs at Public Citizen. "One exception is several anti-disclosure campaign finance provisions that were again included in the funding package."

Though campaign finance riders have been the subject of much controversy in negotiations over government spending in recent years, this time the subject remained fairly low-key. ∎

of other public and private programs. But lawmakers chose to dole out $34 million for the agency in the omnibus, a $2 million increase from enacted levels.

The National Oceanic and Atmospheric Administration would receive $5.7 billion, a $90 million decrease from fiscal 2016 funding levels. The popular Sea Grant program that Trump had also called for eliminating would receive $63 million, and climate research at NOAA would remain flat at $158 million.

NASA, the biggest single component of the bill's science spending, was to receive $19.7 billion in fiscal 2017, an increase of $368 million, while the National Science Foundation would receive $7.5 billion, a $9 million increase from fiscal 2016 levels.

The bill also included $161 million for opioid response programs funded through the subcommittee, an increase of $36 million over the previous year.

The measure retained $385 million for the Legal Services Corp., a program for civil legal aid for the poor that Trump's fiscal 2018 budget sought to eliminate.

The bill included $27 million to reimburse the State Department and local law enforcement for costs associated with protection of Trump from Nov. 9 to Inauguration Day.

In other issues, the fiscal 2017 omnibus included a provision directing the Justice Department to take no action against states where marijuana use for medical purposes is legal.

And it did not include a Republican-backed provision to mandate that any exports to Cuba not be funneled through the island nation's military and security services. The Cuba provision had been included in the House-passed C-J-S spending bill for fiscal 2016.

DEFENSE

The Defense Department received a nearly $15 billion boost in the omnibus spending package, a relatively modest increase. The increase in the Overseas Contingency Operations accounts was stingier than the $30 billion in additional defense spending the Trump administration had proposed several weeks before to pay for planes, ships and other military priorities that did not make the cut for the capped fiscal

2017 defense budget.

But it brought the total defense spending bill to $593 billion — $19.9 billion over fiscal 2016 levels and $16.3 billion more than the Obama administration's request delivered to Capitol Hill in 2016.

The House-Senate defense spending agreement (HR 1301), which the House passed in March, set aside $577.9 billion for defense, but appropriators reached an agreement on that measure before the Trump administration delivered its supplemental request for defense spending. The administration's proposal contained more than $5 billion in duplicative funding already included in the House-passed bill.

The defense portion of the omnibus appeared to closely follow the earlier defense spending agreement for 2017.

The omnibus dropped a House-passed plan from 2016 that would have shortchanged war spending by more than $15 billion in order to use those funds for more weapons and other military programs favored by lawmakers. That maneuver was a non-starter with Democrats, who saw it as an end-run around the budget caps.

Adding in emergency defense funds included in the continuing resolution, the total Pentagon budget for fiscal 2017 would rise to $598.5 billion. That total did not include other security programs, such as military construction and Energy Department-run nuclear weapons projects.

The bill denied cuts to troop levels proposed by the Obama administration and it included an additional $1.6 billion to pay for 3,000 more active-duty and reserve Army soldiers and 1,000 more active-duty Marines. And it would give military personnel a 2.1 percent across-the-board raise, a half-percent higher than requested by President Barack Obama.

The measure would bankroll several weapons identified as "unfunded priorities" by the military service chiefs and favored on Capitol Hill. Total procurement spending came to $123.3 billion, including $108.4 billion in the base budget and $14.9 billion in the overseas accounts. That was $12.3 billion more than the Obama administration's request and $4.7 billion above the previous year's levels.

The bill funded 74 F-35 fighters, 11 more than Obama requested, for a total price tag of $8.2 billion. The F-35 is assembled in the district of

Kay Granger, R-Texas, chairwoman of the House Defense Appropriations Subcommittee, though multiple appropriators from both parties support the stealthy jets.

The measure also provided $1.1 billion for 14 F/A-18E/F Super Hornet fighters, a dozen more than requested.

The bill included $21.2 billion to buy 13 Navy ships, including three DDG-51 guided missile destroyers, three Littoral Combat Ships, one LPD-17 amphibious transport dock ship and a down payment for a polar icebreaker for the Coast Guard.

Several of the ships added to the request — including the LPD-17, an extra destroyer, one more LCS and the polar ice breaker funding — were a possible boon for Senate Appropriations Chairman Thad Cochran's home state of Mississippi, whose shipyard could compete for the work.

Of the $14.8 billion in additional war-related spending added to the bill (about half of what President Donald Trump had sought), $2.5 billion was to be withheld "until the President submits a comprehensive, whole of government strategy for the defeat" of the Islamic State.

The bill demanded "benchmarks for progress" in the war effort and mandated quarterly reports to Congress by the secretaries of Defense and State.

Appropriators' decision to fence off the $2.5 billion until Trump's plan arrived also showed that, despite universal congressional desire to defeat ISIS, lawmakers were not interested in writing a blank check for expanding military operations in the Mideast

Trump had promised during the election campaign to obtain from the Pentagon within 30 days of taking office a plan to defeat ISIS.

"We are going to convene my top generals and give them a simple instruction," Trump said at a Sept. 6 rally. "They will have 30 days to submit to the Oval Office a plan for soundly and quickly defeating ISIS."

In a late January executive order, Trump demanded that the Pentagon give him a preliminary draft of the plan within a month. He received it on time in late February. The plan, though, was not what many people might have had in mind when they heard Trump talk about it during the campaign.

It was not a ready-to-execute military blueprint but was instead a "framework for a broader discussion" of the problem and included non-military components, a Pentagon spokesman told reporters in February.

The February plan was classified secret. Whether or not lawmakers who were cleared to see that secret document had already done so, or had seen subsequent battle plans, the new provision demanding a plan showed that appropriators wanted more information than they had received.

Appropriators were generous toward programs aimed at countering ISIS, despite conditioning some of the aid. The $14.8 billion supplemental came on top of $61.8 billion for overseas contingency operations, which included the campaign against ISIS in Iraq, Syria and beyond.

Appropriators were particularly lavish when it came to a fund to train and equip foreign forces to fight ISIS. The administration had sought in April some $626 million for that fund, even though the fiscal 2017 spending bill (HR 1301), which the House alone passed in March and which became part of the omnibus, already had included $980 million for the train and equip fund. The new bill provided both of those sums to the administration.

ENERGY-WATER

The omnibus increased spending on energy research programs that President Donald Trump had said he wanted to slash.

In total, Energy-Water Appropriations for agencies including the Department of Energy, Army Corps of Engineers and other water projects totaled $37.8 billion, $586 million above the fiscal 2016 spending.

DOE would receive $30.8 billion, an increase of $1.1 billion compared to fiscal 2016. That total was more than Senate and House included in their previously passed fiscal 2017 bills — $30.7 billion and $30 billion, respectively.

The Army Corps would receive $6 billion, including an increase of $49 million compared to fiscal 2016, while the Bureau of Reclamation would receive $1.3 billion for water programs. The bill also omitted money to move forward with the Yucca Mountain permanent nuclear waste repository in Nevada, despite backing from Trump and some lawmakers in Congress.

The omnibus bill appeared to ignore the spending priorities the Trump administration had established in its fiscal 2018 budget proposal — which was outlined even as work on fiscal 2017 wrapped up — that called for reducing or eliminating spending on energy research programs.

Among the key research programs that would be increased were:

The Department of Energy's Office of Energy Efficiency and Renewable Energy would receive $2.1 billion, a $17 million increase over fiscal 2016.

DOE's Office of Science would receive $5.4 billion, up $42 million over fiscal 2016.

DOE's Advanced Research Projects Agency-Energy (ARPA-E) program would receive $306 million, up $15 million over fiscal 2016.

The Trump administration suggested removing funding for ARPA-E, decreasing the Office of Science budget by $900 million and decreasing EERE by an undisclosed amount, although it's part of a $2 billion programmatic decrease.

"The bill," explained the House Appropriations Committee, "prioritizes and increases funding for energy programs that encourage U.S. economic competitiveness and that help advance the nation's goal of an 'all-of-the-above' solution to energy independence."

A large part of DOE has little to do with the generation of energy, but rather with the management and oversight of the nation's nuclear weapons arsenal. The omnibus provided $12.9 billion for nuclear weapon related activities, a $412 million increase compared with fiscal 2016.

Within the nonproliferation account, under the weapons activities budget line, $335 million was set aside, House Appropriations said, "to help fulfill the international commitment by the U.S. to operate a Mixed Oxide (MOX) Fuel Fabrication Facility to dispose of surplus plutonium," at the Savannah River Site in South Carolina.

That project, which would convert weapons-grade plutonium into fuel for nuclear power plants under an agreement with Russia, was over budget and behind schedule. It had been proposed for elimination by the Obama administration, which had been considering other options for meeting the terms of the agreement. Less than a month after the omnibus passed, Trump sent Congress a fiscal 2018 budget request that called for terminating the MOX project.

Absent from the omnibus was any permanent solution to the nuclear waste conundrum. The administration proposed funding to advance work on Yucca Mountain, and the House provided $170 million in its

$1 Billion Plus to Address Addiction

Lawmakers concerned about the spiraling effects of opioid and heroin abuse allocated more than $1 billion in the fiscal 2017 omnibus to fight the addiction crisis gripping many parts of the country.

The funds spanned three bills in the omnibus:

The Labor-HHS-Education title included $801 million;

Commerce-Justice-Science received $276.5 million;

Military Construction-VA, the only one of the 12 appropriations bills that was enacted (PL 114-223) before the start of the fiscal year, received an additional $50 million in the Medical Services account to help address the problem among military veterans.

The opioid epidemic has had a cascading effect on communities and has increased the burden on local law enforcement and public safety departments that must respond to increasing overdose calls.

Billboards could be seen across the Northeast on state and local highways urging individuals to purchase Narcan, an overdose nasal spray that can save a life while emergency services are en route.

At a Senate Appropriations Committee hearing on the problem, Sen. Shelley Moore Capito, R-W.Va., said she had examined Department of Veterans Affairs data that showed veterans with opioid abuse disorders are at higher risk of suicide than those with depression, at a time when lawmakers have injected more money into suicide prevention but have seen no decrease in the suicide rate.

The $801 million in the Labor-HHS-Education title would mostly go to the Substance Abuse and Mental Health Services Administration for response, including $500 million that was authorized in the so-called "Cures" legislation in 2016 (PL 114-255) for a new "State Response to Opioid Abuse" program.

The agreement included:

• A $31 million boost in medication-assisted treatment programs, for a total funding level of $56 million;

• $20 million for programs authorized in a 2014 opioid response law (PL 114-198), including $1 million for increased access to overdose treatment, $12 million to train first responders, $3 million for recovery community-building and $4 million to treat addiction in pregnant women or women who have recently given birth;

• A $50 million boost in prescription drug overdose and heroin abuse programs at the Centers for Disease Control and Prevention to bring the total funding to $126 million;

• A minimum of $50 million to be awarded to Community Health Centers for treatment, prevention, and awareness of opioid abuse;

• $3 million for the Agency for Healthcare Research and Quality related to effective primary care support as well as medical care delivery in rural communities. ■

---

fiscal 2017 bill, but the Senate focused instead on an interim storage approach, allocating $89 million for that purpose. The bill left out the Senate proposal as well.

FINANCIAL SERVICES

Lawmakers spared the IRS but took a cut out of the General Services Administration in a package that put Financial Services spending at $21.5 billion, down $2 billion from fiscal 2016.

The spending agreement cut $1.35 billion from the GSA's Federal Building Fund. The GSA could continue to collect rents, but would be unable to spend the money accumulated in the fund. The agreement cut deeper in the GSA budget than either the Senate or House appropriators had proposed in their versions of the bill.

The IRS, an agency that's long been the target of GOP anger, would see no change from its $11.2 billion funding in fiscal 2016. Treasury Secretary Steven T. Mnuchin said at his confirmation hearing that he was concerned about IRS staffing, which had been slashed since a controversy over the agency's alleged targeting of conservative nonprofit groups. The House had proposed cutting $236 million in fiscal 2017.

Still, as the House Appropriations Committee noted, the IRS' budget was below fiscal 2008 levels, although it "provides sufficient resources to perform its core duties."

The bill also included a bevy of policy riders that were in the 2016 omnibus regarding the IRS, including prohibiting a new rule relating to the tax-exempt status of 501 (c)(4) organizations, and prohibiting the White House from ordering the IRS to determine the tax-exempt status of an organization.

The federal judiciary was the biggest winner, seeing its budget increased 3 percent, to $7.4 billion, from fiscal 2016.

The agreement was also more generous to the Executive Office of the President than the House and Senate had proposed. The package gave the office $709 million in fiscal 2017, more than the $703 million the Senate proposed or the $692 million in the House version.

The District of Columbia received $756 million under the package, another area where the omnibus provided more than Senate and House versions of the bill. The Small Business Administration received $887 million, or $4 million more than the House would have provided.

The total cuts in financial services agencies were 8.5 percent compared to fiscal 2016, but many agencies' budgets lie outside the $21.5 billion spending level. About $14 billion came from funds, such as the Treasury Department's forfeiture fund, rather than from the government's general coffers. The budgets of the Federal Reserve, the Federal Deposit Insurance Corporation, the Office of the Comptroller of the Currency and the Consumer Financial Protection Bureau lie outside the appropriations process.

Negotiators also went with the Senate's recommendation on two agency budgets:

The Securities and Exchange Commission received $1.6 billion, unchanged from fiscal 2016. The House had proposed a $50 million cut.

The Federal Communications Commission got $341 million. The House had proposed $316 million.

What was not in the bill, House Minority Leader Nancy Pelosi, D-Calif., pointed out, were policy riders that would result in "dismantling Dodd-Frank's vital Wall Street consumer protections." Dodd-Frank is the 2010 financial overhaul (PL 111-203) that many Republicans want to dismantle.

In the fiscal 2017 Financial Services bill passed by the House in the summer of 2016, 20 of its pages dealt with overhauling the Con-

sumer Financial Protection Bureau, from eliminating Director Richard Cordray's job and replacing him with a five-person commission, to defunding the bureau's mandatory arbitration rule, which would ban companies from requiring arbitration in consumer contracts.

HOMELAND SECURITY

The Homeland Security Department received $42.4 billion for fiscal 2017, an increase of about $1.45 billion above the previous year's enacted budget The funding was a boost over what the Obama administration sought and would increase spending for major agencies including Customs and Border Protection, Immigration and Customs Enforcement, Transportation Security Administration and the federal cybersecurity activities overseen by DHS.

While the omnibus boosted spending for immigration enforcement, it effectively blocked DHS from using extra border security funds for construction of a border wall that was a cornerstone of Trump's campaign. Trump backed off his demand for wall funding in fiscal 2017, which indicated a likely fight the following year. The omnibus did include $1.5 billion to maintain and improve the existing border fence, deploy unmanned aerial vehicles and other border surveillance technologies as well as hire more Border Patrol agents. Lawmakers in both parties claimed victory in having met their respective goals.

Although no money was included for the wall, Senate Appropriations Chairman Thad Cochran, R-Miss., said the bill provided robust support for border security measures.

Democrats saw the spending package as critical in their efforts to stop Trump's immigration enforcement efforts. House Minority Leader Nancy Pelosi, D-Calif., called it an "immoral and unwise border wall" and noted the omnibus did not "create a cruel new deportation force."

Customs and Border Protection, which oversees construction along the border, would get $11.4 billion, an increase of $226.1 million from the previous year for operations and support. The funds would pay for video surveillance along the border, small unmanned aerial systems and improvements to the agency's current fleet of surveillance drones.

Immigration and Customs Enforcement would receive $6.4 billion, including $617 million for additional detention beds and to pay for the transportation and removal of detained undocumented immigrants.

The funding bill provided $263.6 million for DHS's intelligence efforts and called on the department to implement a program to track fraudulent passports and disrupt transnational criminal networks.

Federal cybersecurity efforts overseen by DHS received $669.4 million, including $9.5 million for information-sharing efforts that help warn state governments of large-scale cyberattacks.

The Coast Guard got $10.5 billion, including $1.37 billion for recapitalization of its fleet of patrol vessels, aircraft and facilities.

The omnibus called on DHS to re-evaluate the Trump administration's decision to abandon the Obama-era Priority Enforcement Program that addresses how the federal government deals with local law enforcement agencies when detaining undocumented immigrants already in custody. The Trump administration had reverted to an earlier program known as Secure Communities.

Trump made enforcement of existing immigration laws a priority and cast a wide net to detain undocumented immigrants with criminal convictions as well as those who commit offenses such as driving under the influence.

The administration also tried to single out localities that don't comply with ICE requests to detain undocumented immigrants held for criminal offenses until the agency could arrest them. After publishing one set of statistics on jurisdictions that did not comply with ICE detention requests, the Trump administration abandoned the effort because the data was flawed.

Lawmakers, citing DHS statistics from 2016, said that the Obama administration's program had elicited better cooperation from local law enforcement agencies.

"ICE should ensure that the reinstatement of the Secure Communities program does not undermine the progress it made through PEP in 2015 and 2016," the omnibus stated. "Specifically, ICE should continue to work" with local law enforcement agencies "that are willing to notify ICE prior to releasing individuals who are enforcement priorities."

The fiscal 2017 spending package also called on DHS to better track visitors who overstay their visas. Although the Trump administration had focused its efforts on those who cross the border illegally, the proportion of those who overstay their visas has been increasing.

INTERIOR-ENVIRONMENT

Republicans largely disregarded President Trump's plan to gut the EPA, agreeing in a deal at the last minute to retain most of the agency's funding and staffing levels.

The omnibus would fund the EPA at $8.06 billion, a reduction of $81.4 million from the fiscal year 2016 enacted level. Congress approved an annualized $8.2 billion for the agency in 2017 under December's continuing resolution (PL 114-254).

Trump took aim at the agency throughout his campaign. In his fiscal 2018 budget proposal, released March 16 as Congress still worked on fiscal 2017 spending, Trump proposed a 31 percent cut in the EPA's funding and called for eliminating about 3,200 jobs. That would bring the agency's budget down to $5.7 billion in fiscal 2018. Trump's budget proposal would also eliminate more than 50 programs at the agency as the new administration seeks to trim the role of the federal government in regulating the environment and eliminate what the White House says is duplication across the EPA.

The EPA dodged those sharp cuts in the omnibus and its staffing was maintained at 15,000 employees.

Overall, the Interior-Environment part of the omnibus provided $32.28 billion for the Interior Department, the EPA and related programs, an increase of $121 million from fiscal 2016. Most of the increase would be directed toward fighting and preventing wildfires, water infrastructure programs to control lead in drinking water, cleaning up Superfund sites, Native American education and health issues and the Bureau of Land Management.

With $2.9 billion, the National Park Service received $81 million above the 2016 level to help it clear a maintenance backlog. Interior Secretary Ryan Zinke, who said he would fight sharp budget cuts at his agency, had said catching up on maintenance was one of his top priorities.

The omnibus boosted funding for the Fish and Wildlife Service to accelerate removal of plants and animals from the Endangered Species list, as well as to control invasive species and illegal wildlife trafficking. The bill maintained a one-year delay on any further Endangered Species Act status "reviews, determinations, and rulemakings" for the greater sage-grouse.

The bill also gave the administration "flexibility" to review and rewrite the Waters of the United States pollution rule, the Clean Power Plan carbon emissions rule, and other environmental regulations. It required the government to report on the backlog of mining permits

waiting to be approved and prohibited it from regulating lead content in ammunition and fishing tackle. The bill also cut funding for EPA's research and regulatory programs as Republicans seek to trim what they view as over-regulation by the agency.

Still, the measure had the support of Democratic leaders who praised it for excluding what they consider "poison pill" riders that could harm the environment and make the bill harder to pass.

LABOR-HHS-EDUCATION

The Health and Human Services Department would receive $2.8 billion more in fiscal 2017 than in the previous year, led by a $2 billion boost for the National Institutes of Health.

Despite the increases for HHS, the overall Labor-HHS-Education portion of the omnibus included $161 billion in discretionary funding, a reduction of $934 million from fiscal 2016.

The higher NIH funding — $34 billion for fiscal 2017 — reflected a bipartisan agreement to provide steady increases for biomedical research. The increase mirrored the $2 billion boost in fiscal 2016.

Health-related groups praised Congress for the increase in NIH funds, but the tardy completion of annual appropriations caused extra work and disruptions throughout the federal government and organizations connected to it, including researchers in academic laboratories. NIH, for example, has to routinely give out instructions about how to parcel out grant money under continuing resolutions.

In addition to NIH, another winner in the spending bill was the Centers for Disease Control and Prevention, which would get a $22 million boost, to $7.3 billion. The agency at the center of global efforts to combat infectious killers such as the Zika and Ebola viruses would get $6.3 billion in appropriated funds and $891 million in transfers from the Prevention and Public Health Fund.

The bill also included a provision to make permanent the health benefits for retired coal mine workers. That provision was sought by Senate Majority Leader Mitch McConnell, R-Ky., as well as lawmakers from both parties who represent coal states. The miners' health benefits would be fully offset. Congress had provided a four-month extension of benefits in 2016.

The spending measure did not defund the women's health organization Planned Parenthood, which many conservatives had hoped to do. The package did rescind the budget for a panel created by the 2010 health law (PL 111-148, PL 111-152) to keep Medicare costs in check, taking back $15 million previously designated for the never-formed Independent Payment Advisory Board. Many Democrats have joined Republicans in opposing the concept behind IPAB.

The Education Department was funded at $68 billion in the omnibus, $1.2 billion below what was enacted in fiscal 2016, and the Labor Department was to receive $12.1 billion, an $83 million decrease from fiscal 2016.

The spending bill reauthorized the D.C. Opportunity Scholarship Program, the only federally funded school voucher program, which serves students in D.C. The program has strong Republican support, although most Democrats, including D.C. Del. Eleanor Holmes Norton, oppose the program. The reauthorization refocused the program on helping students at D.C. schools ranked as the lowest performing based on D.C.'s accountability system.

Year-round Pell Grants also were restored after the option was cut from the grant program several years ago, but $1.3 billion would be taken from the grant's surplus fund, which stood at $8.5 billion at the start of fiscal 2017.

The bill allowed borrowers consolidating student loans to choose which federal servicer will handle their loan. They were currently assigned a servicer through the Education Department. In addition, the department would be required to make performance metrics available to borrowers to help them choose their servicer.

The omnibus would slightly increase funding for the Education Department's Office for Civil Rights from the amount provided in fiscal 2016. Funding for K-12 students with disabilities also would see a minor increase from fiscal 2016 funding levels.

For the Labor Department, the bill would provide $88 million for integrating ex-offenders into the workplace and retraining them for high-demand jobs. Funding for apprenticeships also would go up by about 5.5 percent, or by about $5 million.

LEGISLATIVE BRANCH

The Capitol Police and the Library of Congress both got a boost in the $4.4 billion Legislative Branch title of the omnibus bill — $77 million more than fiscal 2016.

The bill provided $632 million for the Library of Congress, $32 million more than the previous year. The extra funds were to be used to upgrade the library's technology infrastructure to support growing storage needs and increased cybersecurity measures.

The omnibus provided about $1.189 billion for House operations, and $871.2 million for Senate operations.

Report language accompanying the bill included a nod to the 2016 controversy in the Legislative Branch bill over language instructing the library to use terms used in Title 8, U.S. Code as subject headings for library searches - including the term "illegal alien" to describe undocumented immigrants. The fiscal 2017 language instead directed the library to make publicly available its process for changing or adding subject headings.

The Capitol Police would see an $18.3 million boost over fiscal 2016, with $393.3 million provided for the force, which provides security for the Capitol as well as protection for top congressional leaders. The additional funds were slated to boost recruiting, training and administrative needs. Once new officers are fully trained, there is expected to be a reduced need for overtime pay.

The report on the bill also included language instructing the Capitol Police to consider the "family-style neighborhood that the Capitol shares with the surrounding community" and to "forebear enforcement" when encountering snow sledders on Capitol Hill.

The Architect of the Capitol's office, which is responsible for maintaining the Capitol complex and its grounds, would receive $617.9 million under the measure - a $5 million increase from the fiscal 2016 enacted level. This included $20.8 million for the rehabilitation of the Rayburn House Office Building garage and $17 million for the revitalization of historic buildings.

Funding also was included for modernization of the 108-year-old Cannon House Office Building. That project was expected to take a decade and cost nearly $800 million, with $62 million provided for fiscal 2017.

The Government Accountability Office, the independent nonpartisan agency that does investigative and oversight work for Congress, would receive $544.5 million. That was a $13.5 million increase over fiscal 2016 levels.

Funding levels for the Congressional Budget Office was set at $46.5 million, a slight increase from $46 million enacted in fiscal 2016.

Two Legislative Branch agencies slated for the same funding levels

as fiscal 2016 were the Government Publishing Office at $117 million and the Open World Leadership Center at $5.6 million.

House food service programs were noted for inconsistent quality, food variety and management, and the explanatory statement on the bill instructed the chief administrative officer to explore the feasibility of bringing more brand-name food service into the Capitol. In April 2016 a Dunkin' Donuts branch opened in the Longworth House Office Building and could pave the way for more branded options for Capitol staff and visitors.

Concerns about Senate restaurants voiced in the report were not about food offerings, but about the treatment of food service workers. In 2016 the Labor Department found that nearly 700 of the workers had been underpaid. Restaurant Associates was found to have improperly classified workers in positions where they would make lower wages. The back pay due exceeded $1 million. The concerns continue, the omnibus report said.

The report directed the Architect of the Capitol to explore any courses of action available under the Senate food services contract to ensure compliance.

On another issue key for visitors, lawmakers and staff at the Capitol complex, the Architect of the Capitol was trying to make cycling safer and easier with the addition of and connection to bike lanes. The report said that a plan, approved by the Senate Committee on Rules and Administration, would provide protected bike lanes to safely connect riders to Pennsylvania Avenue, the National Mall, the U.S. Capitol, Union Station, and the Metropolitan Branch Trail.

STATE-FOREIGN OPERATIONS

Emergency funding to address an unprecedented level of global hunger driven mostly by war and man-made disasters got a nearly $1 billion boost.

The legislation provided $990 million for famine relief to northern Nigeria, Somalia, South Sudan and Yemen. The United Nations in March had declared it was facing the largest humanitarian crisis since its founding in 1945 with roughly 20 million people spread across the four countries at risk of dying from hunger and starvation.

Most of the new famine relief funding fell under the International Disaster Assistance account, which received a total allocation of over $3.8 billion. The legislation continued fiscal 2016 funding support for refugees under the Migration and Refugee Assistance account with nearly $3.1 billion.

The bill provided a total of $53.1 billion in discretionary funding for the State Department, U.S. Agency for International Development and other related development programs. When emergency famine relief is not counted, the bill was $594 million less than fiscal 2016 levels and contained $36.6 billion in enduring costs and $16.5 billion in Overseas Contingency Operations spending.

The foreign aid bill contained almost none of the cuts sought by Trump, who in December had asked Republicans to delay passage of a final spending bill until he had had a chance to weigh in on its priorities.

Amid growing fears in the humanitarian and international development community that the Trump administration is intent on seeking cuts of nearly one-third from the State-Foreign Operations spending bill in fiscal 2018, Senate Democrats struck a defiant tone in their summary of the omnibus.

"The bill reflects a bipartisan recognition that diplomacy and development are indispensable components of U.S. foreign policy and necessary to effectively project U.S. leadership, promote U.S. ideals and safeguard U.S. security and humanitarian interests," read the Democratic summary. "It represents an implicit rejection of the administration's plan to drastically reduce personnel and programs at the State Department and U.S. Agency for International Development."

Spending bills developed in the summer of 2016 by the House and Senate would each have provided roughly $52.2 billion in diplomacy and development funding compared to the $52.8 billion request from the Obama administration.

Israel continued to receive the largest amount by far of military assistance and would get a small increase of $75 million above the level agreed to in the 2016 Memorandum of Understanding between the U.S. and Israel to nearly $3.2 billion. Sen. Lindsey Graham of South Carolina, chairman of the State-Foreign Operations Appropriations Subcommittee, had sought to increase support for Israel by $300 million.

Support for Jordan remained mostly constant at nearly $1.3 billion.

Notably, Congress did not set specific aid amounts for Afghanistan, Pakistan or Iraq, though the appropriations bill did condition assistance to those countries on improvements in governance, human rights and democracy. The Trump administration in its fiscal 2018 budget outline requested to turn an unspecified amount of the Foreign Military Financing grants that most other countries receive — except Israel — into loans.

The omnibus created a new account, the "Counter Russia Influence Fund," and filled it with $100 million in seed money on top of other bilateral assistance. A passion project of Graham's, the "soft power" account is intended to help counter Russia's influence campaigns in European and Eurasian countries.

State Department operations received a total of $11.8 billion, with $3.7 billion of that amount coming from war spending, $500 million more than fiscal 2016 levels. Meanwhile, USAID operations would see a small increase of about $80 million above current levels to $1.4 billion.

Funding for embassy security overseas would get a nearly $455 million increase to $6.1 billion compared to fiscal 2016 to continue implementing the Benghazi Accountability Review Board's recommendations.

The bill limited U.S. funding for U.N. peacekeeping operations at 25 percent of their costs, an objective pushed by Republicans but that is less than the amount assessed by the United Nations. The legislation also contained no funding for the U.N.'s Green Climate Fund.

TRANSPORTATION-HUD

The omnibus retained funding for transportation programs that Trump had sought to eliminate by the next fiscal year, including $500 million for a competitive grant program and a boost for transit grants.

The bill would sustain the Transportation Investment Generating Economic Recovery, or TIGER program, at the $500 million funding level of fiscal 2016. That money would remain available until September 2020. State or local governments may apply for TIGER grants for portions of highways, bridges, transit programs and other surface transportation infrastructure considered significant for the nation, metropolitan area or region. Trump had targeted the program for elimination in his fiscal 2018 budget request.

Trump campaigned on a pledge to rebuild U.S. infrastructure, promising to invest $1 trillion of public and private money in the system. But his request for fiscal 2018 proposed zeroing out or reducing a few transportation funding programs. The spending bill would preserve

Some Spending Exempt From PAYGO

The omnibus contained language that protected federal programs from sequestration, or across-the-board cuts, in two ways.

Mandatory spending that was put into the $1.07 trillion appropriations bill at the request of House and Senate leaders is exempted from both the pay-as-you go law and a Senate pay-as-you-go rule. That meant the mandatory spending for the retired miners' health care program and Medicaid in Puerto Rico would not be added to the PAYGO scorecard administered by the Office of Management and Budget.

Under the PAYGO law (PL 111-139), if new mandatory spending or tax cuts are not offset and add to the deficit, OMB would order across-the-board spending cuts to reduce the deficit.

The bill included offsets for the new mandatory spending in the form of customs user fees for the miners' health care program, and the rescission of an unobligated balance in the 2010 health care law (PL 111-148, PL 111-152) for Medicaid funding in Puerto Rico.

However, the Congressional Budget Office said in an estimate of the cost of the bill that the rescission would not actually offset the increased Medicaid spending because the unobligated balances that would be canceled would have been spent anyway.

Under normal circumstances, the increased mandatory spending would be entered on the PAYGO scorecard and could have led to a sequester to reduce spending if it increased the deficit. But that didn't happen because the spending in the bill is exempt from PAYGO.

The bill also included a provision that allowed discretionary spending to exceed the statutory caps by up to $2.1 billion if the excess spending was due to a difference in estimates between the CBO and OMB. A similar provision was included in the fiscal 2016 omnibus (PL 114-113).

The CBO scored the discretionary spending in the fiscal 2017 omnibus as within the discretionary caps. However, it was possible that OMB would score the spending as higher based on different technical assumptions.

In case that occurred, the bill provided a $2.1 billion cushion by which scored spending could exceed the caps without triggering across-the-board cuts to federal programs. Lawmakers write legislation to a CBO score, but for the purpose of determining whether there will be across-the-board spending cuts, the OMB score is used.

The caps for base discretionary spending in fiscal 2017 were $551 billion for defense and $518.5 billion for nondefense, for a total of $1.07 trillion. That did not include additional spending for Overseas Contingency Operations and emergencies that is outside the constraints of the caps. ∎

them for another year.

The omnibus also included a $236 million increase in fiscal 2017, to $2.4 billion, in the capital investment grants that the Federal Transit Administration may dole out, and it provides $150 million for Essential Air Service subsidies to air carriers serving small communities — both also Trump targets for elimination in fiscal 2018.

Overall, the omnibus boosted Transportation-HUD spending levels to $57.65 billion, about $350 million more than in fiscal 2016. It raised federal highway and transit formula grants to levels consistent with the December 2015 surface transportation reauthorization bill (PL 114-94), to $43.2 billion for federal-aid highways and $9.3 billion for transit.

The agreement provided $154.8 million to make the entire National Airspace System operate under a satellite navigation system called ADS-B that would replace radar. President Obama's request for the program was $31 million for fiscal 2017.

The ADS-B appropriation was part of an investment in the Federal Aviation Administration's NextGen technology overhaul that totalled more than $1 billion in the omnibus.

The agreement also dropped a rider in the House version of the bill that Senate Democrats said would have killed the California high-speed rail project. The measure would have blocked the Federal Railroad Administration from reimbursing the state for costs on the project and prohibited the agency from conducting oversight. Democrats said the provision would have violated the federal government's grant agreement with California.

Senate Democrats said negotiators dropped a policy rider during final talks that would have pre-empted state laws regarding meal and rest breaks for truck drivers. Trucking groups had fought for the provision, which was included in the House Transportation-HUD Appropriations bill. The measure would have undone state laws in California, for example, that require truckers to spend less time working between rest and meal breaks.

For Housing and Urban Development, the omnibus boosted funding by 1 percent, to $38.8 billion. House appropriators had recommended a 1 percent funding increase, while Senate appropriators pushed for a 2 percent hike.

The deal provided $6.3 billion to HUD for operation, construction and maintenance of public housing. The total includes $25 million for housing agencies to address problems arising from lead-based paint.

As Transportation-HUD Appropriations Subcommittee Chairwoman Susan Collins of Maine had pointed out, HUD has a tough budget to cut since 84 percent of it is for rental assistance, and rents tend to increase from year to year.

Nearly $2.4 billion in federal money would be used for homeless assistance grants, including those aiding homeless youth and veterans.

HUD's Choice Neighborhoods program for community revitalization reached its highest funding level ever, $137.5 million. And funding for the Community Development Block Grant program would remain steady at $3 billion. Trump proposed eliminating it in fiscal 2018. ∎

Fiscal 2018 Efforts Slow to Start; CR Punts Final Decisions Past December

House members and senators were slow to pivot from the fiscal 2017 omnibus appropriations bill signed into law on May 5 to fiscal 2018 spending measures that were supposed to be enacted by Oct. 1.

The congressional agenda was dominated by the health care bill that the House had passed and by news about President Donald Trump's firing of FBI Director James Comey and accompanying revelations about the investigations into Russian interference in the 2016 president election.

Budget committees had not begun marking up their budget resolutions and the Appropriations committees were just starting to hold hearings on the spending requests of government agencies, which were months behind schedule. It appeared increasingly impossible that Congress would meet the deadline for enactment of the 12 annual spending bills.

"I'm very concerned. This will be the latest start since I've been here," said Rep. Harold Rogers of Kentucky, a former chairman of the Appropriations Committee who first came to Congress in 1980. "We haven't received the president's budget yet and the Budget Committee is just now beginning to explore things, so there is no timetable."

None of the Appropriations subcommittees had begun marking up their bills, in part because the Budget committees had not set discretionary spending for fiscal 2018. Without that number, referred to as a 302(a), the Appropriations Committee leaders could not tell each of the 12 subcommittees how much money, in 302(b) allocations, they would be allowed to spend in their respective bills.

Trump, in fact, did not send his fiscal 2018 budget request to Capitol Hill until May 23. It did not matter a great deal, though, because when House appropriators began marking up their bills, they mostly ignored the administration's spending levels.

To make up for the delay, which made the normal appropriations process impractical, House Republicans in late May were considering an ambitious plan to assemble and pass a 12-bill appropriations package ahead of the August recess – effectively an "instant omnibus."

The biggest problem, though, was that such a package would stand little chance in the Senate, where the votes of Democrats would be needed to pass it. In a further complication, Congress needed to extend the federal debt limit so the government could continue to borrow.

Senate Majority Leader Mitch McConnell said on June 13 that he hoped to pass appropriations bills using preliminary spending allocations, which confirmed that both chambers intended to move forward on the spending process without a budget resolution.

"We're going to have to, hopefully sooner rather than later, agree with our Democratic colleagues on what the topline is, what we're going to spend on the discretionary accounts this year. They'll be a part of that, because that's not something we can do Republicans only," McConnell said.

His remarks were some of the most explicit from Republican leaders about the need to come to agreement with Democrats on lifting discretionary spending levels outlined in a 2011 deficit reduction law (PL 112-25), which set spending levels considered untenable by Democrats and defense hawks alike. Trump's director of the Office of

Management and Budget, Mick Mulvaney, meanwhile indicated that the administration would be flexible on the budget totals.

SECURITY 'MINIBUS'

The House on July 27 voted 235-192 to pass a nearly $790 billion "minibus" appropriations package for the military, energy programs and water projects, U.S. Capitol operations, veterans benefits and initial construction of a U.S.-Mexico border wall. (A "minibus" is congressional slang for an abbreviated form of omnibus appropriations bill.)

House members voted largely along party lines to pass the legislation (HR 3219). Most Republicans backed the measure, which was heavy on defense spending, and Democrats were broadly opposed to it because it didn't adhere to the existing budget law (PL 112-25) and would have provided $1.57 billion to begin construction of Trump's wall and more.

In addition to the defense appropriations bill, the minibus included fiscal 2018 Energy-Water (HR 3266), Legislative Branch (HR 3163) and Military Construction-VA (HR 2998) bills.

In the Energy-Water section, Republicans mostly turned away Democrats' attempts to boost funding for renewable energy and efficiency research. Debates also broke out over the Yucca Mountain nuclear waste repository and the Obama administration's Waters of the United States rule.

The Legislative Branch portion of the bill added extra funds for members of Congress to protect themselves, staffers and the Capitol complex. An amendment by Rep. Mia Love, R-Utah, would have allowed members to spend those funds on home security systems.

In the end, though, the Senate didn't even consider the House bill.

As the House Appropriations Committee marked up individual spending bills during the summer, for the most part it ignored the Trump administration's budget request. The five bills released by June 27 proposed spending levels about $26.7 billion more than the White House had requested, sending a clear signal that a GOP Congress would continue to determine spending levels and policy, not a GOP White House.

HOUSE OMNIBUS

The House passed an omnibus appropriations bill for fiscal 2018 on Sept. 14 after two weeks of debate but little prospect of action in the Senate.

The legislation began as an eight-bill consolidated appropriations package that included the Agriculture (HR 3268), Commerce-Justice-Science (HR 3267), Financial Services (HR 3280), Homeland Security (HR 3355), Interior-Environment (HR 3354), Labor-HHS-Education (HR 3358), State-Foreign Operations (HR 3362) and Transportation-HUD (HR 3353) spending bills. It turned into a 12-bill omnibus when the House approved a rule (H Res 500) that rolled the text of the four previously passed spending bills — Defense (HR 3219), Energy-Water (HR 3266), Legislative Branch (HR 3162) and Military Construction-VA (HR 2998) — into the package.

Once again, though, there was scant prospect of action in the Senate,

where Democrats objected to the bill's funding levels and policy riders, and had the votes to block it. The bill violated spending caps in a 2011 budget law (PL 112-25) and, were it to become law, would have triggered the across-the-board spending cuts of sequestration.

The $1.23 trillion omnibus, passed 211-198, would appropriate $621.5 billion for defense and $511 billion for nondefense discretionary programs, including $1.57 billion for President Trump's border wall, despite Trump's campaign pledge that Mexico would foot the bill for the wall. The vote split the parties, with 210 Republicans voting for the package, joined by one Democrat, Collin C. Peterson of Minnesota. Fourteen Republicans, most of them adamant deficit hawks, joined 184 Democrats in opposition.

During the two weeks of floor debate, lawmakers considered 342 amendments on issues ranging from immigration policy to environmental protection to financial regulation.

House Speaker Paul D. Ryan claimed victory, saying it was the first time since 2009 the House had passed all 12 of its spending bills before the start of the fiscal year. "This is a big day in the House of Representatives," he said during a press conference, flanked by Republican appropriators. "We achieved conservative victories for the president's agenda and for our agenda."

Ryan noted though that there was still "a lot of work to do" before Congress enacted a spending bill into law, which would prove to be an understatement.

The panel's ranking Democrat, Nita M. Lowey of New York, sharply criticized the passage of the bill as "inadequate and partisan" and encouraged congressional leaders and the White House to begin working toward a bipartisan agreement on fiscal 2018 spending levels. That would be elusive.

CONTINUING IRRESOLUTION

With little prospect of agreement on an omnibus appropriations bill for fiscal 2018 and time running out in the fiscal year, the House and Senate in early September agreed on a continuing resolution until Dec. 8, which was packaged with a debt limit increase and emergency aid for areas of Texas devastated by Hurricane Harvey in late August.

The $7.85 billion in Hurricane Harvey aid (HR 601) passed the House, 419-3, on Sept. 6.

House Democrats and Republicans supported the stand-alone Harvey aid bill. The House vote was on a resolution to concur in Senate amendments to a House bill (HR 601). Through agreeing to the resolution, the House further amended the bill to insert the text of its own aid bill (HR 3672). This would allow the package to move more quickly in the Senate.

Reps. Justin Amash, R-Mich.; Andy Biggs, R-Ariz.; and Thomas Massie, R-Ky., voted no.

House Appropriations Chairman Rodney Frelinghuysen, R-N.J., and the panel's top Democrat, Nita M. Lowey of New York, both expressed support for the funding bill, which provided $7.4 billion for FEMA's Disaster Relief Fund and $450 million for the Small Business Administration's disaster loan program.

The following day, Sept. 7, the Senate voted 80-17 to pass $15.25 billion in emergency spending for hurricane relief as well as a debt limit suspension and a stopgap spending bill lasting through Dec. 8.

Sen. Rand Paul, R-Ky., proposed an amendment to the legislation that would have paid for the $15.25 billion hurricane aid bill by pulling funds from selected foreign aid accounts. Sen. Ben Sasse, R-Neb., proposed an amendment that would have removed the CR and debt limit

suspension language, returning the package to a stand-alone hurricane relief bill. Neither amendment was adopted.

Despite the concerns, Senate Majority Leader Mitch McConnell and Senate Democratic Leader Charles E. Schumer had urged the bill's passage ahead of the final vote.

"This is a good agreement for the American people and everyone should breathe a sigh of relief," Schumer said. "This agreement takes the threat of a shutdown and default off the table this month and will help us quickly get resources to FEMA and other agencies that are helping with rescue and recovery in the wake of Harvey and will in all likelihood be needed in the wake of Irma as well."

McConnell said the legislative package provided "certainty and stability for first responders, state officials and the many others involved in preparing for and recovering from these storms."

The Senate added another provision to the disaster aid bill, an extension of the National Flood Insurance Program past its Sept. 30 expiration date. The program insures more than 5 million U.S. homes and businesses. The proposal for a short-term extension through early December, overlapping with the three-month continuing resolution, came a day after House Financial Services Chairman Jeb Hensarling said he planned to attach a 3-month extension to an insurance regulation bill (HR 1422).

The real estate industry and local governments had warned that if Congress failed to reauthorize the flood insurance program, created in 1968, it would harm both real estate sales and the housing construction industry.

FINAL ACTION

The House cleared the multi-purpose bill and CR on Sept. 8 on a 316-90 vote, though some Republicans had announced their opposition to the broad measure and voted against it.

"While some have advocated for a 'clean' debt limit increase, this would simply increase the borrowing authority of the government while irresponsibly ignoring the urgency of reforms," Rep. Mark Walker of North Carolina, chairman of the Republican Study Committee wrote. "Worse yet is attaching the debt limit to legislation that continues the status quo or even worsens the trajectory on spending, such as the deal announced yesterday by the President and Congressional Leadership. The RSC Steering Committee opposes this proposal."

MORE DISASTER AID

The Senate on Oct. 26 voted 82-17 to clear a supplemental appropriations bill with $36.5 billion for areas damaged by hurricanes. It was the second such disaster aid package since late August when the first of three hurricanes began wreaking havoc throughout Gulf Coast states, the U.S. Virgin Islands and Puerto Rico. When combined with the first supplemental spending bill (PL 115-56), which appropriated $15.25 billion, the federal government had appropriated $51.75 billion in emergency spending to assist with hurricane and wildfire recovery.

The bill (HR 2266) provided $18.67 billion for FEMA's Disaster Relief Fund, $16 billion in debt forgiveness for the National Flood Insurance Program, $1.27 billion in supplemental nutrition assistance funds for low-income Puerto Rico residents and $576.5 million for wildfire suppression.

Prior to the vote on final passage, the Senate voted 80-19 to waive a point of order raised by Rand Paul, R-Ky., seeking to strike the bill's emergency designation that allowed money to be provided without regard to statutory spending limits.

Senate Minority Leader Charles E. Schumer, D-N.Y., supported the package, but expressed concern that the U.S. Forest Service had to borrow money from other accounts to fund wildfire suppression operations.

"Fire borrowing prevents the agency from carrying out its other missions, including investing in forest fire prevention," Schumer said. "We must take action and provide the Forest Service with long-term wildfire funding fix."

Sen. Patty Murray, D-Wash., urged her colleagues to use this experience to "fix the flawed way this country fights wildfires."

"For far too long the U.S. Forest Service has been forced to use up its budget fighting wildfires every season, only to have no funds left over to work on preventing them," Murray said. "This is a very dangerous cycle and a disservice to so many communities in the West."

Sen. Bill Nelson, D-Fla., expressed concerns about FEMA's ability to process claims, inspect homes and provide mobile homes. During a floor speech, Nelson said that Floridians had experienced lengthy wait times when calling FEMA representatives, a 45-day wait time to have FEMA representatives inspect damaged homes and a lack of enough temporary mobile homes.

"People are suffering and people are hurting and the red tape should not stop anyone in this country from having a safe place to live," Nelson said.

CONTINUING CONFLICT

Congress and the administration made little headway during the autumn months on resolving differences on appropriations, and on Dec. 7, with just one day before the government would have to shut down, lawmakers cleared a two-week continuing resolution to keep things running until Dec. 22.

Trump and congressional leaders appeared no closer to agreement on spending levels or a fiscal 2018 omnibus bill. Ryan said no decisions had been made about how to fund the government after Dec. 22, and conceded that a third continuing resolution would be needed.

"In order to write an omnibus appropriation — that takes weeks to do. And you want to do it right. And you want to do it thoroughly. And that means we have to give the Appropriations Committee enough time to do that. And right now, they don't have that kind of time," Ryan said.

The House passed the two-week stopgap on a 235-193 vote with 18 Republicans voting "no" and 14 Democrats supporting it. About 90 minutes later, the Senate voted 81-14 to pass the legislation, with six Republicans, seven Democrats and one independent — Bernie Sanders of Vermont — voting against the CR.

House debate on the CR (H J Res 123) largely centered around Democratic frustrations that there wasn't a spending agreement yet and Republicans begrudgingly supporting the stopgap bill.

"This resolution is our best and only option at this time," Frelinghuysen said. "Congress must do its job and pass a continuing resolution. And then another one into the new year to keep the government open."

Lowey, the top Democrat on House Appropriations, sharply criticized Republicans for passing a two-week stopgap when neither fiscal 2018 spending levels nor an omnibus could be agreed on in that amount of time.

"The rationale to support a short-term, stopgap continuing resolution is that the parties are engaged in good-faith negotiations to develop a responsible, bipartisan spending package," she said. "Can anyone in this chamber claim that this is the case today?"

Following the House vote, the Senate debated the legislation for about 15 minutes before voting to send the bill to the president's desk.

The top Democrat on the Senate Appropriations Committee, Patrick J. Leahy, of Vermont, was the only senator to speak on the measure during that time. Leahy reiterated his party leadership's demands for a budget deal that provided equal relief from austere statutory defense and nondefense spending caps.

"The continuing resolution before us today allows us more time to reach a bipartisan agreement and keep the government's lights on during negotiations," he said. "I will be joining the distinguished leader in voting for this, but the key to successful negotiations during that time is parity."

House Minority Leader Nancy Pelosi, D-Calif., indicated before votes were cast that her troops were prepared to vote against the interim CR, even while telling reporters that "Democrats have never been in support of shutting down the government and we don't plan on doing so now."

Pelosi maintained that her party's budget priorities, beyond the temporary fix for the Children's Health Insurance Program included in the two-week bill, needed to be addressed.

Among the other items Pelosi mentioned: funding to combat the opioid epidemic and for community health centers, emergency disaster aid, veterans health care and "saving endangered pensions." She also made another pitch for "parity" for defense and nondefense appropriations, or equal funding increases for fiscal 2018 on both sides of the discretionary ledger.

In addition, Pelosi said "we will not leave here" for the Christmas holiday without a fix for young undocumented immigrants enrolled in the Deferred Action for Childhood Arrivals program.

SUPPLEMENTAL AND CR

The House passed an $81 billion disaster supplemental spending bill on Dec. 21 — the third of the year — the same day it passed a continuing resolution to keep the government running through Jan. 19.

House members voted 251-169 for the disaster aid bill after a coalition of Republicans and Democrats from areas hit by one of the worst hurricane seasons on record and wildfires in California pulled the bill across the finish line, despite a Democratic whip effort against the measure due to objections regarding the legislation's treatment of Puerto Rico and the U.S. Virgin Islands, among other issues.

Democrats in the Senate had indicated that the bill would be dead on arrival when Senate Minority Leader Charles E. Schumer, D-N.Y., torpedoed the Republican-written legislation (HR 4667) in floor remarks, calling it "an unacceptable disaster supplemental, which still does not treat fairly California, Puerto Rico and the U.S. Virgin Islands."

Schumer criticized Republicans for not including additional funds for Medicaid, drinking water and infrastructure. He also was critical of the bill for not extending the earned-income tax credit for Puerto Rico.

"Those things must be fixed before a disaster supplemental can move forward," Schumer said. "Because of these inadequacies, the disaster supplemental may have to slip to next year."

During House debate, Rep. José E. Serrano, D-N.Y., said he would oppose the measure since it would give Puerto Rico's oversight board authority over the island territory's disaster recovery plan. Serrano also called for more support for New York and New Jersey, where he said many hurricane victims had flocked for shelter in the wake of the disaster.

In contrast, Rep. Mike Thompson, D-Calif., called the funding pack-

age an "important first step" in a long-term recovery from wildfires that decimated communities in his district.

The bulk of the House's aid package, nearly $54 billion, was split between the Federal Emergency Management Agency's Disaster Relief Fund and Community Development Block Grants administered by the Department of Housing and Urban Development.

The U.S. Army Corps of Engineers would receive $12 billion for repairs to existing projects and flood mitigation studies to try to prevent future damages. The measure also included nearly $3 billion for the Department of Education to help students displaced by the storms, and $2.6 billion for agricultural assistance, including Florida citrus growers who saw crops wiped out.

In all, the measure, combined with already-appropriated funds for hurricane and wildfire relief, would bring total emergency disaster appropriations since September to $133 billion.

The House modified the package slightly with two Republican amendments that gave tax benefits for disaster-afflicted individuals in California and Louisiana as well as another tax provision that would designate Puerto Rico low-income communities as "opportunity zones," making them eligible for a new benefit contained in the comprehensive tax overhaul measure (HR 1).

The Senate did not take up the House's disaster supplemental, however, and it was left behind at year's end.

The supplemental would also modify the federal government's system of preparing for and responding to natural disasters, with a focus on improving pre-disaster planning and mitigation. The disaster funding is designated as emergency funding and is not offset.

After days of wrangling votes and changing plans, the Senate voted 66-32 on Dec. 21 to clear a continuing resolution (HR 1370) that would fund the government through Jan. 19, provide funding for the Children's Health Insurance Program and community health centers through March 31, appropriate $2.1 billion for a private care access pro-

gram for veterans and temporarily extend Section 702 of the Foreign Intelligence Surveillance Act until Jan. 19.

Senate action came just hours after the House voted, 231-188, to pass the measure. Trump signed it the next day.

Two major defense add-ons were also included in the CR: $4 billion for missile defense, including the construction of a missile field in Alaska, and $700 million for Navy ship repairs, each designated as emergency spending to get around budget caps. The stopgap included other "anomalies" — increased funding for certain priorities — related to Coast Guard continuation pay, the Indian Health Service, undocumented immigrants and preparations for a potential influenza pandemic.

The measure also delayed the onset of sequestration for defense and nondefense accounts, since current funding levels were $3 billion and $2 billion over their respective statutory spending caps for fiscal 2018.

For all of the drama about conservatives' objections to the bill, House Republicans were able to muster enough support from their own side for the spending package to send it to the Senate — with 16 GOP members voting "no" and 14 Democrats voting to support the package.

Congressional leaders and the White House still needed to negotiate new fiscal 2018 spending levels to avoid a reduction in discretionary spending, due to the Budget Control Act of 2011 (PL 112-25). Without those numbers, the Appropriations Committee could not write its 12 spending bills and the government would need to either operate under a temporary spending bill or shut down.

In the Senate, there was broad bipartisan support for the stopgap bill, despite Schumer's skepticism and Sen. Rand Paul's objection to including a waiver of "paygo" rules in the stopgap.

In the end, concerns about the deficit and Democrats' concerns about punting numerous legislative issues into 2018 were not enough to prevent the spending bill from passing Congress. ■

Appropriations Bills Left Behind

A late start, an array of other issues and bitter partisanship left the House and Senate Appropriations committees holding hearings and drafting fiscal 2018 bills in the summer when they should've been wrapping things up.

As a result, most of the bills were left by the roadside as Congress drove to pass a continuing resolution that would keep the government funded until mid-January 2018.

Following is a summary of the work done on individual appropriations bills.

AGRICULTURE

E-Cigarette Language a Point of Contention

HOUSE SUBCOMMITTEE

The House Agriculture Appropriations Subcommittee reported out its fiscal 2018 draft bill on June 28, with Democrats lamenting the $20 billion discretionary allocation but relieved that the draft measure rejected most of the Trump administration's budget request for deep cuts or elimination of programs.

Subcommittee ranking member Sanford D. Bishop Jr. and Nita M. Lowey, ranking member on the full House Appropriations Committee, said the subcommittee bill tried to strike a balance. But they used the markup to press Republicans to negotiate with Democrats for a budget that would establish a topline spending number and allow the Appropriations Committee to set overall allocations for subcommittees that might provide additional funding.

"Marking up just one bill at a time without a full list of allocations leaves us effectively working in the dark," said Bishop, D-Ga. "This operational strategy results in an inequitable distribution of funds between defense and nondefense-related accounts."

"Let's cut the charade," added Lowey, D-N.Y.

The panel by voice vote sent the draft bill to the full House Appropriations Committee. The spending bill would provide funding for the Agriculture Department, excluding the Forest Service, the Food and Drug Administration, the Commodity Futures Trading Commission and the Farm Credit Administration.

Under the bill, the FDA would receive a total of $5.1 billion that included $2.75 billion in discretionary funding. The taxpayer funding would be about the same level as in fiscal 2017 but funding from fees would increase by $400 million. The Commodity Futures Trading Commission would receive $248 million, $2 million less than its fiscal 2017 enacted level.

Members offered no amendments during the markup.

"I know you've not been working in the dark. One thing we know is that you've been working together," said Appropriations Chairman Rodney Frelinghuysen, R-N.J., alluding to Bishop's comments about the fiscal 2018 appropriations process.

Subcommittee Chairman Robert B. Aderholt, R-Ala., added he did the best he could with a discretionary spending allocation that was $876 million less than the fiscal 2017 enacted level. The bill also would provide approximately $124 billion in mandatory funding, down from $132.5 billion in fiscal 2017.

Bishop noted that the bill would continue several rural development programs President Donald Trump's fiscal 2018 budget recommended be ended or for which funding be sharply reduced.

Trump's budget proposal led farm groups to question his commitment to rural voters. Adding to the anxiety was a planned reorganization of the Agriculture Department that eliminated the rural development undersecretary's post and moved the agency's missions to USDA Secretary Sonny Perdue's office.

"A major area of bipartisanship is reflected in the fact we did not abandon America's rural communities as proposed in the White House budget request," Bishop said.

Bishop also noted that the bill would keep a school kitchen grant program the Trump administration wanted ended. It would provide money for school cafeterias that need refrigerators, ovens or other equipment to make school lunches that meet federal nutrition standards.

E-Cigarettes

The bill also contained several policy riders, including language to revise the FDA's policies on the regulation of e-cigarettes and other nicotine vapor products, a priority of senior Appropriations Committee member Tom Cole, R-Okla. The bill would allow e-cigarette products currently on the market to be grandfathered in before more stringent regulations take effect over the next few years. The bill would also roll back the FDA's regulation of premium cigars.

Lowey promised to fight the provision at the full committee level, saying the "tobacco language in this bill is a Trojan horse. I urge my colleagues to listen to the science and not fall for this cynical attempt at deregulating tobacco products."

Aderholt and Bishop said they supported the e-cigarette provision because it would protect smaller companies already selling into the market from costly FDA review.

"We want to make sure we protect kids and we are not trying to entice children to get e-cigarettes," Aderholt said. "But at the same time if someone can legally smoke, then certainly it's a great alternative to what's out there now."

The draft bill called for:

· $1.1 billion for the Agricultural Research Service, about $100 million less than fiscal 2017 but $139 million more than the president's budget request.

· $122.7 million for a new rural economic infrastructure grants program intended to consolidate several existing programs.

· $25 million for school kitchen equipment grants, which is less than the $35 million provided in fiscal 2017.

· $1.25 billion for the rural waste and waste water program, the same level as the fiscal 2017 enacted level.

· A $6 million bump in funding for the Food Safety and Inspection Service, which is responsible for overseeing the nation's meat and

poultry slaughter facilities, compared to fiscal 2017. The total for fiscal 2018 would be $1.038 billion.

• $1.6 billion for the Farm Service Agency and farm-related programs in fiscal 2018, $44 million above the president's request, the committee said. The draft bill also included a policy rider prohibiting USDA from closing county Farm Service Agency offices.

• $906 million for the Animal Plant and Health Inspection Service, $96 million more than the president's request but $40 million below the fiscal 2017 enacted level.

• $6.15 billion in discretionary funding for the Women, Infants and Children supplemental nutrition program, the same level as the president's request. The funding was $200 million below the fiscal 2017 enacted level, but a committee release said the lower number reflected an enrollment decline.

• $73.6 billion for the Supplemental Nutrition Assistance Program, which receives mandatory funding, in fiscal 2018. The spending level would be $4.9 billion below fiscal 2017 and $2.6 million below the president's fiscal 2018 request. The committee said the funding would provide benefits for 42 million people projected to participate in SNAP in fiscal 2018, down nearly an estimated 1 million participants from fiscal 2017.

HOUSE COMMITTEE

House appropriators on July 12 approved the fiscal 2018 Agriculture spending bill on a voice vote, but rejected a continuation of the federal ban on horse slaughter, sparred over e-cigarettes and proposed boosting funding for an international school food program.

Overall, the bill would provide $20 billion in discretionary funding for the Agriculture Department, Food and Drug Administration and the Commodity Futures Trading Commission. Money for the U.S. Forest Service, which is part of USDA, is handled by the Interior-Environment Appropriations Subcommittee.

With mandatory spending combined, the bill was $144.9 billion. That was $4.1 billion above the president's request and $8.6 billion below the fiscal 2017 enacted level (PL 115-31).

The full House Appropriations Committee voted out the bill after adopting a manager's package that included changes to the measure as well as accompanying report language. For example, the package increased proposed funding — from $185 million to $201.6 million — for the McGovern-Dole International Food for Education and Child Nutrition program that uses school meals to encourage families in developing nations to send their children to school for an education. The spending would be the same level as enacted for fiscal 2017.

The package also added language to the bill that could hamper the Agriculture Department from finalizing a rule to allow Chinese cooked chicken to be imported into the United States. The rule was an element of the Trump administration's 100-day trade plan with China that included benefits for both countries.

The language would deny funding for carrying out the rule unless USDA's Food Safety and Inspection Service can "ensure that the poultry slaughter inspection system for the PRC (People's Republic of China) is equivalent to that of the U.S." It also included a prohibition on federal nutrition programs buying raw or cooked Chinese chicken and sets out requirements China will have to meet to export cooked chicken to the United States.

The panel approved just two other amendments, both by voice vote: One by Rep. Steve Womack, R-Ark., would put into law sections of a House-passed bill (HR 238) that would require the Commodity Futures Trading Commission to include 12 elements in all cost benefit analysis of its regulations or orders and exempt a company's inter-affiliate transactions from being regulated as swaps.

The second amendment, by Rep. Dan Newhouse, R-Wash., changed bill and report language to make legal foreign workers, primarily temporary agricultural workers brought in through the H-2A visa program, eligible for farm-worker housing currently limited to Americans. Newhouse said the language acknowledges that the pool of U.S. agricultural workers is shrinking and that more farmers are using the H-2A program. New report language said the change in eligibility would apply to housing units currently unoccupied or underutilized.

FDA and E-Cigarettes

The FDA would receive nearly $5.2 billion that included $2.75 billion in discretionary funding. The taxpayer funding is about the same level as in fiscal 2017 but funding from fees would increase by $400 million. The Commodity Futures Trading Commission would receive $248 million, $2 million less than its fiscal 2017 enacted level.

Rep. Robert B. Aderholt, R-Ala., chairman of the Agriculture Subcommittee, and Sanford D. Bishop, Jr., D-Ga., the subcommittee's ranking member, opened the markup noting that they had worked together to produce a bill with bipartisan support despite a lean spending allocation.

The cordial tone did not stop a lengthy debate over an amendment by Rep. Nita M. Lowey of New York, the House Appropriations ranking Democrat, to remove bill language that would allow e-cigarette products currently on the market to be grandfathered in before more stringent regulations take effect over the next few years.

Lowey and others argued that the language would put the FDA permanently behind in trying to regulate e-cigarettes, which she argued are not proven to be safer than conventional cigarettes and which may contain toxic chemicals in addition to nicotine. Teens, she said, may be enticed to smoke e-cigarettes because several companies offer their products in candy-like sweet flavors.

"The FDA would never be able to put the genie back in the bottle," she said.

Rep. Andy Harris, a physician, said no one was arguing that smoking is healthy.

"Smoking is bad," Harris, R-Md., said. However, he cited studies showing e-cigarettes helped conventional smokers cut back on their habit. Others argued that big tobacco companies would be only too happy to have smaller e-cigarettes companies driven out of the market because of the cost of complying with FDA oversight.

The committee rejected Lowey's amendment on a 22-30 vote.

Another long debate ensued over a bipartisan amendment offered by Rep. Lucille Roybal-Allard, D-Calif., to continue a prohibition on the Agriculture Department using funding to put inspectors in slaughter facilities to check horses for disease and drugs before they are slaughtered. The last U.S. processing plant that slaughtered horses to sell overseas for human consumption closed in 2007, but Aderholt noted that 100,000 U.S. horses are sent to either Canada or Mexico for slaughter.

There the slaughter occurs out of the U.S. public view and without the humane standards applied in the United States, he said. Reps. Mark Amodei, R-Nev., and Tom Cole, R-Okla., said alternatives such as horse adoption have not kept up with the wild and domestic horse

populations in their states. Cole said many people may want to adopt a horse, but the cost of feeding and housing one discourages potential adopters.

Roybal-Allard argued that in the United States, horses are treated as companion animals and that slaughtering them for sale as meat overseas was something the American public would not accept.

In a close 25-27 vote, the committee rejected the amendment.

SENATE SUBCOMMITTEE

A Senate appropriations subcommittee quickly voted out a draft fiscal 2018 Agriculture spending bill on July 18, a measure both Republicans and Democrats said reflected their efforts to protect important programs such as farm service offices.

The spending measure rejected the deep cuts requested by President Donald Trump in his fiscal 2018 budget proposal.

Chairman John Hoeven, R-N.D., said he tried to be judicious in spending reductions to maintain the 2014 farm bill (PL 113-79) program priorities and set up a framework for an updated farm bill expected in 2018.

"Although the administration wanted to slash vital housing loan and grant programs, sanitary waste and water programs and rural business programs, this bill rejects those proposals," echoed ranking member Jeff Merkley, D-Ore. "The bill rejects administration proposals to cut hundreds of millions of dollars in conservation assistance that is vital to our farmers to protect the land that they and we rely on."

By voice vote, the Agriculture Appropriations Subcommittee sent the spending measure to the full Appropriations Committee for markup. No amendments were offered.

The draft measure would provide $20.5 billion discretionary funding for the Food and Drug Administration and the Agriculture Department, excluding the U.S. Forest Service, which is funded by the Senate Interior-Environment Appropriations Subcommittee, according to a committee summary. The discretionary funding would be $352 million less than the fiscal 2017 enacted level (PL 115-31).

The bill also would provide $124.9 billion in mandatory funding. The Senate allocation is about $400 million higher than the $20.1 billion in discretionary funding reflected in the House Agriculture spending bill (HR 3268).

After the markup, Hoeven said a manager's package he would offer would reject Agriculture Secretary Sonny Perdue's department reorganization that eliminated the rural development undersecretary post and moved rural development programs under his office to be overseen by an assistant secretary. The shift raised concerns among rural advocates and farm-state lawmakers that rural economic development and related issues were being downgraded in importance.

Hoeven said the provision had bipartisan support because "there is a strong feeling in the committee that we'd like that position in place as part of our emphasis on rural development."

FDA

Under the bill, the Senate would provide the FDA with $1 million in extra discretionary funding compared to House appropriators, with about $2.8 billion. Combined with an expected increase of industry fees, the total FDA budget for fiscal 2018 would be about $5.2 billion, around a $500 million increase over the 2017 enacted levels. That increase would be mostly due to the increased industry fees Congress was in the midst of passing in separate legislation (HR 2430).

Senate appropriators, however, joined with the House in rejecting the administration proposal to further increase industry fees by $1 billion while cutting the discretionary contribution by the same amount.

Unlike the House Agriculture spending bill, the Senate version does not provide funding for the Commodity Futures Trading Commission. In the Senate, the Financial Services Appropriations Subcommittee is responsible for CFTC funding.

The Senate bill, according to the committee, would provide:

· $2.55 billion for the Agricultural Research Service and National Institute of Food and Agriculture. The Agriculture and Food Research Initiative would receive $375 million. Like the House bill, the Senate bill would bar closure of research facilities and would reject a proposal by the Trump administration to close 17 research facilities.

· $1.25 billion for the rural waste and waste water program, the same level as the fiscal 2017 enacted level.

· $1.038 billion for the Food Safety and Inspection Service, which is responsible for overseeing the nation's meat and poultry slaughter facilities.

· $1.5 billion for the Farm Service Agency and farm-related programs in fiscal 2018. The Senate bill, like the House version, also included a rider that would prohibit the USDA from closing county Farm Service Agency offices.

· $953.2 million for the Animal Plant and Health Inspection Service $143.2 million above the president's request and $7 million above the fiscal 2017 enacted level.

· $24 billion in loan authority for the rural single family housing guaranteed loan program, including $1 billion for the direct loan program that provides home loan aid to low-income rural families.

· $6.35 billion in discretionary funding for the Women, Infants and Children supplemental nutrition program, the same level as the president's request. The request reflected expected participation, which was projected to decline.

· $73.6 billion for the Supplemental Nutrition Assistance Program, which receives mandatory funding, in fiscal 2018. The committee said the funding would provide benefits for 42 million people projected to participate in SNAP in fiscal 2018, down nearly an estimated 1 million participants from fiscal 2017.

· $1.6 billion for the Title II Food for Peace humanitarian food aid program and $206.6 million for the McGovern-Dole International Food for Education and Child Nutrition program; the administration had proposed ending both.

SENATE COMMITTEE

Appropriators sent the fiscal 2018 Agriculture spending bill (S 1603) to the full Senate after adding a ban on funding for USDA to inspect horses slated for meat slaughter and preventing the commercial sale of genetically engineered salmon.

The horse slaughter amendment by Sen. Tom Udall, D-N.M., and genetically engineered labeling amendment by Sen. Lisa Murkowski, R-Alaska, were expected and have been included in Agriculture spending bills in prior fiscal years.

The committee adopted both amendments by voice votes. The panel also approved a manager's package that included bill and report language to retain the post of undersecretary for rural development within the USDA. Agriculture Secretary Sonny Perdue's department reorganization was to eliminate the title and move rural development to Perdue's office to be overseen by an assistant secretary.

Overall, of the five amendments offered, three were adopted, one was rejected and one was withdrawn.

The Senate Appropriations Committee voted 31-0 to report out the bill as amended. The spending measure would provide $20.5 billion in discretionary funding and $124.9 billion in mandatory funding to the Agriculture Department and the Food and Drug Administration. The bill's discretionary level was $352 million below the fiscal 2017 level (PL 115-31) and the bill's overall funding was $7.9 billion below the fiscal 2017 enacted amount.

FDA

Under the bill, the Senate would provide the FDA with $1 million in extra discretionary funding compared to House appropriators, with about $2.8 billion. Combined with an expected increase of industry fees of around $2.4 billion, the total FDA budget for fiscal 2018 would be about $5.2 billion, an approximately $500 million increase over the 2017 enacted levels. That increase was mostly due to the increased industry fees.

The Agriculture bill would make cotton farmers eligible for aid under the Price Loss Coverage program in the 2014 farm bill (PL 113-79) by classifying cotton seed as "other oilseed," which is covered by the price loss program. Perdue like his predecessor Tom Vilsack said department lawyers did not think he had the authority to make the reclassification.

Cotton growers complained to sympathetic lawmakers that the farm bill program specifically designed for the cotton industry had proven to be an inadequate financial safety net for long periods of low market prices.

Generally, Senate appropriators said Agriculture Subcommittee Chairman John Hoeven, R-N.D., and ranking member Jeff Merkley, D-Ore., struck a balance despite a funding allocation lower than fiscal 2018. However, Merkley offered an amendment to set a higher funding level in the event congressional Republicans and Democrats reached a deal to replace 2011 spending caps.

The Merkley amendment, rejected by a 15-16 party-line vote, would have added $1.7 billion to the bill.

Cigars

The ongoing tug-of-war over the tobacco-related products subject to a comprehensive FDA review played out during the committee markup.

Sen. Marco Rubio, R-Fla., said that he would push for language that would exempt premium cigars from FDA regulation. Rubio acknowledged that he did not have the votes on the committee for his proposal and said he looked forward to the time when the House and Senate would get together to negotiate their differences. He had the support of Sen. Joe Manchin III, D-W.Va.

"There is no appropriate public health justification to exclude premium cigars from the same regulation as cigarettes," said Sen. Richard J. Durbin of Illinois, the Democratic whip.

Rubio and Manchin argued that the language would only apply to high-quality, hand-rolled cigars. But Durbin argued that it would exempt products also sought by teens. "This definition of premium cigars is not as it has been portrayed. It is a danger to public health," he said.

Udall's horse slaughter ban and Murkowski's genetically engineered salmon amendment generated less discussion.

Udall said slaughtering horses to provide meat for overseas markets clashed with American's views of horses as companion animals. House appropriator Rep. Lucille Roybal-Allard, D-Calif., offered a similar amendment during the July 12 markup of the House Agriculture spending bill, but it was rejected by the House Appropriations Committee by a voice vote.

However, there was bipartisan support to continue a prohibition on the Agriculture Department using funding to put inspectors in horse slaughter facilities, a requirement for plants to operate if they produce meat for human consumption. The last U.S. processing plant that slaughtered horses to sell overseas for human consumption closed in 2007.

Murkowski was successful for a third year running in winning committee support to block the import and sales of genetically engineered salmon, which the FDA approved for human consumption in 2015. The FDA did not require labeling of the fish to identify them as genetically modified products, but Murkowski wanted them labeled. Her amendment would continue an appropriations rider that would prevent the sale for the rest of the fiscal year, or until the FDA puts a labeling requirement in place.

The Alaska congressional delegation was fighting to keep genetically engineered salmon out of the marketplace, arguing that the fast-growing fish could escape into the wild, overwhelm native salmon populations and undermine the state's commercial salmon industry. ∎

COMMERCE-JUSTICE-SCIENCE

House Cardinal Presses NASA Funding

HOUSE SUBCOMMITTEE

House appropriators on June 29 quickly advanced a fiscal 2018 Commerce-Justice-Science spending bill that would provide $54 billion in discretionary funding, including funds to combat terrorism and boost space exploration.

The House Appropriations Commerce-Justice-Science Subcommittee approved the measure on a voice vote and without amendments, saving a broader debate for full committee.

The spending bill, which covers the Justice and Commerce departments and scientific research, among other programs, would provide $2.6 billion less than fiscal 2017 funding (PL 115-31) but $4.8 billion more than President Donald Trump asked for in his budget request, according to the committee.

Democrats expressed concerns about the overall funding level and where cuts were made, including police grant programs, legal representation for the poor and earth sciences.

Subcommittee Chairman John Culberson, R-Texas, said he hoped some of those concerns could be addressed after adoption of a budget resolution and if the subcommittee got a bigger allocation.

"We're counting on a bigger overall budget deal that hopefully will give us a little more room to take care of some of these important things," Culberson said. "But right now, get us out of subcommittee and get us moving down the road. We'll work together."

The measure would provide $29 billion for the Justice Department, the largest component of the bill, as well as $19.9 billion for NASA and $8.3 billion for the Department of Commerce, according to a House summary of the bill.

Culberson highlighted increases of $92 million for the FBI for national security, $65 million for immigration judges for an "intolerable" backlog in cases and $218 million for NASA.

"NASA has had far too much on its plate for too long, and too little funding," Culberson said. "And I'm determined to see that turned around and take NASA above and beyond the glory days of Apollo."

Rep. Jose E. Serrano of New York, the top Democrat on the subcommittee, pointed out that the spending bill "rejects some of the Trump administration's worst proposals," such as cuts to the National Science Foundation and the Minority Business Development Agency.

But Serrano listed a number of concerns with the overall funding level, spending at some agencies and some policy riders.

Among his concerns: an $85 million cut to the Legal Services Corporation for civil legal representation for the poor, a 19 percent cut to National Oceanic and Atmospheric Administration climate research, a $217 million cut to NASA's Earth science program and the elimination of Justice Department grant programs for hiring police and juvenile justice.

He also called a $892 million cut to the Census Bureau "penny-wise and pound foolish," and said he was "troubled" that the bill would fund several Trump administration immigration enforcement priorities, such as more attorneys for securing land along the Southern border for a wall and additional prosecutors focused on criminal immigration.

The bill also contained some policy riders on topics that perennially prompt disagreement among Democrats and Republicans. Culberson said the bill contained Second Amendment protections, while Serrano voiced objections to language that would make permanent four annual gun-related riders.

HOUSE COMMITTEE

The House Appropriations Committee approved an amended fiscal 2018 Commerce-Justice-Science spending bill on July 13, with Republicans rebuffing efforts to add Democratic measures on gun control and President Donald Trump's proposed border wall.

The measure (HR 3267), which covers the Justice and Commerce departments and scientific research among other programs, advanced on a 31-21 vote. It would provide $54 billion in discretionary funding, including funds to boost space exploration and for law enforcement to combat terrorism.

That level would be $2.6 billion less than fiscal 2017 funding (PL 115-31) but $4.8 billion more than Trump asked for in his budget request, according to the committee.

"The bill rightly prioritizes the security of our nation and the enforcement of our laws — cracking down on crime, illegal immigration and terrorism," Chairman Rodney Frelinghuysen, R-N.J., said at the markup. "This is especially critical as we face increased threats here at home."

Rep. John Culberson, R-Texas, the chairman of the Commerce-Justice-Science Subcommittee, touted an increase of $92 million for the FBI to fight terrorism and cybercrime among other priorities, as well as 65 new immigration judges and a $98 million boost to the Drug Enforcement Agency.

Culberson also highlighted the $218 million increase for NASA, which would give the agency $19.9 billion in fiscal 2018 for his goal to return the agency to the "glory days" of the Apollo program and other manned-space exploration missions.

But the subcommittee's top Democrat, Rep. Jose E. Serrano of New York, said the spending bill was not one that Democrats could support in its current form.

"The bill's allocation is simply not adequate given the important programs with urgent funding needs," Serrano said of the reduction from fiscal 2017 levels. "That cut results in the under-funding of crucial economic development, scientific research and justice-related programs."

Among Democrats' concerns:

· $85 million cut to the Legal Services Corporation for civil legal representation for the poor.

· $892 million cut to the Census Bureau as it prepares for the 2020 count.

· A 19 percent cut to climate research at the National Oceanic and Atmospheric Administration.

· $217 million cut to NASA's Earth science program.

· The elimination of Justice Department grant programs for hiring police and juvenile justice.

Serrano offered an amendment to add funding to many of the slashed programs, but Culberson said it couldn't be done under the current allocation for the bill. "We're waiting on that big budget deal

to fill some of these holes," Culberson said before the committee rejected the amendment on a 22-30 vote.

The committee also rejected 21-31 an amendment from Serrano to prevent the Justice Department from spending funds on litigation or an appraisal related to acquisition of land or eminent domain for a wall or fence along the border between Mexico and the United States.

"Federal government should not be in the business of coercing private landowners from giving up their land no matter where it may be," Serrano said. "We should avoid this mess in the first place and stop attacking private land rights."

Culberson called the amendment "a backdoor way of preventing the enforcement of our laws and securing our border" and said the discussion was better reserved for other legislation.

The committee also blocked, 20-32, an amendment from Rep. Nita M. Lowey of New York, the full committee's top Democrat, that would allow the Justice Department to block firearm sales to people on terror watch lists, including what's known as the No-Fly List. Culberson said it would deny Second Amendment rights of Americans without adequate proof, and that the ACLU opposes it.

The committee also rejected on party-line votes, 22-30, two amendments from Rep. Debbie Wasserman Schultz, D-Fla., that sought to strip presidential adviser Jared Kushner of his security clearance. Kushner, Trump's son-in-law, reportedly attended a meeting with Donald Trump Jr. and Paul Manafort, Trump's campaign manager at the time, with a Russian lawyer regarding damaging information about Hillary Clinton.

Wasserman Schultz's amendments would stop funding for security clearances for White House advisers who were under a criminal investigation for aiding a foreign government or had deliberately omitted on security clearance applications any meetings with a hostile foreign government.

SENATE SUBCOMMITTEE

The Senate Commerce-Justice-Science Appropriations Subcommittee on July 25 approved a draft fiscal 2018 spending bill with $53.4 billion in discretionary spending that proposed boosts to the FBI and immigration enforcement but cuts to NASA and scientific research.

The subcommittee advanced the draft bill on a voice vote, but did not make the text public.

The Senate level was $3.2 billion less than fiscal 2017 funding (PL 115-31) but $4.4 billion more than President Donald Trump asked for in his budget request, according to Commerce-Justice-Science Subcommittee Chairman Richard C. Shelby, R-Ala.

"The Committee has made difficult but responsible decisions to produce a bill that strikes a financial balance between the competing priorities of law enforcement, national security, scientific advancement and economic development," Shelby said.

Sen. Jeanne Shaheen of New Hampshire, the subcommittee's top Democrat, called on Congress to strike a new budget deal that would allow more investments in infrastructure, science and law enforcement. She expressed disappointment at $151 million in proposed cuts to the National Science Foundation, funding the agency at $7.3 billion.

"I'm pleased that this legislation rejects most of the egregious cuts and program eliminations proposed in President Trump's budget," Shaheen said. "I appreciate that the bill also includes an increase for programs that fight the ongoing and uncontrolled heroin, opioid and fentanyl crisis."

Under the measure, fiscal 2018 funding for the Justice Department would be $29.1 billion, the Commerce Department would be $9.2 billion, and NASA would be $19.5 billion, a committee press release stated.

Shelby said the bill included funds for cybersecurity, additional assistant U.S. attorneys to tackle violent crime, and 65 additional immigration judges. There was a backlog of deportation and other immigration cases that was expected to take years to resolve.

The bill included the following spending levels compared to fiscal 2017, per a committee summary:

• $76 million less for the Commerce Department, but $51 million more for the Census Bureau as it prepared for the 2020 count.

• $121 million more for the Justice Department, including $213 million more for the FBI and $50 million more for the Drug Enforcement Agency.

• $124 million less for NASA.

The panel's press release said the bill included $56.4 billion in total spending because it included funds from the Crime Victim's Fund, a committee spokesman said.

SENATE COMMITTEE

The Senate Appropriations Committee on July 27 approved an amended $53.4 billion Commerce-Justice-Science spending bill for fiscal 2018 with broad bipartisan support.

Sen. Jeanne Shaheen of New Hampshire, the top Democrat on the subcommittee, urged Republicans to find a budget agreement that would raise discretionary spending limits on the bill. The appropriations measure pays for operations in the Commerce and Justice departments, NASA and other agencies.

The Appropriations Committee had approved temporary allocations for the 12 fiscal 2018 spending bills that kept overall base spending flat.

"Without a new budget deal, we won't be able to move the C-J-S bill on the floor," Shaheen said. "I want us to start talking about responsible funding levels now."

To do so, Shaheen offered an amendment that would add $6.5 billion to the spending bill, contingent on such a budget deal, that is "about necessary, urgent investments in community safety, economic security and scientific innovation."

The amendment would boost funds for line items such as the Census Bureau, weather forecasts, law enforcement and victims' grant programs, infrastructure, the National Science Foundation and space exploration. Committee Republicans rejected Shaheen's amendment 15-16, on a party-line vote.

Sen. Richard C. Shelby, R-Ala., chairman of the Commerce-Justice-Science subcommittee, said there were many programs covered in the bill that deserved strong support, but the measure conformed with the full committee's spending guidance.

"Given the fiscal boundaries that have been set, I believe this bill does a good job of balancing the priorities for our committee members and the nation," Shelby said. "If there is another budget agreement in the future, which we all hope will come about, I want to work with Sen. Shaheen and others to discuss increases for programs in our bill that we all support, just as we worked together on the underlying bill."

The spending bill was advanced on a 30-1 vote, as amended, to the Senate floor. Sen. James Lankford, R-Okla., voted no by proxy.

The funding level represented $3.2 billion less than fiscal 2017 funding (PL 115-31).

The bill included boosts for the FBI and immigration enforcement,

but would cut spending for the Census Bureau, NASA and scientific research.

The committee did not avoid the special counsel investigation into possible connections between Trump's campaign and Russian operatives in the 2016 election. A managers' amendment, adopted without objection, added language to the bill report that directed the leadership of the Justice Department "to adhere faithfully to all of its established processes and regulations regarding the operations of any Special Counsel."

The committee also amended the bill to prevent the Justice Department from spending funds to pursue medical marijuana cases if the targets are following state laws, or to crack down on the cultivation of industrial hemp.

Under the measure, fiscal 2018 funding for the Justice Department would be $29.1 billion, the Commerce Department would be $9.2 billion and NASA would be $19.5 billion, lawmakers said. ■

DEFENSE

Pentagon Bill Goes Sans Senate Markup

HOUSE SUBCOMMITTEE

The House Defense Appropriations Subcommittee approved a bill June 26 that would boost military pay and provide billions more for weapons and Pentagon programs than President Donald Trump requested.

The subcommittee approved the $658.1 billion bill by voice vote in a closed markup. There were no amendments during the markup.

The bill included $584.2 billion in discretionary, base-budget accounts for most Pentagon programs besides military construction. The bill also included $73.9 billion in Overseas Contingency Operations funding, which is an uncapped war fund.

House appropriators marked up their spending bill the same day the draft fiscal 2018 defense authorization was released by House Armed Services Chairman Mac Thornberry, R-Texas. The chairman's mark would authorize a total of $696.5 billion in authorized defense funds for fiscal 2018.

But the defense authorization measure's base budget funding level was not a direct comparison to the appropriations bill because it included funding for defense that appears in other appropriations bills such as Energy-Water and Military Construction-VA.

House members were issuing an opening bid of sorts for a budget deal that would lift or alter the current spending limits for defense and nondefense spending established by the 2011 deficit reduction law (PL 112-25).

HOUSE COMMITTEE

The House Appropriations Committee approved its fiscal 2018 Defense bill by voice vote on June 29. Despite lingering discord over the size of the defense budget, lawmakers adopted just one substantive amendment and a manager's package of mostly small changes to the $658.1 billion measure during a two-hour markup.

The bill (HR 3219) included $584.2 billion in discretionary, base-budget funding, covering most Pentagon programs besides military construction. The bill included $73.9 billion in Overseas Contingency Operations funding. Military construction spending was already agreed to by the panel in the first full committee markup of the year, Military Construction-VA (HR 2998).

The Defense funding level was $68.1 billion above the fiscal 2017 enacted level and $18.4 billion above the president's request.

The lack of a full budget agreement, which had prevented the Appropriations Committee from publicly dividing total discretionary dollars across the 12 spending bills, was a source of frustration for the Defense subcommittee's ranking member, Rep. Peter J. Visclosky of Indiana, and other Democrats.

Visclosky said if a budget agreement wasn't adopted to lift existing spending caps in a 2011 deficit reduction law (PL 112-25), the Department of Defense would face a 13 percent cut under sequestration.

The committee defeated on a 22-30 vote an amendment from Rep. Nita M. Lowey of New York, the committee's top Democrat, that would have established a point of order against the full Appropriations panel considering bills without first agreeing to individual subcommittee allocations.

House Appropriations Chairman Rodney Frelinghuysen, R-N.J., told the committee that budget issues were "through no fault of the committee" and lawmakers needed to continue to forge ahead.

War Authorization

After years of unsuccessful attempts, Rep. Barbara Lee, D-Calif., managed to create an unusual coalition of Republicans and Democrats to require a new Authorization for Use of Military Force within 240 days—eight months—of the bill's enactment. The room erupted in applause when the amendment was adopted on a voice vote.

"This should be bipartisan. This is about our country, this is about our troops and it's about Congress," Lee said, taking "the responsibility to do our jobs."

Before lawmakers agreed to the provision, Republicans on the panel, including Reps. Tom Cole of Oklahoma, Scott Taylor of Virginia and Chris Stewart of Utah, voiced support, suggesting changing political winds in a Congress once hesitant to debate another war authorization and content to expand the 2001 AUMF to today's conflicts.

"If we're going to send people to war, we owe them the support of the Congress of the United States. Our visible support," Cole said.

Granger was the sole dissenting vote, arguing that the provision "cripples our ability to conduct counterterrorism operations against terrorists who pose a threat against United States persons and interests."

Visclosky assured the panel that the amendment did not prescribe policy or hurt the military's ability to deal with threats.

The bill also included a fund of more than $28 billion that could be spent at the discretion of the Defense secretary on the implementation of a National Defense Strategy that the Pentagon was working on.

The National Defense Restoration Fund could cover military

procurement, increased troop levels, research and development, and operations as "deemed by the Secretary of Defense to be in the national security interest of the United States," according to a report accompanying the Defense spending bill.

The National Defense Strategy was expected to be released in September and allow the Defense secretary "to make necessary investments," based on the new strategy, instead of waiting until 2019, House Defense Appropriations Chairwoman Kay Granger, R-Texas, said.

Rep. Peter J. Visclosky of Indiana, the ranking Democrat on the committee, endorsed the fund, which he said allowed Congress to oversee the allocation of the funds. The legislation would require the Pentagon to notify Congress 15 days before accessing the funds.

While members of both parties approved of the new defense fund, the account faced a long road to becoming law and, in fact, had not been enacted by early 2018.

SENATE COMMITTEE

The Senate Appropriations Committee unveiled a Defense spending bill on Nov. 21 and did not mark it up. It would've allocated $650.7 billion — $581.3 billion for core Pentagon and intelligence programs; $64.9 billion for spending labeled as relating to overseas wars; and $4.5 billion in additional funds for missile defense programs.

The draft would allocate nearly $70 billion more than the subcommittee's share of the total amount for defense-related programs the Budget Control Act (PL 112-25) permitted. Its base budget blueprint was even $15.4 billion above President Donald Trump's request, which was about the level that budget negotiators were aiming for as they looked to raise the spending caps.

Yet the $650.7 billion total came in $7.4 billion less than the $658.1 billion House-passed companion appropriations bill (HR 3219).

The Senate's spending plan for defense included $17.7 billion to buy goods and services, mostly weapons, that were not part of the president's budget request but that generals and admirals had sought.

Within that total, the biggest monetary boosts to the president's request included $1.4 billion additional to buy 19 ships instead of the 13 requested. Most of the unrequested ships are relatively small and inexpensive.

The lion's share of the shipbuilding windfall was $1 billion set aside to start building a massive new amphibious ship in Mississippi, home of the committee's chairman, Republican Thad Cochran.

In addition, about $673 million in the bill would be set aside to repair the two Navy destroyers damaged when they collided with merchant ships in the Pacific that summer.

As for aircraft, the panel would add $1 billion to buy eight additional F-35 fighter jets that were not in the administration's request, $739 million for 10 more F/A-18E/F Super Hornet fighters for the Navy than Trump asked for, and $800 million for eight MC-130J special operations planes that were not in the president's request, plus several billion dollars more for 50 or so more helicopters than the White House formally requested.

The committee also planned to allocate $1.5 billion that the administration did not formally seek for a special fund to outfit National Guard and Reserve forces with equipment that would be determined later.

The bill would provide $9.3 billion in total for missile defense programs, a total that included $1.1 billion above the president's request for programs to combat North Korea's ballistic missiles and another $703 million for Israeli antimissile programs — the latter nearly five times the administration's request.

The panel also would add $2.5 billion that was not requested for upgrading facilities across the Defense Department

The committee would bankroll a 9,500-person increase in the required minimum number of total military troops, both active and reservist, a figure known as end strength.

Appropriators would also provide the funds to support a 2.4 percent pay raise for those in uniform, as compared to the president's 2.1 percent request. ■

Energy Research Program Is Targeted

HOUSE SUBCOMMITTEE

The House Energy-Water Appropriations Subcommittee approved a $37.6 billion fiscal 2018 spending bill on June 28 that would have funded many accounts above what the White House proposed but would terminate the popular ARPA-E energy research program.

The subcommittee approved by voice vote its draft fiscal 2018 appropriations bill, the fifth measure taken up by House appropriators as they tried to catch up on their long-delayed spending work.

The measure in total would provide $209 million less than fiscal 2017 funding (PL 115-31) but $3.65 billion more than President Donald Trump asked for in his budget request.

Top Democrats on the panel generally praised the measure while criticizing Republicans for the broader budget uncertainty, as the House GOP conference continued to bicker over a fiscal 2018 budget resolution that would set topline discretionary spending levels for the new fiscal year beginning Oct. 1.

"Unfortunately, to say the process by which this Congress is proceeding currently is in disarray would be understating where we find ourselves," said Rep. Marcy Kaptur, D-Ohio, ranking member on the subcommittee.

Rep. Nita M. Lowey of New York, top Democrat on the full Appropriations Committee, blasted House Republican leaders for the lack of so-called regular order. "There is no budget resolution, no [subcommittee] allocations, no bipartisan discussions to avoid sequestration on defense and nondefense priorities and no plan to avoid a catastrophic debt default," Lowey said.

ARPA-E Cut

Democrats also questioned the proposed elimination of the Advanced Research Project Agency-Energy, or ARPA-E program, which funds experimental energy research.

"While the chairman limited the damage to many accounts, the bill before us shortchanges renewable energy and science by terminating ARPA-E and doing real violence to the Energy Efficiency and Renewable Energy account, which is America's future," Kaptur said.

Lowey said the bill attacked ARPA-E "even though it had successfully propelled American innovation, led to technological advances and created jobs."

Subcommittee Chairman Mike Simpson, R-Idaho, said the bill followed Trump's recommendation to zero out ARPA-E and cut some other programs in order to "reduce federal spending and the size of government." But he pointed out the measure rejected other deep cuts Trump proposed to programs like fossil energy research and development.

The draft legislation also included policy language that would tee up the EPA and Army Corps of Engineers to more easily revoke the Obama administration's "Waters of the United States" pollution rule.

HOUSE COMMITTEE

The House Appropriations Committee approved a $37.6 billion Energy-Water spending bill by voice vote on July 12 after adopting only a minor manager's amendment.

The bill (HR 3266) in total would provide $203 million less than fiscal 2017 funding (PL 115-31), a cut of less than 1 percent, but $3.3 billion — or almost 10 percent — more than Trump sought. The boost largely avoided drastic proposed cuts to energy-related research and development. But not every program escaped intact. In order to fund an almost $1 billion increase in Department of Energy nuclear weapon activities, the House bill would slash renewable and energy efficiency research funding by about the same amount.

"These cuts cede the future to offshore competitors who are co-opting the energy technologies that American taxpayers paid to develop," said Energy-Water's top Democrat, Ohio's Marcy Kaptur.

An amendment by Rep. Matt Cartwright, D-Pa., to restore most of that funding was rejected on a 22-30 vote.

The bill also still would deny funding for ARPA-E. The administration argued that the cut would align with the broader effort to move DOE's responsibilities away from commercializing technology in favor of the basic, or the beginning phases, of scientific research.

While the administration asked for an additional $20 million to close the program in fiscal 2018, the House bill took a faster approach to closing operations, directing the department to use previously appropriated funds.

Democrats also moved to strike all policy riders from the bill, including, most notably, one that could pave the way for an easier repeal of the Army Corps and EPA's joint Clean Water Rule, also known as the "Waters of the United States" rulemaking.

The bill language appeared to exempt the WOTUS repeal from the legal requirements of the Administrative Procedure Act (PL 79-404), the federal law governing how federal agencies propose and issue regulations, including the need for a justification for the withdrawal.

EPA Administrator Scott Pruitt submitted a proposed repeal for the regulation on June 27.

SENATE SUBCOMMITTEE

The Senate Energy-Water Appropriations Subcommittee approved by voice vote on July 18 a spending plan that would provide $38.4 billion for energy and water related programs. That was $4.1 billion more than the Trump administration's request and about $800 million more than proposed in the House's bill. It was $629 million more than what was funded in the fiscal 2017 omnibus spending bill (PL 115-31).

The Army Corps of Engineers would receive $6.2 billion, including an increase of $190 million from fiscal 2017, while the Bureau of Reclamation would receive $1.3 billion for water programs, approximately equaling fiscal 2017. The subcommittee proposed $31.5 billion for the Energy Department, a $700 million increase from fiscal 2017 and $3.5 billion more than the request.

"The Department of Energy's research programs and 17 national laboratories have made the United States a world leader in science technology, which is why we must continue to prioritize spending on these efforts so the United States remains competitive at a time when other countries are investing heavily in research," Energy-Water Chairman Lamar Alexander, R-Tenn., said.

The Department of Energy largely avoided the drastic cuts to research programs proposed by the House and Trump administration. The Senate's bill notably set aside:

• $1.9 billion for Office of Renewable Energy and Efficiency — about $800 million more than the House bill and $1.3 billion more than the request, but $153 million below fiscal 2017.

• $5.6 billion for the Office of Science, which conducts basic research — $158 million more than fiscal 2017 and $1.3 billion more than the request.

• $573 million for the Office of Fossil Energy, which included research in so-called clean coal technology — $95 million less than fiscal 2017 and $293 million more than the request.

The bill would continue funding for the politically popular ARPA-E program, which the House proposed defunding to match the administration's request. The program funds high-potential energy projects that are deemed too experimental for private investment.

The bill set aside $330 million for the program. Congress appropriated $306 million in the fiscal 2017 omnibus spending bill, an increase from the $291 million for the program in fiscal 2016.

Energy-Water lawmakers also included funding to move forward on the nation's nuclear waste stalemate, directing the department to work on temporary storage options, but not Yucca Mountain in Nevada.

The bill contained language to authorize DOE to contract with private companies to store waste on an interim basis while the department worked out whether Yucca Mountain, or some other site, is suitable as a long-term disposal site. Two such companies — one in West Texas and one in southeastern New Mexico — had expressed interest in such a contract.

The Trump administration had made Yucca Mountain a top priority for Energy Secretary Rick Perry's tenure at the department despite bipartisan opposition from elected officials in Nevada. The House included $120 million for efforts to jumpstart the Yucca approval process facility, matching the administration's request.

Nuclear Work

The bill also granted the administration's request to halt construction of a facility in South Carolina to turn weapons grade plutonium into fuel for nuclear power plants. That Mixed Oxide Fuel Fabrication Facility was intended to would convert 34 tons of the plutonium under an arms control agreement with Russia, but is over budget and behind schedule.

As did the Obama administration before it, the Trump Energy Department proposes to instead dilute and dispose of the plutonium at a facility in New Mexico.

The bill also increased funding for the National Nuclear Security Administration, which manages U.S. nuclear weapons, by $747 million to a total of $13.7 billion. Energy-Water's top Democrat, Dianne Feinstein of California, criticized the increase, noting that the boost came at the expense of non-defense projects.

SENATE COMMITTEE

The Energy-Water bill was adopted, 30-11 by the Senate Appropriations Committee on July 20. The bill (S 1609), which rejected most of the research cuts for energy programs proposed in both the administration's request and the House spending bill, maintained funding for the Advanced Research Project Agency-Energy program at a record $330 million and set a path toward temporary storage of high-level nuclear waste.

Sen. Lindsey Graham, R-S.C., cast the dissenting vote on the bill, citing its provision for ending work on the Mixed Oxide Fuel Fabrication Facility (MOX) in his home state as reason for his opposition. Graham offered, and then withdrew, two amendments that would have restored funding to the MOX facility, which the Department of Energy has been building under the terms of a nuclear nonproliferation agreement with Russia to transform 34 metric tons of weapons-grade plutonium into fuel for commercial reactors.

"If this committee breaks this agreement, that would be one of the most serious mistakes in the history of nonproliferation," Graham warned, noting that a change in the agreement would be unlikely to garner Russian support and would effectively end the disarmament agreement.

Building the technology had proven complicated; DOE said it had spent $5 billion on construction over the past decade — the high-end of what initial estimates were for the total project cost — and department officials expected it would cost an additional $12 billion to complete.

In its place, DOE and Senate appropriators decided to go with a "dilute and dispose" method, in which the plutonium would be diluted and buried in a repository in southeastern New Mexico, known as the Waste Isolation Pilot Plant, reserved for defense-related nuclear waste.

Energy-Water Chairman Lamar Alexander, R-Tenn., noted that the decision to move away from MOX was based on choosing a cheaper disposal option compared to the already over-budget, behind-schedule MOX project.

Feinstein said that the multiple analyses by the Department of Energy have concluded the price tag is too high for a nuclear weapons complex that is prioritizing weapons modernization.

Yucca Mountain

A related issue that later complicated negotiations on the "minibus" package of security-related appropriations bills was the Trump administration's wish to restart the Yucca Mountain nuclear waste repository in Nevada.

The project was long blocked by the clout of Nevada Sen. Harry Reid, who led Senate Democrats until his retirement at the end of 2016 and was Senate majority leader from 2007 through 2014. Reid persuaded the Obama administration to drop the project, which is widely opposed in the state.

Without a permanent site for disposing waste from the nation's nuclear power plants, spent radioactive fuel has been accumulating at the plants, one of several factors that have virtually halted the construction of new plants.

"The most important priority now is for Congress to appropriate the funding so that we can reopen the nuclear waste program and finish the Yucca Mountain licensing," Energy Secretary Rick Perry told the House Energy and Commerce Committee. "The sooner that we receive this money, the sooner our scientists and the lawyers can get to work." ∎

House Bill Would Imperil Dodd-Frank

HOUSE SUBCOMMITTEE

The House Financial Services Appropriations Subcommittee approved by voice vote on June 29 a $20.23 billion bill for the Treasury and other agencies over Democratic objections to cuts in small business programs and the Election Assistance Commission, and language to repeal much of the 2010 Dodd-Frank financial regulatory law.

Chairman Tom Graves of Georgia acknowledged that the bill included much of the language from a House bill (HR 10) that would repeal the Dodd-Frank law and he didn't dispute New York Democrat Nita M. Lowey's charge that the bill would "effectively repeal Dodd-Frank." Lowey is ranking member on the Appropriations Committee.

Graves said he was working "hand-in-hand" with the House Financial Services Committee, where the Dodd-Frank repeal bill originated. He said he was "particularly excited about the financial reforms" in the bill and provisions to rein in "the rogue, high-dollar, out-of-control, unaccountable Consumer Financial Protection Bureau" established by Dodd-Frank.

The spending bill would cut $1.28 billion from the fiscal 2017 financial services appropriation (PL 115-31), with the biggest single reduction being $981 million from what the General Services Administration may spend from its Federal Building Fund. The GSA had asked for flat spending from the fund, which is replenished by rents charged to federal agencies, departments and offices.

The bill would cut $149 million from the IRS, leaving a budget of $11.1 billion. It also would cut $31 million, or 14 percent, from the Small Business Administration's Entrepreneurship Development program and 23 percent from the Community Development Financial Institutions program.

"We've had to make a lot of hard decisions," Graves said.

Not only would the subcommittee's bill cut the GSA's building and maintenance plans for 2018, it also would rescind funds from the fiscal 2017 budget for the planned consolidation of FBI headquarters. Graves, who noted that the White House did not seek additional funding for the FBI headquarters, said that rescission was about $200 million.

Graves said he assured GSA Acting Administrator Timothy O. Horne that the cuts did not reflect on the agency and that "this was just merely a math issue."

But subcommittee ranking member Mike Quigley of Illinois complained that the cuts at GSA left the agency with "zero funds to start new construction and only $180 million for repairs and alterations." Quigley complained that the agency faced a "staggering backlog of deferred maintenance projects" even before these cuts.

Democrats, pointing to Russian attempts to influence the 2016 elections, argued against cutting the Election Assistance Commission's funding from $9.6 million to $4 million and against a provision that would zero out the commission after fiscal 2018.

Graves said none of the commission's funding would go to cybersecurity and the agency itself was reportedly hacked the previous year. The commission's main function is to serve as a liaison between the FBI and the Department of Homeland Security, he said.

"I don't think we need an agency to do that," he said, adding that states are in charge of elections.

An amendment offered by Quigley to restore the commission's funding to the White House's requested $9.2 million was defeated on a party-line vote.

The bill included proposed fiscal 2018 cuts to all three offices of inspectors general that oversee the Treasury Department. That contrasts with budget increases for all three that were in the previous year's House and Senate bills and survived in the fiscal 2017 omnibus.

The three IGs — the IG for the Treasury Department; the Treasury Inspector General for Tax Administration, which oversees the IRS; and the Special IG for the Troubled Asset Relief Program — would see their combined budgets go from $248 million to $237 million, a 5 percent reduction.

Quigley called the IG cuts "shortsighted." The goal of the IG offices is to root out waste, fraud and abuse, and the proposed cuts "are not only inconsistent with these goals, but also fiscally irresponsible," he wrote in an email.

HOUSE COMMITTEE

Last-minute changes to the Financial Services bill (HR 3280) approved by the full House Appropriations Committee on July 13 partially restored funding for the Election Assistance Commission and directed the Trump administration to develop a new plan to consolidate the FBI's headquarters.

The committee approved the bill 31-21. It would provide $1.3 billion less than the fiscal 2017 omnibus and $2.5 billion less than the president requested, according to the committee.

Republicans agreed to add $3 million to their $4 million proposal for funding the Election Assistance Commission, created after the 2000 election to assist states. The commission's fiscal 2017 budget was $9.6 million, and Democrats had criticized the proposal to cut it to $4 million in fiscal 2018.

A bipartisan manager's amendment inserted into the bill the requirement that the General Services Administration devise a new plan to consolidate the more than one dozen FBI offices in the Washington area into a single 2.1 million square foot campus. The GSA canceled the $1.4 billion project. The committee rejected an effort to restore $205 million to the project appropriated for fiscal 2017 but that would be rescinded by the bill.

The manager's amendment also inserted provisions similar to those in a measure (HR 1667) that would create a new subchapter in the U.S. Bankruptcy Code to manage the failure of banks with more than $50 billion in assets through the bankruptcy process. The House Judiciary Committee approved that bill in March.

The negotiations added $18 million to IRS Taxpayer Services programs, including the Tax Counseling for the Elderly Program and low-income taxpayer clinic grants.

SENATE BILL

The Senate Appropriations Committee on Nov. 20 released its $20.8 billion fiscal 2018 Financial Services draft bill, saying the measure would appropriate $637 million less than was enacted in fiscal 2017.

The draft text included changes to when and how candidates can coordinate with party committees and would transfer the Consumer Financial Protection Bureau's accounts from the mandatory side to the discretionary side, giving appropriators a chance to exert influence on the agency. Democrats have opposed both.

"In my first year as chair of the Financial Services and General Government Subcommittee, I have worked to produce a funding measure that promotes fiscal responsibility and encourages government efficiency and innovation," subcommittee Chairwoman Shelley Moore Capito, R-W. Va., said in a statement. "Importantly, this bill promotes rural broadband expansion through the FCC and increases critical resources to combat the opioid epidemic through federal drug programs."

Sen. Chris Coons, the top Democrat on the subcommittee, said he was disappointed the spending bill "effectively negates the campaign finance spending limits imposed on coordinated spending by federal candidates and party committees" and "puts in jeopardy continued funding for the Consumer Financial Protection Bureau."

"If the subcommittee had marked-up, I would have offered amendments to provide much-needed funding to states to protect their election systems from outside intrusions and to protect the personal data collected by the new Presidential Advisory Commission on Election Integrity," Coons, D-Del., said in a statement.

The Financial Services legislation was written to fiscal 2017 levels because Congress and the White House had yet to agree to fiscal 2018 spending levels.

The main items in the draft bill included:

- IRS, $11.1 billion, equal to the House's fiscal 2018 bill.
- General Services Administration, $7.8 billion, down slightly from the $7.9 billion in the House bill.
- Federal Judiciary, $7 billion, nearly equal to the House's $7.09 billion.

- Securities and Exchange Commission, $1.8 billion, higher than the $1.6 billion in the House bill.
- Small Business Administration, $886.3 million, slightly higher than the House's $848 million.
- Executive Office of the President, $704 million, higher than the House's $688 million.
- District of Columbia: $704 million, higher than the House's $695.6 million.
- Treasury Department: $347 million, higher than the House's $324 million.
- Federal Communications Commission, $322 million, equal to the House's bill.
- Federal Trade Commission, $306 million, equal to the House's $306 million.

The draft bill would appropriate about $500 million more than the House bill.

The draft did not include a provision that was in the House Financial Services bill that would stop the IRS from enforcing the individual mandate in the 2010 health care bill (PL 111-148, PL 111-152).

The campaign finance provision would effectively loosen rules on coordination between candidates and party committees. Limits on communications expenditures for a campaign would only apply to parties "unless the communication is controlled by, or made at the direction of, the candidate or an authorized committee of the candidate."

Democrats were also opposed to making the CFPB part of discretionary spending and removing a provision from the 2010 Dodd-Frank (PL 111-203) bill that prevents the appropriations committees from intervening in its annual budget request.

"Dodd-Frank created the CFPB with an automatic funding stream, like other financial regulators, in order to protect it from being underfunded and undermined through the annual budget process," stated a Democratic summary. ■

HOMELAND SECURITY

Border Wall Would Get Its First Bricks

HOUSE SUBCOMMITTEE

Democrats indicated their early opposition to the House's fiscal 2018 Homeland Security spending bill (HR 3355) and its funding for President Donald Trump's immigration enforcement priorities, as the $44.3 billion measure was approved by voice vote at a quick Homeland Security Appropriations Subcommittee markup on July 12.

Rep. Nita M. Lowey of New York, the ranking Democrat on the full Appropriations Committee, and Rep. Lucille Roybal Allard of California, the top Democrat on the Homeland Security subcommittee, lambasted Republicans at the markup for putting forth a bill they said was unlikely to garner any Democratic votes.

"One might think the majority would produce bills that could possibly gain support from Democrats by, for example, not funding a wasteful and useless border wall or a deportation force separating children from their families," Lowey said in her prepared remarks.

The bill would provide slightly more money that Trump's $44.1 billion homeland security budget proposal. When disaster funding was

included, the bill's total was $51.1 billion.

The measure included $1.6 billion to begin building Trump's wall on the border with Mexico, plus money for more Immigration and Customs Enforcement officers and immigrant detention beds. The administration said the $1.6 billion would be used to construct the wall's first 74 miles in southern Texas and the San Diego area.

Appropriations Committee Chairman Rodney Frelinghuysen, R-N.J., who had previously raised concerns about the wall's potential price tag, said he now supported it. "I think we need a border wall. It's certainly a priority so, you know, I support the effort and we'll be working to make sure we get it across the finish line," he said.

Roybal-Allard expressed dismay at the inclusion of the immigration funds, saying that under different circumstances she may have supported it because the bill included many provisions she believed were important.

"The truth is that the president's malignant rhetoric on immigration has poisoned the waters on this issue, making anything this administra-

tion poses suspect," she said. "I simply cannot support throwing scarce taxpayer dollars at a campaign promise."

HOUSE COMMITTEE

The House Appropriations Committee on July 18 approved the $44.3 billion bill for the Homeland Security Department. Committee Republicans advanced the bill (HR 3355) on a 33-20 vote despite protests from Democrats who sought to portray myriad line items as misguided or ineffective. Big Democratic targets included $1.6 billion to begin constructing Trump's wall on the U.S.-Mexico border and increased funding for more immigrant detention beds and deportation agents.

The minority party was unsuccessful in rolling back funding for immigration enforcement.

Rep. Lucille Roybal-Allard, D-Calif., offered an amendment that would cancel increases for Customs and Border Protection, known as CBP, and Immigration and Customs Enforcement, known as ICE. She instead would have provided $2.3 billion to the U.S. Coast Guard to build a new fleet of polar ice breaker ships.

Roybal-Allard, the top Democrat on the Homeland Security Subcommittee, called the measure's funding to hire more ICE agents and enlarge detention capacity "alarming." She also described the proposal to fund the Trump administration's border wall project as being rushed, without "a comprehensive plan backed by a clear justification."

Her amendment was defeated 22-30 in a party-line vote.

Other Democrats proposed offsetting the ICE and CBP spending on other priorities. An amendment offered by Rep. Mike Quigley of Illinois would have repurposed the funds as emergency preparedness grants for local first responders, and another offered by Rep. Debbie Wasserman Schultz of Florida would have used the funds to reinstate airport security teams the administration had proposed cutting.

Quigley's amendment was defeated by voice vote; Wasserman Schultz withdrew hers from consideration.

The bill would provide $44.3 billion in overall discretionary funds, slightly above Trump's fiscal 2018 request. When disaster funding is included the bill's total would rise to $51.1 billion.

House Appropriations Chairman Rodney Frelinghuysen, R-N.J., called the spending bill an "ironclad commitment to protecting our homeland." But Rep. Nita M. Lowey of New York, the committee's top Democrat, said the bill "unacceptably provides significant increases" to carry out Trump administration immigration policies that would break up families.

In other action on amendments, Roybal-Allard unsuccessfully tried to force then-Homeland Security Secretary John F. Kelly to continue an Obama-era program that protects undocumented immigrants brought to the U.S. as children.

Kelly raised doubts whether the Trump administration would back the Deferred Action for Childhood Arrivals program, known as DACA, that was being challenged in court by Texas and nine other states. DACA has granted protection from deportation and a two-year work permit to so-called Dreamers since June 2012. Dreamers were brought to the country as minors and have grown up in the United States.

The DACA amendment also was rejected in a 22-30 party-line vote.

Another amendment by Rep. David E. Price, D-N.C., would have reduced funding to hire 1,000 additional Immigration and Customs Enforcement agents and instead used the money to hire more CBP agents for deployment at ports. It was also rejected on a 22-30 vote.

Democrats also unsuccessfully sought to limit the jurisdiction of federal immigration officers by offering an amendment that would prohibit enforcement actions at "sensitive locations" including schools, hospitals and churches, as well as courthouses and motor vehicle offices. The amendment, sponsored by Reps. Jose E. Serrano of New York and Barbara Lee of California, was rejected 22-30.

Rep. John Carter, R-Texas, chairman of the House Appropriations Homeland Security Subcommittee, said Democratic amendments intended to strip money from CBP and ICE to pay for other DHS programs would be wasteful. Carter argued the appropriations committee should not make policy changes in a funding bill, as he believed Democrats were trying to do.

SENATE BILL

The draft Senate bill, released Nov. 21 without a markup, would provide DHS with $1.6 billion that Trump requested in March to construct a wall along 74 miles of the border near San Diego and in southern Texas. The $1.6 billion constituted just a sliver of the massive spending bill, but it was likely to cause the most uproar from Democrats who said the wall — Trump's key campaign promise — would be ineffective and too expensive.

"This is bumper sticker budgeting at its worst," said Sen. Patrick J. Leahy of Vermont, the committee's top Democrat. "Building a wall along our southern border is a waste of taxpayer dollars and an insult to our neighbor to the South."

But the bill's Republican sponsors called it an investment needed to keep the country safe.

"Recent terrorist attacks within the United States demonstrate our need to be constantly vigilant against security threats," Appropriations Chairman Thad Cochran, R-Miss., said in a statement. "I hope this mark sets us on a course to provide the resources required by the Department of Homeland Security to protect the American people."

The draft bill would provide about $44 billion in discretionary funding — around $770 million more than the administration requested — not including $7.4 billion in disaster relief funding and $163 million in Overseas Contingency Operations funding for the Coast Guard exempt from statutory spending caps. A companion bill (HR 3355) passed by the House would provide $45.2 billion in discretionary funds.

Though the bill granted Trump his initial wall funding request, the Senate panel indicated it would require DHS to submit a comprehensive border security plan before additional dollars could be provided. The House bill did not include similar language.

"The committee is disappointed that the department has not submitted a comprehensive border security plan to address known security gaps," according to an explanatory statement released with the draft bill. "Until the department transmits such a plan, as required by [the fiscal 2017 omnibus bill], the committee will continue to recommend funding only for adequately justified investments."

The committee statement made references to language in the fiscal 2017 spending package (PL 115-31) enacted by Congress in May.

The Senate's draft measure also broke with Trump in other areas of immigration policy. For example, it would not increase spending in order to maintain more immigration beds or hire additional Immigration and Customs Enforcement officers. The House bill included funding for an additional 4,676 detention beds, which would bring the nationwide total to 44,000 beds, as well as money to hire 1,000 new ICE officers.

The Senate version also mostly ignored requests to cut funding for various local law enforcement grant programs. ∎

INTERIOR-ENVIRONMENT

Contentious Waters Rule at Issue in Bills

HOUSE SUBCOMMITTEE

The House Interior-Environment Appropriations Subcommittee approved a $31.5 billion fiscal 2018 bill by voice vote on July 12, though Democrats indicated they would not support it without changes.

The bill (HR 3354) would cut spending at the EPA, Interior, and other agencies by 2.5 percent from the $32.3 billion enacted in the fiscal 2017 omnibus bill (PL 115-31).

A rider in the bill would help the Trump administration bypass statutory and regulatory reviews in its efforts to undo the Obama administration's Waters of the United States rule. Another provision would prohibit the Interior Department from proposing any rules that list the greater sage grouse as an endangered species. Still another would preclude the federal government from regulating lead content in ammunition and fishing tackle under the Toxic Substances Control Act (PL 114-182) or any other law.

"These provisions seek to turn back protections for endangered species and undermine clean water and clean air protections," the subcommittee's ranking Democrat, Betty McCollum of Minnesota, said. "They simply do not belong in this bill. They undermine important environmental laws and endanger public health and safety, while benefiting polluters."

Lawmakers had avoided fights over the fiscal 2017 omnibus bill passed with bipartisan support in May by agreeing to keep out contentious riders.

While Republicans ignored the deep cuts President Donald Trump had proposed for EPA, spending levels would still be reduced by 7.4 percent to $7.5 billion, a decrease Democrats said they would not support. The fiscal 2017 omnibus funded the agency at $8.1 billion.

House Appropriations ranking Democrat Nita M. Lowey of New York said the measure ignored the reality of climate change.

"We are at a critical juncture when we should be investing more in preventing climate change and protecting our natural resources, not making draconian cuts that would damage the world around us for generations to come," she said.

But House Appropriations Chairman Rodney Frelinghuysen said Republicans had in the measure "identified opportunities to rein in federal bureaucracy" and "stop harmful and unnecessary regulations that destroy economic opportunity and kill jobs."

HOUSE COMMITTEE

It is normally the GOP attempting to rein in the EPA, but before Republicans on the House Appropriations Committee could approve, 30-21, the Interior-Environment bill on July 18, they had to head off Democrats' amendments to restrict the agency's authority under the Trump administration.

Although outnumbered, committee Democrats pushed multiple amendments to prevent the EPA and the Interior Department, which are funded by the bill, from rolling back safeguards for clean water, endangered species and clean air, all of which had been targeted by the Trump administration and Republican lawmakers who argued that such restrictions were overly burdensome and inhibited job creation.

Republicans defeated, 21-29, an amendment by Mike Quigley, D-Ill., to prevent EPA Administrator Scott Pruitt from closing any of the agency's regional offices. Although the agency had denied reports it planned to close its Region 5 office — which oversees environmental issues in Illinois, Indiana, Ohio, Michigan, Wisconsin and Minnesota — Democrats fear that could change.

"As we have seen, this administration can change its mind in the blink of a tweet," Quigley said.

McCollum urged the panel to adopt the amendment for "comfort language," but the subpanel's chairman, Ken Calvert, said it was unnecessary because the White House's budget request did not propose closing any regional offices.

Democrats also offered an amendment that would require the EPA, Interior Department, Forest Service and other agencies to consult with Congress before undertaking significant staffing changes. Citing reports of impending staff shakeups at Interior and EPA, Democrats argued the amendment would make the government transparent about its intentions.

Interior Secretary Ryan Zinke had said he intended to shed more than 4,000 jobs, partly through reassignments and buyouts. Media reports also indicated Zinke intended to reassign top career employees to new positions. Staff changes also were expected at the EPA.

"We are the purse strings and we have oversight over those changes," said the amendment's sponsor, Rep. Chellie Pingree of Maine, before it was rejected by a voice vote.

The panel also voted, 19-31, to reject an amendment by McCollum to remove language in the bill that would allow the EPA to avoid statutory reviews when withdrawing the Waters of the United States rule. McCollum said the rider would give an unprecedented amount of power to the EPA and would remove important checks and balances in the regulatory process.

"For some of you this rider might be a dream come true for now, but think of the future," she said.

An amendment that would prevent the EPA from going ahead with delaying implementation of ozone regulations was rejected as was another that would force agencies funded by the bill to recognize and prepare for climate change.

Still, the Interior-Environment bill would spare the EPA and other federal agencies funded by the bill from the deep cuts proposed by President Trump. It would fund the EPA at $7.5 billion, down 7.4 percent from the $8.1 billion enacted in the fiscal 2017 omnibus (PL 115-31). The White House had called for cutting the EPA's spending by a third to $5.7 billion.

Federal arts and humanities programs targeted for elimination by the Trump administration would get a lifeline from House appropriators willing to ignore the president's proposal and keep them running.

The Interior-Environment bill included $145 million for the National Endowment for the Arts, a 3.2 percent reduction from fiscal 2017 but more than $116 million above Trump's budget request. The National Endowment for the Humanities would receive $145 million, which was $103.7 million above the White House budget request.

The White House had said it did not consider the activities of those programs" to be core federal responsibilities. "The Heritage Founda-

tion, a conservative think tank that backed Trump's plan to gut the programs, had described them as "welfare for cultural elitists."

SENATE BILL

The Senate's version of the fiscal 2018 Interior-Environment spending bill, released Nov. 20 without a markup, would help the Trump administration withdraw a contentious Obama administration rule that expanded federal jurisdiction over waterways, a provision that was certain to invite criticism from Democrats and environmentalists.

The $32.6 billion measure, which included additional emergency wildfire suppression funds, would finance the agencies at the center of the nation's environment and climate policies.

The bill would allow the EPA to withdraw the Obama administration's Waters of the United States rule without statutory review, which would help the agency dodge providing a legal justification for killing the regulation. The administration would likely still have to contend with lawsuits from environmental groups and Democratic state attorneys general.

Democrats feared the provision, which was also included in the House version of the Interior-Environment bill, would undermine clean water protections and remove key checks and balances in the regulatory process. Republicans have frequently criticized the rule as a federal power grab that infringed on the rights of small land owners and farmers.

The bill would fund the EPA at $7.91 billion, down $149.5 million from the enacted amount in the fiscal 2017 omnibus (PL 115-31). The funding level in the bill, Republicans argued in a summary, was "focused on returning the agency to its core mission of environmental cleanup." Trump proposed cutting EPA's budget by a third to $5.7 billion; House appropriators approved $7.5 billion for the agency.

Democrats were expected to fight over a provision that would prohibit the federal government from regulating the lead content in certain types of ammunition and fishing tackle under the Toxic Substances Control Act (PL 114-182).

The bill also included a frequent rider to prohibit the listing the sage-grouse as an endangered species. It would allow the Fish and Wildlife Service to delist the gray wolf as endangered in some parts of the country.

Senate Appropriations' top Democrat Patrick J. Leahy of Vermont said in a statement that he was disappointed that the bill "has bowed to the anti-science know-nothingism of President Trump by slashing environmental programs and denying the reality of climate change." He also said the measure "falls far short of the funding we need and contains poison pill riders that have no place in the appropriations process."

The measure would allocate $2.94 billion for the National Park Service, an increase of $5.6 million from the previous year, which appropriators said would help address the agency's massive maintenance backlog. It would fund the Forest Service at $5.8 billion. The bill would provide $3.6 billion to fight wildfires, split between the Interior and Agriculture departments. The bill also included $507 million in emergency firefighting funds as Western states grappled with wildfires.

Senate Appropriations Interior-Environment Subcommittee Chairwoman Lisa Murkowski of Alaska said in a statement that the measure would "empower Americans to build our economy" and create healthy communities.

"In this bill, we direct federal resources where they are needed by investing in programs aimed to protect our land and people, enable new infrastructure projects to boost the economy, and help communities provide vital, basic services," Murkowski said.

The measure also would save funding for the National Endowment for the Arts and Humanities, allocating them $149 million each, equal to the fiscal 2017 enacted levels. The Trump administration has proposed eliminating all funding for the programs. ∎

LABOR-HHS-EDUCATION

Boost for NIH Is Endorsed by Lawmakers

HOUSE SUBCOMMITTEE

The House Appropriations Labor-HHS-Education Subcommittee approved a $156 billion fiscal 2018 spending bill on July 13 that would increase funding to the National Institutes of Health while cutting funds for family planning, teacher training programs and the Special Olympics.

The bill was approved on a 9-6 party-line vote.

The largest of the nondefense spending bills, the measure rejected numerous proposals from the Trump administration such as allowing federal funds to pay for students to attend private schools and cutting funding for the NIH, which would see a $1.1 billion increase the next year, bringing its budget to around $35 billion.

Democrats praised certain increases but found plenty to criticize in the bill, such has the elimination of $25 million of Planned Parenthood funding as part of cutting the $286 million in the Title X family planning program in the Department of Health and Human Services. A

proposed $3.3 billion rescission to the Pell Grant surplus fund was also criticized as threatening a program that helps low-income students afford college.

The House proposal cut $542 million from HHS, leaving it with an allocation of $78 billion. The Education Department would be slashed by $2.4 billion to $66 billion for the 2018 fiscal year. The Labor Department's proposed $1 billion cut would leave it with $10.8 billion for the next fiscal year.

The bill contained language that would prevent HHS from using new discretionary funding to implement the 2010 health care law (PL 111-148, PL 111-152), which Republicans were in the middle of trying to gut.

Despite support for the medical research funding, Democrats were critical of the cuts to other public health priorities. Those savings were used to offset the NIH increase. Subcommittee ranking Democrat Rosa DeLauro of Connecticut noted that around $200 million would be cut from the Substance Abuse and Mental Health Services Administration.

"We speak often about the opioid crisis, but when the opportunity arises to take strong action, we fail to fund these priorities in a meaningful way," said DeLauro.

The bill also would cut about $70 million from programs at the Centers for Disease Control and Prevention, targeting chronic disease research and surveillance.

"Even if we invest heavily in research on diabetes, cancer, heart disease and more, cuts to chronic health and tobacco programs at the CDC would mitigate overall improved health outcomes," said Nita M. Lowey of New York, the top Democrat on the full Appropriations committee.

The bulk of the Education Department's decrease would come from the elimination of roughly $2 billion in grants to help train and recruit teachers, as well as develop curriculum.

DeLauro also said the bill would eliminate a dozen education programs, including the Special Olympics and programs to expand reading and arts. However, an additional $100 million was added to a wide-ranging grant program to help provide a variety of services to students, such as mental health services and technology.

Certain job training programs would also be cut under the House's bill.

Several riders would effectively block Labor Department rules that Republicans said harm both business and low-income families seeking retirement planning.

HOUSE COMMITTEE

The House Appropriations Committee approved the bill on July 19 on a 28-22 vote.

"This bill reflects Republican priorities to cut spending and focus investments in programs our people need the most — public health and medical research, biodefense, fundamental education, and proven programs that increase job growth, for example," said committee Chairman Rodney Frelinghuysen, R-N.J. "It also includes important provisions to stop government overreach."

A manager's amendment agreed to by voice vote at the outset of the markup contained a variety of non-controversial changes, including some funding tweaks for health programs including:

· $6 million more for the Centers for Disease Control and Prevention to spend on transmissible diseases that can cause brain damage, like Creutzfeldt-Jakob disease.

· A designation of $1 million for screening and treatment of maternal depression, out of a $100 million HHS grant program for communities with high rates of infant mortality.

· An extra $10 million for an HHS Community Service Block Grant, bringing its total to $617.5 million.

Democrats offered numerous amendments seeking to restore the funding for various health priorities, including mental health and substance abuse treatment, vaccination funding and public health emergencies. They also pushed to restore funding for apprenticeships and teacher training programs facing drastic cuts. The amendments were rejected.

Democrats in both chambers began to dispute some of the proposed cuts—more than 120 House Democrats asked appropriators in a letter not to remove $3.3 billion from the Pell Grant's surplus fund. Although the fund had $8.5 billion, lawmakers were worried the surplus fund wouldn't be able to cover all eligible students if there was an increase in college enrollment.

SENATE SUBCOMMITTEE

The Senate Labor-HHS-Education Appropriations Subcommittee approved by voice vote on Sept. 6 a bipartisan draft bill that would increase funding for the National Institutes of Health by $2 billion and provide more funding to low-income students attending college.

The bill contained $3 billion more than the fiscal 2017 bill, putting funding for the largest nondefense discretionary spending bill at $164.1 billion.

The measure would provide $79.4 billion for HHS, a $1.7 billion boost over fiscal 2017. The Education Department would get $68.3 billion, a $29 million increase, and the Labor Department would receive $12 billion, a $61.5 million decrease from fiscal 2017 levels.

Health and Human Services

The bill would provide $36.1 billion for the National Institutes of Health, a $2 billion increase over its fiscal 2017 levels. That built upon similar increases for each of the previous two years. Alzheimer's research would get the biggest boost at NIH, with a $414 million increase, resulting in $1.8 billion total for those programs.

Additional funding for opioid abuse prevention and treatment would be split between the Centers for Disease Control and Prevention, the Substance Abuse and Mental Health Services Administration and other parts of HHS. The total for opioid-related programs across HHS would be $816 million. Most of that increase was part of a $500 million grant program for states set up by a package of biomedical innovation bills passed in 2016 as the 21st Century Cures Act (PL 114-255).

Senate appropriators rejected the Trump administration's proposed cuts in mental health programs, infectious and chronic disease control and low-income energy assistance. The Senate would sustain most of those programs at fiscal 2017 levels, or increase them slightly, though the House bill did follow through with cuts in many public health areas.

While House Republicans sought to eliminate $287 million in grants to family planning health care providers, the Senate would keep that funding intact and instruct HHS to continue to administer the program consistent with past administrations.

And just days after the administration said it would cut back on funding for outreach and advertisements related to the individual health insurance market, the Senate bill would continue funding for those programs.

Education

Low-income students in higher education as well as elementary, middle and high school would see more funding under the Senate bill than under the House version.

Students attending college and university would see the amount for the maximum Pell Grant increase to $6,020 from the existing level of $5,920. The draft legislation wouldn't continue indexing Pell Grants to inflation, which has been done since 2012. Subcommittee Chairman Roy Blunt, R-Mo., said he felt the issue of whether to tie Pell Grants to inflation should be addressed through an update of the higher education law (PL 110-315).

The Senate bill would rescind $2.6 billion from the Pell Grant surplus, slightly less than the $3.3 billion the House bill would rescind. The Pell Grant program had a surplus of $8.5 billion in June, according to a Congressional Budget Office estimate.

The Senate bill also would require the Education Department to continue to have multiple companies service student loans, a provision

added after the agency announced and then rolled back plans to reduce the number of loan servicers to one.

For low-income students in grades K-12, funding under the Title I program would rise to $15.5 billion, an increase of $25 million from fiscal 2017 funding. Another grant program that allows schools to fund a wide variety of programs from mental health to technology would be increased to $450 million, a $50 million bump from existing funding.

The legislation would provide $367 million for charter schools, an increase of $25 million from fiscal 2017 funding. But it would not fund any of the school choice programs proposed by the Trump administration that would allow public funding to go to private schools.

A grant program to help with teacher education and development that received no funding in the House bill would receive about $2.1 billion in the Senate bill, similar to the program's existing funding levels. The state grant program is aimed at improving teacher quality.

Labor

The Senate bill would create a new $30 million career education program to help unemployed workers in the Appalachian and Delta regions gain skills. The bill would continue funding for federal apprenticeship grants at $95 million, in contrast to House appropriators' plan to cut the program. Apprenticeships have been a top priority for Labor Secretary Alexander Acosta.

Job Corps, a career and technical training program for youth, would be cut by $5 million under the Senate bill and be funded at $1.7 billion. The National Labor Relations Board would continue to be funded at $274 million. The Senate bill did not contain any of the riders in the House bill limiting the actions of the board. Under the House version of the bill, the board would be prevented from enforcing its rulings on Native American tribes and businesses as well as whether two companies can be considered joint employers of a group of workers.

SENATE COMMITTEE

The Senate Appropriations Committee approved the Labor-HHS-Education bill on Sept. 7, voting 29-2 in favor of a measure that would allocate $164.1 billion in discretionary funding to the departments of Health and Human Services, Labor and Education.

The Senate bill would provide $12 billion for the Labor Department, a $61.5 million decrease. The Department of Health and Human Services would receive $79.4 billion, up $1.7 billion from existing levels. The Education Department would get $68.3 billion, a $29 million increase from existing funding levels.

While Senate appropriators were able to compromise on a number of issues, the House version was mostly driven by Republican priorities. For example, House Republicans rejected Democrat-sponsored amendments to increase Pell Grants and eliminate provisions blocking funding to the women's health organization Planned Parenthood.

In contrast, the Senate bill would provide an increase for Pell Grants and would not interfere with funding for Planned Parenthood.

Overall, the bill represented $800 million less in discretionary funding for the three agencies than fiscal 2017 even though the $164.1 billion topline allocation was $3 billion higher than fiscal 2017.

Discretionary spending would be lower overall despite the higher topline discretionary figure because appropriators could not make as many changes to mandatory spending programs as in past years — a vital source of funding and a budgetary maneuver that lawmakers had utilized annually to increase discretionary spending beyond the topline.

Due to increases in mandatory spending for the children's health insurance program, the committee could only free up $4.4 billion in savings that could be funneled into its discretionary spending pot for fiscal 2018, compared to $8.2 billion it was able to offset in fiscal 2017.

Bill Specifics

Health and Human Services:
· The bill would provide $36.1 billion for the National Institutes of Health, a $2 billion increase over fiscal 2017.
· The Centers for Disease Control and Prevention would get about $7.2 billion, a slight increase over 2017 levels.
· Similarly, the Substance Abuse and Mental Health Services Administration would see a small $13 million increase in funding, getting $3.8 billion for fiscal 2018.
· Social service programs would mostly be level with fiscal 2017 or get a slight decrease. The Low Income Home Energy Assistance Program would get $3.4 billion, and the Community Services Block Grant program would receive $700 million.

As in previous years, the bill would prohibit funding it provides from being spent on abortion or health benefits that cover abortion, except in the case of rape, incest or when the mother's life is in danger.

Education:
· The bill would increase the maximum award for a Pell Grant by $100 to $6,020.
· The bill would rescind $2.6 billion from the Pell Grant surplus.
· The bill would restore Pell Grants for students who were defrauded by their college or university.
· The bill would provide $15.5 billion for low-income students in K-12, a $25 million increase.

Labor:
· The bill would create a new $30 million career education program to help unemployed workers in the Appalachian and Delta regions gain skills to help them find work.
· The bill would provide $95 million for apprenticeships. ∎

LEGISLATIVE BRANCH

'Fresh Look at Security' After Shooting

HOUSE SUBCOMMITTEE

The House Legislative Branch Appropriations Subcommittee reported out a $3.58 billion fiscal 2018 bill by voice vote on June 23 that would boost security both at the Capitol and in members' districts.

The meeting was brief and no amendments were offered.

The bill would provide $100 million more than the fiscal 2017 enacted level (PL 115-31) to fund operations in the House, Capitol Police, Library of Congress, Government Accountability Office and other legislative branch agencies. Senate operations are covered by its own bill.

"We are taking a new, fresh look at security," said subcommittee Chairman Kevin Yoder, R-Kan., in light of an attack the week before on House Republicans at a baseball practice in Alexandria, Va., where an assailant shot House Majority Whip Steve Scalise, R-La., two Capitol Police officers and others. The gunman was killed by the security team assigned to Scalise, who in his leadership position had a Capitol Police detail.

Yoder and House Administration Chairman Gregg Harper, R-Miss., collaborated on a plan to increase each member's representational allowance account by $25,000 for official event security in members' districts for the rest of fiscal 2017. The allocations didn't require additional appropriations.

The same level of per-office security funding could be added to MRA accounts for fiscal 2018, Yoder said. "There are enough resources [for] $25,000 next year, if the House Administration Committee so chooses," he said.

The bill would also provide $5 million for the House sergeant-at-arms to enhance district office security, such as cameras and panic buttons.

The bill would boost Capitol Police funding by $29.2 million to $422.5 million for fiscal 2018. "We owe it to the Capitol Police to make sure that they have the necessary resources they need to meet the mission in this increasingly polarized climate," said Yoder.

The subcommittee's ranking Democrat, Tim Ryan of Ohio, supported the increases for Capitol Police and the sergeant-at-arms, but said members needed more information about the full range of options for enhancing security for offices and homes, including information about the cost.

"The scariest part for us is, there used to be this impression by the public that we all had security everywhere we went," Ryan said. "Now everyone knows that isn't the case."

An issue not directly addressed in the bill was security at members' residences. Campaign funds could only be used for residence security under strict guidelines and with permission from the Federal Elections Commission. According to Yoder, the FEC was considering a blanket allowance for campaign funds to be used to secure member residences.

Other Funding

Funding for other Legislative Branch agencies:

• House Operations: The bill contained $1.194 billion for operations of the House, an increase of $5 million from fiscal 2017 enacted levels.

• Architect of the Capitol: The AOC would see a $48.4 million boost over the enacted level to $577.8 million. This included $62 million for the continuation of the restoration and renovation of the Cannon House Office Building, and $31 million for the continuation of the Rayburn House Office Building garage rehabilitation project.

• Library of Congress: The library's budget would be increased by $16 million from fiscal 2017 levels, to $648 million. Language was included that would allow public access to all non-confidential Congressional Research Service reports, a change that government transparency organizations had been pushing.

• Government Accountability Office: The GAO, Congress' watchdog agency, would be funded at $568 million, $450,000 above the fiscal 2017 enacted level.

The bill also:

• Directed the chief administrative officer and the architect of the Capitol to explore adding more branded food options on the House side.

• Discussed efforts to expand the House's child care center and reduce its wait list.

• Suggested the possibility of adding 31 fellowship positions to the 54 two-year fellowships of the Wounded Warrior Program, which staffs congressional offices with wounded veterans.

• Directed the chief administrative officer to "establish a comprehensive wellness program" that would include "nutrition, fitness, general health, and stress management techniques, including meditation."

HOUSE COMMITTEE

The House Appropriations Committee approved the legislative branch bill by voice vote on June 29, after adopting an amendment aimed at combating bias in hiring on Capitol Hill.

The amendment from Rep. Barbara Lee, D-Calif., would require a plan to provide members and their staffs with training to combat unconscious bias in hiring and promotion and with education on the negative impacts of bias.

Lee told the committee that bias training covers not just perceptions of ethnicity or gender but also assumptions about what colleges job applicants have attended and a broad range of issues.

Lawmakers rejected by voice vote an amendment offered by Rep. Betty McCollum, D-Minn., that would direct the Congressional Research Service to submit a plan on how to make the reports public, including cost estimates and how shared websites, rather than just the CRS website, might post the reports. Report language included in the bill would make CRS reports available to the public on the CRS website. "Instead of rushing to impose a burdensome mandate on CRS and its analysts, Congress should hear from the agency itself," McCollum said.

McCollum supported making CRS reports public, but expressed concerns about transforming CRS into a public-facing agency and the strain that could put on the agency's resources. She suggested that reports could be made public on sites that already serve the public, such as Congress.gov.

SENATE COMMITTEE

The Senate Appropriations Committee on July 27 approved a $4.49 billion Legislative Branch spending bill that included an increased allocation for cybersecurity and the protection of senators, their staffs and visitors to the Capitol.

The measure, approved 31-0, would allocate $50 million more than fiscal 2017 enacted levels (PL 115-31) to fund the Senate, House, the Capitol Police, Congressional Budget Office, Library of Congress and other offices.

Of the total spending, $899.8 million would go to Senate operations, an increase of $28.6 million over fiscal 2017. The rest would go to joint and House-only operations, according to a committee statement. The House portion was reserved at $1.32 billion.

"New concerns and challenges require a greater emphasis on the security of those in the Capitol complex," said Appropriations Chairman Thad Cochran, R-Miss.

The Legislative Branch measure would provide $422.5 million for the Capitol Police, a $29.2 million increase over fiscal 2017. The Architect of the Capitol would receive $454 million under the bill, $38.9 million above fiscal 2017. According to the committee statement, funds would prioritize projects that addressed safety protections at the Capitol.

Senators' personal and office expense accounts could see an increase on an effort to improving cybersecurity for members' offices. Senators' salaries, however, would remain frozen under the measure. Salaries have not increased since 2009.

The bill would make non-confidential Congressional Research Service reports available to the public on the Government Publishing Office's website. Confidential reports and information on requests for reports would not be made public.

The House version of the bill had similar report language, although the House bill would make CRS reports available to the public on the CRS website.

The Library of Congress, which CRS operates within, would be funded at $638.9 million, $6.9 million above the fiscal 2017 level. Some of the increase would fund the multi-year process of modernizing its information technology systems.

The Government Accountability Office would be funded at $562.8 million for fiscal 2018 and the Government Publishing Office would see its funding remain unchanged at $117 million.

The Congressional Budget Office would see a $1.6 million increase over fiscal 2017 levels, $1.1 million of which will be used to relocate the CBO data center.

House members rejected two amendments on the floor that would have cut funds and made changes to the CBO's legislative scoring process. ∎

MILITARY CONSTRUCTION-VA

VA Electronic Health Records Prioritized

HOUSE SUBCOMMITTEE

The House Military Construction-VA Appropriations Subcommittee swiftly approved its fiscal 2018 spending bill by voice vote on June 12 with no amendments, saving a broader debate for full committee.

The subcommittee's voice vote on the $88.8 billion measure was the first formal action on an appropriations bill for the new fiscal year. It was $573 million below President Trump's request for all programs included in the bill.

Rep. Charlie Dent, R-Pa., chairman of the subcommittee, said the bill was "solid and fair." He also said the bill would provide funds for an electronic health record update proposed by then-VA Secretary David Shulkin identical to the record system used by the Department of Defense.

But Dent noted "the VA does not yet have an implementation plan" or a cost estimate for the effort, so the committee has "fence[d] 75 percent of EHR funds and all relevant accounts until VA gets us an implementation plan that's in order."

The bill was moving through the process much later than usual — the subcommittee only approved its fiscal 2017 measure at the end of March. Democrats pointed out that the House had no completed budget resolution to go by in fashioning appropriations bills. And they said Republicans should debate the serious spending issues ahead.

"Instead of working constructively, Republicans' markup is just pushing us deeper into the destructive uncertainty and chaos over the budget," House Minority Leader Nancy Pelosi, D-Calif., said in a statement. "Marking up one discretionary bill without any sense of the whole is irresponsible and counterproductive."

HOUSE COMMITTEE

The House Appropriations Committee advanced its bill on June 15 by voice vote, marking the first fiscal 2018 spending measure to be reported out of full committee in either chamber.

Lawmakers also adopted an "interim" discretionary spending allocation for the $88.8 billion measure that House Appropriations Chairman Rodney Frelinghuysen, R-N.J., said in a committee report would "help facilitate floor action" on the bill.

While the markup of the spending measure was fairly cordial, lawmakers split along partisan lines on the decision to move forward with the spending process without a budget or a clear division of discretionary funding among the 12 bills funding the government.

Because the committee moved to apply a discretionary spending level that would be enforceable on the House floor for just one bill funding the government, Democrats questioned what that meant for the other 11 bills and whether those other measures would suffer cuts at the expense of a boost for the first bill.

"While I appreciate the work on this bill, make no mistake. This committee will not return to regular order without addressing the budget caps as we have done every year since sequestration became law," said Nita M. Lowey of New York, the ranking Democrat on Appropriations. She was referring to discretionary spending limits put in

place under a 2011 deficit reduction law (PL 111-25). "I urge the chairman to bring your leadership and the White House to the negotiating table and work with Democrats to raise the budget caps."

In an accompanying report, lawmakers explained in harsh terms their rationale for walling off 75 percent of the $65 million in development funding for an electronic health record overhaul, which VA Secretary David Shulkin had announced would move forward under a sole source contract with Cerner, the same company used by the Defense Department.

"While enthusiastic about the Secretary's choice, the Committee has watched an integrated electronic record emerge and crash multiple times," the committee wrote in its report.

The committee also expressed concern that deteriorating air traffic control towers used by the Defense Department "are unsafe, antiquated, and do not provide adequate control, communications or observation abilities for current air traffic levels at certain levels at certain locations," pointing specifically to the Army's Fort Benning in Georgia. Lawmakers warned that the facility would become "wholly inadequate at the current pace of operations."

Overall, the bill's $88.8 billion would mostly go to the VA, which would be provided $182.3 billion in combined discretionary and mandatory funding, $5.3 billion more than the 2017 level.

The measure also proposed a significant 25 percent or $2.1 billion boost from fiscal 2017 for military construction at a total funding level of $10.2 billion.

The House measure was $573 million below President Donald Trump's request but a significant boost from the $82.5 billion Congress and President Barack Obama agreed to provide in September 2016 (PL 114-223). The measure contained $638 million in Overseas Contingency Operations funding, an account that does not count against discretionary spending caps.

SENATE SUBCOMMITTEE

The Senate Military Construction-VA Appropriations Subcommittee on July 12 approved an $88.9 billion measure to fund veterans programs and military construction. The measure was approved by voice vote and without amendment.

The draft measure would provide an increase of $6.1 billion over existing appropriations (PL 114-223). The measure included $78.4 billion in discretionary funds for the Department of Veterans Affairs, a boost of $4 billion over fiscal 2017.

Military construction would receive $9.5 billion for a total 214 projects, a $1.8 billion increase over enacted levels but $246 million below President Donald Trump's budget request

Included in the military construction funds was $154 million "to provide infrastructure for training, deterrence and the NATO alliance's response to challenges posed by Russia and threats from the Middle East and North Africa."

Sen. Brian Schatz of Hawaii, top Democrat on the subcommittee, praised the typically popular measure as a "bipartisan initial step in the appropriations process" and he said the funding in the bill was a "solid allocation."

But Schatz warned of broader problems ahead if Congress didn't agree on new budget legislation to raise the statutory limits on discretionary spending put in place in 2011 (PL 112-25).

"We are operating in the shadow of BCA," he said, using the shorthand for the 2011 law known as the Budget Control Act. "We'll soon face a reckoning on how we're going to fund all the competing demands on the nondefense side of the budget unless we can lift BCA."

The measure would provide $70.1 billion for veterans medical care, expected to benefit about 9.2 million patients in fiscal 2018. Medical care for veterans of the Iraq and Afghanistan wars would be funded at about $5.5 billion, and $316 million would go toward treating traumatic brain injuries.

At least $180 million was included for processing disability claims. A large portion of those funds would go towards the digital scanning of health records.

The military construction funds included:
- $307 million for European Reassurance Initiative projects.
- $331 million in Overseas Contingency Operations funds for projects in the Middle East.
- $1.4 billion for military family housing.
- $556 million for military medical facilities.
- $249 million for improvements at four overseas military schools.
- $575 million for National Guard and Reserve construction needs.

The bill also would provide $70.7 billion in advance discretionary funds for veterans health care in fiscal 2019, and $107.7 billion in advance mandatory spending for veterans benefits in fiscal 2019.

Arlington National Cemetery would receive $81 million under the bill, and the American Battle Monuments Commission would see $79 million, according to a summary.

Sen. Shelley Moore Capito, R-W.Va., said she was pleased the legislation also would create a pilot program to encourage the use of "agritherapy" among veterans with post-traumatic stress disorder.

Capito said agritherapy is "an issue that I got into when I went to visit a beekeeper who is training veterans who have PTSD in beekeeping and agritherapy, [and] I've really become a believer in this."

She said the bill included "language and some funds for a pilot project on agritherapy for our veterans."

SENATE COMMITTEE

The Senate Appropriations Committee on July 13 unanimously approved an $88.9 billion military construction and VA bill.

The panel approved the measure 31-0 and debated amendments related to medical marijuana for veterans, services for veterans with a less than honorable discharge and more.

Many lawmakers in both parties were hoping for a new deal to raise the defense and nondefense discretionary spending limits for fiscal 2018, prescribed by a 2011 budget law. Appropriators in the House and Senate indicated that if a budget agreement was reached, they would go back and add new funding to the bills they were marking up at lower spending levels.

The committee adopted an amendment from Sens. Steve Daines, R-Mont., and Jeff Merkley, D-Ore., to allow veterans greater access to medical marijuana in states where the substance is legal for health purposes.

The amendment would bar funds from being used to block VA doctors from discussing medical marijuana with veterans or to otherwise interfere with a veteran's ability to participate in a medical marijuana program approved by the state.

Adoption of the provision, on a 24-7 vote, again demonstrated the growing popularity of looser marijuana laws among lawmakers. A similar amendment the previous year from Daines and Merkley was adopted 20-10.

The panel also adopted by voice vote an amendment from Sen. Christopher S. Murphy, D-Conn., that would direct the VA to provide

mental and behavioral health care to veterans who were discharged from the military "under conditions other than honorable."

"These are individuals who did not go through any due process. They were simply given a discharge, likely because of some act that they committed related to their PTSD," Murphy said. Because of that "less than honorable" designation, those veterans could not access needed services from the VA.

He specified that the provision did not apply to those who were dishonorably discharged. It would make VA behavioral health resources available to veterans who had served in combat, were diagnosed with PTSD and had been given "this narrow category of discharge," Murphy said. Murphy also noted the amendment would effectively codify steps that the VA was already taking to help veterans with a less than honorable discharge. ■

STATE-FOREIGN OPERATIONS

Senate More Generous With Foreign Aid

HOUSE SUBCOMMITTEE

The House State-Foreign Operations Appropriations Subcommittee on July 13 approved a $47.4 billion bill for diplomacy and foreign assistance programs that Democrats grudgingly acknowledged was much less draconian than the White House proposal but still far from the policy priorities of the Obama administration.

The subcommittee quickly approved the legislation by voice vote and without amendment.

Overall, the bill would cut State and foreign aid accounts by $10 billion from existing levels. Subcommittee Chairman Harold Rogers, R-Ky., defended the proposed cuts, noting they were $7 billion less than what the Trump administration wanted to cut.

The legislation, Rogers said, "strikes the appropriate balance of fiscal responsibility and support for continued United States' diplomatic management and foreign assistance."

Rep. Nita M. Lowey of New York, the ranking Democrat on Appropriations, said that "while the bill rejects many of the most extreme cuts proposed in the president's budget, the cuts in this bill would make regions less stable and diminish our global leadership by severely reducing or eliminating funding for programs such as multilateral cooperation, international family planning, and climate change."

She thanked Republicans for disregarding the administration's request to end support for a number of taxpayer-funded foreign policy think tanks and development organizations even as many of those organizations, such as the United States Institute of Peace, would see funding reduced.

The measure would protect existing funding levels for democracy promotion programs, basic education, water and sanitation, and women's programs. Lowey applauded those moves while criticizing the bill for proposing to codify a Trump administration order to expand the application of the Mexico City rule to cover all public health programs. The rule prohibits any U.S. foreign aid for nongovernmental organizations that perform or share information about abortions.

The measure included $8.3 billion for global health and more than $5.9 billion for humanitarian assistance.

Funding for the United Nations and its agencies would be cut 18.4 percent, with all funding eliminated for the United Nations Development Program, U.N. Women and several other international organizations.

HOUSE COMMITTEE

The House Appropriations Committee approved the foreign aid and diplomacy bill following a late-night markup on June 19 that lasted for more than two hours and included a number of partisan discussions about the United Nations, access to family planning, and whether federal funds should be spent on hotel properties owned by the president.

The legislation, approved by voice vote, included at least one policy rider Democrats strongly opposed.

The bill would slash $10 billion — a 17 percent reduction from existing levels — in funding for the State Department, U.S. Agency for International Development, and other aid agencies.

The measure would prohibit the secretary of State from implementing any reorganization of the State Department or USAID until the proposed alterations were submitted to congressional oversight committees for review. Multiple news reports had suggested the Trump administration was considering ending or shifting out of the State Department's core missions, such as consular affairs, refugee screening and cybersecurity.

Despite the fraught nature of the geopolitical issues the committee considered, the tone of debate was mostly civil. The tensest moments occurred when the panel discussed relations with Cuba and when Democrats unsuccessfully pushed an amendment that would have prevented State Department funds from being spent on renting rooms at Trump Organization properties.

Rogers argued that the amendment was unnecessary. "The money in our bill can't be spent in violation of the emolument's clause of the Constitution," he said.

Democratic members responded by calling for a committee investigation into news reports of federal funds used in 2017 to pay for rooms at a Trump-branded hotel in Vancouver, Canada, and in support of a company promotion trip taken by the president's younger son, Eric, to Uruguay.

"We have the power of the purse," said Marcy Kaptur, D-Ohio. "We need to know where the money went. Why can't we ask for that?"

Republicans struck down by a vote of 22-30 an amendment from Barbara Lee, D-Calif., to restore $358 million that the legislation proposed cutting from the international organizations and programs account, which funds United Nations activities.

"These U.N. agencies are on the frontline of humanitarian crises and are able to work in areas that the United States cannot," Lee said.

Rogers defended the cuts in funding for the United Nations and other foreign aid programs as necessary given the smaller allocation the subcommittee was given.

Republicans also voted 23-29 to reject an amendment from Lowey to remove language to codify the Trump administration's expansion of the Mexico City rule. Democrats criticized the State Department for enacting the change without first conducting a study about how it would affect access to global health programs.

SENATE SUBCOMMITTEE

Senators indicated on Sept. 6 that they intended to hold the line on foreign aid, approving at the subcommittee level a fiscal 2018 spending bill that was $4 billion larger than its counterpart in the House and nearly $14 billion bigger than what the Trump administration had sought.

Still, the nearly $51.4 billion measure fell $6.1 billion below existing spending levels, which were unusually high to account for an unprecedented worldwide refugee crisis and four near-famine situations, all of which showed no signs of ending anytime soon.

South Carolina Republican Lindsey Graham, chairman of the State-Foreign Operations Appropriations Subcommittee, acknowledged during the 10-minute markup he would have liked the bill, which was closer to fiscal 2016 levels, to have been bigger. But Congress, he said, was waiting to learn Secretary of State Rex Tillerson's options for reorganizing the State Department and the U.S. Agency for International Development, which were due by the middle of September.

"The bottom line is the president's budget was going to cut the State Department by 29 percent," Graham said. "We are trying to restore funding as close to the 2017 levels as possible."

Sen. Patrick J. Leahy of Vermont, the top Democrat on the Appropriations Committee, applauded Graham for seeking to protect as much of the development and diplomacy budget as he did.

"You've reaffirmed Congress's support for international diplomacy and development at a time when they are under assault," Leahy said." I think as chairman, you've done a good job with what we had to spend."

The legislation included $30.4 billion in base-budget funding and $20.8 billion for Overseas Contingency Operations.

With senators leery of potential politically motivated reorganizational changes at Foggy Bottom, the bill would require any proposed changes to first be submitted to Congress' investigative arm, the Government Accountability Office, for review. The legislation also would take away the Trump administration's authority to change certain operating and assistance funding levels and specifically would forbid the use of funds to merge USAID into the State Department.

The legislation would provide more than $6.2 billion in disaster aid and humanitarian assistance, which was $627 million less than existing levels. Still, the figure was nearly $1 billion more than what the administration requested and over $300 million more than what the House was seeking to provide. Humanitarian aid included $3.1 billion for the Migration and Refugee Assistance account and $3.1 billion for the International Disaster Assistance account.

Efforts to counter Russia's malign influence activities were funded at $120 million, $20 million more than existing funding levels. Bipartisan frustration had erupted in the summer when Tillerson reportedly declined to spend $80 million appropriated for fiscal 2017 to counter propaganda by Russia and the Islamic State through the State Department's revamped Global Engagement Center.

The spending measure would continue longtime defense assistance to Israel at $3.1 billion, while Jordan would receive a notable boost of over $220 million compared to existing levels. Jordan would receive $1.5 billion in economic and security assistance.

"It is my view that this bill is national security in another form," Graham said.

Egypt's defense aid would be reduced to just $1 billion, down $300 million from enacted levels. Economic assistance would also be lowered to $75 million, a $37 million cut from appropriated levels. Both Graham and Leahy had criticized Egyptian President Abdel Fattah al-Sisi's crackdown on human rights and democracy activists.

The Trump administration notified Cairo in August that it would lose almost $100 million in 2017 and that another $200 million would be delayed due to the Egyptian government's failure to improve the human rights situation in the country.

The legislation would provide nearly $8.6 billion for global public health programs, $135 million less than existing levels though $2.1 billion more than the 2018 request. The number included over $4.3 billion for the President's Emergency Plan for AIDS Relief and nearly $1.4 billion for the Global Fund to Fight AIDS, tuberculosis and malaria.

SENATE COMMITTEE

A few critical votes from Republicans allowed Democrats to push through amendments on climate change and family planning in the Senate Appropriations Committee before the bill was approved, 31-0, on Sept. 7. The amendments would effectively maintain existing funding levels for international family planning programs and move $10 million from a development assistance account to the U.N. Intergovernmental Panel on Climate Change.

The Senate measure was nearly $51.4 billion, which was $4 billion more than the House version (HR 3362) and almost $14 billion more than what the Trump administration requested. However, the Senate bill was $6.1 billion below fiscal 2017 enacted levels.

A family planning amendment from Sen. Jeanne Shaheen, D-N.H., was adopted by a vote of 16-15 with Republican votes coming from Sens. Susan Collins of Maine and Lisa Murkowski of Alaska. Sen. Joe Manchin III of West Virginia was the only Democrat to oppose.

The measure would repeal the Mexico City policy that blocks federal funding for nongovernmental organizations that provide information about abortions, a policy reinstated by Trump in January. It changed the underlying bill to provide a total of $585 million for bilateral family planning programs and $37.5 million to the U.N. Population Fund.

The House's version of the bill would deny any funding to the U.N. Population Fund and would codify the Trump administration's reinstatement and expansion of the Mexico City rule to cover all public health programs.

The amendment on climate change from Sen. Jeff Merkley, D-Ore., was adopted 16-14-1 with Manchin opposing, Collins and Sen. Lamar Alexander, R-Tenn., supporting and Graham abstaining.

The committee also adopted, by voice vote, an amendment that would deny the sale of equipment to the Turkish president's personal bodyguard. Senators were still outraged by the May incident in which members of President Recep Tayyip Erdogan's personal security detail

attacked pro-democracy protesters outside the Turkish embassy in Washington.

The prohibition, offered by Sen. Chris Van Hollen, D-Md., would remain in place until the State Department certified the Turkish government had made demonstrable progress on human rights.

The spending bill also included a Senate Foreign Relations-

approved measure (HR 1697) that would suspend roughly $328 million in economic support funds for the Palestinian Authority. The funding would be resumed once the Authority ceased payments to the families of those killed or imprisoned for carrying out terrorist attacks on Israelis. The measure, which made limited humanitarian exceptions, would place the withheld funds in an escrow account for one year. ■

TRANSPORTATION-HUD

Committees Differ on TIGER Funding

HOUSE SUBCOMMITTEE

The House Transportation-HUD Appropriations Subcommittee approved its $56.5 billion fiscal 2018 spending bill by voice vote on July 11.

The bill would appropriate discretionary funding for the Department of Transportation at $17.8 billion and the Department of Housing and Urban Development at $38.3 billion. The proposal would be a 2 percent cut in the budgets of the two departments, compared with the $57.65 billion appropriated in the fiscal 2017 omnibus spending bill (PL 115-31). The bill would provide nearly 20 percent more than requested by President Donald Trump.

Subcommittee Chairman Mario Diaz-Balart, R-Fla., noted lawmakers' willingness to provide more than the administration had requested. For example, the Trump administration had proposed cutting all funding for projects in the Federal Transit Administration's Capital Investment Grant program that didn't have fully funded grant agreements, but the House proposal would provide funding to projects still in the works.

"We did not agree with administration's proposal to shut down the Capital Improvement Grant program and instead included funding to keep projects moving through the pipeline," Diaz-Balart said.

Ranking Democrat David E. Price of North Carolina said a bill that funded more than the administration requested was a low bar to clear and that the bill's overall numbers were unacceptable.

The bill adhered to interim discretionary allocations by the House Appropriations Committee. Price said the allocation was "unworkable" and would require unacceptable cuts in key programs at the departments.

He applauded a few funding increases, such as to the Federal Railroad Administration's Federal-State Partnership for State of Good Repair program and other safety programs at transportation agencies. But he said those raises didn't do enough, and he blamed House Republicans majority for not adopting a budget resolution with overall spending levels acceptable to members of both parties.

Following the 18-minute markup, Diaz-Balart told reporters he was faced with tough decisions to meet the spending limit and still fund vital programs. His priorities, he said, were safety programs on the transportation side and housing programs that served "the most vulnerable." He indicated funding for some programs would have to be revisited later in the appropriations process.

"I've got to do with the money that I have," he said. "Look at the bill

— where do I take it out of? It's always easier to just ask for more money. It's a lot more difficult to put together a bill where you have to prioritize, which we've done. I think this is a very good bill. Now, are there areas where we're going to have to revisit? Absolutely."

The Trump administration had recommended zeroing out the Choice Neighborhoods Initiative, which funds local plans to revitalize struggling neighborhoods, but Price thanked Diaz-Balart for the "placeholder" funding of $20 million for the program. The program had a $137.5 million budget in fiscal 2017.

The bill would eliminate funding for the Transportation Investment Generating Economic Recovery, or TIGER, grant program that was popular with lawmakers. The program was funded at $500 million in fiscal 2017.

The bill also would spend $900 million mainly on the Gateway Program of bridges and tunnels connecting New York and New Jersey. With a ban on congressional earmarks, the bill didn't specify the target for that money, but few projects other than Gateway would be able to meet the criteria in the bill.

HOUSE COMMITTEE

The House Appropriations Committee approved, 31-20, a $56.5 billion fiscal 2018 Transportation-HUD spending bill on July 17 that would reduce funding by 2 percent from fiscal 2017 (PL 115-31) and eliminate the popular Transportation Investment Generating Economic Recovery, or TIGER grants.

The bill would provide about 20 percent more funding for the Transportation and Housing and Urban Development departments than President Trump requested.

"We are $1.1 billion below the enacted [2017] level, but $8.6 billion above the budget request," Transportation-HUD Subcommittee Chairman Mario Diaz-Balart, R-Fla., noted during the markup. "We have targeted funding in this bill to essential investments in safety, infrastructure, and housing assistance for our most vulnerable populations. This includes the elderly, the disabled, and our veterans."

Henry Cuellar of Texas was the only Democrat to vote with the Republican majority.

The measure would provide $17.8 billion in discretionary funding for the Department of Transportation and $38.3 billion in net discretionary funding for the Department of Housing and Urban Development. The bill also would fund related independent agencies, including the

Neighborhood Reinvestment Corp., the National Transportation Safety Board and the Federal Maritime Commission.

Democrats criticized Republicans for not allowing more robust spending on infrastructure, and they blasted Trump for not yet introducing an infrastructure plan after promising a package to spend $1 trillion on a wide variety of projects over 10 years.

In the absence of such a plan, Price proposed an amendment that would add $200 billion for transportation and housing infrastructure.

He wanted to add $75 billion for highways and bridges, including $70 billion distributed under existing formulas. It also would appropriate $30 billion to the TIGER grant program that the base bill would eliminate. It would add $10 billion for HUD Community Development Block Grants.

Diaz-Balart opposed the Price amendment, and several other Democrats sought to increase funding for various programs. Each time, he said the amendment would force the bill to exceed the bill's budget allocation, and therefore would stop the bill from being brought to the House floor.

The committee rejected the Price amendment on a party line vote, 21-30.

Each subsequent Democratic amendment to increase funding—including proposals to reinstate funding for TIGER grants, increase funding for transit agencies to install positive train control, and increase funding for veterans housing vouchers and other proposals—was met with the same argument. Each was rejected 21-30.

Appropriators rejected steep budget cuts at HUD recommended by the administration. In particular, they declined to follow the administration's request to zero out grant programs favored by local governments, including the $3.1 billion Community Development Block Grant program and the $950 million HOME Investment Partnerships Program. The bill would instead cut $100 million from each.

SENATE SUBCOMMITTEE

The Senate Transportation-HUD Appropriations Subcommittee approved by voice vote a $60.1 billion draft bill on July 25 that would raise spending across the two departments by about 4 percent and reject the administration's call to eliminate or reduce funding for several programs.

The bill rejected cuts in transportation and HUD programs requested by Trump, including the TIGER grant program, the Essential Air Service subsidy, HUD's Community Development Block Grant and HOME Investment Partnerships programs.

"The bill does not include proposals in the president's budget that would have eliminated or made drastic reductions in some of the most effective programs supported by virtually all members of the subcommittee," Subcommittee Chairwoman Susan Collins, R-Maine, said.

The bill rejected Trump's request to remove the air traffic control system from the Federal Aviation Administration. Collins called the proposal "a solution in search of a problem."

The subcommittee's ranking Democrat, Jack Reed of Rhode Island, praised the measure as a "thoughtful, well-crafted bill put together under very tight allocations that includes priorities of members of both sides of the aisle." But he planned to offer an amendment to increase overall spending.

The Senate bill was about $3.6 billion more than the House Appropriations Committee's $56.5 billion Transportation-HUD spending bill (HR 3353) for fiscal 2018 approved July 17.

Lawmakers provided $57.6 billion for Transportation-HUD in the

fiscal 2017 spending law (PL 115-31).

The Senate bill would provide $19.5 billion in discretionary spending for the Department of Transportation, a 6 percent increase from fiscal 2017. It would also provide $40.2 billion for HUD, a 3.7 percent increase. More than half of the bill would go toward rental assistance, Collins said, though a topline figure for rental assistance was not included in the release.

The administration had sought to cut nearly 20 percent from HUD's discretionary budget.

The Senate bill also included:

• $550 million for TIGER grants, which was $50 million more than the funding in fiscal 2017. The House would eliminate the program.

• $12.1 billion for the Federal Transit Administration, about $380 million more than in the House bill.

• $2.1 billion for the FTA's Capital Investment Grants program that funds new transit programs or expansions to existing ones, $383 million more than the House proposed and $900 million more than the administration's budget request.

• $17 billion for the Federal Aviation Administration, about $4 billion more than was in the House bill.

• $3 billion for HUD's Community Development Block Grant program, consistent with fiscal 2017 and $100 million more than the House proposed.

• $950 million for the HOME Investment Partnerships Program, the same as fiscal 2017 and $100 million more than House appropriators approved.

SENATE COMMITTEE

The Senate Appropriations Committee voted 31-0 on July 27 to approve a $60.1 billion spending bill that would allow airports to raise a fee on airline passengers to fund improvements.

The measure would provide about $3.6 billion more for the departments of Transportation and Housing and Urban Development and other agencies than the House bill (HR 3353). Apart from the topline number, the major differences between Senate and House bills were the funding for the TIGER grant program and for a rail state-of-good-repair program.

Senators would provide $550 million for the TIGER program, a 10 percent increase from the fiscal 2017 level of $500 million. House appropriators would defund the program.

Sen. Susan Collins, R-Maine, who chaired the Transportation-HUD Subcommittee, described the bill as the result of compromise and consensus among members of both parties on the panel.

The bill included a policy rider that would allow airports to raise the Passenger Facility Charge that is added to the price of every ticket. The revenue from the charge is used to fund construction and repair runways and other airport infrastructure. The Senate bill would allow airports to charge up to $8.50 per ticket on passengers' originating flights, a $4 increase from current law.

The change would not affect connecting airports, which could still only charge up to $4.50.

Groups representing airports, including the Airports Council International-North America, touted the measure as a tool to help close the gap between airports' construction needs and available funding.

Airlines and other travelers groups opposed the rider, saying it would add to consumers' cost of air travel and could lead to fewer airline ticket sales.

Despite the unanimous vote, ranking Democrat Jack Reed said

the overall allocation was too low. Reed, of Rhode Island, offered an amendment to increase funding in the bill by $7.7 billion, to about fiscal 2010 levels. Reed's proposal would add $1 billion to TIGER and use another $2 billion to create a discretionary grant program to replace and repair ailing bridges.

Collins said she favored revisiting budget caps to allow more spending on transportation and housing, but said the fiscal 2010 level, enacted as part of an economic stimulus, shouldn't be used as the baseline for spending. Excepting stimulus and sequestration years, the bill was otherwise consistent with gradual increases, she said.

"I don't think we should be using an aberration year — of either the stimulus rollout or sequestration on the other side — as a basis, but rather look at the pattern," she said. "Let me make clear that I, like many around this table, believe that [Budget Control Act, or PL 112-25] caps need to be revisited, and in a responsible way. But to do so requires Congress to act, and that hasn't happened yet."

The committee rejected the amendment on a 15-16 party line vote.

Rep. Mario Diaz-Balart, chairman of the House Transportation-HUD Appropriations Subcommittee, said he saw few substantive differences between his panel's bill and the Senate version, apart from a couple of aviation policy riders.

"We could pretty quickly resolve the differences," Diaz-Balart, R-Fla., said.

Lawmakers provided $57.6 billion for Transportation-HUD in the fiscal 2017 spending. The bill House Appropriations approved July 17 would spend $56.5 billion. ∎

Disaster Relief OK'd After Hurricanes

2017 was the most active hurricane season impacting the United States since 2005, the previous year when any major hurricane (Category 3 or above) made landfall in the United States. In 2017, four hurricanes hit the U.S. (Hurricanes Harvey, Irma, Maria and Nate) — all but Nate being major Category 4 hurricanes at landfall that caused extensive damage. In addition, major wildfires were among the dozens of major disasters declared under the Stafford Act in 2017.

Congress initially enacted two supplemental appropriations bills in response to Trump administration requests made in September 2017 (PL 115-56) and October 2017 (PL 115-72) — providing almost $52 billion in aid (including by canceling $16 billion in Treasury debt incurred by the National Flood Insurance Program so it could continue to borrow to pay claims). The measure also included $4.9 billion in disaster relief loans to Puerto Rico and the U.S. Virgin Islands.

Also, in late September, Congress enacted two bills that provided additional benefits for hurricane victims. The first (PL 115-63) provided certain tax cuts and tax benefits to individuals living in areas impacted by Hurricanes Harvey, Irma and Maria. The second (PL 115-64) required the Education Department to take several actions to make extra federal funding available for student aid and support in areas designated as disaster areas because of the hurricanes, including by waiving non-federal matching fund requirements for two campus-based student aid programs.

The administration in November made a third request for an additional $44 billion in disaster relief funding, and in response the House in December passed legislation (HR 4667) to provide $81 billion in additional disaster aid.

Of the total, almost $54 billion would have gone to two major federal response and recovery program accounts: $27.5 billion for FEMA's Disaster Relief Fund and $26 billion for HUD's Community Development Block Grant Program. Another $12.1 billion would've been for the Army Corps of Engineers to make needed repairs to Corps infrastructure and to undertake dredging and other activities. And it included billions of dollars in aid for agricultural producers and to help get schools up and running again and to support displaced students; dozens of federal agencies would also receive funding to repair damaged equipment and facilities.

The measure was never considered by the Senate, largely due to Democratic objections over inadequate funding for Puerto Rico.

Senate Minority Leader Charles E. Schumer, D-N.Y., blasted the Republican-written bill in floor remarks, calling it "an unacceptable disaster supplemental, which still does not treat fairly California, Puerto Rico and the U.S. Virgin Islands."

Schumer criticized Republicans for not including additional funds for Medicaid, drinking water and infrastructure in the disaster aid package. He was also critical of the bill for not extending the earned-income tax credit for Puerto Rico.

"Those things must be fixed before a disaster supplemental can move forward," Schumer said. "Because of these inadequacies, the disaster supplemental may have to slip to next year."

During House debate, Rep. José E. Serrano, D-N.Y., had said he would oppose the measure since it would give Puerto Rico's oversight board authority over the island territory's disaster recovery plan. Serrano also called for more support for New York and New Jersey, where he said many hurricane victims had flocked for shelter.

In contrast, Rep. Mike Thompson, D-Calif., called the December funding package an "important first step" in a long-term recovery from wildfires that decimated communities in his district. "Folks in California who experienced this terrible disaster need our help," Thompson said.

Congress eventually provided $89.3 billion in additional aid to continue response and recovery from the damage caused by hurricanes, wildfires and other weather events in 2017. But that occurred after the calendar had turned to 2018, and was part of the Bipartisan Budget Act (PL 115-123).

Of the BBA's disaster total, $23.5 billion was for FEMA's Disaster Relief Fund, $28 billion was for the Housing and Urban Development Department's Community Development Block Grant Program, and $17.4 billion was for the Army Corps of Engineers to make needed repairs to Corps infrastructure and to undertake dredging and other activities. It also included $3.7 billion to support Puerto Rico's Medicaid program. ∎

Chapter 3
BANKING & FINANCIAL SERVICES

Trump, Congress Start Whittling Away at Dodd-Frank Financial Regulation Law

Ever since President Barack Obama signed the Wall Street regulation bill known as Dodd-Frank in 2010, Republicans had been working to roll it back, but with little success so long as Obama remained in the White House. During his 2016 presidential campaign, Donald Trump frequently vowed to "dismantle" Dodd-Frank, which he called a "disaster." By the end of his first year in office, Trump could claim some partial successes in overturning administrative rules, but a major overhaul of the law remained on hold.

The 2010 law (PL 111-203), written in the aftermath of the 2008 financial crisis, had passed the House with just three Republican votes. Attempts by GOP leaders in 2016 to change the law fell short of floor action.

By the end of 2017, the House had passed a GOP-written bill to overturn Dodd-Frank. Efforts to find a bipartisan approach stretched into May 2018, when Trump signed a measure (PL 115-74) that made major changes to Dodd-Frank but left its basic structure intact.

HOUSE, SENATE ACTION ON REGULATIONS

The GOP began a piecemeal assault on Dodd-Frank just two weeks after Trump was inaugurated, when the House adopted a resolution under the 1996 Congressional Review Act (PL 104-121) to nullify a Securities and Exchange Commission rule intended to discourage companies from bribing foreign government for rights to extract oil, gas and minerals. The rule had required them to report any such payments.

The House adopted the resolution (H J Res 41) to overturn the SEC rule on Feb. 1, 2017, by a mostly party line 235-187 vote. The Congressional Review Act enables Congress to void regulations that have been finalized in the previous 60 legislative calendar days.

House Banking Chairman Jeb Hensarling, R-Texas, said the bill would rid the country of a "politically driven regulation" that he said gave foreign companies an advantage over American public firms. The rule, Hensarling said, required companies to disclose certain contracts which could be obtained by overseas competitors. U.S. companies, he said, had to shoulder nearly $600 million a year in compliance costs .

The Senate adopted the resolution, 52-47, on Feb. 3 and Trump signed it on Feb. 14.

TRUMP SEEKS MAJOR OVERHAUL

On Feb. 3, Trump directed his Treasury secretary, Steven Mnuchin, to compile a list of all financial laws and regulations he thought reined in economic growth, hampered the competitiveness of businesses or narrowed Americans' ability to make financial decisions. Although Trump's order didn't mention Dodd-Frank, it was clear that the regulatory law was a target.

"We expect to be cutting a lot out of Dodd Frank," Trump said during a meeting with corporate executives, "because frankly I have so many people, friends of mine, that have nice businesses and they can't borrow money. They just can't get any money because the banks just won't let them borrow because of the rules and regulations of Dodd Frank."

Hensarling, who was standing nearby when Trump signed the order, said it closely reflected the Dodd-Frank repeal bill his committee had approved in 2016. Trump's action, he said, showed a desire "to end Wall Street bailouts, end 'too big to fail,' and end top-down regulations."

One of Trump's core principles was to avoid taxpayer funded bailouts of institutions deemed too big to fail. Many congressional Republicans, however, said that Dodd-Frank had encouraged the growth of the biggest financial institutions, making them too big to be allowed to fail.

When he issued his report June 12, however, Mnuchin recommended only some of the most significant changes that Republican lawmakers had been advancing in legislation. Those included giving the president the authority to fire the director of the Consumer Financial Protection Bureau at will, to make "substantial" changes to a rule limiting risky trading by banks, and to reconsider the $50 billion threshold above which banks get extra regulatory scrutiny. In other areas, however, the Treasury secretary took a different tack than the House, He recommended, for example, changing rather than repealing the Volcker rule that bars federally insured banks from risky trading and urging more authority for the Financial Stability Oversight Council.

Among the recommendations in the 149-page report were steps to:

Simplify the risk-based capital requirements for community banks.

Change the CFPB's ability-to-repay and qualified mortgage rules put in place after the financial crisis.

"Significantly streamline" application processes for new banks to get deposit insurance.

Require independent agencies, including financial regulators, to do the kind of cost-benefit analyses for their bigger-impact rules that executive departments are already required to do.

"Comprehensively assess" how the Community Reinvestment Act could be improved.

Provide a regulatory off-ramp for stress testing and living wills for any bank maintaining high levels of capital, such as the 10 percent figure a House bill would use to allow banks to opt out of enhanced Federal Reserve regulation.

Make the Dodd-Frank law's Office of Financial Research part of the Treasury, rather than being independently funded.

Dodd-Frank also established the Financial Stability Oversight Council, a panel of regulators tasked with identifying risks to the financial system. Congressional Republicans have frequently criticized FSOC, saying it has unchecked power and lacks transparency.

But Mnuchin's report recommended that Congress expand FSOC's powers "to play a larger role" in the coordination of what it describes as a fragmented U.S. regulatory system rife with overlap and duplication. As Treasury secretary, Mnuchin chaired the FSOC, which included among its members the heads of the major regulators, including the Federal Reserve, the Securities and Exchange Commission and the Federal Deposit Insurance Corporation.

HOUSE ACTION

Hensarling introduced what he called the "Financial Choice Act" (HR 10) on April 26. It was meant to repeal much of Dodd-Frank and restructure the Consumer Financial Protection Bureau, which had been established by the law. The bill would do away with the Volcker Rule that basically prohibited banks from speculating in the markets and barred them from investing in or running hedge funds and private-equity funds.

Dodd-Frank was designed to prevent the type of practices that led to the financial crisis and the recession it caused. Republicans, though, had long complained that the law stifled the economy because it put too large a regulatory burden on business.

"All of the promises of Dodd-Frank were broken," Hensarling said. "It promised us it would lift the economy, but we are stymied in the weakest and slowest recovery in the post-war era."

But in the view of the Democratic leader in the House, Nancy Pelosi of California, Republicans were forgetting the lessons of the financial crisis.

"House Republicans," she said, "are pushing a dangerous Wall Street-first bill that will drag us straight back into the days of the Great Recession." She described Hensarling's bill as "dastardly" and "malicious."

HOUSE COMMITTEE ACTION

The House Financial Services Committee reported HR 10 on May 3 by a party line vote of 34-26.

The measure was sweeping, changing how the federal government regulates banks and Wall Street and rescinding the Labor Department's fiduciary rule, a requirement that broker-dealers put their clients' interest ahead of their own in giving retirement advice. The measure would undo the Volcker rule's restrictions on proprietary trading at banks and a provision that capped the amount banks could charge retailers in debit card fees. It would accomplish a longtime GOP goal of overhauling the Consumer Financial Protection Bureau.

Partisanship dominated the markup. Panel members rejected 19 Democratic amendments in party line votes.

"I can't do a good James Brown, but I feel good," Hensarling said as he walked down the hall in the Rayburn House Office Building after the vote. "We look forward to taking it to the floor. This economy is poised to take off. It's not going to take off as long as Dodd-Frank in its current form remains on the books."

"It's a bill that I think is going nowhere," Rep. Gregory W. Meeks, a senior Democrat on the committee from New York, said of Hensarling's bill. "I would hope at some point we would be able to sit down and work out what's real."

Debate on the bill ate up 14 hours on the first day of the markup and 13 more the next day, with breaks for floor votes. Democrats tried to delay proceedings, including by asking for a reading of nearly 200 pages that lasted three hours.

The Republicans rejected the following Democratic amendments:

• Eight amendments aimed at maintaining the CFPB's financial independence and enforcement powers.

• An amendment that would delay implementation of the bill until an ethics panel determines whether President Donald Trump and his senior advisers would benefit.

• An amendment that would strike the section of the bill that changes the Federal Reserve's Federal Open Market Committee makeup and how it deliberates.

• Amendments that would rescind the Volcker and fiduciary rules.

• An amendment that would bar banks from enforcing mandatory arbitration clauses in cases where a customer account was fraudulently opened. Wells Fargo had paid the CFPB $100 million after admitting that it opened nearly 2 million bank and credit card accounts without customers' authorization.

• An amendment that would keep the Orderly Liquidation Authority, the Dodd-Frank created mechanism to unwind big failed banks.

• An amendment that would strike changes to Securities and Exchange Commission enforcement procedures and practices.

• An amendment that would delay changes in regulations brought about by the bill until it is determined whether the changes would benefit a creditor listed on any of Trump's last seven tax returns.

The two days of testy debate reached their crescendo over an amendment from Rep. Michael E. Capuano, D-Mass., that Republicans decried as an overtly political attack on Trump. Capuano's amendment would delay implementation of the bill until the Office of Government Ethics determined that the repeal of Dodd-Frank would not financially benefit Trump or others in his administration. Given the extensive financial holdings of Trump and his top advisers, there were fears that an ethics panel probe would delay implementation indefinitely.

Rep. Blaine Luetkemeyer, R-Mo., called the amendment "as partisan as it gets."

Capuano's amendment failed 26-33.

Republicans also rejected an amendment from Rep. Brad Sherman, D-Calif., who wanted to bar banks from forcing customers to accept arbitration to resolve disputes in cases such as Wells Fargo.

CBO ASSESSMENT

The Congressional Budget Office gave Hensarling a boost with a May 18 report that his bill would likely cut the federal budget deficit by more than $24 billion over the 10 years. Hensarling said the CBO score affirmed the Republican contention that the bill would eliminate "forever" the possibility of large bank bailouts.

"The Financial Choice Act is not what Wall Street wants, but it is what Main Street and hardworking taxpayers need," Hensarling said.

CBO estimated the legislation would reduce federal deficits by $24.1 billion over the 2017-2027 period. The office said "direct spending" would be reduced by $30.1 billion and revenues would shrink by $5.9 billion.

CBO cautioned that its estimates were subject to "considerable uncertainty," depending on the probability that a systemically important financial institution would fail. "That probability is small under both current law and under the legislation, but it is hard to predict," CBO wrote.

Hensarling's bill, in part, would repeal the Federal Deposit Insurance Corporation's authority to use the Orderly Liquidation Fund to resolve "strategically important financial institutions," or SIFIs, in danger of collapse. CBO estimated that ending that FDIC authority would reduce deficits by $14.5 billion over the 2018-2027 period.

CBO said the nation's eight largest banks would be unlikely to take advantage of the legislation's provisions that would allow banks to opt out of a number of financial regulations if they chose instead to maintain a leverage ratio of greater than 10 percent. Leverage measures the degree of reliance on debt to fund the bank's assets.

Those banks would, however, get the benefit of repeal of the Volcker rule, a provision that prohibits federally insured banks from

trading with depositors' money. The bill would also rein in the Consumer Financial Protection Bureau, the federal agency that collected $100 million from Wells Fargo after the bank admitted it opened nearly 2 million bank and credit card accounts without customers' knowledge.

CBO said the eight megabanks would likely not make this election "because they would have to raise much more capital." Moreover, those banks would still need to comply with international rule and regulations. "As a result, CBO expects" the global systemically important banks "would be unlikely to choose the alternative regulatory regime authorized by the bill."

CBO noted the eight U.S.-based G-SIBs — JPMorgan Chase, Citigroup, Bank of America, Goldman Sachs, Morgan Stanley, Bank of New York Mellon, State Street, and Wells Fargo — have about half the assets of the U.S. banking industry.

By contrast, smaller community banks — those with assets below $10 billion — would be more likely to opt for the regulatory relief in exchange for meeting and maintaining the 10 percent leverage ratio, according to CBO.

HOUSE ACTION

The House voted 233-186 on June 8 to pass HR 10. Walter B. Jones of North Carolina was the only Republican to vote against the repeal bill, and no Democrats voted for it. Three House Republicans had voted for Dodd-Frank in 2010 and 19 Democrats voted against it.

Democrats said it would end protections put in place after the 2008-9 financial crisis, intimidate regulators by removing their financial independence, and effectively kill a dozen bipartisan provisions by putting them in a bill that Senate Democrats were expected to block.

"I believe it will lead to the next financial crisis," said Rep. Stephen F. Lynch, D-Mass., a member of the Financial Services Committee. "This is an awful bill. This is a real stinker."

In July, Barney Frank, the former chairman of the House Financial Services Committee and co-author of the financial industry law, said he was more worried about what regulators appointed by President Trump might do than he was about what HR 10 would to repeal much of his handiwork.

Topping the former chairman of the House Financial Services Committee's list of concerns was that the Commodity Futures Trading Commission and Securities and Exchange Commission might relax enforcement that required most derivatives to be traded transparently on exchanges.

"They could reduce the pressure to go on exchanges," he told CQ reporters and editors in a July 19 interview. Currently, dealers could make an argument that only "unique" derivative products can be traded over the counter, and Frank said he worried that regulators will see a greater percentage of derivatives qualifying for that exclusion.

The lack of transparency and confusion over commercial and investment bank exposure to derivatives, such as credit default swaps, were causes of panic over foundering firms like Lehman Brothers, which declared bankruptcy in 2008.

A Massachusetts Democrat who teamed with Senate Banking Chairman Chris Dodd, who also retired, to write the law, Frank said

he also worried that Trump regulators might loosen the Volcker Rule in their oversight of big banks.

"None of these [rules] are self-executing," he said. "The Volcker rule was definitions, etc. By another six months, everybody who was administering the Volcker rule will be a Trump person. So expect some relaxation."

SENATE NEGOTIATIONS

Senate Banking Chairman Michael D. Crapo, R-Idaho, launched a bipartisan effort in March with Ohio Democrat Sherrod Brown to develop legislative ideas to boost the economy, which Crapo said would not just be targeted at Dodd-Frank.

Crapo said on June 13 that he hoped to have a financial deregulation bill before year's end. Among its features, he listed:

• Change the $50 billion asset threshold for extra regulatory scrutiny of large banks;

• Remove banks between $10 billion and $50 billion in assets from stress test requirements;

• Exempt banks with less than $10 billion in assets from the Volcker Rule banning trading with depositors' money;

• Restructure of the Consumer Financial Protection Bureau;

• Require new capital requirements, and improvements in the process and transparency of the so-called living will requirements for the biggest banks.

"We will have an easier time getting bipartisan agreement at the smaller size" end of community banking, which many Democrats agree needs regulatory relief, Crapo said. "As you move up the size level for institutions, the ability to get bipartisan agreement diminishes, but it doesn't go away," he said. "Sen. Brown and I are working together and we're approaching it very broadly."

After months of negotiations, though, Crapo said on Nov. 1 that his talks with Brown had ended. "We were unable to reach an agreement," Crapo said, "We did both work hard together in good faith to try to reach one and nothing stops us from continuing to discuss."

Crapo said talks were continuing with other Democrats on the committee and that his objective remained the same. "I want to build a bipartisan bill to achieve significant regulatory reform, and as you know, I call it economic growth," he said.

Brown's statement said that "after working in good faith, it's clear we will not be able to reach a compromise that protects consumers while supporting small banks and credit unions. I continue to support small banks and credit unions, but I cannot agree to gutting protections for working people and taxpayers."

The Crapo-Brown effort included soliciting ideas from industry and other groups about regulatory changes that could encourage economic growth. The committee received more than 100 suggestions from individuals, labor unions, think tanks of all stripes and financial services trade associations.

Crapo referred to the talks as legislative proposals to foster economic growth, rather than following House Republicans' description of their work as a loosening or elimination of regulations.

Relayed to the Senate, the bill was referred to the Banking, Housing and Urban Affairs Committee, where it remained. ∎

Powell Picked to Lead Federal Reserve

The Senate Banking Committee voted 22-1 on Dec. 5 to recommend confirmation of Jerome Powell as the next chairman of the Federal Reserve, succeeding Janet Yellen. New York Democrat Elizabeth Warren voted against the recommendation.

The Senate did not vote on his confirmation before the end of 2017, however, and his nomination was not carried forward via unanimous consent. For that reason, Powell had to be renominated and considered a second time by committee before he was finally confirmed by the Senate on Jan. 23, 2018. Powell has been on the board since 2012.

Banking Chairman Michael D. Crapo, R-Idaho, who had voted against Powell – as well as several other Obama nominees — during his renomination to the Fed board in 2014, backed him this time. "His judgment and expertise will be a continued asset to the board," Crapo said.

Warren, a Massachusetts Democrat, said she was "very concerned that the Fed will systematically roll back" financial regulations. In his confirmation hearing a week earlier and in public comments, Powell said he believes current financial rules "are too demanding" and

should be relaxed, said Warren of Massachusetts.

At his confirmation hearing, Powell described goals similar to Yellen's: "Our aim is to sustain a strong jobs market with inflation moving gradually up toward our target. We expect interest rates to rise somewhat further and the size of our balance sheet to gradually shrink."

He said he was "strongly" committed to transparency and accountability, such as holding news conferences by the chairman after Federal Open Market Committee meetings, instituted by former Fed Chairman Ben Bernanke and continued by Yellen.

Powell also seemed to win favor from Crapo by agreeing that the senator's bank deregulation bill (S 2155) would both provide regulatory relief for small banks while still maintaining regulatory powers over larger banks.

Powell received a 74-21 confirmation vote in 2012, with 20 Republicans and Sen. Bernie Sanders, I-Vt., opposed. Every Democrat backed him, including Senate Banking members Brown, Jon Tester of Montana, Jack Reed of Rhode Island and Mark Warner of Virginia. ∎

Republicans Vote to Strike Finance Rules

Republicans made unprecedented use of the Congressional Review Act in 2017 to nullify several new government rules opposed by section of the finance industry, including those on mandatory arbitration clauses in contracts, the fiduciary duty of investment advisors and the operations of "payday" loan companies.

Under the Congressional Review Act, which was enacted by Republicans who controlled the House and Senate in 1996, Congress has 60 legislative days to rescind a new federal rule.

ARBITRATION

The Senate cleared a resolution on Oct. 24 that, when signed by President Donald Trump, disallowed the Consumer Financial Protection Bureau's rule barring mandatory arbitration clauses in consumer contracts. The rule had been published on July 17.

Vice President Mike Pence cast the tie-breaking vote after two Republicans — Sens. Lindsey Graham of South Carolina and John Kennedy of Louisiana — joined all the Democrats in opposition. The resolution (H J Res 111) was cleared 51-50 nearly three months after the House adopted it on July 25.

The Senate Republicans' timing was complicated by Equifax Inc.'s announcement in September that hackers had gained access to the data of more than 145 million consumers. The company temporarily sought to require consumers to accept arbitration for a product to address the risk posed by the breach.

The thin Republican majority in the Senate also meant that passage would be tougher in that chamber than in the House. Sen. Michael D. Crapo, R-Idaho, the author of the Senate resolution, had said earlier in the summer that the Republicans wouldn't bring the measure to the

floor until they were certain to have the votes.

"I believe the CFPB has gone above and beyond its authority," said Majority Whip John Cornyn, R-Texas, on the floor. "There's no reason for us to enrich a class of lawyers that bring these lawsuits."

The CFPB rule barred consumer contracts with banks, cell phone companies and others from including clauses that waive a consumer's right to join class-action suits, instead offering arbitration as the only option to settle disputes.

"Tonight's vote is a giant setback for every consumer in this country," CFPB Director Richard Cordray said in a statement. "Wall Street won and ordinary people lost. This vote means the courtroom doors will remain closed for groups of people seeking justice and relief when they are wronged by a company. It preserves a two-tiered justice system where banks can have their day in court but deny their customers the same right. It robs consumers of their most effective legal tool against corporate wrongdoing."

Proponents said the rule would expand the legal rights of consumers, since arbitration is expensive, few consumers opt for it and even fewer win their cases.

"Our job is to look out for the people who we serve, not to look out for Wells Fargo, not to look out for Equifax, not to look out for big banks," Sen. Sherrod Brown, D-Ohio, said as the floor debate began.

The American Bankers Association called the vote a win for consumers. "The rule was always going to harm consumers and not help them. Today's vote puts consumers first rather than class-action lawyers," the ABA said in a statement.

A Treasury Department report called the rule a "wealth transfer" to trial lawyers. "The Bureau has not made a reasoned showing that

increased consumer class action litigation will result in a net benefit to consumers or to the public as a whole," the report said.

Supporters of the rule pointed to the actions of Equifax in the wake of the data breach. The company offered a product to protect consumers, but initially said they could have the product only if they agreed to sign an arbitration clause.

Democrats argued that Equifax was using the clause to keep consumers from joining together to sue the company over the breach. Equifax later withdrew that requirement.

Sen. Elizabeth Warren, D-Mass., a defender of both the arbitration rule and the CFPB, accused Republicans of doing the bidding of the banking industry, which has opposed the rule.

On the other side, House Financial Services Chairman Jeb Hensarling, a Texas Republican, said the arbitration rule was the result of an "unholy alliance" between Democrats and trial lawyers. If the rule took effect, Hensarling maintained, consumers' main avenue for redress would be through class-action suits, which would benefit trial lawyers.

A CFPB study of four years of class-action lawsuits in financial services disputes found that out of $2.7 billion in awards to consumers, $424 million in fees went to attorneys – about 16 percent. The study also found that consumers rarely went to arbitration because most disputes with banks and other providers were over amounts far smaller than the cost of arbitration.

PAYDAY LOANS

Republicans were able to delay, but not extinguish a CFPB rule regulating payday lenders. A resolution of disapproval, sponsored by Rep. Dennis A. Ross, R-Fla., and co-sponsored by a number of others including three Democrats, was introduced on Dec. 1.

Though opponents of the rule criticized the government for intervening in a market legal in 35 states, the CFPB had issued a series of reports over five years finding that the industry charged an average annual percentage rate of more than 300 percent — when all fees and interest were counted.

A CFPB study found that four out of five payday loans were re-borrowed within a month, and one out of four initial loans were reborrowed nine times or more, leading opponents to frequently describe the industry as a "debt trap."

Ross' resolution (H J Res 122) would repeal the payday rule under the Congressional Review Act. As with the arbitration rule, consumer groups promised to fight the repeal effort. But, unlike the arbitration rule, Democrats joined in this repeal effort.

One of the Democratic co-sponsors was Rep. Alcee L. Hastings of Florida, who noted that he used a short-term loan to start his law practice and said it was the only credit available to him at the time.

A similar repeal effort did not get underway in the Senate.

Hensarling, who led the arbitration rule repeal effort, described the payday rule as an example of how "unelected, unaccountable government bureaucracy hurts working people."

"Once again we see powerful Washington elites using the guise of 'consumer protection' to actually harm consumers and make life harder for lower and moderate income Americans, who may need a short-term loan to keep their utilities from being cut off or to keep their car on the road so they can get to work," Hensarling said in a statement.

The rule, which wouldn't go fully into effect for 21 months, would regulate payday and auto title lenders whose annual rate of interest

exceeds 36 percent. The CFPB estimated there were 16,000 payday storefronts in the 35 states that allow high-interest, short-term loans typically guaranteed by the borrower's next paycheck.

FIDUCIARY RESPONSIBILITY

The Labor Department on Nov. 27 delayed finalizing a rule requiring broker-dealers dispensing retirement advice to act in the best interest of their clients, potentially giving other regulators a chance to weigh in with their own rules.

Set to take effect for some brokers on Jan. 1, 2018, Labor delayed the so-called fiduciary rule's implementation until July 1, 2019, to sort through all the comments filed by opponents and supporters. The Trump administration said the rule would potentially be damaging to investors but Democrats vehemently supported it as a way to protect retirees.

The Obama-era standard was designed to prevent brokers from taking their own fee income into account when dispensing retirement advice, which is currently allowed as long as the advice is "suitable." The Department of Labor received hundreds of public comments on the issue on both sides.

Business groups and those representing brokers requested a delay.

The U.S. Chamber of Commerce, for example, maintained that 6 million Americans would face higher fees if the standard took effect. The Securities Industry and Financial Markets Association, which represents brokerages, indicated that retirees who prefer to make their own investment decisions would find it cheaper to do so without the rule.

E-Trade Financial Corp. said the rule would make it difficult to offer "robo" advice, where its website is able to offer suggestions based on customer algorithms, it wrote to Labor.

The Financial Services Roundtable, which represents large banks and financial firms, wanted regulators to hold off on enforcement if parties acted in "good faith," and added that more time would be needed to comply with the rule.

The Consumer Federation of America, however, supported the rule, and wanted the Labor Department to ramp up its supervision of firms when they recommend that customer funds move from one account to another, to ensure that the customers get the best deal.

The Labor Department said the delay would give it time to go through all the comments, but also allow other regulators like the Securities and Exchange Commission to weigh in. Many lawmakers say the SEC should be setting policy for brokers.

The rule had been contentious from the start. It was finalized in April 2016 under President Obama. Congress then passed legislation to repeal it, which Obama vetoed. After the election, President Donald Trump asked Labor to conduct a review, with the idea that the rule could be delayed or repealed.

Following Labor's announcement of the delay, consumer advocates and labor unions criticized the decision.

"This is exactly what the industry rule opponents wanted — a best-interest-in-name-only standard that leaves the broker-dealer, insurance, and mutual fund industry free to continue draining retirement savers' hard-earned money with impunity," said the Save Our Retirement Coalition, which includes the AFL-CIO and the Consumer Federation of America.

The House passed legislation to repeal the fiduciary rule as part of a bill (HR 10) to largely repeal many financial regulations enacted in the Dodd-Frank law of 2010. ∎

Cordray Departs Consumer Bureau

Ever since Republicans won control of both houses of Congress in 2014, they had sought to limit the power of the Consumer Financial Protection Bureau and depose its director, Richard Cordray. The bureau, commonly known as the CFPB, was created by the 2010 Dodd-Frank law (PL 111-203) to protect borrowers from the abuses of lenders.

The GOP efforts bore fruit in 2017 when Congress rescinded a CFPB regulation against mandatory arbitration clauses in consumer contracts and delayed a rule requiring broker-dealers dispensing retirement advice to act principally in the best interest of their clients.

Cordray resigned in November to run for governor of Ohio, after he named his chief of staff, Leandra English, as deputy director, which allowed her to become acting director when Cordray's resignation became official. President Donald Trump quickly moved to name his budget director, former Rep. Mick Mulvaney, to the position. English sued, seeking a restraining order to keep Mulvaney from assuming the post, in addition to his duties as budget director.

The battle for control of the CFPB was settled by U.S. District Court Judge Timothy J. Kelly in Washington on Nov. 28 when he denied the request for a temporary restraining order. The decision allowed Mulvaney to remain in a post where he had already implemented what Justice Department attorney Brett Shumate called a "soft freeze" on regulatory actions.

After Trump's inauguration, Cordray's attitude toward the new presidential administration was to proceed with business as usual. His entire tenure, in fact, had been tenuous.

The CFPB had been the brainchild of Sen. Elizabeth Warren, D-Mass., and Cordray's active administration of the bureau won him praise from Democrats. The CFPB said in early 2017 that it had collected and distributed to consumers more than $12 billion in fines and other penalties levied on financial services companies.

Cordray and his agency largely owed their relative independence to the Dodd-Frank stipulation that their budget come from the Federal Reserve, not Congress. Cordray's 2012 nomination to head the CFPB had been held up by Republicans until a compromise was reached in July 2013.

The CFPB encountered another threat when a three-judge panel of the U.S. Court of Appeals for the District of Columbia Circuit ruled in October 2016 that the CFPB's single-director structure was unconstitutional. The panel said Cordray was an "at will" employee, serving at the pleasure of the president, and subject to dismissal without cause. The court echoed the frequent complaint of congressional Republicans, noting that Cordray had "more unilateral authority" than any figure in government other than the president. But the effect of that ruling was put off until after the CFPB exhausted its appeals, and Cordray remained director.

In early January 2017, Republican Sens. Ben Sasse of Nebraska and Mike Lee of Utah wrote Vice President-elect Mike Pence, to suggest that Trump "promptly" dismiss Cordray after the inauguration. Republicans on the House Financial Services Committee turned up the heat on Jan. 18 with a report alleging that Cordray had broken the law when the bureau developed a 2015 rule about regulating the auto lending industry.

Cordray announced on Nov. 15 that he would step down by the end of the month. He had won praise from Democrats for the CFPB's aggressiveness in seeking relief for consumers. In an email to the CFPB staff released by the agency, Cordray cited $12 billion recovered for 30 million consumers and safeguards established to prevent the irrespon-

sible mortgage lending that led Democrats to enact the 2010 overhaul.

After Cordray announced on Nov. 15 that he would resign at the end of the month, the ranking Democrat on House Financial Services, Maxine Waters of California, called Cordray "a true champion for American consumers." Senate Banking ranking Democrat Sherrod Brown of Ohio said that all Americans owed Cordray "a debt of gratitude." But Republicans said Cordray was unaccountable and operated with little oversight.

The chairman of the House Financial Services Committee, Texas Republican Jeb Hensarling, welcomed Cordray's departure in a scathing statement.

"We are long overdue for new leadership at the CFPB, a rogue agency that has done more to hurt consumers than help them," Hensarling said. "The extreme overregulation it imposes on our economy leads to higher costs and less access to financial products and services, particularly for Americans with lower and middle incomes. It has routinely denied market participants their due process rights. All this harm is made even worse by the fact that the CFPB is structurally unconstitutional and completely unaccountable to the American people."

Budget Director Mulvaney, a former House member from South Carolina, had said in 2015, "I don't like the fact CFPB exists."

Mulvaney had confronted Cordray at a March 2016 hearing over features of what was then the bureau's proposed rule to regulate the payday lending industry, aimed at loans charging more than 36 percent annual percentage rates. The final payday lending rule required cooling-off periods between loans so people could not repeatedly borrow money to pay off their last loan.

Mulvaney criticized Cordray in that hearing, saying the director wanted to pre-empt state law in 37 states that allowed short-term, low-dollar payday loans, including Ohio, where Cordray had been attorney general. South Carolina also allowed the high-fee loans with annual percentage rates measured at well above 100 percent.

English, who was named deputy director by Cordray on Nov. 24, said she became acting director when his resignation took effect that midnight and that the Dodd-Frank law spelled out that the deputy director of the CFPB becomes the director in case of a vacancy.

The same day, the Trump administration announced that Mulvaney would replace Cordray on an interim basis. Administration officials told reporters that the Federal Vacancies Act of 1998 (PL 105-227) superseded the Dodd-Frank law. Mulvaney's appointment was limited to 210 days or until a new CFPB director was confirmed. If that nomination were to be rejected or withdrawn, Mulvaney could serve an additional 210 days.

English said in her court filing that the 1998 law did not apply when another statute designates an officer or employee to perform the job. "The President's interpretation of the FVRA [Federal Vacancies Reform Act] runs contrary to Dodd-Frank's later-enacted, more specific, and mandatory text," her filing said.

Judge Kelly's Nov. 28 denial of a request for a temporary restraining order to bar Mulvaney from becoming acting director allowed him to remain in a post. Kelly said he denied the restraining order because English's case would likely not meet the standard of having a "substantial likelihood" of success at trial. The judge also said English's case didn't meet the "irreparable harm" standard. ∎

House Advances CFTC Reauthorization

As one of its first actions, the House voted to reauthorize the Commodity Futures Trading Commission, which polices the futures and over-the-counter derivatives markets. The House passed the bill (HR 238) by 239-182 on Jan. 12, largely along party lines. It stalled in the Senate over Democratic objections over flat multiyear funding levels for CFTC and concerns about exemptions for several CFTC regulations.

House Agriculture Chairman K. Michael Conaway, R-Texas, introduced the bill Jan. 4 and moved it to the floor without formal action by the Agriculture Committee that he chairs. Conway and Democratic counterpart, Collin C. Peterson, D-Minn., sparred over whether the bill would help or undermine the agency's efforts to police the futures and over-the-counter derivatives markets.

Peterson said the bill was part of a general GOP effort to weaken the Dodd-Frank financial overhaul law (PL 111-203) passed in the aftermath of the 2008 recession, the worst U.S. economic downturn since the Great Depression. He said House leaders hurried the 2017 bill without committee action since the House Agriculture Committee has yet to hold its organizational meeting for the 115th Congress. Conaway countered that the committee held hearings in the 114th Congress that produced legislation nearly identical to the current measure.

In floor debate, Conaway, a certified public accountant by profession, argued that exemptions in the bill for non-financial companies would protect them from increased regulatory costs for using the markets to hedge business risks. He said other provisions in the legislation would make the agency more efficient by requiring more in-depth cost benefit analysis of proposed rules.

Peterson and other Democrats voted against the measure because it set annual CFTC funding through fiscal 2021 at $250 million a year, the same amount as appropriators provided in fiscal 2015 and 2016. That, they said, was inadequate for an agency whose responsibilities under Dodd-Frank expanded to oversight of the derivatives market, which has a value of more than $300 trillion.

Derivatives are contracts with values tied to an asset at a designated point in time. The derivative may be tied to a physical commodity, a stock index, an interest rate or some other asset. Unregulated derivatives contributed to the financial turmoil of 2008.

Peterson also objected to provisions in the bill that would limit the CFTC's authority to regulate cross-border derivatives trading. The agency would be required to issue rules that allow U.S. firms to carry out trades in the eight largest foreign markets without U.S. supervision as long as those countries have market oversight equivalent to the United States. He said the provision would encourage banks to shop around for countries with the least stringent review and lead to a "race to the bottom by multi-national banks."

For decades, the CFTC had been of concern mainly to agricultural producers, who used futures contracts to sell future crops. But in recent decades, the derivatives market in financial products had vastly changed the CFTC's oversight role. The Dodd-Frank financial overhaul law expanded CFTC's oversight to include the then unregulated over-the-counter derivatives market. ∎

Comptroller of Currency Confirmed

Broadening the Trump administration's pro-business imprint on financial policy, the Senate confirmed Joseph Otting, a one-time business associate of Treasury Secretary Steven Mnuchin, as Comptroller of the Currency.

The Senate voted 54-43 on Nov. 16 to confirm Otting, whose nomination emerged from the Banking Committee with the support of one Democrat, Sen. Heidi Heitkamp of North Dakota. His confirmation got two Democratic votes on the floor: from Heitkamp and Joe Manchin III of West Virginia. The Office of the Comptroller of the Currency charters, regulates and supervises national banks and federal savings associations.

Senate Banking Committee Chairman Michael D. Crapo of Idaho said Otting's three decades of experience give him the expertise and understanding for the job. "He has touched virtually every segment of the industry," he said.

Democrats had criticized Otting for his actions during and after the financial crisis. He was president and CEO of OneWest Bank, the successor to the failed IndyMac bank that was purchased in 2009 by an investor group led by Mnuchin. Otting faced the same questioning over OneWest's foreclosing on thousands of mortgages during the financial crisis that Mnuchin faced at his confirmation hearing in January.

"Instead of helping families recover from the financial crisis, as CEO of OneWest Bank, he contributed to the devastation," Senate Banking ranking member Sherrod Brown of Ohio said ahead of the committee vote in September.

Otting took over the job from Keith A. Noreika, who was named acting comptroller in May following the May 5 departure of former OCC chief Thomas J. Curry, an appointee of President Barack Obama. For almost all of President Barack Obama's first term, the comptroller's office had been held by Republican holdovers from President George W. Bush's administration because of partisan squabbling engendered by the 2007-08 financial crisis. ∎

Fannie Mae, Freddie Mac Win Reprieve

Days before Christmas and less than two weeks before the mortgage finance giants Fannie Mae and Freddie Mac were scheduled to reduce capital reserves to zero, the two government-sponsored enterprises got a reprieve that allowed them to maintain a capital buffer of $3 billion going into 2018.

The Federal Housing Finance Agency, which oversees Fannie and Freddie as conservator, and the Treasury Department agreed on Dec. 21 to modify the terms of the preferred stock purchase agreements that the federal government used to bail out Freddie and Fannie in 2008, during the subprime mortgage meltdown.

The agreements revised in 2012 required Fannie and Freddie to sweep all profits to the Treasury while retaining an operational capital reserve that was reduced each year and was scheduled to drop to zero on Jan. 1, 2018.

Under the FHFA-Treasury agreement, Fannie and Freddie would still be required to pay quarterly dividends to the Treasury, but also would be permitted to maintain a limited capital buffer of $3 billion, "an amount that should be sufficient to cover income fluctuations in the normal course of business."

The detailed terms of the deal were laid out in "letter agreements" signed by Treasury Secretary Steven Mnuchin and delivered to FHFA Director Melvin L. Watt. ■

Chapter 4

BUDGET

Congressional Budget Office Comes Under Attack From Conservatives

The Congressional Budget Office came under withering criticism from House Republican leaders in March for its assessment that the GOP's plan to repeal and replace the 2010 health care law would cost 24 million Americans their health coverage.

House Speaker Paul D. Ryan, R-Wis., had acknowledged that the plan would leave fewer Americans with health insurance, but the CBO's scoring of the plan, released March 22, in a budget reconciliation bill (HR 1628) that the House was considering startled party leaders.

White House Press Secretary Sean Spicer lambasted the CBO, saying, that "if you're looking to the CBO for accuracy, you're looking in the wrong place." Ryan argued that producing a score that would look good on paper compared to the existing Affordable Care Act was impossible: "So there's no way we can ... compete with on paper a government mandate with coverage."

House Majority Whip Steve Scalise, R-La., said the House wouldn't wait for "unelected bureaucrats" before passing the bill.

Health and Human Services Secretary Tom Price called into question CBO's accuracy by pointing to previous estimates on the 2010 health care law that he said were inaccurate. After the score was released, Price said, "We disagree strenuously with the report that was put out."

"The CBO looked at a portion of our plan, but not the entire plan," Price said during an impromptu news conference with Office of Management and Budget Director Mick Mulvaney, like Price a former House member.

But CBO supporters said they were wrong to attack the nonpartisan agency.

"We need CBO, Washington needs CBO, they all need CBO and they have done nothing to earn this disrespect," said Robert L. Bixby,

A TIMELINE OF BUDGET & APPROPRIATIONS MILESTONES IN 2017

Jan. 12 – Senate voted 51-48 to pass a fiscal 2017 budget resolution (S Con Res 3) with language allowing repeal of substantial sections of the Affordable Care Act through the budget reconciliation process, which would block a Senate filibuster.

March 16 – Trump administration released preliminary fiscal 2018 federal budget request that would increase defense spending by $25 billion and decrease nondefense spending by $15 billion.

March 20 – House Republicans released American Health Care Act of 2017 (HR 1628) to replace the ACA. After failing to gain enough votes for passage, it was withdrawn on March 24. Another attempt was made, which passed the House on May 4, but it died in the Senate.

April 28 – Congress cleared a one-week continuing resolution that extended funding through May 5.

May 4 – Senate cleared Omnibus Consolidated Appropriations Act for fiscal 2017 (HR 244 — PL 115-31) that included all of the remaining appropriations bills for fiscal 2017.

May 23 – President Donald Trump released full $4.1 trillion budget request for fiscal 2018, including a broad outline for tax cuts, a large boost for defense spending, and specific cuts to many domestic and foreign aid programs.

July 27 – House passes a measure (HR 3219) with fiscal 2018 appropriations for four of the 12 annual appropriations bills, with funds for defense, military construction, veterans affairs, legislative branch and energy and water development programs, plus $1.6 billion to begin constructions on President Trump's proposed wall at the Mexican border.

Sept. 8 – Additional disaster funding due to Hurricane Harvey was enacted as part of the Continuing Appropriations Act, 2018 and Supplemental Appropriations for Disaster Relief Requirements Act, 2017 bill (HR 601 – PL 115-56). The measure also suspended the debt limit to prevent a potential default on government debt.

Sept. 14 – House passes $1.23 trillion omnibus appropriations bill (HR 3354), comprising all 12 appropriations bills, following two weeks of debate and consideration of 342 amendments.

Dec. 7 – Senate clears continuing resolution (H J Res 123) extending government funding through Dec. 22.

Dec. 21 – House passes a third disaster aid supplemental bill (HR 4667) for $81 billion following a record hurricane season and wildfires across California. It stalls in the Senate over Democrats' charges of inadequate funding for Puerto Rico and the U.S. Virgin Islands. Some funding shifts to the end-of-year continuing resolution.

Dec. 21 – House clears continuing resolution (HR 1370 – PL 115-90) extending government funding through Jan. 19, 2018.

executive director of the Concord Coalition, a non-partisan group that advocates federal fiscal prudence. "They've done a great job trying to stay nonpartisan and credible. And if you succeed in demolishing the credibility of CBO, well, then what? A scorched earth policy doesn't leave you with much."

Both Republican and Democratic leaders in the House voiced confidence in the CBO after the administration's attacks. When asked at a news conference, Ryan said that he believed in the integrity and the impartiality of CBO and Director Keith Hall.

"Look, I have always had my own complaints about methodology and scorekeeping — we all have our preferences and our opinions about these things," Ryan said, "but it is important that we have a scorekeeper."

Grousing over CBO's budgetary estimates had come from both parties in the past when scores went against them. But the recent complaints from Republicans were unusually fierce, even though CBO Director Keith Hall was a Republican who had been appointed to the jobs by Republican House Speaker John A. Boehner of Ohio and Sen. Orrin G. Hatch, R-Utah, with the full-throated endorsement of then-House Budget Chairman Price.

Later in the year, the House in July rejected two amendments to an appropriations package (HR 3219) that would have cut 50 percent of CBO's funding and eliminated the 89 employees of the agency's budget analysis division. House Budget Chairwoman Diane Black, R-Tenn., opposed the amendments but said she would hold committee hearings later in the year to examine CBO's scoring methods.

Congressional criticism of the CBO continued into the summer, when Republican Sen. Mike Lee of Utah introduced a bill (S 1746) that

would require the CBO to make publicly available the models and data used in its legislative scores.

While acknowledging that Congress needed a scorekeeper to estimate the budgetary effect of legislation, Lee said that "at a bare minimum, that scorekeeper should be forced to show how its models work. Currently the CBO doesn't have to do that."

Hall defended his agency's work at an event at Boston, saying the budget shop did aim for transparency. "We try to document our models as well as we can," he said. "We do a fair amount of presentation on our models. We even write working papers describing our analysis." ■

U.S. Debt Limit Is Again Suspended

After several months of procrastination, recrimination and negotiation, Congress cleared a debt limit suspension on Sept. 8 - good through Dec. 8 - as part of a larger bill (HR 601 - PL 115-56) that extended government funding through Dec. 8 and provided $15.25 billion in emergency aid for victims of Hurricane Harvey and other major disasters.

Ninety Republicans in the House voted against the bill, unhappy that President Donald Trump had opted for a Democratic proposal instead of one put forward by Republican leaders.

Treasury Secretary Steven Mnuchin had set the stage for the agreement in a Sept. 3 television interview when he cautioned that an aid package for storm victims without a debt limit increase could jeopardize the movement of relief funds. Trump later got behind the developing financial package.

The White House had formally asked Congress back on March 9 to either raise or suspend the debt limit, which had last been suspended as part of a budget law (PL 114-74) signed in November 2015.

Because failing to suspend the debt limit carries the risk of a government default, debt limit legislation has long been a bargaining point for other measures. Republicans, for instance, have pushed for spending cuts or changes to entitlement programs in exchange for raising the borrowing ceiling, with varying degrees of success.

Their last victory came in 2011, when a Republican House, Democratic Senate and President Barack Obama agreed on the Budget Control Act (PL 112-25), which set caps on discretionary spending and required at least $1.2 trillion in additional deficit reduction in return for raising the debt limit.

In 2017, Republicans looked at using the fiscal 2018 budget resolution as a vehicle for reconciliation instructions that could be used to overhaul the tax code. The expedited reconciliation process also can be used to make changes in spending and the debt limit.

Of the 29 measures that Congress has passed to raise the debt limit from 1990 through 2017, just four of them were done through reconciliation:

- The Omnibus Budget Reconciliation Act of 1986 (PL 99-509)
- The Omnibus Budget Reconciliation Act of 1990 (PL 101-508)
- The Omnibus Budget Reconciliation Act of 1993 (PL 103-66)
- The Balanced Budget Act of 1997 (PL 105-33)

The 1990 law was a major overhaul of fiscal policy that established tax cuts, tax increases, changes to Medicare, the debt limit increase and discretionary spending levels. Passage of the measure required lawmakers to turn a blind eye, through bipartisan agreement, to provisions that broke the Senate's own rules. And the 1997 bill passed on a widely bipartisan basis in the Senate, by an 85-15 vote.

WORKING IT OUT

The debt ceiling suspension expired March 15. As time ticked away in 2017, Treasury began taking "extraordinary measures" to prevent the debt ceiling from being reached, measures such as suspending the sale of state and local government series securities, which are issued to states and localities to help them conform to certain tax rules.

Through the summer and early fall, Mnuchin periodically asked for a debt limit suspension, warned of the consequences of inaction, but then found new "extraordinary measures" to ward off default.

Lobbyists for financial services and business groups, meanwhile, increased pressure on lawmakers to swiftly extend the debt limit and fund the government without drama. Their main focus was on the debt limit. Without an increase — or suspension — lawmakers would jeopardize the nation's ability to pay its bills. Even just debating the debt limit has caused global stock market losses, and an actual breach of the nation's borrowing authority carries could carry catastrophic consequences.

"We'd like this to be resolved quickly," said Rob Nichols, president of the American Bankers Association and a former Treasury official during the George W. Bush administration. "The whole brinkmanship around the debt ceiling rattles the markets and is counterproductive."

Mnuchin and Senate Majority Leader Mitch McConnell tried to reassure the public and markets that the debt limit would dealt with in time.

"There is zero chance — no chance — we won't raise the debt ceiling. No chance," McConnell declared in late August when he appeared alongside Mnuchin at a business event in Kentucky. "America is not going to default, and we'll get the job done in conjunction with the secretary of the Treasury.

"We're going to get the debt ceiling passed," Mnuchin said. "I think that everybody understands this is not a Republican issue, this is not a Democrat issue. We need to be able to pay our debts.

A few days later, though, Trump criticized McConnell and House Speaker Paul D. Ryan, saying they created a debt ceiling "mess" by refusing his advice.

After the White House and McConnell's office denied a recent New York Times report about tension — including a profanity-filled phone call — between the two, the president started attacking Republican leaders.

"I requested," the president wrote, "that Mitch M & Paul R tie the Debt Ceiling legislation into the popular V.A. Bill (which just passed) for easy approval," the president wrote. "They didn't do it so now we have a big deal with Dems holding them up (as usual) on Debt Ceiling approval. Could have been so easy-now a mess!"

A deal did come to pass in early September, and without further

recrimination, although with some lingering bitterness.

House Freedom Caucus Chairman Mark Meadows, R-N.C., and Republican Study Committee Chairman Mark Walker, R-N.C., both expressed frustration with the agreement.

"Democrats got exactly what they wanted," Meadows said. "It is a three-month CR, three-month debt ceiling to come due a few days before Christmas, which gives them the greatest leverage in the world to get exactly what they want." ■

Spending Caps Deal Evades Congress

Congressional leaders and the White House appeared within reach of a two-year budget agreement in mid-November to raise statutory spending caps, but they were unable to bridge differences over the distribution of discretionary spending and ancillary issues such as immigration and money to build a border wall money sought by President Donald Trump.

It was February 2018 before a new law reset the spending limits.

Under a 2017 Republican proposal, defense caps would have increased by $54 billion and nondefense funds by $37 billion in both fiscal 2018 and 2019. The increase would have been only partially offset. Democrats, however, insisted on the parity for defense and nondefense spending that characterized the 2013 and 2015 budget deals, and they rejected the Republican offer.

Though many Democrats wanted legislation included to resume the Deferred Action for Childhood Arrivals, or DACA, program for the nearly 800,000 immigrants brought to the United States illegally as children, neither that nor money for Trump's border wall was included in the proposal.

The previous budget deal, brokered by then House Speaker John A. Boehner, R-Ohio, and President Barack Obama, raised the caps on spending by $80 billion over fiscal 2016 and 2017. The increase was just barely offset through a combination of mandatory spending cuts, asset sales and fee increases including extending the mandatory sequester an additional year through 2025 — and only after the Congressional Budget Office tweaked its scoring of additional war funding.

Without a budget deal for fiscal 2018, the statutory spending caps would fall from fiscal 2017's $551 billion for defense and $519 billion for nondefense, to $549 billion for defense and $516 billion for nondefense.

The 2011 Budget Control Act (PL 112-25) set limits on discretionary spending through fiscal 2021. Those caps were lowered again when sequestration kicked in after a special congressional "super committee" was unable to reach agreement on a deficit reduction package.

Those who wanted more money for defense were expected to rebel against any deal that raised base defense spending to only $603 billion. The chairmen of the House and Senate Armed Services Committees, Mac Thornberry of Texas and John McCain of Arizona, wanted Congress to appropriate a total of $692.1 billion for the Defense department, including $65.7 billion for overseas war spending, or Overseas

Contingency Operations accounts that are not subject to the caps.

In early December, negotiators moved well north of $200 billion in their discussions of how much to raise discretionary spending caps. The higher numbers under consideration followed an initial GOP offer several weeks earlier to raise defense by $54 billion and nondefense by $37 billion in both fiscal 2018 and 2019 — a $182 billion increase in base discretionary spending.

Democrats then responded with a counteroffer to increase both defense and nondefense by $54 billion each, raising the two-year cost above $200 billion.

The budget deal could have provided more money for nondefense than the numbers would suggest, since it could include the use of some $20 billion in so-called changes in mandatory programs, or CHIMPs, which serve as temporary offsets allowing higher discretionary spending.

Republicans had contemplated even bigger increases — possibly $70 billion or more for defense in 2018 and $80 billion or more for defense in 2019, according to one Republican with knowledge of the talks.

That level of increase would have put defense funding at $619 billion or more in 2018, about halfway between the $603 billion requested by President Donald Trump and the $634 billion agreed to for defense purposes in the defense authorization bill and other legislation.

Democrats remained committed to a dollar-for-dollar increase in nondefense spending compared with defense. Democrats also kept pushing to make DACA permanent, and to include it in a budget deal, but Republicans just as strongly insisted that the issue be considered separately.

By the second week of December, negotiations on a budget deal were losing momentum as Republicans focused on their comprehensive tax code rewrite.

"Unfortunately, it's looking like we may get kicked over into January before all of this can get done," said Senate Majority Whip John Cornyn, R-Texas, adding that "a lot of different pieces" would be catching a ride on some must-pass vehicle once there is an agreement.

Trump signed into law a continuing resolution (PL 115-90) extending federal agencies' budget authority through Dec. 22, to buy time for further talks. Near the end of 2017, the levels were extended in the year-end continuing appropriations law (PL 115-96). ■

Budget Resolutions Begin Process For Tax Overhaul, Health Care Changes

The 115th Congress had barely convened on the third of January when the chairman of the Senate Budget Committee, Republican Michael B. Enzi of Wyoming, rushed to introduce a budget resolution for fiscal year 2017, which by then was three months old. The previous Congress had covered things with a continuing resolution that extended federal spending authority through the end of April.

Enzi was in a hurry for Congress to adopt a budget resolution so it could be used as a vehicle for budget reconciliation instructions to do away with the 2010 health care law that was the signature achievement of President Barack Obama's administration.

By using reconciliation instead of a regular bill, Republicans would be able to repeal core elements of what they derisively called "Obamacare" without having to overcome a Senate filibuster -- the process allows a bill to pass the Senate with a simple majority, but it can only be used if the House and Senate agree to a budget resolution containing reconciliation instructions.

Reconciliation, in fact, would be the GOP's instrument of choice not only to attack the heath care law (PL 111-148, 111-152), but also to pass a major tax cut bill. Though they did not succeed in getting rid of the health care law they did manage the tax cuts, which they then made a central theme of their re-election strategy for the off-year elections of 2018.

Incoming President Donald Trump, meanwhile, put his own theatrical stamp on the budget process, proposing three versions of a fiscal 2018 budget over the course of five months in graduated levels of detail – a budget "outline" on Feb. 27, a "skinny" budget of 62 pages on March 16 and, finally, a full request on May 23, which was late in the process even by the dilatory standards of most new presidents.

Congress, for its part, adopted two budget resolutions almost eight months apart for fiscal 2017 and 2018. House and Senate were unable to agree on a two-year deal to increase spending limits and set overall budget numbers before adjourning in December.

HEALTH CARE BUDGET RESOLUTION

The pared-down, 54-page fiscal blueprint (S Con Res 3) that Enzi introduced contained reconciliation instructions for two committees in the House and two in the Senate to write legislation to dismantle the health care law. The committees had about three and a half weeks to turn in their portions of the repeal to their respective Budget committees, which would then compile the language into a bill.

The budget resolution contained two reserve funds designed to preserve savings from the repeal, which could later be used to offset the cost of replacement legislation. If the savings weren't banked, lawmakers would need to find other offsets for the legislation to avoid running up against Senate rules barring increasing the deficit.

The resolution included exceptions for health care replacement legislation from two Senate rules that prohibit increasing the deficit. That meant the cost of replacement legislation could exceed what would be saved from repealing the existing law.

The Senate voted 51-48 on Jan. 4 to proceed to the budget resolution, setting the gears in motion for repealing the health care law. It

was a significant victory for Republicans, who had voted more than 60 times in the House to dismantle all or part of the law but had gotten no further.

Democrats were united in their opposition to the Republicans' move, and hoped the GOP efforts would rebound on them in the next elections.

One Republican voted against moving the budget resolution forward , Sen. Rand Paul of Kentucky. On the floor, Paul rebuked Republican leaders for writing a budget resolution that would not balance within 10 years and would add trillions of dollars to the national debt.

"What will the first order of business be for the new Republican majority? To pass a budget that never balances. To pass a budget that will add $9.7 trillion of new debt over 10 years," Paul said, noting that he planned to introduce his own budget that would balance within a decade and not add to the national debt. "Is that really what we campaigned on? Is that really what the Republican Party represents?"

Paul said he supported efforts to repeal the health care law, but encouraged Republicans not to forget the debt and the deficit.

Republican Sens. Ted Cruz of Texas, Mike Lee of Utah and Marco Rubio of Florida released a letter prior to the vote saying they would vote for the resolution so as to allow the repeal of the health care law to begin, but noting they did not agree with the numbers.

Kentucky Rep. John Yarmuth, ranking Democrat on the House Budget Committee, and Massachusetts Rep. Richard E. Neal, top Democrat on Ways and Means, requested an analysis of the tax and spending blueprint from the OMB, which was still in President Barack Obama's hands until Trump was inaugurated later in January. The answer from Shaun Donovan, Obama's budget director, was that the budget resolution would hike the national debt by $9.5 trillion.

The blueprint relied on Congressional Budget Office projections of revenue and spending growth over the following 10 years, assuming no changes in existing laws. Recent GOP budget resolutions had assumed trillions of dollars in spending cuts aimed at balancing the budget within a decade.

BUDGET DETAILS

The resolution set budget authority at $3.3 trillion for fiscal 2017, increasing it to $4.1 trillion by fiscal 2022 and $4.9 trillion by fiscal 2026. Those figures were "on-budget," meaning they did not include Social Security and the postal service.

The legislation instructed the House Ways and Means and Energy and Commerce committees as well as Senate Finance and the Health, Education, Labor and Pensions committees to find a minimum of $1 billion each in deficit cuts during the following decade.

Those reconciliation instructions would have allowed those committees to attack portions of the health care law and avoid a filibuster from Democrats.

The resolution added $1 trillion to the annual deficit and a grand total of $9 trillion to the national debt, Senate Minority Leader Charles E. Schumer said in a floor speech.

"To all my deficit hawk friends, your proposal causes a trillion-dollar hole in the budget," the New York Democrat said.

SENATE ADOPTION

Early in the morning of Jan. 12, the Senate voted 51-48 to adopt the budget resolution, following a seven-hour voting session. Paul cast the only Republican vote against it. The chamber considered 19 amendments before the final vote and stymied each one, mostly through procedural votes.

After a relatively uneventful night of debate, the final vote was marked with some drama as Democrats stood up at their desks to explain their votes, an unusual move. "Because there is no replacement, I vote no," said Sen. Claire McCaskill of Missouri. Others said they voted no on behalf of their constituents who they said would lose health care coverage if the law was repealed. Every Democrat was interrupted by the Republican presiding over the chamber, Sen. Cory Gardner of Colorado, who warned that speeches were not allowed during the roll call vote.

The vote-a-rama on amendments started at about 6:20 p.m. on Jan. 11 with a vote on an amendment from Florida Democrat Bill Nelson that would have barred the Senate from taking up legislation to repeal the closing of the coverage gap for the Medicare Part D prescription drug program. Enzi raised a point of order against the amendment, and the chamber voted 47-51 against waiving the point of order, effectively rejecting the amendment. Sixty votes are needed to waive a point of order.

Most amendments were rejected through the same procedural vote. The highly political amendments divided senators nearly along party lines, meaning no amendment came close to the 60 votes needed to waive the point of order. An amendment from Sen. Amy Klobuchar, D-Minn., related to importing prescription drugs from Canada, was rejected 46-52 by a simple roll call vote.

At the end, the budget resolution remained unchanged.

RURAL HOSPITAL ISSUE

One of the rejected amendments came from Sen. Joe Manchin III, D-W.Va. The amendment, blocked on a 51-47 procedural vote, would have barred legislation that reduces federal funds for rural hospitals or imposes financial hardship on hospitals or clinics by reducing insurance coverage in rural communities.

The chamber also voted 48-50 not to waive a point of order raised against an amendment from Wisconsin Democrat Tammy Baldwin related to the provision in the health care law that allows children to stay on their parent's health plan until age 26. The amendment would have barred the Senate from considering legislation that altered the provision or otherwise reduced the number of young Americans enrolled in health insurance.

"The repeal resolution we're debating this week promises relief from Obamacare and provides the tools necessary to immediately repeal this failed law while ensuring a stable transition period to a patient-centered health care system that gives Americans access to quality, affordable health care," Enzi said in a floor speech on Jan. 11.

HOUSE ADOPTION

The House on Jan. 13 adopted a budget resolution aimed at repealing the 2010 health care law, giving the official go-ahead for several committees to write repeal legislation to fulfill Republicans' top goal for the new Congress.

House members voted 227-198 in favor of the budget resolution. Nine Republicans, a mix of centrists and libertarians, voted against the resolution: Justin Amash of Michigan; Charlie Dent and Brian Fitzpatrick of Pennsylvania; Walter B. Jones of North Carolina; John Katko of New York; Raul R. Labrador of Idaho; Tom MacArthur of New Jersey; Thomas Massie of Kentucky; and Tom McClintock of California.

Some of the Republicans, such as Amash, were unhappy with the fiscal outlook included in the budget document, which projected rising deficits over the next 10 years. In a Twitter post before the vote, Amash wrote, "We get the House. We get the Senate. We get the White House. We get a budget that grows debt by $9 trillion?"

Several moderate Republicans, including Dent, were not eager to begin the process of repealing the health care law without a clear alternative ready to go.

Four Republicans who were being tapped for positions in the Trump administration did not vote: Mike Pompeo of Kansas, Tom Price of Georgia, Ryan Zinke of Montana and Mick Mulvaney of South Carolina.

Leading up to the House vote, floor debate was intense at times as Republicans and Democrats volleyed statistics and anecdotes back and forth, painting starkly different views of the landmark health care law.

Republicans blamed the law for rising health care costs, a lack of choice for consumers and an economic burden on small businesses. They sought to portray their repeal efforts as a "rescue mission" for Americans they said were struggling under the law.

"Our experimentation in Soviet-style central planning of our health care system has been an abject failure," said freshman Rep. Jodey C. Arrington of Texas.

Democrats argued just the opposite. They credited the law with expanding coverage and slowing the rise of health care costs. They offered stories of constituents afraid of losing health coverage if the law is repealed and they blasted Republicans for the lack of a clear GOP replacement plan.

After every Republican speaker, Kentucky Rep. John Yarmuth, the Democratic floor manager, noted the number of people in that GOP member's state who would lose health coverage and jobs if the law were repealed.

Rep. Hakeem Jeffries, D-N.Y., said the Republican repeal efforts would benefit "the fat cats who are part of the health care cartel" while leaving many Americans "screwed."

"People in Michigan, Pennsylvania, Wisconsin, Ohio: screwed," Jeffries said. "Seniors in Florida: screwed. People on the West Coast and the East Coast: screwed. People in Appalachia and rural America: screwed."

Summing up the discussion, Rep. Peter Welch, D-Vt., said members were engaging in "the dumbest debate" on "probably the most important issue."

"We say the health care [law] is good, you say it stinks," Welch said.

He added, "You've got some responsibility to show us the beef. Where's the plan? There's a lot of paper over there, but you haven't shown us a plan, and here's why: because when you put pen to paper, all hell is going to break loose on your side."

The final vote followed a vote on a Democratic substitute amendment, which was rejected 149-272. The Democrats' alternative directed Congress to take up legislation related to infrastructure, jobs and taxes, rather than focusing on health care.

TAX BILL BUDGET RESOLUTION

The House adopted a final 2018 budget resolution by a razor-thin margin on Oct. 26, setting the stage for major tax legislation by allowing Republican leaders to write a bill they could pass in the Senate by a simple majority, without the threat of a filibuster. The Senate had adopted the same resolution on Oct. 19 by a 51-49 vote.

The budget resolution (H Con Res 71) was adopted 216-212 even though all Democrats and 20 Republicans voted against it. House Budget Chairman Diane Black, R-Tenn., and GOP leaders were closely watching from the floor as the votes were tallied. The whip count had been somewhat in question as Republicans with constituents that benefitted from the state and local income tax deduction – shorthanded to the SALT deduction in the congressional negotiations – sought to retain it in the tax code.

Lee Zeldin, R-N.Y., for instance, said he voted "no" on the budget over concerns about the fate of the SALT deduction.

With two vacancies in the House and no Democrats supporting the budget, just a handful more GOP "no" votes would have sunk it. Diane Black and Republican leaders came close to the edge with 20 defections, a mix of Northeastern lawmakers from high-tax states and hard-line spending hawks upset about the lack of cuts assumed in the fiscal blueprint.

But Majority Leader Kevin McCarthy, R-Calif., expressed confidence the budget would be adopted, and a planned meeting the day of the vote with those members was cancelled shortly before it was scheduled to begin — indicating there ultimately wasn't too much concern about the final whip count.

FISCAL SPACE FOR TAX CUTS

In addition to opening an expedited path for tax legislation, the budget's reconciliation instructions allowed for up to $1.5 trillion in revenue losses over the following decade.

Republican leaders thought a portion of that money represented the anticipated extension or renewal of dozens of tax provisions — known as "extenders" — that Congress routinely enacts and therefore should be considered part of the baseline. The remainder, about $1 trillion, represented revenue GOP leaders and the White House believed would ultimately be made up for through faster economic growth, resulting in higher tax receipts.

The measure also included reconciliation instructions to the Senate Energy and Natural Resources Committee to find $1 billion in 10-year savings within their jurisdiction, which was expected to come from increased federal oil and gas royalty receipts through opening a protected parcel of Alaska's Arctic National Wildlife Refuge for oil and gas extraction.

Tony Iallonardo, energy communications director for the Wilderness Society, said after the vote that the energy language was "code for ordering up drilling in our nation's most pristine landscape."

During debate, Democrats castigated the budget resolution as a blueprint for spiking deficits without any of the benefits accruing to middle-income households.

"I know my Republican colleagues desperately want to believe the tax cuts in their budget will pay for themselves and usher in a new era of economic growth. But, the record is clear. This approach has failed time and time again," House Budget Committee top Democrat John Yarmuth said on the floor.

The budget resolution, Yarmuth said, should be a way to invest in American families, providing them with a "better and more secure" life. "This budget and the tax code that will follow are a failure on all fronts," Yarmuth continued.

SPENDING CUTS COULD WAIT

The budget that House Republicans adopted was significantly different than the one they had sent to the Senate earlier in October. That budget resolution called for a deficit-neutral tax plan and $203 billion in mandatory spending reductions during a 10-year time frame.

House and Senate leaders employed an unusual truncated process to adopt the budget. After it became clear the Senate's budget would need to carry the day given that chamber's extremely narrow voting margin, there remained discussion of a formal House-Senate conference to at least give the appearance of a negotiation.

But in the interest of shaving as many as two weeks off the start of the tax overhaul effort, Senate Republicans agreed to adopt some largely cosmetic House-backed changes during floor debate and quickly send the measure back to the House for final adoption.

Even though Republicans had campaigned on and called for deficit reductions for years, House Republicans ultimately accepted the Senate's budget, which included instructions to find only $1 billion in 10-year savings — to come from oil and gas drilling royalties, rather than from mandatory spending cuts. The lack of curbs on spending growth would be addressed in the fiscal 2019 budget resolution, GOP leaders said.

For a time, advocates of higher military spending implied they would deny support for the budget resolution unless it assumed higher discretionary spending limits for the Pentagon in fiscal 2018.

Since such resolutions are non-binding, and a change in statutory spending limits with the force of law would be necessary to increase defense appropriations. Senate Armed Services Chairman John McCain, R-Ariz., agreed to stand down in the interest of moving ahead with the tax code rewrite, but with a promise to work out a spending cap deal in the fall.

HOUSE COMMITTEE APPROVAL

Back in the spring, Republican leaders had talked optimistically about finishing a fiscal 2018 budget resolution incorporating reconciliation instructions for a tax bill before summer. The chairwoman of the House Budget Committee, Tennessee Republican Diane Black, even said in April that she hoped to mark up a resolution the week of May 15.

"We are working very hard at looking at every penny that's there to see how we might be able to do that, and we're getting very, very close," she said at the time.

The task, though, proved much more difficult and GOP lawmakers were still working on their budget resolution on May 23 when President Trump issued his full budget request for fiscal 2018. Congress, in fact, faced the real possibility that it would not be able to adopt a budget resolution on time for the second year in a row.

A month later, budget talks were bogged down over demands by some lawmakers that the budget resolution include substantially more money for defense. In a June 22 meeting, Republicans on the House Budget Committee discussed adding $10 billion to the $65 billion the committee had proposed for war funds for the Pentagon. Such spending is not restricted by the caps set in budget law.

Republicans pushed their fiscal 2018 budget resolution through committee on the night of July 19, after weeks of delays, disagreements and a barrage of Democratic amendments. The vote was 22-14, along party lines.

The blueprint set limits on discretionary spending for fiscal 2018, including $621.5 billion for base discretionary defense programs and $511 billion for nondefense discretionary spending. It allowed up to $75 billion in war funding for the military and $12 billion for the State Department and other civilian agencies. War funds are outside the constraints of the statutory caps, and were set at $549 billion for defense and $516 billion for nondefense.

Critically for Republicans, the resolution included reconciliation instructions directing 11 authorizing committees to write legislation to reduce the deficit by a minimum of $203 billion over 10 years. The Ways and Means Committee was expected to produce both a comprehensive tax overhaul as well as legislation to cut mandatory spending programs.

During the daylong markup, Democrats offered 28 amendments — and every one of them was voted down, all but one on party-line votes. The exception was an amendment offered by Barbara Lee, D-Calif., that would've jettisoned the $10 billion addition to war funding put into the budget to assuage those who wanted more defense spending.

Trump had requested $65 billion for the military in the Overseas Contingency Operations account, and that's the amount that an earlier draft of the budget resolution provided. The budget increased that limit to $75 billion. Two Republicans — Mark Sanford of South Carolina and Jason Lewis of Minnesota — joined all 14 Democrats in voting to eliminate the funding. Nineteen Republicans opposed the measure and it fell 16-19.

Most of the Democrats' amendments were aimed at maintaining or strengthening programs they favored, such as the 2010 health care law, Medicaid, the Supplemental Nutrition Assistance Program and foreign aid.

Yarmuth, ranking Democrat on the Budget Committee, proposed striking the reconciliation instructions at the heart of the plan. The Kentucky lawmaker argued that the main purpose of the budget resolution was to facilitate tax cuts for the "wealthiest Americans and corporations."

"By contrast the cuts that will be forced by the reconciliation instructions are cuts that would hurt the most vulnerable citizens in our country," Yarmuth said.

Tom McClintock, R-Calif., defended the reconciliation instructions, saying they were needed in the face of projections that trillion-dollar deficits were returning. "This budget finally uses reconciliation as it was intended," he said. "It doesn't cut spending, it restrains the growth of spending."

Republicans did not offer any amendments. But the fairly uneventful markup took a turn late in the evening when Sanford sought to break what he called the "gentleman's agreement" among GOP members of the committee that they refrain.

As the panel prepared to vote on the final seven amendments offered by Democrats, Sanford tried to propose one of his own that would have effectively prevented the inclusion of a border adjustment tax in a tax overhaul by barring the use of revenue from such a tax from being counted in estimating revenue levels.

To the apparent surprise of just about every member of the committee, Sanford brought up his concern that with a desire for full business expensing as part of a tax overhaul, and the collapse of the health care bill in the Senate, Congress would be headed toward enactment of the border adjustment tax that many Republicans opposed.

"In the last 24 hours health care blew up and in essence that creates more than a trillion-dollar hole in getting to tax reform and I don't know how you do it again without a BAT," he said. The proposed tax would raise $1.2 trillion over a decade, helping to pay for the lowering of tax rates and other tax cuts in the plan.

Black, wielding the gavel, refused to allow Sanford to offer the amendment, since she said it was not on the list of amendments earlier agreed to in a unanimous consent agreement. Two Democrats on the committee urged Black to allow the amendment, to no avail.

SENATE COMMITTEE APPROVAL AND PASSAGE

The Senate Budget Committee approved a draft fiscal 2018 budget resolution, 12-11, on Oct. 5 while earlier the same day the House passed its version in a slim 219-206 vote. House Republicans had already indicated they probably could live with a final product that looked more like the Senate resolution, which did not contain the House's proposed $203 billion in 10-year mandatory spending cuts.

With 52 seats in the Senate, the GOP could only afford to lose two Republican votes and still adopt the budget – and there were several Republican senators who might have given party leaders trouble, including Susan Collins of Maine, Rand Paul of Kentucky, Mike Lee of Utah and John McCain of Arizona.

The Senate resolution included reconciliation instructions for committees to produce tax overhaul legislation that would not lose more than $1.5 trillion in tax revenue over 10 years.

Sen. David Perdue, R-Ga., said he reluctantly supported what he called the "sham" budget resolution only in order to launch the tax overhaul, as the pretense of spending cuts contained in the bill were ultimately meaningless without actual legislation to back them up.

Senate committee members tangled over a flurry of amendments to the resolution, including one that led to an argument over whether the reconciliation instructions in the plan were a "free-range chicken" or some other "critter."

Angus King, I-Maine, offered an amendment to reinstate a rule named after former Senate Budget Chairman Kent Conrad, a North Dakota Democrat, that barred reconciliation legislation that would increase the deficit. The rule had been in effect from 2007 until it was rescinded by Senate Republicans in 2015. King's amendment was rejected.

"If you are going to use reconciliation it ought to be to reduce the deficit," Sheldon Whitehouse, D-R.I., said. He called GOP reconciliation plans "a free-range chicken that can run wherever the majority wants it to."

Whitehouse said the Budget Committee had become a "nullity" when it came to budget policy, adding, "The one thing we do is this reconciliation critter." Whitehouse warned that "one day the worm will turn" and Democrats would be in charge of reconciliation.

Patrick J. Toomey, R-Pa., said reconciliation was "not exactly a free-range chicken." Toomey said. "If we do this tax reform right" it would produce at least $1 trillion in additional revenue from economic growth and reduce the deficit.

The committee approved an amendment from John Kennedy, R-La., to establish a deficit neutral reserve fund to implement work requirements for some recipients of welfare programs not including Social Security, Medicare, unemployment insurance and workers' compensation.

SENATE PASSAGE

The Senate on Oct. 19 adopted a budget resolution (S Con Res 25) that was amended at the 11th hour with the aim of making it acceptable

enough to House Republicans to avoid a conference committee and speed consideration of a tax overhaul. The budget was adopted 51-49.

An amendment offered by Senate Budget Chairman Michael B. Enzi, R-Wyo., modified the House-passed budget resolution, jettisoning reconciliation instructions aimed at getting $203 billion in mandatory spending cuts and replacing the House directive for a deficit-neutral tax cut with one that could add up to $1.5 trillion to the deficit over 10 years, similar to the Senate's.

The Senate approved the amendment 52-48. That version of H Con Res 71 was the one that the House took up and approved on Oct. 26.

The Senate budget retained a reconciliation instruction to its Energy and Natural Resources Committee directing the panel to produce legislation to reduce the deficit by $1 billion, seen by many as a vehicle for opening the Arctic Wildlife Refuge in Alaska to drilling.

The amendment also duplicated within the House budget resolution a reserve fund in the Senate budget that allowed for an appropriations deal to raise the discretionary spending caps, including the Senate notation that the defense cap could be raised to $640 billion for fiscal 2018. As was the case with the Senate rule, the provision would allow the caps to be raised without their additional cost being offset, unlike past budget deals.

Under the Senate resolution, the Finance Committee was asked to write a tax cut that increased the deficit by up to $1.5 trillion over a decade. ■

House Flirts With Earmarks Revival

Ever since House Republicans in 2010 banned earmarks – legislative directions for specific pet projects that for decades had greased the path of highway bills and other legislation – some members of Congress had sought to bring them back.

Many House Republicans thought that allowing earmarks again would help Congress recover power over spending that it had lost to the executive branch, and also help break the gridlock on Capitol Hill.

An incipient effort at the start of the 115th Congress led to meetings and some debate, but congressional leaders were clearly in no hurry to revive a practice that had bought them such bad press for undertakings like the "bridge to nowhere" in Ketchikan, Alaska, in the early 2000s.

At a meeting on Jan. 31, a group of conservative lawmakers had said they strongly opposed modifying or overturning the ban on earmarks in spending bills, saying the prohibition avoided a return to "pork-barrel spending."

The meeting -- hosted by the House Republican Study Committee and Citizens Against Government Waste, a non-profit group that had long opposed earmarks – was called as the House moved closer to a possible vote on overturning the ban.

"I have a sick feeling that there are more than half of the conference who would vote for this if it came back," said Rep. Bill Flores, R-Texas. "So we need to make sure we have grassroots support."

The previous November, in fact, Speaker Paul D. Ryan, R-Wis., had stepped in to prevent Republicans from lifting the earmark ban as part of a rules package for the new Congress. Ryan cautioned against augmenting or lifting the earmarks ban so soon after Donald Trump had campaigned on a "drain the swamp" message.

Ryan promised instead he would organize a thorough review of the ban and hold a floor vote on it during the first quarter of 2017.

In exchange for that promise, Texas Rep. John Culberson, who proposed allowing earmarks for federal, state or local government projects, and Florida Rep. Tom Rooney, who wanted to allow earmarks for Army Corps of Engineer projects, withdrew their amendments to the GOP rules package.

House Rules Committee Chairman Pete Sessions said on Feb. 14 that Republicans were moving forward with plans to review and possibly bring back earmarks later in the year. The committee, Sessions said, planned to hold public hearings on earmarks in the coming months and make a recommendation before the Fourth of July recess.

The revival effort lost steam in the spring, when Sessions said on May 24 that his committee would not produce a report on earmarks by the Fourth of July recess. In fact, it did not appear for the rest of the year. ■

Convention on Balanced Budget Sought

At the start of 2017 more than half the states had taken action to require Congress to put its fiscal house in order by attempting to add a balanced budget amendment to the U.S. Constitution.

It sounds like a pipe dream, but there are some who believe the nation is not far away from its first constitutional convention since 1787. Opinions are sharply divided on whether it would be a tonic for a debt-ridden nation or an opening for far greater constitutional meddling.

Groups promoting the amendment say it would force lawmakers to think more diligently about the budget resolution they are supposed to pass annually. But budget experts and some members of Congress say there could be major consequences to requiring the federal checkbook to balance, especially in times of war or economic downturns, or following costly natural disasters.

House Budget Committee Chairwoman Diane Black, R-Tenn., said she supported a balanced budget amendment, even if it were not written by the committee she led. Black said she was not opposed if states took the lead on the proposal instead of the members of Congress who draft and mark up the annual budget resolution. "The Constitution provides that states can do it," she said in an interview, "and if states have enough support, then I think that is a perfectly acceptable way to move it."

Rep. John Yarmuth, the top Democrat on House Budget, disagreed. He said such an amendment could have severe economic repercussions. "That would be very limiting and potentially dangerous," said Yarmuth, of Kentucky. "There is too much unpredictability in the world and in the country. And the federal government – either rightly or wrongly – is the funder of last resort and the ultimate credit facility for the country."

He said a balanced budget amendment could devastate state governments, on top of problems it might cause at the federal level.

"It would be disastrous for states, because what ultimately happens if you pass [a balanced budget amendment] is that all those spending pressures get pushed down to the states and then they are either going to have to be forced to run huge deficits or cut a lot of services for their citizens," Yarmuth said. "I can't imagine any legislative body — if they think about it — would want to do it."

MAGIC NUMBER 34

By January 2017, 28 state legislatures had passed resolutions calling for a constitutional convention to pass a balanced budget amendment. Thirty-four are needed before Congress would be required to call a convention under Article V of the Constitution. If that were to happen, it would be the first time a constitutional convention has been called to pass an amendment. The 27 amendments to the Constitution have all been proposed by Congress.

While six new resolutions would have given the groups the 34 states they need to hold a convention, New Mexico and Maryland legislators were considering resolutions that would rescind their states' support for a convention. In fact, by May not only Maryland and New Mexico had rescinded their resolutions for calling for a constitutional convention. Nevada had joined them.

Several groups, including the Balanced Budget Amendment Task Force, Citizens for Self-Governance and the American Legislative Exchange Council, known as ALEC, were working with lawmakers in 11 conservative-leaning states — including Arizona, Idaho, Kentucky, Montana, South Carolina and Wyoming — to try to get resolutions calling for a convention passed in 2017. ALEC receives most of its funding from companies or corporate foundations, including Koch Industries, which backs conservative causes; oil giant Exxon Mobil; and AT&T, according to the Center for Media and Democracy. It's also funded from the dues it charges the state lawmakers who join. The Balanced Budget Amendment Task Force is a 501 (c)(4) not-for-profit corporation headquartered in Florida.

If a convention were called, states would send delegations and the convention's delegates would write rules for the convention. They'd also set the threshold for passing a constitutional amendment, write the amendment and vote on passage of that amendment. Then Congress would need to decide how to set up ratification of the amendment.

Congress could opt to send the amendment to state legislatures or Congress could tell each state to call a convention. Either way, 38 states then would have to vote to ratify any balanced budget amendment passed by the convention. Garry W. Banz, a former Oklahoma House member and cofounder of the Balanced Budget Amendment Task Force, was optimistic about the chances of a convention. "My guess is if they like the amendment language they will select what they perceive as the easier of the two methods. If they don't like it, they will choose the more difficult of the two," Banz said of Congress.

State legislatures have ratified 26 of the 27 amendments to the Constitution. The repeal of prohibition — the 21st Amendment — was the only amendment each state called its own convention to ratify.

If an amendment were to be passed by a convention and sent to the states to ratify, it would likely set up an ongoing debate in statehouses throughout the country, which could last for years.

WHY NOT CONGRESS?

Congress could propose a balanced budget amendment on its own, and there were numerous members who supported the idea, but the organizations advocating for a convention didn't hold out much hope.

"It would take an enormous amount of political courage for Congress to police itself in that fashion and there are lots of people who don't believe Congress, as it is today, has the political courage to do that," said Karla Jones, director of international relations and federalism at ALEC. Jones said that supporters of a balanced budget have lost faith in federal lawmakers' ability to budget and spend.

A broad swath of the Republican Party supported a balanced budget amendment to the Constitution. The GOP's 2016 platform included a statement supporting it.

During the 114th Congress, approximately two dozen resolutions were proposed to require balancing the federal budget. One from Sen. Orrin G. Hatch, R-Utah, gained 53 co-sponsors in the Senate — all of them Republicans. On the House side, Rep. Robert W. Goodlatte, R-Va., proposed a resolution that received support from 110 House members, including two Democrats. At least 10 balanced budget resolutions were introduced in 2017.

Even with a unified Republican-led Congress, the way was still difficult. Constitutional amendments require the support of two-thirds of both chambers. With a 52-seat Republican majority in the Senate and

very little support from Democrats in the past, there was little hope for the first session of the 115th Congress.

Even with support in Congress, there could be drawbacks to a balanced budget amendment, budget experts argued.

Marc Goldwein, senior vice president and senior policy director at the nonpartisan Committee for a Responsible Federal Budget, said the real problem with annual, billion-dollar deficits and a $19 trillion national debt lay in mandatory spending.

Budget resolutions set the topline spending number for discretionary spending, but don't control spending on mandatory programs. Budget resolutions can instruct authorizing committees to overhaul those programs, but do not require them to do so. Crucially, congressional budget resolutions are not signed by the president — they can never become law, do not have the binding nature of law and are predominantly used as blueprints for future legislation on taxes and spending. Elements of the budget resolutions Congress does pass can and are often waived by a two-thirds vote.

Goldwein argued that requiring Congress to balance discretionary spending within the budget resolution would not do enough to curb growing entitlement programs, such as Medicare, Medicaid and Social Security. He also said it would not be the best use of energy and resources.

"That process will take a lot of time and I think that might be a lot of steam that could be used to push for fiscal policy," Goldwein said. He supported fiscal targets for Congress, but preferred they should come in the form of a debt-to-gross-domestic-product ratio.

Richard Kogan, a senior fellow at the liberal-leaning Center on Budget and Policy Priorities, worked as a senior adviser at the Office of Management and Budget during the Obama administration and spent 21 years before that working on the House Budget Committee, including as the director of budget policy. He remained opposed to a balanced budget amendment.

A constitutional amendment, he argued, would force spending cuts and tax increases during recessions — exacerbating economic problems. "When the economy slows, federal revenues decline or grow more slowly, spending on social programs rises and deficits rise," Kogan wrote in a paper published in January.

A balanced budget amendment would force policymakers to cut spending, raise taxes or both in that circumstance, he said. "That would launch a vicious spiral of bad economic and fiscal policy," he predicted.

No Limits?

Kogan's paper also anticipated a broader problem. He quoted former Chief Justice Warren Burger, who in 1988 wrote: "[T]here is no way to effectively limit or muzzle the actions of a constitutional convention. The convention could make its own rules and set its own agenda. Congress might try to limit the convention to one amendment or one issue, but there is no way to assure that the convention would obey. After a convention is convened, it will be too late to stop the convention if we don't like its agenda."

There hasn't been a constitutional convention since 1787 — meaning that there isn't much historical precedence or guidance on what a convention could and could not do.

Kogan wrote that any balanced budget amendment convention could expand in scope, just as the 1787 Constitutional Convention did. "Charged with amending the Articles of Confederation to promote trade among the states, the convention instead wrote an entirely new governing document. A convention held today could set its own agenda, too." ■

Chapter 5

CONGRESSIONAL AFFAIRS
& POLITICS

Jobs in Trump's Cabinet, Scandal And Health Issues Spark Turnover

Nine representatives and two senators resigned from Congress in 2017. Some took on new roles in public service, others left amid scandal, and lingering health issues caused a prominent Senate committee chairman to step down.

For five Republican lawmakers with particular policy chops, the election of Donald Trump meant new opportunities at the start of the 115th Congress. The new president turned to Capitol Hill to fill key posts in his Cabinet and White House.

Rep. Mike Pompeo of Kansas, a former Army officer, was sworn in as CIA director on Jan. 23. He was first elected to Congress in 2010.

Sen. Jeff Sessions of Alabama was sworn in as attorney general on Feb. 8. First elected to the Senate in 1996, the former state attorney general was in his fourth Senate term and a senior member of the Judiciary Committee.

Sessions, one of the first members of Congress to endorse Trump for president, advised the campaign in 2016. His decision to recuse himself from the FBI's investigation into Russian meddling in the 2016 election drew fire from Trump, who repeatedly lashed out at the attorney general throughout the year.

Rep. Tom Price of Georgia, an orthopedic surgeon, was sworn in as Health and Human Services secretary on Feb. 10. His confirmation process was dominated by questions about his financial conflicts of interest, including his trade of stocks with pharmaceutical interests. He was forced to resign from the Cabinet post on Sept. 29 following a Politico report that he billed taxpayers for more than $1 million in travel on private and military jets.

Rep. Ryan Zinke of Montana took office as Interior secretary on March 1. First elected to the House in 2014, Zinke was in his second term.

Rep. Mick Mulvaney of South Carolina took office as director of the Office of Management and Budget, a Cabinet-level post in the White House, on Feb. 16. Mulvaney, first elected to the House in 2004, was a member of the hard-line conservative House Freedom Caucus.

SEXUAL MISCONDUCT

Allegations of sexual misconduct forced Reps. John Conyers, D-Mich., Trent Franks, R-Ariz., and Tim Murphy, R-Pa., and Sen. Al Franken, D-Minn., from office in 2017.

Franken announced his resignation on Dec. 7, but it did not take effect until Jan. 2, 2018.

About a week after Franken announced his resignation, Minnesota Gov. Mark Dayton appointed Lt. Gov. Tina Smith to fill the Senate vacancy until a special election in November 2018.

Smith had never held elected office before Dayton asked her to be his running mate in 2014. Prior to that, she was his chief of staff.

Smith's earlier political experience included serving as chief of staff to Minneapolis Mayor R.T. Rybak. She was close to former Vice President Walter F. Mondale and managed his brief campaign for the Senate in 2002 following the death of Democratic Sen. Paul Wellstone in an airplane crash prior to the election.

NEW OPPORTUNITIES

Reps. Jason Chaffetz, R-Utah., and Xavier Becerra, D-Calif., respectively, pursued new opportunities in the private sector and in public service back home.

Chaffetz, chairman of the House Oversight and Government Reform Committee, quit on June 30. Long considered a rising Republican star on Capitol Hill, Chaffetz was a frequent presence on television and used his committee perch to investigate the Obama administration.

He was first elected to Congress in 2008, and his resignation took effect June 30.

"I have long advocated public service should be for a limited time and not a lifetime or full career," said Chaffetz, who joined Fox News as a contributor.

Becerra, the former chairman of the House Democratic Caucus, stepped down Jan. 24 after he was appointed attorney general in his home state. California Gov. Jerry Brown tapped Becerra, a confidant of House Minority Leader Nancy Pelosi, to replace Kamala Harris, who was elected to the U.S. Senate in 2016.

SENATORS WITH HEALTH ISSUES

Two Republican senators in 2017 had extended absences because of medical problems.

Sen. Thad Cochran of Mississippi, 80, announced in September that he was leaving Washington to address a "urological issue."

After returning to the Senate in October, Cochran appeared frail, missed votes intermittently as he continued to recover, and communicated solely through statements sent out by spokesmen. As chairman of the Appropriations Committee, he did not hold a hearing or markup during those months.

Sen. John McCain of Arizona had surgery July 14 to remove a blood clot in his skull above his left eye. Subsequent tests revealed a brain tumor known as a glioblastoma, the Mayo Clinic Hospital in Phoenix said in a statement. McCain, a former prisoner of war in Vietnam, was 80 years old at the time of his diagnosis.

For the remainder of July 2017, he was at the center of the Senate's health care debate. McCain first cast a procedural vote to begin debate on a GOP bill to repeal and replace the 2010 health care law. Then, he cast the key vote against an amendment that would have repealed major parts of the law.

On July 28, McCain's office issued a statement that he would begin a standard post-surgical regimen of targeted radiation and chemotherapy. For the remainder of the year, he made occasional appearances in the Senate.

As chairman of the Armed Services Committee, he continued work on reauthorization of military programs. That measure, which was his chief legislative objective for the year, continued into 2018. ■

Special Election Roundup: GOP Wins Most; Democrats Outperform

The tumult and divisiveness that resulted in Donald Trump's surprise victory over Hillary Clinton for the presidency continued to resonate in 2017. Voters eager to push back on the new administration used special elections for Congress to voice their displeasure with Trump, his policies and style of governing.

There were seven special elections in 2017 for Congress – six for House seats and one for the Senate. Five of those congressional races were the result of Trump tapping Republican incumbents for Cabinet and executive positions in his administration.

Partisan control did not change in any of the six House seats decided by special election. But Democrats won a Senate seat in Alabama for the first time in 25 years – a dramatic victory by Doug Jones over Roy Moore in one of the reddest states in the nation.

Political observers said the special election results portend a tough landscape for Republicans in the 2018 midterm elections. The party of the president in power typically loses House and Senate seats in midterms, but the 2018 congressional races will be viewed even more so as a national referendum on Trump.

The National Republican Congressional Committee, the House's campaign arm, spent money in all but two of the 2017 special election contests in that chamber. The exceptions were in Utah's 3rd District, where GOP Rep. Jason Chaffetz resigned to join the private sector, and in California's 34th District, where Democratic Rep. Xavier Becerra left Congress to become attorney general of his state.

The 2017 results showed there was a voter shift toward Democrats in what should have been comfortable victories for Republicans in the House special elections for Kansas' 4th District, Montana's at-large seat, Georgia's 6th District and South Carolina's 5th District. Trump carried each of those districts by upward of 20 percentage points in 2016. Democrats narrowed the gap and lost those seats by single digits.

The average special election shift was 10 points toward Democrats, according to calculations by National Public Radio. FiveThirtyEight, a website with a focus on politics and opinion poll analysis, calculated what it called the "partisan lean" of a district or state in a "neutral environment" and determined that Democrats outperformed in all of the 2017 special elections. ∎

Senate: Alabama Democrat Doug Jones Scores Upset Victory Over Roy Moore

Democrat Doug Jones, a former U.S. attorney, defeated Roy Moore, a candidate scarred by allegations of sexual abuse and child molestation, for a Senate seat in Alabama that has long been a stronghold for Republicans.

Jones won the Dec. 12 special election by about 2 percentage points over the Republican, according to the state's certified results.

He will serve out the nearly three years remaining on the term of Republican Sen. Jeff Sessions, who resigned in February to become U.S. attorney general. With Jones' victory, Republicans have a narrow 51-49 voting margin in the Senate—whose own rules require bipartisan cooperation for most legislation to pass.

"This entire race has been about dignity and respect," Jones said at his election night victory party in Birmingham, Ala. "This campaign has been about the rule of law. ... This campaign has been about common courtesy and decency, and making sure everyone in this state, regardless of which ZIP code you live in, is going to get a fair shake in life."

Few political observers would have expected voters to choose an ex-federal prosecutor appointed by President Bill Clinton as the replacement for Sessions, a rock-ribbed conservative who was among the first to endorse Trump's presidential aspirations.

But Moore, a former chief justice of the Alabama Supreme Court, could not get past his own controversies or maximize the reluctant support of Trump.

Four women alleged in a Washington Post story published Nov. 9 that Moore inappropriately pursued them when he they were teenagers and he was in his 30s. One of Moore's accusers alleged sexual assault by the GOP Senate nominee. Five women came forward after The Post's blockbuster story, with two also alleging assault by Moore.

Moore said the allegations were "completely false" and "misleading."

ALLEGATIONS AND FALLOUT

Moore was already an unpopular figure among some Republicans in the state, who were turned off by his controversial rhetoric and high-profile defiance of federal orders.

He was twice ousted from the state bench—first in 2003 for refusing to remove a Ten Commandments monument from the courthouse and again in 2016 for ordering judges not to comply with the U.S. Supreme

Court's decision legalizing same-sex marriage across the country.

The allegations of sexual abuse and child molestation were too much for key Republicans such as Sen. Richard C. Shelby, Alabama's senior senator. Shelby said in a Dec. 10 appearance on CNN that he "couldn't vote for Roy Moore" and that he wrote in "a distinguished Republican name. And I think a lot of people could do that."

Support for Moore from the Republican establishment was shaky. After the Post's blockbuster report, Senate Majority Leader Mitch McConnell and Speaker Paul D. Ryan said Moore should step aside. The Republican National Committee and the National Republican Senatorial Committee, the Senate GOP's campaign arm, temporarily withdrew funding from Moore's campaign.

The president, who carried Alabama by about 28 percentage points in 2016, had backed appointed Sen. Luther Strange in the Sept. 26 GOP primary. Following the allegations outlined by the Post, Trump said Moore should withdraw "if the charges are true."

A week before the election, Trump endorsed Moore. The RNC subsequently reinstated its support for Moore, and McConnell said he would "let the people of Alabama decide."

VOTER TURNOUT

In the end, more than 22,000 write-in votes were cast in the race, and they exceeded Jones' margin of victory.

While Jones was helped by the backlash against Moore, he also campaigned strenuously to overcome the state's demographics and racial polarization. Exit polls showed Jones was able to turn out African-American voters and win over more moderate Republicans to build an effective coalition.

Black voters made up 23 percent of registered voters in the state, but accounted for about 30 percent of the electorate in the special election, according to The Washington Post. Seventy-five percent of self-described moderate voters also backed Jones.

Moore did not concede on election night and his campaign filed a lawsuit to delay certifying the result, suggesting voter fraud. Alabama's canvassing board — made up of the governor, secretary of state and attorney general — certified the election results on Dec. 28.

COMMITMENT TO JUSTICE

Jones is the first Democrat to serve in the Senate since Howell Heflin, one of his mentors, retired in 1997. The last time an Alabama Democrat was elected to the Senate was in 1992, when Shelby won his second term. Shelby switched parties in 1994 and became a Republican.

Jones began his career as a staff counsel on the Senate Judiciary Committee for Heflin. He then worked as an assistant U.S. attorney before going into private law practice. Jones served as U.S. attorney for the Northern District of Alabama from 1997 to 2001.

In the landmark case of his legal career, Jones prosecuted two former Ku Klux Klansmen for the 1963 bombing of the 16th Street Baptist Church in Birmingham, which killed four African-American girls. Both were eventually convicted.

As a young law student, he skipped class to watch then-Alabama Attorney General Bill Baxley prosecute the believed orchestrator of the bombing.

Jones said he would continue to prioritize justice issues while in the Senate, including changes to sentencing laws. And Jones told The Economist that he would try to be bipartisan in his Senate work.

"I hope that a voice like mine, a Democrat voice from the South, will be able to reach across that aisle and find that common ground and that middle ground," he said in that November 2017 interview.

GOP PRIMARY: MOORE DEFEATS APPOINTED INCUMBENT

Moore easily defeated appointed Sen. Strange on Sept. 26 for the party's Senate nomination in Alabama, overcoming the incumbent's support from Trump and key GOP figures.

Strange, appointed by Alabama Gov. Bob Bentley in February, was the first incumbent GOP senator to lose a primary since Indiana's Richard G. Lugar was defeated in 2012.

Top Republicans such as Trump and Senate Majority Leader Mitch McConnell were enthusiastic supporters of Strange, who was dogged by questions about his appointment and his ties to McConnell. The Senate Leadership Fund, a super PAC with ties to McConnell, spent millions of dollars to support Strange.

As Alabama's attorney general, Strange was in position to investigate Bentley, who was in the headlines himself for a sex scandal involving a former staffer. [The governor eventually resigned in April.]

Although Trump enjoyed widespread popularity in Alabama, it didn't translate to Strange. He was behind Moore in polling throughout the runoff.

"People can keep that distinction in their head: 'I love President Trump and I'm going to be for him no matter what, but this guy, Sen. Strange, got there in a way I don't approve of so I'm not with the president on that," said Rep. Bradley Byrne, R-Ala., who did not endorse a candidate in the GOP runoff. "I think Sen. Strange would have been far better off doing his local and statewide knitting on issues."

Moore had been elected statewide twice and racked up strong conservative support while serving on the state Supreme Court, where he ignored federal orders on the display of a Ten Commandments statue and on same-sex marriage.

In one fundraising appeal, for example, Moore made clear to his supporters that he was proud that McConnell called him a "conservative rebel" and vowed he would not march lockstep behind the Senate GOP leader's "Big Government, Big Spending" agenda.

In the runoff, Moore was helped by Steve Bannon, a former presidential adviser to Trump who fell out of favor with the White House. Bannon had warned the GOP establishment that their day of "reckoning" would come.

Indeed, Bannon believed Moore's victory in the Alabama GOP Senate primary would lead to a "revolution" by conservative Republicans.

So when Moore won the Senate GOP nomination, there was concern that he would make it even more difficult for McConnell and Republicans to pass legislation in the Senate, where 60 votes are needed to overcome a filibuster and advance bills. At the time of the Alabama Senate GOP runoff, Republicans had a 52-48 voting advantage.

"As a conservative, we expect Roy Moore to vote largely in line with the Republican agenda and certainly President Trump's agenda," said Brian Walsh , a former aide to Senate Majority Whip John Cornyn of Texas, the No. 2 GOP leader behind McConnell.

There were nine Republicans who sought the GOP nomination in the Alabama Senate race. Strange, Moore and Rep. Mo Brooks were considered the top candidates in the field.

Moore and Strange, respectively, were the top two finishers in the first round of voting on Aug. 15. Strange, the incumbent appointed to replace Sessions, never led any primary polls. ■

House: Republican Candidates Claim Victories in Friendly Territory

KANSAS TREASURER ESTES WINS FIRST SPECIAL ELECTION OF TRUMP ERA

Republican Ron Estes, the state treasurer, defeated Democrat James Thompson on April 11 to win a special election in the 4th District of Kansas. Estes succeeded Mike Pompeo, who resigned to become CIA director.

The first congressional election of Donald Trump's presidency was closer than expected, even though Estes won by a margin of 7 percentage points. By comparison, Trump carried the district by 27 points in the 2016 election while Pompeo won re-election by 31 points.

Estes' much narrower margin represented a shift in the district toward Democrats, who were eager to point to the results as a referendum on two unpopular chief executives: Trump and Kansas Gov. Sam Brownback.

Republicans knew there was a problem in the closing days of the race when an internal poll put Estes ahead by just single digits.

Trump and Vice President Mike Pence recorded robocalls for Estes and Speaker Paul D. Ryan sent a fundraising pitch. Sen. Ted Cruz, R-Texas, headlined a rally in Wichita that also included an appearance by a representative of the U.S. Chamber of Commerce.

The National Republican Congressional Committee, the House's campaign arm, and the Congressional Leadership Fund, the super PAC backed by House GOP leadership, also spent money in the race to help Estes.

Republicans were eager to tie Thompson to House Minority Leader Nancy Pelosi, D-Calif. National Democrats largely stayed out of the race and the Democratic Congressional Campaign Committee did not spend any more.

Thompson, meanwhile, tried to tie Estes to Brownback. The governor was deeply unpopular in Kansas after pushing through large tax cuts, privatizing the state's Medicaid system and enacting major changes to welfare programs with the support of the Republican-controlled Legislature.

Trump nominated Brownback, a former member of Congress and U.S. senator, for a State Department post as ambassador at large for religious freedom in July. The Senate Foreign Relations Committee advanced Brownback's nomination, 11-10, on Oct. 26.

A civil engineer by training, Estes earned a master's degree in business administration from Tennessee Technological University before working for several companies including Procter & Gamble, Koch Industries and Bombardier Learjet.

Alluding to his engineering background, Estes said in a March 28 television debate with Thompson and Libertarian Chris Rockhold, "We need more leaders in Washington who will do more with less — and that's how we engineer real change."

During that debate he also said a wall with Mexico, as proposed by Trump, must be part of guarding the border, along with surveillance by unmanned aerial vehicles and the deployment of Border Patrol agents.

Estes also argued the process for foreigners seeking to legally immigrate to the United States should be streamlined.

He served two terms as treasurer of Sedgwick County, Kansas — home to Wichita — before being elected state treasurer in 2010.

In his state treasurer job, he put a priority on alerting Kansans to unclaimed money they may own or may have inherited, such as funds from forgotten bank accounts and the contents of abandoned safe deposit boxes.

The state treasurer's office has custody of such unclaimed assets. In 2016, Estes said his office had returned $100 million in unclaimed property since he became state treasurer.

In January 2017, he launched a new savings program for people with disabilities, which allows them to set aside up to $100,000 for education, job training or other needs without losing benefits and without having to pay taxes on the money they invest. He argued that the program "has the ability to transform the lives of people with disabilities from dependence to independence."

In order to bridge budget gaps, Brownback and the legislature resorted to cutting spending on public schools, transferring money from the state highway fund to the general fund, and deferring contributions to the Kansas Public Employee Retirement System, or KPERS.

As state treasurer, Estes had no authority over taxes and spending, but he did serve as a KPERS trustee. According to The Wichita Eagle, Estes clashed with Brownback over the state's underfunding of KPERS.

GOMEZ WINS BATTLE TO REPLACE BECERRA IN SOUTHERN CALIFORNIA

Assemblyman Jimmy Gomez defeated Robert Lee Ahn on June 7 to win the special election in California's 34th District. Gomez succeeded former Rep. Xavier Becerra, a member of the House Democratic leadership team who resigned to become the state attorney general.

The election featured two Democrats because of California's primary rules, where the top two finishers in the primary advance to a runoff, regardless of party affiliation. Gomez and Ahn were the top two vote-getters in the April 4 primary that featured 23 candidates, nearly all of them Democrats.

The race was a battle over which candidate best represented liberal values.

Gomez said he was the "true progressive" in the race, arguing that he would fight for liberal policies and resist President Donald Trump's administration in Congress.

"Capitulation will lead to failure. So that's why I think there's a big difference between my opponent and myself," Gomez said in a May 25 debate. "I understand the politics of Washington, D.C. You need to hold firm, you need to work with your colleagues and you need to throw elbows."

Gomez, who had the support of Becerra and the California Democratic Party, had name recognition and an advantage over Ahn, a political novice: He already represented half of the district's residents in the state Assembly.

Ahn, a lawyer and former member of the Los Angeles City Planning Commission, sought to portray Gomez as a "professional politician"

funded by special interests. Throughout his campaign, Ahn said he was trying to engage those residents who believe they had no voice in government.

Ahn, whose parents emigrated from South Korea in the 1970s, had an aggressive early vote campaign centered in the Koreatown section of Los Angeles.

Gomez grew up in Southern California, raised by Mexican immigrant parents who often struggled to make ends meet. He worked at Subway and Target after high school, and attended community college before transferring to the University of California, Los Angeles where he earned his bachelor's degree in political science. He later graduated from Harvard with a master's degree in public policy.

Gomez was an aide to a Los Angeles City Council member and to former Rep. Hilda L. Solis. He is also a former political for the United Nurses Associations of California.

Latinos make up 65 percent of the district's residents, according to the Los Angeles Times, but only 38 percent of them are eligible to vote. The district includes the Koreatown section of Los Angeles, as well as areas like Boyle Heights and other communities near downtown where Latinos are an overwhelming majority.

GIANFORTE'S MONTANA VICTORY OVERSHADOWED BY SCUFFLE WITH REPORTER

Republican Greg Gianforte defeated Democrat Rob Quist to win the May 25 special election for Montana's at-large House seat. Gianforte filled the vacancy created by Rob Zinke, who resigned to become Interior secretary.

The state is reliably Republican, but the race had grown closer than expected. Gianforte's altercation with reporter Ben Jacobs of The Guardian on election eve became the talk of the race, sparking a flurry of spending in the latest stages of the race.

Jacobs said on May 24 that he tried to ask Gianforte, a wealthy businessman who had previously run for governor, about the Congressional Budget Office's score of the House GOP's legislation to repeal the 2010 health care law. The reporter tweeted on that Gianforte "bodyslammed" him, and the newspaper later posted audio of the encounter.

Gianforte's campaign that night released a statement with a version of events that did not match the audio recording, and the candidate stayed silent on Election Day. He apologized to Jacobs at his victory celebration.

"Last night, I made a mistake and I took an action I can't take back and I am not proud of what happened," he told supporters in Bozeman, Mont. "I should not have responded the way I did and for that I am sorry."

"That is not the person I am or the leader I will be for Montana," he added.

National Democrats took heat for not investing early in the race.

After Jacobs reported that he was assaulted, groups aligned with Democrats quickly released digital and radio ads using the audio of the attack. But it might have been too late to boost Quist. By the time the polls opened on May 25, about half of the estimated total ballots had already been cast early.

While Quist, a first-time candidate and folk musician, was able to tap into grassroots liberal energy to raise more than $6 million, Gianforte benefited from massive outside spending from GOP groups attacking Quist.

The Congressional Leadership Fund, the super PAC backed by House GOP leadership, spent $2.7 million on the race. Just six months

earlier, Gianforte had lost a bid for Montana governor, underperforming President Donald Trump by double digits. Zinke won re-election last fall by 16 points.

Corry Bliss, the fund's executive director, compared Gianforte to an unpopular incumbent running for re-election. "In this environment, a C-minus candidate isn't going to cut it. So we decided to take this race very seriously from the beginning," Bliss said Thursday. Republicans hammered Quist for his personal financial struggles and tied him to House Minority Leader Nancy Pelosi.

In Montana, the maximum penalty for a misdemeanor assault charge is $500 and six months in jail. A Gallatin County judge on June 12 sentenced Gianforte to 20 hours of anger management counseling and 40 hours of community service after he pleaded guilty.

Gianforte entered his plea after reaching a deal with Jacobs that included an apology and a donation of $50,000 to the Committee to Protect Journalists. In exchange, Jacobs agreed not to file a lawsuit.

"Notwithstanding anyone's statements to the contrary, you did not initiate any physical contact with me, and I had no right to assault you," Gianforte said in his apology.

He was sworn into office on July 21.

Gianforte and his wife founded a software company, where they built their wealth. He was trained as an electrical engineer at the Stevens Institute of Technology in Hoboken, N.J.

He lost a 2016 bid for governor against incumbent Steve Bullock, a Democrat. Gianforte spent $5.8 million of his own money, and lost to Bullock by about 4 percentage points.

THIRD TIME A CHARM FOR HANDEL AS SHE DEFEATS UNEXPECTEDLY STRONG DEMOCRAT

Karen Handel, a Republican, won the June 20 special election over Democrat Jon Ossoff, 52 percent to 48 percent in Georgia's 6th District based in Atlanta's northern suburbs. She is the first Republican woman elected to Congress from Georgia.

The contest to fill the seat vacated by Health and Human Services Secretary Tom Price became the most expensive House race ever, with total spending by all candidates and outside groups reaching about $72.6 million, according to the nonpartisan Center for Responsive Politics.

The contest attracted wide national attention in a way congressional elections rarely do.

President Donald Trump had narrowly won the district by 2 percentage points, but Price had won re-election in 2016 by 23 points. Democrats saw an opportunity to seize on anti-Trump sentiment.

Ossoff, a first-time candidate, built an extensive operation, with a more robust field operation than Handel's campaign.. The national progressive base rallied around him, with groups like End Citizens United and the liberal blog Daily Kos helping him pull in small-dollar contributions.

Republicans turned Ossoff's outside support and fundraising into a central line of attack and tried to paint him as out of touch and too liberal for the district. They also accused him of inflating his national security credentials as a former congressional staffer.

Handel, the former secretary of state of Georgia, had run unsuccessfully for governor in 2010 and Senate in 2014.

The former head of the Fulton County Board of Commissioners, she served as the vice president of the Susan G. Komen Foundation, which supports breast cancer research.

Handel finished second to Ossoff on April 18 in the jungle primary,

outpacing 11 other Republicans. She was the GOP candidate who most distanced herself from Trump during that primary, and she did not fully embrace him in the runoff against Ossoff.

NORMAN WINS SOUTH CAROLINA RACE TO SUCCEED MULVANEY

Republican Ralph Norman won the June 20 special election over Democrat Archie Parnell, 51 percent to 48 percent, in South Carolina's 5th District. Norman, a member of the South Carolina House, replaced Mick Mulvaney, who resigned to become director of the Office of Management and Budget.

Norman's road to victory was not an easy one. He first had to elbow his way through a Republican primary against six other candidates. He won the primary runoff by 221 votes against Tommy Pope, the speaker pro tempore of the South Carolina House.

Parnell, a former Goldman Sachs adviser and tax lawyer, received little campaign support from national Democrats. They had not expected a close contest.

Trump carried the district by nearly 19 points in 2016, and Norman fully embraced the president. He said in an interview before the special election that Trump was still popular in the district. Norman praised Trump's selection of Neil Gorsuch for the Supreme Court and said he'd support a Trump plan for infrastructure spending.

"He's one of these who doesn't give out blank checks," Norman said.

Asked about some of Trump's more controversial measures, such as his executive order to restrict travel from certain Muslim-majority countries, Norman said, "He's right on that, absolutely."

Norman was a developer of hotels, shopping centers and retail stores. In the state House, he was one of only two members in 2013 to vote against South Carolina borrowing $120 million to provide incentives to Boeing so the company would expand its facility in North Charleston. He said he wasn't necessarily opposed to the concept of providing incentives to Boeing to locate manufacturing in his state.

But, he said, "I was against keeping it hidden" and in favor of "knowing where the money went."

CURTIS WINS UTAH SEAT IN CONGRESS FORMERLY HELD BY CHAFFETZ

John Curtis, a Republican, won the Nov. 7 special election in Utah's 3rd District against Democrat Kathie Allen, 58 percent to 27 percent. He replaced Jason Chaffetz, who resigned and became a Fox News contributor.

Curtis, the mayor of Provo since 2009, styled himself as a problem solver. He contrasted himself to the often outspoken Chaffetz. "If someone is expecting me to be a Jason clone, they'll be disappointed," Curtis said.

Curtis' victory was not a surprise in a district where Republicans are a majority of voters. Donald Trump easily carried the district in 2016, but not by a majority.

During the race, Curtis positioned himself as a moderate Republican and defended the productivity of Congress.

"There are many good people back in Washington, D.C., and in many ways the system is working," he said during a debate. Years earlier, he chaired the Utah County Democratic Party. He unsuccessfully sought the Democratic nomination for the Senate in 2000.

In business, Curtis operated a shooting-range manufacturing company with a group of partners. ■

House Majority Whip Scalise Wounded In Shooting During Baseball Practice

House Majority Whip Steve Scalise of Louisiana and four others were seriously wounded in June when a gunman opened fire on an early morning practice of the Republican congressional baseball team.

The gunman, James T. Hodgkinson of Belleville, Ill., was shot and killed by a Capitol Police security detail that was on the scene only because Scalise is a member of the GOP leadership team.

It was more than three months before Scalise, who was shot in the left hip, returned to work in the Capitol, after multiple surgeries and an extended rehabilitation.

In addition to Scalise, those wounded were Zach Barth, a congressional staffer; Matt Mika, a lobbyist for Tyson Foods and former Hill staffer; and Capitol Police officers Crystal Griner and David Bailey.

The practice field at Eugene Simpson Stadium Park in Alexandria, Va., went from bucolic to chaotic in a matter of seconds.

Rep. Mo Brooks, R-Ala., and Sen. Jeff Flake, R-Ariz., described a bloody scene, with lawmakers and staffers scrambling to help the wounded and move others to safety.

"He had crawled into the outfield, leaving a trail of blood, and we started giving him some liquids. I put pressure on his wounds in the hip," said Brooks, who helped administer first aid to Scalise.

Scalise was shot as he stood near second base, then crawled into the outfield as the other players hit the ground.

"There was a blood trail about 10 to 15 yards long from where he was shot to where he crawled into right field," Brooks said.

Hodgkinson reportedly was shooting at players from the dugout, using it for protection as the security detail returned fire.

CONGRESSIONAL RESPONSE

The House canceled floor votes in the wake of the shooting, but the annual Congressional Baseball Game, which raises money for several charities and is sponsored by Roll Call, was played as scheduled at Nationals Park the next night.

The game provided a catharsis for the Hill community and was part of an outpouring of bipartisan concern for Scalise and the other victims.

In the days that followed, President Donald Trump and Vice Presi-

dent Mike Pence, a onetime House colleague of Scalise, visited him in the hospital.

House Speaker Paul D. Ryan, R-Wis., and Minority Leader Nancy Pelosi, D-Calif., both expressed horror at the shooting and praised the response by the Capitol Police both at the site of the attack and in the stepped-up presence at the Capitol in the immediate aftermath.

"An attack on one of us is an attack on all of us," Ryan said as members on both sides of the aisle stood, applauded and cheered.

Hodgkinson had posted anti-Trump views on social media as well as postings in support of Sen. Bernie Sanders, I-Vt., for whom he had volunteered in the 2016 presidential campaign. Sanders condemned the shooting and any violence in support of his political causes.

While the response in support of Scalise was overwhelming, some expressed deep concern that the attack was both a symptom of a political culture grown toxic and reflective of a divide that went beyond politics.

"We're not really a single people anymore," said former Rep. Mickey Edwards, R-Okla. "We are divided by our politics, we are divided by economic status, by race, by geography, by how religious or secular we are."

Other longtime observers of Congress and political scholars said they, too, see a rise in hate-infused rhetoric.

"This tragic shooting shows how far the hatred has gone for some in America," said James A. Thurber, a political science professor at American University.

"Members of Congress practicing for their annual baseball game has always been a way for them to get to know each other better, to build more comity and civility cross-party and cross-chambers. That tradition has been terribly broken with this horrible act of violence."

Thurber said he hoped the "tragedy will help bring members of Congress closer together and cause them to stop using hurtful and polarizing language in campaigns and in governing."

Former Rep. Christopher Shays, a moderate Republican from Connecticut who served from 1987 to 2009, was not optimistic about that changing anytime soon.

"I hate to say it, but I will say it: It's going to continue," Shays said. "And members can't always have security. They just can't. Members can't have security around them all the time, that would just be a killer for our democracy."

PAYING FOR MORE SECURITY

Despite the concerns of those like Shays who worried about added security separating representatives from constituents, lawmakers quickly moved to allow rank-and-file members to spend money from their office accounts on personal security.

Only a small number of members in leadership positions received full-time protective details from the Capitol Police, including the House speaker, majority and minority leaders and whips in both chambers. Other members could receive added protection in response to specific threats, but otherwise spend much of their time outside the Capitol complex, including in their home districts, without protection.

They could hire personal security using their official accounts, known as Members' Representational Allowances, only on a case-by-case basis with approval of the House sergeant-at-arms. MRAs are used for official staff, travel, mail, office equipment and district office rentals. Senators are not permitted to use their Senators' Official Personnel and Office Expense Account for personal security.

There is little doubt that had Scalise and his detail not been at the practice field, the outcome could have been much worse. "He probably saved everybody else's life because if you don't have a leadership person there, there would have been no security there," said Sen. Rand Paul, R-Ky., who was at the practice. "Had they not been there, it would have been a massacre."

Increased spending on security for lawmakers and the Capitol Police was included in the $4.7 billion Legislative Branch portion of the fiscal 2018 omnibus spending law (PL 115-141) enacted in March 2018. The omnibus provided $426.5 million to the Capitol Police, an increase of $33.2 million above the fiscal 2017 enacted level, but $4.2 million below Police Chief Matthew R. Verderosa's budget request submitted in May. Appropriators hoped to address security and protection concerns with $7.5 million for increased training, equipment and technology.

The bill did not include language to allow rank-and-file House members to spend money from their Members' Representational Allowances on personal security expenses. But overall House operations spending would rise by $5 million, to $1.194 billion, which would be used to "enhance security for Members when they are away from the Capitol complex," including enhancements to district office security such as cameras, panic buttons and other security infrastructure.

In addition to the appropriators' actions, the House Administration Committee moved to increase Members' Representational Allowances by $25,000 per member for security purposes in members' districts for the rest of fiscal 2017.

The allocations did not require additional appropriations and were the result of talks between Legislative Branch Appropriations Subcommittee Chairman Kevin Yoder, R-Kan., and Administration Chairman Gregg Harper, R-Miss. If used, the total funds would top more than $11 million.

Citing the attack on Scalise, the Federal Election Commission also moved to allow lawmakers to use campaign funds for "nonstructural" security systems, which would include installation and monitoring costs for cameras, sensors and "removable security devices" at their homes. That is a change from the draft proposed by the FEC ahead of the vote, which said that members could use campaign contributions to install or upgrade residential security systems but did not specify eligible expenditures.

Until the FEC's decision, members could use campaign funds for security only after the FEC granted permission on a case-by-case, threat-specific basis. ∎

Sexual Harassment Accusations Result in Multiple Resignations

Nine members of Congress were accused of sexual harassment in separate incidents. Four of those lawmakers resigned by the end of 2017: Sen. Al Franken, D-Minn., and Reps. John Conyers Jr., D-Mich., Trent Franks, R-Ariz., and Tim Murphy, R-Pa. Three more House members resigned or retired the following year. The two others denied the charges and sought re-election in 2018.

The reports became public during the final three months of 2017, chiefly through news reports, at the time that the "Me Too" movement by victims gained prominence in the entertainment world, the news media and across the nation. The congressional incidents dated back as long as several years, according to the victims who brought the complaints.

The flood of disclosures typically resulted in condemnations of the inappropriate behavior, especially by congressional leaders. The Senate and House passed separate resolutions that sought to prevent sexual harassment in the future, with mandatory education of members and staffers. In response, many members agreed that ethics rules and other congressional procedures had proven inadequate to respond to harassment claims.

RESIGNATIONS

Murphy resigned Oct. 21 following reports that he urged a woman with whom he had an affair to get an abortion. Murphy admitted in September to having an extramarital affair with forensic psychologist Shannon Edwards. Their relationship came to light through Edwards' divorce proceedings. Edwards reportedly said she had met Murphy, a psychologist, while he was advocating for his mental health legislation in 2015.

On Oct. 3, the Pittsburgh Post-Gazette reported details of text messages between the two in which Edwards said Murphy had urged her to have an abortion during what turned out to be an "unfounded pregnancy scare." After the newspaper story, Murphy initially announced that he would not run for re-election but would serve out the rest of his term. Less than 24 hours later, Speaker Paul D. Ryan's office announced that Murphy had submitted a letter of resignation. "I've spoken with Tim quite a bit last couple of days. I think it's appropriate that he moves onto the next chapter of his life, and I think he agrees with that," Ryan, R-Wis., said at a subsequent press conference.

Conyers resigned Dec. 5 over sexual harassment claims. Several days earlier, former Conyers staffer Marion Brown said on NBC that Conyers had frequently propositioned her for sex and inappropriately touched her. "He just violated my body," Brown said. Responding to what he called the "torrent of allegations" against Conyers, Ryan said, "No one should have to endure harassment in any form, in any institution, let alone here in Congress."

In her initial response to the charges, House Minority Leader Nancy Pelosi, D-Calif., in a broadcast interview called Conyers—who served nearly 53 years in the House and was the senior Democrat on the Judiciary Committee—an "icon" who "has done a great deal to protect women." After private discussions among House Democrats, Pelosi read from a prepared statement. The allegations against Conyers were "serious, disappointing and very credible," she said. "The brave women who came forward are owed justice."

Prior to his resignation, Conyers met with the Congressional Black Caucus for what the group's chairman, Rep. Cedric L. Richmond, D-La., called a "very candid" conversation.

Franks resigned Dec. 8 after he had "learned that the Ethics Committee is reviewing an inquiry regarding my discussion of surrogacy with two previous female subordinates, making each feel uncomfortable," he said in a statement the previous day. "In the midst of this current cultural and media climate, I am deeply convinced I would be unable to complete a fair House Ethics investigation before distorted and sensationalized versions of this story would put me, my family, my staff, and my noble colleagues in the House of Representatives through hyperbolized public excoriation."

Franks had met a week earlier with Ryan, who said he found that allegations of misconduct by Franks were "serious and requiring action." Ryan subsequently told Franks that he would refer the matter to the Ethics Committee. He then urged Franks to resign. In a statement issued by his office, Ryan said that he "takes seriously his obligation to ensure a safe workplace in the House." One Arizona Republican said rumors of inappropriate behavior dated back more than five years. Franks had apparently been making plans to run for the Senate in 2012, but abruptly canceled them. "There's been rumors swirling around him for years, at least in 2012," the Republican said.

Franken said on Dec. 7 that he would resign in the face of calls by party colleagues to step down over sexual misconduct allegations. A number of women had come forward to describe incidents that took place prior to his election to the Senate in 2008. In one case, an accuser told Politico that Franken tried to forcibly kiss her after taping his radio show in 2006, telling her, "It's my right as an entertainer." Franken had been a writer for "Saturday Night Live," a long-running comedy program on NBC.

In response, several Democratic senators urged Franken to resign. "As elected officials, we should be held to the highest standards—not the lowest," New York Democratic Sen. Kirsten Gillibrand said in a tweet. "The allegations against Sen. Franken describe behavior that cannot be tolerated."

After his resignation, some senators voiced second thoughts over the handling of the Franken incident. "I have stood for due process throughout my years as a prosecutor and in chairing the Judiciary Committee," Sen. Patrick J. Leahy, D-Vt., said in a statement. "I regret not doing that this time. The Ethics Committee should have been allowed to investigate and make its recommendation."

Franken's official departure came on Jan. 2, 2018, after he delivered a series of final speeches on the Senate floor.

RETIREMENTS

Three other House lawmakers who were the target in 2017 of various sexual harassment allegations responded that they would not seek re-election, though they remained in Congress into 2018.

Rep. Joe L. Barton, R-Texas, announced on Nov. 30 that he would not seek re-election. That followed several days of controversy after The Washington Post reported that Barton in 2015 had reported to Capitol Police a woman who threatened that she would make public a sexually explicit photograph, plus videos and other messages that he had sent to her. The incident reportedly took place when the two of them had ended their relationship, while Barton was separated from his second wife.

After the photo was posted on social media, which Barton described as a "revenge porn" attack, other Texas Republicans urged him to resign. Instead, he decided not to seek another term. "There are enough people who lost faith in me that it's time to step aside and let there be a new voice for the 6th District in Washington, so I am not going to run for re-election," Barton, who served 17 terms, told the Dallas Morning News. "These activities, as unsavory as they may be, were from the past, not the present, and I'm never going to do them again."

Rep. Blake Farenthold, R-Texas, announced on Dec. 14 that he would not seek a fifth term, after the disclosure of a confidential settlement agreement that he had reached in 2015 with Lauren Greene, a former aide who had been fired following her claims of his inappropriate behavior. Politico reported that the little-known congressional Office of Compliance had paid the $84,000 settlement to Greene. Although Farenthold said the Office of Congressional Ethics had recommended dismissal of Greene's complaint, which she filed in 2014, the House Ethics Committee on Dec. 7 unanimously voted to create a subcommittee to investigate Greene's charges.

Farenthold's decision to retire followed two conversations with Speaker Ryan, who voiced support for Farenthold's decision not to seek re-election, in the face of a Republican primary challenge. "I had no idea how to run a congressional office and, as a result, I allowed a workplace culture to take root in my office that was too permissive and decidedly unprofessional," Farenthold said in a video statement. At a press conference that day, Ryan referred to "new stories that are very disconcerting, unacceptable behavior have been alleged," The Texas Tribune reported.

Farenthold initially said he would reimburse the $84,000 to the Treasury, but he subsequently reversed that pledge. He also accelerated his departure date, with his resignation taking effect in April 2018.

Rep. Ruben Kihuen, D-Nev., said on Dec. 16 that he would not seek re-election, amid news reports that he had sexually harassed women while he served in the state Senate and during his campaign in 2016. They included a report by the Nevada Independent that a lobbyist, with whom he did not have a personal relationship, claimed that Kihuen had sent her hundreds of text messages, some of them suggestive, and had touched her inappropriately.

Kihuen, a freshman, initially rejected calls for his resignation by members of the Congressional Hispanic Caucus and said he would welcome an investigation by the Ethics Committee. When he reversed that plan and announced his retirement, he said in a statement, "The allegations that have surfaced would be a distraction from a fair and thorough discussion of the issues in a re-election campaign." In response, one of his accusers, who was not named, told a broadcast station in Las Vegas, "I'm not really comfortable with the fact that my tax money is paying for his salary."

DENIALS

Two other House members rejected accusations that had been made against them and said they would run for re-election in 2018.

The Treasury Department in 2014 paid $220,000 in an undisclosed agreement to settle a lawsuit alleging sexual harassment that involved Rep. Alcee L. Hastings, D-Fla., Roll Call reported on Dec. 8. The suit had been brought by Winsome Packer, a congressional employee as a staff member of the Commission on Security and Cooperation in Europe, also known as the Helsinki Commission. In documents, Packer said Hastings had touched her, made unwanted sexual advances and threatened her job while he served as chairman of the commission. The panel, which promotes international human rights, includes 18 members of Congress plus three executive branch officials.

The $220,000 settlement was approved by the congressional Office of Compliance, the same office that made the payment in the Farenthold case. Roll Call described the Hastings case, and others, as "secretive and convoluted." Hastings said the charges were "ludicrous" and he had not been aware of the settlement agreement with Packer until the day of that news report.

"This matter was handled solely by the Senate Chief Counsel for Employment. At no time was I consulted, nor did I know until after the fact that such a settlement was made," Hastings said in a statement. "I am outraged that any taxpayer dollars were needlessly paid to Ms. Packer." Congressional officials had no comment.

Rep. Robert C. Scott, D-Va., was accused of sexually harassing a former fellow with the Congressional Black Caucus Foundation. M. Reese Everson, who worked in Scott's office during her fellowship in 2013, made the accusations during a Dec. 15 press conference. Scott inappropriately touched her and asked her to flirt with him on a trip to California, she said. After the incident and her attempt to bring it to the attention of other congressional offices, Everson said, "I was retaliated against, I was wrongfully terminated, and I was blackballed and blacklisted."

During the press conference, a former Scott legislative assistant defended Scott, Roll Call reported. "I can tell you there was never a whisper, a hint, a wink or nod," Theresa Thompson said. "The truth will come out." Scott earlier confirmed that Everson had worked in his office. "There have been no credible complaints that I'm aware of," he said.

ENFORCEMENT

Growing anger over the culture of harassment and secrecy on Capitol Hill resulted in a drumbeat to revamp problematic policies that governed the congressional workplace. In the wake of the high-profile resignations and retirement announcements by lawmakers over alleged ethics violations, more than 30 measures to rein in harassment were filed in the waning days of 2017.

A key target of legislative action was the Congressional Accountability Act, which Congress enacted in 1995, setting workplace protections for its offices and establishing the Office of Compliance to enforce them. That existing process has been lengthy, complicated and secretive.

The Office of Compliance gives congressional employees up to 180 days after an alleged incident of harassment to request counseling, which lasts for 30 days. Next come 30 days of mediation if the victim requests it, where the employee and the office can confidentially reach a voluntary settlement.

After at least two months of those steps, the employee can request an administrative proceeding before a hearing officer or file a case in federal district court. That process must begin within a 30- to 90-day window after mediation. Following an administrative hearing, the

employee may appeal to the Office of Compliance board.

In seeking a clampdown on harassment, Speaker Ryan called for a comprehensive review. The House Administration Committee took the lead, as it organized hearings, roundtable discussions with staff and member listening sessions. The House on Nov. 29 approved a resolution (H Res 630) by Rep. Barbara Comstock, R-Va., that required all House members and employees to complete an annual program of training in workplace rights and responsibilities. In December, the Administration Committee approved guidelines.

A bipartisan group of House members prepared sweeping legislation to update the policies governing the congressional workplace. They included House Administration Chairman Gregg Harper, R-Miss., and ranking member Robert A. Brady, D-Pa.; Comstock; Jackie Speier, D-Calif.; and Bradley Byrne, R-Ala. During the hearings, Comstock and Speier described their experiences as former House aides.

The Senate approved by unanimous consent on Nov. 9 its own resolution (S Res 330) by Sen. Amy Klobuchar, D-Minn., to require training for Senators and aides. That action came after nearly 1,500 former staffers signed a letter to congressional leadership saying the existing procedures are "inadequate and need reform." The Senate Rules and Administration Committee was slower to respond with new procedures.

Even with its limited record of policing harassment claims, Congress occasionally has taken action in celebrated cases. Perhaps the most prominent example was Sen. Bob Packwood, R-Ore., who resigned in 1995 as the Senate prepared to consider a resolution for his expulsion. The Senate Ethics Committee had unanimously recommended that action, three years after former aides accused him of unwanted sexual advances. At the time, Packwood chaired the Finance Committee.

In 2006, Rep. Mark Foley, R-Fla., resigned after being accused of sexually harassing teenagers who served as congressional pages, whose job was to deliver messages on the House floor. House leaders ended the page program in 2011. Rep. Eric Massa, D-N.Y., resigned in 2010 after aides accused him of making unwanted sexual overtures.

Affairs with aides led to the resignations of two other Republicans, Rep. Mark Souder of Indiana, in 2010, and Sen. John Ensign of Nevada, in 2011. ■

Nunes Cleared in Ethics Query

The House Ethics Committee announced on Dec. 7 that it had closed its investigation of Intelligence Chairman Devin Nunes, clearing the California Republican of claims that he had made unauthorized disclosures of classified information.

"The committee does not determine whether information is or is not classified ... [so it] sought the analysis of Representative Nunes's statements by classification experts in the intelligence community," Ethics Chairwoman Susan W. Brooks, R-Ind., and ranking member Ted Deutch, D-Fla., said in a statement.

"Based solely on the conclusion of these classification experts that the information that Rep. Nunes disclosed was not classified, the committee will take no further action and consider this matter closed."

The investigation arose after Nunes told reporters at the White House on March 22 that he had reviewed "intelligence reports" indicating that members of President Donald Trump's campaign had been swept up in foreign surveillance by U.S. spy agencies.

Nunes went to the White House to inform Trump about the reports before having briefed the House Intelligence Committee's ranking member, Adam B. Schiff, D-Calif., and other members of the panel, which is investigating Russia's interference in the 2016 election and any potential Trump administration ties to that effort.

That infuriated Democrats and plunged the panel's Russia probe into turmoil. They accused the chairman of working at the administration's behest to try to distract from the investigation into potential Trump-Russia connections.

After the Ethics Committee opened its investigation, Nunes agreed to recuse himself from the Russia investigation. During that time, Texas GOP Rep. K. Michael Conaway led the Intelligence probe.

Nunes had come under intense fire for his leadership of the committee's Russia inquiry. Democrats accused him of acting as a surrogate for the White House and said his close relationship with the administration meant he could not head an impartial investigation into the highly charged question of possible Trump-Russia ties. Several liberal groups, including MoveOn.org, had lodged public complaints against Nunes.

At the time, Nunes described the ethics complaint as "entirely false and politically motivated" from "several left-wing activist groups." He said the allegations against him came "just as the American people are beginning to learn the truth about the improper unmasking of the identities of U.S. citizens and other abuses of power."

But he said it was in the best interest of the committee to remove himself from the Russia inquiry while the Office of Congressional Ethics looks into the claims.

House Speaker Paul D. Ryan, R-Wis., defended Nunes against the allegations of wrongdoing. Asked if Nunes had made some mistakes as the Ethics panel launched its review, Ryan said, "I don't think that's the case, but I think that Chairman Nunes wants to make sure that is not a distraction to a very important investigation."

Following the Ethics Committee's end of its review, Nunes issued a statement thanking the panel "for completely clearing me today of the cloud that was created by this investigation, and for determining that I committed no violation of anything—no violation of House Rules, law, regulations, or any other standards of conduct."

However, the lawmaker complained that the allegations were "obviously frivolous and were rooted in politically motivated complaints filed against me by left-wing activist groups" and expressed dismay that it had taken the Ethics panel "an unbelievable eight months" to dismiss the matter. ■

Jury Deadlocks in Menendez Trial

A federal judge on Nov. 16 declared a mistrial in the corruption case against Sen. Robert Menendez, D-N.J., after saying the jury in New Jersey was hopelessly deadlocked.

In a statement outside the courthouse in Newark, Menendez thanked his supporters, pledged to do more to win back his constituents' trust and had sharp words for his political adversaries. "To those who left me, who abandoned me in my darkest moment, I forgive you. To those who embraced me in my darkest moment, I love you," he said. "To those who were digging my political grave so that they could jump into my seat, I know who you are and I won't forget you," he said.

Prosecutors had charged Menendez with having "sold his office for a lifestyle he couldn't afford" to achieve favors for campaign donor Salomon Melgen, including securing visas for one of Melgen's girlfriends and her sister from the Dominican Republic.

During the opening day of the two-month trial, Menendez's attorney Abbe Lowell told jurors that the senator had been doing "what 535 members of Congress do all the time." Menendez's meetings with executive branch officials could have benefited Melgen, Lowell argued, but they were focused on future policy.

The outcome followed the Supreme Court's March 20 rejection of an appeal from Menendez, who had sought the dismissal of his corruption charges. The one-sentence ruling declined to consider his challenge against improper actions by executive branch prosecutors, including the constitutional requirement that members of Congress "shall not be questioned in any other place" for "any speech or debate in either house." ∎

Change to Filibuster for Supreme Court Nominees Highlights Rules Revisions

Senate Republicans on April 6 invoked the "nuclear option" to change Senate rules to allow a simple majority of senators present to confirm any nominee to the Supreme Court. That step was deployed to limit debate on the nomination of federal appeals Judge Neil Gorsuch, President Donald Trump's pick for a high court seat.

The action was another step toward eliminating centuries-old traditions of open-ended debate that have distinguished the Senate from virtually every other legislative body in the world.

Although Democratic senators objected to ending the filibuster for Supreme Court nominees, Republicans were expanding on changes approved by Senate Democrats in 2013, when they were in the majority and held the White House. At that time, despite heated Republican objections, Democrats revised a Senate rule so that a simple majority vote was required to end debate on Cabinet nominees and federal judges at the district and circuit levels.

In expanding that rule change four years later to include Supreme Court nominees, Senate Majority Leader Mitch McConnell, R-Ky., said Democrats' objections to ending debate on a Supreme Court nominee were unprecedented for the Senate. "There cannot be two sets of standards, one for the nominees of Democratic presidents and another for the nominees of Republican presidents," he said.

Adding to the acrimony between the parties, McConnell had held the Supreme Court seat vacant for more than a year by refusing in 2016 to even hold a hearing for President Barack Obama's nominee, Judge Merrick Garland.

Minority Leader Charles E. Schumer, D-N.Y., in objecting to the rule change, emphasizing the unique responsibility of the Senate for confirming Supreme Court nominees. "When the dust settles, make no mistake about it, it will have been the Republicans who changed the rules on the Supreme Court," Schumer said. "It weakens the standing of the Senate as a whole, as a check on the president's ability to shape the judiciary."

By a party-line vote of 52-48, the chamber voted to bring uniformity to Senate handling of all nominations, which technically overturned the presiding officer's ruling. That effectively lowered the threshold to end debate on a Supreme Court nomination. Subsequently voting to limit debate on Gorsuch were all 52 Republican senators, plus three Democrats: Joe Donnelly of Indiana, Heidi Heitkamp of North Dakota and Joe Manchin III of West Virginia.

On another aspect of Senate filibusters, both parties remained in agreement in 2017: The changes did not affect the rules for debate of legislation.

"There's no sentiment to change the legislative filibuster," McConnell told reporters on April 4. Asked if he was committing to not changing the rules to end debate on legislation while he is the GOP leader, McConnell said, "Correct."

Still, some senators were concerned about the broader implications for the chamber, especially with Trump suggesting in separate tweets that he favored reducing to 51 the vote threshold to limit all debate.

Sen. John McCain, R-Ariz., said he was not terribly optimistic about the legislative filibuster's future. "I can't say with confidence, and I'm afraid we're on a slippery slope," McCain said. "Benjamin Franklin somewhere is turning over because he's the one that advocated for the role of the Senate."

As Schumer noted, recent history shows that once-sacrosanct Senate traditions can be quickly abandoned in the heat of the moment. "Just as it seemed unthinkable decades ago that we would change the rules for nominees, [the April 6] vote is a cautionary tale about how unbridled partisan escalation will overwhelm our basic inclination to work together and frustrate our efforts to pull back," Schumer said.

OFFICE OF CONGRESSIONAL ETHICS

As the 115th Congress prepared to convene, Republicans voted on Jan. 2 to make major revisions in House ethics procedures as part of the package of rules changes that the majority party customarily presents on the opening day of a new Congress. The plan would have reduced the authority of the independent Office of Congressional Ethics, curbed its power to probe potential violations by lawmakers and their aides and renamed it the Office of Congressional Complaint Review.

After a public relations backlash that included criticism from President-elect Donald Trump, House Republicans met privately again on Jan. 3 and voted to restore the ethics office and its authority.

The conflict was an unusual case in which the Republicans' failure to reach their own consensus led to an embarrassing reversal of action even before House members took the oath of office for the new Congress.

"Calmer heads prevailed this morning," said Pennsylvania GOP Rep. Charlie Dent, who was chairman of the House Ethics Committee during the previous Congress. He criticized a provision that would have required the Ethics Committee to have jurisdiction over the independent office. "To me, that was very ambiguous, it was vague," Dent said. "I was not clear how that would work."

House Judiciary Chairman Robert W. Goodlatte, R-Va., the chief proponent of the change, had defended his proposal as a way to keep ethics investigations confidential, with "strong protections against any disclosures to the public or other government entities," he wrote in an op-ed.

Rep. Dave Brat, another Virginia Republican who advocated the rules change, said the ethics office had been used as a "political bludgeon tool to knock each other over the head."

But they were overruled during the follow-up meeting at the Capitol, which lasted less than 10 minutes. Republicans agreed to strip the ethics changes from the rules package amid a firestorm of criticism that members were trying to gut an agency tasked with holding lawmakers accountable.

The episode demonstrated how quickly Democratic lawmakers, progressive organizations and even some conservative-leaning groups could mobilize around efforts to "drain the swamp" and curb influence-peddling and dubious dealings in Congress.

The Office of Congressional Ethics has operated as an independent congressional body that reviews conflicts of interest and other ethics requests made by any member of the public. It has jurisdiction over members of the House only. Under the arrangement, any member of the public may file a request for the OCE to take up a review of a member. The Ethics Committee, by contrast, may only accept requests from other members of Congress.

The office does not have the power to reprimand members. It may only recommend that the Ethics Committee further investigate cases the OCE has reviewed on its own. (Those inquiries may include interviews with members and staff and issuing subpoenas.) The rules also require the Ethics Committee to publicly publish reports submitted by the ethics office after a requisite amount of time.

Public Citizen, a progressive watchdog group, dubbed the proposed change the "Jack Abramoff Restoration Act of 2017." The reference to the convicted lobbyist reflected the genesis of the office, which Democrats formed in 2008 after a series of scandals involving lawmakers of both parties — notably the Abramoff affair — rocked the Capitol.

In reversing their action of the previous evening, Idaho GOP Rep. Mike Simpson said House Republicans were responding to criticism that they were backing off on ethics. "I don't know anybody who's against ethics," Simpson said. "That's not a good campaign slogan. But it ought to be fair, and it ought to be fair to members and the staff."

Trump had weighed in on the prospective change that morning, tweeting that lawmakers should focus on taxes, health care and "other things of far greater importance."

House Majority Leader Kevin McCarthy, R-Calif., said he agreed with Trump. "Any time you want to deal with reforms is probably best in a bipartisan manner," McCarthy said of the reversal.

House Speaker Paul D. Ryan, R-Wis., said in a statement that many members had wanted to overhaul the Office of Congressional Ethics, adding that, even with the proposed changes, the independent agency would still investigate members thoroughly.

Even so, the initial action by the House Republican Conference did not hold up to public scrutiny. "House Republicans showed their true colors last night, and reversing their plans to destroy the Office of Congressional Ethics will not obscure their clear contempt for ethics in the People's House," House Minority Leader Nancy Pelosi, D-Calif., said in a statement.

EARMARK BAN

In another instance of rejecting a proposal to reverse a years-old controversial rules change, House Republican leaders also stifled a move to restore spending earmarks. Instead, the House Rules Committee agreed to hold a series of hearings before making a decision about whether and how to soften the ban on spending for lawmakers' specified projects, which was imposed in 2010.

Rules Chairman Pete Sessions, R-Texas, said many House members were frustrated by the House's lack of control over spending priorities because of the earmark ban, noting that the administration gets to decide how to spend approximately $18 billion of appropriated funds, instead of Congress. "The president of the United States made decisions, including some, excluding others, and I don't think it worked in the best interest," Sessions said.

House GOP leaders decided instead that the Rules Committee should examine a variety of budget perspectives. "We've encouraged our members all along to talk about budget process reforms." Ryan said.

At least some House Republicans continued to support the ban. "I have a sick feeling that there are more than half of the conference who would vote for this if it came back," said Rep. Bill Flores, R-Texas. "So we need to make sure we have grass-roots support."

Some conservative groups continued to support the spending limitation. "Even flirting with bringing back earmarks would be really bad politics," cautioned Tommy Binion, the Heritage Foundation's director of congressional and executive branch relations.

Oddly, during a White House meeting with members of Congress to discuss immigration legislation, Trump encouraged the restoration of congressional authority. "I hear so much about earmarks, the old

earmark system, how there was a great friendliness when you had earmarks, but of course they had other problems with earmarks," Trump said during an exchange. "No? Well, you should do it, and I'm there with you."

He said Congress would have to implement "better controls" and he would expect lawmakers to do it "honestly."

STREAMING ON THE HOUSE FLOOR

House Republicans kept their promise to change House rules to respond to an unusual incident in June 2016, when House Democrats effectively occupied the House chamber overnight to demand gun control. During the sit-in protest, Democrats used their cell phones to record video of their speeches and chants, and took photos of themselves and their colleagues after Republicans turned off the House cameras that provide live floor footage to C-SPAN.

At the time, many Republicans objected to the Democrats' actions, but they took no disciplinary action.

Under the revised rule, the House sergeant-at-arms could fine members up to $2,500 for breaking the rules regarding photography and recording on the House floor. Member salaries could be garnished. Offending members could also be referred to the Ethics Committee for disrupting access to the floor or the official microphones. The rules change did not apply retroactively to the 2016 sit-in.

"These changes will help ensure that order and decorum are preserved in the House of Representatives so lawmakers can do the people's work," said AshLee Strong, a spokeswoman for Ryan.

Drew Hammill, a spokesman for Pelosi, said that "Republicans continue to act as the handmaidens of the gun lobby" and that Democrats would not be silenced on efforts to combat gun violence.

Taking photos or recording video on the House floor has been a longstanding violation of House rules. The fines and other sanctions were a new provision. ■

Chapter 6

DEFENSE, INTELLIGENCE & VETERANS

$692.1 Billion Defense Authorization Increases 'End Strength,' Adds Warships

Congress cleared a $692.1 billion fiscal 2018 defense authorization bill on Nov. 16 after resolving a last-minute Pentagon request that the conference report be modified to allow for emergency access to drugs or medical devices not approved by the Food and Drug Administration (FDA) if they were needed in a future conflict.

The path ultimately was smoothed in the final days by enacting a separate bill (HR 4374 – PL 115-92) allowing expedited FDA approval of medicines and medical devices designed for the battlefield.

The House adopted the conference report for the defense authorization (HR 2810) on Nov. 14 by a 356-70 vote. The Senate cleared it by voice vote on Nov. 16, and President Donald Trump signed the annual measure into law on Dec. 12 (PL 115-91). "We need our military," Trump said. "It's got to be perfecto." Nevertheless, he attached a lengthy signing statement disagreeing with many provisions on grounds that they interfered with his constitutional authority.

The legislation authorized $692.1 billion for the Pentagon, $26.4 billion more than the president's request. The total included $626.4 billion for the Pentagon's "base" budget and $65.7 billion for Overseas Contingency Operations, or war spending, which did not count toward budget caps.

Because the measure had $77.3 billion more than permitted for fiscal year 2018 under the 2011 Budget Control Act (PL 112-25), appropriators would be unable to spend the total authorized in the defense bill unless Congress raised the budget caps to unprecedented levels, or eliminated them completely.

Aside from authorizing spending levels, the bill also set policy for the Defense Department, including authorizing military weapons purchases.

HIGHLIGHTS

The bill authorized 13 new warships, five more than requested by the Trump administration, including an additional Littoral Combat Ship designed for inshore waters, another destroyer, and an extra amphibious assault ship. The bill approved the purchase of 90 new F-35 fighter jets and 24 F/A-18E/F Super Hornets. Missile defense programs would also see a boost, including 28 new interceptors for the system that would aim to shoot down a North Korean missile.

The measure approved an increase in end strength—the mandated minimum number of uniformed personnel — of more than 20,000 above the previous fiscal year's requirement. The increase for all the services combined included a hike of 16,600 in the active forces (of which 7,500 would be active-duty soldiers and 4,000 active-duty

BOX SCORE

BILLS: HR 2810, S 1519 -- fiscal 2018 defense authorization.

LEGISLATIVE ACTION:

HOUSE Committee Armed Services approved HR 2810 on June 28

HOUSE passed HR 2810, 344-81, on July 14.

SENATE Committee Senate Armed Services approved S 1519 on June 28

SENATE passed HR 2810, 89-8, on Sept. 18.

HOUSE adopted conference report on HR 2810, 356-70, on Nov. 14.

SENATE adopted conference report on HR 2810 by voice vote on Nov 16.

PRESIDENT signed HR 2810 on Dec. 12 (PL 115-91).

Marines) and another 3,700 in the Guard and Reserve forces of all the services.

The increase in end strength would be accompanied by a pay bump. The legislation stated that all uniformed personnel would receive a 2.4 percent increase in pay, as compared to the Trump administration's request of 2.1 percent. The actual level, however, would be set by appropriations legislation.

The bill also authorized the continuance of a special supplement to survivor benefits for the families of those killed in the line of duty, at a cost of $2.8 billion over the next decade. The conferees paid for the supplemental survivor benefits by increasing pharmacy copayments for participants in the military's Tricare healthcare network.

"I believe the priorities in this bill are, No. 1 our people, No. 2 readiness and No. 3 missile defense," said House Armed Services Chairman Mac Thornberry, R-Texas.

The bill included a $5.9 billion budget amendment submitted by the White House that covered money for missile-defense programs amid an escalating threat from North Korea, funds to repair two Navy warships that collided with commercial vessels in the Pacific in the summer of 2017, and money to add 3,500 U.S. troops in Afghanistan.

Israel also stood to benefit from provisions in the bill. The U.S. ally was slated to receive $705 million for its missile defenses, nearly five times the Trump administration's request and the second largest annual installment of such aid to date.

Notably absent from the conference report was a measure included in the House-passed version of the authorization bill that would have created a new space-focused military service. A Space Corps had been proposed by Rep. Mike D. Rogers, R-Ala., and Rep. Jim Cooper, D-Tenn., the chairman and ranking member of the House Armed Services Strategic Forces Subcommittee.

The provision was cut during conference committee negotiations, but other space measures were included in the legislation. The conference report eliminated the principal Defense Department space adviser, the Defense space council, and the deputy chief of staff for space operations. The latter had been put in place by Air Force Secretary Heather Wilson in August. The House conference report called the position "a hastily developed half-measure."

HOUSE ACTION
EMERGING THREATS AND CAPABILITIES

The House Armed Services Emerging Threats and Capabilities Subcommittee on June 23 approved its piece of the fiscal 2018 defense authorization bill by voice vote. No amendments were offered in the nine-minute meeting.

The subcommittee, which oversees $68 billion worth of programs, placed a heavy emphasis on strengthening cyber capabilities while increasing oversight on those programs.

The panel said its plans would establish cyber training programs with NATO and Asian allies and would mandate congressional notification for sensitive military cyber operations.

The subcommittee also pushed for the Pentagon to identify cyber vulnerabilities in weapons systems and to strengthen the systems against cyber threats.

The measure authorized $12.3 billion for the U.S. Special Operations Command and required that the committee be notified of any change in presidential policy guidance on direct action by special operations forces.

TACTICAL AIR AND LAND FORCES

The House Armed Services Subcommittee on Tactical Air and Land Forces approved its portion of the authorization bill on June 21 by voice vote with no amendments.

Ohio Republican Michael R. Turner, the subcommittee's chairman, said the panel had sought to authorize funding for many of the military services' $37 billion in wish list items, including: UH-60M Black Hawks, AH-64E Apache, and CH-47 helicopters; F-35 Joint Strike Fighters and F-18 Super Hornets; short-range air defense capabilities; Marine Corps helicopters to include V-22s and AH-1 Vipers; unmanned aircraft systems and upgrades; Army ground combat vehicles and support equipment, and National Guard and Reserve equipment.

The subcommittee authorized procurement of 67 V-22 tilt-rotor aircraft over seven years. It also authorized the purchase of $661 million in parts for F-35 fighter jet exports and would require the Pentagon to certify cost and design stability for those parts.

The subcommittee's portion of the measure expressed concern about what the panel considered to be the slow pace of modernizing Army armored brigade combat teams and developing future vehicles. The full committee's bill would take action to accelerate these programs, aides said.

The panel's report also asked the Pentagon for information about possible plans to discontinue modernization of F-15C fighter jets. And the report requested information about the future of the small-arms and ammunition industries.

READINESS

The House Armed Services Readiness Subcommittee approved its portion of the authorization bill by voice vote on June 22. Six amendments were adopted en bloc during the nine-and-a-half minute meeting, with ranking Democrat Madeleine Z. Bordallo of Guam and Republicans Mike D. Rogers of Alabama and Joe Wilson of South Carolina each offering two amendments.

The panel rejected the Pentagon's request to start a new base-closure round in fiscal 2021. Eschewing politically damaging base closures is a years-long congressional tradition.

MILITARY PERSONNEL

The House Armed Services Military Personnel Subcommittee on June 22 approved its piece of the fiscal 2018 defense authorization bill by voice vote. No amendments were adopted in the eight-and-a-half minute meeting.

The panel's markup recommended a 2.4 percent pay increase for all military personnel, compared to the 2.1 percent raise in the president's

request, as well as a 17,000-soldier increase in the size of the Army.

The Army originally sought an increase in its so-called end strength, but the additional manpower — which would cost some $3.1 billion in fiscal 2018, including money to train and equip the new forces — did not make the president's budget request. The panel supported increasing the size of the Navy (5,000) and the Air Force (5,800), as the president had proposed.

The panel also would crack down on "revenge porn" — the sharing of intimate photos without consent — by making the act a violation of the Uniform Military Code of Justice. The sharing of private photos became a much-publicized issue in the Marine Corps earlier in 2017.

The measure would expand special victims counsel training to consider the challenges of male victims of sexual assault.

The subcommittee aimed to create a process that would allow veterans who suffer from post-traumatic stress disorder or traumatic brain injury to appeal other-than-honorable discharges to allow them easier access to veterans' benefits. The panel would ensure the two boards that consider such appeals utilize the same requirements. The boards would have to consider non-military medical evidence and require what aides called "liberal consideration of evidence" relating to post-traumatic stress or traumatic brain injury.

The subcommittee also recommended increasing annual pilot retention bonuses from $35,000 to $50,000 to hold onto pilots who are leaving the military for commercial airlines.

STRATEGIC FORCES

The Subcommittee on Strategic Forces approved by voice vote on June 22 its portion of the defense authorization bill and called for a $2 billion increase to the president's request for missile defense programs.

The subcommittee's chairman, Alabama Republican Mike D. Rogers, disclosed the proposed funding boost in his opening statement at the markup of his portion of the massive defense bill.

He only noted a few details, including a proposed $550 million increase above the president's request for Israeli antimissile systems.

Rogers also used his opening statement to launch a verbal fusillade at Air Force leaders for resisting the subcommittee's efforts to reorganize the service's space programs. His prepared remarks said he was "pissed," but he altered that during delivery to "outraged."

Members approved by voice vote an amendment by Arizona Republican Trent Franks to require an evaluation of using reusable rockets.

The bigger debates were over amendments that were defeated or withdrawn.

The subcommittee defeated, 8-8, a proposal by Franks that would make an annual Government Accountability Office report on antimissile programs a biannual report.

The panel also rejected by voice vote two amendments by its ranking Democrat, Jim Cooper of Tennessee. One would have removed provisions in the panel's measure that would block dismantlement of nuclear weapons. Another would have struck a provision in the panel's draft barring funding to extend the New START Treaty until the president certifies Russia is complying with the Intermediate Range Nuclear Forces Treaty. The treaty runs through 2021, so the provision would have little practical effect and is principally a message to Russia, members said.

SPACE CORPS

The Strategic Forces Subcommittee chairman's draft contained other noteworthy provisions. It would create a new fighting force called

Space Corps Takes One Small Step

In a bold and even audacious move by a relatively unknown member of Congress, Alabama Republican Mike D. Rogers nevertheless used his perch atop a House Armed Services subcommittee to slip language into the annual Pentagon authorization bill to create an entire new military service focused on space. It almost made it into law.

Moving forward despite fervent objections from the Defense Department and without a full committee hearing or debate, Rogers drafted a new power structure for the military and proposed adding a new member to the exclusive Joint Chiefs of Staff, something that has traditionally only happened after a bruising, years-long turf war.

With the backing of Armed Services leaders, the provision moved rapidly, sailing through the House as part of the massive defense bill (HR 2810) in June, just weeks after his Strategic Forces Subcommittee first approved it.

Air Force Secretary Heather Wilson, who previously represented a New Mexico district in the House as a Republican, opposed it.

"The Pentagon is complicated enough," Wilson said. "This will make it more complex, add more boxes to the organization chart and cost more money. If I had more money, I would put it into lethality, not bureaucracy."

Never mind that the Space Corps proposal, so named by its creator, was dropped from the defense bill in conference after giving some Pentagon leaders heartburn and raising strong objections from senators on the defense committees. Rogers still logged what may be a significant political victory by putting space into the defense spotlight for the first time in years.

The possibility that America could lose its advantage compelled Rogers to pull out the stops for his proposal.

"We as a world have become very dependent on space domestically, commercially, but not only that, militarily," Rogers said. "Space has become an absolutely integral part of our ability to fight and win wars, which is why China and Russia have begun to exert so much influence over that part of their defense budget."

A 2015 Pentagon report outlined China's expanded emphasis on offensive space capabilities, detailing that the People's Liberation Army has developed anti-satellite weapons capable of disabling U.S. satellites. Many of those potential targets are operated by the Air Force and provide the capabilities for the Global Positioning System used by air traffic controllers, power plants and smart phones.

While China continues to increase its war-fighting capabilities in space, Beijing has already proven itself on a smaller scale. A decade ago, when one of its missiles blew up a decrepit Chinese weather satellite, China joined the ranks of Russia and the United States as the only countries to have destroyed space assets.

Russia, always the United States' fiercest competitor in space, displayed its advancements in 2014 by launching two different satellites that tracked and intercepted the communications from European and U.S. military satellites. Experts say these Russian spy machines could also be used to crash into adversary satellites, which could take GPS offline — and, by extension, the terrestrial systems that depend on it. ■

Space Corps in an effort to improve the military's ability to address threats in space.

The Space Corps would be a separate military service responsible for national security space programs for which the Air Force is today responsible, members have said. It would fall under the Department of the Air Force, and its chief would be a member of the Joint Chiefs of Staff. It would be to the Air Force as the Marine Corps is to the Navy, an aide said.

The panel's mark would re-establish U.S. Space Command as a new four-star position under U.S. Strategic Command.

The changes would be "disruptive in the short-term," Rogers said at the markup. He rebutted Air Force Secretary Heather Wilson, who called the proposed reorganization "unnecessary and excessively bureaucratic."

"When I see arguments in the press that we are actually going to set back efforts to respond to adversary space threats, well, I'm outraged," Rogers said. "I've been shocked by the response of the Air Force leadership. ... Maybe we need a Space Force secretary."

Adam Smith of Washington, the ranking Democrat on Armed Services, said before the markup that he supported the Space Corps.

Jim Cooper of Tennessee, the top Democrat on the subcommittee, backed it as well.

MISSILE DEFENSE ADDITIONS

The measure would bar the Pentagon from buying satellite services if there was a threat that they could be compromised by cyber vulnerabilities or because they were launched by, or contained parts from, adversary nations.

Language on Israel's antimissile programs would authorize $705 million for systems in that country that U.S. companies would develop or produce in conjunction with the Israelis.

The measure also would support several Missile Defense Agency priorities that were included in the agency's first-ever unfunded priorities list, including a requirement that the agency begin developing a new system of missile-tracking satellites and procure 24 additional interceptors for Theater High Altitude Area Defense batteries.

The panel also endorsed procurement of 147 PAC-3 MSE interceptors for Patriot antimissile systems that the Defense Department had not requested.

SEAPOWER AND PROJECTION FORCES

The Subcommittee on Seapower and Projection Forces approved by voice vote on June 22 its section of the defense authorization bill, and the panel's chairman recommended a surge in shipbuilding.

Rob Wittman, the Virginia Republican who chairs the panel, said he was urging that the full committee's version of the bill authorize

procurement of several more ships than Trump requested.

Trump's first defense budget was all but bereft of the sizable procurement hikes that he promised on the campaign trail. Administration officials said the buildup would start in fiscal 2019.

Also of concern to shipbuilding advocates on Capitol Hill was the fact that the Navy's "unfunded priorities list" — its compilation of programs that it wants to see funded even though the president's budget did not do so — did not include any major warships.

Wittman, who hails from Navy- and shipbuilding-heavy southern Virginia, clearly wanted to change that. "Today is the first step in our nation's long-term commitment to restoring our readiness," he said.

The administration initially had asked for eight ships and then upped it to nine. But officials had to formally tell Congress how they would pay for the ninth vessel, which would be a second Littoral Combat Ship, or LCS, a small warship capable of multiple missions.

The panel would authorize 13 ships, Wittman said: the nine the administration asked for plus four others. Those four ships included: a third LCS, one destroyer, one amphibious dock landing ship and one expeditionary support base.

Wittman said his measure would expand upon the administration's proposal for several types of aircraft, though he did not quantify. These include, he said, KC-46A tanker jets, C-130J transport aircraft, E-2D command and control planes, and P-8 surveillance and sub-hunting aircraft.

The panel adopted, by voice vote, a block of amendments. One would authorize the Pentagon to use the National Defense Sealift Fund, an account normally used for supply ships, to pay for the construction of icebreakers. A second amendment would exclude icebreakers from a "Buy American" requirement that pertains to certain propulsion systems, since no U.S. companies make the systems in question.

The measure that Wittman put before the panel contained a number of provisions aimed at boosting the size of the Navy's fleet. Realizing that goal would require consistent funding, which appropriators, not authorizers, control.

The subcommittee's portion of the authorization bill would require that the Navy fleet of aircraft carriers must grow from 11 to 12 starting in fiscal 2023.

The panel also urged authorization of construction of aircraft carriers every three years instead of every five. Aides said that such a pace must be maintained to achieve the 355-ship fleet that the Navy wants.

To speed by one year delivery to the fleet of the newest carrier, the USS Gerald R. Ford, the panel would allow the Navy to skip a shock test of the vessel, a grueling trial by fire that gauges a ship's readiness for fighting at sea.

The panel would authorize multiyear procurement of 15 destroyers and 13 attack submarines — more than the Navy asked for in both cases. It also would bar the retirement of cruisers.

HOUSE COMMITTEE ACTION

The House Armed Services Committee approved the fiscal 2018 defense authorization bill with broad bipartisan support just before midnight on June 28, but not before indicating that lawmakers in both parties disagreed with President Trump on issues including defense spending priorities, climate change and his proposed border wall.

In his opening remarks at the panel's markup, Thornberry criticized the Trump administration's budget proposal because it would "cut

missile defense below current spending, cut shipbuilding accounts, add no additional soldiers to the Army, et cetera."

The committee, which reported the bill to the floor on a 60-1 vote, sought to provide the Pentagon with $696.5 billion, including funds for war-related costs, far exceeding the budget caps in place.

Specifically, the proposal included $631.5 billion for base budget accounts and about $65 billion for war spending. The committee tapped $10 billion in Overseas Contingency Operations funding, which is not limited by the 2011 Budget Control Act, to augment the base budget.

The bill was $28.5 billion more than the Trump administration's request, which itself exceeded defense caps by $54 billion. Trump had promised a historic military buildup, but defense hawks on Capitol Hill argued that the proposed boost to the Pentagon's accounts was lackluster.

The policy bill would authorize $21 billion of the $31 billion in the Pentagon's unfunded requirements, including $6 billion for shipbuilding, to help move the Navy toward a 350-ship fleet, Thornberry said.

Rep. Adam Smith of Washington, the committee's ranking Democrat, said the topline proposal was unlikely to become law unless the House voted to significantly lift budget caps.

CLIMATE CHANGE

Despite opposition from some Republicans, the committee adopted by voice vote an amendment by Rep. Jim Langevin, D-R.I., that would require the Pentagon to study the likely effect of climate change in the next two decades on the military's 10 most vulnerable installations around the world.

Calling climate change fundamental to national security, Langevin said that ignoring the "multifaceted threat" could "affect our readiness both tactically and strategically."

Rep. Liz Cheney, R-Wyo., opposed the amendment, saying that there was no evidence that climate change causes wars and "refugees are not leaving their homes because it's hot."

The Intergovernmental Panel on Climate Change in 2014 wrote that there was "justifiable common concern" that climate change increased the chances of armed conflict. The National Academy of Sciences also has linked the Syrian conflict to drought caused by climate change.

The Trump administration had already withdrawn the United States from the Paris climate accord.

BORDER WALL

In a show of bipartisan opposition to the president's proposed wall with Mexico, legislators from border states advanced amendments to block Pentagon funds from being used to build barriers along U.S. borders.

The debate on the amendments prompted Thornberry to remind the committee that the border wall was not in the panel's jurisdiction.

"Just so everyone understands: There is nothing in this bill that has anything to do with a wall on the border," Thornberry said before allowing a vote.

Nonetheless, the committee adopted by voice vote an amendment by Rep. Ruben Gallego, D-Ariz., forbidding the transfer of funds to be used to build any barrier along the U.S.-Mexico border. A substitute amendment by Steve Knight, R-Calif., not to authorize funds for a wall and a perfecting amendment by Beto O'Rourke, D-Texas, prohibiting funds to build a wall on any of America's international borders, were also adopted by voice vote.

SPACE CORPS

In an unusual intraparty spat, Rep. Michael R. Turner, R-Ohio, attempted to block the immediate creation of Space Corps, proposing an amendment to require a Pentagon study of the "strategic need" for the corps before it was organized.

Rogers said it would be "legislative malpractice" to slow-walk the creation of Space Corps, and the amendment was defeated by a voice vote. Thornberry, meanwhile, said Rogers had talked with "an endless number of people" about the idea in the past year.

"I think it's time for this to move forward, even though I completely recognize what the gentleman from Ohio said, this is a significant change," Thornberry said.

Rep. Trent Franks, R-Ariz, advanced an amendment authorizing funds to develop a space-based ballistic missile intercept system, by a 36-26 vote. The amendment received pointed criticism from Rep. Jim Cooper, D-Tenn., who lamented the $30 million to pay for the program. "If you really care about this topic, be a man and raise real money and pay for it." Cooper said.

OTHER ISSUES

Rep. Niki Tsongas, D-Mass., offered an amendment during debate on the Tactical Air and Land portion of the bill that proposed halting further production of the Navy's F/A-18 aircraft until the service addressed problems with the aircraft's on-board oxygen systems. But she withdrew the amendment with the understanding that the Navy would address the issue before the defense authorization bill passed.

Debate on the bill bogged down over the Navy's long-troubled Littoral Combat Ship. The Pentagon's budget proposal included funding for one LCS, although the administration later said it wanted two of the shore-hugging vessels, without explaining how it planned to pay for the additional ship. The committee bill authorized funding for three ships.

Several committee Democrats opposed the additions, arguing that the extra LCS ships were wasteful, especially given their track record of maintenance problems. But an amendment to remove one of the ships from the bill was rejected, 19-43, following a lengthy debate.

Rep. Seth Moulton, D-Mass., a former Marine, took issue with the plan to tap war funds to pay for the LCS. But Thornberry said authorizing three ships would allow the Navy to maintain the production facilities as the service transitions to building frigates.

HOUSE FLOOR ACTION

The House debated more than 200 amendments over three days leading to passage, 344-81, of the $688.5 billion fiscal 2018 defense authorization bill on July 14.

The bill, which authorized $20.5 billion more than President Trump's request and blew past existing budget caps, contained provisions that would create a new space-focused fighting force, prioritize climate change at the Pentagon and push the White House to consider a new Authorization for Use of Military Force, or AUMF, for foreign conflicts.

Despite often raucous debate on the massive policy bill, it drew strong bipartisan support. The vote was the first time in three years that Armed Services Committee ranking member Adam Smith voted for the legislation.

During floor debate, the Washington Democrat emphasized how metastasizing global threats encouraged his vote for the bill.

"U.S. national security is at risk," Smith said. "It is no doubt that [North Korea's] goal is to develop a nuclear missile capable of striking the U.S. … We need to be worried about that. We need to be prepared to stop that."

Armed Services Chairman Mac Thornberry of Texas said the bill would begin to reverse "deep damage" inflicted on the military during years of spending caps. Thornberry also espoused the party-line argument that defense spending increases should not be contingent on similar increases in non-defense discretionary spending.

"We don't tie [the defense budget] to other things," Thornberry said. "The obligations to the men and women who risk their lives stand on their own."

Prior to final passage of the defense bill, lawmakers rejected, 208-217, an amendment from Trent Franks, R-Ariz., that would require a Pentagon study of "violent" Islamic doctrine. The House passed, 235-189, an amendment from Colorado Republican Doug Lamborn that would normalize the operational test and evaluation process for the ballistic missile defense systems.

Among its most noteworthy provisions, the bill authorized the creation of Space Corps, a new fighting force within the Air Force focused entirely on space, despite an objection from Air Force Secretary Heather Wilson and without matching language in the Senate Armed Services' version of the defense authorization bill.

The bill represented a victory for lawmakers concerned about the effects of climate change. On July 13, the House killed an amendment by Rep. Scott Perry, R-Pa., that would have removed language in the defense authorization bill requiring the military to plan for the threat of global warming and rising sea levels.

The House included in the bill an amendment from Oklahoma Republican Tom Cole that would direct the president to send Congress a strategy, budgetary analysis and a report on an AUMF, and legal justification for the new strategy to defeat al-Qaida, the Islamic State and the Taliban.

The language, which Cole called a "baby step" toward requiring a new AUMF, falls short of demanding a new war authorization to replace the two AUMFs from 2001 and 2002 that the U.S. military is currently using to justify ongoing conflicts.

SENATE ACTION
SENATE COMMITTEE ACTION

The Senate Armed Services Committee on June 28 approved a $692 billion defense authorization measure for fiscal 2018 that would add billions for new fighters, ships and other advanced weaponry but made cuts to some struggling programs.

The annual policy bill included $632 billion for the Pentagon's base budget and another $60 billion for Overseas Contingency Operations funding, with the total amount dwarfing the Trump administration's request and exceeding budgetary limits on defense spending.

In its detailed summary of the bill, the committee said it supported another $8 billion in security funding that fell outside the committee's jurisdiction—a figure the committee contended would bring national defense base-budget funding to the $640 billion goal long sought by Senate Armed Services Chairman John McCain, R-Ariz.

The Pentagon's massive F-35 Joint Strike Fighter program was perhaps the biggest winner, with the panel authorizing $10.6 billion for 94 of the stealth fighters for the Air Force, Navy and Marine Corps. The Trump administration had sought $7.5 billion for 70 of the fighters.

The bill would boost the F/A-18E/F Super Hornet fighter jet, another congressional favorite, adding $739 million and 10 aircraft to the administration request for a total of 24 of the aircraft.

A Boost for Military and Medicine

A Pentagon request for expedited FDA approval of medicines and medical devices designed for the battlefield zipped into law in the autumn after briefly holding up the defense authorization.

The Defense Department request surfaced in November as conferees from the House and Senate were wrapping up a final version of the defense authorization bill (HR 2810). A provision was tucked into the conference report to give the Pentagon unprecedented approval over certain drugs and medical devices. That sparked opposition from members who were not part of the defense conference, and they threatened to delay consideration the broader measure.

The solution that leaders came up with was to remove the battlefield medical provision from the conference report and rewrite it to expedite approvals through the Food and Drug Administration. That became a separate bill (HR 4374).

The House passed HR 4374 on Nov. 15 by voice vote and the Senate cleared it by voice vote the next day. President Donald Trump signed it into law (PL 115-92) on Dec. 12.

The drug bill authorized the FDA to expedite the review process for any emergency Defense Department request for the use of unapproved medicines and medical products that would be "reasonably likely" to address military emergencies. It would define such emergencies as situations in which U.S. military personnel are threatened with a biological, chemical, radiological, nuclear or other life-threatening agent.

Rep. Mac Thornberry, R-Texas, the House Armed Services chairman, and Rep. Adam Smith, D-Wash., the committee's ranking member, gave grudging assent to the FDA bill but made clear they were not happy with the agency's slow rate of approving treatments that could save the lives of military personnel. ∎

The committee, which marked up its bill behind closed doors, approved $2.9 billion for 17 KC-46A aerial refueling tankers for the Air Force, an addition of $400 million and two aircraft above the request. The panel also authorized $1.6 billion for 17 MC-130J aircraft, nearly tripling the request.

Shipbuilding programs also came out on top in the Senate bill, which authorized $25 billion for 13 ships in 2018. That came to $5 billion and five ships above the administration's request.

The additional ships included an extra DDG-51 Arleigh-Burke class destroyer and $1 billion in incremental funding for an amphibious assault ship.

The bill did, however, make some cuts to ship programs, including a $94 million reduction in the Littoral Combat Ship program. The shore-hugging vessel, which has a history of cost overruns, schedule delays and technical problems, had long been targeted by McCain.

The panel also trimmed $300 million from aircraft carriers and established a cap of $12 billion for future carriers. McCain criticized the Navy for years for the cost of the new Ford-class carrier fleet.

Army network programs took a hit, with the troubled Warfighter Information Network-Tactical cut by $448 billion.

Meanwhile, the committee sought to move $4.6 billion for the European Deterrence Initiative from war accounts to the base budget. It also authorized $500 million in assistance to Ukraine, including lethal defensive weapons.

Military personnel would receive a 2.1 percent pay raise, matching the administration's request. And the panel approved an increase in Tricare pharmacy co-pays, long a source of contention between the two chambers.

The panel authorized 7,000 troops more than the administration sought. The additional troops include 5,000 for active-duty Army, 1,000 for active-duty Marine Corps, 500 for Army Reserve and 500 for Army National Guard.

In the bill, McCain continued his efforts to pare down the Pentagon bureaucracy, with a 20 percent reduction in deputy assistant secretaries of defense and a 10 percent reduction in senior executive service

personnel. The bill would remove one assistant secretary from each military department.

When the committee's bill was publicly released on July 11, it numbered 932 pages and would set new policy on issues ranging from Arctic military operations to the Army's failed efforts to modernize its ground combat vehicles.

The lengthy report accompanying the bill, meanwhile, touched on many of the panel's pet issues, including oversight of the massive F-35 Joint Strike Fighter program and shipbuilding.

The bill authorized an additional $3.1 billion for 24 more F-35s than the Trump administration requested, but the report demanded that the Defense Department send Congress a report on the affordability of operating and supporting the stealthy jets, which together are estimated to cost some $1 trillion over their life cycle. The panel said it was particularly concerned that the Defense Department's plan to sustain the jet was not linked closely to the military services' budgets, "thus contributing to the lack of transparency and misalignment of responsibility and accountability that has plagued the program from its inception."

In its report, the committee endorsed the Navy's goal of increasing its fleet to 355 ships, but recognized that the service may not have the budget to buy brand-new ships. The committee required the Navy to report on some lower-cost options to achieve that goal, including reactivating old ships and extending the service life of existing vessels.

Several provisions in the bill focused on the Arctic, a growing area of concern for the military as it becomes more navigable and relations with Russia continue to worsen. Among those provisions are a study on the Navy's Arctic capabilities, including any gaps that currently exist, and the authorization, in consultation with the Navy, of six new icebreaker ships for the Coast Guard. The report also directed the Defense Department to conduct an Arctic wargame to assess its strategy, assumptions and capabilities in the region.

The report directed the Defense and Homeland Security departments to recommend to Congress how the Army National Guard and Air National Guard could gain effective unit and individual training

while also enhancing border security.

The bill would expand the special immigrant visa program for Afghan interpreters and others who had assisted the United States, from 11,000 to 15,000 visas. This had been a key area of interest for McCain,

The bill would establish a five-year "period of relief" for active-duty officers to serve as undersecretaries of defense. For some of the department's top jobs, such as the undersecretaries for research, acquisition, personnel and policy, it would narrow the window required for nominees to be retired from the military before taking those posts from seven years to five years. For others, such as the department's comptroller and undersecretary for intelligence positions, it creates a new five-year cooling-off period.

The bill would authorize creation of a new $10 million fund for foreign forces and other groups or individuals supporting Special Operations Forces.

The bill would require the Army to submit to Congress a plan to build a prototype for a new ground combat vehicle, which the service has been unable to get started after several failed attempts, such as the massive (and now canceled) Future Combat Systems.

The plan would include the schedule, key milestones and leadership plan to "rapidly design and build the prototype ground combat vehicle," reflecting McCain's growing impatience with the Army's stalled acquisition efforts.

SENATE FLOOR ACTION

The Senate on Sept. 18 passed HR 2810, amended with its own defense authorization bill (S 1519), 89-8, after truncated debate on the legislation that eschewed roll call votes on a series of high profile and controversial amendments.

The bill, as amended, would authorize $692 billion in discretionary funding for defense programs in fiscal 2018, including $60 billion for Overseas Contingency Operations funds.

Measures that would have ended defense sequestration, shielded transgender troops from expulsion from the military, barred the indefinite detention of American citizens on U.S. soil, and boosted defense spending for medical research did not receive floor votes over the five days of debate on the bill.

The Senate may have moved quickly through the authorization debate so that the chamber could turn to other issues, such as overhauling the tax code, but the defense bill moved too quickly for some frustrated senators who had wanted votes on their amendments.

"I'm very proud of the way this legislation proceeded before the Senate most of the way," McCain said ahead of the vote to limit debate on the bill. "Now I'm not very proud because we are not allowing senators having a vote."

But outstanding issues from the Senate's debate could re-emerge, as McCain vowed to include some of the unconsidered amendments in conference discussions with the House.

Prior to final passage, the Senate adopted a second package of 48 relatively uncontroversial amendments after passing a group of 104 earlier. The 48 included one to authorize spending $600 million not requested by the administration on the Navy's Littoral Combat Ship, a small shore-hugging class of vessel built by two different shipyards, one on Lake Michigan and the other on the Gulf Coast. The program has had troubles in development and early construction. The $600 million would be diverted from what the amendment calls "fuel savings." Appropriators would still have to agree to make the money shift happen.

The amendment had political implications as it might boost the 2018 re-election prospects of some of its sponsors: Michigan Democrat Debbie Stabenow, Wisconsin Democrat Tammy Baldwin and Alabama Republican Luther Strange.

The "no" votes on final passage of the bill were cast by three Republicans — Bob Corker of Tennessee, Mike Lee of Utah, and Rand Paul of Kentucky — and four Democrats — Kirsten Gillibrand of New York, Patrick J. Leahy of Vermont, and Jeff Merkley and Ron Wyden of Oregon — plus independent Bernie Sanders of Vermont.

One of the most contentious debates during the bill's consideration was over Paul's amendment that would have phased out the 2001 and 2002 Authorizations for the Use of Military Force. While the Senate voted, 61-36, to table (or kill) Paul's amendment, the Senate's vote was its first on an AUMF in 15 years

Despite debate between and within both parties over the authorization measure, the overall bill received wide bipartisan support.

"I am pleased, however, that we are able to include several dozens of agreed upon amendments from both Democrats and Republicans," said Jack Reed of Rhode Island, the Senate Armed Services Committee's top Democrat. "In the end, this bill represents a strong, bipartisan effort to provide the military with the resources they need and the support they deserve."

The $692 billion bill, which authorized $24 billion more for the Pentagon than President Trump's request and $3.5 billion more than the House-passed version, included provisions that would require a North Korea strategy, bar the Defense Department from contracting with a Kremlin-linked tech firm and a measure to curb sexual assault in the military.

The North Korea strategy document must describe the nature of that danger as well as Pyongyang's security cooperation with Russia, China and other countries. It must state what the U.S. policy objective is on the peninsula and set forth a "detailed roadmap," including military plans, on how to get there. A classified annex to the report is permitted and the document must be updated quarterly.

The amendment, by Joe Donnelly, D-Ind., was aimed at stimulating public debate on how America could best respond to the challenge of North Korea's nuclear and missile programs.

Donnelly's amendment was one of 104 that the Senate quietly incorporated into the sweeping authorization bill by unanimous consent.

The adopted amendments included another by New Hampshire Democrat Jeanne Shaheen that would bar U.S. government from contracting with Kaspersky Lab, a Russian cybersecurity firm suspected of being a Kremlin agent. Shaheen's amendment would codify and broaden to all U.S. departments and agencies a proposed ban on Kaspersky announced by the Department of Homeland Security that would cover civilian agencies, aides said.

The defense bill also included an amendment by New York Democrat Kirsten Gillibrand that would increase training and require other measures be taken to curb sexual assault at the U.S. Merchant Marine Academy, after a report last year that 63 percent of women and 11 percent of men there had experienced unwanted advances or other sexual harassment.

Another amendment, by Iowa Republican Charles E. Grassley and Delaware Democrat Thomas R. Carper, sought to curtail improper payments by federal departments and agencies by requiring creation of an inter-agency management group to spearhead oversight efforts, and it would mandate greater government use of data analytics and information sharing to solve the problem. Overpayments and underpayments to contractors and people totaled $1.2 trillion across

the federal government between 2003 and 2016, according to the Government Accountability Office. The Pentagon alone paid out $1 billion improperly in fiscal 2016.

CONFERENCE REPORT

The House on Nov. 16 adopted the conference report for the fiscal 2018 defense authorization bill, 356-70, but Senate action was delayed until the chambers passed legislation (HR 4374) to approve drugs and other medical devices for battlefield emergencies. The Senate then adopted the conference report by voice vote the same day.

CONFERENCE AGREEMENT PROVISIONS

The House-Senate conference agreement authorized $692.1 billion for the Pentagon and defense-related programs, $26.4 billion more than the president's overall request and $74.2 billion (12 percent) more than the current level. The total includes $626.4 billion for the Pentagon's base, non-war budget that is subject to spending caps and $65.7 billion for uncapped Overseas Contingency Operations funds for war operations and other anti-terror activities. The base discretionary total was $77.3 billion more than would be permitted for defense spending in FY 2018 by the 2011 Budget Control Act, although that cap applies to appropriations, not authorizations. The measure includes numerous provisions targeting Russia and the Islamic State, new guidelines regarding cybersecurity, and provides a large increase for ballistic missile defense, partly in response to recent actions by North Korea.

U.S. defense spending rose rapidly in response to the 9/11 terrorist attacks in 2001 and subsequent 2003 decision to invade Iraq, with new spending authority increasing from $304 billion in FY 2000 (3 percent of GDP) the year before the 9/11 attack to a high of $721 billion in FY 2010 (4.8 percent of GDP) as the United States engaged militarily in both Afghanistan and Iraq.

Efforts to wind down U.S. operations in those nations were mixed, however, with the U.S. withdrawing almost all of its forces from Iraq before being forced to re-engage and help the new Iraqi government fight the Islamic State after ISIS seized portions of Syria and Iraq in 2014. And in Afghanistan a large contingent of U.S. military forces remains to help bolster the fragile Afghan government, which faces continuing challenges from the Taliban, other terrorist groups, and its own corruption.

The Defense Department estimated that total Pentagon spending for the wars in Afghanistan, Iraq and Syria has been $1.52 trillion, or about $7,740 for each taxpayer. Others said that when associated costs were added, it will be trillions more, particularly with continued and growing spending on veterans pension and medical costs.

While it had been expected that defense funding would be reduced as war-related funding in Iraq and Afghanistan declined and U.S. troops returned home, the continued unrest in the Middle East and emerging threats elsewhere — in particular an increasingly aggressive Russia and China and the growing nuclear threat from North Korea have policymakers rethinking needed defense policy and calling for spending increases.

ISIS & AFGHANISTAN

In addition to funds authorized for continued U.S. combat operations, the conference agreement authorized the president's request for $1.8 billion for the Counter-ISIS Train and Equip fund, the department's effort to arm and train "moderates" in the fight against the Islamic State.

It authorizes the president's request of $4.9 billion to train and equip Afghanistan's national army and other security forces, including the national police. The total includes $3.8 billion for the army and $1.2 billion for Afghanistan's national police.

RUSSIA

In response to past and continued Russian aggression, including in Ukraine and Crimea, the agreement continued to restrict contacts between the United States and Russia and Russia-related nonproliferation programs run by the Energy Department's National Nuclear Security Administration.

It also authorizes $350 million for weapons for Ukraine, requires the National Intelligence Director to report if Russia is complying with the Intermediate Range Nuclear Force Treaty and authorizes additional funding for the European Reassurance Initiative (which involves sending military equipment and additional U.S. forces to Eastern Europe).

MISSILE DEFENSE

The agreement authorizes more than $15 billion for missile defense programs, including funding for Ground-Based Midcourse Defense, European missile defense, THAAD interceptors in Asia, and cooperative programs with Israel. The total was roughly $2.5 billion more than the president's request and $5 billion more than current levels.

It restricted the provision of any missile defense data to Russia and requires the Missile Defense Agency to start designing, developing and testing a space-based anti-missile system. The measure also authorizes funds for an environmental assessment needed to install more advanced medium-range missile defense radar systems on the continental East Coast and in Hawaii.

HEALTH & SURVIVOR BENEFITS

The measure authorized $33.9 billion for defense health care programs, including $396 million in the OCO account. Over the past decade, health care has been one of the fastest rising defense accounts.

The agreement also continues a special supplement to survivor benefits for the families of those killed in the line of duty, at a cost of $2.8 billion over the next decade. To offset that cost, the measure increased the pharmacy copayments that participants in the military's Tricare health network must pay (which would reduce Pentagon spending by $3.4 billion over 10 years).

AIRCRAFT

The measure authorized $19.1 billion for procurement of Navy aircraft and $19.2 billion for Air Force planes, including the following authorizations and provisions:

• F-35 Joint Strike Fighter — $13 billion for procurement of 90 new F-35 planes, continued research and development, and modifications to existing aircraft. The total includes $2.6 billion for 20 unrequested planes.

• P-8A Multimission Maritime Aircraft (Poseidon) — $1.8 billion for 10 Poseidon aircraft, a Boeing 737 commercial derivative that is the Navy's next-generation, maritime, anti-surface warfare surveillance aircraft. The total is $507 million and three more aircraft than requested.

• F-18 Super Hornets — $1.9 billion for 24 F-18 Super Hornet aircraft, the Navy's principal fighter. The total includes $739 million for eight unrequested planes.

• V-22 Osprey — $1.2 billion for 12 V-22 tilt-rotor aircraft for the Ma-

rines, six more than requested.

• KC-46A Aerial Refueling Tanker — $2.9 billion for 17 new refueling aerial tankers, two more than requested.

• A-10 Warthog — Prohibits the retirement of A-10 ground support attack aircraft and authorizes unrequested funds to keep the aircraft operating.

• Army helicopters — $3.1 billion for Army helicopters, including $1.4 billion for 71 AH-64E Apaches, $1.1 billion for 92 UH-60 Blackhawks, $310 million for 10 CH-47F Chinooks, $246 million for 4 MH-47G Chinooks, and $108 million for 13 Light Utility Helicopters.

• Drones — More than $3 billion for new UAVs and related missiles.

SHIPBUILDING

The agreement authorized $26.2 billion for Navy shipbuilding, $6.3 billion more than the request and 50 percent more than the previous level. The total included the following:

• Attack submarines — $5.9 billion for construction and long-lead components for the next boats in the Virginia class of new attack submarines.

• Aircraft carriers — $4.4 billion for the current carrier program, as well as $1.6 billion for nuclear refueling overhauls.

• Littoral Combat Ship — $1.5 million for three Littoral Combat Ships. The president requested funding for only one ship.

• DDG-51 destroyer — $5.3 billion for the next three DDG-51 vessels, including $1.8 billion in extra funds to build the third ship.

• Ship retention — Prohibited the use of funds for the inactivation or storage of Ticonderoga-class cruisers or dock landing ships in FY 2018. The Navy has sought to take 11 cruisers out of service to modernize them.

OTHER PROVISIONS

The measure also did the following:

• Additional personnel — Provided for an increase of 20,300 soldiers and sailors over the president's request, including additional National Guard and Reserve personnel.

• Military pay raise — Supported an average 2.4 percent pay increase for military personnel in fiscal 2018 and extended special pay and bonuses for active-duty and reserve personnel. The president proposed a 2.1 percent increase.

• Armored vehicles — Authorized $2.2 billion for Army ground combat vehicles, including $1.1 billion for Abrams tanks, $622 million for Stryker armored combat vehicles, $445 million for Bradley Fighting Vehicles, and $41 million for Ground Mobility Vehicles.

• Military construction — Authorized $10.7 billion for military construction and family housing.

• Cybersecurity — Authorized $8 billion for various cybersecurity initiatives.

• Energy Department — Authorized $20.6 billion for discretionary defense-related activities at the Energy Department, including $14.1 billion for nuclear weapons laboratories and programs operated by the National Nuclear Security Administration and $5.4 billion for environmental restoration and waste management.

• Base closure — Barred the use of funds for a new round of Base Realignment and Closure. ■

Work on New Authorization for Use Of Military Force Is Sidetracked

More than 15 years after Congress handed the president broad authority to send the military after terrorists who had attacked the United States on Sept. 11, 2001, a group of senators in June of 2017 gamely set off in search of a new Authorization for Use of Military Force that might be less expansive.

The Trump administration was waging an anti-ISIS campaign in the late spring of 2017 under the authority of the 2001 AUMF. Experts in both parties agree the 2001 authorization (PL 107-40) has been stretched beyond almost all legal recognition to justify the occasional air strike on Bashar al-Assad's forces in Syria and even far-flung groups like Al-Shabab in East Africa.

Rather than highlighting their policy differences, as was the case during the previous Congress, Republicans and Democrats on the Senate Foreign Relations Committee thanked one another for their attention to the issue and indicated they were ready to make significant compromises.

Their main focus was a new AUMF proposal from Sens. Jeff Flake, R-Ariz., and Tim Kaine, D-Va., who had co-sponsored an unsuccessful authorization effort in the previous Congress.

The new measure (S J Res 43) specifically authorized military action against al-Qaida, the Taliban and the Islamic State. It also would establish a congressional oversight process for whether other groups or entities could be treated as "associated forces" under the new authorization and if the military campaign expanded beyond certain countries. The measure would replace the 2001 AUMF and expire in five years, absent congressional reauthorization.

"We've struck a pretty decent balance," Flake said. "I hope that we can move forward on that basis."

The following month, after years of failed attempts, Rep. Barbara Lee, D-Calif., managed to put together an unusual coalition of Republicans and Democrats on the House Appropriations Committee to approve an amendment requiring a new Authorization for Use of Military Force within eight months of the bill's enactment.

Lee had voted against the original AUMF and had tried since 2010 to eliminate what she termed the "blank check" lawmakers gave President George W. Bush in the days following the Sept. 11 attacks.

Rules Committee Republicans, however, later quietly removed Lee's amendment from the Defense appropriations bill (HR 3219) — Speaker Paul D. Ryan opposed it — but the repeal order's ability to get the support of all but one Republican appropriator struck observers as

a sign of changing times.

Democrats — and even several Republicans — appeared more willing to work on a compromise AUMF than they were even in 2016, in part because of concerns that Trump could send the country into a war in the Middle East. At the same time, many Republicans were encouraged by the leadership of Defense Secretary James Mattis and National Security Adviser H.R. McMaster and were now willing to debate a new authorization for force.

With most Republicans pushing for a more open-ended authorization and Democrats demanding a sunset clause and prohibitions on a large ground invasion, for years the policy differences appeared too great. One exception was the Senate Foreign Relations Committee's 2013 vote to authorize U.S. military force to punish Syria's Bashar al-Assad regime for its use of chemical weapons, even though Obama ultimately blinked when Assad crossed his "red line."

Sens. Kaine and Flake developed a new proposal that would repeal the 2001 AUMF and a related 2002 authorization that covered the Iraq war. Kaine said he hoped the "renewed energy" around fulfilling Congress' constitutional duty would ultimately produce a concrete result.

On Sept. 7, though, administration officials said Trump would not propose an updated Authorization for Use of Military Force to cover ongoing U.S. operations against groups such as al-Qaida, the Islamic State and others. The White House had concluded it had ample legal authority to continue conducting such military missions.

The news that the administration would not propose a new AUMF came less than an hour after House Speaker Paul D. Ryan said there should be a new one and the administration should take the lead on it. "I think it's in our interest to have a new one; I just want to make sure we have one that works for our warfighters," Ryan had said.

Pressed on what that would entail, Ryan said, "I think the administration should take the lead on what the AUMF looks like."

The Senate on Sept. 18 voted 61-36 to table an amendment to the defense authorization bill (S 1519) by Kentucky Republican Rand Paul that would have rescinded the 2001 Authorization for Use of Military Force in six months.

Paul, a strict constitutionalist, lamented sprawling U.S. military involvement in places like Yemen, Somalia and Libya without congressional authorizations to deploy the military in those countries.

Paul's Kentucky colleague, Senate Majority Leader Mitch McConnell, said that it would be "simply irresponsible" to rescind the AUMF because that would create uncertainty for troops in harm's way.

Democrats were split on the measure. Kaine, long a proponent of a new AUMF, announced his public support for Paul's amendment. On the flip side, Jack Reed of Rhode Island, the top Democrat on the Armed Services Committee, said that a repeal of the AUMFs would strain relations with allies.

"You can't replace something with nothing," Reed said, noting that a repeal could signal to allies that the United States might flee ongoing conflicts.

Discussions continued, though, and in early December a draft AUMF was introduced by a handful of House members, including four Republicans, three Democrats and four combat veterans. The measure (H J Res 118) would repeal the open-ended 2001 and 2002 authorizations to use military force and replace them with an authorization that expires every five years if not renewed by Congress.

The proposed authorization explicitly covered Al Qaeda, the Taliban, the Islamic State and any individuals — but not sovereign nations — who were part of or provided "substantial" support to one of the named terrorist groups and have "engaged in hostilities" against the United States or its armed forces.

"I'm so concerned about the erosion of the balance of power between the executive and the legislative branch," said Rep. Mike Coffman, R-Colo., the primary sponsor of the measure, who served in the Army and Marines in both Iraq wars. "We are allowing this precedent of the imperial presidency."

Coffman told an audience at the Center for Strategic and International Studies that had President Barack Obama requested military authorization before intervening in Libya in 2011, Congress would have refused to provide it, and perhaps the North African nation would not be the widening security vacuum and chaos machine it had become.

Senate Foreign Relations Chairman Bob Corker said on Dec. 13 he thought negotiators had found the right language for a new AUMF and a draft was circulating. "I think we've hit what I hope is a sweet spot," Corker said.

But with concerns mounting about North Korea's war of words with Trump, no bill was marked up by the end of 2017. ∎

Nuclear Questions for Hill and Trump

A blue-ribbon Pentagon board urged the new Trump administration in February to make the U.S. nuclear arsenal more capable of "limited" atomic war, and a month later a National Security Council official said the administration might abandon the goal of nuclear disarmament.

Such steps, along with President Donald Trump's bellicose approach to North Korea's communist regime, led some congressional Democrats to seek a way to curb Trump's nuclear war authority.

Trump had unnerved many longtime Republican and Democratic nuclear policy hands with his off-the-cuff insults of North Korean leader Kim Jong Un, his threats to "totally destroy" the North with "fire and fury," his misunderstanding as a presidential candidate of key characteristics of the U.S. nuclear arsenal and posture, and his reported passing interest early in his presidency in pursuing a massive buildup.

The Defense Science Board, in an unpublished report from December 2016, had urged the president to consider altering existing and planned U.S. armaments to achieve a greater number of lower-yield weapons that could provide a "tailored nuclear option for limited use."

The recommendation was more evolutionary than revolutionary, but it foreshadowed a raging debate just over the horizon.

Fully one-third of the nuclear arsenal was already considered low-yield, defense analysts said, and almost all the newest warheads were being built with less destructive options. But experts on the Pentagon panel and elsewhere said the board's goal was to further increase the number of smaller-scale nuclear weapons — and the ways they could be delivered — in order to deter adversaries, primarily Russia, from using nuclear weapons first.

Critics of such an expansion said that even these less explosive nuclear weapons, which pack only a fraction of the punch of the bombs America dropped on Japan in 1945, can still kill scores of thousands of people and lead to lasting environmental damage. They worry that expanding the inventory of lower-yield warheads—and the means for delivering them—could make atomic war more thinkable and could trigger a cycle of response from adversaries, possibly making nuclear conflict more likely. And, they said, such an expansion would cost a lot of money without necessarily increasing security.

The issue was expected to gain greater prominence in the next several years as an up-to-$1 trillion update of the U.S. nuclear arsenal becomes the biggest Pentagon budget issue. That update, as planned, mostly involves building new versions of the same submarines, bombers, missiles, bombs and warheads.

But any effort to create new weapons, or even to modify existing ones, in order to expand the arsenal of potentially usable nuclear weapons is likely to trigger opposition.

"There's one role, and only one role, for nuclear weapons, and that's deterrence. We cannot, must not, will not ever countenance their actual use," said Sen. Dianne Feinstein, D-Calif. "There's no such thing as limited nuclear war, and for the Pentagon's advisory board to even suggest such a thing is deeply troubling."

"I have no doubt the proposal to research low-yield nuclear weapons is just the first step to actually building them," she added. "I've fought against such reckless efforts in the past and will do so again, with every tool at my disposal."

Conservatives on the congressional defense committees generally supported exploring new nuclear options.

"We know from testimony that Russia, among others, are fielding new nuclear weapons with new capabilities for new employment doctrines," said Mike D. Rogers, R-Ala., chairman of the House Armed Services Strategic Forces Subcommittee. "We would be irresponsible not to evaluate what these developments mean for the U.S. and our modernization programs."

WORRIES ABOUT TRUMP

The Defense Science Board's nuclear recommendation was buried inside a report titled, "Seven Defense Priorities for the New Administration," which also addressed homeland security, protecting information systems and more. The board had made similar nuclear recommendations before, but the new report added volume to a growing chorus of hawkish experts calling for a nuclear arsenal they said would be more "discriminate."

The board's statement came at a pivotal time because Trump rattled many Americans with comments during the campaign about nuclear weapons. He suggested that atomic arms might be an appropriate response to an Islamic State attack and that it's good for a president to be "unpredictable" about nuclear weapons. He also said, referring to nuclear weapons in general, that "the power, the destruction is very important to me."

Trump had mandated a new "nuclear posture review," an assessment of the way forward aimed at ensuring the U.S. nuclear deterrent. The memorandum contained echoes of the Defense Science Board's language. Trump said the review would ensure a "modern, robust, flexible, resilient, ready, and appropriately tailored to deter 21st Century threats and reassure our allies."

A senior administration official said on March 21 that the White House would review whether to back away from longstanding U.S. policy of nuclear disarmament while embarking on the process of updating the country's nuclear arsenal.

"It's not totally obvious that we can continue to have it both ways in that respect for the foreseeable future," said Christopher Ford, senior director on the National Security Council for weapons of mass destruction and counter-proliferation.

Ford, the administration's highest-ranking political appointee focusing on arms control, said at an annual international nuclear policy conference that the White House was studying whether to reaffirm the goal of nuclear disarmament as part of its broader Nuclear Posture Review.

"It is certainly among the conceptual space of options that we're exploring right now," said Ford, a former principal deputy assistant secretary of State focusing on nuclear nonproliferation in the George W. Bush administration.

The United States is legally obligated under the 1968 Nuclear Non-Proliferation Treaty to the goal of total nuclear disarmament. That putative goal has receded and advanced over the years with the change in administrations, according to James Acton, co-director of the Carnegie Endowment for International Peace's nuclear policy program.

FINGERS ON THE TRIGGER

A chorus of Democratic senators and representatives expressed alarm on Oct. 26 about the potential for a U.S. president to begin a nuclear war unilaterally, arguing that such authority should be switched to Congress, particularly with Trump occupying the Oval Office.

Democrats hoped to capitalize on a growing national fear that Trump might lead the country into a nuclear war with North Korea, and they wanted to take away his authority to do so unilaterally.

"This year, the entire world is worried about Donald Trump going nuclear and starting a catastrophic war on the Korean Peninsula," said Sen. Edward J. Markey, a Massachusetts Democrat and leader during the 1980s "Nuclear Freeze" movement, at a conference organized by the anti-nuclear weapons advocacy group, Ploughshares Fund.

"No human being should have the sole authority to initiate a nuclear war," Markey said. "Not any American president and certainly not Donald Trump."

Companion bills had been offered in the House and the Senate that would prohibit the U.S. military from carrying out a first-use nuclear strike absent a declaration of war by Congress. Since they were introduced in January, the measures (HR 669; S 200) from Markey, D-Mass., and Rep. Ted Lieu, D-Calif., had steadily attracted more co-sponsors with over 60 signing-on in the House, including one Republican, Rep. Walter B. Jones of North Carolina.

Congress gave the president the sole ability to launch a nuclear strike in the 1946 Atomic Energy Act but left unresolved the question of whether it was constitutional for a president to order a preemptive nuclear attack if Congress had not declared war.

"This is unconstitutional, undemocratic and simply unbelievable," Markey said.

House Minority Leader Nancy Pelosi of California said in October that it was an "urgent" priority for Democrats to update the "ancient" Atomic Energy Act.

In addition to the Markey-Lieu effort, a flurry of other Democratic bills were in the works that sought to constrain Trump's ability to attack North Korea or to set U.S. nuclear war policy. Sen. Christopher S. Murphy, D-Conn., outlined plans to introduce a bill that would require the president to get authorization from Congress before carrying out

either a conventional or a nuclear preemptive strike on North Korea.

And House Armed Services ranking member Adam Smith, D-Wash., told the conference he planned to offer legislation that would go even further than the Markey-Lieu measures by making a U.S. nuclear first-strike completely illegal.

At a rare Senate hearing on nuclear war powers on Nov. 14, former government and military officials cautioned the Senate against taking any steps that would take away from the president's expansive powers to launch a nuclear weapon, including even when the United States is not under threat of imminent attack.

"We are concerned that the president of the United States is so unstable, is so volatile, has a decision-making process that is so quixotic that he might order a nuclear weapons strike that is widely out of step with U.S. national security interests, so let's just recognize the exceptional nature of this moment, and the discussion that we're having today," said Sen. Christopher S. Murphy, D-Conn. The last time a hearing was held on the president's authority to wage nuclear war was more than 40 years ago. ■

Ship Collisions Unnerve Lawmakers, Spur Study on Readiness Shortfalls

Cultural and structural changes are needed within the Navy to prepare the service to meet rising threats from newer naval powers and to avoid deadly training accidents such as those that plagued the Navy over the summer of 2017, according to a report commissioned by Navy Secretary Richard Spencer and released Dec. 14.

The 96-page "Strategic Readiness Review" report — requested by Spencer following ship collisions that killed 17 sailors involving the Navy's 7th Fleet over the summer — said that everything from increased operational tempo with fewer ships to budget sequestration and defects in a 1986 law known as the Goldwater-Nichols Act contributed to the Navy's current readiness problems.

Spencer, however, was clear that the Navy's readiness shortfalls were the result of years of miscalculations, not one specific policy.

"The readiness consequences identified in this report are not traceable to any single policy or leadership decision," Spencer said. "But rather [they] are the cumulative effects of well-meaning decisions designed to achieve short-term mission requirements that have unintentionally degraded long-term operational capability."

Among the numerous problems that the report's writers link to the Navy's current readiness woes include how the Navy is funded. They bemoaned continuing resolutions — a legislative mechanism that funds the government at the previous year's appropriated levels — as one of the key contributing factors to hampered readiness.

As a military service that relies on expensive, capital-intensive ships, the Navy is hobbled by continuing resolutions, the report said. Without a formal budget enacted every year, funding is often in the wrong appropriations account; shipbuilding cannot be accelerated quickly when needed and new weapons programs cannot begin, the report said.

According to the study, which was conducted by a cadre of former naval officers with input from academics and industry, the Navy has operated under continuing resolutions for 33 of the last 42 years.

The investigators also blamed readiness shortfalls on the 2011 Budget Control Act (PL 112-25), which limits defense spending and implements across-the-board defense cuts when a budget isn't passed.

While blaming congressional action, or inaction, for readiness issues is common in the military, the report also links some of the Navy's structural issues to the 31-year-old Goldwater-Nichols Act, which moved the armed services to more "jointness" or greater cooperation and interoperability among the Army, Navy and Air Force.

In 1986, the Chief of Naval Operations' staff was organized based on naval platforms such as surface ships, submarines or aircraft. Those roles were later reorganized around functional missions, such as manpower and logistics, which matched more closely with the other service branches. As a result, according to the report, the restructuring "reduced the visibility, at the most senior Navy staff, into the readiness conditions of the platforms the Navy operates."

The report also noted that Pentagon staff has grown since Goldwater-Nichols became law, while the ship count has decreased. This changing ratio has led to "ships having to do more in response to more staff demands, which reduces the time available for crews to tend to the operational needs of the ship such as training, readiness, and certifications." The study added, "The growth of the entire staff enterprise has caused a shift from a command-centric to a staff-centric culture in the Navy."

To fix the problem, the investigators suggest Spencer should conduct a " 'clean sheet' review of the administrative chain of command in the Navy to best and most efficiently organize and man headquarters to generate sustainable readiness." ■

FISA Reauthorization Is Tied Up By Concerns Over Privacy

Facing a Dec. 31 deadline, Congress moved in fits and starts to extend the authority of U.S. intelligence agencies to gather phone, email and text data on foreigners — even if they sometimes collect information on Americans, too.

In the end, Congress could pass only a temporary extension during the calendar year. Both chambers and parties were riven by hard-liners on the Intelligence committees who wanted surveillance activities to continue largely unabated, and privacy advocates centered in the Judiciary panels who demanded new restrictions to protect civil liberties.

Facing irreconcilable differences between three different versions of legislation to reauthorize portions of the surveillance act, which would have expired Dec. 31, lawmakers chose a short-term extension of the current statute, enacted in late December as part of a continuing resolution (PL 115-96), with plans to return early in 2018 to consider a revised and more long-term reauthorization of the law.

Several different versions of legislation to reauthorize FISA made their way through Congress before the issue was punted into 2018. The House Intelligence Committee approved its hard-line version (HR 4478) on Dec. 1 by a party-line vote. A version of the bill approved by the Senate Intelligence Committee would give intelligence agencies the most leeway, while a bill backed by Sens. Patrick J. Leahy, D-Vt., Mike Lee, R-Utah, and Ron Wyden, D-Ore., would be more restrictive.

A separate measure (HR 3989) approved by the House Judiciary Committee attempted to strike a balance between those two versions. The differences centered on the degree of freedom the FBI and intelligence agencies would have to search the surveillance database for information on Americans without a warrant, and also on provisions that would end intelligence agencies' ability to engage in so-called incidental collection of information on Americans who are neither senders nor receivers of information from targets.

The issue was not resolved until Jan. 19, 2018, when a compromise version of S 139 (PL 115-118) was signed by President Donald Trump, revising and extending the law for six years through Dec. 31, 2023. For most of 2017, he had insisted that no changes to the law were necessary except an extension, but in the end he accepted the final version of S 139.

The so-called FISA legislation centered on 2008 amendments to the Foreign Intelligence Surveillance Act, known as Section 702, that allow government agents to read emails and text messages in which foreign terrorist suspects are mentioned or involved.

It became controversial in 2013 when Edward Snowden, the National Security Agency whistleblower, revealed that the agency was sometimes scooping up Americans' messages in the dragnet.

The final resolution in 2018 was a setback for digital privacy advocates, who got Congress to prevail in their favor on the previous major piece of privacy legislation in 2015 when it passed antiterrorism legislation (PL 114-23). That law imposed restrictions on bulk metadata collection by the NSA. Metadata includes time, duration, and sender and receiver information on emails and phone calls. It is this data that privacy groups believe should be shielded from federal authorities.

Civil liberties advocates promised to challenge the new law with the intent of preserving Americans' Fourth Amendment rights against unreasonable search and seizure.

The 2018 outcome was a victory for security hawks over civil libertarians. It also marked a win for the House Intelligence Committee over its counterpart, House Judiciary, and a shift in the balance of power on government surveillance from three years prior. A similar gulf divided the Senate Intelligence and Judiciary committees.

This time around, House Judiciary Committee members were deeply divided on reauthorizing the surveillance power that Congress granted in 2008, and that gave the Intelligence panel, which favors broader powers, an edge.

BACKGROUND

The Foreign Intelligence Surveillance Act of 1978 (FISA, PL 95-511) was enacted to limit domestic surveillance in the wake of widespread civil liberties abuses that came to light after congressional investigations of the Nixon administration during and after the Watergate scandal. It established procedures for the physical and electronic surveillance and collection inside the United States of "foreign intelligence information" between "foreign powers" and "agents of foreign powers" (which may include U.S. citizens and permanent residents suspected of espionage or terrorism) — but it generally did not limit U.S. surveillance outside the United States.

The law had been amended several times — including to add judicial oversight by creating the Foreign Intelligence Surveillance Court, often referred to as the "FISA court," as well as congressional oversight through the House and Senate Intelligence Committees — and it provided the legal foundation for certain operations of the National Security Agency (NSA) and other intelligence organizations. It allows intercepts abroad of foreign entities and individuals without a warrant when collecting foreign intelligence, although warrants are required when the target became a U.S. citizen or someone known to be in the United States.

After the 9/11 terrorist attacks, Congress in October 2001 enacted the Patriot Act (PL 107-56), which included a number of new and expanded authorities under FISA to help officials track, arrest and prosecute terrorists and prevent terrorist attacks. At the time, the measure was widely supported in Congress, passing the House by a 357-66 vote and the Senate 98-1. However, the measure soon raised the concerns of civil libertarians about potential loss of privacy and government overreach during investigations.

The 2001 law included specific "sunsets" for many of the new powers, setting them to expire unless Congress acted to extend them. Other counterterrorism authorities, including the so-called "lone wolf" provision, were enacted in a 2004 overhaul (PL 108-458) of the intelligence community that came in the wake of the Sept. 11 Commission's report. Reauthorizations of Patriot Act and FISA authorities have imposed additional oversight requirements and certain restrictions, including through the 2008 FISA Amendments Act (PL 110-261) that strengthened protections for U.S. citizens abroad by requiring the government to obtain an order from the FISA court to target them when

collecting foreign intelligence (previously, the attorney general could issue the order).

Most FISA authorities were extended in 2012 for five years, through Dec. 31, 2017, by the FISA Amendments Act Reauthorization Act (PL 112-238).

In June 2013, Edward Snowden, a former contractor and CIA employee, began releasing through news organizations highly classified documents regarding top-secret NSA data collection programs.

Among the revelations was that the NSA was using its authority for the mass collection of "telephony metadata" from telecommunications companies of most calls made within the United States and to or from foreign countries—including the calls of U.S. citizens. The FISA court had granted a blanket order that telephone companies on an "ongoing, daily basis" provide this metadata information to the NSA, and the NSA was indefinitely storing the data so that it could quickly examine any call connections related to possible terrorism without having to get a warrant for information on a specific target. (Telephone metadata includes the date, time and duration of calls but does not include either content or personal identification information.)

Also revealed was NSA's PRISM "data mining" program, which operated under Section 702 of the FISA Amendments Act and through which the NSA obtained data from electronic service providers on non-U.S. persons who reside outside the United States, including email, chat, photos, videos, stored data and file transfers. The NSA was also found to be tapping into the overseas data hubs of Internet providers without their knowledge.

After Snowden's disclosures that the information of U.S. citizens was being collected, many members and privacy groups called for an end to the practice in order to protect the privacy of Americans, as well as for greater transparency in how U.S. surveillance was being conducted. The National Intelligence director subsequently declassified numerous FISA court opinions and orders, as well as minimization procedures and reviews of programs operated under FISA.

In May 2015, the U.S. Appeals Court for the 2nd Circuit ruled that bulk data collection is illegal and exceeded what Congress authorized under Section 215 of the Patriot Act. Congress subsequently passed the USA FREEDOM Act (PL 114-23) which modified various surveillance authorities and extended certain Patriot Act authorities to December 2019. Notably, it prohibited the NSA from engaging in bulk collection and storage of telephone metadata, instead requiring the NSA to obtain approval from the FISA court to examine the calling records of individual target telephone numbers on a case-by-case basis.

2017 OVERVIEW

During 2017, congressional efforts to enact a long-term extension of FISA authorities were effectively sidetracked because of concerns among privacy advocates and civil libertarians on both sides of the aisle that intelligence and law enforcement agencies need to have more restrictions placed on their ability to access any information on U.S. citizens.

The existing law provided that the FBI, as part of a criminal investigation, could, without a court warrant, search the Section 702 database for any collected emails and phone transcripts of Americans who are suspected of criminal involvement. Privacy advocates argued that this represents a "back-door search loophole" to query information about U.S. citizens and permanent U.S. residents that circumvents the Fourth Amendment's prohibition on unlawful search and seizure.

Months of hearings and draft proposals by multiple committees preceded the start of formal legislative action. At a May 11 hearing before the Senate Intelligence Committee, Director of National Intelligence Dan Coats called Section 702 "an extremely effective tool to protect our nation from terrorist and other threats."

SENATE COMMITTEE ACTION

The Senate Intelligence Committee on Nov. 7 approved a FISA extension (S 2010) that would allow the FBI and intelligence agencies to query the surveillance database without warrants and also allow the NSA to resume collections of "about" communications after first seeking approval from the secret FISA court.

Supporters of the bill argued that current surveillance authority was vital to combating terrorism and must be extended.

Opponents of the measure argued that this so-called "reform" bill was written by the intelligence community, for the intelligence community, which is why it did not accomplish any meaningful changes to Section 702 or to ensure Americans' constitutional right to privacy. The measure, they said, would continue to give the FBI far too much leeway to search the communications records of U.S. citizens that are incidentally collected.

Privacy hawk Sens. Ron Wyden, D-Ore., and Rand Paul, R-Ky., meanwhile, were rounding up cosponsors for competing legislation (S 1997) that would impose the strongest restrictions on the NSA and FBI by requiring warrants for any queries, end the "about" collection, and outlaw use of the foreign surveillance law for purely domestic purposes.

Another bill sponsored by Sen. Tom Cotton, R-Ark., and backed by several national security hawks in the Senate would extend the law with no changes. That was the version favored by the Trump administration. The Cotton bill had the backing of 13 Republican senators, including Intelligence Chairman Richard M. Burr of North Carolina, Armed Services Chairman John McCain of Arizona, and Lindsey Graham of South Carolina, a strong voice on national security matters.

HOUSE JUDICIARY ACTION

The House Judiciary Committee on Nov. 8 approved its bill (HR 3989). The bipartisan measure crafted by Chairman Robert W. Goodlatte, R-Va., and the panel's top Democrat, Rep. John Conyers Jr., would end the NSA's collection practices that sweep up communications about U.S. persons who are neither the sender nor the recipients of messages sent by foreign targets, but contain material about Americans nonetheless. The bill would also place restrictions on how the FBI can access personal data for investigations.

Conyers said that while the bill does not accomplish "every reform I had hoped to see," it nevertheless "represents real, achievable, substantive reform."

The House Judiciary legislation also would end the so-called "about" collection, which refers to data NSA ends up collecting that is neither to nor from an approved foreign target, but communications about that person. Although the NSA has said it had ended the practice, the bill would codify it, sponsors said.

Democrats on the panel all opposed the legislation because it contained language that would restrict a practice called "unmasking" that they said had no place in the bill.

Democrats objected to the unmasking language because they said the provision was motivated by allegations made by President Trump, which were later refuted. Trump claimed that the Obama administration had illegally obtained the names and identities of Trump campaign officials and had later disseminated them through leaks to the

media. A congressional inquiry into the matter concluded that no such illegal unmasking had occurred.

CNN reported in September that Obama administration National Security Adviser Susan Rice told the House Intelligence Committee in a classified briefing that she had sought details from classified reports of Americans who met with Sheikh Mohammed bin Zayed al-Nahyan, the crown prince of the United Arab Emirates, in New York in December 2016. The UAE did not notify the Obama administration of the crown prince's visit to New York during the presidential transition, as is customary, CNN reported.

The unmasking is said to have revealed that retired Army Lt. Gen. Michael Flynn, a Trump campaign adviser who later became national security adviser, Trump's son-in-law Jared Kushner, and Trump campaign chief Steve Bannon met with the crown prince.

At the markup, backers of stronger privacy restrictions, including Republicans and Democrats on the panel such as Reps. Ted Poe, R-Texas, Eric Swalwell, D-Calif., and Sheila Jackson Lee, D-Texas, proposed amendments that would further tighten the ability of intelligence and law enforcement agencies to collect or use data, but those proposals were not adopted.

Those decisions drew condemnation from the ACLU.

"Though this bill has positive elements, it must be improved as it moves forward," the ACLU said in a statement. "Disappointingly, the committee failed to adopt improvements that would help close the 'backdoor search loophole.' The loophole has been used by the government to read and listen to Americans' emails, phone calls, and text messages collected under Section 702 without a warrant."

HOUSE INTELLIGENCE COMMITTEE ACTION

The House Intelligence Committee on Dec. 1 approved by a party-line vote of 13-8 a bill (HR 4478) to reauthorize U.S. intelligence agencies' powers to collect the electronic communications of foreigners who may be working against the interests of the United States.

Democrats on the panel all opposed the legislation because it contained language that would restrict "unmasking" that they said had no place in the bill.

The bill would allow U.S. intelligence agencies and the FBI to query a surveillance database looking for information on Americans without first obtaining a warrant. It would allow the FBI to search and gather information from the database first and later obtain a warrant only if such information is to be used in a criminal case.

The bill included a section spelling out how U.S. officials can request names and identities of Americans whose information is captured by U.S. surveillance while snooping on foreigners.

The bill would require detailed records to be maintained of such unmasking requests authorized by senior officials of agencies, justification for such unmasking, and whether officials making such requests know if the person whose identity they are seeking is a member of a presidential campaign or a president-elect's transition team.

Democrats objected to the language because they said the provision was motivated by allegations made by President Donald Trump, which were later refuted. Trump claimed that the Obama administration had illegally obtained the names and identities of Trump campaign officials and had later disseminated them through leaks to the media. A congressional inquiry into the matter concluded that no such illegal unmasking had occurred.

END-OF-YEAR EXTENSION

In the last month of the session, with the Dec. 31 deadline looming, sponsors jockeyed to get their legislation to the floor. The House Rules Committee scheduled a Dec. 20 hearing to send the Intelligence Committee (HR 4478) version to the floor, but then canceled the meeting. The next day, a short-term extension through Jan. 19, 2018, was put into the stopgap spending bill (HR 1370) and cleared by both chambers. ∎

Intelligence Authorization for Fiscal 2017 Clears, but Not Fiscal 2018

Congress spent the first four months of 2017 finalizing an intelligence policy bill for fiscal 2017 that would establish an executive-branch group to counter Russian assertiveness around the world. For fiscal 2018, the House passed a stand-alone bill, but the Senate did not take it up.

The annual measure, known as the Intelligence Authorization Act, provides policy guidelines for the CIA, FBI, NSA and the rest of the nation's sprawling intelligence community. The House had passed several versions of its bill in 2016, but the Senate didn't clear the measure before the end of the last Congress.

The House Intelligence Committee was hamstrung during the year by an investigation into Russian meddling in the 2016 presidential campaign, an ethics inquiry into Chairman Devin Nunes, R-Calif., that forced him to recuse himself from the Russia probe. Both chambers had to deal with controversies and news breaks concerning surveillance of political campaigns, President Donald Trump's October deci-

sion to decertify the Iran nuclear deal, his verbal jousting with North Korea's leader, and reauthorization of the law governing surveillance of foreign intelligence activities.

Lawmakers finally added the fiscal 2017 intelligence policy bill to the catchall appropriations legislation that cleared May 5. President Donald Trump signed the bill (HR 244 – PL 115-31) the following day, issuing a signing statement that he objected to several provisions that, he contended, infringed on his constitutional authority.

The agreement established an interagency working group within the executive branch to combat Russian efforts to influence events in the United States. Russia has been accused of leaking personal emails from leading political figures in the United States as well as helping to spread "fake news" in order to influence U.S. elections.

The measure directed the group "to counter active measures by Russia to exert covert influence, including by exposing falsehoods, agents of influence, corruption, human rights abuses, terrorism, and

assassinations carried out by the security services or political elites of the Russian Federation or their proxies." The measure required the group to report to Congress within 180 days of enactment on what actions it intends to take.

The agreement required the secretary of State to establish an "advance notification regime" to govern and limit the travel of accredited Russian diplomatic personnel stationed in the United States.

Finally, the agreement required the DNI to report to Congress with an assessment of Russia's war-fighting doctrine, and the extent to which Russian flights under the Open Skies Treaty contribute to that doctrine.

The measure also required the DNI to conduct a prompt declassification review — and, once declassified, make available to the public — intelligence reports prepared by the National Counterterrorism Center regarding the terrorist activities of some detainees who were released or transferred to other nations from the Guantanamo Bay detention facility.

SENATE COMMITTEE ACTION, FISCAL 2017

The Senate Select Committee on Intelligence got off to a quick start in 2017, reporting its bill (S 133) for the current fiscal year on Jan. 20. But it could not get the measure to the floor because of objections that were placed on it for reasons unrelated to the bill itself. The spending bill at the end of the year provided an opportunity to push the measure through.

The most notable provision in the legislation targeted Russia, creating a presidentially-appointed group based within the executive branch that would counter "Russian actions to exert covert influence over peoples and governments."

The legislation included a provision to require the secretary of State, the FBI and the DNI to establish an "advance notification regime" to govern, and would limit the travel of accredited Russian diplomatic staff, according to a House Rules Committee explanation.

A third Russia-related section would have required the DNI to produce a report with an assessment of Russia's war-fighting doctrine, and the extent to which Russian flights under the Open Skies Treaty contribute to that doctrine. The Open Skies Treaty, which took effect in 2002, permits signatories to conduct observation flights over each other's territory. The U.S. and Russia are both members of the treaty.

During the 2016 campaign, Trump spoke in glowing terms about his Russian counterpart, Vladimir Putin, and the FBI was investigating possible links between Trump's associates and the Kremlin as part of the bureau's investigation.

The rest of the year was spent in negotiations between House and Senate leaders leading up to the final agreement on the omnibus appropriations bill.

FISCAL 2018 ACTION
HOUSE COMMITTEE ACTION

The House Intelligence Committee on July 13 approved a bill containing several provisions that would irk the White House, which sought to minimize the role Russia played in the 2016 presidential election and could play again in future elections at home and abroad.

After a closed-door markup, the House Intelligence panel approved the fiscal 2018 Intelligence authorization bill (HR 3180) by voice vote.

The bill would require the DNI to publish online a public advisory on foreign intelligence and cyber threats to election campaigns for national offices and ordered a separate report on efforts by Russia to

influence foreign elections.

"At a time when our nation faces major national security challenges from terrorist groups as well as nation states, it's crucial that the intelligence community receive all the resources it needs to do its job while Congress has the necessary tools to carry out rigorous oversight of its work," Committee Chairman Nunes said in a statement. "This bill will ensure that our intelligence professionals have the biggest chance of success in thwarting foreign threats."

The legislation authorized total funding for the government's 17 intelligence agencies that is "slightly below the president's budget, balancing fiscal discipline and national security," according to a committee news release. The specific topline number is classified. The administration's public budget proposal also did not include a request for the intelligence community.

The Pentagon's Defense Intelligence Agency would see several of its core functions eliminated under the legislation with certain unspecified missions realigned to other parts of the U.S. intelligence community.

Several oversight measures were included in the bill, such as language clarifying that intelligence contractors can meet freely with Congress and requirements for reports on investigations into leaks of classified information, the process for weighing what discovered computer vulnerabilities are publicized or kept secret, and the timeline for processing security clearances.

Another provision sought to reign in the intelligence community's interactions with the entertainment industry. The legislation required the agencies to inform Congress before their organization begins working with TV or movie producers, writers and others on a project.

Such engagements, the explanatory statement said, would "cost taxpayer dollars, raise potential ethics concerns, increase the risk of disclosure of classified information, and consume the time and attention" of members of the intelligence community.

"This bill is the product of months of oversight and examination and a bipartisan commitment to the nation's security," said Rep. Adam B. Schiff of California, ranking member of the Intelligence Committee.

HOUSE FLOOR ACTION

The House on July 28 passed its fiscal 2018 intelligence policy bill, 380-35, after a few procedural hiccups reflective of growing partisan tensions in the chamber, even surrounding a measure that was deliberately designed to be as noncontroversial as possible.

The legislation (HR 3180) was scheduled for floor action four days earlier under suspension of the rules -- a floor procedure that allows quick passage of broadly popular bills. But Democrats rallied at the urging of Minority Leader Nancy Pelosi of California to vote against the measure because they wanted to have a floor debate and the chance to offer amendments, including several targeting the Trump administration. The House Rules Committee then approved a closed rule that did not allow for any amendments.

Democrats had filed a number of amendments related to the Trump White House, including one from Rep. Adriano Espaillat, D-N.Y., that would prevent anyone who has threatened to destroy the government from attending National Security Council meetings. The amendment was directed at President Donald Trumps controversial senior adviser Steve Bannon.

A separate amendment from Rep. Jackie Speier, D-Calif., would have required the White House to submit a report on investigations into unauthorized public disclosures of classified information. The

president himself has been accused of disclosing, via Twitter and to senior Russian government officials, classified information about intelligence operations.

"It's too bad when the minority uses the intelligence authorization bill as part of a political stunt to make what should be a bipartisan process in a bipartisan committee appear partisan," said Liz Cheney, R-Wyo., a Rules Committee member, in floor remarks. She noted the bill advanced out of committee two weeks ago by a unanimous vote and members were given twice as long as last year to review the classified sections of the legislation.

The legislation authorized a classified topline number for fiscal 2018 for the nation's 17 intelligence agencies including the CIA, the National Security Agency, the Defense Intelligence Agency, the FBI, and the Office of the DNI.

The legislation transferred several programs out of DIA to other parts of the intelligence community in order to better focus the Pentagon agency on its core mission of assessing foreign nations' military capabilities.

SENATE COMMITTEE ACTION

The Senate Intelligence Committee on July 27 approved legislation (S 1761) that contains provisions aimed at ensuring tamper-proof future U.S. elections and improving security clearance procedures.

A committee press release announcing approval by a 14-1 was light on details and did not provide a topline funding number for the country' 17 intelligence agencies.

The legislation covered several committee priority areas, including improving the U.S. intelligence community's ability to understand and detect a wide range of cyberattacks, using technology advancements to improve the agility and effectiveness of agencies, and encouraging federal information sharing on threats with state-level election officials. Additionally, the bill included language to prod the intelligence community into being more creative in its approach to satellite systems.

"As a nation, we are facing an unprecedented range of threats," committee Chairman Richard M. Burr, R-N.C., said in a statement, listing state and non-state actors, as well as the committee's ongoing investigation into Russia's interference in the 2016 election.

Added Vice Chairman Mark Warner, D-Va.: "In a year in which intelligence professionals have too often come under unjustified disparagement, they must continue to do what they do best, and the committee has passed a solid, bipartisan bill to give them the resources they need while maintaining strong oversight of their activities."

A provision included in the committee's report would put the DNI in charge of an effort to assess the security and vulnerability of all election systems, in coordination with the heads of CIA, the FBI, the Department of Homeland Security and other intelligence agencies.

The Senate panel also recommended that at least two officials in each state and the District of Columbia get top-secret clearances so they can receive classified briefings from the intelligence community on threats to their election systems.

Having the country's top spy chief study election systems could cause friction with some state officials who have previously bristled at the federal government's efforts to intervene and safeguard the voting machinery.

Making the country's top spy chief responsible for assessing the weakness of election systems didn't mean it was being taken away from the Department of Homeland Security, panel member James Lankford, R-Okla., said. "DHS continues to have the responsibility for securing election systems" but the DNI's role is to ensure that information is being shared, security clearances are in place and whether state officials have all the information they need to make decisions. ■

Bills Cleared to Help Vets on Appeals, Private Medical Care and Education

Congress enacted several major veterans' bills, even as controversy swirled around the Veterans Affairs Department and the speed with which it was advancing Trump administration plans to greatly expand the use of private medical practices to care for veterans – proposals opposed by many veterans' groups.

The VA continued to be plagued by a massive backlog of appeals for veterans' disability benefits, and tensions began to surface within the Trump administration about the performance of VA Secretary David Shulkin, who served as the VA undersecretary for health in President Barack Obama's administration before he was nominated by President Donald Trump to head the agency.

Controversy centered on the VA Choice program, established (in PL 113-146) in the wake of the 2014 scandals at the VA. Choice was supposed to be a temporary program with $10 billion to reimburse private care — a more easily accessible option for veterans who were waiting longer than 30 days, or who had to drive farther than 40 miles for care at a federal facility.

But in subsequent years, neither the administration nor Congress acted like the Choice program was temporary. To avert a shortfall that would have meant the program's extinction, lawmakers plunged $2.1 billion into the program before the August recess with relatively little public debate. Toward the end of the year, another gap in funding loomed.

Trump had a major stake in Veterans Choice, since the final point of a 10-point pledge he made to veterans during the 2016 campaign was this: "Ensure every veteran has the choice to seek care at the VA or at a private service provider of their own choice."

Trump reiterated his support for the program in both his fiscal 2018 budget request, seeking billions of dollars more during the next two years, and during an August event with Shulkin. "We're starting to really get that to a point where Choice is just becoming something that [veterans] are extremely happy about," Trump said.

The four highest-ranking Senate and House Democrats who oversee veterans' programs issued a scathing report in June objecting to Trump's fiscal 2018 budget request for the VA.

The six-page report focused on the White House's proposal to increase funding for VA accounts that pay for use of private health care, which Democrats said would come at the expense of traditional VA facilities.

The report complained about other programs that would be eliminated or slashed in the blueprint. It cited statements critical of the VA budget from AMVETS, Disabled American Veterans, Paralyzed Veterans of America and the American Legion, four influential organizations.

EXTENDING CHOICE

On April 19, Trump signed a bill (S 544 -- PL 115-26) to dramatically expand the Choice program that lets patients seek care from private doctors if they want to bypass the troubled VA system.

The House cleared the measure by voice vote on April 5. The Veterans Choice Improvement Act removed barriers that Congress placed around the original "choice" initiative and eliminates an expiration date that would have shuttered the program in August. Under the 2014 law (PL 113-146), the Veterans Choice Program was set to expire on Aug. 7 or whenever funding runs out, whichever came first.

Progress on the bill was bipartisan. House action came after the Senate passed the legislation (S 544) sponsored by Sen. Jon Tester, D-Mont., by voice vote on April 3.

The House Veterans' Affairs Committee on March 29 had favorably reported nearly identical legislation (HR 369) sponsored by Chairman Phil Roe, R-Tenn. Both the committee bill and the bill voted on by the House would strike the August date and let the program operate until funds are exhausted.

Lawmakers provided the VA the ability to expend the $200 million the Congressional Budget Office estimates would be left in the fund by Aug. 7. The fund was established to reimburse the costs of private care for certain veterans who can demonstrate a hardship, such as living too far from a VA facility or experiencing wait times at the VA longer than 30 days.

The bill also tweaked the Choice law related to the disclosure of records and the payment process.

During debate, Roe warned lawmakers of "potentially tragic consequences" if lawmakers didn't work to swiftly deliver the bill to Trump.

The House VA committee's top Democrat, Rep. Tim Walz, D-Minn., showered Roe with praise for his work to shuttle the bill through. "A sunset that needed to be addressed was handled in a professional manner. … It puts us in a good place," Walz said.

FUNDING PATCH

Shortly before leaving for the August recess, Congress cleared a $2.1 billion funding patch (S 114) for the Choice program. Trump signed it on Aug. 12 (PL 115-46).

The House gave the measure final approval by 414-0 on July 28, four days after the House blocked a different version of the legislation, falling short of the two-thirds majority required under suspension of the rules. The vote was 219-186, undermined by objections raised by some veterans' groups and Democrats.

Key among their objections was that lawmakers included provisions to pay for the $2 billion in new funding. Those pay-fors include extending a reduction in pension payments furnished by the VA for certain nursing facility workers and extending a fee collection requirement for certain VA-guaranteed housing loans.

A letter protesting the pay-fors was signed by AMVETS, Disabled American Veterans, Iraq and Afghanistan Veterans Association, Military Officers Association of America, Military Order of the Purple Heart, Veterans of Foreign Wars, Vietnam Veterans of America and the Wounded Warrior Project. The American Legion and Paralyzed Veterans of America did not sign the letter.

After the initial setback, House Veterans Affairs Chairman Phil Roe, R-Tenn., brought a new package to the House Rules Committee that included not just appropriations for Choice, but also renewals of 28 major medical facility leases that had been sought by lawmakers for years.

The package, swapped out as a substitute amendment to a Senate bill originally related to VA employee bonuses, also included provisions aimed at improving hiring and retention of VA employees.

APPEALS LEGISLATION

On Aug. 23, Trump signed a bipartisan bill (HR 2288 -- PL 115-48) aimed at paring down a backlog of appeals for veterans' disability benefits. The House cleared the measure on Aug. 11. The Senate had passed it by voice vote on Aug. 1, following original House passage by 418-0 on May 23.

The bill essentially created three "lanes" for veterans' appeals as a means to reduce the time a former service member needs to wait for a decision on benefit claims. It was introduced by Rep. Mike Bost, R-Ill., with original cosponsor Rep. Elizabeth Esty, D-Conn.

Veterans' appeals remained a major issue facing the Trump administration. From fiscal 2015 to 2017, pending appeals shot up from approximately 380,000 to 470,000, according to the House veterans' panel. And while Congress had spent hundreds of millions to try to pare down the appeals, the VA estimated that its backlog would take five years to clear even if no new appeals were filed.

'FOREVER GI BILL'

Also on Aug. 16, President Trump signed the "Forever GI Bill" (HR 3218 -- PL 115- 48), which extended education benefits to future veterans for an entire lifetime instead of the previous 15-year window.

The GI Bill, enacted in 1944, provides veterans, their dependents and survivors with education benefits. The last major overhaul was signed in 2011 (PL 111-377).

Also under the measure, veterans who are recipients of a Purple Heart would get full benefits regardless of the amount of time spent on active duty. The bill would also provide additional funds to students studying science, technology, engineering or math while benefits would be restored to veterans who spent their GI Bill aid on now-defunct for-profits schools such as Corinthian Colleges and ITT Technical Institutes.

Hundreds of veterans maxed out their GI Bill benefits attending for-profit schools that either closed or provided them with degrees that proved meaningless during job hunts, according to veteran advocates.

HR 3218 passed the House by 405-0 on July 24; it had been approved by the House Veterans Affairs Committee on July 19. The Senate Veterans Affairs Committee approved a similar measure (S 1598) on July 26 by voice vote, in a markup lasting less than a minute. The Senate cleared the House bill by voice vote on Aug. 2.

VA ACCOUNTABILITY

Congress cleared legislation S 1094 that would expand the VA's ability to fire, demote and suspend employees for misconduct or poor performance. The bill would also establish an office within the VA to receive whistleblower disclosures, track recommendations from audits and investigators, and investigate misconduct, retaliation and poor performance. President Trump signed the measure (PL 115-41) on June 23.

The House cleared the bill by 368-55 on June 13; seven days after the Senate passed it by voice vote. The House had passed a similar version (HR 1259) on March 16 by a vote of 237-178. ∎

Chapter 7

ECONOMIC AFFAIRS

New Administration Freezes Agency Hiring, With Exceptions for Military

Federal workers took it on the chin from the incoming Trump administration, as the new president froze hiring and tried to cut budgets and restrict insurance. Republicans in the House expressed interest in restricting retirement benefits for new employees and making it easier to fire government employees.

One of President Donald Trump's first actions in January was to order an across-the-board hiring freeze of federal civilian employees, exempting only those in the military.

The order allowed department or agency heads to make exceptions for those considered "necessary to meet national security or public safety responsibilities." In addition, the director of the Office of Personnel Management was empowered to grant exemptions if it was determined to be necessary.

In February, the Defense Department issued a sweeping list of jobs exempt from the presidentially mandated federal hiring freeze that covered thousands of positions at military shipyards and depots around the country.

Without the exemptions for positions in depots and shipyards, the hiring freeze could have prompted hundreds of layoffs of temporary and term employees at depots. It also could have stalled ongoing efforts to more rapidly grow a skilled workforce the Defense Department says is critical to boosting the readiness of a force recovering from 15 years of war.

The president's memo directed the Office of Management and Budget to recommend a "long-term plan to reduce the size of the Federal Government's workforce through attrition" within 90 days of the order.

The White House announcement said the federal workforce grew from approximately 1.8 million civilian employees during the Clinton administration to approximately 2.1 million in 2016. Those figures did not include the U.S. Postal Service.

However, there were about 2.1 million civilian federal workers from 1984 through 1993, according to OPM statistics. The decline in the workforce began during the Clinton administration but numbers rose again in the George W. Bush administration.

House Speaker Paul D. Ryan, R-Wis., praised the action. "By instituting a hiring freeze, he has taken a critical first step toward reining in Washington bureaucracy," he said of Trump in a statement. Bills introduced in the House in recent years have proposed thinning the workforce by 10 percent over five years.

Republicans also considered making changes to the generous retirement benefits given federal workers, mainly by looking to shift new employees from a defined benefit into a market-based 401(k). They were also interested in making it easier to fire workers who perform badly.

EXEMPTIONS FOR DEFENSE

In a Feb. 1 memo to senior Pentagon officials, Deputy Defense Secretary Bob Work, a holdover from the Obama administration, explained the exemptions, tasked the department with appropriately implementing the hiring freeze and said he would hold officials accountable for the exemptions they grant.

"This is an opportunity for the Department to assess its most critical missions and requirements, ensuring that the civilian component of our force is assigned and capable of executing our highest priority work, while at the same time gaining full value from every taxpayer dollar we spend on defense," he wrote.

Work told Pentagon officials to apply the exemptions "sparingly" and said they must be prepared to justify exemptions on a "position-by-position basis." Officials with the authority to exempt positions from the freeze were to submit a biweekly report to the Pentagon personnel chief.

Lawmakers had been particularly focused on protecting jobs at military depots and shipyards because of the potential readiness consequences for ground vehicles, aircraft and ships in need of repair and maintenance. Positions at those facilities are the types of industrial jobs that President Donald Trump had said he was trying to protect, and most are in deep-red congressional districts.

But the exemption for shipyards and depots wasn't a blanket one. It pertained only to positions that involve direct management of inventory and direct maintenance of equipment, meaning that some temporary employees faced layoffs, and other positions would not be filled until after the freeze.

'HOLMAN RULE' REVIVED

Federal workers received more unwelcome news in early January when the House revived a 19th-century rule that could make it easier to single out workers, cut pay or eliminate vast swaths of the federal workforce altogether.

And while many conservative Republicans hailed the change, Democrats, worker's unions and even some House Republicans criticized the maneuver, known as the Holman rule for the House member who first drafted it. The rule allowed floor amendments on appropriations bills to target individual salaries or workforce levels.

The Holman rule dates to 1876 and was the brainchild of Rep. William Holman, a Democrat from Indiana. It was meant as a tool to eliminate patronage positions and was last in effect in 1983 when then-House Speaker Thomas P. "Tip" O'Neill had it removed. It was part of the House's official rules package (H Res 5) for the 115th Congress—but for only 2017, on a trial basis.

House Minority Whip Steny H. Hoyer, D-Md., said it allowed "short-sighted and ideologically driven changes to our civil service." Sen. Benjamin L. Cardin, D-Md., called it "outrageous." Norman J. Ornstein, a veteran Congress watcher at the American Enterprise Institute, called the rule "chilling" and probably unconstitutional.

Some members warned that a flurry of such amendments could make it harder to pass appropriations bills.

"That would be a free-for-all, a terrible thing," said Senate Finance Chairman Orrin G. Hatch, R-Utah. "It would cause a lot of discontent. It seems to me it's going to be tough to accomplish anything along

4

those lines."

The man who came up with the idea of reviving the Holman rule, Rep. Morgan Griffith, R-Va., said in an interview that despite the furor, he thought the rule could be an effective tool — not only for cutting spending but also for encouraging responsiveness from agencies.

Ornstein thought that in the end, the rule would be found unconstitutional.

"If you take this to a level where you have Congress singling out individuals because they don't like what they're doing, I think you'd see an immediate constitutional challenge," he said.

The American Federation of Government Employees, which represented 670,000 federal workers, called the rule a violation of due process. "Reviving this rule means lawmakers will be able to vote to cut the pay and jobs of individual workers or groups of workers without getting input from the agencies where these employees work," said J. David Cox Sr., the president of the union. ■

Problems Ahead for 2020 Census

The Census Bureau faced a host of challenges with the decennial 2020 enumeration on the horizon, from budget shortfalls and cost overruns to a shakeup atop the agency with the sudden resignation of Director John H. Thompson, announced in May. There also was apprehension among some groups that President Donald Trump's hard-line stance on immigration could depress census participation, particularly if questions about immigration status were added to the survey.

It all added up to one central fear: a census that would fall short of an accurate count of the population. The data from the periodic survey is used to map congressional districts, inform policymaking and steer billions of dollars in government resources.

The Government Accountability Office placed the 2020 census on its "high-risk list" of programs that are facing peril. There's a precedent — the 2010 census also was designated a high-risk project, as was the 2000 census before it.

This time, the Census Bureau has been readying new technology systems that still needed testing, and a lack of funding already forced the bureau to cancel or scale down some trial runs. "If you don't test those mechanisms, you risk a failed census," said Phil Sparks, communications chief at the Census Bureau during the Clinton administration and a co-director of the Census Project, a coalition of groups that rely on objective census data.

For the first time, the agency plans to let people submit their data online, potentially raising response rates and cutting down on costlier follow-up work with those who don't reply. It also wants to use online technology to verify addresses ahead of the census rather than sending staffers into the streets.

For the follow-up fieldwork contacting "nonresponsive" households, the Census Bureau plans to equip staff members with handheld mobile devices rather than the pen-and-paper system used through the last census. The agency attempted to make that technological jump in 2010. But major problems with the devices were revealed during testing, so following up with nonresponsive households — the bureau's largest and most costly field operation — again used the old paper-based system.

That late decision to abandon the new technology plan raised the cost of the 2010 census by up to $3 billion, according to the Government Accounting Office, making the 2010 test the most expensive ever. Lawmakers fear that costs would again balloon if the same scenario repeats itself.

Census Bureau officials in July indicated they would scrap key portions of the dress rehearsal at two of the three testing sites planned for 2018, citing lack of funding.

"In rural areas, there's lack of broadband, you have particular challenges in terms of addresses, etc., and all of these things needed to be tested because this is a new method of taking the census. And it's apparently not going to be done," Sparks said.

At the top of the list of problems was serial underfunding by lawmakers compared to what the Census Bureau said it needs to adequately prepare for the next census starting April 1, 2020.

Congress appropriated $1.47 billion to the Census Bureau in fiscal 2017, an increase from the previous year but about $160 million less than what the Obama administration had requested. In 2017, the Trump administration and the House and Senate Appropriations committees all proposed giving the Census Bureau about $1.5 billion for fiscal 2018, which began Oct. 1. That would have been a slight increase from current spending — but short of what may be needed as 2020 approaches.

Rep. Nita M. Lowey of New York, top Democrat on the House Appropriations Committee, called the proposed numbers "shockingly insufficient with 2020 looming."

Census analysts said the bureau likely needed $1.8 billion in fiscal 2018, about what the Obama administration had estimated would be needed for fiscal 2018, according to preliminary Census Bureau numbers.

Congress in recent decades has tended to keep census funding low in the early years of the decade and ramp it up later, sometimes to meet a backlog of needs. "In the seventh, eighth, ninth and 10th years of each of the decades, there's a significant ramp-up of both activities and funding in order to prepare for the census," Sparks said. "And that's just not happening under the Trump budget."

At a July 13 Appropriations Committee markup of the Commerce-Justice-Science Appropriations bill, which includes funding for the census, Lowey and other Democrats backed an amendment that would have poured extra money into the Census Bureau, along with other agencies. The proposal was defeated 22-30 on a party-line vote. "We simply do not have the funding available within our allocation," said Rep. John Culberson, R-Texas, chairman. "We're waiting on that bigger budget deal to allow us to fill some of these holes."

Republicans largely focused their attention on cost overruns and other missteps by the agency. For one, the new data-processing system was on track to exceed its projected 10-year costs by $309 million, a 47 percent increase.

"It seems to happen every 10 years," Culberson said. "It's distressing to see the 2020 census look like it's headed the same direction as

the 2010 census, with terrific cost overruns. It's just not acceptable." His Senate counterpart, Republican Richard C. Shelby of Alabama, similarly warned in June that the 2020 census has become a "very expensive item."

Census advocates and Democrats also worried about hostile rhetoric from the Trump administration toward immigrants, and expressed concerns that the new census could include a question about whether residents are U.S. citizens. That might dampen participation in census surveys and potentially skew the data. Censuses historically have undercounted racial minorities and overcounted non-Hispanic white residents, according to analysis from the nonpartisan Congressional Research Service. ■

Troubled National Flood Insurance Program Limps Through Year

Congress passed several extensions of the debt-ridden National Flood Insurance Program, the last in late December after months of deliberations and three major hurricanes failed to produce agreement on a five-year reauthorization of the program. The program was carried into 2018 as part of a year-end continuing appropriations resolution (HR 1370 -- PL 115-960) cleared by Congress on Dec. 22.

Senate Banking Committee Chairman Michael D. Crapo of Idaho and ranking member Sherrod Brown of Ohio had pledged back in March 2017 that they would make a bipartisan effort to reauthorize and possibly overhaul the floor insurance program that was considered essential for some real estate markets.

The program, which at that point owed $24.6 billion to the Treasury and had been widely criticized, was set to expire on Sept. 30. One criticism of the program was that too much premium revenue went to agents who sell the policies.

Roy Wright, a top Federal Emergency Management Agency official, told the Senate Banking Committee on March 14 that not reauthorizing the flood program by the end of September would hurt real estate markets in flood-prone areas.

"When the program lapses we cannot write new policies," said Wright, FEMA's deputy associate administrator for insurance and mitigation. That, he added, would have a "dampening or even an absolute limiting effect" on markets in flood-prone areas.

Wright acknowledged the costliness of the system, which includes hefty state taxes on insurance premiums. He estimated that half the money that goes to private insurers goes to the agents that sell the policies.

"We need to pull down the costs, we need to make this more efficient," Wright said. Part of that effort is using new technologies to draw flood plain maps that better reflect risks, he said.

Crapo said the reauthorization effort would work on improving FEMA's use of technology to create maps that better reflect risk; make greater use of private insurance to give policy holders more options and to share risk between the government and the private sector; and change the length of the reauthorization.

The previous authorization had been enacted in 2012 (PL 112-141).. Set up in the 1960s to abate federal costs for disaster response, the program proved unable to cover its own expenses, particularly over the past dozen years. The program receives premiums from 5.1 million policyholders, but it still has accumulated debt after borrowing $17.5 billion following the 2005 hurricane season that included Hurricane Katrina, $6.25 billion after Hurricane Sandy hit the East Coast in 2012,

and $1.6 billion after floods in 2016, Wright said.

Wright said that $4 billion in claims, largely from flooding in Louisiana and Texas, made 2016 the third-most costly storm season for the program.

Sen. Robert Menendez, D-N.J., complained that more than one-third of premiums went to private insurance companies that sell the policies but bear none of the risk.

HOUSE COMMITTEE ACTION

Republicans pushed a five-year reauthorization of the National Flood Insurance Program through the House Financial Services Committee on June 15 over complaints from Democrats that it would make policies unaffordable for many homeowners.

The bill (HR 2874) was approved 30-26 with every Democrat and Rep. Peter T. King, R-N.Y., voting against it.

Besides extending the program, the bill increased some fees for policyholders and its most controversial aspect barred from the insurance program properties with repeated claims that had been paid and some high value properties. Such properties would instead have been forced to obtain private insurance.

Three Democratic amendments aimed at making major changes to the bill were rejected. The closest vote, 26-28, was on an amendment by Rep. Denny Heck, D-Wash., to remove the bill's phase-out of favorable premiums for policyholders who built homes in flood plains when building codes were more lax.

The panel also approved, 53-0, a measure (HR 2868) that would help cut premiums for those who make efforts to reduce the chance of flood damage, such as by moving heating and ventilation systems to higher floors.

A markup expected to be a bipartisan quickly became contentious as committee members wrangled in a six-hour debate despite a last-minute addition of $1 billion for mitigation programs aimed at addressing a chief concern of Democrats. Rep. Sean P. Duffy, R-Wis., the author of the reauthorization bill, had hoped a manager's amendment, which he said would limit premium increases and fund more than $1 billion of local mitigation projects, would ease concerns from panel members. Democrats, though, said the bills still didn't address concerns about the affordability of the insurance program's policies, the grandfathering in of lower rates for longer-term policyholders and private insurers entering the market and "cherry-picking" the most profitable policies.

According to Duffy, the bills would raise the cost of an average policy from $1,084 in 2016 to $1,126, a 3.9 percent increase that would begin

to address the program's $24.6 billion debt and its annual estimated shortfall of $1.4 billion.

"This isn't extreme. It's common sense," said Duffy, the chairman of the Housing and Insurance Subcommittee.

Rep. Jeb Hensarling, R-Texas, said the bills would move more of the cost of the program to those who benefit from it. He said his Dallas district is more affected by tornadoes, but there is no federal subsidy for insurance against that act of nature.

Democrats complained that many of the main features of Duffy's bill were not shared with them until the previous evening, including the commitment to provide $225 million a year for flood mitigation programs.

The American Bankers Association opposed several provisions in the reauthorization bill, particularly the exclusion from the flood insurance program of properties with lifetime claims amounting to twice a home's value.

HOUSE FLOOR ACTION

The House passed HR 2874 on Nov. 14 by a 237-189 vote. Duffy, the bill's sponsor, Sean P. Duffy, R-Wis., said the flood insurance program's debt was evidence that the status quo "doesn't make sense."

"When do we talk about fixing a program that continues to run deficits?" he asked during floor debate.

Duffy's legislation included provisions designed to reduce the direct taxpayer exposure to flood risk, such as rate increases and coverage caps for repeatedly flooded homes. The measure capped the annual rate increase for NFIP policies at 15 percent, down from the existing 18 percent, so policyholders wouldn't see premiums increase too quickly.

The bill would have authorized the Federal Emergency Management Agency, which oversees the flood program, to perform activities related to flood insurance and flood mitigation, such as making mitigation grants, community flood insurance grants, property buyout programs and flood map funding.

The final version passed by the House also contained the text of six related flood bills (HR 1422, HR 1558, HR 2246, HR 2565, HR 2868, and HR 2875) that had passed the House Financial Services Committee in June.

To shore up support, Republican leaders removed provisions opposed by GOP members from flood-prone districts along the Gulf Coast, the Eastern Seaboard and the Mississippi River. But more than a dozen Republicans still voted against it. Rep. Peter T. King, R-N.Y., whose Long Island district took a hit from 2012's Superstorm Sandy, and Rep. Garret Graves, R-La., were concerned with the higher premiums' effect on consumers.

Most Democrats voted against the bill for concerns over costs. One member referred to the bill's impacts on premiums as "draconian."

SENATE ACTION

Three conflicting bills to reauthorize and update the flood insurance program remained bottled up in the Senate Banking, Housing and Urban Affairs Committee.

S 1313, introduced in June by Sens. Bill Cassidy, R-La., Shelley Moore Capito, R-W.Va., and Kirsten Gillibrand, D-N.Y., included provisions aimed at increasing private participation in flood insurance markets, including one that would increase the eligibility of private policies to cover certain risk classifications.

No privatization provisions, however, were in a reauthorization bill (S 1571) introduced July 17 by Senate Banking, Housing and Urban Affairs Chairman Michael D. Crapo, R-Idaho, and ranking member Sherrod Brown, D-Ohio. Sen. Robert Menendez, D-N.J., called that bill "a wasted opportunity" to change the program with new policy-holder protections and flood mitigation improvements.

Menendez, a critic of government handling of flood insurance, had introduced his own reauthorization measure (S 1368) with such features as caps on premium increases, more transparency requirements, and more money for mitigation assistance.

Menendez had backing from five other senators from flood-prone states: Cory Booker, D-N.J.; John Kennedy, R-La.; Bill Nelson, D-Fla.; Marco Rubio, R-Fla.; and Elizabeth Warren, D-Mass.

Both Menendez's bill and the Crapo-Brown bill reauthorized the program for six years, and both called for more mitigation to reduce the frequency and cost of flood damage. Menendez's bill funded more mitigation programs, including a $1 billion authorization for a Federal Emergency Management Agency program, which was absent from the Crapo-Brown bill.

Menendez's measure included consumer protections and transparency requirements not in the Crapo-Brown bill. He said they would help prevent waste and abuse. His bill imposed a 10 percent cap on rate increases for NFIP policy holders, streamline the claims process, and created a needs-based mitigation assistance loans for homeowners who can't afford premiums.

The Crapo-Brown bill included provisions from the Cassidy-Gillibrand-Capito measure, including a proposed formula adjustment for premium calculations, which the sponsors said would yield lower premiums for less expensive homes. Both bills allowed the Federal Emergency Management Agency, which oversees the NFIP, to reduce risk through reinsurance and catastrophe bonds. ∎

Congress, Administration Move to Roll Back Obama-Era Labor Policies

Both chambers of Congress moved on several fronts to bolster the Trump administration's efforts to empower private employers and to weaken organized labor and its attempts to unionize workers in both the public and private sectors. These legislative efforts carried over into 2018, however, as Democratic opposition kept measures stalled in the Senate because Republicans lacked the 60 votes needed to overcome threatened filibusters.

HOUSE PASSES OVERTIME PAY MEASURE

The House passed a bill on May 2 that would offer private sector workers the choice of compensatory time or overtime pay for extra hours worked, legislation that Republican lawmakers had attempted to pass in previous Congresses.

The bill (HR 1180) passed largely along party lines, 229-197. The Senate did not act on it in 2017.

Republicans said the legislation would allow working parents to have more time with their families. Eligible workers who voluntarily opt to take compensation time instead of overtime would be able to bank an hour and a half for every extra hour worked.

Democrats countered that the measure would deprive workers of power -- for example, they could save up to 160 hours, but couldn't use a single one without their employer's permission.

"Despite what we will hear from the other side of the aisle today, all we are doing is empowering workers with a choice," said Education and the Workforce Committee Chairwoman Virginia Foxx, R-N.C., before the vote. "For some workers, more money in the bank might be the best choice. Nothing, I repeat, nothing will take away that right. But other workers, if given the choice, would seize the opportunity to turn overtime hours into paid time off."

While the bill sailed through the House -- having a hearing, markup and floor vote in the span of a month -- getting the required 60 Senate votes to overcome filibusters loomed as difficult.

Sen. Mike Lee, R-Utah, introduced a companion Senate bill (S 801). It had 18 Republican co-sponsors including Health, Education, Labor and Pensions Chairman Lamar Alexander, R-Tenn, who "hopes to see the bill taken up by the Senate when time allows," said his spokeswoman.

Sen. Patty Murray, D-Wash., the ranking member on the HELP committee, said the bill would hurt workers and urged Republicans to support initiatives such as raising the minimum wage.

"This is nothing but a recycled bad bill that would allow big corporations to make an end-run around giving workers the pay they've earned," she said. "That's wrong, and it's the opposite of what President Trump said he'd do on the campaign trail when he promised to put workers first."

Dozens of workers and labor groups came out against the bill, including the Leadership Conference on Civil and Human Rights and the major union groups AFL-CIO and Service Employees International Union. In a letter to Congress, the groups called the legislation "a smoke-and-mirrors bill that would offer working people a pay cut without any guaranteed flexibility or time off."

Other organizations including free market groups, the Society of Human Resource Management and the pro-business Workforce Fairness Institute, endorsed the legislation.

OBAMA OVERTIME RULE ABANDONED, RECLAIMED

The Labor Department said on June 30 that it would not defend an Obama administration rule to expand overtime pay to more than 4 million people, but officials indicated that they still wanted the ability to establish policies to extend overtime pay to more workers.

At the time the rule was finalized, all workers making less than $23,660 a year had to be paid for overtime. The Obama administration proposed that overtime pay be extended to workers who earned up to $47,476 — a move strongly opposed by businesses, universities and some nonprofit organizations. More than a dozen states and business groups sued the department over the rule.

In a filing at the 5th Circuit Court of Appeals, Labor Department attorneys said they would not defend the higher threshold. Instead, they asked the court to rule on whether the department had the right to set overtime eligibility using a worker's salary.

"The Department has decided not to advocate for the specific salary level ($913 per week) set in the final rule at this time and intends to undertake further rulemaking to determine what the salary level should be," they wrote. "Accordingly, the Department requests that this Court address only the threshold legal question of the Department's statutory authority to set a salary level."

Labor Secretary Alexander Acosta indicated during a Senate hearing earlier in the year that he would not be opposed to raising the salary threshold, although not as high as $47,000.

One of the groups that sued the administration, the National Restaurant Association, supports raising the salary threshold from its current minimum level of $23,660. But businesses have some say in who is eligible for overtime, said Angelo Amador, senior vice president and regulatory counsel with the National Restaurant Association.

Some positions, like a restaurant manager, might need to work more than 40 hours a week. But in rural areas, those positions might make less than $47,476, Amador said. An income threshold that's too high could cause issues for those restaurants, he added.

In August, a Texas federal district court judge blocked implementation of the rule and the Trump administration pledged to rewrite it rather than appeal the case. However, in late October the administration reversed course and decided to appeal the ruling to give the Labor Department more flexibility in rewriting the regulation. A list of regulations the department intends to address in 2018 that was published in December included the overtime pay rule.

HOUSE PASSES BILL TO CURB JOINT EMPLOYER LIABILITY

The House passed a measure Nov. 7 to reverse a National Labor Relations Board ruling, in an effort to undo an Obama-era labor rule. The legislation (HR 3441) would narrow the standard that deems a

company as a joint employer and liable for workers it did not directly hire. It passed on a 242-181 vote.

The NLRB in August 2015 broadened the criteria for when companies and their contractors are considered joint employers of workers and can be held liable and subject to negotiations with a union.

Many House lawmakers and business groups who opposed the NLRB ruling said it lacked clarity over what qualifies a company as a joint employer. Franchisors told the House Education and the Workforce Committee in September that uncertainty about the regulation prevented them from opening up more franchise stores.

"The lines of responsibility for important worker protection are now blurry," Education and the Workforce Chairwoman Virginia Foxx, R-N.C., said during her opening statement at the committee markup, adding that the panel "wouldn't be here today if the overwhelming consensus wasn't that the NLRB and Obama-era bureaucrats made serious mistakes."

Under the bill, only companies with direct and immediate control over workers would be considered employers, returning to the previous standard before the NLRB's 2015 ruling.

While the bill was primarily sponsored and supported by Republicans, it did have some support from Blue Dog Democrats, including Reps. Collin C. Peterson of Minnesota, Henry Cuellar of Texas and Lou Correa of California.

However, most Democrats opposed the bill for "eviscerating workers protections," said Rep. Robert C. Scott of Virginia.

Rep. Jared Polis, D-Colo., said the bill would make it easy for employers to shirk responsibility for workers over whom they might have some control.

"I've been in business, I've used contractors, I've had employees." Polis said. "This bill further blends those lines and actually worsens the situation for many employees by encouraging employers to go with pseudo-contractors instead of taking on the responsibilities of employers themselves."

The Senate did not take up the issue in the first session.

HOUSE PANEL ADVANCES BILLS TO UNDO LABOR BOARD UNION RULINGS

The House Education and the Workforce Committee approved two bills on June 29 that would override various rulings and regulations of the National Labor Relations Board, including ending provisions that make it easier for unions to organize in a workplace.

Each bill was approved along a party-line vote, 22-16. The committee rejected multiple Democratic amendments to the bills.

Committee Chairwoman Virginia Foxx, R-N.C., said that the NLRB was used under the Obama administration as a workaround to further union-friendly measures that couldn't move through Congress.

"Over the years the board has abandoned its role as an impartial referee and launched a concerted effort to boost organized labor," she said. "Unfortunately, the rights of workers – and even Native Americans – were trampled on in the process. We are here today to defend those rights and ensure the law makes it crystal clear that they must be protected."

One bill, HR 2776, would give union elections more time to occur, including with a minimum of 35 days between a petition being filed and an election. Under the NLRB's rule, elections occur on average 23 days after a petition is filed.

Republicans argued that lengthening the time for elections gave employers more time to make their case and workers more time to hear both sides of the argument. Rep. Tim Walberg, R-Mich., a former union member, said workers now have as little as 11 days to decide how they will vote in union elections.

Democrats, such as Rep. Adriano Espaillat, D-N.Y., said the bill was meant to give employers more time to delay union elections, which ultimately plays to the advantage of the employer.

The bill also would block micro-unions, which can be formed with one section of a company's workforce. For example, if all employees at a department store didn't want to unionize, cosmetics and fragrance salespeople could form a smaller union.

The other bill (HR 2775) would allow employees to dictate how unions could contact them. Under the existing regulations, employers were required to give union organizers the email addresses and phone numbers of their workers.

House Panel Approves Bill to Exempt Tribes From NLRB Jurisdiction

The House Education and the Workforce Committee on June 29 approved a bill (HR 986) that would exempt Native American tribes and the businesses they own – including casinos -- from the jurisdiction of the National Labor Relations Board. If enacted, the bill would effectively undo a 2004 ruling from the board.

The measure was approved along a party-line vote, 22-16.

The bill's sponsor, Rep. Todd Rokita, R-Ind., argued that the bill was meant to ensure not only sovereignty for the tribes, but that they were treated the same as state and local governments, which are exempt from NLRB oversight..

Members of Native American tribes told the committee at a March hearing that a 2004 NLRB ruling had infringed on their sovereignty, and several Democrats joined Republicans in supporting the legislation. However, other Democrats said they were opposed to the bill as it would prevent workers in businesses from forming unions.

"We can balance the right to sovereignty with the protection that's due to all Americans if we work at it," said Polis. "But this legislation does not find that balance."

A similar bill in the Senate (S 63) had been approved by the Committee on Indian Affairs by voice vote on Feb. 8. ■

West Virginia Lawmakers Seek More Help for Miner Pension Fund

An issue that had plagued the appropriation process in 2016 re-emerged in early October as West Virginia lawmakers introduced updated legislation to ensure the solvency of a pension fund for retired miners and their spouses. It did not gain a place aboard a year-end continuing resolution, however, and the issue carried over into 2018.

The legislation offered by Republican Sen. Shelley Moore Capito, Democratic Sen. Joe Manchin III and Republican Rep. David B. McKinley, with Vermont Democrat Rep. Peter Welch, (S 1911, HR 3913) would have infused additional federal dollars into the troubled fund, and it could have provided a framework for how the federal government addresses future pension crises.

"After achieving a big victory earlier this year to permanently protect the health care of more than 20,000 retired coal miners, we cannot forget that the hard-earned pension benefits for many more miners are at risk," McKinley said in a statement. "This new legislation will ensure those benefits are there for the men and women who are counting on them."

The pension legislation, along with a separate measure meant to bolster health benefits for the retired miners, had pushed the federal government to the verge of a partial shutdown in December 2016.

The bill would have transferred money to the pension program from two federal accounts. One was the Abandoned Mine Land fund — a source that lawmakers had cited for previous rescue efforts. A second would have been a new federal loan program set up to help troubled pension programs through a 30-year repayment schedule with an interest rate of 1 percent.

The pension fund would have been allowed to borrow up to $600 million a year from the loan pool.

The lawmakers in May had offered similar legislation to shore up the pension program. That bill (S 1105) would have transferred certain funds to the 1974 United Mine Workers of America (UMWA) Pension Plan, mainly drawing from money raised from a four-month extension of certain customs fees. Congress used the same funding offset to save the health care benefits for some 20,000 miners, their spouses and widows in the fiscal 2017 omnibus spending bill.

"I think we have gone about it in a reasonable way," Capito said during a news conference. "It's not like we are saying, 'ok, hand over the money, this is what we have to do.' I think we have tried to work into a loan system where it will eventually be paid back."

The federal government has a long history of contributing to the miners' health and pension benefits. In 1946, when coal was still the nation's biggest energy source, a work stoppage by the union was becoming a national crisis. To end the strike, President Harry Truman nationalized the mines, and an agreement between the mining union, the federal government and the coal companies resulted in a pension and healthcare fund with contributions from taxpayers.

Subsequent changes altered what form and how much the federal government has contributed to the program, but the industry's recent downturn, prompted mostly by market forces from cheap natural gas and a harsh regulatory climate, placed the fund on the verge of insolvency as industry stalwarts teeter on the edge of bankruptcy

Manchin said the pension fund would fail around 2021 or 2022 if not rescued, and its failure would place more than 100,000 former coal miners' pensions at risk. Such a failure could topple the federally managed Pension Benefit Guaranty Corp., the lawmakers predicted, as more beneficiaries move into that backstop for private pension plans.

"Every day that it goes without solving the pension problem, it's another day it's going to cost more," Manchin said.

The average pension pays retirees a monthly installment of $586 and "many thousands receive checks that are under $400 per month," according to United Mine Workers of America President Cecil E. Roberts.

"That may not sound like a lot in Washington, D.C., but it is the difference between buying food or paying the electric bill for these retirees and widows, who live in every state in America," Roberts said in 2016.

The coal state lawmakers ran into a backlash from conservatives who balked at the proposal for fear of the precedent it could set for other struggling industries' pension funds.

Senate Finance Chairman Orrin G. Hatch, R-Utah, said early in 2017 that he supported the health care extension, but he could not get behind the pension fix, mainly due to the high cost. Senate Budget Chairman Michael B. Enzi, R-Wyo., raised similar concerns. ■

Chapter 8

ENERGY & ENVIRONMENT

Trump, Republicans Join Forces to Undo Obama's Environmental Legacy

Republicans used their majority control in the 115th Congress to advance key elements of President Donald Trump's environmental deregulatory agenda, notably his efforts to scrap Obama administration proposals to limit domestic greenhouse gas emissions from coal.

Yet as 2017 ended, opposition from Senate Democrats and disagreements among Republicans left some priorities unfulfilled, among them Trump's plans to slash the size of key federal departments.

Successes for the GOP included opening a portion of the Arctic National Wildlife Refuge to oil and gas exploration, a long-sought goal of Alaska lawmakers. The proposal was included in the 2017 tax overhaul law (PL 115-97).

They also sent to Trump, with the backing of four moderate Senate Democrats, a Congressional Review Act resolution (PL 115-5) rescinding the Obama administration's rule limiting water pollution from mountaintop coal mines.

"In my home state of Kentucky and others across the nation, the stream buffer rule will cause major damage to communities and threaten coal jobs," Majority Leader Mitch McConnell, R-Ky., said on the Senate floor, referring to the coal rule.

They sent two other resolutions to Trump overturning federal land use rules (PL 115-12, PL 115-20).

And the GOP lent legislative support to Trump's plans to replace two of President Barack Obama's most controversial rules, both halted in the federal courts: the Clean Power Plan that would have cut carbon emissions from coal-fired power plants, and the Waters of the United States water pollution regulations, both opposed by a coalition of states.

Those and other efforts, however, were set aside or held over for consideration in 2018. Republicans were unable to send Trump a resolution (H J Res 36) to rescind an Obama rule cutting methane emissions from oil and gas development on federal lands.

That resolution fell short on a procedural vote in the Senate, 49-51, when three Republicans voted against it, including John McCain of Arizona.

Congress also passed omnibus fiscal 2018 appropriations legislation that rejected Trump's proposals to drastically reduce the size of the EPA by a third and make smaller cuts to the Energy and Interior departments.

By the time Trump signed the omnibus in March 2018 (PL 115-141) that reflected a two-year budget agreement, the EPA's funding remained level compared to fiscal 2017, after being reduced slightly in a fiscal 2017 omnibus. The two other departments got increases.

A Trump proposal to put $120 million toward the licensing of the Yucca Mountain nuclear waste dump in Nevada was also taken out of appropriations legislation.

Passage of broader policy legislation remained similarly elusive. A bipartisan Senate energy bill did not get action, though parts relating to forest management were added to the fiscal 2018 omnibus.

House Republicans pushed through a number of bills in committee and on the floor in response to the Obama administration's handling of coal and disapproval of the Keystone XL oil pipeline from Canada, but the Senate did not follow up.

Bills that would have, for instance, sped up the approval of cross-border pipelines (HR 2883) and overhauled the implementation of the Endangered Species Act did not get further action by the end of the year.

Republicans also advanced bills that would limit future moratoriums on federal coal leasing and restrict the use of carbon emissions' social costs to justify federal regulations.

Also left for more debate were proposals to permanently reauthorize the Land and Water Conservation Fund.

The oil lobby's push for Congress to repeal the nation's biofuels law, the Renewable Fuel Standard, got caught up an intraparty conflict among Republicans and did not advance. Ethanol backers, led by Iowa GOP Sen. Charles E. Grassley, kept repeal legislation at bay and successfully pushed Trump to compromise on his proposal to curtail mandated usage in 2018. ■

Water Pollution: One Hit, One Miss

The Obama administration's signature water pollution rule, known as Waters of the United States, or WOTUS, had already been halted by the federal courts when President Donald Trump took office.

But Republicans still had the rule in their sights for a legislative response, along with an Obama environment rule targeting coal mine water pollution, which the Interior Department completed in December 2016.

Lawmakers would first act to repeal Interior's stream protection rule, also known as the stream buffer rule, while saving plans to help the Trump administration repeal WOTUS for the annual appropria-

tions cycle. They would succeed on the former, while the latter effort would ultimately fall short.

CONGRESSIONAL REVIEW ACT RESOLUTION

The stream rule sought to limit water pollution from mountaintop open pit mines. The Obama administration billed it as an overdue response to the contamination of streams and groundwater by mining soils dumped onto mountain slopes, but opponents saw it as a threat to coal mining, particularly in Appalachia.

The House moved first on a resolution of disapproval (H J Res 38)

under the Congressional Review Act, which Congress had used to repeal a regulation just once previously, in 2001.

The resolution, by Rep. Bill Johnson, R-Ohio, would be one of a series of CRA resolutions sent to Trump to overturn Obama regulations and prohibit similar versions in the future.

Johnson called the stream rule "an effort to regulate the coal mining industry right out of business. We could not stand by and allow that to happen."

The House Natural Resources Committee's ranking member, Rep. Raúl M. Grijalva, D-Ariz., said Republicans were showing "slavish deference to corporate and wealthy donor wish lists" at the expense of public health, wildlife and the environment. "These votes are big favors to big industry, and the rest of us are going to pay a heavy price," he said.

Johnson's resolution was quickly swept from its introduction on Jan. 30 through the Rules Committee and to the floor, where it passed on Feb. 1 by a vote of 228-194.

Just nine Republicans voted against passage, while four Democrats voted in favor.

The Trump White House backed the resolution, among others, in a Feb. 2 statement of administration policy.

"The bill disapproves a rule that would establish onerous requirements for coal mining operations, and impose significant compliance burdens on America's coal production. The disapproved rule also duplicates existing protections in the Clean Water Act and is unnecessary given the other Federal and State regulations already in place. The Administration is committed to reviving America's coal mining communities, which have been hurting for too long."

The Senate passed the resolution that same day.

"In my home state of Kentucky and others across the nation, the stream buffer rule will cause major damage to communities and threaten coal jobs," Majority Leader Mitch McConnell, R-Ky., said on the Senate floor.

Senate Energy and Natural Resources ranking member Maria Cantwell, D-Wash., said the rule was needed to address mining's harmful environmental impacts. "There is no reason for us not to set rules and regulations to make sure that the mining industry cleans up their mess," she said.

Four moderate Democrats joined with Republicans to pass the resolution, which needed a simple majority, by a vote of 54-45. They were Joe Manchin III of West Virginia, Heidi Heitkamp of North Dakota, Joe Donnelly of Indiana and Claire McCaskill of Missouri; all four were up for re-election in 2018.

Just one Republican, Susan Collins of Maine, voted against it.

Trump signed the resolution into law (PL 115-5) on Feb. 16. "In other countries, they love their coal, but over here, we haven't treated it with the respect it deserves," he said at the signing ceremony. "This rule would eliminate a major threat to [coal] jobs, and we are going to get rid of that threat immediately."

WOTUS RIDERS

With the WOTUS rule stayed by the federal courts and Trump planning to have the EPA issue a new version that addressed objections by farmers, oil and gas drillers and builders, Republicans added a rider to fiscal 2018 appropriations legislation to speed up the process.

The rider added to the Interior-Environment spending bills in the House and Senate would have let the EPA skip time-consuming regulatory and statutory review processes in withdrawing the rule.

That move drew a warning from a top Appropriations Committee Democrat, who said it would set a bad precedent. "For some of you this rider might be a dream come true for now, but think of the future," House Interior-Environment Appropriations Subcommittee ranking Democrat Betty McCollum of Minnesota said at markup in July.

That same month, the EPA issued a proposal to rescind the rule, complying with Trump's executive order to pull the rule back and reissue it.

Ultimately, the rider language was stripped out of the final omnibus appropriations bill enacted in March 2018 (PL 115-141), at the insistence of Democrats.

"My Democratic colleagues and I worked hard to block a long list of anti-environment provisions that have no place in an appropriations bill," Senate Interior-Environment Appropriations Subcommittee ranking Democrat Tom Udall of New Mexico said.

The bill still included a provision that prohibited the EPA from requiring Clean Water Act permits for certain agricultural provisions. ■

Endangered Species Revamp Stalls

Republican bills in recent years to revamp the Endangered Species Act ran into a predictable fate, falling short in the face of opposition from Senate Democrats and President Barack Obama, particularly during appropriations negotiations.

The election of President Donald Trump was expected to change the dynamic toward an overhaul, but Senate Democrats again held firm, and major proposals were still awaiting action at the end of the year.

The law (PL 93-205) has long been a source of Republican proposals to ease its impact on development, especially in the West. Lawmakers from the region have for years sought to limit protections in particular for the greater sage grouse, a small bird whose habitat in 11 states has been shrinking due to development.

The sage grouse was the subject of a major effort by the Obama administration to broker state-backed conservation plans to avoid listing it as endangered.

"There's too much sand in the gears, and it's just not working the way it was intended to work," Senate Environment and Public Works Chairman John Barrasso, R-Wyo., said about the law in early 2017.

Action was attempted through policy and fiscal 2018 appropriations bills, with some success, but the goal of a major overhaul was not achieved.

REPUBLICAN BILLS

The House Natural Resources Committee on Oct. 4 approved five bills to change the law. One (HR 717), by Rep. Pete Olson, R-Texas,

would require the consideration of the economic impacts before an endangered species listing and would allow a listing to be rejected based on those costs.

Another (HR 1274), by Rep. Dan Newhouse, R-Wash., would mandate that federal agencies share supporting data with states and communities and consider information submitted by state, local and tribal governments.

The others would limit fee recovery by citizens who bring Endangered Species Act lawsuits against the government (HR 3131) and would prohibit the listing of non-native species (HR 2603), which Democrats said could lead to unregulated breeding, trading and hunting of exotic animals in the U.S. and undercut work to combat wildlife trafficking.

Just one Democratic bill (HR 424), by Rep. Collin C. Peterson of Minnesota, was approved. It would direct the Interior Department to reissue rules delisting the gray wolf in the western Great Lakes region and Wyoming.

All were awaiting floor action in early 2018.

For his part, Barrasso held an Environment and Public Works Committee hearing on the law on Feb. 15, but his plan to write a draft bill took until mid-2018, when he released language that would give states more powers.

His panel also approved a bill (S 1514) on July 26 that, among other provisions, would require the Interior Department to delist the gray wolf.

The full Senate later that fall voted on an amendment by Sen. Mike Lee, R-Utah, to the fiscal 2018 House budget resolution (H Con Res 71) that would have prohibited an Endangered Species Act listing for any species in just one state.

Sen. Lamar Alexander, R-Tenn., and Sen. Susan Collins, R-Maine, joined Democrats in voting it down, 49-51.

Appropriations Action

Republicans, as they have in past years, proposed a number of policy provisions related to the law during the fiscal 2018 appropriations process.

Among them was a prohibition on the listing of the sage grouse as endangered, included in the House and Senate draft Interior-Environment spending bills, and language to delist the gray wolf.

Most, however, were dropped in final negotiations. The fiscal 2018 omnibus law (PL 115-141) enacted in March 2018 left out more than a dozen policy riders, including Endangered Species Act provisions that would have prohibited protections for the gray wolf, the lesser prairie chicken and for the Preble's Meadow jumping mouse.

However, the bill retained a provision to limit the Fish and Wildlife Service from reviewing the status of the sage grouse as an endangered species. ∎

Broad Energy Bill Moves Forward

Early in 2017, the leaders of the two key energy committees were optimistic that they could pass broad policy legislation for the first time in a decade.

They were buoyed by passage of energy bills in the House and Senate during the previous Congress that resulted in a conference report, though it was not considered before the end of 2016.

To that end, they launched ambitious initiatives to update federal policies in such areas as the permitting of liquefied natural gas export terminals, nuclear power, conservation and energy efficiency.

The most comprehensive was the 892-page bill (S 1460) by Senate Energy and Natural Resources Chairwoman Lisa Murkowski, R-Alaska, and ranking member Maria Cantwell, D-Wash., which they unveiled in late June.

The bill covered numerous areas under the committee's jurisdiction, including pipeline and hydropower permitting, electricity grid cybersecurity, fossil fuel and renewable energy expansion, national parks maintenance backlogs, and a permanent reauthorization of the Land and Water Conservation Fund.

Murkowski said the bill could move quickly though the Senate on the grounds that the chamber had previously passed many of its provisions.

"When you think about the process we have already been through, and what we have built with this package, this is not brand-new stuff," she said. "What we have done is put [these bills] in a package, and they are ready to go. We need to put a bow on it by passing it again, and hopefully getting it signed into law this time."

But the bill languished in the committee after a hearing in September, though some provisions relating to forest management would be included in the fiscal 2018 appropriations omnibus in March 2018.

Meanwhile, House Energy and Commerce Chairman Greg Walden, R-Ore., took a different tack.

Walden said in June that he was optimistic that a package could be negotiated between the House and Senate. But rather than write his own broad bill, he shepherded a series of individual measures through his committee and the House floor that addressed Republican energy priorities, with an emphasis on reducing permitting timetables for energy and infrastructure projects.

The committee earlier that month approved a slate of energy and infrastructure bills, 11 in all. One (HR 338), by Rep. Bobby L. Rush, D-Ill., would promote workforce training; others sought to improve energy efficiency in public buildings, while seven would extend the license and construction periods for hydroelectric projects.

Later that month the committee approved more sweeping hydropower promotion legislation (HR 3043) by Rep. Cathy McMorris Rodgers, R-Wash., that would consolidate permitting at the Federal Energy Regulatory Commission and included other provisions to speed up approvals.

The bill won House passage, 257-166, in November.

Walden also took up the decades-long debate over spent nuclear fuel disposal. His panel approved a bill (HR 3053) by Rep. John Shimkus, R-Ill., that would set a timetable to finish the review process of the Yucca Mountain nuclear waste site in Nevada.

The committee in June adopted an amendment sought by Democrats that added provisions to authorize interim storage sites. The bill would not get to the House floor until 2018, where it passed and was sent to the Senate. ∎

Hydropower Efforts Are Accelerated

Legislation to speed up federal approval of hydropower dams, a top goal of lawmakers in the Northwest, got a boost in the House, but final action remained to be determined.

The House on Nov. 8 passed a bill (HR 3043) by Rep. Cathy McMorris Rodgers, R-Wash., that would make the Federal Energy Regulatory Commission the lead agency on permitting of new dams and authorize it to set schedules for interagency reviews.

"Licenses are complex, but there's no excuse for a process to take 10 years," McMorris Rodgers said. "It's time to update the approval process and make hydropower production easier and less costly without sacrificing environmental review."

Hydropower makes up about 10 percent of U.S. electricity output.

The bill would also direct coordination between the federal government, states and tribes earlier in the application process, with the goal of avoiding delays later and allow FERC to extend the duration of preliminary permits and time to begin construction. It would also revamp the trial process used to settle disputes and would identify hydropower as a renewable energy source.

Most Democrats did not back the bill, however. Only 26 Democrats voted for it, amid criticism that it would limit state and tribal input and override state environmental laws.

"We cannot allow hydropower facilities to claim a monopoly over our public waterways without mitigating the negative impacts of these facilities on others who rely on these resources and without complying with modern environmental laws," said Rep. Bobby L. Rush of Illinois, the ranking Democrat on the Energy and Commerce Subcommittee on Energy.

The bill came to the floor after an Energy Department report released on Aug. 28 stressed the importance of hydropower, along with coal, natural gas and nuclear plants to a stable domestic electricity grid. The report noted that just 3 percent of existing U.S. dams generate power.

The bill also came to the floor after Energy and Commerce leaders held talks to try to resolve Democratic concerns, without success. Among the issues was the revision to the dispute resolution trials, which Democrats said would give more power to developers.

"It's like having a baseball game where one side gets to pick the venue, change the rules and have family members serve as umpires," a Democratic aide said.

"Both sides of the aisle support hydropower," Rush said. "We tried to come to a bipartisan consensus at the committee level. Unfortunately, I cannot support HR 3043 in its current form."

Energy and Commerce Chairman Greg Walden, R-Ore., said the bill addresses the top problem for hydropower growth: regulatory hurdles and cost. "The licensing of new hydro facilities and the relicensing of existing facilities is both costly and time-consuming. ... We can do better with the hydropower licensing improvements in this bill," he said.

The talks took place after the full committee approved the bill, as amended, by voice vote on June 28.

House passage set up a waiting game into 2018 for McMorris Rodgers and other House backers. Similar provisions were included in a broad energy policy bill (S 1460) by leaders of the Senate Energy and Natural Resources Committee, but that measure had yet to advance to a markup in early 2018. ∎

Federal Lands Issues Prominent

President Barack Obama's use of executive powers to set aside millions of federal acres for conservation and exert greater oversight on other uses incensed Republicans, led by Western lawmakers, who promptly moved to make it harder for future presidents to designate national monuments.

Their biggest goal was to overhaul the Antiquities Act, a 1906 law that gives the president the authority to designate national monuments. Obama used it the most of any president in naming 26 monuments, encompassing some 550 million onshore and offshore acres.

Republicans also wasted little time in sending President Donald Trump a resolution under the Congressional Review Act to rescind a Bureau of Land Management planning rule finalized in December 2016. Congressional critics said it minimized state and local influence and transferred too much power to the federal government.

That rule, known as "Planning 2.0," was targeted by a resolution of disapproval (H J Res 44), which the Senate cleared for Trump, 51-48, on March 7.

The White House supported the resolution, saying in a Feb. 7 statement of administration policy that the BLM rule "does not adequately serve the state and local communities' interests and could potentially dilute their input in planning decisions."

"Don't let the name fool you: This regulation has little to do with improving current policy," Majority Leader Mitch McConnell, R-Ky., said on the Senate floor. "Instead, it really just represents another power grab rushed through by the Obama administration on its way out the door."

Overhauling the Antiquities Act, however, would not be so easy. Lawmakers worked on a bill (HR 3990) by House Natural Resources Chairman Rob Bishop, R-Utah, but it did not get to the House floor by year's end, and the Senate did not take action.

Bishop sought to advance his bill as the Trump administration considered changes to monument designations made over the previous 20 years, following a six-month review. The administration also conducted a review of the Interior Department's offshore oil leasing five-year plan, which limited exploration to existing areas in the Gulf of Mexico and off the coasts of Alaska.

"If we don't reform the Antiquities Act, we will have a replication of failures," Bishop said in August. "If the procedure is flawed, the product is going to be flawed."

He introduced his bill on Oct. 6. It would require monument designations of greater than 10,000 acres to win approval from the affected states, and would prohibit permanent marine monuments, among other provisions.

Bishop said at an Oct. 11 markup that monument designations were no longer being made for their "scientific or architectural value," but for political purposes and in secret. His bill, he said, would fix that process.

But House Natural Resources ranking member Raúl M. Grijalva, D-Ariz., before the markup criticized the bill as poorly drafted.

"They spend years making threats and repeating industry talking points, and when it's time to produce something all they have is a hastily rushed mess with no real debate," Grijalva said in a statement.

The committee approved the bill by a party-line vote of 23-17. The panel also unfavorably reported, 23-17, a resolution (H Res 555) offered by Grijalva that would force the Trump administration to release information on its monuments review and recommendations, which had not yet been made public.

"We'd like to read the final report," Grijalva said. "We'd like to know who they talked to and what they said."

The Bishop bill would not see further action in 2017, but the committee was back at work in December after Trump announced the results of the Interior Department monuments review.

On Dec. 4, Trump said he would reduce two controversial monuments in Utah by a combined total of about 2 million acres: Bears Ears, designated by Obama, and Grand Staircase-Escalante, designated by President Bill Clinton.

The following day the Interior Department announced a proposal to shrink the Cascade-Siskiyou monument in California and Oregon and the Gold Butte monument in Nevada.

The House Natural Resources Subcommittee on Federal Lands held a hearing Dec. 14 on a bill (HR 4558) by Rep. Chris Stewart, R-Utah, that would codify Trump's changes to the Grand Staircase-Escalante monument and create a national park in its new borders. ∎

Methane Rule Survives Repeal Attempts by Republican Majority

Republicans moved quickly in the 115th Congress to approve more than a dozen resolutions under the Congressional Review Act to rescind Obama administration rules, but one that was intended to help the oil and gas industry could not win enough GOP votes in the Senate to get to President Donald Trump's desk.

Separately, a rider to fiscal 2018 appropriations legislation also fell short.

Both actions came in response to a rule the Obama administration issued in its waning days requiring oil and gas drillers on federal lands to capture methane, a potent greenhouse gas, that would otherwise be released into the atmosphere.

Methane releases were a particular problem in the northern Plains states, where there was a lack of infrastructure to ship captured methane to customers.

The venting and flaring rule, issued by the Bureau of Land Management, was opposed by the oil industry and the Trump administration as a regulatory burden that would largely hit small operators and reduce oil and gas production from federal lands.

Trump ordered the Interior Department in March to rework the rule, even as lawmakers continued with the CRA resolution (H J Res 36), which would have also prevented the Interior Department from proposing a similar rule in the future.

HOUSE ACTION

The House in February passed the resolution, 221-191. Four Democrats voted for it, while 11 Republicans voted against, including a number who have called for action to address climate change.

House Natural Resources Chairman Rob Bishop, R-Utah, the resolution's sponsor, argued that the Interior Department should take different actions to lessen emissions, such as faster pipeline permits that would make it easier for operators to get methane gas to market.

"If BLM was consistent in trying to come up with a reasonable solution, they would cut down on the amount of time it takes for the right-of-way permits to go through so you can capture and move [the methane]," Bishop said. "There are other ways of reaching this solution without going through these specific venting and flaring rules."

Speaker Paul D. Ryan, R-Wis., also reiterated industry arguments that the Interior Department lacked the jurisdiction to curb methane releases, saying air pollution was the responsibility of the EPA.

SENATE SURPRISE

Attention turned to the Senate, where two Republicans — Susan Collins of Maine and Lindsey Graham of South Carolina — made it clear early that they were concerned that the resolution would make it impossible for the government to take future steps to address methane releases.

At the same time, backers of the resolution looked to moderate Senate Democrats Heidi Heitkamp of North Dakota, Joe Manchin III of West Virginia and Joe Donnelly of Indiana to offset Republican defections.

Some Republicans, led by Conference Chairman John Thune of South Dakota, also sought to win a promise that the Senate would consider legislation to allow the year-round sale of higher blends of ethanol in gasoline, before they would let the resolution come to a vote.

They held up action until they won that pledge from Majority Leader Mitch McConnell, R-Ky., setting up a vote on May 10. As the vote neared, Sen. Rob Portman, R-Ohio, said he would back the resolution

after Interior Secretary Ryan Zinke told him the department would look for other ways to reduce methane pollution.

That stance raised new questions about the department's potential options given the restrictions on similar regulations imposed under the Congressional Review Act.

The suspense over the outcome was decided by none other than Sen. John McCain, R-Ariz., who unexpectedly voted against the resolution. Collins, Graham and the moderate Democrats also voted to kill the resolution, and it fell short of the simple majority needed, 49-51.

McCain had his own concerns about future work on the issue.

"I join the call for strong action to reduce pollution from venting, flaring and leaks associated with oil and gas production operations on public and Indian land," he said in a statement. "While I am concerned that the BLM rule may be onerous, passage of the resolution would have prevented the federal government, under any administration, from issuing a rule that is 'similar,' according to the plain reading of the Congressional Review Act."

Resolution sponsor John Barrasso, R-Wyo., the chairman of the Senate Environment and Public Works Committee, declared the effort dead, given a deadline to send the resolution to Trump by May 11.

"The vote was today and I don't expect it to change by tomorrow," he told CQ. "That was the final vote."

House Republicans also moved to prohibit the regulation of methane emissions from oil and gas operations via an amendment to the fiscal 2018 Interior-Environment section of the initial omnibus appropriations bill passed on Sept. 14. The amendment by Rep. Markwayne Mullin, R-Okla., was adopted, 218-195.

"This rule is currently facing litigation and uncertainty, and Congress must act to block this job-killing regulation estimated to cost the U.S. economy $530 million annually," Mullin said on the House floor. "Methane emissions from oil and natural gas have significantly declined in recent decades without multiple, overlapping federal regulations, and this is no exception."

Rep. Betty McCollum, D-Minn., the ranking member of the House Interior-Environment Appropriations Subcommittee, responded that the amendment would be a "step backward" from addressing climate change.

"I would like to point out that the rule will prevent the waste of an estimated 65 billion cubic feet of natural gas a year and save the taxpayers $330 million annually, and that is energy that could be put to work here in the United States," she said.

"The public health risks, including more heat waves and drought, as I talked about, the climate change, the health and welfare of our current and future generations must be taken into account. We must take action; we must do something about this."

The Senate, however, did not include the rider in its draft Interior-Environment spending bill released in November, and it was dropped in the final omnibus bill (PL 115-141) enacted in March 2018.

"While I am disappointed that the Interior and Environment bill continues to be the target for poison-pill riders, I am relieved that, once again, we were able to protect our bedrock environment and conservation laws," Senate Interior-Environment Appropriations ranking member Tom Udall, D-N.M., said about the final bill. ■

Ozone Limit Changes Only Rise So High

The deregulatory agenda of congressional Republicans and the Trump administration extended to fighting stricter federal limits on emissions of ground-level ozone, the primary component of smog.

Bills introduced in both chambers would give states eight more years, until 2025, to comply with the most recent standards set by the EPA in 2015. They would also double the interval between regular reviews to every 10 years.

Only the House version (HR 806) advanced to passage, despite Democratic opposition.

The Senate version (S 263) got a hearing before the Environment and Public Works Subcommittee on Clean Air and Nuclear Safety, but no markup was held.

Ozone limits have been the subject of ongoing debates on Capitol Hill and lawsuits in federal courts. Under the Clean Air Act, areas that exceed the limits must write compliance plans.

Business advocates have argued that the 2015 standards would impose high costs on industrial sources and would be difficult, if not impossible, to meet.

They also stressed that EPA did not issue guidance until early 2015 for states to meet the previous, higher limit of 75 parts per billion set in 2008. The new standard lowers the limit to 70 parts per billion.

EPA Administrator Scott Pruitt in June sought to address those complaints by announcing a one-year delay in the Oct. 1 start date for states to comply with the new standard.

But after environmental groups sued in federal court, and then a coalition of 15 states and the District of Columbia filed its own lawsuit, Pruitt in August reversed course and reinstated the original deadline.

Both bills, sponsored by Rep. Pete Olson, R-Texas, and Sen. Shelley Moore Capito, R-W.Va., respectively, reflected those concerns.

During July 18 House floor debate on the Olson bill, Republicans said public health would still be protected, but without damaging the economy.

"We've learned that timelines and procedures established almost 30 years ago can be counterproductive today, resulting in unnecessary costs, regulatory delay and economic uncertainty," Energy and Commerce Environment Subcommittee Chairman John Shimkus, R-Ill., said. The bill "ensures we will continue to deliver effective environmental protections with reforms that will also help expand economic opportunity in communities around the nation," he said.

Democrats, backed by medical and health organizations, argued that the effectiveness of the nation's chief air pollution law was at stake.

"Plain and simple, the bill before us today would undermine the Clean Air Act as a safeguard of our public health law," said Rep. Paul Tonko, D-N.Y.

The House bill passed, 229-199. Democrats offered an amendment to mandate that the bill's provisions would not go into effect if the

EPA's Clean Air Scientific Advisory Committee found that they would increase health risks for children, pregnant women, senior citizens and others. That amendment was defeated, 194-232.

APPROPRIATIONS RIDER

Republicans also included language in the House fiscal 2018 Interior-Environment appropriations bill that would have imposed a similar

10-year delay on implementation of the tougher ozone standard.

That language was part of the initial omnibus appropriations bill (HR 3354) passed by the House on Sept. 14.

The Senate did not include similar language in its Interior-Environment version, released on Nov. 20, and the House rider was ultimately stripped out of the final omnibus (PL 115-141) sent to President Donald Trump on March 23, 2018. ■

ANWR Is OK'd for Oil, Gas Exploration

The success of Republicans in enacting a tax overhaul in 2017 yielded an unexpected victory for members of the Alaska congressional delegation: the opening of a portion of the Arctic National Wildlife Refuge to oil and gas exploration.

The 1.5 million-acre area, known as the coastal plain, had been set aside for potential development in the 1980 law that created the refuge (PL 96-487), subject to approval by Congress.

That approval had been a goal of Alaska politicians ever since, but it never got past opposition from Democrats and some Republicans in Congress, at the urging of environmental groups who said it would put a pristine natural area at risk and add relatively little to the nation's oil production.

The opening of the refuge, known as ANWR, for energy exploration was debated by lawmakers in 2005 and again in 2008, during a time of high gasoline prices.

Advocates got the upper hand when the fiscal 2018 budget resolution (S Con Res 25) included reconciliation instructions to the Senate Energy and Natural Resources Committee to write legislation to raise

$1 billion in federal revenues over 10 years.

Chairwoman Lisa Murkowski, R-Alaska, advanced draft text through the committee in November to open up the area.

"Our text, as you've seen, is four pages, just 587 words total, but I think it presents a tremendous opportunity for both Alaska and the nation," she said at the markup.

Democrats contended that the language would undercut federal environmental protections. Murkowski disagreed.

"It's pretty clear that's what the intent is, to establish [oil and gas drilling], because you're mandating the leasing and you're mandating the money be in the budget and you're mandating oil production happen, so there's no doubt about that," said ranking member Maria Cantwell, D-Wash.

Senate Republicans prevailed, voting 48-52 to reject a Democratic amendment that would have stripped out the language, and the provision was included in the final version of the tax overhaul (HR 1) cleared for President Donald Trump. ■

Brownfields Program Is Reauthorized

After years of unsuccessful attempts, Congress reauthorized the EPA's brownfields program as part of the fiscal 2018 omnibus appropriations law, reflecting a successful bipartisan push in both chambers.

Action started early in the year, with a bill introduced in the Senate (S 822) on April 4, the same day that the House Energy and Commerce Committee held a hearing on a discussion draft bill.

Both made their way through the committee stage by summer, and the House passed its bill before the end of the year.

The program, which was created by the Comprehensive Environmental Response, Compensation, and Liability Act, also known as Superfund, is popular because it provides remediation grants for properties on which potential toxic contamination prevents their redevelopment. The sites' presence can hurt local economies and local real estate values.

The EPA estimates that there are about 450,000 brownfields nationwide awaiting assessment and possible remediation, and more than 1,300 sites are on the EPA's Superfund national priority list. The program has not been reauthorized since 2006.

The main House reauthorization bill (HR 3017), by Rep. David B. McKinley, R-W.Va., was primarily handled by the Energy and Commerce Committee but was also referred to the Transportation and Infrastructure Committee upon introduction on June 22.

The Transportation panel held its own hearing March 28 on the issue of brownfields reauthorization.

The House draft proposed to expand the program to include petroleum sites where no viable responsible party exists; to publicly owned sites acquired before Jan. 11, 2002; and to nonprofits, community development groups, limited liability corporations and limited partnerships.

It also proposed an increase in the cap on each site's grant from $200,000 to $500,000, with the option to waive the limit and grant up to $750,000 per site.

Rep. Paul Tonko, D-N.Y., and Rep. Frank Pallone Jr., D-N.J., the ranking member of the Energy and Commerce Committee, in late March introduced a bill (HR 1747) to raise the caps and increase the total authorization to $600 million fiscal 2023.

The push for a reauthorization came as the Trump administration

proposed cutting the program by 31 percent in its fiscal 2018 budget request.

"We can't continue to expect the same success from a program that is underfunded and lacking the necessary tools to be effective," Pallone said at the April hearing.

Environment Subcommittee Chairman John Shimkus, R-Ill., cautioned against seeking a large increase. "Everybody always wants more money," he said. "And the leveraging is great ... if the federal government got a return on that — not that I'm proposing that," he said. "We've got to be smart in what we're asking for."

Reflecting bipartisan backing, the Energy and Commerce Committee approved McKinley's bill by voice vote on June 28, with language to authorize $250 million annually through fiscal 2022, unchanged from existing levels.

The day before, the Transportation and Infrastructure Committee approved by voice vote a brownfields bill (HR 1758) by Rep. Elizabeth Esty, D-Conn., as amended. Her bill would also set a $250 million annual authorization and raise the per-site cap to $600,000, with an option to raise that to $950,000 by waiver.

The Transportation panel discharged the McKinley bill on Nov. 9, and it won easy passage on the floor, 409-8, on Nov. 30. The final bill raised the cap on grants to sites to $500,000.

"The EPA brownfields program is critical to states and local communities as they address contaminated industrial and commercial properties and return them to productive use," Shimkus said in floor debate. "Cleaning up these sites is great for the economy because brownfields grants can be directly leveraged into jobs, additional redevelopment funds, and increased residential and commercial property values."

Pallone also praised the bill, though he called it a compromise that did not include the level of funding he wanted.

SENATE LEGISLATION AND OMNIBUS

The Senate bill by Sen. James M. Inhofe, R-Okla., also had bipartisan backing. The Environment and Public Works Committee approved it, as amended, by voice vote on July 12.

"We worked very hard on the brownfields bill last year and it was then stopped over in the House, and we have an even better product this year that really is going to provide a capacity to clean up all of these contaminated sites, not just in Massachusetts but all across the country," Sen. Edward J. Markey, D-Mass., said at the markup.

The bill would reauthorize the brownfields program through 2020 at $250 million annually and also raised the cap to $500,000 per site, with exceptions to $650,000.

It did not get a floor vote, but it was incorporated, along with provisions of the McKinley bill, in the final omnibus law (PL 115-141) cleared for President Donald Trump on March 23.

The law set the reauthorization through 2023 and the cap at $500,000, with exceptions for up to $650,000. ∎

Yucca Mountain Proponents Advance Policy Bill; Spending Push Falls Short

The decades-long dispute over the final destination of the nation's spent nuclear fuel stockpile and the Yucca Mountain nuclear waste repository in Nevada again defied a solution in 2017, though a compromise bill advanced out of the House Energy and Commerce Committee with Democratic support.

The Trump administration made it clear early in the year through its fiscal 2018 budget request that it backed the licensing of the controversial Yucca project, which the Obama administration had suspended.

That action, in 2010, was based on opposition from leading politicians in Nevada and the state's congressional delegation. Former Senate Majority Leader Harry Reid, D-Nev., had long vowed to stop the opening of the repository.

Opposition in the state did not wane in the years since, so it was no surprise when Gov. Brian Sandoval, a Republican, and the state's lawmakers in Congress quickly came out against a Yucca discussion draft from Energy and Commerce Environment Subcommittee Chairman John Shimkus, R-Ill., released in April. They said the draft's new infrastructure incentives for the state were uncertain, among other concerns.

In a letter to lawmakers, Sandoval called the measure "fundamentally flawed" and said the incentives "are simply false promises that cannot be guaranteed or enforced."

"My position, and that of the state of Nevada, remains identical to my previous letters to this committee in May 2015, January 2016 and

April 2016: the State of Nevada opposes the project based on scientific, technical and legal merits," Sandoval wrote.

The inclusion of language that would authorize temporary storage facilities for spent fuel, to help speed up its removal from existing and closed nuclear power plants, helped the draft bill win approval from the Environment Subcommittee by voice vote, though not without some Democratic concerns.

"We have jacked around with nuclear waste storage in this country literally for almost 40 years, and we finally have a bipartisan solution — at least it sounds like it," Rep. Joe L. Barton, R-Texas, said. "That is a nontrivial accomplishment."

Just days later, Energy Secretary Rick Perry told the House Energy-Water Appropriations Subcommittee that his department would make the disposal of nuclear waste a priority, whether at a permanent repository or with interim sites. The department's budget proposal included $120 million to restart the Yucca license review at the Nuclear Regulatory Commission.

"We have a moral and national security obligation to come up with a long-term solution, finding the safest repositories available," Perry said. "I understand this is a politically sensitive topic for some, but we can no longer kick the can down the road."

On June 28, the full Energy and Commerce Committee approved the Shimkus bill (HR 3053) by a vote of 49-4, after adding language by Shimkus and Rep. Doris Matsui, D-Calif., that would, among

other provisions, authorize temporary storage at other sites and authorize a pilot Energy Department site, with an authorization of $150 million.

Their amendment also would restore Nevada's air and water pollution permitting authority for the Yucca site, extend the site approval process by a year and expand the total Yucca storage from 70,000 metric tons to 110,000 metric tons. Shimkus said the expansion would ensure that no second permanent repository would be needed.

"Let me be clear, this amendment does not remove the federal government's obligation to fulfill its responsibilities to the ratepayers to get an answer from an independent regulator whether the Yucca Mountain meets all the requirements to serve as a permanent repository," Shimkus said of the compromise.

Matsui praised a provision that would prioritize interim storage for shuttered reactors.

"While I still feel the language is not perfect, I am pleased it provides a light at the end of the tunnel for facilities like Rancho Seco Nuclear Plant that has stored waste onsite for decades," she said. "There are approximately 20 sites [with] similarly situated decommissioned plants across the country. ... They will all be in a better situation to dispose of their spent fuel."

SENATE INACTION

Meanwhile, the Senate did not take up Yucca-related legislation. Senate Energy and Natural Resources Chairwoman Lisa Murkowski, R-Alaska, wrote a bipartisan energy policy bill with ranking member Maria Cantwell, D-Wash., that did not take on nuclear waste storage.

Murkowski said the issue was better addressed through the annual appropriations process, in light of the Trump administration's budget request.

For project backers, that route ended up at a dead end. The House included Trump's request for $120 million in its draft fiscal 2018 omnibus spending bill, but the Senate included just $35 million for interim storage in its spending legislation and none for Yucca.

The final fiscal 2018 omnibus spending bill (PL 115-141), enacted in March 2018, left out both of the House and Senate allocations.

Because of committee jurisdictional issues, the Shimkus policy bill would not get action in 2017. House GOP leaders ultimately brought it to the floor in May 2018, where it passed, 340-72. ∎

Chapter 9

EXECUTIVE BRANCH

Trump Has a Tumultuous First Year

President Donald Trump's tumultuous first year in office included major legislative victories and defeats, an unprecedented revolving door for White House staff, and the launch of an investigation that could potentially threaten the survival of his administration.

The new president's inauguration was perhaps emblematic of the entire first year — marked by historic protests in the streets of Washington and a dispute regarding the size of the crowd that attended the festivities.

In his inaugural address, Trump echoed a familiar theme from his campaign: "We assembled here today are issuing a new decree to be heard in every city, and in every foreign capital and in every hall of power," Trump said. "From this day forward, a new vision will govern our land; from this day forward, it's going to be only America first! America first!"

Shortly after the address, the president signed his first bill into law, a measure that allowed retired Gen. James Mattis to serve as Defense secretary by waiving the legal requirement that he be out of the military for seven years before taking the civilian post.

Inside the White House, Reince Priebus, a leading voice for the GOP establishment in the administration, became chief of staff, although his tenure would be brief. Little more than six months into the Trump era, Priebus was replaced by Homeland Security Secretary John F. Kelly, who proved to be a much more confrontational presence than the former chairman of the Republican National Committee. It was the beginning of an unusually high amount of staff turnover in the administration.

Priebus' position was suspect from the start, in large part because he was meant to be an "equal partner" with Steve Bannon, Trump's campaign CEO who was named chief strategist and senior counselor to the president — although the statement that announced the appointments listed Bannon's name first.

For his part, Bannon lasted just barely longer than Priebus, departing in mid-August after a week in which the president was widely rebuked by Republicans as well as Democrats for his reaction to the deadly violence at a white supremacist rally in Charlottesville, Va.

Deputy Chief of Staff Katie Walsh lasted a little more than two months, departing on March 30. Two months later, communications director Mike Dubke left, to be replaced by Wall Street financier Anthony Scaramucci, who was allowed to bypass Priebus and report directly to the president.

Scaramucci's arrival led to the July 21 resignation of press secretary Sean Spicer. Scaramucci himself lasted less than two weeks, resigning July 31 in the wake of Kelly's ascendancy to chief of staff. That was

shorter even than the tenure of Trump's first national security advisor, Michael Flynn, who lasted just 24 days amid controversy over his contacts with Russian officials, about which he later pleaded guilty of lying to the FBI.

But one constant was family. As bodies came and went around them, the president's daughter Ivanka Trump and son-in-law Jared Kushner sustained and even enhanced their leading, unofficial roles as advisers to the president.

But during Trump's first 100 days, he moved from hard-liner-in-chief to vacillator-in-chief, a not unsurprising development given his vague, detail-free and often contradictory promises during the campaign. Despite the inconsistent rhetoric and head-scratching pivots, a series of policy pronouncements made clear that what one analyst termed the "fundamental contradiction of being both a fire-breathing absolutist and a non-ideological deal-maker" was going to result in a more-or-less standard array of conservative outcomes.

FIRST 100 DAYS

Amid all the personnel churn, there was plenty of policy turmoil as well in an eventful and turbulent first 100 days.

One week after taking office, Trump signed an executive order imposing a 90-day ban on entry into the United States by citizens from Iran, Iraq, Libya, Somalia, Sudan, Syria and Yemen, and halting relocation to the U.S. of refugees from Syria. Within days, multiple district court judges had blocked the order from being carried out, and acting Attorney General Sally Yates was fired Jan. 31 for refusing to enforce the ban. Two days after firing Yates, the administration eased some of the restrictions for green card holders, and on Feb. 16 Trump said he would issue a new order to respond to judicial concerns. That order was released March 6. It excised Iraq from the list of affected countries but failed to satisfy several judges, who continued to block its implementation. The cases would continue to be debated in court throughout the year.

On the last day of January, the president nominated Neil Gorsuch to fill the Supreme Court seat that Senate Republicans had held open for nearly the entire final year of Barack Obama's presidency. Senate Democrats would spend most of the next two months mulling whether they should try to filibuster the nominee.

In the end they did — and Senate Republicans responded by changing Senate rules to eliminate the filibuster for Supreme Court nominees. (The Democrats had already nixed filibusters of lower court nominees in 2013.) Gorsuch was confirmed by a mostly party-line vote of 54-45 on April 7.

Beyond the Gorsuch confirmation, Trump's biggest achievement in

the first 100 days combined executive and legislative action to rescind Obama-era regulations.

Congress used the seldom-employed Congressional Review Act (PL 104-121) to terminate 14 regulations finalized during the final months of the Obama administration, serving as early fulfillment of Trump's campaign promise to reduce government regulations. Marc Short, the administration's legislative affairs chief, said eliminating the rules would save $10 billion over 20 years.

Republicans were successful in 14 of 15 attempts, failing only to roll back a methane emissions rule that makes it harder and more expensive to develop oil and gas on federal lands. Sen. John McCain, R-Ariz., sided with Democrats in voting against the repeal.

In March, Trump issued an executive order that asked federal departments and agencies to come up with plans to restructure operations and streamline programs, with an eye toward delivering government services more efficiently and cutting spending. But both Congress and the administration were looking for ways to expand use of the CRA beyond the rather limited scope that allows targeting of late-stage rules from the previous administration.

BEYOND 100 DAYS

On May 18, Deputy Attorney General Rod J. Rosenstein appointed a special counsel — Robert S. Mueller III, who served as FBI director from 2001 to 2013 — to investigate "any links and/or coordination between the Russian government" and the Trump campaign, as well as "any matters that arose or may arise directly from the investigation."

The investigation would go on to yield several indictments and convictions of both Russians and Trump staffers, and it would still be going strong into 2018.

On June 1, the president announced that the United States would withdraw from the Paris climate agreement. The move was greeted with strong condemnation from Democrats and environmentalists, some of whom had previously complained that the accord was not strong enough.

Elsewhere on the foreign affairs front, in August the president threatened "fire and fury" for North Korea after a news report cited a U.S. intelligence assessment that North Korea had produced a miniaturized nuclear warhead that could be carried by missiles, expanding the range of the country's nuclear weapons arsenal.

A little more than a month later, Trump called North Korean leader Kim Jong Un "rocket man" during a Sept. 19 speech at the United Nations and said the U.S. would "totally destroy North Korea" in the event of an attack by the communist government on democratic South Korea or any other ally.

As much controversy as that speech stirred, it probably was less incendiary than Trump's impromptu remarks following race-fueled clashes in Charlottesville, Va., that involved white supremacists, neo-Nazis and members of the Ku Klux Klan squaring off against anti-fascist militants and a larger contingent of peaceful protesters supporting the planned removal of a statute of Confederate Gen. Robert E. Lee.

After a formal statement in which he called the KKK, neo-Nazis and white supremacist groups "criminals and thugs," Trump followed up the next day by saying there was "blame on both sides" — referring to the "bad" white supremacists and the "very violent" antifa activists who confronted them — and that there were "very fine people" on both sides.

His remarks led to a firestorm of criticism from Democrats and Republicans.

GOP Rep. Ileana Ros-Lehtinen of Florida said placing blame on both sides meant the president had moved "back to relativism when dealing with KKK, Nazi sympathizers, white supremacists? Just no."

Hawaii Democratic Sen. Brian Schatz cited his own Jewish heritage and said of Trump: "Not my president." He added that "words cannot express my disgust and disappointment."

As if to put an exclamation point on the month of August, on the 25th the president pardoned former Maricopa County Sheriff Joe Arpaio, who had been convicted of contempt of court and was awaiting sentencing. Arpaio was a lightning rod for immigration issues when he served as sheriff of Arizona's largest county, gaining a national reputation for his controversial methods of cracking down on illegal immigration and incarcerating immigrants in outdoor camps under harsh conditions. The pardon may have had little practical effect on whether the 85-year-old Arpaio spent much if any time in jail, but it did clear the way for Arpaio to run for the U.S. Senate.

POLICY BATTLES

It was in the traditional legislative arena of Congress where Trump made the least progress, most spectacularly in the failure to fulfill the eight-year-old Republican promise to repeal the 2010 health care law (PL 111-148, PL 111-152) commonly known as Obamacare.

While the inability to pass health care legislation was largely a result of a fractured Republican caucus on the Hill — Deputy House Whip Tom Cole, R-Okla., said Trump "did everything he could" to pass a bill — responsibility for other priorities that fell by the wayside lay squarely in the executive branch.

On Sept. 5, Attorney General Jeff Sessions announced that the administration was ending the Deferred Action for Childhood Arrivals (DACA) program created by executive order by President Barack Obama. Like the travel ban earlier in the year, this was a campaign promise officially met, but it faced multiple legal hurdles and not much in the way of help from Capitol Hill. Trump said the move gave lawmakers six months to find a solution, but congressional efforts to reach an agreement with the administration on the issue went nowhere.

That was pretty much the fate of the president's plans to cut spending, as well.

OMB Director Mick Mulvaney submitted a "skinny budget" in March that provided the barest of outlines for a spending plan, then presented a full budget proposal in May that Congress promptly ignored. By year's end, the government had gone through two shutdown scares and was still operating on a continuing resolution to fund the government. But a budget deal, agreed to in September, at least cleared the way for the administration's biggest win of 2017, an overhaul of the tax system.

Tax cuts were a GOP congressional priority from the start, although it took a while to get going while lawmakers spent much of the summer trying and failing to repeal the health care law.

It took until nearly Christmas for Congress to pass the final tax bill (PL 115-97). That version, which Trump called "so large and so meaningful," made the most significant changes to the tax code in decades. The measure, which passed both chambers with little to no Democratic support, cut rates across the board, nearly doubled the standard deduction and the child tax credit and capped deductions for state income taxes.

The tax bill also accomplished one thing the multiple versions of an Obamacare repeal could not — it got rid of the penalty for not having health insurance coverage, beginning in 2019. ∎

How the President Filled His Cabinet

For all his campaign talk of "draining the swamp" and setting a new tone in Washington, President Donald Trump's Cabinet picks looked a lot like those made by other presidents — with the possible exception that they were considerably more white and male than those of his immediate predecessors.

AGRICULTURE

Former Georgia Gov. Sonny Perdue was among the last Cabinet-level nominees to be tapped, on Jan. 18. At a chummy Senate Agriculture Committee hearing on March 23, lawmakers focused their concerns on trade issues, largely because Trump had promised during the campaign to get tough with U.S. trading partners, including possibly imposing tariffs. Perdue said he would be an advocate for agricultural exports within the administration.

"I plan to be onsite as USDA's chief salesman around the world, to sell these products, to negotiate these deals side by side with USTR, side by side with [Commerce] Secretary Ross and our whole team there [the administration]," he told the committee.

The panel approved Perdue's nomination by voice vote March 30, although Sen. Kirsten Gillibrand, D-N.Y., who made a point of opposing every Trump Cabinet nominee in committee and on the floor, insisted that her opposition be noted, although she did not insist on a recorded vote. In an unusual twist, Perdue's first cousin and former business partner, Sen. David Perdue, R-Ga., did not vote, citing his relationship with the nominee.

Perdue was confirmed by the full Senate on April 24 by a vote of 87-11, one of the wider margins for any of Trump's nominees.

COMMERCE

Wilbur Ross, a billionaire financier, former steel industry executive and, like the president, frequent critic of the North American Free Trade Agreement, was nominated to serve as Commerce secretary on Nov. 30, 2016. Ross ran the private equity firm W.L. Ross & Co. and previously worked with Trump to restructure debt for the Trump Taj Mahal casino and hotel in Atlantic City, N.J.

The Senate Commerce, Science and Transportation Committee approved Ross' nomination by voice vote on Jan. 24, six days after a relatively uneventful confirmation hearing. Ross' backing by the United Steelworkers union dampened any serious Democratic opposition. Ross had won plaudits from the union for his revival of Bethlehem Steel, LTV Steel and Weirton Steel — the combined company, International Steel Group, grew to become the country's biggest steelmaker before it was sold to Mittal Steel in 2005.

Ross was confirmed on Feb. 27 by a vote of 72-27.

DEFENSE

Marine Corps Gen. James Mattis was tapped Dec. 1, 2016, to serve as secretary of Defense. But before he could assume office he had to clear a higher hurdle than simply the Senate confirmation faced by other Cabinet officials — Congress had to pass a bill to create a special exemption from a law that prohibits former military officers from leading the Defense Department within seven years of having served on active duty. Mattis retired only four years earlier, in 2013.

It was not a slam dunk. The House Armed Services Committee broke along party lines, 34-28, to approve the measure, although the vote in the Senate panel was a more comfortable 24-3. The full Senate passed it, 81-17, on Jan. 13, and the House cleared it hours later, 268-151. It was the first bill Trump signed into law.

At his confirmation hearing on Jan. 12, Mattis took issue with Trump's suggestion that he would order U.S. forces to kill terrorists' families. In his written responses to Armed Services Committee questions, Mattis wrote, "The killing of non-combatants in a war against a non-state enemy violates Common Article 3 the Geneva Conventions. Legal questions aside, it is my view that such actions would be self-defeating and a betrayal of our ideals."

The panel approved Mattis' nomination on Jan. 18 by a vote of 26-1, with Gillibrand the lone "no" vote. He was confirmed on Inauguration Day, 98-1, again with the New Yorker casting the lone dissenting vote.

ENERGY

Former Texas Gov. Rick Perry, briefly a rival of Trump's in the 2016 Republican presidential contest, was picked on Dec. 14, 2016, to lead the Energy Department, a federal agency he had once suggested should be eliminated.

That suggestion came up at his confirmation hearing on Jan. 19. He told the Senate Energy and Natural Resources panel that he regretted espousing the idea.

"My past statements made over five years ago about abolishing the Department of Energy do not reflect my current thinking," Perry said. "In fact, after being briefed on so many of the vital functions of the Department of Energy, I regret recommending its elimination."

Perry mollified some members concerned with Trump's stance on global warming, endorsing the idea that human activity is a contributor to climate change. "I believe the climate is changing. I believe some of it is naturally occurring, but some of it is also caused by man-made activity. The question is how do we address it in a thoughtful way that doesn't compromise economic growth, the affordability of energy or American jobs."

The committee approved the nomination, 16-7, on Jan. 31, and the Senate confirmed him, 62-37, on March 2. Among the Democrats voting to confirm Perry was Nevada Sen. Catherine Cortez Masto, who said she thinks he will help her prevent the designation of Nevada's Yucca Mountain as a permanent nuclear waste repository.

EDUCATION

Perhaps no Trump Cabinet nominee roused more vocal opposition than Betsy DeVos, nominated on Nov. 23, 2016, to be Education secretary. A prominent supporter of charter schools, school vouchers and alternatives to public school, DeVos is also a wealthy philanthropist, prominent Republican donor and former chairwoman of the Michigan Republican Party. Her Jan. 31 appearance before the Senate Health, Education, Labor and Pensions Committee drew protesters inside and outside the hearing room.

In addition to dealing with criticisms based on her policy preferences and her lack of experience, The Washington Post reported that DeVos had appeared to commit plagiarism on some of the answers

she submitted to the committee. Sen. Patty Murray, D-Wash., said the answers to committee questions appeared to be "copied and pasted from previous statements, or are simple reiterations of the law and not true responses at all." The panel divided strictly along partisan lines, moving the nomination to the floor by a vote of 12-11.

The division was just as close when the Senate voted on Feb. 7. For the first time in history, the vice president, Mike Pence, was needed to break a tie on a Cabinet nomination. DeVos was confirmed, 51-50, with Republicans Lisa Murkowski of Alaska and Susan Collins of Maine joining with Democrats in opposition. Both cited what they called DeVos' lack of qualifications for the job. Other Republicans countered that she was just the kind of outsider the Education Department needed to challenge the Washington status quo and the Democrat-dominated education establishment.

HEALTH AND HUMAN SERVICES

Rep. Tom Price of Georgia, an orthopedic surgeon and member of the House Republican leadership, was nominated Nov. 29, 2016, to lead the largest civilian department in the federal government.

Controversy swirled around Price's trading of medical industry stocks, and he quickly agreed to divest his holdings in more than 40 companies while denying that he had received or profited from non-public information about any of the companies.

Price endured two Senate hearings — Jan. 18 in front of the Health, Education, Labor and Pensions Committee, and Jan. 24 before the Finance Committee. Finance approved the nomination, 14-0, on Feb. 1. Only Republicans participated in the vote, after the majority amended the committee rules because Democrats boycotted the vote as part of a broad effort to slow confirmation of Trump's nominees.

To further slow things down, Democrats on Feb. 2 forced a vote on a motion to proceed, which was agreed to, 51-48. Price was confirmed Feb. 10 by a party-line vote of 52-47.

But Price's tenure was brief. On Sept. 22, the HHS inspector general's office announced that it would investigate Price's use of private planes for official department business. Six days later, Price said he would stop the practice of using taxpayer-funded private charter flights and that he would reimburse the government for costs he had already racked up. The next day, he resigned.

It took a month and a half for Trump to name a successor. Alex Azar, a drug company executive who had previously served as general counsel and deputy secretary of HHS from 2001 to 2007 and as a clerk for Supreme Court Justice Antonin Scalia, was nominated Nov. 13. The Senate HELP panel quickly held its confirmation hearing, but the Finance Committee's hearing was delayed until 2018.

HOMELAND SECURITY

Retired Marine Corps Gen. John F. Kelly, who served four decades in the military, including seeing combat in Iraq, and closed out his career as commander of the U.S. Southern Command, was nominated Dec. 12, 2016, to lead the Department of Homeland Security.

At his Jan. 10 Senate Homeland Security and Governmental Affairs Committee hearing, Kelly, like Mattis, took issue with several positions laid out by his future boss. While he agreed with Trump's proposal to build a wall on the southern border, he offered different perspectives on issues such as immigration from majority-Muslim countries and the use of "enhanced interrogation techniques" that qualified as torture to extract information from terrorism suspects.

Kelly was confirmed by an 88-11 vote on Inauguration Day.

Kelly served until late July, when Trump named him to replace White House Chief of Staff Reince Priebus.

Kirstjen Nielsen, a top aide to Kelly who had served as his chief of staff at DHS, was announced Oct. 11 as the president's nominee to replace her old boss as Homeland Security secretary. Nielsen was the first nominee to lead DHS to have previously worked at the department.

Nielsen was seen as Kelly's enforcer but had been in her White House job for only a month when tapped to lead Homeland Security. She had previously served as a Senate aide to Republican Connie Mack of Florida and as special assistant on the White House Homeland Security Council in the George W. Bush administration. Previously, she had managed legislative affairs at the Transportation Security Administration.

In the private sector, Nielsen had worked as a lawyer advising companies looking to enter the homeland security market and chaired the World Economic Forum's council on risk.

At her Nov. 8 confirmation hearing, her tone and style echoed Kelly's with direct, blunt answers. When Sen. Claire McCaskill of Missouri, the ranking Democrat on the Homeland Security and Governmental Affairs Committee, asked if she agreed that a 2,000-mile border wall was not necessary to achieve border security, Nielsen was succinct: "Yes, ma'am."

The committee approved her nomination Nov. 1 by a vote of 11-4, and she was confirmed Dec. 5 by a vote of 62-37.

HOUSING AND URBAN DEVELOPMENT

Dr. Ben Carson, another former Trump opponent in the GOP presidential contest, was nominated Dec. 5, 2016, to be secretary of Housing and Urban Development.

Carson was a renowned neurosurgeon who served as director of pediatric neurosurgery at Johns Hopkins University Hospital. But he had never held public office and lacked any obvious qualifications for the HUD job, a point Democrats hammered home at his Senate Banking, Housing, and Urban Affairs Committee confirmation hearing on Jan. 11. They also noted his lack of experience in government and in running a bureaucracy as large as HUD, which has a roughly $50 billion budget and more than 8,000 employees.

Carson responded that brains and hard work would make up for his lack of experience. "A good CEO doesn't necessarily know everything about the business," he told the panel. "But he knows how to pick those people and how to use them."

The committee approved Carson's nomination by voice vote on Jan. 24, and the full Senate confirmed him, 58-41, on March 2, a day after voting 62-37 to cut off debate.

INTERIOR

One-term Rep. Ryan Zinke, R-Mont., was tapped on Dec. 15, 2016, to be Interior secretary. Zinke studied geology at the University of Oregon and spent more than two decades as a Navy SEAL before entering politics as a self-described Theodore Roosevelt Republican.

Democrats voiced their usual concerns about environmental issues at the Senate Energy and Natural Resources Committee hearing on Jan. 17. But there was little real resistance to Zinke. His stated goal of keeping public lands in federal hands made him a palatable choice to most Democrats.

The committee approved the nomination, 16-6, on Jan. 31. After a 67-31 vote to invoke cloture and limit debate on Feb. 27, Zinke was confirmed March 1 by a vote of 68-31.

JUSTICE

Alabama Sen. Jeff Sessions, one of the earliest converts among senior elected Republicans to the candidacy of Donald Trump, was rewarded Nov. 18, 2016, with a nomination to serve as attorney general.

Despite his 20 years in the Senate, Democratic colleagues lashed into Sessions in much the same way senators did in 1986, when charges of racism cost him a federal judgeship. (Sessions at the time labeled the accusations "damnably false.") At his Jan. 10 confirmation hearing before the Judiciary Committee, protesters chanted, "No Trump, no KKK, no fascist USA." Ranking Democrat Dianne Feinstein of California said she had "deep anxiety" about the implications for minorities with Sessions as attorney general and Trump in the White House. "Communities across this country are concerned about whether they will be able to rely on the Department of Justice to protect their rights and freedoms," Feinstein said. Sessions said he would follow the law.

The committee moved the nomination to the Senate floor on Feb. 1 by a party-line vote of 11-9. Once floor debate began, on Feb. 7 Senate Majority Leader Mitch McConnell, R-Ky., and Sen. Elizabeth Warren, D-Mass., clashed when Warren tried to read into the record a 1986 letter by Coretta Scott King, widow of the Rev. Martin Luther King Jr., opposing Sessions' nomination to the federal judgeship. McConnell accused Warren of violating Senate rules by impugning a fellow member.

After Warren's time had expired, McConnell objected to her request that she be allowed to continue. After some procedural maneuvering, the Senate voted 49-43 along party lines to uphold the ruling of the chair that Warren had violated Senate rules. The Senate then rejected on a party-line vote of 43-50 a Democratic motion that Warren be allowed to speak. She was not permitted to speak for the remainder of the confirmation debate.

Later that evening, Sessions was confirmed, 52-47, also along party lines.

LABOR

Alexander Acosta, the dean of Florida International University's law program, was selected by Trump as Labor secretary on Feb. 16, the first Hispanic to be nominated by Trump. The decision came less than a day after his initial choice for the position, Andy Puzder, withdrew from consideration. The fast-food CEO had lost the support of GOP senators after a string of unfavorable news stories, including one that reported he had employed a housekeeper not authorized to work in the country.

In addition to having served as a National Labor Relations Board member, Acosta previously was assistant attorney general for civil rights in the Justice Department under President George W. Bush. In 2006, the Senate confirmed him by voice vote as U.S. attorney for the Southern District of Florida.

Some Democrats voiced concerns that Acosta would not protect workers' rights, that he could be too easily swayed by political pressure and that he was too aligned with Trump's priorities. "Acosta demonstrated neither a willingness nor an interest in challenging the budget or the president's priorities, stressing that his soon-to-be boss guides the ship," said Sen. Richard Blumenthal, D-Conn. "I find that view and perspective alarming."

After a two-day hearing before the HELP Committee on March 21-22, the panel approved the nomination by a party-line vote of 12-11 on March 30.

It took a 61-39 vote April 25 to invoke cloture to move the nomination to the Senate floor. Two days later he was confirmed, 60-38.

STATE

In one of his more outside-the-box choices, Trump picked Exxon Mobil CEO Rex Tillerson to lead the State Department.

Tillerson's Jan. 11 Foreign Relations Committee hearing revealed several differences between the nominee and the president. As Energy Secretary-designate Rick Perry had done, Tillerson said he believes climate change is occurring and humans are playing a role — but also said he would defer to the president's decision about how to address the issue.

Democrats seized on Tillerson's ties to Russian President Vladimir Putin and autocrats in other oil-rich nations, as part of his work for energy giant Exxon. And several heavyweights on the Republican side of the aisle, including Sens. John McCain of Arizona, Lindsey Graham of South Carolina and Marco Rubio of Florida, expressed reservations about his stance on U.S.-Russia relations. Despite those concerns, the committee approved Tillerson's nomination by an 11-10 party-line vote. Floor consideration required a 56-43 cloture vote on Jan. 30 before he was confirmed by the same vote margin on Feb. 1.

TRANSPORTATION

Elaine Chao, a veteran of the confirmation process, was nominated Nov. 29, 2016, to serve as Transportation secretary. The wife of Senate Majority Leader Mitch McConnell, R-Ky., Chao previously served as Labor secretary and Peace Corps director under President George W. Bush.

The Commerce, Science and Transportation Committee's confirmation hearing stirred little controversy. Trump's campaign promise to pump up to $1 trillion into infrastructure was as popular with Democrats as any proposal he made, although the accompanying reductions in regulations to hasten construction and pursue more private financing were not. Chao was expected to play a key role in laying out the nuts and bolts of the plan and said she would form an advisory task force to figure out what the plan would address and how it would be funded.

The committee approved her nomination by voice vote on Jan. 24, and the Senate confirmed her, 93-6, on Jan. 31.

TREASURY

Steve Mnuchin, an investment banker at Goldman Sachs who also gained some notoriety as a Hollywood producer of such films as "Mad Max: Fury Road" and "Suicide Squad" — and as the husband of outspoken model and actress Louise Linton — was named on Nov. 30, 2016, as Trump's choice for Treasury secretary.

At his Jan. 19 confirmation hearing before the Senate Finance Committee, Mnuchin faced tough questions about his tenure at OneWest, a bank that foreclosed on thousands of homes during the housing crisis. "Since I was first nominated to serve as Treasury secretary, I have been maligned as taking advantage of others' hardships in order to earn a buck. Nothing could be further from the truth," he told the committee. Mnuchin said he and others at OneWest had "worked diligently" to help homeowners stay in their houses, extending more than 100,000 loan modifications to people behind on their mortgage payments.

Sen. Elizabeth Warren of Massachusetts and more than 20 other Democratic senators had urged Finance Chairman Orrin G. Hatch, R-Utah, to weigh the foreclosure stories and questioned whether Mnuchin would be able to help "spot and stop the next financial crisis — rather than profiting from it" in his role at Treasury and as the next chairman of the Financial Stability Oversight Council. Senate Minority Leader Charles E. Schumer, D-N.Y., lumped Mnuchin in with a handful of other Trump nominees as members of a "swamp Cabinet, filled with billionaires and bankers that have conflicts of interest and ethical

lapses as far as the eye can see."

At the hearing, Hatch defended the nominee. "No one has credibly alleged that any laws, regulations or industry standards were violated by companies run by Mr. Mnuchin," he said.

On Feb. 1 the committee suspended a rule requiring members of both parties to be present for a vote after Democrats boycotted, and Mnuchin was approved, 14-0. He was confirmed Feb. 13 by a vote of 53-47.

VETERANS AFFAIRS

After a protracted search for a Veterans Affairs secretary, Trump on Jan. 11 nominated David Shulkin, President Barack Obama's VA undersecretary in charge of the Veterans Health Administration.

An internist with 30 years of experience in the hospital industry, Shulkin was the first VA secretary who was not a military veteran. He was also arguably the least contentious of Trump's Cabinet nominees.

The Senate Veterans Affairs Committee held his confirmation hearing on Feb. 1, just three weeks after his nomination. His nomination was approved, 15-0, six days later, and he was confirmed by a unanimous vote of 100-0 on Feb. 13.

EPA

In a move enthusiastically hailed by supporters and loudly decried by detractors, Trump on Dec. 7, 2016, tapped Oklahoma Attorney General Scott Pruitt to be administrator of the EPA, an agency Pruitt had frequently tangled with in court.

At his Jan. 18 confirmation hearing before the Environment and Public Works Committee, Pruitt said he believes the climate is changing and human activity has some impact on it, but he questioned the extent of that impact. At the same time, he said that while he would return most of the authority to regulate clean air and the environment to the states, he believed it was the EPA's responsibility to regulate carbon emissions and told lawmakers he would keep the agency's endangerment finding that the greenhouse gas poses risks to the environment and public health.

"The states are not mere vessels of federal will," Pruitt said. "It matters that the states participate in the way that Congress has directed, and they haven't been able to do so for a number of years."

In response to Democratic demands that he recuse himself from issues over which he had sued the agency as state attorney general — including EPA regulations like the Clean Power Plan, the Clean Water Rule and the Mercury and Air Toxics Standards rule — Pruitt said the agency would judge those instances on a case-by-case basis.

Despite the emotional issues involved, the hearing included few fireworks. But outside the hearing room, environmental advocates and Native American tribal demonstrators got into confrontations with Capitol Police trying to keep them from breaking into the room, while coal miners from West Virginia spent most of the day outside the hearing to show support for Pruitt, who they hoped would help revive their industry.

Democrats boycotted the committee vote, so Republicans moved Pruitt's nomination forward, 11-0, on Feb. 2. He was confirmed by a party-line vote of 52-46 on Feb. 17.

UNITED NATIONS

Nikki Haley, the Republican governor of South Carolina who had little formal experience in foreign relations, was nominated Nov. 23, 2016, to be the U.S. ambassador to the United Nations.

Haley, the first Indian-American chosen to represent the United States at the 193-member United Nations, impressed both Democrats and Republicans during her Jan. 18 confirmation hearing before the Senate Foreign Relations Committee when she firmly supported human rights and international organizations such as NATO.

"She doesn't have substantive foreign policy experience, but I think she has moral fiber," said Sen. Robert Menendez of New Jersey, the ranking Democrat on the committee, noting her call to remove the Confederate flag from the South Carolina capitol in 2015.

The committee approved the nomination by voice vote on Jan. 24, with Democrats Chris Coons of Delaware and Tom Udall of New Mexico registering opposition. She was confirmed, 96-4, later that same day.

OFFICE OF MANAGEMENT AND BUDGET

South Carolina GOP Rep. Mick Mulvaney, a noted fiscal hawk, was nominated Dec. 16, 2016, to be director of the Office of Management and Budget.

Facing two confirmation hearings in one day, Mulvaney endured criticism from Democrats on both the Budget Committee and the Homeland Security and Governmental Affairs Committee over his views on Trump's tax proposals and cutting government aid programs. But Mulvaney's biggest challenge came from Sen. John McCain, R-Ariz., who told his House colleague he was "deeply concerned about your lack of support for the military." McCain lambasted Mulvaney's votes against defense spending bills, saying the nominee had spent "his entire career [in Congress] pitting debt against the military, and each time, for you, the military was less important."

Mulvaney reassured defense advocates on both sides that as OMB director he would support Trump's plans to boost Pentagon spending. But he did not waver in his longtime contention that it was "dishonest" to use Overseas Contingency Operations accounts, or war funds, to pay for Pentagon projects unrelated to ongoing war efforts.

A planned Feb. 1 committee vote was pushed back a day after Democrats complained that the process was moving too quickly. But a day later the Homeland Security and Governmental Affairs Committee voted 8-7 along party lines to take the unusual step of sending the nomination to the full Senate "without recommendation." The Budget Committee approved Mulvaney's nomination by a vote of 12-11, also along party lines.

Further delay followed. It took a 52-48 cloture vote on Feb. 15 to get the nomination onto the floor. Mulvaney was confirmed the next day, 51-49, with McCain siding with the Democrats in opposition.

CIA

Kansas Republican Rep. Mike Pompeo was announced Nov. 18, 2016, as Trump's choice to head the CIA. A former Army tank commander who graduated first in his class at West Point, Pompeo was widely viewed by lawmakers and intelligence officials as a smart and serious individual who had dedicated himself to learning about the spy agencies as a member of the House Intelligence Committee.

At his Senate Intelligence Committee hearing Jan. 12, Pompeo said he would refuse to restart the CIA's "enhanced interrogation" program, in which terrorism suspects had been tortured, if ordered to do so by the president. As a congressman, he had defended CIA officials who carried out the torture of detainees and called those harsh techniques legal. Pompeo also backed intelligence agencies' assessment of Russia's interference in the 2016 U.S. election.

A familiar, if not cozy, atmosphere dominated the exchanges between senators and their House colleague, and the panel approved the nomination by voice vote on Jan. 20. The Senate confirmed him three days later, 66-32. ∎

Turnover in the Trump Administration

NAME	POSITION	NATURE OF PRIOR JOB	NATURE OF DEPARTURE	DATE OF DEPARTURE ANNOUNCEMENT	WHERE TO?
Robin Townley	Senior Director for Africa, NSC	Marines	Resigned Under Pressure (RUP)	2/10/2017	Sonoran Policy Group
Michael Flynn	National Security Adviser	Trump Campaign	RUP	2/13/2017	
Keith Kellogg	Chief of Staff / Executive Secretary, National Security Council	Defense consultant	Promoted	2/13/2017	Acting National Security Adviser
Katie Walsh	Deputy Chief of Staff	Republican National Committee	RUP	3/30/2017	America First Policies
K.T. McFarland	Deputy National Security Adviser	TV analyst	Promoted	5/19/2017	Singapore Ambassador nomination withdrawn
Dina Powell	Assistant to the President and Deputy National Security Adviser	Goldman Sachs	Resigned	12/8/2017	Goldman Sachs
Michael Dubke	Communications Director	Black Rock Group	RUP	5/29/2017	Georgetown University lecturer, Black Rock Group
Sean Spicer	Press Secretary	Republican National Committee	RUP	7/21/2017	Worldwide Speakers Group
Sarah H. Sanders	Deputy Press Secretary	Trump Campaign	Promoted	7/21/2017	Press Secretary
Josh Pitcock	Chief of Staff to the Vice President	Capitol Hill	Resigned	7/28/2017	Oracle
Reince Priebus	Chief of Staff	Republican National Committee	RUP	7/28/2017	Law firm
George Sifakis	Director Public Liaison	Government Relations	RUP	7/31/2017	Ideagen
Ezra Cohen-Watnick	Senior Intelligence Director, NSC	U.S. Government (DIA)	RUP	8/2/2017	Oracle; later hired by Justice Dept.
Steve Bannon	Chief Strategist and Senior Counselor to the President	Media	RUP	8/18/2017	Breitbart News (fired 1/9/18)
George Gigicos	Director of Presidential Advance	Consulting	RUP	8/22/2017	Consulting
Andrea Thompson	National Security Adviser for the Vice President	House Homeland Security Committee Adviser	Promoted	12/12/2017	Under Secretary of State, Arms Control and Intl. Sec.
Anthony Scaramucci	Communications Director	Finance	RUP	7/31/17	
Keith Schiller	Director Oval Office Operations	Trump Organization	RUP	9/20/2017	Private Security Consulting
Tom Price	Secretary of Health and Human Services	U.S. Representative (R-GA)	RUP	9/29/2017	Jackson Healthcare
Greg Katsas	Deputy White House Counsel	Law Firm	Resigned	11/28/2017	Federal Judge, DC Circuit
Omarosa Manigault	Director of Communications, Office of Public Liaison	Reality Television	RUP	12/13/2017	Celebrity Big Brother
Paul Winfree	Deputy Director Domestic Policy Council; Director of Budget Policy	Heritage Foundation	Resigned	12/15/2017	Heritage Foundation
Rick Dearborn	Deputy Chief of Staff	U.S. Senate staff	Resigned	12/23/17	The Cypress Group

Russia Investigation Proves Distraction

Rumblings about Russian interference arose long before former FBI Director Robert S. Mueller III launched his investigation of Trump campaign officials in May.

In the months before the 2016 presidential election, the FBI had been looking into alleged efforts by the Russian government to interfere in the election, and the FBI was working to assess whether any of Donald Trump's associates were aiding the Russian effort.

Once the election was over, the investigation took on a more public face. On Jan. 5, Senate Armed Services Chairman John McCain, R-Ariz., compared Moscow's effort to influence the election to an "act of war." The same day, Director of National Intelligence James R. Clapper Jr. pushed back against President-elect Trump's skepticism about the allegations, saying Moscow had engaged in a wide-ranging effort of interference that included propaganda, cyberattacks and computer hacking, as well as social media interventions. The next day, at Trump Tower in New York, senior U.S. intelligence officials — including FBI Director James Comey — briefed Trump on the intelligence community's conclusions. Within days, the Senate Intelligence Committee said it would investigate possible links between Russian operatives and the Trump campaign.

Some Trump-skeptical lawmakers saw policy implications beyond the possibility of election tampering. McCain suggested that a surge in Russian attacks on Ukrainian forces was a test of the new president by Russian President Vladimir Putin and urged Trump to respond vigorously by providing lethal assistance to Ukraine.

"That this surge of attacks began the day after he talked with you by phone is a clear indication that Vladimir Putin is moving quickly to test you as Commander-in-Chief," McCain wrote to Trump. "America's response will have lasting consequences."

Others echoed the sentiment that Trump could be paralyzed in responding to Russian aggression by his and his aides' relationships with Russian officials.

On the House side, Intelligence Chairman Devin Nunes, R-Calif., said in late February that he had seen no evidence that Trump or his advisers had illegally communicated with Russian officials during the transition but committed his panel to investigate. He temporarily stepped aside following ethics complaints from what he described as "several leftwing activist groups" about his handling of classified information. But he was soon back on the job.

Not so Attorney General Jeff Sessions. On March 2, Sessions, who had been a senior national security adviser to Trump's presidential campaign, recused himself from all campaign-related investigations. The recusal followed press reports that Sessions had met twice during the campaign with Russian Ambassador Sergey Kislyak. Sessions did not disclose those meetings at his confirmation hearing.

Despite all the action on the Russian front in Congress, the media and the White House, it was not until March 20 that Comey confirmed publicly the existence of a counterintelligence investigation into Russian interference. By then, Air Force Gen. Michael Flynn had already resigned as Trump's first national security adviser after less than a month on the job for allegedly lying to senior administration officials about the nature of his communications with Russian officials. In the wake of Sessions' recusal, Deputy Attorney General Rod Rosenstein

was put in charge of the Russia investigation in late April.

One of Rosenstein's first acts was to provide the raw material to justify the firing of Comey. On May 9, Comey was ousted by the president, who cited a memo from Rosenstein that concluded Comey had overstepped his authority when he publicly announced in the summer of 2016 the conclusion of the investigation of Hillary Clinton's use of a private email server while she was secretary of State.

Comey's firing let loose a flood of criticism of Trump. Democrats drew comparisons to the "Saturday Night Massacre" in which President Richard Nixon fired multiple Justice Department officials as part of a plan to rid himself of special prosecutor Archibald Cox. And they insisted the firing meant that an independent counsel was needed to investigate the alleged collusion between the Trump campaign and Russian officials. They would soon get their wish.

On May 17, Rosenstein named Mueller to investigate "any links and/or coordination between the Russian government and individuals associated with" Trump's campaign.

Trump's family was pulled into the probe as well. In July it was revealed that Donald Trump Jr. had engaged in an email exchange during the 2016 campaign concerning a government official in Moscow who wanted to share potentially damaging information about Hillary Clinton. Senate Intelligence Vice Chairman Mark Warner, D-Va., said: "The emails portrayed it as part of a Russian government effort to undermine the Clinton campaign. It appeared that these emails were copied to [Trump son-in-law Jared Kushner] and [then-Trump campaign chairman Paul Manafort], so they've got a lot of explaining to do."

Warner dismissed any defense that Trump Jr. and Kushner had simply made "a rookie mistake," but said he would reserve judgment until he had seen all the evidence. When Kushner testified before Senate Intelligence Committee staffers, he insisted that all of his actions had been both legal and proper. He said he knew little about the agenda for a June 9, 2016, meeting at Trump Tower set up by Donald Trump Jr. with a Russian attorney, and he told the staffers he had left that meeting early. Kushner acknowledged meeting a Russian banker during the transition period to attempt to set up a direct line to Putin, in pursuit of warmer U.S.-Russia relations. Speaking to reporters in a public venue, he said, "I did not collude with Russia, nor do I know of anyone else in the campaign who did so."

As the investigations, recriminations and speculation about the fate of Rosenstein, Mueller and others continued, in September lawmakers got into the act by introducing measures designed to protect Mueller.

A bipartisan proposal (S 1741), by Sens. Thom Tillis, R-N.C., and Chris Coons, D-Del., was aimed at giving a special counsel who is fired the ability to challenge that dismissal in federal court. Another measure (S 1735), from Sens. Lindsey Graham, R-S.C., and Cory Booker, D-N.J., would require a judge to sign off on removing a special counsel.

In October, the Mueller investigation began to bear legal fruit, although not directly related to campaign collusion with Russia. On Oct. 5, former Trump campaign foreign policy adviser George Papadopoulos pleaded guilty to lying to the FBI about contacts with foreign nationals with links to the Russian government. The indictment and plea deal were unsealed Oct. 30. On Dec. 1, Flynn pleaded guilty to lying to investigators about his contacts with Russians. ■

Chapter 10

FOREIGN POLICY & TRADE

Trump Signs Sweeping Sanctions On Russia, Iran and North Korea

Sanctions targeting Russia, Iran and North Korea were rushed into law in late July as Congress sought to wrap up work on the measure before the August recess – and in the process drastically constrain the Trump administration's ability to give Russian President Vladimir Putin relief from U.S. sanctions.

The House passed the measure (HR 3364) by a 419-3 vote on July 25. That was a new bill that combined a Russia-Iran sanctions bill (S 722) the Senate had passed overwhelmingly in June with a North Korea sanctions measure (HR 1644) that the House had previously passed.

The Senate then cleared the measure, 98-2, on July 27. White House Communications Director Anthony Scaramucci brought up the possibility of a veto, saying the president "may sign the sanctions exactly the way they are or he may veto the sanctions and negotiate an even tougher deal against the Russians." President Donald Trump, the ostensible target of the restrictions included in the Russia provisions, signed the measure into law (PL 115-44) on Aug. 2.

Senate Foreign Relations Chairman Bob Corker, R-Tenn., had hoped to strip the North Korea language inserted by the House. But that would have meant returning the bill yet again to the other chamber for another vote. That idea was resisted by both Senate Democrats and House Republicans, who argued that any delay would push final consideration into the fall.

After a full day of negotiations, Corker struck a deal with House Majority Leader Kevin McCarthy, R-Calif., to get the version with sanctions covering all three countries to the president's desk before the summer recess.

In part, Corker was looking out for the institutional interests of the Senate. Senators had spent considerably less time working through sanctions on North Korea than they had on Iran and Russia, and he said that several members of the Foreign Relations and Banking committees had prepared North Korea bills that they would have liked to be included in whatever Congress ultimately passed to tighten the financial screws on the Kim Jong Un regime.

One example: a bill (S 1591) by Senate Banking members Chris Van Hollen, D-Md., and Patrick J. Toomey, R-Pa., that would gradually impose stronger sanctions on foreign banks that do business with North Korea. The legislation, which is modeled on the congressional sanctions that played a major role in prodding Iran to the nuclear negotiating table, would also give Congress the power to block any potential executive branch move to lift sanctions on North Korea.

Corker's viewpoint lost out in the end-of-summer rush. Van Hollen said he preferred to clear the House-passed legislation and deal with his own North Korea measure at a later date.

Van Hollen's Maryland colleague, Foreign Relations ranking Democrat Benjamin L. Cardin, also came out in support of the House version on North Korea, while acknowledging Corker's concerns.

"Should we have had an opportunity in the Senate to debate this, perhaps modify it? Yes," Cardin said.

In effect, it was a two-for-one swap. "I think we have been able to convince the House to go along with us with Russia and Iran; it seems

reasonable for them to ask ... to take their proposal on North Korea," Cardin said.

Beyond a desire to get out of town, lawmakers also expressed a substantive objection to waiting. Democrats, at least, said they were concerned that the president might ease Obama-era sanctions while Congress continued to debate technical details of the sanctions package, which would give Congress the right to review and block any sanctions rollback.

For its part, the House was dead set against taking another pass at the legislation, particularly if it did not include the North Korea language.

Adding a further sense of urgency were reports that the Defense Intelligence Agency believed North Korea could have a reliable nuclear-capable intercontinental ballistic missile as early as 2018, three years earlier than previous estimates.

"Nearly three months ago, the House passed strong North Korea sanctions by a vote of 419-1," said House Foreign Affairs Chairman Ed Royce, R-Calif., who authored the North Korea sanctions language. "The Senate did not take up the bill, even after Kim Jong Un launched a new ICBM that could soon be capable of hitting California. Now the House has acted again, by a vote of 419-3. Further delay on North Korea is completely unacceptable."

BILL DETAILS

The sanctions legislation required the president to submit for congressional review some terminations and waivers of sanctions aimed at Russia. It also specifically required some Obama-era executive order sanctions to remain in effect.

Some cyber- and Ukraine-related sanctions were not included in that requirement.

The bill provided sanctions for activities concerning cybersecurity, crude oil projects, financial institutions, corruption, human rights abuses, evasion of sanctions, transactions with Russian defense or intelligence sectors, export pipelines, privatization of state-owned assets by government officials, and arms transfers to Syria.

On another energy front, the bill required the State Department to work with the government of Ukraine to increase that nation's energy security.

The Treasury Department was required to develop a strategy for combating terrorist financing, and the Treasury secretary was added to the National Security Council.

The North Korea section of the bill gave the president more authority to impose sanctions on anyone in violation of certain U.N. Security Council resolutions.

U.S. financial institutions were barred from having accounts used by foreign financial institutions to provide indirect financial services to North Korea.

The bill also blocked foreign governments that provide North Korea with defense technology or receive any defense-related products or services from North Korea from receiving certain types

of U.S. foreign assistance.

The bill imposed sanctions against North Korean cargo and shipping, goods produced in whole or part by convict or forced labor, and foreigners who employ North Korean forced laborers.

The State Department was required to submit a determination on whether North Korea meets the criteria for designation as a state sponsor of terrorism.

The section targeting Iran directed the president to impose sanctions on the country's ballistic missile and weapons of mass destruction programs, the sale or transfer of military equipment or the provision of related technical or financial assistance, and the Islamic Revolutionary Guard Corps and others outside the country affiliated with the group.

The president was also empowered to impose sanctions against anyone responsible for human rights violations in Iran.

The bill included a provision that allows the president to waive sanctions under certain circumstances. ∎

State Department Restructuring Debated

Nervous about Secretary of State Rex Tillerson's plans for a department-wide reorganization, the Senate Foreign Relations Committee moved to pre-emptively tie his hands by approving an authorization bill that would require the Trump administration to keep the U.S. Agency for International Development a quasi-independent agency.

Although the measure (S 1631) was approved by voice vote, several senators asked to be registered as voting "no." They included Democratic Sens. Tim Kaine of Virginia, Robert Menendez of New Jersey, Christopher S. Murphy of Connecticut and Tom Udall of New Mexico. Republican Rand Paul of Kentucky also asked to be registered as a "no" vote.

The inclusion of amendments directing the continued semi-independence of USAID and forbidding the closing of the Bureau of Democracy, Human Rights, and Labor were adopted over the objections of the committee's Republican and Democratic leaders.

The mini-revolt proved pointless when the Trump administration, which had hinted at the possible merger of USAID into State in its budget proposal, told lawmakers in September that it had no plans to dismantle the agency, although it would continue to look for ways to reorganize the department.

Foreign Relations Chairman Bob Corker of Tennessee and Benjamin L. Cardin of Maryland, the panel's top Democrat, stressed at the July markup the importance of keeping the legislation as controversy-free as possible, to increase its chances of enactment.

Corker said his goal was to gradually build Senate support for floor time on the State authorization measure so that contested amendments could be fully debated, similar to what happens with the annual defense policy bill.

"I think Secretary Tillerson has gone about this in a thoughtful way," Corker said of the reorganization proposals.

The legislation was reported to the Senate floor on Sept. 6, but by year's end had not been considered by the full Senate.

That might have been at least partly a result of two amendments from Menendez included in the measure that would require the continued independence of USAID and enshrining into law the democracy and human rights bureau.

Both amendments were adopted by 11-10 votes in committee, with Sens. Marco Rubio, R-Fla., and Todd Young, R-Ind., joining most Democrats to support the measures that would impose limits to how far any departmental reorganization effort could go.

Menendez said he was frustrated the authorization bill didn't contain many clear-cut directives or authorize a topline funding level.

BILL PROVISIONS

The 90-page authorization legislation included a section dealing with special envoys, which are not Senate-confirmed and have proliferated to 68 positions, plus staff for each office.

The bill would require the roughly 50 special envoy positions that have not been permitted or mandated by Congress to receive Senate confirmation and would cut off funding to those offices whose envoys have not come before the committee for a confirmation hearing.

Citing a recent internal survey of State Department personnel commissioned by Tillerson that found special envoys were associated with unclear chains of command, wasted resources and muddled policy, Corker said "professional staff at the State Department believe these envoys do more harm than good — not every person, but as a group."

In supporting the move to require special envoys to receive Senate confirmation, Cardin noted that any of these positions could currently be eliminated by the secretary of State without congressional input.

At the request of Sen. Jeanne Shaheen, the legislation explicitly preserved the position of ambassador-at-large for Global Women's Issues. The New Hampshire Democrat is the only woman on the Foreign Relations Committee.

The bill also would require State to consult semiannually with appropriate federal agencies regarding the security of U.S. government and nongovernmental information systems used by the department and develop a Bureau of Diplomatic Security training program for detecting classified information leaks.

In another security related provision, the bill would require the department to report to Congress on overseas capital construction and major embassy security upgrade projects, and on any security violations.

It also would require every agency that enters into an international agreement other than a treaty to designate a Chief International Agreements Officer responsible for ensuring State is made aware of the deal. ∎

Lighthizer Takes Winding Road To Job as U.S. Trade Representative

Despite President Donald Trump's repeated attempts to upend trade policy, Congress passed no major legislation in 2017 in response, or to make its own mark. In the end, Congress' only key action on trade came as it vetted Robert E. Lighthizer for the post of U.S. trade representative.

Lighthizer was charged with carrying out Trump's plan to reorganize the way trade policy was made and make good on campaign promises to aggressively promote U.S. products and use the punishment of trade infractions to force concessions from trading partners.

But it was a long, strange trip for Lighthizer, a deputy trade representative during President Ronald Reagan's administration, who was tapped Jan. 3 as Trump's choice for U.S. trade representative. It would be nearly five months between nomination and confirmation, making Lighthizer the last of Trump's Cabinet-level picks to win Senate approval.

Lighthizer, a partner at the law firm of Skadden Arps Slate, Meagher and Flom, spent years representing agricultural, heavy manufacturing and high-tech companies with far-reaching interests in U.S. trade policy. He had also formerly served as board vice chairman of the Overseas Private Investment Corporation (OPIC), which promotes economic growth in developing countries through U.S. investment.

His experience — including a stint as Senate Finance Committee staff director in the early 1980s — played in his favor, as Democrats acknowledged his obvious qualifications for the post. But his long record also created a problem.

Lighthizer needed a congressional waiver to take the USTR post because he had also worked for foreign government entities. But disagreements between Republicans and Democrats on the Senate Finance Committee about how the panel should approve a waiver left his confirmation in limbo.

Two and a half months after Trump tapped him for the post, the committee held a hearing. Chairman Orrin G. Hatch, R-Utah, insisted it was not actually a confirmation hearing. Instead, Hatch said the March 14 meeting was aimed at breaking the impasse on the waiver.

Sen. Ron Wyden of Oregon, the committee's ranking member, and other committee Democrats wanted to approve the waiver, but hoped to attach separate legislation (S 175) that would have provided health and retirement benefits for retired coal miners. Hatch insisted that Lighthizer's nomination, the waiver and the coal miners' issues should be treated separately. The Finance chairman threatened that if Democrats did not agree to drop the coal miners' pension bill, he would move the nominee out of committee with just Republican votes,

as had been done by other panels where Democrats had boycotted the proceedings on Trump nominees.

At the March 14 hearing, Lighthizer tried to assuage the concerns of panel members individually.

He told Sen. Pat Roberts, R-Kan., that the country's agriculture sector would have benefited from the 12-nation Trans-Pacific Partnership trade agreement that the Trump administration withdrew from in January. Lighthizer also said U.S. withdrawal from TPP did not exclude the possibility of reaching bilateral trade agreements with several member nations that could recoup lost benefits. And he assured the Kansan, chairman of the Senate Agriculture Committee, that boosting U.S. agricultural trade would be a priority.

Lighthizer assured Ohio Sens. Sherrod Brown, a Democrat, and Rob Portman, a Republican, that he would tackle the issue of China's government-subsidized overproduction of steel and aluminum.

The Finance Committee members seemed generally satisfied with Lighthizer's performance, but it would still be almost six weeks before the panel would vote.

Negotiations yielded a deal in which the direct linkage between the waiver and the miners' health and retirement benefits was broken. Hatch agreed to support Senate action to extend the benefits, which were scheduled to end April 28. In return, Wyden and other Democrats agreed to end demands that the health benefits and the solvency of a coal miners' pension fund be tied to the waiver.

On April 25 the committee approved the waiver for Lighthizer 26-0, then approved the nomination by the same vote.

It would take another two weeks and two days for the Senate to take up the nomination. But even that final act was not without its share of drama.

Republican Sens. John McCain of Arizona and Ben Sasse of Nebraska broke with their party to oppose Lighthizer. In a lengthy joint statement, the two Republicans said the USTR nominee had not convinced them that he understood the value of trade to their states, and expressed particular concern about plans to renegotiate the 23-year-old North American Free Trade Agreement with Canada and Mexico.

"We fear that you do not have an appreciation for the millions of jobs created by this free trade deal, and that you would not champion agriculture during your time as USTR," McCain and Sasse said in their statement. "Furthermore, we worry that you would not negotiate trade deals that would protect the American consumer and expand economic growth."

But only a handful of Democrats joined McCain and Sasse in opposition. On May 11 senators voted 82-14 to confirm Lighthizer. ■

Lawmakers Lament Trump's Withdrawal From Trans-Pacific Trade Deal

In his Republican National Convention acceptance speech, Donald Trump promised that the United States would "no longer ... enter into these massive deals, with many countries, that are thousands of pages long – and which no one from our country even reads or understands." Three days after taking office, President Donald Trump began making good on that promise.

On Jan. 23, Trump notified the 11 signatories to the Trans-Pacific Partnership trade pact that the United States would be withdrawing from the deal.

The president called the move a "great thing for the American worker," and some Democratic lawmakers offered rare bipartisan praise.

Rep. Richard E. Neal of Massachusetts, top Democrat on the House Ways and Means Committee, said Trump's action opened the door for "new rules and better enforcement to make trade a two-way street, particularly in the Asia-Pacific region."

But critics – mostly Republicans – called withdrawal a serious mistake both economically and strategically.

Sen. John McCain, R-Ariz., chairman of the Senate Armed Services Committee, said leaving the TPP "will forfeit the opportunity to promote American exports, reduce trade barriers, open new markets, and protect American invention and innovation. It will create an opening for China to rewrite the economic rules of the road at the expense of American workers. And it will send a troubling signal of American disengagement in the Asia-Pacific region at a time we can least afford it."

Sen. Ben Sasse, R-Neb., said pro-trade lawmakers like himself needed to do more to explain the benefits of trade.

"It's clear that those of us who believe trade is good for American families have done a terrible job defending trade's historic successes and celebrating its future potential. We have to make the arguments and we have to start now," he said.

Others urged the president to reconsider, keeping some TPP provisions and renegotiating others.

"The TPP agreement contains considerable benefits for the U.S. economy, but it fell short in other ways," Ways and Means Chairman Kevin Brady, R-Texas, and Trade Subcommittee Chairman Dave Reichert, R-Wash., said in a joint statement.

They urged the Trump Administration "to build on the work that has been done, identify what should be improved, and quickly act on a strategy that creates more economic opportunities for America in that region."

Trump gave notice to Australia, Brunei, Canada, Chile, Japan, Malaysia, Mexico, New Zealand, Peru, Singapore and Vietnam that the United States planned to leave the trade pact within six months. The United States signed the agreement in 2015. But, just as with the Paris Climate accord and the Iran nuclear deal, President Barack Obama never sent it to Congress for a vote.

The Trump administration said it preferred to pursue bilateral trade deals with individual countries rather than broad pacts such as TPP and the North American Free Trade Agreement. ■

Chapter 11

HEALTH & EDUCATION

Demise of GOP Health Care Bill Shows The Limits of Unified Government

The scuttling of the Republican attempt to repeal and replace President Barack Obama's signature health care law in 2017 made one thing abundantly clear: The GOP campaign promise that unified government would break the gridlock in the Capitol was vastly oversold.

The bill's demise — after seven years of Republican assurances that, given full control of government, they would repeal the 2010 law — cast doubt on whether the 115th Congress could fulfill its campaign promises beyond a significant tax cut.

In six years of previous attempts, Republicans had never developed replacement legislation, agreeing on general principles but without drafting legislative text for examination. And with Americans fearful they might lose their health care coverage, GOP leaders were relatively cautious in developing their replacement plan.

Facing unified Democratic opposition, Republicans' main challenge was gaining enough GOP support for the legislation to pass, particularly among hardline conservatives who believed it did not go far enough in repealing the 2010 law.

Example A was the year-long conflict between House Freedom Caucus conservatives and Republicans from states that expanded Medicaid under the 2010 health care law.

The House still succeeded in passing a far-reaching bill (HR 1628), but the Senate couldn't come up with a companion measure.

An attempt to cancel the 2010 law while delaying a replacement came to a theatrical end in the early morning hours of July 28 when ailing Sen. John McCain, R-Ariz., turned down his thumb on the effort.

Republicans did salvage one victory in their triumphant tax cut legislation by repealing the 2010 law's mandate requiring individuals to purchase health insurance. And in early 2018, they eliminated a Medicare advisory board that the GOP had portrayed as a potential "death panel" to limit end-of-life treatments.

BACKGROUND

The 2010 Patient Protection and Affordable Care Act (PL 111-148 and PL 111-152) was enacted by Democrats in an effort to expand health care coverage for uninsured Americans through a combination of changes to the employer-based health insurance system, the creation of state-based health insurance exchanges for individuals who don't get insurance through their employers, and expansion of the joint federal-state Medicaid program to cover individuals with incomes up to 138 percent of the federal poverty level.

The law sets minimum federal standards for health insurance and prohibits insurance companies from rejecting individuals based on pre-existing conditions. It requires employers with more than 50 full-time employees to provide health insurance or pay a tax penalty based on the number of workers (a requirement known as the employer mandate). To help sustain the insurance markets and ensure that individuals don't buy insurance just when they get sick, it requires most Americans to obtain and maintain health insurance or face a tax.

To help pay for the law's costs, such as federal subsidies to help make insurance purchased on the state exchanges more affordable, it

provided savings from Medicare (including by reducing federal support for the Medicare Advantage program) and imposed a number of new taxes — including a 3.8 percent net investment income tax and a 0.9-percentage-point increase in the Medicare payroll tax on taxpayers with incomes above certain thresholds, a 2.3 percent tax on many medical devices and a so-called "Cadillac" tax on high-value employer-paid insurance plans.

The law was enacted in response to rapidly growing health care premiums and costs, and it includes elements intended to help restructure the nation's health care delivery system and reduce cost growth (in the jargon of the day, to "bend the cost curve" of future health care costs).

At the time the law was enacted, the Congressional Budget Office (CBO) estimated that by 2016 roughly 21 million people would be purchasing insurance through the exchanges and an additional 17 million would be covered through Medicaid and the Children's Health Insurance Program, known as CHIP.

The Obama administration's most high-profile problem occurred in the fall of 2013 with the launch of state exchanges (also known as marketplaces) to sell health insurance policies. Because 36 states had declined to create their own state-based exchange (many because of GOP opposition to the law within the state), the federal government provided that service for those states through a federal website, HealthCare.gov. But upon its launch, the federal site barely functioned, frequently freezing or crashing and preventing most individuals from purchasing insurance for weeks. The website eventually had to be rebuilt.

In perhaps the most momentous of several cases, the Supreme Court in 2012 upheld the law's individual mandate — but it also allowed states to opt out of the law's expansion of Medicaid. Subsequently, only 31 states and the District of Columbia expanded their Medicaid programs, with 19 states declining to do so, again, largely because of state GOP opposition to the law. As a consequence, only about 11 million low-income individuals had been added to the Medicaid rolls in 2016 as a result of the 2010 law.

CONGRESSIONAL ACTION
BUDGET PRELIMINARIES

Congress wasted no time setting about the business of trying to overturn the 2010 health care law. In what is usually the sleepy first week of a new Congress, the Senate's very first vote set the stage for repeal. It limited debate on a budget resolution that would empower Republicans to send their own legislation to Trump's desk without a single Democratic vote – just like Democrats enacted the 2010 law without any Republican votes.

After 2016's election returns cemented unified control of Congress and the White House, GOP leaders decided to pursue a strategy to target the law by quickly passing a budget resolution (S Con Res 3) for the fiscal 2017 year that would set in motion the reconciliation process, which is used to alter taxes and spending and is not subject to a filibuster in the Senate.

When the Senate agreed 51-48 to the motion, it set up 50 hours of debate on the resolution, followed by in a flurry of votes on amendments, a "vote-a-rama" that allows senators to offer a virtually unlimited number of changes to the resolution, but without real debate.

"In terms of what we can do here most immediately, Obamacare is at the top of the list. It's the very first item we'll consider this session," Senate Majority Leader Mitch McConnell of Kentucky said on the floor.

The resolution would set budget authority at $3.3 trillion for fiscal 2017, increasing it to $4.1 trillion by fiscal 2022 and $4.9 trillion by fiscal 2026. The concurrent resolution would also include reconciliation instructions for the House Energy and Commerce and Ways and Means committees as well as the Senate Finance and Health, Education, Labor and Pensions committees to come up with at least $1 billion each in deficit reduction over a 10-year period to offset the cost of a full-scale repeal.

The Senate adopted S Con Res 3 in the early morning hours of Jan. 12, voting 51-48 following a seven-hour voting session. Sen. Rand Paul of Kentucky cast the only Republican vote against it, on grounds that the budget reconciliation route that his party's leaders had adopted would leave too much of the 2010 law's structure intact. Sen. Dianne Feinstein, D-Calif., was absent after surgery to have a heart pacemaker installed.

The final vote was marked with low-key drama as Democrats stood up at their desks to explain their votes, a highly unusual move. "Because there is no replacement, I vote no," said Sen. Claire McCaskill of Missouri. Others said they voted no on behalf of their constituents who they said would lose health care coverage if the law is repealed. Every Democrat was interrupted by the Republican presiding over the chamber, Sen. Cory Gardner of Colorado, who warned that speeches were not allowed during the roll call vote.

The chamber considered 19 amendments in the vote-a-rama before the final ballot — and stymied each and every one, mostly through procedural votes. But perhaps the key amendment, to delay an initial deadline to write legislation to repeal the 2010 health care law, was withdrawn without a vote. Sen. Bob Corker, R-Tenn., and other moderate GOP senators had proposed pushing back the Jan. 27 deadline for congressional committees to write their implementing legislation. But Corker conceded that the date was not binding, anyway.

The vote marathon wrapped up just after 1 a.m. on Jan. 12. The exercise was largely a political opportunity for Democrats to put their Republican colleagues on the record about a range of health care and budget issues.

Before adoption of the budget blueprint, Sen. Bernie Sanders, I-Vt., the ranking member on the Budget Committee, took a final shot at the budget resolution and Republican efforts to repeal the health care law without a clear replacement.

"If they do that, up to 30 million Americans will lose their health care, with many thousands dying as a result. Because you have no health care and you can't go to a doctor or a hospital, you die," Sanders said. "They have no alternative proposition. They want to kill [the Affordable Care Act], but they have no idea how they're going to bring forth a substitute proposal."

The vote-a-rama started with a vote on an amendment from Florida Democrat Bill Nelson that would have barred the Senate from taking up legislation to repeal the closing of the coverage gap for the Medicare Part D prescription drug program. Enzi raised a point of order against the amendment, and the chamber voted 47-51 against waiving the point of order, effectively rejecting the amendment. Sixty votes are needed to waive the point of order.

Most amendments were rejected through the same procedural vote, with none coming close to the 60-vote threshold. An amendment from Sen. Amy Klobuchar, D-Minn., related to importing prescription drugs from Canada was rejected 46-52.

The Congressional Budget Office slightly dampened GOP enthusiasm Jan. 16 when it released a report estimating that the prior year's attempt by Republicans to dismantle the 2010 health overhaul would increase the number of uninsured individuals by 32 million people and nearly double the premium costs for individual insurance plans in the law's marketplace.

The report, which was requested by Senate Democrats, estimated that a GOP bill cleared in the previous Congress (HR 3762) to repeal the health care law would increase the number of individuals without insurance by 18 million in the first year following enactment. Premiums for plans purchased in the individual marketplace would increase by up to 25 percent in the same time period, CBO found. President Obama vetoed the measure on Jan. 8, in the waning days of his term.

That legislation included an immediate elimination of enforcement of the law's employer and individual mandate penalties. It would have also ended the law's Medicaid expansion and subsidy payments two years after enactment.

HOUSE BUDGET ACTION

The House followed the Senate quickly, adopting S Con Res on Jan. 13 on a 227-198 vote.

Nine Republicans, a mix of centrist and libertarian members, voted against the budget resolution: Reps. Justin Amash of Michigan; Charlie Dent and Brian Fitzpatrick of Pennsylvania; Walter B. Jones of North Carolina; John Katko of New York; Raul R. Labrador of Idaho; Tom MacArthur of New Jersey; Thomas Massie of Kentucky; and Tom McClintock of California.

Some of the Republicans, like Amash, were unhappy with the fiscal outlook included in the budget document, which projected rising deficits over the next 10 years. In a Twitter post before the vote, Amash wrote, "We get the House. We get the Senate. We get the White House. We get a budget that grows debt by $9 trillion?"

Several moderate Republicans, including Dent, were not eager to begin the process of repealing the health care law without a clear alternative ready to go.

Four members who were tapped for positions in the administration of President-elect Trump did not vote: Republicans Mike Pompeo of Kansas, Tom Price of Georgia, Ryan Zinke of Montana and Mick Mulvaney of South Carolina.

House floor debate was intense at times as Republicans and Democrats volleyed statistics and anecdotes back and forth, painting starkly different views of the landmark health care law.

Republicans blamed the law for rising health care costs, a lack of choice for consumers and an economic burden on small businesses. They sought to portray their repeal efforts as a "rescue mission" for Americans struggling under the law.

"Our experimentation in Soviet-style central planning of our health care system has been an abject failure," said freshman Rep. Jodey C. Arrington, R-Texas.

Democrats argued just the opposite. They credited the law with expanding coverage and slowing the rise of health care costs. They offered stories of constituents afraid of losing health coverage if the

law is repealed and they blasted Republicans for the lack of a clear replacement plan.

After every Republican speaker, Kentucky Rep. John Yarmuth, the Democratic floor manager, noted the number of people in that GOP member's state who were estimated to lose health coverage and jobs if the law is repealed.

Final passage of the budget resolution, which did not require presidential approval, cleared the way for consideration of implementing legislation.

RECONCILIATION BILLS

Republicans introduced the two bills that that incorporated the implementing legislation on March 7 and sent them to the House Energy and Commerce Committee and the House Ways and Means Committee. Both panels approved them the following day, as Trump declared his support.

Despite Democrats' protests, both committees approved the measures without an economic analysis from the CBO. That came the following week, when on March 12 the CBO projected that 52 million Americans would be left uninsured under the legislation. The agency also said that insurance premiums would be higher through 2020. Premiums would then be lower compared to the Obama law after 2020.

The House Budget Committee voted 19 to 17 on March 16 to send the combined measure (HR 1628) to the floor. No Democrats supported the bill, and 20 Republicans voted against it.

House Floor Action: Down and Up

House leaders announced they would begin floor action on the bill to the floor during the week of March 20 – and had to beat a hasty retreat on March 24 as leaders abruptly canceled a scheduled vote in the face of rebellion from both extreme conservatives and more moderate Republicans. It was the first of several stinging setbacks for the Trump administration and House leadership.

"This bill is dead," House Energy and Commerce Chairman Greg Walden, R-Ore., told reporters after the announcement was made.

House Speaker Paul D. Ryan rushed to the White House to deliver the news personally to Trump that Republicans did not have the votes to pass the bill. Ryan said that he did not expect the bill "or anything close to it" to survive.

Trump reported that he would "let the marketplaces collapse" under the existing system. In the votes that the House had held since 2010 to repeal Obamacare, totaling more than 60, no more than three Republicans ever bucked leadership before. But until Trump entered the White House, the vote was more a political statement than a realistic chance to reshape the nation's complicated health care system.

To garner support, GOP leaders modified the bill to, among other things, accelerate repeal and further limit the law's Medicaid expansion while allowing states to receive Medicaid funding as a block grant. But those changes were insufficient, with conservatives saying they didn't do enough to reduce insurance premiums and costs and moderates concerned about the impact on constituents.

The next week, however, Trump administration officials and Trump himself began prodding House leaders to do anything to get the bill passed. Negotiators shuttled between the White House and GOP representatives.

On April 20, White House officials declared that they hoped to pass it before Trump's 100th day in office, April 29.

Conservatives negotiated additional changes with Rep. Tom MacArthur, R-N.J., a moderate Republican, and with encouragement from the Trump administration agreed to allow states to opt out of many consumer coverage requirements — including allowing insurers to charge some people more for pre-existing health conditions if the state operates a high-risk pool or risk-sharing program. With a last-minute provision to provide $8 billion to help mitigate the impact of those higher premiums, Republicans could see a pathway to pass the measure.

Conservatives in the Freedom Caucus demanded several major policy changes, including a repeal of the law's so-called essential health benefits.

A few lawmakers were wooed over by last-minute legislative and regulatory sweeteners such as additional funds for mental health services, a change to shift the oversight of health care benefits to the states from the federal government, additional funding for Illinois providers, and an adjustment of New York Medicaid funding that would have relieved burdens on counties.

On April 26, under intense pressure from the White House and GOP leaders, the Freedom Caucus relented after its members were promised an amendment that would allow states to get a waiver that would let them set their own health benefits rules and let insurance companies charge sicker Americans far more for their health coverage.

"While the revised version still does not fully repeal Obamacare, we are prepared to support it to keep our promise to the American people to lower healthcare costs," the group said in a statement.

At the same time, aiming to woo moderate Republicans, former Energy and Commerce chairman Fred Upton, R-Mich., introduced another amendment aimed at addressing concerns that the legislation would leave consumers with pre-existing conditions with unaffordable out-of-pocket costs. His amendment would create a fund of $8 billion that would be available to states from 2018 to 2023. This money would go to states that permit insurers to charge higher premiums to individuals with pre-existing conditions, and would be used to offset those higher costs for these individuals

Upton's amendment ultimately impelled the bill back to the floor. Upton and Missouri Rep. Billy Long switched their stance from opposition to support after Trump accepted the change. The amendment also appeared to win over a few other members who had previously rejected the bill, including David Young of Iowa and Jeff Denham of California.

Before the release of the Upton amendment, roughly two dozen conservative House Freedom Caucus members flipped from a "no" to "yes" vote after winning the inclusion of a plan to let states opt out of insurance regulations that, they said, drove up the costs of insurance premiums.

HOUSE PASSAGE

The House resumed consideration on May 4, passing it 217-214 after making revisions through managers' amendments, changes incorporated into the rule to govern debate, and amendments adopted on the floor. No Democrats supported the bill, and 20 Republicans voted against it.

The only Freedom Caucus member to ultimately vote against the bill was Andy Biggs, R-Ariz. Liberty Caucus members Thomas Massie of Kentucky and Walter B. Jones of North Carolina, who frequently vote against leadership positions, also opposed the bill.

Moments before the main vote, the House voted unanimously to eliminate a provision that would have carved out an exception for congressional members from states that eliminated or modified the existing law's requirements for pre-existing conditions and es-

sential health benefits.

Ryan cast a "yes" vote for the bill. House speakers typically only vote on major legislation. He gave an impassioned speech on the floor before the vote.

"A lot of us have been waiting seven years to cast this vote. Many of us are here because we pledged to pass this very vote," Ryan said. "Are we going to meet this test? Are we going to be men and women of our word? Are we going to keep the promises we made? Or are we going to falter? We will not falter, we will replace, and today is the day that we're going to do this."

House Minority Leader Nancy Pelosi of California, speaking before the vote, called the measure "a stupid bill."

Pelosi said Republicans who flipped their votes from "no" to "yes" did so without valid reason. "The kabuki doesn't kind of play back home and we're going to make sure that people are aware of the inconsistency of it all," Pelosi said.

As the vote tally reached the 216 threshold needed for passage, Republicans clapped and cheered. Democrats responded with a taunting chant, singing, "Nah, nah, nah. Nah, nah, nah. Hey, hey, hey. Goodbye."

Republicans continued their celebration at the White House, rushing off the House floor after the vote to board buses that transported them down Pennsylvania Avenue. They joined President Trump and Vice President Pence in the Rose Garden. "This has brought the Republican Party together. We're going to get this finished," Trump said.

SENATE ACTION

After House passage, Senate leaders said they would need several weeks to craft their own approach to revising the Obama health law. Their task was complicated by the need to tiptoe around the chamber's so-called Byrd rule (named for former Senate Majority Leader Robert C. Byrd, D-W.Va.), which forbids consideration of budget reconciliation provisions that do not affect the federal budget.

Senators were also demanding an economic analysis by the nonpartisan Congressional Budget Office.

Senate Majority Whip John Cornyn, R-Texas, declined to outline a schedule for Senate consideration of the health care reconciliation measure. "There's no timeline. When we get 51 senators, we'll vote," Cornyn said.

In early May, McConnell announced a working group of GOP senators to shepherd the effort, which drew barbs from Democrats because it did not include any women.

On June 19, McConnell sent a draft bill to the Congressional Budget Office for a preliminary estimate, even though some members of the working group reportedly had not seen the draft. Senate leaders said they hoped to pass the measure by June 30.

On June 26, CBO reported that the draft would increase the number of uninsured Americans by 22 million over a decade to 49 million, slightly less than the House bill. The Senate bill would save $321 billion over a decade, $202 billion more than CBO last month said the House bill would.

The effects on coverage would start to occur quickly. In 2018, 15 million more people would be uninsured under the bill than under current law, CBO said.

Under the Senate bill, average premiums for plans for single individuals would be about 20 percent higher in 2018 than under current law, in large part because the penalty for not having insurance would be eliminated, so fewer healthy people would enroll. Premiums would be about 10 percent higher than under current law in 2019, CBO said in its analysis of the Senate bill. Younger people would pay less for plans, CBO said.

But in 2020, the year of the next presidential contest, average premiums for benchmark plans for single individuals would be about 30 percent lower than under current law, CBO said.

Insurance for people who buy it on their own would cover a smaller share of benefits, CBO said. The Senate bill would let states limit the requirements for essential health benefits.

Within a few hours of the release of the bill, several prominent Republican senators spoke against it, and the June 30 deadline faded from sight.

During the next month, as 'yes' votes continued to be elusive, Senate leaders quit searching for a full-scale replacement measure and turned to a fallback strategy – a so-called skinny repeal of the 2010 health care law as a vehicle to get to a conference committee with the House.

A conference was key to senators who were afraid that the House might adopt the narrow repeal in hopes of coming up with a replacement after the 2010 law was nullified.

"If they don't go to conference, then I am not going to vote" for a skinny repeal," said Lindsey Graham, R-S.C.

Many House conservatives did not support the skinny bill. Freedom Caucus chairman Rep. Mark Meadows, R-N.C. told reporters he would favor maintaining the health law over passing a scaled-back bill. The caucus, with roughly three dozen conservatives, could vote as a bloc against starting a conference. That consideration weighed on Senate GOP leaders.

The night of July 27, as floor debate dragged on, McConnell revealed an eight-page scaled-back repeal of the 2010 health care law as an amendment to the House-passed health bill (HR 1628).

The measure would repeal the health law's individual mandate. It would eliminate the law's employer mandate for eight years. It would repeal the law's medical device tax for three years and increase the amount of money an individual can contribute to a health savings account for three years. The amendment would provide additional funding for community health centers, while defunding Planned Parenthood for one year.

It would provide states additional flexibility through waivers that would allow states to roll back certain health care law insurance regulations. However, the bill maintained the current guardrails that states must meet to gain approval for a waiver, which included proving that no fewer people would be covered, and that benefits would not be less comprehensive or less affordable. States would be able to win approval of the waivers for eight years.

An additional 15 million people would be uninsured in 2018 under the proposal, according to a Congressional Budget Office analysis released the same night. Over the next decade, that number would rise to 16 million, according to the analysis. CBO projected that premiums would increase roughly 20 percent compared to current law in all years between 2018 and 2026.

The analysis showed that the amendment would save $135.6 billion over a decade in on-budget savings, just above the $133 billion that GOP senators needed under reconciliation rules that require the Senate version to save as much as the House bill.

Senate leaders announced that there would be a vote on the measure around midnight, which for passage (assuming no Democratic support) would require 50 of the 52 GOP senators to vote for it, with Vice President Mike Pence casting a tiebreaking vote.

SHIFTING SENTIMENTS

Shortly before McConnell introduced the amendment on the floor, two senators who had previously raised concerns about the process said they had been swayed.

"We got assurances. The speaker said I could tell you we got assurance this thing will go to conference," Sen. Ron Johnson, R-Wis., told reporters. Graham also told reporters he would vote to advance the skinny legislation after speaking with Ryan.

Earlier, Graham, Johnson and McCain had slammed the "skinny" repeal measure and said they would not vote to advance the proposal without assurances that the House would vote to enter a conference committee. Graham called the scaled-back repeal a "disaster" and a "fraud."

Ryan released a statement saying the House was "willing" to go to conference on the health bill, but the burden remained on the Senate to show the chamber could pass a bill.

Democrats said it was ludicrous that, just hours before the extended series of votes was set to begin, Senate Republicans still had not unveiled legislative text of what they expect to be the health care bill they would send to the House. After McConnell described the bill, Sen. Patty Murray, D-Wash., made a motion to commit the House bill to the Senate Health, Education, Labor, and Pensions Committee, where she is the ranking member.

"This process is an embarrassment. This is nuclear-grade bonkers," said Chris Murphy, D-Conn.

As Senate GOP leaders sought to persuade another Republican to support the measure, they held open a separate vote on Murray's motion for an hour and three minutes before rejecting it, 48-52.

MCCAIN: THUMBS DOWN

On a dramatic vote in the early morning hours of July 28, the Senate voted down Republicans' latest proposal, 49-51 in a surprising defeat after months of uncertainty. Vice President Pence had arrived at the Capitol before midnight, hoping to cast the tiebreaking vote.

Three Republican senators voted no. Two of them, Susan Collins of Maine and Lisa Murkowski of Alaska, were no surprise; they had announced their positions and voted against previous versions of the bill.

Attention turned to McCain. The 2008 GOP presidential nominee had already scripted an element of drama when he returned to the Capitol earlier in the week, after being diagnosed with brain cancer, to cast an important vote to proceed with the health care debate.

McCain walked into the chamber and doomed the GOP's repeal with a barely audible "no" and flashed his thumb downward. Later, McCain said he opposed the "skinny" repeal bill partly because of how it was built: without hearings, consultation with Democrats or consideration of the recommendations of governors.

"This is clearly a disappointing moment," Majority Leader McConnell said as he pulled the bill from the floor.

"It's time to turn the page," Schumer said, adding, "We are not celebrating. We are relieved." He cited a request from McCain earlier in the week to return to the normal process of working through legislation in public hearings and markups.

President Trump tweeted his disapproval at 2:26 a.m. "3 Republicans and 48 Democrats let the American people down. As I said from the beginning, let ObamaCare implode, then deal. Watch!" he wrote.

House Republicans attending a conference meeting later that morning described a disappointed mood hanging over them as Speaker Ryan read lyrics from the song "The Wreck of the Edmund Fitzgerald." The ballad, by Gordon Lightfoot, is about a Great Lakes shipwreck that the song suggests could have been avoided if the crew had decided to keep sailing through a storm.

Republicans were left with no path forward. "We're back to square one again and time is running out," said Sen. Mike Rounds, R-S.D.

LAST-DITCH EFFORT

A brief breeze of hope for the measure wafted through the Senate in mid-September when Graham, Johnson and and fellow GOP Sens. Bill Cassidy and Dean Heller offered a new proposal drafted by Graham and Cassidy.

It would replace federal funding for the 2010 health care law that covers tax credits, cost-sharing reduction payments and Medicaid expansion with block grants to states, which would expire in 2027. The draft bill also would cap traditional Medicaid spending.

It would repeal the law's individual and employer mandates, a tax on medical devices, and would allow insurers to charge individuals with pre-existing conditions more money for health coverage.

Behind the rush was the advice of the Senate parliamentarian that the budget reconciliation process for fiscal 2017, which would allow the GOP-led Senate to pass a health care bill with only 51 Republican votes, would expire on Sept. 30.

Sen. Rand Paul, R-Ky., slammed the proposal on Twitter, calling it "Obamacare lite" and saying conservatives should not vote for it.

Sen. Mike Lee, R-Utah, who opposed the Senate GOP's primary replacement plan, was "encouraged" by the waiver provisions in the latest draft bill, his spokesman said in a statement.

Arizona Gov. Doug Ducey, a Republican, backed the Graham-Cassidy proposal, raising questions about whether Sen. John McCain, R-Ariz., would favor the plan.

On Sept. 22, McCain announced his opposition.

"I cannot in good conscience vote for the Graham-Cassidy proposal. I believe we could do better working together, Republicans and Democrats, and have not yet really tried," McCain said in a statement. "Nor could I support it without knowing how much it will cost, how it will affect insurance premiums and how many people will be helped or hurt by it."

In the following days, Sens. Collins and Ted Cruz, R-Texas, opposed the latch-ditch effort. Senate leaders backed away from the effort for the rest of the year. "We don't have the votes," said co-author Cassidy.

"The bill's dead," said Sen. John Kennedy, R-La. "It's deader than a doornail." ∎

Provisions of House Health Care Bill

Following are summaries of the major provisions of HR 1628, the American Health Care Act, as it went to the House floor, along with modifications made before final passage on May 4.

BILL AS INITIALLY AMENDED BY RULES COMMITTEE

INSURANCE COVERAGE

The bill effectively repeals the 2010 law's individual and employer mandates and replaces the current income- and cost-based tax subsidies for individuals who purchase health insurance from state exchanges with age-based tax credits. To stabilize premiums, it eliminates certain insurance requirements and creates new rules related to continuous coverage.

The measure repeals the law's requirements that most individuals obtain health insurance or face tax penalties, and that employers with more than 50 employees provide health insurance or face tax penalties, by setting the penalties for violations at $0. CBO estimates that these provisions would reduce revenues by $210 billion over 10 years.

To encourage individuals to maintain insurance coverage, beginning in 2019 it requires insurers to impose a 30 percent surcharge on premiums for 12 months for individuals who go two months or more without health care coverage and then purchase health insurance in that same year.

It allows insurers in non-group and small group markets, beginning in 2018, to charge up to five times more for premiums for older enrollees than younger ones, rather than the three times allowed under current law. And in 2020, it eliminates rules that insurers must offer plans under which the insurance will pick up the cost of at least 60 percent of covered benefits (also known as actuarial value requirement).

The Congressional Budget Office (CBO) and Joint Committee on Taxation (JCT) estimate that coverage provisions in the bill would reduce spending by $1.226 trillion over 10 years and would reduce revenues by $290.9 billion over 10 years.

EMPLOYER MANDATE

The measure effectively repeals the law's requirement that employers with more than 50 employees provide health insurance or face tax penalties, by setting the penalties at $0. (The House in the last Congress attempted to explicitly repeal the mandate, but that would have violated Senate budget rules governing the consideration of reconciliation legislation.)

The employer mandate stipulates that large employers, defined as those with an average of 50 or more employees working at least 30 hours per week, provide health insurance that meets certain affordability and coverage standards or face a tax penalty based on the number of employees. Employers subject to the mandate can incur a penalty for even a single month if one or more of their full-time workers are certified as having received a federal subsidy through a health insurance exchange because the employer either did not offer insurance or offered insurance that was unaffordable.

In determining who is a full-time employee and counts toward the 50-employee threshold, the 2010 health care law defines a full-time employee as someone who works an average of at least 30 hours a week. Also counting toward the 50-employee threshold are the number of a business's "full-time equivalent" employees for each month, which is determined by adding up the hours worked by part-time employees during the month and dividing that sum by 120 (which represents an average of 30 hours a week for four weeks).

For employers that do not offer any insurance, the penalty is $2,000 multiplied by the number of full-time employees in excess of 30. Penalties are also assessed on employers that offer coverage that fails to meet the law's minimum value and affordability standards, where employees instead obtained federally subsidized coverage through a state exchange.

The employer mandate was supposed to become effective for 2014, but in July 2013 the administration postponed implementation until 2015. It subsequently exempted businesses with fewer than 100 employees for an additional year, to 2016, if they certify that they have not reduced their workforce or insurance coverage. For businesses with 100 or more employees, the new rules required employers to provide health insurance to 70 percent of their full-time employees in 2015 and to 95 percent in 2016 and later years.

CBO and JCT have said they expect that any reduction in employer-based insurance would be limited because most companies use a mixed compensation package (wage and non-wage) to attract workers. They further estimate, however, that because employer mandate tax penalties would eventually be passed on to workers in the form of lower wages, repealing the mandate could increase workers' wages and thus their incentive to work.

HEALTH INSURANCE SUBSIDIES

The measure repeals the 2010 law's premium tax credit and cost-sharing reductions that help reduce costs for individuals who purchase insurance through state health care exchanges. The repeal would be effective in 2020. CBO estimates that these provisions would reduce spending by $673 billion over 10 years.

In its place, it provides for an alternative system of refundable tax credits worth $2,000 to $4,000 per person, based on age (but not income) for the purchase of health insurance. The credits would begin to phase out at income levels of $75,000 for individuals and $150,000 for couples, and a family could receive up to $14,000 in tax credits. CBO estimates that the new tax credits would cost $361 billion over 10 years.

Stability Fund

The bill appropriates $100 billion for a Patient and State Stability Fund for grants to states to help stabilize health insurance markets through 2026, including by reducing premiums or by limiting the costs to insurers for enrollees with very high claims. CBO estimates that this provision would increase spending by $80 billion over 10 years.

MEDICAID PROVISIONS

The bill ends additional federal funding for the law's expansion of joint federal-state Medicaid beginning in 2020, as well as the ability of states to extend Medicaid benefits to new enrollees with higher income levels (the law allows states to provide Medicaid benefits to those with incomes up to 138 percent of the federal poverty level). Individuals with higher incomes receiving benefits as of 2019 would be eligible to continue receiving Medicaid services.

Beginning in 2020, it converts Medicaid into a capped entitlement

under which the federal government would provide fixed per capita payments to states, rather than continue to cover a portion of actual medical costs incurred. Payment caps would be based on five categories of beneficiaries, with annual growth limited to no higher than the medical care component of the consumer price index. If states spend more than the cumulative limit, the federal government would provide no additional funding to match that spending.

CBO estimates that the bill's combined changes to the program would reduce direct spending by $880 billion over 10 years and result in 14 million fewer Medicaid enrollees by 2026. By 2026, Medicaid spending would be roughly 25 percent less than current law projections, according to CBO.

The measure also repeals scheduled reductions in payments to Disproportionate Share Hospitals that treat unusually high numbers of patients with little or no health insurance. CBO estimates that this provision would increase spending by $31.2 billion over 10 years.

Affordable Care Act Financing Provisions

The measure repeals or delays more than a dozen taxes that were used to help finance the expansion of health care coverage under the 2010 health care law, with most of the repeals to occur in 2018 (the proposed manager's amendment may make additional modifications, including by making the tax repeals effective for 2017):

Net Investment Tax — Repeals the 3.8 percent tax on net investment income for taxpayers with income over $200,000 or $250,000 for couples (CBO and JCT estimate that this would reduce revenues by $157.6 billion over 10 years).

Medical Device Tax — Repeals the law's 2.3 percent medical device tax that is imposed on a wide array of devices intended for humans, particularly those used in hospitals and doctors' offices (an estimated $19.6 billion reduction in revenues).

Cadillac Tax — Delays until 2025 the law's tax on certain high-value employer-sponsored health insurance plans (an estimated cost of $48.7 billion). (The proposed manager's amendment would delay the tax for an additional year, until 2026.)

Health Insurance Fees — Repeals the health care law's annual fee on health insurers (an estimated $144.7 billion reduction in revenues).

Additional Medicare Tax — Repeals the Medicare hospital payroll tax increase on wages and self-employment income for taxpayers with earned income above $200,000 or $250,000 for couples (an estimated $117.3 billion reduction in revenues).

Chronic Care Tax — Repeals the increased threshold for the itemized deduction of unreimbursed medical expenses, also called the "chronic care" tax. (The proposed manager's amendment would further reduce the threshold to provide savings that could be used by the Senate to enhance the premium tax credits for older individuals.)

The measure also repeals the following tax provisions from the health care law, beginning in 2018.

Flexible Spending Account Limitation — Repeals the limitation ($2,600 for 2017) on contributions to flexible spending accounts under which employees may deposit pre-tax amounts to cover out-of-pocket medical payments (an estimated $18.6 billion cost).

Prescription Medication Fees — Repeals annual industrywide fees levied on companies that manufacture or import brand-name prescription drugs, which are credited to the Medicare Part B trust fund and are scheduled to reach an aggregate level of $4.1 billion in 2018 and then decline to $2.8 billion in later years (an estimated $24.8 billion cost).

Over-the-Counter Medication Coverage — Repeals the treatment of over-the-counter medications as ineligible for coverage through distributions from health savings accounts, medical savings accounts and flexible spending arrangements (an estimated $5.5 billion cost).

Medicare Part D Deduction — Repeals the elimination of the deduction for employers that provide drug benefits to retirees using a Medicare Part D subsidy (an estimated $1.7 billion cost).

Tanning Tax — Repeals the 10 percent excise tax on the use of indoor tanning services that involve ultraviolet radiation (an estimated $600 million cost). (The proposed manager's amendment would accelerate the repeal by just six months, to June 30, 2017, to reflect the quarterly nature of the tax.)

Remuneration Rules — Repeals the special rule for the limitation of the deduction for remuneration for health insurance executives, which involves the deduction of compensation for personal services as an ordinary business expense for certain health insurance providers, to the extent that such remuneration exceeds $500,000 (an estimated $400 million cost).

Health Savings Account Taxes — Repeals the 20 percent tax on distributions from health savings accounts that are not used for qualified medical expenses, allowing it to revert to 10 percent, as well as the 20 percent tax on distributions from Archer medical savings accounts that are not used for qualified medical expenses, allowing it to revert to 15 percent (an estimated $100 million cost).

PLANNED PARENTHOOD & OTHER PROVISIONS

The measure implements a one-year moratorium on federal funding for payments to any entity that performs abortions and receives more than $350 million a year in Medicaid funds — a definition that would apply to Planned Parenthood. CBO estimates that this prohibition would reduce direct spending by $234 million over 10 years, but it could also increase Medicaid spending for additional births, leaving net savings of only $156 million over that period.

To ensure that women who receive non-abortion services from Planned Parenthood can continue to receive those health care services elsewhere, the measure increases by $422 million the amounts provided under existing law to community health centers for FY 2017.

NEW CONTINUOUS COVERAGE INCENTIVE

The 2010 law's individual mandate penalties are intended to encourage individuals to maintain continuous coverage, especially among younger, healthier individuals whose participation is needed to stabilize markets by balancing the market's risk pool of healthy and sick policyholders.

The bill encourages individuals to maintain insurance coverage and limit adverse selection in health care markets by imposing a 30 percent surcharge on individuals who go more than two months (63 days or more) without health care coverage and who then purchase health insurance in that same year. The surcharge would be imposed for 12 months on base premiums and would first be imposed beginning with enrollment for the 2019 benefit year. It would be the same for all market entrants, regardless of health status.

AGE-BASED PREMIUMS & INSURANCE VALUE REQUIREMENTS

The bill allows insurers in non-group and small group markets beginning in 2018 to charge up to five times more for premiums for older enrollees than younger ones. Under current law, insurers can only charge three times more. Republican leaders, citing health economists, say the true cost of care for older individuals is 4.8-to-1.

The measure eliminates rules that insurers must offer plans under which the insurance will pick up the cost of at least 60 percent of covered benefits (also known as actuarial value requirement). This repeal would be effective beginning in 2020. Under the 2010 law, plan issuers are required to label their offerings by metal tier: Bronze, Silver, Gold and Platinum, with the lowest-tier Bronze plans paying 60 percent of covered benefits and higher-tier plans covering higher percentages.

PATIENT STABILITY FUND

The bill appropriates $100 billion for a Patient and State Stability Fund for grants through 2026 to states for activities that help stabilize health insurance markets, particularly on state insurance exchanges—such as by reducing premiums or by limiting insurers' costs of enrollees with very high claims. It appropriates $15 billion for each of 2018 and 2019 and $10 billion each subsequent year through 2026.

If a state chooses not to use the funding for its own program, the funding would become available to the Centers for Medicare & Medicaid Services (CMS) to help stabilize premiums for patients in that state. A state match would be phased-in beginning in 2020, depending on whether a state chooses to use the money for its own program or uses the CMS program.

CBO estimates that these provisions would increase spending by $80 billion over 10 years.

Under the measure, states could use the funds for a variety of reasons, including financial assistance to high-risk individuals who do not have access to employer health coverage and who are seeking coverage through the state's individual market, and incentives to appropriate entities to help stabilize premiums in a state market and thereby reduce the cost of providing coverage for individuals who have a high rate of utilizing health services.

States could also use the funds to reduce out-of-pocket costs such as copayments, coinsurance, premiums and deductibles; to provide payments, directly or indirectly, to health care providers for their services; to promote participation in the state's individual market and small group market; to increase health insurance options; and to promote access to preventive services, dental care services, vision care services, and services for mental health and substance use disorders.

HEALTH SAVINGS ACCOUNTS

The measure nearly doubles the amount of tax-preferred funds that can be placed into health savings accounts (HSAs) each year to $6,550 for an individual and $13,100 for couples. CBO estimates that these provisions would reduce revenues by $19.2 billion over 10 years.

The bill modifies several rules related to health savings accounts (HSAs) in an effort to further promote the use of HSAs, including by nearly doubling the maximum contribution limit, allowing certain couples to divide up their combined catch-up contributions among either of their HSAs and creating a special rule for certain medical expenses incurred before establishment of an HSA. CBO estimates that these provisions would reduce revenues by $19.2 billion over 10 years.

Beginning in 2018, the measure increases the maximum contribution limit for HSAs to equal the sum of the annual deductible and out-of-pocket limitation currently allowed under a high-deductible health plan—resulting in an effective increase of more than 90 percent. Specifically, the sum of the deductible and out-of-pocket expenses would be at least $6,550 for self-only coverage and $13,100

for family coverage.

Under current law, the basic limit on annual contributions to an HSA for self-only coverage is $3,350 for 2016 and $3,400 for 2017. The limit for family coverage is $6,750 for both years.

CBO and JCT estimate that this provision would reduce revenues by $18.6 billion over 10 years.

PREVENTION & PUBLIC HEALTH FUND

The measure repeals the 2010 law's Prevention and Public Health Fund, which is intended to support prevention, wellness and other public-health-related programs authorized under the Public Health Service Act, and it rescinds all unobligated balances at the end of fiscal 2018.

CBO estimates that this provision would reduce direct spending by $8.8 billion over 10 years.

The fund is administered by the Health and Human Services Department (HHS), which issues grants to eligible organizations. Public health activities covered under the fund include prevention research, health screenings and initiatives such as the Community Transformation Grant Program, the Education and Outreach Campaign Regarding Preventive Benefits and immunization programs.

The fund received a permanent annual appropriation under the law, with $1 billion a year provided for fiscal 2016 and 2017; $1.25 billion a year for fiscal 2018 and 2019; $1.5 billion a year for fiscal 2020 and 2021; and $2 billion for fiscal 2022 and each fiscal year thereafter. Under the law, House and Senate Appropriations committees provide funds for eligible activities through annual appropriations acts.

MEDICAID ELIGIBILITY / WORK REQUIREMENTS

The bill includes a number of provisions intended to tighten eligibility for the Medicaid program in all 50 states and thereby reduce state Medicaid spending. CBO estimates that these provisions would reduce direct spending by $7.1 billion over 10 years.

Specifically, it requires individuals to provide documentation of U.S. citizenship or lawful presence in the United States before obtaining Medicaid coverage. Currently, states may enroll individuals who attest to being U.S. citizens or have satisfactory immigration status and then provide them with a reasonable period to provide documentation to verify their status. (A manager's technical amendment would remove the immigration status provisions. Proponents say they would be addressed in separate legislation.)

It requires states, for purposes of determining an individual's adjusted gross income for Medicaid and CHIP eligibility, to consider any monetary winnings from lotteries and other lump sum payments as if they were obtained over multiple months, even if they were obtained in a single month. It counts lottery winnings above $80,000 over multiple months, thus preventing individuals with significant financial wins from joining the Medicaid program, but it also includes a hardship exemption if the denial of coverage would cause an undue medical or financial hardship.

It also limits the effective date for retroactive coverage of Medicaid benefits to the month in which the applicant applied, effective for applications made on or after Oct. 1, 2017, and it repeals the ability of states to substitute a higher home equity limit above the statutory minimum in law for purposes of Medicaid eligibility determinations. In situations where HHS determines that state legislation would be required to amend the state plan, states would have additional time to comply with these requirements.

RESTRUCTURE MEDICAID SUPPORT TO STATES

The Medicaid program is jointly funded by the federal government and states, with the federal government paying states for a specified percentage of the actual cost of services provided to Medicaid beneficiaries. According to HHS's Centers for Medicare & Medicaid Services (CMS), which administers the program, that percentage (known as the Federal Medical Assistance Percentage, or FMAP), varies by state based on criteria such as per capita income. CMS says that the regular average state FMAP is 57 percent but ranges from 50 percent in wealthier states up to 75 percent in states with lower per capita incomes.

As reported, the bill in 2020 converts the program from a open-ended direct reimbursement program based on actual state costs to a reimbursement system that would be capped based on per-enrollee limits — with total allowable federal payments to a state based on the sum of caps for five categories of Medicaid enrollees in the state. (The proposed manager's amendment would also give states the option to receive federal funds through a block grant; see below.)

PER CAPITA PAYMENT LIMITS

Under the measure, the federal government would continue to use FMAP to reimburse states for a portion of their Medicaid expenses, but those federal payments would have cumulative annual caps based on the number of enrollees, regardless of the costs of covering individuals.

The initial overall FY 2020 cap for a state would be set by determining baselines for the five categories of enrollees, based on FY 2016 spending for each category — which would then be added together. Each category amount would be calculated by computing the per capita cost for the category, multiplied by the number of enrollees in that category. The five categories are the elderly, the blind and disabled, children, adults who were not part of a state's Medicaid expansion and those adults who were part of an expanded Medicaid program. Cap amounts would be indexed to inflation, increasing each year by the percentage increase in the medical care component of the consumer price index for all urban consumers (CPI-U).

With a cap in place, federal funds would be provided to states to cover a portion of their Medicaid costs as under the current system, but when cumulative federal spending reaches the cap no further federal spending would be provided. States could, however, continue to fully fund the costs of providing Medicaid services. And if a state receives federal funds for Medicaid beyond its cumulative cap, federal funding for the following year would be reduced by an equal amount.

The measure provides for a temporary increase in federal matching percentages for FY 2018 and FY 2019 to support improvements to Medicaid data reporting systems. And it requires reports regarding medical assistance expenditure data within categories of Medicaid services enrollees in order to better transition the system to a per capita model.

DISPROPORTIONATE SHARE HOSPITALS

The measure repeals scheduled reductions in Medicaid payments to hospitals that treat unusually large numbers of patients with little or no health insurance. CBO estimates that this provision would increase direct spending by $31.2 billion over 10 years.

Disproportionate Share Hospital (DSH) adjustment payments provide additional funding to hospitals that serve a significantly disproportionate number of low-income patients. States receive an annual DSH allotment to cover the costs of designated DSH hospitals that provide care to low-income patients that are not paid by other sources, such as Medicare, Medicaid, the Children's Health Insurance Program or other health insurance.

The allotment is calculated through a statutory formula and includes requirements to ensure that the DSH payments to individual DSH hospitals are not higher than actual uncompensated costs.

The 2010 law modified DSH payments, reducing them as health insurance subsidies and state exchanges became available starting in 2014, with the expectation that more people would have health coverage because of the 2010 law.

Specifically, the bill repeals the Medicaid DSH cuts for non-expansion states in 2018. States that expanded Medicaid would have their DSH cuts repealed in 2020.

CHANGES BEFORE INITIAL FLOOR DEBATE

Following is a summary of changes to HR 1628 made by the House before it was initially brought to the floor in March. The House on March 24 by a 230-194 vote adopted a rule (H Res 228) that automatically modified the bill to incorporate managers' amendments.

MEDICAID CHANGES

One amendment made several major modifications to the Medicaid program and it generally accelerated the repeal of most taxes that finance the 2010 law. Among its provisions, it would give states the option to receive federal Medicaid funds as a block grant rather than through the bill's new per capita payment system; it prevented any additional states from opting into the law's Medicaid expansion; and it allowed states to establish work requirements for Medicaid eligibility.

END MEDICAID EXPANSION

Another amendment would prevent any new states from opting into the law's Medicaid expansion by blocking the higher federal payment rate for otherwise eligible individuals, instead requiring that services for such individuals be reimbursed at the normal federal rate for the state. It also ended after 2017 the state option to cover adults above 138 percent of the federal poverty level, and officially terminated the 2010 law's underlying requirement that states expand Medicaid for certain childless non-disabled, non-elderly, non-pregnant adults up to the 138 percent poverty level.

MEDICAID WORK REQUIREMENTS

The amendment allows states to impose work requirements on non-disabled, non-elderly and non-pregnant adults who wish to receive Medicaid benefits. The work requirements would be modeled after those in the Temporary Assistance for Needy Families (TANF) program and could be satisfied through private or public sector employment, vocational or skills training, education in pursuit of employment, satisfactory attendance at secondary school or in a course of study leading to a GED, job readiness assistance, community service, and providing childcare services for an individual who is participating in a community service program.

It exempts disabled, elderly and pregnant individuals and also provides that a state can not impose a work requirement on the following: children under the age of 19; individuals who are the only parent or caretaker of a child under the age of 6 or who are the only parent or caretaker of a child with a disability; or individuals under the age of 20 who are married or are the head of the household and who maintain satisfactory attendance at school or participate in education directly related to employment.

The amendment provides a 5-percentage-point increase in a state's FMAP for states to administer the requirements.

MEDICAID BLOCK GRANT

The amendment gives states the option to receive federal Medicaid funds as a block grant, rather than through the bill's new per capita payment system, along with greater flexibility in how they use funds.

Block grants would provide a set federal amount for the traditional adult and child populations served in the per capita system, with initial funding for the block grant to be determined using the same type of calculation as for per capita caps. Funding would be indexed to inflation but would not adjust for changes in population. Unused funds would roll over and remain available for as long as the state has a block grant. States could choose block grants for a period of 10 years and could choose to provide health care to either non-expansion adults and children, or just to non-expansion adults.

States choosing block grants must submit a plan to HHS that identifies eligibility under the block grant; certain low-income pregnant women and children in poverty would be automatically eligible. States must outline the types of items and services that will be provided; the amount, duration and scope of the services; any required cost sharing; and the method for delivering care. These items and services, as well as conditions for eligibility, would generally supersede requirements in current law. However, the state program must provide medical assistance for hospital care; surgical care and treatment; medical care and treatment; obstetrical and prenatal care and treatment; prescribed drugs and prosthetics; certain other medical supplies and services; and health care for children under age 18.

DISPROPORTIONATE SHARE HOSPITALS

The amendment places limits on Disproportionate Share Hospitals (DSH) payments to states that require political subdivisions of the state to contribute funds toward Medicaid. The modification is largely aimed at policies in New York that critics say are costly to counties.

Specifically, it provides that for any state with a DSH allotment in 2016 that was more than six times the national average and that requires political subdivisions within the state to contribute funds toward Medicaid, the amount of allowable medical assistance expenditures under the allotment formula would be reduced by the amount required to be contributed by the political subdivisions without reimbursement. The amendment would not apply with respect to state-required contributions from political subdivisions with populations of more than 5 million (i.e., New York City), as well as contributions for certain administrative expenses.

PATIENT AND STATE STABILITY FUND

The amendment allows the Patient and State Stability Fund created by the bill to be used for maternity coverage and newborn care, and it appropriates an additional $15 billion to the fund for 2020 — which could be used only for maternity coverage and newborn care as well as mental health and substance use disorders. It clarifies that mental health and substance use disorder services covered by the fund include direct inpatient and outpatient clinical care for treatment of addiction and mental illness, as well as early identification and intervention for children and young adults with serious mental illness. Funds could also be used to lower costs to individuals who have high costs of health insurance coverage due to the low density population of the state in which they reside.

To offset the increased funding for the Patient and State Stability Fund, the amendment postpones until 2023 the repeal of the additional 0.9 percent Medicare tax on wages and self-employment income for earned income above $200,000 ($250,000 for couples).

TAX REPEALS & OTHER PROVISIONS

The amendment delays the tax on high-value employer sponsored health plans for an additional year, until 2026, but accelerates by a year to immediately repeal most other taxes that finance the 2010 health care law, making the repeals effective for the 2017 tax year.

It creates an American Health Care Implementation Fund within HHS to carry out key policy initiatives created by the bill, including the Medicaid per capita allotment for medical assistance, the Patient and State Stability Fund, and additional modifications to the premium tax credit and the refundable tax credit for health insurance coverage. It appropriates an initial $1 billion for the fund.

Finally, it made technical changes to clarify that the Medicaid per capita allotment growth rate would compound year to year, and to address the needs of states with sicker populations it increases the annual inflation factor for the elderly and disabled categories under the new per capita spending limits by an additional percentage point.

TAX PLACEHOLDER

As reported, the bill would repeal the law's increased threshold of 10 percent of adjusted gross income for the itemized deduction of unreimbursed medical expenses, allowing it to revert to 7.5 percent of adjusted gross income beginning in 2018, and it extends through 2017 a special rule for taxpayers reaching age 65 before the close of the tax year.

The amendment allows the income threshold to be reduced immediately and further lowers it to 5.8 percent — a change intended to serve as a savings placeholder for the Senate to potentially enhance the tax credit for consumers between the ages of 50 and 64 who may face significantly higher premiums under the measure and need additional support.

MINIMUM BENEFITS

Under the current law, the federal government requires that qualified health care plans include 10 essential health benefits. The amendment eliminated that federal requirement in 2018, allowing states to determine which essential health benefits must be included in plans eligible to be purchased using federal tax credits (either the existing premium subsidy system or the bill's replacement tax credit system). However, this federal requirement was restored by the MacArthur amendment (see below), which instead provided for state waivers from essential benefits.

REFUNDABLE TAX CREDIT

The amendment struck the section of the bill that explicitly repealed the premium tax credit and instead formally replaced these provisions with a new refundable tax credit as provided for under the bill. (According to GOP leaders, the changes would preserve the bill's privileged reconciliation status in the Senate and also provide an opportunity for the Senate to modify the bill's tax credits to provide greater support to older low-income individuals.)

As reported, the bill allowed for any excess tax credit to be deposited into an individual's health savings account. The amendment removed this provision.

It eliminated the use of the tax credit for COBRA coverage, which

allows individuals to pay to continue group insurance plans after leaving a job. It also made veterans who are eligible for care through the Veterans Affairs Department, but who have not enrolled, ineligible for the tax credit (as it does not retain the special rule for veterans in the underlying bill).

It provides that requirements for joint filing to claim the credit do not apply to married taxpayers who live apart from their spouse and can't file a joint return because of domestic abuse or spousal abandonment

As reported, the measure directed the Treasury Department to establish a program, building upon existing systems, to deliver the credit to eligible taxpayers. Under the current system, the credit would have been provided by the Treasury Department on a monthly basis to the insurer to help pay for the insurance premium. The amendment modified these provisions, including by requiring the Treasury to prescribe regulations to operate the advance payment program in a manner that protects taxpayer information and provides robust verification.

CONTINUOUS COVERAGE

The amendment removed small group market insurers from provisions requiring imposition of a 30 percent surcharge on individuals who do not maintain continuous coverage. (According to Republican leaders this requirement would be duplicative as the small group market has complied with certain continuous coverage standards, like guaranteed renewability, since the Health Insurance Portability and Accountability Act of 1996.)

MEDICAID

The amendment eliminated bill provisions that would have required individuals to provide documentation of U.S. citizenship or lawful presence in the United States before obtaining Medicaid coverage.

(Under current law, states may enroll individuals who attest to being U.S. citizens or have satisfactory immigration status, and then provide them with a reasonable period to provide documentation to verify their status. The removed provisions are expected to be addressed through separate legislation.)

It also removed the bill's increased civil monetary penalty that the HHS inspector general could levy against parties for intentionally defrauding the Medicaid program.

Finally, it provides that expenditures for childhood vaccines be excluded from the formula for the new Medicaid per capita limits, but requires that all non-DSH supplemental payments be included.

CHANGES BEFORE FINAL PASSAGE

The House on May 4 by a 235-192 vote adopted a second rule (H Res 308) that automatically modified the bill to incorporate three additional amendments; one by Rep. Tom MacArthur, R-N.J., to allow state waivers for insurers from minimum essential benefit standards; one by Fred Upton, R-Mich., to provide $8 billion to help individuals with pre-existing conditions whose insurance premiums increase because of a state waiver; and one by Reps. Gary Palmer, R-Ala., and David Schweikert, R-Ariz., to create a $15 billion federal risk sharing program.

STATE COVERAGE WAIVERS

The MacArthur amendment included a number of provisions intended to help reduce the premiums that insurers charge for health insurance, and thereby make insurance more affordable for most consumers, by allowing states to opt out of certain coverage requirements of the 2010 health care law.

ESSENTIAL HEALTH BENEFITS

The amendment restored federal minimum essential benefit requirements that had been dropped by the earlier manager's amendment, but it allows states to be granted waivers allowing them to exempt insurers from providing those essential health benefits beginning in 2020.

Under the current law, the federal government requires that qualified health care plans include 10 essential health benefits: maternity and newborn care; hospitalization; ambulatory patient services; emergency services; mental health and substance use disorder services, prescription drugs; rehabilitative services and devices; laboratory services; preventive and wellness services and chronic disease management; and pediatric services.

PRE-EXISTING CONDITIONS

The amendment retains the current law's requirement that insurers must offer coverage to people with pre-existing conditions. However, it allows states beginning in 2019 to opt out of parts of the law's "community rating" requirements so insurers can charge higher premiums based on an individual's health status if the individual has a gap in coverage — provided that the state has set up a high-risk pool or reinsurance mechanism to help those who can't otherwise afford coverage, or the state participates in the federal risk-sharing program (see below).

Individuals who maintain continuous health insurance coverage could not be charged premiums based on their health status; their premiums would continue to be calculated under the current law's community rating system.

The amendment explicitly maintains the community rating prohibition on charging higher premiums because of gender.

AGE-RELATED PREMIUMS

The amendment permits states, starting in 2018, to receive waivers and allow insurers to further increase the premiums that older people must pay for health insurance.

Under current law, insurers can charge older individuals no more than three times the amount charged to younger individuals. The bill as reported increased that age rating ratio to 5:1, and the amendment allows even higher levels.

WAIVER PROCESS

In applying to the Health and Human Services Department (HHS) for waivers, states must explain how the waiver will accomplish one or more of the following: reduce average health insurance premiums; increase health insurance enrollment; stabilize the health insurance market; stabilize premiums for individuals with pre-existing conditions; or increase choices of health care plans. All state applications would be automatically approved within 60 days of submission unless HHS notifies the state of reasons for denial within that time period.

Waivers could last for up to 10 years, although states could request a continuation of an existing waiver. Waivers for pre-existing conditions would be terminated immediately if a state ends its risk-sharing program.

Waivers could not be made for health insurance co-ops or multistate plans. Waivers also would not apply with respect to the law's requirement that members of Congress purchase insurance through state health insurance exchanges.

COMMUNITY RATING WAIVERS AID

The Upton amendment added $8 billion to the bill's Patient and State Stability Fund for payments over five years (2018 through 2022) to help individuals with pre-existing conditions whose insurance premiums increase because the state was granted a waiver allowing insurers to raise premiums based on an individual's health status.

Under the amendment, aid is provided only to those states that got a community ratings waiver, with the state to use those funds to provide assistance that reduces the health insurance premiums or other out-of-pocket costs of individuals whose monthly health insurance premiums increased because of their health status (i.e., their pre-existing condition).

FEDERAL RISK SHARING PROGRAM

The Palmer-Schweikert amendment creates a federal invisible risk sharing program and appropriates $15 billion to be available for the program through 2026; unallocated monies from the bill's Patient and State Stability Fund could also be used for the program. Under the program, insurers would receive subsidies to help cover the claims of sick, expensive individuals, with the goal of lowering premiums for all people covered by the insurer.

According to GOP leaders, the amendment was based on a Maine health care law that created invisible high-risk pools. An "invisible" risk sharing program means that neither the health care providers nor the patients receiving care know whether the patients are in the program so there can be no discrimination against these patients by care providers. Such high-risk patients are not removed from the traditional private insurance market; instead, health care insurers are reinsured for the high medical claim costs of those patients.

The amendment requires HHS to establish parameters defining who is automatically eligible for the program based on identified health conditions, as well as a process under which health insurers could qualify individuals who are not automatically eligible. HHS must define operational aspects of the program, including the percentage of insurance premiums that will be paid to insurers and the "attachment" amount (the point at which the health care costs for an individual require repayment under the program).

HHS must define these parameters in consultation with stakeholders, and within 60 days of enactment provide enough detail to specify how the program will operate beginning in plan year 2018. Administration of the program must be transferred to states beginning with plan year 2020. ■

Late-Term Abortion Bill Passes House

The House passed a bill (HR 36) to limit late-term abortions on Oct. 3, 237-189, seeking to claim a victory for anti-abortion groups. A similar measure (S 2311) by Sen. Lindsey Graham, R-S.C., fell nine votes short of the 60 needed for advancement on Jan. 29, 2018.

The House bill authored by Trent Franks, R-Ariz., would prohibit abortions after 20 weeks, with exceptions for cases of rape, incest or endangerment of the woman's life.

Doctors who violated the terms of the bill would face fines or up to a five-year prison sentence. According to the Guttmacher Institute, which tracks family-planning policy, 17 states prohibit abortions after 20 weeks.

"In spite of all the political noise, protecting these helpless little pain-capable unborn children and their mothers is not a Republican issue, or a Democrat issue. It is a test of our basic humanity and who we are as human family," Franks said on the House floor.

Most of the votes fell along party lines, but three Democrats voted for the bill: Daniel Lipinski, D-Ill., Henry Cuellar, D-Texas, and Collin C. Peterson, D-Minn. In addition, two Republicans voted against the bill: Rodney Frelinghuysen, R-N.J. and Charlie Dent, R-Pa.

As a presidential candidate in September 2016, Donald Trump wrote a letter to the leaders of anti-abortion groups outlining four actions he promised to take on abortion issues. One was signing this proposal into law. The administration issued a formal notice of support before the House vote.

The Trump administration had taken steps to please abortion opponents with the appointments of their allies to the Department of Health and Human Services. Those appointments include former Americans United for Life president Charmaine Yoest and Teresa Manning, previously of the Family Research Council.

The Congressional Budget Office estimated that by enacting the legislation, Medicaid costs could increase by $65 million to $335 million over the next 10 years and federal spending between 20018-2027 would rise by $175 million. ■

Children's Health Program Lapses For Two Months Before Renewal

Funding for the Children's Health Insurance Program funding lapsed for two months when the 2018 fiscal year started on Oct. 1, 2017, as its authorization ran out. Two months later, a year-end continuing appropriations bill revived it, and in early 2018, Congress reauthorized the program for six years as part of a budget agreement (PL 115-120).

CHIP has traditionally found bipartisan support from both sides of the aisle. The program was pushed into law by the late Sen. Ted Kennedy, D-Mass., and Senate Finance Chairman Orrin G. Hatch, R-Utah, in 1997 (PL 105-33).

During the Obama administration's most recent renewal in 2015, Congress updated the program five months before the September 2015 deadline.

The biggest holdup in enacting a CHIP renewal was a dispute between Republicans and Democrats over offsets for the cost in the House CHIP bill (HR 3922).

The House and Senate bill (S 1827) mirrored each other in policy, but the House bill was offset with changes to Medicaid and Medicare and cut the Prevention and Public Health fund established under the 2010 health care law (PL 111-148, PL 111-152).

Democrats opposed these offsets and the bill passed the House on Nov. 3 mostly on party lines, 242-174. The Senate measure did not progress to a floor vote.

A December 2017 continuing resolution (PL 115-96) provided appropriations for CHIP that lawmakers expected to cover costs through the first half of the fiscal year, though March 31, 2018. Patient advocates were worried that this money would not actually be enough, but those concerns were addressed a month later when Congress provided more funding.

Children's health advocates expressed dismay over the short-term extensions because they made it hard for states to plan and left families in limbo.

The impasse on CHIP was broken in January 2018 when lawmakers realized that the CHIP renewal costs were lower than originally expected and would actually save money over a decade.

The Congressional Budget Office had estimated that the CHIP provisions over a 10-year period would increase outlays by $7.2 billion but increase revenues by $8.2 billion, resulting in net savings of about $981 million.

The final six-year renewal also temporarily delayed or suspended three taxes imposed under the 2010 health care law: an excise tax on medical devices, a tax on high-cost employer-provided health insurance plans (known as the Cadillac tax), and annual fees on health insurance companies.

MID-YEAR SPARRING

During the year, Democrats and Republicans exchanged jabs over how funding for the program could proceed without addressing funding for Medicaid, the federal-state program that pays for half of the births in the United States as part of its broad mission. Both chambers' evolving measures to repeal the 2010 health law would cap Medicaid funding for the first time since its creation in 1965.

Democrats focused on the issue at a June 23 hearing of the House Energy and Commerce Subcommittee on Health.

"What our Republican colleagues seem to ignore is that our safety net is interconnected. To tear down Medicaid, which is supported by CHIP and community health centers, is misguided and hypocritical," said Energy and Commerce ranking member Frank Pallone Jr., D-N.J.

"It's simple. A strong CHIP program depends on a strong Medicaid program," said Rep. Ben Ray Luján, D-N.M. "You just can't have it both ways."

Committee Republicans countered that these were separate issues. "Medicaid over the next 10 years under our proposal will grow, not be cut," said Rep. Brett Guthrie, R-Ky. The program would grow above its current level, but the House bill would slow its growth by $834 billion over a decade compared to current law.

Seeking to engender bipartisanship in the other wing of the Capitol, Senate Finance Chairman Orrin G. Hatch, R-Utah, turned over the gavel at a Sept. 7 hearing on the topic to ranking member Ron Wyden of Oregon for much of the session.

A week later, Hatch and Wyden announced their support for a five-year extension that would maintain extra money for states — a 23 percentage point federal matching rate increase that was in the 2010 health law — for two more years before phasing it out by 2021. Their bill (S 1827) was introduced Sept. 18.

But an end-of-fiscal-2017 flurry of discussions in both chambers to beat the Sept. 30 deadline foundered as senators were embroiled in efforts to revive the broad Obamacare repeal legislation and to write a massive tax cut measure. The authorization lapsed.

House Republicans said Congress had time beyond the deadline to address the program. "The opportunity to do this is not dire or urgent. In fact, there is money in the bucket right now to fund as it has been," said Rep. Pete Sessions, R-Texas, on the House floor on Sept. 27.

Energy and Commerce Chairman Greg Walden, R-Ore., "indicated that while he does understand the program is scheduled to run through Sept. 30, that the analysis from the nonpartisan Medicaid and CHIP Payment and Access Commission shows that states have enough funds remaining to their accounts to the end of the year," Sessions added.

Federal funding for CHIP and several other programs did expire Sept. 30, raising concerns among state officials and children's advocates about how that might affect the future of CHIP.

The Medicaid and CHIP Payment and Access Commission projected that three states — Arizona, North Carolina and Minnesota — and the District of Columbia could exhaust funding by December. Minnesota state officials warned in August that funding could dry up by the end of September.

The House bill as written would pay for the measure through changes to Medicaid third-party liability, lottery winning calculations and Medicare premium adjustments for higher income persons. For example, Medicare recipients with incomes over $500,000 would be charged higher premiums. In addition, states could prevent lottery

winners from receiving Medicaid benefits, which they estimate would save them $400 million.

House Democrats argued for offsets that would hit the drug industry.

The Senate counterpart bill from Hatch and Wyden did not address CHIP offsets and would increase the deficit by $8.5 billion over five years, according to the Congressional Budget Office.

The Senate Finance Committee approved S 1827 on Oct. 4, by voice vote. Only Sen. Patrick J. Toomey, R-Pa., spoke out against the measure. He said the bill should ensure that money wasn't appropriated to unrelated programs besides CHIP.

The same day, the House Energy and Commerce Committee approved HR 3921 by a 28-23 vote. In a sharp contrast to the bipartisan Senate CHIP markup held earlier Wednesday, the House session was clouded by partisan fallout over offsets.

"The Senate passed the bill on a bipartisan basis this morning. Since when do we do pay-fors here? All of a sudden we're doing pay-fors?" said Rep. Anna G. Eshoo, D-Calif. She noted that Republicans did not propose offsets for some other unrelated bills.

"While some would call these offsets partisan, I'd call them reasonable," responded Walden.

Before floor action in the House, Walden combined the CHIP extension with another bill to extend funding for community health centers and other safety net programs for two years into a new measure (HR 3922).

The new bill, which would renew funding for CHIP for five years like the prior version, would retain most offsets from the two previous bills. But it would eliminate an offset in the original that would have increased Medicare premiums for higher-income seniors.

The new bill would cut the prevention and public health fund more deeply than the original. The updated version would increase the original bill's $6.35 billion cut over 10 years from the health fund to fully offset the bill and compensate for eliminating the Medicare offset.

The new measure would help hospitals by blocking payment cuts that were scheduled for 2018 and 2019 for hospitals that serve a large number of low-income uninsured people, according to a summary.

The House passed the bill 242-174 on Nov. 3, with many Democrats voting "no" because of the offsets.

In December, a temporary extension hitched a ride on the government-wide continuing appropriations bill (H J Res 124). It extended Children's Health Insurance Program funding until March 31 while cutting the Prevention and Public Health Fund that Democrats created in the 2010 health care law — a move that frustrated Democrats and children's advocates.

A state official said the injection of funds was welcome, although a longer-term fix was needed.

"Obviously, we would rather have a permanent long-term funding solution than a short-term CHIP funding bill, but short-term would allow us to keep running the program as usual and not freeze enrollment Jan. 1 or disenroll children Feb. 1," said Cathy Caldwell, director of the Bureau of Children's Health Insurance at the Alabama Department of Public Health. ■

Oft-Maligned Medicare Board Canceled

The House passed a bill on Nov. 2 to repeal the 2010 health care law's Independent Payment Advisory Board by a 307-111 vote. Action carried over into 2018, when the measure was included in budget legislation (HR 1892) to end a brief government shutdown that President Donald Trump signed (PL 115-123) on Feb. 9, 2018.

The board, commonly referred to by its acronym, IPAB, was created under the 2010 health law to identify ways to decrease federal spending on Medicare without affecting coverage or quality. The 15-member board hadn't actually been formed, though, and was not likely to be triggered until 2021, according to a 2017 annual report from the Medicare Trustees.

Ever since 2010, Republicans had expressed outrage about the board, slamming it as a "death panel." Under the health law, it would provide the administration and Congress with cost-cutting recommendations if Medicare spending breached a certain threshold.

Tennessee Rep. Phil Roe, the lead Republican on the House bill (HR 849), said the types of decisions that IPAB would make should be made by elected officials.

"If there are hard decisions to be made on Medicare, Congress should not abdicate that duty to a group of people with no oversight or legal recourse," Roe said on the House floor before the vote. "Those decisions should be made by the people elected as representatives of the people."

The Trump administration declared its support for the measure

Some 76 House Democrats voted with Republicans to pass the bill 307-111 on Nov. 2 over the objections of House Democratic leaders.

The House Ways and Means Committee approved the bill 24-13 on Oct. 4.

In his opening statement, Chairman Kevin Brady, R-Texas, said the advisory board was created to cut Medicare costs but really would be a way to cut corners and remove Congress and the American people from the decision-making process.

"One of our main priorities in health care is to empower patients, families, providers, and states. We want to give the American people — not Washington — more control over their own health care decisions," Brady said.

Under the 2010 health law (PL 111-148, PL 111-152), the payment advisory panel was supposed to be made up of 15 members, such as doctors and policy experts, appointed by the president and confirmed by the Senate. Those members' recommendations to reduce spending would be considered by Congress and acted on by the administration.

While the board could suggest ways to reduce expenses, such as on prescription drug purchases or payments to insurer-run Medicare Advantage plans, the law expressly forbade it from rationing health care.

The nonpartisan Congressional Budget Office estimated that curtailing the advisory board would cost roughly $17.5 billion in foregone Medicare spending reductions through 2027. The House bill did not offset those costs.

Democratic committee members voiced concerns over that lack of offsets and the priority the GOP was placing on it. ■

Medical Liability Measure Passes House; Senate Does Not Take It Up

The House on June 28 passed, 218-210, a controversial bill that would limit medical malpractice lawsuits, overcoming threats from conservative Republicans to spoil a vote on a bill that was a health care priority for GOP leaders. The Senate did not take up the legislation in the face of Democratic opposition.

The bill (HR 1215) would put a $250,000 cap on many awards given to the victims of medical malpractice whose coverage is provided by the federal government in some way. That includes people on Medicare or Medicaid, people receiving subsidies for insurance in the individual market, government employees and veterans.

The cap would be on "non-economic" damages – the awards given for disabilities or physical pain and suffering. The bill would not impose a cap on the award amount for direct monetary losses.

Supporters of the bill argued that medical malpractice awards drive up health costs across the board and that the bill would help bring down costs. Health industry groups such as the American Medical Association and the American Hospital Association supported the bill. According to the hospital association, defending against these lawsuits can cost the health care system between $50 billion to $100 billion a year.

The bill's opponents hoped a combination of conservative Republicans and Democrats would sink its passage. Republicans including Texas Reps. Louie Gohmert and Ted Poe opposed the bill because it would pre-empt the states' ability to enact their own medical malpractice laws. Opposition from those members in a previous session had prevented the bill from even emerging from the Judiciary Committee, but in 2017 Gohmert declined to oppose its journey to the floor.

Nineteen Republicans opposed the bill and no Democrats voted for it. Gohmert and Poe were joined by other members who don't mind bucking leadership, such as Justin Amash of Michigan, Morgan Griffith of Virginia and Walter B. Jones of North Carolina, and moderates like Ileana Ros-Lehtinen of Florida and three Republicans from Pennsylvania.

Republican members trained as medical doctors generally supported the bill. Phil Roe, R-Tenn., an obstetrician and gynecologist, said "the one thing that took away some of the joy of that practice was frivolous lawsuits." Roe argued that before a Tennessee law on medical malpractice suits went into effect, most of the money paid out went to attorneys instead of the victims of malpractice.

Plaintiffs' attorneys opposed the bill. In a letter to House leaders in June, the American Bar Association argued that the caps would harm patients who have been most severely harmed. "Caps diminish access to the courts for low wage earners, like the elderly, children, and women; if economic damages are minor and noneconomic damages are capped, victims are less likely to be able to obtain counsel to represent them in seeking redress," the letter said.

House Democrats seized on data about the extent that medical errors can cause harm. According to a 2016 study by researchers at Johns Hopkins University, medical errors cause 250,000 deaths per year, making it the third-leading cause of death in the United States. Democrats argued the bill would shield negligent doctors as well as drug and medical device companies selling dangerous products.

"Do you want these constant errors to go unrecognized and unreconciled? This bill will do that," said Rep. Sheila Jackson Lee, D-Texas. "This undermines good health care."

Military and veterans groups also opposed the bill.

The House adopted an amendment that would allow physicians to apologize to a patient without having the apology used as evidence against them in court by a vote of 222-197.

An amendment that would limit who could qualify as an expert witness in these cases, putting limits on how far the witness could travel to testify, was adopted by voice vote, as was an amendment to set a statute of limitations for the lawsuits. ■

Perkins Student Loan Program Expires...

A college student loan program with bipartisan support expired on the last day of September after Republican Sen. Lamar Alexander of Tennessee, chairman of the Health, Education, Labor and Pensions Committee, blocked legislation to extend it. The action effectively ended efforts to renew the Perkins Student Loan Program, established in 1957 and named in 1986 for the longtime chairman of the then-Education and Labor Committee, Carl D. Perkins, a former Democratic representative from Kentucky.

The need-based Perkins student loan program provided tens of thousands of college students with a source of financial aid that was a mix of federal dollars and college contributions. Alexander objected on the floor to a bipartisan bill (S 1808) that would have extended the loan program to 2019.

"I object because I think it is time for our country, through legislation by this Congress, to move on to a simplified federal student aid program that has only one federal loan for students, one federal grant for students, and one work-study program for students," Alexander said. He is the former president of the University of Tennessee.

Perkins provided $1.2 billion to 528,000 students in the 2014-15 school year and was supported by colleges and universities as well as lawmakers from both parties. Alexander said that all students who had

a Perkins Loan could keep it for the rest of the school year.

The last time the program was reauthorized, in 2015 (PL 114-105), it had expired for several months before senators reached an agreement to continue it temporarily. As part of the agreement, Perkins aid ended for graduate students in 2016 and required colleges and universities to let undergraduates know that the program would end in October 2017.

The sponsor of the bill, Sen. Tammy Baldwin, D-Wis., had attempted to pass the legislation through an expedited process requiring unanimous consent of all senators. She agreed that the overall federal student aid system needed to be simplified. However, she said, it was not "right or fair to end this program with nothing to replace it to the detriment of students in need."

On Sept. 26, 220 House lawmakers – more than half the body – asked party leaders for a vote on a bipartisan bill (HR 2482) to reauthorize the program for an additional two years. The measure had overwhelming support from Democrats and 53 Republicans also signed on to the bill sponsored by Rep. Elise Stefanik, R-N.Y.

Like Alexander, the chairwoman of the House Education and the Workforce Committee, Virginia Foxx, R-N.C., wanted the federal government to offer students one loan, one grant and one work-study program. The House did not vote on the bill. ∎

...But Update of Related Program For Career Training Is Passed by House

Congress enacted legislation to update career and technical education nationwide, despite mixed signals from the Trump administration on how it wanted to proceed with the programs. The House passed its bill on June 22, but Senate action ceased for a year before it was enacted in mid-2018.

The House bill (HR 2353), sponsored by Rep. Glenn Thompson, R-Pa., updated the 1984 Carl D. Perkins Career and Technical Education Act (PL 109-270) to better align education and training programs with the skills local employers are seeking. The broader Perkins loan program was allowed to expire at the end of September.

Originally, career training programs were associated with manufacturing and construction, but in recent years they also have comprised health care, information technology and other fields with concentrations of higher-skill jobs, such as avionics, that face a paucity of skilled workers.

Money is distributed under the Perkins Act to states and territories

BOX SCORE

BILL: HR 2353 – Job training programs.

LEGISLATIVE ACTION:

House Committee on Education and the Workforce approved HR 2353 on May 17.

House passed HR 2353 by voice vote on June 22.

Senate amended and passed HR 2353 by voice vote on July 23, 2018.

House cleared HR 2353 on July 25, 2018.

President signed HR 2353 (PL 115-224) on July 31, 2018

that issue grants through a designated agency.

The bill reauthorized training programs through fiscal 2024 and gives state agencies more direct control over the programs, including the development of performance metrics.

The bill required that state agencies use performance indicators to assess secondary school training programs, including graduation rates, academic attainment rates and whether students are in postsecondary education, training, military service or unsubsidized employment after leaving high school. Measurements of program quality must also include the attainment of recognized postsecondary credentials or student participation in work-based learning.

TRUMP ADMINISTRATION SIGNALS

House Democrats accused Labor Secretary Alexander Acosta of speaking in contradictions when he came before the Labor-HHS-

Education Appropriations Subcommittee in June to defend President Donald Trump's proposed budget cuts.

Acosta spoke of better aligning "job training, job education and the skills the marketplace demands," but Democrats pointed to White House's fiscal 2018 budget proposal, which sought to slash funding for some of those programs.

Under Trump's budget, the Labor Department's funding would be reduced to $9.7 billion, a $2.4 billion cut from the current level of funding. Some of the programs that would see the largest cuts were meant to prepare kids and adults for the workplace, including a $256 million reduction in the Job Corps program that prepares disadvantaged youth for jobs. The budget proposal would also end a program that helps low-income senior citizens find employment and would slash other job training programs by more than $1 billion dollars.

"You can't cut a program and say you're for a program," said Rep. Rosa DeLauro of Connecticut, the subcommittee's ranking Democrat.

Acosta said the cuts were difficult to make, but he hoped states would pick up the slack and be able to do more with flexibility offered to them.

"There are 37 different programs at DOL, many of those float down to the states," Acosta said. "One element that I think will be helpful to the states is increased flexibility in how to spend the money that they have rather than line item each particular program."

The House Education and the Workforce Committee on May 17 approved HR 2353 by voice vote. ∎

Education Regulations Eliminated

Congress rescinded two Obama administration education rules in early March, voting to eliminate on consecutive days regulations for states to evaluate schools and assess teacher training programs under the 2015 elementary and secondary schools law. President Donald Trump signed both resolutions.

On a 59-40 vote, the Senate on March 8 adopted a resolution (H J Res 58) under the Congressional Review Act to rescind a rule requiring states to report and evaluate teacher training programs. The resolution, which the House on Feb. 7 had adopted, 240-181, also prevented the Education Department from creating a substantially similar rule or regulation in the future.

The regulation, which had been finalized the previous October, required states to annually evaluate and publicly report the effectiveness of teacher preparation programs at higher education institutions with the goal of producing better quality instructors.

On March 9, the Senate adopted a second resolution (H J Res 57) rescinding an education rule that set guidelines for state assessment of schools. The vote was a narrow 50-49. The House had passed it 234-190, also on Feb. 7.

Tennessee Republican Sen. Lamar Alexander, chairman of the Health, Education, Labor and Pensions Committee, had introduced a similar resolution (S J Res 25) on Feb. 28 to end accountability regulation for schools under a new K-12 law but the reaction was more mixed than in the House.

Ohio Republican Rob Portman, for instance, said he wouldn't support the resolution. "These measures balance state flexibility while reinforcing protections for students of color, students with disabilities, and students from low-income families," Portman said in a statement. "We must do more to provide a better education for all students, including those who have been traditionally underserved."

The ranking Democrat on the HELP Committee, Patty Murray of Washington, said that removing the regulation would be "a devastating blow to students across the country."

"Parents, teachers and education advocates did not ask for this regulation to be repealed," she said in a statement. "If Republican leaders choose to bring this up and jam it through the Senate, it would politicize our bipartisan education law, throw state and district planning into chaos, and give Secretary DeVos a blank check to pursue her anti-public education agenda at the expense of our students."

The teacher training regulation had been in the works for several years. It was prompted by people in the education field who said programs to instruct teachers needed increased monitoring, said Elizabeth Ross, managing director of state policy with the National Council on Teacher Quality.

"The biggest benefit of these regulations is the increased data and transparency at the program level. The biggest loss of getting rid of these is the absence of that transparency," she said of the regulation. "It's being collected, but not in a uniform format that is being made publicly available."

At least seven states had no process to evaluate low-performing programs, according to a 2015 Government Accountability Office report. Evaluating educator training programs is a requirement for receiving federal funds under the higher education law.

"If states fail to assess whether [teacher preparation programs] are low-performing, potential teaching candidates may have difficulty identifying low-performing [teacher preparation programs]," the report read. "This could result in teachers who are not fully prepared to educate children."

Teachers unions criticized the regulation when it was finalized because it linked how effective a program was ranked to the test scores of students taught by their teacher graduates. National Education Association President Lily Eskelsen García said too many other factors go into how students perform.

Several education advocacy organizations that support the regulation acknowledged it could have been better, urging Congress to fix it instead of repealing it.

"Using the CRA is a pretty blunt instrument to fix these regulations when they could just go back and re-regulate and try to work things out using a scalpel instead of a hatchet," said Tamara Hiler, senior policy adviser for education at Third Way.

The regulation on school assessments had been targeted by Republicans. Rep. Todd Rokita, R-Ind., said the rule went too far in asserting federal power over decisions that should be left to states.

"The result of the law is less flexibility for state leaders," he said. "Should this rule go forward, more schools would be identified as failing than if the statue was faithfully implemented." ∎

Chapter 12

HOMELAND SECURITY & IMMIGRATION

House Extends Authority of Sprawling Homeland Security Department

The House on July 20 passed legislation (HR 2825) that would specifically authorize the sprawling Department of Homeland Security for the first time since it being created in the wake of the Sept. 11 terrorist attacks.

The measure passed on a vote of 386-41. It followed years of efforts by lawmakers in both parties to provide a single oversight mechanism for the department. Such a step was a key recommendation of the bipartisan 9/11 Commission that has yet to be implemented.

House Homeland Security Chairman Michael McCaul, R-Texas, the bill's sponsor, said the measure would "create efficiencies – eliminate, consolidate and streamline programs," and "hold DHS more accountable."

DHS is composed of 22 agencies, including Immigrations and Customs Enforcement, Customs and Border Protection, the Transportation Security Agency and the Coast Guard. The bill outlines the structural organization of the department and specifies which positions must be filled by presidential appointments. It also would require steps DHS must take while making acquisition decisions and called for increased grant funding by DHS to local law enforcement agencies.

Despite his legislative success, McCaul was unable to amend House rules to bring all of DHS supervision under his committee, another recommendation of the 9/11 commission. However, the eight House committees that oversee various parts of the department agreed in January to coordinate their oversight functions.

In May, the House Judiciary Committee advanced bills to authorize ICE and Citizenship and Immigration Services (HR 2406, HR 2407). The Transportation and Infrastructure Committee marked up related legislation extending the authority of the Coast Guard (HR 2518) and the Federal Emergency Management Agency (HR 2548).

With several Senate committees overseeing DHS, there was no action on companion legislation. ■

House Judiciary Panel Backs Expansion Of Guest Worker Visa Program

The House Judiciary Committee on Oct. 25 approved legislation to expand a federal farmworker visa program that Republicans said would allow agricultural employers to hire tens of thousands of foreign laborers. Democrats objected that the move would drive down wages to the detriment of American workers.

By a 17-16 vote, the panel advanced the bill (HR 4092) to the House floor. It would expand the agricultural guest-worker program by providing year-round visas for up to 450,000 foreign workers — 410,000 for agriculture and 40,000 for meat and poultry processors. Committee Republicans Steve King of Iowa and Louie Gohmert of Texas joined panel Democrats in voting against the bill. Five committee Republicans did not vote.

The bill by Judiciary Chairman Robert W. Goodlatte, R-Va., was crafted to make it attractive to dairy farmers and segments of the agriculture and food industries who said the existing H-2A program is designed for seasonal, short-term employers and not employers who need workers on an extended basis.

The legislation would replace the Labor Department's H-2A visa program for legal, foreign-born, temporary farm laborers, which farm groups and lawmakers say is outdated, involves three government agencies and doesn't always provide American farmers with the workers when needed.

"It's clear that the current program is outdated and broken for American farmers," Goodlatte said in an Oct. 2 statement. "It's well past the time to replace it with a reliable, efficient, and fair program that provides American farmers access to a legal, stable supply of workers, both in the short- and long-term, for seasonal as well as year-round work."

Democrats said the bill's provisions to benefit employers would reduce minimum wages for foreign workers and depress wages for U.S. workers.

"There is no doubt in my mind that if this bill were to become law, employers across the country would immediately begin replacing these workers with foreign guest workers," said Judiciary Committee ranking member John C. Conyers Jr., D-Mich.

Rep. Luis V. Gutierrez, D-Ill., said the committee was wasting its time on a piecemeal approach on immigration and agricultural workers. He said a better approach would be for Republicans to push forward with comprehensive immigration legislation that addresses the estimated 11 million undocumented immigrants living in the United States illegally.

Senate Judiciary Chairman Charles E. Grassley, R-Iowa, was wary of the House Judiciary bill, warning that it could face obstacles in the Senate even as he welcomed Goodlatte's effort to address labor needs in agriculture, which depends on a workforce that is largely comprised of foreign-born workers. "I think we need to do something about agriculture workers, but when you bring something like that up here over in the United States Senate, everybody wants to add everything else on it," Grassley said.

The measure was also referred to the Education and Workforce and Ways and Means Committees because parts of the legislation fall into their jurisdiction. Neither panel took action in 2017. ■

Congress Struggles to Help 'Dreamers' And Boost Immigration Enforcement

Before he took office, President Donald Trump said that he planned to follow up on his promises from the 2016 campaign to address the needs of roughly 740,000 undocumented immigrants, commonly known as "Dreamers," enrolled in President Barack Obama's Deferred Action for Childhood Arrivals (DACA) program.

Under that program, those individuals are protected from deportation and are allowed to work or attend school in the United States provided they meet certain requirements.

"We're going to work something out that's going to make people happy and proud," Trump told "Time" magazine in January, before taking office. "They got brought here at a very young age. They've worked here. They've gone to school here. Some were good students. Some have wonderful jobs. And they're in never-never land."

In the meantime, a bipartisan group of senators was promoting a bill (S 1615) that would allow DACA recipients to receive three years of protected status so they could remain in the United States. Senate Minority Whip Richard J. Durbin, an Illinois Democrat, said passage of the bill would give Congress "a chance to act on the larger immigration issues before us."

But there was little progress on immigration legislation during the subsequent months.

ENFORCEMENT PRIORITIES

The House passed on June 29 a pair of enforcement bills targeting "sanctuary" cities and undocumented immigrants with prior deportation orders. The bills were the first major pieces of immigration legislation taken up by the Republican-led Congress since Trump took office. Unlike Obama, who had threatened to veto such measures, Trump said he would sign both bills.

The measures received scant attention in the Senate. Democrats criticized the measures as racially motivated and aimed at broadly painting immigrants as dangerous, signaling there would not be enough votes to meet the 60-vote threshold required to advance most legislation in the Senate.

House Republicans pushed back on the anti-immigrant narrative, portraying the bills as a way to crack down on criminals and local governments that protect them. They received a boost from Homeland Security Secretary John F. Kelly, who appeared at a news conference with Speaker Paul D. Ryan, R-Wis., to urge final passage.

"The word 'sanctuary' calls to mind some place safe. Instead these cities are places that allow some criminals to go free, undermine federal law enforcement and make our communities less safe," Kelly said.

The sanctuary cities bill (HR 3003) would tighten existing statutes to bar local governments from imposing policies that prohibit police officers "from assisting or cooperating" with federal immigration agents. It would also establish new probable cause standards allowing federal authorities to more easily detain undocumented immigrants held in local jails. The House passed the bill on a nearly party-line vote, 228-195, with three Democrats in favor and seven Republicans opposed.

Some of the cities in question do not consider detainer requests is-

sued by the federal government without an arrest warrant or probable cause. Probable cause would be established if the federal government believes an immigrant is deportable, if they had been recently issued an order of removal, or if an arrest warrant is issued in their name.

The second bill (HR 3004) was named after Kate Steinle, a San Francisco woman who was shot and killed July 1, 2015, by an undocumented criminal with prior deportations. The measure, passed 257-167, would establish new penalties for undocumented immigrants with criminal convictions who re-enter the U.S. illegally after having been previously deported.

Twenty-four House Democrats voted for the measure. Steinle's alleged assailant was found not guilty of assault with a deadly weapon. He was convicted on one count — being a felon in possession of a firearm — after claiming the shooting was unintentional.

The two bills were stand-alone versions of provisions included in a more comprehensive enforcement measure (HR 2431) that was approved in May by the House Judiciary Committee. That measure was sponsored by Judiciary Chairman Robert W. Goodlatte, R-Va. They meshed with Trump's immigration policies, which were rooted in enforcing existing laws. During the 2016 campaign, Trump vilified sanctuary cities and often mentioned by name victims of crimes committed by undocumented immigrants.

PAIRING SECURITY AND 'DREAMER' PROPOSALS

Trump increased the pressure for legislative action on a broader immigration bill when he announced in September that he would end the DACA protections in March 2018 unless Congress enacted an alternative program. His action followed mixed signals by administration officials about the fate of the Obama-era program.

On Sept. 5, the Homeland Security Department announced that it would rescind the 2012 memorandum establishing the Deferred Action for Childhood Arrivals program. The announcement signaled that a program that Trump and other Republicans had derided as an "illegal amnesty" would come to an end.

Trump, who had assured that he would have empathy for Dreamers, said he would give Congress six months to pass legislation that would secure lasting legal status for Dreamers. That kept the door open to what he called an "orderly transition" that "provides minimum disruption."

"As I've said before, we will resolve the DACA issue with heart and compassion — but through the lawful democratic process — while at the same time ensuring that any immigration reform we adopt provides enduring benefits for the American citizens we were elected to serve," Trump said in a statement.

Prospects for a bipartisan agreement appeared to brighten following Trump's Sept. 13 evening meeting at the White House with bipartisan congressional leaders, including Senate Minority Leader Charles E. Schumer and House Minority Leader Nancy Pelosi. According to the Democratic leaders, Trump agreed to pursue a deal that would boost border enforcement in exchange for legal status for Dreamers.

"Both sides agreed that the White House and the Democratic leaders would work out a border security package," Schumer and Pelosi said in a joint statement following the meeting. "Possible proposals were discussed including new technology, drones, air support, sensor equipment, [and] rebuilding roads along the border."

White House officials debated the Democrats' claim that Trump had agreed to table the administration's request for money to build a wall along the U.S.-Mexico border, a nonstarter for Democrats from the beginning.

Many rank-and-file members of both parties quickly dismissed as a bad idea the possibility of pairing border-security measures with steps to replace the DACA program.

Rep. Mo Brooks, R-Ala., said he didn't see a scenario under which he could support legal status for the young undocumented immigrants brought illegally to the United States as children. "There's nowhere near enough border security and long-term immigration controls being implemented to justify ratifying illegal conduct," he said.

Rep. Peter Welch, D-Vt., said Congress would be better to "rip the Band-Aid off" and pass a so-called clean DACA fix. "If we got a Dreamer bill on the floor it would pass, and I think we'd get a lot of Republican votes," he said.

House Democratic leaders and the Congressional Hispanic Caucus advocated specifically for passage of legislation (HR 3440) known as the Dream Act, which would provide conditions under which these young undocumented immigrants could earn legal status and eventually a path to citizenship.

"I don't use that word 'red line' but for me there's no question that we need to pass the Dream Act and it needs to be a clean Dream Act," said Sen. Kamala Harris, D-Calif.

California's Linda T. Sanchez, House Democratic Caucus vice chairwoman and a former Hispanic Caucus chairwoman, dismissed as "a half measure" the legislation (HR 1468) sponsored by Florida GOP Rep. Carlos Curbelo that would provide a path to legal status for Dreamers.

"Creating sort of a second-class citizenship here in the United States for Dreamers is not something CHC is [going to be] part of," Sanchez said of the Curbelo measure.

Curbelo's spokeswoman Joanna Rodriguez disputed that characterization of the bill. The Florida lawmaker's measure "is a permanent legislative solution that would give young immigrants brought to the United States as children three possible pathways into the legal immigration system," she said. "Like any other legal permanent residents, they would be able to apply for citizenship. Naturalization is how Congressman Curbelo's parents and thousands of other immigrants become U.S. citizens every year. There is nothing second-class about it."

Many House Republicans preferred an approach in which border security measures would pass before the DACA piece. "The enforcement needs to happen first before the legalization," said Rep. Lou Barletta, R-Pa., describing enforcement as "securing our borders, cracking down on visa overstays, making E-verify mandatory" for employers.

Rep. Steve King, R-Iowa, said that he told his party's leaders that he didn't see himself voting for any measure that would provide what he saw as amnesty for DACA recipients. He warned that a move in that direction would rile the conservative base. "There's only one thing that cracks President Trump's base and that's if he cracks on immigration," King said.

Senate Judiciary Chairman Charles E. Grassley, R-Iowa, laid out a series of conditions that he said were crucial to securing his vote in favor of a path to legal status for Dreamers. Any deal, he said, must include "robust" border security enhancements, stronger interior enforcement, mandatory E-Verify registration for employers, and an overhaul of the immigration court system and asylum laws.

New doubts about the prospects for an agreement resulted when senior White House and Trump administration officials on Oct. 8 unveiled a sweeping list of demands for immigration overhaul legislation. They told reporters said that Trump wanted the immigration bill to include funding for his proposed U.S.-Mexico border wall, provisions aimed at cracking down on the flow of minors from Central and South America, a new merit-based legal immigration system and changes in the federal grant program for sanctuary cities.

Democratic leaders immediately issued a statement lambasting the administration's demands. The White House "can't be serious about compromise or helping the Dreamers if they begin with a list that is anathema to the Dreamers, to the immigrant community and to the vast majority of Americans," Pelosi and Schumer said.

"We told the president at our meeting that we were open to reasonable border security measures alongside the DREAM Act, but this list goes so far beyond what is reasonable," they said. "If the president was serious about protecting the Dreamers, his staff has not made a good faith effort to do so."

Meanwhile, as discussions continued about a bill to fund the government in fiscal 2018, Trump and Senate Republicans made clear they did not want a legislative fix for Dreamers tacked on to a must-pass appropriations bill. "The president made it very clear he doesn't want to see any DACA solution as part of a year-end package," Sen. David Perdue, R-Ga., said, following a Nov. 2 White House meeting of Republican senators with Trump. ■

Geography of the 'Dreamers'

Where Do They Live?

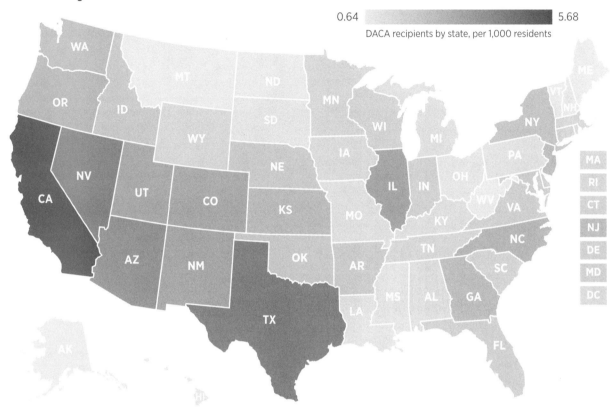

0.64 ▬▬▬▬▬ 5.68

DACA recipients by state, per 1,000 residents

When They Arrived and Where They're From

There have been nearly 790,000 recipients of DACA since the program launched in 2012.

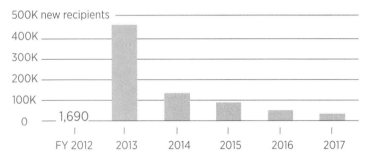

500K new recipients

400K

300K

200K

100K

0 — 1,690

FY 2012 | 2013 | 2014 | 2015 | 2016 | 2017

Most recipients come to the U.S. from Latin American countries

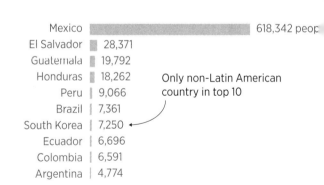

Mexico	618,342 people
El Salvador	28,371
Guatemala	19,792
Honduras	18,262
Peru	9,066
Brazil	7,361
South Korea	7,250
Ecuador	6,696
Colombia	6,591
Argentina	4,774

Only non-Latin American country in top 10

Source: U.S. Citizenship and Immigration Services, Census Bureau, September 2017

Dispute Over Border Wall Funding Slows Progress on Appropriations

As President Donald Trump and Congress deadlocked over broader immigration issues, they made little progress during 2017 on his campaign promise to build a wall along the border with Mexico.

Trump signed an executive order on Jan. 25 that made clear that U.S. taxpayers would foot the bill for the border wall, at least initially, despite his campaign pledge that Mexico would pay for the project. However, Congress would ultimately need to approve funds for the project through the appropriations process. But even in the Republican-controlled House and Senate, there were significant reservations, plus differences over the logistics and costs.

A final price tag would remain murky until the administration hammered out final details, including what material they would use to construct the wall, who would build it and what portions of the southern border it would cover.

When he unveiled the first outline of Trump's fiscal 2018 budget proposal on March 15, Mick Mulvaney, director of the White House Office of Management and Budget, said that $30 billion in supplemental spending for 2017 would include $1.5 billion to build a wall along the U.S.-Mexico border.

The $1.5 billion would be the first installment of a project that could cost taxpayers around $25 billion or more, according to independent estimates.

Mulvaney said at a briefing that the White House was seeking another $2.6 billion to continue building the wall in fiscal 2018. "I think the funding provides for a couple of different pilot cases," he said. "Different kinds of barriers in different kinds of places, as we try to find the most cost-efficient, the safest and also the most effective border protections."

"So the $1.5 billion allows us to start that program. We come along with additional funding, $2.6 billion in 2018, and obviously when we get to the full budget in May, you also start seeing some projections out throughout the 10-year window," he added.

Facing an April 28 deadline to complete a fiscal 2017 spending package, Trump backed off demands to include funding for the wall in that measure. According to an administration official, Trump told conservative media outlets during an April 23 reception that the funding might not be secured until September. But in a tweet the next morning, he wrote, "Don't let the fake media tell you that I have changed my position on the WALL. It will get built and help stop drugs, human trafficking etc."

The deal to fund the government through the end of fiscal 2017 included $1.5 billion for border security technology, border roads and repairs to existing sections of the wall but no new physical barrier between the United States and Mexico. Nearly $350 million was set aside to replace 40 miles of existing fencing with higher, stronger steel structures.

Democrats highlighted that the funding was not dedicated to new wall construction, pointing to language in the measure that specifically blocked spending on new sections of the wall.

In July, House Homeland Security Chairman Michael McCaul, R-Texas, introduced legislation that would authorize $10 billion for a border wall and related technologies as well as money to hire thousands of border and immigration agents. The committee approved the bill (HR 3548) on an 18-12 party-line vote on Oct. 4.

"We have been talking about border security for many years," McCaul said. "Now that we finally have a partner in the White House who has prioritized the issue, it's time for Congress to do its part and get the job done."

Rep. Bennie Thompson of Mississippi, the ranking Democrat on the Homeland Security Committee, called the legislation a "boondoggle that abandons past bipartisan efforts to stop throwing money at the border in an ad hoc way."

Final decisions on spending on fiscal 2018, which began Oct. 1, were delayed as Congress remained deadlocked on immigration legislation. Lawmakers passed a continuing resolution for government financing before Congress adjourned in December 2017. ■

Chapter 13

LEGAL AFFAIRS

Gorsuch Confirmed to Supreme Court

The Senate confirmed Judge Neil Gorsuch in April to the seat on the Supreme Court left vacant by the death of Antonin Scalia 14 months earlier. The partisan battle maintained a tenuous conservative majority and reshaped the Senate's confirmation process for high court nominees.

The vote was 54-45, with three Democrats joining 51 Republicans in voting to confirm. But that narrow margin alone does not begin to convey the partisanship that was on display throughout the process, which began with the nomination of a different judge by a president from a different party.

After Scalia died in February 2016, President Barack Obama the next month nominated Merrick Garland, chief judge on the U.S. Court of Appeals for the District of Columbia, to replace him. A Justice Garland would have tilted the ideological balance of the court leftward, with the liberal Obama appointee replacing the conservative stalwart Scalia.

Senate Republicans balked, refusing to hold a Senate Judiciary Committee hearing on the nomination. It was a political gamble that paid off when Donald Trump was elected president in November 2016. Eleven days after taking the oath of office, he nominated Gorsuch, a 49-year-old judge on the U.S. Court of Appeals for the 10th Circuit.

Democrats promised a fight, and Minority Leader Chuck Schumer, D-N.Y., said "the burden is on Judge Neil Gorsuch to prove himself to be within the legal mainstream and, in this new era, willing to vigorously defend the Constitution from abuses of the executive branch and protect the constitutionally enshrined rights of all Americans. Given his record, I have very serious doubts about Judge Gorsuch's ability to meet this standard."

Undergirding Democrats' opposition to Gorsuch was a festering resentment about Garland. But while they mentioned the abandoned Obama nominee at every opportunity, that complaint gained little traction.

Their larger problem was that they had sown the seeds of their own defeat in 2013, when then-Majority Leader Harry Reid of Nevada pushed through an end to filibusters of nominees for executive branch and lower federal court positions by deploying the so-called nuclear option, which lowered the threshold to limit debate from 60 votes to a simple majority. From that moment, it was only a matter of time before a party in need would deploy the same rule change on behalf of a Supreme Court nominee.

Anticipating the change that would leave them without that arrow in their quiver, Democrats needed unanimity in their own ranks and a couple of Republicans to break with their party. They got neither, largely because of Gorsuch's "extraordinary resume," in Trump's words, and an agreeable judicial temperament left them little at which to aim.

A onetime clerk for Justices Anthony M. Kennedy and fellow Coloradan Byron White, Gorsuch graduated from Columbia University and Harvard Law School, then earned a doctorate in legal philosophy at Oxford. Gorsuch also worked in private practice at a Washington law firm and served in the Justice Department during the George W. Bush administration.

"His academic pedigree is exceptional, to put it mildly," said John Malcolm, director of the legal center at the conservative Heritage Foundation. "He is an outstanding writer, he writes very clearly and with a sense of humor."

His wit was on display when he mentioned during remarks accepting the nomination that he had clerked for White, the last justice from Colorado "and the only justice to lead the NFL in rushing" – in 1938.

At his weeklong confirmation hearing in March, Gorsuch stressed that judges "aren't politicians in robes."

"If I thought that were true, I'd hang up the robe," Gorsuch said told the Senate Judiciary Committee. "Putting on a robe reminds us judges that it's time to lose our egos and open our minds." Judges, he said, occupy a "modest station" in a democracy.

Supportive Republicans asked mostly open-ended questions that gave Gorsuch a chance to talk in broad terms about his judicial philosophy.

But when Democratic senators had the mike, things were different. Dianne Feinstein of California went straight to abortion, the top concern of many of the interest groups weighing in on the nomination, suggesting that Gorsuch's "writings do raise questions," although none of his written decisions in 11 years on the bench directly addressed the issue.

Democrats, divided over whether to launch an all-out assault on Gorsuch and risk an end to the filibuster or save that tactic for a later nominee who might alter the ideological makeup of the court, asked pointed questions but were never able to puncture the nominee's pleasant demeanor or determination to avoid getting dragged into particulars.

"We need to know what you'll do when you're called upon to stand up to this president, or any president, if he claims the power to ignore laws that protect fundamental human rights," Sen. Richard J. Durbin, D-Ill., told Gorsuch. "You're going to have your hands full with this president. He's going to keep you busy."

Grassley had started the hearing off by asking Gorsuch directly about that issue.

"That's a softball, Mr. Chairman," Gorsuch responded. "I have no difficulty ruling for or against any party, other than what the law and the facts in a particular case require."

He also told the panel that nobody in the White House had asked him for any commitments or promises about how he might rule in any case. He said he would never make any such promises.

"I don't believe in litmus tests for judges," Gorsuch said. "I wasn't about to become a party to such a thing."

On Roe v. Wade, the 1973 case that established a woman's right to abortion, Gorsuch called the decision a precedent of the Supreme Court that has been reaffirmed as law, and should be treated as such.

Sen. Patrick J. Leahy, D-Vt., the only sitting senator to have voted on every current Supreme Court justice, pressed Gorsuch on his views about religious tests, mentioning that a Republican lawmaker had said Gorsuch's confirmation would be the best thing to help Trump's efforts aimed at temporarily blocking many immigrants, refugees and travelers from Muslim-majority nations from entering the United States.

"Senator, a lot of people say a lot of silly things," Gorsuch said. "He has no idea how I'd rule in that case. And, senator, I'm not going to say anything here that would give anybody any idea how I would rule in any case like that that could come before the Supreme Court or my court, the 10th Circuit."

He gave similarly noncommittal answers – as has every Supreme Court nominee of the past three decades – during more than 11 hours of questioning on other hot-button issues.

"The bottom line, I think, is that I'd like to convey to you from the bottom of my heart, is that I'm a fair judge," Gorsuch testified. "I can't guarantee you more than that, but I can promise you absolutely nothing less."

When Feinstein pressed for his opinion about a Second Amendment gun rights case, Gorsuch said: "It's not a matter of agreeing or disagreeing, senator, respectfully, it's a matter of it being the law. My job is to apply and enforce the law."

That wasn't enough for Durbin, who told Gorsuch that senators "know your love of fly fishing and rodeos and family," but Democrats are looking for a "beating heart and independent streak."

"I want to try to understand what Neil Gorsuch's heart is leading him to," Durbin told Gorsuch. "You've told us time and time again no place for my heart here. This is all about the facts, this is all about the law."

"I don't buy that. I don't think the decisions of courts are so robotic, so programmatic, that all you need to do is to look at the facts and look at the law and see there's an obvious conclusion," Durbin said. "If that were the case, there would never be a dissent."

Sen. Lindsey Graham, R-S.C., said Democrats were "taking the nomination process to a place it was never intended to go in the Constitution" because they say they won't vote for Gorsuch unless he agrees not to get in the way of their agenda. "If we're going to vote against a nominee because they won't tell us things that we want to hear about issues important to us, then the whole nominating process has become a joke."

On April 3 the committee approved the nomination on a party-line 11-9 vote.

CONFIRMATION VOTE

Gorsuch had been confirmed by voice vote when he joined the 10th circuit in 2006. The partisan committee vote made it clear that such unanimity was not in the offing this time around.

More than 20 progressive advocacy groups warned their Democratic allies that Gorsuch would threaten "the rights of women, LGBTQ people, communities of color, and workers," and they urged a filibuster of the nomination, an all-or-nothing strategy that looked to have little chance of success and carried considerable long-term risk. Democrats knew that a filibuster of Gorsuch, set to replace a fellow conservative on the court, might blow up in their faces should Republicans end the filibuster in response, clearing a path for a future nominee who might be replacing one of the court's reliably liberal justices.

Despite the risk, Schumer got on board quickly and urged others to join him, drawing mock approval from conservatives.

"The fight over abolishing the filibuster for Supreme Court nominees is going to have to be waged some time, and the Gorsuch nomination offers the best possible context for winning that fight," said Ed Whelan, a blogger at National Review and president of the conservative Ethics and Public Policy Center.

For his part, Majority Leader Mitch McConnell, R-Ky., remained cagy about what his response would be.

Sen. Jeff Merkley, D-Ore., held the floor for more than 15 hours to oppose Gorsuch and criticize Republicans for threatening to change Senate rules. And he got in a few jabs about the discarded Garland nomination, saying Republicans "in this chamber decided to steal a Supreme Court seat."

When Democrats forced a cloture vote, the die was cast. Gorsuch supporters fell five votes short of the 60 needed, and Republicans stuck together April 6 on the "nuclear option," ending the filibuster for Supreme Court nominees just as Democrats had done for district and appellate court nominees four years earlier.

In the final confirmation vote on April 7, Gorsuch won the votes of three Democrats — Joe Manchin III of West Virginia, Joe Donnelly of Indiana and Heidi Heitkamp of North Dakota, who also supported cloture — and 51 Republicans. GOP Sen. Johnny Isakson of Georgia was not present for the vote.

It was the lowest vote total for a confirmed justice since Clarence Thomas was confirmed in 1991 on a 52-48 vote.

McConnell said that ending the judicial filibuster would likely be one of the "most consequential decisions I've ever been involved in."

ON THE COURT

Once confirmed, Gorsuch wasted little time at his first oral arguments, quickly showing himself to be an active questioner with a dash of humor and an insistence on hewing closely to legislative text.

His first case lacked the firepower of the sort he had confronted questions about during his confirmation process. Lawyers described Anthony Perry v. Merit Systems Protection Board – about how MSPB cases should traverse the judicial system -- as "unbelievably complicated."

After considerable back and forth about the particulars of the governing law, Gorsuch suggested a way to interpret the statute – and gave a clear indication of his judicial philosophy: "Wouldn't it be a lot easier if we followed the plain text of the statute? What am I missing?"

On a higher profile case – on the topic of religious liberty, something Gorsuch had a track record on as an appellate court judge – he asked few questions and made few comments during oral arguments.

Gorsuch often sided with religious concerns as a federal appeals court judge, including a concurring opinion backing the retail chain Hobby Lobby. The 10th Circuit said — and the Supreme Court affirmed — that Hobby Lobby did not have to offer contraceptive coverage for employees under the 2010 health care law (PL 111-48, PL 111-52) because of the owners' religious beliefs.

In another case, Jason McGehee, et al. v. Asa Hutchinson, Gorsuch joined his conservative colleagues to allow the execution of an Arkansas death row inmate, rejecting concerns that the state was hurrying to carry out eight death sentences in 11 days only because an execution drug was about to expire.

In his first written opinion, Gorsuch delivered some alliteration in a unanimous decision about who qualifies as a debt collector under a 1977 law.

"Disruptive dinnertime calls, downright deceit, and more besides drew Congress's eye to the debt collection industry," Gorsuch wrote.

Gorsuch used that same first opinion to expound on his judicial philosophy of focusing on the text. He waived off arguments about what Congress meant when it wrote the debt collection law: "All of this seems to us quite a lot of speculation."

"And while it is our job to apply faithfully the law Congress has written, it is never our job to rewrite a constitutionally valid statutory text under the banner of speculation about what Congress might have done had it faced a question that, on everyone's account, it never faced," Gorsuch wrote. ■

Contentious Cases Fill Court's Docket

The Supreme Court experienced an eventful year, welcoming a new justice, deciding major cases on generic drugs and free speech, and agreeing to hear high-stakes disputes on gerrymandering, union dues and religious liberty.

Justice Neil Gorsuch joined the court in April, 14 months after the death of Justice Antonin Scalia. His impact was not immediately apparent. But as October approached, it became clear that his presence would make a considerable difference in a number of closely argued cases for his first full term in 2017-18.

FIRST AMENDMENT CASES

As the court wrapped up its 2016-17 term in June with a full complement of justices, it sided with the Asian-American dance-rock band The Slants in ruling that the government can't deny trademark requests as derogatory under a longstanding federal law (PL 79-489). The U.S. Patent and Trademark Office had denied a trademark to The Slants arguing that the reference to persons of Asian ancestry was disparaging.

The decision also appears to benefit the Washington Redskins, which has been in a long-running dispute with some Native American tribes, which contend the team's name is racist. The football team had asked the Supreme Court to take its separate case challenging a ruling that upheld the cancelation of its trademark under the same 1946 law, but the justices did not take that case.

Justice Samuel A. Alito Jr., writing the primary part of the opinion, rejected the idea that the government has an interest in preventing speech expressing ideas that offend, saying that "strikes at the heart of the First Amendment."

"Speech that demeans on the basis of race, ethnicity, gender, religion, age, disability, or any other similar ground is hateful; but the proudest boast of our free speech jurisprudence is that we protect the freedom to express 'the thought that we hate,'" Alito wrote.

No justices dissented in the case, Matal v. Tam, Docket No. 15-1293.

In another First Amendment case, the court unanimously ruled that a 2008 North Carolina law went too far in banning convicted sex offenders from accessing certain websites because it would

freeze out people who had already served their sentences from community discussions, the court ruled.

"On Facebook, for example, users can debate religion and politics with their friends and neighbors or share vacation photos. On LinkedIn, users can look for work, advertise for employees, or review tips on entrepreneurship. And on Twitter, users can petition their elected representatives and otherwise engage with them in a direct manner," Justice Anthony M. Kennedy wrote. "Indeed, Governors in all 50 States and almost every Member of Congress have set up accounts for this purpose."

Kennedy wrote that the decision should not be read to bar states from enacting more specific laws to stop convicted sex offenders from contacting a minor or using a website to gather information about a minor. But foreclosing access to social media altogether prevents exercise of First Amendment rights.

Alito wrote a concurring opinion that agrees with the decision but warned that the main opinion went too far and could be interpreted by some to mean states are largely powerless to restrict dangerous sexual

predators from visiting teenage dating sites.

"I am troubled by the implications of the Court's unnecessary rhetoric," Alito wrote. Chief Justice John G. Roberts Jr. and Justice Clarence Thomas joined in the concurrence.

The case is Packingham v. North Carolina, Docket No. 15-1194.

GENERIC DRUGS

In a pair of rulings, the court handed generic drug makers one full and one partial victory.

A unanimous court said that generic makers of complex biotech treatments do not have to wait 180 days after winning Food and Drug Administration approval before selling their products.

The court also ruled that brand-name drugmakers can't use federal legal remedies to force potential generic competitors to share information about their products. While the decision should help generic drugmakers under federal law, the court is asking a circuit court to decide whether a brand-name company that manufactures the original drug could compel that information-sharing under state laws.

Because the ruling could help so-called biosimilars reach the market six months earlier than they otherwise might have, the makers of the original product would likely lose profits while consumers and insurers could enjoy significant savings. Biosimilars are biological drugs–drugs made from large and generally complex molecules that are produced from living organisms–that are similar to an approved biologic.

"The Supreme Court's ruling on biosimilars will help create more competition among costly biologic medications, which is the key to reducing overall prescription drug costs for consumers, employers, government programs, and others," the Pharmaceutical Care Management Association, which represents the companies that run pharmacy drug benefit programs, said in a statement.

The case is Amgen v. Sandoz.

2017-18 TERM

In a closely watched case that could hinge on the vote of Gorsuch, the court agreed to consider a major labor case that threatened the funding of public-sector unions and promised government workers the chance to keep their jobs without joining a union or paying non-member fees.

The case asks the Supreme Court to overturn a 1977 opinion that allows public-sector unions to collect fees from non-members to cover the union's cost for actions that help all employees. The challenger, Illinois state employee Mark Janus, argues the fees are coerced speech that violates his First Amendment rights.

Unions fear that if non-members don't have to pay fees then fewer would do so, meaning less money for its core functions of collective bargaining. Janus argued that such bargaining by public-sector unions is inherently political because it affects issues such as government spending, taxes and education policy.

The court's decision to hear the case underscored how the Supreme Court, once hamstrung by the absence of a ninth justice, could change direction with Gorsuch on the bench.

The last time the issue was before the court in the 2015-16 term, legal experts predicted that conservative justices would prevail in a case to overturn the court's 1977 ruling in Abood v. Detroit Board of Education.

But that was before Scalia's death in February 2016.

A month later the Supreme Court issued a one-line order that said the court was tied at 4-4. The result affirmed a lower court ruling that continued to allow unions to require the dues.

The case is Janus v. AFSCME, Docket No. 16-1466.

POLITICAL GERRYMANDERING

The court appeared deeply divided during oral arguments in a case that could determine the fate of partisan gerrymandering across the nation.

Paul Smith, representing the Wisconsin voters who challenged a Republican-drawn legislative map in the case, urged the justices to step in and allow federal courts to stop partisan gerrymandering.

But the court's conservative members appeared reluctant to step into what has historically been the political process of redistricting. And the liberal justices grappled for a workable standard for judges to follow when analyzing whether a state's maps give such an advantage to one political party over the other that it violates the Constitution.

Justice Anthony M. Kennedy, thought by many court watchers to be the deciding vote in the case, gave few clues to his thinking during the arguments. Kennedy questioned whether Wisconsin voters have a right to challenge the state's political maps at all, but also asked other questions that made him appear open to the idea that partisan gerrymandering could violate the First Amendment.

The case came to the Supreme Court after a three-judge panel, in a 2-1 vote, struck down Wisconsin's map that used a mechanism known as the "efficiency gap" — which expresses with a number the systematic advantage given to a political party. The case has attracted wide interest just as both parties are mobilizing to influence how maps for Congress and state legislatures are drawn after the 2020 census.

Chief Justice John G. Roberts Jr. expressed concern that the Supreme Court could risk its reputation if it allowed courts to decide partisan gerrymandering cases with a complex formula, since "an intelligent man on the street" is going to say the justices preferred one party over the other.

"We would have to decide in every single case whether Democrats win or Republicans win," Roberts said. "And that's going to come out one case after another as these cases are brought in every state. And that is going to cause very serious harm to the status and integrity of the decisions of this court in the eyes of the country."

The attorney for Wisconsin, Misha Tseytlin, told the justices that allowing courts to hear partisan gerrymandering claims would cause a "redistricting revolution" of litigation across the country.

And Tseytlin said the voters in this case were using "scare tactics" about the future of democracy, since under their own formula the amount of partisan gerrymandering was worse in 1972 than 2014. Of the 17 worst partisan gerrymandering identified by the voters' expert, he said, 10 were drawn by a court or through a process that involved both parties.

The case is Gill v. Whitford, Docket No. 16-116.

PREGNANCY CENTERS

In another hotly contested political issue, the court agreed to hear a case involving a California law that requires religious pregnancy crisis centers to post information on how to obtain a state-funded abortion.

The National Institute of Family and Life Advocates said the law violates the First Amendment rights of more than 110 members that run centers because they were forced to make statements that undermine their religious convictions while other medical and non-medical providers are exempted.

The pregnancy centers said California "now forces licensed centers to communicate the government's message about state-funded abortions to everyone who walks in the door."

The U.S. Court of Appeals for the 9th Circuit upheld the law, finding California has a substantial interest in "the health of its citizens, including ensuring that its citizens have access to and adequate information about constitutionally-protected medical services like abortion."

California had urged the Supreme Court not to hear the case, arguing in a brief that the law educates the 700,000 women who become pregnant each year in the state about public programs, and clears confusion about whether the care and advice comes from a medical professional.

The case is National Institute of Family and Life Advocates v. Becerra, Docket No. 16-1140.

GAY WEDDING CAKES

On another high-profile social issue, the court held oral arguments in a religious freedom case to decide if Masterpiece Cakeshop owner Jack Phillips should be legally required to design a custom wedding cake for a same-sex wedding.

It was the most closely watched case facing the justices in the 2017-18 term and pitted advocates for LGBT rights against the free speech and free exercise rights of those with religious objections.

Dozens of civil rights, religious, legal and other groups filed briefs to sway the justices. People lined up to save a spot in the courtroom days in advance or oral arguments. And lawmakers weighed in at rallies in front of the Supreme Court.

Legal experts said the Supreme Court would be forced to draw a line between protecting the dignity of same-sex couples and protecting an artist and his free speech and religious rights.

The case pitted two of Justice Kennedy's hallmark issues against each other. He authored the court's recent gay rights rulings, including the legalization of same-sex marriage, but has also been a strong defender of free speech and free exercise rights.

The case is Masterpiece Cakeshop et al. v. Colorado Civil Rights Commission et al., Docket No. 16-111.

SOFT MONEY

The court on May 22 upheld the so-called soft money ban on state and local parties, prompting opponents of the restriction to turn their pleas for repeal to Congress.

Although proponents of political money limits cheered the decision, they said that Justice Neil Gorsuch's position on the case confirmed their fears about his campaign finance views.

The ban stemmed from the 2002 McCain-Feingold law (PL 107-155), which prohibited unlimited and unregulated large contributions to party committees known as soft money. The high court affirmed, without hearing oral arguments, a lower court ruling that denied the Louisiana Republican Party's challenge to soft money bans for state and local parties.

"I'm disappointed in the decision, but it's not that big of a surprise," said Hans A. von Spakovsky, a former Federal Election Commission member who manages the Election Law Reform Initiative at the conservative Heritage Foundation. "It's now pretty clear that the court

is just not going to get into this part of McCain-Feingold and if the parties want these provisions to change, they're going to have to go to Congress."

"By rejecting the challenge to political party soft money bans, the Supreme Court has once again affirmed contribution limits as constitutional," said Rep. John Sarbanes of Maryland, chairman of the House›s Democracy Reform Task Force. "Going forward, we must remain vigilant against efforts to further erode reasonable restrictions on big money in politics."

Sarbanes and outside advocates of new restrictions on political money said they were dismayed that Gorsuch, along with conservative Justice Clarence Thomas, went out of his way to say he wanted the court to hear oral arguments on the Louisiana case.

Still, political money and good government groups said the Supreme Court's decision was significant in that it yet again upheld limits on donations to political parties and candidates.

"The most important thing here is the Supreme Court said, 'Yes, we understand these limits are important because there are remaining questions here about corruption and the appearance of corruption,'" said Meredith McGehee, chief of policy, programs and strategy at the bipartisan campaign finance group Issue One. "It's not that parties can corrupt our candidates. The point is to say that parties can be used to circumvent the protections and can be hollowed out just to be these laundromats for large donors to gain influence."

Daniel Weiner, a senior counsel with the Brennan Center for Justice at the New York University School of Law, said the Supreme Court's decision was a good one for those who think decisions about money and politics ought to be made by the legislative branch, not the judicial branch.

The case is Republican Party of Louisiana v. Federal Election Commission, Docket No. 16-865.

SPORTS BETTING

The Supreme Court agreed in June to hear New Jersey's appeal of a lawsuit that sought to overturn the Professional and Amateur Sports Protection Act (PL 102-559). The case was argued in December.

New Jersey lawmakers from both parties have backed legislation in recent years to allow sports betting in the Garden State.

The American Gaming Association launched the American Sports Betting Coalition in June with the goal of persuading Congress to repeal a 1992 law that bans every state but Nevada from allowing sports betting.

The new lobbying group included state and local governments hoping to cash in on the potential bounty of legalized gambling, but also law enforcement associations that favor robust regulations that make it easier to police wagering activating.

The goal of the new coalition was to urge Congress to repeal a 25-year-old law that prohibits nearly all sports betting outside Nevada. A number of states have enacted laws that would permit sports betting in the event the federal law was repealed or overturned in court.

"Big Government's 1992 sports betting prohibition has failed to protect sports, fans and communities," said Geoff Freeman, the casino group's president and chief executive. "We are partnering with local and state elected officials, law enforcement and other diverse interests to tell Washington to get out of the way."

The cases are Governor Christopher J. Christie et al v. National Collegiate Athletic Association et al, Docket No. 16-476, and New Jersey Thoroughbred Horsemen's Association Inc. et al v. National Collegiate Athletic Association et al, Docket No. 16-477. ∎

Shootings Shadow Gun-Related Bills

Congress considered a handful of gun-related measures, including bills that would make it easier to buy noise suppressors and harder to buy bump stocks, the latter of which became a possible area of agreement in the wake of the killing of 58 people in Las Vegas by a shooter who used the device.

The silencer legislation (HR 3668) by Rep. Jeff Duncan, R-S.C., that won committee approval in September had originally been scheduled for consideration in June as a much narrower piece of legislation (HR 367). It was pulled after James Hodgkinson, a volunteer on Sen. Bernie Sanders' 2016 Democratic presidential campaign, shot and critically wounded Rep. Steve Scalise, R-La., during practice for the Congressional Baseball Game.

Duncan's bill was a wide-ranging measure that would require that sales of suppressors, which muffle but don't silence gun discharges, be treated the same as guns; end the requirement to register their purchase; require the attorney general to destroy any existing registrations of silencers in the National Firearms Registration and Transfer Record within a year of the bill becoming law; remove numerous federal restrictions on the sale and import of certain firearms; and lift federal restrictions on some hunting and fishing practices, including which animals can be hunted and what methods can be used. A similar bill (HR 3139) by Rep. Steve

King, R-Iowa, was referred to the Judiciary and Ways and Means committees.

Rep. William Lacy Clay, D-Mo., said the bill was "anti-law enforcement, dangerous and reckless and doesn't deserve our time," and said supporters would "have blood" on their hands.

Democrats also objected to the hunting provisions, which would direct the Interior Department to issue regulations removing the gray wolf from listing under the Endangered Species and block review of the rule by courts.

Another provision would direct the Interior secretary to withdraw rules imposed in 2015 that restricted predator hunting practices in national preserves in Alaska, including hunting wolf and coyote pups and the use of artificial light to take black bear cubs and sows with cubs at dens. The measure also would permit the use of dogs for hunting deer in forests.

Rep. Anthony G. Brown, D-Md., said the "bill is no longer about American hunters or protecting our long tradition and heritage of outdoor shooting. It has become a vehicle to weaken our gun safety laws and boost gun profits as sales are lagging. If the majority wants to roll back gun laws or tell states that the actions they've taken to reduce gun violence are unnecessary, they should do so openly and transparently."

BUMP STOCKS

In the wake of an Oct. 1 shooting in Las Vegas that resulted in 58 killed and hundreds of injured, bipartisan support emerged for addressing access to bump stocks — firearm accessories that effectively convert semiautomatic rifles into automatic weapons.

President Donald Trump said he was open to banning bump stocks, and the National Rifle Association called on the Bureau of Alcohol, Tobacco, Firearms and Explosives to review whether the devices should be subject to additional regulation.

Among the Republican lawmakers expressing support for a legislative remedy were

Reps. Carlos Curbelo of Florida and Lynn Jenkins and Kevin Yoder of Kansas.

Others said the subject at least needed to be looked into, including Speaker of the House Paul Ryan of Wisconsin and two members of the Republican Senate leadership, Majority Whip John Cornyn of Texas and Conference Chairman John Thune of South Dakota.

At the same time, some Democrats who support gun rights were reluctant to immediately endorse an outright ban.

"From the attack that wounded Congressman Scalise to the tragedy in Las Vegas, it is clear that gun violence needs to be addressed," said Rep. Henry Cuellar of Texas. "When the investigation is completed I will be working with my friends on both sides of aisle and in both houses to craft common sense policies to protect Americans and curb gun violence while protecting our constitutional rights."

Stephen Paddock, the 64-year-old Las Vegas gunman, used 12 semiautomatic rifles equipped with bump stocks in the Oct. 1 attack. Semiautomatic rifles require the shooter to manually pull the trigger to fire each round. A bump stock attachment modifies the gun's mechanics so that all a shooter must do to fire a round is apply constant pressure on the trigger.

But simulating automatic fire doesn't necessarily require the purchase of a mechanical device. One stumbling block to any effective legislative or regulatory solution is that bump stock-like fire is relatively easy to devise using ordinary items such as a belt loop or shoulder strap, or even combining a loose hold on the weapon with a rigid finger.

BACKGROUND CHECK REPORTING

Another potential area of bipartisan agreement came with the introduction of legislation (S 2135) that would penalize federal agencies that fail to report to the FBI's National Instant Criminal Background Check System the names of people who should be barred from buying guns.

BOX SCORE

Bills – HR 3668, HR 3139, HR 1181, HR 367, H J Res 40, S 2135, HR 3999, S 1916 – criminal background checks and firearms sales.

LEGISLATIVE ACTION:

House Natural Resources Committee approved HR 3668 on Sept. 13.

House Agriculture Committee, House Judiciary Committee, House Energy and Commerce Committee, House Transportation and Infrastructure Committee, and House Ways and Means Committee discharged HR 3668 pursuant to clause 2 of Rule XIII on Sept. 18.

Bill – HJ Res 40 — Disapproval of firearms purchase limitations for Social Security beneficiaries.

House passed, 235-180, on Feb. 2.

Senate passed, 57-43, on Feb. 15.

President signed Feb. 28 (PL 115-8).

Bill – HR 1181— Disapproval of firearms purchase limitations for veterans.

House Veterans Affairs Committee approved by voice vote on March 8.

House passed, 240-175, on March 16.

The bill was unveiled by Cornyn and Sen. Tim Scott, R-S.C., in the aftermath of the Las Vegas shooting and a Nov. 5 attack at a Baptist church east of San Antonio. A military court had convicted the Texas gunman, Devin Patrick Kelley, in 2012 of beating his wife and stepson, which should have landed him in the background check system. But the court apparently never reported the conviction to the FBI.

In 2011 and 2014, gun control groups started by former New York City Mayor Michael Bloomberg, Mayors Against Illegal Guns and Everytown for Gun Safety published reports warning that many states were not complying with background-check reporting requirements. The groups continue to keep a tally of mental health records reported by each state. New Jersey has reported the most names, 449,153, while New Hampshire has reported only two.

The NRA lined up behind the Cornyn-Scott bill, saying it was all for putting every name in the database that ought to be there.

Considerable debate remained, however, about who fit that description, and in one aspect of that argument, Republican gun-rights supporters and the NRA were joined by the American Civil Liberties Union.

A rule finalized in the last month of President Barack Obama's presidency added the names of people on Social Security disability whom the government had found incapable of managing their own financial affairs to the FBI list of people barred from buying guns.

Gun-rights advocates cried foul, and were joined by the ACLU, which argued that "the rule includes no meaningful due process protections prior to the Social Security Administration's transmittal of names."

In February, both the House and Senate approved a measure (HJ Res 40) to rescind the Social Security Administration regulation. Four Democrats and one independent who caucuses with the Democrats supported the measure in the Senate. All four Democrats -- Joe Donnelly of Indiana, Heidi Heitkamp of North Dakota, Joe Manchin III of West Virginia and Jon Tester of Montana -- are up for re-election in states won by Trump in 2016.

The Veterans Affairs Department had preceded the Social Security Administration in forwarding to the FBI the names of veterans it had deemed incapable of managing their financial affairs. In March, with a dozen Democrats joining all but two Republicans, the House passed a bill (HR 1181) by Veterans Affairs Committee Chairman Phil Roe, R-Tenn., to stop the VA from reporting the names. ∎

Criminal Justice Changes Are Pursued

Just three weeks after taking the oath of office, President Donald Trump signed three executive actions directing the departments of Justice and Homeland Security to crack down on crime. Later in the year, he was working on criminal justice overhaul legislation with senators from both parties.

Early in the year, the president stressed the "menace of rising crime and the threat of deadly terror." He had campaigned as a "law and order" candidate and routinely spoke about rising crime rates in America.

Critics before and after the election pointed to statistics showing a long-term decline in violent crime and contended his administration, including Attorney General Jeff Sessions, was exaggerating the nation's crime problems. The violent crime rate increased slightly in 2016, but remains near the bottom of the nation's 30-year downward trend.

In the three executive actions, Trump:

Directed Justice and Homeland Security to "undertake all necessary and lawful action to break the back of the criminal cartels that have spread across our nation and are destroying the blood of our youth and other people, many other people."

Directed the Justice Department to form a task force on reducing violent crime.

Prioritized the pursuit of "appropriate legislation" to define new crimes, and increase penalties for existing crimes, to prevent violence against federal, state, tribal and local law enforcement officers.

Trump said the message to gang members and drug dealers and drug dealers was that "a new era of justice begins and it begins right now."

SEX-OFFENDER REGISTRY

The following month, the House Judiciary Committee approved three bills aimed at protecting children from sexual abuse.

One measure (HR 1188) would have reauthorized the Sex Offender Management Assistance Program, which provides grants to state and local law enforcement agencies to assist them with tracking registered sex offenders living in their jurisdictions.

The program was initially authorized in 2006 by a law known as the Adam Walsh Child Protection and Safety Act, which provides the current framework for monitoring and registering sex offenders.

The measure, by Wisconsin Republican Jim Sensenbrenner, also would have authorized $60 million for the U.S. Marshals Service to assist state and local law enforcement apprehension of convicted sex offenders who violate registration requirements.

Several of the bill's provisions aimed to modernize the registration system, including provisions that allowed offenders to conduct check-ins through virtual means. Sensenbrenner noted that some of these changes would make it easier for states to comply with federal sex offender registration and notification laws.

BOX SCORE

Bills – S 1917, HR 1188, HR 695, HR 883

LEGISLATIVE ACTION:

House Judiciary Committee approved HR 1188 by voice vote on March 22.

House passed HR 1188 by voice vote under suspension of the rules on May 22.

House Judiciary Committee approved HR 695 on March 22.

House passed HR 695 by voice vote on May 22.

Senate Judiciary Committee approved HR 695 on Oct. 16.

Senate passed HR 695 by voice vote on Oct. 16.

House Judiciary Committee approved HR 883 on March 22.

House passed HR 883 by voice vote on May 22.

The committee's ranking Democrat, John Conyers Jr. of Michigan, expressed overall support but was critical of the "one size-fits-all" approach federal legislation takes on sex offender registration, especially as it applies to juvenile offenders, and noted that "there is still much work to be done."

Another measure (HR 695) would have made permanent a pilot program at the Justice Department to provide criminal background checks through the FBI to non-profit organizations that work with children, the elderly, or individuals with disabilities.

A third measure (HR 883) would have prohibited the recipient of an administrative subpoena, such as an internet service provider, from disclosing the existence of the subpoena during an investigation involving child exploitation. Under current procedures, investigators must apply through the court system for a non-disclosure order. Goodlatte said that revealing the existence of a subpoena "can put a victim in imminent danger, cause the target to flee or destroy evidence, or otherwise endanger the integrity of the investigation."

CRIMINAL JUSTICE OVERHAUL

After the emphasis early in the year on cracking down on crime, lawmakers turned in the fall toward a bipartisan effort to overhaul the federal criminal justice system

The centerpiece was a bill aimed at reducing mandatory minimum sentences for non-violent drug offenders, giving judges more flexibility in sentencing, adding some new mandatory minimums for certain crimes and helping ease the re-entry of released prisoners back into their communities.

The authors included language authorizing $14 million for a two-year commission to review the criminal justice system and make recommendations to Congress and the president, whose support for the effort remained unclear.

In May, the president proposed cutting from $68 million in the fiscal 2017 omnibus package to $48 million in fiscal 2018 a Justice Department grant program that funded just the kind of recidivism-reduction programs the legislation would promote. Majority Whip John Cornyn and others said the proposed cut in Second Chance Act grants would go nowhere.

Senate Judiciary Chairman Charles E. Grassley, R-Iowa, praised the bill (S 1917) for getting rid of unfair mandatory minimums, targeting violent and career criminals, and saving taxpayer dollars on prisons.

"This bill strikes the right balance of improving public safety and ensuring fairness in the criminal justice system," Grassley said, while noting that it was far from a finished product and that lawmakers would "continue to welcome input from stakeholders as we move forward."

The bill drew negative responses from some tough-on-crime Republican senators who had opposed similar legislation in 2016. One

of those had been Jeff Sessions, an Alabama senator in 2016 and now attorney general.

Another hurdle was Utah Republican Orrin Hatch, who insisted that the bill include a provision to establish mens rea, or a "guilty mind" standard, for some federal crimes amid concerns that the criminal code has grown too unwieldy with regulatory crimes. Sessions also insisted that the provision needed to be included.

Senate Democrats opposed that change because they say it would make it easier for white-collar criminals to escape prosecution.

But Cornyn, whose home state of Texas has been a leader on prison reform, was a vocal backer of the bill, which included several provisions that he authored, and it also had support from a varied coalition that included President Barack Obama and Koch Industries, the energy conglomerate founded by conservatives Charles and David Koch.

Another aspect of the debate centered on the opioid crisis, which lent an air of urgency to the debate and was seen as an avenue to win support from the Trump administration.

In an address to an Advancing Justice event in Washington put on by the Charles Koch Institute, Grassley said the Senate bill would free up taxpayer dollars to focus on other important priorities in the criminal justice system, most notably opioid abuse.

"One area where these resources could be effectively deployed is something the president declared a national health emergency today, the opioid crisis," Grassley said. "To tackle the opioid crisis and continue our fight against drug trafficking and violent crime, we need to focus our resources on the most serious offenders." ∎

Change in System to Name Leader Of Copyright Office Is Passed in House

The House moved in April to usurp the authority of the Librarian of Congress to appoint the register of copyrights by easily passing bipartisan legislation that would create a seven-member panel to approve a list of three candidates from which the president would select one to run the U.S. Copyright Office.

The legislation (HR 1695), by Judiciary Committee Chairman Robert W. Goodlatte, R-Va., would have created a 10-year term for the office and hand creative industries a win over public libraries, which prefer the current arrangement.

The nominating panel would have included the Speaker of the House, the president pro tempore of the Senate, the majority and minority leaders of the House and Senate, and the Librarian of Congress.

Goodlatte said the existing system exacerbates disputes between copyright holders and those who use copyrighted material. The goal of his legislation is to reduce such litigation.

BOX SCORE

Bills – HR 1695 -- Change nomination system for register of Copyrights

LEGISLATIVE ACTION:

House Judiciary Committee approved HR 1695 on March 29.

House passed HR 1695, 378-48, on April 26.

Copyright Alliance CEO Keith Kupferschmid says the bill would help begin to "modernize" the Copyright Office by bringing a "more balanced and neutral selection process."

Librarian of Congress Carla Hayden removed Maria Pallante from her role as copyright registrar in October 2016 by transferring her to a non-managerial advisory role, which Pallante refused. She then resigned.

Hayden did not give a reason for Pallante's removal, but advocates for creative industries believe Hayden didn't support Pallante's efforts to strengthen copyright protections.

In opposition to the measure was the Library Copyright Alliance, a group of organizations that represents over 120,000 libraries, which argues that the Goodlatte bill would politicize a position now shielded from politics. ∎

Issues of Abortion, Immigration Both At Play in D.C. Circuit Court Ruling

The volatile issues of abortion and immigration collided when the U.S. Court of Appeals for the District of Columbia Circuit ruled in October that a 17-year-old unaccompanied illegal immigrant in federal custody had the right to an abortion.

The decision by the full court reversed a ruling by a three-judge panel of the D.C. Circuit that had temporarily barred the girl, known as Jane Doe, from having the procedure.

The abortion was subsequently performed, mooting the government's appeal to the Supreme Court.

In the appeals court, the government did not argue or suggest that the teenager's immigration status eliminated her constitutional right to an abortion. Instead, the argument that an abortion was not in her best interests and that the government would have to facilitate the abortion were not sufficient to overcome the right to an abortion guaranteed by Roe v. Wade.

"Surely the mere act of entry into the United States without documentation does not mean that an immigrant's body is no longer her or his own," Judge Patricia Millett wrote in a concurring opinion. "Nor can the sanction for unlawful entry be forcing a child to have a baby. The bedrock protections of the Fifth Amendment's Due Process Clause cannot be that shallow."

In a dissent, Judge Brett Kavanaugh, joined by Judges Karen LeCraft Henderson and Thomas Griffith, wrote that the majority ruling "is ultimately based on a new constitutional principle as novel as it is wrong: a new right for unlawful immigrant minors in U.S. Government detention to obtain immediate abortion on demand, thereby barring any Government efforts to expeditiously transfer the minors to their immigration sponsors before they make that momentous life decision."

Anti-abortion groups also argued that the case would set a new precedent broadening abortion access.

"Expanding a so-called 'right' of a taxpayer-facilitated abortion to apply to any woman who happens to be on U.S. soil goes against the pro-life views of a majority of Americans, and certainly against the views of most Americans who don't want their tax dollars paying to end life," said Kristan Hawkins, president of Students for Life of America.

Cecile Richards, president of Planned Parenthood Federation of America, which supports abortion rights, said "We hope that this ruling sends a strong signal to the Trump administration. Access to safe, legal abortion is the law."

The case is Rochelle Garza v. Eric Hargan, et al., Docket No. 17-5236. ∎

Obama Commutes Manning Sentence

Three days before leaving office, President Barack Obama commuted the prison sentence of Chelsea Manning, the former U.S. Army intelligence analyst convicted in 2013 of handing over secret military and diplomatic documents to WikiLeaks.

Manning, a transgender woman previously known as Bradley Manning, was freed four months later, having served only seven years of a 35-year sentence.

The commutation was loudly criticized by lawmakers from both parties.

"When I was leading soldiers in Afghanistan, Private Manning was undermining us by leaking hundreds of thousands of classified documents to WikiLeaks," said Sen. Tom Cotton, R-Ark., an Army combat veteran and member of the Armed Services Committee. "I don't understand why the president would feel special compassion for someone who endangered the lives of our troops, diplomats, intelligence officers, and allies. We ought not treat a traitor like a martyr."

Sen. John McCain, chairman of the Armed Services Committee, called the commutation a "grave mistake."

Some Democratic senators, including Robert Menendez of New Jersey and Joe Manchin of New Jersey, were also critical of Obama's move.

Others said the original sentence was unprecedented in its severity for the crimes Manning committed.

"Since she was first taken into custody, Chelsea has been subjected to long stretches of solitary confinement — including for attempting suicide — and has been denied access to medically necessary health care," said Chase Strangio, a staff attorney with the American Civil Liberties Union's LGBT Project representing Manning. "This move could quite literally save Chelsea's life, and we are all better off knowing that Chelsea Manning will walk out of prison a free woman, dedicated to making the world a better place and fighting for justice for so many." ∎

Senators Take On Asset Forfeiture

Six senators asked the chairman and ranking member of the Appropriations Commerce-Justice-Science Subcommittee to use the CJS spending bill (S 1662) to block the Justice Department from implementing a pair of civil asset forfeiture programs the federal government operates with state and local law enforcement.

The lawmakers – Republican Sens. Mike Lee of Utah, Rand Paul of Kentucky and Michael D. Crapo of Idaho; Democrats Jeff Merkley of Oregon and Tom Udall of New Mexico; and independent Angus King of Maine – asked CJS Subcommittee Chairman Richard C. Shelby of Alabama and ranking Democrat Jeanne Shaheen of New Hampshire in November to block funding for equitable sharing, which allows state and federal law enforcement agencies to share the proceeds of a seizure, and adoptive forfeiture, in which the federal government takes assets seized by local police, sells them and splits the proceeds.

The six senators said the civil asset forfeiture practices, which include the seizure of assets of people who have not been charged with any crime, "are an obvious violation of the due process protections found in the Fifth Amendment," which bars search and seizure without charge.

Once property is confiscated, the government has to show only that the property was "connected" to a crime to justify keeping it. The burden of proof lies with property owners seeking to get their property returned.

Critics say civil asset forfeiture gives police an incentive to seize property of suspects, both as a way to apply pressure and as a way to fund department activities, so-called policing for profit.

During the Obama administration, the Justice Department took some steps to curb adoptive forfeiture and equitable sharing. But Attorney General Jeff Sessions announced in July that the Justice Department would reverse course and reinstitute the practices.

A number of states have taken steps to restrict asset forfeiture, and the six senators noted that the federal policy allows state law enforcement officers to circumvent some of those limitations.

"This perversely incentivizes local law enforcement to confiscate suspect property even where state laws forbid the practice," their letter states. ∎

BOX SCORE

Bills – S 1662, HR 3354 — Commerce-Justice-Science appropriations, fiscal 2018 omnibus appropriations

LEGISLATIVE ACTION:

Senate Appropriations Committee approved S 1662 on July 27.

House Appropriations Committee approved HR 3354 on July 18.

House passed HR 3354, 211-198, on Sept. 14.

DOJ Oversight Ruling Irks Lawmakers

A May ruling by the Justice Department Office of Legal Counsel that members of Congress who are not chairmen of committees or subcommittees are not guaranteed a response when requesting information from government agencies could have far-reaching consequences for oversight.

Senate Judiciary Chairman Charles E. Grassley, an Iowa Republican, was among those objecting. He sent a letter to President Donald Trump in June asking him to rescind the ruling and received assurances from White House Director of Legislative Affairs Marc Short that the administration would not follow the OLC's interpretation.

OLC nominee Seth Engel said he would review the opinion.

The "de facto result of the DOJ ruling would be to increase and centralize the power of the executive branch," according to Peter Taylor, a senior policy analyst for the Project on Government Oversight, a watchdog group that supports congressional oversight of the executive branch. ∎

Chapter 14

REGULATORY POLICY

GOP Uses Congressional Review Act To Undo Obama-Era Regulations

The Republican majorities in the House and Senate used the arrival of President Donald Trump to the White House for an unprecedented deployment of the 1996 Congressional Review Act to nullify regulations. The CRA allows lawmakers to reverse regulatory actions with simple majorities as long as they do so within 60 days of the rule's submission to Congress.

Fifteen CRA resolutions passed in 2017, all of them to rescind actions taken late in the Obama administration. Congress had used the CRA to block a regulation only once before, in 2001. President Barack Obama vetoed five efforts to do so by the Republican Congress during his presidency.

Republicans in 2017 saw the CRA (PL 104-121) as a tool to line up their legislative agenda with the new president's executive agenda.

Trump himself took executive actions early in his administration to block regulations from taking effect, to review regulations already in effect, and in some cases to shorten the time that executive agencies had to undertake reviews under existing law. Less than two years into his administration, however, the effect of the president's steps is hard to ascertain. Agencies have to follow cumbersome procedures to approve rules; they must follow a similar procedure to undo them.

But the CRA not only nullifies an approved rule, it also prevents the agency from proposing a substantively similar one unless specifically authorized to do so by Congress.

The congressional votes to reverse rules often weren't strictly partisan and at least one involved a regulation approved under the Trump administration – by an agency, the Consumer Financial Protection Bureau, that had enough independence under its Obama-appointed director to be at odds with the Trump White House.

With the arrival of Trump on Jan. 20, 2017, Congress went quickly to work, sending three joint resolutions to Trump within a month.

CORPORATE BRIBERY

The House voted 235-187 on Feb. 1 to pass a resolution (H J Res 41) to nullify a Securities and Exchange Commission requirement that companies that develop oil, natural gas or minerals publicly report payments of at least $100,000 per year per project to foreign governments or the U.S. government. The Senate voted 52-47 on Feb. 3 to clear the resolution. Trump signed it (PL 115-4) on Feb. 14.

The SEC, directed by the 2010 financial overhaul (PL 111-203) to write the rule, didn't finalize it until 2016.

STREAM PROTECTION

Trump signed the next resolution (PL 115-5) enacted under the CRA two days later, on Feb. 16, this time rescinding the Interior Department's stream protection rule requiring coal companies to avoid activity that permanently polluted streams, destroyed drinking water sources, increased flood risk or risked damage to forests. The companies also had to restore mined areas to allow for uses that existed before the mining activity.

The House approved the joint resolution (H J Res 38) 228-194 on Feb. 1. The Senate followed suit the next day with a 54-45 vote.

PROHIBITION ON GUN PURCHASES

The third CRA nullification in February involved the Social Security Administration's rule adding information on mentally impaired Social Security recipients to a list of those prohibited from buying guns. The Obama administration estimated that 75,000 people a year would be added to the National Instant Criminal Background Check System under the rule, and current law prohibits people from buying a gun if they have a mental health issue.

The Senate cleared the resolution (H J Res 40) in a 57-43 vote on Feb. 15. The House voted 235-180 on Feb. 2 to pass it. The president signed it Feb. 28 (PL 115-8).

ALLEGATIONS OF BREAKING LABOR LAW

Trump signed five disapproval resolutions in March, starting with one that nullified a Defense Department, General Services Administration and NASA requirement that companies bidding on federal contracts over $500,000 disclose allegations of labor law violations.

Contractors would have had to report whether they had been accused of violating one of 14 federal labor laws dealing with wages, occupational safety or civil rights in the past three years.

The House voted 236-187 on Feb. 2 to pass the resolution (H J Res 37). The Senate passed it 49-48 on March 6. The president signed it into law (PL 115-11) on March 27.

BUREAU OF LAND MANAGEMENT PROCEDURES

The House passed, 234-186, a resolution (H J Res 44) on Feb. 7 that would nullify the Bureau of Land Management's amendment to agency procedures for developing resource management plans for public lands. The change was designed to add transparency and get more public comment, but Republicans said it centralized land-use decisions in Washington.

The Senate passed the resolution 51-48 on March 7. The president signed it (PL 115-12) on March 27.

TEACHER TRAINING EVALUATION AND SCHOOL PERFORMANCE

Congress voted to rescind two Education Department rules in March: a requirement that states evaluate and publicly report annually on the effectiveness of teacher training programs and a rule on the accountability measures states use to assess school performance.

Republicans and members of teachers unions opposed the department's rule on teacher training programs, saying it didn't fairly evaluate the programs and posed a risk that some would lose federal grant funding for being low performing or at risk.

The House passed the resolution (H J Res 58) 240-181 on Feb. 7. The Senate voted 59-40 on March 8 to do the same and the president signed it into law (PL 115-14) on March 27.

In a parallel action, Congress nullified the department's rule on the measures states should use to keep schools accountable and to rate them. The House voted 234-190 on Feb 7 for the resolution of disapproval (H J Res 57). The Senate passed it 50-49 on March 9 and the president signed it on March 27 (PL 115-13).

DRUG TESTING FOR UNEMPLOYMENT BENEFITS

The Labor Department finalized a rule in August 2016 that limited when states can test for drug use among applicants for unemployment benefits. The rule said testing could be done only on applicants fired for illegal drug use or looking for work in an occupation that regularly tests for drug use.

The House voted 236-189 on Feb. 15 on a resolution (H J Res 42) to nullify the rule. The Senate voted 51-48 on March 14 to do so. The president signed it into law (PL 115-17) on March 31.

LABOR DEPARTMENT RULES

Lawmakers included three more Labor Department rules on the 2017 chopping block, two of which involved private-sector workers and savings plans. The third rule extended the length of time that companies could be fined for not maintaining records of injuries and illness.

The House voted 234-191 on Feb. 15 to rescind a rule exempting certain local government-administered retirement savings plans from some federal regulations governing pension plans. The rule was designed to assist local governments trying to help private-sector workers save for retirement if their employers didn't offer a retirement plan.

The Senate voted 50-49 to approve the resolution (H J Res 67) on March 30 and the president signed the law (PL 115-24) on April 13.

Congress similarly nullified a Labor Department rule that relaxed standards on states offering programs that automatically enrolled private-sector employees in state-administered savings plans.

The House passed the resolution (H J Res 66) 231-193 on Feb. 15. The Senate voted 50-49 on May 3 to do so. The president signed it (PL 115-35) on May 17.

The Occupational Safety and Health Administration put a rule into effect on Jan. 18, 2017, that gave the agency up to five and a half years to cite employers that didn't maintain records of serious injuries and illnesses for five years. The agency previously had six months from a serious injury or illness to issue the citation.

Dozens of trade and business organizations said the rule was an example of federal overreach and said OSHA was trying to sidestep a 2012 federal appeals court ruling that said OSHA should not have cited a company that failed to maintain an injury log for several months because the citation was issued more than six months after the violation.

The House voted 231-191 on March 1 to approve the resolution (H J Res 83). The Senate followed on March 22 with a 50-48 vote. The president signed it into law (PL 115-21) on April 3.

NON-SUBSISTENCE HUNTING

The House voted 225-193 on Feb. 16 to approve a resolution (H J Res 69) rescinding the Interior Department's prohibition on non-subsistence hunting and trapping practices on national wildlife refuges in Alaska. The rule banned traps to hunt bears and the taking of wolves and coyotes during denning season. The Senate approved it 52-47 on March 21 and the president signed the resolution into law (PL 115-20) on April 3.

ISPS AND USE OF DATA

The Senate made the first move on the resolution of disapproval (S J Res 34) of a Federal Communications Commission rule requiring internet service providers to obtain customers' permission to sell personal information and web browsing history to advertisers. The internet service providers called the rule unfair because it didn't apply to sites such as Google and Facebook.

The Senate passed the resolution 50-48 on March 23. The House passed it 215-205 on March 28 and the president signed it (PL 115-22) on April 3.

FAMILY PLANNING FUNDS

Planned Parenthood, a reproductive health provider that's long been a target of Republicans, was at the center of congressional disapproval of a Health and Human Services Department rule. The rule barred states from denying federal family planning funds to the organization and other operators of health centers that provide abortions.

The House approved a resolution negating that rule (H J Res 43) in a 230-188 vote on Feb. 16. Vice President Mike Pence had to break a 50-50 tie in the Senate to clear the resolution on March 30. The president signed the resolution into law (PL 115-23) on April 13.

MANDATORY ARBITRATION

The final nullification under the CRA in 2017 came Nov. 1 when the president signed into law (PL 115-74) a resolution to nullify the Consumer Financial Protection Bureau's ban on mandatory arbitration clauses in consumer contracts. Companies often include such clauses to discourage consumers from joining class-action lawsuits.

The CFPB rule would have affected tens of millions of contracts with banks, cell phone providers and others, according to then-Director Richard Cordray.

The House voted 231-190 on July 25 to approve the resolution (H J Res 111). The Senate voted 50-50 on Oct. 24 to follow suit, with Vice President Mike Pence breaking the tie. Republicans Lindsey Graham of South Carolina and John Kennedy of Louisiana voted with the Democrats.

NULLIFICATION REJECTED

Three Senate Republicans scuttled an effort to repeal an Interior Department rule limiting methane venting and flaring from oil and gas operations on federal land. Sens. John McCain, R-Ariz., Lindsey Graham, R-S.C. and Susan Collins, R-Maine, voted against the motion to proceed to the resolution (H J Res 36) on May 10. The 49-51 vote on the motion effectively killed the resolution.

Interior said the rule would help ensure a fair return for taxpayers, who receive royalties from the sale of oil and gas extracted on federal land, while also helping combat the release of a harmful climate-warming greenhouse gas. Interior estimated the rule would cut methane emissions by 35 percent. ∎

Other Regulatory Efforts: Mixed Results

Separate from using the Congressional Review Act, Congress also turned to the regular legislative process to roll back previously enacted regulations, but with limited results.

For instance, the House cleared a bill (S 496) on April 27 under suspension of the rules to rescind a rule regarding urban planning organizations. The Senate had passed the measure, sponsored by Sen. Tammy Duckworth, D-Ill., on March 8 by unanimous consent. President Donald Trump signed it (PL 115-33) on May 12.

The bill nullified two Department of Transportation agencies' rule requiring metropolitan planning organizations, or MPOs, in a single urban area to merge into one organization or produce unified plans. The rule from the Federal Transit Administration and the Federal Highway Administration also left open the possibility of future changes to the way such bodies are organized.

By undoing the rule legislatively rather than by using the CRA, lawmakers give the agencies a chance to rewrite the rule.

Other proposals, however, did not advance to Trump's desk.

Sen. Lamar Alexander, R-Tenn., introduced a bill (S 1350) that would have rescinded National Labor Relations Board regulations allowing workers to file a petition to form a union and hold an election as soon as 11 days later. The bill would have extended the time to a minimum of 35 days.

The measure was referred to the Senate Health, Education, Labor and Pensions panel, which Alexander led, and was not marked up.

Three House bills sought to make other changes to NLRB rules. None of the bills advanced farther than the committee level.

Rep. Tim Walberg, R-Mich., sponsored a bill (HR 2776) that advanced by a 22-16 vote through the committee on June 29. Two others bills advanced by the same tally: Indiana Republican Todd Rokita's bill (HR 986) exempting Native American tribes and the businesses they own from NLRB jurisdiction and South Carolina Republican Joe Wilson's bill (HR 2775) that would require employers to give the NLRB a list of all employees eligible to vote in a union election within seven days of the NLRB determines the appropriate bargaining unit.

The House sought a more sweeping change to regulatory oversight in a bill (HR 26), dubbed the REINS Act, that would require Congress to approve major federal regulations before they take effect. The House passed the measure quickly after convening the 115th Congress, voting 237-187 on Jan. 5, with two Democrats joining the majority.

The measure would require lawmakers from both chambers to accept or reject within 70 legislative days all rules with an economic impact of more than $100 million. The bill got no action in the Senate.

Rep. Jason Smith, R-Mo., offered a measure (HR 998) that would establish a regulatory review commission to assess existing regulations and recommend which ones can be eliminated or rolled back. The House passed it 240-185 on March 1, and the Senate took no action. ∎

Chapter 15

SCIENCE & TECHNOLOGY

Ambitious Mission Set for NASA In First Reauthorization in Years

Reauthorization of the National Aeronautics and Space Administration has been sporadic for decades, but backers of the agency pushed a bill into law in 2017, the first time since 2010.

Even when not formally reauthorized, the agency has powerful supporters from both parties in Congress. Even newly inaugurated President Donald Trump, who showed little enthusiasm for NASA on the campaign trail, largely spared it from cuts in his first budget request while proposing sharp reductions in other science programs.

Sen. Ted Cruz, R-Texas, sponsored the 2017 reauthorization legislation (S 442) along with three co-sponsors – Sens. John Cornyn, R-Texas, Bill Nelson, D-Fla., and Marco Rubio, R-Fla. Together they represent the Johnson Space Flight Center in Houston and the Kennedy Space Flight Center in Cape Canaveral, Fla., respectively.

"The importance of NASA and space exploration to Houston and the state of Texas cannot be underestimated," said Cruz. "With the passage of this bipartisan legislation, the future of the U.S. space program is now more secure and stable, and we have provided much-needed certainty to the missions of the International Space Station and Johnson Space Center."

Lawmakers sped through the legislation, needing fewer than three weeks to get it from introduction to passage by voice vote in the Senate and under suspension of the rules in the House. The Senate passed the measure on Feb. 17, the same day it was introduced. The House cleared it on March 7. The bill did not have hearings or markups in either chamber.

Trump signed the $19.5 billion reauthorization into law (PL 115-10) on March 21.

Trump's fiscal 2018 budget request asked for $19.1 billion for NASA, only $200 million less than Congress appropriated in fiscal 2017 and a modest paring compared to his proposals for other science programs. The request reflected strong Republican support in Congress, especially among appropriators and leadership.

"You know, in the old days, it was great," Trump said in November 2015 when a boy at a campaign event in New Hampshire asked for his thoughts on NASA. "Right now, we have bigger problems — you understand that? We've got to fix our potholes. You know, we don't exactly have a lot of money."

PAST ATTEMPTS

The 2017 effort was a sharp contrast to the previous Congress. The House passed a NASA reauthorization in early 2015 and the Senate in late 2016 passed a bill that reflected an agreement between House and Senate authorizers. The House, however, never considered the Senate-passed measure before adjourning the 114th Congress.

This year's measure declared that NASA's long-term goal is the expansion of a permanent human presence beyond low Earth orbit. It set the goal of sending a crew to the surface of Mars and allowed for missions to the Moon, asteroids and Martian moons to help achieve that goal.

How realistic the goal is remains a point of disagreement.

The Obama administration had said in 2010 that its plan was send humans to Mars in the 2030s, but in a 2014 report, the National Academies of Science questioned whether NASA could meet that goal. The academies said the agency has an unsustainable and unsafe strategy that will prevent the United States from achieving a human landing on Mars in the foreseeable future.

It also said funding at current levels that does not keep pace with inflation is to "invite failure, disillusionment and the loss of the long-standing international perception that human spaceflight is something the United States does best."

MARS MISSION

The 2017 reauthorization directed NASA to define the capabilities and technologies needed to send humans to Mars in a Human Exploration Road Map and to update the map every two years. The map also has to provide a process for the evolution for the capabilities of the fully integrated Orion crew capsule with the Space Launch System.

The Orion vehicle and the Space Launch System rocket were mandated by the 2010 authorization and were scheduled for the first integrated test flight in fiscal 2018. The agency said in April, a month after the reauthorization, that it expects to be ready for a maiden flight – dubbed Exploration Mission I – by June 2020.

The reauthorization also requires NASA to develop, test and achieve operational readiness of the Space Launch System and make the Orion capsule a priority, as well as report to Congress on the details of components and systems of Orion to ensure it complies with law and the date it is expected to transport crew and cargo to the space station.

The largest single portion – $5.5 billion – of the 2017 reauthorization would go for science programs followed by:
- $5.0 billion for space operations;
- $4.3 billion for space exploration;
- $2.8 billion for safety, security and mission services;
- $686 million for space technology;
- $640 million for aeronautics;
- $388 million for construction and environmental compliance and restoration;
- $115 million for education;
- $37 million for the inspector general.

The reauthorization encompassed more traditional areas of space exploration and technology. The bill, for example, directed the agency to describe capabilities and technologies needed or that could be gained by using the International Space Station, describe a framework for international cooperation and a process for using non-government entities for human exploration of space. ∎

Cyberthreats Grow, but Little Legislation

Cybersecurity questions in 2017 became as prevalent as the internet itself. Not only was special counsel Robert Mueller III appointed in May to investigate Russian meddling in the 2016 election – an election that involved one candidate's campaign emails being hacked and sophisticated use of social media to manipulate voters – but Congress was hearing of threats to many corners of the federal government as well as the private sector.

News over the year gave a flavor:

The Department of Homeland Security designated election systems as critical national infrastructure.

Lawmakers began work on driverless car bills (HR 3388, S 1885) in which cybersecurity and data protection were among the key provisions.

The Internal Revenue Service told students and families in March that it was taking offline a tool that provided income data for an application for federal student aid.

The agency was worried that identify thieves could use the Data Retrieval Tool to obtain data that could be used to file fraudulent tax returns seeking refunds.

The president signed an executive order in May telling federal agency leaders to identify and fix the federal government's cybersecurity weaknesses in line with long-established guidance from the National Institute of Standards and Technology.

The FBI and the Homeland Security Department said in July they were aware of the "potential cyber intrusion affecting entities in the energy sector." They did so after reports from Bloomberg and The New York Times that Russian-backed hacking groups may have targeted nuclear power plants and grid operation system manufacturers and threatened the electric grid.

The Securities and Exchange Commission disclosed in September 2017 that its popular EDGAR database of company securities filings was breached in 2016. Chairman Jay Clayton said he learned of the breach in August 2017. "We are under constant attack," Clayton told the Senate Banking Committee.

The Energy Department urged Congress in January 2017 to bolster national security and cybersecurity protections for the electricity grid and the top Democrat on the Senate Energy and Natural Resources Committee blamed House Republicans for missing a chance to take action in 2016.

House appropriators told the Energy Department in July that it wasn't doing enough to protect its own systems.

The Homeland Security Department ordered antivirus software made by Kaspersky Labs removed from all federal computers in September because it feared Russian intelligence agents could be using the software to gain access to computer systems. The company sued the DHS in December for wrongful termination of contract.

Lawmakers said in November that the Defense Department hadn't done enough to beef up the military's response to proliferating cyber threats and called on President Donald Trump to develop a national policy that spells out U.S. offensive capabilities.

Lawmakers held hearings about a breach at Equifax Inc., a company that sells consumer credit reports, that involved data on more than 145 million people.

CONGRESSIONAL ACTION

Congress remained largely without a legislative response in 2017, clearing no major cybersecurity measures over the course of the year. And as two of the bullet points above indicate, the legislative and executive branches were at odds over which one needed to do more.

Lawmakers did, however, include $8 billion for cybersecurity initivies in the fiscal 2018 defense authorization (HR 2810). The president signed that measure into law on Dec. 12 (PL 115-91).

Members of Congress noted their frustration with the executive branch in the conference report for that bill.

"Over the past five years, Congress has directed the executive branch to develop a national policy and strategy for deterring U.S. adversaries in cyberspace, but that such a policy and strategy have not been adequately addressed by the executive branch," the committee said.

Senior Senate Republicans led the call for legislation to establish a national standard on company requirements to protect data and disclose breaches. Senate Commerce Chairman John Thune, R-S.D., said in November that he would back such a bill. Senate Judiciary Chairman Charles E. Grassley, R-Iowa, said in October he was committed to getting such a bill "over the finish line."

Neither of their committees, however, marked up cybersecurity legislation in the wake of those comments.

Democrats were pushing a range of bills to address private-sector data breaches. Sen. Richard Blumenthal, D-Conn., introduced a measure (S 1900) that would expand the Federal Trade Commission's powers to allow it to investigate any data breach at a company holding consumer data. Massachusetts Sen. Elizabeth Warren offered a bill (S 1816) that would allow consumers to freeze access to their credit files at no cost. Connecticut Democrat Rep. Jim Himes had a similar House bill (HR 3766).

The House passed in January 2018 by voice vote a bill (HR 3202) from Rep. Sheila Jackson Lee, D-Texas, that would expand congressional oversight over the Homeland Security Department's work with the private sector to disclose cyber vulnerabilities.

Under the measure, the department would have to report to Congress annually and include information on how DHS is working with other federal agencies and managers of private cyber infrastructure to mitigate susceptibility to cyber attacks. The House Homeland Security Committee had approved the measure by voice vote on July 26.

Lawmakers were also unable to clear the driverless car bills with provisions on cybersecurity and data privacy. The House passed its version (HR 3388) by voice vote on Sept. 6. But the Senate bill (S 1885) stalled after two Democrats objected.

The House also voted 386-41 in July 2017 to pass a Homeland Security reauthorization (HR 2825) that included provisions on cybersecurity for ports. The Senate Homeland Security and Governmental Affairs Committee advanced the measure in March 2018.

The House bill would codify existing practice under which the Coast Guard is responsible for cybersecurity at U.S. ports. The Coast Guard would have to ensure that cybersecurity is part of the approved facility security plan for each port, and that they will share information regarding cybersecurity risks and incidents with port partners through the National Maritime Advisory Committee. ∎

Narrow Action on Broadband Issues

Lawmakers were largely on the sidelines for two significant government actions on broadband in 2017: the Federal Communications Commission's decisions on so-called net neutrality and on protections for users' data. Congress stepped in on the latter issue after the FCC made the first move.

Republicans were pleased when the FCC voted 3-2 in December to sweep away net neutrality mandates for internet service providers adopted in 2015. Democrats criticized the move. The FCC decision returned regulation of internet service providers to the status before 2015, treating them as information services rather than common carriers and giving the Federal Trade Commission some enforcement authority.

The agency's action removed bans on blocking, degrading or fee-based services for certain applications and websites, but the new rule also required companies to be transparent about blocking, throttling or degrading access, paid prioritization of some sites, and other practices. All those practices are options for treating some providers of content differently from others.

The FCC said the change would unleash investment, while critics said it would mean the end of equal treatment of content. The agency's decision was also expected to raise pressure on Congress for steps to ensure fair consumer access to online entertainment and information.

Congress, however, didn't approve legislation. The deep partisan divide over the issue promised to slow legislative action, but key Republicans vowed to revive bills as the party tried to answer a firestorm of criticism from angry consumers and some online business advocates. Their goal: codify a 2010 FCC order banning website blocking and unreasonable discrimination of content.

Lawmakers did, however, take action on broadband privacy rules, passing a joint resolution in March that effectively codified a March 1 FCC decision. The agency decided to suspend broadband privacy rules due to take effect on March 2. The suspended rule, approved in the Obama administration, would have required internet service providers to get consumers' permission to sell personal data and use information.

The FCC decision to suspend was meant to buy time for the agency to reconsider a plan that internet service providers strongly objected to, saying it would put them at a disadvantage to big content providers such as Google, the search engine that is part of Alphabet Inc., and Facebook Inc., which are able to profit from users' data.

Using the Congressional Review Act that allows Congress to reverse federal regulations, lawmakers effectively nullified the broadband privacy rule before the FCC was able to take a more permanent step. Sen. Jeff Flake, R-Ariz., introduced the resolution (S J Res 34) in the Senate and Rep. Marsha Blackburn, R-Tenn., proposed the House companion (H J Res 86).

The Congressional Review Act not only allows Congress to nullify rules it doesn't like, but prevents the executive branch from reissuing a similar rule. But the thin Republican majority in the Senate meant the party had little room for maneuver. The House vote, in which a handful of Republicans crossed the aisle to vote with the minority, showed that even GOP members might be willing to back the privacy requirements.

The Senate voted 50-48 to pass its resolution on March 23 on a party-line vote. The House cleared it on March 28 in a 215-205 vote that had 15 Republicans joining all the Democrats in voting against. President Trump signed it into law (PL 115-22) on April 3.

RURAL BROADBAND

Among the issues facing Congress is rural broadband. Widely acknowledged as needed for economic vitality, broadband services are harder to deliver profitably in many rural areas than in urban and suburban areas. According to FCC data, in 277 counties, mainly in the West and South, less than 2 percent of the population has access to broadband internet.

Lawmakers have been looking at proposals, including ways to expedite laying of fiber optic cable across public lands and clarifying how the FCC collects data used to distribute universal service funds that subsidize service to low-income and high-cost areas.

The Senate passed a bill (S 19) on Aug. 3 by voice vote that would auction 255 megahertz of spectrum by 2020, a move that was deemed essential for the rollout of 5G broadband, the technology that would underlie the adoption of driverless cars and other advanced applications. The idea of the auction would be to sell nearly 40 percent of that to commercial mobile providers, raising an estimated $20 billion, and hand over another 40 percent to small operators.

FCC Chairman Ajit Pai had told lawmakers on July 25 that the agency needed legislation enacted to have spectrum bidders' deposits held at the Treasury Department, calling it "absolutely critical" for the rollout of 5G technology.

The Senate's bill would direct the FCC and National Telecommunications and Information Administration (NTIA), an arm of the Commerce Department, to make available at least 255 megahertz of spectrum below the frequency of 6000 megahertz for mobile and fixed wireless broadband use. At least 100 megahertz of the space would be devoted to unlicensed providers and at least 100 megahertz to licensed providers for commercial mobile use.

The NTIA would help identify spectrum for commercial use without interfering with federal spectrum users. And the FCC would carry out the spectrum auction, while dealing with administrative issues that could complicate bidding.

"I would like to see the House just pick it up and pass it," Senate Commerce Chairman John Thune, R-S.D., said.

But Rep. Marsha Blackburn, R-Tenn., the chairwoman of the House Energy and Commerce Communications and Technology Subcommittee, said late in the year that she would work on her own bill rather than take up the Senate measure.

Blackburn said she was working on a measure that would try to encourage broadband rollout in rural areas and that could be moved in tandem with the Senate-passed bill. She said she would look at a number of stakeholders beyond the wireless broadband providers covered by the Senate bill.

"We need to get the broadband expansion bill out there and start a movement on that," Blackburn said. "We haven't finished our bill in the House. You see, as soon as we finish tax reform, we're going to pivot or move to doing something on that."

With no bill and seeking a Senate seat in Tennessee, Blackburn appeared with President Donald Trump on a platform in Nashville in

early 2018 where the president talked about "great, great broadband."

Deferring action until March 23, 2018, Congress passed the fiscal 2018 omnibus spending bill (HR 1625) that included broadband provisions. One of them was a requirement that the FCC auction off 255 megahertz of spectrum – as the Senate would have done in the bill passed in August. The spending bill also promoted the use of federal land and facilities for broadband and communications infrastructure and the use of federal-aid highway rights-of-way for expanded broadband deployment.

Within the Rural Utilities Service program, the omnibus bill authorized up to $30 million in loans for the broadband program, and appropriated a separate $600 million for a new broadband loan and grant pilot program for rural areas in which at least 90 percent of households lack broadband with 10 Megabits per second download speeds and 1 Mbps upload speeds.

The Senate, also on March 23, agreed 65-32 to a motion to concur, clearing the measure for the president, who signed it (PL 115-141) the same day. ■

Lack of Broadband Across the United States

While 90 percent of people across the country have access to high speed internet, many of those in rural areas do not. In 277 counties, mainly in the West and South, 2 percent or less of the population has broadband.

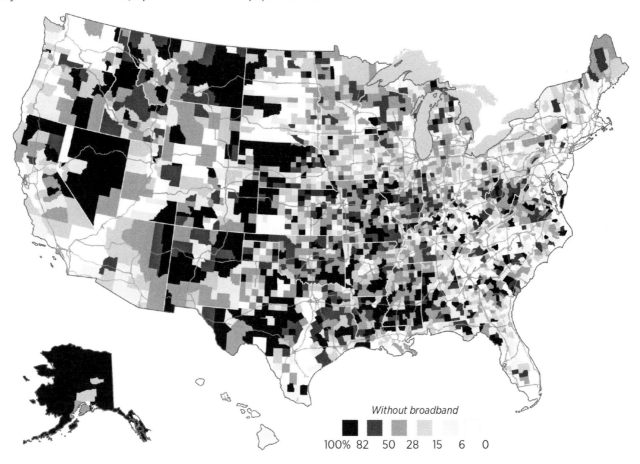

Without broadband

100% 82 50 28 15 6 0

Source: Federal Communications Commission
Randy Leonard/CQ

After Stumbles, FCC Gets New Life

The Federal Communications Commission was reauthorized for two years in the fiscal 2018 spending law (PL 115-141) enacted on March 23, 2018. The bill authorized $333 million for fiscal 2019 and $340 million for 2020. That reauthorization was the first since 1990 (PL 101-396).

The House had worked on a reauthorization in 2017, approving a bill by voice vote in the House Energy and Commerce Communications and Technology Subcommittee on Oct. 11 amid optimism that the chamber would be done by year's end.

"Let's do hope that it is the magic year for getting some of these things across the finish line," said Subcommittee Chairwoman Marsha Blackburn, R-Tenn.

FCC Chairman Ajit Pai had gone before the subcommittee on July 25, 2017, applauding it for work on what was at that time a five-year draft reauthorization. He noted in particular a provision that would allow spectrum bidders' deposits to be held at the Treasury Department, calling it "absolutely critical" for the rollout of 5G technology. "Because without it, the FCC won't be able to launch large spectrum auctions for the foreseeable future," he said.

The full House Energy and Commerce Committee didn't act on the bill (HR 4986) until Feb. 14, 2018. The House had passed it early March under suspension of the rules.

The measure had stumbled between the Oct. 11 subcommittee approval of the draft bill, and the full committee action four months later over a dispute about money to help broadcasters switch channels to accommodate wireless service providers. The draft bill also included language from a FCC process revamp bill (HR 290) passed by the House in January 2017.

Rep. Frank Pallone Jr., D-N.J., the ranking member of the committee, proposed a bill (HR 3347) authorizing $1 billion for a Treasury fund that could be used to compensate broadcasters for moving to a new channel in a reshuffling of spectrum.

Supporters of the Pallone bill said funds are needed to cover the full signal-moving expenses of operators of television stations—such as for new equipment and tower reconfigurations — designed to keep them on the air as they switch channels. The funds also could be used to help multi-channel video distributors and operators of low-power television stations affected by the spectrum reallocation.

The reauthorization included in the omnibus carried a similar provision allowing the Treasury Department leeway to hold spectrum auction deposits, replacing private banks that were spurning the task because of requirements to collateralize and capitalize deposits. Pai had warned lawmakers that the provision had to be in place by May to allow time to set up a spectrum auction planned for November. ∎

House Bill Takes Precedence In Bid to Curb Sex Trafficking

The House and Senate worked on separate bills in the final months of 2017 to curb online sex trafficking. The House version ultimately prevailed and its bill was enacted (PL 115-164) on April 11, 2018.

Rep. Ann Wagner, R-Mo., sponsored the House bill (HR 1865), which was written to hold online businesses responsible for hosting third-party content linked to sex trafficking. Her proposal, however, drew resistance because it was seen as making it too easy to prosecute online businesses.

In the Senate, Rob Portman, R-Ohio, proposed a measure (S 1693), with 70 co-sponsors, that had the backing of the Internet Association, a group that includes Microsoft, Amazon, and Google parent Alphabet.

Both measures would weaken a longstanding liability shield in Section 230 of the 1996 telecommunications law (PL 104-104) that prevents online businesses from being held responsible for third-party material on their websites.

Wagner, whose bill had 174 co-sponsors from both parties, pledged

at the end of November to iron out the problems in talks with House Judiciary Chairman Robert W. Goodlatte, R-Va., and by Dec. 11, the two had done so. The Judiciary Committee approved the amended bill that day by voice vote.

The compromise measure would curb the liability shield to allow prosecutions of online operators for the new criminal offense of intentionally promoting or facilitating prostitution, with a penalty of up to 10 years in prison. It would permit penalties of up to 25 years in prison for aggravated cases. The bill would provide for mandatory restitution and allow victims' civil suits against online operators in prostitution-related cases.

The House passed the bill 388-25 on Feb. 27, 2018. The Senate cleared it, 97-2, on March 21.

Portman's bill advanced through the Senate Commerce, Science and Transportation Committee by voice vote on Nov. 8 but no further action was taken. ∎

Study of Artificial Intelligence Stalls in Both Chambers

Sen. Maria Cantwell, D-Wash., and Rep. John Delaney, D-Md., introduced companion bills (S 2217 and HR 4625) on Dec. 12, 2017, that would instruct the Commerce Department to establish a federal advisory committee to study artificial intelligence and its effect on the economy, workers and privacy.

"We expect that artificial intelligence will be an incredibly transformative force for growth and productivity," Cantwell said in a written statement. "We need to be ready for it."

Lawmakers in both parties were beginning to explore the use of artificial intelligence by a broad range of businesses, including online giants Google (the search engine of parent company Alphabet), Facebook, and automobile manufacturers. But lawmakers have been cautious about proposing legislation that could provide incentives or put limits on the use of artificial intelligence.

Digitized data – the building block of modern artificial intelligence – enables computers to search vast amounts of material and draw conclusions that can have beneficial outcomes as well as potentially unethical or illegal ones.

"Given the many concerns in a field that's advancing so quickly and is so revolutionary, it's hard to believe there is no A.I. policy at the federal level. And that needs to change," said Sen. Brian Schatz at a Dec. 12 hearing of the Senate Commerce Subcommittee on Communications, Technology, Innovation and the Internet. Schatz, D-Hawaii, is the ranking member and Cantwell is also on the panel.

Schatz noted, for example, the potential for artificial intelligence to draw conclusions about religion, marital status or race even though employers aren't allowed to ask such questions.

The federal government will have to decide whether to weigh in not only on how the private sector uses artificial intelligence, but also whether government itself should be deploying it more extensively to provide security, health care and other services.

"It's time to get proactive on artificial intelligence," said Delaney, the co-chairman of the House AI Caucus. "AI is going to reshape our economy the way the steam engine, the transistor or the personal computer did and as a former entrepreneur, I believe the impact will be positive overall."

The Cantwell and Delaney bills would direct the department to establish a 19-member panel to advise the federal government and report to Congress within 18 months on implementation of artificial intelligence techniques, including machine learning and data sifting.

The panel would include five academic experts or researchers, six private industry representatives, two labor organization representatives and six members from civil society, including at least two advocates for civil liberties or civil rights.

The panel's study would examine ways to encourage investment and innovation, job losses and gains, and the effects on privacy rights. It would also provide a means to identify and eliminate bias from algorithms, or computer instructions, used by online businesses to sift data and tailor advertising.

Neither the Senate nor the House marked up the bills.

Artificial intelligence is long established, but has recently moved into the so-called third wave, in which machines understand the context and the environment in which they operate and are able to explain their reasoning and decision making to human operators.

Steven Walker, the director of the Defense Department's Defense Advanced Research Projects Agency, said in March 2018 that the agency has funded more than 50 programs in artificial intelligence since the 1960s.

Technology industry executives were warning that the U.S. was falling behind rivals in the use of artificial intelligence.

"We need to get our act together as a country," said Eric Schmidt, the chairman of Alphabet, in November. He also is chairman of the Defense Innovation Board, an advisory panel tasked with injecting new technology into the Pentagon. "This is that moment when the government collectively with private industry needs to say, 'The technologies are important.'"

He singled out China's ambitions. "It's pretty simple. By 2020 they will have caught up, by 2025 they will be better than us, and by 2030 they will dominate the industries of AI," Schmidt said. "The [Chinese] government said that. Weren't we the one in charge of AI dominance in our country?" ∎

Chapter 16

TAXES

GOP Enacts Sweeping Tax Overhaul, Handing Trump Big Legislative Victory

The most sweeping overhaul of the U.S. tax code since 1986 was signed into law by President Donald Trump on Dec. 22 – giving him and congressional Republicans a signature achievement for 2017 and their first major legislative victory under the unified Republican government.

The Tax Cuts and Jobs Act (PL 115-97) significantly modified both the corporate and individual tax system. It cut the corporate tax rate from 35 percent to 21 percent, bolstered expensing to encourage domestic business investment, and created a new territorial international tax system for U.S. companies with overseas operations. It also provided new breaks for the owners of "pass-through" businesses who pay taxes on their individual returns.

For individuals, it reduced existing tax rates and sought to simply tax filing so that far fewer people would file itemized returns. It doubled the standard deduction and limited itemized deductions. It also doubled the child tax credit and increased the portion that is refundable, while eliminating numerous other deductions and credits.

Republicans used the tax overhaul to also repeal the individual mandate, a pillar of the 2010 health care law, and to achieve a decades-long goal of opening up Alaska's Arctic National Wildlife Refuge to oil and gas drilling.

Trump celebrated the new tax law as "the biggest tax cut in the history of our nation," and he and Republicans argued that it would significantly boost economic growth and create jobs, ensuring that U.S. corporations remain competitive internationally and that businesses and jobs stay in the United States.

They said nearly all Americans would receive a tax cut and that the tax system would be so simplified that individuals and families could file taxes on a form the size of a postcard.

Democrats derided it as a "tax scam," saying it represented a massive giveaway to corporations and the wealthy, including the president, while providing relatively little for middle class families and adding more than a trillion dollars to budget deficits over the next decade. Bernie Sanders, I-Vt., called it "a moral and economic obscenity."

The legislative effort was highly partisan; Republicans developed much of the legislation behind closed doors, and no House or Senate Democrats voted for the measure. It was considered under the budget reconciliation process, which prevented filibusters in the Senate and allowed the tax bill to pass by simple majority vote.

But under that process, in which they could enact legislation adding $1.5 trillion to the deficit over 10 years but none after that, Republicans chose to make the tax cuts for individuals temporary, expiring after eight years, while making the corporate tax cuts permanent.

In developing their tax bill, Congressional Republicans used lessons

BOX SCORE

Bill: HR 1 (PL 115-97)

LEGISLATIVE ACTION:

House passed HR 1 (H Rept 115-409), 227-205, on Nov. 16.

Senate passed HR 1, amended, 51-49, on Dec. 2.

House adopted the conference report (H Rept 115-466), 227-203, on Dec. 19.

Senate adopted a modified conference report, 51-48, on Dec. 20.

House cleared modified conference report on HR 1, 224-201, on Dec. 20.

President signed Dec. 22 (PL 115-97).

learned in their unsuccessful effort to repeal and replace the 2010 health care law. After spending the first four months of the year in heated debate over a controversial border adjustment tax proposal, Republicans pivoted to spend the next five months quietly seeking as much consensus as possible between the White House and House and Senate Republicans on a common framework that both chambers could use in drafting detailed tax overhaul bills.

They then moved with remarkable speed over the last two months of the year to write and pass a tax cut bill the president could sign by the end of the year.

HIGHLIGHTS
INDIVIDUAL TAXES

The bill restructured the individual tax code to reduce taxes for most taxpayers and simplify the process by eliminating or restricting most tax deductions and credits so that fewer taxpayers would choose to itemize.

The modifications became effective for 2018 but were scheduled to expire after eight years – meaning that for 2026 and thereafter the individual tax code would revert to 2017 rates, brackets and standards.

Among the major changes were those that did the following:

Reduced all but one (the 10 percent rate) of the existing seven federal individual income tax rates and increased the threshold income levels at which each rate applies in order to provide a tax cut to those below the new thresholds. The top rate was trimmed from 39.6 percent to 37 percent.

Required that tax brackets each year be adjusted to account for inflation using so-called "chained CPI," which many economists say provides a more accurate estimate of inflation than the standard Consumer Price Index. But because it is usually lower than the existing inflation adjustment, it means tax brackets would not rise as rapidly and more taxpayers could end up with higher tax rates.

Nearly doubled to $12,000 ($24,000 for joint filers) the standard deduction for those who choose not to itemize, but eliminated the personal exemptions (scheduled to be $4,150 per person for 2018) that taxpayers may claim for themselves, their spouses and any dependents to reduce the taxpayer's adjusted gross income in determining taxable income.

Limited to $10,000 a taxpayer's combined itemized deduction for state or local property taxes and state and local income and sales taxes (known in tax jargon as SALT).

Limited a taxpayer's itemized deduction for new mortgage interest to just the interest associated with the first $750,000 of a home loan, including any loan on a second home (down from $1 million), and eliminated the deduction for interest on home equity loans.

Allowed medical expenses that exceed 7.5 percent of adjusted gross income as an itemized deduction (down from the existing 10 percent threshold) for tax years 2017 and 2018.

Doubled from $1,000 to $2,000 the child tax credit and increased from $1,000 to $1,400 the refundable portion of the tax credit; created a $500 per person non-refundable tax credit for dependents other than children; and increased from $75,000 to $200,000 (from $110,000 to $400,0000 for joint filers) the income level eligible for those tax credits.

Increased exemptions from the alternative minimum tax (AMT), a parallel tax system designed to prevent wealthy taxpayers from using loopholes to avoid paying taxes.

Doubled to $11.2 million ($22.4 million for couples) the amount of an estate that would be exempt from the 40 percent estate tax.

Eliminated numerous other tax deductions, credits and exclusions, including the deduction for alimony paid, the personal deduction for moving expenses and the exclusion for employer-provided moving expenses (except for active-duty military in each case), and the exclusion for bicycle commuting.

PASS-THROUGH BUSINESSES

The bill generally allows so-called "pass-through" businesses – where income is not subject to tax at the business level but is taxed as individual income when it is distributed to owners in the form of profits, wages or capital gains – to deduct 20 percent of qualified business income. For qualified income in excess of $157,500 ($315,000 for joint returns), the deduction would be subject to certain limits associated with wages paid.

Pass-through income is generally common for businesses organized as sole proprietorships, partnerships, limited liability companies and S corporations. As with the law's other modifications to individual and family taxes, this tax break would expire after 2025.

The measure provided for the most comprehensive overhaul of corporate taxation since 1986, aiming to boost U.S. competitiveness and increase corporate investment domestically, including by significantly reducing corporate tax rates and increasing the ability of businesses to write off certain expenses, and by establishing a "territorial" tax system that would exempt most income derived overseas from U.S. corporate taxation. Under the law those provisions would be permanent, unlike the tax provisions for individuals.

Specifically, it did the following:

Eliminated the four current corporate tax rates (15 percent, 25 percent, 34 percent and 35 percent) and set a single corporate tax rate at 21 percent.

Repealed the corporate alternative minimum tax.

Allowed businesses through 2022 to immediately expense 100 percent of the cost of assets that are acquired and placed into service by the business, with the percentage phased out over the next four years.

Established a "territorial" tax system to replace the existing system of taxing U.S. corporations on the foreign-source earnings of their foreign subsidiaries. The new system exempts from U.S. taxation 100 percent of the foreign-source portion of dividends paid by a foreign company to a U.S. corporation, if the U.S. company owns 10 percent or more of the foreign entity.

To encourage U.S. companies to repatriate foreign earnings held overseas, established a one-time, 15.5 percent tax on those foreign earnings held as cash or other liquid form and an 8 percent tax for any earnings that were reinvested in illiquid assets, and allowed this repa-triation tax to be payable in escalating installments over eight years.

Included "anti-base erosion" provisions to discourage U.S. companies from moving overseas and shrinking the U.S. corporate tax base.

Included numerous provisions to ease the accounting and tax burden on small businesses.

OTHER TAX PROVISIONS

The law made numerous other tax changes, including those that:

Imposed a 1.4 percent excise tax on the net investment income of private colleges and universities that have at least 500 students and assets valued at $500,000 or more per full-time student.

Restricted the ability of publicly-held corporations to deduct more than $1 million in compensation to executives.

Imposed a 21 percent excise tax on compensation in excess of $1 million for the five highest paid employees of a tax-exempt organization.

Increased from 15 percent to 20 percent the excise tax imposed on the value of stock compensation held by insiders of a U.S. corporation that relocates their headquarters overseas to reduce their tax liability.

Phased out the ability of banks with more than $10 billion in assets to deduct the federal deposit insurance premiums they pay to the Federal Deposit Insurance Corporation (FDIC).

Reduced federal excise taxes on alcohol for two years.

It also included numerous provisions affecting the finances of life insurance and property and casualty insurance companies.

The measure effectively repealed the 2010 health care law's so-called individual mandate, starting January 2019, by setting the tax penalty for failing to obtain health insurance at $0. The individual mandate was intended to ensure that almost everyone, including young healthy individuals, purchase health insurance so there is a broad risk pool and the cost of insurance remains relatively low.

It also ended a 1980 prohibition on oil and gas drilling on the coastal plain of the Arctic National Wildlife Refuge (ANWR) in Alaska, and required the Interior Department to conduct at least two lease sales there: one within four years of enactment and the second within seven years.

COST ESTIMATES

The Joint Committee on Taxation (JCT) estimated that the final agreement would result in net revenue and spending reductions that increase deficits by $1.45 trillion over 10 years and increase debt service costs by $314 billion – thereby increasing deficits by a total of $1.77 trillion over 10 years.

Factoring in estimated macroeconomic effects of the agreement, JCT estimated that the measure would increase economic output so that U.S. gross domestic product (GDP) over the 10-year period would rise by 0.7 percent more than it would have otherwise, resulting in the generation of $451 billion in additional federal revenues to partially offset the bill's revenue losses.

JCT's distributional analysis of changes in after-tax income for taxpayers at various income levels found that virtually everyone would see their income rise for the first couple years because of the tax cuts, with the largest increases (more than 3 percent) occurring for those with income above $200,000. And after-tax income would fall for all income levels below $75,000 in the last two years once the tax cuts expire at the beginning of 2026, with higher-income taxpayers continuing to see their income modestly increase. (A Congressional Research Service report notes that those taxpayers would likely continue to benefit from the corporate tax cut).

Finally, low- and moderate-income taxpayers with incomes below $40,000 would see their income decline in 2023 and later years, partly due to repeal of the 2010 health care law's individual mandate and the likelihood they would no longer be purchasing health insurance and receiving federal subsidies to support those purchases.

According to a Congressional Budget Office (CBO) estimate in November, repeal of the individual mandate would result in $338 billion in savings over 10 years, primarily because fewer people would purchase health insurance and receive the federal subsidies associated with such insurance. CBO also estimated that repeal would cause 13 million fewer people to have health insurance at the end of 10 years, and that health insurance premiums on the individual, non-group insurance market would increase by 10 percent a year as the risk pool shrinks.

BACKGROUND & LEGISLATIVE ACTION

After Congress at the end of the 112th Congress made permanent most of the Bush-era tax cuts for individuals, the focus turned to the need to overhaul the corporate and business tax code.

In particular, there was a desire to update the corporate tax code to make U.S. corporations more competitive internationally -- given that the U.S. corporate tax rate of 35 percent was much higher than most other industrialized nations. Because of the U.S. tax code, many U.S. companies had either moved headquarter operations overseas or were refusing to repatriate more than $2 trillion in overseas earnings in order to avoid U.S. taxation.

It was expected there would be a major bipartisan push in the 115th Congress to restructure corporate and business taxes, but with the election in November 2016 of Donald Trump as president, giving Republicans control of both Congress and the White House, the focus became a more partisan effort to reduce taxes across the board, including for individuals. It took a while, however, for Republicans to agree upon their tax strategy.

INITIAL POSITIONS

Both Trump and House Republicans during their 2016 election campaigns had touted tax cut proposals that would reduce taxes by consolidating the seven existing tax rates (which ranged from 10 percent to 39.6 percent) down to three brackets: 12 percent, 25 percent and 33 percent. Each also proposed significantly raising the standard deduction for taxpayers while restricting or eliminating many itemized deductions.

On the corporate side, Trump had proposed to set a single 15 percent business rate for both corporations and pass-through businesses (such as partnerships, sole proprietorships and S-corporations) where the profits distributed to the business owners are taxed at the individual rate. The House Republicans' "A Better Way" plan, meanwhile, proposed a 20 percent corporate rate and 25 percent for pass-through businesses.

There was some discussion among lawmakers after the 2016 elections of possibly seeking to move bipartisan tax legislation, in particular a limited international corporate tax overhaul package in which the tax revenues from more than $2 trillion in repatriated overseas corporate earnings could be used to pay for improvements to U.S. infrastructure – a concept supported by Trump, who had also campaigned on making major investments in infrastructure.

But GOP conservatives pushed back on the idea of using tax repatriation revenue for infrastructure improvements, saying such revenue should be used as an offset to pay for lower tax rates across the board.

House Ways and Means Chairman Kevin Brady, R-Texas, who wanted to move on the GOP's "Better Way" tax proposals, agreed with conservatives saying that an infrastructure and international tax package should only be a "last resort." Nevertheless, the issue continued to be floated well into the spring of 2017.

House GOP leaders initially set an ambitious agenda under which they envisioned repealing and replacing the 2010 health care law and enacting tax legislation prior to Congress's August recess. By April, however, with the GOP Congress struggling to pass legislation to repeal and replace the 2010 health care law, and with Republicans far from any consensus on what tax legislation to consider, Trump and administration officials moved their deadline for enacting tax legislation to the end of the year. House GOP leaders also eventually adjusted their timeline.

BORDER ADJUSTMENT TAX

Early on, a divide emerged among congressional Republicans and the White House regarding the so-called border adjustment tax included in the House GOP's "Better Way" tax plan.

The House proposal would effectively tax U.S. imports and exempt U.S. exports from tax, and was intended to help discourage U.S. companies from moving overseas, where labor costs and corporate taxes are lower, and shipping their goods back to the United States. Specifically, under the plan U.S., businesses would no longer be able to deduct for tax purposes the cost of imported raw materials, parts or finished goods for use or sale in the United States, while a business's revenue from exports would be excluded from taxable income.

The border adjustment plan was a cornerstone of the House GOP tax proposal because it was estimated to raise $1.2 trillion over 10 years – revenue that would offset the plan's reduced individual and corporate tax rates. House Republicans were calling for any tax package to be revenue neutral, based on macroeconomic, or dynamic, budget scoring (i.e., considering new revenue that could be generated from economic growth prompted by the changes in tax policy) versus traditional, or static, scoring.

But many conservative groups and business interests vehemently opposed the House's border adjustment proposal, saying it would financially harm U.S. retailers and companies that rely on imported goods and raw materials, with those costs being passed on to U.S. consumers in the form of higher prices. Farm interests also expressed concern that agricultural exports could be hit with countervailing duties and other penalties by foreign nations in response to the effective U.S. tax on imports.

Supporters countered that the proposal, also known as a destination-based tax because goods would be taxed based on where they are sold rather than where they are made, would have little impact on consumers because it would cause the value of the U.S. dollar to increase – effectively lowering the price of foreign goods for U.S. importers so that little or no cost would be passed on to consumers. They also argued the border adjustments would emulate the value-added taxes imposed by some nations, which are applied to U.S.-made imports and rebated on the foreign nation's exports.

Treasury Secretary Steven Mnuchin on April 20 said the plan could send adverse ripples through the U.S. economy, regardless of whether it lifts the value of the dollar, and he noted that a stronger dollar would also hurt U.S. exports.

Trump, meanwhile, repeatedly called the proposal "too complicated." A week before he was inaugurated, he said, "Anytime I hear

Tax Law Paves Way for ANWR Drilling

Congressional Republicans and President Donald Trump in 2017 achieved a decades-long GOP goal of opening the Arctic National Wildlife Refuge in Alaska to oil and gas development, by including a bill to open the refuge as part of the enacted tax overhaul.

Oil and gas development in the area had been prohibited since 1980 when Congress designated it as a 19-million-acre wildlife refuge. However, as part of that law (PL 96-487), Congress also allowed for a future vote to permit energy exploration in a 1.5-million-acre section of the refuge known as the "1002" area.

Congressional Republicans for years had unsuccessfully sought to open ANWR to energy development because of the large deposits of oil and gas estimated to be there, but until 2017 they were thwarted by Democrats and environmentally-minded Republicans who wanted to protect the area.

Environmentalists considered the area one of the last pure wilderness regions left in North America which, because of its location, had an extremely sensitive ecosystem that could be severely damaged by development activities. The area was home to migrating caribou, denning polar bears and more than 200 species of migratory birds; many supporters of the refuge described it as the "American Serengeti."

Opening ANWR to energy development was expected to provide a major economic and financial boon to the state of Alaska, where almost 90 percent of the state's budget revenues came from oil activities. Under the enacted law, the state would receive half of all revenues and royalties generated by ANWR oil and gas leasing activities. At the time, the state's economy had been buffeted by a downturn in the world's oil markets and was experiencing high unemployment compared to the rest of the nation.

PATHWAY PROVIDED

Opening ANWR had been a top priority for Alaska lawmakers for decades, and Republican Sen. Lisa Murkowski of Alaska had introduced legislation to allow ANWR drilling in every Congress she had served in since first taking office in 2002.

She said that on election night in November 2016, when Donald Trump won the presidency, she knew her goal could become a reality. "You learn how and when to pick your battles around here. And with President [Barack Obama] in office, it was not going to be a possibility. But when the administration turned, when it was clear that we had majorities, it presents itself as the time, the time to make the effort."

Murkowski, however, in 2005 had seen an effort to open ANWR to drilling fall short, even though Republicans similarly controlled both Congress and the White House.

GOP leaders in 2017 set the stage for passing legislation to allow oil and gas development in ANWR when they initiated the budget reconciliation process to enact an overhaul of the U.S. tax code; legislation considered under the reconciliation process cannot be filibustered, allowing for Senate passage by a simple majority vote.

The final fiscal 2018 budget resolution (H Con Res 71) adopted by the House and Senate included not only reconciliation instructions for enacting a tax overhaul, but also instructions for the Senate Energy and Natural Resources Committee to report legislation producing at least $1 billion in savings over 10 years – which was intended for the ANWR provisions.

At a Nov. 2 hearing on proposals to open ANWR, Murkowski, who was chairwoman of the Energy and Natural Resources Committee, said oil and gas production from the reserve "could raise billions of dollars of revenue for our country every year," once production starts. It was expected there would be little to no actual oil extraction during the first decade, when exploratory activities and the construction of needed production and transportation infrastructure would occur.

PROPOSAL RELEASED; COMMITTEE MARKUP

Murkowski released her legislative proposal on Nov. 8. "This legislation is a tremendous opportunity for both Alaska and our country," she said in a statement. "The legislation I released tonight will put us on a path toward greater prosperity by creating jobs, keeping energy affordable for families and businesses, generating new wealth, and strengthening our security – while reducing the federal deficit not just by $1 billion over 10 years, but tens or even hundreds of billions of dollars over the decades to come."

The Congressional Budget Office estimated it would generate $1.092 billion in federal revenues over 10 years through fee collections for leases for oil and gas drilling rights – thereby meeting the minimum $1 billion in savings required by the budget resolution's reconciliation instructions. Those leases actually would generate nearly $2.2 billion, CBO said, but half was to be provided to the state of Alaska as required by the draft measure.

Specifically, the measure directed the Interior Department to hold at least two competitive lease sales in ANWR's "1002" area of the coastal plain near the Arctic coast, one within four years of enactment and the other within seven years. Each lease sale must provide for at least 400,000 acres that have the highest potential for discovering oil and natural gas, and Interior was required to issue any necessary rights-of-way or easements needed for exploring, developing, or producing oil or gas or for related transport. Up to 2,000 surface acres of federal land could be developed in association with the program, and it set a 16.67 percent royalty rate for oil and gas eventually produced from the leases, with half to be shared with the state of Alaska.

Democrats and environmentalists condemned the proposal and the GOP plans to add it to the tax bill, with Adam Kolton, executive director of the Alaska Wilderness League, saying "It's deplorable that a backdoor budget maneuver is being used to ram Arctic drilling through without a full, fair and open debate."

The Senate Energy and Natural Resources Committee considered the measure on Nov. 15 and approved it by a 13-10 vote, with just one Democrat, Sen. Joe Manchin III of West Virginia, voting with Republicans on approval.

Republicans rejected a series of Democratic amendments, mostly along party lines, that largely sought to prevent drilling in ANWR,

minimize potential impacts on the environment and wildlife, and ensure the proposal would not waive required reviews under the National Environmental Policy Act and Endangered Species Act.

Washington's Maria Cantwell, the panel's top Democrat, and others expressed concern regarding the environmental impact of oil and gas development on the caribou herds that use the area as their principle calving grounds, and on the Alaska native populations that depend on the caribou for food. Republicans countered that improved, modern drilling technology would dramatically reduce any risks to the environment.

Only one amendment was adopted, offered by Louisiana Republican Bill Cassidy and approved on a 13-10 vote. It required that up to 5 million barrels of oil from the Strategic Petroleum Reserve (SPR) be sold to raise a maximum of $325 million for the U.S. Treasury, and it increased for fiscal years 2020 and 2021 the amounts of offshore oil royalties from Gulf of Mexico drilling that could be shared with the four Gulf states for coastal restoration and other activities.

FLOOR CONSIDERATION & FINAL ACTION

The committee's ANWR provisions were subsequently combined with the tax overhaul by the Senate Budget Committee for Senate floor consideration under reconciliation procedures.

On the floor, however, the Energy Committee's provisions had to be modified to comply with Senate reconciliation rules, as well as ensure that the committee's provisions would meet its budget reconciliation requirement of saving $1 billion over 10 years. To do so, GOP leaders as part of a floor amendment increased to 7

million barrels the amount of oil that could be sold from the SPR and increased to $600 million the amount of revenue that could be collected from such sales.

Democrats offered a floor amendment to strike the ANWR provisions, but efforts to waive a budget point of order on the amendment for increasing the deficit was rejected by a 48-52 vote. In trying to rally support for the amendment, Cantwell told senators that "unless you help strike this, you will be joining the ranks of polluters that believe in polluting a wildlife refuge, and you will be joining an administration that I guarantee you is going to go down in history and getting an F in stewardship."

Those ANWR and associated provisions adopted as part of the Senate-passed tax bill were readily agreed to in conference with the House and included in the final tax bill that passed both chambers and was signed into law by the president.

While a number of environmentally-minded House Republicans expressed their opposition to opening ANWR to oil and gas development, their desire to cut taxes and overhaul the tax code overrode those environmental concerns.

Murkowski in a statement said, "This is a watershed moment for Alaska and all of America. We have fought to open the 1002 Area for a very long time, and now, our day has finally arrived. ... Alaskans can now look forward to our best opportunity to refill the Trans-Alaska Pipeline System, thousands of jobs that will pay better wages, and potentially $60 billion in royalties for our state alone. This is a major victory for Alaska that will help us fulfill the promises of our statehood and give us renewed hope for growth and prosperity." ■

border adjustment, I don't love it." Instead, Trump reiterated his campaign call for a "substantial border tax" on U.S. companies that move jobs and operations overseas and seek to import products back into the United States – referencing his ability as president to impose punitive import tariffs on products from other nations.

Trump did briefly warm to the House border proposal in late January when meeting congressional Republicans, with White House spokesman Sean Spicer saying the president was open to "using comprehensive tax reform as means to tax imports from countries that we have a trade deficit from, like Mexico." Spicer on Jan. 26 even suggested that a 20 percent tax on imports (consistent with the House-suggested corporate tax rate associated with the border adjustment plan) could pay for the president's proposed wall on the U.S. border with Mexico, saying such a tax on Mexican imports could raise $10 billion a year "and easily pay for the wall just through that mechanism alone."

In the Senate, where Republicans had only a 52-48 majority, numerous Republicans expressed opposition to the House border adjustment plan. That included Finance Committee Chairman Orrin G. Hatch, R-Utah, who expressed doubt it was viable and early on stated he would develop his own tax plan in the Senate, regardless of what the House passes.

SEEKING A UNIFIED APPROACH

With no consensus among Republicans, the White House on April 26 released a one-page outline of Trump's principles for overhauling the tax code. It made no mention of border adjustments, instead proposing establishment of a territorial international tax system in which U.S. companies would pay tax only on what they earn at home, rather than the existing structure in which they pay tax on income worldwide.

It called for large corporations and small pass-through businesses to both be taxed at a 15 percent rate, and proposed to reduce individual taxes to three rates (10 percent, 25 percent and 35 percent) along with doubling the standard deduction and eliminating most itemized tax deductions, but leaving in place popular deductions for mortgage interest and charitable contributions. He also proposed to eliminate the Alternative Minimum Tax and the estate tax.

Just over a week later, Ways and Means Chairman Brady, who had been hoping to mark up the House's tax bill before the August recess, announced he would not convene a markup until House and Senate Republicans and the White House reached agreement on a "unified plan" for tax legislation. He said such a deal was needed before trying to rally votes in committee and on the House floor.

Republicans said they had learned a lesson from their troubled efforts to repeal and replace the 2010 health care law; that it was important to jointly determine early on the tax framework they wanted to pursue. To develop a common framework, Speaker Paul D. Ryan, R-Wis., and Majority Leader McConnell, along with Brady, Hatch, Treasury Secretary Mnuchin and National Economic Council Director Gary Cohn had begun meeting weekly to seek consensus. The group became known as the "Big Six."

House Ways and Means in mid-May did begin hearings on the House GOP's tax plan, but about the same time the odds against the border adjustment plan continued to grow. Senate Majority Leader Mitch McConnell, R-Ky., in a Bloomberg TV interview stated that the House's "controversial" plan "probably wouldn't pass the Senate," and Mnuchin in meeting with senators on the Finance Committee told them the administration would not push for the House border plan. In early June, the conservative House Freedom Caucus also came out in

opposition to the proposal.

Meanwhile, a growing number of Republicans began voicing support for temporary tax cuts that would add to the deficit and did not have to be offset, similar to those enacted in 2001 and 2003 under President George W. Bush. Rep. Fred Upton, R-Mich., stressed the need for tax cuts to grow the economy. "It may not be revenue-neutral. Getting the economy fixed, and creating jobs, is more important," he said.

The Bush tax cuts had been enacted through the budget reconciliation process, which prohibits increases to the deficit after a budget resolution's budget window (typically a 10-year period after legislation is enacted) and therefore requires out-year offsets if tax cuts are to be made permanent. To lengthen the duration of possible new tax cuts, some Republicans began floating proposals to employ a 20- or 30-year budget window in any budget resolution that would be adopted to activate the budget reconciliation process for new tax legislation.

House GOP leaders, however, continued to press for permanent tax cuts that are fully offset based on dynamic scoring, with Ryan and Brady arguing that that tax cuts with deadlines would have a muted effect on long-range business investment, while permanent tax cuts would prompt the most economic growth. But the likely demise of the House's border adjustment tax, with the $1.2 trillion it would generate as an offset to make the tax package budget neutral, meant Republicans would have to identify new revenue-raising offsets if they wanted a revenue-neutral package.

Adding to the pressure, the Senate on July 13 unveiled a revised version of legislation to repeal the 2010 health care law that did not repeal several taxes created by that 2010 law, including its 3.8 percent net investment income tax and 0.9 percent Medicare payroll surtax. That raised concerns those repeals would need to be included in the tax overhaul legislation, which if the tax package was to be revenue neutral would require GOP leaders to find even more offsets.

On July 27, the day before the House left for its August recess, the Big Six in a joint statement announced that the House's border adjustment tax proposal was being set aside "in order to advance tax reform." They stated that "The goal is a plan that reduces tax rates as much as possible, allows unprecedented capital expensing, places a priority on permanence, and creates a system that encourages American companies to bring back jobs and profits trapped overseas." They also wrote that development of the actual tax legislation would occur in the fall through "regular order," with the House and Senate tax committees developing and drafting the legislation to be considered by each chamber.

During August, with GOP efforts to repeal and replace the health care law effectively dead, Trump took to the road to build public support for overhauling the tax code, saying in an Aug. 30 speech in Springfield, Mo., that he wanted to work with both Republicans and Democrats in Congress on a plan that is "pro-growth, pro-worker and pro-American." He began courting several moderate Democrats who were up for re-election in 2018 in states that Trump had won, bringing Democratic Sen. Heidi Heitkamp of North Dakota onstage with him during a Sept. 6 event in her state. And back in Washington, Trump held meetings with bipartisan groups of lawmakers regarding taxes.

Senate Minority Leader Charles E. Schumer, D-N.Y., said Democrats had three principles they believed should guide an overhaul of the tax code: that it not cut taxes for the top 1 percent of income earners, that it not add to budget deficits, and that it not be considered under the reconciliation process. All but three Senate Democrats in August sent a letter to Trump and GOP leaders outlining those requirements

– with Heitkamp, Joe Donnelly of Indiana, and Joe Manchin III of West Virginia declining to sign the letter.

TAX FRAMEWORK RELEASED

On Sept. 27, the White House and GOP leaders released a 9-page "Unified Framework for Fixing Our Broken Tax Code" that had been negotiated by the Big Six. The framework, the document said, would "achieve pro-American, fiscally-responsible tax reform. This framework will deliver a 21st century tax code that is built for growth, supports middle-class families, defends our workers, protects our jobs, and puts America first."

The framework was intended to provide a common starting point for the House and Senate tax-writing committees to develop overhaul legislation, giving them broad leeway to resolve numerous remaining disputes among Republicans in restructuring the tax code. "The whole point of all of this is the House, the Senate and the White House are starting from the same page and the same outline, and then the tax writers are going to take it from there on the details," Ryan had said earlier in the month.

Under the framework, which included partial details, the corporate tax would be reduced from 35 percent to 20 percent and the corporate AMT would be eliminated. It called for creation of a new territorial international tax system for U.S. companies with overseas operations so they would pay reduced rates on future overseas earnings, while also requiring the repatriation of profits held overseas that would be taxed a single time at reduced rates.

It would cut the top rate pass-through businesses to 25 percent and called for immediate 100 percent expensing of capital investments for all businesses for at least five years, while partially limiting deductions for interest expenses. It also called for eliminating many other business deductions and credits, but retaining the research and development and low-income housing tax incentives.

For individuals, it roughly doubled to $12,000 ($24,000 for joint filers) the standard deduction for taxpayers, while eliminating personal exemption deductions. It called for three individual tax rates (12 percent, 25 percent and 35 percent) instead of the existing seven rates that ranged from 10 percent to 39.6 percent. Senior administration officials told reporters that the Ways and Means and Finance committees had also been given flexibility to add a fourth rate above the 35 percent rate "if they need to, on the wealthiest taxpayers" in order to produce a tax code that is "as progressive as the current system."

The proposal called for eliminating most itemized deductions, including deductions for state and local taxes, while retaining tax incentives for home mortgage interest and charitable contributions, for increasing the $1,000 child tax credit and the income thresholds for households that can claim the credit, and for creating a $500 credit for non-child dependents. It also called for eliminating the individual AMT and the estate tax.

Critics in both parties quickly assailed the framework, with Democrats saying it would disproportionately benefit the wealthy by reducing top tax rates and eliminating the AMT and estate tax. Democrats called the proposed elimination of the SALT deduction an attack on the middle class and said it was targeted toward "blue" (Democratic) states where many taxpayers used the deduction, while Republicans generally countered that any negative impact on the middle class would be mitigated by doubling the standard deduction and increasing the child tax credit.

But eliminating the SALT deduction was problematic for many

Republicans, particularly those from high-tax states such as New York, New Jersey, and California, who said it would result in many of their constituents paying higher taxes. The real estate industry also criticized the proposed SALT elimination, saying the inability to deduct property taxes and any further limits on deducting mortgage interest could discourage homeownership and lower property values.

Trump, meanwhile, touted the framework as one that would primarily benefit the middle class, saying that "We will cut taxes tremendously for the middle class. Not just a little bit, but tremendously." He also insisted that he would not benefit under the GOP tax framework, saying "I think there's very little benefit for people of wealth."

Republicans argued that by eliminating most itemized deductions, the wealthy would not be paying less in taxes overall. Treasury Secretary Mnuchin had been promoting that concept for a couple months, saying that changes to the individual code were focused on providing tax cuts to the middle class and that wealthy families might "have no reduction" because the tax cuts would be "offset by reduced [tax] deductions," including fewer write-offs for state and local taxes.

MOVING TO COMMITTEE MARKUPS

The release of the tax framework freed up the House to vote on its fiscal 2018 budget resolution (H Con Res 71), which had been reported by the House Budget Committee in July and included reconciliation instructions for a revenue-neutral overhaul of the tax code based on dynamic scoring. Hard-line conservatives in the Freedom Caucus had been refusing to vote for the House budget until they could see what was included in the tax framework, fearful that GOP leaders would consider less ambitious tax cuts in order to expedite enactment. The House adopted its budget resolution on Oct. 5 by a 219-206 party-line vote.

The Senate Budget Committee soon after adopted a slimmed-down budget resolution that focused only on activating the budget reconciliation process for considering tax legislation – and which allowed the tax legislation to add $1.5 trillion to the deficit over 10 years using traditional, static budget scoring. The Senate budget also included reconciliation instructions for the Senate Energy and Natural Resources Committee to report out legislation that would reduce the deficit by $1 billion over 10 years, which was intended to allow the tax bill to include provisions opening up a portion of Alaska's Arctic National Wildlife Refuge to oil and gas exploration.

The Senate adopted its budget resolution on Oct. 19 by a 51-49 vote, with the House a week later on Oct. 26 voting 216-212 to adopt the Senate's budget – thereby activating the reconciliation process for tax legislation that could add $1.5 trillion to the deficit over 10 years.

House consideration of the Senate's budget was delayed for several days as House GOP leaders sought to determine whether they had sufficient votes given the opposition of many Republicans to the tax framework's state and local tax deduction elimination. GOP leaders had been so concerned that they began considering alternatives to eliminating the SALT deduction, and also sought the support of moderate Blue Dog Democrats to offset possible GOP losses.

On Oct. 20 Speaker Ryan announced that the House budget when it was unveiled would include a fourth bracket for high-income earners to ensure that middle income taxpayers were the primary beneficiaries of tax cuts. Said Ryan, "The president is the one who has been very insistent that we introduce what we call the fourth bracket, meaning we won't lower taxes for high-income individuals … so that all that revenue goes to the middle class tax cut."

And on Nov. 1, President Trump threw a new element into the mix based on a suggestion from Sen. Tom Cotton, R-Ark. Trump on Twitter floated the idea of including in the tax bill a repeal of the 2010 health care law's individual mandate, which requires that most Americans purchase health insurance or pay a tax penalty.

INITIAL HOUSE DRAFT

Ways and Means Chairman Brady subsequently released a detailed, draft bill on Nov. 2 that generally followed the GOP tax framework. For the fourth tax rate it maintained the existing 39.6 percent top rate, and it modified the proposed elimination of the SALT deduction to allow up to $10,000 deductions for property taxes only, maintaining the proposed elimination of deductions for state and local income taxes.

It reduced allowable deductions for mortgage interest, allowing deductions for interest on new loans of up to $500,000 (down from $1 million) but prohibiting the deduction of mortgage interest on loans for second homes or for interest on home equity loans, which prompted major opposition from the housing industry. It also eliminated the deduction for interest on student loans, and expanded the child tax credit from $1,000 to $1,600 while creating a new $300 credit for each parent or non-child dependent.

For pass-through businesses it established certain "guardrails" to prevent individuals from abusing the system and treating individual income as pass-through income eligible for the reduced 25 percent rate. The National Federal of Independent Business opposed the rate level, saying that "85 to 90 percent of small businesses would not receive a break on their pass-through income, under the bill as currently written," since at their income levels they are already taxed at the 25 percent rate.

And with the border adjustment tax now off the table, other provisions were included to discourage U.S. businesses from moving overseas and reducing the U.S. corporate tax base, but they were so complex that even House tax writers were unable to explain them.

The next day, on Nov. 3, Brady released a substitute that made technical corrections and tweaked the bill to slightly reduce its cost and ensure it would not exceed the $1.5 trillion in on-budget deficits over 10 years allowed for reconciliation under the budget resolution.

Trump labeled the measure the "Cut, Cut, Cut Act" while Democrats blasted it as being primarily a tax cut for the wealthy at the expense of middle-class taxpayers. House Minority Leader Nancy Pelosi, D-Calif., deemed it a "deficit-increasing, job-cutting, tax-cut-for-the-rich bill" that would "plunder the middle class to put into the pocket of the wealthiest one percent more money."

HOUSE WAYS & MEANS MARKUP

The House Ways and Means Committee considered the bill over the course of four days before approving it on Nov. 9 by a 24-16 vote (H Rept 115-409) with no Democratic support.

Democrats criticized the bill for adding $1.5 trillion to the deficit and for projections by the Joint Committee on Taxation that some taxpayers would see tax increases after five years. The JCT's chief of staff confirmed that 38 million households making between $20,000 and $40,000 per year could see their taxes increase starting in 2023 when some tax benefits in the bill would expire.

Republicans argued that that their priority was to modify the tax code to spur economic growth, which they said would create millions of jobs and generate new revenues that would largely offset the supposed $1.5 trillion cost of the bill. Some Republicans and administration

Health Insurance Mandate Defanged

Although congressional Republicans in 2017 were unable to repeal and replace the 2010 health care law, they took advantage of an opportunity when advancing their tax overhaul legislation to effectively repeal a pillar of the health care law: the so-called individual mandate.

The individual mandate required most Americans each year to obtain and maintain health insurance coverage that met certain quality thresholds, or pay a tax penalty for failure to do so. In 2012 the health care law survived a major legal challenge when the Supreme Court, in a 5-to-4 decision, ruled that the individual mandate was constitutional because it falls within Congress' power to tax.

While they acknowledged it to be one of the less popular parts of the health care law, supporters of the law considered it crucial for the stability of health insurance markets and for keeping rates affordable. By requiring younger and healthier individuals to purchase insurance the mandate broadened the individual insurance market's "risk pool," so the market would not be comprised of mostly older and sicker individuals who are more costly to insurers.

In repeated GOP efforts to repeal and replace the health care law since its enactment in 2010, repeal of the individual mandate had been a core element Republicans sought to achieve.

REPEAL INCLUSION PROPOSED

Frustrated by their inability in 2017 to replace the entire 2010 health care law under a unified GOP Congress and White House, conservative Republicans began considering the idea of repealing the individual mandate as part of the tax overhaul as House GOP leaders in October were preparing the details of the tax package to be unveiled for later markup by the Ways and Means Committee.

The proposal got a major boost when Sen. Tom Cotton, R-Ark., in late October suggested the idea to President Donald Trump, and the president on Nov. 1 in a tweet expressed his support for the proposal.

The benefit in repealing the mandate as part of the tax bill, in the eyes of Trump and many Republicans, was that in addition to removing a pillar of the 2010 health law, the budgetary savings from doing so could be used to pay for even deeper tax cuts.

House and Senate GOP tax writers initially discounted the idea, with Ways and Means Chairman Kevin Brady, R-Texas, noting that proposals to kill the mandate hadn't gained 50 votes in the Senate earlier that year, and saying he didn't want its inclusion to sink the tax legislation. And in the Senate, Finance Chairman Orrin G. Hatch, R-Utah, said "We ought to do tax reform, and if we want to do something on health care, then we do that secondly."

There were also concerns that including a repeal of the mandate in the tax bill could stymie separate, bipartisan efforts in the Senate to stabilize the 2010 health care law's insurance markets, which had been disrupted by the president's decision to stop the law's cost-sharing reduction payments And with a narrow 52-48 majority, Senate GOP leaders also wanted to maintain the support of moderate senators Susan Collins, R-Maine, and Lisa Murkowski, R-Alaska, both of whom earlier in the year had voted against GOP plans to overhaul the 2010 health care law and who warned that repealing the mandate as part of the tax bill could complicate its passage.

Consequently, the repeal was not included in either of the initial drafts of the House or Senate tax bills that were unveiled in November. Nor was it added to the House bill by the Ways and Means Committee during that panel's markup of the tax legislation.

But GOP conservatives such as Sen. Ted Cruz of Texas continued to argue that Republicans should end the individual mandate as part of the tax bill, contending the penalty for skipping coverage mostly affected those with middle and lower incomes. "The IRS now fines six-and-a-half million people each year because they don't have enough money to be able to afford health insurance, and I point out that the IRS penalty falls predominantly on the middle- and lower-income Americans," Cruz said.

REPEAL ADDED TO SENATE BILL

With Trump continuing to push for a repeal of the individual mandate to be added to the tax bill, GOP leaders soon changed their minds, particularly as they sought additional savings to allow for deeper tax cuts for individuals.

On Nov. 14, Senate Majority Leader Mitch McConnell announced that repeal of the mandate would be added to the Senate's bill, which was being marked up by the Finance Committee. Republican Conference Chairman John Thune of South Dakota, who served on Senate Finance, said the savings would "be distributed in the form of middle-income tax relief; it will give us even more of an opportunity to really distribute the relief to those middle-income cohorts who could really benefit from it."

Democrats immediately condemned the plan. "Rather than learning the lessons from their failure to repeal health care, Republicans are doubling down on the same partisan strategy that would throw our health care system into chaos," said Senate Minority Leader Charles E. Schumer of New York. "If the American people weren't already outraged by this bill, injecting health care into it will certainly do the trick," he said.

The health care industry also protested the idea, urging Republicans to maintain the mandate until they can pass a comprehensive health care overhaul. America's Health Insurance Plans, the American Medical Association and hospital groups sent a letter to GOP leaders warning of "serious consequences."

"As providers of healthcare and coverage to hundreds of millions of Americans, we are committed to assuring everyone has access to a range of high quality, affordable coverage options so they can access the care they need, regardless of pre-existing conditions," they wrote. "To achieve this critical goal, we are urging you to maintain the individual mandate unless and until Congress can enact a package of reforms to adequately assure a balanced risk pool and prevent extraordinary premium increases."

The Congressional Budget Office (CBO) the prior week had released an update of the projected impact of repealing the individual mandate, estimating it would produce $338 billion in savings over 10 years (mostly because fewer people would purchase insurance and receive federal subsidies for doing so). CBO estimated that 13 million fewer people would be insured after a decade, and that because fewer people would be purchasing insurance, the average insurance

premiums in the individual market would increase by 10 percent in most years over that time period.

The Senate's decision that day also triggered an immediate reaction in the House, where GOP conservatives urged House leaders to add the repeal to the House's tax bill, which was pending House floor consideration.

But while the repeal was added to the Senate's tax bill by the Finance Committee despite vehement Democratic opposition, House GOP leaders declined to add it to their bill for House floor consideration.

House leaders were already concerned regarding opposition by GOP moderates to provisions in the House tax bill that would limit itemized deductions for state and local taxes (SALT), and didn't want to possibly lose any additional GOP votes by adding the mandate repeal.

Senate Republicans defended inclusion of the individual mandate repeal in their tax bill, with Thune at the Senate Finance markup saying: "My understanding is that the individual mandate is a tax collected by the IRS. It seems to me it's perfectly within this committee's jurisdiction."

FINAL ACTIONS

Prior to Senate floor consideration, Collins told reporters that

her concerns about repealing the individual mandate had increased after seeing statistics which showed that repeal would lead to more expensive premiums for middle-class families that make slightly too much to qualify for subsidies – which she said would outweigh the benefits from the tax bill's proposed tax cuts.

But the Senate was able to narrowly pass its tax bill, including the mandate repeal, with McConnell winning Collins' support by promising that other insurance market stabilization measures would later be adopted through separate legislation.

And once the tax bill was in House-Senate conference, it quickly became clear that the House would accept the Senate's individual mandate repeal as part of the final legislation.

As finally adopted by both chambers and enacted into law, the tax overhaul repealed the 2010 health care law's individual mandate.

However, because the tax overhaul was considered through the budget reconciliation process, which prevents filibusters and allows for Senate passage by simple majority vote, the Senate was prohibited by reconciliation rules from actually repealing the individual mandate from the U.S. Code.

Instead, the legislation effectively repealed the mandate by reducing to zero the penalty for failing to have qualified health insurance. Under the measure, that repeal was to become effective on Jan. 1, 2019. ■

officials, including Treasury Secretary Mnuchin, said that the tax cuts could completely pay for themselves through economic growth.

By party-line votes, Republicans rebuffed all the amendments offered by Democrats. Those included amendments to fully restore many deductions and credits the bill would terminate, including itemized deductions for state and local taxes; the tax break for private activity bonds often used to finance projects like hospitals and museums; the deduction for medical expenses that exceed 10 percent of income; wind energy tax credits; and a variety of education tax incentives. Also rejected were Democratic amendments to prevent repeal of the estate tax; further increase the child tax credit and make permanent the proposed $300 family credit for parents and non-child dependents.

Republicans also rejected a Democratic effort to restore the decades-old Johnson amendment, named for a 1954 amendment by then-Sen. Lyndon B. Johnson, that would be terminated by the bill. That provision in law prohibits nonprofit, charitable and related organizations (such as churches) from engaging in political activities.

Republicans offered only two amendments, both by Chairman Brady that were adopted on party-line votes. The first made numerous modifications, including changes to the tax plan's international "base erosion" rules and establishing new eligibility rules for the Earned Income Tax Credit that Brady said were needed to prevent fraud.

His second manager's amendment, adopted the final day, made a variety of changes that on net brought the bill's cost back under $1.5 trillion. It restored the adoption tax credit and moving expense deductions (but only for military families); raised the tax rates that would apply to repatriated overseas profits of U.S. companies, required that business research expenses be amortized over five years beginning in 2023, and effectively raised the excise taxes imposed on payments by U.S. companies to offshore affiliates.

Most importantly, it also addressed concerns by many Republicans and the NFIB regarding the taxation of pass-through businesses by

further reducing the rate that small businesses would pay. Under his amendment, active owners or shareholders who earn less than $150,000 in taxable income would have their first $75,000 in income taxed at a significantly lower rate, starting at 11 percent in 2018 and declining to 9 percent in 2022. This new rate would be applicable to all pass-through businesses, including personal services providers such as doctors, lawyers and accountants (who were excluded under the original bill).

HOUSE FLOOR ACTION

The House passed the bill on Nov. 16 by a 227-205 vote after two days of heated debate in which the two parties reiterated their arguments on the bill.

No Democrats supported the measure, and 13 Republicans – mostly from high-tax states – opposed it, primarily because of the bill's limitation on the SALT deduction. Many other Republicans in the days leading up to the vote said they had reservations regarding the measure, but planned to vote "yes" with the expectation that their concerns would be addressed during House-Senate conference negotiations.

Trump met with House Republicans the morning of the vote to show his support for the measure.

The bill was considered under a closed rule with no amendments permitted, and it was not otherwise modified from the version as reported by the Ways and Means Committee. After Senate Republicans indicated they would be adding repeal of the individual mandate to their version of the tax bill, conservative Republicans called on House leaders to do the same, but GOP leaders said the issue could be addressed in conference with the Senate.

SENATE FINANCE MARKUP

On Nov. 16, the same day the House passed its bill, the Senate Finance Committee approved its version by a 14-12 vote with no Demo-

cratic support, culminating a markup that lasted three days.

Senate Finance Republicans had unveiled an initial outline of their proposal on Nov. 9, the same day that House Ways and Means approved its bill. The Senate proposal was broadly similar to the House-reported bill but had several major differences – including maintaining seven individual tax brackets, although at somewhat lower levels for many with a top rate of 38.5 percent (the House bill included four brackets with the existing top rate of 39.6 percent).

Other differences included a full repeal of the state and local tax deduction; maintaining the existing mortgage interest deduction for loans of up to $1 million; increasing the child tax credit to $1,650 but including no separate credit for parents and non-child dependents; retaining the deduction for medical expenses that exceed 10 percent of adjusted gross income as well as the deduction for student loan interest; and maintaining the estate tax but with higher exemptions.

Unlike the House bill, it also would delay the cut in the corporate tax for one year, until 2019, and would continue to prohibit churches and other tax-exempt nonprofits from engaging in political activities (maintaining the so-called Johnson Amendment).

Committee debate on the bill began on Nov. 14 and immediately became heated because Senate Majority Leader McConnell earlier in the day announced that a revised version of the "chairman's mark" to be unveiled that evening would include provisions to repeal the 2010 health care law's individual mandate, as Trump had been advocating.

In addition to adding the individual mandate repeal – which was estimated to result in savings that could be used to pay for other tax cuts – the revised measure reduced three of the tax rates (from 35 percent, 25 percent and 22.5 percent to 34 percent, 24 percent and 22 percent, respectively) and increased the child tax credit to $2,000 per child.

It also provided for the expiration of most provisions affecting the individual tax code, including rate cuts, after eight years so they wouldn't add to future deficits – while making permanent the reduced 20 percent corporate rate by adding certain long-term tax offsets.

During committee markup, Republicans by party-line votes rejected all Democratic amendments, including those that would have rolled back the bill's tax breaks if they increased deficits, that sought to ensure the bill wouldn't raise taxes on anyone or increase health care premiums or cause anyone to lose insurance, and that would make the individual tax cuts permanent by making the corporate tax cuts temporary. Democrats even offered the House GOP's tax bill as a substitute in order to get GOP senators on the record on the House's bill; it was rejected by a 0-26 vote.

The only amendment adopted was a Hatch manager's amendment that included more than a dozen additional modifications.

ANWR & PREPARING FOR THE FLOOR

Before the tax bill could move to the Senate floor, it had to be merged by the Senate Budget Committee with separate reconciliation provisions to open up a portion of the Arctic National Wildlife Refuge to oil and gas drilling.

The Senate Energy and Natural Resources Committee on Nov. 15 approved such ANWR legislation by a 13-10 vote, which met the budget resolution's reconciliation instructions that it reduce the deficit by at least $1 billion over 10 years. The committee adopted one amendment by Sen. Bill Cassidy, R-La., which required that oil from the Strategic Petroleum Reserve be sold to finance certain Louisiana coastal restoration activities.

As Senate Budget prepared to meet to combine the tax and ANWR

measures into a single reconciliation bill, Senate Republicans had to navigate several obstacles to get the measure to the floor and pass it with their narrow 52-48 majority.

Sen. Ron Johnson, R-Wis., who sat on the Budget Committee, had expressed opposition to the tax bill because he said it was not generous enough to pass-through businesses, saying that the effective tax cut for such businesses was dwarfed by the tax breaks for large companies. Sen. Steve Daines, R-Mont., expressed similar concerns, saying he wanted changes to "ensure Main Street businesses are not put at a competitive disadvantage against large corporations."

Budget Committee member Bob Corker, R-Tenn., also continued to express concerns regarding the bill's fiscal impact. In September Corker had struck an agreement with fellow committee member Patrick J. Toomey, R-Pa., to vote for the fiscal 2018 budget resolution that allowed for tax cuts adding $1.5 trillion to the deficit over 10 years, although he also said his support for a tax cut that adds to the deficit would be contingent on the extent to which it stimulates economic growth and produces new revenue.

Corker, along with Sen. James Lankford, R-Okla., wanted to include a "trigger" mechanism that would automatically increase certain taxes in future years if the bill's tax cuts failed to produce the economic growth and revenues Republicans expected. When the Budget Committee met on Nov. 28, Corker announced that he had reached an agreement with GOP leaders to incorporate a revenue trigger into the measure on the floor.

Consequently, the committee by a party-line 12-11 vote approved the combined measure for Senate floor consideration, with Johnson voting for the measure on the assumption the pass-through issue would also be addressed on the floor.

Separately, Sen. Susan Collins, R-Maine, expressed concern regarding inclusion of the individual mandate repeal, saying it would lead to more expensive insurance premiums for middle-class families that don't qualify for health care tax subsidies, outweighing the benefits of the bill's tax cuts. However, she suggested the issue could be worked out if GOP leaders and Trump agreed to separate legislation that would help stabilize insurance markets and lower health insurance premiums. She also sought to ensure that the bill would be exempted from the statutory pay-as-you-go law (PL 111-139) in order to prevent automatic cuts to Medicare and other programs because the tax bill would add to budget deficits.

Meanwhile, Republican and Democratic Budget staff members began meeting with the Senate Parliamentarian regarding provisions that might violate the Senate's so-called Byrd rule, which bars provisions that are "extraneous" to reconciliation legislation, such as items that do not have a direct budget impact or that affect spending and revenue in ways that are merely "incidental." Provisions that violate the Byrd rule generally must be dropped from the measure.

SENATE FLOOR ACTION

The Senate on Nov. 29 voted 52-48 along party lines to begin consideration of its tax bill, with numerous Republicans voting with the expectation that a McConnell package of modifications would address their specific concerns regarding the bill.

GOP leaders also remained hopeful some Democrats might support the bill. Democratic senators Joe Donnelly of Indiana and Heidi Heitkamp of North Dakota said they were waiting to see a final version of the bill before making a decision. "I'm still trying to see if we can get to yes," Heitkamp said. "We've made some offers. We'll see."

Corker's revenue trigger proposal caused a pause in Senate consideration, however, when the parliamentarian ruled that the proposed trigger would result in a Byrd rule violation. That forced GOP leaders to seek an alternative way to address Corker's concerns, with new proposals being considered – including automatic, future tax increases to raise revenue. Reinforcing Corker's concerns was a new JCT estimate that the Senate's tax plan would lose about $1 trillion in revenue over 10 years, even accounting for economic growth.

After working overnight to work out deals with senators, GOP leaders on Dec. 1 said they had the votes to pass the measure, with Johnson and Daines agreeing to support the measure in return for a more generous tax cut for pass-through businesses. Collins negotiated changes to the bill's SALT deduction to allow $10,000 in property tax deductions, like the House bill, and said she had also secured a commitment for separate legislation to lower health insurance premiums.

Jeff Flake, R-Ariz., offered his support in return for modifications in how capital expensing would be handled to eliminate what he called a "budget gimmick." He also said he had secured a commitment from the White House and GOP leaders to work with him on a legislative fix for "Dreamers" enrolled in the Deferred Action for Childhood Arrivals (DACA) program.

The legislative modifications were unveiled at about 9:30 p.m., and were incorporated into the bill that night by voice as part of a manager's amendment adopted at the end of a vote-a-rama. (Under the budget reconciliation process, Senate floor debate is limited to 20 hours, at the end of which senators are allowed to offer an unlimited number of amendments with virtually no debate –what is known as the "vote-a-rama.")

The adopted manager's amendment also increased exemptions from the AMT for individuals, rather than eliminating it, while retaining the corporate AMT; modified repatriation tax rates for overseas profits to equal the rates in the House bill; allowed medical expenses that exceed 7.5 percent of adjusted gross income as an itemized deduction (down from the existing 10 percent threshold) for tax years 2017 and 2018; and required the sale of oil from the Strategic Petroleum Reserve to ensure that the bill's ANWR provisions achieve the required reconciliation savings, among other provisions. Majority Leader McConnell said the final Senate bill would ease conference negotiations with the House.

However, no trigger deal was worked out for Corker, with GOP conservatives opposing any future tax increases to reduce the bill's revenue losses.

Most other amendments offered were rejected by party-line votes, including a Democratic effort to strip out the ANWR provisions.

The Senate passed the bill at 1:30 am on Saturday, Dec. 2 by a 51-49 vote, with all Democrats and independents voting no.

DEVELOPMENT OF FINAL AGREEMENT

Following Senate passage, informal negotiations quickly began and the two chambers formally moved the bill to conference, seeking to hammer out a compromise.

Despite the final Senate revisions moving towards the House version, the two versions that still had some major differences.

Those major differences included the Senate's one-year delay in cutting the corporate tax and the expiration of individual tax cuts after eight years; differences in individual tax rate structures and the number of tax brackets; the degree to which to modify the mortgage interest deduction and whether to retain the deduction for people with high medical costs; the level of the child tax credit; whether to repeal or limit the estate tax and the AMT; the structure and rate to be used for reducing taxes on pass-through businesses; repealing or preserving the prohibition on political activities by churches; and repeal of the individual mandate and opening up ANWR to oil and gas development – with both the ANWR provisions and individual mandate repeal expected to be accepted by the House.

Given the narrow margin of passage in the Senate, it was expected that in conference the House would have to move towards the Senate's bill in reconciling provisions. A critical consideration during negotiations was that cumulative tax cuts and offsets in the final product could allow no more than $1.5 trillion in added deficits over 10 years, in order for the measure to remain eligible for reconciliation and final Senate passage by simple majority vote.

By Dec. 13, the same day the House-Senate conference committee was scheduled to hold its first meeting, House and Senate Republicans said they had reached an agreement on the broad parameters of the tax code overhaul, the details of which were finalized two days later.

Under the final agreement, the corporate tax rate was permanently set at 21 percent (rather than the 20 percent included in both bills) with the reduced rate from 35 percent to become effective immediately in 2018 (rather than 2019, as in the Senate bill). It fully repealed the corporate AMT, while increasing exemptions so fewer taxpayers would be hit by the individual AMT. And for the one-time repatriation of overseas corporate profits, it established a 15.5 percent tax rate for cash and 8 percent for non-cash assets.

Like the Senate it maintained seven tax brackets but reduced the tax rates for each bracket except the bottom 10 percent bracket; the top bracket was reduced to 37 percent (versus the House's 39.6 percent and the Senate's 38.5 percent). The individual tax cuts would expire after eight years, however. It set the child tax credit at the Senate's level of $2,000 per child, and to garner the support of Sens. Marco Rubio, R-Fla., and Mike Lee, R-Utah, made $1,400 of that tax credit refundable (versus $1,100 in both bills).

For the mortgage interest deduction, it effectively split the difference between House and Senate bills, allowing interest to be deducted on up to $750,000 in loans, including loans on second homes, while eliminating the deductibility of home equity debt. It rejected the House proposal to eventually eliminate the estate tax, but doubled the exemption threshold. And the tax mechanism for pass-through business income merged portions of each chamber's proposals, which Sen. Johnson said he would support, providing a 20 percent deduction for pass-through business income (down from 23 percent in the Senate bill) along with special provisions for companies with few employees and significant depreciable property.

It modified the proposed $10,000 limitation on the SALT deduction to allow that $10,000 cap to apply to a combination of state and local property taxes or income taxes, and not just property taxes. The deductibility of state and local income taxes was important to California, and because three Republicans from California had voted against the original House bill House Majority Leader Kevin McCarthy, R-Calif., had sought to accommodate some ability to deduct state and local income taxes.

Finally, House language to end the ban on political activities by churches and certain other nonprofits was dropped because it did not comply with the Senate's Byrd rule. But as expected, the final measure did include Senate provisions to open ANWR to oil and gas drilling and to effectively repeal the 2010 health care law's individual mandate,

although that repeal would not become effective until 2019.

In a surprise, Corker, who had been the only Republican to oppose the Senate bill, on Dec. 15 said he would support the final agreement despite the fact it would still result in more than $1 trillion in deficits over 10 years.

Corker said the bill was "far from perfect" but that it represented a "once-in-a-generation opportunity to make U.S. businesses domestically more productive and internationally more competitive" and that the nation would be "better off with it." His support effectively ensured that Senate Republicans would have the votes to adopt the conference agreement.

FINAL ACTION

The House acted first on the conference agreement, adopting it on Dec. 19 by a 227-203 vote. Again, no Democrats voted for the measure, with 12 Republicans also opposing it. Of the 13 Republicans who opposed initial House passage, only California's Tom McClintock switched his vote to yes, saying that modifying the $10,000 SALT deduction to include state and local income taxes would help his constituents.

The Senate took up the agreement the same day and passed it shortly after midnight by a party-line 51-48 vote, with Sen. John Mc-Cain, R-Ariz., missing the vote. Before the vote, however, Democrats forced the elimination of several provisions that violated the Byrd Rule. Those dropped provisions related to an excise tax on endowments of small private universities and 529 savings accounts for home-schooling expenses, and the bill's statutory short title – the "Tax Cuts and Jobs Act." A GOP motion to waive the rule, which required 60 votes, failed by a 51-48 vote.

That modification required the House to re-vote on the measure to clear it for the president, which the chamber quickly did on Dec. 20 by a 224-201 vote.

While voting for the agreement, Corker also had to fend off accusations that his vote had been "bought off" by the inclusion of pass-through provisions that benefit wealthy real estate investors such as him and Trump. House and Senate tax writers defended Corker, noting that the provisions had earlier been part of the House bill and were simply included as part of normal conference negotiations.

Trump signed the bill into law on Dec. 22, after the White House initially considered waiting until January to sign it to prevent the measure from triggering automatic spending cuts. Because the legislation would result in $1.46 trillion in deficits over 10 years, the 2010 statutory pay-as-you-go law would require automatic cuts to Medicare and other specified mandatory spending programs over 10 years to offset those revenue losses.

Usually, Congress includes language to waive the 2010 law, but that is not permitted in reconciliation legislation. The White House and lawmakers addressed the issue by including a "paygo" waiver in a separate, four-week stopgap government funding bill (PL 115-96) that also was enacted that week. ■

FINAL BILL: TAX SIDE-BY-SIDE

A side-by-side look at the changes in tax law as initially proposed by the House and Senate and then under the conference agreement between the two chambers and signed into law. Dollar values are displayed as: individual filers/household filers.

PROVISION	HOUSE	SENATE	FINAL BILL
INDIVIDUAL			
Tax brackets	• 12% on taxable income up to $45,000 (individuals)/$90,000 (households) • 25% between $45,000/$90,000 and $200,000/$260,000 • 35% between $200,000/$260,000 and $500,000/$1 million • 39.6% above $500,000/$1 million • Benefit of 12% bracket phases out above $1 million/$1.2 million	• 10% on taxable income up to $9,525/$19,050 • 12% between $9,525/$19,050 and $38,700/$77,400 • 22% between $38,700/$77,400 and $70,000/$140,000 • 24% between $70,000/$140,000 and $160,000/$320,000 • 32% between $160,000/$320,000 and $200,000/$400,000 • 35% between $200,000/$400,000 and $500,000/$1 million • 38.5% on taxable income above $500,000/$1 million • All rates expire after 12/31/25	• 10% on taxable income up to $9,525/$19,050 • 12% between $9,525/%19,050 and $38,700/$77,400 • 22% between $38,700/$77,400 and $82,500/$165,000 • 24% between $82,500/$165,000 and $157,500/$315,000 • 32% between $157,500/$315,000 and $200,000/$400,000 • 35% between $200,000/$400,000 and $500,000/$600,000 • 37% on taxable income above $500,000/$600,000 • All rates expire after 12/31/25
Standard deduction	• Increased to $12,200/$24,400, indexed for inflation after 12/31/18 • Additional standard deduction for elderly and blind repealed	• Increased to $12,000/$24,000, indexed for inflation after 12/31/18 • Additional standard deduction for the elderly and blind is maintained • Expires after 12/31/25	• Same as Senate
Personal exemptions	• Repealed	• Repealed through 12/31/25	• Same as Senate
Alternative inflation measure	• Switch from Consumer Price Index for all urban consumers (CPI-U) to "chained" CPI-U that considers consumer substitution for cheaper goods, beginning after 12/31/17	• Same as House	• Also same as House
Child tax credit	• $1,600 per child under the age of 17 not indexed, refundable up to $1,000 indexed to next $100 • $300 nonrefundable family credit for each parent and non-child dependent, not indexed, expires after 12/31/22 • Increases income threshold to $110,000/$230,000 above which credit phases out • Refundable portion of credit disallowed for taxpayers without valid Social Security Number (SSN), if child does not have SSN, only eligible for $300 nonrefundable credit	• $2,000 per child under the age of 18 (under 17 for 2025 tax year), not indexed, refundable up to $1,000, indexed to next $100 • Refundability threshold lowered to $2,500 in earned income • $500 nonrefundable credit for non-child dependents • Increased phaseout threshold to $500,000/$500,000 • Requires valid SSN for each child to claim refundable portion, otherwise eligible for $500 nonrefundable credit • Expires after 12/31/25	• Generally follows Senate, except refundable portion begins at $1,400 in 2018, income phase-out thresholds are reduced to $200,000/$400,000, and present-law age limit of 17 and under is maintained • Like Senate, requires valid SSN for each child to claim refundable portion, otherwise eligible for $500 nonrefundable credit • Like Senate, expires after 12/31/25
Nonrefundable personal credits	• Elderly and disabled credit and plug-in electric vehicle credit repealed	• No change from present law	• No change from present law

PROVISION	HOUSE	SENATE	FINAL BILL
Education incentives	• Hope credit, lifetime learning credit repealed • Above-the-line deductions for student loan interest and qualified tuition expenses repealed • American Opportunity Tax Credit allowed for fifth year at 50% of prior value (40% for refundable portion) • Valid SSN to claim AOTC required • No new contributions to Coverdell savings accounts, though 529 accounts may receive Coverdell rollovers • Up to $10,000 annual 529 distributions for use in connection with public, private or religious elementary or secondary school, and 529 contributions for unborn children allowed • Exclusions from taxable income for employer education assistance and qualified tuition reduction repealed	• Up to $10,000 annual 529 distributions for use in connection with public, private or religious elementary or secondary school, or home school expenses	• Same as Senate, except home school expenses not eligible for 529 distributions
Pease limitation on itemized deductions, applicable to taxable income above $261,500/$313,800 (indexed)	• Repealed	• Repealed through 12/31/25	• Same as Senate
Mortgage interest deduction	• Deductions for second home, home equity debt repealed • Limit applicability to principal residence debt up to $500,000 • Acquisitions prior to 1/1/18 grandfathered, and refinancings prior to 11/2/17 are grandfathered to the extent the amount of the refinancing does not exceed amount of refinanced debt	• Repeals deduction for home equity debt through 12/31/25	• Reduces limit on deductible mortgage debt to $750,000 for new purchases and refinancings (principal residence or otherwise) entered into after 12/15/17, and repeals deduction for interest paid on home equity debt, through 12/31/25 • Like Senate, keeps deduction for second home
State and local deductions	• Repealed except for property and sales taxes incurred in operating a trade or business, and for up to $10,000 in other property taxes (not indexed)	• Same as House except for expiration after 12/31/25	• Same as House, except limit of up to $10,000 in income, sales and/or property taxes prior to 12/31/25
Charitable deductions	• Increases limit on cash contributions to qualified organizations from 50% to 60% of taxable income • Allows adjustments to vehicle mileage rate in connection with providing volunteer services • Denies deduction for purchases of college athletic seating rights	• Same as House except no change to mileage rate and provisions expire after 12/31/25	• Same as Senate
Other deductions	• Deductions for personal casualty and property losses (except for losses sustained in Hurricanes Harvey/Irma/Maria), tax preparation expenses, medical expenses that exceed 10% of adjusted gross income, alimony payments, moving expenses (except for members of the Armed Forces), and out-of-pocket educator expenses repealed • Includes travel expenses within limit on deduction for wagering losses • No new contributions to Archer Medical Savings Accounts	• Same as House except educator expense deduction is doubled to $500 through 12/31/25 and deductions for all disaster-related personal casualty and property losses, alimony payments, as well as medical expense deduction, are maintained. • Medical expense deduction floor decreased from 10% of adjusted gross income to 7.5% for 2017 and 2018	• Same as Senate except no increase in educator expense deduction and deduction for alimony payments is repealed, effective for settlements executed after Dec. 31, 2018 • Like Senate, deductions for all disaster-related personal casualty and property losses, as well as medical expense deduction, are maintained. • Like Senate, medical expense deduction floor decreased

PROVISION	HOUSE	SENATE	FINAL BILL
Capital gains tax on home sales	• Increases length of time to five of previous eight years taxpayer must own and live in home to qualify for full exclusion of first $250,000/$500,000 profit, otherwise exclusion is reduced • Exclusion can only be used once every five years • Exclusion amount phases out by $1 for every $1 of taxable income above $250,000/$500,000	• Same as House except no phaseout of exclusion amount and limitation expires after 12/31/25	• No change from present law
Exclusions for certain employee fringe benefits	• Exclusions for employee achievement awards, moving expenses and adoption assistance repealed	• Exclusions for bicycle commuting reimbursements and moving expenses repealed, through 12/31/25	• Same as Senate
Dependent care Flexible Spending Accounts	• Repealed after 12/31/22	• No change from present law	• No change from present law
Retirement savings incentives	• Recharacterization of Roth IRA contributions repealed • Reduces minimum age for "in-service" distributions from governmental 457(b) plans to 59.5 • Modifies rules related to hardship withdrawals	• Repeals recharacterization of Roth IRA contributions • Increases limit on amount of public safety volunteer length-of-service awards from $3,000 to $6,000, indexed for inflation	• Same as Senate, except hardship withdrawal provision is not included
Estate, gift and generation-skipping transfer taxes	• Doubles estate and gift tax exemption after 12/31/17 • Repeals estate/GST tax after 12/31/24 • Reduces gift tax from 40% to 35% after 12/31/24	• Doubles estate, gift and GST tax exemption after 12/31/17, through 12/31/25	• Same as Senate
Alternative Minimum Tax	• Repealed	• Exemption amounts increased to $70,300/$109,400, income thresholds above which AMT exemption phases out increased to $156,300/$208,400, effective through 12/31/25	• Same as Senate, except phase-out thresholds are increased to $500,000/$1 million
ACA "individual shared responsibility" payment	• No change from present law	• Repealed after 12/31/18	• Same as Senate
Member of Congress living expenses deduction	• No change from present law	• Repealed	• Same as Senate
Disaster aid	• No change from present law	• Special deductions for personal casualty losses and exemptions from retirement plan withdrawal penalties for individuals in major disaster areas as declared by the president in 2016 under the Stafford Act	• Same as Senate, with clarification that provision applies to losses incurred between 12/31/15 and 1/1/18

BUSINESS

PROVISION	HOUSE	SENATE	FINAL BILL
Corporate tax rate	• Reduced from 35% to 20%, effective after 12/31/17	• Same as House except change is effective after 12/31/18	• Reduced to 21%, effective after 12/31/17, with adjustment for excess tax reserves

PROVISION	HOUSE	SENATE	FINAL BILL
"Pass-through" businesses	• Maximum 25% rate on qualified business income, other than income from personal services (e.g. law, accounting, engineering, financial advisory) • Special rate applicable to 30% of business income, unless business owner elects to apply special capital percentage formula (must elect this formula for five years) • Special 9% rate on first $75,000 of taxable income for all pass-through owners earning up to $150,000, above which the benefit is reduced until it fully phases out at $225,000 taxable income • Special 9 percent rate is phased in over five years, with 11% in 2018-19, 10% in 2020-21, and 9% starting in 2022	• 23% deduction for domestic nonservice income, capped at 50% of taxpayer's total share of W-2 wages paid by the business • Wage cap does not apply if taxable income does not exceed $250,000/$500,000 • Full deduction allowed for services-related income if taxable income does not exceed $250,000/$500,000, phased out over the next $50,000/$100,000 • Active pass-through losses disallowed in excess of $250,000/$500,000 • Publicly traded partnership distributions, agricultural and horticultural cooperatives, and qualified Real Estate Investment Trust and cooperative dividends eligible for deduction • All provisions effective through 12/31/25	• Generally follows Senate, except deduction is equal to 20% and limitation on services-related income and wage cap is phased in beginning at $157,500/$315,000 • Wage cap is modified to equal the greater of 50% of W-2 wages paid or 25% of W-2 wages plus 2.5% of the taxpayers' basis of depreciable property purchases • Definition of services is modified to exclude engineering and architecture and deduction is made available to trusts and estates • Like Senate, active pass-through losses disallowed in excess of $250,000/$500,000 • Like Senate, publicly traded partnership distributions, agricultural and horticultural cooperatives, and qualified Real Estate Investment Trust and cooperative dividends eligible for deduction • Like Senate, all provisions effective through 12/31/25
Corporate Alternative Minimum Tax	• Repealed	• No change from present law	• Repealed
Bonus depreciation	• 100% expensing for qualified property acquired and placed in service and certain plants bearing fruits and nuts planted and grafted between 9/27/17 and 1/1/23 (or 1/1/24 for certain aircraft and longer production period property), applicable to used as well as new property • Public utility and real estate property excluded • Increases from $8,000 to $16,0000 the special depreciation allowance for luxury automobiles	• 100% expensing through 2022, phasing down by 20% each year for next five years through 2027 • Unlike House version, real estate property not excluded and used property is not eligible • Also applicable to film, television and live theater production costs • Maintains $8,000 special depreciation allowance for luxury automobiles, but increases depreciation allowances for taxpayers who do not elect full expensing (e.g. who may be in a loss position) for such vehicles • Removes substantiation requirement for computers and peripheral equipment	• Generally follows Senate, except retains House allowance for used property
Research and experimentation expenses	• Five-year amortization generally required, except for R&E conducted outside the U.S. for which the applicable recovery period is 15 years • Effective after 12/31/22	• Same as House, except provision becomes effective after 12/31/25	• Also same as House, except becomes effective after 12/31/21
Other cost recovery	• No change from present law	• Shortens recovery period for certain farming equipment from seven to five years and repeals 150% declining balance method • Shortens recovery period from 39 years for nonresidential real property and 27.5 years for residential real property to 25 years for each • Shortens recovery period from 15 to 10 years for qualified leasehold, restaurant and retail improvements • For residential rental property covered under the Alternative Depreciation System, normally required for property used outside the U.S., for tax-exempt use or financed by tax-exempt bonds, or for any property whose owner opts out of the net interest expense limitation, the 40-year recovery period is shortened to 30 years	• Generally follows Senate, except maintains current law 39-year and 27.5-year recovery period for nonresidential real property and residential rental property, respectively, and provides for general 15-year recovery period for qualified improvement property

PROVISION	HOUSE	SENATE	FINAL BILL
Sec. 179 expensing limits	• Increased to $5 million, with phaseout beginning at $20 million in total qualified property placed in service • Expanded to include qualified energy efficient heating and air-conditioning property • Expires 12/31/22	• Increased to $1 million, with phaseout beginning at $20 million in total qualified property placed in service • Expanded to include property used to furnish lodging and improvements to nonresidential real property including roofs, heating, ventilation and air-conditioning property, fire protection and alarm systems, and security systems	• Same as Senate
Small business accounting	• Expands ability to use cash method of accounting to all businesses that meet a $25 million gross receipts test for the three prior taxable years	• Same as House except the gross receipts limit is $15 million	• Same as House
Other accounting	• No change from present law	• Generally requires recognition of income in the taxable year in which such income appears in an applicable financial statement such as 10-K filings • Exemptions for certain long-term contracts, income from mortgage servicing rights • Effective date of new financial statement rules delayed one year, to 1/1/19, for income from original issue discount debt instruments issued at less than face value, with six-year adjustment period	• Same as Senate
S corporation conversions to C corporation	• Allows converting S corporation to spread tax impact of switching from cash accounting to accrual accounting method over six years in equal installments (applicable to corporations with greater than $25 million three-year average gross receipts)	• Same as House	• Also same as House
Interest expense deductions	• Limits interest expense deductions to the sum of net interest income plus 30% of adjusted taxable income and any "floor plan financing" interest (common among auto dealers) • Disallowed interest may be carried forward for up to five years • Businesses that meet a three-year, $25 million gross receipts test are exempted, as are real estate businesses and regulated public utilities	• Same as House except adjusted taxable income does not include deductions for depreciation, amortization and depletion, but includes new pass-through deduction • Disallowed interest may be carried forward indefinitely • The gross receipts test is $15 million • Definition of floor plan financing indebtedness includes purchases of vehicles for lease as well as sale, and includes self-propelled vehicles but removes construction equipment from definition • Rural electric cooperatives are also exempt • Farming businesses, including agricultural and horticultural cooperatives, may opt out but must depreciate property over 10 or more years	• Generally follows Senate, except EBITDA basis expires after 12/31/21, after which 30% limit is calculated based on EBIT and follows House on three-year, $25 million gross receipts test
Net operating loss deductions	• Limited to 90% of taxable income, with unlimited carryovers permitted • Carryovers are increased annually • Special carryback provisions are repealed, other than one-year carryback for certain farm or small business losses • Small businesses with no more than $5 million annual gross receipts are exempted	• Limited to 90% of taxable income, declining to 80% after 12/31/22, with unlimited carryovers permitted, except for property and casualty insurance losses for which 20-year carryforwards are maintained • Special carryback provisions are repealed, other than two-year carryback for certain farm or property and casualty insurance losses	• Generally follows Senate, except deduction is limited to 80% beginning after 12/31/17
Like-kind exchanges	• Repealed other than for real property not held primarily for sale	• Same as House	• Also same as House

PROVISION	HOUSE	SENATE	FINAL BILL
Contributions to capital	• Repeals exemption from gross income for contributions to corporations' capital, other than contributions of money or property in exchange for stock or other interests	• No change from present law	• Removes from definition of contribution to capital any contribution in aid of construction or by customer/potential customer, as well as contributions by governmental entities or civic groups
Deduction for local lobbying expenses	• Repealed	• Repealed	• Repealed
Sec. 199 domestic production deduction	• Repealed after 12/31/17	• Repealed after 12/31/17 for noncorporate taxpayers, and after 12/31/18 for C corporations	• Same as House
Employer-provided fringe benefits	• Prohibits business deductions for entertainment expenses, membership dues, parking/transit benefits, on-premises athletic facilities, and food and beverages provided on-premises • Existing 50% deduction limit on business meal expenses would remain	• Same as House except deduction for on-premises athletic facilities would remain, and deduction for food and beverages provided on premises is limited to 50% prior to 12/31/2025, after which deduction would be disallowed • Cash, gift cards and other nontangible personal property no longer deductible forms of employee achievement awards	• Same as Senate
FDIC premiums	• Deduction disallowed for financial institutions with greater than $50 billion in consolidated assets • Limited for institutions with greater than $10 billion in assets • Full deduction allowed for at or below $10 billion assets	• Same as House	• Also same as House
Tax-free rollover of capital gain into Small Business Investment Company	• Repealed	• No change from present law	• Repealed
Capital gains on self-created intangible property	• Repeals preferential rates	• No change from present law	• Same as House
Carried interest	• Holding period for preferential long-term capital gains tax rate increased from one to three years for investment services providers	• Same as House	• Also same as House
Cost basis for securities transactions	• No change	• Switches to "first-in, first-out" method of determining cost basis, rather than at the taxpayer's election under current law, with exemption for mutual funds	• No change from present law
Partnership rules	• Repeal of technical termination of partnerships	• Tightens rules related to sale or exchange of partnership interests, clarifies that charitable contributions and foreign taxes are included in calculation of partners' loss limitations	• Retains House and Senate provisions
Non-disclosure agreements in sexual abuse/harassment cases	• No change from present law	• Denial of deduction for any settlement, payout or attorney fees related to sexual harassment or sexual abuse if such payments are subject to nondisclosure agreement	• Same as Senate
Contingency fees	• Denial of deduction for advances paid to clients	• No change from present law	• No change from present law
Orphan drug credit	• Repealed	• Cuts existing credit from 50% to 27.5%	• Same as Senate except credit is reduced to 25%

PROVISION	HOUSE	SENATE	FINAL BILL
Employer-provided child care credit	• Repealed	• No change from present law	• No change from present law
Historic rehabilitation credit	• Repealed	• Provides 20% credit over five years • Repeals credit for pre-1936 property	• Same as Senate except taxpayer may select 60-month phased rehabilitation period
Work Opportunity Tax Credit	• Repealed	• No change from present law	• No change from present law
New Markets Tax Credit	• Repealed	• No change from present law	• No change from present law
Credit for disabled employee access	• Repealed	• No change from present law/	• No change from present law
FICA tax credit for tipped workers	• Increases threshold above which an employer can claim tip credit to $7.25/hr, in line with federal minimum wage in place for 2017 • Requires employer to allocate tip income among employees in excess of 10% of gross receipts above amounts reported by employees (up from 8% in current law)	• No change from present law	• No change from present law
Famly and medical leave credit	• No change from present law	• Provides credit equal to 12.5% of wages paid during period in which employees are on family or medical leave if payment rate is at least 50% of normal wages • Credit is increased by 0.25 percentage points for each percentage point payment rate rises above 50% • Requires substantiation by Treasury for certain employers claiming credit • Expires after 12/31/19	• Same as Senate
Craft beverage excise taxes	• No change from present law	• Lowers tax rate on beer from $18 per barrel to $16 on first 6 million barrels produced or imported annually, with small brewers taxed at $3.50 per barrel on first 60,000 barrels produced domestically • Removes 250,000 gallon domestic production limitation on wine excise tax credit, and makes sparkling wine producers and importers eligible, with a new tiered credit structure based on volume produced • Allows higher alcohol content wine to qualify for lowest tier excise tax rate • Reduced tax rate on mead and certain carbonated wines, and creates new tiered tax rate structure for distilled spirits • All provisions expire after 12/31/19	• Same as Senate
Aircraft management services	• No change from present law	• Exempts certain payments by aircraft owners for maintenance and support services from air transportation excise taxes	• Same as Senate
Qualified Opportunity Zones	• No change from present law	• Creates deferral of income for capital gains reinvested in a "qualified opportunity fund" which invests in low-income communities	• Same as Senate, with clarification that each state and District of Columbia may submit nominations for a limited number of opportunity zones

PROVISION	HOUSE	SENATE	FINAL BILL
Alaska Native Corporations	• No change from present law	• Allows Alaska Native Corporations to transfer money to settlement trusts established "to promote the health, education and welfare of beneficiaries and to preserve the heritage and culture of Alaska Natives" without recognizing gross income and allowing an ANC to deduct contributions to a settlement trust	• Same as Senate

ENERGY

PROVISION	HOUSE	SENATE	FINAL BILL
Renewable electricity production tax credit	• Eliminates inflation adjustment for facilities which begin construction after date of enactment • Maximum credit is 1.5 cents per kilowatt hour	• No change from present law	• No change from present law
Renewable energy investment tax credit	• Modified to include fiber optic solar, fuel cell, microturbine, geothermal heat pump, small wind and combined heat and power property on same phase out schedule as existing ITC for solar energy property, through 2021 • 10% solar and geothermal ITC is repealed for new projects which begin construction after 2027	• No change from present law	• No change from present law
Residential energy-efficient property credit	• Modified to include geothermal heat pump, small wind and fuel cell property on same phase out schedule as existing residential property credit (through 2021)	• No change from present law	• /No change from present law/
Enhanced oil recovery credit	• Repealed	• No change from present law	• No change from present law/
Marginal oil and gas well credit	• Repealed	• No change from present law	• No change from present law/
Nuclear production tax credit	• Requires allocation of unused megawatt capacity by secretary of the Treasury	• No change from present law	• No change from present law/
Arctic Drilling	• No change from present law	• Repeals prohibition on oil and gas exploration in "1002 Area" of Alaska's Arctic National Wildlife Refuge • Sets 16.67% royalty rate for leases and directs 50% of revenue to Alaska, remainder to federal Treasury, and directs Secretary of Interior to conduct one lease sale within four years and two within seven years after enactment, of least 400,000 acres each • Temporarily increases revenue sharing for Alabama, Mississippi, Texas and Louisiana for fiscal years 2020-21 • Directs Secretary of Energy to draw down and sell seven million barrels of crude oil from Strategic Petroleum Reserve in fiscal 2026-27 for a total of $600 million	• Same as Senate

PROVISION	HOUSE	SENATE	FINAL BILL
INFRASTRUCTURE			
Private activity bonds	• Tax exemption repealed for new bonds issued after 12/31/17	• No change from present law	• No change from present law
Advance refunding bonds	• Exclusion from gross income for interest on bonds issued to advance refund other bonds repealed for new issues after 12/31/17	• Same as House	• Also same as House
Tax credit bonds	• Authority to issue New Clean Renewable Energy Bonds, qualified energy conservation bonds, qualified zone academy bonds and qualified school construction bonds repealed	• No change from present law	• Same as House
Tax-exempt bonds for professional sports stadiums	• Repealed for bonds issued after 11/2/17	• No change from present law	• No change from present law
INSURANCE			
Life insurance / property & casualty insurance modifications	• Includes 8% surtax on life insurance company income • modified discounting and proration rules for property and casualty insurance companies • repeals small life insurance company deduction • aligns accounting treatment of changes in computing life insurance reserves with accounting treatment for other corporations • repeals special rule for distributions to shareholders from pre-1984 policyholders surplus account	• Same as House, but with modified proration rules for life insurers, no modification of discounting rules for P&C insurers • No 8% surtax on life insurer taxable income as in House bill, but would reduce deductible life insurer taxable reserves by 7.13% • Extends amortization period for certain policy acquisition expenses, such as commissions, from 120 to 180 months (60-month amortization of first $5 million in expenses remains in place), and increases percentages of policy acquisition expenses as a share of deductible net premiums	• Generally follows House/Senate, except final agreement drops House's 8% surtax, includes Senate language on proration rules for P&C insurers and modified House language on discounting rules for P&C insurers, increases reduction in deductible life insurer reserves to 7.19% and slightly reduces percentages of policy acquisition expenses as a share of deductible net premiums from Senate version
COMPENSATION			
Employee compensation	• Eliminates exceptions for commissions and performance-based compensation from $1 million annual deduction limit • Expands definition of "covered employee" subject to deduction limitation	• Eliminates exceptions for commissions and performance-based compensation from $1 million annual deduction limit • Expands definition of "covered employee" subject to deduction limitation • With transition rule so that changes do not apply to written binding contracts in effect on 11/2/17 or modified in a material respect after that date	• Generally follows Senate, with modification to transition rule for binding written contracts in place by 11/2/17
Tax-exempt organizations	• 20% excise tax on compensation in excess of $1 million paid to five highest-paid employees	• Same as House	• Generally follows House, except tax rate is 21%, includes narrower definition of "highly compensated employee," and exempts remuneration paid to a licensed medical professional directly related to the performance of medical or veterinary services
Equity grants	• Gives employees option to defer inclusion in income of amounts attributable to stock transferred to the employee	• Same as House	• Generally follows House, with modifications
INTERNATIONAL			
"Territorial" tax regime	• 100% deduction for foreign-source dividends received by domestic corporations	• Same as House	• Also same as House

PROVISION	HOUSE	SENATE	FINAL BILL
Sales or transfers of foreign assets in connection with transition to territorial system	• Limitation on losses incurred upon sale or transfer of foreign branch assets corporations	• Same as House, with additional stipulations that sale of stock held in foreign corporations for one or more years as well as sales of stock in one foreign subsidiary by another foreign subsidiary are also covered by the limitation	• Retains House and Senate provisions
Treatment of deferred foreign income upon transition to territorial regime	• One-time tax on post-1986 earnings and profits indefinitely reinvested abroad and not previously subject to U.S. tax • Tax imposed at a 14% rate for liquid assets and 7% for illiquid assets • Tax payment may spread over eight years in equal installments	• "Deemed" taxes are imposed at rates of 14.49% and 7.49%, respectively • For companies electing installment payments, 8% of tax liability is required for first five years, rising to 15% in year six, 20% in year seven, and 25% in final year • Imposes 35% "recapture" tax on dividends received by companies that enter into inversion transactions within 10 years after date of enactment	• Generally follows Senate, except taxes are imposed at rates of 15.5% and 8% respectively
Modifications to "Subpart F" anti-deferral regime	• Repeals inclusion of certain categories of foreign shipping and oil and gas-related income in Subpart F income • "Look-through" rule for controlled foreign corporations made permanent	• Same as House	• Generally follows House, except conference agreement drops permanent extension of CFC look-through rule
Anti-base erosion provisions	• 10% tax on "foreign high return" income, defined as the excess above the federal short-term rate plus 7%, with the base amount reduced to take into account qualified business asset investment and interest expense • Limits deductible net interest expense of a domestic corporation that is a member of a multinational group to 110% of its share of the worldwide group's net interest expense, with carryforwards of disallowed deductions for five years • Beginning after 12/31/18, imposes 20% excise tax on payments by a domestic corporation to a foreign corporation that are allowed as a deduction or included in costs of goods sold, inventory or as a depreciable or amortizable asset	• 17.5% effective tax rate on new category of "global intangible low-taxed income" or GILTI, defined as aggregate net income over a 10% return on CFC depreciable tangible property, beginning after 12/31/17, reduced to 10% after 12/13/18 and rising to 12.5% beginning after 12/31/25) • Limits deductible net interest expense of a domestic corporation that is a member of a multinational group to 130% of the domestic share of the worldwide group's total indebtedness based on its debt-equity ratio, phasing down to 110% in 2022 in 5% annual increments, with unlimited carryforwards for disallowed deductions • Imposes 10% tax (11% for certain banks and securities dealers) on deductible foreign payments (other than derivatives transactions entered into in the ordinary course of business) from a U.S. corporation, not including cost of goods sold; tax rises to 12.5% (13.5% for certain banks and securities dealers) after 12/31/25 • Restricts certain tax exemptions for foreign insurance income • Increases excise tax on stock compensation of officers of an inverted corporation from 15% to 20%	• Generally follows Senate, except effective tax rate on GILTI ranges from 10.5% to 13.125%, depending on amount of taxes paid overseas, beginning after 12/31/17, rising to 13.125% to 16.406% after 12/31/25 • Removes provisions on excess indebtedness of U.S. member of worldwide group • Tax on base erosion payments is reduced to 5% for one year beginning after 12/31/17, after which it rises to 10%, further rising to 12.5% after 12/31/25 (one percentage point higher in each instance for certain banks and securities dealers)
"Patent box" preferential rate for foreign-derived income from U.S. intellectual property assets	• No change from present law	• Allows reduced rate of 21.875% on foreign-derived intangible income earned from a trade or business operating in the U.S. beginning after 12/31/17, further reduced to 12.5% beginning after 12/31/18, and rising to 15.625% after 12/31/25	• Generally follows Senate, except effective tax rate drops to 13.125% after 12/31/17, and rises to 16.406% after 12/31/25
Special rule for intellectual property transfers	• No change from present law	• Allows for tax-free IP transfers from a controlled foreign corporation to its U.S. parent	• No change from present law
Domestic International Sales Corporation rules	• No change from present law	• Same as House	

PROVISION	HOUSE	SENATE	FINAL BILL
U.S. territories	• Extends Sec. 199 deduction for Puerto Rico activities for one year, retroactive to 1/1/17 • Extends rum "cover over" increase for Puerto Rico and Virgin Islands, and American Samoa economic development credit through 12/31/22	• Removes certain restrictions on the ability of U.S. citizens to claim residence in the U.S. Virgin Islands to benefit from the territory's economic development tax credits • Aligns capital gains tax treatment for USVI residents with treatment of capital gains in Puerto Rico	• No change from present law
Foreign tax credit domestic loss rules	• No change from present law	• Maximum domestic losses creditable for foreign tax credit purposes increased to 100% for pre-2018 losses	• Same as Senate
Insurance	• Restrictions on insurance business exception to passive foreign investment company rules	• Same as House	• Also same as House

TAX-EXEMPT ORGANIZATIONS

PROVISION	HOUSE	SENATE	FINAL BILL
Unrelated Business Taxable Income	• Clarifies that state and local pension plans are subject to UBIT • Provides that UBIT exclusion for fundamental research only applies to research that is publicly available	• Prohibits losses from one unrelated trade or business from being used by a tax-exempt organization to offset gains by another unrelated trade or business	• Same as Senate
Excise taxes	• Replaces two tiers of private foundation excise tax with a single tier at 1.4% on net investment income • Require art museums to provide public access to qualify as a private operating foundation • Impose 1.4% excise tax on net investment income of private colleges and universities with at least 500 students and assets equal to at least $250,000 per student	• Same as House on college/university endowments except requirement is 500 tuition-paying students and assets-per-student threshold is increased to $500,000, and no change to private foundation excise tax or art museum/foundation status	• Generally follows Senate except endowment excise tax applies to colleges/universities with more than 50% of students located in the U.S. and applies to institutions with 500 students (regardless of whether they pay tuition)
Political campaign activity	• Repeals "Johnson Amendment" prohibition on tax-exempt organizations' support for political campaigns, without causing them to lose tax-exempt status	• No change from present law	• No change from present law

Source: House Ways and Means Committee, Senate Finance Committee, Joint Committee on Taxation

Chapter 17

TRANSPORTATION & INFRASTRUCTURE

Trump Infrastructure Plan Sidetracked By Other Priorities, Lack of Specificity

Donald Trump's election provided a surge of optimism to boosters of spending on infrastructure and promised innovative ways to get the private sector to contribute a larger portion of the money. Trump's presidential campaign included a pledge to deliver $1 trillion in infrastructure spending over 10 years from all sources. A campaign white paper called for $167 billion of that to be from the federal government.

Trump's arrival in the White House on Jan. 20, 2017, therefore, was accompanied by hopes that transportation and infrastructure could bridge party differences in a way that repealing the 2010 health care law (PL 111-148, PL 111-152) and tax cuts – two other Trump priorities – wouldn't. Congressional Republicans would back their party's president and Democrats would support legislation to spend more on roads, bridges, tunnels and other things. Or so it was hoped.

"You've got to figure out the pay-fors, things like that, which will come, I believe, in the first hundred days," House Transportation and Infrastructure Chairman Bill Shuster, R-Pa., told reporters on Jan. 4, 2017. "And then I think in the second hundred days will be when we start to put together a big infrastructure package. And that's even bigger than just our committee."

The reality at the end of the year fell far short of those expectations.

Trump's concept carried risks from the start, not least because his infrastructure pledge extended beyond traditional transportation projects to include many other sectors. The president had told voters that he also wanted to boost spending for energy, water, wastewater, broadband and even hospitals for veterans. As Shuster's comment indicated, the wide range of sectors meant many congressional committees would have to participate, adding to the number of moving parts involved in crafting legislation.

The president cited public-private partnerships, asset sales, tax credits and other tools to deliver funds to infrastructure projects. Those ideas raised more potential problems. Each of the tools was suitable to a specific type of infrastructure. Getting members of Congress to go along with the broad package would entail persuading individual members to overlook problems that one part of the plan could create for their district or state or committee because the entirety would deliver benefits.

And in some cases, as with an idea to use tax policy to steer repatriated corporate profits to infrastructure, the concept didn't explain why corporate executives would plow tens or hundreds of billions of dollars into infrastructure sectors in which they had no expertise.

Also lost in the president's broad approach were details about how the $1 trillion would be divided among transportation, energy, water and broadband and other areas -- and how much of the president's promised $167 billion of federal spending would go to each. The private sector already provides energy and broadband services in most areas – and would likely continue to do so with or without federal legislation; the private sector is much less involved in delivering surface transportation.

Republicans on Capitol Hill said the administration would have to lead the effort if anything was to get done. With the benefit of hindsight, their comments also may have signaled skepticism about the idea.

"For the most part, it's probably going to be driven by the administration," Senate Commerce, Science and Transportation Chairman John Thune, R-S.D., told reporters in January. "The big question always is going to be: How do you pay for it? What's the mechanism that they would use? And they've talked about these tax credits, so I want to understand better how that would work."

Trump named Elaine Chao as Transportation secretary, a move that looked like a shrewd step in legislative management. Chao, an experienced Cabinet-level executive, is also the wife of Senate Majority Leader Mitch McConnell, R-Ky. She would understand how to work with Congress. But she also represented only one department component of Trump's infrastructure approach.

Chao was on the Hill in January, saying the administration would form a task force to focus on many financing options for infrastructure.

"In order to take full advantage of the estimated trillions in capital that equity firms, pension funds, and endowments can invest, these partnerships must be incentivized with a bold new vision," she said. "The government does not have the resources to address all the infrastructure needs in our country."

The administration provided a steady stream of promises that big infrastructure decisions were just around the corner, but never did much more than that. Trump's February address to Congress was just one example. Trump said the day before his speech that it would include a "big" announcement on infrastructure. In the event, he repeated his campaign promise.

A SERIES OF FALSE STARTS

The administration's first step toward a proposal came in March, in the so-called skinny budget request for fiscal 2018. Among other things, the request proposed eliminating a federal grant program for transit, a mode of transportation infrastructure that would be very unlikely to attract private investors; canceling another grant program of surface transportation; and eliminating the Essential Air Service that subsidizes flights to small remote airports.

Lawmakers, including Republicans, were dismissive. The administration's first foray into an area that was core to the president's campaign did little to further the infrastructure cause on Capitol Hill. Not only did Trump not offer a plan to get more money to infrastructure, he was in fact offering cuts to transportation programs with powerful congressional support.

The administration disclosed more in its full fiscal 2018 budget request released on May 23 and in a fact sheet released the same day called the "2018 Budget: Infrastructure Initiative." That budget request called for $200 billion in federal spending over a decade, or $33 billion more than indicated during the campaign.

The fact sheet also returned to the breadth of the administration's ambition. It called for spinning off air traffic control from the Federal Aviation Administration, an initiative encouraged by Shuster; selling

electricity transmission assets; reducing restrictions on tolling inter-state highways; giving the Veterans Affairs Department freedom to lease out its unused facilities; increasing the commercial navigation fee on inland waterways; raising the limits on private activity bonds, and increasing some federal programs.

But rather than present a legislative or even regulatory path to deliv-ering on the proposals, the administration largely repeated principles and goals. "We will work to fix underlying incentives, procedures, and policies to spur better infrastructure decisions and outcomes, across a range of sectors," the fact sheet said.

Once again, lawmakers voiced skepticism.

"It's an option to put on the table, but it doesn't work in every state and I doubt if it would work in mine," said Sen. Deb Fischer, R-Neb., of increased tolling. "We don't have the volume necessary to really make a difference on any sections of highway. And in the main regard, it doesn't address the overall problem that we're looking at, which is finding a sustainable revenue source."

The president offered another set of principles on June 5, this time for spinning off air traffic control from the FAA. The principles in-cluded allowing the new nonprofit entity to borrow money, moving the current assets to the new entity and putting it all under the control of a 13-member board.

"I'm still a little skeptical," Sen. James M. Inhofe, R-Okla., said in response. "I'm not sure we have a broken system, as some others are."

Mario Diaz-Balart, R-Fla., the chairman of the House Appropria-tions Transportation-HUD Subcommittee, said it was "highly un-likely" a spinoff bill as described by the administration could pass the House.

On June 8, the White House revisited the $200 billion infrastruc-ture initiative that accompanied the budget, saying in a posting on its website that it would provide $100 billion "for local prioritization of infrastructure needs," $25 billion for rural infrastructure and $15 billion for what the White House called "transformative projects. That left $60 billion of the request still unaccounted for.

The $100 billion would go state and local governments to spend on their own projects, with little input from the federal government, White House spokeswoman Natalie Strom said.

Transportation Secretary Chao, who in April had said a legislative package would come "probably in May, late May, or something like

that," indicated another delay when she spoke to House Transporta-tion-HUD appropriators on June 15. Funding mechanisms would be outlined as part of a full infrastructure proposal sometime this fall, she said, adding that all options remained on the table.

As Congress worked on other legislation in the summer of 2017, the infrastructure initiative drew less attention. Trump drew the spotlight back to infrastructure on Aug. 15, when he signed an executive order designed to speed construction of roads and bridges by putting a single federal authority in charge of approvals for environmental and other permitting requirements.

The order would "hold agencies accountable," Trump said, without being specific about how.

A fact sheet from the White House said the Council on Environmen-tal Quality would develop and implement an action plan to improve environmental reviews and mediate disagreements between agencies. The council would develop criteria for what the fact sheet called "One Federal Decision," which would be applied by a single agency. Other federal agencies would then have 90 days to approve or deny related permits.

Chao's fall deadline to deliver a plan came and went without a proposal. Shuster, who on Jan. 4 was envisioning work on a big infra-structure package within the first 200 days of the administration, went to the White House on Dec. 11 amid reports that the administration had by then moved the deadline to January 2018.

Shuster was circumspect after the meeting.

"Today's meeting with the president was a very positive step for-ward as we begin to work towards improving America's infrastruc-ture," he said in a statement. "We had a good, productive discussion, and I look forward to working with the president, the administration, and my congressional colleagues as we move into the new year to identify specific proposals and priorities."

Ed Mortimer, executive director of transportation infrastructure at the U.S. Chamber of Commerce, agreed the previous false starts may have lessened expectations. But he said a push starting in earnest in January 2018 seemed more real than previous efforts.

Mortimer called an infrastructure package the business commu-nity's "top priority" for the next year, adding the chamber would "be putting the might of our institution behind trying to get this done in 2018." ■

Lawmakers Settle for Six-Month FAA Bill

Lawmakers entered 2017 seeing the Federal Aviation Administra-tion reauthorization as a chance to include policy provisions that were left out of the short-term extension (PL 114-190) enacted in July of the previous year. They had until Sept. 30, 2017, to draft and pass a mea-sure that they hoped would be more comprehensive than a short-term continuation of previous policy.

House Transportation and Infrastructure Chairman Bill Shuster, R-Pa., had the most ambitious goal. He had been pushing since the previous year a spinoff of the air traffic control operation from the FAA. The idea was to set up air traffic control as a separate nonprofit entity that would manage the implementation of the new navigation

system known as NextGen.

Shuster had been unable to get that proposal to the floor in 2016, but President Donald Trump paid lip service to the idea in February 2017, improving its prospects for 2017. The president followed up in June with a statement of principles for the spinoff.

But Shuster's effort was nevertheless going to be uphill. Not only were many in Congress, including Republicans, opposed, but the in-dustry itself was also divided. Airlines backed the spinoff; the general aviation industry opposed it.

Peter DeFazio, D-Ore., the ranking Democrat on Shuster's panel, said he offered Shuster the possibility of including provisions in the

legislation that would change some of the air traffic control system's operations, including overhauls of its acquisition and personnel process, but would keep the system under FAA control.

House members showed more bipartisanship in discussions of streamlining the FAA's oversight of safety and airworthiness of aircraft designs and parts. The agency certifies the equipment and lawmakers said it could do a better job. Lawmakers started hearings in February.

Shuster said government certification is time consuming and a burden for manufacturers, adding that it threatens global competitiveness in the industry. Several countries, including highly industrialized European nations, move through regulation faster than the FAA, he said.

"We've had longstanding leadership in aviation — we invented it. We need to maintain that lead," Shuster said. "It's important that the government agency that oversees this, that regulates it, is just as innovative as our industries have been... I don't want to see aviation industry go the way of electronics, autos, textiles and steel."

DeFazio said certification overhaul provisions would be part of a reauthorization bill – as they were in a 2016 bill that didn't clear.

"We agreed on virtually everything in that bill, with the exception of air traffic organization privatization," DeFazio said. "We have a different chairman in the Senate now, but most of the bill should be pretty easily worked out on a bipartisan basis."

The Senate Commerce, Science and Transportation Committee members were opting for a more traditional aviation bill, seeing little chance that the spinoff would receive approval. But the committee wanted to include drone policy, a reflection of the rapid growth in use of unmanned aerial vehicles and worries about safety and privacy.

The FAA reported in February 2017 that pilots, air traffic controllers, law enforcement agents and citizens reported seeing 1,274 drones from February through September 2016, an increase of 46 percent from the same months of 2015.

So the groundwork was prepared when the House and Senate released their FAA reauthorization bills on June 22.

Shuster introduced a six-year $65.25 billion reauthorization (HR 2997) that included the spinoff. The bill's spending authority was concentrated in the first three years with the final three years reflecting the absence of salaries, operations and maintenance because of the spinoff.

The most significant change from the 2016 bill was in the makeup of the board of directors governing the nonprofit group. Both proposals had 13-member boards, but the 2017 measure gave large passenger airlines, regional airlines and cargo airlines one vote each. The 2016 bill had given airlines four seats, and critics had said that would give airlines too much control.

Senate Commerce, Science and Transportation Chairman John Thune, R-S.D., and ranking member Bill Nelson, D-Fla., introduced a four-year, $68 billion measure (S 1405) that didn't include the spinoff.

The two bills were nearly identical in their funding authority for the first three years: $51.1 billion in the House bill; $51 billion in the Senate bill.

HOUSE COMMITTEE ACTION

Shuster found two Democratic co-sponsors — Reps. Colleen Hanabusa of Hawaii and Kyrsten Sinema of Arizona — for his legislation as well as at least one committee Republican—Sam Graves of Missouri—who had opposed the spinoff the year before.

Advocates of the air traffic control spinoff said the new structure could remove the operation from the congressional budget process. The Trump administration said the new entity would be able to borrow money, thus giving it the ability to manage its own investment in technology. One of the complaints about the FAA has been its inability to properly manage the introduction of NextGen.

Shuster shepherded his bill through committee on June 27 in a 32-25 vote after a nine-hour markup. Todd Rokita, R-Ind., was the only Republican to join Democrats in opposition.

SENATE COMMITTEE ACTION

In the Senate, Thune was also moving quickly. His committee approved the bill by voice vote on June 29. The measure also addressed controversies in the industry by prohibiting airlines from denying boarding to a passenger approved by a gate attendant for boarding, and it removed the limit on compensation to those denied boarding.

Thune received support for an amendment that would allow pilots in training to substitute certain courses and programs for actual flight hours. He said the provision would help regional airlines that struggled to hire enough pilots. Despite Democratic opposition, the committee adopted the amendment by voice vote.

Thune said he was open-minded about adding the spinoff as a floor amendment, but the provision was not in the bill that moved out of committee. Ranking member Bill Nelson, D-Fla., was adamant the spinoff should be left out.

"No matter what happens in the House or how hard various interests press, it's clear that those who support privatization of a public asset, our air space system, the support is not there in this committee or in the Senate," Nelson said. "This idea is simply not there as a sound idea for the safety of travelers and taxpayers, the economy and security of this country."

Thune was also by then warning that the issue could potentially derail a conference on the differing bills before the Sept. 30 expiration.

The Congressional Budget Office weighed in in July, saying the air traffic control spinoff would add $20.7 billion to deficits from 2018 to

2027. The office said that estimate could change dramatically if revenue and budget legislation accompanied the bill.

And at that point, the 2017 effort to enact a long-term reauthorization of the FAA died in Congress.

Advocates for each bill continued to make their cases. Airlines complained that the Senate bill was re-regulating the industry by establishing standards to determine whether fees for baggage, changing reservations and seats and other services were "reasonable." Representatives of the general aviation industry said the spinoff would put air traffic control in the hands of the airlines.

And neither chamber brought a bill to the floor for a vote.

SHORT-TERM EXTENSION

Lawmakers, nevertheless, still faced the need to extend the authorization that was expiring on Sept. 30. And that too turned into an unexpected House legislative battle — although for entirely different reasons.

By the end of August, House Republicans were talking about a short-term extension and on Sept. 22 they were settling on six months. The bill (HR 3823) authorized spending from the aviation trust fund at $1.67 billion for the next half-year, consistent with the fiscal 2017 spending level of $3.35 billion. But the bill also provided aid for victims of hurricanes Harvey, Irma and Maria and include provisions on private flood insurance.

Republican leaders said they would hold a floor vote the following Monday, Sept.25, under suspension of the rules, a procedure that requires two-thirds of members to vote in support.

Democrats then balked, saying the Republicans added non-aviation provisions without their input. With the FAA authorization expiring at midnight the following Saturday, the House was unable to agree on even a short-term extension that could satisfy both parties.

DeFazio took to the floor to blame Shuster for holding up a long-term authorization bill. Stripped of the air traffic control provision, the six-year authorization bill would easily pass, he said.

"That's why we're here today, because the chairman of the committee has stubbornly persisted in attempting to privatize the air traffic control organization of the United States of America," he said.

The Republicans' solution was to set up another vote, but one in which the Rules Committee would first recommend a rule and then send the measure to the floor with a simple majority needed for passage. The Rules Committee recommended a closed rule on Tuesday, Sept. 26.

On Sept. 28, Congress cleared the six-month extension, through March 2018, in several votes.

The House voted first, passing a six-month aviation reauthorization that included flood insurance provisions. The Senate took up the measure in the afternoon and stripped out the flood insurance provisions before passage, requiring the House to act again. The House did so, in the third vote of the day on reauthorizing aviation programs.

"These short-term stopgaps — while necessary — create long-term budget instability, and they contribute to the FAA's overall inability to effectively manage the modernization of our antiquated air traffic control system," Shuster said.

DRONE PROVISIONS LANGUISH

Senate Transportation Chairman John Thune, R-S.D., had said in March that he would like a provision in the aviation bill requiring remote identification standards for new drones to allow law enforcement officials to quickly check registration of any device violating rules. He also said the committee would look at developing safety standards for beyond-line-of-sight operations and other uses that aren't allowed under current law.

Eight months later, with the long-term aviation bill abandoned for the year and a short-term extension enacted, Shuster was admonishing the FAA for moving too slowly with standards for remote identification and tracking of drones.

"Why can't we get that rule in place?" Shuster asked. "Because it seems to me to be the simplest thing to do to be able to start to be able to monitor safety, security, law enforcement and those things."

Ranking member DeFazio said remote identification was key to making drones safe. DeFazio railed against "idiots who have toy drones" and fly them in areas that federal regulations prohibit, such as around airports and in emergency areas.

The administration underscored the interest in drones when President Trump on Oct. 25 directed the establishment of a pilot program for state and local governments to test uses of commercial drones that are illegal under Federal Aviation Administration regulations.

The program would allow state, tribal and local governments to propose using drones beyond a user's sightline, at night and over people. The FAA would use its authority to waive rules for acceptable proposals, according to a White House official, who added drone use was projected to increase five-fold by 2021. ∎

Legislation on Driverless Cars Mulled

Driverless cars have the potential to disrupt large parts of American life. They are also likely to demand a legislative and regulatory response in a country where cars and trucks are pervasive. Autonomous vehicles require fast and reliable communication with one another and with transportation networks. They raise legal and financial questions about who is liable when something goes wrong. And they require a rewriting of laws and regulations that now have built in assumptions, such as that a vehicle will have a steering wheel.

Lawmakers had been paying lip service to the belief that Congress should stay out of the new technology's way and let companies and researchers move forward. But in 2017, members of Congress were starting to declare that they would have to intervene at least in some ways.

"The current regulatory framework simply doesn't work, because it assumes a human [driver]," said Sen. Gary Peters, D-Mich., whose state is home to the big U.S. car companies. "So we need to rewrite all of that. But we also know that that takes years, and this technology isn't waiting years."

Peters said in May that he and Senate Commerce, Science and Transportation Chairman John Thune were working on a bill designed to provide a framework to encourage driverless car technology that

would straddle the current regulations and those that would be needed if such cars become commonplace.

Peters said the Federal Motor Vehicle Safety Standards "are very prescriptive, very specific." The regulations require, for example, that cars and trucks be outfitted with brake pedals and steering wheels, though driverless models may not need those items to steer or stop. Ford Motor Co. aims to have mass-produced autonomous vehicles in 2021, he noted.

Peters said he was disappointed that Congress didn't appropriate money for autonomous vehicle research in the fiscal 2017 omnibus spending bill (PL 115-31) despite President Barrack Obama's request that $200 million go toward the effort.

The National Highway Traffic Safety Administration uses a six-level scale of autonomous adopted in 2016: 0 indicates no automation and the driver performs all tasks; 5 indicates a vehicle that can perform all driving functions under all conditions.

Lawmakers' legislative efforts in 2017 focused on three issues related to self-driving vehicles: exemptions from federal rules to aid development; national uniformity in the rules; and data security. None of the efforts were enacted.

HOUSE LEGISLATIVE ACTION

The House Energy and Committee advanced by a 54-0 vote on July 27 a bill (HR 3388) that would expand the types of exemptions to federal safety standards that the National Highway Traffic Safety Administration could grant to autonomous vehicles — a major issue for cars that wouldn't need components required under existing rules.

The bill would also pre-empt states from creating laws regarding the design, construction or performance of automated vehicles, unless the standards were the same as federal standards. The bill would require any manufacturer of self-driving cars to develop a cybersecurity plan.

Ranking member Rep. Frank Pallone Jr., D-N.J., voiced concerns about the preemption of state laws and regulations, but joined the majority in the vote.

The House passed the bill by voice vote on Sept. 6, 2017.

SENATE COMMITTEE ACTION

In the subsequent weeks, potential obstacles to legislation began to emerge, particularly in the Senate.

Thune and Peters declared in June their "principles" for a bill that they said would be released later in the year. The principles overlapped with the House approach in that they wanted to remove regulatory barriers, define state and federal roles, and strengthen cybersecurity.

But disagreements arose, particularly over whether to include heavy trucks in the legislation. Thune wanted them included, urged to do so by the American Trucking Associations. But Peters favored leaving trucks for later legislation, voicing skepticism that excluding them would make roads less safe. The House bill excluded trucks.

Transportation Secretary Elaine Chao also raised some hackles in September when she unveiled an update to NHTSA and DOT guidance on autonomous vehicles. The new guidance clarified that auto manufacturers and technology developers were not required to submit safety assessments to NHTSA before testing autonomous vehicles.

Sen. Richard Blumenthal, D-Conn., a Senate Commerce member, called the new guidance "anemic" and a "giveaway" to the auto industry.

By the end of the month, on Sept. 28, Thune and Peters released a bill (S 1885) that would exclude trucks weighing more than 10,000 pounds. But the two also noted that the still disagreed on the issue.

"I would argue that it makes sense not to have two safety standards out there, one for trucks and one for automobiles," Thune said. "We want to make sure that we're providing the safest environment for all motorists on the highways, but that's a point that we continue to talk about in terms of the final bill."

Democrats and safety advocates, however, raised additional objections. Sens. Edward J. Markey of Massachusetts and Blumenthal said in early October that they had filed amendments to strengthen provisions on consumer education, cybersecurity, privacy and pre-emption of states' legislation and regulation.

Markey said he wanted the bill to require consumers to have accurate information about when it is safe to let a highly autonomous system take over driving for them, and when they must keep their own hands on the wheel.

Blumenthal, a former state attorney general, said he was bothered by the provision in the bill that would prohibit states and local governments from enacting laws regarding highly autonomous vehicles. States may want to enforce stronger regulations than the federal government.

The panel approved the measure by voice vote on Oct. 4 after Oklahoma Republican James M. Inhofe withdrew an amendment proposing that it include heavy trucks, or those weighing more than 10,000 pounds.

And then the bill stalled, not to get restarted in 2017.

Blumenthal said on Dec. 1 that he and Markey were holding it up to push for measures they felt would improve the safety of highly autonomous vehicles. Blumenthal said he was still pushing for a provision to require autonomous vehicles to allow human drivers to take control. During the markup, he introduced and withdrew an amendment that would have established that requirement. ■

Appendix A

CONGRESS & ITS MEMBERS

Members of the 115th Congress, First Session, an

As of Dec. 31, 2017

REPRESENTATIVES
R 239, D 193
Vacancies: 3 (Arizona 8,
Michigan 13, Pennsylvania 18)

—A—

Abraham, Ralph, R-La. (5)
Adams, Alma, D-N.C. (12)
Aderholt, Robert B., R-Ala. (4)
Aguilar, Pete, D-Calif. (31)
Allen, Rick, R-Ga. (12)
Amash, Justin, R-Mich. (3)
Amodei, Mark, R-Nev. (2)
Arrington, Jodey C., R-Texas (19)

—B—

Babin, Brian, R-Texas (36)
Bacon, Don, R-Neb. (2)
Banks, Jim, R-Ind. (3)
Barletta, Lou, R-Pa. (11)
Barr, Andy, R-Ky. (6)
Barragán, Nanette, D-Calif. (44)
Barton, Joe L., R-Texas (6)
Bass, Karen, D-Calif. (37)
Beatty, Joyce, D-Ohio (3)
Bera, Ami, D-Calif. (7)
Bergman, Jack, R-Mich. (1)
Beyer, Donald S. Jr., D-Va. (8)
Biggs, Andy, R-Ariz. (5)
Bilirakis, Gus, R-Fla. (12)
Bishop, Mike, R-Mich. (8)
Bishop, Rob, R-Utah (1)
Bishop, Sanford D. Jr., D-Ga. (2)
Black, Diane, R-Tenn. (6)
Blackburn, Marsha, R-Tenn. (7)
Blum, Rod, R-Iowa (1)
Blumenauer, Earl, D-Ore. (3)
Blunt Rochester, Lisa, D-Del. AL
Bonamici, Suzanne, D-Ore. (1)
Bost, Mike, R-Ill. (12)
Boyle, Brendan F., D-Pa. (13)
Brady, Kevin, R-Texas (8)
Brady, Robert A., D-Pa. (1)
Brat, Dave, R-Va. (7)
Bridenstine, Jim, R-Okla. (1)
Brooks, Mo, R-Ala. (5)
Brooks, Susan W., R-Ind. (5)
Brown, Anthony G., D-Md. (4)
Brownley, Julia, D-Calif. (26)
Buchanan, Vern, R-Fla. (16)
Buck, Ken, R-Colo. (4)
Bucshon, Larry, R-Ind. (8)
Budd, Ted, R-N.C. (13)
Burgess, Michael C., R-Texas (26)
Bustos, Cheri, D-Ill. (17)
Butterfield, G.K., D-N.C. (1)
Byrne, Bradley, R-Ala. (1)

—C—

Calvert, Ken, R-Calif. (42)
Capuano, Michael E., D-Mass. (7)
Carbajal, Salud, D-Calif. (24)
Cárdenas, Tony, D-Calif. (29)
Carson, André, D-Ind. (7)
Carter, Earl L. "Buddy," R-Ga. (1)
Carter, John, R-Texas (31)
Cartwright, Matt, D-Pa. (17)
Castor, Kathy, D-Fla. (14)
Castro, Joaquin, D-Texas (20)
Chabot, Steve, R-Ohio (1)
Cheney, Liz, R-Wyo. AL
Chu, Judy, D-Calif. (27)
Cicilline, David, D-R.I. (1)
Clark, Katherine M., D-Mass. (5)
Clarke, Yvette D., D-N.Y. (9)
Clay, William Lacy, D-Mo. (1)
Cleaver, Emanuel II, D-Mo. (5)
Clyburn, James E., D-S.C. (6)
Coffman, Mike, R-Colo. (6)
Cohen, Steve, D-Tenn. (9)
Cole, Tom, R-Okla. (4)
Collins, Chris, R-N.Y. (27)
Collins, Doug, R-Ga. (9)
Comer, James R., R-Ky. (1)
Comstock, Barbara, R-Va. (10)
Conaway, K. Michael, R-Texas (11)

Connolly, Gerald E., D-Va. (11)
Cook, Paul, R-Calif. (8)
Cooper, Jim, D-Tenn. (5)
Correa, Lou, D-Calif. (46)
Costa, Jim, D-Calif. (16)
Costello, Ryan A., R-Pa. (6)
Courtney, Joe, D-Conn. (2)
Cramer, Kevin, R-N.D. AL
Crawford, Rick, R-Ark. (1)
Crist, Charlie, D-Fla. (13)
Crowley, Joseph, D-N.Y. (14)
Cuellar, Henry, D-Texas (28)
Culberson, John, R-Texas (7)
Cummings, Elijah E., D-Md. (7)
Curbelo, Carlos, R-Fla. (26)
Curtis, John, R-Utah (3)

—D—

Davidson, Warren, R-Ohio (8)
Davis, Danny K., D-Ill. (7)
Davis, Rodney, R-Ill. (13)
Davis, Susan A., D-Calif. (53)
DeFazio, Peter A., D-Ore. (4)
DeGette, Diana, D-Colo. (1)
Delaney, John, D-Md. (6)
DeLauro, Rosa, D-Conn. (3)
DelBene, Suzan, D-Wash. (1)
Demings, Val B., D-Fla. (10)
Denham, Jeff, R-Calif. (10)
Dent, Charlie, R-Pa. (15)
DeSantis, Ron, R-Fla. (6)
DeSaulnier, Mark, D-Calif. (11)
DesJarlais, Scott, R-Tenn. (4)
Deutch, Ted, D-Fla. (21)
Diaz-Balart, Mario, R-Fla. (25)
Dingell, Debbie, D-Mich. (12)
Doggett, Lloyd, D-Texas (35)
Donovan, Dan, R-N.Y. (11)
Doyle, Mike, D-Pa. (14)
Duffy, Sean P., R-Wis. (7)
Duncan, Jeff, R-S.C. (3)
Duncan, John J. Jr., R-Tenn. (2)
Dunn, Neal, R-Fla. (2)

—E, F—

Ellison, Keith, D-Minn. (5)
Emmer, Tom, R-Minn. (6)
Engel, Eliot L., D-N.Y. (16)
Eshoo, Anna G., D-Calif. (18)
Espaillat, Adriano, D-N.Y. (13)
Esty, Elizabeth, D-Conn. (5)
Estes, Ron, R-Kan. (4)
Farenthold, Blake, R-Texas (27)
Faso, John J., R-N.Y. (19)
Ferguson, Drew, R-Ga. (3)
Fitzpatrick, Brian, R-Pa. (8)
Fleischmann, Chuck, R-Tenn. (3)
Flores, Bill, R-Texas (17)
Fortenberry, Jeff, R-Neb. (1)
Foster, Bill, D-Ill. (11)
Foxx, Virginia, R-N.C. (5)
Frankel, Lois, D-Fla. (22)
Frelinghuysen, Rodney, R-N.J. (11)
Fudge, Marcia L., D-Ohio (11)

—G—

Gabbard, Tulsi, D-Hawaii (2)
Gaetz, Matt, R-Fla. (1)
Gallagher, Mike, R-Wis. (8)
Gallego, Ruben, D-Ariz. (7)
Garamendi, John, D-Calif. (3)
Garrett, Tom, R-Va. (5)
Gianforte, Greg, R-Mt. AL
Gibbs, Bob, R-Ohio (7)
Gohmert, Louie, R-Texas (1)
Gomez, Jimmy, D-Calif. (34)
Gonzalez, Vicente, D-Texas (15)
Goodlatte, Robert W., R-Va. (6)
Gosar, Paul, R-Ariz. (4)
Gottheimer, Josh, D-N.J. (5)
Gowdy, Trey, R-S.C. (4)
Granger, Kay, R-Texas (12)
Graves, Garret, R-La. (6)
Graves, Sam, R-Mo. (6)
Graves, Tom, R-Ga. (14)
Green, Al, D-Texas (9)
Green, Gene, D-Texas (29)
Griffith, Morgan, R-Va. (9)
Grijalva, Raúl M., D-Ariz. (3)

Grothman, Glenn, R-Wis. (6)
Guthrie, Brett, R-Ky. (2)
Gutiérrez, Luis V., D-Ill. (4)

—H—

Hanabusa, Colleen, D-Hawaii (1)
Handel, Karen, R-Ga. (6)
Harper, Gregg, R-Miss. (3)
Harris, Andy, R-Md. (1)
Hartzler, Vicky, R-Mo. (4)
Hastings, Alcee L., D-Fla. (20)
Heck, Denny, D-Wash. (10)
Hensarling, Jeb, R-Texas (5)
Herrera Beutler, Jaime, R-Wash. (3)
Hice, Jody B., R-Ga. (10)
Higgins, Brian, D-N.Y. (26)
Higgins, Clay, R-La. (3)
Hill, French, R-Ark. (2)
Himes, Jim, D-Conn. (4)
Holding, George, R-N.C. (13)
Hollingsworth, Trey, R-Ind. (9)
Hoyer, Steny H., D-Md. (5)
Hudson, Richard, R-N.C. (8)
Huffman, Jared, D-Calif. (2)
Huizenga, Bill, R-Mich. (2)
Hultgren, Randy, R-Ill. (14)
Hunter, Duncan, R-Calif. (50)
Hurd, Will, R-Texas (23)

—I, J—

Issa, Darrell, R-Calif. (49)
Jackson Lee, Sheila, D-Texas (18)
Jayapal, Pramila, D-Wash. (7)
Jeffries, Hakeem, D-N.Y. (8)
Jenkins, Evan, R-W.Va. (3)
Jenkins, Lynn, R-Kan. (2)
Johnson, Bill, R-Ohio (6)
Johnson, Eddie Bernice, D-Texas (30)
Johnson, Hank, D-Ga. (4)
Johnson, Mike, R-La. (4)
Johnson, Sam, R-Texas (3)
Jones, Walter B., R-N.C. (3)
Jordan, Jim, R-Ohio (4)
Joyce, David, R-Ohio (14)

—K—

Kaptur, Marcy, D-Ohio (9)
Katko, John, R-N.Y. (24)
Keating, William, D-Mass. (9)
Kelly, Mike, R-Pa. (3)
Kelly, Robin, D-Ill. (2)
Kelly, Trent, R-Miss. (1)
Kennedy, Joseph P. III, D-Mass. (4)
Khanna, Ro, D-Calif. (17)
Kihuen, Ruben, D-Nev. (4)
Kildee, Dan, D-Mich. (5)
Kilmer, Derek, D-Wash. (6)
Kind, Ron, D-Wis. (3)
King, Peter T., R-N.Y. (2)
King, Steve, R-Iowa (4)
Kinzinger, Adam, R-Ill. (16)
Knight, Steve, R-Calif. (25)
Krishnamoorthi, Raja, D-Ill. (8)
Kuster, Ann McLane, D-N.H. (2)
Kustoff, David, R-Tenn. (8)

—L—

Labrador, Raúl R., R-Idaho (1)
LaHood, Darin, R-Ill (18)
LaMalfa, Doug, R-Calif. (1)
Lamborn, Doug, R-Colo. (5)
Lance, Leonard, R-N.J. (7)
Langevin, Jim, D-R.I. (2)
Larsen, Rick, D-Wash. (2)
Larson, John B., D-Conn. (1)
Latta, Bob, R-Ohio (5)
Lawrence, Brenda, D-Mich. (14)
Lawson, Al, D-Fla. (5)
Lee, Barbara, D-Calif. (13)
Levin, Sander M., D-Mich. (9)
Lewis, Jason, R-Minn. (2)
Lewis, John, D-Ga. (5)
Lieu, Ted, D-Calif. (33)
Lipinski, Daniel, D-Ill. (3)
LoBiondo, Frank A., R-N.J. (2)
Loebsack, Dave, D-Iowa (2)
Lofgren, Zoe, D-Calif. (19)
Long, Billy, R-Mo. (7)
Loudermilk, Barry, R-Ga. (11)
Love, Mia, R-Utah (4)

Lowenthal, Alan, D-Calif. (47)
Lowey, Nita M., D-N.Y. (17)
Lucas, Frank D., R-Okla. (3)
Luetkemeyer, Blaine, R-Mo. (3)
Luján, Ben Ray, D-N.M. (3)
Lujan Grisham, Michelle, D-N.M. (1)
Lynch, Stephen F., D-Mass. (8)

—M—

MacArthur, Tom, R-N.J. (3)
Maloney, Carolyn B., D-N.Y. (12)
Maloney, Sean Patrick, D-N.Y. (18)
Marchant, Kenny, R-Texas (24)
Marshall, Roger, R-Kan. (1)
Marino, Tom, R-Pa. (10)
Massie, Thomas, R-Ky. (4)
Mast, Brian, R-Fla. (18)
Matsui, Doris, D-Calif. (6)
McCarthy, Kevin, R-Calif. (23)
McCaul, Michael, R-Texas (10)
McClintock, Tom, R-Calif. (4)
McCollum, Betty, D-Minn. (4)
McEachin, A. Donald, D-Va. (4)
McGovern, Jim, D-Mass. (2)
McHenry, Patrick T., R-N.C. (10)
McKinley, David B., R-W.Va. (1)
McMorris Rodgers, Cathy, R-Wash. (5)
McNerney, Jerry, D-Calif. (9)
McSally, Martha, R-Ariz. (2)
Meadows, Mark, R-N.C. (11)
Meehan, Patrick, R-Pa. (7)
Meeks, Gregory W., D-N.Y. (5)
Meng, Grace, D-N.Y. (6)
Messer, Luke, R-Ind. (6)
Mitchell, Paul, R-Mich. (10)
Moolenaar, John, R-Mich. (4)
Mooney, Alex X., R-W.Va. (2)
Moore, Gwen, D-Wis. (4)
Moulton, Seth, D-Mass. (6)
Mullin, Markwayne, R-Okla. (2)
Murphy, Stephanie, D-Fla. (7)

—N, O—

Nadler, Jerrold, D-N.Y. (10)
Napolitano, Grace F., D-Calif. (32)
Neal, Richard E., D-Mass. (1)
Newhouse, Dan, R-Wash. (4)
Noem, Kristi, R-S.D. AL
Nolan, Rick, D-Minn. (8)
Norcross, Donald, D-N.J. (1)
Norman, Ralph, R-S.C. (5)
Nunes, Devin, R-Calif. (22)
O'Halleran, Tom, D-Ariz. (1)
O'Rourke, Beto, D-Texas (16)
Olson, Pete, R-Texas (22)

—P—

Palazzo, Steven M., R-Miss. (4)
Pallone, Frank Jr., D-N.J. (6)
Palmer, Gary, R-Ala. (6)
Panetta, Jimmy, D-Calif. (20)
Pascrell, Bill Jr., D-N.J. (9)
Paulsen, Erik, R-Minn. (3)
Payne, Donald M. Jr., D-N.J. (10)
Pearce, Steve, R-N.M. (2)
Pelosi, Nancy, D-Calif. (12)
Perlmutter, Ed, D-Colo. (7)
Perry, Scott, R-Pa. (4)
Peters, Scott, D-Calif. (52)
Peterson, Collin C., D-Minn. (7)
Pingree, Chellie, D-Maine (1)
Pittenger, Robert, R-N.C. (9)
Pocan, Mark, D-Wis. (2)
Poe, Ted, R-Texas (2)
Poliquin, Bruce, R-Maine (2)
Polis, Jared, D-Colo. (2)
Posey, Bill, R-Fla. (8)
Price, David E., D-N.C. (4)

—Q, R—

Quigley, Mike, D-Ill. (5)
Raskin, Jamie, D-Md. (8)
Ratcliffe, John, R-Texas (4)
Reed, Tom, R-N.Y. (23)
Reichert, Dave, R-Wash. (8)
Renacci, James B., R-Ohio (16)
Rice, Kathleen, D-N.Y. (4)
Rice, Tom, R-S.C. (7)
Richmond, Cedric L., D-La. (2)

overnors, Supreme Court and Executive Branch

Roby, Martha, R-Ala. (2)
Roe, Phil, R-Tenn. (1)
Rogers, Harold, R-Ky. (5)
Rogers, Mike D., R-Ala. (3)
Rohrabacher, Dana, R-Calif. (48)
Rokita, Todd, R-Ind. (4)
Rooney, Francis, R-Fla. (19)
Rooney, Tom, R-Fla. (17)
Rosen, Jacky, D-Nev. (3)
Ros-Lehtinen, Ileana, R-Fla. (27)
Roskam, Peter, R-Ill. (6)
Ross, Dennis A., R-Fla. (15)
Rothfus, Keith, R-Pa. (12)
Rouzer, David, R-N.C. (7)
Roybal-Allard, Lucille, D-Calif. (40)
Royce, Ed, R-Calif. (39)
Ruiz, Raul, D-Calif. (36)
Ruppersberger, C.A. Dutch, D-Md. (2)
Rush, Bobby L., D-Ill. (1)
Russell, Steve, R-Okla. (5)
Rutherford, John, R-Fla. (4)
Ryan, Paul D., R-Wis. (1)
Ryan, Tim, D-Ohio (13)

— S —

Sánchez, Linda T., D-Calif. (38)
Sanford, Mark, R-S.C. (1)
Sarbanes, John, D-Md. (3)
Scalise, Steve, R-La. (1)
Schakowsky, Jan, D-Ill. (9)
Schiff, Adam B., D-Calif. (28)
Schneider, Brad, D-Ill. (10)
Schrader, Kurt, D-Ore. (5)
Schweikert, David, R-Ariz. (6)
Scott, Austin, R-Ga. (8)
Scott, David, D-Ga. (13)
Scott, Robert C., D-Va. (3)
Sensenbrenner, Jim, R-Wis. (5)
Serrano, José E., D-N.Y. (15)
Sessions, Pete, R-Texas (32)
Sewell, Terri A., D-Ala. (7)
Shea-Porter, Carol, D-N.H. (1)
Sherman, Brad, D-Calif. (30)
Shimkus, John, R-Ill. (15)
Shuster, Bill, R-Pa. (9)
Simpson, Mike, R-Idaho (2)
Sinema, Kyrsten, D-Ariz. (9)
Sires, Albio, D-N.J. (8)
Slaughter, Louise M., D-N.Y. (25)
Smith, Adam, D-Wash. (9)
Smith, Adrian, R-Neb. (3)
Smith, Christopher H., R-N.J. (4)
Smith, Jason, R-Mo. (8)
Smith, Lamar, R-Texas (21)
Smucker, Lloyd K., R-Pa. (16)
Soto, Darren, D-Fla. (9)
Speier, Jackie, D-Calif. (14)
Stefanik, Elise, R-N.Y. (21)
Stewart, Chris, R-Utah (2)
Stivers, Steve, R-Ohio (15)
Suozzi, Tom, D-N.Y. (3)
Swalwell, Eric, D-Calif. (15)

— T —

Takano, Mark, D-Calif. (41)
Taylor, Scott, R-Va. (2)
Tenney, Claudia, R-N.Y. (22)
Thompson, Bennie, D-Miss. (2)
Thompson, Glenn, R-Pa. (5)
Thompson, Mike, D-Calif. (5)
Thornberry, Mac, R-Texas (13)
Tiberi, Pat, R-Ohio (12)
Tipton, Scott, R-Colo. (3)
Titus, Dina, D-Nev. (1)
Tonko, Paul, D-N.Y. (20)
Torres, Norma J., D-Calif. (35)
Trott, Dave, R-Mich. (11)
Tsongas, Niki, D-Mass. (3)
Turner, Michael R., R-Ohio (10)

— U, V—

Upton, Fred, R-Mich. (6)
Valadao, David, R-Calif. (21)
Vargas, Juan C., D-Calif. (51)
Veasey, Marc, D-Texas (33)
Vela, Filemon, D-Texas (34)
Velázquez, Nydia M., D-N.Y. (7)
Visclosky, Peter J., D-Ind. (1)

— W —

Wagner, Ann, R-Mo. (2)
Walberg, Tim, R-Mich. (7)
Walden, Greg, R-Ore. (2)
Walker, Mark, R-N.C. (6)
Walorski, Jackie, R-Ind. (2)
Walters, Mimi, R-Calif. (45)
Walz, Tim, D-Minn. (1)
Wasserman Schultz, Debbie, D-Fla. (23)
Waters, Maxine, D-Calif. (43)
Watson Coleman, Bonnie, D-N.J. (12)
Weber, Randy, R-Texas (14)
Webster, Daniel, R-Fla. (11)
Welch, Peter, D-Vt. AL
Wenstrup, Brad, R-Ohio (2)
Westerman, Bruce, R-Ark. (4)
Williams, Roger, R-Texas (25)
Wilson, Frederica S., D-Fla. (24)
Wilson, Joe, R-S.C. (2)
Wittman, Rob, R-Va. (1)
Womack, Steve, R-Ark. (3)
Woodall, Rob, R-Ga. (7)

— X, Y, Z —

Yarmuth, John, D-Ky. (3)
Yoder, Kevin, R-Kan. (3)
Yoho, Ted, R-Fla. (3)
Young, David, R-Iowa (3)
Young, Don, R-Alaska AL
Zeldin, Lee, R-N.Y. (1)

DELEGATES
D 4, R 2

Bordallo, Madeleine Z., D-Guam
González-Colón, Jenniffer, R-P.R.
Norton, Eleanor Holmes, D-D.C.
Plaskett, Stacey, D-V.I.
Radewagen, Aumua Amata Coleman, R-A.S.
Sablan, Gregorio Kilili Camacho, D-N. Marianas

SENATE
R 51, D 47, I 2

Alexander, Lamar, R-Tenn.
Baldwin, Tammy, D-Wis.
Barrasso, John, R-Wyo.
Bennet, Michael, D-Colo.
Blumenthal, Richard, D-Conn.
Blunt, Roy, R-Mo.
Booker, Cory, D-N.J.
Boozman, John, R-Ark.
Brown, Sherrod, D-Ohio
Burr, Richard M., R-N.C.
Cantwell, Maria, D-Wash.
Capito, Shelley Moore, R-W.Va.
Cardin, Benjamin L., D-Md.
Carper, Thomas R., D-Del.
Casey, Bob, D-Pa.
Cassidy, Bill, R-La.
Cochran, Thad, R-Miss.
Collins, Susan, R-Maine
Coons, Chris, D-Del.
Corker, Bob, R-Tenn.
Cornyn, John, R-Texas
Cortez Masto, Catherine, D-Nev.
Cotton, Tom, R-Ark.
Crapo, Michael D., R-Idaho
Cruz, Ted, R-Texas
Daines, Steve, R-Mont.
Donnelly, Joe, D-Ind.
Duckworth, Tammy, D-Ill.
Durbin, Richard J., D-Ill.
Enzi, Michael B., R-Wyo.
Ernst, Joni, R-Iowa
Feinstein, Dianne, D-Calif.
Fischer, Deb, R-Neb.
Flake, Jeff, R-Ariz.
Franken, Al D-Minn.
Gardner, Cory, R-Colo.
Gillibrand, Kirsten, D-N.Y.
Graham, Lindsey, R-S.C.
Grassley, Charles E., R-Iowa
Harris, Kamala, D-Calif.
Hassan, Maggie, D-N.H.
Hatch, Orrin G., R-Utah

Heinrich, Martin, D-N.M.
Heitkamp, Heidi, D-N.D.
Heller, Dean, R-Nev.
Hirono, Mazie K., D-Hawaii
Hoeven, John, R-N.D.
Inhofe, James M., R-Okla.
Isakson, Johnny, R-Ga.
Johnson, Ron, R-Wis.
Jones, Doug, D-Ala.
Kaine, Tim, D-Va.
Kennedy, John, R-La.
King, Angus, I-Maine
Klobuchar, Amy, D-Minn.
Lankford, James, R-Okla.
Leahy, Patrick J., D-Vt.
Lee, Mike, R-Utah
Manchin, Joe III, D-W.Va.
Markey, Edward J., D-Mass.
McCain, John, R-Ariz.
McCaskill, Claire, D-Mo.
McConnell, Mitch, R-Ky.
Menendez, Robert, D-N.J.
Merkley, Jeff, D-Ore.
Moran, Jerry, R-Kan.
Murkowski, Lisa, R-Alaska
Murphy, Christopher S., D-Conn.
Murray, Patty, D-Wash.
Nelson, Bill, D-Fla.
Paul, Rand, R-Ky.
Perdue, David, R-Ga.
Peters, Gary, D-Mich.
Portman, Rob, R-Ohio
Reed, Jack, D-R.I.
Risch, Jim, R-Idaho
Roberts, Pat, R-Kan.
Rounds, Mike, R-S.D.
Rubio, Marco, R-Fla.
Sanders, Bernard, I-Vt.
Sasse, Ben, R-Neb.
Schatz, Brian, D-Hawaii
Schumer, Charles E., D-N.Y.
Scott, Tim, R-S.C.
Shaheen, Jeanne, D-N.H.
Shelby, Richard C., R-Ala.
Stabenow, Debbie, D-Mich.
Sullivan, Dan, R-Alaska
Tester, Jon, D-Mont.
Thune, John, R-S.D.
Tillis, Thom, R-N.C.
Toomey, Patrick J., R-Pa.
Udall, Tom, D-N.M.
Van Hollen, Chris, D-Md.
Warner, Mark, D-Va.
Warren, Elizabeth, D-Mass.
Whitehouse, Sheldon, D-R.I.
Wicker, Roger, R-Miss.
Wyden, Ron, D-Ore.
Young, Todd, R-Ind.

GOVERNORS
R 33, D 16, 1 I

Ala. — Kay Ivey, R
Alaska — Bill Walker, I
Ariz. — Doug Ducey, R
Ark. — Asa Hutchinson, R
Calif. — Jerry Brown, D
Colo.   John W. Hickenlooper, D
Conn. — Dannel P. Malloy, D
Del. — John Carney, D
Fla. — Rick Scott, R
Ga. — Nathan Deal, R
Hawaii — David Ige, D
Idaho — C.L. "Butch" Otter, R
Ill. — Bruce Rauner, R
Ind. — Eric Holcomb, R
Iowa — Kim Reynolds, R
Kan. — Sam Brownback, R
Ky. — Matt Bevin, R
La. — John Bel Edwards, D
Maine — Paul R. LePage, R
Md. — Larry Hogan, R
Mass. — Charlie Baker, R
Mich. — Rick Snyder, R
Minn. — Mark Dayton, D
Miss. — Phil Bryant, R
Mo. — Eric Greitens, R
Mont. — Steve Bullock, D
Neb. — Pete Ricketts, R
Nev. — Brian Sandoval, R
N.H. — Chris Sununu, R
N.J. — Chris Christie, R

N.M. — Susana Martinez, R
N.Y. — Andrew M. Cuomo, D
N.C. — Roy Cooper, D
N.D. — Doug Burgum, R
Ohio — John R. Kasich, R
Okla. — Mary Fallin, R
Ore. — Kate Brown, D
Pa. — Tom Wolf, D
R.I. — Gina Raimondo, D
S.C. — Henry McMaster, R
S.D. — Dennis Daugaard, R
Tenn. — Bill Haslam, R
Texas — Greg Abbott, R
Utah — Gary R. Herbert, R
Vt. — Phil Scott, R
Va. — Terry McAuliffe, D
Wash. — Jay Inslee, D
W.Va. — Jim Justice, R
Wis. — Scott Walker, R
Wyo. — Matt Mead, R

SUPREME COURT

John G. Roberts Jr. — Md., Chief Justice
Samuel A. Alito Jr. — N.J.
Stephen G. Breyer — Mass.
Ruth Bader Ginsburg — N.Y.
Neil Gorsuch — Colo.
Elena Kagan — N.Y.
Anthony M. Kennedy — Calif.
Sonia Sotomayor — N.Y.
Clarence Thomas — Ga.

EXECUTIVE BRANCH

President — Donald Trump
Vice President — Mike Pence

SECRETARIES

Agriculture — Sonny Perdue
Attorney General — Jeff Sessions
Commerce — Wilbur Ross
Defense — James Mattis
Education — Betsy DeVos
Energy — Rick Perry
Health and Human Services — Eric D. Hargan (Acting)
Homeland Security — Kirstjen Nielsen
Housing and Urban Development — Ben Carson
Interior — Ryan Zinke
Labor — Alexander Acosta
State — Rex Tillerson
Transportation — Elaine Chao
Treasury — Steven Mnuchin
Veterans Affairs — David Shulkin

OTHER OFFICERS

CIA Director — Mike Pompeo
Director of National Intelligence — Dan Coats
Joint Chiefs of Staff Chairman — Gen. Joseph F. Dunford Jr.
Office of Management and Budget Director — Mick Mulvaney
U.S. Trade Representative — Robert Lighthizer
EPA Administrator — Scott Pruitt
U.N. Ambassador — Nikki Haley
White House Chief of Staff — John F. Kelly
Assistant to the President for National Security Affairs — Lt. Gen. H.R. McMaster
National Economic Council Director — Gary Cohn

Glossary of Congressional Terms

Act — The term for legislation once it has passed both chambers of Congress and has been signed by the president or passed over his veto, thus becoming law. Also used in parliamentary terminology for a bill that has been passed by one house and engrossed. (Also see engrossed bill.)

Adjournment sine die — Adjournment without a fixed day for reconvening; literally, "adjournment without a day." Usually used to connote the final adjournment of a session of Congress. A session can continue until noon Jan. 3 of the following year, when, under the 20th Amendment to the Constitution, it automatically terminates. Both chambers must agree to a concurrent resolution for either chamber to adjourn for more than three days.

Adjournment to a day certain — Adjournment under a motion or resolution that fixes the next time of meeting. Under the Constitution, neither chamber can adjourn for more than three days without the concurrence of the other. A session of Congress is not ended by adjournment to a day certain.

Amendment — A proposal by a member of Congress to alter the language, provisions or stipulations in a bill or in another amendment. An amendment usually is printed, debated and voted upon in the same manner as a bill.

Amendment in the nature of a substitute — Usually an amendment that seeks to replace the entire text of a bill by striking out everything after the enacting clause and inserting a new version of the bill. An amendment in the nature of a substitute can also refer to an amendment that replaces a large portion of the text of a bill.

Appeal — A member's challenge of a ruling or decision made by the presiding officer of the chamber. A senator can appeal to members of the Senate to override the decision. If carried by a majority vote, the appeal nullifies the presiding officer's ruling. In the House, the decision of the speaker traditionally has been final; seldom are there successful appeals to the members to reverse the speaker's stand. To appeal a ruling is considered an attack on the speaker.

Appropriations bill — A bill that gives legal authority to spend or obligate money from the Treasury. The Constitution disallows money to be drawn from the Treasury "but in Consequence of Appropriations made by Law."

By congressional custom, an appropriations bill originates in the House. It is not supposed to be considered by the full House or Senate until a related measure authorizing the spending is enacted. An appropriations bill grants the actual budget authority approved by the authorization bill, though not necessarily the full amount permissible under the authorization.

If the 12 regular appropriations bills are not enacted by the start of the fiscal year, Congress must pass a stopgap spending bill or the departments and agencies covered by the unfinished bills must shut down.

About half of all budget authority, notably that for Social Security and interest on the federal debt, does not require annual appropriations; those programs exist under permanent appropriations. (Also see authorization bill, budget authority, budget process and supplemental appropriations bill.)

Authorization bill — Basic, substantive legislation that establishes or continues the legal operation of a federal program or agency either indefinitely or for a specific period of time, or which sanctions a particular type of obligation or expenditure. Under the rules of both chambers, appropriations for a program or agency may not be considered until the program has been authorized, although this requirement is often waived. An authorization sets the maximum amount that may be appropriated to a program or agency, although sometimes it merely authorizes "such sums as may be necessary." (Also see backdoor spending authority.)

Backdoor spending authority — Budget authority provided in legislation outside the normal appropriations process. The most common forms of backdoor spending are borrowing authority, contract authority, entitlements and loan guarantees that commit the government to payments of principal and interest on loans made by banks or other private lenders. Loan guarantees result in actual outlays only when there is a default by the borrower.

In some cases, such as interest on the public debt, a permanent appropriation is provided that becomes available without further action by Congress.

Bills — Most legislative proposals before Congress are in the form of bills and are designated according to the chamber in which they originate — HR in the House of Representatives or S in the Senate — and by a number assigned in the order in which they are introduced during the two-year period of a congressional term.

"Public bills" address general questions and become public laws if they are cleared by Congress and signed by the president. "Private bills" deal with individual matters, such as claims against the government, immigration and naturalization cases, or land titles, and become private laws if cleared and signed. (Also see private bill, resolution.)

Bills introduced — In both the House and Senate, any number of members may join in introducing a single bill or resolution. The first member listed is the sponsor of the bill, and all subsequent members listed are co-sponsors.

Many bills are committee bills and are introduced under the name of the chairman of the committee or subcommittee. All appropriations bills fall into this category. A committee frequently holds hearings on a number of related bills and may agree to one of them or to an entirely new bill. (Also see clean bill.)

Bills referred — After a bill is introduced, it is referred to the committee or committees that have jurisdiction over the subject with which

the bill is concerned. Under the standing rules of the House and Senate, bills are referred by the speaker in the House and by the presiding officer in the Senate. In practice, the House and Senate parliamentarians act for these officials and refer the vast majority of bills. (Also see discharge a committee.)

Borrowing authority — Statutory authority that permits a federal agency to incur obligations and make payments for specified purposes with borrowed money.

Budget — The document sent to Congress by the president early each year estimating government revenue and expenditures for the ensuing fiscal year.

Budget Act — The common name for the Congressional Budget and Impoundment Control Act of 1974, which established the current budget process and created the Congressional Budget Office. The act also put limits on presidential authority to spend appropriated money. It has undergone several major revisions since 1974. (Also see budget process.)

Budget authority — Authority for federal agencies to enter into obligations that result in immediate or future outlays. The basic forms of budget authority are appropriations, contract authority and borrowing authority. Budget authority may be classified by (1) the period of availability (one-year, multiple-year or without a time limitation), (2) the timing of congressional action (current or permanent) or (3) the manner of determining the amount available (definite or indefinite). (Also see appropriations bill, outlays.)

Budget process — The annual budget process was created by the Congressional Budget and Impoundment Control Act of 1974, with a timetable that was modified in 1990. Under the law, the president must submit his proposed budget by the first Monday in February. Congress is supposed to complete an annual budget resolution by April 15, setting guidelines for congressional action on spending and tax measures. (Also see "cut-as-you-go" rules.)

Budget resolution — A concurrent resolution that is adopted by both chambers of Congress and sets a strict ceiling on discretionary budget authority, along with nonbinding recommendations about how the spending should be allocated. The budget resolution may also contain "reconciliation instructions" requiring authorizing and tax-writing committees to propose changes in existing law to meet deficit reduction goals. If more than one committee is involved, the Budget Committee in each chamber bundles those proposals, without change, into a reconciliation bill and sends it to the floor. The budget resolution is a congressional document and is not sent to the president. (Also see reconciliation.)

By request — A phrase used when a senator or representative introduces a bill at the request of an executive agency or private organization but does not necessarily endorse the legislation.

Calendar — An agenda or list of business awaiting possible action by each chamber. The House uses four legislative calendars. They are the Discharge, House, Private and Union calendars. (Also see individual calendar listings.)

In the Senate, all legislative matters reported from committee go on one calendar. They are listed there in the order in which committees report them or the Senate places them on the calendar, but they may be called up out of order by the majority leader, either by obtaining unanimous consent of the Senate or by a motion to call up a bill. The Senate also has one non-legislative calendar, which is used for treaties and nominations. (Also see Executive Calendar.)

Call of the calendar — Senate bills that are not brought up for debate by a motion, unanimous consent or a unanimous consent agreement are brought before the Senate for action when the calendar listing them is "called." Bills must be called in the order listed. Measures considered by this method usually are noncontroversial, and debate on the bill and any proposed amendments is limited to five minutes for each senator.

Chamber — The meeting place for the membership of either the House or the Senate; also the membership of the House or Senate meeting as such.

Chief administrative officer — An elected officer of the House who, under House rules, has operational and functional responsibility for matters assigned by the House Administration Committee. The office of the chief administrative officer was established under a 1995 change to House rules and replaced the office of director of non-legislative and financial services.

Clean bill — Frequently after a committee has finished a major revision of a bill, one of the committee members, usually the chairman, will assemble the changes and what is left of the original bill into a new measure and introduce it as a "clean bill." The revised measure, which is given a new number, is referred back to the committee, which reports it to the floor for consideration. This often is a time saver, as committee-recommended changes in a clean bill do not have to be considered and voted on by the chamber. Reporting a clean bill also protects committee amendments that could be subject to points of order concerning germaneness.

Clerk of the House — An officer of the House of Representatives who supervises its records and legislative business.

Cloture — The process by which a filibuster can be ended in the Senate other than by unanimous consent. A motion for cloture can apply to any measure before the Senate, including a proposal to change the chamber's rules. To end a filibuster, the cloture motion must obtain the votes of three-fifths of the entire Senate membership (60 if there are no vacancies), except when the filibuster is against a proposal to amend the standing rules of the Senate; then a two-thirds vote of senators present and voting is required.

Under a ruling by the president of the Senate in November 2013 that was upheld by a narrow voting majority of the chamber, the interpretation of the cloture rule was changed as applied to executive branch nominees subject to confirmation and to lower-court judges. Following the reinterpretation, cloture could be imposed on nominees (except for those named to the Supreme Court) by a simple majority vote. The rule was changed again in 2017 to include Supreme Court nominees.

The cloture request is put to a roll call vote one hour after the Senate meets on the second day following introduction of the motion. If approved, cloture limits each senator to one hour of debate. The bill or amendment in question comes to a final vote after 30 hours of consideration, including debate time and the time it takes to conduct roll calls, quorum calls and other procedural motions. (Also see filibuster.)

Committee — A division of the House or Senate that prepares legislation for action by the parent chamber or makes investigations as directed by the parent chamber.

There are several types of committees. Most standing committees are divided into subcommittees, which study legislation, hold hearings and report bills, with or without amendments, to the full committee. Only the full committee can report legislation for action by the House or Senate. (Also see standing, oversight, and select or special committees.)

Committee of the Whole — The working title of what is formally "The Committee of the Whole House [of Representatives] on the State of the Union." The membership is composed of all House members sitting as a committee. Any 100 members who are present on the floor of the chamber to consider legislation constitute a quorum of the committee.

Technically, the Committee of the Whole considers only bills directly or indirectly appropriating money, authorizing appropriations, or involving taxes or charges on the public. Because the Committee of the Whole need number only 100 representatives, a quorum is more readily attained and legislative business is expedited. Before 1971, members' positions were not individually recorded on votes taken in the Committee of the Whole. Periodically, delegates from the District of Columbia and several U.S. territories have been permitted to vote in the Committee of the Whole. A rules change adopted at the beginning of the 112th Congress, removed the permission for delegates to vote. (Also see delegate.)

When the full House resolves itself into the Committee of the Whole, it replaces the speaker with a "chairman." A measure is debated and amendments may be proposed, with votes on amendments as needed. (Also see five-minute rule.)

When the committee completes its work on the measure, it dissolves itself by "rising." The speaker returns, and the chairman of the Committee of the Whole reports to the House that the committee's work has been completed. At this time, members may demand a roll call vote on any amendment adopted in the Committee of the Whole. The final vote is on passage of the legislation.

Committee veto — A requirement added to a few statutes directing that certain policy directives by an executive department or agency be reviewed by certain congressional committees before they are implemented. Under common practice, the government department or agency and the committees involved are expected to reach a consensus before the directives are carried out.

Concurrent resolution — A concurrent resolution, designated H Con Res or S Con Res, must be adopted by both chambers to have

effect, but it is not sent to the president for approval and, therefore, does not have the force of law. A concurrent resolution, for example, is used to fix the time for adjournment of a Congress. It is also used to express the sense of Congress on a foreign policy or domestic issue. The annual budget resolution is a concurrent resolution.

Conference — A meeting between designated representatives of the House and the Senate to reconcile differences between the two chambers on provisions of a bill. House conferees are appointed by the speaker; Senate conferees are appointed by the presiding officer of the Senate.

A majority of the conferees for each chamber must agree on a compromise, reflected in a "conference report," before the final bill can go back to both chambers for approval. When the conference report goes to the floor, it is difficult to amend. If it is not approved by both chambers, the bill may go back to conference under certain situations, or a new conference may be convened. Many rules and informal practices govern the conduct of conference committees.

Bills that are passed by both chambers do not have to be sent to conference. Either chamber may "concur" with the other's amendments, completing action on the legislation, or they may further amend the measure and send it back to the other chamber. Sometimes leaders of the committees of jurisdiction work out an informal compromise instead of having a formal conference. (Also see custody of the papers.)

Confirmations — (See nominations.)

Congressional Record — The daily printed account of proceedings in both the House and Senate chambers, showing substantially verbatim debate and statements and a record of floor action. Highlights of legislative and committee action are given in a Daily Digest section of the Record, and members are entitled to have their extraneous remarks printed in an appendix known as "Extension of Remarks." Members may edit and revise remarks made on the floor during debate.

The Congressional Record provides a way to distinguish remarks spoken on the floor of the House and Senate from undelivered speeches. In the Senate, all speeches, articles and other matter that members insert in the Record without actually reading them on the floor are set off by large black dots, or bullets. However, a loophole allows a member to avoid the bulleting if he or she delivers any portion of the speech in person. In the House, undelivered speeches and other material are printed in a distinctive typeface. The record is also available in electronic form. (Also see Journal.)

Congressional terms of office — Terms normally begin on Jan. 3 of the year following a general election. Terms are two years for representatives and six years for senators. Representatives elected in special elections are sworn in for the remainder of a term. Under most state laws, a person may be appointed to fill a Senate vacancy and serve until a successor is elected; the successor serves until the end of the term applying to the vacant seat.

Continuing resolution — Typically, but not always, a joint resolution, cleared by Congress and signed by the president, is used to

provide new budget authority for federal agencies and programs whose regular appropriations bills have not been enacted. Also known as CRs or continuing appropriations, continuing resolutions are used to keep agencies operating when, as often happens, Congress does not finish the regular appropriations process by the Oct. 1 start of a new fiscal year.

The CR usually specifies a maximum rate at which an agency may incur obligations, based on the rate of the prior year, the president's budget request, or an appropriations bill passed by either or both chambers of Congress but not yet enacted. A CR can be a short-term measure that finances programs temporarily until the regular appropriations bill is enacted, or it can carry spending for the balance of the fiscal year in lieu of regular appropriations bills.

Contract authority — Budget authority contained in an authorization bill that permits the federal government to enter into contracts or other obligations for future payments from money not yet appropriated by Congress. The assumption is that money will be provided in a subsequent appropriations act. (Also see budget authority.)

Correcting recorded votes — Rules prohibit members from changing their votes after the result has been announced. Occasionally, however, a member may announce hours, days or months after a vote has been taken that he or she was "incorrectly recorded." In the Senate, a request to change one's vote almost always receives unanimous consent, as long as it does not change the outcome. In the House, members are prohibited from changing votes if they were tallied by the electronic voting system.

Co-sponsor — (See bills introduced.)

Current services estimates — Estimated budget authority and outlays for federal programs and operations for the forthcoming fiscal year based on continuation of existing levels of service without policy changes but with adjustments for inflation and for demographic changes that affect programs. These estimates, accompanied by the underlying economic and policy assumptions upon which they are based, are transmitted by the president to Congress when the budget is submitted.

Custody of the papers — To reconcile differences between the House and Senate versions of a bill, a conference may be arranged. The chamber with "custody of the papers" — the engrossed bill, engrossed amendments, messages of transmittal — is the only body empowered to request the conference. By custom, the chamber that asks for a conference is the last to act on the conference report.

Custody of the papers sometimes is manipulated to ensure that a particular chamber acts either first or last on the conference report. (Also see conference.)

'Cut-as-you-go' rules — House rules for the 112th Congress made it out of order to consider any legislation, including conference reports, that has the net effect of increasing mandatory spending. The restriction applies to the current year and the following five years, as well as the current year and the following 10 years.

The previous rule, known as "pay as you go," made it out of order to consider legislation, including conference reports, that contained tax provisions or new or expanded entitlement spending that had the net effect of increasing the deficit or reducing the surplus.

Deferral — Executive branch action to defer, or delay, the spending of appropriated money. The 1974 Congressional Budget and Impoundment Control Act requires a special message from the president to Congress reporting a proposed deferral of spending. Deferrals may not extend beyond the end of the fiscal year in which the message is transmitted. A federal district court in 1986 struck down the president's authority to defer spending for policy reasons; the ruling was upheld by a federal appeals court in 1987. Congress can prohibit proposed deferrals by clearing a law doing so; most often, cancellations of proposed deferrals are included in appropriations bills. (Also see rescission.)

Delegate — A nonvoting official representing the District of Columbia, Guam, American Samoa, the U.S. Virgin Islands, the Northern Mariana Islands or Puerto Rico in the House. The first five serve two-year terms. Puerto Rico's nonvoting representative is known as a resident commissioner and serves a four-year term. Delegates may not vote in the full House but are permitted to vote in committees and can introduce and co-sponsor legislation. Periodically, delegates have been permitted to vote in the Committee of the Whole House, where some legislative business is conducted. That permission was eliminated by a House rules change at the beginning of the 112th Congress. (See also Committee of the Whole.)

Dilatory motion — A motion made for the purpose of killing time and preventing action on a bill or amendment. House rules outlaw dilatory motions, but enforcement is largely within the discretion of the speaker or chairman of the Committee of the Whole. The Senate does not have a rule barring dilatory motions except under cloture.

Discharge a committee — Occasionally, attempts are made to relieve a committee of jurisdiction over a bill that is before it. This is attempted more often in the House than in the Senate, and the procedure rarely is successful.

In the House, if a committee does not report a bill within 30 days after the measure is referred to it, any member may file a discharge motion. Once offered, the motion is treated as a petition needing the signatures of a majority of members (218 if there are no vacancies). After the required signatures have been obtained, there is a delay of seven days.

Afterward, on the second and fourth Mondays of each month, except during the last six days of a session, any member who has signed the petition must be recognized, if he or she so desires, to move that the committee be discharged. Debate on the motion to discharge is limited to 20 minutes. If the motion is approved, consideration of the bill becomes a matter of high privilege.

If a resolution to consider a bill is held up in the Rules Committee for more than seven legislative days, any member may enter a motion to discharge the committee. The motion is handled like any other discharge petition in the House. Occasionally, to expedite noncontroversial legislative business, a committee is discharged by unanimous

consent of the House, and a petition is not required. In 1993, the signatures on pending discharge petitions — previously kept secret — were made a matter of public record. (For Senate procedure, see discharge resolution.)

Discharge Calendar — The House calendar to which motions to discharge committees are referred when they have the required number of signatures (218) and are awaiting floor action. (Also see calendar.)

Discharge petition — (See discharge a committee.)

Discharge resolution — In the Senate, a special motion that any senator may introduce to relieve a committee from consideration of a bill before it. The resolution can be called up for Senate approval or disapproval in the same manner as any other Senate business. (For House procedure, see discharge a committee.)

Discretionary spending — Budget authority provided through appropriations bills in amounts determined annually by Congress. In recent years, Congress has established caps on discretionary spending that are enforced through points of order that must be waived to permit action to exceed the cap, or by automatic spending cuts called a sequester. (Also see mandatory spending, sequester.)

Direct spending — (See mandatory spending.)

Division of a question for voting — A practice that is more common in the Senate but also used in the House whereby a member may demand a division of an amendment or a motion for purposes of voting. When the amendment or motion lends itself to such a division, the individual parts are voted on separately.

Emergency spending — Spending that the president and Congress have designated as an emergency requirement. Emergency spending is not subject to limits on discretionary spending set in the budget resolution or to cut-as-you-go rules, which require offsets. The designation is intended for unanticipated items that are not included in the budget for a fiscal year, such as spending to respond to disasters. However, most of the appropriations for the wars in Iraq and Afghanistan have been designated as emergency spending or, more recently, as overseas contingency operations not subject to discretionary spending limits.

Enacting clause — Key phrase in bills beginning, "Be it enacted by the Senate and House of Representatives." A successful motion to strike it from legislation kills the measure.

Engrossed bill — The copy of a bill as passed by one chamber, with the text as amended by floor action and certified by the clerk of the House or the secretary of the Senate.

Enrolled bill — The final copy of a bill that has been passed in identical form by both chambers. It is certified by an officer of the chamber of origin (clerk of the House or secretary of the Senate) and then sent on for the signatures of the House speaker, the Senate president pro tempore and the president of the United States. An enrolled bill is printed on parchment.

Entitlement — A program that guarantees payments to anyone who meets the eligibility criteria set in law. Examples include Social Security, Medicare, Medicaid and food stamps. (Also see mandatory spending.)

Executive Calendar — A nonlegislative calendar in the Senate that lists presidential documents such as treaties and nominations. (Also see calendar.)

Executive document — A document, usually a treaty, sent to the Senate by the president for consideration or approval. Executive documents are referred to committee in the same manner as other measures. Unlike legislative documents, treaties do not die at the end of a Congress but remain "live" proposals until acted on by the Senate or withdrawn by the president.

Executive session — A meeting of a Senate or House committee (or occasionally of either chamber) that only its members may attend. Witnesses regularly appear at committee meetings in executive session — for example, Defense Department officials during presentations of classified defense information. Other members of Congress may be invited, but the public and news media are not allowed to attend.

Filibuster — A time-delaying tactic associated with the Senate and used by a minority in an effort to prevent a vote on a bill, amendment, motion or nomination that probably would prevail if voted upon directly. The most common method is to take advantage of the Senate's rules permitting unlimited debate, but other forms of parliamentary maneuvering may be used. The chamber can vote to invoke cloture to end a filibuster, but that generally requires a majority of 60 votes, and in some cases two-thirds of the chamber. In November 2013, the Senate reinterpreted its cloture rule as it applies to executive branch nominations and lower federal court judges (other than those for the Supreme Court). A simple majority was then all that was required to cut off debate on non-Supreme Court nominations and end a filibuster. In 2017, the Senate voted to apply this rule to Supreme Court nominations as well. (Also see cloture.) The stricter rules of the House make filibusters more difficult, but delaying tactics are employed occasionally through various procedural devices allowed by House rules.

Fiscal year — Financial operations of the government are carried out in a 12-month fiscal year, beginning Oct. 1 and ending Sept. 30. The fiscal year carries the date of the calendar year in which it ends. (From fiscal 1844 to fiscal 1976, the fiscal year began July 1 and ended the following June 30.)

Five-minute rule — A debate-limiting rule of the House that is invoked when the House sits as the Committee of the Whole. Under the rule, a member offering an amendment and a member opposing it are each allowed to speak for five minutes. Debate is then closed. In practice, amendments regularly are debated for more than 10 minutes, with members gaining the floor by offering pro forma amendments or obtaining unanimous consent to speak longer than five minutes. (Also see Committee of the Whole, hour rule, strike out the last word.)

Floor manager — A member who has the task of steering legislation through floor debate and amendment to a final vote in the House

or the Senate. Floor managers usually are chairmen or ranking members of the committee that reported the bill. Managers are responsible for apportioning the debate time granted to supporters of the bill. The ranking minority member of the committee normally apportions time for the minority party's participation in the debate.

Frank — A member's facsimile signature, which is used on envelopes in lieu of stamps for the member's official outgoing mail. The "franking privilege" is the right to send mail postage-free.

Germane — Pertaining to the subject matter of the measure at hand. All House amendments must be germane to the bill being considered. The Senate requires that amendments be germane when they are proposed to general appropriations bills or to bills being considered once cloture has been invoked or, frequently, when the Senate is proceeding under a unanimous consent agreement placing a time limit on consideration of a bill. The 1974 Budget Act also requires that amendments to concurrent budget resolutions be germane.

In the House, floor debate must be germane, and the first three hours of debate each day in the Senate must be germane to the pending business. (Also see cloture.)

Gramm-Rudman Deficit Reduction Act — (See sequester.)

Grandfather clause — A provision that exempts people or other entities already engaged in an activity from new rules or legislation affecting that activity.

Hearings — Committee sessions for taking testimony from witnesses. At hearings on legislation, witnesses usually include specialists, government officials, and spokesmen for individuals or entities affected by the bill or bills under study. Hearings related to special investigations bring forth a variety of witnesses. Committees sometimes use their subpoena power to summon reluctant witnesses. The public and news media may attend open hearings but are barred from closed, or "executive," hearings. The vast majority of hearings are open to the public. (Also see executive session.)

Hold-harmless clause — A provision added to legislation to ensure that recipients of federal money do not receive less in a future year than they did in the current year if a new formula for allocating money authorized in the legislation would result in a reduction to the recipients. This clause has been used most often to soften the impact of sudden reductions in federal grants.

Hopper — A box on the House clerk's desk into which members deposit bills and resolutions to introduce them.

Hour rule — A provision in the rules of the House that permits one hour of debate time for each member on amendments debated in the House of Representatives sitting as the House. Therefore, the House normally amends bills while sitting as the Committee of the Whole, where the five-minute rule on amendments operates.

House as in the Committee of the Whole — A procedure that can be used to expedite consideration of certain measures such as continuing resolutions and, when there is debate, private bills. The pro-

cedure can be invoked only with the unanimous consent of the House or a rule from the Rules Committee and has procedural elements of both the House sitting as the House of Representatives, such as the speaker presiding and the previous question motion being in order, and the House sitting as the Committee of the Whole, with the five-minute rule being in order. (Also see Committee of the Whole.)

House Calendar — A listing for action by the House of public bills and resolutions that do not directly or indirectly appropriate money or raise revenue. (Also see calendar.)

Immunity — The constitutional privilege of members of Congress to make verbal statements on the floor and in committee for which they cannot be sued or arrested for slander or libel. Also, freedom from arrest while traveling to or from sessions of Congress or on official business. Members in this status may be arrested only for treason, felonies or a breach of the peace, as defined by congressional manuals.

Joint committee — A committee composed of a specified number of members of both the House and Senate. A joint committee may be investigative or research-oriented, an example of the latter being the Joint Economic Committee. Others have housekeeping duties; examples include the joint committees on Printing and the Library of Congress. In 2011, Congress convened a Joint Select Committee on Deficit Reduction and charged it with proposing $1.2 trillion in budget savings. The committee did not agree on a plan, and it disbanded in November 2011.

Joint resolution — Like a bill, a joint resolution, designated H J Res or S J Res, requires the approval of both chambers and generally the signature of the president and has the force of law if approved. In most cases, there is no practical difference between a bill and a joint resolution. A joint resolution generally is used to address a limited matter such as a single appropriation.

Joint resolutions also are used to propose amendments to the Constitution. In that case, they require a two-thirds majority in both chambers. They do not require a presidential signature, but they must be ratified by three-fourths of the states to become a part of the Constitution. (Also see concurrent resolution, resolution.)

Journal — The official record of the proceedings of the House and Senate. The Journal records the actions taken in each chamber, but, unlike the Congressional Record, it does not include the substantially verbatim report of speeches, debates, statements and the like.

Law — An act of Congress that has been signed by the president or passed, over his veto, by Congress. Public bills, when signed, become public laws and are cited by the letters PL and a hyphenated number. The number before the hyphen corresponds to the Congress, and the one or more digits after the hyphen refer to the numerical sequence in which the president signed the bills during that Congress. Private bills, when signed, become private laws. (Also see bills, private bill.)

Legislative day — The "day" extending from the time either chamber meets after an adjournment until the time it next adjourns. Because the House normally adjourns from day to day, legislative days and calendar days usually coincide. But in the Senate, a legislative day

may, and frequently does, extend over several calendar days. (Also see recess.)

Line-item veto — Presidential authority to strike individual items from appropriations bills, which presidents since Ulysses S. Grant have sought. Congress gave the president a form of the power in 1996 (PL 104-130), but this "enhanced rescission authority" was struck down by the Supreme Court in 1998 as unconstitutional because it allowed the president to change laws on his own.

Loan guarantees — Loans to third parties for which the federal government guarantees the repayment of principal or interest, in whole or in part, to the lender in the event of default.

Lobby — A group seeking to influence the passage or defeat of legislation. Originally the term referred to people frequenting the lobbies or corridors of legislative chambers to speak to lawmakers.

The definition of a lobby and the activity of lobbying is a matter of differing interpretation. By some definitions, lobbying is limited to direct attempts to influence lawmakers through personal interviews and persuasion. Under other definitions, lobbying includes attempts at indirect, or grass-roots, influence, such as persuading members of a group to write or visit their district's representative and state's senators or attempting to create a climate of opinion favorable to a desired legislative goal.

The right to attempt to influence legislation is based on the First Amendment to the Constitution, which says Congress shall make no law abridging the right of the people "to petition the government for a redress of grievances."

Majority leader — The floor leader for the majority party in each chamber. In the Senate, in consultation with the minority leader, the majority leader directs the legislative schedule for the chamber. This person is also the party's spokesman and chief strategist. In the House, the majority leader is second to the speaker in the majority party's leadership and serves as the party's legislative strategist. (Also see speaker, whip.)

Mandatory spending — Budget authority and outlays often provided under laws other than appropriations acts, although some mandatory spending is provided by annual appropriations (as is all discretionary spending). Mandatory spending, also known as direct spending, covers entitlements and payment of interest on the public debt. (Also see discretionary spending, entitlement.)

Manual — The official handbook in each chamber prescribing in detail its organization, procedures and operations.

Marking up a bill — Going through the contents of a piece of legislation in committee or subcommittee to, for example, consider the provisions, act on amendments to provisions and proposed revisions to the language, and insert new sections and phraseology. If the bill is extensively amended, the committee's version may be introduced as a separate (or "clean") bill, with a new number, before being considered by the full House or Senate. (Also see clean bill.)

Minority leader — The floor leader for the minority party in each chamber.

Morning hour — The time set aside at the beginning of each legislative day for the consideration of regular, routine business. The "hour" is of indefinite duration in the House, where it is rarely used. In the Senate, it is the first two hours of a session following an adjournment, as distinguished from a recess. The morning hour can be terminated earlier if the morning business has been completed.

Business includes such matters as messages from the president, communications from the heads of departments, messages from the House, the presentation of petitions, reports of standing and select committees, and the introduction of bills and resolutions.

During the first hour of the morning hour in the Senate, no motion to proceed to the consideration of any bill on the calendar is in order except by unanimous consent. During the second hour, motions can be made but must be decided without debate. Senate committees may meet while the Senate conducts the morning hour.

Motion — In the House or Senate chamber, a request by a member to institute any one of a wide array of parliamentary actions. He or she "moves" for a certain procedure, such as the consideration of a measure. The precedence of motions, and whether they are debatable, is set forth in the House and Senate rules.

Nominations — Presidential appointments to office subject to Senate confirmation. Although most nominations win quick Senate approval, some are controversial and become the topic of hearings and debate. Sometimes senators object to appointees for patronage reasons — for example, when a nomination to a local federal job is made without consulting the senators of the state concerned. In some situations a senator may object that the nominee is "personally obnoxious" to him. Usually other senators join in blocking such appointments out of courtesy to their colleagues. In recent years, executive branch and judicial nominations have been blocked by filibusters. As a result, the Senate in November 2013 changed its interpretation of the cloture rule used to end filibusters. (Also see cloture, filibuster, senatorial courtesy.)

One-minute speeches — Addresses by House members at the beginning of a legislative day. The speeches may cover any subject but are limited to one minute's duration.

Outlays — Actual spending that flows from the liquidation of budget authority. Outlays associated with appropriations bills and other legislation are estimates of future spending made by the Congressional Budget Office and the White House's Office of Management and Budget. The CBO's estimates govern bills for the purpose of congressional floor debate, while the OMB's numbers govern when it comes to determining whether legislation exceeds spending caps.

Outlays in a given fiscal year may result from budget authority provided in the current year or in previous years. (Also see budget authority, budget process.)

Override a veto — If the president vetoes a bill and sends it back to Congress with his objections, Congress may try to override his veto

and enact the bill into law. Neither chamber is required to attempt to override a veto. The override of a veto requires a recorded vote with a two-thirds majority of those present and voting in each chamber. The question put to each chamber is: "Shall the bill pass, the objections of the president to the contrary notwithstanding?" (Also see pocket veto, veto.)

Oversight committee — A congressional committee or designated subcommittee that is charged with general oversight of one or more federal agencies' programs and activities. Usually, the oversight panel for a particular agency is also the authorizing committee for that agency's programs and operations.

Pair — A voluntary, informal arrangement that two lawmakers, usually on opposite sides of an issue, make on recorded votes. In many cases, the result is to subtract a vote from each side with no effect on the outcome.

Pairs are not authorized in the rules of either chamber, are not counted in tabulating the final result and have no official standing. However, paired members are identified in the Congressional Record, along with their positions on such votes, if known. A member who expects to be absent for a vote can pair with a member who plans to vote, with the latter agreeing to withhold his or her vote.

There are three types of pairs:

(1) A live pair involves a member who is present for a vote and another who is absent. The member in attendance votes and then withdraws the vote, announcing that he or she has a live pair with colleague "X" and stating how the two members would have voted, one in favor, the other opposed. A live pair may affect the outcome of a closely contested vote, since it subtracts one "yea" or one "nay" from the final tally. A live pair may cover one or several specific issues.

(2) A general pair, widely used in the House, does not entail any arrangement between two members and does not affect the vote. Members who expect to be absent notify the clerk that they wish to make a general pair. Each member then is paired with another desiring a pair, and their names are listed in the Congressional Record. The member may or may not be paired with another taking the opposite position, and no indication of how the members would have voted is given.

(3) A specific pair is similar to a general pair, except that the opposing stands of the two members are identified and printed in the Congressional Record.

Petition — A request or plea sent to one or both chambers from an organization or private citizens group seeking support for particular legislation or favorable consideration of a matter not yet receiving congressional attention. Petitions are referred to appropriate committees. In the House, a petition signed by a majority of members (218) can discharge a bill from a committee. (Also see discharge a committee.)

Pocket veto — The act of the president in withholding his approval of a bill after Congress has adjourned. When Congress is in session, a bill becomes law without the president's signature if he does not act upon it within 10 days, excluding Sundays, from the time he receives it. But if Congress adjourns sine die within that 10-day period, the bill, if unsigned, will die even if the president does not formally veto it.

The Supreme Court in 1986 agreed to decide whether the president could pocket veto a bill during recesses and between sessions of the same Congress or only between Congresses. The justices in 1987 declared the case moot, however, because the bill in question was invalid once the case reached the court. The House has treated pocket vetoes between sessions as regular vetoes. (Also see adjournment sine die, veto.)

Point of order — An objection raised by a member that the chamber is departing from rules governing its conduct of business. The objector cites the rule violated, with the chairman sustaining his or her objection if correctly made. The chairman restores order by suspending proceedings of the chamber until it conforms to the prescribed "order of business."

Both chambers have procedures for overcoming a point of order, either by vote or — as is most common in the House — by including language in the rule for floor consideration that waives a point of order against a given bill. (Also see rules.)

President of the Senate — Under the Constitution, the vice president of the United States presides over the Senate. In his absence, the president pro tempore, or a senator designated by the president pro tempore, presides over the chamber.

President pro tempore — The chief officer of the Senate in the absence of the vice president — literally, but loosely, the president for a time. The president pro tempore is elected by his fellow senators. Recent practice has been to elect the senator of the majority party with the longest period of continuous service. The president pro tempore is third in the line of presidential succession, after the vice president and the speaker of the House.

Previous question — A motion for the previous question, when carried, has the effect of cutting off further debate, preventing the offering of further amendments and forcing a vote on the pending matter. In the House, a motion for the previous question is not permitted in the Committee of the Whole, unless a rule governing debate provides otherwise. The motion for the previous question is not in order in the Senate.

Printed amendment — Some House rules guarantee five minutes of floor debate in support and five minutes in opposition, and no other debate time, on amendments printed in the Congressional Record at least one day prior to the amendment's consideration in the Committee of the Whole.

In the Senate, while amendments may be submitted for printing, they have no parliamentary standing or status. An amendment submitted for printing in the Senate, however, may be called up by any senator.

Private bill — A bill dealing with individual matters, such as claims against the government, immigration or land titles. If two members officially object to consideration of a private bill that is before the

chamber, it is recommitted to committee. The backers still have recourse, however. The measure can be put into an omnibus claims bill — several private bills rolled into one. As with any bill, no part of an omnibus claims bill may be deleted without a vote. When the private bill goes back to the House floor in this form, it can be deleted from the omnibus bill only by majority vote.

Private Calendar — The House calendar for private bills. The Private Calendar must be called on the first Tuesday of each month, and the speaker may call it on the third Tuesday of each month, as well. (Also see calendar, private bill.)

Privileged questions — The order in which bills, motions and other legislative measures are considered on the floor of the Senate and House is governed by strict priorities. A motion to table, for instance, is more privileged than a motion to recommit. Thus, if a member moves to recommit a bill to committee for further consideration, another member can supersede the first action by moving to table it, and a vote will occur on the motion to table (or kill) before the motion to recommit. A motion to adjourn is considered "of the highest privilege" and must be considered before virtually any other motion.

Pro forma amendment — (See strike out the last word.)

Pro forma session — A meeting of the House and Senate during which no legislative business is conducted. The sessions are held to satisfy a provision of the Constitution that prohibits either chamber from adjourning for more than three days without the permission of the other chamber. When the House or Senate recesses or adjourns for more than three days, both chambers adopt concurrent resolutions providing for the recess or adjournment. Also, the Senate sometimes holds pro forma sessions during recess periods to prevent the president from making recess appointments.

Public laws — (See law.)

Questions of privilege — These are matters affecting members of Congress individually or collectively. Matters affecting the rights, safety, dignity and integrity of proceedings of the House or Senate as a whole are questions of privilege in both chambers.

Questions involving individual members are called questions of "personal privilege." A member rising to ask a question of personal privilege is given precedence over almost all other proceedings. For instance, if a member feels that he or she has been improperly impugned in comments by another member, he or she can immediately demand to be heard on the floor on a question of personal privilege. An annotation in the House rules points out that the privilege rests primarily on the Constitution, which gives members a conditional immunity from arrest and an unconditional freedom to speak in the House.

In 1993, the House changed its rules to allow the speaker to delay for two legislative days the floor consideration of a resolution raising a question of the privileges of the House unless it is offered by the majority leader or minority leader.

Quorum — The number of members whose presence is necessary for the transaction of business. In the Senate and House, it is a majority of the membership. In the Committee of the Whole, a quorum is 100. If a point of order is made that a quorum is not present, the only business that is in order is either a motion to adjourn or a motion to direct the sergeant at arms to request the attendance of absentees. In practice, however, both chambers conduct much of their business without a quorum present. (Also see Committee of the Whole.)

Quorum call — Procedures used in the House and Senate to establish that a quorum is present. In the House, quorum calls are usually conducted using the electronic voting system, and no roll call is recorded. In the Senate, quorum calls are usually conducted by calling the roll of senators. The House and Senate conduct annual quorum calls at the beginning of each session of Congress. The Senate also uses quorum calls when no senators are speaking on the floor.

Reading of bills — Traditional parliamentary procedure required bills to be read three times before they were passed. This custom is of little modern significance. Normally a bill is considered to have its first reading when it is introduced and printed, by title, in the Congressional Record. In the House, a bill's second reading comes when floor consideration begins. (The actual reading of a bill is most likely to occur at this point if at all.) The second reading in the Senate is supposed to occur on the legislative day after the measure is introduced, but before it is referred to committee. The third reading (again, usually by title) takes place when floor action has been completed on amendments.

Recess — A recess, as distinguished from adjournment, does not end a legislative day and, therefore, does not interrupt unfinished business. The House usually adjourns from day to day. The Senate often recesses, thus meeting on the same legislative day for several calendar days or even weeks at a time. The rules in each chamber set forth certain matters to be taken up and disposed of at the beginning of each legislative day.

Recognition — The power of recognition of a member is lodged in the speaker of the House and the presiding officer of the Senate. The presiding officer names the member to speak first when two or more members simultaneously request recognition. The order of recognition is governed by precedents and tradition for many situations. In the Senate, for instance, the majority leader has the right to be recognized first.

Recommit — A motion to return a bill or joint resolution to committee after the measure has been debated on the floor. In the House, the right to offer a motion to recommit is guaranteed to the minority leader or someone he or she designates, and there must be an opponent.

Under a 2009 House rules change, a motion to recommit with instructions must direct a committee to report the bill back "forthwith" — that is, immediately. Previously, the motion could include the term "promptly," which did not require that the bill be returned to the floor and instead required full committee action.

Reconciliation — The 1974 Budget Act created a reconciliation procedure for bringing existing tax and spending laws into conformity with ceilings set in the congressional budget resolution. Under the procedure, the budget resolution sets specific deficit reduction targets and instructs tax-writing and authorizing committees to propose changes in existing law to meet those targets. If more than one committee is

involved, the Budget committees consolidate the recommendations, without change, into an omnibus reconciliation bill, which then must be considered and approved by both chambers of Congress.

Special rules in the Senate limit debate on a reconciliation bill to 20 hours and bar extraneous or nongermane amendments. (Also see budget resolution, sequester.)

Reconsider a vote — Until it is disposed of, a motion to reconsider the vote by which an action was taken has the effect of putting the action in abeyance. In the Senate, the motion can be made only by a member who voted on the prevailing side of the original question or by a member who did not vote at all. In the House, it can be made only by a member on the prevailing side.

A common practice in the Senate after close votes on an issue is a motion to reconsider, followed by a motion to table the motion to reconsider. On this motion to table, senators vote as they voted on the original question, which allows the motion to table to prevail, assuming there are no switches. That closes the matter, and further motions to reconsider are not entertained.

In the House, as a routine precaution, a motion to reconsider usually is made every time a measure is passed. Such a motion almost always is tabled immediately, thus shutting off the possibility of future reconsideration except by unanimous consent.

Motions to reconsider must be entered in the Senate within the next two days the Senate is in session after the original vote has been taken. In the House, they must be entered either on the same day or the next succeeding day that the House is in session. Sometimes on a close vote, a member — in the Senate, often the majority leader — will switch his or her vote to be eligible to offer a motion to reconsider.

Recorded vote — A vote upon which each member's stand is individually made known. In the Senate, this is accomplished through a roll call of the entire membership, to which each senator on the floor must answer "yea," "nay" or "present." Since January 1973, the House has used an electronic voting system for recorded votes, including "yea" and "nay" votes formerly taken by a call of the roll.

When not required by the Constitution, a recorded vote can be obtained on questions in the House on the demand of one-fifth (44 members) of a quorum or one-fourth (25) of a quorum in the Committee of the Whole. Recorded votes are required in the House for appropriations, budget and tax bills. (Also see "yeas" and "nays.")

Report — Both a verb and a noun as a congressional term. A committee that has been examining a bill referred to it by the parent chamber "reports" its findings and recommendations to the chamber when it completes consideration and returns the measure. The process is called "reporting" a bill. In some cases, a bill is reported without a written report.

A "report" is the document setting forth the committee's explanation of its action. Senate and House reports are numbered separately and are designated S Rept or H Rept. When a committee report is not unanimous, the dissenting committee members may file a statement of their views, called minority or dissenting views and referred to as a minority report. Members in disagreement with some provisions of a bill may file additional or supplementary views. Sometimes a bill or resolution is reported without a committee recommendation.

Legislative committees occasionally submit adverse reports. However, when a committee is opposed to a bill, it usually does not report the bill at all. Some laws require that committee reports — favorable or adverse — be filed.

Rescission — Cancellation of budget authority that was previously appropriated but has not yet been spent.

Resolution — A "simple" resolution, designated H Res or S Res, deals with matters entirely within the prerogatives of a single chamber. It requires neither adoption by the other chamber nor approval by the president, and it does not have the force of law. Most resolutions deal with the rules or procedures of one chamber. They are also used to express the sentiments of a single chamber, such as condolences to the family of a deceased member, or to comment on foreign policy or executive business. A simple resolution is the vehicle for a "rule" from the House Rules Committee. (Also see concurrent and joint resolutions, rules.)

Rider — An amendment, usually not germane, that its sponsor hopes to get through more easily by including it in other legislation. A rider becomes law if the bill to which it is attached is enacted. Amendments providing legislative directives in appropriations bills are examples of riders, although technically legislation is barred from appropriations bills.

The House, unlike the Senate, has a strict germaneness rule; thus, riders usually are Senate devices to get legislation enacted quickly or to bypass lengthy House consideration and, possibly, opposition.

Rules — Each chamber has a body of rules and precedents that govern the conduct of business. These rules deal with issues such as duties of officers, the order of business, admission to the floor, parliamentary procedures on handling amendments and voting, and jurisdictions of committees.

The House re-adopts its rules, usually with some changes, at the beginning of each Congress. Senate rules carry over from one Congress to the next.

In the House, a rule may also be a resolution reported by the Rules Committee to govern the handling of a particular bill on the floor. The committee may report a rule, also called a special order, in the form of a simple resolution. If the House adopts the resolution, the temporary rule becomes as valid as any standing rule and lapses only after action has been completed on the measure to which it pertains.

The rule sets the time limit on general debate. It also may waive points of order against provisions of the bill in question, such as nongermane language, or against certain amendments expected on the floor. It may even forbid all amendments or all amendments except those proposed by the legislative committee that handled the bill. In this instance, it is known as a "closed" rule, as opposed to an "open"

rule, which puts no limitation on floor amendments, thus leaving the bill open to alteration by the adoption of germane amendments. (Also see point of order.)

Secretary of the Senate — Chief administrative officer of the Senate, responsible for overseeing the duties of Senate employees, educating Senate pages, administering oaths, overseeing the registration of lobbyists and handling other tasks necessary for the continuing operation of the Senate. (Also see Clerk of the House.)

Select or special committee — A committee set up for a special purpose and, usually, for a limited time by resolution of either the House or Senate. Most special committees are investigative and lack legislative authority: Legislation is not referred to them, and they cannot report bills to their parent chambers. Each chamber has a Select Committee on Intelligence.

Senatorial courtesy — A general practice with no written rule — sometimes referred to as "the courtesy of the Senate" — applied to consideration of executive nominations. Generally, it means nominees from a state are not to be confirmed unless they have been approved by the senators of the president's party of that state, with other senators following their colleagues' lead in the attitude they take toward consideration of such nominations. (Also see nominations.)

Sequester — Automatic percentage spending cuts for all discretionary spending and some mandatory spending, with exceptions. Under the 1985 Gramm-Rudman anti-deficit law, modified in 1987, a year-end, across-the-board sequester was triggered if the deficit exceeded a preset maximum. The Budget Control Act of 2011 required a $1.2 billion sequester, spread equally over nine years, after a joint deficit reduction committee was unable to agree on savings. For fiscal 2014 and after, the sequester resulted in lower discretionary spending caps and a second across-the-board sequester to enforce those caps. In December 2013, the caps were adjusted higher and the sequester was extended beyond fiscal 2021 for certain spending.

Sine die — (See adjournment sine die.)

Speaker — The presiding officer of the House of Representatives, selected by the majority party's caucus and formally elected by the whole House. While both parties nominate candidates, choice by the majority party is tantamount to election. The speaker is second in the line of presidential succession, after the vice president.

Special session — A session of Congress after it has adjourned sine die, completing its regular session. Special sessions are convened by the president.

Spending authority — The 1974 Budget Act defines spending authority as borrowing authority, contract authority and entitlement authority for which budget authority is not provided in advance by appropriations acts.

Sponsor — (See bills introduced.)

Standing committees — Committees that are permanently established by House and Senate rules. The standing committees are legislative committees: Legislation may be referred to them, and they may report bills and resolutions to their parent chambers.

Standing vote — A nonrecorded vote used in both the House and Senate. (A standing vote is also called a division vote.) Members in favor of a proposal stand and are counted by the presiding officer. Then members opposed stand and are counted. There is no record of how individual members voted.

Statutes at large — A chronological arrangement of the laws enacted in each session of Congress. Though indexed, the laws are not arranged by subject matter, and there is no indication of how they changed previously enacted laws. (Also see law, U.S. Code.)

Strike from the Record — A member of the House who is offended by remarks made on the House floor may move that the offending words be "taken down" for the speaker's cognizance and then expunged from the debate as published in the Congressional Record.

Strike out the last word — A motion whereby a House member is entitled to speak for five minutes on an amendment then being debated by the chamber. A member gains recognition from the chair by moving to "strike out the last word" of the amendment or section of the bill under consideration. The motion is pro forma, requires no vote and does not change the amendment being debated. (Also see five-minute rule.)

Substitute — A motion, amendment or entire bill introduced in place of the pending legislative business. Adoption of the substitute supplants the original text. The substitute may also be amended. (Also see amendment in the nature of a substitute.)

Supplemental appropriations bill — Legislation appropriating money after the regular annual appropriations bill for a federal department or agency has been enacted. In the past, supplemental appropriations bills often arrived about halfway through the fiscal year to pay for urgent needs, such as relief from natural disasters, that Congress and the president did not anticipate (or may not have wanted to finance).

Suspend the rules — A time-saving procedure for passing bills in the House. The wording of the motion, which may be made by any member recognized by the speaker, is "I move to suspend the rules and pass the bill." A favorable vote by two-thirds of those present is required for passage. Debate is limited to 40 minutes, and no amendments from the floor are permitted.

If a two-thirds favorable vote is not attained, the bill may be considered later under regular procedures. The suspension procedure is in order every Monday, Tuesday and Wednesday, and it is intended to be reserved for noncontroversial bills. It also may be used to concur in Senate amendments, adopt conference reports and agree to resolutions.

Table a bill — Motions to table, or to "lay on the table," are used to block or kill amendments or other parliamentary questions. When approved, a tabling motion is considered the final disposition of that issue. One of the most widely used parliamentary procedures, the motion to table is not debatable, and adoption requires a simple majority vote.

In the Senate, however, different language sometimes is used. The motion may be worded to let a bill "lie on the table," perhaps for subsequent "picking up." This motion is more flexible, keeping the bill pending for later action, if desired. Tabling motions on amendments are effective debate-ending devices in the Senate.

Treaties — Executive proposals — in the form of resolutions of ratification — that must be submitted to the Senate for approval by two-thirds of the senators present. Treaties are normally sent to the Foreign Relations Committee for scrutiny before the Senate takes action. Foreign Relations has jurisdiction over all treaties, regardless of the subject matter. Treaties are read three times and debated on the floor in much the same manner as legislative proposals. After approval by the Senate, treaties are formally ratified by the president.

Trust funds — Money collected and used by the federal government for carrying out specific purposes and programs according to terms of a trust agreement or statute such as the Social Security and unemployment compensation trust funds. Such funds are administered by the government in a fiduciary capacity and are not available for the general purposes of the government.

Unanimous consent — A procedure used to expedite floor action. Proceedings of the House or Senate and action on legislation often take place upon the unanimous consent of the chamber, whether or not a rule of the chamber is being violated. It is frequently used in a routine fashion, such as by a senator requesting the unanimous consent of the Senate to have specified members of his or her staff present on the floor during debate on a specific amendment. A single member's objection blocks a unanimous consent request.

Unanimous consent agreement — A device used in the Senate to expedite legislation. Much of the Senate's legislative business, dealing with both minor and controversial issues, is conducted through unanimous consent or unanimous consent agreements. On major legislation, such agreements usually are printed and transmitted to all senators before floor debate. Once agreed to, they are binding on all members unless the Senate, by unanimous consent, agrees to modify them. An agreement may list the order in which various bills are to be considered; specify the length of time for debate on bills and contested amendments and when they are to be voted upon; and, frequently, require that all amendments introduced be germane to the bill under consideration.

In this regard, unanimous consent agreements are similar to the "rules" issued by the House Rules Committee for bills pending in the House. The House rarely sets conditions for floor debate under unanimous consent.

Union Calendar — Bills that directly or indirectly appropriate money or raise revenue are placed on this House calendar according to the date they are reported from committee. (Also see calendar.)

U.S. Code — A consolidation and codification of the general and permanent laws of the United States arranged by subject under 50 titles, the first six dealing with general or political subjects, and the other 44 alphabetically arranged from agriculture to war. The U.S. Code is updated annually, and a new set of bound volumes is published every six years. (Also see law, statutes at large.)

Veto — Disapproval by the president of a bill or joint resolution (other than one proposing an amendment to the Constitution). When Congress is in session, the president must veto a bill within 10 days, excluding Sundays, after he has received it; otherwise, it becomes law without his signature. When the president vetoes a bill, he returns it to the chamber of origin along with a message stating his objections. (Also see pocket veto, override a veto.)

Voice vote — In either the House or Senate, members answer "aye" or "no" in chorus, and the presiding officer decides the result. The term is also used loosely to indicate action by unanimous consent or without objection. (Also see "yeas" and "nays.")

Whip — In effect, the assistant majority or minority leader, in either the House or Senate. His or her job is to help marshal votes in support of party strategy and legislation.

Without objection — Used in lieu of a vote on noncontroversial motions, amendments or bills that may be passed in either chamber if no member voices an objection.

"Yeas" and "nays" — The Constitution requires that "yea" and "nay" votes be taken and recorded when requested by one-fifth of the members present. In the House, the speaker determines whether one-fifth of the members present requested a vote. In the Senate, practice requires only 11 members. The Constitution requires the yeas and nays on a veto override attempt. (Also see recorded vote.)

Yielding — When a member has been recognized to speak, no other member may speak unless he or she obtains permission from the member recognized. This permission is called yielding and usually is requested in the form, "Will the gentleman (or gentlelady) yield to me?" While this activity occasionally is seen in the Senate, the Senate has no rule or practice to parcel out time. In the House, the floor manager of a bill usually apportions debate time by yielding specific amounts of time to members who have requested it. ■

Appendix B

VOTE STUDIES

He Divided, but Conquered

Full control of government gives Trump a record success rate

Donald Trump campaigned as a successful business mogul whose negotiating skills made him uniquely qualified to be a president capable of ending Washington's decades of bitter partisanship to get things done.

Trump, in fact, got his way on almost every vote last year where he publicly stated a position, setting a record for success. The results of votes by both House and Senate combined show he won 98.7 percent of the time on issues he supported. That set a new bicameral record, besting Obama's 96.7 percent success level in 2009 (the last time a president's party controlled both chambers.)

There's a back story to all that winning, of course. Because Trump's party controls the floor in both chambers and is loath to hold votes when facing the prospect of defeat, Republicans were primed somewhat for success. In addition, rules changes for judicial and executive nominees (all of which carry stated presidential positions) removed the threat of a 60-vote threshold for nominations, meaning Republicans could prevail on such votes with only members of their caucus.

Yet even with many advantages, in his first year Trump struggled to claim major legislative victories. And despite boasts that he would unify Washington, his presidency has only intensified a long-developing trend of party warfare.

So far, Trump has not shepherded major bipartisan legislation through the House and Senate. His single big accomplishment is a tax overhaul law that was written exclusively by congressional Republicans and his White House aides, which received nary a Democratic vote on either side of the Capitol. Trump also pushed unsuccessfully to repeal and replace the 2010 health law — working only with Republicans and securing only Republican votes.

Trump has deployed top deputies like his chief of staff, John Kelly, and top domestic policy adviser, Stephen Miller, to strike an immigration deal with Republicans and Democrats. But, so far, they have yet to fashion an agreement.

What's more, when members of both parties had to get together on a government shutdown-ending spending bill late last month, Trump took a back seat. His budget director, Mick Mulvaney, admitted as much on Jan. 23.

"Sometimes not going to the table is one of the best things you can do in a negotiation," Mulvaney told CNN.

Eventually, whether it is on immigration, an infrastructure package or federal spending, the president will have to work across the aisle.

Data of votes cast in 2017, however, show in a stark way that Trump simply has not done that one year into his presidency. CQ has long analyzed how members of both chambers voted when a president's position has been stated publicly. The data show Trump — like his immediate predecessor, Barack Obama — has enjoyed overwhelming support from his own party and staunch opposition from the opposing one.

Republican senators last year voted with Trump 96 percent of the time on legislation or nominations for which his stance was known before members cast their votes. On the House side, GOP members sided with the president 93 percent of the time his view was known.

Both of those scores are historically high, according to data compiled by CQ since 1954 — the highest in that time period for House and Senate Republicans standing by a chief executive. The Senate support level exceeded its previous high in 2001 and 2003, when GOP senators voted with George W. Bush 94 percent of the time.

How the Trump presidency has furthered the trend of partisanship also is reflected in how Democratic members of both chambers voted when they knew his stance beforehand.

House Democrats voted against the president 82 percent of the time, the second-highest opposition score recorded since CQ began tracking the data. The level was behind only the conference's opposition to Bush in 2003 (93 percent). On the Senate side, Democrats voted against Trump's positions 61 percent of the time. That level also is the second-highest, behind only Senate Democrats' 65 percent opposition to the elder George Bush as he was running for re-election in 1992.

The analysis measured 709 House votes and 325 Senate votes. Only 36 votes in the House (5.1 percent) were taken with Trump's stance clear beforehand. That's the lowest since the analysis began. (By comparison, Obama averaged 10 percent on the House side and the younger Bush came in at 8.4 percent.)

Of all Senate votes (117), 36 percent were taken with knowledge of where the president

Perfect Attendance

The count of those who never missed a roll-call vote fell in the House from 16 members in 2016 to 14 members in 2017. The number of senators who cast a "yea" or a "nay" on every recorded vote fell from 18 to 13 members.

HOUSE

Democrats

Levin, Sander M.	Mich.
Schneider, Brad	Ill.

Republicans

Bergman, Jack	Mich.
Conaway, K. Michael	Texas
Fleischmann, Chuck	Tenn.
Foxx, Virginia	N.C.
Latta, Bob	Ohio
LoBiondo, Frank A.	N.J.
McHenry, Patrick T.	N.C.
Moolenaar, John	Mich.
Paulsen, Erik	Minn.
Rothfus, Keith	Pa.
Womack, Steve	Ark.
Young, David	Iowa

SENATE

Independent

King, Angus	Maine

Republicans

Boozman, John	Ark.
Collins, Susan	Maine
Cornyn, John	Texas
Cotton, Tom	Ark.
Daines, Steve	Mont.
Fischer, Deb	Neb.
Gardner, Cory	Colo.
Grassley, Charles E.	Iowa
Kennedy, John	La.
Lankford, James	Okla.
Rounds, Mike	S.D.
Thune, John	S.D.

stood on the issue. For the Senate, that is the highest score for a president's first year since Ronald Reagan's 128 in 1981.

When nominations are weeded out, the Senate voted 23 times knowing Trump's position (10 percent). But only 19.7 percent of Senate votes cast with the president's stance known were not nomination votes, the second-lowest total in three decades.

Senate Republicans opened the floodgates for nominations, giving Trump 94 confirmation floor votes last year, compared to 44 for Obama in the last two years of his presidency while the chamber was under GOP control.

Senate Democrats supported Trump 37 percent of the time when his position was known, the lowest score for either party since the same conference backed George W. Bush only 34 percent of the time in 2008. (By comparison, the lowest rate of support for Obama's known stances by GOP senators was 40 percent in 2013.) Still, Senate Democrats' 2017 score was only the fifth-lowest since the annual analysis started.

For House Democrats, their level of support for Trump was even lower, voting in support of the president's known positions just 16 percent of the time. That is the second-lowest level since 1954, behind only a 7 percent score of support for George W. Bush in 2007 (7 percent).

And while Senate Republicans have been the most outspoken about some of Trump's rhetoric on things like race and his suitability for the presidency, they voted with him at almost every opportunity.

Not only was the 96 percent of presidential support among Senate Republicans their highest ever in CQ's data, the 93 percent among House GOP set a record too.

Perhaps better than any other set of numbers, those seem to underscore how Trump's erratic, nationalist and conservative base-focused presidency has failed to match his campaign-trail rhetoric of becoming a master Washington deal-maker who works with Democrats as often as Republicans.

Nevertheless, the raw numbers show he succeeded in getting his way on nearly all the votes he weighed in on.

Of 117 Senate votes, Trump won 115 times

— his only defeats were the two failed attempts to gut the 2010 health law. That 98.3 percent success rate was second only to Obama's 98.7 percent score in 2009. His two Senate losses were the fewest since Obama's single loss in 2009. (That lone setback was related to a vote on closure of the Guantanamo Bay detention facility in Cuba. Obama pledged to close the facility. The Senate voted to keep it open.)

Trump went 94-0 on nomination votes last year, bested only by Obama's 124 in 2014. Excluding his perfect record on nominations, his 91.3 percent success rate was bested only by Obama, again in 2009, for any president over the past 30 years.

But, notably, the 21 legislative successes ranked 22nd over the same three decades, undercutting Trump's often-stated opinion that he is breaking "all" records when it comes to his legislative agenda.

On the House side, Trump was perfect: 36-0 on votes that members took knowing where he stood.

The 2017 data show Trump's first year only furthered a consistent trend line within the 63-year-old study that reveals a steady progression of partisanship building between Congress and the presidency. During the eight years between John F. Kennedy's inauguration and Lyndon B. Johnson's last day in office, the average Republican member voted with that Democratic duo 41 percent of the time. GOP House members voted with Jimmy Carter 36 percent of the time and with Bill Clinton 31.5 percent of the time. But since Clinton left office, the chasm has only gotten wider. So what changed since 2008, when America elected its first African-American chief executive?

Both political parties became less and less politically diverse; in the past, ideological diversity likely encouraged compromise. Those days appear to be over — at least for now.

The growing distance between the parties in Washington reflects a broader societal trend. A recent Pew Research Center poll found there is a 36 percentage-point chasm between Republicans and those who lean Republican and Democrats and those who lean Democratic. ∎

Guide to the Vote Studies

CQ has analyzed voting patterns of members of Congress since 1945. The three current studies — presidential support, party unity and voting participation — have been conducted in a consistent manner since 1954.

SELECTING VOTES CQ bases its vote studies on all floor votes for which senators and House members were asked to vote "yea" or "nay." In 2017, there were 709 such roll-call votes in the House and 325 in the Senate. The House total excludes one quorum call in 2017.

The House total counts all votes on procedural matters, including votes to approve the journal.

The presidential support and party unity studies are based on a set of votes selected according to the criteria detailed on pages 33 and 38.

INDIVIDUAL SCORES Member scores are based only on the votes each actually cast. This makes individual support and opposition scores total 100 percent. The same method is used to identify the leading scorers on pages 28-29 and 35.

Overall scores To be consistent with previous years, calculations of average scores by chamber and party are based on all eligible votes, whether or not all members cast a "yea" or "nay." The lack of participation by lawmakers in a roll call vote reduces chamber and party average support and opposition scores.

ROUNDING SCORES in the tables that follow are rounded to the nearest percentage point. Scores for the presidential and party support leaders are reported to one decimal point in order to rank them more precisely.

LEADING SCORERS: PRESIDENTIAL SUPPORT

SUPPORT shows those who, in 2017, voted most often for President Donald Trump's position when it was clearly known. **OPPOSITION** shows those who voted most often against his position. Absences do not count. Members with identical scores are listed alphabetically.

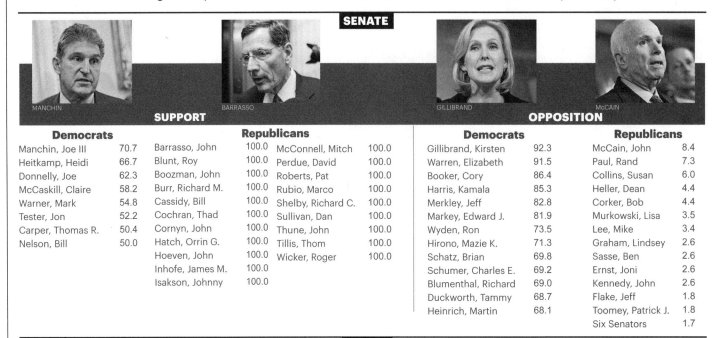

SENATE

MANCHIN — BARRASSO — GILLIBRAND — McCAIN

SUPPORT — **OPPOSITION**

Democrats (Support)

Manchin, Joe III	70.7
Heitkamp, Heidi	66.7
Donnelly, Joe	62.3
McCaskill, Claire	58.2
Warner, Mark	54.8
Tester, Jon	52.2
Carper, Thomas R.	50.4
Nelson, Bill	50.0

Republicans (Support)

Barrasso, John	100.0	McConnell, Mitch	100.0
Blunt, Roy	100.0	Perdue, David	100.0
Boozman, John	100.0	Roberts, Pat	100.0
Burr, Richard M.	100.0	Rubio, Marco	100.0
Cassidy, Bill	100.0	Shelby, Richard C.	100.0
Cochran, Thad	100.0	Sullivan, Dan	100.0
Cornyn, John	100.0	Thune, John	100.0
Hatch, Orrin G.	100.0	Tillis, Thom	100.0
Hoeven, John	100.0	Wicker, Roger	100.0
Inhofe, James M.	100.0		
Isakson, Johnny	100.0		

Democrats (Opposition)

Gillibrand, Kirsten	92.3
Warren, Elizabeth	91.5
Booker, Cory	86.4
Harris, Kamala	85.3
Merkley, Jeff	82.8
Markey, Edward J.	81.9
Wyden, Ron	73.5
Hirono, Mazie K.	71.3
Schatz, Brian	69.8
Schumer, Charles E.	69.2
Blumenthal, Richard	69.0
Duckworth, Tammy	68.7
Heinrich, Martin	68.1

Republicans (Opposition)

McCain, John	8.4
Paul, Rand	7.3
Collins, Susan	6.0
Heller, Dean	4.4
Corker, Bob	4.4
Murkowski, Lisa	3.5
Lee, Mike	3.4
Graham, Lindsey	2.6
Sasse, Ben	2.6
Ernst, Joni	2.6
Kennedy, John	2.6
Flake, Jeff	1.8
Toomey, Patrick J.	1.8
Six Senators	1.7

 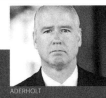  

HOUSE

PETERSON — ADERHOLT — ELLISON — JONES

SUPPORT — **OPPOSITION**

Democrats (Support)

Peterson, Collin C.	61.8
Cuellar, Henry	58.3
Sinema, Kyrsten	45.5
O'Halleran, Tom	38.9
Lipinski, Daniel	33.3
Murphy, Stephanie	31.4
Gottheimer, Josh	30.6
Rosen, Jacky	28.6
Costa, Jim	28.1
Ruiz, Raul	27.8
Schneider, Brad	27.8
Crist, Charlie	27.3
Peters, Scott	25.7
Bishop, Sanford D. Jr.	25.0
Bustos, Cheri	25.0

Republicans (100%)

Aderholt, Robert B.	Dunn, Neal	Pittenger, Robert
Allen, Rick W.	Fleischmann, Chuck	Reed, Tom
Amodei, Mark	Flores, Bill	Rice, Tom
Barletta, Lou	Gowdy, Trey	Rogers, Harold
Bergman, Jack	Granger, Kay	Rutherford, John
Bishop, Mike	Graves, Tom	Scalise, Steve
Bost, Mike	Guthrie, Brett	Scott, Austin
Brady, Kevin	Harper, Gregg	Sessions, Pete
Brooks, Susan W.	Higgins, Clay	Shimkus, John
Buchanan, Vern	Johnson, Bill	Shuster, Bill
Bucshon, Larry	Kelly, Mike	Simpson, Mike
Burgess, Michael C.	Kinzinger, Adam	Smucker, Lloyd K.
Calvert, Ken	Knight, Steve	Stivers, Steve
Carter, John	LaMalfa, Doug	Taylor, Scott
Carter, Earl L. "Buddy"	Lucas, Frank D.	Tenney, Claudia
Chaffetz, Jason	McCarthy, Kevin	Thompson, Glenn
Cole, Tom	McCaul, Michael	Tiberi, Pat
Collins, Chris	McHenry, Patrick T.	Trott, Dave
Conaway, K. Michael	McKinley, David B.	Upton, Fred
Cook, Paul	McMorris Rodgers, Cathy	Valadao, David
Cramer, Kevin	Moolenaar, John	Walberg, Tim
Crawford, Rick	Murphy, Tim	Walden, Greg
Culberson, John	Newhouse, Dan	Walters, Mimi
Davis, Rodney	Nunes, Devin	Wilson, Joe
Denham, Jeff	Paulsen, Erik	Womack, Steve
		Woodall, Rob
		Young, David

Democrats (Opposition)

Ellison, Keith	94.4
Espaillat, Adriano	94.4
Grijalva, Raul M.	94.4
Waters, Maxine	94.4
Gutierrez, Luis V.	94.1
Hastings, Alcee L.	93.9
Cohen, Steve	91.7
DeSaulnier, Mark	91.7
Fudge, Marcia L.	91.7
Jayapal, Pramila	91.7
Lee, Barbara	91.7
Pallone, Frank Jr.	91.7
Raskin, Jamie	91.7
Schakowsky, Jan	91.7
Serrano, Jose E.	91.7
Watson Coleman, Bonnie	91.7
Lewis, John	91.4
Velazquez, Nydia M.	91.4
Wasserman Schultz, Debbie	91.4
Bass, Karen	91.2
Carson, Andre	91.2
Davis, Danny K.	91.2
Deutch, Ted	91.2
Payne, Donald M. Jr.	91.2
Richmond, Cedric L.	90.9
Smith, Adam	90.9
Cummings, Elijah E.	89.7
Pocan, Mark	89.7

Republicans (Opposition)

Jones, Walter B.	46.7
Amash, Justin	36.1
Ros-Lehtinen, Ileana	32.3
Smith, Christopher H.	28.6
LoBiondo, Frank A.	27.8
Massie, Thomas	22.2
Donovan, Dan	22.2
King, Peter T.	19.4
Sanford, Mark	19.4
Curbelo, Carlos	17.1
Biggs, Andy	16.7
Duncan, John J. Jr.	16.7
Fitzpatrick, Brian	16.7
Zeldin, Lee	16.7
Brooks, Mo	15.6
Faso, John J.	13.9
Frelinghuysen, Rodney	13.9
Lance, Leonard	13.9
Meehan, Patrick	13.9
Reichert, Dave	13.9
Stefanik, Elise	13.9
Gosar, Paul	12.9
Griffith, Morgan	11.8
Hollingsworth, Trey	11.4
Seven Representatives	11.1

2017 VOTES: PRESIDENTIAL POSITION

These were the 36 House and 117 Senate roll-call votes in 2017 on which the president took a clear position. A victory is a vote on which the president's position prevailed. For full captions with the president's positions, see CQ.com.

HOUSE

Defense and Foreign Policy

VOTE
NUMBER   DESCRIPTION

1 Victory

136   Appropriations

Domestic Policy

VOTE
NUMBER   DESCRIPTION

31 Victories

65	Abortion funding
73	Environmental regulation
76	Labor regulation
77	Firearms regulation
78	Environmental regulation
83	Public Lands
84	Education policy
85	Education policy
97	Labor regulation
121	Labor regulation
184	Health care policy
186	Health care policy
202	Telecommunications regulation
244	Labor regulation
249	Appropriations
256	Health care policy
306	Health care policy
307	Veterans affairs
337	Tort law
342	Immigration policy
344	Immigration policy
412	Labor regulation
480	Diseaster supplemental
517	Immigration policy
528	Appropriations
542	Appropriations
549	Abortion rights
604	Health care policy
630	Flood insurance
670	Appropriations
708	Appropriations

Economic Policy and Trade

VOTE
NUMBER   DESCRIPTION

4 Victories

72	Financial regulation
637	Tax overhaul
692	Tax overhaul
699	Tax overhaul

House Success

Victories	36
Defeats	0
Total	36
Success rate	**100.0%**

SENATE

Domestic Policy

VOTE
NUMBER   DESCRIPTION

17 Victories

43	Environmental regulation
66	Firearms regulation
81	Labor regulation
82	Public lands
83	Education policy
84	Education policy
87	Labor regulation
93	Labor regulation
99	Labor regulation
109	Senate procedure
120	Labor regulation
121	Appropriations
167	Health care policy
192	Disaster supplemental
219	Budget resolution
311	Appropriations
325	Appropriations

2 Defeats

169	Health care policy
179	Health care policy

Economic Policy and Trade

VOTE
NUMBER   DESCRIPTION

4 Victories

51	Financial regulation
249	Financial regulation
303	Tax overhaul
323	Tax overhaul

Nominations

VOTE
NUMBER   DESCRIPTION

94 Victories

29	James Mattis
30	John F. Kelly
32	Mike Pompeo
33	Nikki R. Haley
35	Elaine L. Chao
36	Rex W. Tillerson
54	Elisabeth Prince DeVos
59	Jeff Sessions
61	Thomas Price
63	Steven T. Mnuchin
64	David J. Shulkin
65	Linda E. McMahon
68	Mick Mulvaney
71	Scott Pruitt
73	Wilbur L. Ross, Jr.
75	Ryan Zinke
77	Benjamin S. Carson, Sr.
79	James Richard Perry
86	Seema Verma
89	Daniel Coats
90	Herbert R. McMaster Jr.
91	Charles R. Breyer and Danny C. Reeves
96	David Friedman
103	Elaine C. Duke
111	Neil M. Gorsuch
112	Sonny Perdue
114	Rod J. Rosenstein
116	R. Alexander Acosta
118	Jay Clayton
122	Heather Wilson
124	Scott Gottlieb
127	Robert Lighthizer
129	Jeffrey A. Rosen
131	Rachel L. Brand
133	Terry Branstad
135	John J. Sullivan
137	Amul R. Thapar
139	Courtney Elwood
141	Scott P. Brown
142	Kenneth P. Rapuano
148	Brock Long
150	Sigal Mandelker
152	Marshall Billingslea
154	Kristine L. Svinicki
156	Neomi Rao
158	David C. Nye
160	William Francis Hagerty IV
162	Patrick M. Shanahan
164	John Kenneth Bush
166	David Bernhardt
181	Christopher A. Wray
182	Kevin Christopher Newsom
184	Marvin Kaplan
186	Dan R. Brouillette
188	Timothy J. Kelly
194	Kevin Allen Hassett
196	Pamela Hughes Patenaude
201	Noel J. Francisco
203	William J. Emanuel
204	Heath P. Tarbert
205	Makan Delrahim
207	Ralph R. Erickson
209	Ajit Varadaraj Pai
211	Eric D. Hargan
213	Randal Quarles
215	Lee Francis Cissna
217	Callista L. Gingrich
218	David Joel Trachtenberg
251	Scott L. Palk
253	Trevor N. McFadden
255	Amy Coney Barrett
257	Joan Louise Larsen
259	Allison H. Eid
261	Stephanos Bibas
262	John H. Gibson II
264	Steven Andrew Engel
266	Peter B. Robb
268	William L. Wehrum
270	Derek Kan
272	Steven Gill Bradbury
274	Mark T. Esper
275	David G. Zatezalo
277	Joseph Otting
280	Donald C. Coggins, Jr.
281	Dabney Langhorne Friedrich
283	Gregory G. Katsas
305	Kirstjen Nielsen
310	Joseph Balash
313	Leonard Steven Grasz
315	Don R. Willett
317	James C. Ho
318	J. Paul Compton, Jr.
319	Owen West
320	Jennifer Gillian Newstead

SENATE SUCCESS

Victories	115
Defeats	2
Total	117
Success rate	**98.3%**
Success rate without nomination	**71.4%**

TOTAL Congress Success

Victories	151
Defeats	2
Total	153
Success rate	**98.7%**

It's All About Togetherness

Senate Republicans set a record for harmony in 2017; The House GOP came close

The chasm between the parties deepened in President Donald Trump's inaugural year as Republicans, working with narrower majorities in both chambers, united to slash taxes, nullify regulations and, in the Senate, confirm nominees.

CQ's annual vote study shows the House in 2017 was more deeply divided than at any time in more than six decades of such analyses. Party unity votes — defined as those with each party's majority on opposing sides — accounted for more than 3 of every 4 roll-call votes. The House had 539 party unity votes.

On the other side of the Capitol, party unity tallies accounted for more than 2 of every 3 Senate roll-call votes, the fifth-highest mark since Congressional Quarterly began the reviews in a consistent manner in 1954. The Senate had 224 party unity votes in 2017.

Senate Republicans stuck with their caucus an average of 97 percent of the time on such votes, an all-time high for either party, surpassing by 3 percentage points the previous record set by Republicans in 2003 and duplicated by Democrats in 2013. Senate Democrats voted with their party an average of 92 percent of the time.

In the House, Republicans were united an average of 92 percent of the time, a notch below their record in 2016, while Democrats voted with their party an average of 93 percent of the time, just above previous high points of 92 percent in 2007, 2008 and 2015.

John J. Pitney Jr., a professor of politics at Claremont McKenna University and a former GOP aide, says that the rise in party unity mirrored a polarization of the electorate and all levels of government, and predicted it would be a kind of template.

"Maybe not at the 97 percent level, but I think we are going to see polarized voting in the House and Senate stretch to the horizon," Pitney says.

From the session's start, Speaker Paul D. Ryan of Wisconsin and Senate Majority Leader Mitch McConnell of Kentucky and their teams worked through an ambitious to-do list, tailoring bills and structuring votes to build consensus within their parties.

The irony of the intense party unity in 2017 is that it wasn't always enough. The majorities, thinner than they were in the previous Congress, especially in the Senate, meant that Republicans had little margin to spare.

Fissures among Senate Republicans unraveled the drive for a filibuster proof reconciliation bill to repeal the 2010 health care overhaul. Even in the House, Republicans needed two runs at the health care bill to get their repeal passed. Party leaders abandoned the vote in the initial run.

Strong Senate GOP unity secured other victories for Trump, such as a resounding December triumph with enactment of a second reconciliation measure to rewrite the tax code, repeal of the individual mandate under the health care law and permit oil drilling in the Arctic National Wildlife Refuge.

Senate Republicans were also able to reverse 15 regulations using the Congressional Review Act in 2017.

Overall, Senate Republicans won 201, or 89.7 percent, of the party unity votes. That was well above the previous top GOP win rate of 83.1 percent in 1981, President Ronald Reagan's first year in office.

And House Republicans won on 90.5 percent of the party unity votes, just a tad less than their record winning percentage in 2016.

In the Senate, McConnell set the stage for the year as Republicans unilaterally ended the filibuster for Supreme Court judges, while leaving it in place for legislation.

The move cleared the way for confirmation of Supreme Court Justice Neil Gorsuch and mirrored the Democrats' use of the same tactic, dubbed the nuclear option, to end filibusters of executive and other judicial nominations in 2013.

Senate Majority Whip John Cornyn, a Texas Republican, links the GOP's tough playbook not to revenge, but to necessity. He points to the Democrats' "monolithic resistance to everything that this president has tried to do or has his name on it" and to near parity in the Senate.

Republicans there have since seen their numbers shrink by one, to 51, following the December election of Democrat Doug Jones from Alabama.

"My hope is that 2018 will be different because, obviously, the margin is thinner, and thankfully there are a number of things we agree on," Cornyn says.

He refers to Trump's expected infrastructure package and possible bipartisan measures dealing with issues such as financial services regulation and criminal justice.

One early test could be on an immigration bill, where some Senate Democrats and Republicans appear to have found common ground. But conservative Republicans and progressive Democrats could nevertheless be tugging them apart.

Republicans like Marco Rubio of Florida say a high level of Senate GOP unity — and division between the parties — might be sustained if the leadership continues its emphasis on moving items with broad GOP support.

"What comes to the floor is so tightly controlled now," Rubio says.

With little room for bipartisan bills or compromise, Senate Minority Whip Richard J. Durbin, the second-ranking Democrat, says frustration was increasing on both sides last year. He predicts more rough patches ahead.

"When Republicans are more Republican, and Democrats are more Democrat, we tend to get very little done," he says.

Durbin links the sour relations between the parties in part to the targeting of vulnerable Democrats.

"Some of it could relate to half of our caucus being up for re-election. Historically — they deny it — but you don't want to give the senator in cycle a good headline or a good result," Durbin says.

Despite the partisanship, some lawmakers found reasons to join

LEADING SCORERS: PARTY UNITY

Support shows those who, in 2017, voted most often with a majority of their party against a majority of the other party. **Opposition** shows those who voted most often against their party in these votes. Absences do not count. Members with identical scores are listed alphabetically.

SENATE

FRANKEN — HOEVEN — HEITKAMP — COLLINS

SUPPORT | **OPPOSITION**

Democrats		Republicans		Democrats		Republicans	
Franken, Al	100.0	Hoeven, John	100.0	Manchin, Joe III	35.9	Collins, Susan	13.4
Cantwell, Maria	99.5	Inhofe, James M.	100.0	Heitkamp, Heidi	30.5	Paul, Rand	7.2
Merkley, Jeff	99.5	Johnson, Ron	100.0	Donnelly, Joe	26.3	McCain, John	7.0
Murray, Patty	99.5	Lankford, James	100.0	McCaskill, Claire	17.8	Heller, Dean	6.5
Van Hollen, Chris	99.5	Rubio, Marco	100.0	Warner, Mark	16.5	Murkowski, Lisa	6.3
Wyden, Ron	99.5	Scott, Tim	100.0	Tester, Jon	12.7	Corker, Bob	3.6
Baldwin, Tammy	99.1	Barrasso, John	99.6	Carper, Thomas R.	11.8	Lee, Mike	3.1
Blumenthal, Richard	99.1	Cotton, Tom	99.6	Nelson, Bill	11.8	Kennedy, John	2.7
Markey, Edward J.	99.1	Crapo, Michael D.	99.6	Bennet, Michael	9.4	Alexander, Lamar	2.3
Schumer, Charles E.	99.1	Ernst, Joni	99.6	Coons, Chris	8.9	Portman, Rob	2.2
Whitehouse, Sheldon	99.1	Risch, Jim	99.6	Cortez Masto, Catherine	6.5	Capito, Shelley Moore	1.8
Harris, Kamala	98.7	Thune, John	99.6	Kaine, Tim	6.3	Graham, Lindsey	1.8
Warren, Elizabeth	98.7	Wicker, Roger	99.6	Shaheen, Jeanne	5.4	Grassley, Charles E.	1.8
						Isakson, Johnny	1.6

HOUSE

GRIJALVA — SCALISE — SINEMA — FITZPATRICK

SUPPORT | **OPPOSITION**

Democrats		Republicans		Democrats		Republicans	
Grijalva, Raúl M.	100.0	Scalise, Steve	100.0	Peterson, Collin C.	32.1	Jones, Walter B.	41.5
Jayapal, Pramila	100.0	Allen, Rick W.	99.8	Sinema, Kyrsten	24.6	Fitzpatrick, Brian	24.2
Lewis, John	100.0	Black, Diane	99.6	Cuellar, Henry	24.0	LoBiondo, Frank A.	20.6
McGovern, Jim	100.0	Chabot, Steve	99.6	Costa, Jim	20.5	Amash, Justin	20.4
Schakowsky, Jan	100.0	Chaffetz, Jason	99.6	Gottheimer, Josh	17.1	Smith, Christopher H.	17.0
Bass, Karen	99.8	Gowdy, Trey	99.6	Murphy, Stephanie	13.8	Ros-Lehtinen, Ileana	16.0
Khanna, Ro	99.8	Johnson, Sam	99.6	Cooper, Jim	13.6	Costello, Ryan A.	16.0
Lee, Barbara	99.8	Ross, Dennis A.	99.6	Schrader, Kurt	13.1	Curbelo, Carlos	15.9
Pallone, Frank Jr.	99.8	Bilirakis, Gus	99.4	O'Halleran, Tom	13.0	Lance, Leonard	15.5
Raskin, Jamie	99.8	DesJarlais, Scott	99.4	Peters, Scott	12.5	Katko, John	14.6
Sarbanes, John	99.8	Ferguson, Drew	99.4	Schneider, Brad	12.1	Faso, John J.	13.6
Slaughter, Louise M.	99.8	Olson, Pete	99.4	Lipinski, Daniel	11.5	Meehan, Patrick	12.7
Tonko, Paul	99.8	Sessions, Pete	99.4	Suozzi, Tom	11.3	Reichert, Dave	12.5
		Webster, Daniel	99.4			MacArthur, Tom	12.2

the other side.

Among Republicans, Susan Collins of Maine scored 87 percent, John McCain of Arizona and Rand Paul of Kentucky both scored 93 percent and Dean Heller of Nevada and Lisa Murkowski of Alaska both scored 94 percent. Heller faces a competitive re-election race this year.

For Senate Democrats, low party unity scores reflected a poten-

tially tough campaign in a red or purple state.

Joe Manchin III of West Virginia scored 64 percent; Heidi Heitkamp of North Dakota, 70 percent; Joe Donnelly of Indiana, 74 percent; Angus King of Maine, an independent who sits with the Democrats, 81 percent; and Claire McCaskill of Missouri, 82 percent. All five are up for re-election in 2018.

In the House, Republicans moved priorities for the most part by

regular order through committee, but also set a modern record with 58 closed rules in the first session of the 115th Congress, beating the previous record of 48 closed rules in 2015.

Rules Chairman Pete Sessions of Texas says the closed-rule milestone was inflated by a drive to reverse pending Obama-era regulations with disapproval resolutions under the Congressional Review Act.

But he attributes the high level of party unity among House Republicans to efforts by party leaders to settle disputes and rally support.

"This was our own internal effort," he says.

Trump did not play a formal role in such consensus-building efforts, but David R. Mayhew, an emeritus professor of political science at Yale University, says the president's stands on certain issues sent a clear message to the party's base and to House conservatives.

"Trump has helped on the House side to keep the tea party people in line, to get them to line up behind Ryan. They can defy Ryan. I think it's hard for them to defy Trump," Mayhew says.

While House Republicans unified behind top priorities, Rep. Louise M. Slaughter of New York, ranking Democrat on Rules, complained in a written statement that the spate of closed rules and other hardball tactics made the first session of the 115th Congress the "most closed" session in history, and prevented Democrats from "doing their job representing their constituents and amending legislation."

As in the Senate, some House members still found room to break ranks.

Among Republicans, Walter B. Jones of North Carolina scored 58 percent; Bryan Fitzpatrick of Pennsylvania, 76 percent; Frank A. LoBiondo of New Jersey, 79 percent; Justin Amash of Michigan, 80 percent; Christopher H. Smith of New Jersey, 83 percent; Ryan A. Costello of Pennsylvania, and Carlos Curbelo and Ileana Ros-Lehtinen, both of Florida, each at 84 percent.

For Democrats, Collin C. Peterson of Minnesota scored 68 percent; Kyrsten Sinema of Arizona, 75 percent; Henry Cuellar of Texas, 76 percent; Jim Costa of California, 80 percent; and Josh Gott-heimer of New Jersey, 83 percent.

As the midterm elections approach, endangered incumbents may feel more pressure to switch sides. But Pitney predicts firm GOP control of floor votes and strong party cohesion on both sides.

"At a time when it's possible that either party could gain control of either chamber, the outcome of the next election is going to shape every roll-call vote," Pitney says. ∎

Appendix C

KEY VOTES

Key Senate and House Votes in 2017

The oldest of CQ Roll Call's annual studies, Key Votes is a selection of the major votes for both House and Senate for the past year. Editors choose the single vote on each issue that best presents a member's stance or that determined the year's legistative outcome. Charts of how each member voted on this list can be found at cq.com.

SENATE VOTES

43. Stream Protection Rule.

Passage of joint resolution (HJ Res 38) nullifying an Office of Surface Mining Reclamation and Enforcement rule requiring surface coal mining operations to avoid disturbing streams and land within 100 feet of streams. Passed, clearing it for the president, 54-45 (R 50-1; D 4-42; I 0-2) on Feb. 2, 2017.

The Interior Department rule finalized in December 2016 was among the first victims of a Republican assault on environmental programs established by Barack Obama's administration. One day after the House voted mainly along party lines to pass a Congressional Review Act resolution nullifying the Stream Protection Rule, the Senate followed suit and sent the bill to President Donald Trump.

The CRA gives Congress authority to block recently finalized regulations. This was just the second time Congress used the law, but many more CRA resolutions were on the GOP agenda in 2017 as part of a systematic plan to roll back rules established by Obama, especially in the environmental arena.

Only one Republican, Susan Collins of Maine, voted with the Democrats, while four Democrats from coal-rich states — all up for re-election in 2018 — went along with the resolution.

Majority Leader Mitch McConnell said the regulation would have a devastating impact in his home state of Kentucky. "One study actually estimated that this regulation would put as many as one-third of coal-related jobs at risk," he said.

54. Confirmation of Betsy DeVos.

Confirmation of Betsy DeVos of Michigan to be secretary of Education. Confirmed, with Vice President Mike Pence casting a "yea" vote to break the tie, by a vote of 50-50 (R 50-2; D 0-46; I 0-2) on Feb. 7, 2017.

Up until February 2017, Trump's nominees for Cabinet positions had mostly sailed through. But many on the left, still smarting from the Democrats' humiliating losses in November 2016, were scouting an opportunity to block someone. At the same time, a host of issues, from Trump's travel ban to his executive orders on refugees, had galvanized many on the left. Phone calls flooded the Capitol urging senators to block Trump's agenda at all costs.

By the end of January, Democratic leaders had changed tack. Senate Minority Leader Charles E. Schumer of New York vowed to attempt to block nearly all of Trump's remaining Cabinet nominees, including Betsy DeVos, Trump's pick to lead the Education Department.

There was only one problem with this new strategy: As the minority party, Democrats had no real chance of stopping any of the nominees, and they had themselves to blame. In 2013, Senate Democrats, frustrated by stalling tactics from Republicans on judicial nominees, eliminated the use of the filibuster — with its 60-vote threshold to

end debate — on all executive branch nominees and judicial picks, with the exception of Supreme Court nominees. McConnell, then the minority leader, warned that Democrats would rue that day.

He was right. In 2017, Democrats could only succeed in blocking Trump's picks by peeling off Republican votes. They almost got there with DeVos, a billionaire Republican donor with no real background in public education.

Democrats called the Michigan native and voucher supporter "uniquely unqualified" and held the Senate floor for 24 hours to decry her nomination. In wee-hour floor speeches they highlighted awkward moments from DeVos' confirmation hearing. One constant trope: her apparent confusion over whether states had discretion in complying with the Individuals with Disabilities Education Act. DeVos sent a letter to Georgia Republican Johnny Isakson clarifying her stance, saying she was "committed to enforcing all federal laws and protecting the hard won rights of students with disabilities."

Ahead of the vote, two moderate Republicans, Collins and Lisa Murkowski of Alaska, said they would vote against DeVos. Democrats needed just one more vote, but they fell short. DeVos squeaked through when Vice President Mike Pence cast the deciding vote to break a 50-50 logjam — the first time a vice president was needed to break a tie on a Cabinet nomination.

57. Elizabeth Warren Ordered to Sit Down.

Affirming the ruling of the chair that one member had broken Senate rules by impugning the motives of another member during debate. Sustained 49-43 (R 49-0; D 0-42; I 0-1) on Feb. 7, 2017.

Republicans en masse endorsed McConnell's extraordinary public shaming of one of the nation's most prominent Democrats, Elizabeth Warren of Massachusetts. It was more than the year's first unmistakable signal that vituperative and sometimes petty partisan skirmishing would continue to define a chamber once revered as "the world's greatest deliberative body."

In hindsight, it also created an early headline in a defining story of 2017: the surge of American women demanding a reckoning for men who have abused their positions of power in the workplace and then retaliated against victims unwilling to stay silent.

The #MeToo movement arrived at the Capitol in an unlikely guise. The debate on the nomination of GOP Sen. Jeff Sessions of Alabama to be Trump's attorney general was supposed to be all about race, given the senator's controversial record on civil rights. But that changed when Warren, already touted by progressives as a 2020 presidential favorite, delivered an impassioned speech against confirmation that quoted Coretta Scott King, the widow of the Rev. Martin Luther King Jr., labeling Sessions a "reprehensible" nominee in 1986 for a federal judgeship.

McConnell demanded Warren be told to take her seat for violating Rule XIX, which says senators may not "directly or indirectly, by any form of words impute to another senator or to other senators any conduct or motive unworthy or unbecoming" of a senator.

"She was warned. She was given an explanation. Nevertheless, she persisted," McConnell intoned—his summation quickly claimed as a meme on all manner of social media excoriations and fundraising appeals from women's rights advocates declaring they were through with being overpowered or shushed.

Democrats warned McConnell had further threatened the fragile state of collegiality and decorum in the Senate by enforcing the rule in a selective and partisan way, noting how GOP senators in previous months had labeled colleagues "liars" and "cancerous."

The Senate vote along party lines had the short-term effect of preventing Warren from speaking more on the floor during the Sessions debate. But she later posted a video of her reading Scott's letter on Facebook, and 2 million watched in a matter of hours.

66. Social Security Gun Rule.

Passage of a joint resolution (HJ Res 40) nullifying a Social Security Administration rule requiring that individuals who need assistance managing their disability benefits because they suffer from a mental impairment be included in the National Instant Criminal Background Check System, barring them from buying guns from licensed gun shops. Passed, clearing it for the president, 57-43 (R 52-0; D 4-42; I 1-1) on Feb. 15, 2017.

After the House advanced a resolution in early February to repeal an Obama administration rule prohibiting Social Security beneficiaries with mental deficiencies from purchasing guns, the Senate approved the measure using the Congressional Review Act, which bars a filibuster and requires only a simple majority.

The vote attracted four Democrats, Joe Donnelly of Indiana, Heidi Heitkamp of North Dakota, Joe Manchin III of West Virginia and Jon Tester of Montana, along with Angus King of Maine, an independent who caucuses with them. They joined a united GOP.

The rule, finalized in December 2016, would have prohibited roughly 75,000 people from buying firearms from gun shops.

In debate ahead of the vote, Republican Charles E. Grassley of Iowa said the rule was "defective" for a number of reasons. "Namely, the regulation does not require the agency to prove a person is dangerous or mentally ill," he said.

In highlighting her support for the rule, Democrat Dianne Feinstein of California took note of a 2011 case in Missouri in which a woman diagnosed with paranoid schizophrenia used her Social Security disability payments to legally buy a gun and later used it to kill her father. The White House weighed in saying "this rule could endanger the Second Amendment rights of law abiding citizens." On Feb. 28, Trump signed the resolution repealing the rule.

What Makes a Key Vote

Since its 1945 founding, CQ Roll Call has selected a series of key votes in Congress on major issues of the year.

A vote is judged to be key by the extent to which it represents:
- a matter of major controversy.
- a matter of presidential or political power.
- a matter of potentially great impact on the nation and the lives of Americans.

For each group of related votes on an issue in each chamber, one key vote is usually chosen — one that, in the opinion of CQ Roll Call editors, was most important in determining the outcome of the issue for the year or best reflected the views of individual lawmakers on that issue.

109. Nuclear Option Vote for Gorsuch.

Rejection of a ruling by the chair that invoking cloture on a Supreme Court nominee requires support from three-fifths of all senators, effectively creating a simple majority threshold for such confirmations. Rejected 48-52 (R 0-52; D 46-0; I 2-0) on April 6, 2017.

This vote cleaved the Senate cleanly into its partisan camps, obliterating the last vestige of a venerated core value: the right of a minority of senators to thwart any presidential nomination.

The moment not only pushed the no-holds-barred nature of partisan combat in Congress to a new level, eliminating the need for cross-aisle consensus in filling seats on the Supreme Court. It also assured confirmation the next day of Neil Gorsuch as the first unambiguously conservative new justice on the court in 11 years.

It was the first legacy-making victory in Congress for Trump, who had courted the cultural and religious right with promises to reshape the federal courts to their liking. The 54-45 confirmation vote also rewarded McConnell for a bold gamble: the unprecedented move to hold a Supreme Court seat vacant for longer than a year.

Those triumphs would not have been possible had not Republicans executed what was ominously dubbed "the nuclear option." A complex procedural maneuver, its use threatened to lay waste to longstanding traditions of deliberation, comity and the rights of the minority party.

The initial seeds for the climactic parliamentary showdown were sown four years earlier, when the power structure was inverted: Obama was president and his fellow Democrats ran the Senate, but their efforts to secure confirmations were routinely stymied by the minority Republicans. To break the logjam, the Democratic majority in November 2013 deployed the first nuclear option, lowering the threshold from a three-fifths majority to a simple majority on motions to invoke cloture and limit debate on all executive branch and judicial nominees—except for the Supreme Court.

"You will regret this, and you may regret it a lot sooner than you think," McConnell warned at the time.

His moment to counterattack opened in February 2016 when Justice Antonin Scalia died after almost three decades as the conservative icon on the court. Ninety minutes after the death was reported, McConnell announced he would block Obama from filling the vacancy during his final year in office, declaring the nomination rightfully belonged to the next president. True to his word, the GOP leader denied so much as a confirmation hearing to Obama's choice, D.C. Circuit Court of Appeals Judge Merrick Garland.

Trump had promised that if elected he would choose from a roster of 21 judges assembled by the right-facing Federalist Society and Heritage Foundation. Twelve days into his presidency he tapped Gorsuch, a highly credentialed and reliably conservative 49-year-old appeals judge on the 10th Circuit.

Democratic leaders lamented the more ideologically extreme aspects of Gorsuch's record, questioned whether he would remain independent of the president who nominated him, and barely hid

their fury that the vacancy still existed. So they launched what they hoped would become the first-ever successful partisan filibuster of a Supreme Court nominee, fully aware McConnell would respond with the final precedent-shattering move of the battle.

Under the longstanding rules, invoking cloture and advancing Gorsuch toward the dispositive vote required eight Democrats to join the Republicans to form a supermajority of 60. But just four broke ranks the morning of April 6, three of them facing re-election races in 2018 in states Trump carried easily: Indiana's Donnelly, North Dakota's Heitkamp and West Virginia's Manchin.

At that point, it took McConnell just an hour to orchestrate a series of procedural steps that changed the rules, climaxing when all 52 GOP senators (but no Democrats) voted in favor of adding Supreme Court picks to the roster of all the other nominees who must win only a simple majority for confirmation.

138. Embassy in Israel.

Adoption of a resolution (S Res 176) reaffirming support for a 1995 law compelling relocation of the United States embassy in Israel to Jerusalem from Tel Aviv. Adopted 90-0 (R 47-0; D 41-0; I 2-0) on June 5, 2017.

The vote was an unambiguous and bipartisan push for Trump to keep one of the most contentious promises of his campaign. He took a fundamental step toward doing so in December, formally recognizing Jerusalem as Israel's capital and launching a several-years-long process for moving the U.S. embassy there.

The move upended seven decades of American foreign policy, annoyed U.S. allies in Europe and the Arab world, and cast serious doubt on prospects for a peace agreement brokered by the Trump administration between the Palestinians and the Israelis. But it was what Congress had officially insisted on for 22 years, since enactment of a law ordering the embassy's relocation from Tel Aviv.

That statute also permitted presidents to postpone the move indefinitely, in six-month increments, if they determined the delay was in the interests of national security. Bill Clinton, George W. Bush and Barack Obama all routinely issued such waivers.

Trump had vowed to end that practice. But on June 1 he signed yet another waiver, deeply disappointing evangelical voters and pro-Israel American Jews. He described the decision as a delay to give the peace process more time, the same rationale of his predecessors. (Like every other country with a diplomatic post in Israel, U.S. envoys are in Tel Aviv to avoid affronting Palestinians, who also eye Jerusalem as the capital of their hoped-for state.)

Senators offered a fresh rejection of those arguments just four days later. The resolution, while technically non-binding, gained significant symbolic weight after not a single Republican nor Democrat voted against it. And when it was time for the next waiver, Trump changed course.

Joining almost all nations in declining to label Jerusalem as Israel's capital, he said, has brought us "no closer to a lasting peace agreement," and "it would be folly to assume that repeating the exact same formula would now produce a different or better result."

175. Russia Sanctions.

Passage of a bill (HR 3364) imposing sanctions on Iran, North Korea and Russia. Passed, clearing it for the president, 98-2 (R 51-1; D 46-0; I 1-1) on July 27, 2017.

Trump's election divided Republicans on Capitol Hill, but they found common cause in new tax legislation and repeal of the 2010 health care law, while rescinding Obama-era regulations.

But Trump and the congressional GOP split, most notably, in July, when the Senate followed the House in passing a bill to slap new sanctions on Russia, Iran and North Korea, and to bar Trump from lifting sanctions on Russia without Congress' say-so.

The Senate vote was 98-2 with no votes only from Republican Rand Paul of Kentucky, an opponent of unilateral sanctions, and independent Bernie Sanders of Vermont, who said he worried the new sanctions would undermine the agreement Obama had reached with Iran to end its nuclear weapons program. The vote followed U.S. intelligence agencies' assessment that Russia had interfered in the 2016 election and marked a rare moment of unity between parties on how best to respond.

Facing a veto-proof majority, Trump waffled about signing it, then did so with a rebuke: "This bill makes it harder for the United States to strike good deals for the American people, and will drive China, Russia and North Korea much closer together," he said.

Foreign Relations Chairman Bob Corker, a Tennessee Republican, led the push for the bill, foreboding his later split with Trump. Corker said he feared that Trump's approach to foreign policy was putting the United States "on the path to World War III."

179. McCain Ends Bid to Repeal Health Care Law.

Rejection of an amendment to a bill (HR 1628) to repeal the 2010 health care law's individual mandate, eliminate the employer mandate through 2024, delay implementation of the medical device tax through 2020 and effectively defund Planned Parenthood for one year. Rejected 49-51 (R 49-3; D 0-46; I 0-2) on July 28, 2017.

No vote in 2017 better symbolized the inability of Republicans to govern than the dramatic "no" vote from Arizona's John McCain that torpedoed the GOP's seven-year quest to repeal Obama's health care overhaul. The rejection of the "skinny" repeal measure was a humiliating setback for Trump as well as McConnell, whose reputation as a master tactician was damaged.

Piecing together repeal legislation was a high-wire act that divided Republicans, especially those from states that expanded Medicaid under the law. Among the vexing issues: how to make up for money lost by repeal of the law's taxes and how to roll back the law's insurance regulations. Democrats made clear they would not participate in eroding the safety net provided by the law.

Senators had already blocked a repeal-and-replace measure in a procedural vote and rejected a partial repeal outright. McConnell's scaled-down repeal offered as an amendment to the House-passed health care bill (HR 1628) was the last option for Republicans to deliver on their No. 1 legislative priority.

Although wavering senators were told it was merely a means to get to conference with the House, its impact was hard to ignore. About 15 million fewer people would have health care coverage the following year than under current law. Premiums were projected to be 20 percent higher, hitting the poor and elderly the hardest.

Collins and Murkowski were adamant they would not vote for repeals that would raise costs, leave more uninsured or make deep cuts to Medicaid. They had voted "no" on the other repeal measures, so it was no surprise when they did the same on the "skinny" repeal.

The linchpin was McCain. The 2008 GOP presidential nominee had already scripted an element of drama when he returned to the Capitol earlier in the week, after being diagnosed with brain cancer, to cast an important vote to proceed with the health care debate.

In a telling sign of what was to come, McCain appealed for bipartisanship and a return to "regular order" by legislating through committees with input from all sides. Just hours after McConnell unveiled his amendment in the wee hours of July 28, all eyes were on McCain, who doomed the GOP's repeal with a barely audible "no" and flashed his thumb downward. Later, McCain said he opposed the "skinny" repeal bill partly because of how it was built: without consultation with Democrats or hearings and without consideration of the recommendations of governors.

192. Disaster Funding.

Motion to concur with an amendment to a bill (HR 601) to make available $15.25 billion in emergency supplemental funding for fiscal 2017 to partially cover the costs of responding to natural disasters, including Hurricane Harvey, and to suspend the public debt limit. Agreed to 80-17 (R 33-17; D 45-0; I 2-0) on Sept. 7, 2017.

Backed into a corner by the president, McConnell went along with a Democratic plan for both funding the government and providing disaster relief to hurricane-ravaged Texas, just as another monster storm was bearing down on Florida.

On Sept. 6, Trump out-maneuvered the savvy Senate majority leader by backing a plan put forward by Schumer and the top Democrat in the House, Nancy Pelosi of California. It called for adding $15.25 billion in disaster aid to a continuing resolution that extended the debt limit and kept the government funded until Dec. 8 — a deal that had been rejected earlier by GOP leadership.

"Look, the president can speak for himself, but his feeling was that we needed to come together to not create a picture of divisiveness at a time of genuine national crisis, and that was the rationale," McConnell said.

Fiscal hard-liners in his party were not pleased, citing the need to find offsets for the increased spending. Rand Paul of Kentucky proposed an amendment to pay for disaster relief with money from foreign aid programs, while Ben Sasse of Nebraska sought to make the bill a stand-alone emergency package without action on the debt and appropriations. Both efforts failed.

In the end 17 Republicans cast the only no votes, including deficit hawks like Corker and McCain.

It would be the first of three emergency aid packages needed as part of fiscal 2017 and 2018 appropriations, with costs piling up to more than $130 billion after Hurricanes Irma and Maria followed in the wake of Harvey, causing severe damage in Florida, Puerto Rico and elsewhere.

The September supplemental would be followed a week later by an omnibus package to finish up fiscal 2017 funding, setting the stage for action in fits and starts on the fiscal 2018 budget.

249. Arbitration Rule.

Passage of a joint resolution (HJ Res 111) nullifying a Consumer Financial Protection Bureau rule that prohibited mandatory arbitration clauses in consumer contracts. Passed, clearing it for the president, 50-50 (R 50-2; D 0-46; I 0-2) with Vice President Mike Pence casting a "yea" vote to break the tie on Oct. 24, 2017.

When the Senate in October passed a resolution rescinding a Consumer Financial Protection Bureau rule barring companies from requiring customers to arbitrate disputes rather than go to court, it marked the 15th time Congress used the Congressional Review Act to overturn a regulation in 2017. But it was the first for a rule made final during the Trump presidency. The act allows Congress to rescind recently finalized rules and bars Senate filibusters.

In creating the CFPB in the 2010 Dodd-Frank financial regulatory law, Congress gave its director a five-year term unaligned with the president's, creating the highly unusual scenario where an executive agency can work at cross-purposes from the White House.

The director appointed by Obama in 2012, former Ohio Attorney General Richard Cordray, had pursued the arbitration rule on the grounds that companies were, increasingly, protecting themselves from litigation by requiring customers to sign contracts barring them from going to court. Most Republicans rejected the agency's concerns as unnecessary and expensive government intrusion.

Still, the vote was a squeaker. Two Republicans, Lindsey Graham of South Carolina and John Kennedy of Louisiana, voted with Democrats, creating a tie that Pence broke.

313. "Not Qualified" Judge Approved.

Confirmation of Omaha attorney Steve Grasz to be a judge on the Eighth U.S. Circuit Court of Appeals. Confirmed 50-48 (R 50-0; D 0-46; I 0-2) on Dec. 12, 2017.

A party-line vote assured a lifetime federal judgeship for a nominee the American Bar Association unanimously rated "not qualified." That had never happened in the three decades the ABA has kept comprehensive ratings of federal court picks. It signaled lost influence of such independent vetting.

The vote also assured that Trump would set a new record (12) for nominees of a first-year president confirmed to the circuit courts, which have the final say on all federal appeals except the 100 or so heard by the Supreme Court each year. Grasz was one of three conservatives endorsed for the appellate bench the week before the Senate went home in December, helping the president fulfill one of his most prominent campaign promises to social conservatives.

Grasz was previously a corporate attorney and a player in conservative political circles in Omaha, and before that spent 11 years as Nebraska's chief deputy attorney general. As the state's attorney and as a member of advocacy groups, he questioned legal precedents supporting abortion and gay rights. It was the first appeals court pick rated unqualified by the ABA since a 2006 George W. Bush nomination, which was withdrawn.

An ABA panel of 15 lawyers from across the country interviewed 180 people before supporting a report that questioned Grasz's ability to judge objectively and "detach himself from his deeply held social agenda and political loyalty."

Instead of giving Republicans on the Judiciary Committee pause, the negative findings prompted several to suggest that the ABA's longstanding role in evaluating nominees may be near its end.

323. Tax Overhaul.

Passage of a bill (HR 1) to overhaul the tax code, lowering the corporate tax rate to 21 percent and individual tax rates through 2025; limiting state and local deductions to $10,000 through 2025; decreasing the limit on deductible mortgage interest through 2025; and creating a new system of taxing U.S. corporations with foreign subsidiaries. Passed 51-48 (R 51-0; D 0-46; I 0-2) on Dec. 20, 2017.

A procedural hiccup did not stop the Senate from passing the final version of the most sweeping tax code changes since 1986. And the party-line, 51-48 vote paved the way for Trump and congressional Republicans to notch their first major legislative victory since assuming unified control of government.

The legislation's scope went beyond cutting taxes for businesses and individuals and eliminating a host of tax perks for targeted constituencies. It also effectively repealed the individual mandate in the 2010 health care law by eliminating the penalty assessed to people who don't obtain health insurance, and opened the pristine Arctic National Wildlife Refuge in Alaska to oil and gas drilling.

Democrats charged that the measure was a boon to big business and wealthy people like Trump at the expense of the middle class. While independent analyses of the measure showed the bill would cut taxes for most Americans, the wealthy would benefit the most.

In the end, the final measure represented a compromise between the House and Senate versions. To keep the 10-year cost of the package under $1.5 trillion, conferees agreed to keep the Senate's framework to let individual tax breaks expire after eight years.

In another change, the refundable portion of the child tax credit was raised to $1,400 of the full $2,000 credit available to families with taxable income. That won over Republican Marco Rubio of Florida, who had been pushing for bigger child tax credits.

The final product moved Corker, the lone Republican holdout when the Senate passed its tax bill on Dec. 1, to the side of supporters. Corker initially warned the tax package would add to the government's red ink and not pay for itself through economic growth.

The glide-path to Trump's desk was derailed temporarily by Democrats, who challenged provisions under the so-called Byrd rule that prohibits the Senate from considering "extraneous matters" in a budget reconciliation bill.

So the parliamentarian nixed provisions that would allow the use of 529 savings accounts for home-schooling expenses and another dealing with an excise tax on investment income of small private universities. Democrats even successfully challenged the GOP's nickname for the bill, "The Tax Cut and Jobs Act," before the Senate passed the final tax bill and sent it back to the House, the last stop before reaching Trump's desk.

HOUSE VOTES

73 Stream Protection Reversal

Passage of joint resolution (HJ Res 38) to nullify an Office of Surface Mining Reclamation and Enforcement rule requiring surface coal-mining operations to avoid disturbing streams and land within 100 feet of streams. Passed 228-194 (R 224-9; D 4-185) on Feb. 1, 2017.

One of the so-called "midnight regulations" of Barack Obama's administration, finalized by the Interior Department in December 2016, was aimed at limiting runoff pollution from open pit coal mines. It would have required coal companies to avoid activities that pollute streams, threaten drinking water or damage forests, and it mandated environmental restoration of mined areas.

Republicans called the rule unnecessary, expensive and duplicative. "Make no mistake about it, this Obama administration rule is not designed to protect streams," said Bill Johnson of Ohio. "Instead, it was an effort to regulate the coal mining industry right out of business. We could not stand by and allow that to happen."

The House voted largely along party lines to pass a Congressional Review Act resolution to prevent the rule's implementation. Nine GOP lawmakers opposed the resolution and four Democrats went along with repeal of the regulation.

This would be among the first of many CRA resolutions advanced by Republicans in 2017 in an effort to nullify President Barack Obama's regulatory legacy. The CRA, devised by then-Speaker Newt Gingrich and the Republican revolutionaries who won the House in 1994, allows Congress to block recently finalized regulations.

Prior to 2017, the review act had only been used once before, in 2001, when Congress rescinded a Labor Department regulation issued at the end of Bill Clinton's presidency mandating protocols to protect workers from ergonomic injuries.

The CRA allows Congress to rescind recently finalized regulations on simple majority votes, with no Senate filibuster permitted. It also bars agencies from pursuing substantially similar rules in the future.

77 Social Security Gun Rule

Passage of a joint resolution (HJ Res 40) to nullify a Social Security Administration rule requiring that individuals who need assistance managing their disability benefits because they suffer from a mental impairment be included in the National Instant Criminal Background Check System, barring them from buying guns from licensed gun shops. Passed 235-180 (R 229-2; D 6-178) on Feb. 2, 2017.

In 2017, Republicans got a chance to roll back a rule finalized by the Obama administration in December 2016 that prohibits Social Security beneficiaries with mental deficiencies from purchasing guns from gun stores. It aimed to make it more difficult for roughly 75,000 people to buy firearms.

But the rule sparked an outcry from gun-rights groups and other, less predictable opponents. The National Rifle Association called it a "last minute, back-door gun grab." The American Civil Liberties Union also came out against the rule, saying it

"reinforces harmful stereotypes" and was a violation of due process.

The regulation was part of a push by Obama in the aftermath of the 2012 shooting at Sandy Hook Elementary School that left 26 dead, including 20 children. The Social Security Administration said that Congress had authorized the regulation in a 2008 law that aimed to stop more mentally ill people from getting guns. It was enacted in response to the shooting at Virginia Tech the prior year in which a mentally ill man, Seung-Hui Cho, killed 32 people.

In the debate leading up to the vote, Michigan Democrat John Conyers Jr. decried the repeal, but nevertheless expressed reservations about the rule: "With regard to issues of public safety, we must recognize that people suffering from mental illness should not be assumed to be dangerous," he said, adding: "If I were proposing such a rule, I cannot say whether this process is exactly what I would recommend."

Only two Republicans voted against the resolution: Dan Donovan and Peter T. King, both of New York. Six moderate Democrats voted in favor, including two with higher-office ambitions in 2018: Kyrsten Sinema of Arizona, who is running for the Senate, and Tim Walz of Minnesota, who is running for governor.

The vote on the rule has taken on greater significance since then. In the aftermath of shootings in Las Vegas in October 2017 that left 58 dead, Jimmy Kimmel, the late-night television host, referenced President Donald Trump signing the resolution overturning the rule, saying that it "made it easier for people with severe mental illness to buy guns legally." And following a February 2018 shooting at a high school in Parkland, Fla., that left 17 dead, Trump tweeted that those who are "mentally disturbed" should be reported to authorities, prompting many to point to the 2017 vote. In both those cases, however, neither shooter would have been subject to the rule.

256   Health Care Law Repeal

Passage of a bill (HR 1628) to repeal and replace the Affordable Care Act. Passed 217-213 (R 217-20; D 0-193) on May 4, 2017.

It seemed like Congress' bid to repeal the 2010 health care law died in March when an unlikely coalition of the most moderate and most conservative House Republicans balked at taking up legislation drafted by GOP leaders, despite Trump's urging. Speaker Paul D. Ryan pulled the measure, rather than face certain defeat.

The moderates worried about the Congressional Budget Office's assessment that replacing the law's mandates and subsidies with tax credits, as GOP leaders proposed, would cause more than 20 million Americans to drop their insurance coverage. Conservatives objected to the credits on the grounds that Republican leaders were proposing to replace one form of subsidies with another.

But after the failure of March, the leaders regrouped with a new pitch for conservatives. Their revised bill offered state governments more flexibility to determine what benefits insurers would have to provide, and to allow them to charge people with pre-existing conditions more.

In the meantime, conservative interest groups and Trump laid into the defectors. Trump, for one, said he'd promote primary challengers to conservatives who'd wavered in fulfilling a 7-year-old pledge to repeal the law.

Moderates continued to object, but conservatives agreed to get behind the renewed effort. When Ryan brought up his revised bill in May, there was no guarantee that the Senate could follow, but the speaker demonstrated that he'd regained control of his caucus.

307   Veterans Affairs Department Accountability

Passage of a bill (S 1094) expanding the VA's ability to fire, demote and suspend employees for misconduct or poor performance. The bill also established a VA office to receive whistle-blower disclosures; track recommendations from audits and investigators; and investigate misconduct, retaliation and poor performance. Passed, clearing it for the president, 368-55 (R 231-1; D 137-54) on June 13, 2017.

In the wake of a long-running scandal about the quality of veterans' care, Congress wanted to make it easier for the Veterans Affairs secretary to fire problem employees and for whistleblowers to come forward.

The bill was arguably the most significant bipartisan legislation that Congress passed in 2017.

Following the overwhelming 368-55 vote, Ryan said the problem at the VA was solved: Such "fiascoes are not going to be tolerated in the future."

In all, 55 members voted against the bill; all but one, Don Young of Alaska, were Democrats.

Opponents expressed concerns about circumventing civil service laws. Several labor groups, including the American Federation of Government Employees, came out against the bill.

Gerald E. Connolly, a Democrat who represents a large number of federal workers in his Northern Virginia district, said he was concerned the bill could lead to weakening worker protections across the federal government. But Connolly ended up voting for the measure.

The entire Democratic leadership voted against the bill, including Minority Leader Nancy Pelosi of California, Minority Whip Steny H. Hoyer of Maryland, Assistant Leader James E. Clyburn of South Carolina and Caucus Chairman Joseph Crowley of New York.

Trump signed the bill 10 days later and has since proposed to expand its disciplinary authorities to other agencies.

337   Curb of Medical Malpractice Lawsuits

Passage of a bill (HR 1215) to limit to $250,000 noneconomic damages awarded in malpractice suits in which the plaintiff's health care was paid for in whole or in part by the federal government, and to establish a statute of limitations. Passed 218-210 (R 218-19; D 0-191) on June 28, 2017.

A longtime Republican goal of capping damages in medical malpractice suits won narrow approval in the House but was destined to die in the Senate, falling short of the 60 votes needed.

The House measure passed despite opposition from 19 Republicans and zero support from Democrats. Conservatives like Louie Gohmert and Ted Poe of Texas voted against the bill,

arguing that it would pre-empt states trying to enact their own medical malpractice laws.

The bill would have put a $250,000 cap on awards to victims of medical malpractice with some level of federal insurance, such as Medicare, Medicaid or veterans' care. The limit would only apply to "noneconomic" damages — such as awards for pain and suffering — and not impose a cap on awards for monetary losses.

The health care industry, including the American Medical Association and the American Hospital Association, generally backed the legislation, saying malpractice suits increase the cost of health care by tens of billions of dollars a year.

Doctors in the House on the GOP side also supported the bill. Phil Roe of Tennessee, an obstetrician and gynecologist, said "the one thing that took away some of the joy of that practice was frivolous lawsuits."

But Democrats were unanimously opposed, taking the position of plaintiffs' attorneys who said the caps would hurt patients who were severely harmed by medical malpractice.

342 Enforcement on 'Sanctuary' Cities

Passage of a bill (HR 3003) to penalize state and local governments that fail to cooperate with federal authorities on enforcement of immigration laws. Passed 228-195 (R 225-7; D 3-188) on June 29, 2017.

In one of the few substantive votes on immigration policy in 2017, the House passed a bill aimed at punishing city, county and state governments that refuse to work with the federal government to deport undocumented immigrants who commit crimes. These jurisdictions are commonly called "sanctuary" cities.

The Republican effort to crack down on sanctuary cities gained momentum after Kate Steinle was shot and killed in 2015 by an undocumented immigrant who had been deported five times. Shortly after taking office, Trump signed an executive order threatening to withhold federal grant money to sanctuary cities. Some of the nation's largest cities, including New York and Los Angeles, have adopted sanctuary status.

The House bill would allow the Homeland Security Department to issue detainers for arrests of undocumented immigrants who commit crimes and revoke eligibility for federal grants to those local jurisdictions that don't comply.

Democrats have argued that the federal government should not deputize local cops as deportation agents, and said the measure could instill fear in immigrant communities. A federal judge, meanwhile, issued an injunction in November permanently blocking Trump's executive order.

369 Transgender Rights in Military

Rejection of a proposal to bar transgender members of the armed forces from receiving medical treatment for gender reassignment; the amendment to the annual defense authorization bill (HR 2810) was rejected 209-214 (R 209-24; D 0-190) on July 13, 2017.

The vote stands as the first in congressional history directly affecting the civil rights of transgender Americans, and their victory was also a rare defeat for social conservatives during a time of Republican control of Congress.

A Defense Department policy set in the closing months of the Obama administration provides gender reassignment surgeries, hormone treatments and other therapies to active duty transgender service members whenever a physician recommends such treatments.

The effort to overturn that decision was led by Vicky Hartzler of Missouri, a Republican member of the Armed Services Committee and one of the most outspoken evangelical Christian culture warriors in the House. Using the military medical system to treat transgender service members is an inappropriate drain on the Pentagon budget, she said, and the long recuperative periods after surgery will result in a dangerous drain in the ranks of deployable soldiers and sailors.

The Human Rights Campaign, the premier LGBTQ lobbying group, derided her proposal as both morally "unconscionable" and an attack on military readiness, by denying necessary health care to several thousand service members. Minority Leader Pelosi labeled it "mean-spirited."

Her fellow Democrats were unified in opposing the amendment. But its defeat was only assured with the additional votes of two dozen Republicans, a roster that went beyond the dwindling ranks of GOP members who have long positioned themselves as cultural moderates.

The vote also presaged the limited political support Trump would receive for his decision, announced on Twitter two weeks later, to seek to ban transgender people from remaining in or enlisting in the military. Three different federal courts blocked his orders from taking effect over the course of the rest of the year, and his allies did not seek again to codify his proposal with legislation.

412 Reversing Ban on Mandatory Arbitration

Passage of a joint resolution (HJ Res 111) nullifying a Consumer Financial Protection Bureau rule that prohibited mandatory arbitration clauses in consumer contracts. Passed 231-190 (R 231-1; D 0-189) on July 25, 2017.

The House moved quickly in July to begin the process of rescinding a Consumer Financial Protection Bureau rule barring companies from requiring their customers to arbitrate disputes, rather than go to court.

The bureau, then still under the control of an Obama appointee, Richard Cordray, issued the rule on July 10. Fifteen days later, the House voted on party lines to rescind the rule using expedited procedures provided for in the 1996 Congressional Review Act.

The only Republican to break with his party on the vote was Walter B. Jones of North Carolina, who is often critical of big business.

The resolution was one of 15 that Republicans passed rescinding Obama-era rules in 2017, but the only one ending a regulation finalized while Trump was president.

It also forebode the coming fight between Cordray and Trump over the leadership of the consumer bureau. Cordray, whose five-year term extended all the way till July 2018, resigned at the end of 2017, but tried to install his deputy as his successor.

Trump appointed his budget director, former South Carolina GOP Rep. Mick Mulvaney. A legal fight ensued. The federal district court and federal appeals court in Washington have sided with Trump and permitted Mulvaney to take the agency's reins.

413　Russia Sanctions

Passage of a bill (HR 3364) imposing sanctions on Iran, North Korea and Russia, passed 419-3 (R 229-3; D 190-0) on July 25, 2017.

The House's passage of legislation imposing new sanctions on the three nations and barring Trump from lifting the sanctions on Russia without Congress' assent marked a rare bipartisan agreement between both chambers.

The overwhelming vote, 419-3, presaged an equally lopsided Senate vote that forced a reluctant Trump to sign legislation that all but ended his bid to improve ties with Russia.

One of the representatives to vote no, John J. Duncan Jr. of Tennessee, shared Trump's view that the United States should be seeking closer ties with Russia to better combat the Islamic State militant group and to seek a peace agreement ending the long civil war in Syria.

The two other objectors, Republicans Justin Amash of Michigan and Thomas Massie of Kentucky, are libertarian-leaning representatives skeptical of using unilateral sanctions as a foreign policy tool.

The vote came only two months after Deputy Attorney General Rod Rosenstein named Robert S. Mueller III as independent counsel to investigate Russian interference in the 2016 elections. U.S. intelligence agencies believe Russia hacked into Democratic Party computers and released emails in an effort to embarrass the Democratic candidate, Hillary Clinton, and bolster Trump.

In retaliation for the Russian interference, Obama had imposed sanctions on Russia in December 2016, booting Russian agents from the country and closing two Russian diplomatic compounds. The sanctions bill codified Obama's executive order and barred Trump from rescinding the sanctions as Trump's first national security adviser, Michael Flynn, had told the Russians he would do.

480　Disaster Funding

Motion to concur with the Senate amendment to a bill (HR 601) making available $15.25 billion in emergency supplemental funding to partially cover costs stemming from natural disasters, including Hurricane Harvey, and to suspend the debt limit. Agreed to, clearing the bill for the president, 316-90 (R 133-90; D 183-0) on Sept. 8, 2017.

After weeks of jabbing congressional Republicans for failing to get any major legislation to his desk, Trump in early September blindsided his own party's leaders by endorsing a Democratic plan for funding the government, raising the debt limit and providing emergency aid to areas slammed by Hurricane Harvey in August.

The president announced the deal with the two top Democrats, Pelosi and Sen. Charles E. Schumer of New York, on Sept. 6, just hours after their proposal had been rejected by Ryan.

GOP leaders, under pressure to deliver disaster relief to Texas and other parts of the South reeling from the hurricane, hastily but begrudgingly went along.

The House voted 419-3 on Sept. 6 to approve $7.85 billion in emergency relief but did not address the debt limit in that bill. The next day the Senate passed the measure, 80-17, as part of a stopgap spending package with the debt limit suspended until Dec. 8 and with the disaster aid increased to $15.25 billion.

That sent the bill back to the House, where it was greeted with derision by conservatives who wanted to address the debt limit and spending for the remainder of fiscal 2017 in separate legislation. Most Republicans, however, said the urgency of the needs outweighed the desire for fiscal restraint.

"Please, please vote for this bill, it is time for us to step up. It is time to set politics aside, and it is time now to focus on the tragedy that is called Harvey and may soon be called Irma," Texas Republican Randy Weber pleaded with his colleagues before the vote, referring to the fact that Hurricane Irma was at that moment heading for the Florida coast.

In the end, 90 Republicans voted against the package, but all House Democrats supported it to send it to Trump's desk for his signature.

549　Abortion Ban

Passage of a bill (HR 549) to prohibit abortions in cases where the probable age of the fetus is 20 weeks or older and to impose criminal penalties on doctors who violate the ban. Passed 237-189 (R 234-2; D 3-187) on Oct. 3, 2017.

Urged on by Trump, abortion opponents in the House made another attempt to restrict the procedure by prohibiting it in cases where the fetus was 20 weeks or older.

They dubbed the legislation the Pain-Capable Unborn Child Protection Act, highlighting the notion that a fetus can feel pain, though that is something abortion rights advocates say has not been scientifically proven. During his 2016 campaign, Trump pledged that if he was elected he would sign such legislation in order to "secure critical pro-life protections."

The bill was passed with only two Republicans opposed and with only three Democrats voting in favor. But there was little hope it would see action in the closely divided Senate, where 60 votes would be needed to bring it to the floor for consideration.

In fact, when a bill to fund the 2010 health care law came up in the Senate in December, House Republicans warned they would not support the measure unless the abortion restrictions were added, but to no avail. Schumer dismissed the threat as "another 11th-hour, partisan demand on a bill that's already been negotiated here in the Senate."

Then in January 2018, the Senate took up the ban on late-term abortions, but fell short of limiting debate in a 51-46 vote.

658　Trump Impeachment

Approval of a motion to table a resolution to impeach Trump. Agreed to 364-58 (R 238-0; D 126-58) on Dec. 6, 2017.

There's probably only one word that simultaneously fires up the liberal base and strikes fear in every leadership Democrat: impeachment.

Even before Donald Trump was inaugurated in 2017 — indeed, even before he secured the Republican nomination in 2016 — many were already starting to mouth the word.

In January 2017, Rep. Jamie Raskin, a freshman Democrat from Maryland, argued on a podcast that if Trump did not divest

his holdings, he would be violating the emoluments clause of the Constitution, which bars federal officials from accepting payment from foreign sources. "If he goes into office and he refuses to divest himself, the moment that the first conflict comes up, that's going to look like an impeachable offense," he said.

When Trump fired his FBI Director, James B. Comey, in May, the impeachment talk heated up again, this time over the question of obstruction of justice.

Three Democrats, Al Green of Texas, Steve Cohen of Tennessee and Brad Sherman of California introduced separate articles of impeachment in the House, but they went nowhere.

Finally, in December, Green's bill to offer articles of impeachment reached the floor, but Republicans killed the effort, getting 126 Democrats to join with every voting Republican to table the motion. "Now is not the time to consider articles of impeachment," Pelosi and Hoyer wrote in December ahead of the vote, without explicitly calling to block the motion. Still, 58 Democrats voted in favor of impeachment, an eyebrow-raising number. Most were from the liberal wing of the party, but some moderates joined them.

As a practical matter, impeachment as a mechanism for removing the president is null and void. Democrats are in the minority in the House and the only way they'll be able to impeach the president is if they win a majority in 2018. But as a campaign matter and a potential litmus test for candidates, it could prove to be a rallying cry and a headache. Democratic leaders fear the impeachment talk could turn off moderate voters, especially in swing districts.

The most visible push for impeachment comes from billionaire Tom Steyer, a Democratic donor, who has spent at least $90 million calling for Trump's removal. Some Democratic candidates in places like California, Florida, Nevada and Wisconsin have pledged that if they win, they'll pursue impeachment. In November 2017, Mary Barzee Flores, a Democrat who is running to replace outgoing GOP Rep. Ileana Ros-Lehtinen in Florida, penned an op-ed in the Miami Herald with this eye-catching headline: "'Impeach Trump' must be Democratic candidates' rallying cry."

692　Tax Code Overhaul

Adoption of the conference report for a bill (HR 1) lowering the corporate tax rate to 21 percent and individual tax rates through 2025; limiting state and local deductions to $10,000 through 2025; decreasing the limit on deductible mortgage interest through 2025; and creating a new system of taxing U.S. corporations with foreign subsidiaries. Adopted 227-203 (R 227-12, D 0-191) on Dec. 19, 2017.

The House cleared the way for Congress' biggest legislative success of 2017 on Nov. 16, when it passed a tax bill that became the basic blueprint for a final measure both chambers cleared the following month. The final House vote came on Dec. 19.

The two House votes were almost identical. In November, it was 227-205, with 13 Republicans from high-tax coastal states objecting to the bill's elimination of the tax deduction for state and local income taxes, a new cap of $10,000 on the property tax deduction, and a provision reducing the amount of mortgage interest that would be deductible on expensive homes.

A month later, the final measure mostly tracked the House's original version. The differences were minor: It reduced the corporate tax rate only to 21 percent, whereas the House initially had proposed 20 percent, and it permitted up to $10,000 in state and local tax deductions, regardless of whether it came from income tax or property tax. The bill also capped the mortgage interest deduction at the first $750,000 in mortgage debt, whereas the House had earlier put the cap at $500,000.

The final vote in December was 227-203 with Republican Tom McClintock of California the only vote-switcher. He moved into the yes column. The level of GOP unity indicated how few of its members now come from the Northeast or California, the regions hardest hit by new limits on itemized deductions.

Not a single Democrat voted for the bill, even those from parts of the country that have the most to gain from the increase the bill provides in the standard deduction: States with no income tax, like Florida, Nevada, Texas and Washington.

Appendix D

TEXTS

Trump Touts 'America First' In First Address as President

Following is the CQ transcript of President Donald Trump's inaugural address, delivered on the West Front of the U.S. Capitol on Friday, Jan. 20, 2017.

Chief Justice Roberts, President Carter, President Clinton, President Bush, President Obama, fellow Americans, and people of the world: thank you.

We, the citizens of America, are now joined in a great national effort to rebuild our country and to restore its promise for all of our people.

Together, we will determine the course of America and the world for years to come.

We will face challenges. We will confront hardships. But we will get the job done.

Every four years, we gather on these steps to carry out the orderly and peaceful transfer of power, and we are grateful to President Obama and First Lady Michelle Obama for their gracious aid throughout this transition. They have been magnificent.

AMERICAN CARNAGE

Today's ceremony, however, has very special meaning. Because today we are not merely transferring power from one Administration to another, or from one party to another — but we are transferring power from Washington, D.C. and giving it back to you, the American People.

For too long, a small group in our nation's Capital has reaped the rewards of government while the people have borne the cost.

Washington flourished - but the people did not share in its wealth.

Politicians prospered - but the jobs left, and the factories closed.

The establishment protected itself, but not the citizens of our country.

Their victories have not been your victories; their triumphs have not been your triumphs; and while they celebrated in our nation's Capital, there was little to celebrate for struggling families all across our land.

That all changes - starting right here, and right now, because this moment is your moment: it belongs to you.

It belongs to everyone gathered here today and everyone watching all across America.

This is your day. This is your celebration.

And this, the United States of America, is your country.

What truly matters is not which party controls our government, but whether our government is controlled by the people.

January 20th 2017, will be remembered as the day the people became the rulers of this nation again.

The forgotten men and women of our country will be forgotten no longer.

Everyone is listening to you now.

You came by the tens of millions to become part of a historic movement the likes of which the world has never seen before.

At the center of this movement is a crucial conviction: that a nation exists to serve its citizens.

Americans want great schools for their children, safe neighborhoods for their families, and good jobs for themselves.

These are the just and reasonable demands of a righteous public.

But for too many of our citizens, a different reality exists: Mothers and children trapped in poverty in our inner cities; rusted-out factories scattered like tombstones across the landscape of our nation; an education system, flush with cash, but which leaves our young and beautiful students deprived of knowledge; and the crime and gangs and drugs that have stolen too many lives and robbed our country of so much unrealized potential.

This American carnage stops right here and stops right now.

We are one nation - and their pain is our pain. Their dreams are our dreams; and their success will be our success. We share one heart, one home, and one glorious destiny.

The oath of office I take today is an oath of allegiance to all Americans.

For many decades, we've enriched foreign industry at the expense of American industry;

Subsidized the armies of other countries while allowing for the very sad depletion of our military;

We've defended other nation's borders while refusing to defend our own;

And spent trillions of dollars overseas while America's infrastructure has fallen into disrepair and decay.

We've made other countries rich while the wealth, strength, and confidence of our country has disappeared over the horizon.

One by one, the factories shuttered and left our shores, with not even a thought about the millions upon millions of American workers left behind.

The wealth of our middle class has been ripped from their homes and then redistributed across the entire world.

AMERICA FIRST

But that is the past. And now we are looking only to the future.

We assembled here today are issuing a new decree to be heard in every city, in every foreign capital, and in every hall of power.

From this day forward, a new vision will govern our land.

From this moment on, it's going to be America First.

Every decision on trade, on taxes, on immigration, on foreign affairs, will be made to benefit American workers and American families.

We must protect our borders from the ravages of other countries making our products, stealing our companies, and destroying our jobs. Protection will lead to great prosperity and strength.

I will fight for you with every breath in my body — and I will never, ever let you down.

America will start winning again, winning like never before.

We will bring back our jobs. We will bring back our borders. We will bring back our wealth. And we will bring back our dreams.

We will build new roads, and highways, and bridges, and airports, and tunnels, and railways all across our wonderful nation.

We will get our people off of welfare and back to work - rebuilding our country with American hands and American labor.

We will follow two simple rules: Buy American and Hire American.

We will seek friendship and goodwill with the nations of the world -

but we do so with the understanding that it is the right of all nations to put their own interests first.

We do not seek to impose our way of life on anyone, but rather to let it shine as an example for everyone to follow.

AMERICAN UNITY

We will reinforce old alliances and form new ones – and unite the civilized world against Radical Islamic Terrorism, which we will eradicate completely from the face of the Earth.

At the bedrock of our politics will be a total allegiance to the United States of America, and through our loyalty to our country, we will rediscover our loyalty to each other.

When you open your heart to patriotism, there is no room for prejudice.

The Bible tells us, "how good and pleasant it is when God's people live together in unity."

We must speak our minds openly, debate our disagreements honestly, but always pursue solidarity.

When America is united, America is totally unstoppable.

There should be no fear – we are protected, and we will always be protected.

We will be protected by the great men and women of our military and law enforcement and, most importantly, we are protected by God.

Finally, we must think big and dream even bigger.

In America, we understand that a nation is only living as long as it is striving.

We will no longer accept politicians who are all talk and no action – constantly complaining but never doing anything about it.

The time for empty talk is over.

Now arrives the hour of action.

Do not let anyone tell you it cannot be done. No challenge can match the heart and fight and spirit of America.

We will not fail. Our country will thrive and prosper again.

We stand at the birth of a new millennium, ready to unlock the mysteries of space, to free the Earth from the miseries of disease, and to harness the energies, industries and technologies of tomorrow.

A new national pride will stir our souls, lift our sights, and heal our divisions.

It is time to remember that old wisdom our soldiers will never forget: that whether we are black or brown or white, we all bleed the same red blood of patriots, we all enjoy the same glorious freedoms, and we all salute the same great American Flag.

And whether a child is born in the urban sprawl of Detroit or the windswept plains of Nebraska, they look up at the same night sky, they fill their heart with the same dreams, and they are infused with the breath of life by the same almighty Creator.

So to all Americans, in every city near and far, small and large, from mountain to mountain, and from ocean to ocean, hear these words:

You will never be ignored again.

Your voice, your hopes, and your dreams, will define our American destiny. And your courage and goodness and love will forever guide us along the way.

Together, We Will Make America Strong Again.

We Will Make America Wealthy Again.

We Will Make America Proud Again.

We Will Make America Safe Again.

And, Yes, Together, We Will Make America Great Again. Thank you, God Bless You, And God Bless America. ■

TOM WILLIAMS/CQ FILE PHOTO

Donald J. Trump speaks after being sworn in as the 45th President of the United States, on the West Front of the Capitol, Jan. 20, 2017.

Trump Speaks to Joint Session A Month After Taking Office

Following is the CQ transcript of President Donald Trump's address to a joint session of Congress on Tuesday, Feb. 28, 2017.

Thank you very much. Mr. Speaker, Mr. Vice President, members of Congress, the first lady of the United States...

... and citizens of America, tonight, as we mark the conclusion of our celebration of Black History Month, we are reminded of our nation's path toward civil rights and the work that still remains to be done.

A MESSAGE OF UNITY AND STRENGTH

Recent threats...

Recent threats targeting Jewish community centers and vandalism of Jewish cemeteries, as well as last week's shooting in Kansas City, remind us that while we may be a nation divided on policies, we are a country that stands united in condemning hate and evil in all of its very ugly forms.

Each American generation passes the torch of truth, liberty and justice, in an unbroken chain all the way down to the present. That torch is now in our hands. And we will use it to light up the world.

I am here tonight to deliver a message of unity and strength, and it is a message deeply delivered from my heart. A new chapter...

... of American greatness is now beginning. A new national pride is sweeping across our nation. And a new surge of optimism is placing impossible dreams firmly within our grasp. What we are witnessing today is the renewal of the American spirit. Our allies will find that America is once again ready to lead.

All the nations of the world — friend or foe — will find that America is strong, America is proud, and America is free. In nine years, the United States will celebrate the 250th anniversary of our founding, 250 years since the day we declared our independence. It will be one of the great milestones in the history of the world.

But what will America look like as we reach our 250th year? What kind of country will we leave for our children? I will not allow the mistakes of recent decades past to define the course of our future.

For too long, we've watched our middle class shrink as we've exported our jobs and wealth to foreign countries. We've financed and built one global project after another, but ignored the fates of our children in the inner cities of Chicago, Baltimore, Detroit, and so many other places throughout our land.

We've defended the borders of other nations, while leaving our own borders wide open, for anyone to cross, and for drugs to pour in at a now unprecedented rate. And we've spent trillions and trillions of dollars overseas, while our infrastructure at home has so badly crumbled.

Then, in 2016, the earth shifted beneath our feet. The rebellion started as a quiet protest, spoken by families of all colors and creeds, families who just wanted a fair shot for their children, and a fair hearing for their concerns.

But then the quiet voices became a loud chorus, as thousands of citizens now spoke out together, from cities small and large, all across our country.

Finally, the chorus became an earthquake, and the people turned out by the tens of millions, and they were all united by one very simple, but crucial demand, that America must put its own citizens first, because only then can we truly make America great again.

Dying industries will come roaring back to life. Heroic veterans will get the care they so desperately need. Our military will be given the resources its brave warriors so richly deserve.

Crumbling infrastructure will be replaced with new roads, bridges, tunnels, airports and railways, gleaming across our very, very beautiful land. Our terrible drug epidemic will slow down and ultimately stop. And our neglected inner cities will see a rebirth of hope, safety, and opportunity.

Above all else, we will keep our promises to the American people.

TOUTING ACCOMPLISHMENTS

Thank you. It's been a little over a month since my inauguration, and I want to take this moment to update the nation on the progress I've made in keeping those promises. Since my election, Ford, Fiat-Chrysler, General Motors, Sprint, Softbank, Lockheed, Intel, Walmart, and many others, have announced that they will invest billions and billions of dollars in the United States and will create tens of thousands of new American jobs.

The stock market has gained almost $3 trillion in value since the election on November 8th, a record. We've saved taxpayers hundreds of millions of dollars by bringing down the price of fantastic — and it is a fantastic — new F-35 jet fighter, and we'll be saving billions more on contracts all across our government.

We have placed a hiring freeze on non-military and non-essential federal workers.

We have begun to drain the swamp of government corruption by imposing a five-year ban on lobbying by executive branch officials — and a lifetime ban...

Thank you. Thank you. And a lifetime ban on becoming lobbyists for a foreign government. We have undertaken a historic effort to massively reduce job-crushing regulations, creating a deregulation task force inside of every government agency...

... and we're imposing a new rule which mandates that for every one new regulation, two old regulations must be eliminated.

We're going to stop the regulations that threaten the future and livelihood of our great coal miners.

We have cleared the way for the construction of the Keystone and Dakota Access Pipelines...

... thereby creating tens of thousands of jobs. And I've issued a new directive that new American pipelines be made with American steel.

We have withdrawn the United States from the job-killing Trans-Pacific Partnership.

And with the help of Prime Minister Justin Trudeau, we have formed a council with our neighbors in Canada to help ensure that women entrepreneurs have access to the networks, markets, and

capital they need to start a business and live out their financial dreams.

IMMIGRATION, BORDER WALL AND TERRORISM

To protect our citizens, I have directed the Department of Justice to form a task force on reducing violent crime. I have further ordered the Departments of Homeland Security and Justice, along with the Department of State and the director of national intelligence, to coordinate an aggressive strategy to dismantle the criminal cartels that have spread all across our nation.

We will stop the drugs from pouring into our country and poisoning our youth, and we will expand treatment for those who have become so badly addicted.

At the same time, my administration has answered the pleas of the American people for immigration enforcement and border security.

By finally enforcing our immigration laws, we will raise wages, help the unemployed, save billions and billions of dollars, and make our communities safer for everyone.

We want all Americans to succeed, but that can't happen in an environment of lawless chaos.

For that reason, we will soon begin the construction of a great, great wall along our southern border.

As we speak tonight, we are removing gang members, drug dealers, and criminals that threaten our communities and prey on our very innocent citizens. Bad ones are going out as I speak, and as I promised throughout the campaign. To any in Congress who do not believe we should enforce our laws, I would ask you this one question: What would you say to the American family that loses their jobs, their income, or their loved one, because America refused to uphold its laws and defend its borders?

Our obligation is to serve, protect, and defend the citizens of the United States. We are also taking strong measures to protect our nation from radical Islamic terrorism.

According to data provided by the Department of Justice, the vast majority of individuals convicted of terrorism and terrorism-related offenses since 9/11 came here from outside of our country. We have seen the attacks at home, from Boston to San Bernardino to the Pentagon and, yes, even the World Trade Center. We have seen the attacks in France, in Belgium, in Germany, and all over the world.

It is not compassionate, but reckless to allow uncontrolled entry from places where proper vetting cannot occur.

Those given the high honor of admission to the United States should support this country and love its people and its values. We cannot allow a beachhead of terrorism to form inside America, and we cannot allow our nation to become a sanctuary for extremists.

That is why my administration has been working on improved vetting procedures, and we will shortly take new steps to keep our nation safe, and to keep those out who will do us harm.

As promised, I directed the Department of Defense to develop a plan to demolish and destroy ISIS, a network of lawless savages that have slaughtered Muslims and Christians, and men, women, and children of all faiths and all beliefs. We will work with our allies, including our friends and allies in the Muslim world, to extinguish this vile enemy from our planet.

I have also imposed new sanctions on entities and individuals who support Iran's ballistic missile program, and reaffirmed our unbreakable alliance with the state of Israel.

REPLACING SCALIA ON THE BENCH

Finally, I have kept my promise to appoint a justice to the United States Supreme Court, from my list of 20 judges, who will defend our Constitution.

I am greatly honored to have Maureen Scalia with us in the gallery tonight.

Thank you, Maureen. Her late, great husband, Antonin Scalia, will forever be a symbol of American justice.

To fill his seat, we have chosen Judge Neil Gorsuch, a man of incredible skill and deep devotion to the law. He was confirmed unanimously by the Court of Appeals, and I am asking the Senate to swiftly approve his nomination.

ADRESSING JOBS, TAX RELIEF AND TARIFFS

Tonight, as I outline the next steps we must take as a country, we must honestly acknowledge the circumstances we inherited. Ninety-four million Americans are out of the labor force. Over 43 million people are now living in poverty. And over 43 million Americans are on food stamps.

More than 1 in 5 people in their prime working years are not working. We have the worst financial recovery in 65 years. In the last 8 years, the past administration has put on more new debt than nearly all of the other presidents combined.

We've lost more than one-fourth of our manufacturing jobs since NAFTA was approved, and we've lost 60,000 factories since China joined the World Trade Organization in 2001. Our trade deficit in goods with the world last year was nearly $800 billion. And overseas, we have inherited a series of tragic foreign policy disasters.

Solving these, and so many other pressing problems, will require us to work past the differences of party. It will require us to tap into the American spirit that has overcome every challenge throughout our long and storied history. But to accomplish our goals at home and abroad, we must restart the engine of the American economy, making it easier for companies to do business in the United States and much, much harder for companies to leave our country.

Right now, American companies are taxed at one of the highest rates anywhere in the world. My economic team is developing historic tax reform that will reduce the tax rate on our companies so they can compete and thrive anywhere and with anyone.

It will be a big, big cut.

At the same time, we will provide massive tax relief for the middle class. We must create a level playing field for American companies and our workers. Have to do it.

Currently, when we ship products out of America, many other countries make us pay very high tariffs and taxes, but when foreign companies ship their products into America, we charge them nothing or almost nothing.

I just met with officials and workers from a great American company, Harley-Davidson. In fact, they proudly displayed five of their magnificent motorcycles, made in the USA, on the front lawn of the White House.

And they wanted me to ride one, and I said, "No, thank you."

At our meeting, I asked them, how are you doing, how is business? They said that it's good. I asked them further, how are you doing with other countries, mainly international sales?

They told me — without even complaining, because they have been so mistreated for so long that they've become used to it — that it's very hard to do business with other countries because they tax our goods at such a high rate. They said that in the case of another country, they taxed their motorcycles at 100 percent.

They weren't even asking for a change. But I am. I believe...

I believe strongly in free trade, but it also has to be fair trade. It's been a long time since we had fair trade.

The first Republican president, Abraham Lincoln, warned that the abandonment of the protective policy by the American government will produce want and ruin among our people."

Lincoln was right, and it's time we heeded his advice and his words.

I am not going to let America and its great companies and workers be taken — advantage of us any longer. They have taken advantage of our country no longer.

I am going to bring back millions of jobs. Protecting our workers also means reforming our system of legal immigration.

The current, outdated system depresses wages for our poorest workers and puts great pressure on taxpayers. Nations around the world, like Canada, Australia, and many others, have a merit-based immigration system.

It's a basic principle that those seeking to enter a country ought to be able to support themselves financially. Yet, in America, we do not enforce this rule, straining the very public resources that our poorest citizens rely upon.

According to the National Academy of Sciences, our current immigration system costs American taxpayers many billions of dollars a year. Switching away from this current system of lower-skilled immigration, and instead adopting a merit-based system, we will have so many more benefits. It will save countless dollars, raise workers' wages, and help struggling families, including immigrant families, enter the middle class. And they will do it quickly, and they will be very, very happy, indeed.

I believe that real and positive immigration reform is possible, as long as we focus on the following goals: To improve jobs and wages for Americans; to strengthen our nation's security; and to restore respect for our laws.

If we are guided by the well-being of American citizens, then I believe Republicans and Democrats can work together to achieve an outcome that has eluded our country for decades.

REINFORCING INFRASTRUCTURE

Another Republican president, Dwight D. Eisenhower, initiated the last truly great national infrastructure program: The building of the interstate highway system. The time has come for a new program of national rebuilding.

America has spent approximately $6 trillion in the Middle East, all the while our infrastructure at home is crumbling.

With the $6 trillion, we could have rebuilt our country twice, and maybe even three times, if we had people who had the ability to negotiate.

To launch our national rebuilding, I will be asking Congress to approve legislation that produces a $1 trillion investment in infrastructure of the United States, financed through both public and private capital, creating millions of new jobs.

This effort will be guided by two core principles: Buy American and hire American.

REPEALING AND REPLACING OBAMACARE

Tonight, I am also calling on this Congress to repeal and replace Obamacare...

... with reforms that expand choice, increase access, lower costs, and at the same time provide better health care.

Mandating every American to buy government-approved health insurance was never the right solution for our country.

The way to make health insurance available to everyone is to lower the cost of health insurance, and that is what we are going to do.

Obamacare premiums nationwide have increased by double and triple digits. As an example, Arizona went up 116 percent last year alone. Governor Matt Bevin of Kentucky just said Obamacare is failing in his state, the state of Kentucky, and it's unsustainable and collapsing.

One third of the counties have only one insurer, and they're losing them fast, they are losing them so fast. They're leaving. And many Americans have no choice at all. There's no choice left.

Remember when you were told that you could keep your doctor and keep your plan? We now know that all of those promises have been totally broken. Obamacare is collapsing, and we must act decisively to protect all Americans.

Action is not a choice; it is a necessity. So I am calling on all Democrats and Republicans in Congress to work with us to save Americans from this imploding Obamacare disaster.

Here are the principles that should guide Congress as we move to create a better health care system for all Americans.

First, we should ensure that Americans with pre-existing conditions have access to coverage and that we have a stable transition for Americans currently enrolled in the health care exchanges.

Secondly, we should help Americans purchase their own coverage, through the use of tax credits and expanded health savings accounts, but it must be the plan they want, not the plan forced on them by our government.

Thirdly, we should give our state governors the resources and flexibility they need with Medicaid to make sure no one is left out.

Fourth, we should implement legal reforms that protect patients and doctors from unnecessary costs that drive up the price of insurance and work to bring down the artificially high price of drugs and bring them down immediately.

And finally, the time has come to give Americans the freedom to purchase health insurance across state lines...

... which will create a truly competitive national marketplace that will bring costs way down and provide far better care. So important.

Everything that is broken in our country can be fixed. Every problem can be solved. And every hurting family can find healing and hope. Our citizens deserve this, and so much more, so why not join forces and finally get the job done and get it done right?

On this and so many other things, Democrats and Republicans should get together and unite for the good of our country and for the good of the American people.

My administration wants to work with members of both parties to make childcare accessible and affordable, to help ensure new parents that they have paid family leave...

... to invest in women's health, and to promote clean air and clean water, and to rebuild our military and our infrastructure.

True love for our people requires us to find common ground, to advance the common good, and to cooperate on behalf of every American child who deserves a much brighter future.

An incredible young woman is with us this evening who should serve as an inspiration to us all. Today is Rare Disease Day, and joining us in the gallery is a rare disease survivor, Megan Crowley. Megan…

Megan was diagnosed with Pompe disease, a rare and serious illness, when she was 15 months old. She was not expected to live past five. On receiving this news, Megan's dad, John, fought with everything he had to save the life of his precious child. He founded a company to look for a cure and helped develop the drug that saved Megan's life. Today she is 20 years old and a sophomore at Notre Dame.

Megan's story is about the unbounded power of a father's love for a daughter. But our slow and burdensome approval process at the Food and Drug Administration keeps too many advances, like the one that saved Megan's life, from reaching those in need.

If we slash the restraints, not just at the FDA but across our government, then we will be blessed with far more miracles just like Megan.

OFFERING A CHOICE IN EDUCATION

In fact, our children will grow up in a nation of miracles. But to achieve this future, we must enrich the mind — and the souls — of every American child. Education is the civil rights issue of our time.

I am calling upon members of both parties to pass an education bill that funds school choice for disadvantaged youth, including millions of African-American and Latino children.

These families should be free to choose the public, private, charter, magnet, religious, or home school that is right for them.

Joining us tonight in the gallery is a remarkable woman, Denisha Merriweather. As a young girl, Denisha struggled in school and failed third grade twice. But then she was able to enroll in a private center for learning, great learning center, with the help of a tax credit and a scholarship program. Today, she is the first in her family to graduate, not just from high school, but from college. Later this year, she will get her master's degree in social work. We want all children to be able to break the cycle of poverty just like Denisha.

TAKING ACTION ON CRIME

But to break the cycle of poverty, we must also break the cycle of violence. The murder rate in 2015 experienced its largest single-year increase in nearly half a century. In Chicago, more than 4,000 people were shot last year alone, and the murder rate so far this year has been even higher. This is not acceptable in our society.

Every American child should be able to grow up in a safe community, to attend a great school, and to have access to a high-paying job.

But to create this future, we must work with — not against — not against — the men and women of law enforcement.

We must build bridges of cooperation and trust, not drive the wedge of disunity and it's — really, it's what it is, division. It's pure, unadulterated division. We have to unify. Police and sheriffs are members of our community. They're friends and neighbors, they're mothers and fathers, sons and daughters, and they leave behind loved ones every day who worry about whether or not they'll come home safe and sound. We must support the incredible men and women of law enforcement.

And we must support the victims of crime. I have ordered the Department of Homeland Security to create an office to serve American victims. The office is called VOICE, Victims of Immigration Crime Engagement.

We are providing a voice to those who have been ignored by our media and silenced by special interests. Joining us…

Joining us in the audience tonight are four very brave Americans whose government failed them. Their names are Jamiel Shaw, Susan Oliver, Jenna Oliver, and Jessica Davis. Jamiel's 17-year-old son was viciously murdered by an illegal immigrant gang member who had just been released from prison. Jamiel Shaw, Jr., was an incredible young man with unlimited potential who was getting ready to go to college where he would have excelled as a great college quarterback.

But he never got the chance. His father, who is in the audience tonight, has become a very good friend of mine. Jamiel, thank you. Thank you.

Also with us are Susan Oliver and Jessica Davis. Their husbands — Deputy Sheriff Danny Oliver and Detective Michael Davis — were slain in the line of duty in California. They were pillars of their community. These brave men were viciously gunned down by an illegal immigrant with a criminal record and two prior deportations. Should have never been in our country.

Sitting with Susan is her daughter, Jenna. Jenna, I want you to know that your father was a hero and that tonight you have the love of an entire country supporting you and praying for you.

To Jamiel, Jenna, Susan and Jessica, I want you to know that we will never stop fighting for justice. Your loved ones will never, ever be forgotten. We will always honor their memory.

REBUILDING THE MILITARY

Finally, to keep America safe, we must provide the men and women of the United States military with the tools they need to prevent war — if they must — they have to fight and they only have to win.

I am sending Congress a budget that rebuilds the military, eliminates the defense sequester…

… and calls for one of the largest increases in national defense spending in American history.

My budget will also increase funding for our veterans. Our veterans have delivered for this nation, and now we must deliver for them.

The challenges we face as a nation are great. But our people are even greater. And none are greater or braver than those who fight for America in uniform.

We are blessed to be joined tonight by Carryn Owens, the widow of U.S. Navy Special Operator, Senior Chief William "Ryan" Owens. Ryan died as he lived, a warrior and a hero, battling against terrorism and securing our nation.

I just spoke to our great General Mattis just now who reconfirmed that, and I quote, "Ryan was a part of a highly successful raid that generated large amounts of vital intelligence that will lead to many more victories in the future against our enemy."

Ryan's legacy is etched into eternity. Thank you.

And Ryan is looking down right now. You know that. And he's very happy, because I think he just broke a record.

For as the Bible teaches us, there is no greater act of love than to lay down one's life for one's friends. Ryan laid down his life for his friends, for his country, and for our freedom. And we will never forget Ryan.

To those allies who wonder what kind of a friend America will be, look no further than the heroes who wear our uniform. Our foreign policy calls for a direct, robust, and meaningful engagement with the world. It is American leadership based on vital security interests that we share with our allies all across the globe.

FORGING A NEW PATH IN FOREIGN POLICY

We strongly support NATO, an alliance forged through the bonds of two world wars, that dethroned fascism...

... and a Cold War and defeated communism.

But our partners must meet their financial obligations. And now, based on our very strong and frank discussions, they are beginning to do just that. In fact, I can tell you the money is pouring in. Very nice.

We expect our partners, whether in NATO, in the Middle East, or in the Pacific, to take a direct and meaningful role in both strategic and military operations, and pay their fair share of the cost. Have to do that.

We will respect historic institutions, but we will respect the foreign rights of all nations. And they have to respect our rights as a nation, also.

Free nations are the best vehicle for expressing the will of the people, and America respects the right of all nations to chart their own path. My job is not to represent the world. My job is to represent the United States of America.

But we know that America is better off when there is less conflict, not more. We must learn from the mistakes of the past. We have seen the war and the destruction that have ravaged and raged throughout the world. All across the world.

The only long-term solution for these humanitarian disasters, in many cases, is to create the conditions where displaced persons can safely return home and begin the long, long process of rebuilding.

America is willing to find new friends, and to forge new partnerships, where shared interests align. We want harmony and stability, not war and conflict. We want peace, wherever peace can be found. America is friends today with former enemies. Some of our closest allies, decades ago, fought on the opposite side of these terrible, terrible wars. This history should give us all faith in the possibilities for a better world.

MAKING AMERICA GREAT AGAIN

Hopefully, the 250th year for America will see a world that is more peaceful, more just, and more free.

On our 100th anniversary in 1876, citizens from across our nation came to Philadelphia to celebrate America's centennial. At that celebration, the country's builders and artists and inventors showed off their wonderful creations. Alexander Graham Bell displayed his telephone for the first time. Remington unveiled the first typewriter. An early attempt was made at electric light. Thomas Edison showed an automatic telegraph and an electric pen. Imagine the wonders our country could know in America's 250th year.

Think of the marvels we could achieve if we simply set free the dreams of our people. Cures to the illnesses that have always plagued us are not too much to hope. American footprints on distant worlds are not too big a dream. Millions lifted from welfare to work is not too much to expect. And streets where mothers are safe from fear — schools where children learn in peace, and jobs where Americans prosper and grow — are not too much to ask.

When we have all of this, we will have made America greater than ever before, for all Americans. This is our vision. This is our mission. But we can only get there together. We are one people, with one destiny.

We all bleed the same blood. We all salute the same great American flag. And we are all made by the same God.

When we fulfill this vision, when we celebrate our 250 years of glorious freedom, we will look back on tonight as when this new chapter of American greatness began. The time for small thinking is over. The time for trivial fights is behind us. We just need the courage to share the dreams that fill our hearts, the bravery to express the hopes that stir our souls, and the confidence to turn those hopes and those dreams into action.

From now on, America will be empowered by our aspirations, not burdened by our fears, inspired by the future, not bound by failures of the past, and guided by a vision, not blinded by our doubts.

I am asking all citizens to embrace this renewal of the American spirit. I am asking all members of Congress to join me in dreaming big, and bold, and daring things for our country. I am asking everyone watching tonight to seize this moment. Believe in yourselves. Believe in your future. And believe, once more, in America.

Thank you, God bless you, and God bless the United States.■

Beshear Calls On Trump to Keep His Word to Families, People

Following is a CQ transcript of the Democratic response to President Donald Trump's address to Congress on Feb 28, 2017. It was delivered by former Kentucky Gov. Steve Beshear.

I'm Steve Beshear. I was governor of Kentucky from 2007 to 2015. Now I'm a private citizen.

I'm here in Lexington, Kentucky — some 400 miles from Washington, — at a diner with some neighbors — Democrats and Republicans — where we just watched the president's address. I'm a proud Democrat, but first and foremost, I'm a proud Republican, and Democrat, and mostly American. And like many of you, I am worried about the future of this nation.

Look, I grew up in Kentucky in a small town called Dawson Springs. My dad and granddad were Baptist preachers. My family owned a funeral home. And my wife, Jane, and I have been married for almost 50 years. I became governor at the start of the global recession, and after eight years, we left things a lot better than we found them.

By being fiscally responsible — I even cut my own pay — we balanced our budget and turned deficits into surpluses without raising taxes. We cut our unemployment rate in half. We made huge gains in high school graduation rates. And we found health coverage for over half a million Kentuckians.

We did that through trust and mutual respect. I listened.

And I built partnerships with business leaders and with Republicans in our legislature. We put people first and politics second.

The America I love allowed a small-town preacher's kid to be elected governor, and it taught me to embrace people who are different from me, not vilify them. The America I love has always been about looking forward, not backward, about working together to find solutions, regardless of party, instead of allowing our differences to divide us and hold us back.

And we Democrats are committed to creating the opportunity for every American to succeed by growing our economy with good-paying jobs, educating and training our people to fill those jobs, giving our businesses the freedom to innovate, keeping our country safe, and providing health care that families can afford and rely on.

CHAMPION THE PEOPLE, NOT WALL STREET

Mr. President, as a candidate, you promised to be a champion for families struggling to make ends meet, and I hope you live up to that promise. But one of your very first executive orders makes it harder for those families to even afford a mortgage. Then you started rolling back rules that provide oversight of the financial industry and safeguard us against another national economic meltdown. And you picked a cabinet of billionaires and Wall Street insiders who want to eviscerate the protections that most Americans count on and that help level the playing field.

That's not being our champion. That's being Wall Street's champion.

EVERY AMERICAN DESERVES AFFORDABLE HEALTH CARE

And even more troubling, you and your Republican allies in Congress seem determined to rip affordable health insurance away from millions of Americans who most need it. Does the Affordable Care Act need some repairs? Sure, it does. But so far, every Republican idea to "replace" the Affordable Care Act would reduce the number of Americans covered, despite your promises to the contrary.

Mr. President, folks here in Kentucky expect you to keep your word. Because this isn't a game. It's life and death for people.

These ideas promise "access" to care but deny the importance of making care affordable and effective. They would charge families more for fewer benefits and put the insurance companies back in control. Behind these ideas is the belief that folks at the lower end of the economic ladder just don't deserve health care, that it's somehow their fault that their employer doesn't offer insurance or that they can't afford to buy expensive health plans.

But just who are these 22 million Americans, including 500,000 people right here in Kentucky, who now have health care that didn't have it before? Look, they're not aliens from some distant planet. They're our friends and our neighbors.

We sit in the bleachers with them on Friday night. We worship in the pews with them on Sunday morning. They're farmers, restaurant workers, part-time teachers, nurses' aides, construction workers, and entrepreneurs working at high-tech start-ups. And before the Affordable Care Act, they woke up every morning and went to work, just hoping and praying they wouldn't get sick, because they knew that they were just one bad diagnosis away from bankruptcy.

You know, in 2010, this country made a commitment, that every American deserved health care they could afford and rely on. And we Democrats are going to do everything in our power to keep President Trump and the Republican Congress from reneging on that commitment. But we're going to need your help by speaking out.

DON'T IGNORE RUSSIAN NATIONAL SECURITY THREAT

Another commitment now being tested is to our national security. Look, make no mistake, I'm a military veteran myself, and I know that protecting America is a president's highest duty. Yet President Trump is ignoring serious threats to our national security from Russia, who's not our friend, while alienating our allies, who've fought with us side by side and are our friends in a dangerous world. His approach makes us less safe and should worry every freedom-loving American.

Instead, President Trump has all but declared war on refugees and immigrants. Look, the president can and should enforce our immigration laws. But we can protect America without abandoning our principles and our moral obligation to help those fleeing war and terror, without tearing families apart, and without needlessly jeopardizing our military men and women fighting overseas.

You know, another Republican president, Ronald Reagan, once said, "In America, our origins matter less than our destination, and that is what democracy is all about."

DON'T ATTACK DISSENT

President Trump also needs to understand that people may disagree with him from time to time, but that doesn't make them his enemies. When the president attacks the loyalty and credibility of our intelligence agencies, the court system, the military, the free press, individual Americans, simply because he doesn't like what they say, he is eroding our democracy. And that's reckless.

Real leaders don't spread derision and division. Real leaders strengthen, they unify, they partner, and they offer real solutions instead of ultimatums and blame.

Look, I may be old-fashioned, but I still believe that dignity, compassion, honesty, and accountability are basic American values. And as a Democrat, I believe that if you work hard, you deserve the opportunity to realize the American dream, regardless of whether you're a coal miner in Kentucky, a teacher in Rhode Island, an autoworker in Detroit, or a software engineer in San Antonio.

Our political system is broken. It's broken because too many of our leaders think it's all about them. They need to remember that they work for us and helping us is their work.

Kentucky made real progress while I was governor because we were motivated by one thing: Helping families. Democrats are trying to bring that same focus back to Washington, D.C. Americans are a diverse people. And we may disagree on a lot of things, but we've always come together when we remember that we are one nation, under God, indivisible, with liberty and justice for all.

Thank you. ∎

Appendix E

PUBLIC LAWS

Laws Enacted in the First Session Of the 115th Congress

■ **PL 115-1** (HR 39) Codify the Presidential Innovation Fellows Program. *Introduced by MCCARTHY, R-Calif., on Jan. 3, 2017. House passed, under suspension of the rules, Jan. 11. Senate passed Jan. 17. President signed Jan. 20, 2017.*

■ **PL 115-2** (S 84) Provide for an exception to a limitation against appointment of persons as Secretary of Defense within seven years of relief from active duty as a regular commissioned officer of the Armed Forces. *Introduced by MCCAIN, R-Ariz., on Jan. 10, 2017. Senate Armed Services reported Jan. 12 (no written report). Senate passed Jan. 12. House passed Jan. 13. President signed Jan. 20, 2017.*

■ **PL 115-3** (HR 72) Authorize the Government Accountability Office (GAO) to obtain federal agency records required to discharge the GAO's duties, including through bringing civil actions to require an agency to produce a record. *Introduced by CARTER, R-Ga., on Jan. 3, 2017. House passed, under suspension of the rules, Jan. 4. Senate Homeland Security and Governmental Affairs discharged Jan. 17. Senate passed Jan. 17. President signed Jan. 31, 2017.*

■ **PL 115-4** (HJ Res 41) Provide for congressional disapproval of a rule submitted by the Securities and Exchange Commission relating to "Disclosure of Payments by Resource Extraction Issuers." *Introduced by HUIZENGA, R-Mich., on Jan. 30, 2017. House passed Feb. 2. Senate passed Feb. 3. President signed Feb. 14, 2017.*

■ **PL 115-5** (HJ Res 38) Disapprove the rule submitted by the Department of the Interior known as the Stream Protection Rule. *Introduced by JOHNSON, R-Ohio, on Jan. 30, 2017. House passed Feb. 1. Senate passed Feb. 2. President signed Feb. 16, 2017.*

■ **PL 115-6** (HR 255) Authorize the National Science Foundation to support entrepreneurial programs for women. *Introduced by ESTY, D-Conn., on Jan. 4, 2017. House passed, under suspension of the rules, Jan. 10. Senate Commerce, Science and Transportation reported Feb. 1 (no written report). Senate passed Feb. 14, 2017. President signed Feb. 28, 2017.*

■ **PL 115-7** (HR 321) Inspire women to enter the aerospace field, including science, technology, engineering, and mathematics, through mentorship and outreach. *Introduced by COMSTOCK, R-Va., on Jan. 5, 2017. House passed, under suspension of the rules, Jan. 10. Senate passed Feb. 14. President signed Feb. 28, 2017.*

■ **PL 115-8** (HJ Res 40) Provide for congressional disapproval under chapter 8 of title 5, United States Code, of the rule submitted by the Social Security Administration relating to Implementation of the NICS Improvement Amendments Act of 2007. *Introduced by JOHNSON, R-Texas, on Jan. 30, 2017. House passed Feb. 2. Senate passed Feb. 15. President signed Feb. 28, 2017.*

■ **PL 115-9** (HR 609) Designate the Department of Veterans Affairs health care center in Center Township, Butler County, Pennsylvania, as the "Abie Abraham VA Clinic." *Introduced by KELLY, R-Pa., on Jan. 23, 2017. House, passed, under suspension of the rules, Feb. 13. Senate Veterans' Affairs discharged Feb. 17. Senate passed Feb. 17. President signed March 13, 2017.*

■ **PL 115-10** (S 442) Authorize the programs of the National Aeronautics and Space Administration. *Introduced by CRUZ, R-Texas, on Feb. 17, 2017. Senate passed Feb. 17. House passed, under suspension of the rules, March 7. President signed March 21, 2017.*

■ **PL 115-11** (HJ Res 37) Disapprove the rule submitted by the Department of Defense, the General Services Administration, and the National Aeronautics and Space Administration relating to the Federal Acquisition Regulation. *Introduced by FOXX, R-N.C., on Jan. 30, 2017. House passed Feb. 2. Senate passed March 6. President signed March 27, 2017.*

■ **PL 115-12** (HJ Res 44) Disapprove the rule submitted by the Department of the Interior relating to Bureau of Land Management regulations that establish the procedures used to prepare, revise, or amend land use plans pursuant to the Federal Land Policy and Management Act of 1976. *Introduced by CHENEY, R-Wyo., on Jan. 30, 2017. House passed Feb. 7. Senate passed March 7. President signed March 27, 2017.*

■ **PL 115-13** (HJ Res 57) Disapprove the rule submitted by the Department of Education relating to accountability and State plans under the Elementary and Secondary Education Act of 1965. *Introduced by ROKITA, R-Ind., on Feb. 1, 2017. House passed Feb. 7. Senate passed March 9. President signed March 27, 2017.*

■ **PL 115-14** (HJ Res 58) Disapprove the rule submitted by the Department of Education relating to teacher preparation issues. *Introduced by GUTHRIE, R-Ky., on Feb. 1, 2017. House passed Feb. 7. Senate passed March 8. President signed March 27, 2017.*

■ **PL 115-15** (S 305) Encourage the display of the flag of the United States on National Vietnam War Veterans Day. *Introduced by TOOMEY, R-Pa., on Feb. 3, 2017. Senate passed Feb. 2. House Judiciary discharged March 21. House passed March 28. President signed March 28, 2017.*

■ **PL 115-16** (HR 1362) Name the Department of Veterans Affairs community-based outpatient clinic in Pago Pago, American Samoa, the Faleomavaega Eni Fa'aua'a Hunkin VA Clinic. *Introduced by RADEWAGEN, R-A.S., on March 6, 2017. House passed, under suspension of the rules, March 7. Senate Veterans' Affairs discharged March 15. Senate passed March 15. President signed March 31, 2017.*

■ **PL 115-17** (HJ Res 42) Disapprove the rule submitted by the Department of Labor relating to drug testing of unemployment compensation applicants. *Introduced by BRADY, R-Texas, on Jan. 30, 2017. House passed Feb. 15. Senate passed March 14. President signed March 31, 2017.*

■ **PL 115-18** (SJ Res 1) Approve the location of a memorial to commemorate and honor the members of the Armed Forces who served on active duty in support of Operation Desert Storm or Operation Desert Shield. *Introduced by BOOZMAN, R-Ark., on Jan. 3, 2017. Senate Energy and Natural Resources discharged March 8. Senate passed March 8. House passed March 15. President signed March 31, 2017.*

■ **PL 115-19** (HR 1228) Provide for the appointment of members of the Board of Directors of the Office of Compliance to replace members whose terms expire during 2017. *Introduced by HARPER, R-Miss., on Feb. 27, 2017. House Administration discharged March 15. House passed March 15. Senate passed March 23. President signed April 3, 2017.*

■ **PL 115-20** (HJ Res 69) Provide for congressional disapproval under chapter 8 of title 5, United States Code, of the final rule of the Department of the Interior relating to "Non-Subsistence Take of Wildlife, and Public Participation and Closure Procedures, on National Wildlife Refuges in Alaska." *Introduced by YOUNG, R-Alaska, on Feb. 7, 2017. House passed Feb. 16. Senate passed March 21. President signed April 3, 2017.*

■ **PL 115-21** (HJ Res 83) Disapprove the rule submitted by the Department of Labor relating to "Clarification of Employer's Continuing Obligation to Make and Maintain an Accurate Record of Each Recordable Injury and Illness." *Introduced by BYRNE, R-Ala., on Feb. 21, 2017. House passed March 1. Senate passed March 22. President signed April 3, 2017.*

■ **PL 115-22** (SJ Res 34) Provide for congressional disapproval under chapter 8 of title 5, United States Code, of the rule submitted by the Federal Communications Commission relating to "Protecting the Privacy of Customers of Broadband and Other Telecommunications Services" *Introduced by FLAKE, R-Ariz., on March 7, 2017. Senate Commerce, Science and Transportation discharged March 15. Senate passed March 15. House passed March 28. President signed April 3, 2017.*

■ **PL 115-23** (HJ Res 43) Provide for congressional disapproval under chapter 8 of title 5, United States Code, of the final rule submitted by Secretary of Health and Human Services relating to compliance with title X requirements by project recipients in selecting subrecipients. *Introduced by BLACK, R-Tenn., on Jan. 30, 2017. House passed Feb. 16. Senate passed March 30. President signed April 13, 2017.*

■ **PL 115-24** (HJ Res 67) Disapprove the rule submitted by the Department of Labor relating to savings arrangements established by qualified State political subdivisions for non-governmental employees. *Introduced by ROONEY, R-Fla., on Feb. 7, 2017. House passed Feb. 15. Senate passed March 30. President signed April 13, 2017.*

■ **PL 115-25** (HR 353) Improve the National Oceanic and Atmospheric Administration's weather research through a focused program of investment on affordable and attainable advances in observational, computing, and modeling capabilities to support substantial improvement in weather forecasting and prediction of high impact weather events, to expand commercial opportunities for the provision of weather data.

Introduced by LUCAS, R-Okla., on Jan. 6, 2017. House passed Jan. 9. Senate passed, amended, March 29. House agreed to Senate amendment April 4. President signed April 18, 2017.

■ **PL 115-26** (S 544) Modify the termination date for the Veterans Choice Program. *Introduced by TESTER, D-Mont., on March 7, 2017. Senate Veterans' Affairs discharged April 3. Senate passed April 3. House passed, under suspension of the rules, April 5. President signed April 19, 2017.*

■ **PL 115-27** (SJ Res 30) Provide for the reappointment of Steve Case as a citizen regent of the Board of Regents of the Smithsonian Institution. *Introduced by PERDUE, R-Ga., on March 2, 2017. Senate Rules and Administration discharged March 27. Senate passed March 27. House Administration discharged April 6. House passed April 6. President signed April 19, 2017.*

■ **PL 115-28** (SJ Res 35) Provide for the appointment of Michael Govan as a citizen regent of the Board of Regents of the Smithsonian Institution. *Introduced by BOOZMAN, R-Ark., on March 8, 2017. Senate Rules and Administration discharged March 27. Senate passed March 27. House Administration discharged April 6. House passed April 6. President signed April 19, 2017.*

■ **PL 115-29** (SJ Res 36) Provide for the appointment of Roger W. Ferguson as a citizen regent of the Board of Regents of the Smithsonian Institution. *Introduced by BOOZMAN, R-Ark., on March 8, 2017. Senate Rules and Administration discharged March 27. Senate passed March 27. House Administration discharged April 6. House passed April 6. President signed April 19, 2017.*

■ **PL 115-30** (HJ Res 99) Make further continuing appropriations for fiscal year 2017. *Introduced by FRELINGHUYSEN, R-N.J., on April 26, 2017. House passed April 26. Senate passed April 28. President signed April 28, 2017.*

■ **PL 115-31** (HR 244) Make appropriations for the fiscal year ending September 30, 2017. *Introduced by COOK, R-Calif., on Jan. 4, 2017. House passed, under suspension of the rules, Feb 13. Senate Health, Education, Labor and Pensions discharged March 21. Senate passed, amended, March 21. House agreed to Senate amendments, with an amendment, May 3. Senate agreed to House amendment May 4.*

■ **PL 115-32** (HR 534) Require the Secretary of State to take such actions as may be necessary for the United States to rejoin the Bureau of International Expositions. *Introduced by EMMER, R-Minn., on Jan. 13, 2017. House passed, under suspension of the rules, April 25. Senate Foreign Relations reported, amended, May 3 (no written report). Senate passed, amended, May 4. House agreed to Senate amendment May 4. President signed May 8, 2017.*

■ **PL 115-33** (S 496) Repeal the rule issued by the Federal Highway Administration and the Federal Transit Administration entitled "Metropolitan Planning Organization Coordination and Planning Area Reform." *Introduced by DUCKWORTH, D-Ill., on March 2, 2017. Senate Banking, Housing and Urban Affairs discharged March 8. Senate passed March 8. House passed, under suspension of the rules, April 27. President signed May 12, 2017.*

■ **PL 115-34** (HR 274) Provide for reimbursement for the use of

modern travel services by Federal employees traveling on official Government business. *Introduced by MOULTON, D-Mass., on Jan. 4, 2017. House passed, under suspension of the rules, Jan. 10. Senate Homeland Security and Governmental Affairs reported April 24 (S Rept 115-31). Senate passed May 2. President signed May 16, 2017.*

■ **PL 115-35** (HJ Res 66) Disapprove the rule submitted by the Department of Labor relating to savings arrangements established by States for non-governmental employees. *Introduced by WALBERG, R-Mich., on Feb. 7, 2017. House passed Feb. 15. Senate passed May 3. President signed May 17, 2017.*

■ **PL 115-36** (S 419) Require adequate reporting on the Public Safety Officers' Benefits program. *Introduced by GRASSLEY, R-Iowa, on Feb. 16, 2017. Senate Judiciary reported March 9 (no written report). Senate passed, amended, May 16. House passed, under suspension of the rules, May 17. President signed June 2, 2017.*

■ **PL 115-37** (S 583) Amend the Omnibus Crime Control and Safe Streets Act of 1968 to authorize COPS grantees to use grant funds to hire veterans as career law enforcement officers. *Introduced by CORNYN, R-Texas, on March 8, 2017. Senate Judiciary reported March 11 (no written report). Senate passed, amended, May 16. House passed May 17. President signed June 2, 2017.*

■ **PL 115-38** (HR 366) Amend the Homeland Security Act of 2002 to direct the Under Secretary for Management of the Department of Homeland Security to make certain improvements in managing the Department's vehicle fleet. *Introduced by PERRY, R-Pa., on Jan. 6, 2017. House passed, under suspension of the rules, Jan. 31. Senate Homeland Security and Governmental Affairs reported, amended, April 24 (S Rept 115-32). Senate passed, amended, May 2. House agreed to Senate amendments May 23. President signed June 6, 2017.*

■ **PL 115-39** (HR 375) Designate the Federal building and United States courthouse located at 719 Church Street in Nashville, Tennessee, as the "Fred D. Thompson Federal Building and United States Courthouse." *Introduced by BLACKBURN, R-Tenn., on Jan. 9, 2017. House Transportation and Infrastructure reported March 7 (H Rept 115-23). House passed, under suspension of the rules, March 7. Senate passed, amended, May 24. President signed June 6, 2017.*

■ **PL 115-40** (HR 657) Extend certain protections against prohibited personnel practices. *Introduced by DUFFY, R-Wis., on Jan. 24, 2017. House Oversight and Government Reform reported, amended, March 29 (H Rept 115-67). House passed, under suspension of the rules, May 1. Senate Homeland Security and Governmental Affairs discharged May 25. Senate passed May 25. President signed June 14, 2017.*

■ **PL 115-41** (S 1094) Improve the accountability of employees of the Department of Veterans Affairs. *Introduced by RUBIO, R-Fla., on May 11, 2017. Senate Veterans' Affairs reported, amended, June 6 (no written report). Senate passed, amended, June 6. House passed June 13. President signed June 23.*

■ **PL 115-42** (S 1083) Provide for stays during a period that the Merit Systems Protection Board lacks a quorum. *Introduced by JOHNSON, R-Wis., on May 10, 2017. Senate Homeland Security and Governmental Affairs discharged May 11. Senate passed May*

11. *House Oversight and Government Reform discharged May 25. House passed, amended, May 25. Senate agreed to House amendment June 14.*

■ **PL 115-43** (HR 1238) Make the Assistant Secretary of Homeland Security for Health Affairs responsible for coordinating the efforts of the Department of Homeland Security related to food, agriculture, and veterinary defense against terrorism. *Introduced by YOUNG, R-Iowa, on Feb. 28, 2017. House Homeland Security, Energy and Commerce, and Agriculture committees discharged March 16. House passed, under suspension of the rules, March 22. Senate Homeland Security and Governmental Affairs discharged May 24. Senate passed, amended, May 24. House agreed to Senate amendments June 20.*

■ **PL 115-44** (HR 3364) Provide congressional review and to counter aggression by the Governments of Iran, the Russian Federation, and North Korea. *Introduced by ROYCE, R-Calif., on July 24, 2017. House passed, under suspension of the rules, July 25. Senate passed July 27. President signed Aug. 2, 2017.*

■ **PL 115-45** (HR 3298) Authorize the Capitol Police Board to make payments from the United States Capitol Police Memorial Fund to employees of the United States Capitol Police who have sustained serious line-of-duty injuries. *Introduced by BARTON, R-Texas, on July 19, 2017. House passed, under suspension of the rules, July 24. Senate Rules and Administration discharged July 27. Senate passed, amended, July 27. House agreed to Senate amendment July 27. President signed Aug. 4, 2017.*

■ **PL 115-46** (S 114) Authorize appropriations and to appropriate amounts for the Veterans Choice Program of the Department of Veterans Affairs, to improve hiring authorities of the Department, to authorize major medical facility leases. *Introduced by HELLER, R-Nev., on Jan. 12, 2017. Senate Veterans' Affairs discharged May 25. Senate passed May 25. House passed, amended, July 28. Senate agreed to House amendments Aug. 1. President signed Aug. 12, 2017.*

■ **PL 115-47** (HR 2210) Designate the community living center of the Department of Veterans Affairs in Butler Township, Butler County, Pennsylvania, as the "Sergeant Joseph George Kusick VA Community Living Center." *Introduced by KELLY, R-Pa., on April 27, 2017. House passed, under suspension of the rules, July 17. Senate passed Aug. 1. President signed Aug. 16, 2017.*

■ **PL 115-48** (HR 3218) Make certain improvements in the laws administered by the Secretary of Veterans Affairs. *Introduced by ROE, R-Tenn., on July 13, 2017. House Veterans Affairs reported, amended, July 24 (H Rept 115-247, Part 1). House Armed Services discharged July 24. House passed July 24. Senate passed Aug. 2. President signed Aug. 16, 2017.*

■ **PL 115-49** (HR 374) Remove the sunset provision of section 203 of Public Law 105-384. *Introduced by HERRERA BEUTLER, R-Wash., on Jan. 9, 2017. House passed, under suspension of the rules, Jan. 30. Senate passed Aug. 3. President signed Aug. 18, 2017.*

■ **PL 115-50** (HR 510) Establish a system for integration of Rapid DNA instruments for use by law enforcement to reduce violent crime and reduce the current DNA analysis backlog. *Introduced by SENSENBRENNER, R-Wis., on Jan. 12, 2017. House Judiciary*

reported May 11 (H Rept 115-117). House passed, under suspension of the rules, May 16. Senate Judiciary discharged Aug. 1. Senate passed Aug. 1. President signed Aug. 18, 2017.

■ **PL 115-51** (HR 873) Authorize the Global War on Terror Memorial Foundation to establish the National Global War on Terrorism Memorial as a commemorative work in the District of Columbia. *Introduced by GALLAGHER, R-Wis., on Feb. 6, 2017. House Natural Resources reported July 28 (H Rept 115-264). House passed, under suspension of the rules, July 28. Senate passed Aug. 3. President signed Aug. 18, 2017.*

■ **PL 115-52** (HR 2430) Revise and extend the user-fee programs for prescription drugs, medical devices, generic drugs, and biosimilar biological products. *Introduced by WALDEN, R-Ore., on May 16, 2017. House Energy and Commerce reported, amended, July 11 (H Rept 115-201). House passed, under suspension of the rules, July 12. Senate passed Aug. 3. President signed Aug. 18, 2017.*

■ **PL 115-53** (HR 339) Amend Public Law 94-241 with respect to the Northern Mariana Islands. *Introduced by SABLAN, D-N. Marianas, on Jan. 5, 2017. House passed, under suspension of the rules, Jan. 30. Senate Energy and Natural Resources discharged Aug. 1. Senate passed, amended, Aug. 1. House agreed to Senate amendment Aug. 11. President signed Aug. 22, 2017.*

■ **PL 115-54** (HJ Res 76) Grant the consent and approval of Congress for the Commonwealth of Virginia, the State of Maryland, and the District of Columbia to enter into a compact relating to the establishment of the Washington Metrorail Safety Commission. *Introduced by HOYER, D-Md., on Feb. 16, 2017. House Judiciary reported, amended, July 17 (H Rept 115-227). House passed, under suspension of the rules, July 17. Senate passed Aug. 4. President signed Aug. 22, 2017.*

■ **PL 115-55** (HR 2288) Grant the consent and approval of Congress for the Commonwealth of Virginia, the State of Maryland, and the District of Columbia to a enter into a compact relating to the establishment of the Washington Metrorail Safety Commission. *Introduced by BOST, R-Ill., on May 2, 2017. House Veterans Affairs reported May 19 (H Rept 115-135). House passed, under suspension of the rules, May 23. Senate Veterans' Affairs discharged Aug. 1. Senate passed, amended, Aug. 1. House agreed to Senate amendments Aug. 11.*

■ **PL 115-56** (HR 601) Enhance the transparency and accelerate the impact of assistance provided under the Foreign Assistance Act of 1961 to promote quality basic education in developing countries, to better enable such countries to achieve universal access to quality basic education and improved learning outcomes, to eliminate duplication and waste. *Introduced by LOWEY, D-Calif., on Jan. 23, 2017. House passed, under suspension of the rules, Jan. 24. Senate Foreign Relations reported, amended, June 5 (no written report). Senate passed, amended, Aug. 1. House agreed to Senate amendments, with an amendment, Sept. 6. Senate agreed to House amendment, with an amendment, Sept. 7.*

■ **PL 115-57** (HR 3732) Provide authority for increased fiscal year 2017 and 2018 payments for temporary assistance to United States citizens returned from foreign countries. *Introduced by REICHERT, R-Wash., on Sept. 11, 2017. House Ways and Means discharged Sept. 11. House Budget discharged Sept. 11. House passed Sept. 11. Senate passed Sept. 11. President signed Sept. 12, 2017.*

■ **PL 115-58** (SJ Res 49) Condemning the violence and domestic terrorist attack that took place during events between August 11 and August 12, 2017 in Charlottesville, Virginia, recognizing first responders, and offering condolences to the family and friends of victims. *Introduced by WARNER, D-Va., on Sept. 6, 2017. Senate passed Sept. 11. House passed Sept. 12. President signed Sept. 14, 2017.*

■ **PL 115-59** (HR 624) Restrict the inclusion of social security account numbers on Federal documents sent by mail, and for other purposes. *Introduced by VALDAO, R-Calif., on Jan. 24, 2017. House Oversight and Government Reform reported, amended, May 23 (H Rept 115-150, Part 1). House Ways and Means discharged May 23. House passed, under suspension of the rules, May 24. Senate passed Sept. 6. President signed Sept. 15, 2017.*

■ **PL 115-60** (S 1616) Award the Congressional Gold Medal to Bob Dole, in recognition for his service to the nation as a soldier, legislator, and statesman. *Introduced by ROBERTS, R-Kan., on July 24, 2017. Senate Banking, Housing and Urban Affairs discharged Aug. 3. Senate passed Aug. 3. House passed, under suspension of the rules, Sept. 5. President signed Sept. 15, 2017.*

■ **PL 115-61** (HR 3110) Amend the Financial Stability Act of 2010 to modify the term of the independent member of the Financial Stability Oversight Council. *Introduced by HULTGREN, R-Ill., on June 29, 2017. House Financial Services reported Sept. 5 (H Rept 115-293). House passed Sept. 5. Senate passed Sept. 19. President signed Sept. 27, 2017.*

■ **PL 115-62** (HR 3819) Extend certain expiring provisions of law administered by the Secretary of Veterans Affairs. *Introduced by MAST, R-Fla., on Sept. 25, 2017. House passed, under suspension of the rules, Sept. 25. Senate passed Sept. 27. President signed Sept. 29, 2017.*

■ **PL 115-63** (HR 3823) Extend authorizations for the airport improvement program, to amend the Internal Revenue Code of 1986 to extend the funding and expenditure authority of the Airport and Airway Trust Fund, to provide disaster tax relief. *Introduced by BRADY, R-Texas, on Sept. 25, 2017. House passed Sept. 28. Senate passed Sept. 28. President signed Sept. 29, 2017.*

■ **PL 115-64** (S 1866) Provide the Secretary of Education with waiver authority for the reallocation rules and authority to extend the deadline by which funds have to be reallocated in the campus-based aid programs under the Higher Education Act of 1965 due to Hurricane Harvey, Hurricane Irma, and Hurricane Maria, to provide equitable services to children and teachers in private schools. *Introduced by ALEXANDER, R-Tenn., on Sept. 26, 2017. Senate passed Sept. 26. House passed, under suspension of the rules, Sept. 28. President signed Sept. 29, 2017.*

■ **PL 115-65** (HR 2519) Require the Secretary of the Treasury to mint commemorative coins in recognition of the 100th anniversary of The American Legion. *Introduced by WALZ, D-Minn., on May 18, 2017. House passed, amended, under suspension of the rules, Sept. 25. Senate passed Sept. 28. President signed Oct. 6, 2017.*

■ **PL 115-66** (S 327) Direct the Securities and Exchange Commission (SEC) to establish and implement a "safe harbor" for certain investment fund research reports published by brokers and dealers. *Introduced by HELLER, R-Nev., on Feb. 7, 2017. Senate Banking, Housing and Urban Affairs reported, amended, March 13 (no written report). Senate passed Sept. 11. House passed Sept. 27. President signed Oct. 6, 2017.*

■ **PL 115-67** (S 810) Facilitate construction of a bridge on certain property in Christian County, Missouri. *Introduced by BLUNT, R-Mo., on April 4, 2017. Senate Environment and Public Works reported, amended, Aug. 2 (S Rept 115-142). Senate passed Aug. 3. House passed Sept. 25. President signed Oct. 6, 2017.*

■ **PL 115-68** (S 1141) Ensure that the United States promotes the meaningful participation of women in mediation and negotiation processes seeking to prevent, mitigate, or resolve violent conflict. *Introduced by SHAHEEN, D-N.H., on May 16, 2017. Senate Foreign Relations reported June 8 (S Rept 115-93). Senate passed Aug. 3. House passed, under suspension of the rules, Sept. 25. President signed Oct. 6, 2017.*

■ **PL 115-69** (HR 1117) Require the Administrator of the Federal Emergency Management Agency to submit a report regarding certain plans regarding assistance to applicants and grantees during the response to an emergency or disaster. *Introduced by HARTZLER, R-Mo., on Feb. 16, 2017. House Transportation and Infrastructure reported, amended, March 9 (H Rept 115-31). House passed, under suspension of the rules, March 27. Senate Homeland Security and Governmental Affairs discharged Sept. 18. Senate passed Oct. 4. President signed Oct. 18, 2017.*

■ **PL 115-70** (S 178) Prevent elder abuse and exploitation and improve the justice system's response to victims in elder abuse and exploitation cases. *Introduced by GRASSLEY, R-Iowa, on Jan. 20, 2017. Senate Judiciary reported March 23 (S Rept 115-9). Senate passed, amended, Aug. 1. House passed, under suspension of the rules, Oct. 3. President signed Oct. 18, 2017.*

■ **PL 115-71** (S 652) Reauthorize a program for early detection, diagnosis, and treatment regarding deaf and hard-of-hearing newborns, infants, and young children. *Introduced by PORTMAN, R-Ohio, on March 15, 2017. Senate Health, Education, Labor and Pensions reported, amended, May 1 (no written report). Senate passed Sept. 6. House passed, under suspension of the rules, Oct. 3. President signed Oct. 18, 2017.*

■ **PL 115-72** (HR 2266) Authorize the appointment of additional bankruptcy judges. *Introduced by CONYERS, D-Mich., on May 1, 2017. House Judiciary reported, amended, May 17 (H Rept 115-130). House passed, under suspension of the rules, May 17. Senate Judiciary discharged Sept. 27. Senate passed, amended, Sept. 27. House agreed to Senate amendment, with an amendment, Oct. 12.*

■ **PL 115-73** (S 585) Provide greater whistleblower protections for Federal employees. *Introduced by JOHNSON, R-Wis., on March 8, 2017. Senate Homeland Security and Governmental Affairs reported, amended, May 4 (S Rept 115-44). Senate passed May 25. House passed Oct. 12. President signed Oct. 26, 2017.*

■ **PL 115-74** (HJ Res 111) Provide for congressional disapproval of the rule submitted by Bureau of Consumer Financial Protection relating to "Arbitration Agreements." *Introduced by ROTHFUS, R-Pa., on July 20, 2017. House passed July 25. Senate passed Oct. 24. President signed Nov. 1, 2017.*

■ **PL 115-75** (HR 1329) Increase the rates of compensation for veterans with service-connected disabilities and the rates of dependency and indemnity compensation for the survivors of certain disabled veterans. *Introduced by BOST, R-Ill., on March 2, 2017. House Veterans Affairs reported, amended, May 19 (H Rept 115-134). House passed, under suspension of the rules, May 23. Senate Veterans' Affairs discharged Oct. 25. Senate passed Oct. 25. President signed Nov. 2, 2017.*

■ **PL 115-76** (HR 1616) Authorize the National Computer Forensics Institute. *Introduced by RATCLIFFE, R-Texas, on March 17, 2017. House passed, under suspension of the rules, May 16. Senate Judiciary discharged Oct. 2. Senate passed, amended, Oct. 2. House agreed to Senate amendment Oct. 12. President signed Nov. 2, 2017.*

■ **PL 115-77** (HR 2989) Establish the Frederick Douglass Bicentennial Commission. *Introduced by NORTON, D-D.C., on June 21, 2017. House Oversight and Government Reform reported, amended, Oct. 5 (H Rept 115-340). House passed, under suspension of the rules, Oct. 18. Senate passed Oct. 18. President signed Nov. 2, 2017.*

■ **PL 115-78** (S 190) Provide for consideration of the extension under the Energy Policy and Conservation Act of nonapplication of No-Load Mode energy efficiency standards to certain security or life safety alarms or surveillance systems. *Introduced by GARDNER, R-Colo., on Jan. 23, 2017 Senate Energy and Natural Resources reported May 24 (S Rept 115-76). Senate passed Aug. 1. House passed, under suspension of the rules, Oct. 11. President signed Nov. 2, 2017.*

■ **PL 115-79** (S 504) Permanently authorize the Asia-Pacific Economic Cooperation Business Travel Card Program. *Introduced by HIRONO, D-Hawaii, on March 2, 2017. Senate Homeland Security and Governmental Affairs reported Aug. 1 (S Rept 115-140). Senate passed, amended, Sept. 26. House passed, under suspension of the rules, Oct. 23. President signed Nov. 2, 2017.*

■ **PL 115-80** (S 920) Establish a National Clinical Care Commission. *Introduced by SHAHEEN, D-N.H., on April 24, 2017. Senate Health, Education, Labor and Pensions reported May 1 (no written report). Senate passed, amended, Sept. 6. House passed, under suspension of the rules, Oct. 11. President signed Nov. 2, 2017.*

■ **PL 115-81** (S 1617) Designate the checkpoint of the United States Border Patrol located on United States Highway 77 North in Sarita, Texas, as the "Javier Vega, Jr. Border Patrol Checkpoint." *Introduced by CORNYN, R-Texas, on July 24, 2017. Senate Homeland Security and Governmental Affairs discharged Aug. 3. Senate passed Aug. 3. House passed, under suspension of the rules, Oct. 10. President signed Nov. 2, 2017.*

■ **PL 115-82** (S 782) Reauthorize the National Internet Crimes Against Children Task Force Program. *Introduced by CORNYN, R-Texas, on July 24, 2017. Senate Judiciary reported June 8 (no written report). Senate passed June 15. House passed, amended, under suspension of the rules, Oct. 3. Senate agreed to House amendment Oct. 26. President signed Nov. 2, 2017.*

■ **PL 115-83** (HR 304) Amend the Controlled Substances Act with regard to the provision of emergency medical services. *Introduced by HUDSON, R-N.C., on Jan. 5, 2017. House passed, under suspension of the rules, Jan. 9. Senate Health, Education, Labor and Pensions discharged Oct. 24. Senate passed, amended, Oct. 24. House agreed to Senate amendment Nov. 2. President signed Nov. 17, 2017.*

■ **PL 115-84** (HR 3031) Provide for flexibility in making withdrawals from a Thrify Savings Plan account. *Introduced by CUMMINGS, D-Md., on June 23, 2017. House Oversight and Government Reform reported, amended, Oct. 10 (H Rept 115-343). House passed Oct. 11. Senate passed Nov. 6. President signed Nov. 17, 2017.*

■ **PL 115-85** (HR 194) Ensure the effective processing of mail by Federal agencies. *Introduced by RUSSELL, R-Okla., on Jan. 3, 2017. House Oversight and Government Reform reported March 29 (H Rept 115-66). House passed, under suspension of the rules, May 17. Senate Homeland Security and Governmental Affairs reported Oct. 19 (no written report). Senate passed Nov. 8. President signed Nov. 21, 2017.*

■ **PL 115-86** (HR 1545) Clarify the authority of the Secretary of Veterans Affairs to disclose certain patient information to State controlled substance monitoring programs. *Introduced by KUSTER, D-N.H., on March 15, 2017. House Veterans Affairs reported May 22 (H Rept 115-144). House passed, under suspension of the rules, May 23. Senate Veterans' Affairs discharged Nov. 15. Senate passed Nov. 15. President signed Nov. 21, 2017.*

■ **PL 115-87** (HR 1679) Ensure that the Federal Emergency Management Agency's current efforts to modernize its grant management system includes applicant accessibility and transparency. *Introduced by GRAVES, R-La., on March 22, 2017. House Transportation and Infrastructure reported May 2 (H Rept 115-107). House passed, under suspension of the rules, May 2. Senate Homeland Security and Governmental Affairs reported Sept. 18 (S Rept 115-159). Senate passed Nov. 13. President signed Nov. 21, 2017.*

■ **PL 115-88** (HR 3243) Eliminate the sunset of certain provisions relating to information technology and extend the sunset relating to the Federal Data Center Consolidation Initiative. *Introduced by CONNOLLY, R-Va., on July 14, 2017. House Oversight and Government Reform reported Oct. 10 (H Rept 115-344). House passed, under suspension of the rules, Oct. 11. Senate passed Nov. 8. President signed Nov. 21, 2017.*

■ **PL 115-89** (HR 3949) Provide for the designation of State approving agencies for multi-State apprenticeship programs for purposes of the educational assistance programs of the Department of Veterans Affairs. *Introduced by KHANNA, D-Calif., on Oct. 4, 2017. House Veterans Affairs reported, amended, Nov. 7 (H Rept 115-398). House passed, under suspension of the rules, Nov. 7. Senate passed Nov. 15. President signed Nov. 21, 2017.*

■ **PL 115-90** (HJ Res 123) Make further continuing appropriations for fiscal year 2018. *Introduced by FRELINGHUYSEN,* R-N.J., on Dec. 4, 2017. House passed Dec. 7. Senate passed Dec. 7. President signed Dec. 8, 2017.

■ **PL 115-91** (HR 2810) Authorize appropriations for fiscal year 2018 for military activities of the Department of Defense, for military construction, and for defense activities of the Department of Energy and to prescribe military personnel strengths for such fiscal year. *Introduced by THORNBERRY, D-Texas, on June 7, 2017. House Armed Services reported, amended, July 6 (H Rept 115-200). House passed July 14. Senate passed, amended, Sept. 18. House agreed to conference report Nov. 14 (H Rept 115-404). Senate agreed to conference report Nov. 16.*

■ **PL 115-92** (HR 4374) Amend the Federal Food, Drug, and Cosmetic Act to authorize additional emergency uses for medical products to reduce deaths and severity of injuries caused by agents of war. *Introduced by WALDEN, R-Ore., on Nov. 13, 2017. House passed, under suspension of the rules, Nov. 15. Senate passed Nov. 16. President signed Dec. 12, 2017.*

■ **PL 115-93** (HR 228) Facilitate the ability of Indian tribes to integrate the employment, training, and related services from diverse Federal sources. *Introduced by YOUNG, R-Alaska, on Jan. 3, 2017. House passed, amended, under suspension of the rules, Feb. 27. Senate passed Nov. 29. President signed Dec. 18, 2017.*

■ **PL 115-94** (S 371) Make technical changes and other improvements to the Department of State Authorities Act. *Introduced by CORKER, R-Tenn., on Feb. 14, 2017. Senate Foreign Relations discharged May 1. Senate passed, amended, May 1. House Foreign Affairs discharged, amended, July 28. House passed, amended, July 28. Senate agreed to House amendment Dec. 4.*

■ **PL 115-95** (S 1266) Authorize the Secretary of Veterans Affairs to enter into contracts with nonprofit organizations to investigate medical centers of the Department of Veterans Affairs. *Introduced by INHOFE, R-Okla., on May 25, 2017. Senate Veterans' Affairs discharged Nov. 9. Senate passed Nov. 9. House passed, under suspension of the rules, Dec. 6. President signed Dec. 20, 2017.*

■ **PL 115-96** (HR 1370) Require the Secretary of Homeland Security to issue Department of Homeland Security-wide guidance and develop training programs as part of the Department of Homeland Security Blue Campaign. *Introduced by MCCAUL, R-Texas, on March 6, 2017. House Homeland Security reported, amended, May 22 (H Rept 115-143). House Judiciary discharged May 22. House passed, under suspension of the rules, May 23. Senate Homeland Security and Governmental Affairs discharged Nov. 6. Senate passed, amended, Nov. 6.*

■ **PL 115-97** (HR 1) Provide for reconciliation pursuant to titles II and V of the concurrent resolution on the budget for fiscal year 2018. *Introduced by BRADY, R-Texas, on Nov. 2, 2017. House Ways and Means reported, amended Nov. 13 (H Rept 115-409). House passed Nov. 16. Senate passed, amended, Dec. 2. Senate receded from its amendment and concurred in the bill with a further amendment Dec 20. House concurred in Senate amendment Dec. 20. President signed Dec. 22, 2017.*

Appendix H

HOUSE ROLL CALL VOTES

VOTES WITH PRESIDENTIAL POSITIONS ARE LISTED ON PAGE B-5

House Roll Call Index by Subject

House Roll Call Index by Bill Number

‖‖ HOUSE VOTES

VOTE NUMBER

1. QUORUM CALL. A quorum was present with 434 members responding. (Not listed at right.)

2. ELECTION OF THE SPEAKER. Nomination of Paul D. Ryan, D-Wis., and Nancy Pelosi, D-Calif., for Speaker of House of Representatives for the 115th Congress. A "Y" on the chart represents a vote for Ryan, an "N" represents a vote for Pelosi, with 4 exceptions. The following two votes were cast for Tim Ryan, D-Ohio: Cooper, D-Tenn.; Rice, D-N.Y. Rep. Massie, R-Ky., cast his vote for Daniel Webster, R-Fla. Rep. Kind, D-Wis., cast a vote for Cooper, D-Tenn. Rep. Sinema cast a vote for Lewis, D-Ga. Ryan elected 239-189 : R 239-0; D 0-189. Jan. 3, 2017.

3. H RES 5. HOUSE ORGANIZING RESOLUTION/MOTION TO TABLE. Mc-Carthy, R-Calif., motion to table (kill) the Norton, D-D.C., motion to refer the resolution that would set the House rules for the 115th Congress to a select committee with instructions that it not be reported back until after the panel has completed a study of and determined whether there is reason to limit delegates' voting rights in the Committee of the Whole. Motion agreed to 228-184 : R 228-0; D 0-184. Jan. 3, 2017.

4. H RES 5. HOUSE ORGANIZING RESOLUTION/PREVIOUS QUESTION. Sessions, R-Texas, motion to order the previous question (thus ending debate and the possibility of amendment) on the resolution (H Res 5) that would establish the rules of the House for the 115th Congress. Motion agreed to 237-193 : R 237-0; D 0-193. Jan. 3, 2017.

5. H RES 5. HOUSE ORGANIZING RESOLUTION/MOTION TO COMMIT. Lewis, D-Ga., motion to commit the resolution to a select committee consisting of the House majority and minority leaders with instructions to report back immediately with an amendment that would remove a proposal that would set monetary fines for using electronic devices on the House floor to take photos or videos. Motion rejected 193-236 : R 0-236; D 193-0. Jan. 3, 2017.

6. H RES 5. HOUSE ORGANIZING RESOLUTION/ADOPTION. Adoption of the resolution that would establish the rules of the House for the 115th Congress. Many of the rules that were in effect at the end of the 114th Congress would carry over. Among the rules changes, it would set monetary fines for using electronic devices on the House floor to take photos or videos. Adopted 234-193 : R 234-3; D 0-190 Jan. 3, 2017.

7. HR 21. REGULATION DISAPPROVAL/RECOMMIT. Castor, D-Fla., motion to recommit the bill to the House Judiciary Committee with instructions to report back immediately with an amendment that would add an exemption to the bill for rules that prohibit health insurance companies from discriminating against individuals based on gender or preexisting conditions. The amendment also would exempt from the measure rules that prohibit higher premiums or out-of-pocket costs for seniors for medication under the Medicare Part D prescription drug program. Motion rejected 183-236 : R 0-235; D 183-1. Jan. 4, 2017.

	2	3	4	5	6	7
ALABAMA						
1 **Byrne**	Y	Y	Y	N	Y	N
2 **Roby**	Y	Y	Y	N	Y	N
3 **Rogers**	Y	Y	Y	N	Y	N
4 **Aderholt**	Y	Y	Y	N	Y	N
5 **Brooks**	Y	Y	Y	N	Y	N
6 **Palmer**	Y	Y	Y	N	Y	N
7 Sewell	N	N	N	Y	N	Y
ALASKA						
AL **Young**	Y	?	Y	N	Y	N
ARIZONA						
1 O'Halleran	N	N	N	Y	N	Y
2 **McSally**	Y	Y	Y	N	Y	N
3 Grijalva	N	N	N	Y	N	Y
4 **Gosar**	Y	Y	Y	N	Y	N
5 **Biggs**	Y	Y	Y	N	Y	N
6 **Schweikert**	Y	Y	Y	N	Y	N
7 Gallego	N	N	N	Y	N	+
8 **Franks**	Y	Y	Y	N	Y	N
9 **Sinema**	C	N	N	Y	N	N
ARKANSAS						
1 **Crawford**	Y	Y	Y	N	Y	N
2 **Hill**	Y	Y	Y	N	Y	N
3 **Womack**	Y	Y	Y	N	Y	N
4 **Westerman**	Y	Y	Y	N	Y	N
CALIFORNIA						
1 **LaMalfa**	Y	Y	Y	N	Y	N
2 Huffman	N	N	N	Y	N	Y
3 Garamendi	N	N	N	Y	N	Y
4 **McClintock**	Y	Y	Y	N	Y	N
5 Thompson	N	N	N	Y	N	Y
6 Matsui	N	N	N	Y	N	Y
7 Bera	N	N	N	Y	N	Y
8 **Cook**	Y	Y	Y	N	Y	N
9 McNerney	N	N	N	Y	N	Y
10 **Denham**	Y	Y	Y	N	Y	N
11 DeSaulnier	N	N	N	Y	N	Y
12 Pelosi	N	N	N	Y	N	Y
13 Lee	N	N	N	Y	N	Y
14 Speier	N	N	N	Y	N	Y
15 Swalwell	N	N	N	Y	N	Y
16 Costa	N	N	N	Y	N	?
17 Khanna	N	N	N	Y	N	Y
18 Eshoo	N	N	N	Y	N	Y
19 Lofgren	N	N	N	Y	N	Y
20 Panetta	N	N	N	Y	N	Y
21 **Valadao**	Y	Y	Y	N	Y	N
22 **Nunes**	Y	Y	Y	N	Y	N
23 **McCarthy**	Y	Y	Y	N	Y	N
24 Carbajal	N	N	N	Y	N	Y
25 **Knight**	Y	Y	Y	N	Y	N
26 Brownley	N	N	N	Y	N	Y
27 Chu	N	N	N	Y	N	Y
28 Schiff	N	N	N	Y	N	Y
29 Cardenas	N	N	N	Y	N	Y
30 Sherman	N	N	N	Y	N	Y
31 Aguilar	N	N	N	Y	N	Y
32 Napolitano	N	N	N	Y	N	Y
33 Lieu	N	N	N	Y	N	Y
34 Becerra	N	N	N	Y	N	+
35 Torres	N	N	N	Y	N	Y
36 Ruiz	N	N	N	Y	N	Y
37 Bass	N	N	N	Y	N	Y
38 Sánchez, Linda	N	N	N	Y	N	Y
39 **Royce**	Y	Y	Y	N	Y	N
40 Roybal-Allard	N	N	N	Y	N	Y
41 Takano	N	N	N	Y	N	Y
42 **Calvert**	Y	Y	Y	N	Y	N
43 Waters	N	N	N	Y	N	?
44 Barragan	N	N	N	Y	N	Y
45 **Walters**	Y	Y	Y	N	Y	N
46 Correa	N	N	N	Y	N	Y
47 Lowenthal	N	N	N	Y	N	Y
48 **Rohrabacher**	Y	Y	Y	?	Y	N
49 **Issa**	Y	?	Y	N	Y	N
50 **Hunter**	Y	Y	Y	N	Y	N
51 Vargas	N	N	N	Y	N	Y
52 Peters	N	N	N	Y	N	Y
53 Davis	N	N	N	Y	N	Y
COLORADO						
1 DeGette	N	N	N	Y	N	Y
2 Polis	N	N	N	Y	N	Y
3 **Tipton**	Y	Y	Y	N	Y	N
4 **Buck**	Y	Y	Y	N	Y	N
5 **Lamborn**	Y	Y	Y	N	Y	N
6 **Coffman**	Y	Y	Y	N	Y	N
7 Perlmutter	N	N	N	Y	–	Y
CONNECTICUT						
1 Larson	N	N	N	Y	N	Y
2 Courtney	N	N	N	Y	N	Y
3 DeLauro	N	N	N	Y	N	Y
4 Himes	N	N	N	Y	N	Y
5 Esty	N	N	N	Y	N	Y
DELAWARE						
AL Blunt Rochester	N	–	N	Y	N	Y
FLORIDA						
1 **Gaetz**	Y	Y	Y	N	Y	N
2 **Dunn**	Y	Y	Y	N	Y	N
3 **Yoho**	Y	Y	Y	N	Y	N
4 **Rutherford**	Y	Y	Y	N	Y	N
5 Lawson	N	N	N	Y	N	Y
6 **DeSantis**	Y	Y	Y	N	Y	N
7 Murphy	N	N	N	Y	N	Y
8 **Posey**	Y	Y	Y	N	Y	N
9 Soto	N	N	N	Y	N	Y
10 Demings	N	N	N	Y	N	Y
11 **Webster**	Y	Y	Y	N	Y	N
12 **Bilirakis**	Y	Y	Y	N	Y	N
13 Crist	N	N	N	Y	N	Y
14 Castor	N	N	N	Y	N	Y
15 **Ross**	Y	Y	Y	N	Y	N
16 **Buchanan**	Y	Y	Y	N	Y	N
17 **Rooney, T.**	Y	?	Y	N	Y	N
18 **Mast**	Y	Y	Y	N	Y	N
19 **Rooney, F.**	Y	Y	Y	N	Y	N
20 Hastings	N	N	N	Y	N	Y
21 Frankel	N	N	N	Y	–	Y
22 Deutch	N	N	N	Y	N	Y
23 Wasserman Schultz	N	N	N	Y	N	Y
24 Wilson	N	N	N	Y	N	Y
25 **Diaz-Balart**	Y	Y	Y	N	Y	N
26 **Curbelo**	Y	Y	Y	N	Y	N
27 **Ros-Lehtinen**	Y	Y	Y	N	Y	N
GEORGIA						
1 **Carter**	Y	Y	Y	N	Y	N
2 Bishop	N	?	N	Y	N	Y
3 **Ferguson**	Y	Y	Y	N	Y	N
4 Johnson	N	N	N	Y	N	Y
5 Lewis	N	N	N	Y	N	Y
6 **Price**	Y	?	?	?	?	?
7 **Woodall**	Y	Y	Y	N	Y	N
8 **Scott, A.**	Y	Y	Y	N	Y	N
9 **Collins**	Y	Y	Y	N	Y	N
10 **Hice**	Y	Y	Y	N	Y	N
11 **Loudermilk**	Y	Y	Y	N	Y	N
12 **Allen**	Y	Y	Y	N	Y	N
13 Scott, D.	N	N	N	Y	N	Y
14 **Graves**	Y	Y	Y	N	Y	N
HAWAII						
1 Hanabusa	N	?	N	Y	N	Y
2 Gabbard	N	N	N	Y	N	Y
IDAHO						
1 **Labrador**	Y	Y	Y	N	Y	N
2 **Simpson**	Y	Y	Y	N	Y	N
ILLINOIS						
1 Rush	N	N	N	Y	?	?
2 Kelly	N	N	N	Y	N	Y
3 Lipinski	N	N	N	Y	N	Y
4 Gutierrez	N	–	N	Y	N	Y
5 Quigley	N	N	N	Y	N	Y
6 **Roskam**	Y	Y	Y	N	Y	N
7 Davis, D.	N	N	N	Y	N	Y
8 Krishnamoorthi	N	N	N	Y	N	Y
9 Schakowsky	N	N	N	Y	N	Y
10 Schneider	N	N	N	Y	N	Y
11 Foster	N	N	N	Y	N	Y
12 **Bost**	Y	Y	Y	N	Y	N
13 **Davis, R.**	Y	Y	Y	N	Y	N
14 **Hultgren**	Y	Y	Y	N	Y	N
15 **Shimkus**	Y	Y	Y	N	Y	N

	2	3	4	5	6	7
16 **Kinzinger**	Y	Y	Y	N	Y	N
17 Bustos	N	N	N	Y	N	Y
18 **LaHood**	Y	Y	Y	N	Y	N
INDIANA						
1 Visclosky	N	N	N	Y	N	Y
2 **Walorski**	Y	Y	Y	N	Y	N
3 **Banks**	Y	Y	Y	N	Y	N
4 **Rokita**	Y	Y	Y	N	Y	N
5 **Brooks**	Y	Y	Y	N	Y	N
6 **Messer**	Y	Y	Y	N	Y	N
7 Carson	N	N	N	Y	N	Y
8 **Bucshon**	Y	Y	Y	N	Y	N
9 **Hollingsworth**	Y	Y	Y	N	Y	N
IOWA						
1 **Blum**	Y	Y	Y	N	Y	N
2 Loebsack	N	N	N	Y	N	Y
3 **Young**	Y	Y	Y	N	Y	N
4 **King**	Y	?	Y	N	Y	N
KANSAS						
1 **Marshall**	Y	Y	Y	N	Y	N
2 **Jenkins**	Y	Y	Y	N	Y	N
3 **Yoder**	Y	Y	Y	N	Y	N
4 **Pompeo**	Y	?	?	?	?	?
KENTUCKY						
1 **Comer**	Y	Y	Y	N	Y	N
2 **Guthrie**	Y	Y	Y	N	Y	N
3 Yarmuth	N	N	N	Y	N	Y
4 **Massie**	C	Y	Y	N	N	N
5 **Rogers**	Y	Y	Y	N	Y	N
6 **Barr**	Y	Y	Y	N	Y	N
LOUISIANA						
1 **Scalise**	Y	Y	Y	N	Y	N
2 Richmond	N	N	N	Y	N	?
3 **Higgins**	Y	Y	Y	N	Y	N
4 **Johnson**	Y	Y	Y	N	Y	N
5 **Abraham**	Y	Y	Y	N	Y	N
6 **Graves**	Y	Y	Y	N	Y	N
MAINE						
1 Pingree	N	N	N	Y	N	Y
2 **Poliquin**	Y	Y	Y	N	Y	N
MARYLAND						
1 **Harris**	Y	Y	Y	N	Y	N
2 Ruppersberger	N	N	N	Y	N	Y
3 Sarbanes	N	N	N	Y	N	Y
4 Brown	N	N	N	Y	N	Y
5 Hoyer	N	N	N	Y	N	Y
6 Delaney	N	N	N	Y	N	Y
7 Cummings	N	N	N	Y	N	Y
8 Raskin	N	N	N	Y	N	Y
MASSACHUSETTS						
1 Neal	N	N	N	Y	N	Y
2 McGovern	N	N	N	Y	N	Y
3 Tsongas	N	N	N	Y	N	Y
4 Kennedy	N	N	N	Y	N	Y
5 Clark	N	N	N	Y	N	Y
6 Moulton	N	N	N	Y	N	Y
7 Capuano	N	N	N	Y	N	Y
8 Lynch	N	?	N	Y	N	Y
9 Keating	N	N	N	Y	N	Y
MICHIGAN						
1 **Bergman**	Y	Y	Y	N	Y	N
2 **Huizenga**	Y	Y	Y	N	Y	N
3 **Amash**	Y	Y	Y	N	N	N
4 **Moolenaar**	Y	Y	Y	N	Y	N
5 Kildee	N	N	N	Y	N	Y
6 **Upton**	Y	Y	Y	N	Y	N
7 **Walberg**	Y	Y	Y	N	Y	N
8 **Bishop**	Y	Y	Y	N	Y	N
9 Levin	N	N	N	Y	N	Y
10 **Mitchell**	Y	Y	Y	N	Y	N
11 **Trott**	Y	Y	Y	N	Y	N
12 Dingell	N	N	N	Y	N	Y
13 Conyers	N	N	N	Y	N	Y
14 Lawrence	N	N	N	Y	N	Y
MINNESOTA						
1 Walz	N	N	N	Y	N	Y
2 **Lewis**	Y	Y	Y	N	Y	N
3 **Paulsen**	Y	Y	Y	N	Y	N
4 McCollum	N	N	N	Y	N	Y
5 Ellison	N	N	N	Y	N	Y
6 **Emmer**	Y	Y	Y	N	Y	N
7 Peterson	N	N	N	Y	N	Y
8 Nolan	N	N	N	Y	N	Y
MISSISSIPPI						
1 **Kelly**	Y	Y	Y	N	Y	N
2 Thompson	N	N	N	Y	N	Y
3 **Harper**	Y	Y	Y	N	Y	N
4 **Palazzo**	Y	Y	Y	N	Y	N
MISSOURI						
1 Clay	N	N	N	Y	N	Y
2 **Wagner**	Y	Y	Y	N	Y	N
3 **Luetkemeyer**	Y	Y	Y	N	Y	N
4 **Hartzler**	Y	Y	Y	N	Y	N
5 Cleaver	N	N	N	Y	N	Y
6 **Graves**	Y	Y	Y	N	Y	N
7 **Long**	Y	Y	Y	N	Y	N
8 **Smith**	Y	Y	Y	N	Y	N
MONTANA						
AL **Zinke**	Y	?	Y	N	Y	N
NEBRASKA						
1 **Fortenberry**	Y	Y	Y	N	Y	N
2 **Bacon**	Y	Y	Y	N	Y	N
3 **Smith**	Y	Y	Y	N	Y	N
NEVADA						
1 Titus	N	N	N	Y	N	Y
2 **Amodei**	Y	Y	Y	N	Y	N
3 Rosen	N	N	N	Y	N	Y
4 Kihuen	N	N	N	Y	N	?
NEW HAMPSHIRE						
1 Shea-Porter	N	N	N	Y	N	Y
2 Kuster	N	N	N	Y	N	Y
NEW JERSEY						
1 Norcross	N	N	N	Y	N	Y
2 **LoBiondo**	Y	Y	Y	N	Y	N
3 **MacArthur**	Y	Y	Y	N	Y	N
4 **Smith**	Y	Y	Y	N	Y	N
5 Gottheimer	N	N	N	Y	N	Y
6 Pallone	N	N	N	Y	N	Y
7 **Lance**	Y	Y	Y	N	Y	N
8 Sires	N	N	N	Y	N	Y
9 Pascrell	N	N	N	Y	N	Y
10 Payne	N	N	N	Y	N	Y
11 **Frelinghuysen**	Y	Y	Y	N	Y	N
12 Watson Coleman	N	N	N	Y	N	Y
NEW MEXICO						
1 Lujan Grisham	N	N	N	Y	N	Y
2 **Pearce**	Y	Y	Y	N	Y	N
3 Luján	N	N	N	Y	N	Y
NEW YORK						
1 **Zeldin**	Y	Y	Y	N	Y	N
2 **King**	Y	Y	Y	N	Y	N
3 Suozzi	N	N	N	Y	N	Y
4 Rice	C	?	N	Y	N	Y
5 Meeks	N	N	N	Y	N	Y
6 Meng	N	N	N	Y	N	Y
7 Velázquez	N	N	N	Y	N	Y
8 Jeffries	N	N	N	Y	N	Y
9 Clarke	N	N	N	Y	N	Y
10 Nadler	N	N	N	Y	N	Y
11 **Donovan**	Y	Y	Y	N	Y	N
12 Maloney, C.	N	N	N	Y	N	Y
13 Espaillat	N	N	N	Y	N	Y
14 Crowley	N	N	N	Y	N	Y
15 Serrano	N	N	N	Y	N	Y
16 Engel	N	N	N	Y	N	Y
17 Lowey	N	N	N	Y	N	Y
18 Maloney, S.P.	N	N	N	Y	N	Y
19 **Faso**	Y	Y	Y	N	Y	N
20 Tonko	N	N	N	Y	N	Y
21 **Stefanik**	Y	Y	Y	N	Y	N
22 **Tenney**	Y	Y	Y	N	Y	N
23 **Reed**	Y	Y	Y	N	Y	N
24 **Katko**	Y	Y	Y	N	Y	N
25 Slaughter	N	N	N	Y	N	Y
26 Higgins	N	?	N	Y	N	Y
27 **Collins**	Y	Y	Y	N	Y	–
NORTH CAROLINA						
1 Butterfield	N	N	N	Y	N	Y
2 **Holding**	Y	Y	Y	N	Y	N
3 **Jones**	Y	?	Y	N	N	N
4 Price	N	N	N	Y	N	Y
%5 **Foxx**	Y	Y	Y	N	Y	N
6 **Walker**	Y	Y	Y	N	Y	N
7 **Rouzer**	Y	Y	Y	N	Y	N
8 **Hudson**	Y	Y	Y	N	Y	N
9 **Pittenger**	Y	Y	Y	N	Y	N
10 **McHenry**	Y	Y	Y	N	Y	N
11 **Meadows**	Y	Y	Y	N	Y	N
12 Adams	N	?	N	Y	N	Y
13 **Budd**	Y	Y	Y	N	Y	N
NORTH DAKOTA						
AL **Cramer**	Y	Y	Y	N	Y	N
OHIO						
1 **Chabot**	Y	Y	Y	N	Y	N
2 **Wenstrup**	Y	Y	Y	N	Y	N
3 Beatty	N	N	N	Y	N	Y
4 **Jordan**	Y	Y	Y	N	Y	N
5 **Latta**	Y	Y	Y	N	Y	N
6 **Johnson**	Y	Y	Y	N	Y	N
7 **Gibbs**	Y	Y	Y	N	Y	N
8 **Davidson**	Y	Y	Y	N	Y	N
9 Kaptur	N	N	N	Y	N	Y
10 **Turner**	Y	Y	Y	N	Y	N
11 Fudge	N	?	N	Y	N	Y
12 **Tiberi**	Y	Y	Y	N	Y	N
13 Ryan	N	N	N	Y	N	Y
14 **Joyce**	Y	Y	Y	N	Y	N
15 **Stivers**	Y	Y	Y	N	Y	N
16 **Renacci**	Y	+	Y	N	Y	N
OKLAHOMA						
1 **Bridenstine**	Y	Y	Y	N	Y	N
2 **Mullin**	Y	Y	Y	N	Y	N
3 **Lucas**	Y	Y	Y	N	Y	N
4 **Cole**	Y	Y	Y	N	Y	N
5 **Russell**	Y	Y	Y	N	Y	N
OREGON						
1 Bonamici	N	N	N	Y	N	Y
2 **Walden**	Y	Y	Y	N	Y	N
3 Blumenauer	N	N	N	Y	N	Y
4 DeFazio	N	N	N	Y	N	Y
5 Schrader	?					
PENNSYLVANIA						
1 Brady	N	N	N	Y	N	Y
2 Evans	N	N	N	Y	N	Y
3 **Kelly**	Y	Y	Y	N	Y	N
4 **Perry**	Y	Y	Y	N	Y	N
5 **Thompson**	Y	Y	Y	N	Y	N
6 **Costello**	Y	Y	Y	N	Y	N
7 **Meehan**	Y	Y	Y	N	Y	N
8 **Fitzpatrick**	Y	Y	Y	N	Y	N
9 **Shuster**	Y	Y	Y	N	Y	N
10 **Marino**	Y	Y	Y	N	Y	N
11 **Barletta**	Y	Y	Y	N	Y	N
12 **Rothfus**	Y	Y	Y	N	Y	N
13 Boyle	N	N	N	Y	N	Y
14 Doyle	N	N	N	Y	N	Y
15 **Dent**	Y	Y	Y	N	Y	N
16 **Smucker**	Y	Y	Y	N	Y	N
17 Cartwright	N	N	N	Y	N	Y
18 **Murphy**	Y	Y	Y	N	Y	N
RHODE ISLAND						
1 Cicilline	N	N	N	Y	N	Y
2 Langevin	N	N	N	Y	N	Y
SOUTH CAROLINA						
1 **Sanford**	Y	Y	Y	N	Y	N
2 **Wilson**	Y	Y	Y	N	Y	N
3 **Duncan**	Y	Y	Y	N	Y	N
4 **Gowdy**	Y	?	Y	N	Y	N
5 **Mulvaney**	Y	?	?	?	?	?
6 Clyburn	N	N	N	Y	N	Y
7 **Rice**	Y	Y	Y	N	Y	N
SOUTH DAKOTA						
AL **Noem**	Y	Y	Y	N	Y	N
TENNESSEE						
1 **Roe**	Y	Y	Y	N	Y	N
2 **Duncan**	Y	Y	Y	N	Y	N
3 **Fleischmann**	Y	Y	Y	N	Y	N
4 **DesJarlais**	Y	Y	Y	N	Y	N
5 Cooper	C	N	N	Y	N	Y
6 **Black**	Y	Y	Y	N	Y	N
7 **Blackburn**	Y	Y	Y	N	Y	N
8 **Kustoff**	Y	Y	Y	N	Y	N
9 Cohen	N	N	N	Y	N	Y
TEXAS						
1 **Gohmert**	Y	Y	Y	N	Y	N
2 **Poe**	Y	Y	Y	N	Y	?
3 **Johnson, S.**	Y	Y	Y	N	Y	N
4 **Ratcliffe**	Y	Y	Y	N	Y	N
5 **Hensarling**	Y	Y	Y	N	Y	N
6 **Barton**	Y	Y	Y	N	Y	N
7 **Culberson**	Y	Y	Y	N	Y	N
8 **Brady**	Y	Y	Y	N	Y	N
9 Green, A.	N	N	N	Y	N	Y
10 **McCaul**	Y	Y	Y	N	Y	N
11 **Conaway**	Y	Y	Y	N	Y	N
12 **Granger**	Y	Y	Y	N	Y	N
13 **Thornberry**	Y	Y	Y	N	Y	N
14 **Weber**	Y	Y	Y	N	Y	N
15 Gonzalez	N	N	N	Y	N	?
16 O'Rourke	N	N	N	Y	N	Y
17 **Flores**	Y	Y	Y	N	Y	N
18 Jackson Lee	N	N	N	Y	N	Y
19 **Arrington**	Y	Y	Y	N	Y	N
20 Castro	N	N	N	Y	N	Y
21 **Smith**	Y	Y	Y	N	Y	N
22 **Olson**	Y	Y	Y	N	Y	N
23 **Hurd**	Y	Y	Y	N	Y	N
24 **Marchant**	Y	?	Y	N	Y	N
25 **Williams**	Y	Y	Y	N	Y	N
26 **Burgess**	Y	Y	Y	N	Y	N
27 **Farenthold**	Y	Y	Y	N	Y	N
28 Cuellar	N	N	N	Y	N	Y
29 Green, G.	N	N	N	Y	N	Y
30 Johnson, E.B.	N	N	N	Y	N	Y
31 **Carter**	Y	Y	Y	N	Y	N
32 **Sessions**	Y	Y	Y	N	Y	N
33 Veasey	N	N	N	Y	N	Y
34 Vela	N	N	N	Y	N	Y
35 Doggett	N	N	N	Y	N	Y
36 **Babin**	Y	Y	Y	N	Y	N
UTAH						
1 **Bishop**	Y	Y	Y	N	Y	N
2 **Stewart**	Y	Y	Y	N	Y	N
3 **Chaffetz**	Y	Y	Y	N	Y	N
4 **Love**	Y	Y	Y	N	Y	N
VERMONT						
AL Welch	N	N	N	Y	N	Y
VIRGINIA						
1 **Wittman**	Y	Y	Y	N	Y	N
2 **Taylor**	Y	Y	Y	N	Y	N
3 Scott	N	N	N	Y	N	Y
4 McEachin	N	N	N	Y	N	Y
5 **Garrett**	Y	Y	Y	N	Y	N
6 **Goodlatte**	Y	Y	Y	N	Y	N
7 **Brat**	Y	Y	Y	N	Y	N
8 Beyer	N	N	N	Y	N	?
9 **Griffith**	Y	Y	Y	N	Y	N
10 **Comstock**	Y	Y	Y	N	Y	N
11 Connolly	N	N	N	Y	N	Y
WASHINGTON						
1 DelBene	N	N	N	Y	N	Y
2 Larsen	N	N	N	Y	N	Y
3 **Herrera Beutler**	Y	Y	Y	N	Y	N
4 **Newhouse**	Y	Y	Y	N	Y	N
5 **McMorris Rodgers**	Y	Y	Y	N	Y	N
6 Kilmer	N	N	N	Y	N	Y
7 Jayapal	N	N	N	Y	N	Y
8 **Reichert**	Y	Y	Y	N	Y	N
9 Smith	N	N	N	Y	N	Y
10 Heck	N	N	N	Y	N	Y
WEST VIRGINIA						
1 **McKinley**	Y	Y	Y	N	Y	N
2 **Mooney**	Y	Y	Y	N	Y	N
3 **Jenkins**	Y	Y	Y	N	Y	N
WISCONSIN						
1 **Ryan**	?					
2 Pocan	N	N	N	Y	N	Y
3 Kind	C	N	N	Y	N	Y
4 Moore	N	N	N	Y	N	Y
5 **Sensenbrenner**	Y	Y	Y	N	Y	N
6 **Grothman**	Y	Y	Y	N	Y	N
7 **Duffy**	Y	Y	Y	N	Y	N
8 **Gallagher**	Y	Y	Y	N	Y	N
WYOMING						
AL **Cheney**	Y	Y	Y	N	Y	N

VOTE NUMBER

8. HR 21. REGULATION DISAPPROVAL/PASSAGE. Passage of the bill that would permit a new Congress to use the procedures under the Congressional Review Act to disapprove, en bloc, multiple regulations issued during the final year of a president's term. Passed 238-184 : R 234-0; D 4-184. Jan. 4, 2017.

9. H RES 22, HR 26, H RES 11. MAJOR RULES APPROVAL AND U.N. SECURITY COUNCIL RESOLUTION/PREVIOUS QUESTION. Collins, R-Ga., motion to order the previous question (thus ending debate and possibility of amendment) on the rule (H Res 22) that would provide for House floor consideration of the bill (HR 26) that would require Congress to approve "major rules" issued by agencies, such as regulations with an annual economic impact of $100 million or more, before they could take effect. The rule would also provide for House floor consideration of the resolution (H Res 11) that would express the House's opposition to the adoption of a U.N. Security Council resolution that criticized continued expansion of Israeli settlements in occupied areas. Motion agreed to 235-188 : R 234-1; D 1-187. Jan. 5, 2017.

10. H RES 22, HR 26, H RES 11. MAJOR RULES APPROVAL AND U.N. SECURITY RESOLUTION/RULE. Adoption of the rule (H Res 22) that would provide for House floor consideration of the bill (HR 26) that would require Congress to approve "major rules" issued by agencies, such as regulations with an annual economic impact of $100 million or more, before they could take effect. The rule would also provide for House floor consideration of the resolution (H Res 11) that would express the House's opposition to the adoption of a U.N. Security Council resolution that criticized continued expansion of Israeli settlements in occupied areas. Adopted 231-187 : R 231-1; D 0-186. Jan. 5, 2017.

11. H RES 11. U.N. SECURITY COUNCIL RESOLUTION/ADOPTION. Adoption of the resolution that would express the House's opposition to a U.N. Security Council resolution that criticized continued expansion of Israeli settlements in occupied areas. Adopted 342-80 : R 233-4; D 109-76. Jan. 5, 2017.

12. HR 26. MAJOR RULES APPROVAL/OFFSETS. Messer, R-Ind., amendment that would require that for new rules, agencies repeal or amend an existing rule or rules to offset any annual costs of the new rule before the new rule could take effect. Adopted in Committee of the Whole 235-185 : R 234-0; D 1-185. Jan. 5, 2017.

13. HR 26. MAJOR RULES APPROVAL/EMISSION IMPACTS. Grijalva, D-Ariz., amendment that would require agencies to include an accounting of greenhouse gas emission impacts associated with a rule in the report that would be required by the bill to be submitted to Congress. The report also would need to include an analysis of the rule's impacts on low-income and rural communities. If a rule would increase carbon equivalent emissions by 25,000 metric tons annually or possibly increase the risk of certain diseases to low-income or rural communities, then the rule would be considered a "major rule." Rejected in Committee of the Whole 193-230 : R 5-229; D 188-1. Jan. 5, 2017.

14. HR 26. MAJOR RULES APPROVAL/DISEASE REDUCTION. Castor, D-Fla., amendment that would exclude rules that would result in reduced incidence of cancer, early death, asthma attacks or respiratory disease in children from the definition of a "major rule." Rejected in Committee of the Whole 190-233 : R 2-232; D 188-1. Jan. 5, 2017.

	8	9	10	11	12	13	14
ALABAMA							
1 **Byrne**	Y	Y	Y	Y	Y	N	N
2 **Roby**	Y	Y	Y	Y	Y	N	N
3 **Rogers**	Y	Y	Y	Y	Y	N	N
4 **Aderholt**	Y	Y	Y	Y	Y	N	N
5 **Brooks**	Y	Y	Y	Y	Y	N	N
6 **Palmer**	Y	Y	Y	Y	Y	N	N
7 Sewell	N	N	Y	N	Y	Y	Y
ALASKA							
AL **Young**	Y	Y	Y	Y	Y	N	N
ARIZONA							
1 O'Halleran	N	N	N	Y	N	Y	Y
2 **McSally**	Y	Y	Y	Y	Y	N	N
3 Grijalva	N	N	N	N	N	Y	Y
4 **Gosar**	Y	Y	Y	Y	Y	N	N
5 **Biggs**	Y	Y	Y	Y	Y	N	N
6 **Schweikert**	Y	Y	Y	Y	Y	N	N
7 Gallego	–	–	–	+	–	+	+
8 **Franks**	Y	Y	Y	+	Y	N	N
9 Sinema	Y	N	N	Y	N	Y	Y
ARKANSAS							
1 **Crawford**	Y	Y	Y	Y	Y	N	N
2 **Hill**	Y	Y	Y	Y	Y	N	N
3 **Womack**	Y	Y	Y	Y	Y	N	N
4 **Westerman**	Y	Y	Y	Y	Y	N	N
CALIFORNIA							
1 **LaMalfa**	Y	Y	Y	Y	Y	N	N
2 Huffman	N	N	N	N	N	Y	Y
3 Garamendi	N	N	N	N	N	Y	Y
4 **McClintock**	Y	Y	Y	Y	Y	N	N
5 Thompson	N	N	N	N	N	Y	Y
6 Matsui	N	N	N	Y	N	Y	Y
7 Bera	N	N	N	N	N	Y	Y
8 **Cook**	Y	Y	Y	Y	Y	N	N
9 McNerney	N	N	N	N	N	Y	Y
10 **Denham**	Y	Y	Y	Y	?	N	?
11 DeSaulnier	N	N	N	N	N	Y	Y
12 Pelosi	N	N	N	N	N	Y	Y
13 Lee	N	N	N	N	N	Y	Y
14 Speier	N	N	N	N	N	Y	Y
15 Swalwell	N	N	N	N	N	Y	Y
16 Costa	N	N	N	Y	N	Y	Y
17 Khanna	N	N	N	Y	N	Y	Y
18 Eshoo	N	N	N	N	N	Y	Y
19 Lofgren	N	N	N	P	N	Y	Y
20 Panetta	N	N	N	Y	N	Y	Y
21 **Valadao**	Y	Y	Y	Y	Y	N	N
22 **Nunes**	Y	Y	Y	Y	Y	N	N
23 **McCarthy**	Y	Y	Y	Y	Y	N	N
24 Carbajal	N	N	N	N	N	Y	Y
25 **Knight**	Y	Y	Y	Y	Y	N	N
26 Brownley	N	N	N	Y	N	Y	Y
27 Chu	N	N	N	N	N	Y	Y
28 Schiff	N	N	N	Y	N	Y	Y
29 Cardenas	N	N	N	Y	N	Y	Y
30 Sherman	N	N	N	Y	N	Y	Y
31 Aguilar	N	N	N	Y	N	Y	Y
32 Napolitano	N	N	N	Y	N	Y	Y
33 Lieu	N	N	N	Y	N	Y	Y
34 Becerra	–	–	–	–	–	+	+
35 Torres	N	N	N	Y	N	Y	?
36 Ruiz	N	N	N	Y	N	Y	Y
37 Bass	N	N	N	N	N	Y	Y
38 Sánchez, Linda	N	N	N	Y	N	Y	Y
39 **Royce**	Y	Y	Y	Y	Y	N	N
40 Roybal-Allard	N	N	N	Y	N	Y	Y
41 Takano	N	N	N	N	N	Y	Y
42 **Calvert**	Y	Y	Y	Y	Y	N	N
43 Waters	?	N	N	N	N	Y	Y
44 Barragan	N	N	N	Y	N	Y	Y
45 **Walters**	Y	Y	Y	Y	Y	N	N
46 Correa	N	N	N	Y	N	Y	Y
47 Lowenthal	N	N	N	N	N	Y	Y
48 **Rohrabacher**	Y	Y	Y	Y	Y	N	N
49 **Issa**	Y	Y	Y	Y	Y	N	N
50 **Hunter**	Y	Y	Y	Y	Y	N	N
51 Vargas	N	N	N	Y	N	Y	Y
52 Peters	N	N	N	Y	N	Y	Y
53 Davis	N	N	N	Y	N	Y	Y

	8	9	10	11	12	13	14
COLORADO							
1 DeGette	N	N	N	N	N	Y	Y
2 Polis	N	N	N	N	N	Y	Y
3 **Tipton**	Y	Y	Y	Y	Y	N	N
4 **Buck**	Y	Y	Y	Y	Y	N	N
5 **Lamborn**	Y	Y	Y	Y	Y	N	N
6 **Coffman**	Y	Y	Y	Y	Y	N	N
7 Perlmutter	N	N	N	Y	N	Y	Y
CONNECTICUT							
1 Larson	N	N	N	N	N	Y	Y
2 Courtney	N	N	N	Y	N	Y	Y
3 DeLauro	N	N	N	N	N	Y	Y
4 Himes	N	N	N	Y	N	Y	Y
5 Esty	N	N	N	Y	N	Y	Y
DELAWARE							
AL Blunt Rochester	N	N	N	N	N	Y	Y
FLORIDA							
1 **Gaetz**	Y	Y	Y	Y	Y	N	N
2 **Dunn**	Y	Y	Y	Y	Y	N	N
3 **Yoho**	Y	Y	Y	Y	Y	N	N
4 **Rutherford**	Y	Y	Y	Y	Y	N	N
5 Lawson	N	–	N	Y	N	Y	Y
6 **DeSantis**	Y	Y	Y	Y	Y	N	N
7 Murphy	N	N	N	Y	N	Y	Y
8 **Posey**	Y	Y	Y	Y	Y	N	N
9 Soto	N	N	N	Y	N	Y	Y
10 Demings	N	N	N	Y	N	Y	Y
11 **Webster**	Y	Y	Y	Y	Y	N	N
12 **Bilirakis**	Y	Y	Y	Y	Y	N	N
13 Crist	N	N	N	+	N	Y	Y
14 Castor	N	N	N	Y	N	Y	Y
15 **Ross**	Y	Y	Y	Y	Y	N	N
16 **Buchanan**	Y	Y	?	Y	Y	N	N
17 **Rooney, T.**	Y	Y	Y	Y	Y	N	N
18 **Mast**	Y	Y	Y	Y	Y	N	N
19 **Rooney, F.**	Y	Y	Y	Y	Y	N	N
20 Hastings	N	N	N	Y	N	Y	Y
21 Frankel	N	N	N	N	N	Y	Y
22 Deutch	N	N	N	N	N	Y	Y
23 Wasserman Schultz	N	N	N	Y	N	Y	Y
24 Wilson	N	N	N	Y	N	Y	Y
25 **Diaz-Balart**	Y	Y	Y	Y	Y	N	N
26 **Curbelo**	Y	Y	Y	Y	Y	N	N
27 **Ros-Lehtinen**	Y	Y	Y	Y	Y	Y	Y
GEORGIA							
1 **Carter**	Y	Y	Y	Y	Y	N	N
2 Bishop	N	N	N	N	N	Y	Y
3 **Ferguson**	Y	Y	Y	Y	Y	N	N
4 Johnson	N	Y	N	N	N	Y	Y
5 Lewis	N	N	N	N	N	Y	Y
6 **Price**	?	?	?	Y	?	?	?
7 **Woodall**	Y	Y	Y	Y	Y	N	N
8 **Scott, A.**	Y	Y	Y	Y	Y	N	N
9 **Collins**	Y	Y	Y	Y	Y	N	N
10 **Hice**	Y	Y	Y	Y	Y	N	N
11 **Loudermilk**	Y	Y	Y	Y	Y	N	N
12 **Allen**	Y	Y	Y	Y	Y	N	N
13 Scott, D.	?	N	N	Y	N	Y	Y
14 **Graves**	Y	Y	Y	Y	Y	N	N
HAWAII							
1 Hanabusa	N	N	N	Y	N	Y	Y
2 Gabbard	N	N	N	N	N	Y	Y
IDAHO							
1 **Labrador**	Y	Y	Y	Y	Y	N	N
2 **Simpson**	Y	Y	Y	Y	Y	N	N
ILLINOIS							
1 Rush	?	?	?	?	?	?	?
2 Kelly	N	N	N	N	N	Y	Y
3 Lipinski	N	N	N	Y	N	Y	Y
4 Gutierroz	N	N	N	–	Y	Y	Y
5 Quigley	N	N	N	Y	N	Y	Y
6 **Roskam**	Y	Y	Y	Y	Y	N	N
7 Davis, D.	N	?	N	N	N	Y	Y
8 Krishnamoorthi	N	N	N	Y	N	Y	Y
9 Schakowsky	N	N	N	N	N	Y	Y
10 Schneider	N	N	N	N	N	Y	Y
11 Foster	N	N	N	N	N	Y	Y
12 **Bost**	Y	Y	Y	Y	Y	N	N
13 **Davis, R.**	Y	Y	Y	Y	Y	N	N
14 **Hultgren**	Y	Y	Y	Y	Y	N	N
15 **Shimkus**	Y	Y	Y	Y	Y	N	N

KEY	Republicans		Democrats		Independents	
Y	Voted for (yea)	X	Paired against	C	Voted "present" to avoid possible conflict of interest
#	Paired for	–	Announced against		
+	Announced for	P	Voted "present"	?	Did not vote or otherwise make a position known
N	Voted against (nay)				

	8	9	10	11	12	13	14
16 **Kinzinger**	Y	Y	Y	Y	Y	N	N
17 Bustos	N	N	N	N	N	Y	Y
18 **LaHood**	Y	Y	Y	Y	Y	N	N
INDIANA							
1 Visclosky	N	N	N	Y	N	Y	Y
2 **Walorski**	Y	Y	Y	Y	Y	N	N
3 **Banks**	Y	Y	Y	Y	Y	N	N
4 **Rokita**	Y	Y	Y	Y	Y	N	N
5 **Brooks**	Y	Y	Y	Y	Y	N	N
6 **Messer**	Y	Y	Y	Y	Y	?	N
7 Carson	N	N	N	N	N	Y	Y
8 **Bucshon**	Y	Y	Y	Y	Y	N	N
9 **Hollingsworth**	Y	Y	Y	Y	Y	N	N
IOWA							
1 **Blum**	Y	Y	Y	Y	Y	N	N
2 Loebsack	N	N	N	N	N	Y	Y
3 **Young**	Y	Y	Y	Y	Y	N	N
4 **King**	Y	Y	Y	Y	Y	N	N
KANSAS							
1 **Marshall**	Y	Y	Y	Y	Y	N	N
2 **Jenkins**	Y	Y	Y	Y	+	–	–
3 **Yoder**	Y	Y	Y	Y	Y	N	N
4 **Pompeo**	?	?	?	?	?	?	?
KENTUCKY							
1 **Comer**	Y	Y	Y	Y	Y	N	N
2 **Guthrie**	Y	Y	Y	Y	Y	N	N
3 Yarmuth	N	N	N	N	N	Y	Y
4 **Massie**	Y	Y	Y	Y	Y	N	N
5 **Rogers**	Y	Y	Y	Y	Y	N	N
6 **Barr**	Y	Y	Y	Y	Y	N	N
LOUISIANA							
1 **Scalise**	Y	Y	Y	Y	Y	N	N
2 Richmond	N	N	?	Y	N	Y	Y
3 **Higgins**	Y	Y	Y	Y	Y	N	N
4 **Johnson**	Y	Y	Y	Y	Y	N	N
5 **Abraham**	Y	Y	Y	Y	Y	N	N
6 **Graves**	Y	Y	Y	Y	Y	N	N
MAINE							
1 Pingree	N	N	N	N	N	Y	Y
2 **Poliquin**	Y	Y	Y	Y	Y	N	N
MARYLAND							
1 **Harris**	Y	Y	Y	Y	Y	N	N
2 Ruppersberger	N	N	N	Y	N	Y	Y
3 Sarbanes	N	N	N	Y	N	Y	Y
4 Brown	N	N	N	Y	N	Y	Y
5 Hoyer	N	N	N	Y	N	Y	Y
6 Delaney	N	N	N	Y	N	Y	Y
7 Cummings	N	N	N	Y	N	Y	Y
8 Raskin	N	N	N	Y	N	Y	Y
MASSACHUSETTS							
1 Neal	N	N	N	Y	N	Y	Y
2 McGovern	N	N	N	Y	N	Y	Y
3 Tsongas	N	N	N	N	N	Y	Y
4 Kennedy	N	N	N	Y	N	Y	Y
5 Clark	N	N	N	N	N	Y	Y
6 Moulton	N	N	N	Y	N	Y	Y
7 Capuano	N	N	N	P	N	Y	Y
8 Lynch	N	N	N	N	N	Y	Y
9 Keating	N	N	N	Y	N	Y	Y
MICHIGAN							
1 **Bergman**	Y	Y	Y	Y	Y	N	N
2 **Huizenga**	Y	Y	Y	Y	Y	N	N
3 **Amash**	Y	Y	Y	N	Y	N	N
4 **Moolenaar**	Y	Y	Y	Y	Y	N	N
5 Kildee	N	N	N	N	N	Y	Y
6 **Upton**	Y	Y	Y	Y	Y	N	N
7 **Walberg**	Y	Y	?	Y	Y	N	N
8 **Bishop**	Y	Y	Y	Y	Y	N	N
9 Levin	N	N	N	Y	N	Y	Y
10 **Mitchell**	Y	Y	Y	Y	Y	N	N
11 **Trott**	Y	Y	Y	Y	Y	N	N
12 Dingell	N	N	N	N	N	Y	Y
13 Conyers	N	N	N	N	N	Y	Y
14 Lawrence	N	N	N	Y	N	Y	Y
MINNESOTA							
1 Walz	N	N	N	Y	N	Y	Y
2 **Lewis**	Y	Y	Y	Y	Y	N	N
3 **Paulsen**	Y	Y	Y	Y	Y	N	N
4 McCollum	N	N	N	N	N	Y	Y
5 Ellison	N	N	N	N	N	Y	N
6 **Emmer**	Y	Y	Y	Y	Y	N	N
7 Peterson	Y	N	N	Y	Y	N	Y
8 Nolan	N	N	N	N	N	Y	Y
MISSISSIPPI							
1 **Kelly**	Y	Y	Y	Y	Y	N	N
2 Thompson	N	N	N	N	N	Y	Y
3 **Harper**	Y	Y	Y	Y	Y	N	N
4 **Palazzo**	Y	Y	Y	Y	Y	N	N
MISSOURI							
1 Clay	N	N	N	N	N	Y	Y
2 **Wagner**	Y	Y	Y	Y	Y	N	N
3 **Luetkemeyer**	Y	Y	Y	Y	Y	N	N
4 **Hartzler**	Y	Y	Y	Y	Y	N	N
5 Cleaver	N	N	N	Y	N	Y	Y
6 **Graves**	Y	Y	Y	Y	Y	N	N
7 **Long**	Y	Y	Y	Y	Y	N	N
8 **Smith**	Y	Y	Y	Y	Y	N	N
MONTANA							
AL **Zinke**	?	?	?	Y	Y	N	N
NEBRASKA							
1 **Fortenberry**	Y	Y	Y	Y	Y	N	N
2 **Bacon**	Y	Y	Y	Y	Y	N	N
3 **Smith**	Y	Y	Y	Y	Y	N	N
NEVADA							
1 Titus	N	N	N	Y	N	Y	Y
2 **Amodei**	Y	Y	Y	Y	Y	N	N
3 Rosen	N	N	N	Y	N	Y	Y
4 Kihuen	N	N	N	N	N	Y	Y
NEW HAMPSHIRE							
1 Shea-Porter	N	N	N	P	N	Y	Y
2 Kuster	N	N	N	N	N	Y	Y
NEW JERSEY							
1 Norcross	N	N	N	Y	N	Y	Y
2 **LoBiondo**	Y	Y	Y	Y	Y	N	N
3 **MacArthur**	Y	Y	Y	Y	Y	N	N
4 **Smith**	Y	Y	Y	Y	Y	N	N
5 Gottheimer	Y	N	N	Y	N	Y	Y
6 Pallone	N	N	N	Y	N	Y	Y
7 **Lance**	Y	Y	Y	Y	Y	N	N
8 Sires	N	N	N	Y	N	Y	Y
9 Pascrell	N	N	N	Y	N	Y	Y
10 Payne	N	N	N	N	N	Y	Y
11 **Frelinghuysen**	Y	Y	Y	Y	Y	N	N
12 Watson Coleman	N	N	N	N	N	Y	Y
NEW MEXICO							
1 Lujan Grisham	N	N	N	Y	N	Y	Y
2 **Pearce**	Y	Y	Y	Y	Y	N	N
3 Luján	N	N	N	Y	?	Y	Y
NEW YORK							
1 **Zeldin**	Y	Y	Y	Y	Y	N	N
2 **King**	Y	Y	Y	Y	Y	N	N
3 Suozzi	N	N	N	Y	–	Y	Y
4 Rice	N	N	N	Y	N	Y	Y
5 Meeks	N	N	?	N	N	Y	Y
6 Meng	N	N	N	Y	N	Y	Y
7 Velázquez	N	N	?	Y	N	Y	Y
8 Jeffries	N	N	N	Y	N	Y	Y
9 Clarke	N	N	N	Y	N	Y	Y
10 Nadler	N	N	N	Y	N	Y	Y
11 **Donovan**	Y	Y	Y	Y	Y	N	N
12 Maloney, C.	N	N	N	Y	N	Y	Y
13 Espaillat	N	N	N	Y	N	Y	Y
14 Crowley	N	N	N	Y	?	Y	Y
15 Serrano	N	N	N	N	N	Y	Y
16 Engel	N	N	N	Y	N	Y	Y
17 Lowey	N	N	N	Y	N	Y	Y
18 Maloney, S.P.	N	N	N	Y	N	Y	Y
19 **Faso**	Y	Y	Y	Y	Y	N	N
20 Tonko	N	N	N	N	N	Y	Y
21 **Stefanik**	Y	Y	Y	Y	Y	Y	N
22 **Tenney**	Y	Y	Y	Y	Y	N	N
23 **Reed**	Y	Y	Y	Y	Y	N	N
24 **Katko**	Y	Y	Y	Y	Y	Y	N
25 Slaughter	N	N	N	N	N	Y	Y
26 Higgins	N	N	N	Y	N	Y	Y
27 **Collins**	+	+	+	+	+	–	–
NORTH CAROLINA							
1 Butterfield	N	N	?	N	N	Y	Y
2 **Holding**	Y	Y	Y	Y	Y	N	N
3 **Jones**	Y	N	N	N	Y	N	Y
4 Price	N	N	N	N	N	Y	Y
5 **Foxx**	Y	Y	Y	Y	Y	N	N
6 **Walker**	Y	Y	Y	Y	Y	N	N
7 **Rouzer**	Y	Y	Y	Y	Y	N	N
8 **Hudson**	Y	Y	Y	Y	Y	N	N
9 **Pittenger**	Y	Y	Y	Y	Y	N	N
10 **McHenry**	Y	Y	Y	Y	Y	N	N
11 **Meadows**	Y	Y	Y	Y	Y	N	N
12 Adams	N	N	N	Y	N	Y	Y
13 **Budd**	Y	Y	Y	Y	Y	N	N
NORTH DAKOTA							
AL **Cramer**	Y	Y	Y	Y	Y	N	N
OHIO							
1 **Chabot**	Y	Y	Y	Y	Y	N	N
2 **Wenstrup**	Y	Y	Y	Y	Y	N	N
3 Beatty	N	N	N	Y	N	Y	Y
4 **Jordan**	Y	Y	Y	Y	Y	N	N
5 **Latta**	Y	Y	Y	Y	Y	N	N
6 **Johnson**	Y	Y	Y	Y	Y	N	N
7 **Gibbs**	Y	Y	Y	Y	Y	N	N
8 **Davidson**	Y	Y	Y	Y	Y	N	N
9 Kaptur	N	N	N	N	N	Y	Y
10 **Turner**	Y	Y	Y	Y	Y	N	N
11 Fudge	N	N	N	Y	N	Y	Y
12 **Tiberi**	Y	Y	Y	Y	Y	N	N
13 Ryan	N	N	N	Y	N	Y	Y
14 **Joyce**	Y	Y	Y	Y	Y	N	N
15 **Stivers**	Y	Y	Y	Y	Y	N	N
16 **Renacci**	Y	Y	Y	Y	Y	N	N
OKLAHOMA							
1 **Bridenstine**	Y	Y	Y	Y	Y	N	N
2 **Mullin**	Y	Y	Y	Y	Y	N	N
3 **Lucas**	Y	Y	Y	Y	Y	N	N
4 **Cole**	Y	Y	Y	Y	Y	N	N
5 **Russell**	Y	Y	Y	Y	Y	N	N
OREGON							
1 Bonamici	N	N	N	Y	N	Y	Y
2 **Walden**	Y	Y	Y	Y	Y	N	N
3 Blumenauer	N	N	N	N	N	Y	Y
4 DeFazio	N	N	N	N	N	Y	Y
5 Schrader							
PENNSYLVANIA							
1 Brady	N	N	N	Y	N	Y	Y
2 Evans	N	N	N	P	N	Y	Y
3 **Kelly**	Y	Y	Y	Y	Y	N	N
4 **Perry**	Y	Y	Y	Y	Y	N	N
5 **Thompson**	Y	Y	Y	Y	Y	N	N
6 **Costello**	Y	Y	Y	Y	Y	N	N
7 **Meehan**	Y	Y	Y	Y	Y	N	N
8 **Fitzpatrick**	Y	Y	Y	Y	Y	Y	N
9 **Shuster**	Y	Y	Y	Y	Y	N	N
10 **Marino**	Y	Y	Y	Y	Y	N	N
11 **Barletta**	Y	Y	Y	Y	Y	N	N
12 **Rothfus**	Y	Y	Y	Y	Y	N	N
13 Boyle	N	N	N	Y	N	Y	Y
14 Doyle	N	N	N	N	N	Y	Y
15 **Dent**	Y	Y	Y	Y	Y	N	N
16 **Smucker**	Y	Y	Y	Y	Y	Y	N
17 Cartwright	N	N	N	Y	N	Y	Y
18 **Murphy**	Y	Y	Y	Y	Y	N	N
RHODE ISLAND							
1 Cicilline	N	N	N	Y	N	Y	Y
2 Langevin	N	N	N	Y	N	Y	Y
SOUTH CAROLINA							
1 **Sanford**	Y	Y	Y	Y	Y	N	N
2 **Wilson**	Y	Y	Y	Y	Y	N	N
3 **Duncan**	Y	Y	Y	Y	Y	N	N
4 **Gowdy**	Y	Y	Y	Y	Y	N	N
5 **Mulvaney**	?	?	?	Y	?	?	?
6 Clyburn	N	N	N	N	N	Y	Y
7 **Rice**	Y	Y	?	Y	Y	N	N
SOUTH DAKOTA							
AL **Noem**	Y	Y	Y	Y	Y	N	N
TENNESSEE							
1 **Roe**	Y	Y	Y	Y	Y	N	N
2 **Duncan**	Y	Y	Y	N	Y	N	N
3 **Fleischmann**	Y	Y	Y	Y	Y	N	N
4 **DesJarlais**	Y	Y	Y	Y	Y	N	N
5 Cooper	N	N	N	Y	N	Y	Y
6 **Black**	Y	Y	Y	Y	Y	N	N
7 **Blackburn**	Y	Y	Y	Y	Y	N	N
8 **Kustoff**	Y	Y	Y	Y	Y	N	N
9 Cohen	N	N	N	N	N	Y	Y
TEXAS							
1 **Gohmert**	Y	Y	Y	N	Y	N	N
2 **Poe**	?	Y	Y	Y	Y	N	N
3 **Johnson, S.**	Y	Y	Y	Y	Y	N	N
4 **Ratcliffe**	Y	Y	Y	Y	Y	N	N
5 **Hensarling**	Y	Y	Y	Y	Y	N	N
6 **Barton**	Y	Y	Y	Y	Y	N	N
7 **Culberson**	Y	Y	Y	Y	Y	N	N
8 **Brady**	Y	Y	Y	Y	Y	N	N
9 Green, A.	N	N	N	N	N	Y	Y
10 **McCaul**	Y	Y	Y	Y	Y	N	N
11 **Conaway**	Y	Y	Y	Y	Y	N	N
12 **Granger**	Y	Y	Y	Y	Y	N	N
13 **Thornberry**	Y	Y	Y	Y	Y	N	N
14 **Weber**	Y	Y	Y	Y	Y	N	N
15 Gonzalez	N	N	N	Y	N	Y	Y
16 O'Rourke	N	N	N	N	N	+	Y
17 **Flores**	Y	Y	Y	Y	Y	N	N
18 Jackson Lee	N	N	N	Y	N	Y	Y
19 **Arrington**	Y	Y	Y	Y	Y	N	N
20 Castro	N	N	N	N	N	Y	Y
21 **Smith**	Y	Y	Y	Y	Y	N	N
22 **Olson**	Y	Y	Y	Y	Y	N	N
23 **Hurd**	Y	Y	Y	Y	Y	N	N
24 **Marchant**	Y	Y	Y	Y	Y	N	N
25 **Williams**	Y	Y	Y	Y	Y	N	N
26 **Burgess**	Y	Y	Y	Y	Y	N	N
27 **Farenthold**	Y	Y	Y	Y	Y	N	N
28 Cuellar	Y	N	N	Y	N	Y	Y
29 Green, G.	N	N	N	Y	N	Y	Y
30 Johnson, E.B.	N	N	N	N	N	Y	Y
31 **Carter**	Y	Y	Y	Y	Y	N	N
32 **Sessions**	Y	Y	Y	Y	Y	N	N
33 Veasey	N	N	N	Y	N	Y	Y
34 Vela	N	N	N	Y	N	Y	Y
35 Doggett	N	N	N	N	N	Y	Y
36 **Babin**	Y	Y	Y	Y	Y	N	N
UTAH							
1 **Bishop**	Y	Y	Y	Y	Y	N	N
2 **Stewart**	Y	Y	Y	Y	Y	N	N
3 **Chaffetz**	Y	Y	Y	Y	Y	N	N
4 **Love**	Y	Y	Y	Y	Y	N	N
VERMONT							
AL Welch	N	N	N	N	N	Y	Y
VIRGINIA							
1 **Wittman**	Y	Y	Y	Y	Y	N	N
2 **Taylor**	Y	Y	Y	Y	Y	N	N
3 Scott	N	N	N	N	N	Y	Y
4 McEachin	N	N	N	Y	N	Y	Y
5 **Garrett**	Y	Y	Y	Y	Y	N	N
6 **Goodlatte**	Y	Y	Y	Y	Y	N	N
7 **Brat**	Y	Y	Y	Y	Y	N	N
8 Beyer	N	N	N	N	N	Y	Y
9 **Griffith**	Y	Y	Y	Y	Y	N	N
10 **Comstock**	Y	Y	Y	Y	Y	N	N
11 Connolly	N	N	N	N	N	Y	Y
WASHINGTON							
1 DelBene	N	N	N	Y	N	Y	Y
2 Larsen	N	N	N	Y	N	Y	Y
3 **Herrera Beutler**	Y	Y	Y	Y	Y	N	N
4 **Newhouse**	Y	Y	Y	Y	Y	N	N
5 **McMorris Rodgers**	Y	Y	Y	Y	Y	N	N
6 Kilmer	N	N	N	Y	N	Y	Y
7 Jayapal	N	N	N	N	N	Y	Y
8 **Reichert**	Y	Y	Y	Y	Y	N	N
9 Smith	N	N	N	Y	N	Y	Y
10 Heck	N	N	N	N	N	Y	Y
WEST VIRGINIA							
1 **McKinley**	Y	Y	Y	Y	Y	N	N
2 **Mooney**	Y	Y	Y	Y	Y	N	N
3 **Jenkins**	Y	Y	Y	Y	Y	N	N
WISCONSIN							
1 **Ryan**							
2 Pocan	N	N	N	N	N	Y	Y
3 Kind	N	N	N	Y	N	Y	Y
4 Moore	N	N	N	N	N	Y	Y
5 **Sensenbrenner**	Y	Y	Y	Y	Y	N	N
6 **Grothman**	Y	Y	Y	Y	Y	N	N
7 **Duffy**	Y	Y	Y	Y	Y	N	N
8 **Gallagher**	Y	Y	Y	Y	Y	N	N
WYOMING							
AL **Cheney**	Y	Y	Y	Y	Y	N	N

VOTE NUMBER

15. HR 26. MAJOR RULES APPROVAL/PUBLIC HEALTH PROTECTION. Cicilline, D-R.I., amendment that would exclude rules related to the protection of public health or safety from the definition of a "major rule." Rejected in Committee of the Whole 186-232 : R 0-231; D 186-1. Jan. 5, 2017.

16. HR 26. MAJOR RULES APPROVAL/LEAD IN DRINKING WATER. Conyers, D-Mich., amendment that would exclude rules that would provide for a reduction in the amount of lead in public drinking water from the definition of a "major rule." Rejected in Committee of the Whole 192-231 : R 3-231; D 189-0. Jan. 5, 2017.

17. HR 26. MAJOR RULES APPROVAL/PRODUCTS FOR YOUNG CHILDREN. Johnson, D-Ga., for Jackson Lee, D-Texas, amendment that would exclude rules related to the safety of products designed to be used or consumed by children younger than 2 years old from the definition of a "major rule." Rejected in Committee of the Whole 190-234 : R 0-234; D 190-0. Jan. 5, 2017.

18. HR 26. MAJOR RULES APPROVAL/NUCLEAR REACTOR SAFETY. Nadler, D-N.Y., amendment that would exclude rules pertaining to nuclear reactor safety standards from the definition of a "major rule." Rejected in Committee of the Whole 194-231 : R 5-230; D 189-1. Jan. 5, 2017.

19. HR 26. MAJOR RULES APPROVAL/PIPELINE SAFETY. McNerney, D-Calif., for Pallone, D-N.J., amendment that would exclude rules intended to either ensure the safety of natural gas or hazardous materials pipelines or to prevent or reduce the impact of spills from such pipelines from the definition of a "major rule." Rejected in Committee of the Whole 190-235 : R 0-235; D 190-0. Jan. 5, 2017.

20. HR 26. MAJOR RULES APPROVAL/OCCUPATIONAL SAFETY. Scott, D-Va., amendment that would exclude from the bill's provisions rules made by the Occupational Safety and Health Administration or the Mine Safety and Health Administration related to the prevention of traumatic injury, cancer or irreversible lung disease. Rejected in Committee of the Whole 193-232 : R 3-232; D 190-0. Jan. 5, 2017.

21. HR 26. MAJOR RULES APPROVAL/EXISTING RULES. King, R-Iowa, amendment that would require each agency annually, for 10 years, to submit to Congress for review at least 10 percent of the agency's existing rules, and would sunset certain rules if Congress had not approved them within 10 years of the bill's enactment. Adopted in Committee of the Whole 230-193 : R 230-4; D 0-189. Jan. 5, 2017.

	15	16	17	18	19	20	21
ALABAMA							
1 Byrne	N	N	N	N	N	N	Y
2 Roby	N	N	N	N	N	N	Y
3 Rogers	N	N	N	N	N	N	Y
4 Aderholt	N	N	N	N	N	N	Y
5 Brooks	N	N	N	N	N	N	Y
6 Palmer	?	N	N	N	N	N	Y
7 Sewell	Y	Y	Y	Y	Y	Y	N
ALASKA							
AL Young	N	N	N	N	N	N	Y
ARIZONA							
1 O'Halleran	Y	Y	Y	Y	Y	Y	N
2 McSally	N	N	N	N	N	N	Y
3 Grijalva	Y	Y	Y	Y	Y	Y	N
4 Gosar	N	N	N	N	N	N	Y
5 Biggs	N	N	N	N	N	N	Y
6 Schweikert	N	N	N	N	N	N	Y
7 Gallego	+	+	+	+	+	+	-
8 Franks	N	N	N	N	N	N	Y
9 Sinema	Y	Y	Y	Y	Y	Y	N
ARKANSAS							
1 Crawford	N	N	?	N	N	N	Y
2 Hill	N	N	N	N	N	N	Y
3 Womack	N	N	N	N	N	N	Y
4 Westerman	N	N	N	N	N	N	Y
CALIFORNIA							
1 LaMalfa	?	N	N	N	N	N	Y
2 Huffman	Y	Y	Y	Y	Y	Y	N
3 Garamendi	Y	Y	Y	Y	Y	Y	N
4 McClintock	N	N	N	N	N	N	Y
5 Thompson	Y	Y	Y	Y	Y	Y	N
6 Matsui	Y	Y	Y	Y	Y	Y	N
7 Bera	Y	Y	Y	Y	Y	Y	N
8 Cook	N	N	N	N	N	N	Y
9 McNerney	Y	Y	Y	Y	Y	Y	N
10 Denham	N	N	N	N	N	N	Y
11 DeSaulnier	Y	Y	Y	Y	Y	Y	N
12 Pelosi	Y	Y	Y	Y	Y	Y	N
13 Lee	Y	Y	Y	Y	Y	Y	N
14 Speier	Y	Y	Y	Y	Y	Y	N
15 Swalwell	Y	Y	Y	Y	Y	Y	N
16 Costa	Y	Y	Y	Y	Y	Y	N
17 Khanna	Y	Y	Y	Y	Y	Y	N
18 Eshoo	Y	Y	Y	Y	Y	Y	N
19 Lofgren	Y	Y	Y	Y	Y	Y	N
20 Panetta	Y	Y	Y	Y	Y	Y	N
21 Valadao	N	N	N	N	N	N	Y
22 Nunes	N	N	N	N	N	N	Y
23 McCarthy	N	N	N	N	N	N	Y
24 Carbajal	Y	Y	Y	Y	Y	Y	N
25 Knight	N	N	N	N	N	N	Y
26 Brownley	Y	Y	Y	Y	Y	Y	N
27 Chu	Y	Y	Y	Y	Y	Y	N
28 Schiff	Y	Y	Y	Y	Y	Y	N
29 Cardenas	Y	Y	Y	Y	Y	Y	N
30 Sherman	Y	Y	Y	Y	Y	Y	N
31 Aguilar	Y	Y	Y	Y	Y	Y	N
32 Napolitano	Y	Y	Y	Y	Y	Y	N
33 Lieu	Y	Y	Y	Y	Y	Y	N
34 Becerra	+	+	+	+	+	+	-
35 Torres	Y	Y	Y	Y	Y	Y	N
36 Ruiz	Y	Y	Y	Y	Y	Y	N
37 Bass	Y	Y	Y	Y	Y	Y	N
38 Sánchez, Linda	Y	?	Y	Y	Y	Y	N
39 Royce	N	N	N	N	N	N	Y
40 Roybal-Allard	Y	Y	Y	Y	Y	Y	N
41 Takano	Y	Y	Y	Y	Y	Y	N
42 Calvert	N	N	N	N	N	N	Y
43 Waters	?	Y	Y	Y	Y	Y	N
44 Barragan	Y	Y	Y	Y	Y	Y	N
45 Walters	N	N	N	N	N	N	Y
46 Correa	Y	Y	Y	Y	Y	Y	N
47 Lowenthal	Y	Y	Y	Y	Y	Y	N
48 Rohrabacher	N	N	N	N	N	N	Y
49 Issa	N	N	N	N	N	N	Y
50 Hunter	N	N	N	N	N	N	Y
51 Vargas	Y	Y	Y	Y	Y	Y	N
52 Peters	Y	Y	Y	Y	Y	Y	N
53 Davis	Y	Y	Y	Y	Y	Y	N

	15	16	17	18	19	20	21
COLORADO							
1 DeGette	Y	Y	Y	Y	Y	Y	N
2 Polis	Y	Y	Y	Y	Y	Y	N
3 Tipton	N	N	N	N	N	N	Y
4 Buck	N	N	N	N	N	N	Y
5 Lamborn	N	N	N	N	N	N	Y
6 Coffman	N	N	N	N	N	N	Y
7 Perlmutter	Y	Y	Y	Y	Y	Y	N
CONNECTICUT							
1 Larson	Y	Y	Y	Y	Y	Y	N
2 Courtney	Y	Y	Y	Y	Y	Y	N
3 DeLauro	Y	Y	Y	Y	Y	Y	N
4 Himes	Y	Y	Y	Y	Y	Y	N
5 Esty	Y	Y	Y	Y	Y	Y	N
DELAWARE							
AL Blunt Rochester	Y	Y	Y	Y	Y	Y	N
FLORIDA							
1 Gaetz	N	N	N	N	N	N	Y
2 Dunn	N	N	N	N	N	N	Y
3 Yoho	N	N	N	N	N	N	Y
4 Rutherford	N	N	N	N	N	N	Y
5 Lawson	Y	Y	Y	Y	Y	Y	N
6 DeSantis	N	N	N	N	N	N	Y
7 Murphy	Y	Y	Y	Y	Y	Y	N
8 Posey	N	N	N	N	N	N	Y
9 Soto	Y	Y	Y	Y	Y	Y	N
10 Demings	Y	Y	Y	Y	Y	Y	N
11 Webster	N	N	N	N	N	N	Y
12 Bilirakis	N	N	N	N	N	N	Y
13 Crist	Y	Y	Y	Y	Y	Y	N
14 Castor	Y	Y	Y	Y	Y	Y	N
15 Ross	N	N	N	N	N	N	Y
16 Buchanan	N	N	N	N	N	N	Y
17 Rooney, T.	N	N	N	N	N	N	Y
18 Mast	N	N	N	N	N	N	Y
19 Rooney, F.	N	N	N	N	N	N	Y
20 Hastings	Y	Y	Y	Y	Y	Y	N
21 Frankel	Y	Y	Y	Y	Y	Y	N
22 Deutch	Y	Y	Y	Y	Y	Y	N
23 Wasserman Schultz	Y	Y	Y	Y	Y	Y	N
24 Wilson	Y	Y	Y	Y	Y	Y	N
25 Diaz-Balart	N	?	N	N	N	N	Y
26 Curbelo	N	N	N	N	N	N	Y
27 Ros-Lehtinen	N	N	N	N	N	N	Y
GEORGIA							
1 Carter	N	N	N	N	N	N	Y
2 Bishop	Y	Y	Y	Y	Y	Y	N
3 Ferguson	N	N	N	N	N	N	Y
4 Johnson	Y	Y	Y	Y	Y	Y	N
5 Lewis	Y	Y	Y	Y	Y	Y	N
6 Price	?	?	?	?	?	?	?
7 Woodall	N	N	N	N	N	N	Y
8 Scott, A.	N	N	N	N	N	N	Y
9 Collins	N	N	N	N	N	N	Y
10 Hice	N	N	N	N	N	N	Y
11 Loudermilk	N	N	N	N	N	N	Y
12 Allen	N	N	N	N	N	N	Y
13 Scott, D.	Y	Y	Y	Y	Y	Y	N
14 Graves	N	N	N	N	N	N	Y
HAWAII							
1 Hanabusa	Y	Y	Y	Y	Y	Y	N
2 Gabbard	Y	Y	Y	Y	Y	Y	N
IDAHO							
1 Labrador	N	N	N	N	N	N	Y
2 Simpson	N	N	N	N	N	N	Y
ILLINOIS							
1 Rush	?	?	?	?	?	?	?
2 Kelly	Y	Y	Y	Y	Y	Y	N
3 Lipinski	Y	Y	Y	Y	Y	Y	N
4 Gutierrez	+	Y	Y	Y	Y	Y	N
5 Quigley	Y	Y	Y	Y	Y	Y	N
6 Roskam	N	N	N	N	N	N	Y
7 Davis, D.	Y	Y	Y	Y	Y	Y	N
8 Krishnamoorthi	Y	Y	Y	Y	Y	Y	N
9 Schakowsky	Y	Y	Y	Y	Y	Y	N
10 Schneider	Y	Y	Y	Y	Y	Y	N
11 Foster	Y	Y	Y	Y	Y	Y	N
12 Bost	N	N	N	N	N	N	Y
13 Davis, R.	N	N	N	N	N	N	Y
14 Hultgren	N	N	N	N	N	N	Y
15 Shimkus	N	N	N	N	N	N	Y

	15	16	17	18	19	20	21
16 **Kinzinger**	N	N	N	N	N	N	Y
17 Bustos	Y	Y	Y	Y	Y	Y	N
18 **LaHood**	N	N	N	N	N	N	Y
INDIANA							
1 Visclosky	Y	Y	Y	Y	Y	Y	N
2 **Walorski**	N	N	N	N	N	N	Y
3 **Banks**	N	N	N	N	N	N	Y
4 **Rokita**	?	N	N	N	N	N	Y
5 **Brooks**	N	N	N	N	N	N	Y
6 **Messer**	N	N	N	N	N	N	Y
7 Carson	Y	Y	Y	Y	Y	Y	N
8 **Bucshon**	N	N	N	N	N	N	Y
9 **Hollingsworth**	N	N	N	N	N	N	Y
IOWA							
1 **Blum**	N	N	N	N	N	N	Y
2 Loebsack	Y	Y	Y	Y	Y	Y	N
3 **Young**	N	N	N	N	N	N	Y
4 **King**	N	N	N	N	N	N	Y
KANSAS							
1 **Marshall**	N	N	N	N	N	N	Y
2 **Jenkins**	–	–	–	–	–	+	–
3 **Yoder**	N	N	N	N	N	N	Y
4 **Pompeo**	?	?	?	?	?	?	?
KENTUCKY							
1 **Comer**	N	N	N	N	N	N	Y
2 **Guthrie**	N	N	N	N	N	N	Y
3 Yarmuth	Y	Y	Y	Y	Y	Y	N
4 **Massie**	N	N	N	N	N	N	Y
5 **Rogers**	N	N	N	N	N	N	Y
6 **Barr**	N	N	N	N	N	N	Y
LOUISIANA							
1 **Scalise**	N	N	N	N	N	N	Y
2 Richmond	Y	Y	Y	Y	Y	Y	N
3 **Higgins**	N	N	N	N	N	N	Y
4 **Johnson**	N	N	N	N	N	N	Y
5 **Abraham**	N	N	N	N	N	N	Y
6 **Graves**	N	N	N	N	N	N	Y
MAINE							
1 Pingree	Y	Y	Y	Y	Y	Y	N
2 **Poliquin**	N	N	N	N	N	N	Y
MARYLAND							
1 **Harris**	N	N	N	N	N	N	Y
2 Ruppersberger	Y	Y	Y	Y	Y	Y	N
3 Sarbanes	Y	Y	Y	Y	Y	Y	N
4 Brown	Y	Y	Y	Y	Y	Y	N
5 Hoyer	Y	Y	Y	Y	Y	Y	N
6 Delaney	Y	Y	Y	Y	Y	Y	N
7 Cummings	Y	Y	Y	Y	Y	Y	N
8 Raskin	Y	Y	Y	Y	Y	Y	N
MASSACHUSETTS							
1 Neal	Y	Y	Y	Y	Y	Y	N
2 McGovern	Y	Y	Y	Y	Y	Y	N
3 Tsongas	Y	Y	Y	Y	Y	Y	N
4 Kennedy	Y	Y	Y	Y	Y	Y	N
5 Clark	Y	Y	Y	Y	Y	Y	N
6 Moulton	Y	Y	Y	Y	Y	Y	N
7 Capuano	Y	Y	Y	Y	Y	Y	N
8 Lynch	Y	Y	Y	Y	Y	Y	N
9 Keating	Y	Y	Y	Y	Y	Y	N
MICHIGAN							
1 **Bergman**	N	N	N	N	N	N	Y
2 **Huizenga**	N	N	N	N	N	N	Y
3 **Amash**	N	N	N	N	N	N	Y
4 **Moolenaar**	N	N	N	N	N	N	Y
5 Kildee	Y	Y	Y	Y	Y	Y	N
6 **Upton**	N	N	N	N	N	N	Y
7 **Walberg**	N	N	N	N	N	N	Y
8 **Bishop**	N	N	N	N	N	N	Y
9 Levin	Y	Y	Y	Y	Y	Y	N
10 **Mitchell**	N	N	N	N	N	N	Y
11 **Trott**	N	N	N	N	N	N	Y
12 Dingell	Y	Y	Y	Y	Y	Y	N
13 Conyers	Y	Y	Y	Y	Y	Y	N
14 Lawrence	Y	Y	Y	Y	Y	Y	N
MINNESOTA							
1 Walz	Y	Y	Y	Y	Y	Y	N
2 **Lewis**	N	N	N	N	N	N	Y
3 **Paulsen**	N	N	N	N	N	N	Y
4 McCollum	Y	Y	Y	Y	Y	Y	N

	15	16	17	18	19	20	21
5 Ellison	Y	Y	Y	Y	Y	Y	N
6 **Emmer**	N	N	N	N	N	N	Y
7 Peterson	N	Y	Y	Y	Y	Y	N
8 Nolan	Y	Y	Y	Y	Y	Y	N
MISSISSIPPI							
1 **Kelly**	N	N	N	N	N	N	Y
2 Thompson	Y	Y	Y	Y	Y	Y	N
3 **Harper**	N	N	N	N	N	N	Y
4 **Palazzo**	N	N	N	N	N	N	Y
MISSOURI							
1 Clay	Y	Y	Y	Y	Y	Y	N
2 **Wagner**	N	N	N	N	N	N	Y
3 **Luetkemeyer**	N	N	N	N	N	N	Y
4 **Hartzler**	N	N	N	N	N	N	Y
5 Cleaver	Y	Y	Y	Y	Y	Y	N
6 **Graves**	N	N	N	N	N	N	Y
7 **Long**	N	N	N	N	N	N	Y
8 **Smith**	N	N	N	N	N	N	Y
MONTANA							
AL **Zinke**	N	N	N	N	N	N	Y
NEBRASKA							
1 **Fortenberry**	N	N	N	N	N	N	Y
2 **Bacon**	N	N	N	N	N	N	Y
3 **Smith**	N	N	N	N	N	N	Y
NEVADA							
1 Titus	Y	Y	Y	Y	Y	Y	N
2 **Amodei**	N	N	N	N	N	N	Y
3 Rosen	Y	Y	Y	Y	Y	Y	N
4 Kihuen	Y	Y	Y	Y	Y	Y	N
NEW HAMPSHIRE							
1 Shea-Porter	Y	Y	Y	Y	Y	Y	N
2 Kuster	Y	Y	Y	Y	Y	Y	N
NEW JERSEY							
1 Norcross	Y	Y	Y	Y	Y	Y	N
2 **LoBiondo**	N	N	N	Y	N	N	N
3 **MacArthur**	N	N	N	N	N	N	Y
4 **Smith**	N	N	N	Y	N	N	N
5 Gottheimer	Y	Y	Y	Y	Y	Y	N
6 Pallone	Y	Y	Y	Y	Y	Y	N
7 **Lance**	N	N	N	N	N	N	Y
8 Sires	Y	Y	Y	Y	Y	Y	N
9 Pascrell	Y	Y	Y	Y	Y	Y	N
10 Payne	Y	Y	Y	Y	Y	Y	N
11 **Frelinghuysen**	N	N	N	N	N	N	Y
12 Watson Coleman	Y	Y	Y	Y	Y	Y	N
NEW MEXICO							
1 Lujan Grisham	Y	Y	Y	Y	Y	Y	N
2 **Pearce**	N	N	N	N	N	N	Y
3 Luján	Y	Y	Y	Y	Y	Y	N
NEW YORK							
1 **Zeldin**	N	N	N	N	N	N	Y
2 **King**	N	N	N	N	N	N	Y
3 Suozzi	Y	Y	Y	Y	Y	Y	N
4 Rice	Y	Y	Y	Y	Y	Y	N
5 Meeks	Y	Y	Y	Y	Y	Y	N
6 Meng	Y	Y	Y	Y	Y	Y	N
7 Velázquez	Y	Y	Y	Y	Y	Y	N
8 Jeffries	Y	Y	Y	Y	Y	Y	N
9 Clarke	Y	Y	Y	Y	Y	Y	N
10 Nadler	Y	Y	Y	Y	Y	Y	N
11 **Donovan**	N	N	N	N	N	N	Y
12 Maloney, C.	Y	Y	Y	Y	Y	Y	N
13 Espaillat	Y	Y	Y	Y	Y	Y	N
14 Crowley	Y	Y	Y	Y	Y	Y	N
15 Serrano	Y	Y	Y	Y	Y	Y	N
16 Engel	Y	Y	Y	Y	Y	Y	N
17 Lowey	Y	Y	Y	Y	Y	Y	N
18 Maloney, S.P.	Y	Y	Y	Y	Y	Y	N
19 **Faso**	N	N	N	N	N	N	Y
20 Tonko	Y	Y	Y	Y	Y	Y	N
21 **Stefanik**	N	Y	N	N	N	N	Y
22 **Tenney**	N	N	N	N	N	N	Y
23 **Reed**	N	N	N	N	N	N	Y
24 **Katko**	N	N	N	N	N	N	Y
25 Slaughter	Y	Y	Y	Y	Y	Y	N
26 Higgins	Y	Y	Y	Y	Y	Y	N
27 **Collins**	–	–	–	–	–	–	+
NORTH CAROLINA							
1 Butterfield	Y	Y	Y	Y	Y	Y	N
2 **Holding**	N	N	N	N	N	N	Y
3 **Jones**	N	Y	N	Y	N	N	Y
4 Price	Y	Y	Y	Y	Y	Y	?

	15	16	17	18	19	20	21
5 **Foxx**	N	N	N	N	N	N	Y
6 **Walker**	N	N	N	N	N	N	Y
7 **Rouzer**	N	N	N	N	N	N	Y
8 **Hudson**	N	N	N	N	N	N	Y
9 **Pittenger**	N	N	N	N	N	N	Y
10 **McHenry**	N	N	N	N	N	N	Y
11 **Meadows**	N	N	N	N	N	N	Y
12 Adams	Y	Y	Y	Y	Y	Y	N
13 **Budd**	N	N	N	N	N	N	Y
NORTH DAKOTA							
AL **Cramer**	N	N	N	N	N	N	Y
OHIO							
1 **Chabot**	N	N	N	N	N	N	Y
2 **Wenstrup**	N	N	N	N	N	N	Y
3 Beatty	Y	Y	Y	Y	Y	Y	N
4 **Jordan**	N	N	N	N	N	N	Y
5 **Latta**	N	N	N	N	N	N	Y
6 **Johnson**	N	N	N	N	N	N	Y
7 **Gibbs**	N	N	N	N	N	N	Y
8 **Davidson**	N	N	N	N	N	N	Y
9 Kaptur	Y	Y	Y	Y	Y	Y	N
10 **Turner**	N	N	N	N	N	N	Y
11 Fudge	Y	Y	Y	Y	Y	Y	N
12 **Tiberi**	N	N	N	N	N	N	Y
13 Ryan	?	Y	Y	Y	Y	Y	N
14 **Joyce**	N	N	N	N	N	N	Y
15 **Stivers**	N	N	N	N	N	N	Y
16 **Renacci**	N	N	N	N	N	N	Y
OKLAHOMA							
1 **Bridenstine**	N	N	N	N	N	N	Y
2 **Mullin**	N	N	N	N	N	N	Y
3 **Lucas**	N	N	N	N	N	N	Y
4 **Cole**	N	N	N	N	N	N	Y
5 **Russell**	N	N	N	N	N	N	Y
OREGON							
1 Bonamici	Y	Y	Y	Y	Y	Y	N
2 **Walden**	N	N	N	N	N	N	Y
3 Blumenauer	Y	Y	Y	N	Y	Y	N
4 DeFazio	Y	Y	Y	Y	Y	Y	N
5 Schrader	I						
PENNSYLVANIA							
1 Brady	Y	Y	Y	Y	Y	Y	N
2 Evans	Y	Y	Y	Y	Y	Y	N
3 **Kelly**	N	N	N	N	N	N	Y
4 **Perry**	N	N	N	N	N	N	Y
5 **Thompson**	N	N	N	N	N	N	Y
6 **Costello**	N	N	N	N	N	N	Y
7 **Meehan**	N	N	N	N	N	N	Y
8 **Fitzpatrick**	N	N	N	N	N	N	Y
9 **Shuster**	N	N	N	N	N	N	Y
10 **Marino**	N	N	N	N	N	N	Y
11 **Barletta**	N	N	N	N	N	N	Y
12 **Rothfus**	N	N	N	N	N	N	Y
13 Boyle	Y	Y	Y	Y	Y	Y	N
14 Doyle	Y	Y	Y	Y	Y	Y	N
15 **Dent**	N	Y	N	N	N	N	Y
16 **Smucker**	N	N	N	N	N	N	N
17 Cartwright	Y	Y	Y	Y	Y	Y	N
18 **Murphy**	N	N	N	N	N	N	Y
RHODE ISLAND							
1 Cicilline	Y	Y	Y	Y	Y	Y	N
2 Langevin	Y	Y	Y	Y	Y	Y	N
SOUTH CAROLINA							
1 **Sanford**	N	N	N	N	N	N	Y
2 **Wilson**	N	N	N	N	N	N	Y
3 **Duncan**	N	N	N	N	N	N	Y
4 **Gowdy**	N	N	N	N	N	N	Y
5 **Mulvaney**	?	?	?	?	?	?	?
6 Clyburn	Y	Y	Y	Y	Y	Y	N
7 **Rice**	N	N	N	N	N	N	Y
SOUTH DAKOTA							
AL **Noem**	N	N	N	N	N	N	Y
TENNESSEE							
1 **Roe**	N	N	N	N	N	N	Y
2 **Duncan**	N	N	N	Y	N	N	Y
3 **Fleischmann**	N	N	N	N	N	N	Y
4 **DesJarlais**	N	N	N	N	N	N	Y
5 Cooper	Y	Y	Y	Y	Y	Y	N
6 **Black**	N	N	N	N	N	N	Y
7 **Blackburn**	N	N	N	N	N	N	Y
8 **Kustoff**	N	N	N	N	N	N	Y
9 Cohen	Y	Y	Y	Y	Y	Y	N

	15	16	17	18	19	20	21
TEXAS							
1 **Gohmert**	N	N	N	N	N	N	Y
2 **Poe**	N	N	N	N	N	N	Y
3 **Johnson, S.**	N	N	N	N	N	N	Y
4 **Ratcliffe**	N	N	N	N	N	N	Y
5 **Hensarling**	N	N	N	N	N	N	Y
6 **Barton**	N	N	N	N	N	N	Y
7 **Culberson**	N	N	N	N	N	N	?
8 **Brady**	N	N	N	N	N	N	Y
9 Green, A.	Y	Y	Y	Y	Y	Y	N
10 **McCaul**	N	N	N	N	N	N	Y
11 **Conaway**	N	N	N	N	N	N	Y
12 **Granger**	N	N	N	N	N	N	Y
13 **Thornberry**	N	N	N	N	N	N	Y
14 **Weber**	N	N	N	N	N	N	Y
15 Gonzalez	Y	Y	Y	Y	Y	Y	N
16 O'Rourke	Y	Y	Y	Y	Y	Y	N
17 **Flores**	N	N	N	N	N	N	Y
18 Jackson Lee	Y	Y	Y	Y	Y	Y	N
19 **Arrington**	N	N	N	N	N	N	Y
20 Castro	Y	Y	Y	Y	Y	Y	N
21 **Smith**	N	N	N	N	N	N	Y
22 **Olson**	N	N	N	N	N	N	Y
23 **Hurd**	N	N	N	N	N	N	Y
24 **Marchant**	N	N	N	N	N	N	Y
25 **Williams**	N	N	N	N	N	N	Y
26 **Burgess**	N	N	N	N	N	N	Y
27 **Farenthold**	N	N	N	N	N	N	Y
28 Cuellar	Y	Y	Y	Y	Y	Y	N
29 Green, G.	Y	Y	Y	Y	Y	Y	N
30 Johnson, E.B.	Y	Y	Y	Y	Y	Y	N
31 **Carter**	N	N	N	N	N	N	Y
32 **Sessions**	N	N	N	N	N	N	Y
33 Veasey	Y	Y	Y	Y	Y	Y	N
34 Vela	Y	Y	Y	Y	Y	Y	N
35 Doggett	Y	Y	Y	Y	Y	Y	N
36 **Babin**	N	N	N	N	N	N	Y
UTAH							
1 **Bishop**	N	N	N	N	N	N	Y
2 **Stewart**	N	N	N	N	N	N	Y
3 **Chaffetz**	N	N	N	N	N	N	Y
4 **Love**	N	N	N	N	N	N	Y
VERMONT							
AL Welch	Y	Y	Y	Y	Y	Y	N
VIRGINIA							
1 **Wittman**	N	N	N	N	N	N	Y
2 **Taylor**	N	N	N	N	N	N	Y
3 Scott	Y	Y	Y	Y	Y	Y	N
4 McEachin	Y	Y	Y	Y	Y	Y	N
5 **Garrett**	N	N	N	N	N	N	Y
6 **Goodlatte**	N	N	N	N	N	N	Y
7 **Brat**	N	N	N	N	N	N	Y
8 Beyer	Y	Y	Y	Y	Y	Y	N
9 **Griffith**	N	N	N	N	N	N	Y
10 **Comstock**	?	N	N	N	N	N	Y
11 Connolly	Y	Y	Y	Y	Y	Y	N
WASHINGTON							
1 DelBene	Y	Y	Y	Y	Y	Y	N
2 Larsen	Y	Y	Y	Y	Y	Y	N
3 **Herrera Beutler**	N	N	N	N	N	N	Y
4 **Newhouse**	N	N	N	N	N	N	Y
5 **McMorris Rodgers**	N	N	N	N	N	N	Y
6 Kilmer	Y	Y	Y	Y	Y	Y	N
7 Jayapal	Y	Y	Y	Y	Y	Y	N
8 **Reichert**	N	N	N	N	N	N	Y
9 Smith	Y	Y	Y	Y	Y	Y	N
10 Heck	Y	Y	Y	Y	Y	Y	N
WEST VIRGINIA							
1 **McKinley**	N	N	N	N	N	Y	Y
2 **Mooney**	N	N	N	N	N	N	Y
3 **Jenkins**	N	N	N	N	N	Y	Y
WISCONSIN							
1 **Ryan**							
2 Pocan	Y	Y	Y	Y	Y	Y	N
3 Kind	Y	Y	Y	Y	Y	Y	N
4 Moore	Y	Y	Y	Y	Y	Y	N
5 **Sensenbrenner**	N	N	N	N	N	N	Y
6 **Grothman**	N	N	N	N	N	N	Y
7 **Duffy**	N	N	N	N	N	N	Y
8 **Gallagher**	N	N	N	N	N	N	Y
WYOMING							
AL **Cheney**	N	N	N	N	N	N	Y

VOTE NUMBER

22. HR 26. MAJOR RULES APPROVAL/RECOMMIT. Murphy, D-Fla., motion to recommit the bill to the House Judiciary Committee with instructions to report back immediately with an amendment that would exempt from the bill any rule prohibiting an insurance issuer from eliminating health coverage for dependents younger than 26 years old. Motion rejected 190-235 : R 0-235; D 190-0. Jan. 5, 2017.

23. HR 26. MAJOR RULES APPROVAL/PASSAGE. Passage of the bill that would require Congress to approve, by enacting legislation, any "major rule" issued by an agency in order for them to take effect. A "major rule" would include any regulation with an annual economic impact of $100 million or more; rules that would significantly harm employment, investment or U.S. economic competitiveness; or rules that would cause a major increase in costs or prices for consumers or industries. The bill also would create an expedited consideration process in both the House and the Senate for joint resolutions of approval. As amended, the measure would require that for new rules, agencies repeal or amend an existing rule or rules to offset any annual costs of the new rule before the new rule could take effect. As amended, it would create a process to sunset existing rules if Congress had not approved them within 10 years of the bill's enactment. Passed 237-187 : R 235-0; D 2-187. Jan. 5, 2017.

24. HR 315. MATERNITY CARE SERVICES/PASSAGE. Burgess, R-Texas, motion to suspend the rules and pass the bill that would require the Health Resources and Services Administration to identify geographic areas within health professional shortages areas that have a shortage of maternity care health professionals, for purposes of assigning such professionals who participate in the National Health Service Corps to these geographic areas. HRSA would need to base the identifications on data it would need to collect comparing the availability of and need for maternal health services in health professional shortage areas. Motion agreed to 405-0 : R 227-0; D 178-0. Jan. 9, 2017.

25. HR 304. PARAMEDICS AND CONTROLLED SUBSTANCES/PASSAGE. Burgess, R-Texas, motion to suspend the rules and pass the bill that would allow for paramedics and other emergency medical services professionals to continue to administer certain controlled substances pursuant to written protocols in which agency medical directors have determined in advance the medical criteria that need to be met, known as standing orders. It also would allow for EMS agencies, for purposes of administering these controlled substances, to register with the Justice Department through a single registration per state instead of requiring separate registrations for each location. Motion agreed to 404-0 : R 225-0; D 179-0. Jan. 9, 2017.

26. HR 79, H RES 33, HR 5. RULE-MAKING PROCESS CHANGES AND SEC GENERAL SOLICITATION/PREVIOUS QUESTION. Collins, R-Ga., motion to order the previous question (thus ending debate and possibility of amendment) on the rule (H Res 33) that would provide for House floor consideration of the bill (HR 79) that would exempt certain events from a Securities and Exchange Commission requirement that calls for verification that attendees are accredited investors, and a bill (HR 5) that would modify the federal rule-making process by codifying certain requirements, including a requirement that agencies estimate the cost of proposed regulations, and would subject rules likely to cost more than $100 million or $1 billion annually to additional procedural steps. Motion agreed to 234-179 : R 233-0; D 1-179. Jan. 10, 2017.

27. HR 79, H RES 33, HR 5. RULE-MAKING PROCESS CHANGES AND SEC GENERAL SOLICITATION/RULE. Adoption of the rule (H Res 33) that would provide for House floor consideration of the bill (HR 79) that would exempt certain events from a Securities and Exchange Commission requirement that calls for verification that attendees are accredited investors, and a bill (HR 5) that would modify the federal rule-making process by codifying certain requirements, including a requirement that agencies estimate the cost of proposed regulations, and would subject rules likely to cost more than $100 million or $1 billion annually to additional procedural steps. Adopted 233-183 : R 233-0; D 0-183. Jan. 10, 2017.

	22	23	24	25	26	27
ALABAMA						
1 Byrne	N	Y	Y	Y	Y	Y
2 Roby	N	Y	Y	Y	Y	Y
3 Rogers	N	Y	Y	Y	Y	Y
4 Aderholt	N	Y	Y	Y	Y	Y
5 Brooks	N	Y	Y	Y	Y	Y
6 Palmer	N	Y	Y	Y	Y	Y
7 Sewell	Y	N	Y	Y	N	N
ALASKA						
AL Young	N	Y	Y	?	Y	Y
ARIZONA						
1 O'Halleran	Y	N	Y	Y	N	N
2 McSally	N	Y	Y	Y	Y	Y
3 Grijalva	Y	N	?	?	N	N
4 Gosar	N	Y	Y	Y	N	Y
5 Biggs	N	Y	Y	Y	Y	Y
6 Schweikert	N	Y	Y	Y	Y	Y
7 Gallego	+	–	Y	Y	N	N
8 Franks	N	Y	Y	Y	Y	Y
9 Sinema	Y	N	Y	Y	N	N
ARKANSAS						
1 Crawford	N	Y	Y	Y	Y	Y
2 Hill	N	Y	Y	Y	Y	Y
3 Womack	N	Y	Y	Y	Y	Y
4 Westerman	N	Y	Y	Y	Y	Y
CALIFORNIA						
1 LaMalfa	N	Y	Y	Y	Y	Y
2 Huffman	Y	N	Y	Y	N	N
3 Garamendi	Y	N	Y	Y	N	N
4 McClintock	N	Y	Y	Y	Y	Y
5 Thompson	Y	N	Y	Y	N	N
6 Matsui	Y	N	Y	Y	N	N
7 Bera	Y	N	Y	Y	N	N
8 Cook	N	Y	Y	Y	Y	Y
9 McNerney	Y	N	Y	Y	N	N
10 Denham	N	Y	Y	Y	Y	Y
11 DeSaulnier	Y	N	Y	Y	N	N
12 Pelosi	Y	N	Y	Y	N	N
13 Lee	Y	N	Y	Y	N	N
14 Speier	Y	N	Y	Y	N	N
15 Swalwell	Y	N	Y	Y	N	N
16 Costa	Y	N	Y	Y	N	N
17 Khanna	Y	N	Y	Y	N	N
18 Eshoo	Y	N	Y	Y	N	N
19 Lofgren	Y	N	Y	Y	N	N
20 Panetta	Y	N	Y	Y	N	N
21 Valadao	N	Y	Y	Y	Y	Y
22 Nunes	N	Y	Y	Y	Y	Y
23 McCarthy	N	Y	Y	Y	Y	Y
24 Carbajal	Y	N	Y	Y	N	N
25 Knight	N	Y	Y	Y	Y	Y
26 Brownley	Y	N	Y	Y	N	N
27 Chu	Y	N	Y	Y	N	N
28 Schiff	Y	N	Y	Y	N	N
29 Cardenas	Y	N	Y	Y	N	N
30 Sherman	Y	N	Y	Y	N	N
31 Aguilar	Y	N	Y	Y	N	N
32 Napolitano	Y	N	Y	Y	N	N
33 Lieu	Y	N	Y	Y	N	N
34 Becerra	+	–	?	?	–	–
35 Torres	Y	N	Y	Y	N	N
36 Ruiz	Y	N	Y	Y	N	N
37 Bass	Y	N	Y	Y	N	N
38 Sánchez, Linda	Y	N	Y	Y	N	N
39 Royce	N	Y	Y	Y	Y	Y
40 Roybal-Allard	Y	N	Y	Y	N	N
41 Takano	Y	N	Y	Y	?	?
42 Calvert	N	Y	Y	Y	Y	Y
43 Waters	Y	N	Y	Y	N	N
44 Barragan	Y	N	Y	Y	N	N
45 Walters	N	Y	Y	Y	Y	Y
46 Correa	Y	N	?	?	N	N
47 Lowenthal	Y	N	Y	Y	N	N
48 Rohrabacher	N	Y	Y	Y	Y	Y
49 Issa	N	Y	Y	Y	Y	Y
50 Hunter	N	Y	Y	Y	Y	Y
51 Vargas	Y	N	Y	Y	N	N
52 Peters	Y	N	Y	Y	N	N
53 Davis	Y	N	Y	Y	N	N

	22	23	24	25	26	27
COLORADO						
1 DeGette	Y	N	Y	Y	N	N
2 Polis	Y	N	Y	Y	N	N
3 Tipton	N	Y	Y	Y	Y	Y
4 Buck	N	Y	Y	Y	Y	Y
5 Lamborn	N	Y	Y	Y	Y	Y
6 Coffman	N	Y	Y	Y	Y	Y
7 Perlmutter	Y	N	+	+	?	?
CONNECTICUT						
1 Larson	Y	N	Y	Y	N	N
2 Courtney	Y	N	Y	Y	N	N
3 DeLauro	Y	N	Y	Y	N	N
4 Himes	Y	N	Y	Y	N	N
5 Esty	Y	N	Y	Y	N	N
DELAWARE						
AL Blunt Rochester	Y	N	+	+	N	N
FLORIDA						
1 Gaetz	N	Y	Y	Y	Y	Y
2 Dunn	N	Y	Y	Y	Y	Y
3 Yoho	N	Y	Y	Y	Y	Y
4 Rutherford	N	Y	Y	Y	Y	Y
5 Lawson	Y	N	Y	Y	N	N
6 DeSantis	N	Y	Y	Y	Y	Y
7 Murphy	Y	N	Y	Y	N	N
8 Posey	N	Y	Y	Y	Y	Y
9 Soto	Y	N	Y	Y	N	N
10 Demings	Y	N	Y	Y	N	N
11 Webster	N	Y	Y	Y	Y	Y
12 Bilirakis	N	Y	Y	Y	Y	Y
13 Crist	Y	N	Y	Y	N	N
14 Castor	Y	N	Y	Y	N	N
15 Ross	N	Y	Y	Y	Y	Y
16 Buchanan	N	Y	?	?	Y	Y
17 Rooney, T.	N	Y	Y	Y	Y	Y
18 Mast	N	Y	Y	Y	Y	Y
19 Rooney, F.	N	Y	Y	Y	Y	Y
20 Hastings	Y	N	Y	Y	N	N
21 Frankel	Y	N	Y	Y	N	N
22 Deutch	Y	N	Y	Y	N	N
23 Wasserman Schultz	Y	N	Y	Y	N	N
24 Wilson	Y	?	Y	Y	–	N
25 Diaz-Balart	N	Y	Y	Y	Y	Y
26 Curbelo	N	Y	Y	Y	Y	Y
27 Ros-Lehtinen	N	Y	?	?	Y	Y
GEORGIA						
1 Carter	N	Y	Y	Y	Y	Y
2 Bishop	Y	N	?	?	N	N
3 Ferguson	N	Y	Y	Y	Y	Y
4 Johnson	Y	N	Y	Y	–	–
5 Lewis	Y	N	Y	Y	N	N
6 Price	?	?	?	?	?	?
7 Woodall	N	Y	Y	Y	Y	Y
8 Scott, A.	N	Y	Y	Y	Y	Y
9 Collins	N	Y	Y	Y	Y	Y
10 Hice	N	Y	Y	Y	Y	Y
11 Loudermilk	N	Y	Y	Y	Y	Y
12 Allen	N	Y	Y	Y	Y	Y
13 Scott, D.	Y	N	Y	Y	N	N
14 Graves	N	Y	Y	Y	Y	Y
HAWAII						
1 Hanabusa	Y	N	Y	Y	N	N
2 Gabbard	Y	N	Y	Y	N	N
IDAHO						
1 Labrador	N	Y	Y	Y	Y	Y
2 Simpson	N	Y	?	?	Y	Y
ILLINOIS						
1 Rush	?	?	?	?	?	?
2 Kelly	Y	N	Y	Y	?	?
3 Lipinski	Y	N	Y	Y	N	N
4 Gutierrez	Y	N	+	+	N	N
5 Quigley	Y	N	Y	Y	N	N
6 Roskam	N	Y	Y	Y	Y	Y
7 Davis, D.	Y	N	?	?	?	?
8 Krishnamoorthi	Y	N	Y	Y	N	N
9 Schakowsky	N	Y	Y	Y	–	–
10 Schneider	Y	N	Y	Y	N	N
11 Foster	Y	N	Y	Y	N	N
12 Bost	N	Y	Y	Y	Y	Y
13 Davis, R.	N	Y	Y	Y	Y	Y
14 Hultgren	N	Y	Y	Y	Y	Y
15 Shimkus	N	Y	Y	Y	Y	Y

	22	23	24	25	26	27
16 **Kinzinger**	N	Y	Y	Y	Y	Y
17 Bustos	Y	N	Y	Y	N	N
18 **LaHood**	N	Y	Y	Y	Y	Y
INDIANA						
1 Visclosky	Y	N	?	?	N	N
2 **Walorski**	N	Y	Y	Y	Y	Y
3 **Banks**	N	Y	Y	Y	Y	Y
4 **Rokita**	N	Y	Y	Y	Y	Y
5 **Brooks**	N	Y	Y	Y	Y	Y
6 **Messer**	N	Y	Y	?	Y	Y
7 Carson	Y	N	Y	Y	N	N
8 **Bucshon**	N	Y	Y	Y	Y	Y
9 **Hollingsworth**	N	Y	Y	Y	Y	Y
IOWA						
1 **Blum**	N	Y	Y	Y	Y	Y
2 Loebsack	Y	N	Y	Y	N	N
3 **Young**	N	Y	Y	Y	Y	Y
4 **King**	N	Y	Y	Y	Y	Y
KANSAS						
1 **Marshall**	N	Y	Y	Y	Y	Y
2 **Jenkins**	–	+	Y	Y	Y	Y
3 **Yoder**	N	Y	Y	Y	Y	Y
4 **Pompeo**	?	?	?	?	?	?
KENTUCKY						
1 **Comer**	N	Y	Y	Y	Y	Y
2 **Guthrie**	N	Y	Y	Y	Y	Y
3 Yarmuth	Y	N	Y	Y	N	N
4 **Massie**	N	Y	Y	Y	Y	Y
5 **Rogers**	N	Y	Y	Y	Y	Y
6 **Barr**	N	Y	Y	Y	Y	Y
LOUISIANA						
1 **Scalise**	N	Y	Y	Y	Y	Y
2 Richmond	Y	N	Y	Y	?	N
3 **Higgins**	N	Y	Y	Y	Y	Y
4 **Johnson**	N	Y	Y	Y	Y	Y
5 **Abraham**	N	Y	Y	Y	Y	Y
6 **Graves**	N	Y	Y	Y	Y	Y
MAINE						
1 Pingree	Y	N	Y	Y	N	N
2 **Poliquin**	N	Y	Y	Y	Y	Y
MARYLAND						
1 **Harris**	N	Y	Y	Y	Y	Y
2 Ruppersberger	Y	N	Y	Y	N	N
3 Sarbanes	Y	N	Y	Y	N	N
4 Brown	Y	N	Y	Y	N	N
5 Hoyer	Y	N	Y	Y	?	N
6 Delaney	Y	N	Y	Y	N	N
7 Cummings	Y	N	Y	Y	N	N
8 Raskin	Y	N	Y	Y	N	N
MASSACHUSETTS						
1 Neal	Y	N	Y	Y	N	N
2 McGovern	Y	N	Y	Y	N	N
3 Tsongas	Y	N	Y	Y	N	N
4 Kennedy	Y	N	Y	Y	N	N
5 Clark	Y	N	Y	Y	N	N
6 Moulton	Y	N	Y	Y	N	N
7 Capuano	Y	N	Y	Y	N	N
8 Lynch	Y	N	Y	Y	N	N
9 Keating	Y	N	Y	Y	N	N
MICHIGAN						
1 **Bergman**	N	Y	Y	Y	Y	Y
2 **Huizenga**	N	Y	Y	Y	Y	Y
3 **Amash**	N	Y	Y	Y	Y	Y
4 **Moolenaar**	N	Y	Y	Y	Y	Y
5 Kildee	Y	N	Y	Y	N	N
6 **Upton**	N	Y	Y	Y	Y	Y
7 **Walberg**	N	Y	Y	Y	Y	Y
8 **Bishop**	N	Y	Y	Y	Y	Y
9 Levin	Y	N	Y	Y	N	N
10 **Mitchell**	N	Y	Y	Y	Y	Y
11 **Trott**	N	Y	Y	Y	Y	Y
12 Dingell	Y	N	Y	Y	?	?
13 Conyers	Y	N	Y	Y	N	N
14 Lawrence	Y	N	Y	Y	N	N
MINNESOTA						
1 Walz	Y	N	Y	Y	N	N
2 **Lewis**	N	Y	Y	Y	Y	Y
3 **Paulsen**	N	Y	Y	Y	Y	Y
4 McCollum	Y	N	Y	Y	N	N

	22	23	24	25	26	27
5 Ellison	Y	N	Y	Y	N	N
6 **Emmer**	N	Y	Y	Y	Y	Y
7 Peterson	Y	Y	Y	Y	N	N
8 Nolan	Y	N	Y	Y	N	N
MISSISSIPPI						
1 **Kelly**	N	Y	Y	Y	Y	Y
2 Thompson	Y	N	Y	Y	N	N
3 **Harper**	N	Y	Y	Y	Y	Y
4 **Palazzo**	N	Y	Y	Y	Y	Y
MISSOURI						
1 Clay	Y	N	Y	Y	N	N
2 **Wagner**	N	Y	?	?	Y	Y
3 **Luetkemeyer**	N	Y	Y	Y	Y	Y
4 **Hartzler**	N	Y	Y	Y	Y	Y
5 Cleaver	Y	N	Y	Y	N	N
6 **Graves**	N	Y	Y	Y	Y	Y
7 **Long**	N	Y	Y	Y	Y	Y
8 **Smith**	N	Y	Y	Y	Y	Y
MONTANA						
AL **Zinke**	N	Y	?	?	?	?
NEBRASKA						
1 **Fortenberry**	N	Y	Y	Y	Y	Y
2 **Bacon**	N	Y	Y	Y	Y	Y
3 **Smith**	N	Y	Y	Y	Y	Y
NEVADA						
1 Titus	Y	N	Y	Y	N	N
2 **Amodei**	N	Y	Y	Y	Y	Y
3 Rosen	Y	N	Y	Y	N	N
4 Kihuen	Y	N	Y	Y	N	N
NEW HAMPSHIRE						
1 Shea-Porter	Y	N	Y	Y	N	N
2 Kuster	Y	N	Y	Y	N	N
NEW JERSEY						
1 Norcross	Y	N	Y	Y	N	N
2 **LoBiondo**	N	Y	Y	Y	Y	Y
3 **MacArthur**	N	Y	Y	Y	Y	Y
4 **Smith**	N	Y	Y	Y	Y	Y
5 Gottheimer	Y	N	Y	Y	N	N
6 Pallone	Y	N	Y	Y	N	N
7 **Lance**	N	Y	Y	Y	Y	Y
8 Sires	Y	N	Y	Y	N	N
9 Pascrell	Y	N	Y	Y	N	N
10 Payne	Y	N	Y	Y	N	N
11 **Frelinghuysen**	N	Y	Y	Y	Y	Y
12 Watson Coleman	Y	N	Y	Y	N	N
NEW MEXICO						
1 Lujan Grisham	Y	N	Y	Y	N	N
2 **Pearce**	N	Y	Y	Y	Y	Y
3 Luján	Y	N	Y	Y	N	N
NEW YORK						
1 **Zeldin**	N	Y	Y	Y	Y	Y
2 **King**	N	Y	Y	Y	Y	Y
3 Suozzi	Y	N	Y	Y	N	N
4 Rice	Y	N	Y	Y	N	N
5 Meeks	Y	N	Y	Y	N	N
6 Meng	Y	N	?	?	N	N
7 Velázquez	Y	N	Y	Y	N	N
8 Jeffries	Y	N	Y	Y	N	N
9 Clarke	Y	N	Y	Y	N	N
10 Nadler	Y	N	Y	Y	N	N
11 **Donovan**	N	Y	Y	Y	Y	Y
12 Maloney, C.	Y	N	Y	Y	N	N
13 Espaillat	Y	N	Y	Y	N	N
14 Crowley	Y	N	Y	Y	–	N
15 Serrano	Y	N	Y	Y	N	N
16 Engel	Y	N	Y	Y	N	N
17 Lowey	Y	N	Y	Y	N	N
18 Maloney, S.P.	Y	N	Y	Y	N	N
19 **Faso**	N	Y	Y	Y	Y	Y
20 Tonko	Y	N	Y	Y	N	N
21 **Stefanik**	N	Y	Y	Y	Y	Y
22 **Tenney**	N	Y	Y	Y	Y	Y
23 **Reed**	N	Y	Y	Y	Y	Y
24 **Katko**	N	Y	Y	Y	Y	Y
25 Slaughter	Y	N	Y	Y	N	N
26 Higgins	Y	N	Y	Y	N	N
27 **Collins**	–	+	Y	Y	Y	Y
NORTH CAROLINA						
1 Butterfield	Y	N	?	?	N	N
2 **Holding**	N	Y	Y	Y	Y	Y
3 **Jones**	N	Y	?	?	?	?
4 Price	Y	N	Y	Y	N	N

	22	23	24	25	26	27
5 **Foxx**	N	Y	Y	Y	Y	Y
6 **Walker**	N	Y	Y	Y	Y	Y
7 **Rouzer**	N	Y	Y	Y	Y	Y
8 **Hudson**	N	Y	Y	Y	Y	Y
9 **Pittenger**	N	Y	Y	Y	Y	Y
10 **McHenry**	N	Y	Y	Y	Y	Y
11 **Meadows**	N	Y	Y	Y	Y	Y
12 Adams	Y	N	Y	Y	N	N
13 **Budd**	N	Y	Y	Y	Y	Y
NORTH DAKOTA						
AL **Cramer**	N	Y	Y	Y	Y	Y
OHIO						
1 **Chabot**	N	Y	Y	Y	Y	Y
2 **Wenstrup**	N	Y	Y	Y	Y	Y
3 Beatty	Y	N	Y	Y	N	N
4 **Jordan**	N	Y	Y	Y	Y	Y
5 **Latta**	N	Y	Y	Y	Y	Y
6 **Johnson**	N	Y	Y	Y	Y	Y
7 **Gibbs**	N	Y	Y	Y	Y	Y
8 **Davidson**	N	Y	Y	Y	Y	Y
9 Kaptur	Y	N	Y	Y	N	N
10 **Turner**	N	Y	Y	Y	Y	Y
11 Fudge	Y	N	Y	Y	N	N
12 **Tiberi**	N	Y	Y	Y	Y	Y
13 Ryan	Y	N	+	+	–	–
14 **Joyce**	N	Y	Y	Y	Y	Y
15 **Stivers**	N	Y	Y	Y	Y	Y
16 **Renacci**	N	Y	Y	Y	Y	Y
OKLAHOMA						
1 **Bridenstine**	N	Y	Y	Y	Y	Y
2 **Mullin**	N	Y	Y	Y	Y	Y
3 **Lucas**	N	Y	Y	Y	Y	Y
4 **Cole**	N	Y	Y	Y	Y	Y
5 **Russell**	N	Y	?	?	Y	Y
OREGON						
1 Bonamici	Y	N	Y	Y	N	N
2 **Walden**	N	Y	Y	Y	Y	Y
3 Blumenauer	Y	N	Y	Y	N	N
4 DeFazio	Y	N	Y	Y	N	N
5 Schrader					N	N
PENNSYLVANIA						
1 Brady	Y	N	Y	Y	N	N
2 Evans	Y	N	Y	Y	N	N
3 **Kelly**	N	Y	Y	Y	Y	Y
4 **Perry**	N	Y	+	+	Y	Y
5 **Thompson**	N	Y	Y	Y	Y	Y
6 **Costello**	N	Y	Y	Y	Y	Y
7 **Meehan**	N	Y	Y	Y	Y	Y
8 **Fitzpatrick**	N	Y	Y	Y	Y	Y
9 **Shuster**	N	Y	Y	Y	Y	Y
10 **Marino**	N	Y	Y	Y	Y	Y
11 **Barletta**	N	Y	Y	Y	Y	Y
12 **Rothfus**	N	Y	Y	Y	Y	Y
13 Boyle	Y	N	+	+	N	N
14 Doyle	Y	N	Y	Y	N	N
15 **Dent**	N	Y	Y	Y	Y	Y
16 **Smucker**	N	Y	Y	Y	Y	Y
17 Cartwright	Y	N	Y	Y	N	N
18 **Murphy**	N	Y	Y	Y	Y	Y
RHODE ISLAND						
1 Cicilline	Y	N	Y	Y	N	N
2 Langevin	Y	N	Y	Y	N	N
SOUTH CAROLINA						
1 **Sanford**	N	Y	Y	Y	Y	Y
2 **Wilson**	N	Y	Y	Y	Y	Y
3 **Duncan**	N	Y	?	?	?	?
4 **Gowdy**	N	Y	Y	Y	Y	Y
5 **Mulvaney**	?	?	?	?	?	?
6 Clyburn	Y	N	Y	Y	N	N
7 **Rice**	N	Y	Y	?	Y	Y
SOUTH DAKOTA						
AL **Noem**	N	Y	Y	Y	Y	Y
TENNESSEE						
1 **Roe**	N	Y	Y	Y	Y	Y
2 **Duncan**	N	Y	Y	Y	Y	Y
3 **Fleischmann**	N	Y	Y	Y	Y	Y
4 **DesJarlais**	N	Y	Y	Y	Y	Y
5 Cooper	Y	N	Y	Y	N	N
6 **Black**	N	Y	Y	Y	Y	Y
7 **Blackburn**	N	Y	Y	Y	Y	Y
8 **Kustoff**	N	Y	Y	Y	Y	Y
9 Cohen	Y	N	Y	Y	N	N

	22	23	24	25	26	27
TEXAS						
1 **Gohmert**	N	Y	Y	Y	Y	Y
2 **Poe**	N	Y	Y	Y	Y	Y
3 **Johnson, S.**	N	Y	Y	Y	Y	Y
4 **Ratcliffe**	N	Y	Y	Y	Y	Y
5 **Hensarling**	N	Y	Y	Y	Y	Y
6 **Barton**	N	Y	Y	Y	Y	Y
7 **Culberson**	N	Y	Y	Y	Y	Y
8 **Brady**	N	Y	?	Y	Y	Y
9 Green, A.	Y	N	Y	Y	N	N
10 **McCaul**	N	Y	Y	Y	Y	?
11 **Conaway**	N	Y	Y	Y	Y	Y
12 **Granger**	N	Y	Y	Y	Y	Y
13 **Thornberry**	N	Y	Y	Y	Y	Y
14 **Weber**	N	Y	Y	Y	Y	Y
15 Gonzalez	Y	N	Y	Y	N	N
16 O'Rourke	Y	N	Y	Y	N	N
17 **Flores**	N	Y	Y	Y	Y	Y
18 Jackson Lee	Y	N	Y	Y	N	N
19 **Arrington**	N	Y	Y	Y	Y	Y
20 Castro	Y	N	Y	Y	N	N
21 **Smith**	N	Y	Y	Y	?	Y
22 **Olson**	N	Y	Y	Y	Y	Y
23 **Hurd**	N	Y	Y	Y	Y	Y
24 **Marchant**	N	Y	Y	Y	Y	Y
25 **Williams**	N	Y	Y	Y	Y	Y
26 **Burgess**	N	Y	Y	Y	Y	Y
27 **Farenthold**	N	Y	Y	Y	Y	Y
28 Cuellar	Y	Y	Y	Y	N	N
29 Green, G.	Y	N	Y	Y	N	N
30 Johnson, E.B.	Y	N	Y	Y	N	N
31 **Carter**	N	Y	Y	Y	Y	Y
32 **Sessions**	N	Y	Y	Y	Y	Y
33 Veasey	Y	N	Y	Y	N	N
34 Vela	Y	N	Y	Y	N	N
35 Doggett	Y	N	Y	Y	N	N
36 **Babin**	N	Y	Y	Y	Y	Y
UTAH						
1 **Bishop**	N	Y	Y	Y	Y	Y
2 **Stewart**	N	Y	Y	Y	Y	Y
3 **Chaffetz**	N	Y	Y	Y	Y	Y
4 **Love**	N	Y	Y	Y	Y	Y
VERMONT						
AL Welch	Y	N	Y	Y	N	N
VIRGINIA						
1 **Wittman**	N	Y	Y	Y	Y	Y
2 **Taylor**	N	Y	Y	Y	Y	Y
3 Scott	Y	N	Y	Y	N	N
4 McEachin	Y	N	Y	Y	N	N
5 **Garrett**	N	Y	Y	Y	Y	Y
6 **Goodlatte**	N	Y	Y	Y	Y	Y
7 **Brat**	N	Y	Y	Y	Y	Y
8 Beyer	Y	N	Y	Y	N	N
9 **Griffith**	N	Y	Y	Y	Y	Y
10 **Comstock**	N	Y	Y	Y	Y	Y
11 Connolly	Y	N	Y	Y	N	N
WASHINGTON						
1 DelBene	Y	N	Y	Y	N	N
2 Larsen	Y	N	Y	Y	N	N
3 **Herrera Beutler**	N	Y	Y	Y	Y	Y
4 **Newhouse**	N	Y	Y	Y	Y	Y
5 **McMorris Rodgers**	N	Y	Y	Y	Y	Y
6 Kilmer	Y	N	Y	Y	N	N
7 Jayapal	Y	N	Y	Y	N	N
8 **Reichert**	N	Y	Y	Y	Y	Y
9 Smith	Y	N	Y	Y	N	N
10 Heck	Y	N	Y	Y	N	N
WEST VIRGINIA						
1 **McKinley**	N	Y	Y	Y	Y	Y
2 **Mooney**	N	Y	Y	Y	Y	Y
3 **Jenkins**	N	Y	Y	Y	Y	Y
WISCONSIN						
1 **Ryan**						
2 Pocan	Y	N	Y	Y	N	N
3 Kind	Y	N	Y	Y	N	N
4 Moore	Y	N	?	Y	N	N
5 **Sensenbrenner**	N	Y	Y	Y	Y	Y
6 **Grothman**	N	Y	Y	Y	Y	Y
7 **Duffy**	N	Y	Y	Y	Y	Y
8 **Gallagher**	N	Y	Y	Y	Y	Y
WYOMING						
AL **Cheney**	N	Y	Y	Y	Y	Y

||| HOUSE VOTES

VOTE NUMBER

28. PROCEDURAL MOTION/APPROVAL OF HOUSE JOURNAL. Approved 248-162 : R 155-77; D 93-85. Jan. 10, 2017.

29. HR 79. SEC GENERAL SOLICITATION/DISCLOSURE. Velazquez, D-N.Y., amendment that would require sponsors of events to provide attendees with a disclosure that would describe the event and the risks of investing in the advertised securities in order for the event to be exempt from the requirement that companies verify that individuals attending are accredited investors. Rejected in Committee of the Whole 167-249 : R 1-234; D 166-15. Jan. 10, 2017.

30. HR 79. SEC GENERAL SOLICITATION/SPONSOR COMPENSATION. Clay, D-Mo., for Waters, D-Calif., amendment that would prohibit sponsors of events from receiving compensation for either introducing investors attending the event to issuers or for negotiating investments in order for the event to be exempt from the requirement that companies verify that individuals attending are accredited investors. Rejected in Committee of the Whole 163-253 : R 0-236; D 163-17. Jan. 10, 2017.

31. HR 79. SEC GENERAL SOLICITATION/PASSAGE. Passage of the bill that would direct the Securities and Exchange Commission to revise regulations to exempt presentations made at certain events where businesses offer unregistered securities in the private market from a requirement that companies verify that individuals attending are accredited investors. The exemption from the verification requirement would apply to presentations made at events sponsored by: government entities, colleges, nonprofit groups, angel investor groups, venture capital associations, trade associations or any additional group that the SEC determines by regulation. Specific information related to the offering of securities could not be distributed at such events, other than information such as the type and amount of securities offered. Passed 344-73 : R 236-0; D 108-73. Jan. 10, 2017.

32. H RES 40, HR 78, HR 238. SEC REGULATION ANALYSIS AND CFTC REAUTHORIZATION/PREVIOUS QUESTION. Newhouse, R-Wash., motion to order the previous question (thus ending debate and possibility of amendment) on the rule (H Res 40) that would provide for House floor consideration of the bill (HR 78) that would require the Securities and Exchange Commission to conduct cost-benefit analyses of proposed regulations and to review existing regulations every five years to determine whether they are excessively burdensome or ineffective. It also would provide for consideration of the bill (HR 238) that would reauthorize operations of the Commodity Futures Trading Commission through fiscal 2021. Motion agreed to 232-168 : R 232-0; D 0-168. Jan. 11, 2017.

33. H RES 40, HR 78, HR 238. SEC REGULATION ANALYSIS AND CFTC RE-AUTHORIZATION/RULE. Adoption of the rule (H Res 40) that would provide for House floor consideration of the bill (HR 78) that would require the Securities and Exchange Commission to conduct cost-benefit analyses of proposed regulations and to review existing regulations every five years to determine whether they are excessively burdensome or ineffective. It also would provide for consideration of the bill (HR 238) that would reauthorize operations of the Commodity Futures Trading Commission through fiscal 2021 and modify how the CFTC should regulate derivatives and swaps. It would grant suspension authority on the legislative day of Jan. 13, 2017. Adopted 233-170 : R 232-1; D 1-169. Jan. 11, 2017.

34. HR 39. PRESIDENTIAL INNOVATION FELLOWS/PASSAGE. Hurd, R-Texas, motion to suspend the rules and pass the bill that would statutorily authorize the Presidential Innovation Fellows program within the General Services Administration. The program's advisory board also would be authorized. Motion agreed to 386-17 : R 217-17; D 169-0. Jan. 11, 2017.

	28	29	30	31	32	33	34
ALABAMA							
1 Byrne	Y	N	N	Y	Y	Y	Y
2 Roby	Y	N	N	Y	Y	Y	Y
3 Rogers	Y	N	N	Y	Y	Y	Y
4 Aderholt	Y	N	N	Y	Y	Y	Y
5 Brooks	Y	N	N	Y	Y	Y	N
6 Palmer	Y	N	N	Y	Y	Y	Y
7 Sewell	N	+	+	+	N	N	Y
ALASKA							
AL Young	N	N	N	Y	Y	Y	Y
ARIZONA							
1 O'Halleran	N	N	N	Y	N	N	Y
2 McSally	N	N	N	Y	Y	Y	Y
3 Grijalva	?	Y	Y	N	N	N	Y
4 Gosar	N	N	N	Y	Y	Y	N
5 Biggs	Y	N	N	Y	Y	Y	Y
6 Schweikert	Y	N	N	Y	Y	Y	Y
7 Gallego	N	Y	Y	N	N	N	Y
8 Franks	Y	N	N	Y	Y	Y	Y
9 Sinema	?	N	N	Y	N	Y	Y
ARKANSAS							
1 Crawford	Y	N	N	Y	Y	Y	Y
2 Hill	N	N	N	Y	Y	Y	Y
3 Womack	Y	N	N	Y	Y	Y	Y
4 Westerman	Y	N	N	Y	Y	Y	Y
CALIFORNIA							
1 LaMalfa	Y	N	N	Y	Y	Y	Y
2 Huffman	Y	Y	Y	N	N	N	Y
3 Garamendi	Y	Y	Y	N	N	N	Y
4 McClintock	Y	N	N	Y	Y	Y	Y
5 Thompson	N	Y	Y	N	N	N	Y
6 Matsui	Y	Y	Y	N	N	N	Y
7 Bera	N	N	Y	N	N	N	Y
8 Cook	Y	N	N	Y	Y	Y	Y
9 McNerney	Y	Y	Y	Y	N	N	Y
10 Denham	N	N	N	Y	Y	Y	Y
11 DeSaulnier	N	Y	Y	N	N	N	Y
12 Pelosi	Y	Y	Y	N	N	N	Y
13 Lee	N	+	+	-	--	-	+
14 Speier	Y	Y	Y	N	N	N	Y
15 Swalwell	N	N	N	N	N	N	Y
16 Costa	N	N	N	Y	N	N	Y
17 Khanna	N	Y	Y	N	N	N	Y
18 Eshoo	Y	Y	Y	N	N	N	Y
19 Lofgren	Y	Y	Y	N	N	N	Y
20 Panetta	Y	Y	N	Y	N	N	Y
21 Valadao	N	N	N	Y	Y	Y	Y
22 Nunes	Y	N	N	Y	Y	Y	Y
23 McCarthy	Y	N	N	Y	Y	Y	Y
24 Carbajal	Y	Y	Y	N	N	N	Y
25 Knight	N	N	N	Y	Y	Y	Y
26 Brownley	N	Y	Y	N	N	N	Y
27 Chu	Y	Y	Y	Y	N	N	Y
28 Schiff	N	Y	Y	N	N	N	Y
29 Cardenas	N	N	Y	N	N	N	Y
30 Sherman	Y	Y	N	Y	N	N	Y
31 Aguilar	N	Y	Y	N	N	N	Y
32 Napolitano	Y	Y	Y	N	N	N	Y
33 Lieu	N	Y	Y	N	N	N	Y
34 Becerra	-	+	+	-	?	?	+
35 Torres	N	Y	Y	N	N	N	Y
36 Ruiz	Y	Y	Y	N	N	N	Y
37 Bass	N	Y	Y	N	?	?	?
38 Sánchez, Linda	?	Y	Y	N	N	N	Y
39 Royce	Y	N	N	Y	Y	Y	Y
40 Roybal-Allard	Y	Y	Y	N	N	N	Y
41 Takano	?	?	?	?	N	N	Y
42 Calvert	Y	N	N	Y	Y	Y	Y
43 Waters	Y	Y	Y	N	N	N	?
44 Barragan	N	Y	Y	N	N	N	Y
45 Walters	Y	N	N	Y	Y	Y	Y
46 Correa	Y	Y	Y	N	N	N	Y
47 Lowenthal	N	Y	Y	N	N	N	Y
48 Rohrabacher	N	N	N	Y	Y	Y	Y
49 Issa	Y	N	N	Y	Y	Y	Y
50 Hunter	Y	N	N	Y	Y	Y	N
51 Vargas	N	Y	Y	N	N	N	Y
52 Peters	N	N	N	Y	N	N	Y
53 Davis	Y	Y	Y	Y	N	N	Y

	28	29	30	31	32	33	34
COLORADO							
1 DeGette	Y	Y	Y	Y	N	N	Y
2 Polis	Y	N	N	Y	N	N	Y
3 Tipton	N	N	N	Y	Y	Y	Y
4 Buck	N	N	N	Y	Y	Y	N
5 Lamborn	Y	N	N	Y	Y	Y	Y
6 Coffman	N	N	N	Y	Y	Y	Y
7 Perlmutter	?	?	?	+	?	?	?
CONNECTICUT							
1 Larson	N	Y	Y	Y	N	N	Y
2 Courtney	Y	Y	Y	N	N	N	Y
3 DeLauro	Y	Y	Y	N	N	N	Y
4 Himes	Y	N	Y	Y	N	N	Y
5 Esty	N	Y	Y	Y	N	N	Y
DELAWARE							
AL Blunt Rochester	Y	Y	Y	Y	N	N	Y
FLORIDA							
1 Gaetz	N	N	N	Y	Y	Y	Y
2 Dunn	Y	N	N	Y	Y	Y	Y
3 Yoho	Y	N	N	Y	Y	Y	Y
4 Rutherford	Y	N	N	Y	Y	Y	+
5 Lawson	Y	Y	Y	N	N	N	Y
6 DeSantis	N	N	N	Y	Y	Y	Y
7 Murphy	Y	N	N	Y	N	N	Y
8 Posey	Y	N	N	Y	Y	Y	Y
9 Soto	Y	Y	Y	Y	N	N	Y
10 Demings	Y	Y	Y	Y	N	N	Y
11 Webster	Y	N	N	Y	Y	Y	Y
12 Bilirakis	Y	N	N	Y	Y	Y	Y
13 Crist	N	Y	Y	Y	N	N	Y
14 Castor	N	Y	Y	Y	N	N	Y
15 Ross	Y	N	N	Y	Y	Y	Y
16 Buchanan	Y	N	N	Y	Y	Y	Y
17 Rooney, T.	Y	N	N	Y	Y	Y	Y
18 Mast	Y	N	N	Y	Y	Y	Y
19 Rooney, F.	Y	N	N	Y	Y	Y	Y
20 Hastings	N	Y	Y	N	N	N	Y
21 Frankel	Y	Y	Y	N	N	N	Y
22 Deutch	Y	Y	Y	Y	N	N	Y
23 Wasserman Schultz	Y	Y	Y	Y	N	N	Y
24 Wilson	N	Y	Y	N	N	N	Y
25 Diaz-Balart	Y	N	N	Y	Y	Y	Y
26 Curbelo	N	N	N	Y	+	Y	Y
27 Ros-Lehtinen	N	N	N	Y	Y	Y	Y
GEORGIA							
1 Carter	N	N	N	Y	Y	Y	Y
2 Bishop	Y	Y	Y	Y	?	?	?
3 Ferguson	Y	N	N	Y	Y	Y	Y
4 Johnson	?	+	+	-	?	?	?
5 Lewis	N	Y	Y	N	?	?	?
6 Price	?	?	?	?	?	?	?
7 Woodall	N	N	N	Y	Y	Y	Y
8 Scott, A.	Y	N	N	Y	Y	Y	Y
9 Collins	N	N	N	Y	Y	Y	Y
10 Hice	Y	N	N	Y	Y	Y	Y
11 Loudermilk	Y	N	N	Y	Y	Y	Y
12 Allen	Y	N	N	Y	Y	Y	Y
13 Scott, D.	Y	Y	Y	Y	N	N	Y
14 Graves	N	N	N	Y	Y	Y	Y
HAWAII							
1 Hanabusa	Y	Y	Y	N	N	N	Y
2 Gabbard	Y	Y	Y	N	N	N	Y
IDAHO							
1 Labrador	Y	N	N	Y	Y	Y	N
2 Simpson	Y	N	N	Y	Y	Y	Y
ILLINOIS							
1 Rush	?	?	?	?	?	?	?
2 Kelly	?	?	?	?	?	?	?
3 Lipinski	Y	Y	Y	Y	N	N	Y
4 Gutierrez	N	Y	+	N	-	N	Y
5 Quigley	Y	Y	Y	N	N	N	Y
6 Roskam	Y	N	Y	Y	Y	Y	Y
7 Davis, D.	?	?	?	?	N	N	Y
8 Krishnamoorthi	Y	Y	Y	N	N	N	Y
9 Schakowsky	-	+	+	-	N	N	Y
10 Schneider	Y	Y	Y	Y	N	N	Y
11 Foster	Y	Y	Y	N	N	N	Y
12 Bost	N	N	N	Y	Y	Y	Y
13 Davis, R.	N	N	N	Y	Y	Y	Y
14 Hultgren	Y	N	N	Y	Y	Y	Y
15 Shimkus	Y	N	N	Y	Y	Y	Y

	28	29	30	31	32	33	34
16 **Kinzinger**	N	N	N	Y	Y	Y	Y
17 Bustos	Y	Y	Y	Y	N	N	Y
18 **LaHood**	N	N	N	Y	Y	Y	Y
INDIANA							
1 Visclosky	N	Y	Y	N	N	N	Y
2 **Walorski**	Y	N	N	Y	Y	Y	Y
3 **Banks**	Y	N	N	Y	Y	Y	Y
4 **Rokita**	N	N	N	Y	Y	Y	Y
5 **Brooks**	Y	N	N	Y	Y	Y	Y
6 **Messer**	Y	N	N	Y	Y	Y	Y
7 Carson	Y	Y	Y	N	N	N	Y
8 **Bucshon**	N	N	N	Y	Y	Y	Y
9 **Hollingsworth**	Y	N	N	Y	Y	Y	Y
IOWA							
1 **Blum**	N	N	N	Y	Y	Y	Y
2 Loebsack	N	Y	Y	Y	N	N	Y
3 **Young**	Y	N	N	Y	Y	Y	Y
4 **King**	Y	N	N	Y	Y	Y	Y
KANSAS							
1 **Marshall**	Y	N	N	Y	Y	Y	Y
2 **Jenkins**	N	N	N	Y	Y	Y	Y
3 **Yoder**	N	N	N	Y	Y	Y	Y
4 **Pompeo**	?	?	?	?	?	?	?
KENTUCKY							
1 **Comer**	Y	N	N	Y	Y	Y	Y
2 **Guthrie**	Y	N	N	Y	Y	Y	Y
3 Yarmuth	Y	Y	Y	Y	N	N	Y
4 **Massie**	Y	N	N	Y	Y	Y	N
5 **Rogers**	Y	N	N	Y	Y	Y	Y
6 **Barr**	Y	N	N	Y	Y	Y	Y
LOUISIANA							
1 **Scalise**	Y	N	N	Y	Y	Y	Y
2 Richmond	N	Y	Y	N	?	?	?
3 **Higgins**	Y	N	N	Y	Y	Y	Y
4 **Johnson**	Y	N	N	Y	Y	Y	Y
5 **Abraham**	Y	N	N	Y	Y	Y	Y
6 **Graves**	N	N	N	Y	Y	Y	Y
MAINE							
1 Pingree	Y	Y	Y	Y	N	N	Y
2 **Poliquin**	N	N	N	Y	Y	Y	Y
MARYLAND							
1 **Harris**	Y	N	N	Y	?	?	?
2 Ruppersberger	Y	Y	Y	Y	N	N	Y
3 Sarbanes	N	Y	Y	N	N	N	Y
4 Brown	Y	Y	Y	Y	–	–	+
5 Hoyer	N	Y	Y	Y	N	N	Y
6 Delaney	N	Y	Y	Y	N	N	Y
7 Cummings	Y	Y	Y	N	N	N	Y
8 Raskin	N	Y	Y	N	N	N	Y
MASSACHUSETTS							
1 Neal	N	Y	Y	N	N	N	Y
2 McGovern	N	Y	Y	N	N	N	Y
3 Tsongas	Y	Y	Y	Y	N	N	Y
4 Kennedy	Y	Y	Y	Y	N	N	Y
5 Clark	N	Y	Y	N	N	N	Y
6 Moulton	Y	N	N	Y	N	N	Y
7 Capuano	N	Y	Y	N	N	N	Y
8 Lynch	N	Y	Y	N	N	N	Y
9 Keating	N	Y	Y	Y	N	N	Y
MICHIGAN							
1 **Bergman**	Y	N	N	Y	Y	Y	Y
2 **Huizenga**	Y	N	N	Y	Y	Y	Y
3 **Amash**	N	N	N	Y	Y	N	N
4 **Moolenaar**	N	N	N	Y	Y	Y	Y
5 Kildee	Y	Y	Y	N	N	N	Y
6 **Upton**	N	N	N	Y	Y	Y	Y
7 **Walberg**	N	N	N	Y	Y	Y	Y
8 **Bishop**	Y	N	N	Y	Y	Y	Y
9 Levin	Y	Y	Y	Y	N	N	Y
10 **Mitchell**	Y	N	N	Y	Y	Y	Y
11 **Trott**	Y	N	N	Y	Y	Y	Y
12 Dingell	?	?	?	?	N	N	Y
13 Conyers	Y	Y	Y	N	N	N	Y
14 Lawrence	Y	Y	Y	Y	N	N	Y
MINNESOTA							
1 Walz	Y	Y	Y	Y	N	N	Y
2 **Lewis**	Y	N	N	Y	Y	Y	Y
3 **Paulsen**	N	N	N	Y	Y	Y	Y
4 McCollum	N	Y	Y	Y	?	N	Y

	28	29	30	31	32	33	34
5 Ellison	Y	Y	Y	N	N	N	Y
6 **Emmer**	Y	N	N	Y	Y	Y	Y
7 Peterson	N	Y	Y	Y	N	N	Y
8 Nolan	N	Y	Y	Y	N	N	Y
MISSISSIPPI							
1 **Kelly**	Y	N	N	Y	Y	Y	Y
2 Thompson	N	Y	Y	N	N	N	Y
3 **Harper**	Y	N	N	Y	Y	Y	Y
4 **Palazzo**	N	N	N	Y	Y	Y	Y
MISSOURI							
1 Clay	N	Y	Y	N	–	–	+
2 **Wagner**	Y	N	N	Y	Y	Y	Y
3 **Luetkemeyer**	Y	N	N	Y	Y	Y	Y
4 **Hartzler**	Y	N	N	Y	Y	Y	Y
5 Cleaver	Y	Y	Y	N	N	N	Y
6 **Graves**	N	N	N	Y	Y	Y	Y
7 **Long**	Y	N	N	Y	Y	Y	Y
8 **Smith**	N	N	N	Y	Y	Y	Y
MONTANA							
AL **Zinke**	?	?	?	?	?	?	?
NEBRASKA							
1 **Fortenberry**	Y	N	N	Y	Y	Y	Y
2 **Bacon**	Y	N	N	Y	Y	Y	Y
3 **Smith**	Y	N	N	Y	Y	Y	Y
NEVADA							
1 Titus	Y	Y	Y	Y	N	N	Y
2 **Amodei**	Y	N	N	Y	Y	Y	Y
3 Rosen	?	N	Y	Y	N	N	Y
4 Kihuen	N	Y	Y	N	N	N	Y
NEW HAMPSHIRE							
1 Shea-Porter	N	Y	Y	Y	N	N	Y
2 Kuster	N	Y	Y	Y	N	N	Y
NEW JERSEY							
1 Norcross	Y	Y	Y	Y	N	N	Y
2 **LoBiondo**	N	N	N	Y	Y	Y	Y
3 **MacArthur**	N	N	N	Y	Y	Y	Y
4 **Smith**	Y	N	N	Y	Y	Y	Y
5 Gottheimer	N	Y	Y	Y	N	N	Y
6 Pallone	N	Y	Y	N	N	N	Y
7 **Lance**	N	N	N	Y	Y	Y	Y
8 Sires	N	Y	Y	N	N	N	Y
9 Pascrell	Y	Y	Y	N	N	N	Y
10 Payne	P	Y	Y	N	?	?	?
11 **Frelinghuysen**	Y	N	N	Y	Y	?	Y
12 Watson Coleman	N	Y	Y	N	?	?	?
NEW MEXICO							
1 Lujan Grisham	Y	Y	Y	Y	N	N	Y
2 **Pearce**	N	N	N	Y	Y	Y	Y
3 Luján	Y	Y	Y	Y	N	N	Y
NEW YORK							
1 **Zeldin**	Y	N	N	Y	Y	Y	Y
2 **King**	Y	N	N	Y	Y	Y	Y
3 Suozzi	N	Y	Y	Y	N	N	Y
4 Rice	N	N	N	Y	N	N	Y
5 Meeks	Y	Y	Y	Y	N	N	Y
6 Meng	Y	Y	Y	Y	N	N	Y
7 Velázquez	N	Y	Y	N	N	N	Y
8 Jeffries	Y	Y	Y	Y	N	N	Y
9 Clarke	N	Y	Y	Y	N	N	Y
10 Nadler	Y	Y	Y	N	?	?	?
11 **Donovan**	Y	N	N	Y	Y	Y	Y
12 Maloney, C.	Y	Y	Y	Y	N	N	Y
13 Espaillat	N	Y	Y	Y	N	N	Y
14 Crowley	N	Y	Y	Y	N	N	Y
15 Serrano	N	Y	Y	Y	N	N	Y
16 Engel	Y	Y	Y	Y	N	N	Y
17 Lowey	N	Y	Y	Y	N	N	Y
18 Maloney, S.P.	N	Y	Y	Y	N	N	Y
19 **Faso**	Y	N	N	Y	Y	Y	Y
20 Tonko	P	Y	Y	Y	N	N	Y
21 **Stefanik**	Y	N	N	Y	Y	Y	Y
22 **Tenney**	Y	N	N	Y	Y	Y	Y
23 **Reed**	N	N	N	Y	Y	Y	Y
24 **Katko**	N	N	N	Y	Y	Y	Y
25 Slaughter	N	Y	Y	Y	N	N	Y
26 Higgins	Y	Y	Y	Y	N	N	Y
27 **Collins**	Y	N	N	Y	Y	Y	Y
NORTH CAROLINA							
1 Butterfield	Y	Y	Y	Y	?	?	?
2 **Holding**	N	N	N	Y	Y	Y	Y
3 **Jones**	?	Y	N	Y	Y	Y	N
4 Price	Y	Y	Y	Y	N	N	Y

	28	29	30	31	32	33	34
5 **Foxx**	N	N	N	Y	Y	Y	Y
6 **Walker**	Y	N	N	Y	Y	Y	Y
7 **Rouzer**	N	N	N	Y	Y	Y	Y
8 **Hudson**	N	N	N	Y	Y	Y	Y
9 **Pittenger**	N	N	N	Y	Y	Y	Y
10 **McHenry**	Y	N	N	Y	Y	Y	Y
11 **Meadows**	Y	N	N	Y	Y	Y	Y
12 Adams	N	Y	Y	Y	N	N	Y
13 **Budd**	Y	N	N	Y	Y	Y	N
NORTH DAKOTA							
AL **Cramer**	Y	N	N	Y	Y	Y	Y
OHIO							
1 **Chabot**	Y	N	N	Y	Y	Y	Y
2 **Wenstrup**	N	N	N	Y	Y	Y	Y
3 Beatty	Y	Y	Y	Y	N	N	Y
4 **Jordan**	N	N	N	Y	Y	Y	N
5 **Latta**	Y	N	N	Y	Y	Y	Y
6 **Johnson**	N	N	N	Y	Y	Y	Y
7 **Gibbs**	Y	N	N	Y	Y	Y	Y
8 **Davidson**	Y	N	N	Y	Y	Y	Y
9 Kaptur	Y	Y	Y	N	N	N	Y
10 **Turner**	N	N	N	Y	Y	Y	Y
11 Fudge	N	Y	Y	N	?	?	?
12 **Tiberi**	N	N	N	Y	Y	Y	Y
13 Ryan	+	+	+	–	–	–	+
14 **Joyce**	N	N	N	Y	Y	Y	Y
15 **Stivers**	N	N	N	Y	Y	Y	Y
16 **Renacci**	N	N	N	Y	Y	Y	Y
OKLAHOMA							
1 **Bridenstine**	Y	N	N	Y	Y	Y	Y
2 **Mullin**	Y	N	N	Y	?	Y	Y
3 **Lucas**	Y	N	N	Y	Y	Y	Y
4 **Cole**	Y	N	N	Y	Y	?	Y
5 **Russell**	Y	N	N	Y	Y	Y	Y
OREGON							
1 Bonamici	Y	Y	Y	N	N	N	Y
2 **Walden**	Y	N	N	Y	Y	Y	Y
3 Blumenauer	Y	Y	Y	N	N	N	Y
4 DeFazio	N	Y	Y	Y	N	N	Y
5 Schrader	N	Y	N	Y	N	N	Y
PENNSYLVANIA							
1 Brady	N	Y	Y	N	N	N	Y
2 Evans	Y	Y	Y	Y	–	–	+
3 **Kelly**	Y	N	N	Y	Y	Y	Y
4 **Perry**	N	N	N	Y	Y	Y	N
5 **Thompson**	N	N	N	Y	Y	Y	Y
6 **Costello**	N	N	N	Y	Y	Y	Y
7 **Meehan**	N	N	N	Y	Y	Y	Y
8 **Fitzpatrick**	N	N	N	Y	Y	Y	Y
9 **Shuster**	Y	N	N	Y	?	Y	Y
10 **Marino**	Y	N	N	Y	Y	Y	Y
11 **Barletta**	Y	N	N	Y	Y	Y	Y
12 **Rothfus**	Y	N	N	Y	Y	Y	Y
13 Boyle	N	Y	Y	Y	N	N	Y
14 Doyle	N	Y	Y	Y	N	N	Y
15 **Dent**	Y	N	N	Y	Y	Y	Y
16 **Smucker**	Y	N	N	Y	Y	Y	Y
17 Cartwright	Y	Y	Y	N	N	N	Y
18 **Murphy**	Y	N	N	Y	Y	Y	Y
RHODE ISLAND							
1 Cicilline	Y	Y	Y	N	N	N	Y
2 Langevin	N	Y	Y	N	N	N	Y
SOUTH CAROLINA							
1 **Sanford**	Y	N	N	Y	Y	Y	N
2 **Wilson**	Y	N	N	Y	Y	Y	Y
3 **Duncan**	?	?	?	?	Y	Y	Y
4 **Gowdy**	Y	N	N	Y	Y	Y	Y
5 **Mulvaney**	?	N	N	Y	?	?	?
6 Clyburn	N	Y	Y	N	?	?	?
7 **Rice**	P	N	N	Y	Y	Y	Y
SOUTH DAKOTA							
AL **Noem**	Y	N	N	Y	Y	Y	Y
TENNESSEE							
1 **Roe**	Y	N	N	Y	Y	Y	Y
2 **Duncan**	Y	N	N	Y	Y	Y	Y
3 **Fleischmann**	Y	N	N	Y	Y	Y	Y
4 **DesJarlais**	Y	N	N	Y	Y	Y	Y
5 Cooper	Y	N	N	Y	N	N	Y
6 **Black**	Y	?	N	Y	Y	Y	Y
7 **Blackburn**	Y	N	N	Y	Y	Y	Y
8 **Kustoff**	Y	N	N	Y	Y	Y	Y
9 Cohen	N	Y	Y	N	N	N	Y

	28	29	30	31	32	33	34
TEXAS							
1 **Gohmert**	?	N	N	Y	Y	Y	N
2 **Poe**	N	N	N	Y	Y	Y	N
3 **Johnson, S.**	Y	N	N	Y	Y	Y	Y
4 **Ratcliffe**	N	N	N	Y	Y	Y	Y
5 **Hensarling**	Y	N	N	Y	Y	Y	Y
6 **Barton**	Y	N	N	Y	Y	Y	Y
7 **Culberson**	Y	N	N	Y	Y	Y	Y
8 **Brady**	Y	N	N	Y	Y	Y	Y
9 Green, A.	Y	Y	Y	N	–	–	+
10 **McCaul**	Y	N	N	Y	Y	Y	Y
11 **Conaway**	N	N	N	Y	Y	Y	Y
12 **Granger**	Y	N	N	Y	Y	Y	Y
13 **Thornberry**	Y	N	N	Y	Y	Y	Y
14 **Weber**	N	N	N	Y	Y	Y	Y
15 Gonzalez	Y	Y	Y	Y	N	N	Y
16 O'Rourke	Y	Y	Y	Y	N	N	Y
17 **Flores**	N	N	N	Y	Y	Y	Y
18 Jackson Lee	N	+	+	+	–	–	+
19 **Arrington**	Y	N	N	Y	Y	Y	Y
20 Castro	N	Y	Y	Y	N	N	Y
21 **Smith**	Y	N	N	Y	Y	Y	Y
22 **Olson**	Y	N	N	Y	Y	Y	Y
23 **Hurd**	N	N	N	Y	Y	Y	Y
24 **Marchant**	N	N	N	Y	Y	Y	Y
25 **Williams**	Y	N	N	Y	Y	Y	Y
26 **Burgess**	N	N	N	Y	Y	Y	Y
27 **Farenthold**	Y	N	N	Y	Y	Y	Y
28 Cuellar	Y	Y	Y	Y	N	N	Y
29 Green, G.	N	Y	Y	N	N	N	Y
30 Johnson, E.B.	Y	Y	Y	N	?	?	?
31 **Carter**	Y	N	N	Y	Y	Y	Y
32 **Sessions**	Y	N	N	Y	Y	Y	Y
33 Veasey	N	Y	Y	Y	N	N	Y
34 Vela	Y	Y	Y	Y	N	N	Y
35 Doggett	Y	Y	Y	N	N	N	Y
36 **Babin**	Y	N	N	Y	Y	Y	Y
UTAH							
1 **Bishop**	Y	N	N	Y	Y	Y	Y
2 **Stewart**	Y	N	N	Y	Y	Y	Y
3 **Chaffetz**	N	N	N	Y	Y	Y	Y
4 **Love**	Y	N	N	Y	Y	Y	Y
VERMONT							
AL Welch	Y	Y	Y	N	N	N	Y
VIRGINIA							
1 **Wittman**	Y	N	N	Y	Y	Y	Y
2 **Taylor**	Y	N	N	Y	Y	Y	Y
3 Scott	Y	Y	Y	N	N	N	Y
4 McEachin	Y	Y	Y	Y	N	N	Y
5 **Garrett**	Y	N	N	Y	Y	Y	Y
6 **Goodlatte**	Y	N	N	Y	Y	Y	Y
7 **Brat**	Y	N	N	Y	Y	Y	N
8 Beyer	N	Y	Y	Y	N	N	Y
9 **Griffith**	N	N	N	Y	Y	Y	N
10 **Comstock**	Y	N	N	Y	Y	Y	Y
11 Connolly	N	Y	Y	Y	N	N	Y
WASHINGTON							
1 DelBene	Y	Y	Y	Y	N	N	Y
2 Larsen	Y	Y	Y	Y	N	N	Y
3 **Herrera Beutler**	N	N	N	Y	Y	Y	Y
4 **Newhouse**	Y	N	N	Y	Y	Y	Y
5 **McMorris Rodgers**	Y	N	N	Y	Y	Y	Y
6 Kilmer	N	Y	Y	Y	N	N	Y
7 Jayapal	N	Y	Y	N	N	N	Y
8 **Reichert**	Y	N	N	Y	Y	Y	Y
9 Smith	Y	Y	Y	N	N	N	Y
10 Heck	Y	Y	Y	Y	N	N	Y
WEST VIRGINIA							
1 **McKinley**	N	N	N	Y	Y	Y	Y
2 **Mooney**	Y	N	N	Y	Y	Y	Y
3 **Jenkins**	N	N	N	Y	Y	Y	Y
WISCONSIN							
1 **Ryan**							
2 Pocan	Y	Y	Y	N	N	N	Y
3 Kind	N	N	N	Y	N	N	Y
4 Moore	N	Y	Y	N	–	–	+
5 **Sensenbrenner**	Y	N	N	Y	Y	Y	Y
6 **Grothman**	Y	N	N	Y	Y	Y	N
7 **Duffy**	N	N	N	Y	Y	Y	Y
8 **Gallagher**	Y	N	N	Y	Y	Y	Y
WYOMING							
AL **Cheney**	Y	N	N	Y	Y	Y	Y

VOTE NUMBER

35. HR 5. RULE-MAKING PROCESS CHANGES/JUDICIAL REVIEW. Goodlatte, R-Va., amendment that would prohibit a court, while reviewing an agency's rule, from interpreting a gap or ambiguity in a rule or law as an implicit delegation of legislative rule-making authority to the agency. Adopted in Committee of the Whole 237-185 : R 234-0; D 3-185. Jan. 11, 2017.

36. HR 5. RULE-MAKING PROCESS CHANGES/RULE ADVOCACY. Peterson, D-Minn., amendment that would prohibit agencies from appealing to the public to advocate in support or against a proposed rule. Adopted in Committee of the Whole 260-161 : R 226-7; D 34-154. Jan. 11, 2017.

37. HR 5. RULE-MAKING PROCESS CHANGES/DISEASE REDUCTION. Castor, D-Fla., amendment that would exempt rules that will result in reduced incidence of cancer, early death or respiratory disease among children or seniors. It would remove the bill's provision that would effectively overturn two Supreme Court decisions that require federal courts to defer to an agency's interpretation of the underlying law or rule when considering challenges to agency rules. Rejected in Committee of the Whole 189-231 : R 2-229; D 187-2. Jan. 11, 2017.

38. HR 5. RULE-MAKING PROCESS CHANGES/FOODBORNE ILLNESS. Cicilline, D-R.I., amendment that would exempt rules related to the prevention of foodborne illness transmission. It would remove the bill's provision that would effectively overturn two Supreme Court decisions that require federal courts to defer to an agency's interpretation of the underlying law or rule when considering challenges to agency rules. Rejected in Committee of the Whole 190-232 : R 1-232; D 189-0. Jan. 11, 2017.

39. HR 5. RULE-MAKING PROCESS CHANGES/EMPLOYMENT AND WAGES. Johnson, D-Ga., amendment that would exempt rules related to improving employment and wages, especially for workers with disabilities or limited English proficiency. It would remove the bill's provision that would effectively overturn two Supreme Court decisions that require federal courts to defer to an agency's interpretation of the underlying law or rule when considering challenges to agency rules. Rejected in Committee of the Whole 188-234 : R 0-233; D 188-1. Jan. 11, 2017.

40. HR 5. RULE-MAKING PROCESS CHANGES/PRODUCTS FOR CHILDREN. Ruiz, D-Calif., amendment that would exempt rules related to the safety of children's toys or products. It would remove the bill's provision that would effectively overturn two Supreme Court decisions that require federal courts to defer to an agency's interpretation of the underlying law or rule when considering challenges to agency rules. Rejected in Committee of the Whole 190-233 : R 2-232; D 188-1. Jan. 11, 2017.

41. HR 5. RULE-MAKING PROCESS CHANGES/OCCUPATIONAL SAFETY. Scott, D-Va., amendment that would exempt rules related to occupational health and safety. It would remove the bill's provision that would effectively overturn two Supreme Court decisions that require federal courts to defer to an agency's interpretation of the underlying law or rule when considering challenges to agency rules. Rejected in Committee of the Whole 195-227 : R 7-226; D 188-1. Jan. 11, 2017.

	35	36	37	38	39	40	41
ALABAMA							
1 **Byrne**	Y	Y	N	N	N	N	N
2 **Roby**	Y	Y	N	N	N	N	N
3 **Rogers**	Y	N	N	N	N	N	N
4 **Aderholt**	Y	Y	N	N	N	N	N
5 **Brooks**	Y	Y	N	N	N	N	N
6 **Palmer**	Y	Y	N	N	N	N	N
7 Sewell	N	N	Y	Y	Y	Y	Y
ALASKA							
AL **Young**	Y	Y	N	N	N	N	N
ARIZONA							
1 O'Halleran	N	Y	Y	Y	Y	Y	Y
2 **McSally**	Y	Y	N	N	N	N	N
3 Grijalva	N	N	Y	Y	Y	Y	Y
4 **Gosar**	Y	Y	N	N	N	N	N
5 **Biggs**	Y	Y	N	N	N	N	N
6 **Schweikert**	Y	Y	N	N	N	N	N
7 Gallego	N	N	Y	Y	Y	Y	Y
8 **Franks**	Y	Y	N	N	N	N	N
9 Sinema	N	Y	Y	Y	Y	Y	Y
ARKANSAS							
1 **Crawford**	Y	Y	N	N	N	N	N
2 **Hill**	Y	Y	N	N	N	N	N
3 **Womack**	Y	Y	N	N	N	N	N
4 **Westerman**	Y	Y	N	N	N	N	N
CALIFORNIA							
1 **LaMalfa**	Y	N	N	N	N	N	N
2 Huffman	N	Y	Y	Y	Y	Y	Y
3 Garamendi	N	N	Y	Y	Y	Y	Y
4 **McClintock**	Y	Y	N	N	N	N	N
5 Thompson	N	N	Y	Y	Y	Y	Y
6 Matsui	N	N	Y	Y	Y	Y	Y
7 Bera	N	Y	Y	Y	Y	Y	Y
8 **Cook**	Y	Y	N	N	N	N	N
9 McNerney	N	N	Y	Y	Y	Y	Y
10 **Denham**	Y	Y	N	N	N	N	N
11 DeSaulnier	N	N	Y	Y	Y	Y	Y
12 Pelosi	?	?	?	?	?	?	?
13 Lee	N	N	Y	Y	Y	Y	Y
14 Speier	N	N	Y	Y	Y	Y	Y
15 Swalwell	N	N	Y	Y	Y	Y	Y
16 Costa	Y	Y	Y	Y	Y	Y	Y
17 Khanna	N	N	Y	Y	Y	Y	Y
18 Eshoo	N	N	Y	Y	Y	Y	Y
19 Lofgren	N	N	Y	Y	Y	Y	Y
20 Panetta	N	N	Y	Y	Y	Y	Y
21 **Valadao**	Y	Y	N	N	N	N	N
22 **Nunes**	Y	Y	N	N	N	N	N
23 **McCarthy**	Y	Y	N	N	N	N	N
24 Carbajal	N	N	Y	Y	Y	Y	Y
25 **Knight**	Y	Y	N	N	N	N	N
26 Brownley	N	N	Y	Y	Y	Y	Y
27 Chu	N	N	Y	Y	Y	Y	Y
28 Schiff	N	N	Y	Y	Y	Y	Y
29 Cardenas	N	N	Y	Y	Y	Y	Y
30 Sherman	N	N	Y	Y	Y	Y	Y
31 Aguilar	N	N	Y	Y	Y	Y	Y
32 Napolitano	N	N	Y	Y	Y	Y	Y
33 Lieu	N	N	Y	Y	Y	Y	Y
34 Becerra	–	–	+	+	+	+	+
35 Torres	N	N	Y	Y	Y	Y	Y
36 Ruiz	N	N	Y	Y	Y	Y	Y
37 Bass	N	N	Y	Y	Y	Y	Y
38 Sánchez, Linda	N	N	Y	Y	Y	Y	Y
39 **Royce**	Y	Y	N	N	N	N	N
40 Roybal-Allard	N	N	Y	Y	Y	Y	Y
41 Takano	N	N	Y	Y	Y	Y	Y
42 **Calvert**	Y	Y	N	N	N	N	N
43 Waters	N	N	Y	Y	Y	Y	Y
44 Barragan	N	N	Y	Y	Y	Y	Y
45 **Walters**	Y	Y	N	N	N	N	N
46 Correa	N	Y	Y	Y	Y	Y	Y
47 Lowenthal	N	N	Y	Y	Y	Y	Y
48 **Rohrabacher**	Y	Y	N	N	N	N	N
49 **Issa**	Y	Y	N	N	N	N	N
50 **Hunter**	Y	Y	N	N	N	N	N
51 Vargas	N	N	Y	Y	Y	Y	Y
52 Peters	N	Y	Y	Y	Y	Y	Y
53 Davis	N	N	Y	Y	Y	Y	Y

	35	36	37	38	39	40	41
COLORADO							
1 DeGette	N	N	Y	Y	Y	Y	Y
2 Polis	N	N	Y	Y	Y	Y	Y
3 **Tipton**	Y	Y	N	N	N	N	Y
4 **Buck**	Y	Y	N	N	N	N	N
5 **Lamborn**	?	?	?	?	?	N	N
6 **Coffman**	Y	Y	N	N	N	N	N
7 Perlmutter	Y	Y	Y	Y	Y	Y	Y
CONNECTICUT							
1 Larson	N	N	Y	Y	Y	Y	Y
2 Courtney	N	N	Y	Y	Y	Y	Y
3 DeLauro	N	N	Y	Y	Y	Y	Y
4 Himes	N	Y	Y	Y	Y	Y	Y
5 Esty	N	N	Y	Y	Y	Y	Y
DELAWARE							
AL Blunt Rochester	N	N	Y	Y	Y	Y	Y
FLORIDA							
1 **Gaetz**	Y	Y	N	N	N	N	N
2 **Dunn**	Y	Y	N	N	N	N	N
3 **Yoho**	Y	Y	N	N	N	N	N
4 **Rutherford**	Y	+	–	–	–	–	–
5 Lawson	N	N	Y	Y	Y	Y	Y
6 **DeSantis**	Y	Y	N	N	N	N	N
7 Murphy	Y	Y	Y	Y	Y	Y	Y
8 **Posey**	Y	Y	N	N	N	N	N
9 Soto	N	N	Y	Y	Y	Y	Y
10 Demings	N	N	Y	Y	Y	Y	Y
11 **Webster**	Y	Y	N	N	N	N	N
12 **Bilirakis**	Y	Y	N	N	N	N	N
13 Crist	N	N	Y	Y	Y	Y	Y
14 Castor	N	N	Y	Y	Y	Y	Y
15 **Ross**	Y	Y	N	N	N	N	N
16 **Buchanan**	Y	Y	N	N	N	N	N
17 **Rooney, T.**	Y	Y	N	N	N	N	N
18 **Mast**	Y	Y	N	N	N	N	N
19 **Rooney, F.**	Y	Y	N	N	N	N	N
20 Hastings	N	N	Y	Y	Y	Y	Y
21 Frankel	N	N	Y	Y	Y	Y	Y
22 Deutch	N	N	Y	Y	Y	Y	Y
23 Wasserman Schultz	N	N	Y	Y	Y	Y	Y
24 Wilson	N	N	Y	Y	Y	Y	Y
25 **Diaz-Balart**	Y	Y	N	N	N	N	N
26 **Curbelo**	Y	Y	N	N	N	N	N
27 **Ros-Lehtinen**	Y	Y	N	N	N	N	N
GEORGIA							
1 **Carter**	Y	Y	N	N	N	N	N
2 Bishop	N	N	Y	Y	Y	Y	Y
3 **Ferguson**	Y	Y	N	N	N	N	N
4 Johnson	N	N	Y	Y	Y	Y	Y
5 Lewis	N	N	Y	Y	Y	Y	Y
6 **Price**	?	?	?	?	?	?	?
7 **Woodall**	Y	Y	N	N	N	N	N
8 **Scott, A.**	Y	Y	N	N	N	N	N
9 **Collins**	Y	Y	N	N	N	N	N
10 **Hice**	Y	Y	N	N	N	N	N
11 **Loudermilk**	Y	Y	N	N	N	N	N
12 **Allen**	Y	Y	N	N	N	N	N
13 Scott, D.	N	Y	Y	Y	Y	Y	Y
14 **Graves**	Y	N	N	N	N	N	N
HAWAII							
1 Hanabusa	N	N	Y	Y	Y	Y	Y
2 Gabbard	N	Y	Y	Y	Y	Y	Y
IDAHO							
1 **Labrador**	Y	Y	N	N	N	N	N
2 **Simpson**	Y	Y	N	N	N	N	N
ILLINOIS							
1 Rush	?	?	?	?	?	?	?
2 Kelly	N	N	Y	Y	Y	Y	Y
3 Lipinski	N	Y	Y	Y	Y	Y	Y
4 Gutierrez	N	N	Y	Y	Y	Y	Y
5 Quigley	N	N	Y	Y	Y	Y	Y
6 **Roskam**	Y	Y	N	N	N	N	N
7 Davis, D.	N	N	Y	Y	Y	Y	Y
8 Krishnamoorthi	N	N	Y	Y	Y	Y	Y
9 Schakowsky	N	N	Y	Y	Y	Y	Y
10 Schneider	N	N	Y	Y	Y	Y	Y
11 Foster	N	N	Y	Y	Y	Y	Y
12 **Bost**	Y	Y	N	N	N	N	N
13 **Davis, R.**	Y	Y	N	N	N	N	N
14 **Hultgren**	Y	Y	N	N	N	N	N
15 **Shimkus**	Y	Y	N	N	N	N	N

	35	36	37	38	39	40	41
16 **Kinzinger**	Y	Y	N	N	N	N	N
17 Bustos	N	Y	Y	Y	Y	Y	Y
18 **LaHood**	Y	Y	N	N	N	N	N
INDIANA							
1 Visclosky	N	N	Y	Y	Y	Y	Y
2 **Walorski**	Y	Y	N	N	N	N	N
3 **Banks**	Y	Y	N	N	N	N	N
4 **Rokita**	Y	N	N	N	N	N	N
5 **Brooks**	Y	Y	N	N	N	N	N
6 **Messer**	Y	Y	N	N	N	N	N
7 Carson	N	N	Y	Y	Y	Y	Y
8 **Bucshon**	Y	Y	N	N	N	N	N
9 **Hollingsworth**	Y	Y	N	N	N	N	N
IOWA							
1 **Blum**	Y	Y	N	N	N	Y	Y
2 Loebsack	N	N	Y	Y	Y	Y	Y
3 **Young**	Y	Y	N	N	N	N	N
4 **King**	Y	Y	N	N	N	N	N
KANSAS							
1 **Marshall**	Y	Y	N	N	N	N	N
2 **Jenkins**	Y	Y	N	N	N	N	N
3 **Yoder**	Y	Y	N	N	N	N	N
4 **Pompeo**	?	?	?	?	?	?	?
KENTUCKY							
1 **Comer**	Y	Y	N	N	N	N	N
2 **Guthrie**	Y	Y	N	N	N	N	N
3 Yarmuth	N	N	Y	Y	Y	Y	Y
4 **Massie**	N	Y	N	N	N	N	N
5 **Rogers**	Y	Y	N	N	N	N	N
6 **Barr**	Y	Y	N	N	N	N	N
LOUISIANA							
1 **Scalise**	Y	Y	N	N	N	N	N
2 Richmond	N	N	Y	Y	Y	Y	Y
3 **Higgins**	Y	Y	N	N	N	N	N
4 **Johnson**	Y	Y	N	N	N	N	N
5 **Abraham**	Y	Y	N	N	N	N	N
6 **Graves**	Y	Y	N	N	N	N	N
MAINE							
1 Pingree	N	N	Y	Y	Y	Y	Y
2 **Poliquin**	Y	Y	N	N	N	N	N
MARYLAND							
1 **Harris**	?	?	?	?	?	?	?
2 Ruppersberger	N	Y	Y	Y	Y	Y	Y
3 Sarbanes	N	N	Y	Y	Y	Y	Y
4 Brown	N	N	Y	Y	Y	Y	Y
5 Hoyer	N	N	Y	Y	Y	Y	Y
6 Delaney	N	Y	Y	Y	Y	Y	Y
7 Cummings	N	N	Y	Y	Y	Y	Y
8 Raskin	N	N	Y	Y	Y	Y	Y
MASSACHUSETTS							
1 Neal	N	Y	Y	Y	Y	Y	Y
2 McGovern	N	N	Y	Y	Y	Y	Y
3 Tsongas	N	N	Y	Y	Y	Y	Y
4 Kennedy	N	N	Y	Y	Y	Y	Y
5 Clark	N	N	Y	Y	Y	Y	Y
6 Moulton	N	N	Y	Y	Y	Y	Y
7 Capuano	N	N	Y	Y	Y	Y	Y
8 Lynch	N	N	Y	Y	Y	Y	Y
9 Keating	N	N	Y	Y	Y	Y	Y
MICHIGAN							
1 **Bergman**	Y	Y	N	N	N	N	N
2 **Huizenga**	Y	Y	N	N	N	N	N
3 **Amash**	Y	Y	N	N	N	N	N
4 **Moolenaar**	Y	Y	N	N	N	N	N
5 Kildee	N	N	Y	Y	Y	Y	Y
6 **Upton**	Y	Y	N	N	N	N	N
7 **Walberg**	Y	Y	N	N	N	N	N
8 **Bishop**	Y	Y	N	N	N	N	N
9 Levin	N	N	Y	Y	Y	Y	Y
10 **Mitchell**	Y	Y	N	N	N	N	N
11 **Trott**	Y	Y	N	N	N	N	N
12 Dingell	N	N	Y	Y	Y	Y	Y
13 Conyers	N	N	Y	Y	Y	Y	Y
14 Lawrence	N	N	Y	Y	Y	Y	Y
MINNESOTA							
1 Walz	N	Y	Y	Y	Y	Y	Y
2 **Lewis**	Y	Y	N	N	N	N	N
3 **Paulsen**	Y	Y	N	N	N	N	N
4 McCollum	N	N	Y	Y	Y	Y	Y

	35	36	37	38	39	40	41
5 Ellison	N	N	Y	Y	Y	Y	Y
6 **Emmer**	Y	Y	N	N	N	N	N
7 Peterson	Y	Y	N	Y	N	N	N
8 Nolan	N	?	Y	Y	Y	Y	Y
MISSISSIPPI							
1 **Kelly**	Y	Y	N	N	N	N	N
2 Thompson	N	N	Y	Y	Y	Y	Y
3 **Harper**	Y	Y	N	N	N	N	N
4 **Palazzo**	Y	Y	N	N	N	N	N
MISSOURI							
1 Clay	N	N	Y	Y	Y	Y	Y
2 **Wagner**	Y	Y	N	N	N	N	N
3 **Luetkemeyer**	Y	Y	N	N	N	N	N
4 **Hartzler**	Y	Y	N	N	N	N	N
5 Cleaver	–	–	+	+	+	+	+
6 **Graves**	Y	Y	N	N	N	N	N
7 **Long**	Y	Y	N	N	N	N	N
8 **Smith**	Y	Y	N	N	N	N	N
MONTANA							
AL **Zinke**	?	?	?	?	?	?	?
NEBRASKA							
1 **Fortenberry**	Y	Y	N	N	N	N	N
2 **Bacon**	Y	Y	N	N	N	N	N
3 **Smith**	Y	Y	N	N	N	N	N
NEVADA							
1 Titus	N	N	Y	Y	Y	Y	Y
2 **Amodei**	Y	Y	N	N	N	N	N
3 Rosen	N	N	Y	Y	Y	Y	Y
4 Kihuen	N	N	Y	Y	Y	Y	Y
NEW HAMPSHIRE							
1 Shea-Porter	N	N	Y	Y	Y	Y	Y
2 Kuster	N	Y	Y	Y	Y	Y	Y
NEW JERSEY							
1 Norcross	N	N	Y	Y	Y	Y	Y
2 **LoBiondo**	Y	Y	N	N	N	N	N
3 **MacArthur**	Y	Y	N	N	N	N	N
4 **Smith**	Y	Y	N	N	N	N	N
5 Gottheimer	N	N	Y	Y	Y	Y	Y
6 Pallone	N	N	Y	Y	Y	Y	Y
7 **Lance**	Y	Y	N	N	N	N	Y
8 Sires	N	N	N	Y	Y	Y	Y
9 Pascrell	N	Y	Y	Y	Y	Y	Y
10 Payne	N	N	Y	Y	Y	Y	Y
11 **Frelinghuysen**	Y	Y	N	N	N	N	N
12 Watson Coleman	N	N	Y	Y	Y	Y	Y
NEW MEXICO							
1 Lujan Grisham	N	N	Y	Y	Y	Y	Y
2 **Pearce**	Y	Y	N	N	N	N	N
3 Luján	N	N	Y	Y	Y	Y	Y
NEW YORK							
1 **Zeldin**	Y	Y	N	N	N	N	N
2 **King**	Y	Y	N	N	N	N	N
3 Suozzi	N	Y	Y	Y	Y	Y	Y
4 Rice	N	N	Y	Y	Y	Y	Y
5 Meeks	N	N	Y	Y	Y	Y	Y
6 Meng	N	N	Y	Y	Y	Y	Y
7 Velázquez	N	N	Y	Y	Y	Y	Y
8 Jeffries	N	N	Y	Y	Y	Y	Y
9 Clarke	N	N	Y	Y	Y	Y	Y
10 Nadler	N	N	Y	Y	Y	Y	Y
11 **Donovan**	Y	Y	N	N	N	N	N
12 Maloney, C.	N	N	Y	Y	Y	Y	Y
13 Espaillat	N	N	Y	Y	Y	Y	Y
14 Crowley	N	Y	Y	Y	Y	Y	Y
15 Serrano	N	N	Y	Y	Y	Y	Y
16 Engel	N	Y	Y	Y	Y	Y	Y
17 Lowey	N	N	Y	Y	Y	Y	Y
18 Maloney, S.P.	N	N	Y	Y	Y	Y	Y
19 **Faso**	Y	Y	N	N	N	N	N
20 Tonko	N	N	Y	Y	Y	Y	Y
21 **Stefanik**	Y	Y	N	N	N	N	N
22 **Tenney**	Y	Y	N	N	N	N	N
23 **Reed**	Y	Y	N	N	N	N	N
24 **Katko**	Y	Y	N	N	N	N	N
25 Slaughter	N	N	Y	Y	Y	Y	Y
26 Higgins	N	N	Y	Y	Y	Y	Y
27 **Collins**	Y	Y	N	N	N	N	N
NORTH CAROLINA							
1 Butterfield	N	N	Y	Y	Y	Y	Y
2 **Holding**	Y	Y	N	N	N	N	N
3 **Jones**	Y	Y	Y	Y	N	Y	Y
4 Price	N	N	Y	Y	Y	Y	Y

	35	36	37	38	39	40	41
5 **Foxx**	Y	Y	N	N	N	N	N
6 **Walker**	Y	Y	N	N	N	N	?
7 **Rouzer**	Y	Y	N	N	N	N	N
8 **Hudson**	Y	Y	N	N	N	N	N
9 **Pittenger**	Y	Y	N	N	N	N	N
10 **McHenry**	Y	Y	N	N	N	N	N
11 **Meadows**	Y	N	N	N	N	N	N
12 Adams	N	N	Y	Y	Y	Y	Y
13 **Budd**	Y	Y	N	N	N	N	N
NORTH DAKOTA							
AL **Cramer**	Y	Y	N	N	N	N	N
OHIO							
1 **Chabot**	Y	Y	N	N	N	N	N
2 **Wenstrup**	Y	Y	N	N	N	N	N
3 Beatty	N	N	Y	Y	Y	Y	Y
4 **Jordan**	Y	Y	N	N	N	N	N
5 **Latta**	Y	Y	N	N	N	N	N
6 **Johnson**	Y	Y	N	N	N	N	N
7 **Gibbs**	Y	Y	N	N	N	N	N
8 **Davidson**	Y	Y	N	N	N	N	N
9 Kaptur	N	Y	Y	Y	Y	Y	Y
10 **Turner**	Y	Y	N	N	N	N	N
11 Fudge	N	Y	Y	Y	Y	Y	Y
12 **Tiberi**	Y	Y	N	N	N	N	N
13 Ryan	–	–	+	+	+	+	+
14 **Joyce**	Y	Y	N	N	N	N	N
15 **Stivers**	Y	Y	?	N	N	N	N
16 **Renacci**	Y	Y	N	N	N	N	N
OKLAHOMA							
1 **Bridenstine**	Y	Y	N	N	N	N	N
2 **Mullin**	Y	Y	N	N	N	N	N
3 **Lucas**	Y	Y	N	N	N	N	N
4 **Cole**	Y	Y	N	N	N	N	N
5 **Russell**	Y	Y	N	N	N	N	N
OREGON							
1 Bonamici	N	N	Y	Y	Y	Y	Y
2 **Walden**	Y	Y	N	N	N	N	N
3 Blumenauer	N	N	Y	Y	Y	Y	Y
4 DeFazio	N	N	Y	Y	Y	Y	Y
5 Schrader	N	Y	Y	Y	Y	Y	Y
PENNSYLVANIA							
1 Brady	N	N	Y	Y	Y	Y	Y
2 Evans	N	N	Y	Y	Y	Y	Y
3 **Kelly**	Y	Y	N	N	N	N	N
4 **Perry**	Y	Y	N	N	N	N	N
5 **Thompson**	Y	Y	N	N	N	N	N
6 **Costello**	Y	Y	N	N	N	N	N
7 **Meehan**	Y	Y	N	N	N	N	N
8 **Fitzpatrick**	Y	N	N	N	N	N	N
9 **Shuster**	Y	Y	N	N	N	N	N
10 **Marino**	Y	Y	N	N	N	N	N
11 **Barletta**	Y	Y	N	N	N	N	N
12 **Rothfus**	Y	Y	N	N	N	N	N
13 Boyle	N	N	Y	Y	Y	Y	Y
14 Doyle	N	N	Y	Y	Y	Y	Y
15 **Dent**	Y	Y	N	N	N	N	N
16 **Smucker**	Y	Y	N	N	N	N	N
17 Cartwright	N	N	Y	Y	Y	Y	Y
18 **Murphy**	Y	Y	N	N	N	N	N
RHODE ISLAND							
1 Cicilline	N	N	Y	Y	Y	Y	Y
2 Langevin	N	N	Y	Y	Y	Y	Y
SOUTH CAROLINA							
1 **Sanford**	Y	Y	N	N	N	N	N
2 **Wilson**	Y	Y	N	N	N	N	N
3 **Duncan**	Y	Y	N	N	N	N	N
4 **Gowdy**	Y	Y	N	N	N	N	N
5 **Mulvaney**	?	?	?	?	?	?	?
6 Clyburn	N	N	Y	Y	Y	Y	Y
7 **Rice**	Y	Y	N	N	N	N	N
SOUTH DAKOTA							
AL **Noem**	Y	Y	N	N	N	N	N
TENNESSEE							
1 **Roe**	Y	Y	N	N	N	N	N
2 **Duncan**	Y	Y	N	N	N	N	N
3 **Fleischmann**	Y	Y	N	N	N	N	N
4 **DesJarlais**	Y	Y	N	N	N	N	N
5 Cooper	N	Y	Y	Y	Y	Y	Y
6 **Black**	Y	Y	N	N	N	N	N
7 **Blackburn**	Y	Y	N	N	N	N	N
8 **Kustoff**	Y	Y	N	N	N	N	N
9 Cohen	N	N	Y	Y	Y	Y	Y

	35	36	37	38	39	40	41
TEXAS							
1 **Gohmert**	Y	Y	N	N	N	N	N
2 **Poe**	Y	Y	N	N	N	N	N
3 **Johnson, S.**	Y	Y	N	N	N	N	N
4 **Ratcliffe**	Y	Y	N	N	N	N	N
5 **Hensarling**	Y	Y	N	N	N	N	N
6 **Barton**	Y	Y	N	N	N	N	N
7 **Culberson**	Y	Y	N	N	N	N	N
8 **Brady**	Y	Y	N	N	N	N	N
9 Green, A.	N	N	Y	Y	Y	Y	Y
10 **McCaul**	Y	N	N	N	N	N	N
11 **Conaway**	Y	Y	N	N	N	N	N
12 **Granger**	Y	Y	N	N	N	N	N
13 **Thornberry**	Y	Y	N	N	N	N	N
14 **Weber**	Y	Y	N	N	N	N	N
15 Gonzalez	?	Y	Y	Y	Y	Y	Y
16 O'Rourke	N	N	Y	Y	Y	Y	Y
17 **Flores**	Y	Y	N	N	N	N	N
18 Jackson Lee	N	N	Y	Y	Y	Y	Y
19 **Arrington**	Y	Y	N	N	N	N	N
20 Castro	N	N	Y	Y	Y	Y	Y
21 **Smith**	Y	Y	N	N	N	N	N
22 **Olson**	Y	Y	N	N	N	N	N
23 **Hurd**	Y	Y	N	N	N	N	N
24 **Marchant**	Y	Y	Y	N	N	N	N
25 **Williams**	Y	Y	N	N	N	N	N
26 **Burgess**	Y	Y	N	N	N	N	N
27 **Farenthold**	Y	Y	N	N	N	N	N
28 Cuellar	N	Y	Y	Y	Y	Y	Y
29 Green, G.	N	N	Y	Y	Y	Y	Y
30 Johnson, E.B.	N	N	Y	Y	Y	Y	Y
31 **Carter**	Y	Y	N	N	N	N	N
32 **Sessions**	Y	Y	N	N	N	N	N
33 Veasey	N	N	Y	Y	Y	Y	Y
34 Vela	N	Y	Y	Y	Y	Y	Y
35 Doggett	N	N	Y	Y	Y	Y	Y
36 **Babin**	Y	Y	N	N	N	N	N
UTAH							
1 **Bishop**	Y	Y	N	N	N	N	N
2 **Stewart**	Y	Y	N	N	N	N	N
3 **Chaffetz**	Y	Y	N	N	N	N	N
4 **Love**	Y	Y	N	N	N	N	N
VERMONT							
AL Welch	N	N	Y	Y	Y	Y	Y
VIRGINIA							
1 **Wittman**	Y	Y	N	N	N	N	N
2 **Taylor**	Y	Y	N	N	N	N	N
3 Scott	N	N	Y	Y	Y	Y	Y
4 McEachin	N	N	Y	Y	Y	Y	Y
5 **Garrett**	Y	Y	N	N	N	N	N
6 **Goodlatte**	Y	Y	?	N	N	N	N
7 **Brat**	Y	Y	N	N	N	N	N
8 Beyer	N	N	Y	Y	Y	Y	Y
9 **Griffith**	Y	Y	N	N	N	N	N
10 **Comstock**	Y	Y	N	N	N	N	N
11 Connolly	N	N	Y	Y	Y	Y	Y
WASHINGTON							
1 DelBene	N	N	Y	Y	Y	Y	Y
2 Larsen	N	N	Y	Y	Y	Y	Y
3 **Herrera Beutler**	Y	Y	N	N	N	N	N
4 **Newhouse**	Y	Y	N	N	N	N	N
5 **McMorris Rodgers**	Y	Y	N	N	N	N	N
6 Kilmer	N	N	Y	Y	Y	Y	Y
7 Jayapal	N	N	Y	Y	Y	Y	Y
8 **Reichert**	Y	Y	N	N	N	N	N
9 Smith	N	N	Y	Y	Y	Y	Y
10 Heck	N	N	Y	Y	Y	Y	Y
WEST VIRGINIA							
1 **McKinley**	Y	Y	N	N	N	N	Y
2 **Mooney**	Y	Y	N	N	N	N	Y
3 **Jenkins**	Y	Y	N	N	N	N	Y
WISCONSIN							
1 **Ryan**							
2 Pocan	N	N	Y	Y	Y	Y	Y
3 Kind	N	N	Y	Y	Y	Y	Y
4 Moore	N	N	Y	Y	Y	Y	Y
5 **Sensenbrenner**	Y	Y	N	N	N	N	N
6 **Grothman**	Y	Y	N	N	N	N	N
7 **Duffy**	Y	Y	N	N	N	N	N
8 **Gallagher**	Y	Y	N	N	N	N	N
WYOMING							
AL **Cheney**	Y	Y	N	N	N	N	N

VOTE NUMBER

42. HR 5. RULE-MAKING PROCESS CHANGES/CHEMICAL SAFETY. Tonko, D-N.Y., amendment that would exempt any rules made under a 2016 chemical safety law. It would remove the bill's provision that would effectively overturn two Supreme Court decisions that require federal courts to defer to an agency's interpretation of the underlying law or rule when considering challenges to agency rules. Rejected in Committee of the Whole 188-235 : R 0-234; D 188-1. Jan. 11, 2017.

43. HR 5. RULE-MAKING PROCESS CHANGES/LAND MANAGEMENT PLANS. Grijalva, D-Ariz., amendment that would remove provisions of the bill that would require the Forest Service and the Bureau of Land Management to conduct regulatory flexibility analyses, which describe the impact on small businesses, for land management plans. Rejected in Committee of the Whole 185-236 : R 0-233; D 185-3. Jan. 11, 2017.

44. HR 5. RULE-MAKING PROCESS CHANGES/RECOMMIT. Demings, D-Fla., motion to recommit the bill to the House Judiciary Committee with instructions to report back immediately with an amendment that would exempt regulations that significantly lower seniors' out-of-pocket costs for prescription drugs under Medicare Part D. It would remove the bill's provision that would effectively overturn two Supreme Court decisions that require federal courts to defer to an agency's interpretation of the underlying law or rule when considering challenges to agency rules. Motion rejected 190-233 : R 0-233; D 190-0. Jan. 11, 2017.

45. HR 5. RULE-MAKING PROCESS CHANGES/PASSAGE. Passage of the bill that would modify the federal rule-making process, including by codifying requirements for agencies to consider costs and benefits of alternatives. The bill would create additional steps that agencies would need to follow when planning "major" rules with annual costs of more than $100 million or "high-impact" rules with annual costs of more than $1 billion. For example, agencies would need to hold an advanced-notice comment period prior to proposing such rules to determine whether to continue the rule-making process. The measure would postpone the effective dates of "high impact" rules until any lawsuits filed within 60 days of the rule's publication in the Federal Register are resolved. It would effectively overturn two Supreme Court decisions that require federal courts to defer to an agency's interpretation of the underlying law or rule when considering legal challenges to rules. It would also require agencies to evaluate the "indirect" impacts of proposed rules on small businesses. Passed 238-183 : R 233-0; D 5-183. Jan. 11, 2017.

46. HR 78. SEC REGULATION ANALYSIS/CONFLICTS OF INTEREST. Green, D-Texas, for Waters, D-Calif., amendment that would require the Securities and Exchange Commission, before issuing a regulation, to identify former employers of commissioners and senior staff that would receive any benefit from a proposed regulation. The commission would need to determine whether the proposal should be amended to remedy a conflict of interest. It also would set similar requirements regarding conflicts of interest related to employers of certain former commissioners and senior staff. Rejected in Committee of the Whole 192-233 : R 1-233; D 191-0. Jan. 12, 2017.

47. HR 78. SEC REGULATION ANALYSIS/FINANCIAL STABILITY. Green, D-Texas, amendment that would exempt regulations issued to maintain or support U.S. financial stability. Rejected in Committee of the Whole 191-232 : R 1-230; D 190-2. Jan. 12, 2017.

48. HR 78. SEC REGULATION ANALYSIS/SEC CHAIRMAN INVESTMENTS. DeSaulnier, D-Calif., amendment that would require the chairman of the Securities and Exchange Commission and the individual's immediate family members divest securities in financial institutions regulated by the commission before the bill's requirements for cost-benefit analysis of new rules and review of existing rules could take effect. Rejected in Committee of the Whole 194-233 : R 2-233; D 192-0. Jan. 12, 2017.

	42	43	44	45	46	47	48
ALABAMA							
1 Byrne	N	N	N	Y	N	N	N
2 Roby	N	N	N	Y	N	N	N
3 Rogers	N	N	N	Y	N	N	N
4 Aderholt	N	N	N	Y	N	N	N
5 Brooks	N	N	N	Y	N	N	N
6 Palmer	N	N	N	Y	N	N	N
7 Sewell	Y	Y	Y	N	Y	Y	Y
ALASKA							
AL Young	N	N	N	Y	N	N	N
ARIZONA							
1 O'Halleran	Y	Y	Y	N	Y	Y	Y
2 McSally	N	N	N	Y	N	N	N
3 Grijalva	Y	Y	Y	N	Y	Y	Y
4 Gosar	N	N	N	Y	N	N	N
5 Biggs	N	N	N	Y	N	N	N
6 Schweikert	N	N	N	Y	N	N	N
7 Gallego	Y	Y	Y	N	Y	Y	Y
8 Franks	N	N	N	Y	N	N	N
9 Sinema	Y	N	Y	N	Y	N	Y
ARKANSAS							
1 Crawford	N	N	N	Y	N	N	N
2 Hill	N	N	N	Y	N	N	N
3 Womack	N	N	N	Y	N	N	N
4 Westerman	N	N	N	Y	N	N	N
CALIFORNIA							
1 LaMalfa	N	N	N	Y	N	?	N
2 Huffman	Y	Y	Y	N	Y	Y	Y
3 Garamendi	Y	Y	Y	N	Y	Y	Y
4 McClintock	N	N	N	Y	N	N	N
5 Thompson	Y	Y	Y	N	Y	Y	Y
6 Matsui	Y	Y	Y	N	Y	Y	Y
7 Bera	Y	Y	Y	N	Y	Y	Y
8 Cook	N	N	N	Y	N	N	N
9 McNerney	Y	Y	Y	N	Y	Y	Y
10 Denham	N	N	N	Y	N	N	N
11 DeSaulnier	Y	Y	Y	N	Y	Y	Y
12 Pelosi	?	?	Y	N	Y	Y	Y
13 Lee	Y	Y	Y	N	Y	Y	Y
14 Speier	Y	Y	Y	N	Y	Y	Y
15 Swalwell	Y	Y	Y	N	Y	Y	Y
16 Costa	Y	N	Y	Y	Y	Y	Y
17 Khanna	Y	Y	Y	N	Y	Y	Y
18 Eshoo	Y	Y	Y	N	Y	Y	Y
19 Lofgren	Y	Y	Y	N	Y	Y	Y
20 Panetta	Y	Y	Y	N	Y	Y	Y
21 Valadao	N	N	N	Y	N	N	N
22 Nunes	N	N	N	Y	N	N	N
23 McCarthy	N	N	N	Y	N	N	N
24 Carbajal	Y	Y	Y	N	Y	Y	Y
25 Knight	N	N	N	Y	N	N	N
26 Brownley	Y	Y	Y	N	Y	Y	Y
27 Chu	Y	Y	Y	N	Y	Y	Y
28 Schiff	Y	Y	Y	N	Y	Y	Y
29 Cardenas	Y	Y	Y	N	Y	Y	Y
30 Sherman	Y	Y	Y	N	Y	Y	Y
31 Aguilar	Y	Y	Y	N	Y	Y	Y
32 Napolitano	Y	Y	Y	N	Y	Y	Y
33 Lieu	Y	Y	Y	N	Y	Y	Y
34 Becerra	+	+	+	–	Y	Y	Y
35 Torres	Y	Y	Y	N	Y	Y	Y
36 Ruiz	Y	Y	Y	N	Y	Y	Y
37 Bass	Y	Y	Y	N	Y	Y	Y
38 Sánchez, Linda	Y	Y	Y	N	Y	Y	Y
39 Royce	N	N	N	Y	N	N	N
40 Roybal-Allard	Y	Y	Y	N	Y	Y	Y
41 Takano	Y	Y	Y	N	Y	Y	Y
42 Calvert	N	N	N	Y	N	N	N
43 Waters	Y	Y	Y	N	Y	Y	Y
44 Barragan	Y	Y	Y	N	Y	Y	Y
45 Walters	N	N	N	Y	N	N	N
46 Correa	Y	Y	Y	N	Y	Y	Y
47 Lowenthal	Y	Y	Y	N	Y	Y	Y
48 Rohrabacher	N	N	N	Y	N	N	N
49 Issa	N	N	N	Y	N	N	N
50 Hunter	N	N	N	Y	N	N	N
51 Vargas	Y	Y	Y	N	Y	Y	Y
52 Peters	Y	Y	Y	N	Y	N	Y
53 Davis	Y	Y	Y	N	Y	Y	Y

	42	43	44	45	46	47	48
COLORADO							
1 DeGette	Y	?	Y	N	Y	Y	Y
2 Polis	Y	Y	Y	N	Y	Y	Y
3 Tipton	N	N	N	Y	N	N	N
4 Buck	N	N	N	Y	N	N	N
5 Lamborn	N	N	N	Y	N	N	N
6 Coffman	N	N	N	Y	N	N	N
7 Perlmutter	Y	Y	Y	N	Y	Y	Y
CONNECTICUT							
1 Larson	Y	Y	Y	N	Y	Y	Y
2 Courtney	Y	Y	Y	N	Y	Y	Y
3 DeLauro	Y	Y	Y	?	Y	Y	Y
4 Himes	Y	Y	Y	N	Y	Y	Y
5 Esty	Y	Y	Y	N	Y	Y	Y
DELAWARE							
AL Blunt Rochester	Y	Y	Y	N	Y	Y	Y
FLORIDA							
1 Gaetz	N	N	N	Y	N	N	N
2 Dunn	N	N	N	Y	N	N	N
3 Yoho	N	N	N	Y	N	N	N
4 Rutherford	–	–	–	+	–	–	–
5 Lawson	Y	Y	Y	N	Y	Y	Y
6 DeSantis	N	N	N	Y	N	N	N
7 Murphy	Y	Y	Y	Y	Y	Y	Y
8 Posey	N	N	N	Y	N	N	N
9 Soto	Y	Y	Y	N	Y	Y	Y
10 Demings	Y	Y	Y	N	Y	Y	Y
11 Webster	N	N	N	Y	N	N	N
12 Bilirakis	N	N	N	Y	N	N	N
13 Crist	Y	Y	Y	N	Y	Y	Y
14 Castor	Y	Y	Y	N	Y	Y	Y
15 Ross	N	N	N	Y	N	N	N
16 Buchanan	N	N	N	Y	N	N	N
17 Rooney, T.	N	N	N	Y	N	N	N
18 Mast	N	N	N	Y	N	N	N
19 Rooney, F.	N	N	N	Y	N	N	N
20 Hastings	Y	Y	Y	N	Y	Y	Y
21 Frankel	Y	Y	Y	N	+	+	+
22 Deutch	Y	Y	Y	N	Y	Y	Y
23 Wasserman Schultz	Y	Y	Y	N	Y	Y	Y
24 Wilson	Y	Y	Y	N	Y	Y	Y
25 Diaz-Balart	N	N	N	Y	N	N	N
26 Curbelo	N	N	N	Y	N	N	N
27 Ros-Lehtinen	N	N	N	Y	N	N	N
GEORGIA							
1 Carter	N	N	N	Y	N	N	N
2 Bishop	Y	Y	Y	N	Y	Y	Y
3 Ferguson	N	N	N	Y	N	N	N
4 Johnson	Y	Y	Y	N	Y	Y	Y
5 Lewis	Y	Y	Y	N	Y	Y	Y
6 Price	?	?	?	?	?	?	?
7 Woodall	N	N	N	Y	N	N	N
8 Scott, A.	N	N	N	Y	N	N	N
9 Collins	N	N	N	Y	N	N	N
10 Hice	N	N	N	Y	N	N	N
11 Loudermilk	N	N	N	Y	N	N	N
12 Allen	N	N	N	Y	N	N	N
13 Scott, D.	Y	Y	Y	N	Y	Y	Y
14 Graves	N	N	N	Y	N	N	N
HAWAII							
1 Hanabusa	Y	Y	Y	N	Y	Y	Y
2 Gabbard	Y	Y	Y	?	Y	Y	Y
IDAHO							
1 Labrador	N	N	N	Y	N	N	N
2 Simpson	N	N	N	Y	N	N	N
ILLINOIS							
1 Rush	?	?	?	?	Y	Y	Y
2 Kelly	Y	Y	Y	N	Y	Y	Y
3 Lipinski	Y	Y	Y	N	Y	Y	Y
4 Gutierrez	Y	Y	Y	N	Y	Y	Y
5 Quigley	Y	Y	Y	N	Y	Y	Y
6 Roskam	N	N	N	Y	N	N	N
7 Davis, D.	Y	Y	Y	N	Y	Y	Y
8 Krishnamoorthi	Y	Y	Y	N	Y	Y	Y
9 Schakowsky	Y	Y	Y	N	Y	Y	Y
10 Schneider	Y	Y	Y	N	Y	Y	Y
11 Foster	Y	Y	Y	N	Y	Y	Y
12 Bost	N	N	N	Y	N	N	N
13 Davis, R.	N	N	N	Y	N	N	N
14 Hultgren	N	N	N	Y	N	N	N
15 Shimkus	N	N	N	Y	N	N	N

	42	43	44	45	46	47	48
16 **Kinzinger**	N	N	N	Y	N	N	N
17 Bustos	Y	Y	Y	N	Y	Y	Y
18 **LaHood**	N	N	N	Y	N	N	N
INDIANA							
1 Visclosky	Y	Y	Y	N	Y	Y	Y
2 **Walorski**	N	N	N	Y	N	N	N
3 **Banks**	N	N	N	Y	N	N	N
4 **Rokita**	N	N	N	Y	N	N	N
5 **Brooks**	N	N	N	Y	N	N	N
6 **Messer**	N	N	N	Y	N	N	N
7 Carson	Y	Y	Y	N	Y	Y	Y
8 **Bucshon**	N	N	N	Y	N	N	N
9 **Hollingsworth**	N	N	N	Y	N	N	N
IOWA							
1 **Blum**	N	N	N	Y	N	N	N
2 Loebsack	Y	Y	Y	N	Y	Y	Y
3 **Young**	N	N	N	Y	N	N	N
4 **King**	N	N	N	Y	N	N	N
KANSAS							
1 **Marshall**	N	N	N	Y	N	N	N
2 **Jenkins**	N	N	N	Y	N	N	N
3 **Yoder**	N	N	N	Y	N	N	N
4 **Pompeo**	?	?	?	?	?	?	?
KENTUCKY							
1 **Comer**	N	N	N	Y	N	N	N
2 **Guthrie**	N	N	N	Y	N	N	N
3 Yarmuth	Y	Y	Y	N	Y	Y	Y
4 **Massie**	N	N	N	Y	N	N	N
5 **Rogers**	N	N	N	Y	N	N	N
6 **Barr**	N	N	N	Y	N	N	N
LOUISIANA							
1 **Scalise**	N	N	N	Y	N	N	N
2 Richmond	Y	Y	Y	N	Y	Y	Y
3 **Higgins**	N	N	N	Y	N	N	N
4 **Johnson**	N	N	N	Y	N	N	N
5 **Abraham**	N	N	N	Y	N	N	N
6 **Graves**	N	N	N	Y	N	N	N
MAINE							
1 Pingree	Y	Y	Y	N	Y	Y	Y
2 **Poliquin**	N	N	N	Y	N	N	N
MARYLAND							
1 **Harris**	?	?	?	?	N	N	N
2 Ruppersberger	Y	Y	Y	N	Y	Y	Y
3 Sarbanes	Y	Y	Y	N	Y	Y	Y
4 Brown	Y	Y	Y	N	Y	Y	Y
5 Hoyer	Y	Y	Y	N	Y	Y	Y
6 Delaney	Y	Y	Y	N	Y	Y	Y
7 Cummings	Y	Y	Y	N	Y	Y	Y
8 Raskin	Y	Y	Y	N	Y	Y	Y
MASSACHUSETTS							
1 Neal	Y	Y	Y	N	?	Y	Y
2 McGovern	Y	Y	Y	N	Y	Y	Y
3 Tsongas	Y	Y	Y	N	Y	Y	Y
4 Kennedy	Y	Y	Y	N	Y	Y	Y
5 Clark	Y	Y	Y	N	Y	Y	Y
6 Moulton	Y	Y	Y	N	Y	Y	Y
7 Capuano	Y	Y	Y	N	Y	Y	Y
8 Lynch	Y	Y	Y	N	Y	Y	Y
9 Keating	Y	Y	Y	N	Y	Y	Y
MICHIGAN							
1 **Bergman**	N	N	N	Y	N	N	N
2 **Huizenga**	N	N	N	Y	N	N	N
3 **Amash**	N	N	N	Y	N	N	N
4 **Moolenaar**	N	N	N	Y	N	N	N
5 Kildee	Y	Y	Y	N	Y	Y	Y
6 **Upton**	N	N	N	Y	N	N	N
7 **Walberg**	N	N	N	Y	N	N	N
8 **Bishop**	N	N	N	Y	N	N	N
9 Levin	Y	Y	Y	N	Y	Y	Y
10 **Mitchell**	N	N	N	Y	N	N	N
11 **Trott**	N	N	N	Y	N	N	N
12 Dingell	Y	Y	Y	N	Y	Y	Y
13 Conyers	Y	Y	Y	N	Y	Y	Y
14 Lawrence	Y	Y	Y	N	Y	Y	Y
MINNESOTA							
1 Walz	Y	Y	Y	N	Y	Y	Y
2 **Lewis**	N	N	N	Y	N	N	N
3 **Paulsen**	N	N	N	Y	N	N	N
4 McCollum	Y	Y	Y	N	Y	Y	Y

	42	43	44	45	46	47	48
5 Ellison	Y	Y	Y	N	Y	Y	Y
6 **Emmer**	N	N	N	Y	N	N	N
7 Peterson	N	N	Y	Y	Y	Y	Y
8 Nolan	Y	Y	Y	N	Y	Y	Y
MISSISSIPPI							
1 **Kelly**	N	N	N	Y	N	N	N
2 Thompson	Y	Y	Y	N	Y	Y	Y
3 **Harper**	N	N	N	Y	N	N	N
4 **Palazzo**	N	N	N	Y	N	N	N
MISSOURI							
1 Clay	Y	Y	Y	N	Y	Y	Y
2 **Wagner**	N	N	N	Y	N	N	N
3 **Luetkemeyer**	N	N	N	Y	N	N	N
4 **Hartzler**	N	N	N	Y	N	N	N
5 Cleaver	+	+	+	–	Y	Y	Y
6 **Graves**	N	N	N	Y	N	N	N
7 **Long**	N	N	N	Y	N	N	N
8 **Smith**	N	N	N	Y	N	N	N
MONTANA							
AL **Zinke**	?	?	?	?	?	?	?
NEBRASKA							
1 **Fortenberry**	N	N	N	Y	N	N	N
2 **Bacon**	N	N	N	Y	N	N	N
3 **Smith**	N	N	N	Y	N	N	N
NEVADA							
1 Titus	Y	Y	Y	N	Y	Y	Y
2 **Amodei**	N	N	N	Y	N	N	N
3 Rosen	Y	Y	Y	N	Y	Y	Y
4 Kihuen	Y	Y	Y	N	Y	Y	Y
NEW HAMPSHIRE							
1 Shea-Porter	Y	Y	Y	N	Y	Y	Y
2 Kuster	Y	Y	Y	N	Y	Y	Y
NEW JERSEY							
1 Norcross	Y	Y	Y	N	Y	Y	Y
2 **LoBiondo**	N	N	N	Y	N	N	N
3 **MacArthur**	N	N	–	Y	N	N	N
4 **Smith**	N	N	N	Y	N	N	N
5 Gottheimer	Y	Y	Y	N	Y	Y	Y
6 Pallone	Y	Y	Y	N	Y	Y	Y
7 **Lance**	N	N	N	Y	N	N	N
8 Sires	Y	Y	Y	N	Y	Y	Y
9 Pascrell	Y	Y	Y	N	Y	Y	Y
10 Payne	Y	Y	Y	N	Y	Y	Y
11 **Frelinghuysen**	N	N	N	Y	N	N	N
12 Watson Coleman	Y	Y	Y	N	Y	Y	Y
NEW MEXICO							
1 Lujan Grisham	Y	Y	Y	N	Y	Y	Y
2 **Pearce**	N	N	N	Y	N	N	N
3 Luján	Y	Y	Y	N	Y	Y	Y
NEW YORK							
1 **Zeldin**	N	N	N	Y	N	N	N
2 **King**	N	N	N	Y	N	N	N
3 Suozzi	Y	Y	Y	N	Y	Y	Y
4 Rice	Y	Y	Y	N	Y	Y	Y
5 Meeks	Y	Y	Y	N	Y	Y	Y
6 Meng	Y	Y	Y	N	Y	Y	Y
7 Velázquez	Y	Y	Y	N	Y	Y	Y
8 Jeffries	Y	Y	Y	N	Y	Y	Y
9 Clarke	Y	Y	Y	N	Y	Y	Y
10 Nadler	Y	Y	Y	N	Y	Y	Y
11 **Donovan**	N	N	N	Y	N	N	N
12 Maloney, C.	Y	Y	Y	N	Y	Y	Y
13 Espaillat	Y	Y	Y	N	Y	Y	Y
14 Crowley	Y	Y	Y	N	Y	Y	Y
15 Serrano	Y	Y	Y	N	Y	Y	Y
16 Engel	Y	Y	Y	N	Y	Y	Y
17 Lowey	Y	Y	Y	N	Y	Y	Y
18 Maloney, S.P.	Y	Y	Y	N	Y	Y	Y
19 **Faso**	N	N	N	Y	N	N	N
20 Tonko	Y	Y	Y	N	Y	Y	Y
21 **Stefanik**	N	N	N	Y	N	N	N
22 **Tenney**	N	N	N	Y	N	N	N
23 **Reed**	N	N	N	Y	N	N	N
24 **Katko**	N	N	N	Y	N	N	N
25 Slaughter	Y	Y	Y	N	Y	Y	Y
26 Higgins	Y	Y	Y	N	Y	Y	Y
27 **Collins**	N	N	N	Y	N	N	N
NORTH CAROLINA							
1 Butterfield	Y	Y	Y	N	Y	Y	Y
2 **Holding**	N	N	N	Y	N	N	N
3 **Jones**	N	N	N	Y	Y	Y	Y
4 Price	Y	Y	Y	N	Y	Y	Y

	42	43	44	45	46	47	48
5 **Foxx**	N	N	N	Y	N	N	N
6 **Walker**	N	N	N	Y	?	N	N
7 **Rouzer**	N	N	N	Y	N	N	N
8 **Hudson**	N	N	N	Y	N	N	N
9 **Pittenger**	N	N	N	Y	N	N	N
10 **McHenry**	N	N	N	Y	N	N	N
11 **Meadows**	N	N	N	Y	N	N	N
12 Adams	Y	Y	Y	N	Y	Y	Y
13 **Budd**	N	N	N	Y	N	N	N
NORTH DAKOTA							
AL **Cramer**	N	N	N	Y	N	?	N
OHIO							
1 **Chabot**	N	N	N	Y	N	N	N
2 **Wenstrup**	N	N	N	Y	N	N	N
3 Beatty	Y	Y	Y	N	Y	Y	Y
4 **Jordan**	N	N	N	Y	N	N	N
5 **Latta**	N	N	N	Y	N	N	N
6 **Johnson**	N	N	N	Y	N	N	N
7 **Gibbs**	N	N	N	Y	N	N	N
8 **Davidson**	N	N	N	Y	N	N	N
9 Kaptur	Y	Y	Y	N	Y	Y	Y
10 **Turner**	N	N	N	Y	N	N	N
11 Fudge	Y	Y	Y	N	Y	Y	Y
12 **Tiberi**	N	N	N	Y	N	N	N
13 Ryan	+	+	+	–	+	+	+
14 **Joyce**	N	N	N	Y	N	N	N
15 **Stivers**	N	N	N	Y	N	N	N
16 **Renacci**	N	N	N	Y	N	N	N
OKLAHOMA							
1 **Bridenstine**	N	N	N	Y	N	N	N
2 **Mullin**	N	N	N	Y	N	N	N
3 **Lucas**	N	N	N	Y	N	N	N
4 **Cole**	N	N	N	Y	N	N	N
5 **Russell**	N	N	N	Y	N	N	N
OREGON							
1 Bonamici	Y	Y	Y	N	Y	Y	Y
2 **Walden**	N	N	N	Y	N	N	N
3 Blumenauer	Y	Y	Y	N	Y	Y	Y
4 DeFazio	Y	Y	Y	N	Y	Y	Y
5 Schrader	Y	Y	Y	Y	Y	Y	Y
PENNSYLVANIA							
1 Brady	Y	Y	Y	N	Y	Y	Y
2 Evans	Y	Y	Y	N	Y	Y	Y
3 **Kelly**	N	N	N	Y	N	N	N
4 **Perry**	N	N	N	Y	N	N	N
5 **Thompson**	N	N	N	Y	N	N	N
6 **Costello**	N	N	N	Y	N	N	N
7 **Meehan**	N	N	N	Y	N	N	N
8 **Fitzpatrick**	N	N	N	Y	N	N	Y
9 **Shuster**	N	N	N	Y	N	N	N
10 **Marino**	N	N	N	Y	N	N	N
11 **Barletta**	N	N	N	Y	N	N	N
12 **Rothfus**	N	N	N	Y	N	N	N
13 Boyle	Y	Y	Y	N	Y	Y	Y
14 Doyle	Y	Y	Y	N	Y	Y	Y
15 **Dent**	N	N	N	Y	N	N	N
16 **Smucker**	N	N	N	Y	N	N	N
17 Cartwright	Y	Y	Y	N	Y	Y	Y
18 **Murphy**	N	N	N	Y	N	N	N
RHODE ISLAND							
1 Cicilline	Y	Y	Y	N	Y	Y	Y
2 Langevin	Y	Y	Y	N	Y	Y	Y
SOUTH CAROLINA							
1 **Sanford**	N	N	N	Y	N	N	N
2 **Wilson**	N	N	N	Y	N	N	N
3 **Duncan**	N	N	N	Y	N	N	N
4 **Gowdy**	N	N	N	Y	N	N	N
5 **Mulvaney**	?	?	?	?	?	?	?
6 Clyburn	Y	Y	Y	N	Y	Y	Y
7 **Rice**	N	N	N	?	N	N	N
SOUTH DAKOTA							
AL **Noem**	N	N	N	Y	N	N	N
TENNESSEE							
1 **Roe**	N	N	N	Y	N	N	N
2 **Duncan**	N	N	N	Y	N	N	N
3 **Fleischmann**	N	N	N	Y	N	N	N
4 **DesJarlais**	N	?	N	Y	N	N	N
5 Cooper	Y	Y	Y	N	Y	Y	Y
6 **Black**	N	N	N	Y	N	N	N
7 **Blackburn**	N	N	N	Y	N	N	N
8 **Kustoff**	N	N	N	Y	N	N	N
9 Cohen	Y	Y	Y	N	Y	Y	Y

	42	43	44	45	46	47	48
TEXAS							
1 **Gohmert**	N	N	N	Y	N	N	N
2 **Poe**	N	N	N	Y	N	N	N
3 **Johnson, S.**	N	N	N	Y	N	N	N
4 **Ratcliffe**	N	N	N	Y	N	N	N
5 **Hensarling**	N	N	N	Y	N	N	N
6 **Barton**	N	N	N	Y	N	N	N
7 **Culberson**	N	N	N	Y	N	N	N
8 **Brady**	N	N	N	Y	N	N	N
9 Green, A.	Y	Y	Y	N	Y	Y	Y
10 **McCaul**	N	N	N	Y	N	N	N
11 **Conaway**	N	N	N	Y	N	N	N
12 **Granger**	N	N	N	Y	N	N	N
13 **Thornberry**	N	N	N	Y	N	N	N
14 **Weber**	N	N	N	Y	N	N	N
15 Gonzalez	Y	Y	Y	N	Y	Y	Y
16 O'Rourke	Y	Y	Y	N	Y	Y	Y
17 **Flores**	N	N	N	Y	N	N	N
18 Jackson Lee	Y	Y	Y	N	Y	Y	Y
19 **Arrington**	N	N	N	Y	N	N	N
20 Castro	Y	Y	Y	N	Y	Y	Y
21 **Smith**	N	N	N	Y	N	N	N
22 **Olson**	N	N	N	Y	N	N	N
23 **Hurd**	N	N	N	Y	N	N	N
24 **Marchant**	N	N	N	Y	N	?	N
25 **Williams**	N	N	N	Y	N	N	N
26 **Burgess**	N	N	N	Y	N	N	N
27 **Farenthold**	N	N	N	Y	N	N	N
28 Cuellar	Y	Y	Y	Y	Y	Y	Y
29 Green, G.	Y	Y	Y	N	Y	Y	Y
30 Johnson, E.B.	Y	Y	Y	N	Y	Y	Y
31 **Carter**	N	N	N	Y	N	N	N
32 **Sessions**	N	N	N	Y	N	N	N
33 Veasey	Y	Y	Y	N	Y	Y	Y
34 Vela	Y	Y	Y	N	Y	Y	Y
35 Doggett	Y	Y	Y	N	Y	Y	Y
36 **Babin**	N	N	N	Y	N	N	N
UTAH							
1 **Bishop**	N	N	N	Y	N	N	N
2 **Stewart**	N	N	N	Y	N	N	N
3 **Chaffetz**	N	N	N	Y	N	N	N
4 **Love**	N	N	N	Y	N	N	N
VERMONT							
AL Welch	Y	Y	Y	N	Y	Y	Y
VIRGINIA							
1 **Wittman**	N	N	N	Y	N	N	N
2 **Taylor**	N	N	N	Y	N	N	N
3 Scott	Y	Y	Y	N	Y	Y	Y
4 McEachin	Y	Y	Y	N	Y	Y	Y
5 **Garrett**	N	N	N	Y	N	N	N
6 **Goodlatte**	N	N	N	Y	N	N	N
7 **Brat**	N	N	N	Y	N	?	N
8 Beyer	Y	Y	Y	N	Y	Y	Y
9 **Griffith**	N	N	N	Y	N	N	N
10 **Comstock**	N	N	N	Y	N	N	N
11 Connolly	Y	Y	Y	N	Y	Y	Y
WASHINGTON							
1 DelBene	Y	Y	Y	N	Y	Y	Y
2 Larsen	Y	Y	Y	N	Y	Y	Y
3 **Herrera Beutler**	N	N	N	Y	N	N	N
4 **Newhouse**	N	N	N	Y	N	N	N
5 **McMorris Rodgers**	N	N	N	Y	N	N	N
6 Kilmer	Y	Y	Y	N	Y	Y	Y
7 Jayapal	Y	Y	Y	N	Y	Y	Y
8 **Reichert**	N	N	N	Y	N	N	N
9 Smith	Y	Y	Y	N	Y	Y	Y
10 Heck	Y	Y	Y	N	Y	Y	Y
WEST VIRGINIA							
1 **McKinley**	N	N	N	Y	N	N	N
2 **Mooney**	N	N	N	Y	N	N	N
3 **Jenkins**	N	N	N	Y	N	N	N
WISCONSIN							
1 **Ryan**							
2 Pocan	Y	Y	Y	N	Y	Y	Y
3 Kind	Y	Y	Y	N	Y	Y	Y
4 Moore	Y	Y	Y	N	Y	Y	Y
5 **Sensenbrenner**	N	N	N	Y	N	N	N
6 **Grothman**	N	N	N	Y	N	N	N
7 **Duffy**	N	N	N	Y	N	N	N
8 **Gallagher**	N	N	N	Y	N	N	N
WYOMING							
AL **Cheney**	N	N	N	Y	N	N	N

‖‖ HOUSE VOTES

VOTE NUMBER

49. HR 78. SEC REGULATION ANALYSIS/ETHICS TRAINING. Raskin, D-Md., amendment that would require the chairman and commissioners of the Securities and Exchange Commission undergo conduct and ethical standards training in relation to prior employment at financial institutions before the bill's requirements for cost-benefit analysis of new rules and review of existing rules could take effect. Rejected in Committee of the Whole 196-231 : R 4-231; D 192-0. Jan. 12, 2017.

50. HR 78. SEC REGULATION ANALYSIS/RECOMMIT. Bustos, D-Ill., motion to recommit the bill to the House Financial Services Committee with instructions to report back immediately with an amendment that would require the Securities and Exchange Commission, in determining the costs and benefits of proposed regulations, to consider whether market participants would have incentive to relocate outside the United States. Motion rejected 195-232 : R 3-232; D 192-0. Jan. 12, 2017.

51. HR 78. SEC REGULATION ANALYSIS/PASSAGE. Passage of the bill that would require the Securities and Exchange Commission to conduct cost-benefit analyses of proposed regulations. It also would direct the commission to assess costs and benefits of alternatives, including the option of not regulating. It would require the SEC to, within two years of issuing rules with an annual cost more than $100 million, review whether these rules have met their goals. It also would require the SEC to periodically review existing rules and modify or repeal those found ineffective or excessively burdensome. Passed 243-184 : R 234-1; D 9-183. Jan. 12, 2017.

52. HR 238. CFTC REAUTHORIZATION/EXCESSIVE SPECULATION. Conaway, R-Texas, amendment that would remove provisions in existing law that specifically designate how the Commodity Futures Trading Commission is to limit excessive speculation. Adopted in Committee of the Whole 236-191 : R 234-1; D 2-190. Jan. 12, 2017.

53. HR 238. CFTC REAUTHORIZATION/RECOMMIT. Langevin, D-R.I., motion to recommit the bill to the House Agriculture Committee with instructions to report back immediately with an amendment that would prohibit the Commodity Futures Trading Commission from considering the swaps regulatory requirements of a foreign nation as comparable to U.S. swaps requirements if that foreign nation had been found by the CFTC, in consultation with the director of national intelligence, to have engaged in cyberattacks targeting U.S. elections. Motion rejected 190-235 : R 0-235; D 190-0. Jan. 12, 2017.

54. HR 238. CFTC REAUTHORIZATION/PASSAGE. Passage of the bill that would reauthorize operations of the Commodity Futures Trading Commission through fiscal 2021 at $250 million annually. It would amend the 2010 Dodd-Frank financial regulatory overhaul to modify and clarify how the commission is to regulate derivatives and swaps. For example, it would modify certain requirements for end users of derivatives, such as farmers and utilities that use derivatives to hedge risk, to ensure they are not subject to the same requirements as entities whose main business derives from swaps. The measure would require the commission to conduct cost-benefit analyses of its proposed rules. As amended, it would exempt all inter-affiliate transactions from being regulated as swaps. Passed 239-182 : R 232-1; D 7-181. Jan. 12, 2017.

55. S 84, S CON RES 3, H RES 48. FISCAL 2017 BUDGET RESOLUTION AND DEFENSE SECRETARY WAIVER/PREVIOUS QUESTION. Woodall, R-Ga., motion to order the previous question (thus ending debate and possibility of amendment) on the rule (H Res 48) that would provide for House floor consideration of a fiscal 2017 budget resolution (S Con Res 3) that would include reconciliation instructions for legislation intended to be used to repeal parts of the 2010 health care overhaul. It also would provide for consideration of a bill (S 84) that would exempt the first person appointed as Defense secretary after the bill's enactment from a requirement for a seven-year waiting period before former servicemembers can be appointed to the position, which would provide a waiver for President-elect Donald Trump's pick for the position, retired Marine Corps Gen. James Mattis. Motion agreed to 234-179 : R 234-0; D 0-179. Jan. 13, 2017.

		49	50	51	52	53	54	55
ALABAMA								
1	Byrne	N	N	Y	Y	N	Y	Y
2	Roby	N	N	Y	Y	N	Y	Y
3	Rogers	N	N	Y	Y	N	Y	Y
4	Aderholt	N	N	Y	Y	N	Y	Y
5	Brooks	N	N	Y	Y	N	Y	Y
6	Palmer	N	N	Y	Y	N	Y	Y
7	Sewell	Y	Y	N	N	Y	N	N
ALASKA								
AL	Young	N	N	Y	Y	N	Y	?
ARIZONA								
1	O'Halleran	Y	Y	N	N	Y	N	N
2	McSally	N	N	Y	Y	N	Y	Y
3	Grijalva	Y	Y	N	N	Y	N	N
4	Gosar	N	N	Y	Y	N	Y	Y
5	Biggs	N	N	Y	Y	N	Y	Y
6	Schweikert	N	N	Y	Y	N	Y	Y
7	Gallego	Y	Y	N	N	Y	N	N
8	Franks	N	N	Y	Y	N	Y	Y
9	Sinema	Y	Y	Y	N	Y	Y	N
ARKANSAS								
1	Crawford	N	N	Y	Y	N	Y	Y
2	Hill	N	N	Y	Y	N	Y	Y
3	Womack	N	N	Y	Y	N	Y	Y
4	Westerman	N	N	Y	Y	N	Y	Y
CALIFORNIA								
1	LaMalfa	N	N	Y	Y	N	Y	Y
2	Huffman	Y	Y	N	Y	Y	N	?
3	Garamendi	Y	Y	N	N	Y	N	N
4	McClintock	N	N	Y	Y	N	Y	Y
5	Thompson	Y	Y	N	N	Y	N	N
6	Matsui	Y	Y	N	N	Y	N	N
7	Bera	Y	Y	N	N	Y	N	N
8	Cook	N	N	Y	Y	N	Y	Y
9	McNerney	Y	Y	N	N	Y	N	N
10	Denham	N	N	Y	Y	N	Y	Y
11	DeSaulnier	Y	Y	N	N	Y	N	N
12	Pelosi	Y	Y	N	N	Y	N	?
13	Lee	Y	Y	N	N	Y	N	N
14	Speier	Y	Y	N	N	Y	N	N
15	Swalwell	Y	Y	N	N	Y	N	N
16	Costa	Y	Y	N	N	Y	N	?
17	Khanna	Y	Y	N	N	Y	N	N
18	Eshoo	Y	Y	N	N	Y	N	N
19	Lofgren	Y	Y	N	N	Y	N	N
20	Panetta	Y	Y	N	N	Y	N	N
21	Valadao	N	N	Y	Y	N	Y	Y
22	Nunes	N	N	Y	Y	N	Y	Y
23	McCarthy	N	N	Y	Y	N	Y	Y
24	Carbajal	Y	Y	N	N	Y	N	N
25	Knight	N	N	Y	Y	N	Y	Y
26	Brownley	Y	Y	N	N	Y	N	N
27	Chu	Y	Y	N	N	Y	?	N
28	Schiff	Y	Y	N	N	Y	N	N
29	Cardenas	Y	Y	Y	N	Y	N	N
30	Sherman	Y	Y	N	N	Y	N	N
31	Aguilar	Y	Y	N	N	Y	N	N
32	Napolitano	Y	Y	N	N	Y	N	N
33	Lieu	Y	Y	N	N	Y	N	N
34	Becerra	Y	Y	N	N	Y	N	N
35	Torres	Y	Y	N	N	Y	N	N
36	Ruiz	Y	Y	N	N	Y	N	N
37	Bass	Y	Y	N	N	Y	N	N
38	Sánchez, Linda	Y	Y	N	N	Y	N	N
39	Royce	N	N	Y	Y	N	Y	Y
40	Roybal-Allard	Y	Y	N	N	Y	N	N
41	Takano	Y	Y	N	N	Y	N	N
42	Calvert	N	N	Y	Y	N	Y	Y
43	Waters	Y	Y	N	N	Y	N	?
44	Barragan	Y	Y	N	N	Y	N	N
45	Walters	N	N	Y	Y	N	Y	Y
46	Correa	Y	Y	N	N	Y	N	N
47	Lowenthal	Y	Y	N	N	Y	N	N
48	Rohrabacher	N	N	Y	Y	N	Y	Y
49	Issa	N	N	Y	Y	N	Y	Y
50	Hunter	N	N	Y	Y	N	Y	Y
51	Vargas	Y	Y	N	N	Y	N	N
52	Peters	Y	Y	N	N	Y	N	N
53	Davis	Y	Y	N	N	Y	N	N
COLORADO								
1	DeGette	Y	Y	N	N	Y	N	N
2	Polis	Y	Y	N	N	Y	N	N
3	Tipton	N	N	Y	Y	N	Y	Y
4	Buck	N	N	Y	Y	N	Y	Y
5	Lamborn	N	N	Y	Y	N	Y	Y
6	Coffman	N	N	Y	Y	N	Y	Y
7	Perlmutter	Y	Y	N	N	Y	N	N
CONNECTICUT								
1	Larson	Y	Y	N	N	Y	N	N
2	Courtney	Y	Y	N	N	Y	N	N
3	DeLauro	Y	Y	N	N	Y	N	N
4	Himes	Y	Y	N	N	Y	N	N
5	Esty	Y	Y	N	N	Y	N	N
DELAWARE								
AL	Blunt Rochester	Y	Y	N	N	Y	N	N
FLORIDA								
1	Gaetz	N	N	Y	Y	N	Y	Y
2	Dunn	N	N	Y	Y	N	Y	Y
3	Yoho	N	N	Y	Y	N	Y	Y
4	Rutherford	-	-	+	-	-	+	+
5	Lawson	Y	Y	N	N	Y	N	N
6	DeSantis	N	N	Y	Y	N	Y	Y
7	Murphy	Y	Y	N	N	Y	N	N
8	Posey	N	N	Y	Y	N	Y	Y
9	Soto	Y	Y	N	N	Y	N	N
10	Demings	Y	Y	N	N	Y	?	N
11	Webster	N	N	Y	Y	N	Y	Y
12	Bilirakis	N	N	Y	Y	N	Y	Y
13	Crist	Y	Y	N	N	Y	N	N
14	Castor	Y	Y	N	N	Y	N	N
15	Ross	N	N	Y	Y	N	Y	Y
16	Buchanan	N	N	Y	Y	N	Y	Y
17	Rooney, T.	N	N	Y	Y	N	Y	Y
18	Mast	N	N	Y	Y	N	Y	Y
19	Rooney, F.	N	N	Y	Y	N	Y	Y
20	Hastings	Y	Y	N	N	Y	N	N
21	Frankel	+	-	-	-	+	-	?
22	Deutch	Y	Y	N	N	Y	N	N
23	Wasserman Schultz	Y	Y	N	N	Y	N	N
24	Wilson	Y	Y	N	N	Y	N	N
25	Diaz-Balart	N	N	Y	Y	N	Y	Y
26	Curbelo	N	N	Y	Y	N	Y	Y
27	Ros-Lehtinen	N	N	Y	Y	N	Y	Y
GEORGIA								
1	Carter	N	N	Y	Y	N	Y	Y
2	Bishop	Y	Y	Y	N	Y	Y	N
3	Ferguson	Y	Y	N	Y	N	Y	Y
4	Johnson	Y	Y	N	N	Y	N	?
5	Lewis	Y	Y	N	N	Y	N	N
6	Price	?	?	?	?	?	?	?
7	Woodall	N	N	Y	Y	N	Y	Y
8	Scott, A.	N	N	Y	Y	N	Y	Y
9	Collins	N	N	Y	Y	N	Y	Y
10	Hice	N	N	Y	Y	N	Y	Y
11	Loudermilk	N	N	Y	Y	N	Y	Y
12	Allen	N	N	Y	Y	N	Y	Y
13	Scott, D.	Y	Y	N	N	Y	Y	N
14	Graves	N	N	Y	Y	N	Y	Y
HAWAII								
1	Hanabusa	Y	Y	N	N	Y	N	N
2	Gabbard	Y	Y	N	N	Y	N	N
IDAHO								
1	Labrador	N	N	Y	Y	N	Y	Y
2	Simpson	N	N	Y	Y	N	Y	Y
ILLINOIS								
1	Rush	Y	Y	N	N	Y	N	?
2	Kelly	Y	Y	N	N	Y	N	N
3	Lipinski	Y	Y	N	N	Y	N	N
4	Gutierrez	Y	Y	N	?	N	N	N
5	Quigley	Y	Y	N	N	Y	N	N
6	Roskam	N	N	Y	Y	N	Y	Y
7	Davis, D.	Y	Y	N	N	Y	N	N
8	Krishnamoorthi	Y	Y	N	N	Y	N	N
9	Schakowsky	Y	Y	N	N	Y	N	N
10	Schneider	Y	Y	N	N	Y	N	N
11	Foster	Y	Y	N	N	Y	N	N
12	Bost	N	N	Y	Y	N	Y	Y
13	Davis, R.	N	N	Y	Y	N	Y	Y
14	Hultgren	N	N	Y	Y	N	Y	Y
15	Shimkus	N	N	Y	Y	N	Y	Y

	49	50	51	52	53	54	55
16 **Kinzinger**	N	N	Y	Y	N	Y	Y
17 Bustos	Y	Y	N	N	Y	N	N
18 **LaHood**	N	N	Y	Y	N	Y	Y
INDIANA							
1 Visclosky	Y	Y	N	N	Y	N	N
2 **Walorski**	N	N	Y	Y	N	Y	Y
3 **Banks**	N	N	Y	Y	N	Y	Y
4 **Rokita**	N	N	Y	Y	N	Y	Y
5 **Brooks**	N	N	Y	Y	N	Y	Y
6 **Messer**	N	N	Y	Y	N	Y	Y
7 Carson	Y	Y	N	N	Y	N	N
8 **Bucshon**	N	N	Y	Y	N	Y	Y
9 **Hollingsworth**	N	N	Y	Y	N	Y	Y
IOWA							
1 **Blum**	N	Y	Y	Y	N	Y	Y
2 Loebsack	Y	Y	N	N	Y	?	N
3 **Young**	N	N	Y	Y	N	Y	Y
4 **King**	N	N	Y	Y	N	Y	Y
KANSAS							
1 **Marshall**	N	N	Y	Y	N	Y	Y
2 **Jenkins**	N	N	Y	Y	N	Y	Y
3 **Yoder**	N	N	Y	Y	N	Y	Y
4 **Pompeo**	?	?	?	?	?	?	?
KENTUCKY							
1 **Comer**	N	N	Y	Y	N	Y	Y
2 **Guthrie**	N	N	Y	Y	N	Y	Y
3 Yarmuth	Y	Y	N	N	Y	N	N
4 **Massie**	N	N	Y	Y	N	Y	Y
5 **Rogers**	N	N	Y	Y	N	Y	Y
6 **Barr**	N	N	Y	Y	N	Y	Y
LOUISIANA							
1 **Scalise**	N	N	Y	Y	N	Y	Y
2 Richmond	Y	Y	N	N	Y	N	N
3 **Higgins**	N	N	Y	Y	N	Y	Y
4 **Johnson**	N	N	Y	Y	N	Y	Y
5 **Abraham**	N	N	Y	Y	N	Y	Y
6 **Graves**	N	N	Y	Y	N	Y	Y
MAINE							
1 Pingree	Y	Y	N	N	Y	N	N
2 **Poliquin**	N	N	Y	Y	N	Y	Y
MARYLAND							
1 **Harris**	N	N	Y	Y	N	Y	Y
2 Ruppersberger	Y	Y	N	N	Y	N	N
3 Sarbanes	Y	Y	N	N	Y	N	N
4 Brown	Y	Y	N	N	Y	N	N
5 Hoyer	Y	Y	N	N	Y	N	N
6 Delaney	Y	Y	N	N	Y	N	N
7 Cummings	Y	Y	N	N	Y	N	N
8 Raskin	Y	Y	N	N	Y	N	N
MASSACHUSETTS							
1 Neal	Y	Y	N	N	Y	N	N
2 McGovern	Y	Y	N	N	Y	N	N
3 Tsongas	Y	Y	N	N	Y	N	N
4 Kennedy	Y	Y	N	N	Y	N	N
5 Clark	Y	Y	N	N	Y	N	N
6 Moulton	Y	Y	N	N	Y	N	N
7 Capuano	Y	Y	N	N	Y	N	N
8 Lynch	Y	Y	N	N	Y	N	N
9 Keating	Y	Y	N	N	Y	N	?
MICHIGAN							
1 **Bergman**	N	N	Y	Y	N	Y	Y
2 **Huizenga**	N	N	Y	Y	N	Y	Y
3 **Amash**	N	N	Y	Y	N	Y	Y
4 **Moolenaar**	N	N	Y	Y	N	Y	Y
5 Kildee	Y	Y	N	N	Y	N	N
6 **Upton**	N	N	Y	Y	N	Y	Y
7 **Walberg**	N	N	Y	Y	N	Y	Y
8 **Bishop**	N	N	Y	Y	N	Y	Y
9 Levin	Y	Y	N	N	Y	N	N
10 **Mitchell**	N	N	Y	Y	N	Y	Y
11 **Trott**	N	N	Y	Y	N	Y	Y
12 Dingell	Y	Y	N	N	Y	N	N
13 Conyers	Y	Y	N	N	Y	N	N
14 Lawrence	Y	Y	N	N	Y	N	N
MINNESOTA							
1 Walz	Y	Y	N	N	Y	N	N
2 **Lewis**	N	N	Y	Y	N	Y	Y
3 **Paulsen**	N	N	Y	Y	N	Y	Y
4 McCollum	Y	Y	N	N	Y	N	N

	49	50	51	52	53	54	55
5 Ellison	Y	Y	N	N	Y	N	N
6 **Emmer**	N	N	Y	Y	N	Y	Y
7 Peterson	Y	Y	N	N	Y	N	N
8 Nolan	Y	Y	N	N	Y	N	N
MISSISSIPPI							
1 **Kelly**	N	N	Y	Y	N	Y	Y
2 Thompson	Y	Y	N	N	Y	N	N
3 **Harper**	N	N	Y	Y	N	Y	Y
4 **Palazzo**	N	N	Y	Y	N	Y	Y
MISSOURI							
1 Clay	Y	Y	N	N	Y	N	N
2 **Wagner**	N	N	Y	Y	N	Y	Y
3 **Luetkemeyer**	N	N	Y	Y	N	Y	Y
4 **Hartzler**	N	N	Y	Y	N	Y	Y
5 Cleaver	Y	Y	N	N	Y	N	N
6 **Graves**	N	N	Y	Y	N	Y	Y
7 **Long**	N	N	Y	Y	N	Y	Y
8 **Smith**	N	N	Y	Y	N	Y	Y
MONTANA							
AL **Zinke**	?	?	?	?	?	?	?
NEBRASKA							
1 **Fortenberry**	N	N	Y	Y	N	Y	Y
2 **Bacon**	N	N	Y	Y	N	Y	Y
3 **Smith**	N	N	Y	Y	N	Y	Y
NEVADA							
1 Titus	Y	Y	N	N	Y	N	N
2 **Amodei**	N	N	Y	Y	N	Y	Y
3 Rosen	Y	Y	Y	N	Y	N	N
4 Kihuen	Y	Y	N	N	Y	N	N
NEW HAMPSHIRE							
1 Shea-Porter	Y	Y	N	N	Y	N	N
2 Kuster	Y	Y	N	N	Y	N	N
NEW JERSEY							
1 Norcross	Y	Y	N	N	Y	N	N
2 **LoBiondo**	N	N	Y	Y	N	Y	Y
3 **MacArthur**	N	N	Y	Y	N	Y	Y
4 **Smith**	N	N	Y	Y	N	Y	Y
5 Gottheimer	Y	Y	Y	N	Y	Y	N
6 Pallone	Y	Y	N	N	Y	N	N
7 **Lance**	N	N	Y	Y	N	Y	Y
8 Sires	Y	Y	N	N	Y	N	N
9 Pascrell	Y	Y	N	N	Y	N	N
10 Payne	Y	Y	N	N	Y	?	N
11 **Frelinghuysen**	N	N	Y	Y	N	Y	Y
12 Watson Coleman	Y	Y	N	N	Y	N	N
NEW MEXICO							
1 Lujan Grisham	Y	Y	N	N	Y	N	N
2 **Pearce**	N	N	Y	Y	N	Y	Y
3 Luján	Y	Y	N	N	Y	N	N
NEW YORK							
1 **Zeldin**	N	N	Y	Y	N	Y	Y
2 **King**	N	N	Y	Y	N	Y	Y
3 Suozzi	Y	Y	Y	N	Y	Y	–
4 Rice	Y	Y	N	N	Y	N	N
5 Meeks	Y	Y	N	N	Y	N	?
6 Meng	Y	Y	N	N	Y	N	N
7 Velázquez	Y	Y	N	N	Y	N	N
8 Jeffries	Y	Y	N	N	Y	N	N
9 Clarke	Y	Y	N	N	Y	N	N
10 Nadler	Y	Y	N	N	Y	N	N
11 **Donovan**	N	N	Y	Y	N	Y	Y
12 Maloney, C.	Y	Y	N	N	?	N	N
13 Espaillat	Y	Y	N	N	Y	N	N
14 Crowley	Y	Y	N	N	Y	N	?
15 Serrano	Y	Y	N	N	Y	N	N
16 Engel	Y	Y	N	N	Y	N	N
17 Lowey	Y	Y	N	N	Y	N	N
18 Maloney, S.P.	Y	Y	N	N	Y	N	N
19 **Faso**	N	N	Y	Y	N	Y	Y
20 Tonko	Y	Y	N	N	Y	N	N
21 **Stefanik**	N	N	Y	Y	N	Y	Y
22 **Tenney**	N	N	Y	Y	N	Y	Y
23 **Reed**	N	N	Y	Y	N	Y	Y
24 **Katko**	N	N	Y	Y	N	Y	Y
25 Slaughter	Y	Y	N	N	Y	N	N
26 Higgins	Y	Y	N	N	Y	N	N
27 **Collins**	N	N	Y	Y	N	Y	Y
NORTH CAROLINA							
1 Butterfield	Y	Y	N	N	Y	N	N
2 **Holding**	N	N	Y	Y	N	Y	Y
3 **Jones**	Y	Y	N	N	N	N	Y
4 Price	Y	Y	N	N	Y	N	N

	49	50	51	52	53	54	55
5 **Foxx**	N	N	Y	Y	N	Y	Y
6 **Walker**	N	N	Y	Y	N	Y	Y
7 **Rouzer**	N	N	Y	Y	N	Y	Y
8 **Hudson**	N	N	Y	Y	N	Y	Y
9 **Pittenger**	N	N	Y	Y	N	Y	Y
10 **McHenry**	N	N	Y	Y	N	Y	Y
11 **Meadows**	N	N	Y	Y	N	Y	Y
12 Adams	Y	Y	N	N	Y	N	N
13 **Budd**	N	N	Y	Y	N	Y	Y
NORTH DAKOTA							
AL **Cramer**	N	N	Y	Y	N	Y	Y
OHIO							
1 **Chabot**	N	N	Y	Y	N	Y	Y
2 **Wenstrup**	N	N	Y	Y	N	Y	Y
3 Beatty	Y	Y	N	N	Y	N	N
4 **Jordan**	N	N	Y	Y	N	Y	Y
5 **Latta**	N	N	Y	Y	N	Y	Y
6 **Johnson**	N	N	Y	Y	N	Y	Y
7 **Gibbs**	N	N	Y	Y	N	Y	Y
8 **Davidson**	N	N	Y	Y	N	Y	Y
9 Kaptur	Y	Y	N	N	Y	N	N
10 **Turner**	N	N	Y	Y	N	Y	Y
11 Fudge	Y	Y	N	N	Y	N	N
12 **Tiberi**	N	N	Y	Y	N	Y	Y
13 Ryan	+	+	–	–	+	–	N
14 **Joyce**	N	N	Y	Y	N	Y	Y
15 **Stivers**	N	N	Y	Y	N	Y	Y
16 **Renacci**	N	N	Y	Y	N	Y	Y
OKLAHOMA							
1 **Bridenstine**	N	N	Y	Y	N	Y	Y
2 **Mullin**	N	N	Y	Y	N	Y	Y
3 **Lucas**	N	N	Y	Y	N	Y	Y
4 **Cole**	N	N	Y	Y	N	Y	Y
5 **Russell**	N	N	Y	Y	N	Y	Y
OREGON							
1 Bonamici	Y	Y	N	N	Y	N	N
2 **Walden**	N	N	Y	Y	N	Y	Y
3 Blumenauer	Y	Y	N	N	Y	N	N
4 DeFazio	Y	Y	N	N	Y	N	N
5 Schrader	Y	Y	Y	N	Y	N	N
PENNSYLVANIA							
1 Brady	Y	Y	N	N	Y	N	N
2 Evans	Y	Y	N	N	Y	N	?
3 **Kelly**	N	N	Y	Y	N	Y	Y
4 **Perry**	N	N	Y	Y	N	Y	Y
5 **Thompson**	N	N	Y	Y	N	Y	Y
6 **Costello**	N	N	Y	Y	N	Y	Y
7 **Meehan**	N	N	Y	Y	N	Y	Y
8 **Fitzpatrick**	Y	N	Y	Y	N	Y	Y
9 **Shuster**	N	N	Y	Y	N	Y	Y
10 **Marino**	N	N	Y	Y	N	Y	Y
11 **Barletta**	N	N	Y	Y	N	Y	Y
12 **Rothfus**	N	N	Y	Y	N	Y	Y
13 Boyle	Y	Y	N	N	Y	N	N
14 Doyle	Y	Y	N	N	Y	N	N
15 **Dent**	Y	N	Y	Y	N	Y	Y
16 **Smucker**	N	N	Y	Y	N	Y	Y
17 Cartwright	Y	Y	N	N	Y	N	N
18 **Murphy**	N	N	Y	Y	N	+	Y
RHODE ISLAND							
1 Cicilline	Y	Y	N	N	Y	N	N
2 Langevin	Y	Y	N	N	Y	N	N
SOUTH CAROLINA							
1 **Sanford**	N	N	Y	Y	N	Y	Y
2 **Wilson**	N	N	Y	Y	N	Y	Y
3 **Duncan**	N	N	Y	Y	N	Y	Y
4 **Gowdy**	N	N	Y	Y	N	Y	Y
5 **Mulvaney**	?	?	?	?	?	?	?
6 Clyburn	Y	Y	N	N	Y	N	N
7 **Rice**	N	N	Y	Y	N	Y	Y
SOUTH DAKOTA							
AL **Noem**	N	N	Y	Y	N	Y	Y
TENNESSEE							
1 **Roe**	N	N	Y	Y	N	Y	Y
2 **Duncan**	N	Y	Y	Y	N	Y	Y
3 **Fleischmann**	N	N	Y	Y	N	Y	Y
4 **DesJarlais**	N	N	Y	Y	N	Y	Y
5 Cooper	Y	Y	N	N	Y	N	N
6 **Black**	N	N	Y	Y	N	Y	Y
7 **Blackburn**	N	N	Y	Y	N	Y	Y
8 **Kustoff**	N	N	Y	Y	N	Y	Y
9 Cohen	Y	Y	N	N	Y	N	N

	49	50	51	52	53	54	55
TEXAS							
1 **Gohmert**	N	N	Y	Y	N	Y	Y
2 **Poe**	N	N	Y	Y	N	Y	Y
3 **Johnson, S.**	N	N	Y	Y	N	Y	Y
4 **Ratcliffe**	N	N	Y	Y	N	Y	Y
5 **Hensarling**	N	N	Y	Y	N	Y	Y
6 **Barton**	N	N	Y	Y	N	Y	Y
7 **Culberson**	N	N	Y	Y	N	Y	Y
8 **Brady**	N	N	Y	Y	N	Y	Y
9 Green, A.	Y	Y	N	N	Y	N	N
10 **McCaul**	N	N	Y	Y	N	Y	Y
11 **Conaway**	N	N	Y	Y	N	Y	Y
12 **Granger**	N	N	Y	Y	N	Y	Y
13 **Thornberry**	N	N	Y	Y	N	Y	Y
14 **Weber**	N	N	Y	Y	N	Y	Y
15 Gonzalez	Y	Y	N	N	Y	N	N
16 O'Rourke	Y	Y	N	N	Y	N	N
17 **Flores**	N	N	Y	Y	N	Y	Y
18 Jackson Lee	Y	Y	N	N	Y	N	N
19 **Arrington**	N	N	Y	Y	N	Y	Y
20 Castro	Y	Y	N	N	Y	N	N
21 **Smith**	N	N	Y	Y	N	Y	Y
22 **Olson**	N	N	Y	Y	N	Y	Y
23 **Hurd**	N	N	Y	Y	N	Y	Y
24 **Marchant**	N	N	Y	Y	N	Y	Y
25 **Williams**	N	N	Y	Y	N	Y	Y
26 **Burgess**	N	N	Y	Y	N	Y	Y
27 **Farenthold**	N	N	Y	Y	N	Y	Y
28 Cuellar	Y	Y	Y	N	Y	Y	N
29 Green, G.	Y	Y	N	N	Y	N	N
30 Johnson, E.B.	Y	Y	N	N	Y	N	N
31 **Carter**	N	N	Y	Y	N	Y	Y
32 **Sessions**	N	N	Y	Y	N	Y	Y
33 Veasey	Y	Y	N	N	Y	N	N
34 Vela	Y	Y	N	N	Y	N	N
35 Doggett	Y	Y	N	N	Y	N	N
36 **Babin**	N	N	Y	Y	N	Y	Y
UTAH							
1 **Bishop**	N	N	Y	Y	N	Y	Y
2 **Stewart**	N	N	Y	Y	N	Y	Y
3 **Chaffetz**	N	N	Y	Y	N	Y	Y
4 **Love**	N	N	Y	Y	N	Y	Y
VERMONT							
AL Welch	Y	Y	N	N	Y	N	N
VIRGINIA							
1 **Wittman**	N	N	Y	Y	N	Y	Y
2 **Taylor**	N	N	Y	Y	N	Y	Y
3 Scott	Y	Y	N	N	Y	N	N
4 McEachin	Y	Y	N	N	Y	N	N
5 **Garrett**	N	N	Y	Y	N	?	Y
6 **Goodlatte**	N	N	Y	Y	N	Y	Y
7 **Brat**	N	N	Y	Y	N	Y	Y
8 Beyer	Y	Y	N	N	Y	N	N
9 **Griffith**	N	N	Y	Y	N	Y	Y
10 **Comstock**	N	N	Y	Y	N	Y	Y
11 Connolly	Y	Y	N	N	Y	N	N
WASHINGTON							
1 DelBene	Y	Y	N	N	Y	N	N
2 Larsen	Y	Y	N	N	Y	N	N
3 **Herrera Beutler**	Y	N	Y	Y	N	Y	Y
4 **Newhouse**	N	N	Y	Y	N	Y	Y
5 **McMorris Rodgers**	N	N	Y	Y	N	Y	Y
6 Kilmer	Y	Y	N	N	Y	N	N
7 Jayapal	Y	Y	N	N	Y	N	N
8 **Reichert**	N	N	Y	Y	N	Y	Y
9 Smith	Y	Y	N	N	Y	N	N
10 Heck	Y	Y	N	N	Y	N	N
WEST VIRGINIA							
1 **McKinley**	N	N	Y	Y	N	Y	Y
2 **Mooney**	N	N	Y	Y	N	Y	Y
3 **Jenkins**	N	N	Y	Y	N	Y	Y
WISCONSIN							
1 **Ryan**							
2 Pocan	Y	Y	N	N	Y	N	N
3 Kind	Y	Y	N	N	Y	N	N
4 Moore	Y	Y	N	N	Y	N	?
5 **Sensenbrenner**	N	N	Y	Y	N	Y	Y
6 **Grothman**	N	N	Y	Y	N	Y	Y
7 **Duffy**	N	N	Y	Y	N	Y	Y
8 **Gallagher**	N	N	Y	Y	N	Y	Y
WYOMING							
AL **Cheney**	N	N	Y	Y	N	Y	Y

VOTE NUMBER

56. S 84, S CON RES 3, H RES 48. FISCAL 2017 BUDGET RESOLUTION AND DEFENSE SECRETARY WAIVER/RULE. Adoption of the rule (H Res 48) that would provide for House floor consideration of a fiscal 2017 budget resolution (S Con Res 3) that would include reconciliation instructions for legislation intended to be used to repeal parts of the 2010 health care overhaul. It also would provide for consideration of a bill (S 84) that would exempt the first person appointed as Defense secretary after the bill's enactment from a requirement for a seven-year waiting period before former servicemembers can be appointed to the position, which would provide a waiver for President-elect Donald Trump's pick for the position, retired Marine Corps Gen. James Mattis. Adopted 235-188 : R 235-0; D 0-188. Jan. 13, 2017.

57. S CON RES 3. FISCAL 2017 BUDGET RESOLUTION/DEMOCRATIC SUBSTITUTE. Yarmuth, D-Ky., substitute amendment that does not contain any reconciliation instructions, and thus would not trigger a process in which the Senate could pass legislation to repeal the 2010 health care law by a simple majority vote. The amendment would allow $3.3 trillion in new budget authority for fiscal 2017 and would provide for the revision of allocations for unspecified legislation related to additional infrastructure investments and tax overhaul if the measure would not increase the deficit. Rejected in Committee of the Whole 149-272 : R 0-235; D 149-37. Jan. 13, 2017.

58. S CON RES 3. FISCAL 2017 BUDGET RESOLUTION/ADOPTION. Adoption of the concurrent resolution that includes reconciliation instructions for the House Energy and Commerce and Ways and Means Committees as well as the Senate Finance and Health, Education, Labor and Pensions Committees to develop legislation to reduce the deficit by at least $1 billion each over a 10-year period by January 27, 2017, which is expected to repeal parts of the 2010 health care law. The concurrent resolution also would set broad spending and revenue targets over the next 10 years. It would allow $3.3 trillion in new budget authority for fiscal 2017. Adopted 227-198 : R 227-9; D 0-189. Jan. 13, 2017.

59. S 84. DEFENSE SECRETARY WAIVER/PASSAGE. Passage of the bill that would allow the first person to be confirmed secretary of Defense after the bill's enactment to serve in the position, even if the individual has not been retired from the military for seven years, so long as the person has been retired for at least three years. The bill would thus provide an exemption for President-elect Donald Trump's pick for the position, retired Marine Corps Gen. James Mattis, from a requirement for a seven-year waiting period before former servicemembers can be appointed to Defense secretary. Passed (thus cleared for the president) 268-151 : R 232-1; D 36-150. Jan. 13, 2017.

60. HR 423. CALLER IDENTIFICATION INFORMATION/PASSAGE. Blackburn, R-Tenn., motion to suspend the rules and pass the bill that would expand an existing prohibition against individuals in the United States causing caller identification services to transmit inaccurate caller identification information with the intent to defraud or harm. Specifically, it would expand the prohibition to cover text messages and individuals outside the United States if the recipient is in the United States. Motion agreed to 398-5 : R 224-5; D 174-0. Jan. 23, 2017.

61. HR 582. MULTILINE TELEPHONE 911 CALLS/PASSAGE. Lance, R-N.J., motion to suspend the rules and pass the bill that would require multiline telephone systems to be configured so that users are able to dial 911 directly, without having to dial an additional digit, such as 9, even if such a code is required to make other calls. Motion agreed to 408-0 : R 229-0; D 179-0. Jan. 23, 2017.

62. H RES 55, HR 7. PERMANENT PROHIBITION ON FEDERAL FUNDING FOR ABORTIONS/PREVIOUS QUESTION. Cheney, R-Wyo., motion to order the previous question (thus ending debate and the possibility of amendment) on the rule (H Res 55) to provide for floor consideration of the bill that would permanently prohibit the use of federal funds to pay for abortion services or health insurance plans that include coverage for abortions. It also would bar the District of Columbia from using its own local funds to provide or pay for abortions. Motion agreed to 233-187 : R 233-0; D 0-187. Jan. 24, 2017.

	56	57	58	59	60	61	62
ALABAMA							
1 Byrne	Y	N	Y	Y	?	?	Y
2 Roby	Y	N	Y	Y	Y	Y	Y
3 Rogers	Y	N	Y	Y	Y	Y	Y
4 Aderholt	Y	N	Y	Y	Y	Y	Y
5 Brooks	Y	N	Y	Y	Y	Y	Y
6 Palmer	Y	N	Y	Y	Y	Y	Y
7 Sewell	N	Y	N	N	Y	N	N
ALASKA							
AL Young	Y	N	Y	Y	Y	Y	Y
ARIZONA							
1 O'Halleran	N	N	Y	Y	Y	Y	N
2 McSally	Y	N	Y	Y	Y	Y	Y
3 Grijalva	N	Y	N	N	?	?	N
4 Gosar	Y	N	Y	Y	Y	Y	Y
5 Biggs	Y	N	Y	Y	Y	Y	Y
6 Schweikert	Y	N	Y	Y	Y	Y	Y
7 Gallego	N	Y	N	N	Y	N	N
8 Franks	Y	N	Y	Y	Y	Y	Y
9 Sinema	N	N	N	Y	Y	Y	N
ARKANSAS							
1 Crawford	Y	N	Y	Y	Y	Y	Y
2 Hill	Y	N	Y	Y	Y	Y	Y
3 Womack	Y	N	Y	Y	Y	Y	Y
4 Westerman	Y	N	Y	Y	Y	Y	Y
CALIFORNIA							
1 LaMalfa	Y	N	Y	Y	Y	Y	Y
2 Huffman	?	Y	N	N	Y	Y	N
3 Garamendi	N	Y	N	N	Y	Y	N
4 McClintock	Y	N	Y	Y	Y	Y	Y
5 Thompson	N	Y	N	Y	Y	Y	N
6 Matsui	N	Y	N	Y	Y	Y	N
7 Bera	N	N	N	Y	Y	Y	N
8 Cook	Y	N	Y	Y	Y	Y	Y
9 McNerney	N	Y	N	Y	Y	Y	N
10 Denham	Y	N	Y	Y	Y	Y	Y
11 DeSaulnier	N	Y	N	Y	Y	Y	N
12 Pelosi	?	Y	N	Y	Y	Y	N
13 Lee	N	Y	N	Y	Y	Y	N
14 Speier	N	Y	N	?	?	N	N
15 Swalwell	N	Y	N	Y	Y	Y	N
16 Costa	N	N	N	Y	Y	Y	N
17 Khanna	N	Y	N	Y	Y	Y	N
18 Eshoo	N	Y	N	Y	Y	Y	N
19 Lofgren	N	N	N	N	Y	Y	N
20 Panetta	N	Y	N	Y	Y	Y	N
21 Valadao	Y	N	Y	Y	Y	Y	Y
22 Nunes	Y	N	Y	Y	Y	Y	Y
23 McCarthy	Y	N	Y	Y	Y	Y	Y
24 Carbajal	N	Y	N	Y	Y	Y	N
25 Knight	Y	N	Y	Y	Y	Y	Y
26 Brownley	N	N	N	Y	Y	Y	N
27 Chu	N	Y	N	Y	Y	Y	N
28 Schiff	N	Y	N	Y	Y	Y	N
29 Cardenas	N	Y	N	Y	Y	Y	N
30 Sherman	N	Y	N	Y	Y	Y	N
31 Aguilar	N	N	N	Y	Y	Y	N
32 Napolitano	N	Y	N	Y	Y	Y	N
33 Lieu	N	?	N	Y	Y	Y	N
34 Becerra	N	Y	N	?	?	?	
35 Torres	N	Y	N	Y	Y	Y	N
36 Ruiz	N	N	N	+	+	N	N
37 Bass	N	Y	N	Y	Y	Y	N
38 Sánchez, Linda	N	Y	N	N	Y	Y	N
39 Royce	Y	N	Y	Y	Y	Y	Y
40 Roybal-Allard	N	Y	N	N	Y	Y	N
41 Takano	N	Y	N	Y	Y	Y	N
42 Calvert	Y	N	Y	Y	Y	Y	Y
43 Waters	N	Y	N	N	Y	Y	N
44 Barragan	N	Y	N	N	Y	Y	N
45 Walters	Y	N	Y	Y	Y	Y	Y
46 Correa	N	Y	N	Y	Y	Y	N
47 Lowenthal	N	Y	N	N	Y	Y	N
48 Rohrabacher	Y	N	Y	Y	Y	Y	Y
49 Issa	Y	N	Y	Y	Y	Y	Y
50 Hunter	Y	N	Y	Y	Y	Y	Y
51 Vargas	N	Y	N	N	Y	Y	N
52 Peters	N	N	N	N	Y	Y	N
53 Davis	N	Y	N	N	Y	N	N

	56	57	58	59	60	61	62
COLORADO							
1 DeGette	N	Y	N	N	Y	Y	N
2 Polis	N	N	N	N	Y	Y	N
3 Tipton	Y	N	Y	Y	Y	Y	Y
4 Buck	Y	N	Y	Y	Y	Y	Y
5 Lamborn	Y	N	Y	Y	Y	Y	Y
6 Coffman	Y	N	Y	Y	Y	Y	+
7 Perlmutter	N	Y	N	Y	Y	Y	N
CONNECTICUT							
1 Larson	N	Y	N	N	?	Y	N
2 Courtney	N	Y	N	N	Y	Y	N
3 DeLauro	N	Y	N	N	Y	Y	N
4 Himes	N	N	N	N	Y	Y	N
5 Esty	N	Y	N	N	Y	Y	N
DELAWARE							
AL Blunt Rochester	N	Y	N	N	Y	Y	N
FLORIDA							
1 Gaetz	Y	N	Y	Y	Y	Y	Y
2 Dunn	Y	N	Y	Y	Y	Y	Y
3 Yoho	Y	N	Y	Y	Y	Y	Y
4 Rutherford	+	–	+	+	Y	Y	Y
5 Lawson	N	Y	N	N	Y	Y	N
6 DeSantis	Y	N	Y	Y	Y	Y	Y
7 Murphy	N	N	N	?	?	N	N
8 Posey	Y	N	Y	Y	Y	Y	Y
9 Soto	N	N	N	Y	Y	Y	N
10 Demings	N	Y	N	N	Y	Y	N
11 Webster	Y	N	Y	+	+	Y	Y
12 Bilirakis	Y	N	Y	Y	Y	Y	Y
13 Crist	N	N	N	Y	Y	Y	N
14 Castor	N	Y	N	N	Y	Y	N
15 Ross	Y	N	Y	Y	Y	Y	Y
16 Buchanan	Y	N	Y	?	Y	Y	Y
17 Rooney, T.	Y	N	Y	Y	Y	Y	Y
18 Mast	Y	N	Y	Y	Y	Y	Y
19 Rooney, F.	Y	N	Y	Y	Y	Y	Y
20 Hastings	N	Y	N	N	Y	Y	N
21 Frankel	?	?	?	?	Y	Y	N
22 Deutch	N	Y	N	N	Y	Y	N
23 Wasserman Schultz	N	Y	N	N	Y	Y	N
24 Wilson	N	+	N	N	Y	N	N
25 Diaz-Balart	Y	N	Y	Y	Y	Y	Y
26 Curbelo	Y	N	Y	Y	Y	Y	Y
27 Ros-Lehtinen	Y	N	Y	Y	Y	Y	Y
GEORGIA							
1 Carter	Y	N	Y	Y	Y	Y	Y
2 Bishop	N	Y	N	N	Y	Y	N
3 Ferguson	Y	N	Y	Y	Y	Y	Y
4 Johnson	N	Y	N	N	Y	Y	N
5 Lewis	N	Y	N	N	Y	Y	N
6 Price	?	?	?	?	?	?	?
7 Woodall	Y	N	Y	Y	Y	Y	Y
8 Scott, A.	Y	N	Y	Y	Y	Y	Y
9 Collins	Y	N	Y	Y	Y	Y	Y
10 Hice	Y	N	Y	Y	Y	Y	Y
11 Loudermilk	Y	N	Y	Y	Y	Y	Y
12 Allen	Y	N	Y	Y	Y	Y	Y
13 Scott, D.	N	Y	N	N	Y	Y	N
14 Graves	Y	N	Y	Y	Y	Y	Y
HAWAII							
1 Hanabusa	N	Y	N	N	Y	Y	N
2 Gabbard	N	Y	N	N	Y	Y	N
IDAHO							
1 Labrador	Y	N	N	Y	N	Y	Y
2 Simpson	Y	N	Y	Y	Y	Y	Y
ILLINOIS							
1 Rush	?	?	?	?	?	?	?
2 Kelly	N	Y	N	N	Y	Y	N
3 Lipinski	N	N	N	P	Y	Y	N
4 Gutierrez	N	Y	N	N	+	N	N
5 Quigley	N	Y	N	N	Y	Y	N
6 Roskam	Y	N	Y	Y	Y	Y	Y
7 Davis, D.	N	Y	N	N	Y	Y	N
8 Krishnamoorthi	N	Y	N	N	Y	Y	N
9 Schakowsky	N	Y	N	N	Y	Y	N
10 Schneider	N	N	N	N	Y	Y	N
11 Foster	N	N	N	N	Y	Y	N
12 Bost	Y	N	Y	Y	Y	Y	Y
13 Davis, R.	Y	N	Y	Y	Y	Y	Y
14 Hultgren	Y	N	Y	Y	Y	Y	Y
15 Shimkus	Y	N	Y	Y	Y	Y	Y

KEY

Republicans	Democrats	Independents
Y Voted for (yea)	X Paired against	C Voted "present" to avoid possible conflict of interest
# Paired for	– Announced against	
+ Announced for	P Voted "present"	? Did not vote or otherwise make a position known
N Voted against (nay)		

	56	57	58	59	60	61	62
16 **Kinzinger**	Y	N	Y	Y	Y	Y	Y
17 Bustos	N	N	N	N	+	+	N
18 **LaHood**	Y	N	Y	Y	Y	Y	Y
INDIANA							
1 Visclosky	N	N	N	N	Y	Y	N
2 **Walorski**	Y	N	Y	Y	Y	Y	Y
3 **Banks**	Y	N	Y	Y	Y	Y	Y
4 **Rokita**	Y	N	Y	Y	Y	Y	Y
5 **Brooks**	Y	N	Y	Y	Y	Y	Y
6 **Messer**	Y	N	Y	Y	Y	?	Y
7 Carson	N	Y	N	N	Y	Y	N
8 **Bucshon**	Y	N	Y	Y	Y	Y	Y
9 **Hollingsworth**	Y	N	Y	Y	Y	Y	Y
IOWA							
1 **Blum**	Y	N	Y	Y	Y	Y	Y
2 Loebsack	N	N	N	Y	Y	Y	N
3 **Young**	Y	N	Y	Y	Y	Y	Y
4 **King**	Y	N	Y	Y	Y	Y	Y
KANSAS							
1 **Marshall**	Y	N	Y	Y	Y	Y	Y
2 **Jenkins**	Y	N	Y	Y	Y	Y	Y
3 **Yoder**	Y	N	Y	Y	Y	Y	Y
KENTUCKY							
1 **Comer**	Y	N	Y	Y	Y	Y	Y
2 **Guthrie**	Y	N	Y	Y	Y	Y	Y
3 Yarmuth	N	Y	N	N	Y	Y	N
4 **Massie**	Y	N	N	Y	N	Y	Y
5 **Rogers**	Y	N	Y	Y	Y	Y	Y
6 **Barr**	Y	N	Y	Y	Y	Y	Y
LOUISIANA							
1 **Scalise**	Y	N	Y	Y	Y	Y	Y
2 Richmond	N	Y	N	N	?	?	N
3 **Higgins**	Y	N	Y	Y	Y	Y	Y
4 **Johnson**	Y	N	Y	Y	Y	Y	Y
5 **Abraham**	Y	N	Y	Y	Y	Y	Y
6 **Graves**	Y	N	Y	Y	Y	Y	Y
MAINE							
1 Pingree	N	Y	N	N	Y	Y	N
2 **Poliquin**	Y	N	Y	Y	Y	Y	Y
MARYLAND							
1 **Harris**	Y	N	Y	Y	Y	Y	Y
2 Ruppersberger	N	Y	N	Y	Y	Y	N
3 Sarbanes	N	Y	N	N	Y	Y	N
4 Brown	N	Y	N	N	Y	Y	N
5 Hoyer	N	Y	N	N	Y	Y	N
6 Delaney	N	N	N	Y	Y	Y	N
7 Cummings	N	Y	N	N	Y	Y	N
8 Raskin	N	Y	N	N	Y	Y	N
MASSACHUSETTS							
1 Neal	N	Y	N	N	Y	Y	N
2 McGovern	N	Y	N	N	Y	Y	N
3 Tsongas	N	N	N	N	Y	Y	N
4 Kennedy	N	Y	N	N	Y	Y	N
5 Clark	N	Y	N	N	Y	Y	N
6 Moulton	N	Y	N	Y	Y	Y	N
7 Capuano	N	Y	N	N	Y	Y	N
8 Lynch	N	Y	N	N	Y	Y	N
9 Keating	N	Y	N	Y	Y	Y	N
MICHIGAN							
1 **Bergman**	Y	N	Y	Y	Y	Y	Y
2 **Huizenga**	Y	N	Y	Y	Y	Y	Y
3 **Amash**	Y	N	N	N	N	Y	Y
4 **Moolenaar**	Y	N	Y	Y	Y	Y	Y
5 Kildee	N	Y	N	N	Y	Y	N
6 **Upton**	Y	N	Y	Y	Y	Y	Y
7 **Walberg**	Y	N	Y	Y	Y	Y	Y
8 **Bishop**	Y	N	Y	Y	+	Y	Y
9 Levin	N	Y	N	N	Y	Y	N
10 **Mitchell**	Y	N	Y	Y	Y	Y	Y
11 **Trott**	Y	N	Y	Y	Y	Y	Y
12 Dingell	N	Y	N	N	Y	Y	N
13 Conyers	N	Y	N	N	?	?	N
14 Lawrence	N	?	N	N	+	+	N
MINNESOTA							
1 Walz	N	N	N	Y	Y	Y	N
2 **Lewis**	Y	N	Y	Y	Y	Y	Y
3 **Paulsen**	Y	N	Y	Y	Y	Y	Y
4 McCollum	N	Y	N	N	Y	Y	N
5 Ellison	N	Y	N	N	Y	Y	N
6 **Emmer**	Y	N	Y	Y	Y	Y	Y
7 Peterson	N	N	N	Y	Y	Y	N
8 Nolan	N	Y	N	Y	Y	Y	N
MISSISSIPPI							
1 **Kelly**	Y	N	Y	Y	Y	Y	Y
2 Thompson	N	Y	N	N	Y	Y	N
3 **Harper**	Y	N	Y	Y	Y	Y	Y
4 **Palazzo**	Y	N	Y	Y	Y	Y	Y
MISSOURI							
1 Clay	N	Y	N	N	Y	Y	N
2 **Wagner**	Y	N	Y	Y	Y	Y	Y
3 **Luetkemeyer**	Y	N	Y	Y	Y	Y	Y
4 **Hartzler**	Y	N	Y	Y	Y	Y	Y
5 Cleaver	N	+	–	–	Y	Y	N
6 **Graves**	Y	N	Y	Y	Y	Y	Y
7 **Long**	Y	N	Y	Y	Y	Y	Y
8 **Smith**	Y	N	Y	Y	Y	Y	Y
MONTANA							
AL **Zinke**	?	?	?	?	?	?	?
NEBRASKA							
1 **Fortenberry**	Y	N	Y	Y	Y	Y	Y
2 **Bacon**	Y	N	Y	Y	Y	Y	Y
3 **Smith**	Y	N	Y	Y	Y	Y	Y
NEVADA							
1 Titus	N	Y	N	N	Y	Y	N
2 **Amodei**	Y	N	Y	Y	Y	Y	Y
3 Rosen	N	N	N	N	Y	Y	N
4 Kihuen	N	Y	N	N	Y	Y	N
NEW HAMPSHIRE							
1 Shea-Porter	N	Y	N	N	Y	Y	N
2 Kuster	N	N	N	Y	Y	Y	N
NEW JERSEY							
1 Norcross	N	Y	N	Y	Y	Y	N
2 **LoBiondo**	Y	N	Y	Y	Y	Y	Y
3 **MacArthur**	Y	N	N	Y	Y	Y	Y
4 **Smith**	Y	N	Y	Y	Y	Y	Y
5 Gottheimer	N	N	N	Y	Y	Y	N
6 Pallone	N	Y	N	N	Y	Y	N
7 **Lance**	Y	N	Y	Y	Y	Y	Y
8 Sires	N	Y	N	Y	Y	Y	N
9 Pascrell	N	Y	N	Y	Y	Y	N
10 Payne	N	Y	N	N	+	+	?
11 **Frelinghuysen**	Y	N	Y	Y	Y	Y	Y
12 Watson Coleman	N	Y	N	N	Y	Y	N
NEW MEXICO							
1 Lujan Grisham	N	Y	N	N	Y	Y	N
2 **Pearce**	Y	N	Y	Y	Y	Y	Y
3 Luján	N	Y	N	N	Y	Y	N
NEW YORK							
1 **Zeldin**	Y	N	Y	Y	Y	Y	Y
2 **King**	Y	N	Y	Y	Y	Y	Y
3 Suozzi	–	N	N	Y	Y	Y	N
4 Rice	N	N	N	N	Y	Y	N
5 Meeks	N	Y	N	N	Y	Y	N
6 Meng	N	Y	N	N	Y	Y	N
7 Velázquez	N	Y	N	N	Y	Y	?
8 Jeffries	N	Y	N	N	Y	Y	N
9 Clarke	N	Y	N	N	?	Y	N
10 Nadler	N	Y	N	N	Y	Y	N
11 **Donovan**	Y	N	Y	Y	Y	Y	Y
12 Maloney, C.	N	Y	N	N	Y	Y	N
13 Espaillat	N	Y	N	N	Y	Y	N
14 Crowley	?	Y	N	N	Y	Y	N
15 Serrano	N	Y	N	N	Y	Y	N
16 Engel	N	Y	N	N	?	Y	N
17 Lowey	N	Y	N	N	Y	Y	N
18 Maloney, S.P.	N	Y	N	Y	Y	Y	N
19 **Faso**	Y	N	Y	Y	Y	Y	Y
20 Tonko	N	Y	N	N	Y	Y	N
21 **Stefanik**	Y	N	Y	Y	Y	Y	Y
22 **Tenney**	Y	N	Y	Y	Y	Y	Y
23 **Reed**	Y	N	Y	Y	Y	Y	Y
24 **Katko**	Y	N	N	Y	Y	Y	Y
25 Slaughter	N	Y	N	N	Y	Y	–
26 Higgins	N	Y	N	N	Y	Y	N
27 **Collins**	Y	N	Y	Y	Y	Y	Y
NORTH CAROLINA							
1 Butterfield	N	Y	N	N	Y	Y	N
2 **Holding**	Y	N	Y	Y	Y	Y	Y
3 **Jones**	Y	N	N	?	?	?	?
4 Price	N	Y	N	N	Y	Y	N
5 **Foxx**	Y	N	Y	Y	Y	Y	Y
6 **Walker**	Y	N	Y	Y	Y	Y	Y
7 **Rouzer**	Y	N	Y	Y	Y	Y	Y
8 **Hudson**	Y	N	Y	Y	Y	Y	Y
9 **Pittenger**	Y	N	Y	Y	Y	Y	Y
10 **McHenry**	Y	N	Y	Y	Y	Y	Y
11 **Meadows**	Y	N	Y	Y	Y	Y	Y
12 Adams	N	Y	N	N	Y	Y	N
13 **Budd**	Y	N	Y	Y	Y	Y	Y
NORTH DAKOTA							
AL **Cramer**	Y	N	Y	Y	Y	Y	Y
OHIO							
1 **Chabot**	Y	N	Y	Y	Y	Y	Y
2 **Wenstrup**	Y	N	Y	Y	Y	Y	Y
3 Beatty	N	Y	N	N	+	Y	N
4 **Jordan**	Y	N	Y	Y	N	Y	Y
5 **Latta**	Y	N	Y	Y	Y	Y	Y
6 **Johnson**	Y	N	Y	Y	Y	Y	Y
7 **Gibbs**	Y	N	Y	Y	Y	Y	Y
8 **Davidson**	Y	N	Y	Y	Y	Y	Y
9 Kaptur	N	Y	N	N	?	?	N
10 **Turner**	Y	N	Y	Y	Y	Y	Y
11 Fudge	N	Y	N	N	Y	Y	N
12 **Tiberi**	Y	N	Y	Y	Y	Y	Y
13 Ryan	N	Y	N	Y	Y	Y	N
14 **Joyce**	Y	N	Y	Y	Y	Y	?
15 **Stivers**	Y	N	Y	Y	Y	Y	Y
16 **Renacci**	Y	N	Y	Y	Y	Y	Y
OKLAHOMA							
1 **Bridenstine**	Y	N	Y	Y	Y	Y	Y
2 **Mullin**	Y	N	Y	Y	Y	Y	Y
3 **Lucas**	Y	N	Y	Y	Y	Y	Y
4 **Cole**	Y	N	Y	Y	Y	Y	Y
5 **Russell**	Y	N	Y	Y	Y	Y	Y
OREGON							
1 Bonamici	N	Y	N	N	Y	Y	N
2 **Walden**	Y	N	Y	Y	Y	Y	Y
3 Blumenauer	N	Y	N	N	+	+	–
4 DeFazio	N	Y	N	Y	Y	Y	N
5 Schrader	N	N	N	N	Y	Y	N
PENNSYLVANIA							
1 Brady	N	Y	N	N	Y	Y	N
2 Evans	N	Y	N	N	Y	Y	N
3 **Kelly**	Y	N	Y	Y	Y	Y	Y
4 **Perry**	Y	N	Y	Y	Y	Y	Y
5 **Thompson**	Y	N	Y	Y	Y	Y	Y
6 **Costello**	Y	N	Y	Y	Y	Y	Y
7 **Meehan**	Y	N	Y	Y	Y	Y	Y
8 **Fitzpatrick**	Y	N	N	Y	Y	Y	Y
9 **Shuster**	Y	N	Y	Y	Y	Y	Y
10 **Marino**	Y	N	Y	Y	Y	Y	Y
11 **Barletta**	Y	N	Y	Y	Y	Y	Y
12 **Rothfus**	Y	N	Y	Y	Y	Y	Y
13 Boyle	N	Y	N	N	Y	Y	N
14 Doyle	N	Y	N	N	Y	Y	N
15 **Dent**	Y	N	N	Y	Y	Y	Y
16 **Smucker**	Y	N	Y	Y	Y	Y	Y
17 Cartwright	N	Y	N	Y	Y	Y	N
18 **Murphy**	Y	N	Y	Y	Y	Y	Y
RHODE ISLAND							
1 Cicilline	N	Y	N	N	Y	Y	N
2 Langevin	N	Y	N	N	Y	Y	N
SOUTH CAROLINA							
1 **Sanford**	Y	N	Y	Y	Y	Y	Y
2 **Wilson**	Y	N	Y	Y	Y	Y	Y
3 **Duncan**	Y	N	Y	Y	?	?	Y
4 **Gowdy**	Y	N	Y	Y	Y	Y	Y
5 **Mulvaney**	?	?	?	?	?	?	?
6 Clyburn	N	?	?	?	?	Y	N
7 **Rice**	Y	N	Y	Y	Y	Y	Y
SOUTH DAKOTA							
AL **Noem**	Y	N	Y	Y	Y	Y	Y
TENNESSEE							
1 **Roe**	Y	N	Y	Y	Y	Y	Y
2 **Duncan**	Y	N	Y	Y	Y	Y	Y
3 **Fleischmann**	Y	N	Y	Y	Y	Y	Y
4 **DesJarlais**	Y	N	Y	Y	Y	Y	Y
5 Cooper	N	N	N	Y	Y	Y	N
6 **Black**	Y	N	Y	Y	Y	Y	Y
7 **Blackburn**	Y	N	Y	Y	Y	Y	Y
8 **Kustoff**	Y	N	Y	Y	Y	Y	Y
9 Cohen	N	Y	N	Y	Y	Y	N
TEXAS							
1 **Gohmert**	Y	N	Y	Y	N	Y	Y
2 **Poe**	Y	N	Y	Y	Y	Y	Y
3 **Johnson, S.**	Y	N	Y	Y	Y	Y	Y
4 **Ratcliffe**	Y	N	Y	Y	Y	Y	Y
5 **Hensarling**	Y	N	Y	Y	Y	Y	Y
6 **Barton**	Y	N	Y	Y	?	?	Y
7 **Culberson**	Y	N	Y	Y	Y	Y	Y
8 **Brady**	Y	N	Y	Y	Y	Y	Y
9 Green, A.	N	Y	N	N	Y	Y	N
10 **McCaul**	Y	N	Y	Y	Y	Y	Y
11 **Conaway**	Y	N	Y	Y	Y	Y	Y
12 **Granger**	Y	N	Y	Y	Y	Y	Y
13 **Thornberry**	Y	N	Y	Y	Y	Y	Y
14 **Weber**	Y	N	Y	Y	Y	Y	Y
15 Gonzalez	N	Y	N	N	Y	Y	N
16 O'Rourke	N	Y	N	N	Y	Y	N
17 **Flores**	Y	N	Y	Y	Y	Y	Y
18 Jackson Lee	N	Y	N	N	Y	Y	N
19 **Arrington**	Y	N	Y	Y	Y	Y	Y
20 Castro	N	Y	N	N	Y	Y	N
21 **Smith**	Y	N	Y	Y	Y	Y	Y
22 **Olson**	Y	N	Y	Y	Y	Y	Y
23 **Hurd**	Y	N	Y	Y	Y	Y	Y
24 **Marchant**	Y	N	Y	Y	Y	Y	Y
25 **Williams**	Y	N	Y	Y	Y	Y	Y
26 **Burgess**	Y	N	Y	Y	Y	Y	Y
27 **Farenthold**	Y	N	Y	Y	Y	Y	Y
28 Cuellar	N	N	N	Y	Y	Y	N
29 Green, G.	N	+	–	–	Y	Y	N
30 Johnson, E.B.	N	Y	N	?	Y	Y	–
31 **Carter**	Y	N	Y	Y	Y	Y	Y
32 **Sessions**	Y	N	Y	Y	Y	Y	Y
33 Veasey	N	Y	N	N	Y	Y	N
34 Vela	N	Y	N	N	Y	Y	N
35 Doggett	N	Y	N	N	Y	Y	N
36 **Babin**	Y	N	Y	Y	Y	Y	Y
UTAH							
1 **Bishop**	Y	N	Y	Y	Y	Y	Y
2 **Stewart**	Y	N	Y	Y	Y	Y	Y
3 **Chaffetz**	Y	N	Y	Y	Y	Y	Y
4 **Love**	Y	N	Y	Y	Y	Y	Y
VERMONT							
AL Welch	N	Y	N	N	Y	Y	N
VIRGINIA							
1 **Wittman**	Y	N	Y	Y	Y	Y	Y
2 **Taylor**	Y	N	Y	Y	Y	Y	Y
3 Scott	N	Y	N	N	Y	Y	N
4 McEachin	N	Y	N	N	Y	Y	N
5 **Garrett**	Y	N	Y	Y	Y	Y	Y
6 **Goodlatte**	Y	N	Y	Y	Y	Y	Y
7 **Brat**	Y	N	Y	Y	Y	Y	Y
8 Beyer	N	Y	N	Y	Y	Y	N
9 **Griffith**	Y	N	Y	Y	Y	Y	Y
10 **Comstock**	Y	N	Y	Y	Y	Y	Y
11 Connolly	N	N	N	Y	Y	Y	N
WASHINGTON							
1 DelBene	N	N	N	N	Y	Y	N
2 Larsen	N	Y	N	N	Y	Y	N
3 **Herrera Beutler**	Y	N	Y	Y	Y	Y	Y
4 **Newhouse**	Y	N	Y	Y	Y	Y	Y
5 **McMorris Rodgers**	Y	N	Y	Y	Y	Y	Y
6 Kilmer	N	N	N	N	Y	Y	N
7 Jayapal	N	Y	N	N	Y	Y	N
8 **Reichert**	Y	N	Y	Y	–	–	Y
9 Smith	N	Y	N	N	Y	Y	N
10 Heck	N	Y	N	N	Y	Y	N
WEST VIRGINIA							
1 **McKinley**	Y	N	Y	Y	Y	Y	Y
2 **Mooney**	Y	N	Y	Y	Y	Y	Y
3 **Jenkins**	Y	N	Y	Y	Y	Y	Y
WISCONSIN							
1 **Ryan**			Y				
2 Pocan	N	Y	N	N	?	?	N
3 Kind	N	N	N	N	Y	Y	N
4 Moore	N	Y	N	N	Y	Y	N
5 **Sensenbrenner**	Y	N	Y	Y	Y	Y	Y
6 **Grothman**	Y	N	Y	Y	Y	Y	Y
7 **Duffy**	Y	N	Y	Y	Y	Y	Y
8 **Gallagher**	Y	N	Y	Y	Y	Y	Y
WYOMING							
AL **Cheney**	Y	N	Y	Y	Y	Y	Y

VOTE NUMBER

63. H RES 55, HR 7. PERMANENT PROHIBITION ON FEDERAL FUNDING FOR ABORTIONS/RULE. Adoption of the rule (H Res 55) that would provide for House floor consideration of the bill (HR 7) that would permanently prohibit the use of federal funds to pay for abortion services or health insurance plans that include coverage for abortions. It also would bar the District of Columbia from using its own local funds to provide or pay for abortions. Adopted 236-183 : R 234-0; D 2-183. Jan. 24, 2017.

64. HR 7. PERMANENT PROHIBITION ON FEDERAL FUNDING FOR ABORTIONS/RECOMMIT. Schakowsky, D-Ill., motion to recommit the bill to the House Energy and Commerce Committee with instructions to report back immediately with an amendment that would state that the bill could not be interpreted to allow health insurance plans to charge women higher premiums than they charge men. Motion rejected 187-235 : R 0-235; D 187-0. Jan. 24, 2017.

65. HR 7. PERMANENT PROHIBITION ON FEDERAL FUNDING FOR ABORTIONS/PASSAGE. Passage of the bill that would permanently prohibit federal funds from being used to pay for abortion services or health insurance plans that include abortion coverage. It also would prohibit the District of Columbia from using its own local funds to provide or pay for abortions. Individuals and small businesses also could not receive tax credits under the 2010 health care law related to purchases of health insurance plans that include abortion coverage. The bill would require the Office of Personnel Management to ensure that, starting in 2018, no multistate qualified health plan offered in a state insurance exchange provides coverage that includes abortion. The provisions would not apply to pregnancies resulting from rape or incest, or to situations where the woman would die unless an abortion is performed. Passed 238-183 : R 235-0; D 3-183. Jan. 24, 2017.

66. HR 374. CRAB FISHERY MANAGEMENT/PASSAGE. McClintock, R-Calif., motion to suspend the rules and pass the bill that would permanently give the states of Washington, Oregon and California the authority to manage the Pacific Dungeness crab fishery in adjacent federal waters. Motion agreed to 388-0 : R 228-0; D 160-0. Jan. 30, 2017.

67. HR 538. OCMULGEE MONUMENT REDESIGNATION AND EXPANSION/PASSAGE. McClintock, R-Calif., motion to suspend the rules and pass the bill that would redesignate the Ocmulgee National Monument in Georgia as the Ocmulgee Mounds National Historical Park. It also would expand the boundary of the park by 2,100 acres, and it would require the National Park Service to only acquire the additional lands by donation or exchange. Motion agreed to 396-8 : R 219-8; D 177-0. Jan. 30, 2017.

68. H RES 70, H J RES 38. STREAM PROTECTION RULE DISAPPROVAL/PREVIOUS QUESTION. Newhouse, R-Wash., motion to order the previous question (thus ending debate and the possibility of amendment) on the rule (H Res 70) that would provide for House floor consideration of the joint resolution (H J Res 38) that would nullify and disapprove of an Office of Surface Mining Reclamation and Enforcement rule that requires surface coal mining operations, to the extent possible, to avoid disturbing streams and land within 100 feet of the streams. Motion agreed to 236-183 : R 235-0; D 1-183. Jan. 31, 2017.

69. H RES 70, H J RES 38. STREAM PROTECTION RULE DISAPPROVAL/RULE. Adoption of the rule (H Res 70) that would provide for House floor consideration of the joint resolution (H J Res 38) would nullify and disapprove of an Office of Surface Mining Reclamation and Enforcement rule that requires surface coal mining operations, to the extent possible, to avoid disturbing streams and land within 100 feet of the streams. Adopted 236-186 : R 236-0; D 0-186. Jan. 31, 2017.

	63	64	65	66	67	68	69
ALABAMA							
1 Byrne	Y	N	Y	Y	Y	Y	Y
2 Roby	Y	N	Y	Y	Y	Y	Y
3 Rogers	Y	N	Y	Y	Y	Y	Y
4 Aderholt	Y	N	Y	Y	Y	Y	Y
5 Brooks	Y	N	Y	Y	Y	Y	Y
6 Palmer	Y	N	Y	Y	Y	Y	Y
7 Sewell	N	Y	N	+	Y	–	N
ALASKA							
AL Young	Y	N	Y	Y	Y	Y	Y
ARIZONA							
1 O'Halleran	N	Y	N	Y	Y	N	N
2 McSally	Y	N	Y	Y	Y	Y	Y
3 Grijalva	N	Y	N	?	?	N	N
4 Gosar	Y	N	Y	Y	Y	Y	Y
5 Biggs	Y	N	Y	Y	Y	Y	Y
6 Schweikert	Y	N	Y	Y	Y	Y	Y
7 Gallego	N	Y	N	+	+	N	N
8 Franks	Y	N	Y	Y	Y	Y	Y
9 Sinema	N	Y	N	Y	Y	N	N
ARKANSAS							
1 Crawford	Y	N	Y	Y	Y	Y	Y
2 Hill	Y	N	Y	Y	Y	Y	Y
3 Womack	Y	N	Y	Y	Y	Y	Y
4 Westerman	Y	N	Y	Y	Y	Y	Y
CALIFORNIA							
1 LaMalfa	Y	N	Y	Y	Y	Y	Y
2 Huffman	–	Y	N	Y	Y	N	N
3 Garamendi	N	Y	N	Y	Y	N	N
4 McClintock	Y	N	Y	Y	Y	Y	Y
5 Thompson	N	Y	N	Y	Y	N	N
6 Matsui	N	Y	N	Y	Y	N	N
7 Bera	N	Y	N	Y	Y	N	N
8 Cook	Y	N	Y	Y	Y	Y	Y
9 McNerney	N	Y	N	Y	Y	N	N
10 Denham	Y	N	Y	Y	Y	Y	Y
11 DeSaulnier	N	Y	N	Y	Y	N	N
12 Pelosi	N	Y	N	?	Y	?	?
13 Lee	N	Y	N	Y	Y	N	N
14 Speier	N	Y	N	Y	Y	N	N
15 Swalwell	N	Y	N	Y	Y	N	N
16 Costa	N	?	?	?	?	N	Y
17 Khanna	N	Y	N	Y	Y	N	N
18 Eshoo	N	Y	N	Y	Y	N	N
19 Lofgren	N	Y	N	Y	Y	–	–
20 Panetta	N	Y	N	Y	Y	N	N
21 Valadao	Y	N	Y	Y	Y	Y	Y
22 Nunes	Y	N	Y	Y	Y	Y	Y
23 McCarthy	Y	N	Y	Y	Y	Y	Y
24 Carbajal	N	Y	N	Y	Y	N	N
25 Knight	Y	N	Y	Y	Y	Y	Y
26 Brownley	N	Y	N	Y	Y	N	N
27 Chu	N	Y	N	?	Y	N	N
28 Schiff	N	Y	N	Y	Y	N	N
29 Cardenas	N	Y	N	Y	Y	N	N
30 Sherman	N	Y	N	Y	Y	N	N
31 Aguilar	N	Y	N	Y	Y	N	N
32 Napolitano	N	Y	N	+	Y	N	N
33 Lieu	N	Y	?	Y	Y	N	N
34 Vacant							
35 Torres	N	Y	N	Y	Y	N	N
36 Ruiz	N	Y	N	Y	Y	N	N
37 Bass	N	Y	N	Y	Y	N	N
38 Sánchez, Linda	N	Y	N	Y	Y	N	N
39 Royce	Y	N	Y	Y	Y	Y	Y
40 Roybal-Allard	N	Y	N	Y	Y	N	N
41 Takano	N	Y	N	Y	Y	N	N
42 Calvert	Y	N	Y	Y	Y	Y	Y
43 Waters	N	Y	N	Y	Y	N	N
44 Barragan	N	Y	N	Y	Y	N	N
45 Walters	Y	N	Y	Y	Y	Y	Y
46 Correa	N	Y	N	Y	Y	N	N
47 Lowenthal	N	Y	N	Y	Y	N	N
48 Rohrabacher	Y	N	Y	Y	Y	Y	Y
49 Issa	Y	N	Y	Y	Y	Y	Y
50 Hunter	Y	N	Y	Y	Y	Y	Y
51 Vargas	N	Y	N	Y	Y	N	N
52 Peters	N	Y	N	Y	Y	N	N
53 Davis	N	Y	N	+	Y	N	N

	63	64	65	66	67	68	69
COLORADO							
1 DeGette	N	Y	N	Y	Y	N	N
2 Polis	N	Y	N	Y	Y	N	N
3 Tipton	Y	N	Y	Y	Y	Y	Y
4 Buck	Y	N	Y	Y	Y	Y	Y
5 Lamborn	Y	N	Y	Y	Y	Y	Y
6 Coffman	+	N	Y	Y	Y	Y	Y
7 Perlmutter	N	Y	N	Y	Y	N	N
CONNECTICUT							
1 Larson	N	Y	N	Y	Y	N	N
2 Courtney	N	Y	N	Y	Y	N	N
3 DeLauro	N	Y	N	Y	Y	N	N
4 Himes	N	Y	N	Y	Y	N	N
5 Esty	N	Y	N	Y	Y	N	N
DELAWARE							
AL Blunt Rochester	N	Y	N	Y	Y	N	N
FLORIDA							
1 Gaetz	Y	N	Y	Y	Y	Y	Y
2 Dunn	Y	N	Y	Y	Y	Y	Y
3 Yoho	Y	N	Y	Y	Y	Y	Y
4 Rutherford	Y	N	Y	Y	Y	Y	Y
5 Lawson	N	Y	N	?	Y	N	N
6 DeSantis	Y	N	Y	Y	Y	Y	Y
7 Murphy	N	Y	N	Y	Y	N	N
8 Posey	Y	N	Y	Y	Y	Y	Y
9 Soto	N	Y	N	Y	Y	N	N
10 Demings	N	Y	N	Y	Y	N	N
11 Webster	Y	N	Y	Y	Y	Y	Y
12 Bilirakis	Y	N	Y	Y	Y	Y	Y
13 Crist	N	Y	N	Y	Y	N	N
14 Castor	N	Y	N	Y	Y	N	N
15 Ross	Y	N	Y	Y	Y	Y	Y
16 Buchanan	Y	N	Y	Y	Y	Y	Y
17 Rooney, T.	Y	N	Y	Y	Y	Y	Y
18 Mast	Y	N	Y	Y	Y	Y	Y
19 Rooney, F.	Y	N	Y	Y	Y	Y	Y
20 Hastings	N	Y	N	Y	Y	N	N
21 Frankel	N	Y	N	Y	Y	N	N
22 Deutch	N	Y	N	Y	Y	N	N
23 Wasserman Schultz	N	Y	N	Y	Y	N	N
24 Wilson	N	Y	N	Y	Y	N	N
25 Diaz-Balart	Y	N	Y	Y	Y	Y	Y
26 Curbelo	Y	N	Y	Y	Y	Y	Y
27 Ros-Lehtinen	Y	N	Y	Y	Y	Y	Y
GEORGIA							
1 Carter	Y	N	Y	Y	Y	Y	Y
2 Bishop	N	Y	N	Y	Y	N	N
3 Ferguson	Y	N	Y	Y	Y	Y	Y
4 Johnson	N	Y	N	?	Y	N	N
5 Lewis	N	Y	N	Y	Y	N	N
6 Price	?	?	?	?	?	?	?
7 Woodall	Y	N	Y	Y	Y	Y	Y
8 Scott, A.	Y	N	Y	Y	Y	Y	Y
9 Collins	Y	N	Y	Y	Y	Y	Y
10 Hice	Y	N	Y	Y	Y	Y	Y
11 Loudermilk	Y	N	Y	Y	Y	Y	Y
12 Allen	Y	N	Y	Y	Y	Y	Y
13 Scott, D.	N	Y	N	Y	Y	N	N
14 Graves	Y	N	Y	Y	Y	Y	Y
HAWAII							
1 Hanabusa	N	Y	N	Y	Y	N	N
2 Gabbard	N	?	?	Y	Y	N	N
IDAHO							
1 Labrador	Y	N	Y	Y	Y	Y	Y
2 Simpson	Y	N	Y	Y	Y	Y	Y
ILLINOIS							
1 Rush	?	?	?	?	?	?	?
2 Kelly	N	Y	N	Y	Y	N	N
3 Lipinski	Y	Y	Y	Y	Y	N	N
4 Gutierrez	N	Y	N	+	+	N	N
5 Quigley	N	Y	N	?	?	?	?
6 Roskam	Y	N	Y	Y	Y	Y	Y
7 Davis, D.	N	Y	N	Y	Y	N	N
8 Krishnamoorthi	N	Y	N	+	Y	N	N
9 Schakowsky	N	Y	N	Y	Y	N	N
10 Schneider	N	Y	N	Y	Y	N	N
11 Foster	N	Y	N	Y	Y	N	N
12 Bost	Y	N	Y	Y	Y	Y	Y
13 Davis, R.	Y	N	Y	Y	Y	Y	Y
14 Hultgren	Y	N	Y	Y	Y	Y	Y
15 Shimkus	Y	N	Y	Y	Y	Y	Y

KEY

Republicans	Democrats	Independents
Y Voted for (yea)	X Paired against	C Voted "present" to avoid possible conflict of interest
# Paired for	– Announced against	
+ Announced for	P Voted "present"	? Did not vote or otherwise make a position known
N Voted against (nay)		

	63	64	65	66	67	68	69
16 **Kinzinger**	Y	N	Y	+	+	Y	Y
17 Bustos	N	Y	N	Y	+	N	N
18 **LaHood**	Y	N	Y	Y	Y	Y	Y
INDIANA							
1 Visclosky	N	Y	N	Y	Y	N	N
2 **Walorski**	Y	N	Y	Y	Y	Y	Y
3 **Banks**	Y	N	Y	Y	Y	Y	Y
4 **Rokita**	Y	N	Y	Y	Y	Y	Y
5 **Brooks**	Y	N	Y	Y	Y	Y	Y
6 **Messer**	Y	N	Y	Y	?	Y	Y
7 Carson	N	Y	N	Y	Y	N	N
8 **Bucshon**	Y	N	Y	Y	Y	Y	Y
9 **Hollingsworth**	Y	N	Y	Y	Y	Y	Y
IOWA							
1 **Blum**	Y	N	Y	Y	Y	Y	Y
2 Loebsack	N	Y	N	Y	Y	N	N
3 **Young**	Y	N	Y	Y	Y	Y	Y
4 **King**	Y	N	Y	Y	Y	Y	Y
KANSAS							
1 **Marshall**	Y	N	Y	Y	Y	Y	Y
2 **Jenkins**	Y	N	Y	Y	Y	Y	Y
3 **Yoder**	Y	N	Y	Y	Y	Y	Y
KENTUCKY							
1 **Comer**	Y	N	Y	Y	Y	Y	Y
2 **Guthrie**	Y	N	Y	Y	Y	Y	Y
3 Yarmuth	N	Y	N	Y	Y	N	N
4 **Massie**	Y	N	Y	Y	N	Y	Y
5 **Rogers**	Y	N	Y	Y	Y	Y	Y
6 **Barr**	Y	N	Y	Y	Y	Y	Y
LOUISIANA							
1 **Scalise**	Y	N	Y	Y	Y	Y	Y
2 Richmond	N	Y	N	Y	Y	N	N
3 **Higgins**	Y	N	Y	Y	Y	Y	Y
4 **Johnson**	Y	N	Y	?	?	Y	Y
5 **Abraham**	Y	N	Y	Y	Y	Y	Y
6 **Graves**	Y	N	Y	Y	Y	Y	Y
MAINE							
1 Pingree	N	Y	N	Y	Y	N	N
2 **Poliquin**	Y	N	Y	Y	Y	Y	Y
MARYLAND							
1 **Harris**	Y	N	Y	Y	Y	Y	Y
2 Ruppersberger	N	Y	N	Y	Y	N	N
3 Sarbanes	N	Y	N	Y	Y	N	N
4 Brown	N	Y	N	Y	Y	N	N
5 Hoyer	N	Y	N	?	Y	N	N
6 Delaney	N	Y	N	Y	Y	N	N
7 Cummings	N	Y	N	Y	Y	N	N
8 Raskin	N	Y	N	Y	Y	N	N
MASSACHUSETTS							
1 Neal	N	Y	N	Y	Y	N	N
2 McGovern	N	Y	N	Y	Y	N	N
3 Tsongas	N	Y	N	Y	Y	N	N
4 Kennedy	N	Y	N	Y	Y	N	N
5 Clark	N	Y	N	?	?	?	?
6 Moulton	N	Y	N	Y	Y	N	N
7 Capuano	N	Y	N	Y	Y	N	N
8 Lynch	N	Y	N	Y	Y	N	N
9 Keating	N	Y	N	Y	Y	N	N
MICHIGAN							
1 **Bergman**	Y	N	Y	Y	Y	Y	Y
2 **Huizenga**	Y	N	Y	+	+	Y	Y
3 **Amash**	Y	N	Y	Y	N	Y	Y
4 **Moolenaar**	Y	N	Y	Y	Y	Y	Y
5 Kildee	N	Y	N	Y	Y	?	?
6 **Upton**	Y	N	Y	Y	Y	Y	Y
7 **Walberg**	Y	N	Y	Y	Y	Y	Y
8 **Bishop**	Y	N	Y	Y	Y	Y	Y
9 Levin	N	Y	N	Y	Y	N	N
10 **Mitchell**	Y	N	Y	Y	Y	Y	Y
11 **Trott**	Y	N	Y	Y	Y	Y	Y
12 Dingell	N	Y	N	Y	Y	N	N
13 Conyers	N	Y	N	Y	Y	N	N
14 Lawrence	N	Y	N	Y	Y	N	N
MINNESOTA							
1 Walz	N	Y	N	Y	Y	N	N
2 **Lewis**	Y	N	Y	Y	Y	Y	Y
3 **Paulsen**	Y	N	Y	Y	Y	Y	Y
4 McCollum	N	Y	N	Y	Y	N	N

	63	64	65	66	67	68	69
5 Ellison	N	Y	N	+	+	N	N
6 **Emmer**	Y	N	Y	Y	Y	Y	Y
7 Peterson	Y	Y	Y	Y	Y	Y	N
8 Nolan	N	Y	N	Y	Y	N	N
MISSISSIPPI							
1 **Kelly**	Y	N	Y	Y	Y	Y	Y
2 Thompson	N	Y	N	Y	Y	N	N
3 **Harper**	Y	N	Y	Y	Y	Y	Y
4 **Palazzo**	Y	N	Y	Y	Y	Y	Y
MISSOURI							
1 Clay	N	Y	N	Y	Y	N	N
2 **Wagner**	Y	N	Y	Y	Y	Y	Y
3 **Luetkemeyer**	Y	N	Y	Y	Y	Y	Y
4 **Hartzler**	Y	N	Y	Y	Y	Y	Y
5 Cleaver	N	Y	N	?	Y	N	N
6 **Graves**	Y	N	Y	Y	Y	Y	Y
7 **Long**	Y	N	Y	Y	Y	Y	Y
8 **Smith**	Y	N	Y	Y	Y	Y	Y
MONTANA							
AL **Zinke**	?	?	?	?	?	?	?
NEBRASKA							
1 **Fortenberry**	Y	N	Y	Y	Y	Y	Y
2 **Bacon**	Y	N	Y	Y	N	Y	Y
3 **Smith**	Y	N	Y	Y	N	Y	Y
NEVADA							
1 Titus	N	Y	N	?	?	?	?
2 **Amodei**	Y	N	Y	Y	Y	Y	Y
3 Rosen	N	Y	N	Y	Y	N	N
4 Kihuen	N	Y	N	Y	Y	N	N
NEW HAMPSHIRE							
1 Shea-Porter	N	Y	N	Y	Y	N	N
2 Kuster	N	Y	N	Y	Y	N	N
NEW JERSEY							
1 Norcross	N	Y	N	Y	Y	N	N
2 **LoBiondo**	Y	N	Y	Y	Y	Y	Y
3 **MacArthur**	Y	N	Y	Y	Y	Y	Y
4 **Smith**	Y	N	Y	Y	Y	Y	Y
5 Gottheimer	N	Y	N	Y	Y	N	N
6 Pallone	N	Y	N	Y	Y	N	N
7 **Lance**	Y	N	Y	Y	Y	Y	Y
8 Sires	N	Y	N	Y	Y	N	N
9 Pascrell	N	Y	N	Y	Y	N	N
10 Payne	?	Y	N	Y	Y	N	N
11 **Frelinghuysen**	Y	N	Y	Y	Y	Y	Y
12 Watson Coleman	N	Y	N	Y	Y	N	N
NEW MEXICO							
1 Lujan Grisham	N	Y	N	Y	Y	N	N
2 **Pearce**	Y	N	Y	Y	Y	Y	Y
3 Luján	N	Y	N	Y	Y	N	N
NEW YORK							
1 **Zeldin**	Y	N	Y	Y	Y	Y	Y
2 **King**	Y	N	Y	Y	Y	Y	Y
3 Suozzi	N	Y	N	Y	Y	N	N
4 Rice	N	Y	N	Y	Y	N	N
5 Meeks	N	Y	N	?	Y	N	N
6 Meng	N	Y	N	?	?	N	N
7 Velázquez	N	Y	N	?	Y	N	N
8 Jeffries	N	Y	N	Y	Y	N	N
9 Clarke	N	Y	N	Y	Y	N	N
10 Nadler	N	Y	N	?	Y	N	N
11 **Donovan**	Y	N	Y	Y	Y	Y	Y
12 Maloney, C.	N	Y	N	Y	Y	N	N
13 Espaillat	N	Y	N	Y	Y	N	N
14 Crowley	N	Y	N	Y	Y	N	N
15 Serrano	N	Y	N	Y	Y	N	N
16 Engel	N	Y	N	Y	Y	?	N
17 Lowey	N	Y	N	Y	Y	N	N
18 Maloney, S.P.	N	Y	N	Y	Y	N	N
19 **Faso**	Y	N	Y	Y	Y	Y	Y
20 Tonko	N	Y	N	+	Y	N	N
21 **Stefanik**	Y	N	Y	Y	Y	Y	Y
22 **Tenney**	Y	N	Y	Y	Y	Y	Y
23 **Reed**	Y	N	Y	Y	Y	Y	Y
24 **Katko**	Y	N	Y	Y	Y	Y	Y
25 Slaughter	–	+	–	+	+	N	N
26 Higgins	N	Y	N	Y	Y	N	N
27 **Collins**	Y	N	Y	Y	Y	Y	Y
NORTH CAROLINA							
1 Butterfield	N	Y	N	?	Y	N	N
2 **Holding**	Y	N	Y	Y	Y	Y	Y
3 **Jones**	?	?	?	Y	N	Y	Y
4 Price	N	Y	N	Y	Y	N	N

	63	64	65	66	67	68	69
5 **Foxx**	Y	N	Y	Y	Y	Y	Y
6 **Walker**	Y	N	Y	Y	Y	Y	Y
7 **Rouzer**	Y	N	Y	Y	Y	Y	Y
8 **Hudson**	Y	N	Y	Y	Y	Y	Y
9 **Pittenger**	Y	N	Y	Y	Y	Y	Y
10 **McHenry**	Y	N	Y	Y	Y	Y	Y
11 **Meadows**	Y	N	Y	Y	Y	Y	Y
12 Adams	N	Y	N	Y	Y	N	N
13 **Budd**	Y	N	Y	Y	Y	Y	Y
NORTH DAKOTA							
AL **Cramer**	Y	N	Y	Y	Y	Y	Y
OHIO							
1 **Chabot**	Y	N	Y	Y	Y	Y	Y
2 **Wenstrup**	Y	N	Y	Y	Y	Y	Y
3 Beatty	N	Y	N	Y	Y	N	N
4 **Jordan**	Y	N	Y	Y	Y	Y	Y
5 **Latta**	Y	N	Y	Y	Y	Y	Y
6 **Johnson**	Y	N	Y	Y	Y	Y	Y
7 **Gibbs**	Y	N	Y	Y	Y	Y	Y
8 **Davidson**	Y	N	Y	Y	Y	Y	Y
9 Kaptur	N	Y	N	Y	Y	N	N
10 **Turner**	Y	N	Y	Y	Y	Y	Y
11 Fudge	N	Y	N	Y	Y	N	N
12 **Tiberi**	Y	N	Y	+	+	Y	Y
13 Ryan	N	Y	N	?	?	N	N
14 **Joyce**	Y	N	Y	Y	Y	Y	Y
15 **Stivers**	Y	N	Y	Y	Y	Y	Y
16 **Renacci**	Y	N	Y	+	+	Y	Y
OKLAHOMA							
1 **Bridenstine**	Y	N	Y	Y	Y	Y	Y
2 **Mullin**	Y	N	Y	Y	Y	Y	Y
3 **Lucas**	Y	N	Y	Y	Y	Y	Y
4 **Cole**	Y	N	Y	Y	Y	Y	Y
5 **Russell**	Y	N	Y	Y	Y	Y	Y
OREGON							
1 Bonamici	N	Y	N	Y	Y	N	N
2 **Walden**	Y	N	Y	Y	Y	Y	Y
3 Blumenauer	–	+	–	Y	Y	N	N
4 DeFazio	N	Y	N	+	+	N	N
5 Schrader	?	Y	N	Y	Y	N	N
PENNSYLVANIA							
1 Brady	N	Y	N	Y	Y	N	N
2 Evans	N	Y	N	Y	Y	N	N
3 **Kelly**	Y	N	Y	Y	Y	Y	Y
4 **Perry**	Y	N	Y	Y	Y	Y	Y
5 **Thompson**	Y	N	Y	Y	Y	Y	Y
6 **Costello**	Y	N	Y	Y	Y	Y	Y
7 **Meehan**	Y	N	Y	Y	Y	Y	Y
8 **Fitzpatrick**	Y	N	Y	Y	Y	Y	Y
9 **Shuster**	Y	N	Y	Y	Y	Y	Y
10 **Marino**	Y	N	Y	Y	Y	Y	Y
11 **Barletta**	Y	N	Y	Y	Y	Y	Y
12 **Rothfus**	Y	N	Y	Y	Y	Y	Y
13 Boyle	N	Y	N	Y	Y	N	N
14 Doyle	N	Y	N	Y	Y	N	N
15 **Dent**	Y	N	Y	Y	Y	Y	Y
16 **Smucker**	Y	N	Y	Y	Y	Y	Y
17 Cartwright	N	Y	N	Y	Y	N	N
18 **Murphy**	Y	N	Y	Y	Y	Y	Y
RHODE ISLAND							
1 Cicilline	N	Y	N	Y	Y	N	N
2 Langevin	N	Y	N	+	Y	N	N
SOUTH CAROLINA							
1 **Sanford**	Y	N	Y	Y	N	Y	Y
2 **Wilson**	Y	N	Y	Y	Y	Y	Y
3 **Duncan**	Y	N	Y	Y	Y	Y	Y
4 **Gowdy**	Y	N	Y	Y	Y	Y	Y
5 **Mulvaney**	?	?	?	?	?	?	?
6 Clyburn	N	Y	N	Y	Y	N	N
7 **Rice**	Y	N	Y	Y	Y	Y	Y
SOUTH DAKOTA							
AL **Noem**	Y	N	Y	Y	Y	Y	Y
TENNESSEE							
1 **Roe**	Y	N	Y	Y	Y	Y	Y
2 **Duncan**	Y	N	Y	Y	N	Y	Y
3 **Fleischmann**	Y	N	Y	Y	Y	Y	Y
4 **DesJarlais**	Y	N	Y	?	?	Y	Y
5 Cooper	N	Y	N	Y	Y	N	N
6 **Black**	Y	N	Y	Y	Y	Y	Y
7 **Blackburn**	Y	N	Y	?	?	Y	Y
8 **Kustoff**	Y	N	Y	Y	Y	Y	Y
9 Cohen	N	Y	N	Y	Y	N	N

	63	64	65	66	67	68	69
TEXAS							
1 **Gohmert**	Y	N	Y	Y	Y	Y	Y
2 **Poe**	Y	N	Y	Y	Y	Y	Y
3 **Johnson, S.**	Y	N	Y	Y	Y	Y	Y
4 **Ratcliffe**	Y	N	Y	Y	Y	Y	Y
5 **Hensarling**	Y	N	Y	Y	Y	Y	Y
6 **Barton**	Y	N	Y	Y	Y	Y	Y
7 **Culberson**	Y	N	Y	Y	Y	Y	Y
8 **Brady**	Y	N	Y	Y	Y	Y	Y
9 Green, A.	N	Y	N	+	+	N	N
10 **McCaul**	Y	N	Y	Y	Y	Y	Y
11 **Conaway**	Y	N	Y	Y	Y	Y	Y
12 **Granger**	Y	N	Y	Y	Y	Y	Y
13 **Thornberry**	Y	N	Y	Y	Y	Y	Y
14 **Weber**	Y	N	Y	Y	Y	Y	Y
15 Gonzalez	N	Y	N	Y	Y	N	N
16 O'Rourke	N	Y	N	Y	Y	N	N
17 **Flores**	Y	N	Y	Y	Y	Y	Y
18 Jackson Lee	N	Y	N	?	Y	N	N
19 **Arrington**	Y	N	Y	Y	Y	Y	Y
20 Castro	N	Y	N	Y	Y	N	N
21 **Smith**	Y	N	Y	Y	Y	?	Y
22 **Olson**	Y	N	Y	Y	Y	Y	Y
23 **Hurd**	Y	N	Y	Y	Y	Y	Y
24 **Marchant**	Y	N	Y	?	?	Y	Y
25 **Williams**	Y	N	Y	Y	Y	Y	Y
26 **Burgess**	Y	N	Y	Y	Y	Y	Y
27 **Farenthold**	Y	N	Y	Y	Y	Y	Y
28 Cuellar	N	Y	Y	Y	Y	N	N
29 Green, G.	N	Y	N	Y	Y	N	N
30 Johnson, E.B.	–	+	–	Y	Y	N	N
31 **Carter**	Y	N	Y	Y	Y	Y	Y
32 **Sessions**	Y	N	Y	Y	Y	Y	Y
33 Veasey	?	Y	N	Y	Y	N	N
34 Vela	N	Y	N	Y	Y	N	N
35 Doggett	N	Y	N	Y	Y	N	N
36 **Babin**	Y	N	Y	Y	Y	Y	Y
UTAH							
1 **Bishop**	Y	N	Y	Y	Y	Y	Y
2 **Stewart**	Y	N	Y	Y	Y	Y	Y
3 **Chaffetz**	Y	N	Y	Y	Y	Y	Y
4 **Love**	Y	N	Y	Y	Y	Y	Y
VERMONT							
AL Welch	N	Y	N	Y	Y	N	N
VIRGINIA							
1 **Wittman**	Y	N	Y	Y	Y	Y	Y
2 **Taylor**	Y	N	Y	Y	Y	Y	Y
3 Scott	N	Y	N	Y	Y	N	N
4 McEachin	N	Y	N	Y	Y	N	N
5 **Garrett**	Y	N	Y	Y	Y	Y	Y
6 **Goodlatte**	Y	N	Y	Y	Y	Y	Y
7 **Brat**	Y	N	Y	Y	N	Y	Y
8 Beyer	N	Y	N	Y	Y	N	N
9 **Griffith**	Y	N	Y	Y	Y	Y	Y
10 **Comstock**	Y	N	Y	Y	Y	Y	Y
11 Connolly	N	Y	N	Y	Y	N	N
WASHINGTON							
1 DelBene	N	Y	N	Y	Y	N	N
2 Larsen	N	Y	N	Y	Y	N	N
3 **Herrera Beutler**	Y	N	Y	Y	Y	Y	Y
4 **Newhouse**	Y	N	Y	Y	Y	Y	Y
5 **McMorris Rodgers**	Y	N	Y	Y	Y	Y	Y
6 Kilmer	N	Y	N	Y	Y	N	N
7 Jayapal	N	Y	N	Y	Y	N	N
8 **Reichert**	Y	N	Y	Y	Y	Y	Y
9 Smith	N	Y	N	Y	Y	N	N
10 Heck	N	Y	N	Y	Y	N	N
WEST VIRGINIA							
1 **McKinley**	Y	N	Y	Y	Y	Y	Y
2 **Mooney**	Y	N	Y	Y	Y	Y	Y
3 **Jenkins**	Y	N	Y	Y	Y	Y	Y
WISCONSIN							
1 **Ryan**							
2 Pocan	N	Y	N	?	?	N	N
3 Kind	N	Y	N	Y	Y	N	N
4 Moore	N	Y	N	Y	Y	N	N
5 **Sensenbrenner**	Y	N	Y	Y	Y	Y	Y
6 **Grothman**	Y	N	Y	Y	Y	Y	Y
7 **Duffy**	Y	N	Y	Y	Y	Y	Y
8 **Gallagher**	Y	N	Y	Y	Y	Y	Y
WYOMING							
AL **Cheney**	Y	N	Y	Y	Y	Y	Y

VOTE NUMBER

70. H J RES 41, H RES 71, H J RES 40. FOREIGN ENERGY DEVELOPMENT DISCLOSURE DISAPPROVAL AND FIREARMS PURCHASE LIMITATION DISAPPROVAL/PREVIOUS QUESTION. Buck, R-Colo., motion to order the previous question (thus ending debate and the possibility of amendment) on the rule (H Res 71) that would provide for House floor consideration of a joint resolution (H J Res 41) that would nullify and disapprove of a Securities and Exchange Commission rule that requires companies that develop oil, natural gas or minerals to publicly report in detail payments to foreign governments or to the U.S. government totaling at least $100,000 annually per project for extraction, exploration or export of these resources. It also would provide for consideration of a joint resolution (H J Res 40) that would nullify and disapprove of a Social Security Administration rule that outlines reporting of information by the agency for inclusion in the National Instant Criminal Background Check System for gun purchases about certain non-elderly individuals with mental impairments who receive disability insurance or Supplemental Security Income benefits and use a "representative payee" because they cannot manage their benefit payments. Motion agreed to 231-191 : R 231-0; D 0-191. Feb. 1, 2017.

71. H J RES 41, H RES 71, H J RES 40. FOREIGN ENERGY DEVELOPMENT DISCLOSURE DISAPPROVAL AND FIREARMS PURCHASE LIMITATION DISAPPROVAL/RULE. Adoption of the rule (H Res 71) that would provide for House floor consideration of a joint resolution (H J Res 41) that would nullify and disapprove of a Securities and Exchange Commission rule that requires companies that develop oil, natural gas or minerals to publicly report in detail payments to foreign governments or to the U.S. government totaling at least $100,000 annually per project for extraction, exploration or export of these resources. It also would provide for consideration of a joint resolution (H J Res 40) that would nullify and disapprove of a Social Security Administration rule that outlines reporting of information by the agency for inclusion in the National Instant Criminal Background Check System for gun purchases about certain non-elderly individuals with mental impairments who receive disability insurance or Supplemental Security Income benefits and use a "representative payee" because they cannot manage their benefit payments. Adopted 231-191 : R 231-0; D 0-191. Feb. 1, 2017.

72. H J RES 41. FOREIGN ENERGY DEVELOPMENT DISCLOSURE DISAPPROVAL/PASSAGE. Passage of the joint resolution that would nullify and disapprove of a Securities and Exchange Commission rule that requires companies that develop oil, natural gas or minerals to publicly report in detail payments to foreign governments or to the U.S. government totaling at least $100,000 annually per project for extraction, exploration or export of these resources. Passed 235-187 : R 230-4; D 5-183. Feb. 1, 2017.

73. H J RES 38. STREAM PROTECTION RULE DISAPPROVAL/PASSAGE. Passage of the joint resolution that would nullify and disapprove of an Office of Surface Mining Reclamation and Enforcement rule that requires surface coal mining operations, to the extent possible, to avoid disturbing streams and land within 100 feet of the streams. The rule also includes provisions related to data collection and restoration and requires native trees and plants to be used to replant reclaimed mine sites. Passed 228-194 : R 224-9; D 4-185. Feb. 1, 2017.

74. H J RES 37, H RES 74, H J RES 36. METHANE LIMITATION DISAPPROVAL AND LABOR LAW VIOLATION DISCLOSURE DISAPPROVAL/PREVIOUS QUESTION. Cole, R-Okla., motion to order the previous question (thus ending debate and the possibility of amendment) on the rule (H Res 74) that would provide for House floor consideration of a joint resolution (H J Res 36) that would nullify a Bureau of Land Management rule that requires oil and gas operators on public and tribal lands to reduce the practice of burning gas by adopting current technologies and to replace outdated equipment to minimize release of gas into the air. It also would provide for consideration of a joint resolution (H J Res 37) that would nullify a Defense Department, General Services Administration and NASA rule that requires companies that bid for federal contracts to disclose whether they have been determined to have violated certain federal labor laws and equivalent state laws. Motion agreed to 230-188 : R 230-0; D 0-188. Feb. 2, 2017.

	70	71	72	73	74
ALABAMA					
1 **Byrne**	Y	Y	Y	Y	Y
2 **Roby**	Y	Y	Y	Y	Y
3 **Rogers**	Y	Y	Y	Y	Y
4 **Aderholt**	Y	Y	Y	Y	Y
5 **Brooks**	Y	Y	Y	Y	Y
6 **Palmer**	Y	Y	Y	Y	Y
7 Sewell	N	N	N	N	N
ALASKA					
AL **Young**	Y	Y	Y	Y	Y
ARIZONA					
1 O'Halleran	N	N	N	N	N
2 **McSally**	Y	Y	Y	Y	Y
3 Grijalva	N	N	N	N	N
4 **Gosar**	Y	Y	Y	Y	Y
5 **Biggs**	Y	Y	Y	Y	Y
6 **Schweikert**	Y	Y	Y	Y	Y
7 Gallego	N	N	N	N	N
8 **Franks**	Y	Y	Y	Y	Y
9 Sinema	N	N	N	N	N
ARKANSAS					
1 **Crawford**	Y	Y	Y	Y	Y
2 **Hill**	Y	Y	Y	Y	Y
3 **Womack**	Y	Y	Y	Y	Y
4 **Westerman**	Y	Y	Y	Y	Y
CALIFORNIA					
1 **LaMalfa**	Y	Y	Y	Y	Y
2 Huffman	N	N	N	N	N
3 Garamendi	N	N	N	N	N
4 **McClintock**	Y	Y	Y	Y	Y
5 Thompson	N	N	N	N	N
6 Matsui	N	N	N	N	N
7 Bera	N	N	N	N	N
8 **Cook**	Y	Y	Y	Y	Y
9 McNerney	N	N	N	N	N
10 **Denham**	Y	Y	Y	Y	Y
11 DeSaulnier	N	N	N	N	N
12 Pelosi	N	N	N	N	N
13 Lee	N	N	N	N	N
14 Speier	N	N	N	N	N
15 Swalwell	N	N	N	N	N
16 Costa	N	N	N	Y	N
17 Khanna	N	N	N	N	N
18 Eshoo	N	N	N	N	N
19 Lofgren	N	N	N	N	N
20 Panetta	N	N	N	N	N
21 **Valadao**	Y	Y	Y	Y	Y
22 **Nunes**	Y	Y	Y	Y	Y
23 **McCarthy**	Y	Y	Y	Y	Y
24 Carbajal	N	N	N	N	N
25 **Knight**	Y	Y	Y	Y	Y
26 Brownley	N	N	N	N	N
27 Chu	N	N	N	N	N
28 Schiff	N	N	N	N	N
29 Cardenas	N	N	N	N	N
30 Sherman	N	N	N	N	N
31 Aguilar	N	N	N	N	N
32 Napolitano	N	N	N	N	N
33 Lieu	N	N	N	N	N
34 Vacant					
35 Torres	N	N	N	N	N
36 Ruiz	N	N	N	N	N
37 Bass	N	N	N	N	N
38 Sánchez, Linda	N	N	N	N	N
39 **Royce**	Y	Y	N	Y	Y
40 Roybal-Allard	N	N	N	N	N
41 Takano	N	N	N	N	N
42 **Calvert**	Y	Y	Y	Y	Y
43 Waters	N	N	N	N	N
44 Barragan	N	N	N	N	N
45 **Walters**	Y	Y	Y	Y	Y
46 Correa	N	N	N	N	N
47 Lowenthal	N	N	N	N	N
48 **Rohrabacher**	Y	Y	Y	Y	Y
49 **Issa**	Y	Y	Y	Y	Y
50 **Hunter**	Y	Y	Y	Y	Y
51 Vargas	N	N	N	N	N
52 Peters	N	N	N	N	N
53 Davis	N	N	N	N	N

	70	71	72	73	74
COLORADO					
1 DeGette	N	N	N	N	N
2 Polis	N	N	N	N	N
3 **Tipton**	Y	Y	Y	Y	Y
4 **Buck**	Y	Y	Y	Y	Y
5 **Lamborn**	Y	Y	Y	Y	Y
6 **Coffman**	Y	Y	Y	Y	Y
7 Perlmutter	N	N	N	N	N
CONNECTICUT					
1 Larson	N	N	N	N	N
2 Courtney	N	N	N	N	N
3 DeLauro	N	N	N	N	N
4 Himes	N	N	N	N	N
5 Esty	N	N	N	N	N
DELAWARE					
AL Blunt Rochester	N	N	N	N	N
FLORIDA					
1 **Gaetz**	Y	Y	Y	Y	Y
2 **Dunn**	Y	Y	Y	Y	Y
3 **Yoho**	Y	Y	Y	Y	Y
4 **Rutherford**	Y	Y	Y	Y	Y
5 Lawson	N	N	N	N	N
6 **DeSantis**	N	N	N	N	N
7 Murphy	N	N	N	N	N
8 **Posey**	Y	Y	Y	Y	Y
9 Soto	N	N	N	N	N
10 Demings	N	N	N	N	N
11 **Webster**	Y	Y	Y	Y	Y
12 **Bilirakis**	Y	Y	Y	Y	Y
13 Crist	N	N	N	N	N
14 Castor	N	N	N	N	N
15 **Ross**	Y	Y	Y	Y	Y
16 **Buchanan**	Y	Y	Y	Y	Y
17 **Rooney, T.**	Y	Y	Y	Y	Y
18 **Mast**	Y	Y	Y	Y	Y
19 **Rooney, F.**	Y	Y	Y	Y	Y
20 Hastings	N	N	N	N	?
21 Frankel	N	N	N	N	N
22 Deutch	N	N	N	N	N
23 Wasserman Schultz	N	N	N	N	N
24 Wilson	N	N	N	N	N
25 **Diaz-Balart**	Y	Y	Y	Y	Y
26 **Curbelo**	Y	Y	Y	N	Y
27 **Ros-Lehtinen**	Y	Y	Y	N	Y
GEORGIA					
1 **Carter**	Y	Y	Y	Y	Y
2 Bishop	N	N	N	Y	N
3 **Ferguson**	Y	Y	Y	Y	Y
4 Johnson	N	N	N	N	N
5 Lewis	N	N	N	N	N
6 **Price**	?	?	?	?	?
7 **Woodall**	Y	Y	Y	Y	Y
8 **Scott, A.**	Y	Y	Y	Y	Y
9 **Collins**	Y	Y	Y	Y	Y
10 **Hice**	Y	Y	Y	Y	Y
11 **Loudermilk**	Y	Y	Y	Y	Y
12 **Allen**	Y	Y	Y	Y	Y
13 Scott, D.	N	N	N	N	N
14 **Graves**	Y	Y	Y	Y	Y
HAWAII					
1 Hanabusa	N	N	N	N	N
2 Gabbard	N	N	N	N	N
IDAHO					
1 **Labrador**	Y	Y	Y	Y	Y
2 **Simpson**	Y	Y	Y	Y	Y
ILLINOIS					
1 Rush	N	N	?	?	?
2 Kelly	N	N	N	N	N
3 Lipinski	N	N	N	N	N
4 Gutierrez	N	N	N	N	N
5 Quigley	N	N	N	N	N
6 **Roskam**	Y	Y	Y	Y	Y
7 Davis, D.	N	N	N	N	N
8 Krishnamoorthi	N	N	N	N	N
9 Schakowsky	N	N	N	N	N
10 Schneider	N	N	N	N	N
11 Foster	N	N	N	N	N
12 **Bost**	Y	Y	Y	Y	Y
13 **Davis, R.**	Y	Y	Y	Y	Y
14 **Hultgren**	Y	Y	Y	Y	Y
15 **Shimkus**	Y	Y	Y	Y	Y

	70	71	72	73	74
16 **Kinzinger**	Y	Y	Y	Y	Y
17 **Bustos**	N	N	N	N	N
18 **LaHood**	Y	Y	Y	Y	Y
INDIANA					
1 Visclosky	N	N	N	N	N
2 **Walorski**	Y	Y	Y	Y	Y
3 **Banks**	Y	Y	Y	Y	Y
4 **Rokita**	Y	Y	Y	Y	Y
5 **Brooks**	Y	Y	Y	Y	Y
6 **Messer**	Y	Y	Y	?	Y
7 Carson	N	N	N	N	N
8 **Bucshon**	Y	Y	Y	Y	?
9 **Hollingsworth**	Y	Y	Y	Y	Y
IOWA					
1 **Blum**	Y	Y	Y	Y	Y
2 Loebsack	N	N	N	N	N
3 **Young**	Y	Y	Y	Y	Y
4 **King**	Y	Y	Y	Y	Y
KANSAS					
1 **Marshall**	Y	Y	Y	Y	Y
2 **Jenkins**	Y	Y	Y	Y	Y
3 **Yoder**	Y	Y	Y	Y	Y
KENTUCKY					
1 **Comer**	Y	Y	Y	Y	Y
2 **Guthrie**	Y	Y	Y	Y	Y
3 Yarmuth	N	N	N	N	N
4 **Massie**	Y	Y	Y	Y	Y
5 **Rogers**	Y	Y	Y	Y	Y
6 **Barr**	Y	Y	Y	Y	Y
LOUISIANA					
1 **Scalise**	Y	Y	Y	Y	Y
2 Richmond	N	N	N	N	N
3 **Higgins**	Y	Y	Y	Y	Y
4 **Johnson**	Y	Y	Y	Y	Y
5 **Abraham**	Y	Y	Y	Y	Y
6 **Graves**	Y	Y	Y	Y	Y
MAINE					
1 Pingree	N	N	N	N	N
2 **Poliquin**	Y	Y	Y	N	Y
MARYLAND					
1 **Harris**	Y	Y	Y	Y	Y
2 Ruppersberger	N	N	N	N	N
3 Sarbanes	N	N	N	N	N
4 Brown	N	N	N	N	N
5 Hoyer	N	N	N	N	N
6 Delaney	N	N	N	N	N
7 Cummings	N	N	N	N	N
8 Raskin	N	N	N	N	N
MASSACHUSETTS					
1 Neal	N	N	N	N	N
2 McGovern	N	N	N	N	N
3 Tsongas	N	N	N	N	N
4 Kennedy	N	N	N	N	N
5 Clark	?	?	?	?	?
6 Moulton	N	N	N	N	N
7 Capuano	N	N	N	N	N
8 Lynch	N	N	N	N	N
9 Keating	N	N	N	N	N
MICHIGAN					
1 **Bergman**	Y	Y	Y	Y	Y
2 **Huizenga**	Y	Y	Y	Y	Y
3 **Amash**	Y	Y	Y	Y	Y
4 **Moolenaar**	Y	Y	Y	Y	Y
5 Kildee	?	?	?	?	N
6 **Upton**	Y	Y	Y	Y	Y
7 **Walberg**	Y	Y	Y	Y	Y
8 **Bishop**	Y	Y	Y	Y	Y
9 Levin	N	N	N	N	N
10 **Mitchell**	Y	Y	Y	Y	Y
11 **Trott**	Y	Y	Y	Y	Y
12 Dingell	N	N	N	N	N
13 Conyers	N	N	N	N	N
14 Lawrence	N	N	N	N	N
MINNESOTA					
1 Walz	N	N	N	N	N
2 **Lewis**	Y	Y	Y	Y	Y
3 **Paulsen**	Y	Y	Y	Y	Y
4 McCollum	N	N	N	N	N

	70	71	72	73	74
5 Ellison	N	N	N	N	N
6 **Emmer**	Y	Y	Y	Y	Y
7 Peterson	N	N	N	Y	N
8 Nolan	N	N	N	N	N
MISSISSIPPI					
1 **Kelly**	Y	Y	Y	Y	Y
2 Thompson	N	N	N	N	N
3 **Harper**	Y	Y	Y	Y	Y
4 **Palazzo**	Y	Y	Y	Y	Y
MISSOURI					
1 Clay	N	N	N	N	N
2 **Wagner**	Y	Y	Y	Y	Y
3 **Luetkemeyer**	Y	Y	Y	Y	Y
4 **Hartzler**	Y	?	Y	Y	Y
5 Cleaver	N	N	N	N	N
6 **Graves**	Y	Y	Y	Y	Y
7 **Long**	Y	Y	Y	Y	Y
8 **Smith**	Y	Y	Y	Y	Y
MONTANA					
AL **Zinke**	?	?	?	?	?
NEBRASKA					
1 **Fortenberry**	Y	Y	Y	Y	Y
2 **Bacon**	Y	Y	Y	Y	Y
3 **Smith**	Y	Y	Y	Y	Y
NEVADA					
1 Titus	N	N	N	N	N
2 **Amodei**	Y	Y	Y	Y	Y
3 Rosen	N	N	N	N	N
4 Kihuen	N	N	N	N	N
NEW HAMPSHIRE					
1 Shea-Porter	N	N	N	N	N
2 Kuster	N	N	N	N	N
NEW JERSEY					
1 Norcross	N	N	N	N	N
2 **LoBiondo**	Y	Y	Y	N	Y
3 **MacArthur**	Y	Y	Y	Y	Y
4 **Smith**	Y	N	N	N	Y
5 Gottheimer	N	N	N	N	N
6 Pallone	N	N	N	N	N
7 **Lance**	Y	Y	Y	Y	Y
8 Sires	N	N	N	N	N
9 Pascrell	N	N	N	N	N
10 Payne	N	N	N	N	N
11 **Frelinghuysen**	Y	Y	Y	Y	Y
12 Watson Coleman	N	N	N	N	N
NEW MEXICO					
1 Lujan Grisham	N	N	N	N	N
2 **Pearce**	Y	Y	Y	Y	Y
3 Luján	N	N	N	N	N
NEW YORK					
1 **Zeldin**	Y	Y	Y	Y	Y
2 **King**	Y	Y	Y	Y	Y
3 Suozzi	N	N	N	N	N
4 Rice	N	N	N	N	N
5 Meeks	N	N	?	?	N
6 Meng	N	N	N	N	N
7 Velázquez	N	N	N	N	N
8 Jeffries	N	N	N	N	N
9 Clarke	N	N	N	N	N
10 Nadler	N	N	N	N	N
11 **Donovan**	Y	Y	Y	Y	Y
12 Maloney, C.	N	N	N	N	N
13 Espaillat	N	N	N	N	N
14 Crowley	N	N	N	N	N
15 Serrano	N	N	N	N	N
16 Engel	N	N	N	N	N
17 Lowey	N	N	N	N	N
18 Maloney, S.P.	N	N	N	N	N
19 **Faso**	Y	Y	Y	Y	Y
20 Tonko	N	N	N	N	N
21 **Stefanik**	Y	Y	Y	Y	Y
22 **Tenney**	Y	Y	Y	Y	Y
23 **Reed**	Y	Y	Y	Y	Y
24 **Katko**	Y	Y	Y	Y	Y
25 Slaughter	N	N	N	N	N
26 Higgins	N	N	N	N	N
27 **Collins**	Y	Y	Y	Y	Y
NORTH CAROLINA					
1 Butterfield	N	N	N	N	N
2 **Holding**	Y	Y	Y	Y	Y
3 **Jones**	Y	N	Y	N	Y
4 Price	N	N	N	N	N

	70	71	72	73	74
5 **Foxx**	Y	Y	Y	Y	Y
6 **Walker**	?	?	?	?	?
7 **Rouzer**	Y	Y	Y	Y	Y
8 **Hudson**	Y	Y	Y	Y	+
9 **Pittenger**	Y	Y	Y	Y	Y
10 **McHenry**	Y	Y	Y	Y	Y
11 **Meadows**	Y	Y	Y	Y	Y
12 Adams	N	N	N	N	N
13 **Budd**	Y	Y	Y	Y	Y
NORTH DAKOTA					
AL **Cramer**	Y	Y	Y	Y	Y
OHIO					
1 **Chabot**	Y	Y	Y	Y	Y
2 **Wenstrup**	Y	Y	Y	Y	Y
3 Beatty	N	N	N	N	N
4 **Jordan**	Y	Y	Y	Y	Y
5 **Latta**	Y	Y	Y	Y	Y
6 **Johnson**	Y	Y	Y	Y	Y
7 **Gibbs**	Y	Y	Y	Y	Y
8 **Davidson**	Y	Y	Y	Y	Y
9 Kaptur	N	N	N	N	N
10 **Turner**	Y	Y	Y	Y	Y
11 Fudge	N	N	N	N	N
12 **Tiberi**	Y	Y	Y	Y	Y
13 Ryan	N	N	N	N	N
14 **Joyce**	Y	Y	Y	Y	Y
15 **Stivers**	Y	Y	Y	Y	Y
16 **Renacci**	Y	Y	Y	Y	Y
OKLAHOMA					
1 **Bridenstine**	Y	Y	Y	Y	Y
2 **Mullin**	Y	Y	Y	Y	Y
3 **Lucas**	Y	Y	Y	Y	Y
4 **Cole**	Y	Y	Y	Y	Y
5 **Russell**	?	?	Y	Y	?
OREGON					
1 Bonamici	N	N	N	N	N
2 **Walden**	Y	Y	Y	Y	Y
3 Blumenauer	N	N	N	N	N
4 DeFazio	N	N	N	N	N
5 Schrader	N	N	N	N	N
PENNSYLVANIA					
1 Brady	N	N	N	N	?
2 Evans	N	N	N	N	N
3 **Kelly**	Y	Y	Y	Y	Y
4 **Perry**	Y	Y	Y	Y	Y
5 **Thompson**	Y	Y	Y	Y	Y
6 **Costello**	Y	Y	Y	Y	Y
7 **Meehan**	Y	Y	Y	Y	+
8 **Fitzpatrick**	Y	Y	N	N	Y
9 **Shuster**	Y	Y	Y	Y	Y
10 **Marino**	Y	Y	Y	Y	Y
11 **Barletta**	Y	Y	Y	Y	Y
12 **Rothfus**	Y	Y	Y	Y	Y
13 Boyle	N	N	N	N	N
14 Doyle	N	N	N	N	N
15 **Dent**	Y	Y	Y	Y	Y
16 **Smucker**	Y	Y	Y	Y	Y
17 Cartwright	N	N	?	N	N
18 **Murphy**	Y	Y	Y	Y	Y
RHODE ISLAND					
1 Cicilline	N	N	N	N	N
2 Langevin	N	N	N	N	N
SOUTH CAROLINA					
1 **Sanford**	Y	Y	Y	N	Y
2 **Wilson**	Y	Y	Y	Y	Y
3 **Duncan**	Y	Y	Y	Y	Y
4 **Gowdy**	Y	Y	Y	Y	Y
5 **Mulvaney**	?	?	?	?	?
6 Clyburn	N	N	N	N	N
7 **Rice**	Y	Y	Y	Y	Y
SOUTH DAKOTA					
AL **Noem**	Y	Y	Y	Y	Y
TENNESSEE					
1 **Roe**	Y	Y	Y	Y	Y
2 **Duncan**	Y	Y	Y	Y	Y
3 **Fleischmann**	Y	Y	Y	Y	Y
4 **DesJarlais**	Y	Y	Y	Y	Y
5 Cooper	N	N	N	N	N
6 **Black**	Y	Y	Y	Y	Y
7 **Blackburn**	?	Y	Y	Y	Y
8 **Kustoff**	Y	Y	Y	Y	Y
9 Cohen	N	N	N	N	N

	70	71	72	73	74
TEXAS					
1 **Gohmert**	Y	Y	Y	Y	Y
2 **Poe**	Y	Y	Y	Y	Y
3 **Johnson, S.**	Y	Y	Y	Y	Y
4 **Ratcliffe**	Y	Y	Y	Y	Y
5 **Hensarling**	Y	Y	Y	Y	Y
6 **Barton**	Y	Y	Y	Y	Y
7 **Culberson**	Y	Y	Y	Y	Y
8 **Brady**	Y	Y	Y	Y	Y
9 Green, A.	N	N	N	N	N
10 **McCaul**	Y	Y	Y	Y	Y
11 **Conaway**	Y	Y	Y	Y	Y
12 **Granger**	Y	Y	Y	Y	Y
13 **Thornberry**	Y	Y	Y	Y	Y
14 **Weber**	Y	Y	Y	Y	Y
15 Gonzalez	N	N	Y	N	N
16 O'Rourke	N	N	N	N	N
17 **Flores**	Y	Y	Y	Y	Y
18 Jackson Lee	N	N	N	N	N
19 **Arrington**	Y	Y	Y	Y	Y
20 Castro	N	N	N	N	N
21 **Smith**	?	?	Y	Y	Y
22 **Olson**	Y	Y	Y	Y	Y
23 **Hurd**	Y	Y	Y	Y	Y
24 **Marchant**	Y	Y	Y	Y	Y
25 **Williams**	Y	Y	Y	Y	Y
26 **Burgess**	Y	Y	Y	Y	Y
27 **Farenthold**	Y	Y	Y	Y	Y
28 Cuellar	N	N	Y	N	N
29 Green, G.	N	N	Y	N	N
30 Johnson, E.B.	N	N	N	N	N
31 **Carter**	Y	Y	Y	Y	Y
32 **Sessions**	Y	Y	Y	Y	Y
33 Veasey	N	N	N	N	N
34 Vela	N	N	Y	N	N
35 Doggett	N	N	N	N	N
36 **Babin**	Y	Y	Y	Y	Y
UTAH					
1 **Bishop**	Y	Y	Y	Y	Y
2 **Stewart**	Y	Y	Y	Y	Y
3 **Chaffetz**	Y	Y	Y	Y	Y
4 **Love**	Y	Y	Y	Y	Y
VERMONT					
AL Welch	N	N	N	N	N
VIRGINIA					
1 **Wittman**	Y	Y	Y	Y	Y
2 **Taylor**	?	?	+	+	Y
3 Scott	N	N	N	N	N
4 McEachin	N	N	N	N	N
5 **Garrett**	Y	Y	Y	Y	Y
6 **Goodlatte**	Y	Y	Y	Y	Y
7 **Brat**	Y	Y	Y	Y	Y
8 Beyer	N	N	N	N	N
9 **Griffith**	Y	Y	Y	Y	Y
10 **Comstock**	Y	Y	Y	Y	Y
11 Connolly	N	N	N	N	N
WASHINGTON					
1 DelBene	N	N	N	N	N
2 Larsen	N	N	N	N	N
3 **Herrera Beutler**	Y	Y	Y	Y	Y
4 **Newhouse**	Y	Y	Y	Y	Y
5 **McMorris Rodgers**	Y	Y	Y	Y	Y
6 Kilmer	N	N	N	N	N
7 Jayapal	N	N	N	N	N
8 **Reichert**	Y	Y	Y	Y	Y
9 Smith	N	N	N	N	N
10 Heck	N	N	N	N	N
WEST VIRGINIA					
1 **McKinley**	Y	Y	Y	Y	Y
2 **Mooney**	Y	Y	Y	Y	Y
3 **Jenkins**	Y	Y	Y	Y	Y
WISCONSIN					
1 **Ryan**					
2 Pocan	N	N	N	N	N
3 Kind	N	N	N	N	N
4 Moore	N	N	N	N	?
5 **Sensenbrenner**	Y	Y	Y	Y	Y
6 **Grothman**	Y	Y	Y	Y	Y
7 **Duffy**	Y	Y	Y	Y	Y
8 **Gallagher**	Y	Y	Y	Y	Y
WYOMING					
AL **Cheney**	Y	Y	Y	Y	Y

VOTE NUMBER

75. H J RES 37, H RES 74, H J RES 36. METHANE LIMITATION DISAPPROVAL AND LABOR LAW VIOLATION DISCLOSURE DISAPPROVAL/RULE. Adoption of the rule (H Res 74) that would provide for House floor consideration of a joint resolution (H J Res 36) that would nullify a Bureau of Land Management rule that requires oil and gas operators on public and tribal lands to reduce the practice of burning gas by adopting current technologies and to replace outdated equipment to minimize release of gas into the air. It also would provide for consideration of a joint resolution (H J Res 37) that would nullify a Defense Department, General Services Administration and NASA rule that requires companies that bid for federal contracts to disclose whether they have been determined to have violated certain federal labor laws and equivalent state laws. Adopted 232-190 : R 232-0; D 0-190. Feb. 2, 2017.

76. H J RES 37. LABOR LAW VIOLATION DISCLOSURE DISAPPROVAL/ PASSAGE. Passage of the joint resolution that would nullify and disapprove of a Defense Department, General Services Administration and NASA rule that requires companies that bid for federal contracts of more than $500,000 to disclose whether they have been determined in the previous three years to have violated certain federal labor laws and equivalent state laws. Passed 236-187 : R 233-1; D 3-186. Feb. 2, 2017.

77. H J RES 40. FIREARMS PURCHASE LIMITATION DISAPPROVAL/ PASSAGE. Passage of the joint resolution that would nullify and disapprove of a Social Security Administration rule that outlines reporting of information by the agency for inclusion in the National Instant Criminal Background Check System for gun purchases about certain non-elderly individuals with mental impairments who receive disability insurance or Supplemental Security Income benefits and use a "representative payee" because they cannot manage their benefit payments. Passed 235-180 : R 229-2; D 6-178. Feb. 2, 2017.

78. H J RES 36. METHANE RELEASE LIMITATION DISAPPROVAL/PASSAGE. Passage of the joint resolution that would nullify a Bureau of Land Management rule that requires oil and gas operators on public lands to take measures that decrease waste of natural gas. The rule requires these operators to reduce the practice of burning gas by adopting current technologies, to replace outdated equipment to minimize release of gas into the air and to periodically inspect their operations for leaks. Passed 221-191 : R 218-11; D 3-180. Feb. 3, 2017.

79. HR 689. COLORADO HEADGATE USAGE/PASSAGE. Lamborn, R-Colo., motion to suspend the rules and pass the bill that would direct the U.S. Forest Service to provide a special use authorization for the town of Minturn, Colorado, to use, maintain and repair a headgate in the Holy Cross Wilderness area and divert water to the Bolts Lake, an off-stream reservoir located outside the boundary of the wilderness area. Motion agreed to 409-1 : R 230-1; D 179-0. Feb. 6, 2017.

80. HR 337. VETERAN CEMETERY EXPANSION/PASSAGE. Lamborn, R-Colo., motion to suspend the rules and pass the bill that would require the Bureau of Land Management to transfer approximately 200 acres of land, in South Dakota, to the Department of Veterans Affairs to accommodate an expansion of the Black Hills National Cemetery. The bill would remove the designated land from the administrative jurisdiction of BLM and laws related to mining, land leasing, mineral leasing and geothermal leasing. The measure would also require the Veterans Affairs Department to reimburse the Department of the Interior for transfer costs, including survey and decontamination costs, and would require the VA to return any portion of the property not intended to be used for cemetery purposes. Motion agreed to 407-0 : R 230-0; D 177-0. Feb. 6, 2017.

	75	76	77	78	79	80
ALABAMA						
1 Byrne	Y	Y	Y	Y	Y	Y
2 Roby	Y	Y	Y	Y	Y	Y
3 Rogers	Y	Y	Y	Y	Y	Y
4 Aderholt	Y	Y	Y	Y	Y	Y
5 Brooks	Y	Y	?	Y	Y	Y
6 Palmer	Y	Y	Y	Y	Y	Y
7 Sewell	N	N	N	Y	Y	Y
ALASKA						
AL Young	Y	Y	Y	Y	Y	Y
ARIZONA						
1 O'Halleran	N	N	Y	N	Y	Y
2 McSally	Y	Y	Y	Y	Y	Y
3 Grijalva	N	N	N	N	?	?
4 Gosar	Y	Y	Y	?	Y	Y
5 Biggs	Y	Y	Y	Y	Y	Y
6 Schweikert	Y	Y	Y	Y	Y	Y
7 Gallego	N	N	N	N	Y	Y
8 Franks	Y	Y	Y	Y	Y	Y
9 Sinema	N	N	Y	N	Y	Y
ARKANSAS						
1 Crawford	Y	Y	Y	Y	Y	Y
2 Hill	Y	Y	Y	Y	Y	Y
3 Womack	Y	Y	Y	Y	Y	Y
4 Westerman	Y	Y	Y	Y	Y	Y
CALIFORNIA						
1 LaMalfa	Y	Y	?	Y	Y	Y
2 Huffman	N	N	N	Y	Y	Y
3 Garamendi	N	N	N	N	Y	Y
4 McClintock	Y	Y	Y	Y	Y	Y
5 Thompson	N	N	N	N	Y	Y
6 Matsui	N	N	N	N	Y	Y
7 Bera	N	N	N	N	Y	Y
8 Cook	Y	Y	Y	Y	Y	Y
9 McNerney	N	N	N	N	Y	Y
10 Denham	Y	Y	Y	Y	Y	Y
11 DeSaulnier	N	N	N	N	Y	Y
12 Pelosi	N	N	N	N	Y	Y
13 Lee	N	N	N	N	Y	Y
14 Speier	N	N	N	N	Y	Y
15 Swalwell	N	N	N	N	Y	Y
16 Costa	N	Y	N	Y	Y	Y
17 Khanna	N	N	N	N	Y	Y
18 Eshoo	N	N	N	N	Y	Y
19 Lofgren	N	N	N	N	Y	Y
20 Panetta	N	N	N	N	Y	Y
21 Valadao	Y	Y	Y	Y	Y	Y
22 Nunes	Y	Y	Y	?	Y	Y
23 McCarthy	Y	Y	Y	Y	Y	Y
24 Carbajal	N	N	N	N	Y	Y
25 Knight	Y	Y	Y	Y	Y	Y
26 Brownley	N	N	N	N	Y	Y
27 Chu	N	N	N	N	Y	Y
28 Schiff	N	N	N	N	Y	Y
29 Cardenas	N	N	N	N	Y	?
30 Sherman	N	N	N	N	Y	Y
31 Aguilar	N	N	N	N	Y	Y
32 Napolitano	N	N	N	N	Y	Y
33 Lieu	N	N	N	N	Y	Y
34 Vacant						
35 Torres	N	N	–	N	Y	Y
36 Ruiz	N	N	N	N	Y	Y
37 Bass	N	N	N	N	Y	Y
38 Sánchez, Linda	N	N	N	N	Y	Y
39 Royce	Y	Y	Y	Y	Y	Y
40 Roybal-Allard	N	N	N	N	Y	Y
41 Takano	N	N	N	N	Y	Y
42 Calvert	Y	Y	Y	Y	Y	Y
43 Waters	N	N	N	N	Y	Y
44 Barragan	N	N	N	N	Y	Y
45 Walters	Y	Y	Y	Y	Y	Y
46 Correa	N	Y	N	N	Y	Y
47 Lowenthal	N	N	N	N	Y	Y
48 Rohrabacher	Y	Y	Y	Y	?	?
49 Issa	Y	Y	Y	Y	Y	Y
50 Hunter	Y	Y	Y	Y	Y	?
51 Vargas	N	N	N	N	Y	Y
52 Peters	N	N	N	N	Y	Y
53 Davis	N	N	N	N	Y	Y

	75	76	77	78	79	80
COLORADO						
1 DeGette	N	N	N	N	Y	Y
2 Polis	N	N	N	N	Y	Y
3 Tipton	Y	Y	Y	Y	Y	Y
4 Buck	Y	Y	Y	Y	Y	Y
5 Lamborn	Y	Y	Y	Y	Y	Y
6 Coffman	Y	Y	Y	Y	Y	Y
7 Perlmutter	N	N	N	N	Y	Y
CONNECTICUT						
1 Larson	N	N	N	N	Y	Y
2 Courtney	N	N	N	N	Y	Y
3 DeLauro	N	N	N	N	Y	Y
4 Himes	N	N	N	N	Y	Y
5 Esty	N	N	N	N	Y	Y
DELAWARE						
AL Blunt Rochester	N	N	N	N	Y	Y
FLORIDA						
1 Gaetz	Y	Y	Y	Y	Y	Y
2 Dunn	Y	Y	Y	Y	Y	Y
3 Yoho	Y	Y	Y	Y	Y	Y
4 Rutherford	Y	Y	Y	Y	Y	Y
5 Lawson	N	N	N	N	Y	Y
6 DeSantis	Y	Y	Y	Y	Y	Y
7 Murphy	N	N	N	N	Y	Y
8 Posey	Y	Y	Y	Y	Y	Y
9 Soto	N	N	N	N	Y	Y
10 Demings	N	N	N	N	Y	Y
11 Webster	Y	Y	Y	Y	Y	Y
12 Bilirakis	Y	Y	Y	Y	Y	Y
13 Crist	N	N	N	N	Y	Y
14 Castor	N	N	N	?	Y	Y
15 Ross	Y	Y	Y	Y	Y	Y
16 Buchanan	Y	Y	Y	Y	Y	Y
17 Rooney, T.	Y	Y	Y	Y	Y	Y
18 Mast	Y	Y	Y	N	Y	Y
19 Rooney, F.	Y	Y	Y	Y	Y	Y
20 Hastings	?	?	?	?	Y	Y
21 Frankel	N	N	–	N	Y	Y
22 Deutch	N	N	N	N	?	?
23 Wasserman Schultz	N	N	N	N	Y	Y
24 Wilson	N	N	N	N	Y	Y
25 Diaz-Balart	Y	Y	Y	Y	Y	Y
26 Curbelo	Y	Y	Y	Y	Y	Y
27 Ros-Lehtinen	Y	N	Y	N	Y	Y
GEORGIA						
1 Carter	Y	Y	Y	Y	Y	Y
2 Bishop	N	N	Y	N	Y	Y
3 Ferguson	Y	Y	Y	Y	Y	Y
4 Johnson	N	N	N	N	Y	?
5 Lewis	N	N	N	N	Y	Y
6 Price	?	?	?	?	?	?
7 Woodall	Y	Y	Y	Y	Y	Y
8 Scott, A.	Y	Y	Y	Y	Y	Y
9 Collins	Y	Y	Y	Y	Y	Y
10 Hice	Y	Y	Y	Y	Y	Y
11 Loudermilk	Y	Y	Y	Y	Y	Y
12 Allen	Y	Y	Y	Y	Y	Y
13 Scott, D.	N	N	N	N	Y	Y
14 Graves	Y	Y	Y	Y	Y	Y
HAWAII						
1 Hanabusa	N	N	N	N	Y	Y
2 Gabbard	N	N	N	N	Y	Y
IDAHO						
1 Labrador	Y	Y	Y	?	Y	Y
2 Simpson	Y	Y	Y	Y	Y	Y
ILLINOIS						
1 Rush	?	?	?	?	?	?
2 Kelly	N	N	N	N	Y	Y
3 Lipinski	N	N	N	N	Y	Y
4 Gutierrez	N	N	N	N	+	+
5 Quigley	N	N	N	N	Y	Y
6 Roskam	Y	Y	Y	Y	Y	Y
7 Davis, D.	N	N	N	N	Y	Y
8 Krishnamoorthi	N	N	N	N	Y	Y
9 Schakowsky	N	N	N	N	Y	Y
10 Schneider	N	N	N	N	Y	Y
11 Foster	N	N	N	N	Y	Y
12 Bost	Y	Y	Y	Y	Y	Y
13 Davis, R.	Y	Y	Y	Y	Y	Y
14 Hultgren	Y	Y	Y	Y	Y	Y
15 Shimkus	Y	Y	Y	Y	Y	Y

	75	76	77	78	79	80
16 **Kinzinger**	Y	Y	Y	Y	Y	Y
17 Bustos	N	N	N	N	Y	Y
18 **LaHood**	Y	Y	Y	Y	Y	Y
INDIANA						
1 Visclosky	N	N	N	N	Y	Y
2 **Walorski**	Y	Y	Y	Y	Y	Y
3 **Banks**	Y	Y	Y	Y	Y	Y
4 **Rokita**	Y	Y	Y	Y	Y	Y
5 **Brooks**	Y	Y	Y	Y	Y	Y
6 **Messer**	Y	Y	Y	Y	Y	?
7 Carson	N	N	N	?	Y	Y
8 **Bucshon**	Y	Y	Y	Y	Y	Y
9 **Hollingsworth**	Y	Y	Y	Y	Y	Y
IOWA						
1 **Blum**	Y	Y	Y	Y	Y	Y
2 Loebsack	N	N	N	N	Y	Y
3 **Young**	Y	Y	Y	Y	Y	Y
4 **King**	Y	Y	Y	Y	Y	Y
KANSAS						
1 **Marshall**	Y	Y	Y	Y	Y	Y
2 **Jenkins**	Y	Y	Y	Y	Y	Y
3 **Yoder**	Y	Y	Y	Y	Y	Y
KENTUCKY						
1 **Comer**	Y	Y	Y	Y	Y	Y
2 **Guthrie**	Y	Y	Y	Y	Y	Y
3 Yarmuth	N	N	N	N	Y	Y
4 **Massie**	Y	Y	Y	Y	Y	Y
5 **Rogers**	Y	Y	Y	Y	Y	Y
6 **Barr**	Y	Y	Y	Y	Y	Y
LOUISIANA						
1 **Scalise**	Y	Y	Y	?	Y	Y
2 Richmond	N	N	N	N	?	?
3 **Higgins**	Y	Y	Y	Y	Y	Y
4 **Johnson**	Y	Y	Y	Y	Y	Y
5 **Abraham**	Y	Y	Y	Y	Y	Y
6 **Graves**	Y	Y	Y	Y	Y	Y
MAINE						
1 Pingree	N	N	–	N	Y	Y
2 **Poliquin**	Y	Y	Y	Y	Y	Y
MARYLAND						
1 **Harris**	Y	Y	Y	Y	Y	Y
2 Ruppersberger	N	N	N	N	Y	Y
3 Sarbanes	N	N	N	N	Y	Y
4 Brown	N	N	N	N	Y	Y
5 Hoyer	N	N	N	N	Y	Y
6 Delaney	N	N	N	N	Y	Y
7 Cummings	N	N	N	N	?	?
8 Raskin	N	N	N	N	Y	Y
MASSACHUSETTS						
1 Neal	N	N	N	N	Y	Y
2 McGovern	N	N	N	N	Y	Y
3 Tsongas	N	N	N	N	Y	Y
4 Kennedy	N	N	N	N	Y	Y
5 Clark	?	?	?	?	Y	Y
6 Moulton	N	N	N	N	Y	Y
7 Capuano	N	N	N	N	Y	Y
8 Lynch	N	N	?	N	?	?
9 Keating	N	N	N	N	Y	Y
MICHIGAN						
1 **Bergman**	Y	Y	Y	Y	Y	Y
2 **Huizenga**	Y	Y	Y	Y	Y	Y
3 **Amash**	Y	Y	Y	Y	N	Y
4 **Moolenaar**	Y	Y	Y	Y	Y	Y
5 Kildee	N	N	N	N	Y	Y
6 **Upton**	Y	Y	Y	Y	Y	Y
7 **Walberg**	Y	Y	Y	Y	Y	Y
8 **Bishop**	Y	Y	Y	Y	Y	Y
9 Levin	N	N	N	N	Y	Y
10 **Mitchell**	Y	Y	Y	Y	Y	Y
11 **Trott**	Y	Y	Y	Y	Y	Y
12 Dingell	N	N	N	N	Y	Y
13 Conyers	N	N	N	N	Y	Y
14 Lawrence	N	N	N	N	Y	Y
MINNESOTA						
1 Walz	N	N	Y	N	Y	Y
2 **Lewis**	Y	Y	Y	Y	Y	Y
3 **Paulsen**	Y	Y	Y	Y	Y	Y
4 McCollum	N	N	N	N	Y	Y

	75	76	77	78	79	80
5 Ellison	N	N	N	N	+	+
6 **Emmer**	Y	Y	Y	Y	Y	Y
7 Peterson	N	?	?	Y	Y	Y
8 Nolan	N	N	N	N	Y	Y
MISSISSIPPI						
1 **Kelly**	Y	Y	Y	Y	Y	Y
2 Thompson	N	N	N	N	Y	Y
3 **Harper**	Y	Y	Y	Y	Y	Y
4 **Palazzo**	Y	Y	Y	Y	Y	Y
MISSOURI						
1 Clay	N	N	N	?	Y	Y
2 **Wagner**	Y	Y	Y	Y	Y	Y
3 **Luetkemeyer**	Y	Y	Y	Y	Y	Y
4 **Hartzler**	Y	Y	Y	Y	Y	Y
5 Cleaver	N	N	N	N	Y	Y
6 **Graves**	Y	Y	Y	Y	Y	Y
7 **Long**	Y	Y	Y	Y	Y	Y
8 **Smith**	Y	Y	Y	Y	Y	Y
MONTANA						
AL **Zinke**	?	?	?	?	?	?
NEBRASKA						
1 **Fortenberry**	Y	Y	Y	Y	Y	Y
2 **Bacon**	Y	Y	Y	Y	Y	Y
3 **Smith**	Y	Y	Y	Y	Y	Y
NEVADA						
1 Titus	N	N	N	N	Y	Y
2 **Amodei**	Y	Y	Y	Y	Y	Y
3 Rosen	N	N	N	N	Y	Y
4 Kihuen	N	N	N	N	Y	Y
NEW HAMPSHIRE						
1 Shea-Porter	N	N	N	N	Y	Y
2 Kuster	N	N	N	N	Y	Y
NEW JERSEY						
1 Norcross	N	N	N	N	Y	Y
2 **LoBiondo**	Y	Y	Y	Y	Y	Y
3 **MacArthur**	Y	Y	Y	Y	Y	Y
4 **Smith**	Y	Y	Y	Y	Y	Y
5 Gottheimer	N	N	N	N	Y	Y
6 Pallone	N	N	N	N	Y	Y
7 **Lance**	Y	Y	Y	Y	Y	Y
8 Sires	N	N	N	N	?	?
9 Pascrell	N	N	N	N	Y	Y
10 Payne	N	N	N	N	Y	Y
11 **Frelinghuysen**	Y	Y	Y	Y	Y	Y
12 Watson Coleman	N	N	N	N	Y	Y
NEW MEXICO						
1 Lujan Grisham	N	N	N	N	Y	Y
2 **Pearce**	Y	Y	Y	Y	Y	Y
3 Luján	N	N	N	N	Y	Y
NEW YORK						
1 **Zeldin**	Y	Y	Y	Y	Y	Y
2 **King**	Y	Y	N	Y	Y	Y
3 Suozzi	N	N	N	N	Y	Y
4 Rice	N	N	N	N	Y	Y
5 Meeks	N	N	N	N	?	?
6 Meng	N	N	N	N	Y	Y
7 Velázquez	N	N	–	N	Y	Y
8 Jeffries	N	N	N	N	?	?
9 Clarke	N	N	N	?	Y	Y
10 Nadler	N	N	N	N	Y	Y
11 **Donovan**	Y	Y	N	Y	Y	Y
12 Maloney, C.	N	N	N	N	Y	Y
13 Espaillat	N	N	N	N	Y	Y
14 Crowley	N	N	N	N	Y	Y
15 Serrano	N	N	N	N	Y	Y
16 Engel	N	N	N	–	Y	Y
17 Lowey	N	N	N	N	Y	Y
18 Maloney, S.P.	N	N	N	N	Y	Y
19 **Faso**	Y	Y	Y	N	Y	Y
20 Tonko	N	N	N	N	Y	Y
21 **Stefanik**	Y	Y	Y	N	Y	Y
22 **Tenney**	Y	Y	Y	Y	Y	Y
23 **Reed**	Y	Y	Y	+	Y	Y
24 **Katko**	Y	Y	Y	N	Y	Y
25 Slaughter	N	N	N	N	Y	Y
26 Higgins	N	N	N	N	Y	Y
27 **Collins**	Y	Y	Y	Y	Y	Y
NORTH CAROLINA						
1 Butterfield	N	N	N	N	Y	Y
2 **Holding**	Y	Y	Y	Y	Y	Y
3 **Jones**	?	?	?	?	Y	Y
4 Price	N	N	N	N	Y	Y

	75	76	77	78	79	80
5 **Foxx**	Y	Y	Y	Y	Y	Y
6 **Walker**	?	?	?	?	Y	Y
7 **Rouzer**	Y	Y	Y	Y	Y	Y
8 **Hudson**	+	Y	Y	Y	Y	Y
9 **Pittenger**	Y	Y	Y	Y	Y	Y
10 **McHenry**	Y	Y	Y	Y	Y	Y
11 **Meadows**	Y	Y	Y	Y	Y	Y
12 Adams	N	N	N	N	Y	Y
13 **Budd**	Y	Y	Y	Y	Y	Y
NORTH DAKOTA						
AL **Cramer**	Y	Y	Y	Y	Y	Y
OHIO						
1 **Chabot**	Y	Y	Y	Y	Y	Y
2 **Wenstrup**	Y	Y	Y	Y	Y	Y
3 Beatty	N	N	N	N	Y	Y
4 **Jordan**	Y	Y	Y	Y	Y	Y
5 **Latta**	Y	Y	Y	Y	Y	Y
6 **Johnson**	Y	Y	Y	Y	Y	Y
7 **Gibbs**	Y	Y	Y	Y	Y	Y
8 **Davidson**	Y	Y	?	Y	Y	Y
9 Kaptur	N	N	N	N	Y	Y
10 **Turner**	Y	Y	Y	Y	Y	Y
11 Fudge	N	N	N	N	Y	Y
12 **Tiberi**	Y	Y	Y	Y	Y	Y
13 Ryan	N	N	N	N	Y	Y
14 **Joyce**	Y	Y	Y	Y	Y	Y
15 **Stivers**	Y	Y	Y	Y	Y	Y
16 **Renacci**	Y	Y	Y	Y	Y	Y
OKLAHOMA						
1 **Bridenstine**	Y	Y	Y	Y	Y	Y
2 **Mullin**	Y	Y	Y	Y	Y	Y
3 **Lucas**	Y	Y	Y	Y	Y	Y
4 **Cole**	Y	Y	Y	Y	Y	Y
5 **Russell**	Y	Y	Y	Y	Y	Y
OREGON						
1 Bonamici	N	N	N	N	Y	Y
2 **Walden**	Y	Y	Y	Y	Y	Y
3 Blumenauer	N	N	N	N	Y	Y
4 DeFazio	N	N	N	N	Y	Y
5 Schrader	N	N	N	N	Y	Y
PENNSYLVANIA						
1 Brady	N	N	N	N	Y	Y
2 Evans	N	N	N	?	Y	Y
3 **Kelly**	Y	Y	Y	Y	Y	Y
4 **Perry**	Y	Y	Y	Y	Y	Y
5 **Thompson**	Y	Y	Y	Y	Y	Y
6 **Costello**	Y	Y	Y	N	Y	Y
7 **Meehan**	Y	Y	Y	N	Y	Y
8 **Fitzpatrick**	Y	Y	Y	N	Y	Y
9 **Shuster**	Y	Y	Y	Y	Y	Y
10 **Marino**	Y	Y	Y	Y	Y	Y
11 **Barletta**	Y	Y	Y	Y	Y	Y
12 **Rothfus**	Y	Y	Y	Y	Y	Y
13 Boyle	N	N	N	N	Y	Y
14 Doyle	N	N	N	N	Y	Y
15 **Dent**	Y	Y	Y	Y	Y	Y
16 **Smucker**	Y	Y	Y	Y	Y	Y
17 Cartwright	N	N	N	N	Y	Y
18 **Murphy**	Y	Y	Y	Y	Y	Y
RHODE ISLAND						
1 Cicilline	N	N	N	N	Y	Y
2 Langevin	N	N	N	N	Y	Y
SOUTH CAROLINA						
1 **Sanford**	Y	Y	Y	N	Y	Y
2 **Wilson**	Y	Y	Y	Y	Y	Y
3 **Duncan**	Y	Y	Y	Y	?	?
4 **Gowdy**	Y	Y	Y	Y	Y	Y
5 **Mulvaney**	?	?	?	?	?	?
6 Clyburn	N	N	N	N	Y	Y
7 **Rice**	Y	Y	Y	Y	Y	Y
SOUTH DAKOTA						
AL **Noem**	Y	Y	Y	Y	Y	Y
TENNESSEE						
1 **Roe**	Y	Y	Y	Y	Y	Y
2 **Duncan**	Y	Y	Y	Y	Y	Y
3 **Fleischmann**	Y	Y	Y	Y	Y	Y
4 **DesJarlais**	Y	Y	Y	Y	Y	Y
5 Cooper	N	N	N	N	Y	Y
6 **Black**	Y	Y	Y	Y	Y	Y
7 **Blackburn**	Y	Y	Y	Y	Y	Y
8 **Kustoff**	Y	Y	Y	Y	Y	Y
9 Cohen	N	N	N	N	Y	Y

	75	76	77	78	79	80
TEXAS						
1 **Gohmert**	Y	Y	Y	Y	Y	Y
2 **Poe**	Y	Y	Y	Y	?	?
3 **Johnson, S.**	Y	Y	Y	Y	Y	Y
4 **Ratcliffe**	Y	Y	Y	Y	Y	Y
5 **Hensarling**	Y	Y	Y	Y	Y	Y
6 **Barton**	Y	Y	Y	Y	Y	Y
7 **Culberson**	Y	Y	Y	Y	Y	Y
8 **Brady**	Y	Y	Y	Y	?	Y
9 Green, A.	N	N	N	N	Y	Y
10 **McCaul**	Y	Y	Y	Y	Y	Y
11 **Conaway**	Y	Y	Y	Y	Y	Y
12 **Granger**	Y	Y	Y	Y	Y	Y
13 **Thornberry**	Y	Y	Y	Y	Y	Y
14 **Weber**	Y	Y	Y	Y	Y	Y
15 Gonzalez	N	N	N	N	Y	Y
16 O'Rourke	N	N	N	N	Y	Y
17 **Flores**	Y	Y	Y	Y	Y	Y
18 Jackson Lee	N	N	N	?	Y	Y
19 **Arrington**	Y	Y	Y	Y	Y	Y
20 Castro	N	N	N	N	Y	Y
21 **Smith**	?	Y	Y	Y	Y	Y
22 **Olson**	Y	Y	Y	Y	Y	Y
23 **Hurd**	Y	Y	Y	Y	Y	Y
24 **Marchant**	Y	Y	Y	Y	Y	Y
25 **Williams**	Y	Y	Y	Y	Y	Y
26 **Burgess**	Y	Y	Y	Y	Y	Y
27 **Farenthold**	Y	Y	Y	Y	Y	Y
28 Cuellar	N	Y	Y	Y	Y	Y
29 Green, G.	N	N	N	N	Y	Y
30 Johnson, E.B.	N	N	N	N	Y	Y
31 **Carter**	Y	Y	Y	Y	Y	Y
32 **Sessions**	Y	Y	Y	Y	?	?
33 Veasey	N	N	N	N	Y	Y
34 Vela	N	N	N	N	Y	Y
35 Doggett	N	N	N	N	Y	Y
36 **Babin**	Y	Y	Y	Y	Y	Y
UTAH						
1 **Bishop**	Y	Y	Y	Y	Y	Y
2 **Stewart**	Y	Y	Y	Y	Y	Y
3 **Chaffetz**	Y	Y	Y	Y	Y	Y
4 **Love**	Y	Y	Y	Y	Y	Y
VERMONT						
AL Welch	N	N	N	N	Y	Y
VIRGINIA						
1 **Wittman**	Y	Y	Y	Y	Y	Y
2 **Taylor**	Y	Y	Y	Y	Y	Y
3 Scott	N	N	N	N	Y	Y
4 McEachin	N	N	N	N	Y	Y
5 **Garrett**	Y	Y	Y	Y	Y	Y
6 **Goodlatte**	Y	Y	Y	Y	Y	Y
7 **Brat**	Y	Y	Y	Y	Y	Y
8 Beyer	N	N	N	N	Y	Y
9 **Griffith**	Y	Y	Y	Y	Y	Y
10 **Comstock**	Y	Y	Y	Y	Y	Y
11 Connolly	N	N	N	N	Y	Y
WASHINGTON						
1 DelBene	N	N	N	N	?	?
2 Larsen	N	N	N	N	Y	Y
3 **Herrera Beutler**	Y	Y	Y	Y	Y	Y
4 **Newhouse**	Y	Y	Y	Y	Y	Y
5 **McMorris Rodgers**	Y	Y	Y	Y	Y	Y
6 Kilmer	N	N	N	N	+	+
7 Jayapal	N	N	N	N	Y	Y
8 **Reichert**	Y	Y	Y	N	Y	Y
9 Smith	N	N	N	N	+	+
10 Heck	N	N	N	N	Y	Y
WEST VIRGINIA						
1 **McKinley**	Y	Y	Y	Y	Y	Y
2 **Mooney**	Y	Y	Y	Y	Y	Y
3 **Jenkins**	Y	Y	Y	Y	Y	Y
WISCONSIN						
1 **Ryan**						
2 Pocan	N	N	N	N	Y	Y
3 Kind	N	N	Y	N	Y	Y
4 Moore	N	N	N	N	Y	Y
5 **Sensenbrenner**	Y	Y	Y	Y	Y	Y
6 **Grothman**	Y	Y	Y	Y	Y	Y
7 **Duffy**	Y	Y	Y	Y	Y	Y
8 **Gallagher**	Y	Y	Y	Y	Y	Y
WYOMING						
AL **Cheney**	Y	Y	Y	Y	Y	Y

VOTE NUMBER

81. H J RES 58, H J RES 57, H J RES 44, H RES 91. Public Land Development Disapproval, Teacher Preparation Disapproval and State Education Plans Disapproval/Previous Question. Byrne, R-Ala., motion to order the previous question (thus ending debate and the possibility of amendment) on the rule (H Res 91) that would provide for House floor consideration of a joint resolution of (H J Res 44) that would nullify and disapprove of a Bureau of Land Management rule that modifies the BLM's process of assessing and planning the development of public lands by increasing public involvement. It would provide for consideration of a joint resolution (H J Res 58) that would nullify an Education Department rule that requires states to annually evaluate the effectiveness of certain teacher preparation programs. It also would provide for consideration of a joint resolution (H J Res 57) that would nullify an Education Department rule that requires states to define and subsequently monitor the performance of low-performing schools. Motion agreed to 234-187 : R 234-0; D 0-187. Feb. 7, 2017.

82. H J RES 58, H J RES 57, H J RES 44, H RES 91. PUBLIC LAND DEVELOPMENT DISAPPROVAL, TEACHER PREPARATION DISAPPROVAL AND STATE EDUCATION PLANS DISAPPROVAL/RULE. Adoption of the rule (H Res 91) that would provide for House floor consideration of a joint resolution of (H J Res 44) that would nullify and disapprove of a Bureau of Land Management rule that modifies the BLM's process of assessing and planning the development of public lands by increasing public involvement. It would provide for consideration of a joint resolution (H J Res 58) that would nullify an Education Department rule that requires states to annually evaluate the effectiveness of certain teacher preparation programs. It also would provide for consideration of a joint resolution (H J Res 57) that would nullify an Education Department rule that requires states to define and subsequently monitor the performance of low-performing schools. Adopted 233-186 : R 233-0; D 0-186. Feb. 7, 2017.

83. H J RES 44. PUBLIC LAND DEVELOPMENT DISAPPROVAL/PASSAGE. Passage of the joint resolution that would nullify and disapprove of a Bureau of Land Management rule that amends the agency's procedures for the development of resource management plans for public lands. The rule directs BLM to design management plans that address resource issues in a number of programs related to wildfire prevention, wildlife habitat protection and demands for renewable and nonrenewable energy. The rule also provides additional opportunities for the public to submit information and comments on a plan revision or amendment. Passed 234-186 : R 230-4; D 4-182. Feb. 7, 2017.

84. H J RES 57. SCHOOL PERFORMANCE ASSESSMENT DISAPPROVAL/PASSAGE. Passage of the joint resolution that would nullify and disapprove of an Education Department rule that requires states to define, subsequently monitor and intervene with schools deemed to be low-performing schools. Under the department's rule, states are required to measure academic achievement through factors such as graduation rates and English proficiency rates. Passed 234-190 : R 234-1; D 0-189. Feb. 7, 2017.

85. H J RES 58. TEACHING PROGRAM EVALUATION DISAPPROVAL/PASSAGE. Passage of the joint resolution that would nullify and disapprove of an Education Department rule that requires states, in evaluating teacher preparation programs at higher education institutions, to annually report on certain factors including placement and retention rates of graduates, student learning outcomes and feedback from graduates and employers on program effectiveness. Under the rule, federal grants for students who commit to teaching at low-income schools for at least four years are to be limited to students in programs rated by states as effective for at least two of the previous three years. Passed 240-181 : R 235-0; D 5-181. Feb. 7, 2017.

86. HR 244. VETERANS' EMPLOYMENT AWARDS/PASSAGE. Bilirakis, R-Fla., motion to suspend the rules and pass the bill that would direct the Department of Labor to establish an award program to recognize employers who recruit, employ and retain veterans. Employers would submit information on a voluntary basis in order to be eligible for a medallion and an award certificate under the program. Motion agreed to 409-1 : R 229-1; D 180-0. Feb. 13, 2017.

		81	82	83	84	85	86
ALABAMA							
1	Byrne	Y	Y	Y	Y	Y	Y
2	Roby	Y	Y	Y	Y	Y	Y
3	Rogers	Y	Y	Y	Y	Y	Y
4	Aderholt	Y	Y	Y	Y	Y	Y
5	Brooks	Y	Y	Y	Y	Y	Y
6	Palmer	Y	Y	Y	Y	Y	Y
7	Sewell	N	N	N	N	N	Y
ALASKA							
AL	Young	Y	Y	Y	Y	Y	Y
ARIZONA							
1	O'Halleran	N	N	N	Y	N	Y
2	McSally	Y	Y	Y	Y	Y	Y
3	Grijalva	N	N	N	N	N	Y
4	Gosar	Y	Y	Y	Y	Y	Y
5	Biggs	Y	Y	Y	Y	Y	Y
6	Schweikert	Y	Y	Y	Y	Y	Y
7	Gallego	N	N	N	N	N	?
8	Franks	Y	Y	Y	Y	Y	Y
9	Sinema	N	N	Y	N	Y	Y
ARKANSAS							
1	Crawford	Y	Y	Y	Y	Y	Y
2	Hill	Y	Y	Y	Y	Y	Y
3	Womack	Y	Y	Y	Y	Y	Y
4	Westerman	Y	Y	Y	Y	Y	Y
CALIFORNIA							
1	LaMalfa	Y	Y	Y	Y	Y	?
2	Huffman	N	N	N	N	N	Y
3	Garamendi	N	N	N	N	N	?
4	McClintock	Y	Y	Y	Y	Y	Y
5	Thompson	N	N	N	N	N	Y
6	Matsui	N	N	N	N	N	Y
7	Bera	N	N	N	N	N	Y
8	Cook	Y	Y	Y	Y	Y	Y
9	McNerney	N	N	N	N	N	Y
10	Denham	Y	Y	Y	Y	Y	Y
11	DeSaulnier	N	N	N	N	N	Y
12	Pelosi	N	N	N	N	N	Y
13	Lee	N	N	N	N	N	Y
14	Speier	N	N	N	N	N	Y
15	Swalwell	N	N	N	N	N	Y
16	Costa	N	N	N	N	N	Y
17	Khanna	N	N	N	N	N	Y
18	Eshoo	N	N	N	N	N	Y
19	Lofgren	N	N	N	N	N	Y
20	Panetta	N	N	N	N	N	Y
21	Valadao	Y	Y	Y	Y	Y	Y
22	Nunes	Y	Y	Y	Y	Y	Y
23	McCarthy	Y	Y	Y	Y	Y	Y
24	Carbajal	N	N	N	N	N	Y
25	Knight	Y	Y	Y	Y	Y	Y
26	Brownley	N	N	N	N	N	Y
27	Chu	N	N	N	N	N	Y
28	Schiff	N	N	N	N	N	Y
29	Cardenas	N	N	N	N	N	Y
30	Sherman	N	N	N	N	N	Y
31	Aguilar	N	N	N	N	N	Y
32	Napolitano	N	N	N	N	N	Y
33	Lieu	N	N	N	N	N	Y
34	Vacant						
35	Torres	N	N	N	N	N	Y
36	Ruiz	N	N	N	N	N	Y
37	Bass	N	N	N	N	N	Y
38	Sánchez, Linda	N	N	N	N	N	Y
39	Royce	Y	Y	Y	Y	Y	Y
40	Roybal-Allard	N	N	N	N	N	Y
41	Takano	N	N	N	N	N	Y
42	Calvert	Y	Y	Y	Y	Y	Y
43	Waters	N	N	N	N	N	?
44	Barragan	N	N	N	N	N	Y
45	Walters	Y	Y	Y	Y	Y	Y
46	Correa	N	N	N	N	N	Y
47	Lowenthal	N	N	N	N	N	Y
48	Rohrabacher	Y	Y	Y	Y	Y	Y
49	Issa	Y	Y	Y	Y	Y	Y
50	Hunter	Y	Y	Y	Y	Y	Y
51	Vargas	N	N	N	N	N	Y
52	Peters	N	N	N	N	N	Y
53	Davis	N	N	N	N	N	Y

		81	82	83	84	85	86
COLORADO							
1	DeGette	N	N	N	N	N	Y
2	Polis	N	N	N	N	N	Y
3	Tipton	Y	Y	Y	Y	Y	Y
4	Buck	Y	Y	Y	Y	Y	Y
5	Lamborn	Y	Y	Y	Y	Y	Y
6	Coffman	Y	Y	Y	Y	Y	Y
7	Perlmutter	N	N	N	N	N	Y
CONNECTICUT							
1	Larson	N	N	N	N	N	Y
2	Courtney	N	N	N	N	N	Y
3	DeLauro	N	N	N	N	N	Y
4	Himes	N	N	N	N	N	Y
5	Esty	N	N	N	N	N	Y
DELAWARE							
AL	Blunt Rochester	N	N	N	N	N	Y
FLORIDA							
1	Gaetz	Y	Y	Y	Y	Y	Y
2	Dunn	Y	Y	Y	Y	Y	Y
3	Yoho	Y	Y	Y	Y	Y	Y
4	Rutherford	Y	Y	Y	Y	Y	Y
5	Lawson	N	N	N	N	N	Y
6	DeSantis	Y	Y	N	Y	Y	Y
7	Murphy	N	N	N	N	Y	Y
8	Posey	Y	Y	Y	Y	Y	Y
9	Soto	N	N	N	N	N	Y
10	Demings	N	N	N	N	N	Y
11	Webster	Y	Y	?	Y	Y	Y
12	Bilirakis	Y	Y	Y	Y	Y	Y
13	Crist	N	N	N	N	N	Y
14	Castor	N	N	N	N	N	Y
15	Ross	Y	Y	Y	Y	Y	Y
16	Buchanan	Y	Y	Y	Y	Y	?
17	Rooney, T.	Y	Y	Y	Y	Y	Y
18	Mast	Y	Y	Y	Y	Y	Y
19	Rooney, F.	Y	Y	Y	Y	Y	Y
20	Hastings	N	?	N	N	N	Y
21	Frankel	N	N	?	N	N	Y
22	Deutch	N	N	N	N	N	Y
23	Wasserman Schultz	N	N	N	N	N	Y
24	Wilson	N	N	–	N	N	Y
25	Diaz-Balart	Y	Y	Y	Y	Y	Y
26	Curbelo	Y	Y	Y	Y	Y	Y
27	Ros-Lehtinen	Y	Y	Y	Y	Y	Y
GEORGIA							
1	Carter	Y	Y	Y	Y	Y	Y
2	Bishop	N	N	N	N	N	Y
3	Ferguson	Y	Y	Y	Y	Y	Y
4	Johnson	N	N	?	N	N	Y
5	Lewis	N	N	N	N	N	Y
7	Woodall	Y	Y	Y	Y	Y	Y
8	Scott, A.	Y	Y	Y	Y	Y	Y
9	Collins	Y	Y	Y	Y	Y	Y
10	Hice	Y	Y	Y	Y	Y	Y
11	Loudermilk	Y	Y	Y	Y	Y	Y
12	Allen	Y	Y	Y	Y	Y	Y
13	Scott, D.	N	N	N	N	?	Y
14	Graves	Y	Y	Y	Y	Y	Y
HAWAII							
1	Hanabusa	N	N	N	N	N	Y
2	Gabbard	N	N	N	N	N	Y
IDAHO							
1	Labrador	Y	Y	Y	Y	Y	Y
2	Simpson	Y	Y	Y	Y	Y	Y
ILLINOIS							
1	Rush	?	?	?	?	?	?
2	Kelly	N	N	N	N	N	Y
3	Lipinski	N	N	N	N	N	Y
4	Gutierrez	N	N	N	N	–	+
5	Quigley	N	N	N	N	N	Y
6	Roskam	Y	Y	Y	Y	Y	Y
7	Davis, D.	N	N	N	N	N	Y
8	Krishnamoorthi	N	N	N	N	N	Y
9	Schakowsky	N	N	N	N	N	Y
10	Schneider	N	N	N	N	N	Y
11	Foster	N	N	N	N	N	Y
12	Bost	Y	Y	Y	Y	Y	Y
13	Davis, R.	Y	Y	Y	Y	Y	Y
14	Hultgren	Y	Y	Y	Y	Y	Y
15	Shimkus	Y	Y	Y	Y	Y	Y

	81	82	83	84	85	86
16 **Kinzinger**	Y	Y	Y	Y	Y	Y
17 Bustos	N	N	N	N	N	Y
18 **LaHood**	Y	Y	Y	Y	Y	Y
INDIANA						
1 Visclosky	N	N	N	N	N	Y
2 **Walorski**	Y	Y	Y	Y	Y	Y
3 **Banks**	Y	Y	Y	Y	Y	Y
4 **Rokita**	Y	Y	Y	Y	Y	Y
5 **Brooks**	Y	Y	Y	Y	Y	Y
6 **Messer**	Y	Y	Y	Y	Y	Y
7 Carson	N	N	N	N	N	Y
8 **Bucshon**	Y	Y	Y	Y	Y	Y
9 **Hollingsworth**	Y	Y	Y	Y	Y	Y
IOWA						
1 **Blum**	Y	Y	Y	Y	Y	Y
2 Loebsack	N	N	N	N	N	Y
3 **Young**	Y	Y	Y	Y	Y	Y
4 **King**	Y	Y	Y	Y	Y	Y
KANSAS						
1 **Marshall**	Y	Y	Y	Y	Y	Y
2 **Jenkins**	Y	Y	Y	Y	Y	+
3 **Yoder**	Y	Y	Y	Y	Y	Y
KENTUCKY						
1 **Comer**	Y	Y	Y	Y	Y	Y
2 **Guthrie**	Y	Y	Y	Y	Y	Y
3 Yarmuth	N	N	N	N	N	Y
4 **Massie**	Y	Y	Y	Y	Y	Y
5 **Rogers**	Y	Y	Y	Y	Y	Y
6 **Barr**	Y	Y	Y	Y	Y	Y
LOUISIANA						
1 **Scalise**	Y	Y	Y	Y	Y	Y
2 Richmond	N	N	N	N	N	Y
3 **Higgins**	Y	Y	Y	Y	Y	Y
4 **Johnson**	Y	Y	Y	Y	Y	Y
5 **Abraham**	Y	Y	Y	Y	Y	Y
6 **Graves**	Y	Y	Y	Y	Y	Y
MAINE						
1 Pingree	N	N	N	N	N	+
2 **Poliquin**	Y	Y	Y	Y	Y	Y
MARYLAND						
1 **Harris**	Y	Y	Y	Y	Y	Y
2 Ruppersberger	N	N	N	N	N	Y
3 Sarbanes	N	N	N	N	N	Y
4 Brown	N	N	N	N	N	Y
5 Hoyer	N	N	N	N	N	Y
6 Delaney	N	N	N	N	N	+
7 Cummings	N	N	N	N	N	Y
8 Raskin	N	N	N	N	N	Y
MASSACHUSETTS						
1 Neal	N	N	N	N	N	Y
2 McGovern	N	N	N	N	N	Y
3 Tsongas	N	N	N	N	N	Y
4 Kennedy	N	N	N	N	N	Y
5 Clark	N	N	N	N	N	Y
6 Moulton	N	N	N	N	N	?
7 Capuano	N	N	N	N	N	Y
8 Lynch	N	N	N	N	N	Y
9 Keating	N	N	N	N	N	Y
MICHIGAN						
1 **Bergman**	Y	Y	Y	Y	Y	Y
2 **Huizenga**	Y	Y	Y	Y	Y	Y
3 **Amash**	Y	Y	Y	Y	Y	N
4 **Moolenaar**	Y	Y	Y	Y	Y	Y
5 Kildee	N	N	N	N	N	Y
6 **Upton**	Y	Y	Y	Y	Y	Y
7 **Walberg**	Y	Y	Y	Y	Y	Y
8 **Bishop**	Y	Y	Y	Y	Y	Y
9 Levin	N	N	N	N	N	Y
10 **Mitchell**	Y	Y	Y	Y	Y	Y
11 **Trott**	Y	Y	Y	Y	Y	Y
12 Dingell	N	N	N	N	N	Y
13 Conyers	N	N	N	N	N	Y
14 Lawrence	N	N	N	N	N	Y
MINNESOTA						
1 Walz	N	N	N	N	N	Y
2 **Lewis**	Y	Y	Y	Y	Y	Y
3 **Paulsen**	Y	Y	Y	Y	Y	Y
4 McCollum	N	N	N	N	N	Y

	81	82	83	84	85	86
%5 Ellison	N	N	N	N	N	+
6 **Emmer**	Y	Y	Y	Y	Y	Y
7 Peterson	N	N	Y	N	N	Y
8 Nolan	N	N	N	N	N	Y
MISSISSIPPI						
1 **Kelly**	Y	Y	Y	Y	Y	Y
2 Thompson	N	N	?	N	N	Y
3 **Harper**	Y	Y	Y	Y	Y	Y
4 **Palazzo**	Y	Y	Y	Y	Y	Y
MISSOURI						
1 Clay	N	N	N	N	N	Y
2 **Wagner**	Y	Y	Y	Y	Y	Y
3 **Luetkemeyer**	Y	Y	Y	Y	Y	Y
4 **Hartzler**	Y	Y	Y	Y	Y	Y
5 Cleaver	N	N	N	N	N	Y
6 **Graves**	Y	Y	Y	Y	Y	Y
7 **Long**	Y	Y	Y	Y	Y	Y
8 **Smith**	Y	Y	Y	Y	Y	Y
MONTANA						
AL **Zinke**	?	?	?	?	?	?
NEBRASKA						
1 **Fortenberry**	Y	Y	Y	Y	Y	Y
2 **Bacon**	Y	Y	Y	Y	Y	Y
3 **Smith**	Y	Y	Y	Y	Y	Y
NEVADA						
1 Titus	N	N	N	N	N	Y
2 **Amodei**	Y	Y	Y	Y	Y	Y
3 Rosen	N	N	N	N	N	Y
4 Kihuen	N	N	N	N	N	Y
NEW HAMPSHIRE						
1 Shea-Porter	N	N	N	N	N	Y
2 Kuster	N	N	N	N	N	Y
NEW JERSEY						
1 Norcross	N	N	N	N	N	Y
2 **LoBiondo**	Y	Y	N	Y	Y	Y
3 **MacArthur**	Y	Y	Y	Y	Y	Y
4 **Smith**	Y	Y	N	Y	Y	Y
5 Gottheimer	N	N	N	N	N	Y
6 Pallone	N	N	N	N	N	Y
7 **Lance**	Y	Y	N	Y	Y	Y
8 Sires	?	?	?	?	?	Y
9 Pascrell	N	N	N	N	N	Y
10 Payne	N	N	N	N	N	Y
11 **Frelinghuysen**	Y	Y	Y	Y	Y	Y
12 Watson Coleman	N	N	N	N	N	Y
NEW MEXICO						
1 Lujan Grisham	N	N	N	N	N	Y
2 **Pearce**	Y	Y	Y	Y	Y	Y
3 Luján	N	N	N	N	N	Y
NEW YORK						
1 **Zeldin**	Y	Y	Y	Y	Y	Y
2 **King**	Y	Y	Y	Y	Y	Y
3 Suozzi	N	N	N	N	N	Y
4 Rice	N	N	N	N	N	Y
5 Meeks	N	N	N	?	N	?
6 Meng	N	N	N	N	N	Y
7 Velázquez	N	N	N	N	N	Y
8 Jeffries	N	N	N	N	N	Y
9 Clarke	N	N	N	N	N	Y
10 Nadler	N	N	N	N	N	Y
11 **Donovan**	Y	Y	Y	Y	Y	Y
12 Maloney, C.	N	N	N	N	N	Y
13 Espaillat	N	N	N	N	N	Y
14 Crowley	N	N	N	N	N	Y
15 Serrano	N	N	N	N	N	Y
16 Engel	N	N	N	N	N	Y
17 Lowey	N	N	N	N	N	Y
18 Maloney, S.P.	N	N	N	N	N	Y
19 **Faso**	Y	Y	Y	Y	Y	+
20 Tonko	N	N	N	N	N	Y
21 **Stefanik**	Y	Y	Y	Y	Y	Y
22 **Tenney**	Y	Y	Y	Y	Y	Y
23 **Reed**	Y	Y	Y	Y	Y	Y
24 **Katko**	Y	Y	Y	Y	Y	Y
25 Slaughter	N	N	N	N	N	Y
26 Higgins	N	N	N	N	?	Y
27 **Collins**	Y	Y	Y	Y	Y	Y
NORTH CAROLINA						
1 Butterfield	N	N	N	N	N	Y
2 **Holding**	Y	Y	Y	Y	Y	Y
3 **Jones**	Y	Y	Y	Y	Y	Y
4 Price	N	N	N	N	N	Y

	81	82	83	84	85	86
5 **Foxx**	Y	Y	Y	Y	Y	Y
6 **Walker**	Y	Y	Y	Y	Y	Y
7 **Rouzer**	Y	Y	Y	Y	Y	Y
8 **Hudson**	Y	Y	Y	Y	Y	Y
9 **Pittenger**	Y	Y	Y	Y	Y	?
10 **McHenry**	Y	Y	Y	Y	Y	Y
11 **Meadows**	Y	Y	Y	Y	Y	Y
12 Adams	N	N	N	N	N	Y
13 **Budd**	Y	Y	Y	Y	Y	Y
NORTH DAKOTA						
AL **Cramer**	Y	Y	Y	Y	Y	Y
OHIO						
1 **Chabot**	Y	Y	Y	Y	Y	Y
2 **Wenstrup**	Y	Y	Y	Y	Y	Y
3 Beatty	–	–	N	N	N	Y
4 **Jordan**	Y	Y	Y	Y	Y	Y
5 **Latta**	Y	Y	Y	Y	Y	Y
6 **Johnson**	Y	Y	Y	Y	Y	Y
7 **Gibbs**	Y	Y	Y	Y	Y	Y
8 **Davidson**	Y	Y	Y	Y	Y	Y
9 Kaptur	N	N	N	N	N	Y
10 **Turner**	Y	Y	Y	Y	Y	Y
11 Fudge	N	N	N	N	N	Y
12 **Tiberi**	Y	Y	Y	Y	Y	Y
13 Ryan	N	N	N	N	N	Y
14 **Joyce**	Y	Y	Y	Y	Y	Y
15 **Stivers**	Y	Y	Y	Y	Y	Y
16 **Renacci**	Y	Y	Y	Y	Y	Y
OKLAHOMA						
1 **Bridenstine**	Y	Y	Y	Y	Y	Y
2 **Mullin**	Y	Y	Y	Y	Y	Y
3 **Lucas**	Y	Y	Y	Y	Y	Y
4 **Cole**	Y	Y	Y	Y	Y	Y
5 **Russell**	Y	Y	Y	Y	Y	Y
OREGON						
1 Bonamici	N	N	N	N	N	Y
2 **Walden**	Y	Y	Y	Y	Y	Y
3 Blumenauer	N	N	N	N	N	Y
4 DeFazio	N	N	N	N	N	Y
5 Schrader	N	N	Y	N	N	Y
PENNSYLVANIA						
1 Brady	N	N	N	N	N	Y
2 Evans	N	N	N	N	N	Y
3 **Kelly**	Y	Y	Y	Y	Y	Y
4 **Perry**	Y	Y	Y	Y	Y	Y
5 **Thompson**	Y	Y	Y	Y	Y	Y
6 **Costello**	Y	Y	Y	Y	Y	Y
7 **Meehan**	Y	Y	Y	N	Y	Y
8 **Fitzpatrick**	Y	Y	N	Y	Y	Y
9 **Shuster**	Y	Y	Y	Y	Y	Y
10 **Marino**	Y	Y	Y	Y	Y	Y
11 **Barletta**	Y	Y	Y	Y	Y	Y
12 **Rothfus**	Y	Y	Y	Y	Y	Y
13 Boyle	N	N	N	N	N	+
14 Doyle	N	N	N	N	N	Y
15 **Dent**	Y	Y	Y	Y	Y	Y
16 **Smucker**	Y	Y	Y	Y	Y	Y
17 Cartwright	N	N	N	N	N	Y
18 **Murphy**	Y	Y	Y	Y	Y	Y
RHODE ISLAND						
1 Cicilline	N	N	N	N	N	Y
2 Langevin	N	N	N	N	N	Y
SOUTH CAROLINA						
1 **Sanford**	Y	Y	Y	Y	Y	Y
2 **Wilson**	Y	Y	Y	Y	Y	Y
3 **Duncan**	Y	Y	Y	Y	Y	Y
4 **Gowdy**	Y	Y	Y	Y	Y	Y
5 **Mulvaney**	?	?	?	?	?	?
6 Clyburn	N	N	N	N	N	Y
7 **Rice**	Y	Y	Y	Y	Y	Y
SOUTH DAKOTA						
AL **Noem**	Y	Y	Y	Y	Y	Y
TENNESSEE						
1 **Roe**	Y	Y	Y	Y	Y	Y
2 **Duncan**	Y	Y	Y	Y	Y	Y
3 **Fleischmann**	Y	Y	Y	Y	Y	Y
4 **DesJarlais**	Y	Y	Y	Y	Y	Y
5 Cooper	?	?	N	N	N	Y
6 **Black**	Y	Y	Y	Y	Y	Y
7 **Blackburn**	Y	Y	Y	Y	Y	Y
8 **Kustoff**	Y	Y	Y	Y	Y	Y
9 Cohen	N	N	N	N	N	Y

	81	82	83	84	85	86
TEXAS						
1 **Gohmert**	Y	Y	Y	Y	Y	Y
2 **Poe**	?	?	?	?	?	Y
3 **Johnson, S.**	Y	Y	Y	Y	Y	Y
4 **Ratcliffe**	Y	Y	Y	Y	Y	Y
5 **Hensarling**	Y	Y	Y	Y	Y	Y
6 **Barton**	Y	Y	Y	Y	Y	Y
7 **Culberson**	Y	Y	Y	Y	Y	Y
8 **Brady**	Y	Y	Y	Y	Y	Y
9 Green, A.	N	N	N	N	N	Y
10 **McCaul**	Y	Y	Y	Y	Y	+
11 **Conaway**	Y	Y	Y	Y	Y	Y
12 **Granger**	Y	Y	Y	Y	Y	Y
13 **Thornberry**	Y	Y	Y	Y	Y	Y
14 **Weber**	Y	Y	Y	Y	Y	Y
15 Gonzalez	N	N	N	N	N	Y
16 O'Rourke	N	N	N	N	N	Y
17 **Flores**	Y	Y	Y	Y	Y	Y
18 Jackson Lee	?	?	N	N	N	Y
19 **Arrington**	Y	Y	Y	Y	Y	Y
20 Castro	N	N	N	N	N	Y
21 **Smith**	Y	Y	Y	Y	Y	Y
22 **Olson**	Y	Y	Y	Y	Y	Y
23 **Hurd**	Y	Y	Y	Y	Y	Y
24 **Marchant**	Y	?	Y	Y	Y	Y
25 **Williams**	Y	Y	Y	Y	Y	Y
26 **Burgess**	Y	Y	Y	Y	Y	Y
27 **Farenthold**	Y	Y	Y	Y	Y	Y
28 Cuellar	N	N	Y	N	N	Y
29 Green, G.	N	N	N	N	N	Y
30 Johnson, E.B.	N	N	N	N	?	Y
31 **Carter**	Y	Y	Y	Y	Y	Y
32 **Sessions**	Y	Y	Y	Y	Y	Y
33 Veasey	N	N	N	N	N	Y
34 Vela	N	N	N	N	N	Y
35 Doggett	N	N	N	N	N	Y
36 **Babin**	Y	Y	Y	Y	Y	Y
UTAH						
1 **Bishop**	Y	Y	Y	Y	Y	Y
2 **Stewart**	Y	Y	Y	Y	Y	Y
3 **Chaffetz**	?	?	Y	Y	Y	Y
4 **Love**	Y	Y	Y	Y	Y	Y
VERMONT						
AL Welch	N	N	N	N	N	+
VIRGINIA						
1 **Wittman**	Y	Y	Y	Y	Y	Y
2 **Taylor**	Y	Y	Y	Y	Y	Y
3 Scott	N	N	N	N	N	Y
4 McEachin	N	N	N	N	N	Y
5 **Garrett**	Y	Y	Y	Y	Y	Y
6 **Goodlatte**	Y	Y	Y	Y	Y	Y
7 **Brat**	Y	Y	Y	Y	Y	Y
8 Beyer	N	N	N	N	N	Y
9 **Griffith**	Y	Y	Y	Y	Y	Y
10 **Comstock**	Y	Y	Y	Y	Y	Y
11 Connolly	N	N	N	N	N	Y
WASHINGTON						
1 DelBene	N	N	N	N	N	Y
2 Larsen	N	N	N	N	N	Y
3 **Herrera Beutler**	Y	Y	Y	Y	Y	Y
4 **Newhouse**	Y	Y	Y	Y	Y	Y
5 **McMorris Rodgers**	Y	Y	Y	Y	Y	Y
6 Kilmer	N	N	N	N	N	Y
7 Jayapal	N	N	N	N	N	Y
8 **Reichert**	Y	Y	Y	Y	Y	Y
9 Smith	–	–	–	–	–	Y
10 Heck	N	N	N	N	Y	Y
WEST VIRGINIA						
1 **McKinley**	Y	Y	Y	Y	Y	Y
2 **Mooney**	Y	Y	Y	Y	Y	Y
3 **Jenkins**	Y	Y	Y	Y	Y	Y
WISCONSIN						
1 **Ryan**						
2 Pocan	N	N	N	N	N	Y
3 Kind	N	N	N	N	N	Y
4 Moore	N	N	N	N	N	+
5 **Sensenbrenner**	Y	Y	Y	Y	Y	Y
6 **Grothman**	Y	Y	Y	Y	Y	Y
7 **Duffy**	Y	Y	Y	Y	Y	Y
8 **Gallagher**	Y	Y	Y	Y	Y	Y
WYOMING						
AL **Cheney**	Y	Y	Y	Y	Y	Y

VOTE NUMBER

87. HR 974. CONTRACTS TO EMPLOYERS OF VETERANS/PASSAGE. Bilirakis, R-Fla., motion to suspend the rules and pass the bill that would authorize the Department of Veterans Affairs, when awarding a contract, to give preference to companies with a high percentage of full-time employees who are veterans. Motion agreed to 407-0 : R 227-0; D 180-0. Feb. 13, 2017.

88. H J RES 42, H RES 99, HR 428. BOUNDARY IDENTIFICATION SURVEY AND UNEMPLOYMENT DRUG TESTING DISAPPROVAL/PREVIOUS QUESTION. Cole, R-Okla., motion to order the previous question (thus ending debate and the possibility of amendment) on the rule (H Res 99) that would provide for House floor consideration of a bill (HR 428) that would authorize $1 million for the Bureau of Land Management to pay for a survey to identify the boundary, with respect to title and ownership, along the Red River on the border between Texas and Oklahoma. It would also provide for consideration of a joint resolution (H J Res 42) that would nullify and disapprove of a Labor Department rule that defines the occupations for which states can require drug tests for individuals applying for unemployment benefits. Motion agreed to 225-189 : R 225-0; D 0-189. Feb. 14, 2017.

89. H J RES 42, H RES 99, HR 428. BOUNDARY IDENTIFICATION SURVEY AND UNEMPLOYMENT DRUG TESTING DISAPPROVAL/RULE. Adoption of the rule (H Res 99) that would provide for House floor consideration of a bill (HR 428) that would authorize $1 million for the Bureau of Land Management to pay for a survey to identify the boundary, with respect to title and ownership, along the Red River on the border between Texas and Oklahoma. It would also provide for consideration of a joint resolution (H J Res 42) that would nullify and disapprove of a Labor Department rule that defines the occupations for which states can require drug tests for individuals applying for unemployment benefits. Adopted 225-187 : R 225-0; D 0-187. Feb. 14, 2017.

90. H J RES 66, H J RES 67, H RES 116. STATE RETIREMENT PLANS DISAPPROVAL AND LOCAL GOVERNMENT RETIREMENT PLANS DISAPPROVAL/PREVIOUS QUESTION. Byrne, R-Ala., motion to order the previous question (thus ending debate and the possibility of amendment) on the rule (H Res 116) that would provide for House floor consideration of a joint resolution (H J Res 66) that would nullify and disapprove of a Labor Department rule that exempts certain state-administered retirement savings plans from select federal regulations if state programs meet certain standards. It would also provide for consideration of a joint resolution (H J Res 67) that would nullify and disapprove of a Labor Department rule that exempts certain local government-administered retirement savings plans for non-government employees from select federal regulations. Motion agreed to 227-188 : R 227-0; D 0-188. Feb. 14, 2017.

91. H J RES 66, H J RES 67, H RES 116. STATE RETIREMENT PLANS DISAPPROVAL AND LOCAL GOVERNMENT RETIREMENT PLANS DISAPPROVAL/RULE. Adoption of the rule (H Res 116) that would provide for House floor consideration of a joint resolution (H J Res 66) that would nullify and disapprove of a Labor Department rule that exempts certain state-administered retirement savings plans from select federal regulations if state programs meet certain standards. It would also provide for consideration of a joint resolution (H J Res 67) that would nullify and disapprove of a Labor Department rule that exempts certain local government-administered retirement savings plans for non-government employees from select federal regulations. Adopted 227-188 : R 227-0; D 0-188. Feb. 14, 2017.

92. HR 428. BOUNDARY IDENTIFICATION SURVEY/PASSAGE. Passage of the bill that would authorize $1 million for the Bureau of Land Management to pay for a survey to identify the boundary, with respect to title and ownership, along the Red River on the border between Texas and Oklahoma. It would require the survey use the gradient boundary method of measurement established in the Supreme Court case Oklahoma v. Texas and that the survey be completed within two years of the bill's enactment. Passed 250-171 : R 235-0; D 15-171. Feb. 14, 2017.

	87	88	89	90	91	92
ALABAMA						
1 **Byrne**	Y	Y	Y	Y	Y	Y
2 **Roby**	Y	Y	Y	Y	Y	Y
3 **Rogers**	Y	Y	Y	Y	Y	Y
4 **Aderholt**	Y	Y	Y	Y	Y	Y
5 **Brooks**	Y	Y	Y	Y	Y	Y
6 **Palmer**	Y	Y	Y	Y	Y	Y
7 Sewell	Y	N	N	N	N	N
ALASKA						
AL **Young**	Y	Y	Y	Y	Y	Y
ARIZONA						
1 O'Halleran	Y	N	N	N	N	N
2 **McSally**	Y	Y	Y	Y	Y	Y
3 Grijalva	Y	N	N	N	N	N
4 **Gosar**	Y	Y	Y	Y	Y	Y
5 **Biggs**	Y	Y	Y	Y	Y	Y
6 **Schweikert**	Y	Y	Y	Y	Y	Y
7 Gallego	?	N	N	N	N	?
8 **Franks**	Y	Y	Y	Y	Y	Y
9 Sinema	Y	N	N	N	N	N
ARKANSAS						
1 **Crawford**	Y	Y	Y	Y	Y	Y
2 **Hill**	Y	Y	Y	Y	Y	Y
3 **Womack**	Y	Y	Y	Y	Y	Y
4 **Westerman**	Y	Y	Y	Y	Y	Y
CALIFORNIA						
1 **LaMalfa**	?	?	Y	Y	Y	Y
2 Huffman	Y	N	N	N	N	N
3 Garamendi	?	N	N	N	N	N
4 **McClintock**	Y	Y	Y	Y	Y	Y
5 Thompson	Y	N	N	N	N	N
6 Matsui	Y	N	N	N	N	N
7 Bera	Y	N	N	N	N	N
8 **Cook**	Y	Y	Y	Y	Y	Y
9 McNerney	Y	N	N	N	N	N
10 **Denham**	Y	Y	Y	Y	Y	Y
11 DeSaulnier	Y	N	N	N	N	N
12 Pelosi	Y	N	N	N	N	N
13 Lee	Y	N	N	N	N	N
14 Speier	Y	N	N	N	N	N
15 Swalwell	Y	N	N	N	N	N
16 Costa	Y	N	N	N	N	N
17 Khanna	Y	N	N	N	N	N
18 Eshoo	Y	N	N	N	N	N
19 Lofgren	Y	N	N	N	N	N
20 Panetta	Y	N	N	N	N	N
21 **Valadao**	Y	Y	Y	Y	Y	Y
22 **Nunes**	Y	Y	Y	Y	Y	Y
23 **McCarthy**	Y	Y	Y	Y	Y	Y
24 Carbajal	Y	N	N	N	N	N
25 **Knight**	Y	Y	Y	Y	Y	Y
26 Brownley	Y	N	N	N	N	N
27 Chu	Y	N	N	N	N	N
28 Schiff	Y	N	N	N	N	N
29 Cardenas	Y	N	N	N	N	N
30 Sherman	Y	N	N	N	N	N
31 Aguilar	Y	N	N	N	N	N
32 Napolitano	Y	N	N	N	N	N
33 Lieu	Y	N	N	N	N	N
34 Vacant						
35 Torres	Y	N	N	N	N	N
36 Ruiz	Y	N	N	N	N	N
37 Bass	Y	N	N	N	N	N
38 Sánchez, Linda	Y	N	N	N	N	N
39 **Royce**	Y	Y	Y	Y	Y	Y
40 Roybal-Allard	Y	N	N	N	N	N
41 Takano	Y	N	N	N	N	N
42 **Calvert**	Y	Y	Y	Y	Y	Y
43 Waters	?	N	N	N	N	N
44 Barragan	Y	N	N	N	N	N
45 **Walters**	Y	Y	Y	Y	Y	Y
46 Correa	Y	N	N	N	N	N
47 Lowenthal	Y	N	N	N	N	N
48 **Rohrabacher**	Y	Y	Y	Y	Y	Y
49 **Issa**	Y	Y	Y	Y	Y	Y
50 **Hunter**	Y	Y	Y	Y	Y	Y
51 Vargas	Y	N	N	N	N	N
52 Peters	Y	N	N	N	N	Y
53 Davis	Y	N	N	N	N	N

	87	88	89	90	91	92
COLORADO						
1 DeGette	Y	N	N	N	N	N
2 Polis	N	N	N	N	N	N
3 **Tipton**	Y	Y	Y	Y	Y	Y
4 **Buck**	Y	Y	Y	Y	Y	Y
5 **Lamborn**	Y	Y	Y	Y	Y	Y
6 **Coffman**	Y	Y	Y	Y	Y	Y
7 Perlmutter	Y	N	N	N	N	N
CONNECTICUT						
1 Larson	Y	N	N	N	N	N
2 Courtney	Y	N	N	N	N	N
3 DeLauro	Y	N	N	N	N	N
4 Himes	Y	N	N	N	N	N
5 Esty	Y	N	N	N	N	N
DELAWARE						
AL Blunt Rochester	Y	N	N	N	N	N
FLORIDA						
1 **Gaetz**	Y	Y	Y	Y	Y	Y
2 **Dunn**	Y	Y	Y	Y	Y	Y
3 **Yoho**	Y	Y	Y	Y	Y	Y
4 **Rutherford**	Y	Y	Y	Y	Y	Y
5 Lawson	Y	N	N	N	N	N
6 **DeSantis**	Y	Y	Y	Y	Y	Y
7 Murphy	Y	N	N	N	N	N
8 **Posey**	Y	Y	Y	Y	Y	Y
9 Soto	Y	N	N	N	N	N
10 Demings	Y	N	N	N	N	?
11 **Webster**	Y	Y	Y	Y	Y	Y
12 **Bilirakis**	Y	Y	Y	Y	Y	Y
13 Crist	Y	N	N	N	N	N
14 Castor	Y	N	N	N	N	N
15 **Ross**	Y	Y	Y	Y	Y	Y
16 **Buchanan**	?	Y	Y	Y	Y	Y
17 **Rooney, T.**	Y	Y	Y	Y	Y	Y
18 **Mast**	Y	Y	Y	Y	Y	Y
19 **Rooney, F.**	Y	Y	Y	Y	Y	Y
20 Hastings	Y	N	N	N	N	N
21 Frankel	Y	N	N	N	N	N
22 Deutch	Y	N	N	N	N	N
23 Wasserman Schultz	Y	N	N	N	N	N
24 Wilson	Y	N	N	N	N	N
25 **Diaz-Balart**	Y	Y	Y	Y	Y	Y
26 **Curbelo**	Y	Y	Y	Y	Y	Y
27 **Ros-Lehtinen**	Y	Y	Y	Y	Y	Y
GEORGIA						
1 **Carter**	Y	Y	Y	Y	Y	Y
2 Bishop	Y	N	N	N	N	N
3 **Ferguson**	Y	Y	Y	Y	Y	Y
4 Johnson	Y	N	N	N	N	N
5 Lewis	Y	N	N	N	N	N
7 **Woodall**	Y	Y	?	?	Y	Y
8 **Scott, A.**	Y	Y	Y	Y	Y	Y
9 **Collins**	Y	Y	Y	Y	Y	Y
10 **Hice**	Y	Y	Y	Y	Y	Y
11 **Loudermilk**	Y	Y	Y	Y	?	Y
12 **Allen**	Y	Y	Y	Y	Y	Y
13 Scott, D.	Y	N	N	N	N	N
14 **Graves**	Y	Y	Y	Y	Y	Y
HAWAII						
1 Hanabusa	Y	N	N	N	N	N
2 Gabbard	Y	N	N	N	N	N
IDAHO						
1 **Labrador**	Y	Y	Y	Y	Y	Y
2 **Simpson**	Y	?	Y	Y	Y	Y
ILLINOIS						
1 Rush	?	?	?	?	?	?
2 Kelly	Y	N	N	N	N	N
3 Lipinski	Y	N	N	N	N	N
4 Gutierrez	+	N	N	N	N	N
5 Quigley	Y	N	N	N	N	N
6 **Roskam**	Y	Y	Y	Y	Y	Y
7 Davis, D.	Y	N	N	N	N	N
8 Krishnamoorthi	Y	N	N	N	N	N
9 Schakowsky	Y	N	N	N	N	N
10 Schneider	Y	N	N	N	N	N
11 Foster	Y	N	N	N	N	N
12 **Bost**	Y	Y	Y	Y	?	Y
13 **Davis, R.**	Y	Y	Y	Y	Y	Y
14 **Hultgren**	Y	Y	Y	Y	Y	Y
15 **Shimkus**	Y	Y	Y	Y	Y	Y

	87	88	89	90	91	92
16 **Kinzinger**	Y	Y	Y	Y	Y	Y
17 Bustos	Y	N	N	N	N	N
18 **LaHood**	Y	Y	Y	Y	Y	Y
INDIANA						
1 Visclosky	Y	–	–	–	–	–
2 **Walorski**	Y	Y	Y	Y	Y	Y
3 **Banks**	Y	Y	Y	Y	Y	Y
4 **Rokita**	Y	Y	Y	Y	Y	Y
5 **Brooks**	Y	Y	Y	Y	Y	Y
6 **Messer**	?	Y	Y	Y	Y	Y
7 Carson	Y	N	N	N	N	N
8 **Bucshon**	Y	Y	Y	Y	Y	Y
9 **Hollingsworth**	Y	Y	Y	Y	Y	Y
IOWA						
1 **Blum**	Y	Y	Y	Y	Y	Y
2 Loebsack	Y	N	N	N	N	N
3 **Young**	Y	Y	Y	Y	Y	Y
4 **King**	Y	Y	Y	Y	Y	Y
KANSAS						
1 **Marshall**	Y	Y	Y	Y	Y	Y
2 **Jenkins**	+	Y	Y	Y	Y	Y
3 **Yoder**	Y	Y	Y	Y	Y	Y
KENTUCKY						
1 **Comer**	Y	Y	Y	Y	Y	Y
2 **Guthrie**	Y	Y	Y	Y	Y	Y
3 Yarmuth	Y	N	N	N	N	N
4 **Massie**	Y	Y	Y	Y	Y	Y
5 **Rogers**	Y	Y	Y	Y	Y	Y
6 **Barr**	Y	Y	Y	Y	Y	Y
LOUISIANA						
1 **Scalise**	Y	Y	Y	Y	Y	Y
2 Richmond	Y	N	N	N	N	N
3 **Higgins**	Y	Y	Y	Y	Y	Y
4 **Johnson**	Y	Y	Y	Y	Y	Y
5 **Abraham**	Y	Y	Y	Y	Y	Y
6 **Graves**	Y	Y	Y	Y	Y	Y
MAINE						
1 Pingree	+	N	N	N	N	N
2 **Poliquin**	Y	Y	Y	Y	Y	Y
MARYLAND						
1 **Harris**	Y	Y	Y	Y	Y	Y
2 Ruppersberger	Y	N	N	N	N	N
3 Sarbanes	Y	N	N	N	N	N
4 Brown	Y	N	N	N	N	N
5 Hoyer	Y	N	N	N	N	N
6 Delaney	+	N	N	N	N	N
7 Cummings	Y	N	N	N	N	N
8 Raskin	Y	N	N	N	N	N
MASSACHUSETTS						
1 Neal	Y	N	N	N	N	N
2 McGovern	Y	N	N	N	N	N
3 Tsongas	Y	N	N	N	N	N
4 Kennedy	Y	N	N	N	N	N
5 Clark	Y	N	N	N	N	N
6 Moulton	?	N	N	N	N	N
7 Capuano	Y	N	N	N	N	N
8 Lynch	Y	N	N	N	N	N
9 Keating	Y	N	N	N	N	N
MICHIGAN						
1 **Bergman**	Y	Y	Y	Y	Y	Y
2 **Huizenga**	Y	+	+	+	+	Y
3 **Amash**	Y	Y	Y	Y	Y	Y
4 **Moolenaar**	Y	Y	Y	Y	Y	Y
5 Kildee	Y	N	N	N	N	N
6 **Upton**	Y	Y	Y	Y	Y	Y
7 **Walberg**	Y	Y	Y	Y	Y	Y
8 **Bishop**	Y	Y	Y	Y	Y	Y
9 Levin	Y	N	N	N	N	N
10 **Mitchell**	Y	Y	Y	Y	Y	Y
11 **Trott**	Y	Y	Y	Y	Y	Y
12 Dingell	Y	N	N	N	N	N
13 Conyers	Y	N	N	N	N	N
14 Lawrence	Y	N	N	N	N	N
MINNESOTA						
1 Walz	Y	N	–	–	–	N
2 **Lewis**	Y	Y	Y	Y	Y	Y
3 **Paulsen**	Y	Y	Y	Y	Y	Y
4 McCollum	Y	N	N	N	N	N

	87	88	89	90	91	92
5 Ellison	+	N	N	N	N	N
6 **Emmer**	Y	+	Y	Y	Y	Y
7 Peterson	Y	N	N	N	N	Y
8 Nolan	Y	N	N	N	N	N
MISSISSIPPI						
1 **Kelly**	Y	Y	Y	Y	Y	Y
2 Thompson	Y	N	N	N	N	N
3 **Harper**	Y	Y	Y	Y	Y	Y
4 **Palazzo**	Y	Y	Y	Y	Y	Y
MISSOURI						
1 Clay	Y	N	N	N	N	N
2 **Wagner**	Y	Y	Y	Y	Y	Y
3 **Luetkemeyer**	Y	Y	Y	Y	Y	Y
4 **Hartzler**	Y	?	?	?	?	Y
5 Cleaver	Y	N	N	N	N	N
6 **Graves**	Y	Y	Y	Y	Y	Y
7 **Long**	Y	Y	Y	Y	Y	Y
8 **Smith**	Y	Y	Y	Y	Y	Y
MONTANA						
AL **Zinke**	?	?	?	?	?	?
NEBRASKA						
1 **Fortenberry**	Y	Y	Y	Y	Y	Y
2 **Bacon**	Y	Y	Y	Y	Y	Y
3 **Smith**	Y	Y	Y	Y	Y	Y
NEVADA						
1 Titus	Y	N	N	N	N	N
2 **Amodei**	Y	Y	Y	Y	Y	Y
3 Rosen	Y	N	–	N	N	N
4 Kihuen	Y	N	N	N	N	N
NEW HAMPSHIRE						
1 Shea-Porter	Y	N	N	N	N	N
2 Kuster	Y	N	N	N	N	N
NEW JERSEY						
1 Norcross	Y	N	N	N	N	N
2 **LoBiondo**	Y	Y	Y	Y	Y	Y
3 **MacArthur**	Y	Y	Y	Y	Y	Y
4 **Smith**	Y	Y	Y	Y	Y	Y
5 Gottheimer	Y	N	N	N	N	Y
6 Pallone	Y	N	N	N	N	N
7 **Lance**	Y	Y	Y	Y	Y	Y
8 Sires	Y	N	N	N	N	N
9 Pascrell	Y	N	N	N	N	N
10 Payne	Y	–	–	–	N	N
11 **Frelinghuysen**	Y	Y	Y	Y	Y	Y
12 Watson Coleman	Y	N	N	N	N	N
NEW MEXICO						
1 Lujan Grisham	Y	N	N	N	N	N
2 **Pearce**	Y	Y	Y	Y	Y	Y
3 Luján	Y	N	N	N	N	N
NEW YORK						
1 **Zeldin**	Y	Y	Y	Y	Y	Y
2 **King**	Y	?	?	?	Y	Y
3 Suozzi	Y	N	N	N	?	N
4 Rice	Y	N	N	N	N	?
5 Meeks	?	N	N	N	N	N
6 Meng	Y	N	N	N	N	N
7 Velázquez	Y	N	N	N	N	N
8 Jeffries	Y	N	N	N	N	N
9 Clarke	Y	N	N	N	N	N
10 Nadler	Y	N	N	N	N	N
11 **Donovan**	Y	Y	Y	Y	Y	Y
12 Maloney, C.	Y	N	N	N	N	N
13 Espaillat	Y	N	N	N	N	N
14 Crowley	Y	N	N	N	N	N
15 Serrano	Y	N	N	N	N	N
16 Engel	Y	N	N	N	N	?
17 Lowey	Y	N	N	N	N	N
18 Maloney, S.P.	Y	N	N	N	N	N
19 **Faso**	+	Y	Y	Y	Y	Y
20 Tonko	Y	N	N	N	N	N
21 **Stefanik**	Y	Y	Y	Y	Y	Y
22 **Tenney**	Y	Y	Y	Y	Y	Y
23 **Reed**	Y	Y	Y	Y	Y	Y
24 **Katko**	Y	Y	Y	Y	Y	Y
25 Slaughter	Y	N	N	N	N	N
26 Higgins	Y	N	N	N	N	N
27 **Collins**	Y	Y	Y	Y	Y	Y
NORTH CAROLINA						
1 Butterfield	Y	N	N	N	N	N
2 **Holding**	Y	Y	Y	Y	Y	Y
3 **Jones**	Y	Y	Y	Y	Y	Y
4 Price	Y	N	N	N	N	N

	87	88	89	90	91	92
5 **Foxx**	Y	Y	Y	Y	Y	Y
6 **Walker**	Y	Y	Y	Y	Y	Y
7 **Rouzer**	Y	Y	Y	Y	Y	Y
8 **Hudson**	Y	Y	Y	Y	Y	Y
9 **Pittenger**	Y	Y	Y	Y	Y	Y
10 **McHenry**	Y	Y	Y	Y	Y	Y
11 **Meadows**	Y	Y	Y	Y	Y	Y
12 Adams	Y	N	N	N	N	N
13 **Budd**	Y	Y	Y	Y	Y	Y
NORTH DAKOTA						
AL **Cramer**	Y	Y	Y	Y	Y	Y
OHIO						
1 **Chabot**	Y	Y	Y	Y	Y	Y
2 **Wenstrup**	Y	Y	Y	Y	Y	Y
3 Beatty	Y	–	–	–	–	–
4 **Jordan**	Y	Y	Y	Y	Y	Y
5 **Latta**	Y	Y	Y	Y	Y	Y
6 **Johnson**	Y	Y	Y	Y	Y	Y
7 **Gibbs**	Y	Y	Y	Y	Y	Y
8 **Davidson**	Y	Y	Y	Y	Y	Y
9 Kaptur	Y	N	N	N	N	N
10 **Turner**	Y	Y	Y	Y	Y	Y
11 Fudge	Y	N	N	N	N	N
12 **Tiberi**	Y	Y	Y	Y	Y	Y
13 Ryan	Y	N	N	N	N	N
14 **Joyce**	Y	Y	Y	Y	Y	Y
15 **Stivers**	Y	Y	Y	Y	Y	Y
16 **Renacci**	Y	Y	Y	Y	Y	Y
OKLAHOMA						
1 **Bridenstine**	Y	Y	Y	Y	Y	Y
2 **Mullin**	Y	Y	Y	Y	Y	Y
3 **Lucas**	Y	Y	Y	Y	Y	Y
4 **Cole**	Y	Y	Y	Y	Y	Y
5 **Russell**	Y	Y	Y	Y	Y	Y
OREGON						
1 Bonamici	Y	N	N	N	N	N
2 **Walden**	Y	Y	Y	Y	Y	Y
3 Blumenauer	Y	N	N	N	N	N
4 DeFazio	Y	N	N	N	N	N
5 Schrader	Y	N	N	N	N	N
PENNSYLVANIA						
1 Brady	Y	N	N	N	N	N
2 Evans	Y	N	N	N	N	N
3 **Kelly**	Y	Y	Y	Y	Y	Y
4 **Perry**	Y	Y	Y	Y	Y	Y
5 **Thompson**	Y	Y	Y	Y	Y	Y
6 **Costello**	Y	Y	Y	Y	Y	Y
7 **Meehan**	Y	Y	Y	Y	Y	Y
8 **Fitzpatrick**	Y	Y	Y	Y	Y	Y
9 **Shuster**	?	?	?	Y	Y	Y
10 **Marino**	Y	Y	Y	Y	Y	Y
11 **Barletta**	Y	Y	Y	Y	Y	Y
12 **Rothfus**	Y	Y	Y	Y	Y	Y
13 Boyle	+	N	N	N	N	N
14 Doyle	Y	N	N	N	N	N
15 **Dent**	Y	Y	Y	Y	Y	Y
16 **Smucker**	Y	Y	Y	Y	Y	Y
17 Cartwright	Y	N	N	N	N	N
18 **Murphy**	Y	Y	Y	Y	Y	Y
RHODE ISLAND						
1 Cicilline	Y	N	N	N	N	N
2 Langevin	Y	N	N	N	N	N
SOUTH CAROLINA						
1 **Sanford**	Y	Y	Y	Y	Y	Y
2 **Wilson**	Y	Y	Y	Y	Y	Y
3 **Duncan**	Y	Y	Y	Y	Y	Y
4 **Gowdy**	Y	Y	Y	Y	Y	Y
5 **Mulvaney**	?	?	?	?	?	?
6 Clyburn	Y	N	N	N	N	N
7 **Rice**	Y	Y	Y	Y	Y	Y
SOUTH DAKOTA						
AL **Noem**	Y	Y	Y	Y	Y	Y
TENNESSEE						
1 **Roe**	Y	Y	+	+	+	Y
2 **Duncan**	?	Y	Y	Y	Y	Y
3 **Fleischmann**	Y	Y	Y	Y	Y	Y
4 **DesJarlais**	Y	Y	Y	Y	Y	Y
5 Cooper	Y	N	N	N	N	N
6 **Black**	Y	Y	Y	Y	Y	Y
7 **Blackburn**	Y	Y	Y	Y	Y	Y
8 **Kustoff**	Y	Y	Y	Y	Y	Y
9 Cohen	Y	N	N	N	N	N

	87	88	89	90	91	92
TEXAS						
1 **Gohmert**	Y	Y	Y	Y	Y	Y
2 **Poe**	Y	Y	Y	Y	Y	Y
3 **Johnson, S.**	Y	Y	Y	Y	Y	Y
4 **Ratcliffe**	?	Y	Y	Y	Y	Y
5 **Hensarling**	Y	?	?	?	?	Y
6 **Barton**	Y	Y	Y	Y	Y	Y
7 **Culberson**	Y	Y	Y	Y	Y	Y
8 **Brady**	Y	Y	Y	Y	Y	Y
9 Green, A.	Y	N	N	N	N	Y
10 **McCaul**	+	+	+	+	+	+
11 **Conaway**	Y	Y	Y	Y	Y	Y
12 **Granger**	Y	Y	Y	Y	Y	Y
13 **Thornberry**	Y	Y	Y	Y	Y	Y
14 **Weber**	Y	Y	Y	Y	Y	Y
15 Gonzalez	Y	N	N	N	N	Y
16 O'Rourke	Y	N	N	N	N	Y
17 **Flores**	Y	Y	Y	Y	Y	Y
18 Jackson Lee	Y	N	N	N	N	Y
19 **Arrington**	Y	Y	Y	Y	Y	Y
20 Castro	Y	N	N	N	N	Y
21 **Smith**	Y	Y	Y	Y	Y	Y
22 **Olson**	Y	Y	Y	Y	Y	Y
23 **Hurd**	Y	Y	Y	Y	Y	Y
24 **Marchant**	Y	Y	Y	Y	Y	Y
25 **Williams**	Y	Y	Y	Y	Y	Y
26 **Burgess**	Y	Y	Y	Y	Y	Y
27 **Farenthold**	Y	Y	Y	Y	Y	Y
28 Cuellar	Y	N	N	N	N	Y
29 Green, G.	Y	N	N	N	N	Y
30 Johnson, E.B.	Y	N	N	N	N	Y
31 **Carter**	Y	Y	Y	Y	Y	Y
32 **Sessions**	Y	Y	Y	Y	Y	Y
33 Veasey	Y	N	N	N	N	Y
34 Vela	Y	N	N	N	N	Y
35 Doggett	Y	N	N	N	N	Y
36 **Babin**	Y	Y	Y	Y	Y	Y
UTAH						
1 **Bishop**	Y	Y	Y	Y	Y	Y
2 **Stewart**	Y	Y	Y	Y	Y	Y
3 **Chaffetz**	Y	Y	Y	Y	Y	Y
4 **Love**	Y	?	?	?	?	Y
VERMONT						
AL Welch	+	N	N	N	N	N
VIRGINIA						
1 **Wittman**	Y	Y	Y	Y	Y	Y
2 **Taylor**	Y	Y	Y	Y	Y	Y
3 Scott	Y	N	N	N	N	N
4 McEachin	Y	N	N	N	N	N
5 **Garrett**	Y	Y	Y	Y	Y	Y
6 **Goodlatte**	Y	Y	Y	Y	Y	Y
7 **Brat**	Y	Y	?	Y	Y	Y
8 Beyer	Y	N	N	N	N	N
9 **Griffith**	Y	Y	Y	Y	Y	Y
10 **Comstock**	Y	Y	Y	Y	Y	Y
11 Connolly	Y	N	N	N	N	N
WASHINGTON						
1 DelBene	Y	N	N	N	N	N
2 Larsen	Y	N	N	N	N	N
3 **Herrera Beutler**	Y	Y	Y	Y	Y	Y
4 **Newhouse**	Y	Y	Y	Y	Y	Y
5 **McMorris Rodgers**	Y	Y	Y	Y	Y	Y
6 Kilmer	Y	N	N	N	N	N
7 Jayapal	Y	N	N	N	N	N
8 **Reichert**	Y	Y	Y	Y	Y	Y
9 Smith	Y	N	N	N	N	N
10 Heck	Y	N	N	N	N	N
WEST VIRGINIA						
1 **McKinley**	Y	Y	Y	Y	Y	Y
2 **Mooney**	Y	Y	Y	Y	Y	Y
3 **Jenkins**	Y	Y	Y	Y	Y	Y
WISCONSIN						
1 **Ryan**						
2 Pocan	Y	N	N	N	N	N
3 Kind	Y	N	N	N	N	N
4 Moore	+	N	N	N	N	N
5 **Sensenbrenner**	Y	Y	Y	Y	Y	Y
6 **Grothman**	Y	Y	Y	Y	Y	Y
7 **Duffy**	Y	?	?	?	?	Y
8 **Gallagher**	Y	Y	Y	Y	Y	Y
WYOMING						
AL **Cheney**	Y	Y	Y	Y	Y	Y

VOTE NUMBER

93. H RES 123, H J RES 69, H J RES 43. Family Planning Funding Disapproval and Alaskan Predator Hunting Disapproval/Previous Question. Burgess, R-Texas, motion to order the previous question (thus ending debate and possibility of amendment) on the rule (H Res 123) that would provide for House floor consideration of the joint resolution (H J Res 43) that would nullify and disapprove of a Health and Human Services Department rule that prevents states from restricting federal family planning funding to a health provider, such as denying funds to a center that provides abortions, for any basis other than its ability to provide health services. It would also provide for consideration of a joint resolution (H J Res 69) that would nullify an Interior Department rule that prohibits certain predator control methods in national wildlife refuges in Alaska. Motion agreed to 233-190 : R 233-0; D 0-190. Feb. 15, 2017.

94. H RES 123, H J RES 69, H J RES 43. FAMILY PLANNING FUNDING DISAPPROVAL AND ALASKAN PREDATOR HUNTING DISAPPROVAL/ RULE. Adoption of the rule (H Res 123) that would provide for House floor consideration of the joint resolution (H J Res 43) that would nullify and disapprove of a Health and Human Services Department rule that prevents states from restricting federal family planning funding to a health provider, such as denying funds to a center that provides abortions, for any basis other than its ability to provide health services. It would also provide for consideration of a joint resolution (H J Res 69) that would nullify an Interior Department rule that prohibits certain predator control methods in national wildlife refuges in Alaska. Adopted 233-188 : R 233-0; D 0-188. Feb. 15, 2017.

95. H J RES 67. LOCAL GOVERNMENT RETIREMENT PLANS DISAPPROVAL/ PASSAGE. Passage of the joint resolution that would nullify and disapprove of a Labor Department rule that exempts certain local government-administered retirement savings plans for non-government employees from select federal regulations governing pension plans. Under the rule, a city or county must have a population at least as large as the least populated state in the nation, and must administer a retirement plan for its own employees for the program to qualify for the exemption. Passed 234-191 : R 233-1; D 1-190. Feb. 15, 2017.

96. H J RES 66. STATE RETIREMENT PLANS DISAPPROVAL/PASSAGE. Passage of the joint resolution that would nullify and disapprove of a Labor Department rule that exempts certain state-administered retirement savings plans from select federal regulations governing pension plans if the state programs meet certain standards. Under the rule, the savings program must be established and administered by the state, and the savings plans must be voluntary for the employee for the program to qualify for the exemption. Passed 231-193 : R 230-3; D 1-190. Feb. 15, 2017.

97. H J RES 42. UNEMPLOYMENT DRUG TESTING DISAPPROVAL/PASSAGE. Passage of the joint resolution that would nullify and disapprove of a Labor Department rule that limits the occupations for which states can require drug tests for individuals applying for unemployment benefits. Under the rule, an individual can be required to be tested for drugs if an individual's typical employment is an occupation for which state or federal laws require an employee to be tested for controlled substances. Passed 236-189 : R 232-1; D 4-188. Feb. 15, 2017.

98. H J RES 69. ALASKAN PREDATOR HUNTING DISAPPROVAL/PASSAGE. Passage of the joint resolution that would nullify and disapprove of an Interior Department rule that prohibits certain predator control methods on federal lands in Alaska. The rule prevents Alaska, which typically has the authority to manage hunting and trapping practices on federal lands within the state, from allowing certain non-subsistence hunting practices on national wildlife refuges. Under the rule, prohibited practices include using traps to hunt bears and the taking of wolves and coyotes during denning season. Passed 225-193 : R 220-10; D 5-183. Feb. 16, 2017.

	93	94	95	96	97	98
ALABAMA						
1 **Byrne**	Y	Y	Y	Y	Y	Y
2 **Roby**	Y	Y	Y	Y	Y	Y
3 **Rogers**	Y	Y	Y	Y	Y	Y
4 **Aderholt**	Y	Y	Y	Y	Y	Y
5 **Brooks**	Y	Y	Y	Y	Y	Y
6 **Palmer**	Y	Y	Y	Y	Y	Y
7 Sewell	N	N	N	N	N	N
ALASKA						
AL **Young**	Y	Y	Y	Y	Y	Y
ARIZONA						
1 O'Halleran	N	N	N	N	N	N
2 **McSally**	Y	Y	Y	Y	Y	N
3 Grijalva	N	N	N	N	N	N
4 **Gosar**	Y	Y	Y	Y	Y	Y
5 **Biggs**	Y	Y	Y	Y	Y	Y
6 **Schweikert**	Y	Y	Y	Y	Y	Y
7 Gallego	N	N	N	N	N	N
8 **Franks**	Y	Y	Y	Y	Y	Y
9 Sinema	N	N	N	N	N	N
ARKANSAS						
1 **Crawford**	Y	Y	Y	Y	Y	Y
2 **Hill**	Y	Y	Y	Y	Y	Y
3 **Womack**	Y	Y	Y	Y	Y	Y
4 **Westerman**	Y	Y	Y	Y	Y	Y
CALIFORNIA						
1 **LaMalfa**	Y	Y	Y	Y	Y	Y
2 Huffman	N	N	N	N	N	N
3 Garamendi	N	N	N	N	N	N
4 **McClintock**	Y	Y	Y	Y	Y	Y
5 Thompson	N	N	N	N	N	N
6 Matsui	N	N	N	N	N	N
7 Bera	N	N	N	N	N	N
8 **Cook**	Y	Y	Y	Y	Y	Y
9 McNerney	N	N	N	N	N	N
10 **Denham**	Y	Y	Y	Y	Y	Y
11 DeSaulnier	N	N	N	N	N	N
12 Pelosi	N	N	N	N	N	N
13 Lee	N	N	N	N	N	N
14 Speier	N	N	N	N	N	N
15 Swalwell	N	N	N	N	N	N
16 Costa	N	N	N	N	N	N
17 Khanna	N	N	N	N	N	N
18 Eshoo	N	N	N	N	N	N
19 Lofgren	N	N	N	N	N	N
20 Panetta	N	N	N	N	N	N
21 **Valadao**	Y	Y	Y	Y	Y	Y
22 **Nunes**	Y	Y	Y	Y	Y	Y
23 **McCarthy**	Y	Y	Y	Y	Y	Y
24 Carbajal	N	N	N	N	N	N
25 **Knight**	Y	Y	Y	Y	Y	Y
26 Brownley	N	N	N	N	N	N
27 Chu	N	N	N	N	N	N
28 Schiff	N	N	N	N	N	N
29 Cardenas	N	N	N	N	N	N
30 Sherman	N	N	N	N	N	N
31 Aguilar	N	N	N	N	N	N
32 Napolitano	N	N	N	N	N	N
33 Lieu	N	N	N	N	N	N
34 Vacant						
35 Torres	N	N	N	N	N	N
36 Ruiz	N	N	N	N	N	N
37 Bass	N	N	N	N	N	?
38 Sánchez, Linda	N	N	N	N	N	N
39 **Royce**	Y	Y	Y	Y	Y	Y
40 Roybal-Allard	N	N	N	N	N	N
41 Takano	N	N	N	N	N	N
42 **Calvert**	Y	Y	Y	Y	Y	Y
43 Waters	N	N	N	N	N	N
44 Barragan	N	N	N	N	N	N
45 **Walters**	Y	Y	Y	Y	Y	Y
46 Correa	N	N	N	N	N	N
47 Lowenthal	N	N	N	N	N	N
48 **Rohrabacher**	Y	Y	Y	Y	Y	Y
49 **Issa**	Y	Y	Y	Y	Y	Y
50 **Hunter**	Y	Y	Y	Y	Y	Y
51 Vargas	N	N	N	N	N	N
52 Peters	N	N	N	N	N	N
53 Davis	N	N	N	N	N	N

	93	94	95	96	97	98
COLORADO						
1 DeGette	N	N	N	N	N	N
2 Polis	N	N	N	N	N	N
3 **Tipton**	Y	Y	Y	Y	Y	Y
4 **Buck**	Y	Y	Y	Y	Y	Y
5 **Lamborn**	Y	Y	Y	Y	Y	Y
6 **Coffman**	Y	Y	Y	Y	Y	Y
7 Perlmutter	N	N	N	N	N	N
CONNECTICUT						
1 Larson	N	N	N	N	N	N
2 Courtney	N	N	N	N	N	N
3 DeLauro	N	N	N	N	N	N
4 Himes	N	N	N	N	N	N
5 Esty	N	N	N	N	N	N
DELAWARE						
AL Blunt Rochester	N	N	N	N	N	N
FLORIDA						
1 **Gaetz**	Y	Y	Y	Y	Y	Y
2 **Dunn**	Y	Y	Y	Y	Y	Y
3 **Yoho**	Y	Y	Y	Y	Y	Y
4 **Rutherford**	Y	Y	Y	Y	Y	Y
5 Lawson	N	N	N	N	N	N
6 **DeSantis**	Y	Y	Y	Y	Y	Y
7 Murphy	N	N	N	N	N	N
8 **Posey**	Y	Y	Y	Y	Y	Y
9 Soto	–	N	N	N	N	N
10 Demings	N	N	N	N	N	N
11 **Webster**	Y	Y	Y	Y	Y	Y
12 **Bilirakis**	Y	Y	Y	Y	Y	Y
13 Crist	N	N	N	N	N	N
14 Castor	N	N	N	N	N	N
15 **Ross**	Y	Y	Y	Y	Y	Y
16 **Buchanan**	Y	Y	Y	Y	Y	Y
17 **Rooney, T.**	Y	Y	Y	Y	Y	Y
18 **Mast**	Y	Y	Y	Y	Y	Y
19 **Rooney, F.**	Y	Y	Y	Y	Y	Y
20 Hastings	N	N	N	N	N	N
21 Frankel	N	N	N	N	N	N
22 Deutch	N	N	N	N	N	N
23 Wasserman Schultz	N	N	N	N	N	N
24 Wilson	N	N	N	N	N	N
25 **Diaz-Balart**	Y	Y	Y	Y	Y	Y
26 **Curbelo**	Y	Y	Y	Y	Y	+
27 **Ros-Lehtinen**	Y	Y	N	N	N	N
GEORGIA						
1 **Carter**	+	+	+	+	+	Y
2 Bishop	N	N	N	N	N	?
3 **Ferguson**	Y	Y	Y	Y	Y	Y
4 Johnson	N	N	N	N	N	N
5 Lewis	N	N	N	N	?	N
7 **Woodall**	Y	Y	Y	Y	Y	Y
8 **Scott, A.**	Y	Y	Y	Y	Y	Y
9 **Collins**	Y	Y	Y	Y	Y	Y
10 **Hice**	Y	Y	Y	Y	Y	Y
11 **Loudermilk**	Y	Y	Y	Y	Y	Y
12 **Allen**	Y	Y	Y	Y	Y	Y
13 Scott, D.	N	N	N	N	N	N
14 **Graves**	Y	Y	Y	Y	Y	Y
HAWAII						
1 Hanabusa	N	N	N	N	N	N
2 Gabbard	N	N	N	N	N	N
IDAHO						
1 **Labrador**	Y	Y	Y	Y	Y	Y
2 **Simpson**	Y	Y	Y	Y	Y	Y
ILLINOIS						
1 Rush	N	N	N	N	N	?
2 Kelly	N	N	N	N	N	N
3 Lipinski	N	N	N	N	N	N
4 Gutierrez	N	N	N	N	N	N
5 Quigley	N	N	N	N	N	N
6 **Roskam**	Y	?	Y	Y	Y	Y
7 Davis, D.	N	N	N	N	N	N
8 Krishnamoorthi	N	N	N	N	N	N
9 Schakowsky	N	N	N	N	N	N
10 Schneider	N	N	N	N	N	N
11 Foster	N	N	N	N	N	N
12 **Bost**	Y	Y	Y	Y	Y	Y
13 **Davis, R.**	+	Y	Y	N	Y	Y
14 **Hultgren**	Y	Y	Y	Y	Y	Y
15 **Shimkus**	Y	Y	Y	Y	Y	Y

	93	94	95	96	97	98
16 **Kinzinger**	Y	Y	Y	Y	Y	Y
17 Bustos	N	N	N	N	N	N
18 **LaHood**	Y	Y	Y	Y	Y	Y
INDIANA						
1 Visclosky	N	N	N	N	N	N
2 **Walorski**	Y	Y	Y	Y	Y	Y
3 **Banks**	Y	Y	Y	Y	Y	Y
4 **Rokita**	Y	Y	Y	Y	Y	Y
5 **Brooks**	Y	Y	Y	Y	Y	Y
6 **Messer**	Y	Y	Y	Y	Y	Y
7 Carson	N	N	N	N	N	N
8 **Bucshon**	Y	Y	Y	Y	Y	Y
9 **Hollingsworth**	Y	Y	Y	Y	Y	Y
IOWA						
1 **Blum**	Y	Y	Y	Y	Y	Y
2 Loebsack	N	N	N	N	N	N
3 **Young**	Y	Y	Y	Y	Y	Y
4 **King**	Y	Y	+	+	Y	Y
KANSAS						
1 **Marshall**	Y	Y	Y	Y	Y	Y
2 **Jenkins**	Y	Y	Y	Y	Y	Y
3 **Yoder**	Y	Y	Y	Y	Y	Y
KENTUCKY						
1 **Comer**	Y	Y	Y	Y	Y	Y
2 **Guthrie**	Y	Y	Y	Y	Y	Y
3 Yarmuth	N	N	N	N	N	N
4 **Massie**	Y	Y	Y	Y	Y	Y
5 **Rogers**	Y	Y	Y	Y	Y	Y
6 **Barr**	Y	Y	Y	Y	Y	Y
LOUISIANA						
1 **Scalise**	Y	Y	Y	Y	Y	Y
2 Richmond	N	N	N	N	N	?
3 **Higgins**	Y	Y	Y	Y	Y	Y
4 **Johnson**	Y	Y	Y	Y	Y	Y
5 **Abraham**	Y	Y	Y	Y	Y	Y
6 **Graves**	Y	Y	Y	Y	Y	Y
MAINE						
1 Pingree	N	N	N	N	N	N
2 **Poliquin**	Y	Y	Y	Y	Y	Y
MARYLAND						
1 **Harris**	Y	Y	Y	Y	Y	Y
2 Ruppersberger	N	N	N	N	N	N
3 Sarbanes	N	N	N	N	N	N
4 Brown	N	N	N	N	N	N
5 Hoyer	N	N	N	N	N	N
6 Delaney	N	N	N	N	N	N
7 Cummings	?	?	N	N	N	N
8 Raskin	N	N	N	N	N	N
MASSACHUSETTS						
1 Neal	N	N	N	N	N	N
2 McGovern	N	N	N	N	N	N
3 Tsongas	N	N	N	N	N	N
4 Kennedy	N	N	N	N	N	N
5 Clark	N	N	N	N	N	N
6 Moulton	N	N	N	N	N	N
7 Capuano	N	N	N	N	N	N
8 Lynch	N	?	N	N	N	N
9 Keating	N	N	N	N	N	N
MICHIGAN						
1 **Bergman**	Y	Y	Y	Y	Y	Y
2 **Huizenga**	Y	Y	Y	Y	Y	Y
3 **Amash**	Y	Y	Y	Y	Y	Y
4 **Moolenaar**	Y	Y	Y	Y	Y	Y
5 Kildee	N	N	N	N	N	N
6 **Upton**	Y	Y	Y	Y	Y	N
7 **Walberg**	Y	Y	Y	Y	Y	Y
8 **Bishop**	Y	Y	Y	Y	Y	Y
9 Levin	N	N	N	N	N	N
10 **Mitchell**	Y	Y	Y	Y	Y	Y
11 **Trott**	Y	Y	Y	Y	Y	+
12 Dingell	N	N	N	N	N	N
13 Conyers	N	N	N	N	N	N
14 Lawrence	N	N	N	N	N	N
MINNESOTA						
1 Walz	N	N	N	N	N	N
2 **Lewis**	Y	Y	Y	Y	Y	Y
3 **Paulsen**	Y	Y	Y	Y	Y	Y
4 McCollum	N	N	N	N	N	N

	93	94	95	96	97	98
5 Ellison	N	N	N	N	N	N
6 **Emmer**	Y	Y	Y	Y	Y	Y
7 Peterson	N	N	N	N	Y	Y
8 Nolan	N	N	N	N	N	N
MISSISSIPPI						
1 **Kelly**	Y	Y	Y	Y	Y	Y
2 Thompson	N	N	N	N	N	N
3 **Harper**	Y	Y	Y	Y	Y	Y
4 **Palazzo**	Y	Y	Y	Y	?	Y
MISSOURI						
1 Clay	N	N	N	N	N	N
2 **Wagner**	Y	Y	Y	Y	Y	Y
3 **Luetkemeyer**	Y	Y	Y	Y	Y	Y
4 **Hartzler**	Y	Y	Y	Y	Y	Y
5 Cleaver	N	N	N	?	N	N
6 **Graves**	Y	Y	Y	Y	Y	Y
7 **Long**	Y	Y	Y	Y	Y	Y
8 **Smith**	Y	Y	Y	Y	Y	Y
MONTANA						
AL **Zinke**	?	?	?	?	?	?
NEBRASKA						
1 **Fortenberry**	Y	Y	Y	Y	Y	Y
2 **Bacon**	Y	Y	Y	Y	Y	Y
3 **Smith**	Y	Y	Y	Y	Y	Y
NEVADA						
1 Titus	N	?	N	N	N	N
2 **Amodei**	Y	Y	Y	Y	Y	?
3 Rosen	N	N	N	N	N	N
4 Kihuen	N	N	N	N	N	N
NEW HAMPSHIRE						
1 Shea-Porter	N	N	N	N	N	N
2 Kuster	N	N	N	N	N	N
NEW JERSEY						
1 Norcross	N	N	N	N	N	N
2 **LoBiondo**	Y	Y	Y	Y	Y	N
3 **MacArthur**	Y	Y	Y	Y	Y	N
4 **Smith**	Y	Y	Y	Y	Y	N
5 Gottheimer	N	N	N	N	N	N
6 Pallone	N	N	N	N	N	N
7 **Lance**	Y	Y	Y	Y	Y	Y
8 Sires	N	N	N	N	N	N
9 Pascrell	N	N	N	N	N	N
10 Payne	–	–	N	N	N	N
11 **Frelinghuysen**	Y	Y	Y	Y	Y	Y
12 Watson Coleman	N	N	N	N	N	N
NEW MEXICO						
1 Lujan Grisham	N	N	N	N	N	N
2 **Pearce**	Y	Y	Y	Y	Y	Y
3 Luján	N	N	N	N	N	N
NEW YORK						
1 **Zeldin**	Y	Y	Y	Y	Y	Y
2 **King**	Y	Y	Y	Y	Y	N
3 Suozzi	N	N	N	N	N	N
4 Rice	N	N	N	N	N	N
5 Meeks	N	N	N	N	N	N
6 Meng	N	N	N	N	N	N
7 Velázquez	N	N	N	N	N	N
8 Jeffries	N	N	N	N	N	N
9 Clarke	N	N	N	N	N	N
10 Nadler	N	N	N	N	N	N
11 **Donovan**	Y	Y	Y	Y	Y	N
12 Maloney, C.	N	N	N	N	N	N
13 Espaillat	N	N	N	N	N	N
14 Crowley	N	N	N	N	N	N
15 Serrano	N	N	N	N	N	N
16 Engel	N	N	N	N	N	N
17 Lowey	N	N	N	N	N	N
18 Maloney, S.P.	N	N	N	N	N	N
19 **Faso**	Y	Y	Y	Y	Y	Y
20 Tonko	N	N	N	–	N	N
21 **Stefanik**	Y	Y	Y	Y	Y	Y
22 **Tenney**	Y	Y	Y	Y	Y	Y
23 **Reed**	Y	Y	Y	Y	Y	Y
24 **Katko**	Y	Y	Y	Y	Y	Y
25 Slaughter	N	N	N	N	N	N
26 Higgins	N	N	N	N	N	N
27 **Collins**	Y	Y	Y	Y	Y	Y
NORTH CAROLINA						
1 Butterfield	N	N	N	N	N	?
2 **Holding**	Y	Y	Y	Y	Y	Y
3 **Jones**	Y	Y	Y	N	Y	Y
4 Price	N	N	N	N	N	N

	93	94	95	96	97	98
5 **Foxx**	Y	Y	Y	Y	Y	Y
6 **Walker**	Y	Y	Y	Y	Y	Y
7 **Rouzer**	Y	Y	Y	Y	Y	Y
8 **Hudson**	Y	Y	Y	Y	Y	Y
9 **Pittenger**	Y	Y	Y	Y	Y	Y
10 **McHenry**	Y	Y	Y	Y	Y	Y
11 **Meadows**	Y	Y	Y	Y	Y	Y
12 Adams	N	N	N	N	N	N
13 **Budd**	Y	Y	Y	Y	Y	Y
NORTH DAKOTA						
AL **Cramer**	Y	Y	Y	Y	Y	Y
OHIO						
1 **Chabot**	Y	Y	Y	Y	Y	Y
2 **Wenstrup**	Y	Y	Y	Y	Y	Y
3 Beatty	N	N	N	N	N	N
4 **Jordan**	Y	Y	Y	Y	Y	Y
5 **Latta**	Y	Y	Y	Y	Y	Y
6 **Johnson**	Y	Y	Y	Y	Y	Y
7 **Gibbs**	Y	Y	Y	Y	Y	Y
8 **Davidson**	Y	Y	Y	Y	Y	Y
9 Kaptur	N	N	?	N	N	N
10 **Turner**	Y	Y	Y	Y	Y	Y
11 Fudge	N	N	N	N	N	N
12 **Tiberi**	Y	Y	Y	Y	Y	Y
13 Ryan	N	N	N	N	N	N
14 **Joyce**	Y	Y	Y	Y	Y	Y
15 **Stivers**	Y	Y	Y	Y	Y	Y
16 **Renacci**	Y	Y	Y	Y	Y	Y
OKLAHOMA						
1 **Bridenstine**	Y	Y	Y	Y	Y	Y
2 **Mullin**	Y	Y	Y	Y	Y	Y
3 **Lucas**	Y	Y	Y	Y	Y	Y
4 **Cole**	Y	Y	Y	Y	Y	Y
5 **Russell**	Y	Y	Y	Y	Y	Y
OREGON						
1 Bonamici	N	N	N	N	N	N
2 **Walden**	Y	Y	Y	Y	Y	Y
3 Blumenauer	N	?	N	N	N	N
4 DeFazio	N	N	N	N	N	N
5 Schrader	N	N	N	N	Y	N
PENNSYLVANIA						
1 Brady	N	N	N	N	N	N
2 Evans	N	N	N	N	N	N
3 **Kelly**	Y	Y	Y	Y	Y	Y
4 **Perry**	Y	Y	Y	Y	Y	Y
5 **Thompson**	Y	Y	Y	Y	Y	Y
6 **Costello**	Y	Y	Y	Y	Y	Y
7 **Meehan**	Y	Y	Y	Y	Y	Y
8 **Fitzpatrick**	Y	Y	Y	Y	Y	N
9 **Shuster**	Y	Y	Y	Y	Y	Y
10 **Marino**	Y	Y	Y	Y	Y	Y
11 **Barletta**	Y	Y	Y	Y	Y	Y
12 **Rothfus**	Y	Y	Y	Y	Y	Y
13 Boyle	N	N	N	N	N	N
14 Doyle	N	N	N	N	N	N
15 **Dent**	Y	Y	Y	Y	Y	Y
16 **Smucker**	Y	Y	Y	Y	Y	Y
17 Cartwright	N	N	N	N	N	N
18 **Murphy**	Y	Y	Y	Y	Y	Y
RHODE ISLAND						
1 Cicilline	N	N	N	N	N	N
2 Langevin	N	N	N	N	N	N
SOUTH CAROLINA						
1 **Sanford**	Y	Y	Y	Y	Y	Y
2 **Wilson**	Y	Y	Y	Y	Y	Y
3 **Duncan**	Y	Y	Y	Y	Y	Y
4 **Gowdy**	Y	Y	Y	Y	Y	Y
5 **Mulvaney**	?	?	?	?	?	
6 Clyburn	N	N	N	N	N	N
7 **Rice**	Y	Y	Y	Y	Y	Y
SOUTH DAKOTA						
AL **Noem**	Y	Y	Y	Y	Y	Y
TENNESSEE						
1 **Roe**	Y	Y	Y	Y	Y	Y
2 **Duncan**	Y	Y	Y	Y	Y	Y
3 **Fleischmann**	Y	Y	Y	Y	Y	Y
4 **DesJarlais**	Y	Y	Y	Y	Y	Y
5 Cooper	N	N	N	N	Y	N
6 **Black**	Y	Y	Y	Y	Y	Y
7 **Blackburn**	Y	Y	Y	Y	Y	Y
8 **Kustoff**	Y	Y	Y	Y	Y	Y
9 Cohen	N	N	N	N	N	N

	93	94	95	96	97	98
TEXAS						
1 **Gohmert**	Y	Y	Y	Y	Y	Y
2 **Poe**	?	?	Y	Y	Y	Y
3 **Johnson, S.**	Y	Y	Y	Y	Y	Y
4 **Ratcliffe**	Y	Y	Y	Y	Y	Y
5 **Hensarling**	Y	Y	Y	Y	Y	Y
6 **Barton**	Y	Y	Y	Y	Y	?
7 **Culberson**	Y	Y	Y	Y	Y	Y
8 **Brady**	Y	Y	Y	Y	Y	Y
9 Green, A.	N	N	N	N	N	N
10 **McCaul**	Y	Y	Y	Y	Y	Y
11 **Conaway**	Y	Y	Y	Y	Y	Y
12 **Granger**	Y	Y	Y	Y	Y	Y
13 **Thornberry**	Y	Y	Y	Y	Y	Y
14 **Weber**	Y	Y	Y	Y	Y	Y
15 Gonzalez	N	N	N	N	N	Y
16 O'Rourke	N	N	N	N	N	N
17 **Flores**	Y	Y	Y	Y	Y	Y
18 Jackson Lee	N	N	N	N	N	N
19 **Arrington**	Y	Y	Y	Y	Y	Y
20 Castro	N	N	N	N	N	N
21 **Smith**	Y	Y	Y	Y	Y	Y
22 **Olson**	Y	Y	Y	Y	Y	?
23 **Hurd**	Y	Y	Y	Y	Y	Y
24 **Marchant**	Y	Y	Y	Y	Y	Y
25 **Williams**	Y	Y	Y	Y	Y	Y
26 **Burgess**	Y	Y	Y	Y	Y	Y
27 **Farenthold**	Y	Y	Y	Y	Y	Y
28 Cuellar	N	N	Y	Y	N	Y
29 Green, G.	N	N	N	N	N	N
30 Johnson, E.B.	N	N	N	N	N	N
31 **Carter**	Y	Y	Y	Y	Y	Y
32 **Sessions**	Y	Y	Y	Y	Y	Y
33 Veasey	N	N	N	N	N	N
34 Vela	N	N	N	N	N	Y
35 Doggett	N	N	N	N	N	N
36 **Babin**	Y	Y	Y	Y	Y	Y
UTAH						
1 **Bishop**	Y	Y	Y	Y	Y	Y
2 **Stewart**	Y	Y	Y	?	?	?
3 **Chaffetz**	Y	Y	Y	Y	Y	Y
4 **Love**	Y	Y	Y	Y	Y	Y
VERMONT						
AL Welch	N	N	N	N	N	N
VIRGINIA						
1 **Wittman**	Y	Y	Y	Y	Y	Y
2 **Taylor**	Y	Y	Y	Y	Y	Y
3 Scott	N	N	N	N	N	N
4 McEachin	N	N	N	N	N	N
5 **Garrett**	Y	Y	Y	Y	Y	Y
6 **Goodlatte**	Y	Y	Y	Y	Y	Y
7 **Brat**	Y	Y	Y	Y	Y	Y
8 Beyer	N	N	?	N	N	N
9 **Griffith**	Y	Y	Y	Y	Y	Y
10 **Comstock**	Y	Y	Y	Y	Y	Y
11 Connolly	N	N	N	N	N	N
WASHINGTON						
1 DelBene	N	N	N	N	N	N
2 Larsen	N	N	N	N	N	N
3 **Herrera Beutler**	Y	Y	Y	Y	Y	Y
4 **Newhouse**	Y	Y	Y	Y	Y	Y
5 **McMorris Rodgers**	Y	Y	Y	Y	Y	Y
6 Kilmer	N	N	N	N	N	N
7 Jayapal	N	N	N	N	N	N
8 **Reichert**	Y	Y	Y	Y	Y	N
9 Smith	N	N	N	N	N	N
10 Heck	N	N	N	N	N	N
WEST VIRGINIA						
1 **McKinley**	Y	Y	Y	Y	Y	Y
2 **Mooney**	Y	Y	Y	Y	Y	Y
3 **Jenkins**	Y	Y	Y	Y	Y	Y
WISCONSIN						
1 **Ryan**						
2 Pocan	N	N	N	N	N	N
3 Kind	N	N	N	N	N	Y
4 Moore	N	N	N	N	N	N
5 **Sensenbrenner**	Y	Y	Y	Y	Y	Y
6 **Grothman**	Y	Y	Y	Y	Y	Y
7 **Duffy**	Y	Y	Y	Y	Y	Y
8 **Gallagher**	Y	Y	Y	Y	Y	Y
WYOMING						
AL **Cheney**	Y	Y	Y	Y	Y	Y

VOTE NUMBER

99. H J RES 43. FAMILY PLANNING FUNDING DISAPPROVAL/PASSAGE. Passage of the joint resolution that would nullify and disapprove of a Health and Human Services Department rule that prevents states from restricting federal family planning funding to a health provider, such as denying funds to a center that provides abortions, for any basis other than its ability to provide health services. Under the rule, HHS can withhold family planning grants to any state that restricts the participation of a health provider in the family planning services grant program. Passed 230-188 : R 228-2; D 2-186. Feb. 16, 2017.

100. HR 699. OREGON LAND EXCHANGE/PASSAGE. McClintock, R-Calif., motion to suspend the rules and pass the bill that would modify the terms of a land exchange between the Forest Service and Mount Hood Meadows ski area in Oregon by reducing the amount of land the Forest Service can convey and modifying the required easements. Motion agreed to 415-1 : R 230-1; D 185-0. Feb. 27, 2017.

101. PRESIDENT'S TAX RETURN DISCLOSURE/MOTION TO TABLE. McCarthy, R-Calif., motion to table (kill) the Pascrell, D-N.J., motion to appeal the ruling of the Chair that the Pascrell resolution related to the disclosure of President Trump's tax returns does not constitute a question of the privileges of the House. Motion agreed to 229-185 : R 229-0; D 0-185. Feb. 27, 2017.

102. HR 863. COLTSVILLE BUILDING REQUIREMENT/PASSAGE. McClintock, R-Calif., motion to suspend the rules and pass the bill that would allow the National Park Service to select an alternate location for park administration and visitor services at Coltsville National Historical Park in Connecticut, rescinding a requirement that had identified a different site for such purposes. Motion agreed to 369-42 : R 185-42; D 184-0. Feb. 27, 2017.

103. H J RES 83, HR 998, H RES 150. REGULATORY REVIEW AND OSHA CITATION DISAPPROVAL/PREVIOUS QUESTION. Collins, R-Ga., motion to order the previous question (thus ending debate and possibility of amendment) on the rule (H Res 150) that would provide for House floor consideration of the bill (HR 998) that would create a commission to review existing federal regulations to identify those that should be repealed in order to reduce costs to the economy. It also would provide for consideration of the joint resolution (H J Res 83) that would nullify and disapprove of an Occupational Safety and Health Administration rule related to citations of employers who do not maintain certain workplace injury or illness records. Motion agreed to 224-191 : R 224-0; D 0-191. Feb. 28, 2017.

104. H J RES 83, HR 998, H RES 150. REGULATORY REVIEW AND OSHA CITATION DISAPPROVAL/RULE. Adoption of the rule (H Res 150) that would provide for House floor consideration of the bill (HR 998) that would create a commission to review existing federal regulations to identify those that should be repealed in order to reduce costs to the economy. It also would provide for consideration of the joint resolution (H J Res 83) that would nullify and disapprove of an Occupational Safety and Health Administration rule related to citations of employers who do not maintain certain workplace injury or illness records. Adopted 225-188 : R 224-0; D 1-188. Feb. 28, 2017.

105. HR 998. REGULATORY REVIEW COMMISSION/PUBLIC HEALTH IMPACT. DeSaulnier, D-Calif., amendment that would require the regulatory review commission, in identifying which rules should be repealed, to consider the extent to which repealing the rule would impact public health. Adopted in Committee of the Whole 348-75 : R 156-75; D 192-0. Feb. 28, 2017.

	99	100	101	102	103	104	105
ALABAMA							
1 Byrne	Y	Y	Y	Y	Y	Y	N
2 Roby	Y	Y	Y	Y	Y	Y	Y
3 Rogers	Y	Y	Y	Y	Y	Y	Y
4 Aderholt	Y	Y	Y	Y	Y	Y	N
5 Brooks	Y	Y	Y	Y	Y	Y	N
6 Palmer	Y	Y	Y	Y	Y	Y	Y
7 Sewell	N	Y	N	Y	N	Y	Y
ALASKA							
AL Young	Y	Y	Y	N	Y	Y	Y
ARIZONA							
1 O'Halleran	N	Y	N	Y	N	N	Y
2 McSally	Y	Y	Y	Y	Y	Y	Y
3 Grijalva	N	?	?	?	N	N	Y
4 Gosar	Y	Y	Y	Y	?	?	N
5 Biggs	Y	Y	Y	N	Y	Y	N
6 Schweikert	Y	Y	Y	Y	Y	Y	Y
7 Gallego	N	Y	N	Y	N	N	Y
8 Franks	Y	Y	Y	Y	Y	Y	Y
9 Sinema	N	Y	N	Y	N	Y	Y
ARKANSAS							
1 Crawford	Y	?	?	?	?	?	?
2 Hill	Y	Y	Y	Y	Y	Y	Y
3 Womack	Y	Y	Y	Y	Y	Y	Y
4 Westerman	Y	Y	Y	Y	Y	Y	Y
CALIFORNIA							
1 LaMalfa	Y	Y	Y	N	Y	Y	N
2 Huffman	N	Y	N	Y	N	N	Y
3 Garamendi	N	Y	N	Y	N	N	Y
4 McClintock	Y	Y	Y	Y	Y	Y	Y
5 Thompson	N	Y	N	Y	N	N	Y
6 Matsui	N	Y	N	Y	N	N	Y
7 Bera	N	Y	N	Y	N	N	Y
8 Cook	Y	Y	Y	Y	Y	Y	N
9 McNerney	N	Y	N	Y	N	N	Y
10 Denham	Y	Y	Y	Y	Y	Y	Y
11 DeSaulnier	N	Y	N	Y	N	N	Y
12 Pelosi	N	Y	N	Y	N	N	Y
13 Lee	N	Y	N	Y	N	N	Y
14 Speier	N	Y	N	Y	N	N	Y
15 Swalwell	N	Y	N	Y	N	N	Y
16 Costa	N	Y	N	Y	N	N	Y
17 Khanna	N	Y	N	Y	N	N	Y
18 Eshoo	N	Y	N	Y	N	N	Y
19 Lofgren	N	+	–	+	N	N	Y
20 Panetta	N	Y	N	Y	N	N	Y
21 Valadao	Y	Y	Y	Y	Y	Y	Y
22 Nunes	Y	Y	Y	Y	Y	Y	N
23 McCarthy	Y	Y	Y	Y	?	?	N
24 Carbajal	N	Y	N	Y	N	N	Y
25 Knight	Y	Y	Y	Y	Y	Y	Y
26 Brownley	N	Y	N	Y	N	N	Y
27 Chu	N	Y	N	Y	N	N	Y
28 Schiff	N	Y	N	Y	N	N	Y
29 Cardenas	N	Y	N	Y	N	N	Y
30 Sherman	N	Y	N	Y	N	N	Y
31 Aguilar	N	Y	N	Y	N	N	Y
32 Napolitano	N	Y	N	Y	N	N	Y
33 Lieu	N	Y	N	Y	N	N	Y
34 Vacant							
35 Torres	N	Y	N	Y	N	N	Y
36 Ruiz	N	Y	N	Y	N	N	Y
37 Bass	?	Y	N	Y	N	N	Y
38 Sánchez, Linda	N	Y	N	Y	N	N	Y
39 Royce	Y	Y	Y	Y	Y	Y	Y
40 Roybal-Allard	N	Y	N	Y	N	N	Y
41 Takano	N	Y	N	Y	N	N	Y
42 Calvert	Y	Y	Y	?	Y	Y	Y
43 Waters	N	Y	N	Y	N	N	Y
44 Barragan	N	Y	N	Y	N	N	Y
45 Walters	Y	Y	Y	Y	Y	Y	Y
46 Correa	N	Y	N	Y	N	N	Y
47 Lowenthal	N	Y	N	Y	N	N	Y
48 Rohrabacher	Y	?	?	?	Y	Y	Y
49 Issa	Y	Y	Y	Y	Y	Y	Y
50 Hunter	Y	?	?	?	Y	Y	Y
51 Vargas	N	Y	N	Y	N	?	Y
52 Peters	N	Y	N	Y	N	N	Y
53 Davis	N	Y	N	Y	N	N	Y

	99	100	101	102	103	104	105
COLORADO							
1 DeGette	N	Y	N	Y	N	N	Y
2 Polis	N	Y	N	Y	N	N	Y
3 Tipton	Y	Y	Y	Y	?	?	Y
4 Buck	Y	Y	Y	N	Y	Y	N
5 Lamborn	Y	Y	Y	Y	Y	Y	Y
6 Coffman	Y	Y	Y	Y	Y	Y	Y
7 Perlmutter	N	Y	N	Y	N	N	Y
CONNECTICUT							
1 Larson	N	Y	N	Y	N	N	Y
2 Courtney	N	Y	N	Y	N	N	Y
3 DeLauro	N	Y	N	Y	N	N	Y
4 Himes	N	Y	N	Y	N	N	Y
5 Esty	N	Y	N	Y	N	N	Y
DELAWARE							
AL Blunt Rochester	N	Y	N	Y	N	N	Y
FLORIDA							
1 Gaetz	Y	Y	Y	Y	Y	Y	N
2 Dunn	Y	Y	Y	Y	Y	Y	Y
3 Yoho	Y	Y	Y	N	Y	Y	Y
4 Rutherford	Y	Y	Y	Y	Y	Y	Y
5 Lawson	N	Y	N	Y	N	N	Y
6 DeSantis	Y	Y	Y	Y	Y	Y	Y
7 Murphy	N	Y	N	Y	N	N	Y
8 Posey	Y	Y	Y	N	Y	Y	N
9 Soto	N	Y	N	Y	N	N	Y
10 Demings	N	Y	N	Y	N	N	Y
11 Webster	Y	Y	Y	N	Y	Y	N
12 Bilirakis	Y	Y	Y	?	Y	Y	Y
13 Crist	N	Y	N	Y	N	N	Y
14 Castor	N	Y	N	Y	N	N	Y
15 Ross	Y	Y	Y	Y	Y	Y	Y
16 Buchanan	Y	Y	Y	Y	Y	Y	Y
17 Rooney, T.	Y	Y	Y	Y	Y	Y	?
18 Mast	Y	Y	Y	Y	Y	Y	Y
19 Rooney, F.	Y	Y	Y	Y	Y	Y	Y
20 Hastings	N	Y	N	Y	N	N	Y
21 Frankel	N	Y	N	Y	N	N	Y
22 Deutch	N	Y	N	Y	N	N	Y
23 Wasserman Schultz	N	Y	N	Y	N	N	Y
24 Wilson	N	?	?	?	N	N	Y
25 Diaz-Balart	Y	Y	Y	Y	Y	Y	Y
26 Curbelo	+	Y	Y	Y	Y	Y	Y
27 Ros-Lehtinen	Y	Y	Y	Y	Y	Y	Y
GEORGIA							
1 Carter	Y	Y	Y	Y	Y	Y	N
2 Bishop	?	Y	N	Y	N	N	Y
3 Ferguson	Y	Y	Y	Y	Y	Y	Y
4 Johnson	N	Y	N	Y	N	N	Y
5 Lewis	N	Y	N	Y	N	N	Y
6 Woodall	Y	Y	Y	Y	Y	Y	Y
7 Scott, A.	Y	Y	Y	N	Y	Y	Y
8 Collins	Y	Y	Y	Y	Y	Y	Y
9 Hice	Y	Y	Y	Y	Y	Y	Y
10 Loudermilk	Y	Y	Y	N	Y	Y	Y
11 Allen	Y	Y	Y	Y	Y	Y	Y
12 Scott, D.	N	Y	N	Y	?	N	Y
13 Graves	Y	Y	Y	Y	Y	Y	N
HAWAII							
1 Hanabusa	N	Y	N	Y	N	N	Y
2 Gabbard	N	Y	N	Y	N	N	Y
IDAHO							
1 Labrador	Y	Y	Y	N	Y	Y	N
2 Simpson	Y	Y	Y	Y	Y	Y	Y
ILLINOIS							
1 Rush	?	?	?	?	?	?	Y
2 Kelly	N	Y	N	Y	N	N	Y
3 Lipinski	Y	Y	N	Y	N	N	Y
4 Gutierrez	N	+	–	+	N	N	Y
5 Quigley	N	Y	N	Y	N	N	Y
6 Roskam	Y	Y	Y	Y	Y	Y	Y
7 Davis, D.	N	Y	N	Y	N	N	Y
8 Krishnamoorthi	N	Y	N	Y	N	N	Y
9 Schakowsky	N	Y	N	Y	N	N	Y
10 Schneider	N	Y	N	Y	N	N	Y
11 Foster	N	Y	N	Y	N	N	Y
12 Bost	Y	Y	Y	Y	Y	Y	Y
13 Davis, R.	Y	Y	Y	Y	Y	Y	+
14 Hultgren	Y	Y	Y	Y	Y	Y	Y
15 Shimkus	Y	Y	Y	Y	Y	Y	Y

KEY	**Republicans**	Democrats	*Independents*	
Y Voted for (yea)		X Paired against		C Voted "present" to avoid possible conflict of interest
# Paired for		– Announced against		
+ Announced for		P Voted "present"		? Did not vote or otherwise make a position known
N Voted against (nay)				

	99	100	101	102	103	104	105
16 **Kinzinger**	Y	Y	Y	Y	Y	Y	Y
17 Bustos	N	Y	N	Y	N	N	Y
18 **LaHood**	Y	Y	Y	Y	Y	Y	N
INDIANA							
1 Visclosky	N	Y	N	Y	N	N	Y
2 **Walorski**	Y	Y	Y	Y	Y	Y	Y
3 **Banks**	Y	Y	Y	Y	Y	Y	N
4 **Rokita**	Y	Y	Y	Y	Y	Y	Y
5 **Brooks**	Y	Y	Y	Y	Y	Y	Y
6 **Messer**	Y	Y	?	?	Y	Y	N
7 Carson	N	Y	N	Y	N	N	Y
8 **Bucshon**	Y	Y	Y	Y	Y	Y	N
9 **Hollingsworth**	Y	Y	Y	Y	Y	Y	N
IOWA							
1 **Blum**	Y	Y	Y	N	Y	Y	Y
2 Loebsack	N	Y	N	Y	N	N	Y
3 **Young**	Y	Y	Y	Y	Y	Y	Y
4 **King**	Y	Y	Y	N	Y	Y	N
KANSAS							
1 **Marshall**	Y	Y	Y	Y	Y	Y	Y
2 **Jenkins**	Y	Y	Y	Y	Y	Y	Y
3 **Yoder**	Y	Y	Y	Y	Y	Y	Y
KENTUCKY							
1 **Comer**	Y	Y	Y	Y	Y	Y	Y
2 **Guthrie**	Y	Y	Y	Y	Y	Y	Y
3 Yarmuth	N	Y	N	Y	N	N	Y
4 **Massie**	Y	Y	Y	N	Y	Y	N
5 **Rogers**	Y	Y	Y	Y	Y	Y	Y
6 **Barr**	Y	Y	Y	Y	Y	Y	N
LOUISIANA							
1 **Scalise**	Y	Y	Y	Y	Y	Y	N
2 Richmond	?	Y	N	Y	N	N	Y
3 **Higgins**	Y	Y	Y	Y	Y	Y	Y
4 **Johnson**	Y	Y	Y	Y	Y	Y	Y
5 **Abraham**	Y	Y	Y	N	Y	Y	N
6 **Graves**	Y	Y	Y	Y	Y	Y	Y
MAINE							
1 Pingree	N	Y	N	Y	N	N	Y
2 **Poliquin**	Y	Y	Y	Y	Y	Y	Y
MARYLAND							
1 **Harris**	Y	Y	Y	Y	Y	Y	N
2 Ruppersberger	N	Y	N	Y	N	N	Y
3 Sarbanes	N	Y	N	Y	N	N	Y
4 Brown	N	Y	N	Y	N	N	Y
5 Hoyer	N	Y	N	Y	N	N	Y
6 Delaney	N	Y	N	Y	N	N	Y
7 Cummings	N	Y	N	Y	N	N	Y
8 Raskin	N	Y	N	Y	N	N	Y
MASSACHUSETTS							
1 Neal	N	Y	N	Y	N	N	Y
2 McGovern	N	Y	N	Y	N	N	Y
3 Tsongas	N	Y	N	Y	N	N	Y
4 Kennedy	N	Y	N	Y	N	N	Y
5 Clark	N	Y	N	Y	N	N	Y
6 Moulton	N	Y	N	Y	N	N	Y
7 Capuano	N	Y	N	Y	N	N	Y
8 Lynch	N	Y	N	Y	N	N	Y
9 Keating	N	Y	N	Y	N	N	Y
MICHIGAN							
1 **Bergman**	Y	Y	Y	Y	Y	Y	Y
2 **Huizenga**	Y	Y	Y	N	Y	Y	Y
3 **Amash**	Y	N	Y	N	Y	Y	Y
4 **Moolenaar**	Y	Y	Y	N	Y	Y	Y
5 Kildee	N	Y	N	Y	N	N	Y
6 **Upton**	Y	Y	Y	Y	Y	Y	Y
7 **Walberg**	Y	Y	Y	N	Y	Y	Y
8 **Bishop**	Y	Y	Y	Y	Y	Y	Y
9 Levin	N	Y	N	Y	N	N	Y
10 **Mitchell**	Y	Y	Y	Y	Y	Y	Y
11 **Trott**	+	Y	Y	Y	Y	Y	Y
12 Dingell	N	Y	N	Y	N	N	Y
13 Conyers	N	Y	N	Y	N	N	Y
14 Lawrence	N	Y	N	Y	N	N	Y
MINNESOTA							
1 Walz	N	Y	N	Y	N	N	Y
2 **Lewis**	Y	Y	Y	Y	Y	Y	Y
3 **Paulsen**	Y	Y	Y	Y	Y	Y	Y
4 McCollum	N	Y	N	Y	N	N	Y

	99	100	101	102	103	104	105
5 Ellison	N	+	–	+	N	N	Y
6 **Emmer**	Y	Y	Y	Y	Y	Y	Y
7 Peterson	Y	Y	N	Y	N	N	Y
8 Nolan	N	Y	N	Y	N	N	Y
MISSISSIPPI							
1 **Kelly**	Y	Y	Y	Y	Y	Y	N
2 Thompson	N	Y	N	Y	N	N	Y
3 **Harper**	Y	Y	Y	Y	Y	Y	Y
4 **Palazzo**	Y	Y	Y	Y	Y	Y	N
MISSOURI							
1 Clay	N	Y	N	Y	N	N	Y
2 **Wagner**	Y	Y	Y	Y	Y	Y	+
3 **Luetkemeyer**	Y	Y	Y	Y	Y	Y	Y
4 **Hartzler**	Y	Y	Y	Y	Y	Y	Y
5 Cleaver	N	Y	N	Y	N	N	Y
6 **Graves**	Y	Y	Y	Y	Y	Y	Y
7 **Long**	Y	Y	Y	Y	Y	Y	Y
8 **Smith**	Y	Y	Y	Y	Y	Y	N
MONTANA							
AL **Zinke**	?	?	?	?	?	?	?
NEBRASKA							
1 **Fortenberry**	Y	Y	Y	Y	Y	Y	Y
2 **Bacon**	Y	Y	Y	Y	Y	Y	Y
3 **Smith**	Y	Y	Y	Y	+	+	N
NEVADA							
1 Titus	N	Y	N	Y	N	N	Y
2 **Amodei**	?	Y	Y	Y	Y	Y	N
3 Rosen	N	Y	N	Y	N	N	Y
4 Kihuen	N	Y	N	Y	N	N	Y
NEW HAMPSHIRE							
1 Shea-Porter	N	Y	N	Y	N	N	Y
2 Kuster	N	Y	N	Y	N	N	Y
NEW JERSEY							
1 Norcross	N	Y	N	Y	N	N	Y
2 **LoBiondo**	Y	Y	Y	Y	Y	Y	Y
3 **MacArthur**	Y	Y	Y	Y	Y	Y	Y
4 **Smith**	Y	Y	Y	Y	Y	Y	Y
5 Gottheimer	N	Y	N	Y	N	N	Y
6 Pallone	N	Y	N	Y	N	N	Y
7 **Lance**	Y	Y	Y	Y	Y	Y	Y
8 Sires	N	Y	N	Y	N	N	Y
9 Pascrell	N	Y	N	Y	N	–	Y
10 Payne	N	Y	N	Y	N	N	Y
11 **Frelinghuysen**	Y	Y	Y	Y	Y	Y	Y
12 Watson Coleman	N	Y	N	Y	N	N	Y
NEW MEXICO							
1 Lujan Grisham	N	Y	N	Y	N	N	Y
2 **Pearce**	Y	Y	Y	Y	Y	Y	N
3 Luján	N	Y	N	Y	N	N	Y
NEW YORK							
1 **Zeldin**	Y	Y	Y	Y	Y	Y	Y
2 **King**	Y	Y	Y	Y	Y	Y	Y
3 Suozzi	N	Y	N	Y	N	N	Y
4 Rice	N	Y	N	Y	N	N	Y
5 Meeks	N	Y	N	Y	N	N	Y
6 Meng	N	?	?	?	N	N	Y
7 Velázquez	N	Y	N	Y	N	N	Y
8 Jeffries	N	Y	N	Y	N	N	Y
9 Clarke	N	Y	N	Y	N	N	Y
10 Nadler	N	Y	N	Y	N	N	Y
11 **Donovan**	Y	Y	Y	Y	Y	Y	Y
12 Maloney, C.	N	Y	N	Y	N	N	Y
13 Espaillat	N	Y	N	Y	N	N	Y
14 Crowley	N	Y	N	Y	N	N	Y
15 Serrano	N	Y	N	Y	N	N	Y
16 Engel	N	Y	N	Y	N	N	Y
17 Lowey	N	Y	N	Y	N	N	Y
18 Maloney, S.P.	N	Y	N	Y	N	N	Y
19 **Faso**	N	Y	Y	Y	Y	Y	Y
20 Tonko	N	Y	N	Y	N	N	Y
21 **Stefanik**	Y	Y	Y	Y	Y	Y	Y
22 **Tenney**	Y	Y	Y	Y	Y	Y	Y
23 **Reed**	Y	+	Y	Y	Y	Y	Y
24 **Katko**	Y	Y	Y	Y	Y	Y	Y
25 Slaughter	N	Y	N	Y	N	N	Y
26 Higgins	N	Y	N	Y	N	N	Y
27 **Collins**	Y	Y	Y	?	Y	Y	Y
NORTH CAROLINA							
1 Butterfield	?	?	?	?	N	N	Y
2 **Holding**	Y	Y	Y	Y	Y	Y	Y
3 **Jones**	Y	Y	P	Y	Y	Y	Y
4 Price	N	Y	N	Y	N	N	Y

	99	100	101	102	103	104	105
5 **Foxx**	Y	Y	Y	Y	Y	Y	Y
6 **Walker**	Y	Y	Y	Y	?	?	N
7 **Rouzer**	Y	Y	Y	Y	Y	Y	Y
8 **Hudson**	Y	Y	Y	Y	?	?	+
9 **Pittenger**	Y	Y	Y	Y	Y	Y	N
10 **McHenry**	Y	Y	Y	Y	Y	Y	Y
11 **Meadows**	Y	Y	Y	N	Y	Y	Y
12 Adams	N	Y	N	Y	N	N	Y
13 **Budd**	Y	Y	Y	Y	Y	Y	N
NORTH DAKOTA							
AL **Cramer**	?	Y	Y	Y	Y	Y	Y
OHIO							
1 **Chabot**	Y	Y	Y	Y	Y	Y	Y
2 **Wenstrup**	Y	Y	Y	Y	Y	Y	Y
3 Beatty	N	Y	N	Y	N	N	Y
4 **Jordan**	Y	Y	Y	N	Y	Y	N
5 **Latta**	Y	Y	Y	Y	Y	Y	Y
6 **Johnson**	Y	Y	Y	Y	Y	Y	Y
7 **Gibbs**	Y	Y	Y	N	?	?	N
8 **Davidson**	Y	Y	Y	N	Y	Y	Y
9 Kaptur	N	Y	N	Y	N	N	Y
10 **Turner**	Y	Y	Y	Y	Y	Y	N
11 Fudge	N	Y	N	Y	N	N	Y
12 **Tiberi**	Y	Y	Y	Y	Y	Y	Y
13 Ryan	N	Y	N	Y	N	N	Y
14 **Joyce**	Y	Y	Y	Y	Y	Y	Y
15 **Stivers**	Y	Y	Y	Y	Y	Y	Y
16 **Renacci**	Y	Y	Y	Y	Y	Y	Y
OKLAHOMA							
1 **Bridenstine**	Y	Y	Y	N	Y	Y	N
2 **Mullin**	Y	Y	Y	Y	Y	Y	Y
3 **Lucas**	Y	Y	Y	Y	Y	Y	N
4 **Cole**	Y	Y	Y	Y	Y	Y	Y
5 **Russell**	Y	Y	Y	N	Y	Y	N
OREGON							
1 Bonamici	N	Y	N	Y	N	N	Y
2 **Walden**	Y	Y	Y	Y	Y	Y	Y
3 Blumenauer	N	Y	N	Y	N	N	Y
4 DeFazio	N	Y	N	Y	N	N	Y
5 Schrader	N	Y	N	Y	N	N	Y
PENNSYLVANIA							
1 Brady	N	Y	N	Y	N	N	Y
2 Evans	N	Y	N	Y	N	N	Y
3 **Kelly**	Y	Y	Y	Y	Y	Y	N
4 **Perry**	Y	Y	Y	Y	Y	Y	N
5 **Thompson**	Y	Y	Y	Y	Y	Y	Y
6 **Costello**	Y	Y	Y	Y	Y	Y	Y
7 **Meehan**	Y	Y	Y	Y	Y	Y	Y
8 **Fitzpatrick**	Y	Y	Y	Y	Y	Y	Y
9 **Shuster**	Y	Y	Y	Y	?	?	Y
10 **Marino**	Y	Y	Y	Y	Y	Y	N
11 **Barletta**	Y	Y	Y	Y	Y	Y	Y
12 **Rothfus**	Y	Y	Y	Y	Y	Y	Y
13 Boyle	N	Y	N	Y	N	N	Y
14 Doyle	N	Y	N	Y	N	N	Y
15 **Dent**	N	Y	Y	Y	Y	Y	Y
16 **Smucker**	Y	Y	Y	Y	Y	Y	Y
17 Cartwright	N	Y	N	Y	N	N	Y
18 **Murphy**	Y	Y	Y	Y	Y	Y	Y
RHODE ISLAND							
1 Cicilline	N	Y	N	Y	N	N	Y
2 Langevin	N	Y	N	Y	N	N	Y
SOUTH CAROLINA							
1 **Sanford**	Y	Y	P	Y	Y	Y	Y
2 **Wilson**	Y	Y	Y	Y	Y	Y	Y
3 **Duncan**	Y	Y	Y	Y	Y	Y	N
4 **Gowdy**	Y	Y	Y	Y	Y	Y	Y
6 Clyburn	N	Y	N	Y	N	N	Y
7 **Rice**	Y	Y	Y	N	Y	Y	Y
SOUTH DAKOTA							
AL **Noem**	Y	Y	Y	Y	Y	Y	N
TENNESSEE							
1 **Roe**	Y	Y	Y	Y	Y	Y	Y
2 **Duncan**	Y	Y	Y	Y	Y	Y	N
3 **Fleischmann**	Y	Y	Y	Y	Y	Y	N
4 **DesJarlais**	Y	Y	Y	N	Y	Y	N
5 Cooper	N	Y	N	Y	N	N	Y
6 **Black**	Y	Y	Y	Y	Y	Y	Y
7 **Blackburn**	Y	Y	Y	Y	Y	Y	Y
8 **Kustoff**	Y	Y	Y	Y	Y	Y	N
9 Cohen	N	Y	N	Y	N	N	Y

	99	100	101	102	103	104	105
TEXAS							
1 **Gohmert**	Y	Y	Y	?	Y	Y	N
2 **Poe**	Y	Y	Y	N	Y	Y	N
3 **Johnson, S.**	Y	Y	Y	Y	Y	Y	N
4 **Ratcliffe**	Y	Y	Y	N	Y	Y	Y
5 **Hensarling**	Y	Y	Y	Y	Y	Y	Y
6 **Barton**	?	?	?	?	?	Y	N
7 **Culberson**	Y	Y	Y	Y	Y	Y	Y
8 **Brady**	Y	Y	Y	Y	+	+	N
9 Green, A.	N	Y	N	Y	N	N	Y
10 **McCaul**	Y	Y	Y	Y	Y	Y	Y
11 **Conaway**	Y	Y	Y	N	Y	Y	Y
12 **Granger**	Y	Y	Y	N	Y	Y	Y
13 **Thornberry**	Y	Y	Y	Y	Y	Y	Y
14 **Weber**	Y	Y	Y	N	Y	Y	N
15 Gonzalez	N	Y	N	Y	N	N	Y
16 O'Rourke	N	Y	N	Y	N	N	Y
17 **Flores**	Y	Y	Y	N	Y	Y	Y
18 Jackson Lee	N	Y	N	Y	N	N	Y
19 **Arrington**	Y	Y	Y	Y	Y	Y	N
20 Castro	N	Y	N	Y	N	N	Y
21 **Smith**	Y	Y	Y	Y	?	?	Y
22 **Olson**	Y	Y	Y	Y	Y	Y	Y
23 **Hurd**	Y	Y	Y	Y	Y	Y	Y
24 **Marchant**	Y	Y	Y	N	Y	Y	Y
25 **Williams**	Y	Y	Y	Y	Y	Y	N
26 **Burgess**	Y	Y	Y	N	Y	Y	N
27 **Farenthold**	Y	Y	Y	Y	Y	Y	Y
28 Cuellar	N	Y	N	Y	N	N	Y
29 Green, G.	N	Y	N	Y	N	N	Y
30 Johnson, E.B.	N	Y	N	Y	N	N	Y
31 **Carter**	Y	Y	Y	N	Y	Y	N
32 **Sessions**	Y	Y	Y	Y	Y	Y	N
33 Veasey	N	Y	N	Y	N	N	Y
34 Vela	N	Y	N	Y	N	N	Y
35 Doggett	N	Y	N	Y	N	N	Y
36 **Babin**	Y	Y	Y	N	Y	Y	N
UTAH							
1 **Bishop**	Y	Y	Y	Y	Y	Y	Y
2 **Stewart**	?	Y	Y	Y	Y	Y	Y
3 **Chaffetz**	Y	Y	Y	Y	Y	Y	Y
4 **Love**	Y	Y	Y	Y	Y	Y	Y
VERMONT							
AL Welch	N	Y	N	?	N	N	Y
VIRGINIA							
1 **Wittman**	Y	Y	Y	Y	Y	Y	N
2 **Taylor**	Y	Y	Y	Y	Y	Y	Y
3 Scott	N	Y	N	Y	N	N	Y
4 McEachin	N	Y	N	Y	N	N	Y
5 **Garrett**	Y	Y	Y	N	Y	Y	N
6 **Goodlatte**	Y	Y	Y	Y	Y	Y	Y
7 **Brat**	Y	Y	Y	N	Y	Y	N
8 Beyer	N	Y	N	Y	N	N	Y
9 **Griffith**	Y	Y	Y	N	Y	Y	Y
10 **Comstock**	Y	Y	Y	Y	?	?	Y
11 Connolly	N	Y	N	Y	N	N	Y
WASHINGTON							
1 DelBene	N	Y	N	Y	N	N	Y
2 Larsen	N	Y	N	Y	N	N	Y
3 **Herrera Beutler**	Y	Y	Y	Y	Y	Y	Y
4 **Newhouse**	Y	Y	Y	Y	Y	Y	Y
5 **McMorris Rodgers**	Y	Y	Y	Y	Y	Y	Y
6 Kilmer	N	Y	N	Y	N	N	Y
7 Jayapal	N	Y	N	Y	N	N	Y
8 **Reichert**	Y	Y	Y	Y	Y	Y	Y
9 Smith	N	Y	N	Y	N	?	Y
10 Heck	N	Y	N	Y	N	N	Y
WEST VIRGINIA							
1 **McKinley**	Y	Y	Y	Y	Y	Y	Y
2 **Mooney**	Y	Y	Y	N	Y	Y	N
3 **Jenkins**	Y	Y	Y	Y	Y	Y	Y
WISCONSIN							
1 **Ryan**							
2 Pocan	N	Y	N	Y	N	N	Y
3 Kind	N	Y	N	Y	N	N	Y
4 Moore	N	Y	N	Y	N	N	?
5 **Sensenbrenner**	Y	Y	Y	Y	Y	Y	N
6 **Grothman**	Y	Y	Y	N	Y	Y	N
7 **Duffy**	Y	Y	Y	Y	Y	Y	Y
8 **Gallagher**	Y	Y	Y	Y	Y	Y	Y
WYOMING							
AL **Cheney**	Y	Y	Y	Y	Y	Y	Y

VOTE NUMBER

106. HR 998. REGULATORY REVIEW COMMISSION/AUTHORIZED FUNDING.
Plaskett, D-V.I., amendment that would remove the bill's authorization of up to $30 million and would prohibit funds authorized or appropriated by other laws from being made available to implement the bill's provisions. Rejected in Committee of the Whole 181-243 : R 0-232; D 181-11. Feb. 28, 2017.

107. HR 998. REGULATORY REVIEW COMMISSION/NATIONAL AIRSPACE.
Krishnamoorthi, D-Ill., amendment that would exempt rules related to the safety of the national airspace system. Rejected in Committee of the Whole 189-234 : R 1-231; D 188-3. Feb. 28, 2017.

108. HR 998. REGULATORY REVIEW COMMISSION/AIRPORT NOISE RESTRICTIONS. Krishnamoorthi, D-Ill., amendment that would exempt rules related to airport noise restrictions. Rejected in Committee of the Whole 192-230 : R 2-229; D 190-1. Feb. 28, 2017.

109. HR 998. REGULATORY REVIEW COMMISSION/STUDENT LOAN BORROWER PROTECTIONS. Bonamici, D-Ore., amendment that would exempt from the bill's provisions rules related to providing consumer protections for student loan borrowers. Rejected in Committee of the Whole 191-235 : R 0-234; D 191-1. March 1, 2017.

110. HR 998. REGULATORY REVIEW COMMISSION/CLEAN AIR ACT ENFORCEMENT. Raskin, D-Md., amendment that would exempt from the bill's provisions rules related to the enforcement of the Clean Air Act. Rejected in Committee of the Whole 189-231 : R 1-229; D 188-2. March 1, 2017.

111. HR 998. REGULATORY REVIEW COMMISSION/TRIBAL SOVEREIGNTY.
Moore, D-Wis., amendment that would exempt from the bill's provisions rules related to federal obligations to tribal governments and rules related to supporting tribal sovereignty. Rejected in Committee of the Whole 197-229 : R 6-229; D 191-0. March 1, 2017.

112. HR 998. REGULATORY REVIEW COMMISSION/WHISTLEBLOWER PROTECTIONS. Cummings, D-Md., amendment that would exempt from the bill's provisions rules related to whistleblower protections and rules related to penalties for retaliation against whistleblowers. Rejected in Committee of the Whole 194-231 : R 4-231; D 190-0. March 1, 2017.

	106	107	108	109	110	111	112
ALABAMA							
1 Byrne	N	N	N	N	N	N	N
2 Roby	N	N	N	N	N	N	N
3 Rogers	N	N	N	N	N	N	N
4 Aderholt	N	N	N	N	N	N	N
5 Brooks	N	N	N	N	N	N	N
6 Palmer	N	N	N	N	N	N	N
7 Sewell	Y	Y	Y	Y	Y	Y	Y
ALASKA							
AL Young	N	N	N	N	N	Y	N
ARIZONA							
1 O'Halleran	N	Y	Y	Y	Y	Y	Y
2 McSally	N	N	N	N	N	N	N
3 Grijalva	Y	Y	Y	Y	Y	Y	Y
4 Gosar	N	N	N	N	N	N	N
5 Biggs	N	N	N	N	N	N	N
6 Schweikert	N	N	N	N	N	N	N
7 Gallego	Y	Y	Y	Y	Y	Y	Y
8 Franks	N	N	N	N	N	N	N
9 Sinema	N	Y	Y	Y	Y	Y	Y
ARKANSAS							
1 Crawford	N	N	N	N	N	N	N
2 Hill	N	N	N	N	N	N	N
3 Womack	N	N	N	N	N	N	N
4 Westerman	N	N	N	N	N	N	N
CALIFORNIA							
1 LaMalfa	N	N	N	N	N	N	N
2 Huffman	Y	Y	Y	Y	Y	Y	Y
3 Garamendi	Y	Y	Y	Y	Y	Y	Y
4 McClintock	N	N	N	N	N	N	N
5 Thompson	Y	Y	Y	Y	Y	Y	Y
6 Matsui	Y	Y	Y	Y	Y	Y	Y
7 Bera	Y	Y	Y	Y	Y	Y	Y
8 Cook	N	N	N	N	N	N	N
9 McNerney	Y	Y	Y	?	Y	Y	Y
10 Denham	N	N	N	N	N	N	N
11 DeSaulnier	Y	Y	Y	Y	Y	Y	Y
12 Pelosi	Y	Y	Y	Y	?	?	?
13 Lee	Y	Y	Y	Y	Y	Y	Y
14 Speier	Y	Y	Y	Y	Y	Y	Y
15 Swalwell	Y	Y	Y	Y	Y	Y	Y
16 Costa	N	N	N	N	N	Y	Y
17 Khanna	Y	Y	Y	Y	Y	Y	Y
18 Eshoo	Y	Y	Y	Y	Y	Y	Y
19 Lofgren	Y	Y	Y	Y	Y	Y	Y
20 Panetta	Y	Y	Y	Y	Y	Y	Y
21 Valadao	N	N	N	N	N	N	N
22 Nunes	N	N	N	N	N	N	N
23 McCarthy	N	N	N	N	N	N	N
24 Carbajal	Y	Y	Y	Y	Y	Y	Y
25 Knight	N	N	N	N	N	N	N
26 Brownley	Y	Y	Y	Y	Y	Y	Y
27 Chu	Y	Y	?	Y	Y	Y	Y
28 Schiff	Y	Y	Y	Y	Y	Y	Y
29 Cardenas	Y	Y	Y	Y	Y	Y	Y
30 Sherman	Y	Y	Y	Y	Y	Y	Y
31 Aguilar	Y	Y	Y	Y	Y	Y	Y
32 Napolitano	Y	Y	Y	Y	Y	Y	Y
33 Lieu	Y	Y	Y	Y	Y	Y	Y
34 Vacant							
35 Torres	Y	Y	Y	Y	Y	Y	Y
36 Ruiz	Y	Y	Y	Y	Y	Y	Y
37 Bass	Y	Y	Y	Y	Y	Y	Y
38 Sánchez, Linda	Y	Y	Y	Y	Y	Y	Y
39 Royce	N	N	N	N	N	N	N
40 Roybal-Allard	Y	Y	Y	Y	Y	Y	Y
41 Takano	Y	Y	Y	Y	Y	Y	Y
42 Calvert	N	N	N	N	N	N	N
43 Waters	Y	Y	Y	Y	Y	Y	Y
44 Barragan	Y	Y	Y	Y	Y	Y	Y
45 Walters	N	N	N	N	N	N	N
46 Correa	Y	Y	Y	Y	Y	Y	Y
47 Lowenthal	Y	Y	Y	Y	Y	Y	?
48 Rohrabacher	N	Y	N	N	N	N	N
49 Issa	N	N	N	N	N	N	N
50 Hunter	N	N	N	N	N	N	N
51 Vargas	Y	Y	Y	Y	Y	Y	Y
52 Peters	N	Y	Y	Y	Y	Y	Y
53 Davis	Y	Y	Y	Y	Y	Y	Y

	106	107	108	109	110	111	112
COLORADO							
1 DeGette	Y	Y	Y	Y	Y	Y	Y
2 Polis	Y	Y	Y	Y	Y	Y	Y
3 Tipton	N	N	N	N	N	N	N
4 Buck	N	N	N	N	N	N	N
5 Lamborn	N	N	N	N	N	N	N
6 Coffman	N	N	N	N	N	N	N
7 Perlmutter	Y	Y	Y	Y	Y	Y	Y
CONNECTICUT							
1 Larson	Y	Y	Y	Y	Y	Y	Y
2 Courtney	Y	Y	Y	Y	Y	Y	Y
3 DeLauro	Y	Y	Y	Y	Y	Y	Y
4 Himes	Y	Y	Y	Y	Y	Y	Y
5 Esty	Y	Y	Y	Y	Y	Y	Y
DELAWARE							
AL Blunt Rochester	Y	Y	Y	Y	Y	Y	Y
FLORIDA							
1 Gaetz	N	N	N	N	N	N	N
2 Dunn	N	N	N	N	N	N	N
3 Yoho	N	N	N	N	N	N	N
4 Rutherford	N	N	N	N	N	N	N
5 Lawson	Y	Y	Y	Y	Y	Y	Y
6 DeSantis	N	N	N	N	N	N	N
7 Murphy	N	Y	Y	Y	Y	Y	Y
8 Posey	N	N	N	N	N	N	N
9 Soto	Y	Y	Y	Y	Y	Y	Y
10 Demings	Y	Y	Y	Y	Y	Y	Y
11 Webster	N	N	N	N	N	N	N
12 Bilirakis	N	N	N	N	N	N	N
13 Crist	Y	Y	Y	Y	Y	Y	Y
14 Castor	Y	Y	Y	Y	Y	Y	Y
15 Ross	N	N	N	N	N	N	N
16 Buchanan	N	N	N	N	N	N	N
17 Rooney, T.	?	?	?	N	N	N	N
18 Mast	N	N	N	N	N	N	N
19 Rooney, F.	N	N	N	N	N	N	N
20 Hastings	Y	Y	Y	Y	Y	Y	Y
21 Frankel	Y	Y	Y	Y	Y	Y	Y
22 Deutch	Y	Y	Y	Y	Y	Y	Y
23 Wasserman Schultz	Y	Y	Y	Y	Y	Y	Y
24 Wilson	Y	Y	Y	Y	Y	Y	Y
25 Diaz-Balart	N	N	N	N	N	N	N
26 Curbelo	N	N	N	N	N	N	N
27 Ros-Lehtinen	N	N	N	N	Y	N	N
GEORGIA							
1 Carter	N	N	N	N	N	N	N
2 Bishop	Y	Y	Y	Y	Y	Y	Y
3 Ferguson	N	N	N	N	N	N	N
4 Johnson	Y	Y	Y	Y	Y	Y	Y
5 Lewis	Y	Y	Y	Y	Y	Y	Y
7 Woodall	N	N	N	N	N	N	N
8 Scott, A.	N	N	N	N	N	N	N
9 Collins	N	N	N	N	N	N	N
10 Hice	N	N	N	N	N	N	N
11 Loudermilk	N	N	N	N	N	N	N
12 Allen	N	N	N	N	N	N	N
13 Scott, D.	Y	Y	Y	Y	Y	?	?
14 Graves	N	N	N	N	N	N	N
HAWAII							
1 Hanabusa	Y	Y	Y	Y	Y	Y	Y
2 Gabbard	Y	Y	Y	Y	Y	Y	Y
IDAHO							
1 Labrador	N	N	N	N	N	N	N
2 Simpson	N	N	N	N	N	N	N
ILLINOIS							
1 Rush	Y	Y	Y	Y	?	Y	Y
2 Kelly	Y	Y	Y	Y	Y	Y	Y
3 Lipinski	Y	Y	Y	Y	Y	Y	Y
4 Gutierrez	Y	Y	Y	Y	Y	Y	Y
5 Quigley	Y	Y	Y	Y	Y	Y	Y
6 Roskam	N	N	N	N	N	N	N
7 Davis, D.	Y	Y	Y	Y	Y	Y	Y
8 Krishnamoorthi	Y	Y	Y	Y	Y	Y	Y
9 Schakowsky	Y	Y	Y	Y	Y	Y	Y
10 Schneider	Y	Y	Y	Y	Y	Y	Y
11 Foster	Y	Y	Y	Y	Y	Y	Y
12 Bost	N	N	N	N	N	N	N
13 Davis, R.	–	–	–	N	N	N	N
14 Hultgren	N	N	N	N	N	N	N
15 Shimkus	N	N	N	N	N	N	N

KEY	Republicans	Democrats	Independents

Y Voted for (yea)	X Paired against	C Voted "present" to avoid possible conflict of interest
# Paired for	– Announced against	
+ Announced for	P Voted "present"	? Did not vote or otherwise make a position known
N Voted against (nay)		

	106	107	108	109	110	111	112
16 **Kinzinger**	N	N	N	N	N	N	N
17 Bustos	Y	Y	Y	Y	Y	Y	Y
18 **LaHood**	N	N	N	N	N	N	N
INDIANA							
1 Visclosky	Y	Y	Y	Y	Y	Y	Y
2 **Walorski**	N	N	N	N	N	N	N
3 **Banks**	N	N	N	N	N	N	N
4 **Rokita**	N	N	N	N	N	N	N
5 **Brooks**	N	N	N	N	N	N	N
6 **Messer**	N	N	N	N	N	N	N
7 Carson	Y	Y	Y	Y	Y	Y	Y
8 **Bucshon**	N	N	N	N	N	N	N
9 **Hollingsworth**	N	N	N	N	N	N	N
IOWA							
1 **Blum**	N	N	N	N	N	N	N
2 Loebsack	Y	Y	Y	Y	Y	Y	Y
3 **Young**	N	N	N	N	N	N	Y
4 **King**	N	N	N	N	N	N	N
KANSAS							
1 **Marshall**	N	N	N	N	N	N	N
2 **Jenkins**	N	N	N	N	N	N	N
3 **Yoder**	N	N	N	N	N	N	N
KENTUCKY							
1 **Comer**	N	N	N	N	N	N	N
2 **Guthrie**	N	N	N	N	N	N	N
3 Yarmuth	Y	Y	Y	Y	Y	Y	Y
4 **Massie**	N	N	N	N	N	N	N
5 **Rogers**	N	N	N	N	N	N	N
6 **Barr**	N	N	N	N	N	N	N
LOUISIANA							
1 **Scalise**	N	N	N	N	N	N	N
2 Richmond	Y	Y	Y	Y	Y	Y	Y
3 **Higgins**	N	N	N	N	N	N	N
4 **Johnson**	N	N	N	N	N	N	N
5 **Abraham**	N	N	N	N	N	N	N
6 **Graves**	N	N	N	N	N	N	N
MAINE							
1 Pingree	Y	Y	Y	Y	Y	Y	Y
2 **Poliquin**	N	N	N	N	N	N	N
MARYLAND							
1 **Harris**	N	N	N	N	N	N	N
2 Ruppersberger	Y	Y	Y	Y	Y	Y	Y
3 Sarbanes	Y	Y	Y	Y	Y	Y	Y
4 Brown	Y	Y	Y	Y	Y	Y	Y
5 Hoyer	Y	Y	Y	Y	Y	Y	Y
6 Delaney	Y	Y	Y	Y	Y	Y	Y
7 Cummings	Y	Y	Y	Y	Y	Y	Y
8 Raskin	Y	Y	Y	Y	Y	Y	Y
MASSACHUSETTS							
1 Neal	Y	Y	Y	Y	Y	Y	Y
2 McGovern	Y	Y	Y	Y	Y	Y	Y
3 Tsongas	Y	Y	Y	Y	Y	Y	Y
4 Kennedy	Y	Y	Y	Y	Y	Y	Y
5 Clark	Y	Y	Y	Y	Y	Y	Y
6 Moulton	Y	Y	Y	Y	Y	Y	Y
7 Capuano	Y	Y	Y	Y	Y	Y	Y
8 Lynch	Y	Y	Y	Y	Y	Y	Y
9 Keating	Y	Y	Y	Y	Y	Y	Y
MICHIGAN							
1 **Bergman**	N	N	N	N	N	N	N
2 **Huizenga**	N	N	N	N	N	N	N
3 **Amash**	N	N	N	N	N	N	N
4 **Moolenaar**	N	N	N	N	N	N	N
5 Kildee	Y	Y	Y	Y	Y	Y	Y
6 **Upton**	N	N	N	N	N	N	N
7 **Walberg**	N	N	N	N	N	N	N
8 **Bishop**	N	N	N	N	N	N	N
9 Levin	Y	Y	Y	Y	Y	Y	Y
10 **Mitchell**	N	N	N	N	N	N	N
11 **Trott**	N	N	N	N	?	N	N
12 Dingell	Y	Y	Y	Y	Y	Y	Y
13 Conyers	Y	Y	Y	Y	Y	Y	Y
14 Lawrence	Y	Y	Y	Y	Y	Y	Y
MINNESOTA							
1 Walz	Y	Y	Y	Y	Y	Y	Y
2 **Lewis**	N	N	N	N	N	N	N
3 **Paulsen**	N	N	N	N	N	N	N
4 McCollum	Y	Y	Y	Y	Y	Y	Y

	106	107	108	109	110	111	112
5 Ellison	Y	Y	Y	Y	Y	Y	Y
6 **Emmer**	N	N	N	N	N	N	N
7 Peterson	N	Y	Y	Y	N	Y	Y
8 Nolan	Y	Y	Y	Y	Y	Y	Y
MISSISSIPPI							
1 **Kelly**	N	N	N	N	N	N	N
2 Thompson	Y	Y	Y	Y	Y	Y	Y
3 **Harper**	N	N	N	N	N	N	N
4 **Palazzo**	N	N	N	N	N	N	N
MISSOURI							
1 Clay	Y	Y	Y	Y	Y	Y	Y
2 **Wagner**	–	–	–	N	N	N	N
3 **Luetkemeyer**	N	N	N	N	N	N	N
4 **Hartzler**	N	N	N	N	N	N	N
5 Cleaver	Y	Y	Y	Y	Y	Y	Y
6 **Graves**	N	N	N	N	N	N	N
7 **Long**	N	N	N	N	N	N	N
8 **Smith**	N	N	N	N	N	N	N
MONTANA							
AL **Zinke**	?	?	?				
NEBRASKA							
1 **Fortenberry**	N	N	N	N	N	N	N
2 **Bacon**	N	N	N	N	N	N	N
3 **Smith**	N	N	N	N	N	N	N
NEVADA							
1 Titus	Y	Y	Y	Y	Y	Y	Y
2 **Amodei**	N	N	N	?	N	N	N
3 Rosen	N	Y	Y	Y	Y	Y	Y
4 Kihuen	Y	Y	Y	Y	Y	Y	Y
NEW HAMPSHIRE							
1 Shea-Porter	Y	Y	Y	Y	Y	Y	Y
2 Kuster	Y	Y	Y	Y	Y	Y	Y
NEW JERSEY							
1 Norcross	Y	Y	Y	Y	Y	Y	Y
2 **LoBiondo**	N	Y	N	N	N	N	N
3 **MacArthur**	N	N	N	N	N	N	N
4 **Smith**	N	N	Y	N	N	N	N
5 Gottheimer	N	Y	Y	Y	Y	Y	Y
6 Pallone	Y	Y	Y	Y	Y	Y	Y
7 **Lance**	N	N	N	N	N	N	N
8 Sires	Y	Y	Y	Y	Y	Y	Y
9 Pascrell	Y	Y	Y	Y	Y	Y	Y
10 Payne	Y	Y	Y	Y	Y	Y	Y
11 **Frelinghuysen**	N	N	N	N	N	N	N
12 Watson Coleman	Y	Y	Y	Y	Y	Y	Y
NEW MEXICO							
1 Lujan Grisham	Y	Y	Y	Y	Y	Y	Y
2 **Pearce**	N	N	N	N	N	N	N
3 Luján	Y	Y	Y	Y	Y	Y	Y
NEW YORK							
1 **Zeldin**	N	N	N	N	N	N	N
2 **King**	N	N	N	N	N	N	N
3 Suozzi	N	N	Y	Y	Y	Y	Y
4 Rice	Y	Y	Y	Y	Y	Y	Y
5 Meeks	Y	Y	Y	Y	Y	Y	Y
6 Meng	Y	Y	Y	Y	Y	Y	Y
7 Velázquez	Y	Y	Y	Y	Y	Y	Y
8 Jeffries	Y	Y	Y	Y	Y	Y	Y
9 Clarke	Y	Y	Y	Y	Y	Y	Y
10 Nadler	Y	Y	Y	Y	Y	Y	Y
11 **Donovan**	N	N	N	N	N	N	N
12 Maloney, C.	Y	Y	Y	Y	Y	Y	Y
13 Espaillat	Y	Y	Y	Y	Y	Y	Y
14 Crowley	Y	Y	Y	Y	Y	Y	Y
15 Serrano	Y	Y	Y	Y	Y	Y	Y
16 Engel	Y	Y	Y	Y	Y	Y	Y
17 Lowey	Y	Y	Y	Y	Y	Y	Y
18 Maloney, S.P.	Y	?	Y	Y	Y	Y	Y
19 **Faso**	N	N	N	N	N	N	N
20 Tonko	Y	Y	Y	Y	Y	Y	Y
21 **Stefanik**	N	N	N	N	N	N	N
22 **Tenney**	N	N	N	N	N	N	N
23 **Reed**	N	N	N	N	N	N	N
24 **Katko**	N	N	N	N	N	N	N
25 Slaughter	Y	Y	Y	Y	Y	Y	Y
26 Higgins	Y	Y	Y	Y	Y	Y	Y
27 **Collins**	N	N	N	N	?	N	N
NORTH CAROLINA							
1 Butterfield	Y	Y	Y	Y	Y	Y	Y
2 **Holding**	N	N	N	N	N	N	N
3 **Jones**	N	N	N	N	N	Y	Y
4 Price	Y	Y	Y	Y	Y	Y	Y

	106	107	108	109	110	111	112
5 **Foxx**	N	N	N	N	N	N	N
6 **Walker**	N	N	N	N	N	N	N
7 **Rouzer**	N	N	N	N	N	N	N
8 **Hudson**	–	–	–	–	–	–	–
9 **Pittenger**	N	N	N	N	N	N	N
10 **McHenry**	N	N	N	N	N	N	N
11 **Meadows**	N	N	N	N	N	N	N
12 Adams	Y	Y	Y	Y	Y	Y	Y
13 **Budd**	N	N	N	N	N	N	N
NORTH DAKOTA							
AL **Cramer**	N	N	N	N	N	N	N
OHIO							
1 **Chabot**	N	N	N	N	N	N	N
2 **Wenstrup**	N	N	N	N	N	N	N
3 Beatty	Y	Y	Y	Y	Y	Y	Y
4 **Jordan**	N	N	N	N	N	N	N
5 **Latta**	N	N	N	N	N	N	N
6 **Johnson**	N	N	N	N	N	N	N
7 **Gibbs**	N	N	N	N	N	N	N
8 **Davidson**	N	N	N	N	N	N	N
9 Kaptur	Y	Y	Y	Y	Y	Y	Y
10 **Turner**	N	N	N	N	N	N	N
11 Fudge	Y	Y	Y	Y	Y	Y	Y
12 **Tiberi**	N	N	N	N	?	N	N
13 Ryan	Y	Y	Y	Y	Y	Y	Y
14 **Joyce**	N	N	N	N	N	N	N
15 **Stivers**	N	N	N	N	?	N	N
16 **Renacci**	N	N	N	N	N	N	N
OKLAHOMA							
1 **Bridenstine**	N	N	N	N	N	N	N
2 **Mullin**	N	N	N	N	N	Y	N
3 **Lucas**	N	N	N	N	N	Y	N
4 **Cole**	N	N	N	N	N	Y	N
5 **Russell**	N	N	N	N	N	N	N
OREGON							
1 Bonamici	Y	Y	Y	Y	Y	Y	Y
2 **Walden**	N	N	N	N	N	N	N
3 Blumenauer	Y	Y	Y	Y	Y	Y	Y
4 DeFazio	Y	Y	Y	Y	Y	Y	Y
5 Schrader	N	Y	Y	Y	Y	Y	Y
PENNSYLVANIA							
1 Brady	Y	Y	Y	Y	Y	Y	Y
2 Evans	Y	Y	Y	Y	Y	Y	Y
3 **Kelly**	N	N	N	N	N	N	N
4 **Perry**	N	N	N	N	N	N	N
5 **Thompson**	N	N	N	N	N	N	N
6 **Costello**	N	N	N	N	N	N	N
7 **Meehan**	N	N	N	N	N	N	N
8 **Fitzpatrick**	N	N	N	N	N	N	Y
9 **Shuster**	N	N	N	N	N	N	N
10 **Marino**	N	N	N	N	N	N	N
11 **Barletta**	N	N	N	N	N	N	N
12 **Rothfus**	N	N	N	N	N	N	N
13 Boyle	Y	Y	Y	Y	Y	Y	Y
14 Doyle	Y	Y	Y	Y	Y	Y	Y
15 **Dent**	N	N	N	N	N	N	N
16 **Smucker**	N	N	N	N	N	N	N
17 Cartwright	Y	Y	Y	Y	Y	Y	Y
18 **Murphy**	N	N	N	N	N	N	N
RHODE ISLAND							
1 Cicilline	Y	Y	Y	Y	Y	Y	Y
2 Langevin	Y	Y	Y	Y	Y	Y	Y
SOUTH CAROLINA							
1 **Sanford**	N	N	N	N	N	N	N
2 **Wilson**	N	N	N	N	N	N	N
3 **Duncan**	N	N	N	N	N	N	N
4 **Gowdy**	N	N	N	N	N	N	N
6 Clyburn	Y	Y	Y	Y	Y	Y	Y
7 **Rice**	N	N	N	N	N	N	N
SOUTH DAKOTA							
AL **Noem**	N	N	N	N	N	N	N
TENNESSEE							
1 **Roe**	N	N	N	N	N	N	N
2 **Duncan**	N	N	N	N	N	N	N
3 **Fleischmann**	N	N	N	N	N	N	N
4 **DesJarlais**	N	N	N	N	N	N	N
5 Cooper	Y	Y	Y	Y	Y	Y	Y
6 **Black**	N	N	N	N	N	N	N
7 **Blackburn**	N	N	N	N	N	N	N
8 **Kustoff**	N	N	N	N	N	N	N
9 Cohen	Y	Y	Y	Y	Y	Y	Y

	106	107	108	109	110	111	112
TEXAS							
1 **Gohmert**	N	N	N	N	N	N	N
2 **Poe**	N	N	N	N	N	N	N
3 **Johnson, S.**	N	N	N	N	N	N	N
4 **Ratcliffe**	N	N	N	N	N	N	N
5 **Hensarling**	N	N	?	N	N	N	N
6 **Barton**	N	N	N	N	N	N	N
7 **Culberson**	N	N	N	N	N	N	N
8 **Brady**	N	N	N	N	N	N	N
9 Green, A.	Y	Y	Y	Y	Y	Y	Y
10 **McCaul**	N	N	N	N	?	N	N
11 **Conaway**	N	N	N	N	N	N	N
12 **Granger**	N	N	N	N	N	N	N
13 **Thornberry**	N	N	N	N	N	N	N
14 **Weber**	N	N	N	N	N	N	N
15 Gonzalez	Y	Y	Y	Y	Y	Y	Y
16 O'Rourke	Y	Y	Y	Y	Y	Y	Y
17 **Flores**	N	N	N	N	N	N	N
18 Jackson Lee	Y	N	Y	Y	Y	Y	Y
19 **Arrington**	N	N	N	N	N	N	N
20 Castro	Y	Y	Y	Y	Y	Y	Y
21 **Smith**	N	N	N	N	N	N	N
22 **Olson**	N	N	N	N	N	N	N
23 **Hurd**	N	N	N	N	N	Y	N
24 **Marchant**	N	N	N	N	N	N	N
25 **Williams**	N	N	N	N	N	N	N
26 **Burgess**	N	N	N	N	N	N	N
27 **Farenthold**	N	N	N	N	N	N	N
28 Cuellar	N	Y	Y	Y	?	Y	Y
29 Green, G.	Y	Y	Y	Y	Y	Y	Y
30 Johnson, E.B.	Y	Y	Y	Y	Y	Y	Y
31 **Carter**	N	N	N	N	N	N	N
32 **Sessions**	N	N	N	N	N	N	N
33 Veasey	Y	Y	Y	Y	Y	Y	Y
34 Vela	Y	Y	Y	Y	Y	Y	Y
35 Doggett	Y	Y	Y	Y	Y	Y	Y
36 **Babin**	N	N	N	N	N	N	N
UTAH							
1 **Bishop**	N	N	N	N	N	N	N
2 **Stewart**	N	N	N	N	N	N	N
3 **Chaffetz**	N	N	N	N	N	N	N
4 **Love**	N	N	N	N	N	N	N
VERMONT							
AL Welch	Y	Y	Y	Y	Y	Y	Y
VIRGINIA							
1 **Wittman**	N	N	N	N	N	N	N
2 **Taylor**	N	N	N	N	N	N	N
3 Scott	Y	Y	Y	Y	Y	Y	Y
4 McEachin	Y	Y	Y	Y	Y	Y	Y
5 **Garrett**	N	N	N	N	N	N	N
6 **Goodlatte**	N	N	N	N	N	N	N
7 **Brat**	N	N	N	N	N	N	N
8 Beyer	Y	Y	Y	Y	Y	Y	Y
9 **Griffith**	N	N	N	N	N	N	N
10 **Comstock**	N	N	N	N	N	N	N
11 Connolly	Y	Y	Y	Y	Y	Y	Y
WASHINGTON							
1 DelBene	Y	Y	Y	Y	Y	Y	Y
2 Larsen	Y	Y	Y	Y	Y	Y	Y
3 **Herrera Beutler**	N	N	N	N	N	N	N
4 **Newhouse**	N	N	N	N	N	N	N
5 **McMorris Rodgers**	N	N	N	N	N	N	N
6 Kilmer	Y	Y	Y	Y	Y	Y	Y
7 Jayapal	Y	Y	Y	Y	Y	Y	Y
8 **Reichert**	N	N	N	N	N	N	N
9 Smith	Y	Y	Y	Y	Y	Y	Y
10 Heck	Y	Y	Y	Y	Y	Y	Y
WEST VIRGINIA							
1 **McKinley**	N	N	N	N	N	N	N
2 **Mooney**	N	N	N	N	N	N	N
3 **Jenkins**	N	N	N	N	N	N	N
WISCONSIN							
1 **Ryan**							
2 Pocan	Y	Y	Y	Y	Y	Y	Y
3 Kind	Y	Y	Y	Y	Y	Y	Y
4 Moore	?	?	?	Y	Y	Y	Y
5 **Sensenbrenner**	N	N	N	N	N	N	N
6 **Grothman**	N	N	N	N	N	N	N
7 **Duffy**	N	N	N	N	N	N	N
8 **Gallagher**	N	N	N	N	N	N	N
WYOMING							
AL **Cheney**	N	N	N	N	N	N	N

VOTE NUMBER

113. HR 998. REGULATORY REVIEW COMMISSION/RECOMMIT. Raskin, D-Md., motion to recommit the bill to the House Oversight and Government Reform Committee with instructions to report it back immediately with an amendment that would exempt from the bill's provisions rules related to laws governing potential conflicts of interest and financial disclosures for executive branch employees, and would exempt rules related to bribery. Motion rejected 190-235 : R 0-235; D 190-0. March 1, 2017.

114. HR 998. REGULATORY REVIEW COMMISSION/PASSAGE. Passage of the bill that would establish a nine-member commission to review existing federal regulations and identify regulations that should be repealed on the basis of reducing costs on the U.S. economy. The commission would identify those regulatory policies that it deems should be repealed immediately, and would set up a "Cut-Go" system that would require agencies to repeal existing rules to offset costs before issuing a new rule. As amended, the commission, in identifying which rules should be repealed, would be required to evaluate the extent to which a repeal of a rule would impact public health. It would bar from membership on the commission individuals who have been registered lobbyists during the previous two years. Passed 240-185 : R 229-5; D 11-180. March 1, 2017.

115. HR 1009, HR 1004, H RES 156. REGULATORY DATABASES AND REGULATORY COST-BENEFIT ANALYSIS/PREVIOUS QUESTION. Sessions, R-Texas, motion to order the previous question (thus ending debate and possibility of amendment) on the rule (H Res 156) that would provide for House floor consideration of the bill (HR 1004) that would require federal agencies to maintain and regularly update detailed online databases of regulatory actions taken and pending before the agency. It would also provide for consideration of the bill (HR 1009) that would require the Office of Management and Budget's Office of Information and Regulatory Affairs to review significant government regulations to insure that they are consistent with relevant laws and do not conflict with regulations issued by other agencies. The bill would define significant regulatory actions as those that are likely to have an annual economic effect of $100 million or more. Motion agreed to 233-189 : R 233-0; D 0-189. March 1, 2017.

116. HR 1009, HR 1004, H RES 156. REGULATORY DATABASES AND REGULATORY COST-BENEFIT ANALYSIS/RULE. Adoption of the rule (H Res 156) that would provide for House floor consideration of the bill (HR 1004) that would require federal agencies to maintain and regularly update detailed online databases of regulatory actions taken and pending before the agency. It would also provide for consideration of the bill (HR 1009) that would require the Office of Management and Budget's Office of Information and Regulatory Affairs to review significant government regulations to insure that they are consistent with relevant laws and do not conflict with regulations issued by other agencies. The bill would define significant regulatory actions as those that are likely to have an annual economic effect of $100 million or more. Adopted 234-180 : R 233-0; D 1-180. March 1, 2017.

117. HR 1009. REGULATORY COST-BENEFIT ANALYSIS/DUPLICITY PREVENTION. Young, R-Iowa, amendment that would require each agency to describe what steps were taken in order to ensure that a new rule or regulation would not be duplicative or conflict with any existing or planned regulatory action. Adopted in Committee of the Whole 265-158 : R 232-0; D 33-158. March 1, 2017.

118. HR 1009. REGULATORY COST-BENEFIT ANALYSIS/RECOMMIT. Cartwright, D-Pa., motion to recommit the bill to the House Oversight and Government Reform Committee with instructions to immediately report it back with an amendment that would exempt the Office of Government Ethics from the Office of Information and Regulatory Affairs' reviews required under the bill. Motion rejected 193-234 : R 1-234; D 192-0. March 1, 2017.

119. HR 1009. REGULATORY COST-BENEFIT ANALYSIS/INDEPENDENT AGENCIES. Connolly, D-Va., amendment that would exempt independent agencies from the Office of Information and Regulatory Affairs' reviews required under the bill. Rejected in Committee of the Whole 188-234 : R 1-232; D 187-2. March 1, 2017.

	113	114	115	116	117	118	119
ALABAMA							
1 **Byrne**	N	Y	Y	Y	Y	N	N
2 **Roby**	N	Y	Y	Y	Y	N	N
3 **Rogers**	N	Y	Y	Y	Y	N	N
4 **Aderholt**	N	Y	Y	Y	Y	N	N
5 **Brooks**	N	Y	Y	Y	Y	N	N
6 **Palmer**	N	Y	Y	Y	Y	N	N
7 Sewell	Y	N	N	N	N	Y	Y
ALASKA							
AL **Young**	N	Y	Y	Y	Y	N	N
ARIZONA							
1 O'Halleran	Y	N	N	Y	Y	Y	Y
2 **McSally**	N	Y	Y	Y	Y	N	Y
3 Grijalva	Y	N	N	N	N	Y	Y
4 **Gosar**	N	Y	Y	Y	Y	N	N
5 **Biggs**	N	N	Y	Y	Y	N	N
6 **Schweikert**	N	Y	Y	Y	Y	N	N
7 Gallego	Y	N	N	Y	Y	Y	Y
8 **Franks**	N	Y	Y	Y	Y	N	N
9 Sinema	Y	Y	N	Y	Y	Y	Y
ARKANSAS							
1 **Crawford**	N	Y	Y	Y	Y	N	N
2 **Hill**	N	Y	Y	Y	Y	N	N
3 **Womack**	N	Y	Y	Y	Y	N	N
4 **Westerman**	N	Y	Y	Y	Y	N	N
CALIFORNIA							
1 **LaMalfa**	N	Y	Y	Y	?	N	N
2 Huffman	Y	N	N	N	N	Y	Y
3 Garamendi	Y	N	N	N	N	Y	Y
4 **McClintock**	N	Y	Y	Y	Y	N	N
5 Thompson	Y	N	N	N	Y	Y	Y
6 Matsui	Y	N	N	N	N	Y	Y
7 Bera	Y	N	N	N	Y	Y	Y
8 **Cook**	N	Y	Y	Y	Y	N	N
9 McNerney	Y	N	N	N	N	Y	Y
10 **Denham**	N	Y	Y	Y	Y	N	N
11 DeSaulnier	Y	N	N	N	N	Y	Y
12 Pelosi	?	?	N	N	N	Y	Y
13 Lee	Y	N	N	N	N	Y	Y
14 Speier	Y	N	N	N	N	Y	Y
15 Swalwell	Y	N	N	N	N	Y	Y
16 Costa	Y	Y	N	?	N	Y	Y
17 Khanna	Y	N	N	N	N	Y	Y
18 Eshoo	Y	N	N	N	N	Y	Y
19 Lofgren	Y	N	N	N	N	Y	Y
20 Panetta	Y	N	N	N	N	Y	Y
21 **Valadao**	N	Y	Y	Y	Y	N	N
22 **Nunes**	N	Y	Y	Y	Y	N	N
23 **McCarthy**	N	Y	Y	Y	Y	N	N
24 Carbajal	Y	N	N	N	N	Y	Y
25 **Knight**	N	Y	Y	Y	Y	N	N
26 Brownley	Y	N	N	N	Y	Y	Y
27 Chu	Y	N	N	N	N	Y	Y
28 Schiff	Y	N	N	N	N	Y	Y
29 Cardenas	Y	N	N	N	N	Y	Y
30 Sherman	Y	N	N	N	N	Y	Y
31 Aguilar	Y	N	N	N	Y	Y	Y
32 Napolitano	Y	N	N	N	N	Y	Y
33 Lieu	Y	N	N	?	N	Y	Y
34 Vacant							
35 Torres	Y	N	N	N	N	Y	Y
36 Ruiz	Y	N	N	N	Y	Y	Y
37 Bass	Y	N	N	?	N	Y	Y
38 Sánchez, Linda	Y	N	N	N	N	Y	Y
39 **Royce**	N	Y	Y	Y	Y	N	N
40 Roybal-Allard	Y	N	N	N	Y	Y	Y
41 Takano	Y	N	N	N	N	Y	Y
42 **Calvert**	N	Y	Y	Y	Y	N	N
43 Waters	Y	N	N	N	N	Y	Y
44 Barragan	Y	N	N	N	N	Y	Y
45 **Walters**	N	Y	Y	Y	Y	N	N
46 Correa	Y	N	N	?	N	Y	Y
47 Lowenthal	Y	N	N	N	N	Y	Y
48 **Rohrabacher**	N	Y	Y	Y	Y	N	N
49 **Issa**	N	Y	Y	Y	Y	N	N
50 **Hunter**	N	Y	Y	Y	Y	N	N
51 Vargas	Y	N	N	N	N	Y	Y
52 Peters	Y	N	N	N	Y	Y	Y
53 Davis	Y	N	N	N	N	Y	Y

	113	114	115	116	117	118	119
COLORADO							
1 DeGette	Y	N	N	N	N	Y	Y
2 Polis	Y	N	N	N	N	Y	Y
3 **Tipton**	N	Y	Y	Y	Y	N	N
4 **Buck**	N	Y	Y	Y	Y	N	N
5 **Lamborn**	N	Y	Y	Y	Y	N	N
6 **Coffman**	N	Y	Y	Y	Y	N	N
7 Perlmutter	Y	N	?	N	Y	Y	Y
CONNECTICUT							
1 Larson	Y	N	N	N	N	Y	Y
2 Courtney	Y	N	N	N	N	Y	Y
3 DeLauro	Y	N	N	N	N	Y	Y
4 Himes	Y	N	N	?	Y	Y	Y
5 Esty	Y	N	N	N	N	Y	Y
DELAWARE							
AL Blunt Rochester	Y	N	N	N	N	Y	Y
FLORIDA							
1 **Gaetz**	N	N	Y	Y	Y	N	N
2 **Dunn**	N	Y	Y	Y	Y	N	N
3 **Yoho**	N	Y	Y	Y	Y	N	N
4 **Rutherford**	N	Y	Y	Y	Y	N	N
5 Lawson	Y	N	N	N	N	Y	Y
6 **DeSantis**	N	Y	Y	Y	Y	N	N
7 Murphy	Y	Y	N	N	Y	Y	Y
8 **Posey**	N	Y	Y	Y	Y	N	N
9 Soto	Y	N	N	N	N	Y	Y
10 Demings	Y	N	N	N	N	Y	Y
11 **Webster**	N	Y	Y	Y	Y	N	N
12 **Bilirakis**	N	Y	Y	Y	Y	N	N
13 Crist	Y	N	N	N	N	Y	Y
14 Castor	Y	N	N	N	N	Y	Y
15 **Ross**	N	Y	Y	Y	Y	N	N
16 **Buchanan**	N	Y	Y	Y	Y	N	N
17 **Rooney, T.**	N	Y	Y	Y	Y	N	N
18 **Mast**	N	Y	Y	Y	Y	N	N
19 **Rooney, F.**	N	Y	Y	Y	Y	N	N
20 Hastings	Y	N	N	N	N	Y	Y
21 Frankel	Y	N	N	N	N	Y	Y
22 Deutch	Y	N	N	N	N	Y	Y
23 Wasserman Schultz	Y	N	N	N	N	Y	Y
24 Wilson	Y	N	N	N	N	Y	Y
25 **Diaz-Balart**	N	Y	Y	Y	Y	N	N
26 **Curbelo**	N	Y	Y	Y	Y	N	N
27 **Ros-Lehtinen**	N	Y	Y	Y	Y	N	N
GEORGIA							
1 **Carter**	N	Y	Y	Y	Y	N	N
2 Bishop	Y	N	N	N	N	Y	Y
3 **Ferguson**	N	Y	Y	Y	Y	N	N
4 Johnson	Y	N	N	N	N	Y	Y
5 Lewis	Y	N	N	N	N	Y	Y
6 **Woodall**	N	Y	Y	Y	Y	N	N
7 **Scott, A.**	N	Y	Y	Y	Y	N	N
8 **Collins**	N	Y	Y	Y	Y	N	N
9 **Hice**	N	Y	Y	Y	Y	N	N
10 **Loudermilk**	N	Y	Y	Y	Y	N	N
11 **Allen**	N	Y	Y	Y	Y	N	N
12 Scott, D.	?	?	?	?	N	Y	Y
13 **Graves**	N	Y	Y	Y	Y	N	N
HAWAII							
1 Hanabusa	Y	N	N	N	N	Y	Y
2 Gabbard	Y	N	N	?	Y	Y	Y
IDAHO							
1 **Labrador**	N	Y	Y	Y	Y	N	N
2 **Simpson**	N	Y	Y	Y	Y	N	N
ILLINOIS							
1 Rush	Y	N	N	N	N	Y	Y
2 Kelly	Y	N	N	N	N	Y	Y
3 Lipinski	Y	N	N	N	Y	Y	Y
4 Gutierrez	Y	N	N	–	N	Y	Y
5 Quigley	Y	N	N	N	N	Y	Y
6 **Roskam**	N	Y	Y	Y	Y	N	N
7 Davis, D.	Y	N	N	N	N	Y	Y
8 Krishnamoorthi	Y	N	N	N	N	Y	Y
9 Schakowsky	Y	N	N	N	N	Y	Y
10 Schneider	Y	N	N	N	N	Y	Y
11 Foster	Y	N	N	N	N	Y	Y
12 **Bost**	N	Y	Y	Y	Y	N	N
13 **Davis, R.**	N	Y	Y	Y	Y	N	N
14 **Hultgren**	N	Y	Y	Y	Y	N	N
15 **Shimkus**	N	Y	Y	Y	Y	N	N

KEY	**Republicans**	Democrats		*Independents*	
Y Voted for (yea)		**X** Paired against		**C** Voted "present" to avoid possible conflict of interest	
# Paired for		**–** Announced against			
+ Announced for		**P** Voted "present"		**?** Did not vote or otherwise make a position known	
N Voted against (nay)					

Member	113	114	115	116	117	118	119
16 **Kinzinger**	N	Y	Y	Y	Y	N	N
17 Bustos	Y	N	N	N	Y	Y	Y
18 **LaHood**	N	Y	Y	Y	Y	N	N
INDIANA							
1 Visclosky	Y	N	N	N	N	Y	Y
2 **Walorski**	N	Y	Y	Y	Y	N	N
3 **Banks**	N	Y	Y	Y	Y	N	N
4 **Rokita**	N	Y	Y	Y	Y	N	N
5 **Brooks**	N	Y	Y	Y	Y	N	N
6 **Messer**	N	Y	Y	Y	Y	N	N
7 Carson	Y	N	N	N	N	Y	Y
8 **Bucshon**	N	Y	Y	Y	Y	N	N
9 **Hollingsworth**	N	Y	Y	Y	Y	N	N
IOWA							
1 **Blum**	N	Y	Y	Y	Y	N	N
2 Loebsack	Y	N	N	N	Y	Y	Y
3 **Young**	N	Y	Y	Y	Y	N	N
4 **King**	N	Y	Y	Y	Y	N	N
KANSAS							
1 **Marshall**	N	Y	+	+	Y	N	N
2 **Jenkins**	N	Y	Y	Y	Y	N	N
3 **Yoder**	N	Y	Y	Y	Y	N	N
KENTUCKY							
1 **Comer**	N	Y	Y	Y	Y	N	N
2 **Guthrie**	N	Y	Y	Y	Y	N	N
3 Yarmuth	Y	N	N	N	N	Y	Y
4 **Massie**	N	N	Y	Y	Y	N	N
5 **Rogers**	N	?	Y	Y	Y	N	N
6 **Barr**	N	Y	Y	Y	Y	N	N
LOUISIANA							
1 **Scalise**	N	Y	Y	Y	Y	N	N
2 Richmond	Y	N	N	N	?	Y	Y
3 **Higgins**	N	Y	Y	Y	Y	N	N
4 **Johnson**	N	Y	Y	Y	Y	N	N
5 **Abraham**	N	Y	Y	Y	Y	N	N
6 **Graves**	N	Y	Y	Y	Y	N	N
MAINE							
1 Pingree	Y	N	N	N	N	Y	Y
2 **Poliquin**	N	Y	Y	Y	Y	N	N
MARYLAND							
1 **Harris**	N	Y	Y	Y	Y	N	N
2 Ruppersberger	Y	N	N	N	N	Y	Y
3 Sarbanes	Y	N	N	N	N	Y	Y
4 Brown	Y	N	N	N	N	Y	Y
5 Hoyer	Y	N	N	N	N	Y	Y
6 Delaney	Y	N	N	N	Y	Y	Y
7 Cummings	Y	N	N	N	N	Y	Y
8 Raskin	Y	N	N	N	N	Y	Y
MASSACHUSETTS							
1 Neal	Y	N	N	N	N	Y	Y
2 McGovern	Y	N	N	N	N	Y	Y
3 Tsongas	Y	N	N	N	N	Y	Y
4 Kennedy	Y	N	N	N	N	Y	Y
5 Clark	Y	N	N	N	N	Y	Y
6 Moulton	Y	N	N	N	Y	Y	Y
7 Capuano	?	N	N	N	N	Y	Y
8 Lynch	Y	N	N	N	N	Y	Y
9 Keating	Y	N	N	N	N	Y	Y
MICHIGAN							
1 **Bergman**	N	Y	Y	Y	Y	N	N
2 **Huizenga**	N	Y	Y	Y	Y	N	N
3 **Amash**	N	Y	Y	Y	Y	N	N
4 **Moolenaar**	N	Y	Y	Y	Y	N	N
5 Kildee	Y	N	N	N	N	Y	Y
6 **Upton**	N	Y	Y	Y	Y	N	N
7 **Walberg**	N	Y	Y	Y	Y	N	N
8 **Bishop**	N	Y	Y	Y	Y	N	N
9 Levin	Y	N	N	N	N	Y	Y
10 **Mitchell**	N	Y	Y	Y	Y	N	N
11 **Trott**	N	Y	Y	Y	Y	N	N
12 Dingell	Y	N	N	N	N	Y	Y
13 Conyers	Y	N	N	N	N	Y	Y
14 Lawrence	Y	N	N	N	N	Y	Y
MINNESOTA							
1 Walz	Y	N	N	N	N	Y	Y
2 **Lewis**	N	Y	Y	Y	Y	N	N
3 **Paulsen**	N	Y	Y	Y	Y	N	N
4 McCollum	Y	N	N	N	N	Y	Y
5 Ellison	Y	N	N	N	N	Y	Y
6 **Emmer**	N	Y	Y	Y	Y	N	N
7 Peterson	Y	Y	N	N	Y	N	Y
8 Nolan	Y	N	N	N	N	Y	Y
MISSISSIPPI							
1 **Kelly**	N	Y	Y	Y	Y	N	N
2 Thompson	Y	N	N	N	N	Y	Y
3 **Harper**	N	Y	Y	Y	Y	N	N
4 **Palazzo**	N	Y	Y	Y	Y	N	N
MISSOURI							
1 Clay	Y	N	N	N	N	Y	Y
2 **Wagner**	N	Y	Y	Y	Y	N	N
3 **Luetkemeyer**	N	Y	Y	Y	Y	N	N
4 **Hartzler**	N	Y	Y	Y	Y	N	N
5 Cleaver	Y	N	N	?	N	Y	Y
6 **Graves**	N	Y	Y	Y	Y	N	N
7 **Long**	N	Y	Y	Y	Y	N	N
8 **Smith**	N	Y	Y	Y	Y	N	N
MONTANA							
AL **Vacant**							
NEBRASKA							
1 **Fortenberry**	N	Y	Y	Y	Y	N	N
2 **Bacon**	N	Y	Y	Y	Y	N	N
3 **Smith**	N	Y	Y	Y	Y	N	N
NEVADA							
1 Titus	Y	N	N	N	N	Y	Y
2 **Amodei**	N	Y	Y	Y	Y	N	N
3 Rosen	Y	Y	N	N	N	Y	Y
4 Kihuen	Y	N	N	N	Y	Y	Y
NEW HAMPSHIRE							
1 Shea-Porter	Y	N	N	N	N	Y	Y
2 Kuster	Y	N	N	N	Y	Y	Y
NEW JERSEY							
1 Norcross	Y	N	N	N	N	Y	Y
2 **LoBiondo**	N	Y	Y	Y	Y	N	N
3 **MacArthur**	N	Y	Y	Y	Y	N	N
4 **Smith**	N	Y	Y	Y	Y	N	N
5 Gottheimer	Y	Y	N	N	Y	Y	Y
6 Pallone	Y	N	N	N	N	Y	Y
7 **Lance**	N	Y	Y	Y	Y	N	N
8 Sires	Y	N	N	N	N	Y	Y
9 Pascrell	Y	N	N	–	N	Y	Y
10 Payne	Y	N	N	N	N	Y	Y
11 **Frelinghuysen**	N	Y	Y	Y	Y	N	N
12 Watson Coleman	Y	N	N	N	N	Y	Y
NEW MEXICO							
1 Lujan Grisham	Y	N	N	N	N	Y	Y
2 **Pearce**	N	Y	Y	Y	Y	N	N
3 Luján	Y	N	N	N	N	Y	Y
NEW YORK							
1 **Zeldin**	N	Y	Y	Y	Y	N	N
2 **King**	N	Y	Y	Y	Y	N	N
3 Suozzi	Y	Y	N	N	Y	Y	Y
4 Rice	Y	N	N	N	N	Y	Y
5 Meeks	Y	N	N	N	N	Y	Y
6 Meng	Y	N	N	N	N	Y	Y
7 Velázquez	Y	N	N	N	N	Y	Y
8 Jeffries	Y	N	N	N	N	Y	Y
9 Clarke	Y	N	N	N	N	Y	Y
10 Nadler	Y	N	N	N	?	?	?
11 **Donovan**	N	Y	Y	Y	Y	N	N
12 Maloney, C.	Y	N	N	N	N	Y	Y
13 Espaillat	Y	N	N	N	N	Y	Y
14 Crowley	Y	N	N	N	N	Y	Y
15 Serrano	Y	N	N	N	N	Y	Y
16 Engel	Y	N	N	N	N	Y	Y
17 Lowey	Y	N	N	N	N	Y	Y
18 Maloney, S.P.	Y	N	N	N	N	Y	Y
19 **Faso**	N	Y	Y	Y	Y	N	N
20 Tonko	Y	N	N	N	N	Y	Y
21 **Stefanik**	N	Y	Y	Y	Y	N	N
22 **Tenney**	N	Y	Y	Y	Y	N	N
23 **Reed**	N	Y	Y	Y	Y	N	N
24 **Katko**	N	Y	Y	Y	Y	N	N
25 Slaughter	Y	N	N	N	N	Y	Y
26 Higgins	Y	N	N	N	N	Y	Y
27 **Collins**	N	Y	Y	Y	Y	N	N
NORTH CAROLINA							
1 Butterfield	Y	N	N	N	N	Y	Y
2 **Holding**	N	Y	Y	Y	Y	N	N
3 **Jones**	N	N	Y	Y	Y	Y	Y
4 Price	Y	N	N	N	N	Y	Y
5 **Foxx**	N	Y	Y	Y	Y	N	N
6 **Walker**	N	Y	Y	Y	Y	N	N
7 **Rouzer**	N	Y	Y	Y	Y	N	N
8 **Hudson**	–	+	+	+	+	–	–
9 **Pittenger**	N	Y	Y	Y	Y	N	N
10 **McHenry**	N	Y	Y	Y	Y	N	N
11 **Meadows**	N	Y	Y	Y	Y	N	N
12 Adams	Y	N	N	N	N	Y	Y
13 **Budd**	N	Y	Y	Y	Y	N	N
NORTH DAKOTA							
AL **Cramer**	N	Y	Y	Y	Y	N	N
OHIO							
1 **Chabot**	N	Y	Y	Y	Y	N	N
2 **Wenstrup**	N	Y	Y	Y	Y	N	N
3 Beatty	Y	N	N	N	N	Y	Y
4 **Jordan**	N	Y	Y	Y	Y	N	N
5 **Latta**	N	Y	Y	Y	Y	N	N
6 **Johnson**	N	Y	Y	Y	Y	N	N
7 **Gibbs**	N	Y	Y	Y	Y	N	N
8 **Davidson**	N	Y	Y	Y	Y	N	N
9 Kaptur	Y	N	N	N	N	Y	Y
10 **Turner**	N	Y	Y	Y	Y	N	N
11 Fudge	Y	N	N	N	N	Y	Y
12 **Tiberi**	N	Y	Y	Y	Y	N	N
13 Ryan	Y	N	N	N	N	Y	Y
14 **Joyce**	N	Y	Y	Y	Y	N	N
15 **Stivers**	N	Y	Y	Y	Y	N	N
16 **Renacci**	N	Y	Y	Y	Y	N	N
OKLAHOMA							
1 **Bridenstine**	N	Y	Y	Y	Y	N	N
2 **Mullin**	N	Y	Y	Y	Y	N	N
3 **Lucas**	N	Y	Y	Y	Y	N	N
4 **Cole**	N	Y	Y	Y	Y	N	N
5 **Russell**	N	Y	Y	Y	Y	N	N
OREGON							
1 Bonamici	Y	N	N	N	N	Y	Y
2 **Walden**	N	Y	Y	Y	?	N	N
3 Blumenauer	Y	N	N	N	N	Y	Y
4 DeFazio	Y	N	N	N	N	Y	Y
5 Schrader	Y	Y	N	N	Y	Y	Y
PENNSYLVANIA							
1 Brady	Y	N	N	N	N	Y	Y
2 Evans	Y	N	N	N	N	Y	Y
3 **Kelly**	N	Y	Y	Y	Y	N	N
4 **Perry**	N	Y	Y	Y	Y	N	N
5 **Thompson**	N	Y	Y	Y	Y	N	N
6 **Costello**	N	Y	Y	Y	Y	N	N
7 **Meehan**	N	Y	Y	Y	Y	N	N
8 **Fitzpatrick**	N	Y	Y	Y	Y	N	N
9 **Shuster**	N	Y	Y	Y	Y	N	N
10 **Marino**	N	Y	Y	Y	Y	N	N
11 **Barletta**	N	Y	Y	Y	Y	N	N
12 **Rothfus**	N	Y	Y	Y	Y	N	N
13 Boyle	Y	N	N	N	N	Y	Y
14 Doyle	Y	N	N	N	N	Y	Y
15 **Dent**	N	Y	Y	Y	Y	N	N
16 **Smucker**	N	Y	Y	Y	Y	N	N
17 Cartwright	Y	N	N	N	N	Y	Y
18 **Murphy**	N	Y	Y	Y	Y	N	N
RHODE ISLAND							
1 Cicilline	Y	N	N	N	N	Y	Y
2 Langevin	Y	N	N	N	N	Y	Y
SOUTH CAROLINA							
1 **Sanford**	N	Y	Y	Y	Y	N	N
2 **Wilson**	N	Y	Y	Y	Y	N	N
3 **Duncan**	N	Y	Y	Y	Y	N	N
4 **Gowdy**	N	Y	Y	Y	Y	N	N
6 Clyburn	Y	N	N	N	N	Y	Y
7 **Rice**	N	Y	Y	Y	Y	N	N
SOUTH DAKOTA							
AL **Noem**	N	Y	Y	Y	Y	N	N
TENNESSEE							
1 **Roe**	N	Y	Y	Y	Y	N	N
2 **Duncan**	N	Y	?	?	Y	N	N
3 **Fleischmann**	N	Y	Y	Y	Y	N	N
4 **DesJarlais**	N	Y	Y	Y	Y	N	N
5 Cooper	Y	N	N	N	Y	N	Y
6 **Black**	N	Y	Y	Y	Y	N	N
7 **Blackburn**	N	Y	Y	Y	Y	N	N
8 **Kustoff**	N	Y	Y	Y	Y	N	N
9 Cohen	Y	N	N	N	Y	Y	Y
TEXAS							
1 **Gohmert**	N	N	Y	Y	Y	N	N
2 **Poe**	N	Y	Y	Y	Y	N	N
3 **Johnson, S.**	N	Y	Y	Y	Y	N	N
4 **Ratcliffe**	N	Y	Y	Y	Y	?	N
5 **Hensarling**	N	Y	Y	Y	Y	N	N
6 **Barton**	N	Y	Y	Y	Y	N	N
7 **Culberson**	N	Y	Y	Y	Y	N	N
8 **Brady**	N	Y	Y	Y	Y	N	N
9 Green, A.	Y	N	–	–	N	Y	Y
10 **McCaul**	N	Y	Y	Y	Y	N	N
11 **Conaway**	N	Y	Y	Y	Y	N	N
12 **Granger**	N	Y	Y	Y	Y	N	N
13 **Thornberry**	N	Y	Y	Y	Y	N	N
14 **Weber**	N	Y	Y	Y	Y	N	N
15 Gonzalez	Y	N	N	N	N	?	Y
16 O'Rourke	Y	N	–	–	N	?	Y
17 **Flores**	N	Y	Y	Y	Y	N	N
18 Jackson Lee	Y	N	N	N	N	Y	Y
19 **Arrington**	N	Y	Y	Y	Y	N	N
20 Castro	Y	N	N	N	N	Y	Y
21 **Smith**	N	Y	Y	Y	Y	N	N
22 **Olson**	N	Y	Y	Y	Y	N	N
23 **Hurd**	N	Y	Y	Y	?	?	N
24 **Marchant**	N	Y	Y	Y	Y	N	N
25 **Williams**	N	Y	Y	Y	Y	N	N
26 **Burgess**	N	Y	Y	Y	Y	N	N
27 **Farenthold**	N	Y	Y	Y	Y	N	N
28 Cuellar	Y	Y	N	N	Y	Y	Y
29 Green, G.	Y	N	N	N	Y	Y	Y
30 Johnson, E.B.	Y	N	N	N	N	Y	Y
31 **Carter**	N	Y	Y	Y	Y	N	N
32 **Sessions**	N	Y	Y	Y	Y	N	N
33 Veasey	Y	N	N	N	N	Y	Y
34 Vela	Y	N	N	N	N	Y	Y
35 Doggett	Y	N	N	N	N	?	Y
36 **Babin**	N	Y	Y	Y	Y	N	N
UTAH							
1 **Bishop**	N	Y	Y	Y	Y	N	N
2 **Stewart**	N	Y	Y	Y	Y	N	N
3 **Chaffetz**	N	Y	Y	Y	Y	N	N
4 **Love**	N	Y	Y	Y	Y	N	N
VERMONT							
AL Welch	Y	N	N	N	N	Y	Y
VIRGINIA							
1 **Wittman**	N	Y	Y	Y	Y	N	N
2 **Taylor**	N	Y	Y	Y	Y	N	N
3 Scott	Y	N	N	N	N	Y	Y
4 McEachin	Y	N	N	N	N	Y	Y
5 **Garrett**	N	Y	Y	Y	Y	N	N
6 **Goodlatte**	N	Y	Y	Y	Y	N	N
7 **Brat**	N	Y	Y	Y	Y	N	N
8 Beyer	Y	N	N	N	Y	Y	Y
9 **Griffith**	N	Y	Y	Y	Y	N	N
10 **Comstock**	N	Y	Y	Y	Y	N	N
11 Connolly	Y	N	N	N	N	Y	Y
WASHINGTON							
1 DelBene	Y	N	N	N	N	Y	Y
2 Larsen	Y	N	N	N	N	Y	Y
3 **Herrera Beutler**	N	Y	Y	Y	Y	N	N
4 **Newhouse**	N	Y	Y	Y	Y	N	N
5 **McMorris Rodgers**	N	Y	Y	Y	Y	N	N
6 Kilmer	Y	N	N	N	N	Y	Y
7 Jayapal	Y	N	N	N	N	Y	Y
8 **Reichert**	N	Y	Y	Y	Y	N	N
9 Smith	Y	N	N	N	N	Y	Y
10 Heck	Y	N	N	N	N	Y	Y
WEST VIRGINIA							
1 **McKinley**	N	Y	Y	Y	Y	N	N
2 **Mooney**	N	Y	Y	Y	Y	N	N
3 **Jenkins**	N	Y	Y	Y	Y	N	N
WISCONSIN							
1 **Ryan**							
2 Pocan	Y	N	N	N	N	Y	Y
3 Kind	Y	N	N	N	Y	Y	Y
4 Moore	Y	N	N	N	N	Y	Y
5 **Sensenbrenner**	N	Y	Y	Y	Y	N	N
6 **Grothman**	N	Y	Y	Y	Y	N	N
7 **Duffy**	N	Y	Y	Y	Y	N	N
8 **Gallagher**	N	Y	Y	Y	Y	N	N
WYOMING							
AL **Cheney**	N	Y	Y	Y	Y	N	N

VOTE NUMBER

120. HR 1009. REGULATORY COST-BENEFIT ANALYSIS/PASSAGE.
Passage of the bill that would require the Office of Management and Budget's Office of Information and Regulatory Affairs to review significant government regulatory actions to insure that they are consistent with relevant laws and do not conflict with regulations issued by other agencies. The bill would define significant regulatory actions as those that are likely to have an annual economic effect of $100 million or more. As amended, it would require OIRA to keep a log of all of its communications with an agency related to a regulation before a regulation is submitted for review. The communications would be required to be published when the regulation is published in the Federal Register. Passed 241-184 : R 234-0; D 7-184. March 1, 2017.

121. H J RES 83. OSHA CITATION DISAPPROVAL/PASSAGE. Passage of a joint resolution that would nullify and disapprove of an Occupational Safety and Health Administration rule that extends, from six months to five years, the period in which OSHA can issue citations to employers who do not maintain workplace injury or illness records. Passed 231-191 : R 227-6; D 4-185. March 1, 2017.

122. HR 1004. REGULATORY DATABASES/PROPAGANDA DEFINITION.
Jackson Lee, D-Texas, amendment that would define the terms propaganda, publicity and advocacy as information or claims that are not widely accepted in the scientific community or not supported by empirical data. Rejected in Committee of the Whole 180-234 : R 0-231; D 180-3. March 2, 2017.

123. HR 1004. REGULATORY DATABASES/DUPLICITY AND OVERLAP.
Farenthold, R-Texas, for Messer, R-Ind., amendment that would require an agency to list regulatory actions issued by the agency, or any other agency, that would duplicate or overlap with the agency's pending regulatory action. Adopted in Committee of the Whole 263-145 : R 224-1; D 39-144. March 2, 2017.

124. HR 1004. REGULATORY DATABASES/FIRST AMENDMENT PROTECTED COMMUNICATIONS. Jackson Lee, D-Texas, amendment that would specify that the bill's restrictions on agency communications would not apply to any communication that would be protected under the First Amendment to the Constitution. Rejected in Committee of the Whole 189-232 : R 5-227; D 184-5. March 2, 2017.

125. HR 1004. REGULATORY INTEGRITY ACT/RECOMMIT. Jayapal, D-Wash., motion to recommit the bill to the House Oversight and Government Reform Committee with instructions to report it back immediately with an amendment that would prohibit the president from making public communications that refer to a business in which the president has an equity interest and would prohibit the president from publically advocating on behalf of such business interests. Motion rejected 189-232 : R 1-231; D 188-1. March 2, 2017.

126. HR 1004. REGULATORY DATABASES/PASSAGE. Passage of the bill that would require federal agencies to maintain and regularly update detailed online databases of regulatory actions taken and pending before the agency. Under the measure, an agency would be required to list whether it is considering alternatives and whether it is accepting comments. It would explicitly prohibit agencies from directly advocating support or opposition for pending regulatory actions in public communications. As amended, the measure would require an agency to list regulatory actions issued by the agency, or any other agency, that would duplicate or overlap with the agency's pending regulatory action. Passed 246-176 : R 231-1; D 15-175. March 2, 2017.

	120	121	122	123	124	125	126
ALABAMA							
1 **Byrne**	Y	Y	N	Y	N	N	Y
2 **Roby**	Y	Y	N	Y	N	N	Y
3 **Rogers**	Y	Y	N	Y	N	N	Y
4 **Aderholt**	Y	Y	N	Y	N	N	Y
5 **Brooks**	Y	Y	N	?	N	N	Y
6 **Palmer**	Y	Y	N	Y	N	N	Y
7 Sewell	N	N	Y	N	Y	Y	N
ALASKA							
AL **Young**	Y	N	?	?	N	N	Y
ARIZONA							
1 O'Halleran	N	N	Y	Y	Y	Y	Y
2 **McSally**	Y	Y	N	Y	N	N	Y
3 Grijalva	N	N	Y	N	Y	Y	N
4 **Gosar**	Y	Y	N	Y	N	N	Y
5 **Biggs**	Y	Y	N	Y	N	N	Y
6 **Schweikert**	Y	Y	N	Y	N	N	Y
7 Gallego	N	N	?	Y	Y	Y	N
8 **Franks**	Y	Y	N	Y	N	N	Y
9 Sinema	Y	Y	Y	Y	Y	Y	Y
ARKANSAS							
1 **Crawford**	Y	Y	N	Y	N	N	Y
2 **Hill**	Y	Y	N	Y	N	N	Y
3 **Womack**	Y	Y	N	Y	N	N	Y
4 **Westerman**	Y	Y	N	Y	N	N	Y
CALIFORNIA							
1 **LaMalfa**	Y	Y	N	Y	N	N	Y
2 Huffman	N	N	Y	N	Y	Y	N
3 Garamendi	N	N	Y	N	Y	Y	N
4 **McClintock**	Y	Y	N	Y	N	N	Y
5 Thompson	N	N	Y	N	Y	Y	N
6 Matsui	N	N	Y	N	Y	Y	N
7 Bera	N	N	Y	Y	Y	Y	N
8 **Cook**	Y	Y	N	Y	N	N	Y
9 McNerney	N	N	Y	N	Y	Y	N
10 **Denham**	Y	Y	N	Y	N	N	Y
11 DeSaulnier	N	N	Y	N	Y	Y	N
12 Pelosi	N	N	Y	N	Y	?	?
13 Lee	N	N	Y	N	Y	Y	N
14 Speier	N	N	Y	N	Y	Y	N
15 Swalwell	N	N	Y	N	Y	Y	N
16 Costa	Y	N	N	Y	Y	Y	Y
17 Khanna	N	N	Y	N	Y	Y	N
18 Eshoo	N	N	Y	N	Y	Y	N
19 Lofgren	N	N	Y	N	Y	Y	N
20 Panetta	N	N	Y	N	Y	Y	Y
21 **Valadao**	Y	Y	N	Y	N	N	Y
22 **Nunes**	Y	Y	N	Y	N	N	Y
23 **McCarthy**	Y	Y	N	Y	N	N	Y
24 Carbajal	N	N	Y	N	Y	Y	N
25 **Knight**	Y	Y	N	Y	N	N	Y
26 Brownley	N	N	Y	N	Y	Y	N
27 Chu	N	N	?	N	Y	Y	N
28 Schiff	N	N	Y	N	Y	Y	N
29 Cardenas	N	N	Y	N	Y	Y	N
30 Sherman	N	N	Y	N	Y	Y	N
31 Aguilar	N	N	Y	N	Y	Y	N
32 Napolitano	N	N	Y	N	Y	Y	N
33 Lieu	N	N	Y	Y	Y	Y	N
34 Vacant							
35 Torres	N	N	Y	N	Y	Y	N
36 Ruiz	N	N	Y	Y	Y	Y	N
37 Bass	N	N	Y	?	?	Y	N
38 Sánchez, Linda	N	N	Y	N	Y	Y	N
39 **Royce**	Y	Y	N	Y	N	N	Y
40 Roybal-Allard	N	N	Y	N	Y	Y	N
41 Takano	N	N	Y	N	Y	Y	N
42 **Calvert**	Y	Y	N	Y	N	N	Y
43 Waters	N	N	Y	?	Y	Y	N
44 Barragan	N	N	Y	N	Y	Y	N
45 **Walters**	Y	Y	N	Y	N	N	Y
46 Correa	N	N	Y	Y	Y	Y	Y
47 Lowenthal	N	N	Y	N	Y	Y	N
48 **Rohrabacher**	Y	Y	N	N	N	N	N
49 **Issa**	Y	Y	N	Y	N	N	Y
50 **Hunter**	Y	Y	N	Y	N	N	Y
51 Vargas	N	N	Y	N	Y	Y	N
52 Peters	N	Y	Y	Y	Y	Y	N
53 Davis	N	N	Y	N	Y	Y	N

	120	121	122	123	124	125	126
COLORADO							
1 DeGette	N	N	Y	N	Y	Y	N
2 Polis	N	N	Y	N	Y	Y	N
3 **Tipton**	Y	Y	N	Y	N	N	Y
4 **Buck**	Y	Y	N	Y	N	N	Y
5 **Lamborn**	Y	Y	N	Y	N	N	Y
6 **Coffman**	Y	Y	N	Y	N	N	Y
7 Perlmutter	N	N	Y	N	Y	Y	N
CONNECTICUT							
1 Larson	N	N	Y	N	Y	Y	N
2 Courtney	N	N	Y	N	Y	Y	N
3 DeLauro	N	N	Y	N	Y	Y	N
4 Himes	N	N	Y	Y	Y	Y	N
5 Esty	N	N	Y	N	Y	Y	N
DELAWARE							
AL Blunt Rochester	N	N	Y	N	Y	Y	N
FLORIDA							
1 **Gaetz**	Y	Y	N	Y	N	N	Y
2 **Dunn**	Y	Y	N	Y	N	N	Y
3 **Yoho**	Y	Y	N	Y	N	N	Y
4 **Rutherford**	?	Y	N	Y	N	N	Y
5 Lawson	N	N	Y	N	Y	Y	N
6 **DeSantis**	Y	Y	N	Y	N	N	Y
7 Murphy	N	N	Y	N	Y	Y	Y
8 **Posey**	Y	Y	N	Y	N	N	Y
9 Soto	N	N	Y	N	Y	Y	N
10 Demings	N	N	Y	N	Y	Y	N
11 **Webster**	Y	Y	N	Y	N	N	Y
12 **Bilirakis**	Y	Y	N	Y	N	N	Y
13 Crist	N	N	Y	Y	Y	?	Y
14 Castor	N	N	Y	N	Y	Y	N
15 **Ross**	Y	Y	N	Y	N	N	Y
16 **Buchanan**	Y	Y	N	Y	N	N	Y
17 **Rooney, T.**	Y	Y	N	Y	N	N	Y
18 **Mast**	Y	Y	N	Y	N	N	Y
19 **Rooney, F.**	Y	Y	N	Y	N	N	Y
20 Hastings	N	N	Y	N	Y	Y	N
21 Frankel	N	N	Y	N	Y	Y	N
22 Deutch	N	N	Y	N	Y	Y	N
23 Wasserman Schultz	N	N	Y	N	Y	Y	N
24 Wilson	N	N	Y	N	Y	Y	N
25 **Diaz-Balart**	Y	Y	N	Y	N	N	Y
26 **Curbelo**	Y	Y	N	Y	N	N	Y
27 **Ros-Lehtinen**	Y	N	N	Y	N	N	Y
GEORGIA							
1 **Carter**	Y	Y	N	Y	N	N	Y
2 Bishop	N	N	Y	Y	Y	Y	N
3 **Ferguson**	Y	Y	N	Y	N	N	Y
4 Johnson	N	N	?	N	Y	Y	N
5 Lewis	N	N	Y	N	Y	Y	N
7 **Woodall**	Y	Y	N	Y	N	N	Y
8 **Scott, A.**	Y	Y	N	Y	N	N	Y
9 **Collins**	Y	Y	N	Y	N	N	Y
10 **Hice**	Y	Y	N	Y	N	N	Y
11 **Loudermilk**	Y	Y	N	Y	N	N	Y
12 **Allen**	Y	Y	N	Y	N	N	Y
13 Scott, D.	N	N	?	?	Y	Y	N
14 **Graves**	Y	Y	N	Y	N	N	Y
HAWAII							
1 Hanabusa	N	N	Y	N	Y	Y	N
2 Gabbard	N	N	Y	Y	Y	Y	N
IDAHO							
1 **Labrador**	Y	Y	N	Y	N	N	Y
2 **Simpson**	Y	Y	N	Y	N	N	Y
ILLINOIS							
1 Rush	N	N	?	?	?	?	?
2 Kelly	N	N	Y	N	Y	Y	N
3 Lipinski	N	N	Y	Y	Y	Y	N
4 Gutierrez	N	–	Y	Y	Y	Y	Y
5 Quigley	N	N	Y	N	Y	Y	N
6 **Roskam**	Y	Y	N	Y	N	N	Y
7 Davis, D.	N	N	Y	N	Y	Y	N
8 Krishnamoorthi	N	N	Y	N	Y	Y	N
9 Schakowsky	N	N	Y	N	Y	Y	N
10 Schneider	N	N	Y	N	Y	Y	N
11 Foster	N	N	Y	N	Y	Y	N
12 **Bost**	Y	Y	N	Y	N	N	Y
13 **Davis, R.**	Y	Y	N	Y	N	N	Y
14 **Hultgren**	Y	Y	N	Y	N	N	Y
15 **Shimkus**	Y	Y	N	Y	N	N	Y

KEY	**Republicans**	Democrats	*Independents*		
Y	Voted for (yea)	X Paired against	C	Voted "present" to avoid possible conflict of interest
#	Paired for	– Announced against		
+	Announced for	P Voted "present"	?	Did not vote or otherwise make a position known
N	Voted against (nay)			

	120	121	122	123	124	125	126
16 **Kinzinger**	Y	Y	N	Y	N	N	Y
17 Bustos	N	N	Y	Y	Y	Y	N
18 **LaHood**	Y	Y	N	Y	N	N	Y
INDIANA							
1 Visclosky	N	N	Y	N	Y	Y	N
2 **Walorski**	Y	Y	N	Y	N	N	Y
3 **Banks**	Y	Y	N	Y	N	N	Y
4 **Rokita**	Y	Y	N	Y	N	N	Y
5 **Brooks**	Y	Y	N	Y	N	N	Y
6 **Messer**	Y	Y	N	Y	N	N	Y
7 Carson	?	N	Y	N	Y	Y	N
8 **Bucshon**	Y	Y	N	Y	N	N	Y
9 **Hollingsworth**	Y	Y	N	Y	Y	N	Y
IOWA							
1 **Blum**	Y	Y	N	Y	N	N	Y
2 Loebsack	N	N	Y	Y	Y	Y	N
3 **Young**	Y	Y	N	Y	N	N	Y
4 **King**	Y	Y	N	Y	N	N	Y
KANSAS							
1 **Marshall**	Y	Y	N	Y	N	N	Y
2 **Jenkins**	Y	Y	N	Y	N	N	Y
3 **Yoder**	Y	Y	N	Y	N	N	Y
KENTUCKY							
1 **Comer**	Y	Y	N	Y	N	N	Y
2 **Guthrie**	Y	Y	N	Y	N	N	Y
3 Yarmuth	N	N	Y	N	Y	Y	N
4 **Massie**	Y	Y	N	Y	N	N	Y
5 **Rogers**	Y	Y	N	?	N	N	Y
6 **Barr**	Y	Y	N	Y	N	N	Y
LOUISIANA							
1 **Scalise**	Y	Y	N	Y	N	N	Y
2 Richmond	N	N	Y	N	Y	Y	N
3 **Higgins**	Y	Y	N	Y	N	N	Y
4 **Johnson**	Y	Y	N	Y	N	N	Y
5 **Abraham**	Y	Y	N	Y	N	N	Y
6 **Graves**	Y	Y	N	Y	N	N	Y
MAINE							
1 Pingree	N	N	Y	N	Y	Y	N
2 **Poliquin**	Y	Y	N	Y	N	N	Y
MARYLAND							
1 **Harris**	Y	Y	N	Y	N	N	Y
2 Ruppersberger	N	N	Y	N	Y	Y	N
3 Sarbanes	N	N	Y	N	Y	Y	N
4 Brown	N	N	+	N	Y	Y	N
5 Hoyer	N	N	Y	N	Y	Y	N
6 Delaney	N	–	Y	Y	Y	Y	N
7 Cummings	N	N	Y	N	Y	Y	N
8 Raskin	N	N	Y	N	Y	Y	N
MASSACHUSETTS							
1 Neal	N	N	Y	N	Y	Y	N
2 McGovern	N	N	?	?	Y	Y	N
3 Tsongas	N	N	Y	N	Y	Y	N
4 Kennedy	N	N	Y	N	Y	Y	N
5 Clark	N	N	Y	N	Y	Y	N
6 Moulton	N	N	Y	Y	Y	Y	N
7 Capuano	N	N	Y	N	Y	Y	N
8 Lynch	N	N	Y	N	Y	Y	N
9 Keating	N	N	Y	?	Y	Y	N
MICHIGAN							
1 **Bergman**	Y	Y	N	Y	N	N	Y
2 **Huizenga**	Y	Y	N	Y	N	N	Y
3 **Amash**	Y	Y	N	Y	N	N	Y
4 **Moolenaar**	Y	Y	N	Y	N	N	Y
5 Kildee	N	N	Y	N	Y	Y	N
6 **Upton**	Y	Y	N	Y	Y	N	Y
7 **Walberg**	Y	Y	N	Y	N	N	Y
8 **Bishop**	Y	Y	N	Y	N	N	Y
9 Levin	N	N	Y	N	Y	Y	N
10 **Mitchell**	Y	Y	N	Y	N	N	Y
11 **Trott**	Y	Y	N	Y	N	N	Y
12 Dingell	N	N	Y	N	Y	Y	N
13 Conyers	N	N	Y	N	Y	Y	N
14 Lawrence	N	N	Y	N	Y	Y	N
MINNESOTA							
1 Walz	N	N	Y	Y	Y	Y	N
2 **Lewis**	Y	Y	N	Y	N	N	Y
3 **Paulsen**	Y	Y	N	Y	N	N	Y
4 McCollum	N	N	Y	N	Y	Y	N

	120	121	122	123	124	125	126
5 Ellison	N	N	Y	N	N	Y	N
6 **Emmer**	Y	Y	N	Y	N	N	Y
7 Peterson	Y	N	N	Y	N	N	Y
8 Nolan	N	N	Y	Y	Y	Y	N
MISSISSIPPI							
1 **Kelly**	Y	Y	N	Y	N	N	Y
2 Thompson	N	N	Y	N	Y	Y	N
3 **Harper**	Y	Y	N	Y	N	N	Y
4 **Palazzo**	Y	Y	N	Y	N	N	Y
MISSOURI							
1 Clay	N	N	Y	N	Y	Y	N
2 **Wagner**	Y	Y	N	Y	N	N	Y
3 **Luetkemeyer**	Y	Y	N	Y	N	N	Y
4 **Hartzler**	Y	Y	N	Y	N	N	Y
5 Cleaver	N	N	Y	N	Y	Y	N
6 **Graves**	Y	Y	N	Y	N	N	Y
7 **Long**	Y	Y	N	Y	N	N	Y
8 **Smith**	Y	Y	N	Y	N	N	Y
MONTANA							
AL **Vacant**							
NEBRASKA							
1 **Fortenberry**	Y	Y	N	Y	N	N	Y
2 **Bacon**	Y	Y	N	Y	N	N	Y
3 **Smith**	Y	Y	N	Y	N	N	Y
NEVADA							
1 Titus	N	N	Y	N	Y	Y	N
2 **Amodei**	Y	Y	N	Y	N	N	Y
3 Rosen	N	N	Y	Y	Y	Y	Y
4 Kihuen	N	N	Y	Y	Y	Y	N
NEW HAMPSHIRE							
1 Shea-Porter	N	N	Y	N	Y	Y	N
2 Kuster	N	N	Y	Y	Y	Y	N
NEW JERSEY							
1 Norcross	N	N	Y	N	Y	Y	N
2 **LoBiondo**	Y	N	N	Y	N	N	Y
3 **MacArthur**	Y	Y	N	Y	N	N	Y
4 **Smith**	Y	N	N	Y	N	N	Y
5 Gottheimer	Y	N	Y	Y	Y	Y	Y
6 Pallone	N	N	Y	N	Y	Y	N
7 **Lance**	Y	Y	N	Y	N	N	Y
8 Sires	N	N	Y	N	Y	Y	N
9 Pascrell	N	N	Y	N	Y	Y	N
10 Payne	N	N	Y	N	Y	Y	N
11 **Frelinghuysen**	Y	Y	N	Y	N	N	Y
12 Watson Coleman	N	N	Y	N	Y	Y	N
NEW MEXICO							
1 Lujan Grisham	N	N	Y	N	Y	Y	N
2 **Pearce**	Y	Y	N	Y	N	N	Y
3 Luján	N	N	Y	N	Y	Y	N
NEW YORK							
1 **Zeldin**	Y	Y	N	Y	N	N	Y
2 **King**	Y	N	N	Y	N	N	Y
3 Suozzi	Y	N	Y	Y	Y	Y	N
4 Rice	N	N	Y	?	Y	Y	N
5 Meeks	N	N	Y	N	Y	Y	N
6 Meng	N	N	Y	N	Y	Y	N
7 Velázquez	N	N	Y	N	Y	Y	N
8 Jeffries	N	N	Y	N	Y	Y	N
9 Clarke	N	N	Y	N	Y	Y	N
10 Nadler	?	?	?	?	?	?	?
11 **Donovan**	Y	N	N	Y	N	N	Y
12 Maloney, C.	N	N	Y	N	N	Y	N
13 Espaillat	N	N	Y	N	Y	Y	N
14 Crowley	N	N	Y	N	Y	Y	N
15 Serrano	N	N	Y	N	Y	Y	N
16 Engel	N	N	Y	N	Y	Y	N
17 Lowey	N	N	Y	N	Y	Y	N
18 Maloney, S.P.	N	N	Y	N	Y	Y	N
19 **Faso**	Y	Y	N	Y	N	N	Y
20 Tonko	N	N	Y	N	Y	Y	N
21 **Stefanik**	Y	Y	N	Y	N	N	Y
22 **Tenney**	Y	Y	N	Y	N	N	Y
23 **Reed**	Y	Y	N	Y	N	N	Y
24 **Katko**	Y	Y	N	Y	N	N	Y
25 Slaughter	N	N	Y	N	Y	Y	N
26 Higgins	N	N	Y	N	Y	Y	N
27 **Collins**	Y	Y	N	Y	N	N	Y
NORTH CAROLINA							
1 Butterfield	N	N	Y	N	Y	Y	N
2 **Holding**	Y	Y	N	Y	N	N	Y
3 **Jones**	Y	Y	N	Y	Y	Y	Y
4 Price	N	N	Y	N	Y	Y	N

	120	121	122	123	124	125	126
5 **Foxx**	Y	Y	N	Y	N	N	Y
6 **Walker**	Y	Y	N	Y	N	N	Y
7 **Rouzer**	Y	Y	N	Y	N	N	Y
8 **Hudson**	+	+	–	+	–	–	+
9 **Pittenger**	Y	?	N	Y	N	N	Y
10 **McHenry**	Y	Y	N	Y	N	N	Y
11 **Meadows**	Y	Y	N	Y	N	N	Y
12 Adams	N	N	Y	N	Y	Y	N
13 **Budd**	Y	Y	N	Y	N	N	Y
NORTH DAKOTA							
AL **Cramer**	Y	Y	N	Y	N	N	Y
OHIO							
1 **Chabot**	Y	Y	N	Y	N	N	Y
2 **Wenstrup**	Y	Y	N	Y	N	N	Y
3 Beatty	N	N	Y	N	Y	Y	N
4 **Jordan**	Y	Y	–	+	–	–	+
5 **Latta**	Y	Y	N	Y	N	N	Y
6 **Johnson**	Y	Y	N	Y	N	N	Y
7 **Gibbs**	Y	Y	N	Y	N	N	Y
8 **Davidson**	Y	Y	N	Y	N	N	Y
9 Kaptur	N	N	Y	N	Y	Y	N
10 **Turner**	Y	Y	N	Y	N	N	Y
11 Fudge	N	N	Y	N	Y	Y	N
12 **Tiberi**	Y	Y	N	Y	Y	N	Y
13 Ryan	N	N	Y	N	Y	Y	N
14 **Joyce**	Y	Y	N	Y	N	N	Y
15 **Stivers**	Y	Y	N	Y	N	N	Y
16 **Renacci**	Y	Y	N	Y	N	N	Y
OKLAHOMA							
1 **Bridenstine**	Y	Y	N	Y	N	N	Y
2 **Mullin**	Y	Y	N	Y	N	N	Y
3 **Lucas**	Y	Y	N	Y	N	N	Y
4 **Cole**	Y	Y	N	Y	N	N	Y
5 **Russell**	Y	Y	N	Y	N	N	Y
OREGON							
1 Bonamici	N	N	Y	N	Y	Y	N
2 **Walden**	Y	Y	N	Y	N	N	Y
3 Blumenauer	N	?	Y	N	Y	Y	N
4 DeFazio	N	N	Y	N	Y	Y	N
5 Schrader	N	N	Y	Y	Y	Y	Y
PENNSYLVANIA							
1 Brady	N	N	Y	N	Y	Y	N
2 Evans	N	N	Y	N	Y	Y	N
3 **Kelly**	Y	Y	N	Y	N	N	Y
4 **Perry**	Y	Y	N	Y	N	N	Y
5 **Thompson**	Y	Y	N	Y	N	N	Y
6 **Costello**	Y	+	N	Y	N	N	Y
7 **Meehan**	Y	Y	N	Y	N	N	Y
8 **Fitzpatrick**	Y	Y	N	+	N	N	Y
9 **Shuster**	Y	Y	N	Y	N	N	Y
10 **Marino**	Y	Y	N	Y	N	N	Y
11 **Barletta**	Y	Y	N	Y	N	N	Y
12 **Rothfus**	Y	Y	N	Y	N	N	Y
13 Boyle	N	N	+	–	Y	Y	N
14 Doyle	N	N	Y	N	Y	Y	N
15 **Dent**	Y	Y	N	Y	N	N	Y
16 **Smucker**	Y	Y	N	Y	N	N	Y
17 Cartwright	N	N	Y	N	Y	Y	N
18 **Murphy**	Y	Y	N	Y	N	N	Y
RHODE ISLAND							
1 Cicilline	N	N	Y	N	Y	Y	N
2 Langevin	N	N	Y	N	Y	Y	N
SOUTH CAROLINA							
1 **Sanford**	Y	Y	N	Y	N	N	Y
2 **Wilson**	Y	Y	N	Y	N	N	Y
3 **Duncan**	Y	Y	N	Y	N	N	Y
4 **Gowdy**	Y	Y	N	Y	N	N	Y
6 Clyburn	N	N	Y	N	Y	Y	N
7 **Rice**	Y	Y	N	Y	N	N	Y
SOUTH DAKOTA							
AL **Noem**	Y	Y	N	Y	N	N	Y
TENNESSEE							
1 **Roe**	Y	Y	N	Y	N	N	Y
2 **Duncan**	Y	Y	N	Y	Y	N	Y
3 **Fleischmann**	Y	Y	N	Y	N	N	Y
4 **DesJarlais**	Y	Y	N	Y	N	N	Y
5 Cooper	Y	N	N	Y	N	Y	Y
6 **Black**	Y	Y	N	Y	N	N	Y
7 **Blackburn**	Y	Y	N	Y	N	N	Y
8 **Kustoff**	Y	Y	N	Y	N	N	Y
9 Cohen	N	N	Y	N	Y	Y	N

	120	121	122	123	124	125	126
TEXAS							
1 **Gohmert**	Y	Y	N	Y	N	N	Y
2 **Poe**	Y	Y	N	?	N	N	Y
3 **Johnson, S.**	Y	Y	N	Y	N	N	Y
4 **Ratcliffe**	Y	Y	N	Y	N	N	Y
5 **Hensarling**	Y	Y	N	Y	N	N	Y
6 **Barton**	Y	Y	N	Y	N	N	Y
7 **Culberson**	Y	Y	N	Y	N	N	Y
8 **Brady**	Y	Y	N	Y	N	N	Y
9 Green, A.	N	N	Y	N	Y	Y	N
10 **McCaul**	Y	Y	N	Y	N	N	Y
11 **Conaway**	Y	Y	N	Y	N	N	Y
12 **Granger**	Y	Y	N	Y	N	N	Y
13 **Thornberry**	Y	Y	N	Y	N	N	Y
14 **Weber**	Y	Y	N	Y	N	N	Y
15 Gonzalez	N	N	Y	Y	Y	Y	N
16 O'Rourke	N	N	Y	Y	Y	Y	N
17 **Flores**	Y	Y	N	Y	N	N	Y
18 Jackson Lee	N	N	Y	N	Y	Y	N
19 **Arrington**	Y	Y	N	Y	N	N	Y
20 Castro	N	N	Y	N	Y	Y	N
21 **Smith**	Y	Y	N	Y	N	N	Y
22 **Olson**	Y	Y	N	Y	N	N	Y
23 **Hurd**	Y	Y	N	Y	N	N	Y
24 **Marchant**	Y	Y	N	?	N	N	Y
25 **Williams**	Y	Y	N	Y	N	N	Y
26 **Burgess**	Y	Y	N	Y	N	N	Y
27 **Farenthold**	Y	Y	N	Y	N	N	Y
28 Cuellar	N	Y	Y	Y	Y	Y	Y
29 Green, G.	N	N	Y	Y	Y	Y	N
30 Johnson, E.B.	N	N	?	?	?	Y	N
31 **Carter**	Y	Y	N	Y	N	N	Y
32 **Sessions**	Y	Y	N	Y	N	N	Y
33 Veasey	N	N	Y	N	Y	Y	N
34 Vela	N	Y	Y	Y	Y	Y	N
35 Doggett	N	N	Y	N	Y	Y	N
36 **Babin**	Y	Y	N	Y	N	N	Y
UTAH							
1 **Bishop**	Y	Y	N	Y	N	N	Y
2 **Stewart**	Y	Y	N	Y	N	N	Y
3 **Chaffetz**	Y	Y	N	Y	N	N	Y
4 **Love**	Y	Y	N	Y	N	N	Y
VERMONT							
AL Welch	N	N	Y	N	Y	Y	N
VIRGINIA							
1 **Wittman**	Y	Y	–	+	–	–	+
2 **Taylor**	Y	Y	–	+	–	–	+
3 Scott	N	N	Y	N	Y	Y	N
4 McEachin	N	N	Y	N	Y	Y	N
5 **Garrett**	Y	Y	N	Y	N	N	Y
6 **Goodlatte**	Y	Y	N	Y	N	N	Y
7 **Brat**	Y	Y	N	Y	N	N	Y
8 Beyer	N	N	Y	N	Y	Y	N
9 **Griffith**	Y	Y	N	Y	N	N	Y
10 **Comstock**	Y	Y	N	?	N	N	Y
11 Connolly	N	N	Y	N	Y	Y	N
WASHINGTON							
1 DelBene	N	N	Y	N	Y	Y	N
2 Larsen	N	N	Y	N	Y	Y	N
3 **Herrera Beutler**	Y	Y	N	Y	N	N	Y
4 **Newhouse**	Y	Y	N	Y	N	N	Y
5 **McMorris Rodgers**	Y	Y	N	Y	N	N	Y
6 Kilmer	N	N	Y	N	Y	Y	N
7 Jayapal	N	N	Y	N	Y	Y	N
8 **Reichert**	Y	Y	N	Y	N	N	Y
9 Smith	N	N	Y	N	Y	Y	N
10 Heck	N	N	Y	N	Y	Y	N
WEST VIRGINIA							
1 **McKinley**	Y	Y	N	Y	N	N	Y
2 **Mooney**	Y	Y	N	Y	N	N	Y
3 **Jenkins**	Y	Y	N	Y	N	N	Y
WISCONSIN							
1 **Ryan**							
2 Pocan	N	N	Y	N	Y	Y	N
3 Kind	N	N	Y	Y	N	Y	N
4 Moore	N	N	Y	N	Y	Y	N
5 **Sensenbrenner**	Y	Y	N	Y	N	N	Y
6 **Grothman**	Y	Y	N	Y	N	N	Y
7 **Duffy**	Y	Y	N	Y	N	N	Y
8 **Gallagher**	Y	Y	N	Y	N	N	Y
WYOMING							
AL **Cheney**	Y	Y	N	Y	N	N	Y

VOTE NUMBER

127. HR 1362. FALEOMAVAEGA ENI FA'AUA'A HUNKIN VA CLINIC/PASSAGE.
Radewagen, R-A.S., motion to suspend the rules and pass the bill that would designate a Veterans Affairs community-based outpatient clinic in Pago Pago, American Samoa, as the "Faleomavaega Eni Fa'aua'a Hunkin VA Clinic." Motion agreed to 411-2 : R 226-2; D 185-0. March 7, 2017.

128. PRESIDENT'S TAX RETURN DISCLOSURE/MOTION TO TABLE.
McCarthy, R-Calif., motion to table (kill) the Eshoo, D-Calif., motion to appeal the ruling of the Chair that the Eshoo resolution related to the disclosure of President Trump's tax returns does not constitute a question of the privileges of the House. Motion agreed to 227-186 : R 226-1; D 1-185. March 7, 2017.

129. HR 725, H RES 175. FRAUDULENT JOINDER/PREVIOUS QUESTION.
Buck, R-Colo., motion to order the previous question (thus ending debate and possibility of amendment) on the rule (H Res 175) that would provide for House floor consideration of the bill that would establish a new standard for determining whether a defendant has been fraudulently included in a lawsuit, for the purpose of deciding whether the case is heard in state court instead of federal court. Motion agreed to 230-184 : R 230-1; D 0-183. March 8, 2017.

130. HR 725, H RES 175. FRAUDULENT JOINDER/RULE. Adoption of the rule (H Res 175) that would provide for House floor consideration of the bill that would establish a new standard for determining whether a defendant has been fraudulently included in a lawsuit, for the purpose of deciding whether the case is heard in state court instead of federal court. Adopted 235-185 : R 234-0; D 1-185. March 8, 2017.

131. H RES 174, HR 1301. FISCAL 2017 DEFENSE APPROPRIATIONS/ PREVIOUS QUESTION. Cheney, R-Wyo., motion to order the previous question (thus ending debate and possibility of amendment) on the rule (H Res 174) that would provide for House floor consideration of the bill that would provide $577.9 billion in discretionary funding for the Defense Department in fiscal 2017. Motion agreed to 232-189 : R 232-1; D 0-188. March 8, 2017.

132. PROCEDURAL MOTION/MOTION TO ADJOURN. Hoyer, D-Md., motion to adjourn. Motion rejected 127-295 : R 0-234; D 127-61. March 8, 2017.

133. H RES 174, HR 1301. FISCAL 2017 DEFENSE APPROPRIATIONS/RULE. Adoption of the rule (H Res 174) that would provide for House floor consideration of the bill that would provide $577.9 billion in discretionary funding for the Defense Department in fiscal 2017. Adopted 233-185 : R 228-3; D 5-182. March 8, 2017.

	127	128	129	130	131	132	133
ALABAMA							
1 Byrne	Y	Y	Y	Y	Y	N	Y
2 Roby	Y	Y	Y	Y	Y	N	Y
3 Rogers	Y	Y	Y	Y	Y	N	Y
4 Aderholt	Y	Y	Y	Y	Y	N	Y
5 Brooks	Y	Y	?	Y	Y	N	Y
6 Palmer	Y	Y	Y	Y	Y	N	Y
7 Sewell	Y	N	N	N	N	Y	N
ALASKA							
AL Young	Y	Y	Y	Y	Y	N	Y
ARIZONA							
1 O'Halleran	Y	N	N	N	Y	N	N
2 McSally	Y	Y	Y	Y	Y	N	Y
3 Grijalva	Y	N	N	N	N	Y	N
4 Gosar	Y	Y	Y	Y	Y	N	Y
5 Biggs	Y	Y	Y	Y	Y	N	Y
6 Schweikert	Y	Y	Y	Y	Y	N	Y
7 Gallego	Y	N	N	N	N	Y	N
8 Franks	Y	Y	Y	Y	Y	N	Y
9 Sinema	Y	Y	N	N	N	N	N
ARKANSAS							
1 Crawford	Y	Y	Y	Y	Y	N	Y
2 Hill	+	?	Y	Y	Y	N	Y
3 Womack	Y	Y	Y	Y	Y	N	Y
4 Westerman	Y	Y	Y	Y	Y	N	Y
CALIFORNIA							
1 LaMalfa	Y	Y	Y	Y	Y	N	Y
2 Huffman	Y	N	N	N	N	N	N
3 Garamendi	Y	N	N	N	Y	N	N
4 McClintock	Y	Y	Y	Y	Y	N	Y
5 Thompson	Y	N	N	N	N	N	N
6 Matsui	Y	N	N	N	Y	N	N
7 Bera	Y	N	N	N	N	N	N
8 Cook	Y	Y	Y	Y	Y	N	Y
9 McNerney	Y	N	N	N	N	Y	N
10 Denham	Y	Y	Y	Y	Y	N	Y
11 DeSaulnier	Y	N	N	N	N	Y	N
12 Pelosi	Y	N	?	N	Y	N	N
13 Lee	Y	N	N	N	N	Y	N
14 Speier	?	?	N	N	N	Y	N
15 Swalwell	Y	N	N	N	N	N	N
16 Costa	Y	N	N	N	Y	N	N
17 Khanna	Y	N	N	N	N	Y	N
18 Eshoo	Y	N	N	N	N	Y	N
19 Lofgren	Y	N	N	N	N	N	N
20 Panetta	Y	N	N	N	Y	N	N
21 Valadao	+	+	Y	Y	Y	N	Y
22 Nunes	Y	Y	Y	Y	Y	N	Y
23 McCarthy	Y	Y	Y	Y	Y	N	Y
24 Carbajal	Y	N	N	N	N	Y	N
25 Knight	Y	Y	Y	Y	Y	N	Y
26 Brownley	Y	N	N	N	N	Y	N
27 Chu	Y	N	N	N	N	Y	N
28 Schiff	Y	N	N	N	N	Y	N
29 Cardenas	Y	N	N	N	N	Y	N
30 Sherman	Y	N	N	N	N	N	N
31 Aguilar	Y	N	N	N	N	Y	N
32 Napolitano	Y	N	N	N	N	N	N
33 Lieu	Y	N	N	N	N	Y	N
34 Vacant							
35 Torres	Y	N	N	N	N	Y	N
36 Ruiz	Y	N	N	N	N	N	N
37 Bass	Y	N	N	N	N	Y	N
38 Sánchez, Linda	Y	N	N	N	N	Y	N
39 Royce	Y	Y	Y	Y	Y	N	Y
40 Roybal-Allard	Y	N	N	N	N	N	N
41 Takano	Y	N	N	N	N	N	N
42 Calvert	Y	Y	Y	Y	Y	N	Y
43 Waters	Y	N	N	N	N	Y	N
44 Barragan	Y	N	N	N	N	Y	N
45 Walters	Y	Y	Y	Y	Y	N	Y
46 Correa	Y	N	N	N	N	Y	N
47 Lowenthal	Y	N	N	N	N	Y	N
48 Rohrabacher	?	?	Y	Y	Y	N	Y
49 Issa	Y	Y	Y	Y	Y	N	Y
50 Hunter	Y	Y	Y	Y	Y	N	?
51 Vargas	Y	N	N	N	N	Y	N
52 Peters	Y	N	N	N	N	N	N
53 Davis	Y	N	N	N	N	N	N

	127	128	129	130	131	132	133
COLORADO							
1 DeGette	Y	N	N	N	N	Y	N
2 Polis	Y	N	N	N	N	N	N
3 Tipton	?	?	Y	Y	Y	N	Y
4 Buck	Y	Y	Y	Y	Y	N	Y
5 Lamborn	Y	Y	Y	Y	Y	N	Y
6 Coffman	Y	Y	Y	Y	Y	N	Y
7 Perlmutter	Y	N	N	N	N	Y	N
CONNECTICUT							
1 Larson	Y	N	N	N	N	Y	N
2 Courtney	Y	N	N	N	N	Y	N
3 DeLauro	Y	N	N	N	N	Y	N
4 Himes	?	?	N	N	N	N	Y
5 Esty	Y	N	N	N	N	N	N
DELAWARE							
AL Blunt Rochester	Y	N	N	N	N	Y	N
FLORIDA							
1 Gaetz	Y	Y	Y	Y	Y	N	Y
2 Dunn	Y	Y	Y	Y	Y	N	?
3 Yoho	Y	Y	Y	Y	Y	N	Y
4 Rutherford	Y	Y	Y	Y	Y	N	Y
5 Lawson	Y	N	N	N	N	N	N
6 DeSantis	Y	Y	Y	Y	Y	N	Y
7 Murphy	Y	N	N	N	N	N	N
8 Posey	Y	Y	Y	Y	Y	N	Y
9 Soto	Y	N	N	N	N	Y	N
10 Demings	Y	N	N	N	N	Y	N
11 Webster	Y	Y	Y	Y	Y	N	Y
12 Bilirakis	Y	Y	Y	Y	Y	N	Y
13 Crist	Y	N	?	N	N	Y	N
14 Castor	Y	N	N	N	N	Y	N
15 Ross	Y	Y	Y	Y	Y	N	Y
16 Buchanan	Y	Y	Y	Y	Y	N	Y
17 Rooney, T.	Y	Y	Y	Y	Y	N	Y
18 Mast	Y	Y	Y	Y	Y	N	Y
19 Rooney, F.	Y	Y	Y	Y	Y	N	Y
20 Hastings	Y	N	N	N	N	Y	N
21 Frankel	Y	N	N	N	N	Y	N
22 Deutch	Y	N	N	N	N	Y	N
23 Wasserman Schultz	Y	N	N	N	N	Y	N
24 Wilson	Y	N	N	N	N	Y	N
25 Diaz-Balart	Y	Y	Y	Y	Y	N	Y
26 Curbelo	Y	Y	Y	Y	Y	N	Y
27 Ros-Lehtinen	Y	Y	Y	Y	Y	N	Y
GEORGIA							
1 Carter	Y	Y	Y	Y	Y	N	Y
2 Bishop	Y	N	?	N	N	Y	N
3 Ferguson	Y	Y	Y	Y	Y	N	Y
4 Johnson	Y	N	N	N	N	Y	N
5 Lewis	Y	N	N	N	N	Y	N
7 Woodall	Y	Y	Y	Y	Y	N	Y
8 Scott, A.	Y	Y	Y	Y	Y	N	Y
9 Collins	Y	Y	Y	Y	Y	N	Y
10 Hice	Y	Y	Y	Y	Y	N	Y
11 Loudermilk	?	Y	Y	Y	Y	N	Y
12 Allen	Y	Y	Y	+	Y	N	Y
13 Scott, D.	Y	N	N	N	N	Y	N
14 Graves	Y	Y	Y	Y	Y	N	Y
HAWAII							
1 Hanabusa	Y	N	N	N	N	Y	N
2 Gabbard	Y	N	N	N	N	N	N
IDAHO							
1 Labrador	Y	Y	Y	Y	Y	N	Y
2 Simpson	Y	Y	Y	Y	Y	N	Y
ILLINOIS							
1 Rush	?	?	N	N	N	Y	N
2 Kelly	Y	N	N	N	N	N	N
3 Lipinski	Y	N	N	N	N	N	N
4 Gutierrez	+	–	N	N	N	N	N
5 Quigley	Y	N	N	N	N	Y	N
6 Roskam	Y	Y	Y	Y	?	N	Y
7 Davis, D.	Y	N	N	N	N	Y	N
8 Krishnamoorthi	Y	N	N	N	N	Y	N
9 Schakowsky	Y	N	N	N	N	Y	N
10 Schneider	Y	N	N	N	N	Y	N
11 Foster	Y	N	N	N	N	N	N
12 Bost	Y	Y	Y	Y	Y	N	Y
13 Davis, R.	Y	Y	Y	Y	Y	N	Y
14 Hultgren	Y	Y	Y	Y	Y	N	Y
15 Shimkus	Y	Y	Y	Y	Y	N	Y

	127	128	129	130	131	132	133
16 **Kinzinger**	Y	Y	Y	Y	Y	N	Y
17 Bustos	Y	N	N	N	N	Y	N
18 **LaHood**	Y	Y	Y	Y	Y	N	Y
INDIANA							
1 Visclosky	Y	N	N	N	N	N	N
2 **Walorski**	Y	Y	Y	Y	Y	N	Y
3 **Banks**	Y	Y	Y	Y	Y	N	Y
4 **Rokita**	Y	Y	Y	Y	Y	N	Y
5 **Brooks**	Y	Y	Y	Y	Y	N	Y
6 **Messer**	Y	Y	Y	Y	Y	N	Y
7 Carson	Y	N	N	N	N	Y	N
8 **Bucshon**	Y	Y	Y	Y	Y	N	Y
9 **Hollingsworth**	Y	Y	Y	Y	Y	N	Y
IOWA							
1 **Blum**	Y	Y	Y	Y	Y	N	Y
2 Loebsack	Y	N	N	N	N	N	N
3 **Young**	Y	Y	Y	Y	Y	N	Y
4 **King**	Y	Y	Y	Y	Y	N	Y
KANSAS							
1 **Marshall**	Y	Y	Y	Y	Y	N	Y
2 **Jenkins**	+	+	+	+	+	–	+
3 **Yoder**	Y	Y	Y	Y	Y	N	Y
KENTUCKY							
1 **Comer**	Y	Y	Y	Y	Y	N	Y
2 **Guthrie**	Y	Y	Y	Y	Y	N	Y
3 Yarmuth	Y	N	N	N	N	Y	N
4 **Massie**	N	Y	Y	Y	Y	N	N
5 **Rogers**	Y	Y	Y	Y	Y	N	Y
6 **Barr**	Y	Y	Y	Y	Y	N	Y
LOUISIANA							
1 **Scalise**	Y	Y	Y	Y	Y	N	Y
2 Richmond	Y	N	N	N	N	Y	N
3 **Higgins**	Y	Y	Y	Y	Y	N	Y
4 **Johnson**	Y	Y	Y	Y	Y	N	Y
5 **Abraham**	Y	Y	Y	Y	Y	N	Y
6 **Graves**	Y	Y	Y	Y	Y	N	Y
MAINE							
1 Pingree	Y	N	N	N	N	Y	N
2 **Poliquin**	Y	Y	Y	Y	Y	N	Y
MARYLAND							
1 **Harris**	Y	Y	Y	Y	Y	N	Y
2 Ruppersberger	Y	N	N	N	N	Y	N
3 Sarbanes	Y	N	N	N	N	Y	N
4 Brown	Y	N	N	N	N	Y	N
5 Hoyer	Y	N	N	N	N	Y	N
6 Delaney	Y	N	N	N	N	Y	Y
7 Cummings	Y	N	?	?	?	?	?
8 Raskin	Y	N	N	N	N	Y	N
MASSACHUSETTS							
1 Neal	Y	N	N	N	N	Y	N
2 McGovern	Y	N	N	N	N	Y	N
3 Tsongas	Y	N	N	N	N	N	N
4 Kennedy	Y	N	N	N	N	Y	N
5 Clark	Y	N	N	N	N	Y	N
6 Moulton	Y	N	N	N	N	N	?
7 Capuano	Y	N	N	N	N	N	N
8 Lynch	Y	N	N	N	N	N	N
9 Keating	Y	N	N	N	N	N	N
MICHIGAN							
1 **Bergman**	Y	Y	Y	Y	Y	N	Y
2 **Huizenga**	Y	Y	Y	Y	Y	N	Y
3 **Amash**	Y	Y	Y	Y	Y	N	N
4 **Moolenaar**	Y	Y	Y	Y	Y	N	Y
5 Kildee	Y	N	N	N	N	N	N
6 **Upton**	Y	Y	Y	Y	Y	N	Y
7 **Walberg**	Y	Y	Y	Y	Y	N	Y
8 **Bishop**	Y	Y	Y	Y	Y	N	Y
9 Levin	Y	N	N	N	N	Y	N
10 **Mitchell**	Y	Y	Y	Y	Y	N	Y
11 **Trott**	Y	Y	Y	Y	Y	N	Y
12 Dingell	Y	N	N	N	N	Y	N
13 Conyers	Y	N	N	N	N	Y	N
14 Lawrence	Y	N	N	N	N	Y	N
MINNESOTA							
1 Walz	Y	N	N	N	N	N	N
2 **Lewis**	Y	Y	Y	Y	Y	N	Y
3 **Paulsen**	Y	Y	Y	Y	Y	N	Y
4 McCollum	Y	N	N	N	N	N	N
5 Ellison	Y	N	N	N	N	Y	N
6 **Emmer**	Y	Y	Y	Y	Y	N	Y
7 Peterson	Y	N	N	N	N	N	N
8 Nolan	?	N	N	N	N	N	N
MISSISSIPPI							
1 **Kelly**	Y	Y	Y	Y	Y	N	Y
2 Thompson	Y	N	N	N	N	Y	N
3 **Harper**	Y	Y	Y	Y	Y	N	Y
4 **Palazzo**	Y	Y	?	Y	Y	N	Y
MISSOURI							
1 Clay	Y	N	N	N	N	Y	N
2 **Wagner**	Y	Y	Y	Y	Y	N	Y
3 **Luetkemeyer**	Y	Y	Y	Y	Y	N	Y
4 **Hartzler**	Y	Y	Y	Y	Y	N	Y
5 Cleaver	+	–	–	–	–	+	–
6 **Graves**	Y	Y	Y	Y	Y	N	Y
7 **Long**	Y	Y	Y	Y	Y	N	Y
8 **Smith**	Y	Y	Y	Y	Y	N	Y
MONTANA							
AL **Vacant**							
NEBRASKA							
1 **Fortenberry**	Y	Y	Y	Y	Y	N	Y
2 **Bacon**	Y	Y	Y	Y	Y	N	Y
3 **Smith**	?	?	Y	Y	Y	N	Y
NEVADA							
1 Titus	?	?	?	?	?	?	?
2 **Amodei**	Y	Y	Y	Y	Y	P	Y
3 Rosen	Y	N	N	N	N	N	N
4 Kihuen	Y	N	N	N	N	Y	N
NEW HAMPSHIRE							
1 Shea-Porter	Y	N	N	N	N	N	N
2 Kuster	Y	N	N	N	N	Y	N
NEW JERSEY							
1 Norcross	Y	N	N	N	N	Y	N
2 **LoBiondo**	Y	Y	Y	Y	Y	N	Y
3 **MacArthur**	Y	Y	Y	Y	Y	N	Y
4 **Smith**	Y	Y	Y	Y	Y	N	?
5 Gottheimer	Y	N	N	N	N	N	Y
6 Pallone	Y	N	N	N	N	Y	N
7 **Lance**	Y	Y	Y	Y	Y	N	Y
8 Sires	Y	N	N	N	N	Y	N
9 Pascrell	Y	N	N	N	N	Y	N
10 Payne	Y	N	N	N	N	Y	N
11 **Frelinghuysen**	Y	Y	Y	Y	Y	N	Y
12 Watson Coleman	Y	N	N	N	N	Y	N
NEW MEXICO							
1 Lujan Grisham	Y	N	N	N	N	N	N
2 **Pearce**	Y	Y	Y	Y	Y	N	Y
3 Luján	Y	N	N	N	N	Y	N
NEW YORK							
1 **Zeldin**	Y	Y	Y	Y	Y	N	Y
2 **King**	Y	Y	Y	Y	Y	N	Y
3 Suozzi	Y	N	N	–	N	Y	N
4 Rice	Y	N	N	N	N	N	N
5 Meeks	Y	N	?	N	N	Y	N
6 Meng	Y	N	N	N	N	Y	N
7 Velázquez	Y	N	N	N	N	Y	N
8 Jeffries	Y	N	?	?	?	?	?
9 Clarke	Y	N	N	N	N	Y	N
10 Nadler	Y	N	N	N	N	Y	N
11 **Donovan**	Y	Y	Y	Y	Y	N	Y
12 Maloney, C.	Y	N	N	N	N	N	N
13 Espaillat	Y	N	N	N	N	Y	N
14 Crowley	Y	N	N	N	N	Y	N
15 Serrano	Y	N	N	N	N	Y	N
16 Engel	Y	N	N	N	N	Y	N
17 Lowey	Y	N	N	N	N	Y	N
18 Maloney, S.P.	Y	N	N	N	N	N	N
19 **Faso**	Y	Y	Y	Y	Y	N	Y
20 Tonko	Y	N	N	N	N	Y	N
21 **Stefanik**	Y	Y	Y	Y	Y	N	Y
22 **Tenney**	Y	Y	Y	Y	Y	N	Y
23 **Reed**	Y	Y	Y	Y	+	N	Y
24 **Katko**	Y	Y	Y	Y	Y	N	Y
25 Slaughter	Y	N	N	N	N	Y	N
26 Higgins	Y	N	N	N	N	Y	N
27 **Collins**	Y	Y	Y	Y	Y	N	Y
NORTH CAROLINA							
1 Butterfield	Y	N	N	N	N	Y	N
2 **Holding**	Y	Y	Y	Y	Y	N	Y
3 **Jones**	Y	N	N	Y	N	N	N
4 Price	Y	N	N	N	N	N	N
5 **Foxx**	Y	Y	Y	Y	Y	N	Y
6 **Walker**	Y	Y	Y	Y	Y	N	Y
7 **Rouzer**	Y	Y	Y	Y	Y	N	Y
8 **Hudson**	Y	Y	Y	Y	Y	N	Y
9 **Pittenger**	Y	Y	+	Y	Y	N	Y
10 **McHenry**	Y	Y	Y	Y	Y	N	Y
11 **Meadows**	Y	Y	Y	Y	Y	N	Y
12 Adams	Y	N	N	N	N	Y	N
13 **Budd**	Y	Y	Y	Y	Y	N	Y
NORTH DAKOTA							
AL **Cramer**	Y	Y	Y	Y	Y	N	Y
OHIO							
1 **Chabot**	Y	Y	Y	Y	Y	N	Y
2 **Wenstrup**	Y	Y	Y	Y	Y	N	Y
3 Beatty	Y	N	N	N	N	Y	N
4 **Jordan**	Y	Y	?	Y	Y	N	Y
5 **Latta**	Y	Y	Y	Y	Y	N	Y
6 **Johnson**	Y	Y	Y	Y	Y	N	Y
7 **Gibbs**	Y	Y	Y	Y	Y	N	Y
8 **Davidson**	Y	Y	Y	Y	Y	N	Y
9 Kaptur	Y	N	N	N	N	Y	N
10 **Turner**	Y	Y	Y	Y	Y	N	Y
11 Fudge	Y	N	N	N	N	Y	N
12 **Tiberi**	Y	Y	Y	Y	Y	N	Y
13 Ryan	Y	N	N	N	N	N	N
14 **Joyce**	Y	Y	Y	Y	Y	N	Y
15 **Stivers**	Y	Y	Y	Y	Y	N	Y
16 **Renacci**	Y	Y	Y	Y	Y	N	Y
OKLAHOMA							
1 **Bridenstine**	Y	Y	Y	Y	Y	N	Y
2 **Mullin**	Y	Y	Y	Y	Y	N	Y
3 **Lucas**	Y	Y	Y	Y	Y	N	Y
4 **Cole**	Y	Y	Y	Y	Y	N	Y
5 **Russell**	Y	Y	Y	Y	Y	N	Y
OREGON							
1 Bonamici	Y	N	N	N	N	N	N
2 **Walden**	Y	Y	Y	Y	Y	N	Y
3 Blumenauer	+	–	N	N	N	N	N
4 DeFazio	Y	N	N	N	N	Y	N
5 Schrader	Y	N	N	N	N	N	N
PENNSYLVANIA							
1 Brady	Y	N	N	N	N	Y	N
2 Evans	Y	N	N	N	N	Y	N
3 **Kelly**	Y	Y	Y	Y	Y	N	Y
4 **Perry**	Y	Y	Y	Y	Y	N	Y
5 **Thompson**	Y	Y	Y	Y	Y	N	Y
6 **Costello**	Y	Y	Y	Y	Y	N	Y
7 **Meehan**	Y	Y	Y	Y	Y	N	Y
8 **Fitzpatrick**	Y	Y	Y	Y	Y	N	Y
9 **Shuster**	Y	Y	Y	Y	Y	N	Y
10 **Marino**	Y	Y	Y	Y	Y	N	Y
11 **Barletta**	Y	Y	Y	Y	Y	N	Y
12 **Rothfus**	Y	Y	Y	Y	Y	N	Y
13 Boyle	Y	N	N	N	N	Y	N
14 Doyle	Y	N	N	N	N	Y	N
15 **Dent**	Y	Y	Y	Y	Y	N	Y
16 **Smucker**	Y	Y	Y	Y	Y	N	Y
17 Cartwright	Y	N	N	N	N	N	N
18 **Murphy**	Y	Y	Y	Y	Y	N	Y
RHODE ISLAND							
1 Cicilline	Y	N	N	N	N	Y	N
2 Langevin	Y	N	N	N	N	Y	N
SOUTH CAROLINA							
1 **Sanford**	N	P	Y	Y	Y	N	Y
2 **Wilson**	Y	Y	Y	Y	Y	N	Y
3 **Duncan**	Y	Y	Y	Y	Y	N	Y
4 **Gowdy**	Y	Y	Y	Y	Y	N	Y
6 Clyburn	Y	N	N	N	N	Y	N
7 **Rice**	Y	Y	Y	Y	Y	N	Y
SOUTH DAKOTA							
AL **Noem**	Y	Y	Y	Y	Y	N	Y
TENNESSEE							
1 **Roe**	Y	Y	Y	Y	Y	N	Y
2 **Duncan**	Y	Y	Y	Y	Y	N	Y
3 **Fleischmann**	Y	Y	Y	Y	Y	N	Y
4 **DesJarlais**	Y	Y	Y	Y	Y	N	Y
5 Cooper	Y	N	N	N	N	Y	Y
6 **Black**	Y	Y	Y	Y	Y	N	Y
7 **Blackburn**	Y	Y	Y	Y	Y	N	Y
8 **Kustoff**	Y	Y	Y	Y	Y	N	Y
9 Cohen	Y	N	N	N	N	Y	N
TEXAS							
1 **Gohmert**	Y	Y	Y	Y	Y	N	Y
2 **Poe**	Y	Y	Y	Y	Y	N	Y
3 **Johnson, S.**	Y	Y	Y	Y	Y	N	Y
4 **Ratcliffe**	Y	Y	Y	Y	Y	N	Y
5 **Hensarling**	Y	Y	Y	Y	Y	N	Y
6 **Barton**	Y	Y	Y	Y	Y	N	Y
7 **Culberson**	+	+	Y	Y	Y	N	Y
8 **Brady**	Y	Y	Y	Y	Y	N	Y
9 Green, A.	Y	N	N	N	N	N	N
10 **McCaul**	Y	Y	Y	Y	Y	N	Y
11 **Conaway**	Y	Y	Y	Y	Y	N	Y
12 **Granger**	Y	Y	Y	Y	Y	N	Y
13 **Thornberry**	Y	Y	Y	Y	Y	N	Y
14 **Weber**	Y	Y	Y	Y	Y	N	Y
15 Gonzalez	Y	N	?	N	N	Y	N
16 O'Rourke	Y	N	N	N	N	N	N
17 **Flores**	Y	Y	Y	Y	Y	N	Y
18 Jackson Lee	Y	N	N	N	N	Y	N
19 **Arrington**	Y	Y	Y	Y	Y	N	Y
20 Castro	Y	N	N	N	N	Y	N
21 **Smith**	Y	Y	Y	Y	Y	N	Y
22 **Olson**	Y	Y	Y	Y	Y	N	Y
23 **Hurd**	Y	Y	Y	Y	Y	N	Y
24 **Marchant**	Y	Y	Y	Y	Y	N	Y
25 **Williams**	Y	Y	Y	Y	Y	N	Y
26 **Burgess**	Y	Y	Y	Y	Y	N	Y
27 **Farenthold**	Y	Y	Y	Y	Y	N	Y
28 Cuellar	Y	N	N	N	N	N	N
29 Green, G.	Y	N	N	N	N	N	N
30 Johnson, E.B.	Y	N	N	N	N	Y	N
31 **Carter**	Y	Y	Y	Y	Y	N	Y
32 **Sessions**	Y	Y	Y	Y	Y	N	Y
33 Veasey	Y	N	N	N	N	Y	N
34 Vela	Y	N	N	N	N	Y	N
35 Doggett	Y	N	N	N	N	Y	N
36 **Babin**	Y	Y	Y	Y	Y	N	Y
UTAH							
1 **Bishop**	Y	Y	Y	Y	Y	N	Y
2 **Stewart**	Y	Y	Y	Y	Y	N	Y
3 **Chaffetz**	Y	Y	Y	Y	Y	N	Y
4 **Love**	Y	Y	Y	Y	Y	N	Y
VERMONT							
AL Welch	Y	N	–	–	–	+	–
VIRGINIA							
1 **Wittman**	Y	Y	Y	Y	Y	N	Y
2 **Taylor**	Y	Y	Y	Y	Y	N	Y
3 Scott	Y	N	N	N	N	N	N
4 McEachin	Y	N	N	N	N	Y	N
5 **Garrett**	Y	?	Y	Y	Y	N	Y
6 **Goodlatte**	Y	Y	Y	Y	Y	N	Y
7 **Brat**	Y	Y	Y	Y	Y	N	Y
8 Beyer	Y	N	N	N	N	Y	N
9 **Griffith**	Y	Y	Y	Y	Y	N	Y
10 **Comstock**	Y	Y	Y	Y	Y	N	Y
11 Connolly	Y	N	N	N	N	N	N
WASHINGTON							
1 DelBene	Y	N	N	N	N	N	N
2 Larsen	Y	N	N	N	N	N	N
3 **Herrera Beutler**	Y	Y	Y	Y	Y	N	Y
4 **Newhouse**	Y	Y	Y	Y	Y	N	Y
5 **McMorris Rodgers**	Y	Y	Y	Y	Y	N	Y
6 Kilmer	Y	N	N	N	N	N	N
7 Jayapal	Y	N	N	N	N	Y	N
8 **Reichert**	Y	Y	Y	Y	Y	N	Y
9 Smith	Y	N	N	N	N	N	N
10 Heck	Y	N	N	N	N	Y	N
WEST VIRGINIA							
1 **McKinley**	Y	Y	Y	Y	Y	N	Y
2 **Mooney**	Y	Y	Y	Y	Y	N	Y
3 **Jenkins**	Y	Y	Y	Y	Y	N	Y
WISCONSIN							
1 **Ryan**							
2 Pocan	Y	N	N	N	N	Y	N
3 Kind	Y	N	N	N	N	N	N
4 Moore	Y	N	?	N	N	Y	N
5 **Sensenbrenner**	Y	Y	Y	Y	Y	N	?
6 **Grothman**	Y	Y	Y	Y	Y	N	Y
7 **Duffy**	Y	Y	Y	Y	Y	N	Y
8 **Gallagher**	Y	Y	Y	Y	Y	N	Y
WYOMING							
AL **Cheney**	Y	Y	Y	Y	Y	N	Y

III HOUSE VOTES

VOTE NUMBER

134. PROCEDURAL MOTION/MOTION TO ADJOURN. McGovern, D-Mass., motion to adjourn. Motion rejected 107-277 : R 0-220; D 107-57. March 8, 2017.

135. PROCEDURAL MOTION/MOTION TO ADJOURN. Takano, D-Calif., motion to adjourn. Motion rejected 114-290 : R 1-226; D 113-64. March 8, 2017.

136. HR 1301. FISCAL 2017 DEFENSE APPROPRIATIONS/PASSAGE. Passage of the bill that would provide $577.9 billion in discretionary funding for the Defense Department in fiscal 2017. The total would include $516.1 billion in base Defense Department funding subject to spending caps. It also would include $61.8 billion in overseas contingency operations funding. The bill would provide approximately $210.1 billion for operations and maintenance, approximately $117.8 billion for procurement, approximately $72.7 billion for research and development and $132.2 billion for military personnel, including a 2.1 percent pay raise. It also would provide roughly $34.1 billion for defense health programs. The measure would prohibit use of funds to construct or modify potential facilities in the United States to house Guantanamo Bay detainees. Passed 371-48 : R 230-5; D 141-43. March 8, 2017.

137. PROCEDURAL MOTION/MOTION TO ADJOURN. Motion agreed to 314-98 : R 205-23; D 109-75. March 8, 2017.

138. HR 720, HR 985, H RES 180. CLASS-ACTION LAWSUIT RESTRICTIONS, ASBESTOS TRUSTS AND FRIVOLOUS LAWSUITS/PREVIOUS QUESTION. Collins, R-Ga., motion to order the previous question (thus ending debate and possibility of amendment) on the rule (H Res 180) that would provide for House floor consideration of the bill (HR 720) that would require federal courts to impose sanctions on parties that file frivolous civil lawsuits. The rule would also provide for consideration of the bill (HR 985) that would prohibit federal courts from certifying proposed classes of individuals for a class-action lawsuit unless each member of the class has suffered the same type and degree of injury. Additionally, the bill would require asbestos trusts to issue quarterly reports on claims made against the trusts and payouts made by the trusts for asbestos-related injuries. Motion agreed to 233-186 : R 233-0; D 0-186. March 9, 2017.

139. HR 720, HR 985, H RES 180. CLASS-ACTION LAWSUIT RESTRICTIONS, ASBESTOS TRUSTS AND FRIVOLOUS LAWSUITS/RULE. Adoption of the rule that would provide for House floor consideration of the bill (HR 720) that would require federal courts to impose sanctions on parties that file frivolous civil lawsuits. The rule would also provide for consideration of the bill (HR 985) that would prohibit federal courts from certifying proposed classes of individuals for a class-action lawsuit unless each member of the class has suffered the same type and degree of injury. Additionally, the bill would require asbestos trusts to issue quarterly reports on claims made against the trusts and payouts made by the trusts for asbestos-related injuries. Adopted 233-184 : R 233-0; D 0-184. March 9, 2017.

140. HR 985. CLASS-ACTION LAWSUIT RESTRICTIONS AND ASBESTOS TRUSTS/COUNSEL AND PLAINTIFF RELATIONSHIP. Deutch, D-Fla., amendment that would remove the bill's prohibition on the use of class counsel if the named plaintiff is a present or former client or has a contractual relationship with the counsel. Rejected in Committee of the Whole 182-227 : R 4-227; D 178-0. March 9, 2017.

	134	135	136	137	138	139	140
ALABAMA							
1 Byrne	N	N	Y	N	Y	Y	N
2 Roby	N	N	Y	Y	Y	Y	N
3 Rogers	N	N	Y	Y	Y	Y	N
4 Aderholt	N	N	Y	Y	Y	Y	N
5 Brooks	N	N	Y	Y	Y	Y	N
6 Palmer	N	N	Y	Y	Y	Y	N
7 Sewell	Y	Y	Y	Y	N	N	Y
ALASKA							
AL Young	N	?	Y	?	Y	Y	N
ARIZONA							
1 O'Halleran	Y	N	Y	N	N	N	Y
2 McSally	N	N	Y	N	Y	Y	N
3 Grijalva	?	?	N	Y	N	N	Y
4 Gosar	?	?	Y	Y	?	?	Y
5 Biggs	N	N	Y	Y	Y	Y	N
6 Schweikert	Y	N	Y	Y	Y	Y	N
7 Gallego	Y	Y	Y	Y	N	N	Y
8 Franks	N	N	Y	N	Y	Y	N
9 Sinema	N	N	Y	N	–	–	+
ARKANSAS							
1 Crawford	N	N	Y	Y	Y	Y	N
2 Hill	N	N	Y	Y	Y	Y	N
3 Womack	N	N	Y	Y	Y	Y	N
4 Westerman	N	N	Y	Y	Y	Y	N
CALIFORNIA							
1 LaMalfa	N	N	Y	Y	Y	Y	N
2 Huffman	N	N	N	N	N	N	Y
3 Garamendi	Y	Y	Y	N	N	N	Y
4 McClintock	N	N	Y	Y	Y	Y	N
5 Thompson	N	N	N	N	N	N	Y
6 Matsui	N	N	Y	Y	N	N	+
7 Bera	N	N	Y	N	N	N	Y
8 Cook	N	N	Y	Y	Y	Y	N
9 McNerney	Y	Y	Y	Y	N	N	Y
10 Denham	N	N	Y	Y	Y	Y	N
11 DeSaulnier	Y	?	N	Y	N	N	Y
12 Pelosi	?	Y	Y	?	N	N	Y
13 Lee	Y	Y	N	Y	N	N	Y
14 Speier	Y	Y	N	Y	N	N	?
15 Swalwell	N	N	Y	N	N	N	Y
16 Costa	Y	?	Y	Y	N	N	Y
17 Khanna	Y	Y	–	Y	N	N	Y
18 Eshoo	Y	Y	Y	Y	N	N	Y
19 Lofgren	N	Y	N	N	?	?	Y
20 Panetta	Y	N	N	N	N	N	Y
21 Valadao	N	N	Y	Y	Y	Y	N
22 Nunes	N	N	Y	Y	Y	Y	N
23 McCarthy	N	N	Y	Y	Y	Y	N
24 Carbajal	Y	N	Y	N	N	N	Y
25 Knight	?	N	Y	Y	Y	Y	N
26 Brownley	Y	Y	N	Y	N	N	Y
27 Chu	Y	Y	N	Y	N	N	Y
28 Schiff	Y	Y	Y	Y	N	N	Y
29 Cardenas	Y	Y	Y	Y	N	N	Y
30 Sherman	N	N	Y	N	N	N	Y
31 Aguilar	N	N	Y	N	N	N	Y
32 Napolitano	Y	N	N	N	N	N	Y
33 Lieu	Y	Y	Y	Y	N	N	Y
34 Vacant							
35 Torres	?	Y	Y	N	N	N	Y
36 Ruiz	N	N	Y	N	N	N	Y
37 Bass	?	?	?	?	N	N	Y
38 Sánchez, Linda	Y	Y	Y	Y	N	N	Y
39 Royce	N	N	Y	Y	Y	Y	N
40 Roybal-Allard	N	N	Y	N	N	N	Y
41 Takano	Y	Y	N	Y	N	N	Y
42 Calvert	N	N	Y	?	Y	Y	N
43 Waters	Y	Y	N	Y	N	N	Y
44 Barragan	+	Y	Y	Y	N	N	Y
45 Walters	N	N	Y	Y	Y	Y	N
46 Correa	Y	N	Y	N	N	N	Y
47 Lowenthal	Y	Y	N	Y	N	N	Y
48 Rohrabacher	N	N	N	Y	Y	Y	N
49 Issa	N	N	Y	Y	Y	Y	N
50 Hunter	N	N	Y	Y	Y	Y	N
51 Vargas	Y	Y	Y	Y	N	N	Y
52 Peters	N	N	Y	N	N	N	Y
53 Davis	N	N	Y	Y	–	–	+

	134	135	136	137	138	139	140
COLORADO							
1 DeGette	Y	Y	N	Y	N	N	?
2 Polis	?	N	N	N	N	N	Y
3 Tipton	N	N	Y	Y	Y	Y	N
4 Buck	N	N	Y	Y	Y	Y	N
5 Lamborn	N	N	Y	Y	Y	Y	N
6 Coffman	N	N	Y	Y	Y	Y	N
7 Perlmutter	N	Y	Y	N	N	N	Y
CONNECTICUT							
1 Larson	Y	N	Y	N	–	–	Y
2 Courtney	N	N	Y	N	N	N	Y
3 DeLauro	Y	Y	Y	N	N	N	Y
4 Himes	Y	Y	Y	?	N	N	Y
5 Esty	N	N	Y	N	N	N	Y
DELAWARE							
AL Blunt Rochester	Y	Y	Y	N	N	N	Y
FLORIDA							
1 Gaetz	N	N	Y	Y	Y	Y	N
2 Dunn	?	N	Y	Y	Y	Y	N
3 Yoho	N	N	Y	Y	Y	Y	N
4 Rutherford	N	N	Y	Y	Y	Y	N
5 Lawson	N	?	Y	N	Y	N	Y
6 DeSantis	N	N	Y	Y	Y	Y	N
7 Murphy	N	N	N	N	N	N	Y
8 Posey	N	N	Y	Y	Y	Y	N
9 Soto	Y	Y	Y	N	N	N	Y
10 Demings	Y	Y	Y	N	N	N	Y
11 Webster	N	N	Y	N	Y	Y	N
12 Bilirakis	N	N	Y	Y	Y	Y	N
13 Crist	N	Y	Y	N	N	N	Y
14 Castor	Y	Y	Y	?	N	N	Y
15 Ross	?	N	Y	Y	Y	Y	N
16 Buchanan	N	N	Y	Y	Y	Y	N
17 Rooney, T.	N	N	Y	Y	Y	Y	N
18 Mast	N	N	Y	Y	Y	Y	N
19 Rooney, F.	N	N	Y	Y	Y	Y	N
20 Hastings	Y	Y	N	Y	N	N	Y
21 Frankel	?	Y	Y	Y	–	–	Y
22 Deutch	–	–	+	N	N	N	Y
23 Wasserman Schultz	N	N	Y	N	N	N	Y
24 Wilson	Y	Y	Y	Y	N	N	+
25 Diaz-Balart	N	N	Y	Y	Y	Y	N
26 Curbelo	N	N	Y	Y	Y	Y	+
27 Ros-Lehtinen	N	N	Y	Y	Y	Y	Y
GEORGIA							
1 Carter	N	N	Y	Y	Y	Y	N
2 Bishop	Y	Y	Y	N	N	N	Y
3 Ferguson	N	N	Y	Y	Y	Y	N
4 Johnson	Y	Y	Y	N	N	N	Y
5 Lewis	?	Y	N	Y	N	N	Y
7 Woodall	N	N	Y	Y	Y	Y	N
8 Scott, A.	N	N	Y	Y	Y	Y	N
9 Collins	N	?	Y	Y	Y	Y	N
10 Hice	N	N	Y	Y	Y	Y	N
11 Loudermilk	N	N	Y	Y	Y	Y	N
12 Allen	N	N	Y	N	Y	Y	N
13 Scott, D.	?	Y	Y	Y	N	N	Y
14 Graves	N	N	Y	Y	Y	Y	N
HAWAII							
1 Hanabusa	?	Y	Y	N	N	N	Y
2 Gabbard	N	N	Y	N	N	N	Y
IDAHO							
1 Labrador	N	N	Y	Y	Y	Y	N
2 Simpson	N	N	Y	N	Y	Y	N
ILLINOIS							
1 Rush	Y	Y	N	Y	?	?	?
2 Kelly	Y	Y	Y	Y	N	N	?
3 Lipinski	N	N	Y	N	N	N	Y
4 Gutierrez	Y	N	Y	N	N	N	Y
5 Quigley	Y	?	Y	Y	N	N	Y
6 Roskam	N	N	Y	Y	Y	Y	N
7 Davis, D.	Y	Y	N	N	N	N	Y
8 Krishnamoorthi	Y	Y	Y	Y	N	N	Y
9 Schakowsky	Y	N	Y	N	N	N	Y
10 Schneider	N	N	Y	N	N	N	Y
11 Foster	Y	Y	Y	N	N	N	Y
12 Bost	N	N	Y	Y	Y	Y	N
13 Davis, R.	N	?	Y	Y	Y	Y	N
14 Hultgren	N	N	Y	Y	Y	Y	N
15 Shimkus	N	N	Y	Y	Y	Y	N

KEY Republicans Democrats *Independents*

Y Voted for (yea)	X Paired against
# Paired for	– Announced against
+ Announced for	P Voted "present"
N Voted against (nay)	C Voted "present" to avoid possible conflict of interest
	? Did not vote or otherwise make a position known

	134	135	136	137	138	139	140
16 **Kinzinger**	?	N	Y	Y	Y	Y	N
17 Bustos	Y	Y	Y	Y	N	N	Y
18 **LaHood**	N	N	Y	Y	Y	Y	N
INDIANA							
1 Visclosky	N	N	Y	N	N	N	Y
2 **Walorski**	N	N	Y	Y	Y	Y	N
3 **Banks**	N	N	Y	Y	Y	Y	N
4 **Rokita**	N	N	Y	N	Y	Y	N
5 **Brooks**	N	N	Y	Y	Y	Y	N
6 **Messer**	N	N	Y	N	Y	Y	N
7 Carson	Y	Y	N	N	N	N	?
8 **Bucshon**	N	N	Y	Y	Y	Y	N
9 **Hollingsworth**	N	N	Y	Y	Y	Y	N
IOWA							
1 **Blum**	N	N	Y	Y	Y	Y	N
2 Loebsack	N	N	Y	?	N	N	Y
3 **Young**	N	N	Y	Y	Y	Y	N
4 **King**	N	N	Y	N	Y	Y	N
KANSAS							
1 **Marshall**	N	N	Y	Y	Y	Y	N
2 **Jenkins**	–	–	+	+	Y	Y	N
3 **Yoder**	N	N	Y	Y	Y	Y	N
KENTUCKY							
1 **Comer**	N	N	Y	Y	Y	Y	N
2 **Guthrie**	N	N	Y	Y	Y	Y	N
3 Yarmuth	Y	Y	Y	Y	N	N	Y
4 **Massie**	N	N	N	Y	Y	Y	N
5 **Rogers**	N	N	Y	Y	Y	Y	N
6 **Barr**	N	N	Y	Y	Y	Y	N
LOUISIANA							
1 **Scalise**	N	N	Y	Y	Y	Y	N
2 Richmond	Y	?	?	Y	N	N	?
3 **Higgins**	N	N	Y	Y	Y	Y	N
4 **Johnson**	N	N	Y	Y	Y	Y	N
5 **Abraham**	N	N	Y	Y	Y	Y	N
6 **Graves**	N	N	Y	Y	Y	Y	N
MAINE							
1 Pingree	Y	Y	Y	Y	N	N	Y
2 **Poliquin**	N	N	Y	Y	Y	Y	N
MARYLAND							
1 **Harris**	N	N	Y	Y	Y	Y	N
2 Ruppersberger	Y	+	Y	Y	N	N	Y
3 Sarbanes	Y	Y	Y	Y	N	N	Y
4 Brown	?	N	Y	Y	N	N	Y
5 Hoyer	Y	Y	Y	Y	N	N	Y
6 Delaney	Y	Y	Y	Y	N	N	Y
7 Cummings	?	Y	Y	N	N	N	Y
8 Raskin	Y	Y	N	Y	N	N	Y
MASSACHUSETTS							
1 Neal	Y	Y	Y	Y	N	N	Y
2 McGovern	Y	Y	N	Y	N	N	Y
3 Tsongas	N	N	Y	N	N	N	Y
4 Kennedy	Y	Y	N	Y	N	N	Y
5 Clark	Y	Y	N	Y	N	N	Y
6 Moulton	N	N	Y	N	N	N	Y
7 Capuano	N	N	N	N	N	N	Y
8 Lynch	N	N	?	N	N	N	Y
9 Keating	N	N	Y	N	N	N	Y
MICHIGAN							
1 **Bergman**	N	N	Y	Y	Y	Y	N
2 **Huizenga**	N	N	Y	Y	Y	Y	N
3 **Amash**	N	N	N	N	Y	Y	N
4 **Moolenaar**	N	N	Y	Y	Y	Y	N
5 Kildee	N	N	Y	N	N	N	Y
6 **Upton**	N	N	Y	Y	Y	Y	N
7 **Walberg**	N	N	Y	Y	Y	Y	N
8 **Bishop**	N	N	Y	Y	Y	Y	N
9 Levin	N	N	Y	Y	N	N	Y
10 **Mitchell**	N	N	Y	Y	Y	Y	N
11 **Trott**	?	N	Y	Y	Y	Y	N
12 Dingell	Y	Y	Y	Y	N	N	Y
13 Conyers	Y	Y	N	?	N	?	Y
14 Lawrence	Y	Y	Y	Y	N	N	Y
MINNESOTA							
1 Walz	N	N	Y	N	N	N	Y
2 **Lewis**	N	N	Y	Y	Y	Y	N
3 **Paulsen**	N	N	Y	Y	Y	Y	N
4 McCollum	?	N	Y	N	N	N	Y

	134	135	136	137	138	139	140
5 Ellison	N	Y	N	N	N	N	Y
6 **Emmer**	N	N	Y	Y	Y	Y	N
7 Peterson	N	N	Y	Y	N	N	Y
8 Nolan	N	N	Y	N	N	N	Y
MISSISSIPPI							
1 **Kelly**	N	N	Y	Y	Y	Y	N
2 Thompson	Y	Y	Y	N	N	N	Y
3 **Harper**	N	N	Y	Y	Y	Y	N
4 **Palazzo**	N	N	Y	Y	Y	Y	N
MISSOURI							
1 Clay	Y	Y	Y	N	N	N	Y
2 **Wagner**	N	?	Y	?	Y	Y	N
3 **Luetkemeyer**	N	N	Y	Y	Y	Y	N
4 **Hartzler**	N	N	Y	Y	Y	Y	N
5 Cleaver	+	+	+	+	N	N	Y
6 **Graves**	N	N	Y	Y	Y	Y	N
7 **Long**	N	N	Y	Y	Y	Y	N
8 **Smith**	N	N	Y	Y	Y	Y	N
MONTANA							
AL **Vacant**							
NEBRASKA							
1 **Fortenberry**	N	N	Y	Y	Y	Y	N
2 **Bacon**	N	N	Y	Y	Y	Y	N
3 **Smith**	N	N	Y	Y	Y	Y	N
NEVADA							
1 Titus	?	?	+	?	?	?	?
2 **Amodei**	N	Y	Y	Y	Y	Y	N
3 Rosen	N	N	Y	N	N	N	Y
4 Kihuen	Y	Y	Y	Y	N	N	Y
NEW HAMPSHIRE							
1 Shea-Porter	N	N	Y	N	N	N	Y
2 Kuster	Y	Y	Y	Y	N	N	Y
NEW JERSEY							
1 Norcross	Y	Y	Y	Y	N	N	Y
2 **LoBiondo**	N	N	Y	Y	Y	Y	N
3 **MacArthur**	N	N	Y	Y	Y	Y	N
4 **Smith**	N	N	Y	N	Y	Y	N
5 Gottheimer	N	N	Y	N	N	N	Y
6 Pallone	Y	Y	N	Y	N	N	Y
7 **Lance**	N	N	Y	Y	Y	Y	N
8 Sires	Y	Y	Y	Y	N	N	Y
9 Pascrell	?	N	Y	Y	N	N	Y
10 Payne	Y	Y	Y	N	N	N	Y
11 **Frelinghuysen**	N	N	Y	Y	Y	Y	N
12 Watson Coleman	Y	Y	N	Y	N	N	Y
NEW MEXICO							
1 Lujan Grisham	N	N	Y	N	N	N	Y
2 **Pearce**	N	N	Y	Y	Y	Y	N
3 Luján	Y	Y	Y	Y	N	N	Y
NEW YORK							
1 **Zeldin**	N	N	Y	Y	Y	Y	N
2 **King**	N	N	Y	Y	Y	Y	N
3 Suozzi	Y	Y	Y	Y	N	N	Y
4 Rice	N	N	Y	Y	N	N	Y
5 Meeks	Y	Y	Y	Y	N	N	Y
6 Meng	Y	Y	Y	Y	N	N	Y
7 Velázquez	Y	Y	N	N	N	N	Y
8 Jeffries	?	Y	Y	Y	N	N	Y
9 Clarke	Y	Y	N	Y	N	N	Y
10 Nadler	Y	Y	Y	Y	N	N	Y
11 **Donovan**	N	N	Y	Y	Y	Y	N
12 Maloney, C.	N	N	N	N	N	N	Y
13 Espaillat	Y	Y	N	Y	N	N	+
14 Crowley	Y	Y	Y	Y	N	N	Y
15 Serrano	Y	Y	N	Y	N	N	Y
16 Engel	Y	Y	Y	Y	N	N	Y
17 Lowey	Y	Y	Y	Y	N	N	Y
18 Maloney, S.P.	N	N	Y	N	N	N	Y
19 **Faso**	N	N	Y	Y	Y	Y	N
20 Tonko	Y	Y	Y	Y	N	N	Y
21 **Stefanik**	N	N	Y	Y	Y	Y	N
22 **Tenney**	N	N	Y	Y	Y	Y	N
23 **Reed**	N	N	Y	Y	Y	Y	N
24 **Katko**	N	N	Y	Y	Y	Y	N
25 Slaughter	Y	Y	Y	Y	N	N	Y
26 Higgins	?	Y	Y	Y	N	N	Y
27 **Collins**	N	N	Y	Y	Y	Y	N
NORTH CAROLINA							
1 Butterfield	Y	Y	Y	N	N	N	Y
2 **Holding**	N	N	Y	N	Y	Y	N
3 **Jones**	N	N	N	Y	Y	Y	Y
4 Price	N	N	Y	N	N	N	Y

	134	135	136	137	138	139	140
5 **Foxx**	N	N	Y	Y	Y	Y	N
6 **Walker**	N	N	Y	Y	Y	Y	N
7 **Rouzer**	N	N	Y	Y	Y	Y	N
8 **Hudson**	N	N	Y	Y	Y	Y	N
9 **Pittenger**	?	N	Y	Y	Y	Y	N
10 **McHenry**	N	N	Y	Y	Y	Y	N
11 **Meadows**	N	N	Y	Y	?	?	N
12 Adams	Y	Y	Y	Y	N	N	Y
13 **Budd**	N	N	Y	Y	Y	Y	N
NORTH DAKOTA							
AL **Cramer**	N	N	Y	Y	Y	Y	N
OHIO							
1 **Chabot**	N	N	Y	Y	Y	Y	N
2 **Wenstrup**	N	N	Y	Y	Y	Y	N
3 Beatty	Y	Y	Y	Y	N	N	Y
4 **Jordan**	N	N	Y	N	?	?	N
5 **Latta**	N	N	Y	Y	Y	Y	N
6 **Johnson**	N	N	Y	Y	Y	Y	N
7 **Gibbs**	N	N	Y	Y	Y	Y	N
8 **Davidson**	?	N	Y	Y	Y	Y	N
9 Kaptur	Y	Y	?	N	N	N	Y
10 **Turner**	N	N	Y	Y	Y	Y	N
11 Fudge	Y	Y	Y	N	N	N	Y
12 **Tiberi**	N	N	Y	Y	Y	Y	N
13 Ryan	N	N	Y	N	N	N	Y
14 **Joyce**	N	N	Y	Y	Y	Y	?
15 **Stivers**	N	N	Y	N	Y	Y	N
16 **Renacci**	N	N	Y	Y	Y	Y	N
OKLAHOMA							
1 **Bridenstine**	N	N	Y	Y	Y	Y	N
2 **Mullin**	N	N	Y	Y	Y	Y	N
3 **Lucas**	N	N	Y	Y	Y	Y	N
4 **Cole**	N	N	Y	N	Y	Y	N
5 **Russell**	N	?	Y	Y	Y	Y	Y
OREGON							
1 Bonamici	N	N	Y	N	N	N	Y
2 **Walden**	N	N	Y	Y	Y	Y	N
3 Blumenauer	?	N	N	N	N	N	Y
4 DeFazio	N	N	N	N	N	N	Y
5 Schrader	N	N	N	N	N	N	Y
PENNSYLVANIA							
1 Brady	Y	Y	Y	Y	N	N	Y
2 Evans	?	Y	Y	Y	N	N	Y
3 **Kelly**	N	N	Y	Y	Y	Y	N
4 **Perry**	N	N	Y	Y	Y	Y	N
5 **Thompson**	N	N	Y	Y	Y	Y	N
6 **Costello**	N	N	Y	Y	Y	Y	N
7 **Meehan**	N	N	Y	Y	Y	Y	N
8 **Fitzpatrick**	N	N	Y	Y	Y	Y	N
9 **Shuster**	?	N	Y	Y	Y	Y	N
10 **Marino**	N	N	Y	Y	Y	Y	N
11 **Barletta**	N	?	Y	Y	Y	Y	–
12 **Rothfus**	N	N	Y	Y	Y	Y	N
13 Boyle	Y	Y	Y	Y	N	–	Y
14 Doyle	Y	Y	Y	Y	N	N	Y
15 **Dent**	?	?	Y	Y	Y	Y	N
16 **Smucker**	N	N	Y	Y	Y	Y	N
17 Cartwright	N	N	Y	N	N	N	Y
18 **Murphy**	N	N	Y	Y	Y	Y	N
RHODE ISLAND							
1 Cicilline	Y	Y	Y	Y	N	N	Y
2 Langevin	Y	Y	Y	Y	N	N	?
SOUTH CAROLINA							
1 **Sanford**	N	N	Y	Y	Y	Y	N
2 **Wilson**	N	N	Y	Y	Y	Y	N
3 **Duncan**	N	N	Y	Y	Y	Y	N
4 **Gowdy**	N	N	Y	Y	Y	Y	N
6 Clyburn	Y	Y	Y	N	N	N	Y
7 **Rice**	N	N	Y	Y	Y	Y	N
SOUTH DAKOTA							
AL **Noem**	N	N	Y	N	Y	Y	N
TENNESSEE							
1 **Roe**	N	N	Y	Y	Y	Y	N
2 **Duncan**	N	N	N	Y	Y	Y	N
3 **Fleischmann**	N	N	Y	Y	Y	Y	N
4 **DesJarlais**	?	N	Y	Y	Y	Y	N
5 Cooper	Y	Y	Y	Y	N	N	Y
6 **Black**	N	N	Y	Y	Y	Y	N
7 **Blackburn**	N	N	Y	Y	Y	Y	N
8 **Kustoff**	N	N	Y	Y	Y	Y	N
9 Cohen	Y	Y	N	N	N	N	Y

	134	135	136	137	138	139	140
TEXAS							
1 **Gohmert**	N	N	Y	N	Y	Y	N
2 **Poe**	N	N	Y	N	Y	Y	N
3 **Johnson, S.**	N	N	Y	Y	Y	Y	N
4 **Ratcliffe**	?	N	Y	N	Y	Y	N
5 **Hensarling**	N	N	Y	Y	Y	Y	N
6 **Barton**	N	N	Y	Y	Y	Y	N
7 **Culberson**	N	N	Y	Y	Y	Y	N
8 **Brady**	N	N	Y	Y	Y	Y	?
9 Green, A.	N	N	Y	N	N	N	Y
10 **McCaul**	N	N	Y	Y	Y	Y	?
11 **Conaway**	N	N	Y	Y	Y	Y	N
12 **Granger**	N	N	Y	Y	Y	Y	N
13 **Thornberry**	N	N	Y	Y	Y	Y	N
14 **Weber**	N	N	Y	N	Y	Y	N
15 Gonzalez	Y	Y	Y	Y	N	N	Y
16 O'Rourke	?	N	Y	N	N	N	Y
17 **Flores**	N	N	Y	Y	Y	Y	N
18 Jackson Lee	Y	Y	Y	Y	N	N	Y
19 **Arrington**	N	N	Y	Y	Y	Y	N
20 Castro	?	Y	Y	Y	N	N	Y
21 **Smith**	N	N	Y	?	Y	Y	N
22 **Olson**	?	N	Y	Y	Y	Y	N
23 **Hurd**	N	N	Y	Y	Y	Y	N
24 **Marchant**	?	N	Y	Y	Y	Y	N
25 **Williams**	N	N	Y	Y	Y	Y	N
26 **Burgess**	N	N	Y	Y	Y	Y	N
27 **Farenthold**	N	N	Y	Y	Y	Y	N
28 Cuellar	N	N	Y	N	N	N	Y
29 Green, G.	N	N	Y	?	N	N	Y
30 Johnson, E.B.	?	Y	Y	Y	N	N	Y
31 **Carter**	N	N	Y	Y	Y	Y	N
32 **Sessions**	N	N	Y	?	Y	Y	N
33 Veasey	Y	Y	Y	N	N	N	Y
34 Vela	?	Y	?	Y	N	N	Y
35 Doggett	Y	Y	Y	Y	N	N	Y
36 **Babin**	N	N	Y	Y	Y	Y	N
UTAH							
1 **Bishop**	N	N	Y	Y	Y	Y	N
2 **Stewart**	N	N	Y	Y	Y	Y	N
3 **Chaffetz**	N	N	Y	Y	Y	Y	N
4 **Love**	N	N	Y	Y	Y	Y	N
VERMONT							
AL Welch	+	+	N	Y	N	N	Y
VIRGINIA							
1 **Wittman**	N	N	Y	Y	Y	Y	N
2 **Taylor**	N	N	Y	N	Y	Y	N
3 Scott	N	N	Y	N	N	N	Y
4 McEachin	Y	Y	Y	Y	N	N	Y
5 **Garrett**	N	N	Y	Y	Y	Y	N
6 **Goodlatte**	N	N	Y	Y	Y	Y	N
7 **Brat**	N	N	Y	Y	Y	Y	N
8 Beyer	?	Y	Y	Y	N	N	Y
9 **Griffith**	N	N	Y	Y	Y	Y	N
10 **Comstock**	N	N	Y	Y	Y	Y	N
11 Connolly	N	N	Y	N	N	N	Y
WASHINGTON							
1 DelBene	N	N	Y	N	N	N	Y
2 Larsen	N	?	Y	N	N	N	Y
3 **Herrera Beutler**	N	N	Y	Y	Y	Y	N
4 **Newhouse**	N	N	Y	Y	Y	Y	N
5 **McMorris Rodgers**	N	N	Y	Y	Y	Y	N
6 Kilmer	N	N	Y	N	N	N	Y
7 Jayapal	Y	Y	N	Y	N	N	?
8 **Reichert**	N	N	Y	Y	Y	Y	N
9 Smith	N	?	Y	N	N	N	Y
10 Heck	?	?	Y	Y	N	N	Y
WEST VIRGINIA							
1 **McKinley**	N	N	Y	Y	Y	Y	N
2 **Mooney**	N	N	Y	N	Y	Y	N
3 **Jenkins**	N	N	Y	?	Y	Y	N
WISCONSIN							
1 **Ryan**							
2 Pocan	?	?	N	Y	N	N	Y
3 Kind	N	N	Y	N	N	N	Y
4 Moore	Y	Y	N	Y	N	N	?
5 **Sensenbrenner**	N	N	Y	Y	Y	Y	N
6 **Grothman**	N	N	Y	Y	Y	Y	N
7 **Duffy**	N	N	Y	?	Y	Y	N
8 **Gallagher**	–	N	Y	Y	Y	Y	N
WYOMING							
AL **Cheney**	N	N	Y	Y	Y	Y	N

VOTE NUMBER

141. HR 985. CLASS-ACTION LAWSUIT RESTRICTIONS AND ASBESTOS TRUSTS/ATTORNEYS' FEE AWARDS. Deutch, D-Fla., amendment that would remove the bill's requirement that attorneys' fee awards to be based on equitable relief. Rejected in Committee of the Whole 189-228 : R 6-227; D 183-1. March 9, 2017.

142. HR 985. CLASS-ACTION LAWSUIT RESTRICTIONS AND ASBESTOS TRUSTS/DISCOVERY PROCEEDINGS. Soto, D-Fla., amendment that would permit discovery proceedings to continue while various legal motions are pending before a court. Rejected in Committee of the Whole 192-230 : R 5-230; D 187-0. March 9, 2017.

143. HR 985. CLASS-ACTION LAWSUIT RESTRICTIONS AND ASBESTOS TRUSTS/ALLEGED FRAUD. Johnson, D-Ga., amendment that would exempt cases related to civil actions alleging fraud from the bill's provisions related to class actions. Rejected in Committee of the Whole 190-230 : R 4-230; D 186-0. March 9, 2017.

144. HR 985. CLASS-ACTION LAWSUIT RESTRICTIONS AND ASBESTOS TRUSTS/CIVIL RIGHTS. Conyers, D-Mich., amendment that would exempt cases related to civil actions alleging violations of civil rights from the bill's provisions related to class actions. Rejected in Committee of the Whole 191-230 : R 5-230; D 186-0. March 9, 2017.

145. HR 985. CLASS-ACTION LAWSUIT RESTRICTIONS AND ASBESTOS TRUSTS/PUBLIC REPORTS. Jackson Lee, D-Texas, amendment that would replace the bill's provisions related to asbestos trusts with a requirement that asbestos trusts provide a report available to the public regarding demands received and payments made. Rejected in Committee of the Whole 193-229 : R 6-229; D 187-0. March 9, 2017.

146. HR 985. CLASS-ACTION LAWSUIT RESTRICTIONS AND ASBESTOS TRUSTS/PUBLIC HOUSING. Espaillat, D-N.Y., amendment that would exempt claimants living in public housing from the bill's provisions related to asbestos trusts. Rejected in Committee of the Whole 193-228 : R 6-228; D 187-0. March 9, 2017.

147. HR 985. CLASS-ACTION LAWSUIT RESTRICTIONS AND ASBESTOS TRUSTS/RECOMMIT. Kildee, D-Mich., motion to recommit the bill to the House Judiciary Committee with instructions to report it back immediately with an amendment that would exempt from the bill's provisions civil actions related to the protection of public drinking water supplies. Motion rejected 188-234 : R 1-234; D 187-0. March 9, 2017.

	141	142	143	144	145	146	147
ALABAMA							
1 Byrne	N	N	N	N	N	N	N
2 Roby	N	N	N	N	N	N	N
3 Rogers	N	N	N	N	N	N	N
4 Aderholt	?	N	N	N	N	N	N
5 Brooks	N	N	N	N	N	N	N
6 Palmer	N	N	N	N	N	N	N
7 Sewell	Y	Y	Y	Y	Y	Y	Y
ALASKA							
AL Young	N	N	N	N	N	N	N
ARIZONA							
1 O'Halleran	Y	Y	Y	Y	Y	Y	Y
2 McSally	N	N	N	N	N	N	N
3 Grijalva	Y	Y	Y	Y	Y	Y	Y
4 Gosar	N	N	N	N	N	N	N
5 Biggs	N	N	N	N	N	N	N
6 Schweikert	N	N	N	N	N	N	N
7 Gallego	Y	Y	Y	Y	Y	Y	Y
8 Franks	N	N	N	N	N	N	N
9 Sinema	+	+	+	+	+	+	+
ARKANSAS							
1 Crawford	N	N	N	N	N	N	N
2 Hill	N	N	N	N	N	N	N
3 Womack	N	N	N	N	N	N	N
4 Westerman	N	N	N	N	N	N	N
CALIFORNIA							
1 LaMalfa	N	N	N	N	N	N	N
2 Huffman	Y	Y	Y	Y	Y	Y	Y
3 Garamendi	Y	Y	Y	Y	Y	Y	Y
4 McClintock	N	N	N	N	N	N	N
5 Thompson	Y	Y	Y	Y	Y	Y	Y
6 Matsui	+	+	+	+	+	+	+
7 Bera	Y	Y	Y	Y	Y	Y	Y
8 Cook	N	N	N	N	N	N	N
9 McNerney	Y	Y	Y	Y	Y	Y	Y
10 Denham	N	N	N	N	N	N	N
11 DeSaulnier	Y	Y	Y	Y	Y	Y	Y
12 Pelosi	Y	Y	Y	Y	Y	Y	Y
13 Lee	Y	Y	Y	Y	Y	Y	Y
14 Speier	Y	Y	Y	Y	Y	Y	Y
15 Swalwell	Y	Y	Y	Y	Y	Y	Y
16 Costa	Y	Y	Y	Y	Y	Y	Y
17 Khanna	Y	Y	Y	Y	Y	Y	Y
18 Eshoo	Y	Y	Y	Y	Y	Y	Y
19 Lofgren	Y	Y	Y	Y	Y	Y	Y
20 Panetta	Y	Y	Y	Y	Y	Y	Y
21 Valadao	N	N	N	N	N	N	N
22 Nunes	N	N	N	N	N	N	N
23 McCarthy	N	N	N	N	N	N	N
24 Carbajal	Y	Y	Y	Y	Y	Y	Y
25 Knight	N	N	N	N	N	N	N
26 Brownley	Y	Y	Y	Y	Y	Y	Y
27 Chu	Y	Y	Y	Y	Y	Y	Y
28 Schiff	Y	Y	Y	Y	Y	Y	Y
29 Cardenas	Y	Y	Y	Y	Y	Y	Y
30 Sherman	Y	Y	Y	Y	Y	Y	Y
31 Aguilar	Y	Y	Y	Y	Y	Y	Y
32 Napolitano	Y	Y	Y	Y	Y	Y	Y
33 Lieu	Y	Y	Y	Y	Y	Y	Y
34 Vacant							
35 Torres	Y	Y	Y	Y	Y	Y	Y
36 Ruiz	Y	Y	Y	Y	Y	Y	Y
37 Bass	Y	Y	Y	Y	Y	Y	Y
38 Sánchez, Linda	Y	Y	Y	Y	Y	Y	Y
39 Royce	N	N	N	N	N	N	N
40 Roybal-Allard	Y	Y	Y	Y	Y	Y	Y
41 Takano	Y	Y	Y	Y	Y	Y	Y
42 Calvert	N	N	N	N	N	N	N
43 Waters	Y	Y	Y	Y	Y	Y	Y
44 Barragan	Y	Y	Y	Y	Y	Y	Y
45 Walters	N	N	N	N	N	N	N
46 Correa	Y	Y	Y	Y	Y	Y	Y
47 Lowenthal	Y	Y	Y	Y	Y	Y	Y
48 Rohrabacher	N	N	N	N	N	N	N
49 Issa	N	N	N	N	N	N	N
50 Hunter	N	N	N	N	N	N	N
51 Vargas	Y	Y	Y	Y	Y	Y	Y
52 Peters	Y	Y	Y	Y	Y	Y	Y
53 Davis	+	+	+	+	+	+	+

	141	142	143	144	145	146	147
COLORADO							
1 DeGette	Y	Y	Y	Y	Y	Y	Y
2 Polis	Y	Y	Y	Y	Y	Y	Y
3 Tipton	N	N	N	N	N	N	N
4 Buck	N	N	N	N	N	N	N
5 Lamborn	N	N	N	N	N	N	N
6 Coffman	N	N	N	N	N	N	N
7 Perlmutter	Y	Y	Y	Y	Y	Y	Y
CONNECTICUT							
1 Larson	Y	Y	?	Y	Y	Y	Y
2 Courtney	Y	Y	Y	Y	Y	Y	Y
3 DeLauro	Y	Y	Y	Y	Y	Y	Y
4 Himes	Y	Y	Y	Y	Y	Y	Y
5 Esty	Y	Y	Y	Y	Y	Y	Y
DELAWARE							
AL Blunt Rochester	Y	Y	Y	Y	Y	Y	Y
FLORIDA							
1 Gaetz	N	N	N	N	N	N	N
2 Dunn	N	N	N	N	N	N	N
3 Yoho	N	N	–	N	N	N	N
4 Rutherford	N	N	N	N	N	N	N
5 Lawson	Y	Y	Y	Y	Y	Y	Y
6 DeSantis	N	N	N	N	N	N	N
7 Murphy	Y	Y	Y	Y	Y	Y	Y
8 Posey	N	N	N	N	N	N	N
9 Soto	Y	Y	Y	Y	Y	Y	Y
10 Demings	Y	Y	Y	Y	Y	Y	Y
11 Webster	N	N	N	N	N	N	N
12 Bilirakis	N	N	N	N	N	N	N
13 Crist	Y	Y	Y	Y	Y	Y	Y
14 Castor	Y	Y	Y	Y	Y	Y	Y
15 Ross	N	N	N	N	N	N	N
16 Buchanan	N	N	N	N	N	N	N
17 Rooney, T.	N	N	N	N	N	N	N
18 Mast	N	N	N	N	N	N	N
19 Rooney, F.	N	N	N	N	N	N	N
20 Hastings	Y	Y	Y	Y	Y	Y	Y
21 Frankel	Y	Y	Y	Y	Y	Y	Y
22 Deutch	Y	Y	Y	Y	Y	Y	Y
23 Wasserman Schultz	Y	Y	Y	Y	Y	Y	Y
24 Wilson	Y	Y	Y	Y	Y	Y	Y
25 Diaz-Balart	N	N	N	N	N	N	N
26 Curbelo	Y	Y	Y	Y	Y	Y	Y
27 Ros-Lehtinen	Y	Y	N	N	Y	N	Y
GEORGIA							
1 Carter	N	N	N	N	N	N	N
2 Bishop	Y	Y	Y	Y	Y	Y	Y
3 Ferguson	N	N	N	N	N	N	N
4 Johnson	Y	Y	Y	Y	Y	Y	Y
5 Lewis	Y	Y	Y	Y	Y	Y	Y
7 Woodall	N	N	N	N	N	N	N
8 Scott, A.	N	N	N	N	N	N	N
9 Collins	N	N	N	N	N	N	N
10 Hice	N	N	N	N	N	N	N
11 Loudermilk	N	N	N	N	N	N	N
12 Allen	N	N	N	N	N	N	N
13 Scott, D.	Y	Y	Y	Y	Y	Y	Y
14 Graves	N	N	N	N	N	N	N
HAWAII							
1 Hanabusa	Y	Y	Y	Y	Y	Y	Y
2 Gabbard	Y	Y	Y	Y	Y	Y	Y
IDAHO							
1 Labrador	N	N	N	N	N	N	N
2 Simpson	N	N	N	N	N	N	N
ILLINOIS							
1 Rush	?	?	?	?	?	?	?
2 Kelly	Y	Y	Y	Y	Y	Y	Y
3 Lipinski	Y	Y	Y	Y	Y	Y	Y
4 Gutierrez	Y	Y	Y	Y	Y	Y	Y
5 Quigley	Y	Y	Y	Y	Y	Y	Y
6 Roskam	N	N	N	N	N	N	N
7 Davis, D.	Y	Y	Y	Y	Y	Y	Y
8 Krishnamoorthi	Y	Y	Y	Y	Y	Y	Y
9 Schakowsky	Y	Y	Y	Y	Y	Y	Y
10 Schneider	Y	Y	Y	Y	Y	Y	Y
11 Foster	Y	Y	Y	Y	Y	Y	Y
12 Bost	N	N	N	N	N	N	N
13 Davis, R.	N	N	N	N	N	N	N
14 Hultgren	N	N	N	N	N	N	N
15 Shimkus	N	N	N	N	N	N	N

KEY	Republicans		Democrats		Independents	
Y	Voted for (yea)	X	Paired against	C	Voted "present" to avoid possible conflict of interest
#	Paired for	–	Announced against		
+	Announced for	P	Voted "present"	?	Did not vote or otherwise make a position known
N	Voted against (nay)				

	141	142	143	144	145	146	147
16 **Kinzinger**	N	N	N	N	N	N	N
17 Bustos	Y	Y	Y	Y	Y	Y	Y
18 **LaHood**	N	N	N	N	N	N	N
INDIANA							
1 Visclosky	Y	Y	Y	Y	Y	Y	Y
2 **Walorski**	N	N	N	N	N	N	N
3 **Banks**	N	N	N	N	N	N	N
4 **Rokita**	N	N	N	N	N	N	N
5 **Brooks**	N	N	N	N	N	N	N
6 **Messer**	N	N	N	N	N	N	N
7 Carson	Y	Y	Y	Y	Y	Y	Y
8 **Bucshon**	N	N	N	N	N	N	N
9 **Hollingsworth**	N	N	N	N	N	N	N
IOWA							
1 **Blum**	N	N	N	N	N	N	N
2 Loebsack	Y	Y	Y	Y	Y	Y	Y
3 **Young**	N	N	N	N	N	N	N
4 **King**	N	N	N	N	N	N	N
KANSAS							
1 **Marshall**	N	N	N	N	N	N	N
2 **Jenkins**	N	N	N	N	N	N	N
3 **Yoder**	N	N	N	N	N	N	N
KENTUCKY							
1 **Comer**	N	N	N	N	N	N	N
2 **Guthrie**	N	N	N	N	N	N	N
3 Yarmuth	Y	Y	Y	Y	Y	Y	Y
4 **Massie**	N	N	N	N	N	N	N
5 **Rogers**	N	N	N	N	N	N	N
6 **Barr**	N	N	N	N	N	N	N
LOUISIANA							
1 **Scalise**	N	N	N	N	N	N	N
2 Richmond	?	?	?	?	?	?	?
3 **Higgins**	N	N	N	N	N	N	N
4 **Johnson**	N	N	N	N	N	N	N
5 **Abraham**	N	N	N	N	N	N	N
6 **Graves**	N	N	N	N	N	N	N
MAINE							
1 Pingree	Y	Y	Y	Y	Y	Y	Y
2 **Poliquin**	N	N	N	N	N	N	N
MARYLAND							
1 **Harris**	N	N	N	N	N	N	N
2 Ruppersberger	Y	Y	Y	Y	Y	Y	Y
3 Sarbanes	Y	Y	Y	Y	Y	Y	Y
4 Brown	Y	Y	Y	Y	Y	Y	Y
5 Hoyer	Y	Y	Y	Y	Y	Y	Y
6 Delaney	Y	Y	Y	Y	Y	Y	Y
7 Cummings	Y	Y	Y	Y	Y	Y	Y
8 Raskin	Y	Y	Y	Y	Y	Y	Y
MASSACHUSETTS							
1 Neal	Y	Y	Y	Y	Y	Y	Y
2 McGovern	Y	Y	Y	Y	Y	Y	Y
3 Tsongas	Y	Y	Y	Y	Y	Y	Y
4 Kennedy	Y	Y	Y	Y	Y	Y	Y
5 Clark	Y	Y	Y	Y	Y	Y	Y
6 Moulton	Y	Y	Y	Y	Y	Y	Y
7 Capuano	Y	Y	Y	Y	Y	Y	Y
8 Lynch	Y	Y	Y	Y	Y	Y	Y
9 Keating	Y	Y	Y	Y	Y	Y	Y
MICHIGAN							
1 **Bergman**	N	N	N	N	N	N	N
2 **Huizenga**	N	N	N	N	N	N	N
3 **Amash**	Y	Y	N	N	N	N	N
4 **Moolenaar**	N	N	N	N	N	N	N
5 Kildee	Y	Y	Y	Y	Y	Y	Y
6 **Upton**	N	N	N	N	N	N	N
7 **Walberg**	N	N	N	N	N	N	N
8 **Bishop**	N	N	N	N	N	N	N
9 Levin	Y	Y	Y	Y	Y	Y	Y
10 **Mitchell**	N	N	N	N	N	N	N
11 **Trott**	N	N	N	N	N	N	N
12 Dingell	Y	Y	Y	Y	Y	Y	Y
13 Conyers	Y	Y	Y	Y	Y	Y	Y
14 Lawrence	Y	Y	Y	Y	Y	Y	Y
MINNESOTA							
1 Walz	Y	Y	Y	Y	Y	Y	Y
2 **Lewis**	N	N	N	N	N	N	N
3 **Paulsen**	N	N	N	N	N	N	N
4 McCollum	Y	Y	Y	Y	Y	Y	Y

	141	142	143	144	145	146	147
5 Ellison	?	Y	Y	Y	Y	Y	Y
6 **Emmer**	N	N	N	N	N	N	N
7 Peterson	Y	Y	Y	Y	Y	Y	Y
8 Nolan	Y	Y	Y	Y	Y	Y	Y
MISSISSIPPI							
1 **Kelly**	N	N	N	N	N	N	N
2 Thompson	Y	Y	Y	Y	Y	Y	Y
3 **Harper**	N	N	N	N	N	N	N
4 **Palazzo**	N	N	N	N	N	N	N
MISSOURI							
1 Clay	Y	Y	Y	?	Y	Y	Y
2 **Wagner**	N	N	N	N	N	N	N
3 **Luetkemeyer**	N	N	N	N	N	N	N
4 **Hartzler**	N	N	N	N	N	N	N
5 Cleaver	?	Y	Y	Y	Y	Y	Y
6 **Graves**	N	N	N	N	N	N	N
7 **Long**	N	N	N	N	N	N	N
8 **Smith**	N	N	N	N	N	N	N
MONTANA							
AL **Vacant**							
NEBRASKA							
1 **Fortenberry**	N	N	N	N	N	N	N
2 **Bacon**	N	N	N	N	N	N	N
3 **Smith**	N	N	N	N	N	N	N
NEVADA							
1 Titus	?	?	?	?	?	?	?
2 **Amodei**	N	N	N	N	N	N	N
3 Rosen	Y	Y	Y	Y	Y	Y	Y
4 Kihuen	Y	Y	Y	Y	Y	Y	Y
NEW HAMPSHIRE							
1 Shea-Porter	Y	Y	Y	Y	Y	Y	Y
2 Kuster	Y	Y	Y	Y	Y	Y	Y
NEW JERSEY							
1 Norcross	Y	Y	Y	Y	Y	Y	Y
2 **LoBiondo**	N	N	N	N	Y	N	N
3 **MacArthur**	N	N	N	N	N	N	N
4 **Smith**	N	N	N	N	N	N	N
5 Gottheimer	Y	Y	Y	Y	Y	Y	Y
6 Pallone	Y	Y	Y	Y	Y	Y	Y
7 **Lance**	N	N	N	N	N	N	N
8 Sires	Y	Y	Y	Y	Y	Y	Y
9 Pascrell	Y	Y	Y	Y	Y	Y	Y
10 Payne	Y	Y	Y	Y	Y	Y	Y
11 **Frelinghuysen**	N	N	N	N	N	N	N
12 Watson Coleman	Y	Y	Y	Y	Y	Y	Y
NEW MEXICO							
1 Lujan Grisham	Y	Y	Y	Y	Y	Y	Y
2 **Pearce**	N	N	N	N	N	N	N
3 Luján	Y	Y	Y	Y	Y	Y	Y
NEW YORK							
1 **Zeldin**	N	N	N	N	N	N	N
2 **King**	N	N	N	N	N	N	N
3 Suozzi	Y	Y	Y	Y	Y	Y	Y
4 Rice	Y	Y	Y	Y	Y	Y	Y
5 Meeks	Y	Y	Y	Y	Y	Y	Y
6 Meng	Y	Y	Y	Y	Y	Y	Y
7 Velázquez	Y	Y	Y	Y	Y	Y	Y
8 Jeffries	Y	Y	Y	Y	Y	Y	Y
9 Clarke	Y	Y	Y	Y	Y	Y	Y
10 Nadler	Y	Y	Y	Y	Y	Y	Y
11 **Donovan**	N	N	N	N	N	N	N
12 Maloney, C.	Y	Y	Y	Y	Y	Y	Y
13 Espaillat	Y	Y	Y	Y	Y	Y	Y
14 Crowley	Y	Y	Y	Y	Y	Y	Y
15 Serrano	N	Y	Y	Y	Y	Y	Y
16 Engel	Y	Y	Y	Y	Y	Y	Y
17 Lowey	Y	Y	Y	Y	Y	Y	Y
18 Maloney, S.P.	Y	Y	Y	Y	Y	Y	Y
19 **Faso**	N	N	Y	Y	N	Y	N
20 Tonko	Y	Y	Y	Y	Y	Y	Y
21 **Stefanik**	N	N	N	N	N	N	N
22 **Tenney**	N	N	N	N	N	N	N
23 **Reed**	N	N	N	N	N	N	N
24 **Katko**	?	N	N	N	N	N	N
25 Slaughter	Y	Y	Y	Y	Y	Y	Y
26 Higgins	Y	Y	Y	Y	Y	Y	Y
27 **Collins**	N	N	N	N	N	N	N
NORTH CAROLINA							
1 Butterfield	Y	Y	Y	Y	Y	Y	Y
2 **Holding**	N	N	N	N	N	N	N
3 **Jones**	Y	Y	Y	Y	Y	Y	Y
4 Price	Y	Y	Y	Y	Y	Y	Y

	141	142	143	144	145	146	147
5 **Foxx**	N	N	N	N	N	N	N
6 **Walker**	N	N	N	N	N	N	N
7 **Rouzer**	N	N	N	N	N	N	N
8 **Hudson**	N	N	N	N	N	N	N
9 **Pittenger**	N	N	N	N	N	N	N
10 **McHenry**	N	N	N	N	N	N	N
11 **Meadows**	N	N	N	N	N	N	N
12 Adams	Y	Y	Y	Y	Y	Y	Y
13 **Budd**	N	N	N	N	N	N	N
NORTH DAKOTA							
AL **Cramer**	N	N	N	N	N	N	N
OHIO							
1 **Chabot**	N	N	N	N	N	N	N
2 **Wenstrup**	N	N	N	N	N	N	N
3 Beatty	Y	Y	Y	Y	Y	Y	Y
4 **Jordan**	N	N	N	N	N	N	N
5 **Latta**	N	N	N	N	N	N	N
6 **Johnson**	N	N	N	N	N	N	N
7 **Gibbs**	N	N	N	N	N	N	N
8 **Davidson**	N	N	N	N	N	N	N
9 Kaptur	?	Y	Y	Y	Y	Y	Y
10 **Turner**	N	N	N	N	N	N	N
11 Fudge	Y	Y	Y	Y	Y	Y	Y
12 **Tiberi**	N	N	N	N	N	N	N
13 Ryan	Y	Y	Y	Y	Y	Y	Y
14 **Joyce**	N	N	N	N	N	?	N
15 **Stivers**	N	N	N	N	N	N	N
16 **Renacci**	N	N	N	N	N	N	N
OKLAHOMA							
1 **Bridenstine**	N	N	N	N	N	N	N
2 **Mullin**	N	N	N	N	N	N	N
3 **Lucas**	N	N	N	N	N	N	N
4 **Cole**	N	N	N	N	N	N	N
5 **Russell**	Y	Y	Y	Y	Y	Y	N
OREGON							
1 Bonamici	Y	Y	Y	Y	Y	Y	Y
2 **Walden**	N	N	N	N	N	N	N
3 Blumenauer	Y	Y	Y	Y	Y	Y	Y
4 DeFazio	Y	Y	Y	Y	Y	Y	Y
5 Schrader	Y	Y	Y	Y	Y	Y	Y
PENNSYLVANIA							
1 Brady	Y	Y	Y	Y	Y	Y	Y
2 Evans	Y	Y	Y	Y	Y	Y	Y
3 **Kelly**	N	N	N	N	N	N	N
4 **Perry**	N	N	N	N	N	N	N
5 **Thompson**	N	N	N	N	N	N	N
6 **Costello**	N	N	N	N	N	N	N
7 **Meehan**	N	N	N	N	N	N	N
8 **Fitzpatrick**	N	N	N	Y	N	N	N
9 **Shuster**	N	N	N	N	N	N	N
10 **Marino**	N	N	N	N	N	N	N
11 **Barletta**	–	–	–	–	–	–	–
12 **Rothfus**	N	N	N	N	N	N	N
13 Boyle	Y	Y	Y	Y	Y	Y	Y
14 Doyle	Y	Y	Y	Y	Y	Y	Y
15 **Dent**	N	N	N	N	N	N	N
16 **Smucker**	N	N	N	N	N	N	N
17 Cartwright	Y	Y	Y	Y	Y	Y	Y
18 **Murphy**	N	N	N	N	N	N	N
RHODE ISLAND							
1 Cicilline	Y	Y	Y	Y	Y	Y	Y
2 Langevin	Y	Y	Y	Y	Y	Y	Y
SOUTH CAROLINA							
1 **Sanford**	N	N	N	N	N	N	N
2 **Wilson**	N	N	N	N	N	N	N
3 **Duncan**	N	N	N	N	N	N	N
4 **Gowdy**	N	N	N	N	N	N	N
6 Clyburn	Y	Y	Y	Y	Y	Y	Y
7 **Rice**	N	N	N	N	N	N	N
SOUTH DAKOTA							
AL **Noem**	N	N	N	N	N	N	N
TENNESSEE							
1 **Roe**	N	N	N	N	N	N	N
2 **Duncan**	N	N	N	N	N	N	N
3 **Fleischmann**	N	N	N	N	N	N	N
4 **DesJarlais**	N	N	N	N	N	N	N
5 Cooper	Y	Y	Y	Y	Y	Y	Y
6 **Black**	N	N	N	N	N	N	N
7 **Blackburn**	N	N	N	N	N	N	N
8 **Kustoff**	N	N	N	N	N	N	N
9 Cohen	Y	Y	Y	Y	Y	Y	Y

	141	142	143	144	145	146	147
TEXAS							
1 **Gohmert**	N	N	N	N	N	N	N
2 **Poe**	N	N	N	N	N	N	N
3 **Johnson, S.**	N	N	N	N	N	N	N
4 **Ratcliffe**	N	N	N	N	N	N	N
5 **Hensarling**	N	N	N	N	N	N	N
6 **Barton**	N	N	N	N	N	N	N
7 **Culberson**	N	N	N	N	N	N	N
8 **Brady**	N	N	N	N	N	N	N
9 Green, A.	Y	Y	Y	Y	Y	Y	Y
10 **McCaul**	N	N	N	N	N	N	N
11 **Conaway**	N	N	N	N	N	N	N
12 **Granger**	N	N	N	N	N	N	N
13 **Thornberry**	N	N	N	N	N	N	N
14 **Weber**	N	N	N	N	N	N	N
15 Gonzalez	Y	Y	Y	Y	Y	Y	Y
16 O'Rourke	Y	Y	Y	Y	Y	Y	Y
17 **Flores**	N	N	N	N	N	N	N
18 Jackson Lee	Y	Y	Y	Y	Y	Y	Y
19 **Arrington**	N	N	N	N	N	N	N
20 Castro	Y	Y	Y	Y	Y	Y	Y
21 **Smith**	N	N	N	N	N	N	N
22 **Olson**	N	N	N	N	N	N	N
23 **Hurd**	N	N	N	N	N	N	N
24 **Marchant**	N	N	N	N	N	N	N
25 **Williams**	N	N	N	N	N	N	N
26 **Burgess**	N	N	N	N	N	N	N
27 **Farenthold**	N	N	N	N	N	N	N
28 Cuellar	Y	Y	Y	Y	Y	Y	Y
29 Green, G.	Y	Y	Y	Y	Y	Y	Y
30 Johnson, E.B.	Y	Y	Y	Y	Y	Y	Y
31 **Carter**	N	N	N	N	N	N	N
32 **Sessions**	N	N	N	N	N	N	N
33 Veasey	Y	Y	Y	Y	Y	Y	Y
34 Vela	Y	Y	Y	Y	Y	Y	Y
35 Doggett	Y	Y	Y	Y	Y	Y	Y
36 **Babin**	N	N	N	N	N	N	N
UTAH							
1 **Bishop**	N	N	N	N	N	N	N
2 **Stewart**	N	N	N	N	N	N	N
3 **Chaffetz**	N	N	N	N	N	N	N
4 **Love**	N	N	N	N	N	N	N
VERMONT							
AL Welch	Y	Y	Y	Y	Y	Y	Y
VIRGINIA							
1 **Wittman**	N	N	N	N	N	N	N
2 **Taylor**	N	N	N	N	N	N	N
3 Scott	Y	Y	Y	Y	Y	Y	Y
4 McEachin	Y	Y	Y	Y	Y	Y	Y
5 **Garrett**	N	N	N	N	N	N	N
6 **Goodlatte**	N	N	N	N	N	N	N
7 **Brat**	N	N	N	N	N	N	N
8 Beyer	Y	Y	Y	Y	Y	Y	Y
9 **Griffith**	N	N	N	N	N	N	N
10 **Comstock**	N	N	N	N	N	N	N
11 Connolly	Y	Y	Y	Y	Y	Y	Y
WASHINGTON							
1 DelBene	Y	Y	Y	Y	Y	Y	Y
2 Larsen	Y	Y	Y	Y	Y	Y	Y
3 **Herrera Beutler**	N	N	N	N	N	N	N
4 **Newhouse**	N	N	N	N	N	N	N
5 **McMorris Rodgers**	N	N	N	N	N	N	N
6 Kilmer	Y	Y	Y	Y	Y	Y	Y
7 Jayapal	Y	Y	Y	Y	Y	Y	Y
8 **Reichert**	N	N	N	N	N	N	N
9 Smith	Y	Y	Y	Y	Y	Y	Y
10 Heck	Y	Y	Y	Y	Y	Y	Y
WEST VIRGINIA							
1 **McKinley**	N	N	N	N	Y	N	N
2 **Mooney**	N	N	N	N	N	N	N
3 **Jenkins**	N	N	N	N	N	N	N
WISCONSIN							
1 **Ryan**							
2 Pocan	Y	Y	Y	Y	Y	Y	Y
3 Kind	Y	Y	Y	Y	Y	Y	Y
4 Moore	Y	Y	Y	Y	Y	Y	Y
5 **Sensenbrenner**	N	N	N	N	N	N	N
6 **Grothman**	N	N	N	N	N	N	N
7 **Duffy**	N	N	N	N	N	N	N
8 **Gallagher**	N	N	N	N	N	N	N
WYOMING							
AL **Cheney**	N	N	N	N	N	N	N

VOTE NUMBER

148. HR 985. CLASS-ACTION LAWSUIT RESTRICTIONS AND ASBESTOS TRUSTS/PASSAGE. Passage of the bill that would prohibit federal courts from certifying proposed classes of individuals for a class-action lawsuit unless each member of the class has suffered the same type and degree of injury. Additionally, the bill would require asbestos trusts to issue quarterly reports on claims made against the trusts and payouts made by the trusts for asbestos-related injuries. Passed 220-201 : R 220-14; D 0-187. March 9, 2017.

149. HR 725. FRAUDULENT JOINDER/PUBLIC HEALTH RISKS. Soto, D-Fla., amendment that would exempt cases in which the plaintiff seeks compensation for public health risks, including byproducts from hydraulic fracturing or water contamination. Rejected in Committee of the Whole 189-233 : R 3-232; D 186-1. March 9, 2017.

150. HR 725. FRAUDULENT JOINDER/BAD FAITH INSURERS. Cartwright, D-Pa., amendment that would exempt cases in which the plaintiff seeks compensation related to the bad faith of an insurer. Rejected in Committee of the Whole 187-229 : R 5-229; D 182-0. March 9, 2017.

151. HR 725. FRAUDULENT JOINDER/RECOMMIT. Kuster, D-N.H., motion to recommit the bill to the House Judiciary Committee with instructions to report it back immediately with an amendment that would exempt from the bill's provisions civil actions related to government ethics. Motion rejected 187-233 : R 1-233; D 186-0. March 9, 2017.

152. HR 725. FRAUDULENT JOINDER/PASSAGE. Passage of the bill that would — for purposes of determining whether certain lawsuits are sent back from federal to state courts — establish a new standard for determining whether a defendant has been fraudulently joined to a case. Under the measure, federal courts would have to deny motions to remand a case back to state court if the court finds that there was fraud in the jurisdictional claim, the plaintiff's claim against that defendant is not possible or plausible under state law, or the plaintiff did not make their claim in good faith. Passed 224-194 : R 224-10; D 0-184. March 9, 2017.

153. HR 720. FRIVOLOUS' LAWSUITS/WITHDRAWAL TIME PERIOD. Soto, D-Fla., that would retain and modify the so-called "safe harbor" clause related to frivolous civil lawsuits by allowing parties to withdraw or correct claims considered frivolous within 14 days of filing. Rejected in Committee of the Whole 181-225 : R 3-224; D 178-1. March, 10, 2017.

154. HR 720. FRIVOLOUS' LAWSUITS/SANCTIONS REMOVAL. Jackson Lee, D-Texas, amendment that would remove the bill's provision that sanctions for frivolous lawsuits would need to include monetary payments to the other party to cover the other party's attorney fees and costs. Rejected in Committee of the Whole 185-225 : R 4-224; D 181-1. March, 10, 2017.

	148	149	150	151	152	153	154
ALABAMA							
1 Byrne	Y	N	N	N	Y	N	N
2 Roby	Y	N	N	N	Y	N	N
3 Rogers	N	N	N	N	Y	N	N
4 Aderholt	Y	N	N	N	Y	N	N
5 Brooks	Y	N	N	N	Y	N	N
6 Palmer	Y	N	N	N	Y	N	N
7 Sewell	N	Y	Y	Y	N	Y	Y
ALASKA							
AL Young	Y	N	N	N	Y	N	N
ARIZONA							
1 O'Halleran	N	Y	Y	Y	N	?	Y
2 McSally	Y	N	N	N	Y	N	N
3 Grijalva	N	Y	Y	Y	N	Y	Y
4 Gosar	Y	N	N	N	Y	N	N
5 Biggs	Y	N	N	N	Y	N	N
6 Schweikert	Y	N	N	N	Y	N	N
7 Gallego	N	Y	Y	Y	N	Y	Y
8 Franks	Y	N	N	N	Y	N	N
9 Sinema	–	+	+	+	–	+	+
ARKANSAS							
1 Crawford	Y	N	N	N	Y	N	N
2 Hill	Y	N	N	N	Y	N	N
3 Womack	Y	N	N	N	Y	N	N
4 Westerman	Y	N	N	N	Y	N	N
CALIFORNIA							
1 LaMalfa	Y	N	N	N	Y	N	N
2 Huffman	N	Y	Y	Y	N	Y	Y
3 Garamendi	N	Y	Y	Y	N	Y	Y
4 McClintock	Y	N	N	N	Y	N	?
5 Thompson	N	Y	Y	Y	N	Y	Y
6 Matsui	–	+	+	+	–	Y	Y
7 Bera	N	Y	Y	Y	N	Y	Y
8 Cook	Y	N	N	N	Y	N	N
9 McNerney	N	Y	Y	Y	N	Y	Y
10 Denham	Y	N	N	N	Y	N	N
11 DeSaulnier	N	Y	Y	Y	N	?	Y
12 Pelosi	N	Y	?	Y	N	Y	Y
13 Lee	N	Y	Y	Y	N	Y	Y
14 Speier	N	Y	Y	Y	N	Y	Y
15 Swalwell	N	Y	Y	Y	N	Y	Y
16 Costa	N	Y	Y	Y	N	N	N
17 Khanna	N	Y	Y	Y	N	Y	Y
18 Eshoo	N	Y	Y	Y	N	Y	Y
19 Lofgren	N	Y	Y	Y	N	Y	Y
20 Panetta	N	Y	Y	Y	N	Y	Y
21 Valadao	Y	N	N	N	Y	N	N
22 Nunes	Y	N	N	N	Y	N	N
23 McCarthy	Y	N	N	N	Y	N	N
24 Carbajal	N	Y	Y	Y	N	Y	Y
25 Knight	Y	N	N	N	Y	N	N
26 Brownley	N	Y	Y	Y	N	Y	Y
27 Chu	N	Y	Y	Y	N	Y	Y
28 Schiff	N	Y	Y	Y	N	Y	Y
29 Cardenas	N	Y	Y	Y	N	Y	Y
30 Sherman	N	Y	Y	Y	N	Y	Y
31 Aguilar	N	Y	Y	Y	N	Y	Y
32 Napolitano	N	Y	Y	Y	N	Y	Y
33 Lieu	N	Y	Y	Y	N	Y	Y
34 Vacant							
35 Torres	N	Y	Y	Y	N	Y	Y
36 Ruiz	N	Y	Y	Y	N	Y	Y
37 Bass	N	Y	Y	Y	N	Y	Y
38 Sánchez, Linda	N	Y	Y	Y	N	Y	Y
39 Royce	Y	N	N	N	Y	N	N
40 Roybal-Allard	N	Y	Y	Y	N	Y	+
41 Takano	N	Y	Y	Y	N	Y	Y
42 Calvert	Y	N	N	N	Y	N	N
43 Waters	N	Y	Y	Y	N	?	Y
44 Barragan	N	Y	Y	Y	N	Y	Y
45 Walters	Y	N	N	N	Y	N	N
46 Correa	N	Y	Y	Y	N	Y	Y
47 Lowenthal	N	Y	Y	Y	N	Y	Y
48 Rohrabacher	Y	N	N	N	Y	N	N
49 Issa	Y	N	N	N	Y	N	N
50 Hunter	Y	N	N	N	Y	N	N
51 Vargas	N	Y	Y	Y	N	Y	Y
52 Peters	N	Y	Y	Y	N	Y	Y
53 Davis	–	+	+	+	–	+	+

	148	149	150	151	152	153	154
COLORADO							
1 DeGette	N	Y	Y	Y	N	Y	Y
2 Polis	N	Y	Y	Y	N	Y	Y
3 Tipton	Y	N	N	N	Y	N	N
4 Buck	Y	N	N	N	Y	?	?
5 Lamborn	Y	N	N	N	Y	N	N
6 Coffman	Y	N	N	N	Y	N	N
7 Perlmutter	N	Y	Y	Y	N	Y	Y
CONNECTICUT							
1 Larson	N	Y	Y	Y	N	Y	Y
2 Courtney	N	Y	Y	Y	N	Y	Y
3 DeLauro	N	Y	Y	Y	N	Y	Y
4 Himes	N	Y	Y	Y	N	Y	Y
5 Esty	N	Y	Y	Y	N	Y	Y
DELAWARE							
AL Blunt Rochester	N	Y	Y	Y	N	Y	Y
FLORIDA							
1 Gaetz	Y	N	N	N	Y	N	?
2 Dunn	Y	N	N	N	Y	N	N
3 Yoho	Y	N	N	N	Y	N	N
4 Rutherford	Y	N	N	N	Y	N	N
5 Lawson	N	Y	Y	Y	N	Y	Y
6 DeSantis	Y	N	N	N	Y	N	N
7 Murphy	N	Y	Y	Y	N	Y	Y
8 Posey	Y	N	N	N	Y	N	N
9 Soto	N	Y	Y	Y	N	Y	Y
10 Demings	N	Y	Y	Y	N	Y	Y
11 Webster	Y	N	N	N	Y	N	N
12 Bilirakis	Y	N	N	N	Y	N	N
13 Crist	N	Y	Y	Y	N	Y	Y
14 Castor	N	Y	Y	Y	N	Y	Y
15 Ross	Y	N	N	N	Y	N	N
16 Buchanan	Y	N	N	N	Y	N	N
17 Rooney, T.	Y	N	?	?	N	N	N
18 Mast	Y	N	N	N	Y	N	N
19 Rooney, F.	Y	N	N	N	Y	N	N
20 Hastings	N	Y	Y	Y	N	Y	Y
21 Frankel	N	Y	Y	Y	N	Y	Y
22 Deutch	N	Y	Y	Y	N	Y	Y
23 Wasserman Schultz	N	Y	Y	Y	N	Y	Y
24 Wilson	N	Y	Y	Y	N	Y	Y
25 Diaz-Balart	N	N	N	N	N	N	N
26 Curbelo	N	Y	Y	Y	N	Y	Y
27 Ros-Lehtinen	N	Y	Y	Y	N	Y	Y
GEORGIA							
1 Carter	Y	N	N	Y	N	–	N
2 Bishop	N	Y	Y	Y	N	Y	Y
3 Ferguson	Y	N	N	N	Y	N	N
4 Johnson	N	Y	Y	Y	N	Y	Y
5 Lewis	N	Y	Y	Y	N	Y	Y
7 Woodall	Y	N	N	N	Y	N	N
8 Scott, A.	Y	N	N	N	Y	N	N
9 Collins	Y	N	N	N	Y	N	N
10 Hice	Y	N	N	N	Y	N	N
11 Loudermilk	Y	N	N	N	Y	N	N
12 Allen	Y	N	N	N	Y	N	N
13 Scott, D.	N	Y	Y	Y	N	Y	Y
14 Graves	Y	N	N	N	Y	N	N
HAWAII							
1 Hanabusa	N	Y	Y	Y	N	Y	Y
2 Gabbard	N	Y	Y	Y	N	Y	Y
IDAHO							
1 Labrador	Y	N	N	N	Y	N	N
2 Simpson	Y	N	N	N	Y	N	N
ILLINOIS							
1 Rush	?	?	?	?	?	?	?
2 Kelly	N	Y	Y	Y	N	Y	Y
3 Lipinski	N	Y	Y	Y	N	Y	Y
4 Gutierrez	N	Y	?	Y	N	Y	Y
5 Quigley	N	Y	Y	Y	N	Y	Y
6 Roskam	Y	N	N	N	Y	N	N
7 Davis, D.	N	Y	Y	Y	N	Y	Y
8 Krishnamoorthi	N	Y	Y	Y	N	Y	Y
9 Schakowsky	N	Y	Y	Y	N	Y	Y
10 Schneider	N	Y	Y	Y	N	Y	Y
11 Foster	N	Y	Y	Y	N	Y	Y
12 Bost	Y	N	N	N	Y	N	N
13 Davis, R.	Y	N	N	N	Y	N	N
14 Hultgren	Y	N	N	N	Y	N	N
15 Shimkus	Y	N	N	N	Y	N	N

KEY	**Republicans**	Democrats	*Independents*
Y Voted for (yea)	X Paired against	C Voted "present" to avoid possible conflict of interest
# Paired for	– Announced against	
+ Announced for	P Voted "present"	? Did not vote or otherwise make a position known
N Voted against (nay)		

	148	149	150	151	152	153	154
16 **Kinzinger**	Y	N	N	N	Y	N	N
17 Bustos	N	Y	Y	Y	N	Y	Y
18 **LaHood**	Y	N	N	N	Y	N	N
INDIANA							
1 Visclosky	N	Y	Y	Y	N	Y	Y
2 **Walorski**	Y	N	N	N	Y	N	N
3 **Banks**	Y	N	N	N	Y	?	N
4 **Rokita**	Y	N	N	N	Y	N	N
5 **Brooks**	Y	N	N	N	Y	N	N
6 **Messer**	Y	N	N	N	Y	N	N
7 Carson	N	Y	Y	Y	N	Y	Y
8 **Bucshon**	Y	N	N	N	Y	N	N
9 **Hollingsworth**	Y	N	N	N	Y	N	N
IOWA							
1 **Blum**	Y	N	N	N	Y	N	N
2 Loebsack	N	Y	Y	Y	N	Y	Y
3 **Young**	Y	N	N	N	Y	N	N
4 **King**	Y	N	–	N	Y	N	N
KANSAS							
1 **Marshall**	Y	N	N	N	Y	N	N
2 **Jenkins**	Y	N	N	N	Y	N	N
3 **Yoder**	Y	N	N	N	Y	N	N
KENTUCKY							
1 **Comer**	Y	N	N	N	Y	N	N
2 **Guthrie**	Y	N	N	N	Y	N	N
3 Yarmuth	N	Y	Y	Y	N	Y	Y
4 **Massie**	N	N	N	N	Y	N	N
5 **Rogers**	Y	N	N	N	Y	N	N
6 **Barr**	Y	N	N	N	Y	N	N
LOUISIANA							
1 **Scalise**	Y	N	N	N	Y	N	N
2 Richmond	?	?	?	?	?	?	?
3 **Higgins**	Y	N	N	N	Y	N	N
4 **Johnson**	Y	N	N	N	Y	N	N
5 **Abraham**	Y	N	N	N	Y	N	N
6 **Graves**	Y	N	N	N	Y	N	N
MAINE							
1 Pingree	N	Y	Y	Y	N	Y	Y
2 **Poliquin**	Y	N	N	N	Y	N	N
MARYLAND							
1 **Harris**	Y	N	N	N	Y	N	N
2 Ruppersberger	N	Y	Y	Y	N	Y	Y
3 Sarbanes	N	Y	Y	Y	N	Y	Y
4 Brown	N	Y	Y	Y	N	Y	Y
5 Hoyer	N	Y	Y	Y	N	Y	Y
6 Delaney	N	Y	Y	Y	N	Y	Y
7 Cummings	N	Y	Y	Y	N	Y	Y
8 Raskin	N	Y	Y	Y	N	Y	Y
MASSACHUSETTS							
1 Neal	N	Y	Y	Y	N	Y	Y
2 McGovern	N	Y	Y	Y	N	Y	Y
3 Tsongas	N	Y	Y	Y	N	Y	Y
4 Kennedy	N	Y	Y	Y	N	Y	Y
5 Clark	N	Y	Y	Y	?	Y	Y
6 Moulton	N	Y	Y	Y	N	Y	Y
7 Capuano	N	Y	Y	Y	N	Y	Y
8 Lynch	N	Y	Y	Y	N	?	Y
9 Keating	N	Y	Y	Y	N	Y	Y
MICHIGAN							
1 **Bergman**	Y	N	N	N	Y	N	N
2 **Huizenga**	Y	N	N	N	Y	N	N
3 **Amash**	N	N	N	N	N	N	–
4 **Moolenaar**	Y	N	N	N	Y	N	N
5 Kildee	N	Y	Y	Y	N	Y	Y
6 **Upton**	Y	N	N	N	Y	N	N
7 **Walberg**	Y	N	N	N	Y	N	N
8 **Bishop**	Y	N	N	N	Y	N	N
9 Levin	N	Y	Y	Y	N	Y	Y
10 **Mitchell**	Y	N	N	N	Y	N	N
11 **Trott**	Y	N	N	N	Y	N	N
12 Dingell	N	Y	Y	Y	N	Y	Y
13 Conyers	N	Y	Y	Y	N	Y	Y
14 Lawrence	N	Y	Y	Y	N	Y	Y
MINNESOTA							
1 Walz	N	Y	Y	Y	N	?	Y
2 **Lewis**	Y	N	N	N	Y	N	N
3 **Paulsen**	Y	N	N	N	Y	N	N
4 McCollum	N	Y	Y	Y	N	Y	Y

	148	149	150	151	152	153	154
5 Ellison	N	Y	Y	Y	N	Y	Y
6 **Emmer**	Y	N	N	N	Y	N	N
7 Peterson	N	Y	Y	Y	N	Y	Y
8 Nolan	N	Y	Y	Y	N	Y	Y
MISSISSIPPI							
1 **Kelly**	Y	N	N	N	Y	N	N
2 Thompson	N	Y	Y	Y	N	Y	Y
3 **Harper**	Y	N	N	N	Y	N	N
4 **Palazzo**	Y	N	N	N	Y	?	N
MISSOURI							
1 Clay	N	Y	Y	Y	N	Y	Y
2 **Wagner**	Y	N	N	N	Y	N	N
3 **Luetkemeyer**	Y	N	N	N	Y	N	N
4 **Hartzler**	Y	N	N	N	Y	N	N
5 Cleaver	N	Y	Y	Y	N	Y	Y
6 **Graves**	Y	N	N	N	Y	N	N
7 **Long**	Y	N	N	N	Y	N	N
8 **Smith**	Y	N	N	N	Y	N	N
MONTANA							
AL **Vacant**							
NEBRASKA							
1 **Fortenberry**	Y	N	N	N	Y	N	N
2 **Bacon**	Y	N	N	N	Y	N	N
3 **Smith**	Y	N	N	N	Y	N	N
NEVADA							
1 Titus	?	?	?	?	?	?	?
2 **Amodei**	Y	N	N	N	Y	N	N
3 Rosen	N	Y	Y	Y	N	Y	Y
4 Kihuen	N	Y	Y	Y	N	Y	Y
NEW HAMPSHIRE							
1 Shea-Porter	N	Y	Y	Y	N	Y	Y
2 Kuster	N	Y	Y	Y	N	+	+
NEW JERSEY							
1 Norcross	N	Y	Y	Y	N	Y	Y
2 **LoBiondo**	N	N	N	N	Y	N	N
3 **MacArthur**	Y	N	N	N	Y	N	N
4 **Smith**	Y	N	N	N	Y	N	N
5 Gottheimer	N	Y	Y	Y	N	Y	Y
6 Pallone	N	Y	Y	Y	N	Y	Y
7 **Lance**	Y	N	N	N	Y	N	N
8 Sires	N	Y	Y	Y	N	Y	Y
9 Pascrell	N	Y	Y	Y	N	Y	Y
10 Payne	N	Y	Y	Y	N	Y	Y
11 **Frelinghuysen**	Y	N	N	N	Y	N	N
12 Watson Coleman	N	Y	Y	Y	N	Y	Y
NEW MEXICO							
1 Lujan Grisham	N	Y	Y	Y	N	Y	Y
2 **Pearce**	Y	N	N	N	Y	N	N
3 Luján	N	Y	Y	Y	N	Y	Y
NEW YORK							
1 **Zeldin**	Y	N	N	N	Y	N	N
2 **King**	Y	N	N	N	Y	N	N
3 Suozzi	N	Y	Y	Y	N	Y	Y
4 Rice	N	Y	Y	Y	N	Y	Y
5 Meeks	N	Y	Y	Y	N	Y	Y
6 Meng	N	Y	Y	Y	N	Y	Y
7 Velázquez	N	Y	Y	Y	N	Y	Y
8 Jeffries	N	Y	Y	Y	N	Y	Y
9 Clarke	N	Y	Y	Y	N	Y	Y
10 Nadler	N	Y	Y	Y	N	Y	Y
11 **Donovan**	Y	N	N	N	Y	N	N
12 Maloney, C.	N	Y	Y	Y	N	Y	Y
13 Espaillat	N	Y	Y	Y	N	Y	Y
14 Crowley	N	Y	Y	Y	N	Y	Y
15 Serrano	N	Y	Y	Y	N	Y	Y
16 Engel	N	Y	Y	Y	N	Y	Y
17 Lowey	N	Y	Y	Y	N	Y	Y
18 Maloney, S.P.	N	Y	Y	Y	?	Y	Y
19 **Faso**	N	N	N	N	Y	N	?
20 Tonko	N	Y	Y	Y	N	Y	Y
21 **Stefanik**	Y	N	N	N	Y	N	N
22 **Tenney**	Y	N	N	N	Y	N	N
23 **Reed**	Y	N	N	N	Y	N	N
24 **Katko**	Y	N	N	N	Y	N	N
25 Slaughter	N	Y	Y	Y	N	Y	Y
26 Higgins	N	Y	Y	Y	N	Y	Y
27 **Collins**	Y	N	N	N	Y	N	N
NORTH CAROLINA							
1 Butterfield	N	Y	Y	Y	N	Y	Y
2 **Holding**	Y	N	N	N	Y	N	N
3 **Jones**	N	Y	Y	Y	N	?	?
4 Price	N	Y	Y	Y	N	Y	Y

	149	150	151	152	153	154	5
Foxx	Y	N	N	N	Y	N	N
6 **Walker**	Y	N	N	N	Y	N	N
7 **Rouzer**	Y	N	N	N	Y	N	N
8 **Hudson**	Y	N	N	N	Y	N	N
9 **Pittenger**	Y	N	N	N	Y	N	N
10 **McHenry**	Y	N	N	N	Y	N	N
11 **Meadows**	Y	N	N	N	Y	N	N
12 Adams	N	Y	Y	Y	N	Y	Y
13 **Budd**	Y	N	N	N	Y	N	N
NORTH DAKOTA							
AL **Cramer**	Y	N	N	N	Y	N	N
OHIO							
1 **Chabot**	Y	N	N	N	Y	N	N
2 **Wenstrup**	Y	N	N	N	Y	N	N
3 Beatty	N	Y	Y	Y	N	Y	Y
4 **Jordan**	Y	N	N	N	Y	N	N
5 **Latta**	Y	N	N	N	Y	N	N
6 **Johnson**	Y	N	N	N	Y	N	N
7 **Gibbs**	Y	N	N	N	Y	N	N
8 **Davidson**	Y	N	N	N	Y	N	N
9 Kaptur	N	Y	Y	Y	N	Y	Y
10 **Turner**	Y	N	N	N	Y	N	N
11 Fudge	N	Y	Y	Y	N	Y	Y
12 **Tiberi**	Y	N	N	N	Y	N	N
13 Ryan	N	Y	?	Y	N	Y	?
14 **Joyce**	Y	N	N	N	Y	N	N
15 **Stivers**	Y	N	N	N	Y	N	N
16 **Renacci**	Y	N	N	N	Y	N	N
OKLAHOMA							
1 **Bridenstine**	Y	N	N	N	Y	N	N
2 **Mullin**	Y	N	N	N	Y	N	N
3 **Lucas**	Y	N	N	N	Y	N	N
4 **Cole**	Y	N	N	N	Y	N	N
5 **Russell**	N	N	N	N	N	Y	Y
OREGON							
1 Bonamici	N	Y	Y	Y	N	Y	Y
2 **Walden**	Y	N	N	N	Y	N	N
3 Blumenauer	N	Y	Y	Y	N	Y	Y
4 DeFazio	N	Y	Y	Y	N	Y	Y
5 Schrader	N	Y	Y	Y	N	Y	Y
PENNSYLVANIA							
1 Brady	N	Y	Y	Y	N	Y	Y
2 Evans	N	Y	Y	Y	N	Y	Y
3 **Kelly**	Y	N	N	N	Y	N	N
4 **Perry**	Y	N	N	N	Y	N	N
5 **Thompson**	Y	N	N	N	Y	N	N
6 **Costello**	Y	N	N	N	Y	N	N
7 **Meehan**	N	N	N	N	Y	N	N
8 **Fitzpatrick**	Y	N	N	N	Y	N	N
9 **Shuster**	Y	N	N	N	Y	N	N
10 **Marino**	Y	N	N	N	Y	N	N
11 **Barletta**	+	–	–	–	+	–	–
12 **Rothfus**	Y	N	N	N	Y	N	N
13 Boyle	N	Y	Y	Y	N	+	+
14 Doyle	N	Y	Y	Y	N	Y	Y
15 **Dent**	Y	N	N	N	Y	N	N
16 **Smucker**	Y	N	N	N	Y	N	N
17 Cartwright	N	Y	Y	Y	N	Y	Y
18 **Murphy**	Y	N	N	N	Y	N	N
RHODE ISLAND							
1 Cicilline	N	Y	Y	Y	N	Y	Y
2 Langevin	N	Y	Y	Y	N	+	Y
SOUTH CAROLINA							
1 **Sanford**	Y	N	N	N	N	N	N
2 **Wilson**	Y	N	N	N	Y	N	N
3 **Duncan**	Y	N	N	N	Y	N	?
4 **Gowdy**	Y	N	N	N	Y	N	N
6 Clyburn	N	Y	Y	Y	N	Y	Y
7 **Rice**	Y	N	N	N	Y	N	N
SOUTH DAKOTA							
AL **Noem**	Y	N	N	N	Y	N	N
TENNESSEE							
1 **Roe**	Y	N	N	N	Y	N	N
2 **Duncan**	N	N	N	N	N	N	N
3 **Fleischmann**	Y	N	N	N	Y	N	N
4 **DesJarlais**	Y	N	N	N	Y	N	N
5 Cooper	N	Y	Y	Y	N	Y	Y
6 **Black**	Y	N	N	N	Y	N	N
7 **Blackburn**	Y	N	N	N	Y	N	N
8 **Kustoff**	Y	N	N	N	Y	N	N
9 Cohen	N	Y	Y	Y	N	Y	Y

	148	149	150	151	152	153	154
TEXAS							
1 **Gohmert**	Y	N	N	N	Y	N	N
2 **Poe**	N	N	N	N	Y	N	N
3 **Johnson, S.**	Y	N	N	N	Y	N	N
4 **Ratcliffe**	Y	N	N	N	Y	N	N
5 **Hensarling**	Y	N	N	N	Y	N	N
6 **Barton**	Y	N	N	N	Y	N	N
7 **Culberson**	Y	N	N	N	Y	N	N
8 **Brady**	Y	N	N	N	Y	N	N
9 Green, A.	N	Y	Y	Y	N	Y	Y
10 **McCaul**	Y	N	N	N	Y	N	N
11 **Conaway**	Y	N	N	N	Y	N	N
12 **Granger**	Y	N	N	N	Y	N	N
13 **Thornberry**	Y	N	N	N	Y	N	N
14 **Weber**	Y	N	N	N	Y	N	N
15 Gonzalez	N	Y	Y	Y	N	Y	Y
16 O'Rourke	N	Y	Y	Y	N	Y	Y
17 **Flores**	Y	N	N	N	Y	N	N
18 Jackson Lee	N	Y	Y	Y	N	Y	Y
19 **Arrington**	Y	N	N	N	Y	N	N
20 Castro	N	Y	Y	Y	N	Y	?
21 **Smith**	Y	N	N	N	Y	N	N
22 **Olson**	Y	N	N	N	Y	N	N
23 **Hurd**	Y	N	N	N	Y	N	N
24 **Marchant**	Y	N	N	N	Y	N	N
25 **Williams**	Y	N	N	N	Y	N	N
26 **Burgess**	Y	N	N	N	Y	N	N
27 **Farenthold**	Y	N	N	N	Y	N	N
28 Cuellar	N	Y	Y	Y	N	Y	Y
29 Green, G.	N	N	?	?	?	Y	Y
30 Johnson, E.B.	N	Y	Y	Y	N	Y	Y
31 **Carter**	Y	N	N	N	Y	N	N
32 **Sessions**	Y	N	N	N	Y	N	N
33 Veasey	N	Y	Y	Y	N	Y	Y
34 Vela	N	Y	Y	Y	N	Y	Y
35 Doggett	N	Y	?	Y	N	Y	Y
36 **Babin**	Y	N	N	N	Y	N	N
UTAH							
1 **Bishop**	Y	N	N	N	Y	?	N
2 **Stewart**	Y	N	N	N	Y	N	N
3 **Chaffetz**	Y	N	N	N	Y	N	N
4 **Love**	Y	N	N	N	Y	N	N
VERMONT							
AL Welch	N	Y	Y	Y	N	Y	Y
VIRGINIA							
1 **Wittman**	Y	N	N	N	Y	N	N
2 **Taylor**	Y	N	N	N	Y	N	N
3 Scott	N	Y	Y	Y	N	Y	Y
4 McEachin	N	Y	Y	Y	N	Y	Y
5 **Garrett**	Y	N	N	N	Y	N	N
6 **Goodlatte**	Y	N	N	N	Y	N	N
7 **Brat**	Y	N	N	N	Y	N	N
8 Beyer	N	Y	Y	Y	N	Y	Y
9 **Griffith**	P	N	Y	N	N	N	Y
10 **Comstock**	Y	N	N	N	Y	–	N
11 Connolly	N	Y	Y	Y	N	Y	Y
WASHINGTON							
1 DelBene	N	Y	Y	Y	N	Y	Y
2 Larsen	N	Y	Y	Y	N	Y	Y
3 **Herrera Beutler**	Y	N	N	N	Y	N	N
4 **Newhouse**	Y	N	N	N	Y	N	N
5 **McMorris Rodgers**	Y	N	N	N	Y	N	N
6 Kilmer	N	Y	Y	Y	N	Y	Y
7 Jayapal	N	Y	Y	Y	N	Y	Y
8 **Reichert**	Y	N	N	N	Y	N	N
9 Smith	N	Y	Y	Y	N	Y	Y
10 Heck	N	Y	Y	Y	N	Y	Y
WEST VIRGINIA							
1 **McKinley**	N	N	N	N	Y	N	N
2 **Mooney**	Y	N	N	N	Y	N	N
3 **Jenkins**	Y	N	N	N	Y	N	N
WISCONSIN							
1 **Ryan**							
2 Pocan	N	Y	Y	Y	N	Y	Y
3 Kind	N	Y	Y	Y	N	Y	Y
4 Moore	N	Y	Y	Y	N	?	?
5 **Sensenbrenner**	Y	N	N	N	Y	N	N
6 **Grothman**	Y	N	N	N	Y	N	N
7 **Duffy**	Y	N	N	N	Y	?	N
8 **Gallagher**	Y	N	N	N	Y	N	N
WYOMING							
AL **Cheney**	Y	N	N	N	Y	N	N

III HOUSE VOTES

VOTE NUMBER

155. HR 720. FRIVOLOUS' LAWSUITS/CIVIL RIGHTS ACTIONS. Conyers, D-Mich., amendment that would exempt from the bill's provisions actions alleging a violation of a constitutional or civil right. Rejected in Committee of the Whole 190-227 : R 5-227; D 185-0. March, 10, 2017.

156. HR 720. FRIVOLOUS' LAWSUITS/WHISTLEBLOWER ACTIONS. Jeffries, D-N.Y., amendment that would exempt from the bill's provisions actions related to federal whistleblower or anti-retaliation laws. Rejected in Committee of the Whole 189-229 : R 4-229; D 185-0. March, 10, 2017.

157. HR 720. FRIVOLOUS' LAWSUITS/RECOMMIT. Lofgren, D-Calif., motion to recommit the bill to the House Judiciary Committee with instructions to report it back immediately with an amendment that would exempt from the bill's provisions any civil action related to the foreign emoluments clause in the Constitution. Motion rejected 186-232 : R 0-232; D 186-0. March, 10, 2017.

158. HR 720. FRIVOLOUS' LAWSUITS/PASSAGE. Passage of the bill that would change federal rules governing civil lawsuits to require federal courts to impose sanctions on parties that file frivolous civil lawsuits. The sanctions would need to include monetary payments to the other party to cover the other party's attorney fees and costs. The bill also would eliminate the so-called "safe harbor" clause by removing the ability of parties to withdraw or correct claims considered frivolous within 21 days of filing. Passed 230-188 : R 227-5; D 3-183. March, 10, 2017.

159. HR 132. OKLAHOMA LAND CONVEYANCE/PASSAGE. Webster, R-Fla., motion to suspend the rules and pass the bill that would require the Bureau of Reclamation to convey all land in the maintenance complex and district office of the federal Arbuckle water project in Oklahoma to the Arbuckle Master Conservancy District in Murray County, Okla. Motion agreed to 407-1 : R 226-1; D 181-0. March, 15, 2017.

160. HR 648. WYOMING DAM AGREEMENT/PASSAGE. Tipton, R-Colo., motion to suspend the rules and pass the bill that would allow the Interior Department to enter into an agreement with the state of Wyoming to expand the storage capacity of the Fontenelle Dam and Reservoir. Motion agreed to 408-0 : R 227-0; D 181-0. March, 15, 2017.

161. PRESIDENT'S TAX RETURN DISCLOSURE/MOTION TO TABLE. McCarthy, R-Calif., motion to table (kill) the Crowley, D-N.Y., motion to appeal the ruling of the Chair that the Crowley resolution related to the disclosure of President Trump's tax returns does not constitute a question of the privileges of the House. Motion agreed to 223-183 : R 223-1; D 0-182. March, 15, 2017.

	155	156	157	158	159	160	161
ALABAMA							
1 Byrne	N	N	N	Y	Y	Y	Y
2 Roby	N	N	N	Y	Y	Y	Y
3 Rogers	N	N	N	Y	Y	Y	Y
4 Aderholt	N	N	N	Y	Y	Y	Y
5 Brooks	N	N	N	Y	Y	Y	Y
6 Palmer	N	N	N	Y	Y	Y	Y
7 Sewell	Y	Y	Y	N	Y	Y	N
ALASKA							
AL Young	N	N	N	Y	Y	Y	Y
ARIZONA							
1 O'Halleran	Y	Y	Y	N	Y	Y	N
2 McSally	N	N	N	Y	Y	Y	Y
3 Grijalva	Y	Y	Y	N	Y	Y	N
4 Gosar	N	N	N	Y	Y	Y	Y
5 Biggs	N	N	N	Y	Y	Y	Y
6 Schweikert	N	N	N	Y	Y	Y	Y
7 Gallego	Y	Y	Y	N	Y	Y	N
8 Franks	N	N	N	Y	Y	Y	Y
9 Sinema	+	+	+	–	Y	Y	N
ARKANSAS							
1 Crawford	N	N	N	Y	Y	Y	Y
2 Hill	N	N	N	Y	Y	Y	Y
3 Womack	N	N	N	Y	Y	Y	Y
4 Westerman	N	N	N	Y	Y	Y	Y
CALIFORNIA							
1 LaMalfa	N	N	N	Y	Y	Y	Y
2 Huffman	Y	Y	Y	N	Y	Y	N
3 Garamendi	Y	Y	Y	N	Y	Y	N
4 McClintock	?	N	N	Y	Y	Y	Y
5 Thompson	Y	Y	Y	N	Y	Y	N
6 Matsui	Y	Y	Y	N	Y	Y	N
7 Bera	Y	Y	Y	N	Y	Y	N
8 Cook	N	N	N	Y	Y	Y	Y
9 McNerney	Y	Y	Y	N	Y	Y	N
10 Denham	N	N	N	Y	Y	Y	Y
11 DeSaulnier	Y	Y	Y	N	Y	Y	N
12 Pelosi	Y	Y	Y	N	Y	Y	N
13 Lee	Y	Y	Y	N	Y	Y	N
14 Speier	Y	Y	Y	N	Y	Y	N
15 Swalwell	Y	Y	Y	N	Y	Y	N
16 Costa	Y	Y	Y	Y	Y	Y	N
17 Khanna	Y	Y	Y	N	Y	Y	N
18 Eshoo	Y	Y	Y	N	Y	Y	N
19 Lofgren	Y	Y	Y	N	Y	Y	N
20 Panetta	Y	Y	Y	N	Y	Y	N
21 Valadao	N	N	N	Y	Y	Y	Y
22 Nunes	N	N	N	Y	Y	Y	Y
23 McCarthy	N	N	N	Y	Y	Y	Y
24 Carbajal	Y	Y	Y	N	Y	Y	N
25 Knight	N	N	N	Y	Y	Y	Y
26 Brownley	Y	Y	Y	N	Y	Y	N
27 Chu	Y	Y	Y	N	Y	Y	N
28 Schiff	Y	Y	Y	N	Y	Y	N
29 Cardenas	Y	Y	Y	N	Y	Y	N
30 Sherman	Y	Y	Y	N	Y	Y	N
31 Aguilar	Y	Y	Y	N	Y	Y	N
32 Napolitano	Y	Y	Y	N	Y	Y	N
33 Lieu	Y	Y	Y	N	Y	Y	N
34 Vacant							
35 Torres	Y	Y	Y	N	Y	Y	N
36 Ruiz	Y	Y	Y	N	Y	Y	N
37 Bass	Y	Y	Y	N	Y	Y	N
38 Sánchez, Linda	Y	Y	Y	N	Y	Y	N
39 Royce	N	N	N	Y	Y	Y	Y
40 Roybal-Allard	Y	Y	Y	N	Y	Y	N
41 Takano	Y	Y	Y	N	Y	Y	N
42 Calvert	N	N	N	Y	Y	Y	Y
43 Waters	Y	Y	Y	N	Y	Y	N
44 Barragan	Y	Y	Y	N	Y	Y	N
45 Walters	N	N	N	Y	Y	Y	Y
46 Correa	Y	Y	Y	N	Y	Y	N
47 Lowenthal	Y	Y	Y	N	Y	Y	N
48 Rohrabacher	N	N	N	Y	?	?	?
49 Issa	N	N	N	Y	Y	Y	Y
50 Hunter	N	N	N	Y	Y	Y	Y
51 Vargas	Y	Y	Y	N	Y	Y	N
52 Peters	Y	Y	Y	N	Y	Y	N
53 Davis	+	+	+	–	Y	Y	N

	155	156	157	158	159	160	161
COLORADO							
1 DeGette	Y	Y	Y	N	Y	Y	N
2 Polis	Y	Y	Y	N	Y	Y	N
3 Tipton	N	N	N	Y	Y	Y	Y
4 Buck	N	N	N	Y	Y	Y	Y
5 Lamborn	N	N	N	Y	Y	Y	Y
6 Coffman	N	N	N	Y	Y	Y	Y
7 Perlmutter	Y	Y	Y	N	Y	Y	N
CONNECTICUT							
1 Larson	Y	Y	Y	N	Y	Y	N
2 Courtney	Y	Y	Y	N	Y	Y	N
3 DeLauro	Y	Y	Y	N	Y	Y	N
4 Himes	Y	Y	Y	N	Y	Y	N
5 Esty	Y	Y	Y	N	Y	Y	N
DELAWARE							
AL Blunt Rochester	Y	Y	Y	N	Y	Y	N
FLORIDA							
1 Gaetz	N	N	N	Y	Y	Y	Y
2 Dunn	N	N	N	Y	Y	Y	Y
3 Yoho	N	–	N	Y	Y	Y	Y
4 Rutherford	N	N	N	Y	Y	Y	Y
5 Lawson	Y	Y	Y	N	Y	Y	N
6 DeSantis	N	N	N	Y	Y	Y	Y
7 Murphy	Y	Y	Y	N	Y	Y	N
8 Posey	N	N	N	Y	Y	Y	Y
9 Soto	Y	Y	Y	N	Y	Y	N
10 Demings	Y	Y	Y	N	Y	Y	N
11 Webster	N	N	N	Y	Y	Y	Y
12 Bilirakis	N	N	N	Y	Y	Y	Y
13 Crist	Y	Y	Y	N	Y	Y	N
14 Castor	Y	Y	Y	N	Y	Y	N
15 Ross	N	N	N	Y	Y	Y	Y
16 Buchanan	N	N	N	Y	Y	Y	Y
17 Rooney, T.	N	N	N	Y	Y	Y	?
18 Mast	N	N	N	Y	Y	Y	Y
19 Rooney, F.	N	N	N	Y	Y	Y	Y
20 Hastings	Y	Y	Y	N	Y	Y	N
21 Frankel	Y	Y	Y	N	Y	Y	N
22 Deutch	Y	Y	Y	N	Y	Y	N
23 Wasserman Schultz	Y	Y	Y	N	Y	Y	N
24 Wilson	Y	Y	Y	N	Y	Y	N
25 Diaz-Balart	N	N	N	Y	Y	Y	Y
26 Curbelo	Y	Y	N	Y	Y	Y	N
27 Ros-Lehtinen	Y	Y	N	Y	Y	Y	Y
GEORGIA							
1 Carter	N	N	N	Y	Y	Y	Y
2 Bishop	Y	Y	Y	N	Y	Y	N
3 Ferguson	N	N	N	Y	Y	Y	Y
4 Johnson	Y	?	Y	N	Y	Y	N
5 Lewis	Y	Y	Y	N	Y	Y	N
7 Woodall	N	N	N	Y	Y	Y	Y
8 Scott, A.	N	N	N	Y	Y	Y	Y
9 Collins	N	N	N	Y	Y	Y	Y
10 Hice	N	N	N	Y	Y	Y	Y
11 Loudermilk	N	N	N	Y	Y	Y	Y
12 Allen	N	N	N	Y	Y	Y	Y
13 Scott, D.	Y	Y	Y	N	Y	?	N
14 Graves	N	N	N	Y	Y	Y	Y
HAWAII							
1 Hanabusa	Y	Y	Y	N	Y	Y	N
2 Gabbard	Y	Y	Y	N	Y	Y	N
IDAHO							
1 Labrador	N	N	N	Y	Y	Y	Y
2 Simpson	N	N	N	Y	Y	Y	Y
ILLINOIS							
1 Rush	?	?	?	?	?	?	?
2 Kelly	Y	Y	Y	N	Y	Y	N
3 Lipinski	Y	Y	Y	N	Y	Y	N
4 Gutierrez	Y	Y	Y	N	Y	Y	N
5 Quigley	Y	Y	Y	N	Y	Y	N
6 Roskam	N	N	N	Y	Y	Y	Y
7 Davis, D.	Y	Y	Y	N	?	?	?
8 Krishnamoorthi	Y	Y	Y	N	Y	Y	N
9 Schakowsky	Y	Y	Y	N	Y	Y	N
10 Schneider	Y	Y	Y	N	Y	Y	N
11 Foster	Y	Y	Y	N	Y	Y	N
12 Bost	N	N	N	Y	Y	Y	Y
13 Davis, R.	N	N	N	Y	Y	Y	Y
14 Hultgren	N	N	N	Y	Y	Y	Y
15 Shimkus	N	N	N	Y	Y	Y	Y

KEY	Republicans	Democrats	Independents
Y	Voted for (yea)	X Paired against	C Voted "present" to avoid possible conflict of interest
#	Paired for	– Announced against	
+	Announced for	P Voted "present"	? Did not vote or otherwise make a position known
N	Voted against (nay)		

	155	156	157	158	159	160	161
16 **Kinzinger**	N	N	N	Y	Y	Y	Y
17 Bustos	Y	Y	Y	N	Y	Y	N
18 **LaHood**	N	N	N	Y	Y	Y	Y
INDIANA							
1 Visclosky	Y	Y	Y	N	Y	Y	N
2 **Walorski**	N	N	N	Y	Y	Y	Y
3 **Banks**	N	N	N	Y	Y	Y	Y
4 **Rokita**	N	N	N	Y	Y	Y	Y
5 **Brooks**	N	N	N	Y	Y	Y	Y
6 **Messer**	N	N	N	Y	Y	Y	Y
7 Carson	Y	Y	Y	N	Y	Y	N
8 **Bucshon**	N	N	N	Y	Y	Y	Y
9 **Hollingsworth**	N	N	N	Y	Y	Y	Y
IOWA							
1 **Blum**	N	N	N	Y	Y	Y	Y
2 Loebsack	Y	Y	Y	N	?	?	?
3 **Young**	N	N	N	Y	Y	Y	Y
4 **King**	N	N	N	Y	Y	Y	Y
KANSAS							
1 **Marshall**	N	N	N	Y	Y	Y	Y
2 **Jenkins**	N	N	N	Y	Y	Y	Y
3 **Yoder**	N	N	N	Y	Y	Y	Y
KENTUCKY							
1 **Comer**	N	N	N	Y	Y	Y	Y
2 **Guthrie**	N	N	N	Y	Y	Y	Y
3 Yarmuth	Y	Y	Y	N	Y	Y	N
4 **Massie**	N	N	N	Y	Y	Y	Y
5 **Rogers**	N	N	N	Y	Y	Y	Y
6 **Barr**	N	N	N	Y	Y	Y	Y
LOUISIANA							
1 **Scalise**	N	N	N	Y	Y	Y	Y
2 Richmond	?	?	?	?	Y	Y	N
3 **Higgins**	N	N	N	Y	Y	Y	Y
4 **Johnson**	N	N	N	Y	Y	Y	Y
5 **Abraham**	N	N	N	Y	Y	Y	Y
6 **Graves**	N	N	N	Y	Y	Y	Y
MAINE							
1 Pingree	Y	Y	Y	N	Y	Y	N
2 **Poliquin**	N	N	N	Y	Y	Y	Y
MARYLAND							
1 **Harris**	N	N	N	Y	Y	Y	Y
2 Ruppersberger	Y	Y	Y	N	Y	Y	N
3 Sarbanes	Y	Y	Y	N	Y	Y	N
4 Brown	Y	Y	Y	N	+	+	+
5 Hoyer	Y	Y	Y	N	Y	Y	N
6 Delaney	Y	Y	Y	N	Y	Y	N
7 Cummings	Y	Y	Y	N	Y	Y	N
8 Raskin	Y	Y	Y	N	Y	Y	N
MASSACHUSETTS							
1 Neal	Y	Y	Y	N	Y	Y	N
2 McGovern	Y	Y	Y	N	Y	Y	N
3 Tsongas	Y	Y	Y	N	Y	Y	N
4 Kennedy	Y	Y	Y	N	Y	Y	N
5 Clark	Y	Y	Y	N	Y	Y	N
6 Moulton	Y	Y	Y	N	Y	Y	N
7 Capuano	Y	Y	Y	N	Y	Y	N
8 Lynch	Y	Y	Y	N	Y	Y	N
9 Keating	Y	Y	Y	N	Y	Y	N
MICHIGAN							
1 **Bergman**	N	N	N	Y	Y	Y	Y
2 **Huizenga**	N	N	N	Y	Y	Y	Y
3 **Amash**	N	N	N	Y	N	Y	Y
4 **Moolenaar**	N	N	N	Y	Y	Y	Y
5 Kildee	Y	Y	Y	N	Y	Y	N
6 **Upton**	N	N	N	Y	Y	Y	Y
7 **Walberg**	N	N	N	Y	Y	Y	Y
8 **Bishop**	N	N	N	Y	Y	Y	Y
9 Levin	Y	Y	Y	N	Y	Y	N
10 **Mitchell**	N	N	N	Y	Y	Y	Y
11 **Trott**	N	N	N	Y	?	?	?
12 Dingell	Y	Y	Y	N	Y	Y	N
13 Conyers	Y	Y	Y	N	Y	Y	N
14 Lawrence	Y	Y	Y	–	Y	Y	N
MINNESOTA							
1 Walz	Y	Y	Y	N	Y	Y	N
2 **Lewis**	N	N	N	Y	Y	Y	Y
3 **Paulsen**	N	N	N	Y	Y	Y	Y
4 McCollum	Y	Y	Y	N	Y	Y	N
5 Ellison	Y	Y	Y	N	Y	Y	N
6 **Emmer**	N	N	N	Y	Y	Y	Y
7 Peterson	Y	Y	Y	Y	Y	Y	N
8 Nolan	Y	Y	Y	N	Y	Y	N
MISSISSIPPI							
1 **Kelly**	N	N	N	Y	Y	Y	Y
2 Thompson	Y	Y	Y	N	Y	Y	N
3 **Harper**	N	N	N	Y	Y	Y	Y
4 **Palazzo**	N	N	N	Y	Y	Y	Y
MISSOURI							
1 Clay	Y	Y	Y	N	Y	Y	N
2 **Wagner**	N	N	N	Y	Y	Y	?
3 **Luetkemeyer**	N	N	N	Y	Y	Y	Y
4 **Hartzler**	N	N	N	Y	Y	Y	Y
5 Cleaver	Y	Y	Y	N	Y	Y	N
6 **Graves**	N	N	N	Y	Y	Y	Y
7 **Long**	N	N	N	Y	Y	Y	Y
8 **Smith**	N	N	N	Y	Y	Y	Y
MONTANA							
AL **Vacant**							
NEBRASKA							
1 **Fortenberry**	N	N	N	Y	Y	Y	Y
2 **Bacon**	N	N	N	Y	Y	Y	Y
3 **Smith**	N	N	N	Y	Y	Y	Y
NEVADA							
1 Titus	?	?	?	?	?	?	?
2 **Amodei**	N	N	N	Y	Y	Y	Y
3 Rosen	Y	Y	Y	N	Y	Y	N
4 Kihuen	Y	Y	Y	N	Y	Y	N
NEW HAMPSHIRE							
1 Shea-Porter	Y	Y	Y	N	Y	Y	N
2 Kuster	+	+	+	N	Y	Y	N
NEW JERSEY							
1 Norcross	Y	Y	Y	N	Y	Y	N
2 **LoBiondo**	N	Y	N	Y	Y	Y	Y
3 **MacArthur**	N	N	N	Y	Y	Y	Y
4 **Smith**	N	N	N	Y	Y	Y	Y
5 Gottheimer	Y	Y	Y	N	Y	Y	N
6 Pallone	Y	Y	Y	N	Y	Y	N
7 **Lance**	N	N	N	Y	Y	Y	Y
8 Sires	Y	Y	Y	N	Y	Y	N
9 Pascrell	Y	Y	Y	N	Y	Y	N
10 Payne	Y	Y	Y	N	?	?	?
11 **Frelinghuysen**	N	N	N	Y	Y	Y	Y
12 Watson Coleman	Y	Y	Y	N	Y	Y	N
NEW MEXICO							
1 Lujan Grisham	Y	Y	Y	N	Y	Y	N
2 **Pearce**	N	N	N	Y	Y	Y	Y
3 Luján	Y	Y	Y	N	Y	Y	N
NEW YORK							
1 **Zeldin**	N	N	N	Y	Y	Y	Y
2 **King**	N	N	N	Y	Y	Y	Y
3 Suozzi	Y	Y	Y	N	Y	Y	N
4 Rice	Y	Y	Y	N	Y	Y	N
5 Meeks	Y	Y	Y	N	Y	Y	N
6 Meng	Y	Y	Y	N	Y	Y	N
7 Velázquez	Y	Y	Y	N	Y	Y	N
8 Jeffries	Y	Y	Y	N	Y	Y	N
9 Clarke	Y	Y	Y	N	Y	Y	N
10 Nadler	Y	Y	Y	N	Y	Y	N
11 **Donovan**	N	N	N	Y	Y	Y	Y
12 Maloney, C.	Y	Y	Y	N	?	Y	N
13 Espaillat	Y	Y	Y	N	Y	Y	N
14 Crowley	Y	Y	Y	N	Y	Y	N
15 Serrano	Y	Y	Y	N	Y	Y	N
16 Engel	Y	Y	Y	N	Y	Y	N
17 Lowey	Y	Y	Y	N	Y	Y	N
18 Maloney, S.P.	Y	Y	Y	N	Y	Y	N
19 **Faso**	N	N	N	Y	Y	Y	Y
20 Tonko	Y	Y	Y	N	Y	Y	N
21 **Stefanik**	N	N	N	Y	Y	Y	Y
22 **Tenney**	N	N	N	Y	Y	Y	Y
23 **Reed**	N	N	N	Y	Y	Y	Y
24 **Katko**	N	N	N	Y	Y	Y	Y
25 Slaughter	Y	Y	Y	N	+	+	–
26 Higgins	Y	Y	Y	N	+	+	–
27 **Collins**	N	N	N	Y	+	+	+
NORTH CAROLINA							
1 Butterfield	Y	Y	Y	N	Y	Y	N
2 **Holding**	N	N	N	Y	Y	Y	Y
3 **Jones**	?	?	?	?	Y	Y	N
4 Price	Y	Y	Y	N	Y	Y	N
5 **Foxx**	N	N	N	Y	Y	Y	Y
6 **Walker**	N	N	N	Y	Y	Y	Y
7 **Rouzer**	N	N	N	Y	Y	Y	Y
8 **Hudson**	N	N	N	Y	Y	Y	Y
9 **Pittenger**	N	N	N	Y	Y	Y	Y
10 **McHenry**	N	N	N	Y	Y	Y	Y
11 **Meadows**	N	N	N	Y	Y	Y	Y
12 Adams	Y	Y	Y	N	Y	Y	N
13 **Budd**	N	N	N	Y	Y	Y	Y
NORTH DAKOTA							
AL **Cramer**	N	N	N	Y	Y	Y	Y
OHIO							
1 **Chabot**	N	N	N	Y	Y	Y	Y
2 **Wenstrup**	N	N	N	Y	Y	Y	Y
3 Beatty	Y	Y	Y	N	Y	Y	N
4 **Jordan**	N	N	N	Y	Y	Y	Y
5 **Latta**	N	N	N	Y	Y	Y	Y
6 **Johnson**	–	N	N	Y	Y	Y	Y
7 **Gibbs**	N	N	N	Y	Y	Y	Y
8 **Davidson**	N	N	N	Y	Y	Y	Y
9 Kaptur	Y	Y	Y	N	Y	Y	N
10 **Turner**	N	N	N	Y	Y	Y	Y
11 Fudge	Y	Y	Y	N	?	?	?
12 **Tiberi**	N	N	N	Y	Y	Y	Y
13 Ryan	Y	Y	Y	N	Y	Y	N
14 **Joyce**	N	N	N	Y	Y	Y	Y
15 **Stivers**	N	N	N	Y	Y	Y	Y
16 **Renacci**	N	N	N	Y	Y	Y	Y
OKLAHOMA							
1 **Bridenstine**	N	N	N	Y	Y	Y	Y
2 **Mullin**	N	N	N	Y	Y	Y	Y
3 **Lucas**	N	N	N	Y	Y	Y	Y
4 **Cole**	N	N	N	Y	Y	Y	Y
5 **Russell**	Y	N	N	N	+	+	+
OREGON							
1 Bonamici	Y	Y	Y	N	Y	Y	N
2 **Walden**	N	N	–	+	Y	Y	Y
3 Blumenauer	Y	Y	Y	N	Y	Y	N
4 DeFazio	Y	Y	Y	N	Y	Y	N
5 Schrader	Y	Y	Y	N	Y	Y	N
PENNSYLVANIA							
1 Brady	Y	Y	Y	N	Y	Y	N
2 Evans	Y	Y	Y	N	Y	Y	N
3 **Kelly**	N	N	N	Y	?	?	?
4 **Perry**	N	N	N	Y	Y	Y	Y
5 **Thompson**	N	N	N	Y	Y	Y	Y
6 **Costello**	N	N	N	Y	Y	Y	Y
7 **Meehan**	N	N	N	Y	Y	Y	Y
8 **Fitzpatrick**	Y	Y	N	Y	Y	Y	Y
9 **Shuster**	N	N	N	Y	Y	Y	Y
10 **Marino**	N	N	N	Y	+	+	+
11 **Barletta**	–	–	–	+	Y	Y	Y
12 **Rothfus**	N	N	N	Y	Y	Y	Y
13 Boyle	+	+	+	–	Y	Y	N
14 Doyle	Y	Y	Y	N	Y	Y	N
15 **Dent**	N	N	N	Y	Y	Y	Y
16 **Smucker**	N	N	N	Y	Y	Y	Y
17 Cartwright	Y	Y	Y	N	Y	Y	N
18 **Murphy**	N	N	N	Y	Y	Y	Y
RHODE ISLAND							
1 Cicilline	Y	Y	Y	N	?	?	?
2 Langevin	Y	Y	Y	N	Y	Y	N
SOUTH CAROLINA							
1 **Sanford**	N	N	N	Y	Y	Y	P
2 **Wilson**	N	N	N	Y	Y	Y	Y
3 **Duncan**	N	N	N	Y	Y	Y	Y
4 **Gowdy**	N	N	N	Y	Y	Y	Y
6 Clyburn	Y	Y	Y	N	Y	Y	N
7 **Rice**	N	N	N	Y	Y	Y	Y
SOUTH DAKOTA							
AL **Noem**	N	N	N	Y	Y	Y	Y
TENNESSEE							
1 **Roe**	N	N	N	Y	Y	Y	Y
2 **Duncan**	N	N	N	Y	Y	Y	Y
3 **Fleischmann**	N	N	N	Y	Y	Y	Y
4 **DesJarlais**	N	N	N	Y	?	?	?
5 Cooper	Y	Y	Y	N	Y	Y	N
6 **Black**	N	N	N	Y	Y	Y	Y
7 **Blackburn**	N	N	N	Y	?	?	?
8 **Kustoff**	N	N	N	N	Y	Y	Y
9 Cohen	Y	Y	Y	N	Y	Y	N
TEXAS							
1 **Gohmert**	N	N	N	Y	Y	Y	Y
2 **Poe**	N	N	N	N	Y	Y	Y
3 **Johnson, S.**	N	N	N	Y	Y	Y	Y
4 **Ratcliffe**	N	N	N	Y	Y	Y	Y
5 **Hensarling**	N	N	N	Y	Y	Y	Y
6 **Barton**	N	N	N	Y	Y	Y	Y
7 **Culberson**	N	N	N	Y	Y	Y	Y
8 **Brady**	N	N	–	+	Y	Y	Y
9 Green, A.	Y	Y	Y	N	Y	Y	N
10 **McCaul**	N	N	N	Y	+	+	+
11 **Conaway**	N	N	N	Y	Y	Y	Y
12 **Granger**	N	N	N	Y	Y	Y	Y
13 **Thornberry**	N	N	N	Y	Y	Y	Y
14 **Weber**	N	N	N	Y	Y	Y	Y
15 Gonzalez	Y	Y	Y	N	Y	Y	N
16 O'Rourke	Y	Y	Y	N	Y	Y	N
17 **Flores**	N	N	N	Y	Y	Y	Y
18 Jackson Lee	Y	Y	Y	N	Y	Y	N
19 **Arrington**	N	N	N	Y	Y	Y	Y
20 Castro	?	Y	Y	N	Y	Y	N
21 **Smith**	N	N	N	Y	Y	Y	Y
22 **Olson**	N	N	N	Y	Y	Y	Y
23 **Hurd**	N	N	N	Y	Y	Y	Y
24 **Marchant**	N	N	N	Y	Y	Y	Y
25 **Williams**	N	N	N	Y	Y	Y	Y
26 **Burgess**	N	N	N	Y	Y	Y	Y
27 **Farenthold**	N	N	N	Y	Y	Y	Y
28 Cuellar	Y	Y	Y	Y	Y	Y	N
29 Green, G.	Y	Y	Y	N	Y	Y	N
30 Johnson, E.B.	Y	Y	Y	N	Y	Y	N
31 **Carter**	N	N	N	Y	Y	Y	Y
32 **Sessions**	N	N	N	Y	Y	Y	Y
33 Veasey	Y	Y	Y	N	Y	Y	N
34 Vela	Y	Y	Y	N	Y	Y	N
35 Doggett	Y	Y	Y	N	Y	Y	N
36 **Babin**	N	N	N	Y	Y	Y	Y
UTAH							
1 **Bishop**	N	N	N	Y	Y	Y	Y
2 **Stewart**	N	N	N	Y	Y	Y	Y
3 **Chaffetz**	N	N	N	Y	Y	Y	Y
4 **Love**	N	N	N	Y	Y	Y	Y
VERMONT							
AL Welch	Y	Y	Y	N	+	+	–
VIRGINIA							
1 **Wittman**	N	N	N	Y	Y	Y	Y
2 **Taylor**	N	N	N	Y	Y	Y	Y
3 Scott	Y	Y	Y	N	Y	Y	N
4 McEachin	Y	Y	Y	N	Y	Y	N
5 **Garrett**	N	N	N	Y	Y	Y	Y
6 **Goodlatte**	N	N	N	Y	Y	Y	Y
7 **Brat**	N	N	N	Y	Y	Y	Y
8 Beyer	Y	Y	Y	N	Y	Y	N
9 **Griffith**	Y	N	N	N	Y	Y	Y
10 **Comstock**	N	N	N	Y	Y	Y	Y
11 Connolly	Y	Y	Y	N	Y	Y	N
WASHINGTON							
1 DelBene	Y	Y	Y	N	Y	Y	N
2 Larsen	Y	Y	Y	N	Y	Y	N
3 **Herrera Beutler**	N	N	N	Y	Y	Y	Y
4 **Newhouse**	N	N	N	Y	Y	Y	Y
5 **McMorris Rodgers**	N	N	N	Y	Y	Y	Y
6 Kilmer	Y	Y	Y	N	Y	Y	N
7 Jayapal	Y	Y	Y	N	Y	Y	N
8 **Reichert**	N	N	N	Y	Y	Y	Y
9 Smith	Y	Y	Y	N	Y	Y	N
10 Heck	Y	Y	Y	N	Y	Y	N
WEST VIRGINIA							
1 **McKinley**	N	N	N	Y	Y	Y	Y
2 **Mooney**	N	N	N	Y	Y	Y	Y
3 **Jenkins**	N	N	N	Y	Y	Y	Y
WISCONSIN							
1 **Ryan**							
2 Pocan	Y	Y	Y	N	Y	Y	N
3 Kind	Y	Y	Y	N	Y	Y	N
4 Moore	Y	Y	Y	N	Y	Y	N
5 **Sensenbrenner**	N	N	N	Y	Y	Y	Y
6 **Grothman**	N	N	N	Y	Y	Y	Y
7 **Duffy**	N	N	N	Y	Y	Y	Y
8 **Gallagher**	N	N	N	Y	Y	Y	Y
WYOMING							
AL **Cheney**	N	N	N	Y	Y	Y	Y

VOTE NUMBER

162. HR 1367, HR 1259, H RES 198, HR 1181. VA MISCONDUCT, VA STAFF-ING PROGRAMS AND VETERAN GUN PURCHASES/PREVIOUS QUESTION. Buck, R-Colo., motion to order the previous question (thus ending debate and possibility of amendment) on the rule that would provide for House floor consideration of a bill (HR 1259) that would expand the Veterans Affairs Department's ability to fire, demote and suspend employees for misconduct; a bill (HR 1367) that would establish various new staffing, recruitment and retention programs at the VA; and a bill (HR 1181) that would prohibit a VA determination that a veteran is mentally incompetent from automatically preventing a veteran from being able to purchase a gun. Motion agreed to 227-185 : R 227-1; D 0-184. March, 16, 2017.

163. HR 1367, HR 1259, H RES 198, HR 1181. VA MISCONDUCT, VA STAFFING PROGRAMS AND VETERAN GUN PURCHASES/RULE. Adoption of rule that would provide for House floor consideration of a bill (HR 1259) that would expand the Veterans Affairs Department's ability to fire, demote and suspend employees for misconduct; a bill (HR 1367) that would establish various new staffing, recruitment and retention programs at the VA; and a bill (HR 1181) that would prohibit a VA determination that a veteran is mentally incompe-tent from automatically preventing the veteran from being able to purchase a gun. Adopted 229-187 : R 229-0; D 0-187. March, 16, 2017.

164. PROCEDURAL MOTION/APPROVAL OF HOUSE JOURNAL. Approved 243-165 : R 153-74; D 90-91. March, 16, 2017.

165. HR 1259. VA MISCONDUCT/SENIOR EXECUTIVE DEMOTION PROCESS. Walz, D-Minn., amendment that would remove the bill's provisions that would expand the Veterans Affairs Department's ability to fire, demote and suspend employees for misconduct, and would alternatively expand the VA's authority to suspend or demote senior executives. It would allow for the removal of non-executives for performance issues occurring only within a preceding two-year period. Rejected in Committee of the Whole 194-223 : R 7-223; D 187-0. March, 16, 2017.

166. HR 1259. VA MISCONDUCT/DANGEROUS EMPLOYEE SUSPENSION. Takano, D-Calif., amendment that would replace the bill's proposed VA employee removal process with an alternative process that would provide for the suspension and removal of Veterans Affairs Department employ-ees for misconduct that is a threat to public health and safety. Suspended employees would be entitled to a written statement of the charges, a hearing and a review of their case. It would also provide for back pay for suspended whistleblowers. Rejected in Committee of the Whole 183-232 : R 0-229; D 183-3. March, 16, 2017.

167. HR 1259. VA MISCONDUCT/RECOMMIT. Kihuen, D-Nev., motion to recommit the bill to the Committee on Veterans' Affairs with instructions to report it back immediately with an amendment that would extend the bill's whistleblower protections to individuals that make disclosures to the central whistleblower office, including those who do so anonymously. It would also exempt veterans and whistleblowers from the bill's provisions that would expand the Veterans Affairs Department's ability to fire, demote and suspend employees for misconduct or poor performance. Motion rejected 189-229 : R 2-229; D 187-0. March, 16, 2017.

168. HR 1259. VA MISCONDUCT/PASSAGE. Passage of the bill that would expand the Veterans Affairs Department's ability to fire, demote and suspend employees for misconduct or poor performance. The measure would autho-rize the VA to recoup any bonus paid to a VA employee if the VA deems it appropriate, and it would require that the employee be given advance notice and the right to appeal the decision. As amended, the measure would require that annual performance reviews for supervisors at the VA include evalua-tions on the supervisor's ability to address poor performance among their employees and would require the VA to provide supervisors with periodic training related to whistleblower rights and effective management tech-niques. Passed 237-178 : R 227-3; D 10-175. March, 16, 2017.

	162	163	164	165	166	167	168
ALABAMA							
1 Byrne	Y	Y	Y	N	N	N	Y
2 Roby	Y	Y	Y	N	N	N	Y
3 Rogers	Y	Y	Y	N	N	N	Y
4 Aderholt	Y	Y	Y	N	N	N	Y
5 Brooks	Y	Y	Y	N	N	N	Y
6 Palmer	Y	Y	Y	N	N	N	Y
7 Sewell	N	N	N	Y	Y	Y	N
ALASKA							
AL Young	Y	Y	Y	Y	N	N	N
ARIZONA							
1 O'Halleran	N	N	N	Y	Y	Y	Y
2 McSally	Y	Y	N	N	N	N	Y
3 Grijalva	N	N	N	Y	Y	Y	N
4 Gosar	Y	Y	N	N	N	N	Y
5 Biggs	Y	Y	N	N	N	N	Y
6 Schweikert	Y	Y	Y	N	N	N	Y
7 Gallego	N	N	N	Y	Y	Y	N
8 Franks	Y	Y	Y	N	N	N	Y
9 Sinema	–	N	Y	Y	N	Y	N
ARKANSAS							
1 Crawford	Y	Y	N	N	N	N	Y
2 Hill	Y	Y	N	N	N	N	Y
3 Womack	Y	Y	Y	N	N	N	Y
4 Westerman	Y	Y	Y	N	N	N	Y
CALIFORNIA							
1 LaMalfa	Y	Y	Y	N	N	N	Y
2 Huffman	N	N	Y	Y	Y	Y	N
3 Garamendi	N	N	N	Y	Y	Y	N
4 McClintock	Y	Y	Y	N	N	N	Y
5 Thompson	N	N	N	Y	Y	Y	N
6 Matsui	N	N	N	Y	Y	Y	N
7 Bera	N	N	N	Y	Y	Y	N
8 Cook	Y	Y	Y	N	N	N	Y
9 McNerney	N	N	Y	Y	Y	Y	N
10 Denham	Y	Y	N	N	N	N	Y
11 DeSaulnier	N	N	N	Y	Y	Y	N
12 Pelosi	N	N	N	Y	Y	Y	N
13 Lee	N	N	N	Y	Y	Y	N
14 Speier	N	N	Y	Y	Y	Y	N
15 Swalwell	N	N	N	Y	Y	Y	N
16 Costa	N	N	N	Y	Y	Y	Y
17 Khanna	N	N	N	Y	Y	Y	N
18 Eshoo	N	N	N	Y	Y	Y	N
19 Lofgren	N	N	N	Y	Y	Y	N
20 Panetta	N	N	N	Y	Y	Y	N
21 Valadao	Y	Y	N	N	N	N	Y
22 Nunes	Y	Y	Y	N	N	N	Y
23 McCarthy	Y	Y	Y	N	N	N	Y
24 Carbajal	N	N	N	Y	Y	Y	N
25 Knight	Y	Y	Y	N	N	N	Y
26 Brownley	N	N	N	Y	Y	Y	N
27 Chu	N	N	N	Y	Y	Y	N
28 Schiff	N	N	N	Y	Y	Y	N
29 Cardenas	N	N	N	Y	Y	Y	N
30 Sherman	N	N	Y	Y	Y	Y	N
31 Aguilar	N	N	N	Y	Y	Y	N
32 Napolitano	N	N	N	Y	Y	Y	N
33 Lieu	N	N	N	Y	Y	Y	N
34 Vacant							
35 Torres	N	N	N	Y	Y	Y	N
36 Ruiz	N	N	N	Y	Y	Y	N
37 Bass	N	N	N	Y	Y	Y	N
38 Sánchez, Linda	N	N	N	Y	Y	Y	N
39 Royce	Y	Y	Y	N	N	N	Y
40 Roybal-Allard	–	N	N	Y	Y	Y	N
41 Takano	N	N	Y	Y	Y	Y	N
42 Calvert	Y	Y	Y	N	N	N	Y
43 Waters	N	N	N	Y	Y	Y	N
44 Barragan	N	N	N	Y	Y	Y	N
45 Walters	Y	Y	Y	N	N	N	Y
46 Correa	N	N	N	Y	Y	Y	N
47 Lowenthal	N	N	N	Y	Y	Y	N
48 Rohrabacher	Y	Y	Y	N	N	N	Y
49 Issa	Y	Y	Y	N	N	N	Y
50 Hunter	Y	Y	Y	N	N	N	Y
51 Vargas	N	N	N	Y	Y	Y	N
52 Peters	N	N	N	Y	Y	Y	N
53 Davis	N	N	Y	Y	Y	Y	N

	162	163	164	165	166	167	168
COLORADO							
1 DeGette	N	N	Y	Y	Y	Y	N
2 Polis	N	N	Y	Y	Y	Y	N
3 Tipton	Y	Y	N	N	N	N	Y
4 Buck	Y	Y	N	N	N	N	Y
5 Lamborn	Y	Y	N	N	N	N	Y
6 Coffman	Y	Y	N	N	N	N	Y
7 Perlmutter	N	N	Y	Y	Y	Y	N
CONNECTICUT							
1 Larson	N	N	Y	Y	Y	Y	N
2 Courtney	N	N	N	Y	Y	Y	N
3 DeLauro	N	N	Y	Y	Y	Y	N
4 Himes	N	N	Y	Y	Y	Y	N
5 Esty	N	N	Y	Y	Y	Y	N
DELAWARE							
AL Blunt Rochester	N	N	Y	Y	Y	Y	N
FLORIDA							
1 Gaetz	Y	Y	N	N	N	N	Y
2 Dunn	Y	Y	Y	N	N	N	Y
3 Yoho	Y	Y	Y	N	N	N	Y
4 Rutherford	Y	Y	Y	N	N	N	Y
5 Lawson	N	N	Y	Y	Y	Y	N
6 DeSantis	Y	Y	N	N	N	N	Y
7 Murphy	N	Y	Y	Y	Y	Y	Y
8 Posey	Y	Y	Y	N	N	N	Y
9 Soto	N	N	Y	Y	Y	Y	N
10 Demings	N	N	Y	Y	Y	Y	N
11 Webster	Y	Y	N	N	N	N	Y
12 Bilirakis	Y	Y	Y	N	N	N	Y
13 Crist	N	N	Y	Y	Y	Y	N
14 Castor	N	N	Y	Y	Y	Y	N
15 Ross	Y	Y	Y	N	N	N	Y
16 Buchanan	Y	Y	Y	N	N	N	Y
17 Rooney, T.	Y	Y	?	N	N	N	Y
18 Mast	Y	Y	Y	N	N	N	Y
19 Rooney, F.	Y	Y	Y	N	N	N	Y
20 Hastings	N	N	N	Y	Y	Y	N
21 Frankel	N	N	Y	Y	Y	Y	N
22 Deutch	?	?	?	?	?	?	?
23 Wasserman Schultz	N	N	Y	Y	Y	Y	N
24 Wilson	–	N	N	Y	Y	Y	N
25 Diaz-Balart	Y	Y	Y	N	N	N	Y
26 Curbelo	N	N	Y	Y	Y	Y	N
27 Ros-Lehtinen	Y	Y	N	N	N	N	Y
GEORGIA							
1 Carter	Y	Y	N	N	N	N	Y
2 Bishop	N	N	N	Y	Y	Y	N
3 Ferguson	Y	Y	Y	N	N	N	Y
4 Johnson	N	N	N	Y	Y	Y	N
5 Lewis	N	N	N	Y	Y	Y	N
6 Woodall	Y	Y	N	N	N	N	Y
7 Scott, A.	Y	Y	N	N	N	N	Y
8 Collins	Y	Y	N	N	N	N	Y
9 Hice	Y	Y	Y	N	N	N	Y
10 Loudermilk	Y	Y	Y	N	N	N	Y
11 Allen	Y	Y	N	N	N	N	Y
12 Scott, D.	N	N	Y	Y	Y	Y	N
13 Graves	Y	Y	N	N	N	N	Y
HAWAII							
1 Hanabusa	N	N	Y	Y	Y	Y	N
2 Gabbard	N	N	Y	Y	Y	Y	N
IDAHO							
1 Labrador	Y	Y	Y	N	N	N	Y
2 Simpson	Y	Y	Y	N	N	N	Y
ILLINOIS							
1 Rush	?	?	?	?	?	?	?
2 Kelly	N	N	Y	Y	Y	Y	N
3 Lipinski	N	N	Y	Y	Y	Y	N
4 Gutierrez	N	N	N	Y	Y	Y	N
5 Quigley	N	N	Y	Y	Y	Y	N
6 Roskam	Y	Y	N	N	N	N	Y
7 Davis, D.	?	?	?	?	?	?	?
8 Krishnamoorthi	N	N	Y	Y	Y	Y	N
9 Schakowsky	N	N	N	Y	Y	Y	N
10 Schneider	N	N	Y	Y	Y	Y	N
11 Foster	N	N	Y	Y	Y	Y	N
12 Bost	Y	Y	N	N	N	N	Y
13 Davis, R.	+	+	Y	N	N	N	Y
14 Hultgren	Y	Y	N	N	N	N	Y
15 Shimkus	Y	Y	Y	N	N	N	Y

	162	163	164	165	166	167	168
16 **Kinzinger**	Y	Y	N	N	N	N	Y
17 Bustos	N	N	Y	Y	Y	Y	N
18 **LaHood**	Y	Y	N	N	N	N	Y
INDIANA							
1 Visclosky	N	N	N	Y	Y	Y	N
2 **Walorski**	+	+	Y	N	N	N	Y
3 **Banks**	Y	Y	Y	N	N	N	Y
4 **Rokita**	Y	Y	N	N	N	N	Y
5 **Brooks**	Y	Y	Y	N	N	N	Y
6 **Messer**	Y	Y	Y	N	N	N	Y
7 Carson	N	N	N	Y	Y	Y	N
8 **Bucshon**	Y	Y	N	N	N	N	Y
9 **Hollingsworth**	Y	Y	Y	N	N	N	Y
IOWA							
1 **Blum**	Y	Y	N	N	N	Y	Y
2 Loebsack	N	N	Y	Y	Y	Y	N
3 **Young**	Y	Y	Y	N	N	N	Y
4 **King**	Y	Y	Y	N	N	N	Y
KANSAS							
1 **Marshall**	Y	Y	Y	N	N	N	Y
2 **Jenkins**	Y	Y	N	N	N	N	Y
3 **Yoder**	Y	Y	N	N	N	N	Y
KENTUCKY							
1 **Comer**	Y	Y	Y	N	N	N	Y
2 **Guthrie**	Y	Y	Y	N	N	N	Y
3 Yarmuth	N	N	Y	Y	Y	Y	N
4 **Massie**	Y	Y	Y	N	N	N	Y
5 **Rogers**	Y	Y	Y	N	N	N	Y
6 **Barr**	Y	Y	Y	N	N	N	Y
LOUISIANA							
1 **Scalise**	Y	Y	Y	N	N	N	Y
2 Richmond	N	N	Y	Y	Y	Y	N
3 **Higgins**	Y	Y	Y	N	N	N	Y
4 **Johnson**	Y	Y	Y	N	N	N	Y
5 **Abraham**	Y	Y	Y	N	N	N	Y
6 **Graves**	+	Y	N	N	N	N	Y
MAINE							
1 Pingree	N	N	Y	Y	Y	Y	N
2 **Poliquin**	Y	Y	N	N	N	N	Y
MARYLAND							
1 **Harris**	Y	?	Y	N	N	N	Y
2 Ruppersberger	N	N	Y	Y	Y	Y	N
3 Sarbanes	N	N	N	Y	Y	Y	N
4 Brown	N	N	Y	Y	Y	Y	N
5 Hoyer	N	N	N	Y	Y	Y	N
6 Delaney	N	N	N	Y	Y	Y	N
7 Cummings	N	N	Y	Y	?	Y	N
8 Raskin	N	N	N	Y	Y	Y	N
MASSACHUSETTS							
1 Neal	N	N	N	Y	Y	Y	N
2 McGovern	N	N	N	Y	Y	Y	N
3 Tsongas	N	N	Y	Y	Y	Y	N
4 Kennedy	N	N	Y	Y	Y	Y	N
5 Clark	N	N	Y	Y	Y	Y	N
6 Moulton	N	N	N	Y	Y	Y	N
7 Capuano	N	N	N	Y	Y	Y	–
8 Lynch	N	N	N	Y	Y	Y	N
9 Keating	N	N	N	Y	Y	Y	N
MICHIGAN							
1 **Bergman**	Y	Y	N	N	N	N	Y
2 **Huizenga**	Y	Y	?	N	N	N	Y
3 **Amash**	Y	Y	N	N	N	N	Y
4 **Moolenaar**	Y	Y	Y	N	N	N	Y
5 Kildee	N	N	Y	Y	Y	Y	N
6 **Upton**	Y	Y	N	N	N	N	Y
7 **Walberg**	Y	Y	N	N	N	N	Y
8 **Bishop**	Y	Y	Y	N	N	N	Y
9 Levin	N	N	N	Y	Y	Y	N
10 **Mitchell**	Y	Y	N	N	N	N	Y
11 **Trott**	Y	Y	Y	N	N	N	Y
12 Dingell	N	N	Y	Y	Y	Y	N
13 Conyers	N	N	?	Y	Y	Y	N
14 Lawrence	N	N	Y	Y	Y	Y	N
MINNESOTA							
1 Walz	N	N	Y	Y	Y	Y	N
2 **Lewis**	Y	Y	Y	N	N	N	Y
3 **Paulsen**	Y	Y	N	N	N	N	Y
4 McCollum	N	N	Y	Y	Y	Y	N
5 Ellison	N	N	Y	Y	Y	Y	N
6 **Emmer**	Y	Y	Y	N	N	N	Y
7 Peterson	N	N	N	Y	Y	Y	N
8 Nolan	N	N	N	Y	Y	Y	N
MISSISSIPPI							
1 **Kelly**	Y	Y	Y	N	N	N	Y
2 Thompson	N	N	N	Y	Y	Y	N
3 **Harper**	Y	Y	Y	N	N	N	Y
4 **Palazzo**	Y	Y	Y	N	N	N	Y
MISSOURI							
1 Clay	N	N	Y	Y	Y	Y	N
2 **Wagner**	Y	Y	Y	N	N	N	Y
3 **Luetkemeyer**	Y	Y	Y	N	N	N	Y
4 **Hartzler**	Y	Y	Y	N	N	N	Y
5 Cleaver	N	N	N	Y	Y	Y	N
6 **Graves**	Y	Y	N	N	N	N	Y
7 **Long**	Y	Y	Y	N	N	N	Y
8 **Smith**	Y	Y	Y	?	N	N	Y
MONTANA							
AL **Vacant**							
NEBRASKA							
1 **Fortenberry**	Y	Y	Y	N	N	N	Y
2 **Bacon**	Y	Y	Y	N	N	N	Y
3 **Smith**	Y	Y	Y	N	N	N	Y
NEVADA							
1 Titus	N	N	Y	Y	Y	Y	N
2 **Amodei**	Y	Y	Y	N	N	N	Y
3 Rosen	N	N	Y	Y	Y	Y	N
4 Kihuen	N	N	N	Y	Y	Y	N
NEW HAMPSHIRE							
1 Shea-Porter	N	N	Y	Y	Y	Y	N
2 Kuster	N	N	N	Y	Y	Y	N
NEW JERSEY							
1 Norcross	N	N	N	Y	Y	Y	N
2 **LoBiondo**	Y	Y	N	Y	N	N	N
3 **MacArthur**	Y	Y	N	N	N	N	Y
4 **Smith**	Y	Y	Y	Y	N	N	N
5 Gottheimer	N	N	N	Y	Y	Y	Y
6 Pallone	N	N	N	Y	Y	Y	N
7 **Lance**	Y	Y	N	N	N	N	Y
8 Sires	N	N	N	Y	Y	Y	N
9 Pascrell	N	N	N	Y	Y	Y	N
10 Payne	?	?	?	?	?	?	?
11 **Frelinghuysen**	Y	Y	Y	N	N	N	Y
12 Watson Coleman	N	N	N	Y	Y	Y	N
NEW MEXICO							
1 Lujan Grisham	N	N	Y	Y	Y	Y	N
2 **Pearce**	Y	Y	N	N	?	N	Y
3 Luján	N	N	Y	Y	Y	Y	N
NEW YORK							
1 **Zeldin**	Y	Y	Y	N	N	N	Y
2 **King**	Y	Y	Y	+	–	–	+
3 Suozzi	N	N	Y	Y	Y	Y	N
4 Rice	N	N	N	Y	Y	Y	N
5 Meeks	N	N	Y	Y	Y	Y	N
6 Meng	N	N	Y	Y	Y	Y	N
7 Velázquez	N	N	N	Y	N	Y	N
8 Jeffries	N	N	N	Y	Y	Y	N
9 Clarke	N	N	N	Y	Y	Y	N
10 Nadler	N	N	Y	Y	Y	Y	N
11 **Donovan**	Y	Y	Y	N	N	N	Y
12 Maloney, C.	N	N	?	Y	Y	Y	N
13 Espaillat	N	N	N	Y	Y	Y	N
14 Crowley	N	N	N	Y	Y	Y	N
15 Serrano	N	N	Y	Y	Y	Y	N
16 Engel	N	N	Y	Y	Y	Y	N
17 Lowey	N	N	N	Y	Y	Y	N
18 Maloney, S.P.	N	N	Y	Y	Y	Y	N
19 **Faso**	Y	Y	?	N	N	N	Y
20 Tonko	N	N	P	Y	Y	Y	N
21 **Stefanik**	Y	Y	Y	N	N	N	Y
22 **Tenney**	Y	Y	Y	N	N	N	Y
23 **Reed**	Y	Y	N	N	N	N	Y
24 **Katko**	Y	Y	N	Y	N	N	Y
25 Slaughter	–	–	–	+	+	+	–
26 Higgins	N	N	N	Y	Y	Y	N
27 **Collins**	+	+	+	–	–	–	+
NORTH CAROLINA							
1 Butterfield	N	N	Y	Y	Y	Y	N
2 **Holding**	Y	Y	N	N	N	N	Y
3 **Jones**	N	Y	Y	Y	N	Y	Y
4 Price	N	N	N	Y	Y	Y	N
5 **Foxx**	Y	Y	N	N	N	N	Y
6 **Walker**	Y	Y	Y	N	N	N	Y
7 **Rouzer**	Y	Y	N	N	N	N	Y
8 **Hudson**	Y	Y	N	N	N	N	Y
9 **Pittenger**	Y	Y	N	N	N	N	Y
10 **McHenry**	Y	Y	Y	N	N	N	Y
11 **Meadows**	Y	Y	Y	N	N	N	Y
12 Adams	N	N	N	Y	Y	Y	N
13 **Budd**	Y	Y	Y	N	N	N	Y
NORTH DAKOTA							
AL **Cramer**	Y	Y	Y	N	N	N	Y
OHIO							
1 **Chabot**	Y	Y	Y	N	N	N	Y
2 **Wenstrup**	Y	Y	N	N	N	N	Y
3 Beatty	N	N	N	Y	Y	Y	N
4 **Jordan**	?	?	?	?	?	?	?
5 **Latta**	Y	Y	Y	N	N	N	Y
6 **Johnson**	Y	Y	N	N	N	N	Y
7 **Gibbs**	Y	Y	N	N	N	N	Y
8 **Davidson**	Y	Y	Y	N	N	N	Y
9 Kaptur	N	N	Y	Y	Y	Y	N
10 **Turner**	Y	Y	N	N	N	N	Y
11 Fudge	?	?	?	Y	Y	Y	N
12 **Tiberi**	Y	Y	N	N	N	N	Y
13 Ryan	N	N	N	Y	Y	Y	N
14 **Joyce**	Y	Y	N	N	N	N	Y
15 **Stivers**	Y	Y	N	N	N	N	Y
16 **Renacci**	Y	Y	N	N	N	N	Y
OKLAHOMA							
1 **Bridenstine**	Y	Y	Y	N	N	N	Y
2 **Mullin**	Y	Y	Y	N	N	N	Y
3 **Lucas**	Y	Y	Y	N	N	N	Y
4 **Cole**	Y	Y	Y	Y	N	N	Y
5 **Russell**	Y	Y	Y	N	N	N	Y
OREGON							
1 Bonamici	N	N	Y	Y	Y	Y	N
2 **Walden**	Y	Y	Y	N	N	N	Y
3 Blumenauer	N	N	?	Y	Y	Y	–
4 DeFazio	N	N	N	Y	Y	Y	N
5 Schrader	N	N	N	Y	Y	Y	N
PENNSYLVANIA							
1 Brady	N	N	N	Y	Y	Y	N
2 Evans	N	N	N	Y	Y	Y	N
3 **Kelly**	?	?	?	?	?	?	?
4 **Perry**	Y	Y	N	N	N	N	Y
5 **Thompson**	Y	Y	N	N	N	N	Y
6 **Costello**	Y	Y	N	N	N	N	Y
7 **Meehan**	Y	Y	Y	N	N	N	Y
8 **Fitzpatrick**	Y	Y	N	N	N	N	Y
9 **Shuster**	Y	Y	Y	N	N	N	Y
10 **Marino**	+	+	+	–	–	–	+
11 **Barletta**	Y	Y	Y	N	N	N	Y
12 **Rothfus**	Y	Y	Y	N	N	N	Y
13 Boyle	N	N	N	Y	Y	Y	N
14 Doyle	N	N	N	Y	Y	Y	N
15 **Dent**	Y	Y	Y	N	N	N	Y
16 **Smucker**	Y	Y	Y	N	N	N	Y
17 Cartwright	N	N	Y	Y	Y	Y	N
18 **Murphy**	Y	Y	Y	N	N	N	Y
RHODE ISLAND							
1 Cicilline	N	N	Y	Y	Y	Y	N
2 Langevin	N	N	N	Y	Y	Y	N
SOUTH CAROLINA							
1 **Sanford**	Y	Y	Y	N	N	N	Y
2 **Wilson**	Y	Y	Y	N	N	N	Y
3 **Duncan**	Y	Y	Y	N	N	N	Y
4 **Gowdy**	Y	Y	Y	N	N	N	Y
6 Clyburn	N	N	N	Y	Y	Y	N
7 **Rice**	Y	Y	N	N	N	N	Y
SOUTH DAKOTA							
AL **Noem**	Y	Y	N	N	N	N	Y
TENNESSEE							
1 **Roe**	Y	Y	Y	N	N	N	Y
2 **Duncan**	Y	Y	Y	N	N	N	Y
3 **Fleischmann**	Y	Y	Y	N	N	N	Y
4 **DesJarlais**	Y	Y	Y	N	N	N	Y
5 Cooper	N	N	Y	Y	Y	Y	N
6 **Black**	Y	Y	Y	N	–	N	Y
7 **Blackburn**	Y	Y	Y	N	N	N	Y
8 **Kustoff**	Y	Y	Y	N	N	N	Y
9 Cohen	N	N	N	Y	Y	Y	N
TEXAS							
1 **Gohmert**	Y	Y	?	N	N	N	Y
2 **Poe**	Y	Y	N	N	N	N	Y
3 **Johnson, S.**	Y	Y	Y	N	N	N	Y
4 **Ratcliffe**	Y	Y	N	N	N	N	Y
5 **Hensarling**	Y	Y	Y	N	N	N	Y
6 **Barton**	Y	Y	Y	N	N	N	Y
7 **Culberson**	Y	Y	Y	N	N	N	Y
8 **Brady**	Y	Y	Y	N	N	N	Y
9 Green, A.	N	N	N	Y	Y	Y	N
10 **McCaul**	Y	Y	N	N	N	N	Y
11 **Conaway**	Y	Y	N	N	N	N	Y
12 **Granger**	Y	Y	Y	N	N	N	Y
13 **Thornberry**	Y	Y	Y	N	N	N	Y
14 **Weber**	Y	Y	N	N	N	N	Y
15 Gonzalez	N	N	?	Y	Y	Y	N
16 O'Rourke	N	N	Y	Y	N	Y	Y
17 **Flores**	Y	Y	N	N	N	N	Y
18 Jackson Lee	N	N	N	Y	Y	Y	N
19 **Arrington**	Y	Y	Y	N	N	N	Y
20 Castro	N	N	Y	Y	Y	Y	Y
21 **Smith**	Y	Y	Y	N	N	N	Y
22 **Olson**	Y	Y	Y	N	N	N	Y
23 **Hurd**	Y	Y	N	N	N	N	Y
24 **Marchant**	Y	Y	?	N	N	N	Y
25 **Williams**	Y	Y	Y	N	N	N	Y
26 **Burgess**	Y	Y	N	N	N	N	Y
27 **Farenthold**	Y	Y	Y	N	N	N	Y
28 Cuellar	N	N	Y	Y	Y	Y	Y
29 Green, G.	N	N	N	Y	Y	Y	N
30 Johnson, E.B.	N	N	N	Y	Y	Y	N
31 **Carter**	Y	Y	Y	N	N	N	Y
32 **Sessions**	Y	Y	Y	N	N	N	Y
33 Veasey	N	N	N	Y	Y	Y	N
34 Vela	N	N	Y	Y	Y	Y	N
35 Doggett	N	N	Y	Y	Y	Y	N
36 **Babin**	Y	Y	Y	N	N	N	Y
UTAH							
1 **Bishop**	Y	Y	Y	N	N	N	?
2 **Stewart**	Y	Y	Y	N	N	N	Y
3 **Chaffetz**	Y	Y	Y	N	N	N	Y
4 **Love**	Y	Y	Y	N	N	N	Y
VERMONT							
AL Welch	N	N	Y	Y	Y	Y	N
VIRGINIA							
1 **Wittman**	Y	Y	Y	N	N	N	Y
2 **Taylor**	Y	Y	Y	N	N	N	Y
3 Scott	N	N	Y	Y	Y	Y	N
4 McEachin	N	N	N	Y	Y	Y	N
5 **Garrett**	Y	Y	Y	N	N	N	Y
6 **Goodlatte**	Y	Y	Y	N	N	N	Y
7 **Brat**	Y	Y	Y	N	N	N	Y
8 Beyer	N	N	N	?	?	?	?
9 **Griffith**	Y	Y	Y	N	N	N	Y
10 **Comstock**	Y	Y	Y	N	N	N	Y
11 Connolly	N	N	N	Y	Y	Y	N
WASHINGTON							
1 DelBene	N	N	Y	Y	Y	Y	N
2 Larsen	N	N	?	Y	Y	Y	N
3 **Herrera Beutler**	Y	Y	N	N	N	N	Y
4 **Newhouse**	Y	Y	Y	N	N	N	Y
5 **McMorris Rodgers**	Y	Y	Y	N	N	N	Y
6 Kilmer	N	N	N	Y	Y	Y	N
7 Jayapal	N	N	N	Y	Y	Y	N
8 **Reichert**	Y	Y	N	N	N	N	Y
9 Smith	N	N	Y	Y	Y	Y	N
10 Heck	N	N	Y	Y	Y	Y	N
WEST VIRGINIA							
1 **McKinley**	Y	Y	N	Y	N	N	Y
2 **Mooney**	Y	Y	Y	N	N	N	Y
3 **Jenkins**	Y	Y	N	N	N	N	Y
WISCONSIN							
1 **Ryan**							
2 Pocan	N	N	Y	Y	Y	Y	N
3 Kind	N	N	N	Y	Y	Y	N
4 Moore	N	N	Y	Y	Y	Y	N
5 **Sensenbrenner**	Y	Y	Y	N	N	N	Y
6 **Grothman**	Y	Y	Y	N	N	N	Y
7 **Duffy**	?	Y	N	N	N	N	Y
8 **Gallagher**	Y	Y	N	N	N	N	Y
WYOMING							
AL **Cheney**	Y	Y	Y	N	N	N	Y

VOTE NUMBER

169. HR 1181. VETERAN GUN PURCHASES/PASSAGE. Passage of the bill that would prohibit a Veterans Affairs Department determination that an individual is mentally incompetent from being used as basis for that individual's inclusion in the National Instant Criminal Background Check System, which would thereby prevent the individual from purchasing a gun. Under the measure, an individual could not be considered to be mentally defective without a judicial authority's finding that the individual poses a danger to himself or herself or others. Passed 240-175 : R 228-2; D 12-173. March, 16, 2017.

170. HR 1367. VA STAFFING PROGRAMS/EXIT SURVEY REPORT. Hanabusa, D-Hawaii, amendment that would require that the report to Congress on voluntary Veterans Affairs Department exit survey results include the total number of employees who voluntarily separated from the VA and the number and percentage of departed employees that took the survey. Adopted in Committee of the Whole 400-8 : R 225-8; D 175-0. March, 17, 2017.

171. HR 1367. VA STAFFING PROGRAMS/PASSAGE. Passage of the bill that would require the Veterans Affairs Inspector General to determine non-clinical VA health care positions that should be eligible for expedited hiring, require annual performance reviews for all political appointees at the VA, and would require the VA to establish a database with information on qualified individuals who previously applied for a position at the VA. The measure would require that the information from the database be used to fill positions that have been vacant for an extended period of time. As amended, it would prohibit the secretary of the VA from appointing former political appointees to non-political positions one grade higher than their last position at the VA without having to go through a competitive selection process. Passed 412-0 : R 232-0; D 180-0. March, 17, 2017.

172. PROCEDURAL MOTION/APPROVAL OF HOUSE JOURNAL. Approved 246-143 : R 137-76; D 109-67. March, 17, 2017.

173. HR 1294. DHS PROGRAM REPORTING REQUIREMENTS/PASSAGE. Rutherford, R-Fla., motion to suspend the rules and pass the bill that would modify reporting requirements for Homeland Security Department major acquisition programs that experience cost overruns or missed deadlines. The measure would require programs with cost or scheduling problems to comply with increasingly stringent reporting requirements depending on the scale of the overrun or delay. If a major acquisition program would fail to meet a cost, schedule or performance threshold, the program's manager would be required to submit a remediation plan to department leadership. Under the measure, a "major acquisition program" would be defined as a program with estimated costs of at least $300 million over its lifespan. Motion agreed to 408-0 : R 227-0; D 181-0. March, 20, 2017.

174. HR 1249. DHS ACQUISITION STRATEGY/PASSAGE. Fitzpatrick, R-Pa., motion to suspend the rules and pass the bill that would require the Homeland Security Department to compose a multiyear acquisition strategy that would include a prioritized list of acquisitions, a plan to inventory the department's investments and assets, and a plan to address funding gaps for major acquisition programs. Under the measure, a "major acquisition program" would be defined as a program with estimated costs of at least $300 million over its lifespan. Motion agreed to 409-0 : R 228-0; D 181-0. March, 20, 2017.

175. HR 1252. DHS ACQUISTION MANAGEMENT/PASSAGE. Higgins, R-La., motion to suspend the rules and pass the bill that would designate the undersecretary for management at the Department of Homeland Security as the chief acquisition officer for the department. The undersecretary would be responsible for advising the department on acquisition management activities and would have acquisition decision authority over major acquisition programs. Under the measure, a "major acquisition program" would be defined as a program with estimated costs of at least $300 million over its lifespan. Motion agreed to 407-1 : R 225-1; D 182-0. March, 20, 2017.

	169	170	171	172	173	174	175
ALABAMA							
1 Byrne	Y	Y	Y	Y	Y	Y	Y
2 Roby	Y	Y	Y	Y	Y	Y	Y
3 Rogers	Y	N	Y	Y	Y	Y	Y
4 Aderholt	Y	Y	Y	Y	Y	Y	Y
5 Brooks	Y	Y	Y	Y	Y	Y	Y
6 Palmer	?	Y	Y	Y	Y	Y	Y
7 Sewell	N	Y	Y	Y	Y	Y	Y
ALASKA							
AL Young	Y	Y	Y	N	Y	Y	Y
ARIZONA							
1 O'Halleran	N	Y	Y	N	Y	Y	Y
2 McSally	Y	Y	Y	N	Y	Y	Y
3 Grijalva	N	Y	Y	N	Y	Y	Y
4 Gosar	Y	Y	Y	N	Y	Y	Y
5 Biggs	Y	Y	Y	N	Y	Y	Y
6 Schweikert	Y	Y	Y	Y	Y	Y	Y
7 Gallego	N	Y	Y	Y	Y	Y	Y
8 Franks	Y	Y	Y	Y	Y	Y	Y
9 Sinema	Y	Y	Y	Y	+	+	+
ARKANSAS							
1 Crawford	Y	Y	Y	Y	Y	Y	Y
2 Hill	Y	Y	Y	N	Y	Y	Y
3 Womack	Y	Y	Y	Y	Y	Y	Y
4 Westerman	Y	Y	Y	N	Y	Y	Y
CALIFORNIA							
1 LaMalfa	Y	Y	Y	?	Y	Y	Y
2 Huffman	N	Y	Y	Y	Y	Y	Y
3 Garamendi	N	Y	Y	Y	Y	Y	Y
4 McClintock	Y	Y	Y	Y	Y	Y	Y
5 Thompson	N	Y	Y	N	Y	Y	Y
6 Matsui	N	Y	Y	N	Y	Y	Y
7 Bera	N	Y	Y	N	Y	Y	Y
8 Cook	Y	Y	Y	Y	Y	Y	Y
9 McNerney	N	Y	Y	Y	Y	Y	Y
10 Denham	Y	Y	Y	N	Y	Y	Y
11 DeSaulnier	N	Y	Y	Y	Y	Y	Y
12 Pelosi	N	?	?	N	Y	Y	Y
13 Lee	N	Y	Y	N	Y	Y	Y
14 Speier	N	Y	Y	Y	Y	Y	Y
15 Swalwell	N	Y	Y	Y	Y	Y	Y
16 Costa	N	Y	Y	N	Y	Y	Y
17 Khanna	N	Y	Y	Y	Y	Y	Y
18 Eshoo	N	Y	Y	Y	Y	Y	Y
19 Lofgren	N	Y	Y	Y	Y	Y	Y
20 Panetta	N	Y	Y	Y	Y	Y	Y
21 Valadao	Y	Y	Y	N	+	+	+
22 Nunes	Y	Y	Y	Y	Y	Y	Y
23 McCarthy	Y	Y	Y	Y	Y	Y	Y
24 Carbajal	N	Y	Y	N	Y	Y	Y
25 Knight	Y	Y	Y	N	Y	Y	Y
26 Brownley	N	Y	Y	N	Y	Y	Y
27 Chu	N	Y	Y	Y	Y	Y	Y
28 Schiff	N	Y	Y	Y	Y	Y	Y
29 Cardenas	N	Y	Y	N	Y	Y	Y
30 Sherman	N	Y	Y	Y	Y	Y	Y
31 Aguilar	N	Y	Y	N	Y	Y	Y
32 Napolitano	N	Y	Y	?	Y	Y	Y
33 Lieu	N	Y	Y	N	Y	Y	Y
34 Vacant							
35 Torres	N	Y	Y	Y	Y	Y	Y
36 Ruiz	N	Y	Y	N	Y	Y	Y
37 Bass	N	Y	Y	N	Y	Y	Y
38 Sánchez, Linda	N	Y	?	N	Y	Y	Y
39 Royce	Y	Y	Y	Y	Y	Y	?
40 Roybal-Allard	N	?	Y	N	Y	Y	Y
41 Takano	N	Y	Y	Y	Y	Y	Y
42 Calvert	Y	Y	Y	Y	Y	Y	Y
43 Waters	N	Y	Y	Y	Y	Y	Y
44 Barragan	N	+	Y	N	Y	Y	Y
45 Walters	Y	Y	Y	Y	Y	Y	Y
46 Correa	Y	Y	Y	Y	Y	Y	Y
47 Lowenthal	N	Y	Y	Y	Y	Y	Y
48 Rohrabacher	Y	Y	Y	N	?	?	?
49 Issa	Y	Y	Y	Y	Y	Y	Y
50 Hunter	Y	Y	Y	Y	Y	Y	Y
51 Vargas	N	?	Y	N	Y	Y	Y
52 Peters	N	Y	Y	N	Y	Y	Y
53 Davis	N	Y	Y	Y	Y	Y	Y

	169	170	171	172	173	174	175
COLORADO							
1 DeGette	N	Y	Y	Y	Y	Y	Y
2 Polis	N	Y	Y	Y	Y	Y	Y
3 Tipton	Y	Y	Y	N	Y	Y	Y
4 Buck	Y	Y	Y	N	Y	Y	Y
5 Lamborn	Y	Y	Y	N	Y	Y	Y
6 Coffman	Y	Y	Y	N	Y	Y	Y
7 Perlmutter	N	Y	Y	Y	Y	Y	Y
CONNECTICUT							
1 Larson	N	Y	Y	Y	Y	Y	Y
2 Courtney	N	Y	Y	Y	Y	Y	Y
3 DeLauro	N	Y	Y	Y	Y	Y	Y
4 Himes	N	Y	Y	Y	Y	Y	Y
5 Esty	N	Y	Y	Y	Y	Y	Y
DELAWARE							
AL Blunt Rochester	N	Y	Y	Y	Y	Y	Y
FLORIDA							
1 Gaetz	Y	N	Y	N	Y	Y	Y
2 Dunn	Y	Y	Y	Y	Y	Y	Y
3 Yoho	Y	Y	Y	N	Y	Y	Y
4 Rutherford	Y	Y	Y	Y	Y	Y	Y
5 Lawson	N	Y	Y	Y	Y	Y	Y
6 DeSantis	Y	Y	Y	N	Y	Y	Y
7 Murphy	N	Y	Y	Y	Y	Y	Y
8 Posey	Y	Y	Y	Y	Y	Y	Y
9 Soto	N	Y	Y	Y	Y	Y	Y
10 Demings	N	Y	Y	Y	Y	Y	Y
11 Webster	Y	Y	Y	?	Y	Y	Y
12 Bilirakis	Y	Y	Y	Y	Y	Y	Y
13 Crist	N	Y	Y	N	Y	Y	Y
14 Castor	N	Y	Y	N	Y	Y	Y
15 Ross	Y	Y	Y	?	Y	Y	Y
16 Buchanan	Y	Y	Y	Y	Y	Y	Y
17 Rooney, T.	Y	Y	Y	Y	Y	Y	Y
18 Mast	Y	Y	Y	N	Y	Y	Y
19 Rooney, F.	Y	Y	Y	Y	Y	Y	Y
20 Hastings	N	Y	Y	Y	Y	Y	Y
21 Frankel	N	Y	Y	Y	Y	Y	Y
22 Deutch	?	?	?	?	?	?	?
23 Wasserman Schultz	?	Y	Y	Y	Y	Y	Y
24 Wilson	N	Y	Y	Y	Y	Y	Y
25 Diaz-Balart	Y	Y	Y	Y	Y	Y	Y
26 Curbelo	Y	Y	Y	Y	Y	Y	Y
27 Ros-Lehtinen	Y	Y	Y	Y	Y	Y	Y
GEORGIA							
1 Carter	Y	Y	Y	N	Y	Y	Y
2 Bishop	Y	Y	Y	N	Y	Y	Y
3 Ferguson	Y	Y	Y	N	Y	Y	Y
4 Johnson	N	Y	Y	Y	Y	Y	Y
5 Lewis	N	Y	Y	Y	Y	Y	Y
7 Woodall	Y	Y	Y	N	Y	Y	Y
8 Scott, A.	Y	Y	Y	N	Y	Y	Y
9 Collins	Y	Y	Y	N	Y	Y	Y
10 Hice	Y	Y	Y	N	Y	Y	Y
11 Loudermilk	Y	Y	Y	N	Y	Y	Y
12 Allen	Y	Y	Y	N	Y	Y	Y
13 Scott, D.	N	Y	Y	Y	Y	Y	Y
14 Graves	Y	Y	Y	N	Y	Y	Y
HAWAII							
1 Hanabusa	N	Y	Y	Y	Y	Y	Y
2 Gabbard	Y	Y	Y	Y	Y	Y	Y
IDAHO							
1 Labrador	Y	Y	Y	Y	Y	Y	Y
2 Simpson	Y	Y	Y	?	Y	Y	Y
ILLINOIS							
1 Rush	?	?	?	?	?	?	?
2 Kelly	N	Y	Y	Y	Y	Y	Y
3 Lipinski	N	Y	Y	Y	Y	Y	Y
4 Gutierrez	N	+	Y	N	+	+	+
5 Quigley	N	Y	Y	?	Y	Y	Y
6 Roskam	Y	Y	Y	Y	Y	Y	Y
7 Davis, D.	?	?	?	?	?	Y	Y
8 Krishnamoorthi	N	Y	Y	Y	Y	Y	Y
9 Schakowsky	N	+	Y	N	Y	Y	Y
10 Schneider	N	Y	Y	Y	Y	Y	Y
11 Foster	N	Y	Y	Y	Y	Y	Y
12 Bost	Y	Y	Y	N	Y	Y	Y
13 Davis, R.	Y	Y	Y	Y	Y	Y	Y
14 Hultgren	Y	Y	Y	Y	Y	Y	Y
15 Shimkus	Y	Y	Y	Y	Y	Y	Y

KEY	**Republicans**	Democrats	*Independents*	
Y Voted for (yea)		**X** Paired against		**C** Voted "present" to avoid possible conflict of interest
# Paired for		**–** Announced against		
+ Announced for		**P** Voted "present"		**?** Did not vote or otherwise make a position known
N Voted against (nay)				

	169	170	171	172	173	174	175
16 **Kinzinger**	Y	Y	Y	N	Y	Y	Y
17 Bustos	N	Y	Y	Y	Y	Y	Y
18 **LaHood**	Y	Y	Y	N	Y	Y	Y
INDIANA							
1 Visclosky	N	Y	Y	N	Y	Y	Y
2 **Walorski**	Y	Y	Y	Y	Y	Y	Y
3 **Banks**	Y	Y	Y	Y	Y	Y	Y
4 **Rokita**	Y	Y	Y	N	Y	Y	Y
5 **Brooks**	Y	Y	Y	Y	Y	Y	Y
6 **Messer**	Y	Y	Y	Y	Y	Y	Y
7 Carson	N	Y	Y	N	Y	Y	Y
8 **Bucshon**	Y	Y	Y	?	Y	Y	Y
9 **Hollingsworth**	Y	Y	Y	Y	Y	Y	Y
IOWA							
1 **Blum**	Y	Y	Y	N	Y	Y	Y
2 Loebsack	N	Y	Y	N	Y	Y	Y
3 **Young**	Y	Y	Y	Y	Y	Y	Y
4 **King**	Y	Y	Y	Y	Y	Y	Y
KANSAS							
1 **Marshall**	Y	Y	Y	Y	Y	Y	Y
2 **Jenkins**	Y	Y	Y	N	Y	Y	Y
3 **Yoder**	Y	Y	Y	N	Y	Y	Y
KENTUCKY							
1 **Comer**	Y	Y	Y	Y	+	+	+
2 **Guthrie**	Y	Y	Y	Y	Y	Y	Y
3 Yarmuth	N	Y	Y	Y	Y	Y	Y
4 **Massie**	Y	Y	Y	Y	Y	Y	Y
5 **Rogers**	Y	Y	Y	Y	Y	Y	Y
6 **Barr**	Y	Y	Y	Y	?	?	?
LOUISIANA							
1 **Scalise**	Y	Y	Y	Y	Y	Y	Y
2 Richmond	N	Y	Y	Y	Y	Y	Y
3 **Higgins**	Y	Y	Y	Y	Y	Y	Y
4 **Johnson**	Y	Y	Y	Y	Y	Y	Y
5 **Abraham**	Y	Y	Y	Y	Y	Y	Y
6 **Graves**	Y	Y	Y	+	Y	Y	Y
MAINE							
1 Pingree	N	Y	Y	Y	Y	Y	Y
2 **Poliquin**	Y	Y	Y	N	Y	Y	Y
MARYLAND							
1 **Harris**	Y	N	Y	Y	Y	Y	Y
2 Ruppersberger	N	Y	Y	Y	Y	Y	Y
3 Sarbanes	N	Y	Y	N	Y	Y	Y
4 Brown	N	Y	Y	?	Y	Y	Y
5 Hoyer	N	Y	Y	N	?	?	?
6 Delaney	N	Y	Y	?	Y	Y	Y
7 Cummings	N	Y	Y	N	Y	Y	Y
8 Raskin	N	Y	Y	N	Y	Y	Y
MASSACHUSETTS							
1 Neal	N	Y	Y	N	Y	Y	Y
2 McGovern	N	Y	Y	N	Y	Y	Y
3 Tsongas	N	Y	Y	Y	?	?	?
4 Kennedy	N	Y	Y	Y	Y	Y	Y
5 Clark	N	Y	Y	Y	Y	Y	Y
6 Moulton	N	Y	Y	Y	Y	Y	Y
7 Capuano	N	Y	Y	N	Y	Y	Y
8 Lynch	N	Y	Y	N	Y	Y	Y
9 Keating	N	Y	Y	Y	Y	Y	Y
MICHIGAN							
1 **Bergman**	Y	Y	Y	N	Y	Y	Y
2 **Huizenga**	Y	Y	Y	N	Y	Y	Y
3 **Amash**	Y	Y	Y	N	Y	Y	Y
4 **Moolenaar**	Y	Y	Y	Y	Y	Y	Y
5 Kildee	N	Y	Y	Y	Y	Y	Y
6 **Upton**	Y	Y	Y	N	Y	Y	Y
7 **Walberg**	Y	Y	Y	N	Y	Y	Y
8 **Bishop**	Y	Y	Y	Y	Y	Y	Y
9 Levin	N	Y	Y	N	Y	Y	Y
10 **Mitchell**	Y	Y	Y	Y	Y	Y	Y
11 **Trott**	Y	Y	Y	Y	Y	Y	Y
12 Dingell	N	Y	Y	Y	Y	Y	Y
13 Conyers	?	Y	Y	Y	Y	Y	Y
14 Lawrence	N	Y	Y	N	Y	Y	Y
MINNESOTA							
1 Walz	Y	Y	Y	Y	Y	Y	Y
2 **Lewis**	Y	Y	Y	Y	Y	Y	Y
3 **Paulsen**	Y	Y	Y	N	Y	Y	Y
4 McCollum	N	Y	Y	Y	Y	Y	Y

	169	170	171	172	173	174	175
5 Ellison	N	Y	Y	Y	Y	Y	Y
6 **Emmer**	Y	Y	Y	Y	Y	Y	Y
7 Peterson	Y	Y	Y	N	Y	Y	Y
8 Nolan	N	Y	Y	N	Y	Y	Y
MISSISSIPPI							
1 **Kelly**	Y	Y	Y	Y	Y	Y	Y
2 Thompson	N	Y	Y	N	Y	Y	Y
3 **Harper**	Y	Y	Y	?	Y	Y	Y
4 **Palazzo**	Y	Y	Y	N	Y	Y	Y
MISSOURI							
1 Clay	N	Y	Y	Y	Y	Y	Y
2 **Wagner**	Y	Y	Y	?	Y	Y	Y
3 **Luetkemeyer**	Y	Y	Y	Y	Y	Y	Y
4 **Hartzler**	Y	Y	Y	Y	Y	Y	Y
5 Cleaver	N	Y	Y	Y	?	?	?
6 **Graves**	Y	Y	Y	N	Y	Y	Y
7 **Long**	Y	Y	Y	Y	Y	Y	Y
8 **Smith**	Y	Y	Y	N	Y	Y	Y
MONTANA							
AL **Vacant**							
NEBRASKA							
1 **Fortenberry**	Y	Y	Y	Y	?	?	?
2 **Bacon**	Y	Y	Y	Y	Y	Y	Y
3 **Smith**	Y	Y	Y	Y	Y	Y	Y
NEVADA							
1 Titus	N	Y	Y	Y	?	?	?
2 **Amodei**	Y	Y	Y	?	Y	Y	Y
3 Rosen	N	Y	Y	N	Y	Y	Y
4 Kihuen	N	Y	Y	N	Y	Y	Y
NEW HAMPSHIRE							
1 Shea-Porter	N	Y	Y	Y	Y	Y	Y
2 Kuster	N	Y	Y	Y	Y	Y	Y
NEW JERSEY							
1 Norcross	N	Y	Y	Y	Y	Y	Y
2 **LoBiondo**	Y	Y	Y	N	Y	Y	Y
3 **MacArthur**	Y	Y	Y	N	?	Y	Y
4 **Smith**	Y	Y	Y	Y	Y	Y	Y
5 Gottheimer	N	Y	Y	N	Y	Y	Y
6 Pallone	N	Y	Y	N	Y	Y	Y
7 **Lance**	N	Y	Y	N	Y	Y	Y
8 Sires	N	Y	Y	N	Y	Y	Y
9 Pascrell	N	Y	Y	?	Y	Y	Y
10 Payne	?	?	?	?	?	?	?
11 **Frelinghuysen**	Y	Y	Y	Y	Y	Y	Y
12 Watson Coleman	N	Y	Y	N	Y	Y	Y
NEW MEXICO							
1 Lujan Grisham	N	Y	Y	Y	Y	Y	Y
2 **Pearce**	Y	Y	Y	?	Y	Y	Y
3 Luján	N	Y	Y	N	Y	Y	Y
NEW YORK							
1 **Zeldin**	Y	Y	Y	Y	Y	Y	Y
2 **King**	–	Y	Y	Y	Y	Y	Y
3 Suozzi	N	Y	Y	Y	+	+	+
4 Rice	N	Y	Y	N	Y	Y	Y
5 Meeks	N	Y	Y	Y	Y	Y	Y
6 Meng	N	Y	Y	Y	Y	Y	Y
7 Velázquez	N	Y	Y	Y	Y	Y	Y
8 Jeffries	N	?	?	?	Y	Y	Y
9 Clarke	N	Y	Y	N	?	?	Y
10 Nadler	N	Y	Y	Y	Y	Y	Y
11 **Donovan**	N	Y	Y	Y	Y	Y	Y
12 Maloney, C.	N	Y	Y	Y	Y	Y	Y
13 Espaillat	N	Y	Y	Y	Y	Y	Y
14 Crowley	N	+	+	N	Y	Y	Y
15 Serrano	N	?	Y	Y	Y	Y	Y
16 Engel	N	Y	+	Y	Y	Y	Y
17 Lowey	N	Y	Y	N	Y	Y	Y
18 Maloney, S.P.	N	Y	Y	N	Y	Y	Y
19 **Faso**	Y	Y	Y	Y	Y	Y	Y
20 Tonko	N	Y	Y	P	Y	Y	Y
21 **Stefanik**	Y	Y	Y	Y	Y	Y	Y
22 **Tenney**	Y	Y	Y	?	Y	Y	Y
23 **Reed**	Y	Y	Y	N	Y	Y	Y
24 **Katko**	Y	Y	Y	?	Y	Y	Y
25 Slaughter	–	+	+	–	+	+	+
26 Higgins	N	+	+	+	Y	Y	Y
27 **Collins**	+	Y	Y	Y	Y	Y	Y
NORTH CAROLINA							
1 Butterfield	N	Y	Y	N	Y	Y	Y
2 **Holding**	Y	Y	Y	N	Y	Y	Y
3 **Jones**	Y	Y	Y	N	Y	Y	N
4 Price	N	Y	Y	N	Y	Y	Y

	169	170	171	172	173	174	175
5 **Foxx**	Y	Y	Y	N	Y	Y	Y
6 **Walker**	Y	Y	Y	Y	Y	Y	Y
7 **Rouzer**	Y	Y	Y	N	Y	Y	Y
8 **Hudson**	Y	Y	Y	N	Y	Y	Y
9 **Pittenger**	Y	Y	Y	N	Y	Y	Y
10 **McHenry**	Y	Y	Y	Y	Y	Y	Y
11 **Meadows**	Y	Y	Y	Y	Y	Y	Y
12 Adams	N	Y	Y	Y	Y	Y	Y
13 **Budd**	Y	Y	Y	Y	Y	Y	Y
NORTH DAKOTA							
AL **Cramer**	Y	Y	Y	Y	Y	Y	Y
OHIO							
1 **Chabot**	Y	Y	Y	Y	Y	Y	Y
2 **Wenstrup**	Y	Y	Y	Y	Y	Y	Y
3 Beatty	N	Y	Y	Y	Y	Y	Y
4 **Jordan**	?	?	?	?	Y	Y	Y
5 **Latta**	Y	Y	Y	Y	Y	Y	Y
6 **Johnson**	Y	Y	Y	N	Y	Y	Y
7 **Gibbs**	Y	Y	Y	N	Y	Y	Y
8 **Davidson**	Y	Y	Y	Y	Y	Y	Y
9 Kaptur	N	Y	Y	Y	Y	Y	Y
10 **Turner**	Y	Y	Y	N	Y	Y	Y
11 Fudge	N	Y	Y	N	Y	Y	Y
12 **Tiberi**	Y	Y	Y	Y	Y	Y	Y
13 Ryan	N	Y	Y	N	Y	Y	Y
14 **Joyce**	Y	Y	Y	?	Y	Y	Y
15 **Stivers**	Y	Y	Y	N	Y	Y	Y
16 **Renacci**	Y	Y	Y	?	+	+	+
OKLAHOMA							
1 **Bridenstine**	Y	Y	Y	Y	Y	Y	Y
2 **Mullin**	Y	Y	Y	Y	Y	Y	Y
3 **Lucas**	Y	Y	Y	Y	Y	Y	Y
4 **Cole**	Y	Y	Y	Y	Y	Y	Y
5 **Russell**	Y	Y	Y	Y	Y	Y	Y
OREGON							
1 Bonamici	N	Y	Y	Y	Y	Y	Y
2 **Walden**	Y	Y	Y	N	Y	Y	Y
3 Blumenauer	N	Y	Y	Y	Y	Y	Y
4 DeFazio	N	Y	Y	N	Y	Y	Y
5 Schrader	Y	Y	Y	N	Y	Y	Y
PENNSYLVANIA							
1 Brady	N	Y	Y	N	Y	Y	Y
2 Evans	N	Y	Y	N	Y	Y	Y
3 **Kelly**	?	?	?	?	Y	Y	Y
4 **Perry**	Y	N	Y	Y	Y	Y	?
5 **Thompson**	Y	Y	Y	N	Y	Y	Y
6 **Costello**	Y	Y	Y	N	Y	Y	Y
7 **Meehan**	Y	Y	Y	Y	Y	Y	Y
8 **Fitzpatrick**	Y	Y	Y	N	Y	Y	Y
9 **Shuster**	Y	Y	Y	Y	Y	Y	Y
10 **Marino**	+	+	+	+	Y	Y	Y
11 **Barletta**	Y	Y	Y	Y	Y	Y	Y
12 **Rothfus**	Y	Y	Y	Y	Y	Y	Y
13 Boyle	N	Y	Y	N	Y	Y	Y
14 Doyle	N	Y	Y	?	Y	Y	Y
15 **Dent**	Y	Y	Y	Y	Y	Y	Y
16 **Smucker**	Y	Y	Y	Y	Y	Y	Y
17 Cartwright	N	Y	Y	Y	Y	Y	Y
18 **Murphy**	Y	Y	Y	N	Y	Y	Y
RHODE ISLAND							
1 Cicilline	N	Y	Y	Y	Y	Y	Y
2 Langevin	N	Y	Y	N	Y	Y	Y
SOUTH CAROLINA							
1 **Sanford**	Y	Y	Y	Y	Y	Y	Y
2 **Wilson**	Y	Y	Y	Y	Y	Y	Y
3 **Duncan**	Y	Y	Y	Y	?	?	?
4 **Gowdy**	Y	Y	Y	Y	Y	Y	Y
6 Clyburn	N	Y	Y	Y	Y	Y	Y
7 **Rice**	Y	Y	Y	P	Y	Y	Y
SOUTH DAKOTA							
AL **Noem**	Y	Y	Y	Y	Y	Y	Y
TENNESSEE							
1 **Roe**	Y	Y	Y	Y	Y	Y	Y
2 **Duncan**	Y	Y	Y	?	Y	Y	Y
3 **Fleischmann**	Y	Y	Y	Y	Y	Y	Y
4 **DesJarlais**	Y	Y	Y	Y	Y	Y	Y
5 Cooper	N	Y	Y	Y	Y	Y	Y
6 **Black**	Y	Y	Y	Y	Y	Y	Y
7 **Blackburn**	Y	Y	Y	?	Y	Y	Y
8 **Kustoff**	Y	Y	Y	Y	Y	Y	Y
9 Cohen	N	Y	Y	N	Y	Y	Y

	169	170	171	172	173	174	175
TEXAS							
1 **Gohmert**	Y	Y	Y	?	Y	Y	Y
2 **Poe**	Y	N	Y	N	Y	Y	Y
3 **Johnson, S.**	Y	Y	Y	Y	Y	Y	Y
4 **Ratcliffe**	Y	Y	Y	N	Y	Y	Y
5 **Hensarling**	Y	Y	Y	Y	Y	Y	Y
6 **Barton**	Y	Y	Y	Y	Y	Y	Y
7 **Culberson**	Y	Y	Y	Y	Y	Y	Y
8 **Brady**	Y	Y	+	Y	Y	Y	Y
9 Green, A.	N	Y	Y	Y	Y	Y	Y
10 **McCaul**	Y	N	Y	Y	Y	Y	Y
11 **Conaway**	Y	Y	Y	N	Y	Y	Y
12 **Granger**	Y	Y	Y	Y	Y	Y	Y
13 **Thornberry**	Y	Y	Y	Y	Y	Y	Y
14 **Weber**	Y	Y	Y	N	Y	Y	Y
15 Gonzalez	Y	?	?	?	Y	Y	Y
16 O'Rourke	N	Y	Y	Y	Y	Y	Y
17 **Flores**	Y	Y	Y	N	Y	Y	Y
18 Jackson Lee	N	?	Y	N	Y	Y	Y
19 **Arrington**	Y	Y	Y	Y	Y	Y	Y
20 Castro	N	Y	Y	Y	Y	Y	Y
21 **Smith**	Y	Y	Y	Y	Y	Y	Y
22 **Olson**	Y	Y	Y	Y	Y	Y	Y
23 **Hurd**	Y	Y	Y	N	Y	Y	Y
24 **Marchant**	Y	Y	Y	N	+	+	+
25 **Williams**	Y	Y	Y	Y	Y	Y	Y
26 **Burgess**	Y	Y	Y	N	Y	Y	Y
27 **Farenthold**	Y	Y	Y	Y	Y	Y	Y
28 Cuellar	Y	Y	Y	Y	Y	Y	Y
29 Green, G.	Y	Y	Y	N	Y	Y	Y
30 Johnson, E.B.	N	Y	Y	Y	Y	Y	Y
31 **Carter**	Y	Y	Y	Y	Y	Y	Y
32 **Sessions**	Y	Y	Y	Y	Y	Y	Y
33 Veasey	N	Y	Y	N	Y	Y	Y
34 Vela	Y	Y	Y	Y	Y	Y	Y
35 Doggett	N	Y	Y	Y	Y	Y	Y
36 **Babin**	Y	Y	Y	Y	Y	Y	Y
UTAH							
1 **Bishop**	Y	Y	Y	Y	Y	Y	Y
2 **Stewart**	Y	N	Y	Y	Y	Y	Y
3 **Chaffetz**	Y	Y	Y	N	Y	Y	Y
4 **Love**	Y	Y	Y	Y	Y	Y	Y
VERMONT							
AL Welch	?	Y	Y	Y	Y	Y	Y
VIRGINIA							
1 **Wittman**	Y	Y	Y	N	Y	Y	Y
2 **Taylor**	Y	N	Y	Y	Y	Y	Y
3 Scott	N	Y	Y	Y	Y	Y	Y
4 McEachin	N	+	+	+	Y	Y	Y
5 **Garrett**	Y	Y	Y	Y	Y	Y	Y
6 **Goodlatte**	Y	Y	Y	Y	Y	Y	Y
7 **Brat**	Y	Y	Y	Y	Y	Y	Y
8 Beyer	?	Y	Y	N	Y	Y	Y
9 **Griffith**	Y	Y	Y	Y	Y	Y	Y
10 **Comstock**	Y	Y	Y	Y	Y	Y	Y
11 Connolly	N	Y	Y	Y	Y	Y	Y
WASHINGTON							
1 DelBene	N	Y	Y	Y	Y	Y	Y
2 Larsen	N	Y	Y	?	Y	Y	Y
3 **Herrera Beutler**	Y	Y	Y	N	Y	Y	Y
4 **Newhouse**	Y	Y	Y	Y	Y	Y	Y
5 **McMorris Rodgers**	Y	Y	Y	Y	Y	Y	Y
6 Kilmer	N	Y	Y	N	Y	Y	Y
7 Jayapal	N	Y	Y	Y	Y	Y	Y
8 **Reichert**	Y	Y	Y	N	Y	Y	Y
9 Smith	N	Y	Y	Y	Y	Y	Y
10 Heck	N	Y	Y	Y	Y	Y	Y
WEST VIRGINIA							
1 **McKinley**	Y	Y	Y	N	Y	Y	Y
2 **Mooney**	Y	Y	Y	Y	Y	Y	Y
3 **Jenkins**	Y	Y	Y	N	Y	Y	Y
WISCONSIN							
1 **Ryan**							
2 Pocan	N	Y	Y	Y	Y	Y	Y
3 Kind	Y	Y	Y	Y	Y	Y	Y
4 Moore	N	Y	Y	Y	Y	Y	Y
5 **Sensenbrenner**	Y	Y	Y	Y	Y	Y	Y
6 **Grothman**	Y	Y	Y	?	Y	Y	Y
7 **Duffy**	Y	Y	Y	N	Y	Y	Y
8 **Gallagher**	Y	Y	Y	N	Y	Y	Y
WYOMING							
AL **Cheney**	Y	Y	Y	Y	Y	Y	Y

VOTE NUMBER

176. HR 372, H RES 209. HEALTH INSURANCE ANTITRUST REGULATION/ PREVIOUS QUESTION. Collins, R-Ga., motion to order the previous question (thus ending debate and possibility of amendment) on the rule (H Res 209) that would provide for House floor consideration of a bill that would eliminate most of the federal antitrust exemptions for health insurance providers that are subject to regulation at the state level. Motion agreed to 231-185 : R 231-1; D 0-184. March, 21, 2017.

177. HR 372, H RES 209. HEALTH INSURANCE ANTITRUST REGULATION/ RULE. Adoption of the rule (H Res 209) that would provide for House floor consideration of a bill that would eliminate most of the federal antitrust exemptions for health insurance providers that are subject to regulation at the state level. The bill would allow federal regulators to take actions against insurers for coordinated activities that could harm consumers. Adopted 234-182 : R 233-0; D 1-182. March, 21, 2017.

178. HR 1353. TSA TECHNOLOGY PLAN REPORT/PASSAGE. Rutherford, R-Fla., motion to suspend the rules and pass the bill that would require the Transportation Security Administration to submit an annual report to Congress on the progress of the TSA's five-year technology investment plan and on any technology acquisitions made by the TSA. The measure would also require the TSA to separately report to Congress on any equipment currently in operation past the end of its anticipated lifespan. Motion agreed to 414-2 : R 233-0; D 181-2. March, 21, 2017.

179. H RES 210, HR 1101. ASSOCIATION HEALTH CARE PLANS/PREVIOUS QUESTION. Byrne, R-Ala., motion to order the previous question (thus ending debate and possibility of amendment) on the rule (H Res 210) that would provide for House floor consideration of the bill that would exempt health care plans sponsored by trade and business associations from most state laws and regulations. Motion agreed to 233-186 : R 233-0; D 0-186. March, 21, 2017.

180. H RES 210, HR 1101. ASSOCIATION HEALTH CARE PLANS/RULE. Adoption of the rule (H Res 210) that would provide for House floor consideration of the bill that would exempt health care plans sponsored by trade and business associations from most state laws and regulations. The bill would allow the association sponsoring a health care plan to have full discretion to choose the health benefits included in the plan, as long as the plan would still meet certain statuary minimums. Adopted 233-186 : R 233-0; D 0-186. March, 21, 2017.

181. HR 1297. DHS REVIEW EXPANSIONS/PASSAGE. Rutherford, R-Fla., motion to suspend the rules and pass the bill that would require the Homeland Security Department quadrennial reviews to include the Homeland Security Advisory Council and the Homeland Security Science and Technology Advisory Committee, and it would also require the reviews to identify resources that are redundant, wasteful or unnecessary. Motion agreed to 415-0 : R 232-0; D 183-0. March, 21, 2017.

182. PRESIDENT'S TAX RETURN DISCLOSURE/MOTION TO TABLE. Cheney, R-Wyo., motion to table (kill) the Polis, D-Colo., motion to appeal the ruling of the Chair that the Polis resolution related to the disclosure of President Trump's tax returns does not constitute a question of the privileges of the House. Motion agreed to 230-189 : R 230-1; D 0-188. March, 22, 2017.

	176	177	178	179	180	181	182
ALABAMA							
1 Byrne	Y	Y	Y	Y	Y	Y	Y
2 Roby	Y	Y	Y	Y	Y	Y	Y
3 Rogers	Y	Y	Y	Y	Y	Y	Y
4 Aderholt	Y	Y	Y	Y	Y	Y	Y
5 Brooks	Y	Y	Y	Y	Y	Y	Y
6 Palmer	Y	Y	Y	Y	Y	Y	Y
7 Sewell	N	N	Y	N	N	Y	N
ALASKA							
AL Young	Y	Y	Y	Y	Y	Y	Y
ARIZONA							
1 O'Halleran	N	N	Y	N	N	Y	N
2 McSally	Y	Y	Y	Y	Y	Y	Y
3 Grijalva	N	N	Y	N	N	Y	N
4 Gosar	Y	Y	Y	Y	Y	Y	Y
5 Biggs	Y	Y	Y	Y	Y	Y	Y
6 Schweikert	Y	?	Y	Y	Y	Y	Y
7 Gallego	N	N	Y	N	N	Y	N
8 Franks	Y	Y	Y	Y	Y	Y	Y
9 Sinema	–	+	+	–	–	+	–
ARKANSAS							
1 Crawford	Y	Y	Y	Y	Y	Y	Y
2 Hill	Y	Y	Y	Y	Y	Y	Y
3 Womack	Y	Y	Y	Y	Y	Y	Y
4 Westerman	Y	Y	Y	Y	Y	Y	Y
CALIFORNIA							
1 LaMalfa	Y	Y	Y	Y	Y	Y	Y
2 Huffman	N	N	Y	N	N	Y	N
3 Garamendi	N	N	Y	N	N	Y	N
4 McClintock	Y	Y	Y	Y	Y	Y	Y
5 Thompson	N	N	Y	N	N	Y	N
6 Matsui	N	N	Y	N	N	Y	N
7 Bera	N	N	Y	N	N	Y	N
8 Cook	Y	Y	Y	Y	Y	Y	Y
9 McNerney	N	N	Y	N	N	Y	N
10 Denham	Y	Y	Y	Y	Y	Y	Y
11 DeSaulnier	N	N	Y	N	N	Y	N
12 Pelosi	N	N	Y	N	N	?	N
13 Lee	N	N	Y	N	N	Y	N
14 Speier	N	N	Y	N	N	Y	N
15 Swalwell	N	N	Y	N	N	Y	N
16 Costa	N	N	Y	N	N	Y	N
17 Khanna	N	N	Y	N	N	Y	N
18 Eshoo	N	N	Y	N	N	Y	N
19 Lofgren	N	N	Y	N	N	Y	N
20 Panetta	N	N	Y	N	N	Y	N
21 Valadao	Y	Y	Y	Y	Y	Y	Y
22 Nunes	Y	Y	Y	Y	Y	Y	Y
23 McCarthy	Y	Y	Y	Y	Y	Y	Y
24 Carbajal	N	N	Y	N	N	Y	N
25 Knight	Y	Y	Y	Y	Y	Y	Y
26 Brownley	N	N	Y	N	N	Y	N
27 Chu	N	N	Y	N	N	Y	N
28 Schiff	N	N	Y	N	N	Y	N
29 Cardenas	N	N	Y	N	N	Y	N
30 Sherman	N	N	Y	N	N	Y	N
31 Aguilar	N	N	Y	N	N	Y	N
32 Napolitano	N	N	N	N	N	Y	N
33 Lieu	N	N	Y	N	N	Y	N
34 Vacant							
35 Torres	N	N	Y	N	N	Y	N
36 Ruiz	N	N	Y	N	N	Y	N
37 Bass	N	N	Y	N	N	Y	N
38 Sánchez, Linda	N	N	Y	N	N	Y	N
39 Royce	Y	Y	Y	Y	Y	Y	Y
40 Roybal-Allard	N	N	Y	N	N	Y	N
41 Takano	N	N	Y	N	N	Y	N
42 Calvert	Y	Y	Y	Y	Y	Y	Y
43 Waters	N	N	Y	N	N	Y	N
44 Barragan	N	N	Y	N	N	Y	N
45 Walters	Y	Y	Y	Y	Y	Y	Y
46 Correa	N	N	Y	N	N	Y	N
47 Lowenthal	N	N	Y	N	N	Y	N
48 Rohrabacher	Y	Y	Y	Y	Y	Y	Y
49 Issa	Y	Y	Y	Y	Y	Y	Y
50 Hunter	Y	Y	Y	Y	Y	Y	Y
51 Vargas	N	N	Y	N	N	Y	N
52 Peters	N	N	Y	N	N	Y	N
53 Davis	N	N	Y	N	N	Y	N

	176	177	178	179	180	181	182
COLORADO							
1 DeGette	N	N	Y	N	N	Y	N
2 Polis	N	N	Y	N	N	Y	N
3 Tipton	Y	Y	Y	Y	Y	Y	Y
4 Buck	Y	Y	Y	Y	Y	Y	Y
5 Lamborn	Y	Y	Y	Y	Y	Y	Y
6 Coffman	Y	Y	Y	Y	Y	Y	Y
7 Perlmutter	N	N	Y	N	N	?	N
CONNECTICUT							
1 Larson	N	N	Y	N	N	Y	N
2 Courtney	N	N	Y	N	N	Y	N
3 DeLauro	N	N	Y	N	N	Y	N
4 Himes	N	N	Y	N	N	Y	N
5 Esty	N	N	Y	N	N	Y	N
DELAWARE							
AL Blunt Rochester	N	N	Y	N	N	Y	N
FLORIDA							
1 Gaetz	Y	Y	Y	Y	+	Y	Y
2 Dunn	Y	Y	Y	Y	Y	Y	Y
3 Yoho	Y	Y	Y	Y	Y	Y	Y
4 Rutherford	Y	Y	Y	Y	Y	Y	Y
5 Lawson	N	N	Y	N	N	Y	N
6 DeSantis	Y	Y	Y	Y	Y	Y	Y
7 Murphy	N	N	Y	N	N	Y	N
8 Posey	Y	Y	Y	Y	Y	Y	Y
9 Soto	N	N	Y	N	N	Y	N
10 Demings	N	N	Y	N	N	Y	N
11 Webster	Y	Y	Y	Y	Y	Y	Y
12 Bilirakis	Y	Y	Y	Y	Y	Y	Y
13 Crist	N	Y	Y	N	N	Y	N
14 Castor	N	N	Y	N	N	Y	N
15 Ross	Y	Y	Y	Y	Y	Y	Y
16 Buchanan	Y	Y	Y	Y	Y	Y	Y
17 Rooney, T.	Y	Y	Y	Y	Y	Y	Y
18 Mast	Y	Y	Y	Y	Y	Y	Y
19 Rooney, F.	Y	Y	Y	Y	Y	Y	Y
20 Hastings	N	N	N	N	N	Y	N
21 Frankel	N	N	Y	N	N	Y	N
22 Deutch	?	?	?	?	?	?	N
23 Wasserman Schultz	N	N	Y	N	N	Y	N
24 Wilson	N	N	Y	N	N	Y	N
25 Diaz-Balart	Y	Y	Y	Y	Y	Y	Y
26 Curbelo	Y	Y	Y	Y	Y	Y	Y
27 Ros-Lehtinen	Y	Y	Y	Y	Y	Y	Y
GEORGIA							
1 Carter	Y	Y	Y	Y	Y	Y	Y
2 Bishop	N	N	Y	N	N	Y	N
3 Ferguson	Y	Y	Y	Y	Y	Y	Y
4 Johnson	N	N	Y	N	N	Y	N
5 Lewis	?	?	?	N	N	Y	N
7 Woodall	Y	Y	Y	Y	Y	Y	Y
8 Scott, A.	Y	Y	Y	Y	Y	Y	Y
9 Collins	Y	Y	Y	Y	Y	Y	Y
10 Hice	Y	Y	Y	Y	Y	Y	Y
11 Loudermilk	Y	Y	Y	Y	Y	Y	Y
12 Allen	+	Y	Y	Y	Y	Y	Y
13 Scott, D.	N	N	Y	N	N	Y	N
14 Graves	Y	Y	Y	Y	Y	Y	Y
HAWAII							
1 Hanabusa	N	N	Y	N	N	Y	N
2 Gabbard	N	N	Y	N	N	Y	N
IDAHO							
1 Labrador	Y	Y	Y	Y	Y	Y	Y
2 Simpson	Y	Y	Y	Y	Y	Y	Y
ILLINOIS							
1 Rush	?	?	?	?	?	?	?
2 Kelly	N	N	Y	N	N	Y	N
3 Lipinski	N	N	Y	N	N	Y	N
4 Gutierrez	N	N	Y	N	N	Y	N
5 Quigley	N	N	Y	N	N	Y	N
6 Roskam	Y	Y	Y	Y	Y	Y	Y
7 Davis, D.	N	N	Y	N	N	Y	N
8 Krishnamoorthi	N	N	Y	N	N	Y	N
9 Schakowsky	N	N	Y	N	N	Y	N
10 Schneider	N	N	Y	N	N	Y	N
11 Foster	N	N	Y	N	N	Y	N
12 Bost	Y	Y	Y	Y	Y	Y	Y
13 Davis, R.	Y	Y	Y	Y	Y	Y	Y
14 Hultgren	Y	Y	Y	Y	Y	Y	Y
15 Shimkus	Y	Y	Y	Y	Y	Y	Y

	176	177	178	179	180	181	182
16 **Kinzinger**	Y	Y	Y	Y	Y	Y	Y
17 Bustos	N	N	Y	N	N	Y	N
18 **LaHood**	Y	Y	Y	Y	Y	Y	Y
INDIANA							
1 Visclosky	N	N	Y	N	N	Y	N
2 **Walorski**	Y	Y	Y	Y	Y	Y	Y
3 **Banks**	Y	Y	Y	Y	Y	Y	Y
4 **Rokita**	Y	Y	?	Y	Y	Y	Y
5 **Brooks**	Y	Y	Y	Y	Y	Y	Y
6 **Messer**	Y	Y	Y	Y	Y	Y	Y
7 Carson	N	N	Y	N	N	Y	N
8 **Bucshon**	Y	Y	Y	Y	Y	Y	Y
9 **Hollingsworth**	Y	Y	Y	Y	Y	Y	Y
IOWA							
1 **Blum**	Y	Y	Y	Y	Y	Y	Y
2 Loebsack	N	N	Y	N	N	Y	N
3 **Young**	Y	Y	Y	Y	Y	Y	Y
4 **King**	Y	Y	Y	Y	Y	Y	+
KANSAS							
1 **Marshall**	Y	Y	Y	Y	Y	Y	Y
2 **Jenkins**	Y	Y	Y	Y	Y	Y	Y
3 **Yoder**	Y	Y	Y	Y	Y	Y	Y
KENTUCKY							
1 **Comer**	Y	Y	Y	Y	Y	Y	Y
2 **Guthrie**	Y	Y	Y	Y	Y	Y	Y
3 Yarmuth	N	N	Y	?	?	?	N
4 **Massie**	Y	Y	Y	Y	Y	Y	Y
5 **Rogers**	Y	Y	Y	Y	Y	Y	Y
6 **Barr**	Y	Y	Y	Y	Y	Y	Y
LOUISIANA							
1 **Scalise**	Y	Y	Y	Y	Y	Y	Y
2 Richmond	N	N	Y	N	N	Y	N
3 **Higgins**	Y	Y	Y	Y	Y	Y	Y
4 **Johnson**	Y	Y	Y	Y	Y	Y	Y
5 **Abraham**	Y	Y	Y	Y	Y	Y	Y
6 **Graves**	Y	Y	Y	Y	Y	Y	Y
MAINE							
1 Pingree	N	N	Y	N	N	Y	N
2 **Poliquin**	Y	Y	Y	Y	Y	Y	Y
MARYLAND							
1 **Harris**	Y	Y	Y	Y	Y	Y	Y
2 Ruppersberger	N	N	Y	N	N	Y	N
3 Sarbanes	N	N	Y	N	N	Y	N
4 Brown	N	N	Y	N	N	+	N
5 Hoyer	N	N	Y	N	N	Y	N
6 Delaney	N	N	Y	N	N	Y	N
7 Cummings	N	N	Y	N	N	Y	N
8 Raskin	N	N	Y	N	N	Y	N
MASSACHUSETTS							
1 Neal	N	N	Y	N	N	Y	N
2 McGovern	N	N	Y	N	N	Y	N
3 Tsongas	?	?	?	?	?	?	?
4 Kennedy	N	N	Y	N	N	Y	N
5 Clark	N	N	Y	N	N	Y	N
6 Moulton	N	N	Y	N	N	Y	N
7 Capuano	N	N	Y	N	N	Y	N
8 Lynch	N	N	Y	N	N	Y	N
9 Keating	N	N	Y	N	N	Y	N
MICHIGAN							
1 **Bergman**	Y	Y	Y	Y	Y	Y	Y
2 **Huizenga**	Y	Y	Y	Y	Y	Y	Y
3 **Amash**	Y	Y	Y	Y	Y	Y	Y
4 **Moolenaar**	Y	Y	Y	Y	Y	Y	Y
5 Kildee	N	N	Y	N	N	Y	N
6 **Upton**	Y	Y	Y	Y	Y	Y	Y
7 **Walberg**	Y	Y	Y	Y	Y	Y	Y
8 **Bishop**	Y	Y	Y	Y	Y	Y	Y
9 Levin	N	N	Y	N	N	Y	N
10 **Mitchell**	Y	Y	Y	Y	Y	Y	Y
11 **Trott**	Y	Y	Y	Y	Y	Y	Y
12 Dingell	N	N	Y	N	N	Y	N
13 Conyers	N	N	Y	N	N	Y	N
14 Lawrence	N	N	Y	N	N	Y	N
MINNESOTA							
1 Walz	N	N	Y	N	N	Y	N
2 **Lewis**	Y	Y	Y	Y	Y	Y	Y
3 **Paulsen**	Y	Y	Y	Y	Y	Y	Y
4 McCollum	N	N	Y	N	N	Y	N

	176	177	178	179	180	181	182
5 Ellison	N	N	Y	N	N	Y	N
6 **Emmer**	?	Y	Y	Y	Y	Y	Y
7 Peterson	N	N	Y	N	N	Y	N
8 Nolan	N	N	Y	N	N	Y	N
MISSISSIPPI							
1 **Kelly**	Y	Y	Y	Y	Y	Y	Y
2 Thompson	?	?	?	N	N	Y	N
3 **Harper**	Y	Y	Y	Y	Y	Y	Y
4 **Palazzo**	Y	Y	Y	Y	Y	Y	Y
MISSOURI							
1 Clay	N	N	Y	N	N	Y	N
2 **Wagner**	Y	Y	Y	Y	Y	Y	Y
3 **Luetkemeyer**	Y	Y	Y	Y	Y	Y	Y
4 **Hartzler**	Y	Y	Y	Y	Y	Y	Y
5 Cleaver	N	N	Y	N	N	Y	N
6 **Graves**	Y	Y	Y	Y	Y	Y	Y
7 **Long**	Y	Y	Y	Y	Y	Y	Y
8 **Smith**	Y	Y	Y	Y	Y	Y	Y
MONTANA							
AL **Vacant**							
NEBRASKA							
1 **Fortenberry**	?	?	?	Y	Y	Y	Y
2 **Bacon**	Y	Y	Y	Y	Y	Y	Y
3 **Smith**	Y	Y	Y	Y	Y	Y	Y
NEVADA							
1 Titus	N	N	Y	N	N	Y	N
2 **Amodei**	Y	Y	Y	Y	Y	Y	Y
3 Rosen	N	N	Y	N	N	Y	N
4 Kihuen	N	N	Y	N	N	Y	N
NEW HAMPSHIRE							
1 Shea-Porter	N	N	Y	N	N	Y	N
2 Kuster	N	N	Y	N	N	Y	N
NEW JERSEY							
1 Norcross	N	?	Y	N	N	Y	N
2 **LoBiondo**	Y	Y	Y	Y	Y	Y	Y
3 **MacArthur**	Y	Y	Y	Y	Y	Y	Y
4 **Smith**	Y	Y	Y	Y	Y	Y	Y
5 Gottheimer	N	N	Y	N	N	Y	N
6 Pallone	N	N	Y	N	N	Y	N
7 **Lance**	Y	Y	Y	Y	Y	Y	Y
8 Sires	N	N	Y	N	N	Y	N
9 Pascrell	N	N	Y	N	N	Y	N
10 Payne	?	?	?	?	?	?	?
11 **Frelinghuysen**	Y	Y	Y	Y	Y	Y	Y
12 Watson Coleman	N	N	Y	N	N	Y	N
NEW MEXICO							
1 Lujan Grisham	N	N	Y	N	N	Y	N
2 **Pearce**	Y	Y	Y	Y	Y	Y	Y
3 Luján	N	N	Y	N	N	Y	N
NEW YORK							
1 **Zeldin**	Y	Y	Y	Y	Y	Y	Y
2 **King**	Y	Y	Y	Y	Y	Y	Y
3 Suozzi	N	N	Y	N	N	Y	N
4 Rice	N	N	Y	N	N	Y	N
5 Meeks	N	N	Y	N	N	Y	N
6 Meng	N	N	Y	N	N	Y	N
7 Velázquez	N	N	Y	N	N	Y	N
8 Jeffries	N	N	Y	N	N	Y	N
9 Clarke	N	N	Y	N	N	Y	N
10 Nadler	N	N	Y	N	N	Y	N
11 **Donovan**	Y	Y	Y	Y	Y	Y	Y
12 Maloney, C.	N	N	Y	N	N	Y	N
13 Espaillat	N	N	Y	N	N	Y	N
14 Crowley	N	N	Y	N	N	Y	N
15 Serrano	N	N	Y	N	N	Y	N
16 Engel	N	N	Y	N	N	Y	N
17 Lowey	N	N	Y	N	N	Y	N
18 Maloney, S.P.	N	N	Y	N	N	Y	N
19 **Faso**	Y	Y	Y	Y	Y	Y	Y
20 Tonko	N	N	Y	N	N	Y	N
21 **Stefanik**	Y	Y	Y	Y	Y	Y	Y
22 **Tenney**	Y	Y	Y	Y	Y	Y	Y
23 **Reed**	Y	Y	Y	Y	Y	Y	Y
24 **Katko**	Y	Y	Y	Y	Y	Y	Y
25 Slaughter	–	–	+	–	–	+	–
26 Higgins	N	N	Y	N	N	Y	N
27 **Collins**	Y	Y	Y	Y	Y	Y	Y
NORTH CAROLINA							
1 Butterfield	N	N	Y	N	N	Y	N
2 **Holding**	Y	Y	Y	Y	Y	Y	Y
3 **Jones**	Y	Y	Y	Y	Y	Y	N
4 Price	N	N	Y	N	N	Y	N

	176	177	178	179	180	181	182
5 **Foxx**	Y	Y	Y	Y	Y	Y	Y
6 **Walker**	Y	Y	Y	Y	Y	Y	Y
7 **Rouzer**	Y	Y	Y	Y	Y	Y	Y
8 **Hudson**	Y	Y	Y	Y	Y	?	Y
9 **Pittenger**	Y	Y	Y	Y	Y	Y	Y
10 **McHenry**	Y	Y	Y	Y	Y	Y	Y
11 **Meadows**	Y	Y	Y	Y	Y	Y	Y
12 Adams	N	N	Y	N	N	Y	N
13 **Budd**	Y	Y	Y	Y	Y	Y	Y
NORTH DAKOTA							
AL **Cramer**	Y	Y	Y	Y	Y	Y	Y
OHIO							
1 **Chabot**	Y	Y	Y	Y	Y	Y	Y
2 **Wenstrup**	Y	Y	Y	Y	Y	Y	Y
3 Beatty	N	N	Y	N	N	Y	N
4 **Jordan**	Y	Y	Y	Y	Y	Y	Y
5 **Latta**	Y	Y	Y	Y	Y	Y	Y
6 **Johnson**	Y	Y	Y	Y	Y	Y	Y
7 **Gibbs**	Y	Y	Y	Y	Y	Y	Y
8 **Davidson**	Y	Y	Y	Y	Y	Y	Y
9 Kaptur	N	N	Y	N	N	Y	N
10 **Turner**	Y	Y	Y	Y	Y	Y	Y
11 Fudge	N	N	Y	N	N	Y	N
12 **Tiberi**	Y	Y	Y	Y	Y	Y	Y
13 Ryan	N	N	Y	N	N	Y	N
14 **Joyce**	Y	Y	Y	Y	Y	Y	Y
15 **Stivers**	Y	Y	Y	Y	Y	Y	Y
16 **Renacci**	Y	Y	Y	Y	Y	Y	Y
OKLAHOMA							
1 **Bridenstine**	Y	Y	Y	?	?	?	Y
2 **Mullin**	Y	Y	Y	Y	Y	Y	Y
3 **Lucas**	Y	Y	Y	Y	Y	Y	Y
4 **Cole**	Y	Y	Y	Y	Y	Y	Y
5 **Russell**	Y	Y	Y	Y	Y	Y	Y
OREGON							
1 Bonamici	N	N	Y	N	N	Y	N
2 **Walden**	Y	Y	Y	Y	Y	Y	Y
3 Blumenauer	N	N	Y	N	N	Y	N
4 DeFazio	N	N	Y	N	N	Y	N
5 Schrader	N	N	Y	N	N	Y	N
PENNSYLVANIA							
1 Brady	N	N	Y	N	N	Y	N
2 Evans	N	N	Y	N	N	Y	N
3 **Kelly**	Y	Y	Y	Y	Y	Y	Y
4 **Perry**	Y	Y	Y	Y	Y	Y	Y
5 **Thompson**	Y	Y	Y	Y	Y	Y	Y
6 **Costello**	Y	Y	Y	Y	Y	Y	Y
7 **Meehan**	Y	Y	Y	Y	Y	Y	Y
8 **Fitzpatrick**	Y	Y	Y	Y	Y	Y	Y
9 **Shuster**	Y	Y	Y	Y	Y	Y	?
10 **Marino**	Y	Y	Y	Y	Y	Y	Y
11 **Barletta**	Y	Y	Y	Y	Y	Y	Y
12 **Rothfus**	Y	Y	Y	Y	Y	Y	Y
13 Boyle	N	N	Y	N	N	Y	N
14 Doyle	N	N	Y	N	N	Y	N
15 **Dent**	Y	Y	Y	Y	Y	Y	Y
16 **Smucker**	Y	Y	Y	Y	Y	Y	Y
17 Cartwright	N	N	Y	N	N	Y	N
18 **Murphy**	Y	Y	Y	Y	Y	Y	Y
RHODE ISLAND							
1 Cicilline	N	N	Y	N	N	Y	N
2 Langevin	N	N	Y	N	N	Y	N
SOUTH CAROLINA							
1 **Sanford**	Y	Y	Y	Y	Y	Y	P
2 **Wilson**	Y	Y	Y	Y	Y	Y	Y
3 **Duncan**	Y	Y	Y	Y	Y	Y	Y
4 **Gowdy**	Y	Y	Y	Y	Y	Y	Y
6 Clyburn	N	N	Y	N	N	Y	N
7 **Rice**	Y	Y	Y	Y	Y	Y	Y
SOUTH DAKOTA							
AL **Noem**	Y	Y	Y	Y	Y	Y	Y
TENNESSEE							
1 **Roe**	Y	Y	Y	Y	Y	Y	Y
2 **Duncan**	Y	Y	Y	Y	Y	Y	Y
3 **Fleischmann**	Y	Y	Y	Y	Y	Y	Y
4 **DesJarlais**	Y	Y	Y	Y	Y	Y	Y
5 Cooper	N	N	Y	N	N	Y	N
6 **Black**	Y	Y	Y	+	Y	Y	Y
7 **Blackburn**	Y	Y	Y	Y	Y	Y	?
8 **Kustoff**	Y	Y	Y	Y	Y	Y	Y
9 Cohen	N	N	Y	N	N	Y	N

	176	177	178	179	180	181	182
TEXAS							
1 **Gohmert**	Y	Y	Y	Y	Y	Y	Y
2 **Poe**	Y	Y	Y	Y	Y	Y	Y
3 **Johnson, S.**	Y	Y	Y	Y	Y	Y	Y
4 **Ratcliffe**	Y	Y	Y	Y	Y	Y	Y
5 **Hensarling**	Y	Y	Y	Y	Y	Y	Y
6 **Barton**	Y	Y	Y	Y	Y	Y	Y
7 **Culberson**	Y	Y	Y	Y	Y	Y	Y
8 **Brady**	Y	Y	Y	Y	Y	+	Y
9 Green, A.	N	N	Y	N	N	Y	N
10 **McCaul**	Y	Y	Y	Y	Y	Y	Y
11 **Conaway**	Y	Y	Y	Y	Y	Y	Y
12 **Granger**	Y	Y	Y	Y	Y	Y	Y
13 **Thornberry**	Y	Y	Y	Y	Y	Y	Y
14 **Weber**	Y	Y	Y	Y	Y	Y	Y
15 Gonzalez	N	N	Y	N	N	Y	N
16 O'Rourke	N	N	Y	N	N	Y	N
17 **Flores**	Y	Y	Y	Y	Y	Y	Y
18 Jackson Lee	N	N	Y	N	N	Y	N
19 **Arrington**	Y	Y	Y	Y	Y	Y	Y
20 Castro	N	N	Y	N	N	Y	N
21 **Smith**	Y	Y	Y	Y	Y	Y	Y
22 **Olson**	Y	Y	Y	Y	Y	Y	Y
23 **Hurd**	Y	Y	Y	Y	Y	Y	Y
24 **Marchant**	+	+	+	+	+	+	Y
25 **Williams**	Y	Y	Y	Y	Y	Y	Y
26 **Burgess**	Y	Y	Y	Y	Y	Y	Y
27 **Farenthold**	Y	Y	Y	Y	Y	Y	Y
28 Cuellar	N	N	Y	N	N	Y	N
29 Green, G.	N	N	Y	N	N	Y	N
30 Johnson, E.B.	N	N	Y	N	N	Y	N
31 **Carter**	Y	Y	Y	Y	Y	Y	Y
32 **Sessions**	Y	Y	Y	Y	Y	Y	Y
33 Veasey	N	N	Y	N	N	Y	N
34 Vela	N	N	Y	N	N	Y	N
35 Doggett	N	N	Y	N	N	Y	N
36 **Babin**	Y	Y	Y	Y	Y	Y	Y
UTAH							
1 **Bishop**	Y	Y	Y	Y	Y	Y	?
2 **Stewart**	Y	Y	Y	Y	Y	Y	Y
3 **Chaffetz**	Y	Y	Y	Y	Y	Y	Y
4 **Love**	Y	Y	Y	Y	Y	Y	Y
VERMONT							
AL Welch	N	N	?	N	N	Y	N
VIRGINIA							
1 **Wittman**	Y	Y	Y	Y	Y	Y	Y
2 **Taylor**	Y	Y	Y	Y	Y	Y	Y
3 Scott	N	N	Y	N	N	Y	N
4 McEachin	N	N	Y	N	N	Y	N
5 **Garrett**	Y	Y	Y	Y	Y	Y	Y
6 **Goodlatte**	Y	Y	Y	Y	Y	Y	Y
7 **Brat**	Y	Y	Y	Y	Y	Y	Y
8 Beyer	?	?	?	N	N	Y	N
9 **Griffith**	Y	Y	Y	Y	Y	Y	Y
10 **Comstock**	Y	Y	Y	Y	Y	Y	Y
11 Connolly	N	N	Y	N	N	Y	N
WASHINGTON							
1 DelBene	N	N	Y	N	N	Y	N
2 Larsen	N	N	Y	N	N	Y	N
3 **Herrera Beutler**	Y	Y	Y	Y	Y	Y	Y
4 **Newhouse**	Y	Y	Y	Y	Y	Y	Y
5 **McMorris Rodgers**	Y	Y	Y	Y	Y	Y	Y
6 Kilmer	N	N	Y	N	N	Y	N
7 Jayapal	N	N	Y	N	N	Y	N
8 **Reichert**	Y	Y	Y	Y	Y	Y	Y
9 Smith	N	N	Y	N	N	Y	N
10 Heck	N	N	Y	N	N	Y	N
WEST VIRGINIA							
1 **McKinley**	Y	Y	Y	Y	Y	Y	Y
2 **Mooney**	Y	Y	Y	Y	Y	Y	Y
3 **Jenkins**	Y	Y	Y	Y	Y	Y	Y
WISCONSIN							
1 **Ryan**							
2 Pocan	N	N	Y	N	N	Y	N
3 Kind	N	N	Y	N	N	Y	N
4 Moore	N	N	Y	N	N	Y	N
5 **Sensenbrenner**	Y	Y	Y	Y	Y	Y	Y
6 **Grothman**	N	Y	Y	Y	Y	Y	Y
7 **Duffy**	Y	Y	Y	Y	Y	Y	Y
8 **Gallagher**	Y	Y	Y	Y	Y	Y	Y
WYOMING							
AL **Cheney**	Y	Y	Y	Y	Y	Y	Y

III HOUSE VOTES

VOTE NUMBER

183. HR 372. HEALTH INSURANCE ANTITRUST REGULATION/RECOMMIT. Rosen, D-Nev., motion to recommit the bill to the House Judiciary Committee and report it back immediately with an amendment that would prohibit companies that issue health insurance from varying the premiums for health insurance by age in a way that would increase health care premiums for individuals over the age of 55 to be more than three times greater than the premiums for individuals under the age of 21. Motion rejected 189-233 : R 2-233; D 187-0. March, 22, 2017.

184. HR 372. HEALTH INSURANCE ANTITRUST REGULATION/PASSAGE. Passage of the bill would eliminate most of the federal antitrust exemptions for health insurance providers that are subject to regulation at the state level. The bill would allow federal regulators to take actions against insurers for co-ordinated activities that could harm consumers. Certain collective insurance industry practices, such as historical data sharing, would still be exempt from federal antitrust laws. Passed 416-7 : R 235-0; D 181-7. March, 22, 2017.

185. HR 1101. ASSOCIATION HEALTH CARE PLANS/RECOMMIT. Shea-Porter, D-N.H., motion to recommit the bill to the House Education and the Workforce Committee with instructions to report it back immediately with an amendment that would require association health plans to provide coverage for substance abuse disorder treatments. Motion rejected 179-233 : R 2-233; D 177-0. March, 22, 2017.

186. HR 1101. ASSOCIATION HEALTH CARE PLANS/PASSAGE. Passage of the bill that would exempt health care plans sponsored by trade and business associations from most state laws and regulations. The bill would allow an association sponsoring a health care plan to have full discretion to choose the health benefits included in the plan, as long as the plan would still meet certain statuary minimums. The sponsored health care plans could not make membership, payment or coverage conditional on factors related to the health of a member company's employees. Passed 236-175 : R 232-0; D 4-175. March, 22, 2017.

187. HR 1238. U.S. AGRICULTURE SYSTEMS DEFENSE/PASSAGE. Donovan, R-N.Y., motion to suspend the rules and pass the bill that would require the Department of Homeland Security to coordinate efforts related to the defense of U.S. food, agriculture, and veterinary systems against terrorism. Motion agreed to 406-6 : R 229-6; D 177-0. March, 22, 2017.

188. H RES 221. SAME-DAY AND SUSPENSION AUTHORITY/PREVIOUS QUESTION. Sessions, R-Texas, motion to order the previous question (thus ending debate and possibility of amendment) on the rule (H Res 221) that would waive, through the legislative day of March 27, 2017, the two-thirds vote requirement to consider legislation on the same day it is reported from the House Rules Committee. It also would provide for consideration of measures under suspension of the rules through March, 26, 2017. Motion agreed to 233-185 : R 233-0; D 0-185. March, 23, 2017.

189. H RES 221. SAME-DAY AND SUSPENSION AUTHORITY/RULE. Adoption of the rule (H Res 221) that would waive, through the legislative day of March 27, 2017, the two-thirds vote requirement to consider legislation on the same day it is reported from the House Rules Committee. It also would provide for consideration of measures under suspension of the rules through the calendar day of March, 26, 2017. Adopted 227-189 : R 227-4; D 0-185. March, 23, 2017.

Member	183	184	185	186	187	188	189
ALABAMA							
1 Byrne	N	Y	N	Y	Y	Y	Y
2 Roby	N	Y	N	Y	Y	Y	Y
3 Rogers	N	Y	N	Y	Y	Y	Y
4 Aderholt	N	Y	N	Y	Y	Y	Y
5 Brooks	N	Y	N	Y	Y	Y	Y
6 Palmer	N	Y	N	Y	Y	Y	Y
7 Sewell	Y	Y	Y	N	Y	N	N
ALASKA							
AL Young	N	Y	N	Y	Y	Y	Y
ARIZONA							
1 O'Halleran	Y	Y	Y	N	Y	N	N
2 McSally	N	Y	N	Y	Y	Y	Y
3 Grijalva	Y	Y	Y	N	Y	N	N
4 Gosar	N	Y	N	Y	Y	Y	Y
5 Biggs	N	Y	N	Y	Y	Y	Y
6 Schweikert	N	Y	N	Y	Y	Y	Y
7 Gallego	Y	N	Y	N	Y	N	N
8 Franks	N	Y	N	Y	Y	Y	?
9 Sinema	+	+	+	+	+	N	N
ARKANSAS							
1 Crawford	N	Y	N	Y	Y	Y	Y
2 Hill	N	Y	N	Y	Y	Y	Y
3 Womack	N	Y	N	Y	Y	Y	Y
4 Westerman	N	Y	N	Y	Y	Y	Y
CALIFORNIA							
1 LaMalfa	N	Y	N	Y	Y	Y	Y
2 Huffman	Y	Y	Y	N	Y	N	N
3 Garamendi	Y	Y	Y	N	Y	N	N
4 McClintock	N	Y	N	Y	Y	Y	Y
5 Thompson	Y	Y	Y	N	Y	N	N
6 Matsui	Y	Y	Y	N	Y	N	N
7 Bera	Y	Y	Y	N	Y	N	N
8 Cook	N	Y	N	Y	Y	Y	Y
9 McNerney	Y	Y	Y	N	Y	N	N
10 Denham	N	Y	N	Y	Y	Y	Y
11 DeSaulnier	Y	Y	Y	N	Y	N	N
12 Pelosi	Y	Y	Y	N	Y	N	N
13 Lee	Y	Y	Y	N	Y	N	N
14 Speier	Y	Y	Y	N	Y	N	N
15 Swalwell	Y	Y	Y	N	Y	N	N
16 Costa	Y	Y	Y	N	Y	N	N
17 Khanna	Y	Y	Y	N	Y	N	N
18 Eshoo	Y	Y	Y	N	Y	N	N
19 Lofgren	Y	Y	Y	N	Y	N	N
20 Panetta	Y	Y	Y	N	Y	N	N
21 Valadao	N	Y	N	Y	Y	Y	Y
22 Nunes	N	Y	?	Y	Y	Y	Y
23 McCarthy	N	Y	N	Y	Y	Y	Y
24 Carbajal	Y	Y	Y	N	Y	N	N
25 Knight	N	Y	N	Y	Y	Y	Y
26 Brownley	Y	Y	Y	N	Y	N	N
27 Chu	Y	Y	Y	N	Y	N	N
28 Schiff	Y	Y	Y	N	Y	N	N
29 Cardenas	Y	Y	Y	N	Y	N	N
30 Sherman	Y	Y	Y	N	Y	N	N
31 Aguilar	Y	Y	Y	N	Y	N	N
32 Napolitano	Y	Y	Y	N	Y	N	N
33 Lieu	Y	Y	?	?	?	?	?
34 Vacant							
35 Torres	Y	Y	Y	N	Y	N	N
36 Ruiz	Y	Y	Y	N	Y	N	N
37 Bass	Y	Y	?	?	?	N	N
38 Sánchez, Linda	Y	Y	Y	N	Y	N	N
39 Royce	N	Y	N	Y	Y	Y	Y
40 Roybal-Allard	Y	Y	Y	N	Y	N	N
41 Takano	Y	Y	?	?	?	?	?
42 Calvert	N	Y	N	Y	Y	Y	Y
43 Waters	Y	N	Y	N	Y	N	N
44 Barragan	Y	Y	Y	N	Y	N	N
45 Walters	N	Y	N	Y	Y	Y	Y
46 Correa	Y	Y	Y	N	Y	N	N
47 Lowenthal	Y	Y	Y	N	Y	N	N
48 Rohrabacher	N	Y	N	Y	Y	Y	Y
49 Issa	N	Y	N	Y	Y	Y	Y
50 Hunter	N	Y	N	Y	Y	Y	Y
51 Vargas	Y	Y	Y	N	Y	N	N
52 Peters	Y	Y	Y	N	Y	N	N
53 Davis	Y	Y	Y	N	Y	N	N
COLORADO							
1 DeGette	Y	Y	Y	N	Y	N	N
2 Polis	Y	Y	Y	N	Y	N	N
3 Tipton	N	Y	N	Y	Y	Y	Y
4 Buck	N	Y	N	Y	Y	Y	Y
5 Lamborn	N	Y	N	Y	Y	Y	Y
6 Coffman	N	Y	N	Y	Y	Y	Y
7 Perlmutter	Y	Y	Y	N	Y	N	N
CONNECTICUT							
1 Larson	Y	Y	+	N	Y	N	N
2 Courtney	Y	Y	Y	N	Y	N	N
3 DeLauro	Y	Y	Y	N	Y	N	N
4 Himes	Y	Y	Y	N	Y	N	N
5 Esty	Y	Y	Y	N	Y	N	N
DELAWARE							
AL Blunt Rochester	Y	Y	Y	N	Y	N	N
FLORIDA							
1 Gaetz	N	Y	N	Y	N	Y	Y
2 Dunn	N	Y	N	Y	Y	Y	Y
3 Yoho	N	Y	N	+	Y	Y	Y
4 Rutherford	N	Y	N	Y	Y	Y	Y
5 Lawson	Y	Y	Y	N	Y	N	N
6 DeSantis	N	Y	N	Y	Y	Y	Y
7 Murphy	Y	Y	Y	N	Y	N	N
8 Posey	N	Y	N	Y	Y	Y	Y
9 Soto	Y	Y	Y	N	Y	N	N
10 Demings	Y	Y	Y	N	Y	N	N
11 Webster	N	Y	N	Y	Y	?	?
12 Bilirakis	N	Y	N	Y	Y	Y	Y
13 Crist	Y	Y	Y	N	Y	N	N
14 Castor	Y	Y	Y	N	Y	N	N
15 Ross	N	Y	N	Y	Y	Y	Y
16 Buchanan	N	Y	N	Y	Y	Y	Y
17 Rooney, T.	N	Y	N	Y	Y	Y	Y
18 Mast	N	Y	N	Y	Y	Y	Y
19 Rooney, F.	N	Y	N	Y	Y	Y	Y
20 Hastings	Y	N	Y	N	Y	N	N
21 Frankel	Y	Y	Y	N	Y	N	N
22 Deutch	Y	Y	Y	N	Y	N	N
23 Wasserman Schultz	Y	Y	Y	N	Y	N	N
24 Wilson	Y	Y	Y	N	Y	N	N
25 Diaz-Balart	N	Y	N	Y	Y	Y	?
26 Curbelo	N	Y	N	Y	Y	Y	Y
27 Ros-Lehtinen	N	Y	N	Y	Y	Y	Y
GEORGIA							
1 Carter	N	Y	N	Y	Y	Y	Y
2 Bishop	Y	Y	Y	N	Y	N	N
3 Ferguson	N	Y	N	Y	Y	Y	Y
4 Johnson	Y	Y	Y	N	Y	N	N
5 Lewis	Y	Y	Y	N	Y	N	N
7 Woodall	N	Y	N	Y	Y	Y	Y
8 Scott, A.	N	Y	N	Y	Y	Y	Y
9 Collins	N	Y	N	Y	Y	Y	Y
10 Hice	N	Y	N	Y	Y	Y	Y
11 Loudermilk	N	Y	N	Y	Y	Y	Y
12 Allen	N	Y	N	Y	Y	Y	Y
13 Scott, D.	Y	Y	Y	N	Y	N	N
14 Graves	N	Y	N	?	Y	Y	Y
HAWAII							
1 Hanabusa	Y	Y	Y	N	Y	N	N
2 Gabbard	Y	Y	Y	N	Y	N	N
IDAHO							
1 Labrador	N	Y	N	Y	Y	Y	Y
2 Simpson	N	Y	N	Y	Y	Y	Y
ILLINOIS							
1 Rush	?	?	?	?	?	?	?
2 Kelly	Y	Y	Y	N	Y	N	N
3 Lipinski	Y	Y	Y	N	Y	N	N
4 Gutierrez	Y	Y	Y	N	Y	N	N
5 Quigley	Y	Y	Y	N	Y	N	N
6 Roskam	N	Y	N	Y	Y	Y	Y
7 Davis, D.	Y	Y	Y	N	Y	N	N
8 Krishnamoorthi	Y	Y	Y	N	Y	N	N
9 Schakowsky	Y	Y	Y	N	Y	N	N
10 Schneider	Y	Y	Y	N	Y	N	N
11 Foster	Y	Y	Y	N	Y	N	N
12 Bost	N	Y	N	Y	Y	Y	Y
13 Davis, R.	N	Y	N	Y	Y	Y	Y
14 Hultgren	N	Y	N	Y	Y	Y	Y
15 Shimkus	N	Y	N	Y	Y	Y	Y

KEY — Republicans   Democrats   *Independents*

- Y Voted for (yea)
- # Paired for
- + Announced for
- N Voted against (nay)
- X Paired against
- – Announced against
- P Voted "present"
- C Voted "present" to avoid possible conflict of interest
- ? Did not vote or otherwise make a position known

	183	184	185	186	187	188	189
16 **Kinzinger**	N	Y	N	Y	Y	Y	Y
17 Bustos	Y	Y	Y	N	Y	N	N
18 **LaHood**	N	Y	N	Y	Y	Y	Y
INDIANA							
1 Visclosky	Y	Y	Y	N	Y	N	N
2 **Walorski**	N	Y	N	Y	Y	Y	Y
3 **Banks**	N	Y	N	Y	Y	Y	Y
4 **Rokita**	N	Y	N	Y	Y	Y	Y
5 **Brooks**	N	Y	N	Y	Y	Y	Y
6 **Messer**	N	Y	N	Y	Y	Y	Y
7 Carson	Y	Y	?	?	?	N	N
8 **Bucshon**	N	Y	N	Y	Y	Y	Y
9 **Hollingsworth**	N	Y	N	Y	Y	Y	Y
IOWA							
1 **Blum**	Y	Y	N	Y	Y	Y	Y
2 Loebsack	Y	Y	Y	N	?	N	N
3 **Young**	N	Y	N	Y	Y	Y	N
4 **King**	–	+	N	Y	Y	Y	Y
KANSAS							
1 **Marshall**	N	Y	N	Y	Y	Y	Y
2 **Jenkins**	N	Y	N	Y	Y	Y	Y
3 **Yoder**	N	Y	N	Y	Y	Y	Y
KENTUCKY							
1 **Comer**	N	Y	N	Y	Y	Y	Y
2 **Guthrie**	N	Y	N	Y	Y	Y	Y
3 Yarmuth	Y	Y	Y	N	Y	N	N
4 **Massie**	N	Y	N	Y	N	Y	N
5 **Rogers**	N	Y	N	Y	Y	Y	Y
6 **Barr**	N	Y	N	Y	Y	Y	Y
LOUISIANA							
1 **Scalise**	N	Y	N	Y	Y	Y	Y
2 Richmond	Y	Y	?	?	?	N	N
3 **Higgins**	N	Y	N	Y	?	Y	Y
4 **Johnson**	N	Y	N	Y	Y	Y	Y
5 **Abraham**	N	Y	N	Y	Y	Y	Y
6 **Graves**	N	Y	N	Y	Y	Y	Y
MAINE							
1 Pingree	Y	Y	Y	N	Y	N	N
2 **Poliquin**	N	Y	N	Y	Y	Y	Y
MARYLAND							
1 **Harris**	N	Y	N	Y	Y	Y	Y
2 Ruppersberger	Y	Y	Y	N	Y	N	N
3 Sarbanes	Y	Y	Y	N	Y	N	N
4 Brown	Y	Y	+	–	+	N	N
5 Hoyer	Y	Y	Y	N	Y	N	N
6 Delaney	Y	Y	Y	N	Y	N	N
7 Cummings	Y	Y	Y	N	Y	N	N
8 Raskin	Y	Y	Y	N	Y	N	N
MASSACHUSETTS							
1 Neal	Y	Y	Y	N	Y	N	N
2 McGovern	Y	Y	Y	N	Y	N	N
3 Tsongas	?	+	?	–	?	?	?
4 Kennedy	Y	Y	Y	N	Y	N	N
5 Clark	Y	Y	Y	N	Y	N	N
6 Moulton	Y	Y	Y	N	Y	N	N
7 Capuano	Y	Y	Y	N	Y	N	N
8 Lynch	Y	Y	Y	N	?	N	N
9 Keating	Y	Y	Y	N	Y	N	N
MICHIGAN							
1 **Bergman**	N	Y	N	Y	Y	Y	Y
2 **Huizenga**	N	Y	N	Y	Y	Y	Y
3 **Amash**	N	Y	N	Y	N	Y	N
4 **Moolenaar**	N	Y	N	Y	Y	Y	Y
5 Kildee	Y	Y	Y	N	Y	N	N
6 **Upton**	N	Y	N	Y	Y	Y	Y
7 **Walberg**	N	Y	N	Y	Y	Y	Y
8 **Bishop**	N	Y	N	Y	Y	Y	Y
9 Levin	Y	Y	Y	N	Y	N	N
10 **Mitchell**	N	Y	N	Y	Y	Y	Y
11 **Trott**	N	Y	N	Y	Y	Y	Y
12 Dingell	Y	Y	Y	N	Y	N	N
13 Conyers	Y	Y	Y	N	Y	N	N
14 Lawrence	Y	Y	+	–	+	N	N
MINNESOTA							
1 Walz	Y	Y	Y	N	Y	N	N
2 **Lewis**	N	Y	N	Y	Y	Y	Y
3 **Paulsen**	N	Y	N	Y	Y	Y	Y
4 McCollum	Y	Y	Y	N	Y	N	N

	183	184	185	186	187	188	189
5 Ellison	Y	Y	Y	N	Y	N	N
6 **Emmer**	N	Y	N	Y	Y	Y	Y
7 Peterson	Y	Y	Y	Y	Y	N	N
8 Nolan	Y	Y	Y	N	Y	N	N
MISSISSIPPI							
1 **Kelly**	N	Y	N	Y	Y	Y	Y
2 Thompson	Y	Y	Y	N	Y	N	N
3 **Harper**	N	Y	N	Y	Y	Y	Y
4 **Palazzo**	N	Y	N	Y	Y	Y	Y
MISSOURI							
1 Clay	Y	Y	Y	N	Y	N	N
2 **Wagner**	N	Y	N	Y	Y	Y	Y
3 **Luetkemeyer**	N	Y	N	Y	Y	Y	Y
4 **Hartzler**	N	Y	N	Y	Y	Y	+
5 Cleaver	Y	Y	Y	N	Y	N	N
6 **Graves**	N	Y	N	Y	Y	Y	Y
7 **Long**	N	Y	N	Y	Y	Y	Y
8 **Smith**	N	Y	N	Y	Y	Y	Y
MONTANA							
AL **Vacant**							
NEBRASKA							
1 **Fortenberry**	N	Y	N	+	Y	Y	Y
2 **Bacon**	N	Y	N	Y	Y	Y	Y
3 **Smith**	N	Y	N	Y	Y	Y	Y
NEVADA							
1 Titus	Y	Y	Y	N	Y	N	N
2 **Amodei**	N	Y	N	Y	Y	Y	Y
3 Rosen	Y	Y	Y	N	Y	N	N
4 Kihuen	Y	Y	Y	N	Y	N	N
NEW HAMPSHIRE							
1 Shea-Porter	Y	Y	Y	N	Y	N	N
2 Kuster	Y	Y	Y	N	Y	N	N
NEW JERSEY							
1 Norcross	Y	Y	Y	N	Y	N	N
2 **LoBiondo**	N	Y	N	Y	Y	Y	Y
3 **MacArthur**	N	Y	N	Y	Y	Y	Y
4 **Smith**	N	Y	N	Y	Y	Y	Y
5 Gottheimer	Y	Y	Y	Y	Y	N	N
6 Pallone	Y	Y	Y	N	Y	N	N
7 **Lance**	N	Y	N	Y	Y	Y	Y
8 Sires	Y	Y	Y	N	Y	N	N
9 Pascrell	Y	Y	Y	N	Y	N	N
10 Payne	?	?	?	?	?	?	?
11 **Frelinghuysen**	N	Y	N	Y	Y	Y	Y
12 Watson Coleman	Y	N	Y	N	Y	N	N
NEW MEXICO							
1 Lujan Grisham	Y	Y	Y	N	Y	N	N
2 **Pearce**	N	Y	N	Y	Y	Y	Y
3 Luján	Y	Y	Y	N	Y	N	N
NEW YORK							
1 **Zeldin**	N	Y	N	Y	Y	Y	Y
2 **King**	N	Y	N	Y	Y	Y	Y
3 Suozzi	Y	Y	Y	N	Y	N	N
4 Rice	Y	Y	Y	N	Y	N	N
5 Meeks	Y	Y	Y	N	Y	?	?
6 Meng	Y	Y	Y	N	Y	N	N
7 Velázquez	Y	Y	Y	N	Y	N	N
8 Jeffries	Y	Y	Y	N	Y	?	?
9 Clarke	Y	Y	Y	N	Y	N	N
10 Nadler	Y	Y	Y	N	Y	N	N
11 **Donovan**	N	Y	N	Y	Y	Y	Y
12 Maloney, C.	?	Y	Y	N	Y	N	N
13 Espaillat	Y	Y	Y	N	Y	N	N
14 Crowley	Y	Y	Y	N	Y	N	N
15 Serrano	Y	Y	Y	N	Y	N	N
16 Engel	Y	Y	Y	N	Y	N	N
17 Lowey	Y	Y	Y	N	Y	N	N
18 Maloney, S.P.	Y	Y	Y	N	Y	N	N
19 **Faso**	N	Y	N	Y	Y	Y	Y
20 Tonko	Y	Y	Y	N	Y	N	N
21 **Stefanik**	N	Y	N	Y	Y	Y	Y
22 **Tenney**	N	Y	N	Y	Y	Y	Y
23 **Reed**	N	Y	N	Y	Y	Y	Y
24 **Katko**	N	Y	N	Y	Y	Y	Y
25 Slaughter	+	+	+	–	+	?	?
26 Higgins	Y	Y	Y	N	Y	N	N
27 **Collins**	N	Y	N	Y	Y	Y	Y
NORTH CAROLINA							
1 Butterfield	Y	Y	Y	N	Y	N	N
2 **Holding**	N	Y	N	Y	Y	Y	Y
3 **Jones**	Y	Y	Y	Y	N	Y	N
4 Price	Y	Y	Y	N	Y	N	N

	184	185	186	187	188	189	5
Foxx	N	Y	N	Y	Y	Y	Y
6 **Walker**	N	Y	N	Y	Y	Y	Y
7 **Rouzer**	N	Y	N	Y	Y	Y	Y
8 **Hudson**	N	Y	N	+	Y	Y	Y
9 **Pittenger**	N	Y	N	Y	Y	Y	Y
10 **McHenry**	N	Y	N	Y	Y	Y	Y
11 **Meadows**	N	Y	N	Y	Y	?	Y
12 Adams	Y	Y	Y	N	Y	N	N
13 **Budd**	N	Y	N	Y	Y	Y	Y
NORTH DAKOTA							
AL **Cramer**	N	Y	N	Y	Y	Y	Y
OHIO							
1 **Chabot**	N	Y	N	Y	Y	Y	Y
2 **Wenstrup**	N	Y	N	Y	Y	Y	Y
3 Beatty	Y	Y	Y	N	Y	N	N
4 **Jordan**	N	Y	N	Y	Y	Y	Y
5 **Latta**	N	Y	N	Y	Y	Y	Y
6 **Johnson**	N	Y	N	Y	Y	Y	Y
7 **Gibbs**	N	Y	N	Y	Y	Y	Y
8 **Davidson**	N	Y	N	Y	Y	Y	Y
9 Kaptur	Y	Y	Y	N	Y	N	N
10 **Turner**	N	Y	N	Y	Y	Y	Y
11 Fudge	Y	N	Y	N	Y	N	N
12 **Tiberi**	N	Y	N	Y	Y	Y	Y
13 Ryan	Y	Y	Y	N	Y	N	N
14 **Joyce**	N	Y	N	Y	Y	Y	Y
15 **Stivers**	N	Y	N	Y	Y	Y	Y
16 **Renacci**	N	Y	N	Y	Y	Y	Y
OKLAHOMA							
1 **Bridenstine**	N	Y	N	Y	Y	Y	Y
2 **Mullin**	N	Y	N	Y	Y	Y	Y
3 **Lucas**	N	Y	N	Y	Y	Y	Y
4 **Cole**	N	Y	N	Y	Y	Y	Y
5 **Russell**	N	Y	N	Y	Y	Y	Y
OREGON							
1 Bonamici	Y	Y	Y	N	Y	N	N
2 **Walden**	N	Y	N	Y	Y	Y	Y
3 Blumenauer	Y	Y	Y	N	Y	N	N
4 DeFazio	Y	Y	Y	N	Y	N	N
5 Schrader	Y	Y	Y	Y	Y	N	N
PENNSYLVANIA							
1 Brady	Y	Y	Y	N	Y	N	N
2 Evans	Y	Y	Y	N	Y	N	N
3 **Kelly**	N	Y	N	Y	Y	Y	Y
4 **Perry**	N	Y	N	Y	Y	Y	Y
5 **Thompson**	N	Y	N	Y	Y	Y	Y
6 **Costello**	N	Y	N	Y	Y	Y	Y
7 **Meehan**	N	Y	N	Y	Y	Y	Y
8 **Fitzpatrick**	N	Y	N	Y	Y	Y	Y
9 **Shuster**	N	Y	N	Y	Y	Y	Y
10 **Marino**	N	Y	N	Y	Y	Y	Y
11 **Barletta**	N	Y	N	Y	Y	Y	Y
12 **Rothfus**	N	Y	N	Y	Y	Y	Y
13 Boyle	Y	Y	Y	N	Y	N	N
14 Doyle	Y	Y	Y	N	Y	N	N
15 **Dent**	N	Y	N	Y	Y	Y	Y
16 **Smucker**	N	Y	N	Y	Y	Y	Y
17 Cartwright	Y	Y	Y	N	Y	N	N
18 **Murphy**	N	Y	N	Y	Y	Y	Y
RHODE ISLAND							
1 Cicilline	Y	Y	Y	N	Y	N	N
2 Langevin	Y	Y	Y	N	Y	N	N
SOUTH CAROLINA							
1 **Sanford**	N	Y	N	Y	N	Y	Y
2 **Wilson**	N	Y	N	Y	Y	Y	Y
3 **Duncan**	N	Y	N	Y	Y	Y	Y
4 **Gowdy**	N	Y	N	Y	Y	Y	Y
6 Clyburn	Y	Y	?	?	?	N	N
7 **Rice**	N	Y	N	Y	Y	Y	Y
SOUTH DAKOTA							
AL **Noem**	N	Y	N	Y	Y	Y	Y
TENNESSEE							
1 **Roe**	N	Y	N	Y	Y	Y	Y
2 **Duncan**	N	Y	Y	Y	Y	Y	Y
3 **Fleischmann**	N	Y	N	Y	Y	Y	Y
4 **DesJarlais**	N	Y	N	Y	Y	Y	Y
5 Cooper	Y	Y	Y	N	Y	N	N
6 **Black**	N	Y	N	Y	Y	Y	Y
7 **Blackburn**	N	Y	N	Y	Y	Y	Y
8 **Kustoff**	N	Y	N	Y	Y	Y	Y
9 Cohen	Y	Y	Y	N	Y	N	N

	183	184	185	186	187	188	189
TEXAS							
1 **Gohmert**	N	Y	N	Y	Y	Y	Y
2 **Poe**	N	Y	N	Y	Y	Y	Y
3 **Johnson, S.**	N	Y	N	Y	Y	Y	Y
4 **Ratcliffe**	N	Y	N	Y	Y	Y	Y
5 **Hensarling**	N	Y	N	Y	Y	Y	Y
6 **Barton**	N	Y	N	Y	Y	Y	Y
7 **Culberson**	N	Y	N	Y	Y	Y	Y
8 **Brady**	N	Y	N	Y	Y	?	Y
9 Green, A.	Y	Y	Y	N	Y	N	N
10 **McCaul**	N	Y	N	Y	Y	Y	Y
11 **Conaway**	N	Y	N	Y	Y	Y	Y
12 **Granger**	N	Y	N	Y	Y	Y	Y
13 **Thornberry**	N	Y	N	Y	Y	Y	Y
14 **Weber**	N	Y	N	Y	Y	Y	Y
15 Gonzalez	Y	Y	Y	N	Y	N	N
16 O'Rourke	Y	Y	Y	N	Y	N	N
17 **Flores**	N	Y	N	Y	Y	Y	Y
18 Jackson Lee	Y	Y	Y	N	Y	N	N
19 **Arrington**	N	Y	N	Y	Y	Y	Y
20 Castro	Y	Y	Y	N	Y	N	N
21 **Smith**	N	Y	N	Y	Y	Y	Y
22 **Olson**	N	Y	N	Y	Y	Y	?
23 **Hurd**	N	Y	N	Y	Y	Y	Y
24 **Marchant**	N	Y	N	Y	Y	Y	Y
25 **Williams**	N	Y	N	Y	Y	Y	Y
26 **Burgess**	N	Y	N	Y	Y	Y	Y
27 **Farenthold**	N	Y	N	Y	Y	Y	Y
28 Cuellar	Y	Y	Y	Y	Y	N	N
29 Green, G.	Y	Y	Y	N	Y	N	N
30 Johnson, E.B.	Y	Y	Y	N	Y	N	N
31 **Carter**	N	Y	N	Y	Y	Y	Y
32 **Sessions**	N	Y	N	Y	Y	Y	Y
33 Veasey	Y	Y	Y	N	Y	N	N
34 Vela	Y	Y	Y	N	Y	N	N
35 Doggett	Y	Y	Y	N	Y	N	N
36 **Babin**	N	Y	N	Y	Y	Y	Y
UTAH							
1 **Bishop**	N	Y	N	Y	Y	Y	Y
2 **Stewart**	N	Y	N	Y	Y	Y	Y
3 **Chaffetz**	N	Y	N	Y	Y	Y	Y
4 **Love**	N	Y	N	Y	Y	Y	Y
VERMONT							
AL Welch	Y	Y	Y	N	Y	N	N
VIRGINIA							
1 **Wittman**	N	Y	N	Y	Y	Y	Y
2 **Taylor**	N	Y	N	Y	Y	Y	Y
3 Scott	Y	Y	Y	N	Y	N	N
4 McEachin	Y	Y	?	N	Y	N	N
5 **Garrett**	N	Y	N	Y	N	Y	Y
6 **Goodlatte**	N	Y	N	Y	Y	Y	Y
7 **Brat**	N	Y	N	Y	Y	Y	Y
8 Beyer	Y	Y	Y	N	Y	N	N
9 **Griffith**	N	Y	N	Y	Y	Y	Y
10 **Comstock**	N	Y	N	Y	Y	Y	Y
11 Connolly	Y	Y	Y	N	Y	N	N
WASHINGTON							
1 DelBene	Y	Y	Y	N	Y	N	N
2 Larsen	Y	Y	Y	N	Y	N	N
3 **Herrera Beutler**	N	Y	N	Y	Y	Y	Y
4 **Newhouse**	N	Y	N	Y	Y	Y	Y
5 **McMorris Rodgers**	N	Y	N	Y	Y	Y	Y
6 Kilmer	Y	Y	Y	N	Y	N	N
7 Jayapal	Y	Y	Y	N	Y	N	N
8 **Reichert**	N	Y	N	Y	Y	Y	Y
9 Smith	Y	N	Y	N	Y	N	N
10 Heck	Y	N	Y	N	Y	N	N
WEST VIRGINIA							
1 **McKinley**	N	Y	N	Y	Y	Y	Y
2 **Mooney**	N	Y	N	Y	Y	Y	Y
3 **Jenkins**	N	Y	N	Y	Y	Y	Y
WISCONSIN							
1 **Ryan**							
2 Pocan	Y	Y	Y	N	Y	N	N
3 Kind	Y	Y	Y	N	Y	N	N
4 Moore	Y	Y	+	–	?	N	N
5 **Sensenbrenner**	N	Y	N	Y	Y	Y	Y
6 **Grothman**	N	Y	N	Y	Y	Y	Y
7 **Duffy**	N	Y	N	Y	Y	Y	Y
8 **Gallagher**	N	Y	N	Y	Y	Y	Y
WYOMING							
AL **Cheney**	N	Y	N	Y	Y	Y	Y

VOTE NUMBER

190. PROCEDURAL MOTION/APPROVAL OF HOUSE JOURNAL. Approved 202-197 : R 132-91; D 70-106. March, 23, 2017.

191. HR 1628, H RES 228. HEALTH CARE MARKETPLACE OVERHAUL/ PREVIOUS QUESTION. Sessions, R-Texas, motion to order the previous question (thus ending debate and possibility of amendment) on the rule (H Res 228) would provide for consideration of the bill that would repeal extensive portions of the 2010 health care overhaul law. Upon adoption, the rule would automatically modify the bill to incorporate amendments that would give states the option of receiving federal Medicaid funding as a block grant with greater state flexibility in how the funds are used, and would require states to establish their own essential health benefits standards. Motion agreed to 236-186 : R 236-0; D 0-186. March, 24, 2017.

192. HR 1628, H RES 228. HEALTH CARE MARKETPLACE OVERHAUL/ RULE. Adoption of the rule (H Res 228) would provide for consideration of the bill that would repeal extensive portions of the 2010 health care overhaul law. Upon adoption, the rule would automatically modify the bill to incorporate amendments that would give states the option of receiving federal Medicaid funding as a block grant with greater state flexibility in how the funds are used, and would require states to establish their own essential health benefits standards. Adopted 230-194 : R 230-6; D 0-188. March, 24, 2017.

193. HR 1365. DHS ACQUISITION PRACTICES/PASSAGE. Donovan, R-N.Y., motion to suspend the rules and pass the bill that would allow the Department of Homeland Security to appoint an individual who would be responsible for managing department acquisition practices through measuring cost, operational efficiency and collaboration with the private sector. Motion agreed to 424-0 : R 236-0; D 188-0. March, 24, 2017.

194. PROCEDURAL MOTION/APPROVAL OF HOUSE JOURNAL. Approved 218-201 : R 153-80; D 65-121. March, 24, 2017.

195. HR 1117. FEMA FUNDING APPLICANT GUIDANCE/PASSAGE. Barletta, R-Pa., motion to suspend the rules and pass the bill that would require the Federal Emergency Management Agency to report to Congress on the agency's plans to provide consistent guidance to funding applicants after a disaster, maintain appropriate documentation and accurately assist funding applicants through the process of obtaining aid from FEMA. Motion agreed to 408-0 : R 225-0; D 183-0. March, 27, 2017.

196. HR 654. FEMA EARTHQUAKE PLAN/PASSAGE. Barletta, R-Pa., motion to suspend the rules and pass the bill that would require the Federal Emergency Management Agency to develop a plan for the purchase and installation of an earthquake early warning system for the "Cascadia Subduction Zone," which includes parts of Washington, Oregon and California. It would also require the president to establish a task force that would recommend what national preparations should be made to plan for, respond to and recover from an earthquake or tsunami event in the Cascadia Subduction Zone. Motion agreed to 395-11 : R 215-11; D 180-0. March, 27, 2017.

	190	191	192	193	194	195	196
ALABAMA							
1 Byrne	Y	Y	Y	Y	Y	Y	Y
2 Roby	Y	Y	Y	Y	Y	Y	Y
3 Rogers	N	Y	Y	Y	N	Y	Y
4 Aderholt	Y	Y	Y	Y	Y	?	?
5 Brooks	Y	Y	N	Y	Y	Y	Y
6 Palmer	N	Y	Y	Y	N	Y	Y
7 Sewell	N	N	N	Y	N	Y	Y
ALASKA							
AL Young	N	Y	Y	Y	N	Y	Y
ARIZONA							
1 O'Halleran	N	N	N	Y	N	Y	Y
2 McSally	Y	Y	Y	Y	N	Y	N
3 Grijalva	?	N	N	Y	N	?	?
4 Gosar	N	Y	N	Y	N	Y	Y
5 Biggs	N	Y	Y	N	Y	Y	Y
6 Schweikert	Y	Y	Y	Y	Y	Y	Y
7 Gallego	Y	N	N	Y	N	Y	Y
8 Franks	N	Y	Y	Y	N	Y	Y
9 Sinema	Y	N	N	Y	Y	Y	Y
ARKANSAS							
1 Crawford	Y	Y	Y	Y	Y	Y	Y
2 Hill	N	Y	Y	Y	N	Y	Y
3 Womack	Y	Y	Y	Y	Y	Y	Y
4 Westerman	Y	Y	Y	Y	Y	Y	Y
CALIFORNIA							
1 LaMalfa	Y	Y	Y	Y	Y	Y	Y
2 Huffman	Y	N	N	Y	Y	?	Y
3 Garamendi	Y	N	N	Y	Y	Y	Y
4 McClintock	Y	Y	Y	Y	Y	Y	Y
5 Thompson	N	N	N	Y	N	Y	Y
6 Matsui	N	N	N	Y	N	Y	Y
7 Bera	Y	N	N	Y	N	Y	Y
8 Cook	Y	Y	Y	Y	Y	Y	Y
9 McNerney	Y	N	N	Y	Y	Y	Y
10 Denham	N	Y	Y	Y	Y	Y	Y
11 DeSaulnier	N	N	N	Y	N	Y	Y
12 Pelosi	N	N	N	Y	N	Y	Y
13 Lee	N	N	N	Y	N	Y	Y
14 Speier	Y	N	N	Y	Y	Y	Y
15 Swalwell	N	N	N	Y	N	Y	Y
16 Costa	N	N	N	Y	N	Y	Y
17 Khanna	N	N	N	Y	N	Y	Y
18 Eshoo	N	N	N	Y	N	Y	Y
19 Lofgren	P	N	N	Y	N	Y	Y
20 Panetta	N	N	N	Y	N	Y	Y
21 Valadao	N	Y	Y	Y	N	Y	Y
22 Nunes	Y	Y	Y	Y	Y	Y	Y
23 McCarthy	Y	Y	Y	Y	Y	Y	Y
24 Carbajal	N	N	N	Y	N	Y	Y
25 Knight	N	Y	Y	Y	Y	Y	Y
26 Brownley	N	N	N	Y	N	Y	Y
27 Chu	Y	N	N	Y	Y	Y	Y
28 Schiff	N	N	N	Y	N	Y	Y
29 Cardenas	N	N	N	Y	?	?	?
30 Sherman	Y	N	N	Y	Y	Y	Y
31 Aguilar	N	N	N	Y	N	Y	Y
32 Napolitano	N	N	N	Y	N	Y	Y
33 Lieu	?	?	?	?	?	Y	Y
34 Vacant							
35 Torres	Y	N	N	Y	Y	Y	Y
36 Ruiz	N	N	N	Y	Y	Y	Y
37 Bass	N	N	N	Y	N	Y	Y
38 Sánchez, Linda	N	N	N	Y	N	Y	Y
39 Royce	Y	Y	Y	Y	Y	Y	Y
40 Roybal-Allard	N	N	N	Y	N	Y	Y
41 Takano	?	?	?	?	?	Y	Y
42 Calvert	Y	Y	Y	Y	Y	Y	Y
43 Waters	N	N	N	Y	N	Y	Y
44 Barragan	N	N	N	Y	N	Y	Y
45 Walters	Y	Y	Y	Y	Y	Y	Y
46 Correa	Y	N	N	Y	Y	Y	Y
47 Lowenthal	Y	N	N	Y	Y	Y	Y
48 Rohrabacher	Y	Y	Y	Y	Y	?	?
49 Issa	?	Y	Y	Y	Y	Y	Y
50 Hunter	Y	Y	Y	Y	Y	Y	N
51 Vargas	N	N	N	Y	N	Y	Y
52 Peters	Y	N	N	Y	N	Y	Y
53 Davis	Y	N	N	Y	Y	Y	Y

	190	191	192	193	194	195	196
COLORADO							
1 DeGette	N	N	N	Y	N	Y	Y
2 Polis	Y	N	N	Y	Y	Y	Y
3 Tipton	N	Y	Y	Y	N	Y	Y
4 Buck	N	Y	Y	Y	N	Y	Y
5 Lamborn	Y	Y	Y	Y	Y	Y	Y
6 Coffman	N	Y	Y	Y	N	Y	Y
7 Perlmutter	Y	N	N	Y	N	Y	Y
CONNECTICUT							
1 Larson	N	N	N	Y	N	Y	Y
2 Courtney	N	N	N	Y	N	Y	Y
3 DeLauro	N	N	N	Y	Y	Y	Y
4 Himes	Y	N	N	Y	Y	Y	Y
5 Esty	Y	N	N	Y	Y	Y	Y
DELAWARE							
AL Blunt Rochester	N	N	N	Y	N	Y	Y
FLORIDA							
1 Gaetz	Y	Y	Y	Y	Y	Y	N
2 Dunn	Y	Y	Y	Y	Y	Y	Y
3 Yoho	N	Y	Y	Y	N	Y	N
4 Rutherford	Y	Y	Y	Y	Y	Y	Y
5 Lawson	N	N	N	Y	Y	Y	Y
6 DeSantis	N	Y	Y	Y	N	Y	Y
7 Murphy	Y	N	N	Y	N	Y	Y
8 Posey	N	Y	Y	Y	Y	Y	Y
9 Soto	Y	N	N	Y	N	Y	Y
10 Demings	Y	N	N	Y	N	Y	Y
11 Webster	?	Y	Y	Y	Y	Y	Y
12 Bilirakis	Y	Y	Y	Y	Y	?	Y
13 Crist	N	N	N	Y	N	Y	Y
14 Castor	N	N	N	Y	N	Y	Y
15 Ross	?	Y	Y	Y	Y	Y	Y
16 Buchanan	N	Y	Y	Y	?	?	Y
17 Rooney, T.	Y	Y	Y	Y	Y	?	Y
18 Mast	N	Y	Y	Y	N	Y	Y
19 Rooney, F.	Y	Y	Y	Y	Y	Y	Y
20 Hastings	N	N	N	Y	N	Y	Y
21 Frankel	Y	N	N	Y	Y	Y	Y
22 Deutch	Y	Y	Y	Y	Y	Y	Y
23 Wasserman Schultz	Y	N	N	Y	Y	Y	Y
24 Wilson	N	N	N	Y	N	Y	?
25 Diaz-Balart	Y	Y	Y	Y	N	Y	Y
26 Curbelo	Y	Y	Y	Y	N	Y	Y
27 Ros-Lehtinen	N	Y	Y	Y	N	?	?
GEORGIA							
1 Carter	N	Y	Y	Y	N	Y	Y
2 Bishop	N	N	N	Y	N	Y	Y
3 Ferguson	Y	Y	Y	Y	Y	Y	Y
4 Johnson	Y	?	N	Y	N	Y	Y
5 Lewis	N	N	N	Y	N	Y	Y
7 Woodall	Y	Y	Y	Y	Y	Y	Y
8 Scott, A.	Y	Y	Y	Y	N	Y	Y
9 Collins	N	Y	Y	Y	N	Y	Y
10 Hice	N	Y	Y	Y	N	Y	Y
11 Loudermilk	Y	Y	Y	Y	Y	Y	Y
12 Allen	Y	Y	Y	Y	Y	Y	Y
13 Scott, D.	Y	N	N	Y	N	Y	Y
14 Graves	N	Y	Y	Y	N	Y	Y
HAWAII							
1 Hanabusa	N	N	N	Y	N	Y	Y
2 Gabbard	Y	N	N	Y	Y	Y	Y
IDAHO							
1 Labrador	Y	Y	Y	Y	Y	Y	Y
2 Simpson	Y	Y	Y	Y	Y	+	+
ILLINOIS							
1 Rush	?	?	?	?	?	?	?
2 Kelly	N	N	N	Y	N	Y	Y
3 Lipinski	Y	N	N	Y	Y	Y	Y
4 Gutierrez	N	N	N	Y	N	+	+
5 Quigley	N	N	N	Y	Y	Y	Y
6 Roskam	N	Y	Y	Y	N	Y	Y
7 Davis, D.	Y	N	N	Y	Y	Y	Y
8 Krishnamoorthi	Y	N	N	Y	N	Y	Y
9 Schakowsky	N	N	N	Y	N	Y	Y
10 Schneider	Y	N	N	Y	Y	Y	Y
11 Foster	Y	N	N	Y	Y	Y	Y
12 Bost	N	Y	N	Y	N	Y	Y
13 Davis, R.	N	Y	Y	Y	N	Y	Y
14 Hultgren	Y	Y	Y	Y	Y	Y	Y
15 Shimkus	Y	Y	Y	Y	Y	Y	Y

	190	191	192	193	194	195	196
16 **Kinzinger**	Y	Y	Y	Y	N	Y	Y
17 Bustos	?	N	N	Y	Y	Y	Y
18 **LaHood**	N	Y	Y	Y	Y	Y	Y
INDIANA							
1 Visclosky	N	N	N	Y	N	+	+
2 **Walorski**	Y	Y	Y	Y	Y	Y	Y
3 **Banks**	Y	Y	Y	Y	Y	Y	Y
4 **Rokita**	N	Y	Y	Y	N	Y	Y
5 **Brooks**	Y	Y	Y	Y	Y	Y	Y
6 **Messer**	Y	Y	Y	Y	Y	Y	Y
7 Carson	N	N	N	Y	N	?	?
8 **Bucshon**	Y	Y	Y	Y	Y	Y	Y
9 **Hollingsworth**	Y	Y	Y	Y	Y	Y	Y
IOWA							
1 **Blum**	N	Y	Y	Y	N	Y	Y
2 Loebsack	?	N	N	Y	N	Y	Y
3 **Young**	Y	Y	Y	Y	Y	Y	Y
4 **King**	Y	Y	Y	Y	Y	Y	Y
KANSAS							
1 **Marshall**	N	Y	Y	Y	Y	Y	Y
2 **Jenkins**	N	Y	Y	Y	N	Y	Y
3 **Yoder**	N	Y	Y	Y	N	+	+
KENTUCKY							
1 **Comer**	N	Y	Y	Y	Y	Y	Y
2 **Guthrie**	Y	Y	Y	Y	Y	Y	Y
3 Yarmuth	Y	N	N	Y	Y	Y	Y
4 **Massie**	Y	Y	N	Y	Y	Y	N
5 **Rogers**	Y	Y	Y	Y	Y	Y	Y
6 **Barr**	Y	Y	Y	Y	N	Y	Y
LOUISIANA							
1 **Scalise**	Y	Y	Y	Y	Y	Y	Y
2 Richmond	P	N	N	Y	N	Y	Y
3 **Higgins**	Y	Y	Y	Y	Y	Y	Y
4 **Johnson**	Y	Y	Y	Y	Y	Y	Y
5 **Abraham**	Y	Y	Y	Y	Y	Y	Y
6 **Graves**	N	Y	Y	Y	N	Y	Y
MAINE							
1 Pingree	Y	N	N	Y	N	Y	Y
2 **Poliquin**	N	Y	Y	Y	N	Y	Y
MARYLAND							
1 **Harris**	Y	Y	Y	Y	Y	Y	Y
2 Ruppersberger	Y	N	N	Y	Y	Y	Y
3 Sarbanes	N	N	N	Y	N	Y	Y
4 Brown	N	N	N	Y	N	Y	Y
5 Hoyer	N	N	N	Y	N	Y	Y
6 Delaney	N	N	N	Y	N	Y	Y
7 Cummings	N	N	N	Y	N	Y	Y
8 Raskin	N	N	N	Y	N	Y	Y
MASSACHUSETTS							
1 Neal	N	N	N	Y	N	Y	Y
2 McGovern	N	N	N	Y	N	Y	Y
3 Tsongas	?	?	?	?	?	Y	Y
4 Kennedy	N	N	N	Y	N	Y	Y
5 Clark	N	N	N	Y	N	Y	Y
6 Moulton	N	N	N	Y	N	Y	Y
7 Capuano	N	N	N	Y	N	Y	Y
8 Lynch	N	N	N	Y	N	Y	Y
9 Keating	N	N	N	Y	N	Y	Y
MICHIGAN							
1 **Bergman**	N	Y	Y	Y	N	Y	Y
2 **Huizenga**	Y	Y	Y	Y	Y	Y	Y
3 **Amash**	N	Y	N	Y	N	Y	N
4 **Moolenaar**	N	Y	Y	Y	Y	Y	Y
5 Kildee	Y	N	N	Y	Y	Y	Y
6 **Upton**	N	Y	Y	Y	N	Y	Y
7 **Walberg**	N	Y	Y	Y	N	Y	Y
8 **Bishop**	N	Y	Y	Y	N	Y	Y
9 Levin	N	N	N	Y	N	Y	Y
10 **Mitchell**	Y	Y	Y	Y	Y	Y	Y
11 **Trott**	Y	Y	Y	Y	Y	Y	Y
12 Dingell	N	N	N	Y	N	Y	Y
13 Conyers	N	N	N	Y	Y	Y	Y
14 Lawrence	N	N	N	Y	N	Y	Y
MINNESOTA							
1 Walz	Y	N	N	Y	Y	Y	Y
2 **Lewis**	N	Y	Y	Y	Y	Y	Y
3 **Paulsen**	N	Y	Y	Y	N	Y	Y
4 McCollum	Y	N	N	Y	+	Y	Y

	190	191	192	193	194	195	196
5 Ellison	Y	N	N	Y	N	Y	Y
6 **Emmer**	Y	Y	Y	Y	Y	Y	Y
7 Peterson	N	N	N	Y	N	Y	Y
8 Nolan	Y	N	N	Y	N	Y	Y
MISSISSIPPI							
1 **Kelly**	Y	Y	Y	Y	Y	Y	Y
2 Thompson	N	N	N	Y	N	Y	Y
3 **Harper**	Y	Y	Y	Y	Y	Y	Y
4 **Palazzo**	Y	Y	Y	Y	Y	Y	Y
MISSOURI							
1 Clay	Y	N	N	Y	Y	Y	Y
2 **Wagner**	Y	Y	Y	Y	Y	Y	Y
3 **Luetkemeyer**	Y	Y	Y	Y	Y	Y	Y
4 **Hartzler**	Y	Y	Y	Y	N	Y	Y
5 Cleaver	N	N	N	Y	N	Y	Y
6 **Graves**	N	Y	Y	Y	Y	Y	Y
7 **Long**	Y	Y	Y	Y	Y	Y	Y
8 **Smith**	N	Y	Y	Y	Y	Y	Y
MONTANA							
AL **Vacant**							
NEBRASKA							
1 **Fortenberry**	Y	Y	Y	Y	Y	Y	Y
2 **Bacon**	Y	Y	Y	Y	Y	Y	Y
3 **Smith**	Y	Y	Y	Y	Y	Y	Y
NEVADA							
1 Titus	Y	N	N	Y	Y	?	?
2 **Amodei**	Y	Y	Y	Y	Y	Y	Y
3 Rosen	Y	N	N	Y	N	Y	Y
4 Kihuen	N	N	N	Y	N	Y	Y
NEW HAMPSHIRE							
1 Shea-Porter	Y	N	N	Y	Y	Y	Y
2 Kuster	Y	N	N	Y	Y	Y	Y
NEW JERSEY							
1 Norcross	N	N	N	Y	N	Y	Y
2 **LoBiondo**	N	Y	Y	Y	N	Y	Y
3 **MacArthur**	?	Y	Y	Y	N	Y	Y
4 **Smith**	Y	Y	Y	Y	Y	Y	Y
5 Gottheimer	N	N	N	Y	Y	Y	Y
6 Pallone	N	N	N	Y	N	Y	Y
7 **Lance**	N	Y	Y	Y	N	Y	Y
8 Sires	N	N	N	Y	N	Y	Y
9 Pascrell	Y	N	N	Y	Y	Y	Y
10 Payne	?	?	?	?	N	Y	Y
11 **Frelinghuysen**	Y	Y	Y	Y	Y	Y	Y
12 Watson Coleman	N	N	N	Y	N	Y	Y
NEW MEXICO							
1 Lujan Grisham	Y	N	N	Y	Y	Y	Y
2 **Pearce**	N	Y	Y	Y	N	Y	Y
3 Luján	N	N	N	Y	N	Y	Y
NEW YORK							
1 **Zeldin**	Y	Y	Y	Y	Y	Y	Y
2 **King**	Y	Y	Y	Y	Y	Y	Y
3 Suozzi	Y	N	N	Y	Y	Y	?
4 Rice	N	N	N	Y	N	Y	Y
5 Meeks	N	N	N	Y	Y	Y	Y
6 Meng	Y	N	N	Y	Y	Y	Y
7 Velázquez	N	N	N	Y	N	Y	Y
8 Jeffries	?	N	N	Y	N	Y	Y
9 Clarke	N	N	N	Y	N	Y	Y
10 Nadler	Y	N	N	Y	Y	Y	Y
11 **Donovan**	Y	Y	Y	Y	Y	Y	Y
12 Maloney, C.	?	N	N	Y	N	?	?
13 Espaillat	N	N	N	Y	N	Y	Y
14 Crowley	N	N	N	Y	N	Y	Y
15 Serrano	Y	N	N	Y	N	Y	Y
16 Engel	Y	N	N	Y	Y	Y	Y
17 Lowey	Y	N	N	Y	Y	Y	Y
18 Maloney, S.P.	N	N	N	Y	N	Y	Y
19 **Faso**	N	Y	Y	Y	Y	Y	Y
20 Tonko	P	N	N	Y	P	Y	Y
21 **Stefanik**	Y	Y	Y	Y	Y	Y	Y
22 **Tenney**	N	Y	Y	Y	Y	Y	Y
23 **Reed**	N	Y	Y	Y	Y	Y	Y
24 **Katko**	N	Y	Y	Y	N	Y	Y
25 Slaughter	?	N	N	Y	Y	+	+
26 Higgins	Y	–	N	Y	N	Y	Y
27 **Collins**	Y	Y	Y	Y	Y	Y	Y
NORTH CAROLINA							
1 Butterfield	N	N	N	Y	N	Y	Y
2 **Holding**	N	Y	Y	Y	N	+	+
3 **Jones**	Y	Y	N	Y	N	Y	N
4 Price	N	N	N	Y	N	Y	Y

	190	191	192	193	194	195	196
5 **Foxx**	N	Y	Y	Y	N	Y	Y
6 **Walker**	N	Y	Y	Y	Y	Y	Y
7 **Rouzer**	N	Y	Y	Y	N	Y	Y
8 **Hudson**	N	Y	Y	Y	N	Y	Y
9 **Pittenger**	?	Y	Y	Y	N	Y	Y
10 **McHenry**	Y	Y	Y	Y	Y	Y	Y
11 **Meadows**	Y	Y	Y	Y	Y	Y	N
12 Adams	N	N	N	Y	N	Y	Y
13 **Budd**	Y	Y	Y	Y	?	Y	Y
NORTH DAKOTA							
AL **Cramer**	Y	Y	Y	Y	Y	Y	Y
OHIO							
1 **Chabot**	Y	Y	Y	Y	Y	Y	Y
2 **Wenstrup**	N	Y	Y	Y	Y	Y	Y
3 Beatty	N	N	N	Y	N	Y	Y
4 **Jordan**	N	Y	Y	Y	N	Y	Y
5 **Latta**	N	Y	Y	Y	Y	Y	Y
6 **Johnson**	N	Y	Y	Y	N	Y	Y
7 **Gibbs**	N	Y	Y	Y	Y	Y	Y
8 **Davidson**	Y	Y	Y	Y	Y	Y	Y
9 Kaptur	N	N	N	Y	N	Y	Y
10 **Turner**	?	Y	Y	Y	N	Y	Y
11 Fudge	N	N	N	Y	N	Y	Y
12 **Tiberi**	N	Y	Y	Y	N	Y	Y
13 Ryan	N	N	N	Y	N	Y	?
14 **Joyce**	N	Y	Y	Y	N	Y	Y
15 **Stivers**	N	Y	Y	Y	N	Y	Y
16 **Renacci**	N	Y	Y	Y	N	Y	Y
OKLAHOMA							
1 **Bridenstine**	Y	Y	Y	Y	Y	Y	Y
2 **Mullin**	Y	Y	Y	Y	Y	Y	Y
3 **Lucas**	Y	Y	Y	Y	Y	Y	Y
4 **Cole**	Y	Y	Y	Y	?	Y	Y
5 **Russell**	Y	Y	Y	Y	Y	Y	Y
OREGON							
1 Bonamici	Y	N	N	Y	Y	Y	Y
2 **Walden**	N	Y	Y	Y	Y	Y	Y
3 Blumenauer	Y	N	N	Y	Y	Y	Y
4 DeFazio	N	N	N	Y	N	Y	Y
5 Schrader	N	N	N	Y	N	Y	Y
PENNSYLVANIA							
1 Brady	N	N	N	Y	N	Y	Y
2 Evans	N	N	N	Y	N	Y	Y
3 **Kelly**	Y	Y	Y	Y	Y	Y	Y
4 **Perry**	?	Y	Y	Y	Y	Y	Y
5 **Thompson**	N	Y	Y	Y	N	Y	Y
6 **Costello**	N	Y	Y	Y	N	Y	Y
7 **Meehan**	N	Y	Y	Y	N	Y	Y
8 **Fitzpatrick**	?	Y	Y	Y	N	Y	Y
9 **Shuster**	Y	Y	Y	Y	Y	Y	Y
10 **Marino**	Y	Y	Y	Y	Y	+	+
11 **Barletta**	Y	Y	Y	Y	Y	Y	Y
12 **Rothfus**	Y	Y	Y	Y	Y	Y	Y
13 Boyle	N	N	N	Y	N	Y	Y
14 Doyle	N	N	N	Y	N	Y	Y
15 **Dent**	Y	Y	Y	Y	Y	Y	Y
16 **Smucker**	Y	Y	Y	Y	Y	Y	Y
17 Cartwright	N	N	N	Y	N	Y	Y
18 **Murphy**	N	Y	Y	Y	Y	Y	Y
RHODE ISLAND							
1 Cicilline	Y	N	N	Y	Y	Y	Y
2 Langevin	N	N	N	Y	N	Y	Y
SOUTH CAROLINA							
1 **Sanford**	N	Y	Y	Y	N	Y	N
2 **Wilson**	?	Y	Y	Y	Y	Y	Y
3 **Duncan**	Y	Y	Y	Y	Y	?	?
4 **Gowdy**	N	Y	Y	Y	Y	Y	Y
6 Clyburn	?	N	N	Y	N	Y	Y
7 **Rice**	P	Y	Y	Y	Y	Y	?
SOUTH DAKOTA							
AL **Noem**	N	Y	Y	Y	N	Y	Y
TENNESSEE							
1 **Roe**	N	Y	Y	Y	N	Y	Y
2 **Duncan**	Y	Y	Y	Y	Y	Y	Y
3 **Fleischmann**	Y	Y	Y	Y	Y	Y	Y
4 **DesJarlais**	Y	Y	Y	Y	Y	Y	Y
5 Cooper	Y	N	N	Y	Y	Y	Y
6 **Black**	Y	Y	Y	Y	Y	Y	Y
7 **Blackburn**	Y	Y	Y	Y	Y	Y	Y
8 **Kustoff**	Y	Y	Y	Y	Y	Y	Y
9 Cohen	?	N	N	Y	N	Y	Y

	190	191	192	193	194	195	196
TEXAS							
1 **Gohmert**	?	Y	N	Y	?	Y	Y
2 **Poe**	N	Y	Y	Y	N	Y	Y
3 **Johnson, S.**	Y	Y	Y	Y	Y	Y	Y
4 **Ratcliffe**	Y	Y	Y	Y	Y	Y	Y
5 **Hensarling**	Y	Y	Y	Y	Y	Y	Y
6 **Barton**	Y	Y	Y	Y	Y	?	Y
7 **Culberson**	Y	Y	Y	Y	Y	Y	Y
8 **Brady**	Y	Y	Y	Y	Y	Y	Y
9 Green, A.	N	N	N	Y	N	Y	Y
10 **McCaul**	Y	Y	Y	Y	Y	Y	Y
11 **Conaway**	N	Y	Y	Y	N	Y	Y
12 **Granger**	Y	Y	Y	Y	Y	Y	Y
13 **Thornberry**	Y	Y	Y	Y	Y	Y	Y
14 **Weber**	N	Y	Y	Y	N	Y	Y
15 Gonzalez	Y	N	N	Y	N	Y	Y
16 O'Rourke	Y	N	N	Y	Y	Y	Y
17 **Flores**	Y	Y	Y	Y	N	Y	Y
18 Jackson Lee	?	N	N	Y	N	Y	Y
19 **Arrington**	Y	Y	Y	Y	Y	Y	Y
20 Castro	Y	N	N	Y	Y	Y	?
21 **Smith**	Y	Y	Y	Y	Y	Y	Y
22 **Olson**	Y	Y	Y	Y	Y	Y	Y
23 **Hurd**	N	Y	Y	Y	N	Y	Y
24 **Marchant**	Y	Y	Y	Y	Y	Y	Y
25 **Williams**	Y	Y	Y	Y	Y	Y	Y
26 **Burgess**	N	Y	Y	Y	N	Y	Y
27 **Farenthold**	Y	Y	Y	Y	Y	Y	Y
28 Cuellar	N	N	N	Y	Y	Y	Y
29 Green, G.	N	N	N	Y	N	Y	Y
30 Johnson, E.B.	N	N	N	Y	N	Y	Y
31 **Carter**	Y	Y	Y	Y	Y	Y	Y
32 **Sessions**	Y	Y	Y	Y	Y	Y	Y
33 Veasey	N	N	N	Y	N	Y	Y
34 Vela	Y	N	N	Y	Y	Y	Y
35 Doggett	Y	N	N	Y	Y	Y	Y
36 **Babin**	N	Y	Y	Y	Y	Y	Y
UTAH							
1 **Bishop**	Y	Y	Y	Y	Y	Y	Y
2 **Stewart**	Y	Y	Y	Y	Y	Y	Y
3 **Chaffetz**	Y	Y	Y	Y	Y	Y	Y
4 **Love**	Y	Y	Y	Y	N	Y	Y
VERMONT							
AL Welch	Y	N	N	Y	Y	Y	Y
VIRGINIA							
1 **Wittman**	N	Y	Y	Y	Y	Y	Y
2 **Taylor**	Y	Y	Y	Y	Y	Y	Y
3 Scott	N	N	N	Y	N	Y	Y
4 McEachin	N	N	N	Y	N	Y	Y
5 **Garrett**	Y	Y	Y	Y	Y	Y	N
6 **Goodlatte**	?	Y	Y	Y	Y	Y	Y
7 **Brat**	Y	Y	Y	Y	Y	Y	Y
8 Beyer	N	N	N	Y	N	Y	Y
9 **Griffith**	N	Y	Y	Y	N	Y	Y
10 **Comstock**	Y	Y	Y	Y	Y	Y	Y
11 Connolly	N	N	N	Y	N	Y	Y
WASHINGTON							
1 DelBene	Y	N	N	Y	Y	Y	Y
2 Larsen	N	N	N	Y	N	Y	Y
3 **Herrera Beutler**	N	Y	Y	Y	N	Y	Y
4 **Newhouse**	Y	Y	Y	Y	Y	Y	Y
5 **McMorris Rodgers**	Y	Y	Y	Y	Y	Y	Y
6 Kilmer	N	N	N	Y	N	Y	Y
7 Jayapal	N	N	N	Y	N	Y	Y
8 **Reichert**	?	Y	Y	Y	N	Y	Y
9 Smith	Y	N	N	Y	Y	Y	Y
10 Heck	Y	N	N	Y	Y	Y	Y
WEST VIRGINIA							
1 **McKinley**	N	Y	Y	Y	N	Y	Y
2 **Mooney**	Y	Y	Y	Y	Y	Y	Y
3 **Jenkins**	N	Y	Y	Y	N	Y	Y
WISCONSIN							
1 **Ryan**							
2 Pocan	Y	N	N	Y	Y	Y	Y
3 Kind	N	N	N	Y	N	Y	Y
4 Moore	N	N	N	Y	N	Y	Y
5 **Sensenbrenner**	Y	Y	Y	Y	Y	Y	Y
6 **Grothman**	N	Y	Y	Y	Y	Y	Y
7 **Duffy**	N	Y	Y	Y	N	Y	Y
8 **Gallagher**	N	Y	Y	Y	N	Y	Y
WYOMING							
AL **Cheney**	Y	Y	Y	Y	Y	Y	Y

⦀ HOUSE VOTES

VOTE NUMBER

197. HR 1430, H RES 229. EPA RULE INFORMATION/PREVIOUS QUESTION. Woodall, R-Ga., motion to order the previous question (thus ending debate and possibility of amendment) on the rule (H Res 229) that would provide for House floor consideration of the bill that would prohibit the EPA from proposing, finalizing or disseminating a rule, regulation or standard unless the scientific and technical information on which the EPA's decisions relied is publicly available for independent analysis. Motion agreed to 231-189 : R 231-0; D 0-189. March, 28, 2017.

198. HR 1430, H RES 229. EPA RULE INFORMATION/RULE. Adoption of the rule (H Res 229) that would provide for House floor consideration of the bill that would prohibit the EPA from proposing, finalizing or disseminating a rule, regulation or standard unless the scientific and technical information on which the EPA's decisions relied is publicly available for independent analysis. Adopted 231-185 : R 230-0; D 1-185. March, 28, 2017.

199. S J RES 34, H RES 230. BROADBAND PRIVACY DISAPPROVAL/ PREVIOUS QUESTION. Burgess, R-Texas, motion to order the previous question (thus ending debate and possibility of amendment) on the rule (H Res 230) that would provide for House floor consideration of the joint resolution (S J Res 34) that would disapprove and nullify a Federal Communications Commission rule that requires broadband internet service providers to obtain affirmative permission from customers to use or share their sensitive information. Motion agreed to 232-184 : R 231-0; D 1-184. March, 28, 2017.

200. S J RES 34, H RES 230. BROADBAND PRIVACY DISAPPROVAL/RULE. Adoption of the rule (H Res 230) that would provide for House floor consideration of the joint resolution (S J Res 34) that would disapprove and nullify a Federal Communications Commission rule that requires broadband internet service providers to obtain affirmative permission from customers to use or share their sensitive information. Adopted 231-189 : R 231-0; D 0-189. March, 28, 2017.

201. PRESIDENT'S TAX RETURN DISCLOSURE/MOTION TO TABLE. Flores, R-Texas, motion to table (kill) the Lofgren, D-Calif., motion to appeal the ruling of the Chair that the Lofgren resolution related to the disclosure of President Trump's tax returns does not constitute a question of the privileges of the House. Motion agreed to 228-190 : R 228-1; D 0-189. March, 28, 2017.

202. S J RES 34. BROADBAND PRIVACY DISAPPROVAL/PASSAGE. Passage of the joint resolution that would disapprove and nullify a Federal Communications Commission rule that requires broadband internet service providers to obtain affirmative permission from customers to use or share their sensitive information, such as web browsing history, geolocation information, content of communications and Social Security numbers; to take reasonable measures to secure customer information; and to notify customers, the commission and law enforcement when a data breach occurs that could result in harm. Passed (thus cleared for the president) 215-205 : R 215-15; D 0-190. March, 28, 2017.

203. H RES 233, HR 1431. EPA SCIENCE ADVISORY BOARD/PREVIOUS QUESTION. Newhouse, R-Wash., motion to order the previous question (thus ending debate and possibility of amendment) on the rule (H Res 233) that would provide for House floor consideration of the bill that would establish a selection process for members of the EPA's Science Advisory Board. Motion agreed to 232-191 : R 232-1; D 0-190. March, 29, 2017.

	197	198	199	200	201	202	203
ALABAMA							
1 **Byrne**	Y	Y	Y	Y	Y	Y	Y
2 **Roby**	Y	Y	Y	Y	Y	Y	Y
3 **Rogers**	Y	?	Y	Y	Y	Y	Y
4 **Aderholt**	Y	Y	Y	Y	Y	Y	Y
5 **Brooks**	Y	Y	Y	Y	Y	N	Y
6 **Palmer**	Y	Y	Y	Y	Y	Y	Y
7 Sewell	N	N	N	N	N	N	N
ALASKA							
AL **Young**	Y	Y	Y	Y	Y	Y	?
ARIZONA							
1 O'Halleran	N	N	N	N	N	N	N
2 **McSally**	Y	Y	Y	Y	Y	Y	Y
3 Grijalva	N	N	N	N	N	N	N
4 **Gosar**	Y	Y	Y	Y	Y	Y	Y
5 **Biggs**	Y	Y	Y	Y	Y	Y	Y
6 **Schweikert**	Y	Y	Y	Y	Y	Y	Y
7 Gallego	N	?	N	N	N	N	N
8 **Franks**	Y	Y	Y	Y	Y	Y	Y
9 Sinema	N	N	N	N	N	N	N
ARKANSAS							
1 **Crawford**	Y	Y	Y	Y	Y	Y	Y
2 **Hill**	Y	Y	Y	Y	Y	–	Y
3 **Womack**	Y	Y	Y	Y	Y	Y	Y
4 **Westerman**	Y	Y	Y	Y	Y	Y	Y
CALIFORNIA							
1 **LaMalfa**	Y	Y	Y	Y	Y	Y	Y
2 Huffman	N	N	N	N	N	N	N
3 Garamendi	N	N	N	N	N	N	N
4 **McClintock**	Y	Y	Y	Y	Y	N	Y
5 Thompson	N	N	N	N	N	N	N
6 Matsui	N	N	N	N	N	N	N
7 Bera	N	N	N	N	N	N	N
8 **Cook**	Y	Y	Y	Y	Y	Y	Y
9 McNerney	N	N	N	N	N	N	N
10 **Denham**	Y	Y	Y	Y	Y	Y	Y
11 DeSaulnier	N	N	N	N	N	N	N
12 Pelosi	N	N	N	N	N	N	N
13 Lee	N	N	N	N	N	N	N
14 Speier	N	N	N	N	N	N	N
15 Swalwell	N	N	N	N	N	N	N
16 Costa	N	Y	N	N	N	N	N
17 Khanna	N	N	N	N	N	N	N
18 Eshoo	N	N	N	N	N	N	N
19 Lofgren	N	N	N	N	N	N	N
20 Panetta	N	N	N	N	N	N	N
21 **Valadao**	Y	Y	Y	Y	Y	Y	Y
22 **Nunes**	Y	Y	Y	Y	Y	Y	Y
23 **McCarthy**	Y	Y	Y	Y	Y	Y	Y
24 Carbajal	N	N	N	N	N	N	N
25 **Knight**	Y	Y	Y	Y	Y	Y	Y
26 Brownley	N	N	N	N	N	N	N
27 Chu	N	N	N	N	N	N	N
28 Schiff	N	N	N	N	N	N	N
29 Cardenas	N	N	N	N	N	N	N
30 Sherman	N	N	N	N	N	N	N
31 Aguilar	N	N	N	N	N	N	N
32 Napolitano	N	N	N	N	N	N	N
33 Lieu	N	N	N	N	N	N	N
34 Vacant							
35 Torres	N	N	N	N	N	N	N
36 Ruiz	N	N	N	N	N	N	N
37 Bass	N	N	N	N	N	N	N
38 Sánchez, Linda	N	N	N	N	N	N	N
39 **Royce**	Y	Y	Y	Y	Y	Y	Y
40 Roybal-Allard	N	N	N	N	N	N	N
41 Takano	N	N	N	N	N	N	N
42 **Calvert**	Y	Y	Y	Y	Y	Y	Y
43 Waters	N	N	N	N	N	N	N
44 Barragan	N	N	N	N	N	N	N
45 **Walters**	Y	Y	Y	Y	Y	Y	Y
46 Correa	N	N	N	N	N	N	N
47 Lowenthal	N	N	N	N	N	N	N
48 **Rohrabacher**	Y	Y	Y	Y	Y	Y	Y
49 **Issa**	Y	Y	Y	Y	Y	Y	Y
50 **Hunter**	Y	Y	Y	Y	Y	Y	Y
51 Vargas	N	N	N	N	N	N	N
52 Peters	N	N	N	N	N	N	N
53 Davis	N	N	N	N	N	N	N

	197	198	199	200	201	202	203
COLORADO							
1 DeGette	N	N	N	N	N	N	N
2 Polis	N	N	N	N	N	N	N
3 **Tipton**	Y	Y	Y	Y	Y	Y	Y
4 **Buck**	Y	Y	Y	Y	Y	Y	Y
5 **Lamborn**	Y	Y	Y	Y	Y	Y	Y
6 **Coffman**	Y	Y	Y	Y	Y	N	Y
7 Perlmutter	N	N	N	N	N	N	N
CONNECTICUT							
1 Larson	N	N	N	N	N	N	N
2 Courtney	N	N	N	N	N	N	N
3 DeLauro	N	N	N	N	N	N	N
4 Himes	N	–	N	N	N	N	N
5 Esty	N	N	N	N	N	N	N
DELAWARE							
AL Blunt Rochester	N	N	N	N	N	N	N
FLORIDA							
1 **Gaetz**	Y	Y	Y	Y	Y	Y	Y
2 **Dunn**	Y	Y	Y	Y	Y	Y	Y
3 **Yoho**	Y	Y	Y	Y	Y	Y	Y
4 **Rutherford**	Y	Y	Y	Y	Y	Y	Y
5 Lawson	N	N	N	N	N	N	N
6 **DeSantis**	Y	Y	Y	Y	Y	Y	Y
7 Murphy	N	N	N	N	N	N	N
8 **Posey**	Y	Y	Y	?	Y	Y	Y
9 Soto	N	N	N	N	N	N	N
10 Demings	N	N	N	N	N	N	N
11 **Webster**	Y	Y	Y	Y	Y	Y	Y
12 **Bilirakis**	Y	Y	Y	Y	Y	Y	Y
13 Crist	N	N	N	N	N	N	N
14 Castor	N	N	N	N	N	N	N
15 **Ross**	Y	Y	Y	Y	Y	Y	Y
16 **Buchanan**	Y	Y	Y	Y	Y	Y	Y
17 **Rooney, T.**	?	?	?	?	Y	Y	Y
18 **Mast**	Y	Y	Y	Y	Y	Y	Y
19 **Rooney, F.**	Y	Y	Y	Y	Y	Y	Y
20 Hastings	N	N	N	N	N	N	N
21 Frankel	N	N	N	N	N	N	N
22 Deutch	N	N	N	N	N	N	N
23 Wasserman Schultz	N	N	N	N	N	N	N
24 Wilson	N	N	N	N	N	N	N
25 **Diaz-Balart**	Y	Y	Y	Y	Y	Y	Y
26 **Curbelo**	Y	Y	Y	Y	Y	Y	Y
27 **Ros-Lehtinen**	?	?	?	?	?	?	Y
GEORGIA							
1 **Carter**	Y	Y	Y	Y	Y	Y	Y
2 Bishop	N	N	N	N	N	N	N
3 **Ferguson**	Y	Y	Y	Y	Y	Y	Y
4 Johnson	N	N	N	N	N	N	N
5 Lewis	N	N	N	N	N	N	N
6 **Woodall**	Y	Y	Y	Y	Y	Y	Y
7 **Scott, A.**	Y	Y	Y	Y	Y	Y	Y
8 **Collins**	Y	Y	Y	Y	Y	Y	Y
9 **Hice**	Y	Y	Y	Y	Y	Y	Y
10 **Loudermilk**	Y	Y	Y	Y	Y	Y	Y
11 **Allen**	Y	Y	Y	Y	Y	Y	Y
12 Scott, D.	?	?	?	?	N	N	N
13 **Graves**	Y	Y	Y	Y	Y	Y	Y
HAWAII							
1 Hanabusa	N	N	N	N	N	N	N
2 Gabbard	N	N	N	N	N	N	N
IDAHO							
1 **Labrador**	Y	Y	Y	Y	Y	Y	Y
2 **Simpson**	+	+	+	+	+	+	Y
ILLINOIS							
1 Rush	?	?	?	?	?	?	?
2 Kelly	N	N	N	N	N	N	N
3 Lipinski	N	N	N	N	N	N	N
4 Gutierrez	N	N	N	N	N	N	N
5 Quigley	N	N	N	N	N	N	N
6 **Roskam**	Y	Y	Y	Y	Y	Y	Y
7 Davis, D.	N	N	N	N	N	N	N
8 Krishnamoorthi	N	N	N	N	N	N	N
9 Schakowsky	N	N	N	N	N	N	N
10 Schneider	N	N	N	N	N	N	N
11 Foster	N	N	N	N	N	N	N
12 **Bost**	Y	Y	Y	Y	Y	Y	Y
13 **Davis, R.**	Y	Y	Y	Y	Y	Y	Y
14 **Hultgren**	Y	Y	Y	Y	Y	Y	Y
15 **Shimkus**	Y	Y	Y	Y	Y	Y	Y

	197	198	199	200	201	202	203
16 **Kinzinger**	Y	Y	Y	Y	Y	Y	Y
17 Bustos	N	N	N	N	N	N	N
18 **LaHood**	Y	Y	Y	Y	Y	Y	Y
INDIANA							
1 Visclosky	N	N	N	N	N	N	N
2 **Walorski**	Y	Y	Y	Y	Y	Y	Y
3 **Banks**	Y	Y	Y	Y	Y	Y	Y
4 **Rokita**	Y	Y	Y	Y	Y	Y	Y
5 **Brooks**	Y	Y	Y	Y	Y	Y	Y
6 **Messer**	Y	Y	Y	Y	Y	Y	Y
7 Carson	N	N	?	N	N	N	N
8 **Bucshon**	Y	Y	Y	Y	Y	Y	Y
9 **Hollingsworth**	Y	Y	Y	Y	Y	Y	Y
IOWA							
1 **Blum**	Y	Y	Y	Y	Y	Y	Y
2 Loebsack	N	N	N	N	N	N	N
3 **Young**	Y	Y	Y	Y	Y	Y	Y
4 **King**	Y	Y	Y	Y	Y	Y	Y
KANSAS							
1 **Marshall**	Y	Y	Y	Y	Y	Y	Y
2 **Jenkins**	Y	Y	Y	Y	Y	Y	Y
3 **Yoder**	Y	Y	Y	Y	Y	N	Y
KENTUCKY							
1 **Comer**	Y	Y	Y	Y	Y	Y	Y
2 **Guthrie**	Y	Y	Y	Y	Y	Y	Y
3 Yarmuth	N	N	N	N	N	N	N
4 **Massie**	Y	Y	Y	Y	Y	Y	Y
5 **Rogers**	Y	Y	Y	Y	Y	Y	Y
6 **Barr**	Y	Y	Y	Y	Y	Y	Y
LOUISIANA							
1 **Scalise**	Y	Y	Y	Y	Y	Y	Y
2 Richmond	N	N	N	N	N	N	N
3 **Higgins**	Y	Y	Y	Y	Y	Y	Y
4 **Johnson**	Y	Y	Y	Y	Y	Y	Y
5 **Abraham**	Y	Y	Y	Y	Y	Y	Y
6 **Graves**	Y	Y	Y	Y	Y	N	Y
MAINE							
1 Pingree	N	N	N	N	N	N	N
2 **Poliquin**	Y	Y	Y	Y	Y	Y	Y
MARYLAND							
1 **Harris**	Y	Y	Y	Y	Y	Y	Y
2 Ruppersberger	N	N	N	N	N	N	N
3 Sarbanes	N	N	N	N	N	N	N
4 Brown	N	N	N	N	N	N	N
5 Hoyer	N	N	N	N	N	N	N
6 Delaney	N	N	N	N	N	N	N
7 Cummings	N	N	N	N	N	N	N
8 Raskin	N	N	N	N	N	N	N
MASSACHUSETTS							
1 Neal	N	N	N	N	N	N	N
2 McGovern	N	N	N	N	N	N	N
3 Tsongas	N	N	N	N	N	N	N
4 Kennedy	N	N	N	N	N	N	N
5 Clark	N	N	N	N	N	N	N
6 Moulton	N	N	N	N	N	N	N
7 Capuano	N	N	N	N	N	N	N
8 Lynch	N	N	N	N	N	N	N
9 Keating	N	N	N	N	N	N	N
MICHIGAN							
1 **Bergman**	Y	Y	Y	Y	Y	Y	Y
2 **Huizenga**	Y	Y	Y	Y	Y	Y	Y
3 **Amash**	Y	Y	Y	Y	Y	N	Y
4 **Moolenaar**	Y	Y	Y	Y	Y	Y	Y
5 Kildee	N	N	N	N	N	N	N
6 **Upton**	Y	Y	Y	Y	Y	Y	Y
7 **Walberg**	Y	Y	Y	Y	Y	Y	Y
8 **Bishop**	Y	Y	Y	Y	Y	Y	Y
9 Levin	N	N	N	N	N	N	N
10 **Mitchell**	Y	Y	Y	Y	Y	Y	Y
11 **Trott**	Y	Y	Y	Y	Y	Y	Y
12 Dingell	N	N	N	N	N	N	N
13 Conyers	N	N	N	N	N	N	N
14 Lawrence	N	N	N	N	N	N	N
MINNESOTA							
1 Walz	N	N	N	N	N	N	N
2 **Lewis**	Y	Y	Y	Y	Y	Y	Y
3 **Paulsen**	Y	Y	Y	Y	Y	Y	Y
4 McCollum	N	N	N	N	N	N	N

	197	198	199	200	201	202	203
5 Ellison	N	N	N	N	N	N	N
6 **Emmer**	Y	Y	Y	Y	Y	Y	Y
7 Peterson	N	N	N	N	N	N	N
8 Nolan	N	N	N	N	?	N	N
MISSISSIPPI							
1 **Kelly**	Y	Y	Y	Y	Y	Y	Y
2 Thompson	N	N	N	N	N	N	N
3 **Harper**	Y	Y	Y	Y	Y	Y	Y
4 **Palazzo**	Y	Y	Y	Y	Y	Y	Y
MISSOURI							
1 Clay	N	N	N	N	N	N	N
2 **Wagner**	Y	Y	Y	Y	Y	Y	Y
3 **Luetkemeyer**	Y	Y	Y	Y	Y	Y	Y
4 **Hartzler**	Y	Y	Y	Y	Y	Y	Y
5 Cleaver	N	?	N	N	N	N	N
6 **Graves**	Y	Y	Y	Y	Y	Y	Y
7 **Long**	Y	Y	Y	Y	Y	Y	Y
8 **Smith**	Y	Y	Y	Y	Y	Y	Y
MONTANA							
AL **Vacant**							
NEBRASKA							
1 **Fortenberry**	Y	Y	Y	Y	Y	Y	Y
2 **Bacon**	Y	Y	Y	Y	Y	Y	Y
3 **Smith**	Y	Y	Y	Y	Y	Y	Y
NEVADA							
1 Titus	N	N	N	N	N	N	N
2 **Amodei**	Y	Y	Y	Y	Y	Y	Y
3 Rosen	N	N	N	N	N	N	N
4 Kihuen	N	N	N	N	N	N	N
NEW HAMPSHIRE							
1 Shea-Porter	N	N	N	N	N	N	N
2 Kuster	N	N	N	N	N	N	N
NEW JERSEY							
1 Norcross	N	N	N	N	N	N	N
2 **LoBiondo**	Y	Y	Y	Y	Y	Y	Y
3 **MacArthur**	Y	Y	Y	Y	Y	Y	Y
4 **Smith**	Y	Y	Y	Y	Y	Y	Y
5 Gottheimer	N	N	N	N	N	N	N
6 Pallone	N	N	N	N	N	N	N
7 **Lance**	Y	Y	Y	Y	Y	Y	Y
8 Sires	N	N	N	N	N	N	N
9 Pascrell	N	N	N	N	N	N	N
10 Payne	N	N	N	N	N	N	N
11 **Frelinghuysen**	Y	Y	Y	Y	Y	Y	Y
12 Watson Coleman	N	N	N	N	N	N	N
NEW MEXICO							
1 Lujan Grisham	N	N	N	N	N	N	N
2 **Pearce**	Y	Y	Y	Y	Y	Y	Y
3 Luján	N	N	N	N	N	N	N
NEW YORK							
1 **Zeldin**	Y	Y	Y	Y	Y	N	Y
2 **King**	Y	Y	Y	Y	Y	Y	Y
3 Suozzi	N	N	?	N	N	N	N
4 Rice	N	N	N	N	N	N	N
5 Meeks	N	N	N	N	N	N	?
6 Meng	N	N	N	N	N	N	N
7 Velázquez	N	N	N	N	N	N	N
8 Jeffries	N	N	N	N	N	N	N
9 Clarke	N	N	N	N	N	N	N
10 Nadler	N	N	N	N	N	N	N
11 **Donovan**	Y	Y	Y	Y	Y	Y	Y
12 Maloney, C.	N	N	N	N	N	N	N
13 Espaillat	N	N	N	N	N	N	N
14 Crowley	N	N	N	N	N	N	N
15 Serrano	N	N	N	N	N	N	N
16 Engel	N	N	N	N	N	N	N
17 Lowey	N	N	N	N	N	N	N
18 Maloney, S.P.	N	N	N	N	N	N	N
19 **Faso**	Y	Y	Y	Y	Y	N	Y
20 Tonko	N	N	N	N	N	–	N
21 **Stefanik**	Y	Y	Y	Y	Y	N	Y
22 **Tenney**	Y	Y	Y	Y	Y	Y	Y
23 **Reed**	Y	Y	Y	Y	Y	Y	Y
24 **Katko**	Y	Y	Y	Y	Y	Y	Y
25 Slaughter	–	–	–	–	–	–	–
26 Higgins	N	N	N	N	N	N	N
27 **Collins**	Y	Y	Y	Y	Y	Y	Y
NORTH CAROLINA							
1 Butterfield	N	N	N	N	N	N	N
2 **Holding**	Y	Y	Y	Y	Y	Y	Y
3 **Jones**	Y	Y	Y	Y	N	N	N
4 Price	?	?	?	?	N	N	N

	197	198	199	200	201	202	203
5 **Foxx**	Y	Y	Y	Y	Y	Y	Y
6 **Walker**	Y	Y	Y	Y	Y	Y	Y
7 **Rouzer**	Y	Y	Y	Y	Y	Y	Y
8 **Hudson**	Y	Y	Y	Y	Y	Y	Y
9 **Pittenger**	?	?	?	?	?	–	Y
10 **McHenry**	Y	Y	Y	Y	Y	Y	Y
11 **Meadows**	Y	Y	Y	Y	Y	Y	Y
12 Adams	N	N	N	N	N	N	N
13 **Budd**	Y	Y	Y	Y	Y	Y	Y
NORTH DAKOTA							
AL **Cramer**	Y	Y	Y	Y	Y	Y	Y
OHIO							
1 **Chabot**	Y	Y	Y	Y	Y	Y	Y
2 **Wenstrup**	Y	Y	Y	Y	Y	Y	Y
3 Beatty	N	N	N	N	N	N	N
4 **Jordan**	Y	Y	Y	Y	Y	Y	Y
5 **Latta**	Y	Y	Y	Y	Y	Y	Y
6 **Johnson**	Y	Y	Y	Y	Y	Y	Y
7 **Gibbs**	Y	Y	Y	Y	Y	Y	Y
8 **Davidson**	Y	Y	Y	Y	Y	N	Y
9 Kaptur	N	N	Y	N	N	N	N
10 **Turner**	Y	Y	Y	Y	Y	Y	Y
11 Fudge	N	N	N	N	N	N	N
12 **Tiberi**	Y	Y	Y	Y	Y	Y	Y
13 Ryan	N	N	N	N	N	N	N
14 **Joyce**	Y	Y	Y	Y	Y	Y	Y
15 **Stivers**	Y	Y	Y	Y	Y	Y	Y
16 **Renacci**	Y	Y	Y	Y	Y	Y	Y
OKLAHOMA							
1 **Bridenstine**	Y	Y	Y	Y	Y	Y	Y
2 **Mullin**	Y	Y	Y	Y	Y	Y	Y
3 **Lucas**	Y	Y	Y	Y	Y	Y	Y
4 **Cole**	Y	Y	Y	Y	Y	Y	Y
5 **Russell**	Y	Y	Y	Y	Y	Y	Y
OREGON							
1 Bonamici	N	N	N	N	N	N	N
2 **Walden**	Y	Y	Y	Y	Y	Y	Y
3 Blumenauer	N	N	N	N	N	N	N
4 DeFazio	N	N	?	N	P	N	N
5 Schrader	N	N	N	N	N	N	N
PENNSYLVANIA							
1 Brady	N	N	N	N	N	N	N
2 Evans	N	N	N	N	N	N	N
3 **Kelly**	Y	Y	Y	Y	Y	Y	Y
4 **Perry**	Y	Y	Y	Y	Y	Y	Y
5 **Thompson**	Y	Y	Y	Y	Y	Y	Y
6 **Costello**	Y	Y	Y	Y	Y	Y	Y
7 **Meehan**	Y	Y	Y	Y	Y	Y	Y
8 **Fitzpatrick**	Y	Y	Y	Y	Y	Y	Y
9 **Shuster**	Y	Y	Y	Y	Y	Y	Y
10 **Marino**	+	+	+	+	+	+	+
11 **Barletta**	Y	Y	Y	Y	Y	Y	Y
12 **Rothfus**	Y	Y	Y	Y	Y	Y	Y
13 Boyle	N	N	N	N	N	N	N
14 Doyle	N	N	N	N	N	N	N
15 **Dent**	Y	Y	Y	Y	Y	Y	Y
16 **Smucker**	Y	Y	Y	Y	Y	Y	Y
17 Cartwright	N	N	N	N	N	N	N
18 **Murphy**	Y	Y	Y	Y	Y	Y	Y
RHODE ISLAND							
1 Cicilline	N	N	N	N	N	N	N
2 Langevin	N	N	N	N	N	N	N
SOUTH CAROLINA							
1 **Sanford**	Y	Y	Y	Y	P	N	Y
2 **Wilson**	Y	Y	Y	Y	Y	Y	Y
3 **Duncan**	Y	Y	Y	Y	Y	Y	Y
4 **Gowdy**	Y	Y	Y	Y	Y	Y	Y
6 Clyburn	N	N	N	N	N	N	N
7 **Rice**	Y	Y	Y	Y	Y	Y	Y
SOUTH DAKOTA							
AL **Noem**	Y	Y	Y	Y	Y	Y	Y
TENNESSEE							
1 **Roe**	Y	Y	Y	Y	Y	Y	Y
2 **Duncan**	Y	Y	Y	Y	Y	N	Y
3 **Fleischmann**	Y	Y	Y	Y	Y	Y	Y
4 **DesJarlais**	Y	Y	Y	Y	Y	Y	Y
5 Cooper	N	N	N	N	N	N	N
6 **Black**	Y	Y	Y	Y	Y	Y	Y
7 **Blackburn**	Y	Y	Y	Y	Y	Y	Y
8 **Kustoff**	Y	Y	Y	Y	Y	Y	Y
9 Cohen	N	N	N	N	N	N	N

	197	198	199	200	201	202	203
TEXAS							
1 **Gohmert**	Y	Y	Y	Y	Y	Y	Y
2 **Poe**	Y	Y	Y	Y	Y	Y	Y
3 **Johnson, S.**	Y	Y	Y	Y	Y	Y	Y
4 **Ratcliffe**	Y	Y	Y	Y	Y	Y	Y
5 **Hensarling**	Y	Y	Y	Y	Y	Y	Y
6 **Barton**	Y	Y	Y	Y	Y	Y	Y
7 **Culberson**	Y	Y	Y	Y	Y	Y	Y
8 **Brady**	Y	Y	Y	Y	Y	Y	Y
9 Green, A.	N	N	N	N	N	N	N
10 **McCaul**	Y	Y	Y	Y	Y	Y	Y
11 **Conaway**	Y	Y	Y	Y	Y	Y	Y
12 **Granger**	Y	Y	Y	Y	Y	Y	Y
13 **Thornberry**	Y	Y	Y	Y	Y	Y	Y
14 **Weber**	Y	Y	Y	Y	Y	Y	Y
15 Gonzalez	N	N	?	N	N	N	N
16 O'Rourke	N	N	N	N	N	N	N
17 **Flores**	Y	Y	Y	Y	Y	Y	Y
18 Jackson Lee	N	N	N	N	N	N	N
19 **Arrington**	Y	Y	Y	Y	Y	Y	Y
20 Castro	N	N	N	N	N	N	N
21 **Smith**	Y	Y	Y	Y	Y	Y	Y
22 **Olson**	Y	Y	Y	Y	Y	Y	Y
23 **Hurd**	Y	Y	Y	Y	Y	Y	Y
24 **Marchant**	Y	Y	Y	Y	Y	Y	Y
25 **Williams**	Y	Y	Y	Y	Y	Y	Y
26 **Burgess**	Y	Y	Y	Y	Y	Y	Y
27 **Farenthold**	Y	Y	Y	Y	Y	Y	Y
28 Cuellar	N	N	N	N	N	N	N
29 Green, G.	N	N	N	N	N	N	N
30 Johnson, E.B.	N	N	N	N	N	N	N
31 **Carter**	Y	Y	Y	Y	Y	Y	Y
32 **Sessions**	Y	Y	Y	Y	Y	Y	Y
33 Veasey	N	N	N	N	N	N	N
34 Vela	N	N	N	N	N	N	N
35 Doggett	N	N	N	N	N	N	N
36 **Babin**	Y	Y	Y	Y	Y	Y	Y
UTAH							
1 **Bishop**	Y	Y	Y	Y	Y	Y	Y
2 **Stewart**	Y	Y	Y	Y	Y	Y	Y
3 **Chaffetz**	Y	Y	Y	Y	Y	Y	Y
4 **Love**	Y	Y	Y	Y	Y	Y	Y
VERMONT							
AL Welch	N	N	N	N	N	N	N
VIRGINIA							
1 **Wittman**	Y	Y	Y	Y	Y	Y	Y
2 **Taylor**	Y	Y	Y	Y	Y	Y	Y
3 Scott	N	N	N	N	N	N	N
4 McEachin	N	N	N	N	N	N	N
5 **Garrett**	Y	Y	Y	Y	Y	Y	Y
6 **Goodlatte**	Y	Y	Y	Y	Y	Y	Y
7 **Brat**	Y	Y	Y	Y	Y	Y	Y
8 Beyer	N	N	N	N	N	N	N
9 **Griffith**	Y	Y	Y	Y	Y	Y	Y
10 **Comstock**	Y	Y	Y	Y	Y	Y	Y
11 Connolly	N	N	N	N	N	N	N
WASHINGTON							
1 DelBene	N	N	N	N	N	N	N
2 Larsen	N	N	N	N	N	N	N
3 **Herrera Beutler**	Y	Y	Y	Y	Y	N	Y
4 **Newhouse**	Y	Y	Y	Y	Y	Y	Y
5 **McMorris Rodgers**	Y	Y	Y	Y	Y	Y	Y
6 Kilmer	N	N	N	N	N	N	N
7 Jayapal	N	N	N	N	N	N	N
8 **Reichert**	Y	Y	Y	Y	Y	N	Y
9 Smith	N	N	N	N	N	N	N
10 Heck	N	N	N	N	N	N	N
WEST VIRGINIA							
1 **McKinley**	Y	Y	Y	Y	Y	Y	Y
2 **Mooney**	Y	Y	Y	Y	Y	Y	Y
3 **Jenkins**	Y	Y	Y	Y	Y	Y	Y
WISCONSIN							
1 **Ryan**							
2 Pocan	N	N	N	N	N	N	N
3 Kind	N	N	N	N	N	N	N
4 Moore	N	N	N	N	N	N	N
5 **Sensenbrenner**	Y	Y	Y	Y	Y	Y	Y
6 **Grothman**	Y	Y	Y	Y	Y	Y	Y
7 **Duffy**	Y	Y	Y	Y	+	+	+
8 **Gallagher**	Y	Y	Y	Y	Y	Y	Y
WYOMING							
AL **Cheney**	Y	Y	Y	Y	Y	Y	Y

VOTE NUMBER

204. HR 1431, H RES 233. EPA SCIENCE ADVISORY BOARD/RULE. Adoption of the rule (H Res 233) that would provide for House floor consideration of the bill that would establish a selection process for members of the EPA's Science Advisory Board. The bill would require board member nominees to disclose financial relationships that would be relevant to EPA advisory activities. Adopted 232-188 : R 231-0; D 1-188. March, 29, 2017.

205. HR 1430. EPA RULE INFORMATION/RECOMMIT. McEachin, D-Va., motion to recommit the bill to the House Science, Space and Technology Committee with instructions to report it back immediately with an amendment that would exempt EPA actions taken in response to a public health threat from the bill's requirement that the scientific information that influenced the EPA's actions must be publicly available. Motion rejected 189-232 : R 1-232; D 188-0. March, 29, 2017.

206. HR 1430. EPA RULE INFORMATION/PASSAGE. Passage of the bill that would prohibit the EPA from proposing, finalizing or disseminating a rule, regulation or standard unless the scientific and technical information on which the EPA's decisions relied is publicly available for independent analysis. It would require any personally identifiable information, trade secrets or sensitive business information to be redacted prior to the publication of the scientific information. Passed 228-194 : R 225-7; D 3-187. March, 29, 2017.

207. HR 1431. EPA SCIENCE ADVISORY BOARD/RECOMMIT. Foster, D-Ill., motion to recommit the bill the House Science, Space and Technology Committee with instructions to report it back immediately with an amendment that would prohibit, both during and for three years following a term on the board, Science Advisory Board members from being employed by any entity with interests before the board. Motion rejected 189-233 : R 1-232; D 188-1. March, 30, 2017.

208. HR 1431. EPA SCIENCE ADVISORY BOARD/PASSAGE. Passage of a bill that would establish a selection process for members of the EPA's Science Advisory Board. The bill would require the board's members represent a variety of scientific and technical viewpoints. It would require board member nominees to disclose financial relationships that would be relevant to EPA advisory activities. It would require the board to generally avoid making policy determinations or recommendations to the EPA. Passed 229-193 : R 227-5; D 2-188. March, 30, 2017.

209. H RES 92. NORTH KOREAN MISSILE PROGRAM/PASSAGE. Royce, R-Calif., motion to suspend the rules and agree to a resolution that would condemn North Korea's development of intercontinental ballistic missiles, would express support for South Korea's deployment of the Terminal High Altitude Area Defense anti-ballistic missile system, and would urge the Chinese government to pressure North Korea to dismantle its nuclear and missile programs. Motion agreed to 398-3 : R 219-3; D 179-0. April 3, 2017.

210. HR 479. NORTH KOREA TERRORISM DESIGNATION/PASSAGE. Royce, R-Calif., motion to suspend the rules and pass the bill that would express the sense of the House of Representatives that the North Korean government likely meets the criteria for designation as a state sponsor of terrorism, and would require the secretary of State to submit a report to Congress on whether the North Korean government meets the criteria for designation as a state sponsor of terrorism. Motion agreed to 394-1 : R 221-1; D 173-0. April 3, 2017.

	204	205	206	207	208	209	210
ALABAMA							
1 Byrne	Y	N	Y	N	Y	Y	Y
2 Roby	Y	N	Y	N	Y	+	+
3 Rogers	Y	N	Y	N	Y	?	?
4 Aderholt	Y	N	Y	N	Y	Y	Y
5 Brooks	Y	N	Y	N	Y	Y	Y
6 Palmer	Y	N	Y	N	Y	Y	Y
7 Sewell	N	Y	N	Y	N	Y	Y
ALASKA							
AL Young	?	?	?	N	Y	Y	Y
ARIZONA							
1 O'Halleran	N	Y	N	Y	N	Y	Y
2 McSally	Y	N	Y	N	Y	Y	Y
3 Grijalva	N	Y	N	Y	N	?	?
4 Gosar	Y	N	Y	N	Y	Y	Y
5 Biggs	Y	N	Y	N	Y	Y	Y
6 Schweikert	Y	N	Y	N	Y	Y	Y
7 Gallego	N	Y	N	Y	N	Y	Y
8 Franks	Y	N	Y	N	Y	Y	Y
9 Sinema	N	Y	N	N	N	Y	Y
ARKANSAS							
1 Crawford	Y	N	Y	N	Y	Y	Y
2 Hill	Y	N	Y	N	Y	Y	Y
3 Womack	Y	N	Y	N	Y	Y	Y
4 Westerman	Y	N	Y	N	Y	Y	Y
CALIFORNIA							
1 LaMalfa	?	N	Y	N	Y	Y	Y
2 Huffman	N	Y	N	Y	N	Y	Y
3 Garamendi	N	Y	N	Y	N	Y	Y
4 McClintock	Y	N	Y	N	Y	?	?
5 Thompson	N	Y	N	Y	N	Y	Y
6 Matsui	N	Y	N	Y	N	Y	Y
7 Bera	N	Y	N	Y	N	Y	Y
8 Cook	Y	N	Y	N	Y	Y	Y
9 McNerney	N	Y	N	Y	N	Y	Y
10 Denham	Y	N	Y	N	Y	Y	Y
11 DeSaulnier	N	Y	N	Y	N	Y	Y
12 Pelosi	N	Y	N	Y	N	Y	?
13 Lee	N	Y	N	Y	N	Y	Y
14 Speier	N	Y	N	Y	N	Y	?
15 Swalwell	N	Y	N	Y	N	Y	Y
16 Costa	N	Y	Y	Y	N	Y	Y
17 Khanna	N	Y	N	Y	N	Y	Y
18 Eshoo	N	Y	N	Y	N	Y	Y
19 Lofgren	N	Y	N	Y	N	Y	?
20 Panetta	N	Y	N	Y	N	Y	Y
21 Valadao	Y	N	Y	N	Y	Y	Y
22 Nunes	Y	N	Y	N	Y	Y	Y
23 McCarthy	Y	N	Y	N	Y	Y	Y
24 Carbajal	N	Y	N	Y	N	Y	Y
25 Knight	Y	N	Y	N	Y	Y	Y
26 Brownley	N	Y	N	Y	N	Y	Y
27 Chu	N	Y	N	Y	N	Y	Y
28 Schiff	N	Y	N	Y	N	Y	Y
29 Cardenas	N	Y	N	Y	N	Y	Y
30 Sherman	N	Y	N	Y	N	Y	Y
31 Aguilar	N	Y	N	Y	N	Y	Y
32 Napolitano	N	Y	N	Y	N	Y	Y
33 Lieu	N	Y	N	Y	N	?	?
34 Vacant							
35 Torres	N	Y	N	Y	N	Y	Y
36 Ruiz	N	Y	N	Y	N	Y	Y
37 Bass	N	Y	N	Y	N	Y	Y
38 Sánchez, Linda	N	Y	N	Y	N	Y	Y
39 Royce	Y	N	Y	N	Y	Y	Y
40 Roybal-Allard	N	Y	N	Y	N	Y	Y
41 Takano	N	Y	N	Y	N	Y	Y
42 Calvert	Y	N	Y	–	+	Y	Y
43 Waters	N	Y	N	Y	N	Y	Y
44 Barragan	N	Y	N	Y	N	Y	Y
45 Walters	Y	N	Y	N	Y	Y	Y
46 Correa	N	Y	N	Y	N	Y	Y
47 Lowenthal	N	Y	N	Y	N	Y	Y
48 Rohrabacher	Y	N	Y	N	Y	Y	Y
49 Issa	Y	N	Y	N	Y	Y	Y
50 Hunter	Y	N	Y	N	Y	Y	Y
51 Vargas	N	Y	N	Y	N	Y	Y
52 Peters	N	Y	N	Y	N	Y	Y
53 Davis	N	Y	N	Y	N	Y	Y

	204	205	206	207	208	209	210
COLORADO							
1 DeGette	N	Y	N	Y	N	Y	Y
2 Polis	N	Y	N	Y	N	Y	?
3 Tipton	Y	N	Y	N	Y	Y	Y
4 Buck	Y	N	Y	N	Y	Y	Y
5 Lamborn	Y	N	Y	N	Y	Y	Y
6 Coffman	Y	N	Y	N	Y	Y	Y
7 Perlmutter	N	Y	N	Y	N	Y	Y
CONNECTICUT							
1 Larson	N	Y	N	Y	N	Y	Y
2 Courtney	N	Y	N	Y	N	Y	Y
3 DeLauro	N	Y	N	Y	N	Y	Y
4 Himes	N	Y	N	Y	N	Y	Y
5 Esty	N	Y	N	Y	N	Y	Y
DELAWARE							
AL Blunt Rochester	N	Y	N	Y	N	Y	Y
FLORIDA							
1 Gaetz	Y	N	Y	N	Y	Y	Y
2 Dunn	Y	N	Y	N	Y	Y	Y
3 Yoho	Y	N	Y	N	Y	?	?
4 Rutherford	Y	N	Y	N	Y	Y	Y
5 Lawson	N	Y	N	Y	N	Y	Y
6 DeSantis	Y	N	Y	N	Y	Y	Y
7 Murphy	N	Y	N	Y	N	+	+
8 Posey	Y	N	Y	N	Y	Y	Y
9 Soto	N	Y	N	Y	N	Y	Y
10 Demings	N	Y	N	Y	N	Y	Y
11 Webster	Y	N	Y	N	Y	Y	Y
12 Bilirakis	Y	N	Y	N	Y	Y	Y
13 Crist	N	Y	N	Y	N	Y	Y
14 Castor	N	Y	N	Y	N	Y	Y
15 Ross	Y	N	Y	N	Y	Y	Y
16 Buchanan	Y	N	Y	N	Y	Y	Y
17 Rooney, T.	Y	N	Y	N	Y	Y	Y
18 Mast	Y	N	Y	N	Y	Y	Y
19 Rooney, F.	Y	N	Y	N	Y	Y	Y
20 Hastings	N	Y	N	Y	N	Y	Y
21 Frankel	N	Y	N	Y	N	Y	Y
22 Deutch	N	Y	N	Y	N	Y	Y
23 Wasserman Schultz	N	Y	N	Y	N	Y	Y
24 Wilson	N	Y	?	N	Y	Y	Y
25 Diaz-Balart	Y	N	Y	N	Y	Y	Y
26 Curbelo	?	N	N	N	N	Y	Y
27 Ros-Lehtinen	Y	N	N	N	N	Y	Y
GEORGIA							
1 Carter	Y	N	Y	N	Y	Y	Y
2 Bishop	N	Y	N	Y	N	?	?
3 Ferguson	Y	N	Y	N	Y	Y	Y
4 Johnson	N	Y	N	Y	N	Y	Y
5 Lewis	N	Y	N	Y	N	Y	Y
7 Woodall	Y	N	Y	N	Y	Y	Y
8 Scott, A.	Y	N	Y	N	Y	Y	Y
9 Collins	Y	N	Y	N	Y	Y	Y
10 Hice	Y	N	Y	N	Y	Y	Y
11 Loudermilk	Y	N	Y	N	Y	Y	Y
12 Allen	Y	N	Y	N	Y	Y	Y
13 Scott, D.	N	Y	N	Y	N	Y	Y
14 Graves	Y	N	Y	N	Y	Y	Y
HAWAII							
1 Hanabusa	N	Y	N	Y	N	Y	Y
2 Gabbard	N	Y	N	Y	N	Y	Y
IDAHO							
1 Labrador	Y	N	Y	N	Y	Y	Y
2 Simpson	Y	N	Y	N	Y	?	?
ILLINOIS							
1 Rush	?	?	?	?	?	Y	Y
2 Kelly	N	Y	N	Y	N	Y	Y
3 Lipinski	N	Y	N	Y	N	Y	Y
4 Gutierrez	N	Y	N	Y	N	+	+
5 Quigley	?	Y	N	?	?	Y	Y
6 Roskam	Y	N	Y	N	Y	Y	Y
7 Davis, D.	N	Y	N	Y	N	?	?
8 Krishnamoorthi	N	Y	N	Y	N	Y	Y
9 Schakowsky	N	Y	N	Y	N	Y	Y
10 Schneider	N	Y	N	Y	N	Y	Y
11 Foster	N	Y	N	Y	N	Y	Y
12 Bost	Y	N	Y	N	Y	Y	Y
13 Davis, R.	Y	N	Y	N	Y	Y	Y
14 Hultgren	Y	N	Y	N	Y	Y	Y
15 Shimkus	Y	N	Y	N	Y	Y	Y

	204	205	206	207	208	209	210
16 **Kinzinger**	Y	N	Y	N	Y	Y	Y
17 Bustos	N	Y	N	Y	N	Y	Y
18 **LaHood**	Y	N	Y	N	Y	Y	Y
INDIANA							
1 Visclosky	N	Y	N	Y	N	+	+
2 **Walorski**	Y	N	Y	N	Y	Y	Y
3 **Banks**	Y	N	Y	N	Y	Y	Y
4 **Rokita**	Y	N	Y	N	Y	Y	Y
5 **Brooks**	Y	N	Y	N	Y	Y	Y
6 **Messer**	Y	N	Y	N	Y	Y	Y
7 Carson	N	?	N	Y	N	Y	Y
8 **Bucshon**	Y	N	Y	N	Y	Y	Y
9 **Hollingsworth**	Y	N	Y	N	Y	Y	Y
IOWA							
1 **Blum**	Y	N	Y	N	Y	Y	Y
2 Loebsack	N	Y	N	Y	N	Y	Y
3 **Young**	Y	N	Y	N	Y	Y	Y
4 **King**	Y	N	Y	N	Y	Y	Y
KANSAS							
1 **Marshall**	Y	N	Y	N	Y	Y	Y
2 **Jenkins**	Y	N	Y	N	Y	Y	Y
3 **Yoder**	Y	N	Y	N	Y	Y	Y
KENTUCKY							
1 **Comer**	Y	N	Y	N	Y	Y	Y
2 **Guthrie**	Y	N	Y	N	Y	Y	Y
3 Yarmuth	N	Y	N	Y	N	Y	Y
4 **Massie**	Y	N	Y	N	Y	N	N
5 **Rogers**	Y	N	Y	N	Y	Y	Y
6 **Barr**	Y	N	Y	N	Y	Y	Y
LOUISIANA							
1 **Scalise**	Y	N	Y	N	Y	Y	Y
2 Richmond	N	Y	N	Y	N	?	?
3 **Higgins**	Y	N	Y	N	Y	Y	Y
4 **Johnson**	Y	N	Y	N	Y	Y	Y
5 **Abraham**	Y	N	Y	N	Y	+	+
6 **Graves**	Y	N	Y	N	Y	Y	Y
MAINE							
1 Pingree	N	Y	N	Y	N	Y	Y
2 **Poliquin**	Y	N	Y	N	Y	Y	Y
MARYLAND							
1 **Harris**	Y	N	Y	N	Y	Y	Y
2 Ruppersberger	N	Y	N	Y	N	Y	Y
3 Sarbanes	N	Y	N	Y	N	Y	Y
4 Brown	N	Y	N	Y	N	Y	Y
5 Hoyer	N	Y	N	Y	N	Y	Y
6 Delaney	N	Y	N	Y	N	Y	Y
7 Cummings	N	Y	N	Y	N	Y	?
8 Raskin	N	Y	N	Y	N	Y	Y
MASSACHUSETTS							
1 Neal	N	Y	N	Y	N	Y	Y
2 McGovern	N	Y	N	Y	N	Y	Y
3 Tsongas	N	Y	N	Y	N	Y	Y
4 Kennedy	N	Y	N	Y	N	Y	Y
5 Clark	N	Y	N	Y	N	Y	Y
6 Moulton	N	Y	N	Y	N	Y	Y
7 Capuano	N	Y	N	Y	N	Y	Y
8 Lynch	N	Y	N	Y	N	Y	Y
9 Keating	N	Y	N	Y	N	Y	Y
MICHIGAN							
1 **Bergman**	Y	N	Y	N	Y	Y	Y
2 **Huizenga**	Y	N	Y	N	Y	Y	Y
3 **Amash**	Y	N	Y	N	Y	N	Y
4 **Moolenaar**	Y	N	Y	N	Y	Y	Y
5 Kildee	N	Y	N	Y	N	Y	Y
6 **Upton**	Y	N	Y	N	Y	Y	Y
7 **Walberg**	Y	N	Y	N	Y	Y	Y
8 **Bishop**	Y	N	Y	N	Y	Y	Y
9 Levin	N	Y	N	Y	N	Y	Y
10 **Mitchell**	Y	N	Y	N	Y	Y	Y
11 **Trott**	Y	N	Y	N	Y	Y	Y
12 Dingell	N	Y	N	Y	N	Y	Y
13 Conyers	N	Y	N	Y	N	Y	Y
14 Lawrence	N	Y	N	Y	N	Y	Y
MINNESOTA							
1 Walz	N	Y	N	Y	N	Y	Y
2 **Lewis**	Y	N	Y	N	Y	Y	Y
3 **Paulsen**	Y	N	Y	N	Y	Y	Y
4 McCollum	N	Y	N	Y	N	Y	Y

	204	205	206	207	208	209	210
5 Ellison	Y	Y	N	Y	N	Y	Y
6 **Emmer**	Y	N	Y	N	Y	Y	Y
7 Peterson	N	Y	Y	Y	Y	Y	Y
8 Nolan	N	Y	N	Y	N	Y	Y
MISSISSIPPI							
1 **Kelly**	Y	N	Y	N	Y	Y	Y
2 Thompson	N	Y	N	Y	N	?	?
3 **Harper**	Y	N	Y	N	Y	Y	Y
4 **Palazzo**	Y	N	Y	N	Y	?	?
MISSOURI							
1 Clay	N	Y	N	Y	N	?	?
2 **Wagner**	Y	N	Y	N	Y	+	Y
3 **Luetkemeyer**	Y	N	Y	N	Y	Y	Y
4 **Hartzler**	Y	N	Y	N	Y	Y	Y
5 Cleaver	N	Y	N	Y	N	Y	Y
6 **Graves**	Y	N	Y	N	Y	Y	Y
7 **Long**	Y	N	Y	N	Y	Y	Y
8 **Smith**	Y	N	Y	N	Y	Y	Y
MONTANA							
AL **Vacant**							
NEBRASKA							
1 **Fortenberry**	Y	N	Y	N	Y	Y	Y
2 **Bacon**	Y	N	Y	N	Y	Y	Y
3 **Smith**	Y	N	Y	N	Y	Y	Y
NEVADA							
1 Titus	N	Y	N	Y	N	Y	Y
2 **Amodei**	Y	N	Y	N	Y	Y	?
3 Rosen	N	Y	N	Y	N	Y	Y
4 Kihuen	N	Y	N	Y	N	Y	Y
NEW HAMPSHIRE							
1 Shea-Porter	N	Y	N	Y	N	Y	Y
2 Kuster	N	Y	N	Y	N	Y	Y
NEW JERSEY							
1 Norcross	N	Y	N	Y	N	Y	Y
2 **LoBiondo**	Y	N	Y	N	Y	Y	Y
3 **MacArthur**	Y	N	Y	N	Y	Y	Y
4 **Smith**	Y	N	Y	N	Y	Y	Y
5 Gottheimer	N	Y	N	Y	N	Y	Y
6 Pallone	N	Y	N	Y	N	Y	Y
7 **Lance**	Y	N	Y	N	Y	Y	Y
8 Sires	N	Y	N	Y	N	Y	Y
9 Pascrell	N	Y	N	Y	N	Y	Y
10 Payne	N	?	?	Y	N	Y	Y
11 **Frelinghuysen**	Y	N	Y	N	Y	Y	Y
12 Watson Coleman	N	Y	N	Y	N	Y	Y
NEW MEXICO							
1 Lujan Grisham	N	Y	N	Y	N	Y	Y
2 **Pearce**	Y	N	Y	N	Y	Y	Y
3 Luján	N	Y	N	Y	N	Y	Y
NEW YORK							
1 **Zeldin**	Y	N	Y	N	Y	Y	Y
2 **King**	Y	N	Y	N	Y	Y	Y
3 Suozzi	N	Y	N	Y	N	Y	Y
4 Rice	N	Y	N	Y	N	Y	Y
5 Meeks	?	Y	N	Y	N	Y	Y
6 Meng	N	Y	N	Y	N	Y	Y
7 Velázquez	N	Y	N	Y	N	Y	Y
8 Jeffries	N	Y	N	Y	N	Y	Y
9 Clarke	N	Y	N	Y	N	Y	Y
10 Nadler	N	Y	N	Y	N	Y	Y
11 **Donovan**	Y	N	Y	N	Y	Y	Y
12 Maloney, C.	N	Y	N	Y	N	Y	Y
13 Espaillat	N	Y	N	Y	N	Y	Y
14 Crowley	N	Y	N	Y	N	Y	Y
15 Serrano	N	Y	N	Y	N	Y	Y
16 Engel	N	Y	N	Y	N	?	?
17 Lowey	N	Y	N	Y	N	Y	Y
18 Maloney, S.P.	N	Y	N	Y	N	Y	Y
19 **Faso**	Y	N	N	N	Y	?	Y
20 Tonko	N	Y	N	Y	N	Y	Y
21 **Stefanik**	Y	N	N	N	N	Y	Y
22 **Tenney**	Y	N	Y	N	Y	Y	Y
23 **Reed**	Y	N	Y	N	Y	Y	Y
24 **Katko**	Y	N	Y	N	Y	Y	Y
25 Slaughter	–	+	–	+	–	+	+
26 Higgins	N	Y	N	Y	N	Y	Y
27 **Collins**	Y	N	Y	N	Y	Y	Y
NORTH CAROLINA							
1 Butterfield	N	Y	N	Y	N	?	?
2 **Holding**	Y	N	Y	N	Y	Y	Y
3 **Jones**	Y	Y	Y	Y	Y	N	Y
4 Price	N	Y	N	Y	N	Y	Y

	204	205	206	207	208	209	210
5 **Foxx**	Y	N	Y	N	Y	Y	Y
6 **Walker**	Y	N	Y	N	Y	Y	Y
7 **Rouzer**	Y	N	Y	N	Y	Y	Y
8 **Hudson**	Y	N	Y	N	Y	Y	Y
9 **Pittenger**	Y	N	Y	N	Y	Y	Y
10 **McHenry**	Y	N	Y	N	Y	Y	Y
11 **Meadows**	Y	N	Y	N	Y	Y	Y
12 Adams	N	Y	N	Y	N	Y	Y
13 **Budd**	Y	N	Y	N	Y	Y	Y
NORTH DAKOTA							
AL **Cramer**	Y	N	Y	N	Y	Y	Y
OHIO							
1 **Chabot**	Y	N	Y	N	Y	Y	Y
2 **Wenstrup**	Y	N	Y	N	Y	Y	Y
3 Beatty	N	Y	N	Y	N	Y	Y
4 **Jordan**	Y	N	Y	N	Y	Y	Y
5 **Latta**	Y	N	Y	N	Y	Y	Y
6 **Johnson**	Y	N	Y	N	Y	Y	Y
7 **Gibbs**	Y	N	Y	N	Y	Y	Y
8 **Davidson**	Y	N	Y	N	Y	Y	Y
9 Kaptur	N	Y	N	Y	N	Y	Y
10 **Turner**	Y	N	Y	N	Y	Y	Y
11 Fudge	N	Y	N	Y	N	Y	Y
12 **Tiberi**	Y	N	Y	N	Y	Y	Y
13 Ryan	N	Y	N	Y	N	Y	Y
14 **Joyce**	Y	N	Y	N	Y	Y	Y
15 **Stivers**	Y	N	Y	N	Y	Y	Y
16 **Renacci**	Y	N	Y	N	Y	Y	Y
OKLAHOMA							
1 **Bridenstine**	Y	N	Y	N	Y	?	?
2 **Mullin**	Y	N	Y	N	?	Y	Y
3 **Lucas**	Y	N	Y	N	Y	Y	Y
4 **Cole**	Y	N	Y	N	Y	Y	Y
5 **Russell**	Y	N	Y	N	Y	Y	Y
OREGON							
1 Bonamici	N	Y	N	Y	N	Y	Y
2 **Walden**	Y	N	Y	N	Y	Y	Y
3 Blumenauer	N	Y	N	Y	N	Y	Y
4 DeFazio	N	Y	N	Y	N	Y	Y
5 Schrader	N	Y	N	Y	Y	Y	Y
PENNSYLVANIA							
1 Brady	N	Y	N	Y	N	Y	Y
2 Evans	N	Y	N	Y	N	Y	Y
3 **Kelly**	Y	N	Y	N	Y	Y	Y
4 **Perry**	Y	N	Y	N	Y	Y	Y
5 **Thompson**	Y	N	Y	N	Y	Y	Y
6 **Costello**	Y	N	N	N	N	Y	Y
7 **Meehan**	Y	N	Y	N	Y	Y	Y
8 **Fitzpatrick**	Y	N	N	N	N	Y	Y
9 **Shuster**	Y	N	Y	N	Y	Y	Y
10 **Marino**	+	–	+	–	+	Y	Y
11 **Barletta**	Y	N	Y	N	Y	?	?
12 **Rothfus**	Y	N	Y	N	Y	Y	Y
13 Boyle	N	Y	N	Y	N	Y	Y
14 Doyle	N	Y	N	Y	N	Y	Y
15 **Dent**	Y	N	Y	N	Y	Y	Y
16 **Smucker**	Y	N	Y	N	Y	Y	Y
17 Cartwright	N	Y	N	Y	N	Y	Y
18 **Murphy**	Y	N	Y	N	Y	Y	Y
RHODE ISLAND							
1 Cicilline	N	Y	N	Y	N	Y	Y
2 Langevin	N	Y	N	Y	N	Y	Y
SOUTH CAROLINA							
1 **Sanford**	Y	N	N	N	Y	Y	Y
2 **Wilson**	Y	N	Y	N	Y	Y	Y
3 **Duncan**	Y	N	Y	N	Y	Y	Y
4 **Gowdy**	Y	N	Y	N	Y	Y	Y
6 Clyburn	N	Y	N	Y	N	Y	?
7 **Rice**	Y	N	Y	N	Y	Y	Y
SOUTH DAKOTA							
AL **Noem**	Y	N	Y	N	Y	Y	Y
TENNESSEE							
1 **Roe**	Y	N	Y	N	Y	Y	Y
2 **Duncan**	Y	N	Y	N	Y	Y	Y
3 **Fleischmann**	Y	N	Y	N	Y	Y	Y
4 **DesJarlais**	Y	N	Y	N	Y	Y	Y
5 Cooper	N	Y	N	Y	N	Y	Y
6 **Black**	Y	N	Y	N	Y	Y	Y
7 **Blackburn**	Y	N	Y	N	Y	Y	Y
8 **Kustoff**	Y	N	Y	N	Y	Y	Y
9 Cohen	N	Y	N	Y	N	Y	Y

	204	205	206	207	208	209	210
TEXAS							
1 **Gohmert**	Y	N	Y	N	Y	?	?
2 **Poe**	Y	N	Y	N	Y	Y	Y
3 **Johnson, S.**	Y	N	Y	N	Y	Y	Y
4 **Ratcliffe**	Y	N	Y	N	Y	Y	Y
5 **Hensarling**	Y	N	Y	N	Y	Y	Y
6 **Barton**	Y	N	Y	N	Y	?	?
7 **Culberson**	Y	N	Y	N	Y	Y	Y
8 **Brady**	Y	N	Y	N	Y	Y	Y
9 Green, A.	N	Y	N	Y	N	Y	Y
10 **McCaul**	Y	N	Y	N	Y	Y	Y
11 **Conaway**	Y	N	Y	N	Y	Y	Y
12 **Granger**	Y	N	Y	N	Y	Y	Y
13 **Thornberry**	Y	N	Y	N	Y	Y	Y
14 **Weber**	Y	N	Y	N	Y	Y	Y
15 Gonzalez	N	Y	N	Y	N	Y	Y
16 O'Rourke	N	Y	N	Y	N	Y	Y
17 **Flores**	Y	N	Y	N	Y	Y	Y
18 Jackson Lee	N	Y	N	Y	N	Y	Y
19 **Arrington**	Y	N	Y	N	Y	Y	Y
20 Castro	N	Y	N	Y	N	Y	Y
21 **Smith**	Y	N	Y	N	Y	Y	Y
22 **Olson**	Y	N	Y	N	Y	Y	Y
23 **Hurd**	Y	N	Y	N	Y	Y	Y
24 **Marchant**	Y	N	?	N	Y	Y	Y
25 **Williams**	Y	N	Y	N	Y	Y	Y
26 **Burgess**	Y	N	Y	N	Y	Y	Y
27 **Farenthold**	Y	N	Y	N	Y	Y	Y
28 Cuellar	N	Y	Y	Y	N	Y	Y
29 Green, G.	N	Y	N	Y	N	Y	Y
30 Johnson, E.B.	N	Y	N	Y	N	Y	Y
31 **Carter**	Y	N	Y	N	Y	Y	Y
32 **Sessions**	Y	N	Y	N	Y	Y	Y
33 Veasey	N	Y	N	Y	N	Y	Y
34 Vela	N	Y	N	Y	N	Y	Y
35 Doggett	N	Y	N	Y	N	Y	Y
36 **Babin**	Y	N	Y	N	Y	Y	Y
UTAH							
1 **Bishop**	Y	N	Y	N	Y	Y	Y
2 **Stewart**	Y	N	Y	N	Y	Y	Y
3 **Chaffetz**	Y	N	Y	N	Y	Y	Y
4 **Love**	Y	N	Y	N	Y	Y	Y
VERMONT							
AL Welch	N	Y	N	Y	N	Y	Y
VIRGINIA							
1 **Wittman**	Y	N	Y	N	Y	Y	Y
2 **Taylor**	Y	N	Y	N	Y	Y	Y
3 Scott	N	Y	N	Y	N	Y	Y
4 McEachin	N	Y	N	Y	N	Y	Y
5 **Garrett**	Y	N	Y	N	Y	Y	Y
6 **Goodlatte**	Y	N	Y	N	Y	Y	Y
7 **Brat**	Y	N	Y	N	Y	Y	Y
8 Beyer	N	Y	N	Y	N	Y	Y
9 **Griffith**	Y	N	Y	N	Y	Y	Y
10 **Comstock**	Y	N	Y	N	Y	Y	?
11 Connolly	N	Y	N	Y	N	Y	Y
WASHINGTON							
1 DelBene	N	Y	N	Y	N	Y	Y
2 Larsen	N	Y	N	Y	N	Y	Y
3 **Herrera Beutler**	Y	N	Y	N	Y	Y	Y
4 **Newhouse**	Y	N	Y	N	Y	Y	Y
5 **McMorris Rodgers**	Y	N	Y	N	Y	Y	Y
6 Kilmer	N	Y	N	Y	N	Y	Y
7 Jayapal	N	Y	N	Y	N	Y	Y
8 **Reichert**	Y	N	Y	N	Y	Y	Y
9 Smith	N	Y	N	Y	N	Y	Y
10 Heck	N	Y	N	Y	N	Y	Y
WEST VIRGINIA							
1 **McKinley**	Y	N	Y	N	Y	Y	Y
2 **Mooney**	Y	N	Y	N	Y	Y	Y
3 **Jenkins**	Y	N	Y	N	Y	+	Y
WISCONSIN							
1 **Ryan**							
2 Pocan	N	Y	N	Y	N	Y	Y
3 Kind	N	Y	N	Y	N	+	+
4 Moore	N	?	N	Y	N	Y	Y
5 **Sensenbrenner**	Y	N	Y	N	Y	Y	Y
6 **Grothman**	Y	N	Y	N	Y	Y	Y
7 **Duffy**	+	–	+	–	+	Y	?
8 **Gallagher**	Y	N	Y	N	Y	Y	Y
WYOMING							
AL **Cheney**	Y	N	Y	N	Y	Y	Y

VOTE NUMBER

211. H RES 241, HR 1304. "STOP-LOSS" INSURANCE DEFINITION/PREVIOUS QUESTION. Byrne, R-Ala., motion to order the previous question (thus ending debate and possibility of amendment) on the rule (H Res 241) that would provide for House floor consideration of the bill that would establish that "stop-loss" insurance, coverage that protects businesses from certain large financial risks associated with providing insurance, would not be considered health care insurance under federal law. Motion agreed to 232-188 : R 232-0; D 0-188. April 4, 2017.

212. H RES 241, HR 1304. "STOP-LOSS" INSURANCE DEFINTION/RULE. Adoption of the rule (H Res 241) that would provide for House floor consideration of the bill that would establish that "stop-loss" insurance, coverage that protects businesses from certain large financial risks associated with providing insurance, would not be considered health care insurance under federal law. Adopted 234-184 : R 232-0; D 2-184. April 4, 2017.

213. H RES 240, HR 1343. SECURITIES SOLD FOR EMPLOYEE COMPENSATION/PREVIOUS QUESTION. Buck, R-Colo., motion to order the previous question (thus ending debate and possibility of amendment) on the rule (H Res 240) that would provide for House floor consideration of the bill that would direct the Securities and Exchange Commission to increase from $5 million to $10 million the annual amount of securities that privately-held companies can sell for employee compensation without needing to disclose certain information to investors. Motion agreed to 229-187 : R 229-1; D 0-186. April 4, 2017.

214. H RES 240, HR 1343. SECURITIES SOLD FOR EMPLOYEE COMPENSATION/RULE. Adoption of the rule (H Res 240) that would provide for House floor consideration of the bill that would direct the Securities and Exchange Commission to increase from $5 million to $10 million the annual amount of securities that privately-held companies can sell for employee compensation without needing to disclose certain information to investors. Adopted 238-177 : R 230-0; D 8-177. April 4, 2017.

215. HR 1343. SECURITIES SOLD FOR EMPLOYEE COMPENSATION/RECOMMIT. Swalwell, D-Calif., motion to recommit the bill to the House Financial Services Committee with instructions to report it back immediately with an amendment that would prevent the bill's provisions from applying to any individual that withheld information from Congress related to an investigation regarding individuals influencing the outcome of the 2016 U.S. presidential election. Motion rejected 185-228 : R 0-228; D 185-0. April 4, 2017.

216. HR 1343. SECURITIES SOLD FOR EMPLOYEE COMPENSATION/PASSAGE. Passage of the bill that would direct the Securities and Exchange Commission to increase from $5 million to $10 million the annual amount of securities that privately-held companies can sell for employee compensation without needing to disclose certain information to investors. Passed 331-87 : R 229-1; D 102-86. April 4, 2017.

217. HR 1219, H RES 242. SMALL BUSINESS VENTURE CAPITAL/PREVIOUS QUESTION. Buck, R-Colo., motion to order the previous question (thus ending debate and possibility of amendment) on the rule (H Res 242) that would provide for House floor consideration of the bill that would increase from 100 to 250 the number of accredited investors who can form a venture capital fund to invest in small businesses. Motion agreed to 231-182 : R 231-1; D 0-181. April 5, 2017.

	211	212	213	214	215	216	217
ALABAMA							
1 Byrne	Y	Y	Y	Y	N	Y	Y
2 Roby	Y	Y	Y	Y	N	Y	Y
3 Rogers	?	?	?	?	?	?	Y
4 Aderholt	Y	Y	Y	Y	N	Y	Y
5 Brooks	Y	Y	Y	Y	N	Y	Y
6 Palmer	Y	Y	Y	Y	N	Y	Y
7 Sewell	N	N	N	N	Y	N	N
ALASKA							
AL Young	Y	Y	Y	Y	N	Y	Y
ARIZONA							
1 O'Halleran	N	N	N	Y	Y	Y	N
2 McSally	Y	Y	Y	Y	N	Y	Y
3 Grijalva	N	N	N	N	Y	N	N
4 Gosar	Y	Y	Y	Y	N	Y	Y
5 Biggs	Y	Y	Y	Y	N	Y	Y
6 Schweikert	Y	Y	Y	Y	N	Y	Y
7 Gallego	N	N	N	N	Y	N	N
8 Franks	Y	Y	Y	Y	N	Y	Y
9 Sinema	N	Y	N	Y	Y	Y	N
ARKANSAS							
1 Crawford	Y	Y	Y	Y	N	Y	Y
2 Hill	Y	Y	Y	Y	N	Y	Y
3 Womack	Y	Y	Y	Y	N	Y	Y
4 Westerman	Y	Y	Y	Y	N	Y	Y
CALIFORNIA							
1 LaMalfa	Y	Y	Y	Y	N	Y	Y
2 Huffman	N	N	N	Y	Y	Y	N
3 Garamendi	N	N	N	N	Y	N	N
4 McClintock	Y	Y	Y	Y	N	Y	Y
5 Thompson	N	N	N	N	Y	Y	N
6 Matsui	N	N	N	N	Y	Y	N
7 Bera	N	N	N	N	Y	Y	N
8 Cook	Y	Y	Y	Y	N	Y	Y
9 McNerney	N	N	N	N	Y	Y	N
10 Denham	Y	Y	Y	Y	N	Y	Y
11 DeSaulnier	N	N	N	N	Y	N	N
12 Pelosi	N	?	?	?	Y	Y	N
13 Lee	N	N	N	N	Y	N	N
14 Speier	N	N	N	N	Y	Y	N
15 Swalwell	N	N	N	N	Y	Y	N
16 Costa	N	N	N	Y	Y	Y	N
17 Khanna	N	N	N	N	Y	N	N
18 Eshoo	N	N	N	N	Y	Y	N
19 Lofgren	N	N	N	N	Y	Y	?
20 Panetta	N	N	N	N	Y	Y	N
21 Valadao	Y	Y	Y	Y	N	Y	Y
22 Nunes	Y	Y	Y	Y	N	Y	Y
23 McCarthy	Y	Y	?	?	N	Y	Y
24 Carbajal	N	N	N	N	Y	Y	N
25 Knight	Y	Y	Y	Y	N	Y	Y
26 Brownley	N	N	N	N	Y	Y	N
27 Chu	N	N	N	N	Y	N	–
28 Schiff	N	N	N	N	Y	N	N
29 Cardenas	N	N	N	N	Y	Y	?
30 Sherman	N	N	N	N	Y	Y	N
31 Aguilar	N	N	N	N	Y	Y	N
32 Napolitano	N	N	N	N	Y	N	N
33 Lieu	N	N	N	N	Y	Y	N
34 Vacant							
35 Torres	N	N	N	N	Y	Y	N
36 Ruiz	N	N	N	N	Y	Y	N
37 Bass	N	N	N	N	Y	Y	N
38 Sánchez, Linda	N	N	N	N	Y	Y	N
39 Royce	Y	Y	Y	Y	N	Y	Y
40 Roybal-Allard	N	N	N	N	Y	Y	N
41 Takano	N	N	N	N	Y	N	N
42 Calvert	Y	Y	Y	Y	N	Y	Y
43 Waters	N	N	N	N	Y	N	N
44 Barragan	N	N	N	N	Y	Y	N
45 Walters	Y	Y	Y	Y	N	Y	Y
46 Correa	N	N	N	N	Y	Y	N
47 Lowenthal	N	N	N	N	Y	N	N
48 Rohrabacher	Y	Y	Y	Y	?	?	Y
49 Issa	Y	Y	Y	Y	N	Y	Y
50 Hunter	Y	Y	Y	Y	N	Y	?
51 Vargas	N	N	N	N	Y	Y	N
52 Peters	N	N	N	Y	Y	Y	N
53 Davis	N	N	N	N	Y	Y	–

	211	212	213	214	215	216	217
COLORADO							
1 DeGette	N	N	N	N	Y	Y	N
2 Polis	N	N	N	N	Y	Y	N
3 Tipton	Y	Y	Y	Y	N	Y	Y
4 Buck	Y	Y	Y	Y	N	Y	Y
5 Lamborn	Y	Y	Y	Y	–	Y	Y
6 Coffman	Y	Y	Y	Y	N	Y	Y
7 Perlmutter	N	N	N	N	Y	Y	N
CONNECTICUT							
1 Larson	N	N	N	N	+	Y	?
2 Courtney	N	N	N	N	Y	Y	N
3 DeLauro	N	N	N	N	Y	Y	N
4 Himes	N	N	N	N	Y	Y	N
5 Esty	N	N	N	N	Y	Y	N
DELAWARE							
AL Blunt Rochester	N	N	N	N	Y	Y	N
FLORIDA							
1 Gaetz	Y	Y	Y	Y	N	Y	Y
2 Dunn	Y	Y	Y	Y	N	Y	Y
3 Yoho	Y	Y	Y	Y	N	Y	Y
4 Rutherford	Y	Y	Y	Y	N	Y	Y
5 Lawson	N	N	N	N	Y	Y	N
6 DeSantis	Y	Y	Y	Y	N	Y	Y
7 Murphy	–	–	–	–	+	+	Y
8 Posey	Y	Y	Y	Y	N	Y	Y
9 Soto	N	N	N	N	Y	Y	N
10 Demings	N	N	N	N	Y	N	N
11 Webster	Y	Y	Y	Y	N	Y	Y
12 Bilirakis	Y	Y	Y	Y	N	Y	Y
13 Crist	N	N	N	N	Y	N	N
14 Castor	N	N	N	N	Y	Y	N
15 Ross	Y	Y	Y	Y	N	Y	Y
16 Buchanan	Y	Y	Y	Y	N	Y	Y
17 Rooney, T.	Y	Y	Y	Y	N	Y	Y
18 Mast	Y	Y	Y	Y	N	Y	Y
19 Rooney, F.	Y	Y	Y	Y	N	Y	Y
20 Hastings	N	N	N	N	Y	Y	N
21 Frankel	N	N	N	N	+	N	N
22 Deutch	N	N	N	N	Y	Y	N
23 Wasserman Schultz	N	N	N	N	Y	Y	N
24 Wilson	N	N	N	N	Y	Y	N
25 Diaz-Balart	Y	Y	Y	Y	N	Y	Y
26 Curbelo	Y	Y	Y	Y	N	Y	Y
27 Ros-Lehtinen	Y	Y	Y	Y	N	Y	Y
GEORGIA							
1 Carter	Y	Y	Y	Y	N	Y	Y
2 Bishop	N	N	N	N	Y	Y	N
3 Ferguson	Y	Y	Y	Y	N	Y	Y
4 Johnson	N	N	N	N	Y	N	N
5 Lewis	N	N	N	N	Y	N	N
6 Woodall	Y	Y	Y	Y	N	Y	Y
7 Scott, A.	Y	Y	Y	Y	N	Y	Y
8 Collins	Y	Y	Y	Y	N	Y	Y
9 Hice	Y	Y	Y	Y	N	Y	Y
10 Loudermilk	Y	Y	Y	Y	N	Y	Y
11 Allen	Y	Y	Y	Y	N	Y	Y
12 Scott, D.	N	N	N	N	Y	Y	N
13 Graves	Y	Y	Y	Y	N	Y	Y
HAWAII							
1 Hanabusa	N	N	N	N	Y	N	N
2 Gabbard	N	N	N	N	Y	N	N
IDAHO							
1 Labrador	Y	Y	Y	Y	N	Y	Y
2 Simpson	Y	Y	Y	Y	N	Y	Y
ILLINOIS							
1 Rush	N	N	N	N	Y	N	N
2 Kelly	N	N	N	–	Y	N	N
3 Lipinski	N	N	N	N	Y	N	N
4 Gutierrez	N	N	N	N	Y	N	N
5 Quigley	N	N	N	N	Y	N	N
6 Roskam	Y	Y	Y	Y	N	Y	Y
7 Davis, D.	?	?	?	?	?	?	?
8 Krishnamoorthi	N	N	N	N	Y	N	N
9 Schakowsky	N	N	N	N	Y	N	N
10 Schneider	N	N	N	N	Y	Y	N
11 Foster	N	N	N	N	Y	Y	N
12 Bost	Y	Y	Y	Y	N	Y	Y
13 Davis, R.	Y	Y	Y	Y	N	Y	Y
14 Hultgren	Y	Y	Y	Y	N	Y	Y
15 Shimkus	Y	Y	Y	Y	N	Y	Y

KEY   **Republicans**   Democrats   *Independents*

- **Y** Voted for (yea)
- **#** Paired for
- **+** Announced for
- **N** Voted against (nay)
- **X** Paired against
- **–** Announced against
- **P** Voted "present"
- **C** Voted "present" to avoid possible conflict of interest
- **?** Did not vote or otherwise make a position known

	211	212	213	214	215	216	217
16 **Kinzinger**	Y	Y	Y	Y	N	Y	Y
17 Bustos	N	N	N	N	Y	Y	N
18 **LaHood**	Y	Y	Y	Y	N	Y	Y
INDIANA							
1 Visclosky	–	–	–	–	+	–	N
2 **Walorski**	Y	Y	Y	Y	N	Y	Y
3 **Banks**	Y	Y	Y	Y	N	Y	Y
4 **Rokita**	Y	Y	Y	Y	N	Y	Y
5 **Brooks**	Y	Y	Y	Y	N	Y	Y
6 **Messer**	Y	Y	Y	Y	N	Y	Y
7 Carson	N	N	N	N	Y	N	N
8 **Bucshon**	Y	Y	Y	Y	N	Y	Y
9 **Hollingsworth**	Y	Y	Y	Y	N	Y	Y
IOWA							
1 **Blum**	Y	Y	Y	Y	N	Y	Y
2 Loebsack	N	N	N	N	Y	Y	N
3 **Young**	Y	Y	Y	Y	N	Y	Y
4 **King**	Y	Y	Y	Y	N	Y	Y
KANSAS							
1 **Marshall**	Y	Y	Y	Y	N	Y	Y
2 **Jenkins**	Y	Y	Y	Y	N	Y	Y
3 **Yoder**	Y	Y	Y	Y	N	Y	Y
KENTUCKY							
1 **Comer**	Y	Y	Y	Y	N	Y	Y
2 **Guthrie**	Y	Y	Y	Y	N	Y	Y
3 Yarmuth	N	N	N	N	Y	Y	N
4 **Massie**	Y	Y	Y	Y	N	Y	Y
5 **Rogers**	Y	Y	Y	Y	N	Y	Y
6 **Barr**	Y	Y	Y	Y	N	Y	Y
LOUISIANA							
1 **Scalise**	Y	Y	Y	Y	N	Y	Y
2 Richmond	N	N	N	N	Y	N	N
3 **Higgins**	Y	Y	Y	Y	N	Y	Y
4 **Johnson**	Y	Y	Y	Y	N	Y	Y
5 **Abraham**	Y	Y	Y	Y	N	Y	Y
6 **Graves**	Y	Y	Y	Y	N	Y	Y
MAINE							
1 Pingree	N	N	N	N	Y	N	N
2 **Poliquin**	Y	Y	Y	Y	N	Y	Y
MARYLAND							
1 **Harris**	Y	Y	Y	Y	N	Y	Y
2 Ruppersberger	N	N	N	N	Y	Y	N
3 Sarbanes	N	N	N	N	Y	N	N
4 Brown	N	N	N	N	Y	Y	N
5 Hoyer	N	?	?	?	Y	Y	?
6 Delaney	N	N	N	Y	Y	Y	N
7 Cummings	N	N	N	N	Y	N	N
8 Raskin	N	N	N	N	Y	N	N
MASSACHUSETTS							
1 Neal	N	N	N	N	Y	Y	N
2 McGovern	N	N	N	N	Y	N	N
3 Tsongas	N	N	N	N	Y	Y	N
4 Kennedy	N	N	N	N	Y	Y	N
5 Clark	N	N	N	N	Y	N	N
6 Moulton	N	N	N	N	Y	Y	N
7 Capuano	N	N	N	N	Y	N	N
8 Lynch	N	N	N	N	Y	N	N
9 Keating	N	N	N	N	Y	Y	N
MICHIGAN							
1 **Bergman**	Y	Y	Y	Y	N	Y	Y
2 **Huizenga**	Y	Y	Y	Y	N	Y	Y
3 **Amash**	Y	Y	Y	Y	N	Y	Y
4 **Moolenaar**	Y	Y	Y	Y	N	Y	Y
5 Kildee	N	N	N	N	Y	N	N
6 **Upton**	Y	Y	Y	Y	N	Y	Y
7 **Walberg**	Y	Y	Y	Y	N	Y	Y
8 **Bishop**	Y	Y	Y	Y	N	Y	Y
9 Levin	N	N	N	N	Y	N	N
10 **Mitchell**	Y	Y	Y	Y	N	Y	Y
11 **Trott**	Y	Y	Y	Y	N	Y	Y
12 Dingell	N	N	N	N	Y	N	N
13 Conyers	N	N	N	N	Y	N	N
14 Lawrence	N	N	N	N	Y	N	N
MINNESOTA							
1 Walz	N	N	N	N	Y	Y	N
2 **Lewis**	Y	Y	Y	Y	N	Y	Y
3 **Paulsen**	Y	Y	Y	Y	N	Y	Y
4 McCollum	N	N	N	N	Y	N	N

	211	212	213	214	215	216	217
5 Ellison	N	N	N	N	Y	N	N
6 **Emmer**	Y	Y	Y	Y	N	Y	Y
7 Peterson	N	N	N	N	Y	Y	N
8 Nolan	N	N	N	N	Y	Y	N
MISSISSIPPI							
1 **Kelly**	Y	Y	Y	Y	N	Y	Y
2 Thompson	N	N	N	N	Y	N	N
3 **Harper**	Y	Y	Y	Y	N	Y	Y
4 **Palazzo**	Y	Y	Y	Y	N	Y	Y
MISSOURI							
1 Clay	N	N	N	N	Y	Y	N
2 **Wagner**	Y	Y	Y	Y	N	Y	Y
3 **Luetkemeyer**	Y	Y	Y	Y	N	Y	Y
4 **Hartzler**	Y	Y	Y	Y	N	Y	Y
5 Cleaver	N	N	N	N	Y	Y	N
6 **Graves**	Y	Y	Y	Y	N	Y	Y
7 **Long**	Y	Y	Y	Y	N	Y	Y
8 **Smith**	Y	Y	Y	Y	N	Y	Y
MONTANA							
AL **Vacant**							
NEBRASKA							
1 **Fortenberry**	Y	Y	Y	Y	N	Y	Y
2 **Bacon**	Y	Y	Y	Y	N	Y	Y
3 **Smith**	Y	Y	Y	Y	N	Y	Y
NEVADA							
1 Titus	N	N	N	N	Y	Y	N
2 **Amodei**	Y	Y	Y	Y	N	Y	Y
3 Rosen	N	N	N	N	Y	Y	N
4 Kihuen	N	N	N	N	Y	Y	N
NEW HAMPSHIRE							
1 Shea-Porter	N	N	N	N	Y	Y	N
2 Kuster	N	N	N	N	Y	Y	N
NEW JERSEY							
1 Norcross	N	N	N	N	Y	Y	N
2 **LoBiondo**	Y	Y	Y	Y	N	Y	Y
3 **MacArthur**	Y	Y	Y	Y	N	Y	Y
4 **Smith**	Y	Y	Y	Y	N	Y	Y
5 Gottheimer	N	Y	N	Y	Y	Y	N
6 Pallone	N	N	N	N	Y	N	N
7 **Lance**	Y	Y	Y	Y	N	Y	Y
8 Sires	N	N	N	N	Y	N	N
9 Pascrell	N	N	N	N	Y	Y	N
10 Payne	N	N	N	N	Y	N	N
11 **Frelinghuysen**	Y	Y	Y	Y	N	Y	Y
12 Watson Coleman	N	N	N	N	Y	N	N
NEW MEXICO							
1 Lujan Grisham	N	N	N	N	Y	N	N
2 **Pearce**	Y	Y	Y	Y	N	Y	Y
3 Luján	N	N	N	N	Y	N	N
NEW YORK							
1 **Zeldin**	Y	Y	Y	Y	N	Y	Y
2 **King**	Y	Y	Y	Y	N	Y	?
3 Suozzi	N	N	N	Y	+	Y	N
4 Rice	N	N	N	N	Y	Y	N
5 Meeks	N	N	N	N	Y	Y	N
6 Meng	N	N	N	N	Y	N	N
7 Velázquez	N	N	N	N	Y	N	N
8 Jeffries	N	N	N	N	Y	N	N
9 Clarke	N	N	N	N	Y	N	N
10 Nadler	N	N	N	N	Y	N	N
11 **Donovan**	Y	Y	Y	Y	N	Y	Y
12 Maloney, C.	N	N	N	N	Y	Y	N
13 Espaillat	N	N	N	N	Y	N	N
14 Crowley	N	N	N	N	Y	Y	N
15 Serrano	N	N	N	N	Y	N	N
16 Engel	N	N	N	N	Y	Y	N
17 Lowey	N	N	N	N	Y	N	?
18 Maloney, S.P.	N	N	N	N	Y	Y	N
19 **Faso**	Y	Y	Y	Y	N	Y	Y
20 Tonko	N	N	N	N	Y	N	N
21 **Stefanik**	Y	Y	Y	Y	N	Y	Y
22 **Tenney**	Y	Y	Y	Y	N	Y	Y
23 **Reed**	Y	Y	Y	Y	N	Y	Y
24 **Katko**	Y	Y	Y	Y	N	Y	Y
25 Slaughter	–	–	–	–	+	+	–
26 Higgins	N	N	N	N	Y	Y	N
27 **Collins**	Y	Y	Y	Y	N	Y	Y
NORTH CAROLINA							
1 Butterfield	N	N	N	N	Y	N	N
2 **Holding**	Y	Y	Y	Y	N	Y	Y
3 **Jones**	Y	Y	N	Y	?	N	N
4 Price	N	N	N	N	Y	Y	N

	211	212	213	214	215	216	217
5 **Foxx**	Y	Y	Y	Y	N	Y	Y
6 **Walker**	Y	Y	Y	Y	N	Y	Y
7 **Rouzer**	Y	Y	Y	Y	N	Y	Y
8 **Hudson**	Y	Y	Y	Y	N	Y	Y
9 **Pittenger**	Y	Y	Y	Y	N	Y	Y
10 **McHenry**	Y	Y	Y	Y	N	Y	Y
11 **Meadows**	Y	Y	Y	Y	N	Y	Y
12 Adams	N	N	N	N	Y	N	N
13 **Budd**	Y	Y	Y	Y	N	Y	Y
NORTH DAKOTA							
AL **Cramer**	Y	Y	Y	Y	N	Y	Y
OHIO							
1 **Chabot**	Y	Y	Y	Y	N	Y	Y
2 **Wenstrup**	Y	Y	Y	Y	N	Y	Y
3 Beatty	N	N	N	N	Y	N	–
4 **Jordan**	Y	Y	Y	Y	N	Y	Y
5 **Latta**	Y	Y	Y	Y	N	Y	Y
6 **Johnson**	Y	Y	Y	Y	N	Y	Y
7 **Gibbs**	Y	Y	Y	Y	N	Y	Y
8 **Davidson**	Y	Y	Y	Y	N	Y	Y
9 Kaptur	N	N	N	N	Y	N	N
10 **Turner**	Y	Y	Y	Y	N	Y	Y
11 Fudge	N	N	N	N	Y	N	N
12 **Tiberi**	Y	Y	Y	Y	N	Y	Y
13 Ryan	N	N	N	N	Y	Y	N
14 **Joyce**	Y	Y	Y	Y	N	Y	Y
15 **Stivers**	Y	Y	Y	Y	N	Y	Y
16 **Renacci**	Y	Y	Y	Y	N	Y	Y
OKLAHOMA							
1 **Bridenstine**	?	?	?	?	?	?	?
2 **Mullin**	Y	Y	Y	Y	N	Y	Y
3 **Lucas**	Y	Y	Y	Y	N	Y	Y
4 **Cole**	Y	Y	Y	Y	N	Y	Y
5 **Russell**	Y	Y	Y	Y	N	Y	Y
OREGON							
1 Bonamici	N	N	N	N	Y	N	N
2 **Walden**	Y	Y	Y	Y	N	Y	Y
3 Blumenauer	N	N	N	N	Y	Y	N
4 DeFazio	N	N	N	N	Y	N	N
5 Schrader	N	N	N	N	Y	Y	N
PENNSYLVANIA							
1 Brady	N	N	N	N	Y	N	N
2 Evans	N	N	N	N	Y	N	N
3 **Kelly**	Y	Y	Y	Y	N	Y	Y
4 **Perry**	Y	Y	Y	Y	N	Y	Y
5 **Thompson**	Y	Y	Y	Y	N	Y	Y
6 **Costello**	Y	Y	Y	Y	N	Y	Y
7 **Meehan**	Y	Y	Y	Y	N	Y	Y
8 **Fitzpatrick**	Y	Y	Y	Y	N	Y	Y
9 **Shuster**	Y	Y	Y	Y	N	Y	Y
10 **Marino**	Y	Y	Y	Y	N	Y	Y
11 **Barletta**	Y	Y	Y	Y	N	Y	Y
12 **Rothfus**	Y	Y	Y	Y	N	Y	Y
13 Boyle	N	N	N	N	Y	Y	N
14 Doyle	N	N	N	N	Y	N	N
15 **Dent**	Y	Y	Y	Y	N	Y	Y
16 **Smucker**	Y	Y	Y	Y	N	Y	Y
17 Cartwright	N	N	N	N	Y	Y	N
18 **Murphy**	Y	Y	Y	Y	N	Y	Y
RHODE ISLAND							
1 Cicilline	N	N	N	N	Y	N	N
2 Langevin	N	N	N	N	Y	N	N
SOUTH CAROLINA							
1 **Sanford**	Y	Y	Y	Y	N	Y	Y
2 **Wilson**	Y	Y	Y	Y	N	Y	Y
3 **Duncan**	Y	Y	Y	Y	N	Y	Y
4 **Gowdy**	Y	Y	Y	Y	N	Y	Y
6 Clyburn	N	N	N	N	Y	N	N
7 **Rice**	Y	Y	Y	Y	N	?	Y
SOUTH DAKOTA							
AL **Noem**	Y	Y	Y	Y	N	Y	Y
TENNESSEE							
1 **Roe**	Y	Y	Y	Y	N	Y	Y
2 **Duncan**	Y	Y	Y	Y	N	Y	Y
3 **Fleischmann**	Y	Y	Y	Y	N	Y	Y
4 **DesJarlais**	Y	Y	Y	Y	N	Y	Y
5 Cooper	N	N	N	N	Y	Y	N
6 **Black**	Y	Y	Y	Y	N	Y	Y
7 **Blackburn**	Y	Y	Y	Y	N	Y	Y
8 **Kustoff**	Y	Y	Y	Y	N	Y	Y
9 Cohen	N	N	N	N	Y	Y	N

	211	212	213	214	215	216	217
TEXAS							
1 **Gohmert**	Y	Y	Y	Y	N	Y	Y
2 **Poe**	Y	Y	Y	Y	?	?	Y
3 **Johnson, S.**	Y	Y	Y	Y	N	Y	Y
4 **Ratcliffe**	Y	Y	Y	Y	N	Y	Y
5 **Hensarling**	Y	Y	Y	Y	N	Y	Y
6 **Barton**	Y	Y	Y	Y	N	Y	Y
7 **Culberson**	Y	Y	Y	Y	N	Y	Y
8 **Brady**	Y	Y	Y	Y	N	Y	Y
9 Green, A.	N	N	N	N	Y	N	–
10 **McCaul**	Y	Y	Y	Y	N	Y	Y
11 **Conaway**	Y	Y	Y	Y	N	Y	Y
12 **Granger**	Y	Y	Y	Y	N	Y	Y
13 **Thornberry**	Y	Y	Y	Y	N	Y	Y
14 **Weber**	Y	Y	Y	Y	N	Y	Y
15 Gonzalez	N	N	N	N	Y	Y	N
16 O'Rourke	N	N	N	N	Y	Y	N
17 **Flores**	Y	Y	Y	Y	N	Y	Y
18 Jackson Lee	N	N	N	N	Y	N	N
19 **Arrington**	Y	Y	Y	Y	N	Y	Y
20 Castro	N	N	N	N	Y	N	N
21 **Smith**	Y	Y	Y	Y	N	Y	Y
22 **Olson**	Y	Y	Y	Y	N	Y	Y
23 **Hurd**	Y	Y	?	?	N	Y	Y
24 **Marchant**	Y	Y	Y	Y	N	Y	Y
25 **Williams**	Y	Y	Y	Y	N	Y	Y
26 **Burgess**	Y	Y	Y	Y	N	Y	Y
27 **Farenthold**	Y	Y	Y	Y	N	Y	Y
28 Cuellar	N	N	N	N	Y	Y	N
29 Green, G.	N	N	N	N	Y	Y	N
30 Johnson, E.B.	N	N	N	N	Y	N	N
31 **Carter**	Y	Y	Y	Y	N	Y	Y
32 **Sessions**	Y	Y	Y	Y	N	Y	Y
33 Veasey	N	N	N	N	Y	Y	N
34 Vela	N	N	N	N	Y	Y	N
35 Doggett	N	N	N	N	Y	N	N
36 **Babin**	Y	Y	Y	Y	N	Y	Y
UTAH							
1 **Bishop**	Y	Y	Y	Y	?	Y	Y
2 **Stewart**	Y	Y	Y	Y	N	Y	?
3 **Chaffetz**	Y	Y	Y	Y	N	Y	Y
4 **Love**	Y	Y	Y	Y	N	Y	Y
VERMONT							
AL Welch	N	N	N	N	Y	N	N
VIRGINIA							
1 **Wittman**	Y	Y	Y	Y	N	Y	Y
2 **Taylor**	Y	Y	Y	Y	N	Y	Y
3 Scott	N	N	N	N	Y	N	N
4 McEachin	?	?	?	?	?	?	?
5 **Garrett**	Y	Y	Y	Y	N	Y	Y
6 **Goodlatte**	Y	Y	Y	Y	N	Y	Y
7 **Brat**	Y	Y	Y	Y	N	Y	Y
8 Beyer	N	N	N	N	Y	Y	N
9 **Griffith**	Y	Y	Y	Y	N	Y	Y
10 **Comstock**	Y	Y	Y	Y	N	Y	Y
11 Connolly	N	N	N	N	Y	Y	N
WASHINGTON							
1 DelBene	N	N	N	N	Y	Y	N
2 Larsen	N	N	N	N	Y	Y	N
3 **Herrera Beutler**	Y	Y	Y	Y	N	Y	Y
4 **Newhouse**	Y	Y	Y	Y	N	Y	Y
5 **McMorris Rodgers**	Y	Y	Y	Y	N	Y	Y
6 Kilmer	N	N	N	N	Y	Y	N
7 Jayapal	N	N	N	N	Y	N	N
8 **Reichert**	Y	Y	Y	Y	N	Y	Y
9 Smith	N	N	N	N	Y	N	N
10 Heck	N	N	N	N	Y	Y	N
WEST VIRGINIA							
1 **McKinley**	Y	Y	Y	Y	N	Y	Y
2 **Mooney**	Y	Y	Y	Y	N	Y	Y
3 **Jenkins**	Y	Y	Y	Y	N	Y	Y
WISCONSIN							
1 **Ryan**							
2 Pocan	N	N	N	N	Y	N	N
3 Kind	N	N	N	N	Y	Y	N
4 Moore	N	N	N	N	Y	N	N
5 **Sensenbrenner**	Y	Y	Y	Y	N	Y	Y
6 **Grothman**	?	?	?	?	?	?	Y
7 **Duffy**	Y	Y	Y	Y	N	Y	Y
8 **Gallagher**	+	+	+	+	N	Y	Y
WYOMING							
AL **Cheney**	Y	Y	Y	Y	N	Y	Y

VOTE NUMBER

218. HR 1219, H RES 242. SMALL BUSINESS VENTURE CAPITAL/RULE. Adoption of the rule (H Res 242) that would provide for House floor consideration of the bill that would increase from 100 to 250 the number of accredited investors who can form a venture capital fund to invest in small businesses. Adopted 240-181 : R 234-0; D 6-181. April 5, 2017.

219. PRESIDENT'S TAX RETURN DISCLOSURE/MOTION TO TABLE. Foxx, R-N.C., motion to table (kill) the Jeffries, D-N.Y., motion to appeal the ruling of the Chair that the Jeffries resolution related to the disclosure of President Trump's tax returns does not constitute a question of the privileges of the House. Motion agreed to 228-185 : R 228-1; D 0-184. April 5, 2017.

220. HR 1304. "STOP LOSS" INSURANCE DEFINITION/PASSAGE. Passage of the bill that would establish that "stop-loss" insurance, coverage that protects businesses from certain large financial risks associated with providing insurance, would not be considered health care insurance under federal law. Passed 400-16 : R 230-0; D 170-16. April 5, 2017.

221. HR 1219. SMALL BUSINESS VENTURE CAPITAL/PASSAGE. Passage of the bill that would increase from 100 to 250 the number of accredited investors who can form a venture capital fund to invest in small businesses. Under the bill, a qualifying venture capital fund could have no more than $10 million in invested capital. Passed 417-3 : R 232-1; D 185-2. April 6, 2017.

222. H RES 187. SOUTH SUDANESE FAMINE/PASSAGE. Royce, R-Calif., motion to suspend the rules and agree to the resolution that would express the sense of the House of Representatives that the administrator of the United States Agency for International Development should continue to respond to the famine in South Sudan through the provision of food and through collaboration with international relief organizations. Motion agreed to 411-2 : R 228-2; D 183-0. April 25, 2017.

223. HR 876. TSA IDENTIFICATION REQUIREMENTS/PASSAGE. Katko, R-N.Y., motion to suspend the rules and pass the bill that would require the Transportation Security Administration to impose additional requirements for airport workers to obtain identification cards for access to secure areas of an airport. It would also require the TSA to identify advanced technologies for securing employee access to all airport areas. Motion agreed to 409-0 : R 228-0; D 181-0. April 25, 2017.

224. HR 1695, H RES 275. REGISTER OF COPYRIGHTS/PREVIOUS QUESTION. Collins, R-Ga., motion to order the previous question (thus ending debate and possibility of amendment) on the rule (H Res 275) that would provide for House floor consideration of the bill that would modify the process for selecting and appointing the U.S. Copyright Office's Register of Copyrights. Motion agreed to 234-191 : R 234-1; D 0-190. April 26, 2017.

	218	219	220	221	222	223	224
ALABAMA							
1 **Byrne**	Y	Y	Y	Y	Y	Y	Y
2 **Roby**	Y	Y	Y	Y	Y	Y	Y
3 **Rogers**	Y	Y	Y	Y	Y	Y	Y
4 **Aderholt**	Y	Y	Y	Y	Y	Y	Y
5 **Brooks**	Y	Y	Y	Y	Y	Y	Y
6 **Palmer**	Y	Y	Y	Y	Y	Y	Y
7 Sewell	N	N	Y	Y	Y	Y	N
ALASKA							
AL **Young**	Y	Y	Y	Y	Y	Y	Y
ARIZONA							
1 O'Halleran	N	N	Y	Y	Y	Y	N
2 **McSally**	Y	Y	Y	Y	Y	Y	Y
3 Grijalva	N	N	N	Y	Y	Y	N
4 **Gosar**	Y	Y	Y	Y	Y	Y	Y
5 **Biggs**	Y	Y	Y	Y	Y	Y	Y
6 **Schweikert**	Y	Y	Y	Y	Y	Y	Y
7 Gallego	N	N	N	Y	Y	Y	N
8 **Franks**	Y	Y	Y	Y	Y	Y	Y
9 Sinema	Y	N	Y	Y	Y	Y	N
ARKANSAS							
1 **Crawford**	Y	Y	Y	Y	Y	Y	Y
2 **Hill**	Y	Y	Y	Y	Y	Y	Y
3 **Womack**	Y	Y	Y	Y	Y	Y	Y
4 **Westerman**	Y	Y	Y	Y	Y	Y	Y
CALIFORNIA							
1 **LaMalfa**	Y	?	Y	Y	Y	Y	Y
2 Huffman	N	N	N	Y	Y	Y	N
3 Garamendi	N	N	Y	Y	Y	Y	N
4 **McClintock**	Y	Y	Y	Y	Y	Y	Y
5 Thompson	N	N	Y	Y	Y	Y	N
6 Matsui	N	N	Y	Y	Y	Y	N
7 Bera	N	N	Y	Y	Y	Y	N
8 **Cook**	Y	Y	Y	Y	Y	Y	Y
9 McNerney	N	N	Y	Y	Y	Y	N
10 **Denham**	Y	Y	Y	Y	Y	Y	Y
11 DeSaulnier	N	N	N	Y	Y	Y	N
12 Pelosi	N	N	?	Y	Y	?	N
13 Lee	N	N	N	Y	?	?	N
14 Speier	N	N	Y	Y	Y	Y	N
15 Swalwell	N	N	Y	Y	Y	Y	N
16 Costa	Y	N	Y	Y	Y	Y	N
17 Khanna	N	N	Y	Y	Y	Y	N
18 Eshoo	N	N	Y	Y	Y	Y	N
19 Lofgren	N	N	Y	Y	Y	Y	N
20 Panetta	N	N	Y	Y	Y	Y	N
21 **Valadao**	Y	Y	Y	Y	Y	Y	Y
22 **Nunes**	Y	Y	Y	Y	Y	Y	Y
23 **McCarthy**	Y	Y	Y	Y	Y	Y	Y
24 Carbajal	N	N	Y	Y	Y	Y	N
25 **Knight**	Y	Y	Y	Y	Y	Y	Y
26 Brownley	N	N	Y	Y	Y	Y	N
27 Chu	N	N	Y	Y	Y	Y	N
28 Schiff	N	N	Y	Y	Y	Y	N
29 Cardenas	N	N	Y	Y	Y	Y	N
30 Sherman	N	N	Y	Y	Y	Y	N
31 Aguilar	N	N	Y	Y	Y	Y	N
32 Napolitano	N	N	Y	Y	Y	Y	N
33 Lieu	N	N	Y	Y	Y	Y	N
34 Vacant							
35 Torres	N	N	Y	Y	Y	Y	N
36 Ruiz	N	N	Y	Y	Y	Y	N
37 Bass	N	N	Y	Y	Y	Y	N
38 Sánchez, Linda	N	–	+	Y	Y	Y	N
39 **Royce**	Y	Y	Y	Y	Y	Y	Y
40 Roybal-Allard	N	N	Y	Y	Y	Y	N
41 Takano	–	N	Y	Y	Y	Y	N
42 **Calvert**	Y	Y	Y	Y	Y	Y	Y
43 Waters	N	N	N	Y	Y	Y	N
44 Barragan	N	N	Y	Y	Y	Y	N
45 **Walters**	Y	Y	Y	Y	Y	Y	Y
46 Correa	N	N	Y	Y	Y	Y	N
47 Lowenthal	N	N	Y	Y	Y	Y	N
48 **Rohrabacher**	Y	Y	Y	Y	?	?	Y
49 **Issa**	Y	Y	Y	Y	Y	Y	Y
50 **Hunter**	Y	Y	Y	Y	Y	Y	Y
51 Vargas	N	N	Y	Y	Y	Y	N
52 Peters	Y	N	Y	Y	Y	Y	N
53 Davis	N	N	Y	Y	Y	Y	N
COLORADO							
1 DeGette	N	N	Y	Y	Y	Y	N
2 Polis	N	N	Y	Y	Y	Y	N
3 **Tipton**	Y	Y	Y	Y	Y	Y	Y
4 **Buck**	Y	Y	Y	Y	Y	Y	Y
5 **Lamborn**	Y	Y	Y	Y	Y	Y	Y
6 **Coffman**	Y	Y	Y	Y	Y	Y	Y
7 Perlmutter	N	N	Y	Y	Y	Y	N
CONNECTICUT							
1 Larson	N	N	Y	Y	Y	+	N
2 Courtney	N	N	Y	Y	Y	Y	N
3 DeLauro	N	N	Y	Y	Y	Y	N
4 Himes	N	N	Y	Y	Y	Y	N
5 Esty	N	N	Y	Y	Y	Y	N
DELAWARE							
AL Blunt Rochester	N	N	Y	Y	Y	Y	N
FLORIDA							
1 **Gaetz**	Y	Y	Y	Y	Y	Y	Y
2 **Dunn**	Y	Y	Y	Y	Y	Y	Y
3 **Yoho**	Y	Y	Y	Y	Y	Y	Y
4 **Rutherford**	Y	Y	Y	Y	Y	Y	Y
5 Lawson	N	N	Y	Y	Y	Y	N
6 **DeSantis**	Y	Y	Y	Y	Y	Y	Y
7 Murphy	N	N	Y	Y	Y	Y	N
8 **Posey**	Y	Y	Y	Y	+	Y	Y
9 Soto	N	N	Y	Y	+	Y	N
10 Demings	N	N	Y	Y	Y	Y	N
11 **Webster**	Y	Y	Y	Y	Y	Y	Y
12 **Bilirakis**	Y	Y	Y	Y	Y	Y	Y
13 Crist	Y	N	Y	Y	Y	Y	N
14 Castor	N	N	Y	Y	Y	Y	N
15 **Ross**	Y	Y	Y	Y	Y	Y	Y
16 **Buchanan**	Y	Y	Y	Y	Y	Y	Y
17 **Rooney, T.**	Y	Y	Y	Y	Y	Y	Y
18 **Mast**	Y	Y	Y	Y	Y	Y	Y
19 **Rooney, F.**	Y	Y	Y	Y	Y	Y	Y
20 Hastings	N	N	Y	Y	Y	Y	N
21 Frankel	N	N	Y	Y	+	+	N
22 Deutch	N	N	Y	Y	Y	Y	N
23 Wasserman Schultz	N	N	Y	Y	?	?	N
24 Wilson	N	N	Y	Y	Y	Y	N
25 **Diaz-Balart**	Y	Y	Y	Y	Y	Y	Y
26 **Curbelo**	Y	Y	Y	Y	Y	Y	Y
27 **Ros-Lehtinen**	Y	Y	Y	Y	Y	Y	Y
GEORGIA							
1 **Carter**	Y	Y	Y	Y	Y	Y	Y
2 Bishop	N	N	Y	Y	+	Y	N
3 **Ferguson**	Y	Y	Y	Y	Y	Y	Y
4 Johnson	N	N	N	Y	Y	Y	N
5 Lewis	N	N	N	Y	Y	Y	N
7 **Woodall**	Y	Y	Y	Y	Y	Y	Y
8 **Scott, A.**	Y	Y	Y	Y	Y	Y	Y
9 **Collins**	Y	?	Y	Y	Y	Y	Y
10 **Hice**	Y	Y	Y	Y	Y	Y	Y
11 **Loudermilk**	Y	Y	Y	Y	?	Y	Y
12 **Allen**	Y	Y	Y	Y	Y	Y	Y
13 Scott, D.	N	N	Y	Y	Y	Y	N
14 **Graves**	Y	Y	Y	Y	Y	Y	Y
HAWAII							
1 Hanabusa	N	N	Y	Y	Y	Y	N
2 Gabbard	N	N	Y	Y	Y	Y	N
IDAHO							
1 **Labrador**	Y	Y	Y	Y	Y	Y	Y
2 **Simpson**	Y	Y	Y	Y	Y	Y	Y
ILLINOIS							
1 Rush	N	N	Y	Y	Y	Y	N
2 Kelly	N	N	Y	Y	Y	Y	N
3 Lipinski	N	N	Y	Y	Y	Y	N
4 Gutierrez	N	N	Y	+	+	Y	N
5 Quigley	N	N	Y	Y	Y	Y	N
6 **Roskam**	Y	Y	Y	Y	Y	Y	Y
7 Davis, D.	?	?	?	?	?	?	N
8 Krishnamoorthi	N	N	Y	Y	Y	Y	N
9 Schakowsky	N	N	N	Y	Y	Y	N
10 Schneider	N	N	Y	Y	Y	Y	N
11 Foster	N	N	Y	Y	Y	Y	N
12 **Bost**	Y	Y	Y	Y	Y	Y	Y
13 **Davis, R.**	Y	Y	Y	Y	Y	Y	Y
14 **Hultgren**	Y	Y	Y	Y	Y	Y	Y
15 **Shimkus**	Y	Y	Y	Y	Y	Y	Y

	218	219	220	221	222	223	224
16 **Kinzinger**	Y	Y	Y	Y	Y	Y	Y
17 Bustos	N	N	Y	Y	Y	Y	N
18 **LaHood**	Y	Y	Y	Y	Y	Y	Y
INDIANA							
1 Visclosky	N	N	N	Y	Y	Y	N
2 **Walorski**	Y	Y	Y	Y	Y	Y	Y
3 **Banks**	Y	Y	Y	Y	Y	Y	Y
4 **Rokita**	Y	Y	Y	Y	Y	Y	Y
5 **Brooks**	Y	Y	Y	Y	Y	Y	Y
6 **Messer**	Y	Y	Y	Y	Y	Y	Y
7 Carson	N	N	Y	Y	Y	Y	N
8 **Bucshon**	Y	Y	Y	Y	Y	Y	Y
9 **Hollingsworth**	Y	Y	Y	Y	Y	Y	Y
IOWA							
1 **Blum**	Y	Y	Y	Y	Y	Y	Y
2 Loebsack	N	N	Y	Y	Y	Y	N
3 **Young**	Y	Y	Y	Y	Y	Y	Y
4 **King**	Y	Y	Y	Y	Y	Y	Y
KANSAS							
1 **Marshall**	Y	Y	Y	Y	Y	Y	Y
2 **Jenkins**	Y	Y	Y	Y	Y	Y	Y
3 **Yoder**	Y	Y	Y	Y	Y	Y	Y
KENTUCKY							
1 **Comer**	Y	Y	Y	Y	Y	Y	Y
2 **Guthrie**	Y	Y	Y	Y	Y	Y	Y
3 Yarmuth	N	?	Y	Y	Y	Y	N
4 **Massie**	Y	Y	Y	Y	N	Y	Y
5 **Rogers**	Y	Y	Y	Y	Y	Y	Y
6 **Barr**	Y	Y	Y	Y	Y	Y	Y
LOUISIANA							
1 **Scalise**	Y	Y	Y	Y	Y	Y	Y
2 Richmond	N	N	Y	Y	Y	Y	N
3 **Higgins**	Y	Y	Y	Y	Y	Y	Y
4 **Johnson**	Y	Y	Y	Y	Y	Y	Y
5 **Abraham**	Y	Y	Y	Y	Y	Y	Y
6 **Graves**	Y	Y	Y	Y	Y	Y	Y
MAINE							
1 Pingree	N	N	Y	Y	Y	Y	N
2 **Poliquin**	Y	Y	+	Y	Y	Y	Y
MARYLAND							
1 **Harris**	Y	Y	Y	Y	Y	Y	Y
2 Ruppersberger	N	N	Y	Y	Y	Y	N
3 Sarbanes	N	N	Y	Y	Y	Y	N
4 Brown	N	N	Y	Y	Y	Y	N
5 Hoyer	?	N	Y	Y	Y	?	N
6 Delaney	N	N	Y	Y	Y	Y	N
7 Cummings	N	N	Y	Y	Y	Y	N
8 Raskin	N	N	N	Y	Y	Y	N
MASSACHUSETTS							
1 Neal	N	N	Y	Y	Y	Y	N
2 McGovern	N	N	Y	Y	Y	Y	N
3 Tsongas	N	N	Y	?	Y	Y	N
4 Kennedy	N	N	Y	Y	Y	Y	N
5 Clark	N	N	Y	Y	Y	Y	N
6 Moulton	N	N	Y	Y	Y	Y	N
7 Capuano	N	N	Y	N	Y	Y	N
8 Lynch	N	N	Y	N	Y	Y	N
9 Keating	N	N	Y	Y	Y	Y	N
MICHIGAN							
1 **Bergman**	Y	Y	Y	Y	Y	Y	Y
2 **Huizenga**	Y	Y	Y	Y	Y	Y	Y
3 **Amash**	Y	Y	Y	N	Y	Y	Y
4 **Moolenaar**	Y	Y	Y	Y	Y	Y	Y
5 Kildee	N	N	Y	Y	Y	Y	N
6 **Upton**	Y	Y	Y	Y	Y	Y	Y
7 **Walberg**	Y	Y	Y	Y	Y	Y	Y
8 **Bishop**	Y	Y	Y	Y	Y	?	Y
9 Levin	N	N	Y	Y	Y	Y	N
10 **Mitchell**	Y	Y	Y	Y	Y	Y	Y
11 **Trott**	Y	Y	Y	Y	Y	Y	Y
12 Dingell	N	N	Y	Y	Y	Y	N
13 Conyers	N	N	N	Y	Y	Y	N
14 Lawrence	N	?	?	Y	Y	Y	N
MINNESOTA							
1 Walz	N	N	Y	Y	Y	Y	N
2 **Lewis**	Y	Y	Y	Y	Y	Y	Y
3 **Paulsen**	Y	Y	Y	Y	Y	Y	Y
4 McCollum	N	N	Y	Y	Y	Y	N

	218	219	220	221	222	223	224
5 Ellison	N	N	Y	Y	Y	Y	N
6 **Emmer**	Y	Y	Y	Y	Y	Y	Y
7 Peterson	N	N	Y	Y	Y	Y	N
8 Nolan	N	N	Y	Y	Y	Y	N
MISSISSIPPI							
1 **Kelly**	Y	Y	Y	Y	Y	Y	Y
2 Thompson	N	N	Y	Y	Y	Y	N
3 **Harper**	Y	Y	Y	Y	Y	Y	Y
4 **Palazzo**	Y	Y	Y	Y	Y	Y	Y
MISSOURI							
1 Clay	N	N	Y	Y	Y	Y	N
2 **Wagner**	Y	Y	Y	Y	Y	Y	Y
3 **Luetkemeyer**	Y	Y	Y	Y	Y	Y	Y
4 **Hartzler**	Y	Y	Y	Y	Y	Y	Y
5 Cleaver	N	N	Y	?	Y	Y	?
6 **Graves**	Y	Y	Y	Y	Y	Y	Y
7 **Long**	Y	Y	Y	Y	Y	Y	Y
8 **Smith**	Y	Y	Y	Y	Y	Y	Y
MONTANA							
AL **Vacant**							
NEBRASKA							
1 **Fortenberry**	Y	Y	Y	Y	Y	Y	Y
2 **Bacon**	Y	Y	Y	Y	Y	Y	Y
3 **Smith**	Y	Y	Y	Y	Y	Y	Y
NEVADA							
1 Titus	N	N	Y	Y	Y	Y	N
2 **Amodei**	Y	Y	Y	Y	Y	Y	Y
3 Rosen	N	N	Y	Y	Y	Y	N
4 Kihuen	N	N	Y	Y	Y	Y	N
NEW HAMPSHIRE							
1 Shea-Porter	N	N	Y	Y	Y	Y	N
2 Kuster	N	N	Y	Y	Y	Y	N
NEW JERSEY							
1 Norcross	N	N	Y	Y	Y	Y	N
2 **LoBiondo**	Y	Y	Y	Y	Y	Y	Y
3 **MacArthur**	Y	Y	Y	Y	Y	Y	Y
4 **Smith**	Y	Y	Y	Y	Y	Y	Y
5 Gottheimer	Y	N	Y	Y	Y	Y	N
6 Pallone	N	N	Y	Y	Y	Y	N
7 **Lance**	Y	Y	Y	Y	Y	Y	Y
8 Sires	N	N	Y	Y	?	?	N
9 Pascrell	N	N	Y	Y	Y	Y	N
10 Payne	N	N	Y	Y	Y	Y	N
11 **Frelinghuysen**	Y	Y	Y	Y	Y	Y	Y
12 Watson Coleman	N	N	N	Y	Y	Y	N
NEW MEXICO							
1 Lujan Grisham	N	N	Y	Y	Y	Y	N
2 **Pearce**	Y	Y	Y	Y	Y	Y	Y
3 Luján	N	N	Y	Y	Y	Y	N
NEW YORK							
1 **Zeldin**	Y	Y	Y	Y	Y	Y	Y
2 **King**	?	?	?	?	Y	Y	Y
3 Suozzi	N	N	Y	Y	Y	Y	N
4 Rice	N	N	Y	Y	Y	Y	N
5 Meeks	N	N	Y	Y	Y	Y	N
6 Meng	N	N	Y	Y	Y	Y	N
7 Velázquez	N	?	Y	Y	Y	Y	N
8 Jeffries	N	N	Y	Y	Y	Y	N
9 Clarke	N	N	Y	Y	Y	Y	N
10 Nadler	N	N	Y	Y	Y	Y	N
11 **Donovan**	Y	Y	Y	Y	Y	Y	Y
12 Maloney, C.	N	N	Y	Y	Y	Y	N
13 Espaillat	N	N	Y	Y	Y	Y	N
14 Crowley	N	N	Y	Y	Y	Y	N
15 Serrano	N	N	Y	Y	Y	Y	N
16 Engel	N	N	Y	Y	Y	Y	N
17 Lowey	N	N	Y	Y	Y	Y	N
18 Maloney, S.P.	N	N	Y	Y	Y	Y	N
19 **Faso**	Y	Y	Y	Y	Y	Y	Y
20 Tonko	N	N	Y	Y	Y	Y	–
21 **Stefanik**	Y	Y	Y	Y	Y	Y	Y
22 **Tenney**	Y	Y	Y	Y	Y	Y	Y
23 **Reed**	Y	Y	Y	Y	Y	Y	Y
24 **Katko**	Y	Y	Y	Y	Y	Y	Y
25 Slaughter	–	–	+	+	+	+	–
26 Higgins	N	N	Y	Y	Y	Y	N
27 **Collins**	Y	Y	Y	Y	Y	Y	Y
NORTH CAROLINA							
1 Butterfield	N	N	Y	Y	Y	Y	N
2 **Holding**	Y	Y	Y	Y	+	+	Y
3 **Jones**	Y	N	Y	Y	N	Y	N
4 Price	N	N	Y	Y	Y	Y	N

	218	219	220	221	222	223	224
5 **Foxx**	Y	Y	Y	Y	Y	Y	Y
6 **Walker**	Y	Y	Y	Y	Y	Y	Y
7 **Rouzer**	Y	Y	Y	Y	Y	Y	Y
8 **Hudson**	Y	Y	Y	Y	Y	?	Y
9 **Pittenger**	Y	Y	Y	Y	Y	Y	Y
10 **McHenry**	Y	Y	Y	Y	Y	Y	Y
11 **Meadows**	Y	Y	Y	Y	Y	Y	Y
12 Adams	N	N	Y	Y	Y	Y	N
13 **Budd**	Y	Y	Y	Y	Y	Y	Y
NORTH DAKOTA							
AL **Cramer**	Y	Y	Y	Y	Y	Y	Y
OHIO							
1 **Chabot**	Y	Y	Y	Y	Y	Y	Y
2 **Wenstrup**	Y	Y	Y	Y	Y	Y	Y
3 Beatty	–	–	+	Y	Y	Y	N
4 **Jordan**	Y	Y	Y	Y	Y	Y	Y
5 **Latta**	Y	Y	Y	Y	Y	Y	Y
6 **Johnson**	Y	Y	Y	Y	Y	Y	Y
7 **Gibbs**	Y	Y	Y	Y	Y	Y	Y
8 **Davidson**	Y	Y	Y	Y	Y	Y	Y
9 Kaptur	N	N	N	Y	Y	Y	N
10 **Turner**	Y	Y	Y	Y	Y	?	Y
11 Fudge	N	N	Y	Y	Y	Y	N
12 **Tiberi**	Y	Y	Y	Y	Y	Y	Y
13 Ryan	N	N	Y	Y	Y	Y	N
14 **Joyce**	Y	Y	Y	Y	Y	?	Y
15 **Stivers**	Y	Y	Y	Y	Y	Y	Y
16 **Renacci**	Y	Y	Y	Y	Y	Y	Y
OKLAHOMA							
1 **Bridenstine**	?	?	?	?	Y	Y	Y
2 **Mullin**	Y	Y	Y	Y	Y	Y	Y
3 **Lucas**	Y	Y	Y	Y	Y	Y	Y
4 **Cole**	Y	Y	Y	Y	Y	Y	Y
5 **Russell**	Y	Y	Y	Y	Y	Y	Y
OREGON							
1 Bonamici	N	N	Y	Y	Y	Y	N
2 **Walden**	Y	Y	Y	Y	Y	Y	Y
3 Blumenauer	N	N	Y	Y	Y	Y	N
4 DeFazio	N	P	Y	Y	Y	Y	N
5 Schrader	N	N	Y	Y	Y	Y	N
PENNSYLVANIA							
1 Brady	N	N	Y	Y	Y	Y	N
2 Evans	N	N	N	?	Y	Y	N
3 **Kelly**	Y	Y	Y	Y	Y	Y	Y
4 **Perry**	Y	Y	Y	Y	Y	Y	Y
5 **Thompson**	Y	Y	Y	Y	Y	Y	Y
6 **Costello**	Y	Y	Y	Y	Y	Y	Y
7 **Meehan**	Y	Y	Y	Y	Y	Y	Y
8 **Fitzpatrick**	Y	Y	Y	Y	Y	Y	Y
9 **Shuster**	Y	Y	Y	Y	Y	Y	Y
10 **Marino**	Y	Y	Y	Y	+	+	+
11 **Barletta**	Y	Y	Y	Y	Y	Y	Y
12 **Rothfus**	Y	Y	Y	Y	Y	Y	Y
13 Boyle	N	N	Y	Y	Y	Y	N
14 Doyle	N	N	Y	Y	Y	Y	N
15 **Dent**	Y	Y	Y	Y	Y	Y	Y
16 **Smucker**	Y	Y	Y	Y	Y	Y	Y
17 Cartwright	N	N	Y	Y	Y	Y	N
18 **Murphy**	Y	Y	Y	Y	Y	Y	Y
RHODE ISLAND							
1 Cicilline	N	N	Y	Y	Y	Y	N
2 Langevin	N	N	Y	Y	Y	Y	N
SOUTH CAROLINA							
1 **Sanford**	Y	P	Y	Y	Y	Y	Y
2 **Wilson**	Y	Y	Y	Y	Y	Y	Y
3 **Duncan**	Y	Y	Y	Y	Y	Y	Y
4 **Gowdy**	Y	Y	Y	Y	Y	Y	Y
6 Clyburn	N	N	Y	Y	Y	Y	N
7 **Rice**	Y	Y	Y	Y	Y	?	Y
SOUTH DAKOTA							
AL **Noem**	Y	Y	Y	Y	Y	Y	Y
TENNESSEE							
1 **Roe**	Y	Y	Y	Y	Y	Y	Y
2 **Duncan**	Y	Y	Y	?	Y	Y	Y
3 **Fleischmann**	Y	Y	Y	Y	Y	Y	Y
4 **DesJarlais**	Y	Y	Y	Y	Y	Y	Y
5 Cooper	N	N	Y	Y	Y	Y	N
6 **Black**	Y	Y	Y	Y	Y	Y	Y
7 **Blackburn**	Y	Y	Y	Y	Y	Y	Y
8 **Kustoff**	Y	Y	Y	Y	Y	Y	Y
9 Cohen	N	N	Y	Y	Y	Y	N

	218	219	220	221	222	223	224
TEXAS							
1 **Gohmert**	Y	Y	Y	Y	Y	Y	Y
2 **Poe**	Y	Y	Y	Y	Y	Y	Y
3 **Johnson, S.**	Y	Y	Y	Y	Y	Y	Y
4 **Ratcliffe**	Y	Y	Y	Y	Y	Y	Y
5 **Hensarling**	Y	Y	Y	Y	Y	Y	Y
6 **Barton**	Y	Y	Y	Y	Y	Y	Y
7 **Culberson**	Y	Y	Y	Y	Y	Y	Y
8 **Brady**	Y	Y	Y	Y	Y	Y	Y
9 Green, A.	N	N	N	Y	Y	Y	N
10 **McCaul**	Y	Y	Y	Y	Y	Y	Y
11 **Conaway**	Y	Y	Y	Y	Y	Y	Y
12 **Granger**	Y	Y	Y	Y	Y	Y	Y
13 **Thornberry**	Y	Y	Y	Y	Y	Y	Y
14 **Weber**	Y	Y	Y	Y	Y	Y	Y
15 Gonzalez	N	N	Y	Y	Y	Y	N
16 O'Rourke	N	N	Y	Y	Y	Y	N
17 **Flores**	Y	Y	Y	Y	Y	Y	Y
18 Jackson Lee	N	N	Y	Y	Y	Y	N
19 **Arrington**	Y	Y	Y	Y	Y	Y	Y
20 Castro	N	N	Y	Y	Y	Y	N
21 **Smith**	Y	Y	?	Y	Y	Y	Y
22 **Olson**	Y	Y	Y	Y	Y	Y	Y
23 **Hurd**	Y	Y	Y	Y	Y	Y	Y
24 **Marchant**	Y	Y	Y	Y	Y	Y	Y
25 **Williams**	Y	?	?	Y	Y	Y	Y
26 **Burgess**	Y	Y	Y	Y	Y	Y	Y
27 **Farenthold**	Y	Y	Y	Y	?	Y	Y
28 Cuellar	N	N	Y	Y	Y	Y	N
29 Green, G.	N	N	Y	Y	Y	Y	N
30 Johnson, E.B.	N	N	Y	Y	Y	Y	N
31 **Carter**	Y	Y	Y	Y	Y	Y	Y
32 **Sessions**	Y	Y	Y	Y	Y	Y	Y
33 Veasey	N	N	Y	Y	Y	Y	N
34 Vela	N	N	Y	Y	Y	Y	N
35 Doggett	N	N	Y	Y	Y	Y	N
36 **Babin**	Y	Y	Y	Y	Y	Y	Y
UTAH							
1 **Bishop**	Y	?	?	Y	Y	Y	Y
2 **Stewart**	Y	Y	Y	Y	Y	Y	Y
3 **Chaffetz**	Y	Y	Y	Y	Y	Y	Y
4 **Love**	Y	Y	Y	Y	Y	Y	Y
VERMONT							
AL Welch	N	N	Y	Y	Y	Y	N
VIRGINIA							
1 **Wittman**	Y	Y	Y	Y	Y	Y	Y
2 **Taylor**	Y	Y	Y	Y	Y	Y	Y
3 Scott	N	N	Y	Y	Y	Y	N
4 McEachin	?	?	?	?	Y	Y	N
5 **Garrett**	Y	Y	Y	Y	Y	Y	Y
6 **Goodlatte**	Y	Y	Y	Y	Y	Y	Y
7 **Brat**	Y	Y	Y	Y	Y	Y	Y
8 Beyer	N	N	Y	Y	Y	Y	N
9 **Griffith**	Y	Y	Y	Y	Y	Y	Y
10 **Comstock**	Y	Y	Y	Y	Y	Y	Y
11 Connolly	N	N	Y	Y	Y	?	N
WASHINGTON							
1 DelBene	N	N	Y	Y	Y	Y	N
2 Larsen	N	N	Y	Y	Y	Y	N
3 **Herrera Beutler**	Y	Y	Y	Y	Y	Y	Y
4 **Newhouse**	Y	Y	Y	Y	?	?	?
5 **McMorris Rodgers**	Y	Y	Y	Y	Y	Y	Y
6 Kilmer	N	N	Y	Y	Y	Y	N
7 Jayapal	N	N	N	Y	Y	Y	N
8 **Reichert**	Y	Y	Y	Y	Y	Y	Y
9 Smith	N	N	Y	Y	Y	Y	N
10 Heck	N	N	Y	Y	Y	Y	N
WEST VIRGINIA							
1 **McKinley**	Y	Y	Y	Y	Y	Y	Y
2 **Mooney**	Y	Y	Y	Y	Y	Y	Y
3 **Jenkins**	Y	Y	Y	Y	Y	Y	Y
WISCONSIN							
1 **Ryan**							
2 Pocan	N	N	Y	Y	Y	Y	N
3 Kind	N	N	Y	Y	Y	Y	N
4 Moore	N	N	Y	Y	+	+	N
5 **Sensenbrenner**	Y	Y	Y	Y	Y	Y	Y
6 **Grothman**	Y	Y	Y	Y	Y	Y	Y
7 **Duffy**	Y	Y	Y	Y	Y	Y	Y
8 **Gallagher**	Y	Y	Y	Y	Y	Y	Y
WYOMING							
AL **Cheney**	Y	Y	Y	Y	Y	Y	Y

VOTE NUMBER

225. HR 1695, H RES 275. REGISTER OF COPYRIGHTS/RULE. Adoption of the rule (H Res 275) that would provide for House floor consideration of the bill that would modify the process for selecting and appointing the U.S. Copyright Office's Register of Copyrights and would limit a Register of Copyrights' term to 10 years. Adopted 237-186 : R 232-0; D 5-186. April 26, 2017.

226. HR 1695. REGISTER OF COPYRIGHTS/CHIEF INFORMATION OFFICER MANAGEMENT. Deutch, D-Fla., amendment that would require that a nominee for the U.S. Copyright Office's Register of Copyrights be capable of identifying and supervising a Chief Information Officer or a similar official that would be responsible for managing modern information technology systems. Adopted 410-14 : R 229-6; D 181-8. April 26, 2017.

227. HR 1695. REGISTER OF COPYRIGHTS/PASSAGE. Passage of the bill that would require the U.S. Copyright Office's Register of Copyrights be recommended by a select panel, nominated by the president and confirmed by the Senate. It would limit a Register of Copyrights' term to 10 years. Passed 378-48 : R 233-2; D 145-46. April 26, 2017.

228. PROCEDURAL MOTION/APPROVAL OF HOUSE JOURNAL. Approved 237-161 : R 137-80; D 100-81. April 26, 2017.

229. HR 1694, H RES 280. MORTGAGE ASSOCIATION OVERSIGHT, SAME-DAY AND SUSPENSION AUTHORITY/PREVIOUS QUESTION. Woodall, R-Ga., motion to order the previous question (thus ending debate and possibility of amendment) on the rule (H Res 280) that would provide for House floor consideration of the bill that would require that Fannie Mae and Freddie Mac comply with the agency requirements of the Freedom of Information Act while they are under the conservatorship of the federal government. It would waive, through the calendar day of April 29, 2017, the two-thirds vote requirement to consider legislation on the same day it is reported from the House Rules Committee. It also would provide for consideration of measures under suspension of the rules through the calendar day of April 29, 2017. Motion agreed to 230-193 : R 230-1; D 0-192. April 27, 2017.

230. HR 1694, H RES 280. MORTGAGE ASSOCIATION OVERSIGHT, SAME-DAY AND SUSPENSION AUTHORITY/RULE. Adoption of the rule (H Res 280) that would provide for House floor consideration of the bill that would require that Fannie Mae and Freddie Mac comply with the agency requirements of the Freedom of Information Act while they are under the conservatorship of the federal government. It would waive, through the calendar day of April 29, 2017, the two-thirds vote requirement to consider legislation on the same day it is reported from the House Rules Committee. It also would provide for consideration of measures under suspension of the rules through the calendar day of April 29, 2017. Adopted 226-192 : R 223-3; D 3-189. April 27, 2017.

231. S 496. URBAN TRANSPORTATION PLANNING/PASSAGE. Lewis, R-Minn., motion to suspend the rules and pass the bill that would repeal the Federal Highway Administration and Federal Transit Administration rule that requires metropolitan planning areas to cover an entire urbanized area, and requires metropolitan planning organizations to adjust their boundaries, merge with other MPOs in the same urbanized area or produce a unified plan for the urbanized area in order to achieve compliance. Motion agreed to, (thus cleared for the president), 417-3 : R 229-0; D 188-3. April 27, 2017.

	225	226	227	228	229	230	231
ALABAMA							
1 Byrne	Y	Y	Y	Y	Y	Y	Y
2 Roby	Y	Y	Y	Y	Y	Y	Y
3 Rogers	Y	Y	Y	Y	Y	Y	Y
4 Aderholt	Y	Y	Y	Y	Y	Y	Y
5 Brooks	Y	Y	Y	Y	Y	Y	Y
6 Palmer	Y	Y	Y	Y	Y	Y	Y
7 Sewell	N	Y	Y	N	N	N	Y
ALASKA							
AL Young	Y	Y	Y	N	Y	Y	Y
ARIZONA							
1 O'Halleran	N	Y	Y	N	N	N	Y
2 McSally	Y	Y	Y	N	Y	Y	Y
3 Grijalva	N	Y	Y	Y	N	N	Y
4 Gosar	Y	Y	Y	Y	Y	Y	Y
5 Biggs	Y	Y	Y	Y	Y	Y	Y
6 Schweikert	Y	Y	Y	Y	Y	Y	Y
7 Gallego	N	Y	N	N	N	N	Y
8 Franks	Y	Y	Y	N	Y	Y	Y
9 Sinema	N	Y	Y	Y	N	Y	Y
ARKANSAS							
1 Crawford	Y	Y	Y	Y	Y	Y	Y
2 Hill	Y	Y	Y	N	Y	Y	Y
3 Womack	Y	Y	Y	Y	Y	Y	Y
4 Westerman	Y	Y	Y	Y	Y	Y	Y
CALIFORNIA							
1 LaMalfa	Y	Y	Y	Y	Y	Y	Y
2 Huffman	N	Y	N	Y	N	N	Y
3 Garamendi	N	Y	Y	?	N	N	Y
4 McClintock	Y	Y	Y	Y	Y	Y	Y
5 Thompson	N	Y	N	N	N	N	Y
6 Matsui	N	Y	N	N	N	N	Y
7 Bera	N	Y	Y	N	N	N	Y
8 Cook	Y	Y	Y	Y	Y	Y	Y
9 McNerney	N	Y	Y	N	N	N	Y
10 Denham	Y	Y	Y	N	Y	Y	Y
11 DeSaulnier	N	N	N	N	N	N	N
12 Pelosi	N	Y	N	N	N	N	Y
13 Lee	N	Y	N	N	N	N	Y
14 Speier	N	Y	N	Y	N	N	Y
15 Swalwell	N	Y	N	N	N	N	Y
16 Costa	N	Y	Y	N	N	N	Y
17 Khanna	N	Y	Y	Y	N	N	Y
18 Eshoo	N	Y	N	Y	N	N	Y
19 Lofgren	N	N	N	N	N	N	N
20 Panetta	N	Y	Y	Y	N	N	Y
21 Valadao	Y	Y	Y	N	Y	+	Y
22 Nunes	Y	Y	Y	Y	Y	Y	Y
23 McCarthy	Y	Y	Y	Y	Y	Y	Y
24 Carbajal	N	Y	N	N	N	N	Y
25 Knight	Y	Y	Y	N	Y	Y	Y
26 Brownley	N	Y	Y	N	N	N	Y
27 Chu	N	Y	Y	N	N	N	Y
28 Schiff	N	Y	Y	N	N	N	Y
29 Cardenas	N	Y	Y	N	N	N	Y
30 Sherman	N	Y	Y	N	N	N	Y
31 Aguilar	N	Y	Y	N	N	N	Y
32 Napolitano	N	Y	Y	N	N	N	Y
33 Lieu	N	Y	Y	N	N	N	Y
34 Vacant							
35 Torres	N	Y	Y	Y	N	N	Y
36 Ruiz	N	Y	Y	N	N	N	Y
37 Bass	N	Y	Y	N	N	N	Y
38 Sánchez, Linda	N	Y	Y	N	N	N	Y
39 Royce	Y	Y	Y	Y	Y	+	Y
40 Roybal-Allard	N	Y	Y	N	N	N	Y
41 Takano	N	Y	N	Y	N	N	Y
42 Calvert	Y	Y	Y	?	Y	Y	Y
43 Waters	N	Y	Y	N	N	N	Y
44 Barragan	N	Y	N	N	N	N	Y
45 Walters	Y	Y	Y	Y	Y	Y	Y
46 Correa	N	Y	N	N	N	N	Y
47 Lowenthal	N	Y	Y	N	N	N	Y
48 Rohrabacher	Y	Y	Y	?	Y	Y	Y
49 Issa	Y	Y	Y	Y	Y	Y	Y
50 Hunter	Y	Y	Y	Y	Y	Y	Y
51 Vargas	N	Y	Y	N	N	N	Y
52 Peters	N	Y	Y	N	N	N	?
53 Davis	N	Y	N	Y	N	N	Y

	225	226	227	228	229	230	231
COLORADO							
1 DeGette	N	Y	N	N	N	N	Y
2 Polis	N	Y	N	N	N	N	Y
3 Tipton	Y	Y	Y	N	Y	Y	Y
4 Buck	Y	Y	Y	N	Y	Y	Y
5 Lamborn	Y	Y	Y	Y	Y	Y	Y
6 Coffman	Y	Y	Y	?	Y	Y	Y
7 Perlmutter	N	Y	Y	N	N	N	Y
CONNECTICUT							
1 Larson	N	Y	Y	N	N	N	Y
2 Courtney	N	Y	Y	N	N	N	Y
3 DeLauro	N	Y	Y	N	N	N	Y
4 Himes	N	Y	Y	N	N	N	Y
5 Esty	N	Y	Y	N	N	N	Y
DELAWARE							
AL Blunt Rochester	N	Y	Y	N	N	N	Y
FLORIDA							
1 Gaetz	Y	N	Y	N	Y	Y	Y
2 Dunn	Y	Y	Y	Y	Y	Y	Y
3 Yoho	Y	Y	Y	?	Y	Y	Y
4 Rutherford	Y	Y	Y	Y	Y	Y	Y
5 Lawson	N	Y	Y	N	N	N	Y
6 DeSantis	Y	Y	Y	N	Y	Y	Y
7 Murphy	N	Y	Y	N	N	N	Y
8 Posey	Y	Y	Y	Y	Y	Y	Y
9 Soto	N	Y	Y	N	N	N	Y
10 Demings	N	Y	?	N	N	N	Y
11 Webster	Y	Y	Y	?	Y	Y	Y
12 Bilirakis	Y	Y	Y	Y	Y	Y	Y
13 Crist	Y	Y	Y	N	N	N	Y
14 Castor	N	Y	N	N	N	N	Y
15 Ross	Y	Y	Y	Y	Y	Y	Y
16 Buchanan	Y	Y	Y	Y	Y	Y	Y
17 Rooney, T.	Y	Y	Y	?	Y	Y	Y
18 Mast	Y	Y	Y	N	Y	Y	Y
19 Rooney, F.	Y	Y	Y	Y	Y	Y	Y
20 Hastings	N	Y	Y	N	N	N	Y
21 Frankel	N	Y	Y	N	N	N	Y
22 Deutch	N	Y	Y	N	N	N	Y
23 Wasserman Schultz	N	Y	Y	N	N	N	Y
24 Wilson	N	Y	Y	N	N	N	Y
25 Diaz-Balart	Y	Y	Y	N	Y	Y	Y
26 Curbelo	Y	Y	Y	Y	Y	Y	Y
27 Ros-Lehtinen	Y	Y	Y	N	Y	Y	Y
GEORGIA							
1 Carter	Y	Y	Y	N	Y	Y	Y
2 Bishop	N	Y	N	N	N	N	Y
3 Ferguson	Y	Y	Y	Y	Y	Y	?
4 Johnson	N	Y	N	N	N	N	Y
5 Lewis	N	Y	N	N	N	N	Y
7 Woodall	Y	Y	Y	Y	Y	Y	Y
8 Scott, A.	Y	Y	Y	Y	Y	Y	Y
9 Collins	Y	Y	Y	N	Y	Y	Y
10 Hice	Y	Y	Y	N	Y	Y	Y
11 Loudermilk	Y	Y	Y	Y	Y	Y	Y
12 Allen	Y	Y	Y	Y	Y	Y	Y
13 Scott, D.	N	Y	Y	N	N	N	Y
14 Graves	Y	Y	Y	N	Y	Y	Y
HAWAII							
1 Hanabusa	N	Y	Y	Y	N	N	Y
2 Gabbard	N	Y	Y	?	N	N	Y
IDAHO							
1 Labrador	Y	Y	Y	Y	Y	Y	Y
2 Simpson	Y	Y	Y	Y	Y	Y	Y
ILLINOIS							
1 Rush	N	N	N	N	N	N	Y
2 Kelly	N	Y	N	N	N	N	Y
3 Lipinski	N	Y	Y	N	N	N	Y
4 Gutierrez	N	Y	N	N	N	N	Y
5 Quigley	N	Y	Y	?	N	N	Y
6 Roskam	Y	Y	Y	Y	Y	Y	Y
7 Davis, D.	N	Y	Y	N	N	N	Y
8 Krishnamoorthi	N	Y	Y	N	N	N	Y
9 Schakowsky	N	Y	N	N	N	N	Y
10 Schneider	Y	Y	Y	N	N	N	Y
11 Foster	N	Y	Y	N	N	N	Y
12 Bost	Y	Y	Y	N	Y	Y	Y
13 Davis, R.	Y	Y	Y	N	Y	Y	Y
14 Hultgren	Y	Y	Y	Y	Y	Y	Y
15 Shimkus	Y	Y	Y	Y	Y	Y	Y

	225	226	227	228	229	230	231
16 **Kinzinger**	Y	Y	Y	N	Y	Y	Y
17 Bustos	N	Y	Y	Y	N	N	Y
18 **LaHood**	Y	Y	Y	N	Y	Y	Y
INDIANA							
1 Visclosky	N	Y	Y	N	N	N	Y
2 **Walorski**	Y	Y	Y	?	?	?	?
3 **Banks**	Y	Y	Y	Y	Y	Y	Y
4 **Rokita**	Y	N	Y	Y	Y	Y	Y
5 **Brooks**	Y	Y	Y	Y	Y	Y	Y
6 **Messer**	Y	Y	Y	?	Y	Y	Y
7 Carson	N	?	Y	Y	N	N	Y
8 **Bucshon**	Y	Y	Y	N	?	?	?
9 **Hollingsworth**	Y	Y	Y	Y	Y	Y	Y
IOWA							
1 **Blum**	Y	Y	Y	N	Y	Y	Y
2 Loebsack	N	Y	Y	N	N	N	Y
3 **Young**	Y	Y	Y	Y	Y	Y	Y
4 **King**	Y	Y	Y	Y	Y	Y	Y
KANSAS							
1 **Marshall**	Y	Y	Y	Y	Y	Y	Y
2 **Jenkins**	Y	Y	Y	N	Y	Y	Y
3 **Yoder**	Y	Y	Y	N	Y	Y	Y
4 **Estes**	Y	Y	Y	Y	Y	Y	Y
KENTUCKY							
1 **Comer**	Y	Y	Y	N	Y	Y	Y
2 **Guthrie**	Y	Y	Y	Y	Y	Y	Y
3 Yarmuth	N	Y	Y	Y	N	N	Y
4 **Massie**	Y	Y	N	Y	Y	N	Y
5 **Rogers**	Y	Y	Y	Y	Y	Y	Y
6 **Barr**	Y	Y	Y	N	Y	Y	Y
LOUISIANA							
1 **Scalise**	Y	Y	Y	Y	Y	Y	Y
2 Richmond	N	N	N	Y	N	N	Y
3 **Higgins**	Y	Y	Y	Y	Y	Y	Y
4 **Johnson**	Y	Y	Y	Y	Y	Y	Y
5 **Abraham**	Y	Y	Y	Y	Y	Y	Y
6 **Graves**	Y	Y	Y	N	Y	Y	?
MAINE							
1 Pingree	N	Y	Y	Y	N	N	Y
2 **Poliquin**	Y	Y	Y	N	Y	Y	Y
MARYLAND							
1 **Harris**	Y	Y	Y	Y	Y	Y	Y
2 Ruppersberger	N	Y	Y	Y	N	N	Y
3 Sarbanes	N	Y	N	N	N	N	Y
4 Brown	N	Y	Y	Y	N	N	Y
5 Hoyer	N	Y	Y	N	N	N	Y
6 Delaney	N	Y	Y	N	N	N	Y
7 Cummings	N	Y	N	N	N	N	Y
8 Raskin	N	Y	Y	N	N	N	Y
MASSACHUSETTS							
1 Neal	N	Y	Y	N	N	N	Y
2 McGovern	N	Y	Y	N	N	N	Y
3 Tsongas	N	Y	Y	Y	N	N	Y
4 Kennedy	N	Y	Y	Y	N	N	Y
5 Clark	N	Y	Y	Y	N	N	Y
6 Moulton	N	Y	Y	Y	N	N	Y
7 Capuano	N	N	N	N	N	N	Y
8 Lynch	N	Y	Y	N	N	N	Y
9 Keating	N	Y	Y	N	N	N	Y
MICHIGAN							
1 **Bergman**	Y	Y	Y	N	Y	Y	Y
2 **Huizenga**	Y	Y	Y	N	Y	Y	Y
3 **Amash**	Y	N	Y	N	Y	N	Y
4 **Moolenaar**	Y	Y	Y	N	Y	Y	Y
5 Kildee	N	Y	Y	Y	N	N	Y
6 **Upton**	Y	Y	Y	N	Y	Y	Y
7 **Walberg**	Y	Y	Y	N	Y	Y	Y
8 **Bishop**	Y	Y	Y	N	Y	Y	Y
9 Levin	N	Y	Y	N	N	N	Y
10 **Mitchell**	Y	Y	Y	Y	Y	Y	Y
11 **Trott**	Y	Y	Y	Y	Y	Y	Y
12 Dingell	N	Y	Y	Y	N	N	Y
13 Conyers	N	Y	Y	Y	N	N	Y
14 Lawrence	N	Y	Y	N	N	N	Y
MINNESOTA							
1 Walz	N	Y	Y	Y	N	N	Y
2 **Lewis**	Y	Y	Y	N	Y	Y	Y
3 **Paulsen**	Y	Y	Y	N	Y	Y	Y
4 McCollum	N	Y	N	Y	N	N	Y

	225	226	227	228	229	230	231
5 Ellison	N	Y	Y	?	N	N	Y
6 **Emmer**	Y	Y	Y	?	Y	Y	Y
7 Peterson	N	Y	Y	N	N	N	Y
8 Nolan	N	Y	Y	?	N	N	Y
MISSISSIPPI							
1 **Kelly**	Y	Y	Y	Y	Y	Y	Y
2 Thompson	N	N	N	N	N	N	Y
3 **Harper**	Y	Y	Y	Y	Y	Y	Y
4 **Palazzo**	Y	Y	Y	Y	Y	Y	Y
MISSOURI							
1 Clay	N	Y	Y	Y	N	N	Y
2 **Wagner**	Y	Y	Y	Y	Y	Y	Y
3 **Luetkemeyer**	Y	Y	Y	Y	Y	Y	Y
4 **Hartzler**	Y	Y	Y	Y	Y	Y	Y
5 Cleaver	N	Y	Y	N	N	N	Y
6 **Graves**	Y	Y	Y	N	Y	Y	Y
7 **Long**	Y	Y	Y	Y	Y	Y	Y
8 **Smith**	Y	Y	Y	N	?	?	?
MONTANA							
AL **Vacant**							
NEBRASKA							
1 **Fortenberry**	Y	Y	Y	Y	Y	Y	Y
2 **Bacon**	Y	Y	Y	Y	Y	Y	Y
3 **Smith**	Y	Y	Y	Y	Y	Y	Y
NEVADA							
1 Titus	N	Y	Y	Y	N	N	Y
2 **Amodei**	Y	Y	Y	Y	Y	Y	Y
3 Rosen	N	Y	N	N	N	N	Y
4 Kihuen	N	Y	Y	N	N	N	Y
NEW HAMPSHIRE							
1 Shea-Porter	N	Y	N	Y	N	N	Y
2 Kuster	Y	Y	Y	Y	N	N	Y
NEW JERSEY							
1 Norcross	N	Y	N	N	N	N	Y
2 **LoBiondo**	Y	Y	Y	N	Y	Y	Y
3 **MacArthur**	Y	Y	Y	N	Y	Y	Y
4 **Smith**	Y	Y	Y	Y	Y	Y	Y
5 Gottheimer	Y	Y	Y	N	N	Y	Y
6 Pallone	N	Y	Y	N	N	N	Y
7 **Lance**	Y	Y	Y	N	Y	Y	Y
8 Sires	N	Y	Y	N	N	N	Y
9 Pascrell	N	?	?	?	N	N	Y
10 Payne	N	Y	N	Y	N	N	Y
11 **Frelinghuysen**	Y	Y	Y	Y	Y	Y	Y
12 Watson Coleman	N	Y	N	N	N	N	Y
NEW MEXICO							
1 Lujan Grisham	N	Y	Y	Y	N	N	Y
2 **Pearce**	Y	Y	Y	N	Y	Y	Y
3 Luján	N	Y	Y	Y	N	N	Y
NEW YORK							
1 **Zeldin**	Y	Y	Y	Y	Y	Y	Y
2 **King**	Y	Y	Y	Y	Y	Y	Y
3 Suozzi	Y	Y	Y	Y	N	Y	Y
4 Rice	N	Y	Y	N	N	N	Y
5 Meeks	N	Y	Y	Y	N	N	Y
6 Meng	N	Y	Y	Y	N	N	Y
7 Velázquez	N	Y	Y	Y	N	N	Y
8 Jeffries	N	?	Y	N	N	N	Y
9 Clarke	N	Y	Y	N	N	N	Y
10 Nadler	N	Y	Y	Y	N	N	Y
11 **Donovan**	Y	Y	Y	Y	Y	Y	Y
12 Maloney, C.	N	Y	Y	Y	N	N	Y
13 Espaillat	N	Y	Y	Y	N	N	Y
14 Crowley	N	Y	Y	Y	N	N	Y
15 Serrano	N	Y	Y	Y	N	N	Y
16 Engel	N	Y	Y	Y	N	N	Y
17 Lowey	N	Y	Y	?	N	N	Y
18 Maloney, S.P.	N	Y	Y	N	N	N	Y
19 **Faso**	Y	Y	Y	N	Y	Y	Y
20 Tonko	–	Y	Y	P	N	N	Y
21 **Stefanik**	Y	Y	Y	Y	Y	Y	Y
22 **Tenney**	Y	Y	Y	Y	Y	Y	Y
23 **Reed**	Y	Y	Y	N	Y	Y	Y
24 **Katko**	Y	Y	Y	Y	Y	Y	Y
25 Slaughter	–	+	+	–	–	–	+
26 Higgins	N	Y	Y	Y	N	N	Y
27 **Collins**	Y	Y	Y	Y	Y	Y	Y
NORTH CAROLINA							
1 Butterfield	N	Y	N	Y	N	N	Y
2 **Holding**	Y	Y	Y	?	Y	Y	Y
3 **Jones**	Y	Y	N	Y	N	N	Y
4 Price	N	Y	N	Y	N	N	Y

	225	226	227	228	229	230	231
5 **Foxx**	Y	Y	Y	N	Y	Y	Y
6 **Walker**	Y	Y	Y	Y	Y	Y	Y
7 **Rouzer**	Y	Y	Y	N	Y	Y	Y
8 **Hudson**	Y	Y	Y	N	Y	Y	Y
9 **Pittenger**	Y	Y	Y	N	Y	Y	Y
10 **McHenry**	Y	Y	Y	Y	Y	Y	Y
11 **Meadows**	Y	Y	Y	Y	Y	Y	Y
12 Adams	N	Y	N	Y	N	N	Y
13 **Budd**	Y	Y	Y	Y	Y	Y	Y
NORTH DAKOTA							
AL **Cramer**	Y	Y	Y	?	Y	Y	Y
OHIO							
1 **Chabot**	Y	Y	Y	Y	Y	Y	Y
2 **Wenstrup**	Y	Y	Y	Y	Y	Y	Y
3 Beatty	N	Y	N	N	N	N	Y
4 **Jordan**	Y	Y	Y	N	Y	Y	Y
5 **Latta**	Y	Y	Y	Y	Y	Y	Y
6 **Johnson**	Y	Y	Y	N	Y	Y	Y
7 **Gibbs**	Y	Y	Y	N	Y	Y	Y
8 **Davidson**	Y	Y	Y	Y	Y	Y	Y
9 Kaptur	N	Y	Y	Y	N	N	Y
10 **Turner**	Y	Y	Y	N	Y	Y	Y
11 Fudge	N	N	N	N	N	N	Y
12 **Tiberi**	Y	Y	Y	N	Y	Y	Y
13 Ryan	N	Y	N	N	N	N	Y
14 **Joyce**	Y	Y	Y	N	Y	Y	Y
15 **Stivers**	Y	Y	Y	N	Y	Y	Y
16 **Renacci**	Y	Y	Y	N	Y	Y	Y
OKLAHOMA							
1 **Bridenstine**	Y	Y	Y	Y	Y	Y	Y
2 **Mullin**	Y	Y	Y	Y	Y	Y	Y
3 **Lucas**	Y	Y	Y	Y	Y	Y	Y
4 **Cole**	+	Y	Y	Y	Y	Y	Y
5 **Russell**	Y	Y	Y	?	Y	Y	Y
OREGON							
1 Bonamici	N	Y	Y	Y	N	N	Y
2 **Walden**	Y	Y	Y	Y	Y	Y	Y
3 Blumenauer	N	Y	N	Y	N	N	N
4 DeFazio	N	Y	N	N	N	N	Y
5 Schrader	N	Y	Y	N	N	N	Y
PENNSYLVANIA							
1 Brady	N	N	N	N	N	N	Y
2 Evans	N	Y	Y	N	N	N	Y
3 **Kelly**	Y	Y	Y	Y	Y	Y	Y
4 **Perry**	Y	Y	Y	N	Y	Y	Y
5 **Thompson**	Y	Y	Y	N	Y	Y	Y
6 **Costello**	Y	Y	Y	N	Y	Y	Y
7 **Meehan**	Y	Y	Y	N	Y	Y	Y
8 **Fitzpatrick**	Y	Y	Y	N	Y	Y	Y
9 **Shuster**	Y	Y	Y	Y	Y	Y	Y
10 **Marino**	+	+	+	+	+	+	+
11 **Barletta**	Y	Y	Y	Y	Y	Y	Y
12 **Rothfus**	Y	Y	Y	Y	Y	Y	Y
13 Boyle	N	Y	N	N	N	N	Y
14 Doyle	N	N	N	N	N	N	Y
15 **Dent**	Y	Y	Y	Y	Y	Y	Y
16 **Smucker**	Y	Y	Y	Y	Y	Y	Y
17 Cartwright	N	Y	N	?	N	N	Y
18 **Murphy**	Y	Y	Y	N	Y	Y	Y
RHODE ISLAND							
1 Cicilline	N	Y	Y	Y	N	N	Y
2 Langevin	N	Y	Y	N	N	N	Y
SOUTH CAROLINA							
1 **Sanford**	Y	Y	Y	Y	Y	Y	Y
2 **Wilson**	Y	Y	Y	Y	Y	Y	Y
3 **Duncan**	Y	N	Y	Y	Y	Y	Y
4 **Gowdy**	Y	Y	Y	Y	Y	Y	Y
6 Clyburn	N	Y	N	N	N	N	Y
7 **Rice**	Y	Y	Y	P	Y	Y	Y
SOUTH DAKOTA							
AL **Noem**	Y	Y	Y	Y	Y	Y	Y
TENNESSEE							
1 **Roe**	Y	Y	Y	Y	Y	Y	Y
2 **Duncan**	?	Y	Y	Y	Y	Y	Y
3 **Fleischmann**	Y	Y	Y	Y	Y	Y	Y
4 **DesJarlais**	Y	Y	Y	Y	Y	Y	Y
5 Cooper	N	Y	Y	Y	N	N	Y
6 **Black**	Y	Y	Y	Y	Y	Y	Y
7 **Blackburn**	Y	Y	Y	Y	Y	Y	Y
8 **Kustoff**	Y	Y	Y	Y	Y	Y	Y
9 Cohen	N	Y	Y	Y	N	N	Y

	225	226	227	228	229	230	231
TEXAS							
1 **Gohmert**	Y	Y	Y	?	Y	Y	Y
2 **Poe**	Y	Y	Y	N	Y	Y	Y
3 **Johnson, S.**	Y	Y	Y	Y	Y	Y	Y
4 **Ratcliffe**	Y	Y	Y	Y	N	Y	Y
5 **Hensarling**	Y	Y	Y	?	Y	Y	Y
6 **Barton**	Y	Y	Y	Y	Y	Y	Y
7 **Culberson**	Y	Y	Y	Y	Y	Y	Y
8 **Brady**	Y	Y	Y	Y	Y	Y	Y
9 Green, A.	N	Y	Y	Y	N	N	Y
10 **McCaul**	Y	Y	Y	Y	Y	Y	Y
11 **Conaway**	Y	Y	Y	N	Y	Y	Y
12 **Granger**	Y	Y	Y	Y	Y	Y	Y
13 **Thornberry**	Y	Y	Y	Y	Y	Y	Y
14 **Weber**	Y	Y	Y	N	Y	Y	Y
15 Gonzalez	N	Y	Y	Y	N	N	Y
16 O'Rourke	N	Y	Y	Y	N	N	Y
17 **Flores**	Y	Y	Y	N	Y	Y	Y
18 Jackson Lee	N	Y	Y	N	N	N	Y
19 **Arrington**	Y	Y	Y	Y	Y	Y	Y
20 Castro	N	Y	Y	Y	N	N	Y
21 **Smith**	Y	Y	Y	Y	Y	Y	Y
22 **Olson**	Y	Y	Y	Y	Y	Y	Y
23 **Hurd**	Y	Y	Y	N	Y	?	Y
24 **Marchant**	?	Y	Y	?	Y	Y	Y
25 **Williams**	Y	Y	Y	Y	Y	Y	Y
26 **Burgess**	Y	Y	Y	N	Y	Y	Y
27 **Farenthold**	Y	Y	Y	Y	Y	Y	Y
28 Cuellar	N	Y	Y	Y	N	N	Y
29 Green, G.	N	Y	Y	N	N	N	Y
30 Johnson, E.B.	N	Y	Y	Y	N	N	Y
31 **Carter**	Y	Y	Y	Y	Y	Y	Y
32 **Sessions**	Y	Y	Y	Y	Y	Y	Y
33 Veasey	N	Y	Y	Y	N	N	Y
34 Vela	N	Y	Y	Y	N	N	Y
35 Doggett	N	Y	Y	Y	N	N	Y
36 **Babin**	Y	Y	Y	N	Y	Y	Y
UTAH							
1 **Bishop**	Y	Y	Y	Y	Y	Y	Y
2 **Stewart**	Y	Y	Y	Y	Y	?	Y
3 **Chaffetz**	Y	Y	Y	Y	?	?	?
4 **Love**	Y	Y	Y	Y	Y	Y	Y
VERMONT							
AL Welch	N	Y	Y	Y	N	N	Y
VIRGINIA							
1 **Wittman**	Y	Y	Y	Y	Y	Y	Y
2 **Taylor**	Y	Y	Y	Y	Y	Y	Y
3 Scott	N	Y	N	Y	N	N	Y
4 McEachin	N	Y	N	N	N	N	Y
5 **Garrett**	Y	Y	Y	Y	Y	Y	Y
6 **Goodlatte**	Y	Y	Y	Y	Y	Y	Y
7 **Brat**	Y	Y	Y	Y	Y	Y	Y
8 Beyer	N	Y	Y	N	N	N	Y
9 **Griffith**	Y	Y	Y	Y	Y	Y	Y
10 **Comstock**	Y	Y	Y	Y	Y	Y	Y
11 Connolly	N	Y	N	N	N	N	Y
ZGDJWASHINGTON							
1 DelBene	N	Y	N	Y	N	N	Y
2 Larsen	N	Y	Y	Y	N	N	Y
3 **Herrera Beutler**	Y	Y	Y	N	Y	Y	Y
4 **Newhouse**	?	?	?	?	?	?	?
5 **McMorris Rodgers**	Y	Y	Y	Y	Y	Y	Y
6 Kilmer	N	Y	Y	N	N	N	Y
7 Jayapal	N	Y	Y	N	N	N	Y
8 **Reichert**	Y	Y	Y	N	Y	Y	Y
9 Smith	N	Y	Y	Y	N	N	Y
10 Heck	N	Y	Y	Y	N	N	Y
WEST VIRGINIA							
1 **McKinley**	Y	Y	Y	N	Y	Y	Y
2 **Mooney**	Y	Y	Y	Y	Y	Y	Y
3 **Jenkins**	Y	Y	Y	?	Y	Y	Y
WISCONSIN							
1 **Ryan**							
2 Pocan	N	Y	Y	Y	N	N	Y
3 Kind	N	Y	Y	N	N	N	Y
4 Moore	N	Y	Y	?	N	N	Y
5 **Sensenbrenner**	Y	Y	Y	Y	Y	Y	Y
6 **Grothman**	Y	N	Y	N	Y	Y	Y
7 **Duffy**	Y	Y	Y	N	Y	Y	Y
8 **Gallagher**	Y	N	Y	N	Y	Y	Y
WYOMING							
AL **Cheney**	Y	Y	Y	Y	Y	+	Y

III HOUSE VOTES

VOTE NUMBER

232. HR 1694. MORTGAGE ASSOCIATION OVERSIGHT/FREEDOM OF INFORMATION ACT EXEMPTIONS. Johnson, D-Ga., amendment that would clarify that all existing exemptions to the Freedom of Information Act would not be impacted by the bill's provisions. Adopted 410-5 : R 227-5; D 183-0. April 27, 2017.

233. HR 1694. MORTGAGE ASSOCIATION OVERSIGHT/PASSAGE. Passage of the bill that would require that Fannie Mae and Freddie Mac comply with the agency requirements of the Freedom of Information Act while they are under the conservatorship of the federal government. It would make records created before, on, or after the bill's date of enactment subject to FOIA requests, including records prior to when the entities were placed under conservatorship. As amended, the bill's provisions would take effect six months after the bill's enactment. Passed 425-0 : R 234-0; D 191-0. April 27, 2017.

234. PROCEDURAL MOTION/APPROVAL OF HOUSE JOURNAL. Approved 249-163 : R 147-83; D 102-80. April 27, 2017.

235. H RES 289, H J RES 99. SHORT-TERM FISCAL 2017 CONTINUING APPROPRIATIONS/RULE. Adoption of the rule (H Res 289) that would provide for House floor consideration of the joint resolution that would extend continuing appropriations for federal government operations through May 5, 2017. It would also provide for an extension, through May 5, 2017, of health care benefits for retired coal miners. Adopted 235-178 : R 225-0; D 10-178. April 28, 2017.

236. H J RES 99. SHORT-TERM FISCAL 2017 CONTINUING APPROPRIATIONS/PASSAGE. Passage of the joint resolution that would extend continuing appropriations for federal government operations through May 5, 2017. It would also provide for an extension, through May 5, of health care benefits for retired coal miners. Passed 382-30 : R 207-16; D 175-14. April 28, 2017.

237. HR 910. SEC SAFE HARBORS/PASSAGE. Hill, R-Ark., motion to suspend the rules and pass the bill that would require the Securities and Exchange Commission to propose and adopt rules that would provide safe harbors for investment fund research reports in regards to exchange traded funds. The investment fund research report would not constitute an offer for sale nor an offer to sell a security that is subject of an offering. The bill would also require the SEC to propose and adopt requirements for the protection of investors and for the promotion of capital formation. Motion agreed to 405-2 : R 224-0; D 181-2. May 1, 2017.

238. HR 1312. SMALL BUSINESS CAPITAL FORMATION FORUM/PASSAGE. Hill, R-Ark., motion to suspend the rules and pass the bill that would require the Securities and Exchange Commission to review the findings and recommendations of the annual Government-Business Forum on Small Business Capital Formation. It also would require the commission to submit a public statement that would assess the findings or recommendations and would disclose what actions, if any, that the SEC plans to take. Motion agreed to 406-0 : R 223-0; D 183-0. May 1, 2017.

	232	233	234	235	236	237	238
ALABAMA							
1 Byrne	Y	Y	Y	Y	Y	Y	Y
2 Roby	Y	Y	Y	Y	Y	Y	Y
3 Rogers	Y	Y	N	Y	Y	Y	Y
4 Aderholt	Y	Y	Y	Y	Y	Y	Y
5 Brooks	Y	Y	Y	Y	Y	Y	Y
6 Palmer	Y	Y	Y	Y	Y	Y	Y
7 Sewell	Y	Y	N	N	Y	Y	Y
ALASKA							
AL Young	Y	Y	N	?	Y	Y	Y
ARIZONA							
1 O'Halleran	Y	Y	N	Y	Y	Y	Y
2 McSally	Y	Y	Y	Y	Y	Y	Y
3 Grijalva	?	Y	P	?	Y	Y	Y
4 Gosar	Y	Y	Y	Y	Y	Y	Y
5 Biggs	Y	Y	Y	Y	Y	Y	Y
6 Schweikert	Y	Y	Y	Y	Y	Y	Y
7 Gallego	Y	Y	Y	N	Y	Y	Y
8 Franks	Y	Y	N	Y	Y	Y	Y
9 Sinema	Y	Y	Y	Y	Y	Y	Y
ARKANSAS							
1 Crawford	Y	Y	Y	Y	Y	Y	Y
2 Hill	Y	Y	N	Y	Y	Y	Y
3 Womack	Y	Y	Y	Y	Y	Y	Y
4 Westerman	Y	Y	Y	Y	Y	Y	Y
CALIFORNIA							
1 LaMalfa	Y	Y	Y	Y	Y	Y	Y
2 Huffman	+	Y	Y	N	Y	N	Y
3 Garamendi	Y	Y	?	N	Y	Y	Y
4 McClintock	Y	Y	Y	Y	Y	Y	Y
5 Thompson	Y	Y	N	N	Y	Y	Y
6 Matsui	Y	Y	N	N	Y	Y	Y
7 Bera	Y	Y	N	N	Y	Y	Y
8 Cook	Y	Y	Y	Y	Y	Y	Y
9 McNerney	Y	Y	Y	N	Y	Y	Y
10 Denham	Y	Y	N	Y	Y	Y	Y
11 DeSaulnier	Y	Y	N	N	Y	Y	Y
12 Pelosi	Y	Y	N	N	Y	Y	Y
13 Lee	Y	Y	N	N	N	Y	Y
14 Speier	Y	Y	N	N	Y	Y	Y
15 Swalwell	Y	Y	N	N	Y	Y	Y
16 Costa	Y	Y	N	Y	Y	Y	Y
17 Khanna	Y	Y	N	N	Y	Y	Y
18 Eshoo	Y	Y	Y	N	Y	Y	Y
19 Lofgren	Y	Y	N	N	Y	Y	Y
20 Panetta	Y	Y	N	N	Y	Y	Y
21 Valadao	Y	Y	N	Y	Y	Y	Y
22 Nunes	Y	Y	Y	Y	Y	Y	Y
23 McCarthy	Y	Y	Y	Y	Y	Y	Y
24 Carbajal	Y	Y	N	N	Y	Y	Y
25 Knight	Y	Y	N	Y	Y	Y	Y
26 Brownley	Y	Y	N	N	Y	Y	Y
27 Chu	Y	Y	Y	N	Y	Y	Y
28 Schiff	Y	Y	N	N	Y	Y	Y
29 Cardenas	?	Y	N	N	N	Y	Y
30 Sherman	Y	Y	N	N	Y	Y	Y
31 Aguilar	Y	Y	N	N	Y	Y	Y
32 Napolitano	+	Y	Y	N	Y	Y	Y
33 Lieu	Y	Y	N	?	?	Y	Y
34 Vacant							
35 Torres	?	Y	?	N	Y	Y	Y
36 Ruiz	Y	Y	N	N	Y	Y	Y
37 Bass	Y	Y	N	N	Y	Y	Y
38 Sánchez, Linda	Y	Y	N	?	?	Y	Y
39 Royce	Y	Y	Y	Y	Y	Y	Y
40 Roybal-Allard	Y	Y	?	N	Y	Y	Y
41 Takano	Y	Y	N	N	Y	Y	Y
42 Calvert	Y	Y	Y	Y	Y	Y	Y
43 Waters	Y	Y	Y	N	Y	Y	Y
44 Barragan	Y	Y	N	N	Y	Y	Y
45 Walters	Y	Y	Y	Y	Y	Y	Y
46 Correa	Y	Y	N	Y	Y	Y	Y
47 Lowenthal	?	Y	N	N	Y	Y	Y
48 Rohrabacher	Y	Y	Y	Y	Y	?	?
49 Issa	Y	Y	Y	Y	Y	Y	Y
50 Hunter	Y	Y	Y	Y	Y	Y	Y
51 Vargas	Y	Y	N	N	Y	Y	Y
52 Peters	Y	Y	N	Y	Y	Y	Y
53 Davis	Y	Y	Y	N	Y	Y	Y

	232	233	234	235	236	237	238
COLORADO							
1 DeGette	Y	Y	Y	N	N	Y	Y
2 Polis	Y	Y	Y	N	Y	Y	Y
3 Tipton	Y	Y	N	Y	Y	Y	Y
4 Buck	Y	Y	N	Y	Y	Y	Y
5 Lamborn	Y	Y	N	Y	Y	Y	Y
6 Coffman	Y	Y	N	Y	Y	Y	Y
7 Perlmutter	Y	Y	Y	N	Y	Y	Y
CONNECTICUT							
1 Larson	Y	Y	N	–	+	Y	Y
2 Courtney	Y	Y	Y	N	Y	Y	Y
3 DeLauro	Y	Y	N	Y	Y	Y	Y
4 Himes	Y	Y	Y	N	Y	Y	Y
5 Esty	Y	Y	Y	N	Y	Y	Y
DELAWARE							
AL Blunt Rochester	Y	Y	Y	N	Y	Y	Y
FLORIDA							
1 Gaetz	N	Y	N	Y	N	Y	Y
2 Dunn	Y	Y	Y	Y	Y	Y	Y
3 Yoho	Y	Y	Y	Y	Y	Y	Y
4 Rutherford	Y	Y	Y	Y	Y	Y	Y
5 Lawson	Y	Y	Y	Y	Y	Y	Y
6 DeSantis	Y	Y	N	Y	Y	Y	Y
7 Murphy	Y	Y	Y	N	Y	Y	Y
8 Posey	N	Y	N	Y	Y	Y	Y
9 Soto	Y	Y	N	N	Y	Y	Y
10 Demings	Y	Y	N	N	Y	Y	Y
11 Webster	N	Y	Y	Y	Y	Y	Y
12 Bilirakis	Y	Y	Y	Y	Y	Y	Y
13 Crist	Y	Y	Y	N	Y	Y	Y
14 Castor	Y	Y	N	N	Y	Y	Y
15 Ross	Y	Y	Y	Y	Y	Y	Y
16 Buchanan	Y	Y	Y	?	?	Y	Y
17 Rooney, T.	Y	Y	Y	Y	Y	?	?
18 Mast	Y	Y	N	Y	Y	Y	Y
19 Rooney, F.	Y	Y	Y	Y	Y	Y	Y
20 Hastings	Y	Y	N	Y	Y	Y	Y
21 Frankel	Y	Y	N	Y	Y	Y	Y
22 Deutch	Y	Y	N	N	Y	?	?
23 Wasserman Schultz	?	?	?	N	Y	Y	Y
24 Wilson	Y	Y	N	N	Y	Y	Y
25 Diaz-Balart	Y	Y	N	Y	Y	Y	Y
26 Curbelo	N	Y	Y	Y	Y	Y	Y
27 Ros-Lehtinen	Y	Y	N	Y	Y	Y	Y
GEORGIA							
1 Carter	Y	Y	N	Y	Y	Y	Y
2 Bishop	Y	Y	N	Y	Y	Y	Y
3 Ferguson	Y	Y	N	Y	Y	Y	Y
4 Johnson	Y	Y	N	Y	Y	Y	Y
5 Lewis	Y	Y	N	N	Y	Y	Y
6 Woodall	Y	Y	N	Y	Y	Y	Y
7 Scott, A.	Y	Y	N	Y	Y	Y	Y
8 Collins	Y	Y	N	Y	Y	Y	Y
9 Hice	Y	Y	N	Y	Y	Y	Y
10 Loudermilk	Y	Y	N	Y	Y	Y	Y
11 Allen	Y	Y	N	Y	Y	Y	Y
12 Scott, D.	Y	Y	N	Y	Y	Y	Y
13 Graves	Y	Y	N	Y	Y	Y	Y
HAWAII							
1 Hanabusa	Y	Y	N	Y	Y	Y	Y
2 Gabbard	Y	Y	Y	N	Y	Y	Y
IDAHO							
1 Labrador	Y	Y	Y	?	?	Y	Y
2 Simpson	Y	Y	Y	Y	Y	Y	Y
ILLINOIS							
1 Rush	Y	Y	N	N	N	Y	Y
2 Kelly	Y	Y	N	N	Y	Y	Y
3 Lipinski	Y	Y	N	Y	Y	Y	Y
4 Gutierrez	Y	Y	N	N	N	Y	Y
5 Quigley	Y	Y	?	N	Y	Y	Y
6 Roskam	Y	Y	N	Y	Y	Y	Y
7 Davis, D.	Y	Y	N	N	Y	Y	Y
8 Krishnamoorthi	Y	Y	N	Y	Y	Y	Y
9 Schakowsky	Y	Y	N	N	Y	Y	Y
10 Schneider	Y	Y	Y	Y	Y	Y	Y
11 Foster	Y	Y	N	Y	Y	Y	Y
12 Bost	Y	Y	N	Y	+	Y	Y
13 Davis, R.	N	Y	N	Y	Y	Y	Y
14 Hultgren	Y	Y	Y	Y	Y	Y	Y
15 Shimkus	Y	Y	Y	Y	Y	Y	Y

	232	233	234	235	236	237	238
16 **Kinzinger**	Y	Y	N	Y	Y	Y	Y
17 Bustos	Y	Y	Y	N	Y	Y	Y
18 **LaHood**	Y	Y	N	Y	Y	Y	Y
INDIANA							
1 Visclosky	Y	Y	N	N	Y	Y	Y
2 **Walorski**	Y	Y	Y	Y	Y	Y	Y
3 **Banks**	Y	Y	Y	Y	Y	Y	Y
4 **Rokita**	Y	Y	?	Y	Y	Y	Y
5 **Brooks**	Y	Y	Y	Y	Y	Y	Y
6 **Messer**	Y	Y	Y	Y	Y	Y	Y
7 Carson	Y	Y	Y	N	Y	Y	Y
8 **Bucshon**	Y	Y	N	Y	Y	Y	Y
9 **Hollingsworth**	Y	Y	Y	Y	N	Y	Y
IOWA							
1 **Blum**	Y	Y	N	Y	Y	Y	Y
2 Loebsack	Y	Y	N	N	Y	Y	Y
3 **Young**	Y	Y	Y	Y	Y	Y	Y
4 **King**	Y	Y	Y	Y	N	Y	Y
KANSAS							
1 **Marshall**	Y	Y	Y	Y	Y	Y	Y
2 **Jenkins**	Y	Y	N	Y	Y	Y	Y
3 **Yoder**	Y	Y	N	Y	Y	Y	Y
4 **Estes**	Y	Y	Y	Y	Y	Y	Y
KENTUCKY							
1 **Comer**	Y	Y	Y	Y	Y	Y	Y
2 **Guthrie**	Y	Y	Y	Y	Y	Y	Y
3 Yarmuth	Y	Y	Y	N	Y	Y	Y
4 **Massie**	Y	Y	Y	Y	N	Y	Y
5 **Rogers**	Y	Y	Y	Y	Y	Y	Y
6 **Barr**	Y	Y	N	Y	Y	Y	Y
LOUISIANA							
1 **Scalise**	Y	Y	Y	Y	Y	Y	Y
2 Richmond	Y	Y	N	N	Y	Y	Y
3 **Higgins**	Y	Y	Y	Y	Y	Y	Y
4 **Johnson**	Y	Y	Y	Y	+	Y	Y
5 **Abraham**	Y	Y	Y	Y	Y	Y	Y
6 **Graves**	Y	Y	N	Y	Y	Y	Y
MAINE							
1 Pingree	Y	Y	Y	N	Y	Y	Y
2 **Poliquin**	Y	Y	N	Y	Y	Y	Y
MARYLAND							
1 **Harris**	Y	Y	Y	Y	Y	Y	Y
2 Ruppersberger	Y	Y	Y	N	Y	Y	Y
3 Sarbanes	Y	Y	N	N	Y	Y	Y
4 Brown	Y	Y	Y	N	Y	Y	Y
5 Hoyer	Y	Y	N	N	Y	Y	Y
6 Delaney	Y	Y	Y	N	Y	Y	Y
7 Cummings	Y	Y	Y	N	Y	Y	Y
8 Raskin	Y	Y	N	N	Y	Y	Y
MASSACHUSETTS							
1 Neal	Y	Y	N	N	Y	Y	Y
2 McGovern	Y	Y	N	N	Y	Y	Y
3 Tsongas	Y	Y	Y	N	Y	Y	Y
4 Kennedy	Y	Y	Y	N	Y	Y	Y
5 Clark	Y	Y	Y	N	Y	Y	Y
6 Moulton	Y	Y	Y	N	Y	Y	Y
7 Capuano	Y	Y	N	N	Y	Y	Y
8 Lynch	Y	Y	N	N	Y	Y	Y
9 Keating	Y	Y	Y	N	Y	Y	Y
MICHIGAN							
1 **Bergman**	Y	Y	N	Y	Y	Y	Y
2 **Huizenga**	Y	Y	N	Y	Y	Y	Y
3 **Amash**	Y	Y	N	Y	N	Y	Y
4 **Moolenaar**	Y	Y	N	Y	Y	Y	Y
5 Kildee	Y	Y	Y	N	Y	?	?
6 **Upton**	Y	Y	N	Y	Y	Y	Y
7 **Walberg**	Y	Y	N	Y	Y	Y	Y
8 **Bishop**	Y	Y	Y	Y	Y	Y	Y
9 Levin	Y	Y	Y	N	Y	Y	Y
10 **Mitchell**	Y	Y	N	Y	Y	Y	Y
11 **Trott**	Y	Y	Y	Y	Y	Y	Y
12 Dingell	Y	Y	Y	N	Y	Y	Y
13 Conyers	Y	Y	Y	N	Y	?	?
14 Lawrence	Y	Y	Y	N	Y	?	?
MINNESOTA							
1 Walz	Y	Y	Y	N	Y	Y	Y
2 **Lewis**	Y	Y	Y	Y	Y	Y	Y
3 **Paulsen**	Y	Y	N	Y	Y	Y	Y
4 McCollum	Y	Y	Y	N	Y	Y	Y
5 Ellison	Y	Y	Y	N	Y	Y	Y
6 **Emmer**	Y	Y	Y	Y	Y	Y	Y
7 Peterson	Y	Y	?	N	Y	Y	Y
8 Nolan	Y	Y	N	N	Y	Y	Y
MISSISSIPPI							
1 **Kelly**	Y	Y	Y	Y	Y	Y	Y
2 Thompson	Y	Y	N	N	Y	Y	Y
3 **Harper**	Y	Y	Y	Y	Y	Y	Y
4 **Palazzo**	Y	Y	Y	Y	Y	Y	Y
MISSOURI							
1 Clay	Y	Y	Y	N	Y	Y	Y
2 **Wagner**	Y	Y	Y	Y	Y	Y	Y
3 **Luetkemeyer**	Y	Y	Y	Y	Y	Y	Y
4 **Hartzler**	Y	Y	N	Y	Y	Y	Y
5 Cleaver	Y	Y	N	N	Y	Y	Y
6 **Graves**	Y	Y	N	Y	Y	Y	Y
7 **Long**	Y	Y	Y	Y	Y	Y	Y
8 **Smith**	Y	Y	N	Y	Y	?	?
MONTANA							
AL **Vacant**							
NEBRASKA							
1 **Fortenberry**	Y	Y	Y	Y	Y	Y	Y
2 **Bacon**	Y	Y	Y	Y	Y	Y	Y
3 **Smith**	Y	Y	Y	Y	Y	Y	Y
NEVADA							
1 Titus	Y	Y	Y	N	Y	Y	Y
2 **Amodei**	Y	Y	Y	Y	Y	?	?
3 Rosen	+	Y	Y	Y	Y	Y	Y
4 Kihuen	Y	Y	N	N	Y	Y	Y
NEW HAMPSHIRE							
1 Shea-Porter	Y	Y	Y	N	Y	Y	Y
2 Kuster	Y	Y	Y	N	Y	Y	Y
NEW JERSEY							
1 Norcross	Y	Y	N	N	Y	Y	Y
2 **LoBiondo**	Y	Y	N	Y	Y	Y	Y
3 **MacArthur**	Y	Y	N	Y	Y	Y	?
4 **Smith**	Y	Y	Y	Y	Y	Y	Y
5 Gottheimer	Y	Y	Y	Y	Y	Y	Y
6 Pallone	Y	Y	N	N	Y	Y	Y
7 **Lance**	Y	Y	N	Y	Y	Y	Y
8 Sires	Y	Y	N	N	Y	Y	Y
9 Pascrell	Y	Y	N	N	Y	Y	Y
10 Payne	Y	Y	Y	N	Y	Y	Y
11 **Frelinghuysen**	Y	Y	Y	Y	Y	Y	Y
12 Watson Coleman	Y	Y	N	N	N	Y	Y
NEW MEXICO							
1 Lujan Grisham	Y	Y	Y	N	N	Y	Y
2 **Pearce**	Y	Y	N	Y	N	Y	Y
3 Luján	Y	Y	Y	N	Y	Y	Y
NEW YORK							
1 **Zeldin**	Y	Y	Y	Y	Y	Y	Y
2 **King**	Y	Y	Y	?	?	Y	Y
3 Suozzi	Y	Y	Y	Y	Y	Y	Y
4 Rice	Y	Y	N	N	Y	Y	Y
5 Meeks	Y	Y	Y	N	Y	Y	Y
6 Meng	Y	Y	Y	N	Y	?	?
7 Velázquez	Y	Y	Y	N	N	Y	Y
8 Jeffries	Y	Y	N	N	Y	Y	Y
9 Clarke	Y	Y	N	N	N	Y	Y
10 Nadler	Y	Y	Y	N	Y	N	Y
11 **Donovan**	Y	Y	Y	Y	Y	Y	Y
12 Maloney, C.	Y	Y	Y	N	Y	?	?
13 Espaillat	Y	Y	N	N	Y	Y	Y
14 Crowley	Y	Y	N	N	Y	Y	Y
15 Serrano	Y	Y	Y	N	Y	Y	Y
16 Engel	Y	Y	Y	N	Y	Y	Y
17 Lowey	Y	Y	Y	N	Y	Y	Y
18 Maloney, S.P.	Y	Y	?	N	Y	Y	Y
19 **Faso**	Y	Y	N	Y	Y	Y	Y
20 Tonko	Y	Y	P	N	Y	Y	Y
21 **Stefanik**	Y	Y	Y	Y	Y	Y	Y
22 **Tenney**	Y	Y	Y	Y	Y	Y	Y
23 **Reed**	Y	Y	N	Y	Y	Y	Y
24 **Katko**	Y	Y	N	Y	Y	Y	Y
25 Slaughter	+	+	–	+	?	+	+
26 Higgins	Y	Y	Y	N	Y	Y	Y
27 **Collins**	Y	Y	Y	Y	Y	Y	Y
NORTH CAROLINA							
1 Butterfield	Y	Y	Y	N	Y	Y	Y
2 **Holding**	Y	Y	N	Y	Y	Y	Y
3 **Jones**	Y	Y	Y	Y	N	?	?
4 Price	Y	Y	Y	N	Y	Y	Y
5 **Foxx**	Y	Y	N	Y	Y	Y	Y
6 **Walker**	Y	Y	Y	Y	Y	Y	?
7 **Rouzer**	Y	Y	N	+	+	Y	Y
8 **Hudson**	+	Y	N	+	+	Y	Y
9 **Pittenger**	Y	Y	N	Y	Y	Y	Y
10 **McHenry**	Y	Y	Y	Y	Y	Y	Y
11 **Meadows**	Y	Y	Y	Y	Y	Y	Y
12 Adams	Y	Y	Y	N	Y	Y	Y
13 **Budd**	Y	Y	Y	Y	Y	Y	Y
NORTH DAKOTA							
AL **Cramer**	Y	Y	Y	Y	Y	Y	Y
OHIO							
1 **Chabot**	Y	Y	Y	Y	Y	Y	Y
2 **Wenstrup**	Y	Y	Y	Y	Y	Y	Y
3 Beatty	Y	Y	Y	N	Y	Y	Y
4 **Jordan**	Y	Y	N	Y	Y	Y	Y
5 **Latta**	Y	Y	N	Y	Y	Y	Y
6 **Johnson**	Y	Y	N	Y	Y	Y	Y
7 **Gibbs**	Y	Y	N	Y	Y	Y	Y
8 **Davidson**	Y	Y	Y	Y	Y	Y	Y
9 Kaptur	Y	Y	Y	N	Y	Y	Y
10 **Turner**	Y	Y	N	Y	Y	Y	Y
11 Fudge	Y	Y	N	N	Y	Y	Y
12 **Tiberi**	Y	Y	Y	Y	Y	Y	Y
13 Ryan	Y	Y	N	N	Y	?	?
14 **Joyce**	Y	Y	N	Y	Y	Y	Y
15 **Stivers**	Y	Y	N	Y	Y	Y	Y
16 **Renacci**	Y	Y	N	Y	N	Y	Y
OKLAHOMA							
1 **Bridenstine**	Y	Y	Y	Y	N	Y	Y
2 **Mullin**	Y	Y	Y	Y	+	Y	Y
3 **Lucas**	Y	Y	Y	Y	Y	Y	Y
4 **Cole**	Y	Y	Y	Y	Y	Y	Y
5 **Russell**	Y	Y	Y	Y	Y	Y	Y
OREGON							
1 Bonamici	Y	Y	Y	N	Y	Y	Y
2 **Walden**	Y	Y	Y	Y	Y	Y	Y
3 Blumenauer	Y	Y	Y	N	Y	Y	Y
4 DeFazio	Y	Y	N	N	N	Y	Y
5 Schrader	Y	Y	N	N	Y	Y	Y
PENNSYLVANIA							
1 Brady	Y	Y	N	N	Y	?	?
2 Evans	Y	Y	N	N	Y	Y	Y
3 **Kelly**	Y	Y	Y	Y	Y	Y	Y
4 **Perry**	Y	Y	Y	Y	Y	Y	Y
5 **Thompson**	Y	Y	N	Y	Y	Y	Y
6 **Costello**	Y	Y	N	Y	Y	Y	Y
7 **Meehan**	Y	Y	N	Y	Y	Y	Y
8 **Fitzpatrick**	Y	Y	N	Y	Y	Y	Y
9 **Shuster**	Y	Y	Y	Y	Y	Y	Y
10 **Marino**	+	+	+	+	+	+	+
11 **Barletta**	Y	Y	Y	Y	Y	Y	Y
12 **Rothfus**	Y	Y	Y	Y	Y	Y	Y
13 Boyle	Y	Y	N	N	N	Y	Y
14 Doyle	Y	Y	N	N	Y	Y	Y
15 **Dent**	Y	Y	Y	Y	Y	Y	Y
16 **Smucker**	Y	Y	?	Y	Y	Y	Y
17 Cartwright	Y	Y	Y	N	Y	Y	Y
18 **Murphy**	Y	Y	Y	Y	Y	Y	Y
RHODE ISLAND							
1 Cicilline	Y	Y	Y	N	Y	Y	Y
2 Langevin	Y	Y	N	N	Y	Y	Y
SOUTH CAROLINA							
1 **Sanford**	Y	Y	Y	Y	Y	Y	Y
2 **Wilson**	Y	Y	Y	Y	Y	Y	Y
3 **Duncan**	?	Y	Y	Y	Y	Y	Y
4 **Gowdy**	Y	Y	Y	Y	Y	Y	Y
6 Clyburn	Y	Y	N	N	Y	Y	Y
7 **Rice**	Y	Y	N	Y	Y	Y	Y
SOUTH DAKOTA							
AL **Noem**	Y	Y	N	Y	Y	Y	Y
TENNESSEE							
1 **Roe**	Y	Y	Y	Y	Y	Y	Y
2 **Duncan**	Y	Y	Y	Y	Y	?	?
3 **Fleischmann**	Y	Y	Y	Y	Y	Y	Y
4 **DesJarlais**	Y	Y	Y	Y	N	Y	Y
5 Cooper	Y	Y	Y	N	Y	Y	Y
6 **Black**	Y	Y	Y	Y	Y	Y	Y
7 **Blackburn**	Y	Y	Y	Y	Y	Y	Y
8 **Kustoff**	Y	Y	Y	Y	Y	Y	Y
9 Cohen	Y	Y	Y	N	Y	Y	Y
TEXAS							
1 **Gohmert**	Y	Y	?	Y	Y	Y	Y
2 **Poe**	Y	Y	N	Y	Y	Y	Y
3 **Johnson, S.**	Y	Y	Y	Y	N	Y	Y
4 **Ratcliffe**	Y	Y	N	Y	N	Y	Y
5 **Hensarling**	Y	Y	Y	Y	Y	Y	Y
6 **Barton**	Y	Y	N	Y	Y	Y	Y
7 **Culberson**	Y	Y	Y	Y	Y	Y	Y
8 **Brady**	Y	Y	Y	Y	Y	Y	Y
9 Green, A.	Y	Y	N	N	Y	Y	Y
10 **McCaul**	Y	Y	Y	Y	Y	Y	Y
11 **Conaway**	Y	Y	N	Y	Y	Y	Y
12 **Granger**	Y	Y	Y	Y	Y	Y	Y
13 **Thornberry**	Y	Y	Y	Y	Y	Y	Y
14 **Weber**	Y	Y	N	Y	Y	Y	Y
15 Gonzalez	Y	Y	Y	N	Y	Y	Y
16 O'Rourke	Y	Y	Y	N	Y	Y	Y
17 **Flores**	Y	Y	N	Y	+	Y	Y
18 Jackson Lee	Y	Y	N	N	Y	Y	Y
19 **Arrington**	Y	Y	Y	Y	Y	+	Y
20 Castro	Y	Y	Y	N	Y	Y	Y
21 **Smith**	Y	Y	Y	Y	Y	Y	Y
22 **Olson**	Y	Y	Y	+	+	?	?
23 **Hurd**	Y	Y	N	Y	Y	?	?
24 **Marchant**	Y	Y	Y	?	Y	Y	Y
25 **Williams**	Y	Y	Y	Y	Y	Y	Y
26 **Burgess**	Y	Y	N	Y	Y	Y	Y
27 **Farenthold**	Y	Y	N	Y	Y	Y	Y
28 Cuellar	Y	Y	Y	N	Y	+	+
29 Green, G.	Y	Y	N	N	Y	Y	Y
30 Johnson, E.B.	Y	Y	Y	N	Y	Y	Y
31 **Carter**	Y	Y	Y	Y	Y	Y	Y
32 **Sessions**	Y	Y	Y	Y	Y	Y	Y
33 Veasey	Y	Y	N	N	Y	Y	Y
34 Vela	Y	Y	N	N	N	Y	Y
35 Doggett	Y	Y	Y	N	Y	Y	Y
36 **Babin**	Y	Y	N	Y	Y	Y	Y
UTAH							
1 **Bishop**	Y	Y	Y	Y	Y	Y	Y
2 **Stewart**	Y	Y	Y	Y	Y	Y	Y
3 **Chaffetz**	?	?	?	?	?	?	?
4 **Love**	Y	Y	Y	Y	Y	Y	Y
VERMONT							
AL Welch	Y	Y	Y	N	Y	Y	Y
VIRGINIA							
1 **Wittman**	Y	Y	Y	Y	N	Y	Y
2 **Taylor**	Y	Y	Y	Y	Y	Y	Y
3 Scott	Y	Y	Y	N	Y	Y	Y
4 McEachin	Y	Y	N	N	Y	Y	Y
5 **Garrett**	Y	Y	Y	Y	N	Y	Y
6 **Goodlatte**	Y	Y	Y	Y	Y	Y	Y
7 **Brat**	Y	Y	Y	+	+	Y	Y
8 Beyer	?	Y	N	N	Y	Y	Y
9 **Griffith**	Y	Y	Y	Y	Y	Y	Y
10 **Comstock**	Y	Y	Y	Y	Y	Y	Y
11 Connolly	Y	Y	N	N	Y	Y	Y
WASHINGTON							
1 DelBene	Y	Y	Y	N	Y	Y	Y
2 Larsen	Y	Y	?	N	Y	Y	Y
3 **Herrera Beutler**	Y	Y	Y	Y	Y	Y	Y
4 **Newhouse**	?	?	?	?	?	?	?
5 **McMorris Rodgers**	Y	Y	Y	Y	Y	Y	Y
6 Kilmer	Y	Y	N	N	Y	Y	Y
7 Jayapal	Y	Y	N	N	Y	Y	Y
8 **Reichert**	Y	Y	Y	Y	Y	Y	Y
9 Smith	Y	Y	Y	N	Y	Y	Y
10 Heck	Y	Y	Y	N	Y	Y	Y
WEST VIRGINIA							
1 **McKinley**	Y	Y	N	Y	Y	Y	Y
2 **Mooney**	Y	Y	Y	Y	N	Y	Y
3 **Jenkins**	Y	Y	N	Y	Y	Y	Y
WISCONSIN							
1 **Ryan**							
2 Pocan	Y	Y	Y	N	Y	Y	Y
3 Kind	Y	Y	N	N	Y	Y	Y
4 Moore	Y	Y	N	N	Y	Y	Y
5 **Sensenbrenner**	Y	Y	Y	Y	N	Y	Y
6 **Grothman**	Y	Y	?	Y	Y	Y	Y
7 **Duffy**	Y	Y	Y	Y	Y	Y	Y
8 **Gallagher**	Y	Y	N	Y	Y	Y	Y
WYOMING							
AL **Cheney**	Y	Y	Y	Y	Y	Y	Y

VOTE NUMBER

239. HR 657. ADVERSE ACTION PROHIBITION EXPANSION/PASSAGE. Comer, R-Ky., motion to suspend the rules and pass the bill that would extend the legal prohibition against federal officials taking or threatening to take adverse personnel actions against an individual to instances in which a federal employee or job applicant refuses to obey an order that would violate a federal rule or regulation, while the current legal prohibition only applies to enacted laws. Motion agreed to 407-0 : R 223-0; D 184-0. May 1, 2017.

240. H RES 299, HR 1180. COMPENSATORY TIME, SAME-DAY AND SUSPENSION AUTHORITY/PREVIOUS QUESTION. Byrne, R-Ala., motion to order the previous question (thus ending debate and possibility of amendment) on the rule (H Res 299) that would provide for House floor consideration of the bill (HR 1180) that would allow private-sector employers to provide non-exempt employees compensatory time off at a rate of 1.5 hours per hour of overtime work. It would waive, through the legislative day of May 5, 2017, the two-thirds vote requirement to consider legislation on the same day it is reported from the House Rules Committee. It also would provide for consideration of measures under suspension of the rules on the legislative days of May 4 and May 5, 2017. Motion agreed to 233-190 : R 233-1; D 0-189. May 2, 2017.

241. H RES 299, HR 1180. COMPENSATORY TIME, SAME-DAY AND SUSPENSION AUTHORITY/RULE. Adoption of the rule (H Res 299) that would provide for House floor consideration of the bill (HR 1180) that would allow private-sector employers to provide non-exempt employees compensatory time off at a rate of 1.5 hours per hour of overtime work. It would waive, through the legislative day of May 5, 2017, the two-thirds vote requirement to consider legislation on the same day it is reported from the House Rules Committee. It also would provide for consideration of measures under suspension of the rules on the legislative days of May 4 and May 5, 2017. Adopted 231-193 : R 231-2; D 0-191. May 2, 2017.

242. HR 1679. FEMA ONLINE INTERFACE/PASSAGE. Barletta, R-Pa., motion to suspend the rules and pass the bill that would require the Federal Emergency Management Agency to create and maintain an online interface in which applicants for federal emergency relief grants could complete forms, submit materials and obtain the status of their applications. Motion agreed to 419-0 : R 230-0; D 189-0. May 2, 2017.

243. HR 1180. COMPENSATORY TIME/RECOMMIT. Scott, D-Va., motion to recommit the bill to the House Education and the Workforce Committee with instructions to report it back immediately with an amendment that would exempt from the bill's provisions employees who receive seven or more sick days from their employer. Motion rejected 192-234 : R 1-234; D 191-0. May 2, 2017.

244. HR 1180. COMPENSATORY TIME/PASSAGE. Passage of the bill that would allow private-sector employers to provide non-exempt employees compensatory time off at a rate of 1.5 hours per hour of overtime work. To be eligible, employees would be required to have worked at least 1,000 hours in a 12-month period. Employees would be limited to 160 hours of compensatory time and employers would be required to provide monetary compensation by Jan. 31, for any unused compensatory time accrued during the preceding year. The bill's provisions would sunset five years after enactment. Passed 229-197 : R 229-6; D 0-191. May 2, 2017.

245. PROCEDURAL MOTION/APPROVAL OF HOUSE JOURNAL. Approved 237-176 : R 142-87; D 95-89. May 2, 2017.

	239	240	241	242	243	244	245
ALABAMA							
1 Byrne	Y	Y	Y	Y	N	Y	Y
2 Roby	Y	Y	Y	Y	N	Y	Y
3 Rogers	Y	Y	Y	Y	N	Y	N
4 Aderholt	Y	Y	Y	Y	N	Y	Y
5 Brooks	Y	Y	Y	Y	N	Y	Y
6 Palmer	Y	Y	Y	Y	N	Y	Y
7 Sewell	Y	N	N	Y	Y	N	N
ALASKA							
AL Young	Y	Y	Y	Y	N	Y	N
ARIZONA							
1 O'Halleran	Y	N	N	Y	Y	N	N
2 McSally	Y	Y	Y	Y	N	Y	N
3 Grijalva	Y	N	N	Y	Y	N	P
4 Gosar	Y	Y	Y	Y	N	Y	N
5 Biggs	Y	Y	Y	Y	N	Y	Y
6 Schweikert	Y	Y	Y	Y	N	Y	Y
7 Gallego	Y	N	N	Y	Y	N	Y
8 Franks	Y	?	?	?	Y	N	Y
9 Sinema	Y	N	N	Y	Y	N	Y
ARKANSAS							
1 Crawford	Y	Y	Y	Y	N	Y	Y
2 Hill	Y	Y	Y	Y	N	Y	Y
3 Womack	Y	Y	Y	Y	N	Y	Y
4 Westerman	Y	Y	Y	Y	N	Y	Y
CALIFORNIA							
1 LaMalfa	Y	Y	Y	Y	N	Y	Y
2 Huffman	Y	N	N	Y	Y	N	Y
3 Garamendi	Y	N	N	Y	Y	N	Y
4 McClintock	Y	Y	Y	Y	N	Y	Y
5 Thompson	Y	N	N	Y	Y	N	N
6 Matsui	Y	N	N	Y	Y	N	N
7 Bera	Y	N	N	Y	Y	N	N
8 Cook	Y	Y	Y	Y	N	Y	Y
9 McNerney	Y	N	N	Y	Y	N	Y
10 Denham	Y	Y	Y	Y	N	Y	N
11 DeSaulnier	Y	N	N	Y	Y	N	N
12 Pelosi	Y	N	N	Y	Y	N	N
13 Lee	Y	N	N	Y	Y	N	N
14 Speier	Y	N	N	Y	Y	N	N
15 Swalwell	Y	N	N	Y	Y	N	N
16 Costa	Y	N	N	Y	Y	N	N
17 Khanna	Y	N	N	Y	Y	N	N
18 Eshoo	Y	N	N	Y	Y	N	N
19 Lofgren	Y	N	N	Y	Y	N	N
20 Panetta	Y	N	N	Y	Y	N	?
21 Valadao	Y	Y	Y	Y	N	Y	N
22 Nunes	Y	Y	Y	Y	N	Y	Y
23 McCarthy	Y	Y	Y	Y	N	Y	Y
24 Carbajal	Y	N	N	Y	Y	N	N
25 Knight	Y	Y	Y	Y	N	Y	N
26 Brownley	Y	N	N	Y	Y	N	N
27 Chu	Y	N	N	Y	Y	N	N
28 Schiff	Y	N	N	Y	Y	N	N
29 Cardenas	Y	N	N	Y	Y	N	N
30 Sherman	Y	N	N	Y	Y	N	N
31 Aguilar	Y	N	N	Y	Y	N	N
32 Napolitano	Y	N	N	Y	Y	N	N
33 Lieu	Y	N	N	Y	Y	N	N
34 Vacant							
35 Torres	Y	N	N	Y	Y	N	N
36 Ruiz	Y	N	N	Y	Y	N	N
37 Bass	Y	N	N	Y	Y	N	N
38 Sánchez, Linda	Y	N	N	Y	Y	N	N
39 Royce	Y	Y	Y	Y	N	Y	Y
40 Roybal-Allard	Y	N	N	Y	Y	N	N
41 Takano	Y	N	N	Y	Y	N	Y
42 Calvert	Y	Y	Y	Y	N	Y	Y
43 Waters	Y	N	N	Y	Y	N	Y
44 Barragan	Y	N	N	Y	Y	N	N
45 Walters	Y	Y	Y	Y	N	Y	Y
46 Correa	Y	N	N	Y	Y	N	Y
47 Lowenthal	Y	N	N	Y	Y	N	Y
48 Rohrabacher	?	Y	Y	Y	N	Y	Y
49 Issa	Y	Y	Y	Y	N	Y	Y
50 Hunter	Y	Y	Y	Y	N	Y	Y
51 Vargas	Y	N	N	Y	Y	N	N
52 Peters	Y	N	N	Y	Y	N	N
53 Davis	Y	N	N	Y	Y	N	Y

	239	240	241	242	243	244	245
COLORADO							
1 DeGette	Y	N	N	Y	Y	N	Y
2 Polis	Y	N	N	Y	Y	N	Y
3 Tipton	?	Y	Y	Y	N	Y	?
4 Buck	Y	Y	Y	Y	N	Y	N
5 Lamborn	Y	Y	Y	Y	N	Y	N
6 Coffman	Y	Y	Y	Y	N	Y	N
7 Perlmutter	Y	N	N	Y	Y	N	?
CONNECTICUT							
1 Larson	Y	N	N	Y	Y	N	Y
2 Courtney	Y	N	N	Y	Y	N	Y
3 DeLauro	Y	N	N	Y	Y	N	Y
4 Himes	Y	N	N	Y	Y	N	Y
5 Esty	Y	N	N	Y	Y	N	Y
DELAWARE							
AL Blunt Rochester	Y	N	N	Y	Y	N	Y
FLORIDA							
1 Gaetz	Y	Y	Y	Y	N	Y	N
2 Dunn	Y	Y	Y	Y	N	Y	Y
3 Yoho	Y	Y	Y	Y	N	Y	Y
4 Rutherford	Y	Y	Y	Y	N	Y	Y
5 Lawson	Y	N	N	Y	Y	N	N
6 DeSantis	Y	Y	Y	Y	N	Y	N
7 Murphy	Y	N	N	Y	Y	N	Y
8 Posey	Y	Y	Y	Y	N	Y	Y
9 Soto	Y	N	N	Y	Y	N	N
10 Demings	Y	N	N	Y	Y	N	N
11 Webster	Y	Y	Y	Y	N	Y	Y
12 Bilirakis	Y	Y	Y	Y	N	Y	Y
13 Crist	Y	N	N	Y	Y	N	N
14 Castor	Y	N	N	Y	Y	N	N
15 Ross	Y	Y	Y	Y	N	Y	Y
16 Buchanan	Y	Y	Y	Y	N	Y	Y
17 Rooney, T.	?	Y	Y	Y	N	Y	Y
18 Mast	Y	Y	Y	Y	N	Y	Y
19 Rooney, F.	Y	Y	Y	Y	N	Y	Y
20 Hastings	Y	N	N	Y	Y	N	Y
21 Frankel	Y	N	N	Y	Y	N	Y
22 Deutch	?	N	N	Y	Y	N	Y
23 Wasserman Schultz	Y	N	N	Y	Y	N	Y
24 Wilson	Y	N	N	Y	Y	N	N
25 Diaz-Balart	Y	Y	Y	Y	N	Y	N
26 Curbelo	Y	Y	Y	Y	N	Y	N
27 Ros-Lehtinen	Y	Y	Y	Y	N	Y	N
GEORGIA							
1 Carter	Y	Y	Y	Y	N	Y	N
2 Bishop	Y	N	N	Y	Y	N	N
3 Ferguson	Y	Y	Y	Y	N	Y	?
4 Johnson	Y	N	N	Y	Y	N	N
5 Lewis	Y	N	N	Y	Y	N	N
7 Woodall	Y	Y	Y	Y	N	Y	N
8 Scott, A.	Y	Y	Y	Y	N	Y	N
9 Collins	Y	Y	Y	Y	N	Y	N
10 Hice	Y	Y	Y	Y	N	Y	N
11 Loudermilk	Y	Y	Y	?	N	Y	Y
12 Allen	Y	Y	Y	Y	N	Y	Y
13 Scott, D.	Y	N	N	Y	Y	N	Y
14 Graves	Y	Y	Y	Y	N	Y	N
HAWAII							
1 Hanabusa	Y	N	N	Y	Y	N	N
2 Gabbard	Y	N	N	Y	Y	N	Y
IDAHO							
1 Labrador	Y	Y	Y	Y	N	Y	Y
2 Simpson	Y	Y	Y	Y	N	Y	Y
ILLINOIS							
1 Rush	Y	N	N	?	Y	N	N
2 Kelly	Y	?	N	Y	Y	N	?
3 Lipinski	Y	N	N	Y	Y	N	Y
4 Gutierrez	Y	N	N	?	Y	N	N
5 Quigley	Y	N	N	Y	Y	N	Y
6 Roskam	Y	Y	Y	Y	N	Y	Y
7 Davis, D.	Y	N	N	Y	Y	N	Y
8 Krishnamoorthi	Y	N	N	Y	Y	N	N
9 Schakowsky	Y	N	N	Y	Y	N	N
10 Schneider	Y	N	N	Y	Y	N	Y
11 Foster	Y	N	N	Y	Y	N	Y
12 Bost	Y	Y	Y	Y	N	Y	N
13 Davis, R.	Y	Y	Y	+	N	Y	N
14 Hultgren	?	Y	Y	Y	N	Y	Y
15 Shimkus	Y	Y	Y	Y	N	Y	Y

KEY	**Republicans**	Democrats	*Independents*
Y Voted for (yea)		X Paired against	C Voted "present" to avoid possible conflict of interest
# Paired for		– Announced against	
+ Announced for		P Voted "present"	? Did not vote or otherwise make a position known
N Voted against (nay)			

	239	240	241	242	243	244	245
16 **Kinzinger**	Y	Y	Y	Y	N	Y	N
17 Bustos	Y	N	N	Y	Y	N	Y
18 **LaHood**	Y	Y	Y	Y	N	Y	N
INDIANA							
1 Visclosky	Y	N	N	Y	Y	N	N
2 **Walorski**	Y	Y	Y	Y	N	Y	N
3 **Banks**	Y	Y	Y	Y	N	Y	Y
4 **Rokita**	Y	Y	Y	Y	N	Y	Y
5 **Brooks**	Y	Y	Y	Y	N	Y	Y
6 **Messer**	Y	Y	Y	Y	N	Y	Y
7 Carson	Y	N	N	Y	Y	N	Y
8 **Bucshon**	Y	Y	Y	Y	N	Y	N
9 **Hollingsworth**	Y	Y	Y	Y	N	Y	Y
IOWA							
1 **Blum**	Y	Y	Y	Y	Y	Y	N
2 Loebsack	Y	N	N	Y	Y	N	N
3 **Young**	Y	Y	Y	Y	N	Y	Y
4 **King**	Y	Y	Y	Y	N	Y	Y
KANSAS							
1 **Marshall**	Y	Y	Y	Y	N	Y	Y
2 **Jenkins**	Y	Y	Y	Y	N	Y	N
3 **Yoder**	Y	Y	Y	Y	N	Y	N
4 **Estes**	Y	Y	Y	Y	N	Y	Y
KENTUCKY							
1 **Comer**	Y	Y	Y	Y	N	Y	N
2 **Guthrie**	Y	Y	Y	Y	N	Y	Y
3 Yarmuth	Y	N	N	Y	Y	N	Y
4 **Massie**	Y	Y	N	Y	N	Y	Y
5 **Rogers**	Y	Y	Y	Y	N	Y	Y
6 **Barr**	Y	Y	Y	Y	N	Y	Y
LOUISIANA							
1 **Scalise**	Y	Y	Y	Y	N	Y	Y
2 Richmond	Y	N	N	Y	Y	N	N
3 **Higgins**	Y	Y	Y	Y	N	Y	Y
4 **Johnson**	Y	Y	Y	Y	N	Y	Y
5 **Abraham**	Y	Y	Y	Y	N	Y	Y
6 **Graves**	Y	Y	Y	Y	N	Y	N
MAINE							
1 Pingree	Y	N	N	Y	Y	N	Y
2 **Poliquin**	Y	Y	Y	Y	N	Y	N
MARYLAND							
1 **Harris**	Y	Y	Y	Y	N	Y	Y
2 Ruppersberger	Y	N	N	Y	Y	N	Y
3 Sarbanes	Y	N	N	Y	Y	N	N
4 Brown	Y	N	N	Y	Y	N	Y
5 Hoyer	Y	N	N	Y	Y	N	N
6 Delaney	Y	N	N	Y	Y	N	N
7 Cummings	Y	N	N	Y	Y	N	N
8 Raskin	Y	N	N	Y	Y	N	Y
MASSACHUSETTS							
1 Neal	Y	N	N	Y	Y	N	N
2 McGovern	Y	N	N	Y	Y	N	N
3 Tsongas	Y	N	N	Y	Y	N	Y
4 Kennedy	Y	N	N	Y	Y	N	Y
5 Clark	Y	N	N	Y	Y	N	Y
6 Moulton	Y	N	N	Y	Y	N	Y
7 Capuano	Y	N	N	Y	Y	N	N
8 Lynch	Y	N	N	Y	Y	N	N
9 Keating	Y	N	N	Y	Y	N	N
MICHIGAN							
1 **Bergman**	Y	Y	Y	Y	N	Y	N
2 **Huizenga**	Y	Y	Y	Y	N	Y	N
3 **Amash**	Y	Y	N	Y	N	Y	N
4 **Moolenaar**	Y	Y	Y	Y	N	Y	Y
5 Kildee	?	N	N	Y	Y	N	Y
6 **Upton**	Y	Y	Y	Y	N	Y	N
7 **Walberg**	?	Y	Y	Y	N	Y	N
8 **Bishop**	Y	Y	Y	Y	N	Y	N
9 Levin	Y	N	N	Y	Y	N	N
10 **Mitchell**	Y	Y	Y	Y	N	Y	Y
11 **Trott**	Y	Y	Y	Y	N	Y	Y
12 Dingell	Y	N	N	Y	Y	N	Y
13 Conyers	?	N	N	Y	Y	N	N
14 Lawrence	Y	N	N	Y	Y	N	N
MINNESOTA							
1 Walz	Y	N	N	Y	Y	N	Y
2 **Lewis**	Y	Y	Y	Y	N	Y	Y
3 **Paulsen**	Y	Y	Y	Y	N	Y	N
4 McCollum	Y	N	N	Y	Y	N	Y
5 Ellison	Y	N	N	Y	Y	N	Y
6 **Emmer**	Y	Y	Y	Y	N	Y	Y
7 Peterson	Y	N	N	Y	Y	N	N
8 Nolan	Y	N	N	Y	Y	N	N
MISSISSIPPI							
1 **Kelly**	Y	Y	Y	Y	N	Y	Y
2 Thompson	Y	N	N	Y	Y	N	N
3 **Harper**	Y	Y	Y	Y	N	Y	Y
4 **Palazzo**	Y	Y	Y	Y	N	Y	Y
MISSOURI							
1 Clay	Y	N	N	Y	Y	N	Y
2 **Wagner**	Y	Y	Y	Y	N	Y	Y
3 **Luetkemeyer**	Y	Y	Y	Y	N	Y	Y
4 **Hartzler**	Y	Y	Y	Y	N	Y	Y
5 Cleaver	Y	N	N	Y	Y	N	Y
6 **Graves**	Y	Y	Y	Y	N	Y	N
7 **Long**	Y	Y	Y	Y	N	Y	Y
8 **Smith**	?	Y	Y	Y	N	Y	N
MONTANA							
AL **Vacant**							
NEBRASKA							
1 **Fortenberry**	Y	Y	Y	Y	N	Y	Y
2 **Bacon**	Y	Y	Y	Y	N	Y	Y
3 **Smith**	Y	Y	Y	Y	N	Y	Y
NEVADA							
1 Titus	Y	N	N	Y	Y	N	Y
2 **Amodei**	?	?	?	?	N	Y	Y
3 Rosen	Y	N	N	Y	Y	N	N
4 Kihuen	Y	N	N	Y	Y	N	N
NEW HAMPSHIRE							
1 Shea-Porter	Y	N	N	Y	Y	N	Y
2 Kuster	Y	N	N	Y	Y	N	Y
NEW JERSEY							
1 Norcross	Y	N	N	Y	Y	N	N
2 **LoBiondo**	Y	Y	Y	Y	N	N	N
3 **MacArthur**	Y	Y	Y	Y	N	N	N
4 **Smith**	Y	Y	Y	Y	N	N	Y
5 Gottheimer	Y	N	N	Y	Y	N	N
6 Pallone	Y	N	N	Y	Y	N	N
7 **Lance**	Y	Y	Y	Y	N	Y	N
8 Sires	Y	N	N	Y	Y	N	N
9 Pascrell	Y	N	N	Y	Y	N	Y
10 Payne	Y	N	N	Y	Y	N	N
11 **Frelinghuysen**	Y	Y	Y	Y	N	Y	?
12 Watson Coleman	Y	N	N	Y	Y	N	N
NEW MEXICO							
1 Lujan Grisham	Y	N	N	Y	Y	N	Y
2 **Pearce**	Y	Y	Y	Y	N	Y	N
3 Luján	Y	N	N	Y	Y	N	Y
NEW YORK							
1 **Zeldin**	Y	Y	Y	Y	N	Y	Y
2 **King**	Y	Y	Y	Y	N	Y	Y
3 Suozzi	Y	N	N	Y	Y	N	Y
4 Rice	Y	N	N	Y	Y	N	N
5 Meeks	Y	N	N	Y	Y	N	Y
6 Meng	?	?	?	?	?	?	?
7 Velázquez	Y	N	N	Y	Y	N	N
8 Jeffries	Y	N	N	Y	Y	N	N
9 Clarke	Y	N	N	Y	Y	N	N
10 Nadler	Y	N	N	Y	Y	N	Y
11 **Donovan**	Y	Y	Y	Y	N	Y	Y
12 Maloney, C.	?	N	N	Y	Y	N	?
13 Espaillat	Y	N	N	Y	Y	N	Y
14 Crowley	Y	N	N	Y	Y	N	N
15 Serrano	Y	N	N	Y	Y	N	Y
16 Engel	Y	N	N	Y	Y	N	Y
17 Lowey	Y	N	N	Y	Y	N	Y
18 Maloney, S.P.	Y	N	N	Y	Y	N	N
19 **Faso**	Y	Y	Y	Y	N	Y	N
20 Tonko	Y	N	N	Y	Y	N	P
21 **Stefanik**	Y	Y	Y	Y	N	Y	Y
22 **Tenney**	Y	Y	Y	Y	N	Y	N
23 **Reed**	Y	Y	Y	Y	?	+	?
24 **Katko**	Y	Y	Y	Y	N	Y	Y
25 Slaughter	+	–	–	+	+	–	–
26 Higgins	Y	N	N	Y	Y	N	Y
27 **Collins**	Y	Y	Y	Y	N	Y	Y
NORTH CAROLINA							
1 Butterfield	Y	N	N	Y	Y	N	Y
2 **Holding**	Y	Y	Y	Y	N	Y	N
3 **Jones**	?	N	Y	Y	N	Y	N
4 Price	Y	N	N	Y	Y	N	Y
5 **Foxx**	Y	Y	Y	Y	N	Y	N
6 **Walker**	Y	Y	Y	Y	N	Y	N
7 **Rouzer**	Y	Y	Y	Y	N	Y	N
8 **Hudson**	Y	Y	Y	Y	N	Y	N
9 **Pittenger**	Y	Y	Y	Y	N	Y	N
10 **McHenry**	Y	Y	Y	Y	N	Y	Y
11 **Meadows**	Y	Y	Y	Y	N	Y	Y
12 Adams	Y	N	N	Y	Y	N	Y
13 **Budd**	Y	Y	Y	Y	N	Y	N
NORTH DAKOTA							
AL **Cramer**	Y	Y	Y	Y	N	Y	Y
OHIO							
1 **Chabot**	Y	Y	Y	Y	N	Y	Y
2 **Wenstrup**	Y	Y	Y	Y	N	Y	Y
3 Beatty	Y	N	N	Y	Y	N	Y
4 **Jordan**	Y	Y	Y	Y	N	Y	N
5 **Latta**	Y	Y	Y	Y	N	Y	Y
6 **Johnson**	Y	Y	Y	Y	N	Y	N
7 **Gibbs**	Y	Y	Y	Y	N	Y	N
8 **Davidson**	Y	Y	Y	Y	N	Y	Y
9 Kaptur	Y	N	N	Y	Y	N	Y
10 **Turner**	Y	Y	Y	Y	N	Y	N
11 Fudge	Y	N	N	Y	Y	N	N
12 **Tiberi**	Y	Y	Y	Y	N	Y	Y
13 Ryan	?	N	N	Y	Y	N	N
14 **Joyce**	Y	Y	Y	Y	N	N	N
15 **Stivers**	Y	Y	Y	Y	N	Y	N
16 **Renacci**	Y	Y	Y	Y	N	Y	Y
OKLAHOMA							
1 **Bridenstine**	Y	Y	Y	Y	N	Y	Y
2 **Mullin**	Y	Y	Y	Y	N	Y	Y
3 **Lucas**	Y	Y	Y	Y	N	Y	Y
4 **Cole**	Y	Y	Y	Y	N	Y	Y
5 **Russell**	Y	Y	Y	Y	N	Y	Y
OREGON							
1 Bonamici	Y	N	N	Y	Y	N	Y
2 **Walden**	Y	Y	Y	Y	N	Y	N
3 Blumenauer	Y	N	N	Y	Y	N	Y
4 DeFazio	Y	N	N	Y	Y	N	N
5 Schrader	Y	N	N	Y	Y	N	N
PENNSYLVANIA							
1 Brady	?	N	N	Y	Y	N	N
2 Evans	Y	N	N	Y	Y	N	N
3 **Kelly**	Y	Y	Y	Y	N	Y	Y
4 **Perry**	Y	Y	Y	Y	N	Y	N
5 **Thompson**	Y	Y	Y	Y	N	Y	N
6 **Costello**	Y	Y	Y	Y	N	Y	N
7 **Meehan**	Y	Y	Y	Y	N	N	N
8 **Fitzpatrick**	Y	Y	Y	Y	N	N	N
9 **Shuster**	Y	Y	Y	Y	N	Y	Y
10 **Marino**	+	Y	Y	Y	N	Y	Y
11 **Barletta**	Y	Y	Y	Y	N	Y	Y
12 **Rothfus**	Y	Y	Y	Y	N	Y	Y
13 Boyle	Y	N	N	Y	Y	N	N
14 Doyle	Y	N	N	Y	Y	N	N
15 **Dent**	Y	Y	Y	Y	N	Y	Y
16 **Smucker**	Y	Y	Y	Y	N	Y	Y
17 Cartwright	Y	N	N	Y	Y	N	Y
18 **Murphy**	Y	Y	Y	Y	N	Y	N
RHODE ISLAND							
1 Cicilline	Y	N	N	Y	Y	N	Y
2 Langevin	Y	N	N	Y	Y	N	N
SOUTH CAROLINA							
1 **Sanford**	Y	Y	Y	Y	N	Y	N
2 **Wilson**	Y	Y	Y	Y	N	Y	Y
3 **Duncan**	Y	Y	Y	Y	N	Y	Y
4 **Gowdy**	Y	Y	Y	Y	N	Y	Y
6 Clyburn	Y	N	N	Y	Y	N	N
7 **Rice**	Y	Y	Y	Y	N	Y	P
SOUTH DAKOTA							
AL **Noem**	Y	Y	Y	Y	N	Y	N
TENNESSEE							
1 **Roe**	Y	Y	Y	Y	N	Y	Y
2 **Duncan**	?	Y	Y	Y	N	Y	Y
3 **Fleischmann**	Y	Y	Y	Y	N	Y	Y
4 **DesJarlais**	Y	Y	Y	Y	N	Y	Y
5 Cooper	Y	N	N	Y	Y	N	Y
6 **Black**	Y	Y	Y	Y	N	Y	Y
7 **Blackburn**	Y	Y	Y	Y	N	Y	Y
8 **Kustoff**	Y	Y	Y	Y	N	Y	Y
9 Cohen	Y	N	N	Y	Y	N	N
TEXAS							
1 **Gohmert**	Y	Y	Y	Y	N	Y	?
2 **Poe**	Y	Y	Y	Y	N	Y	N
3 **Johnson, S.**	Y	Y	Y	Y	N	Y	Y
4 **Ratcliffe**	Y	Y	Y	Y	N	Y	N
5 **Hensarling**	Y	Y	Y	Y	N	Y	Y
6 **Barton**	Y	Y	Y	Y	N	Y	Y
7 **Culberson**	Y	Y	Y	Y	N	Y	Y
8 **Brady**	Y	Y	Y	Y	N	Y	Y
9 Green, A.	Y	N	N	Y	Y	N	Y
10 **McCaul**	Y	Y	Y	Y	N	Y	Y
11 **Conaway**	Y	Y	Y	Y	N	Y	N
12 **Granger**	Y	Y	Y	Y	N	Y	Y
13 **Thornberry**	Y	Y	Y	Y	N	Y	Y
14 **Weber**	Y	Y	Y	Y	N	Y	N
15 Gonzalez	Y	N	N	Y	Y	N	N
16 O'Rourke	Y	N	N	Y	Y	N	Y
17 **Flores**	Y	Y	Y	Y	N	Y	N
18 Jackson Lee	Y	N	N	Y	Y	N	N
19 **Arrington**	Y	Y	Y	Y	N	Y	Y
20 Castro	Y	N	N	Y	Y	N	Y
21 **Smith**	Y	Y	Y	Y	N	Y	Y
22 **Olson**	?	Y	Y	Y	N	Y	Y
23 **Hurd**	?	Y	Y	Y	N	Y	N
24 **Marchant**	Y	Y	Y	Y	N	Y	Y
25 **Williams**	Y	Y	Y	Y	N	Y	Y
26 **Burgess**	Y	Y	Y	Y	N	Y	N
27 **Farenthold**	Y	Y	Y	Y	N	Y	N
28 Cuellar	?	N	N	Y	Y	N	Y
29 Green, G.	Y	N	N	Y	Y	N	N
30 Johnson, E.B.	Y	N	N	Y	Y	N	Y
31 **Carter**	Y	Y	Y	Y	N	Y	Y
32 **Sessions**	Y	Y	Y	Y	N	Y	Y
33 Veasey	Y	N	N	Y	Y	N	N
34 Vela	Y	N	N	Y	Y	N	N
35 Doggett	Y	N	N	Y	Y	N	Y
36 **Babin**	Y	Y	Y	Y	N	Y	N
UTAH							
1 **Bishop**	Y	Y	Y	Y	N	Y	Y
2 **Stewart**	Y	Y	Y	Y	N	Y	Y
3 **Chaffetz**	?	?	?	?	?	?	?
4 **Love**	Y	Y	Y	Y	N	Y	Y
VERMONT							
AL Welch	Y	N	N	Y	Y	N	Y
VIRGINIA							
1 **Wittman**	Y	Y	Y	Y	N	Y	Y
2 **Taylor**	Y	Y	Y	Y	N	Y	Y
3 Scott	Y	N	N	Y	Y	N	Y
4 McEachin	Y	N	N	Y	Y	N	Y
5 **Garrett**	Y	Y	Y	Y	N	Y	Y
6 **Goodlatte**	Y	Y	Y	Y	N	Y	Y
7 **Brat**	Y	Y	Y	Y	N	Y	?
8 Beyer	Y	N	N	Y	Y	N	N
9 **Griffith**	Y	Y	Y	?	N	Y	Y
10 **Comstock**	Y	Y	Y	?	N	Y	Y
11 Connolly	Y	N	N	Y	Y	N	N
WASHINGTON							
1 DelBene	Y	N	N	Y	Y	N	Y
2 Larsen	Y	N	N	Y	Y	N	?
3 **Herrera Beutler**	Y	Y	Y	Y	N	Y	N
4 **Newhouse**	?	Y	Y	Y	N	Y	Y
5 **McMorris Rodgers**	Y	Y	Y	Y	N	Y	Y
6 Kilmer	Y	N	N	Y	Y	N	N
7 Jayapal	Y	N	N	Y	Y	N	N
8 **Reichert**	Y	Y	Y	Y	N	Y	N
9 Smith	Y	N	N	Y	Y	N	Y
10 Heck	Y	N	N	Y	Y	N	Y
WEST VIRGINIA							
1 **McKinley**	Y	Y	Y	Y	N	Y	N
2 **Mooney**	Y	Y	Y	Y	N	Y	Y
3 **Jenkins**	Y	Y	Y	Y	N	Y	N
WISCONSIN							
1 **Ryan**							
2 Pocan	Y	N	N	Y	Y	N	Y
3 Kind	Y	N	N	Y	Y	N	N
4 Moore	Y	N	N	Y	Y	N	Y
5 **Sensenbrenner**	Y	Y	Y	Y	N	Y	Y
6 **Grothman**	Y	Y	+	Y	N	Y	Y
7 **Duffy**	Y	Y	Y	Y	N	Y	N
8 **Gallagher**	Y	Y	Y	Y	N	Y	N
WYOMING							
AL **Cheney**	Y	Y	Y	Y	N	Y	Y

VOTE NUMBER

246. HR 244, H RES 305. FISCAL 2017 OMNIBUS APPROPRIATIONS/ PREVIOUS QUESTION. Cole, R-Okla., motion to order the previous question (thus ending debate and possibility of amendment) on the rule (H Res 305) that would provide for House floor consideration of the Senate amendments to the bill, with House amendment, intended to serve as the legislative vehicle for a measure that would provide $1.16 trillion in discretionary appropriations for federal departments and agencies covered by the 11 unfinished fiscal 2017 spending bills. Motion agreed to 231-192 : R 231-1; D 0-191. May 3, 2017.

247. HR 244, H RES 305. FISCAL 2017 OMNIBUS APPROPRIATIONS/ RULE. Adoption of the rule (H Res 305) that would provide for House floor consideration of the Senate amendments to the bill, with House amendment, intended to serve as the legislative vehicle for a measure that would provide $1.16 trillion in discretionary appropriations for federal departments and agencies covered by the 11 unfinished fiscal 2017 spending bills. Adopted 240-186 : R 233-0; D 7-186. May 3, 2017.

248. HR 1665. FEMA DISASTER RECOMMENDATIONS/PASSAGE. Barletta, R-Pa., motion to suspend the rules and pass the bill that would require the Federal Emergency Management Agency to give greater weight to severe local impact or recent multiple disasters when making recommendations to the president in relation to a major disaster declaration. Motion agreed to 425-0 : R 233-0; D 192-0. May 3, 2017.

249. HR 244. FISCAL 2017 OMNIBUS APPROPRIATIONS/MOTION TO CONCUR. Frelinghuysen, R-N.J., motion to concur in the Senate amendments to the bill with an amendment that would provide $1.16 trillion in discretionary appropriations through Sept. 30, 2017 for federal departments and agencies covered by the remaining 11 fiscal 2017 spending bills. Included in that total is: $20.9 billion for Agriculture, $56.6 billion for Commerce-Justice-Science, $593 billion for Defense, $37.8 billion for Energy-Water, $21.5 billion for Financial Services, $42.4 billion for Homeland Security (including $772 million for improvements and maintenance to existing Customs and Border Protection infrastructure and technology), $32.2 billion for Interior-Environment, $161 billion for Labor-HHS-Education, $4.4 billion for Legislative, $53.1 billion for State-Foreign Operations, and $57.7 billion for Transportation-HUD. The measure would authorize classified amounts of funding for fiscal 2017 for 16 U.S. intelligence agencies and intelligence-related activities of the U.S. government. The measure would provide $608 million for health benefits for retired coal miners and $296 million for Medicaid payments to Puerto Rico. Motion agreed to 309-118 : R 131-103; D 178-15. May 3, 2017.

250. HR 1678. FEMA PAYMENT RECOVERY/PASSAGE. Barletta, R-Pa., motion to suspend the rules and pass the bill that would establish a three-year statute on the Federal Emergency Management Agency's ability to recover a payment made to a state or local government for disaster or emergency assistance. The statute of limitations would apply to assistance provided on or after Jan. 1, 2004. Motion agreed to 423-0 : R 232-0; D 191-0. May 3, 2017.

251. PROCEDURAL MOTION/APPROVAL OF HOUSE JOURNAL. Approved 236-178 : R 136-91; D 100-87. May 3, 2017.

	246	247	248	249	250	251
ALABAMA						
1 **Byrne**	Y	Y	Y	Y	Y	Y
2 **Roby**	Y	Y	Y	Y	Y	Y
3 **Rogers**	Y	Y	Y	N	Y	N
4 **Aderholt**	Y	Y	Y	Y	Y	Y
5 **Brooks**	Y	Y	Y	N	Y	N
6 **Palmer**	Y	Y	Y	N	Y	N
7 Sewell	N	N	Y	Y	Y	N
ALASKA						
AL **Young**	Y	Y	Y	Y	Y	N
ARIZONA						
1 O'Halleran	N	Y	Y	Y	Y	N
2 **McSally**	Y	Y	Y	Y	Y	N
3 Grijalva	N	N	Y	N	?	?
4 **Gosar**	Y	Y	Y	N	Y	Y
5 **Biggs**	Y	Y	Y	N	Y	Y
6 **Schweikert**	Y	Y	Y	N	Y	Y
7 Gallego	N	N	Y	N	Y	N
8 **Franks**	Y	Y	Y	N	Y	N
9 Sinema	N	N	Y	Y	Y	Y
ARKANSAS						
1 **Crawford**	Y	Y	Y	Y	Y	Y
2 **Hill**	Y	Y	Y	Y	Y	Y
3 **Womack**	Y	Y	Y	Y	Y	Y
4 **Westerman**	Y	Y	Y	N	Y	Y
CALIFORNIA						
1 **LaMalfa**	Y	Y	Y	Y	Y	Y
2 Huffman	N	N	Y	Y	Y	Y
3 Garamendi	N	N	Y	Y	Y	N
4 **McClintock**	Y	Y	Y	N	Y	Y
5 Thompson	N	N	Y	Y	Y	N
6 Matsui	N	N	Y	Y	Y	N
7 Bera	N	N	Y	Y	Y	N
8 **Cook**	Y	Y	Y	Y	Y	Y
9 McNerney	N	N	Y	Y	Y	Y
10 **Denham**	Y	Y	Y	Y	Y	N
11 DeSaulnier	N	N	Y	Y	Y	N
12 Pelosi	N	N	Y	Y	Y	N
13 Lee	N	N	Y	Y	Y	N
14 Speier	N	N	Y	Y	Y	N
15 Swalwell	N	N	Y	Y	Y	N
16 Costa	N	N	Y	Y	Y	N
17 Khanna	N	N	Y	Y	Y	N
18 Eshoo	N	N	Y	Y	Y	Y
19 Lofgren	N	N	Y	Y	Y	N
20 Panetta	N	N	Y	Y	Y	N
21 **Valadao**	Y	Y	Y	Y	Y	N
22 **Nunes**	Y	Y	Y	Y	Y	Y
23 **McCarthy**	Y	Y	Y	Y	Y	Y
24 Carbajal	N	N	Y	Y	Y	N
25 **Knight**	Y	Y	Y	Y	Y	N
26 Brownley	N	N	Y	Y	Y	N
27 Chu	N	N	Y	Y	Y	Y
28 Schiff	N	N	Y	Y	Y	Y
29 Cardenas	N	N	Y	N	Y	N
30 Sherman	N	N	Y	Y	Y	Y
31 Aguilar	N	N	Y	Y	Y	N
32 Napolitano	N	N	Y	Y	Y	N
33 Lieu	N	N	Y	N	Y	N
34 Vacant						
35 Torres	N	N	Y	N	Y	N
36 Ruiz	N	N	Y	Y	Y	N
37 Bass	N	N	Y	Y	Y	N
38 Sánchez, Linda	N	N	Y	Y	Y	N
39 **Royce**	Y	Y	Y	Y	Y	Y
40 Roybal-Allard	N	N	Y	Y	Y	N
41 Takano	N	N	Y	Y	Y	Y
42 **Calvert**	Y	Y	Y	Y	Y	Y
43 Waters	N	N	Y	Y	Y	Y
44 Barragan	N	N	Y	N	Y	N
45 **Walters**	Y	Y	Y	Y	Y	Y
46 Correa	N	N	Y	N	Y	Y
47 Lowenthal	N	N	Y	Y	Y	N
48 **Rohrabacher**	Y	Y	Y	Y	Y	N
49 **Issa**	Y	Y	Y	Y	Y	Y
50 **Hunter**	Y	Y	Y	N	Y	N
51 Vargas	N	N	Y	N	Y	N
52 Peters	N	N	Y	Y	Y	N
53 Davis	N	N	Y	Y	Y	N

	246	247	248	249	250	251
COLORADO						
1 DeGette	N	N	Y	Y	Y	?
2 Polis	N	N	Y	Y	Y	Y
3 **Tipton**	Y	Y	Y	N	Y	N
4 **Buck**	Y	Y	Y	N	Y	N
5 **Lamborn**	Y	Y	Y	N	Y	Y
6 **Coffman**	Y	Y	Y	Y	Y	Y
7 Perlmutter	N	N	Y	Y	Y	Y
CONNECTICUT						
1 Larson	–	N	Y	Y	Y	N
2 Courtney	N	N	Y	Y	Y	Y
3 DeLauro	N	N	Y	Y	Y	Y
4 Himes	N	N	Y	Y	Y	Y
5 Esty	N	N	Y	Y	Y	Y
DELAWARE						
AL Blunt Rochester	N	N	Y	Y	Y	Y
FLORIDA						
1 **Gaetz**	Y	Y	Y	N	Y	N
2 **Dunn**	Y	Y	Y	Y	Y	Y
3 **Yoho**	Y	Y	Y	N	Y	Y
4 **Rutherford**	Y	Y	Y	Y	Y	N
5 Lawson	N	N	Y	Y	Y	N
6 **DeSantis**	Y	Y	Y	N	Y	N
7 Murphy	N	N	Y	Y	Y	N
8 **Posey**	Y	Y	Y	N	Y	Y
9 Soto	N	N	Y	Y	Y	N
10 Demings	?	N	Y	Y	Y	N
11 **Webster**	Y	Y	Y	N	Y	Y
12 **Bilirakis**	Y	Y	Y	N	Y	Y
13 Crist	N	N	Y	Y	Y	N
14 Castor	N	N	Y	Y	Y	N
15 **Ross**	Y	Y	Y	Y	Y	Y
16 **Buchanan**	Y	Y	Y	Y	Y	Y
17 **Rooney, T.**	Y	Y	Y	Y	Y	N
18 **Mast**	Y	Y	Y	Y	Y	N
19 **Rooney, F.**	Y	Y	Y	N	Y	?
20 Hastings	N	N	Y	Y	Y	N
21 Frankel	N	N	Y	Y	Y	N
22 Deutch	N	N	Y	Y	Y	Y
23 Wasserman Schultz	N	N	Y	Y	Y	Y
24 Wilson	N	N	Y	Y	Y	?
25 **Diaz-Balart**	Y	Y	Y	Y	?	?
26 **Curbelo**	Y	Y	Y	Y	Y	Y
27 **Ros-Lehtinen**	Y	Y	Y	Y	Y	N
GEORGIA						
1 **Carter**	Y	Y	Y	Y	Y	N
2 Bishop	N	N	Y	?	Y	N
3 **Ferguson**	Y	Y	Y	N	Y	Y
4 Johnson	N	N	Y	Y	Y	N
5 Lewis	N	N	Y	Y	Y	N
7 **Woodall**	Y	Y	Y	Y	Y	Y
8 **Scott, A.**	Y	Y	Y	Y	Y	Y
9 **Collins**	Y	Y	Y	Y	Y	Y
10 **Hice**	Y	Y	Y	N	Y	N
11 **Loudermilk**	Y	Y	Y	N	Y	N
12 **Allen**	Y	Y	Y	Y	Y	Y
13 Scott, D.	N	N	Y	Y	Y	N
14 **Graves**	Y	Y	Y	N	Y	N
HAWAII						
1 Hanabusa	N	N	Y	Y	Y	Y
2 Gabbard	N	N	Y	Y	Y	Y
IDAHO						
1 **Labrador**	Y	Y	Y	N	Y	Y
2 **Simpson**	Y	Y	Y	Y	Y	Y
ILLINOIS						
1 Rush	N	N	Y	N	Y	N
2 Kelly	N	N	Y	Y	Y	N
3 Lipinski	N	Y	Y	Y	Y	Y
4 Gutierrez	N	N	Y	N	Y	N
5 Quigley	N	N	Y	Y	Y	N
6 **Roskam**	Y	Y	Y	Y	Y	Y
7 Davis, D.	N	N	Y	Y	Y	N
8 Krishnamoorthi	N	N	Y	Y	Y	N
9 Schakowsky	N	N	Y	Y	Y	N
10 Schneider	N	N	Y	Y	Y	Y
11 Foster	N	N	Y	Y	Y	N
12 **Bost**	Y	Y	Y	Y	Y	N
13 **Davis, R.**	Y	Y	Y	Y	Y	Y
14 **Hultgren**	Y	Y	Y	N	Y	Y
15 **Shimkus**	Y	Y	Y	Y	Y	Y

	246	247	248	249	250	251
16 **Kinzinger**	Y	Y	Y	Y	Y	N
17 Bustos	N	N	Y	Y	Y	Y
18 **LaHood**	Y	Y	Y	N	Y	N
INDIANA						
1 Visclosky	N	N	Y	Y	Y	N
2 **Walorski**	Y	Y	Y	Y	Y	N
3 **Banks**	Y	Y	Y	N	Y	Y
4 **Rokita**	Y	Y	Y	Y	Y	N
5 **Brooks**	Y	Y	Y	Y	Y	Y
6 **Messer**	Y	Y	Y	N	Y	?
7 Carson	N	N	Y	Y	Y	Y
8 **Bucshon**	Y	Y	Y	Y	Y	N
9 **Hollingsworth**	Y	Y	Y	N	Y	Y
IOWA						
1 **Blum**	Y	Y	Y	N	Y	N
2 Loebsack	N	N	Y	Y	Y	N
3 **Young**	Y	Y	Y	Y	Y	Y
4 **King**	Y	Y	Y	N	Y	Y
KANSAS						
1 **Marshall**	Y	Y	Y	N	Y	Y
2 **Jenkins**	Y	Y	Y	Y	Y	N
3 **Yoder**	Y	Y	Y	Y	Y	N
4 **Estes**	Y	Y	Y	N	Y	Y
KENTUCKY						
1 **Comer**	Y	Y	Y	Y	Y	N
2 **Guthrie**	Y	Y	Y	Y	Y	Y
3 Yarmuth	N	N	Y	Y	Y	Y
4 **Massie**	Y	Y	Y	N	Y	Y
5 **Rogers**	Y	Y	Y	Y	Y	Y
6 **Barr**	Y	Y	Y	Y	Y	Y
LOUISIANA						
1 **Scalise**	Y	Y	Y	Y	Y	Y
2 Richmond	N	N	Y	Y	Y	Y
3 **Higgins**	Y	Y	Y	Y	Y	Y
4 **Johnson**	Y	Y	Y	N	Y	Y
5 **Abraham**	Y	Y	Y	N	Y	Y
6 **Graves**	Y	Y	Y	N	Y	N
MAINE						
1 Pingree	N	N	Y	Y	Y	Y
2 **Poliquin**	?	?	?	?	?	?
MARYLAND						
1 **Harris**	Y	Y	Y	N	Y	Y
2 Ruppersberger	N	N	Y	Y	Y	Y
3 Sarbanes	N	N	Y	Y	Y	N
4 Brown	N	N	Y	Y	Y	Y
5 Hoyer	N	N	Y	Y	Y	N
6 Delaney	N	N	Y	Y	Y	?
7 Cummings	N	N	Y	Y	Y	Y
8 Raskin	N	N	Y	Y	Y	?
MASSACHUSETTS						
1 Neal	N	N	Y	Y	Y	N
2 McGovern	N	N	Y	Y	Y	N
3 Tsongas	N	N	Y	Y	Y	N
4 Kennedy	N	N	Y	Y	Y	Y
5 Clark	N	N	Y	Y	Y	Y
6 Moulton	N	N	Y	Y	Y	Y
7 Capuano	N	N	Y	Y	Y	N
8 Lynch	N	N	Y	Y	Y	N
9 Keating	N	N	Y	Y	Y	N
MICHIGAN						
1 **Bergman**	Y	Y	Y	Y	Y	N
2 **Huizenga**	Y	Y	Y	Y	Y	N
3 **Amash**	Y	Y	Y	N	Y	N
4 **Moolenaar**	Y	Y	Y	Y	Y	N
5 Kildee	N	N	Y	Y	Y	Y
6 **Upton**	Y	Y	Y	Y	Y	N
7 **Walberg**	Y	Y	Y	Y	Y	N
8 **Bishop**	Y	Y	Y	Y	Y	N
9 Levin	N	N	Y	Y	Y	N
10 **Mitchell**	Y	Y	Y	Y	Y	N
11 **Trott**	Y	Y	Y	Y	Y	Y
12 Dingell	N	N	Y	Y	Y	Y
13 Conyers	N	N	Y	Y	Y	N
14 Lawrence	N	N	Y	Y	Y	Y
MINNESOTA						
1 Walz	N	N	Y	Y	Y	Y
2 **Lewis**	Y	Y	Y	N	Y	Y
3 **Paulsen**	Y	Y	Y	Y	Y	N
4 McCollum	N	N	Y	Y	Y	Y
5 Ellison	N	N	Y	N	Y	Y
6 **Emmer**	Y	Y	Y	N	Y	?
7 Peterson	N	N	Y	N	Y	N
8 Nolan	N	N	Y	Y	Y	N
MISSISSIPPI						
1 **Kelly**	Y	Y	Y	N	Y	Y
2 Thompson	N	N	Y	Y	Y	N
3 **Harper**	Y	Y	Y	Y	Y	Y
4 **Palazzo**	Y	Y	Y	Y	Y	Y
MISSOURI						
1 Clay	N	N	Y	Y	Y	Y
2 **Wagner**	Y	Y	Y	N	Y	Y
3 **Luetkemeyer**	Y	Y	Y	Y	Y	Y
4 **Hartzler**	Y	Y	Y	Y	Y	Y
5 Cleaver	N	N	Y	Y	Y	Y
6 **Graves**	Y	Y	Y	Y	Y	N
7 **Long**	Y	Y	Y	N	Y	Y
8 **Smith**	Y	Y	Y	N	Y	Y
MONTANA						
AL **Vacant**						
NEBRASKA						
1 **Fortenberry**	Y	Y	Y	N	Y	Y
2 **Bacon**	Y	Y	Y	Y	Y	Y
3 **Smith**	Y	Y	Y	Y	Y	Y
NEVADA						
1 Titus	N	N	Y	Y	Y	Y
2 **Amodei**	Y	Y	Y	Y	Y	Y
3 Rosen	N	N	Y	Y	Y	Y
4 Kihuen	N	N	Y	Y	Y	N
NEW HAMPSHIRE						
1 Shea-Porter	N	N	Y	Y	Y	Y
2 Kuster	N	N	Y	Y	Y	Y
NEW JERSEY						
1 Norcross	N	N	Y	Y	Y	N
2 **LoBiondo**	Y	Y	Y	Y	Y	N
3 **MacArthur**	Y	Y	Y	Y	Y	N
4 **Smith**	Y	Y	Y	Y	Y	Y
5 Gottheimer	N	Y	Y	Y	Y	Y
6 Pallone	N	N	Y	Y	Y	N
7 **Lance**	Y	Y	Y	Y	Y	N
8 Sires	N	N	Y	Y	Y	N
9 Pascrell	N	N	Y	Y	Y	Y
10 Payne	N	N	Y	Y	Y	N
11 **Frelinghuysen**	Y	Y	Y	Y	Y	Y
12 Watson Coleman	N	N	Y	Y	Y	N
NEW MEXICO						
1 Lujan Grisham	N	N	Y	Y	Y	Y
2 **Pearce**	Y	Y	Y	N	Y	N
3 Luján	N	N	Y	Y	Y	Y
NEW YORK						
1 **Zeldin**	Y	Y	Y	Y	Y	Y
2 **King**	Y	Y	Y	Y	Y	Y
3 Suozzi	N	N	Y	Y	Y	Y
4 Rice	N	N	Y	Y	Y	N
5 Meeks	N	N	Y	Y	Y	N
6 Meng	N	N	Y	Y	Y	Y
7 Velázquez	N	N	Y	Y	Y	N
8 Jeffries	N	N	Y	Y	Y	Y
9 Clarke	N	N	Y	Y	Y	Y
10 Nadler	N	N	Y	Y	Y	Y
11 **Donovan**	Y	Y	Y	Y	Y	Y
12 Maloney, C.	N	N	Y	Y	Y	Y
13 Espaillat	N	N	Y	N	Y	Y
14 Crowley	N	N	Y	Y	Y	N
15 Serrano	N	N	Y	Y	Y	Y
16 Engel	N	N	Y	Y	Y	Y
17 Lowey	N	N	Y	Y	Y	Y
18 Maloney, S.P.	N	N	Y	Y	Y	N
19 **Faso**	Y	Y	Y	Y	Y	N
20 Tonko	N	N	Y	Y	Y	Y
21 **Stefanik**	Y	Y	Y	Y	Y	Y
22 **Tenney**	Y	Y	Y	Y	Y	N
23 **Reed**	Y	Y	Y	Y	Y	N
24 **Katko**	Y	Y	Y	Y	Y	Y
25 Slaughter	N	N	Y	Y	Y	N
26 Higgins	N	N	Y	Y	Y	Y
27 **Collins**	Y	Y	Y	Y	Y	Y
NORTH CAROLINA						
1 Butterfield	N	N	Y	Y	?	?
2 **Holding**	Y	Y	Y	N	Y	?
3 **Jones**	N	Y	Y	N	Y	N
4 Price	N	N	Y	Y	Y	N
5 **Foxx**	Y	Y	Y	N	Y	N
6 **Walker**	Y	Y	Y	N	Y	Y
7 **Rouzer**	Y	Y	Y	N	Y	N
8 **Hudson**	Y	Y	Y	N	Y	N
9 **Pittenger**	Y	Y	Y	+	Y	Y
10 **McHenry**	Y	Y	Y	Y	Y	Y
11 **Meadows**	Y	Y	Y	N	Y	Y
12 Adams	N	N	Y	Y	Y	N
13 **Budd**	Y	Y	Y	N	Y	Y
NORTH DAKOTA						
AL **Cramer**	Y	Y	Y	Y	Y	Y
OHIO						
1 **Chabot**	Y	Y	Y	N	Y	Y
2 **Wenstrup**	Y	Y	Y	N	Y	N
3 Beatty	N	N	Y	Y	Y	Y
4 **Jordan**	Y	Y	Y	N	Y	N
5 **Latta**	Y	Y	Y	N	Y	Y
6 **Johnson**	Y	Y	?	Y	Y	N
7 **Gibbs**	Y	Y	Y	N	Y	N
8 **Davidson**	Y	Y	Y	N	Y	Y
9 Kaptur	N	N	Y	Y	Y	Y
10 **Turner**	Y	Y	Y	Y	Y	N
11 Fudge	N	N	Y	Y	Y	N
12 **Tiberi**	Y	Y	Y	Y	Y	Y
13 Ryan	N	N	Y	Y	Y	N
14 **Joyce**	Y	Y	Y	Y	Y	N
15 **Stivers**	Y	Y	Y	Y	Y	N
16 **Renacci**	Y	Y	Y	N	Y	N
OKLAHOMA						
1 **Bridenstine**	Y	Y	Y	N	Y	Y
2 **Mullin**	Y	Y	Y	N	Y	Y
3 **Lucas**	Y	Y	Y	Y	Y	Y
4 **Cole**	Y	Y	Y	Y	Y	Y
5 **Russell**	Y	Y	Y	N	Y	Y
OREGON						
1 Bonamici	N	N	Y	Y	Y	Y
2 **Walden**	Y	Y	Y	Y	Y	Y
3 Blumenauer	N	N	Y	Y	Y	Y
4 DeFazio	N	N	Y	Y	Y	N
5 Schrader	N	N	Y	Y	Y	N
PENNSYLVANIA						
1 Brady	N	N	Y	Y	Y	N
2 Evans	N	N	Y	Y	Y	Y
3 **Kelly**	Y	Y	Y	Y	Y	Y
4 **Perry**	Y	Y	Y	N	Y	N
5 **Thompson**	Y	Y	Y	Y	Y	N
6 **Costello**	Y	Y	Y	Y	Y	N
7 **Meehan**	Y	Y	Y	Y	Y	N
8 **Fitzpatrick**	Y	Y	Y	Y	Y	N
9 **Shuster**	Y	Y	Y	Y	Y	Y
10 **Marino**	Y	Y	Y	Y	Y	Y
11 **Barletta**	Y	Y	Y	Y	Y	Y
12 **Rothfus**	Y	Y	Y	N	Y	Y
13 Boyle	N	N	Y	Y	Y	N
14 Doyle	N	N	Y	Y	Y	N
15 **Dent**	Y	Y	Y	Y	Y	Y
16 **Smucker**	Y	Y	Y	Y	Y	Y
17 Cartwright	N	N	Y	Y	Y	Y
18 **Murphy**	Y	Y	Y	Y	Y	N
RHODE ISLAND						
1 Cicilline	N	N	Y	Y	Y	Y
2 Langevin	N	N	Y	Y	Y	N
SOUTH CAROLINA						
1 **Sanford**	Y	Y	Y	N	Y	N
2 **Wilson**	Y	Y	Y	Y	Y	Y
3 **Duncan**	Y	?	Y	N	Y	Y
4 **Gowdy**	Y	Y	Y	Y	Y	Y
6 Clyburn	N	N	Y	Y	Y	N
7 **Rice**	Y	Y	Y	Y	Y	Y
SOUTH DAKOTA						
AL **Noem**	Y	Y	Y	N	Y	Y
TENNESSEE						
1 **Roe**	Y	Y	Y	N	Y	N
2 **Duncan**	Y	Y	Y	N	Y	Y
3 **Fleischmann**	Y	Y	Y	Y	Y	Y
4 **DesJarlais**	Y	Y	Y	N	Y	Y
5 Cooper	N	Y	Y	Y	Y	Y
6 **Black**	?	Y	Y	N	Y	Y
7 **Blackburn**	Y	Y	Y	N	Y	N
8 **Kustoff**	Y	Y	Y	N	Y	Y
9 Cohen	N	N	Y	Y	Y	N
TEXAS						
1 **Gohmert**	?	Y	Y	N	Y	?
2 **Poe**	Y	Y	Y	N	Y	N
3 **Johnson, S.**	Y	Y	Y	N	Y	Y
4 **Ratcliffe**	Y	Y	Y	N	Y	N
5 **Hensarling**	Y	Y	Y	Y	Y	Y
6 **Barton**	Y	Y	Y	N	Y	Y
7 **Culberson**	Y	Y	Y	Y	Y	N
8 **Brady**	Y	Y	Y	Y	Y	Y
9 Green, A.	N	N	Y	Y	Y	Y
10 **McCaul**	Y	Y	Y	Y	Y	Y
11 **Conaway**	Y	Y	Y	Y	Y	N
12 **Granger**	Y	Y	Y	Y	Y	Y
13 **Thornberry**	Y	Y	Y	Y	Y	Y
14 **Weber**	Y	Y	Y	N	Y	N
15 Gonzalez	N	N	Y	Y	Y	Y
16 O'Rourke	N	N	Y	Y	Y	Y
17 **Flores**	Y	Y	Y	Y	Y	N
18 Jackson Lee	N	N	Y	Y	Y	N
19 **Arrington**	Y	Y	Y	N	Y	Y
20 Castro	N	N	Y	N	Y	Y
21 **Smith**	Y	Y	Y	N	?	Y
22 **Olson**	Y	Y	Y	N	Y	?
23 **Hurd**	Y	Y	Y	Y	Y	Y
24 **Marchant**	Y	Y	Y	N	Y	N
25 **Williams**	Y	Y	Y	N	Y	Y
26 **Burgess**	Y	Y	Y	Y	Y	N
27 **Farenthold**	Y	Y	Y	N	Y	N
28 Cuellar	N	N	Y	Y	Y	Y
29 Green, G.	N	N	Y	Y	Y	N
30 Johnson, E.B.	N	N	Y	Y	Y	Y
31 **Carter**	Y	Y	Y	Y	Y	Y
32 **Sessions**	Y	Y	Y	Y	Y	Y
33 Veasey	N	N	Y	Y	Y	N
34 Vela	N	N	Y	N	Y	N
35 Doggett	N	N	Y	Y	Y	?
36 **Babin**	Y	Y	Y	N	Y	N
UTAH						
1 **Bishop**	Y	Y	Y	N	Y	Y
2 **Stewart**	Y	Y	Y	N	Y	Y
3 **Chaffetz**	?	?	?	?	?	?
4 **Love**	Y	Y	Y	N	Y	Y
VERMONT						
AL Welch	N	N	Y	Y	Y	Y
VIRGINIA						
1 **Wittman**	Y	Y	Y	N	Y	Y
2 **Taylor**	Y	Y	Y	Y	Y	Y
3 Scott	N	N	Y	Y	Y	Y
4 McEachin	N	N	Y	Y	Y	N
5 **Garrett**	Y	Y	Y	N	Y	N
6 **Goodlatte**	Y	Y	Y	N	Y	Y
7 **Brat**	Y	Y	Y	N	Y	Y
8 Beyer	N	N	Y	Y	Y	N
9 **Griffith**	Y	Y	Y	N	Y	Y
10 **Comstock**	Y	Y	Y	Y	Y	Y
11 Connolly	N	N	Y	Y	Y	N
WASHINGTON						
1 DelBene	N	N	Y	Y	Y	Y
2 Larsen	N	N	Y	Y	Y	N
3 **Herrera Beutler**	Y	Y	Y	Y	Y	N
4 **Newhouse**	?	?	?	?	?	?
5 **McMorris Rodgers**	Y	Y	Y	Y	Y	Y
6 Kilmer	N	N	Y	Y	Y	N
7 Jayapal	N	N	Y	Y	Y	N
8 **Reichert**	Y	Y	Y	Y	Y	Y
9 Smith	N	N	Y	Y	Y	Y
10 Heck	N	N	Y	Y	Y	Y
WEST VIRGINIA						
1 **McKinley**	Y	Y	Y	Y	Y	N
2 **Mooney**	Y	Y	Y	Y	Y	Y
3 **Jenkins**	Y	Y	Y	Y	Y	N
WISCONSIN						
1 **Ryan**				Y		
2 Pocan	N	N	Y	Y	Y	Y
3 Kind	N	N	Y	Y	Y	N
4 Moore	N	N	Y	Y	Y	Y
5 **Sensenbrenner**	Y	Y	Y	N	Y	Y
6 **Grothman**	Y	Y	Y	N	Y	Y
7 **Duffy**	Y	Y	Y	N	Y	N
8 **Gallagher**	Y	Y	Y	N	Y	N
WYOMING						
AL **Cheney**	Y	Y	Y	N	Y	Y

VOTE NUMBER

252. HR 2192, H RES 308, HR 1628. CONGRESSIONAL HEALTH CARE EXEMPTION AND HEALTH CARE MARKETPLACE OVERHAUL/PREVIOUS QUESTION. Collins, R-Ga., motion to order the previous question (thus ending debate and possibility of amendment) on the rule (H Res 308) that would provide for House floor consideration of the bill (HR 2192) that would repeal, if the health care marketplace overhaul measure (HR 1628) is enacted, an exemption for members of Congress and staff from provisions of the health care marketplace overhaul measure that would allow state waivers of certain health insurance minimum benefit and patient protection requirements under the 2010 health care overhaul. It would also provide for House floor consideration of the bill (HR 1628) that would repeal extensive portions of the 2010 health care overhaul law. Upon adoption, the rule would provide for the automatic adoption of amendments to the bill (HR 1628) that would allow states to receive waivers to exempt insurers from having to provide certain minimum benefits, would provide $8 billion over five years for individuals with pre-existing conditions whose insurance premiums increased because the state was granted a waiver to raise premiums based on an individual's health status, and would create a $15 billion federal risk sharing program to cover some of the costs of high medical claims. Motion agreed to 235-193 : R 235-1; D 0-192. May 4, 2017.

253. HR 2192, H RES 308, HR 1628. CONGRESSIONAL HEALTH CARE EXEMPTION AND HEALTH CARE MARKETPLACE OVERHAUL/RULE. Adoption of the rule (H Res 308) that would provide for House floor consideration of the bill (HR 2192) that would repeal, if the health care overhaul measure (HR 1628) is enacted, an exemption for members of Congress and staff from provisions of the health care overhaul measure that would allow state waivers of certain health insurance minimum benefit and patient protection requirements under the 2010 health care overhaul. It would also provide for House floor consideration of the bill (HR 1628) that would repeal extensive portions of the 2010 health care overhaul law. Upon adoption, the rule would provide for the automatic adoption of amendments to the bill (HR 1628) that would allow states to receive waivers to exempt insurers from having to provide certain minimum benefits, would provide $8 billion over five years for individuals with pre-existing conditions whose insurance premiums increased because the state was granted a waiver to raise premiums based on an individual's health status, and would create a $15 billion federal risk sharing program to cover some of the costs of high medical claims. Adopted 235-192 : R 235-1; D 0-191. May 4, 2017.

254. PROCEDURAL MOTION/APPROVAL OF HOUSE JOURNAL. Approved 233-186 : R 166-66; D 67-120. May 4, 2017.

255. HR 2192. CONGRESSIONAL HEALTH CARE EXEMPTION/PASSAGE. Passage of the bill would repeal, if the health care overhaul measure (HR 1628) is enacted, an exemption for members of Congress and staff from provisions of the health care overhaul measure that would allow state waivers of certain health insurance minimum benefit and patient protection requirements under the 2010 health care overhaul. Passed 429-0 : R 237-0; D 192-0. May 4, 2017.

256. HR 1628. HEALTH CARE MARKETPLACE OVERHAUL/PASSAGE. Passage of the bill that would make extensive changes to the 2010 health care overhaul law, by effectively repealing the individual and employer mandates as well as most of the taxes that finance the current system. It would, in 2020, convert Medicaid into a capped entitlement that would provide fixed federal payments to states and end additional federal funding for the 2010 law's joint federal-state Medicaid expansion. It would prohibit federal funding to any entity, such as Planned Parenthood, that performs abortions and receives more than $350 million a year in Medicaid funds. As amended, it would give states the option of receiving federal Medicaid funding as a block grant with greater state flexibility in how the funds are used, and would require states to establish their own essential health benefits standards. It would allow states to receive waivers to exempt insurers from having to provide certain minimum benefits, would provide $8 billion over five years for individuals with pre-existing conditions whose insurance premiums increased because the state was granted a waiver to raise premiums based on an individual's health status, and would create a $15 billion federal risk sharing program to cover some of the costs of high medical claims. Passed 217-213 : R 217-20; D 0-193. May 4, 2017.

	252	253	254	255	256
ALABAMA					
1 Byrne	Y	Y	Y	Y	Y
2 Roby	Y	Y	Y	Y	Y
3 Rogers	Y	Y	N	Y	Y
4 Aderholt	Y	Y	?	Y	Y
5 Brooks	Y	Y	Y	Y	Y
6 Palmer	Y	Y	Y	Y	Y
7 Sewell	N	N	N	Y	N
ALASKA					
AL Young	Y	Y	N	Y	Y
ARIZONA					
1 O'Halleran	N	N	N	Y	N
2 McSally	Y	Y	Y	Y	Y
3 Grijalva	N	N	N	Y	N
4 Gosar	Y	Y	Y	Y	Y
5 Biggs	Y	Y	Y	Y	N
6 Schweikert	Y	Y	Y	Y	Y
7 Gallego	N	N	N	Y	N
8 Franks	Y	Y	N	Y	Y
9 Sinema	N	N	Y	Y	N
ARKANSAS					
1 Crawford	Y	Y	Y	Y	Y
2 Hill	Y	Y	N	Y	Y
3 Womack	Y	Y	Y	Y	Y
4 Westerman	Y	Y	Y	Y	Y
CALIFORNIA					
1 LaMalfa	Y	Y	Y	Y	Y
2 Huffman	N	N	Y	Y	N
3 Garamendi	N	N	Y	Y	N
4 McClintock	Y	Y	Y	Y	Y
5 Thompson	N	N	N	Y	N
6 Matsui	N	N	N	Y	N
7 Bera	N	N	N	Y	N
8 Cook	Y	Y	Y	Y	Y
9 McNerney	N	N	N	Y	N
10 Denham	Y	Y	N	Y	Y
11 DeSaulnier	N	N	N	Y	N
12 Pelosi	N	?	?	Y	N
13 Lee	N	N	N	Y	N
14 Speier	N	N	Y	Y	N
15 Swalwell	N	N	N	Y	N
16 Costa	N	N	N	Y	N
17 Khanna	N	N	N	Y	N
18 Eshoo	N	N	Y	Y	N
19 Lofgren	N	N	N	Y	N
20 Panetta	N	N	N	Y	N
21 Valadao	Y	Y	N	Y	Y
22 Nunes	Y	Y	Y	Y	Y
23 McCarthy	Y	Y	Y	Y	Y
24 Carbajal	N	N	N	Y	N
25 Knight	Y	Y	N	Y	Y
26 Brownley	N	N	N	Y	N
27 Chu	N	N	N	Y	N
28 Schiff	N	N	N	Y	N
29 Cardenas	N	N	N	Y	N
30 Sherman	N	N	N	Y	N
31 Aguilar	N	N	N	Y	N
32 Napolitano	N	N	N	Y	N
33 Lieu	N	N	N	Y	N
34 Vacant					
35 Torres	N	N	N	Y	N
36 Ruiz	N	N	Y	Y	N
37 Bass	N	N	N	Y	N
38 Sánchez, Linda	N	N	N	Y	N
39 Royce	Y	Y	Y	Y	Y
40 Roybal-Allard	N	N	N	Y	N
41 Takano	N	N	Y	Y	N
42 Calvert	Y	Y	Y	Y	Y
43 Waters	N	N	N	Y	N
44 Barragan	N	N	N	Y	N
45 Walters	Y	Y	N	Y	Y
46 Correa	N	N	N	Y	N
47 Lowenthal	N	N	Y	Y	N
48 Rohrabacher	Y	Y	N	Y	Y
49 Issa	Y	Y	N	Y	Y
50 Hunter	Y	Y	Y	Y	Y
51 Vargas	N	N	N	Y	N
52 Peters	N	N	N	Y	N
53 Davis	N	N	Y	Y	N

	252	253	254	255	256
COLORADO					
1 DeGette	N	N	N	Y	N
2 Polis	N	N	Y	Y	N
3 Tipton	Y	Y	N	Y	Y
4 Buck	Y	Y	Y	Y	Y
5 Lamborn	Y	Y	Y	Y	Y
6 Coffman	Y	Y	N	Y	Y
7 Perlmutter	N	N	N	Y	N
CONNECTICUT					
1 Larson	N	N	N	Y	N
2 Courtney	N	N	N	Y	N
3 DeLauro	N	N	+	Y	N
4 Himes	N	N	N	Y	N
5 Esty	N	N	Y	Y	N
DELAWARE					
AL Blunt Rochester	N	N	N	Y	N
FLORIDA					
1 Gaetz	Y	Y	N	Y	Y
2 Dunn	Y	Y	Y	Y	Y
3 Yoho	Y	Y	Y	Y	Y
4 Rutherford	Y	Y	Y	Y	Y
5 Lawson	N	N	N	Y	N
6 DeSantis	Y	Y	Y	Y	Y
7 Murphy	N	N	N	Y	N
8 Posey	Y	Y	Y	Y	Y
9 Soto	N	N	N	Y	N
10 Demings	N	N	N	Y	N
11 Webster	Y	Y	Y	Y	Y
12 Bilirakis	Y	Y	Y	Y	Y
13 Crist	N	N	N	Y	N
14 Castor	N	N	N	Y	N
15 Ross	Y	Y	Y	Y	Y
16 Buchanan	Y	Y	Y	Y	Y
17 Rooney, T.	Y	Y	Y	Y	Y
18 Mast	Y	Y	N	Y	Y
19 Rooney, F.	Y	Y	Y	Y	Y
20 Hastings	N	N	N	Y	N
21 Frankel	N	N	N	Y	N
22 Deutch	N	N	Y	Y	N
23 Wasserman Schultz	N	N	Y	Y	N
24 Wilson	N	N	N	Y	N
25 Diaz-Balart	Y	Y	N	Y	Y
26 Curbelo	Y	Y	Y	Y	Y
27 Ros-Lehtinen	Y	Y	N	Y	N
GEORGIA					
1 Carter	Y	Y	N	Y	Y
2 Bishop	N	N	N	Y	N
3 Ferguson	Y	Y	Y	Y	Y
4 Johnson	N	N	N	Y	N
5 Lewis	N	N	N	Y	N
7 Woodall	Y	Y	N	Y	Y
8 Scott, A.	Y	Y	Y	Y	Y
9 Collins	Y	Y	Y	Y	Y
10 Hice	Y	Y	Y	Y	Y
11 Loudermilk	Y	Y	Y	Y	Y
12 Allen	Y	Y	Y	Y	Y
13 Scott, D.	N	N	Y	Y	N
14 Graves	Y	Y	N	Y	Y
HAWAII					
1 Hanabusa	N	N	N	Y	N
2 Gabbard	N	N	Y	Y	N
IDAHO					
1 Labrador	Y	Y	Y	Y	Y
2 Simpson	Y	Y	Y	Y	Y
ILLINOIS					
1 Rush	N	N	N	Y	N
2 Kelly	N	N	N	Y	N
3 Lipinski	N	N	Y	Y	N
4 Gutierrez	N	N	N	Y	N
5 Quigley	N	N	Y	Y	N
6 Roskam	Y	Y	Y	Y	Y
7 Davis, D.	N	N	N	Y	N
8 Krishnamoorthi	N	N	N	Y	N
9 Schakowsky	N	N	N	Y	N
10 Schneider	N	N	N	Y	N
11 Foster	N	N	N	Y	N
12 Bost	Y	Y	N	Y	Y
13 Davis, R.	Y	Y	N	Y	Y
14 Hultgren	Y	Y	Y	Y	Y
15 Shimkus	Y	Y	Y	Y	Y

KEY	**Republicans**	Democrats	*Independents*	
Y Voted for (yea)		X Paired against		C Voted "present" to avoid possible conflict of interest
# Paired for		- Announced against		
+ Announced for		P Voted "present"		? Did not vote or otherwise make a position known
N Voted against (nay)				

	252	253	254	255	256
16 Kinzinger	Y	Y	N	Y	Y
17 Bustos	N	N	Y	Y	N
18 LaHood	Y	Y	N	Y	Y
INDIANA					
1 Visclosky	N	N	N	Y	N
2 **Walorski**	Y	Y	Y	Y	Y
3 **Banks**	Y	Y	Y	Y	Y
4 **Rokita**	Y	Y	N	Y	Y
5 **Brooks**	Y	Y	Y	Y	Y
6 **Messer**	Y	Y	Y	Y	Y
7 Carson	N	N	N	Y	N
8 **Bucshon**	Y	Y	Y	Y	Y
9 **Hollingsworth**	Y	Y	Y	Y	Y
IOWA					
1 **Blum**	Y	Y	N	Y	Y
2 Loebsack	N	N	N	Y	N
3 **Young**	Y	Y	Y	Y	Y
4 **King**	Y	Y	Y	Y	Y
KANSAS					
1 **Marshall**	Y	Y	N	Y	Y
2 **Jenkins**	Y	Y	N	Y	Y
3 **Yoder**	Y	Y	N	Y	Y
4 **Estes**	Y	Y	Y	Y	Y
KENTUCKY					
1 **Comer**	Y	Y	Y	Y	Y
2 **Guthrie**	Y	Y	Y	Y	Y
3 Yarmuth	N	N	Y	Y	N
4 **Massie**	Y	Y	Y	Y	N
5 **Rogers**	Y	Y	Y	Y	Y
6 **Barr**	Y	Y	Y	Y	Y
LOUISIANA					
1 **Scalise**	Y	Y	Y	Y	Y
2 Richmond	N	N	N	Y	N
3 **Higgins**	Y	Y	Y	Y	Y
4 **Johnson**	Y	Y	Y	Y	Y
5 **Abraham**	Y	Y	Y	Y	Y
6 **Graves**	Y	Y	N	Y	Y
MAINE					
1 Pingree	N	N	Y	Y	N
2 **Poliquin**	Y	Y	N	Y	Y
MARYLAND					
1 **Harris**	Y	Y	Y	Y	Y
2 Ruppersberger	N	N	Y	Y	N
3 Sarbanes	N	N	N	Y	N
4 Brown	N	N	N	Y	N
5 Hoyer	N	N	N	?	N
6 Delaney	N	N	N	Y	N
7 Cummings	N	N	N	Y	N
8 Raskin	N	N	N	Y	N
MASSACHUSETTS					
1 Neal	N	N	N	Y	N
2 McGovern	N	N	N	Y	N
3 Tsongas	N	N	N	Y	N
4 Kennedy	N	N	N	Y	N
5 Clark	N	N	N	Y	N
6 Moulton	N	N	N	Y	N
7 Capuano	N	N	N	Y	N
8 Lynch	N	N	N	Y	N
9 Keating	N	N	N	Y	N
MICHIGAN					
1 **Bergman**	Y	Y	N	Y	Y
2 **Huizenga**	Y	Y	N	Y	Y
3 **Amash**	Y	Y	N	Y	Y
4 **Moolenaar**	Y	Y	Y	Y	Y
5 Kildee	N	N	Y	Y	N
6 **Upton**	Y	Y	N	Y	Y
7 **Walberg**	Y	Y	Y	Y	Y
8 **Bishop**	Y	Y	N	Y	Y
9 Levin	N	N	Y	Y	N
10 **Mitchell**	Y	Y	N	Y	Y
11 **Trott**	Y	Y	N	Y	Y
12 Dingell	N	N	N	Y	N
13 Conyers	N	N	N	Y	N
14 Lawrence	N	N	N	Y	N
MINNESOTA					
1 Walz	N	N	Y	Y	N
2 **Lewis**	Y	Y	Y	Y	Y
3 **Paulsen**	Y	Y	N	Y	Y
4 McCollum	N	N	Y	Y	N
5 Ellison	N	N	Y	Y	N
6 **Emmer**	Y	Y	N	Y	Y
7 Peterson	N	N	N	Y	N
8 Nolan	N	N	?	Y	N
MISSISSIPPI					
1 **Kelly**	Y	Y	Y	Y	Y
2 Thompson	N	N	N	Y	N
3 **Harper**	Y	Y	Y	Y	Y
4 **Palazzo**	Y	Y	Y	Y	Y
MISSOURI					
1 Clay	N	N	Y	Y	N
2 **Wagner**	Y	Y	Y	Y	Y
3 **Luetkemeyer**	Y	Y	Y	Y	Y
4 **Hartzler**	Y	Y	Y	Y	Y
5 Cleaver	N	N	N	Y	N
6 **Graves**	Y	Y	Y	Y	Y
7 **Long**	Y	Y	Y	Y	Y
8 **Smith**	Y	Y	Y	Y	Y
MONTANA					
AL **Vacant**					
NEBRASKA					
1 **Fortenberry**	Y	Y	Y	Y	Y
2 **Bacon**	Y	Y	Y	Y	Y
3 **Smith**	Y	Y	Y	Y	Y
NEVADA					
1 Titus	N	N	Y	Y	N
2 **Amodei**	Y	Y	Y	Y	Y
3 Rosen	N	N	Y	Y	N
4 Kihuen	N	N	N	Y	N
NEW HAMPSHIRE					
1 Shea-Porter	N	N	Y	Y	N
2 Kuster	N	N	Y	Y	N
NEW JERSEY					
1 Norcross	N	N	N	Y	N
2 **LoBiondo**	Y	Y	N	Y	N
3 **MacArthur**	Y	Y	N	Y	Y
4 **Smith**	Y	Y	N	Y	Y
5 Gottheimer	N	N	N	Y	N
6 Pallone	N	N	N	Y	N
7 **Lance**	Y	Y	N	Y	Y
8 Sires	N	N	N	Y	N
9 Pascrell	N	N	N	Y	N
10 Payne	N	N	N	Y	N
11 **Frelinghuysen**	Y	Y	Y	Y	Y
12 Watson Coleman	N	N	N	Y	N
NEW MEXICO					
1 Lujan Grisham	N	N	Y	Y	N
2 **Pearce**	Y	Y	Y	Y	Y
3 Luján	N	N	N	Y	N
NEW YORK					
1 **Zeldin**	Y	Y	Y	Y	Y
2 **King**	Y	Y	Y	Y	Y
3 Suozzi	N	N	Y	Y	N
4 Rice	N	N	Y	Y	N
5 Meeks	N	N	Y	Y	N
6 Meng	N	N	Y	Y	N
7 Velázquez	N	N	N	Y	N
8 Jeffries	N	N	N	Y	N
9 Clarke	N	N	N	Y	N
10 Nadler	N	N	N	Y	N
11 **Donovan**	Y	Y	Y	Y	Y
12 Maloney, C.	N	N	N	Y	N
13 Espaillat	N	N	N	Y	N
14 Crowley	N	N	N	Y	N
15 Serrano	N	N	N	Y	N
16 Engel	?	?	?	Y	N
17 Lowey	N	N	N	Y	N
18 Maloney, S.P.	N	N	N	Y	N
19 **Faso**	Y	Y	N	Y	Y
20 Tonko	N	N	P	Y	N
21 **Stefanik**	Y	Y	N	Y	Y
22 **Tenney**	Y	Y	N	Y	Y
23 **Reed**	Y	Y	N	Y	Y
24 **Katko**	Y	Y	N	Y	Y
25 Slaughter	N	N	N	Y	N
26 Higgins	N	N	N	Y	N
27 **Collins**	Y	Y	Y	Y	Y
NORTH CAROLINA					
1 Butterfield	N	N	?	Y	N
2 **Holding**	Y	Y	N	Y	Y
3 **Jones**	N	N	N	Y	N
4 Price	N	N	N	Y	N
5 **Foxx**	Y	Y	N	Y	Y
6 **Walker**	Y	Y	Y	Y	Y
7 **Rouzer**	Y	Y	N	Y	Y
8 **Hudson**	Y	Y	N	Y	Y
9 **Pittenger**	Y	Y	N	Y	Y
10 **McHenry**	Y	Y	Y	Y	Y
11 **Meadows**	Y	Y	Y	Y	Y
12 Adams	N	N	N	Y	N
13 **Budd**	Y	Y	Y	Y	Y
NORTH DAKOTA					
AL **Cramer**	Y	Y	Y	Y	Y
OHIO					
1 **Chabot**	Y	Y	Y	Y	Y
2 **Wenstrup**	Y	Y	Y	Y	Y
3 Beatty	N	N	N	Y	N
4 **Jordan**	Y	Y	N	Y	Y
5 **Latta**	Y	Y	Y	Y	Y
6 **Johnson**	Y	Y	N	Y	Y
7 **Gibbs**	Y	Y	Y	Y	Y
8 **Davidson**	Y	Y	Y	Y	Y
9 Kaptur	N	N	N	Y	N
10 **Turner**	Y	Y	N	Y	N
11 Fudge	N	N	N	Y	N
12 **Tiberi**	Y	Y	Y	Y	Y
13 Ryan	N	N	N	Y	N
14 **Joyce**	Y	Y	Y	Y	Y
15 **Stivers**	Y	Y	Y	Y	Y
16 **Renacci**	Y	Y	N	Y	Y
OKLAHOMA					
1 **Bridenstine**	Y	Y	Y	Y	Y
2 **Mullin**	Y	Y	Y	Y	Y
3 **Lucas**	Y	Y	Y	Y	Y
4 **Cole**	Y	Y	Y	Y	Y
5 **Russell**	Y	Y	Y	Y	Y
OREGON					
1 Bonamici	N	N	Y	Y	N
2 **Walden**	Y	Y	Y	Y	Y
3 Blumenauer	N	N	Y	Y	N
4 DeFazio	N	N	N	Y	N
5 Schrader	N	N	N	Y	N
PENNSYLVANIA					
1 Brady	N	N	N	Y	N
2 Evans	N	N	Y	Y	N
3 **Kelly**	Y	Y	Y	Y	Y
4 **Perry**	Y	Y	Y	Y	Y
5 **Thompson**	Y	Y	Y	Y	Y
6 **Costello**	Y	Y	Y	Y	Y
7 **Meehan**	Y	Y	?	Y	N
8 **Fitzpatrick**	Y	Y	N	Y	Y
9 **Shuster**	Y	Y	Y	Y	Y
10 **Marino**	Y	Y	Y	Y	Y
11 **Barletta**	Y	Y	Y	Y	Y
12 **Rothfus**	Y	Y	Y	Y	Y
13 Boyle	N	N	N	Y	N
14 Doyle	N	N	N	Y	N
15 **Dent**	Y	Y	Y	Y	N
16 **Smucker**	Y	Y	Y	Y	Y
17 Cartwright	N	N	Y	Y	N
18 **Murphy**	Y	Y	Y	Y	Y
RHODE ISLAND					
1 Cicilline	N	N	N	Y	N
2 Langevin	N	N	N	Y	N
SOUTH CAROLINA					
1 **Sanford**	Y	Y	N	Y	Y
2 **Wilson**	Y	Y	Y	Y	Y
3 **Duncan**	Y	Y	Y	Y	Y
4 **Gowdy**	Y	Y	Y	Y	Y
6 Clyburn	N	N	N	Y	N
7 **Rice**	Y	Y	P	Y	Y
SOUTH DAKOTA					
AL **Noem**	Y	Y	Y	Y	Y
TENNESSEE					
1 **Roe**	Y	Y	Y	Y	Y
2 **Duncan**	Y	Y	Y	Y	Y
3 **Fleischmann**	Y	Y	Y	Y	Y
4 **DesJarlais**	Y	Y	Y	Y	Y
5 Cooper	N	N	Y	Y	N
6 **Black**	Y	Y	Y	Y	Y
7 **Blackburn**	Y	Y	Y	Y	Y
8 **Kustoff**	Y	Y	Y	Y	Y
9 Cohen	N	N	N	Y	N
TEXAS					
1 **Gohmert**	Y	Y	?	Y	Y
2 **Poe**	Y	Y	N	Y	Y
3 **Johnson, S.**	Y	Y	Y	Y	Y
4 **Ratcliffe**	Y	Y	N	Y	Y
5 **Hensarling**	Y	Y	N	Y	Y
6 **Barton**	Y	Y	Y	Y	Y
7 **Culberson**	Y	Y	Y	Y	Y
8 **Brady**	Y	Y	Y	Y	Y
9 Green, A.	N	N	N	Y	N
10 **McCaul**	Y	Y	Y	Y	Y
11 **Conaway**	Y	Y	Y	Y	Y
12 **Granger**	Y	Y	Y	Y	Y
13 **Thornberry**	Y	Y	Y	Y	Y
14 **Weber**	Y	Y	Y	Y	Y
15 Gonzalez	N	N	Y	Y	N
16 O'Rourke	N	N	Y	Y	N
17 **Flores**	Y	Y	N	Y	Y
18 Jackson Lee	N	N	N	Y	N
19 **Arrington**	Y	Y	Y	Y	Y
20 Castro	N	N	Y	Y	N
21 **Smith**	Y	Y	Y	Y	Y
22 **Olson**	Y	Y	Y	Y	Y
23 **Hurd**	Y	Y	N	Y	Y
24 **Marchant**	Y	Y	Y	Y	Y
25 **Williams**	Y	Y	Y	Y	Y
26 **Burgess**	Y	Y	Y	Y	Y
27 **Farenthold**	Y	Y	Y	Y	Y
28 Cuellar	N	N	N	Y	N
29 Green, G.	N	N	N	Y	N
30 Johnson, E.B.	N	N	N	Y	N
31 **Carter**	Y	Y	Y	Y	Y
32 **Sessions**	Y	Y	Y	Y	Y
33 Veasey	N	N	N	Y	N
34 Vela	N	N	N	Y	N
35 Doggett	N	N	N	Y	N
36 **Babin**	Y	Y	Y	Y	Y
UTAH					
1 **Bishop**	Y	Y	Y	Y	Y
2 **Stewart**	Y	Y	Y	Y	Y
3 **Chaffetz**	Y	Y	Y	Y	Y
4 **Love**	Y	Y	Y	Y	Y
VERMONT					
AL Welch	N	N	N	Y	N
VIRGINIA					
1 **Wittman**	Y	Y	Y	Y	Y
2 **Taylor**	Y	Y	Y	Y	Y
3 Scott	N	N	Y	Y	N
4 McEachin	N	N	Y	Y	N
5 **Garrett**	Y	Y	Y	Y	Y
6 **Goodlatte**	Y	Y	Y	Y	Y
7 **Brat**	Y	Y	Y	Y	Y
8 Beyer	N	N	Y	Y	N
9 **Griffith**	Y	Y	Y	Y	Y
10 **Comstock**	Y	Y	N	Y	Y
11 Connolly	N	N	N	Y	N
WASHINGTON					
1 DelBene	N	N	Y	Y	N
2 Larsen	N	N	Y	Y	N
3 **Herrera Beutler**	Y	Y	Y	Y	N
4 **Newhouse**	?	?	?	?	?
5 **McMorris Rodgers**	Y	Y	Y	Y	Y
6 Kilmer	N	N	N	Y	N
7 Jayapal	N	N	N	Y	N
8 **Reichert**	Y	Y	N	Y	Y
9 Smith	N	N	Y	Y	N
10 Heck	N	N	Y	Y	N
WEST VIRGINIA					
1 **McKinley**	Y	Y	N	Y	Y
2 **Mooney**	Y	Y	Y	Y	Y
3 **Jenkins**	Y	Y	N	Y	Y
WISCONSIN					
1 **Ryan**				Y	Y
2 Pocan	N	N	N	Y	N
3 Kind	N	N	N	Y	N
4 Moore	N	N	N	Y	N
5 **Sensenbrenner**	Y	Y	Y	Y	Y
6 **Grothman**	Y	Y	Y	Y	Y
7 **Duffy**	Y	Y	Y	Y	Y
8 **Gallagher**	Y	Y	N	Y	Y
WYOMING					
AL **Cheney**	Y	Y	Y	Y	Y

VOTE NUMBER

257. HR 1644. NORTH KOREAN SANCTIONS/PASSAGE. Royce, R-Calif., motion to suspend the rules and pass the bill that would mandate sanctions against any foreign person who buys certain minerals or metals from North Korea or provides certain types of fuel for military use to the country. The bill would require U.S. financial institutions to terminate any correspondent accounts used to do business with foreign financial institutions if the account provides financial services to the North Korean government. Motion agreed to 419-1 : R 232-1; D 187-0. May 4, 2017.

258. HR 1616. NATIONAL COMPUTER FORENSICS INSTITUTE AUTHORIZATION/PASSAGE. Goodlatte, R-Va., motion to suspend the rules and pass the bill that would formally authorize, for fiscal 2017 through fiscal 2022, the National Computer Forensics Institute within the Homeland Security Department to educate and train state and local law enforcement officers, prosecutors and judges on cybercrime and electronic crimes. It would require the institute to disseminate homeland security information related to the investigation and prevention of cybercrime and electronic crimes. Motion agreed to 408-3 : R 224-3; D 184-0. May 16, 2017.

259. H RES 323, HR 115. DEATH SENTENCE AGGRAVATING FACTOR EXPANSION/PREVIOUS QUESTION. Buck, R-Colo., motion to order the previous question (thus ending debate and possibility of amendment) on the rule (H Res 323) that would provide for House floor consideration of the bill that would require courts and juries to consider if a defendant killed or attempted to kill a state law enforcement officer, local law enforcement officer or first responder as an aggravating factor when determining whether to impose the death sentence on a defendant. Motion agreed to 230-189 : R 230-1; D 0-188. May 17, 2017.

260. H RES 323, HR 115. DEATH SENTENCE AGGRAVATING FACTOR EXPANSION/RULE. Adoption of the rule (H Res 323) that would provide for House floor consideration of the bill that would provide for House floor consideration of the bill that would require courts and juries to consider if a defendant killed or attempted to kill a state law enforcement officer, local law enforcement officer or first responder as an aggravating factor when determining whether to impose the death sentence on a defendant. Adopted 233-184 : R 231-0; D 2-184. May 17, 2017.

261. PRESIDENT'S TAX RETURN DISCLOSURE/MOTION TO TABLE. Rothfus, R-Pa., motion to table (kill) the Pascrell, D-N.J., motion to appeal the ruling of the Chair that the Pascrell resolution related to the disclosure of President Trump's tax returns does not constitute a question of the privileges of the House. Motion agreed to 229-188 : R 229-1; D 0-187. May 17, 2017.

262. HR 1177. CITY OF OLD TOWN, MAINE LAND USE RESTRICTIONS/PASSAGE. Davis, R-Ill., motion to suspend the rules and pass the bill that would require the secretary of Agriculture, if requested by the City of Old Town, Maine, to remove restrictions on the use of land previously transferred to the city for its airport. Motion agreed to 418-1 : R 231-1; D 187-0. May 17, 2017.

263. HR 1039, H RES 324. PROBATION OFFICER ARREST AUTHORITY/PREVIOUS QUESTION. Collins, R-Ga., motion to order the previous question (thus ending debate and possibility of amendment) on the rule (H Res 324) that would provide for House floor consideration of the bill that would authorize probation officers, during the course of their official duties, to arrest an individual without a warrant if there is probable cause that the individual has assaulted or impeded the officer. Motion agreed to 226-188 : R 226-1; D 0-187. May 18, 2017.

	257	258	259	260	261	262	263
ALABAMA							
1 **Byrne**	Y	Y	Y	Y	Y	Y	Y
2 **Roby**	Y	Y	Y	Y	Y	Y	Y
3 **Rogers**	Y	Y	Y	Y	Y	Y	Y
4 **Aderholt**	?	Y	Y	Y	Y	Y	Y
5 **Brooks**	Y	?	Y	Y	Y	Y	Y
6 **Palmer**	Y	Y	Y	Y	Y	Y	Y
7 Sewell	Y	Y	N	N	N	Y	N
ALASKA							
AL **Young**	Y	Y	Y	Y	Y	Y	Y
ARIZONA							
1 O'Halleran	Y	Y	N	N	N	Y	N
2 **McSally**	Y	Y	Y	Y	Y	Y	Y
3 Grijalva	Y	?	N	N	N	Y	N
4 **Gosar**	Y	Y	Y	Y	Y	Y	Y
5 **Biggs**	Y	Y	Y	Y	Y	Y	Y
6 **Schweikert**	Y	Y	Y	Y	Y	Y	Y
7 Gallego	Y	Y	N	N	N	Y	N
8 **Franks**	Y	Y	Y	?	Y	Y	Y
9 Sinema	Y	+	N	N	N	Y	N
ARKANSAS							
1 **Crawford**	Y	Y	Y	Y	Y	Y	?
2 **Hill**	Y	Y	Y	Y	Y	Y	Y
3 **Womack**	Y	Y	Y	Y	Y	Y	Y
4 **Westerman**	Y	Y	Y	Y	Y	Y	Y
CALIFORNIA							
1 **LaMalfa**	Y	Y	Y	Y	Y	Y	Y
2 Huffman	Y	Y	N	N	N	Y	N
3 Garamendi	Y	Y	N	N	N	Y	N
4 **McClintock**	Y	Y	Y	Y	Y	Y	Y
5 Thompson	Y	Y	N	N	N	Y	N
6 Matsui	Y	Y	N	N	N	Y	N
7 Bera	Y	Y	N	N	N	Y	N
8 **Cook**	Y	Y	Y	Y	Y	Y	Y
9 McNerney	Y	Y	N	N	N	Y	N
10 **Denham**	Y	Y	Y	Y	Y	Y	Y
11 DeSaulnier	Y	Y	N	N	N	Y	N
12 Pelosi	Y	?	?	?	?	?	N
13 Lee	Y	Y	N	N	N	Y	N
14 Speier	Y	Y	N	N	N	Y	–
15 Swalwell	Y	Y	N	N	N	Y	–
16 Costa	Y	Y	N	N	N	Y	N
17 Khanna	Y	Y	N	N	N	Y	N
18 Eshoo	Y	Y	N	N	N	Y	N
19 Lofgren	Y	Y	N	N	N	Y	N
20 Panetta	Y	Y	N	N	N	Y	N
21 **Valadao**	Y	Y	Y	Y	Y	Y	Y
22 **Nunes**	Y	Y	Y	Y	?	?	Y
23 **McCarthy**	Y	Y	Y	Y	Y	Y	Y
24 Carbajal	Y	Y	N	N	N	Y	N
25 **Knight**	Y	Y	Y	Y	Y	Y	?
26 Brownley	Y	Y	N	N	N	Y	N
27 Chu	Y	Y	?	?	N	Y	N
28 Schiff	Y	Y	N	N	?	?	N
29 Cardenas	Y	Y	N	N	N	Y	N
30 Sherman	Y	Y	N	N	N	Y	N
31 Aguilar	Y	Y	N	N	N	Y	N
32 Napolitano	Y	?	–	–	–	+	–
33 Lieu	Y	?	?	?	N	Y	N
34 Vacant							
35 Torres	?	Y	N	N	N	Y	N
36 Ruiz	Y	Y	N	N	N	Y	N
37 Bass	Y	Y	N	N	N	Y	N
38 Sánchez, Linda	Y	Y	N	N	N	Y	N
39 **Royce**	Y	Y	Y	Y	Y	Y	Y
40 Roybal-Allard	Y	?	N	N	N	Y	N
41 Takano	Y	Y	N	?	N	Y	N
42 **Calvert**	Y	Y	Y	Y	Y	Y	Y
43 Waters	Y	Y	N	N	N	Y	N
44 Barragan	Y	Y	N	N	N	Y	N
45 **Walters**	Y	Y	Y	Y	Y	Y	Y
46 Correa	Y	Y	N	N	N	Y	N
47 Lowenthal	Y	Y	N	N	N	Y	N
48 **Rohrabacher**	Y	?	Y	Y	Y	Y	Y
49 **Issa**	Y	Y	Y	Y	Y	Y	Y
50 **Hunter**	Y	?	Y	Y	Y	Y	Y
51 Vargas	Y	Y	N	N	N	Y	N
52 Peters	Y	Y	N	N	N	Y	N
53 Davis	Y	Y	N	N	N	Y	N

	257	258	259	260	261	262	263
COLORADO							
1 DeGette	Y	Y	N	N	N	Y	N
2 Polis	Y	Y	N	N	N	Y	N
3 **Tipton**	Y	Y	Y	Y	Y	Y	Y
4 **Buck**	Y	Y	Y	Y	Y	Y	Y
5 **Lamborn**	Y	Y	Y	Y	Y	Y	Y
6 **Coffman**	Y	Y	Y	Y	Y	Y	Y
7 Perlmutter	Y	?	N	N	N	Y	N
CONNECTICUT							
1 Larson	Y	Y	N	N	N	Y	N
2 Courtney	Y	Y	N	N	N	Y	N
3 DeLauro	Y	Y	N	N	N	Y	N
4 Himes	Y	Y	N	N	N	Y	N
5 Esty	Y	Y	N	N	N	Y	N
DELAWARE							
AL Blunt Rochester	Y	Y	N	N	N	Y	N
FLORIDA							
1 **Gaetz**	Y	Y	Y	Y	Y	Y	Y
2 **Dunn**	Y	Y	Y	Y	Y	Y	Y
3 **Yoho**	Y	Y	Y	Y	Y	Y	Y
4 **Rutherford**	Y	Y	Y	Y	Y	Y	Y
5 Lawson	Y	Y	N	N	N	Y	N
6 **DeSantis**	Y	Y	Y	?	Y	Y	Y
7 Murphy	Y	Y	N	Y	N	Y	N
8 **Posey**	Y	Y	Y	Y	Y	Y	Y
9 Soto	Y	Y	N	N	N	Y	N
10 Demings	Y	Y	N	N	N	Y	N
11 **Webster**	Y	Y	Y	Y	Y	Y	Y
12 **Bilirakis**	Y	Y	Y	Y	Y	Y	Y
13 Crist	Y	Y	N	N	N	Y	N
14 Castor	?	Y	N	N	N	Y	N
15 **Ross**	Y	Y	Y	Y	Y	Y	Y
16 **Buchanan**	Y	Y	Y	Y	Y	Y	Y
17 **Rooney, T.**	Y	?	Y	Y	Y	Y	?
18 **Mast**	Y	Y	Y	Y	Y	Y	Y
19 **Rooney, F.**	Y	Y	Y	Y	Y	Y	Y
20 Hastings	Y	Y	N	N	N	Y	N
21 Frankel	+	Y	N	N	N	Y	N
22 Deutch	Y	Y	N	N	N	Y	N
23 Wasserman Schultz	Y	Y	N	N	N	Y	N
24 Wilson	Y	Y	N	N	N	Y	N
25 **Diaz-Balart**	Y	Y	Y	Y	Y	Y	Y
26 **Curbelo**	Y	Y	Y	Y	Y	Y	Y
27 **Ros-Lehtinen**	Y	Y	Y	Y	Y	Y	Y
GEORGIA							
1 **Carter**	Y	Y	Y	Y	Y	Y	Y
2 Bishop	Y	Y	N	N	N	Y	N
3 **Ferguson**	Y	Y	Y	Y	Y	Y	Y
4 Johnson	Y	Y	N	N	N	Y	N
5 Lewis	Y	Y	N	N	N	Y	N
7 **Woodall**	Y	Y	Y	Y	Y	Y	Y
8 **Scott, A.**	Y	Y	Y	Y	Y	Y	Y
9 **Collins**	Y	Y	Y	Y	Y	Y	Y
10 **Hice**	Y	Y	Y	Y	Y	Y	Y
11 **Loudermilk**	Y	Y	Y	Y	Y	Y	Y
12 **Allen**	Y	Y	Y	Y	Y	Y	Y
13 Scott, D.	Y	Y	N	N	N	Y	N
14 **Graves**	Y	Y	Y	Y	Y	Y	Y
HAWAII							
1 Hanabusa	Y	Y	N	N	N	Y	N
2 Gabbard	Y	Y	N	N	N	Y	N
IDAHO							
1 **Labrador**	Y	Y	Y	Y	Y	Y	Y
2 **Simpson**	Y	Y	Y	Y	Y	Y	Y
ILLINOIS							
1 Rush	Y	Y	N	N	N	Y	N
2 Kelly	Y	Y	N	N	N	Y	N
3 Lipinski	Y	Y	N	N	N	Y	N
4 Gutierrez	Y	?	?	?	?	?	?
5 Quigley	Y	Y	N	N	N	Y	N
6 **Roskam**	Y	Y	Y	Y	Y	Y	Y
7 Davis, D.	Y	Y	N	N	N	Y	N
8 Krishnamoorthi	Y	Y	N	N	N	Y	N
9 Schakowsky	Y	Y	N	N	N	Y	N
10 Schneider	Y	Y	N	N	N	Y	N
11 Foster	Y	Y	N	N	N	Y	N
12 **Bost**	Y	Y	Y	Y	Y	Y	Y
13 **Davis, R.**	Y	Y	Y	Y	Y	Y	Y
14 **Hultgren**	Y	Y	Y	Y	Y	Y	Y
15 **Shimkus**	Y	Y	Y	Y	Y	Y	Y

	257	258	259	260	261	262	263
16 **Kinzinger**	Y	Y	Y	Y	Y	Y	Y
17 Bustos	Y	Y	N	N	N	Y	N
18 **LaHood**	Y	Y	Y	Y	Y	Y	Y
INDIANA							
1 Visclosky	Y	Y	N	N	N	Y	N
2 **Walorski**	Y	Y	Y	Y	Y	Y	Y
3 **Banks**	Y	Y	Y	Y	Y	Y	Y
4 **Rokita**	Y	Y	Y	Y	Y	Y	?
5 **Brooks**	Y	Y	Y	Y	Y	Y	Y
6 **Messer**	Y	Y	Y	Y	Y	Y	Y
7 Carson	Y	Y	N	N	N	Y	N
8 **Bucshon**	Y	Y	Y	Y	Y	Y	Y
9 **Hollingsworth**	Y	Y	Y	Y	Y	Y	Y
IOWA							
1 **Blum**	Y	Y	Y	Y	Y	Y	Y
2 Loebsack	Y	Y	N	N	N	Y	N
3 **Young**	Y	Y	Y	Y	Y	Y	Y
4 **King**	Y	Y	Y	Y	Y	Y	Y
KANSAS							
1 **Marshall**	Y	Y	Y	Y	Y	Y	Y
2 **Jenkins**	Y	Y	Y	Y	Y	Y	Y
3 **Yoder**	Y	Y	Y	Y	Y	Y	Y
4 **Estes**	Y	Y	Y	Y	Y	Y	Y
KENTUCKY							
1 **Comer**	Y	Y	Y	Y	Y	Y	Y
2 **Guthrie**	Y	Y	Y	Y	Y	Y	Y
3 Yarmuth	Y	Y	N	N	N	Y	N
4 **Massie**	N	N	Y	Y	Y	Y	Y
5 **Rogers**	Y	Y	Y	Y	Y	Y	Y
6 **Barr**	Y	Y	Y	Y	Y	Y	Y
LOUISIANA							
1 **Scalise**	Y	Y	Y	Y	Y	Y	Y
2 Richmond	Y	Y	N	N	N	Y	N
3 **Higgins**	Y	Y	Y	Y	Y	Y	Y
4 **Johnson**	Y	Y	Y	Y	Y	Y	Y
5 **Abraham**	Y	Y	Y	Y	Y	Y	Y
6 **Graves**	Y	Y	Y	Y	Y	Y	Y
MAINE							
1 Pingree	Y	Y	N	N	N	Y	N
2 **Poliquin**	Y	Y	Y	Y	Y	Y	Y
MARYLAND							
1 **Harris**	Y	Y	Y	?	Y	Y	Y
2 Ruppersberger	Y	Y	N	N	N	Y	N
3 Sarbanes	Y	Y	N	N	N	Y	N
4 Brown	Y	Y	N	N	N	Y	N
5 Hoyer	Y	Y	N	N	N	Y	N
6 Delaney	Y	Y	N	N	N	Y	N
7 Cummings	Y	Y	N	N	N	Y	N
8 Raskin	?	Y	N	N	N	Y	N
MASSACHUSETTS							
1 Neal	Y	Y	N	N	N	Y	N
2 McGovern	Y	Y	N	N	N	Y	N
3 Tsongas	Y	Y	N	N	N	Y	N
4 Kennedy	Y	Y	N	N	N	Y	N
5 Clark	Y	Y	N	N	N	Y	N
6 Moulton	Y	Y	N	N	N	Y	N
7 Capuano	Y	Y	N	N	N	Y	N
8 Lynch	Y	Y	N	N	N	Y	N
9 Keating	Y	Y	N	N	N	Y	N
MICHIGAN							
1 **Bergman**	Y	Y	Y	Y	Y	Y	Y
2 **Huizenga**	Y	Y	Y	Y	Y	Y	Y
3 **Amash**	Y	N	Y	Y	Y	N	Y
4 **Moolenaar**	Y	Y	Y	Y	Y	Y	Y
5 Kildee	Y	Y	N	N	N	Y	N
6 **Upton**	Y	Y	Y	Y	Y	Y	Y
7 **Walberg**	Y	Y	Y	Y	Y	Y	Y
8 **Bishop**	?	Y	Y	Y	Y	Y	Y
9 Levin	Y	Y	N	N	N	Y	N
10 **Mitchell**	Y	Y	Y	Y	Y	Y	Y
11 **Trott**	Y	Y	Y	Y	Y	Y	Y
12 Dingell	Y	Y	N	N	N	Y	N
13 Conyers	Y	Y	N	N	N	Y	N
14 Lawrence	Y	Y	N	N	N	Y	N
MINNESOTA							
1 Walz	Y	Y	N	N	N	Y	N
2 **Lewis**	Y	Y	Y	Y	Y	Y	Y
3 **Paulsen**	Y	Y	Y	Y	Y	Y	Y
4 McCollum	Y	Y	N	N	N	Y	N

	257	258	259	260	261	262	263
5 Ellison	Y	Y	N	?	N	Y	N
6 **Emmer**	Y	Y	Y	Y	Y	Y	Y
7 Peterson	Y	Y	N	N	N	Y	N
8 Nolan	Y	Y	N	N	N	Y	N
MISSISSIPPI							
1 **Kelly**	Y	Y	Y	Y	Y	Y	Y
2 Thompson	Y	Y	N	N	N	Y	N
3 **Harper**	Y	Y	Y	Y	Y	Y	Y
4 **Palazzo**	Y	Y	Y	Y	Y	Y	Y
MISSOURI							
1 Clay	Y	Y	N	N	N	Y	N
2 **Wagner**	Y	Y	Y	Y	Y	Y	Y
3 **Luetkemeyer**	Y	Y	Y	Y	Y	Y	Y
4 **Hartzler**	Y	Y	Y	Y	Y	Y	Y
5 Cleaver	Y	Y	N	N	N	Y	N
6 **Graves**	Y	Y	Y	Y	Y	Y	Y
7 **Long**	Y	Y	Y	Y	Y	Y	Y
8 **Smith**	Y	Y	Y	Y	Y	Y	Y
MONTANA							
AL **Vacant**							
NEBRASKA							
1 **Fortenberry**	Y	Y	Y	Y	Y	Y	Y
2 **Bacon**	Y	Y	Y	Y	Y	Y	Y
3 **Smith**	Y	Y	Y	Y	Y	Y	Y
NEVADA							
1 Titus	Y	Y	N	N	N	Y	N
2 **Amodei**	Y	Y	Y	Y	Y	Y	Y
3 Rosen	Y	Y	N	N	N	Y	N
4 Kihuen	Y	Y	N	N	N	Y	N
NEW HAMPSHIRE							
1 Shea-Porter	Y	Y	N	N	N	Y	N
2 Kuster	Y	Y	N	N	N	Y	N
NEW JERSEY							
1 Norcross	Y	Y	N	N	N	Y	N
2 **LoBiondo**	Y	Y	Y	Y	Y	Y	Y
3 **MacArthur**	Y	Y	Y	Y	Y	Y	Y
4 **Smith**	Y	Y	Y	Y	Y	Y	Y
5 Gottheimer	Y	Y	N	N	N	Y	N
6 Pallone	Y	Y	N	N	N	Y	N
7 **Lance**	Y	Y	Y	Y	Y	Y	Y
8 Sires	Y	Y	N	N	N	Y	N
9 Pascrell	Y	Y	N	N	N	Y	N
10 Payne	Y	Y	N	N	?	?	N
11 **Frelinghuysen**	Y	Y	Y	Y	Y	Y	Y
12 Watson Coleman	Y	Y	N	N	N	Y	N
NEW MEXICO							
1 Lujan Grisham	Y	Y	N	N	N	Y	N
2 **Pearce**	Y	Y	Y	Y	Y	Y	Y
3 Luján	Y	Y	N	N	N	Y	N
NEW YORK							
1 **Zeldin**	Y	Y	Y	Y	Y	Y	Y
2 **King**	Y	Y	Y	Y	Y	Y	Y
3 Suozzi	Y	Y	N	N	N	Y	N
4 Rice	Y	Y	N	N	N	Y	N
5 Meeks	Y	Y	N	N	N	Y	?
6 Meng	Y	Y	N	N	N	Y	N
7 Velázquez	Y	Y	N	N	N	Y	N
8 Jeffries	Y	Y	N	N	N	Y	N
9 Clarke	Y	Y	N	N	N	Y	N
10 Nadler	Y	Y	N	N	N	Y	N
11 **Donovan**	Y	Y	Y	Y	Y	Y	Y
12 Maloney, C.	Y	Y	N	N	N	Y	N
13 Espaillat	Y	Y	N	N	N	Y	N
14 Crowley	Y	Y	N	N	N	Y	N
15 Serrano	Y	Y	N	N	N	Y	N
16 Engel	Y	Y	N	N	N	Y	N
17 Lowey	Y	Y	N	N	N	Y	N
18 Maloney, S.P.	Y	Y	N	N	N	Y	N
19 **Faso**	Y	Y	Y	Y	Y	Y	Y
20 Tonko	Y	Y	N	N	N	Y	N
21 **Stefanik**	Y	Y	Y	Y	Y	Y	Y
22 **Tenney**	+	Y	Y	Y	Y	Y	Y
23 **Reed**	Y	Y	Y	Y	Y	Y	Y
24 **Katko**	Y	Y	Y	Y	Y	Y	Y
25 Slaughter	Y	Y	N	N	N	Y	N
26 Higgins	?	Y	N	N	–	+	N
27 **Collins**	Y	Y	Y	Y	Y	Y	Y
NORTH CAROLINA							
1 Butterfield	?	Y	N	N	N	Y	N
2 **Holding**	Y	Y	Y	Y	Y	Y	Y
3 **Jones**	Y	N	N	Y	N	Y	N
4 Price	Y	Y	N	N	N	Y	N

	257	258	259	260	261	262	263
5 **Foxx**	Y	Y	Y	Y	Y	Y	Y
6 **Walker**	Y	Y	Y	Y	Y	Y	Y
7 **Rouzer**	Y	Y	Y	Y	Y	Y	Y
8 **Hudson**	Y	Y	Y	Y	Y	Y	Y
9 **Pittenger**	Y	Y	Y	Y	Y	Y	+
10 **McHenry**	Y	Y	Y	Y	Y	Y	Y
11 **Meadows**	Y	Y	Y	Y	Y	Y	Y
12 Adams	Y	Y	N	N	N	Y	N
13 **Budd**	Y	Y	Y	Y	Y	Y	Y
NORTH DAKOTA							
AL **Cramer**	Y	Y	Y	Y	Y	Y	Y
OHIO							
1 **Chabot**	Y	Y	Y	Y	Y	Y	Y
2 **Wenstrup**	Y	Y	Y	Y	Y	Y	Y
3 Beatty	Y	Y	N	N	N	Y	N
4 **Jordan**	Y	Y	Y	Y	Y	Y	Y
5 **Latta**	Y	Y	Y	Y	Y	Y	Y
6 **Johnson**	Y	Y	Y	Y	Y	Y	Y
7 **Gibbs**	Y	Y	Y	Y	Y	Y	Y
8 **Davidson**	Y	Y	Y	Y	Y	Y	Y
9 Kaptur	Y	Y	N	N	N	Y	N
10 **Turner**	Y	Y	Y	Y	Y	Y	Y
11 Fudge	Y	Y	N	N	N	Y	N
12 **Tiberi**	Y	?	Y	Y	Y	Y	Y
13 Ryan	Y	Y	N	N	N	Y	N
14 **Joyce**	Y	Y	Y	Y	Y	Y	Y
15 **Stivers**	Y	Y	Y	Y	Y	Y	Y
16 **Renacci**	Y	Y	Y	Y	Y	Y	Y
OKLAHOMA							
1 **Bridenstine**	Y	Y	Y	Y	Y	Y	Y
2 **Mullin**	Y	Y	Y	Y	Y	Y	Y
3 **Lucas**	Y	Y	Y	Y	Y	Y	Y
4 **Cole**	Y	Y	+	+	+	+	+
5 **Russell**	Y	Y	Y	Y	Y	Y	Y
OREGON							
1 Bonamici	Y	Y	N	N	N	Y	N
2 **Walden**	Y	Y	Y	Y	Y	Y	Y
3 Blumenauer	Y	Y	N	N	N	Y	N
4 DeFazio	Y	Y	N	N	N	Y	N
5 Schrader	Y	Y	N	N	N	Y	N
PENNSYLVANIA							
1 Brady	Y	?	N	N	N	Y	N
2 Evans	Y	Y	N	N	N	Y	N
3 **Kelly**	Y	Y	Y	Y	Y	Y	Y
4 **Perry**	Y	Y	Y	Y	Y	Y	Y
5 **Thompson**	Y	Y	Y	Y	Y	Y	Y
6 **Costello**	Y	Y	Y	Y	Y	Y	Y
7 **Meehan**	Y	Y	Y	Y	Y	Y	Y
8 **Fitzpatrick**	Y	Y	Y	Y	Y	Y	Y
9 **Shuster**	Y	Y	?	Y	Y	Y	Y
10 **Marino**	Y	?	Y	Y	Y	Y	Y
11 **Barletta**	Y	Y	Y	Y	Y	Y	Y
12 **Rothfus**	Y	Y	Y	Y	Y	Y	Y
13 Boyle	Y	Y	N	N	N	Y	N
14 Doyle	Y	Y	N	N	N	Y	N
15 **Dent**	Y	Y	Y	Y	Y	Y	Y
16 **Smucker**	Y	Y	Y	Y	Y	Y	Y
17 Cartwright	Y	Y	N	N	N	Y	N
18 **Murphy**	Y	Y	Y	Y	Y	Y	Y
RHODE ISLAND							
1 Cicilline	Y	Y	N	N	N	Y	N
2 Langevin	Y	Y	N	N	N	Y	N
SOUTH CAROLINA							
1 **Sanford**	Y	Y	Y	Y	P	Y	Y
2 **Wilson**	Y	Y	Y	Y	Y	Y	Y
3 **Duncan**	Y	Y	Y	Y	Y	Y	Y
4 **Gowdy**	Y	Y	Y	Y	Y	Y	Y
6 Clyburn	Y	Y	N	N	N	Y	N
7 **Rice**	Y	Y	Y	Y	Y	Y	Y
SOUTH DAKOTA							
AL **Noem**	Y	Y	Y	Y	Y	Y	Y
TENNESSEE							
1 **Roe**	Y	Y	Y	Y	Y	Y	Y
2 **Duncan**	Y	Y	Y	Y	Y	Y	Y
3 **Fleischmann**	Y	Y	Y	Y	Y	Y	Y
4 **DesJarlais**	Y	Y	Y	Y	Y	Y	Y
5 Cooper	Y	Y	N	N	N	Y	N
6 **Black**	Y	Y	Y	Y	Y	Y	Y
7 **Blackburn**	Y	Y	Y	Y	Y	Y	Y
8 **Kustoff**	Y	Y	Y	Y	Y	Y	Y
9 Cohen	Y	Y	N	N	N	Y	N

	257	258	259	260	261	262	263
TEXAS							
1 **Gohmert**	Y	Y	Y	Y	Y	Y	Y
2 **Poe**	Y	?	Y	Y	Y	Y	Y
3 **Johnson, S.**	Y	?	?	?	?	?	?
4 **Ratcliffe**	Y	Y	Y	Y	Y	Y	Y
5 **Hensarling**	Y	Y	Y	Y	Y	Y	Y
6 **Barton**	Y	Y	Y	Y	Y	Y	Y
7 **Culberson**	Y	Y	Y	Y	Y	Y	Y
8 **Brady**	Y	Y	Y	Y	Y	Y	Y
9 Green, A.	Y	Y	N	N	N	Y	N
10 **McCaul**	Y	Y	Y	Y	Y	Y	Y
11 **Conaway**	Y	Y	Y	Y	Y	Y	Y
12 **Granger**	Y	Y	Y	Y	Y	Y	Y
13 **Thornberry**	Y	Y	Y	Y	Y	Y	Y
14 **Weber**	Y	Y	Y	Y	Y	Y	Y
15 Gonzalez	Y	Y	N	N	N	Y	N
16 O'Rourke	Y	Y	N	N	N	Y	N
17 **Flores**	Y	Y	Y	Y	Y	Y	Y
18 Jackson Lee	Y	Y	N	N	N	Y	N
19 **Arrington**	Y	Y	Y	Y	Y	Y	Y
20 Castro	Y	Y	N	N	N	Y	N
21 **Smith**	Y	Y	Y	Y	Y	Y	Y
22 **Olson**	Y	Y	Y	Y	Y	Y	Y
23 **Hurd**	Y	Y	Y	Y	Y	Y	Y
24 **Marchant**	Y	Y	Y	Y	Y	Y	Y
25 **Williams**	Y	Y	Y	Y	Y	Y	Y
26 **Burgess**	Y	Y	Y	Y	Y	Y	Y
27 **Farenthold**	Y	Y	Y	Y	Y	Y	Y
28 Cuellar	Y	Y	N	N	N	Y	N
29 Green, G.	Y	Y	N	N	N	Y	N
30 Johnson, E.B.	Y	Y	N	N	N	Y	N
31 **Carter**	Y	Y	Y	Y	Y	Y	Y
32 **Sessions**	Y	Y	Y	Y	Y	Y	?
33 Veasey	Y	Y	N	N	N	Y	N
34 Vela	Y	Y	N	N	N	Y	N
35 Doggett	Y	Y	N	N	N	Y	N
36 **Babin**	Y	Y	Y	Y	Y	Y	Y
UTAH							
1 **Bishop**	Y	Y	Y	Y	Y	Y	Y
2 **Stewart**	Y	Y	Y	Y	Y	Y	Y
3 **Chaffetz**	Y	?	?	?	?	?	?
4 **Love**	Y	Y	Y	Y	Y	Y	Y
VERMONT							
AL Welch	Y	Y	N	N	N	Y	N
VIRGINIA							
1 **Wittman**	Y	Y	Y	Y	Y	Y	Y
2 **Taylor**	Y	Y	Y	Y	Y	Y	Y
3 Scott	Y	Y	N	N	N	Y	N
4 McEachin	Y	Y	N	N	N	Y	?
5 **Garrett**	Y	Y	?	Y	Y	Y	Y
6 **Goodlatte**	Y	Y	Y	Y	Y	Y	Y
7 **Brat**	Y	Y	Y	Y	Y	Y	Y
8 Beyer	Y	Y	N	N	N	Y	N
9 **Griffith**	Y	Y	Y	Y	Y	Y	Y
10 **Comstock**	Y	Y	Y	Y	Y	Y	Y
11 Connolly	Y	Y	N	N	N	Y	N
WASHINGTON							
1 DelBene	Y	Y	N	N	N	Y	N
2 Larsen	Y	Y	N	N	N	Y	N
3 **Herrera Beutler**	Y	Y	Y	Y	Y	Y	Y
4 **Newhouse**	?	?	?	?	?	?	?
5 **McMorris Rodgers**	Y	Y	Y	Y	Y	Y	Y
6 Kilmer	Y	Y	N	N	N	Y	N
7 Jayapal	Y	Y	N	N	N	Y	N
8 **Reichert**	Y	Y	Y	Y	Y	Y	Y
9 Smith	Y	Y	N	N	N	Y	N
10 Heck	Y	Y	N	N	N	Y	N
WEST VIRGINIA							
1 **McKinley**	Y	Y	Y	Y	Y	Y	Y
2 **Mooney**	Y	Y	Y	Y	Y	Y	Y
3 **Jenkins**	Y	Y	Y	Y	Y	Y	Y
WISCONSIN							
1 **Ryan**							
2 Pocan	Y	Y	N	N	N	Y	N
3 Kind	Y	Y	N	N	N	Y	N
4 Moore	Y	Y	N	N	N	Y	N
5 **Sensenbrenner**	Y	Y	Y	Y	Y	Y	Y
6 **Grothman**	Y	Y	Y	Y	Y	Y	Y
7 **Duffy**	Y	Y	Y	Y	Y	Y	Y
8 **Gallagher**	Y	Y	Y	Y	Y	Y	Y
WYOMING							
AL **Cheney**	Y	Y	Y	Y	Y	Y	Y

⫿ HOUSE VOTES

VOTE NUMBER

264. HR 1039, H RES 324. PROBATION OFFICER ARREST AUTHORITY/ RULE. Adoption of the rule (H Res 324) that would provide for House floor consideration of the bill that would authorize probation officers, during the course of their official duties, to arrest an individual without a warrant if there is probable cause that the individual has assaulted or impeded the officer. Adopted 230-184 : R 227-0; D 3-184. May 18, 2017.

265. HR 115. DEATH SENTENCE AGGRAVATING FACTOR EXPANSION/ PASSAGE. Passage of the bill that would require courts and juries to consider if a defendant killed or attempted to kill a state law enforcement officer, local law enforcement officer or first responder as an aggravating factor when determining whether to impose the death sentence on a defendant. Passed 271-143 : R 223-4; D 48-139. May 18, 2017.

266. HR 1892. HALF-STAFF FLAGS/PASSAGE. Goodlatte, R-Va., motion to suspend the rules and pass the bill that would allow the governor of a state, territory, possession or the mayor of the District of Columbia to order that the United States flag be flown at half-staff to honor the death of a first responder who dies while serving in the line of duty. Motion agreed to 411-1 : R 224-0; D 187-1. May 18, 2017.

267. HR 1039. PROBATION OFFICER ARREST AUTHORITY/GAO REPORT AND SUNSET PROVISIONS. Jackson Lee, D-Texas, amendment that would require the Government Accountability Office to report to Congress on the results of the bill's expansion of arrest authority for probation officers, including if any harm resulted from the exercise of the expanded authority. It would also sunset the bill's expanded arrest authority 30 months after the bill's enactment. Rejected in Committee of the Whole 178-229 : R 7-218; D 171-11. May 19, 2017.

268. HR 1039. PROBATION OFFICER ARREST AUTHORITY/PASSAGE. Passage of the bill that would authorize probation officers, during the course of their official duties, to arrest an individual without a warrant if there is probable cause that the individual has assaulted or impeded the officer. It would require the Administrative Office of the United States Courts to issue rules and regulations governing probation officers' use of expanded arrest authority. Passed 229-177 : R 192-33; D 37-144. May 19, 2017.

269. HR 1862. ILLICIT SEXUAL CONDUCT DEFINITION/PASSAGE. Goodlatte, R-Va., motion to suspend the rules and pass the bill that would expand the definition of illicit sexual conduct related to the transportation of a minor abroad to include improper conduct with a minor, not just a sexual act. It would modify that a conviction for coercion or enticement of a minor into any criminal sexual activity would be subject to a mandatory minimum sentence of life imprisonment. Motion agreed to 372-30 : R 219-2; D 153-28. May 22, 2017.

270. HR 1842. REPEAT OFFENDER PENALTIES/PASSAGE. Goodlatte, R-Va., motion to suspend the rules and pass the bill that would subject a sex offender who has not properly registered in the sex offenders registry and who commits a violent crime under state law to the same enhanced penalty that would be required if the crime had been committed under federal law. It would uniformly clarify that individuals convicted for child sexual exploitation and aggravated sexual abuse offenses under military law would be considered a repeat offender if they commit similar crimes under federal or state law. Motion agreed to 371-30 : R 218-2; D 153-28. May 22, 2017.

	264	265	266	267	268	269	270
ALABAMA							
1 **Byrne**	Y	Y	Y	N	Y	Y	Y
2 **Roby**	Y	Y	Y	N	Y	Y	Y
3 **Rogers**	Y	Y	Y	N	Y	Y	Y
4 **Aderholt**	Y	Y	Y	N	Y	Y	Y
5 **Brooks**	Y	Y	Y	N	Y	?	?
6 **Palmer**	Y	Y	Y	N	Y	Y	Y
7 Sewell	N	N	Y	Y	N	Y	Y
ALASKA							
AL **Young**	Y	Y	Y	N	Y	Y	Y
ARIZONA							
1 O'Halleran	Y	Y	Y	Y	Y	Y	Y
2 **McSally**	Y	Y	Y	N	Y	Y	Y
3 Grijalva	N	N	?	Y	N	Y	Y
4 **Gosar**	Y	Y	Y	N	N	Y	Y
5 **Biggs**	Y	Y	Y	N	Y	Y	Y
6 **Schweikert**	Y	Y	Y	N	Y	Y	Y
7 Gallego	N	N	Y	N	Y	N	Y
8 **Franks**	?	Y	Y	N	Y	Y	Y
9 Sinema	N	Y	Y	Y	Y	Y	Y
ARKANSAS							
1 **Crawford**	?	?	?	?	?	Y	Y
2 **Hill**	Y	Y	Y	N	N	Y	Y
3 **Womack**	Y	Y	Y	N	Y	Y	Y
4 **Westerman**	Y	Y	Y	N	Y	Y	Y
CALIFORNIA							
1 **LaMalfa**	Y	Y	Y	N	Y	Y	Y
2 Huffman	N	N	Y	Y	N	N	N
3 Garamendi	N	Y	Y	Y	Y	Y	Y
4 **McClintock**	Y	Y	Y	N	Y	Y	Y
5 Thompson	N	Y	Y	Y	N	Y	Y
6 Matsui	N	N	Y	Y	N	Y	Y
7 Bera	N	Y	Y	Y	N	Y	N
8 **Cook**	Y	Y	Y	N	Y	Y	Y
9 McNerney	N	N	Y	Y	N	Y	Y
10 **Denham**	Y	Y	Y	N	Y	Y	Y
11 DeSaulnier	N	N	Y	Y	N	N	N
12 Pelosi	N	N	Y	Y	N	Y	Y
13 Lee	N	N	Y	?	?	N	N
14 Speier	–	N	Y	Y	Y	Y	Y
15 Swalwell	–	+	+	+	–	+	+
16 Costa	N	Y	Y	?	?	Y	Y
17 Khanna	N	N	Y	Y	N	N	N
18 Eshoo	N	N	Y	Y	Y	Y	Y
19 Lofgren	N	N	Y	?	?	Y	Y
20 Panetta	N	Y	Y	Y	N	Y	Y
21 **Valadao**	Y	Y	Y	N	Y	+	+
22 **Nunes**	Y	Y	Y	N	Y	Y	Y
23 **McCarthy**	Y	Y	Y	N	Y	Y	Y
24 Carbajal	N	Y	Y	Y	N	Y	Y
25 **Knight**	Y	Y	Y	N	Y	Y	Y
26 Brownley	N	N	Y	Y	N	Y	Y
27 Chu	N	N	Y	Y	N	N	N
28 Schiff	N	Y	Y	Y	N	Y	Y
29 Cardenas	N	N	Y	?	?	Y	Y
30 Sherman	N	N	Y	Y	N	Y	Y
31 Aguilar	N	Y	Y	Y	N	Y	Y
32 Napolitano	–	–	+	?	?	Y	Y
33 Lieu	N	N	Y	Y	N	Y	Y
34 Vacant							
35 Torres	N	N	Y	Y	N	Y	Y
36 Ruiz	N	Y	Y	Y	N	Y	Y
37 Bass	N	N	Y	Y	N	N	N
38 Sánchez, Linda	N	N	Y	Y	N	Y	Y
39 **Royce**	Y	Y	Y	N	Y	Y	Y
40 Roybal-Allard	N	N	Y	Y	N	Y	Y
41 Takano	N	N	Y	Y	N	N	N
42 **Calvert**	Y	Y	Y	N	Y	Y	Y
43 Waters	N	N	Y	Y	N	N	N
44 Barragan	N	N	Y	Y	N	Y	Y
45 **Walters**	Y	Y	Y	N	Y	Y	Y
46 Correa	N	Y	Y	Y	Y	Y	Y
47 Lowenthal	N	N	Y	Y	N	Y	Y
48 **Rohrabacher**	Y	Y	Y	N	N	?	?
49 **Issa**	Y	Y	Y	N	Y	Y	Y
50 **Hunter**	Y	Y	Y	N	Y	Y	Y
51 Vargas	N	N	Y	Y	N	Y	Y
52 Peters	N	Y	Y	Y	N	Y	Y
53 Davis	N	N	Y	Y	N	Y	Y

	264	265	266	267	268	269	270
COLORADO							
1 DeGette	N	N	Y	Y	N	Y	Y
2 Polis	N	N	Y	Y	N	?	?
3 **Tipton**	Y	Y	Y	N	N	Y	Y
4 **Buck**	Y	Y	?	N	Y	Y	Y
5 **Lamborn**	Y	Y	Y	N	N	Y	Y
6 **Coffman**	Y	Y	Y	N	Y	Y	Y
7 Perlmutter	N	Y	Y	N	Y	Y	Y
CONNECTICUT							
1 Larson	N	N	Y	?	?	Y	Y
2 Courtney	N	N	Y	Y	Y	Y	Y
3 DeLauro	N	N	Y	Y	Y	Y	Y
4 Himes	N	N	Y	N	Y	Y	Y
5 Esty	N	N	Y	Y	N	?	?
DELAWARE							
AL Blunt Rochester	N	N	Y	Y	N	Y	Y
FLORIDA							
1 **Gaetz**	Y	Y	Y	N	Y	Y	Y
2 **Dunn**	Y	Y	Y	N	Y	Y	Y
3 **Yoho**	Y	Y	Y	N	Y	Y	Y
4 **Rutherford**	Y	Y	Y	N	Y	Y	Y
5 Lawson	N	Y	Y	Y	N	Y	Y
6 **DeSantis**	Y	Y	Y	N	Y	Y	Y
7 Murphy	N	Y	Y	N	Y	Y	Y
8 **Posey**	Y	Y	Y	N	Y	Y	Y
9 Soto	N	Y	Y	Y	N	Y	Y
10 Demings	N	N	Y	?	Y	Y	Y
11 **Webster**	Y	Y	Y	N	Y	Y	Y
12 **Bilirakis**	Y	Y	Y	N	Y	Y	Y
13 Crist	N	N	Y	Y	N	Y	Y
14 Castor	N	N	Y	Y	N	Y	Y
15 **Ross**	Y	Y	Y	N	Y	Y	Y
16 **Buchanan**	Y	Y	Y	N	Y	?	?
17 **Rooney, T.**	?	+	+	N	Y	Y	Y
18 **Mast**	Y	Y	Y	N	Y	Y	Y
19 **Rooney, F.**	Y	Y	Y	N	Y	Y	Y
20 Hastings	N	N	N	Y	N	N	Y
21 Frankel	N	N	Y	Y	N	Y	Y
22 Deutch	N	N	Y	Y	N	?	?
23 Wasserman Schultz	N	N	Y	Y	N	Y	Y
24 Wilson	N	+	Y	Y	N	Y	Y
25 **Diaz-Balart**	Y	Y	Y	N	Y	Y	Y
26 **Curbelo**	Y	+	+	?	?	Y	Y
27 **Ros-Lehtinen**	Y	Y	Y	N	Y	Y	Y
GEORGIA							
1 **Carter**	Y	Y	Y	N	Y	Y	Y
2 Bishop	N	Y	Y	Y	N	Y	Y
3 **Ferguson**	Y	Y	Y	N	Y	Y	Y
4 Johnson	N	N	Y	Y	N	N	N
5 Lewis	N	N	Y	Y	N	?	?
7 **Woodall**	Y	Y	Y	N	Y	Y	Y
8 **Scott, A.**	Y	Y	Y	N	Y	Y	Y
9 **Collins**	Y	Y	Y	N	Y	Y	Y
10 **Hice**	Y	Y	Y	N	Y	Y	Y
11 **Loudermilk**	Y	Y	Y	N	Y	Y	Y
12 **Allen**	Y	Y	Y	N	Y	Y	Y
13 Scott, D.	N	N	Y	N	Y	Y	Y
14 **Graves**	Y	Y	Y	N	Y	Y	Y
HAWAII							
1 Hanabusa	N	N	Y	Y	N	Y	Y
2 Gabbard	N	N	Y	Y	N	Y	Y
IDAHO							
1 **Labrador**	Y	Y	Y	N	Y	?	?
2 **Simpson**	Y	Y	Y	N	Y	Y	Y
ILLINOIS							
1 Rush	N	N	Y	Y	N	Y	Y
2 Kelly	N	N	Y	Y	N	Y	Y
3 Lipinski	N	Y	Y	Y	Y	Y	Y
4 Gutierrez	?	?	?	?	?	–	–
5 Quigley	N	Y	Y	Y	Y	Y	Y
6 **Roskam**	Y	Y	Y	N	Y	Y	Y
7 Davis, D.	N	N	Y	N	Y	Y	Y
8 Krishnamoorthi	N	Y	Y	N	Y	Y	Y
9 Schakowsky	N	N	Y	Y	N	N	N
10 Schneider	N	N	Y	Y	N	Y	Y
11 Foster	N	N	Y	N	Y	Y	Y
12 **Bost**	Y	Y	Y	N	Y	Y	Y
13 **Davis, R.**	Y	Y	Y	N	Y	Y	Y
14 **Hultgren**	Y	Y	Y	N	Y	Y	Y
15 **Shimkus**	Y	Y	Y	N	Y	Y	Y

	264	265	266	267	268	269	270
16 **Kinzinger**	Y	Y	Y	N	Y	Y	Y
17 Bustos	N	Y	Y	Y	N	Y	Y
18 **LaHood**	Y	Y	Y	N	Y	Y	Y
INDIANA							
1 Visclosky	N	N	Y	Y	N	Y	Y
2 **Walorski**	Y	Y	Y	N	Y	Y	Y
3 **Banks**	Y	Y	Y	N	N	Y	Y
4 **Rokita**	Y	Y	Y	N	N	Y	Y
5 **Brooks**	Y	Y	Y	N	Y	Y	Y
6 **Messer**	Y	Y	Y	N	N	Y	Y
7 Carson	N	N	Y	Y	N	Y	Y
8 **Bucshon**	Y	Y	Y	N	Y	Y	Y
9 **Hollingsworth**	Y	Y	Y	N	Y	Y	Y
IOWA							
1 **Blum**	Y	Y	Y	N	Y	Y	Y
2 Loebsack	N	N	Y	Y	N	Y	Y
3 **Young**	Y	Y	Y	N	Y	Y	Y
4 **King**	Y	Y	Y	N	Y	Y	Y
KANSAS							
1 **Marshall**	Y	Y	Y	N	Y	Y	Y
2 **Jenkins**	Y	Y	Y	N	N	Y	Y
3 **Yoder**	Y	Y	Y	N	Y	Y	Y
4 **Estes**	Y	Y	Y	N	Y	Y	Y
KENTUCKY							
1 **Comer**	Y	Y	Y	N	N	Y	Y
2 **Guthrie**	Y	Y	Y	N	Y	Y	Y
3 Yarmuth	N	N	Y	Y	N	Y	Y
4 **Massie**	Y	N	Y	Y	N	N	N
5 **Rogers**	Y	Y	Y	N	Y	Y	Y
6 **Barr**	Y	Y	Y	N	Y	Y	Y
LOUISIANA							
1 **Scalise**	Y	Y	Y	N	Y	Y	Y
2 Richmond	N	N	Y	?	?	N	N
3 **Higgins**	Y	Y	Y	N	Y	Y	Y
4 **Johnson**	Y	Y	Y	N	Y	Y	Y
5 **Abraham**	Y	Y	Y	N	Y	Y	Y
6 **Graves**	Y	Y	Y	N	Y	Y	Y
MAINE							
1 Pingree	N	N	Y	Y	N	Y	Y
2 **Poliquin**	Y	Y	Y	N	Y	Y	Y
MARYLAND							
1 **Harris**	Y	Y	Y	N	Y	Y	Y
2 Ruppersberger	N	Y	Y	Y	N	Y	Y
3 Sarbanes	N	N	Y	Y	N	Y	Y
4 Brown	N	N	Y	Y	N	Y	Y
5 Hoyer	N	N	Y	Y	N	Y	Y
6 Delaney	N	N	Y	Y	Y	Y	Y
7 Cummings	N	N	Y	Y	N	?	?
8 Raskin	N	N	Y	Y	N	Y	Y
MASSACHUSETTS							
1 Neal	N	N	Y	Y	Y	Y	Y
2 McGovern	N	N	Y	Y	N	N	N
3 Tsongas	N	N	Y	Y	N	Y	Y
4 Kennedy	N	N	Y	Y	N	Y	Y
5 Clark	N	N	Y	Y	N	Y	Y
6 Moulton	N	N	Y	Y	N	Y	Y
7 Capuano	N	N	Y	Y	N	N	N
8 Lynch	N	Y	Y	Y	Y	?	Y
9 Keating	N	N	Y	Y	Y	Y	Y
MICHIGAN							
1 **Bergman**	Y	Y	Y	N	Y	Y	Y
2 **Huizenga**	Y	Y	Y	N	Y	+	+
3 **Amash**	Y	N	Y	Y	N	N	N
4 **Moolenaar**	Y	Y	Y	N	Y	Y	Y
5 Kildee	N	N	Y	Y	N	Y	Y
6 **Upton**	Y	Y	Y	N	Y	Y	Y
7 **Walberg**	Y	Y	Y	N	Y	Y	Y
8 **Bishop**	Y	Y	Y	N	Y	Y	?
9 Levin	N	N	Y	Y	N	Y	Y
10 **Mitchell**	Y	N	Y	N	Y	Y	Y
11 **Trott**	Y	Y	Y	N	Y	Y	Y
12 Dingell	N	N	Y	Y	N	Y	Y
13 Conyers	N	N	Y	Y	N	N	N
14 Lawrence	N	N	Y	Y	N	Y	Y
MINNESOTA							
1 Walz	N	N	Y	Y	N	Y	Y
2 **Lewis**	Y	Y	Y	N	N	Y	Y
3 **Paulsen**	Y	Y	Y	N	Y	Y	Y
4 McCollum	N	N	Y	Y	N	Y	Y

	264	265	266	267	268	269	270
5 Ellison	N	N	Y	Y	N	N	N
6 **Emmer**	Y	Y	Y	N	Y	Y	Y
7 Peterson	N	Y	Y	N	Y	Y	Y
8 Nolan	N	N	Y	Y	N	Y	Y
MISSISSIPPI							
1 **Kelly**	Y	Y	Y	N	N	Y	Y
2 Thompson	N	Y	Y	?	?	Y	Y
3 **Harper**	Y	Y	Y	N	Y	Y	Y
4 **Palazzo**	Y	Y	Y	N	Y	Y	Y
MISSOURI							
1 Clay	N	N	Y	?	?	Y	Y
2 **Wagner**	Y	Y	Y	?	?	Y	Y
3 **Luetkemeyer**	Y	Y	Y	N	Y	Y	Y
4 **Hartzler**	Y	Y	Y	N	Y	Y	Y
5 Cleaver	N	N	Y	Y	N	Y	Y
6 **Graves**	Y	Y	Y	N	Y	+	+
7 **Long**	Y	Y	Y	N	Y	Y	Y
8 **Smith**	Y	Y	Y	N	N	Y	Y
MONTANA							
AL **Vacant**							
NEBRASKA							
1 **Fortenberry**	Y	Y	Y	N	Y	Y	Y
2 **Bacon**	Y	Y	Y	N	Y	Y	Y
3 **Smith**	Y	Y	Y	N	Y	Y	Y
NEVADA							
1 Titus	N	N	Y	Y	N	Y	Y
2 **Amodei**	Y	Y	Y	N	Y	Y	Y
3 Rosen	N	Y	Y	Y	Y	Y	Y
4 Kihuen	N	N	Y	Y	N	Y	Y
NEW HAMPSHIRE							
1 Shea-Porter	N	N	Y	Y	N	Y	Y
2 Kuster	N	N	Y	Y	N	Y	Y
NEW JERSEY							
1 Norcross	N	Y	Y	Y	N	Y	Y
2 **LoBiondo**	Y	Y	Y	N	Y	Y	Y
3 **MacArthur**	Y	Y	Y	N	Y	Y	Y
4 **Smith**	Y	N	Y	N	Y	Y	Y
5 Gottheimer	Y	Y	Y	N	Y	Y	Y
6 Pallone	N	N	Y	Y	N	Y	Y
7 **Lance**	Y	Y	Y	N	Y	Y	Y
8 Sires	N	N	Y	N	Y	Y	Y
9 Pascrell	Y	Y	Y	N	Y	?	?
10 Payne	N	N	Y	Y	N	?	?
11 **Frelinghuysen**	Y	Y	Y	N	Y	Y	Y
12 Watson Coleman	N	N	Y	Y	N	N	N
NEW MEXICO							
1 Lujan Grisham	N	N	Y	Y	N	Y	Y
2 **Pearce**	Y	Y	Y	N	Y	Y	Y
3 Luján	N	N	Y	Y	N	Y	Y
NEW YORK							
1 **Zeldin**	Y	Y	Y	N	Y	Y	Y
2 **King**	Y	Y	Y	N	Y	Y	Y
3 Suozzi	N	–	Y	Y	Y	Y	Y
4 Rice	N	N	Y	Y	N	Y	Y
5 Meeks	N	N	Y	N	N	Y	Y
6 Meng	N	Y	Y	Y	N	Y	Y
7 Velázquez	N	N	Y	Y	N	Y	Y
8 Jeffries	N	N	Y	Y	N	Y	Y
9 Clarke	N	N	Y	Y	N	N	N
10 Nadler	N	N	Y	Y	N	N	N
11 **Donovan**	Y	Y	Y	N	Y	Y	Y
12 Maloney, C.	N	N	Y	Y	N	Y	Y
13 Espaillat	N	N	Y	Y	N	Y	N
14 Crowley	N	N	Y	Y	N	Y	Y
15 Serrano	N	N	Y	Y	N	Y	Y
16 Engel	N	N	Y	Y	N	Y	Y
17 Lowey	N	N	Y	Y	N	Y	Y
18 Maloney, S.P.	N	Y	Y	Y	N	Y	Y
19 **Faso**	Y	Y	Y	N	Y	Y	Y
20 Tonko	N	N	Y	Y	N	Y	Y
21 **Stefanik**	Y	Y	Y	N	Y	Y	Y
22 **Tenney**	Y	Y	Y	N	Y	Y	Y
23 **Reed**	Y	Y	Y	N	Y	Y	Y
24 **Katko**	Y	Y	Y	?	?	Y	Y
25 Slaughter	N	N	Y	Y	N	Y	Y
26 Higgins	N	Y	Y	Y	Y	Y	Y
27 **Collins**	Y	Y	Y	N	Y	+	+
NORTH CAROLINA							
1 Butterfield	N	N	Y	Y	N	Y	Y
2 **Holding**	?	Y	Y	N	Y	Y	Y
3 **Jones**	Y	Y	Y	Y	N	Y	Y
4 Price	N	N	Y	Y	N	Y	Y

	264	265	266	267	268	269	270
5 **Foxx**	Y	Y	Y	N	Y	Y	Y
6 **Walker**	Y	Y	?	N	Y	Y	Y
7 **Rouzer**	Y	Y	Y	N	Y	Y	Y
8 **Hudson**	Y	Y	Y	N	Y	Y	Y
9 **Pittenger**	+	Y	Y	N	Y	Y	Y
10 **McHenry**	Y	Y	Y	N	Y	Y	Y
11 **Meadows**	Y	Y	Y	N	N	Y	Y
12 Adams	N	N	Y	Y	N	Y	Y
13 **Budd**	Y	Y	Y	N	Y	Y	Y
NORTH DAKOTA							
AL **Cramer**	Y	Y	Y	N	Y	Y	Y
OHIO							
1 **Chabot**	Y	Y	Y	N	Y	Y	Y
2 **Wenstrup**	Y	Y	Y	N	Y	Y	Y
3 Beatty	N	N	Y	Y	N	Y	Y
4 **Jordan**	Y	Y	Y	N	N	Y	Y
5 **Latta**	Y	Y	Y	N	Y	Y	Y
6 **Johnson**	Y	Y	Y	N	Y	Y	Y
7 **Gibbs**	Y	Y	Y	N	Y	Y	Y
8 **Davidson**	Y	Y	Y	N	N	Y	Y
9 Kaptur	N	N	Y	Y	Y	Y	Y
10 **Turner**	Y	Y	Y	N	Y	Y	Y
11 Fudge	N	N	Y	Y	N	N	N
12 **Tiberi**	Y	Y	Y	N	Y	+	+
13 Ryan	N	N	Y	Y	N	Y	Y
14 **Joyce**	Y	Y	Y	N	Y	Y	Y
15 **Stivers**	Y	Y	Y	N	Y	Y	Y
16 **Renacci**	Y	Y	Y	N	Y	Y	Y
OKLAHOMA							
1 **Bridenstine**	Y	Y	Y	N	N	Y	Y
2 **Mullin**	Y	Y	Y	N	Y	Y	Y
3 **Lucas**	Y	Y	Y	N	Y	Y	Y
4 **Cole**	–	+	+	?	?	Y	Y
5 **Russell**	Y	?	?	?	?	Y	Y
OREGON							
1 Bonamici	N	N	Y	Y	N	Y	Y
2 **Walden**	Y	Y	Y	N	Y	Y	Y
3 Blumenauer	N	N	Y	Y	N	Y	Y
4 DeFazio	N	N	Y	Y	Y	Y	Y
5 Schrader	N	Y	Y	Y	Y	Y	Y
PENNSYLVANIA							
1 Brady	N	N	Y	Y	N	Y	Y
2 Evans	N	N	Y	Y	N	N	N
3 **Kelly**	Y	Y	Y	N	Y	Y	Y
4 **Perry**	Y	Y	Y	N	N	Y	Y
5 **Thompson**	Y	Y	Y	N	Y	Y	Y
6 **Costello**	Y	Y	Y	N	Y	Y	Y
7 **Meehan**	Y	Y	Y	N	Y	Y	Y
8 **Fitzpatrick**	Y	Y	Y	N	Y	Y	Y
9 **Shuster**	Y	Y	Y	N	Y	Y	Y
10 **Marino**	Y	Y	Y	N	Y	Y	Y
11 **Barletta**	Y	Y	Y	N	Y	Y	Y
12 **Rothfus**	Y	Y	Y	N	Y	Y	Y
13 Boyle	?	N	Y	Y	Y	Y	Y
14 Doyle	N	N	Y	Y	N	Y	Y
15 **Dent**	Y	Y	Y	N	Y	Y	Y
16 **Smucker**	Y	Y	Y	N	Y	Y	Y
17 Cartwright	N	Y	Y	Y	Y	Y	Y
18 **Murphy**	Y	Y	Y	N	Y	Y	Y
RHODE ISLAND							
1 Cicilline	N	N	Y	Y	N	?	?
2 Langevin	N	N	Y	Y	Y	Y	Y
SOUTH CAROLINA							
1 **Sanford**	Y	Y	Y	Y	N	Y	Y
2 **Wilson**	Y	Y	Y	N	Y	Y	Y
3 **Duncan**	Y	Y	Y	?	?	Y	Y
4 **Gowdy**	Y	Y	Y	N	Y	Y	Y
6 Clyburn	N	N	Y	Y	N	N	N
7 **Rice**	Y	Y	Y	N	Y	Y	Y
SOUTH DAKOTA							
AL **Noem**	Y	Y	?	?	?	Y	Y
TENNESSEE							
1 **Roe**	Y	Y	Y	N	Y	Y	Y
2 **Duncan**	Y	Y	Y	N	N	Y	Y
3 **Fleischmann**	Y	Y	Y	N	Y	Y	Y
4 **DesJarlais**	Y	Y	Y	N	Y	Y	Y
5 Cooper	N	N	Y	Y	N	Y	Y
6 **Black**	Y	Y	Y	N	Y	+	+
7 **Blackburn**	Y	Y	Y	?	?	Y	Y
8 **Kustoff**	Y	Y	Y	N	Y	Y	Y
9 Cohen	N	N	Y	Y	N	Y	Y

	264	265	266	267	268	269	270
TEXAS							
1 **Gohmert**	Y	?	?	N	Y	Y	Y
2 **Poe**	Y	Y	Y	N	Y	Y	Y
3 **Johnson, S.**	?	?	?	?	?	?	?
4 **Ratcliffe**	Y	Y	Y	N	Y	Y	Y
5 **Hensarling**	Y	Y	Y	N	Y	Y	Y
6 **Barton**	Y	Y	Y	N	Y	Y	Y
7 **Culberson**	Y	Y	Y	N	Y	Y	Y
8 **Brady**	Y	Y	Y	N	Y	Y	Y
9 Green, A.	N	N	Y	Y	N	Y	Y
10 **McCaul**	Y	Y	Y	N	Y	Y	Y
11 **Conaway**	Y	Y	Y	N	Y	Y	Y
12 **Granger**	Y	Y	Y	N	Y	+	+
13 **Thornberry**	Y	Y	Y	N	Y	Y	Y
14 **Weber**	Y	Y	Y	N	Y	Y	Y
15 Gonzalez	N	Y	Y	Y	N	Y	Y
16 O'Rourke	N	Y	Y	Y	N	Y	Y
17 **Flores**	Y	Y	Y	N	Y	Y	Y
18 Jackson Lee	N	N	Y	Y	N	N	P
19 **Arrington**	Y	Y	Y	N	Y	Y	Y
20 Castro	N	N	Y	Y	N	Y	Y
21 **Smith**	Y	Y	Y	N	Y	?	?
22 **Olson**	Y	Y	Y	N	Y	Y	Y
23 **Hurd**	Y	Y	Y	N	Y	Y	Y
24 **Marchant**	Y	Y	Y	N	Y	Y	Y
25 **Williams**	Y	Y	Y	N	Y	Y	Y
26 **Burgess**	Y	Y	Y	N	Y	Y	Y
27 **Farenthold**	Y	Y	Y	N	Y	Y	Y
28 Cuellar	N	Y	Y	Y	Y	Y	Y
29 Green, G.	N	Y	Y	Y	N	Y	Y
30 Johnson, E.B.	N	N	Y	Y	N	Y	N
31 **Carter**	Y	Y	Y	N	Y	?	?
32 **Sessions**	?	?	?	N	Y	Y	Y
33 Veasey	N	N	Y	Y	N	Y	Y
34 Vela	N	Y	Y	N	Y	Y	Y
35 Doggett	N	N	Y	Y	N	Y	Y
36 **Babin**	Y	Y	Y	N	N	Y	Y
UTAH							
1 **Bishop**	Y	Y	Y	N	Y	Y	Y
2 **Stewart**	Y	Y	Y	N	Y	Y	Y
3 **Chaffetz**	?	?	?	?	?	?	?
4 **Love**	Y	Y	Y	N	Y	Y	Y
VERMONT							
AL Welch	N	N	Y	N	N	Y	Y
VIRGINIA							
1 **Wittman**	Y	Y	Y	N	N	Y	Y
2 **Taylor**	Y	Y	Y	N	Y	Y	Y
3 Scott	N	N	Y	Y	N	N	N
4 McEachin	?	?	?	Y	N	N	N
5 **Garrett**	Y	Y	Y	N	N	Y	Y
6 **Goodlatte**	Y	Y	Y	N	Y	Y	Y
7 **Brat**	Y	Y	Y	N	N	Y	Y
8 Beyer	N	N	Y	Y	N	N	Y
9 **Griffith**	Y	Y	Y	Y	N	Y	Y
10 **Comstock**	Y	Y	Y	N	Y	Y	Y
11 Connolly	N	N	Y	Y	N	Y	Y
WASHINGTON							
1 DelBene	N	N	Y	Y	N	Y	Y
2 Larsen	N	N	Y	Y	N	Y	Y
3 **Herrera Beutler**	Y	Y	Y	N	Y	Y	Y
4 **Newhouse**	?	?	?	?	?	?	?
5 **McMorris Rodgers**	Y	Y	Y	N	Y	Y	Y
6 Kilmer	N	Y	Y	Y	N	Y	Y
7 Jayapal	N	N	Y	Y	N	N	N
8 **Reichert**	Y	Y	Y	N	Y	Y	Y
9 Smith	N	N	Y	Y	N	N	N
10 Heck	N	Y	Y	Y	N	Y	Y
WEST VIRGINIA							
1 **McKinley**	Y	Y	Y	N	Y	Y	Y
2 **Mooney**	Y	Y	Y	Y	N	Y	Y
3 **Jenkins**	Y	Y	Y	N	Y	Y	Y
WISCONSIN							
1 **Ryan**							
2 Pocan	N	N	Y	Y	N	Y	Y
3 Kind	N	Y	Y	Y	Y	?	?
4 Moore	N	N	Y	Y	N	Y	N
5 **Sensenbrenner**	Y	Y	Y	N	Y	Y	Y
6 **Grothman**	Y	Y	Y	N	Y	Y	Y
7 **Duffy**	Y	Y	Y	N	Y	Y	Y
8 **Gallagher**	Y	Y	Y	N	Y	Y	Y
WYOMING							
AL **Cheney**	Y	Y	Y	N	Y	Y	Y

VOTE NUMBER

271. HR 953, H RES 348. PESTICIDE PERMITS/PREVIOUS QUESTION. Woodall, R-Ga., motion to order the previous question (thus ending debate and possibility of amendment) on the rule (H Res 348) that would provide for House floor consideration of the bill that would modify existing law to prohibit the EPA and state governments from requiring a permit for the use of registered pesticides in certain circumstances. Motion agreed to 229-191 : R 229-1; D 0-190. May 23, 2017.

272. HR 953, H RES 348. PESTICIDE PERMITS/RULE. Adoption of the rule (H Res 348) that would provide for House floor consideration of the bill that would modify existing law to prohibit the EPA and state governments from requiring a permit for the use of registered pesticides in certain circumstances. Adopted 232-189 : R 230-0; D 2-189. May 23, 2017.

273. HR 2288. VA BENEFITS APPEALS/PASSAGE. Roe, R-Tenn., motion to suspend the rules and pass the bill that would create three new options for appealing VA disability benefits decisions and would require the VA to develop a comprehensive plan to implement the new system. Motion agreed to 418-0 : R 232-0; D 186-0. May 23, 2017.

274. PRESIDENT'S TAX RETURN DISCLOSURE/MOTION TO TABLE. Buck, R-Colo., motion to table (kill) the Sanchez, D-Calif., motion to appeal the ruling of the Chair that the Sanchez resolution related to the disclosure of President Trump's text returns does not constitute a question of the privileges of the House. Motion agreed to 225-187 : R 225-1; D 0-186. May 24, 2017.

275. H RES 352, HR 1761, HR 1973. CHILD ABUSE REPORTING AND CHILD PORNOGRAPHY CRIMES/PREVIOUS QUESTION. Buck, R-Colo., motion to order the previous question (thus ending debate and possibility of amendment) on the rule (H Res 352) that would provide for House floor consideration of the bill (HR 1973) that would require adults authorized to interact with minors or amateur athletes to report any suspected incidents of child abuse to the sport's governing body. It would also provide for consideration of the bill (HR 1761) that would make the production of child pornography a crime regardless of whether the conduct with the minor was initiated for the purposes of producing such content. Motion agreed to 231-188 : R 230-1; D 1-187. May 24, 2017.

276. H RES 352, HR 1761, HR 1973. CHILD ABUSE REPORTING AND CHILD PORNOGRAPHY CRIMES/RULE. Adoption of the rule (H Res 352) that would provide for House floor consideration of the bill (HR 1973) that would require adults authorized to interact with minors or amateur athletes to report any suspected incidents of child abuse to the sport's governing body. It would also provide for consideration of the bill (HR 1761) that would make the production of child pornography a crime regardless of whether the conduct with the minor was initiated for the purposes of producing such content. Adopted 239-179 : R 229-0; D 10-179. May 24, 2017.

277. HR 2052. WRONGFUL DISTRIBUTION OF INTIMATE IMAGES/PASSAGE. McSally, R-Ariz., motion to suspend the rules and pass the bill that would amend the Uniform Code of Military Justice to prohibit the wrongful distribution of intimate visual images of the private area of another person, and would subject individuals guilty of taking such actions to punishment by a court-martial. Motion agreed to 418-0 : R 230-0; D 188-0. May 24, 2017.

	271	272	273	274	275	276	277
ALABAMA							
1 Byrne	Y	Y	Y	Y	Y	Y	Y
2 Roby	Y	Y	Y	Y	Y	Y	Y
3 Rogers	Y	Y	Y	Y	Y	Y	Y
4 Aderholt	Y	Y	Y	Y	Y	Y	Y
5 Brooks	Y	Y	Y	Y	Y	Y	Y
6 Palmer	Y	Y	Y	Y	Y	Y	Y
7 Sewell	N	N	Y	N	N	N	Y
ALASKA							
AL Young	Y	Y	Y	Y	Y	Y	Y
ARIZONA							
1 O'Halleran	N	N	Y	N	N	Y	Y
2 McSally	Y	Y	Y	?	?	?	?
3 Grijalva	N	N	Y	N	N	N	Y
4 Gosar	Y	Y	Y	Y	Y	Y	Y
5 Biggs	Y	Y	Y	Y	Y	Y	Y
6 Schweikert	Y	Y	Y	Y	Y	Y	Y
7 Gallego	N	N	Y	N	N	N	Y
8 Franks	Y	Y	Y	Y	Y	Y	Y
9 Sinema	N	Y	Y	?	N	Y	Y
ARKANSAS							
1 Crawford	Y	Y	Y	Y	Y	Y	Y
2 Hill	Y	Y	Y	Y	Y	Y	Y
3 Womack	Y	Y	Y	Y	Y	Y	Y
4 Westerman	Y	Y	Y	Y	Y	Y	Y
CALIFORNIA							
1 LaMalfa	Y	Y	Y	Y	Y	Y	Y
2 Huffman	N	N	Y	N	N	N	Y
3 Garamendi	N	N	Y	N	N	N	Y
4 McClintock	Y	Y	Y	Y	Y	Y	Y
5 Thompson	N	N	Y	N	N	N	Y
6 Matsui	N	N	Y	N	N	N	Y
7 Bera	N	N	Y	N	N	N	Y
8 Cook	Y	Y	Y	Y	Y	Y	Y
9 McNerney	N	N	Y	N	N	N	Y
10 Denham	Y	Y	Y	Y	Y	Y	Y
11 DeSaulnier	N	N	Y	N	N	N	Y
12 Pelosi	N	N	Y	N	N	N	Y
13 Lee	N	N	Y	N	N	N	Y
14 Speier	N	N	Y	N	N	N	Y
15 Swalwell	N	N	+	-	-	-	+
16 Costa	N	Y	Y	N	Y	Y	Y
17 Khanna	N	N	Y	N	N	N	Y
18 Eshoo	N	N	Y	N	N	N	Y
19 Lofgren	N	N	Y	N	N	N	Y
20 Panetta	N	N	Y	N	N	N	Y
21 Valadao	Y	Y	Y	Y	Y	Y	Y
22 Nunes	Y	Y	Y	Y	Y	Y	Y
23 McCarthy	Y	Y	Y	Y	Y	Y	Y
24 Carbajal	N	N	Y	N	N	N	Y
25 Knight	Y	Y	Y	Y	Y	Y	Y
26 Brownley	N	N	Y	N	N	N	Y
27 Chu	N	N	Y	N	N	N	Y
28 Schiff	N	N	Y	N	N	N	Y
29 Cardenas	N	N	Y	N	N	N	Y
30 Sherman	N	N	Y	N	N	N	Y
31 Aguilar	N	N	Y	N	N	N	Y
32 Napolitano	N	N	Y	N	N	N	Y
33 Lieu	N	N	?	N	N	N	Y
34 Vacant							
35 Torres	N	N	Y	N	N	N	Y
36 Ruiz	N	N	Y	N	N	N	Y
37 Bass	N	N	Y	N	N	N	Y
38 Sánchez, Linda	N	N	Y	N	N	N	Y
39 Royce	Y	Y	Y	Y	Y	Y	Y
40 Roybal-Allard	-	N	Y	N	N	N	Y
41 Takano	N	N	Y	N	N	N	Y
42 Calvert	Y	Y	Y	Y	Y	Y	Y
43 Waters	N	N	Y	N	N	N	Y
44 Barragan	N	N	Y	N	N	N	Y
45 Walters	Y	Y	Y	Y	Y	Y	Y
46 Correa	N	N	Y	N	N	Y	Y
47 Lowenthal	N	N	Y	N	N	N	Y
48 Rohrabacher	Y	Y	Y	Y	Y	Y	Y
49 Issa	Y	Y	Y	Y	Y	Y	Y
50 Hunter	Y	Y	Y	Y	Y	Y	Y
51 Vargas	N	N	Y	N	N	N	Y
52 Peters	N	N	Y	N	N	N	Y
53 Davis	N	N	Y	N	N	N	Y

	271	272	273	274	275	276	277
COLORADO							
1 DeGette	N	N	Y	N	N	N	Y
2 Polis	N	N	Y	N	N	N	Y
3 Tipton	Y	Y	Y	Y	Y	Y	Y
4 Buck	Y	Y	Y	Y	Y	Y	Y
5 Lamborn	Y	Y	Y	Y	Y	Y	Y
6 Coffman	Y	Y	Y	Y	Y	Y	Y
7 Perlmutter	N	N	Y	N	N	N	Y
CONNECTICUT							
1 Larson	N	N	Y	N	N	N	Y
2 Courtney	N	N	Y	N	N	N	Y
3 DeLauro	N	N	Y	N	N	N	Y
4 Himes	N	N	Y	N	N	N	Y
5 Esty	N	N	Y	N	N	N	Y
DELAWARE							
AL Blunt Rochester	N	N	Y	N	N	N	Y
FLORIDA							
1 Gaetz	Y	?	Y	Y	Y	Y	Y
2 Dunn	Y	Y	Y	Y	Y	Y	?
3 Yoho	Y	Y	Y	Y	Y	Y	Y
4 Rutherford	Y	Y	Y	Y	Y	Y	Y
5 Lawson	N	N	Y	N	N	N	Y
6 DeSantis	Y	Y	Y	Y	Y	Y	Y
7 Murphy	N	N	Y	N	N	N	Y
8 Posey	Y	Y	Y	Y	Y	Y	Y
9 Soto	N	N	Y	N	N	N	Y
10 Demings	N	N	Y	N	N	N	Y
11 Webster	Y	Y	Y	Y	Y	Y	Y
12 Bilirakis	Y	Y	Y	Y	Y	Y	Y
13 Crist	N	N	Y	N	N	N	Y
14 Castor	N	N	Y	N	N	N	Y
15 Ross	Y	Y	Y	Y	Y	Y	Y
16 Buchanan	Y	Y	Y	Y	Y	Y	Y
17 Rooney, T.	Y	Y	Y	Y	Y	Y	Y
18 Mast	Y	Y	Y	Y	Y	Y	Y
19 Rooney, F.	Y	Y	Y	Y	Y	Y	Y
20 Hastings	N	N	Y	N	N	N	Y
21 Frankel	N	N	Y	N	N	N	Y
22 Deutch	?	?	?	N	N	N	Y
23 Wasserman Schultz	?	?	?	N	N	N	Y
24 Wilson	N	N	Y	N	N	N	Y
25 Diaz-Balart	Y	Y	Y	Y	Y	Y	Y
26 Curbelo	Y	Y	Y	Y	Y	Y	Y
27 Ros-Lehtinen	Y	Y	Y	Y	Y	Y	Y
GEORGIA							
1 Carter	Y	Y	Y	Y	Y	Y	Y
2 Bishop	N	N	Y	?	?	N	Y
3 Ferguson	Y	Y	Y	Y	Y	Y	Y
4 Johnson	N	N	Y	N	N	N	Y
5 Lewis	N	N	Y	N	N	N	Y
7 Woodall	Y	Y	Y	Y	Y	Y	Y
8 Scott, A.	Y	Y	Y	Y	Y	Y	Y
9 Collins	Y	Y	Y	Y	Y	Y	Y
10 Hice	?	?	?	Y	Y	Y	Y
11 Loudermilk	Y	Y	Y	?	?	?	?
12 Allen	Y	Y	Y	Y	Y	Y	Y
13 Scott, D.	N	N	Y	N	N	N	Y
14 Graves	Y	Y	Y	Y	Y	Y	Y
HAWAII							
1 Hanabusa	N	N	Y	N	N	N	Y
2 Gabbard	N	N	Y	N	N	N	Y
IDAHO							
1 Labrador	Y	Y	Y	Y	Y	Y	Y
2 Simpson	?	Y	Y	Y	Y	Y	Y
ILLINOIS							
1 Rush	N	N	Y	N	N	N	Y
2 Kelly	N	N	Y	N	N	N	Y
3 Lipinski	N	N	Y	N	N	N	Y
4 Gutierrez	N	N	Y	N	N	N	Y
5 Quigley	N	N	Y	N	N	N	Y
6 Roskam	Y	Y	Y	Y	Y	Y	Y
7 Davis, D.	N	N	Y	N	N	N	Y
8 Krishnamoorthi	N	N	Y	N	N	N	Y
9 Schakowsky	N	N	Y	N	N	N	Y
10 Schneider	N	N	Y	N	N	N	Y
11 Foster	N	N	Y	N	N	N	Y
12 Bost	Y	Y	Y	Y	Y	Y	Y
13 Davis, R.	Y	Y	Y	Y	Y	Y	Y
14 Hultgren	Y	Y	Y	Y	Y	Y	Y
15 Shimkus	Y	Y	Y	Y	Y	Y	Y

KEY	**Republicans**	Democrats	*Independents*
Y Voted for (yea)	X Paired against		C Voted "present" to avoid possible conflict of interest
# Paired for	- Announced against		
+ Announced for	P Voted "present"		? Did not vote or otherwise make a position known
N Voted against (nay)			

	271	272	273	274	275	276	277
16 **Kinzinger**	Y	Y	Y	Y	Y	Y	Y
17 Bustos	N	N	Y	N	N	N	Y
18 **LaHood**	Y	Y	Y	Y	Y	Y	Y
INDIANA							
1 Visclosky	N	N	Y	N	N	N	Y
2 **Walorski**	Y	Y	Y	Y	Y	Y	Y
3 **Banks**	Y	Y	Y	Y	Y	Y	Y
4 **Rokita**	Y	Y	Y	Y	Y	Y	Y
5 **Brooks**	Y	Y	Y	?	Y	Y	Y
6 **Messer**	Y	Y	Y	Y	Y	Y	Y
7 Carson	N	N	Y	N	N	N	Y
8 **Bucshon**	Y	Y	Y	Y	Y	Y	Y
9 **Hollingsworth**	Y	Y	Y	Y	Y	?	Y
IOWA							
1 **Blum**	Y	Y	Y	Y	Y	Y	Y
2 Loebsack	N	N	Y	N	N	N	Y
3 **Young**	Y	Y	Y	Y	Y	Y	Y
4 **King**	Y	Y	Y	Y	Y	Y	Y
KANSAS							
1 **Marshall**	Y	Y	Y	Y	Y	Y	Y
2 **Jenkins**	Y	Y	Y	Y	Y	Y	Y
3 **Yoder**	Y	Y	Y	Y	Y	Y	Y
4 **Estes**	Y	Y	Y	Y	Y	Y	Y
KENTUCKY							
1 **Comer**	Y	Y	Y	Y	Y	Y	Y
2 **Guthrie**	Y	Y	Y	Y	Y	Y	Y
3 Yarmuth	N	N	Y	N	N	N	Y
4 **Massie**	Y	Y	Y	Y	Y	Y	Y
5 **Rogers**	Y	Y	Y	Y	Y	Y	Y
6 **Barr**	Y	Y	Y	Y	Y	Y	Y
LOUISIANA							
1 **Scalise**	Y	Y	Y	Y	Y	Y	Y
2 Richmond	N	N	Y	N	N	N	Y
3 **Higgins**	Y	Y	Y	Y	Y	Y	Y
4 **Johnson**	Y	Y	Y	Y	Y	Y	Y
5 **Abraham**	Y	Y	Y	Y	Y	Y	Y
6 **Graves**	Y	Y	Y	?	?	?	?
MAINE							
1 Pingree	N	N	Y	N	N	N	Y
2 **Poliquin**	Y	Y	Y	Y	Y	Y	Y
MARYLAND							
1 **Harris**	Y	Y	Y	Y	Y	Y	Y
2 Ruppersberger	N	N	Y	N	N	N	Y
3 Sarbanes	N	N	Y	N	N	N	Y
4 Brown	N	N	Y	N	N	N	Y
5 Hoyer	N	N	Y	N	N	N	Y
6 Delaney	N	N	Y	N	N	N	Y
7 Cummings	N	N	Y	?	?	?	?
8 Raskin	N	N	Y	N	N	N	Y
MASSACHUSETTS							
1 Neal	N	N	Y	N	N	N	Y
2 McGovern	N	N	Y	N	N	N	Y
3 Tsongas	N	N	Y	N	N	N	Y
4 Kennedy	N	N	Y	N	N	N	Y
5 Clark	N	N	Y	N	N	N	Y
6 Moulton	N	N	Y	N	N	N	Y
7 Capuano	N	N	Y	N	N	N	Y
8 Lynch	N	N	Y	N	N	N	Y
9 Keating	N	N	Y	N	N	N	Y
MICHIGAN							
1 **Bergman**	Y	Y	Y	Y	Y	Y	Y
2 **Huizenga**	?	?	?	Y	Y	Y	Y
3 **Amash**	Y	Y	Y	Y	Y	Y	Y
4 **Moolenaar**	Y	Y	Y	Y	Y	Y	Y
5 Kildee	N	N	Y	N	N	N	Y
6 **Upton**	Y	Y	Y	Y	Y	Y	Y
7 **Walberg**	Y	Y	Y	Y	Y	Y	Y
8 **Bishop**	Y	Y	Y	Y	Y	Y	Y
9 Levin	N	N	Y	N	N	N	Y
10 **Mitchell**	Y	Y	Y	Y	Y	Y	Y
11 **Trott**	Y	Y	Y	Y	Y	Y	Y
12 Dingell	N	N	Y	N	N	N	Y
13 Conyers	N	N	Y	N	N	N	Y
14 Lawrence	N	N	Y	N	N	N	Y
MINNESOTA							
1 Walz	N	N	Y	N	N	N	Y
2 **Lewis**	Y	Y	Y	Y	Y	Y	Y
3 **Paulsen**	Y	Y	Y	Y	Y	Y	Y
4 McCollum	N	N	Y	N	N	N	Y
5 Ellison	N	N	Y	?	N	N	Y
6 **Emmer**	Y	Y	Y	Y	Y	Y	Y
7 Peterson	N	N	Y	N	N	Y	Y
8 Nolan	N	N	Y	N	N	N	Y
MISSISSIPPI							
1 **Kelly**	Y	Y	Y	Y	Y	Y	Y
2 Thompson	N	N	Y	N	N	N	Y
3 **Harper**	Y	Y	Y	Y	Y	Y	Y
4 **Palazzo**	Y	Y	Y	Y	Y	Y	Y
MISSOURI							
1 Clay	N	N	Y	N	N	N	Y
2 **Wagner**	Y	Y	Y	Y	Y	Y	Y
3 **Luetkemeyer**	Y	Y	Y	Y	Y	Y	Y
4 **Hartzler**	Y	Y	Y	Y	Y	Y	Y
5 Cleaver	N	N	?	N	N	N	Y
6 **Graves**	Y	Y	Y	Y	Y	Y	Y
7 **Long**	Y	Y	Y	Y	Y	Y	Y
8 **Smith**	Y	Y	Y	Y	Y	Y	Y
MONTANA							
AL **Vacant**							
NEBRASKA							
1 **Fortenberry**	Y	Y	Y	Y	Y	Y	Y
2 **Bacon**	Y	Y	Y	Y	Y	Y	Y
3 **Smith**	Y	Y	Y	Y	Y	Y	Y
NEVADA							
1 Titus	N	N	Y	N	N	N	Y
2 **Amodei**	Y	Y	Y	Y	Y	Y	Y
3 Rosen	N	N	Y	N	N	Y	Y
4 Kihuen	N	N	Y	N	N	N	Y
NEW HAMPSHIRE							
1 Shea-Porter	N	N	Y	N	N	N	Y
2 Kuster	N	N	Y	N	N	N	Y
NEW JERSEY							
1 Norcross	N	N	Y	N	N	N	Y
2 **LoBiondo**	Y	Y	Y	Y	Y	Y	Y
3 **MacArthur**	Y	Y	Y	Y	Y	Y	Y
4 **Smith**	Y	Y	Y	Y	Y	Y	Y
5 Gottheimer	N	N	Y	N	N	Y	Y
6 Pallone	N	N	Y	N	N	N	Y
7 **Lance**	Y	Y	Y	Y	Y	Y	Y
8 Sires	N	N	Y	N	N	N	Y
9 Pascrell	N	N	Y	N	N	N	Y
10 Payne	N	N	Y	N	N	N	Y
11 **Frelinghuysen**	Y	Y	Y	Y	Y	Y	Y
12 Watson Coleman	N	N	Y	N	N	N	Y
NEW MEXICO							
1 Lujan Grisham	N	N	Y	N	N	N	Y
2 **Pearce**	Y	Y	Y	Y	Y	Y	Y
3 Luján	N	N	Y	N	N	N	Y
NEW YORK							
1 **Zeldin**	Y	Y	Y	Y	Y	Y	Y
2 **King**	Y	Y	Y	Y	Y	Y	Y
3 Suozzi	N	N	Y	N	N	N	Y
4 Rice	N	N	?	N	N	N	Y
5 Meeks	N	N	Y	N	N	N	Y
6 Meng	N	N	Y	N	N	N	Y
7 Velázquez	N	N	Y	?	?	?	?
8 Jeffries	N	N	Y	N	N	N	Y
9 Clarke	N	N	Y	N	N	N	Y
10 Nadler	N	N	Y	N	N	N	Y
11 **Donovan**	Y	Y	Y	Y	Y	Y	Y
12 Maloney, C.	N	N	Y	?	?	?	?
13 Espaillat	N	N	Y	N	N	N	Y
14 Crowley	N	N	Y	N	N	N	Y
15 Serrano	N	N	Y	N	N	N	Y
16 Engel	N	N	Y	N	N	N	Y
17 Lowey	N	N	Y	N	N	N	Y
18 Maloney, S.P.	N	N	Y	N	N	N	Y
19 **Faso**	Y	Y	Y	Y	Y	Y	Y
20 Tonko	N	N	Y	N	N	N	Y
21 **Stefanik**	Y	Y	Y	Y	Y	Y	Y
22 **Tenney**	Y	Y	Y	Y	Y	Y	Y
23 **Reed**	Y	Y	Y	Y	Y	Y	Y
24 **Katko**	Y	Y	Y	Y	Y	Y	Y
25 Slaughter	N	N	Y	N	N	N	Y
26 Higgins	N	N	Y	N	N	N	Y
27 **Collins**	Y	Y	Y	Y	Y	Y	Y
NORTH CAROLINA							
1 Butterfield	N	N	Y	N	N	N	Y
2 **Holding**	Y	Y	Y	Y	Y	Y	Y
3 **Jones**	N	Y	Y	N	N	Y	Y
4 Price	N	N	Y	N	N	N	Y
5 **Foxx**	Y	Y	Y	Y	Y	Y	Y
6 **Walker**	Y	Y	Y	Y	Y	Y	Y
7 **Rouzer**	Y	Y	Y	Y	Y	Y	Y
8 **Hudson**	Y	Y	Y	Y	Y	Y	Y
9 **Pittenger**	Y	Y	Y	Y	Y	Y	Y
10 **McHenry**	Y	Y	Y	Y	Y	Y	Y
11 **Meadows**	Y	Y	Y	Y	Y	Y	Y
12 Adams	N	N	Y	N	N	N	Y
13 **Budd**	Y	Y	Y	Y	Y	Y	Y
NORTH DAKOTA							
AL **Cramer**	Y	Y	Y	Y	Y	Y	Y
OHIO							
1 **Chabot**	Y	Y	Y	Y	Y	Y	Y
2 **Wenstrup**	Y	Y	Y	Y	Y	Y	Y
3 Beatty	N	N	Y	N	N	N	Y
4 **Jordan**	Y	Y	Y	Y	Y	Y	Y
5 **Latta**	Y	Y	Y	Y	Y	Y	Y
6 **Johnson**	Y	Y	Y	?	Y	Y	Y
7 **Gibbs**	Y	Y	Y	Y	Y	Y	Y
8 **Davidson**	Y	Y	Y	Y	Y	Y	Y
9 Kaptur	N	N	Y	N	N	N	Y
10 **Turner**	Y	Y	Y	Y	Y	Y	Y
11 Fudge	N	N	?	N	N	N	Y
12 **Tiberi**	?	?	+	Y	Y	Y	Y
13 Ryan	N	N	Y	N	N	N	Y
14 **Joyce**	Y	Y	Y	Y	Y	Y	Y
15 **Stivers**	Y	Y	Y	Y	Y	Y	Y
16 **Renacci**	Y	Y	Y	Y	Y	Y	Y
OKLAHOMA							
1 **Bridenstine**	Y	Y	Y	Y	Y	Y	Y
2 **Mullin**	Y	Y	Y	Y	Y	Y	Y
3 **Lucas**	Y	Y	Y	Y	Y	Y	Y
4 **Cole**	Y	Y	Y	Y	Y	Y	Y
5 **Russell**	Y	Y	Y	Y	Y	Y	Y
OREGON							
1 Bonamici	N	N	Y	N	N	N	Y
2 **Walden**	Y	Y	Y	Y	Y	Y	Y
3 Blumenauer	N	N	Y	N	N	N	Y
4 DeFazio	N	N	Y	N	N	N	Y
5 Schrader	N	N	Y	N	N	N	Y
PENNSYLVANIA							
1 Brady	N	N	Y	N	N	N	Y
2 Evans	N	N	Y	N	N	N	Y
3 **Kelly**	Y	Y	Y	Y	Y	Y	Y
4 **Perry**	Y	Y	Y	Y	Y	Y	Y
5 **Thompson**	Y	Y	Y	?	Y	Y	Y
6 **Costello**	Y	Y	Y	Y	Y	Y	Y
7 **Meehan**	Y	Y	Y	Y	Y	Y	Y
8 **Fitzpatrick**	Y	Y	Y	Y	Y	Y	Y
9 **Shuster**	Y	Y	Y	Y	Y	Y	Y
10 **Marino**	Y	Y	Y	Y	Y	Y	Y
11 **Barletta**	Y	Y	Y	Y	Y	Y	Y
12 **Rothfus**	Y	Y	Y	Y	Y	Y	Y
13 Boyle	N	N	Y	N	N	N	Y
14 Doyle	N	N	Y	N	N	N	Y
15 **Dent**	Y	Y	Y	Y	Y	Y	Y
16 **Smucker**	Y	Y	Y	Y	Y	Y	Y
17 Cartwright	N	N	Y	N	N	N	Y
18 **Murphy**	Y	Y	Y	Y	Y	Y	Y
RHODE ISLAND							
1 Cicilline	N	N	Y	N	N	N	Y
2 Langevin	N	N	Y	N	N	N	Y
SOUTH CAROLINA							
1 **Sanford**	Y	Y	Y	P	Y	Y	Y
2 **Wilson**	Y	Y	Y	Y	Y	Y	Y
3 **Duncan**	Y	Y	Y	Y	Y	Y	Y
4 **Gowdy**	Y	Y	Y	Y	Y	Y	Y
6 Clyburn	N	N	Y	N	N	N	Y
7 **Rice**	Y	Y	Y	Y	Y	Y	Y
SOUTH DAKOTA							
AL **Noem**	Y	Y	Y	Y	Y	Y	Y
TENNESSEE							
1 **Roe**	Y	Y	Y	Y	Y	Y	Y
2 **Duncan**	Y	Y	Y	Y	Y	Y	Y
3 **Fleischmann**	Y	Y	Y	Y	Y	Y	Y
4 **DesJarlais**	Y	Y	Y	Y	Y	Y	Y
5 Cooper	N	N	Y	N	N	N	Y
6 **Black**	?	?	?	?	?	?	?
7 **Blackburn**	Y	Y	Y	Y	Y	Y	Y
8 **Kustoff**	Y	Y	Y	Y	Y	Y	Y
9 Cohen	N	N	Y	N	N	N	Y
TEXAS							
1 **Gohmert**	Y	Y	Y	Y	Y	Y	Y
2 **Poe**	Y	Y	Y	Y	Y	Y	Y
3 **Johnson, S.**	?	?	?	?	?	?	?
4 **Ratcliffe**	Y	Y	Y	Y	Y	Y	Y
5 **Hensarling**	Y	Y	Y	Y	Y	Y	Y
6 **Barton**	Y	Y	Y	Y	Y	Y	Y
7 **Culberson**	Y	Y	Y	Y	Y	Y	Y
8 **Brady**	Y	Y	Y	Y	Y	Y	Y
9 Green, A.	N	N	Y	N	N	N	Y
10 **McCaul**	Y	Y	Y	Y	Y	Y	Y
11 **Conaway**	Y	Y	Y	Y	Y	Y	Y
12 **Granger**	Y	Y	Y	Y	Y	Y	Y
13 **Thornberry**	Y	Y	Y	Y	Y	Y	Y
14 **Weber**	Y	Y	Y	Y	Y	Y	Y
15 Gonzalez	N	N	Y	N	N	N	Y
16 O'Rourke	N	N	Y	N	N	N	Y
17 **Flores**	Y	Y	Y	Y	Y	Y	Y
18 Jackson Lee	N	N	Y	N	N	N	Y
19 **Arrington**	Y	Y	Y	Y	Y	Y	Y
20 Castro	N	N	Y	N	N	N	Y
21 **Smith**	Y	Y	Y	Y	Y	Y	Y
22 **Olson**	Y	Y	Y	Y	Y	Y	Y
23 **Hurd**	Y	Y	Y	Y	Y	Y	Y
24 **Marchant**	Y	Y	Y	Y	Y	Y	Y
25 **Williams**	Y	Y	Y	Y	Y	Y	Y
26 **Burgess**	Y	Y	Y	?	Y	Y	Y
27 **Farenthold**	Y	Y	Y	Y	Y	Y	Y
28 Cuellar	N	N	Y	N	N	N	Y
29 Green, G.	N	N	Y	N	N	N	Y
30 Johnson, E.B.	N	N	Y	N	N	N	Y
31 **Carter**	Y	Y	Y	Y	Y	Y	Y
32 **Sessions**	Y	Y	Y	Y	Y	Y	Y
33 Veasey	N	N	Y	N	N	N	Y
34 Vela	N	N	Y	N	N	N	Y
35 Doggett	N	N	Y	N	N	N	Y
36 **Babin**	Y	Y	Y	Y	Y	Y	Y
UTAH							
1 **Bishop**	Y	Y	Y	Y	Y	Y	Y
2 **Stewart**	Y	Y	Y	Y	Y	Y	Y
3 **Chaffetz**	Y	Y	Y	Y	Y	Y	Y
4 **Love**	Y	Y	Y	Y	Y	Y	Y
VERMONT							
AL Welch	N	N	Y	N	N	N	Y
VIRGINIA							
1 **Wittman**	Y	Y	Y	Y	Y	Y	Y
2 **Taylor**	Y	Y	Y	Y	Y	Y	Y
3 Scott	N	N	Y	N	N	N	Y
4 McEachin	N	N	Y	N	N	N	?
5 **Garrett**	Y	Y	Y	Y	Y	?	Y
6 **Goodlatte**	Y	Y	Y	Y	Y	Y	Y
7 **Brat**	Y	Y	Y	Y	Y	Y	Y
8 Beyer	N	N	Y	N	N	N	Y
9 **Griffith**	Y	Y	Y	Y	Y	Y	Y
10 **Comstock**	Y	Y	Y	Y	Y	Y	Y
11 Connolly	N	N	Y	N	N	N	Y
WASHINGTON							
1 DelBene	N	N	Y	N	N	N	Y
2 Larsen	N	N	Y	N	N	N	Y
3 **Herrera Beutler**	Y	Y	Y	Y	Y	Y	Y
4 **Newhouse**	?	?	?	?	?	?	?
5 **McMorris Rodgers**	Y	Y	Y	Y	Y	Y	Y
6 Kilmer	N	N	Y	N	N	N	Y
7 Jayapal	N	N	Y	N	N	N	Y
8 **Reichert**	Y	Y	Y	Y	Y	Y	Y
9 Smith	N	N	Y	N	N	N	Y
10 Heck	N	N	Y	N	N	N	Y
WEST VIRGINIA							
1 **McKinley**	Y	Y	Y	Y	Y	Y	Y
2 **Mooney**	Y	Y	Y	Y	Y	Y	Y
3 **Jenkins**	Y	Y	Y	Y	Y	Y	Y
WISCONSIN							
1 **Ryan**							
2 Pocan	N	N	Y	N	N	N	Y
3 Kind	N	N	Y	N	N	Y	Y
4 Moore	N	N	Y	N	N	N	Y
5 **Sensenbrenner**	Y	Y	Y	Y	Y	Y	Y
6 **Grothman**	Y	Y	Y	Y	Y	Y	Y
7 **Duffy**	Y	Y	Y	Y	Y	Y	Y
8 **Gallagher**	Y	Y	Y	Y	Y	Y	Y
WYOMING							
AL **Cheney**	Y	Y	Y	Y	Y	Y	Y

⫼ HOUSE VOTES

VOTE NUMBER

278. HR 467. VA APPOINTMENT COMPLIANCE/PASSAGE. Roe, R-Tenn., motion to suspend the rules and pass the bill that would direct the secretary of Veterans Affairs to ensure that directors of VA medical facilities annually certify that the facility is in full compliance with laws and regulations related to veterans' scheduling of appointments to receive hospital care and medical services. Motion agreed to 419-0 : R 230-0; D 189-0. May 24, 2017.

279. HR 953. PESTICIDE PERMITS/TOXIC INGREDIENTS. Esty, D-Conn., amendment that would require that the bill's provisions related to permit exemptions not apply to ingredients or chemicals in pesticides that contain certain toxic pollutants and hazardous substances previously established by federal law. Rejected in Committee of the Whole 191-229 : R 9-223; D 182-6. May 24, 2017.

280. HR 953. PESTICIDE PERMITS/FISHERY IMPACT. Huffman, D-Calif., amendment that would clarify that none of the bill's provisions would prevent the EPA or a state from requiring a permit under the Federal Water Pollution Control Act for the use of a pesticide that would have a negative impact on fisheries. Rejected in Committee of the Whole 189-230 : R 5-225; D 184-5. May 24, 2017.

281. HR 953. PESTICIDE PERMITS/RECOMMIT. McGovern, D-Mass., motion to recommit the bill to the House Transportation and Infrastructure Committee with instructions to report it back immediately with an amendment that would exempt from the bill's provisions a discharge of a pesticide if its manufacturer or distributor made a political contribution to the president or to any federal official responsible for its registration, regulation or the approval of its use. Motion rejected 183-230 : R 1-228; D 182-2. May 24, 2017.

282. HR 953. PESTICIDE PERMITS/PASSAGE. Passage of the bill that would prohibit the EPA and states from requiring permits for the point source use of a pesticide registered under the Federal Insecticide, Fungicide, and Rodenticide Act. It would prohibit the EPA or states from requiring a Federal Water Pollution Control Act permit for the use of registered pesticides near navigable waters. Passed 256-165 : R 231-1; D 25-164. May 24, 2017.

283. HR 1761. CHILD PORNOGRAPHY CRIMES/LIMITATION ON IMPRISONMENT. Jackson Lee, D-Texas, amendment that would limit, to one year, a term of imprisonment for individuals convicted of child pornography crimes who are 19 years old or younger and the minor involved is 15 years old or older, as long as the minor was not more than four years younger than the individual who committed the violation and the sexual conduct that occurred was consensual. Rejected in Committee of the Whole 180-238 : R 2-231; D 178-7. May 25, 2017.

284. HR 1761. CHILD PORNOGRAPHY CRIMES/PASSAGE. Passage of the bill that would make the production of child pornography a crime regardless of whether the sexual conduct with the minor was initiated for the purposes of producing such content. The bill would establish new offenses that could be prosecuted as child pornography and subjected to the same mandatory minimum prison sentences as current child pornography crimes, including live streaming a child engaged in sexually-explicit conduct, whether produced domestically or abroad. Passed 368-51 : R 231-2; D 137-49. May 25, 2017.

	278	279	280	281	282	283	284
ALABAMA							
1 **Byrne**	Y	N	N	N	Y	N	Y
2 **Roby**	Y	N	N	N	Y	N	Y
3 **Rogers**	Y	N	N	N	Y	N	Y
4 **Aderholt**	Y	N	N	N	Y	N	Y
5 **Brooks**	Y	N	N	N	Y	N	Y
6 **Palmer**	Y	N	N	N	Y	N	Y
7 Sewell	Y	Y	Y	Y	Y	Y	Y
ALASKA							
AL **Young**	Y	N	N	N	Y	N	Y
ARIZONA							
1 O'Halleran	Y	N	Y	Y	Y	Y	Y
2 **McSally**	?	?	?	?	?	–	+
3 Grijalva	Y	Y	Y	Y	N	Y	N
4 **Gosar**	Y	N	N	N	Y	N	Y
5 **Biggs**	Y	N	N	N	Y	N	Y
6 **Schweikert**	Y	N	N	N	Y	N	Y
7 Gallego	Y	Y	Y	Y	N	Y	Y
8 **Franks**	Y	N	N	?	Y	N	Y
9 Sinema	Y	Y	Y	Y	Y	Y	Y
ARKANSAS							
1 **Crawford**	Y	N	N	N	Y	N	Y
2 **Hill**	Y	N	N	N	Y	N	Y
3 **Womack**	Y	N	N	N	Y	N	Y
4 **Westerman**	Y	N	N	N	Y	N	Y
CALIFORNIA							
1 **LaMalfa**	Y	N	N	N	Y	N	Y
2 Huffman	Y	Y	Y	Y	N	Y	N
3 Garamendi	Y	Y	Y	Y	N	Y	Y
4 **McClintock**	Y	N	N	N	Y	N	Y
5 Thompson	Y	Y	Y	Y	N	Y	Y
6 Matsui	Y	Y	Y	Y	N	Y	Y
7 Bera	Y	Y	Y	Y	N	N	Y
8 **Cook**	Y	N	N	N	Y	N	Y
9 McNerney	Y	Y	Y	Y	N	Y	Y
10 **Denham**	Y	N	N	N	Y	N	Y
11 DeSaulnier	Y	Y	Y	Y	N	Y	N
12 Pelosi	Y	Y	Y	Y	N	Y	Y
13 Lee	Y	Y	Y	Y	N	Y	N
14 Speier	Y	Y	Y	Y	N	Y	Y
15 Swalwell	+	+	+	+	–	–	+
16 Costa	Y	N	N	?	Y	N	Y
17 Khanna	Y	Y	Y	Y	N	Y	N
18 Eshoo	Y	Y	Y	Y	N	Y	Y
19 Lofgren	Y	Y	Y	Y	N	Y	Y
20 Panetta	Y	Y	Y	Y	N	Y	Y
21 **Valadao**	Y	N	N	N	Y	N	Y
22 **Nunes**	Y	N	N	N	Y	N	Y
23 **McCarthy**	Y	N	N	N	Y	N	Y
24 Carbajal	Y	Y	Y	Y	N	Y	Y
25 **Knight**	Y	N	N	N	Y	N	Y
26 Brownley	Y	Y	Y	Y	N	Y	Y
27 Chu	Y	Y	Y	Y	N	Y	N
28 Schiff	Y	Y	Y	Y	N	Y	Y
29 Cardenas	Y	Y	Y	?	N	Y	N
30 Sherman	Y	Y	Y	?	N	Y	N
31 Aguilar	Y	Y	Y	Y	N	Y	Y
32 Napolitano	Y	Y	Y	Y	N	Y	Y
33 Lieu	Y	Y	Y	Y	N	Y	Y
34 Vacant							
35 Torres	Y	Y	Y	Y	N	Y	Y
36 Ruiz	Y	Y	Y	Y	N	Y	Y
37 Bass	Y	Y	Y	Y	N	Y	N
38 Sánchez, Linda	Y	Y	Y	Y	N	Y	Y
39 **Royce**	Y	N	N	N	Y	N	Y
40 Roybal-Allard	Y	Y	Y	Y	N	Y	Y
41 Takano	Y	Y	Y	Y	N	Y	N
42 **Calvert**	Y	N	N	N	Y	N	Y
43 Waters	Y	Y	Y	?	N	Y	N
44 Barragan	Y	Y	Y	Y	N	Y	N
45 **Walters**	Y	N	N	N	Y	N	Y
46 Correa	Y	Y	Y	Y	N	Y	Y
47 Lowenthal	Y	Y	Y	Y	N	Y	N
48 **Rohrabacher**	Y	N	N	N	Y	N	Y
49 **Issa**	Y	N	N	N	Y	N	Y
50 **Hunter**	Y	N	N	N	Y	N	Y
51 Vargas	Y	Y	Y	Y	N	Y	Y
52 Peters	Y	Y	Y	Y	N	Y	Y
53 Davis	Y	Y	Y	Y	N	Y	+

	278	279	280	281	282	283	284
COLORADO							
1 DeGette	Y	Y	Y	Y	N	Y	Y
2 Polis	Y	Y	Y	Y	N	Y	Y
3 **Tipton**	Y	N	N	N	Y	N	Y
4 **Buck**	Y	N	N	N	Y	N	Y
5 **Lamborn**	Y	N	N	N	Y	N	Y
6 **Coffman**	Y	N	N	N	Y	N	Y
7 Perlmutter	Y	?	Y	Y	N	Y	Y
CONNECTICUT							
1 Larson	Y	Y	Y	Y	N	Y	Y
2 Courtney	Y	Y	Y	Y	N	Y	Y
3 DeLauro	Y	Y	Y	Y	N	Y	Y
4 Himes	Y	Y	Y	Y	N	Y	Y
5 Esty	Y	Y	Y	Y	N	Y	Y
DELAWARE							
AL Blunt Rochester	Y	Y	Y	Y	Y	Y	Y
FLORIDA							
1 **Gaetz**	Y	N	N	N	Y	N	Y
2 **Dunn**	Y	N	N	N	Y	N	Y
3 **Yoho**	Y	N	N	N	Y	N	Y
4 **Rutherford**	Y	N	N	N	Y	N	Y
5 Lawson	Y	Y	Y	Y	Y	Y	Y
6 **DeSantis**	Y	N	N	N	Y	N	Y
7 Murphy	Y	Y	Y	Y	N	Y	Y
8 **Posey**	Y	N	N	N	Y	N	Y
9 Soto	Y	Y	Y	Y	N	Y	Y
10 Demings	Y	Y	Y	Y	N	Y	Y
11 **Webster**	Y	N	N	N	Y	N	Y
12 **Bilirakis**	Y	N	N	N	Y	N	Y
13 Crist	Y	Y	Y	Y	N	Y	Y
14 Castor	Y	Y	Y	Y	N	Y	Y
15 **Ross**	Y	N	N	N	Y	N	Y
16 **Buchanan**	Y	N	N	N	Y	N	Y
17 **Rooney, T.**	Y	N	N	N	Y	N	Y
18 **Mast**	Y	N	N	N	Y	N	Y
19 **Rooney, F.**	Y	N	N	N	Y	N	Y
20 Hastings	Y	Y	Y	Y	N	Y	N
21 Frankel	Y	Y	Y	Y	N	Y	Y
22 Deutch	Y	Y	Y	Y	N	Y	Y
23 Wasserman Schultz	Y	Y	Y	Y	N	Y	N
24 Wilson	Y	Y	Y	Y	N	Y	N
25 **Diaz-Balart**	Y	N	N	N	Y	N	Y
26 **Curbelo**	Y	N	N	N	Y	N	Y
27 **Ros-Lehtinen**	Y	N	N	N	Y	N	Y
GEORGIA							
1 **Carter**	Y	N	N	N	Y	N	Y
2 Bishop	Y	Y	Y	Y	Y	Y	Y
3 **Ferguson**	Y	N	N	N	Y	N	Y
4 Johnson	Y	Y	Y	Y	N	?	N
5 Lewis	Y	Y	Y	Y	N	Y	N
7 **Woodall**	Y	N	N	N	Y	N	Y
8 **Scott, A.**	Y	N	N	N	Y	N	Y
9 **Collins**	Y	N	N	N	Y	N	Y
10 **Hice**	Y	N	N	N	Y	N	Y
11 **Loudermilk**	?	N	N	N	Y	N	Y
12 **Allen**	Y	N	N	N	Y	N	Y
13 Scott, D.	Y	Y	Y	Y	Y	Y	Y
14 **Graves**	Y	N	N	N	Y	N	Y
HAWAII							
1 Hanabusa	Y	Y	Y	Y	N	Y	Y
2 Gabbard	Y	Y	Y	Y	N	Y	Y
IDAHO							
1 **Labrador**	Y	N	N	N	Y	Y	Y
2 **Simpson**	Y	N	N	N	Y	N	Y
ILLINOIS							
1 Rush	Y	Y	Y	Y	N	Y	N
2 Kelly	Y	Y	Y	Y	N	Y	Y
3 Lipinski	Y	Y	Y	Y	N	Y	Y
4 Gutierrez	Y	Y	Y	Y	N	Y	N
5 Quigley	Y	Y	Y	Y	N	?	Y
6 **Roskam**	Y	N	N	N	Y	N	Y
7 Davis, D.	Y	Y	Y	Y	N	Y	N
8 Krishnamoorthi	Y	Y	Y	Y	N	Y	Y
9 Schakowsky	Y	Y	Y	Y	N	Y	N
10 Schneider	Y	Y	Y	Y	N	Y	Y
11 Foster	Y	Y	Y	Y	N	Y	Y
12 **Bost**	Y	N	N	N	Y	N	Y
13 **Davis, R.**	Y	N	N	N	Y	N	Y
14 **Hultgren**	Y	N	N	N	Y	N	Y
15 **Shimkus**	Y	N	N	N	Y	N	Y

KEY	Republicans	Democrats	Independents
Y Voted for (yea)	**X** Paired against		**C** Voted "present" to avoid possible conflict of interest
# Paired for	**–** Announced against		
+ Announced for	**P** Voted "present"		**?** Did not vote or otherwise make a position known
N Voted against (nay)			

	278	279	280	281	282	283	284
16 **Kinzinger**	Y	N	N	N	Y	N	Y
17 Bustos	Y	Y	Y	Y	Y	Y	Y
18 **LaHood**	Y	N	N	N	Y	N	Y
INDIANA							
1 Visclosky	Y	Y	Y	Y	N	Y	Y
2 **Walorski**	Y	N	N	N	Y	N	Y
3 **Banks**	Y	N	N	N	Y	N	Y
4 **Rokita**	Y	N	N	N	Y	N	Y
5 **Brooks**	Y	N	N	N	Y	N	Y
6 **Messer**	Y	N	N	N	Y	N	Y
7 Carson	Y	Y	Y	Y	Y	Y	Y
8 **Bucshon**	Y	N	N	N	Y	N	Y
9 **Hollingsworth**	Y	N	N	N	Y	N	Y
IOWA							
1 **Blum**	Y	N	N	N	Y	N	Y
2 Loebsack	Y	Y	Y	Y	Y	Y	Y
3 **Young**	Y	N	N	N	Y	N	Y
4 **King**	Y	N	N	N	Y	N	Y
KANSAS							
1 **Marshall**	Y	N	N	N	Y	N	Y
2 **Jenkins**	Y	N	N	N	Y	N	Y
3 **Yoder**	Y	N	N	N	Y	N	Y
4 **Estes**	Y	N	N	N	Y	N	Y
KENTUCKY							
1 **Comer**	Y	N	N	N	Y	N	Y
2 **Guthrie**	Y	N	N	N	Y	N	Y
3 Yarmuth	Y	Y	Y	Y	N	Y	Y
4 **Massie**	Y	N	N	N	Y	N	N
5 **Rogers**	Y	N	N	N	Y	N	Y
6 **Barr**	Y	N	N	N	Y	N	Y
LOUISIANA							
1 **Scalise**	Y	N	N	N	Y	N	Y
2 Richmond	Y	Y	Y	Y	N	Y	N
3 **Higgins**	Y	N	N	N	Y	N	Y
4 **Johnson**	Y	N	N	N	Y	N	Y
5 **Abraham**	Y	N	N	N	Y	N	Y
6 **Graves**	?	?	?	?	?	N	Y
MAINE							
1 Pingree	Y	Y	Y	Y	N	Y	Y
2 **Poliquin**	Y	N	N	N	Y	N	Y
MARYLAND							
1 **Harris**	Y	N	N	N	Y	N	Y
2 Ruppersberger	Y	Y	Y	Y	N	Y	Y
3 Sarbanes	Y	Y	Y	Y	N	Y	Y
4 Brown	Y	Y	Y	Y	N	Y	Y
5 Hoyer	Y	Y	Y	Y	N	Y	Y
6 Delaney	Y	Y	Y	Y	N	Y	Y
7 Cummings	?	?	?	?	?	?	?
8 Raskin	Y	Y	Y	Y	N	Y	Y
MASSACHUSETTS							
1 Neal	Y	Y	Y	Y	N	Y	Y
2 McGovern	Y	Y	Y	Y	N	Y	N
3 Tsongas	Y	Y	Y	Y	N	Y	Y
4 Kennedy	Y	Y	Y	Y	N	Y	Y
5 Clark	Y	Y	Y	Y	N	Y	Y
6 Moulton	Y	Y	Y	Y	N	Y	Y
7 Capuano	Y	Y	Y	Y	N	Y	Y
8 Lynch	Y	Y	Y	Y	N	Y	Y
9 Keating	Y	Y	Y	Y	N	Y	Y
MICHIGAN							
1 **Bergman**	Y	N	N	N	Y	N	Y
2 **Huizenga**	Y	N	N	N	Y	N	Y
3 **Amash**	Y	N	N	N	Y	Y	N
4 **Moolenaar**	Y	N	N	N	Y	N	Y
5 Kildee	Y	Y	Y	Y	N	Y	Y
6 **Upton**	Y	N	N	N	Y	N	Y
7 **Walberg**	Y	N	N	N	Y	N	Y
8 **Bishop**	Y	N	N	N	Y	N	Y
9 Levin	Y	Y	Y	Y	N	Y	Y
10 **Mitchell**	Y	N	N	N	Y	N	Y
11 **Trott**	Y	N	N	N	Y	N	Y
12 Dingell	Y	Y	Y	Y	N	Y	Y
13 Conyers	Y	Y	Y	Y	N	Y	N
14 Lawrence	Y	Y	Y	Y	N	Y	Y
MINNESOTA							
1 Walz	Y	N	N	Y	Y	Y	Y
2 **Lewis**	Y	N	N	N	Y	N	Y
3 **Paulsen**	Y	N	N	N	Y	N	Y
4 McCollum	Y	Y	Y	Y	N	Y	Y

	278	279	280	281	282	283	284
5 Ellison	Y	Y	Y	Y	N	Y	N
6 **Emmer**	Y	N	N	N	Y	N	Y
7 Peterson	Y	N	N	N	Y	N	Y
8 Nolan	Y	N	N	Y	Y	+	+
MISSISSIPPI							
1 **Kelly**	Y	N	N	N	Y	N	Y
2 Thompson	Y	Y	Y	Y	N	Y	Y
3 **Harper**	Y	N	N	N	Y	N	Y
4 **Palazzo**	Y	N	N	N	Y	N	Y
MISSOURI							
1 Clay	Y	Y	Y	Y	N	Y	N
2 **Wagner**	Y	N	N	N	Y	N	Y
3 **Luetkemeyer**	Y	N	N	N	Y	N	Y
4 **Hartzler**	Y	N	N	N	Y	N	Y
5 Cleaver	Y	Y	Y	Y	N	Y	N
6 **Graves**	Y	N	N	N	Y	N	Y
7 **Long**	Y	N	N	N	Y	N	Y
8 **Smith**	Y	N	N	N	Y	N	Y
MONTANA							
AL **Vacant**							
NEBRASKA							
1 **Fortenberry**	Y	N	N	N	Y	N	Y
2 **Bacon**	Y	N	N	N	Y	N	Y
3 **Smith**	Y	N	N	N	Y	N	Y
NEVADA							
1 Titus	Y	Y	Y	Y	N	Y	Y
2 **Amodei**	Y	N	N	N	Y	N	Y
3 Rosen	Y	Y	Y	Y	N	Y	Y
4 Kihuen	Y	?	?	?	?	?	?
NEW HAMPSHIRE							
1 Shea-Porter	Y	Y	Y	Y	N	Y	Y
2 Kuster	Y	Y	Y	Y	Y	Y	Y
NEW JERSEY							
1 Norcross	Y	Y	Y	Y	N	Y	Y
2 **LoBiondo**	Y	Y	N	N	Y	N	Y
3 **MacArthur**	Y	N	N	N	Y	N	Y
4 **Smith**	Y	Y	Y	N	Y	N	Y
5 Gottheimer	Y	Y	Y	Y	N	N	Y
6 Pallone	Y	Y	Y	Y	N	Y	N
7 **Lance**	Y	Y	N	N	Y	N	Y
8 Sires	Y	Y	Y	Y	N	Y	Y
9 Pascrell	Y	Y	Y	Y	N	Y	Y
10 Payne	Y	Y	Y	Y	N	Y	N
11 **Frelinghuysen**	Y	N	N	N	Y	N	Y
12 Watson Coleman	Y	Y	Y	Y	N	Y	N
NEW MEXICO							
1 Lujan Grisham	Y	Y	Y	Y	N	Y	Y
2 **Pearce**	Y	N	N	N	Y	N	Y
3 Luján	Y	Y	Y	Y	N	Y	Y
NEW YORK							
1 **Zeldin**	Y	N	N	N	Y	N	Y
2 **King**	Y	N	N	N	Y	N	Y
3 Suozzi	Y	Y	Y	Y	N	Y	Y
4 Rice	Y	Y	Y	Y	N	Y	Y
5 Meeks	Y	Y	Y	Y	N	?	?
6 Meng	Y	Y	Y	Y	N	Y	Y
7 Velázquez	?	Y	Y	Y	N	Y	Y
8 Jeffries	Y	Y	Y	Y	N	Y	Y
9 Clarke	Y	Y	Y	Y	N	Y	N
10 Nadler	Y	Y	Y	?	N	Y	N
11 **Donovan**	Y	N	N	N	Y	N	Y
12 Maloney, C.	?	?	?	?	?	?	?
13 Espaillat	Y	Y	Y	Y	N	Y	Y
14 Crowley	Y	Y	Y	Y	N	Y	Y
15 Serrano	Y	Y	Y	Y	N	Y	Y
16 Engel	Y	Y	Y	Y	N	Y	Y
17 Lowey	Y	Y	Y	Y	N	Y	Y
18 Maloney, S.P.	Y	Y	Y	Y	Y	Y	Y
19 **Faso**	Y	N	N	N	Y	N	Y
20 Tonko	Y	Y	Y	Y	N	Y	Y
21 **Stefanik**	Y	N	N	N	Y	N	Y
22 **Tenney**	Y	N	N	N	Y	N	Y
23 **Reed**	Y	N	N	N	Y	N	Y
24 **Katko**	Y	N	N	N	Y	N	Y
25 Slaughter	Y	Y	Y	Y	N	Y	Y
26 Higgins	Y	Y	Y	Y	N	Y	Y
27 **Collins**	Y	N	N	N	Y	N	Y
NORTH CAROLINA							
1 Butterfield	Y	Y	Y	Y	Y	Y	Y
2 **Holding**	Y	N	N	N	Y	N	Y
3 **Jones**	Y	Y	Y	Y	Y	N	Y
4 Price	Y	Y	Y	Y	N	Y	Y

	278	279	280	281	282	283	284
5 **Foxx**	Y	N	N	N	Y	N	Y
6 **Walker**	Y	N	N	N	Y	N	Y
7 **Rouzer**	Y	N	N	N	Y	N	Y
8 **Hudson**	Y	N	N	N	Y	N	Y
9 **Pittenger**	Y	N	N	N	Y	N	Y
10 **McHenry**	Y	N	N	N	Y	N	Y
11 **Meadows**	Y	N	N	N	Y	N	Y
12 Adams	Y	Y	Y	Y	N	Y	Y
13 **Budd**	Y	N	N	N	Y	N	Y
NORTH DAKOTA							
AL **Cramer**	Y	N	N	N	Y	N	Y
OHIO							
1 **Chabot**	Y	N	N	N	Y	N	Y
2 **Wenstrup**	Y	N	N	N	Y	N	Y
3 Beatty	Y	Y	Y	Y	N	Y	Y
4 **Jordan**	Y	N	N	N	Y	N	Y
5 **Latta**	Y	N	N	N	Y	N	Y
6 **Johnson**	Y	N	N	N	Y	N	Y
7 **Gibbs**	Y	N	N	N	Y	N	Y
8 **Davidson**	Y	N	N	?	Y	N	Y
9 Kaptur	Y	Y	Y	Y	N	Y	Y
10 **Turner**	Y	N	N	N	Y	N	Y
11 Fudge	Y	Y	Y	Y	N	Y	N
12 **Tiberi**	Y	N	N	N	Y	N	Y
13 Ryan	Y	Y	Y	Y	N	Y	Y
14 **Joyce**	Y	Y	Y	N	Y	N	Y
15 **Stivers**	Y	N	N	N	Y	N	Y
16 **Renacci**	Y	N	N	N	Y	N	Y
OKLAHOMA							
1 **Bridenstine**	Y	N	N	N	Y	N	Y
2 **Mullin**	Y	N	N	N	Y	N	Y
3 **Lucas**	Y	N	N	N	Y	N	Y
4 **Cole**	Y	N	N	N	Y	N	Y
5 **Russell**	Y	N	N	N	Y	N	Y
OREGON							
1 Bonamici	Y	Y	Y	Y	N	Y	N
2 **Walden**	Y	N	N	N	Y	N	Y
3 Blumenauer	Y	Y	Y	Y	N	Y	N
4 DeFazio	Y	Y	Y	Y	N	Y	Y
5 Schrader	Y	N	N	N	Y	N	Y
PENNSYLVANIA							
1 Brady	Y	Y	Y	Y	N	Y	Y
2 Evans	Y	Y	Y	Y	N	Y	N
3 **Kelly**	Y	N	N	N	Y	N	Y
4 **Perry**	Y	N	N	N	Y	N	Y
5 **Thompson**	Y	N	N	N	Y	N	Y
6 **Costello**	Y	Y	Y	N	Y	N	Y
7 **Meehan**	Y	Y	N	N	Y	N	Y
8 **Fitzpatrick**	Y	Y	Y	N	N	N	Y
9 **Shuster**	Y	N	N	N	Y	N	Y
10 **Marino**	Y	N	N	N	Y	N	Y
11 **Barletta**	Y	N	N	N	Y	N	Y
12 **Rothfus**	Y	N	N	N	Y	N	Y
13 Boyle	Y	Y	Y	Y	N	Y	Y
14 Doyle	Y	Y	Y	Y	N	Y	Y
15 **Dent**	Y	N	N	N	Y	N	Y
16 **Smucker**	Y	N	N	N	Y	N	Y
17 Cartwright	Y	Y	Y	Y	N	Y	Y
18 **Murphy**	Y	N	N	N	Y	N	Y
RHODE ISLAND							
1 Cicilline	Y	Y	Y	Y	N	Y	Y
2 Langevin	Y	Y	Y	Y	N	Y	Y
SOUTH CAROLINA							
1 **Sanford**	Y	N	N	N	Y	N	Y
2 **Wilson**	Y	N	?	?	Y	N	Y
3 **Duncan**	Y	N	N	N	Y	N	Y
4 **Gowdy**	Y	N	N	N	Y	N	Y
6 Clyburn	Y	Y	Y	Y	N	Y	N
7 **Rice**	Y	N	N	N	Y	N	Y
SOUTH DAKOTA							
AL **Noem**	Y	N	N	N	Y	N	Y
TENNESSEE							
1 **Roe**	Y	N	N	N	Y	N	Y
2 **Duncan**	Y	N	N	N	Y	N	Y
3 **Fleischmann**	Y	N	N	N	Y	N	Y
4 **DesJarlais**	?	N	N	N	Y	N	Y
5 Cooper	Y	Y	Y	Y	N	Y	Y
6 **Black**	?	?	?	?	?	N	Y
7 **Blackburn**	Y	N	N	N	Y	N	Y
8 **Kustoff**	Y	N	N	N	Y	?	?
9 Cohen	Y	Y	Y	Y	N	Y	Y

	278	279	280	281	282	283	284
TEXAS							
1 **Gohmert**	Y	N	N	N	Y	N	Y
2 **Poe**	Y	N	N	N	Y	N	Y
3 **Johnson, S.**	?	?	?	?	?	?	?
4 **Ratcliffe**	Y	N	N	N	Y	N	Y
5 **Hensarling**	Y	N	N	N	Y	N	Y
6 **Barton**	Y	N	N	N	Y	N	Y
7 **Culberson**	Y	N	N	N	Y	N	Y
8 **Brady**	Y	N	?	N	Y	N	Y
9 Green, A.	Y	Y	Y	Y	N	Y	N
10 **McCaul**	Y	N	N	N	Y	N	Y
11 **Conaway**	Y	N	N	N	Y	N	Y
12 **Granger**	Y	N	N	N	Y	N	Y
13 **Thornberry**	Y	N	N	N	Y	N	Y
14 **Weber**	Y	N	N	N	Y	N	Y
15 Gonzalez	Y	Y	Y	Y	Y	Y	Y
16 O'Rourke	Y	Y	Y	Y	N	Y	Y
17 **Flores**	Y	N	N	N	Y	N	Y
18 Jackson Lee	Y	Y	Y	Y	N	Y	N
19 **Arrington**	Y	N	N	N	Y	N	Y
20 Castro	Y	Y	Y	Y	N	Y	N
21 **Smith**	Y	N	N	N	Y	N	Y
22 **Olson**	Y	N	N	N	Y	N	Y
23 **Hurd**	Y	N	N	N	Y	N	Y
24 **Marchant**	Y	N	N	N	Y	N	Y
25 **Williams**	Y	N	N	N	Y	N	Y
26 **Burgess**	Y	N	N	N	Y	N	Y
27 **Farenthold**	Y	N	N	N	Y	N	Y
28 Cuellar	Y	Y	Y	Y	Y	Y	Y
29 Green, G.	Y	Y	Y	?	N	Y	Y
30 Johnson, E.B.	Y	Y	Y	Y	N	Y	N
31 **Carter**	Y	N	N	N	Y	N	Y
32 **Sessions**	Y	N	N	N	Y	N	Y
33 Veasey	Y	Y	Y	Y	N	Y	N
34 Vela	Y	Y	Y	Y	Y	Y	Y
35 Doggett	Y	Y	Y	Y	N	Y	Y
36 **Babin**	Y	N	N	N	Y	N	Y
UTAH							
1 **Bishop**	Y	N	N	N	Y	N	Y
2 **Stewart**	Y	N	N	N	Y	N	Y
3 **Chaffetz**	Y	N	N	N	Y	N	Y
4 **Love**	Y	N	N	N	Y	N	Y
VERMONT							
AL Welch	Y	Y	Y	Y	Y	Y	Y
VIRGINIA							
1 **Wittman**	Y	N	N	N	Y	N	Y
2 **Taylor**	Y	N	N	N	Y	N	Y
3 Scott	Y	Y	Y	Y	N	Y	N
4 McEachin	Y	Y	Y	Y	N	Y	N
5 **Garrett**	Y	N	N	N	Y	N	Y
6 **Goodlatte**	Y	N	N	N	Y	N	Y
7 **Brat**	Y	N	N	N	Y	N	Y
8 Beyer	Y	Y	Y	Y	N	Y	N
9 **Griffith**	Y	N	N	N	Y	N	Y
10 **Comstock**	Y	N	N	N	Y	N	Y
11 Connolly	Y	Y	Y	Y	N	Y	Y
WASHINGTON							
1 DelBene	Y	Y	Y	Y	Y	Y	Y
2 Larsen	Y	Y	Y	Y	N	Y	Y
3 **Herrera Beutler**	Y	N	N	N	Y	N	Y
4 **Newhouse**	?	?	?	?	?	?	?
5 **McMorris Rodgers**	Y	N	N	N	Y	N	Y
6 Kilmer	Y	Y	Y	Y	N	Y	Y
7 Jayapal	Y	Y	Y	Y	N	Y	N
8 **Reichert**	Y	N	N	N	Y	N	Y
9 Smith	Y	Y	Y	Y	N	Y	N
10 Heck	Y	Y	Y	Y	N	Y	Y
WEST VIRGINIA							
1 **McKinley**	Y	N	N	N	Y	N	Y
2 **Mooney**	Y	N	N	N	Y	N	Y
3 **Jenkins**	Y	N	N	N	Y	N	Y
WISCONSIN							
1 **Ryan**							
2 Pocan	Y	Y	Y	Y	N	Y	N
3 Kind	Y	Y	Y	Y	Y	Y	Y
4 Moore	Y	Y	Y	Y	N	Y	N
5 **Sensenbrenner**	Y	N	N	N	Y	N	Y
6 **Grothman**	Y	N	N	N	Y	N	Y
7 **Duffy**	Y	N	N	N	Y	N	Y
8 **Gallagher**	Y	N	N	N	Y	N	Y
WYOMING							
AL **Cheney**	Y	N	N	N	Y	N	Y

VOTE NUMBER

285. HR 1973. CHILD ABUSE REPORTING/PASSAGE. Passage of the bill that would require adults authorized to interact with minors or amateur athletes to report any suspected incidents of child abuse to the sport's governing body. It would shield sports organizations from legal liability if they investigate and resolve any such suspected incidents, and would allow victims who suffer a personal injury as a result of such abuse to file civil lawsuits in district court against their assailant. Passed 415-3 : R 231-2; D 184-1. May 25, 2017.

286. H RES 354. CONDEMN VIOLENCE AGAINST PROTESTERS/ADOPTION. Royce, R-Calif., motion to suspend the rules and agree to the resolution that would condemn the violence against peaceful protesters outside the Turkish Ambassador's residence on May 16, 2017, and would state that any Turkish security officers who participated in the suppression of the peaceful protest should be charged and prosecuted under U.S. law. Motion agreed to 397-0 : R 224-0; D 173-0. June 6, 2017.

287. H RES 355. CONDEMN UK TERRORIST ATTACKS/ADOPTION. Royce, R-Calif., motion to suspend the rules and agree to the resolution would condemn the terrorist attacks in Manchester, United Kingdom, on May 22, 2017, and in London, United Kingdom, on June 3, 2017, and would reaffirm the commitment of the United States to the multilateral, global fight against Islamist terrorist groups. Motion agreed to 397-0 : R 221-0; D 176-0. June 6, 2017.

288. HR 2213, H RES 374. CBP POLYGRAPH WAIVER/PREVIOUS QUESTION. Cheney, R-Wyo., motion to order the previous question (thus ending debate and possibility of amendment) on the rule (H Res 374) that would provide for House floor consideration of the bill (HR 2213) that would authorize the commissioner of U.S. Customs and Border Protection to waive the requirement that applicants for law enforcement positions at CBP undergo polygraph examinations for certain applicants that have previously undergone a polygraph examination or a background investigation. Motion agreed to 228-189 : R 228-1; D 0-188. June 7, 2017.

289. HR 2213, H RES 374. CBP POLYGRAPH WAIVER/RULE. Adoption of the rule (H Res 374) that would provide for House floor consideration of the bill (HR 2213) that would authorize the commissioner of U.S. Customs and Border Protection to waive the requirement that applicants for law enforcement positions at CBP undergo polygraph examinations for certain applicants that have previously undergone a polygraph examination or a background investigation. Adopted 231-185 : R 231-0; D 0-185. June 7, 2017.

290. H RES 375, HR 10. FINANCIAL REGULATION RESTRUCTURING/ PREVIOUS QUESTION. Buck, R-Colo., motion to order the previous question (thus ending debate and possibility of amendment) on the rule (H Res 375) that would provide for House floor consideration of the bill (HR 10) that would overhaul financial industry regulations and repeal many provisions of the 2010 Dodd-Frank law. Motion agreed to 228-185 : R 227-1; D 1-184. June 7, 2017.

291. H RES 375, HR 10. FINANCIAL REGULATION RESTRUCTURING/ RULE. Adoption of the rule (H Res 375) that would overhaul financial industry regulations and repeal many provisions of the 2010 Dodd-Frank law. It would convert the Consumer Financial Protection Bureau into an executive agency, modify operations at the Federal Reserve and at the Securities and Exchange Commission, modify regulations governing the amount of capital that banks are required to maintain, and repeal the prohibition on banking entities engaging in proprietary trading. Adopted 231-188 : R 230-1; D 1-187. June 7, 2017.

	285	286	287	288	289	290	291
ALABAMA							
1 **Byrne**	Y	Y	Y	Y	Y	Y	Y
2 **Roby**	Y	Y	Y	Y	Y	Y	Y
3 **Rogers**	Y	Y	Y	Y	Y	Y	Y
4 **Aderholt**	Y	?	?	?	?	?	?
5 **Brooks**	Y	?	?	Y	Y	Y	Y
6 **Palmer**	Y	Y	Y	Y	Y	Y	Y
7 Sewell	Y	Y	Y	N	N	N	N
ALASKA							
AL **Young**	Y	Y	Y	Y	Y	Y	Y
ARIZONA							
1 O'Halleran	Y	Y	Y	N	N	N	N
2 **McSally**	+	Y	Y	Y	Y	Y	Y
3 Grijalva	Y	Y	Y	N	N	N	N
4 **Gosar**	Y	Y	Y	Y	Y	Y	Y
5 **Biggs**	Y	Y	Y	Y	Y	Y	Y
6 **Schweikert**	Y	Y	Y	Y	Y	Y	Y
7 Gallego	Y	Y	Y	N	N	N	N
8 **Franks**	Y	Y	Y	Y	Y	Y	Y
9 Sinema	Y	Y	Y	N	N	N	N
ARKANSAS							
1 **Crawford**	Y	Y	Y	Y	Y	Y	Y
2 **Hill**	Y	Y	Y	Y	Y	Y	Y
3 **Womack**	Y	Y	Y	Y	Y	Y	Y
4 **Westerman**	Y	Y	Y	Y	Y	Y	Y
CALIFORNIA							
1 **LaMalfa**	Y	Y	Y	Y	Y	Y	Y
2 Huffman	Y	Y	Y	N	N	N	N
3 Garamendi	Y	Y	Y	N	N	N	N
4 **McClintock**	Y	Y	Y	Y	Y	Y	Y
5 Thompson	Y	Y	Y	N	N	N	N
6 Matsui	Y	Y	Y	N	N	N	N
7 Bera	Y	Y	Y	N	N	N	N
8 **Cook**	Y	Y	Y	Y	Y	Y	Y
9 McNerney	Y	Y	Y	N	N	N	N
10 **Denham**	Y	Y	Y	Y	Y	Y	Y
11 DeSaulnier	Y	Y	Y	N	N	N	N
12 Pelosi	Y	Y	Y	N	N	?	N
13 Lee	Y	Y	Y	N	N	N	N
14 Speier	+	+	+	N	N	N	N
15 Swalwell	+	Y	Y	N	N	N	N
16 Costa	Y	Y	Y	N	N	N	N
17 Khanna	Y	Y	Y	N	N	N	N
18 Eshoo	Y	Y	Y	N	N	N	N
19 Lofgren	Y	Y	Y	N	N	N	N
20 Panetta	Y	Y	Y	N	N	N	N
21 **Valadao**	Y	Y	Y	Y	Y	Y	Y
22 **Nunes**	Y	Y	Y	Y	Y	Y	Y
23 **McCarthy**	Y	Y	Y	Y	Y	Y	Y
24 Carbajal	Y	Y	Y	N	N	N	N
25 **Knight**	Y	Y	Y	Y	Y	Y	Y
26 Brownley	Y	Y	Y	N	N	N	N
27 Chu	Y	Y	Y	N	N	N	N
28 Schiff	Y	Y	Y	N	N	N	N
29 Cardenas	Y	Y	Y	N	N	N	N
30 Sherman	Y	Y	Y	N	-	-	N
31 Aguilar	Y	Y	Y	N	N	N	N
32 Napolitano	Y	+	+	-	-	-	-
33 Lieu	Y	?	?	N	N	N	N
34 Vacant							
35 Torres	Y	Y	Y	N	N	N	N
36 Ruiz	Y	?	Y	N	N	N	N
37 Bass	Y	?	Y	N	N	N	N
38 Sánchez, Linda	Y	Y	Y	N	N	N	N
39 **Royce**	Y	Y	Y	Y	Y	Y	Y
40 Roybal-Allard	Y	Y	Y	N	N	N	N
41 Takano	Y	Y	Y	N	N	N	N
42 **Calvert**	Y	Y	Y	Y	Y	Y	Y
43 Waters	Y	?	?	N	N	N	N
44 Barragan	Y	Y	Y	N	N	N	N
45 **Walters**	Y	Y	Y	Y	Y	Y	Y
46 Correa	Y	Y	Y	N	N	N	N
47 Lowenthal	Y	Y	Y	N	N	N	N
48 **Rohrabacher**	Y	?	?	Y	Y	Y	Y
49 **Issa**	Y	Y	Y	Y	Y	Y	Y
50 **Hunter**	Y	Y	Y	Y	Y	Y	Y
51 Vargas	Y	Y	Y	N	N	N	N
52 Peters	Y	Y	Y	N	N	N	N
53 Davis	Y	Y	Y	N	N	N	N

	285	286	287	288	289	290	291
COLORADO							
1 DeGette	Y	Y	Y	N	N	N	N
2 Polis	Y	Y	Y	N	N	N	N
3 **Tipton**	Y	Y	Y	Y	Y	Y	Y
4 **Buck**	Y	Y	Y	Y	Y	Y	Y
5 **Lamborn**	Y	Y	Y	Y	Y	Y	Y
6 **Coffman**	Y	Y	Y	Y	Y	Y	Y
7 Perlmutter	Y	Y	Y	N	N	N	N
CONNECTICUT							
1 Larson	Y	?	Y	N	?	N	N
2 Courtney	Y	Y	Y	N	N	N	N
3 DeLauro	Y	Y	Y	N	N	N	N
4 Himes	Y	Y	Y	N	N	N	N
5 Esty	Y	Y	Y	N	N	N	N
DELAWARE							
AL Blunt Rochester	Y	Y	Y	N	N	N	N
FLORIDA							
1 **Gaetz**	Y	Y	Y	Y	Y	Y	Y
2 **Dunn**	Y	Y	Y	Y	Y	Y	Y
3 **Yoho**	Y	Y	Y	Y	Y	Y	Y
4 **Rutherford**	Y	Y	Y	Y	Y	Y	Y
5 Lawson	Y	Y	Y	N	N	N	N
6 **DeSantis**	Y	Y	Y	Y	Y	Y	Y
7 Murphy	Y	Y	Y	N	N	N	N
8 **Posey**	Y	Y	Y	Y	Y	Y	Y
9 Soto	Y	Y	Y	N	N	N	N
10 Demings	Y	Y	Y	N	N	N	N
11 **Webster**	Y	+	+	Y	Y	Y	Y
12 **Bilirakis**	Y	Y	Y	Y	Y	Y	Y
13 Crist	Y	Y	Y	N	N	N	N
14 Castor	Y	Y	Y	N	N	N	N
15 **Ross**	Y	?	?	Y	Y	Y	Y
16 **Buchanan**	Y	?	?	Y	Y	Y	Y
17 **Rooney, T.**	Y	Y	Y	Y	Y	+	Y
18 **Mast**	Y	Y	Y	Y	Y	Y	Y
19 **Rooney, F.**	Y	?	?	Y	Y	Y	Y
20 Hastings	N	Y	Y	N	N	N	N
21 Frankel	Y	Y	Y	N	N	N	N
22 Deutch	Y	Y	Y	N	N	N	N
23 Wasserman Schultz	Y	Y	Y	N	N	N	N
24 Wilson	Y	Y	Y	N	N	N	N
25 **Diaz-Balart**	Y	Y	Y	Y	Y	Y	Y
26 **Curbelo**	Y	Y	Y	Y	Y	Y	Y
27 **Ros-Lehtinen**	Y	Y	Y	Y	Y	Y	Y
GEORGIA							
1 **Carter**	Y	Y	Y	Y	Y	Y	Y
2 Bishop	Y	Y	Y	N	N	N	N
3 **Ferguson**	Y	Y	Y	Y	Y	Y	Y
4 Johnson	Y	Y	Y	N	N	N	N
5 Lewis	Y	?	?	N	N	N	N
6 **Woodall**	Y	Y	Y	Y	Y	?	Y
7 **Scott, A.**	Y	Y	Y	Y	Y	Y	Y
8 **Collins**	Y	Y	Y	Y	Y	Y	Y
9 **Hice**	Y	Y	Y	Y	Y	Y	Y
10 **Loudermilk**	Y	Y	Y	Y	Y	Y	Y
11 **Allen**	Y	Y	Y	Y	Y	Y	Y
12 Scott, D.	Y	Y	Y	N	N	N	N
13 **Graves**	Y	Y	Y	Y	Y	Y	Y
HAWAII							
1 Hanabusa	Y	Y	Y	N	N	N	N
2 Gabbard	Y	Y	Y	N	N	N	N
IDAHO							
1 **Labrador**	Y	Y	Y	Y	Y	Y	Y
2 **Simpson**	Y	Y	Y	Y	Y	Y	Y
ILLINOIS							
1 Rush	Y	?	?	N	N	N	N
2 Kelly	Y	Y	Y	N	N	N	N
3 Lipinski	Y	Y	Y	N	N	N	N
4 Gutierrez	Y	+	+	N	N	N	N
5 Quigley	Y	Y	Y	N	N	N	N
6 **Roskam**	Y	Y	Y	Y	Y	Y	Y
7 Davis, D.	Y	Y	Y	N	N	N	N
8 Krishnamoorthi	Y	Y	Y	N	N	N	N
9 Schakowsky	Y	Y	Y	N	N	N	N
10 Schneider	Y	Y	Y	N	N	N	N
11 Foster	Y	Y	Y	N	N	N	N
12 **Bost**	Y	Y	Y	Y	Y	Y	Y
13 **Davis, R.**	Y	Y	?	Y	Y	Y	Y
14 **Hultgren**	Y	Y	Y	Y	Y	Y	Y
15 **Shimkus**	Y	Y	Y	Y	Y	Y	Y

KEY	**Republicans**	Democrats	*Independents*
Y Voted for (yea)		X Paired against	C Voted "present" to avoid possible conflict of interest
# Paired for		- Announced against	
+ Announced for		P Voted "present"	? Did not vote or otherwise make a position known
N Voted against (nay)			

	285	286	287	288	289	290	291
16 **Kinzinger**	Y	Y	Y	Y	Y	Y	Y
17 Bustos	Y	Y	Y	N	N	N	N
18 **LaHood**	Y	Y	Y	Y	Y	Y	Y
INDIANA							
1 Visclosky	Y	Y	Y	N	N	N	N
2 **Walorski**	Y	Y	Y	Y	Y	Y	Y
3 **Banks**	Y	Y	Y	Y	Y	Y	Y
4 **Rokita**	Y	Y	Y	?	Y	Y	Y
5 **Brooks**	Y	Y	Y	Y	Y	Y	Y
6 **Messer**	Y	Y	Y	Y	Y	Y	Y
7 Carson	Y	Y	Y	N	N	N	N
8 **Bucshon**	Y	Y	Y	Y	Y	Y	Y
9 **Hollingsworth**	Y	Y	Y	Y	Y	Y	Y
IOWA							
1 **Blum**	Y	Y	Y	Y	Y	Y	Y
2 Loebsack	Y	Y	Y	N	N	N	N
3 **Young**	Y	Y	Y	Y	Y	Y	Y
4 **King**	Y	Y	Y	Y	Y	Y	Y
KANSAS							
1 **Marshall**	Y	Y	Y	Y	Y	Y	Y
2 **Jenkins**	Y	Y	Y	Y	Y	Y	Y
3 **Yoder**	Y	Y	Y	Y	Y	Y	Y
4 **Estes**	Y	Y	Y	Y	Y	Y	Y
KENTUCKY							
1 **Comer**	Y	Y	Y	Y	Y	Y	Y
2 **Guthrie**	Y	Y	Y	Y	Y	Y	Y
3 Yarmuth	Y	Y	Y	N	N	N	N
4 **Massie**	N	Y	Y	Y	Y	Y	Y
5 **Rogers**	Y	Y	Y	Y	Y	Y	Y
6 **Barr**	Y	Y	Y	Y	Y	Y	Y
LOUISIANA							
1 **Scalise**	Y	Y	Y	Y	Y	Y	Y
2 Richmond	Y	Y	Y	N	N	N	N
3 **Higgins**	Y	Y	Y	Y	Y	Y	Y
4 **Johnson**	Y	Y	Y	Y	Y	Y	Y
5 **Abraham**	Y	Y	Y	Y	Y	Y	Y
6 **Graves**	Y	Y	Y	Y	Y	Y	Y
MAINE							
1 Pingree	Y	Y	Y	N	N	N	N
2 **Poliquin**	Y	Y	Y	Y	Y	Y	Y
MARYLAND							
1 **Harris**	Y	Y	Y	Y	Y	Y	Y
2 Ruppersberger	Y	Y	Y	N	N	N	N
3 Sarbanes	Y	Y	Y	N	N	N	N
4 Brown	Y	Y	Y	N	N	N	N
5 Hoyer	Y	Y	Y	N	N	N	N
6 Delaney	Y	Y	Y	?	?	N	N
7 Cummings	?	?	?	?	?	?	?
8 Raskin	Y	Y	Y	N	N	N	N
MASSACHUSETTS							
1 Neal	Y	Y	Y	N	N	N	N
2 McGovern	Y	Y	Y	N	N	N	N
3 Tsongas	Y	Y	Y	N	N	N	N
4 Kennedy	Y	Y	Y	N	N	N	N
5 Clark	Y	Y	Y	N	N	N	N
6 Moulton	Y	Y	Y	N	N	N	N
7 Capuano	Y	Y	Y	N	N	N	N
8 Lynch	Y	Y	Y	N	N	N	N
9 Keating	Y	Y	Y	N	N	N	Y
MICHIGAN							
1 **Bergman**	Y	Y	Y	Y	Y	Y	Y
2 **Huizenga**	Y	Y	Y	Y	Y	Y	Y
3 **Amash**	N	Y	Y	Y	Y	Y	Y
4 **Moolenaar**	Y	Y	Y	Y	Y	Y	Y
5 Kildee	Y	Y	Y	N	N	N	N
6 **Upton**	Y	Y	Y	Y	Y	Y	Y
7 **Walberg**	Y	Y	Y	Y	Y	Y	Y
8 **Bishop**	Y	Y	Y	Y	Y	Y	Y
9 Levin	Y	Y	Y	N	N	N	N
10 **Mitchell**	Y	Y	Y	Y	Y	Y	Y
11 **Trott**	Y	Y	Y	Y	Y	Y	Y
12 Dingell	Y	Y	Y	N	N	N	N
13 Conyers	Y	Y	Y	N	N	N	N
14 Lawrence	Y	Y	Y	N	N	N	N
MINNESOTA							
1 Walz	Y	Y	Y	N	N	N	N
2 **Lewis**	Y	Y	Y	Y	Y	Y	Y
3 **Paulsen**	Y	Y	Y	Y	Y	Y	Y
4 McCollum	Y	Y	Y	N	N	N	N

	285	286	287	288	289	290	291
5 Ellison	Y	+	+	N	N	?	N
6 **Emmer**	Y	Y	Y	Y	Y	Y	Y
7 Peterson	Y	Y	Y	N	N	Y	N
8 Nolan	+	Y	Y	N	N	N	N
MISSISSIPPI							
1 **Kelly**	Y	Y	Y	Y	Y	Y	Y
2 Thompson	Y	Y	Y	N	N	N	N
3 **Harper**	Y	Y	Y	Y	Y	Y	Y
4 **Palazzo**	Y	Y	Y	Y	Y	Y	Y
MISSOURI							
1 Clay	Y	Y	Y	N	N	N	N
2 **Wagner**	Y	Y	Y	Y	Y	Y	Y
3 **Luetkemeyer**	Y	Y	Y	Y	Y	Y	Y
4 **Hartzler**	Y	Y	Y	Y	Y	Y	Y
5 Cleaver	Y	Y	Y	N	N	N	N
6 **Graves**	Y	Y	Y	Y	Y	Y	Y
7 **Long**	Y	Y	Y	Y	Y	Y	Y
8 **Smith**	Y	Y	Y	Y	Y	Y	Y
MONTANA							
AL **Vacant**							
NEBRASKA							
1 **Fortenberry**	Y	Y	Y	Y	Y	Y	Y
2 **Bacon**	Y	Y	Y	Y	Y	Y	Y
3 **Smith**	Y	Y	Y	Y	Y	Y	Y
NEVADA							
1 Titus	Y	Y	Y	N	N	N	N
2 **Amodei**	Y	Y	Y	Y	Y	Y	Y
3 Rosen	Y	Y	Y	N	N	N	N
4 Kihuen	?	?	?	N	N	N	N
NEW HAMPSHIRE							
1 Shea-Porter	Y	Y	Y	N	N	N	N
2 Kuster	Y	Y	Y	N	N	N	N
NEW JERSEY							
1 Norcross	Y	Y	Y	N	N	N	N
2 **LoBiondo**	Y	Y	Y	Y	Y	Y	Y
3 **MacArthur**	Y	Y	Y	Y	Y	Y	Y
4 **Smith**	Y	Y	Y	Y	Y	Y	Y
5 Gottheimer	Y	Y	Y	N	N	N	N
6 Pallone	Y	?	Y	N	N	N	N
7 **Lance**	Y	Y	Y	Y	Y	Y	Y
8 Sires	Y	Y	Y	N	N	N	N
9 Pascrell	Y	Y	Y	N	N	N	N
10 Payne	Y	Y	Y	N	N	N	N
11 **Frelinghuysen**	Y	Y	Y	Y	Y	Y	Y
12 Watson Coleman	Y	Y	Y	N	N	N	N
NEW MEXICO							
1 Lujan Grisham	Y	Y	Y	N	N	N	N
2 **Pearce**	Y	Y	Y	Y	Y	Y	Y
3 Luján	Y	Y	Y	N	N	N	N
NEW YORK							
1 **Zeldin**	Y	+	+	Y	Y	Y	Y
2 **King**	Y	Y	Y	Y	Y	Y	Y
3 Suozzi	Y	Y	Y	N	N	N	N
4 Rice	Y	Y	Y	N	N	N	N
5 Meeks	?	?	?	N	N	N	N
6 Meng	Y	Y	Y	N	N	N	N
7 Velázquez	Y	Y	Y	N	N	N	N
8 Jeffries	Y	Y	Y	N	N	N	N
9 Clarke	Y	Y	Y	N	N	N	N
10 Nadler	Y	Y	Y	N	N	N	N
11 **Donovan**	Y	Y	Y	Y	Y	Y	Y
12 Maloney, C.	?	Y	Y	N	N	N	N
13 Espaillat	Y	Y	Y	N	N	N	N
14 Crowley	Y	Y	Y	N	N	N	N
15 Serrano	Y	Y	Y	N	N	N	N
16 Engel	Y	?	?	?	?	?	?
17 Lowey	Y	Y	Y	N	N	N	N
18 Maloney, S.P.	Y	Y	Y	N	N	N	N
19 **Faso**	Y	Y	Y	Y	Y	Y	Y
20 Tonko	Y	Y	Y	N	N	N	N
21 **Stefanik**	Y	Y	Y	Y	Y	Y	Y
22 **Tenney**	Y	Y	Y	Y	Y	Y	Y
23 **Reed**	Y	Y	Y	Y	Y	Y	Y
24 **Katko**	Y	Y	Y	Y	Y	Y	Y
25 Slaughter	Y	Y	Y	N	N	N	N
26 Higgins	?	+	+	N	N	N	N
27 **Collins**	Y	Y	Y	Y	Y	Y	Y
NORTH CAROLINA							
1 Butterfield	Y	Y	Y	N	N	N	N
2 **Holding**	Y	Y	Y	Y	Y	Y	Y
3 **Jones**	Y	Y	Y	N	Y	N	N
4 Price	Y	Y	Y	N	N	N	N

	285	286	287	288	289	290	291
5 **Foxx**	Y	Y	Y	Y	Y	Y	Y
6 **Walker**	Y	Y	Y	Y	Y	Y	Y
7 **Rouzer**	Y	Y	Y	Y	Y	Y	Y
8 **Hudson**	Y	Y	Y	Y	Y	Y	Y
9 **Pittenger**	Y	Y	Y	Y	Y	Y	Y
10 **McHenry**	Y	Y	Y	Y	Y	Y	Y
11 **Meadows**	Y	Y	Y	Y	Y	Y	Y
12 Adams	Y	Y	Y	N	N	N	N
13 **Budd**	Y	Y	Y	Y	Y	Y	Y
NORTH DAKOTA							
AL **Cramer**	Y	Y	Y	Y	Y	Y	Y
OHIO							
1 **Chabot**	Y	Y	Y	Y	Y	Y	Y
2 **Wenstrup**	Y	Y	Y	Y	Y	Y	Y
3 Beatty	Y	Y	Y	N	N	N	N
4 **Jordan**	Y	Y	Y	Y	Y	Y	Y
5 **Latta**	Y	Y	Y	Y	Y	Y	Y
6 **Johnson**	Y	Y	Y	Y	Y	Y	Y
7 **Gibbs**	Y	Y	Y	Y	Y	Y	Y
8 **Davidson**	Y	Y	Y	Y	Y	Y	Y
9 Kaptur	Y	Y	Y	N	N	N	N
10 **Turner**	Y	Y	Y	Y	Y	Y	Y
11 Fudge	Y	Y	Y	N	N	N	N
12 **Tiberi**	Y	Y	Y	Y	Y	Y	Y
13 Ryan	Y	Y	Y	N	N	N	N
14 **Joyce**	Y	Y	Y	Y	Y	Y	Y
15 **Stivers**	Y	Y	Y	Y	Y	Y	Y
16 **Renacci**	Y	+	+	Y	Y	Y	Y
OKLAHOMA							
1 **Bridenstine**	Y	Y	Y	Y	Y	Y	Y
2 **Mullin**	Y	Y	Y	Y	Y	Y	Y
3 **Lucas**	Y	Y	Y	Y	Y	Y	Y
4 **Cole**	Y	Y	Y	Y	Y	Y	Y
5 **Russell**	Y	Y	Y	Y	Y	Y	Y
OREGON							
1 Bonamici	Y	Y	Y	N	N	N	N
2 **Walden**	Y	Y	Y	Y	Y	Y	Y
3 Blumenauer	Y	+	+	N	N	N	N
4 DeFazio	Y	Y	Y	N	N	N	N
5 Schrader	Y	Y	Y	N	N	N	N
PENNSYLVANIA							
1 Brady	Y	Y	Y	N	N	N	N
2 Evans	Y	Y	Y	N	N	N	N
3 **Kelly**	Y	Y	Y	Y	Y	Y	Y
4 **Perry**	Y	Y	Y	Y	Y	Y	Y
5 **Thompson**	Y	Y	Y	Y	Y	Y	Y
6 **Costello**	Y	Y	Y	Y	Y	Y	Y
7 **Meehan**	Y	Y	Y	Y	Y	Y	Y
8 **Fitzpatrick**	Y	Y	Y	Y	Y	Y	Y
9 **Shuster**	Y	Y	Y	Y	Y	Y	Y
10 **Marino**	Y	+	+	+	+	+	+
11 **Barletta**	Y	?	?	Y	Y	Y	Y
12 **Rothfus**	Y	Y	Y	Y	Y	Y	Y
13 Boyle	Y	Y	Y	N	N	N	N
14 Doyle	Y	Y	Y	N	N	N	N
15 **Dent**	Y	Y	Y	Y	Y	Y	Y
16 **Smucker**	Y	Y	Y	Y	Y	Y	Y
17 Cartwright	Y	Y	Y	N	N	N	N
18 **Murphy**	Y	Y	Y	Y	Y	Y	Y
RHODE ISLAND							
1 Cicilline	Y	Y	Y	N	N	N	N
2 Langevin	Y	Y	Y	N	N	N	N
SOUTH CAROLINA							
1 **Sanford**	Y	Y	Y	Y	Y	Y	Y
2 **Wilson**	Y	Y	Y	Y	Y	Y	Y
3 **Duncan**	Y	Y	Y	Y	Y	Y	Y
4 **Gowdy**	Y	Y	Y	Y	Y	Y	Y
6 Clyburn	Y	?	?	?	?	?	?
7 **Rice**	Y	Y	Y	Y	Y	Y	Y
SOUTH DAKOTA							
AL **Noem**	Y	Y	Y	Y	Y	Y	Y
TENNESSEE							
1 **Roe**	Y	Y	Y	Y	Y	Y	Y
2 **Duncan**	Y	Y	Y	Y	Y	Y	Y
3 **Fleischmann**	Y	Y	Y	Y	Y	Y	Y
4 **DesJarlais**	Y	Y	Y	Y	Y	Y	Y
5 Cooper	Y	Y	Y	N	N	N	N
6 **Black**	Y	Y	Y	Y	Y	Y	Y
7 **Blackburn**	Y	Y	Y	Y	Y	Y	Y
8 **Kustoff**	?	Y	Y	Y	Y	Y	Y
9 Cohen	Y	Y	Y	N	N	N	N

	285	286	287	288	289	290	291
TEXAS							
1 **Gohmert**	Y	Y	Y	?	Y	Y	Y
2 **Poe**	Y	Y	?	Y	Y	Y	Y
3 **Johnson, S.**	?	?	?	?	?	?	?
4 **Ratcliffe**	Y	?	?	Y	Y	Y	Y
5 **Hensarling**	Y	Y	Y	Y	Y	Y	Y
6 **Barton**	Y	Y	Y	Y	Y	Y	Y
7 **Culberson**	Y	Y	Y	Y	Y	Y	Y
8 **Brady**	Y	Y	Y	Y	Y	?	Y
9 Green, A.	Y	Y	Y	N	–	?	N
10 **McCaul**	Y	Y	Y	Y	Y	Y	Y
11 **Conaway**	Y	Y	Y	Y	Y	Y	Y
12 **Granger**	Y	Y	Y	Y	Y	Y	Y
13 **Thornberry**	Y	Y	?	Y	Y	Y	Y
14 **Weber**	Y	Y	Y	Y	Y	Y	Y
15 Gonzalez	Y	Y	Y	N	N	N	N
16 O'Rourke	Y	Y	Y	N	N	N	N
17 **Flores**	Y	Y	Y	Y	Y	Y	Y
18 Jackson Lee	Y	Y	Y	N	N	N	N
19 **Arrington**	Y	Y	Y	Y	Y	Y	Y
20 Castro	Y	Y	Y	N	N	N	N
21 **Smith**	Y	Y	Y	?	?	?	?
22 **Olson**	Y	Y	Y	Y	Y	Y	Y
23 **Hurd**	Y	Y	Y	Y	Y	Y	Y
24 **Marchant**	Y	Y	Y	Y	Y	Y	Y
25 **Williams**	Y	Y	Y	Y	Y	Y	Y
26 **Burgess**	Y	Y	Y	Y	Y	Y	Y
27 **Farenthold**	Y	Y	Y	Y	Y	Y	Y
28 Cuellar	Y	Y	Y	N	N	N	N
29 Green, G.	Y	Y	Y	N	N	N	N
30 Johnson, E.B.	Y	Y	Y	N	N	N	N
31 **Carter**	Y	Y	Y	Y	Y	Y	Y
32 **Sessions**	Y	Y	Y	Y	Y	Y	Y
33 Veasey	Y	Y	Y	N	N	N	N
34 Vela	Y	Y	Y	N	N	N	N
35 Doggett	Y	Y	Y	N	N	N	N
36 **Babin**	Y	Y	Y	+	+	+	+
UTAH							
1 **Bishop**	Y	Y	Y	Y	Y	Y	Y
2 **Stewart**	Y	Y	Y	Y	Y	Y	Y
3 **Chaffetz**	Y	Y	Y	Y	Y	Y	Y
4 **Love**	Y	Y	Y	Y	Y	Y	Y
VERMONT							
AL Welch	Y	Y	Y	N	N	N	N
VIRGINIA							
1 **Wittman**	Y	Y	Y	Y	Y	Y	Y
2 **Taylor**	Y	Y	Y	Y	Y	Y	Y
3 Scott	Y	Y	Y	N	N	N	N
4 McEachin	Y	Y	Y	N	N	N	?
5 **Garrett**	Y	Y	Y	Y	Y	Y	Y
6 **Goodlatte**	Y	Y	Y	Y	Y	Y	Y
7 **Brat**	Y	Y	Y	Y	Y	Y	Y
8 Beyer	Y	Y	Y	N	N	N	N
9 **Griffith**	Y	Y	Y	Y	Y	Y	Y
10 **Comstock**	Y	Y	Y	Y	Y	Y	Y
11 Connolly	Y	Y	Y	N	N	N	N
WASHINGTON							
1 DelBene	Y	Y	Y	N	N	N	N
2 Larsen	Y	?	?	N	N	N	N
3 **Herrera Beutler**	Y	Y	Y	Y	Y	Y	Y
4 **Newhouse**	?	Y	Y	Y	Y	Y	Y
5 **McMorris Rodgers**	Y	Y	Y	Y	Y	Y	Y
6 Kilmer	Y	Y	Y	N	N	N	N
7 Jayapal	Y	Y	Y	N	N	N	N
8 **Reichert**	Y	Y	Y	+	+	+	+
9 Smith	Y	Y	Y	N	N	N	N
10 Heck	Y	Y	Y	N	N	N	N
WEST VIRGINIA							
1 **McKinley**	Y	Y	Y	Y	Y	Y	Y
2 **Mooney**	Y	Y	Y	Y	Y	Y	Y
3 **Jenkins**	Y	Y	Y	Y	Y	Y	Y
WISCONSIN							
1 **Ryan**							
2 Pocan	Y	Y	Y	N	N	N	N
3 Kind	Y	Y	Y	N	N	N	N
4 Moore	Y	?	?	N	N	N	N
5 **Sensenbrenner**	Y	Y	Y	Y	Y	Y	Y
6 **Grothman**	Y	Y	Y	Y	Y	Y	Y
7 **Duffy**	Y	Y	Y	Y	Y	Y	Y
8 **Gallagher**	Y	Y	Y	Y	Y	Y	Y
WYOMING							
AL **Cheney**	Y	Y	Y	Y	Y	Y	Y

VOTE NUMBER

292. PRESIDENT'S TAX RETURN DISCLOSURE/MOTION TO TABLE. McCaul, R-Texas, motion to table (kill) the Capuano, D-Mass., motion to appeal the ruling of the Chair that the Capuano resolution related to the disclosure of President Trump's tax returns does not constitute a question of the privileges of the House. Motion agreed to 228-186 : R 227-1; D 1-185. June 7, 2017.

293. HR 2213. CBP POLYGRAPH WAIVER/PROGRAM EVALUATION AND CERTIFICATION. Lujan Grisham, D-N.M., amendment that would delay enactment of the bill's provisions until the commissioner of U.S. Customs and Border Protection has conducted an evaluation and pilot program of the Test for Espionage, Sabotage, and Corruption and the Homeland Security Department has certified that the waivers provided under the bill would not endanger national security. Rejected in Committee of the Whole 179-238 : R 3-227; D 176-11. June 7, 2017.

294. HR 2213. CBP POLYGRAPH WAIVER/PASSAGE. Passage of the bill that would authorize the commissioner of U.S. Customs and Border Protection to waive the requirement that applicants for law enforcement positions at CBP undergo polygraph examinations for specific groups of applicants. Certain veterans and law enforcement officers who have already passed a polygraph examination or stringent background investigation could be exempt from the polygraph requirement. Passed 282-137 : R 231-0; D 51-137. June 7, 2017.

295. HR 10. FINANCIAL REGULATION RESTRUCTURING/MEETING ATTENDANCE AND APPROPRIATIONS PROCESS CLARIFICATION. Hensarling, R-Texas, amendment that would only allow members of the authorization and oversight committees of the House and Senate to attend meetings of the Financial Stability Oversight Council if the meetings are open to the public. It would also clarify the appropriations funding process for the Federal Deposit Insurance Corporation and National Credit Union Administration. Adopted in Committee of the Whole 232-185 : R 231-1; D 1-184. June 8, 2017.

296. HR 10. FINANCIAL REGULATION RESTRUCTURING/"WELL-KNOWN SEASONED ISSUERS" CLASSIFICATION. Hollingsworth, R-Ind., amendment that would allow certain closed-end companies registered as investment companies to be considered "well-known seasoned issuers" under federal regulations. Adopted in Committee of the Whole 231-180 : R 228-1; D 3-179. June 8, 2017.

297. HR 10. FINANCIAL REGULATION RESTRUCTURING/MUTUAL HOLDING COMPANY VALUATION. Faso, R-N.Y., amendment that would modify federal regulations governing the valuation process for mutual holding companies in the event of a full conversion from mutual-form to stock-form of ownership. Adopted in Committee of the Whole 235-184 : R 233-1; D 2-183. June 8, 2017.

298. HR 10. FINANCIAL REGULATION RESTRUCTURING/AGENCY LEASING NEEDS. Buck, R-Colo., amendment that would require the General Services Administration to report to Congress on the Consumer Law Enforcement Agency's real estate leasing needs, as impacted by the bill's changes to the agency's structure. It would authorize the GSA to sell the current CLEA building if it no longer fits the needs of the CLEA or the needs of another government agency. Adopted in Committee of the Whole 233-185 : R 232-1; D 1-184. June 8, 2017.

	292	293	294	295	296	297	298
ALABAMA							
1 Byrne	Y	N	Y	Y	Y	Y	Y
2 Roby	Y	N	Y	Y	Y	Y	Y
3 Rogers	Y	N	Y	Y	Y	Y	Y
4 Aderholt	?	?	?	Y	Y	Y	Y
5 Brooks	Y	N	Y	Y	Y	Y	Y
6 Palmer	Y	N	Y	Y	Y	Y	Y
7 Sewell	N	Y	N	N	N	N	N
ALASKA							
AL Young	Y	N	Y	Y	Y	Y	Y
ARIZONA							
1 O'Halleran	N	N	N	N	N	N	N
2 McSally	Y	N	Y	Y	Y	Y	Y
3 Grijalva	N	Y	N	N	N	N	N
4 Gosar	Y	N	Y	Y	Y	Y	Y
5 Biggs	Y	N	Y	Y	Y	Y	Y
6 Schweikert	Y	N	Y	Y	Y	Y	Y
7 Gallego	N	Y	N	N	N	N	N
8 Franks	Y	N	Y	Y	Y	Y	Y
9 Sinema	N	N	Y	N	N	N	N
ARKANSAS							
1 Crawford	Y	N	Y	Y	Y	Y	Y
2 Hill	Y	N	Y	Y	Y	Y	Y
3 Womack	Y	N	Y	Y	Y	Y	Y
4 Westerman	Y	N	Y	Y	Y	Y	Y
CALIFORNIA							
1 LaMalfa	Y	N	Y	?	Y	Y	Y
2 Huffman	N	Y	N	N	N	N	N
3 Garamendi	N	Y	N	N	N	N	N
4 McClintock	Y	N	Y	Y	Y	Y	Y
5 Thompson	N	Y	N	N	N	N	N
6 Matsui	N	Y	N	N	N	N	N
7 Bera	N	Y	N	N	N	N	N
8 Cook	Y	N	Y	Y	Y	Y	Y
9 McNerney	N	Y	N	N	N	N	N
10 Denham	Y	N	Y	Y	Y	Y	Y
11 DeSaulnier	N	Y	N	N	N	N	N
12 Pelosi	N	Y	N	N	N	N	N
13 Lee	N	Y	N	N	N	N	N
14 Speier	N	Y	N	N	N	N	N
15 Swalwell	N	Y	N	N	N	N	N
16 Costa	N	N	Y	–	–	–	–
17 Khanna	N	Y	N	N	N	N	N
18 Eshoo	N	Y	N	N	N	N	N
19 Lofgren	N	Y	N	N	N	N	N
20 Panetta	N	Y	N	N	N	N	N
21 Valadao	Y	N	Y	Y	Y	Y	Y
22 Nunes	Y	N	Y	Y	Y	Y	Y
23 McCarthy	Y	N	Y	Y	Y	Y	Y
24 Carbajal	N	Y	N	N	N	N	N
25 Knight	Y	N	Y	Y	Y	Y	Y
26 Brownley	N	Y	N	N	N	N	N
27 Chu	N	Y	N	N	N	N	N
28 Schiff	N	Y	N	N	N	N	N
29 Cardenas	N	Y	N	N	N	N	N
30 Sherman	N	Y	N	N	N	N	N
31 Aguilar	N	Y	N	–	–	–	–
32 Napolitano	?	?	+	–	–	–	–
33 Lieu	N	Y	N	N	N	N	N
34 Vacant							
35 Torres	N	Y	N	N	N	N	N
36 Ruiz	N	Y	N	N	N	N	N
37 Bass	N	Y	N	N	N	N	N
38 Sánchez, Linda	N	Y	N	N	N	N	N
39 Royce	Y	N	Y	Y	Y	Y	Y
40 Roybal-Allard	N	Y	N	N	N	N	N
41 Takano	N	Y	N	N	N	N	N
42 Calvert	Y	N	Y	Y	Y	Y	Y
43 Waters	N	Y	N	N	N	N	N
44 Barragan	N	Y	N	N	N	N	N
45 Walters	Y	N	Y	Y	Y	Y	Y
46 Correa	N	Y	N	N	N	N	N
47 Lowenthal	N	Y	N	N	N	N	N
48 Rohrabacher	Y	N	Y	Y	Y	Y	Y
49 Issa	Y	N	Y	Y	Y	Y	Y
50 Hunter	Y	N	Y	Y	Y	Y	Y
51 Vargas	N	Y	N	N	N	N	N
52 Peters	N	Y	N	N	N	N	N
53 Davis	N	Y	N	N	N	N	N
COLORADO							
1 DeGette	N	Y	N	N	N	N	N
2 Polis	N	Y	N	N	?	N	N
3 Tipton	Y	N	Y	Y	Y	Y	Y
4 Buck	Y	N	Y	Y	Y	Y	Y
5 Lamborn	Y	N	Y	Y	?	Y	Y
6 Coffman	Y	N	Y	Y	Y	Y	Y
7 Perlmutter	N	Y	N	N	N	N	N
CONNECTICUT							
1 Larson	N	Y	N	N	N	N	N
2 Courtney	N	Y	N	N	N	N	N
3 DeLauro	N	Y	N	N	N	N	N
4 Himes	N	Y	N	N	N	N	N
5 Esty	N	Y	N	N	N	N	N
DELAWARE							
AL Blunt Rochester	N	Y	Y	N	N	N	N
FLORIDA							
1 Gaetz	Y	N	Y	Y	Y	Y	Y
2 Dunn	Y	N	Y	?	Y	Y	Y
3 Yoho	Y	N	Y	Y	Y	Y	Y
4 Rutherford	Y	N	Y	Y	Y	Y	Y
5 Lawson	N	Y	N	N	N	N	N
6 DeSantis	Y	N	Y	Y	Y	Y	Y
7 Murphy	N	Y	N	N	N	N	N
8 Posey	Y	N	Y	Y	Y	Y	Y
9 Soto	N	Y	N	N	N	N	N
10 Demings	N	Y	N	N	N	N	N
11 Webster	Y	N	Y	Y	Y	Y	Y
12 Bilirakis	Y	N	Y	Y	Y	Y	Y
13 Crist	N	Y	N	N	N	N	N
14 Castor	N	Y	N	N	N	N	N
15 Ross	Y	N	Y	Y	Y	Y	Y
16 Buchanan	Y	N	Y	Y	Y	Y	Y
17 Rooney, T.	Y	N	Y	Y	Y	Y	Y
18 Mast	Y	N	Y	Y	Y	Y	Y
19 Rooney, F.	Y	N	Y	Y	Y	Y	Y
20 Hastings	N	Y	N	N	N	N	N
21 Frankel	N	Y	N	N	N	N	N
22 Deutch	N	Y	N	N	N	N	N
23 Wasserman Schultz	N	Y	N	N	N	N	N
24 Wilson	N	Y	N	N	N	N	N
25 Diaz-Balart	Y	N	Y	Y	Y	Y	Y
26 Curbelo	Y	N	Y	Y	Y	Y	Y
27 Ros-Lehtinen	Y	N	Y	Y	Y	Y	Y
GEORGIA							
1 Carter	Y	N	Y	Y	Y	Y	Y
2 Bishop	N	Y	N	N	N	N	N
3 Ferguson	Y	N	Y	Y	Y	Y	Y
4 Johnson	N	Y	N	N	N	N	N
5 Lewis	N	Y	N	N	N	N	N
7 Woodall	Y	N	Y	Y	Y	Y	Y
8 Scott, A.	Y	N	Y	Y	Y	Y	Y
9 Collins	Y	N	Y	Y	Y	Y	Y
10 Hice	Y	N	Y	Y	Y	Y	Y
11 Loudermilk	Y	N	Y	Y	Y	Y	Y
12 Allen	Y	N	Y	Y	Y	Y	Y
13 Scott, D.	N	Y	N	N	N	N	N
14 Graves	Y	N	Y	Y	Y	Y	Y
HAWAII							
1 Hanabusa	N	Y	N	N	N	N	N
2 Gabbard	N	Y	N	N	N	N	N
IDAHO							
1 Labrador	Y	N	Y	Y	Y	Y	Y
2 Simpson	Y	N	Y	Y	Y	Y	Y
ILLINOIS							
1 Rush	N	Y	N	N	N	N	N
2 Kelly	N	Y	N	N	N	N	N
3 Lipinski	N	Y	N	N	N	N	N
4 Gutierrez	N	Y	N	N	N	N	N
5 Quigley	N	Y	N	N	N	N	N
6 Roskam	Y	N	Y	Y	Y	Y	Y
7 Davis, D.	N	Y	N	N	N	N	N
8 Krishnamoorthi	N	Y	N	N	N	N	N
9 Schakowsky	N	Y	N	N	N	N	N
10 Schneider	N	Y	N	N	N	N	N
11 Foster	N	Y	N	N	N	N	N
12 Bost	Y	N	Y	Y	Y	Y	Y
13 Davis, R.	Y	N	Y	Y	Y	Y	Y
14 Hultgren	Y	N	Y	Y	Y	Y	Y
15 Shimkus	Y	N	Y	Y	Y	Y	Y

KEY	Republicans	Democrats	Independents
Y Voted for (yea)	X Paired against		C Voted "present" to avoid possible conflict of interest
# Paired for	– Announced against		
+ Announced for	P Voted "present"		? Did not vote or otherwise make a position known
N Voted against (nay)			

	292	293	294	295	296	297	298
16 **Kinzinger**	Y	N	Y	Y	Y	Y	Y
17 Bustos	N	Y	Y	N	N	N	N
18 **LaHood**	Y	N	Y	Y	Y	Y	Y
INDIANA							
1 Visclosky	N	Y	N	N	N	N	N
2 **Walorski**	Y	N	Y	Y	Y	Y	Y
3 **Banks**	Y	N	Y	Y	Y	Y	Y
4 **Rokita**	Y	N	Y	Y	Y	Y	Y
5 **Brooks**	Y	N	Y	Y	Y	Y	Y
6 **Messer**	Y	N	Y	Y	Y	Y	Y
7 Carson	N	Y	N	N	N	N	N
8 **Bucshon**	Y	N	Y	Y	Y	Y	Y
9 **Hollingsworth**	Y	N	Y	Y	Y	Y	Y
IOWA							
1 **Blum**	Y	N	Y	Y	Y	Y	Y
2 Loebsack	N	Y	Y	N	N	N	N
3 **Young**	Y	N	Y	Y	Y	Y	Y
4 **King**	Y	N	Y	Y	Y	Y	Y
KANSAS							
1 **Marshall**	Y	N	Y	Y	Y	Y	Y
2 **Jenkins**	Y	N	Y	Y	Y	Y	Y
3 **Yoder**	Y	N	Y	Y	Y	Y	Y
4 **Estes**	Y	N	Y	Y	Y	Y	Y
KENTUCKY							
1 **Comer**	Y	N	Y	Y	Y	Y	Y
2 **Guthrie**	Y	N	Y	Y	Y	Y	Y
3 Yarmuth	N	Y	N	N	N	N	N
4 **Massie**	Y	N	Y	Y	Y	Y	Y
5 **Rogers**	Y	N	Y	Y	Y	Y	Y
6 **Barr**	Y	N	Y	Y	Y	Y	Y
LOUISIANA							
1 **Scalise**	Y	N	Y	Y	Y	Y	Y
2 Richmond	?	Y	Y	N	N	N	N
3 **Higgins**	Y	N	Y	Y	Y	Y	Y
4 **Johnson**	Y	N	Y	Y	Y	Y	Y
5 **Abraham**	Y	N	Y	Y	Y	Y	Y
6 **Graves**	Y	N	Y	Y	Y	Y	Y
MAINE							
1 Pingree	N	Y	Y	N	N	N	N
2 **Poliquin**	Y	N	Y	Y	Y	Y	Y
MARYLAND							
1 **Harris**	Y	N	Y	Y	Y	Y	Y
2 Ruppersberger	N	Y	Y	N	N	N	N
3 Sarbanes	N	Y	N	N	N	N	N
4 Brown	N	Y	N	N	N	N	N
5 Hoyer	N	Y	N	N	N	N	N
6 Delaney	N	Y	Y	N	N	N	N
7 Cummings	?	?	?	?	?	?	?
8 Raskin	N	Y	N	N	N	N	N
MASSACHUSETTS							
1 Neal	N	Y	N	N	N	N	N
2 McGovern	N	Y	N	N	N	N	N
3 Tsongas	N	Y	N	N	N	N	N
4 Kennedy	N	Y	N	N	N	N	N
5 Clark	N	Y	N	N	N	N	N
6 Moulton	N	Y	N	N	N	N	N
7 Capuano	N	Y	N	N	N	N	N
8 Lynch	N	Y	Y	N	?	N	N
9 Keating	N	Y	Y	N	N	N	N
MICHIGAN							
1 **Bergman**	Y	N	Y	Y	Y	Y	Y
2 **Huizenga**	Y	N	Y	Y	Y	Y	Y
3 **Amash**	Y	Y	Y	Y	Y	Y	Y
4 **Moolenaar**	Y	N	Y	Y	Y	Y	Y
5 Kildee	N	Y	N	N	N	N	N
6 **Upton**	Y	N	Y	Y	Y	Y	Y
7 **Walberg**	Y	N	Y	Y	Y	Y	Y
8 **Bishop**	Y	N	Y	Y	Y	Y	Y
9 Levin	N	Y	N	N	N	N	N
10 **Mitchell**	Y	N	Y	Y	Y	Y	Y
11 **Trott**	Y	N	Y	Y	Y	Y	Y
12 Dingell	N	Y	N	N	N	N	N
13 Conyers	N	Y	N	N	N	N	N
14 Lawrence	N	Y	N	N	N	N	N
MINNESOTA							
1 Walz	N	Y	Y	N	N	N	N
2 **Lewis**	Y	N	Y	Y	Y	Y	Y
3 **Paulsen**	Y	N	Y	Y	Y	Y	Y
4 McCollum	N	Y	N	N	N	N	N
5 Ellison	N	Y	N	N	N	N	N
6 **Emmer**	Y	N	Y	Y	Y	Y	Y
7 Peterson	Y	N	Y	N	N	N	N
8 Nolan	N	Y	Y	N	N	N	N
MISSISSIPPI							
1 **Kelly**	Y	N	Y	Y	Y	Y	Y
2 Thompson	N	Y	Y	N	N	N	N
3 **Harper**	Y	N	Y	Y	Y	Y	Y
4 **Palazzo**	Y	N	Y	Y	Y	Y	Y
MISSOURI							
1 Clay	N	Y	N	N	N	N	N
2 **Wagner**	Y	N	Y	Y	Y	Y	Y
3 **Luetkemeyer**	Y	N	Y	Y	Y	Y	Y
4 **Hartzler**	Y	N	Y	Y	Y	Y	Y
5 Cleaver	N	Y	Y	N	N	N	N
6 **Graves**	Y	N	Y	Y	Y	Y	Y
7 **Long**	Y	N	Y	Y	Y	Y	Y
8 **Smith**	Y	N	Y	Y	Y	Y	Y
MONTANA							
AL **Vacant**							
NEBRASKA							
1 **Fortenberry**	Y	N	Y	Y	Y	Y	Y
2 **Bacon**	Y	N	Y	Y	Y	Y	Y
3 **Smith**	Y	N	Y	Y	+	Y	Y
NEVADA							
1 Titus	N	Y	Y	N	N	N	N
2 **Amodei**	Y	N	Y	Y	Y	Y	Y
3 Rosen	N	N	Y	N	N	N	N
4 Kihuen	N	Y	N	N	N	N	N
NEW HAMPSHIRE							
1 Shea-Porter	N	Y	N	N	N	N	N
2 Kuster	N	Y	Y	N	N	N	N
NEW JERSEY							
1 Norcross	N	Y	N	N	N	N	N
2 **LoBiondo**	Y	N	Y	Y	Y	Y	Y
3 **MacArthur**	Y	N	Y	Y	Y	Y	Y
4 **Smith**	Y	Y	Y	Y	Y	Y	Y
5 Gottheimer	N	N	Y	N	Y	N	N
6 Pallone	N	Y	N	N	N	N	N
7 **Lance**	Y	N	Y	Y	Y	Y	Y
8 Sires	N	Y	N	N	N	N	N
9 Pascrell	N	Y	N	N	N	N	N
10 Payne	N	Y	N	N	N	N	N
11 **Frelinghuysen**	Y	N	Y	Y	Y	Y	Y
12 Watson Coleman	N	Y	Y	N	N	N	N
NEW MEXICO							
1 Lujan Grisham	N	Y	N	N	N	N	N
2 **Pearce**	Y	N	Y	Y	Y	Y	Y
3 Luján	N	Y	N	N	N	N	N
NEW YORK							
1 **Zeldin**	Y	N	Y	Y	Y	Y	Y
2 **King**	Y	N	Y	Y	Y	Y	Y
3 Suozzi	N	Y	Y	N	N	N	N
4 Rice	N	Y	Y	N	N	N	N
5 Meeks	N	Y	Y	N	N	N	N
6 Meng	N	Y	N	N	N	N	N
7 Velázquez	N	Y	N	N	N	N	N
8 Jeffries	N	Y	N	N	N	N	N
9 Clarke	N	Y	N	N	N	N	N
10 Nadler	N	Y	N	N	N	N	N
11 **Donovan**	Y	N	Y	Y	Y	Y	Y
12 Maloney, C.	N	Y	N	?	?	?	?
13 Espaillat	N	Y	N	N	N	N	N
14 Crowley	N	Y	N	N	N	N	N
15 Serrano	N	Y	N	N	N	N	N
16 Engel	?	?	?	?	?	?	?
17 Lowey	N	Y	N	N	N	N	N
18 Maloney, S.P.	N	Y	Y	N	N	N	N
19 **Faso**	Y	N	Y	Y	Y	Y	Y
20 Tonko	N	Y	N	N	N	N	N
21 **Stefanik**	Y	N	Y	Y	Y	Y	Y
22 **Tenney**	Y	N	Y	Y	Y	Y	Y
23 **Reed**	Y	N	Y	Y	Y	Y	Y
24 **Katko**	Y	N	Y	Y	Y	Y	Y
25 Slaughter	N	Y	N	N	N	N	N
26 Higgins	N	Y	Y	N	N	N	N
27 **Collins**	Y	N	Y	Y	Y	Y	Y
NORTH CAROLINA							
1 Butterfield	N	Y	N	N	N	N	N
2 **Holding**	Y	N	Y	Y	Y	Y	Y
3 **Jones**	N	N	Y	N	N	N	N
4 Price	N	Y	N	N	N	N	N
5 **Foxx**	Y	N	Y	Y	Y	Y	Y
6 **Walker**	Y	N	Y	Y	Y	Y	Y
7 **Rouzer**	Y	N	Y	Y	Y	Y	Y
8 **Hudson**	Y	N	Y	Y	Y	Y	Y
9 **Pittenger**	Y	N	Y	Y	Y	Y	Y
10 **McHenry**	Y	N	Y	Y	Y	Y	Y
11 **Meadows**	Y	N	Y	Y	?	Y	Y
12 Adams	N	Y	N	N	N	N	N
13 **Budd**	Y	N	Y	Y	Y	Y	Y
NORTH DAKOTA							
AL **Cramer**	Y	N	Y	Y	Y	Y	Y
OHIO							
1 **Chabot**	Y	N	Y	Y	Y	Y	Y
2 **Wenstrup**	Y	N	Y	Y	Y	Y	Y
3 Beatty	N	Y	Y	N	N	N	N
4 **Jordan**	Y	N	Y	Y	Y	Y	Y
5 **Latta**	Y	N	Y	Y	Y	Y	Y
6 **Johnson**	Y	N	Y	Y	Y	Y	Y
7 **Gibbs**	Y	N	Y	Y	Y	Y	Y
8 **Davidson**	Y	N	Y	Y	Y	Y	Y
9 Kaptur	N	N	N	N	N	N	N
10 **Turner**	Y	N	Y	Y	Y	Y	Y
11 Fudge	N	Y	Y	N	N	N	N
12 **Tiberi**	Y	N	Y	Y	Y	Y	Y
13 Ryan	N	Y	N	N	N	N	N
14 **Joyce**	Y	N	Y	Y	Y	Y	Y
15 **Stivers**	Y	N	Y	Y	Y	Y	Y
16 **Renacci**	Y	N	Y	Y	Y	Y	Y
OKLAHOMA							
1 **Bridenstine**	Y	N	Y	Y	Y	Y	Y
2 **Mullin**	Y	N	Y	Y	Y	Y	Y
3 **Lucas**	Y	N	Y	Y	Y	Y	Y
4 **Cole**	Y	N	Y	Y	+	Y	Y
5 **Russell**	Y	N	Y	Y	Y	Y	Y
OREGON							
1 Bonamici	N	Y	N	N	N	N	N
2 **Walden**	Y	N	Y	Y	Y	Y	Y
3 Blumenauer	N	Y	N	N	N	N	N
4 DeFazio	–	+	–	–	–	–	–
5 Schrader	N	Y	Y	N	N	N	N
PENNSYLVANIA							
1 Brady	N	Y	N	N	N	N	N
2 Evans	N	Y	N	N	N	N	N
3 **Kelly**	Y	N	Y	Y	Y	Y	Y
4 **Perry**	Y	N	Y	Y	Y	Y	Y
5 **Thompson**	Y	N	Y	Y	Y	Y	Y
6 **Costello**	Y	N	Y	Y	Y	Y	Y
7 **Meehan**	Y	N	Y	Y	Y	Y	Y
8 **Fitzpatrick**	Y	N	Y	Y	Y	Y	Y
9 **Shuster**	Y	N	Y	Y	Y	Y	?
10 **Marino**	+	+	+	+	+	+	+
11 **Barletta**	Y	N	Y	Y	Y	Y	Y
12 **Rothfus**	Y	N	Y	Y	Y	Y	Y
13 Boyle	N	Y	N	N	N	N	N
14 Doyle	N	Y	N	N	N	N	N
15 **Dent**	Y	N	Y	Y	Y	Y	Y
16 **Smucker**	Y	N	Y	Y	Y	Y	Y
17 Cartwright	N	Y	Y	N	N	N	N
18 **Murphy**	Y	N	Y	Y	Y	Y	Y
RHODE ISLAND							
1 Cicilline	N	Y	N	N	N	N	N
2 Langevin	N	Y	Y	N	N	N	N
SOUTH CAROLINA							
1 **Sanford**	P	N	Y	Y	Y	Y	Y
2 **Wilson**	Y	N	Y	Y	Y	Y	Y
3 **Duncan**	Y	N	Y	Y	Y	Y	Y
4 **Gowdy**	Y	N	Y	Y	Y	Y	Y
6 Clyburn	?	?	?	?	?	?	?
7 **Rice**	Y	N	Y	Y	Y	Y	Y
SOUTH DAKOTA							
AL **Noem**	Y	N	Y	Y	Y	Y	Y
TENNESSEE							
1 **Roe**	Y	N	Y	Y	Y	Y	Y
2 **Duncan**	Y	N	Y	Y	Y	Y	Y
3 **Fleischmann**	Y	N	Y	Y	Y	Y	Y
4 **DesJarlais**	Y	N	Y	Y	Y	Y	Y
5 Cooper	N	Y	Y	N	Y	N	N
6 **Black**	Y	N	Y	Y	Y	Y	Y
7 **Blackburn**	Y	N	Y	Y	Y	Y	Y
8 **Kustoff**	Y	N	Y	Y	Y	Y	Y
9 Cohen	N	Y	N	N	N	N	N
TEXAS							
1 **Gohmert**	Y	N	Y	Y	Y	Y	Y
2 **Poe**	Y	Y	Y	Y	Y	Y	Y
3 **Johnson, S.**	?	?	?	?	?	?	?
4 **Ratcliffe**	Y	N	Y	Y	Y	Y	Y
5 **Hensarling**	Y	N	Y	Y	Y	Y	Y
6 **Barton**	Y	N	Y	Y	Y	Y	Y
7 **Culberson**	Y	N	Y	Y	Y	Y	Y
8 **Brady**	+	–	Y	Y	Y	Y	Y
9 Green, A.	N	Y	N	N	?	N	N
10 **McCaul**	Y	N	Y	Y	Y	Y	Y
11 **Conaway**	Y	N	Y	Y	Y	Y	Y
12 **Granger**	Y	N	Y	Y	Y	Y	Y
13 **Thornberry**	Y	N	Y	Y	Y	Y	Y
14 **Weber**	Y	N	Y	Y	Y	Y	Y
15 Gonzalez	N	N	Y	N	N	Y	N
16 O'Rourke	N	Y	Y	N	N	N	N
17 **Flores**	Y	N	Y	Y	Y	Y	Y
18 Jackson Lee	–	+	N	N	N	N	N
19 **Arrington**	Y	N	Y	Y	Y	Y	Y
20 Castro	N	Y	N	N	N	N	N
21 **Smith**	?	?	?	Y	Y	Y	Y
22 **Olson**	Y	N	Y	Y	Y	Y	Y
23 **Hurd**	Y	N	Y	Y	Y	Y	Y
24 **Marchant**	Y	N	Y	Y	Y	Y	Y
25 **Williams**	Y	N	Y	Y	Y	Y	Y
26 **Burgess**	Y	N	Y	Y	Y	Y	Y
27 **Farenthold**	Y	N	Y	Y	Y	Y	Y
28 Cuellar	N	N	Y	Y	Y	Y	Y
29 Green, G.	N	Y	Y	N	N	N	N
30 Johnson, E.B.	N	Y	N	N	N	N	N
31 **Carter**	Y	N	Y	Y	Y	Y	Y
32 **Sessions**	Y	N	Y	Y	Y	Y	Y
33 Veasey	N	Y	Y	N	N	N	N
34 Vela	N	N	Y	N	N	N	N
35 Doggett	N	Y	N	N	N	N	N
36 **Babin**	+	–	+	Y	Y	Y	Y
UTAH							
1 **Bishop**	Y	N	Y	Y	?	Y	Y
2 **Stewart**	Y	N	Y	Y	Y	Y	Y
3 **Chaffetz**	Y	N	Y	Y	Y	Y	Y
4 **Love**	Y	N	Y	Y	Y	Y	Y
VERMONT							
AL Welch	N	Y	N	N	N	N	N
VIRGINIA							
1 **Wittman**	Y	N	Y	Y	Y	Y	Y
2 **Taylor**	Y	N	Y	Y	Y	Y	Y
3 Scott	N	Y	N	N	N	N	N
4 McEachin	N	Y	Y	N	N	N	N
5 **Garrett**	Y	N	Y	Y	Y	Y	Y
6 **Goodlatte**	Y	N	Y	Y	Y	Y	Y
7 **Brat**	Y	N	Y	Y	Y	Y	Y
8 Beyer	N	Y	N	N	N	N	N
9 **Griffith**	Y	N	Y	Y	Y	Y	Y
10 **Comstock**	Y	N	Y	Y	Y	Y	Y
11 Connolly	N	Y	N	N	N	N	N
WASHINGTON							
1 DelBene	N	Y	N	N	N	N	N
2 Larsen	N	Y	N	N	N	N	N
3 **Herrera Beutler**	Y	N	Y	Y	Y	Y	Y
4 **Newhouse**	Y	N	Y	Y	Y	Y	Y
5 **McMorris Rodgers**	Y	N	Y	Y	Y	Y	Y
6 Kilmer	N	Y	N	N	N	N	N
7 Jayapal	N	Y	N	N	N	N	N
8 **Reichert**	+	–	+	+	+	+	+
9 Smith	N	Y	N	N	N	N	N
10 Heck	N	Y	N	N	N	N	N
WEST VIRGINIA							
1 **McKinley**	Y	N	Y	Y	Y	Y	Y
2 **Mooney**	Y	N	Y	Y	Y	Y	Y
3 **Jenkins**	Y	N	Y	Y	Y	Y	Y
WISCONSIN							
1 **Ryan**							
2 Pocan	N	Y	N	N	N	N	N
3 Kind	N	Y	Y	N	N	N	N
4 Moore	N	Y	N	N	N	N	N
5 **Sensenbrenner**	Y	N	Y	Y	Y	Y	Y
6 **Grothman**	?	N	Y	Y	Y	Y	Y
7 **Duffy**	Y	N	Y	Y	Y	Y	Y
8 **Gallagher**	Y	N	Y	Y	Y	Y	Y
WYOMING							
AL **Cheney**	Y	N	Y	Y	Y	Y	Y

VOTE NUMBER

299. HR 10. FINANCIAL REGULATION RESTRUCTURING/PASSAGE.
Passage of the bill that would overhaul financial industry regulations and repeal many provisions of the 2010 Dodd-Frank law. It would convert the Consumer Financial Protection Bureau into an executive agency funded by annual appropriations and would modify operations at the Federal Reserve and at the Securities and Exchange Commission. It would repeal the prohibition on banking entities engaging in proprietary trading and would modify regulations governing the amount of capital that banks are required to maintain. It would also nullify the Labor Department's April 2016 "fiduciary" rule regarding standards for individuals who provide retirement investment advice to act in the best interests of their clients. Passed 233-186 : R 233-1; D 0-185. June 8, 2017.

300. HR 2292. CANNONSVILLE RESERVOIR HYDROPOWER DEADLINE EXTENSION/PASSAGE. Upton, R-Mich., motion to suspend the rules and pass the bill that would allow the Federal Energy Regulatory Commission to extend the deadline for construction to begin on the hydroelectric project at the Cannonsville Reservoir on the West Branch of the Delaware River in Delaware County, N.Y. The bill would allow the commission to extend the deadline by up to three consecutive two-year periods, and would also allow the commission to renew the license if it should expire. Motion agreed to 400-1 : R 222-1; D 178-0. June 12, 2017.

301. HR 2457. J. BENNETT JOHNSTON WATERWAY HYDROPOWER DEADLINE EXTENSION/PASSAGE. Upton, R-Mich., motion to suspend the rules and pass the bill that would allow the Federal Energy Regulatory Commission to extend the deadline for construction to begin on three Army Corps of Engineers hydroelectric projects on the Red River in Louisiana. The bill would allow the commission to extend the deadline by up to three consecutive two-year segments, and would also allow the commission to renew the license if it should expire. The bill would also waive the requirement that the licensee pay annual charges to the commission until the project commences construction. Motion agreed to 402-1 : R 221-1; D 181-0. June 12, 2017.

302. HR 2581, H RES 378, S 1094. HEALTH INSURANCE TAX CREDIT VERIFICATION AND VA ACCOUNTABILITY/PREVIOUS QUESTION. Buck, R-Colo., motion to order the previous question (thus ending debate and possibility of amendment) on the rule (H Res 378) that would provide for consideration of the bill (HR 2581) that would prohibit the advance payment of health insurance premium tax credits to individuals that apply for the credits unless the Treasury Department receives confirmation from the Health and Human Services Department that such an individual's status as a citizens or lawfully present alien has been verified, and providing for consideration of the bill (S 1094) that would expand the VA's ability to fire, demote and suspend employees for misconduct or poor performance. Motion agreed to 229-189 : R 229-1; D 0-188. June 13, 2017.

303. HR 2581, H RES 378, S 1094. HEALTH INSURANCE TAX CREDIT VERIFICATION AND VA ACCOUNTABILITY/RULE. Adoption of the rule (H Res 378) that would provide for consideration of the bill (HR 2581) that would prohibit the advance payment of health insurance premium tax credits to individuals that apply for the credits unless the Treasury Department receives confirmation from the Health and Human Services Department that such an individual's status as a citizens or lawfully present alien has been verified, and providing for consideration of the bill (S 1094) that would expand the VA's ability to fire, demote and suspend employees for misconduct or poor performance. Adopted 229-190 : R 229-0; D 0-190. June 13, 2017.

304. PROCEDURAL MOTION/APPROVAL OF HOUSE JOURNAL. Approved 238-166 : R 147-76; D 91-90. June 13, 2017.

	299	300	301	302	303	304
ALABAMA						
1 **Byrne**	Y	Y	Y	Y	Y	Y
2 **Roby**	Y	Y	Y	Y	Y	Y
3 **Rogers**	Y	Y	Y	Y	Y	Y
4 **Aderholt**	Y	Y	Y	Y	Y	Y
5 **Brooks**	Y	?	?	?	?	?
6 **Palmer**	Y	Y	Y	Y	Y	Y
7 Sewell	N	Y	Y	N	N	N
ALASKA						
AL **Young**	Y	Y	Y	Y	Y	N
ARIZONA						
1 O'Halleran	N	Y	Y	N	N	N
2 **McSally**	Y	Y	Y	Y	Y	N
3 Grijalva	N	Y	Y	N	N	?
4 **Gosar**	Y	Y	Y	Y	Y	N
5 **Biggs**	Y	Y	Y	Y	Y	N
6 **Schweikert**	Y	Y	Y	Y	Y	Y
7 Gallego	N	Y	Y	N	N	N
8 **Franks**	Y	Y	Y	Y	Y	N
9 Sinema	N	Y	Y	N	N	N
ARKANSAS						
1 **Crawford**	Y	Y	Y	Y	Y	Y
2 **Hill**	Y	Y	Y	Y	Y	Y
3 **Womack**	Y	Y	Y	Y	Y	Y
4 **Westerman**	Y	Y	Y	Y	Y	Y
CALIFORNIA						
1 **LaMalfa**	Y	Y	Y	Y	Y	Y
2 Huffman	N	Y	Y	N	N	Y
3 Garamendi	N	Y	Y	N	N	Y
4 **McClintock**	Y	Y	Y	Y	Y	Y
5 Thompson	N	Y	Y	N	N	N
6 Matsui	N	Y	Y	N	N	N
7 Bera	N	Y	Y	N	N	?
8 **Cook**	Y	Y	Y	Y	Y	Y
9 McNerney	N	Y	Y	N	N	Y
10 **Denham**	Y	Y	Y	Y	Y	Y
11 DeSaulnier	N	Y	Y	N	N	Y
12 Pelosi	N	Y	Y	?	?	?
13 Lee	N	Y	Y	N	N	N
14 Speier	N	Y	Y	N	N	Y
15 Swalwell	N	Y	Y	N	N	Y
16 Costa	–	Y	Y	N	N	N
17 Khanna	N	Y	Y	N	N	N
18 Eshoo	N	Y	Y	N	N	?
19 Lofgren	N	+	+	N	N	N
20 Panetta	N	Y	Y	N	N	Y
21 **Valadao**	Y	Y	Y	Y	Y	N
22 **Nunes**	Y	Y	Y	Y	Y	Y
23 **McCarthy**	Y	Y	Y	Y	Y	Y
24 Carbajal	N	Y	Y	N	N	N
25 **Knight**	Y	Y	Y	Y	Y	Y
26 Brownley	N	Y	Y	N	N	N
27 Chu	N	Y	Y	N	N	Y
28 Schiff	N	Y	Y	N	N	N
29 Cardenas	N	Y	Y	N	N	N
30 Sherman	N	Y	Y	N	N	Y
31 Aguilar	–	Y	Y	N	N	N
32 Napolitano	–	+	+	–	–	?
33 Lieu	N	?	?	N	N	N
34 Vacant						
35 Torres	N	Y	Y	N	N	Y
36 Ruiz	N	Y	Y	N	N	N
37 Bass	N	Y	Y	N	N	N
38 Sánchez, Linda	N	Y	Y	N	N	N
39 **Royce**	Y	Y	Y	Y	Y	+
40 Roybal-Allard	N	Y	Y	N	N	N
41 Takano	N	Y	Y	N	N	Y
42 **Calvert**	Y	Y	Y	Y	Y	Y
43 Waters	N	Y	Y	N	N	N
44 Barragan	N	Y	Y	N	N	N
45 **Walters**	Y	Y	Y	Y	Y	Y
46 Correa	N	Y	Y	N	N	N
47 Lowenthal	N	Y	Y	?	N	N
48 **Rohrabacher**	Y	?	?	Y	Y	N
49 **Issa**	Y	Y	Y	Y	Y	?
50 **Hunter**	Y	Y	Y	Y	Y	Y
51 Vargas	N	Y	Y	N	N	N
52 Peters	N	Y	Y	N	N	N
53 Davis	N	Y	Y	N	N	Y

	299	300	301	302	303	304
COLORADO						
1 DeGette	N	Y	Y	N	N	Y
2 Polis	N	?	?	N	N	Y
3 **Tipton**	Y	Y	Y	Y	Y	N
4 **Buck**	Y	Y	Y	Y	Y	N
5 **Lamborn**	Y	Y	Y	Y	Y	Y
6 **Coffman**	Y	Y	Y	Y	Y	N
7 Perlmutter	N	Y	Y	N	N	N
CONNECTICUT						
1 Larson	N	Y	Y	N	N	N
2 Courtney	N	Y	Y	N	N	N
3 DeLauro	N	Y	Y	N	N	N
4 Himes	N	Y	Y	N	N	N
5 Esty	N	Y	Y	N	N	N
DELAWARE						
AL Blunt Rochester	N	Y	Y	N	N	N
FLORIDA						
1 **Gaetz**	Y	Y	Y	Y	Y	N
2 **Dunn**	Y	Y	Y	Y	Y	Y
3 **Yoho**	Y	Y	Y	Y	Y	?
4 **Rutherford**	Y	Y	Y	Y	Y	Y
5 Lawson	N	?	Y	N	N	N
6 **DeSantis**	Y	?	?	Y	Y	N
7 Murphy	N	Y	Y	N	N	Y
8 **Posey**	Y	Y	Y	Y	Y	Y
9 Soto	N	Y	Y	N	N	N
10 Demings	N	Y	Y	N	N	N
11 **Webster**	Y	Y	Y	Y	Y	Y
12 **Bilirakis**	Y	Y	Y	Y	Y	Y
13 Crist	N	Y	Y	N	N	N
14 Castor	N	Y	Y	N	N	N
15 **Ross**	Y	Y	Y	Y	Y	Y
16 **Buchanan**	Y	Y	Y	Y	Y	Y
17 **Rooney, T.**	Y	Y	Y	Y	Y	Y
18 **Mast**	Y	Y	Y	Y	Y	Y
19 **Rooney, F.**	Y	Y	Y	Y	Y	Y
20 Hastings	N	Y	Y	N	N	N
21 Frankel	N	Y	Y	N	N	?
22 Deutch	N	Y	Y	N	N	N
23 Wasserman Schultz	N	Y	Y	N	N	N
24 Wilson	N	Y	Y	N	N	N
25 **Diaz-Balart**	Y	Y	Y	Y	Y	N
26 **Curbelo**	Y	+	+	Y	Y	N
27 **Ros-Lehtinen**	Y	Y	Y	Y	Y	N
GEORGIA						
1 **Carter**	Y	Y	Y	Y	Y	N
2 Bishop	N	Y	Y	N	N	Y
3 **Ferguson**	Y	Y	Y	Y	Y	Y
4 Johnson	N	Y	Y	N	N	Y
5 Lewis	N	?	?	N	N	N
7 **Woodall**	Y	Y	Y	Y	Y	N
8 **Scott, A.**	Y	Y	Y	Y	Y	N
9 **Collins**	Y	Y	Y	Y	Y	N
10 **Hice**	Y	Y	Y	Y	Y	Y
11 **Loudermilk**	Y	Y	Y	Y	Y	Y
12 **Allen**	Y	Y	Y	Y	Y	Y
13 Scott, D.	N	Y	Y	N	N	Y
14 **Graves**	Y	Y	Y	Y	Y	N
HAWAII						
1 Hanabusa	N	Y	Y	N	N	Y
2 Gabbard	N	Y	Y	N	N	Y
IDAHO						
1 **Labrador**	Y	Y	Y	Y	Y	?
2 **Simpson**	Y	Y	Y	Y	Y	Y
ILLINOIS						
1 Rush	N	Y	Y	N	N	Y
2 Kelly	N	Y	Y	N	N	?
3 Lipinski	N	?	?	N	N	N
4 Gutierrez	N	+	+	N	N	N
5 Quigley	N	Y	Y	N	N	N
6 **Roskam**	Y	Y	Y	Y	Y	Y
7 Davis, D.	N	Y	Y	N	N	Y
8 Krishnamoorthi	N	Y	Y	N	N	N
9 Schakowsky	N	Y	Y	N	N	N
10 Schneider	N	Y	Y	N	N	N
11 Foster	N	Y	Y	N	N	N
12 **Bost**	Y	Y	Y	Y	Y	N
13 **Davis, R.**	Y	Y	Y	Y	Y	N
14 **Hultgren**	Y	Y	Y	Y	Y	Y
15 **Shimkus**	Y	Y	Y	Y	Y	Y

	299	300	301	302	303	304
16 **Kinzinger**	Y	Y	Y	Y	Y	N
17 Bustos	N	Y	Y	N	N	Y
18 **LaHood**	Y	Y	Y	Y	Y	N
INDIANA						
1 Visclosky	N	Y	Y	N	N	N
2 **Walorski**	Y	Y	Y	Y	Y	Y
3 **Banks**	Y	Y	Y	Y	Y	Y
4 **Rokita**	Y	Y	Y	Y	Y	N
5 **Brooks**	Y	Y	Y	Y	Y	Y
6 **Messer**	Y	Y	Y	Y	Y	Y
7 Carson	N	Y	Y	N	N	Y
8 **Bucshon**	Y	Y	Y	Y	Y	Y
9 **Hollingsworth**	Y	Y	Y	Y	Y	Y
IOWA						
1 **Blum**	Y	?	?	Y	Y	N
2 Loebsack	N	Y	Y	N	N	N
3 **Young**	Y	Y	Y	Y	Y	Y
4 **King**	Y	Y	Y	Y	Y	Y
KANSAS						
1 **Marshall**	Y	Y	Y	Y	Y	Y
2 **Jenkins**	Y	Y	Y	Y	Y	N
3 **Yoder**	Y	Y	Y	Y	Y	N
4 **Estes**	Y	Y	Y	Y	Y	Y
KENTUCKY						
1 **Comer**	Y	Y	Y	Y	Y	N
2 **Guthrie**	Y	Y	Y	Y	Y	Y
3 Yarmuth	N	Y	Y	N	N	Y
4 **Massie**	Y	Y	Y	Y	Y	Y
5 **Rogers**	Y	Y	Y	Y	Y	Y
6 **Barr**	Y	Y	Y	Y	Y	Y
LOUISIANA						
1 **Scalise**	Y	Y	Y	Y	Y	Y
2 Richmond	N	Y	Y	N	N	Y
3 **Higgins**	Y	Y	Y	+	+	Y
4 **Johnson**	Y	Y	Y	Y	Y	Y
5 **Abraham**	Y	Y	Y	Y	Y	Y
6 **Graves**	Y	Y	Y	Y	Y	N
MAINE						
1 Pingree	N	?	?	N	N	Y
2 **Poliquin**	Y	Y	Y	Y	Y	N
MARYLAND						
1 **Harris**	Y	?	?	Y	Y	Y
2 Ruppersberger	N	Y	Y	N	N	Y
3 Sarbanes	N	Y	Y	N	N	N
4 Brown	N	Y	Y	N	N	Y
5 Hoyer	N	Y	Y	N	N	N
6 Delaney	N	Y	Y	N	N	N
7 Cummings	?	?	?	?	?	?
8 Raskin	N	Y	Y	N	N	?
MASSACHUSETTS						
1 Neal	N	Y	Y	N	N	N
2 McGovern	N	Y	Y	?	N	N
3 Tsongas	N	Y	Y	N	N	Y
4 Kennedy	N	Y	Y	N	N	N
5 Clark	N	Y	Y	N	N	N
6 Moulton	N	Y	Y	N	N	Y
7 Capuano	N	Y	Y	N	N	N
8 Lynch	N	Y	Y	N	N	N
9 Keating	N	Y	Y	N	N	N
MICHIGAN						
1 **Bergman**	Y	Y	Y	Y	Y	Y
2 **Huizenga**	Y	Y	Y	Y	+	Y
3 **Amash**	Y	N	N	Y	Y	N
4 **Moolenaar**	Y	Y	Y	Y	Y	Y
5 Kildee	N	Y	Y	N	N	Y
6 **Upton**	Y	Y	Y	Y	Y	N
7 **Walberg**	Y	Y	Y	Y	Y	N
8 **Bishop**	Y	Y	Y	Y	Y	Y
9 Levin	N	Y	Y	N	N	N
10 **Mitchell**	Y	Y	Y	Y	Y	Y
11 **Trott**	Y	Y	Y	Y	Y	Y
12 Dingell	N	Y	Y	N	N	Y
13 Conyers	N	Y	Y	N	N	N
14 Lawrence	N	Y	Y	N	N	N
MINNESOTA						
1 Walz	N	Y	Y	N	N	Y
2 **Lewis**	Y	Y	Y	Y	Y	Y
3 **Paulsen**	Y	Y	Y	Y	Y	N
4 McCollum	N	Y	Y	N	N	Y

	299	300	301	302	303	304
5 Ellison	N	Y	Y	N	N	N
6 **Emmer**	Y	Y	Y	Y	Y	Y
7 Peterson	N	Y	Y	N	N	N
8 Nolan	N	Y	Y	N	N	N
MISSISSIPPI						
1 **Kelly**	Y	Y	Y	Y	Y	Y
2 Thompson	N	Y	Y	N	N	N
3 **Harper**	Y	Y	Y	Y	Y	Y
4 **Palazzo**	Y	Y	Y	Y	Y	Y
MISSOURI						
1 Clay	N	Y	Y	N	N	Y
2 **Wagner**	Y	Y	Y	Y	Y	?
3 **Luetkemeyer**	Y	Y	Y	Y	Y	Y
4 **Hartzler**	Y	Y	Y	Y	Y	Y
5 Cleaver	N	Y	Y	N	N	Y
6 **Graves**	Y	Y	Y	Y	Y	N
7 **Long**	Y	Y	Y	Y	Y	Y
8 **Smith**	Y	Y	Y	Y	Y	N
MONTANA						
AL **Vacant**						
NEBRASKA						
1 **Fortenberry**	Y	Y	Y	Y	Y	Y
2 **Bacon**	Y	Y	Y	Y	Y	Y
3 **Smith**	Y	Y	Y	Y	Y	Y
NEVADA						
1 Titus	N	Y	Y	N	N	Y
2 **Amodei**	Y	Y	Y	Y	Y	Y
3 Rosen	N	Y	Y	N	N	N
4 Kihuen	N	Y	Y	N	N	N
NEW HAMPSHIRE						
1 Shea-Porter	N	Y	Y	N	N	Y
2 Kuster	N	Y	Y	N	N	Y
NEW JERSEY						
1 Norcross	N	Y	Y	N	N	N
2 **LoBiondo**	Y	Y	Y	Y	Y	N
3 **MacArthur**	Y	Y	Y	Y	Y	N
4 **Smith**	Y	Y	Y	Y	Y	Y
5 Gottheimer	N	Y	Y	N	N	Y
6 Pallone	N	Y	Y	N	N	N
7 **Lance**	Y	Y	Y	Y	Y	N
8 Sires	N	Y	Y	N	N	?
9 Pascrell	N	Y	Y	N	N	Y
10 Payne	N	Y	Y	N	N	N
11 **Frelinghuysen**	Y	Y	?	Y	Y	Y
12 Watson Coleman	N	Y	Y	N	N	N
NEW MEXICO						
1 Lujan Grisham	N	Y	Y	N	N	Y
2 **Pearce**	Y	Y	Y	Y	Y	Y
3 Luján	N	Y	Y	N	N	Y
NEW YORK						
1 **Zeldin**	Y	Y	Y	Y	Y	Y
2 **King**	Y	Y	Y	Y	Y	Y
3 Suozzi	N	Y	Y	N	N	Y
4 Rice	N	Y	Y	N	N	N
5 Meeks	N	Y	Y	N	N	Y
6 Meng	N	?	?	N	N	Y
7 Velázquez	N	Y	Y	N	N	Y
8 Jeffries	N	Y	Y	N	N	Y
9 Clarke	N	Y	Y	N	N	N
10 Nadler	N	Y	Y	N	N	Y
11 **Donovan**	Y	Y	Y	Y	Y	Y
12 Maloney, C.	?	?	Y	N	N	N
13 Espaillat	N	Y	Y	N	N	N
14 Crowley	N	Y	Y	N	N	N
15 Serrano	N	Y	Y	N	N	Y
16 Engel	–	?	?	N	N	Y
17 Lowey	N	Y	Y	N	N	N
18 Maloney, S.P.	N	Y	Y	N	N	N
19 **Faso**	Y	Y	Y	Y	Y	N
20 Tonko	N	Y	Y	N	N	P
21 **Stefanik**	Y	Y	Y	Y	Y	Y
22 **Tenney**	Y	Y	Y	Y	Y	Y
23 **Reed**	Y	Y	Y	Y	Y	N
24 **Katko**	Y	Y	Y	Y	Y	Y
25 Slaughter	N	Y	Y	N	N	?
26 Higgins	N	Y	Y	N	N	Y
27 **Collins**	Y	Y	Y	Y	Y	Y
NORTH CAROLINA						
1 Butterfield	N	Y	Y	N	N	Y
2 **Holding**	Y	Y	Y	Y	Y	N
3 **Jones**	N	Y	Y	N	Y	N
4 Price	N	Y	Y	N	N	N

	299	300	301	302	303	304
5 **Foxx**	Y	Y	Y	Y	Y	N
6 **Walker**	Y	Y	Y	Y	Y	Y
7 **Rouzer**	Y	Y	Y	Y	Y	N
8 **Hudson**	Y	Y	Y	Y	Y	N
9 **Pittenger**	Y	Y	Y	Y	Y	N
10 **McHenry**	Y	Y	Y	Y	Y	Y
11 **Meadows**	Y	Y	Y	Y	Y	Y
12 Adams	N	Y	Y	N	N	Y
13 **Budd**	Y	Y	Y	Y	Y	Y
NORTH DAKOTA						
AL **Cramer**	Y	Y	Y	Y	Y	Y
OHIO						
1 **Chabot**	Y	Y	Y	Y	Y	Y
2 **Wenstrup**	Y	Y	Y	Y	Y	Y
3 Beatty	N	Y	Y	N	N	Y
4 **Jordan**	Y	Y	Y	Y	Y	N
5 **Latta**	Y	Y	Y	Y	Y	N
6 **Johnson**	Y	Y	Y	Y	Y	N
7 **Gibbs**	Y	Y	Y	Y	Y	N
8 **Davidson**	Y	Y	Y	Y	Y	Y
9 Kaptur	N	Y	Y	N	N	Y
10 **Turner**	Y	Y	Y	Y	Y	N
11 Fudge	N	Y	Y	N	N	N
12 **Tiberi**	Y	+	+	Y	Y	?
13 Ryan	N	Y	Y	N	N	Y
14 **Joyce**	Y	Y	Y	Y	Y	N
15 **Stivers**	Y	Y	Y	Y	Y	N
16 **Renacci**	Y	+	+	Y	Y	N
OKLAHOMA						
1 **Bridenstine**	Y	Y	Y	Y	Y	Y
2 **Mullin**	Y	Y	Y	Y	Y	Y
3 **Lucas**	Y	Y	Y	Y	Y	Y
4 **Cole**	Y	Y	Y	Y	Y	Y
5 **Russell**	Y	Y	Y	Y	Y	Y
OREGON						
1 Bonamici	N	Y	Y	N	N	Y
2 **Walden**	Y	Y	Y	Y	Y	Y
3 Blumenauer	N	Y	Y	N	N	Y
4 DeFazio	–	Y	Y	N	N	N
5 Schrader	N	Y	Y	N	N	N
PENNSYLVANIA						
1 Brady	N	Y	Y	N	N	N
2 Evans	N	Y	Y	N	N	N
3 **Kelly**	Y	Y	Y	Y	Y	Y
4 **Perry**	Y	Y	Y	Y	Y	N
5 **Thompson**	Y	Y	Y	Y	Y	N
6 **Costello**	Y	Y	Y	Y	Y	N
7 **Meehan**	Y	Y	Y	Y	Y	Y
8 **Fitzpatrick**	Y	Y	Y	Y	Y	N
9 **Shuster**	Y	Y	Y	Y	Y	Y
10 **Marino**	+	Y	Y	Y	Y	Y
11 **Barletta**	Y	Y	Y	Y	Y	Y
12 **Rothfus**	Y	Y	Y	Y	Y	Y
13 Boyle	N	Y	Y	N	N	N
14 Doyle	N	?	?	N	N	N
15 **Dent**	Y	Y	Y	Y	Y	Y
16 **Smucker**	Y	Y	Y	Y	Y	Y
17 Cartwright	N	Y	Y	N	N	Y
18 **Murphy**	Y	Y	Y	Y	Y	N
RHODE ISLAND						
1 Cicilline	N	Y	Y	N	N	Y
2 Langevin	N	Y	Y	N	N	N
SOUTH CAROLINA						
1 **Sanford**	Y	Y	Y	Y	Y	N
2 **Wilson**	Y	Y	Y	Y	Y	Y
3 **Duncan**	Y	Y	Y	Y	Y	Y
4 **Gowdy**	Y	Y	Y	Y	Y	Y
6 Clyburn	?	Y	Y	N	N	Y
7 **Rice**	Y	Y	Y	Y	Y	P
SOUTH DAKOTA						
AL **Noem**	Y	?	?	Y	Y	Y
TENNESSEE						
1 **Roe**	Y	Y	Y	Y	Y	Y
2 **Duncan**	Y	Y	Y	Y	Y	Y
3 **Fleischmann**	Y	Y	Y	Y	Y	Y
4 **DesJarlais**	Y	Y	Y	Y	Y	Y
5 Cooper	N	Y	Y	N	N	Y
6 **Black**	Y	Y	Y	Y	Y	Y
7 **Blackburn**	Y	Y	Y	Y	Y	Y
8 **Kustoff**	Y	Y	Y	Y	Y	Y
9 Cohen	N	Y	Y	N	N	N

	299	300	301	302	303	304
TEXAS						
1 **Gohmert**	Y	Y	Y	Y	Y	?
2 **Poe**	Y	?	?	Y	Y	N
3 **Johnson, S.**	?	?	?	?	?	?
4 **Ratcliffe**	Y	Y	Y	Y	Y	N
5 **Hensarling**	Y	Y	Y	Y	Y	Y
6 **Barton**	Y	Y	Y	Y	Y	N
7 **Culberson**	Y	Y	Y	Y	Y	Y
8 **Brady**	Y	Y	Y	Y	Y	Y
9 Green, A.	N	Y	Y	N	N	Y
10 **McCaul**	Y	Y	Y	Y	Y	Y
11 **Conaway**	Y	Y	Y	Y	Y	N
12 **Granger**	Y	+	+	+	+	+
13 **Thornberry**	Y	Y	Y	Y	Y	Y
14 **Weber**	Y	Y	Y	?	?	?
15 Gonzalez	N	Y	Y	N	N	N
16 O'Rourke	N	Y	Y	N	N	Y
17 **Flores**	Y	Y	Y	Y	Y	N
18 Jackson Lee	N	Y	Y	N	N	N
19 **Arrington**	Y	Y	Y	Y	Y	Y
20 Castro	N	Y	Y	N	N	Y
21 **Smith**	Y	Y	Y	Y	Y	Y
22 **Olson**	Y	Y	Y	Y	Y	Y
23 **Hurd**	Y	Y	Y	Y	Y	N
24 **Marchant**	Y	Y	Y	Y	Y	Y
25 **Williams**	Y	Y	Y	Y	Y	Y
26 **Burgess**	Y	Y	Y	Y	Y	N
27 **Farenthold**	Y	Y	Y	Y	Y	N
28 Cuellar	N	Y	Y	N	N	Y
29 Green, G.	N	Y	Y	N	N	N
30 Johnson, E.B.	N	Y	Y	N	N	Y
31 **Carter**	Y	?	?	Y	Y	Y
32 **Sessions**	Y	Y	Y	Y	Y	Y
33 Veasey	N	Y	Y	N	N	N
34 Vela	N	Y	Y	N	N	N
35 Doggett	N	Y	Y	N	N	Y
36 **Babin**	Y	Y	Y	Y	Y	Y
UTAH						
1 **Bishop**	Y	?	?	Y	Y	Y
2 **Stewart**	Y	Y	Y	Y	Y	Y
3 **Chaffetz**	Y	Y	Y	Y	Y	Y
4 **Love**	Y	Y	Y	Y	Y	Y
VERMONT						
AL Welch	N	Y	Y	N	N	Y
VIRGINIA						
1 **Wittman**	Y	Y	Y	Y	Y	Y
2 **Taylor**	Y	Y	Y	+	+	+
3 Scott	N	Y	Y	N	N	Y
4 McEachin	N	?	Y	N	N	Y
5 **Garrett**	Y	Y	Y	Y	Y	Y
6 **Goodlatte**	Y	Y	Y	Y	Y	Y
7 **Brat**	Y	Y	Y	Y	Y	Y
8 Beyer	N	Y	Y	N	N	N
9 **Griffith**	Y	Y	Y	?	?	?
10 **Comstock**	Y	Y	Y	Y	Y	Y
11 Connolly	N	Y	Y	N	N	N
WASHINGTON						
1 DelBene	N	Y	Y	N	N	Y
2 Larsen	N	Y	Y	N	N	Y
3 **Herrera Beutler**	Y	Y	Y	Y	Y	N
4 **Newhouse**	Y	Y	Y	Y	Y	Y
5 **McMorris Rodgers**	Y	Y	Y	Y	Y	Y
6 Kilmer	N	Y	Y	N	N	N
7 Jayapal	N	Y	Y	N	N	N
8 **Reichert**	+	Y	Y	Y	Y	Y
9 Smith	N	Y	Y	N	N	Y
10 Heck	N	Y	Y	N	N	Y
WEST VIRGINIA						
1 **McKinley**	Y	Y	Y	Y	Y	N
2 **Mooney**	Y	Y	Y	Y	Y	Y
3 **Jenkins**	Y	Y	Y	Y	Y	N
WISCONSIN						
1 **Ryan**						
2 Pocan	N	Y	Y	N	N	Y
3 Kind	N	Y	Y	N	N	N
4 Moore	N	Y	Y	N	N	N
5 **Sensenbrenner**	Y	Y	Y	Y	Y	Y
6 **Grothman**	Y	Y	Y	Y	Y	N
7 **Duffy**	Y	Y	Y	Y	Y	Y
8 **Gallagher**	Y	Y	Y	Y	Y	N
WYOMING						
AL **Cheney**	Y	Y	Y	Y	Y	Y

⫶ HOUSE VOTES

VOTE NUMBER

305. HR 2581. HEALTH INSURANCE TAX CREDIT VERIFICATION/ RECOMMIT. Sanchez, D-Calif., motion to recommit the bill to the House Committee on Ways and Means with instructions to report it back immediately with an amendment that would exempt individuals under 1-year-old from the bill's prohibition on the advance payment of health insurance premium tax credits unless the Treasury Department has received confirmation of the individuals' status as a citizen or lawfully present alien has been verified. Motion rejected 193-231 : R 2-231; D 191-0. June 13, 2017.

306. HR 2581. HEALTH INSURANCE TAX CREDIT VERIFICATION/PASSAGE. Passage of the bill that would prohibit the advance payment of health insurance premium tax credits to individuals that apply for the credits unless the Treasury Department receives confirmation from the Health and Human Services Department that such an individual's status as a citizens or lawfully present alien has been verified. If the American Health Care Act (HR 1628) is enacted, the bill (HR 2581) would make verification of an individual's status mandatory in order to receive advance payment of the new health insurance premium tax credit created by the American Health Care Act, and would also provide an exemption from the American Health Care Act's continuous coverage requirements for individuals who experience delays in coverage as a result of the verification process. Passed 238-184 : R 231-1; D 7-183. June 13, 2017.

307. S 1094. VA ACCOUNTABILITY/PASSAGE. Passage of the bill that would expand the VA's ability to fire, demote and suspend employees for misconduct or poor performance. The bill would authorize the VA to recoup any bonus or relocation expense paid to a VA employee if it deems it appropriate. It would require that the employee be given advance notice and would allow the employee the right to appeal the disciplinary action through procedures set by collective bargaining. The bill would also establish an office within the VA to receive whistleblower disclosures, track recommendations from audits and investigators, and investigate misconduct, retaliation and poor performance. Passed (thus cleared for the president) 368-55 : R 231-1; D 137-54. June 13, 2017.

308. HR 2579. HEALTH CARE TAX CREDIT EXPANSION/PASSAGE. Passage of the bill that would modify the definition of a "qualified health plan" to allow, beginning in 2020, for new tax credits proposed by the American Health Care Act (HR 1628) to be used by individuals or families to pay for continued group health coverage under COBRA, provided that the AHCA is enacted into law. The measure would also apply to continuation coverage as part of church-based group health plans, but the tax credit could not be utilized for a health flex spending account under the bill's provisions. Passed 267-144 : R 226-0; D 41-144. June 15, 2017.

309. HR 2847. FOSTER CARE BENEFITS EXPANSION/PASSAGE. Walorski, R-Ind., motion to suspend the rules and pass the bill that would extend the cutoff age from 21 to 23 for an individual in foster care to be eligible for assistance under the John H. Chafee Foster Care Independence program. It would require that all individuals who have been in foster care at 14-years-old or thereafter be eligible for aid under the program, and it would increase the age limit to 26-years-old for an individual to use the program's education and training vouchers. Motion agreed to 391-8 : R 217-8; D 174-0. June 20, 2017.

310. HR 2866. FOSTER FAMILY HOME LICENSING STANDARDS/PASSAGE. Kelly, R-Pa., motion to suspend the rules and pass the bill that would require the Health and Human Services Department to identify national model standards for the licensing of foster family homes by Oct. 2018. The bill would require states to provide, by April 2019, information to the department addressing whether their licensing standards are in accordance with the national model identified by the department. Specifically, states would have to indicate as to whether they utilize their authority to waive non-safety standards when licensing relatives as foster families for children. Motion agreed to 382-19 : R 206-19; D 176-0. June 20, 2017.

	305	306	307	308	309	310
ALABAMA						
1 Byrne	N	Y	Y	Y	Y	Y
2 Roby	N	Y	Y	Y	Y	Y
3 Rogers	N	Y	Y	Y	Y	Y
4 Aderholt	N	Y	Y	Y	?	Y
5 Brooks	N	Y	Y	Y	?	?
6 Palmer	N	Y	Y	Y	Y	N
7 Sewell	Y	N	Y	N	Y	Y
ALASKA						
AL Young	N	Y	N	Y	Y	Y
ARIZONA						
1 O'Halleran	Y	Y	Y	Y	Y	Y
2 McSally	N	Y	Y	Y	Y	Y
3 Grijalva	Y	N	N	N	Y	Y
4 Gosar	N	Y	Y	Y	Y	N
5 Biggs	N	Y	Y	Y	N	N
6 Schweikert	N	Y	Y	Y	Y	Y
7 Gallego	Y	N	N	N	Y	Y
8 Franks	N	Y	Y	Y	Y	Y
9 Sinema	Y	Y	Y	Y	Y	Y
ARKANSAS						
1 Crawford	N	Y	Y	Y	Y	Y
2 Hill	N	Y	Y	Y	Y	Y
3 Womack	N	Y	Y	Y	Y	Y
4 Westerman	N	Y	Y	Y	Y	Y
CALIFORNIA						
1 LaMalfa	N	Y	Y	Y	Y	Y
2 Huffman	Y	N	N	N	Y	Y
3 Garamendi	Y	N	N	N	Y	Y
4 McClintock	N	Y	Y	Y	N	Y
5 Thompson	Y	N	N	N	Y	Y
6 Matsui	Y	N	N	N	Y	Y
7 Bera	Y	N	Y	Y	Y	Y
8 Cook	N	Y	Y	Y	Y	Y
9 McNerney	Y	N	N	N	Y	Y
10 Denham	N	Y	Y	Y	Y	Y
11 DeSaulnier	Y	N	N	N	Y	Y
12 Pelosi	Y	N	N	N	?	?
13 Lee	Y	N	N	N	Y	Y
14 Speier	Y	N	N	N	?	?
15 Swalwell	Y	N	N	N	Y	Y
16 Costa	Y	N	Y	Y	Y	Y
17 Khanna	Y	N	N	N	Y	Y
18 Eshoo	Y	N	N	N	Y	Y
19 Lofgren	Y	N	N	N	Y	Y
20 Panetta	Y	N	N	N	Y	Y
21 Valadao	N	Y	Y	Y	Y	Y
22 Nunes	N	Y	Y	Y	Y	Y
23 McCarthy	N	Y	Y	Y	Y	Y
24 Carbajal	Y	N	N	N	Y	Y
25 Knight	N	Y	Y	Y	Y	Y
26 Brownley	Y	N	N	N	Y	Y
27 Chu	Y	N	N	N	Y	Y
28 Schiff	Y	N	N	N	Y	Y
29 Cardenas	Y	N	N	N	Y	Y
30 Sherman	Y	–	Y	N	Y	Y
31 Aguilar	Y	N	N	N	Y	Y
32 Napolitano	+	–	–	–	+	+
33 Lieu	Y	N	N	Y	Y	Y
34 Vacant						
35 Torres	Y	N	N	N	Y	Y
36 Ruiz	Y	N	Y	Y	Y	Y
37 Bass	Y	N	N	N	Y	Y
38 Sánchez, Linda	Y	N	N	N	?	?
39 Royce	N	Y	Y	Y	Y	Y
40 Roybal-Allard	Y	N	N	N	Y	Y
41 Takano	Y	N	N	N	Y	Y
42 Calvert	N	Y	Y	Y	Y	Y
43 Waters	Y	N	N	N	+	+
44 Barragan	Y	N	N	N	Y	Y
45 Walters	N	Y	Y	Y	Y	Y
46 Correa	Y	N	Y	Y	Y	Y
47 Lowenthal	Y	N	Y	N	?	?
48 Rohrabacher	N	Y	Y	Y	?	?
49 Issa	N	Y	Y	Y	Y	Y
50 Hunter	N	Y	Y	Y	Y	Y
51 Vargas	Y	N	N	N	Y	Y
52 Peters	Y	N	Y	Y	Y	Y
53 Davis	Y	N	N	Y	N	Y

	305	306	307	308	309	310
COLORADO						
1 DeGette	Y	N	N	N	Y	Y
2 Polis	Y	N	N	N	Y	Y
3 Tipton	N	Y	Y	Y	Y	Y
4 Buck	N	Y	Y	Y	N	N
5 Lamborn	N	Y	Y	Y	Y	Y
6 Coffman	N	Y	Y	Y	Y	Y
7 Perlmutter	Y	N	N	N	Y	Y
CONNECTICUT						
1 Larson	Y	N	N	N	Y	Y
2 Courtney	Y	N	Y	Y	Y	Y
3 DeLauro	Y	N	N	N	Y	Y
4 Himes	Y	N	Y	Y	?	?
5 Esty	Y	N	Y	Y	Y	Y
DELAWARE						
AL Blunt Rochester	Y	N	Y	?	Y	Y
FLORIDA						
1 Gaetz	N	Y	Y	Y	Y	N
2 Dunn	N	Y	Y	Y	Y	Y
3 Yoho	N	Y	Y	Y	N	Y
4 Rutherford	N	Y	Y	Y	Y	Y
5 Lawson	Y	N	Y	Y	Y	Y
6 DeSantis	N	Y	Y	Y	Y	Y
7 Murphy	Y	N	Y	Y	Y	Y
8 Posey	N	Y	Y	Y	+	+
9 Soto	Y	N	N	Y	Y	Y
10 Demings	Y	N	N	N	Y	Y
11 Webster	N	Y	Y	Y	Y	Y
12 Bilirakis	N	Y	Y	Y	Y	Y
13 Crist	Y	N	N	Y	Y	Y
14 Castor	Y	N	N	Y	Y	Y
15 Ross	N	Y	Y	Y	Y	Y
16 Buchanan	N	Y	Y	Y	Y	Y
17 Rooney, T.	N	Y	Y	Y	Y	Y
18 Mast	N	Y	Y	Y	Y	Y
19 Rooney, F.	N	Y	Y	Y	Y	Y
20 Hastings	Y	N	N	N	Y	Y
21 Frankel	Y	N	N	Y	Y	Y
22 Deutch	Y	N	N	N	Y	Y
23 Wasserman Schultz	Y	N	N	?	Y	Y
24 Wilson	Y	N	N	?	?	Y
25 Diaz-Balart	N	Y	Y	Y	Y	Y
26 Curbelo	N	Y	Y	Y	Y	Y
27 Ros-Lehtinen	N	Y	Y	Y	Y	Y
GEORGIA						
1 Carter	N	Y	Y	Y	Y	Y
2 Bishop	Y	N	Y	Y	Y	Y
3 Ferguson	N	Y	Y	Y	Y	Y
4 Johnson	Y	N	N	N	Y	Y
5 Lewis	Y	N	N	N	?	?
7 Woodall	N	Y	Y	Y	Y	Y
8 Scott, A.	N	Y	Y	Y	Y	Y
9 Collins	N	Y	Y	Y	Y	Y
10 Hice	N	Y	Y	Y	Y	Y
11 Loudermilk	N	Y	Y	Y	Y	Y
12 Allen	N	Y	Y	Y	Y	Y
13 Scott, D.	Y	N	Y	N	Y	Y
14 Graves	N	Y	Y	Y	Y	Y
HAWAII						
1 Hanabusa	Y	N	N	N	Y	Y
2 Gabbard	Y	N	Y	N	?	?
IDAHO						
1 Labrador	N	Y	Y	?	N	N
2 Simpson	N	Y	Y	?	Y	Y
ILLINOIS						
1 Rush	Y	N	N	N	Y	Y
2 Kelly	Y	N	N	N	Y	Y
3 Lipinski	Y	N	Y	Y	Y	Y
4 Gutierrez	Y	N	N	N	+	+
5 Quigley	Y	N	N	N	Y	Y
6 Roskam	N	Y	Y	Y	Y	Y
7 Davis, D.	Y	N	N	Y	Y	Y
8 Krishnamoorthi	Y	N	Y	Y	Y	Y
9 Schakowsky	Y	N	N	N	Y	Y
10 Schneider	Y	N	Y	Y	Y	Y
11 Foster	Y	N	Y	Y	Y	Y
12 Bost	N	Y	Y	Y	Y	Y
13 Davis, R.	N	Y	Y	Y	Y	Y
14 Hultgren	N	Y	Y	Y	Y	Y
15 Shimkus	N	Y	Y	Y	Y	Y

KEY

Republicans	Democrats	*Independents*

Y Voted for (yea)	X Paired against	C Voted "present" to avoid possible conflict of interest
# Paired for	– Announced against	
+ Announced for	P Voted "present"	? Did not vote or otherwise make a position known
N Voted against (nay)		

	305	306	307	308	309	310
16 **Kinzinger**	N	Y	Y	Y	Y	Y
17 Bustos	Y	N	Y	Y	Y	Y
18 **LaHood**	N	Y	Y	Y	Y	Y
INDIANA						
1 Visclosky	Y	N	Y	N	Y	Y
2 **Walorski**	N	Y	Y	Y	Y	Y
3 **Banks**	N	Y	Y	Y	Y	Y
4 **Rokita**	N	Y	Y	Y	Y	Y
5 **Brooks**	N	Y	Y	Y	Y	Y
6 **Messer**	N	Y	Y	Y	Y	Y
7 Carson	Y	N	N	N	Y	Y
8 **Bucshon**	N	Y	Y	Y	Y	Y
9 **Hollingsworth**	N	Y	Y	Y	Y	Y
IOWA						
1 **Blum**	N	Y	Y	Y	Y	Y
2 Loebsack	Y	N	Y	Y	Y	Y
3 **Young**	N	Y	Y	Y	Y	Y
4 **King**	N	Y	Y	Y	Y	Y
KANSAS						
1 **Marshall**	N	Y	Y	Y	Y	Y
2 **Jenkins**	N	Y	Y	Y	Y	Y
3 **Yoder**	N	Y	Y	Y	Y	Y
4 **Estes**	N	Y	Y	Y	Y	Y
KENTUCKY						
1 **Comer**	N	Y	Y	Y	Y	Y
2 **Guthrie**	N	Y	Y	Y	Y	Y
3 Yarmuth	Y	N	Y	Y	Y	Y
4 **Massie**	N	Y	Y	Y	Y	N
5 **Rogers**	N	Y	Y	Y	Y	Y
6 **Barr**	N	Y	Y	Y	Y	Y
LOUISIANA						
1 **Scalise**	N	Y	Y	+	+	+
2 Richmond	Y	N	N	N	Y	Y
3 **Higgins**	N	Y	Y	Y	Y	Y
4 **Johnson**	N	Y	Y	?	Y	Y
5 **Abraham**	N	Y	Y	Y	Y	Y
6 **Graves**	N	Y	Y	Y	Y	Y
MAINE						
1 Pingree	Y	N	Y	N	?	?
2 **Poliquin**	N	Y	Y	Y	Y	Y
MARYLAND						
1 **Harris**	N	Y	Y	?	Y	Y
2 Ruppersberger	Y	N	Y	N	Y	Y
3 Sarbanes	Y	N	Y	N	Y	Y
4 Brown	Y	N	N	N	Y	Y
5 Hoyer	Y	N	N	N	Y	Y
6 Delaney	Y	N	Y	Y	Y	Y
7 Cummings	?	?	?	?	?	?
8 Raskin	Y	N	N	N	Y	Y
MASSACHUSETTS						
1 Neal	Y	N	Y	N	Y	Y
2 McGovern	Y	N	Y	N	Y	Y
3 Tsongas	Y	N	Y	N	Y	Y
4 Kennedy	Y	N	Y	N	?	?
5 Clark	Y	N	Y	N	Y	Y
6 Moulton	Y	N	Y	N	Y	Y
7 Capuano	Y	N	Y	N	Y	Y
8 Lynch	Y	Y	N	Y	Y	Y
9 Keating	Y	N	Y	N	Y	Y
MICHIGAN						
1 **Bergman**	N	Y	Y	Y	Y	Y
2 **Huizenga**	N	Y	Y	Y	Y	Y
3 **Amash**	N	Y	Y	Y	N	N
4 **Moolenaar**	N	Y	Y	Y	Y	Y
5 Kildee	Y	N	Y	N	Y	Y
6 **Upton**	N	Y	Y	Y	Y	Y
7 **Walberg**	N	Y	Y	Y	Y	Y
8 **Bishop**	N	Y	Y	Y	Y	Y
9 Levin	Y	N	N	N	Y	Y
10 **Mitchell**	N	Y	Y	Y	Y	Y
11 **Trott**	N	Y	Y	Y	Y	Y
12 Dingell	Y	N	Y	N	Y	Y
13 Conyers	Y	N	Y	N	Y	Y
14 Lawrence	Y	N	Y	N	Y	Y
MINNESOTA						
1 Walz	Y	N	Y	?	Y	Y
2 **Lewis**	N	+	Y	Y	Y	Y
3 **Paulsen**	N	Y	Y	Y	Y	Y
4 McCollum	Y	N	Y	N	Y	Y

	305	306	307	308	309	310
5 Ellison	Y	N	N	N	Y	Y
6 **Emmer**	N	Y	Y	Y	Y	Y
7 Peterson	Y	Y	Y	Y	Y	Y
8 Nolan	Y	N	Y	N	Y	Y
MISSISSIPPI						
1 **Kelly**	N	Y	Y	Y	Y	Y
2 Thompson	Y	N	N	N	Y	Y
3 **Harper**	N	Y	Y	Y	Y	Y
4 **Palazzo**	N	Y	Y	Y	Y	Y
MISSOURI						
1 Clay	Y	N	Y	N	Y	Y
2 **Wagner**	N	Y	Y	Y	?	?
3 **Luetkemeyer**	N	Y	Y	Y	Y	Y
4 **Hartzler**	N	Y	Y	Y	Y	Y
5 Cleaver	Y	N	Y	N	Y	Y
6 **Graves**	N	Y	Y	Y	Y	Y
7 **Long**	N	Y	Y	Y	Y	Y
8 **Smith**	N	Y	Y	Y	Y	Y
MONTANA						
AL **Vacant**						
NEBRASKA						
1 **Fortenberry**	N	Y	Y	Y	Y	Y
2 **Bacon**	N	Y	Y	Y	Y	Y
3 **Smith**	N	Y	Y	Y	Y	Y
NEVADA						
1 Titus	Y	N	Y	N	Y	Y
2 **Amodei**	N	Y	Y	Y	Y	Y
3 Rosen	Y	N	Y	Y	Y	Y
4 Kihuen	Y	N	Y	Y	Y	Y
NEW HAMPSHIRE						
1 Shea-Porter	Y	N	Y	Y	+	+
2 Kuster	Y	N	Y	N	Y	Y
NEW JERSEY						
1 Norcross	Y	N	N	?	Y	Y
2 **LoBiondo**	N	Y	Y	Y	Y	Y
3 **MacArthur**	N	Y	Y	Y	Y	Y
4 **Smith**	N	Y	Y	Y	?	?
5 Gottheimer	Y	N	Y	Y	Y	Y
6 Pallone	Y	N	N	N	Y	Y
7 **Lance**	N	Y	Y	Y	Y	Y
8 Sires	Y	N	Y	N	Y	Y
9 Pascrell	Y	N	Y	N	Y	Y
10 Payne	Y	N	N	?	Y	Y
11 **Frelinghuysen**	N	Y	Y	Y	Y	Y
12 Watson Coleman	Y	N	N	N	Y	Y
NEW MEXICO						
1 Lujan Grisham	Y	N	Y	Y	Y	Y
2 **Pearce**	N	Y	Y	Y	Y	Y
3 Luján	Y	N	Y	N	Y	Y
NEW YORK						
1 **Zeldin**	N	Y	Y	Y	Y	Y
2 **King**	N	Y	Y	Y	Y	Y
3 Suozzi	Y	N	N	Y	Y	Y
4 Rice	Y	N	N	Y	?	Y
5 Meeks	Y	N	Y	N	Y	Y
6 Meng	Y	N	Y	N	Y	Y
7 Velázquez	Y	N	N	N	Y	Y
8 Jeffries	Y	N	N	N	Y	Y
9 Clarke	Y	N	N	N	Y	Y
10 Nadler	Y	N	N	N	Y	Y
11 **Donovan**	N	Y	Y	Y	Y	Y
12 Maloney, C.	Y	N	Y	N	Y	Y
13 Espaillat	Y	N	N	N	Y	Y
14 Crowley	Y	N	N	N	Y	Y
15 Serrano	Y	N	N	N	Y	Y
16 Engel	Y	N	N	N	Y	Y
17 Lowey	Y	N	Y	N	Y	Y
18 Maloney, S.P.	Y	N	Y	Y	Y	Y
19 **Faso**	N	Y	Y	Y	Y	Y
20 Tonko	Y	N	Y	N	Y	Y
21 **Stefanik**	N	Y	Y	Y	Y	Y
22 **Tenney**	N	Y	Y	Y	Y	Y
23 **Reed**	N	Y	Y	+	Y	Y
24 **Katko**	N	Y	Y	Y	Y	Y
25 Slaughter	Y	N	Y	N	Y	Y
26 Higgins	Y	N	Y	N	Y	Y
27 **Collins**	N	Y	Y	Y	Y	Y
NORTH CAROLINA						
1 Butterfield	Y	N	Y	N	Y	Y
2 **Holding**	N	Y	Y	Y	Y	Y
3 **Jones**	Y	Y	Y	Y	Y	N
4 Price	Y	N	Y	N	Y	Y

	305	306	307	308	309	310
5 **Foxx**	N	Y	Y	Y	Y	Y
6 **Walker**	N	Y	Y	Y	Y	Y
7 **Rouzer**	N	Y	Y	+	Y	Y
8 **Hudson**	N	Y	Y	Y	Y	Y
9 **Pittenger**	N	Y	Y	Y	Y	Y
10 **McHenry**	N	Y	Y	Y	Y	Y
11 **Meadows**	N	Y	Y	Y	Y	Y
12 Adams	Y	N	Y	N	Y	Y
13 **Budd**	N	Y	Y	Y	Y	Y
NORTH DAKOTA						
AL **Cramer**	N	Y	Y	Y	Y	Y
OHIO						
1 **Chabot**	N	Y	Y	Y	Y	Y
2 **Wenstrup**	N	Y	Y	Y	Y	Y
3 Beatty	Y	N	Y	N	Y	Y
4 **Jordan**	N	Y	Y	Y	Y	N
5 **Latta**	N	Y	Y	Y	Y	Y
6 **Johnson**	N	Y	Y	Y	Y	Y
7 **Gibbs**	N	Y	Y	Y	Y	N
8 **Davidson**	N	Y	Y	Y	Y	Y
9 Kaptur	Y	Y	Y	N	Y	Y
10 **Turner**	N	Y	Y	Y	Y	Y
11 Fudge	Y	N	N	N	?	?
12 **Tiberi**	N	Y	Y	Y	Y	Y
13 Ryan	Y	N	Y	N	Y	Y
14 **Joyce**	N	Y	Y	Y	Y	Y
15 **Stivers**	N	Y	Y	Y	Y	Y
16 **Renacci**	N	Y	Y	Y	+	+
OKLAHOMA						
1 **Bridenstine**	N	Y	Y	Y	Y	Y
2 **Mullin**	N	Y	Y	Y	Y	Y
3 **Lucas**	N	Y	Y	Y	Y	Y
4 **Cole**	N	Y	Y	+	Y	Y
5 **Russell**	N	Y	Y	Y	Y	Y
OREGON						
1 Bonamici	Y	N	Y	N	Y	Y
2 **Walden**	N	Y	Y	Y	Y	Y
3 Blumenauer	Y	N	Y	N	Y	Y
4 DeFazio	Y	Y	Y	Y	Y	Y
5 Schrader	Y	N	Y	N	Y	Y
PENNSYLVANIA						
1 Brady	Y	N	Y	N	Y	Y
2 Evans	Y	N	N	N	Y	Y
3 **Kelly**	N	Y	Y	Y	Y	Y
4 **Perry**	N	Y	Y	Y	Y	Y
5 **Thompson**	N	Y	Y	Y	Y	Y
6 **Costello**	N	Y	Y	Y	Y	Y
7 **Meehan**	N	Y	Y	Y	Y	Y
8 **Fitzpatrick**	N	Y	Y	Y	Y	Y
9 **Shuster**	N	Y	Y	Y	Y	Y
10 **Marino**	N	Y	Y	Y	Y	Y
11 **Barletta**	N	Y	Y	Y	Y	Y
12 **Rothfus**	N	Y	Y	Y	Y	Y
13 Boyle	Y	N	Y	N	Y	Y
14 Doyle	Y	N	Y	N	Y	Y
15 **Dent**	N	Y	Y	Y	Y	Y
16 **Smucker**	N	Y	Y	Y	Y	Y
17 Cartwright	Y	N	Y	N	Y	Y
18 **Murphy**	N	Y	Y	Y	Y	Y
RHODE ISLAND						
1 Cicilline	Y	N	Y	N	?	?
2 Langevin	Y	N	Y	N	Y	Y
SOUTH CAROLINA						
1 **Sanford**	N	Y	Y	Y	N	N
2 **Wilson**	N	Y	Y	Y	Y	Y
3 **Duncan**	N	Y	Y	Y	Y	Y
4 **Gowdy**	N	Y	Y	Y	Y	Y
6 Clyburn	Y	N	N	N	Y	Y
7 **Rice**	N	Y	Y	Y	Y	Y
SOUTH DAKOTA						
AL **Noem**	N	Y	Y	Y	Y	Y
TENNESSEE						
1 **Roe**	N	Y	Y	Y	Y	Y
2 **Duncan**	Y	Y	Y	Y	Y	Y
3 **Fleischmann**	N	Y	Y	Y	Y	Y
4 **DesJarlais**	N	Y	Y	Y	Y	Y
5 Cooper	Y	N	Y	N	Y	Y
6 **Black**	N	Y	Y	Y	Y	Y
7 **Blackburn**	N	Y	+	Y	Y	Y
8 **Kustoff**	N	Y	Y	Y	Y	Y
9 Cohen	Y	N	N	Y	Y	Y

	305	306	307	308	309	310
TEXAS						
1 **Gohmert**	N	Y	Y	?	Y	N
2 **Poe**	N	Y	Y	Y	Y	N
3 **Johnson, S.**	?	?	?	?	?	?
4 **Ratcliffe**	N	Y	Y	Y	Y	N
5 **Hensarling**	N	Y	Y	Y	Y	Y
6 **Barton**	N	Y	Y	Y	?	Y
7 **Culberson**	N	Y	Y	Y	Y	Y
8 **Brady**	N	Y	Y	Y	Y	Y
9 Green, A.	Y	N	N	N	Y	Y
10 **McCaul**	N	Y	Y	Y	Y	Y
11 **Conaway**	N	Y	Y	Y	Y	Y
12 **Granger**	–	+	+	Y	Y	Y
13 **Thornberry**	N	Y	Y	Y	Y	Y
14 **Weber**	?	?	?	?	?	?
15 Gonzalez	Y	N	Y	Y	Y	Y
16 O'Rourke	Y	N	Y	Y	Y	Y
17 **Flores**	N	Y	Y	Y	Y	Y
18 Jackson Lee	Y	N	N	N	Y	Y
19 **Arrington**	N	Y	Y	Y	Y	Y
20 Castro	Y	N	Y	N	Y	Y
21 **Smith**	N	Y	Y	Y	Y	Y
22 **Olson**	N	Y	Y	Y	Y	Y
23 **Hurd**	N	Y	Y	Y	Y	Y
24 **Marchant**	N	Y	Y	Y	?	?
25 **Williams**	N	Y	Y	Y	Y	Y
26 **Burgess**	N	Y	Y	Y	Y	Y
27 **Farenthold**	N	Y	Y	Y	Y	Y
28 Cuellar	Y	Y	Y	Y	Y	Y
29 Green, G.	Y	N	Y	N	Y	Y
30 Johnson, E.B.	Y	N	N	N	Y	Y
31 **Carter**	N	Y	Y	Y	Y	Y
32 **Sessions**	N	Y	Y	Y	Y	Y
33 Veasey	Y	N	Y	N	Y	Y
34 Vela	Y	N	Y	?	Y	Y
35 Doggett	Y	N	Y	N	Y	Y
36 **Babin**	N	Y	Y	Y	Y	+
UTAH						
1 **Bishop**	N	Y	Y	Y	Y	Y
2 **Stewart**	N	Y	Y	Y	Y	Y
3 **Chaffetz**	N	Y	Y	Y	Y	Y
4 **Love**	N	Y	Y	Y	Y	Y
VERMONT						
AL Welch	Y	N	Y	N	Y	Y
VIRGINIA						
1 **Wittman**	N	Y	Y	Y	Y	Y
2 **Taylor**	N	Y	Y	Y	Y	Y
3 Scott	Y	N	N	Y	Y	Y
4 McEachin	Y	N	N	N	Y	Y
5 **Garrett**	N	Y	Y	Y	Y	N
6 **Goodlatte**	N	Y	Y	Y	Y	Y
7 **Brat**	N	Y	Y	Y	N	N
8 Beyer	Y	N	N	N	Y	Y
9 **Griffith**	?	?	?	Y	Y	Y
10 **Comstock**	N	Y	Y	Y	Y	Y
11 Connolly	Y	N	Y	N	Y	Y
WASHINGTON						
1 DelBene	Y	N	Y	N	Y	Y
2 Larsen	Y	N	Y	N	+	+
3 **Herrera Beutler**	N	Y	Y	Y	Y	Y
4 **Newhouse**	N	Y	Y	Y	Y	Y
5 **McMorris Rodgers**	N	Y	Y	Y	Y	Y
6 Kilmer	Y	N	Y	N	Y	Y
7 Jayapal	Y	N	N	N	Y	Y
8 **Reichert**	N	Y	Y	Y	Y	Y
9 Smith	Y	N	N	N	Y	Y
10 Heck	Y	N	Y	N	Y	Y
WEST VIRGINIA						
1 **McKinley**	N	Y	Y	Y	Y	Y
2 **Mooney**	N	Y	Y	Y	Y	N
3 **Jenkins**	N	Y	Y	Y	Y	Y
WISCONSIN						
1 **Ryan**						
2 Pocan	Y	N	N	N	Y	Y
3 Kind	Y	N	Y	Y	Y	Y
4 Moore	Y	N	Y	N	Y	Y
5 **Sensenbrenner**	N	Y	Y	Y	Y	Y
6 **Grothman**	N	Y	Y	Y	Y	N
7 **Duffy**	N	Y	Y	Y	Y	Y
8 **Gallagher**	N	Y	Y	Y	Y	Y
WYOMING						
AL **Cheney**	N	Y	Y	Y	Y	+

VOTE NUMBER

311. PRESIDENT'S TAX RETURN DISCLOSURE/MOTION TO TABLE.
Newhouse, R-Wash., motion to table (kill) the Doggett, D-Texas., motion to appeal the ruling of the Chair that the Doggett resolution related to the disclosure of President Trump's tax returns does not constitute a question of the privileges of the House. Motion agreed to 227-188 : R 227-1; D 0-187. June 21, 2017.

312. HR 1654, HR 1873, H RES 392. FEDERAL LANDS VEGETATION AND SURFACE WATER STORAGE/PREVIOUS QUESTION. Newhouse, R-Wash., motion to order the previous question (thus ending debate and possibility of amendment) on the rule (H Res 392) that would provide for consideration of the bill (HR 1873) that would allow utilities to submit long-term plans to the Forest Service and Bureau of Land Management for advance approval of vegetation management and other maintenance activities on electricity rights-of-way on federal lands. The rule would also provide for consideration of the bill (HR 1654) that would establish the Bureau of Reclamation in the Interior Department as the lead agency for the coordination of all reviews, analyses, opinions, statements, permits, licenses or other approvals or decisions required by federal law in order to construct new or expanded surface water storage projects on federal lands. Motion agreed to 229-186 : R 229-1; D 0-185. June 21, 2017.

313. HR 1654, HR 1873, H RES 392. FEDERAL LANDS VEGETATION AND SURFACE WATER STORAGE/RULE. Adoption of the rule (H Res 392) that would provide for consideration of the bill (HR 1873) that would allow utilities to submit long-term plans to the Forest Service and Bureau of Land Management for advance approval of vegetation management and other maintenance activities on electricity rights-of-way on federal lands. The rule would also provide for consideration of the bill (HR 1654) that would establish the Bureau of Reclamation in the Interior Department as the lead agency for the coordination of all reviews, analyses, opinions, statements, permits, licenses or other approvals or decisions required by federal law in order to construct new or expanded surface water storage projects on federal lands. Adopted 230-185 : R 228-0; D 2-185. June 21, 2017.

314. HR 1873. FEDERAL LANDS VEGETATION MANAGEMENT PROTOCOL/ SUBMITTED PLAN REQUIREMENTS. Carbajal, D-Calif., amendment that would require (rather than allow) utilities to submit long-term plans to the Forest Service and Bureau of Land Management for advance approval of vegetation management and other maintenance activities on electricity rights-of-way on federal lands, and would remove the bill's provision that would prohibit the secretaries of the Agriculture Department and Interior Department from having the authority to modify electric system reliability and fire safety requirements for such plans. Rejected in Committee of the Whole 171-243 : R 0-229; D 171-14. June 21, 2017.

315. HR 1873. FEDERAL LANDS VEGETATION MANAGEMENT PROTOCOL/ PASSAGE. Passage of the bill that would allow utilities to submit long-term plans to the Forest Service and Bureau of Land Management for advance approval of vegetation management and other maintenance activities on electricity right-of-ways on federal lands. The bill would allow for utilities to conduct vegetation management and control activities on such electricity right-of-ways three days after notifying the relevant agency, if the relevant trees or other vegetation within or adjacent to it do not meet legal clearance requirements, and would exempt utilities from liability for wildfires caused by trees or vegetation contacting an electric line if the relevant agency failed to grant approval for the removal the vegetation. Passed 300-118 : R 231-0; D 69-118. June 21, 2017.

	311	312	313	314	315
ALABAMA					
1 **Byrne**	Y	Y	Y	N	Y
2 **Roby**	Y	Y	Y	N	Y
3 **Rogers**	Y	Y	Y	N	Y
4 **Aderholt**	?	?	?	?	?
5 **Brooks**	Y	Y	Y	N	Y
6 **Palmer**	Y	Y	Y	N	Y
7 Sewell	N	N	N	Y	N
ALASKA					
AL **Young**	Y	Y	Y	N	Y
ARIZONA					
1 O'Halleran	N	N	N	Y	N
2 **McSally**	Y	Y	Y	N	Y
3 Grijalva	N	N	N	Y	N
4 **Gosar**	Y	Y	Y	N	Y
5 **Biggs**	Y	Y	Y	N	Y
6 **Schweikert**	Y	Y	Y	N	Y
7 Gallego	N	N	N	Y	N
8 **Franks**	Y	Y	Y	N	Y
9 Sinema	N	N	Y	Y	Y
ARKANSAS					
1 **Crawford**	Y	Y	Y	N	Y
2 **Hill**	Y	Y	Y	N	Y
3 **Womack**	Y	Y	Y	N	Y
4 **Westerman**	Y	Y	Y	N	Y
CALIFORNIA					
1 **LaMalfa**	Y	Y	Y	N	Y
2 Huffman	N	N	N	Y	N
3 Garamendi	N	N	N	Y	Y
4 **McClintock**	Y	Y	Y	N	Y
5 Thompson	N	N	N	Y	Y
6 Matsui	N	N	N	Y	Y
7 Bera	N	N	N	Y	Y
8 **Cook**	Y	Y	Y	N	Y
9 McNerney	N	N	N	Y	Y
10 **Denham**	Y	Y	Y	N	Y
11 DeSaulnier	N	N	N	Y	N
12 Pelosi	N	N	N	Y	N
13 Lee	N	N	N	Y	N
14 Speier	N	N	N	Y	N
15 Swalwell	N	N	N	Y	N
16 Costa	N	N	N	N	Y
17 Khanna	N	N	N	Y	N
18 Eshoo	N	N	N	Y	Y
19 Lofgren	N	N	N	Y	N
20 Panetta	N	N	N	Y	Y
21 **Valadao**	Y	Y	Y	N	Y
22 **Nunes**	Y	Y	Y	N	Y
23 **McCarthy**	Y	Y	Y	N	Y
24 Carbajal	N	N	N	Y	N
25 **Knight**	Y	Y	Y	N	Y
26 Brownley	N	N	N	Y	Y
27 Chu	N	N	N	Y	N
28 Schiff	N	N	N	Y	N
29 Cardenas	N	N	N	Y	Y
30 Sherman	N	N	N	Y	N
31 Aguilar	N	N	N	Y	Y
32 Napolitano	–	–	–	+	+
33 Lieu	N	N	N	Y	N
34 Vacant					
35 Torres	N	N	N	Y	Y
36 Ruiz	N	N	N	Y	Y
37 Bass	N	N	N	Y	N
38 Sánchez, Linda	N	N	N	Y	N
39 **Royce**	Y	Y	Y	N	Y
40 Roybal-Allard	N	N	N	Y	N
41 Takano	N	N	N	Y	N
42 **Calvert**	Y	Y	Y	N	Y
43 Waters	N	N	N	Y	N
44 Barragan	N	N	N	Y	N
45 **Walters**	Y	Y	Y	N	Y
46 Correa	N	N	N	Y	Y
47 Lowenthal	N	N	N	Y	N
48 **Rohrabacher**	Y	Y	Y	N	Y
49 **Issa**	Y	Y	Y	N	Y
50 **Hunter**	Y	Y	Y	N	Y
51 Vargas	N	N	N	Y	N
52 Peters	N	N	N	N	Y
53 Davis	N	N	N	Y	N

	311	312	313	314	315
COLORADO					
1 DeGette	N	N	N	Y	N
2 Polis	N	N	N	Y	N
3 **Tipton**	Y	Y	Y	N	Y
4 **Buck**	Y	Y	Y	N	Y
5 **Lamborn**	Y	Y	Y	N	Y
6 **Coffman**	Y	Y	Y	N	Y
7 Perlmutter	N	N	N	Y	N
CONNECTICUT					
1 Larson	N	N	N	Y	Y
2 Courtney	N	N	N	Y	Y
3 DeLauro	N	N	N	Y	Y
4 Himes	N	N	N	Y	Y
5 Esty	N	N	N	Y	Y
DELAWARE					
AL Blunt Rochester	N	N	N	Y	N
FLORIDA					
1 **Gaetz**	Y	Y	Y	N	Y
2 **Dunn**	Y	Y	Y	N	Y
3 **Yoho**	Y	Y	Y	N	Y
4 **Rutherford**	Y	Y	Y	N	Y
5 Lawson	N	N	N	Y	Y
6 **DeSantis**	Y	Y	Y	N	Y
7 Murphy	N	N	N	Y	Y
8 **Posey**	Y	Y	Y	N	Y
9 Soto	N	N	N	Y	Y
10 Demings	N	N	N	Y	N
11 **Webster**	Y	Y	Y	N	Y
12 **Bilirakis**	Y	Y	Y	N	Y
13 Crist	N	N	N	Y	Y
14 Castor	N	N	N	Y	N
15 **Ross**	Y	Y	Y	N	Y
16 **Buchanan**	Y	Y	Y	N	Y
17 **Rooney, T.**	Y	Y	Y	N	Y
18 **Mast**	Y	Y	Y	N	Y
19 **Rooney, F.**	Y	Y	Y	N	Y
20 Hastings	N	N	N	Y	N
21 Frankel	N	N	N	Y	N
22 Deutch	N	N	N	Y	N
23 Wasserman Schultz	N	N	N	Y	N
24 Wilson	?	?	?	?	?
25 **Diaz-Balart**	Y	Y	Y	N	Y
26 **Curbelo**	Y	Y	Y	N	Y
27 **Ros-Lehtinen**	Y	Y	Y	N	Y
GEORGIA					
1 **Carter**	Y	Y	Y	N	Y
2 Bishop	N	N	N	Y	Y
3 **Ferguson**	Y	Y	Y	N	Y
4 Johnson	N	N	N	Y	N
5 Lewis	N	N	N	Y	N
7 **Woodall**	Y	Y	Y	N	Y
8 **Scott, A.**	Y	Y	Y	N	Y
9 **Collins**	Y	Y	Y	N	Y
10 **Hice**	Y	Y	Y	N	Y
11 **Loudermilk**	Y	Y	Y	N	Y
12 **Allen**	Y	Y	Y	N	Y
13 Scott, D.	N	?	N	Y	Y
14 **Graves**	Y	Y	Y	N	Y
HAWAII					
1 Hanabusa	N	N	N	Y	N
2 Gabbard	?	?	?	?	?
IDAHO					
1 **Labrador**	Y	Y	Y	N	Y
2 **Simpson**	Y	Y	Y	N	Y
ILLINOIS					
1 Rush	N	N	N	Y	N
2 Kelly	N	N	N	Y	N
3 Lipinski	N	N	N	Y	Y
4 Gutierrez	N	N	N	Y	N
5 Quigley	N	N	N	Y	N
6 **Roskam**	Y	Y	Y	N	Y
7 Davis, D.	N	N	N	Y	N
8 Krishnamoorthi	N	N	N	Y	Y
9 Schakowsky	N	N	N	Y	N
10 Schneider	N	N	N	Y	Y
11 Foster	N	N	N	Y	Y
12 **Bost**	Y	Y	Y	N	Y
13 **Davis, R.**	Y	Y	Y	N	Y
14 **Hultgren**	Y	Y	Y	N	Y
15 **Shimkus**	Y	Y	Y	N	Y

	311	312	313	314	315
16 Kinzinger	Y	Y	Y	N	Y
17 Bustos	N	N	N	Y	Y
18 LaHood	Y	Y	Y	N	Y
INDIANA					
1 Visclosky	N	N	N	Y	N
2 Walorski	Y	Y	Y	N	Y
3 Banks	Y	Y	Y	N	Y
4 Rokita	Y	Y	Y	N	Y
5 Brooks	Y	Y	Y	N	Y
6 Messer	Y	Y	Y	N	Y
7 Carson	N	N	N	Y	N
8 Bucshon	Y	Y	Y	N	Y
9 Hollingsworth	Y	Y	Y	N	Y
IOWA					
1 Blum	Y	?	?	?	?
2 Loebsack	N	N	N	Y	Y
3 Young	Y	Y	Y	N	Y
4 King	Y	Y	Y	N	Y
KANSAS					
1 Marshall	Y	Y	Y	N	Y
2 Jenkins	Y	Y	Y	N	Y
3 Yoder	Y	Y	Y	N	Y
4 Estes	Y	Y	Y	N	Y
KENTUCKY					
1 Comer	Y	Y	Y	N	Y
2 Guthrie	Y	Y	Y	N	Y
3 Yarmuth	N	N	N	Y	N
4 Massie	Y	Y	Y	N	Y
5 Rogers	Y	Y	Y	N	Y
6 Barr	Y	Y	Y	N	Y
LOUISIANA					
1 Scalise	+	+	+	-	+
2 Richmond	N	N	N	Y	N
3 Higgins	Y	Y	Y	N	Y
4 Johnson	Y	Y	Y	N	Y
5 Abraham	Y	Y	Y	N	Y
6 Graves	Y	Y	Y	N	Y
MAINE					
1 Pingree	N	N	N	Y	N
2 Poliquin	Y	Y	Y	N	Y
MARYLAND					
1 Harris	Y	Y	Y	N	Y
2 Ruppersberger	N	N	N	Y	N
3 Sarbanes	N	N	N	Y	N
4 Brown	N	N	N	Y	Y
5 Hoyer	N	N	N	Y	N
6 Delaney	N	N	N	Y	Y
7 Cummings	?	?	?	?	?
8 Raskin	N	N	N	Y	N
MASSACHUSETTS					
1 Neal	N	N	N	Y	N
2 McGovern	N	N	N	Y	N
3 Tsongas	N	N	N	Y	N
4 Kennedy	N	N	N	Y	N
5 Clark	N	N	N	Y	N
6 Moulton	N	N	N	Y	Y
7 Capuano	N	N	N	Y	N
8 Lynch	N	N	N	?	N
9 Keating	N	N	N	Y	N
MICHIGAN					
1 Bergman	Y	Y	Y	N	Y
2 Huizenga	Y	Y	Y	N	Y
3 Amash	Y	Y	Y	N	Y
4 Moolenaar	Y	Y	Y	N	Y
5 Kildee	N	N	N	Y	N
6 Upton	Y	Y	Y	N	Y
7 Walberg	Y	Y	Y	N	Y
8 Bishop	Y	Y	Y	N	Y
9 Levin	N	N	N	Y	N
10 Mitchell	Y	Y	Y	N	Y
11 Trott	Y	Y	Y	N	Y
12 Dingell	N	N	N	Y	N
13 Conyers	N	N	N	Y	N
14 Lawrence	N	N	N	Y	N
MINNESOTA					
1 Walz	N	N	N	Y	N
2 Lewis	Y	Y	Y	N	Y
3 Paulsen	Y	Y	Y	N	Y
4 McCollum	N	N	N	Y	N

	311	312	313	314	315
5 Ellison	N	N	N	Y	N
6 Emmer	Y	Y	Y	N	Y
7 Peterson	N	N	N	Y	N
8 Nolan	N	N	N	Y	Y
MISSISSIPPI					
1 Kelly	Y	Y	Y	N	Y
2 Thompson	N	N	N	Y	N
3 Harper	Y	Y	Y	N	Y
4 Palazzo	Y	Y	Y	N	Y
MISSOURI					
1 Clay	N	N	N	Y	N
2 Wagner	Y	Y	Y	N	Y
3 Luetkemeyer	Y	Y	Y	N	Y
4 Hartzler	Y	Y	Y	N	Y
5 Cleaver	N	N	N	Y	N
6 Graves	Y	Y	Y	N	Y
7 Long	+	+	+	-	+
8 Smith	Y	Y	Y	N	Y
MONTANA					
AL Gianforte		Y	Y	Y	N	Y
NEBRASKA					
1 Fortenberry	Y	Y	Y	N	Y
2 Bacon	Y	Y	Y	N	Y
3 Smith	Y	Y	Y	N	Y
NEVADA					
1 Titus	N	N	N	Y	N
2 Amodei	Y	Y	Y	N	Y
3 Rosen	N	N	N	Y	Y
4 Kihuen	N	N	N	Y	Y
NEW HAMPSHIRE					
1 Shea-Porter	N	N	N	Y	Y
2 Kuster	N	N	N	Y	Y
NEW JERSEY					
1 Norcross	N	N	N	Y	N
2 LoBiondo	Y	Y	Y	N	Y
3 MacArthur	Y	Y	Y	N	Y
4 Smith	Y	Y	Y	N	Y
5 Gottheimer	N	N	N	Y	Y
6 Pallone	N	N	N	Y	N
7 Lance	Y	Y	Y	N	Y
8 Sires	N	N	N	Y	Y
9 Pascrell	N	N	N	Y	Y
10 Payne	N	N	N	Y	N
11 Frelinghuysen	Y	Y	Y	N	Y
12 Watson Coleman	N	N	N	Y	N
NEW MEXICO					
1 Lujan Grisham	N	N	N	Y	Y
2 Pearce	Y	Y	Y	N	Y
3 Luján	N	N	N	Y	Y
NEW YORK					
1 Zeldin	Y	Y	Y	N	Y
2 King	Y	Y	Y	N	Y
3 Suozzi	N	N	N	Y	N
4 Rice	N	N	N	Y	N
5 Meeks	N	N	N	Y	N
6 Meng	N	N	N	Y	N
7 Velázquez	N	N	N	Y	N
8 Jeffries	N	N	N	Y	N
9 Clarke	N	N	N	Y	N
10 Nadler	N	N	N	Y	N
11 Donovan	Y	Y	Y	N	Y
12 Maloney, C.	N	N	N	Y	N
13 Espaillat	N	N	N	Y	N
14 Crowley	N	N	N	Y	N
15 Serrano	N	N	N	Y	N
16 Engel	N	N	N	Y	N
17 Lowey	N	N	N	Y	N
18 Maloney, S.P.	N	N	N	Y	N
19 Faso	Y	Y	Y	N	Y
20 Tonko	N	N	N	Y	N
21 Stefanik	Y	Y	Y	N	Y
22 Tenney	Y	Y	Y	N	Y
23 Reed	Y	Y	Y	N	Y
24 Katko	Y	Y	Y	N	Y
25 Slaughter	N	N	N	Y	N
26 Higgins	-	-	-	+	-
27 Collins	Y	Y	Y	N	Y
NORTH CAROLINA					
1 Butterfield	N	N	N	Y	N
2 Holding	Y	Y	Y	N	Y
3 Jones	N	N	Y	N	Y
4 Price	N	N	N	Y	N

	311	312	313	314	315
5 Foxx	Y	Y	Y	N	Y
6 Walker	Y	Y	Y	N	Y
7 Rouzer	Y	Y	Y	N	Y
8 Hudson	Y	Y	Y	N	Y
9 Pittenger	Y	Y	Y	N	Y
10 McHenry	Y	Y	Y	N	Y
11 Meadows	Y	Y	Y	N	Y
12 Adams	N	N	N	Y	N
13 Budd	Y	Y	Y	N	Y
NORTH DAKOTA					
AL Cramer	Y	Y	Y	?	Y
OHIO					
1 Chabot	Y	Y	Y	N	Y
2 Wenstrup	Y	Y	Y	N	Y
3 Beatty	N	N	N	Y	N
4 Jordan	Y	Y	Y	N	Y
5 Latta	Y	Y	Y	N	Y
6 Johnson	Y	Y	Y	N	Y
7 Gibbs	Y	Y	Y	N	Y
8 Davidson	Y	Y	Y	N	Y
9 Kaptur	N	N	N	Y	N
10 Turner	Y	Y	Y	N	Y
11 Fudge	N	N	N	Y	N
12 Tiberi	Y	Y	Y	N	Y
13 Ryan	N	N	N	?	N
14 Joyce	Y	Y	Y	N	Y
15 Stivers	Y	Y	Y	N	Y
16 Renacci	Y	Y	Y	N	Y
OKLAHOMA					
1 Bridenstine	Y	Y	Y	N	Y
2 Mullin	Y	Y	Y	N	Y
3 Lucas	Y	Y	Y	N	Y
4 Cole	Y	Y	Y	N	Y
5 Russell	Y	Y	Y	N	Y
OREGON					
1 Bonamici	N	N	N	Y	Y
2 Walden	Y	Y	Y	N	Y
3 Blumenauer	N	N	N	Y	N
4 DeFazio	N	N	N	Y	N
5 Schrader	N	N	Y	N	Y
PENNSYLVANIA					
1 Brady	N	N	N	N	Y
2 Evans	N	N	N	Y	N
3 Kelly	Y	Y	Y	N	Y
4 Perry	Y	Y	Y	N	Y
5 Thompson	Y	Y	Y	N	Y
6 Costello	Y	Y	Y	N	Y
7 Meehan	Y	Y	?	N	Y
8 Fitzpatrick	Y	Y	Y	N	Y
9 Shuster	Y	Y	Y	N	Y
10 Marino	Y	Y	Y	N	Y
11 Barletta	Y	Y	Y	N	Y
12 Rothfus	Y	Y	Y	N	Y
13 Boyle	N	N	N	Y	N
14 Doyle	N	N	N	Y	N
15 Dent	Y	Y	Y	N	Y
16 Smucker	Y	Y	Y	N	Y
17 Cartwright	N	N	N	Y	N
18 Murphy	Y	Y	Y	N	Y
RHODE ISLAND					
1 Cicilline	N	N	N	Y	N
2 Langevin	N	N	N	Y	Y
SOUTH CAROLINA					
1 Sanford	P	Y	Y	N	Y
2 Wilson	Y	Y	Y	N	Y
3 Duncan	Y	Y	Y	N	Y
4 Gowdy	Y	Y	Y	N	Y
6 Clyburn	N	N	N	Y	N
7 Rice	Y	Y	Y	N	Y
SOUTH DAKOTA					
AL Noem	Y	Y	Y	?	Y
TENNESSEE					
1 Roe	Y	Y	Y	N	Y
2 Duncan	Y	Y	Y	N	Y
3 Fleischmann	Y	Y	Y	N	Y
4 DesJarlais	Y	Y	Y	N	Y
5 Cooper	N	N	N	Y	Y
6 Black	Y	Y	Y	N	Y
7 Blackburn	Y	Y	Y	N	Y
8 Kustoff	Y	Y	Y	N	Y
9 Cohen	N	N	N	Y	N

	311	312	313	314	315
TEXAS					
1 Gohmert	Y	Y	Y	N	Y
2 Poe	Y	Y	Y	N	Y
3 Johnson, S.	?	?	?	?	?
4 Ratcliffe	Y	Y	Y	N	Y
5 Hensarling	Y	Y	Y	N	Y
6 Barton	Y	Y	Y	N	Y
7 Culberson	Y	Y	Y	N	Y
8 Brady	Y	Y	Y	N	Y
9 Green, A.	N	N	N	Y	N
10 McCaul	Y	Y	Y	N	Y
11 Conaway	Y	Y	Y	N	Y
12 Granger	Y	Y	+	N	Y
13 Thornberry	Y	Y	Y	N	Y
14 Weber	?	?	?	?	?
15 Gonzalez	N	N	N	Y	N
16 O'Rourke	N	N	N	Y	N
17 Flores	Y	Y	Y	N	Y
18 Jackson Lee	N	N	N	Y	N
19 Arrington	Y	Y	Y	N	Y
20 Castro	N	N	N	Y	N
21 Smith	Y	Y	Y	N	Y
22 Olson	Y	Y	Y	N	Y
23 Hurd	Y	Y	Y	N	Y
24 Marchant	Y	Y	Y	N	Y
25 Williams	Y	Y	Y	N	Y
26 Burgess	Y	Y	Y	N	Y
27 Farenthold	Y	Y	Y	N	Y
28 Cuellar	N	N	N	Y	N
29 Green, G.	N	?	N	Y	N
30 Johnson, E.B.	N	N	N	Y	N
31 Carter	Y	Y	Y	N	Y
32 Sessions	Y	Y	Y	N	Y
33 Veasey	N	N	N	Y	N
34 Vela	N	N	N	Y	Y
35 Doggett	N	N	N	Y	N
36 Babin	Y	Y	Y	N	Y
UTAH					
1 Bishop	Y	Y	Y	N	Y
2 Stewart	?	Y	Y	N	Y
3 Chaffetz	?	?	?	N	Y
4 Love	Y	Y	Y	N	Y
VERMONT					
AL Welch	N	N	N	Y	N
VIRGINIA					
1 Wittman	Y	Y	Y	N	Y
2 Taylor	Y	Y	Y	N	Y
3 Scott	N	N	N	Y	N
4 McEachin	N	N	N	Y	N
5 Garrett	Y	Y	Y	N	Y
6 Goodlatte	Y	Y	Y	N	Y
7 Brat	Y	Y	Y	N	Y
8 Beyer	N	N	N	Y	N
9 Griffith	Y	Y	Y	N	Y
10 Comstock	+	+	+	-	+
11 Connolly	N	N	N	Y	Y
WASHINGTON					
1 DelBene	N	N	N	Y	N
2 Larsen	-	-	-	+	-
3 Herrera Beutler	Y	Y	Y	N	Y
4 Newhouse	Y	Y	Y	N	Y
5 McMorris Rodgers	Y	Y	Y	N	Y
6 Kilmer	N	N	N	Y	N
7 Jayapal	N	N	N	Y	N
8 Reichert	Y	Y	Y	N	Y
9 Smith	N	N	N	Y	N
10 Heck	N	N	N	Y	Y
WEST VIRGINIA					
1 McKinley	Y	Y	Y	N	Y
2 Mooney	Y	Y	Y	N	Y
3 Jenkins	Y	Y	Y	N	Y
WISCONSIN					
1 Ryan					
2 Pocan	N	N	N	Y	N
3 Kind	N	N	N	Y	N
4 Moore	N	N	N	Y	N
5 Sensenbrenner	Y	Y	Y	N	Y
6 Grothman	Y	Y	Y	N	Y
7 Duffy	Y	Y	Y	N	Y
8 Gallagher	Y	Y	Y	N	Y
WYOMING					
AL Cheney	Y	Y	Y	N	Y

VOTE NUMBER

316. HR 2353, HR 2842, H RES 396. STATE COORDINATED TEMPORARY EMPLOYMENT SUBSIDIES AND TECHNICAL EDUCATION/PREVIOUS QUESTION. Cole, R-Okla., motion to order the previous question (thus ending debate and possibility of amendment) on the rule (H Res 396) that would provide for House floor consideration of the bill (HR 2842) that would authorize state demonstration projects within the Temporary Assistance for Needy Families program to temporarily subsidize employment for TANF beneficiaries with willing employers, and would require $100 million in existing TANF funding to be used for grants to states to implement such programs. The rule would also provide for consideration of the bill (HR 2353) to reauthorize and modify career and technical education programs for skilled-labor positions under suspension of the rules, through the legislative day of June 22, 2017. Motion agreed to 226-184 : R 226-0; D 0-184. June 22, 2017.

317. HR 2353, HR 2842, H RES 396. STATE COORDINATED TEMPORARY EMPLOYMENT SUBSIDIES AND TECHNICAL EDUCATION/RULE. Adoption of the rule (H Res 396) that would provide for consideration of the bill (HR 2842) that would authorize state demonstration projects within the Temporary Assistance for Needy Families program to temporarily subsidize employment for TANF beneficiaries with willing employers, and would require $100 million in existing TANF funding to be used for grants to states to implement such programs. The rule would also provide for consideration of the bill (HR 2353) to reauthorize and modify career and technical education programs for skilled-labor positions under suspension of the rules, through the legislative day of June 22, 2017. Adopted 233-179 : R 228-0; D 5-179. June 22, 2017.

318. HR 1654. SURFACE WATER STORAGE PERMITTING/COMMERCIAL FISHERIES PROTECTION. Lowenthal, D-Calif., amendment that would specify that the bill's provisions would not apply to any project that the Interior Department has determined may cause harm to commercial fisheries. Rejected in Committee of the Whole 179-232 : R 2-228; D 177-4. June 22, 2017.

319. HR 1654. SURFACE WATER STORAGE PERMITTING/PASSAGE.
Passage of the bill that would establish the Bureau of Reclamation in the Interior Department as the lead agency for the coordination of all reviews, analyses, opinions, statements, permits, licenses or other approvals or decisions required by federal law in order to construct new or expanded surface water storage projects on federal lands. The bill would require the bureau to work with all agencies considering an aspect of a project application to establish a schedule for the review and approval process, including a deadline for a final decision, and would require the bureau to prepare a unified environmental review document that would incorporate a single environmental record on which all cooperating agencies would be required to base project approval decisions. Passed 233-180 : R 225-5; D 8-175. June 22, 2017.

320. HR 2842. STATE COORDINATED TEMPORARY EMPLOYMENT SUBSIDIES/PREVIOUS TRAINING EMPLOYMENT STATISTICS.
Krishnamoorthi, D-Ill., amendment that would require a state include the percentage of individuals that receive subsidized employment to work in an area matching their previous training and work experience in its annual report to the Health and Human Services Department on the outcomes of its demonstration projects. Adopted in Committee of the Whole 380-32 : R 197-32; D 183-0. June 23, 2017.

321. HR 2842. STATE COORDINATED TEMPORARY EMPLOYMENT SUBSIDIES/CONCURRENT BENEFIT ENROLLMENT STATISTICS REPORTING. Davidson, R-Ohio, amendment that would require a state to include the number of eligible individuals that concurrently received both subsidized employment and other federal or state means-tested benefits in its annual report to the Health and Human Services Department on the outcomes of its demonstration projects. Adopted in Committee of the Whole 264-147: R 224-4; D 40-143. June 23, 2017.

	316	317	318	319	320	321
ALABAMA						
1 **Byrne**	Y	Y	N	Y	Y	Y
2 **Roby**	Y	Y	N	Y	Y	Y
3 **Rogers**	Y	Y	?	Y	?	Y
4 **Aderholt**	Y	?	N	Y	Y	Y
5 **Brooks**	Y	Y	N	Y	N	Y
6 **Palmer**	Y	Y	N	Y	Y	Y
7 Sewell	N	N	Y	N	Y	N
ALASKA						
AL **Young**	Y	Y	N	Y	Y	Y
ARIZONA						
1 O'Halleran	N	N	Y	N	Y	N
2 **McSally**	Y	Y	N	Y	Y	Y
3 Grijalva	N	N	Y	N	Y	N
4 **Gosar**	Y	Y	?	?	?	?
5 **Biggs**	Y	Y	N	Y	N	Y
6 **Schweikert**	Y	Y	N	Y	Y	Y
7 Gallego	N	N	Y	N	Y	N
8 **Franks**	Y	Y	N	Y	Y	Y
9 Sinema	N	Y	Y	Y	Y	Y
ARKANSAS						
1 **Crawford**	Y	Y	N	Y	Y	Y
2 **Hill**	Y	Y	N	Y	Y	Y
3 **Womack**	Y	Y	N	Y	Y	Y
4 **Westerman**	Y	Y	N	Y	Y	Y
CALIFORNIA						
1 **LaMalfa**	Y	Y	N	Y	?	?
2 Huffman	N	N	Y	N	Y	N
3 Garamendi	N	N	Y	N	Y	N
4 **McClintock**	Y	Y	N	Y	Y	Y
5 Thompson	N	N	Y	N	Y	N
6 Matsui	N	N	Y	N	Y	N
7 Bera	N	N	Y	N	Y	Y
8 **Cook**	Y	Y	N	Y	Y	Y
9 McNerney	N	N	Y	N	Y	N
10 **Denham**	Y	Y	N	Y	Y	Y
11 DeSaulnier	N	N	Y	N	Y	N
12 Pelosi	N	N	?	?	?	?
13 Lee	N	N	Y	N	Y	N
14 Speier	N	N	Y	N	?	?
15 Swalwell	N	N	Y	N	Y	N
16 Costa	N	Y	Y	Y	Y	Y
17 Khanna	N	N	Y	N	Y	N
18 Eshoo	N	N	Y	N	Y	N
19 Lofgren	N	N	Y	N	Y	N
20 Panetta	N	N	Y	N	Y	N
21 **Valadao**	Y	Y	N	Y	Y	Y
22 **Nunes**	Y	Y	N	Y	Y	Y
23 **McCarthy**	Y	Y	N	Y	Y	Y
24 Carbajal	N	N	Y	N	Y	N
25 **Knight**	Y	Y	N	Y	Y	Y
26 Brownley	N	N	Y	N	Y	N
27 Chu	N	N	Y	N	Y	N
28 Schiff	N	N	Y	N	Y	N
29 Cardenas	N	N	Y	N	Y	N
30 Sherman	N	N	Y	N	Y	N
31 Aguilar	N	N	Y	N	Y	N
32 Napolitano	–	–	+	N	+	N
33 Lieu	?	?	?	?	?	?
34 Vacant						
35 Torres	N	N	Y	N	Y	N
36 Ruiz	N	–	Y	N	Y	N
37 Bass	N	N	Y	N	Y	N
38 Sánchez, Linda	N	N	Y	N	Y	N
39 Royce	Y	Y	N	Y	Y	Y
40 Roybal-Allard	N	N	Y	N	Y	N
41 Takano	N	N	Y	N	Y	N
42 Calvert	Y	Y	N	Y	Y	Y
43 Waters	N	N	?	?	Y	N
44 Barragan	N	N	Y	N	Y	N
45 **Walters**	Y	Y	N	Y	Y	Y
46 Correa	N	N	Y	Y	Y	N
47 Lowenthal	N	N	Y	N	Y	N
48 **Rohrabacher**	Y	Y	N	Y	Y	Y
49 **Issa**	Y	Y	?	?	Y	Y
50 **Hunter**	Y	Y	N	Y	Y	Y
51 Vargas	N	N	Y	N	Y	N
52 Peters	N	N	Y	N	Y	N
53 Davis	N	N	Y	N	Y	N

	316	317	318	319	320	321
COLORADO						
1 DeGette	N	N	Y	N	Y	N
2 Polis	N	N	Y	N	Y	N
3 **Tipton**	Y	Y	N	Y	Y	Y
4 **Buck**	Y	Y	N	Y	Y	Y
5 **Lamborn**	Y	Y	N	Y	Y	Y
6 **Coffman**	Y	Y	N	Y	Y	Y
7 Perlmutter	N	N	Y	N	Y	N
CONNECTICUT						
1 Larson	N	N	Y	N	Y	N
2 Courtney	N	N	Y	N	Y	N
3 DeLauro	?	N	Y	N	Y	N
4 Himes	N	N	Y	N	Y	N
5 Esty	N	N	Y	N	Y	Y
DELAWARE						
AL Blunt Rochester	N	N	Y	N	Y	N
FLORIDA						
1 **Gaetz**	Y	Y	N	Y	N	N
2 **Dunn**	Y	Y	N	Y	Y	Y
3 **Yoho**	Y	Y	N	Y	N	Y
4 **Rutherford**	Y	Y	N	Y	Y	Y
5 Lawson	N	N	Y	N	Y	N
6 **DeSantis**	Y	Y	N	Y	Y	Y
7 Murphy	N	N	Y	N	Y	Y
8 **Posey**	Y	Y	N	Y	N	Y
9 Soto	N	N	Y	N	Y	N
10 Demings	N	N	Y	N	Y	N
11 **Webster**	Y	Y	N	Y	Y	Y
12 **Bilirakis**	Y	Y	N	Y	Y	Y
13 Crist	N	N	Y	N	Y	Y
14 Castor	N	N	Y	N	Y	N
15 **Ross**	Y	Y	N	Y	Y	Y
16 **Buchanan**	Y	Y	N	Y	Y	Y
17 **Rooney, T.**	Y	Y	N	Y	Y	Y
18 **Mast**	Y	Y	N	Y	Y	Y
19 **Rooney, F.**	Y	Y	N	Y	Y	Y
20 Hastings	N	?	Y	N	Y	N
21 Frankel	N	N	Y	N	Y	N
22 Deutch	N	N	Y	N	Y	N
23 Wasserman Schultz	?	?	?	?	?	?
24 Wilson	N	N	Y	N	Y	N
25 **Diaz-Balart**	Y	Y	N	Y	Y	Y
26 **Curbelo**	Y	Y	N	Y	Y	Y
27 **Ros-Lehtinen**	Y	Y	N	Y	Y	Y
GEORGIA						
1 **Carter**	Y	Y	N	Y	Y	Y
2 Bishop	N	N	Y	Y	Y	N
3 **Ferguson**	Y	Y	N	Y	Y	Y
4 Johnson	N	N	Y	N	Y	N
5 Lewis	N	N	Y	N	Y	N
7 **Woodall**	Y	Y	N	Y	Y	Y
8 **Scott, A.**	Y	Y	N	Y	Y	Y
9 **Collins**	Y	Y	N	Y	Y	Y
10 **Hice**	Y	Y	N	Y	Y	Y
11 **Loudermilk**	Y	Y	N	Y	Y	Y
12 **Allen**	Y	Y	N	Y	Y	Y
13 Scott, D.	N	N	Y	N	Y	N
14 **Graves**	Y	Y	N	Y	N	Y
HAWAII						
1 Hanabusa	N	N	Y	N	Y	N
2 Gabbard	?	?	?	?	?	?
IDAHO						
1 **Labrador**	Y	Y	N	Y	Y	Y
2 **Simpson**	Y	Y	N	Y	Y	Y
ILLINOIS						
1 Rush	N	N	Y	N	Y	N
2 Kelly	N	N	Y	N	Y	N
3 Lipinski	N	N	Y	N	Y	N
4 Gutierrez	N	N	?	N	Y	N
5 Quigley	N	N	Y	N	Y	N
6 **Roskam**	?	Y	N	Y	Y	Y
7 Davis, D.	N	N	Y	N	Y	N
8 **Krishnamoorthi**	N	N	Y	N	Y	N
9 Schakowsky	N	N	Y	N	Y	N
10 Schneider	N	N	Y	N	Y	N
11 Foster	N	N	Y	N	Y	N
12 **Bost**	Y	Y	N	Y	Y	Y
13 **Davis, R.**	Y	Y	N	Y	Y	Y
14 **Hultgren**	Y	Y	N	Y	Y	Y
15 **Shimkus**	Y	Y	N	Y	Y	Y

	316	317	318	319	320	321
16 **Kinzinger**	Y	Y	N	Y	Y	Y
17 Bustos	N	N	Y	N	Y	Y
18 **LaHood**	Y	Y	N	Y	Y	Y
INDIANA						
1 Visclosky	N	N	Y	N	Y	N
2 **Walorski**	Y	Y	N	Y	Y	Y
3 **Banks**	?	Y	N	Y	N	Y
4 **Rokita**	Y	Y	N	Y	Y	Y
5 **Brooks**	Y	Y	N	Y	Y	Y
6 **Messer**	?	?	N	Y	N	Y
7 Carson	N	N	Y	N	Y	N
8 **Bucshon**	Y	Y	N	Y	Y	Y
9 **Hollingsworth**	Y	Y	N	Y	Y	Y
IOWA						
1 **Blum**	Y	Y	N	Y	Y	Y
2 Loebsack	N	N	Y	N	Y	Y
3 **Young**	Y	Y	N	Y	Y	Y
4 **King**	Y	Y	N	Y	Y	Y
KANSAS						
1 **Marshall**	Y	Y	N	Y	Y	Y
2 **Jenkins**	Y	Y	N	Y	Y	Y
3 **Yoder**	Y	Y	N	Y	Y	Y
4 **Estes**	Y	Y	N	Y	Y	Y
KENTUCKY						
1 **Comer**	Y	Y	N	Y	Y	Y
2 **Guthrie**	Y	Y	N	Y	Y	Y
3 Yarmuth	N	N	Y	N	Y	N
4 **Massie**	Y	Y	N	Y	N	Y
5 **Rogers**	Y	Y	N	Y	Y	Y
6 **Barr**	Y	Y	N	Y	N	Y
LOUISIANA						
1 **Scalise**	+	+	–	+	+	+
2 Richmond	N	N	Y	N	?	N
3 **Higgins**	Y	Y	N	Y	Y	Y
4 **Johnson**	?	Y	N	Y	Y	Y
5 **Abraham**	Y	Y	N	Y	Y	Y
6 **Graves**	Y	Y	N	Y	Y	Y
MAINE						
1 Pingree	N	N	Y	N	Y	N
2 **Poliquin**	Y	Y	N	Y	Y	Y
MARYLAND						
1 **Harris**	Y	Y	N	Y	N	Y
2 Ruppersberger	N	N	Y	N	Y	N
3 Sarbanes	N	N	Y	N	Y	Y
4 Brown	N	N	Y	N	Y	N
5 Hoyer	N	N	Y	N	Y	N
6 Delaney	N	N	Y	N	Y	N
7 Cummings	?	?	?	?	?	?
8 Raskin	N	N	Y	N	Y	N
MASSACHUSETTS						
1 Neal	N	N	Y	N	Y	?
2 McGovern	N	N	Y	N	Y	N
3 Tsongas	N	N	Y	N	Y	N
4 Kennedy	N	N	Y	N	Y	N
5 Clark	N	N	Y	N	Y	N
6 Moulton	N	N	Y	N	Y	Y
7 Capuano	N	N	Y	N	Y	N
8 Lynch	N	N	Y	N	Y	N
9 Keating	?	N	Y	N	Y	N
MICHIGAN						
1 **Bergman**	Y	Y	N	Y	Y	Y
2 **Huizenga**	Y	Y	N	Y	Y	Y
3 **Amash**	Y	Y	N	N	N	N
4 **Moolenaar**	Y	Y	N	Y	Y	Y
5 Kildee	N	N	Y	N	Y	N
6 **Upton**	Y	Y	N	Y	Y	Y
7 **Walberg**	Y	Y	N	Y	Y	Y
8 **Bishop**	Y	Y	N	Y	Y	Y
9 Levin	N	N	Y	N	Y	N
10 **Mitchell**	Y	Y	N	Y	Y	Y
11 **Trott**	Y	Y	N	Y	Y	Y
12 Dingell	N	N	Y	N	Y	N
13 Conyers	N	N	Y	N	Y	N
14 Lawrence	N	N	Y	N	Y	N
MINNESOTA						
1 Walz	N	N	Y	N	Y	N
2 **Lewis**	Y	Y	N	Y	Y	Y
3 **Paulsen**	Y	Y	N	Y	Y	Y
4 McCollum	N	N	Y	N	Y	N
5 Ellison	N	N	Y	N	Y	N
6 **Emmer**	Y	Y	N	Y	Y	Y
7 Peterson	N	N	N	Y	Y	Y
8 Nolan	N	N	Y	N	Y	N
MISSISSIPPI						
1 **Kelly**	Y	Y	N	Y	N	Y
2 Thompson	N	N	?	N	Y	N
3 **Harper**	Y	Y	N	Y	Y	Y
4 **Palazzo**	Y	Y	N	Y	N	Y
MISSOURI						
1 Clay	N	N	Y	N	Y	N
2 **Wagner**	Y	Y	N	Y	Y	Y
3 **Luetkemeyer**	Y	Y	N	Y	Y	Y
4 **Hartzler**	Y	Y	N	Y	Y	Y
5 Cleaver	N	N	Y	N	Y	N
6 **Graves**	Y	Y	N	Y	Y	Y
7 **Long**	+	+	–	+	+	+
8 **Smith**	Y	Y	N	Y	Y	Y
MONTANA						
AL **Gianforte**	Y	Y	N	Y	Y	Y
NEBRASKA						
1 **Fortenberry**	Y	Y	N	Y	Y	Y
2 **Bacon**	Y	Y	N	Y	Y	Y
3 **Smith**	Y	Y	N	Y	Y	Y
NEVADA						
1 Titus	N	N	Y	N	Y	N
2 **Amodei**	Y	Y	N	Y	Y	Y
3 Rosen	N	N	Y	N	Y	Y
4 Kihuen	N	N	Y	N	Y	Y
NEW HAMPSHIRE						
1 Shea-Porter	N	N	Y	N	Y	Y
2 Kuster	N	N	Y	N	Y	Y
NEW JERSEY						
1 Norcross	N	N	Y	N	Y	N
2 **LoBiondo**	Y	Y	N	N	Y	Y
3 **MacArthur**	Y	Y	N	Y	Y	Y
4 **Smith**	Y	Y	N	N	Y	Y
5 Gottheimer	N	Y	Y	Y	Y	Y
6 Pallone	N	N	Y	N	Y	N
7 **Lance**	?	?	N	Y	Y	Y
8 Sires	N	N	Y	N	Y	N
9 Pascrell	N	N	Y	N	Y	N
10 Payne	N	N	Y	N	Y	N
11 **Frelinghuysen**	Y	Y	N	Y	Y	Y
12 Watson Coleman	N	N	Y	N	Y	N
NEW MEXICO						
1 Lujan Grisham	N	N	Y	N	Y	N
2 **Pearce**	Y	Y	N	Y	N	Y
3 Luján	N	N	Y	N	Y	N
NEW YORK						
1 **Zeldin**	Y	Y	N	Y	Y	Y
2 **King**	Y	Y	N	Y	Y	Y
3 Suozzi	N	N	Y	N	Y	Y
4 Rice	N	N	Y	N	Y	N
5 Meeks	?	?	?	?	Y	N
6 Meng	N	N	Y	N	Y	N
7 Velázquez	N	N	Y	N	Y	N
8 Jeffries	N	N	Y	N	Y	N
9 Clarke	N	N	Y	N	Y	N
10 Nadler	N	N	Y	N	Y	N
11 **Donovan**	Y	Y	N	Y	Y	Y
12 Maloney, C.	N	N	Y	N	Y	N
13 Espaillat	N	N	Y	N	Y	N
14 Crowley	N	N	Y	N	Y	Y
15 Serrano	N	N	Y	N	Y	N
16 Engel	N	N	Y	N	?	?
17 Lowey	N	N	Y	N	Y	N
18 Maloney, S.P.	N	N	Y	Y	Y	N
19 **Faso**	Y	Y	N	Y	Y	Y
20 Tonko	N	N	Y	N	Y	Y
21 **Stefanik**	Y	Y	N	Y	Y	Y
22 **Tenney**	Y	Y	N	Y	Y	Y
23 **Reed**	Y	Y	N	Y	Y	Y
24 **Katko**	Y	Y	N	N	Y	Y
25 Slaughter	N	N	Y	N	Y	N
26 Higgins	N	N	Y	N	Y	N
27 **Collins**	Y	Y	N	Y	Y	Y
NORTH CAROLINA						
1 Butterfield	N	N	Y	N	Y	N
2 **Holding**	Y	Y	N	Y	Y	Y
3 **Jones**	Y	Y	N	Y	N	Y
4 Price	N	N	Y	N	Y	N
5 **Foxx**	Y	Y	N	Y	Y	Y
6 **Walker**	Y	Y	N	Y	Y	Y
7 **Rouzer**	Y	Y	N	Y	Y	Y
8 **Hudson**	Y	Y	N	Y	Y	Y
9 **Pittenger**	Y	Y	N	Y	Y	Y
10 **McHenry**	Y	Y	N	Y	Y	Y
11 **Meadows**	Y	Y	N	Y	Y	Y
12 Adams	N	N	Y	N	Y	N
13 **Budd**	Y	Y	N	Y	Y	Y
NORTH DAKOTA						
AL **Cramer**	Y	Y	N	Y	Y	Y
OHIO						
1 **Chabot**	Y	Y	N	Y	Y	Y
2 **Wenstrup**	+	+	N	Y	Y	Y
3 Beatty	N	N	Y	N	Y	N
4 **Jordan**	Y	Y	N	Y	Y	Y
5 **Latta**	Y	Y	N	Y	Y	Y
6 **Johnson**	Y	Y	N	Y	Y	Y
7 **Gibbs**	Y	Y	N	Y	Y	Y
8 **Davidson**	Y	Y	N	Y	Y	Y
9 Kaptur	N	N	Y	N	Y	N
10 **Turner**	Y	Y	N	Y	Y	Y
11 Fudge	N	N	Y	N	Y	N
12 **Tiberi**	?	?	?	+	?	?
13 Ryan	N	N	Y	N	Y	N
14 **Joyce**	Y	Y	N	Y	Y	Y
15 **Stivers**	Y	Y	N	Y	Y	Y
16 **Renacci**	Y	Y	Y	Y	?	?
OKLAHOMA						
1 **Bridenstine**	Y	Y	N	Y	?	?
2 **Mullin**	Y	Y	N	Y	Y	Y
3 **Lucas**	Y	Y	N	Y	Y	Y
4 **Cole**	Y	Y	N	Y	Y	Y
5 **Russell**	Y	Y	N	Y	Y	Y
OREGON						
1 Bonamici	N	N	Y	N	Y	N
2 **Walden**	Y	Y	N	Y	Y	Y
3 Blumenauer	N	N	Y	N	Y	N
4 DeFazio	N	N	Y	N	Y	N
5 Schrader	N	N	Y	N	Y	Y
PENNSYLVANIA						
1 Brady	N	N	Y	N	Y	N
2 Evans	N	N	Y	N	Y	Y
3 **Kelly**	Y	Y	N	Y	Y	Y
4 **Perry**	+	+	N	Y	N	Y
5 **Thompson**	Y	Y	N	Y	Y	Y
6 **Costello**	Y	Y	N	Y	Y	Y
7 **Meehan**	Y	Y	N	Y	Y	Y
8 **Fitzpatrick**	Y	Y	Y	N	Y	Y
9 **Shuster**	Y	Y	N	Y	Y	Y
10 **Marino**	Y	Y	N	Y	Y	Y
11 **Barletta**	Y	Y	N	Y	Y	Y
12 **Rothfus**	Y	Y	N	Y	Y	Y
13 Boyle	N	N	Y	N	Y	N
14 Doyle	N	N	Y	N	Y	N
15 **Dent**	Y	Y	N	Y	Y	Y
16 **Smucker**	Y	Y	N	Y	Y	Y
17 Cartwright	N	N	Y	N	Y	N
18 **Murphy**	Y	Y	N	Y	Y	Y
RHODE ISLAND						
1 Cicilline	N	N	Y	N	Y	N
2 Langevin	N	N	Y	N	Y	N
SOUTH CAROLINA						
1 **Sanford**	Y	Y	N	Y	Y	Y
2 **Wilson**	Y	Y	N	Y	Y	Y
3 **Duncan**	Y	Y	N	Y	N	Y
4 **Gowdy**	Y	Y	N	Y	Y	Y
6 Clyburn	N	N	Y	N	Y	N
7 **Rice**	Y	Y	N	Y	Y	Y
SOUTH DAKOTA						
AL **Noem**	Y	Y	N	Y	Y	Y
TENNESSEE						
1 **Roe**	Y	Y	N	Y	Y	Y
2 **Duncan**	Y	Y	N	Y	Y	Y
3 **Fleischmann**	Y	Y	N	Y	Y	Y
4 **DesJarlais**	Y	Y	N	Y	N	Y
5 Cooper	N	N	Y	N	Y	Y
6 **Black**	Y	Y	N	Y	Y	Y
7 **Blackburn**	Y	Y	N	Y	Y	Y
8 **Kustoff**	Y	Y	N	Y	Y	Y
9 Cohen	N	N	Y	N	Y	N
TEXAS						
1 **Gohmert**	Y	Y	N	Y	N	N
2 **Poe**	Y	Y	N	Y	N	Y
3 **Johnson, S.**	?	?	?	?	?	?
4 **Ratcliffe**	Y	Y	N	Y	Y	Y
5 **Hensarling**	Y	Y	N	Y	Y	Y
6 **Barton**	Y	Y	N	Y	N	Y
7 **Culberson**	Y	Y	N	Y	Y	Y
8 **Brady**	Y	Y	N	Y	Y	Y
9 Green, A.	N	N	Y	N	Y	N
10 **McCaul**	Y	Y	N	Y	Y	Y
11 **Conaway**	Y	Y	N	Y	Y	Y
12 **Granger**	Y	Y	+	+	Y	Y
13 **Thornberry**	Y	Y	N	Y	Y	Y
14 **Weber**	Y	Y	N	Y	N	Y
15 Gonzalez	N	N	Y	N	Y	N
16 O'Rourke	N	N	Y	N	Y	Y
17 **Flores**	Y	Y	N	Y	Y	Y
18 Jackson Lee	N	N	Y	N	Y	N
19 **Arrington**	Y	Y	N	Y	Y	Y
20 Castro	N	N	?	N	Y	N
21 **Smith**	Y	Y	N	Y	Y	Y
22 **Olson**	Y	Y	N	Y	N	Y
23 **Hurd**	Y	Y	N	Y	Y	Y
24 **Marchant**	Y	Y	N	Y	N	Y
25 **Williams**	Y	Y	N	Y	Y	Y
26 **Burgess**	Y	Y	N	Y	N	Y
27 **Farenthold**	Y	Y	N	Y	N	Y
28 Cuellar	N	N	N	Y	Y	Y
29 Green, G.	N	N	Y	N	Y	Y
30 Johnson, E.B.	N	N	Y	N	Y	N
31 **Carter**	Y	Y	N	Y	Y	Y
32 **Sessions**	Y	Y	N	Y	Y	Y
33 Veasey	N	N	Y	N	Y	N
34 Vela	N	N	Y	N	Y	Y
35 Doggett	N	N	Y	?	Y	N
36 **Babin**	Y	Y	N	Y	N	Y
UTAH						
1 **Bishop**	?	?	N	Y	N	?
2 **Stewart**	Y	Y	N	Y	Y	Y
3 **Chaffetz**	Y	Y	N	Y	Y	Y
4 **Love**	Y	Y	N	Y	Y	Y
VERMONT						
AL Welch	N	N	Y	N	Y	N
VIRGINIA						
1 **Wittman**	Y	Y	N	Y	N	Y
2 **Taylor**	Y	Y	N	Y	Y	Y
3 Scott	N	N	Y	N	Y	N
4 McEachin	N	N	Y	N	Y	N
5 **Garrett**	Y	Y	N	Y	?	?
6 **Goodlatte**	Y	Y	N	Y	Y	Y
7 **Brat**	Y	Y	N	Y	N	Y
8 Beyer	N	N	Y	N	Y	Y
9 **Griffith**	Y	Y	N	Y	Y	Y
10 **Comstock**	Y	Y	N	Y	Y	Y
11 Connolly	N	N	Y	N	Y	N
WASHINGTON						
1 DelBene	N	N	Y	N	Y	N
2 Larsen	–	–	+	–	+	–
3 **Herrera Beutler**	Y	Y	N	Y	Y	Y
4 **Newhouse**	Y	Y	N	Y	Y	Y
5 **McMorris Rodgers**	Y	Y	N	Y	Y	Y
6 Kilmer	N	N	Y	N	Y	Y
7 Jayapal	N	N	Y	N	Y	N
8 **Reichert**	Y	Y	N	Y	Y	Y
9 Smith	N	N	Y	N	Y	N
10 Heck	N	N	Y	N	Y	N
WEST VIRGINIA						
1 **McKinley**	Y	Y	N	Y	Y	Y
2 **Mooney**	Y	Y	N	Y	Y	Y
3 **Jenkins**	Y	Y	N	Y	Y	Y
WISCONSIN						
1 **Ryan**						
2 Pocan	N	N	Y	N	Y	N
3 Kind	N	N	Y	N	Y	Y
4 Moore	N	N	Y	N	Y	N
5 **Sensenbrenner**	Y	Y	N	Y	Y	Y
6 **Grothman**	Y	Y	N	Y	Y	Y
7 **Duffy**	Y	Y	N	Y	Y	Y
8 **Gallagher**	Y	Y	N	Y	N	N
WYOMING						
AL **Cheney**	Y	Y	N	Y	Y	Y

III HOUSE VOTES

VOTE NUMBER

322. HR 2842. STATE COORDINATED TEMPORARY EMPLOYMENT SUBSIDIES/PASSAGE. Passage of the bill that would authorize state demonstration projects within the Temporary Assistance for Needy Families program to temporarily subsidize employment for program beneficiaries with willing employers and would require $100 million in existing TANF funding must be used for grants to states to implement such programs. The bill would require at least one of the state projects that receives funding to be an apprenticeship program, and would require at least $15 million of the existing TANF funding to be used for programs that offer career pathway services. Passed 377-34 : R 214-13; D 163-21. June 23, 2017.

323. HR 2547. COMMERCIAL VEHICLE LICENSURE MEDICAL REVIEW/ PASSAGE. Graves, R-Mo., motion to suspend the rules and pass the bill that would allow certain medical professionals within the VA health care system, including physicians, nurses and physician assistants, to be eligible to be certified to conduct medical examinations required for a veteran to obtain a commercial driver's license. Motion agreed to 409-0 : R 228-0; D 181-0. June 26, 2017.

324. HR 2258. ACTIVE DUTY COMMERCIAL VEHICLE LICENSURE BENEFIT EXPANSION/PASSAGE. Graves, R-Mo., motion to suspend the rules and pass the bill that would allow active duty members of the armed forces and military reservists to be exempt from certain driving test requirements when obtaining a commercial driver's license, if such individuals have experience driving vehicles similar to commercial motor vehicles as a part of their military service. The bill would codify a proposed rule change from the Federal Motor Carrier Safety Administration, expanding the group eligible for the licensure benefit beyond veterans only. Motion agreed to 409-0 : R 228-0; D 181-0. June 26, 2017.

325. H RES 382, HR 1215. MEDICAL MALPRACTICE LAWSUIT LIMITATION/ PREVIOUS QUESTION. Buck, R-Colo., motion to order the previous question (thus ending debate and possibility of amendment) on the rule (H Res 382) that would provide for House floor consideration of the bill (HR 1215) that would limit to $250,000 the non-economic damages that could be awarded in a medical malpractice lawsuit where the plaintiff's health care was paid for in whole or in part via a federal program, subsidy or tax benefit, and would establish a statute of limitations for initiating such lawsuits of either three years following the plaintiff's injury or one year after the plaintiff discovers such injury, whichever occurs first. Motion agreed to 234-184 : R 234-0; D 0-184. June 27, 2017.

326. H RES 382, HR 1215. MEDICAL MALPRACTICE LAWSUIT LIMITATION/ RULE. Adoption of the rule (H Res 382) that would provide for consideration of the bill (HR 1215) that would limit to $250,000 the non-economic damages that could be awarded in a medical malpractice lawsuit where the plaintiff's health care was paid for in whole or in part via a federal program, subsidy or tax benefit, and would establish a statute of limitations for initiating such lawsuits of either three years following the plaintiff's injury or one year after the plaintiff discovers such injury, whichever occurs first. Adopted 235-186 : R 235-0; D 0-186. June 27, 2017.

327. PROCEDURAL MOTION/APPROVAL OF HOUSE JOURNAL. Approved 238-178 : R 145-86; D 93-92. June 27, 2017.

328. H RES 397. NATO COLLECTIVE DEFENSE/PASSAGE. Royce, R-Calif., motion to suspend the rules and agree to the resolution that would reaffirm the United States' commitment to NATO's principle of collective defense as outlined in Article 5 of the North Atlantic Treaty. The resolution would welcome the Republic of Montenegro as the 29th member of the NATO Alliance. Motion agreed to 423-4 : R 232-4; D 191-0. June 27, 2017.

	322	323	324	325	326	327	328
ALABAMA							
1 **Byrne**	Y	Y	Y	Y	Y	Y	Y
2 **Roby**	Y	Y	Y	Y	Y	Y	Y
3 **Rogers**	Y	Y	Y	Y	Y	N	Y
4 **Aderholt**	Y	Y	Y	Y	Y	Y	Y
5 **Brooks**	N	?	?	Y	Y	Y	Y
6 **Palmer**	Y	Y	Y	Y	Y	Y	Y
7 Sewell	Y	Y	Y	–	N	N	Y
ALASKA							
AL **Young**	Y	Y	Y	Y	Y	N	Y
ARIZONA							
1 O'Halleran	Y	Y	Y	?	N	N	Y
2 **McSally**	Y	Y	Y	Y	Y	N	Y
3 Grijalva	Y	Y	Y	N	N	N	Y
4 **Gosar**	?	Y	Y	Y	Y	Y	Y
5 **Biggs**	N	Y	Y	Y	Y	N	N
6 **Schweikert**	Y	Y	Y	Y	Y	Y	Y
7 Gallego	N	Y	N	N	N	N	Y
8 **Franks**	Y	Y	Y	Y	Y	N	Y
9 Sinema	Y	Y	Y	N	N	N	Y
ARKANSAS							
1 **Crawford**	Y	Y	Y	Y	Y	Y	Y
2 **Hill**	Y	Y	Y	Y	Y	Y	Y
3 **Womack**	Y	Y	Y	Y	Y	Y	Y
4 **Westerman**	Y	Y	Y	Y	Y	N	Y
CALIFORNIA							
1 **LaMalfa**	?	Y	Y	Y	Y	Y	Y
2 Huffman	Y	Y	Y	N	N	Y	Y
3 Garamendi	Y	Y	Y	N	N	Y	Y
4 **McClintock**	Y	Y	Y	Y	Y	Y	Y
5 Thompson	Y	Y	Y	N	N	N	Y
6 Matsui	Y	Y	N	N	N	N	Y
7 Bera	Y	Y	Y	N	N	N	Y
8 **Cook**	Y	Y	Y	Y	Y	Y	Y
9 McNerney	Y	Y	Y	N	N	N	Y
10 **Denham**	Y	Y	Y	Y	Y	N	Y
11 DeSaulnier	Y	Y	Y	N	N	Y	Y
12 Pelosi	?	Y	Y	N	?	?	Y
13 Lee	Y	Y	Y	N	N	N	Y
14 Speier	?	Y	Y	N	N	N	Y
15 Swalwell	Y	Y	Y	N	N	N	Y
16 Costa	Y	Y	Y	N	N	N	Y
17 Khanna	Y	Y	Y	N	N	N	Y
18 Eshoo	Y	Y	Y	N	N	Y	Y
19 Lofgren	Y	Y	Y	N	N	N	Y
20 Panetta	Y	Y	Y	N	N	Y	Y
21 **Valadao**	Y	Y	Y	Y	Y	Y	Y
22 **Nunes**	Y	Y	Y	Y	Y	Y	Y
23 **McCarthy**	Y	Y	Y	Y	Y	Y	Y
24 Carbajal	Y	Y	Y	N	N	N	Y
25 **Knight**	Y	Y	Y	Y	Y	Y	Y
26 Brownley	Y	Y	Y	N	N	N	Y
27 Chu	Y	Y	Y	N	N	N	Y
28 Schiff	Y	Y	Y	N	N	N	Y
29 Cardenas	Y	Y	Y	N	N	N	Y
30 Sherman	Y	Y	Y	N	N	N	Y
31 Aguilar	Y	Y	Y	N	N	N	Y
32 Napolitano	+	+	+	–	–	?	+
33 Lieu	?	Y	Y	N	N	N	Y
34 Vacant							
35 Torres	Y	Y	Y	N	N	Y	Y
36 Ruiz	Y	?	?	N	N	N	Y
37 Bass	Y	Y	Y	N	N	N	Y
38 Sánchez, Linda	Y	Y	Y	N	N	N	Y
39 **Royce**	Y	Y	Y	Y	Y	Y	Y
40 Roybal-Allard	Y	Y	Y	N	N	N	Y
41 Takano	Y	Y	Y	N	N	N	Y
42 **Calvert**	Y	Y	Y	Y	Y	Y	Y
43 Waters	Y	Y	Y	N	N	N	Y
44 Barragan	Y	Y	Y	N	N	N	Y
45 **Walters**	Y	Y	Y	Y	Y	Y	Y
46 Correa	Y	Y	Y	N	N	N	Y
47 Lowenthal	Y	Y	Y	N	N	N	Y
48 **Rohrabacher**	Y	?	?	Y	Y	Y	Y
49 **Issa**	Y	Y	Y	Y	Y	Y	Y
50 **Hunter**	Y	Y	Y	Y	Y	?	Y
51 Vargas	Y	Y	Y	N	N	N	Y
52 Peters	Y	Y	Y	N	N	N	Y
53 Davis	Y	Y	Y	N	N	Y	Y

	322	323	324	325	326	327	328
COLORADO							
1 DeGette	Y	Y	Y	N	N	Y	Y
2 Polis	Y	Y	Y	N	N	Y	Y
3 **Tipton**	Y	Y	Y	Y	Y	N	Y
4 **Buck**	Y	Y	Y	Y	Y	N	Y
5 **Lamborn**	Y	Y	Y	Y	Y	N	Y
6 **Coffman**	Y	Y	Y	Y	Y	N	Y
7 Perlmutter	Y	Y	Y	N	N	N	Y
CONNECTICUT							
1 Larson	Y	Y	Y	N	N	Y	Y
2 Courtney	Y	Y	Y	N	N	Y	Y
3 DeLauro	Y	Y	Y	–	–	–	Y
4 Himes	Y	Y	Y	N	?	Y	Y
5 Esty	Y	Y	Y	N	N	N	Y
DELAWARE							
AL Blunt Rochester	Y	Y	Y	N	N	Y	Y
FLORIDA							
1 **Gaetz**	Y	Y	Y	Y	Y	N	Y
2 **Dunn**	Y	Y	Y	Y	Y	Y	Y
3 **Yoho**	N	Y	Y	Y	Y	Y	Y
4 **Rutherford**	Y	Y	Y	Y	Y	Y	Y
5 Lawson	Y	Y	Y	N	N	N	Y
6 **DeSantis**	Y	Y	Y	Y	Y	N	Y
7 Murphy	Y	Y	Y	N	N	N	Y
8 **Posey**	Y	Y	Y	Y	Y	N	Y
9 Soto	Y	Y	Y	N	N	N	Y
10 Demings	Y	Y	Y	N	N	N	Y
11 **Webster**	Y	Y	Y	Y	Y	N	Y
12 **Bilirakis**	Y	Y	Y	Y	Y	N	Y
13 Crist	Y	Y	Y	N	N	N	Y
14 Castor	Y	Y	Y	N	N	N	Y
15 **Ross**	Y	Y	Y	Y	Y	Y	Y
16 **Buchanan**	Y	?	?	Y	Y	Y	Y
17 **Rooney, T.**	Y	Y	Y	Y	Y	Y	Y
18 **Mast**	Y	Y	Y	Y	Y	Y	Y
19 **Rooney, F.**	Y	Y	Y	Y	Y	Y	Y
20 Hastings	Y	Y	Y	N	N	N	Y
21 Frankel	Y	Y	Y	N	N	N	Y
22 Deutch	Y	Y	Y	N	N	N	Y
23 Wasserman Schultz	?	Y	Y	N	N	N	Y
24 Wilson	Y	Y	Y	N	N	N	Y
25 **Diaz-Balart**	Y	Y	Y	Y	Y	N	Y
26 **Curbelo**	Y	Y	Y	Y	Y	N	Y
27 **Ros-Lehtinen**	Y	Y	Y	Y	Y	N	Y
GEORGIA							
1 **Carter**	Y	Y	Y	Y	Y	N	Y
2 Bishop	Y	Y	Y	N	N	N	Y
3 **Ferguson**	Y	Y	Y	Y	Y	N	Y
4 Johnson	Y	Y	Y	N	N	N	Y
5 Lewis	Y	Y	Y	N	N	N	Y
7 **Woodall**	Y	Y	Y	Y	Y	N	Y
8 **Scott, A.**	Y	Y	Y	Y	Y	N	Y
9 **Collins**	Y	Y	Y	Y	Y	N	Y
10 **Hice**	Y	Y	Y	Y	?	N	Y
11 **Loudermilk**	Y	Y	Y	Y	Y	N	Y
12 **Allen**	Y	Y	Y	Y	Y	N	Y
13 Scott, D.	Y	Y	Y	N	N	N	Y
14 **Graves**	Y	Y	Y	Y	Y	N	Y
HAWAII							
1 Hanabusa	Y	Y	Y	N	N	N	Y
2 Gabbard	?	Y	Y	N	N	Y	Y
IDAHO							
1 **Labrador**	N	?	?	Y	Y	Y	Y
2 **Simpson**	Y	Y	Y	Y	Y	Y	Y
ILLINOIS							
1 Rush	Y	?	?	N	N	N	Y
2 Kelly	Y	Y	Y	N	N	N	Y
3 Lipinski	Y	Y	Y	N	N	N	Y
4 Gutierrez	Y	+	+	N	N	N	Y
5 Quigley	Y	Y	Y	N	N	Y	Y
6 **Roskam**	Y	Y	Y	Y	Y	Y	Y
7 Davis, D.	Y	Y	Y	N	N	N	Y
8 Krishnamoorthi	Y	Y	Y	N	N	N	Y
9 Schakowsky	Y	Y	Y	N	N	N	Y
10 Schneider	Y	Y	Y	N	N	N	Y
11 Foster	Y	Y	Y	N	N	N	Y
12 **Bost**	Y	Y	Y	Y	Y	Y	Y
13 **Davis, R.**	Y	Y	Y	Y	Y	Y	Y
14 **Hultgren**	Y	Y	Y	Y	Y	Y	Y
15 **Shimkus**	Y	Y	Y	Y	Y	Y	Y

KEY	Republicans	Democrats	Independents	
Y Voted for (yea)	**X** Paired against		**C** Voted "present" to avoid possible conflict of interest	
# Paired for	**–** Announced against			
+ Announced for	**P** Voted "present"		**?** Did not vote or otherwise make a position known	
N Voted against (nay)				

	322	323	324	325	326	327	328
16 **Kinzinger**	Y	Y	?	Y	Y	N	Y
17 Bustos	Y	Y	Y	N	N	Y	Y
18 **LaHood**	Y	Y	Y	Y	Y	N	Y
INDIANA							
1 Visclosky	Y	Y	Y	N	N	N	Y
2 **Walorski**	Y	Y	Y	Y	Y	Y	Y
3 **Banks**	Y	Y	Y	Y	Y	Y	Y
4 **Rokita**	Y	Y	Y	Y	Y	N	Y
5 **Brooks**	Y	Y	Y	Y	Y	Y	Y
6 **Messer**	Y	Y	Y	Y	Y	Y	Y
7 Carson	Y	Y	Y	N	N	N	Y
8 **Bucshon**	Y	?	?	Y	Y	Y	Y
9 **Hollingsworth**	Y	Y	Y	Y	Y	Y	Y
IOWA							
1 **Blum**	Y	Y	Y	Y	Y	N	Y
2 Loebsack	Y	Y	Y	?	N	N	Y
3 **Young**	Y	Y	Y	Y	Y	Y	Y
4 **King**	Y	Y	Y	Y	Y	Y	Y
KANSAS							
1 **Marshall**	Y	Y	Y	Y	Y	N	Y
2 **Jenkins**	Y	Y	Y	Y	Y	N	Y
3 **Yoder**	Y	Y	Y	Y	Y	N	Y
4 **Estes**	Y	Y	Y	Y	Y	Y	Y
KENTUCKY							
1 **Comer**	Y	Y	Y	Y	Y	N	Y
2 **Guthrie**	Y	Y	Y	Y	Y	Y	Y
3 Yarmuth	Y	Y	Y	?	N	Y	Y
4 **Massie**	N	Y	Y	Y	Y	Y	N
5 **Rogers**	Y	Y	Y	Y	Y	Y	Y
6 **Barr**	Y	Y	Y	Y	Y	N	Y
LOUISIANA							
1 **Scalise**	+	+	+	+	+	+	+
2 Richmond	Y	?	Y	N	N	N	Y
3 **Higgins**	Y	Y	Y	Y	Y	Y	Y
4 **Johnson**	Y	Y	Y	Y	Y	Y	Y
5 **Abraham**	Y	Y	Y	Y	Y	Y	Y
6 **Graves**	Y	Y	Y	Y	Y	N	Y
MAINE							
1 Pingree	Y	?	?	N	N	Y	Y
2 **Poliquin**	Y	Y	Y	Y	Y	Y	Y
MARYLAND							
1 **Harris**	Y	Y	Y	Y	Y	Y	Y
2 Ruppersberger	Y	Y	Y	N	N	Y	Y
3 Sarbanes	Y	Y	Y	N	N	N	Y
4 Brown	Y	Y	Y	N	N	Y	Y
5 Hoyer	Y	Y	Y	N	N	N	Y
6 Delaney	Y	Y	Y	N	N	N	Y
7 Cummings	?	?	?	?	?	?	?
8 Raskin	Y	Y	Y	N	N	N	Y
MASSACHUSETTS							
1 Neal	?	?	?	?	?	?	Y
2 McGovern	Y	Y	Y	N	N	N	Y
3 Tsongas	Y	Y	Y	N	N	Y	Y
4 Kennedy	Y	Y	Y	N	N	Y	Y
5 Clark	Y	Y	Y	N	N	Y	Y
6 Moulton	Y	Y	Y	N	N	Y	Y
7 Capuano	Y	Y	Y	N	N	N	Y
8 Lynch	Y	Y	Y	N	N	N	Y
9 Keating	Y	Y	Y	N	N	N	Y
MICHIGAN							
1 **Bergman**	Y	Y	Y	Y	Y	Y	Y
2 **Huizenga**	Y	Y	Y	Y	Y	N	Y
3 **Amash**	N	Y	Y	Y	Y	N	Y
4 **Moolenaar**	Y	Y	Y	Y	Y	Y	Y
5 Kildee	Y	Y	Y	N	N	Y	Y
6 **Upton**	Y	Y	Y	Y	Y	N	Y
7 **Walberg**	Y	Y	Y	Y	Y	N	Y
8 **Bishop**	Y	Y	Y	Y	Y	N	Y
9 Levin	Y	Y	Y	N	N	N	Y
10 **Mitchell**	Y	Y	Y	Y	Y	N	Y
11 **Trott**	Y	Y	Y	Y	Y	Y	Y
12 Dingell	Y	Y	Y	N	N	Y	Y
13 Conyers	Y	Y	Y	N	N	N	Y
14 Lawrence	Y	Y	Y	N	N	N	Y
MINNESOTA							
1 Walz	Y	?	?	N	N	Y	Y
2 **Lewis**	Y	Y	Y	Y	Y	Y	Y
3 **Paulsen**	Y	Y	Y	Y	Y	N	Y
4 McCollum	Y	Y	Y	N	N	Y	Y

	322	323	324	325	326	327	328
5 Ellison	Y	Y	Y	N	N	P	Y
6 **Emmer**	Y	Y	Y	Y	Y	N	Y
7 Peterson	Y	Y	Y	N	N	N	Y
8 Nolan	Y	Y	Y	N	N	N	Y
MISSISSIPPI							
1 **Kelly**	Y	Y	Y	Y	Y	Y	Y
2 Thompson	Y	Y	Y	N	N	N	Y
3 **Harper**	Y	Y	Y	Y	Y	Y	Y
4 **Palazzo**	Y	Y	Y	Y	Y	Y	Y
MISSOURI							
1 Clay	Y	Y	Y	N	N	Y	Y
2 **Wagner**	Y	Y	Y	Y	Y	Y	Y
3 **Luetkemeyer**	Y	Y	Y	Y	Y	Y	Y
4 **Hartzler**	Y	Y	Y	Y	Y	Y	Y
5 Cleaver	Y	Y	Y	N	N	Y	Y
6 **Graves**	Y	Y	Y	Y	Y	N	Y
7 **Long**	?	+	+	+	+	+	+
8 **Smith**	Y	Y	Y	Y	Y	N	Y
MONTANA							
AL **Gianforte**	Y	Y	Y	Y	Y	Y	Y
NEBRASKA							
1 **Fortenberry**	Y	Y	Y	Y	Y	Y	Y
2 **Bacon**	Y	Y	Y	Y	Y	Y	Y
3 **Smith**	Y	Y	Y	Y	Y	Y	Y
NEVADA							
1 Titus	N	Y	Y	N	N	Y	Y
2 **Amodei**	Y	Y	Y	Y	Y	Y	Y
3 Rosen	Y	Y	Y	N	N	N	Y
4 Kihuen	Y	Y	Y	N	N	N	Y
NEW HAMPSHIRE							
1 Shea-Porter	Y	Y	Y	N	N	Y	Y
2 Kuster	Y	Y	Y	N	N	Y	Y
NEW JERSEY							
1 Norcross	Y	Y	Y	N	N	N	Y
2 **LoBiondo**	Y	Y	Y	Y	Y	N	Y
3 **MacArthur**	Y	Y	Y	Y	Y	N	Y
4 **Smith**	Y	Y	Y	Y	Y	Y	Y
5 Gottheimer	Y	Y	Y	N	N	Y	Y
6 Pallone	Y	Y	Y	N	N	N	Y
7 **Lance**	Y	Y	Y	Y	Y	N	Y
8 Sires	Y	Y	Y	N	N	N	Y
9 Pascrell	Y	Y	Y	N	N	N	Y
10 Payne	Y	Y	Y	N	N	N	Y
11 **Frelinghuysen**	Y	Y	Y	Y	Y	Y	Y
12 Watson Coleman	Y	Y	Y	N	N	N	Y
NEW MEXICO							
1 Lujan Grisham	Y	Y	Y	N	N	Y	Y
2 **Pearce**	Y	Y	Y	Y	Y	N	Y
3 Luján	Y	Y	Y	N	N	Y	Y
NEW YORK							
1 **Zeldin**	Y	Y	Y	Y	Y	Y	Y
2 **King**	Y	Y	Y	Y	Y	Y	Y
3 Suozzi	N	Y	Y	N	N	N	Y
4 Rice	N	Y	Y	N	N	N	Y
5 Meeks	N	Y	Y	N	N	Y	Y
6 Meng	N	?	?	N	N	Y	Y
7 Velázquez	N	?	?	N	N	N	Y
8 Jeffries	N	Y	Y	N	N	Y	Y
9 Clarke	N	Y	Y	N	N	N	Y
10 Nadler	N	Y	Y	N	N	Y	Y
11 **Donovan**	Y	Y	Y	Y	Y	Y	Y
12 Maloney, C.	N	Y	Y	N	N	N	Y
13 Espaillat	N	Y	Y	N	N	N	Y
14 Crowley	N	Y	Y	N	N	Y	Y
15 Serrano	N	Y	Y	N	N	Y	Y
16 Engel	N	Y	Y	N	N	Y	Y
17 Lowey	N	Y	Y	N	N	?	Y
18 Maloney, S.P.	N	Y	Y	N	N	N	Y
19 **Faso**	Y	Y	Y	Y	Y	N	Y
20 Tonko	N	Y	Y	N	N	P	Y
21 **Stefanik**	Y	Y	Y	Y	Y	Y	Y
22 **Tenney**	Y	Y	Y	Y	Y	N	Y
23 **Reed**	Y	Y	Y	Y	Y	N	Y
24 **Katko**	Y	Y	Y	Y	Y	N	Y
25 Slaughter	N	Y	Y	N	N	N	Y
26 Higgins	N	Y	Y	N	N	Y	Y
27 **Collins**	Y	Y	Y	Y	Y	Y	Y
NORTH CAROLINA							
1 Butterfield	Y	?	?	N	N	Y	Y
2 **Holding**	Y	Y	Y	Y	Y	N	Y
3 **Jones**	N	Y	Y	Y	Y	Y	N
4 Price	Y	Y	Y	N	N	N	Y

	322	323	324	325	326	327	328
5 **Foxx**	Y	Y	Y	Y	Y	N	Y
6 **Walker**	Y	Y	Y	Y	Y	Y	Y
7 **Rouzer**	Y	Y	Y	Y	Y	N	Y
8 **Hudson**	Y	Y	+	Y	Y	N	Y
9 **Pittenger**	Y	Y	Y	Y	Y	N	Y
10 **McHenry**	Y	Y	Y	Y	Y	Y	Y
11 **Meadows**	Y	Y	Y	Y	Y	Y	Y
12 Adams	Y	Y	Y	N	N	Y	Y
13 **Budd**	N	Y	Y	Y	Y	Y	Y
NORTH DAKOTA							
AL **Cramer**	Y	Y	Y	Y	Y	Y	Y
OHIO							
1 **Chabot**	Y	Y	Y	Y	Y	Y	Y
2 **Wenstrup**	Y	Y	Y	Y	Y	Y	Y
3 Beatty	Y	Y	Y	N	N	N	Y
4 **Jordan**	Y	Y	Y	Y	Y	N	Y
5 **Latta**	Y	Y	Y	Y	Y	Y	Y
6 **Johnson**	Y	Y	Y	Y	Y	N	Y
7 **Gibbs**	Y	Y	Y	Y	Y	N	Y
8 **Davidson**	Y	Y	Y	Y	Y	Y	Y
9 Kaptur	Y	Y	Y	N	N	Y	Y
10 **Turner**	Y	+	+	Y	Y	N	Y
11 Fudge	Y	Y	Y	N	N	N	Y
12 **Tiberi**	+	Y	Y	Y	Y	Y	Y
13 Ryan	Y	Y	Y	N	N	N	Y
14 **Joyce**	Y	Y	Y	Y	Y	N	Y
15 **Stivers**	Y	Y	Y	?	?	?	?
16 **Renacci**	?	Y	Y	?	?	?	?
OKLAHOMA							
1 **Bridenstine**	?	Y	Y	Y	Y	Y	Y
2 **Mullin**	Y	Y	Y	Y	Y	Y	Y
3 **Lucas**	Y	+	+	Y	Y	Y	Y
4 **Cole**	Y	Y	Y	Y	Y	Y	Y
5 **Russell**	Y	Y	Y	Y	Y	Y	Y
OREGON							
1 Bonamici	Y	Y	Y	N	N	Y	Y
2 **Walden**	Y	Y	Y	Y	Y	N	Y
3 Blumenauer	Y	Y	Y	N	N	Y	Y
4 DeFazio	Y	Y	Y	N	N	N	Y
5 Schrader	Y	Y	Y	N	N	N	Y
PENNSYLVANIA							
1 Brady	Y	Y	Y	N	N	N	Y
2 Evans	Y	Y	Y	N	N	N	Y
3 **Kelly**	Y	Y	Y	Y	Y	Y	Y
4 **Perry**	N	Y	Y	Y	Y	N	Y
5 **Thompson**	Y	Y	Y	Y	Y	N	Y
6 **Costello**	Y	Y	Y	Y	Y	N	Y
7 **Meehan**	Y	Y	Y	Y	Y	Y	Y
8 **Fitzpatrick**	Y	Y	Y	Y	Y	N	Y
9 **Shuster**	Y	Y	Y	Y	Y	Y	Y
10 **Marino**	Y	Y	Y	Y	Y	Y	Y
11 **Barletta**	Y	Y	Y	Y	Y	Y	Y
12 **Rothfus**	Y	Y	Y	Y	Y	Y	Y
13 Boyle	Y	Y	Y	N	N	N	Y
14 Doyle	Y	Y	Y	N	N	N	Y
15 **Dent**	Y	Y	Y	Y	Y	Y	Y
16 **Smucker**	Y	Y	Y	Y	Y	Y	Y
17 Cartwright	Y	Y	Y	N	N	Y	Y
18 **Murphy**	Y	Y	Y	Y	Y	N	Y
RHODE ISLAND							
1 Cicilline	Y	Y	Y	N	N	Y	Y
2 Langevin	Y	Y	Y	N	N	N	Y
SOUTH CAROLINA							
1 **Sanford**	N	Y	Y	Y	Y	N	Y
2 **Wilson**	Y	Y	Y	Y	Y	Y	Y
3 **Duncan**	Y	Y	Y	Y	Y	Y	Y
4 **Gowdy**	Y	Y	Y	Y	Y	Y	Y
6 Clyburn	Y	Y	Y	N	N	Y	Y
7 **Rice**	Y	Y	Y	Y	Y	Y	Y
SOUTH DAKOTA							
AL **Noem**	Y	Y	Y	Y	Y	Y	Y
TENNESSEE							
1 **Roe**	Y	Y	Y	Y	Y	N	Y
2 **Duncan**	Y	Y	Y	Y	Y	Y	N
3 **Fleischmann**	Y	Y	Y	Y	Y	Y	Y
4 **DesJarlais**	Y	Y	Y	Y	Y	Y	Y
5 Cooper	Y	Y	Y	N	N	Y	Y
6 **Black**	Y	Y	Y	Y	Y	?	Y
7 **Blackburn**	Y	Y	Y	Y	Y	N	Y
8 **Kustoff**	Y	Y	Y	Y	Y	Y	Y
9 Cohen	Y	Y	Y	N	N	N	Y

	322	323	324	325	326	327	328
TEXAS							
1 **Gohmert**	N	Y	Y	Y	Y	?	Y
2 **Poe**	Y	Y	Y	Y	Y	N	Y
3 **Johnson, S.**	?	Y	Y	Y	Y	Y	Y
4 **Ratcliffe**	Y	Y	Y	Y	Y	N	Y
5 **Hensarling**	Y	Y	Y	Y	Y	Y	Y
6 **Barton**	Y	Y	Y	Y	Y	Y	Y
7 **Culberson**	Y	Y	Y	Y	Y	Y	Y
8 **Brady**	Y	Y	Y	Y	Y	Y	Y
9 Green, A.	Y	Y	Y	N	N	Y	Y
10 **McCaul**	Y	Y	Y	Y	Y	Y	Y
11 **Conaway**	Y	Y	Y	Y	Y	N	Y
12 **Granger**	?	Y	Y	?	Y	Y	Y
13 **Thornberry**	Y	Y	Y	Y	Y	Y	Y
14 **Weber**	Y	Y	Y	Y	Y	N	Y
15 Gonzalez	Y	Y	Y	N	N	Y	Y
16 O'Rourke	Y	Y	Y	N	N	Y	Y
17 **Flores**	Y	Y	Y	?	Y	N	Y
18 Jackson Lee	Y	Y	Y	N	N	N	Y
19 **Arrington**	Y	Y	Y	Y	Y	Y	Y
20 Castro	Y	Y	Y	N	N	Y	Y
21 **Smith**	Y	Y	Y	Y	Y	Y	Y
22 **Olson**	?	Y	Y	Y	Y	Y	Y
23 **Hurd**	Y	Y	Y	Y	Y	N	Y
24 **Marchant**	Y	?	?	Y	Y	N	Y
25 **Williams**	Y	Y	Y	Y	Y	Y	Y
26 **Burgess**	Y	Y	Y	Y	Y	?	Y
27 **Farenthold**	Y	Y	Y	Y	Y	Y	Y
28 Cuellar	Y	Y	Y	N	N	Y	Y
29 Green, G.	Y	Y	Y	N	N	N	Y
30 Johnson, E.B.	Y	Y	Y	N	N	Y	Y
31 **Carter**	Y	Y	Y	Y	Y	Y	Y
32 **Sessions**	Y	Y	Y	Y	Y	?	Y
33 Veasey	Y	Y	Y	N	N	N	Y
34 Vela	Y	Y	Y	N	?	N	Y
35 Doggett	N	Y	Y	N	N	Y	Y
36 **Babin**	N	Y	Y	Y	Y	Y	Y
UTAH							
1 **Bishop**	Y	Y	Y	Y	Y	Y	Y
2 **Stewart**	Y	Y	Y	Y	Y	Y	Y
3 **Chaffetz**	Y	Y	Y	Y	Y	Y	Y
4 **Love**	Y	Y	Y	Y	Y	N	Y
VERMONT							
AL Welch	Y	Y	Y	N	N	Y	Y
VIRGINIA							
1 **Wittman**	Y	Y	Y	Y	Y	N	Y
2 **Taylor**	Y	Y	Y	Y	Y	Y	Y
3 Scott	Y	Y	Y	N	N	Y	Y
4 McEachin	Y	Y	Y	N	N	Y	Y
5 **Garrett**	?	Y	Y	Y	Y	N	Y
6 **Goodlatte**	Y	Y	Y	Y	Y	Y	Y
7 **Brat**	N	Y	Y	Y	Y	Y	Y
8 Beyer	Y	Y	?	N	N	N	Y
9 **Griffith**	Y	Y	Y	Y	Y	Y	Y
10 **Comstock**	Y	Y	Y	Y	Y	Y	Y
11 Connolly	Y	Y	Y	N	N	N	Y
WASHINGTON							
1 DelBene	Y	Y	Y	N	N	Y	Y
2 Larsen	+	Y	Y	N	N	Y	Y
3 **Herrera Beutler**	Y	Y	Y	Y	Y	N	Y
4 **Newhouse**	Y	Y	Y	Y	Y	Y	Y
5 **McMorris Rodgers**	Y	Y	Y	Y	Y	Y	Y
6 Kilmer	Y	Y	Y	N	N	N	Y
7 Jayapal	Y	Y	Y	–	N	N	Y
8 **Reichert**	Y	Y	Y	Y	Y	N	Y
9 Smith	Y	Y	Y	N	N	Y	Y
10 Heck	Y	Y	Y	N	N	Y	Y
WEST VIRGINIA							
1 **McKinley**	Y	Y	Y	Y	Y	N	Y
2 **Mooney**	Y	Y	Y	Y	Y	Y	Y
3 **Jenkins**	Y	Y	Y	Y	Y	N	Y
WISCONSIN							
1 **Ryan**							
2 Pocan	Y	Y	Y	N	N	Y	Y
3 Kind	Y	Y	Y	N	N	N	Y
4 Moore	Y	Y	Y	N	N	N	Y
5 **Sensenbrenner**	Y	Y	Y	Y	Y	Y	Y
6 **Grothman**	Y	Y	Y	Y	Y	Y	Y
7 **Duffy**	Y	Y	Y	Y	Y	Y	Y
8 **Gallagher**	Y	Y	Y	Y	Y	N	Y
WYOMING							
AL **Cheney**	Y	Y	Y	Y	Y	Y	Y

III HOUSE VOTES

VOTE NUMBER

329. HR 497. SANTA ANA RIVER WASH PLAN LAND EXCHANGE ACT/ PASSAGE. Cook, R-Calif., motion to suspend the rules and pass the bill that would require the Bureau of Land Management to exchange 327 acres of its land for 310 acres of land currently owned by the San Bernardino Valley Water Conservation District in California if such action were to be requested by the water district. Motion agreed to 424-0 : R 235-0; D 189-0. June 27, 2017.

330. HR 220. KODIAK REFUGE HYDROELECTRIC EXPANSION/PASSAGE. Cook, R-Calif., motion to suspend the rules and pass the bill that would allow the Kodiak Electric Association to use up to 20 acres of federal land within the Kodiak National Wildlife Refuge for an expansion of the Terror Lake Hydroelectric Project. The bill would require no further approval of the land use by the Interior Department. Motion agreed to 424-1 : R 235-1; D 189-0. June 27, 2017.

331. HR 3003, H RES 414. IMMIGRATION LAW ENFORCEMENT COMPLIANCE/PREVIOUS QUESTION. Collins, R-Ga., motion to order the previous question (thus ending debate and possibility of amendment) on the rule (H Res 414) that would provide for House floor consideration of the bill (HR 3003) that would prohibit federal, state and local governments from restricting any federal, state, or local government entity or official from complying with immigration laws or from assisting federal law enforcement in its enforcement of such laws. Motion agreed to 235-190 : R 235-0; D 0-190. June 28, 2017.

332. HR 3003, H RES 414. IMMIGRATION LAW ENFORCEMENT COMPLIANCE/RULE. Adoption of the rule (H Res 414) that would provide for House floor consideration of the bill (HR 3003) that would prohibit federal, state and local governments from restricting any federal, state, or local government entity or official from complying with immigration laws or from assisting federal law enforcement in its enforcement of such laws. Adopted 235-190 : R 235-0; D 0-190. June 28, 2017.

333. PROCEDURAL MOTION/APPROVAL OF HOUSE JOURNAL. Approved 232-183 : R 144-88; D 88-95. June 28, 2017.

334. HR 1215. MEDICAL MALPRACTICE LAWSUIT LIMITATION/ ADMISSIBLE EVIDENCE. Hudson, R-N.C., amendment that would prohibit an apology by a health care provider or by an employee of a health care provider from being admissible as evidence of an admission of liability in a health care liability case. The amendment would also prohibit a health care professional from being qualified to testify as an expert witness in a medical malpractice case unless the individual meets certain professional qualifications and specialization requirements relevant to the provision or use of the health care services or medical products for which the case was brought. Adopted in Committee of the Whole 222-197 : R 215-17; D 7-180. June 28, 2017.

335. HR 1215. MEDICAL MALPRACTICE LAWSUIT LIMITATION/CLINICAL GUIDELINES LIABILITY. Barr, R-Ky., amendment that would provide an affirmative defense to defendants in health care liability cases if they can show they complied with approved clinical practice guidelines and such guidelines applicable to the provision or use of the health care services or medical products for which the case was brought. Rejected in Committee of the Whole 116-310 : R 107-129; D 9-181. June 28, 2017.

	329	330	331	332	333	334	335
ALABAMA							
1 Byrne	Y	Y	Y	Y	Y	Y	N
2 Roby	Y	Y	Y	Y	Y	Y	N
3 Rogers	Y	Y	Y	Y	N	?	N
4 Aderholt	Y	Y	Y	Y	Y	Y	Y
5 Brooks	Y	Y	Y	Y	N	N	Y
6 Palmer	Y	Y	Y	Y	N	Y	N
7 Sewell	Y	Y	N	N	N	N	N
ALASKA							
AL Young	Y	Y	Y	Y	N	Y	Y
ARIZONA							
1 O'Halleran	Y	Y	N	N	N	N	N
2 McSally	Y	Y	Y	Y	N	Y	N
3 Grijalva	Y	Y	N	N	?	N	N
4 Gosar	Y	Y	Y	Y	Y	Y	Y
5 Biggs	Y	Y	Y	Y	Y	Y	N
6 Schweikert	Y	Y	Y	Y	Y	Y	N
7 Gallego	Y	Y	N	N	N	N	N
8 Franks	Y	Y	Y	Y	N	Y	Y
9 Sinema	Y	Y	N	N	N	N	Y
ARKANSAS							
1 Crawford	Y	Y	Y	Y	Y	Y	N
2 Hill	Y	Y	Y	Y	Y	Y	N
3 Womack	Y	Y	Y	Y	Y	Y	N
4 Westerman	Y	Y	Y	Y	N	Y	N
CALIFORNIA							
1 LaMalfa	Y	Y	Y	Y	Y	Y	Y
2 Huffman	Y	Y	N	N	Y	N	N
3 Garamendi	Y	Y	N	N	Y	N	?
4 McClintock	Y	Y	Y	Y	Y	Y	N
5 Thompson	Y	Y	N	N	N	N	N
6 Matsui	Y	Y	N	N	N	N	N
7 Bera	Y	Y	N	N	N	Y	Y
8 Cook	Y	Y	Y	Y	Y	Y	N
9 McNerney	Y	Y	N	N	Y	?	N
10 Denham	Y	Y	Y	Y	Y	Y	N
11 DeSaulnier	Y	Y	N	N	Y	N	N
12 Pelosi	Y	Y	?	N	Y	N	N
13 Lee	Y	Y	N	N	N	N	N
14 Speier	Y	Y	N	N	Y	N	N
15 Swalwell	Y	Y	N	N	N	N	N
16 Costa	Y	Y	N	N	N	N	N
17 Khanna	Y	Y	N	N	N	N	N
18 Eshoo	Y	Y	N	N	Y	N	N
19 Lofgren	Y	Y	N	N	N	N	N
20 Panetta	Y	Y	N	N	Y	N	N
21 Valadao	Y	Y	Y	Y	Y	Y	Y
22 Nunes	Y	Y	Y	Y	Y	Y	Y
23 McCarthy	Y	Y	Y	Y	Y	Y	N
24 Carbajal	Y	Y	N	N	N	N	N
25 Knight	Y	Y	Y	Y	Y	Y	N
26 Brownley	Y	Y	N	N	Y	N	N
27 Chu	Y	Y	N	N	Y	N	N
28 Schiff	Y	Y	N	N	N	N	N
29 Cardenas	Y	Y	N	N	N	N	N
30 Sherman	Y	Y	N	N	Y	N	N
31 Aguilar	Y	Y	N	N	N	N	N
32 Napolitano	+	+	-	-	?	-	-
33 Lieu	Y	Y	N	N	N	N	N
34 Vacant							
35 Torres	Y	Y	N	N	N	N	N
36 Ruiz	Y	Y	N	N	N	Y	Y
37 Bass	Y	Y	N	N	N	N	N
38 Sánchez, Linda	Y	Y	N	-	N	N	N
39 Royce	Y	Y	Y	Y	Y	Y	N
40 Roybal-Allard	Y	Y	N	N	N	N	N
41 Takano	Y	Y	N	N	Y	N	N
42 Calvert	Y	Y	Y	Y	Y	Y	N
43 Waters	Y	Y	N	N	N	N	N
44 Barragan	Y	Y	N	N	N	N	N
45 Walters	Y	Y	Y	Y	Y	Y	N
46 Correa	Y	Y	N	N	N	Y	N
47 Lowenthal	Y	Y	N	N	Y	N	N
48 Rohrabacher	Y	Y	Y	Y	Y	Y	Y
49 Issa	Y	Y	Y	Y	Y	Y	N
50 Hunter	Y	Y	Y	Y	Y	Y	Y
51 Vargas	Y	Y	N	N	N	N	N
52 Peters	Y	Y	N	N	?	Y	Y
53 Davis	Y	Y	N	N	Y	N	N
COLORADO							
1 DeGette	Y	Y	N	N	Y	N	N
2 Polis	Y	Y	N	N	Y	N	N
3 Tipton	Y	Y	Y	Y	N	Y	N
4 Buck	Y	Y	Y	Y	Y	Y	Y
5 Lamborn	Y	Y	Y	Y	Y	Y	Y
6 Coffman	Y	Y	Y	Y	N	Y	N
7 Perlmutter	Y	Y	N	N	Y	N	N
CONNECTICUT							
1 Larson	Y	Y	N	N	N	N	N
2 Courtney	Y	Y	N	N	Y	N	N
3 DeLauro	Y	Y	N	N	Y	N	N
4 Himes	Y	?	N	N	Y	N	N
5 Esty	Y	Y	N	N	Y	N	N
DELAWARE							
AL Blunt Rochester	Y	Y	N	N	Y	N	N
FLORIDA							
1 Gaetz	Y	Y	Y	Y	N	Y	Y
2 Dunn	Y	Y	Y	Y	Y	Y	Y
3 Yoho	Y	Y	Y	Y	Y	Y	N
4 Rutherford	Y	Y	Y	Y	N	Y	N
5 Lawson	Y	Y	N	N	N	N	N
6 DeSantis	Y	Y	Y	Y	N	Y	Y
7 Murphy	Y	Y	N	N	Y	N	N
8 Posey	Y	Y	Y	Y	Y	Y	N
9 Soto	Y	Y	N	N	N	N	N
10 Demings	Y	Y	N	N	Y	N	N
11 Webster	Y	Y	Y	Y	Y	Y	Y
12 Bilirakis	Y	Y	Y	Y	Y	Y	Y
13 Crist	Y	Y	N	N	N	N	N
14 Castor	Y	Y	N	N	N	N	N
15 Ross	Y	Y	Y	Y	Y	Y	Y
16 Buchanan	Y	Y	Y	Y	Y	Y	N
17 Rooney, T.	Y	Y	Y	Y	Y	Y	N
18 Mast	Y	Y	Y	Y	Y	Y	Y
19 Rooney, F.	Y	Y	Y	Y	Y	Y	N
20 Hastings	Y	Y	N	N	Y	N	N
21 Frankel	Y	Y	N	N	Y	N	N
22 Deutch	Y	Y	N	N	Y	N	N
23 Wasserman Schultz	Y	Y	N	N	Y	N	N
24 Wilson	Y	Y	N	N	?	N	N
25 Diaz-Balart	Y	Y	Y	N	N	N	N
26 Curbelo	Y	Y	Y	Y	N	N	N
27 Ros-Lehtinen	Y	Y	Y	Y	N	N	N
GEORGIA							
1 Carter	Y	Y	Y	Y	N	Y	Y
2 Bishop	Y	Y	N	N	N	N	N
3 Ferguson	Y	Y	Y	Y	N	Y	N
4 Johnson	Y	Y	N	N	Y	N	N
5 Lewis	Y	Y	N	N	N	N	N
6 Handel	Y	Y	Y	Y	Y	Y	N
7 Woodall	Y	Y	Y	Y	N	Y	N
8 Scott, A.	Y	Y	Y	Y	Y	Y	Y
9 Collins	Y	Y	Y	Y	Y	Y	N
10 Hice	Y	Y	Y	Y	Y	Y	Y
11 Loudermilk	Y	Y	Y	Y	Y	Y	Y
12 Allen	Y	Y	Y	Y	Y	Y	Y
13 Scott, D.	Y	Y	N	N	Y	N	N
14 Graves	Y	Y	Y	Y	N	Y	N
HAWAII							
1 Hanabusa	Y	Y	N	N	N	N	N
2 Gabbard	Y	Y	N	N	Y	N	N
IDAHO							
1 Labrador	Y	Y	Y	Y	Y	Y	Y
2 Simpson	Y	Y	Y	Y	Y	Y	Y
ILLINOIS							
1 Rush	Y	Y	N	N	N	N	N
2 Kelly	Y	Y	N	N	N	N	N
3 Lipinski	Y	Y	N	N	Y	N	N
4 Gutierrez	Y	Y	N	N	N	N	N
5 Quigley	Y	Y	N	N	Y	N	N
6 Roskam	Y	Y	Y	Y	?	Y	Y
7 Davis, D.	Y	Y	N	N	N	N	N
8 Krishnamoorthi	Y	Y	N	N	Y	N	N
9 Schakowsky	Y	Y	N	N	N	N	N
10 Schneider	Y	Y	N	N	Y	N	N
11 Foster	Y	Y	N	N	Y	N	N
12 Bost	Y	Y	Y	Y	Y	Y	N
13 Davis, R.	Y	Y	Y	Y	N	Y	N
14 Hultgren	Y	Y	Y	Y	Y	Y	N
15 Shimkus	Y	Y	Y	Y	Y	Y	N

	329	330	331	332	333	334	335
16 **Kinzinger**	Y	Y	Y	Y	N	Y	N
17 Bustos	Y	Y	N	N	Y	N	N
18 **LaHood**	Y	Y	Y	Y	N	Y	N
INDIANA							
1 Visclosky	Y	Y	N	N	N	N	N
2 **Walorski**	Y	Y	Y	Y	Y	Y	N
3 **Banks**	Y	Y	Y	Y	Y	Y	N
4 **Rokita**	Y	Y	Y	Y	Y	Y	Y
5 **Brooks**	Y	Y	Y	Y	Y	Y	N
6 **Messer**	Y	Y	Y	Y	Y	Y	N
7 Carson	Y	Y	N	N	N	N	N
8 **Bucshon**	Y	Y	Y	Y	N	Y	Y
9 **Hollingsworth**	Y	Y	Y	Y	Y	Y	Y
IOWA							
1 **Blum**	Y	Y	Y	Y	N	Y	N
2 Loebsack	Y	Y	N	N	N	N	N
3 **Young**	Y	Y	Y	Y	Y	Y	Y
4 **King**	Y	Y	Y	Y	Y	Y	Y
KANSAS							
1 **Marshall**	Y	Y	Y	Y	Y	Y	Y
2 **Jenkins**	Y	Y	Y	Y	N	Y	Y
3 **Yoder**	Y	Y	Y	Y	N	Y	Y
4 **Estes**	Y	Y	Y	Y	Y	Y	N
KENTUCKY							
1 **Comer**	Y	Y	Y	Y	N	Y	N
2 **Guthrie**	Y	Y	Y	Y	Y	Y	Y
3 Yarmuth	Y	Y	N	N	Y	N	N
4 **Massie**	Y	Y	Y	Y	Y	N	N
5 **Rogers**	Y	Y	Y	Y	Y	Y	Y
6 **Barr**	Y	Y	Y	Y	Y	Y	Y
LOUISIANA							
1 **Scalise**	+	+	+	+	+	+	+
2 Richmond	Y	Y	N	N	N	N	N
3 **Higgins**	Y	Y	Y	Y	Y	Y	N
4 **Johnson**	Y	Y	Y	Y	Y	Y	Y
5 **Abraham**	Y	Y	Y	Y	Y	Y	Y
6 **Graves**	Y	Y	Y	Y	N	Y	Y
MAINE							
1 Pingree	Y	Y	N	N	Y	N	N
2 **Poliquin**	Y	Y	Y	Y	N	Y	N
MARYLAND							
1 **Harris**	Y	Y	Y	Y	Y	Y	Y
2 Ruppersberger	Y	Y	N	N	Y	N	N
3 Sarbanes	Y	Y	N	N	N	N	N
4 Brown	Y	Y	N	N	Y	N	N
5 Hoyer	Y	Y	N	N	N	N	N
6 Delaney	Y	Y	N	N	?	N	N
7 Cummings	?	?	?	?	?	?	?
8 Raskin	?	Y	N	N	Y	N	N
MASSACHUSETTS							
1 Neal	Y	Y	N	N	N	N	N
2 McGovern	Y	Y	N	N	N	N	N
3 Tsongas	Y	Y	N	N	Y	N	N
4 Kennedy	Y	Y	N	N	Y	N	N
5 Clark	Y	Y	N	N	N	N	N
6 Moulton	Y	Y	N	N	Y	N	N
7 Capuano	Y	Y	N	N	N	N	N
8 Lynch	Y	Y	N	N	N	N	N
9 Keating	Y	Y	N	N	N	N	N
MICHIGAN							
1 **Bergman**	Y	Y	Y	Y	Y	Y	Y
2 **Huizenga**	Y	Y	Y	Y	Y	Y	Y
3 **Amash**	Y	N	Y	Y	N	N	N
4 **Moolenaar**	Y	Y	Y	Y	N	Y	N
5 Kildee	Y	Y	N	N	Y	N	N
6 **Upton**	Y	Y	Y	Y	N	Y	N
7 **Walberg**	Y	Y	Y	Y	N	Y	Y
8 **Bishop**	Y	Y	Y	Y	N	Y	N
9 Levin	Y	Y	N	N	N	N	N
10 **Mitchell**	Y	Y	Y	Y	Y	Y	N
11 **Trott**	Y	Y	Y	Y	Y	Y	N
12 Dingell	Y	Y	N	N	N	N	N
13 Conyers	Y	Y	N	N	Y	N	N
14 Lawrence	Y	Y	N	N	Y	N	N
MINNESOTA							
1 Walz	Y	Y	N	N	Y	N	N
2 **Lewis**	Y	Y	Y	Y	Y	Y	N
3 **Paulsen**	Y	Y	Y	Y	N	Y	N
4 McCollum	Y	Y	N	N	Y	N	N

	329	330	331	332	333	334	335
5 Ellison	Y	Y	N	N	Y	N	N
6 **Emmer**	Y	Y	Y	Y	N	Y	N
7 Peterson	Y	Y	N	N	N	Y	N
8 Nolan	Y	Y	N	N	N	N	N
MISSISSIPPI							
1 **Kelly**	Y	Y	Y	Y	Y	Y	N
2 Thompson	Y	Y	N	N	N	N	N
3 **Harper**	Y	Y	Y	Y	Y	Y	N
4 **Palazzo**	Y	Y	Y	Y	Y	Y	N
MISSOURI							
1 Clay	Y	Y	N	N	Y	N	N
2 **Wagner**	Y	Y	Y	Y	Y	Y	Y
3 **Luetkemeyer**	Y	Y	Y	Y	Y	Y	N
4 **Hartzler**	Y	Y	Y	Y	N	Y	N
5 Cleaver	Y	Y	N	N	N	N	N
6 **Graves**	Y	Y	Y	Y	N	Y	Y
7 **Long**	+	+	+	+	+	+	–
8 **Smith**	Y	Y	Y	Y	N	Y	Y
MONTANA							
AL **Gianforte**	Y	Y	Y	Y	Y	Y	Y
NEBRASKA							
1 **Fortenberry**	Y	Y	Y	Y	Y	Y	Y
2 **Bacon**	Y	Y	Y	Y	Y	Y	N
3 **Smith**	Y	Y	Y	Y	Y	Y	Y
NEVADA							
1 Titus	Y	Y	N	N	Y	N	N
2 **Amodei**	Y	Y	Y	Y	Y	?	Y
3 Rosen	Y	Y	N	N	N	Y	Y
4 Kihuen	Y	Y	N	N	N	N	N
NEW HAMPSHIRE							
1 Shea-Porter	Y	Y	N	N	Y	N	N
2 Kuster	Y	Y	N	N	Y	N	N
NEW JERSEY							
1 Norcross	Y	Y	N	N	?	N	N
2 **LoBiondo**	Y	Y	Y	Y	N	N	N
3 **MacArthur**	Y	Y	Y	Y	N	Y	Y
4 **Smith**	Y	Y	Y	Y	Y	N	N
5 Gottheimer	Y	Y	N	N	Y	N	N
6 Pallone	Y	Y	N	N	N	N	N
7 **Lance**	Y	Y	Y	Y	N	Y	N
8 Sires	Y	Y	N	N	N	N	N
9 Pascrell	Y	Y	N	N	Y	N	N
10 Payne	Y	Y	N	N	N	N	N
11 **Frelinghuysen**	Y	Y	Y	Y	Y	Y	N
12 Watson Coleman	Y	Y	N	N	N	N	N
NEW MEXICO							
1 Lujan Grisham	Y	Y	N	N	Y	N	N
2 **Pearce**	Y	Y	Y	Y	N	Y	Y
3 Luján	Y	Y	N	N	N	N	N
NEW YORK							
1 **Zeldin**	Y	Y	Y	Y	Y	Y	N
2 **King**	Y	Y	Y	Y	Y	Y	N
3 Suozzi	Y	Y	N	N	Y	N	N
4 Rice	Y	Y	N	N	N	N	N
5 Meeks	Y	Y	N	N	Y	?	N
6 Meng	Y	Y	N	N	Y	N	N
7 Velázquez	Y	Y	N	N	N	N	N
8 Jeffries	Y	Y	N	N	Y	N	N
9 Clarke	Y	Y	N	N	N	N	N
10 Nadler	Y	Y	N	N	Y	N	N
11 **Donovan**	Y	Y	Y	Y	Y	Y	N
12 Maloney, C.	Y	Y	N	N	Y	N	N
13 Espaillat	Y	Y	N	N	N	N	N
14 Crowley	Y	Y	N	N	N	N	N
15 Serrano	Y	Y	N	N	Y	N	N
16 Engel	?	?	N	N	Y	N	N
17 Lowey	Y	Y	N	N	Y	N	N
18 Maloney, S.P.	Y	Y	N	N	N	N	N
19 **Faso**	Y	Y	Y	Y	N	Y	N
20 Tonko	Y	Y	N	N	P	N	N
21 **Stefanik**	Y	Y	Y	Y	Y	Y	N
22 **Tenney**	Y	Y	Y	Y	N	Y	Y
23 **Reed**	Y	Y	Y	Y	N	Y	N
24 **Katko**	Y	Y	Y	Y	Y	Y	N
25 Slaughter	Y	Y	N	N	N	N	N
26 Higgins	Y	Y	N	N	N	N	N
27 **Collins**	Y	Y	Y	+	Y	Y	N
NORTH CAROLINA							
1 Butterfield	Y	Y	N	N	Y	N	N
2 **Holding**	Y	Y	Y	Y	N	Y	Y
3 **Jones**	Y	Y	Y	Y	?	?	N
4 Price	Y	Y	N	N	N	N	N

	329	330	331	332	333	334	335
5 **Foxx**	Y	Y	Y	Y	N	Y	Y
6 **Walker**	Y	Y	Y	Y	Y	Y	Y
7 **Rouzer**	+	Y	Y	Y	N	Y	Y
8 **Hudson**	Y	Y	Y	Y	N	Y	Y
9 **Pittenger**	Y	Y	Y	Y	N	Y	N
10 **McHenry**	Y	Y	Y	Y	Y	Y	N
11 **Meadows**	Y	Y	Y	Y	Y	Y	Y
12 Adams	Y	Y	N	N	N	N	N
13 **Budd**	Y	Y	Y	Y	N	Y	Y
NORTH DAKOTA							
AL **Cramer**	Y	Y	Y	Y	Y	Y	N
OHIO							
1 **Chabot**	Y	Y	Y	Y	Y	Y	N
2 **Wenstrup**	Y	Y	Y	Y	Y	Y	Y
3 Beatty	Y	Y	N	N	N	N	N
4 **Jordan**	Y	Y	Y	Y	N	Y	N
5 **Latta**	Y	Y	Y	Y	Y	Y	N
6 **Johnson**	Y	Y	Y	Y	N	Y	N
7 **Gibbs**	Y	Y	Y	Y	N	Y	N
8 **Davidson**	Y	Y	Y	Y	Y	N	Y
9 Kaptur	Y	Y	N	N	N	N	Y
10 **Turner**	Y	Y	Y	Y	Y	N	N
11 Fudge	Y	Y	N	N	N	N	N
12 **Tiberi**	Y	Y	Y	Y	N	Y	Y
13 Ryan	Y	Y	N	N	N	N	N
14 **Joyce**	Y	Y	Y	Y	N	Y	Y
15 **Stivers**	?	?	?	?	?	?	?
16 **Renacci**	?	?	?	?	?	?	?
OKLAHOMA							
1 **Bridenstine**	Y	Y	Y	Y	Y	Y	N
2 **Mullin**	Y	Y	Y	Y	Y	Y	Y
3 **Lucas**	Y	Y	Y	Y	Y	Y	N
4 **Cole**	Y	Y	Y	Y	Y	Y	Y
5 **Russell**	Y	Y	Y	Y	Y	N	N
OREGON							
1 Bonamici	Y	Y	N	N	Y	N	N
2 **Walden**	Y	Y	Y	Y	N	Y	N
3 Blumenauer	Y	Y	N	N	Y	N	N
4 DeFazio	Y	Y	N	N	N	N	N
5 Schrader	Y	Y	N	N	N	N	Y
PENNSYLVANIA							
1 Brady	Y	Y	N	N	N	N	N
2 Evans	Y	Y	N	N	Y	N	N
3 **Kelly**	Y	Y	Y	Y	Y	Y	Y
4 **Perry**	Y	Y	Y	Y	N	N	N
5 **Thompson**	Y	Y	Y	Y	N	Y	Y
6 **Costello**	Y	Y	Y	Y	N	Y	Y
7 **Meehan**	Y	Y	Y	Y	Y	Y	Y
8 **Fitzpatrick**	Y	Y	Y	Y	N	Y	Y
9 **Shuster**	Y	Y	Y	Y	Y	Y	N
10 **Marino**	Y	Y	Y	Y	Y	Y	Y
11 **Barletta**	Y	Y	Y	Y	Y	Y	Y
12 **Rothfus**	Y	Y	Y	Y	Y	Y	Y
13 Boyle	Y	Y	N	N	N	N	N
14 Doyle	Y	Y	N	N	N	N	N
15 **Dent**	Y	Y	Y	Y	Y	Y	Y
16 **Smucker**	Y	Y	Y	Y	Y	Y	Y
17 Cartwright	Y	Y	N	N	Y	N	N
18 **Murphy**	Y	Y	Y	Y	N	Y	N
RHODE ISLAND							
1 Cicilline	Y	Y	N	N	Y	N	N
2 Langevin	Y	Y	N	N	N	–	N
SOUTH CAROLINA							
1 **Sanford**	Y	Y	Y	Y	N	N	N
2 **Wilson**	Y	Y	Y	Y	Y	Y	Y
3 **Duncan**	Y	Y	Y	Y	Y	Y	Y
4 **Gowdy**	Y	Y	Y	Y	Y	Y	N
5 **Norman**	Y	Y	Y	Y	Y	Y	Y
6 Clyburn	Y	Y	N	N	N	N	N
7 **Rice**	Y	Y	Y	Y	P	Y	Y
SOUTH DAKOTA							
AL **Noem**	Y	Y	Y	Y	Y	Y	N
TENNESSEE							
1 **Roe**	Y	Y	Y	Y	Y	Y	Y
2 **Duncan**	Y	Y	Y	Y	Y	N	N
3 **Fleischmann**	Y	Y	Y	Y	Y	Y	Y
4 **DesJarlais**	Y	Y	Y	Y	Y	Y	Y
5 Cooper	Y	Y	N	N	Y	N	N
6 **Black**	Y	Y	Y	Y	Y	?	N
7 **Blackburn**	Y	Y	Y	Y	Y	Y	N
8 **Kustoff**	Y	Y	Y	Y	Y	Y	Y
9 Cohen	Y	Y	N	N	N	N	N

	329	330	331	332	333	334	335
TEXAS							
1 **Gohmert**	Y	Y	Y	Y	?	Y	N
2 **Poe**	Y	Y	Y	Y	N	N	N
3 **Johnson, S.**	Y	Y	Y	Y	Y	Y	N
4 **Ratcliffe**	Y	Y	Y	Y	N	Y	N
5 **Hensarling**	Y	Y	Y	Y	Y	Y	N
6 **Barton**	Y	Y	Y	Y	Y	Y	N
7 **Culberson**	Y	Y	Y	Y	Y	Y	N
8 **Brady**	Y	Y	Y	Y	Y	Y	N
9 Green, A.	Y	Y	N	N	Y	N	N
10 **McCaul**	Y	Y	Y	Y	Y	Y	Y
11 **Conaway**	Y	Y	Y	Y	N	Y	N
12 **Granger**	Y	Y	Y	Y	Y	Y	N
13 **Thornberry**	Y	Y	Y	Y	Y	Y	N
14 **Weber**	Y	Y	Y	Y	N	Y	N
15 Gonzalez	Y	Y	N	N	N	N	N
16 O'Rourke	Y	Y	N	N	Y	N	N
17 **Flores**	Y	Y	Y	Y	N	Y	N
18 Jackson Lee	Y	Y	N	N	N	N	N
19 **Arrington**	Y	Y	Y	Y	Y	Y	N
20 Castro	Y	Y	N	N	Y	N	N
21 **Smith**	Y	Y	Y	Y	Y	Y	N
22 **Olson**	Y	Y	Y	Y	Y	Y	N
23 **Hurd**	Y	Y	Y	Y	N	Y	N
24 **Marchant**	Y	Y	Y	Y	Y	Y	Y
25 **Williams**	Y	Y	Y	Y	Y	Y	Y
26 **Burgess**	Y	Y	Y	Y	N	Y	N
27 **Farenthold**	Y	Y	Y	Y	Y	Y	Y
28 Cuellar	Y	Y	N	N	Y	Y	Y
29 Green, G.	Y	Y	N	N	N	N	N
30 Johnson, E.B.	Y	Y	N	N	N	–	N
31 **Carter**	Y	Y	Y	Y	Y	Y	N
32 **Sessions**	Y	Y	Y	Y	Y	Y	Y
33 Veasey	Y	Y	N	N	N	N	N
34 Vela	Y	Y	N	N	N	N	N
35 Doggett	Y	Y	N	N	?	N	N
36 **Babin**	Y	Y	Y	Y	N	Y	N
UTAH							
1 **Bishop**	Y	Y	Y	Y	Y	Y	Y
2 **Stewart**	Y	Y	Y	Y	Y	Y	Y
3 **Chaffetz**	Y	Y	Y	Y	N	Y	N
4 **Love**	Y	Y	Y	Y	N	Y	N
VERMONT							
AL Welch	Y	Y	N	N	Y	N	N
VIRGINIA							
1 **Wittman**	Y	Y	Y	Y	N	Y	N
2 **Taylor**	Y	Y	Y	Y	Y	Y	N
3 Scott	Y	Y	N	N	Y	N	N
4 McEachin	Y	Y	N	N	Y	N	N
5 **Garrett**	Y	Y	Y	Y	Y	N	N
6 **Goodlatte**	Y	Y	Y	Y	Y	Y	N
7 **Brat**	Y	Y	Y	Y	Y	Y	N
8 Beyer	Y	Y	N	N	N	N	N
9 **Griffith**	Y	Y	Y	Y	Y	N	N
10 **Comstock**	Y	Y	?	Y	Y	Y	Y
11 Connolly	Y	Y	N	N	N	N	N
WASHINGTON							
1 DelBene	Y	Y	N	N	Y	N	N
2 Larsen	Y	Y	N	N	Y	N	N
3 **Herrera Beutler**	Y	Y	Y	Y	N	Y	N
4 **Newhouse**	Y	Y	Y	Y	Y	Y	N
5 **McMorris Rodgers**	Y	Y	Y	Y	Y	Y	Y
6 Kilmer	Y	Y	N	N	N	N	N
7 Jayapal	Y	Y	N	N	N	N	N
8 **Reichert**	Y	Y	Y	Y	N	Y	N
9 Smith	Y	Y	N	N	Y	N	N
10 Heck	Y	Y	N	N	Y	N	N
WEST VIRGINIA							
1 **McKinley**	Y	Y	Y	Y	N	Y	N
2 **Mooney**	Y	Y	Y	Y	Y	Y	Y
3 **Jenkins**	Y	Y	Y	Y	N	Y	Y
WISCONSIN							
1 **Ryan**							
2 Pocan	Y	Y	N	N	Y	N	N
3 Kind	Y	Y	N	N	N	N	N
4 Moore	Y	Y	N	N	N	N	N
5 **Sensenbrenner**	Y	Y	Y	Y	Y	Y	N
6 **Grothman**	Y	Y	Y	Y	N	Y	N
7 **Duffy**	Y	Y	Y	Y	Y	Y	Y
8 **Gallagher**	Y	Y	Y	Y	N	Y	Y
WYOMING							
AL **Cheney**	Y	Y	Y	Y	Y	Y	Y

VOTE NUMBER

336. HR 1215. MEDICAL MALPRACTICE LAWSUIT LIMITATION/RECOMMIT. Kuster, D-N.H., motion to recommit the bill to the House Judiciary Committee with instructions to report it back immediately with an amendment that would modify the bill's definition of "health care lawsuits" to not include a claim or action related to the "grossly negligent" prescription of opioids. Motion rejected 191-235 : R 0-235; D 191-0. June 28, 2017.

337. HR 1215. MEDICAL MALPRACTICE LAWSUIT LIMITATION/PASSAGE. Passage of the bill that would limit to $250,000 the non-economic damages that can be awarded in a medical malpractice lawsuit in which the plaintiff's health care was paid for in whole or in part via a federal program, subsidy or tax benefit, and would establish a statute of limitations for initiating such lawsuits of either three years following the plaintiff's injury, or one year after the plaintiff discovers such injury, whichever occurs first. The bill would also prohibit a health care provider that prescribes or dispenses a FDA-approved medical product from being named as a party in either a product liability lawsuit involving the product or a class action lawsuit against the manufacturer, distributor or seller of such product. Passed 218-210 : R 218-19; D 0-191. June 28, 2017.

338. HR 1500. EMMET PARK DESIGNATION/PASSAGE. Cook, R-Calif., motion to suspend the rules and pass the bill that would redesignate the Washington, D.C. property currently designated by the National Park Service as reservation 302 as "Robert Emmet Park," and would allow the Interior Department to place signage on or near the park that includes information on Robert Emmet and the history of the statue of Robert Emmet located on the property. Motion agreed to 423-0 : R 233-0; D 190-0. June 28, 2017.

339. H RES 415, HR 3004. UNDOCUMENTED IMMIGRANT SENTENCING GUIDELINES/PREVIOUS QUESTION. Sessions, R-Texas, motion to order the previous question (thus ending debate and possibility of amendment) on the rule (H Res 415) that would provide for House floor consideration of the bill (HR 3004) that would establish specific possible fines and prison sentences for undocumented immigrants convicted of certain criminal offenses and who illegally return to the United States despite having been previously deported or otherwise excluded from the country. Motion agreed to 235-190 : R 235-1; D 0-189. June 29, 2017.

340. H RES 415, HR 3004. UNDOCUMENTED IMMIGRANT SENTENCING GUIDELINES/RULE. Adoption of the rule (H Res 415) that would provide for House floor consideration of the bill (HR 3004) that would establish specific possible fines and prison sentences for undocumented immigrants convicted of certain criminal offenses and who illegally return to the United States despite having been previously deported or otherwise excluded from the country. Adopted 236-191 : R 236-0; D 0-191. June 29, 2017.

341. HR 3003. IMMIGRATION LAW ENFORCEMENT COMPLIANCE/ RECOMMIT. Demings, D-Fla., motion to recommit the bill to the House Judiciary Committee with instructions to report it back immediately with an amendment that would exempt state or local governments from the bill's noncompliance provisions if such governments certify to the attorney general that complying with the bill's provisions would endanger public safety. Motion rejected 181-230 : R 0-230; D 181-0. June 29, 2017.

342. HR 3003. IMMIGRATION LAW ENFORCEMENT COMPLIANCE/ PASSAGE. Passage of the bill that would prohibit federal, state and local governments from restricting any federal, state, or local government entity or official from complying with immigration laws or from assisting federal law enforcement entities or officials in their enforcement of such laws. The bill would allow the Homeland Security Department to issue detainers for arrests of individuals in violation of "any criminal or motor vehicle law" in cases where there is probable cause to believe such individual is an "inadmissible or deportable alien," and would revoke eligibility for certain federal law enforcement grants for states and cities found not to be in compliance with the bill's provisions. Passed 228-195 : R 225-7; D 3-188. June 29, 2017.

	336	337	338	339	340	341	342
ALABAMA							
1 **Byrne**	N	Y	Y	Y	Y	N	Y
2 **Roby**	N	Y	Y	Y	Y	N	Y
3 **Rogers**	N	Y	Y	Y	Y	N	Y
4 **Aderholt**	N	Y	Y	Y	Y	N	Y
5 **Brooks**	N	Y	Y	Y	Y	N	Y
6 **Palmer**	N	Y	Y	Y	Y	N	Y
7 Sewell	Y	N	Y	N	N	Y	N
ALASKA							
AL **Young**	N	Y	Y	Y	Y	N	Y
ARIZONA							
1 O'Halleran	Y	N	Y	N	N	Y	N
2 **McSally**	N	N	Y	Y	Y	N	Y
3 Grijalva	Y	N	Y	N	N	Y	N
4 **Gosar**	N	Y	Y	Y	Y	?	?
5 **Biggs**	N	Y	Y	Y	Y	N	Y
6 **Schweikert**	N	Y	Y	Y	Y	N	Y
7 Gallego	Y	N	Y	N	N	Y	N
8 **Franks**	N	Y	Y	?	?	N	Y
9 Sinema	Y	N	Y	N	N	Y	N
ARKANSAS							
1 **Crawford**	N	Y	Y	Y	Y	N	Y
2 **Hill**	N	Y	Y	Y	Y	N	Y
3 **Womack**	N	Y	Y	Y	Y	N	Y
4 **Westerman**	N	Y	Y	Y	Y	N	Y
CALIFORNIA							
1 **LaMalfa**	N	Y	Y	Y	Y	N	Y
2 Huffman	Y	N	Y	N	N	?	N
3 Garamendi	Y	N	Y	N	N	Y	N
4 **McClintock**	N	Y	Y	Y	Y	N	Y
5 Thompson	Y	N	Y	N	N	Y	N
6 Matsui	Y	N	Y	N	N	Y	N
7 Bera	Y	N	Y	N	N	Y	N
8 **Cook**	N	Y	Y	Y	Y	N	Y
9 McNerney	Y	N	Y	N	N	Y	N
10 **Denham**	N	Y	Y	Y	Y	N	Y
11 DeSaulnier	Y	N	Y	N	N	Y	N
12 Pelosi	Y	N	Y	N	N	Y	N
13 Lee	Y	N	Y	N	N	Y	N
14 Speier	Y	N	Y	N	N	Y	N
15 Swalwell	Y	N	Y	N	N	Y	N
16 Costa	Y	N	Y	N	N	Y	N
17 Khanna	Y	N	Y	N	N	Y	N
18 Eshoo	Y	N	Y	N	N	Y	N
19 Lofgren	Y	N	Y	N	N	Y	N
20 Panetta	Y	N	Y	N	N	Y	N
21 **Valadao**	N	Y	Y	Y	Y	N	Y
22 **Nunes**	N	Y	Y	Y	Y	–	+
23 **McCarthy**	N	Y	Y	Y	Y	N	Y
24 Carbajal	Y	N	Y	N	N	Y	N
25 **Knight**	N	Y	Y	Y	Y	N	Y
26 Brownley	Y	N	Y	N	N	Y	N
27 Chu	Y	N	Y	N	N	Y	N
28 Schiff	Y	N	Y	N	N	Y	N
29 Cardenas	Y	N	Y	N	N	Y	N
30 Sherman	Y	N	Y	N	N	Y	N
31 Aguilar	Y	N	Y	N	N	Y	N
32 Napolitano	+	–	+	–	–	+	–
33 Lieu	Y	N	Y	N	N	Y	N
34 Vacant							
35 Torres	Y	N	Y	N	N	Y	N
36 Ruiz	Y	N	Y	N	N	Y	N
37 Bass	Y	N	Y	N	N	Y	N
38 Sánchez, Linda	Y	N	Y	N	N	Y	N
39 **Royce**	N	Y	Y	Y	Y	N	Y
40 Roybal-Allard	Y	N	Y	N	N	Y	N
41 Takano	Y	N	Y	N	N	Y	N
42 **Calvert**	N	Y	Y	Y	Y	N	Y
43 Waters	Y	N	Y	N	N	Y	N
44 Barragan	Y	N	Y	N	N	Y	N
45 **Walters**	N	Y	Y	Y	Y	N	Y
46 Correa	Y	N	Y	N	N	Y	N
47 Lowenthal	Y	N	Y	N	N	Y	N
48 **Rohrabacher**	N	Y	Y	Y	Y	N	Y
49 **Issa**	N	Y	Y	Y	Y	N	Y
50 **Hunter**	N	Y	Y	Y	Y	N	Y
51 Vargas	Y	N	Y	N	N	Y	N
52 Peters	Y	N	Y	N	N	Y	N
53 Davis	Y	N	Y	N	N	Y	N

	336	337	338	339	340	341	342
COLORADO							
1 DeGette	Y	N	Y	N	N	Y	N
2 Polis	Y	N	Y	N	N	Y	N
3 **Tipton**	N	Y	Y	Y	Y	N	Y
4 **Buck**	N	Y	Y	Y	Y	N	Y
5 **Lamborn**	N	Y	Y	Y	Y	N	Y
6 **Coffman**	N	Y	Y	Y	Y	N	Y
7 Perlmutter	Y	N	Y	N	N	Y	N
CONNECTICUT							
1 Larson	Y	N	Y	N	N	?	N
2 Courtney	Y	N	Y	N	N	Y	N
3 DeLauro	Y	N	Y	N	N	Y	N
4 Himes	Y	N	Y	N	N	Y	N
5 Esty	Y	N	Y	N	N	Y	N
DELAWARE							
AL Blunt Rochester	Y	N	Y	N	N	Y	N
FLORIDA							
1 **Gaetz**	N	Y	Y	Y	Y	N	Y
2 **Dunn**	N	Y	Y	Y	Y	N	Y
3 **Yoho**	N	Y	Y	Y	Y	N	Y
4 **Rutherford**	N	Y	Y	Y	Y	N	Y
5 Lawson	Y	N	Y	N	N	Y	N
6 **DeSantis**	N	Y	Y	Y	Y	N	Y
7 Murphy	Y	N	Y	N	N	Y	N
8 **Posey**	N	Y	Y	Y	Y	N	Y
9 Soto	Y	N	Y	N	N	Y	N
10 Demings	Y	N	Y	N	N	Y	N
11 **Webster**	N	Y	Y	Y	Y	N	Y
12 **Bilirakis**	N	Y	Y	Y	Y	N	Y
13 Crist	Y	N	Y	N	N	Y	N
14 Castor	Y	N	?	N	N	Y	N
15 **Ross**	N	Y	Y	Y	Y	N	Y
16 **Buchanan**	N	Y	Y	Y	Y	N	Y
17 **Rooney, T.**	N	Y	Y	Y	Y	N	Y
18 **Mast**	N	Y	Y	Y	Y	N	Y
19 **Rooney, F.**	N	Y	Y	Y	Y	N	Y
20 Hastings	Y	N	Y	N	N	Y	N
21 Frankel	Y	N	Y	N	N	+	N
22 Deutch	Y	N	Y	N	N	Y	N
23 Wasserman Schultz	Y	N	Y	N	N	Y	N
24 Wilson	Y	N	Y	N	N	Y	N
25 **Diaz-Balart**	N	Y	Y	Y	Y	N	Y
26 **Curbelo**	N	Y	Y	Y	Y	N	N
27 **Ros-Lehtinen**	N	N	Y	Y	Y	N	N
GEORGIA							
1 **Carter**	N	Y	Y	Y	Y	N	Y
2 Bishop	Y	N	Y	N	N	Y	N
3 **Ferguson**	N	Y	Y	Y	Y	N	Y
4 Johnson	Y	N	Y	N	N	Y	N
5 Lewis	Y	N	Y	N	N	Y	N
6 **Handel**	N	Y	Y	Y	Y	N	Y
7 **Woodall**	N	Y	?	Y	Y	N	Y
8 **Scott, A.**	N	Y	Y	Y	Y	N	Y
9 **Collins**	N	Y	Y	Y	Y	N	Y
10 **Hice**	N	Y	Y	Y	Y	N	Y
11 **Loudermilk**	N	Y	Y	Y	Y	N	Y
12 **Allen**	N	Y	Y	Y	Y	N	Y
13 Scott, D.	Y	N	Y	N	N	Y	N
14 **Graves**	N	Y	Y	Y	Y	N	Y
HAWAII							
1 Hanabusa	Y	N	Y	N	N	Y	N
2 Gabbard	Y	N	Y	N	N	Y	N
IDAHO							
1 **Labrador**	N	Y	Y	Y	Y	N	Y
2 **Simpson**	N	Y	Y	Y	Y	N	Y
ILLINOIS							
1 Rush	Y	N	Y	N	N	?	N
2 Kelly	Y	N	Y	N	N	Y	N
3 Lipinski	Y	N	Y	N	N	Y	N
4 Gutierrez	Y	N	Y	?	N	Y	N
5 Quigley	Y	N	Y	N	N	Y	N
6 **Roskam**	N	Y	Y	Y	Y	N	Y
7 Davis, D.	Y	N	Y	N	N	Y	N
8 Krishnamoorthi	Y	N	Y	N	N	Y	N
9 Schakowsky	Y	N	Y	N	N	Y	N
10 Schneider	Y	N	Y	N	N	Y	N
11 Foster	Y	N	Y	N	N	Y	N
12 **Bost**	N	Y	Y	Y	Y	N	Y
13 **Davis, R.**	N	Y	Y	Y	Y	N	Y
14 **Hultgren**	N	Y	Y	Y	Y	N	Y
15 **Shimkus**	N	Y	Y	Y	Y	N	Y

	336	337	338	339	340	341	342
16 **Kinzinger**	N	Y	Y	Y	Y	N	Y
17 Bustos	Y	N	Y	N	N	Y	N
18 **LaHood**	N	Y	Y	Y	Y	N	Y
INDIANA							
1 Visclosky	Y	N	Y	N	N	Y	N
2 **Walorski**	N	Y	Y	Y	Y	N	Y
3 **Banks**	N	Y	Y	Y	Y	N	Y
4 **Rokita**	N	Y	Y	Y	Y	N	Y
5 **Brooks**	N	Y	Y	Y	Y	N	Y
6 **Messer**	N	Y	Y	Y	Y	N	Y
7 Carson	Y	N	Y	N	N	?	N
8 **Bucshon**	N	Y	Y	Y	Y	N	Y
9 **Hollingsworth**	N	Y	Y	Y	Y	N	Y
IOWA							
1 **Blum**	N	Y	Y	Y	Y	N	Y
2 Loebsack	Y	N	Y	N	N	Y	N
3 **Young**	N	Y	Y	Y	Y	N	Y
4 **King**	N	Y	Y	Y	Y	N	Y
KANSAS							
1 **Marshall**	N	Y	Y	Y	Y	N	Y
2 **Jenkins**	N	Y	Y	Y	Y	N	Y
3 **Yoder**	N	Y	Y	Y	Y	N	Y
4 **Estes**	N	Y	Y	Y	Y	N	Y
KENTUCKY							
1 **Comer**	N	Y	Y	Y	Y	N	Y
2 **Guthrie**	N	Y	Y	Y	Y	N	Y
3 Yarmuth	Y	N	Y	N	N	Y	N
4 **Massie**	N	N	Y	Y	Y	N	Y
5 **Rogers**	N	Y	Y	Y	Y	N	Y
6 **Barr**	N	Y	Y	Y	Y	N	Y
LOUISIANA							
1 **Scalise**	–	+	+	+	+	–	+
2 Richmond	Y	N	Y	N	N	Y	N
3 **Higgins**	N	Y	Y	Y	Y	N	Y
4 **Johnson**	N	Y	Y	Y	Y	N	Y
5 **Abraham**	N	Y	Y	Y	Y	N	Y
6 **Graves**	N	Y	Y	Y	Y	N	Y
MAINE							
1 Pingree	Y	N	Y	N	N	Y	N
2 **Poliquin**	N	Y	Y	Y	Y	N	Y
MARYLAND							
1 **Harris**	N	Y	Y	Y	Y	N	Y
2 Ruppersberger	Y	N	Y	N	N	Y	N
3 Sarbanes	Y	N	Y	N	N	Y	N
4 Brown	Y	N	Y	N	N	Y	N
5 Hoyer	Y	N	Y	N	N	Y	N
6 Delaney	Y	N	Y	N	N	Y	N
7 Cummings	?	?	?	?	?	?	?
8 Raskin	Y	N	Y	N	N	Y	N
MASSACHUSETTS							
1 Neal	Y	N	Y	N	N	Y	N
2 McGovern	Y	N	Y	N	N	Y	N
3 Tsongas	Y	N	Y	N	N	Y	N
4 Kennedy	Y	N	Y	N	N	Y	N
5 Clark	Y	N	Y	N	N	Y	N
6 Moulton	Y	N	Y	N	N	Y	N
7 Capuano	Y	N	Y	N	N	Y	N
8 Lynch	Y	N	Y	N	N	Y	N
9 Keating	Y	N	Y	N	N	Y	N
MICHIGAN							
1 **Bergman**	N	Y	Y	Y	Y	N	Y
2 **Huizenga**	N	Y	Y	Y	Y	+	Y
3 **Amash**	N	N	Y	Y	Y	N	N
4 **Moolenaar**	N	Y	Y	Y	Y	N	Y
5 Kildee	Y	N	Y	N	N	Y	N
6 **Upton**	N	Y	Y	Y	Y	N	Y
7 **Walberg**	N	Y	Y	Y	Y	N	Y
8 **Bishop**	N	Y	Y	Y	Y	N	Y
9 Levin	Y	N	Y	N	N	Y	N
10 **Mitchell**	N	Y	Y	Y	Y	N	Y
11 **Trott**	N	Y	Y	Y	Y	N	Y
12 Dingell	Y	N	Y	N	N	Y	N
13 Conyers	Y	N	Y	N	N	Y	N
14 Lawrence	Y	N	Y	N	N	Y	N
MINNESOTA							
1 Walz	Y	N	Y	N	N	Y	N
2 **Lewis**	N	Y	Y	Y	Y	N	Y
3 **Paulsen**	N	Y	Y	Y	Y	N	Y
4 McCollum	Y	N	Y	N	N	Y	N

	336	337	338	339	340	341	342
5 Ellison	Y	N	Y	N	N	Y	N
6 **Emmer**	N	N	Y	Y	Y	N	Y
7 Peterson	Y	N	Y	N	N	Y	Y
8 Nolan	Y	N	Y	N	N	Y	N
MISSISSIPPI							
1 **Kelly**	N	Y	Y	Y	Y	N	Y
2 Thompson	Y	N	Y	N	N	Y	N
3 **Harper**	N	Y	Y	Y	Y	N	Y
4 **Palazzo**	N	Y	Y	Y	Y	N	Y
MISSOURI							
1 Clay	Y	N	Y	N	N	Y	N
2 **Wagner**	N	Y	Y	Y	Y	N	Y
3 **Luetkemeyer**	N	Y	Y	Y	Y	N	Y
4 **Hartzler**	N	Y	Y	Y	Y	N	Y
5 Cleaver	Y	N	Y	N	N	Y	N
6 **Graves**	N	Y	Y	Y	Y	N	Y
7 **Long**	–	+	+	+	+	–	+
8 **Smith**	N	Y	Y	Y	Y	N	Y
MONTANA							
AL **Gianforte**	N	Y	Y	Y	Y	N	Y
NEBRASKA							
1 **Fortenberry**	N	Y	Y	Y	Y	N	Y
2 **Bacon**	N	Y	Y	Y	Y	N	Y
3 **Smith**	N	Y	Y	Y	Y	N	Y
NEVADA							
1 Titus	Y	N	Y	N	N	Y	N
2 **Amodei**	N	Y	Y	Y	Y	N	Y
3 Rosen	Y	N	Y	N	N	Y	N
4 Kihuen	Y	N	Y	N	N	Y	N
NEW HAMPSHIRE							
1 Shea-Porter	Y	N	Y	N	N	Y	N
2 Kuster	Y	N	Y	N	N	Y	N
NEW JERSEY							
1 Norcross	Y	N	Y	N	N	Y	N
2 **LoBiondo**	N	Y	Y	Y	Y	N	Y
3 **MacArthur**	N	Y	Y	Y	Y	N	Y
4 **Smith**	N	Y	Y	Y	Y	N	+
5 Gottheimer	Y	N	Y	N	N	Y	N
6 Pallone	Y	N	Y	N	N	Y	N
7 **Lance**	N	Y	Y	Y	Y	N	Y
8 Sires	Y	N	Y	N	N	Y	N
9 Pascrell	Y	N	Y	N	N	Y	N
10 Payne	Y	N	Y	N	N	Y	N
11 **Frelinghuysen**	N	Y	Y	Y	Y	N	Y
12 Watson Coleman	Y	N	Y	N	N	Y	N
NEW MEXICO							
1 Lujan Grisham	Y	N	Y	N	N	Y	N
2 **Pearce**	N	Y	Y	Y	Y	N	Y
3 Luján	Y	N	Y	N	N	Y	N
NEW YORK							
1 **Zeldin**	N	Y	Y	Y	Y	N	Y
2 **King**	N	Y	Y	Y	Y	N	N
3 Suozzi	Y	N	Y	N	N	Y	N
4 Rice	Y	N	Y	N	N	Y	N
5 Meeks	Y	N	Y	N	N	?	N
6 Meng	Y	N	Y	N	N	Y	N
7 Velázquez	Y	N	Y	N	N	Y	N
8 Jeffries	Y	N	Y	N	N	Y	N
9 Clarke	Y	N	Y	N	N	Y	N
10 Nadler	Y	N	Y	N	N	Y	N
11 **Donovan**	N	Y	Y	Y	Y	N	N
12 Maloney, C.	Y	N	Y	N	N	Y	N
13 Espaillat	Y	N	Y	N	N	Y	N
14 Crowley	Y	N	Y	N	N	Y	N
15 Serrano	Y	N	Y	N	N	Y	N
16 Engel	Y	N	Y	?	N	Y	N
17 Lowey	Y	N	Y	N	N	Y	N
18 Maloney, S.P.	Y	N	Y	N	N	Y	N
19 **Faso**	N	Y	Y	Y	Y	N	Y
20 Tonko	Y	N	Y	N	N	Y	N
21 **Stefanik**	N	Y	Y	Y	Y	N	Y
22 **Tenney**	N	Y	Y	Y	Y	N	Y
23 **Reed**	N	Y	Y	Y	Y	N	Y
24 **Katko**	N	Y	Y	Y	Y	?	Y
25 Slaughter	Y	N	Y	N	N	Y	N
26 Higgins	Y	N	Y	N	N	Y	N
27 **Collins**	N	Y	Y	Y	Y	N	Y
NORTH CAROLINA							
1 Butterfield	Y	N	Y	N	N	Y	N
2 **Holding**	N	Y	Y	Y	Y	N	Y
3 **Jones**	N	N	Y	N	Y	N	Y
4 Price	Y	N	Y	N	N	Y	N

	336	337	338	339	340	341	342
5 **Foxx**	N	Y	Y	Y	Y	N	Y
6 **Walker**	N	Y	Y	Y	Y	?	Y
7 **Rouzer**	N	Y	Y	Y	Y	N	Y
8 **Hudson**	N	Y	Y	Y	Y	N	Y
9 **Pittenger**	N	Y	?	Y	Y	N	Y
10 **McHenry**	N	Y	Y	Y	Y	N	Y
11 **Meadows**	N	Y	Y	Y	Y	N	+
12 Adams	Y	N	Y	N	N	Y	N
13 **Budd**	N	Y	Y	Y	Y	N	Y
NORTH DAKOTA							
AL **Cramer**	N	Y	Y	Y	Y	N	Y
OHIO							
1 **Chabot**	N	Y	Y	Y	Y	N	Y
2 **Wenstrup**	N	Y	Y	Y	Y	N	Y
3 Beatty	Y	N	Y	N	N	+	N
4 **Jordan**	N	Y	Y	Y	Y	N	Y
5 **Latta**	N	Y	Y	Y	Y	N	Y
6 **Johnson**	N	Y	Y	Y	Y	N	Y
7 **Gibbs**	N	Y	Y	Y	Y	N	Y
8 **Davidson**	N	Y	Y	Y	Y	N	Y
9 Kaptur	Y	N	Y	N	N	Y	N
10 **Turner**	N	Y	Y	Y	Y	N	Y
11 Fudge	Y	N	Y	N	N	Y	N
12 **Tiberi**	N	Y	Y	Y	Y	N	Y
13 Ryan	Y	N	Y	N	N	Y	N
14 **Joyce**	N	Y	Y	Y	Y	N	Y
15 **Stivers**	?	?	?	?	?	?	?
16 **Renacci**	?	?	?	Y	Y	N	Y
OKLAHOMA							
1 **Bridenstine**	N	Y	Y	Y	Y	N	Y
2 **Mullin**	N	Y	Y	Y	Y	N	Y
3 **Lucas**	N	Y	Y	Y	Y	N	Y
4 **Cole**	N	Y	Y	Y	Y	N	Y
5 **Russell**	N	N	Y	Y	Y	N	Y
OREGON							
1 Bonamici	Y	N	Y	N	N	Y	N
2 **Walden**	N	Y	Y	Y	Y	N	Y
3 Blumenauer	Y	N	Y	N	N	Y	N
4 DeFazio	Y	N	Y	N	N	Y	N
5 Schrader	Y	N	Y	N	N	Y	N
PENNSYLVANIA							
1 Brady	Y	N	Y	N	N	Y	N
2 Evans	Y	N	Y	N	N	Y	N
3 **Kelly**	N	Y	Y	Y	Y	N	Y
4 **Perry**	N	Y	Y	Y	Y	N	Y
5 **Thompson**	N	Y	Y	Y	Y	N	Y
6 **Costello**	N	N	Y	Y	Y	N	Y
7 **Meehan**	N	N	Y	Y	Y	N	Y
8 **Fitzpatrick**	N	Y	Y	Y	Y	N	Y
9 **Shuster**	N	Y	Y	Y	Y	N	Y
10 **Marino**	N	N	Y	Y	Y	N	Y
11 **Barletta**	N	Y	Y	Y	Y	N	Y
12 **Rothfus**	N	Y	Y	Y	Y	N	Y
13 Boyle	Y	N	Y	N	N	Y	N
14 Doyle	Y	N	Y	N	N	Y	N
15 **Dent**	N	Y	Y	Y	Y	N	Y
16 **Smucker**	N	Y	Y	Y	Y	N	Y
17 Cartwright	Y	N	Y	N	N	Y	Y
18 **Murphy**	N	Y	Y	Y	Y	N	Y
RHODE ISLAND							
1 Cicilline	Y	N	Y	N	N	Y	N
2 Langevin	Y	N	Y	N	N	Y	N
SOUTH CAROLINA							
1 **Sanford**	N	Y	Y	Y	Y	N	Y
2 **Wilson**	N	Y	Y	Y	Y	N	Y
3 **Duncan**	N	Y	Y	Y	Y	N	Y
4 **Gowdy**	N	Y	Y	Y	Y	N	Y
5 **Norman**	N	Y	Y	Y	Y	N	Y
6 Clyburn	Y	N	Y	N	N	Y	N
7 **Rice**	N	Y	Y	Y	Y	N	Y
SOUTH DAKOTA							
AL **Noem**	N	Y	Y	Y	Y	N	Y
TENNESSEE							
1 **Roe**	N	Y	Y	Y	Y	N	Y
2 **Duncan**	N	N	Y	Y	Y	N	Y
3 **Fleischmann**	N	Y	Y	Y	Y	N	Y
4 **DesJarlais**	N	Y	Y	Y	Y	N	Y
5 Cooper	Y	N	Y	N	N	Y	N
6 **Black**	N	Y	Y	Y	Y	N	Y
7 **Blackburn**	N	Y	Y	Y	Y	N	Y
8 **Kustoff**	N	N	Y	Y	Y	N	Y
9 Cohen	Y	N	Y	N	N	Y	N

	336	337	338	339	340	341	342
TEXAS							
1 **Gohmert**	N	N	Y	Y	Y	N	Y
2 **Poe**	N	N	Y	Y	Y	N	Y
3 **Johnson, S.**	N	Y	Y	Y	Y	N	Y
4 **Ratcliffe**	N	Y	Y	Y	Y	N	Y
5 **Hensarling**	N	Y	Y	Y	Y	N	Y
6 **Barton**	N	Y	Y	Y	Y	N	Y
7 **Culberson**	N	Y	Y	Y	Y	N	Y
8 **Brady**	–	Y	Y	Y	Y	N	Y
9 Green, A.	Y	N	Y	N	N	Y	N
10 **McCaul**	N	Y	Y	Y	Y	N	Y
11 **Conaway**	N	Y	Y	Y	Y	N	Y
12 **Granger**	N	Y	Y	Y	Y	N	Y
13 **Thornberry**	N	Y	Y	Y	Y	N	Y
14 **Weber**	N	Y	Y	Y	Y	N	Y
15 Gonzalez	Y	N	Y	N	N	Y	N
16 O'Rourke	Y	N	Y	N	N	Y	N
17 **Flores**	N	Y	Y	Y	Y	N	Y
18 Jackson Lee	Y	N	Y	N	N	Y	N
19 **Arrington**	N	Y	Y	Y	Y	N	Y
20 Castro	Y	N	Y	N	N	Y	N
21 **Smith**	N	Y	Y	Y	Y	N	Y
22 **Olson**	N	Y	Y	Y	Y	N	Y
23 **Hurd**	N	Y	Y	Y	Y	N	Y
24 **Marchant**	N	Y	Y	Y	Y	N	Y
25 **Williams**	N	Y	Y	Y	Y	N	Y
26 **Burgess**	N	Y	?	Y	Y	N	Y
27 **Farenthold**	N	Y	Y	Y	Y	N	Y
28 Cuellar	Y	N	Y	N	N	Y	Y
29 Green, G.	Y	N	Y	N	N	Y	N
30 Johnson, E.B.	Y	N	Y	N	N	Y	N
31 **Carter**	N	Y	Y	Y	Y	N	Y
32 **Sessions**	N	Y	Y	Y	Y	N	Y
33 Veasey	Y	N	Y	N	N	Y	N
34 Vela	Y	N	Y	N	N	Y	N
35 Doggett	Y	N	Y	N	N	Y	N
36 **Babin**	N	Y	Y	Y	Y	N	Y
UTAH							
1 **Bishop**	N	Y	Y	Y	Y	?	Y
2 **Stewart**	N	Y	Y	Y	Y	N	Y
3 **Chaffetz**	N	Y	Y	Y	Y	?	?
4 **Love**	N	Y	Y	Y	Y	N	Y
VERMONT							
AL Welch	Y	N	Y	N	N	Y	N
VIRGINIA							
1 **Wittman**	N	Y	Y	Y	Y	N	Y
2 **Taylor**	N	Y	Y	Y	Y	N	Y
3 Scott	Y	N	Y	N	N	Y	N
4 McEachin	Y	N	Y	N	N	Y	N
5 **Garrett**	N	N	Y	Y	Y	N	Y
6 **Goodlatte**	N	Y	Y	Y	Y	N	Y
7 **Brat**	N	Y	Y	Y	Y	N	Y
8 Beyer	Y	N	Y	N	N	?	N
9 **Griffith**	N	N	Y	Y	Y	N	Y
10 **Comstock**	N	Y	Y	Y	Y	N	Y
11 Connolly	Y	N	Y	N	N	Y	N
WASHINGTON							
1 DelBene	Y	N	Y	N	N	Y	N
2 Larsen	Y	N	Y	N	N	?	N
3 **Herrera Beutler**	N	Y	Y	Y	Y	N	Y
4 **Newhouse**	N	Y	Y	Y	Y	N	Y
5 **McMorris Rodgers**	N	Y	Y	Y	Y	N	Y
6 Kilmer	Y	N	Y	N	N	Y	N
7 Jayapal	Y	N	Y	N	N	Y	N
8 **Reichert**	N	Y	Y	Y	Y	N	N
9 Smith	Y	N	Y	N	N	+	N
10 Heck	Y	N	Y	N	N	Y	N
WEST VIRGINIA							
1 **McKinley**	N	Y	Y	Y	Y	N	Y
2 **Mooney**	N	Y	Y	Y	Y	N	Y
3 **Jenkins**	N	Y	Y	Y	Y	N	Y
WISCONSIN							
1 **Ryan**		Y					
2 Pocan	Y	N	Y	N	N	Y	N
3 Kind	Y	N	Y	N	N	Y	N
4 Moore	Y	N	Y	N	N	Y	N
5 **Sensenbrenner**	N	Y	Y	Y	Y	N	Y
6 **Grothman**	N	Y	Y	Y	Y	N	Y
7 **Duffy**	N	Y	Y	Y	Y	N	Y
8 **Gallagher**	N	Y	Y	Y	Y	N	Y
WYOMING							
AL **Cheney**	N	Y	Y	Y	Y	N	Y

VOTE NUMBER

343. HR 3004. UNDOCUMENTED IMMIGRANT SENTENCING GUIDE-LINES/RECOMMIT. Lofgren, D-Calif., motion to recommit the bill to the House Judiciary Committee with instructions to report it back immediately with an amendment that would exempt from the bill's provisions victims of sex trafficking that voluntarily present themselves at a port of entry and request protection. Motion rejected 193-232 : R 2-232; D 191-0. June 29, 2017.

344. HR 3004. UNDOCUMENTED IMMIGRANT SENTENCING GUIDE-LINES/PASSAGE. Passage of the bill that would establish specific possible fines and prison sentences for undocumented immigrants convicted of certain criminal offenses and who illegally return to the United States despite having been previously deported or otherwise excluded from the country. The bill would establish maximum sentences for such individuals with varying criminal histories, including a 10-year maximum sentence for illegal immigrants who reattempt to enter the country after three or more deportations, even if such individuals have not been convicted of any other crimes. Passed 257-167 : R 233-1; D 24-166. June 29, 2017.

345. HR 1397. MOORE COLONIAL FARM LAND CONVEYANCE/PASSAGE. LaHood, R-Ill., motion to suspend the rules and pass the bill that would allow the Interior Department to transfer administrative jurisdiction of .342 acres of its land within the boundary of the Claude Moore Colonial Farm to the Transportation Department, and would allow the Transportation Department to transfer .479 acres of Transportation Department land within the boundary of the Federal Highway Administration's Turner-Fairbank Highway Research Center to the Interior Department. Motion agreed to 406-0 : R 226-0; D 180-0. July 11, 2017.

346. HR 1719. MUIR HISTORIC SITE EXPANSION/PASSAGE. LaHood, R-Ill., motion to suspend the rules and pass the bill that would allow the Interior Department to acquire approximately 44 acres of land in Martinez, Calif., from the Muir Heritage Land Trust to be administered as part of the John Muir National Historic Site, and would allow the department to adjust the boundaries of the historic site to include the acquired land. Motion agreed to 401-15 : R 216-15; D 185-0. July 11, 2017.

347. HR 2810, HR 23, H RES 431. FISCAL 2018 DEFENSE AUTHORIZATION AND CALIFORNIA DROUGHT PROTECTION/PREVIOUS QUESTION. Byrne, R-Ala., motion to order the previous question (thus ending debate and possibility of amendment) on the rule (H Res 431) that would provide for House floor consideration of the bill (HR 2810) that would authorize $688.3 billion in discretionary funding for defense programs in fiscal 2018. The total would include $74.6 billion for Overseas Contingency Operations funds, including $10 billion for non-war, base defense budget needs. The rule would also provide for consideration of the bill (HR 23) that would require the Interior Department to take certain actions to increase the availability of water in California's Central Valley when water levels are low. Motion agreed to 234-183 : R 234-0; D 0-183. July 12, 2017.

348. HR 2810, HR 23, H RES 431. FISCAL 2018 DEFENSE AUTHORIZATION AND CALIFORNIA DROUGHT PROTECTION/RULE. Adoption of the rule (H Res 431) that would provide for House floor consideration of the bill (HR 2810) that would authorize $688.3 billion in discretionary funding for defense programs in fiscal 2018. The total would include $74.6 billion for Overseas Contingency Operations funds, including $10 billion for non-war, base defense budget needs. The rule would also provide for consideration of the bill (HR 23) that would require the Interior Department to take certain actions to increase the availability of water in California's Central Valley when water levels are low. Adopted 232-187 : R 232-1; D 0-186. July 12, 2017.

	343	344	345	346	347	348
ALABAMA						
1 Byrne	N	Y	Y	Y	Y	Y
2 Roby	N	Y	Y	Y	Y	Y
3 Rogers	N	Y	Y	Y	Y	Y
4 Aderholt	N	Y	Y	Y	Y	Y
5 Brooks	N	Y	Y	Y	Y	Y
6 Palmer	N	Y	Y	Y	Y	Y
7 Sewell	Y	N	Y	Y	N	N
ALASKA						
AL Young	N	Y	Y	Y	Y	Y
ARIZONA						
1 O'Halleran	Y	Y	Y	Y	N	N
2 McSally	N	Y	Y	Y	Y	Y
3 Grijalva	Y	N	?	Y	N	N
4 Gosar	?	?	?	?	Y	Y
5 Biggs	N	Y	Y	N	Y	Y
6 Schweikert	N	Y	?	Y	Y	Y
7 Gallego	Y	N	Y	N	N	N
8 Franks	N	Y	Y	Y	Y	Y
9 Sinema	Y	Y	Y	Y	N	N
ARKANSAS						
1 Crawford	N	Y	Y	Y	Y	Y
2 Hill	N	Y	Y	Y	Y	Y
3 Womack	N	Y	Y	Y	Y	Y
4 Westerman	N	Y	Y	Y	Y	Y
CALIFORNIA						
1 LaMalfa	N	Y	Y	Y	Y	Y
2 Huffman	Y	N	Y	Y	N	N
3 Garamendi	Y	N	Y	Y	N	N
4 McClintock	N	Y	Y	Y	Y	Y
5 Thompson	Y	N	Y	Y	N	N
6 Matsui	Y	N	Y	Y	N	N
7 Bera	Y	N	Y	N	N	N
8 Cook	N	Y	Y	Y	Y	Y
9 McNerney	Y	N	Y	Y	N	N
10 Denham	N	Y	Y	Y	Y	Y
11 DeSaulnier	Y	N	Y	Y	N	N
12 Pelosi	Y	N	Y	Y	?	?
13 Lee	Y	N	Y	Y	N	N
14 Speier	Y	Y	Y	Y	N	N
15 Swalwell	Y	Y	Y	Y	N	N
16 Costa	Y	N	Y	Y	?	?
17 Khanna	Y	N	Y	Y	-	-
18 Eshoo	Y	N	Y	Y	N	N
19 Lofgren	Y	N	Y	Y	N	N
20 Panetta	Y	N	Y	Y	N	N
21 Valadao	N	Y	Y	Y	Y	Y
22 Nunes	-	+	Y	Y	Y	Y
23 McCarthy	N	Y	Y	Y	Y	Y
24 Carbajal	Y	N	Y	Y	N	N
25 Knight	N	Y	Y	Y	Y	Y
26 Brownley	Y	N	Y	Y	N	N
27 Chu	Y	N	Y	Y	N	N
28 Schiff	Y	N	Y	-	N	N
29 Cardenas	Y	N	Y	Y	N	N
30 Sherman	Y	N	Y	Y	N	N
31 Aguilar	Y	N	Y	Y	N	N
32 Napolitano	+	-	?	?	-	-
33 Lieu	Y	N	?	?	?	?
35 Torres	Y	N	Y	Y	?	N
36 Ruiz	Y	N	Y	Y	N	N
37 Bass	Y	N	Y	Y	N	N
38 Sánchez, Linda	Y	N	Y	Y	N	N
39 Royce	N	Y	Y	Y	Y	Y
40 Roybal-Allard	Y	N	Y	Y	N	N
41 Takano	Y	N	Y	Y	N	N
42 Calvert	N	Y	Y	Y	Y	Y
43 Waters	Y	N	Y	Y	N	N
44 Barragan	Y	N	Y	Y	N	N
45 Walters	N	Y	Y	Y	Y	Y
46 Correa	Y	N	Y	Y	N	N
47 Lowenthal	Y	N	Y	Y	N	N
48 Rohrabacher	N	Y	?	?	Y	Y
49 Issa	N	Y	Y	Y	Y	Y
50 Hunter	N	Y	Y	Y	Y	Y
51 Vargas	Y	N	Y	Y	N	N
52 Peters	Y	N	Y	Y	N	N
53 Davis	Y	N	Y	Y	N	N
COLORADO						
1 DeGette	Y	N	Y	Y	N	N
2 Polis	Y	N	Y	Y	N	N
3 Tipton	N	Y	Y	Y	Y	Y
4 Buck	N	Y	Y	Y	Y	Y
5 Lamborn	N	Y	Y	Y	Y	Y
6 Coffman	N	Y	Y	Y	Y	Y
7 Perlmutter	Y	N	?	?	N	N
CONNECTICUT						
1 Larson	Y	Y	?	Y	N	N
2 Courtney	Y	Y	Y	Y	N	N
3 DeLauro	Y	N	Y	Y	N	N
4 Himes	Y	N	Y	Y	N	N
5 Esty	Y	Y	Y	Y	N	N
DELAWARE						
AL Blunt Rochester	Y	N	Y	Y	N	N
FLORIDA						
1 Gaetz	N	Y	?	Y	Y	Y
2 Dunn	N	Y	Y	Y	Y	Y
3 Yoho	N	Y	Y	N	Y	Y
4 Rutherford	N	Y	Y	Y	Y	Y
5 Lawson	Y	N	Y	Y	N	N
6 DeSantis	N	Y	Y	Y	Y	Y
7 Murphy	Y	Y	Y	Y	N	N
8 Posey	N	Y	Y	Y	Y	Y
9 Soto	Y	N	Y	Y	N	N
10 Demings	Y	N	Y	Y	N	N
11 Webster	N	Y	Y	Y	Y	Y
12 Bilirakis	N	Y	Y	Y	Y	Y
13 Crist	Y	Y	Y	Y	N	N
14 Castor	Y	N	Y	Y	N	N
15 Ross	N	Y	Y	Y	Y	Y
16 Buchanan	N	Y	Y	Y	Y	Y
17 Rooney, T.	N	Y	?	?	Y	Y
18 Mast	N	Y	Y	Y	Y	Y
19 Rooney, F.	N	Y	Y	Y	Y	Y
20 Hastings	Y	N	Y	Y	N	N
21 Frankel	Y	N	Y	Y	N	N
22 Deutch	Y	N	Y	Y	N	N
23 Wasserman Schultz	Y	N	Y	Y	N	N
24 Wilson	Y	N	Y	Y	N	N
25 Diaz-Balart	N	Y	Y	Y	Y	Y
26 Curbelo	N	Y	Y	Y	Y	Y
27 Ros-Lehtinen	N	Y	Y	Y	Y	Y
GEORGIA						
1 Carter	N	Y	Y	Y	Y	Y
2 Bishop	Y	N	Y	Y	N	N
3 Ferguson	N	Y	Y	Y	Y	Y
4 Johnson	Y	N	Y	Y	N	N
5 Lewis	Y	N	Y	Y	N	N
6 Handel	N	Y	Y	Y	Y	Y
7 Woodall	N	Y	Y	Y	Y	Y
8 Scott, A.	N	Y	Y	Y	Y	Y
9 Collins	N	Y	?	Y	Y	Y
10 Hice	N	Y	Y	Y	Y	Y
11 Loudermilk	N	Y	Y	Y	Y	Y
12 Allen	N	Y	Y	Y	Y	Y
13 Scott, D.	Y	N	Y	Y	N	N
14 Graves	N	Y	Y	Y	Y	Y
HAWAII						
1 Hanabusa	Y	N	Y	Y	N	N
2 Gabbard	Y	N	Y	Y	N	N
IDAHO						
1 Labrador	N	Y	Y	Y	Y	Y
2 Simpson	N	Y	Y	Y	Y	Y
ILLINOIS						
1 Rush	Y	N	Y	Y	N	N
2 Kelly	Y	N	Y	Y	N	N
3 Lipinski	Y	Y	Y	Y	N	N
4 Gutierrez	Y	N	+	+	N	N
5 Quigley	Y	N	Y	Y	N	N
6 Roskam	N	Y	Y	Y	Y	Y
7 Davis, D.	Y	N	Y	Y	N	N
8 Krishnamoorthi	Y	N	Y	Y	N	N
9 Schakowsky	Y	N	Y	Y	N	N
10 Schneider	Y	N	Y	Y	N	N
11 Foster	Y	N	Y	Y	N	N
12 Bost	N	Y	Y	Y	Y	Y
13 Davis, R.	N	Y	Y	Y	Y	Y
14 Hultgren	N	Y	Y	Y	Y	Y
15 Shimkus	N	Y	Y	Y	Y	Y

KEY	**Republicans**	Democrats	*Independents*
Y Voted for (yea)	X Paired against	C Voted "present" to avoid possible conflict of interest
# Paired for	- Announced against	
+ Announced for	P Voted "present"	? Did not vote or otherwise make a position known
N Voted against (nay)		

	343	344	345	346	347	348
16 **Kinzinger**	N	Y	Y	Y	Y	Y
17 Bustos	Y	N	Y	Y	N	N
18 **LaHood**	N	Y	Y	Y	Y	Y
INDIANA						
1 Visclosky	Y	N	Y	Y	N	N
2 **Walorski**	N	Y	Y	Y	Y	Y
3 **Banks**	N	Y	Y	Y	Y	Y
4 **Rokita**	N	Y	Y	Y	Y	Y
5 **Brooks**	N	Y	Y	Y	Y	Y
6 **Messer**	N	Y	Y	Y	Y	Y
7 Carson	Y	N	Y	Y	N	N
8 **Bucshon**	N	Y	Y	Y	?	Y
9 **Hollingsworth**	N	Y	Y	Y	Y	Y
IOWA						
1 **Blum**	Y	Y	Y	Y	Y	Y
2 Loebsack	Y	N	Y	Y	N	N
3 **Young**	N	Y	Y	Y	Y	Y
4 **King**	N	Y	Y	Y	Y	Y
KANSAS						
1 **Marshall**	N	Y	Y	Y	Y	Y
2 **Jenkins**	N	Y	Y	Y	Y	Y
3 **Yoder**	N	Y	Y	Y	Y	Y
4 **Estes**	N	Y	Y	Y	Y	Y
KENTUCKY						
1 **Comer**	N	Y	Y	Y	Y	Y
2 **Guthrie**	N	Y	Y	Y	+	+
3 Yarmuth	Y	N	Y	Y	N	N
4 **Massie**	N	Y	Y	N	Y	Y
5 **Rogers**	N	Y	Y	Y	Y	Y
6 **Barr**	N	Y	Y	Y	?	?
LOUISIANA						
1 **Scalise**	–	+	+	+	+	+
2 Richmond	Y	N	Y	Y	N	N
3 **Higgins**	N	Y	Y	Y	Y	Y
4 **Johnson**	N	Y	Y	Y	Y	Y
5 **Abraham**	N	Y	Y	Y	Y	Y
6 **Graves**	N	Y	Y	Y	Y	Y
MAINE						
1 Pingree	Y	N	Y	Y	N	N
2 **Poliquin**	N	Y	Y	Y	Y	Y
MARYLAND						
1 **Harris**	N	Y	Y	N	Y	Y
2 Ruppersberger	Y	Y	Y	Y	N	N
3 Sarbanes	Y	N	Y	Y	N	N
4 Brown	Y	N	Y	Y	N	N
5 Hoyer	Y	N	?	Y	N	N
6 Delaney	Y	N	Y	Y	N	N
7 Cummings	?	?	?	?	?	?
8 Raskin	Y	N	?	?	N	N
MASSACHUSETTS						
1 Neal	Y	N	Y	Y	N	N
2 McGovern	Y	N	Y	Y	N	N
3 Tsongas	Y	N	Y	Y	N	N
4 Kennedy	Y	N	Y	Y	N	N
5 Clark	Y	N	Y	Y	N	N
6 Moulton	Y	N	Y	Y	N	N
7 Capuano	Y	N	Y	Y	N	N
8 Lynch	Y	Y	Y	Y	N	N
9 Keating	Y	Y	Y	Y	N	N
MICHIGAN						
1 **Bergman**	N	Y	Y	Y	Y	Y
2 **Huizenga**	N	Y	Y	Y	Y	Y
3 **Amash**	N	N	Y	N	Y	Y
4 **Moolenaar**	N	Y	Y	Y	Y	Y
5 Kildee	Y	N	Y	Y	N	N
6 **Upton**	N	Y	Y	Y	Y	Y
7 **Walberg**	N	Y	Y	Y	Y	Y
8 **Bishop**	N	Y	Y	Y	Y	Y
9 Levin	Y	N	Y	Y	N	N
10 **Mitchell**	N	Y	Y	Y	Y	Y
11 **Trott**	N	Y	Y	Y	Y	Y
12 Dingell	Y	N	Y	Y	N	N
13 Conyers	Y	N	Y	Y	N	N
14 Lawrence	Y	N	Y	Y	N	N
MINNESOTA						
1 Walz	Y	N	Y	Y	N	N
2 **Lewis**	N	Y	Y	Y	Y	Y
3 **Paulsen**	N	Y	Y	Y	Y	Y
4 McCollum	Y	N	Y	Y	N	N

	343	344	345	346	347	348
5 Ellison	Y	N	Y	Y	N	N
6 **Emmer**	N	Y	Y	Y	Y	Y
7 Peterson	Y	Y	Y	Y	N	N
8 Nolan	Y	N	Y	Y	N	N
MISSISSIPPI						
1 **Kelly**	N	Y	Y	Y	Y	Y
2 Thompson	Y	N	Y	Y	N	N
3 **Harper**	N	Y	Y	Y	Y	Y
4 **Palazzo**	N	Y	Y	Y	Y	Y
MISSOURI						
1 Clay	Y	N	Y	Y	N	N
2 **Wagner**	N	Y	Y	Y	Y	Y
3 **Luetkemeyer**	N	Y	Y	Y	Y	Y
4 **Hartzler**	N	Y	Y	Y	Y	Y
5 Cleaver	Y	N	?	Y	N	N
6 **Graves**	N	Y	Y	Y	Y	Y
7 **Long**	–	+	Y	Y	Y	Y
8 **Smith**	N	Y	Y	Y	Y	Y
MONTANA						
AL **Gianforte**	N	Y	Y	Y	Y	Y
NEBRASKA						
1 **Fortenberry**	N	Y	Y	Y	Y	Y
2 **Bacon**	N	Y	Y	Y	Y	Y
3 **Smith**	N	Y	Y	Y	Y	Y
NEVADA						
1 Titus	Y	N	?	?	N	N
2 **Amodei**	N	Y	Y	Y	Y	Y
3 Rosen	Y	N	Y	Y	N	N
4 Kihuen	Y	N	Y	Y	N	N
NEW HAMPSHIRE						
1 Shea-Porter	Y	N	Y	Y	–	–
2 Kuster	Y	Y	Y	Y	N	N
NEW JERSEY						
1 Norcross	Y	N	Y	Y	N	N
2 **LoBiondo**	N	Y	Y	Y	Y	Y
3 **MacArthur**	N	Y	Y	Y	Y	Y
4 **Smith**	N	Y	Y	Y	Y	Y
5 Gottheimer	Y	Y	Y	Y	N	N
6 Pallone	Y	N	Y	Y	N	N
7 **Lance**	N	Y	Y	Y	Y	Y
8 Sires	Y	N	Y	Y	?	N
9 Pascrell	Y	N	Y	Y	N	N
10 Payne	Y	N	Y	Y	N	N
11 **Frelinghuysen**	N	Y	Y	Y	Y	Y
12 Watson Coleman	Y	N	Y	Y	N	N
NEW MEXICO						
1 Lujan Grisham	Y	N	Y	Y	N	N
2 **Pearce**	N	Y	?	?	Y	Y
3 Luján	Y	N	Y	Y	N	N
NEW YORK						
1 **Zeldin**	N	Y	Y	Y	Y	Y
2 **King**	N	Y	Y	Y	Y	Y
3 Suozzi	Y	N	Y	Y	N	N
4 Rice	Y	N	Y	Y	N	N
5 Meeks	Y	N	Y	Y	N	N
6 Meng	Y	N	Y	Y	N	N
7 Velázquez	Y	N	Y	Y	N	N
8 Jeffries	Y	N	Y	Y	N	N
9 Clarke	Y	N	Y	Y	N	N
10 Nadler	Y	N	Y	Y	N	N
11 **Donovan**	N	Y	Y	Y	Y	Y
12 Maloney, C.	Y	N	Y	Y	N	N
13 Espaillat	Y	N	Y	Y	N	N
14 Crowley	Y	N	Y	Y	–	–
15 Serrano	Y	N	Y	Y	N	N
16 Engel	Y	N	Y	Y	N	N
17 Lowey	Y	N	Y	Y	N	N
18 Maloney, S.P.	Y	N	Y	Y	N	N
19 **Faso**	N	Y	Y	Y	Y	Y
20 Tonko	Y	N	Y	Y	N	N
21 **Stefanik**	N	Y	Y	Y	Y	Y
22 **Tenney**	N	Y	Y	Y	Y	Y
23 **Reed**	N	Y	Y	Y	Y	Y
24 **Katko**	N	Y	Y	Y	Y	Y
25 Slaughter	Y	N	Y	Y	N	N
26 Higgins	Y	Y	Y	Y	N	N
27 **Collins**	N	Y	Y	Y	Y	Y
NORTH CAROLINA						
1 Butterfield	Y	N	?	?	N	N
2 **Holding**	N	Y	Y	Y	Y	Y
3 **Jones**	Y	Y	Y	N	Y	Y
4 Price	Y	N	Y	Y	N	N

	343	344	345	346	347	348
5 **Foxx**	N	Y	Y	Y	Y	Y
6 **Walker**	N	Y	Y	Y	Y	Y
7 **Rouzer**	N	Y	Y	N	Y	Y
8 **Hudson**	N	Y	Y	Y	Y	Y
9 **Pittenger**	N	Y	Y	Y	Y	Y
10 **McHenry**	N	Y	Y	Y	Y	Y
11 **Meadows**	N	Y	Y	Y	Y	Y
12 Adams	Y	N	Y	Y	N	N
13 **Budd**	N	Y	Y	N	Y	Y
NORTH DAKOTA						
AL **Cramer**	N	Y	Y	Y	Y	Y
OHIO						
1 **Chabot**	N	Y	Y	Y	Y	Y
2 **Wenstrup**	N	Y	Y	Y	Y	Y
3 Beatty	Y	N	Y	Y	N	N
4 **Jordan**	N	Y	Y	N	Y	Y
5 **Latta**	N	Y	Y	Y	Y	Y
6 **Johnson**	N	Y	Y	Y	Y	Y
7 **Gibbs**	N	Y	Y	Y	Y	Y
8 **Davidson**	N	Y	Y	Y	Y	Y
9 Kaptur	Y	N	Y	Y	N	N
10 **Turner**	N	Y	Y	Y	Y	Y
11 Fudge	Y	N	Y	Y	N	N
12 **Tiberi**	N	Y	Y	Y	Y	Y
13 Ryan	Y	N	Y	Y	N	N
14 **Joyce**	N	Y	Y	Y	Y	Y
15 **Stivers**	?	?	Y	Y	Y	Y
16 **Renacci**	N	Y	Y	Y	Y	Y
OKLAHOMA						
1 **Bridenstine**	N	Y	Y	Y	Y	Y
2 **Mullin**	N	Y	Y	Y	Y	Y
3 **Lucas**	N	Y	Y	Y	Y	Y
4 **Cole**	N	Y	Y	Y	Y	Y
5 **Russell**	N	Y	Y	Y	Y	Y
OREGON						
1 Bonamici	Y	N	Y	Y	N	N
2 **Walden**	N	Y	Y	Y	Y	Y
3 Blumenauer	Y	N	Y	Y	N	N
4 DeFazio	Y	Y	Y	Y	N	N
5 Schrader	Y	N	Y	Y	N	N
PENNSYLVANIA						
1 Brady	Y	N	Y	Y	N	N
2 Evans	Y	N	Y	Y	N	N
3 **Kelly**	N	Y	Y	Y	Y	Y
4 **Perry**	N	Y	Y	Y	Y	Y
5 **Thompson**	N	Y	Y	Y	Y	Y
6 **Costello**	N	Y	Y	Y	Y	Y
7 **Meehan**	N	Y	Y	Y	Y	Y
8 **Fitzpatrick**	N	Y	Y	Y	Y	Y
9 **Shuster**	N	Y	Y	Y	Y	Y
10 **Marino**	N	Y	Y	Y	Y	Y
11 **Barletta**	N	Y	Y	Y	Y	?
12 **Rothfus**	N	Y	Y	Y	Y	Y
13 Boyle	Y	N	Y	Y	N	N
14 Doyle	Y	N	Y	Y	N	N
15 **Dent**	N	Y	Y	Y	Y	Y
16 **Smucker**	N	Y	?	Y	Y	Y
17 Cartwright	Y	Y	Y	Y	N	N
18 **Murphy**	N	Y	Y	Y	Y	Y
RHODE ISLAND						
1 Cicilline	Y	N	Y	Y	N	N
2 Langevin	Y	Y	Y	Y	N	N
SOUTH CAROLINA						
1 **Sanford**	N	Y	Y	Y	Y	Y
2 **Wilson**	N	Y	Y	Y	Y	Y
3 **Duncan**	N	Y	Y	Y	Y	Y
4 **Gowdy**	N	Y	Y	Y	Y	Y
5 **Norman**	N	Y	Y	Y	Y	Y
6 Clyburn	Y	N	Y	Y	N	N
7 **Rice**	N	Y	Y	Y	Y	Y
SOUTH DAKOTA						
AL **Noem**	N	Y	Y	Y	Y	Y
TENNESSEE						
1 **Roe**	N	Y	Y	Y	Y	Y
2 **Duncan**	N	Y	?	?	Y	Y
3 **Fleischmann**	N	Y	Y	Y	Y	Y
4 **DesJarlais**	N	Y	Y	Y	Y	Y
5 Cooper	Y	Y	Y	Y	N	N
6 **Black**	N	Y	Y	Y	Y	Y
7 **Blackburn**	N	Y	Y	Y	Y	Y
8 **Kustoff**	N	Y	Y	Y	Y	Y
9 Cohen	Y	N	Y	Y	N	N

	343	344	345	346	347	348
TEXAS						
1 **Gohmert**	N	Y	Y	Y	Y	N
2 **Poe**	N	Y	Y	Y	Y	Y
3 **Johnson, S.**	N	Y	?	?	?	?
4 **Ratcliffe**	N	Y	Y	Y	Y	Y
5 **Hensarling**	N	Y	Y	Y	Y	?
6 **Barton**	N	Y	Y	Y	Y	Y
7 **Culberson**	N	Y	Y	Y	Y	Y
8 **Brady**	N	Y	Y	Y	Y	Y
9 Green, A.	Y	N	Y	Y	N	N
10 **McCaul**	N	Y	Y	Y	Y	Y
11 **Conaway**	N	Y	Y	Y	Y	Y
12 **Granger**	N	Y	Y	Y	Y	Y
13 **Thornberry**	N	Y	Y	Y	Y	Y
14 **Weber**	N	Y	Y	N	Y	Y
15 Gonzalez	Y	N	Y	Y	N	N
16 O'Rourke	Y	N	Y	Y	N	N
17 **Flores**	N	Y	Y	Y	Y	Y
18 Jackson Lee	Y	N	Y	Y	N	N
19 **Arrington**	N	Y	Y	Y	Y	Y
20 Castro	Y	N	Y	Y	N	N
21 **Smith**	N	Y	Y	Y	Y	Y
22 **Olson**	N	Y	Y	Y	Y	Y
23 **Hurd**	N	Y	+	+	Y	Y
24 **Marchant**	N	Y	Y	Y	Y	Y
25 **Williams**	N	Y	Y	Y	Y	Y
26 **Burgess**	N	Y	Y	Y	Y	Y
27 **Farenthold**	N	Y	Y	Y	Y	Y
28 Cuellar	Y	Y	Y	Y	N	N
29 Green, G.	Y	N	Y	Y	N	N
30 Johnson, E.B.	Y	N	Y	Y	N	N
31 **Carter**	N	Y	Y	Y	Y	Y
32 **Sessions**	N	Y	Y	Y	Y	Y
33 Veasey	Y	N	Y	Y	N	N
34 Vela	Y	N	Y	Y	N	N
35 Doggett	Y	N	Y	Y	N	N
36 **Babin**	N	Y	Y	N	Y	Y
UTAH						
1 **Bishop**	N	Y	Y	Y	Y	Y
2 **Stewart**	N	Y	Y	Y	Y	Y
4 **Love**	N	Y	Y	Y	Y	Y
VERMONT						
AL Welch	Y	N	Y	Y	N	N
VIRGINIA						
1 **Wittman**	N	Y	Y	Y	Y	Y
2 **Taylor**	N	Y	Y	Y	Y	Y
3 Scott	Y	N	Y	Y	N	N
4 McEachin	Y	?	Y	Y	N	N
5 **Garrett**	N	Y	?	N	Y	Y
6 **Goodlatte**	N	Y	Y	Y	Y	Y
7 **Brat**	N	Y	Y	N	Y	Y
8 Beyer	Y	N	Y	Y	N	N
9 **Griffith**	N	Y	Y	N	Y	Y
10 **Comstock**	N	Y	Y	Y	Y	Y
11 Connolly	Y	N	Y	Y	N	N
WASHINGTON						
1 DelBene	Y	N	Y	Y	N	N
2 Larsen	Y	N	Y	Y	N	N
3 **Herrera Beutler**	N	Y	Y	Y	Y	Y
4 **Newhouse**	N	Y	Y	Y	Y	Y
5 **McMorris Rodgers**	N	Y	Y	Y	Y	Y
6 Kilmer	Y	N	Y	Y	N	N
7 Jayapal	Y	N	Y	Y	N	N
8 **Reichert**	N	Y	Y	Y	Y	Y
9 Smith	Y	N	Y	Y	N	N
10 Heck	Y	N	Y	Y	N	N
WEST VIRGINIA						
1 **McKinley**	N	Y	Y	Y	Y	Y
2 **Mooney**	N	Y	Y	N	Y	Y
3 **Jenkins**	N	Y	Y	Y	Y	Y
WISCONSIN						
1 **Ryan**						
2 Pocan	Y	N	Y	Y	N	N
3 Kind	Y	Y	Y	Y	N	N
4 Moore	Y	N	+	+	N	N
5 **Sensenbrenner**	N	Y	Y	Y	Y	Y
6 **Grothman**	N	Y	Y	Y	Y	Y
7 **Duffy**	N	Y	Y	Y	Y	Y
8 **Gallagher**	N	Y	Y	Y	Y	Y
WYOMING						
AL **Cheney**	N	Y	Y	Y	Y	Y

III HOUSE VOTES

VOTE NUMBER

349. HR 1492. ADMINISTRATION OF CONTROLLED SUBSTANCES ACROSS STATE LINES/PASSAGE. Burgess, R-Texas, motion to suspend the rules and pass the bill that would establish a separate Drug Enforcement Administration registration process for medical practitioners under the Controlled Substances Act, which would allow such registered medical professionals to transport and administer controlled substances to patients in a state other than the one in which the medical professional's principal place of business or professional practice is located. The bill would require that registered medical practitioners limit the time of transport and administration of any controlled substance to no more than 72 hours, after which the controlled substances would have to be returned to their originally registered location. Motion agreed to 416-2 : R 230-2; D 186-0. July 12, 2017.

350. HR 23. MUNICIPAL WASTEWATER RECYCLING EXPANSION/ADOPTION. DeSaulnier, D-Calif., amendment that would require the Interior Department to review available and new technologies and programs for capturing and recycling municipal wastewater for the purposes of providing drinking water and energy, and would require the department to report on the feasibility of expanding the implementation of such technologies and programs among contractors with the Central Valley Project. Rejected in Committee of the Whole 201-221 : R 12-221; D 189-0. July 12, 2017.

351. HR 23. NATIONAL INTERAGENCY FIRE CENTER EXEMPTION/ RECOMMIT. Carbajal, D-Calif., motion to recommit the bill to the House Natural Resources Committee with instructions to report it back immediately with an amendment that would exempt the National Interagency Fire Center from any of the bill's provisions that would impair the center's ability to ensure that there is an adequate supply of water to fight wildfires. Motion rejected 189-230 : R 2-230; D 187-0. July 12, 2017.

352. HR 23. CALIFORNIA DROUGHT PREVENTION/PASSAGE. Passage of the bill that would require the Interior Department to take certain actions to increase the availability of water for agricultural and other purposes in California's Central Valley, including a requirement that the maximum amount of water practicable would have to be provided to all individuals or districts that receive water through the Central Valley Project. The bill would require the department to expedite reviews of all applications for water transfers in the Central Valley and would require the department to make a determination on an application for a water transfer in the Central Valley within 45 days of the application's submission. The bill would establish the Bureau of Reclamation as the lead federal agency for the coordination of all reviews, approvals or decisions required by federal law for the construction of new or expanded surface water storage projects on federal lands. Passed 230-190 : R 226-7; D 4-183. July 12, 2017.

353. PROCEDURAL MOTION/MOTION TO ADJOURN. Motion rejected 77-326 : R 2-224; D 75-102. July 13, 2017.

354. H RES 440, HR 2810. FISCAL 2018 DEFENSE AUTHORIZATION/ PREVIOUS QUESTION. Byrne, R-Ala., motion to order the previous question (thus ending debate and the possibility of amendment) on the rule (H Res 440) providing for further House floor consideration of the bill (HR 2810) that would authorize $688.3 billion in discretionary funding for defense programs in fiscal 2018. The total would include $74.6 billion for Overseas Contingency Operations funds, including $10 billion for non-war, base defense budget needs. Motion agreed to 234-187 : R 234-0; D 0-187. July 13, 2017.

355. H RES 440, HR 2810. FISCAL 2018 DEFENSE AUTHORIZATION/RULE. Adoption of the rule (H Res 440) that would provide for further House floor consideration of the bill (HR 2810) that would authorize $688.3 billion in discretionary funding for defense programs in fiscal 2018. The total would include $74.6 billion for Overseas Contingency Operations funds, including $10 billion for non-war, base defense budget needs. Adopted 230-190 : R 229-3; D 1-187. July 13, 2017.

	349	350	351	352	353	354	355
ALABAMA							
1 Byrne	Y	N	N	Y	N	Y	Y
2 Roby	Y	N	N	Y	N	Y	Y
3 Rogers	Y	N	N	Y	N	Y	Y
4 Aderholt	Y	N	N	Y	N	Y	Y
5 Brooks	Y	N	N	Y	N	Y	Y
6 Palmer	Y	N	N	Y	N	Y	?
7 Sewell	Y	Y	Y	N	?	N	N
ALASKA							
AL Young	Y	N	N	Y	Y	Y	Y
ARIZONA							
1 O'Halleran	Y	Y	Y	N	N	N	N
2 McSally	Y	Y	N	Y	N	Y	Y
3 Grijalva	Y	Y	Y	N	?	N	N
4 Gosar	Y	N	N	Y	N	Y	Y
5 Biggs	Y	N	N	Y	N	Y	Y
6 Schweikert	Y	N	N	Y	N	Y	Y
7 Gallego	Y	Y	Y	N	Y	N	N
8 Franks	Y	N	N	Y	N	Y	Y
9 Sinema	Y	Y	Y	N	N	N	N
ARKANSAS							
1 Crawford	Y	N	N	Y	N	Y	Y
2 Hill	Y	N	N	Y	N	Y	Y
3 Womack	Y	N	N	Y	N	Y	Y
4 Westerman	Y	N	N	Y	N	Y	Y
CALIFORNIA							
1 LaMalfa	Y	Y	N	Y	N	Y	Y
2 Huffman	Y	Y	Y	N	?	N	N
3 Garamendi	Y	Y	Y	N	N	N	N
4 McClintock	Y	N	N	Y	N	Y	Y
5 Thompson	Y	Y	Y	N	N	N	N
6 Matsui	Y	Y	Y	N	N	N	N
7 Bera	Y	Y	Y	N	N	N	N
8 Cook	Y	N	N	Y	N	Y	Y
9 McNerney	Y	Y	Y	N	N	N	N
10 Denham	Y	N	N	Y	N	Y	Y
11 DeSaulnier	Y	Y	Y	N	N	N	N
12 Pelosi	Y	Y	Y	N	N	N	N
13 Lee	Y	Y	Y	N	N	N	N
14 Speier	Y	Y	Y	N	N	N	N
15 Swalwell	Y	Y	Y	N	N	N	N
16 Costa	?	Y	Y	Y	?	N	N
17 Khanna	+	+	+	-	Y	N	N
18 Eshoo	Y	Y	Y	N	N	N	N
19 Lofgren	Y	Y	Y	N	N	N	N
20 Panetta	Y	Y	Y	N	N	N	N
21 Valadao	Y	N	N	Y	N	Y	Y
22 Nunes	Y	N	N	Y	N	Y	Y
23 McCarthy	Y	N	N	Y	N	Y	Y
24 Carbajal	Y	Y	Y	N	N	N	N
25 Knight	Y	N	N	Y	N	Y	Y
26 Brownley	Y	Y	Y	N	N	N	N
27 Chu	Y	Y	Y	N	?	N	N
28 Schiff	Y	Y	Y	N	N	N	N
29 Cardenas	Y	Y	Y	N	N	N	N
30 Sherman	Y	Y	Y	N	N	N	N
31 Aguilar	Y	Y	Y	N	N	N	N
32 Napolitano	+	+	+	-	?	?	?
33 Lieu	?	?	?	?	?	?	?
34 Gomez	Y	Y	Y	N	N	N	N
35 Torres	Y	Y	Y	N	N	N	N
36 Ruiz	Y	Y	Y	N	N	N	N
37 Bass	Y	Y	Y	N	N	N	N
38 Sánchez, Linda	Y	Y	Y	N	N	N	N
39 Royce	Y	N	N	Y	?	Y	Y
40 Roybal-Allard	Y	Y	Y	N	N	N	N
41 Takano	Y	Y	Y	N	Y	N	N
42 Calvert	Y	N	N	Y	N	Y	Y
43 Waters	Y	Y	Y	N	Y	N	N
44 Barragan	Y	Y	Y	N	Y	N	N
45 Walters	Y	N	N	Y	N	Y	Y
46 Correa	Y	Y	Y	N	N	N	N
47 Lowenthal	Y	Y	Y	N	N	N	N
48 Rohrabacher	Y	N	N	Y	N	Y	Y
49 Issa	Y	N	N	Y	N	Y	Y
50 Hunter	Y	N	N	Y	N	Y	Y
51 Vargas	Y	Y	Y	N	Y	N	N
52 Peters	Y	Y	Y	N	N	?	N
53 Davis	Y	Y	Y	N	N	N	N

	349	350	351	352	353	354	355
COLORADO							
1 DeGette	Y	Y	Y	N	N	N	N
2 Polis	Y	Y	Y	N	N	N	N
3 Tipton	Y	N	N	Y	N	Y	Y
4 Buck	Y	N	N	Y	N	Y	Y
5 Lamborn	Y	N	N	Y	N	Y	Y
6 Coffman	Y	N	N	Y	N	Y	Y
7 Perlmutter	Y	Y	Y	N	N	N	N
CONNECTICUT							
1 Larson	Y	Y	Y	N	N	N	N
2 Courtney	Y	Y	+	-	N	N	N
3 DeLauro	Y	Y	Y	N	N	N	N
4 Himes	Y	+	Y	N	N	N	N
5 Esty	Y	Y	Y	N	N	N	N
DELAWARE							
AL Blunt Rochester	Y	Y	Y	N	N	N	N
FLORIDA							
1 Gaetz	Y	N	N	Y	N	Y	Y
2 Dunn	Y	N	N	Y	N	Y	Y
3 Yoho	Y	N	N	Y	N	Y	Y
4 Rutherford	Y	N	N	Y	N	Y	Y
5 Lawson	Y	Y	Y	N	Y	N	N
6 DeSantis	Y	N	N	Y	N	Y	Y
7 Murphy	Y	Y	Y	N	N	N	N
8 Posey	Y	N	N	Y	N	Y	Y
9 Soto	Y	Y	Y	N	N	N	N
10 Demings	Y	Y	Y	N	N	N	N
11 Webster	Y	N	N	Y	N	Y	Y
12 Bilirakis	Y	N	N	Y	N	Y	Y
13 Crist	Y	Y	Y	N	N	N	N
14 Castor	Y	Y	Y	N	N	N	N
15 Ross	Y	N	N	Y	N	Y	Y
16 Buchanan	Y	N	N	Y	N	Y	Y
17 Rooney, T.	Y	N	N	Y	?	Y	Y
18 Mast	Y	N	N	Y	N	Y	Y
19 Rooney, F.	Y	N	N	Y	N	Y	Y
20 Hastings	Y	Y	Y	N	N	N	N
21 Frankel	Y	Y	Y	N	N	N	N
22 Deutch	Y	Y	Y	N	N	N	N
23 Wasserman Schultz	Y	Y	Y	N	N	N	N
24 Wilson	Y	Y	Y	N	N	N	N
25 Diaz-Balart	Y	N	N	Y	N	Y	Y
26 Curbelo	Y	N	N	Y	N	Y	Y
27 Ros-Lehtinen	Y	N	N	Y	N	Y	Y
GEORGIA							
1 Carter	Y	N	N	Y	N	Y	Y
2 Bishop	Y	Y	Y	N	N	N	N
3 Ferguson	Y	N	N	Y	N	Y	Y
4 Johnson	Y	Y	Y	N	Y	N	N
5 Lewis	Y	Y	Y	N	Y	N	N
6 Handel	Y	N	N	Y	N	Y	Y
7 Woodall	Y	N	N	Y	N	Y	Y
8 Scott, A.	Y	N	N	Y	N	Y	Y
9 Collins	Y	N	N	Y	N	Y	Y
10 Hice	Y	N	N	Y	N	Y	Y
11 Loudermilk	Y	N	N	Y	N	Y	Y
12 Allen	Y	N	N	Y	N	Y	Y
13 Scott, D.	Y	Y	Y	N	N	N	N
14 Graves	Y	N	N	Y	N	Y	Y
HAWAII							
1 Hanabusa	Y	Y	Y	N	N	N	N
2 Gabbard	Y	Y	Y	N	N	N	N
IDAHO							
1 Labrador	Y	N	N	Y	N	Y	Y
2 Simpson	Y	N	N	Y	N	Y	Y
ILLINOIS							
1 Rush	Y	Y	Y	N	?	N	N
2 Kelly	Y	Y	Y	N	N	N	N
3 Lipinski	Y	Y	Y	N	N	N	N
4 Cutierrez	I	Y	Y	Y	Y	N	N
5 Quigley	Y	Y	Y	N	N	N	N
6 Roskam	Y	N	N	Y	N	?	+
7 Davis, D.	Y	Y	Y	N	N	N	N
8 Krishnamoorthi	Y	Y	Y	N	N	N	N
9 Schakowsky	Y	Y	Y	N	N	N	N
10 Schneider	Y	Y	Y	N	N	N	N
11 Foster	Y	Y	Y	N	N	N	N
12 Bost	Y	N	N	Y	N	Y	Y
13 Davis, R.	Y	-	-	+	-	+	+
14 Hultgren	Y	N	N	Y	N	Y	Y
15 Shimkus	Y	N	N	Y	N	Y	Y

KEY   **Republicans**   Democrats   *Independents*

Y Voted for (yea)	X Paired against	C Voted "present" to avoid possible conflict of interest
# Paired for	– Announced against	
+ Announced for	P Voted "present"	? Did not vote or otherwise make a position known
N Voted against (nay)		

	349	350	351	352	353	354	355
16 **Kinzinger**	Y	N	N	Y	N	Y	Y
17 Bustos	Y	Y	Y	N	N	N	N
18 **LaHood**	+	N	N	Y	N	Y	Y
INDIANA							
1 Visclosky	Y	Y	Y	N	N	N	N
2 **Walorski**	Y	N	N	Y	N	Y	Y
3 **Banks**	Y	N	N	Y	N	Y	Y
4 **Rokita**	Y	N	N	Y	N	Y	Y
5 **Brooks**	Y	N	N	Y	N	Y	Y
6 **Messer**	Y	N	N	Y	N	Y	Y
7 Carson	Y	Y	Y	N	Y	N	N
8 **Bucshon**	Y	N	N	Y	N	Y	Y
9 **Hollingsworth**	Y	N	N	Y	N	Y	Y
IOWA							
1 **Blum**	Y	N	Y	Y	N	Y	Y
2 Loebsack	Y	Y	Y	N	N	N	N
3 **Young**	Y	N	N	Y	N	Y	Y
4 **King**	Y	N	N	Y	N	Y	Y
KANSAS							
1 **Marshall**	Y	N	N	Y	N	Y	Y
2 **Jenkins**	Y	N	N	Y	N	Y	Y
3 **Yoder**	Y	N	N	Y	N	Y	Y
4 **Estes**	Y	N	N	Y	N	Y	Y
KENTUCKY							
1 **Comer**	Y	N	N	Y	N	Y	Y
2 **Guthrie**	+	–	–	+	N	Y	Y
3 Yarmuth	Y	Y	Y	N	N	N	N
4 **Massie**	N	N	N	N	N	Y	N
5 **Rogers**	Y	N	N	Y	N	Y	Y
6 **Barr**	?	?	?	?	N	Y	Y
LOUISIANA							
1 **Scalise**	+	–	–	+	–	+	+
2 Richmond	Y	Y	Y	N	Y	N	N
3 **Higgins**	Y	N	N	Y	N	Y	Y
4 **Johnson**	Y	N	N	Y	N	Y	Y
5 **Abraham**	Y	N	N	Y	N	Y	Y
6 **Graves**	Y	N	N	Y	N	Y	Y
MAINE							
1 Pingree	Y	Y	Y	N	Y	N	N
2 **Poliquin**	Y	N	N	Y	N	Y	Y
MARYLAND							
1 **Harris**	Y	N	N	Y	N	Y	Y
2 Ruppersberger	Y	Y	Y	N	N	N	N
3 Sarbanes	Y	Y	Y	N	Y	N	N
4 Brown	Y	Y	Y	N	N	N	N
5 Hoyer	Y	Y	Y	N	?	N	N
6 Delaney	Y	Y	Y	N	Y	N	N
7 Cummings	?	?	?	?	?	?	?
8 Raskin	Y	Y	Y	N	Y	N	N
MASSACHUSETTS							
1 Neal	Y	Y	Y	N	Y	N	N
2 McGovern	Y	Y	Y	N	Y	N	N
3 Tsongas	Y	Y	Y	N	N	N	N
4 Kennedy	Y	Y	Y	N	Y	N	N
5 Clark	Y	Y	Y	N	Y	N	N
6 Moulton	Y	Y	Y	N	Y	N	N
7 Capuano	Y	Y	Y	N	N	N	N
8 Lynch	Y	Y	Y	N	N	N	N
9 Keating	Y	Y	Y	N	N	N	N
MICHIGAN							
1 **Bergman**	Y	N	N	Y	N	Y	Y
2 **Huizenga**	Y	N	N	Y	N	Y	Y
3 **Amash**	Y	N	N	N	N	Y	N
4 **Moolenaar**	Y	N	N	Y	N	Y	Y
5 Kildee	Y	Y	Y	N	N	N	N
6 **Upton**	Y	N	N	Y	N	Y	Y
7 **Walberg**	Y	N	N	Y	N	Y	Y
8 **Bishop**	Y	N	N	Y	N	Y	Y
9 Levin	Y	Y	Y	N	Y	N	N
10 **Mitchell**	Y	N	N	Y	N	Y	Y
11 **Trott**	Y	N	N	Y	N	Y	Y
12 Dingell	Y	Y	Y	N	N	N	N
13 Conyers	Y	Y	Y	N	Y	N	N
14 Lawrence	Y	Y	Y	N	Y	N	N
MINNESOTA							
1 Walz	Y	Y	Y	N	Y	N	N
2 **Lewis**	Y	N	N	Y	N	Y	Y
3 **Paulsen**	Y	Y	N	Y	N	Y	Y
4 McCollum	Y	Y	Y	N	N	N	N
5 Ellison	Y	Y	Y	N	Y	N	N
6 **Emmer**	Y	N	N	Y	N	Y	Y
7 Peterson	Y	Y	Y	Y	N	N	N
8 Nolan	Y	Y	Y	N	N	N	N
MISSISSIPPI							
1 **Kelly**	Y	N	N	Y	N	Y	Y
2 Thompson	Y	Y	Y	N	Y	N	N
3 **Harper**	Y	N	N	Y	N	Y	Y
4 **Palazzo**	Y	N	N	Y	N	Y	Y
MISSOURI							
1 Clay	Y	Y	Y	N	Y	N	N
2 **Wagner**	Y	N	N	Y	N	Y	Y
3 **Luetkemeyer**	Y	N	N	Y	N	Y	Y
4 **Hartzler**	Y	N	N	Y	N	Y	Y
5 Cleaver	Y	Y	+	–	–	–	–
6 **Graves**	Y	N	N	Y	N	Y	Y
7 **Long**	Y	N	N	Y	N	Y	Y
8 **Smith**	Y	N	N	Y	N	Y	Y
MONTANA							
AL **Gianforte**	Y	N	N	Y	N	Y	Y
NEBRASKA							
1 **Fortenberry**	Y	N	N	Y	N	Y	Y
2 **Bacon**	Y	N	N	Y	N	Y	Y
3 **Smith**	Y	N	N	Y	N	Y	Y
NEVADA							
1 Titus	Y	Y	Y	N	?	N	N
2 **Amodei**	Y	N	N	Y	N	Y	Y
3 Rosen	Y	Y	Y	N	N	N	N
4 Kihuen	Y	Y	Y	N	N	N	N
NEW HAMPSHIRE							
1 Shea-Porter	+	Y	Y	N	–	N	N
2 Kuster	Y	Y	Y	N	N	N	N
NEW JERSEY							
1 Norcross	Y	Y	Y	N	N	N	N
2 **LoBiondo**	Y	Y	N	Y	N	Y	Y
3 **MacArthur**	Y	N	N	Y	N	Y	Y
4 **Smith**	Y	Y	N	Y	N	Y	Y
5 Gottheimer	Y	Y	Y	N	N	N	N
6 Pallone	Y	Y	Y	N	Y	N	N
7 **Lance**	Y	N	N	Y	N	Y	Y
8 Sires	Y	Y	Y	N	N	N	N
9 Pascrell	Y	Y	Y	N	Y	N	N
10 Payne	Y	Y	Y	N	Y	N	N
11 **Frelinghuysen**	Y	N	N	Y	N	Y	Y
12 Watson Coleman	Y	Y	Y	N	Y	N	N
NEW MEXICO							
1 Lujan Grisham	Y	Y	Y	N	N	N	N
2 **Pearce**	Y	N	N	Y	N	Y	Y
3 Luján	Y	Y	Y	N	N	N	N
NEW YORK							
1 **Zeldin**	Y	N	N	Y	N	Y	Y
2 **King**	Y	N	N	Y	N	Y	Y
3 Suozzi	Y	Y	Y	N	N	N	N
4 Rice	Y	Y	Y	N	Y	N	N
5 Meeks	Y	Y	Y	N	N	N	N
6 Meng	Y	Y	Y	N	N	N	N
7 Velázquez	Y	Y	Y	N	Y	N	N
8 Jeffries	Y	Y	Y	N	N	N	N
9 Clarke	Y	Y	Y	N	Y	N	N
10 Nadler	Y	Y	?	N	Y	N	N
11 **Donovan**	Y	N	N	Y	N	Y	Y
12 Maloney, C.	Y	Y	Y	N	Y	N	N
13 Espaillat	Y	Y	Y	N	Y	N	N
14 Crowley	+	Y	Y	N	Y	N	N
15 Serrano	Y	Y	Y	N	Y	N	N
16 Engel	Y	Y	Y	N	Y	N	N
17 Lowey	Y	Y	Y	N	Y	N	N
18 Maloney, S.P.	Y	Y	Y	N	N	N	N
19 **Faso**	Y	N	N	Y	N	Y	Y
20 Tonko	Y	Y	Y	N	N	N	N
21 **Stefanik**	Y	N	N	Y	N	Y	Y
22 **Tenney**	Y	N	N	Y	N	Y	Y
23 **Reed**	?	N	N	Y	N	Y	Y
24 **Katko**	Y	Y	N	Y	N	Y	Y
25 Slaughter	Y	Y	Y	N	Y	N	N
26 Higgins	Y	Y	Y	N	N	N	N
27 **Collins**	Y	N	N	Y	N	Y	Y
NORTH CAROLINA							
1 Butterfield	Y	Y	Y	?	N	N	N
2 **Holding**	Y	N	N	Y	N	Y	Y
3 **Jones**	Y	Y	Y	N	Y	Y	N
4 Price	Y	Y	Y	N	N	?	?
5 **Foxx**	Y	N	N	Y	N	Y	Y
6 **Walker**	Y	N	N	Y	N	Y	Y
7 **Rouzer**	Y	N	N	Y	N	Y	Y
8 **Hudson**	Y	N	–	Y	N	Y	Y
9 **Pittenger**	Y	N	N	Y	N	Y	Y
10 **McHenry**	Y	N	N	Y	N	Y	Y
11 **Meadows**	Y	N	N	Y	N	Y	Y
12 Adams	Y	Y	Y	N	Y	N	N
13 **Budd**	Y	N	N	Y	N	Y	Y
NORTH DAKOTA							
AL **Cramer**	Y	N	N	Y	N	Y	Y
OHIO							
1 **Chabot**	Y	N	N	Y	N	Y	Y
2 **Wenstrup**	Y	N	N	Y	N	Y	Y
3 Beatty	Y	Y	Y	N	Y	N	N
4 **Jordan**	Y	N	N	Y	N	Y	Y
5 **Latta**	Y	N	N	Y	N	Y	Y
6 **Johnson**	Y	N	N	Y	N	Y	Y
7 **Gibbs**	Y	N	N	Y	N	Y	Y
8 **Davidson**	?	N	N	Y	N	Y	Y
9 Kaptur	Y	Y	Y	N	Y	N	N
10 **Turner**	Y	N	N	Y	N	Y	Y
11 Fudge	Y	Y	Y	N	Y	N	N
12 **Tiberi**	Y	N	N	Y	N	Y	Y
13 Ryan	Y	Y	Y	N	N	N	N
14 **Joyce**	Y	N	N	Y	N	Y	Y
15 **Stivers**	Y	N	N	Y	N	Y	Y
16 **Renacci**	Y	N	N	Y	N	Y	Y
OKLAHOMA							
1 **Bridenstine**	Y	N	N	Y	N	Y	Y
2 **Mullin**	Y	N	N	Y	N	Y	Y
3 **Lucas**	Y	N	N	Y	N	Y	Y
4 **Cole**	Y	N	N	Y	N	Y	Y
5 **Russell**	Y	N	N	Y	?	Y	Y
OREGON							
1 Bonamici	Y	Y	Y	N	Y	N	N
2 **Walden**	Y	N	N	Y	N	Y	Y
3 Blumenauer	Y	Y	Y	N	N	N	N
4 DeFazio	Y	Y	Y	N	?	N	N
5 Schrader	Y	Y	Y	N	?	N	N
PENNSYLVANIA							
1 Brady	Y	Y	Y	N	N	N	N
2 Evans	Y	Y	Y	N	Y	N	N
3 **Kelly**	Y	N	N	Y	N	Y	Y
4 **Perry**	Y	N	N	Y	N	Y	Y
5 **Thompson**	Y	N	N	Y	?	Y	Y
6 **Costello**	Y	N	N	Y	N	Y	Y
7 **Meehan**	Y	N	N	Y	–	Y	Y
8 **Fitzpatrick**	Y	Y	N	N	N	Y	Y
9 **Shuster**	Y	N	N	Y	?	Y	Y
10 **Marino**	Y	N	N	Y	N	Y	Y
11 **Barletta**	Y	N	N	Y	?	Y	Y
12 **Rothfus**	Y	N	N	Y	N	Y	Y
13 Boyle	Y	Y	Y	N	N	N	N
14 Doyle	Y	Y	Y	N	?	N	N
15 **Dent**	Y	Y	N	Y	N	Y	Y
16 **Smucker**	Y	N	N	Y	N	Y	Y
17 Cartwright	Y	Y	Y	N	N	N	N
18 **Murphy**	Y	N	N	Y	?	Y	Y
RHODE ISLAND							
1 Cicilline	Y	Y	Y	N	Y	N	N
2 Langevin	Y	Y	Y	N	N	N	N
SOUTH CAROLINA							
1 **Sanford**	Y	N	N	N	?	?	?
2 **Wilson**	Y	N	N	Y	N	Y	Y
3 **Duncan**	Y	N	N	Y	N	Y	Y
4 **Gowdy**	Y	N	N	Y	N	Y	Y
5 **Norman**	Y	N	N	Y	N	Y	Y
6 Clyburn	Y	Y	Y	N	Y	N	N
7 **Rice**	Y	N	N	Y	N	Y	Y
SOUTH DAKOTA							
AL **Noem**	Y	N	N	Y	N	Y	Y
TENNESSEE							
1 **Roe**	Y	N	N	Y	N	Y	Y
2 **Duncan**	Y	N	N	Y	N	Y	Y
3 **Fleischmann**	Y	N	N	Y	N	Y	Y
4 **DesJarlais**	Y	N	N	Y	N	Y	Y
5 Cooper	Y	Y	Y	N	N	N	Y
6 **Black**	Y	N	N	Y	N	Y	Y
7 **Blackburn**	Y	N	N	Y	N	Y	Y
8 **Kustoff**	Y	N	N	Y	N	Y	Y
9 Cohen	Y	Y	Y	N	N	N	N
TEXAS							
1 **Gohmert**	N	N	N	Y	N	Y	Y
2 **Poe**	Y	N	N	Y	N	Y	Y
3 **Johnson, S.**	?	?	?	?	?	?	?
4 **Ratcliffe**	Y	N	N	Y	N	Y	Y
5 **Hensarling**	Y	N	N	Y	N	Y	Y
6 **Barton**	Y	N	N	Y	N	Y	Y
7 **Culberson**	Y	N	N	Y	N	Y	Y
8 **Brady**	Y	N	N	Y	N	Y	Y
9 Green, A.	Y	Y	Y	N	N	N	N
10 **McCaul**	Y	N	N	Y	N	Y	Y
11 **Conaway**	Y	N	N	Y	N	Y	Y
12 **Granger**	Y	N	N	Y	N	Y	Y
13 **Thornberry**	Y	N	N	Y	N	Y	Y
14 **Weber**	Y	N	N	Y	N	Y	Y
15 Gonzalez	Y	Y	Y	N	Y	N	N
16 O'Rourke	Y	Y	Y	N	N	N	N
17 **Flores**	Y	N	N	Y	N	Y	Y
18 Jackson Lee	Y	Y	Y	N	Y	N	N
19 **Arrington**	Y	N	N	Y	N	Y	+
20 Castro	Y	Y	Y	N	Y	N	N
21 **Smith**	Y	N	N	Y	N	Y	Y
22 **Olson**	Y	N	N	Y	N	Y	Y
23 **Hurd**	Y	N	N	Y	N	Y	Y
24 **Marchant**	Y	N	N	Y	N	Y	Y
25 **Williams**	Y	N	N	Y	N	Y	Y
26 **Burgess**	Y	N	N	Y	N	Y	Y
27 **Farenthold**	Y	N	N	Y	N	Y	Y
28 Cuellar	Y	Y	Y	Y	N	N	N
29 Green, G.	Y	Y	Y	N	N	N	N
30 Johnson, E.B.	Y	Y	Y	N	Y	N	N
31 **Carter**	Y	N	N	Y	N	Y	Y
32 **Sessions**	Y	N	N	Y	N	Y	Y
33 Veasey	Y	Y	Y	N	N	N	N
34 Vela	Y	Y	Y	N	N	N	N
35 Doggett	Y	Y	Y	N	Y	N	N
36 **Babin**	Y	N	N	Y	N	Y	Y
UTAH							
1 **Bishop**	Y	N	N	Y	?	Y	Y
2 **Stewart**	Y	N	N	Y	N	Y	Y
4 **Love**	Y	N	N	Y	N	Y	Y
VERMONT							
AL Welch	Y	Y	Y	N	N	N	N
VIRGINIA							
1 **Wittman**	Y	N	N	Y	N	Y	Y
2 **Taylor**	Y	N	N	Y	N	Y	Y
3 Scott	Y	Y	Y	N	N	N	N
4 McEachin	Y	Y	Y	N	N	N	N
5 **Garrett**	Y	N	N	N	N	Y	Y
6 **Goodlatte**	Y	N	N	Y	N	Y	Y
7 **Brat**	Y	N	N	Y	N	Y	Y
8 Beyer	Y	Y	Y	N	Y	N	N
9 **Griffith**	Y	N	N	Y	N	Y	Y
10 **Comstock**	Y	N	N	Y	N	Y	Y
11 Connolly	Y	Y	Y	N	N	N	N
WASHINGTON							
1 DelBene	Y	Y	Y	N	N	N	N
2 Larsen	Y	Y	Y	N	?	N	N
3 **Herrera Beutler**	Y	N	N	Y	N	Y	Y
4 **Newhouse**	Y	N	N	Y	N	Y	Y
5 **McMorris Rodgers**	Y	N	N	Y	N	Y	Y
6 Kilmer	Y	Y	Y	N	N	N	N
7 Jayapal	Y	Y	Y	N	Y	N	N
8 **Reichert**	Y	Y	N	Y	N	Y	Y
9 Smith	Y	Y	Y	N	N	N	N
10 Heck	Y	Y	Y	N	Y	N	N
WEST VIRGINIA							
1 **McKinley**	Y	N	N	Y	N	Y	Y
2 **Mooney**	Y	N	N	Y	N	Y	Y
3 **Jenkins**	Y	N	N	Y	N	Y	Y
WISCONSIN							
1 **Ryan**							
2 Pocan	Y	Y	Y	N	Y	N	N
3 Kind	Y	Y	Y	N	N	N	N
4 Moore	Y	Y	Y	N	Y	?	?
5 **Sensenbrenner**	Y	N	N	Y	N	Y	Y
6 **Grothman**	Y	N	N	Y	N	Y	Y
7 **Duffy**	Y	N	N	Y	N	Y	Y
8 **Gallagher**	Y	N	N	Y	N	Y	Y
WYOMING							
AL **Cheney**	Y	–	–	+	N	Y	Y

III HOUSE VOTES

VOTE NUMBER

356. HR 2810. FISCAL 2018 DEFENSE AUTHORIZATION/MILITARY BIOFUEL PROHIBITION. Conaway, R-Texas, amendment that would prohibit the Defense Department from entering into any new contracts, making any awards, or expending any funds with respect to drop-in biofuels or biorefineries. Rejected in Committee of the Whole 198-225 : R 194-40; D 4-185. July 13, 2017.

357. HR 2810. FISCAL 2018 DEFENSE AUTHORIZATION/PRESIENTIAL ONE PERCENT REDUCTION DIRECTIVE. Polis, D-Colo., amendment that would direct the president to make reductions in amounts authorized by the bill as the president considers appropriate to reach a total reduction of one percent of the funds authorized by the bill. Military, reserve and National Guard personnel accounts and the Defense Health Program account would not be eligible for such reductions. Rejected in Committee of the Whole 73-351 : R 4-231; D 69-120. July 13, 2017.

358. HR 2810. FISCAL 2018 DEFENSE AUTHORIZATION/DEFENSE AND NON-DEFENSE DISCRETIONARY SPENDING PARITY. Jayapal, D-Wash., for Pocan, D-Wis., amendment that would express the sense of Congress that any increase of the combined amount authorized for National Defense Budget and Overseas Contingency Operations should be matched by a dollar-for-dollar increase of the annual amounts authorized for the federal non-defense discretionary budget. Rejected in Committee of the Whole 179-245 : R 2-233; D 177-12. July 13, 2017.

359. HR 2810. FISCAL 2018 DEFENSE AUTHORIZATION/GUANTANAMO BAY DETAINEES TRANSFER AND RELEASE PROCEDURES. Nadler, D N.Y., amendment that would remove the bill's prohibition on the use of funds for the transfer or release of individuals detained at Guantanamo Bay to the United States. Rejected in Committee of the Whole 167-257 : R 3-232; D 164-25. July 13, 2017.

360. HR 2810. FISCAL 2018 DEFENSE AUTHORIZATION/INTERMEDIATE RANGE NUCLEAR MISSILE SYSTEM APPROVAL REQUIREMENT. Blumenauer, D-Ore., amendment that would prohibit the Department of Defense from developing and funding an intermediate range ground-launched missile system until the secretary of Defense has certified to Congress that such missile system is preferred for ensuring that the North Atlantic Treaty Organization's deterrence and defense posture remains credible in the face of a Russian intermediate ground-launched missile system, and the secretary of State has certified to Congress that such missile system is necessary to the secretary's efforts to return Russia to full compliance with the INF treaty. Rejected in Committee of the Whole 173-249 : R 1-234; D 172-15. July 13, 2017.

361. HR 2810. FISCAL 2018 DEFENSE AUTHORIZATION/NUCLEAR ARSENAL COST ESTIMATE PERIOD EXTENSION. Aguilar, D-Calif., amendment that would extend a Congressional Budget Office cost estimate review on the fielding, maintaining, modernization, replacement and life extension of nuclear weapons and nuclear weapons delivery systems from covering a 10-year period to covering a 30-year period. Rejected in Committee of the Whole 188-235 : R 7-227; D 181-8. July 13, 2017.

362. HR 2810. FISCAL 2018 DEFENSE AUTHORIZATION/NUCLEAR ARSENAL COST ESTIMATE PERIOD OPTIONAL EXTENSION. Rogers, R-Ky., amendment that would allow the secretary of Defense to include information in the annual report on the plan for US nuclear systems on the cost of fielding, maintaining, modernizing and replacing nuclear weapons and nuclear weapons delivery systems past a 10 year period. Adopted in Committee of the Whole 253-172 : R 233-2; D 20-170. July 13, 2017.

	356	357	358	359	360	361	362
ALABAMA							
1 Byrne	Y	N	N	N	N	N	Y
2 Roby	Y	N	N	N	N	N	Y
3 Rogers	Y	N	N	N	N	N	Y
4 Aderholt	Y	N	N	N	N	N	Y
5 Brooks	Y	N	N	N	N	N	Y
6 Palmer	Y	N	N	N	N	N	Y
7 Sewell	N	N	Y	N	Y	Y	N
ALASKA							
AL Young	Y	N	N	N	N	N	Y
ARIZONA							
1 O'Halleran	N	N	Y	N	N	N	Y
2 McSally	N	N	N	N	N	N	Y
3 Grijalva	N	Y	Y	Y	Y	Y	N
4 Gosar	Y	N	N	N	N	N	Y
5 Biggs	Y	N	N	N	N	N	Y
6 Schweikert	Y	N	N	N	N	N	Y
7 Gallego	N	N	Y	Y	Y	Y	Y
8 Franks	Y	N	N	N	N	N	Y
9 Sinema	N	N	N	N	N	N	Y
ARKANSAS							
1 Crawford	Y	N	N	N	N	N	Y
2 Hill	Y	N	N	N	N	N	Y
3 Womack	Y	N	N	N	N	N	Y
4 Westerman	Y	N	N	N	N	N	Y
CALIFORNIA							
1 LaMalfa	Y	N	N	N	N	N	Y
2 Huffman	N	Y	Y	Y	Y	Y	N
3 Garamendi	N	Y	Y	Y	Y	Y	N
4 McClintock	Y	N	N	N	N	N	Y
5 Thompson	N	N	Y	Y	Y	Y	N
6 Matsui	N	N	Y	Y	Y	Y	N
7 Bera	N	N	N	Y	N	N	Y
8 Cook	N	N	N	N	N	N	Y
9 McNerney	N	N	Y	Y	Y	Y	N
10 Denham	Y	N	N	N	N	N	Y
11 DeSaulnier	N	Y	Y	Y	Y	Y	N
12 Pelosi	N	Y	Y	Y	Y	Y	N
13 Lee	N	Y	Y	Y	Y	Y	N
14 Speier	N	Y	Y	Y	Y	Y	N
15 Swalwell	N	N	Y	Y	Y	Y	N
16 Costa	N	N	Y	Y	Y	Y	Y
17 Khanna	N	Y	Y	Y	Y	Y	N
18 Eshoo	N	Y	Y	Y	Y	Y	N
19 Lofgren	N	Y	Y	Y	Y	Y	N
20 Panetta	N	Y	Y	Y	Y	Y	N
21 Valadao	Y	N	N	N	N	N	Y
22 Nunes	Y	N	N	N	N	N	Y
23 McCarthy	Y	N	N	N	N	N	Y
24 Carbajal	N	N	Y	Y	+	Y	N
25 Knight	Y	N	N	N	N	N	Y
26 Brownley	N	N	Y	N	Y	Y	Y
27 Chu	N	Y	Y	Y	Y	Y	N
28 Schiff	N	N	Y	Y	Y	Y	N
29 Cardenas	N	Y	Y	Y	Y	Y	N
30 Sherman	N	Y	Y	Y	Y	Y	N
31 Aguilar	N	N	Y	N	Y	Y	N
32 Napolitano	-	+	+	+	+	+	-
33 Lieu	?	?	?	?	?	?	?
34 Gomez	N	N	Y	Y	Y	Y	N
35 Torres	N	N	Y	Y	Y	Y	N
36 Ruiz	N	N	Y	Y	Y	Y	N
37 Bass	N	Y	Y	Y	Y	Y	N
38 Sánchez, Linda	N	Y	Y	Y	Y	Y	N
39 Royce	Y	N	N	N	N	N	Y
40 Roybal-Allard	N	Y	Y	Y	Y	Y	N
41 Takano	N	Y	Y	Y	Y	Y	N
42 Calvert	Y	N	N	N	N	N	Y
43 Waters	N	Y	Y	Y	Y	Y	N
44 Barragan	N	Y	Y	Y	Y	Y	N
45 Walters	Y	N	N	N	N	N	Y
46 Correa	N	N	N	N	N	Y	N
47 Lowenthal	N	Y	Y	Y	Y	Y	N
48 Rohrabacher	Y	N	N	N	N	N	Y
49 Issa	Y	N	N	N	N	N	Y
50 Hunter	Y	N	N	N	N	N	Y
51 Vargas	N	N	Y	Y	Y	Y	N
52 Peters	N	N	N	Y	N	Y	N
53 Davis	N	N	Y	Y	Y	Y	N
COLORADO							
1 DeGette	N	N	Y	Y	Y	Y	N
2 Polis	N	Y	Y	Y	Y	Y	N
3 Tipton	Y	N	N	N	N	N	Y
4 Buck	Y	N	N	N	N	N	Y
5 Lamborn	Y	N	N	N	N	N	Y
6 Coffman	Y	N	N	N	N	N	Y
7 Perlmutter	N	N	Y	Y	Y	Y	N
CONNECTICUT							
1 Larson	N	N	Y	Y	Y	Y	N
2 Courtney	N	N	Y	Y	Y	Y	N
3 DeLauro	N	N	Y	Y	Y	Y	N
4 Himes	N	N	Y	Y	Y	Y	N
5 Esty	N	N	Y	Y	Y	Y	N
DELAWARE							
AL Blunt Rochester	N	N	Y	Y	Y	Y	N
FLORIDA							
1 Gaetz	Y	N	N	N	N	N	Y
2 Dunn	Y	N	N	N	N	N	Y
3 Yoho	Y	N	N	N	N	N	Y
4 Rutherford	Y	N	N	N	N	N	Y
5 Lawson	N	Y	N	Y	N	Y	Y
6 DeSantis	Y	N	N	N	N	N	Y
7 Murphy	N	N	Y	Y	Y	Y	N
8 Posey	Y	N	N	N	N	N	Y
9 Soto	N	N	Y	Y	Y	Y	N
10 Demings	N	N	Y	Y	Y	Y	N
11 Webster	Y	N	N	N	N	N	Y
12 Bilirakis	Y	N	N	N	N	N	Y
13 Crist	N	N	Y	Y	Y	Y	N
14 Castor	N	Y	Y	Y	Y	Y	N
15 Ross	Y	N	N	N	N	N	Y
16 Buchanan	Y	N	N	N	N	N	Y
17 Rooney, T.	Y	N	N	N	N	N	Y
18 Mast	Y	N	N	N	N	N	Y
19 Rooney, F.	Y	N	N	N	N	N	Y
20 Hastings	N	Y	Y	Y	Y	Y	N
21 Frankel	N	N	Y	Y	Y	Y	N
22 Deutch	N	N	Y	Y	Y	Y	N
23 Wasserman Schultz	N	N	Y	Y	Y	Y	N
24 Wilson	N	Y	Y	Y	Y	Y	N
25 Diaz-Balart	Y	N	N	N	N	N	Y
26 Curbelo	Y	N	N	N	N	N	Y
27 Ros-Lehtinen	N	N	N	N	N	N	Y
GEORGIA							
1 Carter	Y	N	N	N	N	N	Y
2 Bishop	N	N	Y	Y	Y	Y	N
3 Ferguson	Y	N	N	N	N	N	Y
4 Johnson	N	N	Y	Y	Y	Y	N
5 Lewis	N	Y	Y	Y	Y	Y	N
6 Handel	Y	N	N	N	N	N	Y
7 Woodall	Y	N	N	N	N	N	Y
8 Scott, A.	Y	N	N	N	N	N	Y
9 Collins	Y	N	N	N	N	N	Y
10 Hice	Y	N	N	N	N	N	Y
11 Loudermilk	Y	N	N	N	N	N	Y
12 Allen	Y	N	N	N	N	N	Y
13 Scott, D.	N	N	Y	N	Y	Y	Y
14 Graves	Y	N	N	N	N	N	Y
HAWAII							
1 Hanabusa	N	N	Y	Y	Y	Y	N
2 Gabbard	N	N	Y	Y	Y	Y	N
IDAHO							
1 Labrador	Y	N	N	N	N	N	Y
2 Simpson	Y	N	N	N	N	N	Y
ILLINOIS							
1 Rush	N	Y	Y	Y	Y	Y	N
2 Kelly	N	Y	Y	Y	Y	Y	N
3 Lipinski	N	N	Y	Y	Y	Y	N
4 Gutierrez	N	Y	Y	Y	Y	Y	N
5 Quigley	N	Y	Y	Y	Y	Y	N
6 Roskam	Y	N	N	N	N	-	Y
7 Davis, D.	N	Y	Y	Y	Y	Y	N
8 Krishnamoorthi	N	N	Y	Y	Y	Y	N
9 Schakowsky	N	Y	Y	Y	Y	Y	N
10 Schneider	N	N	Y	Y	Y	Y	N
11 Foster	N	N	Y	Y	Y	Y	N
12 Bost	Y	N	N	N	N	N	Y
13 Davis, R.	-	-	-	-	-	-	-
14 Hultgren	Y	N	N	N	N	N	Y
15 Shimkus	N	N	N	N	N	N	Y

	356	357	358	359	360	361	362
16 **Kinzinger**	N	N	N	N	N	N	Y
17 Bustos	N	N	Y	Y	Y	Y	N
18 **LaHood**	Y	N	N	N	N	N	Y
INDIANA							
1 Visclosky	N	N	Y	Y	Y	Y	N
2 **Walorski**	Y	N	N	N	N	N	Y
3 **Banks**	Y	N	N	N	N	N	Y
4 **Rokita**	Y	N	N	N	N	N	Y
5 **Brooks**	N	N	N	N	N	N	Y
6 **Messer**	N	N	N	N	N	N	Y
7 Carson	N	Y	Y	Y	Y	Y	N
8 **Bucshon**	Y	N	N	N	N	N	Y
9 **Hollingsworth**	N	N	N	N	N	N	Y
IOWA							
1 **Blum**	N	N	N	N	N	N	Y
2 Loebsack	N	N	Y	Y	Y	Y	N
3 **Young**	N	N	N	N	N	N	Y
4 **King**	N	N	N	N	N	N	N
KANSAS							
1 **Marshall**	Y	N	N	N	N	N	Y
2 **Jenkins**	Y	N	N	N	N	N	Y
3 **Yoder**	N	N	N	N	N	N	Y
4 **Estes**	N	N	N	N	N	N	Y
KENTUCKY							
1 **Comer**	N	N	N	N	N	N	Y
2 **Guthrie**	Y	N	N	N	N	N	Y
3 Yarmuth	N	N	Y	Y	Y	Y	N
4 **Massie**	Y	N	N	N	N	Y	Y
5 **Rogers**	Y	N	N	N	N	N	Y
6 **Barr**	Y	N	N	N	N	N	Y
LOUISIANA							
1 **Scalise**	+	–	–	–	–	–	+
2 Richmond	N	N	Y	Y	Y	Y	N
3 **Higgins**	N	N	N	N	N	N	Y
4 **Johnson**	Y	N	N	N	N	N	Y
5 **Abraham**	Y	N	N	N	N	N	Y
6 **Graves**	Y	N	N	N	N	N	Y
MAINE							
1 Pingree	N	Y	Y	Y	Y	Y	N
2 **Poliquin**	N	N	N	N	N	N	Y
MARYLAND							
1 **Harris**	Y	N	N	N	N	N	Y
2 Ruppersberger	N	N	Y	N	Y	Y	N
3 Sarbanes	N	Y	Y	Y	Y	Y	N
4 Brown	N	N	Y	Y	Y	Y	N
5 Hoyer	N	N	Y	Y	Y	Y	N
6 Delaney	N	N	Y	Y	Y	Y	Y
7 Cummings	?	?	?	?	?	?	?
8 Raskin	N	Y	Y	Y	Y	Y	N
MASSACHUSETTS							
1 Neal	N	N	Y	Y	Y	Y	N
2 McGovern	N	Y	Y	Y	Y	Y	N
3 Tsongas	N	Y	Y	Y	Y	Y	N
4 Kennedy	N	N	Y	Y	Y	Y	N
5 Clark	N	Y	Y	Y	Y	Y	N
6 Moulton	N	N	N	Y	Y	Y	N
7 Capuano	N	N	Y	Y	Y	Y	N
8 Lynch	N	N	Y	Y	Y	Y	N
9 Keating	N	N	Y	Y	Y	Y	N
MICHIGAN							
1 **Bergman**	Y	N	N	N	N	N	Y
2 **Huizenga**	Y	N	N	N	N	N	Y
3 **Amash**	Y	N	N	Y	Y	Y	Y
4 **Moolenaar**	Y	N	N	N	N	N	Y
5 Kildee	N	Y	Y	Y	Y	Y	N
6 **Upton**	Y	N	N	N	N	N	Y
7 **Walberg**	Y	N	N	N	N	N	Y
8 **Bishop**	Y	N	N	N	N	N	Y
9 Levin	N	Y	Y	Y	Y	Y	N
10 **Mitchell**	Y	N	N	N	N	N	Y
11 **Trott**	Y	N	N	N	N	N	Y
12 Dingell	N	N	Y	Y	Y	Y	N
13 Conyers	N	Y	Y	Y	Y	Y	N
14 Lawrence	N	N	Y	Y	Y	Y	N
MINNESOTA							
1 Walz	N	N	Y	Y	Y	Y	N
2 **Lewis**	Y	N	N	N	N	N	Y
3 **Paulsen**	N	N	N	N	N	N	Y
4 McCollum	N	N	Y	Y	Y	Y	N

	356	357	358	359	360	361	362
5 Ellison	N	Y	Y	Y	Y	Y	N
6 **Emmer**	N	N	N	N	N	N	Y
7 Peterson	N	N	Y	Y	Y	N	N
8 Nolan	N	N	Y	Y	Y	Y	N
MISSISSIPPI							
1 **Kelly**	Y	N	N	N	N	N	Y
2 Thompson	N	N	Y	Y	Y	Y	N
3 **Harper**	Y	N	N	N	N	N	Y
4 **Palazzo**	Y	N	N	N	N	N	Y
MISSOURI							
1 Clay	N	Y	Y	Y	Y	Y	N
2 **Wagner**	Y	N	N	N	N	N	Y
3 **Luetkemeyer**	Y	N	N	N	N	N	Y
4 **Hartzler**	Y	N	N	N	N	N	N
5 Cleaver	–	–	+	+	+	+	–
6 **Graves**	N	N	N	N	N	N	Y
7 **Long**	Y	N	N	N	N	N	Y
8 **Smith**	N	N	N	N	N	N	Y
MONTANA							
AL **Gianforte**	Y	N	N	N	N	N	Y
NEBRASKA							
1 **Fortenberry**	N	N	N	N	N	N	Y
2 **Bacon**	N	N	N	N	N	N	Y
3 **Smith**	N	N	N	N	N	N	Y
NEVADA							
1 Titus	N	N	Y	Y	Y	Y	N
2 **Amodei**	Y	N	N	N	N	N	Y
3 Rosen	N	N	N	N	N	Y	N
4 Kihuen	N	N	Y	Y	?	Y	N
NEW HAMPSHIRE							
1 Shea-Porter	N	N	Y	N	Y	Y	N
2 Kuster	N	N	Y	Y	Y	Y	N
NEW JERSEY							
1 Norcross	N	N	Y	Y	Y	Y	N
2 **LoBiondo**	N	N	N	N	N	N	Y
3 **MacArthur**	Y	N	N	N	N	N	Y
4 **Smith**	Y	N	N	N	N	N	Y
5 Gottheimer	N	N	N	N	N	N	Y
6 Pallone	N	Y	Y	Y	Y	Y	N
7 **Lance**	Y	N	N	N	N	Y	Y
8 Sires	N	N	Y	N	Y	Y	N
9 Pascrell	N	N	Y	Y	Y	Y	N
10 Payne	N	N	Y	Y	Y	Y	N
11 **Frelinghuysen**	Y	N	N	N	N	N	Y
12 Watson Coleman	N	Y	Y	N	Y	Y	N
NEW MEXICO							
1 Lujan Grisham	N	N	Y	Y	Y	N	Y
2 **Pearce**	Y	N	N	N	N	N	Y
3 Luján	N	N	Y	Y	Y	N	Y
NEW YORK							
1 **Zeldin**	Y	N	N	N	N	N	Y
2 **King**	N	N	N	N	N	N	Y
3 Suozzi	N	N	Y	N	Y	Y	Y
4 Rice	N	N	Y	Y	Y	Y	N
5 Meeks	N	Y	Y	Y	Y	Y	N
6 Meng	N	N	Y	Y	Y	Y	N
7 Velázquez	N	Y	Y	Y	Y	Y	N
8 Jeffries	N	Y	Y	Y	Y	Y	N
9 Clarke	N	Y	Y	Y	Y	Y	N
10 Nadler	N	Y	Y	Y	Y	Y	N
11 **Donovan**	Y	N	N	N	N	N	Y
12 Maloney, C.	N	Y	Y	Y	Y	Y	N
13 Espaillat	N	Y	Y	Y	Y	Y	N
14 Crowley	N	Y	Y	Y	Y	Y	N
15 Serrano	N	Y	Y	Y	Y	Y	N
16 Engel	N	Y	Y	Y	N	Y	N
17 Lowey	N	N	Y	Y	Y	Y	N
18 Maloney, S.P.	N	N	Y	N	N	Y	N
19 **Faso**	Y	N	N	N	N	N	Y
20 Tonko	N	Y	Y	Y	Y	Y	N
21 **Stefanik**	N	N	N	N	N	N	Y
22 **Tenney**	Y	N	N	N	N	N	Y
23 **Reed**	N	N	N	N	N	N	Y
24 **Katko**	N	N	N	N	N	N	Y
25 Slaughter	N	Y	Y	Y	Y	Y	N
26 Higgins	N	N	Y	Y	N	Y	Y
27 **Collins**	Y	N	N	N	N	N	Y
NORTH CAROLINA							
1 Butterfield	N	N	Y	Y	Y	Y	N
2 **Holding**	Y	N	N	N	N	N	Y
3 **Jones**	Y	Y	Y	Y	N	Y	Y
4 Price	N	N	Y	Y	Y	Y	N

		357	358	359	360	361	362
5 **Foxx**	Y	N	N	N	N	N	Y
6 **Walker**	Y	N	N	N	N	N	Y
7 **Rouzer**	Y	N	N	N	N	N	Y
8 **Hudson**	Y	N	N	N	N	N	Y
9 **Pittenger**	Y	N	N	N	N	N	Y
10 **McHenry**	Y	N	N	N	N	N	Y
11 **Meadows**	Y	N	N	N	N	N	Y
12 Adams	N	N	Y	Y	Y	Y	N
13 **Budd**	Y	N	N	N	N	N	Y
NORTH DAKOTA							
AL **Cramer**	N	N	N	N	N	N	Y
OHIO							
1 **Chabot**	Y	N	N	N	N	N	Y
2 **Wenstrup**	Y	N	N	N	N	N	Y
3 Beatty	N	N	Y	Y	Y	Y	N
4 **Jordan**	Y	N	N	N	N	N	Y
5 **Latta**	Y	N	N	N	N	N	Y
6 **Johnson**	Y	N	N	N	N	N	Y
7 **Gibbs**	N	N	N	N	N	N	Y
8 **Davidson**	Y	N	N	N	N	N	Y
9 Kaptur	N	Y	Y	Y	Y	Y	N
10 **Turner**	Y	N	N	N	N	N	Y
11 Fudge	N	N	Y	Y	Y	Y	N
12 **Tiberi**	Y	N	N	N	N	N	Y
13 Ryan	N	N	Y	Y	Y	Y	N
14 **Joyce**	Y	N	N	N	N	N	Y
15 **Stivers**	Y	N	N	N	N	N	Y
16 **Renacci**	Y	N	N	N	N	N	Y
OKLAHOMA							
1 **Bridenstine**	Y	N	N	N	N	N	Y
2 **Mullin**	Y	N	N	N	N	N	Y
3 **Lucas**	Y	N	N	N	N	N	Y
4 **Cole**	Y	N	N	N	N	N	Y
5 **Russell**	Y	N	N	N	N	N	Y
OREGON							
1 Bonamici	N	Y	Y	Y	Y	Y	N
2 **Walden**	N	N	N	N	N	N	Y
3 Blumenauer	N	Y	Y	Y	Y	Y	N
4 DeFazio	N	Y	Y	Y	Y	Y	N
5 Schrader	N	N	Y	Y	Y	Y	N
PENNSYLVANIA							
1 Brady	N	N	Y	Y	Y	Y	N
2 Evans	N	Y	Y	Y	Y	Y	N
3 **Kelly**	Y	N	N	N	N	N	Y
4 **Perry**	Y	N	N	N	N	N	Y
5 **Thompson**	Y	N	N	N	N	N	Y
6 **Costello**	N	N	N	N	N	N	Y
7 **Meehan**	Y	N	N	N	N	N	Y
8 **Fitzpatrick**	N	N	N	N	N	N	Y
9 **Shuster**	Y	N	N	N	N	N	Y
10 **Marino**	Y	N	N	N	N	N	Y
11 **Barletta**	Y	N	N	N	N	N	Y
12 **Rothfus**	Y	N	N	N	N	N	Y
13 Boyle	N	N	Y	Y	N	Y	N
14 Doyle	N	N	Y	Y	Y	Y	N
15 **Dent**	Y	N	N	N	N	N	Y
16 **Smucker**	Y	N	N	N	N	N	Y
17 Cartwright	N	N	Y	Y	Y	Y	N
18 **Murphy**	N	N	N	N	N	N	Y
RHODE ISLAND							
1 Cicilline	N	N	Y	Y	Y	Y	N
2 Langevin	N	N	Y	Y	Y	Y	N
SOUTH CAROLINA							
1 **Sanford**	?	?	?	?	?	?	?
2 **Wilson**	Y	N	N	N	N	N	Y
3 **Duncan**	Y	N	N	N	N	N	Y
4 **Gowdy**	Y	N	N	N	N	N	Y
5 **Norman**	Y	N	N	N	N	N	Y
6 Clyburn	N	Y	Y	Y	Y	Y	N
7 **Rice**	Y	N	N	N	N	N	Y
SOUTH DAKOTA							
AL **Noem**	N	N	N	N	N	N	Y
TENNESSEE							
1 **Roe**	Y	N	N	N	N	N	Y
2 **Duncan**	Y	Y	Y	Y	N	Y	Y
3 **Fleischmann**	Y	N	N	N	N	N	Y
4 **DesJarlais**	Y	N	N	N	N	N	Y
5 Cooper	N	N	N	Y	N	N	Y
6 **Black**	Y	N	N	N	N	N	Y
7 **Blackburn**	Y	N	N	N	N	N	Y
8 **Kustoff**	Y	N	N	N	N	N	Y
9 Cohen	N	Y	Y	N	Y	Y	N

	356	357	358	359	360	361	362
TEXAS							
1 **Gohmert**	Y	N	N	N	N	N	Y
2 **Poe**	Y	N	N	N	N	N	Y
3 **Johnson, S.**	?	?	?	?	?	?	?
4 **Ratcliffe**	Y	N	N	N	N	N	Y
5 **Hensarling**	Y	N	N	N	N	N	Y
6 **Barton**	Y	N	N	N	N	N	Y
7 **Culberson**	Y	N	N	N	N	N	Y
8 **Brady**	Y	N	N	N	N	N	Y
9 Green, A.	N	N	Y	Y	Y	Y	N
10 **McCaul**	Y	N	N	N	N	N	Y
11 **Conaway**	Y	N	N	N	N	N	Y
12 **Granger**	Y	N	N	N	N	N	Y
13 **Thornberry**	Y	N	N	N	N	N	Y
14 **Weber**	Y	N	N	N	N	N	Y
15 Gonzalez	N	N	Y	N	N	Y	Y
16 O'Rourke	N	N	N	Y	Y	Y	N
17 **Flores**	Y	N	N	N	N	N	Y
18 Jackson Lee	N	Y	Y	Y	Y	Y	N
19 **Arrington**	Y	N	N	N	N	N	Y
20 Castro	N	N	Y	Y	Y	Y	N
21 **Smith**	Y	N	N	N	N	N	Y
22 **Olson**	Y	N	N	N	N	N	Y
23 **Hurd**	Y	N	N	N	N	N	Y
24 **Marchant**	Y	N	N	N	N	N	Y
25 **Williams**	Y	N	N	N	N	N	Y
26 **Burgess**	Y	N	N	N	N	N	Y
27 **Farenthold**	Y	N	N	N	N	N	Y
28 Cuellar	Y	N	Y	N	Y	Y	N
29 Green, G.	Y	N	Y	N	N	Y	N
30 Johnson, E.B.	N	N	Y	Y	Y	Y	N
31 **Carter**	Y	N	N	N	N	N	Y
32 **Sessions**	Y	N	N	N	N	N	Y
33 Veasey	N	N	N	Y	Y	Y	N
34 Vela	Y	N	Y	N	N	Y	N
35 Doggett	N	N	Y	Y	Y	Y	N
36 **Babin**	Y	N	N	N	N	N	Y
UTAH							
1 **Bishop**	Y	N	N	N	N	N	Y
2 **Stewart**	Y	N	N	N	N	N	Y
4 **Love**	Y	N	N	N	N	N	Y
VERMONT							
AL Welch	N	Y	Y	Y	Y	Y	N
VIRGINIA							
1 **Wittman**	Y	N	N	N	N	N	Y
2 **Taylor**	Y	N	N	N	N	N	Y
3 Scott	Y	N	Y	Y	Y	Y	N
4 McEachin	N	N	Y	Y	Y	Y	N
5 **Garrett**	Y	N	N	N	N	N	Y
6 **Goodlatte**	Y	N	N	N	N	N	Y
7 **Brat**	Y	N	N	N	N	N	Y
8 Beyer	N	N	Y	Y	Y	Y	N
9 **Griffith**	Y	N	N	N	N	N	Y
10 **Comstock**	Y	N	N	N	N	N	Y
11 Connolly	N	N	Y	Y	Y	Y	N
WASHINGTON							
1 DelBene	N	N	Y	Y	Y	Y	N
2 Larsen	N	N	Y	Y	Y	Y	N
3 **Herrera Beutler**	Y	N	N	N	N	N	Y
4 **Newhouse**	Y	N	N	N	N	N	Y
5 **McMorris Rodgers**	Y	N	N	N	N	N	Y
6 Kilmer	N	N	Y	Y	Y	Y	N
7 Jayapal	N	Y	Y	Y	Y	Y	N
8 **Reichert**	N	N	N	N	N	N	Y
9 Smith	N	Y	Y	Y	Y	Y	Y
10 Heck	N	N	Y	N	Y	Y	N
WEST VIRGINIA							
1 **McKinley**	Y	N	N	N	N	N	Y
2 **Mooney**	Y	N	N	N	N	Y	Y
3 **Jenkins**	Y	N	N	N	N	N	Y
WISCONSIN							
1 **Ryan**							
2 Pocan	N	Y	Y	Y	Y	Y	N
3 Kind	N	N	Y	Y	Y	Y	N
4 Moore	?	?	?	?	?	?	N
5 **Sensenbrenner**	Y	Y	N	N	N	Y	Y
6 **Grothman**	?	N	N	N	N	N	Y
7 **Duffy**	Y	N	N	N	N	N	Y
8 **Gallagher**	Y	N	N	N	N	N	Y
WYOMING							
AL **Cheney**	Y	N	N	N	N	N	Y

III HOUSE VOTES

VOTE NUMBER

363. HR 2810. FISCAL 2018 DEFENSE AUTHORIZATION/NUCLEAR ARSENAL MODERNIZATION PLAN MODIFICATION. Garamendi, D-Calif., amendment that would require that the federally mandated annual report regarding the nuclear weapons stockpile, complex, delivery systems and the nuclear weapons command and control system to include a detailed plan to sustain, life-extend, modernize or replace the nuclear weapons and bombs in the nuclear weapons stockpile, and would extend the scope of the report from covering a 10-year period to covering a 25-year period. Rejected in Committee of the Whole 192-232 : R 6-229; D 186-3. July 13, 2017.

364. HR 2810. FISCAL 2018 DEFENSE AUTHORIZATION/NUCLEAR POSTURE REVIEW REQUIREMENT. Blumenauer, D-Ore., amendment that would limit funding to $95.6 million for development of the long range stand-off weapon and $220.3 million for the W80-4 warhead until the secretary of Defense, in consultation with other federal agencies, submits to Congress a nuclear posture review including a detailed assessment of the long range standoff weapon's capabilities. Rejected in Committee of the Whole 169-254 : R 2-232; D 167-22. July 13, 2017.

365. HR 2810. FISCAL 2018 DEFENSE AUTHORIZATION/BASE REALIGNMENT AND CLOSURE REPETITION. McClintock, R-Calif., amendment that would eliminate the bill's prohibition on conducting an additional round of base realignment and closure. Rejected in Committee of the Whole 175-248 : R 95-140; D 80-108. July 13, 2017.

366. HR 2810. FISCAL 2018 DEFENSE AUTHORIZATION/ICEBREAKER FLEET EXPANSION. Garamendi, D-Calif., amendment that would eliminate the bill's provision that would prohibit defense department funds authorized in the bill from being used to procure a new Coast Guard icebreaker. Rejected in Committee of the Whole 198-220 : R 20-213; D 178-7. July 13, 2017.

367. HR 2810. FISCAL 2018 DEFENSE AUTHORIZATION/ALTERNATIVE ENERGY QUALIFICATION REQUIREMENT. Buck, R-Colo., amendment that would prohibit funds authorized by the bill from being used by the Defense Department to purchase alternative energy unless such energy is equivalent in its cost and capabilities to conventional energy. The bill would require the Defense Department to complete a cost competitiveness calculation in order to determine the cost and capabilities of such energy sources. Rejected in Committee of the Whole 203-218 : R 202-32; D 1-186. July 13, 2017.

368. HR 2810. FISCAL 2018 DEFENSE AUTHORIZATION/CLIMATE CHANGE VULNERABILITIES REPORT. Perry, R-Pa., amendment that would eliminate the bill's provision that would express the sense of Congress that climate change is a direct threat to national security, and would eliminate the provision that would require the secretary of Defense to report to Congress on vulnerabilities to military installations and combatant commands resulting from climate change-related effects. Rejected in Committee of the Whole 185-234 : R 185-46; D 0-188. July 13, 2017.

369. HR 2810. FISCAL 2018 DEFENSE AUTHORIZATION/GENDER TRANSITION TREATMENT PROHIBITION. Hartzler, R-Mo., amendment that would prohibit the use of Defense Department funds to provide medical treatment (other than mental health treatment) related to gender transition to a person entitled to military medical care under current law. Rejected in Committee of the Whole 209-214 : R 209-24; D 0-190. July 13, 2017.

	363	364	365	366	367	368	369
ALABAMA							
1 Byrne	N	N	N	Y	Y	Y	Y
2 Roby	N	N	N	Y	N	Y	Y
3 Rogers	N	N	N	Y	Y	Y	Y
4 Aderholt	N	N	Y	N	Y	Y	Y
5 Brooks	N	N	Y	N	Y	Y	Y
6 Palmer	N	N	Y	N	Y	Y	Y
7 Sewell	Y	Y	N	Y	N	N	N
ALASKA							
AL Young	N	N	N	Y	Y	Y	Y
ARIZONA							
1 O'Halleran	Y	N	N	Y	N	N	N
2 McSally	N	N	N	N	Y	N	Y
3 Grijalva	Y	Y	N	Y	N	N	N
4 Gosar	N	N	Y	N	Y	Y	Y
5 Biggs	N	N	Y	N	Y	Y	Y
6 Schweikert	N	N	Y	N	Y	Y	Y
7 Gallego	Y	Y	N	Y	N	N	N
8 Franks	N	N	N	N	Y	Y	Y
9 Sinema	Y	N	N	N	N	N	N
ARKANSAS							
1 Crawford	N	N	N	Y	N	Y	Y
2 Hill	N	N	Y	N	Y	Y	Y
3 Womack	N	N	Y	N	Y	Y	Y
4 Westerman	N	N	Y	N	Y	Y	Y
CALIFORNIA							
1 LaMalfa	N	N	Y	N	Y	Y	Y
2 Huffman	Y	Y	Y	?	N	N	N
3 Garamendi	Y	Y	N	Y	N	N	N
4 McClintock	N	N	Y	Y	Y	Y	Y
5 Thompson	Y	Y	Y	Y	N	N	N
6 Matsui	Y	Y	Y	Y	N	N	N
7 Bera	Y	Y	Y	Y	N	N	N
8 Cook	N	N	N	N	N	Y	N
9 McNerney	Y	Y	N	Y	N	N	N
10 Denham	N	N	Y	N	Y	N	N
11 DeSaulnier	Y	Y	N	Y	N	N	N
12 Pelosi	Y	Y	Y	Y	N	N	N
13 Lee	Y	Y	N	Y	N	N	N
14 Speier	Y	Y	N	Y	?	N	N
15 Swalwell	Y	Y	N	Y	N	N	N
16 Costa	Y	Y	N	Y	N	N	N
17 Khanna	Y	Y	Y	Y	N	N	N
18 Eshoo	Y	Y	N	Y	N	N	N
19 Lofgren	Y	Y	Y	Y	N	N	N
20 Panetta	Y	Y	N	Y	N	N	N
21 Valadao	N	N	N	N	Y	Y	?
22 Nunes	N	N	N	N	Y	Y	Y
23 McCarthy	N	N	N	N	N	Y	Y
24 Carbajal	Y	Y	N	Y	N	N	N
25 Knight	N	N	N	Y	N	N	N
26 Brownley	Y	Y	N	Y	N	N	N
27 Chu	Y	Y	Y	Y	N	N	N
28 Schiff	Y	Y	N	Y	N	N	N
29 Cardenas	Y	Y	Y	Y	N	N	N
30 Sherman	Y	Y	Y	Y	N	N	N
31 Aguilar	Y	N	N	Y	N	N	N
32 Napolitano	+	+	-	+	-	-	-
33 Lieu	?	?	?	?	?	?	-
34 Gomez	Y	Y	N	Y	N	N	N
35 Torres	Y	Y	N	Y	N	N	N
36 Ruiz	Y	Y	N	Y	N	N	N
37 Bass	Y	Y	N	Y	N	N	N
38 Sánchez, Linda	Y	Y	N	Y	N	N	N
39 Royce	N	N	Y	N	Y	N	Y
40 Roybal-Allard	Y	Y	N	Y	N	N	N
41 Takano	Y	Y	N	Y	N	N	N
42 Calvert	N	N	N	N	Y	Y	Y
43 Waters	Y	Y	N	Y	N	N	N
44 Barragan	Y	Y	N	Y	N	N	N
45 Walters	N	N	N	N	Y	N	Y
46 Correa	Y	N	N	Y	N	N	N
47 Lowenthal	Y	Y	N	Y	N	N	N
48 Rohrabacher	N	Y	N	Y	Y	Y	Y
49 Issa	N	N	N	Y	N	N	N
50 Hunter	N	N	N	Y	Y	Y	Y
51 Vargas	Y	Y	N	Y	N	N	N
52 Peters	Y	N	N	Y	N	N	N
53 Davis	Y	Y	Y	Y	N	N	N

	363	364	365	366	367	368	369
COLORADO							
1 DeGette	Y	Y	Y	Y	N	N	N
2 Polis	Y	Y	Y	N	N	N	N
3 Tipton	N	N	Y	N	Y	Y	Y
4 Buck	N	N	Y	N	Y	Y	Y
5 Lamborn	N	N	N	N	Y	Y	Y
6 Coffman	N	N	Y	N	Y	N	N
7 Perlmutter	Y	Y	Y	Y	N	N	N
CONNECTICUT							
1 Larson	Y	Y	N	Y	N	N	N
2 Courtney	Y	Y	N	Y	N	N	N
3 DeLauro	Y	Y	N	Y	N	N	N
4 Himes	Y	Y	N	Y	N	N	N
5 Esty	Y	Y	Y	Y	N	N	N
DELAWARE							
AL Blunt Rochester	Y	Y	N	Y	N	N	N
FLORIDA							
1 Gaetz	N	N	N	N	Y	Y	Y
2 Dunn	N	N	N	Y	Y	Y	Y
3 Yoho	N	N	Y	N	Y	Y	Y
4 Rutherford	N	N	N	N	Y	Y	Y
5 Lawson	Y	N	Y	N	N	N	N
6 DeSantis	N	N	Y	N	Y	Y	Y
7 Murphy	Y	N	Y	N	N	N	N
8 Posey	N	N	N	N	Y	Y	Y
9 Soto	Y	N	N	Y	N	N	N
10 Demings	Y	Y	N	Y	N	N	N
11 Webster	N	N	Y	N	Y	Y	Y
12 Bilirakis	N	N	N	?	Y	Y	Y
13 Crist	Y	N	N	Y	N	N	N
14 Castor	Y	Y	Y	Y	N	N	N
15 Ross	N	N	N	N	Y	Y	Y
16 Buchanan	N	N	N	N	N	Y	Y
17 Rooney, T.	N	N	N	Y	Y	Y	Y
18 Mast	N	N	N	Y	Y	Y	Y
19 Rooney, F.	N	N	Y	N	Y	Y	Y
20 Hastings	Y	Y	N	Y	N	N	N
21 Frankel	?	?	?	Y	N	N	N
22 Deutch	Y	Y	Y	Y	N	N	N
23 Wasserman Schultz	Y	Y	Y	Y	N	N	N
24 Wilson	Y	Y	N	Y	N	N	N
25 Diaz-Balart	N	N	N	Y	N	N	Y
26 Curbelo	N	N	N	N	N	N	N
27 Ros-Lehtinen	N	N	N	N	N	N	N
GEORGIA							
1 Carter	N	N	N	Y	Y	Y	Y
2 Bishop	Y	Y	N	Y	N	N	N
3 Ferguson	N	N	N	Y	Y	Y	Y
4 Johnson	Y	Y	Y	Y	N	N	N
5 Lewis	Y	Y	Y	Y	N	N	N
6 Handel	N	N	N	Y	Y	Y	Y
7 Woodall	N	N	Y	N	Y	Y	Y
8 Scott, A.	N	N	N	Y	Y	Y	Y
9 Collins	N	N	Y	N	Y	Y	Y
10 Hice	N	N	N	Y	Y	Y	Y
11 Loudermilk	N	N	N	Y	Y	Y	Y
12 Allen	N	N	N	Y	Y	Y	Y
13 Scott, D.	Y	Y	N	Y	N	N	N
14 Graves	N	N	Y	N	Y	Y	Y
HAWAII							
1 Hanabusa	Y	Y	N	Y	N	N	N
2 Gabbard	Y	Y	Y	Y	N	N	N
IDAHO							
1 Labrador	N	N	Y	?	?	?	?
2 Simpson	N	N	N	N	Y	Y	Y
ILLINOIS							
1 Rush	Y	Y	Y	?	N	N	N
2 Kelly	Y	Y	Y	Y	N	N	N
3 Lipinski	Y	Y	Y	Y	N	N	N
4 Gutierrez	Y	N	Y	Y	—	N	N
5 Quigley	Y	Y	Y	Y	N	N	N
6 Roskam	N	N	Y	N	Y	Y	Y
7 Davis, D.	Y	Y	?	?	?	?	N
8 Krishnamoorthi	Y	Y	Y	Y	N	N	N
9 Schakowsky	Y	Y	Y	Y	N	N	N
10 Schneider	Y	Y	N	N	N	N	N
11 Foster	Y	Y	Y	Y	N	N	N
12 Bost	N	N	N	N	N	Y	Y
13 Davis, R.	-	-	-	-	-	-	-
14 Hultgren	N	N	Y	N	Y	Y	Y
15 Shimkus	N	N	N	N	N	Y	Y

	363	364	365	366	367	368	369
16 **Kinzinger**	N	N	N	Y	N	N	Y
17 Bustos	Y	Y	N	Y	N	N	N
18 **LaHood**	N	N	Y	N	Y	Y	Y
INDIANA							
1 Visclosky	Y	Y	Y	N	N	N	N
2 **Walorski**	N	N	N	N	Y	Y	Y
3 **Banks**	N	N	N	N	Y	Y	Y
4 **Rokita**	N	N	Y	N	Y	Y	Y
5 **Brooks**	N	N	N	N	Y	Y	Y
6 **Messer**	N	N	Y	N	Y	Y	Y
7 Carson	Y	N	Y	Y	N	N	N
8 **Bucshon**	N	N	N	N	Y	Y	Y
9 **Hollingsworth**	N	N	Y	N	Y	N	Y
IOWA							
1 **Blum**	N	N	N	N	N	Y	Y
2 Loebsack	Y	Y	N	Y	N	N	N
3 **Young**	N	N	Y	N	N	N	Y
4 **King**	N	N	N	N	N	Y	Y
KANSAS							
1 **Marshall**	N	N	N	N	N	Y	Y
2 **Jenkins**	N	N	N	N	Y	Y	Y
3 **Yoder**	N	N	N	N	Y	Y	Y
4 **Estes**	N	N	Y	N	N	Y	Y
KENTUCKY							
1 **Comer**	N	N	Y	N	Y	Y	Y
2 **Guthrie**	N	N	Y	N	Y	Y	Y
3 Yarmuth	Y	Y	N	Y	N	N	N
4 **Massie**	Y	?	Y	Y	Y	Y	Y
5 **Rogers**	N	N	N	N	Y	Y	Y
6 **Barr**	N	N	Y	N	Y	Y	Y
LOUISIANA							
1 **Scalise**	–	–	–	+	+	+	+
2 Richmond	Y	Y	N	Y	N	N	N
3 **Higgins**	N	N	N	N	Y	Y	Y
4 **Johnson**	N	N	N	N	Y	Y	Y
5 **Abraham**	N	N	N	N	Y	Y	Y
6 **Graves**	N	N	N	Y	Y	N	Y
MAINE							
1 Pingree	Y	Y	N	Y	N	N	N
2 **Poliquin**	N	N	N	N	Y	N	Y
MARYLAND							
1 **Harris**	N	N	Y	N	Y	Y	Y
2 Ruppersberger	Y	N	Y	Y	N	N	N
3 Sarbanes	Y	Y	Y	Y	N	N	N
4 Brown	Y	Y	Y	Y	N	N	N
5 Hoyer	Y	Y	N	Y	N	N	N
6 Delaney	Y	Y	Y	Y	N	N	N
7 Cummings	?	?	?	?	?	?	?
8 Raskin	Y	Y	Y	Y	N	N	N
MASSACHUSETTS							
1 Neal	Y	Y	N	Y	N	N	N
2 McGovern	Y	Y	Y	Y	N	N	N
3 Tsongas	Y	Y	Y	Y	N	N	N
4 Kennedy	Y	Y	Y	Y	N	N	N
5 Clark	Y	Y	N	Y	N	N	N
6 Moulton	Y	Y	Y	Y	N	N	N
7 Capuano	Y	Y	N	Y	N	N	N
8 Lynch	Y	Y	N	Y	N	N	N
9 Keating	Y	Y	N	Y	N	N	N
MICHIGAN							
1 **Bergman**	N	N	Y	N	Y	Y	N
2 **Huizenga**	N	N	Y	N	Y	Y	Y
3 **Amash**	Y	Y	Y	N	Y	Y	N
4 **Moolenaar**	N	N	N	N	Y	Y	Y
5 Kildee	Y	Y	Y	Y	N	N	N
6 **Upton**	N	N	N	N	Y	N	Y
7 **Walberg**	N	N	N	N	Y	Y	Y
8 **Bishop**	N	N	Y	N	Y	N	Y
9 Levin	Y	Y	Y	Y	N	N	N
10 **Mitchell**	N	N	N	N	Y	Y	Y
11 **Trott**	N	N	N	N	Y	Y	Y
12 Dingell	Y	Y	N	Y	N	N	N
13 Conyers	Y	Y	Y	Y	N	N	N
14 Lawrence	Y	Y	Y	Y	N	N	N
MINNESOTA							
1 Walz	Y	Y	Y	Y	N	N	N
2 **Lewis**	N	N	Y	Y	N	Y	Y
3 **Paulsen**	N	N	Y	N	N	N	Y
4 McCollum	Y	Y	Y	Y	N	N	N

	363	364	365	366	367	368	369
5 Ellison	Y	Y	Y	Y	N	N	N
6 **Emmer**	N	N	Y	N	N	Y	Y
7 Peterson	Y	N	Y	Y	N	N	N
8 Nolan	Y	Y	Y	Y	N	N	N
MISSISSIPPI							
1 **Kelly**	N	N	N	N	Y	Y	Y
2 Thompson	Y	Y	N	Y	N	N	N
3 **Harper**	N	N	N	N	Y	Y	Y
4 **Palazzo**	N	N	N	Y	Y	Y	Y
MISSOURI							
1 Clay	Y	Y	Y	Y	N	N	N
2 **Wagner**	N	N	Y	N	Y	Y	Y
3 **Luetkemeyer**	N	N	N	N	Y	Y	Y
4 **Hartzler**	N	N	N	N	Y	Y	Y
5 Cleaver	+	+	–	+	–	–	–
6 **Graves**	N	N	N	N	Y	Y	Y
7 **Long**	N	N	N	N	Y	Y	Y
8 **Smith**	N	N	N	N	Y	Y	Y
MONTANA							
AL **Gianforte**	N	N	N	N	Y	Y	Y
NEBRASKA							
1 **Fortenberry**	N	N	N	N	N	N	Y
2 **Bacon**	N	N	N	N	N	N	Y
3 **Smith**	N	N	N	N	N	Y	Y
NEVADA							
1 Titus	Y	Y	Y	Y	N	N	N
2 **Amodei**	N	N	N	N	Y	N	Y
3 Rosen	Y	Y	N	Y	N	N	N
4 Kihuen	Y	Y	Y	Y	N	N	N
NEW HAMPSHIRE							
1 Shea-Porter	Y	Y	N	Y	N	N	N
2 Kuster	Y	Y	N	Y	N	N	N
NEW JERSEY							
1 Norcross	Y	Y	N	Y	N	N	N
2 **LoBiondo**	N	N	N	Y	N	N	N
3 **MacArthur**	N	N	N	N	Y	N	N
4 **Smith**	N	N	N	Y	N	N	Y
5 Gottheimer	Y	N	N	Y	N	N	N
6 Pallone	Y	Y	N	Y	N	N	N
7 **Lance**	N	N	Y	N	Y	N	N
8 Sires	Y	Y	N	Y	N	N	N
9 Pascrell	Y	Y	N	Y	N	N	N
10 Payne	Y	Y	N	Y	N	N	N
11 **Frelinghuysen**	N	N	N	N	Y	Y	Y
12 Watson Coleman	Y	Y	N	Y	N	N	N
NEW MEXICO							
1 Lujan Grisham	N	N	N	Y	N	N	N
2 **Pearce**	N	N	N	N	Y	Y	Y
3 Luján	N	N	N	Y	N	N	N
NEW YORK							
1 **Zeldin**	N	N	Y	N	Y	N	Y
2 **King**	N	N	N	N	Y	Y	Y
3 Suozzi	Y	N	Y	Y	N	N	N
4 Rice	Y	Y	Y	Y	N	N	N
5 Meeks	Y	Y	N	Y	N	N	N
6 Meng	Y	Y	N	Y	N	N	N
7 Velázquez	Y	Y	N	Y	N	N	N
8 Jeffries	Y	Y	N	Y	N	N	N
9 Clarke	Y	Y	N	Y	N	N	N
10 Nadler	Y	Y	Y	Y	N	N	N
11 **Donovan**	N	N	N	N	Y	Y	Y
12 Maloney, C.	Y	Y	Y	Y	N	N	N
13 Espaillat	Y	Y	N	Y	N	N	N
14 Crowley	Y	Y	Y	Y	N	N	N
15 Serrano	Y	Y	N	Y	N	N	N
16 Engel	Y	N	N	Y	N	N	N
17 Lowey	Y	Y	Y	Y	N	N	N
18 Maloney, S.P.	Y	N	N	Y	N	N	N
19 **Faso**	N	N	Y	N	N	N	N
20 Tonko	Y	Y	N	Y	N	N	N
21 **Stefanik**	N	N	N	N	N	N	N
22 **Tenney**	N	N	N	N	Y	N	N
23 **Reed**	N	N	N	N	N	N	N
24 **Katko**	N	N	N	N	N	N	N
25 Slaughter	Y	Y	N	Y	N	N	N
26 Higgins	Y	Y	N	Y	N	N	N
27 **Collins**	N	N	N	N	Y	Y	Y
NORTH CAROLINA							
1 Butterfield	Y	Y	N	Y	N	N	N
2 **Holding**	N	N	N	N	Y	Y	Y
3 **Jones**	Y	N	N	N	Y	Y	Y
4 Price	Y	Y	Y	Y	N	N	N

	363	364	365	366	367	368	369
5 **Foxx**	N	N	Y	N	Y	Y	Y
6 **Walker**	N	N	Y	N	Y	Y	Y
7 **Rouzer**	N	N	N	N	Y	Y	Y
8 **Hudson**	N	N	Y	N	Y	?	Y
9 **Pittenger**	N	N	Y	N	Y	Y	Y
10 **McHenry**	N	N	N	N	Y	Y	Y
11 **Meadows**	N	N	Y	N	Y	Y	Y
12 Adams	Y	Y	N	Y	N	N	N
13 **Budd**	N	N	Y	N	Y	Y	Y
NORTH DAKOTA							
AL **Cramer**	N	N	N	N	Y	Y	Y
OHIO							
1 **Chabot**	N	N	Y	N	Y	Y	Y
2 **Wenstrup**	N	N	Y	N	Y	Y	Y
3 Beatty	Y	Y	N	Y	N	N	N
4 **Jordan**	N	N	Y	N	Y	Y	Y
5 **Latta**	N	N	N	N	Y	Y	Y
6 **Johnson**	N	N	N	N	Y	Y	Y
7 **Gibbs**	N	N	N	N	Y	Y	Y
8 **Davidson**	N	N	Y	N	Y	Y	Y
9 Kaptur	Y	Y	N	Y	N	?	N
10 **Turner**	N	N	N	N	Y	Y	Y
11 Fudge	Y	Y	N	Y	N	N	N
12 **Tiberi**	N	N	N	N	Y	Y	Y
13 Ryan	Y	Y	N	Y	N	N	N
14 **Joyce**	N	N	N	N	N	N	Y
15 **Stivers**	N	N	N	N	Y	Y	Y
16 **Renacci**	N	N	N	N	Y	Y	Y
OKLAHOMA							
1 **Bridenstine**	N	N	Y	Y	Y	N	Y
2 **Mullin**	N	N	N	N	Y	Y	Y
3 **Lucas**	N	N	N	N	Y	Y	Y
4 **Cole**	N	N	N	N	Y	Y	Y
5 **Russell**	N	N	N	N	Y	Y	Y
OREGON							
1 Bonamici	Y	Y	Y	Y	N	N	N
2 **Walden**	N	N	Y	N	Y	N	Y
3 Blumenauer	Y	Y	Y	Y	N	N	N
4 DeFazio	Y	Y	Y	Y	N	N	N
5 Schrader	Y	Y	Y	Y	N	N	N
PENNSYLVANIA							
1 Brady	Y	Y	N	Y	N	N	N
2 Evans	Y	Y	N	Y	N	N	N
3 **Kelly**	N	N	N	N	Y	Y	Y
4 **Perry**	N	N	Y	N	Y	Y	Y
5 **Thompson**	N	N	Y	N	Y	N	Y
6 **Costello**	N	N	N	Y	N	N	N
7 **Meehan**	N	N	N	N	Y	N	Y
8 **Fitzpatrick**	N	N	Y	N	N	N	N
9 **Shuster**	N	N	N	Y	N	?	N
10 **Marino**	N	N	N	N	Y	Y	Y
11 **Barletta**	N	N	N	N	Y	Y	Y
12 **Rothfus**	N	N	Y	N	Y	Y	Y
13 Boyle	Y	Y	N	Y	N	N	N
14 Doyle	Y	Y	N	Y	N	N	N
15 **Dent**	N	N	Y	Y	N	N	N
16 **Smucker**	N	N	N	N	Y	Y	Y
17 Cartwright	Y	Y	N	Y	N	N	N
18 **Murphy**	N	N	N	N	Y	Y	Y
RHODE ISLAND							
1 Cicilline	Y	Y	Y	Y	N	N	N
2 Langevin	Y	N	Y	Y	N	N	N
SOUTH CAROLINA							
1 **Sanford**	?	?	?	?	?	?	?
2 **Wilson**	N	N	N	N	Y	Y	Y
3 **Duncan**	N	N	Y	N	Y	Y	Y
4 **Gowdy**	N	N	Y	N	Y	Y	Y
5 **Norman**	N	N	Y	N	Y	Y	Y
6 Clyburn	Y	Y	N	?	N	N	N
7 **Rice**	N	N	Y	N	Y	Y	Y
SOUTH DAKOTA							
AL **Noem**	N	N	N	N	N	Y	Y
TENNESSEE							
1 **Roe**	N	N	Y	N	Y	Y	Y
2 **Duncan**	Y	N	Y	Y	Y	Y	Y
3 **Fleischmann**	N	N	Y	N	Y	Y	Y
4 **DesJarlais**	N	N	Y	N	Y	Y	Y
5 Cooper	N	N	Y	Y	N	N	N
6 **Black**	N	N	N	N	Y	Y	Y
7 **Blackburn**	N	N	N	N	Y	Y	Y
8 **Kustoff**	N	N	Y	N	Y	Y	Y
9 Cohen	Y	Y	N	Y	N	N	N

	363	364	365	366	367	368	369
TEXAS							
1 **Gohmert**	N	N	N	N	Y	Y	Y
2 **Poe**	N	N	N	N	Y	Y	Y
3 **Johnson, S.**	?	?	?	?	?	?	?
4 **Ratcliffe**	N	N	Y	N	Y	Y	Y
5 **Hensarling**	N	N	Y	N	Y	Y	Y
6 **Barton**	N	N	N	N	Y	Y	Y
7 **Culberson**	N	N	N	Y	Y	Y	Y
8 **Brady**	N	N	N	N	Y	Y	Y
9 Green, A.	Y	Y	N	Y	N	N	N
10 **McCaul**	N	N	N	N	Y	Y	Y
11 **Conaway**	N	N	N	N	Y	Y	Y
12 **Granger**	N	N	N	N	Y	Y	Y
13 **Thornberry**	N	N	N	N	Y	Y	Y
14 **Weber**	N	N	N	N	Y	Y	Y
15 Gonzalez	Y	Y	N	?	N	N	N
16 O'Rourke	Y	Y	Y	Y	N	N	N
17 **Flores**	N	N	Y	N	Y	Y	Y
18 Jackson Lee	Y	Y	N	N	N	N	N
19 **Arrington**	N	N	N	N	Y	Y	Y
20 Castro	Y	Y	Y	Y	N	N	N
21 **Smith**	N	N	N	N	Y	Y	Y
22 **Olson**	N	N	N	N	Y	Y	Y
23 **Hurd**	N	N	N	N	Y	Y	Y
24 **Marchant**	N	N	Y	N	Y	Y	Y
25 **Williams**	N	N	Y	N	Y	Y	Y
26 **Burgess**	N	N	Y	N	Y	Y	Y
27 **Farenthold**	N	N	N	N	Y	Y	Y
28 Cuellar	Y	N	N	Y	N	N	N
29 Green, G.	Y	Y	N	Y	N	N	N
30 Johnson, E.B.	Y	Y	N	Y	N	N	N
31 **Carter**	N	N	N	N	Y	Y	Y
32 **Sessions**	N	N	Y	N	Y	Y	Y
33 Veasey	Y	N	N	Y	N	N	N
34 Vela	Y	Y	N	Y	Y	N	N
35 Doggett	Y	Y	Y	Y	N	N	N
36 **Babin**	N	N	N	N	Y	Y	Y
UTAH							
1 **Bishop**	N	N	N	N	Y	?	Y
2 **Stewart**	N	N	Y	N	Y	Y	Y
4 **Love**	N	N	Y	N	Y	N	Y
VERMONT							
AL Welch	Y	Y	Y	Y	N	N	N
VIRGINIA							
1 **Wittman**	N	N	N	N	Y	Y	Y
2 **Taylor**	N	N	Y	N	Y	N	Y
3 Scott	Y	Y	N	N	N	N	N
4 McEachin	Y	Y	Y	Y	N	N	N
5 **Garrett**	N	N	N	Y	Y	Y	Y
6 **Goodlatte**	N	N	Y	N	Y	Y	Y
7 **Brat**	N	N	Y	N	Y	Y	Y
8 Beyer	Y	Y	N	N	N	N	N
9 **Griffith**	N	N	Y	N	Y	Y	Y
10 **Comstock**	N	N	N	N	Y	N	N
11 Connolly	Y	Y	Y	Y	N	N	N
WASHINGTON							
1 DelBene	Y	Y	Y	Y	N	N	N
2 Larsen	Y	Y	Y	Y	N	N	N
3 **Herrera Beutler**	N	N	Y	N	Y	Y	Y
4 **Newhouse**	N	N	Y	N	Y	Y	Y
5 **McMorris Rodgers**	N	N	N	N	Y	Y	Y
6 Kilmer	Y	Y	Y	Y	N	N	N
7 Jayapal	Y	Y	Y	Y	N	N	N
8 **Reichert**	N	N	N	N	N	N	N
9 Smith	Y	Y	Y	Y	N	N	N
10 Heck	Y	Y	Y	Y	N	N	N
WEST VIRGINIA							
1 **McKinley**	N	N	Y	N	Y	Y	Y
2 **Mooney**	Y	N	N	N	Y	Y	Y
3 **Jenkins**	N	N	N	N	Y	Y	Y
WISCONSIN							
1 **Ryan**							
2 Pocan	Y	Y	Y	Y	N	N	N
3 Kind	Y	Y	N	Y	N	N	N
4 Moore	Y	Y	Y	Y	N	N	N
5 **Sensenbrenner**	Y	N	Y	Y	Y	Y	Y
6 **Grothman**	N	N	Y	N	Y	Y	Y
7 **Duffy**	N	N	N	N	Y	Y	Y
8 **Gallagher**	N	N	Y	N	Y	N	Y
WYOMING							
AL **Cheney**	N	N	N	N	Y	Y	Y

VOTE NUMBER

370. HR 2810. FISCAL 2018 DEFENSE AUTHORIZATION/PREVAILING WAGE DETERMINATION METHOD. Gosar, R-Ariz., amendment that would require any determination of prevailing wage under the bill to be conducted by the secretary of Labor, through the Bureau of Labor Statistics, using surveys that utilize random statistical sampling techniques. Rejected in Committee of the Whole 183-242 : R 183-51; D 0-191. July 13, 2017.

371. HR 2810. FISCAL 2018 DEFENSE AUTHORIZATION/ATHLETIC DEFERMENT PROHIBITION FOR SERVICE ACADEMY GRADUATES. Rooney, R-Fla., amendment that would eliminate the bill's provision that would prohibit student-athletes graduating from service academies from seeking a deferment of service in order to pursue professional athletic careers. Rejected in Committee of the Whole 107-318 : R 46-188; D 61-130. July 13, 2017.

372. HR 2810. FISCAL 2018 DEFENSE AUTHORIZATION/TERRORIST MESSAGING ASSESSMENT. Franks, R-Ariz., amendment that would require the secretary of Defense to conduct two concurrent strategic assessments of the use of violent or unorthodox Islamic religious doctrine to support extremist or terrorist messaging and justification, and would require the secretary to submit to Congress the results of the assessments. Rejected in Committee of the Whole 208-217 : R 208-27; D 0-190. July 14, 2017.

373. HR 2810. FISCAL 2018 DEFENSE AUTHORIZATION/BALLISTIC MISSILE DEFENSE OPERATIONAL TEST NORMALIZATION. Lamborn, R-Colo., amendment that would normalize the operational test and evaluation processes for the ballistic missile defense system by confirming the condition for proceeding below low-rate initial production in line with all other major defense acquisition programs. Adopted in Committee of the Whole 235-189 : R 231-3; D 4-186. July 14, 2017.

374. HR 2810. FISCAL 2018 DEFENSE AUTHORIZATION/RECREATIONAL VESSEL DESIGNATION. Byrne, R-Ala., for Frankel, D-Fla., amendment that would classify a vessel being repaired or dismantled as a "recreational vessel" if it shares elements of design and construction with traditional recreational vessels and is not normally engaged in military or commercial undertakings while it is in operation. Adopted in Committee of the Whole 244-181 : R 229-6; D 15-175. July 14, 2017.

375. HR 2810. FISCAL 2018 DEFENSE AUTHORIZATION/CLAIMS LIMITATION FOR FOREIGN NATIONAL SEAMEN. Hunter, R-Calif., amendment that would prohibit a claim for damages related to personal injury, illness, or death of a seaman that is a foreign national on a foreign passenger vessel from being brought under federal law if the seaman was not a legal resident of the U.S. at the time of the claim and the harm arose outside U.S. waters. Adopted in Committee of the Whole 234-190 : R 234-1; D 0-189. July 14, 2017.

376. HR 2810. FISCAL 2018 DEFENSE AUTHORIZATION/RADIATION-EXPOSED VETERANS SERVICE MEDAL. McGovern, D-Mass., amendment that would require the secretary of Defense to design and produce a military service medal to honor retired or former members of the armed forces who are radiation-exposed veterans, and would designate the medal as the "Atomic Veterans Service Medal." Adopted in Committee of the Whole 424-0 : R 234-0; D 190-0. July 14, 2017.

	370	371	372	373	374	375	376
ALABAMA							
1 **Byrne**	Y	N	Y	Y	Y	Y	Y
2 **Roby**	Y	Y	Y	Y	Y	Y	Y
3 **Rogers**	Y	N	Y	Y	Y	Y	Y
4 **Aderholt**	Y	N	Y	Y	Y	Y	Y
5 **Brooks**	Y	N	Y	Y	Y	Y	Y
6 **Palmer**	Y	N	Y	Y	Y	Y	Y
7 Sewell	N	N	N	N	N	N	Y
ALASKA							
AL **Young**	N	N	N	Y	Y	Y	Y
ARIZONA							
1 O'Halleran	N	N	N	N	N	N	Y
2 **McSally**	Y	N	Y	Y	Y	Y	Y
3 Grijalva	N	N	N	N	N	N	Y
4 **Gosar**	Y	N	Y	Y	Y	Y	Y
5 **Biggs**	Y	N	Y	Y	Y	Y	Y
6 **Schweikert**	Y	N	Y	Y	Y	Y	Y
7 Gallego	N	N	N	N	N	N	Y
8 **Franks**	Y	N	Y	Y	Y	Y	Y
9 Sinema	N	Y	N	Y	N	N	Y
ARKANSAS							
1 **Crawford**	Y	N	Y	Y	Y	Y	Y
2 **Hill**	Y	N	N	Y	Y	Y	Y
3 **Womack**	Y	Y	Y	Y	Y	Y	Y
4 **Westerman**	Y	N	Y	Y	Y	Y	Y
CALIFORNIA							
1 **LaMalfa**	Y	Y	Y	Y	Y	Y	Y
2 Huffman	N	N	N	N	N	N	Y
3 Garamendi	N	N	N	Y	N	Y	N
4 **McClintock**	Y	N	Y	Y	Y	Y	Y
5 Thompson	N	N	N	N	N	N	Y
6 Matsui	N	N	N	N	N	N	Y
7 Bera	N	Y	N	N	N	N	Y
8 **Cook**	N	Y	Y	Y	Y	Y	Y
9 McNerney	N	N	N	N	N	N	Y
10 **Denham**	Y	N	Y	Y	Y	Y	Y
11 DeSaulnier	N	N	N	N	N	N	Y
12 Pelosi	N	N	N	N	N	N	Y
13 Lee	N	N	N	N	N	N	Y
14 Speier	N	N	N	N	N	N	Y
15 Swalwell	N	Y	N	N	N	N	Y
16 Costa	N	N	N	N	N	N	Y
17 Khanna	N	N	N	N	N	N	Y
18 Eshoo	N	N	N	N	N	N	Y
19 Lofgren	N	N	N	N	N	N	Y
20 Panetta	N	N	N	N	N	N	Y
21 **Valadao**	N	N	Y	Y	Y	Y	Y
22 **Nunes**	Y	Y	Y	Y	Y	Y	Y
23 **McCarthy**	Y	N	Y	Y	Y	Y	Y
24 Carbajal	N	N	N	N	N	N	Y
25 **Knight**	Y	N	Y	Y	Y	Y	Y
26 Brownley	N	N	N	N	N	N	Y
27 Chu	N	N	N	N	N	N	Y
28 Schiff	N	Y	N	N	N	N	Y
29 Cardenas	N	N	N	N	N	N	Y
30 Sherman	N	N	N	N	N	N	Y
31 Aguilar	N	Y	N	N	N	N	Y
32 Napolitano	–	–	–	–	–	–	+
33 Lieu	N	N	N	N	N	N	Y
34 Gomez	N	N	N	N	N	N	Y
35 Torres	N	N	N	N	N	N	Y
36 Ruiz	N	N	N	Y	N	N	Y
37 Bass	N	Y	N	N	N	N	Y
38 Sánchez, Linda	N	N	N	N	N	N	Y
39 **Royce**	Y	N	Y	Y	Y	Y	Y
40 Roybal-Allard	N	N	N	N	N	N	Y
41 Takano	N	N	N	N	N	N	Y
42 **Calvert**	Y	N	Y	Y	Y	Y	Y
43 Waters	N	N	N	N	N	N	Y
44 Barragan	N	N	N	N	N	N	Y
45 **Walters**	Y	N	Y	Y	Y	Y	Y
46 Correa	N	N	N	N	N	N	Y
47 Lowenthal	N	N	N	N	N	N	Y
48 **Rohrabacher**	Y	N	Y	Y	Y	Y	Y
49 **Issa**	Y	N	Y	Y	Y	Y	Y
50 **Hunter**	N	Y	N	Y	N	Y	Y
51 Vargas	N	Y	N	Y	N	Y	Y
52 Peters	N	Y	N	N	N	N	Y
53 Davis	N	N	N	N	N	N	Y

	370	371	372	373	374	375	376
COLORADO							
1 DeGette	N	Y	N	N	N	N	Y
2 Polis	N	N	N	N	N	N	Y
3 **Tipton**	Y	Y	Y	Y	Y	Y	Y
4 **Buck**	Y	N	Y	Y	Y	Y	Y
5 **Lamborn**	Y	Y	Y	?	Y	Y	Y
6 **Coffman**	Y	N	Y	Y	Y	Y	Y
7 Perlmutter	N	N	N	N	N	?	Y
CONNECTICUT							
1 Larson	N	Y	N	N	N	N	Y
2 Courtney	N	Y	N	N	N	N	Y
3 DeLauro	N	N	N	N	N	N	Y
4 Himes	N	N	N	N	N	N	Y
5 Esty	N	N	N	N	N	N	Y
DELAWARE							
AL Blunt Rochester	N	Y	N	N	N	N	Y
FLORIDA							
1 **Gaetz**	N	Y	Y	Y	Y	Y	Y
2 **Dunn**	Y	Y	Y	Y	Y	Y	Y
3 **Yoho**	Y	N	Y	Y	Y	Y	Y
4 **Rutherford**	Y	N	Y	Y	Y	Y	Y
5 Lawson	N	Y	N	N	N	N	Y
6 **DeSantis**	Y	Y	Y	Y	Y	Y	Y
7 Murphy	N	Y	N	Y	N	Y	Y
8 **Posey**	Y	N	Y	Y	Y	Y	Y
9 Soto	N	N	N	N	N	N	Y
10 Demings	N	Y	N	N	N	N	Y
11 **Webster**	Y	Y	Y	Y	Y	Y	Y
12 **Bilirakis**	Y	N	+	+	+	+	+
13 Crist	N	N	N	N	N	N	Y
14 Castor	N	N	N	N	N	N	Y
15 **Ross**	Y	Y	Y	Y	Y	Y	Y
16 **Buchanan**	Y	N	Y	Y	Y	Y	Y
17 **Rooney, T.**	Y	Y	Y	Y	Y	Y	Y
18 **Mast**	N	Y	Y	Y	Y	Y	Y
19 **Rooney, F.**	Y	N	Y	Y	Y	Y	Y
20 Hastings	N	Y	N	N	Y	N	Y
21 Frankel	N	N	N	N	N	N	Y
22 Deutch	N	Y	N	N	N	N	Y
23 Wasserman Schultz	N	Y	N	N	N	N	Y
24 Wilson	N	N	N	N	N	N	Y
25 **Diaz-Balart**	N	Y	Y	Y	Y	Y	Y
26 **Curbelo**	N	N	Y	Y	Y	Y	Y
27 **Ros-Lehtinen**	N	Y	N	Y	Y	Y	Y
GEORGIA							
1 **Carter**	Y	N	Y	Y	Y	Y	Y
2 Bishop	N	Y	N	N	N	N	Y
3 **Ferguson**	Y	N	Y	Y	Y	Y	Y
4 Johnson	N	N	N	N	N	N	Y
5 Lewis	N	N	N	N	N	N	Y
6 **Handel**	Y	N	Y	Y	Y	Y	Y
7 **Woodall**	Y	N	Y	Y	Y	Y	Y
8 **Scott, A.**	Y	N	Y	Y	Y	Y	Y
9 **Collins**	Y	N	Y	Y	Y	Y	Y
10 **Hice**	Y	N	Y	Y	Y	Y	Y
11 **Loudermilk**	Y	N	Y	Y	Y	Y	Y
12 **Allen**	Y	N	Y	Y	Y	Y	Y
13 Scott, D.	N	Y	N	N	N	N	Y
14 **Graves**	Y	N	Y	Y	Y	Y	Y
HAWAII							
1 Hanabusa	N	N	N	N	N	N	Y
2 Gabbard	N	N	N	N	N	N	Y
IDAHO							
1 **Labrador**	?	?	?	?	?	?	?
2 **Simpson**	N	N	Y	Y	Y	Y	Y
ILLINOIS							
1 Rush	N	N	N	N	N	N	Y
2 Kelly	N	Y	N	N	N	N	Y
3 Lipinski	N	Y	N	N	N	N	Y
4 Gutierrez	N	Y	N	N	N	N	Y
5 Quigley	N	N	N	N	N	N	Y
6 **Roskam**	N	N	Y	Y	Y	Y	Y
7 Davis, D.	N	Y	N	N	N	N	Y
8 Krishnamoorthi	N	Y	N	N	N	N	Y
9 Schakowsky	N	N	N	N	N	N	Y
10 Schneider	N	N	N	N	N	N	Y
11 Foster	N	N	N	N	N	N	Y
12 **Bost**	Y	N	Y	Y	Y	Y	Y
13 **Davis, R.**	–	+	Y	Y	Y	Y	Y
14 **Hultgren**	N	N	Y	Y	Y	Y	Y
15 **Shimkus**	N	Y	Y	Y	Y	Y	Y

	370	371	372	373	374	375	376
16 **Kinzinger**	N	Y	Y	Y	Y	Y	Y
17 Bustos	N	Y	N	N	N	N	Y
18 **LaHood**	N	Y	Y	Y	Y	Y	Y
INDIANA							
1 Visclosky	N	N	N	N	N	N	Y
2 **Walorski**	Y	N	Y	Y	Y	Y	Y
3 **Banks**	Y	N	Y	Y	Y	Y	Y
4 **Rokita**	Y	N	Y	Y	Y	Y	Y
5 **Brooks**	Y	N	Y	Y	Y	Y	Y
6 **Messer**	Y	Y	Y	Y	Y	Y	Y
7 Carson	N	Y	N	N	N	N	Y
8 **Bucshon**	Y	N	Y	Y	Y	Y	Y
9 **Hollingsworth**	Y	N	Y	Y	Y	Y	Y
IOWA							
1 **Blum**	Y	N	Y	Y	Y	Y	Y
2 Loebsack	N	N	N	N	N	N	Y
3 **Young**	Y	N	Y	Y	Y	Y	Y
4 **King**	Y	N	Y	Y	Y	Y	Y
KANSAS							
1 **Marshall**	Y	N	Y	Y	Y	Y	Y
2 **Jenkins**	Y	N	Y	Y	Y	Y	Y
3 **Yoder**	Y	Y	Y	Y	Y	Y	Y
4 **Estes**	Y	N	Y	Y	Y	Y	Y
KENTUCKY							
1 **Comer**	Y	Y	Y	Y	Y	Y	Y
2 **Guthrie**	Y	Y	Y	Y	Y	Y	Y
3 Yarmuth	N	N	N	N	N	N	Y
4 **Massie**	Y	N	Y	Y	Y	Y	Y
5 **Rogers**	Y	Y	Y	Y	Y	Y	Y
6 **Barr**	Y	N	Y	Y	Y	Y	Y
LOUISIANA							
1 **Scalise**	+	–	+	+	+	+	+
2 Richmond	N	Y	N	N	N	N	Y
3 **Higgins**	Y	N	Y	Y	Y	Y	Y
4 **Johnson**	Y	N	Y	Y	Y	Y	Y
5 **Abraham**	Y	N	Y	Y	Y	Y	Y
6 **Graves**	Y	N	Y	Y	Y	Y	Y
MAINE							
1 Pingree	N	Y	N	N	N	N	Y
2 **Poliquin**	Y	N	Y	Y	Y	Y	Y
MARYLAND							
1 **Harris**	Y	N	Y	Y	Y	Y	Y
2 Ruppersberger	N	Y	N	Y	N	N	Y
3 Sarbanes	N	N	N	N	N	N	Y
4 Brown	N	N	N	N	N	N	Y
5 Hoyer	N	Y	N	N	N	N	Y
6 Delaney	N	N	N	N	N	N	Y
7 Cummings	?	?	?	?	?	?	?
8 Raskin	N	N	N	N	N	N	Y
MASSACHUSETTS							
1 Neal	N	N	N	N	N	N	Y
2 McGovern	N	N	N	N	N	N	Y
3 Tsongas	N	N	N	N	N	N	Y
4 Kennedy	N	N	N	N	N	N	Y
5 Clark	N	N	N	N	N	N	Y
6 Moulton	N	N	N	N	N	N	Y
7 Capuano	N	N	N	N	N	N	Y
8 Lynch	N	N	N	N	N	N	Y
9 Keating	N	N	N	N	N	N	Y
MICHIGAN							
1 **Bergman**	Y	N	Y	Y	Y	Y	Y
2 **Huizenga**	Y	N	Y	Y	Y	Y	Y
3 **Amash**	Y	N	N	N	Y	N	Y
4 **Moolenaar**	Y	N	Y	Y	Y	Y	Y
5 Kildee	N	N	N	N	N	N	Y
6 **Upton**	N	Y	N	Y	Y	Y	Y
7 **Walberg**	Y	N	Y	Y	Y	Y	Y
8 **Bishop**	Y	N	Y	Y	Y	Y	Y
9 Levin	N	N	N	N	N	N	Y
10 **Mitchell**	Y	N	Y	Y	Y	Y	Y
11 **Trott**	Y	N	Y	Y	Y	Y	Y
12 Dingell	N	N	N	N	N	N	Y
13 Conyers	N	Y	N	N	N	N	Y
14 Lawrence	N	Y	N	N	N	N	Y
MINNESOTA							
1 Walz	N	Y	N	N	N	N	Y
2 **Lewis**	N	N	N	Y	Y	Y	Y
3 **Paulsen**	Y	N	N	Y	Y	Y	Y
4 McCollum	N	N	N	N	N	N	Y
5 Ellison	N	N	N	N	N	N	Y
6 **Emmer**	N	N	Y	Y	Y	Y	Y
7 Peterson	N	N	N	N	N	N	Y
8 Nolan	N	N	N	N	N	N	Y
MISSISSIPPI							
1 **Kelly**	Y	N	Y	Y	Y	Y	Y
2 Thompson	N	Y	N	N	Y	N	Y
3 **Harper**	Y	N	Y	Y	Y	Y	Y
4 **Palazzo**	Y	N	Y	Y	Y	Y	Y
MISSOURI							
1 Clay	N	Y	N	N	N	N	Y
2 **Wagner**	Y	N	Y	Y	Y	Y	Y
3 **Luetkemeyer**	Y	N	Y	Y	Y	Y	Y
4 **Hartzler**	Y	N	Y	Y	Y	Y	Y
5 Cleaver	–	+	–	–	–	–	+
6 **Graves**	Y	Y	Y	Y	Y	Y	Y
7 **Long**	Y	N	Y	Y	Y	Y	Y
8 **Smith**	Y	N	Y	Y	Y	Y	Y
MONTANA							
AL **Gianforte**	Y	N	Y	Y	Y	Y	Y
NEBRASKA							
1 **Fortenberry**	Y	N	Y	Y	Y	Y	Y
2 **Bacon**	Y	N	Y	Y	Y	Y	Y
3 **Smith**	Y	N	Y	Y	Y	Y	Y
NEVADA							
1 Titus	N	Y	N	N	N	N	Y
2 **Amodei**	Y	Y	Y	Y	Y	Y	Y
3 Rosen	N	N	N	N	N	N	Y
4 Kihuen	N	N	N	N	N	N	Y
NEW HAMPSHIRE							
1 Shea-Porter	N	N	N	N	Y	N	Y
2 Kuster	N	N	N	N	Y	N	Y
NEW JERSEY							
1 Norcross	N	N	N	N	N	N	Y
2 **LoBiondo**	N	N	N	Y	Y	Y	Y
3 **MacArthur**	N	N	Y	Y	Y	Y	Y
4 **Smith**	N	N	Y	Y	N	Y	Y
5 Gottheimer	N	N	N	N	N	N	Y
6 Pallone	N	N	N	N	N	N	Y
7 **Lance**	N	N	Y	Y	Y	Y	Y
8 Sires	N	Y	N	N	N	N	Y
9 Pascrell	N	N	N	N	N	N	Y
10 Payne	N	Y	N	N	N	N	Y
11 **Frelinghuysen**	Y	N	Y	Y	Y	Y	Y
12 Watson Coleman	N	Y	N	N	N	N	Y
NEW MEXICO							
1 Lujan Grisham	N	N	N	N	N	N	Y
2 **Pearce**	Y	Y	Y	N	Y	Y	Y
3 Luján	N	N	N	N	N	N	Y
NEW YORK							
1 **Zeldin**	N	N	Y	Y	Y	Y	Y
2 **King**	N	N	Y	Y	Y	Y	Y
3 Suozzi	N	N	N	N	N	N	Y
4 Rice	N	N	N	N	N	N	Y
5 Meeks	N	N	?	?	?	?	?
6 Meng	N	N	N	N	N	N	Y
7 Velázquez	N	Y	N	N	N	N	Y
8 Jeffries	N	Y	N	N	N	N	Y
9 Clarke	N	Y	N	N	N	N	Y
10 Nadler	N	N	N	N	N	N	Y
11 **Donovan**	N	N	Y	Y	Y	Y	Y
12 Maloney, C.	N	N	N	N	N	N	Y
13 Espaillat	N	N	N	N	N	N	Y
14 Crowley	N	Y	N	N	N	N	Y
15 Serrano	N	N	N	N	N	N	Y
16 Engel	N	N	N	N	N	N	Y
17 Lowey	N	N	N	N	N	N	Y
18 Maloney, S.P.	N	Y	N	Y	N	N	Y
19 **Faso**	N	N	N	Y	Y	Y	Y
20 Tonko	N	N	N	N	N	N	Y
21 **Stefanik**	N	N	Y	Y	Y	Y	Y
22 **Tenney**	Y	N	Y	Y	Y	Y	Y
23 **Reed**	N	N	Y	Y	Y	Y	Y
24 **Katko**	N	N	N	Y	N	Y	Y
25 Slaughter	N	N	N	N	N	N	Y
26 Higgins	N	N	N	N	N	N	Y
27 **Collins**	Y	N	N	Y	Y	Y	Y
NORTH CAROLINA							
1 Butterfield	N	Y	N	N	N	N	Y
2 **Holding**	Y	N	Y	Y	Y	Y	Y
3 **Jones**	Y	Y	?	?	?	?	?
4 Price	N	N	N	N	N	N	Y
5 **Foxx**	Y	N	Y	Y	Y	Y	Y
6 **Walker**	Y	N	Y	Y	Y	Y	Y
7 **Rouzer**	Y	N	Y	Y	Y	Y	Y
8 **Hudson**	Y	N	Y	Y	Y	Y	Y
9 **Pittenger**	Y	N	Y	Y	Y	Y	Y
10 **McHenry**	Y	N	Y	Y	Y	Y	Y
11 **Meadows**	Y	N	Y	Y	Y	Y	Y
12 Adams	N	Y	N	N	N	N	Y
13 **Budd**	Y	N	Y	Y	Y	Y	Y
NORTH DAKOTA							
AL **Cramer**	Y	Y	Y	Y	Y	Y	Y
OHIO							
1 **Chabot**	Y	N	Y	Y	Y	Y	Y
2 **Wenstrup**	Y	N	Y	Y	Y	Y	Y
3 Beatty	N	Y	N	N	N	N	Y
4 **Jordan**	Y	N	Y	Y	Y	Y	Y
5 **Latta**	Y	N	Y	Y	Y	Y	Y
6 **Johnson**	N	N	Y	Y	Y	Y	Y
7 **Gibbs**	Y	N	Y	Y	Y	Y	Y
8 **Davidson**	Y	Y	Y	Y	Y	Y	Y
9 Kaptur	N	N	N	N	N	N	Y
10 **Turner**	N	N	N	Y	Y	Y	Y
11 Fudge	N	Y	N	N	N	N	Y
12 **Tiberi**	N	Y	Y	Y	Y	Y	Y
13 Ryan	N	Y	N	N	N	N	Y
14 **Joyce**	N	N	N	Y	N	Y	Y
15 **Stivers**	N	N	N	Y	Y	Y	Y
16 **Renacci**	N	Y	Y	Y	Y	Y	Y
OKLAHOMA							
1 **Bridenstine**	Y	Y	Y	Y	Y	Y	Y
2 **Mullin**	Y	N	Y	Y	Y	Y	Y
3 **Lucas**	Y	N	Y	Y	Y	Y	Y
4 **Cole**	Y	N	Y	Y	Y	Y	Y
5 **Russell**	Y	N	N	Y	Y	Y	Y
OREGON							
1 Bonamici	N	N	N	N	N	N	Y
2 **Walden**	N	N	N	Y	Y	Y	Y
3 Blumenauer	N	N	N	N	N	N	Y
4 DeFazio	N	N	N	N	N	N	Y
5 Schrader	N	N	N	N	N	N	Y
PENNSYLVANIA							
1 Brady	N	N	N	N	N	N	Y
2 Evans	N	Y	N	N	N	N	Y
3 **Kelly**	N	Y	Y	Y	Y	Y	Y
4 **Perry**	Y	N	Y	Y	Y	Y	Y
5 **Thompson**	Y	N	Y	Y	Y	Y	Y
6 **Costello**	N	Y	N	Y	Y	Y	Y
7 **Meehan**	N	N	N	Y	Y	Y	Y
8 **Fitzpatrick**	N	N	N	Y	N	Y	Y
9 **Shuster**	N	N	Y	Y	Y	Y	Y
10 **Marino**	N	Y	Y	Y	Y	Y	Y
11 **Barletta**	N	Y	Y	Y	Y	Y	Y
12 **Rothfus**	Y	N	Y	Y	Y	Y	Y
13 Boyle	N	N	N	N	N	N	Y
14 Doyle	N	N	N	N	N	N	Y
15 **Dent**	Y	N	N	Y	Y	Y	Y
16 **Smucker**	Y	N	Y	Y	Y	Y	Y
17 Cartwright	N	N	N	N	N	N	Y
18 **Murphy**	N	N	Y	Y	N	Y	Y
RHODE ISLAND							
1 Cicilline	N	N	N	N	N	N	Y
2 Langevin	N	N	N	N	N	N	Y
SOUTH CAROLINA							
1 **Sanford**	?	?	N	N	Y	Y	Y
2 **Wilson**	Y	N	Y	Y	Y	Y	Y
3 **Duncan**	Y	N	Y	Y	Y	Y	Y
4 **Gowdy**	Y	Y	Y	Y	Y	Y	Y
5 **Norman**	Y	N	Y	Y	Y	Y	Y
6 Clyburn	N	Y	N	N	N	N	Y
7 **Rice**	Y	Y	Y	Y	Y	Y	Y
SOUTH DAKOTA							
AL **Noem**	Y	N	Y	Y	Y	Y	Y
TENNESSEE							
1 **Roe**	Y	N	Y	Y	Y	Y	Y
2 **Duncan**	Y	N	Y	Y	Y	Y	Y
3 **Fleischmann**	Y	N	Y	Y	Y	Y	Y
4 **DesJarlais**	Y	N	Y	Y	Y	Y	Y
5 Cooper	N	Y	N	N	N	N	Y
6 **Black**	Y	N	Y	Y	Y	Y	Y
7 **Blackburn**	Y	N	Y	Y	Y	Y	Y
8 **Kustoff**	Y	N	Y	Y	Y	Y	Y
9 Cohen	N	N	N	N	N	N	Y
TEXAS							
1 **Gohmert**	Y	N	Y	Y	Y	Y	Y
2 **Poe**	Y	N	Y	Y	Y	Y	Y
3 **Johnson, S.**	?	?	Y	Y	Y	Y	Y
4 **Ratcliffe**	Y	N	Y	Y	Y	Y	Y
5 **Hensarling**	Y	N	Y	Y	Y	Y	Y
6 **Barton**	Y	N	Y	Y	Y	Y	Y
7 **Culberson**	Y	N	Y	Y	Y	Y	Y
8 **Brady**	Y	N	Y	Y	Y	Y	Y
9 Green, A.	N	N	N	N	N	N	Y
10 **McCaul**	Y	N	Y	Y	Y	Y	Y
11 **Conaway**	Y	Y	Y	Y	Y	Y	Y
12 **Granger**	Y	N	Y	Y	Y	Y	Y
13 **Thornberry**	Y	N	Y	Y	Y	Y	Y
14 **Weber**	Y	N	Y	Y	Y	Y	Y
15 Gonzalez	N	Y	N	N	N	N	Y
16 O'Rourke	N	N	N	N	N	N	Y
17 **Flores**	Y	N	Y	Y	Y	Y	Y
18 Jackson Lee	N	Y	N	N	Y	N	Y
19 **Arrington**	Y	N	Y	Y	Y	Y	Y
20 Castro	N	N	N	N	N	N	Y
21 **Smith**	Y	N	Y	Y	Y	Y	Y
22 **Olson**	Y	N	Y	Y	Y	Y	Y
23 **Hurd**	Y	N	Y	Y	Y	Y	Y
24 **Marchant**	Y	N	Y	Y	Y	Y	Y
25 **Williams**	Y	N	Y	Y	Y	Y	Y
26 **Burgess**	Y	N	Y	Y	Y	Y	Y
27 **Farenthold**	Y	N	Y	Y	Y	Y	Y
28 Cuellar	N	N	N	N	N	N	Y
29 Green, G.	N	N	N	N	N	N	Y
30 Johnson, E.B.	N	N	N	N	Y	N	Y
31 **Carter**	Y	N	Y	Y	Y	Y	Y
32 **Sessions**	Y	N	Y	Y	Y	Y	Y
33 Veasey	N	N	N	N	N	N	Y
34 Vela	N	N	N	N	Y	N	Y
35 Doggett	N	N	N	N	N	N	Y
36 **Babin**	Y	N	Y	Y	Y	Y	Y
UTAH							
1 **Bishop**	Y	N	Y	Y	Y	Y	Y
2 **Stewart**	Y	N	Y	Y	Y	Y	Y
4 **Love**	Y	Y	Y	Y	Y	Y	Y
VERMONT							
AL Welch	N	N	N	N	N	N	Y
VIRGINIA							
1 **Wittman**	Y	Y	Y	Y	Y	Y	Y
2 **Taylor**	Y	N	Y	Y	Y	Y	Y
3 Scott	N	N	N	N	N	N	Y
4 McEachin	N	N	N	N	N	N	Y
5 **Garrett**	Y	Y	Y	Y	Y	Y	Y
6 **Goodlatte**	Y	N	Y	Y	Y	Y	Y
7 **Brat**	Y	N	Y	Y	Y	Y	Y
8 Beyer	N	N	N	N	N	N	Y
9 **Griffith**	Y	N	Y	Y	Y	Y	Y
10 **Comstock**	Y	N	N	Y	Y	Y	Y
11 Connolly	N	N	N	N	N	N	Y
WASHINGTON							
1 DelBene	N	Y	N	N	N	N	Y
2 Larsen	N	Y	N	N	N	N	Y
3 **Herrera Beutler**	Y	N	Y	Y	Y	Y	Y
4 **Newhouse**	N	N	N	Y	Y	Y	Y
5 **McMorris Rodgers**	N	N	Y	Y	Y	Y	Y
6 Kilmer	N	Y	N	N	N	N	Y
7 Jayapal	N	N	N	N	N	N	Y
8 **Reichert**	N	N	N	Y	Y	Y	Y
9 Smith	N	N	N	N	N	N	Y
10 Heck	N	Y	N	N	N	N	Y
WEST VIRGINIA							
1 **McKinley**	N	Y	Y	Y	Y	Y	Y
2 **Mooney**	Y	Y	Y	Y	Y	Y	Y
3 **Jenkins**	Y	N	Y	Y	Y	Y	Y
WISCONSIN							
1 **Ryan**							
2 Pocan	N	N	N	N	N	N	Y
3 Kind	N	Y	N	N	N	N	Y
4 Moore	N	Y	N	N	N	N	Y
5 **Sensenbrenner**	Y	N	Y	Y	N	Y	Y
6 **Grothman**	Y	N	Y	Y	Y	Y	Y
7 **Duffy**	N	N	Y	Y	Y	Y	Y
8 **Gallagher**	Y	N	Y	Y	Y	Y	Y
WYOMING							
AL **Cheney**	Y	N	Y	Y	Y	Y	Y

VOTE NUMBER

377. HR 2810. FISCAL 2018 DEFENSE AUTHORIZATION/RECOMMIT. Lujan Grisham, D-N.M., motion to recommit the bill to the House Armed Services Committee with instructions to report it back immediately with an amendment that would prohibit funds authorized by the bill from being used to plan, develop, or construct any barriers, including walls or fences, along "the international border of the United States." Motion rejected 190-235 : R 0-235; D 190-0. July 14, 2017.

378. HR 2810. FISCAL 2018 DEFENSE AUTHORIZATION/PASSAGE. Passage of the bill that would authorize $688.3 billion in discretionary funding for defense programs in fiscal 2018. The total would include $74.6 billion for Overseas Contingency Operations funds, of which $10 billion would be used for non-war, base defense budget needs; $239.7 billion for operations and maintenance; $10.2 billion for military construction; $142.9 billion for military personnel; and $33.9 billion for defense health care programs. It would authorize $12.5 billion for procurement of F-35 planes, research and development, as well as modifications to existing aircraft, and would prohibit the retirement of the A-10 bomber fleet. The bill would require the Defense Department to submit to Congress a report on vulnerabilities to military installations resulting from climate change over the next 20 years, and would express the sense of Congress that climate change is a "direct threat" to U.S. national security. The bill would also require the Air Force to establish, by 2019, the Space Corps, a fighting force to improve the U.S. military's ability to address threats in space. Passed 344-81 : R 227-8; D 117-73. July 14, 2017.

379. HR 2210. SERGEANT JOSEPH GEORGE KUSICK VA COMMUNITY LIVING CENTER/PASSAGE. Dunn, R-Fla., motion to suspend the rules and pass the bill that would designate the VA's community living center in Butler Township, Butler County, Pa., as the "Sergeant Joseph George Kusick VA Community Living Center." Motion agreed to 401-0 : R 224-0; D 177-0. July 17, 2017.

380. H J RES 92. WMATA BOARD APPOINTEE PROTOCOL/PASSAGE. Goodlatte, R-Va., motion to suspend the rules and pass the joint resolution that would grant congressional approval to amendments made by Virginia, Maryland and the District of Columbia to the Washington Area Transit Regulation Compact regarding the appointment of federal directors to the Washington Metropolitan Area Transit Authority's board of directors. Motion agreed to 402-0 : R 224-0; D 178-0. July 17, 2017.

381. H J RES 76. WASHINGTON METRORAIL SAFETY COMMISSION/PASSAGE. Goodlatte, R-Va., motion to suspend the rules and pass the joint resolution that would grant congressional approval to the Commonwealth of Virginia, the state of Maryland and the District of Columbia to enter into an interstate compact, which would establish the Washington Metrorail Safety Commission. The commission would act as the safety oversight authority for the Washington Metropolitan Area Transit Authority, with safety, regulatory and enforcement authority over the Metrorail system operated by WMATA. Motion agreed to 399-5 : R 221-5; D 178-0. July 17, 2017.

382. H RES 451, HR 806. OZONE STANDARDS IMPLEMENTATION/PREVIOUS QUESTION. Burgess, R-Texas, motion to order the previous question (thus ending debate and the possibility of amendment) on the rule (H Res 451) that would provide for House floor consideration of the bill (HR 806) that would extend for eight years the deadline for the EPA to implement new National Ambient Air Quality Standards for ground-level ozone. The bill would not limit the authority of state or local governments to require more stringent emissions standards, but it would prohibit EPA from proposing new standards for ground-level ozone before 2025. Motion agreed to 231-188 : R 231-0; D 0-188. July 18, 2017.

383. H RES 451, HR 806. OZONE STANDARDS IMPLIMENTATION/RULE. Adoption of the rule (H Res 451) that would provide for House floor consideration of the bill (HR 806) that would extend for eight years the deadline for the Environmental Protection Agency to implement new National Ambient Air Quality Standards for ground-level ozone. The bill would not limit the authority of state or local governments to require more stringent emissions standards, but it would prohibit EPA from proposing new standards for ground-level ozone before 2025. Adopted 235-188 : R 234-0; D 1-188. July 18, 2017.

	377	378	379	380	381	382	383
ALABAMA							
1 Byrne	N	Y	Y	Y	Y	Y	Y
2 Roby	N	Y	Y	Y	Y	Y	Y
3 Rogers	N	Y	Y	Y	Y	Y	Y
4 Aderholt	N	Y	Y	Y	Y	Y	Y
5 Brooks	N	Y	?	?	?	?	?
6 Palmer	N	Y	Y	Y	Y	?	Y
7 Sewell	Y	Y	Y	Y	Y	N	N
ALASKA							
AL Young	N	Y	Y	Y	Y	Y	Y
ARIZONA							
1 O'Halleran	Y	Y	Y	Y	Y	N	N
2 McSally	N	Y	Y	Y	Y	Y	Y
3 Grijalva	Y	N	?	?	?	N	N
4 Gosar	N	Y	Y	Y	Y	Y	Y
5 Biggs	N	Y	Y	Y	Y	Y	Y
6 Schweikert	N	Y	Y	Y	Y	Y	Y
7 Gallego	Y	Y	Y	Y	Y	N	N
8 Franks	N	Y	Y	Y	Y	Y	Y
9 Sinema	Y	Y	Y	Y	Y	N	N
ARKANSAS							
1 Crawford	N	Y	Y	Y	Y	Y	Y
2 Hill	N	Y	Y	Y	Y	Y	Y
3 Womack	N	Y	Y	Y	Y	Y	Y
4 Westerman	N	Y	Y	Y	Y	Y	Y
CALIFORNIA							
1 LaMalfa	N	Y	Y	Y	Y	Y	Y
2 Huffman	Y	N	Y	Y	Y	N	N
3 Garamendi	Y	Y	Y	Y	Y	N	N
4 McClintock	N	N	Y	Y	Y	Y	Y
5 Thompson	Y	N	Y	Y	Y	N	N
6 Matsui	Y	Y	Y	Y	Y	N	N
7 Bera	Y	Y	Y	Y	Y	N	N
8 Cook	N	Y	Y	Y	Y	Y	Y
9 McNerney	Y	Y	?	?	?	N	N
10 Denham	N	Y	Y	Y	Y	Y	Y
11 DeSaulnier	Y	N	Y	Y	Y	N	N
12 Pelosi	Y	Y	Y	Y	Y	N	N
13 Lee	Y	N	Y	Y	Y	N	N
14 Speier	Y	N	Y	Y	Y	N	N
15 Swalwell	Y	N	Y	Y	Y	N	N
16 Costa	Y	Y	Y	Y	Y	N	N
17 Khanna	Y	N	Y	Y	Y	N	N
18 Eshoo	Y	N	Y	Y	Y	N	N
19 Lofgren	Y	N	Y	Y	Y	N	N
20 Panetta	Y	Y	Y	Y	Y	N	N
21 Valadao	N	Y	Y	Y	Y	Y	Y
22 Nunes	N	Y	Y	Y	Y	Y	Y
23 McCarthy	N	Y	Y	Y	Y	Y	Y
24 Carbajal	Y	Y	Y	Y	Y	N	N
25 Knight	N	Y	+	+	+	Y	Y
26 Brownley	Y	Y	Y	Y	Y	N	N
27 Chu	Y	N	Y	Y	Y	N	N
28 Schiff	Y	Y	Y	Y	Y	N	N
29 Cardenas	Y	Y	Y	Y	Y	N	N
30 Sherman	Y	N	Y	Y	Y	N	N
31 Aguilar	Y	Y	Y	Y	Y	N	N
32 Napolitano	+	-	?	?	?	?	?
33 Lieu	Y	N	Y	Y	Y	N	N
34 Gomez	Y	N	Y	Y	Y	N	N
35 Torres	Y	Y	Y	Y	Y	N	N
36 Ruiz	Y	Y	Y	Y	Y	N	N
37 Bass	Y	N	Y	Y	Y	N	N
38 Sánchez, Linda	Y	N	Y	Y	Y	N	N
39 Royce	N	Y	Y	Y	Y	Y	Y
40 Roybal-Allard	Y	Y	Y	Y	Y	N	N
41 Takano	Y	N	Y	Y	Y	N	N
42 Calvert	N	Y	Y	Y	Y	Y	Y
43 Waters	Y	Y	Y	Y	Y	N	N
44 Barragan	Y	N	Y	Y	Y	N	N
45 Walters	N	Y	Y	Y	Y	Y	Y
46 Correa	Y	Y	Y	Y	Y	N	N
47 Lowenthal	Y	N	Y	Y	Y	N	N
48 Rohrabacher	N	Y	?	?	Y	Y	Y
49 Issa	N	Y	Y	Y	Y	Y	Y
50 Hunter	N	Y	Y	Y	Y	Y	Y
51 Vargas	Y	N	?	?	?	N	N
52 Peters	Y	Y	Y	Y	Y	N	N
53 Davis	Y	Y	Y	Y	Y	N	N

	377	378	379	380	381	382	383
COLORADO							
1 DeGette	Y	N	Y	Y	Y	N	N
2 Polis	Y	N	Y	Y	Y	N	N
3 Tipton	N	Y	?	?	?	Y	Y
4 Buck	N	Y	Y	Y	Y	Y	Y
5 Lamborn	N	Y	Y	Y	Y	Y	Y
6 Coffman	N	Y	Y	Y	Y	Y	Y
7 Perlmutter	Y	Y	Y	Y	Y	N	N
CONNECTICUT							
1 Larson	Y	Y	Y	Y	Y	N	N
2 Courtney	Y	Y	Y	Y	Y	N	N
3 DeLauro	Y	Y	Y	Y	Y	N	N
4 Himes	Y	Y	Y	Y	Y	N	N
5 Esty	Y	Y	Y	Y	Y	N	N
DELAWARE							
AL Blunt Rochester	Y	Y	Y	Y	Y	N	N
FLORIDA							
1 Gaetz	N	Y	Y	Y	Y	Y	Y
2 Dunn	N	Y	Y	Y	Y	Y	Y
3 Yoho	N	Y	Y	Y	Y	Y	Y
4 Rutherford	N	Y	Y	Y	Y	Y	Y
5 Lawson	Y	Y	Y	Y	Y	N	N
6 DeSantis	N	Y	?	?	?	?	Y
7 Murphy	Y	Y	Y	Y	Y	N	N
8 Posey	N	Y	Y	Y	Y	Y	Y
9 Soto	Y	Y	Y	Y	Y	N	N
10 Demings	Y	Y	Y	Y	Y	N	N
11 Webster	N	Y	+	+	+	Y	Y
12 Bilirakis	-	+	Y	Y	Y	Y	Y
13 Crist	Y	Y	Y	Y	Y	N	N
14 Castor	Y	Y	Y	Y	Y	N	N
15 Ross	N	Y	Y	Y	Y	Y	Y
16 Buchanan	N	Y	Y	Y	Y	Y	Y
17 Rooney, T.	N	Y	Y	Y	Y	Y	Y
18 Mast	N	Y	?	?	?	Y	Y
19 Rooney, F.	N	Y	?	?	?	Y	Y
20 Hastings	Y	Y	Y	Y	Y	N	N
21 Frankel	Y	Y	Y	Y	Y	N	N
22 Deutch	Y	Y	Y	Y	Y	N	N
23 Wasserman Schultz	Y	Y	Y	Y	Y	N	N
24 Wilson	Y	Y	Y	Y	Y	N	N
25 Diaz-Balart	N	Y	Y	Y	Y	Y	Y
26 Curbelo	N	Y	Y	Y	Y	Y	Y
27 Ros-Lehtinen	N	Y	Y	Y	Y	Y	Y
GEORGIA							
1 Carter	N	Y	Y	Y	Y	Y	Y
2 Bishop	Y	Y	Y	Y	Y	N	N
3 Ferguson	N	Y	Y	Y	Y	Y	Y
4 Johnson	Y	N	Y	Y	Y	N	N
5 Lewis	Y	N	Y	Y	Y	N	N
6 Handel	N	Y	Y	Y	Y	Y	Y
7 Woodall	N	Y	Y	Y	Y	Y	Y
8 Scott, A.	N	Y	Y	Y	Y	Y	Y
9 Collins	N	Y	Y	Y	Y	Y	Y
10 Hice	N	Y	Y	Y	Y	Y	Y
11 Loudermilk	N	Y	Y	Y	Y	Y	Y
12 Allen	N	Y	Y	Y	Y	Y	Y
13 Scott, D.	Y	Y	Y	Y	Y	N	N
14 Graves	N	Y	Y	Y	Y	Y	Y
HAWAII							
1 Hanabusa	Y	Y	Y	Y	Y	N	N
2 Gabbard	Y	N	Y	Y	Y	N	N
IDAHO							
1 Labrador	?	?	Y	Y	Y	?	?
2 Simpson	N	Y	Y	Y	Y	Y	Y
ILLINOIS							
1 Rush	Y	Y	?	?	?	N	N
2 Kelly	Y	N	Y	Y	Y	N	N
3 Lipinski	Y	Y	Y	Y	Y	N	N
4 Cutierrez	Y	N	+	+	+	N	N
5 Quigley	Y	Y	Y	Y	Y	N	N
6 Roskam	N	Y	Y	Y	Y	Y	Y
7 Davis, D.	Y	Y	Y	Y	Y	?	?
8 Krishnamoorthi	Y	Y	Y	Y	Y	N	N
9 Schakowsky	Y	N	Y	Y	Y	N	N
10 Schneider	Y	Y	Y	Y	Y	N	N
11 Foster	Y	Y	Y	Y	Y	N	N
12 Bost	N	Y	Y	Y	Y	Y	Y
13 Davis, R.	N	Y	Y	Y	Y	Y	Y
14 Hultgren	N	Y	?	Y	Y	Y	Y
15 Shimkus	N	Y	Y	Y	Y	Y	Y

	377	378	379	380	381	382	383
16 **Kinzinger**	N	Y	Y	Y	Y	Y	Y
17 Bustos	Y	Y	Y	Y	Y	N	N
18 **LaHood**	N	Y	Y	Y	Y	Y	Y
INDIANA							
1 Visclosky	Y	N	+	Y	Y	N	N
2 **Walorski**	N	Y	Y	Y	Y	Y	Y
3 **Banks**	N	Y	Y	Y	Y	Y	Y
4 **Rokita**	N	Y	Y	Y	Y	Y	Y
5 **Brooks**	N	Y	Y	Y	Y	Y	Y
6 **Messer**	N	Y	Y	Y	Y	Y	Y
7 Carson	Y	N	Y	Y	Y	N	N
8 **Bucshon**	N	Y	Y	Y	Y	Y	Y
9 **Hollingsworth**	N	Y	Y	Y	Y	Y	Y
IOWA							
1 **Blum**	N	Y	Y	Y	Y	Y	Y
2 Loebsack	Y	Y	Y	Y	Y	N	N
3 **Young**	N	Y	Y	Y	Y	Y	Y
4 **King**	N	Y	Y	Y	Y	Y	Y
KANSAS							
1 **Marshall**	N	Y	Y	Y	Y	Y	Y
2 **Jenkins**	N	Y	Y	Y	Y	Y	Y
3 **Yoder**	N	Y	Y	Y	Y	Y	Y
4 **Estes**	N	Y	Y	+	Y	Y	Y
KENTUCKY							
1 **Comer**	N	Y	Y	Y	Y	Y	Y
2 **Guthrie**	N	Y	Y	Y	Y	Y	Y
3 Yarmuth	Y	N	Y	Y	Y	N	N
4 **Massie**	N	N	Y	Y	N	Y	Y
5 **Rogers**	N	Y	Y	Y	Y	Y	Y
6 **Barr**	N	Y	Y	Y	Y	Y	Y
LOUISIANA							
1 **Scalise**	–	+	+	+	+	+	+
2 Richmond	Y	N	Y	Y	Y	N	N
3 **Higgins**	N	Y	?	?	?	Y	Y
4 **Johnson**	N	Y	?	?	?	Y	Y
5 **Abraham**	N	Y	Y	Y	Y	Y	Y
6 **Graves**	N	Y	Y	Y	Y	+	Y
MAINE							
1 Pingree	Y	Y	Y	Y	Y	N	N
2 **Poliquin**	N	Y	Y	Y	Y	Y	Y
MARYLAND							
1 **Harris**	N	N	Y	Y	Y	Y	Y
2 Ruppersberger	Y	Y	Y	Y	Y	N	?
3 Sarbanes	Y	Y	Y	Y	Y	N	N
4 Brown	Y	Y	Y	Y	Y	N	N
5 Hoyer	Y	Y	Y	Y	Y	N	N
6 Delaney	Y	Y	Y	Y	Y	N	N
7 Cummings	?	?	?	?	?	?	?
8 Raskin	Y	N	Y	Y	Y	N	N
MASSACHUSETTS							
1 Neal	Y	N	Y	Y	Y	N	N
2 McGovern	Y	N	Y	Y	Y	N	N
3 Tsongas	Y	N	Y	Y	Y	N	N
4 Kennedy	Y	N	Y	Y	Y	N	N
5 Clark	Y	N	Y	Y	Y	N	N
6 Moulton	Y	Y	Y	Y	Y	N	N
7 Capuano	Y	N	Y	Y	Y	N	N
8 Lynch	Y	Y	Y	Y	Y	N	N
9 Keating	Y	Y	Y	Y	Y	N	N
MICHIGAN							
1 **Bergman**	N	Y	Y	Y	Y	Y	Y
2 **Huizenga**	N	Y	Y	Y	Y	Y	Y
3 **Amash**	N	N	Y	Y	N	Y	Y
4 **Moolenaar**	N	Y	Y	Y	Y	Y	Y
5 Kildee	Y	N	Y	Y	Y	N	N
6 **Upton**	N	Y	Y	Y	Y	Y	Y
7 **Walberg**	N	Y	Y	Y	Y	Y	Y
8 **Bishop**	N	Y	Y	Y	Y	Y	Y
9 Levin	Y	N	Y	Y	Y	N	N
10 **Mitchell**	N	Y	Y	Y	Y	Y	Y
11 **Trott**	N	Y	Y	Y	Y	Y	Y
12 Dingell	Y	Y	Y	Y	Y	N	N
13 Conyers	Y	N	?	?	?	N	N
14 Lawrence	Y	N	Y	Y	Y	N	N
MINNESOTA							
1 Walz	Y	Y	Y	Y	Y	N	N
2 **Lewis**	N	Y	Y	Y	Y	Y	Y
3 **Paulsen**	N	Y	Y	Y	Y	Y	Y
4 McCollum	Y	Y	Y	Y	Y	N	N

	377	378	379	380	381	382	383
5 Ellison	Y	N	Y	Y	Y	N	N
6 **Emmer**	N	Y	Y	Y	Y	Y	Y
7 Peterson	Y	Y	Y	Y	Y	N	N
8 Nolan	Y	Y	Y	Y	Y	N	N
MISSISSIPPI							
1 **Kelly**	N	Y	Y	Y	Y	Y	Y
2 Thompson	Y	Y	Y	Y	Y	N	N
3 **Harper**	N	Y	Y	Y	Y	Y	Y
4 **Palazzo**	N	Y	Y	Y	Y	Y	Y
MISSOURI							
1 Clay	Y	Y	Y	Y	Y	N	N
2 **Wagner**	N	Y	Y	Y	Y	Y	Y
3 **Luetkemeyer**	N	Y	Y	Y	Y	Y	Y
4 **Hartzler**	N	Y	Y	Y	Y	Y	Y
5 Cleaver	+	+	Y	Y	Y	N	N
6 **Graves**	N	Y	Y	Y	Y	Y	Y
7 **Long**	N	Y	Y	Y	Y	Y	Y
8 **Smith**	N	Y	Y	Y	Y	Y	Y
MONTANA							
AL **Gianforte**	N	Y	Y	Y	Y	Y	Y
NEBRASKA							
1 **Fortenberry**	N	Y	Y	Y	Y	Y	Y
2 **Bacon**	N	Y	Y	Y	Y	Y	Y
3 **Smith**	N	Y	Y	Y	Y	Y	Y
NEVADA							
1 Titus	Y	Y	Y	Y	Y	N	N
2 **Amodei**	N	Y	Y	Y	Y	Y	Y
3 Rosen	Y	Y	Y	Y	Y	N	N
4 Kihuen	Y	Y	Y	Y	Y	N	N
NEW HAMPSHIRE							
1 Shea-Porter	Y	Y	Y	Y	Y	?	N
2 Kuster	Y	Y	Y	Y	Y	N	N
NEW JERSEY							
1 Norcross	Y	Y	Y	Y	Y	N	N
2 **LoBiondo**	N	Y	Y	Y	Y	Y	Y
3 **MacArthur**	N	Y	Y	Y	Y	Y	Y
4 **Smith**	N	Y	Y	Y	Y	Y	Y
5 Gottheimer	Y	Y	Y	Y	Y	N	N
6 Pallone	Y	N	Y	Y	Y	N	N
7 **Lance**	N	Y	Y	Y	Y	Y	Y
8 Sires	Y	Y	?	?	?	N	N
9 Pascrell	Y	Y	Y	Y	Y	N	N
10 Payne	Y	N	Y	Y	Y	N	N
11 **Frelinghuysen**	N	Y	Y	Y	Y	Y	Y
12 Watson Coleman	Y	N	Y	Y	Y	N	N
NEW MEXICO							
1 Lujan Grisham	Y	Y	Y	Y	Y	N	N
2 **Pearce**	N	Y	Y	Y	Y	Y	Y
3 Luján	Y	Y	Y	Y	Y	N	N
NEW YORK							
1 **Zeldin**	N	Y	Y	Y	Y	Y	Y
2 **King**	N	Y	Y	Y	Y	Y	Y
3 Suozzi	Y	Y	Y	Y	Y	N	N
4 Rice	Y	Y	?	?	?	N	N
5 Meeks	?	?	?	?	?	N	N
6 Meng	Y	N	Y	Y	Y	N	N
7 Velázquez	Y	N	Y	Y	Y	N	N
8 Jeffries	Y	N	Y	Y	Y	N	N
9 Clarke	Y	N	+	+	+	N	N
10 Nadler	Y	N	Y	Y	Y	N	N
11 **Donovan**	N	Y	Y	Y	Y	Y	Y
12 Maloney, C.	Y	Y	Y	Y	Y	N	N
13 Espaillat	Y	N	?	?	?	N	N
14 Crowley	Y	N	Y	Y	Y	N	N
15 Serrano	Y	N	Y	Y	Y	N	N
16 Engel	Y	Y	Y	Y	Y	N	N
17 Lowey	Y	Y	Y	Y	Y	N	N
18 Maloney, S.P.	Y	Y	?	?	?	N	N
19 **Faso**	N	Y	Y	Y	Y	Y	Y
20 Tonko	Y	N	Y	Y	Y	N	N
21 **Stefanik**	N	Y	Y	Y	Y	Y	Y
22 **Tenney**	N	Y	Y	Y	Y	Y	Y
23 **Reed**	N	Y	Y	Y	Y	Y	Y
24 **Katko**	N	Y	Y	Y	Y	Y	Y
25 Slaughter	Y	N	+	+	+	N	N
26 Higgins	Y	Y	Y	Y	Y	N	N
27 **Collins**	N	Y	Y	Y	Y	Y	Y
NORTH CAROLINA							
1 Butterfield	Y	N	Y	Y	Y	N	N
2 **Holding**	N	Y	Y	Y	Y	Y	Y
3 **Jones**	?	?	Y	Y	N	Y	Y
4 Price	Y	N	Y	Y	Y	N	N

	377	378	379	380	381	382	383
5 **Foxx**	N	Y	Y	Y	Y	Y	Y
6 **Walker**	N	Y	Y	Y	Y	Y	Y
7 **Rouzer**	N	Y	Y	Y	Y	Y	Y
8 **Hudson**	N	Y	Y	Y	Y	Y	Y
9 **Pittenger**	N	Y	Y	Y	Y	Y	Y
10 **McHenry**	N	Y	Y	Y	Y	Y	Y
11 **Meadows**	N	Y	Y	Y	Y	Y	Y
12 Adams	Y	N	Y	Y	Y	N	N
13 **Budd**	N	Y	Y	Y	Y	Y	Y
NORTH DAKOTA							
AL **Cramer**	N	Y	Y	Y	Y	Y	Y
OHIO							
1 **Chabot**	N	Y	Y	Y	Y	Y	Y
2 **Wenstrup**	N	Y	Y	Y	Y	Y	Y
3 Beatty	Y	Y	Y	Y	Y	N	N
4 **Jordan**	N	Y	Y	Y	Y	Y	Y
5 **Latta**	N	Y	Y	Y	Y	Y	Y
6 **Johnson**	N	Y	Y	Y	Y	Y	Y
7 **Gibbs**	N	Y	Y	Y	Y	Y	Y
8 **Davidson**	N	Y	Y	Y	Y	Y	Y
9 Kaptur	Y	Y	Y	Y	Y	N	N
10 **Turner**	N	Y	Y	Y	Y	Y	Y
11 Fudge	Y	N	Y	Y	Y	N	N
12 **Tiberi**	N	Y	Y	Y	Y	Y	Y
13 Ryan	Y	Y	?	?	?	N	N
14 **Joyce**	N	Y	Y	?	Y	Y	Y
15 **Stivers**	N	Y	Y	Y	Y	Y	Y
16 **Renacci**	N	Y	Y	Y	Y	Y	Y
OKLAHOMA							
1 **Bridenstine**	N	Y	Y	Y	Y	Y	Y
2 **Mullin**	N	Y	Y	Y	Y	Y	Y
3 **Lucas**	N	Y	Y	Y	Y	Y	Y
4 **Cole**	N	Y	Y	Y	Y	Y	Y
5 **Russell**	N	Y	Y	Y	Y	Y	Y
OREGON							
1 Bonamici	Y	N	Y	Y	Y	N	N
2 **Walden**	N	Y	Y	Y	Y	Y	Y
3 Blumenauer	Y	N	Y	Y	Y	N	N
4 DeFazio	Y	N	Y	Y	Y	N	N
5 Schrader	Y	N	Y	Y	Y	N	N
PENNSYLVANIA							
1 Brady	Y	Y	Y	Y	Y	N	N
2 Evans	Y	Y	Y	Y	Y	N	N
3 **Kelly**	N	Y	Y	Y	Y	Y	Y
4 **Perry**	N	Y	Y	Y	Y	Y	Y
5 **Thompson**	N	Y	Y	Y	Y	Y	Y
6 **Costello**	N	Y	Y	Y	Y	Y	Y
7 **Meehan**	N	Y	Y	Y	Y	Y	Y
8 **Fitzpatrick**	N	Y	Y	Y	Y	Y	Y
9 **Shuster**	N	Y	Y	Y	Y	Y	Y
10 **Marino**	N	Y	+	+	+	Y	Y
11 **Barletta**	N	Y	Y	Y	Y	Y	Y
12 **Rothfus**	N	Y	Y	Y	Y	Y	Y
13 Boyle	Y	Y	Y	Y	Y	N	N
14 Doyle	Y	N	Y	Y	Y	N	N
15 **Dent**	N	Y	Y	Y	Y	Y	Y
16 **Smucker**	N	Y	Y	Y	Y	Y	Y
17 Cartwright	Y	Y	Y	Y	Y	N	N
18 **Murphy**	N	Y	Y	Y	Y	Y	Y
RHODE ISLAND							
1 Cicilline	Y	N	Y	Y	Y	N	N
2 Langevin	Y	Y	Y	Y	Y	N	N
SOUTH CAROLINA							
1 **Sanford**	N	Y	Y	Y	N	Y	Y
2 **Wilson**	N	Y	Y	Y	Y	Y	Y
3 **Duncan**	N	Y	Y	Y	Y	Y	Y
4 **Gowdy**	N	Y	Y	Y	Y	Y	Y
5 **Norman**	N	Y	Y	Y	Y	Y	Y
6 Clyburn	Y	Y	Y	Y	Y	N	N
7 **Rice**	N	Y	Y	Y	Y	Y	?
SOUTH DAKOTA							
AL **Noem**	N	Y	Y	Y	Y	Y	Y
TENNESSEE							
1 **Roe**	N	Y	Y	Y	Y	Y	Y
2 **Duncan**	N	N	Y	Y	Y	Y	Y
3 **Fleischmann**	N	Y	Y	Y	Y	Y	Y
4 **DesJarlais**	N	Y	Y	Y	Y	Y	Y
5 Cooper	Y	Y	Y	Y	Y	N	N
6 **Black**	N	Y	Y	Y	Y	Y	Y
7 **Blackburn**	N	Y	Y	Y	Y	Y	Y
8 **Kustoff**	N	Y	Y	Y	Y	Y	Y
9 Cohen	Y	N	Y	Y	Y	N	N

	377	378	379	380	381	382	383
TEXAS							
1 **Gohmert**	N	N	Y	Y	Y	Y	Y
2 **Poe**	N	Y	Y	Y	Y	Y	Y
3 **Johnson, S.**	N	Y	?	?	?	?	?
4 **Ratcliffe**	N	Y	Y	Y	Y	Y	Y
5 **Hensarling**	N	Y	Y	Y	Y	Y	Y
6 **Barton**	N	Y	Y	Y	Y	Y	Y
7 **Culberson**	N	Y	Y	Y	Y	?	Y
8 **Brady**	N	Y	Y	Y	Y	Y	Y
9 Green, A.	Y	Y	Y	Y	Y	N	N
10 **McCaul**	N	Y	Y	Y	Y	Y	Y
11 **Conaway**	N	Y	Y	Y	Y	Y	Y
12 **Granger**	N	Y	Y	Y	Y	Y	Y
13 **Thornberry**	N	Y	Y	Y	Y	Y	Y
14 **Weber**	N	Y	Y	Y	Y	Y	Y
15 Gonzalez	Y	Y	Y	Y	Y	N	N
16 O'Rourke	Y	Y	Y	Y	Y	N	N
17 **Flores**	N	Y	Y	Y	Y	Y	Y
18 Jackson Lee	Y	Y	Y	Y	Y	–	–
19 **Arrington**	N	Y	Y	Y	Y	Y	Y
20 Castro	Y	Y	Y	Y	Y	N	N
21 **Smith**	N	Y	Y	Y	Y	Y	Y
22 **Olson**	N	Y	Y	Y	Y	Y	Y
23 **Hurd**	N	Y	Y	Y	Y	Y	Y
24 **Marchant**	N	Y	Y	Y	Y	Y	Y
25 **Williams**	N	Y	Y	Y	Y	Y	Y
26 **Burgess**	N	Y	Y	Y	Y	Y	Y
27 **Farenthold**	N	Y	Y	Y	Y	Y	Y
28 Cuellar	Y	Y	Y	Y	Y	N	N
29 Green, G.	Y	Y	Y	Y	Y	N	N
30 Johnson, E.B.	Y	Y	Y	Y	Y	N	N
31 **Carter**	N	Y	Y	Y	Y	Y	Y
32 **Sessions**	N	Y	Y	Y	Y	Y	Y
33 Veasey	Y	Y	Y	Y	Y	N	N
34 Vela	Y	N	Y	Y	Y	N	N
35 Doggett	Y	Y	Y	Y	Y	N	N
36 **Babin**	N	Y	Y	Y	Y	Y	Y
UTAH							
1 **Bishop**	N	Y	Y	Y	Y	Y	Y
2 **Stewart**	N	Y	Y	Y	Y	Y	Y
4 **Love**	N	Y	Y	Y	Y	Y	Y
VERMONT							
AL Welch	Y	N	Y	Y	Y	N	N
VIRGINIA							
1 **Wittman**	N	Y	Y	Y	Y	Y	Y
2 **Taylor**	N	Y	Y	Y	Y	Y	Y
3 Scott	Y	Y	Y	Y	Y	N	N
4 McEachin	Y	Y	Y	Y	Y	N	N
5 **Garrett**	N	N	?	Y	Y	Y	Y
6 **Goodlatte**	N	Y	Y	Y	Y	Y	Y
7 **Brat**	N	Y	Y	Y	Y	Y	Y
8 Beyer	Y	Y	Y	Y	Y	N	N
9 **Griffith**	N	N	Y	Y	Y	Y	Y
10 **Comstock**	N	Y	Y	Y	Y	Y	Y
11 Connolly	Y	Y	Y	Y	Y	N	N
WASHINGTON							
1 DelBene	Y	Y	Y	Y	Y	N	N
2 Larsen	Y	Y	Y	Y	Y	?	N
3 **Herrera Beutler**	N	Y	Y	Y	Y	Y	Y
4 **Newhouse**	N	Y	Y	Y	Y	Y	Y
5 **McMorris Rodgers**	N	Y	Y	Y	Y	Y	Y
6 Kilmer	Y	Y	Y	Y	Y	N	N
7 Jayapal	Y	N	Y	Y	Y	N	N
8 **Reichert**	N	Y	Y	Y	Y	Y	Y
9 Smith	Y	Y	Y	Y	Y	N	N
10 Heck	Y	Y	Y	Y	Y	N	N
WEST VIRGINIA							
1 **McKinley**	N	Y	Y	Y	Y	Y	Y
2 **Mooney**	N	Y	Y	Y	N	Y	Y
3 **Jenkins**	N	Y	Y	Y	Y	Y	Y
WISCONSIN							
1 **Ryan**							
2 Pocan	Y	N	Y	Y	Y	N	N
3 Kind	Y	Y	Y	Y	Y	N	N
4 Moore	Y	N	Y	Y	Y	N	N
5 **Sensenbrenner**	N	Y	Y	Y	Y	Y	Y
6 **Grothman**	N	Y	Y	Y	Y	Y	Y
7 **Duffy**	N	Y	Y	Y	Y	Y	Y
8 **Gallagher**	N	Y	Y	Y	Y	Y	Y
WYOMING							
AL **Cheney**	N	Y	Y	Y	Y	Y	Y

⦀ HOUSE VOTES

VOTE NUMBER

384. HR 2786. SMALL CONDUIT HYDROPOWER FACILITY LICENSING REQUIREMENT/PASSAGE. Upton, R-Mich., motion to suspend the rules and pass the bill that would eliminate the five megawatt limit on the size of small conduit hydropower facilities that can be built or operated without a federal license. Motion agreed to 420-2 : R 234-1; D 186-1. July 18, 2017.

385. HR 806. OZONE STANDARDS IMPLEMENTATION/HEALTH IMPACT EVALUATION. Castor, D-Fla., amendment that would prohibit an extension of the deadline for the EPA to implement new national ambient air quality standards if the Clean Air Scientific Advisory Committee finds that such changes could increase health risks to vulnerable populations, including children, seniors and pregnant women. Rejected in Committee of the Whole 194-232 : R 5-230; D 189-2. July 18, 2017.

386. HR 806. OZONE STANDARDS IMPLEMENTATION/TECHNOLOGICAL FEASIBILITY CONSIDERATION. Tonko, D-N.Y., amendment that would remove the bill's provision that would allow the EPA to consider "likely technological feasibility" as a factor when establishing and revising the national primary ambient air quality standard for pollutants. Rejected in Committee of the Whole 182-241 : R 4-230; D 178-11. July 18, 2017.

387. HR 806. OZONE STANDARDS IMPLEMENTATION/EXTERNAL FACTORS IN NON-ATTAINMENT AREAS. Beyer, D-Va., amendment that would allow the Environmental Protection Agency to sanction any state that has a "severe" or "extreme" non-attainment area, as defined under the Clean Air Act, regardless of whether the non-attainment designation resulted from an event or source outside the non-attainment area. Rejected in Committee of the Whole 191-235 : R 6-230; D 185-5. July 18, 2017.

388. HR 806. OZONE STANDARDS IMPLEMENTATION/HYDROGEN SULFIDE HAZARD. Polis, D-Colo., amendment that would require the EPA to issue a rule adding hydrogen sulfide to the list of hazardous air pollutants. Rejected in Committee of the Whole 186-242 : R 0-236; D 186-6. July 18, 2017.

389. HR 806. OZONE STANDARDS IMPLEMENTATION/AUTHORIZATION OF ADDITIONAL FUNDS. McNerney, D-Calif., amendment that would remove the bill's provision that would prohibit additional funds from being authorized by the bill to carry out the bill's requirements. Rejected in Committee of the Whole 190-236 : R 2-233; D 188-3. July 18, 2017.

390. HR 806. OZONE STANDARDS IMPLEMENTATION/RECOMMIT. Cartwright, D-Pa., motion to recommit the bill to the House Energy and Commerce Committee with instructions to report it back immediately with an amendment that would prohibit implementation of the bill's provisions if the Clean Air Scientific Advisory Committee, in consultation with the Congressional Budget Office, finds such implementation could increase various health risks for individuals without access to "affordable, comprehensive" health insurance. Motion rejected 191-235 : R 2-234; D 189-1. July 18, 2017.

	384	385	386	387	388	389	390
ALABAMA							
1 Byrne	Y	N	N	N	N	N	N
2 Roby	Y	N	N	N	N	N	N
3 Rogers	Y	N	N	N	N	N	N
4 Aderholt	Y	N	N	N	N	N	N
5 Brooks	?	N	N	N	N	N	N
6 Palmer	Y	N	N	N	N	N	N
7 Sewell	Y	Y	N	Y	Y	Y	Y
ALASKA							
AL Young	Y	N	N	N	N	N	N
ARIZONA							
1 O'Halleran	Y	Y	Y	N	Y	Y	Y
2 McSally	Y	N	N	N	N	N	N
3 Grijalva	Y	Y	Y	Y	Y	Y	Y
4 Gosar	Y	N	N	N	N	N	N
5 Biggs	Y	N	N	N	N	N	N
6 Schweikert	Y	N	N	N	N	N	N
7 Gallego	Y	Y	Y	Y	Y	Y	Y
8 Franks	Y	N	N	N	N	N	N
9 Sinema	Y	N	N	N	Y	N	Y
ARKANSAS							
1 Crawford	Y	N	N	N	N	N	N
2 Hill	Y	N	N	N	N	N	N
3 Womack	Y	N	N	N	N	N	N
4 Westerman	Y	N	N	N	N	N	N
CALIFORNIA							
1 LaMalfa	Y	N	N	N	N	N	N
2 Huffman	Y	Y	Y	Y	Y	Y	Y
3 Garamendi	Y	Y	Y	Y	Y	Y	Y
4 McClintock	Y	N	N	N	N	N	N
5 Thompson	Y	Y	Y	Y	Y	Y	Y
6 Matsui	Y	Y	Y	Y	Y	Y	Y
7 Bera	Y	Y	Y	Y	Y	Y	Y
8 Cook	Y	N	N	N	N	N	N
9 McNerney	Y	Y	Y	Y	Y	Y	Y
10 Denham	Y	N	N	N	N	N	N
11 DeSaulnier	Y	Y	Y	Y	Y	Y	Y
12 Pelosi	Y	?	?	Y	Y	?	Y
13 Lee	Y	Y	Y	Y	Y	Y	Y
14 Speier	Y	Y	Y	Y	Y	Y	Y
15 Swalwell	Y	Y	Y	Y	Y	Y	Y
16 Costa	Y	Y	Y	N	N	Y	Y
17 Khanna	Y	Y	Y	Y	Y	Y	Y
18 Eshoo	Y	Y	Y	Y	Y	Y	Y
19 Lofgren	Y	Y	Y	Y	Y	Y	Y
20 Panetta	Y	Y	Y	Y	Y	Y	Y
21 Valadao	Y	N	N	N	N	N	N
22 Nunes	Y	N	N	N	N	N	N
23 McCarthy	Y	N	N	N	N	N	N
24 Carbajal	Y	Y	Y	Y	Y	Y	Y
25 Knight	Y	N	N	N	N	N	N
26 Brownley	Y	Y	Y	Y	Y	Y	Y
27 Chu	Y	Y	Y	Y	Y	Y	Y
28 Schiff	Y	Y	Y	Y	Y	Y	Y
29 Cardenas	Y	Y	Y	Y	Y	Y	Y
30 Sherman	Y	Y	Y	Y	Y	Y	Y
31 Aguilar	Y	Y	Y	Y	Y	Y	Y
32 Napolitano	?	+	+	+	+	+	+
33 Lieu	Y	Y	Y	Y	Y	Y	Y
34 Gomez	Y	Y	Y	Y	Y	Y	Y
35 Torres	Y	Y	Y	Y	Y	Y	Y
36 Ruiz	Y	Y	Y	Y	Y	Y	Y
37 Bass	Y	Y	Y	Y	Y	Y	Y
38 Sánchez, Linda	Y	Y	Y	Y	Y	Y	Y
39 Royce	Y	N	N	N	N	N	N
40 Roybal-Allard	Y	Y	Y	Y	Y	Y	Y
41 Takano	Y	Y	Y	Y	Y	Y	Y
42 Calvert	Y	N	N	N	N	N	N
43 Waters	Y	Y	Y	Y	Y	Y	Y
44 Barragan	Y	Y	Y	Y	Y	Y	Y
45 Walters	Y	N	N	N	N	N	N
46 Correa	Y	Y	Y	Y	Y	Y	Y
47 Lowenthal	Y	Y	Y	Y	Y	Y	Y
48 Rohrabacher	Y	N	N	N	N	N	N
49 Issa	Y	N	N	N	N	N	N
50 Hunter	Y	N	N	N	N	N	N
51 Vargas	Y	Y	Y	Y	Y	Y	Y
52 Peters	Y	Y	Y	Y	Y	Y	Y
53 Davis	Y	Y	Y	Y	Y	Y	Y

	384	385	386	387	388	389	390
COLORADO							
1 DeGette	Y	Y	Y	Y	Y	Y	Y
2 Polis	N	Y	Y	Y	Y	Y	Y
3 Tipton	Y	N	N	N	N	N	N
4 Buck	Y	N	N	N	N	N	N
5 Lamborn	Y	N	N	N	N	N	N
6 Coffman	N	N	N	N	N	N	N
7 Perlmutter	Y	Y	Y	Y	Y	Y	Y
CONNECTICUT							
1 Larson	Y	Y	Y	Y	Y	Y	Y
2 Courtney	Y	Y	Y	Y	Y	Y	Y
3 DeLauro	Y	Y	Y	Y	Y	Y	Y
4 Himes	Y	Y	Y	Y	Y	Y	Y
5 Esty	Y	Y	Y	Y	Y	Y	Y
DELAWARE							
AL Blunt Rochester	Y	Y	Y	Y	Y	Y	Y
FLORIDA							
1 Gaetz	Y	N	N	N	N	N	N
2 Dunn	Y	N	N	N	N	N	N
3 Yoho	Y	N	N	N	N	N	N
4 Rutherford	Y	N	N	N	N	N	N
5 Lawson	Y	Y	Y	Y	Y	Y	Y
6 DeSantis	Y	N	N	N	N	N	N
7 Murphy	Y	N	Y	Y	Y	Y	Y
8 Posey	Y	N	N	N	N	N	N
9 Soto	Y	Y	Y	Y	Y	Y	Y
10 Demings	Y	Y	Y	Y	Y	Y	Y
11 Webster	Y	N	N	N	N	N	N
12 Bilirakis	Y	N	N	N	N	N	N
13 Crist	Y	Y	Y	Y	Y	Y	Y
14 Castor	Y	Y	Y	Y	Y	Y	Y
15 Ross	Y	N	N	N	N	N	N
16 Buchanan	Y	N	N	N	N	N	N
17 Rooney, T.	Y	N	N	N	N	N	N
18 Mast	Y	Y	Y	N	N	N	N
19 Rooney, F.	Y	N	N	N	N	N	N
20 Hastings	Y	Y	Y	Y	Y	Y	Y
21 Frankel	Y	Y	Y	Y	Y	Y	Y
22 Deutch	Y	Y	Y	Y	Y	Y	Y
23 Wasserman Schultz	Y	Y	Y	Y	Y	Y	Y
24 Wilson	Y	Y	Y	Y	Y	Y	Y
25 Diaz-Balart	Y	N	N	N	N	N	N
26 Curbelo	Y	N	N	N	Y	N	N
27 Ros-Lehtinen	Y	N	Y	N	N	N	N
GEORGIA							
1 Carter	Y	N	N	N	N	N	N
2 Bishop	Y	Y	N	Y	Y	Y	Y
3 Ferguson	Y	N	N	N	N	N	N
4 Johnson	Y	Y	Y	Y	Y	Y	Y
5 Lewis	Y	Y	Y	Y	Y	Y	Y
6 Handel	Y	N	N	N	N	N	N
7 Woodall	Y	N	N	N	N	N	N
8 Scott, A.	Y	N	N	N	N	N	N
9 Collins	Y	N	N	N	N	N	N
10 Hice	Y	N	N	N	N	N	N
11 Loudermilk	Y	N	N	N	N	N	N
12 Allen	Y	N	N	N	N	N	N
13 Scott, D.	?	Y	Y	Y	Y	Y	Y
14 Graves	Y	N	N	N	N	N	N
HAWAII							
1 Hanabusa	Y	Y	Y	Y	Y	Y	Y
2 Gabbard	Y	Y	Y	Y	Y	Y	Y
IDAHO							
1 Labrador	?	?	?	?	?	?	?
2 Simpson	Y	N	N	N	N	N	N
ILLINOIS							
1 Rush	Y	Y	Y	Y	Y	Y	Y
2 Kelly	Y	Y	Y	Y	Y	Y	Y
3 Lipinski	Y	Y	Y	Y	Y	Y	Y
4 Gutierrez	Y	Y	Y	Y	Y	Y	Y
5 Quigley	Y	Y	Y	Y	Y	Y	Y
6 Roskam	Y	N	N	N	N	N	N
7 Davis, D.	?	Y	Y	Y	Y	Y	Y
8 Krishnamoorthi	Y	Y	Y	Y	Y	Y	Y
9 Schakowsky	Y	Y	Y	Y	Y	Y	Y
10 Schneider	Y	Y	Y	Y	Y	Y	Y
11 Foster	Y	Y	Y	Y	Y	Y	Y
12 Bost	Y	N	N	N	N	N	N
13 Davis, R.	Y	N	N	N	N	N	N
14 Hultgren	Y	N	N	N	N	N	N
15 Shimkus	Y	N	N	N	N	N	N

	384	385	386	387	388	389	390
16 **Kinzinger**	Y	N	N	N	N	N	N
17 Bustos	Y	Y	Y	Y	Y	Y	Y
18 **LaHood**	Y	N	N	N	N	N	N
INDIANA							
1 Visclosky	Y	Y	Y	Y	Y	Y	Y
2 **Walorski**	Y	N	N	N	N	N	N
3 **Banks**	Y	N	N	N	N	N	N
4 **Rokita**	Y	N	N	N	N	N	N
5 **Brooks**	Y	N	N	N	N	N	N
6 **Messer**	Y	N	N	N	N	N	N
7 Carson	Y	Y	Y	Y	Y	Y	Y
8 **Bucshon**	Y	N	N	N	N	N	N
9 **Hollingsworth**	Y	N	N	N	N	N	N
IOWA							
1 **Blum**	Y	N	N	N	N	N	Y
2 Loebsack	Y	Y	Y	Y	Y	Y	Y
3 **Young**	Y	N	N	N	N	N	N
4 **King**	Y	N	N	N	N	N	N
KANSAS							
1 **Marshall**	Y	N	N	N	N	N	N
2 **Jenkins**	Y	N	N	N	N	N	N
3 **Yoder**	Y	N	N	N	N	N	N
4 **Estes**	Y	N	N	N	N	N	N
KENTUCKY							
1 **Comer**	Y	N	N	N	N	N	N
2 **Guthrie**	Y	N	N	N	N	N	N
3 Yarmuth	?	Y	Y	Y	Y	Y	Y
4 **Massie**	Y	N	N	N	N	N	N
5 **Rogers**	Y	N	N	N	N	N	N
6 **Barr**	Y	N	N	N	N	N	N
LOUISIANA							
1 **Scalise**	+	–	–	–	–	–	–
2 Richmond	Y	Y	Y	Y	Y	Y	Y
3 **Higgins**	Y	N	N	N	N	N	N
4 **Johnson**	Y	N	N	N	N	N	N
5 **Abraham**	Y	N	N	N	N	N	N
6 **Graves**	Y	N	N	N	N	N	N
MAINE							
1 Pingree	Y	Y	Y	Y	Y	Y	Y
2 **Poliquin**	Y	Y	N	N	N	N	N
MARYLAND							
1 **Harris**	Y	N	N	N	N	N	N
2 Ruppersberger	Y	Y	Y	Y	Y	Y	?
3 Sarbanes	Y	Y	Y	Y	Y	Y	Y
4 Brown	Y	Y	Y	Y	Y	Y	Y
5 Hoyer	Y	Y	Y	Y	Y	Y	Y
6 Delaney	Y	Y	Y	Y	Y	Y	Y
7 Cummings	?	?	?	?	?	?	?
8 Raskin	Y	Y	Y	Y	Y	Y	Y
MASSACHUSETTS							
1 Neal	Y	Y	Y	Y	Y	Y	Y
2 McGovern	Y	Y	Y	Y	Y	Y	Y
3 Tsongas	Y	Y	Y	Y	Y	Y	Y
4 Kennedy	Y	Y	Y	Y	Y	Y	Y
5 Clark	Y	Y	Y	Y	Y	Y	Y
6 Moulton	Y	Y	Y	Y	Y	Y	Y
7 Capuano	Y	Y	Y	Y	Y	Y	Y
8 Lynch	Y	Y	Y	Y	Y	Y	Y
9 Keating	Y	Y	Y	Y	Y	Y	Y
MICHIGAN							
1 **Bergman**	Y	N	N	N	N	N	N
2 **Huizenga**	Y	N	N	N	N	N	N
3 **Amash**	Y	N	N	N	N	N	N
4 **Moolenaar**	Y	N	N	N	N	N	N
5 Kildee	Y	Y	Y	Y	Y	Y	Y
6 **Upton**	Y	N	N	N	N	N	N
7 **Walberg**	Y	N	N	N	N	N	N
8 **Bishop**	Y	N	N	N	N	N	N
9 Levin	Y	Y	Y	Y	Y	Y	Y
10 **Mitchell**	Y	N	N	N	N	N	N
11 **Trott**	Y	N	N	N	N	N	N
12 Dingell	Y	Y	Y	Y	Y	Y	Y
13 Conyers	Y	Y	Y	Y	Y	Y	Y
14 Lawrence	Y	Y	Y	Y	Y	Y	Y
MINNESOTA							
1 Walz	Y	Y	Y	Y	Y	Y	Y
2 **Lewis**	Y	N	N	N	N	N	N
3 **Paulsen**	Y	N	N	N	N	N	N
4 McCollum	Y	Y	Y	Y	Y	Y	Y

	384	385	386	387	388	389	390
5 Ellison	Y	Y	N	Y	Y	Y	Y
6 **Emmer**	Y	N	N	N	N	N	N
7 Peterson	Y	N	N	N	N	N	N
8 Nolan	Y	Y	Y	Y	Y	Y	Y
MISSISSIPPI							
1 **Kelly**	Y	N	N	N	N	N	N
2 Thompson	Y	Y	Y	Y	Y	Y	Y
3 **Harper**	Y	N	N	N	N	N	N
4 **Palazzo**	Y	N	N	N	N	N	N
MISSOURI							
1 Clay	Y	Y	Y	Y	Y	Y	Y
2 **Wagner**	Y	N	N	N	N	N	N
3 **Luetkemeyer**	Y	N	N	N	N	N	N
4 **Hartzler**	Y	N	N	N	N	N	N
5 Cleaver	Y	Y	N	Y	Y	Y	Y
6 **Graves**	Y	N	N	N	N	N	N
7 **Long**	Y	N	N	N	N	N	N
8 **Smith**	Y	N	N	N	N	N	N
MONTANA							
AL **Gianforte**	Y	N	N	N	N	N	N
NEBRASKA							
1 **Fortenberry**	Y	N	N	N	N	N	N
2 **Bacon**	Y	N	N	N	N	N	N
3 **Smith**	Y	N	N	N	N	N	N
NEVADA							
1 Titus	Y	Y	Y	Y	Y	Y	Y
2 **Amodei**	Y	N	N	N	N	N	N
3 Rosen	Y	Y	Y	Y	Y	Y	Y
4 Kihuen	Y	Y	Y	Y	Y	Y	Y
NEW HAMPSHIRE							
1 Shea-Porter	Y	Y	Y	Y	Y	Y	Y
2 Kuster	Y	Y	Y	Y	Y	Y	Y
NEW JERSEY							
1 Norcross	Y	Y	Y	Y	Y	Y	Y
2 **LoBiondo**	Y	N	N	N	N	N	N
3 **MacArthur**	Y	N	N	N	N	N	N
4 **Smith**	Y	N	N	N	N	N	N
5 Gottheimer	Y	Y	N	Y	Y	Y	Y
6 Pallone	Y	Y	Y	Y	Y	Y	Y
7 **Lance**	Y	N	N	N	N	N	N
8 Sires	Y	Y	Y	Y	Y	Y	Y
9 Pascrell	Y	Y	Y	Y	Y	Y	Y
10 Payne	Y	Y	Y	Y	Y	Y	Y
11 **Frelinghuysen**	Y	N	N	N	N	N	N
12 Watson Coleman	Y	Y	Y	Y	Y	Y	Y
NEW MEXICO							
1 Lujan Grisham	Y	Y	Y	Y	Y	Y	Y
2 **Pearce**	Y	N	N	N	N	N	N
3 Luján	Y	Y	Y	Y	Y	Y	Y
NEW YORK							
1 **Zeldin**	Y	N	N	N	N	N	N
2 **King**	Y	N	N	N	N	N	N
3 Suozzi	Y	Y	Y	Y	Y	Y	Y
4 Rice	Y	Y	Y	Y	Y	Y	Y
5 Meeks	Y	Y	Y	Y	Y	Y	Y
6 Meng	Y	Y	Y	Y	Y	Y	Y
7 Velázquez	Y	Y	Y	Y	Y	Y	Y
8 Jeffries	Y	Y	Y	Y	Y	Y	Y
9 Clarke	Y	Y	Y	Y	Y	Y	Y
10 Nadler	Y	Y	Y	Y	Y	Y	Y
11 **Donovan**	Y	N	N	N	N	N	N
12 Maloney, C.	Y	Y	Y	Y	Y	Y	Y
13 Espaillat	Y	Y	Y	Y	Y	Y	Y
14 Crowley	Y	Y	Y	Y	Y	Y	Y
15 Serrano	Y	Y	Y	Y	Y	Y	Y
16 Engel	Y	Y	Y	Y	Y	Y	Y
17 Lowey	Y	Y	Y	Y	Y	Y	Y
18 Maloney, S.P.	Y	Y	Y	Y	Y	Y	Y
19 **Faso**	Y	N	Y	N	N	N	N
20 Tonko	Y	Y	Y	Y	Y	Y	Y
21 **Stefanik**	Y	N	N	Y	N	N	N
22 **Tenney**	Y	N	N	N	N	N	N
23 **Reed**	Y	N	N	N	N	N	N
24 **Katko**	Y	N	N	N	N	N	N
25 Slaughter	Y	Y	Y	Y	Y	Y	Y
26 Higgins	Y	Y	Y	Y	Y	Y	Y
27 **Collins**	Y	N	N	N	N	N	N
NORTH CAROLINA							
1 Butterfield	Y	Y	Y	Y	Y	Y	Y
2 **Holding**	Y	N	N	N	N	N	N
3 **Jones**	Y	Y	N	N	N	N	Y
4 Price	Y	Y	Y	Y	Y	Y	Y

	384	385	386	387	388	389	390
5 **Foxx**	Y	N	N	N	N	N	N
6 **Walker**	Y	N	N	N	N	N	N
7 **Rouzer**	Y	N	N	N	N	N	N
8 **Hudson**	Y	N	N	N	N	N	N
9 **Pittenger**	Y	N	N	N	N	N	N
10 **McHenry**	Y	N	N	N	N	N	N
11 **Meadows**	Y	N	N	N	N	N	N
12 Adams	Y	Y	Y	Y	Y	Y	Y
13 **Budd**	Y	N	N	N	N	N	N
NORTH DAKOTA							
AL **Cramer**	Y	N	N	N	N	N	N
OHIO							
1 **Chabot**	Y	N	N	N	N	N	N
2 **Wenstrup**	Y	N	N	N	N	N	N
3 Beatty	Y	Y	+	+	Y	Y	Y
4 **Jordan**	Y	N	N	N	N	N	N
5 **Latta**	Y	N	N	N	N	N	N
6 **Johnson**	Y	N	N	N	N	N	N
7 **Gibbs**	Y	N	N	N	N	N	N
8 **Davidson**	Y	N	N	N	N	N	N
9 Kaptur	Y	Y	?	Y	Y	Y	Y
10 **Turner**	Y	N	N	N	N	N	N
11 Fudge	Y	Y	Y	Y	Y	Y	Y
12 **Tiberi**	Y	N	N	N	N	N	N
13 Ryan	Y	Y	Y	Y	Y	Y	Y
14 **Joyce**	Y	N	N	N	N	?	N
15 **Stivers**	Y	N	N	N	N	N	N
16 **Renacci**	Y	N	N	N	N	N	N
OKLAHOMA							
1 **Bridenstine**	Y	N	N	N	N	N	N
2 **Mullin**	Y	N	N	N	N	N	N
3 **Lucas**	Y	N	N	N	N	N	N
4 **Cole**	Y	N	N	N	N	N	N
5 **Russell**	Y	N	N	N	N	N	N
OREGON							
1 Bonamici	Y	Y	Y	Y	Y	Y	Y
2 **Walden**	Y	N	N	N	N	N	N
3 Blumenauer	Y	Y	Y	Y	Y	Y	Y
4 DeFazio	Y	Y	Y	Y	Y	Y	Y
5 Schrader	Y	Y	N	Y	Y	Y	Y
PENNSYLVANIA							
1 Brady	Y	Y	Y	Y	Y	Y	Y
2 Evans	Y	Y	Y	Y	Y	Y	Y
3 **Kelly**	Y	N	N	N	N	N	N
4 **Perry**	Y	N	N	N	N	N	N
5 **Thompson**	Y	N	N	N	N	N	N
6 **Costello**	Y	N	N	N	N	N	N
7 **Meehan**	Y	N	N	N	N	N	N
8 **Fitzpatrick**	Y	Y	N	Y	N	N	N
9 **Shuster**	Y	N	N	N	N	N	N
10 **Marino**	Y	N	N	N	N	N	N
11 **Barletta**	Y	N	N	N	N	N	N
12 **Rothfus**	Y	N	N	N	N	N	N
13 Boyle	Y	Y	Y	Y	Y	Y	Y
14 Doyle	Y	Y	Y	Y	Y	Y	Y
15 **Dent**	Y	N	N	Y	N	N	N
16 **Smucker**	Y	N	N	N	N	N	N
17 Cartwright	Y	Y	Y	Y	Y	Y	Y
18 **Murphy**	Y	N	N	N	N	N	N
RHODE ISLAND							
1 Cicilline	+	Y	Y	Y	Y	Y	Y
2 Langevin	Y	Y	Y	Y	Y	Y	Y
SOUTH CAROLINA							
1 **Sanford**	Y	N	N	N	N	N	N
2 **Wilson**	Y	N	N	N	N	N	N
3 **Duncan**	Y	N	N	N	N	N	N
4 **Gowdy**	Y	N	N	N	N	N	N
5 **Norman**	Y	N	N	N	N	N	N
6 Clyburn	Y	Y	Y	Y	Y	Y	Y
7 **Rice**	Y	N	N	N	N	N	N
SOUTH DAKOTA							
AL **Noem**	Y	N	N	N	N	N	N
TENNESSEE							
1 **Roe**	Y	N	N	N	N	N	N
2 **Duncan**	Y	N	N	N	N	N	N
3 **Fleischmann**	Y	N	N	N	N	N	N
4 **DesJarlais**	Y	N	?	N	N	N	N
5 Cooper	Y	Y	Y	Y	Y	Y	Y
6 **Black**	Y	N	N	N	N	N	N
7 **Blackburn**	Y	N	N	N	N	N	N
8 **Kustoff**	Y	N	N	N	N	N	N
9 Cohen	Y	Y	Y	Y	Y	Y	Y

	384	385	386	387	388	389	390
TEXAS							
1 **Gohmert**	Y	N	N	N	N	N	N
2 **Poe**	Y	N	N	N	N	N	N
3 **Johnson, S.**	Y	N	N	N	N	N	N
4 **Ratcliffe**	Y	?	?	N	N	N	N
5 **Hensarling**	Y	N	N	N	N	N	N
6 **Barton**	Y	N	N	N	N	N	N
7 **Culberson**	Y	N	N	N	N	N	N
8 **Brady**	?	N	N	N	N	N	N
9 Green, A.	Y	Y	Y	Y	Y	Y	Y
10 **McCaul**	Y	N	N	N	N	N	N
11 **Conaway**	Y	N	N	N	N	N	N
12 **Granger**	Y	–	–	–	–	–	–
13 **Thornberry**	Y	N	N	N	N	N	N
14 **Weber**	Y	N	N	N	N	N	N
15 Gonzalez	Y	Y	N	Y	N	Y	Y
16 O'Rourke	Y	Y	Y	Y	Y	Y	Y
17 **Flores**	Y	N	N	N	N	N	N
18 Jackson Lee	+	Y	Y	Y	Y	Y	Y
19 **Arrington**	Y	N	N	N	N	N	N
20 Castro	Y	Y	Y	Y	Y	Y	Y
21 **Smith**	Y	N	N	N	N	N	N
22 **Olson**	Y	N	N	N	N	N	N
23 **Hurd**	Y	N	N	N	N	N	N
24 **Marchant**	Y	N	N	N	N	N	N
25 **Williams**	Y	N	N	N	N	N	N
26 **Burgess**	Y	N	N	N	N	N	N
27 **Farenthold**	Y	N	N	N	N	N	N
28 Cuellar	Y	Y	Y	Y	N	N	Y
29 Green, G.	Y	Y	N	N	N	Y	Y
30 Johnson, E.B.	Y	Y	Y	Y	Y	Y	Y
31 **Carter**	Y	N	N	N	N	N	N
32 **Sessions**	Y	N	N	N	N	N	N
33 Veasey	Y	Y	Y	Y	N	Y	Y
34 Vela	Y	Y	Y	Y	Y	Y	Y
35 Doggett	Y	Y	Y	Y	Y	Y	Y
36 **Babin**	Y	N	N	N	N	N	N
UTAH							
1 **Bishop**	Y	N	N	N	N	N	N
2 **Stewart**	Y	N	N	N	N	N	N
4 **Love**	Y	N	N	N	N	N	N
VERMONT							
AL Welch	Y	Y	Y	Y	Y	Y	?
VIRGINIA							
1 **Wittman**	Y	N	N	N	N	N	N
2 **Taylor**	Y	N	N	N	N	N	N
3 Scott	Y	Y	Y	Y	Y	Y	Y
4 McEachin	Y	Y	Y	Y	Y	Y	Y
5 **Garrett**	Y	N	N	N	N	N	N
6 **Goodlatte**	Y	N	N	N	N	N	N
7 **Brat**	Y	N	N	N	N	N	N
8 Beyer	Y	Y	Y	Y	Y	Y	Y
9 **Griffith**	Y	N	N	N	N	N	N
10 **Comstock**	Y	N	N	N	N	N	N
11 Connolly	Y	Y	Y	Y	Y	Y	Y
WASHINGTON							
1 DelBene	Y	Y	Y	Y	Y	Y	Y
2 Larsen	Y	Y	Y	Y	Y	Y	Y
3 **Herrera Beutler**	Y	N	N	N	N	N	N
4 **Newhouse**	Y	N	N	N	N	N	N
5 **McMorris Rodgers**	Y	N	N	N	N	N	N
6 Kilmer	Y	Y	Y	Y	Y	Y	Y
7 Jayapal	Y	Y	Y	Y	Y	Y	Y
8 **Reichert**	Y	Y	N	N	N	N	N
9 Smith	Y	Y	Y	?	Y	Y	Y
10 Heck	Y	Y	Y	Y	Y	Y	Y
WEST VIRGINIA							
1 **McKinley**	Y	N	N	N	N	N	N
2 **Mooney**	Y	N	N	N	N	N	N
3 **Jenkins**	Y	N	N	N	N	N	N
WISCONSIN							
1 **Ryan**							
2 Pocan	Y	Y	Y	Y	Y	Y	Y
3 Kind	Y	Y	Y	Y	Y	Y	Y
4 Moore	Y	Y	Y	Y	Y	Y	Y
5 **Sensenbrenner**	Y	N	N	N	N	N	N
6 **Grothman**	Y	N	N	N	N	N	N
7 **Duffy**	Y	N	N	N	N	N	N
8 **Gallagher**	Y	N	N	N	N	N	N
WYOMING							
AL **Cheney**	Y	N	N	N	N	N	N

||| HOUSE VOTES

VOTE NUMBER

391. HR 806. OZONE STANDARDS IMPLEMENTATION/PASSAGE. Passage of the bill that would extend for eight years the deadline for the EPA to implement new National Ambient Air Quality Standards for ground-level ozone (the EPA issued such deadlines on Oct. 26, 2015). The bill would require the EPA to review the national ambient air quality standards for each pollutant every ten years, instead of every five, and would require the agency to evaluate possible adverse effects of standard changes, including effects related to public health, welfare and economics, prior to establishing or revising a national ambient air quality standard. Passed 229-199 : R 225-11; D 4-188. July 18, 2017.

392. PRESIDENT'S TAX RETURN DISCLOSURE/MOTION TO TABLE. Cheney, R-Wyo., motion to table (kill) the Cicilline, D-R.I., motion to appeal the ruling of the Chair that the Cicilline resolution related to the disclosure of President Trump's tax returns does not constitute a question of the privileges of the House. Motion agreed to 235-190 : R 235-1; D 0-189. July 19, 2017.

393. HR 2910, H RES 454, HR 2825, HR 218, HR 2883. ENERGY REGULATORY POLICY, HOMELAND SECURITY DEPARTMENT REAUTHORIZATION, AND KING COVE ACCESS ROAD/PREVIOUS QUESTION. Cheney, R-Wyo., motion to order the previous question (thus ending debate and possibility of amendment) on the rule (H Res 454) that would provide for House floor consideration of the bill (HR 2910) that would establish the Federal Energy Regulatory Commission as the lead agency for the permitting of proposals to build or expand natural gas pipelines, would provide for consideration of the bill (HR 2883) that would establish a new system for the approval and permitting of border-crossing oil and gas pipelines and electrical transmission lines, and would provide for consideration of the bill (HR 218) that would require the Interior Department to convey to the state of Alaska, if requested, 206 acres of federal land within the Izembek National Wildlife Refuge and Izembek Wilderness for the purpose of constructing a single-lane gravel road between the towns of King Cove and Cold Bay, Alaska. The rule would also provide for a motion to suspend the rules and pass the DHS Authorization Act (HR 2825), as amended. Motion agreed to 236-192 : R 236-1; D 0-191. July 19, 2017.

394. HR 2910, H RES 454, HR 2825, HR 218, HR 2883. ENERGY REGULATORY POLICY, HOMELAND SECURITY DEPARTMENT REAUTHORIZATION, AND KING COVE ACCESS ROAD/RULE. Adoption of the rule (H Res 454) that would provide for House floor consideration of the bill (HR 2910) that would establish the Federal Energy Regulatory Commission as the lead agency for the permitting of proposals to build or expand natural gas pipelines, would provide for consideration of the bill (HR 2883) that would establish a new system for the approval and permitting of border-crossing oil and gas pipelines and electrical transmission lines, and would provide for consideration of the bill (HR 218) that would require the Interior Department to convey to the state of Alaska, if requested, 206 acres of federal land within the Izembek National Wildlife Refuge and Izembek Wilderness for the purpose of constructing a single-lane gravel road between the towns of King Cove and Cold Bay, Alaska. The rule would also provide for a motion to suspend the rules and pass the DHS Authorization Act (HR 2825), as amended. Adopted 234-194 : R 234-2; D 0-192. July 19, 2017.

395. HR 2883. CROSS-BORDER ENERGY INFRASTRUCTURE/STATE DEPARTMENT PERMITTING AUTHORITY. Engel, D-N.Y., amendment that would establish the State Department as the agency of jurisdiction with respect to permitting authority for cross-border oil pipelines. Rejected in Committee of the Whole 182-246 : R 2-234; D 180-12. July 19, 2017.

396. HR 2883. CROSS-BORDER ENERGY INFRASTRUCTURE/ CONSERVATION AND RECREATION EXEMPTION. Tsongas, D-Mass., amendment that would prohibit the Federal Energy Regulatory Commission from issuing a certificate of crossing for an oil or natural gas pipeline project if any part of such facility would be located on lands required, by federal, state, or local law, to be managed for natural resource conservation or recreation. Rejected in Committee of the Whole 179-247 : R 0-234; D 179-13. July 19, 2017.

	391	392	393	394	395	396
ALABAMA						
1 Byrne	Y	Y	Y	Y	N	N
2 Roby	Y	Y	Y	Y	N	N
3 Rogers	Y	Y	Y	Y	N	N
4 Aderholt	Y	Y	Y	Y	N	N
5 Brooks	Y	Y	Y	Y	N	N
6 Palmer	Y	Y	Y	Y	N	N
7 Sewell	N	N	N	N	Y	Y
ALASKA						
AL Young	Y	Y	Y	Y	N	N
ARIZONA						
1 O'Halleran	N	N	N	N	Y	Y
2 McSally	Y	Y	Y	Y	N	N
3 Grijalva	N	N	N	N	Y	Y
4 Gosar	Y	Y	Y	Y	N	N
5 Biggs	Y	Y	Y	Y	N	N
6 Schweikert	Y	Y	Y	Y	N	N
7 Gallego	N	N	N	N	Y	Y
8 Franks	Y	Y	Y	Y	N	N
9 Sinema	N	N	N	N	Y	N
ARKANSAS						
1 Crawford	Y	Y	Y	Y	N	N
2 Hill	Y	Y	Y	Y	N	N
3 Womack	Y	Y	Y	Y	N	N
4 Westerman	Y	Y	Y	Y	N	N
CALIFORNIA						
1 LaMalfa	Y	Y	Y	Y	N	N
2 Huffman	N	?	N	N	Y	Y
3 Garamendi	N	N	N	N	Y	Y
4 McClintock	Y	Y	Y	Y	N	N
5 Thompson	N	N	N	N	Y	Y
6 Matsui	N	N	N	N	Y	Y
7 Bera	N	N	N	N	Y	Y
8 Cook	Y	Y	Y	Y	N	N
9 McNerney	N	N	N	N	Y	Y
10 Denham	Y	Y	Y	Y	N	N
11 DeSaulnier	N	N	N	N	Y	Y
12 Pelosi	N	N	N	N	Y	Y
13 Lee	N	N	N	N	Y	Y
14 Speier	N	N	N	N	Y	Y
15 Swalwell	N	N	N	N	Y	Y
16 Costa	Y	N	N	N	N	N
17 Khanna	N	N	N	N	Y	Y
18 Eshoo	N	N	N	N	Y	Y
19 Lofgren	N	N	N	N	Y	Y
20 Panetta	N	N	N	N	Y	Y
21 Valadao	Y	Y	Y	Y	N	N
22 Nunes	Y	Y	Y	Y	N	N
23 McCarthy	Y	Y	Y	Y	N	N
24 Carbajal	N	N	N	N	Y	Y
25 Knight	Y	Y	Y	Y	N	N
26 Brownley	N	N	N	N	Y	Y
27 Chu	N	N	N	N	Y	Y
28 Schiff	N	N	N	N	Y	Y
29 Cardenas	N	N	N	N	Y	Y
30 Sherman	N	N	N	N	Y	Y
31 Aguilar	N	N	N	N	Y	Y
32 Napolitano	-	?	?	?	+	+
33 Lieu	N	N	N	N	Y	Y
34 Gomez	N	-	N	N	Y	Y
35 Torres	N	N	N	N	Y	Y
36 Ruiz	N	N	N	N	Y	Y
37 Bass	N	N	N	N	Y	Y
38 Sánchez, Linda	N	N	N	N	Y	Y
39 Royce	Y	Y	Y	Y	Y	N
40 Roybal-Allard	N	N	N	N	Y	Y
41 Takano	N	N	N	N	Y	Y
42 Calvert	Y	Y	Y	Y	N	N
43 Waters	N	N	N	N	Y	Y
44 Barragan	N	N	N	N	Y	Y
45 Walters	Y	Y	Y	Y	N	N
46 Correa	N	N	N	N	N	N
47 Lowenthal	N	N	N	N	Y	Y
48 Rohrabacher	Y	Y	Y	Y	N	N
49 Issa	Y	Y	Y	Y	N	N
50 Hunter	Y	Y	Y	Y	Y	N
51 Vargas	N	N	N	N	Y	Y
52 Peters	N	N	N	N	Y	Y
53 Davis	N	N	N	N	Y	Y

	391	392	393	394	395	396
COLORADO						
1 DeGette	N	N	N	N	Y	Y
2 Polis	N	N	N	N	Y	Y
3 Tipton	Y	Y	Y	Y	N	N
4 Buck	Y	Y	Y	Y	N	N
5 Lamborn	Y	Y	Y	Y	N	N
6 Coffman	Y	Y	Y	Y	N	N
7 Perlmutter	N	N	N	N	Y	Y
CONNECTICUT						
1 Larson	N	N	N	N	Y	Y
2 Courtney	N	N	N	N	Y	Y
3 DeLauro	N	N	N	N	Y	Y
4 Himes	N	N	N	N	Y	Y
5 Esty	N	N	N	N	Y	Y
DELAWARE						
AL Blunt Rochester	N	N	N	N	Y	Y
FLORIDA						
1 Gaetz	Y	Y	Y	Y	N	N
2 Dunn	Y	Y	Y	Y	N	N
3 Yoho	Y	Y	Y	Y	N	N
4 Rutherford	Y	Y	Y	Y	N	N
5 Lawson	N	N	N	N	Y	N
6 DeSantis	Y	Y	Y	Y	N	N
7 Murphy	N	N	N	N	Y	Y
8 Posey	Y	Y	Y	Y	N	N
9 Soto	N	N	N	N	Y	Y
10 Demings	N	N	N	N	Y	Y
11 Webster	Y	Y	Y	Y	N	N
12 Bilirakis	Y	Y	Y	Y	N	N
13 Crist	N	N	N	N	Y	Y
14 Castor	N	N	N	N	Y	Y
15 Ross	Y	Y	Y	Y	N	N
16 Buchanan	Y	Y	Y	Y	N	N
17 Rooney, T.	Y	Y	Y	Y	N	N
18 Mast	N	Y	Y	Y	N	N
19 Rooney, F.	Y	Y	Y	Y	N	N
20 Hastings	N	N	N	N	Y	Y
21 Frankel	N	N	N	N	Y	Y
22 Deutch	N	N	N	N	Y	Y
23 Wasserman Schultz	N	N	N	N	Y	Y
24 Wilson	N	N	N	N	Y	Y
25 Diaz-Balart	Y	Y	Y	Y	N	N
26 Curbelo	N	Y	Y	Y	N	N
27 Ros-Lehtinen	N	Y	Y	Y	N	N
GEORGIA						
1 Carter	Y	Y	Y	Y	N	N
2 Bishop	Y	N	N	N	Y	Y
3 Ferguson	Y	Y	Y	Y	N	N
4 Johnson	N	N	N	N	Y	Y
5 Lewis	N	N	N	N	Y	Y
6 Handel	Y	Y	Y	Y	N	N
7 Woodall	Y	Y	Y	Y	N	N
8 Scott, A.	Y	Y	Y	Y	N	N
9 Collins	Y	Y	Y	Y	N	N
10 Hice	Y	Y	Y	Y	N	N
11 Loudermilk	Y	Y	Y	Y	N	N
12 Allen	Y	Y	Y	Y	N	N
13 Scott, D.	N	N	N	N	Y	Y
14 Graves	Y	Y	Y	Y	N	N
HAWAII						
1 Hanabusa	N	N	N	N	Y	Y
2 Gabbard	N	N	N	N	Y	Y
IDAHO						
1 Labrador	?	?	?	?	?	?
2 Simpson	Y	Y	Y	Y	N	N
ILLINOIS						
1 Rush	N	N	N	N	Y	Y
2 Kelly	N	N	N	N	Y	Y
3 Lipinski	N	N	N	N	Y	Y
4 Gutierrez	N	N	N	N	Y	Y
5 Quigley	N	N	N	N	Y	Y
6 Roskam	Y	Y	Y	Y	N	N
7 Davis, D.	N	N	N	N	Y	Y
8 Krishnamoorthi	N	N	N	N	Y	Y
9 Schakowsky	N	N	N	N	Y	Y
10 Schneider	N	N	N	N	Y	Y
11 Foster	N	N	N	N	Y	Y
12 Bost	Y	Y	Y	Y	N	N
13 Davis, R.	Y	Y	Y	Y	N	N
14 Hultgren	Y	Y	Y	Y	N	N
15 Shimkus	Y	Y	Y	Y	N	N

KEY	**Republicans**	Democrats	*Independents*		
Y Voted for (yea)		X Paired against		C Voted "present" to avoid possible conflict of interest	
# Paired for		– Announced against			
+ Announced for		P Voted "present"		? Did not vote or otherwise make a position known	
N Voted against (nay)					

	391	392	393	394	395	396
16 **Kinzinger**	Y	Y	Y	Y	N	N
17 Bustos	N	N	N	N	Y	Y
18 **LaHood**	Y	Y	Y	Y	N	N
INDIANA						
1 Visclosky	N	N	N	N	Y	Y
2 **Walorski**	Y	Y	Y	Y	N	N
3 **Banks**	Y	Y	Y	Y	N	N
4 **Rokita**	Y	Y	Y	Y	N	N
5 **Brooks**	Y	Y	Y	Y	N	N
6 **Messer**	Y	Y	Y	Y	N	N
7 Carson	N	N	N	N	Y	Y
8 **Bucshon**	Y	Y	Y	Y	N	N
9 **Hollingsworth**	Y	Y	Y	Y	N	N
IOWA						
1 **Blum**	Y	Y	Y	Y	N	N
2 Loebsack	N	N	N	N	Y	Y
3 **Young**	Y	Y	Y	Y	N	N
4 **King**	Y	Y	Y	Y	N	N
KANSAS						
1 **Marshall**	Y	Y	Y	Y	N	N
2 **Jenkins**	Y	Y	Y	Y	N	N
3 **Yoder**	Y	Y	Y	Y	N	N
4 **Estes**	Y	Y	Y	Y	N	N
KENTUCKY						
1 **Comer**	Y	Y	Y	Y	N	N
2 **Guthrie**	Y	Y	Y	Y	N	N
3 Yarmuth	N	N	N	N	Y	Y
4 **Massie**	Y	Y	Y	N	N	N
5 **Rogers**	Y	Y	Y	Y	N	N
6 **Barr**	Y	Y	Y	Y	N	N
LOUISIANA						
1 **Scalise**	+	+	+	+	–	–
2 Richmond	N	N	N	N	Y	Y
3 **Higgins**	Y	Y	Y	Y	N	N
4 **Johnson**	Y	Y	Y	Y	N	N
5 **Abraham**	Y	Y	Y	Y	N	N
6 **Graves**	Y	Y	Y	Y	N	N
MAINE						
1 Pingree	N	N	N	N	Y	Y
2 **Poliquin**	N	Y	Y	Y	N	N
MARYLAND						
1 **Harris**	Y	Y	Y	Y	N	N
2 Ruppersberger	N	N	N	N	Y	Y
3 Sarbanes	N	N	N	N	Y	Y
4 Brown	N	N	N	N	Y	Y
5 Hoyer	N	N	N	N	Y	Y
6 Delaney	N	N	N	N	Y	Y
7 Cummings	?	?	?	?	?	?
8 Raskin	N	N	N	N	Y	Y
MASSACHUSETTS						
1 Neal	N	N	N	N	Y	Y
2 McGovern	N	N	N	N	Y	Y
3 Tsongas	N	N	N	N	Y	Y
4 Kennedy	N	N	N	N	Y	Y
5 Clark	N	N	N	N	Y	Y
6 Moulton	N	N	N	N	Y	Y
7 Capuano	N	N	N	N	Y	Y
8 Lynch	N	N	N	N	Y	Y
9 Keating	N	N	N	N	Y	Y
MICHIGAN						
1 **Bergman**	Y	Y	Y	Y	N	N
2 **Huizenga**	Y	Y	Y	Y	N	N
3 **Amash**	Y	Y	Y	N	N	N
4 **Moolenaar**	Y	Y	Y	Y	N	N
5 Kildee	N	N	N	N	Y	Y
6 **Upton**	Y	Y	Y	Y	N	N
7 **Walberg**	Y	Y	Y	Y	N	N
8 **Bishop**	Y	Y	Y	Y	N	N
9 Levin	N	N	N	N	Y	Y
10 **Mitchell**	Y	Y	Y	Y	N	N
11 **Trott**	Y	Y	Y	Y	N	N
12 Dingell	N	N	N	N	Y	Y
13 Conyers	N	N	N	N	Y	Y
14 Lawrence	N	N	N	N	Y	Y
MINNESOTA						
1 Walz	N	N	N	N	Y	Y
2 **Lewis**	Y	Y	Y	Y	N	N
3 **Paulsen**	Y	Y	Y	Y	N	N
4 McCollum	N	N	N	N	Y	Y
5 Ellison	N	N	N	N	Y	Y
6 **Emmer**	Y	Y	Y	Y	N	N
7 Peterson	Y	N	N	N	N	N
8 Nolan	N	N	N	N	Y	Y
MISSISSIPPI						
1 **Kelly**	Y	Y	Y	Y	N	N
2 Thompson	N	N	N	N	Y	Y
3 **Harper**	Y	Y	Y	Y	N	N
4 **Palazzo**	Y	Y	Y	Y	N	N
MISSOURI						
1 Clay	N	N	N	N	Y	Y
2 **Wagner**	Y	Y	Y	Y	N	N
3 **Luetkemeyer**	Y	Y	Y	Y	N	N
4 **Hartzler**	Y	Y	Y	Y	N	N
5 Cleaver	N	N	N	N	Y	Y
6 **Graves**	Y	Y	Y	Y	N	N
7 **Long**	Y	Y	Y	Y	N	N
8 **Smith**	Y	Y	Y	Y	N	N
MONTANA						
AL **Gianforte**	Y	Y	Y	Y	N	N
NEBRASKA						
1 **Fortenberry**	Y	Y	Y	Y	N	N
2 **Bacon**	Y	Y	Y	Y	N	N
3 **Smith**	Y	Y	Y	Y	N	N
NEVADA						
1 Titus	N	N	N	N	Y	Y
2 **Amodei**	Y	Y	Y	Y	N	N
3 Rosen	N	N	N	N	Y	Y
4 Kihuen	N	N	N	N	Y	Y
NEW HAMPSHIRE						
1 Shea-Porter	N	N	N	N	Y	Y
2 Kuster	N	N	N	N	Y	Y
NEW JERSEY						
1 Norcross	N	N	N	N	Y	N
2 **LoBiondo**	N	Y	Y	Y	N	N
3 **MacArthur**	Y	Y	Y	Y	N	N
4 **Smith**	N	Y	Y	Y	N	N
5 Gottheimer	N	N	N	N	N	Y
6 Pallone	N	N	N	N	Y	Y
7 **Lance**	Y	Y	Y	Y	N	N
8 Sires	N	N	N	N	Y	Y
9 Pascrell	N	N	N	N	Y	Y
10 Payne	N	N	N	N	Y	Y
11 **Frelinghuysen**	Y	Y	Y	Y	N	N
12 Watson Coleman	N	N	N	N	Y	Y
NEW MEXICO						
1 Lujan Grisham	N	N	N	N	Y	Y
2 **Pearce**	Y	Y	Y	Y	N	N
3 Luján	N	N	N	N	Y	Y
NEW YORK						
1 **Zeldin**	Y	Y	Y	Y	N	N
2 **King**	Y	Y	Y	Y	N	N
3 Suozzi	N	N	N	N	Y	Y
4 Rice	N	N	N	N	Y	Y
5 Meeks	N	N	N	N	Y	Y
6 Meng	N	N	N	N	Y	Y
7 Velázquez	N	N	N	N	Y	Y
8 Jeffries	N	N	N	N	Y	Y
9 Clarke	N	N	N	N	Y	Y
10 Nadler	N	N	N	N	Y	Y
11 **Donovan**	Y	Y	Y	Y	N	N
12 Maloney, C.	N	N	N	N	Y	Y
13 Espaillat	N	N	N	N	Y	Y
14 Crowley	N	N	N	N	Y	Y
15 Serrano	N	N	N	N	Y	Y
16 Engel	N	N	N	N	Y	Y
17 Lowey	N	N	N	N	Y	Y
18 Maloney, S.P.	N	N	N	N	Y	Y
19 **Faso**	N	Y	Y	Y	N	N
20 Tonko	N	N	N	N	Y	Y
21 **Stefanik**	N	Y	Y	Y	N	N
22 **Tenney**	Y	Y	Y	Y	–	–
23 **Reed**	Y	Y	Y	Y	N	N
24 **Katko**	Y	Y	Y	Y	N	N
25 Slaughter	N	N	N	N	Y	Y
26 Higgins	N	N	N	N	Y	Y
27 **Collins**	Y	Y	Y	Y	N	N
NORTH CAROLINA						
1 Butterfield	N	N	N	N	Y	Y
2 **Holding**	Y	Y	Y	Y	N	N
3 **Jones**	Y	N	N	Y	N	N
4 Price	N	N	N	N	Y	Y
5 **Foxx**	Y	Y	Y	Y	N	N
6 **Walker**	Y	Y	Y	Y	N	N
7 **Rouzer**	Y	Y	Y	Y	N	N
8 **Hudson**	Y	Y	Y	Y	N	–
9 **Pittenger**	Y	Y	Y	Y	N	N
10 **McHenry**	Y	Y	Y	Y	N	N
11 **Meadows**	Y	Y	Y	Y	N	N
12 Adams	N	N	N	N	Y	Y
13 **Budd**	Y	Y	Y	Y	N	N
NORTH DAKOTA						
AL **Cramer**	Y	Y	Y	Y	N	N
OHIO						
1 **Chabot**	Y	Y	Y	Y	N	N
2 **Wenstrup**	Y	Y	Y	Y	N	N
3 Beatty	N	N	N	N	Y	Y
4 **Jordan**	Y	Y	Y	Y	N	N
5 **Latta**	Y	Y	Y	Y	N	N
6 **Johnson**	Y	Y	Y	Y	N	N
7 **Gibbs**	Y	Y	Y	Y	N	N
8 **Davidson**	Y	Y	Y	Y	N	N
9 Kaptur	N	N	N	N	Y	Y
10 **Turner**	Y	Y	Y	?	N	N
11 Fudge	N	N	N	N	Y	Y
12 **Tiberi**	Y	Y	Y	Y	N	N
13 Ryan	N	N	N	N	Y	Y
14 **Joyce**	Y	Y	Y	Y	N	N
15 **Stivers**	Y	Y	Y	Y	N	N
16 **Renacci**	Y	Y	Y	Y	N	N
OKLAHOMA						
1 **Bridenstine**	Y	Y	Y	Y	N	N
2 **Mullin**	Y	Y	Y	Y	N	N
3 **Lucas**	Y	Y	Y	Y	N	N
4 **Cole**	Y	Y	Y	Y	N	N
5 **Russell**	Y	Y	Y	Y	N	N
OREGON						
1 Bonamici	N	N	N	N	Y	Y
2 **Walden**	Y	Y	Y	Y	N	N
3 Blumenauer	N	N	N	N	Y	Y
4 DeFazio	N	N	N	N	Y	Y
5 Schrader	N	N	N	N	N	N
PENNSYLVANIA						
1 Brady	N	N	N	N	N	N
2 Evans	N	N	N	N	Y	Y
3 **Kelly**	Y	Y	Y	Y	N	N
4 **Perry**	Y	Y	Y	Y	N	N
5 **Thompson**	Y	Y	Y	Y	N	N
6 **Costello**	Y	Y	Y	Y	N	N
7 **Meehan**	Y	Y	Y	Y	N	N
8 **Fitzpatrick**	N	Y	Y	Y	N	N
9 **Shuster**	Y	Y	Y	Y	N	N
10 **Marino**	Y	Y	Y	Y	N	N
11 **Barletta**	Y	Y	Y	Y	N	N
12 **Rothfus**	Y	Y	Y	Y	N	N
13 Boyle	N	N	N	N	Y	Y
14 Doyle	N	N	N	N	Y	N
15 **Dent**	Y	Y	Y	Y	N	N
16 **Smucker**	Y	Y	Y	Y	N	N
17 Cartwright	N	N	N	N	Y	Y
18 **Murphy**	Y	Y	Y	Y	N	N
RHODE ISLAND						
1 Cicilline	N	N	N	N	Y	Y
2 Langevin	N	N	N	N	Y	Y
SOUTH CAROLINA						
1 **Sanford**	N	P	Y	Y	N	N
2 **Wilson**	Y	Y	Y	Y	N	N
3 **Duncan**	Y	Y	Y	Y	N	N
4 **Gowdy**	Y	Y	Y	Y	N	N
5 **Norman**	Y	Y	Y	Y	N	N
6 Clyburn	N	N	N	N	Y	Y
7 **Rice**	Y	Y	Y	Y	N	N
SOUTH DAKOTA						
AL **Noem**	Y	Y	Y	Y	N	N
TENNESSEE						
1 **Roe**	Y	Y	Y	Y	N	N
2 **Duncan**	Y	Y	Y	Y	N	N
3 **Fleischmann**	Y	Y	Y	Y	N	N
4 **DesJarlais**	Y	Y	Y	Y	N	N
5 Cooper	N	N	N	N	Y	Y
6 **Black**	Y	Y	Y	Y	N	N
7 **Blackburn**	Y	Y	Y	Y	N	N
8 **Kustoff**	Y	Y	Y	Y	N	N
9 Cohen	N	N	N	N	N	Y
TEXAS						
1 **Gohmert**	Y	Y	Y	Y	N	N
2 **Poe**	Y	Y	Y	Y	N	N
3 **Johnson, S.**	Y	Y	Y	Y	N	N
4 **Ratcliffe**	Y	Y	Y	Y	N	N
5 **Hensarling**	Y	Y	Y	Y	N	N
6 **Barton**	Y	Y	Y	Y	N	N
7 **Culberson**	Y	Y	Y	Y	N	N
8 **Brady**	Y	Y	Y	Y	N	N
9 Green, A.	N	N	N	N	Y	Y
10 **McCaul**	Y	Y	Y	Y	N	N
11 **Conaway**	Y	Y	Y	Y	N	N
12 **Granger**	+	Y	Y	Y	N	N
13 **Thornberry**	Y	Y	Y	Y	N	N
14 **Weber**	Y	Y	Y	Y	N	N
15 Gonzalez	N	N	N	N	N	N
16 O'Rourke	N	N	N	N	Y	Y
17 **Flores**	Y	Y	Y	Y	N	N
18 Jackson Lee	N	N	N	N	Y	Y
19 **Arrington**	Y	Y	Y	Y	N	N
20 Castro	N	N	N	N	Y	Y
21 **Smith**	Y	Y	Y	Y	N	N
22 **Olson**	Y	Y	Y	Y	N	N
23 **Hurd**	Y	Y	Y	Y	N	N
24 **Marchant**	Y	Y	Y	Y	N	N
25 **Williams**	Y	Y	Y	Y	N	N
26 **Burgess**	Y	Y	Y	Y	N	N
27 **Farenthold**	Y	Y	Y	Y	N	N
28 Cuellar	Y	N	N	N	N	N
29 Green, G.	N	N	N	N	N	N
30 Johnson, E.B.	N	N	N	N	Y	Y
31 **Carter**	Y	Y	Y	Y	N	N
32 **Sessions**	Y	Y	Y	Y	N	N
33 Veasey	N	N	N	N	N	N
34 Vela	N	N	N	N	N	N
35 Doggett	N	N	N	N	Y	Y
36 **Babin**	Y	Y	Y	Y	N	N
UTAH						
1 **Bishop**	Y	Y	Y	Y	N	N
2 **Stewart**	Y	Y	Y	Y	N	N
4 **Love**	Y	Y	Y	Y	N	N
VERMONT						
AL Welch	N	N	N	N	Y	Y
VIRGINIA						
1 **Wittman**	Y	Y	Y	Y	N	?
2 **Taylor**	Y	Y	Y	Y	N	N
3 Scott	N	N	N	N	Y	Y
4 McEachin	N	?	?	N	Y	Y
5 **Garrett**	Y	Y	Y	Y	N	N
6 **Goodlatte**	Y	Y	Y	Y	N	N
7 **Brat**	Y	Y	Y	Y	N	N
8 Beyer	N	N	N	N	Y	Y
9 **Griffith**	Y	Y	Y	Y	N	N
10 **Comstock**	Y	Y	Y	Y	N	N
11 Connolly	N	N	N	N	Y	Y
WASHINGTON						
1 DelBene	N	N	N	N	Y	Y
2 Larsen	N	N	N	N	Y	Y
3 **Herrera Beutler**	Y	Y	Y	Y	N	N
4 **Newhouse**	Y	Y	Y	Y	N	N
5 **McMorris Rodgers**	Y	Y	Y	Y	N	N
6 Kilmer	N	N	N	N	Y	Y
7 Jayapal	N	N	N	N	Y	Y
8 **Reichert**	N	Y	Y	Y	Y	N
9 Smith	N	N	N	N	Y	Y
10 Heck	N	N	N	N	Y	Y
WEST VIRGINIA						
1 **McKinley**	Y	Y	Y	Y	N	N
2 **Mooney**	Y	Y	Y	Y	N	N
3 **Jenkins**	Y	Y	Y	Y	N	N
WISCONSIN						
1 **Ryan**						
2 Pocan	N	N	N	N	Y	Y
3 Kind	N	N	N	N	Y	Y
4 Moore	N	N	N	N	Y	Y
5 **Sensenbrenner**	Y	Y	Y	Y	N	N
6 **Grothman**	Y	Y	Y	Y	N	N
7 **Duffy**	Y	Y	Y	Y	N	N
8 **Gallagher**	Y	Y	Y	Y	N	N
WYOMING						
AL **Cheney**	Y	Y	Y	Y	N	N

VOTE NUMBER

397. HR 2883. CROSS-BORDER ENERGY INFRASTRUCTURE/RECOMMIT.
O'Halleran, D-Ariz., motion to recommit the bill to the House Energy and Commerce Committee with instructions to report it back immediately with an amendment that would require, as a condition of issuing a certificate of crossing, that all iron and steel products used in the construction, connection, operation, and maintenance of a border-crossing facility would be produced in the United States. Motion rejected 193-232 : R 2-232; D 191-0. July 19, 2017.

398. HR 2883. CROSS-BORDER ENERGY INFRASTRUCTURE/PASSAGE.
Passage of the bill that would establish a new system for the approval and permitting of border-crossing oil and gas pipelines and electrical transmission lines. The bill would require sponsors of border-crossing oil pipelines and electricity transmission facilities that cross the U.S. borders into Canada and Mexico to receive a "certificate of crossing" from the relevant federal agency in order to build or modify their projects, thereby eliminating the need for a presidential permit. The bill would eliminate the requirement under current law that the Energy Department approve the transmission of electricity from the U.S. to another country. Passed 254-175 : R 237-0; D 17-175. July 19, 2017.

399. HR 2910. FEDERAL ENERGY REGULATORY COMMISSION AGENCY COORDINATING AUTHORITY/CONSERVATION AND RECREATION EXEMPTION. Tsongas, D-Mass., amendment that would prohibit the Federal Energy Regulatory Commission from issuing a certificate of public convenience and necessity to an oil or natural gas pipeline project if any part of such facility would be located on lands required, by federal, state, or local law, to be managed for natural resource conservation or recreation. Rejected in Committee of the Whole 180-249 : R 1-236; D 179-13. July 19, 2017.

400. HR 2910. FEDERAL ENERGY REGULATORY COMMISSION AGENCY COORDINATING AUTHORITY/SUPPLEMENTAL ENVIRONMENTAL REPORTS. Beyer, D-Va., amendment that would require the Federal Energy Regulatory Commission, when conducting a project-related review under the National Environmental Policy Act, to prepare a supplement to its environmental impact statement in certain cases, such as if the commission makes a substantial change to the proposed action related to environmental concerns, or if there were to be "significant new circumstances or information" related to environmental concerns with bearing on the application. Rejected in Committee of the Whole 192-236 : R 3-233; D 189-3. July 19, 2017.

401. HR 2910. FEDERAL ENERGY REGULATORY COMMISSION AGENCY COORDINATION AUTHORITY/RECOMMIT. Watson Coleman, D-N.J., motion to recommit the bill to the House Energy and Commerce Committee with instructions to report it back immediately with an amendment that would prohibit approval of an application for a certificate of public convenience and necessity under the Natural Gas Act unless the applicant agrees not to exercise its eminent domain authority under such law. Motion rejected 189-239 : R 1-235; D 188-4. July 19, 2017.

402. HR 2910. FEDERAL ENERGY REGULATORY COMMISSION AGENCY COORDINATING AUTHORITY/PASSAGE. Passage of the bill that would establish the Federal Energy Regulatory Commission as the sole lead agency for the permitting of proposals to build or expand natural gas pipelines. The bill would require the commission to set deadlines by which federal agencies would need to take certain actions as part of the pipeline project proposal review process and would, in the event an agency fails to meet a deadline set by the commission, require the head of the agency to notify Congress and set forth a recommended implementation plan for the completion of the action. Passed 248-179 : R 235-1; D 13-178. July 19, 2017.

	397	398	399	400	401	402
ALABAMA						
1 **Byrne**	N	Y	N	N	N	Y
2 **Roby**	N	Y	N	N	N	Y
3 **Rogers**	N	Y	N	N	N	Y
4 **Aderholt**	N	Y	N	N	N	Y
5 **Brooks**	N	Y	N	N	N	Y
6 **Palmer**	N	Y	N	N	N	Y
7 Sewell	Y	N	Y	Y	Y	N
ALASKA						
AL **Young**	N	Y	N	N	N	Y
ARIZONA						
1 O'Halleran	Y	N	Y	Y	Y	Y
2 **McSally**	N	Y	N	N	N	Y
3 Grijalva	Y	N	Y	Y	Y	N
4 **Gosar**	N	Y	N	N	N	Y
5 **Biggs**	N	Y	N	N	N	Y
6 **Schweikert**	N	Y	N	N	N	Y
7 Gallego	Y	N	Y	Y	Y	N
8 **Franks**	N	Y	N	N	N	Y
9 Sinema	Y	N	N	Y	Y	Y
ARKANSAS						
1 **Crawford**	N	Y	N	N	N	Y
2 **Hill**	N	Y	N	N	N	Y
3 **Womack**	N	Y	N	N	N	Y
4 **Westerman**	N	Y	N	N	N	Y
CALIFORNIA						
1 **LaMalfa**	N	Y	N	N	N	Y
2 Huffman	Y	N	Y	Y	Y	N
3 Garamendi	Y	N	Y	Y	Y	N
4 **McClintock**	N	Y	N	N	N	Y
5 Thompson	Y	N	Y	Y	Y	N
6 Matsui	Y	N	Y	Y	Y	N
7 Bera	Y	N	Y	Y	Y	N
8 **Cook**	N	Y	N	N	N	Y
9 McNerney	Y	N	Y	Y	Y	N
10 **Denham**	N	Y	N	N	N	Y
11 DeSaulnier	Y	N	Y	Y	Y	N
12 Pelosi	?	N	Y	Y	Y	N
13 Lee	Y	N	Y	Y	Y	N
14 Speier	Y	N	Y	Y	Y	N
15 Swalwell	Y	N	Y	Y	Y	N
16 Costa	Y	Y	N	N	Y	N
17 Khanna	Y	N	Y	Y	Y	N
18 Eshoo	Y	N	Y	Y	Y	N
19 Lofgren	Y	N	Y	Y	Y	N
20 Panetta	Y	N	Y	Y	Y	N
21 **Valadao**	?	Y	N	N	?	Y
22 **Nunes**	N	Y	N	N	N	Y
23 **McCarthy**	N	Y	N	N	N	Y
24 Carbajal	Y	N	Y	Y	Y	N
25 **Knight**	N	Y	N	N	N	Y
26 Brownley	Y	N	Y	Y	Y	N
27 Chu	Y	N	Y	Y	Y	N
28 Schiff	Y	N	Y	Y	Y	N
29 Cardenas	Y	N	Y	Y	Y	N
30 Sherman	Y	N	Y	Y	Y	N
31 Aguilar	Y	N	Y	Y	Y	N
32 Napolitano	+	-	+	+	+	-
33 Lieu	Y	N	Y	Y	Y	N
34 Gomez	Y	N	Y	Y	Y	N
35 Torres	Y	N	Y	Y	Y	N
36 Ruiz	Y	N	Y	Y	Y	N
37 Bass	Y	N	Y	Y	Y	N
38 Sánchez, Linda	Y	N	Y	Y	Y	N
39 **Royce**	N	Y	N	N	N	Y
40 Roybal-Allard	Y	N	Y	Y	Y	N
41 Takano	Y	N	Y	Y	Y	N
42 **Calvert**	N	Y	N	?	N	Y
43 Waters	Y	N	Y	Y	Y	N
44 Barragan	Y	N	Y	Y	Y	N
45 **Walters**	N	Y	N	N	N	Y
46 Correa	Y	Y	Y	Y	Y	Y
47 Lowenthal	Y	N	Y	Y	Y	N
48 **Rohrabacher**	N	Y	N	N	N	Y
49 **Issa**	N	Y	N	N	N	Y
50 **Hunter**	N	Y	N	N	N	Y
51 Vargas	Y	N	Y	Y	Y	N
52 Peters	Y	N	Y	Y	Y	N
53 Davis	Y	N	Y	Y	Y	N

	397	398	399	400	401	402
COLORADO						
1 DeGette	Y	N	Y	Y	Y	N
2 Polis	Y	N	Y	Y	Y	N
3 **Tipton**	N	Y	N	N	N	Y
4 **Buck**	N	Y	N	N	N	Y
5 **Lamborn**	N	Y	N	N	N	Y
6 **Coffman**	N	Y	N	N	N	Y
7 Perlmutter	Y	N	Y	Y	Y	N
CONNECTICUT						
1 Larson	Y	N	Y	Y	Y	N
2 Courtney	Y	N	Y	Y	Y	N
3 DeLauro	Y	N	Y	Y	Y	N
4 Himes	Y	N	Y	Y	Y	N
5 Esty	Y	N	Y	Y	Y	N
DELAWARE						
AL Blunt Rochester	Y	N	Y	Y	Y	N
FLORIDA						
1 **Gaetz**	N	Y	N	N	N	Y
2 **Dunn**	N	Y	N	N	N	Y
3 **Yoho**	N	Y	N	N	N	Y
4 **Rutherford**	N	Y	N	N	N	Y
5 Lawson	Y	N	Y	Y	Y	N
6 **DeSantis**	N	Y	N	N	N	Y
7 Murphy	Y	N	Y	Y	Y	N
8 **Posey**	N	Y	N	N	N	Y
9 Soto	Y	N	Y	Y	Y	N
10 Demings	Y	N	Y	Y	Y	N
11 **Webster**	N	Y	N	N	N	Y
12 **Bilirakis**	N	Y	N	N	N	Y
13 Crist	Y	N	Y	Y	Y	N
14 Castor	Y	N	Y	Y	Y	N
15 **Ross**	N	Y	N	N	N	Y
16 **Buchanan**	N	Y	N	N	N	Y
17 **Rooney, T.**	N	Y	N	N	N	Y
18 **Mast**	N	Y	N	N	N	Y
19 **Rooney, F.**	N	Y	N	N	N	Y
20 Hastings	Y	N	Y	Y	Y	N
21 Frankel	Y	N	Y	Y	Y	N
22 Deutch	Y	N	Y	Y	Y	N
23 Wasserman Schultz	Y	N	Y	Y	Y	N
24 Wilson	Y	N	Y	Y	Y	N
25 **Diaz-Balart**	N	Y	N	N	N	Y
26 **Curbelo**	N	Y	N	N	N	Y
27 **Ros-Lehtinen**	N	Y	N	N	N	?
GEORGIA						
1 **Carter**	N	Y	N	N	N	Y
2 Bishop	Y	Y	Y	Y	Y	N
3 **Ferguson**	N	Y	N	N	N	Y
4 Johnson	Y	N	Y	Y	Y	N
5 Lewis	Y	N	Y	Y	Y	N
6 **Handel**	N	Y	N	N	N	Y
7 **Woodall**	N	Y	N	N	N	Y
8 **Scott, A.**	N	Y	N	N	N	Y
9 **Collins**	N	Y	N	N	N	Y
10 **Hice**	N	Y	N	N	N	Y
11 **Loudermilk**	N	Y	N	N	N	Y
12 **Allen**	N	Y	N	N	N	Y
13 Scott, D.	Y	N	Y	Y	Y	N
14 **Graves**	N	Y	N	N	N	Y
HAWAII						
1 Hanabusa	Y	N	Y	Y	Y	N
2 Gabbard	Y	N	Y	Y	Y	N
IDAHO						
1 **Labrador**	?	?	?	?	?	?
2 **Simpson**	N	Y	N	N	N	Y
ILLINOIS						
1 Rush	Y	N	Y	Y	Y	N
2 Kelly	Y	N	Y	Y	Y	N
3 Lipinski	Y	N	Y	Y	Y	N
4 Gutierrez	Y	N	Y	Y	Y	N
5 Quigley	Y	N	Y	Y	Y	N
6 **Roskam**	N	Y	N	N	N	Y
7 Davis, D.	Y	N	Y	Y	Y	N
8 Krishnamoorthi	Y	N	Y	Y	Y	N
9 Schakowsky	Y	N	Y	Y	Y	N
10 Schneider	Y	N	Y	Y	Y	N
11 Foster	Y	N	Y	Y	Y	N
12 **Bost**	N	Y	N	N	N	Y
13 **Davis, R.**	N	Y	N	N	N	Y
14 **Hultgren**	N	Y	N	N	N	Y
15 **Shimkus**	N	Y	N	N	N	Y

KEY	**Republicans**	Democrats	*Independents*
Y Voted for (yea)	X Paired against	C Voted "present" to avoid possible conflict of interest
# Paired for	– Announced against	
+ Announced for	P Voted "present"	? Did not vote or otherwise make a position known
N Voted against (nay)		

	397	398	399	400	401	402
16 **Kinzinger**	N	Y	N	N	N	Y
17 Bustos	Y	N	Y	Y	Y	N
18 **LaHood**	N	Y	N	N	N	Y
INDIANA						
1 Visclosky	Y	N	Y	Y	Y	N
2 **Walorski**	N	Y	N	N	N	Y
3 **Banks**	N	Y	N	N	N	Y
4 **Rokita**	N	Y	N	N	N	Y
5 **Brooks**	N	Y	N	N	N	Y
6 **Messer**	N	Y	N	N	N	Y
7 Carson	Y	N	Y	Y	Y	N
8 **Bucshon**	N	Y	N	N	N	Y
9 **Hollingsworth**	N	Y	N	N	N	Y
IOWA						
1 **Blum**	N	Y	N	N	N	Y
2 Loebsack	Y	N	Y	Y	Y	?
3 **Young**	N	Y	N	N	N	Y
4 **King**	N	Y	N	N	N	Y
KANSAS						
1 **Marshall**	N	Y	N	N	N	Y
2 **Jenkins**	N	Y	N	N	N	Y
3 **Yoder**	N	Y	N	N	N	Y
4 **Estes**	N	Y	N	N	N	Y
KENTUCKY						
1 **Comer**	N	Y	N	N	N	Y
2 **Guthrie**	N	Y	N	N	N	Y
3 Yarmuth	Y	N	Y	Y	Y	N
4 **Massie**	N	Y	N	N	N	Y
5 **Rogers**	?	Y	N	N	N	Y
6 **Barr**	N	Y	N	N	N	Y
LOUISIANA						
1 **Scalise**	–	+	–	–	–	+
2 Richmond	Y	Y	Y	Y	Y	N
3 **Higgins**	N	Y	N	N	N	Y
4 **Johnson**	N	Y	N	N	N	Y
5 **Abraham**	N	Y	N	N	N	Y
6 **Graves**	N	Y	N	N	N	Y
MAINE						
1 Pingree	Y	N	Y	Y	Y	N
2 **Poliquin**	N	Y	N	N	N	Y
MARYLAND						
1 **Harris**	N	Y	N	Y	N	Y
2 Ruppersberger	Y	N	Y	Y	Y	N
3 Sarbanes	Y	N	Y	Y	Y	N
4 Brown	Y	N	Y	Y	Y	N
5 Hoyer	Y	N	Y	Y	Y	N
6 Delaney	Y	N	Y	Y	Y	N
7 Cummings	?	?	?	?	?	?
8 Raskin	Y	N	Y	Y	Y	N
MASSACHUSETTS						
1 Neal	Y	N	Y	Y	Y	N
2 McGovern	Y	N	Y	Y	Y	N
3 Tsongas	Y	N	Y	Y	Y	N
4 Kennedy	Y	N	Y	Y	Y	N
5 Clark	Y	N	Y	Y	Y	N
6 Moulton	Y	N	Y	Y	Y	N
7 Capuano	Y	N	Y	Y	Y	N
8 Lynch	Y	N	Y	Y	Y	N
9 Keating	Y	N	Y	Y	Y	N
MICHIGAN						
1 **Bergman**	N	Y	N	N	N	Y
2 **Huizenga**	N	Y	N	N	N	Y
3 **Amash**	N	Y	N	N	N	Y
4 **Moolenaar**	N	Y	N	N	N	Y
5 Kildee	Y	N	Y	Y	Y	N
6 **Upton**	N	Y	N	N	N	Y
7 **Walberg**	N	Y	N	N	N	Y
8 **Bishop**	N	Y	N	N	N	Y
9 Levin	Y	N	Y	Y	Y	N
10 **Mitchell**	N	Y	N	N	N	Y
11 **Trott**	N	Y	N	N	N	Y
12 Dingell	Y	N	Y	Y	Y	N
13 Conyers	Y	N	Y	Y	Y	N
14 Lawrence	Y	N	Y	Y	Y	N
MINNESOTA						
1 Walz	Y	N	Y	Y	Y	N
2 **Lewis**	N	Y	N	N	N	Y
3 **Paulsen**	N	Y	N	N	N	Y
4 McCollum	Y	N	Y	Y	Y	N

	397	398	399	400	401	402
5 Ellison	Y	N	Y	Y	Y	N
6 **Emmer**	N	Y	N	N	N	Y
7 Peterson	Y	Y	N	N	N	Y
8 Nolan	Y	N	Y	Y	Y	N
MISSISSIPPI						
1 **Kelly**	N	Y	N	N	N	Y
2 Thompson	Y	N	Y	Y	Y	N
3 **Harper**	N	Y	N	N	N	Y
4 **Palazzo**	N	Y	N	N	N	Y
MISSOURI						
1 Clay	Y	N	Y	Y	Y	N
2 **Wagner**	N	Y	N	N	N	Y
3 **Luetkemeyer**	N	Y	N	N	N	Y
4 **Hartzler**	N	Y	N	N	N	Y
5 Cleaver	Y	N	Y	Y	Y	N
6 **Graves**	N	Y	N	N	N	Y
7 **Long**	N	Y	N	N	N	Y
8 **Smith**	N	Y	N	N	N	Y
MONTANA						
AL **Gianforte**	N	Y	N	N	N	Y
NEBRASKA						
1 **Fortenberry**	N	Y	N	N	N	Y
2 **Bacon**	N	Y	N	N	N	Y
3 **Smith**	N	Y	N	N	N	Y
NEVADA						
1 Titus	Y	N	Y	Y	Y	N
2 **Amodei**	N	Y	N	N	N	Y
3 Rosen	Y	N	Y	Y	Y	N
4 Kihuen	Y	N	Y	Y	Y	N
NEW HAMPSHIRE						
1 Shea-Porter	Y	N	Y	Y	Y	N
2 Kuster	Y	N	Y	Y	Y	N
NEW JERSEY						
1 Norcross	Y	Y	N	Y	Y	Y
2 **LoBiondo**	N	Y	N	N	N	Y
3 **MacArthur**	N	Y	N	N	N	Y
4 **Smith**	N	Y	N	N	N	Y
5 Gottheimer	Y	Y	Y	N	Y	N
6 Pallone	Y	N	Y	Y	Y	N
7 **Lance**	N	Y	N	N	N	N
8 Sires	Y	N	Y	Y	Y	N
9 Pascrell	Y	N	Y	Y	Y	N
10 Payne	Y	N	Y	Y	Y	N
11 **Frelinghuysen**	N	Y	N	N	N	Y
12 Watson Coleman	Y	N	Y	Y	Y	N
NEW MEXICO						
1 Lujan Grisham	Y	N	Y	Y	Y	N
2 **Pearce**	N	Y	N	N	N	Y
3 Luján	Y	N	Y	Y	Y	N
NEW YORK						
1 **Zeldin**	N	Y	N	N	N	Y
2 **King**	N	Y	N	N	N	Y
3 Suozzi	Y	N	Y	Y	Y	N
4 Rice	Y	N	Y	Y	Y	N
5 Meeks	Y	N	Y	Y	Y	N
6 Meng	Y	N	Y	Y	Y	N
7 Velázquez	Y	N	Y	Y	Y	N
8 Jeffries	Y	N	Y	Y	Y	N
9 Clarke	Y	N	Y	Y	Y	N
10 Nadler	Y	N	Y	Y	Y	N
11 **Donovan**	N	Y	N	N	N	Y
12 Maloney, C.	Y	N	Y	Y	Y	N
13 Espaillat	Y	N	Y	Y	Y	N
14 Crowley	Y	N	Y	Y	Y	N
15 Serrano	Y	N	Y	Y	Y	N
16 Engel	Y	N	Y	Y	Y	N
17 Lowey	Y	N	Y	Y	Y	N
18 Maloney, S.P.	Y	N	Y	Y	Y	N
19 **Faso**	N	Y	N	N	N	Y
20 Tonko	Y	N	Y	Y	Y	N
21 **Stefanik**	N	Y	N	N	N	Y
22 **Tenney**	N	Y	N	N	N	Y
23 **Reed**	–	Y	N	N	N	Y
24 **Katko**	N	Y	N	N	N	Y
25 Slaughter	Y	N	Y	Y	Y	N
26 Higgins	Y	N	Y	Y	Y	N
27 **Collins**	N	Y	N	N	N	Y
NORTH CAROLINA						
1 Butterfield	Y	N	Y	Y	Y	N
2 **Holding**	N	Y	N	N	N	Y
3 **Jones**	Y	Y	N	N	Y	Y
4 Price	Y	N	Y	Y	Y	N

	397	398	399	400	401	402
5 **Foxx**	N	Y	N	N	N	Y
6 **Walker**	N	Y	N	N	N	Y
7 **Rouzer**	N	Y	N	N	N	Y
8 **Hudson**	N	Y	N	N	N	Y
9 **Pittenger**	N	Y	N	N	N	Y
10 **McHenry**	N	Y	N	N	N	Y
11 **Meadows**	N	Y	N	N	N	Y
12 Adams	Y	N	Y	Y	Y	N
13 **Budd**	N	Y	N	N	N	Y
NORTH DAKOTA						
AL **Cramer**	N	Y	N	N	N	Y
OHIO						
1 **Chabot**	N	Y	N	N	N	Y
2 **Wenstrup**	N	Y	N	N	N	Y
3 Beatty	Y	N	Y	Y	Y	N
4 **Jordan**	N	Y	N	N	N	Y
5 **Latta**	N	Y	N	N	N	Y
6 **Johnson**	N	Y	N	N	N	Y
7 **Gibbs**	N	Y	N	N	N	Y
8 **Davidson**	N	Y	N	N	N	Y
9 Kaptur	Y	N	Y	Y	Y	N
10 **Turner**	N	Y	N	N	N	Y
11 Fudge	Y	N	Y	Y	Y	N
12 **Tiberi**	N	Y	N	N	N	Y
13 Ryan	Y	N	N	Y	Y	N
14 **Joyce**	N	Y	N	N	N	Y
15 **Stivers**	N	Y	N	N	N	Y
16 **Renacci**	N	Y	N	N	N	Y
OKLAHOMA						
1 **Bridenstine**	N	Y	N	N	N	Y
2 **Mullin**	N	Y	N	N	N	Y
3 **Lucas**	N	Y	N	N	N	Y
4 **Cole**	N	Y	N	N	N	Y
5 **Russell**	N	Y	N	N	N	Y
OREGON						
1 Bonamici	Y	N	Y	Y	Y	N
2 **Walden**	N	Y	N	N	N	Y
3 Blumenauer	Y	N	Y	Y	Y	N
4 DeFazio	Y	N	Y	Y	Y	N
5 Schrader	Y	Y	N	Y	N	Y
PENNSYLVANIA						
1 Brady	Y	Y	N	Y	Y	Y
2 Evans	Y	N	Y	Y	Y	N
3 **Kelly**	N	Y	N	N	N	Y
4 **Perry**	N	Y	N	N	N	Y
5 **Thompson**	N	Y	N	N	N	Y
6 **Costello**	N	Y	N	N	N	Y
7 **Meehan**	N	Y	N	N	N	Y
8 **Fitzpatrick**	N	Y	Y	N	N	Y
9 **Shuster**	N	Y	N	N	N	Y
10 **Marino**	N	Y	N	N	N	Y
11 **Barletta**	N	Y	N	N	N	Y
12 **Rothfus**	N	Y	N	N	N	Y
13 Boyle	Y	N	N	Y	Y	Y
14 Doyle	Y	N	Y	Y	Y	N
15 **Dent**	N	Y	N	N	N	Y
16 **Smucker**	N	Y	N	N	N	Y
17 Cartwright	Y	N	Y	Y	Y	N
18 **Murphy**	N	Y	N	N	N	Y
RHODE ISLAND						
1 Cicilline	Y	N	Y	Y	Y	N
2 Langevin	Y	N	Y	Y	Y	N
SOUTH CAROLINA						
1 **Sanford**	N	Y	N	N	N	Y
2 **Wilson**	N	Y	N	N	N	Y
3 **Duncan**	N	Y	N	N	N	Y
4 **Gowdy**	N	Y	N	N	N	Y
5 **Norman**	N	Y	N	N	N	Y
6 Clyburn	Y	N	Y	Y	Y	N
7 **Rice**	N	Y	N	N	N	Y
SOUTH DAKOTA						
AL **Noem**	N	Y	N	N	N	Y
TENNESSEE						
1 **Roe**	N	Y	N	N	N	Y
2 **Duncan**	Y	Y	N	N	N	Y
3 **Fleischmann**	N	Y	N	N	N	Y
4 **DesJarlais**	N	Y	N	N	N	Y
5 Cooper	Y	N	Y	Y	Y	N
6 **Black**	N	Y	N	N	N	Y
7 **Blackburn**	N	Y	N	N	N	Y
8 **Kustoff**	N	Y	N	N	N	Y
9 Cohen	Y	N	Y	Y	Y	N

	397	398	399	400	401	402
TEXAS						
1 **Gohmert**	N	Y	N	N	N	Y
2 **Poe**	N	Y	N	N	N	Y
3 **Johnson, S.**	N	Y	N	N	N	Y
4 **Ratcliffe**	N	Y	N	N	N	Y
5 **Hensarling**	N	Y	N	N	N	Y
6 **Barton**	N	Y	N	N	N	Y
7 **Culberson**	N	Y	N	N	N	Y
8 **Brady**	N	Y	N	N	N	Y
9 Green, A.	Y	N	Y	Y	Y	N
10 **McCaul**	N	Y	N	N	N	Y
11 **Conaway**	N	Y	N	N	N	Y
12 **Granger**	N	Y	N	N	N	Y
13 **Thornberry**	N	Y	N	N	N	Y
14 **Weber**	N	Y	N	N	N	Y
15 Gonzalez	Y	Y	N	Y	Y	Y
16 O'Rourke	Y	N	Y	Y	Y	N
17 **Flores**	N	Y	N	N	N	Y
18 Jackson Lee	Y	Y	Y	Y	Y	N
19 **Arrington**	N	Y	N	N	N	Y
20 Castro	Y	N	Y	Y	Y	N
21 **Smith**	N	Y	N	N	N	Y
22 **Olson**	N	Y	N	N	N	Y
23 **Hurd**	N	Y	N	N	N	Y
24 **Marchant**	N	Y	N	N	N	Y
25 **Williams**	N	Y	N	N	N	Y
26 **Burgess**	N	Y	N	N	N	Y
27 **Farenthold**	N	Y	N	N	N	Y
28 Cuellar	Y	Y	N	Y	Y	Y
29 Green, G.	Y	Y	N	Y	N	Y
30 Johnson, E.B.	Y	N	Y	Y	Y	N
31 **Carter**	N	Y	N	N	N	Y
32 **Sessions**	N	Y	N	N	N	Y
33 Veasey	Y	Y	N	Y	Y	N
34 Vela	Y	Y	N	Y	Y	Y
35 Doggett	Y	N	Y	Y	Y	N
36 **Babin**	N	Y	N	N	N	Y
UTAH						
1 **Bishop**	N	Y	N	N	N	Y
2 **Stewart**	N	Y	N	N	N	Y
4 **Love**	N	Y	N	N	N	Y
VERMONT						
AL Welch	Y	N	Y	Y	Y	N
VIRGINIA						
1 **Wittman**	N	Y	N	N	N	Y
2 **Taylor**	N	Y	N	N	N	Y
3 Scott	Y	N	Y	Y	Y	N
4 McEachin	Y	N	Y	Y	Y	N
5 **Garrett**	N	Y	N	N	N	Y
6 **Goodlatte**	N	Y	N	Y	N	Y
7 **Brat**	N	Y	N	N	N	Y
8 Beyer	Y	N	Y	Y	Y	N
9 **Griffith**	N	Y	N	Y	N	Y
10 **Comstock**	N	Y	N	N	N	Y
11 Connolly	Y	N	Y	Y	Y	N
WASHINGTON						
1 DelBene	Y	N	Y	Y	Y	N
2 Larsen	Y	N	Y	Y	Y	N
3 **Herrera Beutler**	N	Y	N	N	N	Y
4 **Newhouse**	N	Y	N	N	N	Y
5 **McMorris Rodgers**	N	Y	N	N	N	Y
6 Kilmer	Y	N	Y	Y	Y	N
7 Jayapal	Y	N	Y	Y	Y	N
8 **Reichert**	N	Y	N	N	N	Y
9 Smith	Y	N	Y	Y	Y	N
10 Heck	Y	N	Y	Y	Y	N
WEST VIRGINIA						
1 **McKinley**	N	Y	N	N	N	Y
2 **Mooney**	N	Y	N	N	N	Y
3 **Jenkins**	N	Y	N	N	N	Y
WISCONSIN						
1 **Ryan**						
2 Pocan	Y	N	Y	Y	Y	N
3 Kind	Y	N	Y	Y	Y	N
4 Moore	Y	N	Y	Y	Y	N
5 **Sensenbrenner**	N	Y	N	N	N	Y
6 **Grothman**	N	Y	N	N	N	Y
7 **Duffy**	N	Y	N	N	N	Y
8 **Gallagher**	N	Y	N	N	N	Y
WYOMING						
AL **Cheney**	N	Y	N	N	N	Y

VOTE NUMBER

403. HR 2825. HOMELAND SECURITY REAUTHORIZATION/PASSAGE.
McCaul, R-Texas, motion to suspend the rules and pass the bill that would authorize funding through fiscal 2019 to U.S. Coast Guard programs and activities, including $7.3 billion in fiscal 2018 and $7.5 billion in fiscal 2019 for operations and maintenance and $1.9 billion each year for infrastructure; would authorize funding through fiscal 2020 to Federal Emergency Management Agency programs and activities at $1.05 billion for fiscal 2018, $1.07 billion for fiscal 2019 and $1.08 billion for fiscal 2020; and would authorize funding through fiscal 2022 to multiple Homeland Security Department grant programs, including $200 million annually in funding through fiscal 2022 to the Transit Security Grant Program and $200 million annually in funding to the Port Security Grant Program. The bill would require the department to establish and carry out a grant program for emergency response providers to prevent, prepare for, and respond to terrorist attacks and would authorize $39 million in funding through fiscal 2022 for the program. The bill would also require the department to establish and carry a grant program that would provide grants to eligible non-profit organizations for activities related to security enhancement and protection against terrorist attacks and would authorize $50 million in funding through fiscal 2022 for the program. The bill would formally establish U.S. Immigration and Customs Enforcement and U.S. Citizenship and Immigration Services and would establish a headquarters office for the Homeland Security Department and the offices which make up the headquarters, as well as other offices at the department. Motion agreed to 386-41 : R 227-9; D 159-32. July 20, 2017.

404. HR 218. KING COVE LAND EXCHANGE/FEDERAL MITIGATION REQUIREMENTS. Tsongas, D-Mass., amendment that would include in the bill's road requirements a provision that would require the implementation of previous federal mitigation requirements established by the Omnibus Public Land Management Act of 2009, related to the movement of wildlife and tidal flows, for the purpose of constructing a single-lane gravel road between King Cove, Alaska, and Cold Bay, Alaska. Rejected in Committee of the Whole 190-234 : R 0-233; D 190-1. July 20, 2017.

405. HR 218. KING COVE LAND EXCHANGE/DEPARTMENT OF INTERIOR APPROPRIATIONS REPAYMENT REQUIREMENT. Grijalva, D-Ariz., amendment that would prohibit implementation of the bill's provisions until the state of Alaska has repaid $20 million to the federal government in funds appropriated and loaned to the state of Alaska under the Department of the Interior and Related Agencies Appropriations Act of 1999, for the purpose of construction of an unpaved road, a dock, and marine facilities and equipment on King Cove Corporation lands in King Cove, Alaska. Rejected in Committee of the Whole 167-260 : R 0-236; D 167-24. July 20, 2017.

406. HR 218. KING COVE LAND EXCHANGE/PASSAGE. Passage of the bill that would require the Interior Department to convey to the state of Alaska, if requested, 206 acres of federal land within the Izembek National Wildlife Refuge and Izembek Wilderness for the purpose of constructing a single-lane gravel road between the towns of King Cove and Cold Bay, Alaska. Passed 248-179 : R 233-3; D 15-176. July 20, 2017.

407. HR 3180. FISCAL 2018 INTELLIGENCE AUTHORIZATION/PASSAGE.
Nunes, R-Calif., motion to suspend the rules and pass the bill that would authorize classified amounts of funding through fiscal 2018 for 16 U.S. intelligence agencies and intelligence-related activities, including the Office of the National Intelligence Director, the CIA and the National Security Agency. The bill would authorize $527 million in fiscal 2018 in funding to the Intelligence Community Management Account and would authorize $514 million through fiscal 2018 in funding to the CIA Retirement and Disability Fund. The bill would require the director of National Intelligence to submit to Congress multiple reports regarding Russia's campaigns directed at foreign elections and its efforts related to cyber influence, including an analytical assessment of the most significant Russian influence campaigns, if any, conducted during the three years prior to the bill's enactment. Motion rejected 241-163 : R 211-10; D 30-153. July 24, 2017.

	403	404	405	406	407
ALABAMA					
1 **Byrne**	Y	N	N	Y	Y
2 **Roby**	Y	N	N	Y	Y
3 **Rogers**	Y	N	N	Y	Y
4 **Aderholt**	Y	N	N	Y	Y
5 **Brooks**	Y	N	N	Y	?
6 **Palmer**	Y	N	N	Y	Y
7 Sewell	Y	Y	Y	N	N
ALASKA					
AL **Young**	Y	N	N	Y	Y
ARIZONA					
1 O'Halleran	Y	Y	N	N	Y
2 **McSally**	Y	N	N	Y	Y
3 Grijalva	N	Y	Y	N	N
4 **Gosar**	Y	N	N	Y	Y
5 **Biggs**	N	N	N	Y	Y
6 **Schweikert**	Y	N	N	Y	Y
7 Gallego	N	Y	Y	N	N
8 **Franks**	Y	N	N	Y	Y
9 Sinema	Y	Y	N	N	Y
ARKANSAS					
1 **Crawford**	Y	N	N	Y	?
2 **Hill**	Y	N	N	Y	Y
3 **Womack**	Y	N	N	Y	Y
4 **Westerman**	Y	N	N	Y	Y
CALIFORNIA					
1 **LaMalfa**	Y	N	N	Y	Y
2 Huffman	Y	Y	Y	N	N
3 Garamendi	Y	Y	Y	N	Y
4 **McClintock**	Y	N	N	Y	Y
5 Thompson	Y	Y	Y	N	N
6 Matsui	Y	Y	Y	N	N
7 Bera	Y	Y	Y	N	Y
8 **Cook**	Y	N	N	Y	Y
9 McNerney	Y	Y	Y	N	Y
10 **Denham**	Y	N	N	Y	Y
11 DeSaulnier	Y	Y	Y	N	N
12 Pelosi	Y	Y	Y	N	N
13 Lee	N	Y	Y	N	N
14 Speier	Y	Y	Y	N	N
15 Swalwell	Y	Y	Y	N	N
16 Costa	Y	Y	Y	N	Y
17 Khanna	Y	Y	Y	N	N
18 Eshoo	Y	Y	Y	N	N
19 Lofgren	Y	Y	Y	N	N
20 Panetta	Y	Y	Y	N	N
21 **Valadao**	Y	N	N	Y	Y
22 **Nunes**	Y	N	N	Y	Y
23 **McCarthy**	Y	N	N	Y	Y
24 Carbajal	Y	Y	Y	N	Y
25 **Knight**	Y	N	N	Y	Y
26 Brownley	Y	Y	Y	N	Y
27 Chu	Y	Y	Y	N	N
28 Schiff	Y	Y	Y	N	N
29 Cardenas	N	Y	Y	N	N
30 Sherman	Y	Y	Y	N	N
31 Aguilar	Y	Y	N	N	Y
32 Napolitano	-	+	+	-	-
33 Lieu	Y	Y	Y	N	N
34 Gomez	Y	Y	Y	N	N
35 Torres	Y	Y	Y	N	N
36 Ruiz	Y	Y	Y	N	Y
37 Bass	N	Y	Y	N	?
38 Sánchez, Linda	Y	Y	Y	N	N
39 **Royce**	Y	N	N	Y	Y
40 Roybal-Allard	Y	Y	Y	N	N
41 Takano	N	Y	Y	N	N
42 **Calvert**	Y	N	N	Y	Y
43 Waters	N	Y	Y	N	?
44 Barragan	Y	Y	Y	N	N
45 **Walters**	Y	N	N	Y	Y
46 Correa	Y	Y	Y	N	Y
47 Lowenthal	Y	Y	Y	N	N
48 **Rohrabacher**	Y	N	N	Y	?
49 **Issa**	Y	N	N	Y	Y
50 **Hunter**	Y	N	N	Y	Y
51 Vargas	N	Y	Y	N	?
52 Peters	Y	Y	Y	N	N
53 Davis	Y	Y	Y	N	N
COLORADO					
1 DeGette	Y	Y	Y	N	N
2 Polis	N	Y	Y	N	N
3 **Tipton**	Y	N	N	Y	Y
4 **Buck**	Y	N	N	Y	Y
5 **Lamborn**	Y	N	N	Y	Y
6 **Coffman**	Y	N	N	Y	Y
7 Perlmutter	Y	Y	Y	N	N
CONNECTICUT					
1 Larson	Y	Y	Y	N	N
2 Courtney	Y	Y	Y	N	N
3 DeLauro	Y	Y	Y	N	N
4 Himes	Y	Y	Y	N	N
5 Esty	Y	Y	Y	N	N
DELAWARE					
AL Blunt Rochester	Y	Y	Y	N	N
FLORIDA					
1 **Gaetz**	Y	N	N	Y	Y
2 **Dunn**	Y	N	N	Y	Y
3 **Yoho**	Y	N	N	Y	Y
4 **Rutherford**	Y	N	N	Y	Y
5 Lawson	Y	Y	Y	N	N
6 **DeSantis**	Y	N	N	Y	Y
7 Murphy	Y	Y	Y	N	N
8 **Posey**	Y	N	N	Y	Y
9 Soto	Y	Y	Y	N	N
10 Demings	Y	Y	Y	N	N
11 **Webster**	?	N	N	Y	Y
12 **Bilirakis**	Y	N	N	Y	Y
13 Crist	Y	Y	Y	N	N
14 Castor	Y	Y	Y	N	N
15 **Ross**	Y	N	N	Y	Y
16 **Buchanan**	Y	N	N	Y	Y
17 **Rooney, T.**	Y	N	N	Y	+
18 **Mast**	Y	N	N	Y	Y
19 **Rooney, F.**	Y	N	N	Y	Y
20 Hastings	Y	Y	Y	N	N
21 Frankel	Y	Y	Y	N	N
22 Deutch	Y	Y	Y	N	N
23 Wasserman Schultz	Y	Y	Y	N	N
24 Wilson	Y	Y	Y	N	N
25 **Diaz-Balart**	Y	N	N	Y	Y
26 **Curbelo**	Y	N	N	Y	Y
27 **Ros-Lehtinen**	Y	N	N	Y	Y
GEORGIA					
1 **Carter**	Y	N	N	Y	Y
2 Bishop	Y	Y	Y	N	Y
3 **Ferguson**	Y	N	N	Y	Y
4 Johnson	N	Y	Y	N	-
5 Lewis	Y	Y	Y	N	N
6 **Handel**	Y	N	N	Y	Y
7 **Woodall**	Y	?	N	Y	Y
8 **Scott, A.**	Y	N	N	Y	Y
9 **Collins**	Y	N	N	Y	Y
10 **Hice**	Y	N	N	Y	Y
11 **Loudermilk**	Y	N	N	Y	Y
12 **Allen**	Y	N	N	Y	Y
13 Scott, D.	Y	Y	Y	N	N
14 **Graves**	Y	N	N	Y	Y
HAWAII					
1 Hanabusa	Y	Y	N	N	N
2 Gabbard	Y	Y	N	Y	N
IDAHO					
1 **Labrador**	?	?	?	?	N
2 **Simpson**	Y	N	N	Y	Y
ILLINOIS					
1 Rush	Y	Y	Y	N	N
2 Kelly	Y	Y	Y	N	N
3 Lipinski	Y	Y	N	N	Y
4 Gutierrez	N	Y	Y	N	N
5 Quigley	Y	Y	Y	N	N
6 **Roskam**	Y	N	N	Y	Y
7 Davis, D.	N	Y	Y	N	?
8 Krishnamoorthi	Y	Y	Y	N	N
9 Schakowsky	N	Y	Y	N	N
10 Schneider	Y	Y	Y	N	Y
11 Foster	Y	Y	Y	N	N
12 **Bost**	Y	N	N	Y	Y
13 **Davis, R.**	Y	?	N	Y	Y
14 **Hultgren**	Y	N	N	Y	?
15 **Shimkus**	Y	N	N	Y	Y

KEY	Republicans	Democrats	Independents

Y Voted for (yea)	X Paired against	C Voted "present" to avoid possible conflict of interest
# Paired for	– Announced against	? Did not vote or otherwise make a position known
+ Announced for	P Voted "present"	
N Voted against (nay)		

	403	404	405	406	407
16 Kinzinger	Y	N	N	Y	Y
17 Bustos	Y	Y	Y	N	Y
18 LaHood	Y	N	N	Y	Y
INDIANA					
1 Visclosky	Y	Y	Y	N	N
2 Walorski	Y	N	N	Y	Y
3 Banks	Y	N	N	Y	Y
4 Rokita	Y	N	N	Y	Y
5 Brooks	Y	N	N	Y	Y
6 Messer	Y	N	N	Y	Y
7 Carson	Y	Y	Y	Y	N
8 Bucshon	Y	N	N	Y	Y
9 Hollingsworth	Y	N	N	Y	Y
IOWA					
1 Blum	Y	N	N	Y	Y
2 Loebsack	Y	Y	N	N	Y
3 Young	Y	N	N	Y	Y
4 King	Y	N	N	Y	Y
KANSAS					
1 Marshall	Y	N	N	Y	Y
2 Jenkins	Y	N	N	Y	Y
3 Yoder	Y	N	N	Y	Y
4 Estes	Y	N	N	Y	Y
KENTUCKY					
1 Comer	Y	N	N	Y	Y
2 Guthrie	Y	N	N	Y	Y
3 Yarmuth	Y	Y	Y	N	N
4 Massie	N	N	N	N	N
5 Rogers	Y	N	N	Y	Y
6 Barr	Y	N	N	Y	Y
LOUISIANA					
1 Scalise	+	−	−	+	+
2 Richmond	?	?	?	?	N
3 Higgins	Y	N	N	Y	Y
4 Johnson	Y	N	N	Y	Y
5 Abraham	Y	N	N	Y	Y
6 Graves	Y	N	N	Y	Y
MAINE					
1 Pingree	Y	Y	Y	N	N
2 Poliquin	Y	N	N	Y	Y
MARYLAND					
1 Harris	Y	N	N	Y	Y
2 Ruppersberger	Y	Y	Y	N	N
3 Sarbanes	Y	Y	Y	N	N
4 Brown	Y	Y	Y	N	N
5 Hoyer	Y	Y	Y	N	N
6 Delaney	Y	Y	Y	N	N
7 Cummings	?	?	?	?	?
8 Raskin	Y	Y	Y	N	N
MASSACHUSETTS					
1 Neal	Y	Y	Y	N	N
2 McGovern	N	Y	Y	N	N
3 Tsongas	Y	Y	Y	N	N
4 Kennedy	Y	Y	Y	N	N
5 Clark	Y	Y	Y	N	N
6 Moulton	Y	Y	Y	N	N
7 Capuano	Y	Y	Y	N	N
8 Lynch	Y	Y	N	N	N
9 Keating	Y	Y	Y	N	Y
MICHIGAN					
1 Bergman	Y	N	N	Y	Y
2 Huizenga	Y	N	N	Y	Y
3 Amash	N	N	N	N	N
4 Moolenaar	Y	N	N	Y	Y
5 Kildee	Y	Y	Y	N	N
6 Upton	Y	N	N	Y	Y
7 Walberg	Y	N	N	Y	Y
8 Bishop	Y	N	N	Y	Y
9 Levin	Y	Y	Y	N	N
10 Mitchell	Y	N	N	Y	Y
11 Trott	Y	N	N	Y	Y
12 Dingell	Y	Y	Y	N	N
13 Conyers	N	Y	Y	N	N
14 Lawrence	Y	Y	Y	N	−
MINNESOTA					
1 Walz	Y	Y	Y	N	N
2 Lewis	Y	N	N	Y	Y
3 Paulsen	Y	N	N	Y	Y
4 McCollum	Y	Y	Y	N	N

	403	404	405	406	407
5 Ellison	N	Y	Y	N	N
6 Emmer	Y	N	N	Y	Y
7 Peterson	Y	N	Y	Y	Y
8 Nolan	Y	Y	Y	N	N
MISSISSIPPI					
1 Kelly	Y	N	N	Y	Y
2 Thompson	Y	Y	Y	N	N
3 Harper	Y	N	N	Y	Y
4 Palazzo	Y	N	N	Y	?
MISSOURI					
1 Clay	Y	Y	Y	Y	N
2 Wagner	Y	?	?	?	Y
3 Luetkemeyer	Y	N	N	Y	Y
4 Hartzler	Y	N	N	Y	Y
5 Cleaver	Y	Y	Y	N	N
6 Graves	Y	N	N	Y	+
7 Long	Y	N	N	Y	?
8 Smith	Y	N	N	Y	?
MONTANA					
AL Gianforte	Y	N	N	Y	Y
NEBRASKA					
1 Fortenberry	Y	N	N	Y	Y
2 Bacon	Y	N	N	Y	Y
3 Smith	Y	N	N	Y	Y
NEVADA					
1 Titus	Y	Y	Y	N	N
2 Amodei	Y	N	N	Y	Y
3 Rosen	Y	Y	N	Y	Y
4 Kihuen	Y	Y	Y	N	Y
NEW HAMPSHIRE					
1 Shea-Porter	Y	Y	N	N	Y
2 Kuster	Y	Y	Y	N	Y
NEW JERSEY					
1 Norcross	Y	Y	Y	N	Y
2 LoBiondo	Y	N	N	Y	Y
3 MacArthur	Y	N	N	Y	Y
4 Smith	Y	N	N	Y	Y
5 Gottheimer	Y	Y	N	Y	Y
6 Pallone	Y	Y	Y	N	N
7 Lance	Y	N	N	Y	Y
8 Sires	Y	Y	Y	N	N
9 Pascrell	Y	Y	Y	N	N
10 Payne	Y	Y	Y	N	N
11 Frelinghuysen	Y	N	N	Y	Y
12 Watson Coleman	Y	Y	Y	N	N
NEW MEXICO					
1 Lujan Grisham	Y	Y	Y	N	Y
2 Pearce	Y	N	N	Y	Y
3 Luján	Y	Y	Y	N	N
NEW YORK					
1 Zeldin	Y	N	N	Y	Y
2 King	Y	N	N	Y	Y
3 Suozzi	Y	Y	N	N	Y
4 Rice	Y	Y	Y	N	N
5 Meeks	Y	Y	Y	N	N
6 Meng	N	Y	Y	N	N
7 Velázquez	N	Y	Y	N	N
8 Jeffries	N	Y	Y	N	N
9 Clarke	N	Y	Y	N	N
10 Nadler	N	Y	Y	N	N
11 Donovan	Y	N	N	Y	Y
12 Maloney, C.	Y	Y	Y	N	N
13 Espaillat	N	Y	Y	N	N
14 Crowley	N	Y	Y	N	−
15 Serrano	N	Y	Y	N	N
16 Engel	Y	Y	Y	N	N
17 Lowey	Y	Y	Y	N	N
18 Maloney, S.P.	Y	Y	N	Y	N
19 Faso	Y	N	N	Y	Y
20 Tonko	Y	Y	Y	N	N
21 Stefanik	Y	N	N	Y	Y
22 Tenney	Y	N	N	Y	Y
23 Reed	Y	N	N	Y	Y
24 Katko	Y	N	N	Y	Y
25 Slaughter	Y	Y	Y	N	N
26 Higgins	Y	Y	Y	N	N
27 Collins	Y	N	N	Y	Y
NORTH CAROLINA					
1 Butterfield	Y	Y	Y	N	N
2 Holding	Y	N	N	Y	Y
3 Jones	N	N	N	Y	N
4 Price	Y	Y	Y	N	N

	403	404	405	406	407
5 Foxx	Y	N	N	Y	Y
6 Walker	Y	N	N	Y	Y
7 Rouzer	Y	N	N	Y	Y
8 Hudson	Y	N	N	Y	Y
9 Pittenger	Y	N	N	Y	Y
10 McHenry	Y	N	N	Y	Y
11 Meadows	Y	N	N	Y	Y
12 Adams	Y	Y	Y	N	N
13 Budd	Y	N	N	Y	Y
NORTH DAKOTA					
AL Cramer	Y	N	N	Y	Y
OHIO					
1 Chabot	Y	N	N	Y	Y
2 Wenstrup	Y	N	N	Y	Y
3 Beatty	Y	Y	Y	N	N
4 Jordan	Y	N	N	Y	Y
5 Latta	Y	N	N	Y	Y
6 Johnson	Y	N	N	Y	Y
7 Gibbs	Y	N	N	Y	Y
8 Davidson	N	N	N	Y	Y
9 Kaptur	N	Y	Y	N	N
10 Turner	Y	N	Y	Y	Y
11 Fudge	Y	Y	Y	N	N
12 Tiberi	Y	N	N	Y	Y
13 Ryan	Y	Y	N	N	N
14 Joyce	Y	N	N	Y	Y
15 Stivers	Y	N	N	Y	Y
16 Renacci	Y	N	N	Y	+
OKLAHOMA					
1 Bridenstine	Y	N	N	Y	Y
2 Mullin	Y	N	N	Y	Y
3 Lucas	Y	N	N	Y	Y
4 Cole	Y	N	N	Y	Y
5 Russell	Y	N	N	Y	Y
OREGON					
1 Bonamici	Y	Y	Y	N	N
2 Walden	Y	N	N	Y	Y
3 Blumenauer	N	Y	Y	N	N
4 DeFazio	Y	Y	Y	N	N
5 Schrader	N	Y	Y	N	Y
PENNSYLVANIA					
1 Brady	Y	Y	Y	N	N
2 Evans	Y	Y	Y	N	N
3 Kelly	Y	N	N	Y	Y
4 Perry	Y	N	N	Y	Y
5 Thompson	Y	N	N	Y	Y
6 Costello	Y	N	N	Y	+
7 Meehan	Y	N	N	Y	Y
8 Fitzpatrick	Y	N	N	Y	Y
9 Shuster	Y	?	N	Y	Y
10 Marino	Y	N	N	Y	Y
11 Barletta	Y	N	N	Y	Y
12 Rothfus	Y	N	N	Y	Y
13 Boyle	Y	Y	Y	N	N
14 Doyle	Y	Y	Y	N	N
15 Dent	Y	N	N	Y	Y
16 Smucker	Y	N	N	Y	Y
17 Cartwright	Y	Y	Y	N	N
18 Murphy	Y	N	N	Y	Y
RHODE ISLAND					
1 Cicilline	Y	Y	Y	N	N
2 Langevin	Y	Y	Y	N	N
SOUTH CAROLINA					
1 Sanford	N	N	N	Y	Y
2 Wilson	Y	N	N	Y	Y
3 Duncan	Y	N	N	Y	Y
4 Gowdy	Y	N	N	Y	Y
5 Norman	Y	N	N	Y	Y
6 Clyburn	Y	Y	Y	N	N
7 Rice	Y	N	N	Y	Y
SOUTH DAKOTA					
AL Noem	Y	N	N	Y	Y
TENNESSEE					
1 Roe	Y	N	N	Y	Y
2 Duncan	N	N	N	Y	Y
3 Fleischmann	Y	N	N	Y	Y
4 DesJarlais	Y	N	N	Y	Y
5 Cooper	Y	Y	Y	N	N
6 Black	Y	N	N	Y	Y
7 Blackburn	Y	N	N	Y	Y
8 Kustoff	Y	N	N	Y	Y
9 Cohen	Y	Y	Y	N	N

	403	404	405	406	407
TEXAS					
1 Gohmert	N	N	N	Y	N
2 Poe	Y	N	N	Y	?
3 Johnson, S.	Y	N	N	Y	Y
4 Ratcliffe	Y	N	N	Y	Y
5 Hensarling	Y	N	N	Y	Y
6 Barton	Y	N	N	Y	Y
7 Culberson	Y	N	N	Y	Y
8 Brady	Y	N	N	Y	Y
9 Green, A.	N	Y	Y	N	N
10 McCaul	Y	N	N	Y	+
11 Conaway	Y	N	N	Y	Y
12 Granger	Y	N	N	Y	Y
13 Thornberry	Y	N	N	Y	Y
14 Weber	Y	N	N	Y	Y
15 Gonzalez	Y	Y	Y	Y	N
16 O'Rourke	Y	Y	Y	Y	N
17 Flores	Y	N	N	Y	Y
18 Jackson Lee	Y	Y	Y	N	N
19 Arrington	Y	N	N	Y	Y
20 Castro	N	Y	Y	N	N
21 Smith	Y	N	N	Y	Y
22 Olson	Y	N	N	Y	Y
23 Hurd	Y	N	N	Y	Y
24 Marchant	Y	N	N	Y	Y
25 Williams	Y	N	N	Y	+
26 Burgess	Y	N	N	Y	Y
27 Farenthold	Y	N	N	Y	Y
28 Cuellar	Y	Y	Y	N	N
29 Green, G.	Y	Y	Y	N	N
30 Johnson, E.B.	Y	Y	N	Y	N
31 Carter	Y	N	N	Y	Y
32 Sessions	Y	N	N	Y	Y
33 Veasey	N	Y	N	Y	N
34 Vela	Y	Y	Y	Y	N
35 Doggett	N	Y	Y	N	N
36 Babin	Y	N	N	Y	Y
UTAH					
1 Bishop	Y	N	N	Y	Y
2 Stewart	Y	N	N	Y	?
4 Love	Y	N	N	Y	Y
VERMONT					
AL Welch	Y	Y	Y	N	−
VIRGINIA					
1 Wittman	Y	N	N	Y	Y
2 Taylor	Y	N	N	Y	Y
3 Scott	Y	Y	Y	N	N
4 McEachin	Y	Y	Y	N	N
5 Garrett	Y	N	N	Y	Y
6 Goodlatte	Y	N	N	Y	Y
7 Brat	N	N	N	Y	Y
8 Beyer	Y	Y	Y	N	N
9 Griffith	Y	N	N	Y	Y
10 Comstock	Y	N	N	Y	Y
11 Connolly	Y	Y	Y	N	N
WASHINGTON					
1 DelBene	Y	Y	Y	N	N
2 Larsen	Y	Y	Y	N	N
3 Herrera Beutler	Y	N	N	Y	Y
4 Newhouse	Y	N	N	Y	Y
5 McMorris Rodgers	Y	N	N	Y	Y
6 Kilmer	Y	Y	Y	N	N
7 Jayapal	N	Y	Y	N	N
8 Reichert	Y	N	N	Y	Y
9 Smith	Y	Y	Y	N	N
10 Heck	Y	Y	Y	N	N
WEST VIRGINIA					
1 McKinley	Y	N	N	Y	?
2 Mooney	Y	N	N	Y	?
3 Jenkins	Y	N	N	Y	+
WISCONSIN					
1 Ryan					
2 Pocan	Y	Y	Y	N	N
3 Kind	Y	Y	Y	N	N
4 Moore	Y	Y	Y	N	N
5 Sensenbrenner	Y	N	N	Y	Y
6 Grothman	Y	N	N	Y	Y
7 Duffy	Y	N	N	Y	Y
8 Gallagher	Y	N	N	Y	Y
WYOMING					
AL Cheney	Y	N	N	Y	Y

VOTE NUMBER

408. S 114. VETERANS CHOICE FUND AUTHORIZATION/PASSAGE. Roe, R-Tenn., motion to suspend the rules and pass the bill that would make available an additional $2 billion in funding for the Veterans Choice Fund, without fiscal year limitation. The bill would extend until Dec. 31, 2027, the current cap on per-month payment of VA pensions to certain veterans residing at VA nursing care facilities, as well as the VA's authority to collect fees for VA housing loans and the VA's authority to obtain and use income information from the Social Security Administration and the IRS to validate an application for VA benefits. Motion rejected 219-186 : R 217-4; D 2-182. July 24, 2017.

409. HR 3218. VETERANS EDUCATION BENEFITS INDEFINITE EXTENSION/ PASSAGE. Roe, R-Tenn., motion to suspend the rules and pass the bill that would eliminate the 15-year time limit to use Post-9/11 GI Bill education benefits for all existing and future servicemembers, as well as for veterans who left active duty after 2012, and would effectively increase GI Bill funding for Reservists and Guardsmen, dependents, and surviving spouses and dependents. The bill would require the VA to provide additional GI Bill benefits to student veterans completing a STEM degree and would restore eligibility for educational assistance to certain servicemembers whose schools close in the middle of a semester. Motion agreed to 405-0 : R 221-0; D 184-0. July 24, 2017.

410. H RES 468, H J RES 111. CFPB ARBITRATION RULE DISAPPROVAL/ PREVIOUS QUESTION. Buck, R-Colo., motion to order the previous question (thus ending debate and the possibility of amendment) on the rule (H Res 468) that would provide for House floor consideration of the joint resolution (H J Res 111) that would nullify and disapprove of a Consumer Financial Protection Bureau rule that prohibits mandatory arbitration clauses in certain consumer contracts. Motion agreed to 229-184 : R 229-0; D 0-184. July 25, 2017.

411. H RES 468, H J RES 111. CFPB ARBITRATION RULE DISAPPROVAL/ RULE. Adoption of the rule (H Res 468) that would provide for House floor consideration of the joint resolution (H J Res 111) that would nullify and disapprove of a Consumer Financial Protection Bureau rule that prohibits mandatory arbitration clauses in certain consumer contracts. Adopted 233-188 : R 233-0; D 0-188. July 25, 2017.

412. H J RES 111. CFPB ARBITRATION RULE DISAPPROVAL/PASSAGE. Passage of the joint resolution that would nullify and disapprove of a Consumer Financial Protection Bureau rule that prohibits mandatory arbitration clauses in consumer contracts related to financial services and products. Passed 231-190 : R 231-1; D 0-189. July 25, 2017.

413. HR 3364. SANCTIONS ON RUSSIA, IRAN AND NORTH KOREA/PASSAGE. Royce, R-Calif., motion to suspend the rules and pass the bill that would codify certain existing sanctions on Russia, including various sanctions tied to Russia's aggression in Ukraine, Moscow's annexation of Crimea, and malicious cyber activities relating to the 2016 U.S. elections. The bill would establish multiple new sanctions on Russia, including sanctions on entities conducting malicious cyber activity on behalf of the Russian government and entities which conduct business with the Russian intelligence and defense sectors. The bill would impose various new or expanded sanctions against Iran, including sanctions on persons that engage in or pose a risk of materially contributing to Iran's ballistic missile program and sanctions on officials, agents or affiliates of Iran's Islamic Revolutionary Guard Corps. The bill would also impose multiple new or expanded sanctions on North Korea, including sanctions against entities that purchase certain metals or minerals from North Korea, and would require the secretary of State to make a determination as to whether North Korea constitutes a "state sponsor of terrorism." Passed 419-3 : R 229-3; D 190-0. July 25, 2017.

414. HR 3219, H RES 473. FISCAL 2018 MINIBUS APPROPRIATIONS/ PREVIOUS QUESTION. Cole, R-Okla., motion to order the previous question (thus ending debate and possibility of amendment) on the rule (H Res 473) that would provide for House floor consideration of the bill (HR 3219) that would make certain appropriations for the fiscal year ending Sept. 30, 2018, and would provide for consideration of amendments to the Legislative Branch, Military Construction and Veterans Affairs, and Energy and Water divisions of the bill. Motion agreed to 230-193 : R 230-2; D 0-191. July 26, 2017.

	408	409	410	411	412	413	414
ALABAMA							
1 Byrne	Y	Y	Y	Y	Y	Y	Y
2 Roby	Y	Y	Y	Y	Y	Y	Y
3 Rogers	Y	Y	Y	Y	Y	Y	Y
4 Aderholt	Y	Y	Y	Y	Y	Y	Y
5 Brooks	?	?	?	?	Y	Y	Y
6 Palmer	Y	Y	Y	Y	?	?	?
7 Sewell	N	Y	N	N	N	Y	N
ALASKA							
AL Young	Y	Y	Y	Y	Y	Y	Y
ARIZONA							
1 O'Halleran	N	Y	N	N	N	Y	N
2 McSally	Y	Y	Y	Y	Y	Y	Y
3 Grijalva	N	Y	N	N	N	Y	N
4 Gosar	Y	Y	Y	Y	Y	Y	Y
5 Biggs	Y	Y	Y	Y	Y	Y	Y
6 Schweikert	N	Y	Y	Y	Y	Y	Y
7 Gallego	N	Y	N	N	N	Y	N
8 Franks	Y	Y	Y	Y	Y	Y	Y
9 Sinema	Y	Y	N	N	N	Y	N
ARKANSAS							
1 Crawford	?	?	Y	Y	Y	Y	Y
2 Hill	Y	Y	Y	Y	Y	Y	Y
3 Womack	Y	Y	Y	Y	Y	Y	Y
4 Westerman	Y	Y	Y	Y	Y	Y	+
CALIFORNIA							
1 LaMalfa	Y	Y	Y	Y	Y	Y	Y
2 Huffman	N	Y	N	N	N	Y	N
3 Garamendi	N	Y	N	N	N	Y	N
4 McClintock	Y	Y	Y	Y	Y	Y	Y
5 Thompson	N	Y	N	N	N	Y	N
6 Matsui	N	Y	N	N	N	Y	N
7 Bera	N	Y	N	N	N	Y	N
8 Cook	Y	Y	Y	Y	Y	Y	Y
9 McNerney	N	Y	N	N	N	Y	N
10 Denham	Y	Y	Y	Y	Y	Y	Y
11 DeSaulnier	N	Y	N	N	N	Y	N
12 Pelosi	N	Y	N	N	N	Y	N
13 Lee	N	Y	N	N	N	Y	N
14 Speier	N	Y	N	N	N	Y	N
15 Swalwell	N	Y	N	N	N	Y	N
16 Costa	Y	Y	N	N	N	Y	N
17 Khanna	N	Y	N	N	N	Y	N
18 Eshoo	N	Y	N	N	N	Y	N
19 Lofgren	N	Y	N	N	N	Y	N
20 Panetta	N	Y	N	N	N	Y	N
21 Valadao	Y	Y	Y	Y	Y	Y	Y
22 Nunes	Y	Y	Y	Y	Y	Y	Y
23 McCarthy	Y	Y	Y	Y	Y	Y	Y
24 Carbajal	N	Y	N	N	N	Y	N
25 Knight	Y	Y	Y	Y	Y	Y	Y
26 Brownley	N	Y	N	N	N	Y	N
27 Chu	N	Y	N	N	N	Y	N
28 Schiff	N	Y	N	N	N	Y	N
29 Cardenas	N	Y	N	N	N	Y	N
30 Sherman	N	Y	N	N	N	Y	N
31 Aguilar	N	Y	N	N	N	Y	N
32 Napolitano	-	+	-	-	-	+	-
33 Lieu	N	Y	N	N	N	Y	N
34 Gomez	N	Y	N	N	N	Y	N
35 Torres	N	Y	N	N	N	Y	N
36 Ruiz	N	Y	N	N	N	Y	N
37 Bass	?	?	?	?	N	Y	N
38 Sánchez, Linda	N	Y	N	N	N	Y	N
39 Royce	Y	Y	Y	Y	Y	Y	Y
40 Roybal-Allard	N	Y	N	N	N	Y	N
41 Takano	N	Y	N	N	N	Y	N
42 Calvert	Y	Y	Y	Y	Y	Y	Y
43 Waters	N	Y	N	N	N	Y	N
44 Barragan	N	Y	N	N	N	Y	N
45 Walters	Y	Y	Y	Y	Y	Y	Y
46 Correa	N	Y	N	N	N	Y	N
47 Lowenthal	N	Y	N	N	N	Y	N
48 Rohrabacher	?	?	Y	Y	Y	Y	Y
49 Issa	Y	Y	Y	Y	Y	Y	Y
50 Hunter	Y	Y	Y	Y	Y	Y	Y
51 Vargas	?	?	N	N	N	Y	N
52 Peters	N	Y	N	N	N	Y	N
53 Davis	N	Y	N	N	N	Y	N

	408	409	410	411	412	413	414
COLORADO							
1 DeGette	N	Y	N	N	N	Y	N
2 Polis	N	Y	N	N	N	Y	N
3 Tipton	Y	Y	Y	Y	Y	Y	Y
4 Buck	Y	Y	Y	Y	Y	Y	Y
5 Lamborn	Y	Y	Y	Y	Y	Y	Y
6 Coffman	Y	Y	Y	Y	Y	Y	Y
7 Perlmutter	N	Y	N	N	N	Y	N
CONNECTICUT							
1 Larson	N	Y	N	N	N	Y	N
2 Courtney	N	Y	N	N	N	Y	N
3 DeLauro	N	Y	N	N	N	Y	N
4 Himes	N	Y	N	N	N	Y	N
5 Esty	N	Y	N	N	N	Y	N
DELAWARE							
AL Blunt Rochester	N	Y	N	N	N	Y	N
FLORIDA							
1 Gaetz	Y	Y	Y	Y	Y	Y	Y
2 Dunn	Y	Y	Y	Y	Y	Y	Y
3 Yoho	Y	Y	Y	Y	Y	Y	Y
4 Rutherford	Y	Y	Y	Y	Y	Y	Y
5 Lawson	N	Y	N	N	-	Y	N
6 DeSantis	Y	Y	Y	Y	Y	Y	Y
7 Murphy	N	Y	N	N	N	Y	N
8 Posey	Y	Y	Y	Y	Y	Y	Y
9 Soto	N	Y	N	N	N	Y	N
10 Demings	N	Y	N	N	N	Y	N
11 Webster	Y	Y	Y	Y	Y	Y	Y
12 Bilirakis	Y	Y	Y	Y	Y	Y	Y
13 Crist	N	Y	N	N	N	Y	N
14 Castor	N	Y	N	N	N	Y	N
15 Ross	Y	Y	Y	Y	Y	Y	Y
16 Buchanan	Y	Y	Y	Y	?	Y	Y
17 Rooney, T.	+	+	Y	Y	Y	Y	Y
18 Mast	Y	Y	Y	Y	Y	Y	Y
19 Rooney, F.	Y	Y	Y	Y	Y	Y	Y
20 Hastings	N	Y	N	N	N	Y	N
21 Frankel	N	Y	-	N	N	Y	N
22 Deutch	N	Y	N	N	N	Y	N
23 Wasserman Schultz	N	Y	N	N	N	Y	N
24 Wilson	N	Y	N	N	N	Y	N
25 Diaz-Balart	Y	Y	Y	Y	Y	Y	Y
26 Curbelo	Y	Y	Y	Y	Y	Y	Y
27 Ros-Lehtinen	Y	Y	Y	Y	Y	Y	Y
GEORGIA							
1 Carter	Y	Y	Y	Y	Y	Y	Y
2 Bishop	N	Y	N	N	N	Y	N
3 Ferguson	Y	Y	Y	Y	Y	Y	Y
4 Johnson	-	+	N	N	N	Y	N
5 Lewis	N	Y	N	N	N	Y	N
6 Handel	Y	Y	Y	Y	Y	Y	Y
7 Woodall	Y	Y	Y	Y	Y	Y	Y
8 Scott, A.	Y	Y	Y	Y	Y	Y	Y
9 Collins	Y	Y	Y	Y	Y	Y	Y
10 Hice	Y	Y	Y	Y	Y	Y	Y
11 Loudermilk	Y	Y	Y	Y	Y	Y	Y
12 Allen	Y	Y	Y	Y	Y	Y	Y
13 Scott, D.	N	Y	N	N	N	Y	N
14 Graves	Y	Y	Y	Y	Y	Y	Y
HAWAII							
1 Hanabusa	N	Y	N	N	N	Y	N
2 Gabbard	N	Y	N	N	N	Y	N
IDAHO							
1 Labrador	Y	Y	Y	Y	Y	Y	Y
2 Simpson	Y	Y	Y	Y	Y	Y	Y
ILLINOIS							
1 Rush	N	Y	N	N	N	Y	N
2 Kelly	N	Y	N	N	N	Y	N
3 Lipinski	N	Y	N	N	N	Y	N
4 Gutierrez	-	+	N	N	N	Y	N
5 Quigley	N	Y	N	N	N	Y	N
6 Roskam	Y	Y	Y	Y	Y	Y	Y
7 Davis, D.	?	?	?	?	?	?	N
8 Krishnamoorthi	N	Y	N	N	N	Y	N
9 Schakowsky	N	Y	N	N	N	Y	N
10 Schneider	N	Y	N	N	N	Y	N
11 Foster	N	Y	N	N	N	Y	N
12 Bost	Y	Y	Y	Y	Y	Y	Y
13 Davis, R.	Y	Y	Y	Y	Y	Y	Y
14 Hultgren	?	?	Y	Y	Y	Y	Y
15 Shimkus	Y	Y	Y	Y	Y	Y	Y

KEY	**Republicans**	Democrats	*Independents*		
Y Voted for (yea)		**X** Paired against		**C** Voted "present" to avoid possible conflict of interest	
# Paired for		**–** Announced against		**?** Did not vote or otherwise make a position known	
+ Announced for		**P** Voted "present"			
N Voted against (nay)					

	408	409	410	411	412	413	414
16 **Kinzinger**	Y	Y	Y	Y	Y	Y	Y
17 Bustos	N	Y	N	N	N	Y	N
18 **LaHood**	Y	Y	Y	Y	Y	Y	Y
INDIANA							
1 Visclosky	N	Y	N	N	N	Y	N
2 **Walorski**	Y	Y	Y	Y	Y	Y	Y
3 **Banks**	Y	Y	Y	Y	Y	Y	Y
4 **Rokita**	Y	Y	Y	Y	Y	Y	Y
5 **Brooks**	Y	Y	Y	Y	Y	Y	Y
6 **Messer**	Y	Y	Y	Y	Y	Y	Y
7 Carson	N	Y	N	N	N	Y	N
8 **Bucshon**	Y	Y	Y	Y	Y	Y	Y
9 **Hollingsworth**	Y	Y	Y	Y	Y	Y	?
IOWA							
1 **Blum**	Y	Y	Y	Y	Y	Y	Y
2 Loebsack	N	Y	N	N	N	Y	N
3 **Young**	Y	Y	Y	Y	Y	Y	Y
4 **King**	Y	Y	Y	Y	Y	Y	Y
KANSAS							
1 **Marshall**	Y	Y	Y	Y	Y	Y	Y
2 **Jenkins**	Y	Y	Y	Y	Y	Y	Y
3 **Yoder**	Y	Y	Y	Y	Y	Y	Y
4 **Estes**	Y	Y	Y	Y	Y	Y	Y
KENTUCKY							
1 **Comer**	Y	Y	Y	Y	Y	Y	Y
2 **Guthrie**	Y	Y	Y	Y	Y	Y	Y
3 Yarmuth	N	Y	N	N	N	Y	N
4 **Massie**	N	Y	Y	Y	Y	N	N
5 **Rogers**	Y	Y	Y	Y	Y	Y	Y
6 **Barr**	Y	Y	Y	Y	Y	Y	Y
LOUISIANA							
1 **Scalise**	+	+	+	+	+	+	+
2 Richmond	N	Y	?	N	N	Y	N
3 **Higgins**	Y	Y	Y	Y	Y	Y	Y
4 **Johnson**	Y	Y	Y	Y	Y	Y	Y
5 **Abraham**	Y	Y	Y	Y	Y	Y	Y
6 **Graves**	Y	Y	Y	Y	Y	Y	Y
MAINE							
1 Pingree	N	Y	N	N	N	Y	N
2 **Poliquin**	Y	Y	Y	Y	Y	Y	Y
MARYLAND							
1 **Harris**	Y	Y	Y	Y	Y	Y	Y
2 Ruppersberger	N	Y	N	N	N	Y	N
3 Sarbanes	N	Y	N	N	N	Y	N
4 Brown	N	Y	N	N	N	Y	N
5 Hoyer	N	Y	N	N	N	Y	N
6 Delaney	N	Y	N	N	N	Y	N
7 Cummings	?	?	?	?	?	?	?
8 Raskin	N	Y	N	N	N	Y	N
MASSACHUSETTS							
1 Neal	N	Y	N	N	N	Y	N
2 McGovern	N	Y	N	N	N	Y	N
3 Tsongas	N	Y	N	N	N	Y	N
4 Kennedy	N	Y	N	N	N	Y	N
5 Clark	N	Y	N	N	N	Y	N
6 Moulton	N	Y	N	N	N	Y	N
7 Capuano	N	Y	N	N	N	Y	N
8 Lynch	N	Y	N	N	N	Y	N
9 Keating	N	Y	N	N	N	Y	N
MICHIGAN							
1 **Bergman**	Y	Y	Y	Y	Y	Y	Y
2 **Huizenga**	Y	Y	Y	Y	Y	Y	Y
3 **Amash**	Y	Y	Y	Y	Y	N	Y
4 **Moolenaar**	Y	Y	Y	Y	Y	Y	Y
5 Kildee	N	Y	N	N	N	Y	N
6 **Upton**	Y	Y	Y	Y	Y	Y	Y
7 **Walberg**	Y	Y	Y	Y	Y	Y	Y
8 **Bishop**	Y	Y	Y	Y	Y	Y	Y
9 Levin	N	Y	N	N	N	Y	N
10 **Mitchell**	Y	Y	Y	Y	Y	Y	Y
11 **Trott**	Y	Y	Y	Y	Y	Y	Y
12 Dingell	N	Y	N	N	N	Y	N
13 Conyers	N	Y	N	N	N	Y	N
14 Lawrence	–	+	N	N	N	Y	N
MINNESOTA							
1 Walz	N	Y	N	N	N	Y	N
2 **Lewis**	Y	Y	Y	Y	Y	Y	Y
3 **Paulsen**	Y	Y	Y	Y	Y	Y	Y
4 McCollum	N	Y	N	N	N	Y	N

	408	409	410	411	412	413	414
5 Ellison	N	Y	N	N	N	Y	N
6 **Emmer**	Y	Y	Y	Y	Y	Y	Y
7 Peterson	N	Y	N	N	N	Y	N
8 Nolan	N	Y	N	N	N	Y	N
MISSISSIPPI							
1 **Kelly**	Y	Y	Y	Y	Y	Y	Y
2 Thompson	N	Y	N	N	N	Y	N
3 **Harper**	Y	Y	Y	Y	Y	Y	Y
4 **Palazzo**	?	?	Y	Y	Y	Y	Y
MISSOURI							
1 Clay	N	Y	N	N	N	Y	N
2 **Wagner**	Y	Y	Y	Y	Y	Y	Y
3 **Luetkemeyer**	Y	Y	Y	Y	Y	Y	Y
4 **Hartzler**	Y	Y	Y	Y	Y	Y	Y
5 Cleaver	N	Y	N	N	N	Y	N
6 **Graves**	+	+	+	+	+	+	+
7 **Long**	Y	Y	Y	Y	Y	Y	Y
8 **Smith**	?	?	Y	Y	Y	Y	Y
MONTANA							
AL **Gianforte**	Y	Y	Y	Y	Y	Y	Y
NEBRASKA							
1 **Fortenberry**	Y	Y	Y	Y	Y	Y	Y
2 **Bacon**	Y	Y	Y	Y	Y	Y	Y
3 **Smith**	Y	Y	Y	Y	Y	Y	Y
NEVADA							
1 Titus	N	Y	N	N	N	Y	N
2 **Amodei**	Y	Y	Y	Y	Y	Y	Y
3 Rosen	N	Y	N	N	N	Y	N
4 Kihuen	N	Y	N	N	N	Y	N
NEW HAMPSHIRE							
1 Shea-Porter	N	Y	N	N	N	Y	N
2 Kuster	N	Y	N	N	N	Y	–
NEW JERSEY							
1 Norcross	N	Y	N	N	N	Y	N
2 **LoBiondo**	Y	Y	Y	Y	Y	Y	Y
3 **MacArthur**	Y	Y	Y	Y	Y	Y	Y
4 **Smith**	Y	Y	Y	Y	Y	Y	Y
5 Gottheimer	N	Y	N	N	N	Y	N
6 Pallone	N	Y	N	N	N	Y	N
7 **Lance**	Y	Y	Y	Y	Y	Y	Y
8 Sires	N	Y	N	N	N	Y	N
9 Pascrell	N	Y	N	N	N	Y	N
10 Payne	N	Y	N	N	N	Y	N
11 **Frelinghuysen**	Y	Y	Y	Y	Y	Y	Y
12 Watson Coleman	N	Y	N	N	N	Y	N
NEW MEXICO							
1 Lujan Grisham	N	Y	N	N	N	Y	N
2 **Pearce**	Y	Y	Y	Y	Y	Y	Y
3 Luján	N	Y	N	N	N	Y	N
NEW YORK							
1 **Zeldin**	Y	Y	Y	Y	Y	Y	Y
2 **King**	Y	Y	Y	Y	Y	Y	Y
3 Suozzi	N	Y	N	N	N	Y	N
4 Rice	N	Y	N	N	N	Y	N
5 Meeks	N	Y	N	N	N	Y	N
6 Meng	N	Y	N	N	N	Y	N
7 Velázquez	N	Y	N	N	N	Y	N
8 Jeffries	N	Y	N	N	N	Y	N
9 Clarke	N	Y	N	N	N	Y	N
10 Nadler	N	Y	N	N	N	Y	N
11 **Donovan**	Y	Y	Y	Y	Y	Y	Y
12 Maloney, C.	N	Y	N	N	N	Y	N
13 Espaillat	N	Y	N	N	N	Y	N
14 Crowley	–	+	–	–	–	+	N
15 Serrano	N	Y	N	N	N	Y	N
16 Engel	N	Y	N	N	N	Y	N
17 Lowey	N	Y	N	N	N	Y	N
18 Maloney, S.P.	N	Y	N	N	N	Y	N
19 **Faso**	Y	Y	Y	Y	Y	Y	Y
20 Tonko	N	Y	N	N	N	Y	N
21 **Stefanik**	Y	Y	Y	Y	Y	Y	Y
22 **Tenney**	Y	Y	Y	Y	Y	Y	Y
23 **Reed**	Y	Y	Y	Y	Y	Y	Y
24 **Katko**	Y	Y	Y	Y	Y	Y	Y
25 Slaughter	N	Y	N	N	N	Y	N
26 Higgins	N	Y	N	N	N	Y	N
27 **Collins**	Y	Y	Y	Y	Y	Y	Y
NORTH CAROLINA							
1 Butterfield	N	Y	N	N	N	Y	N
2 **Holding**	Y	Y	Y	Y	Y	Y	Y
3 **Jones**	N	Y	Y	Y	N	Y	N
4 Price	N	Y	N	N	N	Y	N

	408	409	410	411	412	413	414
5 **Foxx**	Y	Y	Y	Y	Y	Y	Y
6 **Walker**	Y	Y	Y	Y	Y	Y	Y
7 **Rouzer**	Y	Y	Y	Y	Y	Y	Y
8 **Hudson**	Y	Y	Y	Y	Y	Y	Y
9 **Pittenger**	Y	Y	Y	Y	Y	Y	Y
10 **McHenry**	Y	Y	Y	Y	Y	Y	Y
11 **Meadows**	Y	Y	?	?	?	?	Y
12 Adams	N	Y	N	N	N	Y	N
13 **Budd**	Y	Y	Y	Y	Y	?	Y
NORTH DAKOTA							
AL **Cramer**	Y	Y	?	Y	Y	Y	Y
OHIO							
1 **Chabot**	Y	Y	Y	Y	Y	Y	Y
2 **Wenstrup**	Y	Y	Y	Y	Y	Y	Y
3 Beatty	N	Y	N	N	N	Y	N
4 **Jordan**	Y	Y	Y	Y	Y	Y	Y
5 **Latta**	Y	Y	Y	Y	Y	Y	Y
6 **Johnson**	Y	Y	Y	Y	Y	Y	Y
7 **Gibbs**	Y	Y	Y	Y	Y	Y	Y
8 **Davidson**	Y	Y	Y	Y	Y	Y	Y
9 Kaptur	N	Y	N	N	N	Y	N
10 **Turner**	Y	Y	Y	Y	Y	Y	Y
11 Fudge	N	Y	?	N	N	Y	N
12 **Tiberi**	Y	Y	Y	Y	Y	Y	Y
13 Ryan	N	Y	N	N	N	Y	N
14 **Joyce**	Y	Y	Y	Y	Y	Y	Y
15 **Stivers**	Y	Y	Y	Y	Y	Y	Y
16 **Renacci**	+	+	+	+	+	+	Y
OKLAHOMA							
1 **Bridenstine**	Y	Y	Y	Y	Y	Y	Y
2 **Mullin**	Y	Y	Y	Y	Y	Y	Y
3 **Lucas**	Y	Y	Y	Y	Y	Y	Y
4 **Cole**	Y	Y	Y	Y	Y	Y	Y
5 **Russell**	Y	Y	Y	Y	Y	Y	Y
OREGON							
1 Bonamici	N	Y	N	N	N	Y	N
2 **Walden**	Y	Y	Y	Y	Y	Y	Y
3 Blumenauer	N	Y	N	N	N	Y	N
4 DeFazio	N	Y	N	N	N	Y	N
5 Schrader	N	Y	N	N	N	Y	N
PENNSYLVANIA							
1 Brady	N	Y	N	N	N	Y	N
2 Evans	N	Y	N	N	N	Y	N
3 **Kelly**	Y	Y	Y	Y	Y	Y	Y
4 **Perry**	Y	Y	Y	Y	Y	Y	Y
5 **Thompson**	Y	Y	Y	Y	Y	Y	Y
6 **Costello**	+	+	?	?	?	?	Y
7 **Meehan**	Y	Y	Y	Y	Y	Y	Y
8 **Fitzpatrick**	Y	Y	Y	Y	Y	Y	Y
9 **Shuster**	Y	Y	Y	Y	Y	Y	Y
10 **Marino**	Y	Y	Y	Y	Y	Y	Y
11 **Barletta**	Y	Y	Y	Y	Y	Y	Y
12 **Rothfus**	Y	Y	Y	Y	Y	Y	Y
13 Boyle	N	Y	N	N	N	Y	N
14 Doyle	N	Y	N	N	N	Y	N
15 **Dent**	Y	Y	Y	Y	Y	Y	Y
16 **Smucker**	Y	Y	Y	Y	Y	Y	Y
17 Cartwright	N	Y	N	N	N	Y	N
18 **Murphy**	Y	Y	Y	Y	Y	Y	Y
RHODE ISLAND							
1 Cicilline	N	Y	N	N	N	Y	N
2 Langevin	N	Y	–	N	N	Y	N
SOUTH CAROLINA							
1 **Sanford**	Y	Y	Y	Y	Y	Y	Y
2 **Wilson**	Y	Y	Y	Y	Y	Y	Y
3 **Duncan**	Y	Y	?	Y	Y	Y	Y
4 **Gowdy**	Y	Y	Y	Y	Y	Y	Y
5 **Norman**	Y	Y	Y	Y	Y	Y	Y
6 Clyburn	N	Y	N	N	N	Y	N
7 **Rice**	Y	Y	Y	Y	Y	Y	Y
SOUTH DAKOTA							
AL **Noem**	Y	Y	Y	Y	Y	Y	Y
TENNESSEE							
1 **Roe**	Y	Y	Y	Y	Y	Y	Y
2 **Duncan**	Y	Y	Y	Y	Y	N	Y
3 **Fleischmann**	Y	Y	Y	Y	Y	Y	Y
4 **DesJarlais**	Y	Y	Y	Y	Y	Y	Y
5 Cooper	N	Y	N	N	N	Y	N
6 **Black**	Y	Y	Y	Y	Y	Y	Y
7 **Blackburn**	Y	Y	Y	Y	Y	Y	Y
8 **Kustoff**	Y	Y	Y	Y	Y	Y	Y
9 Cohen	N	Y	N	N	N	Y	N

	408	409	410	411	412	413	414
TEXAS							
1 **Gohmert**	Y	Y	Y	Y	Y	Y	Y
2 **Poe**	?	?	Y	Y	Y	Y	Y
3 **Johnson, S.**	Y	Y	Y	Y	Y	Y	Y
4 **Ratcliffe**	Y	Y	Y	Y	Y	Y	Y
5 **Hensarling**	Y	Y	Y	Y	Y	Y	Y
6 **Barton**	Y	Y	Y	Y	Y	Y	Y
7 **Culberson**	Y	Y	Y	Y	Y	Y	Y
8 **Brady**	Y	Y	Y	Y	Y	Y	Y
9 Green, A.	N	Y	?	?	N	Y	N
10 **McCaul**	+	+	Y	Y	Y	Y	Y
11 **Conaway**	Y	Y	Y	Y	Y	Y	Y
12 **Granger**	Y	Y	Y	Y	Y	Y	Y
13 **Thornberry**	Y	Y	Y	Y	Y	Y	Y
14 **Weber**	Y	Y	Y	Y	Y	Y	Y
15 Gonzalez	N	Y	N	N	N	Y	N
16 O'Rourke	N	Y	N	N	N	Y	N
17 **Flores**	Y	Y	Y	Y	Y	Y	Y
18 Jackson Lee	N	Y	N	N	N	Y	N
19 **Arrington**	Y	Y	Y	Y	Y	Y	Y
20 Castro	N	Y	N	N	N	Y	N
21 **Smith**	Y	Y	Y	Y	Y	Y	Y
22 **Olson**	Y	Y	Y	Y	Y	Y	Y
23 **Hurd**	Y	Y	Y	Y	Y	Y	Y
24 **Marchant**	Y	Y	Y	Y	Y	Y	Y
25 **Williams**	+	+	Y	Y	Y	Y	Y
26 **Burgess**	Y	Y	Y	Y	Y	Y	Y
27 **Farenthold**	Y	Y	Y	Y	Y	Y	Y
28 Cuellar	N	Y	N	N	N	Y	N
29 Green, G.	N	Y	N	N	N	Y	N
30 Johnson, E.B.	N	Y	N	N	N	Y	N
31 **Carter**	Y	Y	Y	Y	Y	Y	Y
32 **Sessions**	Y	Y	Y	Y	Y	Y	Y
33 Veasey	N	Y	N	N	N	Y	N
34 Vela	N	Y	N	N	N	Y	N
35 Doggett	N	Y	N	N	N	Y	N
36 **Babin**	Y	Y	Y	Y	Y	Y	Y
UTAH							
1 **Bishop**	Y	Y	Y	Y	Y	Y	Y
2 **Stewart**	?	?	Y	Y	Y	Y	Y
4 **Love**	Y	Y	Y	Y	Y	Y	Y
VERMONT							
AL Welch	–	+	N	N	N	Y	N
VIRGINIA							
1 **Wittman**	Y	Y	+	Y	Y	Y	Y
2 **Taylor**	Y	Y	Y	Y	Y	Y	Y
3 Scott	N	Y	N	N	N	Y	N
4 McEachin	N	Y	N	N	N	Y	N
5 **Garrett**	Y	Y	Y	Y	Y	Y	Y
6 **Goodlatte**	Y	Y	Y	Y	Y	Y	Y
7 **Brat**	Y	Y	Y	Y	Y	Y	+
8 Beyer	N	Y	N	N	N	Y	N
9 **Griffith**	Y	Y	Y	Y	Y	Y	Y
10 **Comstock**	Y	Y	Y	Y	Y	Y	?
11 Connolly	N	Y	N	N	N	Y	N
WASHINGTON							
1 DelBene	N	Y	N	N	N	Y	N
2 Larsen	N	Y	N	N	N	Y	N
3 **Herrera Beutler**	Y	Y	Y	Y	Y	Y	Y
4 **Newhouse**	Y	Y	Y	Y	Y	Y	Y
5 **McMorris Rodgers**	Y	Y	Y	Y	Y	Y	Y
6 Kilmer	N	Y	N	N	N	Y	N
7 Jayapal	N	Y	N	N	N	Y	N
8 **Reichert**	Y	Y	Y	Y	Y	Y	Y
9 Smith	N	Y	N	N	N	Y	N
10 Heck	N	Y	N	N	N	Y	N
WEST VIRGINIA							
1 **McKinley**	?	?	Y	Y	Y	Y	Y
2 **Mooney**	+	+	Y	Y	Y	Y	Y
3 **Jenkins**	+	+	Y	Y	Y	Y	Y
WISCONSIN							
1 **Ryan**							
2 Pocan	N	Y	N	N	N	Y	N
3 Kind	N	Y	N	N	N	Y	N
4 Moore	N	Y	N	N	N	Y	N
5 **Sensenbrenner**	Y	Y	Y	Y	Y	Y	Y
6 **Grothman**	Y	Y	Y	Y	Y	Y	Y
7 **Duffy**	Y	Y	Y	Y	Y	Y	Y
8 **Gallagher**	Y	Y	Y	Y	Y	Y	Y
WYOMING							
AL **Cheney**	Y	Y	+	Y	Y	Y	Y

VOTE NUMBER

415. HR 3219, H RES 473. FISCAL 2018 MINIBUS APPROPRIATIONS/RULE. Adoption of the rule (H Res 473) providing for consideration of the bill (HR 3219) that would make certain appropriations for the fiscal year ending Sept. 30, 2018, and would provide for consideration of amendments to the Legislative Branch, Military Construction and Veterans Affairs, and Energy and Water divisions of the bill. Adopted 232-192 : R 230-3; D 2-189. July 26, 2017.

416. HR 3219. FISCAL 2018 MINIBUS APPROPRIATIONS/CONGRESSIONAL BUDGET OFFICE FUNDING REDUCTION. Perry, R-Pa., amendment that would decrease by $25.4 million funding for staffing and operations at the Congressional Budget Office. Rejected in Committee of the Whole 107-314 : R 107-124; D 0-190. July 26, 2017.

417. HR 3219. FISCAL 2018 MINIBUS APPROPRIATIONS/CONGRESSIONAL BUDGET ANALYSIS AUTHORITY. Griffith, R-Va., amendment that would eliminate the budget analysis division of the Congressional Budget Office and would transfer the responsibilities of the division to the CBO's office of the director. Rejected in Committee of the Whole 116-309 : R 116-120; D 0-189. July 26, 2017.

418. HR 3219. FISCAL 2018 MINIBUS APPROPRIATIONS/TECHNOLOGY ASSESSMENT REINSTATEMENT. Takano, D-Calif., amendment that would provide $2.5 million in funding for salaries and expenses in what would become the Office of Technology Assessment, and would reduce by $2.6 million funding to the capital construction and operations account of the Architect of the Capitol. Rejected in Committee of the Whole 191-236 : R 13-223; D 178-13. July 26, 2017.

419. HR 3219. FISCAL 2018 MINIBUS APPROPRIATIONS/PREVAILING WAGE REQUIREMENTS PROHIBITION. King, R-Iowa, amendment that would prohibit funds made available in the bill from being used to implement, administer or enforce prevailing wage requirements associated with the Davis-Bacon Act, which specify the basis for wages paid to employees by companies under contract with the federal government. Rejected in Committee of the Whole 178-249 : R 178-58; D 0-191. July 26, 2017.

420. HR 3219. FISCAL 2018 MINIBUS APPROPRIATIONS/RENEWABLE ENERGY PRIORITIZATION. Castor, D-Fla., amendment that would increase by $177 million funding to the Energy Efficiency and Renewable Energy account and would reduce by $355 million funding to the Fossil Fuel Research and Development account. Rejected in Committee of the Whole 181-246 : R 10-226; D 171-20. July 26, 2017.

421. HR 3219. FISCAL 2018 MINIBUS APPROPRIATIONS/RENEWABLE ENERGY ACQUISITIONS. Norcross, D-N.J., amendment that would increase by $161.7 million funding to the Office of Energy Efficiency and Renewable Energy for facility acquisition, construction or expansion, and would reduce by $323.5 million funding to the Energy Department Fossil Energy Research and Development account. Rejected in Committee of the Whole 186-241 : R 12-224; D 174-17. July 26, 2017.

	415	416	417	418	419	420	421
ALABAMA							
1 Byrne	Y	Y	Y	N	Y	N	N
2 Roby	Y	N	N	N	Y	N	N
3 Rogers	Y	N	N	N	Y	N	N
4 Aderholt	Y	?	N	N	Y	N	N
5 Brooks	Y	Y	Y	N	Y	N	Y
6 Palmer	?	Y	Y	N	Y	N	N
7 Sewell	N	N	N	Y	N	Y	Y
ALASKA							
AL Young	Y	Y	Y	N	N	N	N
ARIZONA							
1 O'Halleran	N	N	N	Y	N	Y	Y
2 McSally	Y	N	N	N	Y	N	N
3 Grijalva	N	N	N	Y	N	Y	Y
4 Gosar	Y	Y	Y	N	Y	N	N
5 Biggs	Y	Y	Y	N	Y	N	N
6 Schweikert	Y	N	N	N	Y	N	N
7 Gallego	N	N	N	Y	N	Y	Y
8 Franks	+	Y	Y	N	Y	N	N
9 Sinema	Y	N	N	Y	N	N	N
ARKANSAS							
1 Crawford	Y	N	N	Y	Y	N	N
2 Hill	Y	N	N	N	Y	N	N
3 Womack	Y	N	N	N	Y	N	N
4 Westerman	Y	Y	Y	N	Y	N	N
CALIFORNIA							
1 LaMalfa	Y	Y	Y	N	Y	N	N
2 Huffman	N	N	N	Y	N	Y	Y
3 Garamendi	N	N	N	Y	N	Y	Y
4 McClintock	Y	N	N	Y	N	N	N
5 Thompson	N	N	N	Y	N	Y	Y
6 Matsui	N	N	N	Y	N	Y	Y
7 Bera	N	N	N	Y	N	Y	Y
8 Cook	Y	N	N	N	N	N	N
9 McNerney	N	N	N	Y	N	Y	Y
10 Denham	Y	N	N	N	N	N	N
11 DeSaulnier	N	N	N	Y	N	Y	Y
12 Pelosi	N	N	N	Y	N	Y	Y
13 Lee	N	N	N	Y	N	Y	Y
14 Speier	N	N	N	Y	N	Y	Y
15 Swalwell	N	N	N	Y	N	Y	Y
16 Costa	N	N	N	Y	N	N	N
17 Khanna	N	N	N	Y	N	Y	Y
18 Eshoo	N	N	N	Y	N	Y	Y
19 Lofgren	N	N	N	Y	N	Y	Y
20 Panetta	N	N	N	Y	N	Y	Y
21 Valadao	Y	N	N	N	N	N	N
22 Nunes	Y	N	N	N	Y	N	N
23 McCarthy	Y	N	N	N	Y	N	N
24 Carbajal	N	N	N	Y	N	Y	Y
25 Knight	Y	N	N	N	N	N	N
26 Brownley	N	N	N	Y	N	Y	Y
27 Chu	N	N	N	Y	N	Y	Y
28 Schiff	N	N	N	Y	N	Y	Y
29 Cardenas	N	N	N	Y	N	Y	Y
30 Sherman	N	N	N	Y	N	Y	Y
31 Aguilar	N	N	N	Y	N	Y	Y
32 Napolitano	–	–	–	+	N	+	+
33 Lieu	N	N	N	Y	N	Y	Y
34 Gomez	N	N	N	Y	N	Y	Y
35 Torres	N	N	N	Y	N	Y	Y
36 Ruiz	N	N	N	Y	N	Y	Y
37 Bass	N	N	N	Y	N	Y	Y
38 Sánchez, Linda	N	N	N	Y	N	Y	Y
39 Royce	Y	?	Y	N	Y	N	N
40 Roybal-Allard	N	N	N	Y	N	Y	Y
41 Takano	N	N	N	Y	N	Y	Y
42 Calvert	Y	N	N	N	Y	N	N
43 Waters	N	N	N	Y	N	Y	Y
44 Barragan	N	N	N	Y	N	Y	Y
45 Walters	Y	N	N	N	Y	N	N
46 Correa	N	N	N	Y	N	N	N
47 Lowenthal	N	N	N	Y	N	Y	Y
48 Rohrabacher	Y	Y	Y	N	Y	N	N
49 Issa	Y	N	N	N	Y	N	N
50 Hunter	Y	Y	Y	N	N	N	N
51 Vargas	N	N	N	Y	N	Y	Y
52 Peters	N	N	N	Y	N	Y	Y
53 Davis	N	N	N	Y	N	Y	Y
COLORADO							
1 DeGette	N	N	N	Y	N	Y	Y
2 Polis	N	N	N	Y	N	Y	Y
3 Tipton	Y	N	N	N	Y	N	N
4 Buck	Y	Y	Y	N	Y	N	N
5 Lamborn	Y	Y	Y	N	Y	N	N
6 Coffman	Y	N	N	N	Y	N	N
7 Perlmutter	N	N	N	Y	N	Y	Y
CONNECTICUT							
1 Larson	N	N	N	Y	N	N	N
2 Courtney	N	N	N	Y	N	N	N
3 DeLauro	N	N	N	Y	N	N	N
4 Himes	N	N	N	Y	N	N	N
5 Esty	N	N	N	Y	N	N	N
DELAWARE							
AL Blunt Rochester	N	N	N	Y	N	Y	Y
FLORIDA							
1 Gaetz	Y	Y	Y	N	Y	N	N
2 Dunn	Y	Y	Y	N	Y	N	N
3 Yoho	Y	Y	Y	N	Y	N	N
4 Rutherford	Y	N	N	N	Y	N	N
5 Lawson	N	N	N	Y	N	Y	Y
6 DeSantis	Y	Y	Y	N	Y	N	N
7 Murphy	N	N	N	Y	N	Y	Y
8 Posey	Y	Y	Y	N	Y	N	N
9 Soto	N	N	N	Y	N	Y	Y
10 Demings	N	N	N	Y	N	Y	Y
11 Webster	Y	Y	Y	N	Y	N	N
12 Bilirakis	Y	N	N	Y	N	N	N
13 Crist	N	N	N	Y	N	Y	Y
14 Castor	N	N	N	Y	N	Y	Y
15 Ross	Y	N	N	N	Y	N	N
16 Buchanan	Y	N	N	N	Y	N	N
17 Rooney, T.	Y	N	N	N	Y	N	N
18 Mast	Y	N	N	N	Y	N	N
19 Rooney, F.	Y	Y	Y	N	Y	N	N
20 Hastings	N	N	N	Y	N	Y	Y
21 Frankel	N	N	N	Y	N	Y	Y
22 Deutch	N	N	N	Y	N	Y	Y
23 Wasserman Schultz	N	N	N	Y	N	Y	Y
24 Wilson	N	N	N	Y	N	Y	Y
25 Diaz-Balart	Y	N	N	N	N	N	N
26 Curbelo	Y	N	N	Y	N	Y	Y
27 Ros-Lehtinen	Y	N	N	Y	N	Y	Y
GEORGIA							
1 Carter	Y	Y	Y	N	Y	N	N
2 Bishop	N	N	N	Y	N	Y	Y
3 Ferguson	Y	Y	Y	N	Y	N	N
4 Johnson	N	N	N	Y	N	Y	Y
5 Lewis	N	N	N	Y	N	Y	Y
6 Handel	Y	N	N	N	Y	N	N
7 Woodall	Y	N	N	N	Y	N	N
8 Scott, A.	Y	Y	Y	N	Y	N	N
9 Collins	Y	N	N	N	Y	N	N
10 Hice	Y	Y	Y	N	Y	N	N
11 Loudermilk	Y	?	Y	Y	Y	N	N
12 Allen	Y	Y	Y	N	Y	N	N
13 Scott, D.	N	N	N	Y	N	Y	Y
14 Graves	Y	Y	Y	N	Y	N	N
HAWAII							
1 Hanabusa	N	N	N	Y	N	Y	Y
2 Gabbard	N	N	N	N	N	Y	Y
IDAHO							
1 Labrador	Y	Y	Y	N	Y	N	N
2 Simpson	Y	N	N	N	N	N	N
ILLINOIS							
1 Rush	N	N	N	Y	N	Y	Y
2 Kelly	N	N	N	Y	N	Y	Y
3 Lipinski	N	N	N	Y	N	Y	Y
4 Gutierrez	N	N	N	Y	N	Y	Y
5 Quigley	N	N	N	Y	N	Y	Y
6 Roskam	Y	N	N	N	N	N	N
7 Davis, D.	N	N	N	Y	N	Y	Y
8 Krishnamoorthi	N	N	N	Y	N	Y	Y
9 Schakowsky	N	N	N	Y	N	Y	Y
10 Schneider	N	N	N	Y	N	N	N
11 Foster	N	N	N	Y	N	Y	Y
12 Bost	Y	N	N	N	N	N	N
13 Davis, R.	Y	N	N	N	N	N	N
14 Hultgren	Y	N	N	N	N	N	N
15 Shimkus	Y	N	N	N	N	N	N

	415	416	417	418	419	420	421
16 **Kinzinger**	Y	N	N	N	N	N	N
17 Bustos	N	N	N	Y	N	Y	Y
18 **LaHood**	Y	Y	Y	N	N	N	N
INDIANA							
1 Visclosky	N	N	N	Y	N	Y	Y
2 **Walorski**	Y	N	N	N	Y	N	N
3 **Banks**	Y	Y	Y	N	Y	N	N
4 **Rokita**	Y	Y	Y	N	Y	N	N
5 **Brooks**	Y	N	N	N	Y	N	N
6 **Messer**	Y	Y	Y	N	Y	N	N
7 Carson	N	N	N	Y	N	Y	Y
8 **Bucshon**	Y	N	N	N	N	N	N
9 **Hollingsworth**	?	?	?	?	?	?	?
IOWA							
1 **Blum**	Y	?	Y	N	Y	Y	Y
2 Loebsack	N	N	N	Y	N	Y	Y
3 **Young**	Y	N	Y	N	Y	Y	Y
4 **King**	Y	Y	Y	N	Y	Y	Y
KANSAS							
1 **Marshall**	Y	Y	Y	N	Y	N	N
2 **Jenkins**	Y	N	N	N	Y	N	N
3 **Yoder**	Y	N	N	N	Y	N	N
4 **Estes**	Y	Y	Y	N	Y	N	N
KENTUCKY							
1 **Comer**	Y	Y	Y	N	Y	N	N
2 **Guthrie**	Y	N	N	N	Y	N	N
3 Yarmuth	N	N	N	Y	N	Y	Y
4 **Massie**	N	Y	Y	N	Y	N	N
5 **Rogers**	Y	N	N	N	Y	N	N
6 **Barr**	Y	Y	Y	N	Y	N	N
LOUISIANA							
1 **Scalise**	+	–	–	–	+	–	–
2 Richmond	N	N	N	Y	N	N	N
3 **Higgins**	Y	N	Y	N	Y	N	N
4 **Johnson**	Y	N	Y	N	Y	N	N
5 **Abraham**	Y	Y	Y	N	Y	N	N
6 **Graves**	Y	N	N	N	Y	N	N
MAINE							
1 Pingree	N	N	N	Y	N	Y	Y
2 **Poliquin**	Y	N	N	N	N	N	N
MARYLAND							
1 **Harris**	Y	Y	Y	N	Y	N	N
2 Ruppersberger	N	N	N	Y	N	Y	Y
3 Sarbanes	N	N	N	Y	N	Y	Y
4 Brown	N	N	N	Y	N	Y	Y
5 Hoyer	N	N	N	Y	N	Y	Y
6 Delaney	N	N	N	Y	N	Y	Y
7 Cummings	?	?	?	?	?	?	?
8 Raskin	N	N	N	Y	N	Y	Y
MASSACHUSETTS							
1 Neal	N	N	N	N	N	Y	Y
2 McGovern	N	N	N	Y	N	Y	Y
3 Tsongas	N	N	N	Y	N	Y	Y
4 Kennedy	N	N	N	Y	N	Y	Y
5 Clark	N	N	N	Y	N	Y	Y
6 Moulton	N	N	N	Y	N	Y	Y
7 Capuano	N	N	N	N	N	Y	Y
8 Lynch	N	N	N	Y	N	Y	Y
9 Keating	N	N	N	Y	N	Y	Y
MICHIGAN							
1 **Bergman**	Y	N	N	N	Y	N	N
2 **Huizenga**	Y	Y	Y	N	Y	N	N
3 **Amash**	N	N	Y	Y	Y	Y	Y
4 **Moolenaar**	Y	N	N	N	Y	N	N
5 Kildee	N	N	N	Y	N	Y	Y
6 **Upton**	Y	N	N	N	N	N	N
7 **Walberg**	Y	Y	Y	N	Y	N	N
8 **Bishop**	Y	N	N	N	Y	N	N
9 Levin	N	N	N	Y	N	Y	Y
10 **Mitchell**	Y	N	N	N	Y	N	N
11 **Trott**	Y	N	N	N	Y	N	N
12 Dingell	N	N	N	Y	N	Y	Y
13 Conyers	N	N	N	Y	N	Y	Y
14 Lawrence	N	N	N	Y	N	Y	Y
MINNESOTA							
1 Walz	N	N	N	Y	N	Y	Y
2 **Lewis**	Y	N	N	N	N	N	N
3 **Paulsen**	Y	N	N	N	Y	N	N
4 McCollum	N	N	N	N	N	Y	Y

	415	416	417	418	419	420	421
5 Ellison	N	N	N	Y	N	Y	Y
6 **Emmer**	Y	N	N	N	N	N	N
7 Peterson	N	N	N	N	N	N	N
8 Nolan	?	N	N	Y	N	Y	Y
MISSISSIPPI							
1 **Kelly**	Y	Y	Y	N	Y	N	N
2 Thompson	N	N	N	Y	N	N	N
3 **Harper**	Y	N	Y	N	Y	N	N
4 **Palazzo**	Y	Y	N	N	Y	N	N
MISSOURI							
1 Clay	N	N	N	Y	N	Y	Y
2 **Wagner**	Y	Y	Y	N	Y	N	N
3 **Luetkemeyer**	Y	Y	Y	N	Y	N	N
4 **Hartzler**	Y	N	N	N	Y	N	N
5 Cleaver	N	N	N	Y	N	Y	Y
6 **Graves**	+	N	N	N	N	N	N
7 **Long**	Y	N	N	N	Y	N	N
8 **Smith**	Y	Y	Y	N	Y	N	N
MONTANA							
AL **Gianforte**	Y	N	N	N	N	N	N
NEBRASKA							
1 **Fortenberry**	Y	N	N	N	Y	N	N
2 **Bacon**	Y	Y	N	N	Y	N	N
3 **Smith**	Y	N	N	N	Y	N	N
NEVADA							
1 Titus	N	N	N	Y	N	Y	Y
2 **Amodei**	Y	N	N	N	N	N	N
3 Rosen	N	N	N	Y	N	Y	Y
4 Kihuen	N	N	N	Y	N	Y	Y
NEW HAMPSHIRE							
1 Shea-Porter	N	N	N	Y	N	Y	Y
2 Kuster	N	N	N	Y	N	Y	Y
NEW JERSEY							
1 Norcross	N	N	N	N	N	Y	Y
2 **LoBiondo**	Y	N	N	N	N	N	N
3 **MacArthur**	?	N	N	N	N	N	N
4 **Smith**	Y	N	N	N	N	N	N
5 Gottheimer	Y	N	N	N	N	Y	Y
6 Pallone	N	N	N	Y	N	Y	Y
7 **Lance**	Y	N	N	N	Y	N	N
8 Sires	N	N	N	N	N	Y	Y
9 Pascrell	N	N	N	N	N	Y	Y
10 Payne	N	N	N	Y	N	Y	Y
11 **Frelinghuysen**	Y	N	N	N	Y	N	N
12 Watson Coleman	N	N	N	Y	N	Y	Y
NEW MEXICO							
1 Lujan Grisham	N	N	N	Y	N	Y	Y
2 **Pearce**	Y	Y	Y	N	Y	N	N
3 Luján	N	N	N	Y	N	Y	Y
NEW YORK							
1 **Zeldin**	Y	Y	Y	N	N	N	N
2 **King**	Y	N	N	N	N	N	N
3 Suozzi	N	N	N	Y	N	Y	Y
4 Rice	N	N	N	Y	N	Y	Y
5 Meeks	N	N	N	Y	N	Y	Y
6 Meng	N	N	N	Y	N	Y	Y
7 Velázquez	N	N	N	Y	N	Y	Y
8 Jeffries	N	?	?	?	?	?	?
9 Clarke	N	N	N	Y	N	Y	Y
10 Nadler	N	N	N	Y	N	Y	Y
11 **Donovan**	Y	N	N	N	N	N	N
12 Maloney, C.	N	N	?	N	N	Y	Y
13 Espaillat	N	N	N	Y	N	Y	Y
14 Crowley	N	N	N	Y	N	Y	Y
15 Serrano	N	N	N	Y	N	Y	Y
16 Engel	N	N	N	Y	N	Y	Y
17 Lowey	N	N	N	Y	N	Y	Y
18 Maloney, S.P.	N	N	N	Y	N	Y	Y
19 **Faso**	Y	N	N	N	N	N	N
20 Tonko	N	N	N	Y	N	Y	Y
21 **Stefanik**	Y	N	N	N	N	N	N
22 **Tenney**	Y	N	N	N	N	N	N
23 **Reed**	Y	N	N	N	N	N	N
24 **Katko**	Y	N	N	N	N	Y	Y
25 Slaughter	N	N	N	Y	N	Y	Y
26 Higgins	N	N	N	Y	N	Y	Y
27 **Collins**	Y	N	N	N	Y	N	N
NORTH CAROLINA							
1 Butterfield	N	N	N	Y	N	Y	Y
2 **Holding**	Y	N	N	N	Y	N	N
3 **Jones**	N	N	N	N	Y	N	N
4 Price	N	N	N	Y	N	Y	Y

	415	416	417	418	419	420	421
5 **Foxx**	Y	N	N	N	Y	N	N
6 **Walker**	Y	N	N	N	Y	N	N
7 **Rouzer**	Y	Y	Y	N	Y	N	N
8 **Hudson**	Y	Y	Y	N	Y	N	N
9 **Pittenger**	Y	Y	Y	N	Y	N	N
10 **McHenry**	Y	N	N	N	Y	N	N
11 **Meadows**	Y	Y	Y	N	Y	N	N
12 Adams	N	N	N	Y	N	Y	Y
13 **Budd**	Y	Y	Y	N	Y	N	N
NORTH DAKOTA							
AL **Cramer**	Y	Y	Y	N	Y	N	N
OHIO							
1 **Chabot**	Y	Y	Y	N	Y	N	N
2 **Wenstrup**	Y	Y	Y	N	Y	N	N
3 Beatty	N	N	N	Y	N	N	Y
4 **Jordan**	Y	Y	Y	N	Y	N	N
5 **Latta**	Y	Y	Y	N	Y	N	N
6 **Johnson**	Y	N	N	N	N	N	N
7 **Gibbs**	Y	Y	Y	N	Y	N	N
8 **Davidson**	Y	Y	Y	N	Y	N	N
9 Kaptur	N	N	N	Y	N	N	N
10 **Turner**	Y	N	N	N	N	N	N
11 Fudge	N	N	N	Y	N	Y	Y
12 **Tiberi**	Y	N	N	N	N	N	N
13 Ryan	N	–	–	Y	N	Y	Y
14 **Joyce**	Y	N	N	N	N	N	N
15 **Stivers**	Y	N	N	N	N	N	N
16 **Renacci**	Y	Y	Y	N	N	N	N
OKLAHOMA							
1 **Bridenstine**	Y	Y	Y	N	Y	N	N
2 **Mullin**	Y	Y	Y	N	Y	N	N
3 **Lucas**	Y	Y	Y	N	Y	N	N
4 **Cole**	Y	N	N	N	Y	N	N
5 **Russell**	Y	N	N	Y	Y	N	N
OREGON							
1 Bonamici	N	N	N	Y	N	Y	Y
2 **Walden**	Y	N	N	N	N	N	N
3 Blumenauer	N	N	N	Y	N	Y	Y
4 DeFazio	N	N	N	Y	N	Y	Y
5 Schrader	N	N	N	N	N	Y	Y
PENNSYLVANIA							
1 Brady	N	N	N	N	N	Y	Y
2 Evans	N	N	N	Y	N	Y	Y
3 **Kelly**	Y	N	N	N	N	N	N
4 **Perry**	Y	Y	Y	N	Y	N	N
5 **Thompson**	Y	N	N	N	Y	N	N
6 **Costello**	Y	–	–	–	–	–	–
7 **Meehan**	Y	N	N	N	N	N	N
8 **Fitzpatrick**	Y	N	N	N	N	Y	Y
9 **Shuster**	Y	N	N	N	N	N	N
10 **Marino**	Y	Y	N	N	N	N	N
11 **Barletta**	Y	N	N	N	N	N	N
12 **Rothfus**	Y	Y	Y	N	Y	N	N
13 Boyle	N	N	N	Y	N	Y	Y
14 Doyle	N	N	N	Y	N	N	N
15 **Dent**	Y	N	N	N	Y	N	N
16 **Smucker**	Y	N	N	N	Y	N	N
17 Cartwright	N	N	N	Y	N	Y	Y
18 **Murphy**	Y	+	Y	N	N	N	N
RHODE ISLAND							
1 Cicilline	N	N	N	Y	N	Y	Y
2 Langevin	N	N	N	Y	N	Y	Y
SOUTH CAROLINA							
1 **Sanford**	Y	N	N	N	Y	Y	Y
2 **Wilson**	Y	Y	Y	N	Y	N	N
3 **Duncan**	Y	Y	Y	N	Y	N	N
4 **Gowdy**	Y	Y	Y	N	Y	N	N
5 **Norman**	Y	Y	Y	Y	Y	N	N
6 Clyburn	N	N	N	Y	N	Y	Y
7 **Rice**	Y	N	N	N	Y	N	Y
SOUTH DAKOTA							
AL **Noem**	Y	N	N	N	Y	N	N
TENNESSEE							
1 **Roe**	Y	N	N	N	Y	N	N
2 **Duncan**	Y	Y	Y	N	Y	N	N
3 **Fleischmann**	Y	N	N	N	Y	N	N
4 **DesJarlais**	Y	Y	Y	N	Y	N	N
5 Cooper	N	N	N	Y	N	Y	Y
6 **Black**	Y	N	N	N	Y	N	N
7 **Blackburn**	Y	Y	Y	N	Y	N	N
8 **Kustoff**	Y	N	N	N	Y	N	N
9 Cohen	N	N	N	Y	N	Y	Y

	415	416	417	418	419	420	421
TEXAS							
1 **Gohmert**	Y	Y	Y	N	Y	N	N
2 **Poe**	Y	Y	Y	N	Y	N	N
3 **Johnson, S.**	Y	Y	Y	N	Y	N	N
4 **Ratcliffe**	Y	Y	Y	N	Y	N	N
5 **Hensarling**	Y	Y	Y	N	Y	N	N
6 **Barton**	Y	Y	Y	N	Y	N	N
7 **Culberson**	Y	Y	N	N	Y	N	N
8 **Brady**	Y	N	N	N	Y	N	N
9 Green, A.	N	N	N	Y	N	Y	Y
10 **McCaul**	Y	Y	Y	Y	Y	N	N
11 **Conaway**	Y	N	N	N	Y	N	N
12 **Granger**	Y	N	N	Y	Y	N	N
13 **Thornberry**	Y	N	N	N	Y	N	N
14 **Weber**	Y	Y	Y	N	Y	N	N
15 Gonzalez	N	N	N	Y	N	N	N
16 O'Rourke	N	N	N	Y	N	Y	Y
17 **Flores**	Y	Y	Y	N	Y	N	N
18 Jackson Lee	N	N	N	Y	N	Y	Y
19 **Arrington**	Y	N	N	N	Y	N	N
20 Castro	N	N	N	Y	N	Y	Y
21 **Smith**	Y	N	N	Y	Y	N	N
22 **Olson**	Y	Y	Y	N	Y	N	N
23 **Hurd**	Y	N	N	N	Y	N	N
24 **Marchant**	Y	Y	Y	Y	Y	N	N
25 **Williams**	Y	Y	Y	N	Y	N	N
26 **Burgess**	Y	Y	Y	N	Y	N	N
27 **Farenthold**	Y	Y	Y	Y	Y	N	N
28 Cuellar	N	N	N	Y	N	N	N
29 Green, G.	N	N	N	N	N	N	N
30 Johnson, E.B.	N	N	N	Y	N	Y	Y
31 **Carter**	Y	N	N	N	Y	N	N
32 **Sessions**	Y	N	N	N	Y	N	N
33 Veasey	N	N	N	Y	N	N	Y
34 Vela	N	N	N	Y	N	Y	Y
35 Doggett	N	N	N	Y	N	Y	Y
36 **Babin**	Y	Y	Y	N	Y	N	N
UTAH							
1 **Bishop**	Y	Y	Y	N	Y	N	N
2 **Stewart**	Y	Y	Y	N	Y	N	N
4 **Love**	Y	Y	Y	N	Y	N	N
VERMONT							
AL Welch	N	N	N	Y	N	Y	Y
VIRGINIA							
1 **Wittman**	Y	Y	Y	N	Y	N	N
2 **Taylor**	Y	N	Y	N	Y	N	N
3 Scott	N	N	N	Y	N	Y	Y
4 McEachin	N	N	N	Y	N	Y	Y
5 **Garrett**	Y	Y	Y	N	Y	N	N
6 **Goodlatte**	Y	Y	Y	N	Y	N	N
7 **Brat**	Y	Y	Y	N	Y	N	N
8 Beyer	N	N	N	Y	N	Y	Y
9 **Griffith**	Y	Y	Y	N	Y	N	N
10 **Comstock**	Y	N	N	N	Y	N	N
11 Connolly	N	N	N	Y	N	Y	Y
WASHINGTON							
1 DelBene	N	N	N	Y	N	Y	Y
2 Larsen	N	N	N	Y	N	N	Y
3 **Herrera Beutler**	Y	N	N	N	Y	N	N
4 **Newhouse**	Y	N	N	N	N	N	N
5 **McMorris Rodgers**	Y	N	N	N	Y	N	N
6 Kilmer	N	N	N	Y	N	Y	Y
7 Jayapal	N	N	N	Y	N	Y	Y
8 **Reichert**	Y	N	N	N	N	Y	Y
9 Smith	N	N	N	Y	N	Y	Y
10 Heck	N	N	N	Y	N	Y	Y
WEST VIRGINIA							
1 **McKinley**	Y	Y	Y	N	N	N	N
2 **Mooney**	Y	Y	Y	N	Y	N	N
3 **Jenkins**	Y	Y	Y	N	N	N	N
WISCONSIN							
1 **Ryan**							
2 Pocan	N	N	N	Y	N	Y	Y
3 Kind	N	N	N	Y	N	Y	Y
4 Moore	N	N	N	Y	N	Y	Y
5 **Sensenbrenner**	Y	Y	Y	N	Y	N	N
6 **Grothman**	Y	Y	Y	N	Y	N	N
7 **Duffy**	Y	Y	Y	N	N	N	N
8 **Gallagher**	Y	Y	Y	N	Y	N	N
WYOMING							
AL **Cheney**	Y	Y	Y	N	Y	N	N

VOTE NUMBER

422. HR 3219. FISCAL 2018 MINIBUS APPROPRIATIONS/RENEWABLE ENERGY RESEARCH EXPANSION. Esty, D-Conn., amendment that would increase by $20 million funding for facility acquisition, construction or expansion in the Office of Energy Efficiency and Renewable Energy, and would reduce by $40 million funding to the Fossil Energy Research and Development account. Rejected in Committee of the Whole 203-224 : R 21-215; D 182-9. July 26, 2017.

423. HR 3219. FISCAL 2018 MINIBUS APPROPRIATIONS/NUCLEAR NON-PROLIFERATION PRIORITIZATION. Garamendi, D-Calif., amendment that would increase by $118 million funding to the National Nuclear Security Administration defense nuclear nonproliferation account, and would decrease funding for weapons activities at National Nuclear Security Administration by the same amount. Rejected in Committee of the Whole 180-247 : R 1-235; D 179-12. July 26, 2017.

424. HR 3219. FISCAL 2018 MINIBUS APPROPRIATIONS/COASTAL AND MARINE PLANNING ALLOWANCE. Pingree, D-Maine, amendment that would eliminate the bill's provision that would prohibit funding made available by the bill from being used to further implement the coastal and marine spatial planning and ecosystem-based management components of the National Ocean Policy developed under a 2010 executive order. Rejected in Committee of the Whole 192-235 : R 3-233; D 189-2. July 26, 2017.

425. HR 3219. FISCAL 2018 MINIBUS APPROPRIATIONS/CORPS CIVIL INVESTIGATIONS. Jackson Lee, D-Texas, amendment that would reduce by $3 million, and increase by the same amount, funding to the Army Corps of Engineers Investigations account. Adopted in Committee of the Whole 234-192 : R 51-185; D 183-7. July 26, 2017.

426. H RES 478, HR 3219. FISCAL 2018 MINIBUS APPROPRIATIONS/PREVIOUS QUESTION. Newhouse, R-Wash., motion to order the previous question (thus limiting debate and possibility of amendment) on the rule (H Res 478) that would provide for further House floor consideration of the bill making certain appropriations for fiscal 2018 (HR 3219), would provide for consideration of amendments to the Defense division of the bill, and would provide for consideration of motions to suspend the rules through July 28, 2017. Motion agreed to 233-185 : R 233-1; D 0-184. July 27, 2017.

427. H RES 478, HR 3219. FISCAL 2018 MINIBUS APPROPRIATIONS/RULE. Adoption of the rule (H Res 478) that would provide for further House floor consideration of the bill that would make certain appropriations for fiscal 2018 (HR 3219), would provide for consideration of amendments to the Defense division of the bill; and would provide for consideration of motions to suspend the rules through the legislative day of July 28, 2017. The rule would also automatically modify the fiscal 2018 minibus to include an amendment that would provide $1.6 billion in funding to U.S. Customs and Border Protection for procurement, construction and improvement of a barrier along the southern U.S. border. Adopted 230-196 : R 230-5; D 0-191. July 27, 2017.

428. HR 3219. FISCAL 2018 MINIBUS APPROPRIATIONS/ENERGY AND WATER DIVISION REDUCTION. Blackburn, R-Tenn., amendment that would reduce by one percent all discretionary spending provided for in the Energy and Water division of the bill. Rejected in Committee of the Whole 140-285 : R 139-96; D 1-189. July 27, 2017.

	422	423	424	425	426	427	428
ALABAMA							
1 Byrne	N	N	N	N	Y	Y	N
2 Roby	N	N	N	N	Y	Y	N
3 Rogers	N	N	N	N	?	Y	N
4 Aderholt	N	N	N	N	Y	Y	N
5 Brooks	Y	N	N	N	Y	Y	N
6 Palmer	N	N	N	N	Y	Y	Y
7 Sewell	Y	Y	Y	N	N	N	N
ALASKA							
AL Young	N	N	N	N	Y	Y	N
ARIZONA							
1 O'Halleran	Y	N	Y	N	N	N	N
2 McSally	N	N	N	Y	Y	Y	Y
3 Grijalva	Y	Y	Y	Y	N	N	N
4 Gosar	N	N	N	N	Y	Y	Y
5 Biggs	N	N	N	N	Y	Y	Y
6 Schweikert	N	N	N	N	Y	Y	Y
7 Gallego	Y	Y	Y	N	N	N	N
8 Franks	N	N	N	N	Y	Y	N
9 Sinema	Y	N	Y	N	N	N	N
ARKANSAS							
1 Crawford	N	N	N	N	Y	Y	Y
2 Hill	N	N	N	N	Y	Y	N
3 Womack	N	N	N	N	Y	Y	N
4 Westerman	N	N	N	N	Y	Y	Y
CALIFORNIA							
1 LaMalfa	N	N	N	N	Y	Y	Y
2 Huffman	Y	Y	Y	N	N	N	N
3 Garamendi	Y	Y	Y	Y	N	N	N
4 McClintock	N	N	N	N	Y	Y	Y
5 Thompson	Y	Y	Y	N	N	N	N
6 Matsui	Y	Y	Y	N	N	N	N
7 Bera	Y	Y	Y	N	N	N	N
8 Cook	N	N	N	N	Y	Y	N
9 McNerney	Y	Y	Y	N	N	N	N
10 Denham	N	N	N	N	Y	Y	N
11 DeSaulnier	Y	Y	Y	N	N	N	N
12 Pelosi	Y	Y	Y	?	N	N	N
13 Lee	Y	Y	Y	N	N	N	N
14 Speier	Y	Y	Y	–	N	N	N
15 Swalwell	Y	N	Y	N	N	N	N
16 Costa	Y	Y	Y	N	N	N	N
17 Khanna	Y	Y	Y	N	N	N	N
18 Eshoo	Y	Y	Y	N	N	N	N
19 Lofgren	Y	Y	Y	N	N	N	N
20 Panetta	Y	Y	Y	N	N	N	N
21 Valadao	N	N	N	N	Y	Y	N
22 Nunes	N	N	N	N	Y	Y	N
23 McCarthy	N	N	N	N	Y	Y	Y
24 Carbajal	Y	Y	Y	N	N	N	N
25 Knight	N	N	N	N	Y	Y	N
26 Brownley	Y	Y	Y	N	N	N	N
27 Chu	Y	Y	Y	N	N	N	N
28 Schiff	Y	Y	Y	Y	N	N	N
29 Cardenas	Y	Y	Y	N	N	N	N
30 Sherman	Y	Y	Y	N	N	N	N
31 Aguilar	Y	Y	Y	N	N	N	N
32 Napolitano	+	+	+	+	–	–	–
33 Lieu	Y	Y	Y	N	N	N	N
34 Gomez	Y	Y	Y	N	N	N	N
35 Torres	Y	Y	Y	?	N	N	N
36 Ruiz	Y	Y	Y	N	N	N	N
37 Bass	Y	Y	Y	N	N	N	N
38 Sánchez, Linda	Y	Y	Y	N	N	N	N
39 Royce	N	N	N	N	Y	Y	Y
40 Roybal-Allard	Y	Y	Y	N	N	N	N
41 Takano	Y	Y	Y	N	N	N	N
42 Calvert	N	N	N	N	Y	Y	N
43 Waters	Y	Y	Y	N	N	N	N
44 Barragan	Y	Y	Y	N	N	N	N
45 Walters	N	N	N	N	Y	Y	N
46 Correa	N	Y	Y	N	N	N	N
47 Lowenthal	Y	Y	Y	N	N	N	N
48 Rohrabacher	N	N	N	N	Y	Y	N
49 Issa	N	N	N	N	Y	?	Y
50 Hunter	N	N	N	N	Y	Y	N
51 Vargas	Y	Y	Y	N	N	N	N
52 Peters	Y	Y	Y	N	N	N	N
53 Davis	Y	Y	Y	Y	N	N	N

	422	423	424	425	426	427	428
COLORADO							
1 DeGette	Y	Y	Y	Y	N	N	N
2 Polis	Y	Y	Y	Y	N	N	N
3 Tipton	N	N	N	Y	Y	Y	N
4 Buck	N	N	N	N	Y	Y	Y
5 Lamborn	N	N	N	N	Y	Y	Y
6 Coffman	Y	N	Y	Y	Y	Y	N
7 Perlmutter	Y	Y	Y	N	N	N	N
CONNECTICUT							
1 Larson	Y	Y	Y	N	N	N	N
2 Courtney	Y	Y	Y	N	N	N	N
3 DeLauro	Y	Y	Y	N	N	N	N
4 Himes	Y	Y	Y	N	N	N	N
5 Esty	Y	Y	Y	N	N	N	N
DELAWARE							
AL Blunt Rochester	Y	Y	Y	N	N	N	N
FLORIDA							
1 Gaetz	N	N	N	N	Y	Y	N
2 Dunn	N	N	N	N	Y	Y	Y
3 Yoho	N	N	N	N	Y	Y	Y
4 Rutherford	N	N	N	N	Y	Y	N
5 Lawson	Y	Y	Y	N	N	N	N
6 DeSantis	N	N	N	Y	Y	Y	Y
7 Murphy	Y	Y	Y	Y	N	N	N
8 Posey	N	N	N	N	Y	Y	N
9 Soto	Y	Y	Y	N	N	N	N
10 Demings	Y	Y	Y	N	N	N	N
11 Webster	N	N	N	N	Y	Y	Y
12 Bilirakis	N	N	N	N	Y	Y	N
13 Crist	Y	N	Y	N	N	N	N
14 Castor	Y	Y	Y	N	N	N	N
15 Ross	N	N	N	N	Y	Y	N
16 Buchanan	N	N	N	N	Y	Y	N
17 Rooney, T.	N	N	N	N	Y	Y	N
18 Mast	Y	N	N	N	Y	Y	Y
19 Rooney, F.	N	N	N	N	Y	Y	Y
20 Hastings	Y	Y	Y	N	N	N	N
21 Frankel	Y	Y	Y	N	N	N	N
22 Deutch	Y	Y	Y	N	N	N	N
23 Wasserman Schultz	Y	Y	Y	N	N	N	N
24 Wilson	Y	Y	Y	N	N	N	N
25 Diaz-Balart	N	N	N	Y	Y	Y	N
26 Curbelo	N	N	N	Y	Y	Y	N
27 Ros-Lehtinen	N	N	N	Y	Y	Y	N
GEORGIA							
1 Carter	N	N	N	N	Y	Y	Y
2 Bishop	Y	Y	Y	N	N	N	N
3 Ferguson	N	N	N	N	Y	Y	Y
4 Johnson	Y	Y	Y	N	N	N	N
5 Lewis	Y	Y	Y	N	N	N	N
6 Handel	N	N	N	N	Y	Y	Y
7 Woodall	N	N	N	N	Y	Y	Y
8 Scott, A.	N	N	N	N	Y	Y	N
9 Collins	N	N	Y	?	Y	Y	Y
10 Hice	N	N	N	N	Y	Y	Y
11 Loudermilk	N	N	N	N	Y	Y	Y
12 Allen	N	N	N	N	Y	Y	Y
13 Scott, D.	Y	Y	Y	N	N	N	N
14 Graves	N	N	N	N	Y	Y	N
HAWAII							
1 Hanabusa	Y	Y	Y	N	N	N	N
2 Gabbard	Y	Y	Y	N	N	N	N
IDAHO							
1 Labrador	N	N	N	N	Y	Y	Y
2 Simpson	N	N	N	Y	Y	Y	N
ILLINOIS							
1 Rush	Y	Y	Y	?	N	N	N
2 Kelly	Y	Y	Y	N	N	N	N
3 Lipinski	Y	Y	Y	N	N	N	N
4 Gutierrez	Y	Y	Y	N	N	N	N
5 Quigley	Y	Y	Y	N	N	N	N
6 Roskam	N	N	N	N	?	?	?
7 Davis, D.	Y	Y	Y	N	N	N	N
8 Krishnamoorthi	Y	Y	Y	N	N	N	N
9 Schakowsky	Y	Y	Y	N	N	N	N
10 Schneider	Y	Y	Y	N	N	N	N
11 Foster	Y	Y	Y	N	N	N	N
12 Bost	N	N	N	N	Y	Y	N
13 Davis, R.	N	N	N	N	Y	Y	?
14 Hultgren	N	N	N	N	Y	Y	N
15 Shimkus	N	N	N	N	Y	Y	N

	422	423	424	425	426	427	428
16 **Kinzinger**	N	N	N	Y	Y	Y	N
17 Bustos	Y	Y	Y	Y	N	N	N
18 **LaHood**	N	N	N	N	Y	Y	Y
INDIANA							
1 Visclosky	Y	Y	Y	Y	N	N	N
2 **Walorski**	N	N	N	Y	Y	Y	Y
3 **Banks**	N	N	N	N	Y	Y	Y
4 **Rokita**	N	N	N	N	Y	Y	Y
5 **Brooks**	N	N	N	Y	Y	Y	Y
6 **Messer**	N	N	N	N	Y	Y	Y
7 Carson	Y	Y	Y	Y	N	N	N
8 **Bucshon**	N	N	N	N	Y	Y	Y
9 **Hollingsworth**	?	?	?	?	?	?	?
IOWA							
1 **Blum**	Y	N	N	N	Y	Y	Y
2 Loebsack	Y	Y	Y	Y	N	N	N
3 **Young**	Y	N	N	Y	Y	Y	Y
4 **King**	Y	N	N	N	Y	Y	Y
KANSAS							
1 **Marshall**	N	N	N	N	Y	Y	Y
2 **Jenkins**	N	N	N	N	Y	Y	Y
3 **Yoder**	N	N	N	N	Y	Y	N
4 **Estes**	N	N	N	N	Y	Y	Y
KENTUCKY							
1 **Comer**	N	N	N	N	Y	Y	Y
2 **Guthrie**	N	N	N	N	Y	Y	Y
3 Yarmuth	Y	Y	Y	Y	N	N	N
4 **Massie**	N	N	N	N	Y	N	Y
5 **Rogers**	N	N	N	N	Y	Y	N
6 **Barr**	N	N	N	N	Y	Y	N
LOUISIANA							
1 **Scalise**	–	–	–	+	+	+	+
2 Richmond	N	Y	Y	N	N	N	N
3 **Higgins**	N	N	N	N	Y	Y	N
4 **Johnson**	N	N	N	Y	Y	Y	N
5 **Abraham**	N	N	N	Y	Y	Y	N
6 **Graves**	N	N	N	Y	Y	Y	Y
MAINE							
1 Pingree	Y	Y	Y	Y	N	N	N
2 **Poliquin**	Y	N	Y	N	Y	Y	Y
MARYLAND							
1 **Harris**	N	N	N	N	Y	Y	Y
2 Ruppersberger	Y	N	Y	Y	N	N	N
3 Sarbanes	Y	Y	Y	Y	?	N	P
4 Brown	Y	Y	Y	Y	N	N	N
5 Hoyer	Y	N	Y	Y	N	N	N
6 Delaney	Y	Y	Y	Y	N	N	N
7 Cummings	?	?	?	?	?	?	?
8 Raskin	Y	Y	Y	Y	N	N	N
MASSACHUSETTS							
1 Neal	Y	Y	Y	Y	N	N	N
2 McGovern	Y	Y	Y	Y	N	N	N
3 Tsongas	Y	Y	Y	Y	N	N	N
4 Kennedy	Y	Y	Y	Y	N	N	N
5 Clark	Y	Y	Y	Y	N	N	N
6 Moulton	Y	Y	Y	Y	N	N	N
7 Capuano	Y	Y	Y	Y	N	N	N
8 Lynch	Y	Y	Y	Y	N	N	N
9 Keating	Y	Y	Y	Y	N	N	N
MICHIGAN							
1 **Bergman**	N	N	N	N	Y	Y	N
2 **Huizenga**	N	N	N	N	Y	Y	Y
3 **Amash**	Y	Y	N	N	Y	N	Y
4 **Moolenaar**	N	N	N	N	Y	Y	N
5 Kildee	Y	Y	Y	Y	N	N	N
6 **Upton**	Y	N	N	Y	Y	Y	Y
7 **Walberg**	N	N	N	N	Y	Y	Y
8 **Bishop**	N	N	N	N	Y	Y	N
9 Levin	Y	Y	Y	Y	N	N	N
10 **Mitchell**	N	N	N	N	Y	Y	Y
11 **Trott**	N	N	N	Y	Y	Y	N
12 Dingell	Y	Y	Y	Y	N	N	N
13 Conyers	Y	Y	Y	Y	N	N	N
14 Lawrence	Y	Y	Y	Y	N	N	N
MINNESOTA							
1 Walz	Y	Y	Y	Y	N	N	N
2 **Lewis**	N	N	N	N	Y	Y	Y
3 **Paulsen**	N	N	N	Y	Y	Y	Y
4 McCollum	Y	Y	Y	Y	N	N	N
5 Ellison	Y	Y	Y	Y	N	N	N
6 **Emmer**	N	N	N	N	Y	Y	N
7 Peterson	N	N	N	N	N	N	N
8 Nolan	Y	Y	Y	Y	?	N	N
MISSISSIPPI							
1 **Kelly**	N	N	N	N	Y	Y	Y
2 Thompson	Y	Y	Y	Y	N	N	N
3 **Harper**	N	N	N	N	Y	Y	N
4 **Palazzo**	N	N	N	N	Y	Y	Y
MISSOURI							
1 Clay	Y	Y	Y	Y	N	N	N
2 **Wagner**	N	N	N	Y	Y	Y	Y
3 **Luetkemeyer**	N	N	N	N	Y	Y	N
4 **Hartzler**	N	N	N	Y	Y	Y	N
5 Cleaver	Y	Y	Y	Y	N	N	N
6 **Graves**	N	N	N	N	Y	Y	N
7 **Long**	N	N	N	N	Y	Y	Y
8 **Smith**	N	N	N	N	Y	Y	Y
MONTANA							
AL **Gianforte**	N	N	N	N	Y	Y	N
NEBRASKA							
1 **Fortenberry**	Y	N	Y	Y	Y	Y	N
2 **Bacon**	Y	N	N	N	Y	Y	N
3 **Smith**	N	N	N	N	Y	Y	Y
NEVADA							
1 Titus	Y	Y	Y	Y	N	N	N
2 **Amodei**	N	N	N	N	Y	Y	N
3 Rosen	Y	Y	Y	Y	N	N	N
4 Kihuen	Y	Y	Y	Y	N	N	N
NEW HAMPSHIRE							
1 Shea-Porter	Y	Y	Y	Y	N	N	N
2 Kuster	Y	Y	Y	Y	N	N	N
NEW JERSEY							
1 Norcross	Y	Y	Y	Y	N	N	N
2 **LoBiondo**	Y	N	N	Y	Y	Y	N
3 **MacArthur**	N	N	N	Y	Y	Y	N
4 **Smith**	Y	N	N	N	Y	Y	N
5 Gottheimer	Y	N	Y	N	N	N	N
6 Pallone	Y	Y	Y	Y	N	N	N
7 **Lance**	N	N	N	N	Y	Y	Y
8 Sires	Y	Y	Y	Y	N	N	N
9 Pascrell	Y	Y	Y	Y	?	N	N
10 Payne	Y	Y	Y	Y	N	N	N
11 **Frelinghuysen**	N	N	N	N	Y	Y	N
12 Watson Coleman	Y	Y	Y	Y	N	N	N
NEW MEXICO							
1 Lujan Grisham	Y	N	Y	Y	N	N	N
2 **Pearce**	N	N	N	N	Y	N	N
3 Luján	Y	N	Y	Y	N	N	N
NEW YORK							
1 **Zeldin**	N	N	N	N	Y	Y	Y
2 **King**	N	N	N	Y	Y	Y	N
3 Suozzi	Y	Y	Y	Y	N	N	N
4 Rice	Y	Y	Y	Y	N	N	N
5 Meeks	Y	Y	Y	Y	N	N	N
6 Meng	Y	Y	Y	Y	N	N	N
7 Velázquez	Y	Y	Y	Y	N	N	N
8 Jeffries	?	?	?	?	N	N	N
9 Clarke	Y	Y	Y	Y	N	N	N
10 Nadler	Y	Y	Y	Y	N	N	N
11 **Donovan**	N	N	N	Y	Y	Y	N
12 Maloney, C.	Y	Y	Y	Y	N	N	N
13 Espaillat	Y	Y	Y	Y	N	N	N
14 Crowley	Y	Y	Y	Y	N	N	N
15 Serrano	Y	Y	Y	Y	N	N	N
16 Engel	Y	Y	Y	Y	N	N	N
17 Lowey	Y	Y	Y	Y	–	N	N
18 Maloney, S.P.	Y	N	Y	N	N	N	N
19 **Faso**	N	N	N	Y	Y	Y	N
20 Tonko	Y	Y	Y	Y	N	N	N
21 **Stefanik**	Y	N	N	N	Y	Y	N
22 **Tenney**	N	N	N	Y	Y	Y	N
23 **Reed**	Y	N	N	N	Y	Y	N
24 **Katko**	Y	N	N	Y	Y	Y	N
25 Slaughter	Y	Y	Y	Y	N	N	N
26 Higgins	Y	Y	Y	Y	N	N	N
27 **Collins**	N	N	N	N	Y	Y	N
NORTH CAROLINA							
1 Butterfield	Y	Y	Y	Y	N	N	N
2 **Holding**	N	N	N	N	Y	Y	Y
3 **Jones**	N	N	N	N	N	N	Y
4 Price	Y	Y	Y	Y	N	N	N
5 **Foxx**	N	N	N	N	Y	Y	Y
6 **Walker**	N	N	N	Y	Y	Y	Y
7 **Rouzer**	N	N	N	N	Y	Y	Y
8 **Hudson**	N	N	N	N	Y	Y	Y
9 **Pittenger**	N	N	N	N	Y	Y	N
10 **McHenry**	N	N	N	N	Y	Y	Y
11 **Meadows**	N	N	N	N	Y	Y	Y
12 Adams	Y	Y	Y	Y	N	N	N
13 **Budd**	N	N	N	N	Y	Y	Y
NORTH DAKOTA							
AL **Cramer**	N	N	N	N	Y	Y	Y
OHIO							
1 **Chabot**	N	N	N	N	Y	Y	Y
2 **Wenstrup**	N	N	N	N	Y	Y	Y
3 Beatty	N	Y	Y	Y	N	N	N
4 **Jordan**	N	N	N	N	Y	Y	Y
5 **Latta**	N	N	N	N	Y	Y	Y
6 **Johnson**	N	N	N	N	Y	Y	Y
7 **Gibbs**	N	N	N	N	Y	Y	Y
8 **Davidson**	N	N	N	N	Y	Y	Y
9 Kaptur	Y	Y	Y	Y	N	N	N
10 **Turner**	N	N	N	N	Y	Y	N
11 Fudge	N	Y	Y	N	N	N	N
12 **Tiberi**	N	N	N	N	Y	Y	N
13 Ryan	Y	Y	Y	Y	–	–	–
14 **Joyce**	N	N	N	N	Y	Y	N
15 **Stivers**	N	N	N	Y	Y	Y	N
16 **Renacci**	N	N	N	N	Y	Y	N
OKLAHOMA							
1 **Bridenstine**	N	N	N	N	Y	Y	Y
2 **Mullin**	N	N	N	N	Y	Y	Y
3 **Lucas**	N	N	N	N	Y	Y	Y
4 **Cole**	N	N	N	N	Y	Y	N
5 **Russell**	N	N	N	N	Y	Y	Y
OREGON							
1 Bonamici	Y	Y	Y	Y	N	N	N
2 **Walden**	N	N	N	N	Y	Y	N
3 Blumenauer	Y	Y	Y	Y	N	N	N
4 DeFazio	Y	Y	Y	Y	N	N	N
5 Schrader	Y	Y	Y	Y	N	N	N
PENNSYLVANIA							
1 Brady	Y	Y	Y	Y	N	N	N
2 Evans	Y	Y	Y	Y	N	N	N
3 **Kelly**	N	N	N	N	Y	Y	N
4 **Perry**	N	N	N	N	Y	Y	Y
5 **Thompson**	N	N	N	N	Y	Y	N
6 **Costello**	–	–	–	+	Y	Y	N
7 **Meehan**	N	N	N	Y	Y	Y	N
8 **Fitzpatrick**	Y	N	Y	Y	Y	Y	N
9 **Shuster**	N	N	N	N	Y	Y	Y
10 **Marino**	N	N	N	N	Y	Y	N
11 **Barletta**	N	N	N	N	Y	Y	N
12 **Rothfus**	N	N	N	N	Y	Y	Y
13 Boyle	Y	Y	Y	Y	N	N	N
14 Doyle	Y	Y	Y	Y	N	N	N
15 **Dent**	N	N	N	Y	Y	Y	N
16 **Smucker**	N	N	N	N	Y	Y	N
17 Cartwright	Y	Y	Y	Y	N	N	N
18 **Murphy**	N	N	N	N	Y	Y	N
RHODE ISLAND							
1 Cicilline	Y	Y	Y	Y	N	N	N
2 Langevin	Y	Y	Y	Y	N	N	N
SOUTH CAROLINA							
1 **Sanford**	Y	N	N	N	Y	Y	Y
2 **Wilson**	N	N	N	N	Y	Y	N
3 **Duncan**	N	N	N	N	Y	Y	Y
4 **Gowdy**	N	N	N	N	Y	Y	Y
5 **Norman**	N	N	N	N	Y	Y	Y
6 Clyburn	Y	Y	Y	Y	N	N	N
7 **Rice**	Y	N	N	Y	Y	Y	Y
SOUTH DAKOTA							
AL **Noem**	N	N	N	N	Y	Y	N
TENNESSEE							
1 **Roe**	N	N	N	N	Y	Y	Y
2 **Duncan**	N	N	N	N	Y	Y	Y
3 **Fleischmann**	N	N	N	N	Y	Y	N
4 **DesJarlais**	N	N	N	N	Y	Y	Y
5 Cooper	Y	N	Y	Y	N	N	N
6 **Black**	N	N	N	N	Y	Y	Y
7 **Blackburn**	N	N	N	N	Y	Y	Y
8 **Kustoff**	N	N	N	N	Y	Y	Y
9 Cohen	Y	Y	Y	Y	N	N	N
TEXAS							
1 **Gohmert**	N	N	N	N	Y	Y	Y
2 **Poe**	N	N	N	Y	Y	Y	Y
3 **Johnson, S.**	N	N	N	N	Y	Y	Y
4 **Ratcliffe**	N	N	N	N	Y	Y	Y
5 **Hensarling**	N	N	N	N	Y	Y	Y
6 **Barton**	N	N	N	N	Y	Y	Y
7 **Culberson**	N	N	N	Y	Y	Y	Y
8 **Brady**	N	N	N	N	Y	Y	Y
9 Green, A.	Y	Y	Y	Y	N	N	N
10 **McCaul**	N	N	N	Y	Y	Y	Y
11 **Conaway**	N	N	N	N	Y	Y	Y
12 **Granger**	N	N	N	Y	Y	Y	N
13 **Thornberry**	N	N	N	N	Y	Y	N
14 **Weber**	N	N	N	Y	Y	Y	Y
15 Gonzalez	N	Y	N	Y	N	N	N
16 O'Rourke	Y	Y	Y	Y	N	N	N
17 **Flores**	N	N	N	Y	Y	Y	Y
18 Jackson Lee	Y	Y	Y	Y	N	N	N
19 **Arrington**	N	N	N	N	Y	Y	N
20 Castro	Y	Y	Y	Y	N	N	N
21 **Smith**	N	N	N	Y	Y	Y	N
22 **Olson**	N	N	N	Y	Y	Y	Y
23 **Hurd**	N	N	N	Y	Y	N	Y
24 **Marchant**	N	N	N	Y	Y	Y	Y
25 **Williams**	N	N	N	N	Y	Y	Y
26 **Burgess**	N	N	N	N	Y	Y	Y
27 **Farenthold**	N	N	N	Y	Y	Y	Y
28 Cuellar	N	Y	Y	Y	N	N	N
29 Green, G.	N	Y	Y	Y	N	N	N
30 Johnson, E.B.	Y	Y	Y	Y	N	N	N
31 **Carter**	N	N	N	N	Y	Y	N
32 **Sessions**	N	N	N	N	Y	Y	Y
33 Veasey	N	Y	Y	Y	N	N	N
34 Vela	Y	Y	Y	Y	N	N	N
35 Doggett	Y	Y	Y	Y	N	N	N
36 **Babin**	N	N	N	N	Y	Y	Y
UTAH							
1 **Bishop**	N	N	N	N	Y	Y	N
2 **Stewart**	N	N	N	N	Y	Y	Y
4 **Love**	N	N	N	N	Y	Y	Y
VERMONT							
AL Welch	Y	Y	Y	Y	N	N	N
VIRGINIA							
1 **Wittman**	N	N	N	N	Y	Y	Y
2 **Taylor**	N	N	N	N	Y	Y	N
3 Scott	Y	Y	Y	Y	N	N	N
4 McEachin	Y	Y	Y	Y	N	N	N
5 **Garrett**	N	N	N	N	Y	Y	Y
6 **Goodlatte**	N	N	N	N	Y	Y	Y
7 **Brat**	N	N	N	N	Y	Y	Y
8 Beyer	Y	Y	Y	Y	N	N	N
9 **Griffith**	N	N	N	N	Y	Y	Y
10 **Comstock**	N	N	N	N	Y	Y	N
11 Connolly	Y	Y	Y	Y	N	N	N
WASHINGTON							
1 DelBene	Y	Y	Y	Y	N	N	N
2 Larsen	Y	Y	Y	Y	N	N	N
3 **Herrera Beutler**	N	N	N	Y	Y	Y	N
4 **Newhouse**	N	N	N	N	Y	Y	N
5 **McMorris Rodgers**	N	N	N	N	Y	Y	Y
6 Kilmer	Y	Y	Y	Y	N	N	N
7 Jayapal	Y	Y	Y	Y	N	N	N
8 **Reichert**	Y	N	N	N	Y	Y	N
9 Smith	Y	Y	Y	Y	N	N	N
10 Heck	Y	Y	Y	Y	N	N	N
WEST VIRGINIA							
1 **McKinley**	N	N	N	Y	Y	Y	N
2 **Mooney**	N	N	N	Y	Y	Y	Y
3 **Jenkins**	N	N	N	Y	Y	Y	N
WISCONSIN							
1 **Ryan**							
2 Pocan	Y	Y	Y	Y	N	N	N
3 Kind	Y	Y	Y	N	N	N	N
4 Moore	Y	Y	Y	Y	N	N	N
5 **Sensenbrenner**	N	N	N	N	Y	Y	Y
6 **Grothman**	N	N	N	N	Y	Y	Y
7 **Duffy**	N	N	N	N	Y	Y	Y
8 **Gallagher**	N	N	N	N	Y	Y	N
WYOMING							
AL **Cheney**	N	N	N	N	Y	Y	N

VOTE NUMBER

429. HR 3219. FISCAL 2018 MINIBUS APPROPRIATIONS/ENERGY CONSERVATION RULE PROHIBITION. Perry, R-Pa., amendment that would prohibit funding made available by the bill from being used to implement or enforce the Energy Department rule entitled "Energy Conservation Program: Test Procedures for Central Air Conditioners and Heat Pumps," published on Jan. 5, 2017. Rejected in Committee of the Whole 177-248 : R 177-57; D 0-191. July 27, 2017.

430. HR 3219. FISCAL 2018 MINIBUS APPROPRIATIONS/NAVAL ENVIRONMENTAL RESTORATION. Suozzi, D-N.Y., amendment that would increase funding for Naval environmental restoration operations by $34.7 million, and would decrease by an equivalent amount funding for Defense Department-wide operations and maintenance. Adopted in Committee of the Whole 214-211 : R 25-209; D 189-2. July 27, 2017.

431. HR 3219. FISCAL 2018 MINIBUS APPROPRIATIONS/NAVAL AND AIR FORCE ENVIRONMENTAL RESTORATION. Boyle, D-Pa., amendment that would increase by $30 million funding for Navy environmental restoration operations, would increase by $30 million funding to Air Force environmental restoration, and would reduce by $60 million funding to Defense Department-wide operation and maintenance. Adopted in Committee of the Whole 256-169 : R 68-166; D 188-3. July 27, 2017.

432. HR 3219. FISCAL 2018 MINIBUS APPROPRIATIONS/GUANTANAMO BAY DETAINEE TRANSFER. Nadler, D-N.Y., amendment that would eliminate the bill's provision that would prohibit the use of funding made available by the bill to transfer or release, or assist in the transfer or release, to or within the U.S. of Khalid Sheikh Mohammed or any other detainee who is not a U.S. citizen and is held at Guantanamo Bay. The amendment would eliminate a provision that would prohibit funds from being used to construct, acquire or modify any facility in the U.S. to house a prisoner transferred from Guantanamo Bay. Rejected in Committee of the Whole 172-252 : R 3-230; D 169-22. July 27, 2017.

433. HR 3219. FISCAL 2018 MINIBUS APPROPRIATIONS/PUBLIC-PRIVATE COMPETITION PROHIBITION. Cartwright, D-Pa., amendment that would prohibit funding made available by the bill from being used to begin, continue, process, or approve of a public-private competition regarding converting any function performed by federal employees to contractor performance. Adopted in Committee of the Whole 253-172 : R 62-172; D 191-0. July 27, 2017.

434. HR 3219. FISCAL 2018 MINIBUS APPROPRIATIONS/RECOMMIT. Roybal-Allard, D-Calif., motion to recommit the bill to the House Appropriations Committee with instructions to report it back immediately with an amendment that would eliminate the bill's provision related to providing funding to U.S. Customs and Border Protection for procurement, construction and improvement of a barrier along the southern U.S. border. Motion rejected 193-234 : R 1-234; D 192-0. July 27, 2017.

435. HR 3219. FISCAL 2018 MINIBUS APPROPRIATIONS/PASSAGE. Passage of the bill that would provide $788 billion in discretionary funding for fiscal 2018 to various departments, agencies and legislative operations, including $658.1 billion in funding for Defense programs; $88.8 billion in net appropriations subject to discretionary caps for fiscal 2018 that would provide funding for military construction activities and for VA programs and activities; $37.6 billion in net appropriations subject to discretionary caps for fiscal 2018 that would provide funding for the Energy Department, Army Corps of Engineers, Bureau of Reclamation and related agencies; and $3.6 billion in funding fiscal 2018 for operations of the House of Representatives, joint House-Senate items and legislative branch entities such as the Library of Congress, the Capitol Police, and the Government Accountability Office. The bill would provide $1.6 billion in funding to U.S. Customs and Border Protection for procurement, construction and improvement of a barrier along the southern U.S. border. Passed 235-192 : R 230-5; D 5-187. July 27, 2017.

	429	430	431	432	433	434	435
ALABAMA							
1 Byrne	Y	N	Y	N	N	N	Y
2 Roby	Y	N	N	N	N	N	Y
3 Rogers	N	N	N	Y	N	Y	Y
4 Aderholt	Y	N	N	Y	N	N	Y
5 Brooks	Y	N	N	N	N	N	Y
6 Palmer	Y	?	?	?	?	N	Y
7 Sewell	N	Y	Y	N	Y	Y	N
ALASKA							
AL Young	Y	N	Y	N	Y	N	Y
ARIZONA							
1 O'Halleran	N	Y	Y	N	Y	Y	Y
2 McSally	Y	N	N	N	N	N	Y
3 Grijalva	N	Y	Y	Y	Y	Y	N
4 Gosar	Y	N	N	N	N	N	Y
5 Biggs	Y	N	N	N	N	N	Y
6 Schweikert	Y	N	Y	N	N	N	Y
7 Gallego	N	Y	Y	Y	Y	Y	N
8 Franks	Y	N	Y	N	N	N	Y
9 Sinema	N	Y	Y	N	Y	Y	Y
ARKANSAS							
1 Crawford	Y	N	N	N	N	N	Y
2 Hill	Y	N	N	N	N	N	Y
3 Womack	Y	N	N	N	N	N	Y
4 Westerman	Y	N	N	Y	N	Y	Y
CALIFORNIA							
1 LaMalfa	N	N	N	N	N	N	Y
2 Huffman	N	Y	Y	Y	Y	Y	N
3 Garamendi	N	Y	Y	Y	Y	Y	N
4 McClintock	Y	N	N	N	N	N	Y
5 Thompson	N	Y	Y	Y	Y	Y	N
6 Matsui	N	Y	Y	Y	Y	Y	N
7 Bera	N	Y	Y	Y	Y	Y	N
8 Cook	N	Y	N	Y	N	N	Y
9 McNerney	N	Y	Y	Y	Y	Y	N
10 Denham	N	N	N	Y	N	N	Y
11 DeSaulnier	N	Y	Y	Y	Y	Y	N
12 Pelosi	N	Y	Y	Y	Y	Y	N
13 Lee	N	Y	Y	Y	Y	Y	N
14 Speier	N	Y	Y	Y	Y	Y	N
15 Swalwell	N	Y	Y	Y	Y	Y	N
16 Costa	N	Y	Y	Y	Y	Y	N
17 Khanna	N	Y	Y	Y	Y	Y	N
18 Eshoo	N	Y	Y	Y	Y	Y	N
19 Lofgren	N	Y	Y	Y	Y	Y	N
20 Panetta	N	Y	Y	Y	Y	Y	N
21 Valadao	N	N	N	N	N	N	Y
22 Nunes	Y	N	N	N	N	N	Y
23 McCarthy	Y	N	N	N	N	N	Y
24 Carbajal	N	Y	Y	Y	Y	Y	N
25 Knight	N	N	Y	N	N	N	Y
26 Brownley	N	Y	Y	Y	Y	Y	N
27 Chu	N	Y	Y	Y	Y	Y	N
28 Schiff	N	Y	Y	Y	Y	Y	N
29 Cardenas	N	Y	Y	N	Y	Y	N
30 Sherman	N	Y	Y	Y	Y	Y	N
31 Aguilar	N	Y	Y	N	Y	Y	N
32 Napolitano	–	+	+	+	+	+	–
33 Lieu	N	Y	Y	Y	Y	Y	N
34 Gomez	N	Y	Y	Y	Y	Y	N
35 Torres	N	Y	Y	Y	Y	Y	N
36 Ruiz	N	Y	Y	N	Y	Y	N
37 Bass	N	Y	Y	Y	Y	Y	N
38 Sánchez, Linda	N	Y	Y	Y	Y	Y	N
39 Royce	Y	N	Y	N	N	N	Y
40 Roybal-Allard	N	Y	Y	Y	Y	Y	N
41 Takano	N	Y	Y	Y	Y	Y	N
42 Calvert	Y	N	N	N	N	N	Y
43 Waters	N	Y	Y	Y	Y	Y	N
44 Barragan	N	Y	Y	Y	Y	Y	N
45 Walters	N	N	N	N	N	N	Y
46 Correa	N	Y	N	Y	N	Y	N
47 Lowenthal	N	Y	Y	Y	Y	Y	N
48 Rohrabacher	Y	N	N	N	N	N	Y
49 Issa	Y	N	Y	N	N	N	Y
50 Hunter	Y	N	Y	N	N	N	Y
51 Vargas	N	Y	Y	Y	Y	Y	N
52 Peters	N	Y	Y	Y	Y	Y	N
53 Davis	N	Y	Y	Y	Y	Y	N

	429	430	431	432	433	434	435
COLORADO							
1 DeGette	N	Y	Y	Y	Y	Y	N
2 Polis	N	Y	Y	Y	Y	Y	N
3 Tipton	Y	N	N	N	N	N	Y
4 Buck	Y	N	N	N	N	N	Y
5 Lamborn	Y	N	N	N	N	N	Y
6 Coffman	Y	N	Y	N	N	N	Y
7 Perlmutter	N	Y	Y	Y	Y	Y	N
CONNECTICUT							
1 Larson	N	Y	Y	Y	Y	Y	N
2 Courtney	N	Y	Y	Y	Y	Y	N
3 DeLauro	N	Y	Y	Y	Y	Y	N
4 Himes	N	Y	Y	Y	Y	Y	N
5 Esty	N	Y	Y	Y	Y	Y	N
DELAWARE							
AL Blunt Rochester	N	Y	Y	Y	Y	Y	N
FLORIDA							
1 Gaetz	Y	N	N	N	N	N	Y
2 Dunn	N	N	Y	N	Y	N	Y
3 Yoho	Y	N	N	N	N	N	Y
4 Rutherford	N	N	N	N	N	N	Y
5 Lawson	N	Y	Y	Y	Y	Y	N
6 DeSantis	Y	N	N	N	N	N	Y
7 Murphy	N	Y	Y	Y	Y	Y	N
8 Posey	N	N	N	N	N	Y	Y
9 Soto	N	Y	Y	Y	Y	Y	N
10 Demings	N	Y	Y	Y	Y	Y	N
11 Webster	Y	N	N	N	N	N	Y
12 Bilirakis	N	N	N	N	N	N	Y
13 Crist	N	Y	Y	Y	Y	Y	N
14 Castor	N	Y	Y	Y	Y	Y	N
15 Ross	Y	N	N	N	N	N	Y
16 Buchanan	Y	N	N	N	N	N	Y
17 Rooney, T.	N	N	N	N	N	N	Y
18 Mast	Y	Y	N	N	Y	N	Y
19 Rooney, F.	N	N	Y	N	N	N	Y
20 Hastings	N	Y	Y	Y	Y	Y	N
21 Frankel	N	Y	Y	Y	Y	Y	N
22 Deutch	N	Y	Y	Y	Y	Y	N
23 Wasserman Schultz	N	Y	Y	Y	Y	Y	N
24 Wilson	N	Y	Y	Y	Y	Y	N
25 Diaz-Balart	Y	N	N	N	N	N	Y
26 Curbelo	N	Y	N	Y	N	N	Y
27 Ros-Lehtinen	N	Y	Y	N	Y	N	Y
GEORGIA							
1 Carter	N	N	N	N	N	N	Y
2 Bishop	N	Y	Y	Y	Y	Y	Y
3 Ferguson	Y	N	N	N	N	N	Y
4 Johnson	N	Y	Y	Y	Y	Y	N
5 Lewis	N	Y	Y	Y	Y	Y	N
6 Handel	N	N	N	N	N	N	Y
7 Woodall	?	N	N	Y	N	N	Y
8 Scott, A.	Y	N	N	N	N	N	Y
9 Collins	Y	N	N	N	N	N	Y
10 Hice	Y	N	N	N	N	N	Y
11 Loudermilk	Y	N	N	N	N	N	Y
12 Allen	Y	N	N	N	N	N	Y
13 Scott, D.	N	Y	Y	Y	Y	Y	N
14 Graves	Y	N	N	N	N	N	Y
HAWAII							
1 Hanabusa	N	Y	Y	Y	Y	Y	N
2 Gabbard	N	Y	Y	Y	Y	Y	N
IDAHO							
1 Labrador	Y	N	N	N	N	N	Y
2 Simpson	Y	Y	N	N	N	N	Y
ILLINOIS							
1 Rush	N	Y	Y	Y	Y	Y	N
2 Kelly	N	Y	Y	Y	Y	Y	N
3 Lipinski	N	Y	Y	Y	Y	Y	N
4 Gutierrez	N	Y	Y	Y	Y	Y	N
5 Quigley	N	Y	Y	Y	Y	Y	N
6 Roskam	?	?	?	?	?	?	?
7 Davis, D.	N	Y	Y	Y	Y	Y	N
8 Krishnamoorthi	N	Y	Y	Y	Y	Y	N
9 Schakowsky	N	Y	Y	Y	Y	Y	N
10 Schneider	N	Y	Y	Y	Y	Y	N
11 Foster	N	Y	Y	Y	Y	Y	N
12 Bost	N	N	N	N	Y	N	Y
13 Davis, R.	N	N	N	N	N	N	Y
14 Hultgren	Y	N	N	N	N	N	Y
15 Shimkus	Y	N	N	N	N	N	Y

	429	430	431	432	433	434	435
16 **Kinzinger**	N	N	N	N	N	N	Y
17 Bustos	N	Y	Y	Y	Y	Y	N
18 **LaHood**	Y	N	N	N	N	N	Y
INDIANA							
1 Visclosky	N	Y	Y	Y	Y	Y	N
2 **Walorski**	Y	N	N	N	N	N	Y
3 **Banks**	Y	N	N	N	N	N	Y
4 **Rokita**	Y	N	N	N	N	N	Y
5 **Brooks**	Y	N	N	N	N	N	Y
6 **Messer**	Y	N	N	N	N	N	Y
7 Carson	N	Y	Y	Y	Y	Y	N
8 **Bucshon**	Y	N	N	N	N	N	Y
9 **Hollingsworth**	?	?	?	?	?	?	?
IOWA							
1 **Blum**	N	N	N	N	N	N	Y
2 Loebsack	N	Y	Y	Y	Y	Y	N
3 **Young**	Y	Y	N	N	Y	N	Y
4 **King**	Y	N	N	N	N	N	Y
KANSAS							
1 **Marshall**	Y	N	N	N	N	N	Y
2 **Jenkins**	Y	N	N	N	N	N	Y
3 **Yoder**	Y	N	Y	N	N	N	Y
4 **Estes**	Y	N	N	N	N	N	Y
KENTUCKY							
1 **Comer**	Y	N	N	N	N	N	Y
2 **Guthrie**	N	N	N	N	N	N	Y
3 Yarmuth	N	Y	Y	Y	Y	Y	N
4 **Massie**	Y	N	N	N	N	N	N
5 **Rogers**	Y	N	N	N	N	N	Y
6 **Barr**	Y	N	N	N	N	N	Y
LOUISIANA							
1 **Scalise**	+	–	–	–	–	–	+
2 Richmond	N	Y	Y	Y	Y	Y	N
3 **Higgins**	Y	N	N	N	N	N	Y
4 **Johnson**	Y	N	N	N	N	N	Y
5 **Abraham**	Y	N	Y	N	Y	N	Y
6 **Graves**	Y	N	N	N	N	N	Y
MAINE							
1 Pingree	N	Y	Y	Y	Y	Y	N
2 **Poliquin**	Y	N	N	N	N	N	Y
MARYLAND							
1 **Harris**	Y	N	N	N	N	N	Y
2 Ruppersberger	N	Y	Y	N	Y	Y	N
3 Sarbanes	N	Y	Y	Y	Y	Y	N
4 Brown	N	Y	Y	Y	Y	Y	N
5 Hoyer	N	Y	Y	Y	Y	Y	N
6 Delaney	N	Y	Y	Y	Y	Y	N
7 Cummings	?	?	?	?	?	?	?
8 Raskin	N	Y	Y	Y	Y	Y	N
MASSACHUSETTS							
1 Neal	N	Y	Y	Y	Y	Y	N
2 McGovern	N	Y	Y	Y	Y	Y	N
3 Tsongas	N	Y	Y	Y	Y	Y	N
4 Kennedy	N	Y	Y	Y	Y	Y	N
5 Clark	N	Y	Y	Y	Y	Y	N
6 Moulton	N	Y	Y	Y	Y	Y	N
7 Capuano	N	Y	Y	Y	Y	Y	N
8 Lynch	N	Y	Y	Y	Y	Y	N
9 Keating	N	Y	Y	Y	Y	Y	N
MICHIGAN							
1 **Bergman**	Y	N	Y	N	Y	N	Y
2 **Huizenga**	Y	N	N	N	N	N	Y
3 **Amash**	Y	N	N	Y	N	N	N
4 **Moolenaar**	N	N	N	N	N	N	Y
5 Kildee	N	Y	Y	Y	Y	Y	N
6 **Upton**	N	N	Y	N	N	N	Y
7 **Walberg**	N	N	Y	N	N	N	Y
8 **Bishop**	N	N	N	N	N	N	Y
9 Levin	N	Y	Y	Y	Y	Y	N
10 **Mitchell**	Y	N	N	N	N	N	Y
11 **Trott**	Y	N	N	N	N	N	Y
12 Dingell	N	Y	Y	Y	Y	Y	N
13 Conyers	N	Y	Y	Y	Y	Y	N
14 Lawrence	N	Y	Y	Y	Y	Y	N
MINNESOTA							
1 Walz	N	Y	Y	Y	Y	Y	N
2 **Lewis**	Y	N	N	N	N	N	Y
3 **Paulsen**	N	N	N	N	Y	N	Y
4 McCollum	N	Y	Y	Y	Y	Y	N
5 Ellison	N	Y	Y	Y	Y	Y	N
6 **Emmer**	Y	N	N	N	N	N	Y
7 Peterson	N	N	N	N	Y	Y	N
8 Nolan	N	Y	Y	Y	Y	Y	N
MISSISSIPPI							
1 **Kelly**	Y	N	N	N	N	N	Y
2 Thompson	N	Y	Y	Y	Y	Y	N
3 **Harper**	N	N	N	N	N	N	Y
4 **Palazzo**	Y	N	N	N	Y	N	Y
MISSOURI							
1 Clay	N	Y	Y	Y	Y	Y	N
2 **Wagner**	Y	N	N	N	N	N	Y
3 **Luetkemeyer**	Y	N	N	N	N	N	Y
4 **Hartzler**	Y	N	Y	N	N	N	Y
5 Cleaver	N	Y	Y	Y	Y	Y	N
6 **Graves**	Y	N	N	N	N	N	Y
7 **Long**	Y	N	N	N	N	N	Y
8 **Smith**	Y	N	N	N	N	N	Y
MONTANA							
AL **Gianforte**	Y	N	N	N	N	N	Y
NEBRASKA							
1 **Fortenberry**	N	?	?	?	?	?	?
2 **Bacon**	Y	N	Y	N	N	N	Y
3 **Smith**	Y	N	N	N	N	N	Y
NEVADA							
1 Titus	N	Y	Y	Y	Y	Y	N
2 **Amodei**	Y	N	N	N	N	N	Y
3 Rosen	N	Y	Y	N	Y	Y	N
4 Kihuen	N	Y	Y	Y	Y	Y	N
NEW HAMPSHIRE							
1 Shea-Porter	N	Y	Y	Y	Y	Y	N
2 Kuster	N	Y	Y	Y	Y	Y	N
NEW JERSEY							
1 Norcross	N	Y	Y	Y	Y	Y	N
2 **LoBiondo**	N	Y	N	N	Y	N	Y
3 **MacArthur**	N	N	Y	N	N	N	Y
4 **Smith**	N	Y	Y	N	Y	N	Y
5 Gottheimer	N	Y	Y	N	Y	Y	Y
6 Pallone	N	Y	Y	Y	Y	Y	N
7 **Lance**	N	N	N	N	Y	N	Y
8 Sires	N	Y	Y	N	Y	Y	N
9 Pascrell	N	Y	Y	Y	Y	Y	N
10 Payne	N	Y	Y	Y	Y	Y	N
11 **Frelinghuysen**	Y	N	N	N	N	N	Y
12 Watson Coleman	N	Y	Y	Y	Y	Y	N
NEW MEXICO							
1 Lujan Grisham	N	Y	Y	Y	Y	Y	N
2 **Pearce**	Y	N	N	N	Y	N	Y
3 Luján	N	Y	Y	Y	Y	Y	N
NEW YORK							
1 **Zeldin**	Y	Y	Y	N	Y	N	Y
2 **King**	Y	Y	Y	N	Y	N	Y
3 Suozzi	N	Y	Y	N	Y	Y	N
4 Rice	N	Y	Y	Y	Y	Y	N
5 Meeks	N	Y	Y	Y	Y	Y	N
6 Meng	N	Y	Y	Y	Y	Y	N
7 Velázquez	N	Y	Y	Y	Y	Y	N
8 Jeffries	N	Y	Y	Y	Y	Y	N
9 Clarke	N	Y	Y	Y	Y	Y	N
10 Nadler	N	Y	Y	Y	Y	Y	N
11 **Donovan**	N	Y	N	N	Y	N	Y
12 Maloney, C.	N	Y	Y	N	Y	Y	N
13 Espaillat	N	Y	Y	Y	Y	Y	N
14 Crowley	N	Y	Y	Y	Y	Y	N
15 Serrano	N	Y	Y	Y	Y	Y	N
16 Engel	N	N	Y	Y	Y	Y	N
17 Lowey	N	Y	Y	Y	Y	Y	N
18 Maloney, S.P.	N	Y	Y	N	Y	Y	N
19 **Faso**	N	Y	Y	N	Y	N	Y
20 Tonko	N	Y	Y	Y	Y	Y	N
21 **Stefanik**	N	Y	Y	N	Y	N	Y
22 **Tenney**	N	Y	Y	N	Y	N	Y
23 **Reed**	N	Y	Y	N	Y	N	Y
24 **Katko**	N	Y	Y	N	Y	N	Y
25 Slaughter	N	Y	Y	Y	Y	Y	N
26 Higgins	N	Y	Y	Y	Y	Y	N
27 **Collins**	N	N	N	N	N	N	Y
NORTH CAROLINA							
1 Butterfield	N	Y	Y	Y	Y	Y	N
2 **Holding**	Y	N	N	N	N	N	Y
3 **Jones**	Y	Y	Y	N	Y	Y	N
4 Price	N	Y	Y	Y	Y	Y	N
5 **Foxx**	Y	N	N	N	N	N	Y
6 **Walker**	Y	N	N	N	N	N	Y
7 **Rouzer**	Y	N	N	N	N	N	Y
8 **Hudson**	N	N	N	N	N	N	Y
9 **Pittenger**	Y	N	N	N	N	N	Y
10 **McHenry**	Y	N	N	N	N	N	Y
11 **Meadows**	Y	N	N	N	N	N	Y
12 Adams	N	Y	Y	Y	Y	Y	N
13 **Budd**	Y	N	N	N	N	N	Y
NORTH DAKOTA							
AL **Cramer**	Y	N	N	N	N	N	Y
OHIO							
1 **Chabot**	Y	N	N	N	N	N	Y
2 **Wenstrup**	Y	N	Y	N	N	N	Y
3 Beatty	N	Y	Y	Y	Y	Y	N
4 **Jordan**	Y	N	N	N	N	N	Y
5 **Latta**	N	N	Y	N	N	N	Y
6 **Johnson**	N	N	N	N	N	N	Y
7 **Gibbs**	Y	N	Y	N	N	N	Y
8 **Davidson**	Y	N	N	N	N	N	Y
9 Kaptur	N	Y	Y	Y	Y	Y	N
10 **Turner**	Y	N	Y	N	N	N	Y
11 Fudge	N	Y	Y	Y	Y	Y	N
12 **Tiberi**	N	Y	N	N	N	N	Y
13 Ryan	–	–	–	–	–	Y	N
14 **Joyce**	N	N	N	N	N	N	Y
15 **Stivers**	Y	N	N	N	N	N	Y
16 **Renacci**	Y	N	N	N	N	N	Y
OKLAHOMA							
1 **Bridenstine**	Y	N	N	N	Y	N	Y
2 **Mullin**	Y	N	N	N	Y	N	Y
3 **Lucas**	Y	N	N	N	Y	N	Y
4 **Cole**	N	N	N	N	Y	N	Y
5 **Russell**	Y	N	Y	N	Y	N	Y
OREGON							
1 Bonamici	N	Y	Y	Y	Y	Y	N
2 **Walden**	N	N	N	N	N	N	Y
3 Blumenauer	N	Y	Y	Y	Y	Y	N
4 DeFazio	N	Y	Y	Y	Y	Y	N
5 Schrader	N	Y	Y	Y	Y	Y	N
PENNSYLVANIA							
1 Brady	N	Y	Y	Y	Y	Y	N
2 Evans	N	Y	Y	Y	Y	Y	N
3 **Kelly**	Y	N	Y	N	Y	N	Y
4 **Perry**	Y	N	N	N	N	N	Y
5 **Thompson**	N	N	Y	N	Y	N	Y
6 **Costello**	N	Y	Y	N	Y	N	Y
7 **Meehan**	Y	Y	Y	N	Y	N	Y
8 **Fitzpatrick**	N	Y	Y	N	Y	N	Y
9 **Shuster**	Y	Y	Y	N	Y	N	Y
10 **Marino**	Y	N	Y	N	Y	N	Y
11 **Barletta**	Y	N	Y	N	Y	N	Y
12 **Rothfus**	Y	N	Y	N	N	N	Y
13 Boyle	N	Y	Y	Y	Y	Y	N
14 Doyle	N	Y	Y	Y	Y	Y	N
15 **Dent**	Y	N	Y	N	Y	N	Y
16 **Smucker**	N	N	Y	N	N	N	Y
17 Cartwright	N	Y	Y	Y	Y	Y	N
18 **Murphy**	Y	N	Y	N	Y	N	Y
RHODE ISLAND							
1 Cicilline	N	Y	Y	Y	Y	Y	N
2 Langevin	N	Y	Y	Y	Y	Y	N
SOUTH CAROLINA							
1 **Sanford**	Y	N	Y	Y	N	N	N
2 **Wilson**	Y	N	N	N	N	N	Y
3 **Duncan**	Y	N	N	N	N	N	Y
4 **Gowdy**	Y	N	N	N	N	N	Y
5 **Norman**	Y	N	N	N	N	N	Y
6 Clyburn	N	Y	Y	Y	Y	Y	N
7 **Rice**	Y	N	N	N	N	N	Y
SOUTH DAKOTA							
AL **Noem**	Y	N	N	N	N	N	Y
TENNESSEE							
1 **Roe**	N	N	N	N	N	N	Y
2 **Duncan**	Y	N	N	Y	N	N	N
3 **Fleischmann**	Y	Y	Y	N	N	N	Y
4 **DesJarlais**	Y	N	N	N	N	N	Y
5 Cooper	N	Y	N	Y	Y	Y	N
6 **Black**	Y	N	N	N	N	N	Y
7 **Blackburn**	N	N	N	N	N	N	Y
8 **Kustoff**	Y	N	N	N	N	N	Y
9 Cohen	N	Y	Y	Y	Y	Y	N
TEXAS							
1 **Gohmert**	Y	N	N	N	N	N	Y
2 **Poe**	Y	N	N	N	N	N	Y
3 **Johnson, S.**	Y	N	N	N	N	N	Y
4 **Ratcliffe**	Y	N	N	N	Y	N	Y
5 **Hensarling**	Y	N	N	N	Y	N	Y
6 **Barton**	Y	N	N	N	N	N	Y
7 **Culberson**	N	N	N	N	N	N	Y
8 **Brady**	?	N	N	N	N	N	Y
9 Green, A.	N	Y	Y	Y	Y	Y	N
10 **McCaul**	Y	N	N	N	N	N	Y
11 **Conaway**	Y	N	Y	N	N	N	Y
12 **Granger**	Y	N	N	N	N	N	Y
13 **Thornberry**	Y	N	Y	N	N	N	Y
14 **Weber**	Y	N	N	N	N	N	Y
15 Gonzalez	N	Y	Y	N	Y	Y	N
16 O'Rourke	N	Y	Y	Y	Y	Y	N
17 **Flores**	N	N	N	N	N	N	Y
18 Jackson Lee	N	Y	Y	Y	Y	Y	N
19 **Arrington**	Y	N	N	N	N	N	Y
20 Castro	N	Y	Y	Y	Y	Y	N
21 **Smith**	Y	N	Y	N	N	N	Y
22 **Olson**	Y	N	N	N	N	N	Y
23 **Hurd**	Y	N	Y	N	N	N	Y
24 **Marchant**	Y	N	N	N	N	N	Y
25 **Williams**	Y	N	N	N	N	N	Y
26 **Burgess**	Y	N	N	N	N	N	Y
27 **Farenthold**	Y	N	N	N	N	N	Y
28 Cuellar	N	Y	Y	N	Y	Y	N
29 Green, G.	N	Y	N	N	Y	Y	N
30 Johnson, E.B.	N	Y	Y	Y	Y	Y	N
31 **Carter**	Y	N	N	N	N	N	Y
32 **Sessions**	Y	N	N	N	N	N	Y
33 Veasey	N	Y	Y	Y	Y	Y	N
34 Vela	N	Y	Y	Y	Y	Y	N
35 Doggett	N	Y	Y	Y	Y	Y	N
36 **Babin**	Y	N	N	?	N	N	Y
UTAH							
1 **Bishop**	Y	N	N	N	Y	N	Y
2 **Stewart**	Y	N	N	N	Y	N	Y
4 **Love**	Y	N	N	N	Y	N	Y
VERMONT							
AL Welch	N	Y	Y	Y	Y	Y	N
VIRGINIA							
1 **Wittman**	Y	N	N	N	Y	N	Y
2 **Taylor**	Y	N	N	N	N	N	Y
3 Scott	N	Y	Y	Y	Y	Y	N
4 McEachin	N	Y	Y	Y	Y	Y	N
5 **Garrett**	Y	N	N	N	N	N	Y
6 **Goodlatte**	Y	N	Y	N	N	N	Y
7 **Brat**	Y	N	N	N	N	N	Y
8 Beyer	N	Y	Y	Y	Y	Y	N
9 **Griffith**	N	N	N	N	N	N	Y
10 **Comstock**	N	Y	Y	N	Y	N	Y
11 Connolly	N	Y	Y	Y	Y	Y	N
WASHINGTON							
1 DelBene	N	Y	Y	Y	Y	Y	N
2 Larsen	N	Y	Y	Y	Y	Y	N
3 **Herrera Beutler**	Y	N	N	N	Y	N	Y
4 **Newhouse**	Y	N	N	N	Y	N	Y
5 **McMorris Rodgers**	Y	N	Y	N	N	N	Y
6 Kilmer	N	Y	Y	Y	Y	Y	N
7 Jayapal	N	Y	Y	Y	Y	Y	N
8 **Reichert**	N	N	N	N	N	N	Y
9 Smith	N	Y	Y	Y	Y	Y	N
10 Heck	N	Y	Y	Y	Y	Y	N
WEST VIRGINIA							
1 **McKinley**	N	N	Y	N	Y	N	Y
2 **Mooney**	Y	N	Y	N	N	N	Y
3 **Jenkins**	Y	N	N	N	N	N	Y
WISCONSIN							
1 **Ryan**							
2 Pocan	N	Y	Y	Y	Y	Y	N
3 Kind	N	Y	Y	Y	Y	Y	N
4 Moore	N	Y	Y	Y	Y	Y	N
5 **Sensenbrenner**	Y	N	Y	N	N	N	Y
6 **Grothman**	Y	N	N	N	N	N	Y
7 **Duffy**	Y	N	N	N	N	N	Y
8 **Gallagher**	N	N	N	N	N	N	Y
WYOMING							
AL **Cheney**	Y	N	N	N	N	N	Y

⦀ HOUSE VOTES

VOTE NUMBER

436. HR 3180, H RES 481. FISCAL 2018 INTELLIGENCE AUTHORIZATION AND SAME-DAY AUTHORITY/RULE. Adoption of the rule (H Res 481) that would provide for House floor consideration of the bill (HR 3180) that would authorize classified amounts of funding through fiscal 2018 for 16 U.S. intelligence agencies and intelligence-related activities, including the Office of the National Intelligence Director, the CIA and the National Security Agency. The rule would waive, through the legislative day of August 1, 2017, the two-thirds vote requirement to consider legislation on the same day it is reported from the House Rules Committee. Adopted 224-186 : R 223-3; D 1-183. July 28, 2017.

437. HR 3180. FISCAL 2018 INTELLIGENCE AUTHORIZATION/PASSAGE. Passage of the bill that would authorize classified amounts of funding through fiscal 2018 for 16 U.S. intelligence agencies and intelligence-related activities, including the Office of the National Intelligence Director, the CIA and the National Security Agency. The bill would authorize $527 million in fiscal 2018 in funding to the Intelligence Community Management Account and would authorize $514 million through fiscal 2018 in funding to the CIA Retirement and Disability Fund. The bill would require the Director of National Intelligence to submit to Congress multiple reports regarding Russia's campaigns directed at foreign elections and its efforts related to cyber influence, including an analytical assessment of the most significant Russian influence campaigns, if any, conducted during the three years prior to the bill's enactment. Passed 380-35 : R 223-6; D 157-29. July 28, 2017.

438. S 114. VETERANS CHOICE FUND AUTHORIZATION/PASSAGE. Passage of the bill that would make available an additional $2.1 billion in funding for the Veterans Choice Fund, without fiscal year limitation. The bill would extend until Sept. 30, 2027, the current cap on per-month payment of VA pensions to certain veterans residing at VA nursing care facilities, as well as the VA's authority to collect fees for VA housing loans and the VA's authority to obtain and use income information from the Social Security Administration and the IRS to validate an application for VA benefits. Passed 414-0 : R 228-0; D 186-0. July 28, 2017.

439. HR 3110. FINANCIAL STABILITY OVERSIGHT COUNCIL MEMBERSHIP/PASSAGE. Hultgren, R-Ill., motion to suspend the rules and pass the bill that would allow an independent member of the Financial Stability Oversight Council to continue to serve on the council for a period of up to 18 months if a successor is not appointed and confirmed by the end of the current member's term of service. Motion agreed to 407-1 : R 226-1; D 181-0. Sept. 5, 2017.

440. HR 2864. SEC REDUCED FILING REQUIREMENTS/PASSAGE. Hultgren, R-Ill., motion to suspend the rules and pass the bill that would direct the Securities and Exchange Commission to modify a regulation, known as Regulation A-Plus, that reduces filing requirements for certain companies not fully registered with the SEC. Doing so would allow fully registered small public companies to issue securities under the same terms that apply to companies subject to the reduced SEC filing requirement. Motion agreed to 403-3 : R 225-2; D 178-1. Sept. 5, 2017.

441. H RES 502, HR 601. EMERGENCY HURRICANE HARVEY SUPPLEMENTAL APPROPRIATIONS/ADOPTION. Frelinghuysen, R-N.J., motion to suspend the rules and agree to the resolution that would provide for the House to concur in the Senate amendments to a bill (HR 601) that would codify practices and programs at the United States Agency for International Development related to U.S. education assistance abroad, with further amendment that would appropriate $7.9 billion in emergency supplemental funding for fiscal 2017 as an initial payment to cover the costs of responding to Hurricane Harvey. The total would include $7.4 billion for the Homeland Security Department's Disaster Relief Fund, which will be used by the Federal Emergency Management Agency to support ongoing hurricane response efforts. It would also include $450 million for the Small Business Administration's disaster loan program to assist small businesses and homeowners. Motion agreed to 419-3 : R 229-3; D 190-0. Sept. 6, 2017.

	436	437	438	439	440	441
ALABAMA						
1 Byrne	Y	Y	Y	Y	Y	Y
2 Roby	Y	Y	Y	Y	Y	Y
3 Rogers	Y	Y	Y	Y	Y	Y
4 Aderholt	Y	Y	Y	Y	Y	Y
5 Brooks	Y	Y	Y	Y	Y	Y
6 Palmer	Y	Y	Y	Y	Y	Y
7 Sewell	N	Y	Y	Y	Y	Y
ALASKA						
AL Young	?	Y	Y	Y	Y	Y
ARIZONA						
1 O'Halleran	N	Y	Y	Y	Y	Y
2 McSally	Y	Y	Y	Y	Y	Y
3 Grijalva	N	N	Y	?	?	Y
4 Gosar	Y	Y	Y	Y	Y	Y
5 Biggs	Y	Y	Y	Y	Y	N
6 Schweikert	Y	Y	Y	Y	Y	Y
7 Gallego	N	Y	Y	Y	Y	Y
8 Franks	Y	Y	Y	Y	Y	Y
9 Sinema	N	Y	Y	Y	Y	Y
ARKANSAS						
1 Crawford	Y	Y	Y	Y	Y	Y
2 Hill	Y	Y	Y	Y	Y	Y
3 Womack	Y	Y	Y	Y	Y	Y
4 Westerman	Y	Y	Y	Y	Y	Y
CALIFORNIA						
1 LaMalfa	Y	Y	Y	Y	Y	Y
2 Huffman	N	N	Y	Y	Y	Y
3 Garamendi	N	Y	Y	Y	Y	Y
4 McClintock	Y	Y	Y	Y	Y	Y
5 Thompson	N	Y	Y	Y	Y	Y
6 Matsui	N	Y	Y	Y	Y	Y
7 Bera	N	Y	Y	Y	Y	Y
8 Cook	Y	Y	Y	Y	Y	Y
9 McNerney	N	Y	Y	Y	Y	Y
10 Denham	Y	Y	Y	Y	Y	Y
11 DeSaulnier	N	Y	Y	Y	Y	Y
12 Pelosi	N	Y	Y	Y	Y	Y
13 Lee	N	N	Y	Y	Y	Y
14 Speier	N	?	?	Y	Y	Y
15 Swalwell	N	Y	Y	Y	Y	Y
16 Costa	Y	?	?	?	?	?
17 Khanna	N	N	Y	Y	Y	Y
18 Eshoo	N	Y	Y	Y	Y	Y
19 Lofgren	N	N	Y	Y	Y	Y
20 Panetta	N	Y	Y	Y	Y	Y
21 Valadao	Y	Y	Y	Y	Y	Y
22 Nunes	Y	Y	Y	Y	Y	Y
23 McCarthy	Y	Y	Y	Y	Y	Y
24 Carbajal	N	Y	Y	Y	Y	Y
25 Knight	Y	Y	Y	Y	Y	Y
26 Brownley	N	Y	Y	Y	Y	Y
27 Chu	N	N	Y	Y	Y	Y
28 Schiff	N	Y	Y	Y	Y	Y
29 Cardenas	N	Y	Y	Y	Y	Y
30 Sherman	N	Y	Y	Y	Y	Y
31 Aguilar	N	Y	Y	Y	?	Y
32 Napolitano	–	+	+	?	?	Y
33 Lieu	N	Y	Y	Y	Y	Y
34 Gomez	N	N	Y	Y	Y	Y
35 Torres	N	Y	Y	Y	Y	Y
36 Ruiz	N	Y	Y	Y	Y	Y
37 Bass	?	N	?	Y	Y	Y
38 Sánchez, Linda	N	Y	Y	Y	Y	Y
39 Royce	Y	Y	Y	Y	Y	Y
40 Roybal-Allard	N	Y	Y	Y	Y	Y
41 Takano	N	N	Y	Y	Y	Y
42 Calvert	Y	Y	Y	Y	Y	Y
43 Waters	?	?	Y	Y	Y	Y
44 Barragan	N	Y	Y	Y	Y	Y
45 Walters	Y	Y	Y	Y	Y	Y
46 Correa	N	Y	Y	Y	Y	Y
47 Lowenthal	N	Y	Y	Y	Y	Y
48 Rohrabacher	Y	Y	Y	Y	Y	Y
49 Issa	Y	Y	Y	Y	Y	?
50 Hunter	?	Y	Y	Y	Y	Y
51 Vargas	N	Y	Y	Y	Y	Y
52 Peters	N	Y	Y	Y	Y	Y
53 Davis	N	Y	Y	Y	Y	Y

	436	437	438	439	440	441
COLORADO						
1 DeGette	N	Y	Y	?	?	?
2 Polis	N	N	Y	Y	Y	Y
3 Tipton	Y	Y	Y	Y	Y	Y
4 Buck	Y	Y	Y	Y	Y	Y
5 Lamborn	Y	Y	Y	Y	Y	Y
6 Coffman	Y	Y	Y	Y	Y	Y
7 Perlmutter	N	Y	Y	Y	Y	Y
CONNECTICUT						
1 Larson	N	+	+	Y	Y	Y
2 Courtney	N	Y	Y	Y	Y	Y
3 DeLauro	N	Y	Y	?	?	Y
4 Himes	N	Y	Y	Y	Y	Y
5 Esty	N	Y	Y	Y	Y	Y
DELAWARE						
AL Blunt Rochester	N	Y	Y	Y	Y	Y
FLORIDA						
1 Gaetz	Y	Y	Y	Y	Y	Y
2 Dunn	Y	Y	Y	Y	Y	Y
3 Yoho	Y	Y	Y	Y	Y	Y
4 Rutherford	Y	Y	Y	Y	Y	Y
5 Lawson	N	Y	Y	Y	Y	Y
6 DeSantis	Y	Y	Y	Y	Y	Y
7 Murphy	N	Y	Y	Y	Y	Y
8 Posey	Y	Y	Y	Y	?	Y
9 Soto	N	Y	Y	Y	Y	Y
10 Demings	N	Y	Y	Y	Y	Y
11 Webster	?	?	?	Y	Y	Y
12 Bilirakis	Y	Y	Y	Y	Y	Y
13 Crist	N	Y	Y	Y	Y	Y
14 Castor	N	Y	Y	Y	Y	Y
15 Ross	Y	Y	Y	Y	Y	Y
16 Buchanan	Y	Y	Y	Y	Y	Y
17 Rooney, T.	?	Y	Y	Y	Y	Y
18 Mast	Y	Y	Y	Y	Y	Y
19 Rooney, F.	Y	Y	Y	Y	Y	Y
20 Hastings	N	Y	Y	Y	Y	Y
21 Frankel	N	Y	Y	Y	Y	Y
22 Deutch	N	Y	Y	Y	Y	Y
23 Wasserman Schultz	N	Y	Y	Y	Y	Y
24 Wilson	N	Y	Y	Y	Y	Y
25 Diaz-Balart	Y	Y	Y	Y	Y	Y
26 Curbelo	Y	Y	Y	Y	Y	Y
27 Ros-Lehtinen	Y	Y	Y	Y	Y	Y
GEORGIA						
1 Carter	Y	Y	Y	?	Y	Y
2 Bishop	N	Y	Y	Y	Y	Y
3 Ferguson	Y	Y	Y	Y	Y	Y
4 Johnson	N	N	Y	Y	Y	Y
5 Lewis	N	N	Y	Y	Y	Y
6 Handel	Y	Y	Y	Y	Y	Y
7 Woodall	Y	Y	Y	Y	Y	Y
8 Scott, A.	Y	Y	Y	Y	Y	Y
9 Collins	Y	Y	Y	Y	Y	Y
10 Hice	Y	Y	Y	Y	Y	Y
11 Loudermilk	Y	Y	Y	Y	Y	Y
12 Allen	Y	Y	Y	Y	Y	Y
13 Scott, D.	N	Y	Y	Y	Y	Y
14 Graves	Y	Y	Y	Y	Y	Y
HAWAII						
1 Hanabusa	N	Y	Y	Y	Y	Y
2 Gabbard	N	N	Y	Y	Y	Y
IDAHO						
1 Labrador	Y	N	Y	Y	Y	Y
2 Simpson	Y	Y	Y	Y	Y	Y
ILLINOIS						
1 Rush	N	Y	Y	Y	Y	Y
2 Kelly	N	Y	Y	Y	Y	Y
3 Lipinski	N	Y	Y	Y	Y	Y
4 Gutierrez	?	N	Y	?	?	Y
5 Quigley	N	Y	Y	Y	Y	Y
6 Roskam	?	?	?	Y	Y	Y
7 Davis, D.	N	Y	Y	Y	Y	Y
8 Krishnamoorthi	N	Y	Y	Y	Y	Y
9 Schakowsky	N	N	Y	Y	Y	Y
10 Schneider	N	Y	Y	Y	Y	Y
11 Foster	N	Y	Y	Y	Y	Y
12 Bost	Y	Y	Y	Y	Y	Y
13 Davis, R.	Y	Y	Y	Y	Y	Y
14 Hultgren	Y	Y	Y	Y	Y	Y
15 Shimkus	Y	Y	Y	?	?	Y

KEY	Republicans	Democrats	Independents
Y Voted for (yea)		**X** Paired against	**C** Voted "present" to avoid possible conflict of interest
# Paired for		**–** Announced against	
+ Announced for		**P** Voted "present"	**?** Did not vote or otherwise make a position known
N Voted against (nay)			

	436	437	438	439	440	441
16 **Kinzinger**	Y	Y	Y	Y	Y	Y
17 Bustos	N	Y	Y	Y	Y	Y
18 **LaHood**	Y	Y	Y	Y	Y	Y
INDIANA						
1 Visclosky	N	Y	Y	Y	Y	Y
2 **Walorski**	Y	Y	Y	Y	Y	Y
3 **Banks**	Y	Y	Y	Y	Y	Y
4 **Rokita**	Y	Y	Y	Y	Y	Y
5 **Brooks**	Y	Y	Y	Y	Y	Y
6 **Messer**	Y	Y	Y	?	?	Y
7 Carson	N	Y	Y	Y	Y	Y
8 **Bucshon**	Y	Y	Y	Y	Y	Y
9 **Hollingsworth**	?	?	?	Y	Y	Y
IOWA						
1 **Blum**	Y	Y	Y	Y	Y	Y
2 Loebsack	N	Y	Y	Y	Y	Y
3 **Young**	Y	Y	Y	Y	Y	Y
4 **King**	Y	Y	Y	Y	Y	Y
KANSAS						
1 **Marshall**	Y	Y	Y	Y	Y	Y
2 **Jenkins**	Y	Y	Y	Y	Y	Y
3 **Yoder**	Y	Y	Y	Y	Y	Y
4 **Estes**	Y	Y	Y	Y	Y	Y
KENTUCKY						
1 **Comer**	Y	Y	Y	Y	Y	Y
2 **Guthrie**	Y	Y	Y	Y	Y	Y
3 Yarmuth	N	Y	Y	Y	Y	Y
4 **Massie**	N	N	Y	Y	Y	N
5 **Rogers**	Y	Y	Y	Y	Y	Y
6 **Barr**	Y	Y	Y	Y	Y	Y
LOUISIANA						
1 **Scalise**	+	+	+	+	+	+
2 Richmond	?	Y	Y	Y	Y	Y
3 **Higgins**	Y	Y	Y	?	?	?
4 **Johnson**	Y	Y	Y	Y	Y	Y
5 **Abraham**	Y	Y	Y	Y	Y	Y
6 **Graves**	Y	Y	Y	Y	Y	Y
MAINE						
1 Pingree	N	Y	Y	Y	Y	Y
2 **Poliquin**	Y	Y	Y	Y	Y	Y
MARYLAND						
1 **Harris**	Y	Y	Y	Y	Y	Y
2 Ruppersberger	N	Y	Y	Y	Y	Y
3 Sarbanes	N	Y	Y	Y	Y	Y
4 Brown	N	Y	Y	Y	Y	Y
5 Hoyer	N	Y	Y	Y	Y	Y
6 Delaney	N	Y	Y	Y	Y	Y
7 Cummings	?	?	?	?	?	?
8 Raskin	N	Y	Y	Y	Y	Y
MASSACHUSETTS						
1 Neal	N	Y	Y	Y	Y	Y
2 McGovern	N	N	Y	Y	Y	Y
3 Tsongas	N	Y	Y	Y	Y	Y
4 Kennedy	N	Y	Y	Y	Y	Y
5 Clark	N	N	Y	Y	Y	Y
6 Moulton	N	Y	Y	Y	Y	Y
7 Capuano	N	N	Y	Y	Y	Y
8 Lynch	N	Y	Y	Y	Y	Y
9 Keating	N	Y	Y	Y	Y	Y
MICHIGAN						
1 **Bergman**	Y	Y	Y	Y	Y	Y
2 **Huizenga**	Y	Y	Y	Y	Y	Y
3 **Amash**	N	N	Y	Y	Y	N
4 **Moolenaar**	Y	Y	Y	Y	Y	Y
5 Kildee	N	Y	Y	Y	Y	Y
6 **Upton**	Y	Y	Y	Y	Y	Y
7 **Walberg**	Y	Y	Y	Y	Y	Y
8 **Bishop**	Y	Y	Y	Y	Y	Y
9 Levin	N	Y	Y	Y	Y	Y
10 **Mitchell**	Y	Y	Y	Y	Y	Y
11 **Trott**	Y	Y	Y	Y	Y	Y
12 Dingell	N	Y	Y	Y	Y	Y
13 Conyers	?	N	Y	Y	Y	Y
14 Lawrence	N	Y	Y	Y	Y	Y
MINNESOTA						
1 Walz	N	Y	Y	Y	Y	Y
2 **Lewis**	Y	Y	Y	Y	Y	Y
3 **Paulsen**	Y	Y	Y	Y	Y	Y
4 McCollum	N	Y	Y	Y	Y	Y

	436	437	438	439	440	441
5 Ellison	N	N	Y	Y	Y	Y
6 **Emmer**	Y	Y	Y	Y	Y	Y
7 Peterson	N	Y	Y	Y	Y	Y
8 Nolan	N	Y	Y	Y	Y	Y
MISSISSIPPI						
1 **Kelly**	Y	Y	Y	Y	Y	Y
2 Thompson	N	Y	Y	Y	Y	Y
3 **Harper**	Y	Y	Y	Y	Y	Y
4 **Palazzo**	Y	Y	Y	Y	Y	Y
MISSOURI						
1 Clay	?	?	?	Y	Y	Y
2 **Wagner**	Y	Y	Y	Y	Y	Y
3 **Luetkemeyer**	Y	Y	Y	Y	Y	Y
4 **Hartzler**	Y	Y	Y	Y	N	Y
5 Cleaver	N	Y	Y	Y	Y	Y
6 **Graves**	?	?	?	Y	Y	Y
7 **Long**	Y	Y	Y	Y	Y	Y
8 **Smith**	Y	Y	Y	Y	Y	Y
MONTANA						
AL **Gianforte**	Y	Y	Y	?	?	Y
NEBRASKA						
1 **Fortenberry**	Y	Y	Y	Y	Y	Y
2 **Bacon**	Y	Y	Y	Y	Y	Y
3 **Smith**	Y	Y	Y	Y	Y	Y
NEVADA						
1 Titus	N	Y	Y	Y	Y	Y
2 **Amodei**	Y	Y	Y	Y	Y	Y
3 Rosen	N	Y	Y	Y	Y	Y
4 Kihuen	N	Y	Y	Y	Y	Y
NEW HAMPSHIRE						
1 Shea-Porter	N	Y	Y	?	?	Y
2 Kuster	N	Y	Y	Y	Y	Y
NEW JERSEY						
1 Norcross	N	Y	Y	Y	Y	Y
2 **LoBiondo**	Y	Y	Y	Y	Y	Y
3 **MacArthur**	Y	Y	Y	Y	Y	Y
4 **Smith**	Y	Y	Y	Y	Y	Y
5 Gottheimer	N	Y	Y	Y	Y	Y
6 Pallone	N	Y	Y	Y	Y	Y
7 **Lance**	Y	Y	Y	Y	Y	Y
8 Sires	N	Y	Y	Y	Y	Y
9 Pascrell	N	Y	Y	Y	Y	Y
10 Payne	N	Y	Y	Y	Y	Y
11 **Frelinghuysen**	Y	Y	Y	Y	Y	Y
12 Watson Coleman	N	Y	Y	Y	Y	Y
NEW MEXICO						
1 Lujan Grisham	?	?	?	Y	Y	Y
2 **Pearce**	Y	Y	Y	Y	Y	Y
3 Luján	N	Y	Y	Y	Y	Y
NEW YORK						
1 **Zeldin**	+	+	+	Y	Y	Y
2 **King**	?	?	?	Y	Y	Y
3 Suozzi	N	Y	Y	?	?	?
4 Rice	N	Y	Y	Y	Y	Y
5 Meeks	N	Y	Y	Y	Y	Y
6 Meng	N	Y	Y	?	?	Y
7 Velázquez	N	N	Y	Y	Y	Y
8 Jeffries	N	Y	Y	Y	Y	Y
9 Clarke	N	N	Y	Y	Y	Y
10 Nadler	N	Y	Y	Y	Y	Y
11 **Donovan**	?	?	?	Y	Y	Y
12 Maloney, C.	N	Y	Y	Y	Y	Y
13 Espaillat	N	Y	Y	Y	Y	Y
14 Crowley	N	Y	Y	Y	Y	Y
15 Serrano	N	Y	Y	Y	Y	Y
16 Engel	?	Y	Y	Y	Y	Y
17 Lowey	N	Y	Y	Y	Y	Y
18 Maloney, S.P.	N	Y	Y	Y	Y	Y
19 **Faso**	Y	Y	Y	Y	Y	Y
20 Tonko	N	Y	Y	Y	Y	Y
21 **Stefanik**	Y	Y	Y	Y	Y	Y
22 **Tenney**	Y	Y	Y	Y	Y	Y
23 **Reed**	Y	Y	Y	Y	Y	Y
24 **Katko**	Y	Y	Y	Y	Y	Y
25 Slaughter	N	Y	Y	Y	Y	Y
26 Higgins	N	Y	Y	?	?	Y
27 **Collins**	?	?	?	Y	Y	Y
NORTH CAROLINA						
1 Butterfield	N	Y	Y	Y	Y	Y
2 **Holding**	Y	Y	Y	Y	Y	Y
3 **Jones**	N	N	Y	Y	N	Y
4 Price	N	Y	Y	Y	Y	Y

	436	437	438	439	440	441
5 **Foxx**	Y	Y	Y	Y	Y	Y
6 **Walker**	Y	Y	Y	Y	Y	Y
7 **Rouzer**	Y	Y	Y	Y	Y	Y
8 **Hudson**	Y	Y	Y	Y	Y	Y
9 **Pittenger**	Y	Y	Y	Y	Y	Y
10 **McHenry**	Y	Y	Y	Y	Y	Y
11 **Meadows**	Y	Y	Y	Y	Y	Y
12 Adams	N	Y	Y	Y	Y	Y
13 **Budd**	Y	Y	Y	Y	Y	Y
NORTH DAKOTA						
AL **Cramer**	Y	Y	Y	Y	Y	?
OHIO						
1 **Chabot**	Y	Y	Y	Y	Y	Y
2 **Wenstrup**	Y	Y	Y	Y	Y	Y
3 Beatty	N	Y	Y	Y	Y	Y
4 **Jordan**	Y	Y	Y	Y	Y	Y
5 **Latta**	Y	Y	Y	Y	Y	Y
6 **Johnson**	Y	Y	Y	Y	Y	Y
7 **Gibbs**	Y	Y	Y	Y	Y	Y
8 **Davidson**	Y	Y	Y	Y	Y	Y
9 Kaptur	N	Y	Y	Y	Y	Y
10 **Turner**	Y	Y	Y	Y	Y	Y
11 Fudge	N	Y	Y	Y	Y	Y
12 **Tiberi**	Y	Y	Y	Y	Y	Y
13 Ryan	N	Y	Y	Y	Y	Y
14 **Joyce**	Y	Y	Y	Y	Y	Y
15 **Stivers**	Y	Y	Y	Y	Y	Y
16 **Renacci**	Y	Y	Y	?	?	Y
OKLAHOMA						
1 **Bridenstine**	Y	Y	Y	?	?	?
2 **Mullin**	Y	Y	Y	Y	Y	Y
3 **Lucas**	Y	Y	Y	Y	Y	Y
4 **Cole**	Y	Y	Y	Y	Y	Y
5 **Russell**	Y	Y	Y	Y	Y	Y
OREGON						
1 Bonamici	N	Y	Y	?	?	Y
2 **Walden**	Y	Y	Y	Y	Y	Y
3 Blumenauer	N	N	Y	Y	Y	Y
4 DeFazio	N	Y	Y	Y	Y	Y
5 Schrader	N	Y	Y	Y	Y	Y
PENNSYLVANIA						
1 Brady	N	Y	Y	Y	Y	Y
2 Evans	N	Y	Y	Y	Y	Y
3 **Kelly**	Y	Y	Y	Y	Y	Y
4 **Perry**	Y	Y	Y	Y	Y	Y
5 **Thompson**	Y	Y	Y	Y	Y	Y
6 **Costello**	+	+	+	Y	Y	Y
7 **Meehan**	Y	Y	Y	Y	Y	Y
8 **Fitzpatrick**	Y	Y	Y	Y	Y	Y
9 **Shuster**	Y	Y	Y	Y	Y	Y
10 **Marino**	Y	Y	Y	Y	Y	Y
11 **Barletta**	Y	Y	Y	Y	Y	Y
12 **Rothfus**	Y	Y	Y	Y	Y	Y
13 Boyle	N	Y	Y	Y	Y	Y
14 Doyle	N	Y	Y	Y	Y	Y
15 **Dent**	Y	Y	Y	Y	Y	Y
16 **Smucker**	Y	Y	Y	Y	Y	Y
17 Cartwright	N	Y	Y	Y	Y	Y
18 **Murphy**	Y	Y	Y	Y	Y	Y
RHODE ISLAND						
1 Cicilline	N	Y	Y	Y	Y	Y
2 Langevin	N	Y	Y	Y	Y	Y
SOUTH CAROLINA						
1 **Sanford**	Y	N	Y	Y	Y	Y
2 **Wilson**	Y	Y	Y	Y	Y	Y
3 **Duncan**	Y	Y	Y	Y	Y	Y
4 **Gowdy**	Y	Y	Y	Y	Y	Y
5 **Norman**	Y	Y	Y	Y	Y	Y
6 Clyburn	N	Y	Y	Y	Y	Y
7 **Rice**	Y	Y	Y	Y	Y	Y
SOUTH DAKOTA						
AL **Noem**	Y	Y	Y	Y	Y	Y
TENNESSEE						
1 **Roe**	Y	Y	Y	Y	Y	Y
2 **Duncan**	Y	N	Y	Y	Y	?
3 **Fleischmann**	Y	Y	Y	Y	Y	Y
4 **DesJarlais**	Y	Y	Y	Y	Y	Y
5 Cooper	N	Y	Y	Y	?	Y
6 **Black**	Y	Y	Y	Y	Y	Y
7 **Blackburn**	Y	Y	Y	Y	Y	Y
8 **Kustoff**	Y	Y	Y	Y	Y	Y
9 Cohen	N	Y	Y	Y	Y	Y

	436	437	438	439	440	441
TEXAS						
1 **Gohmert**	Y	Y	Y	N	Y	Y
2 **Poe**	Y	Y	Y	?	?	Y
3 **Johnson, S.**	Y	Y	Y	Y	Y	Y
4 **Ratcliffe**	Y	Y	Y	Y	Y	Y
5 **Hensarling**	Y	Y	Y	Y	Y	Y
6 **Barton**	Y	Y	Y	Y	Y	Y
7 **Culberson**	Y	Y	Y	Y	Y	Y
8 **Brady**	Y	Y	Y	Y	Y	Y
9 Green, A.	N	Y	Y	Y	Y	Y
10 **McCaul**	Y	Y	Y	Y	Y	Y
11 **Conaway**	Y	Y	Y	Y	Y	Y
12 **Granger**	Y	Y	Y	Y	Y	Y
13 **Thornberry**	Y	Y	Y	Y	Y	Y
14 **Weber**	Y	Y	Y	Y	Y	Y
15 Gonzalez	N	Y	Y	?	?	Y
16 O'Rourke	N	N	Y	Y	Y	Y
17 **Flores**	Y	Y	Y	Y	Y	Y
18 Jackson Lee	N	Y	Y	Y	Y	Y
19 **Arrington**	Y	Y	Y	Y	Y	Y
20 Castro	N	Y	Y	Y	Y	Y
21 **Smith**	Y	Y	Y	Y	Y	Y
22 **Olson**	Y	Y	Y	+	+	Y
23 **Hurd**	Y	Y	Y	Y	Y	Y
24 **Marchant**	Y	Y	Y	Y	Y	Y
25 **Williams**	Y	Y	Y	Y	Y	Y
26 **Burgess**	Y	Y	Y	Y	Y	Y
27 **Farenthold**	Y	Y	Y	Y	Y	Y
28 Cuellar	N	Y	Y	Y	Y	Y
29 Green, G.	N	Y	Y	Y	Y	Y
30 Johnson, E.B.	N	Y	Y	Y	Y	Y
31 **Carter**	Y	Y	Y	Y	Y	Y
32 **Sessions**	Y	Y	Y	Y	Y	Y
33 Veasey	N	Y	Y	Y	Y	Y
34 Vela	N	Y	Y	Y	N	Y
35 Doggett	N	Y	Y	Y	Y	Y
36 **Babin**	Y	Y	Y	Y	Y	Y
UTAH						
1 **Bishop**	Y	Y	Y	Y	Y	Y
2 **Stewart**	Y	Y	Y	Y	Y	Y
4 **Love**	Y	Y	Y	Y	Y	Y
VERMONT						
AL Welch	N	N	Y	Y	Y	Y
VIRGINIA						
1 **Wittman**	Y	Y	Y	Y	Y	Y
2 **Taylor**	Y	Y	?	Y	Y	Y
3 Scott	N	Y	Y	Y	Y	Y
4 McEachin	N	Y	Y	Y	Y	Y
5 **Garrett**	Y	Y	Y	?	?	?
6 **Goodlatte**	Y	Y	Y	Y	Y	Y
7 **Brat**	Y	Y	Y	Y	Y	Y
8 Beyer	N	Y	Y	Y	Y	Y
9 **Griffith**	Y	Y	Y	Y	Y	Y
10 **Comstock**	Y	Y	Y	Y	Y	Y
11 Connolly	N	Y	Y	Y	Y	Y
WASHINGTON						
1 DelBene	N	N	Y	Y	Y	Y
2 Larsen	N	Y	Y	Y	Y	Y
3 **Herrera Beutler**	Y	Y	Y	?	?	Y
4 **Newhouse**	Y	Y	Y	Y	Y	Y
5 **McMorris Rodgers**	Y	Y	Y	Y	Y	Y
6 Kilmer	N	Y	Y	Y	Y	Y
7 Jayapal	N	N	Y	Y	Y	Y
8 **Reichert**	Y	Y	Y	Y	Y	Y
9 Smith	N	N	Y	Y	Y	Y
10 Heck	N	Y	Y	Y	Y	Y
WEST VIRGINIA						
1 **McKinley**	Y	Y	Y	Y	Y	Y
2 **Mooney**	Y	Y	Y	Y	Y	Y
3 **Jenkins**	Y	Y	Y	Y	Y	Y
WISCONSIN						
1 **Ryan**						
2 Pocan	N	N	Y	Y	Y	Y
3 Kind	N	Y	Y	Y	Y	Y
4 Moore	N	Y	Y	Y	Y	Y
5 **Sensenbrenner**	Y	Y	Y	Y	Y	Y
6 **Grothman**	Y	Y	Y	Y	Y	Y
7 **Duffy**	Y	Y	Y	Y	Y	Y
8 **Gallagher**	Y	Y	Y	Y	Y	Y
WYOMING						
AL **Cheney**	Y	Y	Y	Y	Y	Y

VOTE NUMBER

442. H RES 500, HR 3354. FISCAL 2018 OMNIBUS APPROPRIATIONS LEGISLATIVE VEHICLE/PREVIOUS QUESTION. Cole, R-Okla., motion to order the previous question (thus limiting debate and possibility of amendment) on the rule (H Res 500) that would provide for House floor consideration of the fiscal 2018 Interior-Environment appropriations bill (HR 3354), which is the legislative vehicle for an omnibus appropriations package which would include: eight of the 12 fiscal 2018 appropriations measures and the text of the minibus appropriations package (HR 3219) passed on July 27, 2017. Motion agreed to 233-187 : R 233-0; D 0-187. Sept. 6, 2017.

443. H RES 500, HR 3354. FISCAL 2018 OMNIBUS APPROPRIATIONS LEGISLATIVE VEHICLE/RULE. Adoption of the rule (H Res 500) that would provide for House floor consideration of the fiscal 2018 Interior-Environment appropriations bill (HR 3354), which is the legislative vehicle for an omnibus appropriations package which would include: eight of the 12 fiscal 2018 appropriations measures and the text of the minibus appropriations package (HR 3219) passed on July 27, 2017. The rule would waive, through the legislative day of September 9, 2017, the two-thirds vote requirement to consider legislation on the same day it is reported from the House Rules Committee. The rule would also provide for motions to suspend the rules through the legislative day of September 9, 2017. Adopted 230-191 : R 230-3; D 0-188. Sept. 6, 2017.

444. PROCEDURAL MOTION/APPROVAL OF HOUSE JOURNAL. Approved 230-182 : R 145-85; D 85-97. Sept. 6, 2017.

445. HR 3354. FISCAL 2018 OMNIBUS APPROPRIATIONS LEGISLATIVE VEHICLE/PREVAILING WAGE REQUIREMENTS — AGRICULTURE DEPARTMENT. King, R-Iowa, amendment that would prohibit funds made available in the bill for the Agriculture Department and related agencies from being used to implement, administer or enforce Davis-Bacon Act prevailing wage requirements. Rejected in Committee of the Whole 176-241 : R 176-54; D 0-187. Sept. 6, 2017.

446. HR 3354. FISCAL 2018 OMNIBUS APPROPRIATIONS LEGISLATIVE VEHICLE/COMPOUNDED DRUG REGULATIONS. Carter, R-Ga., amendment that would prohibit funds provided by the bill from being used by the Food and Drug Administration to finalize, implement or enforce a 2015 draft standard memorandum of understanding between the FDA and states related to distributions of compounded human drugs. Rejected in Committee of the Whole 141-279 : R 136-96; D 5-183. Sept. 6, 2017.

447. HR 3354. FISCAL 2018 OMNIBUS APPROPRIATIONS LEGISLATIVE VEHICLE/ESSENTIAL AIR SERVICE PROGRAM. McClintock, R-Calif., amendment that would decrease funding to the Essential Air Service program by $150 million and would transfer the savings to the spending reduction account. Rejected in Committee of the Whole 140-280 : R 136-96; D 4-184. Sept. 6, 2017.

448. HR 3354. FISCAL 2018 OMNIBUS APPROPRIATIONS LEGISLATIVE VEHICLE/NEW FIXED GUIDEWAY GRANT INCREASE. Budd, R-N.C., amendment that would decrease funding for the Federal-State Partnership for State of Good Repair grants by $474 million, would increase funding for fixed guideway investment grants by $1, would increase funding for new fixed guideway grants by $400 million and would decrease funding for small start projects by the same amount. Rejected in Committee of the Whole 159-260 : R 155-76; D 4-184. Sept. 6, 2017.

	442	443	444	445	446	447	448
ALABAMA							
1 Byrne	Y	Y	Y	Y	Y	Y	Y
2 Roby	Y	Y	Y	Y	Y	Y	Y
3 Rogers	Y	Y	N	Y	Y	Y	N
4 Aderholt	Y	Y	Y	Y	Y	N	N
5 Brooks	Y	Y	Y	Y	Y	Y	Y
6 Palmer	Y	Y	Y	Y	Y	Y	Y
7 Sewell	N	N	N	N	N	N	N
ALASKA							
AL Young	Y	Y	N	N	N	N	N
ARIZONA							
1 O'Halleran	N	N	N	N	N	N	N
2 McSally	Y	Y	N	Y	Y	Y	Y
3 Grijalva	N	N	?	N	N	N	N
4 Gosar	Y	Y	N	Y	Y	N	Y
5 Biggs	Y	Y	Y	Y	Y	N	Y
6 Schweikert	Y	Y	Y	Y	Y	Y	Y
7 Gallego	N	N	N	N	N	N	N
8 Franks	Y	Y	N	?	?	?	?
9 Sinema	N	N	N	N	N	N	Y
ARKANSAS							
1 Crawford	Y	Y	N	Y	Y	N	Y
2 Hill	Y	Y	Y	Y	Y	N	Y
3 Womack	Y	Y	N	Y	Y	Y	Y
4 Westerman	Y	Y	Y	Y	Y	N	Y
CALIFORNIA							
1 LaMalfa	Y	Y	Y	Y	Y	N	Y
2 Huffman	N	N	Y	?	?	?	?
3 Garamendi	N	N	Y	N	N	N	N
4 McClintock	Y	Y	Y	Y	Y	Y	Y
5 Thompson	N	N	N	N	N	N	N
6 Matsui	N	N	N	N	N	N	N
7 Bera	N	N	N	N	N	N	N
8 Cook	Y	Y	N	N	N	Y	N
9 McNerney	N	N	Y	N	N	N	N
10 Denham	Y	Y	N	N	N	Y	N
11 DeSaulnier	N	N	N	N	N	N	N
12 Pelosi	N	N	Y	N	N	N	N
13 Lee	N	N	N	N	N	N	N
14 Speier	N	N	Y	N	N	N	N
15 Swalwell	N	N	Y	N	N	N	N
16 Costa	?	?	?	?	?	?	?
17 Khanna	N	N	Y	N	N	N	N
18 Eshoo	N	N	N	N	N	N	N
19 Lofgren	N	N	Y	N	N	N	N
20 Panetta	N	N	Y	N	N	N	N
21 Valadao	Y	Y	N	N	N	N	N
22 Nunes	Y	Y	Y	Y	Y	N	Y
23 McCarthy	Y	Y	Y	Y	Y	N	Y
24 Carbajal	N	N	N	N	N	N	N
25 Knight	Y	Y	N	Y	N	N	N
26 Brownley	N	N	N	N	N	N	N
27 Chu	N	N	Y	N	N	N	N
28 Schiff	N	N	N	N	N	N	N
29 Cardenas	N	N	N	N	N	N	N
30 Sherman	N	N	N	N	N	N	N
31 Aguilar	N	N	N	N	N	N	N
32 Napolitano	N	N	Y	N	N	N	N
33 Lieu	N	N	N	?	?	?	?
34 Gomez	N	N	N	N	N	N	N
35 Torres	N	N	N	N	N	N	N
36 Ruiz	N	N	Y	N	N	N	N
37 Bass	N	N	N	N	N	N	N
38 Sánchez, Linda	N	N	N	N	N	N	N
39 Royce	Y	Y	Y	Y	N	Y	Y
40 Roybal-Allard	N	N	?	N	N	N	N
41 Takano	N	N	N	N	N	N	N
42 Calvert	Y	Y	Y	Y	Y	Y	N
43 Waters	N	N	Y	N	N	N	N
44 Barragan	N	N	N	N	N	N	N
45 Walters	Y	Y	Y	Y	N	Y	Y
46 Correa	N	N	N	N	N	N	N
47 Lowenthal	N	N	N	N	N	N	N
48 Rohrabacher	Y	Y	N	Y	Y	Y	Y
49 Issa	Y	Y	Y	Y	Y	Y	Y
50 Hunter	Y	Y	Y	Y	N	Y	Y
51 Vargas	N	N	N	N	N	N	N
52 Peters	N	N	N	N	N	N	N
53 Davis	N	N	Y	N	N	N	N

	442	443	444	445	446	447	448
COLORADO							
1 DeGette	?	?	?	?	?	?	?
2 Polis	N	N	Y	N	N	N	N
3 Tipton	Y	Y	N	Y	Y	N	Y
4 Buck	Y	Y	N	Y	N	Y	Y
5 Lamborn	Y	Y	Y	Y	N	Y	Y
6 Coffman	Y	Y	N	Y	Y	N	Y
7 Perlmutter	N	N	Y	N	N	N	N
CONNECTICUT							
1 Larson	N	N	Y	N	N	N	N
2 Courtney	N	N	Y	N	N	N	N
3 DeLauro	N	N	Y	N	N	N	N
4 Himes	N	N	Y	N	N	Y	N
5 Esty	N	N	N	N	N	N	N
DELAWARE							
AL Blunt Rochester	N	N	Y	N	N	N	N
FLORIDA							
1 Gaetz	Y	Y	N	Y	N	Y	Y
2 Dunn	Y	Y	Y	Y	Y	Y	Y
3 Yoho	Y	Y	N	Y	Y	N	N
4 Rutherford	Y	Y	N	Y	Y	N	N
5 Lawson	N	N	N	N	N	N	N
6 DeSantis	Y	Y	N	Y	N	N	N
7 Murphy	N	N	Y	N	N	N	N
8 Posey	Y	Y	Y	Y	Y	Y	Y
9 Soto	N	N	Y	N	N	N	N
10 Demings	N	N	Y	N	N	N	N
11 Webster	Y	Y	Y	Y	Y	Y	Y
12 Bilirakis	Y	Y	Y	Y	N	Y	Y
13 Crist	N	N	N	N	N	N	N
14 Castor	N	N	N	N	Y	N	N
15 Ross	?	?	?	?	?	?	?
16 Buchanan	Y	Y	Y	Y	N	Y	Y
17 Rooney, T.	Y	Y	Y	Y	Y	Y	Y
18 Mast	Y	Y	N	Y	N	Y	Y
19 Rooney, F.	Y	Y	?	Y	Y	N	Y
20 Hastings	N	N	N	N	N	N	N
21 Frankel	N	N	N	N	N	N	N
22 Deutch	N	N	Y	N	N	N	N
23 Wasserman Schultz	?	?	?	?	?	?	?
24 Wilson	N	N	?	N	N	N	N
25 Diaz-Balart	Y	Y	N	N	N	N	N
26 Curbelo	Y	Y	N	?	?	?	?
27 Ros-Lehtinen	Y	?	?	?	?	?	?
GEORGIA							
1 Carter	Y	Y	N	Y	Y	Y	Y
2 Bishop	N	N	Y	N	N	N	N
3 Ferguson	Y	Y	Y	Y	Y	Y	Y
4 Johnson	N	N	N	N	N	N	N
5 Lewis	N	N	N	N	N	N	N
6 Handel	Y	Y	Y	Y	Y	Y	Y
7 Woodall	Y	Y	N	Y	Y	Y	Y
8 Scott, A.	Y	Y	Y	Y	Y	Y	Y
9 Collins	Y	Y	Y	Y	Y	Y	Y
10 Hice	Y	Y	N	Y	Y	Y	Y
11 Loudermilk	Y	Y	N	Y	Y	Y	Y
12 Allen	Y	Y	Y	Y	Y	Y	Y
13 Scott, D.	N	N	Y	N	N	N	N
14 Graves	Y	Y	Y	Y	Y	Y	Y
HAWAII							
1 Hanabusa	N	N	Y	N	N	N	N
2 Gabbard	N	N	Y	N	N	N	N
IDAHO							
1 Labrador	Y	Y	Y	Y	Y	Y	Y
2 Simpson	Y	Y	Y	Y	N	N	N
ILLINOIS							
1 Rush	N	N	Y	?	N	N	N
2 Kelly	N	N	N	N	N	N	N
3 Lipinski	N	N	Y	N	N	N	N
4 Gutierrez	N	N	N	N	N	N	N
5 Quigley	N	N	Y	N	N	N	N
6 Roskam	Y	Y	N	N	N	Y	Y
7 Davis, D.	N	N	N	N	N	N	N
8 Krishnamoorthi	N	N	Y	N	N	N	N
9 Schakowsky	N	N	N	N	N	N	N
10 Schneider	N	N	Y	N	N	N	N
11 Foster	N	N	Y	N	N	N	N
12 Bost	Y	Y	N	N	N	N	N
13 Davis, R.	Y	Y	N	Y	N	N	N
14 Hultgren	Y	Y	Y	N	Y	Y	Y
15 Shimkus	Y	Y	Y	N	N	N	N

	442	443	444	445	446	447	448
16 **Kinzinger**	Y	Y	N	N	N	N	N
17 Bustos	N	N	Y	N	N	N	N
18 **LaHood**	Y	Y	N	N	Y	N	Y
INDIANA							
1 Visclosky	N	N	N	N	N	N	N
2 **Walorski**	Y	Y	Y	Y	N	Y	Y
3 **Banks**	Y	Y	Y	Y	Y	Y	Y
4 **Rokita**	Y	Y	Y	Y	Y	Y	Y
5 **Brooks**	Y	Y	Y	?	N	Y	Y
6 **Messer**	Y	Y	Y	Y	N	Y	Y
7 Carson	N	N	N	N	N	N	N
8 **Bucshon**	Y	Y	Y	N	N	N	N
9 **Hollingsworth**	Y	Y	Y	Y	Y	Y	Y
IOWA							
1 **Blum**	Y	Y	N	Y	Y	N	Y
2 Loebsack	N	N	N	N	N	N	N
3 **Young**	Y	Y	Y	Y	Y	Y	N
4 **King**	Y	Y	Y	Y	Y	N	Y
KANSAS							
1 **Marshall**	Y	Y	N	Y	Y	N	Y
2 **Jenkins**	Y	Y	N	Y	N	N	Y
3 **Yoder**	Y	Y	N	Y	N	Y	Y
4 **Estes**	Y	Y	Y	Y	Y	N	Y
KENTUCKY							
1 **Comer**	Y	Y	N	Y	Y	N	Y
2 **Guthrie**	Y	Y	N	Y	N	N	Y
3 Yarmuth	N	N	?	N	N	N	N
4 **Massie**	Y	N	Y	Y	Y	Y	Y
5 **Rogers**	Y	Y	Y	Y	Y	N	N
6 **Barr**	Y	Y	Y	Y	N	N	Y
LOUISIANA							
1 **Scalise**	+	+	+	+	+	+	–
2 Richmond	N	N	Y	N	N	N	N
3 **Higgins**	Y	Y	Y	Y	Y	Y	Y
4 **Johnson**	Y	Y	N	Y	Y	Y	Y
5 **Abraham**	Y	Y	Y	Y	Y	N	Y
6 **Graves**	Y	Y	N	Y	Y	Y	Y
MAINE							
1 Pingree	N	N	Y	N	N	N	N
2 **Poliquin**	Y	Y	N	Y	Y	N	Y
MARYLAND							
1 **Harris**	Y	Y	Y	Y	N	Y	Y
2 Ruppersberger	N	N	Y	N	Y	N	N
3 Sarbanes	N	N	N	N	N	N	N
4 Brown	N	N	Y	N	N	N	N
5 Hoyer	N	N	N	N	N	N	N
6 Delaney	N	N	N	N	N	N	N
7 Cummings	?	?	?	?	?	?	?
8 Raskin	N	N	N	N	N	N	N
MASSACHUSETTS							
1 Neal	N	N	N	N	N	N	N
2 McGovern	N	N	N	N	N	N	N
3 Tsongas	N	N	Y	N	N	N	N
4 Kennedy	N	N	N	N	N	N	N
5 Clark	N	N	Y	N	N	N	N
6 Moulton	N	N	Y	N	N	N	N
7 Capuano	N	N	N	N	N	N	N
8 Lynch	N	N	N	N	N	N	N
9 Keating	N	N	N	N	N	N	N
MICHIGAN							
1 **Bergman**	Y	Y	Y	Y	N	N	Y
2 **Huizenga**	Y	Y	N	Y	N	Y	Y
3 **Amash**	Y	N	N	Y	Y	Y	Y
4 **Moolenaar**	Y	Y	N	Y	N	N	N
5 Kildee	N	N	Y	N	N	N	N
6 **Upton**	Y	Y	Y	N	N	N	N
7 **Walberg**	Y	Y	Y	Y	N	Y	Y
8 **Bishop**	Y	Y	N	Y	N	Y	Y
9 Levin	N	N	N	N	N	N	N
10 **Mitchell**	Y	Y	Y	Y	N	N	Y
11 **Trott**	Y	Y	Y	Y	N	Y	N
12 Dingell	N	N	Y	N	N	N	N
13 Conyers	N	N	Y	N	N	N	N
14 Lawrence	N	N	Y	N	N	N	N
MINNESOTA							
1 Walz	N	N	Y	N	N	N	N
2 **Lewis**	Y	Y	Y	N	Y	Y	Y
3 **Paulsen**	Y	Y	N	Y	N	Y	Y
4 McCollum	N	N	Y	N	N	N	N

	442	443	444	445	446	447	448
5 Ellison	N	N	N	N	N	N	N
6 **Emmer**	Y	Y	Y	N	N	Y	Y
7 Peterson	N	N	N	N	N	N	N
8 Nolan	N	N	N	N	N	N	N
MISSISSIPPI							
1 **Kelly**	Y	Y	Y	Y	Y	N	Y
2 Thompson	N	N	N	N	N	N	N
3 **Harper**	Y	Y	Y	Y	N	N	Y
4 **Palazzo**	Y	Y	Y	Y	Y	N	N
MISSOURI							
1 Clay	N	N	Y	N	N	N	N
2 **Wagner**	Y	Y	Y	Y	N	Y	Y
3 **Luetkemeyer**	Y	Y	Y	Y	N	N	Y
4 **Hartzler**	Y	Y	Y	Y	N	N	Y
5 Cleaver	N	N	N	N	N	N	N
6 **Graves**	Y	Y	N	N	N	N	Y
7 **Long**	Y	Y	Y	Y	N	N	Y
8 **Smith**	Y	Y	N	Y	N	N	Y
MONTANA							
AL **Gianforte**	Y	Y	Y	N	Y	N	N
NEBRASKA							
1 **Fortenberry**	Y	Y	Y	Y	N	N	N
2 **Bacon**	Y	Y	Y	Y	N	N	Y
3 **Smith**	Y	Y	Y	Y	N	N	Y
NEVADA							
1 Titus	N	N	Y	N	N	N	N
2 **Amodei**	Y	Y	Y	Y	Y	N	N
3 Rosen	N	N	N	N	N	N	N
4 Kihuen	N	N	N	N	N	N	N
NEW HAMPSHIRE							
1 Shea-Porter	N	N	Y	N	N	N	N
2 Kuster	N	N	Y	N	N	N	N
NEW JERSEY							
1 Norcross	N	N	N	N	N	N	N
2 **LoBiondo**	Y	Y	N	N	Y	N	N
3 **MacArthur**	Y	Y	N	N	N	N	N
4 **Smith**	Y	Y	Y	N	N	N	N
5 Gottheimer	N	N	N	N	N	N	N
6 Pallone	N	N	N	N	N	N	N
7 **Lance**	Y	Y	N	N	N	Y	N
8 Sires	N	N	N	N	N	N	N
9 Pascrell	N	N	N	N	N	N	N
10 Payne	N	N	N	N	N	N	N
11 **Frelinghuysen**	Y	Y	Y	Y	Y	N	N
12 Watson Coleman	N	N	N	N	N	N	N
NEW MEXICO							
1 Lujan Grisham	N	N	Y	N	N	N	N
2 **Pearce**	Y	Y	N	Y	Y	N	Y
3 Luján	N	N	Y	N	N	N	N
NEW YORK							
1 **Zeldin**	Y	Y	Y	N	N	Y	N
2 **King**	Y	Y	Y	N	N	N	N
3 Suozzi	?	?	?	N	N	N	N
4 Rice	N	N	N	N	N	N	N
5 Meeks	N	N	Y	N	N	N	N
6 Meng	N	N	Y	N	N	N	N
7 Velázquez	N	N	Y	N	N	N	N
8 Jeffries	N	N	N	N	N	N	N
9 Clarke	N	N	?	N	N	N	N
10 Nadler	N	N	Y	N	N	N	N
11 **Donovan**	Y	Y	Y	N	N	N	N
12 Maloney, C.	N	N	Y	N	N	N	N
13 Espaillat	N	N	N	N	N	N	N
14 Crowley	N	N	N	N	N	N	N
15 Serrano	N	N	Y	N	N	N	N
16 Engel	N	N	Y	N	N	N	N
17 Lowey	N	N	Y	N	N	N	N
18 Maloney, S.P.	N	N	N	N	N	N	N
19 **Faso**	Y	Y	Y	N	N	N	N
20 Tonko	N	N	P	N	N	N	N
21 **Stefanik**	Y	Y	Y	N	N	N	N
22 **Tenney**	Y	Y	N	N	N	N	N
23 **Reed**	Y	Y	N	N	Y	Y	N
24 **Katko**	Y	Y	N	N	N	N	N
25 Slaughter	N	N	N	N	N	N	N
26 Higgins	?	?	?	N	N	N	N
27 **Collins**	Y	Y	Y	Y	N	Y	N
NORTH CAROLINA							
1 Butterfield	N	N	Y	N	N	N	N
2 **Holding**	Y	Y	N	Y	N	Y	N
3 **Jones**	Y	N	N	Y	Y	Y	Y
4 Price	N	N	Y	N	N	N	N

	442	443	444	445	446	447	448
5 **Foxx**	Y	Y	N	Y	Y	Y	Y
6 **Walker**	Y	Y	N	Y	N	Y	Y
7 **Rouzer**	Y	Y	N	Y	N	Y	Y
8 **Hudson**	Y	Y	N	Y	Y	Y	Y
9 **Pittenger**	Y	Y	N	?	Y	Y	Y
10 **McHenry**	Y	Y	Y	Y	Y	Y	N
11 **Meadows**	Y	Y	Y	Y	Y	Y	Y
12 Adams	N	N	Y	N	N	N	N
13 **Budd**	Y	Y	Y	Y	N	Y	Y
NORTH DAKOTA							
AL **Cramer**	?	?	?	Y	N	N	N
OHIO							
1 **Chabot**	Y	Y	Y	Y	Y	Y	Y
2 **Wenstrup**	Y	Y	Y	Y	N	Y	Y
3 Beatty	N	N	N	N	N	N	N
4 **Jordan**	Y	Y	N	Y	Y	Y	Y
5 **Latta**	Y	Y	N	Y	N	Y	Y
6 **Johnson**	Y	Y	N	N	N	N	N
7 **Gibbs**	Y	Y	Y	Y	N	N	Y
8 **Davidson**	Y	Y	Y	Y	Y	Y	Y
9 Kaptur	N	N	Y	N	N	N	N
10 **Turner**	Y	Y	Y	N	N	N	N
11 Fudge	N	N	N	N	N	N	N
12 **Tiberi**	Y	Y	N	N	N	Y	N
13 Ryan	N	N	N	N	N	N	N
14 **Joyce**	Y	Y	N	N	N	N	N
15 **Stivers**	Y	Y	N	N	N	N	N
16 **Renacci**	Y	Y	N	N	Y	Y	Y
OKLAHOMA							
1 **Bridenstine**	?	?	?	?	?	?	?
2 **Mullin**	Y	Y	Y	Y	N	N	Y
3 **Lucas**	Y	Y	Y	Y	N	N	N
4 **Cole**	Y	Y	Y	Y	Y	N	N
5 **Russell**	Y	Y	Y	Y	Y	Y	Y
OREGON							
1 Bonamici	N	N	Y	N	N	N	N
2 **Walden**	Y	Y	Y	N	N	N	N
3 Blumenauer	N	N	Y	N	N	N	N
4 DeFazio	N	N	N	N	N	N	N
5 Schrader	N	N	N	N	N	N	N
PENNSYLVANIA							
1 Brady	N	N	N	N	N	N	N
2 Evans	N	N	Y	N	N	N	N
3 **Kelly**	Y	Y	Y	N	N	N	Y
4 **Perry**	Y	Y	Y	Y	Y	Y	Y
5 **Thompson**	Y	Y	N	Y	Y	N	N
6 **Costello**	Y	Y	N	N	N	Y	N
7 **Meehan**	Y	Y	Y	N	N	N	N
8 **Fitzpatrick**	Y	Y	N	N	N	N	N
9 **Shuster**	Y	Y	Y	N	N	N	N
10 **Marino**	Y	Y	Y	N	Y	N	N
11 **Barletta**	Y	Y	Y	N	Y	N	N
12 **Rothfus**	Y	Y	Y	Y	N	N	Y
13 Boyle	N	N	N	N	N	N	N
14 Doyle	N	N	N	N	N	N	N
15 **Dent**	Y	Y	Y	Y	N	N	N
16 **Smucker**	Y	Y	Y	Y	N	N	N
17 Cartwright	N	N	Y	N	N	N	N
18 **Murphy**	Y	Y	Y	N	N	N	N
RHODE ISLAND							
1 Cicilline	N	N	Y	N	N	N	N
2 Langevin	N	N	N	N	N	N	N
SOUTH CAROLINA							
1 **Sanford**	Y	Y	Y	Y	Y	Y	Y
2 **Wilson**	Y	Y	Y	Y	Y	Y	Y
3 **Duncan**	Y	Y	Y	Y	Y	Y	Y
4 **Gowdy**	Y	Y	Y	Y	Y	Y	Y
5 **Norman**	Y	Y	Y	Y	Y	Y	Y
6 Clyburn	N	N	Y	N	N	N	N
7 **Rice**	Y	Y	P	Y	N	Y	Y
SOUTH DAKOTA							
AL **Noem**	Y	Y	Y	Y	Y	N	Y
TENNESSEE							
1 **Roe**	Y	Y	Y	Y	Y	Y	Y
2 **Duncan**	Y	Y	Y	Y	Y	Y	Y
3 **Fleischmann**	Y	Y	Y	Y	N	N	N
4 **DesJarlais**	Y	Y	Y	Y	Y	Y	Y
5 Cooper	N	N	Y	N	N	Y	N
6 **Black**	Y	Y	Y	Y	Y	Y	Y
7 **Blackburn**	Y	Y	N	Y	Y	Y	Y
8 **Kustoff**	Y	Y	Y	Y	N	N	Y
9 Cohen	N	N	N	N	N	N	N

	442	443	444	445	446	447	448
TEXAS							
1 **Gohmert**	Y	Y	?	Y	Y	Y	Y
2 **Poe**	Y	Y	Y	Y	Y	Y	Y
3 **Johnson, S.**	Y	Y	Y	Y	Y	Y	Y
4 **Ratcliffe**	Y	Y	N	Y	Y	Y	Y
5 **Hensarling**	Y	Y	Y	Y	Y	Y	Y
6 **Barton**	Y	Y	Y	Y	Y	Y	Y
7 **Culberson**	Y	Y	Y	Y	Y	Y	N
8 **Brady**	Y	Y	Y	Y	Y	Y	?
9 Green, A.	N	N	Y	N	N	N	N
10 **McCaul**	Y	Y	Y	Y	Y	Y	Y
11 **Conaway**	Y	Y	N	Y	Y	Y	Y
12 **Granger**	?	Y	Y	Y	Y	Y	N
13 **Thornberry**	Y	Y	Y	Y	Y	Y	Y
14 **Weber**	Y	Y	N	Y	Y	Y	Y
15 Gonzalez	N	N	N	N	N	N	N
16 O'Rourke	N	N	Y	N	N	N	N
17 **Flores**	Y	Y	N	Y	N	Y	Y
18 Jackson Lee	?	N	N	N	N	N	N
19 **Arrington**	Y	Y	Y	Y	Y	Y	Y
20 Castro	N	N	Y	N	N	N	N
21 **Smith**	Y	Y	Y	Y	Y	Y	Y
22 **Olson**	Y	Y	Y	Y	Y	Y	Y
23 **Hurd**	Y	Y	N	Y	N	N	N
24 **Marchant**	Y	Y	Y	Y	Y	Y	Y
25 **Williams**	Y	Y	Y	Y	N	Y	Y
26 **Burgess**	Y	Y	N	Y	Y	Y	N
27 **Farenthold**	Y	Y	Y	Y	Y	Y	Y
28 Cuellar	N	N	Y	N	Y	N	N
29 Green, G.	N	N	N	N	N	N	N
30 Johnson, E.B.	N	N	N	N	N	N	N
31 **Carter**	Y	Y	Y	Y	Y	Y	N
32 **Sessions**	Y	Y	Y	Y	Y	Y	Y
33 Veasey	N	N	N	N	N	N	N
34 Vela	N	N	N	N	N	N	N
35 Doggett	N	N	Y	N	N	N	N
36 **Babin**	Y	Y	N	Y	Y	Y	Y
UTAH							
1 **Bishop**	Y	Y	Y	Y	Y	N	N
2 **Stewart**	Y	Y	Y	Y	Y	Y	N
4 **Love**	Y	Y	N	Y	Y	Y	Y
VERMONT							
AL Welch	N	N	Y	N	N	N	N
VIRGINIA							
1 **Wittman**	Y	Y	N	Y	Y	Y	Y
2 **Taylor**	Y	Y	Y	N	Y	N	Y
3 Scott	N	N	Y	N	N	N	N
4 McEachin	N	N	Y	N	N	N	N
5 **Garrett**	?	?	?	?	?	?	?
6 **Goodlatte**	Y	Y	Y	Y	Y	Y	Y
7 **Brat**	Y	Y	Y	Y	Y	Y	Y
8 Beyer	N	N	N	N	N	N	N
9 **Griffith**	Y	Y	Y	Y	Y	Y	Y
10 **Comstock**	Y	Y	Y	Y	Y	N	N
11 Connolly	N	N	N	N	N	N	N
WASHINGTON							
1 DelBene	N	N	Y	N	N	N	N
2 Larsen	N	N	Y	N	N	N	N
3 **Herrera Beutler**	Y	Y	N	Y	Y	Y	N
4 **Newhouse**	Y	Y	Y	N	N	Y	N
5 **McMorris Rodgers**	Y	Y	Y	Y	Y	Y	Y
6 Kilmer	N	N	N	N	N	N	N
7 Jayapal	N	N	N	N	N	N	N
8 **Reichert**	Y	Y	Y	N	N	N	N
9 Smith	N	N	Y	N	N	N	Y
10 Heck	N	N	Y	N	N	N	N
WEST VIRGINIA							
1 **McKinley**	Y	Y	N	N	N	N	Y
2 **Mooney**	Y	Y	Y	Y	Y	N	Y
3 **Jenkins**	Y	Y	N	N	Y	N	Y
WISCONSIN							
1 **Ryan**							
2 Pocan	N	N	Y	N	Y	N	N
3 Kind	N	N	N	N	N	N	N
4 Moore	N	N	N	N	N	N	N
5 **Sensenbrenner**	Y	Y	Y	Y	Y	Y	Y
6 **Grothman**	Y	Y	N	Y	Y	Y	Y
7 **Duffy**	Y	Y	Y	N	N	N	Y
8 **Gallagher**	Y	Y	N	Y	Y	Y	Y
WYOMING							
AL **Cheney**	Y	Y	Y	Y	Y	N	Y

VOTE NUMBER

449. HR 3354. FISCAL 2018 OMNIBUS APPROPRIATIONS LEGISLATIVE VEHICLE/AMTRAK FUNDING ELIMINATION. Brooks, R-Ala., amendment that would eliminate $1.1 billion in funding for grants to the National Railroad Passenger Corporation (operating as Amtrak). Rejected in Committee of the Whole 128-293 : R 128-105; D 0-188. Sept. 6, 2017.

450. HR 3354. FISCAL 2018 OMNIBUS APPROPRIATIONS LEGISLATIVE VEHICLE/NEIGHBORHOOD REINVESTMENT CORPORATION. Rosen, D-Nev., amendment that would decrease funding for the Department of Housing and Urban Development administrative support offices by $47 million, decrease HUD Office CFO funding by $4 million, decrease HUD Office of General Counsel funding by $8 million, decrease HUD Office of Administration funding by $32.7 million, decrease HUD Office of the Chief Procurement Office funding by $1.9 million, decrease HUD Office of Strategic Planning and Management funding by $475,000 and increase the Neighborhood Reinvestment Corporation funding by $35 million. Rejected in Committee of the Whole 200-220 : R 16-216; D 184-4. Sept. 6, 2017.

451. HR 3354. FISCAL 2018 OMNIBUS APPROPRIATIONS LEGISLATIVE VEHICLE/SECTION 8 HOUSING CONTRACT DECREASE. Grothman, R-Wis., amendment that would decrease the funding for the Public and Indian Housing Tenant-Based Rental Assistance Program of expiring section 8 housing tenant-based annual contributions contracts by $177 million and would transfer the savings to the spending reduction account. Rejected in Committee of the Whole 124-295 : R 124-108; D 0-187. Sept. 6, 2017.

452. HR 3354. FISCAL 2018 OMNIBUS APPROPRIATIONS LEGISLATIVE VEHICLE/RENTAL ASSISTANCE SUBSIDY DECREASE. Grothman, R-Wis., amendment that would decrease funding for project based rental assistance subsidy contracts by $266 million and would transfer the savings to the spending reduction account. Rejected in Committee of the Whole 139-282 : R 139-94; D 0-188. Sept. 6, 2017.

453. HR 3354. FISCAL 2018 OMNIBUS APPROPRIATIONS LEGISLATIVE VEHICLE/PREVAILING WAGE REQUIREMENT — TRANSPORTATION AND HOUSING. King, R-Iowa, amendment that would prohibit funds appropriated to the Departments of Transportation, Housing and Urban Development and related agencies from being used to implement, administer, or enforce the Davis-Bacon Act prevailing wage requirement. Rejected in Committee of the Whole 180-241 : R 180-53; D 0-188. Sept. 6, 2017.

454. HR 3354. FISCAL 2018 OMNIBUS APPROPRIATIONS LEGISLATIVE VEHICLE/HOUSING AND URBAN DEVELOPMENT DECREASE. Grothman, R-Wis., amendment that would reduce the bill's funding for the Department of Housing and Urban Development by two percent. Rejected in Committee of the Whole 140-280 : R 140-92; D 0-188. Sept. 6, 2017.

455. HR 3354. FISCAL 2018 OMNIBUS APPROPRIATIONS LEGISLATIVE VEHICLE/IMMIGRATION STATUS INFORMATION. Smith, R-Mo., amendment that would prohibit state and local government entities from receiving Housing and Urban Development Department funding if the state or local entity prohibits or restricts any government entity from reporting to Immigration and Naturalization Service with information regarding the citizenship or immigration status, lawful or unlawful, of any individual. Adopted in Committee of the Whole 225-195 : R 224-8; D 1-187. Sept. 6, 2017.

	449	450	451	452	453	454	455
ALABAMA							
1 Byrne	Y	N	Y	Y	Y	Y	Y
2 Roby	Y	N	N	N	Y	N	Y
3 Rogers	Y	N	N	N	Y	N	Y
4 Aderholt	Y	N	N	N	Y	N	Y
5 Brooks	Y	N	Y	Y	Y	Y	Y
6 Palmer	Y	N	Y	Y	Y	Y	Y
7 Sewell	N	Y	N	N	N	N	N
ALASKA							
AL Young	N	N	N	N	N	N	Y
ARIZONA							
1 O'Halleran	N	Y	N	N	N	N	N
2 McSally	Y	N	N	N	Y	N	Y
3 Grijalva	N	Y	N	N	N	N	N
4 Gosar	Y	N	Y	Y	Y	Y	Y
5 Biggs	Y	N	Y	Y	Y	Y	Y
6 Schweikert	Y	N	N	Y	Y	Y	Y
7 Gallego	N	Y	N	N	N	N	N
8 Franks	Y	N	Y	Y	Y	Y	Y
9 Sinema	N	Y	N	N	N	N	N
ARKANSAS							
1 Crawford	Y	N	Y	Y	Y	Y	Y
2 Hill	N	N	Y	Y	Y	Y	Y
3 Womack	N	N	Y	Y	Y	Y	Y
4 Westerman	Y	N	Y	Y	Y	Y	Y
CALIFORNIA							
1 LaMalfa	N	N	Y	Y	Y	Y	Y
2 Huffman	?	?	?	?	?	?	?
3 Garamendi	N	Y	N	N	N	N	N
4 McClintock	Y	N	Y	Y	Y	Y	Y
5 Thompson	N	Y	N	N	N	N	N
6 Matsui	N	Y	N	N	N	N	N
7 Bera	N	Y	N	N	N	N	N
8 Cook	N	N	N	N	N	N	Y
9 McNerney	N	Y	N	N	N	N	N
10 Denham	N	N	N	N	N	N	Y
11 DeSaulnier	N	Y	N	N	N	N	N
12 Pelosi	N	Y	N	N	N	N	N
13 Lee	N	Y	N	N	N	N	N
14 Speier	N	Y	N	N	N	N	N
15 Swalwell	N	Y	N	N	N	N	N
16 Costa	?	?	?	?	?	?	?
17 Khanna	N	Y	N	N	N	N	N
18 Eshoo	N	Y	N	N	N	N	N
19 Lofgren	N	Y	N	N	N	N	N
20 Panetta	N	Y	N	N	N	N	N
21 Valadao	N	N	N	N	N	N	N
22 Nunes	N	N	N	N	Y	N	Y
23 McCarthy	N	N	N	Y	Y	Y	Y
24 Carbajal	N	Y	N	N	N	N	N
25 Knight	N	N	N	N	N	N	N
26 Brownley	N	Y	N	N	N	N	N
27 Chu	N	Y	N	N	N	N	N
28 Schiff	N	Y	N	N	N	N	N
29 Cardenas	N	Y	N	N	N	N	N
30 Sherman	N	Y	N	N	N	N	N
31 Aguilar	N	Y	N	N	N	N	N
32 Napolitano	N	Y	N	N	N	N	N
33 Lieu	?	?	?	?	?	?	?
34 Gomez	N	Y	N	N	N	N	N
35 Torres	N	Y	N	N	N	N	N
36 Ruiz	N	Y	N	N	N	N	N
37 Bass	N	Y	N	N	N	N	N
38 Sánchez, Linda	N	Y	N	N	N	N	N
39 Royce	Y	N	Y	Y	Y	Y	Y
40 Roybal-Allard	N	Y	N	N	N	N	N
41 Takano	N	Y	N	N	N	N	N
42 Calvert	N	N	N	N	Y	Y	Y
43 Waters	N	Y	N	N	N	N	N
44 Barragan	N	Y	N	N	N	N	N
45 Walters	N	N	Y	Y	Y	Y	Y
46 Correa	N	Y	N	N	N	N	N
47 Lowenthal	N	Y	N	N	N	N	N
48 Rohrabacher	Y	N	Y	Y	Y	Y	Y
49 Issa	Y	N	N	N	Y	N	Y
50 Hunter	Y	N	Y	Y	N	Y	Y
51 Vargas	N	Y	N	N	N	N	N
52 Peters	N	Y	N	N	N	N	N
53 Davis	N	Y	N	N	N	N	N

	449	450	451	452	453	454	455
COLORADO							
1 DeGette	?	?	?	?	?	?	?
2 Polis	N	Y	N	N	N	N	N
3 Tipton	N	N	N	N	Y	N	Y
4 Buck	Y	N	Y	Y	Y	Y	Y
5 Lamborn	Y	N	Y	Y	Y	Y	Y
6 Coffman	Y	N	Y	Y	Y	N	Y
7 Perlmutter	N	Y	N	N	N	N	N
CONNECTICUT							
1 Larson	N	Y	N	N	N	N	N
2 Courtney	N	Y	N	N	N	N	N
3 DeLauro	N	Y	N	N	N	N	N
4 Himes	N	Y	N	N	N	N	N
5 Esty	N	Y	N	N	N	N	N
DELAWARE							
AL Blunt Rochester	N	Y	N	N	N	N	N
FLORIDA							
1 Gaetz	Y	N	Y	Y	Y	Y	Y
2 Dunn	N	N	Y	Y	Y	Y	Y
3 Yoho	Y	N	Y	Y	Y	Y	Y
4 Rutherford	N	N	N	N	Y	N	Y
5 Lawson	N	Y	N	N	N	N	N
6 DeSantis	Y	N	Y	Y	Y	Y	Y
7 Murphy	N	Y	N	N	N	N	N
8 Posey	Y	N	Y	Y	Y	Y	Y
9 Soto	N	Y	N	N	N	N	N
10 Demings	N	Y	N	N	N	N	N
11 Webster	Y	N	Y	Y	Y	Y	Y
12 Bilirakis	Y	N	Y	Y	Y	?	Y
13 Crist	N	Y	N	N	N	N	N
14 Castor	N	Y	N	N	N	N	N
15 Ross	?	?	?	?	?	?	?
16 Buchanan	N	N	N	N	N	N	N
17 Rooney, T.	N	N	N	N	N	N	N
18 Mast	Y	N	N	N	Y	N	Y
19 Rooney, F.	Y	N	Y	Y	Y	Y	Y
20 Hastings	N	Y	N	N	N	N	N
21 Frankel	N	Y	N	N	N	N	N
22 Deutch	N	Y	N	N	N	N	N
23 Wasserman Schultz	?	?	?	?	?	?	?
24 Wilson	N	Y	N	N	N	N	N
25 Diaz-Balart	N	N	N	N	N	N	Y
26 Curbelo	?	?	?	?	?	?	?
27 Ros-Lehtinen	?	?	?	?	?	?	?
GEORGIA							
1 Carter	Y	N	N	Y	Y	Y	Y
2 Bishop	N	Y	N	N	N	N	N
3 Ferguson	N	Y	Y	Y	Y	Y	Y
4 Johnson	N	Y	N	N	N	N	N
5 Lewis	N	Y	N	N	N	N	N
6 Handel	N	N	N	N	Y	N	Y
7 Woodall	Y	N	Y	Y	Y	Y	Y
8 Scott, A.	N	N	Y	Y	Y	N	Y
9 Collins	Y	N	N	Y	Y	Y	Y
10 Hice	Y	N	Y	Y	Y	Y	Y
11 Loudermilk	Y	N	Y	Y	Y	Y	Y
12 Allen	Y	N	Y	Y	Y	Y	Y
13 Scott, D.	N	Y	?	N	N	N	N
14 Graves	Y	N	Y	Y	Y	Y	Y
HAWAII							
1 Hanabusa	N	Y	N	N	N	N	N
2 Gabbard	N	Y	N	N	N	N	N
IDAHO							
1 Labrador	Y	N	Y	Y	Y	Y	Y
2 Simpson	N	N	N	N	N	N	Y
ILLINOIS							
1 Rush	N	Y	N	N	N	N	N
2 Kelly	N	Y	N	N	N	N	N
3 Lipinski	N	Y	N	N	N	N	N
4 Gutierrez	N	Y	N	N	N	N	N
5 Quigley	N	Y	N	N	N	N	N
6 Roskam	N	N	N	N	N	N	N
7 Davis, D.	N	Y	N	N	N	N	N
8 Krishnamoorthi	N	Y	N	N	N	N	N
9 Schakowsky	N	Y	N	N	N	N	N
10 Schneider	N	Y	N	N	N	N	N
11 Foster	N	Y	N	N	N	N	N
12 Bost	N	N	N	N	N	N	Y
13 Davis, R.	N	N	N	N	N	N	Y
14 Hultgren	N	N	N	N	Y	N	Y
15 Shimkus	N	N	N	N	N	N	Y

	449	450	451	452	453	454	455
16 **Kinzinger**	N	N	N	N	N	N	Y
17 Bustos	N	Y	N	N	N	N	N
18 **LaHood**	N	N	Y	Y	N	Y	Y
INDIANA							
1 Visclosky	N	Y	N	N	N	N	N
2 **Walorski**	Y	N	N	Y	Y	Y	Y
3 **Banks**	Y	N	Y	Y	Y	Y	Y
4 **Rokita**	Y	N	Y	Y	Y	Y	Y
5 **Brooks**	N	N	N	N	Y	N	Y
6 **Messer**	Y	N	Y	Y	Y	Y	Y
7 Carson	N	Y	N	N	N	N	N
8 **Bucshon**	N	N	N	N	N	N	Y
9 **Hollingsworth**	Y	N	Y	Y	Y	N	Y
IOWA							
1 **Blum**	Y	N	Y	Y	Y	Y	Y
2 Loebsack	N	Y	N	N	N	N	N
3 **Young**	Y	N	Y	N	Y	Y	Y
4 **King**	Y	N	Y	Y	Y	Y	Y
KANSAS							
1 **Marshall**	Y	Y	Y	Y	Y	Y	Y
2 **Jenkins**	N	N	N	Y	Y	Y	Y
3 **Yoder**	Y	N	Y	Y	Y	Y	Y
4 **Estes**	N	N	Y	Y	Y	Y	Y
KENTUCKY							
1 **Comer**	Y	N	Y	Y	Y	Y	Y
2 **Guthrie**	Y	N	Y	Y	Y	Y	Y
3 Yarmuth	N	Y	N	N	N	N	N
4 **Massie**	Y	N	Y	Y	Y	Y	Y
5 **Rogers**	N	N	N	N	Y	N	Y
6 **Barr**	Y	N	Y	Y	Y	Y	Y
LOUISIANA							
1 **Scalise**	+	–	+	+	+	+	+
2 Richmond	N	Y	N	N	N	N	N
3 **Higgins**	Y	N	Y	Y	Y	Y	Y
4 **Johnson**	Y	N	Y	Y	Y	Y	Y
5 **Abraham**	N	N	Y	Y	Y	Y	Y
6 **Graves**	Y	N	Y	Y	Y	Y	Y
MAINE							
1 Pingree	N	Y	N	N	N	N	N
2 **Poliquin**	N	N	N	N	Y	N	Y
MARYLAND							
1 **Harris**	Y	N	Y	Y	Y	Y	Y
2 Ruppersberger	N	Y	N	N	N	N	N
3 Sarbanes	N	Y	N	N	N	N	N
4 Brown	N	Y	N	N	N	N	N
5 Hoyer	N	Y	N	N	N	N	N
6 Delaney	N	Y	N	N	N	N	N
7 Cummings	?	?	?	?	?	?	?
8 Raskin	N	Y	N	N	N	N	N
MASSACHUSETTS							
1 Neal	N	Y	N	N	N	N	N
2 McGovern	N	Y	N	N	N	N	N
3 Tsongas	N	Y	N	N	N	N	N
4 Kennedy	N	Y	N	N	N	N	N
5 Clark	N	Y	N	N	N	N	N
6 Moulton	N	Y	N	N	N	N	N
7 Capuano	N	Y	N	N	N	N	N
8 Lynch	N	Y	N	N	N	N	N
9 Keating	N	Y	N	N	N	N	N
MICHIGAN							
1 **Bergman**	Y	N	N	Y	Y	Y	Y
2 **Huizenga**	Y	N	Y	Y	Y	Y	Y
3 **Amash**	Y	Y	Y	Y	Y	Y	Y
4 **Moolenaar**	N	N	N	N	Y	N	Y
5 Kildee	N	Y	N	N	N	N	N
6 **Upton**	N	N	N	N	N	Y	Y
7 **Walberg**	N	N	N	Y	Y	Y	Y
8 **Bishop**	N	N	Y	Y	Y	Y	Y
9 Levin	N	Y	N	N	N	N	N
10 **Mitchell**	N	N	N	N	Y	N	Y
11 **Trott**	Y	N	N	N	Y	N	Y
12 Dingell	N	Y	N	N	N	N	N
13 Conyers	N	Y	N	N	N	N	N
14 Lawrence	N	Y	N	N	N	N	N
MINNESOTA							
1 Walz	N	Y	N	N	N	N	N
2 **Lewis**	N	N	Y	Y	N	Y	Y
3 **Paulsen**	N	N	N	N	Y	Y	Y
4 McCollum	N	Y	N	N	N	N	N
5 Ellison	N	Y	N	N	N	N	N
6 **Emmer**	Y	N	Y	N	N	Y	Y
7 Peterson	N	Y	N	N	N	N	N
8 Nolan	N	Y	N	N	N	N	N
MISSISSIPPI							
1 **Kelly**	Y	N	N	Y	Y	Y	Y
2 Thompson	N	Y	N	N	N	N	N
3 **Harper**	N	N	Y	N	Y	Y	Y
4 **Palazzo**	N	N	N	N	Y	N	?
MISSOURI							
1 Clay	N	Y	N	N	N	N	N
2 **Wagner**	Y	N	Y	Y	Y	Y	Y
3 **Luetkemeyer**	Y	N	Y	N	Y	N	Y
4 **Hartzler**	Y	N	Y	Y	Y	N	Y
5 Cleaver	N	Y	N	N	N	N	N
6 **Graves**	Y	N	Y	Y	N	Y	Y
7 **Long**	N	N	N	N	Y	Y	Y
8 **Smith**	Y	N	Y	Y	Y	Y	Y
MONTANA							
AL **Gianforte**	N	N	N	N	N	N	Y
NEBRASKA							
1 **Fortenberry**	N	Y	N	N	Y	N	Y
2 **Bacon**	Y	N	N	N	Y	Y	Y
3 **Smith**	Y	N	Y	Y	Y	Y	Y
NEVADA							
1 Titus	N	Y	N	N	N	N	N
2 **Amodei**	N	N	N	N	Y	N	Y
3 Rosen	N	Y	N	N	N	N	N
4 Kihuen	N	Y	N	N	N	N	N
NEW HAMPSHIRE							
1 Shea-Porter	N	Y	N	N	N	N	N
2 Kuster	N	Y	N	N	N	N	N
NEW JERSEY							
1 Norcross	N	Y	N	N	N	N	N
2 **LoBiondo**	N	Y	N	N	N	N	N
3 **MacArthur**	N	N	N	N	N	N	Y
4 **Smith**	N	Y	N	N	N	N	Y
5 Gottheimer	N	Y	N	N	N	N	N
6 Pallone	N	Y	N	N	N	N	N
7 **Lance**	N	N	N	N	N	N	Y
8 Sires	N	Y	N	N	N	N	N
9 Pascrell	N	Y	N	N	N	N	N
10 Payne	N	Y	N	N	N	N	N
11 **Frelinghuysen**	N	N	N	N	Y	N	Y
12 Watson Coleman	N	Y	N	N	N	N	N
NEW MEXICO							
1 Lujan Grisham	N	Y	N	N	N	N	N
2 **Pearce**	Y	N	N	N	Y	N	Y
3 Luján	N	Y	N	N	N	N	N
NEW YORK							
1 **Zeldin**	N	Y	Y	Y	N	Y	Y
2 **King**	N	N	N	N	N	N	N
3 Suozzi	N	Y	N	N	N	N	N
4 Rice	N	Y	N	N	N	N	N
5 Meeks	N	Y	N	N	N	N	N
6 Meng	N	Y	N	N	N	N	N
7 Velázquez	N	Y	N	N	N	N	N
8 Jeffries	N	Y	N	N	N	N	N
9 Clarke	N	Y	N	N	N	N	N
10 Nadler	N	Y	N	N	N	N	N
11 **Donovan**	N	N	N	N	N	N	N
12 Maloney, C.	N	Y	N	N	N	N	N
13 Espaillat	N	Y	N	N	N	N	N
14 Crowley	N	Y	N	N	N	N	N
15 Serrano	N	Y	N	N	N	N	N
16 Engel	N	N	N	N	N	N	N
17 Lowey	N	Y	N	N	N	N	N
18 Maloney, S.P.	N	Y	N	N	N	N	N
19 **Faso**	N	N	N	N	N	N	Y
20 Tonko	N	Y	N	N	N	N	N
21 **Stefanik**	N	N	N	N	N	N	Y
22 **Tenney**	N	N	N	N	N	N	Y
23 **Reed**	N	Y	N	N	N	N	Y
24 **Katko**	N	N	N	N	N	N	Y
25 Slaughter	N	Y	N	N	N	N	N
26 Higgins	N	Y	N	N	N	N	N
27 **Collins**	N	N	N	N	Y	N	Y
NORTH CAROLINA							
1 Butterfield	N	Y	N	N	N	N	N
2 **Holding**	Y	N	Y	Y	Y	Y	Y
3 **Jones**	N	N	N	Y	Y	Y	Y
4 Price	N	Y	N	N	N	N	N
%5 **Foxx**	Y	N	Y	Y	Y	Y	Y
6 **Walker**	N	N	Y	Y	Y	Y	Y
7 **Rouzer**	Y	N	Y	Y	Y	Y	Y
8 **Hudson**	Y	N	Y	Y	Y	Y	Y
9 **Pittenger**	Y	N	Y	Y	Y	Y	Y
10 **McHenry**	Y	N	Y	Y	Y	Y	Y
11 **Meadows**	Y	N	Y	Y	Y	Y	Y
12 Adams	N	Y	N	N	N	N	N
13 **Budd**	Y	N	Y	Y	Y	Y	Y
NORTH DAKOTA							
AL **Cramer**	N	N	N	N	Y	N	Y
OHIO							
1 **Chabot**	Y	N	Y	Y	Y	Y	Y
2 **Wenstrup**	Y	N	Y	Y	Y	N	Y
3 Beatty	N	Y	N	N	N	N	N
4 **Jordan**	Y	N	Y	Y	Y	Y	Y
5 **Latta**	Y	N	Y	Y	Y	Y	Y
6 **Johnson**	N	N	N	N	N	N	Y
7 **Gibbs**	Y	N	Y	Y	Y	N	Y
8 **Davidson**	Y	N	Y	Y	Y	Y	Y
9 Kaptur	N	Y	N	N	N	N	N
10 **Turner**	N	N	N	N	N	N	Y
11 Fudge	N	Y	N	N	N	N	N
12 **Tiberi**	N	N	N	N	N	N	N
13 Ryan	N	Y	N	N	N	N	N
14 **Joyce**	N	N	N	N	N	N	Y
15 **Stivers**	N	N	N	N	N	N	Y
16 **Renacci**	N	N	Y	Y	N	N	Y
OKLAHOMA							
1 **Bridenstine**	?	?	?	?	?	?	?
2 **Mullin**	Y	N	N	Y	Y	Y	Y
3 **Lucas**	N	N	N	N	Y	N	Y
4 **Cole**	N	N	N	N	Y	N	Y
5 **Russell**	Y	N	Y	Y	Y	Y	Y
OREGON							
1 Bonamici	N	Y	N	N	N	N	N
2 **Walden**	N	N	N	N	N	N	N
3 Blumenauer	N	Y	N	N	N	N	N
4 DeFazio	N	Y	N	N	N	N	N
5 Schrader	N	Y	N	N	N	N	N
PENNSYLVANIA							
1 Brady	N	Y	N	N	N	N	N
2 Evans	N	N	N	N	N	N	N
3 **Kelly**	N	N	N	N	N	N	Y
4 **Perry**	Y	N	Y	Y	Y	Y	Y
5 **Thompson**	N	N	N	N	Y	N	Y
6 **Costello**	N	Y	N	N	N	N	Y
7 **Meehan**	N	Y	Y	N	N	N	Y
8 **Fitzpatrick**	N	N	N	N	N	N	Y
9 **Shuster**	N	N	?	N	N	N	Y
10 **Marino**	N	N	N	N	Y	N	Y
11 **Barletta**	N	N	N	N	N	N	Y
12 **Rothfus**	N	N	N	N	Y	N	Y
13 Boyle	N	Y	N	N	N	N	N
14 Doyle	N	Y	N	N	N	N	N
15 **Dent**	N	Y	N	N	Y	N	Y
16 **Smucker**	N	N	N	N	Y	N	Y
17 Cartwright	N	Y	N	N	N	N	N
18 **Murphy**	N	Y	N	N	N	N	Y
RHODE ISLAND							
1 Cicilline	N	Y	N	N	N	N	N
2 Langevin	N	Y	N	N	N	N	N
SOUTH CAROLINA							
1 **Sanford**	Y	N	Y	Y	Y	Y	Y
2 **Wilson**	Y	N	Y	Y	Y	Y	Y
3 **Duncan**	Y	N	Y	Y	Y	Y	Y
4 **Gowdy**	Y	N	Y	Y	Y	Y	Y
5 **Norman**	Y	N	Y	Y	Y	Y	Y
6 Clyburn	N	Y	N	N	N	N	N
7 **Rice**	Y	N	Y	Y	Y	Y	Y
SOUTH DAKOTA							
AL **Noem**	Y	N	N	N	Y	N	Y
TENNESSEE							
1 **Roe**	Y	N	N	Y	Y	N	Y
2 **Duncan**	N	N	Y	Y	Y	Y	Y
3 **Fleischmann**	N	N	N	N	Y	N	Y
4 **DesJarlais**	Y	N	Y	Y	Y	Y	Y
5 Cooper	N	Y	N	N	N	N	N
6 **Black**	Y	N	N	Y	Y	Y	Y
7 **Blackburn**	Y	N	Y	Y	Y	Y	Y
8 **Kustoff**	N	N	Y	Y	Y	Y	Y
9 Cohen	N	Y	N	N	N	N	N
TEXAS							
1 **Gohmert**	N	?	Y	Y	Y	Y	Y
2 **Poe**	Y	N	N	N	Y	Y	Y
3 **Johnson, S.**	Y	N	Y	Y	Y	Y	Y
4 **Ratcliffe**	Y	N	Y	Y	Y	Y	Y
5 **Hensarling**	Y	N	Y	Y	Y	Y	Y
6 **Barton**	Y	N	N	Y	Y	Y	Y
7 **Culberson**	Y	N	Y	Y	Y	Y	Y
8 **Brady**	N	Y	Y	Y	Y	Y	Y
9 Green, A.	N	Y	N	N	N	N	N
10 **McCaul**	N	N	N	N	Y	N	Y
11 **Conaway**	Y	N	Y	Y	Y	Y	Y
12 **Granger**	N	N	N	Y	Y	Y	Y
13 **Thornberry**	N	N	N	N	Y	N	Y
14 **Weber**	Y	N	Y	Y	Y	Y	Y
15 Gonzalez	N	Y	N	N	N	N	N
16 O'Rourke	N	Y	N	N	N	N	N
17 **Flores**	Y	N	Y	Y	Y	Y	Y
18 Jackson Lee	N	Y	N	N	N	N	N
19 **Arrington**	Y	N	Y	Y	Y	Y	Y
20 Castro	N	Y	N	N	N	N	N
21 **Smith**	Y	N	Y	Y	Y	Y	Y
22 **Olson**	Y	N	Y	Y	Y	Y	Y
23 **Hurd**	N	N	N	N	Y	N	Y
24 **Marchant**	Y	N	Y	Y	Y	Y	Y
25 **Williams**	Y	Y	Y	Y	Y	N	Y
26 **Burgess**	Y	N	Y	Y	Y	N	Y
27 **Farenthold**	Y	N	Y	Y	Y	Y	Y
28 Cuellar	N	Y	N	N	N	N	Y
29 Green, G.	N	Y	N	N	N	N	N
30 Johnson, E.B.	N	Y	N	N	N	N	N
31 **Carter**	Y	N	N	Y	Y	Y	Y
32 **Sessions**	Y	N	N	Y	Y	Y	Y
33 Veasey	N	Y	N	N	N	N	N
34 Vela	N	Y	N	N	N	N	N
35 Doggett	N	Y	N	N	N	N	N
36 **Babin**	Y	N	Y	Y	Y	Y	Y
UTAH							
1 **Bishop**	Y	N	N	Y	Y	Y	Y
2 **Stewart**	Y	N	N	Y	Y	Y	Y
4 **Love**	N	N	Y	N	Y	Y	Y
VERMONT							
AL Welch	N	Y	N	N	N	N	N
VIRGINIA							
1 **Wittman**	Y	N	Y	Y	Y	Y	Y
2 **Taylor**	Y	N	N	Y	Y	Y	N
3 Scott	N	Y	N	N	N	N	N
4 McEachin	N	Y	N	N	N	N	N
5 **Garrett**	?	?	?	?	?	?	?
6 **Goodlatte**	N	N	Y	Y	Y	Y	Y
7 **Brat**	Y	N	Y	Y	Y	Y	Y
8 Beyer	N	N	N	N	N	N	N
9 **Griffith**	N	N	Y	Y	Y	Y	Y
10 **Comstock**	N	N	N	N	Y	N	Y
11 Connolly	N	N	N	N	N	N	N
WASHINGTON							
1 DelBene	N	Y	N	N	N	N	N
2 Larsen	N	Y	N	N	N	N	N
3 **Herrera Beutler**	N	N	N	N	Y	N	Y
4 **Newhouse**	N	N	N	N	N	N	Y
5 **McMorris Rodgers**	N	N	Y	N	Y	N	Y
6 Kilmer	N	Y	N	N	N	N	N
7 Jayapal	N	Y	N	N	N	N	N
8 **Reichert**	N	N	N	N	N	N	N
9 Smith	N	Y	N	N	N	N	N
10 Heck	N	Y	N	N	N	N	N
WEST VIRGINIA							
1 **McKinley**	N	Y	N	N	N	N	Y
2 **Mooney**	Y	Y	Y	Y	Y	Y	Y
3 **Jenkins**	N	Y	N	N	N	N	Y
WISCONSIN							
1 **Ryan**							
2 Pocan	N	Y	N	N	N	N	N
3 Kind	N	Y	N	N	N	N	N
4 Moore	N	Y	N	N	N	N	N
5 **Sensenbrenner**	Y	N	Y	Y	Y	Y	Y
6 **Grothman**	Y	N	Y	Y	Y	Y	Y
7 **Duffy**	Y	N	N	N	N	N	Y
8 **Gallagher**	Y	N	N	Y	Y	Y	Y
WYOMING							
AL **Cheney**	Y	N	Y	Y	Y	Y	Y

VOTE NUMBER

456. HR 3354. FISCAL 2018 OMNIBUS APPROPRIATIONS LEGISLATIVE VEHICLE/ELECTRONIC LOGGING DEVICES. Babin, R-Texas, amendment that would prohibit any of the bill's funding for the Department of Transportation from being used to enforce a regulation that certain commercial vehicles must use an electronic logging devices. Rejected in Committee of the Whole 173-246 : R 165-67; D 8-179. Sept. 6, 2017.

457. H RES 504, HR 3354. FISCAL 2018 OMNIBUS APPROPRIATIONS LEGISLATIVE VEHICLE/PREVIOUS QUESTION. Woodall, R-Ga., motion to order the previous question (thus limiting debate and possibility of amendment) on the rule (H Res 504) that would provide for further House floor consideration of the fiscal 2018 Interior-Environment appropriations bill (HR 3354), which is the legislative vehicle for an omnibus appropriations package which would include: eight of the 12 fiscal 2018 appropriations measures and the text of the minibus appropriations package (HR 3219) passed on July 27, 2017. Motion agreed to 227-186 : R 227-0; D 0-186. Sept. 7, 2017.

458. H RES 504, HR 3354. FISCAL 2018 OMNIBUS APPROPRIATIONS LEGISLATIVE VEHICLE/RULE. Adoption of the rule (H Res 504) that would provide for House floor consideration of the fiscal 2018 Interior-Environment appropriations bill (HR 3354), which is the legislative vehicle for an omnibus appropriations package which would include: eight of the 12 fiscal 2018 appropriations measures and the text of the minibus appropriations package (HR 3219) passed on July 27, 2017. Adopted 222-190 : R 222-4; D 0-186. Sept. 7, 2017.

459. HR 3354. FISCAL 2018 OMNIBUS APPROPRIATIONS LEGISLATIVE VEHICLE/CBP OPERATIONS AND SUPPORT. Castro, D-Texas, amendment that would increase by $5 million, and decrease by the same amount, funding to the Customs and Border Protection Operations and Support account. Rejected in Committee of the Whole 205-207 : R 20-207; D 185-0. Sept. 7, 2017.

460. HR 3354. FISCAL 2018 OMNIBUS APPROPRIATIONS LEGISLATIVE VEHICLE/COAST GUARD ACQUISITION $850 MILLION INCREASE. Roybal-Allard, D-Calif., amendment that would increase by $850 million funding to the Coast Guard Acquisition, Construction, and Improvements account (for icebreakers), and would decrease funding to the Immigration and Customs Enforcement Operations and Support account by the same amount. Rejected in Committee of the Whole 170-241 : R 1-226; D 169-15. Sept. 7, 2017.

461. HR 3354. FISCAL 2018 OMNIBUS APPROPRIATIONS LEGISLATIVE VEHICLE/IMMIGRATION AND CUSTOMS ENFORCEMENT OPERATIONS. Castro, D-Texas, amendment that would increase by $10 million, and would decrease by the same amount, funding to the Immigration and Customs Enforcement Operations and Support account. Rejected in Committee of the Whole 203-211 : R 17-210; D 186-1. Sept. 7, 2017.

462. HR 3354. FISCAL 2018 OMNIBUS APPROPRIATIONS LEGISLATIVE VEHICLE/COAST GUARD ACQUISITION $100 MILLION INCREASE. Correa, D-Calif., amendment that would increase by $100 million funding to the Coast Guard Acquisition, Construction, and Improvements account, and would decrease funding to the Immigration and Customs Enforcement Operations and Support account by the same amount. Rejected in Committee of the Whole 182-229 : R 0-224; D 182-5. Sept. 7, 2017.

	456	457	458	459	460	461	462
ALABAMA							
1 Byrne	Y	Y	Y	N	N	N	N
2 Roby	N	Y	Y	N	N	N	N
3 Rogers	Y	Y	Y	N	N	N	N
4 Aderholt	N	Y	Y	N	N	N	N
5 Brooks	Y	Y	Y	N	N	N	N
6 Palmer	Y	Y	Y	N	N	N	N
7 Sewell	N	N	N	Y	Y	Y	Y
ALASKA							
AL Young	N	Y	N	N	Y	N	N
ARIZONA							
1 O'Halleran	N	N	N	Y	N	Y	Y
2 McSally	N	Y	Y	N	N	N	N
3 Grijalva	N	N	N	Y	Y	Y	Y
4 Gosar	Y	Y	Y	N	N	N	N
5 Biggs	N	Y	Y	N	N	N	N
6 Schweikert	N	Y	Y	N	N	Y	N
7 Gallego	N	N	N	Y	Y	Y	Y
8 Franks	Y	Y	Y	N	N	N	N
9 Sinema	N	N	N	Y	N	Y	Y
ARKANSAS							
1 Crawford	N	Y	Y	N	N	N	N
2 Hill	N	Y	Y	N	N	N	N
3 Womack	N	Y	Y	N	N	N	N
4 Westerman	N	Y	Y	N	N	N	N
CALIFORNIA							
1 LaMalfa	Y	?	?	N	N	N	N
2 Huffman	?	N	N	Y	Y	Y	Y
3 Garamendi	Y	N	N	Y	Y	Y	Y
4 McClintock	Y	Y	Y	N	N	N	N
5 Thompson	N	N	N	Y	Y	Y	Y
6 Matsui	N	N	N	Y	Y	Y	Y
7 Bera	N	N	N	Y	N	Y	Y
8 Cook	Y	Y	Y	N	N	N	N
9 McNerney	N	Y	N	Y	Y	Y	N
10 Denham	N	Y	N	N	N	N	N
11 DeSaulnier	N	N	N	Y	Y	Y	Y
12 Pelosi	N	N	?	?	?	Y	Y
13 Lee	N	N	N	Y	Y	Y	Y
14 Speier	N	N	N	Y	Y	Y	Y
15 Swalwell	N	N	N	Y	Y	Y	Y
16 Costa	?	?	?	?	?	?	?
17 Khanna	N	N	N	Y	Y	Y	Y
18 Eshoo	N	N	N	Y	Y	Y	Y
19 Lofgren	N	N	N	Y	Y	Y	Y
20 Panetta	N	N	N	Y	Y	Y	Y
21 Valadao	Y	Y	Y	N	N	N	N
22 Nunes	Y	Y	Y	N	N	N	N
23 McCarthy	N	Y	Y	N	N	N	N
24 Carbajal	N	N	N	Y	Y	Y	Y
25 Knight	N	Y	Y	N	N	N	N
26 Brownley	N	N	N	Y	Y	Y	Y
27 Chu	N	N	N	Y	Y	Y	Y
28 Schiff	N	N	N	Y	Y	Y	Y
29 Cardenas	N	N	N	Y	Y	Y	Y
30 Sherman	N	N	N	Y	Y	Y	Y
31 Aguilar	N	N	N	Y	Y	Y	Y
32 Napolitano	N	N	N	Y	Y	Y	Y
33 Lieu	?	N	N	Y	Y	Y	Y
34 Gomez	N	N	N	Y	Y	Y	Y
35 Torres	N	N	N	Y	Y	Y	Y
36 Ruiz	N	N	N	Y	Y	Y	Y
37 Bass	N	N	N	Y	Y	Y	Y
38 Sánchez, Linda	N	N	N	Y	Y	Y	Y
39 Royce	Y	Y	Y	N	N	N	N
40 Roybal-Allard	N	N	N	Y	Y	Y	Y
41 Takano	N	N	N	Y	Y	Y	Y
42 Calvert	Y	Y	Y	N	N	N	N
43 Waters	N	N	N	Y	Y	Y	Y
44 Barragan	N	N	N	Y	Y	Y	Y
45 Walters	Y	Y	Y	N	N	N	N
46 Correa	N	N	N	Y	Y	Y	Y
47 Lowenthal	N	?	N	Y	Y	Y	Y
48 Rohrabacher	Y	Y	N	N	N	N	N
49 Issa	Y	Y	Y	N	N	N	N
50 Hunter	Y	Y	Y	N	N	N	N
51 Vargas	N	N	N	Y	Y	Y	Y
52 Peters	N	N	N	Y	N	Y	Y
53 Davis	N	N	N	Y	Y	Y	Y

	456	457	458	459	460	461	462
COLORADO							
1 DeGette	?	?	?	?	?	?	?
2 Polis	Y	N	N	Y	Y	Y	Y
3 Tipton	Y	Y	Y	N	N	N	N
4 Buck	Y	Y	Y	N	N	N	N
5 Lamborn	Y	Y	Y	N	N	N	N
6 Coffman	Y	Y	Y	N	Y	N	Y
7 Perlmutter	N	N	N	Y	Y	Y	Y
CONNECTICUT							
1 Larson	N	N	N	Y	Y	Y	Y
2 Courtney	N	N	N	Y	Y	Y	Y
3 DeLauro	N	N	N	Y	Y	Y	Y
4 Himes	N	N	N	Y	Y	Y	Y
5 Esty	N	N	N	Y	Y	Y	Y
DELAWARE							
AL Blunt Rochester	N	N	N	Y	Y	Y	Y
FLORIDA							
1 Gaetz	Y	Y	Y	N	N	N	N
2 Dunn	Y	Y	Y	N	N	N	N
3 Yoho	Y	Y	Y	N	N	N	N
4 Rutherford	N	Y	Y	N	N	N	N
5 Lawson	N	N	N	Y	Y	Y	Y
6 DeSantis	Y	?	?	?	?	?	?
7 Murphy	N	N	N	Y	Y	Y	Y
8 Posey	Y	?	?	?	?	?	?
9 Soto	N	N	N	Y	Y	Y	Y
10 Demings	?	N	N	Y	Y	Y	Y
11 Webster	Y	?	?	?	?	?	?
12 Bilirakis	Y	Y	Y	N	N	N	N
13 Crist	N	?	?	?	?	?	?
14 Castor	N	N	N	Y	N	Y	Y
15 Ross	?	?	?	?	?	?	?
16 Buchanan	N	Y	Y	N	N	N	N
17 Rooney, T.	Y	Y	Y	N	N	N	N
18 Mast	Y	Y	Y	N	N	N	N
19 Rooney, F.	Y	Y	Y	N	N	N	N
20 Hastings	N	N	N	Y	Y	Y	Y
21 Frankel	N	N	N	Y	Y	Y	Y
22 Deutch	N	?	?	?	?	?	?
23 Wasserman Schultz	?	?	?	?	?	?	?
24 Wilson	N	N	N	Y	Y	Y	Y
25 Diaz-Balart	N	?	?	?	?	?	?
26 Curbelo	?	?	?	?	?	?	?
27 Ros-Lehtinen	?	?	?	?	?	?	?
GEORGIA							
1 Carter	N	Y	Y	N	N	N	N
2 Bishop	N	N	N	Y	Y	Y	Y
3 Ferguson	Y	Y	Y	N	N	N	N
4 Johnson	N	N	N	Y	Y	Y	Y
5 Lewis	N	N	N	Y	Y	Y	Y
6 Handel	Y	Y	Y	N	N	N	N
7 Woodall	N	Y	Y	N	N	N	N
8 Scott, A.	Y	Y	Y	N	N	N	N
9 Collins	Y	Y	Y	N	N	N	N
10 Hice	Y	Y	Y	N	N	N	N
11 Loudermilk	Y	Y	Y	N	N	N	N
12 Allen	Y	Y	Y	N	N	N	N
13 Scott, D.	N	N	N	Y	Y	Y	Y
14 Graves	Y	Y	Y	N	N	N	N
HAWAII							
1 Hanabusa	N	N	N	Y	Y	Y	Y
2 Gabbard	N	N	N	Y	Y	Y	Y
IDAHO							
1 Labrador	Y	Y	Y	N	N	N	N
2 Simpson	N	Y	Y	N	N	N	N
ILLINOIS							
1 Rush	N	N	N	Y	?	Y	Y
2 Kelly	N	N	N	Y	Y	Y	Y
3 Lipinski	N	N	N	Y	N	Y	Y
4 Gutierrez	N	N	N	Y	Y	Y	Y
5 Quigley	N	N	N	Y	Y	Y	Y
6 Roskam	N	Y	Y	N	N	N	N
7 Davis, D.	N	N	N	Y	Y	Y	Y
8 Krishnamoorthi	N	N	N	Y	Y	Y	Y
9 Schakowsky	N	N	N	Y	Y	Y	Y
10 Schneider	N	N	N	Y	Y	Y	Y
11 Foster	N	N	N	Y	Y	Y	Y
12 Bost	Y	Y	Y	N	N	N	N
13 Davis, R.	N	Y	Y	N	N	N	N
14 Hultgren	Y	Y	Y	N	N	N	N
15 Shimkus	Y	Y	Y	N	N	N	N

KEY Republicans   Democrats   *Independents*

Y	Voted for (yea)	X	Paired against	C	Voted "present" to avoid possible conflict of interest
#	Paired for	–	Announced against	?	Did not vote or otherwise make a position known
+	Announced for	P	Voted "present"		
N	Voted against (nay)				

	456	457	458	459	460	461	462
16 **Kinzinger**	N	Y	Y	N	N	N	N
17 Bustos	N	N	N	Y	N	Y	Y
18 **LaHood**	Y	Y	Y	N	N	N	N
INDIANA							
1 Visclosky	N	N	N	Y	Y	Y	Y
2 **Walorski**	Y	Y	Y	N	N	N	N
3 **Banks**	Y	Y	Y	N	N	N	N
4 **Rokita**	Y	Y	Y	N	N	N	N
5 **Brooks**	N	Y	Y	N	N	N	N
6 **Messer**	N	Y	Y	N	N	N	N
7 Carson	N	N	N	Y	Y	Y	Y
8 **Bucshon**	N	Y	Y	Y	N	N	N
9 **Hollingsworth**	Y	Y	Y	N	N	N	N
IOWA							
1 **Blum**	Y	Y	Y	N	N	N	N
2 Loebsack	N	N	N	Y	N	Y	Y
3 **Young**	Y	Y	Y	N	N	N	N
4 **King**	Y	Y	Y	N	N	N	N
KANSAS							
1 **Marshall**	Y	Y	Y	N	N	N	N
2 **Jenkins**	Y	Y	Y	N	N	N	N
3 **Yoder**	Y	Y	Y	N	N	N	N
4 **Estes**	Y	Y	Y	N	N	N	N
KENTUCKY							
1 **Comer**	Y	Y	Y	N	N	N	N
2 **Guthrie**	Y	Y	Y	N	N	N	N
3 Yarmuth	N	N	N	Y	Y	Y	Y
4 **Massie**	N	Y	Y	Y	N	N	N
5 **Rogers**	Y	Y	Y	N	N	N	N
6 **Barr**	Y	Y	Y	N	N	N	N
LOUISIANA							
1 **Scalise**	+	+	+	–	–	–	+
2 Richmond	N	N	N	Y	Y	Y	Y
3 **Higgins**	Y	Y	Y	N	N	N	N
4 **Johnson**	Y	Y	Y	N	N	N	N
5 **Abraham**	Y	Y	Y	N	N	N	N
6 **Graves**	Y	Y	Y	N	N	N	N
MAINE							
1 Pingree	N	N	N	Y	Y	Y	Y
2 **Poliquin**	Y	Y	Y	N	N	N	N
MARYLAND							
1 **Harris**	Y	Y	Y	N	N	N	N
2 Ruppersberger	N	N	N	Y	Y	Y	Y
3 Sarbanes	N	N	N	Y	Y	Y	Y
4 Brown	N	N	N	Y	Y	Y	Y
5 Hoyer	N	N	N	Y	Y	Y	Y
6 Delaney	N	N	N	Y	Y	Y	Y
7 Cummings	?	?	?	?	?	?	?
8 Raskin	N	N	N	Y	Y	Y	Y
MASSACHUSETTS							
1 Neal	N	N	N	Y	Y	Y	Y
2 McGovern	N	N	N	Y	Y	Y	Y
3 Tsongas	N	?	?	?	?	?	?
4 Kennedy	N	N	N	Y	Y	Y	Y
5 Clark	N	N	N	Y	Y	Y	Y
6 Moulton	N	N	N	Y	Y	Y	Y
7 Capuano	N	N	N	Y	Y	Y	Y
8 Lynch	N	N	N	Y	N	Y	N
9 Keating	N	N	N	Y	Y	Y	Y
MICHIGAN							
1 **Bergman**	Y	Y	Y	N	N	N	N
2 **Huizenga**	Y	Y	Y	N	N	N	N
3 **Amash**	Y	Y	N	N	N	N	N
4 **Moolenaar**	Y	Y	Y	N	N	N	N
5 Kildee	N	N	N	Y	Y	Y	Y
6 **Upton**	N	Y	Y	Y	N	N	N
7 **Walberg**	N	Y	Y	N	N	N	N
8 **Bishop**	Y	Y	Y	N	N	N	N
9 Levin	N	N	N	Y	Y	Y	Y
10 **Mitchell**	N	Y	Y	N	N	N	N
11 **Trott**	N	Y	Y	N	N	N	N
12 Dingell	N	N	N	Y	Y	Y	Y
13 Conyers	N	N	N	Y	Y	Y	Y
14 Lawrence	N	N	N	Y	Y	Y	Y
MINNESOTA							
1 Walz	Y	N	N	Y	Y	Y	Y
2 **Lewis**	Y	Y	Y	Y	N	N	N
3 **Paulsen**	N	Y	Y	N	N	N	N
4 McCollum	N	N	N	Y	Y	Y	Y

	456	457	458	459	460	461	462
5 Ellison	N	N	N	Y	Y	Y	Y
6 **Emmer**	N	Y	Y	N	N	N	N
7 Peterson	Y	N	N	Y	N	N	Y
8 Nolan	Y	N	N	Y	?	Y	Y
MISSISSIPPI							
1 **Kelly**	Y	Y	Y	N	N	N	N
2 Thompson	N	N	N	Y	Y	Y	Y
3 **Harper**	N	Y	Y	N	N	N	N
4 **Palazzo**	N	Y	Y	N	N	N	N
MISSOURI							
1 Clay	N	N	N	Y	Y	Y	Y
2 **Wagner**	N	?	?	?	?	?	?
3 **Luetkemeyer**	Y	Y	Y	N	N	N	N
4 **Hartzler**	Y	Y	Y	N	N	N	N
5 Cleaver	N	N	N	Y	Y	Y	Y
6 **Graves**	Y	Y	Y	N	N	N	N
7 **Long**	N	Y	Y	N	N	N	N
8 **Smith**	Y	Y	Y	N	N	N	N
MONTANA							
AL **Gianforte**	Y	Y	Y	N	N	N	N
NEBRASKA							
1 **Fortenberry**	N	Y	Y	N	N	N	N
2 **Bacon**	Y	Y	Y	N	N	N	N
3 **Smith**	Y	Y	Y	N	N	N	N
NEVADA							
1 Titus	N	N	N	Y	Y	Y	Y
2 **Amodei**	N	Y	Y	N	N	N	N
3 Rosen	N	N	N	Y	Y	Y	Y
4 Kihuen	N	N	N	Y	Y	Y	Y
NEW HAMPSHIRE							
1 Shea-Porter	N	N	N	Y	Y	Y	Y
2 Kuster	N	N	N	Y	Y	Y	Y
NEW JERSEY							
1 Norcross	N	N	N	Y	Y	Y	Y
2 **LoBiondo**	N	Y	Y	Y	N	Y	N
3 **MacArthur**	Y	Y	Y	Y	N	Y	N
4 **Smith**	N	Y	Y	Y	N	Y	N
5 Gottheimer	N	N	N	Y	Y	Y	Y
6 Pallone	N	N	N	Y	Y	Y	Y
7 **Lance**	N	Y	Y	Y	N	Y	N
8 Sires	N	N	N	Y	Y	Y	Y
9 Pascrell	N	N	N	Y	Y	Y	Y
10 Payne	N	N	N	Y	Y	Y	Y
11 **Frelinghuysen**	N	Y	Y	N	N	N	N
12 Watson Coleman	N	N	N	Y	Y	Y	Y
NEW MEXICO							
1 Lujan Grisham	N	N	N	Y	Y	Y	Y
2 **Pearce**	Y	Y	Y	N	N	N	N
3 Luján	N	N	N	Y	Y	Y	Y
NEW YORK							
1 **Zeldin**	Y	Y	Y	N	N	N	N
2 **King**	N	Y	Y	N	N	N	N
3 Suozzi	N	N	N	Y	N	Y	Y
4 Rice	N	N	N	Y	Y	Y	Y
5 Meeks	N	N	N	Y	Y	Y	Y
6 Meng	N	N	N	Y	Y	Y	Y
7 Velázquez	N	N	N	Y	Y	Y	Y
8 Jeffries	N	N	N	Y	Y	Y	Y
9 Clarke	N	N	N	Y	Y	Y	Y
10 Nadler	N	N	N	Y	Y	Y	Y
11 **Donovan**	N	Y	Y	N	N	N	N
12 Maloney, C.	N	N	N	?	Y	Y	Y
13 Espaillat	N	N	N	Y	Y	Y	Y
14 Crowley	N	N	N	Y	Y	Y	Y
15 Serrano	N	N	N	Y	Y	Y	Y
16 Engel	N	N	N	Y	Y	Y	Y
17 Lowey	N	N	N	Y	Y	Y	Y
18 Maloney, S.P.	N	N	N	Y	N	Y	Y
19 **Faso**	Y	Y	Y	N	N	N	N
20 Tonko	N	N	N	Y	Y	Y	Y
21 **Stefanik**	N	Y	Y	N	N	N	N
22 **Tenney**	Y	Y	Y	N	N	N	N
23 **Reed**	Y	Y	Y	Y	N	N	N
24 **Katko**	N	Y	Y	Y	N	Y	N
25 Slaughter	N	N	N	Y	Y	Y	Y
26 Higgins	N	N	N	Y	N	Y	Y
27 **Collins**	N	Y	Y	N	N	N	N
NORTH CAROLINA							
1 Butterfield	N	N	N	Y	Y	Y	Y
2 **Holding**	Y	Y	Y	N	N	N	N
3 **Jones**	Y	Y	N	N	N	N	N
4 Price	N	N	N	Y	Y	Y	Y

	456	457	458	459	460	461	462
5 **Foxx**	Y	Y	Y	N	N	N	N
6 **Walker**	Y	Y	Y	N	N	N	N
7 **Rouzer**	N	Y	Y	N	N	N	N
8 **Hudson**	Y	Y	Y	N	N	N	N
9 **Pittenger**	Y	Y	Y	N	N	N	N
10 **McHenry**	N	Y	Y	N	N	N	N
11 **Meadows**	N	Y	?	?	?	?	?
12 Adams	N	N	N	Y	Y	Y	Y
13 **Budd**	Y	Y	Y	N	N	N	N
NORTH DAKOTA							
AL **Cramer**	Y	Y	Y	N	N	N	N
OHIO							
1 **Chabot**	Y	Y	Y	N	N	N	N
2 **Wenstrup**	Y	Y	Y	N	N	N	N
3 Beatty	N	N	N	Y	Y	Y	Y
4 **Jordan**	N	Y	Y	N	N	N	N
5 **Latta**	N	Y	Y	N	N	N	N
6 **Johnson**	Y	Y	Y	N	N	N	N
7 **Gibbs**	Y	Y	Y	N	N	N	N
8 **Davidson**	Y	Y	Y	N	N	N	N
9 Kaptur	N	N	N	Y	Y	Y	Y
10 **Turner**	N	Y	Y	N	N	N	N
11 Fudge	N	N	N	Y	Y	Y	Y
12 **Tiberi**	Y	Y	Y	N	N	N	N
13 Ryan	N	N	N	Y	Y	Y	Y
14 **Joyce**	N	Y	Y	N	N	N	N
15 **Stivers**	Y	Y	Y	N	N	N	N
16 **Renacci**	N	Y	Y	N	N	N	N
OKLAHOMA							
1 **Bridenstine**	?	?	?	?	?	?	?
2 **Mullin**	?	Y	Y	N	N	N	N
3 **Lucas**	Y	Y	Y	N	N	N	N
4 **Cole**	N	Y	Y	N	N	N	N
5 **Russell**	Y	Y	Y	N	N	N	N
OREGON							
1 Bonamici	N	N	N	Y	Y	Y	Y
2 **Walden**	Y	Y	Y	N	N	N	N
3 Blumenauer	N	N	N	Y	Y	Y	Y
4 DeFazio	N	N	N	Y	Y	Y	Y
5 Schrader	N	N	N	Y	Y	Y	Y
PENNSYLVANIA							
1 Brady	N	N	N	Y	Y	Y	Y
2 Evans	N	N	N	Y	Y	Y	Y
3 **Kelly**	Y	Y	Y	N	N	N	N
4 **Perry**	Y	Y	Y	N	N	N	N
5 **Thompson**	Y	Y	Y	N	N	N	N
6 **Costello**	Y	Y	Y	Y	N	Y	N
7 **Meehan**	Y	Y	Y	Y	N	Y	N
8 **Fitzpatrick**	N	Y	Y	Y	N	Y	N
9 **Shuster**	N	Y	Y	N	N	N	?
10 **Marino**	Y	Y	Y	N	N	N	N
11 **Barletta**	N	Y	Y	N	N	N	N
12 **Rothfus**	Y	Y	Y	N	N	N	N
13 Boyle	N	N	N	Y	Y	Y	Y
14 Doyle	N	N	N	Y	Y	Y	Y
15 **Dent**	Y	Y	Y	N	N	N	N
16 **Smucker**	Y	Y	Y	N	N	N	N
17 Cartwright	N	N	N	Y	Y	Y	Y
18 **Murphy**	Y	Y	Y	N	N	N	N
RHODE ISLAND							
1 Cicilline	N	N	N	Y	Y	Y	Y
2 Langevin	N	N	N	Y	Y	Y	Y
SOUTH CAROLINA							
1 **Sanford**	Y	Y	Y	N	N	N	N
2 **Wilson**	Y	Y	Y	N	N	N	N
3 **Duncan**	Y	Y	Y	N	N	N	N
4 **Gowdy**	Y	Y	Y	N	N	N	N
5 **Norman**	Y	Y	Y	N	N	Y	N
6 Clyburn	N	N	N	Y	Y	Y	Y
7 **Rice**	N	Y	Y	N	N	N	N
SOUTH DAKOTA							
AL **Noem**	Y	Y	Y	N	N	N	N
TENNESSEE							
1 **Roe**	Y	Y	Y	N	N	N	N
2 **Duncan**	Y	Y	Y	N	N	N	N
3 **Fleischmann**	N	Y	Y	N	N	N	N
4 **DesJarlais**	Y	Y	Y	N	N	N	N
5 Cooper	N	N	N	Y	N	Y	Y
6 **Black**	Y	Y	Y	N	N	N	N
7 **Blackburn**	N	Y	Y	N	N	N	N
8 **Kustoff**	Y	Y	Y	N	N	N	N
9 Cohen	N	N	N	Y	Y	Y	Y

	456	457	458	459	460	461	462
TEXAS							
1 **Gohmert**	Y	Y	Y	N	N	N	N
2 **Poe**	N	Y	Y	Y	N	Y	N
3 **Johnson, S.**	N	Y	Y	N	N	N	N
4 **Ratcliffe**	Y	Y	Y	N	N	N	N
5 **Hensarling**	Y	Y	Y	N	N	N	?
6 **Barton**	Y	Y	Y	Y	N	Y	N
7 **Culberson**	Y	Y	Y	N	N	N	N
8 **Brady**	Y	Y	Y	N	N	N	N
9 Green, A.	N	N	N	Y	Y	Y	Y
10 **McCaul**	Y	Y	Y	N	N	N	N
11 **Conaway**	Y	Y	Y	N	N	N	N
12 **Granger**	Y	Y	Y	N	N	N	N
13 **Thornberry**	Y	Y	Y	N	N	N	N
14 **Weber**	Y	Y	Y	N	N	N	N
15 Gonzalez	N	N	N	Y	Y	Y	Y
16 O'Rourke	N	N	N	Y	Y	Y	Y
17 **Flores**	Y	Y	Y	N	N	N	N
18 Jackson Lee	N	N	N	Y	Y	Y	Y
19 **Arrington**	Y	Y	Y	N	N	N	N
20 Castro	N	N	N	Y	Y	Y	Y
21 **Smith**	Y	Y	Y	N	N	N	N
22 **Olson**	Y	Y	Y	N	N	N	N
23 **Hurd**	Y	Y	Y	N	N	N	N
24 **Marchant**	Y	Y	Y	N	N	N	N
25 **Williams**	Y	Y	Y	N	N	N	N
26 **Burgess**	Y	Y	Y	Y	N	N	N
27 **Farenthold**	Y	Y	Y	Y	N	N	N
28 Cuellar	N	N	N	Y	Y	Y	N
29 Green, G.	Y	N	N	Y	Y	Y	Y
30 Johnson, E.B.	N	N	N	Y	Y	Y	Y
31 **Carter**	Y	Y	Y	N	N	N	N
32 **Sessions**	Y	Y	Y	N	N	N	N
33 Veasey	N	N	N	Y	Y	Y	Y
34 Vela	Y	N	N	Y	Y	Y	N
35 Doggett	N	N	N	Y	Y	Y	Y
36 **Babin**	Y	Y	Y	N	N	N	N
UTAH							
1 **Bishop**	Y	Y	Y	N	N	N	N
2 **Stewart**	Y	Y	Y	N	N	N	N
4 **Love**	Y	Y	Y	N	N	N	N
VERMONT							
AL Welch	N	N	N	Y	Y	Y	Y
VIRGINIA							
1 **Wittman**	Y	Y	Y	N	N	N	N
2 **Taylor**	Y	Y	Y	N	N	N	N
3 Scott	N	N	N	Y	Y	Y	N
4 McEachin	N	N	N	Y	Y	Y	Y
5 **Garrett**	?	?	?	?	?	?	?
6 **Goodlatte**	Y	Y	Y	N	N	N	N
7 **Brat**	Y	Y	Y	N	N	N	?
8 Beyer	N	N	N	Y	Y	Y	Y
9 **Griffith**	Y	Y	Y	N	N	N	N
10 **Comstock**	Y	Y	Y	N	N	N	N
11 Connolly	N	N	N	Y	Y	Y	Y
WASHINGTON							
1 DelBene	N	N	N	Y	Y	Y	Y
2 Larsen	N	N	N	Y	Y	Y	Y
3 **Herrera Beutler**	Y	Y	Y	Y	N	Y	N
4 **Newhouse**	Y	Y	Y	N	N	N	N
5 **McMorris Rodgers**	Y	Y	Y	N	N	N	N
6 Kilmer	N	N	N	Y	Y	Y	Y
7 Jayapal	N	N	N	Y	Y	Y	Y
8 **Reichert**	N	Y	Y	N	N	N	N
9 Smith	N	N	N	Y	Y	Y	Y
10 Heck	N	N	N	Y	Y	Y	Y
WEST VIRGINIA							
1 **McKinley**	Y	Y	Y	N	N	N	N
2 **Mooney**	Y	Y	Y	N	N	N	N
3 **Jenkins**	Y	Y	Y	N	N	N	N
WISCONSIN							
1 **Ryan**							
2 Pocan	N	N	N	Y	Y	Y	Y
3 Kind	Y	N	N	Y	Y	Y	Y
4 Moore	N	N	N	Y	Y	Y	Y
5 **Sensenbrenner**	Y	Y	Y	N	N	N	N
6 **Grothman**	Y	Y	Y	N	N	N	N
7 **Duffy**	Y	Y	Y	N	N	N	N
8 **Gallagher**	N	Y	Y	N	N	N	N
WYOMING							
AL **Cheney**	Y	Y	Y	N	N	N	N

VOTE NUMBER

463. HR 3354. FISCAL 2018 OMNIBUS APPROPRIATIONS LEGISLATIVE VEHICLE/ICEBREAKER FUNDING. Hunter, R-Calif., amendment that would increase by $5 million funding for the Coast Guard Research, Development, Test and Evaluating account (for icebreakers), and would decrease funding for the Coast Guard Operating Expenses account by the same amount. Adopted in Committee of the Whole 245-168 : R 215-12; D 30-156. Sept. 7, 2017.

464. HR 3354. FISCAL 2018 OMNIBUS APPROPRIATIONS LEGISLATIVE VEHICLE/PREVAILING WAGE REQUIREMENTS — HOMELAND SECURITY. King, R-Iowa, amendment, as modified, that would prohibit funding made available in the bill for the Department of Homeland Security and related agencies from being used to implement, administer or enforce the Davis-Bacon Act prevailing wage requirements. Rejected in Committee of the Whole 173-240 : R 173-54; D 0-186. Sept. 7, 2017.

465. HR 3354. FISCAL 2018 OMNIBUS APPROPRIATIONS LEGISLATIVE VEHICLE/PRIVATE IMMIGRATION DETENTION FACILITIES. Castro, D-Texas, amendment that would prohibit funds appropriated to the Department of Homeland Security to be used to enter into contracts with privatized immigration detention facilities. Rejected in Committee of the Whole 183-230 : R 0-227; D 183-3. Sept. 7, 2017.

466. HR 3354. FISCAL 2018 OMNIBUS APPROPRIATIONS LEGISLATIVE VEHICLE/DETENTION FACILITY CONSTRUCTION. Jayapal, D-Wash., amendment that would prohibit funds appropriated to the Department of Homeland Security for use in the construction or expansion of detention facilities. Rejected in Committee of the Whole 180-230 : R 0-225; D 180-5. Sept. 7, 2017.

467. HR 3354. FISCAL 2018 OMNIBUS APPROPRIATIONS LEGISLATIVE VEHICLE/NARCOTICS CONTROL. Rothfus, R-Pa., amendment that would increase by $30 million funding for the International Narcotics Control and Law Enforcement and decrease funding for the Fulbright Program by the same amount. Rejected in Committee of the Whole 163-248 : R 163-62; D 0-186. Sept. 7, 2017.

468. HR 3354. FISCAL 2018 OMNIBUS APPROPRIATIONS LEGISLATIVE VEHICLE/WESTERN HEMISPHERE REGIONAL COOPERATION. Scott, R-Ga., amendment that would increase funding for Western Hemisphere Regional Cooperation by $10 million, and would decrease funding for international multilateral organizations by the same amount. Adopted in Committee of the Whole 217-193 : R 213-11; D 4-182. Sept. 7, 2017.

469. HR 3354. FISCAL 2018 OMNIBUS APPROPRIATIONS LEGISLATIVE VEHICLE/ECONOMIC SUPPORT FUND DECREASE. Grothman, R-Wis., amendment that would decrease funding for the Economic Support Fund by $12 million and would transfer the savings to the spending reduction account. Rejected in Committee of the Whole 105-307 : R 105-121; D 0-186. Sept. 7, 2017.

	463	464	465	466	467	468	469
ALABAMA							
1 Byrne	Y	Y	N	N	Y	Y	N
2 Roby	Y	Y	N	N	N	Y	N
3 Rogers	N	Y	N	N	Y	Y	N
4 Aderholt	Y	Y	N	N	Y	Y	N
5 Brooks	N	Y	N	N	Y	Y	Y
6 Palmer	Y	Y	N	N	N	Y	Y
7 Sewell	N	N	Y	Y	N	N	N
ALASKA							
AL Young	Y	N	N	N	N	Y	Y
ARIZONA							
1 O'Halleran	N	N	Y	Y	N	N	N
2 McSally	Y	Y	N	N	Y	Y	N
3 Grijalva	N	N	Y	Y	N	N	N
4 Gosar	Y	Y	N	N	Y	Y	Y
5 Biggs	Y	Y	N	N	Y	Y	Y
6 Schweikert	Y	Y	N	N	N	Y	N
7 Gallego	Y	N	Y	Y	N	N	N
8 Franks	Y	Y	N	N	Y	Y	Y
9 Sinema	Y	N	Y	N	N	N	N
ARKANSAS							
1 Crawford	Y	Y	N	N	Y	Y	N
2 Hill	Y	Y	N	N	N	Y	Y
3 Womack	Y	Y	N	N	N	Y	N
4 Westerman	Y	Y	N	N	N	Y	N
CALIFORNIA							
1 LaMalfa	Y	Y	N	N	Y	Y	Y
2 Huffman	N	N	Y	Y	N	N	N
3 Garamendi	N	N	Y	Y	N	N	N
4 McClintock	Y	Y	N	N	Y	Y	Y
5 Thompson	N	N	Y	Y	N	N	N
6 Matsui	N	N	Y	Y	N	N	N
7 Bera	Y	N	Y	Y	N	N	N
8 Cook	Y	N	N	N	Y	Y	N
9 McNerney	Y	N	Y	Y	N	N	N
10 Denham	Y	N	N	N	Y	Y	N
11 DeSaulnier	N	N	Y	Y	N	N	N
12 Pelosi	?	?	?	?	N	N	N
13 Lee	N	N	Y	Y	N	N	N
14 Speier	N	N	Y	Y	N	N	N
15 Swalwell	N	N	Y	Y	N	N	N
16 Costa	?	?	?	?	?	?	?
17 Khanna	N	N	Y	Y	N	N	N
18 Eshoo	N	N	Y	Y	N	N	N
19 Lofgren	N	N	Y	Y	N	N	N
20 Panetta	N	N	Y	Y	N	N	N
21 Valadao	Y	N	N	N	Y	Y	N
22 Nunes	Y	Y	N	N	Y	Y	N
23 McCarthy	Y	Y	N	N	Y	Y	N
24 Carbajal	N	N	Y	Y	N	N	N
25 Knight	Y	Y	N	N	Y	Y	N
26 Brownley	Y	N	Y	Y	N	N	N
27 Chu	N	N	Y	Y	N	N	N
28 Schiff	N	N	Y	Y	N	N	N
29 Cardenas	N	N	Y	Y	N	N	N
30 Sherman	Y	N	Y	Y	N	N	N
31 Aguilar	Y	N	Y	Y	N	N	N
32 Napolitano	N	N	Y	Y	N	N	N
33 Lieu	N	N	Y	Y	N	N	N
34 Gomez	N	N	Y	Y	N	N	N
35 Torres	N	N	Y	Y	N	N	N
36 Ruiz	N	N	Y	Y	N	N	N
37 Bass	N	N	Y	Y	N	N	N
38 Sánchez, Linda	N	N	Y	Y	N	N	N
39 Royce	Y	Y	N	N	Y	Y	N
40 Roybal-Allard	N	N	Y	Y	N	N	N
41 Takano	N	N	Y	Y	N	N	N
42 Calvert	Y	Y	N	N	N	Y	N
43 Waters	N	N	Y	Y	N	N	N
44 Barragan	N	N	Y	Y	N	N	N
45 Walters	Y	Y	N	N	Y	Y	Y
46 Correa	Y	N	Y	Y	N	N	N
47 Lowenthal	N	N	Y	Y	N	N	N
48 Rohrabacher	Y	Y	N	N	N	Y	Y
49 Issa	Y	Y	N	N	Y	Y	N
50 Hunter	Y	Y	N	N	Y	Y	Y
51 Vargas	N	N	Y	Y	N	N	N
52 Peters	Y	N	Y	Y	N	N	N
53 Davis	N	N	Y	Y	N	N	N

	463	464	465	466	467	468	469
COLORADO							
1 DeGette	?	?	?	?	?	?	?
2 Polis	N	N	Y	Y	N	N	N
3 Tipton	Y	Y	N	N	Y	Y	Y
4 Buck	Y	Y	N	N	Y	Y	Y
5 Lamborn	Y	Y	N	N	Y	Y	Y
6 Coffman	Y	N	N	N	Y	Y	N
7 Perlmutter	Y	N	Y	N	N	N	N
CONNECTICUT							
1 Larson	N	N	Y	N	N	N	N
2 Courtney	Y	N	Y	N	N	N	N
3 DeLauro	N	N	Y	N	N	N	N
4 Himes	N	N	Y	Y	N	N	N
5 Esty	N	N	Y	Y	N	N	N
DELAWARE							
AL Blunt Rochester	N	N	Y	Y	N	N	N
FLORIDA							
1 Gaetz	Y	Y	N	N	Y	Y	Y
2 Dunn	Y	Y	N	N	Y	Y	Y
3 Yoho	Y	Y	N	N	Y	Y	Y
4 Rutherford	N	N	N	?	?	?	?
5 Lawson	N	N	Y	?	?	?	?
6 DeSantis	?	?	?	?	?	?	?
7 Murphy	Y	N	Y	N	N	N	N
8 Posey	?	?	?	?	?	?	?
9 Soto	N	N	Y	Y	N	N	N
10 Demings	N	N	Y	Y	N	N	N
11 Webster	?	?	?	?	?	?	?
12 Bilirakis	Y	Y	N	N	Y	Y	N
13 Crist	?	?	?	?	?	?	?
14 Castor	N	N	Y	?	N	N	N
15 Ross	?	?	?	?	?	?	?
16 Buchanan	Y	Y	N	N	?	?	?
17 Rooney, T.	Y	Y	N	N	Y	Y	N
18 Mast	Y	N	N	N	N	N	N
19 Rooney, F.	Y	N	N	N	Y	Y	Y
20 Hastings	N	N	Y	Y	N	N	N
21 Frankel	N	N	Y	Y	N	N	N
22 Deutch	?	?	?	?	?	?	?
23 Wasserman Schultz	?	?	?	?	?	?	?
24 Wilson	N	N	Y	Y	N	N	N
25 Diaz-Balart	?	?	?	?	?	?	?
26 Curbelo	?	?	?	?	?	?	?
27 Ros-Lehtinen	?	?	?	?	?	?	?
GEORGIA							
1 Carter	Y	Y	N	N	Y	Y	Y
2 Bishop	N	N	Y	N	N	N	N
3 Ferguson	Y	Y	N	N	Y	Y	N
4 Johnson	Y	N	Y	N	N	N	N
5 Lewis	N	N	Y	N	N	N	N
6 Handel	Y	Y	N	N	Y	Y	Y
7 Woodall	Y	N	N	N	Y	Y	N
8 Scott, A.	Y	N	N	N	Y	Y	N
9 Collins	Y	Y	N	N	Y	Y	Y
10 Hice	Y	Y	N	N	Y	Y	Y
11 Loudermilk	Y	Y	N	N	Y	Y	Y
12 Allen	Y	Y	N	N	Y	Y	Y
13 Scott, D.	N	N	Y	N	N	N	N
14 Graves	Y	Y	N	N	Y	Y	N
HAWAII							
1 Hanabusa	N	N	Y	N	N	N	N
2 Gabbard	Y	N	Y	N	N	N	N
IDAHO							
1 Labrador	N	Y	N	N	Y	Y	Y
2 Simpson	Y	N	N	N	N	Y	N
ILLINOIS							
1 Rush	N	N	Y	Y	N	N	N
2 Kelly	N	N	Y	N	N	N	N
3 Lipinski	N	N	Y	N	N	N	N
4 Gutierrez	N	N	Y	Y	N	N	N
5 Quigley	N	N	Y	N	N	N	N
6 Roskam	Y	Y	N	N	N	N	N
7 Davis, D.	N	N	Y	N	N	N	N
8 Krishnamoorthi	N	N	Y	Y	N	N	N
9 Schakowsky	N	N	Y	Y	N	N	N
10 Schneider	N	N	Y	Y	N	N	N
11 Foster	N	N	Y	Y	N	N	N
12 Bost	Y	N	N	N	Y	Y	N
13 Davis, R.	Y	N	N	N	Y	Y	N
14 Hultgren	Y	N	N	N	Y	Y	Y
15 Shimkus	Y	N	N	N	N	Y	N

	463	464	465	466	467	468	469
16 **Kinzinger**	Y	N	N	N	Y	Y	N
17 Bustos	N	N	Y	Y	N	N	N
18 **LaHood**	Y	N	N	N	N	Y	N
INDIANA							
1 Visclosky	N	N	Y	Y	N	N	N
2 **Walorski**	Y	Y	N	N	Y	Y	N
3 **Banks**	Y	Y	N	N	Y	Y	Y
4 **Rokita**	Y	Y	N	N	Y	Y	Y
5 **Brooks**	Y	Y	N	N	Y	Y	N
6 **Messer**	Y	Y	N	N	Y	Y	Y
7 Carson	N	N	Y	Y	N	N	N
8 **Bucshon**	Y	N	N	N	Y	Y	N
9 **Hollingsworth**	N	Y	N	N	Y	Y	N
IOWA							
1 **Blum**	Y	Y	N	N	Y	Y	Y
2 Loebsack	N	N	Y	Y	N	N	N
3 **Young**	Y	Y	N	N	Y	Y	N
4 **King**	Y	Y	N	N	Y	Y	Y
KANSAS							
1 **Marshall**	Y	Y	N	N	Y	Y	Y
2 **Jenkins**	Y	Y	N	N	N	N	N
3 **Yoder**	Y	Y	N	N	Y	Y	N
4 **Estes**	Y	Y	N	N	Y	Y	N
KENTUCKY							
1 **Comer**	Y	Y	N	N	Y	Y	Y
2 **Guthrie**	Y	Y	N	N	Y	Y	Y
3 Yarmuth	N	N	Y	Y	N	N	N
4 **Massie**	Y	Y	N	N	N	Y	Y
5 **Rogers**	Y	Y	N	N	N	Y	N
6 **Barr**	Y	Y	N	N	Y	Y	N
LOUISIANA							
1 **Scalise**	+	+	–	–	+	+	+
2 Richmond	Y	N	Y	Y	N	N	N
3 **Higgins**	Y	Y	N	N	Y	Y	Y
4 **Johnson**	N	Y	N	N	Y	Y	Y
5 **Abraham**	Y	Y	N	N	Y	Y	Y
6 **Graves**	Y	Y	N	N	Y	Y	Y
MAINE							
1 Pingree	N	N	Y	Y	N	N	N
2 **Poliquin**	Y	Y	N	N	Y	Y	N
MARYLAND							
1 **Harris**	Y	Y	N	N	Y	Y	Y
2 Ruppersberger	N	N	Y	Y	N	N	N
3 Sarbanes	N	N	Y	Y	N	N	N
4 Brown	N	N	Y	Y	N	N	N
5 Hoyer	N	N	Y	Y	N	N	N
6 Delaney	N	N	Y	Y	N	N	N
7 Cummings	?	?	?	?	?	?	?
8 Raskin	N	N	Y	Y	N	N	N
MASSACHUSETTS							
1 Neal	N	N	Y	Y	N	N	N
2 McGovern	N	N	Y	Y	N	N	N
3 Tsongas	?	?	?	?	?	?	?
4 Kennedy	N	N	Y	Y	N	N	N
5 Clark	N	N	Y	Y	N	N	N
6 Moulton	N	N	Y	Y	N	N	N
7 Capuano	N	N	Y	Y	N	N	N
8 Lynch	N	N	Y	Y	N	N	N
9 Keating	N	N	Y	Y	N	N	N
MICHIGAN							
1 **Bergman**	Y	Y	N	N	N	Y	Y
2 **Huizenga**	Y	Y	N	N	Y	Y	N
3 **Amash**	N	Y	N	N	N	N	Y
4 **Moolenaar**	Y	Y	N	N	N	Y	N
5 Kildee	N	N	Y	Y	N	N	N
6 **Upton**	Y	N	N	N	N	Y	N
7 **Walberg**	Y	Y	N	N	Y	Y	Y
8 **Bishop**	Y	Y	N	N	N	Y	Y
9 Levin	N	N	Y	Y	N	N	N
10 **Mitchell**	Y	Y	N	N	Y	Y	N
11 **Trott**	Y	Y	N	N	N	Y	N
12 Dingell	N	N	Y	Y	N	N	N
13 Conyers	N	N	Y	Y	N	N	N
14 Lawrence	N	N	Y	Y	N	N	N
MINNESOTA							
1 Walz	N	N	Y	Y	N	N	N
2 **Lewis**	Y	N	N	N	Y	Y	Y
3 **Paulsen**	Y	Y	N	N	N	N	N
4 McCollum	N	N	Y	Y	N	N	N

	463	464	465	466	467	468	469
5 Ellison	N	N	Y	Y	N	N	N
6 **Emmer**	Y	N	N	?	Y	Y	N
7 Peterson	N	N	N	N	N	N	N
8 Nolan	N	N	Y	Y	N	N	N
MISSISSIPPI							
1 **Kelly**	Y	Y	N	N	N	Y	Y
2 Thompson	N	N	Y	Y	N	N	N
3 **Harper**	Y	Y	N	N	N	Y	N
4 **Palazzo**	Y	Y	N	N	Y	Y	Y
MISSOURI							
1 Clay	N	N	Y	Y	N	N	N
2 **Wagner**	?	?	?	?	Y	Y	N
3 **Luetkemeyer**	Y	Y	N	N	Y	Y	N
4 **Hartzler**	Y	Y	N	N	Y	Y	Y
5 Cleaver	N	N	Y	Y	N	N	N
6 **Graves**	Y	Y	N	N	Y	Y	Y
7 **Long**	N	Y	N	N	N	N	Y
8 **Smith**	Y	Y	N	N	Y	Y	Y
MONTANA							
AL **Gianforte**	Y	N	N	N	Y	Y	Y
NEBRASKA							
1 **Fortenberry**	Y	Y	N	N	N	N	N
2 **Bacon**	Y	Y	N	N	N	Y	N
3 **Smith**	Y	Y	N	N	Y	Y	N
NEVADA							
1 Titus	N	N	Y	Y	N	N	N
2 **Amodei**	Y	N	N	N	N	Y	N
3 Rosen	N	N	Y	Y	N	N	N
4 Kihuen	N	N	Y	Y	N	N	N
NEW HAMPSHIRE							
1 Shea-Porter	N	N	Y	Y	N	N	N
2 Kuster	N	N	Y	Y	N	N	N
NEW JERSEY							
1 Norcross	N	N	Y	Y	N	N	N
2 **LoBiondo**	Y	N	N	N	N	Y	N
3 **MacArthur**	Y	N	N	N	N	N	N
4 **Smith**	Y	N	N	N	Y	Y	N
5 Gottheimer	Y	N	Y	Y	N	Y	N
6 Pallone	N	N	Y	Y	N	N	N
7 **Lance**	Y	N	N	N	Y	Y	N
8 Sires	N	N	Y	Y	N	N	N
9 Pascrell	N	N	Y	Y	N	N	N
10 Payne	Y	N	Y	Y	N	N	N
11 **Frelinghuysen**	Y	Y	N	N	N	N	N
12 Watson Coleman	N	N	Y	Y	N	N	N
NEW MEXICO							
1 Lujan Grisham	N	N	Y	Y	N	N	N
2 **Pearce**	Y	Y	N	N	N	Y	Y
3 Luján	N	N	Y	Y	N	N	N
NEW YORK							
1 **Zeldin**	Y	N	N	N	Y	Y	N
2 **King**	Y	N	N	N	N	Y	N
3 Suozzi	Y	N	Y	Y	N	N	N
4 Rice	N	N	Y	Y	N	N	N
5 Meeks	Y	N	Y	Y	N	N	N
6 Meng	N	N	Y	Y	N	N	N
7 Velázquez	N	N	Y	Y	N	N	N
8 Jeffries	Y	N	Y	Y	N	N	N
9 Clarke	Y	N	Y	Y	N	N	N
10 Nadler	N	N	Y	Y	N	N	N
11 **Donovan**	Y	N	N	N	N	Y	N
12 Maloney, C.	N	N	Y	Y	N	N	N
13 Espaillat	N	N	Y	Y	N	Y	N
14 Crowley	N	N	Y	Y	N	N	N
15 Serrano	N	N	Y	Y	N	N	N
16 Engel	Y	N	Y	Y	N	N	N
17 Lowey	N	N	Y	Y	N	N	N
18 Maloney, S.P.	N	N	Y	Y	N	N	N
19 **Faso**	Y	N	N	N	Y	Y	Y
20 Tonko	N	N	Y	Y	N	N	N
21 **Stefanik**	Y	N	N	N	Y	Y	N
22 **Tenney**	Y	N	N	N	Y	Y	N
23 **Reed**	Y	N	N	N	Y	Y	N
24 **Katko**	Y	N	N	N	Y	Y	N
25 Slaughter	N	N	Y	Y	N	N	N
26 Higgins	N	N	Y	Y	N	N	N
27 **Collins**	Y	Y	N	N	Y	Y	N
NORTH CAROLINA							
1 Butterfield	N	N	Y	Y	N	N	N
2 **Holding**	Y	Y	N	N	Y	Y	Y
3 **Jones**	Y	Y	N	N	N	Y	Y
4 Price	N	N	Y	Y	N	N	N

	463	464	465	466	467	468	469
5 **Foxx**	Y	Y	N	N	Y	Y	N
6 **Walker**	Y	Y	N	N	Y	Y	Y
7 **Rouzer**	Y	Y	N	N	Y	Y	Y
8 **Hudson**	Y	Y	N	N	Y	Y	Y
9 **Pittenger**	Y	Y	N	N	Y	Y	Y
10 **McHenry**	Y	Y	N	N	Y	Y	N
11 **Meadows**	?	?	?	?	Y	Y	Y
12 Adams	N	N	Y	Y	N	N	N
13 **Budd**	N	Y	N	N	Y	Y	Y
NORTH DAKOTA							
AL **Cramer**	Y	Y	N	N	Y	Y	N
OHIO							
1 **Chabot**	Y	Y	N	N	Y	Y	N
2 **Wenstrup**	Y	Y	N	N	Y	Y	N
3 Beatty	N	N	Y	Y	N	N	N
4 **Jordan**	Y	Y	N	N	Y	Y	Y
5 **Latta**	Y	Y	N	N	Y	Y	Y
6 **Johnson**	Y	N	N	N	Y	Y	N
7 **Gibbs**	Y	Y	N	N	Y	Y	Y
8 **Davidson**	N	Y	N	N	Y	Y	Y
9 Kaptur	N	N	Y	Y	N	N	N
10 **Turner**	Y	N	N	N	Y	Y	N
11 Fudge	N	N	Y	Y	N	N	N
12 **Tiberi**	Y	N	N	N	Y	Y	N
13 Ryan	N	N	Y	Y	N	N	N
14 **Joyce**	Y	N	N	N	N	Y	N
15 **Stivers**	Y	N	N	N	N	Y	N
16 **Renacci**	Y	N	N	N	Y	Y	Y
OKLAHOMA							
1 **Bridenstine**	?	?	?	?	?	?	?
2 **Mullin**	Y	Y	N	N	Y	Y	Y
3 **Lucas**	Y	Y	N	N	N	Y	N
4 **Cole**	Y	Y	N	?	N	Y	N
5 **Russell**	Y	Y	N	N	Y	Y	Y
OREGON							
1 Bonamici	N	N	Y	Y	N	N	N
2 **Walden**	Y	N	N	N	Y	Y	N
3 Blumenauer	N	N	Y	Y	N	N	N
4 DeFazio	N	N	Y	Y	N	N	N
5 Schrader	N	N	Y	Y	N	Y	N
PENNSYLVANIA							
1 Brady	N	N	Y	Y	N	N	N
2 Evans	N	N	Y	Y	N	N	N
3 **Kelly**	Y	N	N	N	Y	Y	N
4 **Perry**	Y	Y	N	N	Y	Y	Y
5 **Thompson**	Y	Y	N	N	N	Y	N
6 **Costello**	Y	N	N	N	N	Y	Y
7 **Meehan**	Y	N	N	N	N	Y	N
8 **Fitzpatrick**	Y	N	N	N	N	N	N
9 **Shuster**	Y	N	N	N	Y	Y	Y
10 **Marino**	Y	N	N	N	?	?	N
11 **Barletta**	Y	N	N	N	Y	Y	N
12 **Rothfus**	Y	Y	N	N	Y	Y	N
13 Boyle	N	N	Y	Y	N	N	N
14 Doyle	N	N	Y	Y	N	N	N
15 **Dent**	Y	Y	N	N	N	N	N
16 **Smucker**	Y	Y	N	N	Y	Y	N
17 Cartwright	N	N	Y	Y	N	N	N
18 **Murphy**	Y	N	N	N	Y	Y	N
RHODE ISLAND							
1 Cicilline	N	N	Y	Y	N	N	N
2 Langevin	N	N	Y	Y	N	N	N
SOUTH CAROLINA							
1 **Sanford**	Y	Y	N	N	N	Y	Y
2 **Wilson**	Y	Y	N	N	Y	Y	N
3 **Duncan**	Y	Y	N	N	Y	Y	Y
4 **Gowdy**	Y	Y	N	N	Y	Y	Y
5 **Norman**	Y	Y	N	N	Y	Y	Y
6 Clyburn	N	N	Y	Y	N	N	N
7 **Rice**	Y	Y	N	N	Y	Y	N
SOUTH DAKOTA							
AL **Noem**	Y	Y	N	N	Y	Y	Y
TENNESSEE							
1 **Roe**	Y	Y	N	N	Y	Y	N
2 **Duncan**	Y	Y	N	N	Y	Y	Y
3 **Fleischmann**	Y	Y	N	N	Y	Y	N
4 **DesJarlais**	Y	Y	N	N	Y	Y	N
5 Cooper	N	N	Y	Y	N	N	N
6 **Black**	Y	Y	N	N	Y	Y	Y
7 **Blackburn**	Y	Y	N	N	Y	Y	Y
8 **Kustoff**	Y	Y	N	N	Y	Y	N
9 Cohen	Y	N	Y	Y	N	N	N

	463	464	465	466	467	468	469
TEXAS							
1 **Gohmert**	Y	Y	N	N	Y	Y	Y
2 **Poe**	Y	Y	N	N	Y	Y	Y
3 **Johnson, S.**	Y	Y	N	N	Y	Y	Y
4 **Ratcliffe**	Y	Y	N	N	Y	Y	Y
5 **Hensarling**	Y	Y	N	N	Y	Y	Y
6 **Barton**	Y	Y	N	N	Y	Y	Y
7 **Culberson**	Y	Y	N	N	N	Y	N
8 **Brady**	Y	Y	N	N	N	Y	N
9 Green, A.	N	N	Y	Y	N	N	N
10 **McCaul**	Y	Y	N	N	Y	Y	N
11 **Conaway**	Y	Y	N	N	Y	Y	Y
12 **Granger**	Y	Y	N	N	Y	Y	N
13 **Thornberry**	Y	Y	N	N	Y	Y	N
14 **Weber**	Y	Y	N	N	Y	Y	N
15 Gonzalez	N	N	Y	Y	N	N	N
16 O'Rourke	N	N	Y	Y	N	N	N
17 **Flores**	Y	Y	N	N	N	Y	N
18 Jackson Lee	N	N	Y	Y	N	N	N
19 **Arrington**	Y	Y	N	N	Y	Y	Y
20 Castro	N	N	Y	Y	N	N	N
21 **Smith**	Y	Y	N	N	Y	Y	N
22 **Olson**	Y	Y	N	N	Y	Y	N
23 **Hurd**	Y	Y	N	N	N	Y	N
24 **Marchant**	Y	Y	N	N	Y	Y	N
25 **Williams**	Y	Y	N	N	Y	Y	Y
26 **Burgess**	Y	Y	N	N	Y	Y	Y
27 **Farenthold**	Y	Y	N	N	Y	Y	N
28 Cuellar	N	N	N	N	N	N	N
29 Green, G.	N	N	Y	Y	N	N	N
30 Johnson, E.B.	N	N	Y	Y	N	N	N
31 **Carter**	Y	Y	N	N	N	?	N
32 **Sessions**	Y	Y	N	N	Y	Y	N
33 Veasey	N	N	Y	Y	N	N	N
34 Vela	N	N	Y	Y	N	Y	N
35 Doggett	N	N	Y	Y	N	N	N
36 **Babin**	Y	Y	N	N	Y	Y	N
UTAH							
1 **Bishop**	Y	Y	N	N	Y	Y	N
2 **Stewart**	Y	Y	N	N	Y	Y	N
4 **Love**	Y	Y	N	N	Y	Y	Y
VERMONT							
AL Welch	N	N	Y	Y	N	N	N
VIRGINIA							
1 **Wittman**	Y	Y	N	N	Y	Y	Y
2 **Taylor**	Y	Y	N	N	Y	Y	Y
3 Scott	Y	N	Y	Y	N	N	N
4 McEachin	Y	N	Y	Y	N	N	N
5 **Garrett**	?	?	?	?	?	?	?
6 **Goodlatte**	N	Y	N	N	Y	Y	Y
7 **Brat**	Y	Y	N	N	Y	Y	Y
8 Beyer	Y	N	Y	Y	N	N	N
9 **Griffith**	Y	Y	N	N	Y	Y	Y
10 **Comstock**	Y	Y	N	N	N	Y	N
11 Connolly	Y	N	Y	Y	N	N	N
WASHINGTON							
1 DelBene	Y	N	Y	Y	N	N	N
2 Larsen	N	N	Y	Y	N	N	N
3 **Herrera Beutler**	Y	Y	N	N	N	Y	N
4 **Newhouse**	Y	N	N	N	Y	Y	N
5 **McMorris Rodgers**	Y	Y	N	N	Y	Y	Y
6 Kilmer	N	N	Y	Y	N	N	N
7 Jayapal	N	N	Y	Y	N	N	N
8 **Reichert**	Y	N	N	N	Y	Y	N
9 Smith	Y	N	Y	Y	N	N	N
10 Heck	N	N	Y	Y	N	N	N
WEST VIRGINIA							
1 **McKinley**	Y	N	N	N	Y	Y	N
2 **Mooney**	Y	Y	N	N	Y	Y	Y
3 **Jenkins**	Y	N	N	N	Y	Y	N
WISCONSIN							
1 **Ryan**							
2 Pocan	N	N	Y	Y	N	N	N
3 Kind	Y	N	Y	Y	N	N	N
4 Moore	N	N	Y	Y	N	N	N
5 **Sensenbrenner**	Y	Y	N	N	Y	Y	Y
6 **Grothman**	Y	N	N	N	Y	Y	Y
7 **Duffy**	Y	N	N	N	Y	Y	N
8 **Gallagher**	Y	Y	N	N	Y	Y	N
WYOMING							
AL **Cheney**	Y	Y	N	N	Y	Y	Y

⫼ HOUSE VOTES

VOTE NUMBER

470. HR 3354. FISCAL 2018 OMNIBUS APPROPRIATIONS LEGISLATIVE VEHICLE/UN HUMAN RIGHTS CONTRIBUTIONS. Yoho, Fla., for Ros-Lehtinen, R-Fla., amendment that would prohibit funds from being used to make contributions to the United Nations Human Rights Council, the United Nations Office of the United Nations High Commissioner for Human Rights, and the United Nations Relief and Works Agency. Rejected in Committee of the Whole 199-212 : R 196-29; D 3-183. Sept. 7, 2017.

471. HR 3354. FISCAL 2018 OMNIBUS APPROPRIATIONS LEGISLATIVE VEHICLE/EPA SUPERFUND SITES. Grijalva, D-Ariz., amendment that would increase funding for EPA Superfund sites by $12 million, and would decrease funding for the Bureau of Land Management's oil and gas program by the same amount. Rejected in Committee of the Whole 191-221 : R 9-217; D 182-4. Sept. 7, 2017.

472. HR 3354. FISCAL 2018 OMNIBUS APPROPRIATIONS LEGISLATIVE VEHICLE/ABANDONED MINE RECLAMATION. Thompson, R-Pa., amendment that would increase funds for reclamation of abandoned mine lands and other related activities by $32.5 million, and would decrease EPA funding by the same amount. Adopted in Committee of the Whole 207-205 : R 198-28; D 9-177. Sept. 7, 2017.

473. HR 3354. FISCAL 2018 OMNIBUS APPROPRIATIONS LEGISLATIVE VEHICLE/EPA FUNDING INCREASE. Grijalva, D-Ariz., amendment that would decrease the Department of the Interior Office of the Secretary funding by $1 million, and would increase funding for the EPA by the same amount. Rejected in Committee of the Whole 190-218 : R 9-213; D 181-5. Sept. 7, 2017.

474. HR 3354. FISCAL 2018 OMNIBUS APPROPRIATIONS LEGISLATIVE VEHICLE/EPA OPERATIONS AND MAINTENANCE. Biggs, R-Ariz., amendment that would decrease the EPA operations and maintenance funding by $10.2 million and would transfer the savings to the spending reduction account. Rejected in Committee of the Whole 184-228 : R 184-42; D 0-186. Sept. 7, 2017.

475. HR 3354. FISCAL 2018 OMNIBUS APPROPRIATIONS LEGISLATIVE VEHICLE/EPA STATE GRANTS. Lujan, D-N.M., amendment that would increase by $6 million, and decrease by the same amount, funding to EPA state and tribal assistance grants for environmental programs and infrastructure assistance. Adopted in Committee of the Whole 220-191 : R 35-191; D 185-0. Sept. 7, 2017.

476. HR 3354. FISCAL 2018 OMNIBUS APPROPRIATIONS LEGISLATIVE VEHICLE/OZONE STANDARDS. Ellison, D-Minn., amendment that would eliminate the bill's provision that would delay the implementation date for national ambient air quality standards for ozone until 2026. Rejected in Committee of the Whole 194-218 : R 11-215; D 183-3. Sept. 7, 2017.

	470	471	472	473	474	475	476
ALABAMA							
1 Byrne	Y	N	Y	N	Y	N	N
2 Roby	N	N	Y	N	Y	N	N
3 Rogers	Y	N	Y	N	Y	N	N
4 Aderholt	N	N	Y	N	Y	N	N
5 Brooks	Y	N	Y	N	Y	N	N
6 Palmer	Y	N	Y	N	Y	N	N
7 Sewell	N	Y	N	Y	N	Y	Y
ALASKA							
AL Young	Y	N	Y	N	Y	N	N
ARIZONA							
1 O'Halleran	N	Y	N	Y	N	Y	Y
2 McSally	Y	N	Y	Y	Y	Y	N
3 Grijalva	N	Y	N	Y	N	Y	Y
4 Gosar	Y	N	Y	N	Y	N	N
5 Biggs	Y	N	Y	N	Y	N	N
6 Schweikert	Y	N	Y	N	Y	N	N
7 Gallego	N	Y	N	Y	N	Y	Y
8 Franks	Y	N	N	N	Y	N	N
9 Sinema	Y	Y	N	Y	N	Y	Y
ARKANSAS							
1 Crawford	Y	N	Y	N	Y	N	N
2 Hill	Y	N	Y	N	Y	N	N
3 Womack	Y	N	Y	N	Y	N	N
4 Westerman	Y	N	Y	N	Y	N	N
CALIFORNIA							
1 LaMalfa	Y	N	Y	N	Y	Y	N
2 Huffman	N	Y	N	Y	N	Y	Y
3 Garamendi	N	Y	N	Y	N	Y	Y
4 McClintock	Y	N	Y	N	Y	Y	Y
5 Thompson	N	Y	N	Y	N	Y	Y
6 Matsui	N	Y	N	Y	N	Y	Y
7 Bera	N	N	N	Y	N	Y	Y
8 Cook	Y	N	Y	N	Y	N	N
9 McNerney	N	Y	N	Y	N	Y	Y
10 Denham	N	N	N	Y	N	N	N
11 DeSaulnier	N	Y	N	Y	N	Y	Y
12 Pelosi	N	Y	N	Y	N	Y	Y
13 Lee	N	Y	N	Y	N	Y	Y
14 Speier	N	Y	N	Y	N	Y	Y
15 Swalwell	N	Y	N	Y	N	Y	Y
16 Costa	?	?	?	?	?	?	?
17 Khanna	N	Y	N	Y	N	Y	Y
18 Eshoo	N	Y	N	Y	N	Y	Y
19 Lofgren	N	Y	N	Y	N	Y	Y
20 Panetta	N	Y	N	Y	N	Y	Y
21 Valadao	N	N	Y	N	Y	N	N
22 Nunes	Y	N	Y	N	Y	N	N
23 McCarthy	Y	N	Y	N	Y	N	N
24 Carbajal	N	Y	N	Y	N	Y	Y
25 Knight	Y	N	N	N	N	N	N
26 Brownley	N	Y	N	Y	N	Y	Y
27 Chu	N	Y	N	Y	N	Y	Y
28 Schiff	N	Y	N	Y	N	Y	Y
29 Cardenas	N	Y	N	Y	N	Y	Y
30 Sherman	N	Y	N	Y	N	Y	Y
31 Aguilar	N	Y	N	Y	N	Y	Y
32 Napolitano	N	Y	N	Y	N	Y	Y
33 Lieu	N	Y	N	Y	N	Y	Y
34 Gomez	N	Y	N	Y	N	Y	Y
35 Torres	N	Y	N	Y	N	Y	Y
36 Ruiz	N	Y	N	Y	N	Y	Y
37 Bass	N	Y	N	Y	N	Y	Y
38 Sánchez, Linda	N	Y	N	Y	N	Y	Y
39 Royce	Y	N	Y	N	Y	N	N
40 Roybal-Allard	N	Y	N	Y	N	Y	Y
41 Takano	N	Y	N	Y	N	Y	Y
42 Calvert	Y	N	Y	N	Y	N	N
43 Waters	N	Y	N	Y	N	Y	Y
44 Barragan	N	Y	N	Y	N	Y	Y
45 Walters	Y	N	N	N	Y	N	N
46 Correa	N	Y	N	Y	N	Y	Y
47 Lowenthal	N	Y	N	Y	N	Y	Y
48 Rohrabacher	Y	N	Y	N	Y	N	N
49 Issa	Y	N	Y	N	Y	N	N
50 Hunter	Y	N	Y	N	Y	N	N
51 Vargas	N	Y	N	Y	N	Y	Y
52 Peters	N	Y	N	Y	N	Y	Y
53 Davis	N	Y	N	Y	N	Y	Y

	470	471	472	473	474	475	476
COLORADO							
1 DeGette	?	?	?	?	?	?	?
2 Polis	N	Y	N	Y	N	Y	N
3 Tipton	Y	N	Y	N	N	Y	N
4 Buck	Y	N	Y	N	Y	Y	N
5 Lamborn	Y	N	Y	N	Y	Y	N
6 Coffman	Y	N	Y	N	Y	N	N
7 Perlmutter	N	Y	N	Y	N	Y	Y
CONNECTICUT							
1 Larson	N	Y	Y	Y	N	Y	Y
2 Courtney	N	Y	N	Y	N	Y	Y
3 DeLauro	N	Y	N	Y	N	Y	Y
4 Himes	N	Y	N	Y	N	Y	Y
5 Esty	N	Y	N	Y	N	Y	Y
DELAWARE							
AL Blunt Rochester	N	Y	N	Y	N	Y	Y
FLORIDA							
1 Gaetz	Y	N	N	N	Y	N	N
2 Dunn	Y	N	Y	N	Y	N	N
3 Yoho	Y	N	Y	N	Y	N	N
4 Rutherford	?	?	?	?	?	?	?
5 Lawson	?	?	?	?	?	?	?
6 DeSantis	?	?	?	?	?	?	?
7 Murphy	N	Y	N	Y	N	Y	Y
8 Posey	?	?	?	?	?	?	?
9 Soto	N	Y	N	Y	N	Y	Y
10 Demings	N	Y	N	Y	N	Y	Y
11 Webster	?	?	?	?	?	?	?
12 Bilirakis	?	?	?	?	?	?	?
13 Crist	N	Y	N	Y	N	Y	Y
14 Castor	N	Y	N	Y	N	Y	Y
15 Ross	?	?	?	?	?	?	?
16 Buchanan	?	?	?	?	?	?	?
17 Rooney, T.	N	N	Y	N	Y	N	N
18 Mast	Y	N	Y	N	Y	N	Y
19 Rooney, F.	?	N	N	Y	N	N	N
20 Hastings	N	Y	N	Y	N	Y	Y
21 Frankel	N	Y	N	Y	N	Y	Y
22 Deutch	?	?	?	?	?	?	?
23 Wasserman Schultz	?	?	?	?	?	?	?
24 Wilson	N	Y	N	Y	N	Y	Y
25 Diaz-Balart	?	?	?	?	?	?	?
26 Curbelo	?	?	?	?	?	?	?
27 Ros-Lehtinen	?	?	?	?	?	?	?
GEORGIA							
1 Carter	Y	N	Y	N	Y	N	N
2 Bishop	N	Y	N	Y	N	Y	Y
3 Ferguson	Y	N	Y	N	Y	N	N
4 Johnson	N	Y	N	Y	N	Y	Y
5 Lewis	N	Y	N	Y	N	Y	Y
6 Handel	Y	N	Y	N	Y	N	N
7 Woodall	Y	N	Y	N	Y	N	N
8 Scott, A.	Y	N	Y	N	Y	N	N
9 Collins	Y	N	Y	N	Y	N	N
10 Hice	Y	N	Y	N	Y	N	N
11 Loudermilk	Y	N	Y	?	Y	N	N
12 Allen	Y	N	Y	N	Y	N	N
13 Scott, D.	N	Y	N	Y	N	Y	Y
14 Graves	Y	N	Y	N	Y	N	N
HAWAII							
1 Hanabusa	N	Y	N	Y	N	Y	Y
2 Gabbard	N	Y	N	Y	N	Y	Y
IDAHO							
1 Labrador	Y	N	Y	?	Y	N	N
2 Simpson	Y	N	Y	N	N	N	N
ILLINOIS							
1 Rush	N	Y	N	Y	N	Y	Y
2 Kelly	N	Y	N	Y	N	?	Y
3 Lipinski	N	Y	N	Y	N	Y	Y
4 Gutierrez	N	Y	N	Y	N	Y	Y
5 Quigley	N	Y	N	Y	N	Y	Y
6 Roskam	Y	N	N	N	Y	N	N
7 Davis, D.	N	Y	N	Y	N	Y	Y
8 Krishnamoorthi	N	Y	N	Y	N	Y	Y
9 Schakowsky	N	Y	N	Y	N	Y	Y
10 Schneider	N	Y	N	Y	N	Y	Y
11 Foster	N	Y	N	Y	N	Y	Y
12 Bost	Y	N	Y	N	N	N	N
13 Davis, R.	N	Y	N	Y	N	N	N
14 Hultgren	N	Y	N	N	N	N	N
15 Shimkus	Y	N	Y	N	N	N	N

	470	471	472	473	474	475	476
16 **Kinzinger**	N	N	Y	N	N	Y	N
17 Bustos	N	Y	N	Y	N	Y	Y
18 **LaHood**	Y	N	Y	?	Y	N	N
INDIANA							
1 Visclosky	N	Y	N	Y	N	Y	Y
2 **Walorski**	Y	N	Y	N	Y	N	N
3 **Banks**	Y	N	Y	N	Y	N	N
4 **Rokita**	Y	N	Y	N	Y	Y	N
5 **Brooks**	N	N	Y	N	N	N	N
6 **Messer**	Y	N	Y	N	Y	N	N
7 Carson	N	Y	N	Y	N	Y	Y
8 **Bucshon**	N	N	Y	N	Y	N	N
9 **Hollingsworth**	Y	N	Y	N	Y	N	N
IOWA							
1 **Blum**	Y	N	Y	N	Y	Y	N
2 Loebsack	N	Y	N	Y	N	Y	Y
3 **Young**	Y	N	Y	N	Y	Y	N
4 **King**	Y	N	Y	N	Y	N	N
KANSAS							
1 **Marshall**	Y	N	Y	N	Y	N	N
2 **Jenkins**	Y	N	Y	N	Y	N	N
3 **Yoder**	Y	N	Y	N	Y	N	N
4 **Estes**	Y	N	Y	N	Y	N	N
KENTUCKY							
1 **Comer**	Y	N	Y	N	Y	N	N
2 **Guthrie**	Y	N	Y	N	Y	N	N
3 Yarmuth	N	Y	N	Y	N	Y	Y
4 **Massie**	Y	N	Y	N	Y	N	N
5 **Rogers**	N	N	Y	N	Y	N	N
6 **Barr**	Y	N	Y	N	Y	N	N
LOUISIANA							
1 **Scalise**	+	–	+	–	+	–	–
2 Richmond	N	Y	N	Y	N	Y	Y
3 **Higgins**	Y	N	Y	N	Y	N	N
4 **Johnson**	Y	N	Y	N	Y	N	N
5 **Abraham**	Y	N	Y	N	Y	N	N
6 **Graves**	Y	N	Y	N	N	N	N
MAINE							
1 Pingree	N	Y	N	Y	N	Y	Y
2 **Poliquin**	N	N	Y	N	N	N	Y
MARYLAND							
1 **Harris**	Y	N	Y	N	Y	N	N
2 Ruppersberger	N	Y	N	Y	N	Y	Y
3 Sarbanes	N	Y	N	Y	N	Y	Y
4 Brown	N	Y	N	Y	N	Y	Y
5 Hoyer	N	Y	N	Y	N	Y	Y
6 Delaney	N	Y	N	Y	N	Y	Y
7 Cummings	?	?	?	?	?	?	?
8 Raskin	N	Y	N	Y	N	Y	Y
MASSACHUSETTS							
1 Neal	N	Y	N	Y	N	Y	Y
2 McGovern	N	Y	N	Y	N	Y	Y
3 Tsongas	?	?	?	?	?	?	?
4 Kennedy	N	Y	N	Y	N	Y	Y
5 Clark	N	Y	N	Y	N	Y	Y
6 Moulton	N	Y	N	Y	N	Y	Y
7 Capuano	N	Y	N	Y	N	Y	Y
8 Lynch	N	Y	N	Y	N	Y	Y
9 Keating	N	Y	N	Y	N	Y	Y
MICHIGAN							
1 **Bergman**	Y	N	Y	N	N	Y	N
2 **Huizenga**	Y	N	Y	N	Y	N	N
3 **Amash**	N	N	N	N	Y	Y	N
4 **Moolenaar**	Y	N	N	N	Y	N	N
5 Kildee	N	Y	N	Y	N	Y	Y
6 **Upton**	N	N	Y	N	N	Y	N
7 **Walberg**	Y	N	Y	N	Y	N	N
8 **Bishop**	Y	N	Y	N	Y	N	N
9 Levin	N	Y	N	Y	N	Y	Y
10 **Mitchell**	Y	N	Y	N	Y	N	N
11 **Trott**	N	N	Y	N	Y	N	N
12 Dingell	N	Y	N	Y	N	Y	Y
13 Conyers	N	Y	N	Y	N	Y	Y
14 Lawrence	N	Y	N	Y	N	Y	Y
MINNESOTA							
1 Walz	N	Y	N	Y	N	Y	Y
2 **Lewis**	Y	N	N	N	Y	N	N
3 **Paulsen**	Y	N	N	Y	N	Y	N
4 McCollum	N	Y	N	Y	N	Y	Y

	470	471	472	473	474	475	476
5 Ellison	N	Y	N	Y	N	Y	Y
6 **Emmer**	Y	N	N	N	Y	N	N
7 Peterson	N	N	Y	N	N	Y	N
8 Nolan	N	Y	N	Y	N	Y	Y
MISSISSIPPI							
1 **Kelly**	Y	N	Y	N	Y	N	N
2 Thompson	N	Y	N	Y	N	Y	Y
3 **Harper**	Y	N	Y	N	Y	N	N
4 **Palazzo**	Y	N	Y	N	Y	N	N
MISSOURI							
1 Clay	N	Y	N	Y	N	Y	Y
2 **Wagner**	Y	N	N	N	Y	N	N
3 **Luetkemeyer**	Y	N	Y	N	Y	N	N
4 **Hartzler**	Y	N	Y	N	Y	N	N
5 Cleaver	N	Y	N	Y	N	Y	Y
6 **Graves**	Y	N	Y	N	Y	N	N
7 **Long**	Y	N	Y	?	Y	N	N
8 **Smith**	Y	N	Y	N	Y	N	N
MONTANA							
AL **Gianforte**	Y	N	Y	N	Y	Y	N
NEBRASKA							
1 **Fortenberry**	N	N	N	N	N	N	N
2 **Bacon**	Y	N	Y	N	Y	Y	N
3 **Smith**	Y	N	Y	N	Y	N	N
NEVADA							
1 Titus	N	Y	N	Y	N	Y	Y
2 **Amodei**	N	N	Y	N	Y	N	N
3 Rosen	N	Y	N	Y	N	Y	Y
4 Kihuen	N	Y	N	Y	N	Y	Y
NEW HAMPSHIRE							
1 Shea-Porter	N	Y	N	Y	N	Y	Y
2 Kuster	N	Y	N	Y	N	Y	Y
NEW JERSEY							
1 Norcross	N	Y	N	Y	N	Y	Y
2 **LoBiondo**	Y	Y	Y	N	N	N	Y
3 **MacArthur**	N	N	N	N	N	N	Y
4 **Smith**	Y	Y	N	Y	N	N	Y
5 Gottheimer	Y	Y	N	Y	N	Y	Y
6 Pallone	N	Y	N	Y	N	Y	Y
7 **Lance**	Y	Y	N	Y	N	Y	Y
8 Sires	N	Y	N	Y	N	Y	Y
9 Pascrell	N	Y	N	Y	N	Y	Y
10 Payne	N	Y	N	Y	N	Y	Y
11 **Frelinghuysen**	Y	N	Y	N	N	N	N
12 Watson Coleman	N	Y	N	Y	N	Y	Y
NEW MEXICO							
1 Lujan Grisham	N	N	N	Y	N	Y	Y
2 **Pearce**	Y	N	Y	N	Y	N	N
3 Luján	N	Y	N	Y	N	Y	Y
NEW YORK							
1 **Zeldin**	Y	N	N	N	N	N	N
2 **King**	Y	Y	Y	N	N	N	N
3 Suozzi	Y	Y	N	N	Y	Y	Y
4 Rice	N	Y	N	Y	N	Y	Y
5 Meeks	N	Y	N	Y	N	Y	N
6 Meng	N	Y	N	Y	N	Y	Y
7 Velázquez	N	Y	N	Y	N	Y	Y
8 Jeffries	N	Y	N	Y	N	Y	Y
9 Clarke	N	Y	N	Y	N	Y	Y
10 Nadler	N	Y	N	Y	N	Y	Y
11 **Donovan**	Y	Y	Y	N	N	N	N
12 Maloney, C.	N	Y	N	Y	N	Y	Y
13 Espaillat	N	Y	N	Y	N	Y	Y
14 Crowley	N	Y	N	Y	N	Y	Y
15 Serrano	N	Y	N	N	N	Y	Y
16 Engel	N	Y	N	Y	N	Y	Y
17 Lowey	N	Y	N	Y	N	Y	Y
18 Maloney, S.P.	N	Y	N	Y	N	Y	Y
19 **Faso**	Y	Y	Y	N	N	N	Y
20 Tonko	N	Y	N	Y	N	Y	Y
21 **Stefanik**	Y	N	Y	N	N	Y	Y
22 **Tenney**	Y	N	Y	N	Y	N	N
23 **Reed**	Y	N	Y	N	Y	N	N
24 **Katko**	Y	N	Y	N	N	N	N
25 Slaughter	N	Y	N	Y	N	Y	Y
26 Higgins	N	Y	N	Y	N	Y	Y
27 **Collins**	N	N	Y	N	Y	N	N
NORTH CAROLINA							
1 Butterfield	N	Y	N	Y	N	Y	Y
2 **Holding**	Y	N	Y	N	Y	N	N
3 **Jones**	Y	Y	Y	Y	Y	N	N
4 Price	N	Y	N	Y	N	Y	Y

	470	471	472	473	474	475	476
5 **Foxx**	Y	N	Y	N	Y	N	N
6 **Walker**	Y	N	N	N	Y	N	N
7 **Rouzer**	Y	N	Y	N	Y	N	N
8 **Hudson**	Y	N	Y	N	Y	N	N
9 **Pittenger**	Y	N	Y	N	Y	N	N
10 **McHenry**	N	N	Y	N	Y	N	N
11 **Meadows**	Y	N	N	N	Y	N	N
12 Adams	N	Y	N	Y	N	Y	Y
13 **Budd**	Y	N	Y	N	Y	N	N
NORTH DAKOTA							
AL **Cramer**	N	N	Y	N	Y	N	N
OHIO							
1 **Chabot**	Y	N	Y	N	Y	N	N
2 **Wenstrup**	Y	N	Y	N	Y	N	N
3 Beatty	N	Y	N	Y	N	Y	Y
4 **Jordan**	Y	N	Y	N	Y	N	N
5 **Latta**	Y	N	Y	N	Y	N	N
6 **Johnson**	Y	N	Y	N	Y	N	N
7 **Gibbs**	Y	N	Y	N	Y	N	N
8 **Davidson**	Y	N	Y	N	Y	N	N
9 Kaptur	N	Y	N	Y	N	Y	Y
10 **Turner**	Y	N	Y	N	N	N	N
11 Fudge	N	Y	N	Y	N	Y	Y
12 **Tiberi**	Y	N	Y	N	Y	N	N
13 Ryan	N	Y	Y	Y	N	Y	Y
14 **Joyce**	Y	N	Y	N	N	N	N
15 **Stivers**	Y	N	Y	N	N	N	N
16 **Renacci**	Y	N	Y	N	Y	N	N
OKLAHOMA							
1 **Bridenstine**	?	?	?	?	?	?	?
2 **Mullin**	Y	N	Y	N	Y	N	N
3 **Lucas**	N	N	Y	N	Y	N	N
4 **Cole**	N	N	Y	N	N	Y	N
5 **Russell**	Y	N	Y	N	Y	N	N
OREGON							
1 Bonamici	N	Y	N	Y	N	Y	Y
2 **Walden**	Y	N	Y	N	N	N	N
3 Blumenauer	N	Y	N	Y	N	Y	Y
4 DeFazio	N	Y	Y	Y	N	Y	Y
5 Schrader	N	Y	N	N	N	Y	Y
PENNSYLVANIA							
1 Brady	N	Y	Y	Y	N	Y	Y
2 Evans	N	Y	N	Y	N	Y	Y
3 **Kelly**	Y	N	Y	N	Y	N	N
4 **Perry**	Y	N	Y	N	Y	N	N
5 **Thompson**	Y	N	Y	N	Y	N	N
6 **Costello**	N	Y	Y	Y	N	N	N
7 **Meehan**	N	N	N	Y	N	Y	N
8 **Fitzpatrick**	N	Y	N	Y	N	Y	Y
9 **Shuster**	Y	N	Y	N	N	N	N
10 **Marino**	Y	N	Y	N	Y	N	N
11 **Barletta**	Y	N	Y	N	Y	N	N
12 **Rothfus**	Y	N	Y	N	Y	N	N
13 Boyle	N	Y	Y	N	N	Y	Y
14 Doyle	N	Y	Y	Y	N	Y	Y
15 **Dent**	N	N	Y	N	N	N	N
16 **Smucker**	Y	N	Y	N	Y	N	N
17 Cartwright	N	Y	Y	Y	N	Y	Y
18 **Murphy**	Y	N	Y	N	N	N	N
RHODE ISLAND							
1 Cicilline	N	Y	N	Y	N	Y	Y
2 Langevin	N	Y	N	Y	N	Y	Y
SOUTH CAROLINA							
1 **Sanford**	Y	N	N	N	Y	N	Y
2 **Wilson**	Y	N	Y	N	Y	N	N
3 **Duncan**	Y	N	Y	N	Y	Y	N
4 **Gowdy**	Y	N	Y	N	Y	N	N
5 **Norman**	Y	N	N	N	Y	N	N
6 Clyburn	N	Y	N	Y	N	Y	Y
7 **Rice**	N	N	Y	N	Y	N	N
SOUTH DAKOTA							
AL **Noem**	Y	N	Y	N	Y	N	N
TENNESSEE							
1 **Roe**	Y	N	Y	N	Y	N	N
2 **Duncan**	Y	N	Y	N	Y	N	N
3 **Fleischmann**	Y	N	Y	N	Y	N	N
4 **DesJarlais**	Y	N	Y	N	Y	N	N
5 Cooper	N	Y	N	Y	N	Y	Y
6 **Black**	Y	N	Y	N	Y	N	N
7 **Blackburn**	Y	N	Y	N	Y	N	N
8 **Kustoff**	N	N	Y	N	Y	N	N
9 Cohen	N	Y	N	Y	N	Y	Y

	470	471	472	473	474	475	476
TEXAS							
1 **Gohmert**	Y	N	Y	N	Y	Y	N
2 **Poe**	Y	N	Y	N	Y	Y	N
3 **Johnson, S.**	Y	N	Y	N	Y	N	N
4 **Ratcliffe**	Y	N	Y	N	Y	N	N
5 **Hensarling**	Y	N	Y	N	Y	N	N
6 **Barton**	Y	N	Y	N	Y	N	N
7 **Culberson**	Y	N	Y	N	Y	N	N
8 **Brady**	Y	N	Y	N	Y	N	N
9 Green, A.	N	Y	N	Y	N	Y	Y
10 **McCaul**	Y	N	Y	N	Y	N	N
11 **Conaway**	Y	N	Y	N	Y	N	N
12 **Granger**	Y	N	Y	N	Y	N	N
13 **Thornberry**	Y	N	Y	N	Y	N	N
14 **Weber**	Y	N	Y	N	Y	N	N
15 Gonzalez	N	Y	N	Y	N	Y	Y
16 O'Rourke	N	Y	N	Y	N	Y	Y
17 **Flores**	Y	N	Y	N	Y	N	N
18 Jackson Lee	N	Y	N	Y	N	Y	Y
19 **Arrington**	Y	N	Y	N	Y	N	N
20 Castro	N	Y	N	Y	N	Y	Y
21 **Smith**	Y	N	Y	N	Y	N	N
22 **Olson**	Y	N	Y	N	Y	N	N
23 **Hurd**	Y	N	Y	N	N	N	N
24 **Marchant**	Y	N	Y	N	Y	N	N
25 **Williams**	Y	N	Y	N	Y	N	N
26 **Burgess**	Y	N	Y	N	Y	Y	N
27 **Farenthold**	Y	N	Y	N	Y	N	N
28 Cuellar	N	N	Y	Y	N	Y	N
29 Green, G.	N	Y	N	Y	N	Y	Y
30 Johnson, E.B.	N	Y	N	Y	N	Y	Y
31 **Carter**	N	N	Y	N	Y	N	N
32 **Sessions**	Y	N	Y	N	Y	Y	N
33 Veasey	N	Y	N	Y	N	Y	Y
34 Vela	N	Y	N	Y	N	Y	Y
35 Doggett	N	Y	N	Y	N	Y	Y
36 **Babin**	Y	N	Y	N	Y	N	N
UTAH							
1 **Bishop**	Y	N	Y	N	Y	N	N
2 **Stewart**	Y	N	Y	N	Y	N	N
4 **Love**	Y	N	Y	N	Y	N	N
VERMONT							
AL Welch	N	Y	N	Y	N	Y	Y
VIRGINIA							
1 **Wittman**	Y	N	Y	N	Y	N	N
2 **Taylor**	Y	N	Y	N	Y	N	N
3 Scott	N	Y	N	Y	N	Y	Y
4 McEachin	N	Y	N	Y	N	Y	Y
5 **Garrett**	?	?	?	?	?	?	?
6 **Goodlatte**	Y	N	Y	N	Y	N	N
7 **Brat**	Y	N	N	N	Y	N	N
8 Beyer	N	Y	N	Y	N	Y	Y
9 **Griffith**	Y	N	Y	N	Y	N	N
10 **Comstock**	Y	N	N	N	N	N	N
11 Connolly	N	Y	N	Y	N	Y	Y
WASHINGTON							
1 DelBene	N	Y	N	Y	N	Y	Y
2 Larsen	N	Y	N	Y	N	Y	Y
3 **Herrera Beutler**	Y	N	Y	N	N	N	N
4 **Newhouse**	Y	N	Y	N	Y	Y	N
5 **McMorris Rodgers**	Y	N	Y	N	Y	N	N
6 Kilmer	N	Y	N	Y	N	Y	Y
7 Jayapal	N	Y	N	Y	N	Y	Y
8 **Reichert**	Y	N	Y	N	N	N	Y
9 Smith	N	Y	N	Y	N	Y	Y
10 Heck	N	Y	N	Y	N	Y	Y
WEST VIRGINIA							
1 **McKinley**	Y	N	Y	N	Y	Y	N
2 **Mooney**	Y	N	Y	N	Y	Y	N
3 **Jenkins**	Y	N	Y	N	Y	Y	N
WISCONSIN							
1 **Ryan**							
2 Pocan	N	Y	N	Y	N	Y	Y
3 Kind	N	Y	N	Y	N	Y	Y
4 Moore	N	Y	N	Y	N	Y	Y
5 **Sensenbrenner**	Y	N	Y	N	Y	N	N
6 **Grothman**	Y	N	Y	N	Y	Y	N
7 **Duffy**	Y	N	Y	N	Y	N	N
8 **Gallagher**	Y	N	Y	N	Y	N	N
WYOMING							
AL **Cheney**	Y	N	N	N	Y	N	N

VOTE NUMBER

477. HR 3354. FISCAL 2018 OMNIBUS APPROPRIATIONS LEGISLATIVE VEHICLE/MARINE POLICY IMPLEMENTATION. Lowenthal, D-Calif., amendment that would eliminate the bill's provision that would prohibit funding made available by the bill from being used to further implement the coastal and marine spatial planning and ecosystem-based management components of the National Ocean Policy. Rejected in Committee of the Whole 189-220 : R 6-219; D 183-1. Sept. 7, 2017.

478. HR 3354. FISCAL 2018 OMNIBUS APPROPRIATIONS LEGISLATIVE VEHICLE/ALASKA WILDLIFE MANAGEMENT RULE. Young, R-Alaska, amendment that would prohibit funds made available by the bill from being used to implement a rule by the National Park Service related to wildlife management practices on national preserves in Alaska. Adopted in Committee of the Whole 215-196 : R 210-15; D 5-181. Sept. 7, 2017.

479. HR 3354. FISCAL 2018 OMNIBUS APPROPRIATIONS LEGISLATIVE VEHICLE/CHESAPEAKE BAY WATERSHED. Goodlatte, R-Va., amendment that would prohibit the EPA from using funds made available by the bill to take "backstop" actions against any of the six states in the Chesapeake Bay Watershed in the event that a state does not meet the goals mandated by the EPA's Chesapeake Bay Total Maximum Daily Load. Adopted in Committee of the Whole 214-197 : R 213-13; D 1-184. Sept. 7, 2017.

480. HR 601. FISCAL 2017 DISASTER SUPPLEMENTAL APPROPRIATIONS, DEBT LIMIT, CONTINUING APPROPRIATIONS/MOTION TO CONCUR. Frelinghuysen, R-N.J., motion to concur in the Senate amendment to the House amendment to the Senate amendment to the bill that would make available $15.25 billion in emergency supplemental funding for fiscal 2017 to partially cover the costs of responding to multiple natural disasters, including Hurricane Harvey. The measure would suspend the public debt limit from the bill's date of enactment until Dec. 8, 2017, and would provide for government operations to be funded at fiscal 2017 levels until Dec. 8, 2017. Motion agreed to, (thus cleared for the president), 316-90 : R 133-90; D 183-0. Sept. 8, 2017.

481. HR 3354. FISCAL 2018 OMNIBUS APPROPRIATIONS LEGISLATIVE VEHICLE/ONE PERCENT REDUCTION. Blackburn, R-Tenn., amendment that would reduce all funds appropriated in Interior division of the bill by one percent. Rejected in Committee of the Whole 156-248 : R 154-68; D 2-180. Sept. 8, 2017.

482. HR 3354. FISCAL 2018 OMNIBUS APPROPRIATIONS LEGISLATIVE VEHICLE/EPA CRIMINAL ENFORCEMENT. Palmer, R-Ala., amendment that would prohibit the use of funds by the EPA to enforce the EPA's Criminal Enforcement Division. Rejected in Committee of the Whole 178-227 : R 177-45; D 1-182. Sept. 8, 2017.

483. HR 3354. FISCAL 2018 OMNIBUS APPROPRIATIONS LEGISLATIVE VEHICLE/HYDRAULIC FRACTURING PERMITS. Carbajal, D-Calif., amendment that would prohibit funds to process any application under the Outer Continental Shelf Lands Act for a permit to drill or a permit to modify, that would authorize use of hydraulic fracturing or acid well stimulation treatment in the Pacific Outer Continental Shelf. Rejected in Committee of the Whole 177-230 : R 4-220; D 173-10. Sept. 8, 2017.

	477	478	479	480	481	482	483
ALABAMA							
1 Byrne	N	Y	N	Y	N	Y	N
2 Roby	N	Y	Y	N	N	Y	N
3 Rogers	N	Y	Y	Y	Y	Y	N
4 Aderholt	N	Y	Y	Y	N	Y	N
5 Brooks	N	Y	Y	N	Y	Y	N
6 Palmer	N	Y	N	Y	N	Y	N
7 Sewell	Y	N	N	Y	N	N	Y
ALASKA							
AL Young	N	Y	Y	Y	N	Y	N
ARIZONA							
1 O'Halleran	Y	N	N	Y	N	N	Y
2 McSally	N	N	Y	Y	N	Y	N
3 Grijalva	Y	N	N	N	N	N	Y
4 Gosar	N	Y	N	Y	N	Y	N
5 Biggs	N	Y	N	Y	N	Y	N
6 Schweikert	N	Y	N	Y	N	Y	N
7 Gallego	Y	N	N	N	N	N	Y
8 Franks	N	Y	Y	N	Y	N	N
9 Sinema	Y	N	N	Y	N	N	N
ARKANSAS							
1 Crawford	N	Y	Y	Y	Y	Y	N
2 Hill	N	Y	Y	N	Y	Y	N
3 Womack	N	Y	Y	Y	Y	Y	N
4 Westerman	N	Y	Y	N	Y	Y	N
CALIFORNIA							
1 LaMalfa	N	Y	Y	Y	Y	Y	N
2 Huffman	Y	N	N	Y	N	N	Y
3 Garamendi	Y	N	N	Y	N	N	N
4 McClintock	N	Y	N	Y	N	Y	N
5 Thompson	Y	N	N	Y	N	N	Y
6 Matsui	Y	N	N	Y	N	N	Y
7 Bera	Y	N	N	Y	N	N	Y
8 Cook	N	Y	N	Y	Y	Y	N
9 McNerney	Y	N	N	Y	N	N	Y
10 Denham	N	N	N	Y	Y	Y	N
11 DeSaulnier	Y	N	N	Y	N	N	Y
12 Pelosi	Y	N	N	Y	N	N	Y
13 Lee	Y	N	N	N	N	N	Y
14 Speier	Y	N	N	Y	N	N	Y
15 Swalwell	Y	N	N	Y	N	N	Y
16 Costa	?	?	?	?	?	?	?
17 Khanna	Y	N	N	Y	N	N	Y
18 Eshoo	Y	N	N	Y	N	N	Y
19 Lofgren	Y	N	N	Y	N	N	Y
20 Panetta	Y	N	N	Y	N	N	Y
21 Valadao	N	Y	Y	Y	N	Y	N
22 Nunes	N	Y	Y	Y	Y	Y	N
23 McCarthy	N	Y	Y	Y	Y	Y	N
24 Carbajal	Y	N	N	Y	N	N	Y
25 Knight	N	Y	Y	Y	N	Y	N
26 Brownley	Y	N	N	Y	N	N	Y
27 Chu	Y	N	N	Y	N	N	Y
28 Schiff	Y	N	N	Y	N	N	Y
29 Cardenas	Y	N	N	Y	N	N	Y
30 Sherman	Y	N	N	Y	N	N	Y
31 Aguilar	Y	N	N	Y	N	N	Y
32 Napolitano	Y	N	N	Y	N	N	Y
33 Lieu	Y	N	N	Y	N	N	Y
34 Gomez	Y	N	N	Y	N	N	Y
35 Torres	Y	N	N	Y	N	N	Y
36 Ruiz	Y	N	N	Y	N	N	Y
37 Bass	Y	N	N	Y	N	N	Y
38 Sánchez, Linda	Y	N	N	Y	N	N	Y
39 Royce	N	Y	Y	Y	N	N	N
40 Roybal-Allard	Y	N	N	Y	N	N	Y
41 Takano	Y	N	N	Y	N	N	Y
42 Calvert	N	Y	Y	Y	N	N	N
43 Waters	Y	N	N	Y	N	N	Y
44 Barragan	Y	N	N	Y	N	N	Y
45 Walters	N	Y	Y	Y	Y	Y	N
46 Correa	Y	N	N	Y	N	Y	Y
47 Lowenthal	Y	N	N	Y	N	N	Y
48 Rohrabacher	N	Y	Y	Y	N	Y	N
49 Issa	N	Y	Y	Y	Y	Y	N
50 Hunter	N	Y	Y	Y	N	Y	N
51 Vargas	Y	N	N	Y	N	N	Y
52 Peters	Y	N	N	Y	N	N	Y
53 Davis	Y	N	N	Y	N	N	Y

	477	478	479	480	481	482	483
COLORADO							
1 DeGette	?	?	?	?	?	?	?
2 Polis	Y	N	N	Y	N	N	Y
3 Tipton	N	Y	Y	N	N	Y	N
4 Buck	N	Y	Y	N	Y	Y	N
5 Lamborn	N	Y	Y	N	Y	Y	N
6 Coffman	N	Y	Y	Y	Y	Y	N
7 Perlmutter	Y	N	N	Y	N	N	Y
CONNECTICUT							
1 Larson	Y	N	N	Y	N	N	Y
2 Courtney	Y	N	N	Y	N	N	Y
3 DeLauro	Y	N	N	?	?	?	?
4 Himes	Y	N	N	Y	N	N	Y
5 Esty	Y	N	N	Y	N	N	Y
DELAWARE							
AL Blunt Rochester	Y	N	N	Y	N	N	Y
FLORIDA							
1 Gaetz	N	?	Y	N	Y	Y	N
2 Dunn	N	Y	Y	?	?	?	?
3 Yoho	N	Y	Y	N	Y	Y	N
4 Rutherford	?	?	?	?	?	?	?
5 Lawson	?	?	?	?	?	?	?
6 DeSantis	?	?	?	?	?	?	?
7 Murphy	Y	N	N	?	?	?	?
8 Posey	?	?	?	?	?	?	?
9 Soto	Y	N	N	Y	N	N	Y
10 Demings	Y	N	N	Y	N	N	Y
11 Webster	?	?	?	?	?	?	?
12 Bilirakis	?	?	?	?	?	?	?
13 Crist	?	?	?	?	?	?	?
14 Castor	Y	N	N	Y	N	N	Y
15 Ross	?	?	?	?	?	?	?
16 Buchanan	?	?	?	?	?	?	?
17 Rooney, T.	N	Y	Y	Y	N	Y	N
18 Mast	Y	Y	Y	Y	N	Y	N
19 Rooney, F.	N	Y	Y	Y	Y	Y	N
20 Hastings	Y	N	N	Y	N	N	Y
21 Frankel	Y	N	N	Y	N	N	Y
22 Deutch	?	?	?	?	?	?	?
23 Wasserman Schultz	?	?	?	?	?	?	?
24 Wilson	Y	N	N	Y	N	N	Y
25 Diaz-Balart	?	?	?	?	?	?	?
26 Curbelo	?	?	?	?	?	?	?
27 Ros-Lehtinen	?	?	?	?	?	?	?
GEORGIA							
1 Carter	N	Y	Y	Y	Y	Y	N
2 Bishop	Y	N	N	N	N	N	N
3 Ferguson	N	Y	Y	Y	Y	Y	N
4 Johnson	Y	N	N	Y	N	N	Y
5 Lewis	Y	N	N	N	N	N	Y
6 Handel	N	Y	Y	Y	Y	Y	N
7 Woodall	N	Y	Y	Y	Y	Y	N
8 Scott, A.	N	Y	Y	Y	Y	Y	N
9 Collins	N	Y	Y	Y	N	Y	N
10 Hice	N	Y	Y	Y	N	Y	N
11 Loudermilk	N	Y	Y	N	Y	?	N
12 Allen	N	Y	Y	N	Y	Y	N
13 Scott, D.	Y	N	N	Y	N	N	Y
14 Graves	N	Y	Y	Y	N	Y	N
HAWAII							
1 Hanabusa	Y	N	N	Y	N	N	Y
2 Gabbard	Y	N	N	Y	N	N	Y
IDAHO							
1 Labrador	N	Y	Y	?	Y	Y	N
2 Simpson	N	Y	Y	Y	N	N	N
ILLINOIS							
1 Rush	Y	N	N	Y	N	N	Y
2 Kelly	Y	N	N	Y	N	N	Y
3 Lipinski	Y	N	N	Y	N	N	Y
4 Gutierrez	Y	N	N	Y	N	N	Y
5 Quigley	Y	N	N	Y	N	N	Y
6 Roskam	N	Y	Y	N	N	Y	N
7 Davis, D.	Y	N	N	?	?	?	?
8 Krishnamoorthi	Y	N	N	Y	N	N	Y
9 Schakowsky	Y	N	N	Y	N	N	Y
10 Schneider	Y	N	N	Y	N	N	Y
11 Foster	Y	N	N	Y	N	N	Y
12 Bost	N	Y	Y	Y	N	N	N
13 Davis, R.	N	Y	Y	N	N	N	N
14 Hultgren	N	Y	Y	N	Y	N	N
15 Shimkus	N	Y	Y	Y	Y	Y	N

KEY	**Republicans**	Democrats	*Independents*	
Y	Voted for (yea)	X Paired against	C Voted "present" to avoid possible conflict of interest	
#	Paired for	– Announced against		
+	Announced for	P Voted "present"	? Did not vote or otherwise make a position known	
N	Voted against (nay)			

	477	478	479	480	481	482	483
16 **Kinzinger**	N	Y	Y	Y	N	N	N
17 Bustos	Y	N	N	Y	N	N	Y
18 **LaHood**	N	Y	Y	N	Y	Y	N
INDIANA							
1 Visclosky	Y	N	N	Y	N	N	Y
2 **Walorski**	N	Y	Y	N	Y	Y	N
3 **Banks**	N	Y	Y	N	Y	Y	N
4 **Rokita**	N	Y	Y	N	Y	Y	N
5 **Brooks**	?	Y	Y	Y	Y	N	N
6 **Messer**	N	Y	Y	N	Y	Y	N
7 Carson	Y	N	N	Y	N	N	Y
8 **Bucshon**	N	Y	Y	Y	Y	N	N
9 **Hollingsworth**	N	Y	Y	N	N	N	N
IOWA							
1 **Blum**	N	Y	Y	Y	Y	Y	N
2 Loebsack	Y	N	N	Y	N	N	Y
3 **Young**	N	Y	Y	N	Y	Y	N
4 **King**	N	Y	Y	Y	Y	Y	N
KANSAS							
1 **Marshall**	N	Y	Y	Y	Y	Y	N
2 **Jenkins**	N	Y	Y	N	Y	Y	N
3 **Yoder**	N	Y	Y	N	Y	Y	N
4 **Estes**	N	Y	Y	N	Y	Y	N
KENTUCKY							
1 **Comer**	N	Y	Y	N	Y	Y	N
2 **Guthrie**	N	Y	Y	Y	Y	Y	N
3 Yarmuth	Y	N	N	Y	N	N	Y
4 **Massie**	N	Y	Y	N	Y	Y	N
5 **Rogers**	N	Y	Y	Y	N	N	N
6 **Barr**	N	Y	Y	N	Y	Y	N
LOUISIANA							
1 **Scalise**	–	+	+	+	?	?	?
2 Richmond	Y	N	N	?	?	?	?
3 **Higgins**	N	Y	Y	Y	Y	Y	N
4 **Johnson**	N	Y	Y	Y	Y	Y	N
5 **Abraham**	N	Y	Y	Y	Y	Y	N
6 **Graves**	N	Y	Y	Y	Y	Y	N
MAINE							
1 Pingree	Y	N	N	Y	N	N	Y
2 **Poliquin**	Y	Y	Y	Y	Y	N	N
MARYLAND							
1 **Harris**	N	Y	N	N	Y	Y	N
2 Ruppersberger	?	N	N	Y	N	N	Y
3 Sarbanes	Y	N	N	Y	N	N	Y
4 Brown	Y	N	N	Y	N	N	Y
5 Hoyer	Y	N	N	Y	N	N	Y
6 Delaney	Y	N	N	Y	N	N	Y
7 Cummings	?	?	?	?	?	?	?
8 Raskin	Y	N	N	Y	N	N	Y
MASSACHUSETTS							
1 Neal	Y	N	N	Y	N	N	Y
2 McGovern	Y	N	N	Y	N	N	Y
3 Tsongas	?	?	?	Y	N	N	Y
4 Kennedy	Y	N	N	Y	N	N	Y
5 Clark	Y	N	N	Y	N	N	Y
6 Moulton	Y	N	N	Y	N	N	Y
7 Capuano	Y	N	N	Y	N	N	Y
8 Lynch	Y	N	N	Y	N	N	Y
9 Keating	Y	N	N	Y	N	N	Y
MICHIGAN							
1 **Bergman**	N	Y	Y	Y	Y	Y	N
2 **Huizenga**	N	Y	Y	N	Y	Y	N
3 **Amash**	N	Y	Y	N	Y	Y	N
4 **Moolenaar**	N	Y	Y	Y	N	N	N
5 Kildee	Y	N	N	Y	N	N	Y
6 **Upton**	N	N	Y	Y	Y	N	N
7 **Walberg**	N	Y	Y	Y	Y	Y	N
8 **Bishop**	N	Y	Y	Y	Y	Y	N
9 Levin	Y	N	N	Y	N	N	Y
10 **Mitchell**	N	Y	Y	Y	Y	Y	N
11 **Trott**	N	Y	Y	Y	Y	Y	N
12 Dingell	Y	N	N	Y	N	N	Y
13 Conyers	Y	N	N	Y	N	N	Y
14 Lawrence	Y	N	N	Y	N	N	Y
MINNESOTA							
1 Walz	Y	N	N	Y	N	N	Y
2 **Lewis**	N	Y	Y	Y	N	Y	N
3 **Paulsen**	N	Y	N	Y	Y	Y	N
4 McCollum	Y	N	N	Y	N	N	Y
5 Ellison	Y	N	N	Y	N	N	Y
6 **Emmer**	N	Y	Y	N	Y	Y	N
7 Peterson	N	Y	Y	Y	N	N	N
8 Nolan	?	N	N	Y	N	N	Y
MISSISSIPPI							
1 **Kelly**	N	Y	Y	N	Y	Y	N
2 Thompson	Y	N	N	Y	N	N	Y
3 **Harper**	N	Y	Y	Y	N	Y	N
4 **Palazzo**	N	Y	Y	Y	Y	Y	N
MISSOURI							
1 Clay	Y	N	N	Y	N	N	Y
2 **Wagner**	N	Y	Y	N	Y	Y	N
3 **Luetkemeyer**	N	Y	Y	N	N	Y	N
4 **Hartzler**	N	Y	Y	N	Y	N	N
5 Cleaver	Y	N	N	Y	N	N	Y
6 **Graves**	N	Y	Y	N	Y	Y	N
7 **Long**	N	Y	Y	N	Y	Y	N
8 **Smith**	N	Y	Y	N	Y	Y	N
MONTANA							
AL **Gianforte**	N	Y	Y	Y	N	Y	N
NEBRASKA							
1 **Fortenberry**	Y	Y	Y	Y	N	N	N
2 **Bacon**	N	Y	Y	N	Y	Y	N
3 **Smith**	N	Y	Y	N	Y	Y	N
NEVADA							
1 Titus	Y	N	N	Y	N	N	Y
2 **Amodei**	N	Y	Y	Y	N	Y	N
3 Rosen	Y	N	N	Y	N	N	Y
4 Kihuen	Y	N	N	Y	N	N	Y
NEW HAMPSHIRE							
1 Shea-Porter	Y	N	N	Y	N	N	Y
2 Kuster	Y	N	N	Y	N	N	Y
NEW JERSEY							
1 Norcross	Y	N	N	Y	N	N	Y
2 **LoBiondo**	N	N	N	Y	N	N	N
3 **MacArthur**	N	N	N	Y	?	N	N
4 **Smith**	N	N	N	Y	N	N	N
5 Gottheimer	Y	N	N	Y	N	N	Y
6 Pallone	Y	N	N	Y	N	N	Y
7 **Lance**	N	N	N	Y	Y	N	N
8 Sires	Y	N	N	Y	N	N	Y
9 Pascrell	Y	N	N	Y	N	N	Y
10 Payne	Y	N	N	Y	N	N	Y
11 **Frelinghuysen**	N	Y	Y	Y	N	N	N
12 Watson Coleman	Y	N	N	Y	N	N	Y
NEW MEXICO							
1 Lujan Grisham	Y	N	N	Y	N	N	Y
2 **Pearce**	N	Y	Y	N	Y	Y	N
3 Luján	Y	N	N	Y	N	N	Y
NEW YORK							
1 **Zeldin**	N	Y	Y	N	Y	?	N
2 **King**	N	N	Y	Y	N	Y	N
3 Suozzi	Y	N	N	Y	N	N	Y
4 Rice	Y	N	N	Y	N	N	Y
5 Meeks	Y	N	N	Y	N	N	Y
6 Meng	Y	N	N	Y	N	N	Y
7 Velázquez	Y	N	N	Y	N	N	Y
8 Jeffries	Y	N	N	Y	N	N	Y
9 Clarke	Y	N	N	Y	N	N	Y
10 Nadler	Y	N	N	Y	N	N	Y
11 **Donovan**	N	N	Y	Y	N	N	N
12 Maloney, C.	Y	N	N	Y	N	N	Y
13 Espaillat	Y	N	N	Y	N	N	Y
14 Crowley	Y	N	N	Y	N	N	Y
15 Serrano	Y	N	N	Y	N	N	Y
16 Engel	Y	N	N	Y	N	N	Y
17 Lowey	Y	N	N	Y	N	N	Y
18 Maloney, S.P.	Y	N	N	Y	N	N	Y
19 **Faso**	N	Y	N	Y	N	N	N
20 Tonko	Y	N	N	Y	N	N	Y
21 **Stefanik**	Y	Y	Y	Y	N	N	N
22 **Tenney**	N	N	Y	Y	N	Y	N
23 **Reed**	N	Y	Y	Y	N	N	N
24 **Katko**	N	Y	Y	Y	N	Y	N
25 Slaughter	Y	N	N	Y	N	N	Y
26 Higgins	Y	N	N	Y	N	N	Y
27 **Collins**	N	Y	Y	Y	N	Y	N
NORTH CAROLINA							
1 Butterfield	Y	N	N	Y	N	N	Y
2 **Holding**	N	Y	Y	N	Y	Y	N
3 **Jones**	N	Y	Y	?	?	?	?
4 Price	Y	N	N	Y	N	N	Y
5 **Foxx**	N	Y	Y	N	N	Y	N
6 **Walker**	N	Y	Y	N	Y	Y	N
7 **Rouzer**	N	Y	Y	N	Y	Y	N
8 **Hudson**	N	Y	Y	N	Y	Y	N
9 **Pittenger**	N	Y	Y	Y	Y	Y	N
10 **McHenry**	N	Y	Y	Y	Y	Y	N
11 **Meadows**	N	Y	Y	N	Y	Y	N
12 Adams	Y	N	N	Y	N	N	Y
13 **Budd**	N	Y	Y	N	Y	Y	N
NORTH DAKOTA							
AL **Cramer**	N	Y	Y	Y	Y	Y	N
OHIO							
1 **Chabot**	N	Y	Y	Y	Y	Y	N
2 **Wenstrup**	N	Y	Y	N	Y	Y	N
3 Beatty	Y	N	N	Y	N	N	Y
4 **Jordan**	N	Y	Y	N	Y	Y	N
5 **Latta**	N	Y	Y	Y	Y	Y	N
6 **Johnson**	N	Y	Y	Y	Y	Y	N
7 **Gibbs**	N	Y	Y	Y	Y	Y	N
8 **Davidson**	N	Y	Y	N	Y	Y	N
9 Kaptur	Y	N	N	Y	?	N	Y
10 **Turner**	N	Y	Y	N	N	N	N
11 Fudge	Y	N	N	Y	N	N	Y
12 **Tiberi**	N	Y	Y	Y	N	Y	N
13 Ryan	Y	N	N	Y	N	N	Y
14 **Joyce**	N	Y	N	Y	N	N	N
15 **Stivers**	N	Y	Y	Y	N	Y	N
16 **Renacci**	N	Y	Y	N	N	Y	N
OKLAHOMA							
1 **Bridenstine**	?	?	?	?	?	?	?
2 **Mullin**	N	Y	Y	N	Y	Y	N
3 **Lucas**	N	Y	Y	Y	Y	N	N
4 **Cole**	N	Y	Y	Y	N	N	N
5 **Russell**	N	Y	Y	N	Y	Y	N
OREGON							
1 Bonamici	Y	N	N	Y	N	N	Y
2 **Walden**	N	Y	Y	Y	N	N	N
3 Blumenauer	Y	N	N	Y	N	N	Y
4 DeFazio	Y	N	N	Y	N	N	Y
5 Schrader	Y	N	N	Y	N	N	Y
PENNSYLVANIA							
1 Brady	Y	N	N	Y	N	N	Y
2 Evans	Y	N	N	Y	N	N	Y
3 **Kelly**	N	Y	Y	Y	N	Y	N
4 **Perry**	N	Y	Y	N	Y	Y	N
5 **Thompson**	N	Y	Y	Y	N	Y	N
6 **Costello**	Y	N	Y	Y	N	N	Y
7 **Meehan**	N	N	N	Y	N	N	N
8 **Fitzpatrick**	Y	N	N	Y	N	N	Y
9 **Shuster**	N	Y	Y	Y	?	Y	N
10 **Marino**	N	Y	Y	Y	N	Y	N
11 **Barletta**	N	Y	Y	Y	N	N	N
12 **Rothfus**	N	Y	Y	N	N	Y	N
13 Boyle	Y	N	N	Y	N	N	Y
14 Doyle	Y	N	N	Y	N	N	Y
15 **Dent**	N	Y	Y	Y	N	Y	N
16 **Smucker**	N	Y	Y	Y	N	Y	N
17 Cartwright	Y	N	N	Y	N	N	Y
18 **Murphy**	N	Y	Y	Y	N	N	N
RHODE ISLAND							
1 Cicilline	Y	N	N	Y	N	N	Y
2 Langevin	Y	N	N	Y	N	N	Y
SOUTH CAROLINA							
1 **Sanford**	N	Y	Y	N	Y	Y	Y
2 **Wilson**	N	Y	Y	Y	Y	Y	N
3 **Duncan**	N	Y	Y	N	Y	Y	N
4 **Gowdy**	N	Y	Y	Y	Y	Y	N
5 **Norman**	N	Y	Y	N	Y	Y	N
6 Clyburn	Y	N	N	Y	N	N	Y
7 **Rice**	N	Y	Y	Y	Y	Y	N
SOUTH DAKOTA							
AL **Noem**	N	Y	Y	N	N	Y	N
TENNESSEE							
1 **Roe**	N	Y	Y	Y	Y	N	N
2 **Duncan**	N	Y	Y	N	Y	Y	N
3 **Fleischmann**	N	Y	Y	Y	N	Y	N
4 **DesJarlais**	N	Y	Y	N	Y	Y	N
5 Cooper	Y	N	N	Y	Y	N	N
6 **Black**	N	Y	Y	N	Y	Y	N
7 **Blackburn**	N	Y	Y	N	Y	Y	N
8 **Kustoff**	N	Y	Y	N	Y	Y	N
9 Cohen	Y	N	N	Y	N	N	Y
TEXAS							
1 **Gohmert**	N	Y	Y	Y	Y	Y	N
2 **Poe**	N	Y	Y	Y	Y	Y	N
3 **Johnson, S.**	N	Y	Y	N	Y	Y	N
4 **Ratcliffe**	N	Y	Y	Y	Y	Y	N
5 **Hensarling**	N	Y	Y	N	Y	Y	N
6 **Barton**	N	Y	Y	N	Y	N	N
7 **Culberson**	N	Y	Y	Y	Y	N	N
8 **Brady**	N	Y	Y	Y	Y	Y	N
9 Green, A.	Y	N	N	Y	N	N	N
10 **McCaul**	N	Y	Y	Y	Y	Y	N
11 **Conaway**	N	Y	Y	Y	Y	Y	N
12 **Granger**	N	Y	Y	Y	N	Y	N
13 **Thornberry**	N	Y	Y	N	Y	Y	N
14 **Weber**	N	Y	Y	Y	Y	Y	N
15 Gonzalez	Y	Y	N	Y	N	N	N
16 O'Rourke	Y	N	N	Y	N	N	Y
17 **Flores**	N	Y	Y	Y	Y	Y	N
18 Jackson Lee	Y	N	N	Y	N	N	N
19 **Arrington**	N	Y	Y	Y	Y	Y	N
20 Castro	Y	N	N	Y	N	N	Y
21 **Smith**	N	Y	Y	Y	Y	Y	N
22 **Olson**	N	Y	Y	Y	Y	Y	N
23 **Hurd**	N	Y	Y	Y	Y	Y	N
24 **Marchant**	N	Y	Y	Y	Y	Y	N
25 **Williams**	N	Y	Y	Y	Y	Y	N
26 **Burgess**	N	Y	Y	Y	Y	Y	N
27 **Farenthold**	N	Y	Y	Y	Y	Y	N
28 Cuellar	Y	Y	N	Y	N	N	N
29 Green, G.	Y	Y	N	Y	N	N	N
30 Johnson, E.B.	Y	N	N	Y	N	N	Y
31 **Carter**	N	Y	Y	Y	Y	Y	N
32 **Sessions**	N	Y	Y	Y	Y	Y	N
33 Veasey	Y	N	N	Y	N	N	Y
34 Vela	Y	N	N	Y	Y	Y	N
35 Doggett	Y	N	N	Y	N	N	Y
36 **Babin**	N	Y	Y	Y	Y	Y	N
UTAH							
1 **Bishop**	N	Y	Y	Y	Y	Y	N
2 **Stewart**	N	Y	Y	N	Y	Y	N
4 **Love**	N	Y	Y	Y	Y	Y	N
VERMONT							
AL Welch	Y	N	N	Y	N	N	Y
VIRGINIA							
1 **Wittman**	N	Y	N	N	Y	Y	N
2 **Taylor**	N	Y	N	Y	Y	Y	N
3 Scott	Y	N	N	Y	N	N	Y
4 McEachin	Y	N	N	Y	N	N	Y
5 **Garrett**	?	?	?	?	?	?	?
6 **Goodlatte**	N	Y	Y	N	Y	Y	N
7 **Brat**	N	Y	Y	N	Y	Y	N
8 Beyer	Y	N	N	Y	N	N	Y
9 **Griffith**	N	Y	Y	N	Y	Y	N
10 **Comstock**	N	Y	N	Y	N	N	N
11 Connolly	Y	N	N	Y	N	N	Y
WASHINGTON							
1 DelBene	Y	N	N	Y	N	N	Y
2 Larsen	Y	N	N	Y	N	N	Y
3 **Herrera Beutler**	N	Y	Y	N	N	N	N
4 **Newhouse**	N	Y	Y	Y	N	Y	N
5 **McMorris Rodgers**	N	Y	Y	Y	Y	Y	N
6 Kilmer	Y	N	N	Y	N	N	Y
7 Jayapal	Y	N	N	Y	N	N	Y
8 **Reichert**	N	N	Y	Y	N	N	N
9 Smith	Y	N	N	Y	N	N	Y
10 Heck	Y	N	N	Y	N	N	Y
WEST VIRGINIA							
1 **McKinley**	N	Y	Y	Y	N	Y	N
2 **Mooney**	N	Y	Y	N	Y	Y	N
3 **Jenkins**	N	Y	Y	N	N	Y	N
WISCONSIN							
1 **Ryan**							
2 Pocan	Y	N	N	Y	N	N	Y
3 Kind	Y	Y	N	Y	N	N	Y
4 Moore	Y	N	N	Y	N	N	Y
5 **Sensenbrenner**	N	Y	Y	Y	Y	Y	N
6 **Grothman**	N	Y	Y	Y	Y	Y	N
7 **Duffy**	N	Y	Y	N	Y	Y	N
8 **Gallagher**	N	Y	Y	N	N	Y	N
WYOMING							
AL **Cheney**	N	Y	Y	N	N	Y	N

VOTE NUMBER

484. HR 3354. FISCAL 2018 OMNIBUS APPROPRIATIONS LEGISLATIVE VEHICLE/BLM NATURAL GAS FLARING RULES. Pearce, R-N.M. amendment that would prohibit the use of funds to finalize, implement, or enforce the Bureau of Land Management's rule aimed to reduce waste of natural gas from venting, flaring, and leaks during oil and natural gas production activities on onshore federal and Indian (other than Osage Tribe) leases. Adopted in Committee of the Whole 216-186 : R 214-8; D 2-178. Sept. 8, 2017.

485. HR 2611. LITTLE ROCK CENTRAL HIGH SCHOOL NATIONAL HISTORIC SITE/PASSAGE. Bishop, R-Utah, motion to suspend the rules and pass the bill that would modify the boundary of the Little Rock Central High School National Historic Site to include seven residences on South Park Street in Little Rock, Ark., and would authorize the secretary of the Interior to enter into cooperative agreements with the owners of the seven residences to provide technical assistance related to the preservation and interpretation of the properties. Motion agreed to 390-0 : R 214-0; D 176-0. Sept. 12, 2017.

486. H RES 513, HR 3697. CRIMINAL GANG MEMBERS/PREVIOUS QUESTION. Collins, R-Ga., motion to order the previous question (thus limiting debate and possibility of amendment) on the rule (H Res 513) that would provide for House floor consideration of the bill (HR 3697) that would define a criminal gang as a group of five or more persons that has the primary purpose of the commission of one or more certain criminal offenses and would prohibit individuals defined as foreign criminal gang members from entering the United States. Motion agreed to 222-184 : R 222-0; D 0-184. Sept. 13, 2017.

487. H RES 513, HR 3697. CRIMINAL GANG MEMBERS/RULE. Adoption of the rule (H Res 513) that would provide for House floor consideration of the bill (HR 3697) that would define a criminal gang as a group of five or more persons that has the primary purpose of the commission of one or more certain criminal offenses and would prohibit individuals defined as foreign criminal gang members from entering the United States. Adopted 222-186 : R 222-0; D 0-186. Sept. 13, 2017.

488. HR 3354. FISCAL 2018 OMNIBUS APPROPRIATIONS LEGISLATIVE VEHICLE/GREENHOUSE GAS EMISSIONS. Mullin, R-Okla., amendment that would prohibit the use of funds appropriated by the bill to enforce rules relating to source performance standards for greenhouse gas emissions and volatile organic compound emissions from the oil and natural gas sector. Adopted in Committee of the Whole 218-195 : R 215-11; D 3-184. Sept. 13, 2017.

489. HR 3354. FISCAL 2018 OMNIBUS APPROPRIATIONS LEGISLATIVE VEHICLE/SOCIAL COST OF CARBON. Mullin, R-Okla., amendment that would prohibit the use of funds appropriated by the bill to implement any rules or regulations that rely on certain studies related to the "social cost of carbon." Adopted in Committee of the Whole 225-186 : R 221-5; D 4-181. Sept. 13, 2017.

490. HR 3354. FISCAL 2018 OMNIBUS APPROPRIATIONS LEGISLATIVE VEHICLE/EPA REGIONAL OFFICES. Polis, D-Colo., amendment that would prohibit the use of funds made appropriated by the bill to close or consolidate any regional office of the EPA. Rejected in Committee of the Whole 201-212 : R 17-209; D 184-3. Sept. 13, 2017.

	484	485	486	487	488	489	490
ALABAMA							
1 Byrne	Y	Y	Y	Y	Y	Y	N
2 Roby	Y	Y	Y	Y	Y	Y	N
3 Rogers	Y	Y	Y	Y	Y	Y	N
4 Aderholt	Y	Y	Y	Y	Y	Y	N
5 Brooks	Y	Y	Y	Y	Y	Y	N
6 Palmer	Y	Y	?	Y	Y	Y	N
7 Sewell	N	Y	N	N	N	N	Y
ALASKA							
AL Young	Y	Y	Y	Y	Y	Y	N
ARIZONA							
1 O'Halleran	N	Y	N	N	N	N	Y
2 McSally	Y	Y	Y	Y	Y	Y	N
3 Grijalva	N	?	N	N	N	N	Y
4 Gosar	Y	Y	Y	Y	Y	Y	N
5 Biggs	Y	Y	Y	Y	Y	Y	N
6 Schweikert	Y	Y	Y	Y	Y	Y	N
7 Gallego	N	Y	N	N	N	N	Y
8 Franks	Y	Y	Y	Y	Y	Y	N
9 Sinema	N	Y	N	N	N	N	Y
ARKANSAS							
1 Crawford	Y	Y	Y	Y	Y	Y	N
2 Hill	Y	Y	Y	Y	Y	Y	N
3 Womack	Y	Y	Y	Y	Y	Y	N
4 Westerman	Y	Y	Y	Y	Y	Y	N
CALIFORNIA							
1 LaMalfa	Y	Y	Y	Y	Y	Y	N
2 Huffman	N	Y	N	N	N	N	Y
3 Garamendi	N	Y	N	N	N	N	Y
4 McClintock	Y	Y	Y	Y	Y	Y	N
5 Thompson	N	Y	N	N	N	N	Y
6 Matsui	N	Y	N	N	N	N	Y
7 Bera	N	Y	N	N	N	N	Y
8 Cook	Y	?	Y	Y	Y	Y	N
9 McNerney	N	Y	N	N	N	N	Y
10 Denham	Y	Y	Y	Y	Y	Y	N
11 DeSaulnier	N	Y	N	N	N	N	Y
12 Pelosi	N	Y	N	N	N	N	Y
13 Lee	N	Y	N	N	N	N	Y
14 Speier	N	Y	N	N	N	N	Y
15 Swalwell	N	Y	N	N	N	N	Y
16 Costa	?	?	?	?	?	?	?
17 Khanna	N	Y	N	N	N	N	Y
18 Eshoo	N	Y	N	N	N	N	Y
19 Lofgren	N	Y	N	N	N	N	Y
20 Panetta	N	Y	N	N	N	N	Y
21 Valadao	Y	Y	Y	Y	Y	Y	N
22 Nunes	Y	Y	Y	Y	Y	Y	N
23 McCarthy	Y	Y	Y	Y	Y	Y	N
24 Carbajal	N	Y	N	N	N	N	Y
25 Knight	Y	Y	Y	Y	N	Y	N
26 Brownley	N	Y	N	N	N	N	Y
27 Chu	N	Y	N	N	N	N	Y
28 Schiff	N	Y	N	N	N	N	Y
29 Cardenas	N	Y	N	N	N	N	Y
30 Sherman	N	Y	N	N	N	N	Y
31 Aguilar	N	Y	N	N	N	N	Y
32 Napolitano	N	Y	N	N	N	N	Y
33 Lieu	N	Y	N	N	N	N	Y
34 Gomez	N	Y	N	N	N	N	Y
35 Torres	N	Y	N	N	N	N	Y
36 Ruiz	N	Y	N	N	N	N	Y
37 Bass	N	Y	N	N	N	N	Y
38 Sánchez, Linda	N	Y	N	N	N	N	Y
39 Royce	Y	Y	Y	Y	Y	Y	N
40 Roybal-Allard	N	Y	N	N	N	N	Y
41 Takano	N	Y	N	N	N	N	Y
42 Calvert	Y	Y	Y	Y	Y	Y	N
43 Waters	N	Y	N	N	N	N	Y
44 Barragan	N	Y	N	N	N	N	Y
45 Walters	Y	Y	Y	Y	Y	Y	N
46 Correa	N	Y	N	N	N	N	Y
47 Lowenthal	N	Y	N	N	N	N	Y
48 Rohrabacher	Y	Y	Y	Y	Y	Y	N
49 Issa	Y	Y	Y	Y	Y	Y	N
50 Hunter	Y	Y	Y	Y	Y	Y	N
51 Vargas	N	Y	N	N	N	N	Y
52 Peters	N	Y	N	N	N	N	N
53 Davis	N	Y	N	N	N	N	Y
COLORADO							
1 DeGette	?	Y	N	N	N	N	Y
2 Polis	N	Y	N	N	N	N	Y
3 Tipton	Y	Y	Y	Y	Y	Y	Y
4 Buck	Y	Y	Y	Y	Y	Y	N
5 Lamborn	Y	Y	Y	Y	Y	Y	N
6 Coffman	Y	Y	Y	Y	Y	Y	N
7 Perlmutter	N	Y	N	N	N	N	Y
CONNECTICUT							
1 Larson	?	Y	N	N	N	N	Y
2 Courtney	?	Y	N	N	N	N	Y
3 DeLauro	?	+	–	–	–	–	+
4 Himes	N	Y	N	N	N	N	Y
5 Esty	N	Y	N	N	N	N	Y
DELAWARE							
AL Blunt Rochester	N	Y	N	N	N	N	Y
FLORIDA							
1 Gaetz	Y	Y	Y	Y	Y	Y	N
2 Dunn	?	Y	Y	Y	Y	Y	N
3 Yoho	Y	Y	Y	Y	Y	Y	N
4 Rutherford	?	+	+	+	Y	Y	N
5 Lawson	?	?	?	?	?	?	?
6 DeSantis	?	?	?	?	?	?	?
7 Murphy	?	Y	N	N	N	N	Y
8 Posey	?	?	?	?	?	?	?
9 Soto	N	Y	N	N	N	N	Y
10 Demings	N	+	–	–	N	N	Y
11 Webster	?	?	?	?	Y	Y	N
12 Bilirakis	?	?	Y	Y	Y	Y	N
13 Crist	?	N	N	N	N	N	Y
14 Castor	N	?	?	?	?	?	?
15 Ross	?	?	?	?	?	?	?
16 Buchanan	?	?	Y	Y	Y	Y	N
17 Rooney, T.	Y	Y	Y	Y	Y	Y	N
18 Mast	N	?	Y	Y	N	Y	Y
19 Rooney, F.	Y	?	?	?	?	?	?
20 Hastings	N	Y	N	N	N	N	Y
21 Frankel	N	Y	N	N	N	N	Y
22 Deutch	?	Y	N	N	N	N	Y
23 Wasserman Schultz	?	?	N	N	N	N	Y
24 Wilson	N	Y	N	N	N	N	Y
25 Diaz-Balart	?	?	?	?	?	?	?
26 Curbelo	?	?	?	?	?	?	?
27 Ros-Lehtinen	?	?	?	?	?	?	?
GEORGIA							
1 Carter	Y	?	Y	Y	Y	Y	N
2 Bishop	Y	Y	N	N	N	?	Y
3 Ferguson	Y	Y	Y	Y	Y	Y	N
4 Johnson	N	Y	N	N	N	N	Y
5 Lewis	N	Y	N	N	N	N	Y
6 Handel	Y	Y	Y	Y	Y	Y	N
7 Woodall	Y	Y	Y	Y	Y	Y	N
8 Scott, A.	Y	?	Y	Y	Y	Y	N
9 Collins	?	Y	Y	Y	Y	Y	N
10 Hice	Y	Y	Y	Y	Y	Y	N
11 Loudermilk	Y	?	?	?	?	?	?
12 Allen	Y	Y	Y	Y	Y	Y	N
13 Scott, D.	N	Y	N	N	N	N	Y
14 Graves	Y	Y	Y	Y	Y	Y	N
HAWAII							
1 Hanabusa	N	Y	N	N	N	N	Y
2 Gabbard	N	Y	N	N	N	N	Y
IDAHO							
1 Labrador	Y	?	Y	Y	Y	Y	N
2 Simpson	Y	Y	Y	Y	Y	Y	N
ILLINOIS							
1 Rush	N	Y	N	N	N	N	Y
2 Kelly	N	Y	N	N	N	N	Y
3 Lipinski	N	Y	N	N	N	N	Y
4 Gutierrez	N	Y	N	N	N	N	Y
5 Quigley	N	Y	N	N	N	N	Y
6 Roskam	Y	Y	Y	Y	Y	Y	N
7 Davis, D.	?	Y	N	N	N	N	Y
8 Krishnamoorthi	N	Y	N	N	N	N	Y
9 Schakowsky	N	Y	N	N	N	N	Y
10 Schneider	N	Y	N	N	N	N	Y
11 Foster	N	Y	N	N	N	N	Y
12 Bost	Y	Y	Y	Y	Y	Y	N
13 Davis, R.	Y	Y	Y	Y	Y	Y	N
14 Hultgren	Y	Y	Y	Y	Y	Y	N
15 Shimkus	Y	Y	Y	Y	Y	Y	N

KEY	Republicans	Democrats	Independents
Y Voted for (yea)		**X** Paired against	**C** Voted "present" to avoid possible conflict of interest
# Paired for		**–** Announced against	
+ Announced for		**P** Voted "present"	**?** Did not vote or otherwise make a position known
N Voted against (nay)			

	484	485	486	487	488	489	490
16 **Kinzinger**	Y	Y	Y	Y	Y	Y	N
17 Bustos	N	Y	N	N	N	N	Y
18 **LaHood**	Y	Y	Y	Y	Y	Y	N
INDIANA							
1 Visclosky	N	Y	N	N	N	N	Y
2 **Walorski**	Y	Y	Y	Y	Y	Y	N
3 **Banks**	Y	Y	Y	Y	Y	Y	N
4 **Rokita**	Y	Y	Y	Y	Y	Y	N
5 **Brooks**	Y	Y	Y	Y	Y	Y	N
6 **Messer**	Y	?	Y	Y	Y	Y	N
7 Carson	N	Y	N	N	N	N	Y
8 **Bucshon**	Y	Y	Y	Y	Y	Y	N
9 **Hollingsworth**	Y	Y	Y	Y	Y	Y	N
IOWA							
1 **Blum**	Y	Y	Y	Y	Y	Y	N
2 Loebsack	N	Y	N	N	N	N	Y
3 **Young**	Y	Y	Y	Y	Y	Y	N
4 **King**	Y	Y	Y	Y	Y	Y	N
KANSAS							
1 **Marshall**	Y	Y	Y	Y	Y	Y	N
2 **Jenkins**	Y	Y	Y	Y	Y	Y	N
3 **Yoder**	Y	Y	Y	Y	Y	Y	N
4 **Estes**	Y	Y	Y	Y	Y	Y	N
KENTUCKY							
1 **Comer**	Y	Y	Y	Y	Y	Y	N
2 **Guthrie**	Y	Y	Y	Y	Y	Y	N
3 Yarmuth	N	Y	N	N	N	N	Y
4 **Massie**	Y	Y	Y	Y	Y	Y	N
5 **Rogers**	Y	Y	Y	Y	Y	Y	N
6 **Barr**	Y	Y	Y	Y	Y	Y	N
LOUISIANA							
1 **Scalise**	?	?	?	?	?	?	?
2 Richmond	?	Y	N	N	N	N	Y
3 **Higgins**	Y	Y	Y	Y	Y	Y	N
4 **Johnson**	Y	Y	Y	Y	Y	Y	N
5 **Abraham**	Y	Y	Y	Y	Y	Y	N
6 **Graves**	Y	Y	Y	Y	Y	Y	N
MAINE							
1 Pingree	N	Y	N	N	N	N	Y
2 **Poliquin**	Y	Y	Y	Y	Y	Y	Y
MARYLAND							
1 **Harris**	Y	Y	Y	Y	Y	Y	N
2 Ruppersberger	N	Y	N	N	N	N	Y
3 Sarbanes	N	Y	N	N	N	N	Y
4 Brown	N	Y	N	N	N	N	Y
5 Hoyer	N	Y	N	N	N	?	Y
6 Delaney	N	Y	N	N	N	N	Y
7 Cummings	?	Y	N	N	N	N	Y
8 Raskin	N	Y	N	N	N	N	Y
MASSACHUSETTS							
1 Neal	N	Y	N	N	N	N	Y
2 McGovern	N	Y	N	N	N	N	Y
3 Tsongas	N	?	N	N	N	N	Y
4 Kennedy	N	Y	N	N	N	N	Y
5 Clark	N	Y	N	N	N	N	Y
6 Moulton	N	Y	N	N	N	N	Y
7 Capuano	N	Y	N	N	N	N	Y
8 Lynch	Y	Y	N	N	N	N	Y
9 Keating	N	Y	N	N	N	N	Y
MICHIGAN							
1 **Bergman**	Y	Y	Y	Y	Y	N	N
2 **Huizenga**	Y	Y	Y	Y	Y	Y	N
3 **Amash**	Y	Y	Y	Y	Y	Y	N
4 **Moolenaar**	Y	Y	Y	Y	Y	Y	N
5 Kildee	N	Y	N	N	N	N	Y
6 **Upton**	Y	Y	Y	Y	Y	Y	Y
7 **Walberg**	Y	Y	Y	Y	Y	Y	N
8 **Bishop**	Y	Y	Y	Y	Y	Y	N
9 Levin	N	Y	N	N	N	N	Y
10 **Mitchell**	Y	Y	?	?	Y	Y	N
11 **Trott**	Y	Y	Y	Y	Y	Y	N
12 Dingell	N	Y	N	N	N	N	Y
13 Conyers	N	Y	N	N	N	N	Y
14 Lawrence	N	Y	N	N	N	N	Y
MINNESOTA							
1 Walz	N	Y	N	N	N	N	Y
2 **Lewis**	Y	Y	Y	Y	Y	Y	N
3 **Paulsen**	Y	Y	Y	Y	Y	Y	N
4 McCollum	N	Y	N	N	N	N	Y

	484	485	486	487	488	489	490
5 Ellison	N	Y	N	N	N	N	Y
6 **Emmer**	Y	Y	Y	Y	Y	Y	N
7 Peterson	N	Y	N	N	Y	Y	N
8 Nolan	N	Y	N	N	N	N	Y
MISSISSIPPI							
1 **Kelly**	Y	Y	Y	Y	Y	Y	N
2 Thompson	N	Y	N	N	N	N	Y
3 **Harper**	Y	Y	Y	Y	Y	Y	N
4 **Palazzo**	Y	Y	Y	Y	Y	Y	N
MISSOURI							
1 Clay	N	Y	N	N	N	N	Y
2 **Wagner**	Y	Y	Y	Y	Y	Y	N
3 **Luetkemeyer**	Y	Y	Y	Y	Y	Y	N
4 **Hartzler**	Y	Y	Y	Y	Y	Y	N
5 Cleaver	N	Y	N	N	N	N	Y
6 **Graves**	Y	?	+	+	+	+	–
7 **Long**	Y	Y	Y	Y	Y	Y	N
8 **Smith**	Y	Y	Y	Y	Y	Y	N
MONTANA							
AL **Gianforte**	Y	Y	Y	Y	Y	Y	N
NEBRASKA							
1 **Fortenberry**	Y	Y	Y	Y	Y	Y	Y
2 **Bacon**	Y	Y	Y	Y	Y	Y	N
3 **Smith**	Y	Y	Y	Y	Y	Y	N
NEVADA							
1 Titus	N	?	N	N	N	N	Y
2 **Amodei**	Y	Y	Y	Y	Y	Y	N
3 Rosen	N	Y	N	N	N	N	Y
4 Kihuen	N	Y	N	N	N	N	Y
NEW HAMPSHIRE							
1 Shea-Porter	N	Y	N	N	N	N	Y
2 Kuster	N	Y	N	N	N	N	Y
NEW JERSEY							
1 Norcross	N	Y	N	N	N	N	Y
2 **LoBiondo**	Y	Y	Y	Y	Y	Y	Y
3 **MacArthur**	Y	Y	Y	Y	Y	Y	Y
4 **Smith**	Y	Y	Y	Y	N	Y	Y
5 Gottheimer	N	Y	N	N	N	N	Y
6 Pallone	N	Y	N	N	N	N	Y
7 **Lance**	Y	Y	Y	Y	Y	Y	Y
8 Sires	N	Y	N	N	N	N	Y
9 Pascrell	N	Y	N	N	N	N	Y
10 Payne	N	Y	N	N	N	N	Y
11 **Frelinghuysen**	Y	Y	Y	Y	Y	Y	N
12 Watson Coleman	N	Y	N	N	?	?	?
NEW MEXICO							
1 Lujan Grisham	N	Y	N	N	N	N	Y
2 **Pearce**	Y	Y	Y	Y	Y	Y	N
3 Luján	N	Y	N	N	N	N	Y
NEW YORK							
1 **Zeldin**	Y	Y	Y	Y	Y	Y	N
2 **King**	Y	Y	Y	Y	Y	Y	N
3 Suozzi	N	Y	N	N	N	N	Y
4 Rice	N	Y	N	N	N	N	Y
5 Meeks	N	Y	N	N	N	N	Y
6 Meng	N	Y	N	N	N	N	Y
7 Velázquez	N	Y	N	N	N	N	Y
8 Jeffries	N	Y	N	N	N	N	Y
9 Clarke	N	?	N	N	N	N	Y
10 Nadler	N	Y	N	N	N	N	Y
11 **Donovan**	Y	Y	Y	Y	Y	Y	N
12 Maloney, C.	N	?	?	?	N	N	Y
13 Espaillat	N	Y	N	N	N	N	Y
14 Crowley	N	?	?	N	N	N	Y
15 Serrano	N	Y	N	N	N	N	Y
16 Engel	N	Y	?	N	N	N	Y
17 Lowey	N	Y	N	N	N	N	Y
18 Maloney, S.P.	N	Y	N	N	N	N	Y
19 **Faso**	N	Y	Y	Y	N	N	N
20 Tonko	N	Y	N	N	N	N	Y
21 **Stefanik**	N	Y	Y	Y	N	N	Y
22 **Tenney**	Y	Y	Y	Y	Y	Y	N
23 **Reed**	Y	Y	Y	Y	Y	Y	N
24 **Katko**	N	Y	Y	Y	N	Y	N
25 Slaughter	N	Y	N	N	N	N	Y
26 Higgins	N	Y	N	N	N	N	Y
27 **Collins**	Y	Y	Y	Y	Y	Y	N
NORTH CAROLINA							
1 Butterfield	N	?	N	N	N	N	Y
2 **Holding**	Y	Y	Y	Y	Y	Y	N
3 **Jones**	?	Y	Y	Y	Y	Y	N
4 Price	N	Y	N	N	N	N	Y

	484	485	486	487	488	489	490
5 **Foxx**	Y	Y	Y	Y	Y	Y	N
6 **Walker**	Y	Y	Y	Y	Y	Y	N
7 **Rouzer**	Y	Y	Y	Y	Y	Y	N
8 **Hudson**	Y	Y	Y	Y	Y	Y	N
9 **Pittenger**	Y	Y	Y	Y	Y	Y	N
10 **McHenry**	Y	Y	Y	Y	Y	Y	N
11 **Meadows**	Y	Y	Y	Y	Y	Y	N
12 Adams	N	Y	N	N	N	N	Y
13 **Budd**	Y	Y	Y	Y	Y	Y	N
NORTH DAKOTA							
AL **Cramer**	Y	Y	Y	Y	Y	Y	N
OHIO							
1 **Chabot**	Y	Y	Y	Y	Y	Y	N
2 **Wenstrup**	Y	Y	Y	Y	Y	Y	N
3 Beatty	N	Y	N	N	N	N	Y
4 **Jordan**	Y	Y	Y	Y	Y	Y	N
5 **Latta**	Y	Y	Y	Y	Y	Y	N
6 **Johnson**	Y	Y	Y	Y	Y	Y	N
7 **Gibbs**	Y	Y	Y	Y	Y	Y	N
8 **Davidson**	Y	Y	Y	Y	Y	Y	N
9 Kaptur	N	Y	N	N	N	N	Y
10 **Turner**	Y	Y	Y	Y	Y	Y	N
11 Fudge	N	Y	N	N	N	N	Y
12 **Tiberi**	Y	?	?	?	?	?	?
13 Ryan	N	?	N	N	N	N	Y
14 **Joyce**	Y	Y	Y	Y	Y	Y	N
15 **Stivers**	Y	Y	Y	Y	Y	Y	Y
16 **Renacci**	Y	Y	Y	Y	Y	Y	N
OKLAHOMA							
1 **Bridenstine**	?	?	?	?	?	?	?
2 **Mullin**	Y	Y	Y	Y	Y	Y	N
3 **Lucas**	Y	Y	Y	Y	Y	Y	N
4 **Cole**	Y	Y	Y	Y	Y	Y	N
5 **Russell**	Y	Y	Y	Y	Y	Y	N
OREGON							
1 Bonamici	N	Y	N	N	N	N	Y
2 **Walden**	Y	Y	Y	Y	Y	Y	N
3 Blumenauer	N	Y	N	N	N	N	Y
4 DeFazio	N	Y	N	N	N	N	Y
5 Schrader	N	?	N	N	N	N	N
PENNSYLVANIA							
1 Brady	N	Y	N	N	N	N	Y
2 Evans	N	Y	N	N	N	N	Y
3 **Kelly**	Y	Y	Y	Y	Y	Y	N
4 **Perry**	Y	Y	Y	?	Y	Y	N
5 **Thompson**	Y	Y	Y	Y	Y	Y	N
6 **Costello**	N	Y	Y	Y	N	N	Y
7 **Meehan**	Y	Y	Y	Y	N	Y	Y
8 **Fitzpatrick**	N	Y	Y	Y	N	N	Y
9 **Shuster**	Y	Y	Y	Y	Y	Y	N
10 **Marino**	Y	?	Y	Y	Y	Y	N
11 **Barletta**	Y	Y	Y	Y	Y	Y	N
12 **Rothfus**	Y	Y	Y	Y	Y	Y	N
13 Boyle	N	Y	N	N	N	N	Y
14 Doyle	N	Y	N	N	N	N	Y
15 **Dent**	Y	Y	Y	Y	Y	Y	Y
16 **Smucker**	Y	Y	Y	Y	Y	Y	N
17 Cartwright	N	Y	N	N	N	N	Y
18 **Murphy**	?	Y	Y	Y	Y	Y	N
RHODE ISLAND							
1 Cicilline	N	Y	N	N	N	N	Y
2 Langevin	N	Y	N	N	N	N	Y
SOUTH CAROLINA							
1 **Sanford**	N	Y	Y	Y	N	Y	Y
2 **Wilson**	Y	Y	Y	Y	Y	Y	N
3 **Duncan**	Y	Y	Y	Y	Y	Y	N
4 **Gowdy**	Y	Y	Y	Y	Y	Y	N
5 **Norman**	Y	Y	Y	Y	Y	Y	N
6 Clyburn	N	Y	?	?	?	?	?
7 **Rice**	Y	Y	Y	Y	Y	Y	N
SOUTH DAKOTA							
AL **Noem**	Y	Y	Y	Y	Y	Y	N
TENNESSEE							
1 **Roe**	Y	Y	Y	Y	Y	Y	N
2 **Duncan**	Y	Y	Y	Y	Y	Y	N
3 **Fleischmann**	Y	Y	Y	Y	Y	Y	N
4 **DesJarlais**	Y	Y	Y	Y	Y	Y	N
5 Cooper	N	Y	N	N	N	N	Y
6 **Black**	Y	Y	Y	Y	Y	Y	N
7 **Blackburn**	Y	Y	Y	Y	Y	Y	N
8 **Kustoff**	Y	Y	Y	Y	Y	Y	N
9 Cohen	N	Y	N	N	N	N	Y

	484	485	486	487	488	489	490
TEXAS							
1 **Gohmert**	Y	Y	Y	Y	Y	Y	N
2 **Poe**	Y	?	?	?	?	?	?
3 **Johnson, S.**	Y	Y	Y	Y	Y	Y	N
4 **Ratcliffe**	Y	Y	Y	Y	Y	Y	N
5 **Hensarling**	Y	Y	Y	Y	Y	Y	N
6 **Barton**	Y	Y	Y	Y	Y	Y	N
7 **Culberson**	Y	Y	Y	Y	Y	Y	N
8 **Brady**	Y	Y	Y	Y	Y	Y	N
9 Green, A.	N	Y	N	N	N	N	Y
10 **McCaul**	Y	Y	Y	Y	Y	Y	N
11 **Conaway**	Y	Y	Y	Y	Y	Y	Y
12 **Granger**	Y	Y	Y	Y	Y	Y	N
13 **Thornberry**	Y	Y	Y	Y	Y	Y	N
14 **Weber**	Y	Y	Y	Y	Y	Y	N
15 Gonzalez	N	Y	N	N	Y	Y	Y
16 O'Rourke	N	Y	N	N	N	N	Y
17 **Flores**	Y	Y	Y	Y	Y	Y	N
18 Jackson Lee	?	Y	N	N	N	N	Y
19 **Arrington**	Y	Y	Y	Y	Y	Y	N
20 Castro	N	Y	N	N	N	N	Y
21 **Smith**	Y	Y	Y	Y	Y	Y	N
22 **Olson**	Y	Y	Y	Y	Y	Y	N
23 **Hurd**	Y	Y	Y	Y	Y	Y	N
24 **Marchant**	Y	Y	Y	Y	Y	Y	N
25 **Williams**	Y	Y	Y	Y	Y	Y	N
26 **Burgess**	Y	Y	Y	Y	Y	Y	N
27 **Farenthold**	Y	Y	Y	Y	Y	Y	N
28 Cuellar	N	Y	N	N	Y	Y	Y
29 Green, G.	N	Y	N	N	N	Y	Y
30 Johnson, E.B.	N	Y	N	N	N	N	Y
31 **Carter**	Y	Y	Y	Y	Y	Y	N
32 **Sessions**	Y	Y	Y	Y	Y	Y	N
33 Veasey	N	Y	N	N	N	N	Y
34 Vela	N	Y	N	N	N	N	Y
35 Doggett	N	Y	N	N	N	N	Y
36 **Babin**	Y	Y	Y	Y	Y	Y	N
UTAH							
1 **Bishop**	Y	Y	Y	Y	Y	Y	N
2 **Stewart**	Y	Y	Y	Y	Y	Y	N
4 **Love**	Y	Y	Y	Y	Y	Y	N
VERMONT							
AL Welch	N	Y	N	N	N	N	Y
VIRGINIA							
1 **Wittman**	Y	Y	Y	Y	Y	Y	N
2 **Taylor**	Y	Y	Y	Y	Y	Y	N
3 Scott	N	Y	N	N	N	N	Y
4 McEachin	N	Y	?	?	?	?	?
5 **Garrett**	?	?	?	?	?	?	?
6 **Goodlatte**	Y	Y	Y	Y	Y	Y	N
7 **Brat**	Y	Y	Y	Y	Y	Y	N
8 Beyer	N	Y	N	N	N	N	Y
9 **Griffith**	Y	Y	Y	Y	Y	Y	N
10 **Comstock**	Y	Y	Y	Y	Y	Y	N
11 Connolly	N	Y	N	N	N	N	Y
WASHINGTON							
1 DelBene	N	Y	N	N	N	N	Y
2 Larsen	N	Y	N	N	N	N	Y
3 **Herrera Beutler**	Y	Y	Y	Y	Y	Y	N
4 **Newhouse**	Y	Y	Y	Y	Y	Y	N
5 **McMorris Rodgers**	Y	Y	Y	Y	Y	Y	N
6 Kilmer	N	Y	N	N	N	N	Y
7 Jayapal	N	Y	N	N	N	N	Y
8 **Reichert**	N	Y	Y	Y	N	Y	N
9 Smith	N	Y	N	N	N	N	Y
10 Heck	N	Y	N	N	N	N	Y
WEST VIRGINIA							
1 **McKinley**	Y	Y	Y	Y	Y	Y	N
2 **Mooney**	Y	Y	Y	Y	Y	Y	N
3 **Jenkins**	Y	Y	Y	Y	Y	Y	N
WISCONSIN							
1 **Ryan**							
2 Pocan	N	Y	N	N	N	N	Y
3 Kind	N	Y	N	N	N	N	Y
4 Moore	N	Y	N	N	N	N	Y
5 **Sensenbrenner**	Y	Y	Y	Y	Y	Y	N
6 **Grothman**	Y	Y	Y	Y	Y	Y	N
7 **Duffy**	Y	Y	Y	Y	Y	Y	N
8 **Gallagher**	Y	Y	Y	Y	Y	Y	N
WYOMING							
AL **Cheney**	Y	Y	Y	Y	Y	Y	N

VOTE NUMBER

491. HR 3354. FISCAL 2018 OMNIBUS APPROPRIATIONS LEGISLATIVE VEHICLE/FEDERAL LAND TRANSFERS. Polis, D-Colo., amendment that would prohibit the use of funds appropriated by the bill to pursue any extra-legal ways to transfer federal lands to private owners in contravention of existing law. Rejected in Committee of the Whole 198-212 : R 13-211; D 185-1. Sept. 13, 2017.

492. HR 3354. FISCAL 2018 OMNIBUS APPROPRIATIONS LEGISLATIVE VEHICLE/EPA FUNDING REDUCTION. Norman, R-S.C., amendment that would reduce funding for the EPA by $1.8 million. Rejected in Committee of the Whole 151-260 : R 150-75; D 1-185. Sept. 13, 2017.

493. HR 3354. FISCAL 2018 OMNIBUS APPROPRIATIONS LEGISLATIVE VEHICLE/NIST MANUFACTURING PARTNERSHIP. Torres, D-Calif., amendment that would decrease funding for the the Department of Justice's salaries and expenses by $5 million and would increase funding for the National Institute of Standards and Technology's Hollings Manufacturing Extension Partnership by the same amount. Adopted in Committee of the Whole 279-137 : R 90-136; D 189-1. Sept. 13, 2017.

494. HR 3354. FISCAL 2018 OMNIBUS APPROPRIATIONS LEGISLATIVE VEHICLE/ATF FUNDING REDUCTION. Grothman, R-Wis., amendment that would decrease funding for the Department of Justice's Bureau of Alcohol, Tobacco, Firearms and Explosives by $64.7 million, and would and transfer the savings to the department's spending reduction account. Rejected in Committee of the Whole 98-313 : R 95-127; D 3-186. Sept. 13, 2017.

495. HR 3354. FISCAL 2018 OMNIBUS APPROPRIATIONS LEGISLATIVE VEHICLE/EMPLOYEE EARNINGS INFORMATION. Scott, D-Va., for DeLauro, D-Conn., amendment that would allow funds appropriated to the Equal Employment Opportunity Commission to be used for the collection of information from employers related to employees' earning and hours worked. Rejected in Committee of the Whole 192-223 : R 3-223; D 189-0. Sept. 13, 2017.

496. HR 3354. FISCAL 2018 OMNIBUS APPROPRIATIONS LEGISLATIVE VEHICLE/SUBSISTENCE FEE PROHIBITION. Norton, D-D.C., amendment that would prohibit funds appropriated by the bill to be used to require individuals who reside in a halfway house or on home confinement to pay a subsistence fee. Rejected in Committee of the Whole 189-225 : R 3-222; D 186-3. Sept. 13, 2017.

497. HR 3354. FISCAL 2018 OMNIBUS APPROPRIATIONS LEGISLATIVE VEHICLE/OCEAN, COASTS AND LAKES STEWARDSHIP POLICY. Flores, R-Texas, for Byrne, R-Ala., amendment that would prohibit funds appropriated by the bill to be used to implement, administer or enforce the National Ocean Policy, related to the stewardship of oceans, coasts and the Great Lakes. Adopted in Committee of the Whole 216-199 : R 214-11; D 2-188. Sept. 13, 2017.

	491	492	493	494	495	496	497
ALABAMA							
1 Byrne	N	Y	N	N	N	N	Y
2 Roby	N	Y	N	N	N	N	Y
3 Rogers	N	Y	Y	N	N	N	Y
4 Aderholt	N	Y	N	N	N	N	Y
5 Brooks	N	N	N	N	N	N	Y
6 Palmer	N	Y	N	Y	N	Y	Y
7 Sewell	Y	N	Y	N	Y	Y	N
ALASKA							
AL Young	N	Y	?	?	?	?	Y
ARIZONA							
1 O'Halleran	Y	N	Y	Y	Y	Y	N
2 McSally	N	N	Y	N	N	N	Y
3 Grijalva	Y	N	Y	N	Y	Y	N
4 Gosar	N	Y	N	Y	N	N	Y
5 Biggs	N	Y	N	Y	N	N	Y
6 Schweikert	N	Y	N	Y	N	N	Y
7 Gallego	Y	N	Y	N	Y	Y	N
8 Franks	N	Y	N	Y	N	Y	Y
9 Sinema	Y	N	Y	N	Y	Y	N
ARKANSAS							
1 Crawford	N	Y	N	N	N	N	Y
2 Hill	N	N	N	N	N	N	Y
3 Womack	N	Y	N	N	N	N	Y
4 Westerman	N	Y	N	Y	N	N	Y
CALIFORNIA							
1 LaMalfa	N	Y	N	Y	N	N	Y
2 Huffman	Y	N	Y	N	Y	Y	N
3 Garamendi	Y	N	Y	N	Y	Y	N
4 McClintock	N	Y	N	Y	N	N	Y
5 Thompson	Y	N	Y	N	Y	Y	N
6 Matsui	Y	N	Y	N	Y	Y	N
7 Bera	Y	N	Y	N	Y	Y	N
8 Cook	N	N	Y	N	N	N	Y
9 McNerney	Y	N	Y	N	Y	Y	N
10 Denham	N	N	N	N	N	N	Y
11 DeSaulnier	Y	N	Y	N	Y	Y	N
12 Pelosi	Y	N	Y	N	Y	Y	N
13 Lee	Y	N	Y	N	Y	Y	N
14 Speier	Y	N	Y	N	Y	Y	N
15 Swalwell	Y	N	Y	N	Y	Y	N
16 Costa	?	?	?	?	?	?	?
17 Khanna	Y	N	Y	N	Y	Y	N
18 Eshoo	Y	N	Y	N	Y	Y	N
19 Lofgren	Y	N	Y	N	Y	Y	N
20 Panetta	Y	N	Y	N	Y	Y	N
21 Valadao	N	N	N	N	N	N	Y
22 Nunes	N	N	N	N	N	N	Y
23 McCarthy	N	N	N	N	N	N	Y
24 Carbajal	Y	N	Y	N	Y	Y	N
25 Knight	N	N	N	N	N	N	Y
26 Brownley	Y	N	Y	N	Y	Y	N
27 Chu	Y	N	Y	N	Y	?	N
28 Schiff	Y	N	Y	N	Y	Y	N
29 Cardenas	Y	N	Y	N	Y	Y	N
30 Sherman	Y	N	Y	N	Y	Y	N
31 Aguilar	Y	N	Y	N	Y	Y	N
32 Napolitano	Y	N	Y	N	Y	Y	N
33 Lieu	Y	N	Y	N	Y	Y	N
34 Gomez	Y	N	Y	N	Y	Y	N
35 Torres	Y	N	Y	N	Y	Y	N
36 Ruiz	Y	N	Y	N	Y	Y	N
37 Bass	Y	N	Y	N	Y	Y	N
38 Sánchez, Linda	Y	N	Y	N	Y	Y	N
39 Royce	N	Y	Y	N	N	N	Y
40 Roybal-Allard	Y	N	Y	N	Y	Y	N
41 Takano	Y	N	Y	N	Y	Y	N
42 Calvert	N	N	Y	N	N	N	Y
43 Waters	Y	N	Y	N	Y	Y	N
44 Barragan	Y	N	Y	N	Y	Y	N
45 Walters	N	Y	N	Y	N	N	Y
46 Correa	Y	N	Y	N	Y	Y	N
47 Lowenthal	Y	N	Y	N	Y	Y	N
48 Rohrabacher	N	N	Y	N	N	N	Y
49 Issa	N	N	Y	N	N	N	Y
50 Hunter	N	Y	Y	Y	N	N	Y
51 Vargas	Y	N	Y	N	Y	Y	N
52 Peters	Y	N	Y	N	Y	Y	N
53 Davis	Y	N	Y	N	Y	Y	N
COLORADO							
1 DeGette	Y	N	Y	Y	Y	Y	N
2 Polis	Y	N	Y	Y	Y	Y	N
3 Tipton	Y	N	N	N	N	N	Y
4 Buck	N	Y	N	Y	N	N	Y
5 Lamborn	N	Y	N	Y	N	N	Y
6 Coffman	N	N	Y	N	N	N	Y
7 Perlmutter	Y	N	Y	N	Y	N	N
CONNECTICUT							
1 Larson	Y	N	Y	N	Y	Y	N
2 Courtney	Y	N	Y	N	Y	Y	N
3 DeLauro	+	–	+	–	+	+	–
4 Himes	Y	N	Y	N	Y	Y	N
5 Esty	Y	N	Y	N	Y	Y	N
DELAWARE							
AL Blunt Rochester	Y	N	Y	N	Y	Y	N
FLORIDA							
1 Gaetz	N	Y	N	Y	N	Y	Y
2 Dunn	Y	Y	N	Y	N	N	Y
3 Yoho	N	Y	N	Y	N	N	Y
4 Rutherford	N	N	N	N	N	N	Y
5 Lawson	?	?	?	?	?	?	?
6 DeSantis	N	Y	N	Y	N	N	Y
7 Murphy	Y	N	Y	N	Y	Y	N
8 Posey	?	?	?	?	?	?	?
9 Soto	Y	N	Y	N	Y	Y	N
10 Demings	Y	N	Y	N	Y	Y	N
11 Webster	N	N	N	N	N	N	Y
12 Bilirakis	N	Y	N	N	N	N	Y
13 Crist	Y	N	Y	N	Y	Y	N
14 Castor	?	?	N	Y	N	Y	N
15 Ross	?	?	?	?	?	?	?
16 Buchanan	N	N	Y	N	N	N	Y
17 Rooney, T.	N	N	N	N	N	N	Y
18 Mast	N	N	N	N	N	N	N
19 Rooney, F.	?	?	?	?	?	?	?
20 Hastings	Y	N	Y	N	Y	Y	N
21 Frankel	Y	N	Y	–	+	Y	N
22 Deutch	Y	N	Y	N	Y	Y	N
23 Wasserman Schultz	Y	N	Y	N	Y	Y	N
24 Wilson	Y	N	Y	N	Y	Y	Y
25 Diaz-Balart	?	?	?	?	?	?	?
26 Curbelo	?	?	Y	N	N	N	N
27 Ros-Lehtinen	?	?	?	?	?	?	?
GEORGIA							
1 Carter	N	Y	N	Y	N	N	Y
2 Bishop	Y	N	Y	N	Y	Y	N
3 Ferguson	N	Y	N	N	N	N	Y
4 Johnson	Y	N	Y	N	Y	Y	N
5 Lewis	Y	N	Y	N	Y	Y	N
6 Handel	N	Y	N	N	N	N	Y
7 Woodall	N	N	N	N	N	N	Y
8 Scott, A.	N	Y	N	Y	N	N	Y
9 Collins	N	N	N	N	N	N	Y
10 Hice	N	Y	N	N	N	N	Y
11 Loudermilk	?	?	?	?	?	?	?
12 Allen	N	Y	N	N	N	N	Y
13 Scott, D.	Y	N	Y	N	Y	Y	N
14 Graves	N	Y	N	Y	N	?	N
HAWAII							
1 Hanabusa	Y	N	Y	N	Y	Y	N
2 Gabbard	Y	N	Y	N	Y	Y	N
IDAHO							
1 Labrador	N	Y	N	Y	N	N	Y
2 Simpson	Y	N	Y	N	N	N	Y
ILLINOIS							
1 Rush	Y	N	Y	N	Y	Y	N
2 Kelly	Y	N	Y	N	Y	Y	N
3 Lipinski	Y	N	Y	N	Y	Y	N
4 Gutierrez	Y	N	Y	N	Y	Y	N
5 Quigley	Y	N	Y	N	Y	Y	N
6 Roskam	N	N	N	N	N	N	Y
7 Davis, D.	Y	N	Y	N	Y	Y	N
8 Krishnamoorthi	Y	N	Y	N	Y	Y	N
9 Schakowsky	Y	N	Y	N	Y	Y	N
10 Schneider	Y	N	Y	N	Y	Y	N
11 Foster	Y	N	Y	N	Y	Y	N
12 Bost	N	N	N	N	N	N	Y
13 Davis, R.	N	N	Y	N	N	N	Y
14 Hultgren	N	Y	N	Y	N	N	Y
15 Shimkus	N	N	Y	N	N	N	Y

	491	492	493	494	495	496	497
16 **Kinzinger**	N	Y	Y	N	N	N	Y
17 Bustos	Y	N	Y	N	Y	Y	N
18 **LaHood**	N	?	N	Y	N	N	Y
INDIANA							
1 Visclosky	Y	N	Y	N	Y	Y	N
2 **Walorski**	N	Y	N	N	N	N	Y
3 **Banks**	N	Y	Y	Y	N	N	Y
4 **Rokita**	N	N	N	Y	N	N	Y
5 **Brooks**	Y	N	Y	N	N	N	Y
6 **Messer**	N	Y	Y	Y	N	N	Y
7 Carson	Y	N	Y	N	Y	Y	N
8 **Bucshon**	N	N	Y	N	N	N	Y
9 **Hollingsworth**	N	Y	Y	N	N	N	Y
IOWA							
1 **Blum**	N	Y	Y	Y	N	N	Y
2 Loebsack	Y	N	Y	N	Y	Y	N
3 **Young**	N	Y	Y	Y	N	N	Y
4 **King**	N	Y	N	Y	N	N	Y
KANSAS							
1 **Marshall**	N	Y	Y	Y	N	N	Y
2 **Jenkins**	N	Y	N	Y	N	N	Y
3 **Yoder**	N	Y	N	Y	N	N	Y
4 **Estes**	N	Y	N	Y	N	N	Y
KENTUCKY							
1 **Comer**	N	Y	N	Y	N	N	N
2 **Guthrie**	N	Y	N	Y	N	N	Y
3 Yarmuth	Y	N	Y	N	Y	Y	N
4 **Massie**	N	Y	N	Y	N	N	Y
5 **Rogers**	N	N	Y	N	N	N	Y
6 **Barr**	N	Y	N	Y	N	N	Y
LOUISIANA							
1 **Scalise**	?	?	?	?	?	?	?
2 Richmond	Y	N	N	N	Y	Y	N
3 **Higgins**	N	Y	N	N	N	N	Y
4 **Johnson**	N	Y	N	N	N	N	Y
5 **Abraham**	N	Y	N	Y	N	N	Y
6 **Graves**	N	Y	N	N	N	N	Y
MAINE							
1 Pingree	Y	N	Y	N	Y	Y	N
2 **Poliquin**	N	N	Y	N	N	N	N
MARYLAND							
1 **Harris**	N	Y	N	Y	N	N	Y
2 Ruppersberger	Y	N	Y	N	Y	Y	N
3 Sarbanes	Y	N	Y	N	Y	Y	N
4 Brown	Y	N	Y	N	Y	Y	N
5 Hoyer	Y	N	Y	N	Y	Y	N
6 Delaney	Y	N	Y	N	Y	Y	N
7 Cummings	Y	N	Y	N	Y	Y	N
8 Raskin	Y	N	Y	N	Y	Y	N
MASSACHUSETTS							
1 Neal	Y	N	Y	N	Y	Y	N
2 McGovern	Y	N	Y	N	Y	Y	N
3 Tsongas	Y	N	Y	N	Y	Y	N
4 Kennedy	Y	N	Y	N	Y	Y	N
5 Clark	Y	N	Y	N	Y	Y	N
6 Moulton	Y	N	Y	N	Y	Y	N
7 Capuano	Y	N	Y	N	Y	Y	N
8 Lynch	Y	N	Y	N	Y	Y	N
9 Keating	Y	N	Y	N	Y	Y	N
MICHIGAN							
1 **Bergman**	N	N	N	N	N	N	Y
2 **Huizenga**	N	Y	Y	N	N	N	Y
3 **Amash**	N	Y	N	Y	N	Y	Y
4 **Moolenaar**	N	N	Y	N	N	N	Y
5 Kildee	Y	N	Y	N	Y	Y	N
6 **Upton**	N	N	Y	N	N	N	Y
7 **Walberg**	N	Y	Y	N	N	N	Y
8 **Bishop**	N	N	Y	N	N	N	Y
9 Levin	Y	N	Y	N	Y	Y	N
10 **Mitchell**	N	N	Y	N	N	N	Y
11 **Trott**	N	N	Y	N	N	N	Y
12 Dingell	Y	N	Y	N	Y	Y	N
13 Conyers	Y	N	Y	N	Y	Y	N
14 Lawrence	Y	N	Y	N	Y	Y	N
MINNESOTA							
1 Walz	Y	N	Y	N	Y	Y	N
2 **Lewis**	N	Y	N	Y	N	N	Y
3 **Paulsen**	N	N	Y	N	N	N	Y
4 McCollum	Y	N	Y	N	Y	Y	N
5 Ellison	Y	N	Y	N	Y	Y	N
6 **Emmer**	N	Y	Y	Y	N	N	Y
7 Peterson	N	Y	Y	N	Y	Y	Y
8 Nolan	Y	N	Y	N	Y	Y	N
MISSISSIPPI							
1 **Kelly**	N	Y	N	Y	N	N	Y
2 Thompson	Y	N	Y	N	Y	Y	N
3 **Harper**	N	Y	N	N	N	N	Y
4 **Palazzo**	N	Y	N	N	N	N	Y
MISSOURI							
1 Clay	Y	N	Y	N	Y	Y	N
2 **Wagner**	N	Y	N	N	N	N	Y
3 **Luetkemeyer**	N	Y	Y	N	N	N	Y
4 **Hartzler**	N	Y	Y	N	N	N	Y
5 Cleaver	Y	N	Y	N	Y	Y	N
6 **Graves**	–	+	+	–	–	–	+
7 **Long**	N	Y	N	Y	N	N	Y
8 **Smith**	N	Y	N	Y	N	N	Y
MONTANA							
AL **Gianforte**	Y	N	N	Y	N	N	Y
NEBRASKA							
1 **Fortenberry**	Y	N	Y	N	N	N	N
2 **Bacon**	N	N	Y	Y	N	N	Y
3 **Smith**	N	Y	Y	Y	N	N	Y
NEVADA							
1 Titus	Y	N	Y	N	Y	Y	N
2 **Amodei**	N	N	?	N	N	N	Y
3 Rosen	Y	N	Y	N	Y	Y	N
4 Kihuen	Y	N	Y	N	Y	Y	N
NEW HAMPSHIRE							
1 Shea-Porter	Y	N	Y	N	Y	Y	N
2 Kuster	Y	N	Y	N	Y	Y	N
NEW JERSEY							
1 Norcross	Y	N	Y	N	Y	Y	N
2 **LoBiondo**	N	N	Y	N	N	N	Y
3 **MacArthur**	N	N	Y	N	N	N	Y
4 **Smith**	N	N	Y	N	N	N	Y
5 Gottheimer	Y	N	Y	N	Y	Y	N
6 Pallone	Y	N	Y	N	Y	Y	N
7 **Lance**	Y	N	Y	N	N	N	Y
8 Sires	Y	N	Y	N	Y	Y	N
9 Pascrell	Y	N	Y	N	Y	Y	N
10 Payne	Y	N	Y	N	Y	Y	N
11 **Frelinghuysen**	N	N	N	N	N	N	Y
12 Watson Coleman	?	?	Y	N	Y	Y	N
NEW MEXICO							
1 Lujan Grisham	Y	N	Y	N	Y	Y	N
2 **Pearce**	N	N	N	N	N	N	Y
3 Luján	Y	N	Y	N	Y	Y	N
NEW YORK							
1 **Zeldin**	N	Y	N	N	N	N	Y
2 **King**	N	N	Y	N	N	N	Y
3 Suozzi	Y	N	Y	N	Y	Y	N
4 Rice	Y	N	Y	N	Y	Y	N
5 Meeks	Y	N	Y	N	Y	Y	N
6 Meng	Y	N	Y	N	Y	Y	N
7 Velázquez	Y	N	Y	N	Y	Y	N
8 Jeffries	Y	N	Y	N	Y	Y	N
9 Clarke	Y	N	Y	N	Y	Y	N
10 Nadler	Y	N	Y	N	Y	Y	N
11 **Donovan**	N	N	N	N	N	N	N
12 Maloney, C.	Y	N	Y	N	Y	Y	N
13 Espaillat	Y	N	Y	N	Y	Y	N
14 Crowley	Y	N	Y	N	Y	Y	N
15 Serrano	Y	N	Y	N	Y	Y	N
16 Engel	Y	N	Y	N	Y	Y	N
17 Lowey	Y	N	Y	N	Y	Y	N
18 Maloney, S.P.	Y	N	Y	N	Y	Y	N
19 **Faso**	N	N	Y	N	N	N	Y
20 Tonko	Y	N	Y	N	Y	Y	N
21 **Stefanik**	Y	N	Y	N	N	N	N
22 **Tenney**	N	Y	N	N	N	N	Y
23 **Reed**	N	N	Y	N	N	N	Y
24 **Katko**	Y	N	Y	N	N	N	Y
25 Slaughter	Y	N	Y	N	Y	Y	N
26 Higgins	Y	N	Y	N	Y	Y	N
27 **Collins**	N	N	N	N	N	N	Y
NORTH CAROLINA							
1 Butterfield	Y	N	Y	N	Y	Y	N
2 **Holding**	N	Y	N	Y	N	N	Y
3 **Jones**	Y	Y	Y	Y	N	N	Y
4 Price	Y	N	Y	N	Y	Y	N
5 **Foxx**	N	Y	N	N	N	N	Y
6 **Walker**	N	Y	N	Y	N	N	Y
7 **Rouzer**	N	N	N	N	N	N	Y
8 **Hudson**	?	Y	Y	Y	N	N	Y
9 **Pittenger**	N	Y	N	N	N	N	Y
10 **McHenry**	N	Y	N	N	N	N	Y
11 **Meadows**	N	Y	N	Y	N	N	Y
12 Adams	Y	N	Y	N	Y	Y	N
13 **Budd**	N	Y	N	Y	N	N	Y
NORTH DAKOTA							
AL **Cramer**	N	Y	N	N	N	N	Y
OHIO							
1 **Chabot**	N	Y	N	Y	N	N	Y
2 **Wenstrup**	N	Y	N	Y	N	N	Y
3 Beatty	Y	N	Y	N	Y	Y	N
4 **Jordan**	N	Y	N	Y	N	N	Y
5 **Latta**	N	Y	Y	Y	N	N	Y
6 **Johnson**	N	Y	Y	N	N	N	Y
7 **Gibbs**	N	Y	Y	N	N	N	Y
8 **Davidson**	N	Y	N	Y	N	N	Y
9 Kaptur	Y	N	Y	N	Y	Y	N
10 **Turner**	N	N	N	N	Y	N	Y
11 Fudge	Y	N	Y	N	Y	Y	N
12 **Tiberi**	?	?	?	?	?	?	?
13 Ryan	Y	N	Y	N	Y	Y	N
14 **Joyce**	N	N	Y	N	N	N	Y
15 **Stivers**	N	N	Y	N	N	N	Y
16 **Renacci**	N	Y	Y	N	N	N	Y
OKLAHOMA							
1 **Bridenstine**	?	?	?	?	?	?	?
2 **Mullin**	N	Y	N	Y	N	N	Y
3 **Lucas**	N	N	N	N	N	N	Y
4 **Cole**	N	N	N	N	N	N	Y
5 **Russell**	N	Y	N	Y	N	N	Y
OREGON							
1 Bonamici	Y	N	Y	N	Y	Y	N
2 **Walden**	N	N	N	N	N	N	Y
3 Blumenauer	Y	N	Y	N	Y	Y	N
4 DeFazio	Y	N	Y	N	Y	Y	N
5 Schrader	Y	N	Y	N	Y	N	N
PENNSYLVANIA							
1 Brady	Y	N	Y	N	Y	Y	N
2 Evans	Y	N	Y	N	Y	Y	N
3 **Kelly**	N	Y	Y	N	N	N	Y
4 **Perry**	N	Y	Y	Y	N	N	Y
5 **Thompson**	N	N	Y	N	N	N	Y
6 **Costello**	Y	N	Y	N	N	N	N
7 **Meehan**	Y	N	Y	N	N	N	Y
8 **Fitzpatrick**	Y	N	Y	N	Y	N	N
9 **Shuster**	N	Y	N	?	N	N	Y
10 **Marino**	N	N	Y	?	N	N	Y
11 **Barletta**	N	Y	Y	N	N	N	Y
12 **Rothfus**	N	N	Y	N	N	N	Y
13 Boyle	Y	N	Y	N	Y	Y	N
14 Doyle	Y	N	Y	N	Y	Y	N
15 **Dent**	N	N	Y	N	N	?	?
16 **Smucker**	N	N	Y	N	N	N	Y
17 Cartwright	Y	N	Y	N	Y	Y	N
18 **Murphy**	N	N	Y	N	N	N	Y
RHODE ISLAND							
1 Cicilline	Y	N	Y	N	Y	Y	N
2 Langevin	Y	N	Y	N	Y	Y	N
SOUTH CAROLINA							
1 **Sanford**	N	Y	N	Y	N	N	Y
2 **Wilson**	N	Y	Y	Y	N	N	Y
3 **Duncan**	N	Y	Y	Y	N	N	Y
4 **Gowdy**	N	Y	N	N	N	N	Y
5 **Norman**	N	Y	Y	Y	N	N	Y
6 Clyburn	?	?	?	?	?	?	?
7 **Rice**	N	Y	N	Y	N	N	Y
SOUTH DAKOTA							
AL **Noem**	N	Y	N	N	N	N	Y
TENNESSEE							
1 **Roe**	N	Y	N	Y	N	N	Y
2 **Duncan**	N	Y	Y	Y	N	N	Y
3 **Fleischmann**	N	Y	N	N	N	N	Y
4 **DesJarlais**	N	Y	N	N	N	N	Y
5 Cooper	Y	N	Y	N	Y	Y	N
6 **Black**	N	Y	N	Y	N	N	Y
7 **Blackburn**	N	Y	N	Y	N	N	Y
8 **Kustoff**	N	Y	N	N	N	N	Y
9 Cohen	Y	N	Y	N	Y	Y	N
TEXAS							
1 **Gohmert**	N	Y	N	N	N	N	Y
2 **Poe**	?	?	N	Y	N	N	Y
3 **Johnson, S.**	N	Y	N	N	N	N	Y
4 **Ratcliffe**	N	Y	N	N	N	N	Y
5 **Hensarling**	N	Y	N	N	N	N	Y
6 **Barton**	N	N	Y	Y	N	N	Y
7 **Culberson**	N	Y	N	N	N	N	Y
8 **Brady**	N	N	N	N	N	N	Y
9 Green, A.	Y	N	Y	N	Y	Y	N
10 **McCaul**	N	Y	N	N	N	N	Y
11 **Conaway**	N	Y	N	N	N	N	Y
12 **Granger**	N	Y	N	N	N	N	Y
13 **Thornberry**	N	Y	N	N	N	N	Y
14 **Weber**	N	Y	N	Y	N	N	Y
15 Gonzalez	?	?	Y	Y	Y	Y	N
16 O'Rourke	Y	N	Y	N	Y	Y	N
17 **Flores**	N	Y	N	N	N	N	Y
18 Jackson Lee	Y	N	Y	N	Y	Y	N
19 **Arrington**	N	Y	N	N	N	N	Y
20 Castro	Y	N	Y	N	Y	Y	N
21 **Smith**	N	Y	N	N	N	N	Y
22 **Olson**	N	Y	N	N	N	N	Y
23 **Hurd**	N	N	Y	N	N	N	Y
24 **Marchant**	N	Y	Y	N	N	N	Y
25 **Williams**	N	Y	N	Y	N	N	Y
26 **Burgess**	N	Y	N	N	N	N	Y
27 **Farenthold**	N	Y	N	Y	N	N	Y
28 Cuellar	Y	N	Y	N	Y	Y	N
29 Green, G.	Y	N	Y	N	Y	Y	N
30 Johnson, E.B.	Y	N	Y	N	Y	Y	N
31 **Carter**	N	Y	N	N	N	N	Y
32 **Sessions**	N	Y	N	N	N	N	Y
33 Veasey	Y	N	Y	N	Y	Y	N
34 Vela	Y	N	Y	N	Y	Y	N
35 Doggett	Y	N	Y	N	Y	Y	N
36 **Babin**	N	Y	N	Y	N	N	Y
UTAH							
1 **Bishop**	N	Y	Y	Y	N	N	Y
2 **Stewart**	N	Y	Y	N	N	N	Y
4 **Love**	N	Y	N	Y	N	N	Y
VERMONT							
AL Welch	Y	N	Y	N	Y	Y	N
VIRGINIA							
1 **Wittman**	N	Y	N	Y	N	N	Y
2 **Taylor**	N	Y	N	N	N	N	Y
3 Scott	Y	N	Y	N	Y	Y	N
4 McEachin	?	?	Y	N	Y	Y	N
5 **Garrett**	?	?	?	?	?	?	?
6 **Goodlatte**	N	Y	N	?	N	N	?
7 **Brat**	N	Y	N	Y	N	N	Y
8 Beyer	Y	N	Y	N	Y	Y	N
9 **Griffith**	N	Y	N	Y	N	N	Y
10 **Comstock**	?	Y	Y	N	?	N	Y
11 Connolly	Y	N	Y	N	Y	Y	N
WASHINGTON							
1 DelBene	Y	N	Y	N	Y	Y	N
2 Larsen	Y	N	Y	N	Y	Y	N
3 **Herrera Beutler**	N	N	Y	N	N	N	Y
4 **Newhouse**	N	Y	N	?	N	N	Y
5 **McMorris Rodgers**	N	Y	Y	Y	N	N	Y
6 Kilmer	Y	N	Y	N	Y	Y	N
7 Jayapal	Y	N	Y	N	Y	Y	N
8 **Reichert**	N	N	N	N	N	N	Y
9 Smith	Y	N	Y	N	Y	Y	N
10 Heck	Y	N	Y	N	Y	Y	N
WEST VIRGINIA							
1 **McKinley**	N	Y	Y	N	N	N	Y
2 **Mooney**	N	Y	Y	Y	N	N	Y
3 **Jenkins**	N	Y	Y	N	N	N	Y
WISCONSIN							
1 **Ryan**							
2 Pocan	Y	N	Y	N	Y	Y	N
3 Kind	Y	N	Y	N	Y	Y	N
4 Moore	Y	N	Y	N	Y	Y	N
5 **Sensenbrenner**	N	Y	N	Y	N	N	Y
6 **Grothman**	N	Y	Y	Y	N	N	Y
7 **Duffy**	N	Y	Y	N	N	N	Y
8 **Gallagher**	N	Y	Y	Y	N	N	Y
WYOMING							
AL **Cheney**	N	Y	N	Y	N	N	Y

VOTE NUMBER

498. HR 3354. FISCAL 2018 OMNIBUS APPROPRIATIONS LEGISLATIVE VEHICLE/IMMIGRATION STATUS INFORMATION. Buck, R-Colo., amendment that would prohibit funds appropriated by the bill to be used to violate the federal government's ability to send or receive information regarding the citizenship or immigration status of an individual. Adopted in Committee of the Whole 226-191 : R 222-6; D 4-185. Sept. 13, 2017.

499. HR 3354. FISCAL 2018 OMNIBUS APPROPRIATIONS LEGISLATIVE VEHICLE/YOUTH EMPLOYMENT ACTIVITIES. Kildee, D-Mich., amendment that would increase funding for the Department of Labor's youth employment activities by $10 million, and would decrease funding for the department's salaries and expenses by the same amount. Adopted in Committee of the Whole 247-170 : R 57-170; D 190-0. Sept. 13, 2017.

500. HR 3354. FISCAL 2018 OMNIBUS APPROPRIATIONS LEGISLATIVE VEHICLE/WORKER PROTECTION AGENCIES. Pocan, D-Wis., for DeLauro, D-Conn., amendment that would increase funding for the Labor, Health and Human Services and Education Departments' worker protection agencies by $149 million, and would decrease funding to the departments' program administration funds by $164 million. Rejected in Committee of the Whole 199-219 : R 10-218; D 189-1. Sept. 13, 2017.

501. HR 3354. FISCAL 2018 OMNIBUS APPROPRIATIONS LEGISLATIVE VEHICLE/DEPARTMENT OF LABOR MANAGEMENT. Meng, D-N.Y., amendment that would decrease funding for the Bureau of Labor Statistics by $1.1 million, and increase funding for the departments of management within the Department of Labor by the same amount. Adopted in Committee of the Whole 220-198 : R 30-198; D 190-0. Sept. 13, 2017.

502. HR 3354. FISCAL 2018 OMNIBUS APPROPRIATIONS LEGISLATIVE VEHICLE/MATERNAL AND CHILD HEALTH SERVICE GRANTS. Kildee, D-Mich., amendment that would increase funding for Maternal and Child Health Service block grants by $25 million, and would decrease funding for the office of the Secretary of the Department of Health and Human Services by the same amount. Adopted in Committee of the Whole 243-175 : R 53-175; D 190-0. Sept. 13, 2017.

503. HR 3354. FISCAL 2018 OMNIBUS APPROPRIATIONS LEGISLATIVE VEHICLE/SUBSTANCE ABUSE AND MENTAL HEALTH SERVICES. Clark, D-Mass., for DeLauro, D-Conn., amendment that would increase funding for the Substance Abuse and Mental Health Services Administration by $231.3 million, would decrease funding for the Office of the Secretary of the Department of Health and Human Services by $219.6 million, and would decrease funding for the Department of Management of the Department of Education by $11.7 million. Adopted in Committee of the Whole 225-192 : R 38-189; D 187-3. Sept. 13, 2017.

504. HR 3354. FISCAL 2018 OMNIBUS APPROPRIATIONS LEGISLATIVE VEHICLE/MEDICARE ACCESS FOR MENTAL DISORDERS. Murphy, R-Pa., amendment that would increase funding related to access to Medicare for mental and substance use disorders by $5 million. Rejected in Committee of the Whole 198-219 : R 131-96; D 67-123. Sept. 13, 2017.

	498	499	500	501	502	503	504
ALABAMA							
1 Byrne	Y	N	N	N	N	N	Y
2 Roby	Y	N	N	N	N	N	N
3 Rogers	Y	N	N	N	N	N	Y
4 Aderholt	Y	N	N	N	N	N	N
5 Brooks	Y	N	N	N	N	N	N
6 Palmer	Y	N	N	N	N	N	Y
7 Sewell	N	Y	Y	Y	Y	Y	Y
ALASKA							
AL Young	Y	N	Y	N	N	N	N
ARIZONA							
1 O'Halleran	N	Y	Y	Y	Y	Y	Y
2 McSally	Y	Y	N	Y	Y	N	Y
3 Grijalva	N	Y	Y	Y	Y	Y	N
4 Gosar	Y	N	N	N	N	N	N
5 Biggs	Y	N	N	N	N	N	N
6 Schweikert	Y	N	Y	N	N	N	N
7 Gallego	N	Y	Y	Y	Y	Y	N
8 Franks	Y	N	N	N	N	N	N
9 Sinema	N	Y	Y	Y	Y	Y	Y
ARKANSAS							
1 Crawford	Y	N	N	N	N	N	Y
2 Hill	Y	N	N	N	N	N	Y
3 Womack	Y	N	N	N	N	N	N
4 Westerman	Y	N	N	N	N	Y	N
CALIFORNIA							
1 LaMalfa	Y	N	N	N	N	N	Y
2 Huffman	N	Y	Y	Y	Y	Y	N
3 Garamendi	N	Y	Y	Y	Y	Y	Y
4 McClintock	Y	N	N	N	N	N	N
5 Thompson	N	Y	Y	Y	Y	Y	Y
6 Matsui	N	Y	Y	Y	Y	Y	N
7 Bera	N	Y	Y	Y	Y	Y	Y
8 Cook	Y	N	N	Y	N	N	N
9 McNerney	N	Y	Y	Y	Y	Y	Y
10 Denham	Y	N	N	Y	N	N	N
11 DeSaulnier	N	Y	Y	Y	Y	Y	N
12 Pelosi	N	Y	Y	Y	Y	Y	N
13 Lee	N	Y	Y	Y	Y	Y	Y
14 Speier	N	Y	Y	Y	Y	Y	N
15 Swalwell	N	Y	Y	Y	Y	Y	N
16 Costa	?	?	?	?	?	?	?
17 Khanna	N	Y	Y	Y	Y	Y	N
18 Eshoo	N	Y	Y	Y	Y	Y	Y
19 Lofgren	N	Y	Y	Y	Y	Y	N
20 Panetta	N	Y	Y	Y	Y	Y	Y
21 Valadao	Y	N	N	N	N	N	N
22 Nunes	Y	N	N	N	N	N	N
23 McCarthy	Y	N	N	N	N	N	Y
24 Carbajal	N	Y	Y	Y	Y	Y	N
25 Knight	Y	N	N	N	N	N	N
26 Brownley	N	Y	Y	Y	Y	Y	Y
27 Chu	N	Y	Y	Y	Y	Y	N
28 Schiff	N	Y	Y	Y	Y	Y	N
29 Cardenas	N	Y	Y	Y	Y	Y	N
30 Sherman	N	Y	Y	Y	Y	Y	Y
31 Aguilar	N	Y	Y	Y	Y	Y	Y
32 Napolitano	N	Y	Y	Y	Y	Y	N
33 Lieu	N	Y	Y	Y	Y	Y	N
34 Gomez	N	Y	Y	Y	Y	Y	N
35 Torres	N	Y	Y	Y	Y	Y	Y
36 Ruiz	N	Y	Y	Y	Y	Y	N
37 Bass	N	Y	Y	Y	Y	Y	Y
38 Sánchez, Linda	N	Y	Y	Y	Y	Y	N
39 Royce	Y	Y	N	Y	N	Y	Y
40 Roybal-Allard	N	Y	Y	Y	Y	Y	N
41 Takano	N	Y	Y	Y	Y	Y	N
42 Calvert	Y	N	N	Y	N	N	N
43 Waters	N	Y	Y	Y	Y	Y	N
44 Barragan	N	Y	Y	Y	Y	Y	N
45 Walters	Y	N	N	N	N	N	Y
46 Correa	N	Y	Y	Y	Y	Y	N
47 Lowenthal	N	Y	Y	Y	Y	Y	N
48 Rohrabacher	Y	N	N	N	N	N	N
49 Issa	Y	N	N	N	N	N	N
50 Hunter	Y	N	N	N	N	N	Y
51 Vargas	N	Y	Y	Y	Y	Y	N
52 Peters	N	Y	Y	Y	Y	Y	Y
53 Davis	N	Y	Y	Y	Y	Y	N
COLORADO							
1 DeGette	N	Y	Y	Y	Y	Y	N
2 Polis	N	Y	Y	Y	Y	Y	N
3 Tipton	Y	N	N	Y	Y	Y	Y
4 Buck	Y	N	N	Y	N	Y	Y
5 Lamborn	Y	N	N	N	N	N	N
6 Coffman	Y	N	N	N	N	N	N
7 Perlmutter	N	Y	Y	Y	Y	Y	Y
CONNECTICUT							
1 Larson	N	Y	Y	Y	Y	Y	Y
2 Courtney	N	Y	Y	Y	Y	Y	Y
3 DeLauro	–	+	+	+	+	+	–
4 Himes	N	Y	Y	Y	Y	Y	Y
5 Esty	N	Y	Y	Y	Y	Y	Y
DELAWARE							
AL Blunt Rochester	N	Y	Y	Y	Y	Y	N
FLORIDA							
1 Gaetz	Y	N	N	N	N	N	Y
2 Dunn	Y	N	N	N	N	N	Y
3 Yoho	Y	N	N	N	N	N	Y
4 Rutherford	Y	N	N	N	N	N	Y
5 Lawson	?	?	?	?	?	?	?
6 DeSantis	Y	N	N	N	N	N	N
7 Murphy	N	Y	Y	Y	Y	Y	N
8 Posey	?	?	?	?	?	?	?
9 Soto	N	Y	Y	Y	Y	Y	N
10 Demings	N	Y	Y	Y	Y	Y	N
11 Webster	Y	N	N	N	N	N	Y
12 Bilirakis	Y	N	N	N	N	N	Y
13 Crist	N	Y	Y	Y	Y	Y	N
14 Castor	N	Y	Y	Y	Y	Y	N
15 Ross	?	?	?	?	?	?	?
16 Buchanan	Y	Y	N	N	N	N	Y
17 Rooney, T.	Y	N	N	Y	N	N	Y
18 Mast	Y	N	N	Y	N	N	Y
19 Rooney, F.	?	?	?	?	?	?	?
20 Hastings	N	Y	Y	Y	Y	Y	N
21 Frankel	N	Y	Y	Y	Y	Y	N
22 Deutch	N	Y	Y	Y	Y	Y	Y
23 Wasserman Schultz	N	Y	Y	Y	Y	Y	N
24 Wilson	N	Y	Y	Y	Y	Y	N
25 Diaz-Balart	?	?	?	?	?	?	?
26 Curbelo	N	Y	N	Y	Y	Y	Y
27 Ros-Lehtinen	?	?	?	?	?	?	?
GEORGIA							
1 Carter	Y	N	N	N	N	N	Y
2 Bishop	N	Y	Y	Y	Y	Y	Y
3 Ferguson	Y	N	N	N	N	N	Y
4 Johnson	N	Y	Y	Y	Y	Y	Y
5 Lewis	N	Y	Y	Y	Y	Y	Y
6 Handel	Y	N	N	N	N	N	Y
7 Woodall	Y	N	N	N	N	N	N
8 Scott, A.	Y	N	N	N	N	N	N
9 Collins	Y	N	N	N	N	N	Y
10 Hice	Y	N	N	N	N	N	N
11 Loudermilk	?	?	?	?	?	?	?
12 Allen	Y	N	N	N	N	N	N
13 Scott, D.	N	Y	Y	Y	Y	Y	N
14 Graves	Y	N	N	N	N	N	N
HAWAII							
1 Hanabusa	N	Y	Y	Y	Y	Y	Y
2 Gabbard	N	Y	Y	Y	Y	Y	Y
IDAHO							
1 Labrador	N	N	N	N	N	N	N
2 Simpson	Y	N	N	N	N	N	N
ILLINOIS							
1 Rush	N	Y	Y	Y	Y	Y	N
2 Kelly	N	Y	Y	Y	Y	Y	Y
3 Lipinski	N	Y	Y	Y	Y	Y	Y
4 Gutierrez	N	Y	Y	Y	Y	Y	Y
5 Quigley	N	Y	Y	Y	Y	Y	Y
6 Roskam	Y	Y	N	Y	N	Y	Y
7 Davis, D.	N	Y	Y	Y	Y	Y	Y
8 Krishnamoorthi	N	Y	Y	Y	Y	Y	N
9 Schakowsky	N	Y	Y	Y	Y	Y	Y
10 Schneider	N	Y	Y	Y	Y	Y	Y
11 Foster	N	Y	Y	Y	Y	Y	Y
12 Bost	Y	N	N	N	N	N	Y
13 Davis, R.	Y	?	N	Y	Y	Y	Y
14 Hultgren	Y	N	N	N	N	N	Y
15 Shimkus	Y	N	N	N	N	N	Y

	498	499	500	501	502	503	504
16 **Kinzinger**	Y	N	N	N	Y	N	Y
17 Bustos	N	Y	Y	Y	Y	Y	N
18 **LaHood**	Y	Y	N	N	N	Y	Y
INDIANA							
1 Visclosky	N	Y	Y	Y	Y	Y	Y
2 **Walorski**	Y	Y	N	N	N	N	Y
3 **Banks**	Y	N	N	N	N	N	N
4 **Rokita**	Y	Y	N	N	N	N	Y
5 **Brooks**	Y	N	N	N	Y	Y	Y
6 **Messer**	Y	Y	N	N	Y	Y	Y
7 Carson	N	Y	Y	Y	Y	Y	N
8 **Bucshon**	Y	N	N	Y	Y	Y	Y
9 **Hollingsworth**	Y	Y	N	N	Y	N	N
IOWA							
1 **Blum**	Y	Y	Y	N	Y	Y	Y
2 Loebsack	N	Y	Y	Y	Y	Y	Y
3 **Young**	Y	Y	N	N	N	N	Y
4 **King**	Y	N	N	N	N	N	Y
KANSAS							
1 **Marshall**	Y	Y	N	N	N	N	N
2 **Jenkins**	Y	N	N	N	N	N	Y
3 **Yoder**	Y	N	N	N	N	N	Y
4 **Estes**	Y	N	N	N	N	N	Y
KENTUCKY							
1 **Comer**	Y	N	N	N	N	N	N
2 **Guthrie**	Y	N	N	N	N	N	Y
3 Yarmuth	N	Y	Y	Y	Y	Y	N
4 **Massie**	Y	N	N	Y	N	N	N
5 **Rogers**	Y	N	N	N	N	N	N
6 **Barr**	Y	N	N	N	N	N	Y
LOUISIANA							
1 **Scalise**	?	?	?	?	?	?	?
2 Richmond	N	Y	Y	Y	Y	Y	Y
3 **Higgins**	Y	Y	N	N	N	N	Y
4 **Johnson**	Y	N	N	N	N	N	Y
5 **Abraham**	Y	N	N	N	Y	N	Y
6 **Graves**	Y	N	N	Y	N	Y	Y
MAINE							
1 Pingree	N	Y	Y	Y	Y	Y	N
2 **Poliquin**	Y	Y	N	N	N	N	Y
MARYLAND							
1 **Harris**	Y	N	N	N	N	N	N
2 Ruppersberger	N	Y	Y	Y	Y	Y	N
3 Sarbanes	N	Y	Y	Y	Y	Y	N
4 Brown	N	Y	Y	Y	Y	Y	Y
5 Hoyer	N	Y	Y	Y	Y	N	N
6 Delaney	N	Y	Y	Y	Y	Y	Y
7 Cummings	N	Y	Y	Y	Y	Y	N
8 Raskin	N	Y	Y	Y	Y	Y	N
MASSACHUSETTS							
1 Neal	N	Y	Y	Y	Y	Y	N
2 McGovern	N	Y	Y	Y	Y	Y	N
3 Tsongas	N	Y	Y	Y	Y	Y	N
4 Kennedy	N	Y	Y	Y	Y	Y	N
5 Clark	N	Y	Y	Y	Y	Y	N
6 Moulton	N	Y	Y	Y	Y	Y	N
7 Capuano	N	Y	Y	Y	Y	Y	N
8 Lynch	Y	Y	Y	Y	Y	Y	Y
9 Keating	N	Y	Y	Y	Y	Y	N
MICHIGAN							
1 **Bergman**	Y	Y	N	N	Y	N	Y
2 **Huizenga**	Y	N	N	N	N	N	Y
3 **Amash**	Y	N	Y	N	N	N	N
4 **Moolenaar**	Y	N	N	N	N	N	N
5 Kildee	N	Y	Y	Y	Y	Y	N
6 **Upton**	Y	Y	N	N	Y	Y	Y
7 **Walberg**	Y	N	N	N	N	N	Y
8 **Bishop**	Y	Y	N	N	Y	N	Y
9 Levin	N	Y	Y	Y	Y	Y	N
10 **Mitchell**	Y	N	N	N	N	N	Y
11 **Trott**	Y	Y	N	N	Y	N	Y
12 Dingell	N	Y	Y	Y	Y	Y	N
13 Conyers	N	Y	Y	Y	Y	Y	N
14 Lawrence	N	Y	Y	Y	Y	Y	Y
MINNESOTA							
1 Walz	N	Y	Y	Y	Y	Y	N
2 **Lewis**	Y	N	N	N	N	N	N
3 **Paulsen**	Y	Y	N	Y	Y	Y	Y
4 McCollum	N	Y	Y	Y	Y	Y	N

	498	499	500	501	502	503	504
5 Ellison	N	Y	Y	Y	Y	Y	N
6 **Emmer**	Y	Y	N	N	N	N	N
7 Peterson	Y	Y	Y	Y	Y	Y	Y
8 Nolan	N	Y	Y	Y	Y	Y	Y
MISSISSIPPI							
1 **Kelly**	Y	N	N	N	N	N	N
2 Thompson	N	Y	Y	Y	Y	Y	Y
3 **Harper**	Y	N	N	N	N	N	Y
4 **Palazzo**	Y	N	N	N	N	N	N
MISSOURI							
1 Clay	N	Y	Y	Y	Y	Y	N
2 **Wagner**	Y	N	N	N	N	N	Y
3 **Luetkemeyer**	Y	N	N	N	Y	N	Y
4 **Hartzler**	Y	N	N	N	N	N	Y
5 Cleaver	N	Y	Y	Y	Y	Y	Y
6 **Graves**	+	-	-	-	-	-	-
7 **Long**	Y	N	N	N	N	N	N
8 **Smith**	Y	N	N	N	N	N	Y
MONTANA							
AL **Gianforte**	Y	N	N	N	N	N	Y
NEBRASKA							
1 **Fortenberry**	Y	N	N	Y	N	Y	Y
2 **Bacon**	Y	Y	N	N	Y	N	Y
3 **Smith**	Y	Y	N	N	N	N	N
NEVADA							
1 Titus	N	Y	Y	Y	Y	Y	N
2 **Amodei**	Y	N	N	N	N	N	Y
3 Rosen	N	Y	Y	Y	Y	Y	N
4 Kihuen	N	Y	Y	Y	Y	Y	N
NEW HAMPSHIRE							
1 Shea-Porter	N	Y	Y	Y	Y	Y	Y
2 Kuster	N	Y	Y	Y	Y	Y	Y
NEW JERSEY							
1 Norcross	N	Y	Y	Y	Y	Y	N
2 **LoBiondo**	N	Y	Y	Y	Y	Y	Y
3 **MacArthur**	Y	Y	N	N	Y	N	Y
4 **Smith**	Y	Y	Y	Y	Y	Y	Y
5 Gottheimer	N	Y	Y	Y	Y	Y	Y
6 Pallone	N	Y	Y	Y	Y	Y	N
7 **Lance**	Y	Y	Y	Y	Y	Y	Y
8 Sires	N	Y	Y	Y	Y	Y	N
9 Pascrell	N	Y	Y	Y	Y	Y	N
10 Payne	N	Y	Y	Y	Y	Y	N
11 **Frelinghuysen**	Y	N	N	Y	N	N	N
12 Watson Coleman	N	Y	Y	Y	Y	Y	N
NEW MEXICO							
1 Lujan Grisham	N	Y	Y	Y	Y	Y	N
2 **Pearce**	Y	Y	N	N	Y	N	Y
3 Luján	N	Y	Y	Y	Y	Y	N
NEW YORK							
1 **Zeldin**	Y	Y	N	Y	Y	Y	Y
2 **King**	N	Y	Y	Y	N	N	Y
3 Suozzi	N	Y	Y	Y	Y	Y	Y
4 Rice	N	Y	Y	Y	Y	Y	N
5 Meeks	N	Y	Y	Y	Y	Y	Y
6 Meng	N	Y	Y	Y	Y	Y	N
7 Velázquez	N	Y	Y	Y	Y	Y	N
8 Jeffries	N	Y	Y	Y	Y	Y	Y
9 Clarke	N	Y	Y	Y	Y	Y	N
10 Nadler	N	Y	Y	Y	Y	Y	N
11 **Donovan**	N	N	N	Y	N	N	Y
12 Maloney, C.	N	Y	Y	Y	Y	Y	N
13 Espaillat	N	Y	Y	Y	Y	Y	N
14 Crowley	N	Y	Y	Y	Y	Y	N
15 Serrano	N	Y	Y	Y	Y	Y	N
16 Engel	N	Y	Y	Y	Y	Y	N
17 Lowey	N	Y	Y	Y	Y	Y	N
18 Maloney, S.P.	N	Y	Y	Y	Y	Y	N
19 **Faso**	Y	Y	N	Y	Y	Y	Y
20 Tonko	N	Y	Y	Y	Y	Y	N
21 **Stefanik**	Y	Y	N	N	N	Y	Y
22 **Tenney**	Y	N	N	N	N	N	Y
23 **Reed**	Y	Y	N	Y	Y	Y	Y
24 **Katko**	Y	Y	Y	Y	Y	Y	Y
25 Slaughter	N	Y	Y	Y	Y	Y	N
26 Higgins	N	Y	Y	Y	Y	Y	N
27 **Collins**	Y	N	N	N	N	N	Y
NORTH CAROLINA							
1 Butterfield	N	Y	Y	Y	Y	Y	Y
2 **Holding**	Y	N	N	N	N	N	N
3 **Jones**	Y	Y	Y	N	Y	Y	Y
4 Price	N	Y	Y	Y	Y	Y	N

	498	499	500	501	502	503	504
5 **Foxx**	Y	N	N	N	N	N	N
6 **Walker**	Y	N	N	N	N	N	N
7 **Rouzer**	Y	N	N	N	N	N	Y
8 **Hudson**	Y	Y	N	N	N	N	Y
9 **Pittenger**	Y	N	N	N	N	N	N
10 **McHenry**	Y	N	N	N	N	N	Y
11 **Meadows**	Y	N	N	N	N	N	N
12 Adams	N	Y	Y	Y	Y	Y	Y
13 **Budd**	Y	N	N	N	N	N	N
NORTH DAKOTA							
AL **Cramer**	Y	N	N	N	N	N	N
OHIO							
1 **Chabot**	Y	N	N	N	N	N	N
2 **Wenstrup**	Y	N	N	N	N	N	Y
3 Beatty	N	Y	Y	Y	Y	Y	Y
4 **Jordan**	Y	N	N	N	N	N	N
5 **Latta**	Y	N	N	N	N	N	Y
6 **Johnson**	Y	N	N	N	N	N	Y
7 **Gibbs**	Y	N	N	N	N	N	Y
8 **Davidson**	Y	N	N	N	N	N	N
9 Kaptur	N	Y	Y	Y	Y	Y	Y
10 **Turner**	Y	Y	N	N	Y	Y	Y
11 Fudge	N	Y	Y	Y	Y	Y	Y
12 **Tiberi**	?	?	?	?	?	?	?
13 Ryan	?	Y	Y	Y	Y	Y	N
14 **Joyce**	Y	N	N	N	N	N	N
15 **Stivers**	Y	Y	N	N	Y	Y	Y
16 **Renacci**	Y	N	N	N	N	N	Y
OKLAHOMA							
1 **Bridenstine**	?	?	?	?	?	?	?
2 **Mullin**	Y	N	N	N	N	N	Y
3 **Lucas**	Y	N	N	N	N	N	N
4 **Cole**	Y	N	N	N	N	N	N
5 **Russell**	Y	N	N	N	N	N	N
OREGON							
1 Bonamici	N	Y	Y	Y	Y	Y	Y
2 **Walden**	Y	Y	N	N	Y	N	Y
3 Blumenauer	N	Y	Y	Y	Y	Y	Y
4 DeFazio	N	Y	Y	Y	Y	Y	Y
5 Schrader	N	Y	Y	Y	Y	Y	Y
PENNSYLVANIA							
1 Brady	N	Y	Y	Y	Y	Y	N
2 Evans	N	Y	Y	Y	Y	Y	N
3 **Kelly**	Y	Y	N	N	N	N	Y
4 **Perry**	Y	Y	N	N	N	N	N
5 **Thompson**	Y	N	N	N	Y	N	Y
6 **Costello**	Y	Y	N	Y	Y	Y	Y
7 **Meehan**	Y	Y	N	N	Y	Y	Y
8 **Fitzpatrick**	Y	Y	Y	Y	Y	Y	Y
9 **Shuster**	Y	N	N	N	N	N	Y
10 **Marino**	Y	N	N	N	N	?	?
11 **Barletta**	Y	Y	N	N	Y	Y	Y
12 **Rothfus**	Y	Y	N	N	N	N	Y
13 Boyle	N	Y	Y	Y	Y	Y	N
14 Doyle	N	Y	Y	Y	Y	Y	N
15 **Dent**	Y	Y	N	Y	Y	Y	Y
16 **Smucker**	Y	N	N	N	N	N	Y
17 Cartwright	Y	Y	Y	Y	Y	Y	N
18 **Murphy**	Y	Y	N	N	Y	Y	Y
RHODE ISLAND							
1 Cicilline	N	Y	Y	Y	Y	Y	N
2 Langevin	N	Y	Y	Y	Y	Y	N
SOUTH CAROLINA							
1 **Sanford**	Y	N	N	N	N	N	Y
2 **Wilson**	Y	N	N	N	N	N	Y
3 **Duncan**	Y	N	N	N	N	N	N
4 **Gowdy**	Y	N	N	N	N	N	Y
5 **Norman**	Y	N	N	N	N	N	N
6 Clyburn	?	?	?	?	?	?	?
7 **Rice**	Y	N	N	N	Y	N	Y
SOUTH DAKOTA							
AL **Noem**	Y	N	N	N	N	Y	Y
TENNESSEE							
1 **Roe**	Y	N	N	N	Y	Y	Y
2 **Duncan**	Y	N	N	N	N	N	N
3 **Fleischmann**	Y	N	N	N	N	N	N
4 **DesJarlais**	Y	N	N	N	N	N	N
5 Cooper	N	Y	Y	Y	Y	Y	Y
6 **Black**	Y	N	N	N	N	N	N
7 **Blackburn**	Y	N	N	N	N	N	N
8 **Kustoff**	Y	N	N	N	N	N	N
9 Cohen	N	Y	Y	Y	Y	Y	N

	498	499	500	501	502	503	504
TEXAS							
1 **Gohmert**	Y	N	N	N	N	N	Y
2 **Poe**	Y	N	N	N	N	N	N
3 **Johnson, S.**	Y	N	N	N	N	N	N
4 **Ratcliffe**	Y	N	N	N	N	N	N
5 **Hensarling**	Y	N	N	N	N	N	N
6 **Barton**	Y	N	N	Y	Y	N	N
7 **Culberson**	Y	N	N	N	N	N	N
8 **Brady**	Y	N	N	N	N	N	N
9 Green, A.	N	Y	Y	Y	Y	Y	Y
10 **McCaul**	Y	N	N	N	N	N	N
11 **Conaway**	Y	N	N	N	N	N	N
12 **Granger**	Y	N	N	N	N	N	N
13 **Thornberry**	Y	N	N	N	N	N	Y
14 **Weber**	Y	N	N	N	N	N	N
15 Gonzalez	N	Y	Y	Y	Y	Y	Y
16 O'Rourke	N	Y	Y	Y	Y	Y	Y
17 **Flores**	Y	N	N	N	N	N	N
18 Jackson Lee	N	Y	Y	Y	Y	Y	Y
19 **Arrington**	Y	N	N	N	N	N	N
20 Castro	N	Y	Y	Y	Y	Y	N
21 **Smith**	Y	N	N	N	N	N	N
22 **Olson**	Y	N	N	N	N	N	N
23 **Hurd**	Y	Y	N	N	N	N	N
24 **Marchant**	Y	N	N	N	N	N	N
25 **Williams**	Y	N	N	N	N	N	N
26 **Burgess**	Y	N	N	N	N	N	Y
27 **Farenthold**	Y	N	N	N	N	N	Y
28 Cuellar	Y	Y	Y	Y	Y	Y	Y
29 Green, G.	N	Y	Y	Y	Y	Y	Y
30 Johnson, E.B.	N	Y	Y	Y	Y	Y	Y
31 **Carter**	Y	N	N	N	N	N	N
32 **Sessions**	Y	N	N	N	N	N	N
33 Veasey	N	Y	Y	Y	Y	Y	N
34 Vela	N	Y	Y	Y	Y	Y	Y
35 Doggett	N	Y	Y	Y	Y	Y	N
36 **Babin**	Y	N	N	N	N	N	N
UTAH							
1 **Bishop**	Y	Y	N	N	Y	N	Y
2 **Stewart**	Y	N	N	N	N	N	N
4 **Love**	Y	N	N	N	Y	N	N
VERMONT							
AL Welch	N	Y	Y	Y	Y	Y	N
VIRGINIA							
1 **Wittman**	Y	N	N	N	N	N	N
2 **Taylor**	Y	N	N	N	Y	N	N
3 Scott	N	Y	Y	Y	Y	Y	N
4 McEachin	N	Y	Y	Y	Y	Y	N
5 **Garrett**	?	?	?	?	?	?	?
6 **Goodlatte**	Y	N	N	N	N	N	N
7 **Brat**	Y	N	N	N	N	N	N
8 Beyer	N	Y	N	Y	Y	Y	N
9 **Griffith**	Y	N	N	N	N	N	Y
10 **Comstock**	Y	N	N	N	N	N	N
11 Connolly	N	Y	Y	Y	Y	Y	N
WASHINGTON							
1 DelBene	N	Y	Y	Y	Y	Y	Y
2 Larsen	N	Y	Y	Y	Y	Y	Y
3 **Herrera Beutler**	Y	Y	N	Y	Y	N	Y
4 **Newhouse**	Y	N	N	N	N	N	Y
5 **McMorris Rodgers**	Y	N	N	N	N	N	Y
6 Kilmer	N	Y	Y	Y	Y	Y	N
7 Jayapal	N	Y	Y	Y	Y	Y	N
8 **Reichert**	N	Y	N	N	Y	Y	Y
9 Smith	N	Y	Y	Y	Y	Y	Y
10 Heck	N	Y	Y	Y	Y	Y	N
WEST VIRGINIA							
1 **McKinley**	Y	N	N	N	Y	Y	Y
2 **Mooney**	Y	Y	N	N	Y	Y	Y
3 **Jenkins**	Y	N	N	N	Y	Y	Y
WISCONSIN							
1 **Ryan**							
2 Pocan	N	Y	Y	Y	Y	Y	N
3 Kind	N	Y	Y	Y	Y	Y	Y
4 Moore	N	Y	Y	Y	Y	Y	N
5 **Sensenbrenner**	Y	Y	N	N	Y	Y	N
6 **Grothman**	Y	N	N	N	N	N	N
7 **Duffy**	Y	N	N	N	N	N	N
8 **Gallagher**	Y	N	N	N	Y	N	Y
WYOMING							
AL **Cheney**	Y	N	N	N	N	N	Y

⦀ HOUSE VOTES

VOTE NUMBER

505. HR 3354. FISCAL 2018 OMNIBUS APPROPRIATIONS LEGISLATIVE VEHICLE/PEER SUPPORT PROGRAMS. Lujan, D-N.M., amendment that would decrease and then increase funding for the Office of the Secretary of the Department of Health and Human Services by $2 million (related to peer support programs). Adopted in Committee of the Whole 213-205 : R 23-205; D 190-0. Sept. 13, 2017.

506. HR 3354. FISCAL 2018 OMNIBUS APPROPRIATIONS LEGISLATIVE VEHICLE/ACADEMIC YEAR FUNDING, 2018-2019. Lowey, D-N.Y., for De-Lauro, D-Conn., amendment that would increase funding for school improvement activities by $100 million, would increase funding for school improvement for the academic year 2018-2019 by $100 million, would increase funding for integrated student supports and specialized instructional support services by $100 million, and would decrease funding for the Department of Management of the Department of Education by $100 million. Adopted in Committee of the Whole 228-188 : R 39-187; D 189-1. Sept. 13, 2017.

507. HR 3354. FISCAL 2018 OMNIBUS APPROPRIATIONS LEGISLATIVE VEHICLE/MAGNET SCHOOLS. Courtney, D-Conn., amendment that would increase, then decrease, funding for education innovation and improvement by $1.2 million (related to magnet schools). Rejected in Committee of the Whole 204-212 : R 19-208; D 185-4. Sept. 13, 2017.

508. HR 3354. FISCAL 2018 OMNIBUS APPROPRIATIONS LEGISLATIVE VEHICLE/ADULT EDUCATION. Lewis, R-Minn., amendment that would increase funding for adult education by $70.2 million and would decrease funding for higher education by the same amount. Rejected in Committee of the Whole 153-263 : R 149-77; D 4-186. Sept. 13, 2017.

509. HR 3354. FISCAL 2018 OMNIBUS APPROPRIATIONS LEGISLATIVE VEHICLE/DEPARTMENT OF EDUCATION FUNDING REDUCTION. Grothman, R-Wis., amendment that would decrease funding for the Student Aid Administration by $34 million, would decrease funding for the Department of Education's program administration by $8.6 million, would decrease funding for the Office of Inspector General of the Department of Education by $1.1 million, and would transfer the balance of the saving to the spending reduction account. Rejected in Committee of the Whole 131-285 : R 131-96; D 0-189. Sept. 13, 2017.

510. HR 3354. FISCAL 2018 OMNIBUS APPROPRIATIONS LEGISLATIVE VEHICLE/NATIONAL LABOR RELATIONS BOARD. Grothman, R-Wis., amendment decrease the salaries and expenses of the National Labor Relations Board by $99 million and would transfer the savings to the spending reduction account. Rejected in Committee of the Whole 175-241 : R 175-52; D 0-189. Sept. 13, 2017.

511. HR 3354. FISCAL 2018 OMNIBUS APPROPRIATIONS LEGISLATIVE VEHICLE/COAL MINE SAFETY AND HEALTH. Meadows, R-N.C., amendment that would reduce the funding for the Coal Mine Safety and Health program by 10 percent. Rejected in Committee of the Whole 178-238 : R 177-49; D 1-189. Sept. 13, 2017.

	505	506	507	508	509	510	511
ALABAMA							
1 Byrne	N	N	N	Y	Y	Y	N
2 Roby	N	N	N	N	N	Y	Y
3 Rogers	N	N	N	N	Y	N	Y
4 Aderholt	N	N	N	N	N	Y	Y
5 Brooks	N	N	N	Y	Y	Y	Y
6 Palmer	N	N	N	Y	Y	Y	Y
7 Sewell	Y	Y	Y	N	N	N	N
ALASKA							
AL Young	N	Y	N	N	N	N	N
ARIZONA							
1 O'Halleran	Y	Y	Y	N	N	N	N
2 McSally	Y	N	N	N	N	Y	N
3 Grijalva	Y	Y	Y	N	N	N	N
4 Gosar	N	N	N	Y	Y	Y	Y
5 Biggs	N	N	N	Y	Y	Y	Y
6 Schweikert	N	N	Y	Y	Y	Y	Y
7 Gallego	Y	Y	Y	N	N	N	N
8 Franks	N	N	N	Y	Y	Y	Y
9 Sinema	Y	Y	Y	N	N	N	Y
ARKANSAS							
1 Crawford	N	N	N	N	Y	Y	Y
2 Hill	N	N	N	N	Y	Y	Y
3 Womack	N	N	N	N	N	Y	Y
4 Westerman	N	N	N	Y	Y	Y	Y
CALIFORNIA							
1 LaMalfa	N	N	N	N	Y	Y	Y
2 Huffman	Y	Y	Y	N	N	N	N
3 Garamendi	Y	Y	Y	N	N	N	N
4 McClintock	N	N	N	Y	Y	Y	Y
5 Thompson	Y	Y	Y	N	N	N	N
6 Matsui	Y	Y	Y	N	N	N	N
7 Bera	Y	Y	Y	N	N	N	N
8 Cook	N	N	N	N	N	N	Y
9 McNerney	Y	Y	Y	N	N	N	N
10 Denham	N	N	N	N	N	N	Y
11 DeSaulnier	Y	Y	Y	N	N	N	N
12 Pelosi	Y	Y	Y	N	N	N	N
13 Lee	Y	Y	Y	N	N	N	N
14 Speier	Y	Y	Y	N	N	N	N
15 Swalwell	Y	Y	Y	N	N	N	N
16 Costa	?	?	?	?	?	?	?
17 Khanna	Y	Y	Y	N	N	N	N
18 Eshoo	Y	Y	Y	N	N	N	N
19 Lofgren	Y	Y	?	N	N	N	N
20 Panetta	Y	Y	Y	N	N	N	N
21 Valadao	N	N	N	N	N	N	Y
22 Nunes	N	N	N	N	N	N	N
23 McCarthy	N	N	N	Y	Y	Y	N
24 Carbajal	Y	Y	N	N	N	N	N
25 Knight	N	N	N	N	N	N	Y
26 Brownley	Y	Y	Y	N	N	N	N
27 Chu	Y	Y	Y	N	N	N	N
28 Schiff	Y	Y	Y	N	N	N	N
29 Cardenas	Y	Y	Y	N	N	N	N
30 Sherman	Y	Y	Y	N	N	N	N
31 Aguilar	Y	Y	Y	N	N	N	N
32 Napolitano	Y	Y	Y	N	N	N	N
33 Lieu	Y	Y	Y	N	N	N	N
34 Gomez	Y	Y	Y	N	N	N	N
35 Torres	Y	Y	Y	N	N	N	N
36 Ruiz	Y	Y	Y	N	N	N	N
37 Bass	Y	Y	Y	N	N	N	N
38 Sánchez, Linda	Y	Y	Y	N	N	N	N
39 Royce	N	N	N	Y	Y	Y	N
40 Roybal-Allard	Y	Y	Y	N	N	N	N
41 Takano	Y	Y	Y	N	N	N	N
42 Calvert	N	N	N	N	N	N	Y
43 Waters	Y	Y	Y	N	N	N	N
44 Barragan	Y	Y	Y	N	N	N	N
45 Walters	N	N	N	Y	Y	Y	Y
46 Correa	Y	Y	Y	N	N	N	N
47 Lowenthal	Y	Y	Y	N	N	N	N
48 Rohrabacher	N	N	N	Y	Y	Y	Y
49 Issa	N	N	N	N	N	Y	N
50 Hunter	N	N	N	Y	Y	Y	Y
51 Vargas	Y	Y	Y	N	N	N	N
52 Peters	Y	Y	Y	N	N	N	N
53 Davis	Y	Y	Y	N	N	N	N

	505	506	507	508	509	510	511
COLORADO							
1 DeGette	Y	Y	Y	N	N	N	N
2 Polis	Y	Y	Y	N	N	N	N
3 Tipton	N	Y	Y	Y	N	Y	Y
4 Buck	Y	N	N	Y	Y	Y	Y
5 Lamborn	N	N	N	Y	Y	Y	Y
6 Coffman	N	N	N	N	N	Y	N
7 Perlmutter	Y	Y	Y	N	N	N	N
CONNECTICUT							
1 Larson	Y	Y	Y	N	N	N	N
2 Courtney	Y	Y	Y	N	N	N	N
3 DeLauro	+	+	+	-	-	-	-
4 Himes	Y	Y	Y	N	N	N	N
5 Esty	Y	Y	Y	N	N	N	N
DELAWARE							
AL Blunt Rochester	Y	Y	Y	N	N	N	N
FLORIDA							
1 Gaetz	N	Y	N	N	Y	Y	Y
2 Dunn	N	N	N	Y	Y	Y	Y
3 Yoho	N	N	N	Y	Y	Y	Y
4 Rutherford	N	N	N	N	Y	N	Y
5 Lawson	?	?	?	?	?	?	?
6 DeSantis	N	N	N	Y	Y	Y	Y
7 Murphy	Y	Y	N	N	N	N	N
8 Posey	?	?	?	?	?	?	?
9 Soto	Y	Y	Y	N	N	N	N
10 Demings	Y	Y	Y	N	N	N	N
11 Webster	N	N	N	Y	Y	Y	Y
12 Bilirakis	N	N	N	Y	Y	Y	Y
13 Crist	Y	Y	Y	N	N	N	N
14 Castor	Y	Y	Y	N	N	N	N
15 Ross	?	?	?	?	?	?	?
16 Buchanan	N	N	N	Y	Y	Y	Y
17 Rooney, T.	N	N	N	N	N	N	N
18 Mast	Y	Y	N	Y	N	Y	N
19 Rooney, F.	?	?	?	?	?	?	?
20 Hastings	Y	Y	Y	N	N	N	N
21 Frankel	Y	Y	Y	N	N	N	N
22 Deutch	Y	Y	Y	N	N	N	N
23 Wasserman Schultz	Y	Y	Y	N	N	N	N
24 Wilson	Y	Y	Y	N	N	N	N
25 Diaz-Balart	?	?	?	?	?	?	?
26 Curbelo	Y	Y	Y	N	N	N	N
27 Ros-Lehtinen	?	?	?	?	?	?	?
GEORGIA							
1 Carter	N	N	N	Y	Y	Y	Y
2 Bishop	Y	Y	Y	N	N	N	N
3 Ferguson	N	N	N	Y	N	Y	Y
4 Johnson	Y	Y	Y	N	N	N	N
5 Lewis	Y	Y	Y	N	N	N	N
6 Handel	N	N	N	Y	Y	Y	Y
7 Woodall	N	N	N	Y	Y	Y	Y
8 Scott, A.	N	N	N	Y	Y	Y	Y
9 Collins	N	N	N	Y	Y	Y	Y
10 Hice	N	N	N	Y	Y	Y	Y
11 Loudermilk	?	?	?	?	?	?	?
12 Allen	N	N	N	Y	Y	Y	Y
13 Scott, D.	Y	Y	Y	N	N	N	N
14 Graves	N	N	N	Y	Y	Y	Y
HAWAII							
1 Hanabusa	Y	Y	Y	N	N	N	N
2 Gabbard	Y	Y	Y	N	N	N	N
IDAHO							
1 Labrador	N	N	N	N	Y	Y	Y
2 Simpson	N	N	N	N	N	N	N
ILLINOIS							
1 Rush	Y	Y	Y	N	N	N	N
2 Kelly	Y	Y	Y	N	N	N	N
3 Lipinski	Y	Y	Y	N	N	N	N
4 Gutierrez	Y	Y	Y	N	N	N	N
5 Quigley	Y	Y	Y	N	N	N	N
6 Roskam	N	N	N	N	N	N	Y
7 Davis, D.	Y	Y	Y	N	N	N	N
8 Krishnamoorthi	Y	Y	Y	N	N	N	N
9 Schakowsky	Y	Y	Y	N	N	N	N
10 Schneider	Y	Y	Y	N	N	N	N
11 Foster	Y	Y	Y	N	N	N	N
12 Bost	N	N	N	N	N	N	Y
13 Davis, R.	N	N	N	Y	N	N	N
14 Hultgren	N	N	N	Y	N	Y	Y
15 Shimkus	N	N	N	Y	N	N	Y

	505	506	507	508	509	510	511
16 **Kinzinger**	N	N	N	N	N	N	N
17 Bustos	Y	Y	Y	N	N	N	N
18 **LaHood**	N	N	N	Y	Y	Y	Y
INDIANA							
1 Visclosky	Y	Y	Y	N	N	N	N
2 **Walorski**	N	N	N	Y	N	Y	Y
3 **Banks**	N	N	N	Y	Y	Y	Y
4 **Rokita**	N	N	N	Y	Y	Y	Y
5 **Brooks**	Y	Y	N	Y	N	Y	N
6 **Messer**	N	N	N	Y	Y	Y	Y
7 Carson	Y	Y	Y	N	N	N	N
8 **Bucshon**	N	N	N	N	N	Y	Y
9 **Hollingsworth**	N	Y	N	Y	Y	Y	Y
IOWA							
1 **Blum**	N	Y	N	P	Y	Y	Y
2 Loebsack	Y	Y	Y	N	N	N	N
3 **Young**	N	N	N	Y	Y	Y	Y
4 **King**	N	N	N	Y	Y	Y	Y
KANSAS							
1 **Marshall**	N	N	N	Y	Y	Y	Y
2 **Jenkins**	N	N	N	N	Y	Y	N
3 **Yoder**	N	N	N	Y	N	Y	N
4 **Estes**	N	N	N	Y	Y	Y	Y
KENTUCKY							
1 **Comer**	N	N	N	Y	Y	Y	Y
2 **Guthrie**	N	N	N	Y	Y	Y	N
3 Yarmuth	Y	Y	Y	N	N	N	N
4 **Massie**	N	N	N	Y	Y	Y	Y
5 **Rogers**	N	Y	N	N	N	N	Y
6 **Barr**	N	Y	N	Y	Y	Y	Y
LOUISIANA							
1 **Scalise**	?	?	?	?	?	?	?
2 Richmond	Y	Y	Y	N	N	N	N
3 **Higgins**	N	N	N	Y	N	Y	Y
4 **Johnson**	N	Y	N	Y	Y	Y	Y
5 **Abraham**	N	N	N	Y	N	Y	Y
6 **Graves**	N	N	N	Y	Y	Y	Y
MAINE							
1 Pingree	Y	Y	Y	N	N	N	N
2 **Poliquin**	N	Y	N	Y	N	N	Y
MARYLAND							
1 **Harris**	N	N	N	Y	Y	Y	Y
2 Ruppersberger	Y	Y	Y	N	N	N	N
3 Sarbanes	Y	Y	Y	N	N	N	N
4 Brown	Y	Y	Y	N	N	N	N
5 Hoyer	Y	Y	Y	N	N	N	N
6 Delaney	Y	Y	Y	N	N	N	N
7 Cummings	Y	Y	Y	N	N	N	N
8 Raskin	Y	Y	Y	N	N	N	N
MASSACHUSETTS							
1 Neal	Y	Y	Y	N	N	N	N
2 McGovern	Y	Y	Y	N	N	N	N
3 Tsongas	Y	Y	Y	N	N	N	N
4 Kennedy	Y	Y	Y	N	N	N	N
5 Clark	Y	Y	Y	N	N	N	N
6 Moulton	Y	Y	Y	N	N	N	N
7 Capuano	Y	Y	Y	N	N	N	N
8 Lynch	Y	Y	N	N	N	N	N
9 Keating	Y	Y	Y	N	N	N	N
MICHIGAN							
1 **Bergman**	N	N	N	Y	Y	Y	N
2 **Huizenga**	N	N	N	N	Y	Y	P
3 **Amash**	N	N	N	N	Y	Y	Y
4 **Moolenaar**	N	N	N	Y	N	N	N
5 Kildee	Y	Y	Y	N	N	N	N
6 **Upton**	Y	Y	N	N	N	Y	N
7 **Walberg**	N	N	N	Y	N	Y	Y
8 **Bishop**	N	N	N	Y	Y	Y	Y
9 Levin	Y	Y	Y	N	N	N	N
10 **Mitchell**	N	N	N	Y	N	Y	Y
11 **Trott**	Y	N	N	Y	N	Y	N
12 Dingell	Y	Y	Y	N	N	N	N
13 Conyers	Y	Y	Y	N	N	N	N
14 Lawrence	Y	Y	Y	N	N	N	N
MINNESOTA							
1 Walz	Y	Y	Y	N	N	N	N
2 **Lewis**	N	N	N	Y	Y	Y	Y
3 **Paulsen**	Y	N	N	N	N	Y	N
4 McCollum	Y	Y	Y	N	N	N	N

	505	506	507	508	509	510	511
5 Ellison	Y	Y	Y	N	N	N	N
6 **Emmer**	N	N	N	Y	Y	Y	Y
7 Peterson	Y	Y	Y	Y	N	N	N
8 Nolan	Y	Y	Y	N	N	N	N
MISSISSIPPI							
1 **Kelly**	N	N	N	Y	Y	Y	Y
2 Thompson	Y	Y	Y	N	N	N	N
3 **Harper**	N	N	N	N	N	Y	N
4 **Palazzo**	N	N	N	Y	Y	Y	Y
MISSOURI							
1 Clay	Y	Y	Y	N	N	N	N
2 **Wagner**	N	N	N	Y	Y	Y	Y
3 **Luetkemeyer**	N	Y	Y	Y	N	Y	Y
4 **Hartzler**	N	N	N	N	Y	Y	Y
5 Cleaver	Y	Y	Y	N	N	N	N
6 **Graves**	–	–	+	+	+	+	+
7 **Long**	N	N	N	N	Y	Y	Y
8 **Smith**	N	N	N	N	Y	Y	Y
MONTANA							
AL **Gianforte**	N	N	N	Y	Y	Y	Y
NEBRASKA							
1 **Fortenberry**	N	N	N	N	N	N	N
2 **Bacon**	N	N	N	N	Y	Y	Y
3 **Smith**	N	N	N	N	Y	Y	Y
NEVADA							
1 Titus	Y	Y	Y	N	N	N	N
2 **Amodei**	N	N	N	N	N	N	Y
3 Rosen	Y	Y	Y	N	N	N	N
4 Kihuen	Y	Y	Y	N	N	N	N
NEW HAMPSHIRE							
1 Shea-Porter	Y	Y	Y	N	N	N	N
2 Kuster	Y	Y	Y	N	N	N	N
NEW JERSEY							
1 Norcross	Y	Y	Y	N	N	N	N
2 **LoBiondo**	N	Y	Y	N	N	N	N
3 **MacArthur**	N	N	N	N	N	N	N
4 **Smith**	N	Y	Y	N	N	N	N
5 Gottheimer	Y	Y	Y	N	N	N	N
6 Pallone	Y	Y	Y	N	N	N	N
7 **Lance**	N	Y	Y	N	N	N	N
8 Slres	Y	Y	Y	N	N	N	N
9 Pascrell	Y	Y	Y	N	?	N	N
10 Payne	Y	Y	Y	N	N	N	N
11 **Frelinghuysen**	N	N	N	N	N	N	Y
12 Watson Coleman	Y	Y	Y	N	N	N	N
NEW MEXICO							
1 Lujan Grisham	Y	Y	Y	N	N	N	N
2 **Pearce**	Y	N	N	N	Y	Y	Y
3 Luján	Y	Y	Y	N	N	N	N
NEW YORK							
1 **Zeldin**	N	Y	N	Y	N	Y	Y
2 **King**	N	Y	N	N	N	N	N
3 Suozzi	Y	Y	Y	N	N	N	N
4 Rice	Y	Y	Y	N	N	N	N
5 Meeks	Y	Y	Y	N	N	N	N
6 Meng	Y	Y	Y	N	N	N	N
7 Velázquez	Y	Y	Y	N	N	N	N
8 Jeffries	Y	Y	Y	N	N	N	N
9 Clarke	Y	Y	Y	N	N	N	N
10 Nadler	Y	Y	Y	N	N	N	N
11 **Donovan**	N	Y	N	N	N	N	N
12 Maloney, C.	Y	Y	Y	N	N	N	N
13 Espaillat	Y	Y	Y	N	N	N	N
14 Crowley	Y	Y	Y	N	N	N	N
15 Serrano	Y	Y	Y	N	N	N	N
16 Engel	Y	Y	Y	N	N	N	N
17 Lowey	Y	Y	Y	N	N	N	N
18 Maloney, S.P.	Y	Y	Y	N	N	N	N
19 **Faso**	N	Y	N	Y	N	N	N
20 Tonko	Y	Y	Y	N	N	N	N
21 **Stefanik**	N	Y	N	N	N	N	N
22 **Tenney**	N	Y	N	Y	N	N	Y
23 **Reed**	Y	N	N	Y	N	N	N
24 **Katko**	Y	Y	Y	Y	N	N	N
25 Slaughter	Y	Y	Y	N	N	N	N
26 Higgins	Y	Y	Y	N	N	N	N
27 **Collins**	N	N	N	N	N	N	Y
NORTH CAROLINA							
1 Butterfield	Y	Y	Y	N	N	N	N
2 **Holding**	N	N	N	Y	Y	Y	Y
3 **Jones**	Y	Y	N	Y	Y	Y	Y
4 Price	Y	Y	Y	N	N	N	N

	505	506	507	508	509	510	511
5 **Foxx**	N	N	N	Y	N	N	N
6 **Walker**	N	N	N	Y	Y	Y	Y
7 **Rouzer**	N	N	N	Y	Y	Y	Y
8 **Hudson**	N	N	N	Y	Y	Y	Y
9 **Pittenger**	N	N	N	Y	Y	Y	N
10 **McHenry**	N	N	N	Y	N	Y	Y
11 **Meadows**	N	Y	N	N	Y	Y	Y
12 Adams	Y	Y	Y	N	N	N	N
13 **Budd**	N	N	N	Y	Y	Y	Y
NORTH DAKOTA							
AL **Cramer**	N	N	N	Y	N	N	Y
OHIO							
1 **Chabot**	N	N	N	Y	Y	Y	Y
2 **Wenstrup**	Y	N	N	Y	Y	Y	Y
3 Beatty	Y	Y	Y	N	N	N	N
4 **Jordan**	N	N	N	Y	Y	Y	Y
5 **Latta**	N	N	N	Y	N	Y	Y
6 **Johnson**	N	N	N	N	Y	Y	Y
7 **Gibbs**	N	N	N	Y	Y	Y	Y
8 **Davidson**	N	N	N	Y	Y	Y	Y
9 Kaptur	Y	Y	Y	N	N	N	N
10 **Turner**	N	N	N	Y	N	N	Y
11 Fudge	Y	Y	Y	N	N	N	N
12 **Tiberi**	?	?	?	?	?	?	?
13 Ryan	Y	Y	Y	N	N	N	N
14 **Joyce**	N	N	N	N	N	N	Y
15 **Stivers**	N	Y	N	N	N	N	Y
16 **Renacci**	N	N	N	Y	Y	Y	Y
OKLAHOMA							
1 **Bridenstine**	?	?	?	?	?	?	?
2 **Mullin**	N	N	N	N	Y	Y	Y
3 **Lucas**	N	N	N	N	N	N	Y
4 **Cole**	N	N	N	N	N	N	Y
5 **Russell**	N	N	N	Y	Y	Y	Y
OREGON							
1 Bonamici	Y	Y	Y	N	N	N	N
2 **Walden**	Y	N	N	N	N	N	N
3 Blumenauer	Y	Y	Y	N	N	N	N
4 DeFazio	Y	Y	Y	N	N	N	N
5 Schrader	Y	Y	Y	N	N	?	N
PENNSYLVANIA							
1 Brady	Y	Y	Y	N	N	N	N
2 Evans	Y	Y	Y	N	N	N	N
3 **Kelly**	N	N	N	Y	N	Y	Y
4 **Perry**	N	N	N	Y	Y	Y	Y
5 **Thompson**	N	Y	N	N	N	N	N
6 **Costello**	Y	Y	Y	Y	N	N	N
7 **Meehan**	N	N	N	N	N	N	N
8 **Fitzpatrick**	Y	Y	Y	Y	N	N	N
9 **Shuster**	N	N	N	N	N	N	Y
10 **Marino**	N	Y	N	N	N	N	Y
11 **Barletta**	N	Y	N	Y	N	N	Y
12 **Rothfus**	N	N	N	N	Y	Y	Y
13 Boyle	Y	Y	Y	N	N	N	N
14 Doyle	Y	Y	Y	N	N	N	N
15 **Dent**	N	Y	N	N	N	N	N
16 **Smucker**	N	N	N	Y	N	Y	Y
17 Cartwright	Y	Y	Y	N	N	N	N
18 **Murphy**	N	N	N	Y	N	N	Y
RHODE ISLAND							
1 Cicilline	Y	Y	Y	N	N	N	N
2 Langevin	Y	Y	Y	N	N	N	N
SOUTH CAROLINA							
1 **Sanford**	N	N	N	Y	Y	Y	Y
2 **Wilson**	N	N	N	N	Y	N	Y
3 **Duncan**	N	N	N	Y	Y	Y	Y
4 **Gowdy**	N	N	N	Y	N	Y	Y
5 **Norman**	N	N	N	N	Y	Y	Y
6 Clyburn	?	?	?	?	?	?	?
7 **Rice**	N	Y	N	Y	Y	Y	Y
SOUTH DAKOTA							
AL **Noem**	N	N	N	Y	Y	Y	Y
TENNESSEE							
1 **Roe**	N	N	N	Y	Y	Y	Y
2 **Duncan**	N	N	N	Y	Y	Y	Y
3 **Fleischmann**	N	N	N	N	N	Y	Y
4 **DesJarlais**	N	N	N	Y	Y	Y	Y
5 Cooper	Y	Y	N	N	N	N	N
6 **Black**	N	?	?	?	?	?	?
7 **Blackburn**	N	N	N	Y	Y	Y	Y
8 **Kustoff**	N	N	N	Y	Y	Y	Y
9 Cohen	Y	Y	Y	N	N	N	N

	505	506	507	508	509	510	511
TEXAS							
1 **Gohmert**	N	N	N	N	Y	Y	Y
2 **Poe**	N	N	Y	Y	Y	Y	Y
3 **Johnson, S.**	N	N	N	Y	Y	Y	Y
4 **Ratcliffe**	N	N	N	N	Y	Y	Y
5 **Hensarling**	N	N	N	Y	Y	Y	N
6 **Barton**	N	N	N	Y	N	Y	Y
7 **Culberson**	N	N	N	Y	Y	Y	Y
8 **Brady**	N	N	N	Y	N	Y	Y
9 Green, A.	Y	Y	Y	N	N	N	N
10 **McCaul**	N	N	Y	Y	Y	Y	Y
11 **Conaway**	N	N	N	N	Y	Y	Y
12 **Granger**	N	N	N	Y	N	Y	Y
13 **Thornberry**	N	N	N	N	Y	Y	Y
14 **Weber**	N	N	Y	Y	Y	Y	Y
15 Gonzalez	Y	Y	Y	N	N	N	N
16 O'Rourke	Y	Y	Y	N	N	N	N
17 **Flores**	N	N	N	Y	Y	Y	Y
18 Jackson Lee	Y	Y	Y	N	N	N	N
19 **Arrington**	N	N	N	Y	Y	Y	Y
20 Castro	Y	Y	Y	N	N	N	N
21 **Smith**	N	Y	Y	Y	Y	Y	Y
22 **Olson**	N	N	Y	Y	Y	Y	Y
23 **Hurd**	Y	Y	N	N	N	Y	Y
24 **Marchant**	N	N	N	Y	Y	Y	Y
25 **Williams**	N	N	N	Y	N	Y	Y
26 **Burgess**	N	N	N	Y	Y	Y	Y
27 **Farenthold**	N	N	N	Y	Y	Y	Y
28 Cuellar	Y	Y	Y	N	N	N	N
29 Green, G.	Y	Y	Y	N	N	N	N
30 Johnson, E.B.	Y	Y	Y	N	N	N	N
31 **Carter**	N	N	N	Y	N	Y	Y
32 **Sessions**	N	N	N	Y	Y	Y	Y
33 Veasey	Y	Y	Y	N	N	N	N
34 Vela	Y	Y	Y	Y	N	N	N
35 Doggett	Y	Y	Y	N	N	N	N
36 **Babin**	N	N	N	Y	Y	Y	N
UTAH							
1 **Bishop**	N	N	N	N	Y	Y	Y
2 **Stewart**	N	N	N	N	Y	Y	Y
4 **Love**	N	N	N	N	Y	Y	Y
VERMONT							
AL Welch	Y	Y	Y	N	N	N	N
VIRGINIA							
1 **Wittman**	N	N	N	Y	Y	Y	Y
2 **Taylor**	N	Y	N	Y	Y	Y	Y
3 Scott	Y	Y	Y	N	N	N	N
4 McEachin	Y	Y	Y	N	N	N	N
5 **Garrett**	?	?	?	?	?	?	?
6 **Goodlatte**	N	N	N	Y	Y	Y	Y
7 **Brat**	N	?	N	Y	Y	Y	Y
8 Beyer	Y	N	Y	N	N	N	N
9 **Griffith**	N	N	N	Y	Y	Y	Y
10 **Comstock**	N	N	N	N	N	Y	N
11 Connolly	Y	Y	Y	N	N	N	N
WASHINGTON							
1 DelBene	Y	Y	Y	N	N	N	N
2 Larsen	Y	Y	Y	N	N	N	N
3 **Herrera Beutler**	Y	Y	Y	Y	N	N	N
4 **Newhouse**	N	N	N	N	N	Y	Y
5 **McMorris Rodgers**	N	N	N	Y	Y	Y	Y
6 Kilmer	Y	Y	Y	N	N	N	N
7 Jayapal	Y	Y	Y	N	N	N	N
8 **Reichert**	Y	Y	Y	N	N	N	N
9 Smith	Y	Y	Y	N	N	N	N
10 Heck	Y	Y	Y	N	N	N	N
WEST VIRGINIA							
1 **McKinley**	N	N	Y	N	N	N	Y
2 **Mooney**	Y	N	N	Y	Y	Y	Y
3 **Jenkins**	Y	N	Y	N	N	Y	Y
WISCONSIN							
1 **Ryan**							
2 Pocan	Y	Y	Y	N	N	N	N
3 Kind	Y	Y	Y	N	N	N	N
4 Moore	Y	Y	Y	N	N	N	N
5 **Sensenbrenner**	N	N	N	Y	Y	Y	Y
6 **Grothman**	N	N	N	Y	Y	Y	Y
7 **Duffy**	N	N	N	Y	N	Y	Y
8 **Gallagher**	N	N	N	Y	Y	Y	Y
WYOMING							
AL **Cheney**	N	N	N	N	N	Y	Y

VOTE NUMBER

512. HR 3354. FISCAL 2018 OMNIBUS APPROPRIATIONS LEGISLATIVE VEHICLE/REPRESENTATION-CASE PROCEDURES RULE ENFORCEMENT. Walberg, R-Mich., amendment that would prohibit any funds appropriated by the bill from being used to implement a 2014 National Labor Relations Board final rule governing representation-case procedures. Adopted in Committee of the Whole 221-196 : R 220-7; D 1-189. Sept. 13, 2017.

513. HR 3354. FISCAL 2018 OMNIBUS APPROPRIATIONS LEGISLATIVE VEHICLE/ONE PERCENT CUT. Blackburn, R-Tenn., amendment that would provide for a one percent cut to all funds appropriated by the bill to the Labor Department, Health and Human Services Department and the Education Department. Rejected in Committee of the Whole 156-260 : R 156-70; D 0-190. Sept. 13, 2017.

514. HR 3354. FISCAL 2018 OMNIBUS APPROPRIATIONS LEGISLATIVE VEHICLE/FAIR LABOR STANDARDS ACT VIOLATORS. Ellison, D-Minn., amendment that would prohibit funding appropriated by the bill from being used to enter into contracts with federal contractors who have willfully or repeatedly violated the Fair Labor Standards Act. Rejected in Committee of the Whole 191-226 : R 3-224; D 188-2. Sept. 13, 2017.

515. HR 3354. FISCAL 2018 OMNIBUS APPROPRIATIONS LEGISLATIVE VEHICLE/WORKPLACE INJURY RULE. Gibbs, R-Ohio, amendment that would prohibit funds appropriated by the bill from being using to implement, administer or enforce Department of Labor regulations concerned with workplace injuries and illness, that were published May 12, 2016. Adopted in Committee of the Whole 215-201 : R 214-13; D 1-188. Sept. 13, 2017.

516. HR 3697. CRIMINAL GANG MEMBERS/RECOMMIT. Beyer, D-Va., motion to recommit the bill to the House Judiciary Committee with instructions to report it back immediately with an amendment that would prohibit the bill's provisions from being used to authorize the deportation of an undocumented immigrant for action taken on behalf of a religious organization with the primary purpose of providing humanitarian aid. Motion rejected 184-220 : R 0-220; D 184-0. Sept. 14, 2017.

517. HR 3697. CRIMINAL GANG MEMBERS/PASSAGE. Passage of the bill that would define a criminal gang as a group of five or more persons that has the primary purpose of the commission of one or more certain criminal offenses and would prohibit individuals defined as foreign criminal gang members from entering the United States. It would prohibit a criminal gang member, who is not a U.S. citizen or U.S. national, from being eligible for certain immigration benefits such as asylum, special immigrant juvenile status, and temporary protected status. Passed 233-175 : R 222-1; D 11-174. Sept. 14, 2017.

518. HR 3354. FISCAL 2018 OMNIBUS APPROPRIATIONS LEGISLATIVE VEHICLE/DC REPRODUCTIVE HEALTH LAW. Palmer, R-Ala., amendment that would prohibit any funds appropriated by the bill from being used to implement the District of Columbia's Reproductive Health Non-Discrimination Amendment Act. Adopted in Committee of the Whole 214-194 : R 212-11; D 2-183. Sept. 14, 2017.

	512	513	514	515	516	517	518
ALABAMA							
1 Byrne	Y	Y	N	Y	N	Y	Y
2 Roby	Y	N	N	Y	N	Y	Y
3 Rogers	Y	Y	N	Y	N	Y	Y
4 Aderholt	Y	N	N	Y	N	Y	Y
5 Brooks	Y	Y	N	Y	N	Y	Y
6 Palmer	Y	Y	N	Y	N	Y	Y
7 Sewell	N	N	Y	N	Y	N	N
ALASKA							
AL Young	N	N	N	N	N	Y	Y
ARIZONA							
1 O'Halleran	N	N	Y	N	Y	Y	N
2 McSally	Y	Y	N	Y	N	Y	N
3 Grijalva	N	N	Y	N	Y	N	N
4 Gosar	Y	Y	N	Y	?	?	?
5 Biggs	Y	Y	N	Y	N	Y	Y
6 Schweikert	Y	Y	N	Y	N	Y	Y
7 Gallego	N	N	Y	N	Y	N	N
8 Franks	Y	Y	N	Y	N	Y	Y
9 Sinema	N	N	Y	N	+	Y	N
ARKANSAS							
1 Crawford	Y	Y	N	Y	N	Y	Y
2 Hill	Y	Y	N	Y	N	Y	Y
3 Womack	Y	N	N	Y	N	Y	Y
4 Westerman	Y	Y	N	Y	N	Y	Y
CALIFORNIA							
1 LaMalfa	Y	Y	N	Y	N	Y	Y
2 Huffman	N	N	Y	N	Y	N	N
3 Garamendi	N	N	Y	N	Y	N	N
4 McClintock	Y	Y	N	Y	N	Y	Y
5 Thompson	N	N	Y	N	Y	N	N
6 Matsui	N	N	Y	N	Y	N	N
7 Bera	N	N	Y	N	Y	N	N
8 Cook	Y	N	N	Y	N	Y	Y
9 McNerney	N	N	Y	N	Y	N	N
10 Denham	Y	N	N	Y	N	Y	Y
11 DeSaulnier	N	N	Y	N	Y	N	N
12 Pelosi	N	N	Y	N	Y	?	?
13 Lee	N	N	Y	N	Y	N	N
14 Speier	N	N	Y	N	Y	N	N
15 Swalwell	N	N	Y	N	Y	N	N
16 Costa	?	?	?	?	?	?	?
17 Khanna	N	N	Y	N	Y	N	N
18 Eshoo	N	N	Y	N	Y	N	N
19 Lofgren	N	N	Y	N	Y	N	N
20 Panetta	N	N	Y	N	Y	N	N
21 Valadao	Y	N	N	Y	N	Y	Y
22 Nunes	Y	N	N	Y	N	Y	Y
23 McCarthy	Y	Y	N	Y	N	Y	Y
24 Carbajal	N	N	N	Y	Y	N	N
25 Knight	Y	N	N	Y	N	Y	Y
26 Brownley	N	N	Y	N	Y	N	N
27 Chu	N	N	Y	N	?	N	N
28 Schiff	N	N	Y	N	Y	N	N
29 Cardenas	N	N	Y	N	?	N	N
30 Sherman	N	N	Y	N	Y	N	N
31 Aguilar	N	N	Y	N	Y	N	N
32 Napolitano	N	N	Y	N	Y	N	N
33 Lieu	N	N	Y	N	Y	N	N
34 Gomez	N	N	Y	N	Y	N	N
35 Torres	N	N	Y	N	Y	N	N
36 Ruiz	N	N	Y	N	Y	N	N
37 Bass	N	N	Y	N	Y	N	N
38 Sánchez, Linda	N	N	Y	N	Y	N	N
39 Royce	Y	Y	N	Y	N	Y	Y
40 Roybal-Allard	N	N	Y	N	Y	N	N
41 Takano	N	N	Y	N	Y	N	N
42 Calvert	Y	N	N	Y	N	Y	Y
43 Waters	N	N	Y	N	Y	N	N
44 Barragan	N	N	Y	N	Y	N	N
45 Walters	Y	Y	N	Y	N	Y	Y
46 Correa	N	N	Y	N	Y	N	N
47 Lowenthal	N	N	Y	N	Y	N	N
48 Rohrabacher	Y	Y	N	Y	N	Y	Y
49 Issa	Y	Y	N	Y	N	Y	Y
50 Hunter	Y	Y	N	Y	N	Y	Y
51 Vargas	N	N	Y	N	Y	N	N
52 Peters	N	N	Y	N	Y	N	N
53 Davis	N	N	Y	N	Y	N	N

	512	513	514	515	516	517	518
COLORADO							
1 DeGette	N	N	Y	N	Y	N	N
2 Polis	N	N	Y	N	Y	N	N
3 Tipton	Y	Y	N	Y	N	Y	Y
4 Buck	Y	Y	N	Y	N	Y	Y
5 Lamborn	Y	Y	N	Y	N	Y	Y
6 Coffman	Y	Y	N	Y	N	Y	Y
7 Perlmutter	N	N	Y	N	Y	N	N
CONNECTICUT							
1 Larson	N	N	Y	N	+	–	–
2 Courtney	N	N	Y	N	Y	N	N
3 DeLauro	–	–	+	N	+	–	–
4 Himes	N	N	Y	N	Y	N	N
5 Esty	N	N	Y	N	Y	N	N
DELAWARE							
AL Blunt Rochester	N	N	Y	N	Y	N	N
FLORIDA							
1 Gaetz	Y	Y	N	Y	N	Y	Y
2 Dunn	Y	Y	N	Y	N	Y	Y
3 Yoho	Y	Y	N	Y	–	+	+
4 Rutherford	Y	N	N	Y	–	+	+
5 Lawson	?	?	?	?	?	?	?
6 DeSantis	Y	Y	N	Y	N	Y	Y
7 Murphy	N	N	Y	N	Y	N	N
8 Posey	?	?	?	?	?	?	?
9 Soto	N	N	Y	N	Y	N	N
10 Demings	N	N	Y	N	Y	N	N
11 Webster	Y	Y	N	Y	N	Y	Y
12 Bilirakis	Y	Y	N	Y	N	Y	Y
13 Crist	N	N	Y	N	?	?	?
14 Castor	N	N	Y	N	Y	N	N
15 Ross	?	?	?	?	?	?	?
16 Buchanan	Y	Y	N	Y	N	Y	Y
17 Rooney, T.	Y	N	N	Y	?	?	?
18 Mast	Y	N	Y	N	Y	N	Y
19 Rooney, F.	?	?	?	?	?	?	?
20 Hastings	N	N	Y	N	Y	N	N
21 Frankel	N	N	Y	N	?	?	?
22 Deutch	N	N	Y	N	Y	N	N
23 Wasserman Schultz	N	N	Y	N	Y	N	N
24 Wilson	N	N	Y	N	Y	N	N
25 Diaz-Balart	?	?	?	?	?	?	?
26 Curbelo	Y	N	N	Y	N	Y	N
27 Ros-Lehtinen	?	?	?	?	?	?	?
GEORGIA							
1 Carter	Y	Y	N	Y	–	+	+
2 Bishop	N	N	Y	N	Y	N	N
3 Ferguson	Y	Y	N	Y	N	Y	Y
4 Johnson	N	N	Y	N	Y	N	N
5 Lewis	N	N	Y	N	Y	N	N
6 Handel	Y	Y	N	Y	N	Y	Y
7 Woodall	Y	Y	N	Y	N	Y	Y
8 Scott, A.	Y	Y	N	Y	N	Y	Y
9 Collins	Y	Y	N	Y	N	Y	Y
10 Hice	Y	Y	N	Y	N	Y	Y
11 Loudermilk	?	?	?	?	?	?	?
12 Allen	Y	Y	N	Y	N	Y	Y
13 Scott, D.	N	N	Y	N	Y	N	N
14 Graves	Y	Y	N	Y	N	Y	Y
HAWAII							
1 Hanabusa	N	N	Y	N	Y	N	N
2 Gabbard	N	N	Y	N	Y	N	N
IDAHO							
1 Labrador	Y	Y	N	Y	N	Y	Y
2 Simpson	Y	N	N	Y	N	Y	Y
ILLINOIS							
1 Rush	N	N	Y	N	Y	N	N
2 Kelly	N	N	Y	N	Y	N	N
3 Lipinski	N	N	Y	N	Y	Y	Y
4 Gutierrez	N	N	Y	N	Y	N	N
5 Quigley	N	N	Y	N	Y	N	N
6 Roskam	N	N	Y	N	Y	N	N
7 Davis, D.	N	N	Y	N	Y	N	N
8 Krishnamoorthi	N	N	Y	N	Y	N	N
9 Schakowsky	N	N	Y	N	Y	N	N
10 Schneider	N	N	Y	N	Y	N	N
11 Foster	N	N	Y	N	Y	N	N
12 Bost	Y	N	N	Y	N	Y	Y
13 Davis, R.	Y	N	N	Y	N	Y	Y
14 Hultgren	Y	Y	N	Y	N	Y	Y
15 Shimkus	Y	Y	N	Y	N	Y	Y

	512	513	514	515	516	517	518
16 **Kinzinger**	Y	N	N	Y	N	Y	Y
17 Bustos	N	N	Y	N	Y	N	N
18 **LaHood**	Y	Y	N	Y	N	Y	Y
INDIANA							
1 Visclosky	N	N	Y	N	Y	N	N
2 **Walorski**	Y	Y	N	Y	N	Y	Y
3 **Banks**	Y	Y	N	Y	N	Y	Y
4 **Rokita**	Y	Y	N	Y	N	Y	Y
5 **Brooks**	Y	Y	N	Y	N	Y	Y
6 **Messer**	Y	Y	N	Y	N	Y	Y
7 Carson	N	N	Y	N	Y	N	N
8 **Bucshon**	Y	Y	N	Y	N	Y	Y
9 **Hollingsworth**	Y	N	N	Y	N	Y	Y
IOWA							
1 **Blum**	Y	Y	N	N	N	Y	Y
2 Loebsack	N	N	Y	N	Y	N	N
3 **Young**	Y	Y	N	Y	N	Y	Y
4 **King**	Y	Y	N	Y	N	Y	Y
KANSAS							
1 **Marshall**	Y	Y	N	Y	N	Y	Y
2 **Jenkins**	Y	Y	N	Y	N	Y	Y
3 **Yoder**	Y	Y	N	Y	N	Y	Y
4 **Estes**	Y	Y	N	Y	N	Y	Y
KENTUCKY							
1 **Comer**	Y	Y	N	Y	N	Y	Y
2 **Guthrie**	Y	Y	N	Y	N	Y	Y
3 Yarmuth	N	N	Y	N	Y	N	N
4 **Massie**	Y	Y	N	Y	N	Y	Y
5 **Rogers**	Y	N	N	Y	N	Y	Y
6 **Barr**	Y	N	N	Y	N	Y	Y
LOUISIANA							
1 **Scalise**	?	?	?	?	?	?	?
2 Richmond	N	N	Y	N	Y	N	N
3 **Higgins**	Y	Y	N	Y	N	Y	Y
4 **Johnson**	Y	Y	N	Y	N	Y	Y
5 **Abraham**	Y	Y	N	Y	N	Y	Y
6 **Graves**	Y	Y	N	Y	N	Y	Y
MAINE							
1 Pingree	N	N	Y	N	Y	N	N
2 **Poliquin**	Y	Y	N	Y	N	Y	N
MARYLAND							
1 **Harris**	Y	Y	N	Y	N	Y	Y
2 Ruppersberger	N	N	Y	N	Y	N	N
3 Sarbanes	N	N	Y	N	Y	N	N
4 Brown	N	N	Y	N	Y	N	N
5 Hoyer	N	N	Y	N	Y	N	N
6 Delaney	N	N	Y	N	Y	N	N
7 Cummings	N	N	Y	N	Y	N	N
8 Raskin	N	N	Y	N	Y	N	N
MASSACHUSETTS							
1 Neal	N	N	Y	N	Y	N	N
2 McGovern	N	N	Y	N	Y	N	N
3 Tsongas	N	N	Y	N	Y	N	N
4 Kennedy	N	N	Y	N	Y	N	N
5 Clark	N	N	Y	N	Y	N	N
6 Moulton	N	N	Y	N	Y	N	N
7 Capuano	N	N	Y	N	Y	N	N
8 Lynch	N	N	Y	N	Y	N	N
9 Keating	N	N	Y	N	Y	N	N
MICHIGAN							
1 **Bergman**	Y	Y	N	Y	N	Y	Y
2 **Huizenga**	Y	Y	N	Y	N	Y	Y
3 **Amash**	Y	Y	N	Y	N	N	Y
4 **Moolenaar**	Y	N	N	Y	N	Y	Y
5 Kildee	N	N	Y	N	Y	N	N
6 **Upton**	Y	Y	N	Y	N	Y	Y
7 **Walberg**	Y	Y	N	Y	N	Y	Y
8 **Bishop**	Y	Y	N	Y	N	Y	Y
9 Levin	N	N	Y	N	Y	N	N
10 **Mitchell**	Y	Y	N	Y	N	Y	Y
11 **Trott**	Y	N	N	Y	N	Y	Y
12 Dingell	N	N	Y	N	Y	N	N
13 Conyers	N	N	Y	N	Y	N	N
14 Lawrence	N	N	Y	N	Y	N	N
MINNESOTA							
1 Walz	N	N	Y	N	Y	N	N
2 **Lewis**	Y	Y	N	Y	N	Y	Y
3 **Paulsen**	Y	N	N	Y	N	Y	Y
4 McCollum	N	N	Y	N	Y	N	N
5 Ellison	N	N	Y	N	Y	N	N
6 **Emmer**	Y	Y	Y	Y	N	Y	Y
7 Peterson	N	N	Y	Y	Y	Y	Y
8 Nolan	N	N	Y	N	Y	N	N
MISSISSIPPI							
1 **Kelly**	Y	Y	N	Y	N	Y	Y
2 Thompson	N	N	Y	N	Y	N	N
3 **Harper**	Y	N	N	Y	N	Y	Y
4 **Palazzo**	Y	Y	N	Y	N	Y	Y
MISSOURI							
1 Clay	N	N	Y	N	Y	N	N
2 **Wagner**	Y	Y	N	Y	N	Y	Y
3 **Luetkemeyer**	Y	N	N	Y	N	Y	Y
4 **Hartzler**	Y	Y	N	Y	N	Y	Y
5 Cleaver	N	N	Y	N	+	–	–
6 **Graves**	+	+	–	+	?	?	?
7 **Long**	Y	Y	N	Y	N	Y	Y
8 **Smith**	Y	Y	N	Y	N	Y	Y
MONTANA							
AL **Gianforte**	Y	Y	N	Y	N	Y	Y
NEBRASKA							
1 **Fortenberry**	Y	N	N	Y	N	Y	Y
2 **Bacon**	Y	Y	Y	Y	N	Y	Y
3 **Smith**	Y	?	N	Y	N	Y	Y
NEVADA							
1 Titus	N	N	Y	N	Y	N	N
2 **Amodei**	Y	N	N	Y	N	Y	Y
3 Rosen	N	N	Y	N	Y	Y	N
4 Kihuen	N	N	Y	N	Y	Y	N
NEW HAMPSHIRE							
1 Shea-Porter	N	N	Y	N	Y	N	N
2 Kuster	N	N	Y	N	Y	N	N
NEW JERSEY							
1 Norcross	N	N	Y	N	Y	N	N
2 **LoBiondo**	N	N	N	N	N	Y	Y
3 **MacArthur**	N	N	N	N	N	Y	Y
4 **Smith**	N	N	N	N	N	Y	Y
5 Gottheimer	N	N	Y	N	Y	Y	N
6 Pallone	N	N	Y	N	Y	N	N
7 **Lance**	Y	Y	N	N	N	Y	Y
8 Sires	N	N	Y	N	Y	N	N
9 Pascrell	N	N	Y	N	Y	N	N
10 Payne	N	N	Y	N	Y	N	N
11 **Frelinghuysen**	Y	N	N	Y	N	Y	Y
12 Watson Coleman	N	N	Y	N	Y	N	N
NEW MEXICO							
1 Lujan Grisham	N	N	Y	N	Y	N	N
2 **Pearce**	Y	N	N	Y	N	Y	Y
3 Luján	N	N	Y	N	Y	N	N
NEW YORK							
1 **Zeldin**	Y	Y	N	Y	N	Y	Y
2 **King**	N	N	N	Y	N	Y	Y
3 Suozzi	N	N	Y	N	Y	N	N
4 Rice	N	N	Y	N	Y	N	N
5 Meeks	N	N	Y	N	Y	N	N
6 Meng	N	N	Y	N	Y	N	N
7 Velázquez	N	N	Y	N	Y	N	N
8 Jeffries	N	N	Y	N	Y	N	N
9 Clarke	N	N	Y	N	Y	N	N
10 Nadler	N	N	Y	N	Y	N	N
11 **Donovan**	N	N	N	N	N	Y	Y
12 Maloney, C.	N	N	Y	N	Y	N	N
13 Espaillat	N	N	Y	N	Y	N	N
14 Crowley	N	N	Y	N	Y	N	N
15 Serrano	N	N	Y	N	Y	N	N
16 Engel	N	N	Y	N	Y	N	N
17 Lowey	N	N	Y	N	Y	N	N
18 Maloney, S.P.	N	N	Y	N	Y	N	N
19 **Faso**	Y	N	N	N	N	Y	Y
20 Tonko	N	N	Y	N	Y	N	N
21 **Stefanik**	Y	N	N	Y	N	Y	N
22 **Tenney**	Y	N	N	Y	N	Y	Y
23 **Reed**	Y	N	N	Y	N	Y	N
24 **Katko**	Y	N	N	N	N	Y	N
25 Slaughter	N	N	Y	N	Y	N	N
26 Higgins	N	N	Y	N	Y	N	N
27 **Collins**	Y	N	N	Y	N	Y	Y
NORTH CAROLINA							
1 Butterfield	N	N	Y	N	Y	N	N
2 **Holding**	Y	Y	N	Y	N	Y	Y
3 **Jones**	Y	Y	N	N	N	Y	Y
4 Price	N	N	Y	N	Y	N	N
5 **Foxx**	Y	N	N	Y	N	Y	Y
6 **Walker**	Y	Y	N	Y	N	Y	Y
7 **Rouzer**	Y	Y	N	Y	N	Y	Y
8 **Hudson**	Y	Y	N	Y	N	Y	Y
9 **Pittenger**	Y	Y	N	Y	N	Y	Y
10 **McHenry**	Y	Y	N	Y	N	Y	Y
11 **Meadows**	Y	Y	N	Y	N	Y	Y
12 Adams	N	N	Y	N	Y	N	N
13 **Budd**	Y	Y	N	Y	N	Y	Y
NORTH DAKOTA							
AL **Cramer**	Y	Y	N	Y	N	Y	Y
OHIO							
1 **Chabot**	Y	Y	N	Y	N	Y	Y
2 **Wenstrup**	Y	Y	N	Y	N	Y	Y
3 Beatty	N	N	Y	N	Y	N	N
4 **Jordan**	Y	Y	N	Y	N	Y	Y
5 **Latta**	Y	Y	N	Y	N	Y	Y
6 **Johnson**	Y	Y	N	Y	N	Y	Y
7 **Gibbs**	Y	Y	N	Y	N	Y	Y
8 **Davidson**	Y	Y	N	Y	N	Y	Y
9 Kaptur	N	N	Y	N	Y	N	N
10 **Turner**	Y	N	N	Y	N	Y	Y
11 Fudge	N	N	Y	N	Y	N	N
12 **Tiberi**	?	?	?	?	?	+	?
13 Ryan	N	N	Y	N	Y	N	N
14 **Joyce**	Y	N	N	Y	N	Y	Y
15 **Stivers**	Y	N	N	Y	N	Y	Y
16 **Renacci**	Y	N	N	Y	N	Y	Y
OKLAHOMA							
1 **Bridenstine**	?	?	?	?	?	?	?
2 **Mullin**	Y	Y	N	Y	N	Y	Y
3 **Lucas**	Y	Y	N	Y	N	Y	Y
4 **Cole**	Y	N	N	Y	N	Y	Y
5 **Russell**	Y	Y	N	Y	N	Y	Y
OREGON							
1 Bonamici	N	N	Y	N	Y	N	N
2 **Walden**	Y	N	N	Y	N	Y	Y
3 Blumenauer	N	N	Y	N	Y	N	N
4 DeFazio	N	N	Y	N	Y	N	N
5 Schrader	N	N	Y	N	Y	N	N
PENNSYLVANIA							
1 Brady	N	N	Y	N	Y	N	N
2 Evans	N	N	Y	N	Y	N	N
3 **Kelly**	Y	N	N	Y	N	Y	Y
4 **Perry**	Y	Y	N	Y	N	Y	Y
5 **Thompson**	Y	N	N	Y	N	Y	Y
6 **Costello**	Y	N	N	Y	N	Y	N
7 **Meehan**	Y	N	N	Y	N	Y	N
8 **Fitzpatrick**	N	N	N	N	N	Y	N
9 **Shuster**	Y	Y	N	Y	N	Y	Y
10 **Marino**	Y	N	N	Y	N	Y	Y
11 **Barletta**	Y	N	N	Y	N	Y	Y
12 **Rothfus**	Y	Y	N	Y	N	Y	Y
13 Boyle	N	N	Y	N	Y	N	N
14 Doyle	N	N	Y	N	Y	N	N
15 **Dent**	Y	N	N	Y	N	Y	N
16 **Smucker**	Y	N	N	Y	N	Y	Y
17 Cartwright	N	N	Y	N	Y	N	N
18 **Murphy**	Y	N	N	Y	N	Y	Y
RHODE ISLAND							
1 Cicilline	N	N	Y	N	Y	N	N
2 Langevin	N	N	Y	N	Y	N	N
SOUTH CAROLINA							
1 **Sanford**	Y	Y	N	Y	N	Y	Y
2 **Wilson**	Y	Y	N	Y	N	Y	Y
3 **Duncan**	Y	Y	N	Y	N	Y	Y
4 **Gowdy**	Y	Y	N	Y	N	Y	Y
5 **Norman**	Y	Y	N	Y	N	Y	Y
6 Clyburn	?	?	?	?	?	?	?
7 **Rice**	Y	Y	N	Y	N	Y	Y
SOUTH DAKOTA							
AL **Noem**	Y	Y	N	Y	N	Y	Y
TENNESSEE							
1 **Roe**	Y	Y	N	Y	N	Y	Y
2 **Duncan**	Y	Y	Y	Y	N	Y	Y
3 **Fleischmann**	Y	N	N	Y	N	Y	Y
4 **DesJarlais**	Y	Y	N	Y	N	Y	Y
5 Cooper	N	N	Y	?	Y	N	N
6 **Black**	?	?	?	?	N	Y	Y
7 **Blackburn**	Y	Y	N	Y	N	Y	Y
8 **Kustoff**	Y	Y	N	Y	N	Y	Y
9 Cohen	N	N	Y	N	Y	N	N
TEXAS							
1 **Gohmert**	Y	Y	N	Y	N	Y	Y
2 **Poe**	Y	Y	N	Y	N	Y	Y
3 **Johnson, S.**	Y	Y	N	Y	N	Y	Y
4 **Ratcliffe**	Y	Y	N	Y	N	Y	Y
5 **Hensarling**	Y	Y	N	Y	N	Y	Y
6 **Barton**	Y	Y	N	Y	N	Y	Y
7 **Culberson**	Y	N	N	N	N	Y	Y
8 **Brady**	Y	Y	N	Y	N	Y	Y
9 Green, A.	N	N	Y	N	Y	N	N
10 **McCaul**	Y	Y	N	Y	N	Y	Y
11 **Conaway**	Y	Y	N	Y	N	Y	Y
12 **Granger**	Y	N	N	Y	N	Y	Y
13 **Thornberry**	Y	Y	N	Y	N	Y	Y
14 **Weber**	Y	Y	N	Y	N	Y	Y
15 Gonzalez	N	N	N	N	Y	N	N
16 O'Rourke	N	N	Y	N	Y	N	N
17 **Flores**	Y	Y	N	Y	N	Y	Y
18 Jackson Lee	N	N	Y	N	Y	N	N
19 **Arrington**	Y	Y	N	Y	N	Y	Y
20 Castro	N	N	Y	N	Y	N	N
21 **Smith**	Y	Y	N	Y	N	Y	Y
22 **Olson**	Y	Y	N	Y	?	Y	Y
23 **Hurd**	Y	Y	N	Y	N	Y	Y
24 **Marchant**	Y	Y	N	Y	N	Y	Y
25 **Williams**	Y	Y	N	Y	N	Y	Y
26 **Burgess**	Y	Y	N	Y	N	Y	Y
27 **Farenthold**	Y	Y	N	Y	N	Y	Y
28 Cuellar	Y	N	Y	N	Y	Y	N
29 Green, G.	N	N	Y	N	Y	N	N
30 Johnson, E.B.	N	N	Y	N	Y	N	N
31 **Carter**	Y	N	N	Y	N	Y	Y
32 **Sessions**	Y	Y	N	Y	N	Y	Y
33 Veasey	N	N	Y	N	Y	N	N
34 Vela	N	N	Y	N	Y	N	N
35 Doggett	N	N	Y	N	Y	N	N
36 **Babin**	Y	Y	N	Y	N	Y	Y
UTAH							
1 **Bishop**	Y	Y	N	Y	N	Y	Y
2 **Stewart**	Y	Y	N	Y	N	Y	Y
4 **Love**	Y	Y	N	Y	N	Y	Y
VERMONT							
AL Welch	N	N	Y	N	Y	N	N
VIRGINIA							
1 **Wittman**	Y	Y	N	Y	N	Y	Y
2 **Taylor**	Y	Y	N	Y	N	Y	Y
3 Scott	N	N	Y	N	Y	N	N
4 McEachin	N	N	Y	N	Y	N	N
5 **Garrett**	?	?	?	?	?	?	?
6 **Goodlatte**	Y	Y	N	Y	N	Y	Y
7 **Brat**	Y	Y	N	Y	N	Y	Y
8 Beyer	N	N	Y	N	Y	N	N
9 **Griffith**	Y	Y	N	Y	?	Y	Y
10 **Comstock**	Y	N	N	Y	N	Y	Y
11 Connolly	N	N	Y	N	Y	N	N
WASHINGTON							
1 DelBene	N	N	Y	N	Y	N	N
2 Larsen	N	N	Y	N	Y	N	N
3 **Herrera Beutler**	Y	N	N	Y	N	Y	Y
4 **Newhouse**	Y	N	N	Y	N	Y	Y
5 **McMorris Rodgers**	Y	Y	N	Y	N	Y	Y
6 Kilmer	N	N	Y	N	Y	N	N
7 Jayapal	N	N	Y	N	Y	N	N
8 **Reichert**	Y	N	N	Y	N	Y	Y
9 Smith	N	N	Y	N	Y	N	N
10 Heck	N	N	Y	N	Y	N	N
WEST VIRGINIA							
1 **McKinley**	Y	N	N	Y	N	Y	Y
2 **Mooney**	Y	Y	N	Y	N	Y	Y
3 **Jenkins**	Y	N	N	Y	N	Y	Y
WISCONSIN							
1 **Ryan**							
2 Pocan	N	N	Y	N	Y	N	N
3 Kind	N	N	Y	N	Y	N	N
4 Moore	N	N	Y	N	Y	N	N
5 **Sensenbrenner**	Y	Y	N	Y	N	Y	Y
6 **Grothman**	Y	Y	N	Y	N	Y	Y
7 **Duffy**	Y	Y	N	Y	?	Y	Y
8 **Gallagher**	Y	N	N	Y	N	Y	Y
WYOMING							
AL **Cheney**	Y	N	N	Y	N	Y	Y

III HOUSE VOTES

VOTE NUMBER

519. HR 3354. FISCAL 2018 OMNIBUS APPROPRIATIONS LEGISLATIVE VEHICLE/IRS OPERATIONS. Gohmert, R-Texas, for Posey, R-Fla., amendment that would decrease funding for Internal Revenue Service operations support by $165,300, and would transfer the savings to the spending reduction account. Rejected in Committee of the Whole 186-223 : R 186-37; D 0-186. Sept. 14, 2017.

520. HR 3354. FISCAL 2018 OMNIBUS APPROPRIATIONS LEGISLATIVE VEHICLE/DC BUDGET AUTONOMY. Norton, D-D.C., amendment that would eliminate the bill's repeal of the District of Columbia's budget autonomy. Rejected in Committee of the Whole 186-222 : R 0-222; D 186-0. Sept. 14, 2017.

521. HR 3354. FISCAL 2018 OMNIBUS APPROPRIATIONS LEGISLATIVE VEHICLE/CFPB APPROPRIATIONS PROCESS INTEGRATION. Ellison, D-Minn., amendment that would eliminate the bill's provision that would incorporate the Consumer Financial Protection Bureau into the regular appropriations process. Rejected in Committee of the Whole 183-226 : R 2-221; D 181-5. Sept. 14, 2017.

522. HR 3354. FISCAL 2018 OMNIBUS APPROPRIATIONS LEGISLATIVE VEHICLE/MANUFACTURED HOUSING. Ellison, D-Minn., amendment that would eliminate the bill's provisions related to manufactured housing mortgages, manufacturers and retailers. Rejected in Committee of the Whole 163-245 : R 1-222; D 162-23. Sept. 14, 2017.

523. HR 3354. FISCAL 2018 OMNIBUS APPROPRIATIONS LEGISLATIVE VEHICLE/SMALL DOLLAR CREDIT REGULATION. Ellison, D-Minn., amendment that would eliminate the bill's provision that would remove the Consumer Financial Protection Bureau's authority to regulate certain types of small dollar credit, such as payday loans and vehicle loans. Rejected in Committee of the Whole 186-221 : R 4-218; D 182-3. Sept. 14, 2017.

524. HR 3354. FISCAL 2018 OMNIBUS APPROPRIATIONS LEGISLATIVE VEHICLE/10 PERCENT SALARY DECREASE. Mitchell, R-Mich., amendment that would decrease funding for all departmental salary and expense accounts under the Financial Services and General Government Appropriations section of the bill by 10 percent and would transfer the savings to the spending reduction account. Rejected in Committee of the Whole 166-241 : R 166-56; D 0-185. Sept. 14, 2017.

525. HR 3354. FISCAL 2018 OMNIBUS APPROPRIATIONS LEGISLATIVE VEHICLE/SEC CONFLICT MATERIALS RULE. Huizenga, R-Mich., amendment that would prohibit funds appropriated by the bill from being used to implement, administer or enforce a Securities Exchange Commission rule related to conflict materials. Adopted in Committee of the Whole 211-195 : R 211-10; D 0-185. Sept. 14, 2017.

	519	520	521	522	523	524	525
ALABAMA							
1 **Byrne**	Y	N	N	N	N	Y	Y
2 **Roby**	Y	N	N	N	N	N	Y
3 **Rogers**	Y	N	N	N	N	N	Y
4 **Aderholt**	Y	N	N	N	N	N	Y
5 **Brooks**	Y	N	N	N	N	N	Y
6 **Palmer**	Y	N	N	N	N	Y	Y
7 Sewell	N	Y	Y	N	Y	N	N
ALASKA							
AL **Young**	Y	N	N	N	N	Y	Y
ARIZONA							
1 O'Halleran	N	Y	Y	N	Y	N	N
2 **McSally**	Y	N	N	N	N	N	Y
3 Grijalva	N	Y	Y	Y	Y	N	N
4 **Gosar**	?	?	?	?	?	?	?
5 **Biggs**	Y	N	N	N	N	N	Y
6 **Schweikert**	Y	N	N	N	N	N	Y
7 Gallego	N	Y	Y	N	Y	N	N
8 **Franks**	Y	N	N	N	N	Y	Y
9 Sinema	N	Y	Y	N	Y	N	N
ARKANSAS							
1 **Crawford**	Y	N	N	N	N	Y	Y
2 **Hill**	Y	N	N	N	N	Y	Y
3 **Womack**	Y	N	N	N	N	Y	Y
4 **Westerman**	Y	N	N	N	N	Y	Y
CALIFORNIA							
1 **LaMalfa**	Y	N	N	N	N	Y	Y
2 Huffman	N	Y	Y	Y	Y	N	N
3 Garamendi	N	Y	Y	Y	Y	N	N
4 **McClintock**	Y	N	N	N	N	Y	Y
5 Thompson	N	Y	Y	Y	Y	N	N
6 Matsui	N	Y	Y	Y	Y	N	N
7 Bera	N	Y	Y	Y	Y	N	N
8 **Cook**	Y	N	N	N	N	N	Y
9 McNerney	N	Y	Y	Y	Y	N	N
10 **Denham**	Y	N	N	N	N	N	Y
11 DeSaulnier	N	Y	Y	Y	Y	N	N
12 Pelosi	N	Y	Y	Y	Y	N	N
13 Lee	N	Y	Y	Y	Y	N	N
14 Speier	N	Y	Y	Y	Y	N	N
15 Swalwell	N	Y	Y	Y	Y	N	N
16 Costa	?	?	?	?	?	?	?
17 Khanna	N	Y	Y	Y	Y	N	N
18 Eshoo	N	Y	Y	Y	Y	N	N
19 Lofgren	N	Y	Y	Y	Y	N	N
20 Panetta	N	Y	Y	N	Y	N	N
21 **Valadao**	Y	N	N	N	N	N	Y
22 **Nunes**	Y	N	N	N	N	N	Y
23 **McCarthy**	Y	N	N	N	N	Y	Y
24 Carbajal	N	Y	Y	N	Y	N	N
25 **Knight**	Y	N	N	N	N	N	Y
26 Brownley	N	Y	Y	Y	Y	N	N
27 Chu	N	Y	Y	Y	Y	N	N
28 Schiff	N	Y	Y	Y	Y	N	N
29 Cardenas	N	Y	Y	Y	Y	N	N
30 Sherman	N	Y	Y	N	Y	N	N
31 Aguilar	N	Y	Y	Y	Y	N	N
32 Napolitano	N	Y	Y	Y	Y	N	N
33 Lieu	N	Y	Y	Y	Y	N	N
34 Gomez	N	Y	Y	Y	Y	N	N
35 Torres	N	Y	Y	Y	Y	N	N
36 Ruiz	N	Y	Y	Y	Y	N	N
37 Bass	N	Y	Y	Y	Y	N	N
38 Sánchez, Linda	N	Y	Y	Y	Y	N	N
39 **Royce**	Y	N	N	N	N	Y	N
40 Roybal-Allard	N	Y	Y	Y	Y	N	N
41 Takano	N	Y	Y	Y	Y	N	N
42 **Calvert**	Y	N	N	N	N	N	Y
43 Waters	N	Y	Y	Y	Y	N	N
44 Barragan	N	Y	Y	Y	Y	N	N
45 **Walters**	Y	N	N	N	N	Y	Y
46 Correa	N	Y	Y	N	Y	N	N
47 Lowenthal	N	Y	Y	Y	Y	N	N
48 **Rohrabacher**	Y	N	N	N	N	Y	Y
49 **Issa**	Y	N	N	N	N	Y	Y
50 **Hunter**	Y	N	N	N	N	Y	Y
51 Vargas	N	Y	Y	Y	Y	N	N
52 Peters	N	Y	N	Y	Y	N	N
53 Davis	N	Y	Y	Y	Y	N	N

	519	520	521	522	523	524	525
COLORADO							
1 DeGette	N	Y	Y	Y	Y	N	N
2 Polis	N	Y	Y	Y	Y	N	N
3 **Tipton**	Y	N	N	N	N	Y	Y
4 **Buck**	Y	N	N	N	N	Y	Y
5 **Lamborn**	Y	N	N	N	N	Y	Y
6 **Coffman**	Y	N	N	N	N	Y	Y
7 Perlmutter	N	Y	Y	N	Y	N	N
CONNECTICUT							
1 Larson	-	+	+	+	+	-	-
2 Courtney	N	Y	Y	Y	Y	N	N
3 DeLauro	-	+	+	-	+	+	-
4 Himes	N	Y	Y	Y	Y	N	N
5 Esty	N	Y	Y	Y	Y	N	N
DELAWARE							
AL **Blunt Rochester**	N	Y	Y	Y	Y	N	N
FLORIDA							
1 **Gaetz**	Y	N	N	N	N	Y	Y
2 **Dunn**	Y	N	N	N	N	N	Y
3 **Yoho**	+	-	-	-	-	+	+
4 **Rutherford**	+	-	-	-	-	+	+
5 Lawson	?	?	?	?	?	?	?
6 **DeSantis**	Y	N	N	N	N	Y	Y
7 Murphy	N	Y	N	N	Y	N	N
8 **Posey**	?	?	?	?	?	?	?
9 Soto	N	Y	Y	Y	Y	N	N
10 Demings	N	Y	Y	Y	Y	N	N
11 **Webster**	Y	N	N	N	N	Y	Y
12 **Bilirakis**	Y	N	N	N	N	N	Y
13 **Crist**	?	?	?	?	?	?	?
14 Castor	N	Y	Y	Y	Y	N	N
15 **Ross**	?	?	?	?	?	?	?
16 **Buchanan**	N	Y	N	N	Y	N	N
17 **Rooney, T.**	?	?	?	?	?	?	?
18 **Mast**	Y	N	N	N	N	Y	Y
19 **Rooney, F.**	?	?	?	?	?	?	?
20 Hastings	N	Y	Y	N	Y	N	N
21 Frankel	?	?	?	?	?	?	?
22 Deutch	N	Y	Y	Y	Y	N	N
23 Wasserman Schultz	N	Y	Y	Y	Y	N	N
24 Wilson	N	Y	Y	Y	Y	N	N
25 **Diaz-Balart**	?	?	?	?	?	?	?
26 **Curbelo**	N	N	N	N	N	N	N
27 **Ros-Lehtinen**	?	?	?	?	?	?	?
GEORGIA							
1 **Carter**	+	-	-	-	-	+	+
2 Bishop	N	Y	Y	Y	Y	N	N
3 **Ferguson**	Y	N	N	N	N	Y	Y
4 Johnson	N	Y	Y	Y	Y	N	N
5 Lewis	N	Y	Y	Y	Y	N	N
6 **Handel**	Y	N	N	N	N	Y	Y
7 **Woodall**	Y	N	N	N	N	Y	Y
8 **Scott, A.**	Y	N	N	N	N	Y	Y
9 **Collins**	Y	N	N	N	N	Y	Y
10 **Hice**	Y	N	N	N	N	Y	Y
11 **Loudermilk**	?	?	?	?	?	?	?
12 **Allen**	Y	N	N	N	N	Y	Y
13 Scott, D.	N	Y	Y	Y	Y	N	N
14 **Graves**	Y	N	N	N	N	Y	Y
HAWAII							
1 Hanabusa	N	Y	Y	Y	Y	N	N
2 Gabbard	N	Y	Y	Y	Y	N	N
IDAHO							
1 **Labrador**	Y	N	N	N	N	Y	Y
2 **Simpson**	N	N	N	N	N	N	Y
ILLINOIS							
1 Rush	N	Y	Y	Y	Y	N	N
2 Kelly	N	Y	Y	Y	Y	N	N
3 Lipinski	N	Y	Y	Y	Y	N	N
4 Gutierrez	N	Y	Y	Y	Y	N	N
5 Quigley	N	Y	Y	Y	Y	N	N
6 **Roskam**	N	N	N	N	N	Y	N
7 Davis, D.	N	Y	Y	Y	Y	N	N
8 Krishnamoorthi	N	Y	Y	Y	Y	N	N
9 Schakowsky	N	Y	Y	Y	Y	N	N
10 Schneider	N	Y	Y	Y	Y	N	N
11 Foster	N	Y	Y	Y	Y	N	N
12 **Bost**	N	N	N	N	N	N	Y
13 **Davis, R.**	N	N	N	N	N	Y	N
14 **Hultgren**	Y	N	N	N	N	Y	Y
15 **Shimkus**	N	N	N	N	N	Y	Y

KEY	Republicans	Democrats	Independents
Y	Voted for (yea)	X	Paired against	C	Voted "present" to avoid possible conflict of interest
#	Paired for	-	Announced against	
+	Announced for	P	Voted "present"	?	Did not vote or otherwise make a position known
N	Voted against (nay)		

	519	520	521	522	523	524	525
16 **Kinzinger**	Y	N	N	N	N	Y	Y
17 Bustos	N	Y	Y	Y	Y	N	N
18 **LaHood**	Y	N	N	N	N	Y	Y
INDIANA							
1 Visclosky	N	Y	Y	Y	Y	N	N
2 **Walorski**	Y	N	N	N	N	Y	Y
3 **Banks**	Y	N	N	N	N	Y	Y
4 **Rokita**	Y	N	N	N	N	Y	Y
5 **Brooks**	Y	N	N	N	N	Y	Y
6 **Messer**	Y	N	N	N	N	Y	Y
7 Carson	N	Y	Y	Y	Y	N	N
8 **Bucshon**	N	N	N	N	N	Y	Y
9 **Hollingsworth**	Y	N	N	N	N	Y	Y
IOWA							
1 **Blum**	Y	N	N	N	N	Y	Y
2 Loebsack	N	Y	Y	Y	Y	N	N
3 **Young**	Y	N	N	N	N	Y	Y
4 **King**	Y	N	N	N	N	Y	Y
KANSAS							
1 **Marshall**	Y	N	N	N	N	Y	Y
2 **Jenkins**	Y	N	N	N	N	Y	Y
3 **Yoder**	Y	N	N	N	N	Y	Y
4 **Estes**	Y	N	N	N	N	Y	Y
KENTUCKY							
1 **Comer**	Y	N	N	N	N	Y	Y
2 **Guthrie**	Y	N	N	N	N	Y	Y
3 Yarmuth	N	Y	Y	Y	Y	N	N
4 **Massie**	Y	N	N	N	N	N	Y
5 **Rogers**	N	N	N	N	N	N	Y
6 **Barr**	Y	N	N	N	N	Y	Y
LOUISIANA							
1 **Scalise**	?	?	?	?	?	?	?
2 Richmond	N	Y	Y	Y	Y	N	N
3 **Higgins**	Y	N	N	N	N	Y	Y
4 **Johnson**	Y	N	N	N	N	Y	Y
5 **Abraham**	Y	N	N	N	N	Y	Y
6 **Graves**	Y	N	N	N	N	Y	Y
MAINE							
1 Pingree	N	Y	Y	Y	Y	N	N
2 **Poliquin**	Y	N	Y	N	Y	Y	Y
MARYLAND							
1 **Harris**	Y	N	N	N	N	Y	Y
2 Ruppersberger	N	Y	Y	Y	Y	N	N
3 Sarbanes	N	Y	Y	Y	Y	N	N
4 Brown	N	Y	Y	Y	Y	N	N
5 Hoyer	N	Y	Y	Y	Y	N	N
6 Delaney	N	Y	Y	N	Y	N	N
7 Cummings	N	Y	Y	Y	Y	N	N
8 Raskin	N	Y	Y	Y	Y	N	N
MASSACHUSETTS							
1 Neal	N	Y	Y	Y	Y	N	N
2 McGovern	N	Y	Y	Y	Y	N	N
3 Tsongas	N	Y	Y	Y	Y	N	N
4 Kennedy	N	Y	Y	Y	Y	N	N
5 Clark	N	Y	Y	Y	Y	N	N
6 Moulton	N	Y	Y	N	Y	N	N
7 Capuano	N	Y	Y	Y	Y	N	N
8 Lynch	N	Y	Y	Y	Y	N	N
9 Keating	N	Y	Y	Y	Y	N	N
MICHIGAN							
1 **Bergman**	Y	N	N	N	N	Y	Y
2 **Huizenga**	Y	N	N	N	N	Y	Y
3 **Amash**	Y	N	N	N	N	Y	Y
4 **Moolenaar**	N	N	N	N	N	Y	Y
5 Kildee	N	Y	Y	Y	Y	N	N
6 **Upton**	Y	N	N	N	N	Y	Y
7 **Walberg**	Y	N	N	N	N	Y	Y
8 **Bishop**	Y	N	N	N	N	Y	Y
9 Levin	N	Y	Y	Y	Y	N	N
10 **Mitchell**	Y	N	N	N	N	Y	Y
11 **Trott**	Y	N	N	N	N	N	Y
12 Dingell	N	Y	Y	Y	Y	N	N
13 Conyers	N	Y	Y	Y	Y	N	N
14 Lawrence	N	Y	Y	Y	Y	N	N
MINNESOTA							
1 Walz	N	Y	Y	Y	Y	N	N
2 **Lewis**	Y	N	N	N	N	Y	Y
3 **Paulsen**	Y	N	N	N	N	Y	Y
4 McCollum	N	Y	Y	Y	Y	N	N

	519	520	521	522	523	524	525
5 Ellison	N	Y	Y	Y	Y	N	N
6 **Emmer**	Y	N	N	N	N	Y	Y
7 Peterson	N	Y	Y	N	N	N	N
8 Nolan	N	Y	Y	Y	Y	N	N
MISSISSIPPI							
1 **Kelly**	Y	N	N	N	N	Y	Y
2 Thompson	N	Y	Y	Y	Y	N	N
3 **Harper**	Y	N	N	N	N	N	Y
4 **Palazzo**	Y	N	N	N	N	Y	Y
MISSOURI							
1 Clay	N	Y	Y	Y	Y	N	N
2 **Wagner**	Y	N	N	N	N	Y	Y
3 **Luetkemeyer**	Y	N	N	N	N	N	Y
4 **Hartzler**	Y	N	N	N	N	Y	Y
5 Cleaver	–	+	+	+	+	+	–
6 **Graves**	?	?	?	?	?	?	?
7 **Long**	Y	N	N	N	N	Y	Y
8 **Smith**	Y	N	N	N	N	Y	Y
MONTANA							
AL **Gianforte**	Y	N	N	N	N	Y	Y
NEBRASKA							
1 **Fortenberry**	N	N	N	N	N	N	N
2 **Bacon**	Y	N	N	N	N	Y	Y
3 **Smith**	Y	N	N	N	N	Y	Y
NEVADA							
1 Titus	N	Y	Y	Y	Y	N	N
2 **Amodei**	N	N	N	N	N	N	Y
3 Rosen	N	Y	Y	N	Y	N	N
4 Kihuen	N	Y	Y	N	Y	N	N
NEW HAMPSHIRE							
1 Shea-Porter	N	Y	Y	Y	Y	N	N
2 Kuster	N	Y	Y	Y	Y	N	N
NEW JERSEY							
1 Norcross	N	Y	Y	Y	Y	N	N
2 **LoBiondo**	N	N	N	N	N	N	N
3 **MacArthur**	N	N	N	N	N	N	N
4 **Smith**	Y	N	N	N	N	N	N
5 Gottheimer	N	Y	Y	N	Y	N	N
6 Pallone	N	Y	Y	Y	Y	N	N
7 **Lance**	N	N	N	N	N	N	N
8 Sires	N	Y	Y	Y	Y	N	N
9 Pascrell	N	Y	Y	Y	Y	N	N
10 Payne	N	Y	Y	Y	Y	N	N
11 **Frelinghuysen**	N	N	N	N	N	N	N
12 Watson Coleman	N	Y	Y	Y	Y	N	N
NEW MEXICO							
1 Lujan Grisham	N	Y	Y	Y	Y	N	N
2 **Pearce**	Y	N	N	N	N	N	Y
3 Luján	N	Y	Y	Y	Y	N	N
NEW YORK							
1 **Zeldin**	Y	N	N	N	N	Y	Y
2 **King**	N	N	N	N	N	N	Y
3 Suozzi	N	Y	Y	N	Y	N	N
4 Rice	N	Y	Y	N	Y	N	N
5 Meeks	N	Y	Y	Y	Y	N	N
6 Meng	N	Y	Y	Y	Y	N	N
7 Velázquez	N	Y	Y	Y	Y	N	N
8 Jeffries	N	Y	Y	Y	Y	N	N
9 Clarke	N	Y	Y	Y	Y	N	N
10 Nadler	N	Y	Y	Y	Y	N	N
11 **Donovan**	N	N	N	N	N	N	Y
12 Maloney, C.	N	Y	Y	Y	Y	N	N
13 Espaillat	N	Y	Y	Y	Y	N	N
14 Crowley	N	Y	Y	Y	Y	N	N
15 Serrano	N	Y	Y	Y	Y	N	N
16 Engel	N	Y	Y	Y	Y	N	N
17 Lowey	N	Y	Y	Y	Y	N	N
18 Maloney, S.P.	N	Y	Y	Y	Y	N	N
19 **Faso**	N	N	N	N	N	N	Y
20 Tonko	N	Y	Y	Y	Y	N	N
21 **Stefanik**	N	N	N	N	N	N	Y
22 **Tenney**	Y	N	N	N	N	Y	Y
23 **Reed**	N	N	N	N	N	N	Y
24 **Katko**	N	N	N	N	N	N	Y
25 Slaughter	N	Y	Y	Y	Y	N	N
26 Higgins	N	Y	Y	Y	Y	N	N
27 **Collins**	Y	N	N	N	N	N	Y
NORTH CAROLINA							
1 Butterfield	N	Y	Y	Y	Y	N	N
2 **Holding**	Y	N	N	N	N	Y	Y
3 **Jones**	Y	N	Y	Y	Y	Y	N
4 Price	N	Y	Y	Y	Y	N	N

	519	520	521	522	523	524	525
5 **Foxx**	N	N	N	N	N	N	Y
6 **Walker**	Y	N	N	N	N	Y	Y
7 **Rouzer**	Y	N	N	N	N	Y	Y
8 **Hudson**	Y	N	N	N	N	Y	Y
9 **Pittenger**	Y	N	N	N	N	Y	Y
10 **McHenry**	Y	N	N	N	N	Y	Y
11 **Meadows**	Y	N	N	N	N	Y	Y
12 Adams	N	Y	Y	Y	Y	N	N
13 **Budd**	Y	N	N	N	N	Y	Y
NORTH DAKOTA							
AL **Cramer**	Y	N	N	N	N	N	Y
OHIO							
1 **Chabot**	Y	N	N	N	N	Y	Y
2 **Wenstrup**	Y	N	N	N	N	Y	Y
3 Beatty	N	Y	Y	Y	Y	N	N
4 **Jordan**	Y	N	N	N	N	Y	Y
5 **Latta**	Y	N	N	N	N	Y	Y
6 **Johnson**	Y	N	N	N	N	Y	Y
7 **Gibbs**	Y	N	N	N	N	Y	Y
8 **Davidson**	Y	N	N	N	N	Y	Y
9 Kaptur	N	Y	Y	Y	Y	N	N
10 **Turner**	Y	N	N	N	N	N	Y
11 Fudge	N	Y	Y	Y	Y	N	N
12 **Tiberi**	?	?	?	?	?	?	?
13 Ryan	N	Y	Y	Y	Y	N	N
14 **Joyce**	Y	N	N	N	N	N	Y
15 **Stivers**	Y	N	N	N	N	Y	Y
16 **Renacci**	N	N	N	N	N	N	Y
OKLAHOMA							
1 **Bridenstine**	?	?	?	?	?	?	?
2 **Mullin**	Y	N	N	N	N	Y	Y
3 **Lucas**	Y	N	N	N	N	N	Y
4 **Cole**	N	N	N	N	N	N	Y
5 **Russell**	Y	N	N	N	N	Y	Y
OREGON							
1 Bonamici	N	Y	Y	Y	Y	N	N
2 **Walden**	N	N	N	N	N	Y	Y
3 Blumenauer	N	Y	Y	Y	Y	N	N
4 DeFazio	N	Y	Y	N	Y	N	N
5 Schrader	N	Y	Y	Y	?	N	?
PENNSYLVANIA							
1 Brady	N	Y	Y	Y	Y	N	N
2 Evans	N	Y	Y	Y	Y	N	N
3 **Kelly**	N	N	N	N	N	N	Y
4 **Perry**	Y	N	N	N	N	Y	Y
5 **Thompson**	N	N	N	N	N	N	Y
6 **Costello**	N	N	N	N	N	N	N
7 **Meehan**	N	N	N	N	N	N	Y
8 **Fitzpatrick**	N	N	N	N	N	N	N
9 **Shuster**	N	N	N	N	N	Y	Y
10 **Marino**	N	N	N	N	N	?	?
11 **Barletta**	N	N	N	N	N	N	Y
12 **Rothfus**	Y	N	N	N	N	Y	Y
13 Boyle	N	Y	Y	Y	Y	N	N
14 Doyle	N	Y	Y	Y	Y	N	N
15 **Dent**	N	N	N	N	N	N	Y
16 **Smucker**	Y	N	N	N	N	Y	Y
17 Cartwright	N	Y	Y	Y	Y	N	N
18 **Murphy**	N	N	N	N	N	N	Y
RHODE ISLAND							
1 Cicilline	N	Y	Y	Y	Y	N	N
2 Langevin	N	Y	Y	Y	Y	N	N
SOUTH CAROLINA							
1 **Sanford**	Y	N	N	N	N	Y	Y
2 **Wilson**	Y	N	N	N	N	Y	Y
3 **Duncan**	Y	N	N	N	N	Y	Y
4 **Gowdy**	Y	N	N	N	N	Y	Y
5 **Norman**	Y	N	N	N	N	Y	Y
6 Clyburn	?	?	?	?	?	?	?
7 **Rice**	Y	N	N	N	N	Y	?
SOUTH DAKOTA							
AL **Noem**	Y	N	N	N	N	Y	Y
TENNESSEE							
1 **Roe**	Y	N	N	N	N	Y	Y
2 **Duncan**	Y	N	N	N	N	Y	Y
3 **Fleischmann**	Y	N	N	N	N	N	Y
4 **DesJarlais**	Y	N	N	N	N	Y	Y
5 Cooper	N	Y	N	N	Y	N	N
6 **Black**	Y	N	N	N	N	Y	Y
7 **Blackburn**	Y	N	N	N	N	Y	Y
8 **Kustoff**	Y	N	N	N	N	Y	Y
9 Cohen	N	Y	Y	Y	Y	N	N

	519	520	521	522	523	524	525
TEXAS							
1 **Gohmert**	Y	N	N	N	N	Y	Y
2 **Poe**	Y	N	N	N	N	Y	Y
3 **Johnson, S.**	Y	N	N	N	N	Y	Y
4 **Ratcliffe**	Y	N	N	N	N	Y	Y
5 **Hensarling**	Y	N	N	N	N	Y	Y
6 **Barton**	Y	N	N	N	N	Y	Y
7 **Culberson**	Y	N	N	N	N	Y	Y
8 **Brady**	Y	?	N	N	N	N	Y
9 Green, A.	N	Y	Y	Y	Y	N	N
10 **McCaul**	Y	N	N	N	N	Y	Y
11 **Conaway**	Y	N	N	N	N	Y	Y
12 **Granger**	Y	N	N	N	N	Y	Y
13 **Thornberry**	Y	N	N	N	N	Y	Y
14 **Weber**	Y	N	N	N	N	Y	Y
15 Gonzalez	N	Y	Y	Y	Y	N	N
16 O'Rourke	N	Y	Y	Y	Y	N	N
17 **Flores**	Y	N	N	N	N	Y	Y
18 Jackson Lee	N	Y	Y	Y	Y	N	N
19 **Arrington**	Y	N	N	N	?	Y	Y
20 Castro	N	Y	Y	Y	Y	N	N
21 **Smith**	Y	N	N	N	N	Y	Y
22 **Olson**	Y	N	N	N	N	Y	Y
23 **Hurd**	Y	N	N	N	N	N	Y
24 **Marchant**	Y	N	N	N	N	Y	Y
25 **Williams**	Y	N	N	N	N	Y	Y
26 **Burgess**	Y	N	N	N	N	Y	Y
27 **Farenthold**	Y	N	N	N	N	Y	Y
28 Cuellar	N	Y	N	Y	N	N	N
29 Green, G.	N	Y	Y	Y	Y	N	N
30 Johnson, E.B.	N	Y	Y	Y	Y	N	N
31 **Carter**	Y	N	N	N	N	Y	Y
32 **Sessions**	Y	N	N	N	N	Y	Y
33 Veasey	N	Y	Y	Y	Y	N	N
34 Vela	N	Y	Y	?	Y	N	N
35 Doggett	N	Y	Y	Y	Y	N	N
36 **Babin**	Y	N	N	N	N	Y	Y
UTAH							
1 **Bishop**	Y	N	N	N	N	Y	Y
2 **Stewart**	Y	N	N	N	N	Y	Y
4 **Love**	Y	N	N	N	N	Y	Y
VERMONT							
AL Welch	N	Y	Y	Y	Y	?	N
VIRGINIA							
1 **Wittman**	Y	N	N	N	N	Y	Y
2 **Taylor**	Y	N	N	N	N	Y	Y
3 Scott	N	Y	Y	Y	Y	N	N
4 McEachin	N	Y	Y	Y	Y	N	N
5 **Garrett**	?	?	?	?	?	?	?
6 **Goodlatte**	Y	N	N	N	N	Y	Y
7 **Brat**	Y	N	N	N	N	Y	Y
8 Beyer	N	Y	Y	Y	Y	N	N
9 **Griffith**	Y	N	N	N	N	Y	Y
10 **Comstock**	N	N	N	N	N	N	Y
11 Connolly	N	Y	Y	Y	Y	N	N
WASHINGTON							
1 DelBene	N	Y	Y	Y	Y	N	N
2 Larsen	N	Y	Y	Y	Y	N	N
3 **Herrera Beutler**	Y	N	N	N	N	Y	Y
4 **Newhouse**	Y	N	N	N	N	Y	Y
5 **McMorris Rodgers**	Y	N	N	N	N	Y	Y
6 Kilmer	N	Y	Y	Y	Y	N	N
7 Jayapal	N	Y	Y	Y	Y	N	N
8 **Reichert**	N	N	N	N	N	N	Y
9 Smith	N	Y	Y	Y	Y	N	N
10 Heck	N	Y	Y	Y	Y	N	N
WEST VIRGINIA							
1 **McKinley**	Y	N	N	N	N	N	Y
2 **Mooney**	Y	N	N	N	N	Y	Y
3 **Jenkins**	Y	N	N	N	N	Y	Y
WISCONSIN							
1 **Ryan**							
2 Pocan	N	Y	Y	Y	Y	N	N
3 Kind	N	Y	Y	N	Y	N	N
4 Moore	N	Y	Y	Y	Y	N	N
5 **Sensenbrenner**	Y	N	N	N	N	Y	Y
6 **Grothman**	Y	N	N	N	Y	Y	Y
7 **Duffy**	Y	N	N	N	N	Y	Y
8 **Gallagher**	Y	N	N	N	N	Y	Y
WYOMING							
AL **Cheney**	Y	N	N	N	N	Y	Y

VOTE NUMBER

526. HR 3354. FISCAL 2018 OMNIBUS APPROPRIATIONS LEGISLATIVE VEHICLE/IDENTITY THEFT CASEWORK. Jackson Lee, D-Texas, amendment that would increase funding for the Taxpayer Advocate Service's identity theft casework by $500,000, and would decrease funding for IRS operational support by $1 million. Adopted in Committee of the Whole 265-143 : R 82-140; D 183-3. Sept. 14, 2017.

527. HR 3354. FISCAL 2018 OMNIBUS APPROPRIATIONS/RECOMMIT. Jackson Lee, D-Texas, motion to recommit the bill to the House Appropriations Committee with instructions to report it back immediately with an amendment that would increase funding for the Federal Emergency Management Agency's National Predisaster Mitigation Fund by $2.4 billion, would eliminate $1.6 billion in funding to U.S. Customs and Border Protection for procurement, construction and improvement of a barrier along the southern U.S. border, and would decrease funding for U.S. Immigration and Customs Enforcement operations by $849.5 million. Motion rejected 186-223 : R 0-223; D 186-0. Sept. 14, 2017.

528. HR 3354. FISCAL 2018 OMNIBUS APPROPRIATIONS/PASSAGE. Passage of the bill, as amended, that would provide $1.23 trillion for federal departments and agencies covered by the 12 unfinished fiscal 2018 spending bills, including $621.5 billion for defense and $511 billion for nondefense discretionary spending. Passed 211-198 : R 210-14; D 1-184. Sept. 14, 2017.

529. HR 3284. COUNTERTERRORISM AWARENESS WORKSHOPS/PASSAGE. Fitzpatrick, R-Pa., motion to suspend the rules and pass the bill that would authorize $1 million for certain counterterrorism training programs, known as the Joint Counterterrorism Awareness Workshop Series, carried out by the Federal Emergency Management Agency in consultation with the National Counterterrorism Center and the FBI. Motion agreed to 398-4 : R 216-4; D 182-0. Sept. 14, 2017.

530. HR 3823. FAA SHORT TERM REAUTHORIZATION, FLOOD INSURANCE AND HURRICANE TAX ADJUSTMENTS/PASSAGE. Curbelo, R-Fla., motion to suspend the rules and pass the bill that would extend through March 31, 2018, various expiring authorities, programs and activities for the Federal Aviation Administration. It would also extend multiple health care programs, would establish the basis for the development of a private flood insurance market, and would modify tax provisions for individuals living in areas impacted by Hurricanes Harvey, Irma and Maria. Motion rejected 245-171 : R 219-8; D 26-163. Sept. 25, 2017.

531. HR 2061. NORTH KOREAN REFUGEE ASSISTANCE FUNDING REAUTHORIZATION/PASSAGE. Royce, R-Calif., motion to suspend the rules and pass the bill that would extend, through fiscal 2022, the current authorization of $20 million annually for North Korean refugee assistance. It would also authorize, through fiscal 2022, $3 million annually for actions related to increasing the availability of information inside North Korea. It would require the State Department to submit a report to Congress that would include a plan for reuniting North Korean refugees with their families. Motion agreed to 415-0 : R 227-0; D 188-0. Sept. 25, 2017.

532. H RES 533, HR 2824, HR 2792. MATERNAL AND INFANT HOME VISIT PROGRAM AND PAROLE VIOLATORS' BENEFITS REVOCATION/PREVIOUS QUESTION. Burgess, R-Texas, motion to order the previous question (thus limiting debate and possibility of amendment) on the rule (H Res 533) that would provide for House floor consideration of the bill (HR 2824), that would authorize, through fiscal 2022, $400 million a year for the Maternal, Infant and Early Childhood Home Visiting program created under the 2010 health care overhaul, and for consideration of the bill (HR 2792), that would prohibit, beginning in 2021, the payment of Social Security benefits to an individual who is the subject of an outstanding arrest warrant for committing a felony or for violating a condition of parole or probation. Motion agreed to 230-189 : R 230-0; D 0-189. Sept. 26, 2017.

	526	527	528	529	530	531	532
ALABAMA							
1 Byrne	N	N	Y	Y	Y	Y	Y
2 Roby	N	N	Y	Y	Y	Y	Y
3 Rogers	N	N	Y	Y	Y	Y	Y
4 Aderholt	N	N	Y	Y	?	?	Y
5 Brooks	N	N	N	Y	Y	Y	Y
6 Palmer	N	N	Y	Y	Y	Y	Y
7 Sewell	Y	Y	N	Y	N	Y	N
ALASKA							
AL Young	N	N	Y	Y	Y	Y	Y
ARIZONA							
1 O'Halleran	Y	Y	Y	Y	Y	Y	N
2 McSally	Y	N	Y	Y	Y	Y	Y
3 Grijalva	Y	Y	N	Y	N	Y	N
4 Gosar	?	?	?	?	Y	Y	Y
5 Biggs	N	N	N	Y	Y	Y	Y
6 Schweikert	N	N	Y	Y	Y	Y	Y
7 Gallego	Y	Y	N	Y	N	Y	N
8 Franks	N	N	Y	Y	Y	Y	Y
9 Sinema	N	Y	N	Y	Y	Y	N
ARKANSAS							
1 Crawford	N	N	Y	Y	Y	Y	Y
2 Hill	N	N	Y	Y	Y	Y	Y
3 Womack	N	N	Y	Y	Y	Y	Y
4 Westerman	N	N	Y	Y	Y	Y	Y
CALIFORNIA							
1 LaMalfa	N	N	Y	Y	Y	Y	Y
2 Huffman	Y	Y	N	Y	N	Y	N
3 Garamendi	Y	Y	N	Y	N	Y	N
4 McClintock	Y	N	Y	Y	Y	Y	Y
5 Thompson	Y	Y	N	Y	N	Y	N
6 Matsui	Y	Y	N	Y	N	Y	N
7 Bera	Y	Y	N	Y	N	Y	N
8 Cook	N	N	Y	Y	Y	Y	Y
9 McNerney	Y	Y	N	Y	N	Y	N
10 Denham	N	N	Y	Y	Y	Y	Y
11 DeSaulnier	Y	Y	N	Y	N	Y	N
12 Pelosi	Y	Y	N	Y	N	Y	N
13 Lee	Y	Y	N	Y	N	Y	N
14 Speier	Y	Y	N	Y	N	Y	N
15 Swalwell	Y	Y	N	Y	N	Y	N
16 Costa	?	?	?	?	Y	Y	N
17 Khanna	Y	Y	N	Y	N	Y	N
18 Eshoo	Y	Y	N	Y	N	Y	N
19 Lofgren	Y	Y	N	Y	N	Y	N
20 Panetta	Y	Y	N	Y	N	Y	N
21 Valadao	N	N	Y	Y	Y	Y	Y
22 Nunes	N	N	Y	Y	Y	Y	Y
23 McCarthy	N	N	Y	Y	Y	Y	Y
24 Carbajal	Y	Y	N	Y	N	Y	N
25 Knight	N	N	Y	Y	Y	Y	Y
26 Brownley	Y	Y	N	Y	N	Y	N
27 Chu	Y	Y	N	Y	N	Y	N
28 Schiff	Y	Y	N	Y	N	Y	N
29 Cardenas	Y	Y	N	Y	N	Y	N
30 Sherman	Y	Y	N	Y	N	Y	N
31 Aguilar	Y	Y	N	Y	N	Y	N
32 Napolitano	Y	Y	N	Y	?	?	N
33 Lieu	Y	Y	N	Y	N	Y	N
34 Gomez	Y	Y	N	Y	N	Y	N
35 Torres	Y	Y	N	Y	N	Y	N
36 Ruiz	Y	Y	N	Y	Y	Y	N
37 Bass	Y	Y	N	Y	N	Y	N
38 Sánchez, Linda	Y	Y	N	Y	N	Y	N
39 Royce	Y	N	Y	Y	Y	Y	Y
40 Roybal-Allard	Y	Y	–	Y	N	Y	N
41 Takano	Y	Y	N	Y	N	Y	N
42 Calvert	N	N	Y	Y	Y	Y	Y
43 Waters	Y	Y	N	Y	N	Y	N
44 Barragan	Y	Y	N	Y	N	Y	N
45 Walters	N	N	Y	Y	Y	Y	Y
46 Correa	Y	Y	N	Y	N	Y	N
47 Lowenthal	Y	Y	N	Y	N	Y	N
48 Rohrabacher	Y	N	Y	Y	?	?	Y
49 Issa	N	N	Y	Y	Y	Y	Y
50 Hunter	Y	N	Y	Y	Y	Y	Y
51 Vargas	Y	Y	N	Y	N	Y	N
52 Peters	Y	Y	N	Y	N	Y	N
53 Davis	Y	Y	N	Y	N	Y	N

	526	527	528	529	530	531	532
COLORADO							
1 DeGette	Y	Y	N	Y	N	Y	N
2 Polis	Y	Y	N	Y	N	Y	N
3 Tipton	Y	N	Y	Y	Y	Y	Y
4 Buck	Y	N	N	Y	Y	Y	Y
5 Lamborn	Y	N	Y	Y	Y	Y	Y
6 Coffman	N	N	Y	Y	Y	Y	Y
7 Perlmutter	Y	Y	N	Y	N	Y	N
CONNECTICUT							
1 Larson	+	+	–	+	N	Y	N
2 Courtney	Y	Y	N	Y	N	Y	N
3 DeLauro	+	+	–	+	N	Y	N
4 Himes	Y	Y	N	?	N	Y	N
5 Esty	Y	Y	N	Y	N	Y	N
DELAWARE							
AL Blunt Rochester	Y	Y	N	Y	–	+	Y
FLORIDA							
1 Gaetz	Y	N	Y	Y	Y	Y	Y
2 Dunn	N	N	Y	Y	Y	Y	Y
3 Yoho	+	–	+	+	Y	Y	Y
4 Rutherford	–	–	+	+	Y	Y	Y
5 Lawson	?	?	?	?	Y	Y	N
6 DeSantis	Y	N	N	Y	Y	Y	Y
7 Murphy	Y	Y	N	Y	N	Y	N
8 Posey	?	?	?	?	Y	Y	Y
9 Soto	Y	Y	N	Y	N	Y	N
10 Demings	Y	Y	N	Y	N	Y	N
11 Webster	N	N	Y	Y	Y	Y	Y
12 Bilirakis	N	N	Y	Y	Y	Y	Y
13 Crist	?	?	?	?	Y	Y	N
14 Castor	Y	Y	N	Y	N	Y	N
15 Ross	?	?	?	?	Y	Y	Y
16 Buchanan	?	?	?	?	Y	Y	Y
17 Rooney, T.	?	?	?	?	Y	Y	Y
18 Mast	N	N	Y	Y	Y	Y	Y
19 Rooney, F.	?	?	?	?	Y	Y	Y
20 Hastings	Y	Y	N	Y	N	Y	N
21 Frankel	?	?	?	?	N	Y	N
22 Deutch	Y	Y	N	Y	N	Y	N
23 Wasserman Schultz	Y	Y	N	Y	N	Y	N
24 Wilson	Y	Y	N	Y	N	Y	N
25 Diaz-Balart	?	?	?	?	Y	Y	Y
26 Curbelo	N	N	Y	Y	Y	Y	Y
27 Ros-Lehtinen	?	?	?	?	?	?	?
GEORGIA							
1 Carter	–	–	+	+	Y	Y	Y
2 Bishop	Y	Y	N	Y	N	Y	N
3 Ferguson	N	N	Y	Y	Y	Y	Y
4 Johnson	Y	Y	N	Y	N	Y	N
5 Lewis	Y	Y	N	Y	N	Y	N
6 Handel	N	N	Y	Y	Y	Y	Y
7 Woodall	N	N	Y	Y	Y	Y	Y
8 Scott, A.	N	N	Y	Y	Y	Y	Y
9 Collins	N	N	Y	Y	Y	Y	Y
10 Hice	N	N	Y	Y	Y	Y	Y
11 Loudermilk	?	?	?	?	Y	Y	Y
12 Allen	N	N	Y	Y	Y	Y	Y
13 Scott, D.	Y	Y	N	Y	N	Y	N
14 Graves	N	N	Y	Y	Y	Y	N
HAWAII							
1 Hanabusa	Y	Y	N	Y	?	?	?
2 Gabbard	Y	Y	N	Y	?	?	N
IDAHO							
1 Labrador	N	N	Y	Y	Y	Y	Y
2 Simpson	Y	N	Y	Y	Y	Y	Y
ILLINOIS							
1 Rush	Y	Y	N	Y	N	Y	N
2 Kelly	Y	Y	N	Y	N	Y	N
3 Lipinski	Y	Y	N	Y	N	Y	N
4 Gutierrez	Y	Y	N	Y	N	Y	N
5 Quigley	Y	Y	N	Y	N	Y	N
6 Roskam	Y	Y	N	Y	N	Y	Y
7 Davis, D.	Y	Y	N	Y	N	Y	N
8 Krishnamoorthi	Y	Y	N	Y	N	Y	N
9 Schakowsky	Y	Y	N	Y	N	Y	N
10 Schneider	Y	Y	N	Y	N	Y	N
11 Foster	Y	Y	N	Y	N	Y	N
12 Bost	N	N	Y	?	Y	Y	Y
13 Davis, R.	N	N	Y	Y	Y	Y	Y
14 Hultgren	Y	N	Y	Y	Y	Y	Y
15 Shimkus	Y	N	Y	Y	?	?	Y

	526	527	528	529	530	531	532
16 **Kinzinger**	Y	N	Y	Y	Y	Y	Y
17 Bustos	Y	Y	N	Y	N	Y	N
18 **LaHood**	Y	N	Y	Y	Y	Y	Y
INDIANA							
1 Visclosky	Y	Y	N	Y	N	Y	N
2 **Walorski**	N	N	Y	Y	Y	Y	Y
3 **Banks**	N	N	Y	Y	Y	Y	Y
4 **Rokita**	Y	N	N	Y	Y	Y	Y
5 **Brooks**	N	N	Y	Y	Y	Y	Y
6 **Messer**	Y	N	N	Y	Y	Y	?
7 Carson	Y	Y	N	Y	N	Y	N
8 **Bucshon**	Y	N	Y	Y	Y	Y	Y
9 **Hollingsworth**	Y	N	Y	Y	Y	Y	Y
IOWA							
1 **Blum**	Y	N	Y	Y	Y	Y	Y
2 Loebsack	Y	Y	N	Y	Y	Y	N
3 **Young**	Y	N	Y	Y	Y	Y	Y
4 **King**	Y	N	Y	Y	Y	Y	Y
KANSAS							
1 **Marshall**	N	N	Y	Y	Y	Y	Y
2 **Jenkins**	N	N	Y	Y	Y	Y	Y
3 **Yoder**	Y	N	Y	Y	Y	Y	Y
4 **Estes**	N	N	Y	Y	N	Y	Y
KENTUCKY							
1 **Comer**	N	N	Y	Y	Y	Y	Y
2 **Guthrie**	N	N	Y	Y	Y	Y	Y
3 Yarmuth	Y	Y	N	Y	N	Y	?
4 **Massie**	N	N	N	N	Y	Y	Y
5 **Rogers**	N	N	Y	Y	Y	Y	Y
6 **Barr**	N	N	Y	Y	Y	Y	Y
LOUISIANA							
1 **Scalise**	?	?	?	?	?	?	?
2 Richmond	Y	Y	N	Y	N	Y	N
3 **Higgins**	Y	N	Y	Y	Y	Y	Y
4 **Johnson**	Y	N	Y	Y	Y	Y	Y
5 **Abraham**	N	N	Y	Y	N	Y	Y
6 **Graves**	N	N	Y	Y	N	Y	Y
MAINE							
1 Pingree	Y	Y	N	Y	N	Y	N
2 **Poliquin**	Y	N	Y	Y	Y	Y	Y
MARYLAND							
1 **Harris**	N	N	Y	Y	Y	Y	Y
2 Ruppersberger	Y	Y	N	Y	N	Y	N
3 Sarbanes	Y	Y	N	Y	N	Y	N
4 Brown	Y	Y	N	Y	N	Y	N
5 Hoyer	N	Y	N	Y	N	Y	N
6 Delaney	Y	Y	N	Y	N	?	N
7 Cummings	Y	Y	N	Y	N	Y	N
8 Raskin	Y	Y	N	Y	N	Y	N
MASSACHUSETTS							
1 Neal	Y	Y	N	Y	N	Y	N
2 McGovern	Y	Y	N	Y	N	Y	N
3 Tsongas	Y	Y	N	Y	N	Y	N
4 Kennedy	Y	Y	N	Y	N	Y	N
5 Clark	Y	Y	N	Y	N	Y	N
6 Moulton	Y	Y	N	Y	N	Y	N
7 Capuano	Y	Y	N	Y	N	Y	N
8 Lynch	Y	Y	N	Y	N	Y	N
9 Keating	Y	Y	N	Y	N	Y	N
MICHIGAN							
1 **Bergman**	Y	N	Y	Y	Y	Y	Y
2 **Huizenga**	N	N	Y	Y	Y	Y	Y
3 **Amash**	Y	N	N	N	N	Y	Y
4 **Moolenaar**	Y	N	Y	Y	Y	Y	Y
5 Kildee	Y	Y	N	Y	N	Y	N
6 **Upton**	Y	N	Y	Y	Y	Y	Y
7 **Walberg**	Y	N	Y	Y	Y	Y	Y
8 **Bishop**	N	N	Y	Y	?	Y	Y
9 Levin	Y	Y	N	Y	N	Y	N
10 **Mitchell**	N	N	Y	Y	Y	Y	Y
11 **Trott**	N	N	Y	Y	Y	Y	Y
12 Dingell	Y	Y	N	Y	N	Y	–
13 Conyers	Y	Y	N	Y	N	Y	N
14 Lawrence	Y	Y	N	Y	N	Y	N
MINNESOTA							
1 Walz	Y	Y	N	Y	N	Y	N
2 **Lewis**	N	N	Y	Y	Y	Y	Y
3 **Paulsen**	Y	N	Y	Y	Y	Y	Y
4 McCollum	Y	Y	N	Y	N	Y	N

	526	527	528	529	530	531	532
5 Ellison	Y	Y	N	Y	N	Y	N
6 **Emmer**	Y	N	Y	Y	Y	Y	Y
7 Peterson	Y	Y	Y	Y	Y	Y	N
8 Nolan	Y	Y	N	Y	N	Y	N
MISSISSIPPI							
1 **Kelly**	N	N	Y	Y	Y	Y	Y
2 Thompson	Y	Y	N	Y	N	Y	N
3 **Harper**	N	N	Y	Y	Y	Y	Y
4 **Palazzo**	N	N	Y	Y	Y	Y	Y
MISSOURI							
1 Clay	Y	Y	N	Y	N	Y	N
2 **Wagner**	N	N	Y	Y	Y	Y	Y
3 **Luetkemeyer**	N	N	Y	Y	Y	Y	Y
4 **Hartzler**	N	N	Y	Y	Y	Y	Y
5 Cleaver	+	+	–	?	N	Y	N
6 **Graves**	?	?	?	?	Y	Y	Y
7 **Long**	N	N	Y	Y	Y	Y	+
8 **Smith**	N	N	Y	Y	Y	Y	Y
MONTANA							
AL **Gianforte**	Y	N	Y	Y	Y	Y	Y
NEBRASKA							
1 **Fortenberry**	Y	N	Y	Y	Y	Y	Y
2 **Bacon**	Y	N	Y	Y	Y	Y	Y
3 **Smith**	Y	N	Y	Y	Y	Y	Y
NEVADA							
1 Titus	Y	Y	N	Y	N	Y	N
2 **Amodei**	Y	N	Y	Y	Y	Y	Y
3 Rosen	Y	Y	N	Y	Y	Y	N
4 Kihuen	Y	Y	N	Y	Y	Y	N
NEW HAMPSHIRE							
1 Shea-Porter	Y	Y	N	Y	Y	Y	N
2 Kuster	Y	Y	N	Y	Y	Y	N
NEW JERSEY							
1 Norcross	Y	Y	N	Y	N	Y	N
2 **LoBiondo**	Y	N	N	Y	Y	Y	Y
3 **MacArthur**	Y	N	Y	Y	Y	Y	Y
4 **Smith**	Y	N	Y	Y	Y	Y	Y
5 Gottheimer	Y	Y	N	Y	N	Y	N
6 Pallone	Y	Y	N	Y	N	Y	N
7 **Lance**	Y	N	Y	Y	Y	Y	Y
8 Sires	Y	Y	N	Y	N	Y	N
9 Pascrell	Y	Y	N	Y	N	Y	N
10 Payne	Y	Y	N	Y	N	Y	?
11 **Frelinghuysen**	N	N	Y	Y	Y	Y	Y
12 Watson Coleman	Y	Y	N	Y	N	Y	N
NEW MEXICO							
1 Lujan Grisham	Y	Y	N	Y	N	Y	N
2 **Pearce**	N	N	Y	Y	Y	Y	Y
3 Luján	Y	Y	N	Y	N	Y	N
NEW YORK							
1 **Zeldin**	N	N	Y	Y	Y	Y	Y
2 **King**	Y	N	Y	Y	Y	Y	Y
3 Suozzi	Y	Y	N	Y	Y	Y	N
4 Rice	Y	Y	N	Y	N	Y	N
5 Meeks	Y	Y	N	Y	N	Y	N
6 Meng	Y	Y	N	Y	N	Y	N
7 Velázquez	Y	Y	N	Y	N	Y	N
8 Jeffries	Y	Y	N	Y	N	Y	N
9 Clarke	Y	Y	N	Y	N	Y	N
10 Nadler	Y	Y	N	Y	N	Y	N
11 **Donovan**	Y	N	Y	Y	Y	Y	Y
12 Maloney, C.	Y	Y	N	Y	N	Y	N
13 Espaillat	Y	Y	N	?	N	Y	N
14 Crowley	Y	Y	N	Y	N	Y	N
15 Serrano	Y	Y	N	Y	N	Y	N
16 Engel	Y	Y	N	Y	N	Y	N
17 Lowey	Y	Y	N	Y	N	Y	N
18 Maloney, S.P.	Y	Y	N	Y	Y	Y	N
19 **Faso**	Y	N	Y	Y	Y	Y	Y
20 Tonko	Y	Y	N	Y	N	Y	N
21 **Stefanik**	Y	N	Y	Y	Y	Y	Y
22 **Tenney**	Y	N	Y	Y	Y	Y	Y
23 **Reed**	Y	N	Y	Y	Y	Y	Y
24 **Katko**	N	N	N	Y	Y	Y	Y
25 Slaughter	Y	Y	N	Y	N	Y	N
26 Higgins	Y	Y	N	Y	N	Y	N
27 **Collins**	N	N	Y	Y	Y	Y	Y
NORTH CAROLINA							
1 Butterfield	Y	Y	N	Y	N	Y	N
2 **Holding**	N	N	Y	Y	Y	Y	Y
3 **Jones**	Y	N	N	N	N	Y	Y
4 Price	Y	Y	N	Y	N	Y	N

	526	527	528	529	530	531	532
5 **Foxx**	N	N	Y	Y	Y	Y	Y
6 **Walker**	N	N	Y	Y	Y	Y	Y
7 **Rouzer**	N	N	Y	Y	Y	Y	Y
8 **Hudson**	N	N	Y	Y	Y	Y	Y
9 **Pittenger**	N	N	Y	Y	Y	Y	Y
10 **McHenry**	Y	N	Y	Y	Y	Y	Y
11 **Meadows**	N	N	Y	Y	Y	Y	?
12 Adams	Y	Y	N	Y	N	Y	N
13 **Budd**	N	N	Y	Y	Y	Y	Y
NORTH DAKOTA							
AL **Cramer**	N	N	Y	Y	Y	Y	Y
OHIO							
1 **Chabot**	N	N	Y	Y	Y	Y	Y
2 **Wenstrup**	N	N	Y	Y	Y	Y	Y
3 Beatty	Y	Y	N	Y	N	Y	N
4 **Jordan**	N	N	Y	Y	Y	Y	Y
5 **Latta**	N	N	Y	Y	Y	Y	Y
6 **Johnson**	Y	N	Y	Y	Y	Y	Y
7 **Gibbs**	N	N	Y	Y	Y	Y	Y
8 **Davidson**	N	N	Y	N	Y	Y	Y
9 Kaptur	Y	Y	N	Y	N	Y	N
10 **Turner**	N	N	Y	Y	Y	Y	Y
11 Fudge	Y	Y	N	Y	?	?	N
12 **Tiberi**	?	?	+	+	+	+	?
13 Ryan	Y	Y	N	Y	N	Y	N
14 **Joyce**	Y	N	Y	Y	Y	Y	Y
15 **Stivers**	N	N	Y	?	Y	Y	Y
16 **Renacci**	N	N	Y	Y	Y	Y	Y
OKLAHOMA							
1 **Bridenstine**	?	?	?	?	?	?	?
2 **Mullin**	N	N	Y	Y	Y	Y	Y
3 **Lucas**	N	N	Y	Y	Y	Y	Y
4 **Cole**	N	N	Y	Y	Y	Y	Y
5 **Russell**	N	N	Y	Y	Y	Y	Y
OREGON							
1 Bonamici	Y	Y	N	Y	N	Y	N
2 **Walden**	Y	N	Y	Y	Y	Y	Y
3 Blumenauer	Y	Y	N	Y	N	Y	N
4 DeFazio	Y	Y	N	Y	N	Y	N
5 Schrader	Y	Y	N	Y	N	Y	N
PENNSYLVANIA							
1 Brady	Y	Y	N	Y	N	Y	N
2 Evans	Y	Y	N	Y	N	Y	N
3 **Kelly**	Y	N	Y	Y	Y	Y	Y
4 **Perry**	N	N	Y	Y	Y	Y	Y
5 **Thompson**	Y	N	Y	Y	Y	Y	Y
6 **Costello**	N	N	Y	Y	Y	Y	Y
7 **Meehan**	Y	N	Y	Y	Y	Y	Y
8 **Fitzpatrick**	Y	N	Y	Y	Y	Y	Y
9 **Shuster**	Y	N	Y	Y	Y	Y	Y
10 **Marino**	?	N	Y	Y	Y	Y	Y
11 **Barletta**	Y	N	Y	Y	Y	Y	Y
12 **Rothfus**	N	N	Y	Y	Y	Y	Y
13 Boyle	Y	Y	N	Y	N	Y	N
14 Doyle	Y	Y	N	Y	N	Y	N
15 **Dent**	Y	N	Y	Y	Y	Y	Y
16 **Smucker**	N	N	Y	Y	Y	Y	Y
17 Cartwright	Y	Y	N	Y	N	Y	N
18 **Murphy**	Y	N	Y	Y	Y	Y	Y
RHODE ISLAND							
1 Cicilline	Y	Y	N	?	N	Y	N
2 Langevin	Y	Y	N	Y	N	Y	N
SOUTH CAROLINA							
1 **Sanford**	Y	N	N	Y	N	Y	Y
2 **Wilson**	N	N	Y	Y	Y	Y	Y
3 **Duncan**	N	N	Y	Y	Y	Y	Y
4 **Gowdy**	N	N	Y	Y	Y	Y	Y
5 **Norman**	Y	N	Y	Y	Y	Y	Y
6 Clyburn	?	?	?	?	N	Y	N
7 **Rice**	N	N	Y	Y	Y	Y	Y
SOUTH DAKOTA							
AL **Noem**	N	N	Y	Y	Y	Y	Y
TENNESSEE							
1 **Roe**	N	N	Y	Y	Y	Y	Y
2 **Duncan**	Y	N	N	Y	Y	Y	Y
3 **Fleischmann**	Y	N	Y	Y	Y	Y	Y
4 **DesJarlais**	N	N	Y	Y	Y	Y	Y
5 Cooper	Y	Y	N	Y	N	Y	N
6 **Black**	N	N	Y	Y	Y	Y	Y
7 **Blackburn**	N	N	Y	Y	Y	Y	Y
8 **Kustoff**	N	N	Y	Y	Y	Y	Y
9 Cohen	Y	Y	N	Y	N	Y	N

	526	527	528	529	530	531	532
TEXAS							
1 **Gohmert**	N	N	Y	Y	Y	Y	Y
2 **Poe**	N	N	Y	Y	Y	Y	Y
3 **Johnson, S.**	N	N	Y	Y	?	?	?
4 **Ratcliffe**	N	N	Y	Y	Y	Y	Y
5 **Hensarling**	N	N	Y	Y	Y	Y	Y
6 **Barton**	Y	N	Y	Y	Y	Y	Y
7 **Culberson**	Y	N	Y	Y	Y	Y	Y
8 **Brady**	N	N	Y	Y	Y	Y	Y
9 Green, A.	Y	Y	N	Y	Y	Y	N
10 **McCaul**	N	N	Y	Y	Y	Y	Y
11 **Conaway**	N	N	Y	Y	Y	Y	Y
12 **Granger**	N	N	Y	Y	+	+	+
13 **Thornberry**	N	N	Y	Y	Y	Y	Y
14 **Weber**	N	N	Y	Y	Y	Y	Y
15 Gonzalez	Y	Y	N	Y	Y	Y	N
16 O'Rourke	Y	Y	N	Y	N	Y	N
17 **Flores**	N	N	Y	Y	?	?	Y
18 Jackson Lee	Y	Y	N	Y	Y	Y	N
19 **Arrington**	Y	N	Y	Y	Y	Y	Y
20 Castro	Y	Y	N	Y	N	Y	N
21 **Smith**	N	N	Y	Y	Y	Y	Y
22 **Olson**	N	N	Y	Y	Y	Y	Y
23 **Hurd**	Y	N	Y	Y	Y	Y	Y
24 **Marchant**	N	N	Y	Y	Y	Y	Y
25 **Williams**	Y	N	Y	Y	Y	Y	Y
26 **Burgess**	Y	N	Y	Y	Y	Y	Y
27 **Farenthold**	Y	N	Y	Y	Y	Y	Y
28 Cuellar	Y	Y	N	Y	Y	Y	N
29 Green, G.	Y	Y	N	Y	Y	Y	N
30 Johnson, E.B.	Y	Y	N	Y	N	Y	–
31 **Carter**	N	N	Y	Y	Y	Y	Y
32 **Sessions**	N	N	Y	Y	Y	Y	Y
33 Veasey	Y	Y	N	Y	N	Y	N
34 Vela	Y	Y	N	?	N	Y	N
35 Doggett	Y	Y	N	Y	N	Y	N
36 **Babin**	N	N	Y	Y	Y	Y	Y
UTAH							
1 **Bishop**	N	N	Y	Y	Y	Y	Y
2 **Stewart**	Y	N	Y	Y	Y	Y	Y
4 **Love**	N	N	Y	Y	Y	Y	Y
VERMONT							
AL Welch	Y	Y	N	Y	N	Y	N
VIRGINIA							
1 **Wittman**	N	N	Y	Y	Y	Y	Y
2 **Taylor**	N	N	Y	Y	Y	Y	Y
3 Scott	Y	Y	N	Y	N	Y	N
4 McEachin	Y	Y	N	Y	N	Y	N
5 **Garrett**	?	?	?	?	Y	Y	Y
6 **Goodlatte**	N	N	Y	Y	Y	Y	Y
7 **Brat**	N	N	Y	Y	Y	Y	Y
8 Beyer	Y	Y	N	Y	N	Y	N
9 **Griffith**	Y	N	Y	Y	Y	?	Y
10 **Comstock**	N	N	Y	Y	Y	Y	Y
11 Connolly	Y	Y	N	Y	Y	Y	N
WASHINGTON							
1 DelBene	Y	Y	N	Y	N	Y	N
2 Larsen	Y	Y	N	Y	N	Y	N
3 **Herrera Beutler**	Y	N	Y	Y	Y	Y	Y
4 **Newhouse**	N	N	Y	Y	Y	Y	Y
5 **McMorris Rodgers**	Y	N	Y	Y	Y	Y	Y
6 Kilmer	Y	Y	N	Y	N	Y	N
7 Jayapal	Y	Y	N	Y	N	Y	N
8 **Reichert**	N	N	Y	Y	Y	Y	Y
9 Smith	Y	Y	N	Y	N	Y	N
10 Heck	Y	Y	N	Y	N	Y	N
WEST VIRGINIA							
1 **McKinley**	Y	N	Y	Y	Y	Y	Y
2 **Mooney**	Y	N	Y	Y	Y	Y	Y
3 **Jenkins**	Y	N	Y	Y	Y	Y	Y
WISCONSIN							
1 **Ryan**			Y				
2 Pocan	Y	Y	N	Y	N	Y	N
3 Kind	Y	Y	N	Y	N	Y	N
4 Moore	Y	Y	N	Y	N	Y	N
5 **Sensenbrenner**	Y	N	N	Y	N	Y	Y
6 **Grothman**	N	N	Y	Y	N	Y	Y
7 **Duffy**	Y	N	Y	?	?	?	Y
8 **Gallagher**	N	N	Y	Y	Y	Y	Y
WYOMING							
AL **Cheney**	N	N	Y	Y	Y	Y	Y

VOTE NUMBER

533. H RES 533, HR 2824, HR 2792. MATERNAL AND INFANT HOME VISIT PROGRAM AND PAROLE VIOLATORS' BENEFITS REVOCATION/RULE. Adoption of the rule (H Res 533) that would provide for House floor consideration of the bill (HR 2824), that would authorize, through fiscal 2022, $400 million a year for the Maternal, Infant and Early Childhood Home Visiting program created under the 2010 health care overhaul, and for consideration of the bill (HR 2792), that would prohibit, beginning in 2021, the payment of Social Security benefits to an individual who is the subject of an outstanding arrest warrant for committing a felony or for violating a condition of parole or probation. The rule would also provide for the text of the Control Unlawful Fugitive Felons Act (HR 2792), as passed by the House, if passed by the House, to be incorporated into the text of the Increasing Opportunity through Evidence-Based Home Visiting Act (HR 2824) during the engrossment of HR 2824. Adopted 230-190 : R 230-0; D 0-190. Sept. 26, 2017.

534. PROCEDURAL MOTION/APPROVAL OF HOUSE JOURNAL. Approved 214-199 : R 136-91; D 78-108. Sept. 26, 2017.

535. HR 2824. MATERNAL AND INFANT HOME VISIT PROGRAM/ EMPLOYMENT BENCHMARKS. Pascrell, D-N.J., amendment that would remove the bill's provision that would require states or other eligible entities to track whether the home visit program increases employment and earnings as a measure of the program goals. Rejected in Committee of the Whole 191-231 : R 1-231; D 190-0. Sept. 26, 2017.

536. HR 2824. MATERNAL AND INFANT HOME VISIT PROGRAM/RECOMMIT. DelBene, D-Wash., motion to recommit the bill to the House Ways and Means Committee with instructions to report it back immediately with an amendment that would eliminate the bill's provisions that would require entities that receive grants under the Maternal, Infant and Early Childhood Home Visiting program to continue to demonstrate improvements in applicable benchmarks and guidelines. Motion rejected 191-232 : R 0-232; D 191-0. Sept. 26, 2017.

537. HR 2824. MATERNAL AND INFANT HOME VISIT PROGRAM/PASSAGE. Passage of the bill that would authorize, through fiscal 2022, $400 million a year for the Maternal, Infant and Early Childhood Home Visiting program created under the 2010 health care overhaul. The bill would require entities that receive grants under the Maternal, Infant and Early Childhood Home Visiting program to continue to demonstrate improvements in applicable benchmarks and guidelines. Passed 214-209 : R 212-20; D 2-189. Sept. 26, 2017.

538. HR 3823, H RES 538. FAA SHORT TERM REAUTHORIZATION, FLOOD INSURANCE AND HURRICANE TAX ADJUSTMENTS/PREVIOUS QUESTION. Sessions, R-Texas, motion to order the previous question (thus limiting debate and possibility of amendment) on the rule (H Res 538) that would provide for House floor consideration of the bill (HR 3823) that would extend through March 31, 2018, various expiring authorities, programs and activities for the Federal Aviation Administration. The measure would also extend multiple health care programs, would establish the basis for the development of a private flood insurance market, and would modify tax provisions for individuals living in areas impacted by Hurricanes Harvey, Irma and Maria. The rule would also provide for motions to suspend the rules on the legislative day of September 28, 2017. Motion agreed to 223-187 : R 223-0; D 0-187. Sept. 27, 2017.

539. HR 3823, H RES 538. FAA SHORT TERM REAUTHORIZATION, FLOOD INSURANCE AND HURRICANE TAX ADJUSTMENTS/RULE. Adoption of the rule (H Res 538) that would provide for House floor consideration of the bill (HR 3823) that would extend through March 31, 2018, various expiring authorities, programs and activities for the Federal Aviation Administration. The measure would also extend multiple health care programs, would establish the basis for the development of a private flood insurance market, and would modify tax provisions for individuals living in areas impacted by Hurricanes Harvey, Irma and Maria. The rule would also provide for motions to suspend the rules on the legislative day of September 28, 2017. Adopted 223-190 : R 218-7; D 5-183. Sept. 27, 2017.

	533	534	535	536	537	538	539
ALABAMA							
1 Byrne	Y	Y	N	N	Y	Y	Y
2 Roby	Y	Y	N	N	Y	Y	Y
3 Rogers	Y	N	N	N	Y	Y	Y
4 Aderholt	Y	Y	N	N	Y	Y	Y
5 Brooks	Y	Y	N	N	N	Y	Y
6 Palmer	Y	N	N	N	Y	Y	Y
7 Sewell	N	N	Y	N	N	N	N
ALASKA							
AL Young	Y	N	N	N	Y	Y	Y
ARIZONA							
1 O'Halleran	N	N	Y	Y	N	N	Y
2 McSally	Y	N	N	N	Y	Y	Y
3 Grijalva	N	N	Y	N	N	N	N
4 Gosar	Y	N	N	N	N	N	N
5 Biggs	Y	N	N	N	N	N	N
6 Schweikert	Y	N	N	Y	N	Y	Y
7 Gallego	N	N	Y	N	N	N	N
8 Franks	Y	N	N	N	Y	Y	Y
9 Sinema	N	N	Y	N	N	N	N
ARKANSAS							
1 Crawford	Y	Y	N	N	Y	Y	?
2 Hill	Y	Y	N	N	Y	Y	Y
3 Womack	Y	Y	N	N	Y	Y	Y
4 Westerman	Y	Y	N	N	Y	Y	Y
CALIFORNIA							
1 LaMalfa	Y	Y	N	N	Y	Y	Y
2 Huffman	N	Y	Y	Y	N	N	N
3 Garamendi	N	Y	Y	Y	N	N	N
4 McClintock	Y	Y	N	N	Y	Y	Y
5 Thompson	N	N	Y	Y	N	N	N
6 Matsui	N	N	Y	Y	N	N	N
7 Bera	N	N	Y	Y	N	N	N
8 Cook	Y	Y	N	N	Y	Y	Y
9 McNerney	N	Y	Y	Y	N	N	N
10 Denham	Y	N	N	N	Y	Y	Y
11 DeSaulnier	N	N	Y	Y	N	N	N
12 Pelosi	N	Y	?	Y	N	N	N
13 Lee	N	N	Y	Y	N	N	N
14 Speier	N	N	Y	Y	N	N	N
15 Swalwell	N	N	Y	Y	N	N	N
16 Costa	N	N	Y	Y	N	N	Y
17 Khanna	N	N	Y	Y	N	N	N
18 Eshoo	N	N	Y	Y	N	N	N
19 Lofgren	N	N	Y	Y	N	N	N
20 Panetta	N	N	Y	Y	N	N	N
21 Valadao	Y	N	N	N	Y	Y	Y
22 Nunes	Y	Y	N	N	Y	Y	Y
23 McCarthy	Y	Y	N	N	Y	Y	Y
24 Carbajal	N	N	Y	Y	N	N	N
25 Knight	Y	N	N	N	Y	Y	Y
26 Brownley	N	N	Y	Y	N	N	N
27 Chu	N	Y	Y	Y	N	N	N
28 Schiff	N	N	Y	Y	N	N	N
29 Cardenas	N	N	Y	Y	N	N	N
30 Sherman	N	Y	Y	Y	N	N	N
31 Aguilar	N	N	Y	Y	N	N	N
32 Napolitano	N	N	Y	Y	N	N	N
33 Lieu	N	N	Y	Y	N	N	?
34 Gomez	N	N	Y	Y	N	N	N
35 Torres	N	?	Y	Y	N	N	N
36 Ruiz	N	N	Y	Y	N	N	N
37 Bass	N	N	Y	Y	N	N	N
38 Sánchez, Linda	N	N	Y	Y	N	N	N
39 Royce	Y	Y	N	N	Y	Y	Y
40 Roybal-Allard	N	N	Y	Y	N	N	N
41 Takano	N	Y	Y	Y	N	N	N
42 Calvert	Y	Y	N	N	Y	Y	Y
43 Waters	N	N	Y	Y	N	N	N
44 Barragan	N	N	Y	Y	N	N	N
45 Walters	Y	Y	N	N	Y	Y	Y
46 Correa	N	N	Y	Y	N	N	N
47 Lowenthal	N	Y	Y	Y	N	N	N
48 Rohrabacher	Y	N	N	N	Y	Y	Y
49 Issa	Y	Y	N	N	Y	Y	Y
50 Hunter	Y	Y	N	N	Y	Y	Y
51 Vargas	N	N	Y	Y	N	N	N
52 Peters	N	N	Y	Y	N	N	N
53 Davis	N	Y	Y	Y	N	N	N

	533	534	535	536	537	538	539
COLORADO							
1 DeGette	N	Y	Y	Y	N	N	N
2 Polis	N	Y	Y	Y	N	N	N
3 Tipton	Y	N	N	N	Y	Y	Y
4 Buck	Y	N	N	N	Y	Y	Y
5 Lamborn	Y	Y	N	N	Y	Y	Y
6 Coffman	Y	N	N	N	Y	Y	Y
7 Perlmutter	N	Y	Y	Y	N	N	N
CONNECTICUT							
1 Larson	N	N	Y	Y	N	N	N
2 Courtney	Y	Y	Y	N	N	N	N
3 DeLauro	N	Y	Y	Y	N	N	N
4 Himes	N	Y	Y	Y	N	N	N
5 Esty	N	N	Y	Y	N	N	N
DELAWARE							
AL Blunt Rochester	N	N	Y	Y	N	N	N
FLORIDA							
1 Gaetz	Y	N	N	N	N	Y	Y
2 Dunn	Y	?	N	N	Y	Y	Y
3 Yoho	Y	Y	N	N	Y	+	Y
4 Rutherford	Y	Y	N	N	Y	Y	Y
5 Lawson	N	N	Y	Y	N	N	N
6 DeSantis	Y	N	N	N	Y	Y	Y
7 Murphy	N	Y	Y	N	N	Y	N
8 Posey	Y	N	N	N	Y	Y	Y
9 Soto	N	N	Y	Y	N	N	N
10 Demings	N	Y	Y	Y	N	N	N
11 Webster	Y	Y	N	N	Y	Y	Y
12 Bilirakis	Y	Y	N	N	Y	Y	Y
13 Crist	N	N	Y	Y	N	N	N
14 Castor	N	N	Y	Y	N	N	N
15 Ross	Y	N	N	N	Y	Y	Y
16 Buchanan	Y	Y	N	N	Y	Y	Y
17 Rooney, T.	Y	Y	N	N	Y	Y	Y
18 Mast	Y	N	N	N	Y	Y	Y
19 Rooney, F.	Y	Y	N	N	?	Y	Y
20 Hastings	N	N	Y	Y	N	N	N
21 Frankel	N	Y	Y	Y	N	N	N
22 Deutch	N	Y	Y	Y	N	N	N
23 Wasserman Schultz	N	Y	Y	Y	N	N	N
24 Wilson	N	Y	Y	Y	N	N	N
25 Diaz-Balart	Y	N	N	N	Y	Y	Y
26 Curbelo	Y	N	N	N	Y	Y	Y
27 Ros-Lehtinen	?	?	?	?	?	?	?
GEORGIA							
1 Carter	Y	N	N	N	Y	Y	Y
2 Bishop	N	N	Y	Y	N	N	N
3 Ferguson	Y	Y	N	N	Y	Y	Y
4 Johnson	N	Y	Y	Y	N	?	N
5 Lewis	N	N	Y	Y	N	N	N
6 Handel	Y	N	N	N	Y	Y	Y
7 Woodall	Y	N	N	N	Y	Y	Y
8 Scott, A.	Y	Y	N	N	Y	Y	Y
9 Collins	Y	N	N	N	Y	Y	Y
10 Hice	Y	N	N	N	Y	Y	Y
11 Loudermilk	Y	N	N	N	Y	Y	?
12 Allen	Y	N	N	N	Y	Y	Y
13 Scott, D.	N	Y	Y	Y	N	N	N
14 Graves	Y	N	N	N	Y	Y	Y
HAWAII							
1 Hanabusa	?	?	?	?	?	?	?
2 Gabbard	N	Y	Y	Y	N	N	N
IDAHO							
1 Labrador	Y	Y	N	N	Y	Y	Y
2 Simpson	Y	Y	N	N	Y	Y	Y
ILLINOIS							
1 Rush	N	N	Y	Y	N	-	N
2 Kelly	N	N	Y	Y	N	N	N
3 Lipinski	N	Y	Y	Y	N	N	N
4 Gutierrez	N	N	Y	Y	N	-	-
5 Quigley	N	?	Y	Y	N	N	N
6 Roskam	Y	Y	N	N	Y	?	Y
7 Davis, D.	N	Y	Y	Y	N	N	N
8 Krishnamoorthi	N	Y	Y	Y	N	N	N
9 Schakowsky	N	N	Y	Y	N	N	N
10 Schneider	N	Y	Y	Y	N	N	N
11 Foster	N	Y	Y	Y	N	N	N
12 Bost	Y	N	N	N	Y	Y	Y
13 Davis, R.	Y	N	N	Y	Y	Y	Y
14 Hultgren	Y	Y	N	N	Y	Y	Y
15 Shimkus	Y	Y	N	N	Y	Y	Y

	533	534	535	536	537	538	539
16 **Kinzinger**	Y	N	N	N	Y	Y	Y
17 Bustos	N	Y	Y	Y	N	N	N
18 **LaHood**	Y	N	N	N	Y	Y	Y
INDIANA							
1 Visclosky	N	N	Y	Y	N	N	N
2 **Walorski**	Y	Y	N	N	Y	+	+
3 **Banks**	Y	Y	N	N	Y	Y	Y
4 **Rokita**	Y	N	N	N	Y	Y	Y
5 **Brooks**	Y	Y	N	N	Y	+	+
6 **Messer**	Y	Y	N	N	Y	?	?
7 Carson	N	N	Y	Y	N	N	N
8 **Bucshon**	Y	N	N	N	Y	?	Y
9 **Hollingsworth**	Y	Y	N	N	Y	Y	Y
IOWA							
1 **Blum**	Y	N	N	N	Y	Y	Y
2 Loebsack	N	N	Y	Y	N	N	N
3 **Young**	Y	Y	N	N	N	Y	Y
4 **King**	Y	Y	N	N	Y	Y	Y
KANSAS							
1 **Marshall**	Y	Y	N	N	Y	Y	Y
2 **Jenkins**	Y	N	N	N	Y	Y	Y
3 **Yoder**	Y	N	N	N	Y	Y	Y
4 **Estes**	Y	Y	N	N	Y	Y	Y
KENTUCKY							
1 **Comer**	Y	N	N	N	Y	Y	Y
2 **Guthrie**	Y	Y	N	N	Y	Y	Y
3 Yarmuth	?	?	Y	Y	N	N	N
4 **Massie**	Y	Y	N	N	N	Y	N
5 **Rogers**	Y	Y	N	N	N	Y	Y
6 **Barr**	Y	N	N	N	Y	Y	Y
LOUISIANA							
1 **Scalise**	?	?	?	?	?	?	?
2 Richmond	N	Y	Y	Y	N	N	N
3 **Higgins**	Y	Y	N	N	Y	Y	Y
4 **Johnson**	Y	Y	N	N	Y	Y	Y
5 **Abraham**	Y	Y	N	N	Y	Y	Y
6 **Graves**	Y	N	N	N	Y	Y	Y
MAINE							
1 Pingree	N	Y	Y	Y	N	N	N
2 **Poliquin**	Y	N	N	N	Y	Y	Y
MARYLAND							
1 **Harris**	Y	Y	N	N	N	Y	Y
2 Ruppersberger	N	Y	Y	Y	N	N	N
3 Sarbanes	N	N	Y	Y	N	N	N
4 Brown	N	Y	Y	Y	N	N	N
5 Hoyer	N	N	Y	Y	N	N	N
6 Delaney	N	Y	Y	Y	N	N	N
7 Cummings	N	Y	Y	Y	N	N	N
8 Raskin	N	N	Y	Y	N	N	N
MASSACHUSETTS							
1 Neal	N	N	Y	Y	N	N	N
2 McGovern	N	N	Y	Y	N	N	N
3 Tsongas	N	Y	Y	Y	N	N	N
4 Kennedy	N	N	Y	Y	N	N	N
5 Clark	N	N	Y	Y	N	–	N
6 Moulton	N	Y	Y	Y	N	N	N
7 Capuano	N	N	Y	Y	N	N	N
8 Lynch	N	N	Y	Y	N	N	N
9 Keating	N	N	Y	Y	N	N	N
MICHIGAN							
1 **Bergman**	Y	N	N	N	Y	Y	Y
2 **Huizenga**	Y	Y	N	N	Y	Y	Y
3 **Amash**	Y	N	N	N	N	Y	N
4 **Moolenaar**	Y	N	N	N	Y	Y	Y
5 Kildee	N	Y	Y	Y	N	N	N
6 **Upton**	Y	N	N	N	Y	Y	Y
7 **Walberg**	Y	N	N	N	Y	Y	Y
8 **Bishop**	Y	N	N	N	Y	Y	Y
9 Levin	N	N	Y	Y	N	N	N
10 **Mitchell**	Y	Y	N	N	Y	Y	Y
11 **Trott**	Y	Y	N	N	Y	Y	Y
12 Dingell	N	N	Y	Y	N	N	N
13 Conyers	N	Y	Y	Y	N	N	N
14 Lawrence	N	N	Y	Y	N	N	N
MINNESOTA							
1 Walz	N	Y	Y	Y	N	?	?
2 **Lewis**	Y	Y	N	N	Y	Y	Y
3 **Paulsen**	Y	N	N	N	Y	Y	Y
4 McCollum	N	Y	Y	Y	N	N	N

	533	534	535	536	537	538	539
5 Ellison	N	Y	Y	Y	N	N	–
6 **Emmer**	Y	Y	N	N	Y	Y	Y
7 Peterson	N	N	Y	Y	Y	N	N
8 Nolan	N	N	Y	Y	N	N	N
MISSISSIPPI							
1 **Kelly**	Y	Y	N	N	Y	Y	Y
2 Thompson	N	N	Y	Y	N	N	N
3 **Harper**	Y	Y	N	N	Y	Y	Y
4 **Palazzo**	Y	Y	N	N	Y	Y	Y
MISSOURI							
1 Clay	N	Y	Y	Y	N	N	N
2 **Wagner**	Y	Y	N	N	Y	Y	Y
3 **Luetkemeyer**	Y	Y	N	N	Y	Y	Y
4 **Hartzler**	Y	N	N	N	Y	Y	Y
5 Cleaver	N	N	Y	Y	N	N	N
6 **Graves**	Y	N	N	N	Y	Y	Y
7 **Long**	+	+	–	–	+	+	+
8 **Smith**	Y	N	N	N	Y	Y	Y
MONTANA							
AL **Gianforte**	Y	Y	N	N	Y	Y	Y
NEBRASKA							
1 **Fortenberry**	Y	Y	N	N	Y	Y	Y
2 **Bacon**	Y	Y	N	N	Y	Y	Y
3 **Smith**	Y	Y	N	N	Y	Y	Y
NEVADA							
1 Titus	N	Y	Y	Y	N	N	N
2 **Amodei**	Y	Y	N	N	Y	Y	Y
3 Rosen	N	N	Y	Y	N	N	N
4 Kihuen	N	N	Y	Y	N	N	N
NEW HAMPSHIRE							
1 Shea-Porter	N	Y	Y	Y	N	N	N
2 Kuster	N	Y	Y	Y	N	N	N
NEW JERSEY							
1 Norcross	N	N	Y	Y	N	N	N
2 **LoBiondo**	Y	N	N	N	Y	Y	Y
3 **MacArthur**	Y	N	N	N	Y	Y	Y
4 **Smith**	Y	Y	N	N	Y	Y	Y
5 Gottheimer	N	N	Y	Y	N	N	N
6 Pallone	N	N	Y	Y	N	N	N
7 **Lance**	Y	N	N	N	Y	Y	Y
8 Sires	N	N	Y	Y	N	N	N
9 Pascrell	N	N	Y	Y	N	N	N
10 Payne	?	?	?	?	?	N	N
11 **Frelinghuysen**	Y	Y	N	N	Y	Y	Y
12 Watson Coleman	N	N	Y	Y	N	N	N
NEW MEXICO							
1 Lujan Grisham	N	Y	Y	Y	N	N	N
2 **Pearce**	Y	N	N	N	Y	Y	Y
3 Luján	N	Y	Y	Y	N	N	N
NEW YORK							
1 **Zeldin**	Y	Y	N	N	Y	Y	Y
2 **King**	Y	Y	N	N	Y	Y	Y
3 Suozzi	N	N	Y	Y	N	N	Y
4 Rice	N	N	Y	Y	N	N	N
5 Meeks	N	Y	Y	Y	N	N	N
6 Meng	N	Y	Y	Y	N	N	N
7 Velázquez	N	Y	Y	Y	N	N	N
8 Jeffries	N	N	Y	Y	N	N	N
9 Clarke	N	N	Y	Y	N	N	N
10 Nadler	N	Y	Y	Y	N	N	N
11 **Donovan**	Y	Y	N	N	Y	Y	Y
12 Maloney, C.	N	Y	Y	Y	N	N	N
13 Espaillat	N	N	Y	Y	N	N	N
14 Crowley	N	N	Y	Y	N	N	N
15 Serrano	N	Y	Y	Y	N	N	N
16 Engel	N	Y	Y	Y	N	N	N
17 Lowey	N	Y	Y	Y	N	N	N
18 Maloney, S.P.	N	N	Y	Y	N	N	N
19 **Faso**	Y	Y	N	N	Y	Y	Y
20 Tonko	N	P	Y	Y	N	N	N
21 **Stefanik**	Y	Y	N	N	Y	Y	Y
22 **Tenney**	Y	N	N	N	Y	Y	Y
23 **Reed**	Y	N	N	N	Y	Y	Y
24 **Katko**	Y	N	N	N	Y	Y	Y
25 Slaughter	N	N	Y	Y	N	N	N
26 Higgins	N	Y	Y	Y	N	N	N
27 **Collins**	Y	Y	N	N	Y	Y	Y
NORTH CAROLINA							
1 Butterfield	N	?	Y	Y	N	N	N
2 **Holding**	Y	N	N	N	Y	Y	Y
3 **Jones**	Y	Y	Y	N	N	Y	N
4 Price	N	N	Y	Y	N	N	N

	533	534	535	536	537	538	539
5 **Foxx**	Y	N	N	N	Y	Y	Y
6 **Walker**	Y	Y	N	N	Y	Y	Y
7 **Rouzer**	Y	N	N	N	Y	Y	Y
8 **Hudson**	Y	N	N	N	Y	Y	Y
9 **Pittenger**	Y	N	N	N	Y	Y	Y
10 **McHenry**	Y	Y	N	N	Y	Y	Y
11 **Meadows**	?	?	N	N	Y	Y	Y
12 Adams	N	N	Y	Y	N	N	N
13 **Budd**	Y	Y	N	N	Y	Y	Y
NORTH DAKOTA							
AL **Cramer**	Y	Y	N	N	Y	Y	Y
OHIO							
1 **Chabot**	Y	Y	N	N	Y	Y	Y
2 **Wenstrup**	Y	Y	N	N	Y	Y	Y
3 Beatty	N	N	Y	Y	N	N	N
4 **Jordan**	Y	N	N	N	N	Y	N
5 **Latta**	Y	Y	N	N	Y	Y	Y
6 **Johnson**	Y	N	N	N	Y	Y	Y
7 **Gibbs**	Y	N	N	N	Y	Y	Y
8 **Davidson**	Y	N	N	N	Y	Y	Y
9 Kaptur	N	Y	Y	Y	N	N	N
10 **Turner**	Y	N	N	N	Y	Y	Y
11 Fudge	N	N	Y	Y	N	N	N
12 **Tiberi**	?	?	?	?	+	?	?
13 Ryan	N	N	Y	Y	N	N	N
14 **Joyce**	Y	N	N	N	Y	Y	Y
15 **Stivers**	Y	N	N	N	Y	Y	Y
16 **Renacci**	Y	N	N	N	Y	Y	Y
OKLAHOMA							
1 **Bridenstine**	?	?	?	?	?	?	?
2 **Mullin**	Y	Y	N	N	Y	Y	Y
3 **Lucas**	Y	Y	N	N	Y	Y	Y
4 **Cole**	Y	Y	N	N	Y	Y	Y
5 **Russell**	Y	Y	N	N	Y	Y	Y
OREGON							
1 Bonamici	N	Y	Y	Y	N	N	N
2 **Walden**	Y	Y	N	N	Y	Y	Y
3 Blumenauer	N	Y	Y	Y	N	N	N
4 DeFazio	N	N	Y	Y	N	N	N
5 Schrader	N	N	Y	Y	N	N	N
PENNSYLVANIA							
1 Brady	N	N	Y	Y	N	N	N
2 Evans	N	N	Y	Y	N	N	N
3 **Kelly**	Y	Y	N	N	Y	Y	Y
4 **Perry**	Y	N	N	N	N	Y	N
5 **Thompson**	Y	N	N	N	Y	Y	Y
6 **Costello**	Y	Y	N	N	Y	Y	Y
7 **Meehan**	Y	Y	N	N	Y	Y	Y
8 **Fitzpatrick**	Y	N	N	N	Y	Y	Y
9 **Shuster**	Y	Y	N	N	Y	Y	Y
10 **Marino**	Y	Y	N	N	Y	Y	Y
11 **Barletta**	Y	Y	N	N	Y	Y	Y
12 **Rothfus**	Y	Y	N	N	Y	Y	Y
13 Boyle	N	N	Y	Y	N	N	N
14 Doyle	N	N	Y	Y	N	N	N
15 **Dent**	Y	Y	N	N	Y	Y	Y
16 **Smucker**	Y	N	N	N	Y	Y	Y
17 Cartwright	N	Y	Y	Y	N	N	N
18 **Murphy**	Y	N	N	N	Y	Y	Y
RHODE ISLAND							
1 Cicilline	N	Y	Y	Y	N	N	N
2 Langevin	N	N	Y	Y	N	N	N
SOUTH CAROLINA							
1 **Sanford**	Y	Y	N	N	Y	Y	Y
2 **Wilson**	Y	Y	N	N	Y	Y	Y
3 **Duncan**	Y	Y	N	N	Y	Y	Y
4 **Gowdy**	Y	Y	N	N	Y	Y	Y
5 **Norman**	Y	Y	N	N	Y	Y	Y
6 Clyburn	N	N	Y	Y	N	N	N
7 **Rice**	Y	Y	N	N	Y	Y	Y
SOUTH DAKOTA							
AL **Noem**	Y	Y	N	N	Y	Y	Y
TENNESSEE							
1 **Roe**	Y	N	N	N	Y	Y	Y
2 **Duncan**	Y	Y	N	N	N	Y	Y
3 **Fleischmann**	Y	Y	N	N	Y	Y	Y
4 **DesJarlais**	Y	Y	N	N	Y	Y	Y
5 Cooper	N	Y	Y	Y	N	N	N
6 **Black**	?	?	N	N	Y	Y	Y
7 **Blackburn**	Y	N	N	N	Y	Y	Y
8 **Kustoff**	Y	Y	N	N	Y	Y	Y
9 Cohen	N	Y	Y	Y	N	N	N

	533	534	535	536	537	538	539
TEXAS							
1 **Gohmert**	Y	?	N	N	Y	Y	Y
2 **Poe**	Y	N	N	N	Y	Y	Y
3 **Johnson, S.**	?	?	?	?	?	?	?
4 **Ratcliffe**	Y	N	N	N	Y	Y	Y
5 **Hensarling**	Y	Y	N	N	Y	Y	Y
6 **Barton**	Y	Y	N	N	Y	Y	Y
7 **Culberson**	Y	Y	N	N	Y	Y	Y
8 **Brady**	Y	Y	N	N	Y	Y	Y
9 Green, A.	N	N	Y	Y	N	N	N
10 **McCaul**	Y	?	N	N	Y	Y	Y
11 **Conaway**	Y	N	N	N	Y	Y	Y
12 **Granger**	+	–	–	–	+	+	+
13 **Thornberry**	Y	Y	N	N	Y	Y	Y
14 **Weber**	Y	N	N	N	Y	Y	Y
15 Gonzalez	N	N	Y	Y	N	N	N
16 O'Rourke	N	Y	Y	Y	N	N	N
17 **Flores**	Y	N	N	N	Y	Y	Y
18 Jackson Lee	N	N	Y	Y	N	N	N
19 **Arrington**	Y	Y	N	N	Y	Y	Y
20 Castro	N	Y	Y	Y	N	N	N
21 **Smith**	Y	Y	N	N	Y	Y	Y
22 **Olson**	Y	Y	N	N	Y	Y	Y
23 **Hurd**	Y	Y	N	N	Y	Y	Y
24 **Marchant**	Y	Y	N	N	Y	Y	Y
25 **Williams**	Y	Y	N	N	Y	Y	Y
26 **Burgess**	Y	N	N	N	Y	Y	Y
27 **Farenthold**	Y	Y	N	N	Y	Y	Y
28 Cuellar	N	Y	Y	Y	Y	N	N
29 Green, G.	N	N	Y	Y	N	N	N
30 Johnson, E.B.	–	–	+	+	–	–	–
31 **Carter**	Y	N	N	N	Y	Y	Y
32 **Sessions**	Y	Y	N	N	Y	Y	Y
33 Veasey	N	N	Y	Y	N	N	N
34 Vela	N	N	Y	Y	N	N	N
35 Doggett	N	Y	Y	Y	N	N	N
36 **Babin**	Y	N	N	N	Y	Y	Y
UTAH							
1 **Bishop**	Y	Y	N	N	Y	?	?
2 **Stewart**	Y	Y	N	N	Y	Y	Y
4 **Love**	Y	Y	N	N	Y	Y	Y
VERMONT							
AL Welch	N	Y	Y	Y	N	N	N
VIRGINIA							
1 **Wittman**	Y	Y	N	N	Y	Y	Y
2 **Taylor**	Y	Y	N	N	Y	Y	Y
3 Scott	N	Y	Y	Y	N	N	N
4 McEachin	N	N	Y	Y	N	N	N
5 **Garrett**	Y	N	N	N	N	Y	Y
6 **Goodlatte**	Y	Y	N	N	Y	Y	Y
7 **Brat**	Y	Y	N	N	N	Y	Y
8 Beyer	N	N	Y	Y	N	N	N
9 **Griffith**	Y	Y	N	N	N	Y	Y
10 **Comstock**	Y	Y	N	N	Y	Y	Y
11 Connolly	N	N	Y	Y	N	N	N
WASHINGTON							
1 DelBene	N	Y	Y	Y	N	N	N
2 Larsen	N	Y	Y	Y	N	N	N
3 **Herrera Beutler**	Y	N	N	N	Y	Y	Y
4 **Newhouse**	Y	Y	N	N	Y	Y	Y
5 **McMorris Rodgers**	Y	Y	N	N	Y	Y	Y
6 Kilmer	N	N	Y	Y	N	N	N
7 Jayapal	N	N	Y	Y	N	N	N
8 **Reichert**	Y	N	N	N	Y	Y	Y
9 Smith	N	Y	Y	Y	N	N	N
10 Heck	N	Y	Y	Y	N	N	N
WEST VIRGINIA							
1 **McKinley**	Y	N	N	N	Y	Y	Y
2 **Mooney**	Y	Y	N	N	Y	Y	Y
3 **Jenkins**	Y	N	N	N	Y	Y	Y
WISCONSIN							
1 **Ryan**							
2 Pocan	N	Y	Y	Y	N	N	N
3 Kind	N	N	Y	Y	N	N	N
4 Moore	N	Y	Y	Y	N	N	N
5 **Sensenbrenner**	Y	N	N	N	Y	Y	Y
6 **Grothman**	Y	N	N	N	Y	+	Y
7 **Duffy**	Y	N	N	N	Y	Y	Y
8 **Gallagher**	Y	N	N	N	Y	Y	Y
WYOMING							
AL **Cheney**	Y	N	N	N	Y	Y	Y

VOTE NUMBER

540. H RES 311. ASEAN SUPPORT AND COOPERATION/PASSAGE. Royce, R-Calif., motion to suspend the rules and agree to the resolution that would express the House of Representative's support for the relationship between the United States and Association of Southeast Asian Nations, and would express support for cooperation with ASEAN to eliminate trade barriers and implement counter-terrorism measures. Motion agreed to 413-0 : R 225-0; D 188-0. Sept. 27, 2017.

541. HR 3823. FAA SHORT TERM REAUTHORIZATION, FLOOD INSURANCE AND HURRICANE TAX ADJUSTMENTS/RECOMMIT. Nadler, D-N.Y., motion to recommit the bill to the House Ways and Means Committee with instructions to report it back immediately with an amendment that would require the secretary of the Treasury to pay to the U.S. Virgin Islands and Puerto Rico amounts equal to 400 percent of the loss in revenues from Hurricanes Harvey, Irma and Maria for the repair of infrastructure and the payment of health care costs on the islands. It would also modify corporate taxes and charitable contribution limitations in relation to disaster relief. Motion rejected 188-227 : R 0-227; D 188-0. Sept. 28, 2017.

542. HR 3823. FAA SHORT TERM REAUTHORIZATION, FLOOD INSURANCE AND HURRICANE TAX ADJUSTMENTS/PASSAGE. Passage of the bill that would extend through March 31, 2018, various expiring authorities, programs and activities for the Federal Aviation Administration. The measure would also extend multiple health care programs and would establish the basis for the development of a private flood insurance market. It would modify tax provisions for individuals living in areas impacted by Hurricanes Harvey, Irma and Maria, and would allow the federal government to reimburse the governments of Puerto Rico and the U.S. Virgin Islands for any disaster tax relief that those islands provide their citizens. Passed 264-155 : R 221-7; D 43-148. Sept. 28, 2017.

543. HR 2792. PAROLE VIOLATORS' BENEFITS REVOCATION/PASSAGE. Passage of the bill that would prohibit, beginning in 2021, the payment of Social Security benefits to an individual who is the subject of an outstanding arrest warrant for committing a felony or for violating a condition of parole or probation. Passed 244-171 : R 223-3; D 21-168. Sept. 28, 2017.

544. HR 1547. UDALL PARK INTEREST CONVEYANCE/PASSAGE. Thompson, R-Pa., motion to suspend the rules and pass the bill that would require the Interior Department to convey to the city of Tucson, Ariz., the federal government's reversionary interest in Tucson's Udall Park. Motion agreed to 401-0 : R 229-0; D 172-0. Oct. 2, 2017.

545. HR 965. SAINT-GAUDENS NATIONAL HISTORICAL PARK DESIGNATION /PASSAGE. Thompson, R-Pa., motion to suspend the rules and pass the bill that would redesignate the Saint-Gaudens National Historic Site in Sullivan County, N.H., as the Saint-Gaudens National Historical Park. Motion agreed to 401-0 : R 229-0; D 172-0. Oct. 2, 2017.

546. H RES 548, HR 36. TWENTY-WEEK ABORTION BAN/PREVIOUS QUESTION. Cheney, R-Wyo., motion to order the previous question (thus ending debate and possibility of amendment) on the rule (H Res 548) that would provide for House floor consideration of the bill (HR 36) that would prohibit abortions in cases where the probable age of the fetus is 20 weeks or later and would impose criminal penalties on doctors who violate the ban, with certain exceptions. Motion agreed to 233-184 : R 233-0; D 0-184. Oct. 3, 2017.

	540	541	542	543	544	545	546
ALABAMA							
1 Byrne	Y	N	Y	Y	Y	Y	Y
2 Roby	Y	N	Y	Y	Y	Y	Y
3 Rogers	Y	N	Y	Y	Y	Y	Y
4 Aderholt	Y	N	Y	Y	Y	Y	Y
5 Brooks	Y	N	Y	Y	Y	Y	Y
6 Palmer	Y	N	Y	Y	Y	Y	Y
7 Sewell	Y	Y	N	N	Y	N	N
ALASKA							
AL Young	Y	N	Y	Y	Y	Y	Y
ARIZONA							
1 O'Halleran	Y	Y	Y	Y	Y	Y	N
2 McSally	Y	N	Y	Y	Y	Y	Y
3 Grijalva	Y	Y	N	N	Y	N	N
4 Gosar	Y	N	Y	Y	Y	Y	Y
5 Biggs	Y	N	Y	Y	Y	Y	Y
6 Schweikert	Y	N	Y	Y	Y	Y	Y
7 Gallego	Y	Y	N	N	Y	N	N
8 Franks	Y	N	Y	Y	Y	Y	Y
9 Sinema	Y	Y	Y	Y	Y	Y	N
ARKANSAS							
1 Crawford	Y	N	Y	Y	Y	Y	Y
2 Hill	Y	N	Y	Y	Y	Y	Y
3 Womack	Y	N	Y	Y	Y	Y	Y
4 Westerman	Y	N	Y	Y	Y	Y	Y
CALIFORNIA							
1 LaMalfa	Y	N	Y	Y	Y	Y	Y
2 Huffman	Y	Y	N	N	Y	N	N
3 Garamendi	Y	Y	N	N	Y	N	N
4 McClintock	Y	N	Y	Y	Y	Y	Y
5 Thompson	Y	Y	N	N	Y	N	N
6 Matsui	Y	Y	N	N	Y	N	N
7 Bera	Y	Y	Y	Y	Y	Y	N
8 Cook	Y	N	Y	Y	Y	Y	Y
9 McNerney	Y	Y	Y	N	Y	Y	N
10 Denham	Y	N	Y	Y	Y	Y	Y
11 DeSaulnier	Y	Y	N	N	Y	N	N
12 Pelosi	Y	Y	N	N	Y	N	N
13 Lee	Y	Y	N	N	Y	N	N
14 Speier	Y	Y	N	N	Y	Y	?
15 Swalwell	Y	Y	N	N	Y	Y	N
16 Costa	Y	Y	N	N	Y	Y	N
17 Khanna	Y	Y	N	N	Y	N	N
18 Eshoo	Y	Y	N	N	Y	N	N
19 Lofgren	Y	Y	N	N	Y	N	N
20 Panetta	Y	Y	N	N	Y	Y	N
21 Valadao	Y	N	Y	Y	Y	Y	Y
22 Nunes	Y	N	Y	Y	Y	Y	Y
23 McCarthy	Y	N	Y	Y	Y	Y	Y
24 Carbajal	Y	Y	Y	N	Y	Y	N
25 Knight	Y	N	Y	Y	Y	Y	Y
26 Brownley	Y	Y	Y	N	Y	Y	N
27 Chu	Y	Y	N	N	Y	Y	N
28 Schiff	Y	Y	N	N	Y	Y	N
29 Cardenas	Y	Y	N	N	Y	Y	N
30 Sherman	Y	Y	N	N	Y	Y	N
31 Aguilar	Y	Y	N	N	Y	Y	N
32 Napolitano	Y	Y	N	N	Y	Y	N
33 Lieu	Y	Y	N	N	Y	Y	N
34 Gomez	Y	Y	N	N	Y	Y	N
35 Torres	Y	Y	N	N	Y	Y	N
36 Ruiz	Y	Y	Y	Y	Y	Y	N
37 Bass	Y	Y	N	N	Y	Y	N
38 Sánchez, Linda	Y	Y	N	N	Y	Y	N
39 Royce	Y	N	Y	Y	Y	Y	Y
40 Roybal-Allard	Y	Y	N	N	Y	Y	N
41 Takano	Y	Y	N	N	Y	Y	N
42 Calvert	Y	N	Y	Y	Y	Y	Y
43 Waters	Y	Y	N	N	Y	Y	N
44 Barragan	Y	Y	N	N	Y	Y	N
45 Walters	Y	N	Y	Y	Y	Y	Y
46 Correa	Y	Y	Y	Y	Y	Y	N
47 Lowenthal	Y	Y	N	N	Y	Y	N
48 Rohrabacher	Y	N	Y	Y	?	?	Y
49 Issa	Y	N	Y	Y	Y	Y	Y
50 Hunter	Y	N	Y	Y	Y	Y	Y
51 Vargas	Y	Y	N	N	Y	Y	N
52 Peters	Y	Y	Y	N	Y	Y	N
53 Davis	Y	Y	N	N	Y	Y	N
COLORADO							
1 DeGette	Y	Y	N	N	Y	Y	N
2 Polis	Y	Y	N	N	Y	Y	N
3 Tipton	Y	N	Y	Y	Y	Y	Y
4 Buck	Y	N	Y	Y	Y	Y	Y
5 Lamborn	Y	N	Y	Y	Y	Y	Y
6 Coffman	Y	N	Y	Y	Y	Y	Y
7 Perlmutter	Y	Y	N	N	Y	Y	N
CONNECTICUT							
1 Larson	Y	Y	N	–	Y	Y	N
2 Courtney	Y	Y	N	N	Y	Y	N
3 DeLauro	Y	Y	N	N	Y	Y	N
4 Himes	Y	Y	N	N	Y	Y	N
5 Esty	Y	Y	N	N	Y	Y	N
DELAWARE							
AL Blunt Rochester	Y	Y	N	N	Y	Y	N
FLORIDA							
1 Gaetz	Y	N	Y	Y	Y	Y	Y
2 Dunn	Y	N	Y	Y	Y	Y	Y
3 Yoho	Y	N	Y	Y	Y	Y	Y
4 Rutherford	Y	N	Y	Y	Y	Y	Y
5 Lawson	Y	Y	Y	N	Y	Y	N
6 DeSantis	Y	Y	Y	N	Y	Y	N
7 Murphy	Y	Y	Y	N	Y	Y	N
8 Posey	Y	N	Y	Y	Y	Y	Y
9 Soto	Y	Y	Y	N	?	?	N
10 Demings	Y	Y	N	N	Y	Y	N
11 Webster	Y	N	Y	Y	Y	Y	Y
12 Bilirakis	Y	N	Y	Y	Y	Y	Y
13 Crist	Y	Y	N	N	?	?	N
14 Castor	Y	Y	N	N	Y	Y	N
15 Ross	Y	N	Y	Y	Y	Y	Y
16 Buchanan	Y	N	Y	?	?	?	Y
17 Rooney, T.	Y	N	Y	Y	Y	Y	Y
18 Mast	Y	N	Y	Y	Y	Y	Y
19 Rooney, F.	?	?	?	?	Y	Y	Y
20 Hastings	Y	Y	N	N	Y	Y	N
21 Frankel	Y	Y	N	N	Y	Y	N
22 Deutch	Y	Y	N	N	Y	Y	?
23 Wasserman Schultz	Y	Y	N	N	Y	Y	N
24 Wilson	Y	?	N	N	Y	Y	N
25 Diaz-Balart	Y	N	Y	Y	Y	Y	Y
26 Curbelo	Y	N	Y	Y	Y	Y	Y
27 Ros-Lehtinen	?	?	?	?	Y	Y	Y
GEORGIA							
1 Carter	Y	N	Y	Y	Y	Y	Y
2 Bishop	Y	Y	N	N	Y	Y	N
3 Ferguson	Y	N	Y	Y	Y	Y	Y
4 Johnson	Y	?	N	N	Y	Y	N
5 Lewis	Y	Y	N	N	Y	Y	N
6 Handel	Y	N	Y	Y	Y	Y	Y
7 Woodall	Y	N	Y	Y	Y	Y	Y
8 Scott, A.	Y	N	Y	Y	Y	Y	Y
9 Collins	Y	N	Y	?	Y	Y	Y
10 Hice	Y	N	Y	Y	Y	Y	Y
11 Loudermilk	Y	N	Y	Y	Y	Y	?
12 Allen	Y	N	Y	Y	Y	Y	Y
13 Scott, D.	Y	Y	N	N	Y	Y	N
14 Graves	Y	N	Y	Y	Y	Y	Y
HAWAII							
1 Hanabusa	?	Y	N	N	Y	Y	N
2 Gabbard	Y	Y	Y	N	Y	Y	N
IDAHO							
1 Labrador	Y	N	Y	Y	Y	Y	Y
2 Simpson	Y	N	Y	Y	?	?	Y
ILLINOIS							
1 Rush	Y	Y	N	N	Y	Y	N
2 Kelly	Y	Y	N	N	Y	Y	N
3 Lipinski	Y	Y	Y	Y	Y	Y	N
4 Gutierrez	+	Y	N	N	+	+	?
5 Quigley	Y	Y	N	N	Y	Y	N
6 Roskam	Y	N	Y	Y	Y	Y	Y
7 Davis, D.	Y	Y	N	N	Y	Y	N
8 Krishnamoorthi	Y	Y	N	N	Y	Y	N
9 Schakowsky	Y	Y	N	N	Y	Y	N
10 Schneider	Y	Y	Y	N	Y	Y	N
11 Foster	Y	Y	N	N	Y	Y	N
12 Bost	Y	N	Y	Y	Y	Y	Y
13 Davis, R.	Y	N	Y	Y	Y	Y	Y
14 Hultgren	Y	N	Y	Y	Y	Y	Y
15 Shimkus	Y	N	Y	Y	Y	Y	Y

KEY	Republicans	Democrats	Independents

Y	Voted for (yea)	X	Paired against	C	Voted "present" to avoid possible conflict of interest
#	Paired for	–	Announced against	?	Did not vote or otherwise make a position known
+	Announced for	P	Voted "present"		
N	Voted against (nay)				

	540	541	542	543	544	545	546
16 **Kinzinger**	Y	N	Y	Y	Y	Y	Y
17 Bustos	Y	Y	Y	Y	Y	Y	N
18 **LaHood**	Y	N	Y	Y	Y	Y	Y
INDIANA							
1 Visclosky	Y	Y	N	N	Y	Y	N
2 **Walorski**	+	N	Y	Y	Y	Y	Y
3 **Banks**	Y	N	Y	Y	Y	Y	Y
4 **Rokita**	Y	N	Y	Y	Y	Y	Y
5 **Brooks**	+	N	Y	Y	Y	Y	Y
6 **Messer**	?	N	Y	Y	Y	Y	Y
7 Carson	Y	Y	N	N	Y	Y	N
8 **Bucshon**	Y	N	Y	Y	Y	Y	Y
9 **Hollingsworth**	Y	N	?	Y	Y	Y	Y
IOWA							
1 **Blum**	Y	N	Y	Y	Y	Y	Y
2 Loebsack	Y	Y	Y	Y	Y	Y	N
3 **Young**	Y	N	Y	Y	Y	Y	Y
4 **King**	Y	N	Y	Y	Y	Y	Y
KANSAS							
1 **Marshall**	Y	N	Y	Y	Y	Y	Y
2 **Jenkins**	Y	N	Y	Y	+	+	Y
3 **Yoder**	Y	N	Y	Y	Y	Y	Y
4 **Estes**	Y	N	Y	Y	Y	Y	Y
KENTUCKY							
1 **Comer**	Y	N	Y	Y	Y	Y	Y
2 **Guthrie**	Y	N	Y	Y	Y	Y	Y
3 Yarmuth	Y	Y	N	N	?	?	N
4 **Massie**	Y	N	Y	N	Y	Y	Y
5 **Rogers**	Y	N	Y	Y	Y	Y	Y
6 **Barr**	Y	N	Y	Y	Y	Y	Y
LOUISIANA							
1 **Scalise**	?	?	Y	Y	Y	Y	Y
2 Richmond	Y	?	N	N	?	Y	?
3 **Higgins**	Y	N	Y	Y	Y	Y	Y
4 **Johnson**	Y	N	N	Y	Y	Y	Y
5 **Abraham**	Y	N	N	Y	Y	Y	Y
6 **Graves**	Y	N	N	Y	Y	Y	Y
MAINE							
1 Pingree	Y	Y	N	N	Y	Y	N
2 **Poliquin**	Y	N	Y	Y	Y	Y	Y
MARYLAND							
1 **Harris**	Y	N	Y	Y	Y	Y	Y
2 Ruppersberger	Y	Y	Y	N	Y	+	N
3 Sarbanes	Y	Y	N	N	Y	Y	N
4 Brown	Y	Y	N	N	Y	Y	N
5 Hoyer	?	Y	N	N	Y	Y	N
6 Delaney	Y	Y	Y	N	Y	Y	N
7 Cummings	Y	Y	N	N	Y	Y	N
8 Raskin	Y	Y	N	N	Y	Y	N
MASSACHUSETTS							
1 Neal	Y	Y	N	N	Y	Y	N
2 McGovern	Y	Y	N	N	Y	Y	N
3 Tsongas	Y	Y	N	N	?	?	N
4 Kennedy	Y	Y	N	N	Y	Y	N
5 Clark	Y	Y	N	N	Y	Y	N
6 Moulton	Y	Y	Y	N	Y	Y	N
7 Capuano	Y	Y	N	N	Y	Y	N
8 Lynch	Y	Y	N	Y	Y	Y	N
9 Keating	?	Y	Y	Y	Y	Y	N
MICHIGAN							
1 **Bergman**	Y	N	Y	Y	Y	Y	Y
2 **Huizenga**	Y	N	Y	Y	Y	Y	Y
3 **Amash**	Y	N	N	N	Y	Y	Y
4 **Moolenaar**	Y	N	Y	Y	Y	Y	Y
5 Kildee	Y	Y	N	N	Y	Y	N
6 **Upton**	Y	N	Y	Y	Y	Y	Y
7 **Walberg**	Y	N	Y	Y	Y	Y	Y
8 **Bishop**	Y	N	Y	Y	Y	Y	Y
9 Levin	Y	Y	N	N	Y	Y	N
10 **Mitchell**	Y	N	Y	Y	Y	Y	Y
11 **Trott**	Y	N	Y	Y	Y	Y	Y
12 Dingell	Y	Y	N	N	Y	Y	N
13 Conyers	Y	Y	N	N	Y	Y	N
14 Lawrence	Y	Y	N	N	Y	Y	N
MINNESOTA							
1 Walz	?	?	–	–	Y	Y	N
2 **Lewis**	Y	N	Y	Y	Y	Y	Y
3 **Paulsen**	Y	N	Y	Y	Y	Y	Y
4 McCollum	Y	Y	N	N	Y	Y	N

	540	541	542	543	544	545	546
5 Ellison	Y	Y	N	N	Y	Y	N
6 **Emmer**	Y	N	Y	Y	Y	Y	Y
7 Peterson	Y	Y	Y	Y	Y	Y	N
8 Nolan	Y	Y	N	N	Y	Y	N
MISSISSIPPI							
1 **Kelly**	Y	N	Y	Y	Y	Y	Y
2 Thompson	Y	Y	N	N	Y	Y	?
3 **Harper**	Y	N	Y	Y	Y	Y	Y
4 **Palazzo**	Y	N	Y	Y	Y	Y	Y
MISSOURI							
1 Clay	Y	Y	N	N	Y	Y	N
2 **Wagner**	Y	?	?	?	Y	Y	Y
3 **Luetkemeyer**	Y	N	Y	Y	Y	Y	Y
4 **Hartzler**	Y	N	Y	Y	Y	Y	Y
5 Cleaver	Y	Y	N	N	Y	Y	N
6 **Graves**	Y	N	Y	Y	Y	Y	Y
7 **Long**	+	–	+	+	+	+	+
8 **Smith**	Y	N	Y	Y	Y	Y	Y
MONTANA							
AL **Gianforte**	Y	N	Y	Y	Y	Y	Y
NEBRASKA							
1 **Fortenberry**	Y	N	Y	Y	Y	Y	Y
2 **Bacon**	Y	N	Y	Y	Y	Y	Y
3 **Smith**	Y	N	Y	Y	Y	Y	Y
NEVADA							
1 Titus	Y	Y	N	N	+	+	–
2 **Amodei**	Y	N	Y	Y	Y	Y	Y
3 Rosen	Y	Y	Y	Y	+	+	–
4 Kihuen	Y	Y	Y	N	?	?	?
NEW HAMPSHIRE							
1 Shea-Porter	Y	Y	Y	N	Y	Y	N
2 Kuster	Y	Y	Y	N	Y	Y	N
NEW JERSEY							
1 Norcross	Y	Y	N	N	Y	Y	N
2 **LoBiondo**	Y	N	Y	Y	Y	Y	Y
3 **MacArthur**	Y	N	Y	Y	Y	Y	Y
4 **Smith**	Y	?	Y	Y	Y	Y	Y
5 Gottheimer	Y	Y	N	Y	Y	Y	N
6 Pallone	Y	Y	N	N	Y	Y	N
7 **Lance**	Y	N	Y	Y	Y	Y	Y
8 Sires	Y	Y	N	N	?	?	N
9 Pascrell	Y	+	–	–	Y	Y	N
10 Payne	Y	Y	N	N	Y	Y	N
11 **Frelinghuysen**	Y	N	Y	Y	Y	Y	Y
12 Watson Coleman	Y	Y	N	N	Y	Y	N
NEW MEXICO							
1 Lujan Grisham	Y	Y	N	N	Y	Y	N
2 **Pearce**	Y	N	Y	Y	?	?	Y
3 Luján	Y	Y	N	N	Y	Y	N
NEW YORK							
1 **Zeldin**	Y	N	Y	Y	Y	Y	Y
2 **King**	Y	N	Y	Y	Y	Y	Y
3 Suozzi	Y	Y	Y	Y	Y	Y	N
4 Rice	Y	Y	N	N	Y	Y	N
5 Meeks	Y	Y	N	N	Y	Y	N
6 Meng	Y	Y	N	N	?	?	N
7 Velázquez	Y	Y	N	N	Y	Y	N
8 Jeffries	Y	Y	N	N	Y	Y	N
9 Clarke	Y	Y	N	N	?	?	N
10 Nadler	Y	Y	N	N	Y	Y	N
11 **Donovan**	Y	N	Y	Y	Y	Y	Y
12 Maloney, C.	Y	Y	N	N	Y	Y	N
13 Espaillat	Y	Y	N	N	Y	Y	N
14 Crowley	Y	Y	N	N	+	+	–
15 Serrano	Y	Y	N	N	Y	Y	N
16 Engel	Y	Y	N	N	Y	Y	N
17 Lowey	Y	Y	N	N	Y	Y	N
18 Maloney, S.P.	Y	Y	Y	N	Y	Y	N
19 **Faso**	Y	N	Y	Y	Y	Y	Y
20 Tonko	Y	Y	N	N	Y	Y	N
21 **Stefanik**	Y	N	Y	Y	Y	Y	Y
22 **Tenney**	Y	N	Y	Y	Y	Y	Y
23 **Reed**	Y	N	Y	Y	Y	Y	Y
24 **Katko**	Y	N	Y	Y	?	?	Y
25 Slaughter	Y	Y	N	N	Y	Y	N
26 Higgins	Y	Y	N	N	Y	Y	N
27 **Collins**	Y	N	Y	Y	Y	Y	Y
NORTH CAROLINA							
1 Butterfield	Y	Y	N	N	?	?	N
2 **Holding**	Y	N	Y	Y	Y	Y	Y
3 **Jones**	Y	N	N	Y	Y	Y	Y
4 Price	Y	Y	N	N	Y	Y	N

	540	541	542	543	544	545	546
5 **Foxx**	Y	N	Y	Y	Y	Y	Y
6 **Walker**	Y	N	Y	Y	Y	Y	Y
7 **Rouzer**	Y	N	Y	Y	Y	Y	Y
8 **Hudson**	+	N	Y	Y	Y	Y	Y
9 **Pittenger**	Y	N	Y	Y	Y	Y	Y
10 **McHenry**	Y	N	Y	Y	Y	Y	Y
11 **Meadows**	Y	N	Y	Y	Y	?	Y
12 Adams	Y	Y	N	N	Y	Y	N
13 **Budd**	Y	N	Y	Y	Y	Y	Y
NORTH DAKOTA							
AL **Cramer**	Y	N	Y	?	Y	Y	Y
OHIO							
1 **Chabot**	Y	N	Y	Y	Y	Y	Y
2 **Wenstrup**	Y	N	Y	Y	Y	Y	Y
3 Beatty	Y	Y	N	N	Y	Y	N
4 **Jordan**	Y	N	Y	Y	Y	Y	Y
5 **Latta**	Y	N	Y	Y	Y	Y	Y
6 **Johnson**	Y	N	Y	Y	Y	Y	?
7 **Gibbs**	Y	N	Y	Y	Y	Y	Y
8 **Davidson**	Y	N	Y	Y	Y	Y	Y
9 Kaptur	Y	Y	N	N	?	?	N
10 **Turner**	Y	N	Y	Y	Y	Y	Y
11 Fudge	Y	Y	N	N	Y	?	N
12 **Tiberi**	+	?	+	+	Y	Y	Y
13 Ryan	Y	Y	N	N	?	?	N
14 **Joyce**	Y	N	Y	Y	Y	Y	Y
15 **Stivers**	Y	N	Y	Y	Y	Y	Y
16 **Renacci**	Y	N	Y	Y	Y	Y	Y
OKLAHOMA							
1 **Bridenstine**	?	?	?	?	?	?	?
2 **Mullin**	Y	N	Y	Y	Y	Y	Y
3 **Lucas**	Y	N	Y	Y	Y	Y	Y
4 **Cole**	Y	N	Y	Y	Y	Y	Y
5 **Russell**	Y	N	Y	Y	Y	Y	Y
OREGON							
1 Bonamici	Y	Y	N	N	Y	Y	N
2 **Walden**	Y	N	Y	Y	Y	Y	Y
3 Blumenauer	Y	Y	N	N	Y	?	N
4 DeFazio	Y	Y	N	N	+	+	N
5 Schrader	Y	Y	Y	Y	Y	Y	N
PENNSYLVANIA							
1 Brady	Y	Y	N	N	Y	Y	N
2 Evans	Y	Y	N	N	Y	Y	N
3 **Kelly**	Y	N	Y	Y	Y	Y	Y
4 **Perry**	Y	N	Y	Y	Y	Y	Y
5 **Thompson**	Y	N	Y	Y	Y	Y	Y
6 **Costello**	Y	N	Y	Y	Y	Y	Y
7 **Meehan**	Y	N	Y	Y	Y	Y	Y
8 **Fitzpatrick**	Y	N	Y	Y	Y	Y	Y
9 **Shuster**	Y	N	Y	Y	Y	Y	Y
10 **Marino**	Y	N	Y	Y	Y	Y	Y
11 **Barletta**	Y	–	+	+	Y	Y	Y
12 **Rothfus**	Y	N	Y	Y	Y	Y	Y
13 Boyle	Y	Y	N	Y	Y	Y	N
14 Doyle	Y	Y	N	N	Y	Y	N
15 **Dent**	Y	N	Y	Y	Y	Y	Y
16 **Smucker**	Y	N	Y	Y	Y	Y	Y
17 Cartwright	Y	Y	N	N	Y	Y	N
18 **Murphy**	Y	N	Y	Y	Y	Y	Y
RHODE ISLAND							
1 Cicilline	Y	Y	N	N	Y	Y	N
2 Langevin	Y	Y	N	N	+	Y	N
SOUTH CAROLINA							
1 **Sanford**	Y	N	N	Y	Y	Y	Y
2 **Wilson**	Y	N	Y	Y	Y	Y	Y
3 **Duncan**	Y	N	Y	Y	Y	Y	Y
4 **Gowdy**	Y	N	Y	Y	Y	Y	Y
5 **Norman**	Y	N	Y	Y	Y	Y	Y
6 Clyburn	Y	Y	N	N	Y	Y	N
7 **Rice**	Y	N	Y	Y	Y	Y	Y
SOUTH DAKOTA							
AL **Noem**	Y	N	Y	Y	Y	Y	Y
TENNESSEE							
1 **Roe**	Y	N	Y	Y	Y	Y	Y
2 **Duncan**	Y	N	Y	Y	Y	Y	Y
3 **Fleischmann**	Y	N	Y	Y	Y	Y	Y
4 **DesJarlais**	Y	N	Y	Y	?	?	?
5 Cooper	Y	Y	N	N	Y	Y	N
6 **Black**	Y	N	Y	Y	Y	Y	Y
7 **Blackburn**	Y	N	Y	Y	Y	Y	Y
8 **Kustoff**	Y	N	Y	Y	Y	Y	Y
9 Cohen	Y	Y	N	N	Y	Y	N

	540	541	542	543	544	545	546
TEXAS							
1 **Gohmert**	Y	N	Y	Y	Y	Y	Y
2 **Poe**	Y	N	Y	Y	Y	Y	Y
3 **Johnson, S.**	?	?	?	?	Y	Y	Y
4 **Ratcliffe**	Y	N	Y	Y	Y	Y	Y
5 **Hensarling**	Y	N	Y	Y	Y	Y	Y
6 **Barton**	Y	N	Y	Y	Y	Y	Y
7 **Culberson**	Y	N	Y	Y	Y	Y	Y
8 **Brady**	Y	N	Y	Y	Y	Y	Y
9 Green, A.	Y	Y	Y	N	Y	Y	N
10 **McCaul**	Y	N	Y	Y	Y	Y	Y
11 **Conaway**	Y	N	Y	Y	Y	Y	Y
12 **Granger**	+	–	+	+	Y	Y	Y
13 **Thornberry**	Y	N	Y	Y	Y	Y	Y
14 **Weber**	Y	N	Y	Y	Y	Y	Y
15 Gonzalez	Y	Y	Y	N	Y	Y	N
16 O'Rourke	Y	Y	N	N	Y	Y	N
17 **Flores**	Y	N	Y	Y	Y	Y	Y
18 Jackson Lee	Y	Y	Y	N	Y	Y	N
19 **Arrington**	Y	N	Y	Y	Y	Y	Y
20 Castro	Y	Y	N	N	Y	Y	N
21 **Smith**	Y	N	Y	Y	Y	Y	Y
22 **Olson**	Y	N	Y	Y	Y	Y	Y
23 **Hurd**	Y	N	Y	Y	Y	Y	Y
24 **Marchant**	?	N	Y	Y	Y	Y	Y
25 **Williams**	Y	N	Y	Y	Y	Y	Y
26 **Burgess**	Y	N	Y	Y	Y	Y	Y
27 **Farenthold**	Y	N	Y	Y	Y	Y	Y
28 Cuellar	Y	Y	Y	Y	Y	Y	N
29 Green, G.	Y	Y	Y	N	Y	Y	N
30 Johnson, E.B.	+	+	–	–	?	?	?
31 **Carter**	Y	N	Y	Y	Y	Y	Y
32 **Sessions**	Y	N	Y	Y	Y	Y	Y
33 Veasey	Y	Y	N	N	Y	Y	N
34 Vela	Y	Y	Y	N	Y	Y	N
35 Doggett	Y	Y	N	N	Y	Y	N
36 **Babin**	Y	N	Y	Y	Y	Y	Y
UTAH							
1 **Bishop**	?	?	?	?	Y	Y	Y
2 **Stewart**	Y	N	Y	Y	Y	Y	Y
4 **Love**	Y	N	Y	Y	Y	Y	Y
VERMONT							
AL Welch	Y	Y	N	N	Y	Y	N
VIRGINIA							
1 **Wittman**	Y	N	Y	Y	Y	Y	Y
2 **Taylor**	Y	N	Y	Y	Y	Y	Y
3 Scott	Y	Y	N	–	Y	Y	N
4 McEachin	Y	Y	N	N	Y	Y	N
5 **Garrett**	Y	N	Y	?	Y	Y	+
6 **Goodlatte**	Y	N	Y	Y	Y	Y	Y
7 **Brat**	Y	N	Y	Y	Y	Y	Y
8 Beyer	Y	Y	N	N	Y	Y	N
9 **Griffith**	Y	N	Y	N	Y	Y	Y
10 **Comstock**	Y	N	Y	Y	Y	Y	Y
11 Connolly	Y	Y	Y	N	?	?	N
WASHINGTON							
1 DelBene	Y	Y	N	N	Y	Y	N
2 Larsen	Y	Y	N	N	Y	Y	N
3 **Herrera Beutler**	Y	N	Y	Y	Y	Y	Y
4 **Newhouse**	Y	N	Y	Y	Y	Y	Y
5 **McMorris Rodgers**	Y	N	Y	Y	Y	Y	Y
6 Kilmer	Y	Y	N	N	Y	Y	N
7 Jayapal	Y	Y	N	N	Y	Y	N
8 **Reichert**	Y	N	Y	Y	Y	Y	Y
9 Smith	Y	Y	N	N	Y	Y	N
10 Heck	Y	Y	N	N	Y	Y	N
WEST VIRGINIA							
1 **McKinley**	Y	N	Y	Y	Y	Y	Y
2 **Mooney**	Y	N	Y	Y	Y	Y	Y
3 **Jenkins**	Y	N	Y	Y	Y	Y	Y
WISCONSIN							
1 **Ryan**							
2 Pocan	Y	Y	N	N	Y	Y	N
3 Kind	Y	Y	Y	Y	Y	Y	N
4 Moore	Y	Y	N	N	Y	Y	N
5 **Sensenbrenner**	Y	N	Y	Y	Y	Y	Y
6 **Grothman**	Y	N	N	Y	Y	Y	Y
7 **Duffy**	Y	N	Y	Y	Y	Y	Y
8 **Gallagher**	Y	N	Y	Y	Y	Y	Y
WYOMING							
AL **Cheney**	Y	N	Y	Y	Y	Y	Y

VOTE NUMBER

547. H RES 548, HR 36. TWENTY-WEEK ABORTION BAN/RULE. Adoption of the rule (H Res 548) that would provide for House floor consideration of the bill (HR 36) that would prohibit abortions in cases where the probable age of the fetus is 20 weeks or later and would impose criminal penalties on doctors who violate the ban, with certain exceptions. Adopted 233-187 : R 232-0; D 1-187. Oct. 3, 2017.

548. HR 36. TWENTY-WEEK ABORTION BAN/RECOMMIT. Brownley, D-Calif., motion to recommit the bill to the House Judiciary Committee with instructions to report it back immediately with an amendment that would add an exception to the 20-week abortion ban for abortions necessary to save the health of the pregnant woman. Motion rejected 187-238 : R 0-236; D 187-2. Oct. 3, 2017.

549. HR 36. TWENTY-WEEK ABORTION BAN/PASSAGE. Passage of the bill that would prohibit abortions in cases where the probable age of the fetus is 20 weeks or later and would impose criminal penalties on doctors who violate the ban. It would provide exceptions for cases in which the woman's life is in danger as well as for pregnancies that are a result of rape against an adult woman, if the woman received counseling or medical treatment for the rape at least 48 hours prior to the abortion. An exception would be provided for pregnancies resulting from rape or incest against a minor if the rape or incest had been previously reported to law enforcement or another government agency authorized to act on reports of child abuse. The bill would require a second doctor trained in neonatal resuscitation to be present for abortions where the fetus has the "potential" to survive outside the womb. Passed 237-189 : R 234-2; D 3-187. Oct. 3, 2017.

550. S 782. INTERNET CRIMES AGAINST CHILDREN TASK FORCE/PASSAGE. Goodlatte, R-Va., motion to suspend the rules and pass the bill that would reauthorize, through fiscal 2022, $60 million annually for the Justice Department's Internet Crimes Against Children Task Force program. Motion agreed to 417-3 : R 231-2; D 186-1. Oct. 3, 2017.

551. H CON RES 71, H RES 553. FISCAL 2018 BUDGET RESOLUTION/ PREVIOUS QUESTION. Woodall, R-Ga., motion to order the previous question (thus ending debate and possibility of amendment) on the rule (H Res 553) that would provide for House floor consideration of the fiscal 2018 budget resolution (H Con Res 71). Motion agreed to 231-189 : R 231-0; D 0-189. Oct. 4, 2017.

552. H CON RES 71, H RES 553. FISCAL 2018 BUDGET RESOLUTION/RULE. Adoption of the rule (H Res 553) that would provide for House floor consideration of the fiscal 2018 budget resolution (H Con Res 71). Adopted 232-188 : R 232-0; D 0-188. Oct. 4, 2017.

553. H CON RES 71. FISCAL 2018 BUDGET RESOLUTION/CONGRESSIONAL PROGRESSIVE CAUCUS SUBSTITUTE. Grijalva, D-Ariz., for Pocan, D-Wis., substitute amendment that would provide for $3.8 trillion in new budget authority in fiscal 2018, not including off-budget accounts. It would raise overall spending by $3.5 trillion over 10 years and would increase revenues by $8.2 trillion over the same period through policies that would increase taxes for corporations and high-income individuals. It would repeal the Budget Control Act sequester and caps on discretionary spending, would modify the tax code by adding five higher marginal tax rates, would create a public insurance option to be sold within the current health insurance exchanges and would call for implementation of comprehensive immigration overhaul. Rejected in Committee of the Whole 108-314 : R 0-235; D 108-79. Oct. 4, 2017.

	547	548	549	550	551	552	553
ALABAMA							
1 Byrne	Y	N	Y	Y	Y	Y	N
2 Roby	Y	N	Y	Y	Y	Y	N
3 Rogers	Y	N	Y	Y	Y	Y	N
4 Aderholt	Y	N	Y	Y	Y	Y	N
5 Brooks	Y	N	Y	Y	Y	Y	N
6 Palmer	Y	N	Y	?	Y	Y	N
7 Sewell	N	Y	N	Y	N	N	N
ALASKA							
AL Young	Y	N	Y	Y	Y	Y	N
ARIZONA							
1 O'Halleran	N	Y	N	Y	N	N	N
2 McSally	Y	N	Y	Y	Y	Y	N
3 Grijalva	N	Y	N	Y	N	N	Y
4 Gosar	Y	N	Y	Y	Y	Y	N
5 Biggs	Y	N	Y	?	Y	Y	N
6 Schweikert	Y	N	Y	Y	Y	Y	N
7 Gallego	N	Y	N	Y	N	N	Y
8 Franks	Y	N	Y	Y	Y	Y	N
9 Sinema	N	Y	N	Y	N	N	N
ARKANSAS							
1 Crawford	Y	N	Y	Y	Y	Y	N
2 Hill	Y	N	Y	Y	Y	Y	N
3 Womack	Y	N	Y	Y	Y	Y	N
4 Westerman	Y	N	Y	Y	Y	Y	N
CALIFORNIA							
1 LaMalfa	Y	N	Y	Y	Y	Y	N
2 Huffman	N	Y	N	Y	N	N	Y
3 Garamendi	N	Y	N	Y	N	N	N
4 McClintock	Y	N	Y	Y	Y	Y	N
5 Thompson	N	Y	N	Y	N	N	N
6 Matsui	N	Y	N	Y	N	N	N
7 Bera	N	Y	N	Y	N	N	N
8 Cook	Y	N	Y	Y	Y	Y	N
9 McNerney	N	Y	N	Y	N	N	N
10 Denham	Y	N	Y	Y	Y	Y	N
11 DeSaulnier	N	Y	N	Y	N	N	Y
12 Pelosi	N	Y	N	Y	?	N	?
13 Lee	N	Y	N	Y	N	N	Y
14 Speier	N	Y	N	Y	N	N	N
15 Swalwell	N	Y	N	Y	N	N	N
16 Costa	N	Y	N	Y	N	N	N
17 Khanna	N	Y	N	Y	N	N	Y
18 Eshoo	N	Y	N	Y	N	N	N
19 Lofgren	N	Y	N	Y	N	N	Y
20 Panetta	N	Y	N	Y	N	N	Y
21 Valadao	Y	N	Y	Y	Y	Y	N
22 Nunes	Y	N	Y	Y	Y	Y	N
23 McCarthy	Y	N	Y	?	?	Y	N
24 Carbajal	N	Y	N	Y	N	N	N
25 Knight	Y	N	Y	Y	Y	Y	N
26 Brownley	N	Y	N	Y	N	N	N
27 Chu	N	Y	N	Y	N	N	Y
28 Schiff	N	Y	N	Y	N	N	N
29 Cardenas	N	Y	N	Y	N	N	Y
30 Sherman	N	Y	N	Y	N	N	Y
31 Aguilar	N	Y	N	Y	N	N	N
32 Napolitano	N	Y	N	Y	N	N	+
33 Lieu	N	Y	N	Y	N	N	Y
34 Gomez	N	Y	N	Y	N	N	Y
35 Torres	N	Y	N	Y	N	N	Y
36 Ruiz	N	Y	N	Y	N	N	N
37 Bass	N	Y	N	Y	N	N	Y
38 Sánchez, Linda	N	Y	N	Y	N	N	Y
39 Royce	Y	N	Y	Y	Y	Y	N
40 Roybal-Allard	N	Y	N	Y	N	N	Y
41 Takano	N	Y	N	Y	N	N	Y
42 Calvert	Y	N	Y	Y	Y	Y	N
43 Waters	N	Y	N	Y	N	N	Y
44 Barragan	N	Y	N	Y	N	N	Y
45 Walters	Y	N	Y	Y	Y	Y	N
46 Correa	N	Y	N	Y	N	N	N
47 Lowenthal	N	Y	N	Y	N	N	Y
48 Rohrabacher	Y	N	Y	Y	Y	Y	N
49 Issa	Y	N	Y	Y	Y	Y	N
50 Hunter	Y	N	Y	Y	Y	Y	N
51 Vargas	N	Y	N	Y	N	N	Y
52 Peters	N	Y	N	Y	N	N	N
53 Davis	N	Y	N	Y	N	N	N

	547	548	549	550	551	552	553
COLORADO							
1 DeGette	N	Y	N	Y	N	N	N
2 Polis	N	Y	N	N	N	N	N
3 Tipton	Y	N	Y	Y	Y	Y	N
4 Buck	Y	N	Y	Y	Y	Y	N
5 Lamborn	Y	N	Y	Y	Y	Y	N
6 Coffman	Y	N	Y	Y	Y	Y	N
7 Perlmutter	N	Y	N	N	N	N	N
CONNECTICUT							
1 Larson	N	Y	N	N	N	N	N
2 Courtney	N	Y	N	N	N	N	N
3 DeLauro	N	Y	N	N	N	N	N
4 Himes	N	+	–	+	N	N	N
5 Esty	N	Y	N	N	N	N	N
DELAWARE							
AL Blunt Rochester	N	Y	N	Y	N	N	?
FLORIDA							
1 Gaetz	Y	N	Y	Y	Y	Y	N
2 Dunn	Y	N	Y	Y	Y	Y	N
3 Yoho	Y	N	Y	Y	Y	Y	N
4 Rutherford	Y	N	Y	Y	Y	Y	N
5 Lawson	N	Y	N	Y	N	N	N
6 DeSantis	Y	N	Y	Y	Y	Y	N
7 Murphy	N	Y	N	Y	N	N	N
8 Posey	Y	N	Y	Y	Y	Y	N
9 Soto	N	Y	N	Y	N	N	Y
10 Demings	N	Y	N	Y	N	N	N
11 Webster	Y	N	Y	Y	Y	Y	N
12 Bilirakis	Y	N	Y	Y	Y	Y	N
13 Crist	N	Y	N	Y	N	N	N
14 Castor	N	Y	N	Y	N	N	N
15 Ross	Y	N	Y	Y	Y	Y	N
16 Buchanan	Y	N	Y	Y	Y	Y	N
17 Rooney, T.	Y	N	Y	Y	Y	Y	?
18 Mast	Y	N	Y	Y	Y	Y	N
19 Rooney, F.	Y	N	Y	?	Y	Y	N
20 Hastings	N	Y	N	N	N	N	N
21 Frankel	N	Y	N	Y	N	N	Y
22 Deutch	?	Y	N	Y	N	N	N
23 Wasserman Schultz	N	Y	N	Y	N	N	Y
24 Wilson	N	Y	N	Y	N	N	Y
25 Diaz-Balart	Y	N	Y	Y	Y	Y	N
26 Curbelo	Y	N	Y	Y	Y	Y	N
27 Ros-Lehtinen	Y	N	Y	Y	Y	Y	N
GEORGIA							
1 Carter	Y	N	Y	Y	Y	Y	N
2 Bishop	N	Y	N	Y	N	N	N
3 Ferguson	Y	N	Y	Y	Y	Y	N
4 Johnson	N	Y	N	Y	N	N	Y
5 Lewis	N	Y	N	Y	N	N	N
6 Handel	Y	N	Y	Y	Y	Y	N
7 Woodall	Y	N	Y	Y	Y	Y	N
8 Scott, A.	Y	N	Y	Y	Y	Y	N
9 Collins	Y	N	Y	Y	Y	Y	N
10 Hice	Y	N	Y	Y	Y	Y	N
11 Loudermilk	?	?	?	?	?	?	N
12 Allen	Y	N	Y	Y	Y	Y	N
13 Scott, D.	N	Y	N	Y	N	?	Y
14 Graves	Y	N	Y	Y	Y	Y	N
HAWAII							
1 Hanabusa	N	Y	N	?	N	N	N
2 Gabbard	N	Y	N	Y	N	N	Y
IDAHO							
1 Labrador	Y	N	Y	Y	Y	Y	N
2 Simpson	Y	N	Y	Y	Y	Y	N
ILLINOIS							
1 Rush	N	Y	N	Y	N	N	Y
2 Kelly	N	Y	N	Y	N	N	Y
3 Lipinski	Y	N	Y	Y	N	N	N
4 Gutierrez	N	Y	N	Y	N	N	Y
5 Quigley	N	Y	N	Y	N	N	N
6 Roskam	Y	N	Y	Y	Y	Y	N
7 Davis, D.	N	Y	N	Y	N	N	Y
8 Krishnamoorthi	N	Y	N	Y	N	N	N
9 Schakowsky	N	Y	N	Y	N	N	Y
10 Schneider	N	Y	N	Y	N	N	N
11 Foster	N	+	N	Y	N	N	N
12 Bost	Y	N	Y	Y	Y	Y	N
13 Davis, R.	Y	N	Y	Y	Y	Y	N
14 Hultgren	Y	N	Y	Y	Y	?	N
15 Shimkus	Y	N	Y	Y	Y	Y	N

	547	548	549	550	551	552	553
16 **Kinzinger**	Y	N	Y	Y	Y	Y	N
17 Bustos	N	Y	N	Y	N	N	N
18 **LaHood**	Y	N	Y	Y	Y	Y	N
INDIANA							
1 Visclosky	N	Y	N	Y	N	N	N
2 **Walorski**	Y	N	Y	Y	Y	Y	N
3 **Banks**	Y	N	Y	Y	Y	Y	N
4 **Rokita**	Y	N	Y	Y	Y	Y	N
5 **Brooks**	Y	N	Y	Y	Y	Y	N
6 **Messer**	Y	N	Y	Y	Y	Y	N
7 Carson	N	Y	N	Y	N	N	Y
8 **Bucshon**	Y	N	Y	Y	Y	Y	N
9 **Hollingsworth**	Y	N	Y	Y	Y	Y	N
IOWA							
1 **Blum**	Y	N	Y	Y	Y	Y	N
2 Loebsack	N	Y	N	Y	N	N	N
3 **Young**	Y	N	Y	Y	Y	Y	N
4 **King**	Y	N	Y	Y	Y	Y	N
KANSAS							
1 **Marshall**	Y	N	Y	Y	Y	Y	N
2 **Jenkins**	Y	N	Y	Y	Y	Y	N
3 **Yoder**	Y	N	Y	Y	Y	Y	N
4 **Estes**	Y	N	Y	Y	Y	Y	N
KENTUCKY							
1 **Comer**	Y	N	Y	Y	Y	Y	N
2 **Guthrie**	Y	N	Y	Y	Y	Y	N
3 Yarmuth	N	Y	N	Y	N	N	Y
4 **Massie**	Y	N	Y	N	Y	Y	N
5 **Rogers**	Y	N	Y	Y	Y	Y	N
6 **Barr**	Y	N	Y	Y	Y	Y	N
LOUISIANA							
1 **Scalise**	Y	N	Y	Y	+	+	N
2 Richmond	N	Y	N	Y	N	N	Y
3 **Higgins**	Y	N	Y	Y	Y	Y	N
4 **Johnson**	Y	N	Y	Y	Y	Y	N
5 **Abraham**	Y	N	Y	Y	Y	Y	N
6 **Graves**	Y	N	Y	Y	Y	Y	N
MAINE							
1 Pingree	N	Y	N	Y	N	N	Y
2 **Poliquin**	Y	N	Y	Y	Y	Y	N
MARYLAND							
1 **Harris**	Y	N	Y	Y	Y	Y	N
2 Ruppersberger	N	Y	N	Y	N	N	N
3 Sarbanes	N	Y	N	Y	N	N	Y
4 Brown	N	Y	N	Y	N	N	Y
5 Hoyer	N	Y	N	Y	N	N	N
6 Delaney	N	Y	N	Y	N	N	N
7 Cummings	N	Y	N	Y	N	N	Y
8 Raskin	N	Y	N	Y	N	N	Y
MASSACHUSETTS							
1 Neal	N	Y	N	Y	N	N	N
2 McGovern	N	Y	N	Y	N	N	Y
3 Tsongas	N	Y	N	Y	N	N	N
4 Kennedy	N	Y	N	Y	N	N	Y
5 Clark	N	Y	N	Y	N	N	Y
6 Moulton	N	Y	N	Y	N	N	N
7 Capuano	N	Y	N	Y	N	N	Y
8 Lynch	N	Y	N	Y	N	N	Y
9 Keating	N	Y	N	Y	N	N	N
MICHIGAN							
1 **Bergman**	Y	N	Y	Y	Y	Y	N
2 **Huizenga**	Y	N	Y	Y	Y	Y	N
3 **Amash**	Y	N	Y	N	Y	Y	N
4 **Moolenaar**	Y	N	Y	Y	Y	Y	N
5 Kildee	N	Y	N	Y	N	N	Y
6 **Upton**	Y	N	Y	Y	Y	Y	N
7 **Walberg**	Y	N	Y	Y	Y	Y	N
8 **Bishop**	Y	N	Y	Y	Y	Y	N
9 Levin	N	Y	N	Y	N	N	N
10 **Mitchell**	Y	N	Y	Y	Y	Y	N
11 **Trott**	Y	N	Y	Y	Y	Y	N
12 Dingell	N	Y	N	Y	N	N	Y
13 Conyers	N	Y	N	Y	N	N	Y
14 Lawrence	N	Y	N	Y	N	N	Y
MINNESOTA							
1 Walz	N	Y	N	Y	N	N	N
2 **Lewis**	Y	N	Y	Y	Y	Y	N
3 **Paulsen**	Y	N	Y	Y	Y	Y	N
4 McCollum	N	Y	N	Y	N	N	Y

	547	548	549	550	551	552	553
5 Ellison	N	Y	N	Y	N	N	Y
6 **Emmer**	Y	N	Y	Y	Y	Y	N
7 Peterson	N	N	N	Y	N	N	N
8 Nolan	N	Y	N	Y	N	N	Y
MISSISSIPPI							
1 **Kelly**	Y	N	Y	Y	Y	Y	N
2 Thompson	N	Y	N	Y	N	N	Y
3 **Harper**	Y	N	Y	Y	Y	Y	N
4 **Palazzo**	Y	N	Y	Y	Y	Y	N
MISSOURI							
1 Clay	N	Y	N	Y	N	N	Y
2 **Wagner**	Y	N	Y	Y	Y	Y	N
3 **Luetkemeyer**	Y	N	Y	Y	Y	Y	N
4 **Hartzler**	Y	N	Y	Y	Y	Y	N
5 Cleaver	N	Y	N	Y	N	N	Y
6 **Graves**	Y	N	Y	Y	Y	Y	N
7 **Long**	+	–	+	+	+	+	–
8 **Smith**	Y	N	Y	Y	Y	Y	N
MONTANA							
AL **Gianforte**	Y	N	Y	Y	Y	Y	N
NEBRASKA							
1 **Fortenberry**	Y	N	Y	Y	Y	Y	N
2 **Bacon**	Y	N	Y	Y	Y	Y	N
3 **Smith**	Y	N	Y	Y	Y	Y	N
NEVADA							
1 Titus	–	+	–	+	–	–	+
2 **Amodei**	Y	N	Y	Y	?	?	N
3 Rosen	–	+	–	+	–	–	–
4 Kihuen	?	?	?	?	?	?	?
NEW HAMPSHIRE							
1 Shea-Porter	N	Y	N	Y	N	N	N
2 Kuster	N	Y	N	Y	N	N	N
NEW JERSEY							
1 Norcross	N	Y	N	Y	N	N	Y
2 **LoBiondo**	Y	N	Y	Y	Y	Y	N
3 **MacArthur**	Y	N	Y	Y	Y	Y	N
4 **Smith**	Y	N	Y	Y	Y	Y	N
5 Gottheimer	N	Y	N	Y	N	N	N
6 Pallone	N	Y	N	Y	N	N	Y
7 **Lance**	Y	N	Y	Y	Y	Y	N
8 Sires	N	Y	N	Y	N	N	Y
9 Pascrell	N	Y	N	Y	N	N	Y
10 Payne	N	Y	N	Y	N	N	Y
11 **Frelinghuysen**	Y	N	N	Y	Y	Y	N
12 Watson Coleman	N	Y	N	Y	N	N	Y
NEW MEXICO							
1 Lujan Grisham	N	Y	N	Y	N	N	N
2 **Pearce**	Y	N	Y	Y	Y	Y	N
3 Luján	N	Y	N	Y	N	N	Y
NEW YORK							
1 **Zeldin**	Y	N	Y	Y	Y	Y	N
2 **King**	Y	N	Y	Y	Y	Y	N
3 Suozzi	N	Y	N	Y	N	N	N
4 Rice	N	Y	N	Y	N	N	N
5 Meeks	N	Y	N	?	N	N	Y
6 Meng	N	Y	N	Y	N	N	Y
7 Velázquez	N	Y	N	Y	N	N	Y
8 Jeffries	N	Y	N	Y	N	N	Y
9 Clarke	N	Y	N	Y	N	N	Y
10 Nadler	N	Y	N	Y	N	N	Y
11 **Donovan**	Y	N	Y	Y	Y	Y	N
12 Maloney, C.	N	Y	N	Y	N	N	Y
13 Espaillat	N	Y	N	Y	N	N	Y
14 Crowley	–	Y	N	Y	N	N	Y
15 Serrano	N	Y	N	Y	N	N	Y
16 Engel	N	Y	N	Y	N	N	Y
17 Lowey	N	Y	N	Y	N	N	Y
18 Maloney, S.P.	N	Y	N	Y	N	N	N
19 **Faso**	Y	N	Y	Y	Y	Y	N
20 Tonko	N	Y	N	?	N	N	Y
21 **Stefanik**	Y	N	Y	Y	Y	Y	N
22 **Tenney**	Y	N	Y	Y	Y	Y	N
23 **Reed**	Y	N	Y	Y	Y	Y	N
24 **Katko**	Y	N	Y	Y	Y	Y	N
25 Slaughter	N	Y	N	Y	N	N	Y
26 Higgins	N	Y	N	Y	N	N	Y
27 **Collins**	Y	N	Y	Y	Y	Y	N
NORTH CAROLINA							
1 Butterfield	N	Y	N	Y	N	N	Y
2 **Holding**	Y	N	Y	Y	Y	Y	N
3 **Jones**	Y	N	Y	?	Y	Y	N
4 Price	N	Y	N	Y	N	N	Y

	547	548	549	550	551	552	553
5 **Foxx**	Y	N	Y	Y	Y	Y	N
6 **Walker**	Y	N	Y	Y	Y	Y	N
7 **Rouzer**	Y	N	Y	Y	Y	Y	N
8 **Hudson**	Y	N	Y	Y	Y	Y	N
9 **Pittenger**	Y	N	Y	Y	Y	Y	N
10 **McHenry**	Y	N	Y	Y	Y	Y	N
11 **Meadows**	Y	N	Y	Y	Y	Y	N
12 Adams	N	Y	N	Y	N	N	Y
13 **Budd**	Y	N	Y	Y	Y	Y	N
NORTH DAKOTA							
AL **Cramer**	Y	N	Y	Y	Y	Y	N
OHIO							
1 **Chabot**	Y	N	Y	Y	Y	Y	N
2 **Wenstrup**	Y	N	Y	Y	Y	Y	N
3 Beatty	N	Y	N	Y	N	N	Y
4 **Jordan**	Y	N	Y	Y	Y	Y	N
5 **Latta**	Y	N	Y	Y	Y	Y	N
6 **Johnson**	?	N	Y	Y	Y	Y	N
7 **Gibbs**	Y	N	Y	Y	Y	Y	N
8 **Davidson**	Y	N	Y	Y	Y	Y	N
9 Kaptur	N	Y	N	Y	N	N	Y
10 **Turner**	Y	N	Y	Y	Y	Y	N
11 Fudge	N	Y	N	Y	N	N	Y
12 **Tiberi**	Y	N	Y	Y	Y	Y	N
13 Ryan	N	Y	N	Y	N	N	Y
14 **Joyce**	Y	N	Y	Y	Y	Y	N
15 **Stivers**	Y	N	Y	Y	Y	Y	N
16 **Renacci**	Y	N	Y	Y	Y	Y	N
OKLAHOMA							
1 **Bridenstine**	?	?	?	?	?	?	?
2 **Mullin**	Y	N	Y	Y	Y	Y	N
3 **Lucas**	Y	N	Y	Y	Y	Y	N
4 **Cole**	Y	N	Y	Y	Y	Y	N
5 **Russell**	Y	N	Y	Y	Y	Y	N
OREGON							
1 Bonamici	N	Y	N	Y	N	N	N
2 **Walden**	Y	N	Y	Y	Y	Y	N
3 Blumenauer	N	Y	N	Y	N	N	Y
4 DeFazio	N	Y	N	Y	N	N	Y
5 Schrader	N	Y	N	Y	N	?	N
PENNSYLVANIA							
1 Brady	N	Y	N	Y	N	N	Y
2 Evans	N	Y	N	Y	N	N	Y
3 **Kelly**	Y	N	Y	Y	Y	Y	N
4 **Perry**	Y	N	Y	Y	Y	Y	N
5 **Thompson**	Y	N	Y	Y	Y	Y	N
6 **Costello**	Y	N	Y	Y	Y	Y	N
7 **Meehan**	Y	N	Y	Y	Y	Y	N
8 **Fitzpatrick**	Y	N	Y	Y	Y	Y	N
9 **Shuster**	Y	N	Y	Y	Y	Y	N
10 **Marino**	Y	N	Y	Y	Y	Y	N
11 **Barletta**	Y	N	Y	Y	Y	Y	N
12 **Rothfus**	Y	N	Y	Y	Y	Y	N
13 Boyle	N	Y	N	Y	N	N	Y
14 Doyle	N	Y	N	Y	?	?	+
15 **Dent**	Y	N	N	Y	Y	Y	N
16 **Smucker**	+	N	Y	Y	Y	Y	N
17 Cartwright	N	Y	N	Y	N	N	N
18 **Murphy**	Y	N	Y	Y	Y	Y	–
RHODE ISLAND							
1 Cicilline	N	Y	N	Y	N	N	N
2 Langevin	N	Y	N	Y	N	N	N
SOUTH CAROLINA							
1 **Sanford**	Y	N	Y	Y	Y	Y	N
2 **Wilson**	Y	N	Y	Y	Y	Y	N
3 **Duncan**	Y	N	Y	Y	Y	Y	N
4 **Gowdy**	Y	N	Y	Y	Y	Y	N
5 **Norman**	Y	N	Y	Y	Y	Y	N
6 Clyburn	N	Y	N	Y	N	N	Y
7 **Rice**	Y	N	Y	Y	Y	Y	N
SOUTH DAKOTA							
AL **Noem**	Y	N	Y	Y	Y	Y	N
TENNESSEE							
1 **Roe**	Y	N	Y	Y	Y	Y	N
2 **Duncan**	Y	N	Y	Y	Y	Y	N
3 **Fleischmann**	Y	N	Y	Y	Y	Y	N
4 **DesJarlais**	?	N	Y	Y	Y	Y	N
5 Cooper	N	Y	N	Y	N	N	N
6 **Black**	Y	N	Y	Y	Y	Y	N
7 **Blackburn**	Y	N	Y	Y	Y	Y	N
8 **Kustoff**	Y	N	Y	Y	Y	Y	N
9 Cohen	N	Y	N	Y	N	N	Y

	547	548	549	550	551	552	553
TEXAS							
1 **Gohmert**	Y	N	Y	Y	Y	Y	N
2 **Poe**	Y	N	Y	Y	?	Y	N
3 **Johnson, S.**	Y	N	Y	Y	Y	Y	N
4 **Ratcliffe**	Y	N	Y	Y	Y	Y	N
5 **Hensarling**	Y	N	Y	Y	Y	Y	N
6 **Barton**	Y	N	Y	Y	Y	Y	N
7 **Culberson**	Y	N	Y	Y	Y	Y	N
8 **Brady**	Y	N	Y	Y	Y	Y	N
9 Green, A.	N	Y	N	Y	N	N	Y
10 **McCaul**	Y	N	Y	Y	Y	Y	N
11 **Conaway**	Y	N	Y	Y	Y	Y	N
12 **Granger**	Y	N	Y	Y	Y	Y	N
13 **Thornberry**	Y	N	Y	Y	Y	Y	N
14 **Weber**	Y	N	Y	Y	Y	Y	N
15 Gonzalez	N	Y	N	Y	N	N	N
16 O'Rourke	N	Y	N	Y	N	N	N
17 **Flores**	Y	N	Y	Y	Y	Y	N
18 Jackson Lee	N	Y	N	Y	N	N	Y
19 **Arrington**	Y	N	Y	Y	Y	Y	N
20 Castro	N	Y	N	Y	N	N	N
21 **Smith**	Y	N	Y	Y	Y	Y	N
22 **Olson**	Y	N	Y	Y	Y	Y	N
23 **Hurd**	Y	N	Y	Y	Y	Y	N
24 **Marchant**	?	N	Y	Y	Y	Y	N
25 **Williams**	Y	N	Y	Y	Y	Y	N
26 **Burgess**	Y	N	Y	Y	Y	Y	N
27 **Farenthold**	Y	N	Y	Y	Y	Y	N
28 Cuellar	N	Y	Y	Y	N	N	N
29 Green, G.	N	Y	N	Y	N	N	N
30 Johnson, E.B.	?	Y	N	Y	N	N	Y
31 **Carter**	Y	N	Y	Y	Y	Y	N
32 **Sessions**	Y	N	Y	Y	Y	Y	N
33 Veasey	N	Y	N	Y	N	N	N
34 Vela	N	Y	N	Y	N	N	Y
35 Doggett	N	Y	N	Y	N	N	Y
36 **Babin**	Y	N	Y	Y	Y	Y	N
UTAH							
1 **Bishop**	Y	N	Y	Y	Y	Y	N
2 **Stewart**	Y	N	Y	Y	Y	Y	N
4 **Love**	Y	N	Y	Y	Y	Y	N
VERMONT							
AL Welch	N	Y	N	Y	N	N	Y
VIRGINIA							
1 **Wittman**	Y	N	Y	Y	Y	Y	N
2 **Taylor**	Y	N	Y	Y	Y	Y	N
3 Scott	N	Y	N	Y	N	N	Y
4 McEachin	N	Y	N	Y	N	N	Y
5 **Garrett**	Y	N	Y	Y	Y	Y	N
6 **Goodlatte**	Y	N	Y	Y	Y	Y	N
7 **Brat**	Y	N	Y	Y	Y	Y	N
8 Beyer	N	Y	N	Y	N	N	Y
9 **Griffith**	Y	N	Y	Y	Y	Y	N
10 **Comstock**	Y	N	Y	Y	Y	Y	N
11 Connolly	N	Y	N	Y	N	N	N
WASHINGTON							
1 DelBene	N	Y	N	Y	N	N	N
2 Larsen	N	Y	N	Y	N	N	N
3 **Herrera Beutler**	Y	N	Y	Y	Y	Y	N
4 **Newhouse**	Y	N	Y	Y	Y	Y	N
5 **McMorris Rodgers**	Y	N	Y	Y	Y	Y	N
6 Kilmer	N	Y	N	Y	N	N	N
7 Jayapal	N	Y	N	Y	N	N	Y
8 **Reichert**	Y	N	Y	Y	Y	Y	N
9 Smith	N	Y	N	Y	N	N	Y
10 Heck	N	Y	N	Y	N	N	N
WEST VIRGINIA							
1 **McKinley**	Y	N	Y	Y	Y	Y	N
2 **Mooney**	Y	N	Y	Y	Y	Y	N
3 **Jenkins**	Y	N	Y	Y	Y	Y	N
WISCONSIN							
1 **Ryan**							
2 Pocan	N	Y	N	Y	N	N	Y
3 Kind	N	Y	N	Y	N	N	N
4 Moore	N	Y	N	Y	N	N	Y
5 **Sensenbrenner**	Y	N	Y	Y	Y	Y	N
6 **Grothman**	Y	N	Y	Y	Y	Y	N
7 **Duffy**	Y	N	Y	Y	Y	Y	N
8 **Gallagher**	Y	N	Y	Y	Y	Y	N
WYOMING							
AL **Cheney**	Y	N	Y	Y	Y	Y	N

VOTE NUMBER

554. H CON RES 71. FISCAL 2018 BUDGET RESOLUTION/CONGRESSIONAL BLACK CAUCUS SUBSTITUTE. Scott, D-Va., substitute amendment that would provide for $3.8 trillion in new budget authority in fiscal 2018, not including off-budget accounts. It would increase spending by $1 trillion over five years and would provide for a number of revenue-raising options, totaling $10.9 trillion, that could be used to raise at least $3.9 trillion in additional revenues over 10 years. It would repeal the Budget Control Act sequester and caps on discretionary spending, would end defense funding through the Overseas Contingency Operations account, would create a public insurance option to be sold within the current health insurance exchanges, would call for implementation of comprehensive immigration overhaul and would include $200 billion for hurricane recovery in Texas, Florida, Puerto Rico and the U.S. Virgin Islands. Rejected in Committee of the Whole 130-292 : R 0-235; D 130-57. Oct. 4, 2017.

555. H CON RES 71. FISCAL 2018 BUDGET RESOLUTION/REPUBLICAN STUDY COMMITTEE SUBSTITUTE. McClintock, R-Calif., substitute amendment that would provide for $2.9 trillion in new budget authority in fiscal 2018. It would balance the budget by fiscal 2023 by reducing spending by $10.1 trillion over 10 years. It would cap total discretionary spending at $1.06 trillion for fiscal 2018 and would assume no separate Overseas Contingency Operations funding for fiscal 2018 or subsequent years and would incorporate funding related to war or terror into the base defense account. It would assume repeal of the 2010 health care overhaul and would convert Medicaid and the Children's Health Insurance Program into a single block grant program. It would require that off budget programs, such as Social Security, the U.S. Postal Service, and Fannie Mae and Freddie Mac, be included in the budget. Rejected in Committee of the Whole 139-281 : R 139-95; D 0-186. Oct. 5, 2017.

556. H CON RES 71. FISCAL 2018 BUDGET RESOLUTION/DEMOCRATIC CAUCUS SUBSTITUTE. Yarmuth, D-Ky., substitute amendment that would provide for $3.4 trillion in new budget authority in fiscal 2018, not including off-budget accounts. It would repeal the Budget Control Act sequester and caps on discretionary spending and would provide an additional $54 billion for both defense and non-defense spending in fiscal 2018. It would allow for Overseas Contingency Operations funding at the level requested by the president, but would prevent the use of OCO funding for base defense needs. It would assume $160 billion in Medicare savings through efficiency programs. It would call for an increase in the minimum wage, would assume the implementation of a comprehensive immigration overhaul and it would call for the enactment of legislation to expand paid sick leave. Rejected in Committee of the Whole 156-268 : R 0-236; D 156-32. Oct. 5, 2017.

557. H CON RES 71. FISCAL 2018 BUDGET RESOLUTION/ADOPTION. Adoption of the concurrent resolution that would provide for $3.2 trillion in new budget authority in fiscal 2018, not including off-budget accounts. It would assume $1.22 trillion in discretionary spending in fiscal 2018. It would assume the repeal of the 2010 health care overhaul law. It would also propose reducing spending on mandatory programs such as Medicare and Medicaid and changing programs such as the Supplemental Nutrition Assistance Program (also known as food stamps). It would call for restructuring Medicare into a "premium support" system beginning in 2024. I would also require the House Ways and Means Committee to report out legislation under the budget reconciliation process that would provide for a revenue-neutral, comprehensive overhaul of the U.S. tax code and would include instructions to 11 House committees to trigger the budget reconciliation process to cut mandatory spending. The concurrent resolution would assume that, over 10 years, base (non-Overseas Contingency Operations) discretionary defense spending would be increased by a total of $929 billion over the Budget Control Act caps and non-defense spending be reduced by $1.3 trillion. Adopted 219-206 : R 219-18; D 0-188. Oct. 5, 2017.

558. HR 1858. STAFF SERGEANT RYAN SCOTT OSTROM POST OFFICE/ PASSAGE. Gianforte, R-Mont., motion to suspend the rules and pass the bill that would designate the facility of the United States Postal Service located at 4514 Williamson Trail in Liberty, Pa., as the "Staff Sergeant Ryan Scott Ostrom Post Office." Motion agreed to 397-0 : R 222-0; D 175-0. Oct. 10, 2017.

	554	555	556	557	558
ALABAMA					
1 Byrne	N	Y	N	Y	Y
2 Roby	N	N	N	Y	Y
3 Rogers	N	N	N	Y	Y
4 Aderholt	N	N	N	Y	Y
5 Brooks	N	Y	N	Y	Y
6 Palmer	N	Y	N	Y	Y
7 Sewell	Y	N	Y	N	Y
ALASKA					
AL Young	N	?	N	Y	Y
ARIZONA					
1 O'Halleran	N	N	N	N	Y
2 McSally	N	N	N	Y	Y
3 Grijalva	Y	N	Y	N	?
4 Gosar	N	Y	N	Y	Y
5 Biggs	N	Y	N	Y	Y
6 Schweikert	N	Y	N	Y	Y
7 Gallego	Y	N	Y	N	Y
8 Franks	N	Y	N	Y	Y
9 Sinema	N	N	N	N	Y
ARKANSAS					
1 Crawford	N	N	N	Y	Y
2 Hill	N	Y	N	Y	Y
3 Womack	N	N	N	Y	Y
4 Westerman	N	Y	N	Y	Y
CALIFORNIA					
1 LaMalfa	N	Y	N	Y	Y
2 Huffman	Y	N	Y	N	+
3 Garamendi	N	N	Y	N	Y
4 McClintock	N	Y	N	Y	Y
5 Thompson	N	N	Y	N	+
6 Matsui	Y	N	Y	N	Y
7 Bera	N	N	N	N	Y
8 Cook	N	N	N	Y	Y
9 McNerney	N	N	Y	N	Y
10 Denham	N	N	Y	N	?
11 DeSaulnier	Y	N	Y	N	Y
12 Pelosi	?	N	Y	N	Y
13 Lee	Y	N	Y	N	Y
14 Speier	Y	N	Y	N	Y
15 Swalwell	N	N	Y	N	Y
16 Costa	N	N	N	N	Y
17 Khanna	Y	N	Y	N	Y
18 Eshoo	Y	N	Y	N	Y
19 Lofgren	Y	N	Y	N	Y
20 Panetta	Y	N	Y	N	Y
21 Valadao	N	N	N	Y	?
22 Nunes	N	N	N	Y	Y
23 McCarthy	N	N	N	Y	?
24 Carbajal	N	Y	Y	N	Y
25 Knight	N	N	N	Y	+
26 Brownley	N	N	N	N	Y
27 Chu	Y	N	Y	N	Y
28 Schiff	Y	N	Y	N	Y
29 Cardenas	Y	N	Y	N	Y
30 Sherman	Y	N	Y	N	Y
31 Aguilar	N	N	Y	N	Y
32 Napolitano	+	-	+	-	Y
33 Lieu	Y	N	Y	N	Y
34 Gomez	Y	N	Y	N	Y
35 Torres	N	N	Y	N	Y
36 Ruiz	N	N	N	N	Y
37 Bass	Y	N	Y	N	Y
38 Sánchez, Linda	Y	N	Y	N	Y
39 Royce	N	N	N	Y	Y
40 Roybal-Allard	Y	-	Y	N	Y
41 Takano	Y	N	Y	N	Y
42 Calvert	N	Y	N	Y	Y
43 Waters	Y	N	Y	N	Y
44 Barragan	Y	N	Y	N	Y
45 Walters	N	Y	N	Y	Y
46 Correa	N	N	Y	N	Y
47 Lowenthal	Y	N	Y	N	Y
48 Rohrabacher	N	Y	N	Y	?
49 Issa	N	N	N	Y	Y
50 Hunter	N	N	N	Y	Y
51 Vargas	Y	N	Y	N	Y
52 Peters	N	N	N	N	Y
53 Davis	N	N	Y	N	+

	554	555	556	557	558
COLORADO					
1 DeGette	N	N	Y	N	Y
2 Polis	N	N	Y	N	Y
3 Tipton	N	Y	N	Y	Y
4 Buck	N	Y	N	N	Y
5 Lamborn	N	Y	N	Y	Y
6 Coffman	N	Y	N	Y	Y
7 Perlmutter	N	N	Y	N	Y
CONNECTICUT					
1 Larson	Y	N	Y	N	Y
2 Courtney	N	N	Y	N	Y
3 DeLauro	Y	N	Y	N	Y
4 Himes	N	N	N	N	Y
5 Esty	N	N	Y	N	Y
DELAWARE					
AL Blunt Rochester	?	N	Y	N	Y
FLORIDA					
1 Gaetz	N	Y	N	Y	Y
2 Dunn	N	Y	N	Y	Y
3 Yoho	N	Y	N	Y	Y
4 Rutherford	N	N	N	Y	Y
5 Lawson	Y	N	Y	N	Y
6 DeSantis	N	?	?	?	Y
7 Murphy	N	Y	N	Y	Y
8 Posey	N	Y	N	Y	Y
9 Soto	N	N	Y	N	Y
10 Demings	Y	N	Y	N	Y
11 Webster	N	Y	N	Y	?
12 Bilirakis	N	N	N	Y	Y
13 Crist	N	N	N	N	Y
14 Castor	Y	N	Y	N	Y
15 Ross	N	Y	N	Y	Y
16 Buchanan	N	N	N	Y	Y
17 Rooney, T.	?	Y	N	Y	Y
18 Mast	N	N	N	Y	Y
19 Rooney, F.	N	Y	N	Y	Y
20 Hastings	Y	N	Y	N	?
21 Frankel	Y	N	Y	N	Y
22 Deutch	N	N	Y	N	Y
23 Wasserman Schultz	Y	N	Y	N	Y
24 Wilson	Y	N	Y	N	?
25 Diaz-Balart	N	N	N	Y	Y
26 Curbelo	N	N	N	Y	Y
27 Ros-Lehtinen	N	N	N	N	Y
GEORGIA					
1 Carter	N	Y	N	Y	Y
2 Bishop	Y	N	Y	N	Y
3 Ferguson	N	Y	N	Y	Y
4 Johnson	Y	N	Y	N	Y
5 Lewis	Y	N	Y	N	Y
6 Handel	N	Y	N	Y	Y
7 Woodall	N	Y	N	Y	Y
8 Scott, A.	N	Y	N	Y	Y
9 Collins	N	Y	N	Y	Y
10 Hice	N	Y	N	Y	Y
11 Loudermilk	N	Y	N	Y	Y
12 Allen	N	Y	N	Y	Y
13 Scott, D.	Y	N	Y	N	Y
14 Graves	N	Y	N	Y	Y
HAWAII					
1 Hanabusa	N	N	Y	N	?
2 Gabbard	Y	N	Y	N	Y
IDAHO					
1 Labrador	N	Y	N	Y	?
2 Simpson	N	N	N	Y	Y
ILLINOIS					
1 Rush	N	N	Y	N	Y
2 Kelly	Y	N	Y	N	Y
3 Lipinski	N	N	N	N	Y
4 Gutierrez	Y	N	Y	N	+
5 Quigley	N	N	Y	N	?
6 Roskam	N	N	N	Y	Y
7 Davis, D.	Y	N	Y	N	Y
8 Krishnamoorthi	Y	N	Y	N	Y
9 Schakowsky	Y	N	Y	N	Y
10 Schneider	N	N	N	N	Y
11 Foster	N	N	N	N	Y
12 Bost	N	N	N	Y	Y
13 Davis, R.	N	N	N	Y	Y
14 Hultgren	N	Y	N	Y	Y
15 Shimkus	N	Y	N	Y	?

	554	555	556	557	558
16 Kinzinger	N	N	N	Y	Y
17 Bustos	N	N	N	N	Y
18 LaHood	N	Y	N	Y	Y
INDIANA					
1 Visclosky	N	N	N	N	?
2 Walorski	N	Y	N	Y	Y
3 Banks	N	Y	N	Y	Y
4 Rokita	N	Y	N	Y	Y
5 Brooks	N	N	N	Y	Y
6 Messer	N	Y	N	Y	Y
7 Carson	Y	N	Y	N	Y
8 Bucshon	N	Y	N	Y	Y
9 Hollingsworth	N	Y	N	Y	Y
IOWA					
1 Blum	N	N	N	N	N
2 Loebsack	N	N	N	N	N
3 Young	N	N	N	Y	Y
4 King	N	N	N	Y	Y
KANSAS					
1 Marshall	N	N	N	Y	Y
2 Jenkins	N	Y	N	Y	Y
3 Yoder	N	Y	N	Y	Y
4 Estes	N	Y	N	Y	Y
KENTUCKY					
1 Comer	N	Y	N	Y	Y
2 Guthrie	N	Y	N	Y	Y
3 Yarmuth	Y	N	Y	N	?
4 Massie	N	Y	N	N	Y
5 Rogers	N	N	N	Y	Y
6 Barr	N	Y	N	Y	Y
LOUISIANA					
1 Scalise	N	Y	N	Y	Y
2 Richmond	Y	N	N	N	Y
3 Higgins	N	Y	N	Y	Y
4 Johnson	N	Y	N	Y	Y
5 Abraham	N	Y	N	Y	Y
6 Graves	N	Y	N	Y	Y
MAINE					
1 Pingree	Y	N	Y	N	?
2 Poliquin	N	N	N	Y	Y
MARYLAND					
1 Harris	N	Y	N	Y	Y
2 Ruppersberger	N	N	Y	N	Y
3 Sarbanes	Y	?	Y	N	Y
4 Brown	Y	N	Y	N	Y
5 Hoyer	Y	N	Y	N	Y
6 Delaney	N	N	N	N	Y
7 Cummings	Y	N	Y	N	Y
8 Raskin	Y	N	Y	N	Y
MASSACHUSETTS					
1 Neal	Y	N	Y	N	Y
2 McGovern	Y	N	Y	N	Y
3 Tsongas	Y	N	Y	N	?
4 Kennedy	Y	N	Y	N	Y
5 Clark	Y	N	Y	N	Y
6 Moulton	Y	N	Y	N	Y
7 Capuano	Y	N	Y	N	Y
8 Lynch	Y	N	Y	N	Y
9 Keating	N	N	Y	N	Y
MICHIGAN					
1 Bergman	N	Y	N	Y	Y
2 Huizenga	N	Y	N	Y	Y
3 Amash	N	Y	N	Y	Y
4 Moolenaar	N	Y	N	Y	Y
5 Kildee	Y	N	Y	N	Y
6 Upton	N	N	N	Y	Y
7 Walberg	N	Y	N	Y	Y
8 Bishop	N	Y	N	Y	Y
9 Levin	N	N	Y	N	Y
10 Mitchell	N	Y	N	Y	Y
11 Trott	N	N	N	Y	Y
12 Dingell	Y	N	Y	N	Y
13 Conyers	N	N	Y	N	Y
14 Lawrence	Y	N	Y	N	Y
MINNESOTA					
1 Walz	Y	?	?	?	?
2 Lewis	N	Y	N	Y	Y
3 Paulsen	N	N	N	Y	Y
4 McCollum	Y	N	Y	N	Y

	554	555	556	557	558
5 Ellison	Y	N	Y	N	Y
6 Emmer	N	Y	N	Y	Y
7 Peterson	N	N	N	N	Y
8 Nolan	Y	N	Y	N	Y
MISSISSIPPI					
1 Kelly	N	Y	N	Y	Y
2 Thompson	Y	N	N	N	Y
3 Harper	N	Y	N	Y	Y
4 Palazzo	N	N	N	Y	Y
MISSOURI					
1 Clay	Y	N	Y	N	Y
2 Wagner	N	N	N	Y	Y
3 Luetkemeyer	N	N	N	Y	Y
4 Hartzler	N	N	N	Y	Y
5 Cleaver	Y	N	Y	N	?
6 Graves	N	Y	N	Y	Y
7 Long	–	Y	N	Y	+
8 Smith	N	Y	N	Y	Y
MONTANA					
AL Gianforte	N	N	N	Y	Y
NEBRASKA					
1 Fortenberry	N	N	N	Y	Y
2 Bacon	N	N	N	Y	Y
3 Smith	N	Y	N	Y	Y
NEVADA					
1 Titus	+	–	+	–	+
2 Amodei	N	Y	N	Y	Y
3 Rosen	–	–	–	–	Y
4 Kihuen	?	?	?	?	Y
NEW HAMPSHIRE					
1 Shea-Porter	N	N	Y	N	Y
2 Kuster	N	N	N	N	Y
NEW JERSEY					
1 Norcross	Y	N	Y	N	Y
2 LoBiondo	N	N	N	N	Y
3 MacArthur	N	N	N	N	Y
4 Smith	N	N	N	N	Y
5 Gottheimer	N	N	N	N	Y
6 Pallone	Y	N	Y	N	Y
7 Lance	N	N	N	N	Y
8 Sires	Y	N	Y	N	Y
9 Pascrell	Y	N	Y	N	Y
10 Payne	Y	N	N	N	Y
11 Frelinghuysen	N	–	N	Y	Y
12 Watson Coleman	Y	N	Y	N	Y
NEW MEXICO					
1 Lujan Grisham	Y	N	Y	N	Y
2 Pearce	N	N	N	Y	Y
3 Luján	Y	N	Y	N	Y
NEW YORK					
1 Zeldin	N	Y	N	Y	Y
2 King	N	N	N	N	Y
3 Suozzi	N	N	N	N	Y
4 Rice	N	N	N	N	Y
5 Meeks	Y	N	Y	N	Y
6 Meng	Y	N	Y	N	Y
7 Velázquez	Y	N	Y	N	Y
8 Jeffries	Y	N	Y	N	Y
9 Clarke	Y	N	Y	N	Y
10 Nadler	Y	N	Y	N	?
11 Donovan	N	N	N	N	Y
12 Maloney, C.	Y	N	Y	N	Y
13 Espaillat	Y	N	Y	N	?
14 Crowley	Y	N	Y	N	Y
15 Serrano	Y	N	Y	N	Y
16 Engel	Y	N	Y	N	Y
17 Lowey	Y	N	Y	N	Y
18 Maloney, S.P.	N	N	N	N	Y
19 Faso	N	N	N	Y	Y
20 Tonko	Y	N	Y	N	Y
21 Stefanik	N	N	N	N	Y
22 Tenney	N	N	N	Y	Y
23 Reed	N	N	N	Y	Y
24 Katko	N	N	N	N	Y
25 Slaughter	Y	N	Y	N	Y
26 Higgins	Y	N	Y	N	Y
27 Collins	N	N	N	Y	Y
NORTH CAROLINA					
1 Butterfield	Y	N	Y	N	Y
2 Holding	N	Y	N	Y	Y
3 Jones	N	N	N	N	Y
4 Price	Y	N	Y	N	Y

	554	555	556	557	558
5 Foxx	N	N	N	Y	Y
6 Walker	N	Y	N	Y	Y
7 Rouzer	N	Y	N	Y	+
8 Hudson	N	Y	N	Y	Y
9 Pittenger	N	Y	N	Y	Y
10 McHenry	N	Y	N	Y	Y
11 Meadows	N	Y	N	Y	Y
12 Adams	Y	N	Y	N	Y
13 Budd	N	Y	N	Y	Y
NORTH DAKOTA					
AL Cramer	N	N	N	Y	Y
OHIO					
1 Chabot	N	Y	N	Y	Y
2 Wenstrup	N	Y	N	Y	Y
3 Beatty	Y	N	Y	N	+
4 Jordan	N	Y	N	Y	Y
5 Latta	N	Y	N	Y	Y
6 Johnson	N	N	N	Y	?
7 Gibbs	N	Y	N	Y	Y
8 Davidson	N	Y	N	Y	Y
9 Kaptur	Y	N	Y	N	Y
10 Turner	N	N	N	Y	Y
11 Fudge	Y	N	Y	N	Y
12 Tiberi	N	N	N	Y	Y
13 Ryan	N	Y	N	Y	Y
14 Joyce	N	Y	N	Y	Y
15 Stivers	N	N	N	Y	Y
16 Renacci	N	Y	N	Y	+
OKLAHOMA					
1 Bridenstine	?	?	?	?	?
2 Mullin	N	Y	N	Y	Y
3 Lucas	N	N	N	Y	Y
4 Cole	N	Y	N	Y	Y
5 Russell	N	N	N	Y	Y
OREGON					
1 Bonamici	N	N	N	Y	N
2 Walden	N	N	N	Y	?
3 Blumenauer	Y	N	Y	N	Y
4 DeFazio	Y	N	Y	N	Y
5 Schrader	N	N	N	N	Y
PENNSYLVANIA					
1 Brady	Y	N	Y	N	Y
2 Evans	Y	N	Y	N	Y
3 Kelly	N	Y	N	Y	Y
4 Perry	N	Y	N	Y	Y
5 Thompson	N	N	N	Y	Y
6 Costello	N	N	N	N	Y
7 Meehan	N	N	N	N	Y
8 Fitzpatrick	N	N	N	N	Y
9 Shuster	N	N	N	Y	Y
10 Marino	N	N	N	Y	Y
11 Barletta	N	N	N	Y	Y
12 Rothfus	N	N	N	Y	Y
13 Boyle	Y	N	Y	N	Y
14 Doyle	+	?	+	–	Y
15 Dent	N	N	N	N	Y
16 Smucker	N	Y	N	Y	?
17 Cartwright	Y	N	Y	N	Y
18 Murphy	–	–	–	+	Y
RHODE ISLAND					
1 Cicilline	Y	N	Y	N	Y
2 Langevin	N	N	Y	N	Y
SOUTH CAROLINA					
1 Sanford	N	Y	N	Y	Y
2 Wilson	N	Y	N	Y	Y
3 Duncan	N	N	N	Y	Y
4 Gowdy	N	Y	N	Y	Y
5 Norman	N	N	Y	Y	Y
6 Clyburn	Y	N	Y	N	Y
7 Rice	N	Y	N	Y	Y
SOUTH DAKOTA					
AL Noem	N	N	N	Y	Y
TENNESSEE					
1 Roe	N	N	N	Y	Y
2 Duncan	N	N	N	Y	Y
3 Fleischmann	N	Y	N	Y	Y
4 DesJarlais	N	Y	N	Y	?
5 Cooper	N	N	N	N	Y
6 Black	N	Y	N	Y	Y
7 Blackburn	N	Y	N	Y	Y
8 Kustoff	N	Y	N	Y	Y
9 Cohen	Y	N	Y	N	Y

	554	555	556	557	558
TEXAS					
1 Gohmert	N	Y	N	Y	Y
2 Poe	N	Y	N	Y	Y
3 Johnson, S.	N	Y	N	Y	Y
4 Ratcliffe	N	Y	N	Y	Y
5 Hensarling	N	Y	N	Y	Y
6 Barton	N	Y	N	Y	Y
7 Culberson	N	Y	N	Y	Y
8 Brady	N	Y	N	Y	Y
9 Green, A.	Y	N	Y	N	Y
10 McCaul	N	Y	N	Y	Y
11 Conaway	N	N	N	Y	Y
12 Granger	N	N	N	Y	Y
13 Thornberry	N	N	N	Y	+
14 Weber	N	Y	N	Y	Y
15 Gonzalez	Y	N	Y	N	Y
16 O'Rourke	N	N	Y	N	Y
17 Flores	N	Y	N	Y	Y
18 Jackson Lee	Y	N	Y	N	Y
19 Arrington	N	Y	N	Y	Y
20 Castro	Y	N	Y	N	Y
21 Smith	N	Y	N	Y	Y
22 Olson	N	N	N	Y	Y
23 Hurd	N	N	N	Y	Y
24 Marchant	N	Y	N	Y	Y
25 Williams	N	Y	N	Y	Y
26 Burgess	N	Y	N	Y	Y
27 Farenthold	N	N	N	N	Y
28 Cuellar	N	N	N	N	Y
29 Green, G.	Y	N	Y	N	Y
30 Johnson, E.B.	Y	N	Y	N	Y
31 Carter	N	Y	N	Y	Y
32 Sessions	N	Y	N	Y	Y
33 Veasey	Y	N	Y	N	Y
34 Vela	Y	N	Y	N	Y
35 Doggett	Y	N	Y	N	Y
36 Babin	N	Y	N	Y	Y
UTAH					
1 Bishop	N	Y	N	Y	Y
2 Stewart	N	Y	N	Y	Y
4 Love	N	Y	N	Y	Y
VERMONT					
AL Welch	Y	N	Y	N	Y
VIRGINIA					
1 Wittman	N	N	N	Y	Y
2 Taylor	N	Y	N	Y	Y
3 Scott	Y	N	Y	N	Y
4 McEachin	Y	N	Y	N	Y
5 Garrett	N	Y	N	Y	Y
6 Goodlatte	N	Y	N	Y	Y
7 Brat	N	Y	N	Y	Y
8 Beyer	Y	N	Y	N	Y
9 Griffith	N	N	N	Y	Y
10 Comstock	N	N	N	N	Y
11 Connolly	Y	N	Y	N	Y
WASHINGTON					
1 DelBene	N	N	Y	N	Y
2 Larsen	N	Y	N	Y	Y
3 Herrera Beutler	N	N	N	Y	Y
4 Newhouse	N	Y	N	Y	Y
5 McMorris Rodgers	N	Y	N	Y	Y
6 Kilmer	N	N	Y	N	Y
7 Jayapal	Y	N	Y	N	Y
8 Reichert	N	N	N	Y	Y
9 Smith	Y	N	Y	N	Y
10 Heck	Y	N	Y	N	Y
WEST VIRGINIA					
1 McKinley	N	N	N	Y	Y
2 Mooney	N	N	N	Y	Y
3 Jenkins	N	N	N	Y	Y
WISCONSIN					
1 Ryan			Y		
2 Pocan	Y	N	Y	N	Y
3 Kind	N	N	N	N	Y
4 Moore	Y	N	Y	N	Y
5 Sensenbrenner	N	Y	N	Y	Y
6 Grothman	N	N	N	Y	Y
7 Duffy	N	N	N	Y	Y
8 Gallagher	N	N	N	Y	Y
WYOMING					
AL Cheney	N	N	N	Y	Y

VOTE NUMBER

559. HR 2464. JOHN FITZGERALD KENNEDY POST OFFICE/PASSAGE. Gianforte, R-Mont., motion to suspend the rules and pass the bill that would designate the facility of the United States Postal Service located at 25 New Chardon Street Lobby in Boston, Mass., as the "John Fitzgerald Kennedy Post Office." Motion agreed to 395-0 : R 220-0; D 175-0. Oct. 10, 2017.

560. H RES 562, S 585. FEDERAL WHISTLEBLOWER RETALIATION PENALTIES AND SUSPENSION AUTHORITY/PREVIOUS QUESTION. Collins, R-Ga., motion to order the previous question (thus limiting debate and possibility of amendment) on the rule (H Res 562) that would provide for House floor consideration of the bill (S 585) that would set specific penalties for federal supervisors who retaliate against an employee who discloses waste, fraud or abuse, and would require the VA to develop a plan to protect the medical records of employees. The rule would also provide for motions to suspend the rules on the legislative days of Oct. 12 and 13, 2017. Motion agreed to 227-190: R 227-0; D 0-190. Oct. 11, 2017.

561. H RES 562, S 585. FEDERAL WHISTLEBLOWER RETALIATION PENALTIES AND SUSPENSION AUTHORITY/RULE. Adoption of the rule (H Res 562) that would set specific penalties for federal supervisors who retaliate against an employee who discloses waste, fraud or abuse. It would also require the VA to develop a plan to protect the medical records of employees and would prohibit VA employees from accessing medical files for demographic information when another non-medical database is available. The rule would also provide for motions to suspend the rules on the legislative days of Oct. 12 and 13, 2017. Adopted 234-185 : R 227-2; D 7-183. Oct. 11, 2017.

562. HR 452. SPECIALIST JEFFREY L. WHITE, JR. POST OFFICE/PASSAGE. Gianforte, R-Mont., motion to suspend the rules and pass the bill that would designate the facility of the United States Postal Service located at 324 West Saint Louis Street, in Pacific, Mo., as the "Specialist Jeffrey L. White, Jr. Post Office." Motion agreed to 418-0 : R 227-0; D 191-0. Oct. 11, 2017.

563. HR 3243. FEDERAL INFORMATION TECHNOLOGY REQUIREMENTS/ PASSAGE. Russell, R-Okla., motion to suspend the rules and pass the bill that would eliminate the sunset dates for certain federal information technology requirements, including those related to data center consolidation, transparency and risk management of major federal IT investments, thereby keeping such requirements in place after Dec. 2019. Motion agreed to 418-0 : R 227-0; D 191-0. Oct. 11, 2017.

564. HR 2810. FISCAL 2018 NATIONAL DEFENSE AUTHORIZATION/ MOTION TO INSTRUCT. Langevin, D-R.I., motion to instruct House conferees to disagree with subsection (c) of section 336 of the Senate amendment to the bill, to recede from section 1064 of the House bill and to disagree with section 1087 of the Senate amendment to the bill. Motion rejected 184-237 : R 1-231; D 183-6. Oct. 12, 2017.

565. HR 2810. FISCAL 2018 NATIONAL DEFENSE AUTHORIZATION/ MOTION TO CLOSE. Thornberry, R-Texas, motion that the meetings of the conference between the House and the Senate on the bill may be closed to the public at such times as classified national security information may be discussed, provided that any sitting member of Congress shall be entitled to attend any meeting of the conference. Motion agreed to 414-8 : R 228-5; D 186-3. Oct. 12, 2017.

	559	560	561	562	563	564	565
ALABAMA							
1 Byrne	Y	Y	Y	Y	Y	N	Y
2 Roby	Y	Y	Y	Y	Y	N	Y
3 Rogers	Y	Y	Y	Y	Y	N	Y
4 Aderholt	Y	Y	Y	Y	Y	N	Y
5 Brooks	Y	Y	Y	Y	Y	N	Y
6 Palmer	Y	Y	Y	Y	Y	N	Y
7 Sewell	Y	N	N	Y	Y	Y	Y
ALASKA							
AL Young	Y	Y	Y	Y	Y	N	Y
ARIZONA							
1 O'Halleran	Y	N	N	Y	Y	Y	Y
2 McSally	Y	Y	Y	Y	Y	N	Y
3 Grijalva	?	N	N	Y	Y	Y	N
4 Gosar	Y	Y	Y	Y	Y	N	Y
5 Biggs	Y	Y	Y	Y	Y	N	Y
6 Schweikert	Y	Y	Y	Y	Y	N	Y
7 Gallego	Y	N	N	Y	Y	Y	Y
8 Franks	Y	Y	Y	Y	Y	N	Y
9 Sinema	Y	N	Y	Y	Y	N	Y
ARKANSAS							
1 Crawford	Y	Y	Y	Y	Y	N	Y
2 Hill	Y	Y	Y	Y	Y	N	Y
3 Womack	Y	Y	Y	Y	Y	N	Y
4 Westerman	Y	Y	Y	Y	Y	N	Y
CALIFORNIA							
1 LaMalfa	Y	Y	Y	Y	Y	N	Y
2 Huffman	+	–	–	+	+	+	+
3 Garamendi	Y	N	N	Y	Y	Y	Y
4 McClintock	Y	Y	Y	Y	Y	N	Y
5 Thompson	+	–	–	+	+	+	+
6 Matsui	Y	N	N	Y	Y	Y	Y
7 Bera	Y	N	N	Y	Y	Y	Y
8 Cook	Y	Y	Y	Y	Y	N	Y
9 McNerney	Y	N	N	Y	Y	Y	Y
10 Denham	?	Y	Y	Y	Y	N	Y
11 DeSaulnier	Y	N	N	Y	Y	Y	Y
12 Pelosi	Y	N	N	Y	Y	Y	Y
13 Lee	Y	N	N	Y	Y	Y	Y
14 Speier	Y	N	N	Y	Y	Y	Y
15 Swalwell	Y	N	N	Y	Y	Y	Y
16 Costa	Y	N	N	Y	Y	Y	Y
17 Khanna	Y	N	N	Y	Y	Y	Y
18 Eshoo	Y	N	N	Y	Y	+	+
19 Lofgren	Y	N	N	Y	Y	Y	Y
20 Panetta	Y	N	N	Y	Y	Y	Y
21 Valadao	?	Y	Y	Y	Y	N	Y
22 Nunes	Y	Y	Y	Y	Y	N	Y
23 McCarthy	?	Y	Y	Y	Y	N	Y
24 Carbajal	Y	N	N	Y	Y	Y	Y
25 Knight	+	Y	Y	Y	?	N	Y
26 Brownley	Y	N	N	Y	Y	Y	Y
27 Chu	Y	N	N	Y	Y	Y	Y
28 Schiff	Y	N	N	Y	Y	Y	Y
29 Cardenas	Y	N	N	Y	Y	Y	Y
30 Sherman	Y	N	N	Y	Y	Y	Y
31 Aguilar	Y	N	N	Y	Y	Y	Y
32 Napolitano	Y	N	N	Y	Y	Y	Y
33 Lieu	Y	N	N	Y	Y	Y	Y
34 Gomez	Y	N	N	Y	Y	Y	Y
35 Torres	Y	N	N	Y	Y	Y	Y
36 Ruiz	Y	N	N	Y	Y	Y	Y
37 Bass	Y	N	N	Y	Y	Y	Y
38 Sánchez, Linda	Y	N	N	Y	Y	Y	Y
39 Royce	Y	Y	Y	Y	Y	N	Y
40 Roybal-Allard	Y	N	N	Y	Y	Y	Y
41 Takano	Y	N	N	Y	Y	Y	Y
42 Calvert	Y	Y	Y	Y	Y	N	Y
43 Waters	Y	N	N	Y	Y	Y	Y
44 Barragan	Y	N	N	Y	Y	Y	Y
45 Walters	Y	Y	Y	Y	Y	N	Y
46 Correa	Y	N	N	Y	Y	Y	Y
47 Lowenthal	Y	N	N	Y	Y	Y	Y
48 Rohrabacher	?	Y	Y	Y	Y	N	Y
49 Issa	Y	Y	Y	Y	Y	N	Y
50 Hunter	Y	Y	Y	Y	Y	N	Y
51 Vargas	Y	N	N	Y	Y	Y	Y
52 Peters	Y	N	Y	Y	Y	Y	Y
53 Davis	Y	N	N	Y	Y	Y	Y

	559	560	561	562	563	564	565
COLORADO							
1 DeGette	Y	N	N	Y	Y	Y	Y
2 Polis	Y	N	N	Y	Y	Y	Y
3 Tipton	Y	Y	Y	Y	Y	N	Y
4 Buck	Y	Y	Y	Y	Y	N	Y
5 Lamborn	Y	Y	Y	Y	Y	N	Y
6 Coffman	Y	Y	Y	Y	Y	N	Y
7 Perlmutter	Y	N	N	Y	Y	Y	Y
CONNECTICUT							
1 Larson	Y	N	N	Y	Y	Y	Y
2 Courtney	Y	N	N	Y	Y	Y	Y
3 DeLauro	Y	N	N	Y	Y	Y	Y
4 Himes	Y	N	N	Y	Y	Y	Y
5 Esty	Y	N	N	Y	Y	Y	Y
DELAWARE							
AL Blunt Rochester	Y	N	N	Y	Y	Y	Y
FLORIDA							
1 Gaetz	Y	Y	Y	Y	Y	N	Y
2 Dunn	Y	Y	Y	Y	Y	N	Y
3 Yoho	Y	Y	Y	Y	Y	N	Y
4 Rutherford	Y	Y	Y	Y	Y	N	Y
5 Lawson	Y	N	N	Y	Y	Y	Y
6 DeSantis	Y	Y	Y	Y	Y	N	Y
7 Murphy	Y	N	N	Y	Y	Y	Y
8 Posey	Y	Y	Y	Y	Y	N	Y
9 Soto	Y	N	N	Y	Y	Y	Y
10 Demings	Y	N	N	Y	Y	Y	Y
11 Webster	?	?	Y	Y	Y	N	Y
12 Bilirakis	Y	Y	Y	Y	Y	N	Y
13 Crist	Y	N	Y	Y	Y	Y	Y
14 Castor	Y	N	N	Y	Y	Y	Y
15 Ross	Y	Y	Y	Y	Y	N	Y
16 Buchanan	Y	Y	?	Y	Y	N	Y
17 Rooney, T.	Y	Y	Y	Y	Y	N	Y
18 Mast	Y	Y	Y	Y	Y	N	Y
19 Rooney, F.	Y	Y	Y	Y	Y	N	Y
20 Hastings	?	N	N	Y	Y	Y	Y
21 Frankel	Y	N	N	Y	Y	Y	Y
22 Deutch	Y	N	N	Y	Y	Y	Y
23 Wasserman Schultz	Y	N	N	Y	Y	Y	Y
24 Wilson	?	N	N	Y	Y	Y	Y
25 Diaz-Balart	Y	Y	Y	Y	Y	N	Y
26 Curbelo	Y	Y	Y	?	Y	N	Y
27 Ros-Lehtinen	Y	Y	Y	Y	Y	N	Y
GEORGIA							
1 Carter	Y	Y	Y	Y	Y	N	Y
2 Bishop	Y	N	N	Y	Y	Y	Y
3 Ferguson	Y	Y	Y	Y	Y	N	Y
4 Johnson	Y	N	N	Y	Y	Y	Y
5 Lewis	Y	N	N	Y	Y	Y	Y
6 Handel	Y	Y	Y	Y	Y	N	Y
7 Woodall	Y	Y	Y	Y	Y	N	Y
8 Scott, A.	Y	Y	Y	Y	Y	N	Y
9 Collins	Y	Y	Y	Y	Y	N	Y
10 Hice	Y	Y	Y	Y	Y	N	Y
11 Loudermilk	Y	Y	Y	Y	Y	N	Y
12 Allen	Y	Y	Y	Y	Y	N	Y
13 Scott, D.	Y	N	N	Y	Y	Y	Y
14 Graves	Y	Y	Y	Y	Y	N	Y
HAWAII							
1 Hanabusa	?	?	?	Y	Y	Y	Y
2 Gabbard	Y	N	N	Y	Y	Y	Y
IDAHO							
1 Labrador	?	Y	Y	Y	Y	N	N
2 Simpson	Y	Y	Y	Y	Y	N	Y
ILLINOIS							
1 Rush	Y	N	N	Y	Y	Y	Y
2 Kelly	Y	N	N	Y	Y	Y	Y
3 Lipinski	Y	N	N	Y	Y	Y	Y
4 Gutierrez	+	N	N	Y	Y	Y	Y
5 Quigley	?	N	N	Y	Y	Y	Y
6 Roskam	Y	Y	Y	Y	Y	N	Y
7 Davis, D.	Y	N	N	Y	Y	Y	Y
8 Krishnamoorthi	Y	N	N	Y	Y	Y	Y
9 Schakowsky	Y	N	N	Y	Y	Y	Y
10 Schneider	Y	N	N	Y	Y	Y	Y
11 Foster	Y	N	N	Y	Y	Y	Y
12 Bost	Y	Y	Y	Y	Y	N	Y
13 Davis, R.	Y	Y	Y	Y	Y	N	Y
14 Hultgren	Y	Y	Y	Y	Y	N	Y
15 Shimkus	?	Y	Y	Y	Y	N	Y

KEY	Republicans		Democrats		Independents	
Y	Voted for (yea)	X	Paired against	C	Voted "present" to avoid possible conflict of interest
#	Paired for	–	Announced against		
+	Announced for	P	Voted "present"	?	Did not vote or otherwise make a position known
N	Voted against (nay)				

	559	560	561	562	563	564	565
16 **Kinzinger**	Y	Y	Y	Y	Y	N	Y
17 Bustos	Y	N	N	Y	Y	Y	Y
18 **LaHood**	Y	Y	Y	Y	Y	N	Y
INDIANA							
1 Visclosky	?	N	N	Y	Y	Y	Y
2 **Walorski**	Y	Y	Y	Y	Y	N	Y
3 **Banks**	Y	Y	Y	Y	Y	N	Y
4 **Rokita**	Y	Y	Y	Y	Y	N	Y
5 **Brooks**	Y	Y	Y	Y	Y	N	Y
6 **Messer**	Y	Y	Y	Y	Y	N	Y
7 Carson	Y	N	N	Y	Y	Y	Y
8 **Bucshon**	Y	Y	Y	Y	Y	N	Y
9 **Hollingsworth**	Y	Y	Y	Y	Y	N	Y
IOWA							
1 **Blum**	Y	Y	Y	Y	Y	N	Y
2 Loebsack	Y	N	N	Y	Y	Y	Y
3 **Young**	Y	Y	Y	Y	Y	N	Y
4 **King**	Y	Y	Y	Y	Y	N	Y
KANSAS							
1 **Marshall**	Y	Y	Y	Y	Y	N	Y
2 **Jenkins**	Y	Y	Y	Y	Y	N	Y
3 **Yoder**	Y	Y	Y	Y	Y	N	Y
4 **Estes**	Y	Y	Y	Y	Y	N	Y
KENTUCKY							
1 **Comer**	Y	Y	Y	Y	Y	N	Y
2 **Guthrie**	Y	Y	Y	Y	Y	N	Y
3 Yarmuth	?	N	N	Y	Y	Y	Y
4 **Massie**	Y	Y	N	Y	Y	N	N
5 **Rogers**	Y	Y	Y	Y	Y	N	Y
6 **Barr**	Y	Y	Y	Y	Y	N	Y
LOUISIANA							
1 **Scalise**	Y	Y	Y	Y	Y	N	Y
2 Richmond	Y	N	N	Y	Y	Y	Y
3 **Higgins**	Y	Y	Y	Y	Y	N	Y
4 **Johnson**	Y	Y	Y	Y	Y	N	Y
5 **Abraham**	Y	Y	Y	Y	Y	N	Y
6 **Graves**	Y	Y	Y	Y	Y	N	Y
MAINE							
1 Pingree	?	N	N	Y	Y	Y	Y
2 **Poliquin**	Y	Y	Y	Y	Y	N	Y
MARYLAND							
1 **Harris**	Y	Y	Y	Y	Y	N	Y
2 Ruppersberger	Y	N	N	Y	Y	Y	Y
3 Sarbanes	Y	N	N	Y	Y	Y	Y
4 Brown	Y	N	N	Y	Y	Y	Y
5 Hoyer	Y	N	N	Y	Y	Y	Y
6 Delaney	Y	N	N	Y	Y	Y	Y
7 Cummings	Y	N	N	Y	Y	Y	Y
8 Raskin	Y	N	N	Y	Y	Y	Y
MASSACHUSETTS							
1 Neal	Y	N	N	Y	Y	Y	Y
2 McGovern	Y	N	N	Y	Y	Y	Y
3 Tsongas	?	N	N	Y	Y	Y	Y
4 Kennedy	Y	N	N	Y	Y	Y	Y
5 Clark	Y	N	N	Y	Y	Y	Y
6 Moulton	Y	N	N	Y	Y	Y	Y
7 Capuano	Y	N	N	Y	Y	Y	Y
8 Lynch	Y	N	N	Y	Y	Y	Y
9 Keating	Y	N	N	Y	Y	Y	Y
MICHIGAN							
1 **Bergman**	Y	Y	Y	Y	Y	N	Y
2 **Huizenga**	Y	Y	Y	Y	Y	N	Y
3 **Amash**	Y	Y	N	Y	Y	N	N
4 **Moolenaar**	Y	Y	Y	Y	Y	N	Y
5 Kildee	Y	N	N	Y	Y	Y	Y
6 **Upton**	Y	Y	Y	Y	Y	N	Y
7 **Walberg**	Y	Y	Y	Y	Y	N	Y
8 **Bishop**	Y	Y	Y	Y	Y	N	Y
9 Levin	Y	N	N	Y	Y	Y	Y
10 **Mitchell**	Y	Y	Y	Y	Y	N	Y
11 **Trott**	Y	Y	Y	Y	Y	N	Y
12 Dingell	Y	N	N	Y	Y	Y	Y
13 Conyers	Y	N	N	Y	Y	Y	Y
14 Lawrence	?	N	N	+	+	+	+
MINNESOTA							
1 Walz	?	N	N	Y	Y	Y	Y
2 **Lewis**	Y	Y	Y	Y	Y	N	Y
3 **Paulsen**	Y	Y	Y	Y	Y	N	Y
4 McCollum	Y	N	N	Y	Y	Y	Y

	559	560	561	562	563	564	565
5 Ellison	Y	N	N	Y	Y	Y	Y
6 **Emmer**	Y	Y	Y	Y	Y	N	Y
7 Peterson	Y	N	N	Y	Y	N	Y
8 Nolan	Y	N	N	Y	Y	Y	Y
MISSISSIPPI							
1 **Kelly**	Y	Y	Y	Y	Y	N	Y
2 Thompson	Y	N	N	Y	Y	Y	Y
3 **Harper**	Y	Y	Y	Y	Y	N	Y
4 **Palazzo**	Y	Y	Y	Y	Y	–	+
MISSOURI							
1 Clay	Y	N	N	Y	Y	Y	Y
2 **Wagner**	Y	Y	Y	Y	Y	N	Y
3 **Luetkemeyer**	Y	Y	Y	Y	Y	N	Y
4 **Hartzler**	Y	Y	Y	Y	Y	N	Y
5 Cleaver	Y	N	N	Y	Y	Y	Y
6 **Graves**	Y	Y	Y	Y	Y	N	Y
7 **Long**	+	+	+	+	+	–	+
8 **Smith**	Y	Y	Y	Y	Y	N	Y
MONTANA							
AL **Gianforte**	Y	Y	Y	Y	Y	N	Y
NEBRASKA							
1 **Fortenberry**	Y	Y	Y	Y	Y	N	Y
2 **Bacon**	Y	Y	Y	Y	Y	N	Y
3 **Smith**	Y	Y	Y	Y	Y	N	Y
NEVADA							
1 Titus	+	N	N	Y	Y	Y	Y
2 **Amodei**	Y	Y	Y	Y	Y	N	Y
3 Rosen	Y	N	N	Y	Y	Y	Y
4 Kihuen	Y	N	N	Y	Y	Y	Y
NEW HAMPSHIRE							
1 Shea-Porter	Y	N	N	Y	Y	Y	Y
2 Kuster	Y	N	N	Y	Y	Y	Y
NEW JERSEY							
1 Norcross	Y	N	N	Y	Y	Y	Y
2 **LoBiondo**	Y	Y	Y	Y	Y	N	Y
3 **MacArthur**	Y	Y	Y	Y	Y	N	Y
4 **Smith**	Y	Y	Y	Y	Y	N	Y
5 Gottheimer	Y	N	N	Y	Y	Y	Y
6 Pallone	Y	N	N	Y	Y	Y	Y
7 **Lance**	Y	Y	Y	Y	Y	N	Y
8 Sires	Y	N	N	Y	Y	Y	Y
9 Pascrell	Y	N	N	Y	Y	Y	Y
10 Payne	Y	N	N	Y	Y	Y	Y
11 **Frelinghuysen**	Y	Y	Y	Y	Y	N	Y
12 Watson Coleman	Y	N	N	Y	Y	Y	Y
NEW MEXICO							
1 Lujan Grisham	Y	N	N	Y	Y	Y	Y
2 **Pearce**	Y	Y	Y	Y	Y	N	Y
3 Luján	Y	N	N	Y	Y	Y	Y
NEW YORK							
1 **Zeldin**	Y	Y	Y	Y	Y	N	Y
2 **King**	Y	Y	Y	Y	Y	N	Y
3 Suozzi	Y	N	N	Y	Y	Y	Y
4 Rice	Y	N	N	Y	Y	Y	Y
5 Meeks	Y	N	N	Y	Y	Y	Y
6 Meng	Y	N	N	Y	Y	Y	Y
7 Velázquez	Y	N	N	Y	Y	Y	Y
8 Jeffries	Y	N	N	Y	Y	Y	Y
9 Clarke	Y	N	N	Y	Y	Y	Y
10 Nadler	?	N	N	Y	Y	Y	Y
11 **Donovan**	Y	Y	Y	Y	Y	N	Y
12 Maloney, C.	Y	N	N	Y	Y	Y	Y
13 Espaillat	?	N	N	Y	Y	Y	Y
14 Crowley	Y	N	N	Y	Y	Y	Y
15 Serrano	Y	N	N	Y	Y	Y	Y
16 Engel	Y	N	N	Y	Y	Y	Y
17 Lowey	Y	N	N	Y	Y	Y	Y
18 Maloney, S.P.	Y	N	N	Y	Y	Y	Y
19 **Faso**	Y	Y	Y	Y	Y	N	Y
20 Tonko	Y	N	N	Y	Y	Y	Y
21 **Stefanik**	Y	Y	Y	Y	Y	N	Y
22 **Tenney**	Y	Y	Y	Y	Y	N	Y
23 **Reed**	Y	Y	Y	Y	Y	N	Y
24 **Katko**	Y	Y	Y	Y	Y	N	Y
25 Slaughter	Y	N	N	Y	Y	Y	Y
26 Higgins	Y	N	N	Y	Y	Y	Y
27 **Collins**	Y	Y	Y	Y	Y	N	Y
NORTH CAROLINA							
1 Butterfield	?	N	N	Y	Y	Y	Y
2 **Holding**	Y	Y	Y	Y	Y	N	Y
3 **Jones**	Y	Y	Y	Y	Y	Y	N
4 Price	Y	N	N	Y	Y	Y	Y

	559	560	561	562	563	564	565
5 **Foxx**	Y	Y	Y	Y	Y	N	Y
6 **Walker**	Y	Y	Y	Y	Y	N	Y
7 **Rouzer**	+	Y	Y	Y	Y	N	Y
8 **Hudson**	Y	Y	Y	Y	Y	N	Y
9 **Pittenger**	Y	Y	Y	Y	Y	N	Y
10 **McHenry**	Y	Y	Y	Y	Y	N	Y
11 **Meadows**	Y	Y	Y	Y	Y	N	Y
12 Adams	Y	N	N	Y	Y	Y	Y
13 **Budd**	Y	Y	Y	Y	Y	N	Y
NORTH DAKOTA							
AL **Cramer**	Y	Y	Y	Y	Y	N	Y
OHIO							
1 **Chabot**	Y	Y	Y	Y	Y	N	Y
2 **Wenstrup**	Y	Y	Y	Y	Y	N	Y
3 Beatty	+	N	N	Y	Y	Y	Y
4 **Jordan**	Y	Y	Y	Y	Y	?	Y
5 **Latta**	Y	Y	Y	Y	Y	N	Y
6 **Johnson**	?	Y	Y	Y	Y	N	Y
7 **Gibbs**	Y	Y	Y	Y	Y	N	Y
8 **Davidson**	Y	Y	Y	Y	Y	N	Y
9 Kaptur	Y	N	N	Y	Y	Y	Y
10 **Turner**	Y	Y	Y	Y	Y	N	Y
11 Fudge	Y	N	N	Y	Y	Y	Y
12 **Tiberi**	Y	Y	Y	Y	Y	N	Y
13 Ryan	Y	N	N	Y	Y	Y	Y
14 **Joyce**	Y	Y	Y	Y	Y	N	Y
15 **Stivers**	Y	Y	Y	Y	Y	N	Y
16 **Renacci**	+	Y	Y	Y	Y	?	?
OKLAHOMA							
1 **Bridenstine**	?	?	?	?	?	?	?
2 **Mullin**	Y	Y	Y	Y	Y	N	Y
3 **Lucas**	Y	Y	Y	Y	Y	N	Y
4 **Cole**	Y	Y	Y	Y	Y	N	Y
5 **Russell**	Y	Y	Y	Y	Y	N	Y
OREGON							
1 Bonamici	Y	N	N	Y	Y	Y	Y
2 **Walden**	?	Y	Y	Y	Y	N	Y
3 Blumenauer	Y	N	N	Y	Y	Y	N
4 DeFazio	Y	N	N	Y	Y	Y	N
5 Schrader	Y	N	N	Y	Y	N	Y
PENNSYLVANIA							
1 Brady	Y	N	N	Y	Y	Y	Y
2 Evans	Y	N	N	Y	Y	Y	Y
3 **Kelly**	Y	?	?	?	?	N	Y
4 **Perry**	Y	+	+	+	+	N	Y
5 **Thompson**	Y	Y	Y	Y	Y	N	Y
6 **Costello**	Y	Y	Y	Y	Y	N	Y
7 **Meehan**	Y	?	?	?	?	N	Y
8 **Fitzpatrick**	Y	Y	Y	Y	Y	N	Y
9 **Shuster**	Y	Y	Y	Y	Y	N	Y
10 **Marino**	Y	?	?	?	?	?	?
11 **Barletta**	Y	?	?	?	?	N	Y
12 **Rothfus**	Y	Y	Y	Y	Y	N	Y
13 Boyle	Y	N	N	Y	Y	Y	Y
14 Doyle	Y	N	N	Y	Y	Y	Y
15 **Dent**	Y	Y	Y	Y	Y	N	Y
16 **Smucker**	?	?	?	?	?	N	Y
17 Cartwright	Y	N	N	Y	Y	Y	Y
18 **Murphy**	Y	Y	Y	Y	Y	N	Y
RHODE ISLAND							
1 Cicilline	Y	N	N	Y	Y	Y	Y
2 Langevin	Y	N	N	Y	Y	Y	Y
SOUTH CAROLINA							
1 **Sanford**	Y	Y	Y	Y	Y	N	N
2 **Wilson**	Y	Y	Y	Y	Y	N	Y
3 **Duncan**	Y	Y	Y	Y	Y	N	Y
4 **Gowdy**	Y	Y	Y	Y	Y	N	Y
5 **Norman**	Y	Y	Y	Y	Y	N	Y
6 Clyburn	Y	N	N	Y	Y	?	?
7 **Rice**	Y	Y	Y	Y	Y	N	Y
SOUTH DAKOTA							
AL **Noem**	Y	Y	Y	Y	Y	N	Y
TENNESSEE							
1 **Roe**	Y	Y	Y	Y	Y	N	Y
2 **Duncan**	Y	Y	Y	Y	Y	N	Y
3 **Fleischmann**	Y	Y	Y	Y	Y	N	Y
4 **DesJarlais**	?	?	?	Y	Y	N	Y
5 Cooper	Y	N	N	Y	Y	N	Y
6 **Black**	Y	Y	Y	Y	Y	?	?
7 **Blackburn**	?	Y	Y	Y	Y	N	Y
8 **Kustoff**	Y	Y	Y	Y	Y	N	Y
9 Cohen	Y	N	N	Y	Y	Y	Y

	559	560	561	562	563	564	565
TEXAS							
1 **Gohmert**	Y	Y	Y	Y	Y	N	Y
2 **Poe**	Y	Y	Y	Y	Y	N	Y
3 **Johnson, S.**	Y	Y	Y	Y	Y	N	Y
4 **Ratcliffe**	Y	Y	Y	Y	Y	N	Y
5 **Hensarling**	Y	Y	Y	Y	Y	N	Y
6 **Barton**	Y	Y	Y	Y	Y	N	Y
7 **Culberson**	Y	Y	Y	Y	Y	N	Y
8 **Brady**	Y	Y	Y	Y	Y	N	Y
9 Green, A.	Y	N	N	Y	Y	Y	Y
10 **McCaul**	Y	?	Y	Y	?	N	Y
11 **Conaway**	Y	Y	Y	Y	Y	N	Y
12 **Granger**	Y	Y	Y	+	+	N	Y
13 **Thornberry**	+	Y	Y	Y	Y	N	Y
14 **Weber**	Y	Y	Y	Y	Y	N	Y
15 Gonzalez	Y	N	N	Y	Y	Y	Y
16 O'Rourke	Y	N	N	Y	Y	Y	Y
17 **Flores**	Y	Y	Y	?	?	N	Y
18 Jackson Lee	Y	N	N	Y	Y	Y	Y
19 **Arrington**	Y	Y	Y	Y	Y	N	Y
20 Castro	Y	N	N	Y	Y	Y	Y
21 **Smith**	Y	Y	Y	Y	Y	N	Y
22 **Olson**	Y	Y	Y	?	Y	N	Y
23 **Hurd**	Y	Y	Y	Y	Y	N	Y
24 **Marchant**	Y	?	Y	Y	Y	N	Y
25 **Williams**	Y	Y	Y	Y	Y	N	Y
26 **Burgess**	Y	Y	Y	Y	Y	N	Y
27 **Farenthold**	Y	Y	Y	Y	Y	N	Y
28 Cuellar	Y	N	N	Y	Y	N	Y
29 Green, G.	Y	N	N	Y	Y	Y	Y
30 Johnson, E.B.	Y	N	N	Y	Y	Y	Y
31 **Carter**	Y	Y	Y	Y	Y	N	Y
32 **Sessions**	Y	Y	Y	Y	Y	N	Y
33 Veasey	Y	N	N	Y	Y	Y	Y
34 Vela	Y	N	N	Y	Y	Y	Y
35 Doggett	Y	N	N	Y	Y	Y	Y
36 **Babin**	Y	Y	Y	Y	Y	N	Y
UTAH							
1 **Bishop**	Y	Y	Y	Y	Y	N	Y
2 **Stewart**	Y	Y	Y	Y	Y	N	Y
4 **Love**	Y	Y	Y	Y	Y	N	Y
VERMONT							
AL Welch	Y	N	N	Y	Y	Y	Y
VIRGINIA							
1 **Wittman**	Y	Y	Y	Y	Y	N	Y
2 **Taylor**	+	Y	Y	Y	Y	N	Y
3 Scott	Y	N	N	Y	Y	Y	Y
4 McEachin	Y	N	N	Y	Y	Y	Y
5 **Garrett**	Y	Y	Y	Y	Y	N	Y
6 **Goodlatte**	Y	Y	Y	Y	Y	N	Y
7 **Brat**	Y	Y	Y	Y	Y	N	Y
8 Beyer	Y	N	N	Y	Y	Y	Y
9 **Griffith**	Y	Y	Y	Y	Y	N	Y
10 **Comstock**	Y	Y	Y	Y	Y	N	Y
11 Connolly	Y	?	?	Y	Y	Y	Y
WASHINGTON							
1 DelBene	Y	N	N	Y	Y	Y	Y
2 Larsen	Y	N	N	Y	Y	Y	Y
3 **Herrera Beutler**	Y	Y	Y	Y	Y	N	Y
4 **Newhouse**	Y	Y	Y	Y	Y	N	Y
5 **McMorris Rodgers**	Y	Y	Y	Y	Y	N	Y
6 Kilmer	Y	N	N	Y	Y	Y	Y
7 Jayapal	Y	N	N	Y	Y	Y	Y
8 **Reichert**	Y	Y	Y	Y	Y	N	Y
9 Smith	Y	N	N	Y	Y	Y	Y
10 Heck	Y	N	N	Y	Y	Y	Y
WEST VIRGINIA							
1 **McKinley**	Y	Y	Y	Y	Y	N	Y
2 **Mooney**	Y	Y	Y	Y	Y	N	Y
3 **Jenkins**	Y	Y	Y	Y	Y	N	Y
WISCONSIN							
1 **Ryan**							
2 Pocan	Y	N	N	Y	Y	Y	Y
3 Kind	Y	N	N	Y	Y	N	Y
4 Moore	Y	N	N	Y	Y	Y	Y
5 **Sensenbrenner**	Y	Y	Y	Y	Y	N	Y
6 **Grothman**	Y	Y	Y	Y	Y	N	Y
7 **Duffy**	Y	Y	Y	Y	Y	N	Y
8 **Gallagher**	Y	Y	Y	Y	Y	N	Y
WYOMING							
AL **Cheney**	Y	Y	Y	Y	Y	N	Y

VOTE NUMBER

566. H RES 569. EMERGENCY HURRICANE AND WILDFIRE DISASTER APPROPRIATIONS LEGISLATIVE VEHICLE/ADOPTION. Frelinghuysen, R-N.J., motion to suspend the rules and agree to the resolution (H Res 569) that would provide that upon agreeing to the resolution, the House will have been considered to have concurred in the Senate amendment to the bill (HR 2266) with a House amendment that would make available $36.5 billion in emergency supplemental funding for fiscal 2018 to partially cover the costs of responding to multiple natural disasters, including hurricanes and wildfires. The measure would include $18.7 billion for the Federal Emergency Management Agency's Disaster Relief Fund - $4.9 billion of which would be used for disaster relief loans to Puerto Rico and the U.S. Virgin Islands. It would also cancel $16 billion of the Treasury debt incurred by FEMA's National Flood Insurance Program, would release $1.2 billion in contingency reserves from the Supplemental Nutrition Assistance Program for use in Puerto Rico would provide $577 million in funding to fight wildfires. Motion agreed to 353-69 : R 164-69; D 189-0. Oct. 12, 2017.

567. S 585. FEDERAL WHISTLEBLOWER RETALIATION PENALTIES/ RECOMMIT. O'Halleran, D-Ariz., motion to recommit the bill to the House Oversight and Government Reform Committee with instructions to report it back immediately with an amendment that would extend the bill's provisions to apply to any federal employee disclosure regarding the violation of any law or regulation related to travel by the head of an agency or a political appointee. Motion rejected 190-232 : R 1-232; D 189-0. Oct. 12, 2017.

568. S 585. FEDERAL WHISTLEBLOWER RETALIATION PENALTIES/ PASSAGE. Passage of the bill that would set specific penalties for federal supervisors who retaliate against an employee who discloses waste, fraud or abuse. It would require a supervisor to be suspended for at least three days for an initial offense, and would require a supervisor to be fired for a second offense. It would also require the VA to develop a plan to protect the medical records of employees and would prohibit VA employees from accessing medical files for demographic information when another non-medical database is available. Passed (thus cleared for the president) 420-0 : R 232-0; D 188-0. Oct. 12, 2017.

569. HR 3551. C-TPAT PROGRAM TIERS/PASSAGE. McSally, R-Ariz., motion to suspend the rules and pass the bill that would establish three tiers of program participation within the Customs Trade Partnership Against Terrorism program and would designate the program as the authorized economic operator program for the United States, as defined by the World Customs Organization. It would also create the position of director for C-TPAT. The director would be responsible for establishing the minimum-security criteria necessary for program participation and would also be responsible for ensuring that program participants receive tangible benefits for their voluntary participation in the program. Motion agreed to 402-1 : R 222-1; D 180-0. Oct. 23, 2017.

570. S 504. APEC BUSINESS TRAVEL CARDS AUTHORIZATION/PASSAGE. McSally, R-Ariz., motion to suspend the rules and pass the bill that would permanently authorize the Homeland Security Department to issue Asia-Pacific Economic Cooperation business travel cards to certain U.S. citizens with business or government engagements in the Asia-Pacific region. The measure would also modify APEC's administration and financing. Motion agreed to 401-2 : R 220-2; D 181-0. Oct. 23, 2017.

571. PROCEDURAL MOTION/APPROVAL OF HOUSE JOURNAL. Approved 236-158 : R 134-83; D 102-75. Oct. 23, 2017.

	566	567	568	569	570	571
ALABAMA						
1 **Byrne**	Y	N	Y	Y	Y	Y
2 **Roby**	Y	N	Y	Y	Y	Y
3 **Rogers**	Y	N	Y	Y	Y	N
4 **Aderholt**	Y	N	Y	Y	Y	Y
5 **Brooks**	N	N	Y	Y	Y	Y
6 **Palmer**	N	N	Y	Y	Y	N
7 Sewell	Y	Y	Y	Y	Y	N
ALASKA						
AL **Young**	Y	N	Y	Y	Y	N
ARIZONA						
1 **O'Halleran**	Y	Y	Y	Y	Y	N
2 **McSally**	Y	N	Y	Y	Y	Y
3 **Grijalva**	Y	Y	Y	Y	Y	?
4 **Gosar**	N	N	Y	Y	Y	N
5 **Biggs**	N	N	Y	Y	Y	N
6 **Schweikert**	N	N	Y	Y	Y	Y
7 **Gallego**	Y	Y	Y	Y	Y	N
8 **Franks**	N	N	Y	?	?	?
9 **Sinema**	Y	Y	Y	Y	Y	N
ARKANSAS						
1 **Crawford**	Y	N	Y	Y	Y	Y
2 **Hill**	N	N	Y	Y	Y	Y
3 **Womack**	Y	N	Y	Y	Y	Y
4 **Westerman**	Y	N	Y	Y	Y	N
CALIFORNIA						
1 **LaMalfa**	Y	N	Y	Y	Y	Y
2 Huffman	+	+	+	Y	Y	Y
3 **Garamendi**	Y	Y	Y	Y	Y	Y
4 **McClintock**	Y	N	Y	Y	Y	Y
5 Thompson	+	+	+	Y	Y	N
6 Matsui	Y	Y	Y	Y	Y	N
7 Bera	Y	Y	Y	Y	Y	N
8 **Cook**	Y	N	Y	Y	Y	Y
9 McNerney	Y	Y	Y	Y	Y	Y
10 **Denham**	Y	N	Y	Y	Y	N
11 DeSaulnier	Y	Y	Y	Y	Y	Y
12 Pelosi	Y	Y	Y	Y	Y	Y
13 Lee	Y	Y	Y	Y	Y	N
14 Speier	Y	Y	Y	Y	Y	Y
15 Swalwell	Y	Y	Y	Y	Y	N
16 Costa	Y	Y	Y	Y	Y	N
17 Khanna	Y	Y	Y	Y	Y	Y
18 Eshoo	+	+	+	Y	Y	Y
19 Lofgren	Y	Y	Y	Y	Y	N
20 Panetta	Y	Y	Y	Y	Y	N
21 **Valadao**	Y	N	Y	Y	Y	N
22 **Nunes**	Y	N	Y	Y	Y	Y
23 **McCarthy**	Y	N	Y	Y	Y	Y
24 Carbajal	Y	Y	Y	Y	Y	N
25 **Knight**	Y	N	Y	Y	Y	N
26 Brownley	Y	Y	Y	Y	Y	N
27 Chu	Y	Y	Y	Y	Y	Y
28 Schiff	Y	Y	Y	Y	Y	Y
29 Cardenas	Y	Y	Y	Y	Y	Y
30 Sherman	Y	Y	Y	Y	Y	Y
31 Aguilar	Y	Y	Y	Y	Y	N
32 Napolitano	Y	Y	Y	Y	Y	Y
33 Lieu	Y	Y	Y	Y	Y	Y
34 Gomez	Y	Y	Y	Y	Y	N
35 Torres	Y	Y	Y	Y	Y	Y
36 Ruiz	Y	Y	Y	Y	Y	N
37 Bass	Y	Y	Y	?	?	?
38 Sánchez, Linda	Y	Y	Y	Y	Y	N
39 **Royce**	Y	N	Y	Y	Y	Y
40 Roybal-Allard	Y	Y	Y	Y	Y	N
41 Takano	Y	Y	Y	Y	Y	Y
42 **Calvert**	Y	N	Y	Y	Y	Y
43 Waters	Y	Y	Y	Y	Y	Y
44 Barragan	Y	Y	Y	Y	Y	N
45 **Walters**	Y	N	Y	Y	Y	Y
46 Correa	Y	Y	Y	Y	Y	N
47 Lowenthal	Y	Y	Y	?	?	?
48 **Rohrabacher**	Y	N	Y	Y	Y	N
49 **Issa**	Y	N	Y	Y	Y	Y
50 **Hunter**	Y	N	Y	Y	Y	Y
51 Vargas	Y	Y	Y	Y	Y	N
52 Peters	Y	Y	Y	Y	Y	N
53 Davis	Y	Y	Y	Y	Y	Y

	566	567	568	569	570	571
COLORADO						
1 DeGette	Y	Y	Y	Y	Y	Y
2 Polis	Y	Y	Y	Y	Y	N
3 **Tipton**	Y	N	Y	Y	Y	N
4 **Buck**	N	N	Y	Y	Y	N
5 **Lamborn**	N	N	Y	Y	Y	Y
6 **Coffman**	Y	N	Y	Y	Y	N
7 Perlmutter	Y	Y	Y	Y	Y	Y
CONNECTICUT						
1 Larson	Y	Y	Y	Y	Y	N
2 Courtney	Y	Y	Y	Y	Y	Y
3 DeLauro	Y	Y	Y	Y	Y	Y
4 Himes	Y	Y	Y	Y	Y	Y
5 Esty	Y	Y	Y	Y	Y	N
DELAWARE						
AL Blunt Rochester	Y	Y	Y	Y	Y	Y
FLORIDA						
1 **Gaetz**	Y	N	Y	Y	Y	N
2 **Dunn**	Y	N	Y	Y	Y	Y
3 **Yoho**	Y	N	Y	Y	Y	Y
4 **Rutherford**	Y	N	Y	Y	Y	N
5 Lawson	Y	Y	Y	Y	Y	N
6 **DeSantis**	Y	N	?	?	?	?
7 Murphy	Y	Y	Y	Y	Y	Y
8 **Posey**	Y	N	Y	Y	Y	Y
9 Soto	Y	Y	Y	Y	Y	N
10 Demings	Y	Y	Y	Y	Y	N
11 **Webster**	Y	N	Y	Y	Y	Y
12 **Bilirakis**	Y	N	Y	Y	Y	Y
13 Crist	Y	Y	Y	Y	Y	N
14 Castor	Y	Y	Y	Y	Y	N
15 **Ross**	Y	N	?	?	?	?
16 **Buchanan**	Y	N	?	?	?	?
17 **Rooney, T.**	Y	N	Y	Y	Y	?
18 **Mast**	Y	N	Y	Y	Y	N
19 **Rooney, F.**	Y	N	Y	Y	Y	Y
20 Hastings	Y	Y	Y	Y	Y	Y
21 Frankel	Y	Y	Y	?	Y	Y
22 Deutch	Y	Y	Y	Y	Y	Y
23 Wasserman Schultz	Y	Y	Y	Y	Y	Y
24 Wilson	Y	Y	Y	?	?	?
25 **Diaz-Balart**	Y	N	Y	Y	Y	N
26 **Curbelo**	Y	N	Y	Y	Y	N
27 **Ros-Lehtinen**	Y	N	Y	Y	Y	N
GEORGIA						
1 **Carter**	Y	N	Y	Y	Y	N
2 Bishop	Y	Y	Y	Y	Y	Y
3 **Ferguson**	Y	N	Y	Y	Y	N
4 Johnson	Y	Y	Y	Y	Y	Y
5 Lewis	Y	Y	Y	Y	Y	N
6 **Handel**	Y	N	Y	Y	Y	Y
7 **Woodall**	Y	N	Y	Y	Y	Y
8 **Scott, A.**	Y	N	Y	Y	Y	N
9 **Collins**	Y	N	Y	Y	Y	N
10 **Hice**	N	N	Y	Y	Y	Y
11 **Loudermilk**	N	N	Y	Y	Y	Y
12 **Allen**	Y	N	Y	Y	Y	Y
13 Scott, D.	Y	Y	?	Y	Y	Y
14 **Graves**	Y	N	Y	Y	Y	N
HAWAII						
1 Hanabusa	Y	Y	Y	Y	Y	N
2 Gabbard	Y	Y	Y	Y	Y	Y
IDAHO						
1 **Labrador**	Y	N	Y	Y	Y	Y
2 **Simpson**	Y	N	Y	Y	Y	Y
ILLINOIS						
1 Rush	Y	Y	Y	?	?	?
2 Kelly	Y	Y	Y	Y	Y	N
3 Lipinski	Y	Y	Y	Y	Y	Y
4 Gutierrez	Y	Y	Y	+	+	–
5 Quigley	Y	Y	Y	Y	Y	?
6 **Roskam**	Y	N	Y	Y	Y	Y
7 Davis, D.	Y	Y	Y	Y	Y	Y
8 Krishnamoorthi	Y	Y	Y	Y	Y	Y
9 Schakowsky	Y	Y	Y	Y	Y	N
10 Schneider	Y	Y	Y	Y	Y	Y
11 Foster	Y	Y	Y	Y	Y	Y
12 **Bost**	Y	N	Y	Y	Y	Y
13 **Davis, R.**	Y	N	Y	Y	Y	Y
14 **Hultgren**	Y	N	Y	Y	Y	Y
15 **Shimkus**	Y	N	Y	Y	Y	Y

	566	567	568	569	570	571
16 **Kinzinger**	Y	N	Y	Y	Y	N
17 Bustos	Y	Y	Y	Y	Y	Y
18 **LaHood**	Y	N	Y	Y	Y	N
INDIANA						
1 Visclosky	Y	Y	Y	Y	Y	N
2 **Walorski**	N	N	Y	Y	Y	Y
3 **Banks**	N	N	Y	Y	Y	Y
4 **Rokita**	N	N	Y	Y	Y	Y
5 **Brooks**	Y	N	Y	Y	Y	Y
6 **Messer**	N	N	Y	Y	Y	Y
7 Carson	Y	Y	Y	+	+	+
8 **Bucshon**	Y	N	Y	Y	Y	N
9 **Hollingsworth**	Y	N	Y	Y	Y	Y
IOWA						
1 **Blum**	N	Y	Y	Y	Y	N
2 Loebsack	Y	Y	Y	Y	Y	N
3 **Young**	Y	N	Y	Y	Y	Y
4 **King**	Y	N	Y	Y	Y	Y
KANSAS						
1 **Marshall**	Y	N	Y	Y	Y	N
2 **Jenkins**	Y	N	Y	Y	Y	N
3 **Yoder**	Y	N	Y	Y	Y	N
4 **Estes**	Y	N	Y	Y	Y	Y
KENTUCKY						
1 **Comer**	N	N	Y	Y	Y	N
2 **Guthrie**	Y	N	Y	Y	Y	Y
3 Yarmuth	Y	Y	Y	?	?	?
4 **Massie**	N	N	Y	Y	Y	Y
5 **Rogers**	Y	N	Y	Y	Y	Y
6 **Barr**	N	N	Y	Y	Y	N
LOUISIANA						
1 **Scalise**	Y	N	Y	Y	Y	Y
2 Richmond	Y	Y	Y	Y	Y	N
3 **Higgins**	Y	N	Y	Y	Y	Y
4 **Johnson**	N	N	Y	Y	Y	Y
5 **Abraham**	Y	N	Y	Y	Y	Y
6 **Graves**	Y	N	Y	Y	Y	N
MAINE						
1 Pingree	Y	Y	Y	?	?	?
2 **Poliquin**	Y	N	Y	Y	Y	N
MARYLAND						
1 **Harris**	N	N	Y	Y	Y	Y
2 Ruppersberger	Y	Y	Y	Y	Y	?
3 Sarbanes	Y	Y	Y	Y	Y	N
4 Brown	Y	Y	Y	Y	Y	Y
5 Hoyer	Y	Y	Y	Y	Y	Y
6 Delaney	Y	Y	Y	Y	Y	N
7 Cummings	Y	Y	Y	Y	Y	Y
8 Raskin	Y	Y	Y	Y	Y	N
MASSACHUSETTS						
1 Neal	Y	Y	Y	Y	Y	N
2 McGovern	Y	Y	Y	Y	Y	N
3 Tsongas	Y	Y	Y	Y	Y	Y
4 Kennedy	Y	Y	Y	Y	Y	Y
5 Clark	Y	Y	Y	Y	Y	N
6 Moulton	Y	Y	Y	Y	Y	Y
7 Capuano	Y	Y	Y	Y	Y	N
8 Lynch	Y	Y	Y	Y	Y	N
9 Keating	Y	Y	Y	Y	Y	N
MICHIGAN						
1 **Bergman**	N	N	Y	Y	Y	N
2 **Huizenga**	Y	N	Y	+	+	+
3 **Amash**	N	N	Y	N	Y	N
4 **Moolenaar**	Y	N	Y	Y	Y	Y
5 Kildee	Y	Y	Y	Y	Y	Y
6 **Upton**	Y	N	Y	Y	Y	N
7 **Walberg**	Y	N	Y	Y	Y	N
8 **Bishop**	N	N	Y	Y	Y	N
9 Levin	Y	Y	Y	Y	Y	Y
10 **Mitchell**	Y	N	Y	Y	Y	Y
11 **Trott**	Y	N	Y	?	?	?
12 Dingell	Y	Y	Y	Y	Y	Y
13 Conyers	Y	Y	Y	Y	Y	Y
14 Lawrence	+	+	+	Y	Y	Y
MINNESOTA						
1 Walz	Y	Y	Y	Y	Y	Y
2 **Lewis**	N	N	Y	Y	Y	Y
3 **Paulsen**	Y	N	Y	Y	Y	N
4 McCollum	Y	Y	Y	Y	Y	Y
5 Ellison	Y	Y	Y	Y	Y	Y
6 **Emmer**	N	N	Y	Y	Y	Y
7 Peterson	Y	Y	Y	Y	Y	Y
8 Nolan	Y	Y	Y	Y	Y	N
MISSISSIPPI						
1 **Kelly**	N	N	Y	Y	Y	Y
2 Thompson	Y	Y	Y	Y	Y	N
3 **Harper**	Y	N	Y	Y	Y	Y
4 **Palazzo**	+	–	+	Y	Y	N
MISSOURI						
1 Clay	Y	Y	Y	?	?	?
2 **Wagner**	Y	N	Y	Y	Y	Y
3 **Luetkemeyer**	Y	N	Y	Y	Y	Y
4 **Hartzler**	Y	N	Y	Y	Y	Y
5 Cleaver	Y	Y	Y	Y	Y	Y
6 **Graves**	Y	N	Y	Y	Y	N
7 **Long**	+	–	+	+	+	+
8 **Smith**	N	N	Y	Y	Y	N
MONTANA						
AL **Gianforte**	Y	N	Y	Y	Y	Y
NEBRASKA						
1 **Fortenberry**	Y	N	Y	Y	Y	Y
2 **Bacon**	Y	N	Y	Y	Y	Y
3 **Smith**	Y	N	Y	Y	Y	Y
NEVADA						
1 Titus	Y	Y	Y	Y	Y	Y
2 **Amodei**	Y	N	Y	Y	Y	Y
3 Rosen	Y	Y	Y	Y	Y	N
4 Kihuen	Y	Y	Y	Y	Y	N
NEW HAMPSHIRE						
1 Shea-Porter	Y	Y	Y	Y	Y	Y
2 Kuster	Y	Y	Y	Y	Y	Y
NEW JERSEY						
1 Norcross	Y	Y	Y	Y	Y	N
2 **LoBiondo**	Y	N	Y	Y	Y	N
3 **MacArthur**	Y	N	Y	Y	Y	N
4 **Smith**	Y	N	Y	Y	Y	Y
5 Gottheimer	Y	Y	Y	Y	Y	Y
6 Pallone	Y	Y	Y	Y	Y	N
7 **Lance**	Y	N	Y	Y	Y	N
8 Sires	Y	Y	Y	?	?	?
9 Pascrell	Y	Y	Y	Y	Y	Y
10 Payne	Y	Y	Y	Y	Y	Y
11 **Frelinghuysen**	Y	N	Y	Y	Y	Y
12 Watson Coleman	Y	Y	Y	Y	Y	Y
NEW MEXICO						
1 Lujan Grisham	Y	Y	Y	Y	Y	Y
2 **Pearce**	N	N	Y	Y	Y	N
3 Luján	Y	Y	Y	Y	Y	Y
NEW YORK						
1 **Zeldin**	Y	N	Y	Y	Y	Y
2 **King**	Y	N	Y	Y	Y	Y
3 Suozzi	Y	Y	Y	Y	Y	N
4 Rice	Y	Y	Y	Y	Y	N
5 Meeks	Y	Y	Y	Y	Y	Y
6 Meng	Y	Y	Y	Y	Y	Y
7 Velázquez	Y	Y	Y	Y	Y	N
8 Jeffries	Y	Y	Y	Y	Y	Y
9 Clarke	Y	Y	Y	Y	Y	N
10 Nadler	Y	Y	Y	Y	Y	Y
11 **Donovan**	Y	N	Y	Y	Y	Y
12 Maloney, C.	Y	Y	Y	Y	Y	Y
13 Espaillat	Y	Y	Y	Y	Y	Y
14 Crowley	Y	Y	Y	Y	Y	N
15 Serrano	Y	Y	Y	Y	Y	Y
16 Engel	Y	Y	Y	Y	Y	Y
17 Lowey	Y	Y	Y	Y	Y	Y
18 Maloney, S.P.	Y	Y	Y	Y	Y	N
19 **Faso**	Y	N	Y	Y	Y	N
20 Tonko	Y	Y	Y	Y	Y	P
21 **Stefanik**	Y	N	Y	Y	Y	Y
22 **Tenney**	Y	N	Y	Y	Y	N
23 **Reed**	Y	N	Y	Y	Y	N
24 **Katko**	Y	N	Y	Y	Y	N
25 Slaughter	Y	Y	Y	Y	Y	N
26 Higgins	Y	Y	Y	Y	Y	Y
27 **Collins**	Y	N	Y	Y	Y	Y
NORTH CAROLINA						
1 Butterfield	Y	Y	Y	?	?	?
2 **Holding**	N	N	Y	Y	Y	N
3 **Jones**	N	N	Y	Y	N	?
4 Price	Y	Y	Y	Y	Y	Y
5 **Foxx**	N	N	Y	Y	Y	N
6 **Walker**	N	N	Y	Y	Y	Y
7 **Rouzer**	N	N	Y	Y	Y	N
8 **Hudson**	N	N	Y	Y	Y	N
9 **Pittenger**	N	N	Y	Y	?	N
10 **McHenry**	Y	N	Y	Y	Y	Y
11 **Meadows**	N	N	Y	Y	Y	Y
12 Adams	Y	Y	Y	Y	Y	Y
13 **Budd**	N	N	Y	Y	Y	Y
NORTH DAKOTA						
AL **Cramer**	Y	N	Y	Y	Y	Y
OHIO						
1 **Chabot**	N	N	Y	Y	Y	Y
2 **Wenstrup**	N	N	Y	Y	Y	Y
3 Beatty	Y	Y	Y	Y	Y	Y
4 **Jordan**	N	N	Y	Y	Y	N
5 **Latta**	Y	N	Y	Y	Y	Y
6 **Johnson**	Y	N	Y	Y	Y	N
7 **Gibbs**	N	N	Y	Y	Y	Y
8 **Davidson**	N	N	Y	Y	Y	Y
9 Kaptur	Y	Y	Y	Y	Y	Y
10 **Turner**	Y	N	Y	Y	Y	N
11 Fudge	Y	Y	Y	Y	Y	N
12 **Tiberi**	Y	N	Y	Y	Y	Y
13 Ryan	Y	Y	Y	?	?	?
14 **Joyce**	Y	N	Y	Y	Y	N
15 **Stivers**	Y	N	Y	Y	Y	N
16 **Renacci**	?	?	?	+	+	–
OKLAHOMA						
1 **Bridenstine**	?	?	?	?	?	?
2 **Mullin**	N	N	Y	Y	Y	?
3 **Lucas**	Y	N	Y	Y	Y	Y
4 **Cole**	Y	N	Y	Y	Y	Y
5 **Russell**	Y	N	Y	Y	Y	Y
OREGON						
1 Bonamici	Y	Y	Y	Y	Y	Y
2 **Walden**	Y	N	Y	Y	Y	Y
3 Blumenauer	Y	Y	Y	+	+	+
4 DeFazio	Y	Y	Y	Y	Y	N
5 Schrader	Y	Y	Y	Y	Y	N
PENNSYLVANIA						
1 Brady	Y	Y	Y	Y	Y	N
2 Evans	Y	Y	Y	Y	Y	Y
3 **Kelly**	Y	N	Y	Y	Y	Y
4 **Perry**	N	N	Y	Y	Y	N
5 **Thompson**	Y	N	Y	Y	Y	N
6 **Costello**	Y	N	Y	Y	Y	N
7 **Meehan**	Y	N	Y	Y	Y	N
8 **Fitzpatrick**	Y	N	Y	Y	Y	N
9 **Shuster**	Y	N	Y	Y	Y	Y
10 **Marino**	?	?	?	Y	Y	Y
11 **Barletta**	Y	N	Y	?	?	?
12 **Rothfus**	N	N	Y	Y	Y	Y
13 Boyle	Y	Y	Y	Y	Y	N
14 Doyle	Y	Y	Y	Y	Y	Y
15 **Dent**	Y	N	Y	Y	Y	Y
16 **Smucker**	Y	N	Y	Y	Y	Y
17 Cartwright	Y	Y	Y	Y	Y	Y
RHODE ISLAND						
1 Cicilline	Y	Y	Y	Y	Y	Y
2 Langevin	Y	Y	Y	Y	Y	N
SOUTH CAROLINA						
1 **Sanford**	N	N	Y	Y	Y	Y
2 **Wilson**	Y	N	Y	Y	Y	Y
3 **Duncan**	N	N	Y	Y	Y	Y
4 **Gowdy**	Y	N	Y	Y	Y	Y
5 **Norman**	N	N	Y	Y	Y	Y
6 Clyburn	?	?	?	Y	Y	Y
7 **Rice**	Y	N	Y	Y	Y	P
SOUTH DAKOTA						
AL **Noem**	N	N	Y	Y	Y	N
TENNESSEE						
1 **Roe**	Y	N	Y	Y	Y	Y
2 **Duncan**	N	N	Y	Y	Y	Y
3 **Fleischmann**	Y	N	Y	Y	Y	Y
4 **DesJarlais**	N	N	Y	Y	Y	Y
5 Cooper	Y	Y	Y	Y	Y	Y
6 **Black**	?	?	?	Y	Y	Y
7 **Blackburn**	N	N	Y	?	?	?
8 **Kustoff**	N	N	Y	Y	Y	Y
9 Cohen	Y	Y	Y	Y	Y	N
TEXAS						
1 **Gohmert**	N	N	Y	Y	N	?
2 **Poe**	Y	N	Y	Y	Y	N
3 **Johnson, S.**	Y	N	Y	Y	Y	Y
4 **Ratcliffe**	N	N	Y	Y	Y	N
5 **Hensarling**	N	N	Y	Y	Y	Y
6 **Barton**	N	N	Y	Y	Y	N
7 **Culberson**	Y	N	Y	+	+	+
8 **Brady**	Y	N	Y	Y	Y	Y
9 Green, A.	Y	Y	Y	Y	Y	Y
10 **McCaul**	Y	N	Y	Y	Y	Y
11 **Conaway**	Y	N	Y	Y	Y	N
12 **Granger**	Y	N	Y	?	?	?
13 **Thornberry**	Y	N	Y	Y	Y	Y
14 **Weber**	Y	N	Y	Y	Y	N
15 Gonzalez	Y	Y	Y	Y	Y	Y
16 O'Rourke	Y	Y	Y	Y	Y	Y
17 **Flores**	Y	N	Y	Y	Y	N
18 Jackson Lee	Y	Y	Y	Y	Y	N
19 **Arrington**	Y	N	Y	Y	Y	Y
20 Castro	Y	Y	Y	Y	Y	Y
21 **Smith**	Y	N	Y	Y	Y	Y
22 **Olson**	Y	N	Y	Y	Y	Y
23 **Hurd**	Y	N	Y	Y	Y	Y
24 **Marchant**	N	N	Y	Y	Y	Y
25 **Williams**	N	N	Y	?	?	?
26 **Burgess**	Y	N	Y	Y	Y	?
27 **Farenthold**	Y	N	Y	Y	Y	Y
28 Cuellar	Y	Y	Y	Y	Y	Y
29 Green, G.	Y	Y	Y	Y	Y	N
30 Johnson, E.B.	Y	Y	Y	Y	Y	N
31 **Carter**	Y	N	Y	Y	Y	Y
32 **Sessions**	Y	N	Y	Y	Y	Y
33 Veasey	Y	Y	Y	Y	Y	N
34 Vela	Y	Y	Y	Y	Y	Y
35 Doggett	Y	Y	Y	Y	Y	Y
36 **Babin**	Y	N	Y	Y	Y	N
UTAH						
1 **Bishop**	Y	N	Y	Y	Y	Y
2 **Stewart**	N	N	Y	Y	Y	Y
4 **Love**	Y	N	Y	Y	Y	Y
VERMONT						
AL Welch	Y	Y	Y	Y	Y	Y
VIRGINIA						
1 **Wittman**	Y	N	Y	Y	Y	Y
2 **Taylor**	Y	N	Y	Y	Y	Y
3 Scott	Y	Y	Y	Y	Y	Y
4 McEachin	Y	Y	Y	Y	Y	Y
5 **Garrett**	N	N	Y	Y	Y	Y
6 **Goodlatte**	N	N	?	Y	Y	Y
7 **Brat**	N	N	Y	Y	Y	Y
8 Beyer	Y	Y	Y	Y	Y	Y
9 **Griffith**	N	N	Y	Y	Y	Y
10 **Comstock**	Y	N	Y	Y	Y	Y
11 Connolly	Y	Y	Y	Y	Y	N
WASHINGTON						
1 DelBene	Y	Y	Y	Y	Y	Y
2 Larsen	Y	Y	Y	Y	Y	Y
3 **Herrera Beutler**	Y	N	Y	Y	Y	N
4 **Newhouse**	Y	N	Y	Y	Y	Y
5 **McMorris Rodgers**	Y	N	Y	Y	Y	Y
6 Kilmer	Y	Y	Y	Y	Y	N
7 Jayapal	Y	Y	Y	Y	Y	Y
8 **Reichert**	Y	N	Y	Y	Y	N
9 Smith	Y	Y	Y	Y	Y	Y
10 Heck	Y	Y	Y	Y	Y	Y
WEST VIRGINIA						
1 **McKinley**	Y	N	Y	Y	Y	N
2 **Mooney**	N	N	Y	Y	Y	Y
3 **Jenkins**	Y	N	Y	Y	Y	N
WISCONSIN						
1 **Ryan**						
2 Pocan	Y	Y	Y	Y	Y	Y
3 Kind	Y	Y	Y	Y	Y	N
4 Moore	Y	Y	Y	Y	Y	Y
5 **Sensenbrenner**	N	N	Y	Y	Y	Y
6 **Grothman**	Y	N	Y	Y	Y	N
7 **Duffy**	N	N	Y	+	+	–
8 **Gallagher**	N	N	Y	Y	Y	N
WYOMING						
AL **Cheney**	Y	N	Y	Y	Y	N

VOTE NUMBER

572. HR 469, HR 732, H RES 577. THIRD PARTY SETTLEMENTS AND CONSENT DECREES NOTICE/PREVIOUS QUESTION. Collins, R-Ga., motion to order the previous question (thus ending debate and the possibility of amendment) on the rule (H Res 577) that would provide for House floor consideration of the bill (HR 732) that would prohibit settlement agreements involving the U.S. government from requiring the non-governmental party to make a payment or loan to any party other than the U.S. government. It would also provide for consideration of the bill (HR 469) that would require the federal government to provide advance public notice when it plans to enter into discussions regarding consent decrees and would codify and expand certain disclosure practices with regard to the Treasury Department's Judgment Fund payments. Motion agreed to 228-189 : R 228-0; D 0-189. Oct. 24, 2017.

573. HR 469, HR 732, H RES 577. THIRD PARTY SETTLEMENTS AND CONSENT DECREES NOTICE/RULE. Adoption of the rule that would provide for House floor consideration of the bill (HR 732) that would prohibit settlement agreements involving the U.S. government from requiring the non-governmental party to make a payment or loan to any party other than the U.S. government. It would also provide for consideration of the bill (HR 469) that would require the federal government to provide advance public notice when it plans to enter into discussions regarding consent decrees and would codify and expand certain disclosure practices with regard to the Treasury Department's Judgment Fund payments. Adopted 227-190 : R 227-0; D 0-190. Oct. 24, 2017.

574. HR 2142. CHEMICAL SCREENING DEVICES/PASSAGE. Fitzpatrick, R-Pa., motion to suspend the rules and pass the bill that would authorize $9 million for U.S. Customs and Border Protection to purchase additional chemical screening devices that could determine the presence of synthetic opioids or other narcotics. The authorized funding could also be used to hire personnel and scientists to operate the screening devices and interpret the data collected by the devices. Motion agreed to 412-3 : R 226-2; D 186-1. Oct. 24, 2017.

575. HR 732. THIRD PARTY SETTLEMENTS/DISCRIMINATION. Cohen, D-Tenn., amendment that would exempt, from the bill's provisions, settlement agreements related to discrimination based on race, religion, national origin or any other protected category. Rejected in Committee of the Whole 187-233 : R 0-230; D 187-3. Oct. 24, 2017.

576. HR 732. THIRD PARTY SETTLEMENTS/VEHICLE EMISSIONS CONTROL SYSTEM. Johnson, D-Ga., amendment that would exempt, from the bill's provisions, settlement agreements related to indirect harm caused by unlawful conduct, including the intentional bypassing, defeating or rendering inoperative a required element of a vehicle's emissions control system. Rejected in Committee of the Whole 183-235 : R 0-229; D 183-6. Oct. 24, 2017.

577. HR 732. THIRD PARTY SETTLEMENTS/STATE RESTITUTION. Jackson Lee, D-Texas, amendment that would exempt, from the bill's provisions, settlement agreements related to providing restitution for a state. Rejected in Committee of the Whole 185-234 : R 0-229; D 185-5. Oct. 24, 2017.

578. HR 732. THIRD PARTY SETTLEMENTS/RESIDENTIAL MORTGAGE-BACKED SECURITIES. Cicilline, D-R.I., amendment that would exempt, from the bill's provisions, settlement agreements related to predatory or fraudulent conduct involving residential mortgage-backed securities. Rejected in Committee of the Whole 189-231 : R 3-227; D 186-4. Oct. 24, 2017.

	572	573	574	575	576	577	578
ALABAMA							
1 Byrne	Y	Y	Y	N	N	N	N
2 Roby	Y	Y	Y	N	N	N	N
3 Rogers	Y	Y	Y	N	N	N	N
4 Aderholt	Y	Y	Y	N	N	N	N
5 Brooks	Y	?	Y	N	N	N	N
6 Palmer	Y	Y	Y	N	N	N	N
7 Sewell	N	N	Y	Y	Y	Y	Y
ALASKA							
AL Young	Y	Y	Y	N	N	N	N
ARIZONA							
1 O'Halleran	N	N	Y	Y	Y	Y	Y
2 McSally	Y	Y	Y	N	N	N	N
3 Grijalva	N	N	Y	Y	Y	Y	Y
4 Gosar	Y	Y	Y	N	N	N	N
5 Biggs	Y	Y	Y	N	N	N	N
6 Schweikert	Y	Y	Y	N	N	N	N
7 Gallego	N	N	Y	Y	Y	Y	Y
8 Franks	Y	Y	Y	N	N	N	N
9 Sinema	N	N	Y	N	N	N	N
ARKANSAS							
1 Crawford	Y	Y	Y	N	N	N	N
2 Hill	Y	Y	Y	N	N	N	N
3 Womack	Y	Y	Y	N	N	N	N
4 Westerman	Y	Y	Y	N	N	N	N
CALIFORNIA							
1 LaMalfa	Y	Y	Y	N	N	N	N
2 Huffman	N	N	Y	Y	Y	Y	Y
3 Garamendi	N	N	Y	Y	Y	Y	Y
4 McClintock	Y	Y	Y	N	N	N	N
5 Thompson	N	N	Y	Y	Y	Y	Y
6 Matsui	N	N	Y	Y	Y	Y	Y
7 Bera	N	N	Y	Y	Y	Y	Y
8 Cook	Y	Y	Y	N	N	N	N
9 McNerney	N	N	Y	Y	Y	Y	Y
10 Denham	Y	Y	Y	N	N	N	N
11 DeSaulnier	N	N	Y	Y	Y	Y	Y
12 Pelosi	N	N	Y	Y	Y	Y	Y
13 Lee	N	N	Y	Y	Y	Y	Y
14 Speier	N	N	Y	Y	Y	Y	Y
15 Swalwell	N	N	Y	Y	Y	Y	Y
16 Costa	N	N	Y	Y	Y	Y	Y
17 Khanna	N	N	Y	Y	Y	Y	Y
18 Eshoo	N	N	Y	Y	Y	Y	Y
19 Lofgren	N	N	Y	Y	Y	Y	Y
20 Panetta	N	N	Y	Y	Y	Y	Y
21 Valadao	Y	Y	Y	N	N	N	N
22 Nunes	Y	Y	Y	N	N	N	N
23 McCarthy	Y	Y	Y	N	N	N	N
24 Carbajal	N	N	Y	Y	Y	Y	Y
25 Knight	Y	Y	Y	N	N	N	N
26 Brownley	N	N	Y	Y	Y	Y	Y
27 Chu	N	N	Y	Y	Y	Y	Y
28 Schiff	N	N	Y	Y	Y	Y	Y
29 Cardenas	N	N	Y	Y	Y	Y	Y
30 Sherman	N	N	N	Y	Y	Y	Y
31 Aguilar	N	N	Y	Y	Y	Y	Y
32 Napolitano	N	N	Y	Y	Y	Y	Y
33 Lieu	N	N	Y	Y	Y	Y	Y
34 Gomez	N	N	Y	Y	Y	Y	Y
35 Torres	N	N	Y	Y	Y	Y	Y
36 Ruiz	N	N	Y	Y	Y	Y	Y
37 Bass	?	?	?	?	?	?	?
38 Sánchez, Linda	N	N	Y	Y	Y	Y	Y
39 Royce	Y	Y	Y	N	N	N	N
40 Roybal-Allard	N	N	Y	Y	Y	Y	Y
41 Takano	N	N	Y	Y	Y	Y	Y
42 Calvert	Y	Y	Y	N	N	N	N
43 Waters	N	N	Y	Y	Y	Y	Y
44 Barragan	?	?	?	?	?	?	?
45 Walters	Y	Y	Y	N	N	N	N
46 Correa	N	N	Y	Y	Y	Y	Y
47 Lowenthal	?	?	?	?	?	?	?
48 Rohrabacher	Y	Y	Y	N	N	N	N
49 Issa	Y	Y	Y	N	N	N	N
50 Hunter	Y	Y	?	N	N	N	N
51 Vargas	N	N	Y	Y	Y	Y	Y
52 Peters	N	N	Y	N	N	N	N
53 Davis	N	N	Y	Y	Y	Y	Y

	572	573	574	575	576	577	578
COLORADO							
1 DeGette	N	N	Y	Y	Y	Y	Y
2 Polis	N	N	Y	Y	Y	Y	Y
3 Tipton	Y	Y	Y	N	N	N	N
4 Buck	Y	Y	Y	N	N	N	N
5 Lamborn	Y	Y	Y	N	N	N	N
6 Coffman	Y	Y	Y	N	N	N	N
7 Perlmutter	N	N	Y	Y	Y	Y	Y
CONNECTICUT							
1 Larson	N	N	Y	Y	Y	Y	Y
2 Courtney	N	N	Y	Y	Y	Y	Y
3 DeLauro	N	N	Y	Y	Y	Y	Y
4 Himes	N	N	Y	Y	Y	Y	Y
5 Esty	N	N	Y	Y	Y	Y	Y
DELAWARE							
AL Blunt Rochester	N	N	Y	Y	Y	Y	Y
FLORIDA							
1 Gaetz	Y	Y	Y	N	N	N	N
2 Dunn	Y	Y	Y	N	N	N	N
3 Yoho	Y	Y	Y	N	N	N	N
4 Rutherford	Y	Y	Y	N	N	N	N
5 Lawson	N	N	Y	Y	Y	Y	Y
6 DeSantis	Y	Y	?	N	N	N	N
7 Murphy	N	N	Y	Y	Y	Y	Y
8 Posey	Y	Y	Y	N	N	N	N
9 Soto	N	N	Y	Y	Y	Y	Y
10 Demings	N	N	Y	Y	Y	Y	Y
11 Webster	Y	Y	Y	N	N	N	N
12 Bilirakis	Y	Y	Y	N	N	N	N
13 Crist	N	N	Y	Y	Y	Y	Y
14 Castor	N	N	Y	Y	Y	Y	Y
15 Ross	Y	Y	Y	N	N	N	N
16 Buchanan	?	?	?	N	N	N	N
17 Rooney, T.	Y	Y	Y	N	N	N	N
18 Mast	Y	Y	Y	N	N	N	N
19 Rooney, F.	Y	?	Y	N	N	N	N
20 Hastings	N	N	Y	Y	Y	Y	Y
21 Frankel	N	N	?	Y	N	Y	Y
22 Deutch	N	N	Y	Y	Y	Y	Y
23 Wasserman Schultz	N	N	Y	Y	Y	Y	Y
24 Wilson	?	?	?	?	?	?	?
25 Diaz-Balart	Y	Y	Y	N	N	N	N
26 Curbelo	Y	Y	Y	N	N	N	N
27 Ros-Lehtinen	Y	Y	Y	N	N	N	N
GEORGIA							
1 Carter	Y	Y	Y	N	N	N	N
2 Bishop	N	N	Y	Y	Y	Y	Y
3 Ferguson	Y	Y	Y	N	N	N	N
4 Johnson	N	N	Y	Y	Y	Y	Y
5 Lewis	N	N	Y	Y	Y	Y	Y
6 Handel	Y	Y	Y	N	N	N	N
7 Woodall	Y	Y	Y	N	N	N	N
8 Scott, A.	Y	Y	Y	N	N	?	N
9 Collins	Y	Y	Y	N	N	N	N
10 Hice	Y	Y	Y	N	N	N	N
11 Loudermilk	Y	?	Y	N	N	N	N
12 Allen	Y	Y	Y	N	N	N	N
13 Scott, D.	N	N	Y	Y	Y	Y	Y
14 Graves	Y	Y	Y	N	N	N	N
HAWAII							
1 Hanabusa	N	N	Y	Y	Y	Y	Y
2 Gabbard	N	N	Y	Y	Y	Y	Y
IDAHO							
1 Labrador	Y	Y	Y	N	N	N	N
2 Simpson	Y	Y	Y	N	N	N	N
ILLINOIS							
1 Rush	N	N	Y	Y	Y	Y	Y
2 Kelly	N	N	Y	Y	Y	Y	Y
3 Lipinski	N	N	Y	Y	Y	Y	Y
4 Gutierrez	N	N	Y	Y	Y	Y	Y
5 Quigley	N	N	Y	Y	Y	Y	Y
6 Roskam	?	Y	Y	N	N	N	N
7 Davis, D.	N	N	Y	Y	Y	Y	Y
8 Krishnamoorthi	N	N	Y	Y	Y	Y	Y
9 Schakowsky	N	N	Y	Y	Y	Y	Y
10 Schneider	N	N	Y	Y	Y	Y	Y
11 Foster	N	N	Y	Y	Y	Y	Y
12 Bost	Y	Y	Y	N	N	N	N
13 Davis, R.	Y	Y	Y	N	N	N	N
14 Hultgren	Y	Y	Y	N	N	N	N
15 Shimkus	Y	Y	Y	N	N	N	N

	572	573	574	575	576	577	578
16 **Kinzinger**	Y	Y	Y	N	N	N	N
17 Bustos	N	N	Y	Y	Y	Y	Y
18 **LaHood**	Y	Y	Y	N	N	N	N
INDIANA							
1 Visclosky	N	N	Y	Y	Y	Y	Y
2 **Walorski**	Y	Y	Y	N	N	N	N
3 **Banks**	Y	Y	Y	N	N	N	N
4 **Rokita**	Y	Y	Y	N	N	N	N
5 **Brooks**	Y	Y	Y	N	N	N	N
6 **Messer**	Y	Y	Y	N	N	N	N
7 Carson	?	N	Y	Y	Y	Y	Y
8 **Bucshon**	Y	Y	Y	N	N	N	N
9 **Hollingsworth**	Y	Y	Y	N	N	N	N
IOWA							
1 **Blum**	Y	Y	Y	N	N	N	N
2 Loebsack	N	N	Y	Y	Y	Y	Y
3 **Young**	Y	Y	Y	N	N	N	N
4 **King**	Y	Y	Y	N	N	N	N
KANSAS							
1 **Marshall**	Y	Y	Y	N	N	N	N
2 **Jenkins**	Y	Y	Y	N	N	N	N
3 **Yoder**	Y	Y	Y	N	N	N	N
4 **Estes**	Y	Y	Y	N	N	N	N
KENTUCKY							
1 **Comer**	Y	Y	Y	N	N	N	N
2 **Guthrie**	Y	Y	Y	N	N	N	N
3 Yarmuth	N	N	Y	Y	Y	Y	Y
4 **Massie**	Y	Y	Y	N	N	N	N
5 **Rogers**	Y	Y	Y	N	N	N	N
6 **Barr**	Y	Y	Y	N	N	N	N
LOUISIANA							
1 **Scalise**	Y	Y	Y	–	–	–	–
2 Richmond	N	N	Y	Y	Y	Y	Y
3 **Higgins**	Y	Y	Y	N	N	N	N
4 **Johnson**	Y	Y	Y	N	N	N	N
5 **Abraham**	Y	Y	Y	N	N	N	N
6 **Graves**	Y	Y	Y	N	N	N	N
MAINE							
1 Pingree	N	N	Y	Y	Y	Y	Y
2 **Poliquin**	Y	Y	Y	N	N	N	N
MARYLAND							
1 **Harris**	Y	Y	Y	N	N	N	N
2 Ruppersberger	N	N	Y	Y	Y	Y	Y
3 Sarbanes	N	N	Y	Y	Y	Y	Y
4 Brown	N	N	Y	Y	Y	Y	Y
5 Hoyer	N	N	Y	Y	Y	Y	Y
6 Delaney	N	N	Y	Y	Y	Y	Y
7 Cummings	N	N	Y	Y	Y	Y	Y
8 Raskin	N	N	Y	Y	Y	Y	Y
MASSACHUSETTS							
1 Neal	N	N	Y	Y	Y	Y	Y
2 McGovern	N	N	Y	Y	Y	Y	Y
3 Tsongas	N	N	Y	Y	Y	Y	Y
4 Kennedy	N	N	Y	Y	Y	Y	Y
5 Clark	N	N	Y	Y	Y	Y	Y
6 Moulton	N	N	Y	Y	Y	Y	Y
7 Capuano	N	N	Y	Y	Y	Y	Y
8 Lynch	N	N	Y	Y	Y	Y	Y
9 Keating	N	N	Y	Y	Y	Y	Y
MICHIGAN							
1 **Bergman**	Y	Y	Y	N	N	N	N
2 **Huizenga**	+	+	+	–	–	–	–
3 **Amash**	Y	Y	N	N	N	N	N
4 **Moolenaar**	Y	Y	Y	N	N	N	N
5 Kildee	N	N	Y	Y	Y	Y	Y
6 **Upton**	Y	Y	Y	N	N	N	N
7 **Walberg**	Y	Y	Y	N	N	N	N
8 **Bishop**	Y	Y	Y	N	N	N	N
9 Levin	N	N	Y	Y	Y	Y	Y
10 **Mitchell**	Y	Y	Y	N	N	N	N
11 **Trott**	?	?	?	?	?	?	?
12 Dingell	N	N	Y	Y	Y	Y	Y
13 Conyers	N	N	Y	Y	Y	Y	Y
14 Lawrence	N	N	Y	Y	Y	Y	Y
MINNESOTA							
1 Walz	N	N	Y	Y	Y	Y	Y
2 **Lewis**	Y	Y	Y	N	N	N	N
3 **Paulsen**	Y	Y	Y	N	N	N	N
4 McCollum	N	N	Y	Y	Y	Y	Y

	572	573	574	575	576	577	578
5 Ellison	N	N	Y	Y	Y	Y	Y
6 **Emmer**	Y	Y	Y	N	N	N	N
7 Peterson	N	N	Y	Y	N	N	N
8 Nolan	N	N	Y	Y	Y	Y	Y
MISSISSIPPI							
1 **Kelly**	Y	Y	Y	N	N	N	N
2 Thompson	N	N	Y	Y	Y	Y	Y
3 **Harper**	Y	Y	Y	N	N	N	N
4 **Palazzo**	Y	Y	Y	N	N	N	N
MISSOURI							
1 Clay	N	N	Y	Y	Y	Y	Y
2 **Wagner**	Y	Y	Y	N	N	N	N
3 **Luetkemeyer**	Y	Y	Y	N	N	N	N
4 **Hartzler**	Y	Y	Y	N	N	N	N
5 Cleaver	N	N	Y	Y	Y	Y	Y
6 **Graves**	Y	Y	Y	N	N	N	N
7 **Long**	+	+	+	–	–	–	–
8 **Smith**	Y	Y	Y	N	N	N	N
MONTANA							
AL **Gianforte**	Y	Y	Y	N	N	N	N
NEBRASKA							
1 **Fortenberry**	Y	Y	Y	N	N	N	N
2 **Bacon**	Y	Y	Y	N	N	N	N
3 **Smith**	Y	Y	Y	N	N	N	N
NEVADA							
1 Titus	N	N	Y	Y	Y	Y	Y
2 **Amodei**	Y	Y	Y	N	N	N	N
3 Rosen	N	N	Y	Y	Y	Y	Y
4 Kihuen	N	N	Y	Y	Y	Y	Y
NEW HAMPSHIRE							
1 Shea-Porter	N	N	Y	Y	?	Y	Y
2 Kuster	N	N	Y	Y	Y	Y	Y
NEW JERSEY							
1 Norcross	N	N	Y	Y	Y	Y	Y
2 **LoBiondo**	Y	Y	Y	N	N	N	N
3 **MacArthur**	Y	Y	Y	N	N	N	?
4 **Smith**	Y	Y	Y	N	N	N	N
5 Gottheimer	N	N	Y	Y	N	N	Y
6 Pallone	N	N	Y	Y	Y	Y	Y
7 **Lance**	Y	Y	Y	N	N	N	N
8 Sires	N	N	Y	Y	Y	Y	Y
9 Pascrell	N	N	Y	Y	Y	Y	Y
10 Payne	N	N	Y	Y	Y	Y	Y
11 **Frelinghuysen**	Y	Y	Y	N	N	N	N
12 Watson Coleman	N	N	Y	Y	Y	Y	Y
NEW MEXICO							
1 Lujan Grisham	N	N	Y	Y	Y	Y	Y
2 **Pearce**	Y	Y	Y	N	N	N	N
3 Luján	N	N	Y	Y	Y	Y	Y
NEW YORK							
1 **Zeldin**	Y	Y	Y	N	N	N	N
2 **King**	Y	Y	Y	N	N	N	N
3 Suozzi	N	N	Y	Y	Y	Y	Y
4 Rice	N	N	Y	Y	Y	Y	Y
5 Meeks	N	N	Y	Y	Y	Y	Y
6 Meng	N	N	Y	Y	Y	Y	Y
7 Velázquez	N	N	Y	Y	Y	Y	Y
8 Jeffries	N	N	Y	Y	Y	Y	Y
9 Clarke	N	N	Y	Y	Y	Y	Y
10 Nadler	N	N	Y	Y	Y	Y	Y
11 **Donovan**	Y	Y	Y	N	N	N	N
12 Maloney, C.	N	N	Y	Y	Y	Y	Y
13 Espaillat	N	N	Y	Y	Y	Y	Y
14 Crowley	N	N	Y	Y	Y	Y	Y
15 Serrano	N	N	Y	Y	Y	Y	Y
16 Engel	N	N	Y	Y	Y	Y	Y
17 Lowey	N	N	Y	Y	Y	Y	Y
18 Maloney, S.P.	N	N	Y	Y	Y	Y	Y
19 **Faso**	Y	Y	Y	N	N	N	N
20 Tonko	N	N	Y	Y	Y	Y	Y
21 **Stefanik**	Y	Y	Y	N	N	N	N
22 **Tenney**	Y	Y	Y	N	N	N	N
23 **Reed**	+	Y	Y	N	N	N	N
24 **Katko**	Y	Y	Y	N	N	N	N
25 Slaughter	N	N	Y	Y	Y	Y	Y
26 Higgins	N	N	Y	Y	Y	Y	Y
27 **Collins**	Y	Y	Y	N	N	N	N
NORTH CAROLINA							
1 Butterfield	N	N	Y	Y	Y	Y	Y
2 **Holding**	Y	Y	Y	N	N	N	N
3 **Jones**	Y	Y	N	N	N	N	Y
4 Price	N	N	Y	Y	Y	Y	Y

	572	573	574	575	576	577	578
5 **Foxx**	Y	Y	Y	N	N	N	N
6 **Walker**	Y	Y	Y	N	N	N	N
7 **Rouzer**	Y	Y	Y	N	N	N	N
8 **Hudson**	Y	Y	Y	N	N	N	N
9 **Pittenger**	Y	Y	Y	N	N	N	N
10 **McHenry**	Y	Y	Y	N	N	N	N
11 **Meadows**	Y	Y	Y	N	N	N	N
12 Adams	N	N	Y	Y	Y	Y	Y
13 **Budd**	Y	Y	Y	N	N	N	N
NORTH DAKOTA							
AL **Cramer**	Y	Y	Y	N	N	N	N
OHIO							
1 **Chabot**	Y	Y	Y	N	N	N	N
2 **Wenstrup**	Y	Y	Y	N	N	N	N
3 Beatty	N	N	Y	Y	Y	Y	Y
4 **Jordan**	Y	Y	Y	N	N	N	N
5 **Latta**	Y	Y	Y	N	N	N	N
6 **Johnson**	Y	Y	Y	N	N	N	N
7 **Gibbs**	Y	Y	Y	N	N	N	N
8 **Davidson**	Y	Y	Y	N	N	N	N
9 Kaptur	N	N	Y	Y	Y	Y	Y
10 **Turner**	Y	Y	Y	N	N	N	N
11 Fudge	N	N	Y	Y	Y	Y	Y
12 **Tiberi**	Y	Y	Y	N	N	N	N
13 Ryan	N	N	Y	Y	Y	Y	Y
14 **Joyce**	Y	Y	Y	?	?	?	N
15 **Stivers**	Y	Y	Y	N	N	N	N
16 **Renacci**	Y	Y	Y	N	N	N	N
OKLAHOMA							
1 **Bridenstine**	?	?	?	?	?	?	?
2 **Mullin**	Y	Y	Y	N	N	N	N
3 **Lucas**	Y	Y	Y	N	N	N	N
4 **Cole**	Y	Y	Y	N	N	N	N
5 **Russell**	Y	Y	Y	N	N	N	N
OREGON							
1 Bonamici	N	N	Y	Y	Y	Y	Y
2 **Walden**	Y	Y	Y	N	N	N	N
3 Blumenauer	N	N	Y	Y	Y	Y	Y
4 DeFazio	N	N	Y	Y	Y	Y	Y
5 Schrader	N	N	Y	Y	Y	Y	Y
PENNSYLVANIA							
1 Brady	N	N	Y	Y	Y	Y	Y
2 Evans	N	N	Y	Y	Y	Y	Y
3 **Kelly**	Y	Y	Y	N	N	N	N
4 **Perry**	Y	Y	Y	N	N	N	N
5 **Thompson**	Y	Y	Y	N	N	N	N
6 **Costello**	Y	Y	Y	N	N	N	N
7 **Meehan**	Y	Y	Y	N	N	N	N
8 **Fitzpatrick**	Y	Y	Y	N	N	N	N
9 **Shuster**	Y	Y	Y	N	N	N	N
10 **Marino**	Y	Y	Y	N	N	N	N
11 **Barletta**	?	?	?	?	?	?	?
12 **Rothfus**	Y	Y	Y	N	N	N	N
13 Boyle	N	N	Y	Y	Y	Y	Y
14 Doyle	N	N	Y	Y	Y	Y	Y
15 **Dent**	Y	Y	Y	N	N	N	N
16 **Smucker**	Y	Y	Y	N	N	N	N
17 Cartwright	N	N	Y	Y	Y	Y	Y
RHODE ISLAND							
1 Cicilline	N	N	Y	Y	Y	Y	Y
2 Langevin	N	N	Y	Y	Y	Y	Y
SOUTH CAROLINA							
1 **Sanford**	Y	Y	Y	N	N	N	N
2 **Wilson**	Y	Y	Y	N	N	N	N
3 **Duncan**	Y	Y	Y	N	N	N	N
4 **Gowdy**	Y	Y	Y	N	N	N	N
5 **Norman**	Y	Y	Y	N	N	N	N
6 Clyburn	N	N	Y	Y	Y	Y	Y
7 **Rice**	Y	Y	Y	N	N	N	N
SOUTH DAKOTA							
AL **Noem**	Y	Y	Y	N	N	N	N
TENNESSEE							
1 **Roe**	Y	Y	Y	N	N	N	N
2 **Duncan**	Y	Y	Y	N	N	N	N
3 **Fleischmann**	Y	Y	Y	N	N	N	N
4 **DesJarlais**	Y	Y	Y	N	N	N	N
5 Cooper	N	N	Y	N	N	N	N
6 **Black**	Y	Y	Y	N	N	N	N
7 **Blackburn**	Y	Y	Y	N	N	N	N
8 **Kustoff**	Y	Y	Y	N	N	N	N
9 Cohen	N	N	Y	Y	Y	Y	Y

	572	573	574	575	576	577	578
TEXAS							
1 **Gohmert**	Y	Y	Y	N	N	N	N
2 **Poe**	Y	Y	Y	N	N	N	N
3 **Johnson, S.**	Y	Y	Y	N	N	N	N
4 **Ratcliffe**	Y	Y	Y	N	N	N	N
5 **Hensarling**	Y	Y	Y	N	N	N	N
6 **Barton**	Y	Y	Y	N	N	N	N
7 **Culberson**	Y	Y	Y	N	N	N	N
8 **Brady**	Y	Y	Y	N	N	N	N
9 Green, A.	N	N	Y	Y	Y	Y	Y
10 **McCaul**	Y	Y	Y	N	N	N	N
11 **Conaway**	Y	Y	Y	N	N	N	N
12 **Granger**	Y	Y	Y	N	N	N	N
13 **Thornberry**	Y	Y	Y	N	N	N	N
14 **Weber**	Y	Y	Y	N	N	N	N
15 Gonzalez	N	N	Y	Y	Y	Y	Y
16 O'Rourke	N	N	Y	Y	Y	Y	Y
17 **Flores**	Y	Y	Y	N	N	N	N
18 Jackson Lee	N	N	Y	Y	Y	Y	Y
19 **Arrington**	Y	Y	Y	N	N	N	N
20 Castro	N	N	Y	Y	Y	Y	Y
21 **Smith**	Y	Y	Y	N	N	N	N
22 **Olson**	Y	Y	Y	N	N	N	N
23 **Hurd**	Y	Y	Y	N	N	N	N
24 **Marchant**	?	Y	Y	N	N	N	N
25 **Williams**	Y	Y	Y	N	N	N	N
26 **Burgess**	?	?	?	?	?	?	?
27 **Farenthold**	Y	Y	Y	N	N	N	N
28 Cuellar	N	N	Y	Y	Y	Y	Y
29 Green, G.	N	N	Y	Y	Y	Y	Y
30 Johnson, E.B.	N	N	Y	Y	Y	Y	Y
31 **Carter**	Y	Y	Y	N	N	N	N
32 **Sessions**	Y	Y	Y	N	N	N	N
33 Veasey	N	N	Y	Y	Y	Y	Y
34 Vela	N	N	Y	Y	Y	Y	Y
35 Doggett	N	N	?	Y	Y	Y	Y
36 **Babin**	Y	Y	Y	N	N	N	N
UTAH							
1 **Bishop**	Y	Y	Y	N	N	N	N
2 **Stewart**	Y	Y	Y	N	N	N	N
4 **Love**	Y	Y	Y	N	N	N	N
VERMONT							
AL Welch	N	N	Y	Y	Y	Y	Y
VIRGINIA							
1 **Wittman**	Y	Y	Y	N	N	N	N
2 **Taylor**	Y	Y	Y	N	N	N	N
3 Scott	N	N	Y	Y	Y	Y	Y
4 McEachin	N	N	Y	Y	Y	Y	Y
5 **Garrett**	Y	Y	Y	N	N	N	N
6 **Goodlatte**	Y	Y	Y	N	N	N	N
7 **Brat**	Y	Y	Y	N	N	N	N
8 Beyer	N	N	?	Y	Y	Y	Y
9 **Griffith**	Y	?	Y	N	P	N	Y
10 **Comstock**	Y	Y	?	N	N	N	N
11 Connolly	N	N	Y	Y	Y	Y	Y
WASHINGTON							
1 DelBene	N	N	Y	Y	Y	Y	Y
2 Larsen	N	N	Y	Y	Y	Y	Y
3 **Herrera Beutler**	Y	Y	Y	N	N	N	N
4 **Newhouse**	Y	Y	Y	N	N	N	N
5 **McMorris Rodgers**	Y	Y	Y	N	N	N	N
6 Kilmer	N	N	Y	Y	Y	Y	Y
7 Jayapal	N	N	Y	Y	Y	Y	Y
8 **Reichert**	Y	Y	Y	N	N	N	N
9 Smith	N	N	Y	Y	Y	Y	Y
10 Heck	N	N	Y	Y	Y	Y	Y
WEST VIRGINIA							
1 **McKinley**	Y	Y	Y	N	N	N	N
2 **Mooney**	Y	Y	Y	N	N	N	N
3 **Jenkins**	Y	Y	Y	N	N	N	N
WISCONSIN							
1 **Ryan**							
2 Pocan	N	N	Y	Y	Y	Y	Y
3 Kind	N	N	Y	Y	Y	Y	Y
4 Moore	N	N	Y	Y	Y	Y	Y
5 **Sensenbrenner**	Y	Y	Y	N	N	N	N
6 **Grothman**	Y	Y	Y	N	N	N	N
7 **Duffy**	Y	Y	Y	N	N	N	N
8 **Gallagher**	Y	Y	Y	N	N	N	N
WYOMING							
AL **Cheney**	Y	Y	Y	N	N	N	N

VOTE NUMBER

579. HR 732. THIRD PARTY SETTLEMENTS/LEAD IN DRINKING WATER. Conyers, D-Mich., amendment that would exempt, from the bill's provisions, settlements related to indirect harm from unlawful conduct that results in an increase in the amount of lead in public drinking water. Rejected in Committee of the Whole 191-229 : R 4-226; D 187-3. Oct. 24, 2017.

580. HR 732. THIRD PARTY SETTLEMENTS/PASSAGE. Passage of the bill that would prohibit settlement agreements involving the U.S. government from requiring the non-governmental party to make a payment or loan to any party other than the U.S. government. Prohibitions would not apply if the payment or loan under the settlement is for restitution to affected parties or is a direct remedy for actual harm. Passed 238-183 : R 231-0; D 7-183. Oct. 24, 2017.

581. HR 3898. EXPANDED NORTH KOREAN SANCTIONS/PASSAGE. Barr, R-Ky., motion to suspend the rules and pass the bill that would expand existing sanctions related to North Korea by imposing financial sanctions on individuals and entities that provide or facilitate financial transactions with or on behalf of North Korea, or that facilitate the import or export of bulk cash, goods and services to North Korea. It would require various penalties for violations of the expanded sanctions, including financial fines and prison sentences of up to 20 years. Motion agreed to 415-2 : R 228-2; D 187-0. Oct. 24, 2017.

582. H RES 580, H CON RES 71. FISCAL 2018 BUDGET RESOLUTION/ PREVIOUS QUESTION. Woodall, R-Ga., motion to order the previous question (thus ending debate and the possibility of amendment) on the rule (H Res 580) that would provide for House floor consideration of the Senate amendment to the fiscal 2018 budget resolution (H Con Res 71). Motion agreed to 229-188 : R 229-1; D 0-187. Oct. 25, 2017.

583. H RES 580, H CON RES 71. FISCAL 2018 HOUSE BUDGET RESOLUTION/ RULE. Adoption of the rule (H Res 580) that would provide for House floor consideration of the fiscal 2018 budget resolution (H Con Res 71) that would provide for $3.1 trillion in new budget authority in fiscal 2018, not including off-budget accounts. Adopted 233-188 : R 233-1; D 0-187. Oct. 25, 2017.

584. PROCEDURAL MOTION/APPROVAL OF HOUSE JOURNAL. Approved 230-180 : R 146-82; D 84-98. Oct. 25, 2017.

585. HR 469. CONSENT DECREES NOTICE/HIGH-SPEED BROADBAND. Johnson, D-Ga., amendment that would exempt, from the bill's provisions that would require advance public notice for certain settlement agreements, settlement agreements pertaining to deadlines set by Congress related to improving access to affordable high-speed broadband in under-served markets. Rejected in Committee of the Whole 185-231 : R 0-230; D 185-1. Oct. 25, 2017.

	579	580	581	582	583	584	585
ALABAMA							
1 Byrne	N	Y	Y	Y	Y	Y	N
2 Roby	N	Y	Y	Y	Y	Y	N
3 Rogers	N	Y	Y	Y	Y	N	N
4 Aderholt	N	Y	Y	Y	Y	Y	N
5 Brooks	N	Y	Y	Y	Y	Y	N
6 Palmer	N	Y	Y	Y	Y	Y	N
7 Sewell	Y	N	Y	N	N	N	Y
ALASKA							
AL Young	N	Y	Y	Y	Y	N	N
ARIZONA							
1 O'Halleran	Y	N	Y	N	N	N	Y
2 McSally	N	Y	Y	Y	Y	N	N
3 Grijalva	Y	N	Y	N	N	?	Y
4 Gosar	N	Y	Y	Y	Y	N	N
5 Biggs	N	Y	Y	Y	Y	N	N
6 Schweikert	N	Y	Y	Y	Y	N	N
7 Gallego	Y	N	Y	N	N	Y	Y
8 Franks	N	Y	Y	Y	Y	N	N
9 Sinema	N	Y	Y	N	N	N	Y
ARKANSAS							
1 Crawford	N	Y	Y	Y	Y	Y	N
2 Hill	N	Y	Y	Y	Y	Y	N
3 Womack	N	Y	Y	Y	Y	Y	N
4 Westerman	N	Y	Y	Y	Y	Y	N
CALIFORNIA							
1 LaMalfa	N	Y	Y	Y	Y	Y	N
2 Huffman	Y	N	Y	N	N	Y	+
3 Garamendi	Y	N	Y	N	N	Y	Y
4 McClintock	N	Y	Y	Y	Y	Y	N
5 Thompson	Y	N	Y	–	–	–	+
6 Matsui	Y	N	Y	N	N	N	Y
7 Bera	Y	N	Y	N	N	N	Y
8 Cook	N	Y	Y	Y	Y	Y	N
9 McNerney	Y	N	Y	N	N	Y	Y
10 Denham	N	Y	Y	Y	Y	N	?
11 DeSaulnier	Y	N	Y	N	N	Y	Y
12 Pelosi	Y	N	Y	N	N	N	Y
13 Lee	Y	N	Y	N	N	N	Y
14 Speier	Y	N	Y	N	N	N	Y
15 Swalwell	Y	N	+	N	N	N	Y
16 Costa	Y	N	Y	N	N	N	Y
17 Khanna	Y	N	Y	N	N	N	Y
18 Eshoo	Y	N	Y	N	N	N	Y
19 Lofgren	Y	N	Y	N	N	N	Y
20 Panetta	Y	N	Y	N	N	N	Y
21 Valadao	N	Y	Y	Y	Y	N	N
22 Nunes	N	Y	Y	Y	Y	N	N
23 McCarthy	N	Y	Y	Y	Y	N	N
24 Carbajal	Y	N	Y	N	N	N	Y
25 Knight	N	Y	Y	Y	Y	N	N
26 Brownley	Y	N	Y	N	N	N	Y
27 Chu	Y	N	Y	N	N	Y	Y
28 Schiff	Y	N	Y	N	N	Y	Y
29 Cardenas	Y	N	Y	N	N	N	Y
30 Sherman	Y	N	Y	N	N	Y	Y
31 Aguilar	Y	N	Y	N	N	N	Y
32 Napolitano	Y	N	Y	N	N	N	Y
33 Lieu	Y	N	Y	N	N	N	Y
34 Gomez	Y	N	Y	N	N	N	Y
35 Torres	Y	N	Y	N	N	N	Y
36 Ruiz	Y	N	Y	N	N	N	Y
37 Bass	?	?	?	N	N	N	Y
38 Sánchez, Linda	Y	N	Y	N	N	N	Y
39 Royce	N	Y	Y	Y	Y	Y	N
40 Roybal-Allard	Y	N	Y	N	N	N	Y
41 Takano	Y	N	Y	N	N	N	Y
42 Calvert	N	Y	Y	Y	Y	Y	N
43 Waters	Y	N	Y	N	N	N	Y
44 Barragan	?	?	?	N	N	N	Y
45 Walters	N	Y	Y	Y	Y	Y	N
46 Correa	Y	Y	Y	N	N	N	Y
47 Lowenthal	?	?	?	?	?	?	?
48 Rohrabacher	N	Y	Y	Y	Y	Y	N
49 Issa	N	Y	Y	Y	Y	Y	N
50 Hunter	N	Y	Y	Y	Y	Y	N
51 Vargas	Y	N	Y	N	N	N	Y
52 Peters	N	Y	Y	N	N	N	Y
53 Davis	Y	N	Y	N	N	Y	Y

	579	580	581	582	583	584	585
COLORADO							
1 DeGette	Y	N	Y	N	N	Y	Y
2 Polis	Y	N	Y	N	N	Y	Y
3 Tipton	N	Y	Y	Y	Y	N	N
4 Buck	N	Y	Y	Y	Y	N	N
5 Lamborn	N	Y	Y	Y	Y	N	N
6 Coffman	N	Y	Y	Y	Y	N	N
7 Perlmutter	Y	N	Y	N	N	Y	Y
CONNECTICUT							
1 Larson	Y	N	Y	–	–	+	Y
2 Courtney	Y	N	Y	N	N	?	Y
3 DeLauro	Y	N	Y	N	N	?	Y
4 Himes	Y	N	Y	N	N	Y	Y
5 Esty	Y	N	Y	N	N	N	Y
DELAWARE							
AL Blunt Rochester	Y	N	Y	N	N	N	Y
FLORIDA							
1 Gaetz	N	Y	?	Y	Y	N	N
2 Dunn	N	Y	Y	Y	Y	Y	N
3 Yoho	N	Y	Y	Y	Y	N	N
4 Rutherford	N	Y	Y	Y	Y	Y	N
5 Lawson	Y	N	Y	N	?	Y	Y
6 DeSantis	N	Y	Y	Y	Y	N	N
7 Murphy	Y	N	Y	N	N	N	Y
8 Posey	N	Y	Y	Y	Y	N	N
9 Soto	Y	N	Y	N	N	N	Y
10 Demings	Y	N	Y	N	N	Y	Y
11 Webster	N	Y	?	?	?	?	?
12 Bilirakis	N	Y	Y	Y	Y	Y	N
13 Crist	Y	N	Y	N	N	N	Y
14 Castor	Y	N	Y	N	N	N	Y
15 Ross	N	Y	Y	Y	Y	Y	N
16 Buchanan	N	Y	Y	Y	Y	Y	N
17 Rooney, T.	N	Y	Y	Y	Y	Y	?
18 Mast	N	Y	Y	Y	Y	N	N
19 Rooney, F.	N	Y	?	Y	Y	?	N
20 Hastings	Y	N	Y	N	N	N	Y
21 Frankel	Y	N	Y	N	N	N	Y
22 Deutch	Y	N	Y	N	N	N	Y
23 Wasserman Schultz	Y	N	Y	N	N	N	Y
24 Wilson	?	?	?	?	?	?	?
25 Diaz-Balart	N	Y	Y	Y	Y	N	N
26 Curbelo	N	Y	Y	Y	Y	N	N
27 Ros-Lehtinen	N	Y	Y	Y	Y	?	N
GEORGIA							
1 Carter	N	Y	Y	Y	Y	N	N
2 Bishop	Y	N	Y	N	N	?	Y
3 Ferguson	N	Y	Y	Y	Y	Y	N
4 Johnson	Y	N	Y	N	N	N	Y
5 Lewis	Y	N	Y	N	N	N	Y
6 Handel	N	Y	Y	Y	Y	Y	N
7 Woodall	N	Y	Y	Y	Y	Y	N
8 Scott, A.	N	Y	Y	Y	Y	N	N
9 Collins	N	Y	Y	Y	Y	Y	N
10 Hice	N	Y	Y	Y	Y	Y	N
11 Loudermilk	N	Y	Y	Y	Y	Y	N
12 Allen	N	Y	Y	Y	Y	Y	N
13 Scott, D.	Y	N	Y	N	N	Y	Y
14 Graves	N	Y	Y	Y	Y	Y	N
HAWAII							
1 Hanabusa	Y	N	Y	N	N	Y	Y
2 Gabbard	Y	N	Y	N	N	Y	Y
IDAHO							
1 Labrador	N	Y	Y	Y	Y	N	N
2 Simpson	N	Y	Y	Y	Y	Y	N
ILLINOIS							
1 Rush	Y	N	Y	N	N	N	Y
2 Kelly	Y	N	Y	N	N	N	Y
3 Lipinski	Y	N	Y	N	N	N	Y
4 Gutierrez	Y	N	Y	?	N	N	Y
5 Quigley	Y	N	Y	N	N	?	Y
6 Roskam	N	Y	Y	Y	Y	Y	N
7 Davis, D.	Y	N	Y	N	N	N	Y
8 Krishnamoorthi	Y	N	Y	N	N	Y	Y
9 Schakowsky	Y	N	Y	N	N	N	Y
10 Schneider	Y	N	Y	N	N	N	Y
11 Foster	Y	N	Y	N	N	N	Y
12 Bost	N	Y	Y	Y	Y	Y	N
13 Davis, R.	N	Y	Y	Y	Y	N	N
14 Hultgren	N	Y	Y	Y	Y	Y	N
15 Shimkus	N	Y	Y	Y	Y	Y	N

KEY	Republicans	Democrats	Independents
Y Voted for (yea)	**X** Paired against		**C** Voted "present" to avoid possible conflict of interest
# Paired for	**–** Announced against		
+ Announced for	**P** Voted "present"		**?** Did not vote or otherwise make a position known
N Voted against (nay)			

	579	580	581	582	583	584	585
16 **Kinzinger**	N	Y	Y	Y	Y	N	N
17 Bustos	Y	N	Y	N	N	N	Y
18 **LaHood**	N	Y	Y	Y	Y	N	N
INDIANA							
1 Visclosky	Y	N	Y	N	N	N	Y
2 **Walorski**	N	Y	Y	Y	Y	Y	N
3 **Banks**	N	Y	Y	Y	Y	Y	N
4 **Rokita**	N	Y	Y	Y	Y	Y	N
5 **Brooks**	N	Y	Y	Y	Y	Y	N
6 **Messer**	N	Y	Y	Y	Y	Y	N
7 Carson	Y	N	Y	N	N	Y	Y
8 **Bucshon**	N	Y	Y	Y	Y	N	N
9 **Hollingsworth**	N	Y	Y	Y	Y	Y	N
IOWA							
1 **Blum**	N	Y	Y	Y	Y	N	N
2 Loebsack	Y	N	Y	N	N	N	Y
3 **Young**	N	Y	Y	Y	Y	Y	N
4 **King**	N	Y	Y	Y	Y	Y	N
KANSAS							
1 **Marshall**	N	Y	Y	Y	Y	Y	N
2 **Jenkins**	N	Y	Y	Y	Y	N	N
3 **Yoder**	N	Y	Y	Y	Y	N	N
4 **Estes**	N	Y	Y	Y	Y	Y	N
KENTUCKY							
1 **Comer**	N	Y	Y	Y	Y	N	N
2 **Guthrie**	N	Y	Y	Y	Y	Y	N
3 Yarmuth	Y	N	Y	N	N	Y	Y
4 **Massie**	N	Y	N	Y	Y	Y	N
5 **Rogers**	N	Y	Y	Y	Y	Y	N
6 **Barr**	N	Y	Y	Y	Y	Y	N
LOUISIANA							
1 **Scalise**	–	+	+	Y	Y	Y	N
2 Richmond	Y	N	Y	?	?	?	?
3 **Higgins**	N	Y	Y	Y	Y	Y	N
4 **Johnson**	N	Y	Y	Y	Y	Y	N
5 **Abraham**	N	Y	Y	Y	Y	Y	N
6 **Graves**	N	Y	Y	Y	Y	N	N
MAINE							
1 Pingree	Y	N	Y	N	N	Y	Y
2 **Poliquin**	N	Y	Y	Y	Y	N	N
MARYLAND							
1 **Harris**	N	Y	Y	Y	Y	Y	N
2 Ruppersberger	Y	N	Y	N	N	?	Y
3 Sarbanes	Y	N	Y	N	N	N	Y
4 Brown	Y	N	Y	N	N	Y	Y
5 Hoyer	Y	N	Y	N	N	N	Y
6 Delaney	Y	N	Y	N	N	N	Y
7 Cummings	Y	N	Y	N	N	N	Y
8 Raskin	Y	N	Y	N	N	N	Y
MASSACHUSETTS							
1 Neal	Y	N	Y	N	N	N	Y
2 McGovern	Y	N	Y	N	N	N	Y
3 Tsongas	Y	N	Y	N	N	Y	Y
4 Kennedy	Y	N	Y	N	N	Y	Y
5 Clark	Y	N	Y	N	N	N	Y
6 Moulton	Y	N	Y	N	N	Y	Y
7 Capuano	Y	N	Y	N	N	N	Y
8 Lynch	Y	N	Y	N	N	N	+
9 Keating	Y	N	Y	N	N	Y	Y
MICHIGAN							
1 **Bergman**	N	Y	Y	Y	Y	N	N
2 **Huizenga**	–	+	+	Y	Y	Y	N
3 **Amash**	N	Y	N	Y	Y	N	N
4 **Moolenaar**	N	Y	Y	Y	Y	Y	N
5 Kildee	Y	N	Y	N	N	Y	Y
6 **Upton**	N	Y	Y	Y	Y	N	N
7 **Walberg**	N	Y	Y	Y	Y	N	N
8 **Bishop**	N	Y	Y	Y	Y	N	N
9 Levin	Y	N	Y	N	N	N	Y
10 **Mitchell**	N	Y	Y	Y	Y	N	N
11 **Trott**	?	?	?	Y	Y	Y	N
12 Dingell	Y	N	Y	N	N	Y	Y
13 Conyers	Y	N	?	N	N	Y	Y
14 Lawrence	Y	N	Y	N	N	N	Y
MINNESOTA							
1 Walz	Y	N	Y	N	N	Y	Y
2 **Lewis**	N	Y	Y	Y	Y	Y	N
3 **Paulsen**	N	Y	Y	Y	Y	N	N
4 McCollum	Y	N	Y	N	N	Y	Y

	579	580	581	582	583	584	585
5 Ellison	Y	N	Y	N	N	N	Y
6 **Emmer**	N	Y	Y	Y	Y	Y	N
7 Peterson	Y	Y	Y	N	N	N	Y
8 Nolan	Y	N	Y	N	N	N	Y
MISSISSIPPI							
1 **Kelly**	N	Y	Y	Y	Y	Y	N
2 Thompson	Y	N	Y	N	N	N	Y
3 **Harper**	N	Y	Y	Y	Y	Y	N
4 **Palazzo**	N	Y	Y	Y	Y	Y	N
MISSOURI							
1 Clay	Y	N	Y	N	N	Y	Y
2 **Wagner**	N	Y	Y	Y	Y	Y	N
3 **Luetkemeyer**	N	Y	Y	Y	Y	Y	N
4 **Hartzler**	N	Y	Y	Y	Y	N	N
5 Cleaver	Y	N	Y	N	N	Y	Y
6 **Graves**	N	Y	Y	Y	Y	N	N
7 **Long**	–	+	+	+	+	+	N
8 **Smith**	N	Y	Y	Y	Y	Y	N
MONTANA							
AL **Gianforte**	N	Y	Y	Y	Y	Y	N
NEBRASKA							
1 **Fortenberry**	N	Y	Y	Y	Y	Y	?
2 **Bacon**	N	Y	Y	Y	Y	Y	N
3 **Smith**	N	Y	Y	?	?	?	?
NEVADA							
1 Titus	Y	N	Y	N	N	Y	Y
2 **Amodei**	N	Y	Y	?	Y	Y	N
3 Rosen	Y	N	Y	N	N	N	Y
4 Kihuen	Y	N	Y	N	N	N	Y
NEW HAMPSHIRE							
1 Shea-Porter	Y	N	Y	N	N	Y	Y
2 Kuster	Y	N	Y	N	N	Y	Y
NEW JERSEY							
1 Norcross	Y	N	Y	N	N	N	Y
2 **LoBiondo**	Y	Y	Y	Y	Y	N	N
3 **MacArthur**	N	Y	Y	Y	Y	N	N
4 **Smith**	Y	Y	Y	Y	Y	Y	N
5 Gottheimer	Y	Y	?	N	N	N	Y
6 Pallone	Y	N	Y	N	N	N	Y
7 **Lance**	N	Y	Y	Y	Y	N	N
8 Sires	Y	N	Y	N	N	N	Y
9 Pascrell	Y	N	Y	N	N	Y	Y
10 Payne	Y	N	Y	N	N	N	Y
11 **Frelinghuysen**	Y	Y	Y	Y	Y	?	N
12 Watson Coleman	Y	N	Y	N	N	N	Y
NEW MEXICO							
1 Lujan Grisham	Y	N	Y	N	N	Y	Y
2 **Pearce**	N	Y	Y	Y	Y	Y	N
3 Luján	Y	N	Y	N	N	N	Y
NEW YORK							
1 **Zeldin**	N	Y	Y	Y	Y	Y	N
2 **King**	N	Y	Y	Y	Y	Y	N
3 Suozzi	Y	N	Y	N	N	N	Y
4 Rice	Y	N	Y	N	N	N	Y
5 Meeks	Y	N	Y	N	N	Y	Y
6 Meng	Y	N	Y	N	N	?	Y
7 Velázquez	Y	N	Y	N	N	N	Y
8 Jeffries	Y	N	Y	N	N	N	+
9 Clarke	Y	N	Y	N	N	N	Y
10 Nadler	Y	N	Y	N	N	Y	Y
11 **Donovan**	N	Y	Y	Y	Y	Y	N
12 Maloney, C.	Y	N	Y	N	N	Y	Y
13 Espaillat	Y	N	Y	?	N	Y	Y
14 Crowley	Y	N	Y	N	N	N	Y
15 Serrano	Y	N	Y	N	N	N	Y
16 Engel	Y	N	Y	N	N	Y	Y
17 Lowey	Y	N	Y	N	N	N	Y
18 Maloney, S.P.	Y	N	Y	N	N	N	Y
19 **Faso**	N	Y	Y	Y	Y	N	N
20 Tonko	Y	N	Y	N	N	P	Y
21 **Stefanik**	N	Y	Y	Y	Y	Y	N
22 **Tenney**	N	Y	Y	Y	Y	Y	N
23 **Reed**	N	Y	Y	Y	Y	N	N
24 **Katko**	N	Y	Y	Y	Y	Y	N
25 Slaughter	Y	N	Y	N	N	N	Y
26 Higgins	Y	N	Y	N	N	N	Y
27 **Collins**	N	Y	Y	Y	Y	Y	N
NORTH CAROLINA							
1 Butterfield	Y	N	Y	N	N	Y	Y
2 **Holding**	N	Y	Y	Y	Y	N	N
3 **Jones**	Y	Y	Y	N	N	N	N
4 Price	Y	N	Y	N	N	N	Y

	579	580	581	582	583	584	585
5 **Foxx**	N	Y	Y	Y	Y	N	N
6 **Walker**	N	Y	Y	Y	Y	Y	N
7 **Rouzer**	N	Y	Y	Y	Y	N	N
8 **Hudson**	N	Y	Y	Y	Y	N	?
9 **Pittenger**	N	Y	Y	Y	Y	N	N
10 **McHenry**	N	Y	Y	Y	Y	Y	N
11 **Meadows**	N	Y	Y	Y	Y	Y	N
12 Adams	Y	N	Y	N	N	Y	Y
13 **Budd**	N	Y	Y	Y	Y	Y	N
NORTH DAKOTA							
AL **Cramer**	N	Y	Y	Y	Y	Y	N
OHIO							
1 **Chabot**	N	Y	Y	Y	Y	Y	N
2 **Wenstrup**	N	Y	Y	Y	Y	N	N
3 Beatty	Y	N	Y	N	N	Y	Y
4 **Jordan**	N	Y	Y	Y	Y	N	N
5 **Latta**	N	Y	Y	Y	Y	Y	N
6 **Johnson**	N	Y	Y	Y	Y	N	N
7 **Gibbs**	N	Y	Y	Y	Y	Y	N
8 **Davidson**	N	Y	Y	Y	Y	Y	N
9 Kaptur	Y	N	Y	N	N	Y	?
10 **Turner**	N	Y	Y	Y	Y	N	N
11 Fudge	Y	N	Y	N	N	N	Y
12 **Tiberi**	N	Y	Y	Y	Y	Y	N
13 Ryan	Y	N	Y	N	N	N	Y
14 **Joyce**	N	Y	Y	Y	Y	N	N
15 **Stivers**	N	Y	Y	Y	Y	N	N
16 **Renacci**	N	Y	Y	Y	Y	N	N
OKLAHOMA							
1 **Bridenstine**	?	?	?	?	?	?	?
2 **Mullin**	N	Y	Y	Y	Y	Y	N
3 **Lucas**	N	Y	Y	Y	Y	Y	N
4 **Cole**	N	Y	Y	Y	Y	Y	N
5 **Russell**	N	Y	Y	Y	Y	Y	N
OREGON							
1 Bonamici	Y	N	Y	N	N	Y	Y
2 **Walden**	N	Y	Y	Y	Y	Y	N
3 Blumenauer	Y	N	Y	N	N	Y	Y
4 DeFazio	Y	N	Y	N	N	N	Y
5 Schrader	Y	N	Y	N	?	N	N
PENNSYLVANIA							
1 Brady	Y	N	Y	N	N	N	Y
2 Evans	Y	N	Y	N	N	Y	Y
3 **Kelly**	N	Y	Y	Y	Y	Y	N
4 **Perry**	N	Y	Y	Y	Y	N	N
5 **Thompson**	N	Y	Y	Y	Y	N	N
6 **Costello**	N	Y	Y	Y	Y	N	N
7 **Meehan**	N	Y	Y	Y	Y	Y	N
8 **Fitzpatrick**	N	Y	Y	Y	Y	N	N
9 **Shuster**	N	Y	Y	Y	Y	Y	N
10 **Marino**	N	Y	Y	Y	Y	Y	N
11 **Barletta**	?	?	?	Y	Y	Y	N
12 **Rothfus**	N	Y	Y	Y	Y	Y	N
13 Boyle	Y	N	Y	N	N	N	Y
14 Doyle	Y	N	Y	N	N	N	Y
15 **Dent**	N	Y	Y	Y	Y	Y	N
16 **Smucker**	N	Y	Y	Y	Y	N	N
17 Cartwright	Y	N	Y	N	N	Y	Y
RHODE ISLAND							
1 Cicilline	Y	N	Y	N	N	Y	Y
2 Langevin	Y	N	Y	N	N	N	Y
SOUTH CAROLINA							
1 **Sanford**	N	Y	Y	Y	Y	Y	N
2 **Wilson**	N	Y	Y	Y	Y	Y	N
3 **Duncan**	N	Y	Y	Y	Y	Y	N
4 **Gowdy**	N	Y	Y	Y	Y	Y	N
5 **Norman**	N	Y	Y	Y	Y	Y	N
6 Clyburn	Y	N	Y	N	N	N	Y
7 **Rice**	N	Y	Y	Y	Y	P	N
SOUTH DAKOTA							
AL **Noem**	N	Y	Y	Y	Y	Y	N
TENNESSEE							
1 **Roe**	N	Y	Y	Y	Y	Y	N
2 **Duncan**	N	Y	Y	Y	Y	Y	N
3 **Fleischmann**	N	Y	Y	Y	Y	Y	N
4 **DesJarlais**	N	Y	Y	Y	Y	Y	N
5 Cooper	N	Y	Y	N	N	Y	Y
6 **Black**	N	Y	Y	Y	Y	Y	N
7 **Blackburn**	N	Y	Y	Y	Y	Y	N
8 **Kustoff**	N	Y	Y	Y	Y	Y	N
9 Cohen	Y	N	Y	N	N	Y	Y

	579	580	581	582	583	584	585
TEXAS							
1 **Gohmert**	N	Y	Y	Y	Y	?	N
2 **Poe**	N	Y	Y	Y	Y	N	N
3 **Johnson, S.**	N	Y	Y	Y	Y	Y	?
4 **Ratcliffe**	N	Y	Y	Y	Y	Y	N
5 **Hensarling**	N	Y	Y	Y	Y	Y	N
6 **Barton**	N	Y	Y	Y	Y	N	N
7 **Culberson**	N	Y	Y	Y	Y	Y	N
8 **Brady**	N	Y	Y	Y	Y	Y	N
9 Green, A.	Y	N	Y	N	N	N	Y
10 **McCaul**	N	Y	Y	Y	Y	Y	N
11 **Conaway**	N	Y	Y	Y	Y	Y	N
12 **Granger**	N	Y	Y	Y	Y	Y	N
13 **Thornberry**	N	Y	Y	Y	Y	Y	N
14 **Weber**	N	Y	Y	Y	Y	N	N
15 Gonzalez	Y	N	Y	N	N	N	Y
16 O'Rourke	Y	N	Y	N	N	Y	Y
17 **Flores**	N	Y	Y	Y	Y	N	N
18 Jackson Lee	Y	N	Y	N	N	N	Y
19 **Arrington**	N	Y	Y	Y	Y	Y	N
20 Castro	Y	N	Y	N	N	Y	Y
21 **Smith**	N	Y	Y	Y	Y	Y	N
22 **Olson**	N	Y	Y	Y	Y	Y	N
23 **Hurd**	N	Y	Y	Y	Y	N	N
24 **Marchant**	N	Y	Y	Y	Y	Y	N
25 **Williams**	N	Y	Y	Y	Y	Y	N
26 **Burgess**	?	?	?	Y	Y	N	N
27 **Farenthold**	N	Y	Y	Y	Y	?	N
28 Cuellar	Y	Y	Y	N	N	Y	Y
29 Green, G.	Y	N	Y	N	N	N	Y
30 Johnson, E.B.	Y	N	Y	N	N	N	Y
31 **Carter**	N	Y	Y	Y	Y	Y	N
32 **Sessions**	N	Y	Y	Y	Y	Y	N
33 Veasey	Y	N	Y	N	N	N	Y
34 Vela	Y	N	Y	N	N	Y	Y
35 Doggett	Y	N	Y	N	N	Y	Y
36 **Babin**	N	Y	Y	Y	Y	N	N
UTAH							
1 **Bishop**	N	Y	Y	?	Y	Y	N
2 **Stewart**	N	Y	Y	Y	Y	Y	N
4 **Love**	N	Y	Y	Y	Y	Y	N
VERMONT							
AL Welch	Y	N	Y	N	N	Y	Y
VIRGINIA							
1 **Wittman**	N	Y	Y	Y	Y	N	N
2 **Taylor**	N	Y	Y	Y	Y	Y	N
3 Scott	Y	N	Y	N	N	Y	Y
4 McEachin	Y	N	Y	N	N	Y	Y
5 **Garrett**	N	Y	Y	?	Y	N	N
6 **Goodlatte**	N	Y	Y	Y	Y	Y	N
7 **Brat**	N	Y	Y	Y	Y	Y	N
8 Beyer	Y	N	Y	N	N	N	Y
9 **Griffith**	N	Y	Y	Y	Y	Y	N
10 **Comstock**	?	Y	Y	Y	Y	Y	N
11 Connolly	Y	N	Y	N	N	N	Y
WASHINGTON							
1 DelBene	Y	N	Y	N	N	Y	Y
2 Larsen	Y	N	Y	N	N	Y	Y
3 **Herrera Beutler**	N	Y	Y	Y	Y	Y	N
4 **Newhouse**	N	Y	Y	Y	Y	Y	N
5 **McMorris Rodgers**	N	Y	Y	Y	Y	Y	N
6 Kilmer	Y	N	Y	N	N	N	Y
7 Jayapal	Y	N	Y	N	N	N	Y
8 **Reichert**	N	Y	Y	Y	Y	Y	N
9 Smith	Y	N	Y	N	N	Y	Y
10 Heck	Y	N	Y	N	N	Y	Y
WEST VIRGINIA							
1 **McKinley**	N	Y	Y	Y	Y	N	N
2 **Mooney**	N	Y	Y	Y	Y	Y	N
3 **Jenkins**	N	Y	Y	Y	Y	N	N
WISCONSIN							
1 **Ryan**							
2 Pocan	Y	N	Y	N	N	Y	Y
3 Kind	Y	N	Y	N	N	N	Y
4 Moore	Y	N	Y	N	N	N	Y
5 **Sensenbrenner**	N	Y	Y	Y	Y	Y	N
6 **Grothman**	N	Y	Y	Y	Y	Y	N
7 **Duffy**	N	Y	Y	Y	Y	N	N
8 **Gallagher**	N	Y	Y	Y	Y	N	N
WYOMING							
AL **Cheney**	N	Y	Y	Y	Y	N	N

III HOUSE VOTES

VOTE NUMBER

586. HR 469. CONSENT DECREES NOTICE/AIR AND WATER QUALITY IMPROVEMENT. McEachin, D-Va., amendment that would exempt, from the bill's provisions that would require advance public notice for certain settlement agreements, settlement agreements related to improvement or maintenance of air or water quality. Rejected in Committee of the Whole 187-226 : R 3-226; D 184-0. Oct. 25, 2017.

587. HR 469. CONSENT DECREES NOTICE/ASSISTANT ATTORNEY GENERALS' SETTLEMENT PROCESS. Cartwright, D-Pa., amendment that would exempt, from the bill's provisions that would require advance public notice for certain settlement agreements, settlement agreements entered into by the assistant attorney generals under the process, known as the Meese Policy, for assistant attorney generals to accept, recommend acceptance, or reject settlement offers. Rejected in Committee of the Whole 186-232 : R 0-232; D 186-0. Oct. 25, 2017.

588. HR 469. CONSENT DECREES NOTICE/PASSAGE. Passage of the bill, as amended, that would require the federal government to provide advance public notice when it plans to enter into discussions regarding consent decrees and would codify and expand certain disclosure practices with regard to the Treasury Department's Judgment Fund payments. It would also allow counsel for the House of Representatives to intervene or appear as amicus curiae in any federal, state or local court. It would establish a new reporting deadline for the attorney general to inform Congress whether the Justice Department will contest, or refrain from defending, the constitutionality of a provision of federal law in court. Passed 234-187 : R 232-0; D 2-187. Oct. 25, 2017.

589. H CON RES 71. FISCAL 2018 BUDGET RESOLUTION/MOTION TO CONCUR. Black, R-Tenn., motion to concur in the Senate amendment to the concurrent resolution that would provide for $3.1 trillion in new budget authority in fiscal 2018, not including off-budget accounts. It would allow the cap on defense spending to be raised to $640 billion for fiscal 2018, without the need for offsets. It would require the Senate Finance Committee to report legislation under the budget reconciliation process that would increase the deficit by no more than $1.5 trillion over the period of fiscal 2018 through fiscal 2027. It would also instruct the Senate Energy and Natural Resources Committee to report legislation under the budget reconciliation process that would reduce the deficit by $1 billion over the period of fiscal 2018 through fiscal 2027. The concurrent resolution would authorize the establishment of various reserve funds, including a deficit-neutral reserve fund related to repealing or replacing the 2010 health care overhaul law, and a revenue-neutral reserve fund related to modifying the federal tax system. Motion agreed to 216-212 : R 216-20; D 0-192. Oct. 26, 2017.

590. HR 1698. IRANIAN BALLISTIC MISSILE PROGRAM SANCTIONS/ PASSAGE. Royce, R-Calif., motion to suspend the rules and pass the bill that would expand certain existing sanctions and mandate new sanctions on Iran related to country's ballistic missile program. It would impose sanctions on individuals that support Iran's ballistic missile program and on foreign persons who provide significant financial services to supporters of the program. It would also classify the transfer of certain traditional arms, such as anti-missile air defense systems, as sanctionable offenses. Motion agreed to 423-2 : R 232-2; D 191-0. Oct. 26, 2017.

591. HR 2521. PEANUT STANDARDS BOARD/PASSAGE. Crawford, R-Ark., motion to suspend the rules and pass the bill that would add South Carolina to the Virginia/Carolina peanut producing region of the department of Agriculture's Peanut Standards Board. Motion agreed to 394-1 : R 218-0; D 176-1. Oct. 31, 2017.

	586	587	588	589	590	591
ALABAMA						
1 **Byrne**	N	N	Y	Y	Y	Y
2 **Roby**	N	N	Y	Y	Y	Y
3 **Rogers**	N	N	Y	Y	Y	Y
4 **Aderholt**	N	N	Y	Y	Y	Y
5 **Brooks**	N	N	Y	Y	Y	Y
6 **Palmer**	N	N	Y	Y	Y	Y
7 Sewell	Y	Y	N	N	Y	Y
ALASKA						
AL **Young**	N	N	Y	Y	Y	Y
ARIZONA						
1 O'Halleran	Y	Y	N	N	Y	Y
2 **McSally**	N	N	Y	Y	Y	Y
3 Grijalva	Y	Y	N	N	Y	?
4 **Gosar**	N	N	Y	Y	Y	Y
5 **Biggs**	N	N	Y	Y	Y	Y
6 **Schweikert**	N	N	Y	Y	Y	Y
7 Gallego	Y	Y	N	N	Y	Y
8 **Franks**	N	N	Y	Y	Y	?
9 Sinema	Y	Y	N	N	Y	Y
ARKANSAS						
1 **Crawford**	N	N	Y	Y	Y	Y
2 **Hill**	N	N	Y	Y	Y	+
3 **Womack**	N	N	Y	Y	Y	Y
4 **Westerman**	N	N	Y	Y	Y	+
CALIFORNIA						
1 **LaMalfa**	N	N	Y	Y	Y	Y
2 Huffman	+	+	N	N	Y	Y
3 Garamendi	Y	Y	N	N	Y	?
4 **McClintock**	N	N	Y	Y	Y	Y
5 Thompson	+	+	-	-	+	Y
6 Matsui	Y	Y	N	N	Y	Y
7 Bera	Y	Y	N	N	Y	Y
8 **Cook**	N	N	Y	Y	Y	Y
9 McNerney	Y	Y	N	N	Y	Y
10 **Denham**	?	N	Y	Y	N	Y
11 DeSaulnier	Y	Y	N	N	Y	Y
12 Pelosi	Y	Y	N	N	Y	Y
13 Lee	Y	Y	N	N	Y	Y
14 Speier	Y	Y	N	N	Y	Y
15 Swalwell	Y	Y	N	N	Y	Y
16 Costa	Y	Y	N	N	Y	Y
17 Khanna	Y	Y	N	N	Y	Y
18 Eshoo	Y	Y	N	N	Y	Y
19 Lofgren	Y	Y	N	N	Y	Y
20 Panetta	Y	Y	N	N	Y	Y
21 **Valadao**	N	N	Y	Y	Y	Y
22 **Nunes**	N	N	Y	Y	Y	Y
23 **McCarthy**	N	N	Y	Y	Y	Y
24 Carbajal	Y	Y	N	N	Y	Y
25 **Knight**	N	N	Y	Y	Y	Y
26 Brownley	Y	Y	N	N	Y	Y
27 Chu	Y	Y	N	N	Y	Y
28 Schiff	Y	Y	N	N	Y	Y
29 Cardenas	Y	Y	N	N	Y	Y
30 Sherman	Y	Y	N	N	Y	Y
31 Aguilar	Y	Y	N	N	Y	?
32 Napolitano	Y	Y	N	N	Y	Y
33 Lieu	Y	Y	N	N	Y	Y
34 Gomez	Y	Y	N	N	Y	Y
35 Torres	Y	Y	N	N	Y	Y
36 Ruiz	Y	Y	N	N	Y	Y
37 Bass	Y	Y	N	N	Y	Y
38 Sánchez, Linda	Y	Y	N	N	Y	Y
39 **Royce**	N	N	Y	Y	Y	Y
40 Roybal-Allard	Y	Y	N	N	Y	Y
41 Takano	Y	Y	N	N	Y	Y
42 **Calvert**	N	N	Y	Y	Y	Y
43 Waters	Y	Y	N	N	Y	Y
44 Barragan	Y	Y	N	N	Y	?
45 **Walters**	N	N	Y	Y	Y	Y
46 Correa	Y	Y	N	N	Y	Y
47 Lowenthal	?	?	-	N	Y	Y
48 **Rohrabacher**	N	N	Y	Y	Y	?
49 **Issa**	N	N	Y	Y	Y	Y
50 **Hunter**	N	N	Y	Y	Y	Y
51 Vargas	Y	Y	N	N	Y	Y
52 Peters	Y	Y	N	N	Y	Y
53 Davis	Y	Y	N	N	Y	Y

	586	587	588	589	590	591
COLORADO						
1 DeGette	Y	Y	N	N	Y	?
2 Polis	Y	Y	N	N	Y	+
3 **Tipton**	N	N	Y	Y	Y	Y
4 **Buck**	N	N	Y	Y	Y	Y
5 **Lamborn**	N	N	Y	Y	Y	Y
6 **Coffman**	N	N	Y	Y	Y	Y
7 Perlmutter	Y	Y	N	N	Y	Y
CONNECTICUT						
1 Larson	Y	Y	N	N	Y	Y
2 Courtney	Y	Y	N	N	Y	Y
3 DeLauro	Y	Y	N	N	Y	Y
4 Himes	Y	Y	N	N	Y	Y
5 Esty	Y	Y	N	N	Y	Y
DELAWARE						
AL Blunt Rochester	Y	Y	N	N	Y	Y
FLORIDA						
1 **Gaetz**	N	N	Y	N	Y	Y
2 **Dunn**	N	N	Y	Y	Y	Y
3 **Yoho**	-	N	Y	Y	Y	Y
4 **Rutherford**	N	N	Y	Y	Y	Y
5 Lawson	Y	Y	N	N	Y	Y
6 **DeSantis**	N	N	Y	Y	Y	Y
7 Murphy	Y	Y	N	N	Y	Y
8 **Posey**	N	N	Y	Y	Y	Y
9 Soto	Y	Y	N	N	Y	Y
10 Demings	Y	Y	N	N	Y	Y
11 **Webster**	-	-	+	+	+	Y
12 **Bilirakis**	N	N	Y	Y	Y	Y
13 Crist	Y	Y	N	N	Y	Y
14 Castor	Y	Y	N	N	Y	Y
15 **Ross**	N	N	Y	Y	Y	Y
16 **Buchanan**	N	N	Y	Y	Y	Y
17 **Rooney, T.**	?	?	?	Y	Y	Y
18 **Mast**	N	N	Y	Y	Y	Y
19 **Rooney, F.**	N	N	Y	Y	Y	Y
20 Hastings	Y	Y	N	N	Y	Y
21 Frankel	Y	Y	N	N	Y	Y
22 Deutch	Y	Y	N	N	Y	Y
23 Wasserman Schultz	Y	Y	N	N	Y	Y
24 Wilson	?	?	?	?	?	Y
25 **Diaz-Balart**	N	N	Y	Y	Y	Y
26 **Curbelo**	N	N	Y	Y	Y	Y
27 **Ros-Lehtinen**	N	N	Y	Y	Y	?
GEORGIA						
1 **Carter**	N	N	Y	Y	Y	Y
2 Bishop	Y	Y	N	N	Y	Y
3 **Ferguson**	N	N	Y	Y	Y	Y
4 Johnson	Y	Y	N	N	Y	Y
5 Lewis	Y	Y	N	N	Y	Y
6 **Handel**	N	N	Y	Y	Y	Y
7 **Woodall**	N	N	Y	Y	Y	Y
8 **Scott, A.**	N	N	Y	Y	Y	Y
9 **Collins**	N	N	Y	Y	Y	Y
10 **Hice**	N	N	Y	Y	Y	Y
11 **Loudermilk**	N	N	Y	Y	Y	Y
12 **Allen**	N	N	Y	Y	Y	Y
13 Scott, D.	Y	Y	N	N	Y	Y
14 **Graves**	N	N	Y	Y	Y	Y
HAWAII						
1 Hanabusa	Y	Y	N	N	Y	Y
2 Gabbard	Y	Y	N	N	Y	Y
IDAHO						
1 **Labrador**	N	N	Y	Y	Y	Y
2 **Simpson**	N	N	Y	Y	Y	?
ILLINOIS						
1 Rush	Y	Y	N	N	Y	Y
2 Kelly	Y	Y	N	N	Y	Y
3 Lipinski	Y	Y	N	N	Y	Y
4 Gutierrez	Y	Y	N	N	Y	+
5 Quigley	Y	Y	N	N	Y	Y
6 **Roskam**	N	N	Y	N	Y	Y
7 Davis, D.	Y	Y	N	N	Y	Y
8 Krishnamoorthi	Y	Y	N	N	Y	Y
9 Schakowsky	Y	Y	N	N	Y	Y
10 Schneider	Y	Y	N	N	Y	Y
11 Foster	Y	Y	N	N	Y	Y
12 **Bost**	N	N	Y	Y	Y	Y
13 **Davis, R.**	N	N	Y	Y	Y	Y
14 **Hultgren**	N	N	Y	Y	Y	Y
15 **Shimkus**	N	N	Y	Y	Y	Y

	586	587	588	589	590	591
16 **Kinzinger**	N	N	Y	Y	Y	Y
17 Bustos	Y	Y	N	N	Y	Y
18 **LaHood**	N	N	Y	Y	Y	Y
INDIANA						
1 Visclosky	Y	Y	N	N	Y	Y
2 **Walorski**	N	N	Y	Y	Y	Y
3 **Banks**	N	N	Y	Y	Y	Y
4 **Rokita**	N	N	Y	Y	Y	+
5 **Brooks**	N	N	Y	Y	Y	Y
6 **Messer**	N	N	Y	Y	Y	Y
7 Carson	Y	Y	N	N	Y	Y
8 **Bucshon**	N	N	Y	Y	Y	Y
9 **Hollingsworth**	N	N	Y	Y	Y	Y
IOWA						
1 **Blum**	N	N	Y	Y	Y	Y
2 Loebsack	Y	Y	N	N	Y	Y
3 **Young**	N	N	Y	Y	Y	Y
4 **King**	N	N	Y	Y	Y	Y
KANSAS						
1 **Marshall**	N	N	Y	Y	Y	Y
2 **Jenkins**	N	N	Y	N	Y	Y
3 **Yoder**	N	N	Y	Y	Y	+
4 **Estes**	N	N	Y	Y	Y	Y
KENTUCKY						
1 **Comer**	N	N	Y	Y	Y	Y
2 **Guthrie**	N	N	Y	Y	Y	Y
3 Yarmuth	Y	Y	N	N	Y	Y
4 **Massie**	N	N	Y	N	N	Y
5 **Rogers**	N	N	Y	Y	Y	Y
6 **Barr**	N	N	Y	Y	Y	?
LOUISIANA						
1 **Scalise**	N	N	Y	Y	Y	Y
2 Richmond	?	?	?	N	Y	Y
3 **Higgins**	N	N	Y	Y	Y	Y
4 **Johnson**	N	N	Y	Y	Y	Y
5 **Abraham**	N	N	Y	Y	Y	Y
6 **Graves**	N	N	Y	Y	Y	Y
MAINE						
1 Pingree	Y	Y	N	N	Y	Y
2 **Poliquin**	N	N	Y	Y	Y	Y
MARYLAND						
1 **Harris**	N	N	Y	Y	Y	Y
2 Ruppersberger	Y	Y	N	N	Y	?
3 Sarbanes	Y	Y	N	N	Y	Y
4 Brown	Y	Y	N	N	Y	Y
5 Hoyer	Y	Y	N	N	Y	Y
6 Delaney	Y	Y	N	N	Y	Y
7 Cummings	Y	Y	N	N	Y	Y
8 Raskin	Y	Y	N	N	Y	Y
MASSACHUSETTS						
1 Neal	Y	Y	N	N	Y	Y
2 McGovern	Y	Y	N	N	Y	Y
3 Tsongas	Y	Y	N	N	Y	Y
4 Kennedy	Y	Y	N	N	Y	Y
5 Clark	Y	Y	N	N	Y	Y
6 Moulton	Y	Y	N	N	Y	Y
7 Capuano	Y	Y	N	N	Y	Y
8 Lynch	+	Y	N	N	Y	Y
9 Keating	Y	Y	N	N	Y	Y
MICHIGAN						
1 **Bergman**	N	N	Y	Y	Y	Y
2 **Huizenga**	N	N	Y	Y	Y	Y
3 **Amash**	N	N	Y	N	Y	Y
4 **Moolenaar**	N	N	Y	Y	Y	Y
5 Kildee	Y	Y	N	N	Y	Y
6 **Upton**	N	N	Y	Y	Y	Y
7 **Walberg**	N	N	Y	Y	Y	Y
8 **Bishop**	N	N	Y	Y	Y	Y
9 Levin	Y	Y	N	N	Y	Y
10 **Mitchell**	N	N	Y	Y	Y	Y
11 **Trott**	N	N	Y	Y	Y	Y
12 Dingell	Y	Y	N	N	Y	Y
13 Conyers	Y	Y	N	N	Y	Y
14 Lawrence	Y	Y	N	N	Y	Y
MINNESOTA						
1 Walz	Y	Y	N	N	Y	Y
2 **Lewis**	N	N	Y	Y	Y	Y
3 **Paulsen**	N	N	Y	Y	Y	Y
4 McCollum	Y	Y	N	N	Y	Y

	586	587	588	589	590	591
5 Ellison	Y	Y	N	N	Y	Y
6 **Emmer**	N	N	Y	Y	Y	Y
7 Peterson	Y	Y	Y	N	Y	Y
8 Nolan	Y	Y	N	N	Y	Y
MISSISSIPPI						
1 **Kelly**	N	N	Y	Y	Y	Y
2 Thompson	Y	Y	N	N	Y	Y
3 **Harper**	N	N	Y	Y	Y	Y
4 **Palazzo**	N	N	Y	Y	Y	Y
MISSOURI						
1 Clay	Y	Y	N	N	Y	Y
2 **Wagner**	N	N	Y	Y	Y	Y
3 **Luetkemeyer**	N	N	Y	Y	Y	Y
4 **Hartzler**	N	N	Y	Y	Y	Y
5 Cleaver	Y	Y	N	N	Y	Y
6 **Graves**	N	N	Y	Y	Y	Y
7 **Long**	N	N	Y	Y	Y	Y
8 **Smith**	N	N	Y	Y	Y	Y
MONTANA						
AL **Gianforte**	N	N	Y	Y	Y	?
NEBRASKA						
1 **Fortenberry**	?	?	?	Y	Y	Y
2 **Bacon**	N	N	Y	Y	Y	Y
3 **Smith**	?	?	?	?	?	Y
NEVADA						
1 Titus	Y	Y	N	N	Y	Y
2 **Amodei**	N	N	Y	Y	Y	Y
3 Rosen	Y	Y	N	N	Y	Y
4 Kihuen	Y	Y	N	N	Y	Y
NEW HAMPSHIRE						
1 Shea-Porter	Y	Y	N	N	Y	Y
2 Kuster	Y	?	N	N	Y	Y
NEW JERSEY						
1 Norcross	Y	Y	N	N	Y	Y
2 **LoBiondo**	Y	N	Y	N	Y	Y
3 **MacArthur**	N	N	Y	N	Y	Y
4 **Smith**	Y	N	Y	N	Y	Y
5 Gottheimer	Y	Y	N	N	Y	Y
6 Pallone	Y	Y	N	N	Y	Y
7 **Lance**	N	N	Y	N	Y	Y
8 Sires	Y	Y	N	N	Y	Y
9 Pascrell	?	Y	N	N	Y	?
10 Payne	Y	Y	N	N	Y	Y
11 **Frelinghuysen**	N	N	Y	Y	Y	?
12 Watson Coleman	Y	Y	N	N	Y	Y
NEW MEXICO						
1 Lujan Grisham	Y	Y	N	N	Y	Y
2 **Pearce**	N	N	Y	Y	Y	Y
3 Luján	Y	Y	N	N	Y	Y
NEW YORK						
1 **Zeldin**	N	N	Y	N	Y	Y
2 **King**	N	N	Y	N	Y	Y
3 Suozzi	Y	Y	N	N	Y	Y
4 Rice	Y	Y	N	N	Y	Y
5 Meeks	Y	Y	N	N	Y	Y
6 Meng	Y	Y	N	N	Y	?
7 Velázquez	Y	Y	N	N	Y	?
8 Jeffries	+	+	–	N	Y	Y
9 Clarke	Y	Y	N	N	Y	Y
10 Nadler	Y	Y	N	N	Y	Y
11 **Donovan**	N	N	Y	N	Y	Y
12 Maloney, C.	Y	Y	N	N	Y	Y
13 Espaillat	Y	Y	N	N	Y	Y
14 Crowley	Y	Y	N	N	Y	Y
15 Serrano	Y	Y	N	N	Y	Y
16 Engel	Y	Y	N	N	Y	Y
17 Lowey	Y	Y	N	N	Y	Y
18 Maloney, S.P.	Y	Y	N	N	Y	Y
19 **Faso**	N	N	Y	N	Y	Y
20 Tonko	Y	Y	N	N	Y	Y
21 **Stefanik**	N	N	Y	N	Y	Y
22 **Tenney**	N	N	Y	N	Y	Y
23 **Reed**	N	N	Y	Y	Y	Y
24 **Katko**	N	N	Y	N	Y	Y
25 Slaughter	Y	Y	N	N	Y	Y
26 Higgins	Y	Y	N	N	Y	Y
27 **Collins**	N	N	Y	Y	Y	Y
NORTH CAROLINA						
1 Butterfield	Y	Y	N	N	Y	?
2 **Holding**	N	N	Y	Y	Y	Y
3 **Jones**	Y	N	Y	N	Y	Y
4 Price	Y	Y	N	N	Y	Y

	586	587	588	589	590	591
5 **Foxx**	N	N	Y	Y	Y	Y
6 **Walker**	N	N	Y	Y	Y	Y
7 **Rouzer**	N	N	Y	Y	Y	Y
8 **Hudson**	?	N	Y	Y	Y	Y
9 **Pittenger**	N	N	Y	Y	Y	Y
10 **McHenry**	N	N	Y	Y	Y	Y
11 **Meadows**	N	N	Y	Y	Y	Y
12 Adams	Y	Y	N	N	Y	Y
13 **Budd**	N	N	Y	Y	Y	Y
NORTH DAKOTA						
AL **Cramer**	N	N	Y	Y	Y	Y
OHIO						
1 **Chabot**	N	N	Y	Y	Y	Y
2 **Wenstrup**	N	N	Y	Y	Y	Y
3 Beatty	Y	Y	N	N	Y	Y
4 **Jordan**	N	N	Y	Y	Y	Y
5 **Latta**	N	N	Y	Y	Y	Y
6 **Johnson**	N	N	Y	Y	Y	Y
7 **Gibbs**	N	N	Y	Y	Y	Y
8 **Davidson**	N	N	Y	Y	Y	Y
9 Kaptur	Y	Y	N	N	Y	Y
10 **Turner**	N	N	Y	Y	Y	Y
11 Fudge	Y	Y	N	N	Y	Y
12 **Tiberi**	N	N	Y	Y	Y	Y
13 Ryan	Y	?	N	N	Y	?
14 **Joyce**	N	N	Y	Y	Y	Y
15 **Stivers**	N	N	Y	Y	Y	Y
16 **Renacci**	N	N	Y	Y	Y	Y
OKLAHOMA						
1 **Bridenstine**	?	?	?	Y	?	?
2 **Mullin**	N	N	Y	Y	Y	Y
3 **Lucas**	N	N	Y	Y	Y	Y
4 **Cole**	N	N	Y	Y	Y	Y
5 **Russell**	N	N	Y	Y	Y	Y
OREGON						
1 Bonamici	Y	Y	N	N	Y	Y
2 **Walden**	N	N	Y	Y	Y	Y
3 Blumenauer	?	Y	N	N	Y	N
4 DeFazio	Y	Y	N	N	Y	Y
5 Schrader	Y	Y	N	N	Y	Y
PENNSYLVANIA						
1 Brady	Y	Y	N	N	Y	Y
2 Evans	Y	Y	N	N	Y	Y
3 **Kelly**	N	N	Y	Y	Y	Y
4 **Perry**	N	N	Y	Y	Y	Y
5 **Thompson**	N	N	Y	Y	Y	Y
6 **Costello**	N	N	Y	Y	Y	Y
7 **Meehan**	N	N	Y	Y	Y	Y
8 **Fitzpatrick**	N	N	Y	N	Y	Y
9 **Shuster**	N	N	Y	Y	Y	Y
10 **Marino**	N	N	Y	Y	Y	Y
11 **Barletta**	N	N	Y	Y	Y	Y
12 **Rothfus**	N	N	Y	Y	Y	Y
13 Boyle	Y	Y	N	N	Y	Y
14 Doyle	Y	Y	N	N	Y	Y
15 **Dent**	N	N	Y	Y	Y	Y
16 **Smucker**	N	N	Y	Y	Y	Y
17 Cartwright	Y	Y	N	N	Y	Y
RHODE ISLAND						
1 Cicilline	Y	Y	N	N	?	Y
2 Langevin	Y	Y	N	N	Y	Y
SOUTH CAROLINA						
1 **Sanford**	N	N	Y	N	Y	Y
2 **Wilson**	N	N	Y	Y	Y	Y
3 **Duncan**	N	N	Y	Y	Y	Y
4 **Gowdy**	N	N	Y	Y	Y	Y
5 **Norman**	N	N	Y	Y	Y	Y
6 Clyburn	Y	Y	N	N	Y	Y
7 **Rice**	N	N	Y	Y	Y	Y
SOUTH DAKOTA						
AL **Noem**	N	N	Y	Y	Y	Y
TENNESSEE						
1 **Roe**	N	N	Y	Y	Y	Y
2 **Duncan**	N	N	Y	N	N	Y
3 **Fleischmann**	N	N	Y	Y	Y	Y
4 **DesJarlais**	N	N	Y	Y	Y	?
5 Cooper	Y	Y	N	N	Y	Y
6 **Black**	N	N	Y	Y	Y	Y
7 **Blackburn**	N	N	Y	Y	Y	?
8 **Kustoff**	N	N	Y	Y	Y	Y
9 Cohen	Y	Y	N	N	Y	Y

	586	587	588	589	590	591
TEXAS						
1 **Gohmert**	N	N	Y	Y	Y	Y
2 **Poe**	N	N	Y	Y	Y	Y
3 **Johnson, S.**	?	?	?	?	?	Y
4 **Ratcliffe**	N	N	Y	Y	Y	Y
5 **Hensarling**	N	N	Y	Y	Y	Y
6 **Barton**	N	N	Y	Y	Y	Y
7 **Culberson**	N	N	Y	Y	Y	Y
8 **Brady**	N	N	Y	Y	Y	Y
9 Green, A.	Y	Y	N	N	Y	Y
10 **McCaul**	N	N	Y	Y	Y	Y
11 **Conaway**	N	N	Y	Y	Y	Y
12 **Granger**	N	N	Y	Y	Y	Y
13 **Thornberry**	N	N	Y	Y	Y	+
14 **Weber**	N	N	Y	Y	Y	Y
15 Gonzalez	Y	Y	N	N	Y	+
16 O'Rourke	Y	Y	N	N	Y	Y
17 **Flores**	N	N	Y	Y	Y	Y
18 Jackson Lee	Y	Y	N	N	Y	Y
19 **Arrington**	N	N	Y	Y	Y	Y
20 Castro	?	Y	N	N	Y	Y
21 **Smith**	N	N	Y	Y	Y	Y
22 **Olson**	N	N	Y	Y	Y	Y
23 **Hurd**	N	N	Y	Y	Y	+
24 **Marchant**	N	N	Y	Y	Y	Y
25 **Williams**	N	N	Y	Y	Y	Y
26 **Burgess**	N	N	Y	Y	Y	Y
27 **Farenthold**	N	N	Y	Y	Y	Y
28 Cuellar	Y	Y	Y	N	Y	Y
29 Green, G.	Y	Y	N	N	Y	Y
30 Johnson, E.B.	Y	Y	N	N	Y	Y
31 **Carter**	N	N	Y	Y	Y	Y
32 **Sessions**	N	N	Y	Y	Y	Y
33 Veasey	Y	Y	N	N	Y	?
34 Vela	Y	Y	N	N	Y	Y
35 Doggett	Y	Y	N	N	Y	Y
36 **Babin**	N	N	Y	Y	Y	Y
UTAH						
1 **Bishop**	N	N	Y	Y	Y	Y
2 **Stewart**	N	N	Y	Y	Y	Y
4 **Love**	N	N	Y	Y	Y	?
VERMONT						
AL Welch	Y	Y	N	N	Y	Y
VIRGINIA						
1 **Wittman**	N	N	Y	Y	Y	Y
2 **Taylor**	N	N	Y	Y	Y	Y
3 Scott	Y	Y	N	N	Y	Y
4 McEachin	Y	Y	N	N	Y	Y
5 **Garrett**	N	N	Y	Y	Y	Y
6 **Goodlatte**	N	N	Y	Y	Y	Y
7 **Brat**	N	N	Y	Y	Y	Y
8 Beyer	Y	Y	N	N	Y	Y
9 **Griffith**	N	N	Y	Y	Y	?
10 **Comstock**	N	N	Y	Y	Y	Y
11 Connolly	Y	Y	N	N	Y	Y
WASHINGTON						
1 DelBene	Y	Y	N	N	Y	Y
2 Larsen	Y	Y	N	N	Y	Y
3 **Herrera Beutler**	N	N	Y	Y	Y	Y
4 **Newhouse**	N	N	Y	Y	Y	Y
5 **McMorris Rodgers**	N	N	Y	Y	Y	Y
6 Kilmer	Y	Y	N	N	Y	Y
7 Jayapal	Y	Y	N	N	Y	Y
8 **Reichert**	N	N	Y	Y	Y	Y
9 Smith	Y	Y	N	N	Y	Y
10 Heck	Y	Y	N	N	Y	Y
WEST VIRGINIA						
1 **McKinley**	N	N	Y	Y	Y	Y
2 **Mooney**	N	N	Y	Y	Y	+
3 **Jenkins**	N	N	Y	Y	Y	Y
WISCONSIN						
1 **Ryan**				Y		
2 Pocan	Y	Y	N	N	Y	+
3 Kind	Y	Y	N	N	Y	Y
4 Moore	Y	Y	N	N	Y	+
5 **Sensenbrenner**	N	N	Y	Y	Y	Y
6 **Grothman**	N	N	Y	Y	Y	Y
7 **Duffy**	N	N	Y	Y	Y	+
8 **Gallagher**	N	N	Y	Y	Y	Y
WYOMING						
AL **Cheney**	N	N	Y	Y	Y	Y

VOTE NUMBER

592. HR 2936, H RES 595. WILDFIRE FUNDING AND ENVIRONMENTAL REVIEWS/PREVIOUS QUESTION. Newhouse, R-Wash., motion to order the previous question (thus ending debate and the possibility of amendment) on the rule (H Res 595) that would provide for House floor consideration of the bill (HR 2936) that would allow for a presidential declaration of a major disaster with regard to wildfires and would modify the disaster cap under the Budget Control Act to account for expected wildfire funding needs. It would also include various categorical exclusions from certain environmental reviews. Motion agreed to 232-184 : R 232-0; D 0-184. Nov. 1, 2017.

593. HR 2936, H RES 595. WILDFIRE FUNDING AND ENVIRONMENTAL REVIEWS/RULE. Adoption of the rule (H Res 595) that would provide for House floor consideration of the bill (HR 2936) that would allow for a presidential declaration of a major disaster with regard to wildfires, which would allow for the release of funding from Federal Emergency Management Agency's Disaster Relief Fund to fight major wildfires, and would modify the disaster cap under the Budget Control Act to account for expected wildfire funding needs. It would also include various categorical exclusions from certain environmental reviews. Adopted 232-184 : R 231-0; D 1-184. Nov. 1, 2017.

594. HR 2936. WILDFIRE FUNDING AND ENVIRONMENTAL REVIEWS/ FOREST MANAGEMENT DISPUTE ARBITRATION. Khanna, D-Calif., amendment that would eliminate the forest management dispute arbitration pilot program that would be established under the bill. Rejected in Committee of the Whole 189-232 : R 5-227; D 184-5. Nov. 1, 2017.

595. HR 2936. WILDFIRE FUNDING AND ENVIRONMENTAL REVIEWS/ ENDANGERED SPECIES ACT PROCEDURES. O'Halleran, D-Ariz., amendment that would eliminate the bill's provisions that would modify review periods and procedures under the Endangered Species Act and would consider any changes to a forest plan as a major federal action that would require an environmental impact statement. Rejected in Committee of the Whole 194-226 : R 6-225; D 188-1. Nov. 1, 2017.

596. HR 2936. WILDFIRE FUNDING AND ENVIRONMENTAL REVIEWS/ NEW MEXICO PILOT PROGRAM. Pearce, R-N.M., amendment that would authorize the secretary of Agriculture, through the chief of the Forest Service, to establish a pilot program within certain national forests in the state of New Mexico to demonstrate techniques related to thinning forests, watershed improvement and habitat restoration. Adopted in Committee of the Whole 236-184 : R 229-3; D 7-181. Nov. 1, 2017.

597. HR 2936. WILDFIRE FUNDING AND ENVIRONMENTAL REVIEWS/ RECOMMIT. O'Halleran, D-Ariz., motion to recommit the bill to the House Natural Resources Committee with instructions to report it back immediately with an amendment that would reauthorize, through 2020, the program that allows counties adjacent to National Forest Service lands to receive a percentage of the agency's timber sales revenues equal to their average payment in previous years, and would also require any forest management plan to include strategies for climate change mitigation. Motion rejected 189-230: R 2-230; D 187-0. Nov. 1, 2017.

598. HR 2936. WILDFIRE FUNDING AND ENVIRONMENTAL REVIEWS/ PASSAGE. Passage of the bill that would allow for a presidential declaration of a major disaster with regard to wildfires, which would allow for the release of funding from Federal Emergency Management Agency's Disaster Relief Fund to fight major wildfires, and would modify the disaster cap under the Budget Control Act to account for expected wildfire funding needs. It would also exempt various forest management activities from filing environmental impact statements and would provide for expedited timber salvage operations and reforestation activities after catastrophic events. It would prohibit any court from issuing restraining orders or injunctions against salvage operations or reforestation activities undertaken in response to a large-scale catastrophic event. Passed 232-188 : R 222-9; D 10-179. Nov. 1, 2017.

	592	593	594	595	596	597	598
ALABAMA							
1 Byrne	Y	Y	N	N	Y	N	Y
2 Roby	Y	Y	N	N	Y	N	Y
3 Rogers	Y	Y	N	N	Y	N	Y
4 Aderholt	Y	Y	N	N	Y	N	Y
5 Brooks	?	?	?	?	?	?	?
6 Palmer	Y	Y	N	N	Y	N	Y
7 Sewell	N	N	Y	Y	N	Y	Y
ALASKA							
AL Young	Y	Y	N	N	Y	N	Y
ARIZONA							
1 O'Halleran	N	N	Y	Y	N	Y	N
2 McSally	Y	Y	N	N	Y	N	Y
3 Grijalva	N	N	Y	Y	N	Y	N
4 Gosar	Y	Y	N	N	Y	N	Y
5 Biggs	Y	Y	N	N	Y	N	Y
6 Schweikert	Y	Y	N	N	Y	N	Y
7 Gallego	N	N	Y	Y	N	Y	Y
8 Franks	Y	Y	N	N	Y	N	Y
9 Sinema	N	N	Y	Y	N	Y	Y
ARKANSAS							
1 Crawford	Y	Y	N	N	Y	N	Y
2 Hill	+	+	-	-	+	-	+
3 Womack	Y	Y	N	N	Y	N	Y
4 Westerman	Y	Y	N	N	Y	N	Y
CALIFORNIA							
1 LaMalfa	Y	Y	N	N	Y	N	Y
2 Huffman	N	N	Y	Y	N	Y	N
3 Garamendi	?	?	?	?	?	?	?
4 McClintock	Y	Y	N	N	Y	N	Y
5 Thompson	N	N	Y	Y	N	Y	N
6 Matsui	N	N	Y	Y	N	Y	N
7 Bera	N	N	Y	Y	N	Y	N
8 Cook	Y	Y	N	N	Y	N	Y
9 McNerney	N	N	Y	Y	N	Y	N
10 Denham	Y	Y	N	N	Y	N	Y
11 DeSaulnier	N	N	Y	Y	N	Y	N
12 Pelosi	N	N	Y	Y	N	?	N
13 Lee	N	N	Y	Y	N	Y	N
14 Speier	N	N	Y	Y	N	I	N
15 Swalwell	N	N	Y	Y	N	Y	N
16 Costa	N	N	Y	Y	N	Y	Y
17 Khanna	N	N	Y	Y	N	Y	N
18 Eshoo	N	N	Y	Y	N	Y	N
19 Lofgren	N	N	Y	Y	N	Y	N
20 Panetta	N	N	Y	Y	N	Y	N
21 Valadao	Y	Y	N	N	Y	N	Y
22 Nunes	Y	Y	N	N	Y	N	Y
23 McCarthy	Y	Y	N	N	Y	N	Y
24 Carbajal	N	N	Y	Y	N	Y	N
25 Knight	Y	Y	N	N	Y	N	Y
26 Brownley	N	N	Y	Y	N	Y	N
27 Chu	N	N	Y	Y	N	Y	N
28 Schiff	N	N	Y	Y	N	Y	N
29 Cardenas	N	N	Y	Y	N	Y	N
30 Sherman	N	N	Y	Y	-	Y	N
31 Aguilar	N	N	Y	Y	N	Y	N
32 Napolitano	N	N	Y	Y	N	Y	N
33 Lieu	N	N	Y	Y	N	Y	N
34 Gomez	?	?	?	?	?	?	?
35 Torres	N	N	Y	Y	N	Y	N
36 Ruiz	N	N	Y	Y	N	Y	N
37 Bass	N	N	Y	Y	N	Y	N
38 Sánchez, Linda	N	N	Y	Y	N	Y	N
39 Royce	Y	Y	N	N	Y	N	Y
40 Roybal-Allard	N	N	Y	Y	N	Y	N
41 Takano	N	N	Y	Y	N	Y	N
42 Calvert	Y	Y	N	N	Y	N	Y
43 Waters	N	N	Y	Y	N	Y	N
44 Barragan	?	?	?	?	?	?	?
45 Walters	Y	Y	N	N	Y	N	Y
46 Correa	N	N	Y	Y	N	Y	N
47 Lowenthal	N	N	Y	Y	N	Y	N
48 Rohrabacher	Y	Y	N	N	Y	N	Y
49 Issa	Y	Y	N	N	Y	N	Y
50 Hunter	Y	Y	N	N	Y	N	Y
51 Vargas	N	N	Y	Y	N	Y	N
52 Peters	N	N	Y	Y	N	Y	N
53 Davis	N	N	Y	Y	N	Y	N

	592	593	594	595	596	597	598
COLORADO							
1 DeGette	?	?	Y	Y	N	Y	N
2 Polis	-	-	Y	Y	N	Y	N
3 Tipton	Y	Y	N	N	Y	N	Y
4 Buck	Y	Y	N	N	Y	N	Y
5 Lamborn	Y	Y	N	N	Y	N	Y
6 Coffman	Y	Y	N	N	Y	N	Y
7 Perlmutter	N	N	Y	Y	N	Y	N
CONNECTICUT							
1 Larson	N	N	Y	Y	N	Y	N
2 Courtney	N	N	Y	Y	N	Y	N
3 DeLauro	N	N	Y	Y	N	Y	N
4 Himes	N	N	Y	Y	N	Y	N
5 Esty	N	N	Y	Y	N	Y	N
DELAWARE							
AL Blunt Rochester	N	N	Y	Y	N	Y	N
FLORIDA							
1 Gaetz	Y	Y	Y	N	Y	N	Y
2 Dunn	Y	Y	N	N	Y	N	Y
3 Yoho	Y	Y	N	N	Y	N	Y
4 Rutherford	Y	Y	N	N	Y	N	Y
5 Lawson	N	N	Y	Y	N	Y	N
6 DeSantis	Y	Y	N	N	Y	N	Y
7 Murphy	N	N	Y	Y	N	Y	N
8 Posey	Y	Y	N	N	Y	N	Y
9 Soto	N	N	Y	Y	N	Y	N
10 Demings	N	N	Y	Y	N	Y	N
11 Webster	Y	Y	N	N	Y	N	Y
12 Bilirakis	Y	Y	N	N	Y	N	Y
13 Crist	N	N	Y	Y	N	Y	N
14 Castor	N	N	Y	Y	N	Y	N
15 Ross	Y	Y	N	N	Y	N	Y
16 Buchanan	Y	Y	N	N	Y	N	Y
17 Rooney, T.	Y	Y	?	?	?	?	?
18 Mast	Y	Y	N	N	Y	N	Y
19 Rooney, F.	Y	Y	N	N	Y	N	Y
20 Hastings	N	N	Y	Y	N	Y	N
21 Frankel	N	N	Y	Y	N	Y	N
22 Deutch	N	N	Y	Y	N	Y	N
23 Wasserman Schultz	N	N	Y	Y	N	Y	N
24 Wilson	N	N	Y	Y	N	Y	N
25 Diaz-Balart	Y	Y	N	N	Y	N	Y
26 Curbelo	Y	Y	N	N	Y	N	Y
27 Ros-Lehtinen	Y	Y	N	N	Y	N	Y
GEORGIA							
1 Carter	Y	Y	N	N	Y	N	Y
2 Bishop	N	N	Y	Y	N	Y	Y
3 Ferguson	Y	Y	N	N	Y	N	Y
4 Johnson	N	N	Y	Y	N	Y	N
5 Lewis	N	N	Y	Y	N	Y	N
6 Handel	Y	Y	N	N	Y	N	Y
7 Woodall	Y	Y	N	N	Y	N	Y
8 Scott, A.	Y	Y	N	N	Y	N	Y
9 Collins	Y	Y	N	N	Y	N	Y
10 Hice	Y	Y	N	N	Y	N	Y
11 Loudermilk	Y	Y	N	N	Y	N	Y
12 Allen	Y	Y	N	N	Y	N	Y
13 Scott, D.	N	N	Y	Y	N	Y	N
14 Graves	Y	Y	N	N	Y	N	Y
HAWAII							
1 Hanabusa	N	N	Y	Y	N	Y	N
2 Gabbard	N	N	Y	Y	N	Y	N
IDAHO							
1 Labrador	Y	Y	N	N	Y	N	Y
2 Simpson	Y	Y	N	N	Y	N	Y
ILLINOIS							
1 Rush	N	N	Y	Y	N	Y	N
2 Kelly	N	N	Y	Y	N	Y	N
3 Lipinski	N	N	Y	Y	N	Y	N
4 Gutierrez	N	N	Y	Y	N	Y	N
5 Quigley	N	N	Y	Y	N	Y	N
6 Roskam	Y	Y	N	N	Y	N	Y
7 Davis, D.	N	N	Y	Y	N	Y	N
8 Krishnamoorthi	N	N	Y	Y	N	Y	N
9 Schakowsky	N	N	Y	Y	N	Y	N
10 Schneider	N	N	Y	Y	N	Y	N
11 Foster	N	N	Y	Y	N	Y	N
12 Bost	Y	Y	N	N	Y	N	Y
13 Davis, R.	Y	Y	N	N	Y	N	Y
14 Hultgren	Y	Y	N	N	Y	N	Y
15 Shimkus	Y	Y	N	N	Y	N	Y

KEY	**Republicans**	Democrats	*Independents*
Y Voted for (yea)		X Paired against	C Voted "present" to avoid possible conflict of interest
# Paired for		– Announced against	
+ Announced for		P Voted "present"	? Did not vote or otherwise make a position known
N Voted against (nay)			

	592	593	594	595	596	597	598
16 **Kinzinger**	Y	Y	N	N	Y	N	Y
17 Bustos	N	N	Y	Y	N	Y	N
18 **LaHood**	Y	Y	N	N	Y	N	Y
INDIANA							
1 Visclosky	N	N	Y	Y	N	Y	N
2 **Walorski**	Y	Y	N	N	Y	N	Y
3 **Banks**	Y	Y	N	N	Y	N	Y
4 **Rokita**	Y	Y	N	N	Y	N	Y
5 **Brooks**	Y	Y	N	N	Y	N	Y
6 **Messer**	Y	Y	N	N	Y	N	Y
7 Carson	N	N	Y	Y	N	Y	N
8 **Bucshon**	Y	Y	N	N	Y	N	Y
9 **Hollingsworth**	Y	Y	N	N	Y	N	Y
IOWA							
1 **Blum**	Y	Y	N	N	Y	Y	Y
2 Loebsack	N	N	Y	Y	N	Y	N
3 **Young**	Y	Y	N	N	Y	N	Y
4 **King**	Y	Y	N	N	Y	N	Y
KANSAS							
1 **Marshall**	Y	Y	N	N	Y	N	Y
2 **Jenkins**	Y	Y	N	N	Y	N	Y
3 **Yoder**	Y	Y	N	N	Y	N	Y
4 **Estes**	Y	Y	N	N	Y	N	Y
KENTUCKY							
1 **Comer**	Y	Y	N	N	Y	N	N
2 **Guthrie**	Y	Y	N	N	Y	N	Y
3 Yarmuth	N	N	Y	Y	N	Y	N
4 **Massie**	Y	Y	N	N	Y	N	Y
5 **Rogers**	Y	Y	N	N	Y	N	Y
6 **Barr**	Y	Y	N	N	Y	N	Y
LOUISIANA							
1 **Scalise**	Y	Y	–	–	+	–	+
2 Richmond	N	N	Y	Y	N	Y	N
3 **Higgins**	Y	Y	N	N	Y	N	Y
4 **Johnson**	Y	Y	N	N	Y	N	Y
5 **Abraham**	Y	Y	N	N	Y	N	Y
6 **Graves**	Y	Y	N	?	Y	N	Y
MAINE							
1 Pingree	N	N	Y	Y	N	Y	N
2 **Poliquin**	Y	Y	N	N	Y	N	Y
MARYLAND							
1 **Harris**	Y	Y	N	N	Y	N	Y
2 Ruppersberger	N	N	Y	Y	N	Y	N
3 Sarbanes	N	N	Y	Y	N	Y	N
4 Brown	N	N	Y	Y	Y	Y	N
5 Hoyer	N	N	Y	Y	N	Y	N
6 Delaney	N	N	Y	Y	N	Y	N
7 Cummings	?	?	?	?	?	?	?
8 Raskin	N	N	Y	Y	N	Y	N
MASSACHUSETTS							
1 Neal	N	N	Y	Y	N	Y	N
2 McGovern	N	N	Y	Y	N	Y	N
3 Tsongas	N	N	Y	Y	N	Y	N
4 Kennedy	N	N	Y	Y	N	Y	N
5 Clark	N	N	Y	Y	N	Y	N
6 Moulton	N	N	Y	Y	N	Y	N
7 Capuano	N	N	Y	Y	N	Y	N
8 Lynch	N	N	Y	Y	Y	Y	N
9 Keating	N	N	Y	Y	N	Y	N
MICHIGAN							
1 **Bergman**	Y	Y	N	N	Y	N	Y
2 **Huizenga**	Y	Y	N	N	Y	N	Y
3 **Amash**	Y	Y	Y	N	N	N	N
4 **Moolenaar**	Y	Y	N	N	Y	N	Y
5 Kildee	N	N	Y	Y	N	Y	N
6 **Upton**	Y	Y	N	N	Y	N	Y
7 **Walberg**	Y	Y	N	N	Y	N	Y
8 **Bishop**	Y	Y	N	N	Y	N	Y
9 Levin	N	N	Y	Y	N	Y	N
10 **Mitchell**	Y	Y	N	N	Y	N	Y
11 **Trott**	Y	Y	N	N	Y	N	Y
12 Dingell	N	N	Y	Y	N	Y	N
13 Conyers	N	N	Y	Y	N	Y	N
14 Lawrence	N	N	Y	Y	N	Y	N
MINNESOTA							
1 Walz	N	N	Y	Y	N	Y	N
2 **Lewis**	Y	Y	N	N	Y	N	Y
3 **Paulsen**	Y	Y	N	N	Y	N	Y
4 McCollum	N	N	Y	Y	N	Y	N
5 Ellison	N	N	Y	Y	N	Y	N
6 **Emmer**	Y	Y	N	N	Y	N	Y
7 Peterson	N	N	N	Y	Y	Y	Y
8 Nolan	N	N	N	Y	N	Y	Y
MISSISSIPPI							
1 **Kelly**	Y	Y	N	N	Y	N	Y
2 Thompson	N	N	Y	Y	N	Y	N
3 **Harper**	Y	Y	N	N	Y	N	Y
4 **Palazzo**	Y	Y	N	N	Y	N	Y
MISSOURI							
1 Clay	N	N	Y	Y	N	Y	N
2 **Wagner**	Y	Y	N	N	Y	N	Y
3 **Luetkemeyer**	Y	Y	N	N	Y	N	Y
4 **Hartzler**	Y	Y	N	N	Y	N	Y
5 Cleaver	N	N	Y	Y	N	Y	N
6 **Graves**	Y	Y	N	N	Y	N	Y
7 **Long**	Y	Y	N	N	Y	N	Y
8 **Smith**	Y	Y	N	N	Y	N	Y
MONTANA							
AL **Gianforte**	Y	Y	N	N	Y	N	Y
NEBRASKA							
1 **Fortenberry**	Y	Y	N	N	Y	N	Y
2 **Bacon**	Y	Y	N	N	Y	N	Y
3 **Smith**	?	?	?	?	?	?	?
NEVADA							
1 Titus	N	N	Y	Y	N	Y	N
2 **Amodei**	Y	Y	N	N	Y	N	Y
3 Rosen	N	N	Y	Y	N	Y	N
4 Kihuen	N	N	Y	Y	N	Y	N
NEW HAMPSHIRE							
1 Shea-Porter	N	N	Y	Y	N	Y	N
2 Kuster	N	N	Y	Y	N	Y	Y
NEW JERSEY							
1 Norcross	N	N	Y	Y	N	Y	N
2 **LoBiondo**	Y	Y	N	Y	Y	N	N
3 **MacArthur**	Y	Y	N	N	Y	N	Y
4 **Smith**	Y	Y	N	Y	Y	N	N
5 Gottheimer	N	N	Y	Y	N	Y	N
6 Pallone	N	N	Y	Y	N	Y	N
7 **Lance**	Y	Y	Y	Y	N	N	N
8 Sires	N	N	Y	Y	N	Y	N
9 Pascrell	N	N	Y	Y	N	Y	N
10 Payne	N	N	Y	Y	N	Y	N
11 **Frelinghuysen**	Y	Y	N	N	Y	N	Y
12 Watson Coleman	N	N	Y	Y	N	Y	N
NEW MEXICO							
1 Lujan Grisham	N	N	Y	Y	N	Y	N
2 **Pearce**	Y	Y	N	N	Y	N	Y
3 Luján	N	N	Y	Y	N	Y	N
NEW YORK							
1 **Zeldin**	Y	Y	N	N	Y	N	Y
2 **King**	Y	Y	N	N	Y	N	Y
3 Suozzi	N	N	Y	Y	N	Y	N
4 Rice	N	N	Y	Y	N	Y	N
5 Meeks	N	N	Y	Y	N	Y	N
6 Meng	N	N	Y	Y	N	Y	N
7 Velázquez	N	N	Y	Y	N	Y	N
8 Jeffries	N	N	Y	Y	N	Y	N
9 Clarke	N	N	Y	Y	N	Y	N
10 Nadler	?	?	Y	Y	N	Y	N
11 **Donovan**	Y	Y	N	N	Y	N	Y
12 Maloney, C.	N	N	Y	Y	N	Y	N
13 Espaillat	N	N	Y	Y	N	Y	N
14 Crowley	N	N	Y	Y	N	Y	N
15 Serrano	N	N	Y	Y	N	Y	N
16 Engel	N	N	Y	Y	N	Y	N
17 Lowey	N	N	Y	Y	N	Y	N
18 Maloney, S.P.	N	N	Y	Y	N	Y	N
19 **Faso**	Y	Y	N	N	Y	N	+
20 Tonko	N	N	Y	Y	N	Y	N
21 **Stefanik**	Y	Y	N	N	Y	N	Y
22 **Tenney**	Y	Y	N	N	Y	N	Y
23 **Reed**	Y	Y	N	N	Y	N	Y
24 **Katko**	Y	Y	N	N	Y	N	Y
25 Slaughter	N	N	Y	Y	N	Y	N
26 Higgins	N	N	Y	Y	N	Y	N
27 **Collins**	Y	?	N	N	Y	N	Y
NORTH CAROLINA							
1 Butterfield	N	N	Y	Y	N	Y	N
2 **Holding**	Y	Y	N	N	Y	N	Y
3 **Jones**	Y	Y	Y	N	Y	Y	Y
4 Price	N	N	Y	Y	N	Y	N
5 **Foxx**	Y	Y	N	N	Y	N	Y
6 **Walker**	Y	Y	N	N	Y	N	Y
7 **Rouzer**	Y	Y	N	N	Y	N	Y
8 **Hudson**	Y	Y	N	N	Y	N	Y
9 **Pittenger**	Y	Y	N	N	Y	N	Y
10 **McHenry**	Y	Y	N	N	Y	N	Y
11 **Meadows**	Y	Y	N	N	Y	N	Y
12 Adams	N	N	Y	Y	N	Y	N
13 **Budd**	Y	Y	N	N	Y	N	Y
NORTH DAKOTA							
AL **Cramer**	Y	Y	N	N	Y	N	Y
OHIO							
1 **Chabot**	Y	Y	N	N	Y	N	Y
2 **Wenstrup**	Y	Y	N	N	Y	N	Y
3 Beatty	N	N	Y	Y	N	Y	N
4 **Jordan**	Y	Y	N	N	Y	N	Y
5 **Latta**	Y	Y	N	N	Y	N	Y
6 **Johnson**	Y	Y	N	N	Y	N	Y
7 **Gibbs**	Y	Y	N	N	Y	N	Y
8 **Davidson**	Y	Y	N	N	Y	N	Y
9 Kaptur	N	N	Y	Y	N	Y	N
10 **Turner**	Y	Y	N	N	Y	N	Y
11 Fudge	N	N	Y	Y	N	Y	N
12 **Tiberi**	Y	Y	N	N	Y	N	Y
13 Ryan	N	N	Y	Y	N	Y	N
14 **Joyce**	Y	Y	N	N	Y	N	Y
15 **Stivers**	Y	Y	N	N	Y	N	Y
16 **Renacci**	Y	Y	N	N	Y	N	Y
OKLAHOMA							
1 **Bridenstine**	?	?	?	?	?	?	?
2 **Mullin**	Y	Y	N	N	Y	N	Y
3 **Lucas**	Y	Y	N	N	Y	N	Y
4 **Cole**	Y	Y	N	N	Y	N	Y
5 **Russell**	Y	Y	N	N	Y	N	Y
OREGON							
1 Bonamici	N	N	Y	Y	N	Y	N
2 **Walden**	Y	Y	N	N	Y	N	Y
3 Blumenauer	N	N	Y	Y	N	Y	N
4 DeFazio	N	N	Y	Y	N	Y	N
5 Schrader	N	Y	N	N	Y	Y	Y
PENNSYLVANIA							
1 Brady	N	N	Y	Y	N	Y	N
2 Evans	N	N	Y	Y	N	Y	N
3 **Kelly**	Y	Y	N	N	Y	N	Y
4 **Perry**	+	+	N	N	Y	N	Y
5 **Thompson**	Y	Y	N	N	Y	N	Y
6 **Costello**	Y	Y	N	Y	Y	N	N
7 **Meehan**	Y	Y	N	N	Y	N	Y
8 **Fitzpatrick**	Y	Y	Y	Y	N	N	N
9 **Shuster**	Y	Y	N	N	Y	N	Y
10 **Marino**	Y	Y	N	N	Y	N	Y
11 **Barletta**	Y	Y	N	N	Y	N	Y
12 **Rothfus**	Y	Y	N	N	Y	N	Y
13 Boyle	N	N	Y	Y	N	Y	N
14 Doyle	N	N	Y	Y	N	Y	N
15 **Dent**	Y	Y	N	Y	Y	N	Y
16 **Smucker**	Y	Y	N	N	Y	N	Y
17 Cartwright	N	N	Y	Y	N	Y	N
RHODE ISLAND							
1 Cicilline	N	N	Y	Y	N	Y	N
2 Langevin	N	N	Y	Y	N	Y	N
SOUTH CAROLINA							
1 **Sanford**	Y	Y	N	N	Y	N	N
2 **Wilson**	Y	Y	N	N	Y	N	Y
3 **Duncan**	Y	Y	N	N	Y	N	Y
4 **Gowdy**	Y	Y	N	N	Y	N	Y
5 **Norman**	Y	Y	N	N	Y	N	Y
6 Clyburn	?	?	Y	Y	N	Y	N
7 **Rice**	Y	Y	N	N	Y	N	Y
SOUTH DAKOTA							
AL **Noem**	Y	Y	N	N	Y	N	Y
TENNESSEE							
1 **Roe**	Y	Y	N	N	Y	N	Y
2 **Duncan**	Y	Y	N	N	Y	N	Y
3 **Fleischmann**	Y	Y	N	N	Y	N	Y
4 **DesJarlais**	?	?	N	N	Y	N	Y
5 Cooper	N	N	Y	Y	N	Y	N
6 **Black**	Y	Y	N	N	Y	N	Y
7 **Blackburn**	Y	Y	N	N	Y	N	Y
8 **Kustoff**	Y	Y	N	N	Y	N	Y
9 Cohen	N	N	Y	Y	N	Y	N
TEXAS							
1 **Gohmert**	Y	Y	N	N	Y	N	Y
2 **Poe**	Y	Y	N	N	Y	N	Y
3 **Johnson, S.**	Y	Y	N	N	Y	N	Y
4 **Ratcliffe**	Y	Y	N	N	Y	N	Y
5 **Hensarling**	Y	Y	N	N	Y	N	Y
6 **Barton**	Y	Y	N	N	Y	N	Y
7 **Culberson**	Y	Y	N	N	Y	N	Y
8 **Brady**	Y	Y	N	N	Y	N	Y
9 Green, A.	N	N	Y	Y	N	Y	N
10 **McCaul**	Y	Y	N	N	Y	N	Y
11 **Conaway**	Y	Y	N	N	Y	N	Y
12 **Granger**	Y	Y	N	N	Y	N	Y
13 **Thornberry**	Y	Y	N	N	Y	N	Y
14 **Weber**	Y	Y	N	N	Y	N	Y
15 Gonzalez	N	N	Y	Y	Y	Y	N
16 O'Rourke	N	N	Y	Y	N	Y	N
17 **Flores**	Y	Y	N	N	Y	N	Y
18 Jackson Lee	–	N	Y	Y	N	Y	N
19 **Arrington**	Y	Y	N	N	Y	N	Y
20 Castro	N	N	Y	Y	N	Y	N
21 **Smith**	Y	Y	N	N	Y	N	Y
22 **Olson**	Y	Y	N	N	Y	N	Y
23 **Hurd**	Y	Y	N	N	Y	N	Y
24 **Marchant**	Y	Y	N	N	Y	N	Y
25 **Williams**	Y	Y	N	N	Y	N	Y
26 **Burgess**	Y	Y	N	N	Y	N	Y
27 **Farenthold**	Y	Y	N	N	Y	N	Y
28 Cuellar	N	N	N	Y	Y	Y	Y
29 Green, G.	N	N	Y	Y	N	Y	N
30 Johnson, E.B.	N	N	Y	Y	N	Y	N
31 **Carter**	Y	Y	N	N	Y	N	Y
32 **Sessions**	Y	Y	N	N	Y	N	Y
33 Veasey	N	N	Y	Y	N	Y	N
34 Vela	N	N	Y	Y	N	Y	N
35 Doggett	N	N	Y	Y	N	Y	N
36 **Babin**	Y	Y	N	N	Y	N	Y
UTAH							
1 **Bishop**	Y	Y	N	N	Y	N	Y
2 **Stewart**	Y	Y	N	N	Y	N	Y
4 **Love**	Y	Y	N	N	Y	N	Y
VERMONT							
AL Welch	N	N	Y	Y	N	Y	N
VIRGINIA							
1 **Wittman**	Y	Y	N	N	Y	N	Y
2 **Taylor**	Y	Y	N	N	Y	N	Y
3 Scott	N	N	Y	Y	N	Y	N
4 McEachin	N	N	Y	Y	N	Y	N
5 **Garrett**	Y	Y	N	N	Y	N	Y
6 **Goodlatte**	Y	Y	N	N	Y	N	Y
7 **Brat**	Y	Y	N	N	Y	N	Y
8 Beyer	N	N	Y	Y	N	Y	N
9 **Griffith**	Y	Y	N	N	Y	N	Y
10 **Comstock**	Y	Y	N	N	Y	N	Y
11 Connolly	N	N	Y	Y	N	Y	N
WASHINGTON							
1 DelBene	N	N	Y	Y	N	Y	N
2 Larsen	N	N	Y	Y	N	Y	N
3 **Herrera Beutler**	Y	Y	N	N	Y	N	Y
4 **Newhouse**	Y	Y	N	N	Y	N	Y
5 **McMorris Rodgers**	Y	Y	N	N	Y	N	Y
6 Kilmer	N	N	Y	Y	N	Y	N
7 Jayapal	N	N	Y	Y	N	Y	N
8 **Reichert**	Y	Y	N	N	Y	N	Y
9 Smith	N	N	Y	Y	N	Y	N
10 Heck	N	N	Y	Y	N	Y	N
WEST VIRGINIA							
1 **McKinley**	Y	Y	N	N	Y	N	Y
2 **Mooney**	Y	Y	N	N	Y	N	Y
3 **Jenkins**	Y	Y	N	N	Y	N	Y
WISCONSIN							
1 **Ryan**							
2 Pocan	–	–	+	+	+	+	–
3 Kind	N	N	Y	Y	N	Y	N
4 Moore	N	N	Y	Y	N	Y	N
5 **Sensenbrenner**	Y	Y	N	N	Y	N	N
6 **Grothman**	Y	Y	N	N	Y	N	Y
7 **Duffy**	Y	Y	N	N	Y	N	Y
8 **Gallagher**	Y	Y	N	N	Y	N	Y
WYOMING							
AL **Cheney**	Y	Y	N	N	Y	N	Y

III HOUSE VOTES

VOTE NUMBER

599. HR 3903. SEC DRAFT REGISTRATION STATEMENTS/PASSAGE.
Huizenga, R-Mich., motion to suspend the rules and pass the bill that would authorize the Securities Exchange Commission to issue regulations that would allow companies of any size to confidentially submit draft registration statements to the SEC for review prior to going public. Motion agreed to 419-0 : R 232-0; D 187-0. Nov. 1, 2017.

600. H RES 600, HR 849. INDEPENDENT PAYMENT ADVISORY BOARD REPEAL/PREVIOUS QUESTION. Burgess, R-Texas, motion to order the previous question (thus ending debate and the possibility of amendment) on the rule (H Res 600) that would provide for House floor consideration of the bill (HR 849) that would repeal provisions of the 2010 health care overhaul that provide for the creation of the Independent Payment Advisory Board. Motion agreed to 230-193 : R 230-1; D 0-192. Nov. 2, 2017.

601. H RES 600, HR 849. INDEPENDENT PAYMENT ADVISORY BOARD REPEAL/RULE. Adoption of the rule (H Res 600) that would provide for House floor consideration of the bill (HR 849) that would repeal provisions of the 2010 health care overhaul that provide for the creation of the Independent Payment Advisory Board. Adopted 240-178 : R 229-0; D 11-178. Nov. 2, 2017.

602. HR 3922, H RES 601. CHIP AND COMMUNITY HEALTH CENTERS FUNDING REAUTHORIZATION/PREVIOUS QUESTION. Burgess, R-Texas, motion to order the previous question (thus ending debate and the possibility of amendment) on the rule (H Res 601) that would provide for House floor consideration of the bill (HR 3922) that would extend funding for the Children's Health Insurance Program, community health centers and other public health programs. It would also provide for up to $1 billion in additional Medicaid funding to Puerto Rico. Motion agreed to 230-191 : R 230-1; D 0-190. Nov. 2, 2017.

603. HR 3922, H RES 601. CHIP AND COMMUNITY HEALTH CENTERS FUNDING REAUTHORIZATION/RULE. Adoption of the rule (H Res 601) that would provide for House floor consideration of the bill (HR 3922) that would extend funding for the Children's Health Insurance Program for five years, community health centers for two years and other public health programs for two years. It would also provide for up to $1 billion in additional Medicaid funding to Puerto Rico. Adopted 231-192 : R 231-0; D 0-192. Nov. 2, 2017.

604. HR 849. INDEPENDENT PAYMENT ADVISORY BOARD REPEAL/PASSAGE. Passage of the bill that would repeal provisions of the 2010 health care overhaul that provide for the creation of Independent Payment Advisory Board, which would recommend cost-cutting measures if Medicare spending exceeds a target growth rate. It would restore the Medicare Payment Advisory Commission, which would make non-binding recommendations related to controlling health care costs associated with Medicare. Passed 307-111 : R 231-0; D 76-111. Nov. 2, 2017.

605. HR 3922. CHIP AND COMMUNITY HEALTH CENTERS FUNDING REAUTHORIZATION/RECOMMIT. Clyburn, D-S.C., motion to recommit the bill to the House Energy and Commerce Committee with instructions to report it back immediately with an amendment that would modify the Medicare Advantage payment system to offset the funding in the measure. Motion rejected 187-231 : R 0-231; D 187-0. Nov. 3, 2017.

	599	600	601	602	603	604	605
ALABAMA							
1 Byrne	Y	Y	Y	Y	Y	Y	N
2 Roby	Y	Y	Y	Y	Y	Y	N
3 Rogers	Y	Y	Y	Y	Y	Y	N
4 Aderholt	Y	Y	Y	Y	Y	Y	?
5 Brooks	?	?	?	?	?	?	?
6 Palmer	Y	Y	Y	Y	Y	Y	N
7 Sewell	Y	N	N	N	N	Y	Y
ALASKA							
AL Young	Y	Y	Y	Y	Y	Y	N
ARIZONA							
1 O'Halleran	Y	N	N	N	N	Y	Y
2 McSally	Y	Y	Y	Y	Y	Y	?
3 Grijalva	?	N	N	N	N	N	Y
4 Gosar	Y	Y	Y	Y	Y	Y	N
5 Biggs	Y	Y	Y	Y	Y	Y	N
6 Schweikert	Y	Y	Y	Y	Y	Y	N
7 Gallego	Y	N	N	N	N	Y	Y
8 Franks	Y	Y	Y	Y	Y	Y	N
9 Sinema	Y	N	Y	N	N	+	Y
ARKANSAS							
1 Crawford	Y	Y	Y	Y	Y	Y	N
2 Hill	+	Y	Y	Y	Y	Y	N
3 Womack	Y	Y	Y	Y	Y	Y	N
4 Westerman	Y	Y	Y	Y	Y	Y	N
CALIFORNIA							
1 LaMalfa	Y	Y	Y	Y	Y	Y	?
2 Huffman	Y	N	N	N	N	N	Y
3 Garamendi	?	N	N	N	N	N	Y
4 McClintock	Y	Y	Y	Y	Y	Y	N
5 Thompson	Y	N	N	N	N	N	Y
6 Matsui	Y	N	N	N	N	N	Y
7 Bera	Y	N	N	N	N	Y	Y
8 Cook	Y	Y	Y	Y	Y	Y	N
9 McNerney	Y	N	N	N	N	Y	Y
10 Denham	Y	Y	Y	Y	Y	Y	N
11 DeSaulnier	Y	N	N	N	N	N	Y
12 Pelosi	Y	N	N	N	N	N	Y
13 Lee	Y	N	?	N	N	N	Y
14 Speier	Y	N	N	N			Y
15 Swalwell	Y	N	N	N	N	N	Y
16 Costa	Y	N	N	N	N	N	Y
17 Khanna	Y	N	N	N	N	N	Y
18 Eshoo	Y	N	N	N	N	N	Y
19 Lofgren	Y	N	N	N	N	Y	Y
20 Panetta	Y	N	N	N	N	N	Y
21 Valadao	Y	Y	Y	Y	Y	Y	N
22 Nunes	Y	Y	Y	Y	Y	+	Y
23 McCarthy	Y	Y	Y	Y	Y	Y	N
24 Carbajal	Y	N	N	N	N	Y	Y
25 Knight	Y	Y	Y	Y	Y	Y	N
26 Brownley	Y	N	N	N	N	Y	Y
27 Chu	Y	N	N	N	N	N	Y
28 Schiff	Y	N	N	N	N	N	Y
29 Cardenas	Y	N	N	N	N	Y	Y
30 Sherman	Y	N	N	N	N	N	Y
31 Aguilar	Y	N	N	N	N	Y	Y
32 Napolitano	Y	N	N	N	N	N	Y
33 Lieu	Y	N	N	N	N	N	Y
34 Gomez	?	N	N	N	N	N	Y
35 Torres	Y	N	N	N	N	N	Y
36 Ruiz	Y	N	Y	N	N	Y	Y
37 Bass	Y	N	N	N	N	N	Y
38 Sánchez, Linda	Y	N	N	N	N	N	Y
39 Royce	Y	Y	Y	Y	Y	Y	N
40 Roybal-Allard	Y	N	N	N	N	N	Y
41 Takano	Y	N	N	N	N	N	Y
42 Calvert	Y	Y	Y	Y	Y	Y	N
43 Waters	Y	N	N	N	N	N	Y
44 Barragan	?	N	N	N	N	Y	Y
45 Walters	Y	Y	Y	Y	Y	Y	N
46 Correa	Y	N	N	N	N	N	Y
47 Lowenthal	Y	N	N	N	N	N	Y
48 Rohrabacher	Y	Y	Y	Y	Y	Y	N
49 Issa	Y	Y	Y	Y	Y	Y	N
50 Hunter	Y	Y	Y	Y	Y	Y	N
51 Vargas	Y	N	N	N	N	Y	Y
52 Peters	Y	?	?	?	?	+	?
53 Davis	Y	N	N	N	N	Y	Y

	599	600	601	602	603	604	605
COLORADO							
1 DeGette	Y	N	N	N	N	Y	Y
2 Polis	Y	N	N	N	N	Y	Y
3 Tipton	Y	Y	Y	Y	Y	Y	N
4 Buck	Y	Y	Y	Y	Y	Y	N
5 Lamborn	Y	Y	Y	Y	Y	Y	N
6 Coffman	Y	Y	Y	Y	Y	Y	N
7 Perlmutter	Y	N	N	N	N	N	Y
CONNECTICUT							
1 Larson	Y	N	N	N	N	Y	Y
2 Courtney	Y	N	N	N	N	N	Y
3 DeLauro	Y	N	N	N	N	N	Y
4 Himes	Y	N	N	N	N	N	Y
5 Esty	Y	N	N	N	N	Y	Y
DELAWARE							
AL Blunt Rochester	Y	N	N	N	N	Y	Y
FLORIDA							
1 Gaetz	Y	Y	Y	Y	Y	Y	N
2 Dunn	Y	Y	Y	Y	Y	Y	N
3 Yoho	Y	Y	Y	Y	Y	Y	N
4 Rutherford	Y	Y	Y	Y	Y	Y	N
5 Lawson	Y	N	N	N	N	N	Y
6 DeSantis	Y	Y	Y	Y	Y	Y	N
7 Murphy	Y	N	N	N	N	N	Y
8 Posey	Y	Y	Y	Y	Y	Y	N
9 Soto	Y	N	N	N	N	N	Y
10 Demings	Y	N	N	N	N	N	Y
11 Webster	Y	Y	Y	Y	Y	Y	N
12 Bilirakis	Y	Y	Y	Y	Y	Y	N
13 Crist	Y	N	N	N	N	N	Y
14 Castor	Y	N	N	N	N	N	Y
15 Ross	Y	Y	Y	Y	Y	Y	N
16 Buchanan	Y	Y	Y	Y	Y	Y	N
17 Rooney, T.	?	Y	Y	Y	Y	Y	N
18 Mast	Y	Y	Y	Y	Y	Y	N
19 Rooney, F.	Y	Y	Y	Y	Y	Y	N
20 Hastings	Y	N	N	N	N	N	Y
21 Frankel	Y	N	N	N	N	N	Y
22 Deutch	Y	N	N	N	N	N	Y
23 Wasserman Schultz	Y	N	N	N	N	N	Y
24 Wilson	Y	N	N	N	N	–	+
25 Diaz-Balart	Y	Y	Y	Y	Y	Y	N
26 Curbelo	Y	Y	Y	Y	Y	Y	N
27 Ros-Lehtinen	Y	Y	Y	Y	Y	Y	N
GEORGIA							
1 Carter	Y	Y	Y	Y	Y	Y	N
2 Bishop	Y	N	N	N	N	Y	?
3 Ferguson	Y	Y	Y	Y	Y	Y	N
4 Johnson	Y	N	N	N	N	Y	Y
5 Lewis	Y	N	N	N	N	N	Y
6 Handel	Y	Y	Y	Y	Y	Y	N
7 Woodall	Y	Y	Y	Y	Y	Y	N
8 Scott, A.	Y	Y	Y	Y	Y	Y	N
9 Collins	Y	Y	Y	Y	Y	Y	N
10 Hice	Y	Y	Y	Y	Y	Y	N
11 Loudermilk	Y	Y	Y	Y	Y	Y	N
12 Allen	Y	Y	Y	Y	Y	Y	N
13 Scott, D.	Y	N	?	N	N	?	Y
14 Graves	Y	Y	Y	Y	Y	Y	N
HAWAII							
1 Hanabusa	Y	N	N	N	N	N	Y
2 Gabbard	Y	N	N	N	N	Y	Y
IDAHO							
1 Labrador	Y	Y	Y	Y	Y	Y	N
2 Simpson	Y	Y	Y	Y	Y	+	N
ILLINOIS							
1 Rush	Y	N	N	?	N	Y	Y
2 Kelly	Y	N	N	N	N	N	Y
3 Lipinski	Y	N	N	N	N	N	Y
4 Gutierrez	Y	N	N	N	N	N	+
5 Quigley	Y	N	N	N	N	N	Y
6 Roskam	Y	Y	Y	Y	Y	Y	N
7 Davis, D.	Y	N	N	N	N	N	Y
8 Krishnamoorthi	Y	N	N	N	N	Y	Y
9 Schakowsky	Y	N	N	N	N	N	Y
10 Schneider	Y	N	Y	N	N	Y	Y
11 Foster	Y	N	N	N	N	N	Y
12 Bost	Y	Y	Y	Y	Y	Y	N
13 Davis, R.	Y	Y	Y	Y	Y	Y	N
14 Hultgren	Y	Y	Y	Y	Y	Y	N
15 Shimkus	Y	Y	Y	Y	Y	Y	N

	599	600	601	602	603	604	605
16 **Kinzinger**	Y	Y	Y	Y	Y	Y	N
17 Bustos	Y	N	N	N	N	Y	Y
18 **LaHood**	Y	Y	Y	Y	Y	Y	N
INDIANA							
1 Visclosky	Y	N	N	N	N	N	Y
2 **Walorski**	Y	Y	Y	Y	Y	Y	N
3 **Banks**	Y	Y	Y	Y	Y	Y	N
4 **Rokita**	Y	Y	Y	Y	Y	Y	N
5 **Brooks**	Y	Y	Y	Y	Y	Y	N
6 **Messer**	Y	Y	Y	Y	Y	Y	N
7 Carson	Y	N	N	N	N	N	Y
8 **Bucshon**	Y	Y	Y	Y	Y	Y	N
9 **Hollingsworth**	Y	Y	Y	Y	Y	Y	N
IOWA							
1 **Blum**	Y	Y	Y	Y	Y	Y	N
2 Loebsack	Y	N	N	N	N	N	Y
3 **Young**	Y	Y	Y	Y	Y	Y	N
4 **King**	Y	Y	Y	Y	Y	Y	N
KANSAS							
1 **Marshall**	Y	Y	Y	Y	Y	Y	N
2 **Jenkins**	Y	Y	Y	Y	Y	Y	N
3 **Yoder**	Y	Y	Y	Y	Y	Y	N
4 **Estes**	Y	Y	Y	Y	Y	Y	N
KENTUCKY							
1 **Comer**	Y	Y	Y	Y	Y	Y	N
2 **Guthrie**	Y	Y	Y	Y	Y	Y	N
3 Yarmuth	Y	N	N	N	N	N	Y
4 **Massie**	Y	Y	Y	Y	Y	Y	N
5 **Rogers**	Y	Y	Y	Y	Y	Y	N
6 **Barr**	Y	?	?	?	?	Y	N
LOUISIANA							
1 **Scalise**	+	Y	Y	Y	Y	?	N
2 Richmond	Y	N	N	N	N	Y	Y
3 **Higgins**	Y	Y	Y	Y	Y	Y	N
4 **Johnson**	Y	Y	Y	Y	Y	Y	N
5 **Abraham**	Y	Y	Y	Y	Y	Y	N
6 **Graves**	Y	Y	Y	Y	Y	Y	N
MAINE							
1 Pingree	Y	N	N	N	N	N	Y
2 **Poliquin**	Y	Y	Y	Y	Y	Y	N
MARYLAND							
1 **Harris**	Y	Y	Y	Y	Y	Y	N
2 Ruppersberger	Y	N	N	N	N	Y	Y
3 Sarbanes	Y	N	N	N	N	N	Y
4 Brown	Y	N	N	N	N	N	Y
5 Hoyer	Y	N	?	N	N	N	Y
6 Delaney	Y	N	N	N	N	N	Y
7 Cummings	?	N	N	N	N	N	Y
8 Raskin	Y	N	N	N	N	N	Y
MASSACHUSETTS							
1 Neal	Y	N	N	N	N	N	Y
2 McGovern	Y	N	N	N	N	N	Y
3 Tsongas	Y	N	N	N	N	N	Y
4 Kennedy	Y	N	N	N	N	N	Y
5 Clark	Y	N	N	N	N	N	Y
6 Moulton	Y	N	N	N	N	Y	Y
7 Capuano	Y	N	N	N	N	N	Y
8 Lynch	Y	N	N	N	N	Y	Y
9 Keating	Y	N	N	N	N	Y	Y
MICHIGAN							
1 **Bergman**	Y	Y	Y	Y	Y	Y	N
2 **Huizenga**	Y	Y	Y	Y	Y	Y	N
3 **Amash**	Y	Y	Y	Y	Y	Y	N
4 **Moolenaar**	Y	Y	Y	Y	Y	Y	N
5 Kildee	Y	N	N	N	N	N	Y
6 **Upton**	Y	?	?	?	?	?	?
7 **Walberg**	Y	Y	Y	Y	Y	Y	N
8 **Bishop**	Y	Y	Y	Y	Y	Y	N
9 Levin	Y	N	N	N	N	N	Y
10 **Mitchell**	Y	Y	Y	Y	Y	Y	N
11 **Trott**	Y	Y	Y	Y	Y	Y	N
12 Dingell	Y	N	N	N	N	N	Y
13 Conyers	Y	N	N	N	N	N	Y
14 Lawrence	Y	N	N	N	N	Y	Y
MINNESOTA							
1 Walz	Y	N	N	N	N	N	Y
2 **Lewis**	Y	Y	Y	Y	Y	Y	N
3 **Paulsen**	Y	Y	Y	Y	Y	Y	N
4 McCollum	Y	N	N	N	N	N	Y

	599	600	601	602	603	604	605
5 Ellison	Y	N	N	N	N	N	Y
6 **Emmer**	Y	Y	Y	Y	Y	Y	N
7 Peterson	Y	N	Y	?	N	Y	Y
8 Nolan	Y	N	N	N	N	Y	Y
MISSISSIPPI							
1 **Kelly**	Y	Y	Y	Y	Y	Y	N
2 Thompson	Y	N	N	N	N	N	Y
3 **Harper**	Y	Y	Y	Y	Y	Y	N
4 **Palazzo**	Y	Y	Y	Y	Y	Y	N
MISSOURI							
1 Clay	Y	N	N	N	N	N	Y
2 **Wagner**	Y	Y	Y	Y	Y	Y	N
3 **Luetkemeyer**	Y	Y	Y	Y	Y	Y	N
4 **Hartzler**	Y	Y	Y	Y	Y	Y	N
5 Cleaver	Y	N	N	N	N	N	Y
6 **Graves**	Y	Y	Y	Y	Y	Y	N
7 **Long**	Y	Y	Y	Y	Y	Y	N
8 **Smith**	Y	Y	Y	Y	Y	Y	N
MONTANA							
AL **Gianforte**	Y	Y	Y	Y	Y	Y	N
NEBRASKA							
1 **Fortenberry**	Y	Y	Y	Y	Y	Y	N
2 **Bacon**	Y	Y	Y	Y	Y	Y	N
3 **Smith**	?	Y	Y	Y	Y	Y	N
NEVADA							
1 Titus	Y	N	N	N	N	N	Y
2 **Amodei**	Y	Y	Y	Y	Y	Y	N
3 Rosen	Y	N	Y	N	N	Y	Y
4 Kihuen	Y	N	N	N	N	Y	Y
NEW HAMPSHIRE							
1 Shea-Porter	Y	N	N	N	N	Y	Y
2 Kuster	Y	N	N	N	N	Y	Y
NEW JERSEY							
1 Norcross	Y	N	N	N	N	Y	Y
2 **LoBiondo**	Y	Y	Y	Y	Y	Y	N
3 **MacArthur**	Y	Y	Y	Y	Y	Y	N
4 **Smith**	Y	Y	Y	Y	Y	Y	N
5 Gottheimer	Y	N	Y	N	N	Y	Y
6 Pallone	Y	N	N	N	N	N	Y
7 **Lance**	Y	Y	Y	Y	Y	Y	N
8 Sires	Y	N	N	N	N	Y	Y
9 Pascrell	Y	N	N	N	N	Y	Y
10 Payne	Y	N	N	N	N	N	Y
11 **Frelinghuysen**	Y	Y	Y	Y	Y	Y	N
12 Watson Coleman	Y	N	N	N	N	Y	Y
NEW MEXICO							
1 Lujan Grisham	Y	N	N	N	N	Y	Y
2 **Pearce**	Y	Y	Y	Y	Y	Y	N
3 Luján	Y	N	N	N	N	N	Y
NEW YORK							
1 **Zeldin**	Y	Y	Y	Y	Y	Y	N
2 **King**	Y	Y	Y	Y	Y	Y	N
3 Suozzi	Y	N	Y	N	N	Y	Y
4 Rice	Y	N	N	N	N	N	Y
5 Meeks	Y	N	N	N	N	Y	Y
6 Meng	Y	N	N	N	N	Y	Y
7 Velázquez	Y	N	N	N	N	N	Y
8 Jeffries	Y	N	N	N	N	N	Y
9 Clarke	Y	N	N	N	N	Y	Y
10 Nadler	Y	N	N	N	N	N	Y
11 **Donovan**	Y	Y	Y	Y	Y	Y	N
12 Maloney, C.	Y	N	N	N	N	N	Y
13 Espaillat	Y	N	N	N	N	N	Y
14 Crowley	Y	N	N	N	N	N	Y
15 Serrano	Y	N	N	N	N	N	Y
16 Engel	Y	N	N	N	N	N	Y
17 Lowey	Y	N	N	N	N	N	Y
18 Maloney, S.P.	Y	N	N	N	N	Y	Y
19 **Faso**	Y	Y	Y	Y	Y	Y	N
20 Tonko	Y	N	N	N	N	N	Y
21 **Stefanik**	Y	Y	Y	Y	Y	Y	N
22 **Tenney**	Y	Y	Y	Y	Y	Y	N
23 **Reed**	Y	Y	Y	Y	+	Y	N
24 **Katko**	Y	Y	Y	Y	Y	Y	N
25 Slaughter	Y	N	N	N	N	N	Y
26 Higgins	Y	N	N	N	N	N	Y
27 **Collins**	Y	Y	Y	Y	Y	Y	N
NORTH CAROLINA							
1 Butterfield	Y	N	N	N	N	Y	Y
2 **Holding**	Y	Y	Y	Y	Y	Y	N
3 **Jones**	Y	N	Y	N	Y	Y	N
4 Price	Y	N	N	N	N	N	Y

	599	600	601	602	603	604	605
5 **Foxx**	Y	Y	Y	Y	Y	Y	N
6 **Walker**	Y	Y	Y	Y	Y	Y	N
7 **Rouzer**	Y	Y	Y	Y	Y	Y	N
8 **Hudson**	Y	Y	Y	Y	Y	Y	N
9 **Pittenger**	Y	Y	Y	Y	Y	Y	N
10 **McHenry**	Y	Y	Y	Y	Y	Y	N
11 **Meadows**	Y	Y	Y	Y	Y	Y	N
12 Adams	Y	N	N	N	N	N	Y
13 **Budd**	Y	Y	Y	Y	Y	Y	N
NORTH DAKOTA							
AL **Cramer**	Y	Y	Y	Y	Y	Y	N
OHIO							
1 **Chabot**	Y	Y	Y	Y	Y	Y	N
2 **Wenstrup**	Y	Y	Y	Y	Y	Y	N
3 Beatty	Y	N	N	N	N	Y	Y
4 **Jordan**	Y	Y	Y	Y	Y	Y	N
5 **Latta**	Y	Y	Y	Y	Y	Y	N
6 **Johnson**	Y	Y	Y	Y	Y	Y	N
7 **Gibbs**	Y	Y	Y	Y	Y	Y	N
8 **Davidson**	Y	Y	Y	Y	Y	Y	N
9 Kaptur	Y	N	N	N	N	N	Y
10 **Turner**	Y	Y	Y	Y	Y	Y	N
11 Fudge	Y	N	N	N	N	N	Y
12 **Tiberi**	Y	Y	Y	Y	Y	Y	N
13 Ryan	Y	N	N	N	N	N	Y
14 **Joyce**	Y	Y	Y	Y	Y	Y	N
15 **Stivers**	Y	Y	Y	Y	Y	Y	N
16 **Renacci**	Y	Y	Y	Y	Y	Y	N
OKLAHOMA							
1 **Bridenstine**	?	?	?	?	?	?	?
2 **Mullin**	Y	Y	Y	Y	Y	Y	N
3 **Lucas**	Y	Y	Y	Y	Y	Y	N
4 **Cole**	Y	Y	Y	Y	Y	Y	N
5 **Russell**	Y	Y	Y	Y	Y	Y	N
OREGON							
1 Bonamici	Y	N	N	N	N	N	Y
2 **Walden**	Y	Y	Y	Y	Y	Y	N
3 Blumenauer	Y	N	N	N	N	N	Y
4 DeFazio	Y	N	N	N	N	Y	Y
5 Schrader	Y	N	N	N	N	N	Y
PENNSYLVANIA							
1 Brady	Y	N	N	N	N	N	Y
2 Evans	Y	N	N	N	N	N	Y
3 **Kelly**	Y	Y	Y	Y	Y	Y	N
4 **Perry**	Y	Y	Y	Y	Y	Y	N
5 **Thompson**	Y	Y	Y	Y	Y	Y	N
6 **Costello**	Y	Y	Y	Y	Y	Y	N
7 **Meehan**	Y	Y	Y	Y	Y	Y	N
8 **Fitzpatrick**	Y	Y	Y	Y	Y	Y	N
9 **Shuster**	Y	Y	Y	Y	Y	Y	N
10 **Marino**	Y	Y	Y	Y	Y	Y	N
11 **Barletta**	Y	Y	Y	Y	Y	Y	N
12 **Rothfus**	Y	Y	Y	Y	Y	Y	N
13 Boyle	Y	N	N	N	N	Y	Y
14 Doyle	Y	N	N	N	N	N	Y
15 **Dent**	Y	Y	Y	Y	Y	Y	N
16 **Smucker**	Y	Y	Y	Y	Y	Y	N
17 Cartwright	Y	N	N	N	N	N	Y
RHODE ISLAND							
1 Cicilline	Y	N	N	N	N	N	Y
2 Langevin	Y	N	N	N	N	N	Y
SOUTH CAROLINA							
1 **Sanford**	Y	Y	Y	Y	Y	Y	N
2 **Wilson**	Y	Y	Y	Y	Y	Y	N
3 **Duncan**	Y	Y	Y	Y	Y	Y	N
4 **Gowdy**	Y	?	?	?	?	Y	N
5 **Norman**	Y	Y	Y	Y	Y	Y	N
6 Clyburn	Y	N	N	N	N	N	Y
7 **Rice**	Y	Y	Y	Y	Y	Y	N
SOUTH DAKOTA							
AL **Noem**	Y	Y	Y	Y	Y	Y	N
TENNESSEE							
1 **Roe**	Y	Y	Y	Y	Y	Y	N
2 **Duncan**	Y	Y	Y	Y	Y	Y	N
3 **Fleischmann**	Y	Y	Y	Y	Y	Y	N
4 **DesJarlais**	Y	Y	Y	Y	Y	Y	N
5 Cooper	Y	N	N	N	N	N	Y
6 **Black**	Y	?	?	?	?	+	?
7 **Blackburn**	Y	Y	Y	Y	Y	Y	N
8 **Kustoff**	Y	Y	Y	Y	Y	Y	N
9 Cohen	Y	N	N	N	N	N	Y

	599	600	601	602	603	604	605
TEXAS							
1 **Gohmert**	Y	Y	Y	Y	Y	Y	N
2 **Poe**	Y	Y	Y	Y	Y	Y	N
3 **Johnson, S.**	Y	Y	Y	Y	Y	Y	?
4 **Ratcliffe**	Y	Y	Y	Y	Y	Y	N
5 **Hensarling**	Y	?	?	?	Y	Y	N
6 **Barton**	Y	Y	Y	Y	Y	Y	N
7 **Culberson**	Y	Y	Y	Y	Y	Y	N
8 **Brady**	Y	Y	Y	Y	Y	Y	N
9 Green, A.	Y	N	N	N	N	N	Y
10 **McCaul**	Y	Y	Y	Y	Y	Y	N
11 **Conaway**	Y	Y	Y	Y	Y	Y	N
12 **Granger**	Y	Y	Y	Y	Y	Y	N
13 **Thornberry**	Y	Y	Y	Y	Y	Y	N
14 **Weber**	Y	Y	Y	Y	Y	Y	N
15 Gonzalez	Y	N	N	N	N	Y	Y
16 O'Rourke	Y	N	N	N	N	Y	Y
17 **Flores**	Y	Y	Y	Y	Y	Y	N
18 Jackson Lee	Y	N	N	N	N	N	+
19 **Arrington**	Y	Y	Y	Y	Y	Y	N
20 Castro	Y	N	N	N	N	Y	Y
21 **Smith**	Y	Y	Y	Y	Y	Y	N
22 **Olson**	Y	Y	Y	Y	Y	Y	N
23 **Hurd**	Y	Y	Y	Y	Y	Y	N
24 **Marchant**	Y	Y	?	Y	Y	Y	N
25 **Williams**	Y	Y	Y	Y	Y	Y	N
26 **Burgess**	Y	Y	Y	Y	Y	Y	N
27 **Farenthold**	Y	Y	Y	Y	Y	Y	N
28 Cuellar	Y	N	N	N	N	Y	Y
29 Green, G.	Y	N	N	N	N	Y	Y
30 Johnson, E.B.	Y	N	N	N	N	?	?
31 **Carter**	Y	Y	Y	Y	Y	Y	N
32 **Sessions**	Y	Y	Y	Y	Y	Y	N
33 Veasey	Y	N	N	N	N	Y	Y
34 Vela	Y	N	N	N	N	Y	Y
35 Doggett	Y	N	N	N	N	N	Y
36 **Babin**	Y	Y	Y	Y	Y	Y	N
UTAH							
1 **Bishop**	Y	Y	Y	Y	Y	Y	N
2 **Stewart**	Y	Y	?	Y	Y	Y	N
4 **Love**	Y	Y	Y	Y	Y	Y	N
VERMONT							
AL Welch	Y	N	N	N	N	N	Y
VIRGINIA							
1 **Wittman**	Y	Y	Y	Y	Y	Y	N
2 **Taylor**	Y	Y	Y	Y	Y	Y	N
3 Scott	Y	N	N	N	N	N	Y
4 McEachin	Y	N	N	N	N	N	Y
5 **Garrett**	Y	Y	Y	Y	Y	Y	N
6 **Goodlatte**	Y	Y	Y	Y	Y	Y	N
7 **Brat**	Y	Y	Y	Y	Y	Y	N
8 Beyer	Y	N	N	N	N	N	Y
9 **Griffith**	Y	Y	Y	Y	Y	Y	N
10 **Comstock**	Y	Y	Y	Y	Y	Y	N
11 Connolly	Y	N	N	N	N	Y	Y
WASHINGTON							
1 DelBene	Y	N	N	N	N	N	Y
2 Larsen	Y	N	N	N	N	N	Y
3 **Herrera Beutler**	Y	Y	Y	Y	Y	Y	N
4 **Newhouse**	Y	Y	Y	Y	Y	Y	N
5 **McMorris Rodgers**	Y	Y	Y	Y	Y	Y	N
6 Kilmer	Y	N	N	N	N	N	Y
7 Jayapal	Y	N	N	N	N	N	Y
8 **Reichert**	Y	Y	Y	Y	Y	Y	N
9 Smith	Y	N	N	N	N	N	Y
10 Heck	Y	N	N	N	N	N	Y
WEST VIRGINIA							
1 **McKinley**	Y	Y	Y	Y	Y	Y	N
2 **Mooney**	Y	Y	Y	Y	Y	Y	N
3 **Jenkins**	Y	Y	Y	Y	Y	Y	N
WISCONSIN							
1 **Ryan**							
2 Pocan	+	–	–	–	–	+	+
3 Kind	Y	N	N	N	N	N	Y
4 Moore	?	N	N	N	N	N	Y
5 **Sensenbrenner**	Y	Y	Y	Y	Y	Y	N
6 **Grothman**	Y	Y	Y	Y	Y	Y	N
7 **Duffy**	Y	Y	Y	Y	Y	Y	N
8 **Gallagher**	Y	Y	Y	Y	Y	Y	N
WYOMING							
AL **Cheney**	Y	Y	Y	Y	Y	Y	N

ⅠⅠⅠ HOUSE VOTES

VOTE NUMBER

606. HR 3922. CHIP AND COMMUNITY HEALTH CENTERS FUNDING REAUTHORIZATION/PASSAGE. Passage of the bill, as amended, that would extend funding for the Children's Health Insurance Program through fiscal 2022, and would increase funding from $21.5 billion in fiscal 2018 to $25.9 billion in fiscal 2022. It would also provide $3.6 billion annually for community health centers through fiscal 2019, and would extend funding for a number of other public health programs through fiscal 2019. It would provide for up to $1 billion in additional Medicaid funding to Puerto Rico and would eliminate, through fiscal 2019, scheduled cuts in Medicaid funding to hospitals that serve large numbers of uninsured and low-income patients. It would reduce spending from the Prevention and Public Health Fund through fiscal 2026, would require high-income individuals enrolled in Medicare parts B and D to pay the entirety of their premiums for these services and would shorten the grace period for certain missed payments on federally subsidized health insurance plans purchased through state exchanges to offset the cost of the measure's funding for CHIP, community health centers and other health programs. Passed 242-174 : R 227-3; D 15-171. Nov. 3, 2017.

607. HR 3562. VA HOUSING ADAPTATION ASSISTANCE ADMINISTRATION/PASSAGE. Roe, R-Tenn., motion to suspend the rules and pass the bill that would transfer the administration of VA housing adaptation assistance for independent living from rehabilitation and employment counselors to VA housing adaption agents and would cap the payments for independent living modifications to homes that can be made for each beneficiary at $77,307, which would be adjusted annually for inflation at the beginning of every fiscal year. Motion agreed to 400-0 : R 223-0; D 177-0. Nov. 6, 2017.

608. HR 1066. VA EFFECTIVENESS REPORT/PASSAGE. Roe, R-Tenn., motion to suspend the rules and pass the bill that would require the VA to submit a report to Congress on the organizational structure of the department, and therein make recommendations for legislation that the secretary of the VA would consider appropriate to improve department effectiveness and accountability. Motion agreed to 399-0 : R 223-0; D 176-0. Nov. 6, 2017.

609. PROCEDURAL MOTION/APPROVAL OF HOUSE JOURNAL. Approved 222-169 : R 134-86; D 88-83. Nov. 6, 2017.

610. HR 3043, HR 3441, H RES 607. HYDROPOWER REGULATION AND JOINT EMPLOYER DEFINITION/PREVIOUS QUESTION. Byrne, R-Ala., motion to order the previous question (thus ending debate and the possibility of amendment) on the rule (H Res 607) that would provide for House floor consideration of the bill (HR 3043) that would specify a variety of timeframes and procedures for the Federal Energy Regulatory Commission to follow in carrying out required permitting and licensing activities for non-federal hydropower projects. It would also provide for consideration of the bill (HR 3441) that would modify the statutory definition of joint employer. Motion agreed to 233-182 : R 232-1; D 1-181. Nov. 7, 2017.

611. HR 3043, HR 3441, H RES 607. HYDROPOWER REGULATION AND JOINT EMPLOYER DEFINITION/RULE. Adoption of the rule (H Res 607) that would provide for House floor consideration of the bill (HR 3043) that would specify a variety of timeframes and procedures for the Federal Energy Regulatory Commission to follow in carrying out required permitting and licensing activities for non-federal hydropower projects. It would also provide for consideration of the bill (HR 3441) that would modify the statutory definition of joint employer to clarify that an employer must have actual, direct and immediate control over employees to be considered a joint employer. Adopted 233-182 : R 233-0; D 0-182. Nov. 7, 2017.

612. PROCEDURAL MOTION/APPROVAL OF HOUSE JOURNAL. Approved 225-184 : R 144-87; 81-97. Nov. 7, 2017.

	606	607	608	609	610	611	612
ALABAMA							
1 **Byrne**	Y	Y	Y	Y	Y	Y	Y
2 **Roby**	Y	Y	Y	Y	Y	Y	Y
3 **Rogers**	Y	Y	Y	N	Y	Y	N
4 **Aderholt**	?	Y	Y	Y	Y	Y	Y
5 **Brooks**	?	Y	Y	N	Y	Y	N
6 **Palmer**	Y	Y	Y	N	Y	N	N
7 Sewell	N	Y	Y	N	N	N	N
ALASKA							
AL **Young**	Y	?	?	?	Y	Y	N
ARIZONA							
1 O'Halleran	Y	Y	Y	N	N	N	N
2 **McSally**	Y	Y	Y	N	Y	Y	N
3 Grijalva	N	Y	Y	?	N	N	?
4 **Gosar**	Y	Y	Y	N	Y	Y	N
5 **Biggs**	N	Y	Y	N	Y	N	N
6 **Schweikert**	Y	Y	Y	Y	Y	Y	Y
7 Gallego	N	Y	Y	N	N	N	N
8 **Franks**	Y	Y	Y	Y	Y	Y	Y
9 Sinema	Y	Y	Y	N	N	N	N
ARKANSAS							
1 **Crawford**	Y	Y	Y	Y	Y	Y	Y
2 **Hill**	Y	Y	Y	N	Y	Y	Y
3 **Womack**	Y	Y	Y	Y	Y	Y	Y
4 **Westerman**	Y	Y	Y	Y	Y	Y	Y
CALIFORNIA							
1 **LaMalfa**	+	Y	Y	Y	Y	Y	Y
2 Huffman	N	Y	Y	Y	?	?	?
3 Garamendi	N	Y	Y	N	N	N	Y
4 **McClintock**	Y	Y	Y	Y	Y	Y	Y
5 Thompson	N	Y	Y	N	N	N	N
6 Matsui	N	Y	Y	N	N	N	N
7 Bera	Y	Y	Y	N	N	N	N
8 **Cook**	Y	Y	Y	Y	Y	Y	Y
9 McNerney	N	?	?	?	N	N	Y
10 **Denham**	Y	Y	Y	N	Y	Y	N
11 DeSaulnier	N	Y	Y	N	N	N	N
12 Pelosi	N	Y	Y	N	N	N	Y
13 Lee	N	Y	Y	N	N	N	N
14 Speier	–	Y	Y	N	N	N	Y
15 Swalwell	N	Y	Y	N	N	N	N
16 Costa	Y	Y	Y	N	N	N	N
17 Khanna	N	Y	Y	N	N	N	N
18 Eshoo	N	Y	Y	N	N	N	Y
19 Lofgren	N	Y	Y	N	N	N	N
20 Panetta	N	Y	Y	N	N	N	N
21 **Valadao**	Y	?	?	?	Y	Y	N
22 **Nunes**	Y	Y	Y	Y	Y	Y	Y
23 **McCarthy**	Y	Y	Y	Y	Y	Y	Y
24 Carbajal	Y	Y	Y	N	N	N	N
25 **Knight**	Y	Y	Y	N	Y	Y	N
26 Brownley	N	Y	Y	N	N	N	N
27 Chu	N	Y	Y	N	N	N	Y
28 Schiff	N	Y	Y	N	N	N	N
29 Cardenas	N	Y	Y	N	N	N	N
30 Sherman	N	Y	Y	N	N	N	Y
31 Aguilar	N	Y	Y	N	N	N	N
32 Napolitano	N	Y	Y	N	N	N	N
33 Lieu	N	Y	Y	N	N	N	N
34 Gomez	N	Y	Y	N	N	N	N
35 Torres	N	Y	Y	N	N	N	N
36 Ruiz	N	Y	Y	N	N	N	N
37 Bass	N	Y	Y	N	N	N	N
38 Sánchez, Linda	N	Y	Y	N	N	N	N
39 **Royce**	Y	Y	Y	Y	Y	Y	Y
40 Roybal-Allard	N	+	+	–	–	–	–
41 Takano	N	Y	Y	N	N	N	Y
42 **Calvert**	Y	Y	Y	Y	Y	Y	Y
43 Waters	N	Y	Y	N	N	N	N
44 Barragan	N	Y	Y	N	N	N	N
45 **Walters**	Y	Y	Y	Y	Y	Y	Y
46 Correa	Y	Y	Y	N	N	N	N
47 Lowenthal	N	Y	Y	N	N	N	Y
48 **Rohrabacher**	Y	?	?	?	Y	Y	N
49 **Issa**	Y	Y	Y	Y	Y	Y	Y
50 **Hunter**	Y	Y	Y	N	Y	Y	N
51 Vargas	N	Y	Y	N	N	N	N
52 Peters	+	Y	Y	N	N	N	N
53 Davis	N	Y	Y	N	N	N	Y

	606	607	608	609	610	611	612
COLORADO							
1 DeGette	N	Y	Y	N	N	N	Y
2 Polis	N	+	+	?	?	?	?
3 **Tipton**	Y	Y	Y	N	Y	Y	N
4 **Buck**	Y	Y	Y	N	Y	N	N
5 **Lamborn**	Y	Y	Y	Y	Y	Y	Y
6 **Coffman**	Y	Y	Y	N	Y	N	N
7 Perlmutter	N	?	?	?	N	N	Y
CONNECTICUT							
1 Larson	N	Y	?	N	N	N	Y
2 Courtney	N	Y	Y	N	N	N	N
3 DeLauro	N	Y	Y	N	N	N	Y
4 Himes	N	Y	Y	N	N	N	N
5 Esty	N	Y	Y	N	N	N	N
DELAWARE							
AL Blunt Rochester	N	Y	Y	N	N	N	N
FLORIDA							
1 **Gaetz**	Y	Y	Y	N	Y	Y	N
2 **Dunn**	Y	Y	Y	?	Y	Y	Y
3 **Yoho**	Y	Y	Y	Y	Y	Y	N
4 **Rutherford**	Y	Y	Y	N	Y	Y	Y
5 Lawson	N	Y	Y	N	N	N	N
6 **DeSantis**	Y	Y	Y	N	Y	N	N
7 Murphy	Y	Y	Y	Y	N	N	Y
8 **Posey**	Y	Y	Y	Y	Y	N	N
9 Soto	N	Y	Y	N	N	N	N
10 Demings	N	Y	Y	N	N	N	N
11 **Webster**	Y	Y	Y	Y	Y	Y	Y
12 **Bilirakis**	Y	Y	Y	Y	Y	Y	Y
13 Crist	N	Y	Y	N	N	N	N
14 Castor	N	Y	Y	N	N	N	N
15 **Ross**	Y	Y	Y	Y	Y	Y	Y
16 **Buchanan**	Y	Y	Y	Y	Y	Y	Y
17 **Rooney, T.**	Y	Y	Y	N	Y	Y	N
18 **Mast**	Y	Y	Y	N	Y	Y	N
19 **Rooney, F.**	Y	Y	Y	Y	Y	Y	N
20 Hastings	N	?	?	?	?	?	N
21 Frankel	N	Y	Y	N	N	N	Y
22 Deutch	N	Y	Y	N	N	N	N
23 Wasserman Schultz	N	Y	Y	N	N	N	N
24 Wilson	–	+	+	+	–	–	–
25 **Diaz-Balart**	Y	?	?	?	Y	Y	Y
26 **Curbelo**	Y	Y	Y	Y	Y	Y	Y
27 **Ros-Lehtinen**	Y	Y	Y	N	Y	Y	N
GEORGIA							
1 **Carter**	Y	Y	Y	N	Y	Y	N
2 Bishop	?	Y	Y	N	N	N	Y
3 **Ferguson**	Y	Y	Y	N	Y	Y	Y
4 Johnson	N	Y	Y	?	?	?	?
5 Lewis	N	Y	Y	N	N	N	N
6 **Handel**	Y	Y	Y	Y	Y	Y	Y
7 **Woodall**	Y	Y	Y	N	Y	Y	N
8 **Scott, A.**	Y	Y	Y	Y	Y	Y	Y
9 **Collins**	Y	Y	Y	?	Y	Y	N
10 **Hice**	Y	Y	Y	N	Y	Y	N
11 **Loudermilk**	Y	Y	Y	Y	Y	Y	Y
12 **Allen**	Y	Y	Y	Y	Y	Y	Y
13 Scott, D.	N	Y	Y	N	N	N	Y
14 **Graves**	Y	Y	Y	N	Y	Y	N
HAWAII							
1 Hanabusa	N	Y	Y	N	N	N	Y
2 Gabbard	N	Y	Y	N	N	N	Y
IDAHO							
1 **Labrador**	Y	Y	Y	Y	Y	Y	Y
2 **Simpson**	Y	Y	Y	Y	Y	Y	Y
ILLINOIS							
1 Rush	N	Y	Y	N	N	N	N
2 Kelly	N	Y	Y	N	N	N	N
3 Lipinski	Y	Y	Y	N	N	N	Y
4 Gutierrez	–	?	?	?	N	N	N
5 Quigley	N	Y	Y	?	N	N	Y
6 **Roskam**	Y	Y	Y	Y	Y	Y	Y
7 Davis, D.	N	Y	Y	N	N	N	Y
8 Krishnamoorthi	N	Y	Y	N	N	N	N
9 Schakowsky	N	Y	Y	N	N	N	N
10 Schneider	N	Y	Y	N	N	N	N
11 Foster	N	Y	Y	N	N	N	Y
12 **Bost**	Y	Y	Y	N	Y	Y	N
13 **Davis, R.**	Y	Y	Y	N	Y	Y	N
14 **Hultgren**	Y	Y	Y	Y	Y	Y	Y
15 **Shimkus**	Y	Y	Y	Y	Y	Y	Y

KEY — Republicans — Democrats — *Independents*

Y Voted for (yea)	**X** Paired against	**C** Voted "present" to avoid possible conflict of interest
# Paired for	**–** Announced against	
+ Announced for	**P** Voted "present"	**?** Did not vote or otherwise make a position known
N Voted against (nay)		

	606	607	608	609	610	611	612
16 **Kinzinger**	Y	Y	Y	N	Y	Y	N
17 Bustos	N	Y	Y	Y	N	N	Y
18 **LaHood**	Y	Y	Y	N	Y	Y	N
INDIANA							
1 Visclosky	N	Y	Y	?	N	N	N
2 **Walorski**	Y	Y	Y	Y	Y	Y	Y
3 **Banks**	Y	Y	Y	Y	Y	Y	Y
4 **Rokita**	Y	Y	Y	N	Y	Y	N
5 **Brooks**	Y	Y	Y	Y	Y	Y	Y
6 **Messer**	Y	?	?	?	Y	Y	Y
7 Carson	N	Y	Y	Y	N	N	N
8 **Bucshon**	Y	Y	Y	Y	Y	Y	Y
9 **Hollingsworth**	Y	Y	Y	Y	Y	Y	Y
IOWA							
1 **Blum**	Y	Y	Y	N	Y	Y	N
2 Loebsack	Y	Y	Y	N	N	N	N
3 **Young**	Y	Y	Y	Y	Y	Y	Y
4 **King**	Y	Y	Y	Y	Y	Y	Y
KANSAS							
1 **Marshall**	Y	Y	Y	Y	Y	Y	Y
2 **Jenkins**	Y	Y	Y	N	Y	Y	N
3 **Yoder**	Y	Y	Y	N	Y	Y	N
4 **Estes**	Y	Y	Y	Y	Y	Y	Y
KENTUCKY							
1 **Comer**	Y	Y	Y	Y	Y	Y	Y
2 **Guthrie**	Y	Y	Y	Y	Y	Y	Y
3 Yarmuth	N	Y	Y	Y	N	N	Y
4 **Massie**	N	Y	Y	Y	Y	Y	Y
5 **Rogers**	Y	Y	Y	Y	Y	Y	Y
6 **Barr**	Y	Y	Y	Y	Y	Y	Y
LOUISIANA							
1 **Scalise**	Y	Y	Y	Y	Y	+	+
2 Richmond	N	Y	Y	Y	N	N	N
3 **Higgins**	Y	Y	Y	Y	Y	Y	Y
4 **Johnson**	Y	Y	Y	Y	Y	Y	Y
5 **Abraham**	Y	Y	Y	Y	Y	Y	Y
6 **Graves**	Y	Y	Y	N	Y	Y	N
MAINE							
1 Pingree	N	Y	Y	Y	N	N	Y
2 **Poliquin**	Y	Y	Y	N	Y	Y	N
MARYLAND							
1 **Harris**	Y	Y	Y	Y	Y	Y	Y
2 Ruppersberger	N	Y	Y	Y	N	N	Y
3 Sarbanes	N	Y	Y	N	N	N	N
4 Brown	N	Y	Y	Y	N	N	Y
5 Hoyer	N	Y	Y	N	?	?	?
6 Delaney	N	+	+	–	N	N	N
7 Cummings	N	Y	Y	Y	?	?	?
8 Raskin	N	Y	Y	N	N	N	N
MASSACHUSETTS							
1 Neal	N	Y	Y	N	N	N	N
2 McGovern	N	Y	Y	N	N	N	N
3 Tsongas	N	Y	Y	Y	N	N	Y
4 Kennedy	N	Y	Y	Y	N	N	Y
5 Clark	N	?	?	?	N	N	N
6 Moulton	N	Y	Y	Y	N	N	Y
7 Capuano	N	Y	Y	N	N	N	N
8 Lynch	N	Y	Y	N	N	N	N
9 Keating	N	Y	Y	N	N	N	Y
MICHIGAN							
1 **Bergman**	Y	Y	Y	N	Y	Y	N
2 **Huizenga**	Y	Y	Y	Y	Y	Y	N
3 **Amash**	N	Y	Y	N	Y	Y	N
4 **Moolenaar**	Y	Y	Y	Y	Y	Y	Y
5 Kildee	N	Y	Y	Y	N	N	Y
6 **Upton**	?	?	?	?	Y	Y	Y
7 **Walberg**	Y	Y	Y	N	Y	Y	N
8 **Bishop**	Y	Y	Y	N	Y	Y	N
9 Levin	N	Y	Y	Y	N	N	N
10 **Mitchell**	Y	Y	Y	N	Y	Y	Y
11 **Trott**	Y	Y	Y	Y	Y	Y	Y
12 Dingell	N	Y	Y	N	N	N	Y
13 Conyers	N	Y	Y	Y	N	N	N
14 Lawrence	N	Y	Y	N	N	N	Y
MINNESOTA							
1 Walz	N	Y	Y	Y	N	N	Y
2 **Lewis**	Y	Y	Y	Y	Y	Y	Y
3 **Paulsen**	Y	Y	Y	N	Y	Y	N
4 McCollum	N	Y	Y	Y	N	N	Y

	606	607	608	609	610	611	612
5 Ellison	N	Y	Y	P	N	N	P
6 **Emmer**	Y	Y	Y	Y	Y	Y	Y
7 Peterson	Y	Y	Y	N	Y	N	N
8 Nolan	N	Y	Y	N	N	N	N
MISSISSIPPI							
1 **Kelly**	Y	Y	Y	Y	Y	Y	Y
2 Thompson	N	?	?	?	?	?	?
3 **Harper**	Y	Y	Y	Y	Y	Y	Y
4 **Palazzo**	Y	Y	Y	N	Y	Y	N
MISSOURI							
1 Clay	N	Y	Y	Y	N	N	Y
2 **Wagner**	Y	Y	Y	Y	Y	Y	Y
3 **Luetkemeyer**	Y	Y	Y	Y	Y	Y	Y
4 **Hartzler**	Y	Y	Y	N	Y	Y	Y
5 Cleaver	N	Y	Y	Y	N	N	Y
6 **Graves**	Y	Y	Y	N	Y	Y	N
7 **Long**	Y	Y	Y	Y	Y	Y	Y
8 **Smith**	Y	Y	Y	N	Y	Y	N
MONTANA							
AL **Gianforte**	Y	Y	Y	Y	Y	Y	Y
NEBRASKA							
1 **Fortenberry**	Y	Y	Y	Y	Y	Y	Y
2 **Bacon**	Y	Y	Y	Y	Y	Y	Y
3 **Smith**	Y	Y	Y	Y	Y	Y	Y
NEVADA							
1 Titus	N	Y	Y	Y	N	N	Y
2 **Amodei**	Y	Y	Y	Y	Y	Y	Y
3 Rosen	Y	Y	Y	N	N	N	Y
4 Kihuen	N	Y	Y	N	N	N	N
NEW HAMPSHIRE							
1 Shea-Porter	N	Y	Y	Y	N	N	Y
2 Kuster	N	Y	Y	Y	N	N	Y
NEW JERSEY							
1 Norcross	N	Y	Y	N	N	N	N
2 **LoBiondo**	Y	Y	Y	N	Y	Y	N
3 **MacArthur**	Y	Y	Y	N	Y	Y	N
4 **Smith**	Y	Y	Y	Y	Y	Y	Y
5 Gottheimer	N	Y	Y	N	N	N	N
6 Pallone	N	Y	Y	N	N	N	N
7 **Lance**	Y	Y	Y	N	Y	Y	N
8 Sires	N	Y	Y	N	N	N	N
9 Pascrell	N	Y	Y	Y	N	N	?
10 Payne	N	Y	Y	N	N	N	N
11 **Frelinghuysen**	Y	Y	Y	Y	Y	Y	Y
12 Watson Coleman	N	Y	Y	N	N	N	N
NEW MEXICO							
1 Lujan Grisham	N	Y	Y	Y	N	N	Y
2 **Pearce**	Y	Y	Y	N	Y	Y	N
3 Luján	N	Y	Y	N	N	N	+
NEW YORK							
1 **Zeldin**	Y	Y	Y	Y	Y	Y	Y
2 **King**	Y	Y	Y	N	Y	Y	Y
3 Suozzi	N	Y	Y	N	N	N	N
4 Rice	N	Y	Y	N	N	N	N
5 Meeks	N	?	?	?	N	N	Y
6 Meng	N	Y	Y	Y	N	N	Y
7 Velázquez	N	Y	Y	N	N	N	N
8 Jeffries	N	Y	Y	N	N	N	Y
9 Clarke	N	Y	Y	N	N	N	N
10 Nadler	N	Y	Y	Y	N	N	Y
11 **Donovan**	Y	Y	Y	Y	Y	Y	Y
12 Maloney, C.	N	?	?	?	N	N	Y
13 Espaillat	N	Y	Y	N	N	N	N
14 Crowley	N	Y	Y	N	N	N	N
15 Serrano	N	Y	Y	Y	N	N	N
16 Engel	N	Y	Y	N	N	N	Y
17 Lowey	N	Y	Y	Y	N	N	Y
18 Maloney, S.P.	N	?	?	?	N	N	N
19 **Faso**	Y	Y	Y	Y	Y	Y	N
20 Tonko	N	Y	Y	P	N	N	P
21 **Stefanik**	Y	Y	Y	Y	Y	Y	Y
22 **Tenney**	Y	Y	Y	N	Y	Y	N
23 **Reed**	Y	Y	Y	N	Y	Y	N
24 **Katko**	Y	Y	Y	N	Y	Y	N
25 Slaughter	N	Y	Y	N	N	N	N
26 Higgins	N	Y	Y	Y	N	N	N
27 **Collins**	Y	Y	Y	Y	Y	Y	Y
NORTH CAROLINA							
1 Butterfield	N	Y	Y	Y	N	N	Y
2 **Holding**	Y	Y	Y	N	Y	Y	N
3 **Jones**	Y	?	?	?	N	Y	N
4 Price	N	Y	Y	N	N	N	N

	606	607	608	609	610	611	612
5 **Foxx**	Y	Y	Y	N	Y	Y	N
6 **Walker**	Y	Y	Y	Y	Y	Y	Y
7 **Rouzer**	Y	Y	Y	N	Y	Y	N
8 **Hudson**	Y	Y	Y	N	+	+	–
9 **Pittenger**	Y	Y	Y	N	Y	Y	N
10 **McHenry**	Y	Y	Y	Y	Y	Y	Y
11 **Meadows**	Y	Y	Y	Y	Y	Y	Y
12 Adams	N	Y	Y	N	N	N	Y
13 **Budd**	Y	Y	Y	N	Y	Y	Y
NORTH DAKOTA							
AL **Cramer**	Y	Y	Y	Y	Y	Y	Y
OHIO							
1 **Chabot**	Y	Y	Y	Y	Y	Y	Y
2 **Wenstrup**	Y	Y	Y	Y	Y	Y	Y
3 Beatty	N	Y	Y	Y	N	N	Y
4 **Jordan**	Y	Y	Y	N	Y	Y	N
5 **Latta**	Y	Y	Y	N	Y	Y	Y
6 **Johnson**	Y	Y	Y	N	Y	Y	N
7 **Gibbs**	Y	Y	Y	Y	Y	Y	N
8 **Davidson**	Y	Y	Y	Y	Y	Y	Y
9 Kaptur	N	Y	Y	Y	N	N	Y
10 **Turner**	Y	Y	Y	N	Y	Y	N
11 Fudge	N	Y	Y	N	N	N	N
12 **Tiberi**	Y	Y	Y	Y	Y	Y	Y
13 Ryan	N	Y	Y	N	N	N	N
14 **Joyce**	Y	Y	Y	N	Y	Y	N
15 **Stivers**	Y	Y	Y	N	Y	Y	N
16 **Renacci**	Y	Y	Y	N	Y	Y	N
OKLAHOMA							
1 **Bridenstine**	?	?	?	?	?	?	?
2 **Mullin**	Y	Y	Y	Y	Y	Y	Y
3 **Lucas**	Y	Y	Y	Y	Y	Y	Y
4 **Cole**	Y	Y	Y	Y	Y	Y	Y
5 **Russell**	Y	Y	Y	Y	Y	Y	Y
OREGON							
1 Bonamici	N	Y	Y	Y	N	N	Y
2 **Walden**	Y	Y	Y	Y	Y	Y	Y
3 Blumenauer	N	Y	Y	Y	N	N	Y
4 DeFazio	N	Y	Y	N	N	N	N
5 Schrader	Y	Y	Y	N	N	N	N
PENNSYLVANIA							
1 Brady	N	Y	Y	N	?	?	?
2 Evans	N	Y	Y	Y	N	N	Y
3 **Kelly**	Y	Y	Y	Y	Y	Y	Y
4 **Perry**	Y	Y	Y	N	Y	Y	N
5 **Thompson**	Y	Y	Y	N	Y	Y	N
6 **Costello**	Y	Y	Y	N	Y	Y	N
7 **Meehan**	Y	Y	Y	N	Y	Y	Y
8 **Fitzpatrick**	Y	Y	Y	N	Y	Y	N
9 **Shuster**	Y	Y	Y	Y	Y	Y	Y
10 **Marino**	Y	Y	Y	Y	Y	Y	Y
11 **Barletta**	Y	Y	Y	Y	Y	Y	Y
12 **Rothfus**	Y	Y	Y	Y	Y	Y	Y
13 Boyle	N	+	+	?	N	N	N
14 Doyle	N	Y	Y	Y	N	N	N
15 **Dent**	Y	Y	Y	Y	Y	Y	Y
16 **Smucker**	Y	Y	Y	N	Y	Y	N
17 Cartwright	N	Y	Y	Y	N	N	Y
RHODE ISLAND							
1 Cicilline	N	Y	Y	Y	N	N	Y
2 Langevin	N	+	+	–	N	N	N
SOUTH CAROLINA							
1 **Sanford**	Y	Y	Y	Y	Y	Y	Y
2 **Wilson**	Y	Y	Y	Y	Y	Y	Y
3 **Duncan**	Y	Y	Y	Y	Y	Y	Y
4 **Gowdy**	Y	?	?	?	Y	Y	Y
5 **Norman**	Y	Y	Y	Y	Y	Y	Y
6 Clyburn	N	Y	Y	N	N	N	N
7 **Rice**	Y	Y	Y	P	?	Y	P
SOUTH DAKOTA							
AL **Noem**	Y	Y	Y	N	Y	Y	N
TENNESSEE							
1 **Roe**	Y	Y	Y	N	Y	Y	Y
2 **Duncan**	Y	Y	Y	Y	Y	Y	Y
3 **Fleischmann**	Y	Y	Y	Y	Y	Y	Y
4 **DesJarlais**	Y	+	+	?	?	?	?
5 Cooper	N	Y	Y	Y	N	N	Y
6 **Black**	+	Y	Y	Y	Y	Y	Y
7 **Blackburn**	Y	+	+	N	Y	Y	Y
8 **Kustoff**	Y	Y	Y	Y	Y	Y	Y
9 Cohen	N	Y	Y	Y	N	N	Y

	606	607	608	609	610	611	612
TEXAS							
1 **Gohmert**	Y	?	Y	?	Y	Y	?
2 **Poe**	Y	Y	Y	N	Y	Y	N
3 **Johnson, S.**	?	Y	Y	Y	Y	Y	Y
4 **Ratcliffe**	Y	Y	Y	N	Y	Y	N
5 **Hensarling**	Y	Y	Y	Y	Y	Y	Y
6 **Barton**	Y	Y	Y	Y	Y	Y	Y
7 **Culberson**	Y	Y	Y	Y	Y	Y	Y
8 **Brady**	Y	Y	Y	?	Y	Y	Y
9 Green, A.	N	Y	Y	Y	N	N	Y
10 **McCaul**	Y	Y	Y	Y	Y	Y	Y
11 **Conaway**	Y	Y	Y	N	Y	Y	N
12 **Granger**	Y	+	+	+	Y	Y	Y
13 **Thornberry**	Y	?	?	?	Y	Y	Y
14 **Weber**	Y	Y	Y	N	Y	Y	N
15 Gonzalez	N	Y	Y	N	N	N	N
16 O'Rourke	N	Y	Y	Y	N	N	Y
17 **Flores**	Y	Y	Y	N	Y	Y	N
18 Jackson Lee	–	Y	Y	N	N	N	N
19 **Arrington**	Y	Y	Y	Y	Y	Y	Y
20 Castro	N	Y	Y	Y	N	N	Y
21 **Smith**	Y	Y	Y	Y	Y	Y	Y
22 **Olson**	Y	Y	Y	Y	Y	Y	Y
23 **Hurd**	Y	Y	Y	Y	Y	Y	N
24 **Marchant**	Y	Y	Y	N	Y	Y	N
25 **Williams**	?	Y	Y	Y	Y	Y	Y
26 **Burgess**	Y	Y	Y	N	Y	Y	N
27 **Farenthold**	Y	Y	Y	Y	Y	Y	Y
28 Cuellar	Y	Y	Y	Y	N	N	N
29 Green, G.	N	Y	Y	N	N	N	N
30 Johnson, E.B.	?	+	+	–	–	–	–
31 **Carter**	Y	Y	Y	N	Y	Y	Y
32 **Sessions**	Y	Y	Y	Y	Y	Y	Y
33 Veasey	N	Y	Y	N	N	N	N
34 Vela	N	Y	Y	Y	N	N	Y
35 Doggett	N	Y	Y	Y	N	N	Y
36 **Babin**	Y	Y	Y	N	Y	Y	N
UTAH							
1 **Bishop**	Y	Y	Y	Y	Y	Y	Y
2 **Stewart**	Y	Y	Y	Y	Y	Y	Y
4 **Love**	Y	Y	Y	Y	Y	Y	N
VERMONT							
AL Welch	N	Y	Y	Y	N	N	Y
VIRGINIA							
1 **Wittman**	Y	Y	Y	Y	Y	Y	Y
2 **Taylor**	Y	Y	Y	Y	Y	Y	Y
3 Scott	N	Y	Y	Y	N	N	Y
4 McEachin	N	Y	Y	Y	N	N	Y
5 **Garrett**	Y	+	+	+	?	?	?
6 **Goodlatte**	Y	Y	Y	Y	Y	Y	Y
7 **Brat**	Y	Y	Y	Y	Y	Y	Y
8 Beyer	N	Y	Y	N	N	N	N
9 **Griffith**	Y	Y	Y	Y	Y	Y	Y
10 **Comstock**	Y	Y	Y	Y	Y	Y	Y
11 Connolly	N	Y	Y	N	N	N	N
WASHINGTON							
1 DelBene	N	Y	Y	Y	N	N	Y
2 Larsen	N	Y	Y	?	N	N	N
3 **Herrera Beutler**	Y	Y	Y	Y	Y	Y	N
4 **Newhouse**	Y	Y	?	Y	Y	Y	Y
5 **McMorris Rodgers**	Y	Y	Y	Y	Y	Y	Y
6 Kilmer	N	Y	Y	N	N	N	N
7 Jayapal	N	Y	Y	N	N	N	N
8 **Reichert**	Y	Y	Y	Y	Y	Y	N
9 Smith	N	Y	Y	Y	N	N	Y
10 Heck	N	Y	Y	Y	N	N	Y
WEST VIRGINIA							
1 **McKinley**	Y	Y	Y	N	Y	Y	N
2 **Mooney**	Y	Y	Y	Y	Y	Y	Y
3 **Jenkins**	Y	Y	Y	N	Y	Y	N
WISCONSIN							
1 **Ryan**							
2 Pocan	–	+	+	+	–	–	+
3 Kind	Y	Y	Y	N	N	N	N
4 Moore	N	Y	Y	Y	N	N	N
5 **Sensenbrenner**	Y	Y	Y	Y	Y	Y	Y
6 **Grothman**	Y	Y	Y	Y	Y	Y	Y
7 **Duffy**	Y	Y	Y	N	Y	Y	N
8 **Gallagher**	Y	Y	Y	N	Y	Y	N
WYOMING							
AL **Cheney**	Y	Y	Y	N	Y	Y	N

VOTE NUMBER

613. HR 3441. JOINT EMPLOYER DEFINITION/RECOMMIT. Bonamici, D-Ore., motion to recommit the bill to the House Education and the Workforce Committee with instructions to report it back immediately with an amendment that would require a franchisor to be treated as a joint employer if a franchisee violates labor laws at the direction of the franchisor. Motion rejected 186-235 : R 1-233; D 185-2. Nov. 7, 2017.

614. HR 3441. JOINT EMPLOYER DEFINITION/PASSAGE. Passage of the bill that would define a joint employer as an entity with actual, direct and immediate control over employees, with significant control over essential terms of employment such as hiring, determining pay and benefits, day-to-day supervision of employees, and assigning individual work schedules. Passed 242-181 : R 234-0; D 8-181. Nov. 7, 2017.

615. HR 3911. CREDIT RATING ORGANIZATION EXAMINATIONS/PASSAGE. Huizenga, R-Mich., motion to suspend the rules and pass the bill that would authorize the Securities and Exchange Commission to modify the requirements for annual credit rating organization examinations as appropriate for each organization reviewed. Motion agreed to 389-32 : R 232-1; D 157-31. Nov. 7, 2017.

616. H RES 609, HR 2201. SECURITIES REGULATIONS EXEMPTIONS/ PREVIOUS QUESTION. Buck, R-Colo., motion to order the previous question (thus ending debate and the possibility of amendment) on the rule (H Res 609) that would provide for House floor consideration of the bill (HR 2201) that would require an issuer of securities to meet a specific set of criteria in order for the issuer's transactions to constitute a sale of "nonpublic" securities that are exempt from registration with the Securities and Exchange Commission and from state regulation. Motion agreed to 224-190 : R 224-0; D 0-190. Nov. 8, 2017.

617. H RES 609, HR 2201. SECURITIES REGULATIONS EXEMPTIONS/RULE. Adoption of the rule (H Res 609) that would provide for House floor consideration of the bill (HR 2201) that would require an issuer of securities to meet a specific set of criteria in order for the issuer's transactions to constitute a sale of "nonpublic" securities that are exempt from registration with the Securities and Exchange Commission and from state regulation. Adopted 233-190 : R 233-0; D 0-190. Nov. 8, 2017.

618. HR 4173. VETERANS CRISIS LINE REPORT/PASSAGE. Bilirakis, R-Fla., motion to suspend the rules and pass the bill that would require the VA to conduct a study on the outcomes and efficacy of the Veterans Crisis Line and report to Congress with its findings by March 1, 2020. Motion agreed to 420-0 : R 230-0; D 190-0. Nov. 8, 2017.

619. HR 3043. HYDROPOWER REGULATION/AGENCY COORDINATION RULE. Rush, D-Ill., amendment that would replace the entirety of the bill's provisions with a requirement that a number of federal agencies work alongside other stakeholders, including tribal organizations, to develop a rule that would provide a new process for coordinated federal hydropower project licensing. Rejected in Committee of the Whole 185-234 : R 4-229; D 181-5. Nov. 8, 2017.

	613	614	615	616	617	618	619
ALABAMA							
1 **Byrne**	N	Y	Y	Y	Y	Y	N
2 **Roby**	N	Y	Y	Y	Y	Y	N
3 **Rogers**	N	Y	Y	Y	Y	Y	N
4 **Aderholt**	N	Y	Y	?	?	Y	N
5 **Brooks**	N	Y	Y	Y	Y	Y	N
6 **Palmer**	N	Y	Y	Y	Y	Y	N
7 Sewell	Y	N	Y	N	N	Y	Y
ALASKA							
AL **Young**	N	Y	Y	Y	Y	Y	Y
ARIZONA							
1 O'Halleran	Y	N	Y	N	N	Y	Y
2 **McSally**	N	Y	Y	Y	Y	Y	N
3 Grijalva	Y	N	N	N	N	Y	Y
4 **Gosar**	N	Y	Y	?	Y	Y	N
5 **Biggs**	N	Y	Y	Y	Y	Y	N
6 **Schweikert**	N	Y	Y	Y	Y	Y	N
7 Gallego	Y	N	N	N	N	Y	Y
8 **Franks**	N	Y	Y	Y	Y	+	N
9 Sinema	Y	N	Y	N	N	Y	Y
ARKANSAS							
1 **Crawford**	N	Y	Y	Y	Y	Y	N
2 **Hill**	N	Y	Y	Y	Y	Y	N
3 **Womack**	N	Y	Y	Y	Y	Y	N
4 **Westerman**	N	Y	Y	Y	Y	Y	N
CALIFORNIA							
1 **LaMalfa**	N	Y	Y	?	Y	Y	N
2 Huffman	Y	N	N	N	N	Y	Y
3 Garamendi	Y	N	Y	N	N	Y	Y
4 **McClintock**	N	Y	Y	Y	Y	Y	N
5 Thompson	Y	N	Y	N	N	Y	Y
6 Matsui	Y	N	Y	N	N	Y	Y
7 Bera	Y	Y	Y	N	N	Y	Y
8 **Cook**	N	Y	Y	Y	Y	Y	N
9 McNerney	Y	N	Y	N	N	Y	N
10 **Denham**	N	Y	Y	Y	Y	Y	N
11 DeSaulnier	Y	N	N	N	N	Y	Y
12 Pelosi	?	N	Y	N	N	Y	?
13 Lee	Y	N	Y	N	N	Y	Y
14 Speier	Y	N	N	N	N	Y	Y
15 Swalwell	Y	N	Y	N	N	Y	Y
16 Costa	N	Y	Y	N	N	Y	N
17 Khanna	Y	N	N	N	N	Y	Y
18 Eshoo	Y	N	Y	N	N	Y	Y
19 Lofgren	Y	N	Y	N	N	Y	Y
20 Panetta	Y	N	Y	N	N	Y	Y
21 **Valadao**	N	Y	Y	Y	Y	Y	N
22 **Nunes**	N	Y	Y	Y	Y	Y	N
23 **McCarthy**	N	Y	Y	Y	Y	Y	N
24 Carbajal	Y	N	Y	N	N	Y	Y
25 **Knight**	N	Y	Y	Y	Y	Y	N
26 Brownley	Y	N	Y	N	N	Y	Y
27 Chu	Y	N	N	N	N	Y	Y
28 Schiff	Y	N	Y	N	N	Y	Y
29 Cardenas	Y	N	Y	N	N	Y	Y
30 Sherman	Y	N	Y	N	N	Y	Y
31 Aguilar	Y	N	Y	N	N	Y	Y
32 Napolitano	Y	N	Y	N	N	Y	Y
33 Lieu	Y	N	N	N	N	Y	Y
34 Gomez	Y	N	Y	N	N	Y	Y
35 Torres	Y	N	Y	N	N	Y	Y
36 Ruiz	Y	N	Y	N	N	Y	Y
37 Bass	Y	N	Y	N	N	Y	Y
38 Sánchez, Linda	Y	N	Y	N	N	Y	Y
39 **Royce**	N	Y	Y	Y	Y	Y	N
40 Roybal-Allard	+	-	-	-	-	+	+
41 Takano	Y	N	Y	N	N	Y	Y
42 **Calvert**	N	Y	Y	Y	Y	Y	N
43 Waters	Y	N	Y	N	N	Y	Y
44 Barragan	Y	N	Y	N	N	Y	Y
45 **Walters**	N	Y	Y	Y	Y	Y	N
46 Correa	Y	Y	Y	N	N	Y	Y
47 Lowenthal	Y	N	N	N	N	Y	Y
48 **Rohrabacher**	N	Y	Y	Y	Y	Y	N
49 **Issa**	N	Y	Y	Y	Y	Y	N
50 **Hunter**	N	Y	Y	Y	Y	Y	N
51 Vargas	Y	N	Y	N	N	Y	Y
52 Peters	Y	Y	Y	N	N	Y	N
53 Davis	Y	N	Y	N	N	Y	Y

	613	614	615	616	617	618	619
COLORADO							
1 DeGette	Y	N	Y	N	N	Y	Y
2 Polis	Y	N	N	N	N	Y	Y
3 **Tipton**	N	Y	Y	Y	Y	Y	N
4 **Buck**	N	Y	Y	Y	Y	Y	N
5 **Lamborn**	N	Y	Y	Y	Y	Y	N
6 **Coffman**	N	Y	Y	+	Y	Y	N
7 Perlmutter	Y	N	Y	N	N	Y	Y
CONNECTICUT							
1 Larson	Y	N	Y	N	N	Y	Y
2 Courtney	Y	N	Y	N	N	Y	Y
3 DeLauro	Y	N	Y	N	N	Y	Y
4 Himes	Y	N	Y	N	N	Y	Y
5 Esty	Y	N	Y	N	N	Y	Y
DELAWARE							
AL Blunt Rochester	Y	N	Y	N	N	Y	Y
FLORIDA							
1 **Gaetz**	N	Y	Y	Y	Y	Y	N
2 **Dunn**	N	Y	Y	Y	Y	Y	N
3 **Yoho**	N	Y	Y	Y	Y	Y	N
4 **Rutherford**	N	Y	Y	Y	Y	Y	N
5 Lawson	Y	N	Y	N	N	Y	+
6 **DeSantis**	N	Y	Y	Y	Y	Y	N
7 Murphy	Y	N	Y	N	N	Y	Y
8 **Posey**	N	Y	Y	Y	Y	Y	N
9 Soto	Y	N	Y	N	N	Y	Y
10 Demings	Y	N	Y	N	N	Y	Y
11 **Webster**	N	Y	Y	Y	Y	Y	N
12 **Bilirakis**	N	Y	Y	Y	Y	Y	N
13 Crist	Y	N	Y	N	N	Y	Y
14 Castor	Y	N	Y	N	N	Y	Y
15 **Ross**	N	Y	Y	Y	Y	Y	N
16 **Buchanan**	N	Y	Y	Y	Y	Y	N
17 **Rooney, T.**	N	Y	Y	?	Y	Y	N
18 **Mast**	N	Y	Y	Y	Y	Y	N
19 **Rooney, F.**	N	Y	Y	Y	Y	Y	N
20 Hastings	Y	N	Y	N	N	Y	Y
21 Frankel	Y	N	Y	N	N	Y	Y
22 Deutch	Y	N	N	N	N	Y	Y
23 Wasserman Schultz	Y	N	N	N	N	Y	Y
24 Wilson	Y	N	Y	N	N	Y	Y
25 **Diaz-Balart**	N	Y	Y	Y	Y	Y	N
26 **Curbelo**	N	Y	Y	Y	Y	Y	N
27 **Ros-Lehtinen**	N	Y	Y	Y	Y	Y	N
GEORGIA							
1 **Carter**	N	Y	Y	Y	Y	Y	N
2 Bishop	Y	N	Y	N	N	Y	Y
3 **Ferguson**	N	Y	Y	Y	Y	Y	N
4 Johnson	Y	N	Y	N	N	Y	Y
5 Lewis	Y	N	Y	N	N	Y	Y
6 **Handel**	N	Y	Y	Y	Y	Y	N
7 **Woodall**	N	Y	Y	Y	Y	Y	N
8 **Scott, A.**	N	Y	Y	Y	Y	Y	N
9 **Collins**	N	Y	Y	Y	Y	Y	N
10 **Hice**	N	Y	Y	Y	Y	Y	N
11 **Loudermilk**	N	Y	Y	Y	Y	Y	N
12 **Allen**	N	Y	Y	Y	Y	?	N
13 Scott, D.	Y	N	Y	N	N	Y	?
14 **Graves**	N	Y	Y	Y	Y	Y	N
HAWAII							
1 Hanabusa	Y	N	Y	N	N	Y	Y
2 Gabbard	Y	N	N	N	N	Y	Y
IDAHO							
1 **Labrador**	N	Y	Y	Y	Y	Y	N
2 **Simpson**	N	Y	Y	Y	Y	Y	N
ILLINOIS							
1 Rush	Y	N	Y	N	N	Y	Y
2 Kelly	Y	N	Y	N	N	Y	Y
3 Lipinski	Y	N	Y	N	N	Y	Y
4 Gutierrez	Y	N	N	N	N	Y	Y
5 Quigley	Y	N	N	N	N	Y	Y
6 **Roskam**	N	Y	Y	Y	Y	?	N
7 Davis, D.	Y	N	Y	N	N	Y	Y
8 Krishnamoorthi	Y	N	Y	N	N	Y	Y
9 Schakowsky	Y	N	N	N	N	Y	Y
10 Schneider	Y	N	Y	N	N	Y	Y
11 Foster	Y	N	Y	N	N	Y	Y
12 **Bost**	N	Y	Y	Y	Y	Y	N
13 **Davis, R.**	N	Y	Y	Y	Y	Y	N
14 **Hultgren**	N	Y	Y	Y	Y	Y	N
15 **Shimkus**	N	Y	Y	Y	Y	Y	N

KEY | Republicans | Democrats | *Independents*

Y Voted for (yea)	**X** Paired against
# Paired for	**–** Announced against
+ Announced for	**P** Voted "present"
N Voted against (nay)	**C** Voted "present" to avoid possible conflict of interest
	? Did not vote or otherwise make a position known

	613	614	615	616	617	618	619
16 **Kinzinger**	N	Y	Y	Y	Y	Y	N
17 Bustos	+	N	Y	N	N	Y	Y
18 **LaHood**	N	Y	Y	Y	Y	Y	N
INDIANA							
1 Visclosky	Y	N	Y	N	N	Y	Y
2 **Walorski**	N	Y	Y	Y	Y	Y	N
3 **Banks**	N	Y	Y	Y	Y	Y	N
4 **Rokita**	N	Y	Y	Y	Y	Y	N
5 **Brooks**	N	Y	Y	Y	Y	Y	N
6 **Messer**	N	Y	Y	Y	Y	?	N
7 Carson	Y	N	N	N	N	Y	Y
8 **Bucshon**	N	Y	Y	Y	Y	Y	N
9 **Hollingsworth**	N	Y	Y	Y	Y	Y	N
IOWA							
1 **Blum**	N	Y	Y	Y	Y	Y	N
2 Loebsack	Y	N	Y	N	N	Y	Y
3 **Young**	N	Y	Y	Y	Y	Y	N
4 **King**	N	Y	Y	Y	Y	Y	N
KANSAS							
1 **Marshall**	N	Y	Y	Y	Y	Y	N
2 **Jenkins**	N	Y	Y	Y	Y	Y	N
3 **Yoder**	N	Y	Y	Y	Y	Y	N
4 **Estes**	N	Y	Y	Y	Y	Y	N
KENTUCKY							
1 **Comer**	N	Y	Y	Y	Y	Y	N
2 **Guthrie**	N	Y	Y	Y	Y	Y	N
3 Yarmuth	Y	N	Y	N	N	Y	Y
4 **Massie**	N	Y	Y	Y	Y	Y	N
5 **Rogers**	N	Y	Y	Y	Y	Y	N
6 **Barr**	N	Y	Y	Y	Y	Y	N
LOUISIANA							
1 **Scalise**	N	Y	Y	Y	Y	Y	–
2 Richmond	Y	N	Y	N	N	Y	Y
3 **Higgins**	N	Y	Y	Y	Y	Y	N
4 **Johnson**	N	Y	Y	Y	Y	Y	N
5 **Abraham**	N	Y	Y	Y	Y	Y	N
6 **Graves**	N	Y	Y	Y	Y	Y	N
MAINE							
1 Pingree	Y	N	N	N	N	Y	Y
2 **Poliquin**	N	Y	Y	Y	Y	Y	N
MARYLAND							
1 **Harris**	N	Y	Y	Y	Y	Y	N
2 Ruppersberger	Y	N	Y	N	N	Y	Y
3 Sarbanes	Y	N	Y	N	N	Y	Y
4 Brown	Y	N	Y	N	N	Y	Y
5 Hoyer	Y	N	Y	N	N	Y	Y
6 Delaney	Y	N	Y	N	N	Y	Y
7 Cummings	Y	N	N	N	N	Y	Y
8 Raskin	Y	N	Y	N	N	Y	Y
MASSACHUSETTS							
1 Neal	Y	N	Y	N	N	Y	Y
2 McGovern	Y	N	N	N	N	Y	Y
3 Tsongas	Y	N	Y	N	N	Y	Y
4 Kennedy	Y	N	Y	N	N	Y	Y
5 Clark	Y	N	Y	N	N	Y	+
6 Moulton	Y	N	Y	N	N	Y	Y
7 Capuano	Y	N	Y	N	N	Y	Y
8 Lynch	Y	N	Y	N	N	Y	Y
9 Keating	Y	N	Y	N	N	Y	Y
MICHIGAN							
1 **Bergman**	N	Y	Y	Y	Y	Y	N
2 **Huizenga**	N	Y	Y	Y	Y	Y	N
3 **Amash**	N	Y	Y	Y	Y	Y	N
4 **Moolenaar**	N	Y	Y	Y	Y	Y	N
5 Kildee	Y	N	Y	N	N	Y	Y
6 **Upton**	N	Y	Y	Y	Y	Y	N
7 **Walberg**	N	Y	Y	Y	Y	Y	N
8 **Bishop**	N	Y	Y	Y	Y	Y	N
9 Levin	Y	N	Y	N	N	Y	Y
10 **Mitchell**	N	Y	Y	?	?	?	?
11 **Trott**	N	Y	Y	Y	Y	Y	N
12 Dingell	Y	N	Y	N	N	Y	Y
13 Conyers	Y	N	Y	N	N	Y	Y
14 Lawrence	Y	N	Y	N	N	Y	Y
MINNESOTA							
1 Walz	Y	N	Y	N	N	Y	Y
2 **Lewis**	N	Y	Y	Y	Y	Y	N
3 **Paulsen**	N	Y	Y	Y	Y	Y	N
4 McCollum	Y	N	Y	N	N	Y	Y

	613	614	615	616	617	618	619
5 Ellison	+	–	?	N	N	Y	Y
6 **Emmer**	N	Y	Y	Y	Y	Y	N
7 Peterson	Y	Y	Y	N	N	Y	N
8 Nolan	Y	N	Y	N	N	Y	Y
MISSISSIPPI							
1 **Kelly**	N	Y	Y	Y	Y	Y	N
2 Thompson	Y	N	Y	N	N	Y	Y
3 **Harper**	N	Y	Y	Y	Y	Y	N
4 **Palazzo**	N	Y	Y	Y	Y	Y	N
MISSOURI							
1 Clay	Y	N	Y	N	N	Y	Y
2 **Wagner**	N	Y	Y	Y	Y	Y	N
3 **Luetkemeyer**	N	Y	Y	Y	Y	Y	N
4 **Hartzler**	N	Y	Y	Y	Y	Y	N
5 Cleaver	Y	N	Y	N	N	Y	Y
6 **Graves**	N	Y	Y	Y	Y	Y	N
7 **Long**	N	Y	Y	Y	Y	Y	N
8 **Smith**	N	Y	Y	Y	Y	Y	N
MONTANA							
AL **Gianforte**	N	Y	Y	Y	Y	Y	N
NEBRASKA							
1 **Fortenberry**	N	Y	?	Y	Y	Y	N
2 **Bacon**	N	Y	Y	Y	Y	Y	N
3 **Smith**	N	Y	Y	Y	Y	Y	N
NEVADA							
1 Titus	Y	N	N	N	N	Y	Y
2 **Amodei**	N	Y	Y	Y	Y	Y	N
3 Rosen	Y	N	Y	N	N	Y	Y
4 Kihuen	Y	N	Y	N	N	Y	Y
NEW HAMPSHIRE							
1 Shea-Porter	Y	N	Y	N	N	Y	Y
2 Kuster	Y	N	Y	N	N	Y	Y
NEW JERSEY							
1 Norcross	Y	N	Y	N	N	Y	Y
2 **LoBiondo**	N	Y	Y	Y	Y	Y	N
3 **MacArthur**	N	Y	Y	Y	Y	Y	N
4 **Smith**	N	Y	Y	Y	Y	Y	N
5 Gottheimer	N	N	Y	N	N	Y	Y
6 Pallone	Y	N	Y	N	N	Y	Y
7 **Lance**	N	Y	Y	Y	Y	Y	N
8 Sires	Y	N	Y	N	N	Y	Y
9 Pascrell	Y	N	Y	N	N	Y	Y
10 Payne	Y	N	Y	N	N	Y	Y
11 **Frelinghuysen**	N	Y	Y	Y	Y	Y	N
12 Watson Coleman	Y	N	N	N	N	Y	Y
NEW MEXICO							
1 Lujan Grisham	Y	N	Y	N	N	Y	Y
2 **Pearce**	N	Y	Y	Y	Y	Y	N
3 Luján	Y	N	Y	N	N	Y	Y
NEW YORK							
1 **Zeldin**	N	Y	Y	Y	Y	Y	N
2 **King**	N	Y	Y	Y	Y	Y	N
3 Suozzi	Y	N	Y	N	N	Y	Y
4 Rice	Y	N	Y	N	N	Y	Y
5 Meeks	Y	N	Y	N	N	Y	Y
6 Meng	Y	N	Y	N	N	Y	Y
7 Velázquez	Y	N	Y	N	N	Y	Y
8 Jeffries	Y	N	Y	N	N	Y	Y
9 Clarke	Y	N	N	N	N	Y	Y
10 Nadler	Y	N	N	N	N	Y	Y
11 **Donovan**	N	Y	Y	Y	Y	Y	N
12 Maloney, C.	Y	N	Y	N	N	Y	Y
13 Espaillat	Y	N	N	N	N	Y	Y
14 Crowley	Y	N	Y	N	N	Y	Y
15 Serrano	Y	N	Y	N	N	Y	Y
16 Engel	Y	N	Y	N	N	Y	Y
17 Lowey	Y	N	Y	N	N	Y	Y
18 Maloney, S.P.	Y	N	Y	N	N	Y	Y
19 **Faso**	N	Y	Y	Y	Y	Y	N
20 Tonko	Y	N	Y	N	N	Y	Y
21 **Stefanik**	N	Y	Y	Y	Y	Y	N
22 **Tenney**	N	Y	Y	Y	Y	Y	N
23 **Reed**	N	Y	Y	Y	Y	Y	N
24 **Katko**	N	Y	Y	Y	Y	Y	N
25 Slaughter	Y	N	Y	N	N	Y	Y
26 Higgins	Y	N	Y	N	N	Y	Y
27 **Collins**	N	Y	Y	Y	Y	Y	N
NORTH CAROLINA							
1 Butterfield	Y	N	Y	N	N	Y	Y
2 **Holding**	N	Y	Y	Y	Y	Y	N
3 **Jones**	Y	Y	N	Y	Y	Y	Y
4 Price	Y	N	Y	N	N	Y	Y

	613	614	615	616	617	618	619
5 **Foxx**	N	Y	Y	Y	Y	Y	N
6 **Walker**	N	Y	Y	?	Y	Y	N
7 **Rouzer**	N	Y	Y	Y	Y	Y	N
8 **Hudson**	–	+	+	Y	Y	Y	N
9 **Pittenger**	N	Y	Y	Y	Y	Y	N
10 **McHenry**	N	Y	Y	Y	Y	Y	N
11 **Meadows**	N	Y	Y	Y	Y	Y	N
12 Adams	Y	N	Y	N	N	Y	Y
13 **Budd**	N	Y	Y	Y	Y	Y	N
NORTH DAKOTA							
AL **Cramer**	N	Y	Y	Y	Y	Y	N
OHIO							
1 **Chabot**	N	Y	Y	Y	Y	Y	N
2 **Wenstrup**	N	Y	Y	Y	Y	Y	N
3 Beatty	Y	N	Y	N	N	Y	Y
4 **Jordan**	N	Y	Y	Y	Y	Y	N
5 **Latta**	N	Y	Y	Y	Y	Y	N
6 **Johnson**	N	Y	Y	Y	Y	Y	N
7 **Gibbs**	N	Y	Y	Y	Y	Y	N
8 **Davidson**	N	Y	Y	Y	Y	Y	N
9 Kaptur	Y	N	Y	N	N	Y	Y
10 **Turner**	N	Y	Y	Y	Y	Y	N
11 Fudge	Y	N	Y	N	N	Y	Y
12 **Tiberi**	N	Y	Y	Y	Y	Y	N
13 Ryan	Y	N	Y	N	N	Y	Y
14 **Joyce**	N	Y	Y	Y	Y	Y	N
15 **Stivers**	N	Y	Y	Y	Y	Y	N
16 **Renacci**	N	Y	Y	Y	Y	Y	N
OKLAHOMA							
1 **Bridenstine**	?	?	?	?	?	?	?
2 **Mullin**	N	Y	Y	Y	Y	Y	Y
3 **Lucas**	N	Y	Y	Y	Y	Y	N
4 **Cole**	N	Y	Y	Y	Y	Y	Y
5 **Russell**	N	Y	Y	Y	Y	Y	N
OREGON							
1 Bonamici	Y	N	N	N	N	Y	Y
2 **Walden**	N	Y	Y	Y	Y	Y	N
3 Blumenauer	Y	N	N	N	N	Y	Y
4 DeFazio	Y	N	Y	N	N	Y	Y
5 Schrader	Y	Y	Y	N	N	Y	N
PENNSYLVANIA							
1 Brady	?	?	?	N	N	Y	Y
2 Evans	Y	N	Y	N	N	Y	Y
3 **Kelly**	N	Y	Y	Y	Y	Y	N
4 **Perry**	N	Y	Y	Y	Y	Y	N
5 **Thompson**	N	Y	Y	Y	Y	Y	N
6 **Costello**	N	Y	Y	Y	Y	Y	N
7 **Meehan**	N	Y	Y	Y	Y	Y	N
8 **Fitzpatrick**	N	Y	Y	Y	Y	Y	N
9 **Shuster**	N	Y	Y	Y	Y	Y	N
10 **Marino**	N	Y	Y	Y	Y	Y	N
11 **Barletta**	N	Y	Y	Y	Y	Y	N
12 **Rothfus**	N	Y	Y	Y	Y	Y	N
13 Boyle	Y	N	Y	N	N	Y	Y
14 Doyle	Y	N	Y	N	N	Y	Y
15 **Dent**	N	Y	Y	Y	Y	Y	N
16 **Smucker**	N	Y	Y	Y	Y	Y	N
17 Cartwright	Y	N	Y	N	N	Y	Y
RHODE ISLAND							
1 Cicilline	Y	N	N	N	N	Y	Y
2 Langevin	Y	N	Y	N	N	Y	Y
SOUTH CAROLINA							
1 **Sanford**	N	Y	Y	+	+	+	N
2 **Wilson**	N	Y	Y	Y	Y	Y	N
3 **Duncan**	N	Y	Y	Y	Y	Y	N
4 **Gowdy**	N	Y	Y	Y	Y	Y	N
5 **Norman**	N	Y	Y	?	Y	Y	N
6 Clyburn	Y	N	Y	N	N	Y	Y
7 **Rice**	N	Y	Y	Y	Y	Y	N
SOUTH DAKOTA							
AL **Noem**	N	Y	Y	Y	Y	Y	N
TENNESSEE							
1 **Roe**	N	Y	Y	Y	Y	Y	N
2 **Duncan**	N	Y	Y	Y	Y	Y	N
3 **Fleischmann**	N	Y	Y	Y	Y	Y	N
4 **DesJarlais**	N	Y	Y	Y	Y	Y	N
5 Cooper	Y	N	Y	N	N	Y	Y
6 **Black**	?	?	?	Y	Y	Y	N
7 **Blackburn**	N	Y	Y	Y	Y	Y	N
8 **Kustoff**	N	Y	Y	Y	Y	Y	N
9 Cohen	Y	N	Y	N	N	Y	Y

	613	614	615	616	617	618	619
TEXAS							
1 **Gohmert**	N	Y	Y	Y	Y	Y	N
2 **Poe**	N	Y	Y	Y	Y	Y	N
3 **Johnson, S.**	N	Y	Y	Y	Y	Y	?
4 **Ratcliffe**	N	Y	Y	Y	Y	Y	N
5 **Hensarling**	N	Y	Y	Y	Y	Y	N
6 **Barton**	N	Y	Y	Y	Y	Y	N
7 **Culberson**	N	Y	Y	Y	Y	Y	N
8 **Brady**	N	Y	Y	Y	Y	Y	N
9 Green, A.	Y	N	Y	N	N	Y	Y
10 **McCaul**	N	Y	Y	Y	Y	Y	N
11 **Conaway**	N	Y	Y	Y	Y	Y	N
12 **Granger**	N	Y	Y	Y	Y	Y	N
13 **Thornberry**	N	Y	Y	Y	Y	Y	N
14 **Weber**	N	Y	Y	Y	Y	Y	N
15 Gonzalez	Y	N	Y	N	N	Y	Y
16 O'Rourke	Y	N	Y	N	N	Y	Y
17 **Flores**	N	Y	Y	Y	Y	Y	N
18 Jackson Lee	Y	N	Y	N	N	Y	Y
19 **Arrington**	N	Y	Y	Y	Y	Y	N
20 Castro	Y	N	N	N	N	Y	Y
21 **Smith**	N	Y	Y	Y	Y	Y	N
22 **Olson**	N	Y	Y	Y	Y	Y	N
23 **Hurd**	N	Y	Y	+	+	+	–
24 **Marchant**	N	Y	Y	Y	Y	Y	N
25 **Williams**	N	Y	Y	Y	Y	Y	N
26 **Burgess**	N	Y	Y	Y	Y	Y	N
27 **Farenthold**	N	Y	Y	Y	Y	Y	N
28 Cuellar	Y	Y	Y	?	–	+	+
29 Green, G.	Y	N	Y	N	N	Y	Y
30 Johnson, E.B.	+	–	+	–	–	+	+
31 **Carter**	N	Y	Y	Y	Y	Y	N
32 **Sessions**	N	Y	Y	Y	Y	Y	N
33 Veasey	Y	N	Y	N	N	Y	Y
34 Vela	Y	N	Y	N	N	Y	Y
35 Doggett	Y	N	Y	N	N	Y	Y
36 **Babin**	N	Y	Y	?	Y	Y	N
UTAH							
1 **Bishop**	N	Y	Y	Y	Y	Y	N
2 **Stewart**	N	Y	Y	Y	Y	Y	N
4 **Love**	N	Y	Y	Y	Y	Y	N
VERMONT							
AL Welch	Y	N	N	N	N	Y	Y
VIRGINIA							
1 **Wittman**	N	Y	Y	Y	Y	Y	N
2 **Taylor**	N	Y	Y	Y	Y	Y	N
3 Scott	Y	N	?	N	N	Y	Y
4 McEachin	Y	N	Y	N	N	Y	Y
5 **Garrett**	–	+	+	Y	Y	Y	N
6 **Goodlatte**	N	Y	Y	Y	Y	Y	N
7 **Brat**	N	Y	Y	Y	Y	Y	N
8 Beyer	Y	N	Y	N	N	Y	Y
9 **Griffith**	N	Y	Y	Y	Y	Y	N
10 **Comstock**	N	Y	Y	Y	Y	Y	N
11 Connolly	Y	N	Y	N	N	Y	Y
WASHINGTON							
1 DelBene	Y	N	Y	N	N	Y	Y
2 Larsen	Y	N	Y	N	N	Y	Y
3 **Herrera Beutler**	N	Y	Y	Y	Y	Y	N
4 **Newhouse**	N	Y	Y	Y	Y	Y	N
5 **McMorris Rodgers**	N	Y	Y	Y	Y	Y	N
6 Kilmer	Y	N	Y	N	N	Y	Y
7 Jayapal	Y	N	N	N	N	Y	Y
8 **Reichert**	N	Y	Y	Y	Y	Y	N
9 Smith	Y	N	N	N	N	Y	Y
10 Heck	Y	N	Y	N	N	Y	Y
WEST VIRGINIA							
1 **McKinley**	N	Y	Y	Y	Y	Y	N
2 **Mooney**	N	Y	Y	Y	Y	Y	N
3 **Jenkins**	N	Y	Y	Y	Y	Y	N
WISCONSIN							
1 **Ryan**							
2 Pocan	+	–	?	–	–	+	+
3 Kind	Y	N	Y	N	N	Y	Y
4 Moore	Y	N	Y	N	N	Y	Y
5 **Sensenbrenner**	N	Y	Y	Y	Y	Y	N
6 **Grothman**	N	Y	Y	+	Y	Y	N
7 **Duffy**	N	Y	Y	Y	Y	Y	N
8 **Gallagher**	N	Y	Y	Y	Y	Y	N
WYOMING							
AL **Cheney**	N	Y	Y	+	Y	Y	N

VOTE NUMBER

620. HR 3043. HYDROPOWER REGULATION/PASSAGE. Passage of the bill that would specify a variety of timeframes and procedures for the Federal Energy Regulatory Commission to follow in carrying out required permitting and licensing activities for non-federal hydropower projects and would make FERC the lead agency for coordinating all applicable federal authorizations. It would extend, from three years to four, the duration of a preliminary permit for proposed non-federal hydropower projects and would allow project sponsors to initiate construction up to 10 years after a proposed project receives a license from FERC. Passed 257-166 : R 231-3; D 26-163. Nov. 8, 2017.

621. HR 3705. VA DEBT NOTICES/PASSAGE. Bilirakis, R-Fla., motion to suspend the rules and pass the bill that would require the secretary of the VA to develop a standard letter and notification process for contacting veterans who owe debts to the VA. Motion agreed to 422-0 : R 233-0; D 189-0. Nov. 8, 2017.

622. HR 2201. SECURITIES REGULATIONS EXEMPTIONS/PASSAGE. Passage of the bill that would require an issuer of securities to meet a specific set of criteria in order for the issuer's transactions to constitute a sale of "nonpublic" securities that are exempt from registration with the Securities and Exchange Commission and from state regulation. It would require each purchaser to have a substantive pre-existing relationship with an officer or certain shareholders of the issuer, permit no more than 35 purchasers under the exemption over the preceding 12 months, and would cap, at $500,000, the total aggregate amount of securities sold in the 12-month period preceding the transaction. Passed 232-188 : R 232-1; D 0-187. Nov. 9, 2017.

623. H RES 599. CONFLICT IN YEMEN/ADOPTION. Adoption of the resolution that would state that the House of Representatives condemns the targeting of civilian populations in Yemen, condemns Iranian activities in Yemen, and supports the Saudi-led Arab Coalition's commitment to abide by their no-strike list. Adopted 366-30 : R 203-19; D 163-11. Nov. 13, 2017.

624. HR 3071. FEDERAL EQUIPMENT ACQUISITION/PASSAGE. Hice, R-Ga., motion to suspend the rules and pass the bill that would require federal agencies to consider equipment rentals in all cost-effectiveness analyses for equipment acquisition. Motion agreed to 396-0 : R 221-0; D 175-0. Nov. 13, 2017.

625. PROCEDURAL MOTION/APPROVAL OF HOUSE JOURNAL. Approved 220-165 : R 132-85; D 88-80. Nov. 13, 2017.

626. HR 2874, H RES 616, HR 2810. FISCAL 2018 DEFENSE AUTHORIZATION AND FLOOD INSURANCE REAUTHORIZATION/ PREVIOUS QUESTION. Byrne, R-Ala., motion to order the previous question (thus ending debate and the possibility of amendment) on the rule (H Res 616) that would provide for House floor consideration of the conference report to accompany the bill (HR 2810) that would authorize $692.1 billion for defense programs in fiscal 2018. It would also provide for consideration of the bill (HR 2874) that would reauthorize the National Flood Insurance Program through fiscal 2022 and would modify several aspects of the program. Motion agreed to 234-189 : R 234-0; D 0-189. Nov. 14, 2017.

	620	621	622	623	624	625	626
ALABAMA							
1 Byrne	Y	Y	Y	Y	Y	Y	Y
2 Roby	Y	Y	Y	Y	Y	Y	Y
3 Rogers	Y	Y	Y	Y	Y	N	Y
4 Aderholt	Y	Y	Y	Y	Y	Y	Y
5 Brooks	Y	Y	Y	Y	Y	Y	Y
6 Palmer	Y	Y	Y	Y	Y	N	Y
7 Sewell	Y	Y	N	Y	Y	N	N
ALASKA							
AL Young	Y	Y	Y	Y	Y	N	Y
ARIZONA							
1 O'Halleran	N	Y	N	Y	Y	N	N
2 McSally	Y	Y	Y	Y	Y	N	Y
3 Grijalva	N	Y	N	Y	Y	?	N
4 Gosar	Y	Y	Y	N	Y	N	Y
5 Biggs	Y	Y	Y	N	Y	N	Y
6 Schweikert	Y	Y	Y	Y	Y	Y	Y
7 Gallego	N	Y	N	Y	Y	N	N
8 Franks	Y	Y	Y	?	?	?	Y
9 Sinema	N	Y	N	Y	Y	N	N
ARKANSAS							
1 Crawford	Y	Y	Y	Y	Y	Y	Y
2 Hill	Y	Y	Y	Y	Y	Y	Y
3 Womack	Y	Y	Y	Y	Y	Y	Y
4 Westerman	Y	Y	Y	Y	Y	Y	Y
CALIFORNIA							
1 LaMalfa	Y	Y	Y	Y	Y	Y	Y
2 Huffman	N	Y	N	+	+	+	N
3 Garamendi	N	Y	N	Y	Y	N	N
4 McClintock	Y	Y	Y	Y	Y	Y	Y
5 Thompson	N	Y	N	Y	Y	N	N
6 Matsui	N	Y	N	Y	Y	N	N
7 Bera	N	Y	N	Y	Y	N	N
8 Cook	Y	Y	Y	Y	Y	Y	Y
9 McNerney	Y	Y	N	Y	Y	N	N
10 Denham	Y	Y	Y	Y	Y	N	Y
11 DeSaulnier	N	Y	N	Y	Y	N	N
12 Pelosi	N	Y	N	Y	Y	Y	?
13 Lee	N	Y	N	N	Y	N	N
14 Speier	N	Y	N	Y	Y	N	N
15 Swalwell	N	Y	N	N	Y	N	N
16 Costa	Y	Y	N	Y	Y	N	N
17 Khanna	N	Y	N	Y	Y	N	N
18 Eshoo	N	Y	N	Y	Y	N	N
19 Lofgren	N	Y	N	Y	Y	N	N
20 Panetta	Y	Y	N	Y	Y	N	N
21 Valadao	Y	Y	Y	Y	Y	N	Y
22 Nunes	Y	Y	Y	Y	Y	Y	Y
23 McCarthy	Y	Y	Y	Y	Y	Y	Y
24 Carbajal	N	Y	N	Y	Y	N	N
25 Knight	Y	Y	Y	Y	Y	N	Y
26 Brownley	N	Y	N	Y	Y	N	N
27 Chu	N	Y	N	Y	Y	Y	N
28 Schiff	N	Y	N	Y	Y	Y	N
29 Cardenas	N	Y	N	Y	Y	N	N
30 Sherman	N	Y	N	Y	Y	N	N
31 Aguilar	N	Y	N	Y	Y	N	N
32 Napolitano	N	Y	N	Y	Y	N	N
33 Lieu	N	Y	N	?	?	?	N
34 Gomez	N	Y	N	Y	Y	N	N
35 Torres	Y	Y	N	Y	Y	Y	N
36 Ruiz	N	Y	N	Y	Y	N	N
37 Bass	N	Y	N	N	Y	N	N
38 Sánchez, Linda	N	Y	N	Y	Y	N	N
39 Royce	Y	Y	Y	Y	Y	Y	Y
40 Roybal-Allard	–	+	–	Y	Y	N	N
41 Takano	N	Y	N	Y	Y	?	N
42 Calvert	Y	Y	Y	Y	Y	Y	Y
43 Waters	N	Y	N	?	?	?	N
44 Barragan	N	Y	N	Y	Y	N	N
45 Walters	Y	Y	Y	Y	Y	Y	Y
46 Correa	Y	Y	N	Y	Y	N	N
47 Lowenthal	N	Y	N	Y	Y	N	N
48 Rohrabacher	Y	Y	Y	?	?	?	Y
49 Issa	Y	Y	Y	Y	Y	Y	Y
50 Hunter	Y	Y	Y	N	Y	N	Y
51 Vargas	N	Y	N	Y	Y	N	N
52 Peters	Y	Y	N	Y	Y	N	N
53 Davis	N	Y	N	Y	Y	Y	N

	620	621	622	623	624	625	626
COLORADO							
1 DeGette	N	Y	N	Y	Y	Y	N
2 Polis	N	Y	N	?	?	?	N
3 Tipton	Y	Y	Y	Y	Y	N	Y
4 Buck	Y	Y	Y	Y	Y	N	Y
5 Lamborn	Y	Y	Y	Y	Y	Y	Y
6 Coffman	Y	Y	Y	Y	Y	N	Y
7 Perlmutter	N	Y	N	Y	Y	Y	N
CONNECTICUT							
1 Larson	N	Y	N	Y	Y	N	N
2 Courtney	N	Y	N	Y	Y	Y	N
3 DeLauro	N	Y	N	Y	Y	N	N
4 Himes	N	Y	N	Y	Y	Y	N
5 Esty	N	Y	N	Y	Y	N	N
DELAWARE							
AL Blunt Rochester	N	Y	N	Y	Y	N	N
FLORIDA							
1 Gaetz	Y	Y	Y	Y	Y	N	Y
2 Dunn	Y	Y	Y	Y	Y	Y	Y
3 Yoho	Y	Y	Y	Y	Y	N	Y
4 Rutherford	Y	Y	Y	Y	Y	Y	Y
5 Lawson	N	Y	N	Y	Y	N	N
6 DeSantis	Y	Y	Y	?	?	?	Y
7 Murphy	N	Y	N	Y	Y	N	N
8 Posey	Y	Y	Y	Y	Y	Y	Y
9 Soto	N	Y	N	Y	Y	N	N
10 Demings	N	Y	N	Y	Y	N	N
11 Webster	Y	Y	Y	?	Y	Y	Y
12 Bilirakis	Y	Y	Y	Y	Y	Y	Y
13 Crist	N	Y	N	Y	Y	N	N
14 Castor	N	Y	N	Y	Y	N	N
15 Ross	Y	Y	Y	Y	Y	Y	Y
16 Buchanan	Y	Y	Y	Y	Y	Y	Y
17 Rooney, T.	Y	Y	?	Y	Y	Y	Y
18 Mast	Y	Y	Y	Y	Y	N	Y
19 Rooney, F.	Y	Y	Y	Y	Y	Y	Y
20 Hastings	N	Y	N	Y	Y	N	N
21 Frankel	N	Y	N	Y	Y	N	N
22 Deutch	N	Y	N	Y	Y	N	N
23 Wasserman Schultz	N	Y	N	Y	Y	Y	N
24 Wilson	N	Y	N	Y	Y	?	N
25 Diaz-Balart	Y	Y	Y	Y	Y	N	Y
26 Curbelo	Y	Y	Y	Y	Y	N	Y
27 Ros-Lehtinen	Y	Y	Y	Y	Y	N	Y
GEORGIA							
1 Carter	Y	Y	Y	Y	Y	N	Y
2 Bishop	Y	Y	N	Y	Y	?	N
3 Ferguson	Y	Y	Y	Y	Y	Y	Y
4 Johnson	N	Y	N	P	Y	N	N
5 Lewis	N	Y	N	Y	Y	N	N
6 Handel	Y	Y	Y	Y	Y	Y	Y
7 Woodall	Y	Y	Y	Y	Y	N	?
8 Scott, A.	Y	Y	Y	Y	Y	Y	Y
9 Collins	Y	Y	Y	Y	Y	N	Y
10 Hice	Y	Y	Y	Y	Y	N	Y
11 Loudermilk	Y	Y	Y	Y	Y	N	Y
12 Allen	Y	Y	Y	Y	Y	Y	Y
13 Scott, D.	Y	Y	N	Y	Y	N	N
14 Graves	Y	Y	Y	Y	Y	N	Y
HAWAII							
1 Hanabusa	N	Y	N	Y	Y	Y	N
2 Gabbard	N	Y	N	N	Y	Y	N
IDAHO							
1 Labrador	Y	Y	Y	?	?	?	Y
2 Simpson	Y	Y	Y	Y	Y	Y	Y
ILLINOIS							
1 Rush	N	Y	N	?	?	?	?
2 Kelly	N	Y	N	Y	Y	N	N
3 Lipinski	N	Y	N	?	?	?	N
4 Gutierrez	N	Y	N	+	–	–	N
5 Quigley	N	Y	N	Y	Y	?	N
6 Roskam	Y	Y	Y	Y	Y	Y	Y
7 Davis, D.	N	Y	N	?	?	?	N
8 Krishnamoorthi	N	Y	N	Y	Y	Y	N
9 Schakowsky	N	Y	N	N	Y	N	N
10 Schneider	N	Y	N	Y	Y	N	N
11 Foster	N	Y	N	Y	Y	N	N
12 Bost	Y	Y	Y	Y	Y	N	Y
13 Davis, R.	Y	Y	Y	Y	Y	N	Y
14 Hultgren	Y	Y	Y	Y	Y	Y	Y
15 Shimkus	Y	Y	Y	Y	Y	Y	Y

	620	621	622	623	624	625	626
16 **Kinzinger**	Y	Y	Y	N	Y	N	Y
17 Bustos	Y	Y	N	Y	Y	Y	N
18 **LaHood**	Y	?	Y	Y	Y	N	Y
INDIANA							
1 Visclosky	N	Y	N	–	+	–	–
2 **Walorski**	Y	Y	Y	Y	Y	Y	Y
3 **Banks**	Y	Y	Y	Y	Y	Y	Y
4 **Rokita**	Y	Y	Y	Y	Y	N	Y
5 **Brooks**	Y	Y	Y	Y	Y	Y	Y
6 **Messer**	Y	Y	Y	Y	Y	Y	Y
7 Carson	N	Y	N	Y	Y	Y	N
8 **Bucshon**	Y	Y	Y	Y	Y	Y	Y
9 **Hollingsworth**	Y	Y	Y	Y	Y	Y	Y
IOWA							
1 **Blum**	Y	Y	Y	?	?	?	Y
2 Loebsack	Y	Y	N	?	?	?	N
3 **Young**	Y	Y	Y	Y	Y	Y	Y
4 **King**	Y	Y	Y	Y	Y	Y	Y
KANSAS							
1 **Marshall**	Y	Y	Y	Y	Y	Y	Y
2 **Jenkins**	Y	Y	Y	Y	Y	N	Y
3 **Yoder**	Y	Y	Y	Y	Y	N	Y
4 **Estes**	Y	Y	Y	Y	Y	Y	Y
KENTUCKY							
1 **Comer**	Y	Y	Y	Y	Y	N	Y
2 **Guthrie**	Y	Y	Y	Y	Y	Y	Y
3 Yarmuth	N	Y	N	Y	Y	Y	N
4 **Massie**	Y	Y	Y	N	Y	Y	Y
5 **Rogers**	Y	Y	Y	Y	Y	Y	Y
6 **Barr**	Y	Y	Y	Y	Y	Y	Y
LOUISIANA							
1 **Scalise**	+	+	Y	Y	Y	Y	Y
2 Richmond	N	Y	?	?	?	?	N
3 **Higgins**	Y	Y	Y	Y	?	Y	Y
4 **Johnson**	Y	Y	Y	Y	Y	Y	Y
5 **Abraham**	Y	Y	Y	Y	Y	Y	Y
6 **Graves**	Y	Y	Y	Y	Y	N	Y
MAINE							
1 Pingree	N	Y	N	Y	Y	Y	N
2 **Poliquin**	Y	Y	Y	Y	Y	N	Y
MARYLAND							
1 **Harris**	N	Y	Y	N	Y	Y	Y
2 Ruppersberger	N	Y	N	Y	Y	Y	N
3 Sarbanes	N	Y	N	Y	Y	N	N
4 Brown	N	Y	N	Y	Y	Y	N
5 Hoyer	N	Y	N	Y	Y	N	N
6 Delaney	N	Y	N	+	+	–	N
7 Cummings	N	Y	N	Y	Y	N	N
8 Raskin	N	Y	N	N	Y	N	N
MASSACHUSETTS							
1 Neal	N	Y	N	Y	Y	N	N
2 McGovern	N	Y	N	Y	Y	N	–
3 Tsongas	N	Y	N	?	?	?	N
4 Kennedy	N	Y	N	Y	Y	Y	N
5 Clark	–	+	–	Y	Y	N	N
6 Moulton	N	Y	N	Y	Y	Y	N
7 Capuano	N	Y	N	Y	Y	N	N
8 Lynch	N	Y	N	Y	Y	N	N
9 Keating	N	Y	N	Y	Y	N	N
MICHIGAN							
1 **Bergman**	Y	Y	Y	Y	Y	N	Y
2 **Huizenga**	Y	Y	Y	Y	Y	N	Y
3 **Amash**	Y	Y	Y	N	Y	N	Y
4 **Moolenaar**	Y	Y	Y	Y	Y	Y	Y
5 Kildee	N	Y	N	Y	Y	Y	N
6 **Upton**	Y	Y	Y	Y	Y	N	Y
7 **Walberg**	Y	Y	Y	Y	Y	N	Y
8 **Bishop**	Y	Y	Y	Y	Y	N	Y
9 Levin	N	Y	N	Y	Y	Y	N
10 **Mitchell**	?	?	Y	Y	Y	Y	Y
11 **Trott**	Y	Y	Y	?	?	?	Y
12 Dingell	N	Y	N	Y	Y	Y	N
13 Conyers	N	Y	N	Y	Y	Y	N
14 Lawrence	N	Y	N	Y	Y	Y	N
MINNESOTA							
1 Walz	N	Y	–	?	+	?	N
2 **Lewis**	Y	Y	Y	Y	Y	Y	Y
3 **Paulsen**	Y	Y	Y	Y	Y	N	Y
4 McCollum	N	Y	N	Y	Y	Y	N

	620	621	622	623	624	625	626
5 Ellison	N	Y	N	N	Y	N	N
6 **Emmer**	Y	Y	Y	Y	Y	Y	Y
7 Peterson	Y	Y	N	Y	Y	Y	N
8 Nolan	Y	Y	N	Y	Y	N	N
MISSISSIPPI							
1 **Kelly**	Y	Y	Y	Y	Y	Y	Y
2 Thompson	N	Y	N	Y	Y	N	N
3 **Harper**	Y	Y	Y	Y	Y	Y	Y
4 **Palazzo**	Y	Y	+	Y	Y	N	Y
MISSOURI							
1 Clay	N	Y	N	Y	?	?	N
2 **Wagner**	Y	Y	Y	Y	Y	Y	Y
3 **Luetkemeyer**	Y	Y	Y	Y	Y	Y	Y
4 **Hartzler**	Y	Y	Y	Y	Y	?	Y
5 Cleaver	N	Y	N	Y	Y	Y	N
6 **Graves**	Y	Y	Y	+	+	–	Y
7 **Long**	Y	Y	Y	Y	Y	Y	Y
8 **Smith**	Y	Y	Y	Y	Y	N	Y
MONTANA							
AL **Gianforte**	Y	Y	Y	Y	Y	Y	Y
NEBRASKA							
1 **Fortenberry**	Y	Y	Y	Y	Y	Y	Y
2 **Bacon**	Y	Y	Y	Y	Y	Y	Y
3 **Smith**	Y	Y	Y	Y	Y	Y	Y
NEVADA							
1 Titus	N	Y	N	Y	Y	Y	N
2 **Amodei**	Y	Y	Y	Y	Y	Y	Y
3 Rosen	N	Y	N	Y	Y	N	N
4 Kihuen	N	Y	N	Y	Y	N	N
NEW HAMPSHIRE							
1 Shea-Porter	N	Y	N	Y	Y	Y	N
2 Kuster	N	Y	N	Y	Y	Y	N
NEW JERSEY							
1 Norcross	Y	Y	N	Y	Y	N	N
2 **LoBiondo**	Y	Y	Y	Y	Y	N	Y
3 **MacArthur**	Y	Y	Y	Y	Y	N	Y
4 **Smith**	Y	Y	Y	Y	Y	Y	Y
5 Gottheimer	N	Y	N	Y	Y	N	N
6 Pallone	N	Y	N	Y	Y	N	N
7 **Lance**	Y	Y	Y	Y	Y	N	Y
8 Sires	N	Y	N	?	?	?	N
9 Pascrell	N	Y	N	Y	Y	N	N
10 Payne	N	Y	N	Y	Y	N	N
11 **Frelinghuysen**	Y	Y	Y	Y	Y	Y	Y
12 Watson Coleman	N	Y	N	N	Y	N	N
NEW MEXICO							
1 Lujan Grisham	N	Y	N	Y	Y	Y	N
2 **Pearce**	Y	Y	Y	Y	Y	N	Y
3 Luján	N	Y	N	Y	Y	Y	N
NEW YORK							
1 **Zeldin**	Y	Y	Y	N	Y	Y	Y
2 **King**	Y	Y	Y	Y	Y	Y	Y
3 Suozzi	N	Y	N	Y	Y	N	N
4 Rice	N	Y	N	Y	Y	N	N
5 Meeks	N	Y	N	Y	Y	Y	N
6 Meng	N	Y	N	+	Y	Y	N
7 Velázquez	N	Y	N	Y	Y	N	N
8 Jeffries	N	Y	N	Y	Y	N	N
9 Clarke	N	Y	N	N	Y	N	N
10 Nadler	N	Y	N	Y	Y	Y	N
11 **Donovan**	Y	Y	Y	Y	Y	Y	Y
12 Maloney, C.	N	Y	N	Y	Y	Y	N
13 Espaillat	Y	Y	N	Y	Y	N	N
14 Crowley	N	Y	N	Y	Y	N	N
15 Serrano	N	Y	N	Y	Y	N	N
16 Engel	N	Y	N	Y	Y	Y	N
17 Lowey	N	Y	N	Y	Y	Y	N
18 Maloney, S.P.	N	Y	N	?	Y	N	N
19 **Faso**	Y	Y	Y	Y	Y	N	Y
20 Tonko	N	Y	N	Y	Y	P	N
21 **Stefanik**	Y	Y	Y	Y	Y	Y	Y
22 **Tenney**	Y	Y	Y	Y	Y	N	Y
23 **Reed**	Y	Y	Y	Y	Y	N	Y
24 **Katko**	Y	Y	Y	Y	Y	N	Y
25 Slaughter	N	Y	N	Y	Y	N	N
26 Higgins	N	Y	N	Y	Y	Y	N
27 **Collins**	Y	Y	Y	Y	Y	Y	Y
NORTH CAROLINA							
1 Butterfield	N	Y	N	Y	Y	Y	N
2 **Holding**	Y	Y	Y	Y	Y	N	Y
3 **Jones**	N	Y	N	N	Y	Y	Y
4 Price	N	Y	N	Y	Y	N	N

	620	621	622	623	624	625	626
5 **Foxx**	Y	Y	Y	Y	Y	N	Y
6 **Walker**	Y	Y	Y	Y	Y	Y	Y
7 **Rouzer**	Y	Y	Y	Y	Y	N	Y
8 **Hudson**	Y	Y	Y	Y	Y	N	Y
9 **Pittenger**	Y	Y	Y	Y	Y	N	Y
10 **McHenry**	Y	Y	Y	Y	Y	Y	Y
11 **Meadows**	Y	Y	Y	Y	Y	Y	Y
12 Adams	N	Y	N	Y	Y	N	N
13 **Budd**	Y	Y	Y	Y	Y	Y	Y
NORTH DAKOTA							
AL **Cramer**	Y	Y	Y	Y	Y	Y	Y
OHIO							
1 **Chabot**	Y	Y	Y	Y	Y	Y	Y
2 **Wenstrup**	Y	Y	Y	Y	Y	N	Y
3 Beatty	N	Y	N	Y	Y	Y	N
4 **Jordan**	Y	Y	Y	N	Y	N	Y
5 **Latta**	Y	Y	Y	Y	Y	N	Y
6 **Johnson**	Y	Y	Y	Y	Y	N	Y
7 **Gibbs**	Y	Y	Y	Y	Y	N	Y
8 **Davidson**	Y	Y	Y	N	Y	Y	Y
9 Kaptur	N	Y	N	Y	Y	Y	N
10 **Turner**	Y	Y	Y	Y	Y	N	Y
11 Fudge	N	Y	N	Y	Y	N	N
12 **Tiberi**	Y	Y	Y	?	?	?	Y
13 Ryan	Y	Y	N	Y	Y	N	N
14 **Joyce**	Y	Y	Y	Y	Y	N	Y
15 **Stivers**	Y	Y	Y	Y	Y	N	Y
16 **Renacci**	Y	Y	Y	+	+	–	Y
OKLAHOMA							
1 **Bridenstine**	?	?	?	?	?	?	?
2 **Mullin**	Y	Y	Y	Y	Y	Y	Y
3 **Lucas**	Y	Y	Y	Y	Y	Y	Y
4 **Cole**	N	Y	Y	Y	Y	Y	Y
5 **Russell**	Y	Y	Y	Y	Y	Y	Y
OREGON							
1 Bonamici	N	Y	N	Y	Y	Y	N
2 **Walden**	Y	Y	Y	Y	Y	Y	Y
3 Blumenauer	N	Y	N	Y	Y	Y	N
4 DeFazio	N	Y	N	Y	?	?	N
5 Schrader	Y	Y	N	Y	Y	N	N
PENNSYLVANIA							
1 Brady	Y	Y	N	Y	Y	N	N
2 Evans	Y	Y	N	Y	Y	Y	N
3 **Kelly**	Y	Y	Y	Y	Y	Y	Y
4 **Perry**	Y	Y	Y	N	Y	N	Y
5 **Thompson**	Y	Y	Y	Y	Y	N	Y
6 **Costello**	Y	Y	Y	Y	Y	N	Y
7 **Meehan**	Y	Y	Y	Y	Y	N	Y
8 **Fitzpatrick**	Y	Y	Y	Y	Y	N	Y
9 **Shuster**	Y	Y	Y	Y	Y	?	Y
10 **Marino**	Y	Y	Y	Y	Y	Y	Y
11 **Barletta**	Y	Y	Y	Y	Y	Y	Y
12 **Rothfus**	Y	Y	Y	N	Y	Y	Y
13 Boyle	Y	Y	N	Y	Y	N	N
14 Doyle	Y	Y	N	Y	Y	N	N
15 **Dent**	Y	Y	Y	?	?	?	?
16 **Smucker**	Y	Y	Y	Y	Y	Y	Y
17 Cartwright	N	Y	N	Y	Y	Y	N
RHODE ISLAND							
1 Cicilline	N	Y	N	Y	Y	Y	N
2 Langevin	N	Y	N	Y	Y	Y	N
SOUTH CAROLINA							
1 **Sanford**	Y	Y	Y	N	Y	N	Y
2 **Wilson**	Y	Y	Y	Y	Y	Y	Y
3 **Duncan**	Y	Y	Y	Y	Y	Y	Y
4 **Gowdy**	Y	Y	Y	Y	Y	Y	Y
5 **Norman**	Y	Y	Y	Y	Y	Y	Y
6 Clyburn	N	Y	N	Y	Y	Y	N
7 **Rice**	Y	Y	Y	Y	Y	P	Y
SOUTH DAKOTA							
AL **Noem**	Y	Y	Y	Y	Y	Y	Y
TENNESSEE							
1 **Roe**	Y	Y	Y	Y	Y	Y	Y
2 **Duncan**	Y	Y	Y	N	Y	Y	Y
3 **Fleischmann**	Y	Y	Y	Y	Y	Y	Y
4 **DesJarlais**	Y	Y	Y	Y	Y	Y	Y
5 Cooper	N	Y	N	Y	Y	Y	N
6 **Black**	Y	Y	Y	Y	Y	?	?
7 **Blackburn**	Y	Y	Y	?	?	?	Y
8 **Kustoff**	Y	Y	Y	Y	Y	Y	Y
9 Cohen	N	Y	N	Y	Y	Y	N

	620	621	622	623	624	625	626
TEXAS							
1 **Gohmert**	Y	Y	Y	?	Y	?	Y
2 **Poe**	Y	Y	Y	?	?	?	Y
3 **Johnson, S.**	Y	Y	Y	?	?	?	?
4 **Ratcliffe**	Y	Y	Y	Y	Y	N	Y
5 **Hensarling**	Y	Y	Y	Y	Y	Y	Y
6 **Barton**	Y	Y	Y	Y	Y	Y	Y
7 **Culberson**	Y	Y	Y	Y	Y	Y	Y
8 **Brady**	Y	Y	Y	Y	Y	?	Y
9 Green, A.	N	Y	N	Y	Y	Y	N
10 **McCaul**	Y	Y	Y	Y	Y	Y	Y
11 **Conaway**	Y	Y	Y	Y	Y	N	Y
12 **Granger**	Y	Y	?	Y	Y	Y	Y
13 **Thornberry**	Y	Y	Y	Y	Y	Y	Y
14 **Weber**	Y	Y	Y	N	Y	N	Y
15 Gonzalez	Y	Y	N	Y	Y	N	N
16 O'Rourke	N	Y	N	+	+	+	N
17 **Flores**	Y	Y	Y	Y	Y	N	Y
18 Jackson Lee	N	Y	N	Y	Y	N	N
19 **Arrington**	Y	Y	Y	Y	Y	Y	Y
20 Castro	N	Y	N	Y	Y	Y	N
21 **Smith**	Y	Y	Y	Y	Y	Y	Y
22 **Olson**	Y	Y	Y	Y	Y	Y	Y
23 **Hurd**	+	+	+	Y	Y	N	Y
24 **Marchant**	Y	Y	Y	Y	Y	N	Y
25 **Williams**	Y	Y	Y	Y	Y	Y	Y
26 **Burgess**	Y	Y	Y	Y	Y	N	Y
27 **Farenthold**	Y	Y	Y	Y	Y	Y	Y
28 Cuellar	+	+	–	Y	Y	Y	N
29 Green, G.	Y	Y	N	Y	Y	?	N
30 Johnson, E.B.	–	+	?	Y	Y	N	N
31 **Carter**	Y	Y	Y	Y	Y	Y	Y
32 **Sessions**	Y	Y	Y	Y	Y	Y	Y
33 Veasey	Y	Y	N	Y	Y	N	N
34 Vela	Y	Y	N	Y	Y	Y	N
35 Doggett	N	Y	N	N	Y	Y	N
36 **Babin**	Y	Y	Y	Y	Y	N	Y
UTAH							
1 **Bishop**	Y	Y	Y	Y	Y	Y	Y
2 **Stewart**	Y	Y	Y	?	?	?	Y
4 **Love**	Y	Y	Y	Y	Y	Y	Y
VERMONT							
AL Welch	N	Y	N	Y	Y	Y	N
VIRGINIA							
1 **Wittman**	Y	Y	Y	Y	?	Y	Y
2 **Taylor**	Y	Y	Y	N	Y	Y	Y
3 Scott	N	Y	N	Y	Y	Y	N
4 McEachin	N	Y	N	Y	Y	Y	N
5 **Garrett**	Y	Y	Y	Y	Y	N	Y
6 **Goodlatte**	Y	Y	Y	Y	Y	Y	Y
7 **Brat**	Y	Y	Y	Y	Y	Y	Y
8 Beyer	N	Y	N	Y	Y	N	N
9 **Griffith**	Y	Y	Y	N	Y	Y	Y
10 **Comstock**	Y	Y	Y	Y	Y	Y	Y
11 Connolly	N	Y	N	Y	Y	N	N
WASHINGTON							
1 DelBene	N	Y	N	Y	Y	Y	N
2 Larsen	N	Y	N	Y	Y	Y	N
3 **Herrera Beutler**	Y	Y	Y	Y	Y	N	Y
4 **Newhouse**	Y	Y	Y	Y	Y	Y	Y
5 **McMorris Rodgers**	Y	Y	Y	Y	Y	Y	Y
6 Kilmer	N	Y	N	Y	Y	N	N
7 Jayapal	N	Y	N	N	Y	N	N
8 **Reichert**	Y	Y	Y	Y	Y	?	Y
9 Smith	N	Y	N	N	Y	Y	N
10 Heck	N	Y	N	Y	Y	Y	N
WEST VIRGINIA							
1 **McKinley**	Y	Y	Y	Y	Y	N	Y
2 **Mooney**	Y	Y	Y	Y	Y	Y	Y
3 **Jenkins**	Y	Y	Y	Y	Y	N	Y
WISCONSIN							
1 **Ryan**							
2 Pocan	–	+	–	+	+	+	–
3 Kind	N	Y	N	Y	Y	N	N
4 Moore	N	Y	N	Y	Y	Y	N
5 **Sensenbrenner**	Y	Y	Y	Y	Y	Y	Y
6 **Grothman**	Y	Y	Y	Y	Y	N	Y
7 **Duffy**	Y	Y	Y	Y	Y	N	Y
8 **Gallagher**	Y	Y	Y	Y	Y	N	Y
WYOMING							
AL **Cheney**	Y	Y	Y	N	Y	Y	Y

VOTE NUMBER

627. HR 2874, H RES 616, HR 2810. FISCAL 2018 DEFENSE AUTHORIZATION AND FLOOD INSURANCE REAUTHORIZATION/RULE. Adoption of the rule (H Res 616) that would provide for House floor consideration of the conference report to accompany the bill (HR 2810) that would authorize $692.1 billion for defense programs in fiscal 2018. It would also provide for consideration of the bill (HR 2874) that would reauthorize the National Flood Insurance Program through fiscal 2022 and would modify several aspects of the program. The rule would require the House clerk to not transmit to the Senate a message that the House has adopted the conference report to accompany the fiscal 2018 defense authorization (HR 2810) until the House receives a message from the Senate that the Senate has passed a bill (HR 4374), without amendment, that would authorize the Food and Drug Administration to expedite consideration of certain medical products at the Pentagon's request. Adopted 233-187 : R 229-2; D 4-185. Nov. 14, 2017.

628. PROCEDURAL MOTION/APPROVAL OF HOUSE JOURNAL. Approved 224-190 : R 138-90; D 86-100. Nov. 14, 2017.

629. HR 2874. FLOOD INSURANCE REAUTHORIZATION/RECOMMIT. Pascrell, D-N.J., motion to recommit the bill to the House Financial Services Committee with instructions to report it back immediately with an amendment that would prevent the bill's provisions from taking effect unless the Federal Emergency Management Agency certifies the resolution of all claims for losses resulting from Hurricane Sandy of 2012 that were covered under the National Flood Insurance Program. Motion rejected 190-236 : R 0-236; D 190-0. Nov. 14, 2017.

630. HR 2874. FLOOD INSURANCE REAUTHORIZATION/PASSAGE. Passage of the bill, as amended, that would reauthorize the National Flood Insurance Program through fiscal 2022 and would make modifications to the program, including: raise annual surcharges and reserve fund assessments on federal flood insurance policyholders, raise rates on properties that incur multiple losses, establish an annual deductible for severe and extreme repetitive loss properties and end the requirement that flood insurance be purchased for commercial and multifamily properties located in flood risk zones. It would also require that flood insurance provided by private sector carriers be accepted by Federal Emergency Management Agency and considered as meeting the National Flood Insurance Program's mandatory flood insurance purchase requirements, and would allow private insurers and any other interested party to review FEMA information regarding its assessments of flood risk. Passed 237-189 : R 222-14; D 15-175. Nov. 14, 2017.

631. HR 2810. FISCAL 2018 NATIONAL DEFENSE AUTHORIZATION/ CONFERENCE REPORT. Adoption of the conference report on the bill that would authorize $692.1 billion for defense programs in fiscal 2018, including $65.7 billion for overseas operations in Afghanistan, Iraq and Syria, and for the general war on terror. It would authorize $241.2 billion for operations and maintenance; $146.2 billion for military personnel; $10.7 billion for military construction and family housing; $15 billion for ballistic-missile defense; and $33.9 billion for defense health care programs, including $396 million from the overseas operations account. It would prohibit the use of funds for a new round of base closures. It would authorize $8 billion for various cybersecurity programs, would require the president to develop a national policy for the United States related to cybersecurity and would withhold certain funds made available for White House staff until the president would submit such national policy to Congress. The bill would authorize a 2.4 percent pay raise for military personnel. It would prohibit detainees at Guantanamo Bay, Cuba, from being transferred to U.S. soil, and would prohibit the closing of the main base and detention facility at Guantanamo. It would extend, through 2018, the authority for several bonus and special payments for military members. Adopted (thus sent to the Senate) 356-70 : R 229-7; D 127-63. Nov. 14, 2017.

	627	628	629	630	631
ALABAMA					
1 Byrne	Y	Y	N	Y	Y
2 Roby	Y	Y	N	Y	Y
3 Rogers	Y	N	N	Y	Y
4 Aderholt	Y	Y	N	Y	Y
5 Brooks	Y	Y	N	Y	Y
6 Palmer	Y	Y	N	Y	Y
7 Sewell	N	N	Y	N	Y
ALASKA					
AL Young	Y	N	N	Y	Y
ARIZONA					
1 O'Halleran	N	N	Y	N	Y
2 McSally	Y	N	N	Y	Y
3 Grijalva	N	N	Y	N	–
4 Gosar	Y	N	N	Y	Y
5 Biggs	Y	N	N	Y	Y
6 Schweikert	Y	Y	N	Y	Y
7 Gallego	N	N	Y	N	Y
8 Franks	Y	Y	N	Y	Y
9 Sinema	N	N	Y	Y	Y
ARKANSAS					
1 Crawford	Y	Y	N	Y	Y
2 Hill	Y	N	N	Y	Y
3 Womack	Y	Y	N	Y	Y
4 Westerman	Y	Y	N	Y	Y
CALIFORNIA					
1 LaMalfa	Y	Y	N	Y	Y
2 Huffman	N	Y	Y	Y	N
3 Garamendi	N	Y	Y	N	Y
4 McClintock	Y	Y	N	Y	Y
5 Thompson	N	N	Y	N	N
6 Matsui	N	N	Y	N	N
7 Bera	N	N	Y	N	Y
8 Cook	Y	Y	N	Y	Y
9 McNerney	N	Y	Y	N	Y
10 Denham	Y	N	N	Y	Y
11 DeSaulnier	N	Y	Y	N	N
12 Pelosi	?	?	?	?	?
13 Lee	N	Y	Y	N	N
14 Speier	N	Y	Y	N	N
15 Swalwell	N	N	Y	N	N
16 Costa	N	N	Y	N	Y
17 Khanna	N	N	Y	N	N
18 Eshoo	N	Y	Y	N	N
19 Lofgren	N	N	Y	N	N
20 Panetta	N	N	Y	N	Y
21 Valadao	Y	N	N	Y	Y
22 Nunes	Y	N	N	Y	Y
23 McCarthy	Y	Y	N	Y	Y
24 Carbajal	N	N	Y	N	Y
25 Knight	Y	N	N	Y	Y
26 Brownley	N	N	Y	N	Y
27 Chu	N	Y	Y	N	N
28 Schiff	N	N	Y	N	Y
29 Cardenas	N	Y	Y	N	Y
30 Sherman	N	Y	Y	Y	Y
31 Aguilar	N	N	Y	N	Y
32 Napolitano	N	Y	Y	N	N
33 Lieu	N	N	Y	N	N
34 Gomez	N	N	Y	N	N
35 Torres	N	N	Y	N	N
36 Ruiz	N	N	Y	N	Y
37 Bass	N	N	Y	N	N
38 Sánchez, Linda	N	N	Y	N	Y
39 Royce	Y	Y	N	Y	Y
40 Roybal-Allard	N	N	Y	N	Y
41 Takano	N	Y	Y	N	N
42 Calvert	Y	Y	N	Y	Y
43 Waters	N	Y	Y	N	Y
44 Barragan	N	N	Y	N	N
45 Walters	Y	Y	N	Y	Y
46 Correa	N	N	Y	Y	Y
47 Lowenthal	N	Y	Y	N	N
48 Rohrabacher	Y	Y	N	Y	Y
49 Issa	Y	N	N	Y	Y
50 Hunter	Y	Y	N	Y	Y
51 Vargas	N	N	Y	N	N
52 Peters	N	N	Y	Y	Y
53 Davis	N	Y	Y	N	Y

	627	628	629	630	631
COLORADO					
1 DeGette	N	Y	Y	N	N
2 Polis	N	Y	Y	N	N
3 Tipton	Y	N	N	Y	Y
4 Buck	Y	N	N	Y	Y
5 Lamborn	Y	Y	N	Y	Y
6 Coffman	Y	N	N	Y	Y
7 Perlmutter	N	Y	Y	N	Y
CONNECTICUT					
1 Larson	N	?	N	Y	N
2 Courtney	N	Y	N	Y	Y
3 DeLauro	N	Y	Y	N	Y
4 Himes	N	Y	Y	N	Y
5 Esty	N	N	Y	N	Y
DELAWARE					
AL Blunt Rochester	N	N	Y	N	Y
FLORIDA					
1 Gaetz	Y	N	N	Y	Y
2 Dunn	Y	Y	N	Y	Y
3 Yoho	Y	N	N	Y	Y
4 Rutherford	Y	Y	N	Y	Y
5 Lawson	N	N	Y	N	Y
6 DeSantis	Y	N	N	Y	Y
7 Murphy	Y	Y	N	Y	N
8 Posey	Y	N	N	Y	Y
9 Soto	N	N	Y	N	Y
10 Demings	N	N	Y	N	Y
11 Webster	Y	Y	N	Y	Y
12 Bilirakis	Y	Y	N	Y	Y
13 Crist	N	N	Y	N	Y
14 Castor	N	N	Y	N	Y
15 Ross	Y	Y	N	Y	Y
16 Buchanan	Y	Y	N	Y	Y
17 Rooney, T.	Y	N	N	Y	Y
18 Mast	Y	N	N	Y	Y
19 Rooney, F.	Y	Y	N	Y	Y
20 Hastings	N	Y	Y	N	Y
21 Frankel	N	Y	Y	N	Y
22 Deutch	N	Y	Y	N	Y
23 Wasserman Schultz	N	Y	Y	N	Y
24 Wilson	N	N	Y	N	Y
25 Diaz-Balart	?	N	N	N	Y
26 Curbelo	Y	N	N	N	Y
27 Ros-Lehtinen	Y	N	N	N	Y
GEORGIA					
1 Carter	Y	N	N	Y	Y
2 Bishop	N	N	Y	N	Y
3 Ferguson	Y	Y	N	Y	Y
4 Johnson	N	Y	Y	N	N
5 Lewis	N	N	Y	N	N
6 Handel	Y	Y	N	Y	Y
7 Woodall	?	?	N	Y	Y
8 Scott, A.	Y	Y	N	Y	Y
9 Collins	Y	N	N	Y	Y
10 Hice	Y	N	N	Y	Y
11 Loudermilk	Y	Y	N	Y	Y
12 Allen	Y	Y	N	Y	Y
13 Scott, D.	N	N	Y	N	Y
14 Graves	Y	N	N	Y	Y
HAWAII					
1 Hanabusa	N	Y	Y	N	Y
2 Gabbard	N	Y	Y	N	N
IDAHO					
1 Labrador	Y	Y	N	Y	N
2 Simpson	Y	Y	N	Y	Y
ILLINOIS					
1 Rush	?	?	Y	N	Y
2 Kelly	N	N	Y	N	Y
3 Lipinski	N	Y	Y	Y	Y
4 Gutierrez	N	N	Y	N	N
5 Quigley	N	Y	Y	N	Y
6 Roskam	Y	Y	N	Y	Y
7 Davis, D.	N	Y	Y	N	N
8 Krishnamoorthi	N	Y	Y	N	Y
9 Schakowsky	N	Y	Y	N	N
10 Schneider	Y	Y	Y	Y	Y
11 Foster	N	Y	Y	N	Y
12 Bost	Y	?	N	Y	Y
13 Davis, R.	Y	N	N	Y	Y
14 Hultgren	Y	Y	N	Y	Y
15 Shimkus	Y	Y	N	Y	Y

	627	628	629	630	631
16 Kinzinger	Y	N	N	Y	Y
17 Bustos	N	Y	Y	N	Y
18 LaHood	Y	N	N	Y	Y
INDIANA					
1 Visclosky	–	–	Y	N	N
2 Walorski	Y	Y	N	Y	Y
3 Banks	Y	Y	Y	N	Y
4 Rokita	Y	N	N	Y	Y
5 Brooks	Y	Y	N	Y	Y
6 Messer	Y	Y	N	Y	Y
7 Carson	N	Y	Y	N	N
8 Bucshon	Y	Y	N	Y	Y
9 Hollingsworth	Y	Y	N	Y	Y
IOWA					
1 Blum	Y	N	N	Y	Y
2 Loebsack	N	N	Y	N	Y
3 Young	Y	Y	N	Y	Y
4 King	Y	Y	N	Y	Y
KANSAS					
1 Marshall	Y	N	N	Y	Y
2 Jenkins	Y	N	N	Y	Y
3 Yoder	Y	N	N	Y	Y
4 Estes	Y	Y	N	Y	Y
KENTUCKY					
1 Comer	Y	N	N	Y	Y
2 Guthrie	Y	Y	N	Y	Y
3 Yarmuth	N	Y	Y	N	N
4 Massie	N	Y	N	N	N
5 Rogers	Y	Y	N	Y	Y
6 Barr	Y	N	N	Y	Y
LOUISIANA					
1 Scalise	Y	Y	N	Y	Y
2 Richmond	N	N	Y	N	Y
3 Higgins	Y	Y	N	Y	Y
4 Johnson	Y	Y	N	Y	Y
5 Abraham	Y	Y	N	N	Y
6 Graves	Y	N	N	N	Y
MAINE					
1 Pingree	N	Y	Y	N	Y
2 Poliquin	Y	N	N	Y	Y
MARYLAND					
1 Harris	Y	Y	N	Y	Y
2 Ruppersberger	N	Y	Y	N	N
3 Sarbanes	N	N	Y	N	Y
4 Brown	N	Y	Y	N	Y
5 Hoyer	N	?	Y	N	Y
6 Delaney	N	N	Y	N	Y
7 Cummings	N	Y	Y	N	Y
8 Raskin	N	N	Y	N	N
MASSACHUSETTS					
1 Neal	N	N	Y	N	Y
2 McGovern	–	?	+	–	–
3 Tsongas	N	N	Y	N	Y
4 Kennedy	N	Y	Y	N	N
5 Clark	N	N	Y	N	Y
6 Moulton	N	Y	Y	N	Y
7 Capuano	N	N	Y	N	N
8 Lynch	N	N	Y	N	N
9 Keating	N	Y	Y	N	Y
MICHIGAN					
1 Bergman	Y	N	N	Y	Y
2 Huizenga	Y	N	N	Y	Y
3 Amash	N	N	N	N	N
4 Moolenaar	Y	N	N	Y	Y
5 Kildee	N	Y	Y	N	N
6 Upton	Y	N	N	Y	Y
7 Walberg	Y	N	N	Y	Y
8 Bishop	Y	N	N	Y	Y
9 Levin	N	N	Y	N	N
10 Mitchell	Y	N	N	Y	Y
11 Trott	Y	Y	N	Y	Y
12 Dingell	N	Y	Y	N	Y
13 Conyers	N	N	Y	N	N
14 Lawrence	N	Y	Y	N	Y
MINNESOTA					
1 Walz	N	Y	Y	N	Y
2 Lewis	Y	Y	N	Y	Y
3 Paulsen	Y	N	N	Y	Y
4 McCollum	N	Y	Y	N	Y

	627	628	629	630	631
5 Ellison	N	Y	Y	N	N
6 Emmer	Y	Y	N	Y	Y
7 Peterson	N	N	Y	Y	Y
8 Nolan	N	N	Y	Y	Y
MISSISSIPPI					
1 Kelly	Y	Y	N	Y	Y
2 Thompson	N	N	Y	N	Y
3 Harper	Y	Y	N	Y	Y
4 Palazzo	Y	N	N	N	Y
MISSOURI					
1 Clay	N	Y	Y	Y	Y
2 Wagner	Y	Y	N	Y	Y
3 Luetkemeyer	Y	Y	N	Y	Y
4 Hartzler	Y	Y	N	Y	Y
5 Cleaver	N	N	Y	N	N
6 Graves	Y	N	N	Y	Y
7 Long	Y	Y	N	Y	Y
8 Smith	Y	Y	N	Y	Y
MONTANA					
AL Gianforte	Y	Y	N	Y	Y
NEBRASKA					
1 Fortenberry	Y	Y	N	Y	Y
2 Bacon	Y	Y	N	Y	Y
3 Smith	Y	+	N	Y	Y
NEVADA					
1 Titus	N	Y	Y	Y	Y
2 Amodei	Y	Y	N	Y	Y
3 Rosen	Y	N	Y	Y	Y
4 Kihuen	N	N	Y	N	Y
NEW HAMPSHIRE					
1 Shea-Porter	N	Y	Y	N	Y
2 Kuster	N	Y	Y	N	Y
NEW JERSEY					
1 Norcross	N	N	Y	N	Y
2 LoBiondo	Y	N	N	N	Y
3 MacArthur	Y	N	Y	Y	Y
4 Smith	Y	N	N	N	Y
5 Gottheimer	N	N	Y	N	Y
6 Pallone	N	Y	Y	N	N
7 Lance	Y	N	Y	N	Y
8 Sires	N	N	Y	N	N
9 Pascrell	N	N	Y	N	N
10 Payne	N	N	Y	N	N
11 Frelinghuysen	Y	Y	N	Y	Y
12 Watson Coleman	N	N	N	N	N
NEW MEXICO					
1 Lujan Grisham	N	Y	Y	N	Y
2 Pearce	Y	N	N	Y	Y
3 Luján	N	Y	Y	N	Y
NEW YORK					
1 Zeldin	Y	Y	N	Y	Y
2 King	Y	Y	N	N	Y
3 Suozzi	Y	N	Y	N	Y
4 Rice	N	N	Y	N	Y
5 Meeks	N	N	Y	N	Y
6 Meng	N	Y	Y	N	Y
7 Velázquez	N	N	Y	N	N
8 Jeffries	N	N	Y	N	Y
9 Clarke	N	N	Y	N	N
10 Nadler	N	N	Y	N	N
11 Donovan	Y	Y	N	N	Y
12 Maloney, C.	N	Y	?	N	Y
13 Espaillat	N	N	Y	N	N
14 Crowley	N	N	Y	N	Y
15 Serrano	N	N	Y	N	N
16 Engel	N	N	Y	N	Y
17 Lowey	N	Y	Y	N	Y
18 Maloney, S.P.	N	N	Y	N	Y
19 Faso	Y	N	N	Y	Y
20 Tonko	N	P	Y	N	Y
21 Stefanik	Y	Y	N	N	Y
22 Tenney	Y	N	N	Y	Y
23 Reed	Y	N	N	Y	Y
24 Katko	Y	N	N	Y	Y
25 Slaughter	N	N	Y	N	N
26 Higgins	N	Y	Y	N	Y
27 Collins	Y	Y	N	Y	Y
NORTH CAROLINA					
1 Butterfield	N	Y	N	Y	Y
2 Holding	+	N	N	Y	Y
3 Jones	Y	N	N	N	N
4 Price	N	N	Y	N	N

	627	628	629	630	631
5 Foxx	Y	N	N	Y	Y
6 Walker	Y	Y	N	Y	Y
7 Rouzer	Y	N	N	Y	Y
8 Hudson	Y	N	N	Y	Y
9 Pittenger	Y	N	N	Y	Y
10 McHenry	Y	Y	N	Y	Y
11 Meadows	Y	Y	N	Y	Y
12 Adams	N	Y	Y	N	Y
13 Budd	Y	Y	N	Y	Y
NORTH DAKOTA					
AL Cramer	Y	Y	N	Y	Y
OHIO					
1 Chabot	Y	Y	N	Y	Y
2 Wenstrup	Y	Y	N	Y	Y
3 Beatty	N	Y	Y	N	Y
4 Jordan	Y	N	N	Y	Y
5 Latta	Y	Y	N	Y	Y
6 Johnson	Y	N	N	Y	Y
7 Gibbs	Y	Y	N	Y	Y
8 Davidson	Y	N	N	Y	Y
9 Kaptur	N	Y	Y	N	Y
10 Turner	Y	?	N	Y	Y
11 Fudge	N	N	Y	N	Y
12 Tiberi	Y	Y	N	Y	Y
13 Ryan	N	N	Y	N	Y
14 Joyce	Y	N	Y	Y	Y
15 Stivers	Y	N	N	Y	Y
16 Renacci	Y	Y	N	Y	Y
OKLAHOMA					
1 Bridenstine	?	?	?	?	?
2 Mullin	Y	Y	N	Y	Y
3 Lucas	Y	Y	N	Y	Y
4 Cole	?	Y	N	Y	Y
5 Russell	Y	Y	N	Y	Y
OREGON					
1 Bonamici	N	Y	Y	N	Y
2 Walden	Y	Y	N	Y	Y
3 Blumenauer	N	Y	Y	Y	N
4 DeFazio	N	N	Y	N	N
5 Schrader	N	N	Y	N	N
PENNSYLVANIA					
1 Brady	N	N	Y	N	Y
2 Evans	N	N	Y	N	Y
3 Kelly	Y	Y	N	Y	Y
4 Perry	Y	N	N	Y	Y
5 Thompson	Y	N	N	Y	Y
6 Costello	Y	N	N	Y	Y
7 Meehan	Y	N	N	Y	Y
8 Fitzpatrick	Y	N	N	Y	Y
9 Shuster	Y	N	N	Y	Y
10 Marino	Y	N	N	Y	Y
11 Barletta	Y	Y	N	Y	Y
12 Rothfus	Y	Y	N	Y	Y
13 Boyle	N	N	Y	N	Y
14 Doyle	N	N	Y	N	Y
15 Dent	?	?	?	?	?
16 Smucker	Y	N	N	Y	Y
17 Cartwright	N	Y	Y	N	Y
RHODE ISLAND					
1 Cicilline	N	Y	Y	N	Y
2 Langevin	N	N	Y	N	Y
SOUTH CAROLINA					
1 Sanford	Y	N	N	Y	Y
2 Wilson	Y	Y	N	Y	Y
3 Duncan	Y	N	N	Y	Y
4 Gowdy	Y	Y	N	Y	Y
5 Norman	Y	Y	N	Y	Y
6 Clyburn	N	N	Y	N	Y
7 Rice	Y	Y	N	Y	Y
SOUTH DAKOTA					
AL Noem	Y	Y	N	Y	Y
TENNESSEE					
1 Roe	Y	N	N	Y	Y
2 Duncan	Y	Y	N	Y	N
3 Fleischmann	Y	Y	N	Y	Y
4 DesJarlais	Y	Y	N	Y	Y
5 Cooper	N	Y	Y	N	Y
6 Black	?	?	N	Y	Y
7 Blackburn	Y	Y	N	Y	Y
8 Kustoff	Y	Y	N	Y	Y
9 Cohen	N	Y	Y	N	N

	627	628	629	630	631
TEXAS					
1 Gohmert	Y	?	N	Y	Y
2 Poe	Y	N	N	Y	Y
3 Johnson, S.	?	?	?	?	?
4 Ratcliffe	Y	Y	N	Y	Y
5 Hensarling	Y	Y	N	Y	Y
6 Barton	Y	Y	N	Y	Y
7 Culberson	Y	Y	N	Y	Y
8 Brady	Y	Y	N	Y	Y
9 Green, A.	N	N	Y	N	Y
10 McCaul	Y	N	N	Y	Y
11 Conaway	Y	N	N	Y	Y
12 Granger	Y	N	N	Y	Y
13 Thornberry	Y	N	N	Y	Y
14 Weber	Y	N	N	Y	Y
15 Gonzalez	N	N	Y	N	Y
16 O'Rourke	N	Y	Y	N	Y
17 Flores	Y	N	N	Y	Y
18 Jackson Lee	N	N	Y	N	Y
19 Arrington	Y	N	N	Y	Y
20 Castro	N	Y	Y	N	Y
21 Smith	Y	N	N	Y	Y
22 Olson	Y	N	N	Y	Y
23 Hurd	Y	N	N	Y	Y
24 Marchant	Y	N	N	Y	Y
25 Williams	Y	N	N	Y	Y
26 Burgess	Y	N	N	Y	Y
27 Farenthold	Y	N	N	Y	Y
28 Cuellar	N	Y	Y	N	Y
29 Green, G.	N	N	Y	N	Y
30 Johnson, E.B.	N	Y	Y	N	Y
31 Carter	Y	Y	N	Y	Y
32 Sessions	Y	Y	N	Y	Y
33 Veasey	N	N	Y	N	Y
34 Vela	N	N	Y	N	Y
35 Doggett	N	Y	Y	Y	Y
36 Babin	Y	Y	N	Y	Y
UTAH					
1 Bishop	Y	Y	N	Y	Y
2 Stewart	Y	Y	N	Y	Y
3 Curtis	Y	Y	N	Y	Y
4 Love	Y	Y	N	Y	Y
VERMONT					
AL Welch	N	N	Y	N	N
VIRGINIA					
1 Wittman	Y	N	N	Y	Y
2 Taylor	Y	Y	N	Y	Y
3 Scott	N	Y	Y	N	Y
4 McEachin	N	Y	Y	?	Y
5 Garrett	Y	?	N	Y	N
6 Goodlatte	Y	Y	N	Y	Y
7 Brat	Y	?	N	Y	Y
8 Beyer	N	N	Y	N	Y
9 Griffith	Y	Y	N	Y	N
10 Comstock	Y	Y	N	Y	Y
11 Connolly	N	N	Y	N	Y
WASHINGTON					
1 DelBene	N	Y	Y	N	Y
2 Larsen	N	Y	Y	N	Y
3 Herrera Beutler	Y	N	N	Y	Y
4 Newhouse	Y	N	N	Y	Y
5 McMorris Rodgers	Y	Y	N	Y	Y
6 Kilmer	N	N	Y	N	Y
7 Jayapal	N	N	Y	N	N
8 Reichert	Y	Y	N	Y	Y
9 Smith	N	N	Y	N	Y
10 Heck	N	Y	Y	N	Y
WEST VIRGINIA					
1 McKinley	Y	N	N	Y	Y
2 Mooney	Y	Y	N	Y	Y
3 Jenkins	Y	N	N	Y	Y
WISCONSIN					
1 Ryan					
2 Pocan	–	+	+	–	–
3 Kind	N	N	Y	N	Y
4 Moore	N	Y	N	N	N
5 Sensenbrenner	Y	Y	N	Y	Y
6 Grothman	Y	N	N	Y	Y
7 Duffy	Y	N	N	Y	Y
8 Gallagher	Y	N	N	Y	Y
WYOMING					
AL Cheney	Y	Y	N	Y	Y

VOTE NUMBER

632. HR 1, H RES 619. TAX OVERHAUL/PREVIOUS QUESTION. Sessions, R-Texas, motion to order the previous question (thus ending debate and the possibility of amendment) on the rule (H Res 619) that would provide for House floor consideration of the bill (HR 1) that would revise the federal income tax system by: lowering individual and corporate tax rates; consolidating the current seven tax income rates into four rates; eliminating the deduction for state and local income taxes; limiting certain deductions for property taxes and home mortgages; and creating a new system of taxing U.S. corporations with foreign subsidiaries. Motion agreed to 234-193 : R 234-1; D 0-192. Nov. 15, 2017.

633. HR 1, H RES 619. TAX OVERHAUL/RULE. Adoption of the rule (H Res 619) that would provide for House floor consideration of the bill (HR 1) that would revise the federal income tax system by: lowering individual and corporate tax rates; consolidating the current seven tax income rates into four rates; eliminating the deduction for state and local income taxes; limiting certain deductions for property taxes and home mortgages; and creating a new system of taxing U.S. corporations with foreign subsidiaries. Adopted 235-191 : R 235-0; D 0-191. Nov. 15, 2017.

634. HR 2331. MOBILE-FRIENDLY GOVERNMENT WEBSITES/PASSAGE. Hice, R-Ga., motion to suspend the rules and pass the bill that would require new or redesigned public federal agency websites to be configured for viewing and access on a smartphone, tablet or other similar mobile device. Motion agreed to 423-0 : R 234-0; D 189-0. Nov. 15, 2017.

635. HR 3821. ZACK T. ADDINGTON POST OFFICE/PASSAGE. Comer, R-Ky., motion to suspend the rules and pass the bill that would designate the postal facility at 430 Main Street in Clermont, Ga., as the "Zack T. Addington Post Office." Motion agreed to 420-0 : R 230-0; D 190-0. Nov. 15, 2017.

636. HR 2672. SGT. DOUGLAS J. RINEY POST OFFICE/PASSAGE. Comer, R-Ky., motion to suspend the rules and pass the bill that would designate the postal facility at 520 Carter Street in Fairview, Ill., as the "Sgt. Douglas J. Riney Post Office." Motion agreed to 423-0 : R 231-0; D 192-0. Nov. 15, 2017.

637. HR 1. TAX OVERHAUL/PASSAGE. Passage of the bill that would revise the federal income tax system by: lowering individual and corporate tax rates; consolidating the current seven tax income rates into four rates; eliminating the deduction for state and local income taxes; limiting certain deductions for property taxes and home mortgages; and creating a new system of taxing U.S. corporations with foreign subsidiaries. Specifically, it would eliminate personal exemptions and would nearly double the standard deduction. It would raise the child tax credit through 2022, repeal the alternative minimum tax, repeal the estate tax in 2025 and reduce the gift tax rate in 2025. It would establish a new top tax rate for pass-through business income and would modify tax credits related to energy production. Passed 227-205 : R 227-13; D 0-192. Nov. 16, 2017.

638. HR 2768. FOWLER AND BOSKOFF PEAKS DESIGNATION/PASSAGE. Tipton, R-Colo., motion to suspend the rules and pass the bill that would designate specified mountain peaks in the Uncompahgre National Forest in the state of Colorado as "Fowler Peak" and "Boskoff Peak." Motion agreed to 409-0 : R 225-0; D 184-0. Nov. 28, 2017.

	632	633	634	635	636	637	638
ALABAMA							
1 Byrne	Y	Y	Y	Y	Y	Y	Y
2 Roby	Y	Y	Y	Y	Y	Y	Y
3 Rogers	Y	Y	Y	Y	Y	Y	Y
4 Aderholt	Y	Y	Y	Y	Y	Y	Y
5 Brooks	?	?	?	Y	Y	Y	Y
6 Palmer	Y	Y	Y	Y	Y	Y	Y
7 Sewell	N	N	Y	Y	Y	N	+
ALASKA							
AL Young	Y	Y	Y	Y	Y	Y	Y
ARIZONA							
1 O'Halleran	N	N	Y	Y	Y	N	Y
2 McSally	Y	Y	Y	Y	Y	Y	Y
3 Grijalva	N	N	Y	Y	Y	N	Y
4 Gosar	Y	Y	Y	Y	Y	Y	Y
5 Biggs	Y	Y	Y	Y	Y	Y	Y
6 Schweikert	Y	Y	Y	Y	Y	Y	Y
7 Gallego	N	N	Y	Y	Y	N	Y
8 Franks	Y	Y	Y	Y	Y	Y	Y
9 Sinema	N	N	Y	Y	Y	N	Y
ARKANSAS							
1 Crawford	Y	Y	Y	Y	Y	Y	Y
2 Hill	Y	Y	Y	Y	Y	Y	Y
3 Womack	Y	Y	Y	Y	Y	Y	Y
4 Westerman	Y	Y	Y	Y	Y	Y	Y
CALIFORNIA							
1 LaMalfa	Y	Y	Y	Y	Y	Y	Y
2 Huffman	N	N	Y	Y	Y	N	Y
3 Garamendi	N	N	Y	Y	Y	N	Y
4 McClintock	Y	Y	Y	Y	Y	Y	Y
5 Thompson	N	N	Y	Y	Y	N	Y
6 Matsui	N	N	Y	Y	Y	N	Y
7 Bera	N	N	Y	Y	Y	N	Y
8 Cook	Y	Y	Y	Y	Y	Y	Y
9 McNerney	N	N	Y	Y	Y	N	Y
10 Denham	Y	Y	Y	Y	Y	Y	Y
11 DeSaulnier	N	N	Y	Y	Y	N	Y
12 Pelosi	N	?	?	?	Y	N	Y
13 Lee	N	N	Y	Y	Y	N	Y
14 Speier	N	N	Y	Y	Y	N	Y
15 Swalwell	N	N	Y	Y	Y	N	Y
16 Costa	N	N	Y	Y	Y	N	Y
17 Khanna	N	N	Y	Y	Y	N	Y
18 Eshoo	N	N	Y	Y	Y	N	Y
19 Lofgren	N	N	Y	Y	Y	N	Y
20 Panetta	N	N	Y	Y	Y	N	Y
21 Valadao	Y	Y	Y	Y	Y	Y	Y
22 Nunes	Y	Y	Y	Y	Y	Y	Y
23 McCarthy	Y	Y	Y	Y	Y	Y	Y
24 Carbajal	N	N	Y	Y	Y	N	Y
25 Knight	Y	Y	Y	Y	Y	Y	Y
26 Brownley	N	N	Y	Y	Y	N	Y
27 Chu	N	N	Y	Y	Y	N	Y
28 Schiff	N	N	Y	Y	Y	N	Y
29 Cardenas	N	N	Y	Y	Y	N	Y
30 Sherman	N	N	Y	Y	Y	N	Y
31 Aguilar	N	N	Y	Y	Y	N	Y
32 Napolitano	N	N	Y	Y	Y	N	Y
33 Lieu	N	N	Y	Y	Y	N	Y
34 Gomez	N	N	Y	Y	Y	N	Y
35 Torres	N	N	Y	Y	Y	N	Y
36 Ruiz	N	N	Y	Y	Y	N	Y
37 Bass	N	N	Y	Y	Y	N	Y
38 Sánchez, Linda	N	N	Y	Y	Y	N	Y
39 Royce	Y	Y	Y	Y	Y	Y	Y
40 Roybal-Allard	N	N	Y	Y	Y	N	Y
41 Takano	N	N	Y	Y	Y	N	Y
42 Calvert	Y	Y	Y	Y	Y	Y	Y
43 Waters	N	N	Y	Y	Y	N	Y
44 Barragan	N	N	Y	Y	Y	N	Y
45 Walters	Y	Y	Y	Y	Y	Y	Y
46 Correa	N	N	Y	Y	Y	N	Y
47 Lowenthal	N	N	Y	Y	Y	N	Y
48 Rohrabacher	Y	Y	Y	Y	Y	N	?
49 Issa	Y	Y	Y	Y	Y	N	Y
50 Hunter	Y	Y	Y	Y	Y	Y	Y
51 Vargas	N	N	Y	Y	Y	N	Y
52 Peters	N	N	Y	Y	Y	N	Y
53 Davis	N	N	Y	Y	Y	N	Y

	632	633	634	635	636	637	638
COLORADO							
1 DeGette	N	N	Y	Y	Y	N	Y
2 Polis	N	N	Y	Y	Y	N	Y
3 Tipton	Y	Y	Y	Y	Y	Y	Y
4 Buck	Y	Y	Y	Y	Y	Y	Y
5 Lamborn	Y	Y	Y	Y	Y	Y	Y
6 Coffman	Y	Y	Y	Y	Y	Y	Y
7 Perlmutter	N	N	Y	Y	Y	N	Y
CONNECTICUT							
1 Larson	N	N	Y	Y	Y	N	Y
2 Courtney	N	N	Y	Y	Y	N	Y
3 DeLauro	N	N	Y	Y	Y	N	Y
4 Himes	N	N	Y	Y	Y	N	Y
5 Esty	N	N	Y	Y	Y	N	Y
DELAWARE							
AL Blunt Rochester	N	N	Y	Y	Y	N	Y
FLORIDA							
1 Gaetz	Y	Y	Y	Y	Y	Y	Y
2 Dunn	Y	Y	Y	Y	Y	Y	Y
3 Yoho	Y	Y	Y	Y	Y	Y	Y
4 Rutherford	Y	Y	Y	Y	Y	Y	Y
5 Lawson	N	N	Y	Y	Y	N	Y
6 DeSantis	Y	Y	Y	?	Y	Y	?
7 Murphy	N	N	Y	Y	Y	N	Y
8 Posey	Y	Y	Y	Y	Y	Y	?
9 Soto	N	N	Y	Y	Y	N	Y
10 Demings	N	N	Y	Y	Y	N	Y
11 Webster	Y	Y	Y	Y	Y	Y	Y
12 Bilirakis	Y	Y	Y	Y	Y	Y	Y
13 Crist	N	N	Y	Y	Y	N	Y
14 Castor	N	N	Y	Y	Y	N	?
15 Ross	Y	Y	Y	Y	Y	Y	Y
16 Buchanan	Y	Y	Y	?	Y	Y	Y
17 Rooney, T.	Y	Y	Y	Y	Y	Y	Y
18 Mast	Y	Y	Y	Y	Y	Y	Y
19 Rooney, F.	Y	Y	Y	Y	Y	Y	?
20 Hastings	N	N	Y	Y	Y	N	Y
21 Frankel	N	N	Y	Y	Y	N	Y
22 Deutch	N	N	Y	Y	Y	N	Y
23 Wasserman Schultz	N	N	Y	Y	Y	N	Y
24 Wilson	N	N	Y	Y	Y	–	Y
25 Diaz-Balart	Y	Y	Y	Y	Y	Y	Y
26 Curbelo	Y	Y	Y	Y	Y	Y	Y
27 Ros-Lehtinen	Y	Y	Y	Y	Y	Y	Y
GEORGIA							
1 Carter	Y	Y	Y	Y	Y	Y	Y
2 Bishop	N	N	Y	Y	Y	N	Y
3 Ferguson	Y	Y	Y	Y	Y	Y	Y
4 Johnson	N	N	Y	Y	Y	N	Y
5 Lewis	N	N	Y	Y	Y	N	Y
6 Handel	Y	Y	Y	Y	Y	Y	Y
7 Woodall	Y	Y	Y	Y	Y	Y	Y
8 Scott, A.	Y	Y	Y	Y	Y	Y	Y
9 Collins	Y	Y	Y	Y	Y	Y	Y
10 Hice	Y	Y	Y	Y	Y	Y	Y
11 Loudermilk	Y	Y	Y	Y	Y	Y	Y
12 Allen	Y	Y	Y	Y	Y	Y	Y
13 Scott, D.	N	N	Y	Y	Y	N	Y
14 Graves	Y	Y	Y	Y	Y	Y	Y
HAWAII							
1 Hanabusa	N	N	Y	Y	Y	N	Y
2 Gabbard	N	N	Y	Y	Y	N	Y
IDAHO							
1 Labrador	Y	Y	Y	Y	Y	Y	?
2 Simpson	Y	Y	Y	Y	Y	Y	Y
ILLINOIS							
1 Rush	N	N	Y	Y	Y	N	?
2 Kelly	N	N	Y	Y	Y	N	Y
3 Lipinski	N	N	Y	Y	Y	N	Y
4 Gutierrez	N	N	Y	Y	Y	N	+
5 Quigley	N	N	Y	Y	Y	N	Y
6 Roskam	Y	Y	Y	?	Y	Y	Y
7 Davis, D.	N	N	Y	Y	Y	N	Y
8 Krishnamoorthi	N	N	?	Y	Y	N	Y
9 Schakowsky	N	N	Y	Y	Y	N	Y
10 Schneider	N	N	Y	Y	Y	N	Y
11 Foster	N	N	Y	Y	Y	N	Y
12 Bost	Y	Y	Y	Y	Y	Y	Y
13 Davis, R.	Y	Y	Y	Y	Y	Y	Y
14 Hultgren	Y	Y	Y	Y	Y	Y	Y
15 Shimkus	Y	Y	Y	Y	Y	Y	?

KEY	Republicans	Democrats	Independents
Y Voted for (yea)		X Paired against	C Voted "present" to avoid possible conflict of interest
# Paired for		– Announced against	
+ Announced for		P Voted "present"	? Did not vote or otherwise make a position known
N Voted against (nay)			

	632	633	634	635	636	637	638
16 **Kinzinger**	Y	Y	Y	Y	Y	Y	Y
17 Bustos	N	N	Y	Y	Y	N	Y
18 **LaHood**	Y	Y	Y	Y	Y	Y	Y
INDIANA							
1 Visclosky	N	N	Y	Y	Y	N	Y
2 **Walorski**	Y	Y	Y	Y	Y	Y	Y
3 **Banks**	Y	Y	Y	Y	Y	Y	Y
4 **Rokita**	Y	Y	Y	Y	Y	Y	Y
5 **Brooks**	Y	Y	Y	Y	Y	Y	Y
6 **Messer**	Y	Y	Y	Y	Y	Y	?
7 Carson	N	N	Y	Y	Y	N	Y
8 **Bucshon**	Y	Y	Y	Y	Y	Y	Y
9 **Hollingsworth**	Y	Y	Y	Y	Y	Y	Y
IOWA							
1 **Blum**	Y	Y	Y	Y	Y	Y	Y
2 Loebsack	N	N	Y	Y	Y	N	Y
3 **Young**	Y	Y	Y	Y	Y	Y	Y
4 **King**	Y	Y	Y	Y	Y	Y	Y
KANSAS							
1 **Marshall**	Y	Y	Y	Y	Y	Y	Y
2 **Jenkins**	Y	Y	Y	Y	Y	Y	Y
3 **Yoder**	Y	Y	Y	Y	Y	Y	Y
4 **Estes**	Y	Y	Y	Y	Y	Y	Y
KENTUCKY							
1 **Comer**	Y	Y	Y	Y	Y	Y	Y
2 **Guthrie**	Y	Y	Y	Y	Y	Y	Y
3 Yarmuth	N	N	Y	Y	Y	N	Y
4 **Massie**	Y	Y	Y	Y	Y	Y	Y
5 **Rogers**	Y	Y	Y	Y	Y	Y	Y
6 **Barr**	Y	Y	Y	Y	Y	Y	Y
LOUISIANA							
1 **Scalise**	Y	Y	Y	Y	Y	Y	Y
2 Richmond	N	N	Y	Y	Y	N	Y
3 **Higgins**	Y	Y	Y	Y	Y	Y	Y
4 **Johnson**	Y	Y	Y	Y	Y	Y	Y
5 **Abraham**	Y	Y	Y	Y	Y	Y	Y
6 **Graves**	Y	Y	Y	Y	Y	Y	Y
MAINE							
1 Pingree	N	N	Y	Y	Y	N	Y
2 **Poliquin**	Y	Y	Y	Y	Y	Y	Y
MARYLAND							
1 **Harris**	Y	Y	Y	Y	Y	Y	Y
2 Ruppersberger	N	N	Y	Y	Y	N	Y
3 Sarbanes	N	N	Y	Y	Y	N	Y
4 Brown	N	N	Y	Y	Y	N	Y
5 Hoyer	N	N	Y	Y	Y	N	Y
6 Delaney	N	N	Y	Y	Y	N	+
7 Cummings	N	N	Y	Y	Y	N	Y
8 Raskin	N	N	Y	Y	Y	N	Y
MASSACHUSETTS							
1 Neal	N	N	Y	Y	Y	N	Y
2 McGovern	–	–	+	+	+	N	Y
3 Tsongas	N	N	Y	Y	Y	N	?
4 Kennedy	N	N	Y	Y	Y	N	?
5 Clark	N	N	Y	Y	Y	N	Y
6 Moulton	N	N	Y	Y	Y	N	Y
7 Capuano	N	N	Y	Y	Y	N	Y
8 Lynch	N	N	Y	Y	Y	N	Y
9 Keating	N	N	Y	Y	Y	N	Y
MICHIGAN							
1 **Bergman**	Y	Y	Y	Y	Y	Y	Y
2 **Huizenga**	Y	Y	Y	Y	Y	Y	Y
3 **Amash**	Y	Y	Y	Y	Y	Y	Y
4 **Moolenaar**	Y	Y	Y	Y	Y	Y	Y
5 Kildee	N	N	Y	Y	Y	N	Y
6 **Upton**	Y	Y	Y	Y	Y	Y	Y
7 **Walberg**	Y	Y	Y	Y	Y	Y	Y
8 **Bishop**	Y	Y	Y	Y	Y	Y	Y
9 Levin	N	N	Y	Y	Y	N	Y
10 **Mitchell**	Y	Y	Y	Y	Y	Y	Y
11 **Trott**	Y	Y	Y	Y	Y	Y	Y
12 Dingell	N	N	Y	Y	Y	N	Y
13 Conyers	N	N	Y	Y	Y	N	?
14 Lawrence	N	N	Y	Y	Y	N	Y
MINNESOTA							
1 Walz	N	N	Y	Y	Y	N	Y
2 **Lewis**	Y	Y	Y	Y	Y	Y	Y
3 **Paulsen**	Y	Y	Y	Y	Y	Y	Y
4 McCollum	N	N	Y	Y	Y	N	Y

	632	633	634	635	636	637	638
5 Ellison	N	N	Y	Y	Y	N	Y
6 **Emmer**	Y	Y	Y	Y	Y	Y	Y
7 Peterson	N	N	Y	Y	Y	N	Y
8 Nolan	N	N	Y	Y	Y	N	Y
MISSISSIPPI							
1 **Kelly**	Y	Y	Y	Y	Y	Y	Y
2 Thompson	N	N	Y	Y	Y	N	Y
3 **Harper**	Y	Y	Y	Y	Y	Y	Y
4 **Palazzo**	Y	Y	Y	Y	Y	Y	Y
MISSOURI							
1 Clay	N	N	Y	Y	Y	N	Y
2 **Wagner**	Y	Y	Y	Y	Y	Y	Y
3 **Luetkemeyer**	Y	Y	Y	Y	Y	Y	Y
4 **Hartzler**	Y	Y	Y	Y	Y	Y	Y
5 Cleaver	N	N	Y	Y	Y	N	Y
6 **Graves**	Y	Y	Y	Y	Y	Y	Y
7 **Long**	Y	Y	Y	Y	Y	Y	Y
8 **Smith**	Y	Y	Y	Y	Y	Y	Y
MONTANA							
AL **Gianforte**	Y	Y	Y	Y	Y	Y	Y
NEBRASKA							
1 **Fortenberry**	Y	Y	Y	Y	Y	Y	Y
2 **Bacon**	Y	Y	Y	Y	Y	Y	Y
3 **Smith**	Y	Y	Y	Y	Y	Y	Y
NEVADA							
1 Titus	N	N	Y	Y	Y	N	Y
2 **Amodei**	Y	Y	Y	Y	Y	Y	Y
3 Rosen	N	N	Y	Y	Y	N	Y
4 Kihuen	N	N	?	Y	Y	N	Y
NEW HAMPSHIRE							
1 Shea-Porter	N	N	Y	Y	Y	N	Y
2 Kuster	N	N	Y	Y	Y	N	Y
NEW JERSEY							
1 Norcross	N	N	Y	Y	Y	N	Y
2 **LoBiondo**	Y	Y	Y	Y	Y	N	Y
3 **MacArthur**	Y	Y	Y	Y	Y	Y	Y
4 **Smith**	Y	Y	Y	Y	Y	N	Y
5 Gottheimer	N	N	Y	Y	Y	N	Y
6 Pallone	N	N	Y	Y	Y	N	Y
7 **Lance**	Y	Y	Y	Y	Y	N	Y
8 Sires	N	N	Y	Y	Y	N	Y
9 Pascrell	N	N	Y	Y	Y	N	Y
10 Payne	N	N	Y	Y	Y	N	Y
11 **Frelinghuysen**	Y	Y	Y	Y	Y	N	Y
12 Watson Coleman	N	N	Y	Y	Y	N	Y
NEW MEXICO							
1 Lujan Grisham	N	N	Y	Y	Y	N	Y
2 **Pearce**	Y	Y	Y	Y	Y	Y	Y
3 Luján	N	N	Y	Y	Y	N	Y
NEW YORK							
1 **Zeldin**	Y	Y	Y	Y	Y	N	Y
2 **King**	Y	Y	Y	Y	Y	N	Y
3 Suozzi	N	N	Y	Y	Y	N	Y
4 Rice	N	N	Y	Y	Y	N	Y
5 Meeks	N	N	Y	Y	Y	N	Y
6 Meng	N	N	Y	Y	Y	N	Y
7 Velázquez	N	N	Y	Y	Y	N	Y
8 Jeffries	N	N	Y	Y	Y	N	Y
9 Clarke	N	N	Y	Y	Y	N	Y
10 Nadler	N	N	Y	Y	Y	N	Y
11 **Donovan**	Y	Y	Y	Y	Y	N	Y
12 Maloney, C.	N	N	Y	Y	Y	N	Y
13 Espaillat	N	N	Y	Y	Y	N	Y
14 Crowley	N	N	Y	Y	Y	N	Y
15 Serrano	N	N	Y	Y	Y	N	Y
16 Engel	N	N	Y	Y	Y	N	Y
17 Lowey	N	N	Y	Y	Y	N	Y
18 Maloney, S.P.	N	N	Y	Y	Y	N	Y
19 **Faso**	Y	Y	Y	Y	Y	N	Y
20 Tonko	N	N	Y	Y	Y	N	Y
21 **Stefanik**	Y	Y	Y	Y	Y	N	Y
22 **Tenney**	Y	Y	Y	Y	Y	Y	Y
23 **Reed**	Y	Y	Y	Y	Y	Y	Y
24 **Katko**	Y	Y	Y	Y	Y	N	Y
25 Slaughter	N	N	Y	Y	Y	N	Y
26 Higgins	N	N	Y	Y	Y	N	Y
27 **Collins**	Y	Y	Y	Y	Y	Y	Y
NORTH CAROLINA							
1 Butterfield	N	N	Y	Y	Y	N	?
2 **Holding**	Y	Y	Y	Y	Y	Y	Y
3 **Jones**	N	Y	Y	Y	Y	N	Y
4 Price	N	N	Y	?	Y	N	Y

	632	633	634	635	636	637	638
5 **Foxx**	Y	Y	Y	Y	Y	Y	Y
6 **Walker**	Y	Y	Y	Y	Y	Y	Y
7 **Rouzer**	Y	Y	Y	Y	Y	Y	Y
8 **Hudson**	Y	Y	Y	Y	+	Y	Y
9 **Pittenger**	Y	Y	Y	Y	Y	Y	+
10 **McHenry**	Y	Y	Y	Y	Y	Y	Y
11 **Meadows**	Y	Y	Y	Y	Y	Y	Y
12 Adams	N	N	Y	Y	Y	N	Y
13 **Budd**	Y	Y	Y	Y	Y	Y	Y
NORTH DAKOTA							
AL **Cramer**	Y	Y	Y	Y	Y	Y	Y
OHIO							
1 **Chabot**	Y	Y	Y	Y	Y	Y	Y
2 **Wenstrup**	Y	Y	Y	Y	Y	Y	Y
3 Beatty	N	N	Y	Y	Y	N	Y
4 **Jordan**	Y	Y	Y	?	Y	Y	Y
5 **Latta**	Y	Y	Y	Y	Y	Y	Y
6 **Johnson**	Y	Y	Y	Y	Y	Y	Y
7 **Gibbs**	Y	Y	Y	Y	Y	Y	Y
8 **Davidson**	Y	Y	Y	Y	Y	Y	Y
9 Kaptur	N	N	Y	Y	Y	N	Y
10 **Turner**	Y	Y	Y	Y	Y	Y	Y
11 Fudge	N	N	Y	Y	Y	N	Y
12 **Tiberi**	Y	Y	Y	Y	Y	Y	Y
13 Ryan	N	N	Y	Y	Y	N	Y
14 **Joyce**	Y	Y	Y	Y	Y	Y	Y
15 **Stivers**	Y	Y	Y	Y	Y	Y	?
16 **Renacci**	?	?	?	?	?	Y	+
OKLAHOMA							
1 **Bridenstine**	?	?	?	?	?	Y	?
2 **Mullin**	Y	Y	Y	Y	Y	Y	Y
3 **Lucas**	Y	Y	Y	Y	Y	Y	?
4 **Cole**	Y	Y	Y	Y	Y	Y	Y
5 **Russell**	Y	Y	Y	+	+	Y	Y
OREGON							
1 Bonamici	N	N	Y	Y	Y	N	Y
2 **Walden**	Y	Y	Y	Y	Y	Y	Y
3 Blumenauer	N	N	Y	Y	Y	N	Y
4 DeFazio	N	N	Y	Y	Y	N	Y
5 Schrader	N	N	Y	Y	Y	N	Y
PENNSYLVANIA							
1 Brady	N	N	Y	Y	Y	N	Y
2 Evans	N	N	Y	Y	Y	N	Y
3 **Kelly**	Y	Y	Y	Y	Y	Y	Y
4 **Perry**	Y	Y	Y	Y	Y	Y	Y
5 **Thompson**	Y	Y	Y	Y	Y	Y	Y
6 **Costello**	Y	Y	Y	Y	Y	Y	Y
7 **Meehan**	Y	Y	Y	Y	Y	Y	Y
8 **Fitzpatrick**	Y	Y	Y	Y	Y	Y	Y
9 **Shuster**	Y	Y	Y	Y	Y	Y	Y
10 **Marino**	Y	Y	Y	Y	Y	Y	Y
11 **Barletta**	Y	Y	Y	Y	Y	Y	Y
12 **Rothfus**	Y	Y	Y	Y	Y	Y	Y
13 Boyle	N	N	Y	Y	Y	N	Y
14 Doyle	N	N	Y	Y	Y	N	Y
15 **Dent**	Y	Y	Y	Y	Y	Y	Y
16 **Smucker**	Y	Y	Y	Y	Y	Y	Y
17 Cartwright	N	N	Y	Y	Y	N	Y
RHODE ISLAND							
1 Cicilline	N	N	Y	Y	Y	N	Y
2 Langevin	N	N	Y	Y	Y	N	Y
SOUTH CAROLINA							
1 **Sanford**	Y	Y	Y	Y	Y	Y	Y
2 **Wilson**	Y	Y	Y	Y	Y	Y	Y
3 **Duncan**	Y	Y	Y	Y	Y	Y	Y
4 **Gowdy**	Y	Y	Y	Y	Y	Y	Y
5 **Norman**	Y	Y	Y	Y	Y	Y	Y
6 Clyburn	N	N	Y	Y	Y	N	Y
7 **Rice**	Y	Y	Y	Y	Y	Y	Y
SOUTH DAKOTA							
AL **Noem**	Y	Y	Y	Y	Y	Y	Y
TENNESSEE							
1 **Roe**	Y	Y	?	Y	Y	Y	Y
2 **Duncan**	Y	Y	Y	Y	Y	Y	Y
3 **Fleischmann**	Y	Y	Y	Y	Y	Y	Y
4 **DesJarlais**	Y	Y	Y	Y	Y	Y	Y
5 Cooper	N	N	Y	Y	Y	N	Y
6 **Black**	Y	Y	Y	Y	Y	Y	?
7 **Blackburn**	Y	Y	Y	Y	Y	Y	Y
8 **Kustoff**	Y	Y	Y	Y	Y	Y	Y
9 Cohen	N	N	Y	Y	Y	N	Y

	632	633	634	635	636	637	638
TEXAS							
1 **Gohmert**	Y	Y	Y	Y	Y	Y	Y
2 **Poe**	Y	Y	Y	Y	Y	Y	Y
3 **Johnson, S.**	?	?	?	?	?	Y	Y
4 **Ratcliffe**	Y	Y	Y	Y	Y	Y	Y
5 **Hensarling**	Y	Y	Y	Y	Y	Y	Y
6 **Barton**	Y	Y	Y	?	?	Y	Y
7 **Culberson**	Y	Y	Y	Y	Y	Y	Y
8 **Brady**	Y	Y	Y	Y	Y	Y	Y
9 Green, A.	N	N	Y	Y	Y	N	Y
10 **McCaul**	Y	Y	Y	Y	Y	Y	Y
11 **Conaway**	Y	Y	Y	Y	Y	Y	Y
12 **Granger**	Y	Y	Y	+	+	Y	Y
13 **Thornberry**	Y	Y	Y	Y	Y	Y	Y
14 **Weber**	Y	Y	Y	Y	Y	Y	Y
15 Gonzalez	N	N	Y	Y	Y	N	Y
16 O'Rourke	N	N	Y	Y	Y	N	Y
17 **Flores**	Y	Y	Y	Y	Y	Y	Y
18 Jackson Lee	N	N	Y	Y	Y	N	Y
19 **Arrington**	Y	Y	Y	Y	Y	Y	Y
20 Castro	N	N	Y	Y	Y	N	Y
21 **Smith**	Y	Y	Y	Y	Y	Y	Y
22 **Olson**	Y	Y	Y	Y	Y	Y	Y
23 **Hurd**	Y	Y	Y	Y	Y	Y	Y
24 **Marchant**	Y	Y	Y	Y	Y	Y	Y
25 **Williams**	Y	Y	Y	Y	Y	Y	Y
26 **Burgess**	Y	Y	Y	Y	Y	Y	Y
27 **Farenthold**	Y	Y	Y	Y	Y	Y	Y
28 Cuellar	N	N	Y	Y	Y	N	Y
29 Green, G.	N	N	Y	Y	Y	N	Y
30 Johnson, E.B.	N	N	Y	Y	Y	N	Y
31 **Carter**	Y	Y	Y	Y	Y	Y	Y
32 **Sessions**	Y	Y	Y	Y	Y	Y	Y
33 Veasey	N	N	Y	Y	Y	N	Y
34 Vela	N	N	Y	Y	Y	N	Y
35 Doggett	N	N	Y	Y	Y	N	Y
36 **Babin**	Y	Y	Y	Y	Y	Y	Y
UTAH							
1 **Bishop**	Y	Y	Y	Y	Y	Y	Y
2 **Stewart**	Y	Y	Y	Y	Y	Y	Y
3 **Curtis**	Y	Y	Y	Y	Y	Y	Y
4 **Love**	Y	Y	Y	Y	Y	Y	Y
VERMONT							
AL Welch	N	N	Y	Y	Y	N	Y
VIRGINIA							
1 **Wittman**	Y	Y	Y	Y	Y	Y	Y
2 **Taylor**	Y	Y	Y	Y	Y	Y	Y
3 Scott	N	N	Y	Y	Y	N	Y
4 McEachin	N	N	Y	Y	Y	N	Y
5 **Garrett**	Y	Y	Y	Y	Y	Y	Y
6 **Goodlatte**	Y	Y	Y	Y	Y	Y	Y
7 **Brat**	Y	Y	Y	Y	Y	Y	Y
8 Beyer	N	N	Y	Y	Y	N	Y
9 **Griffith**	Y	Y	Y	Y	Y	Y	Y
10 **Comstock**	Y	Y	Y	Y	Y	Y	Y
11 Connolly	N	N	Y	Y	Y	N	Y
WASHINGTON							
1 DelBene	N	N	Y	Y	Y	N	Y
2 Larsen	N	N	Y	Y	Y	N	Y
3 **Herrera Beutler**	Y	Y	Y	Y	Y	Y	+
4 **Newhouse**	Y	Y	Y	Y	Y	Y	Y
5 **McMorris Rodgers**	Y	Y	Y	Y	Y	Y	Y
6 Kilmer	N	N	Y	Y	Y	N	Y
7 Jayapal	N	N	Y	Y	Y	N	Y
8 **Reichert**	Y	Y	Y	Y	Y	Y	Y
9 Smith	N	N	Y	Y	Y	N	Y
10 Heck	N	N	Y	Y	Y	N	Y
WEST VIRGINIA							
1 **McKinley**	Y	Y	Y	Y	Y	Y	Y
2 **Mooney**	Y	Y	Y	Y	Y	Y	Y
3 **Jenkins**	Y	Y	Y	Y	Y	Y	Y
WISCONSIN							
1 **Ryan**						Y	
2 Pocan	–	–	+	+	+	+	+
3 Kind	N	N	Y	Y	Y	N	Y
4 Moore	N	N	Y	Y	Y	N	Y
5 **Sensenbrenner**	Y	Y	Y	Y	Y	Y	Y
6 **Grothman**	Y	Y	Y	Y	Y	Y	Y
7 **Duffy**	Y	Y	Y	Y	Y	Y	Y
8 **Gallagher**	Y	Y	Y	Y	Y	Y	Y
WYOMING							
AL **Cheney**	Y	Y	Y	Y	Y	Y	Y

VOTE NUMBER

639. HR 3115. POLYMET MINING LAND EXCHANGE/PASSAGE. Tipton, R-Colo., motion to suspend the rules and pass the bill that would require the secretary of the Interior to exchange 6,650 acres of land within the Superior National Forest in Minnesota for 6,690 acres currently owned by PolyMet Mining Company. The bill would waive PolyMet's right to a cash equalization payment for the value of the land. Motion agreed to 309-99 : R 220-4; D 89-95. Nov. 28, 2017.

640. HR 3017, HR 3905, H RES 631. EPA BROWNFIELDS AND NATIONAL FOREST MINING/PREVIOUS QUESTION. Cheney, R-Wyo., motion to order the previous question (thus ending debate and the possibility of amendment) on the rule (H Res 631) that would provide for House floor consideration of the bill (HR 3017) that would reauthorize the EPA's brownfields program through fiscal year 2022. It would provide for consideration of the bill (HR 3905) that would require congressional approval of any mineral withdrawal or national monument designation involving the National Forest System lands in the State of Minnesota. Motion agreed to 227-189 : R 227-1; D 0-188. Nov. 29, 2017.

641. HR 3017, HR 3905, H RES 631. EPA BROWNFIELDS AND NATIONAL FOREST MINING/RULE. Adoption of the rule (H Res 631) that would provide for House floor consideration of the bill (HR 3017) that would reauthorize the EPA's brownfields program through fiscal year 2022. It would provide for consideration of the bill (HR 3905) that would require congressional approval of any mineral withdrawal or national monument designation involving the National Forest System lands in the state of Minnesota. Adopted 228-186 : R 228-0; D 0-186. Nov. 29, 2017.

642. HR 3905. NATIONAL FOREST MINING/NATIONAL FOREST MINERAL LEASE ROYALTIES. Grijalva, D-Ariz., amendment that would set a royalty rate for mineral leases in the Superior National Forest at no less than 16.66 percent. Rejected in Committee of the Whole 182-237 : R 1-230; D 181-7. Nov. 30, 2017.

643. HR 3905. NATIONAL FOREST MINING/PASSAGE. Passage of the bill that would prohibit the designation of national monuments and the withdrawal of lands in the National Forest System in the state of Minnesota from mineral and geothermal leases without the approval of Congress. It would designate any mineral leases issued within the boundaries of the National Forest System lands in Minnesota as indeterminate preference right leases. Passed 216-204 : R 208-22; D 8-182. Nov. 30, 2017.

644. H RES 635, HR 1699, HR 4182. FEDERAL WORKFORCE PROBATION AND HOME LENDING REGULATION/PREVIOUS QUESTION. Woodall, R-Ga., motion to order the previous question (thus ending debate and the possibility of amendment) on the rule (H Res 635) that would provide for House floor consideration of the bill (HR 4182), that would change the probationary period for certain federal employees in new or promoted positions and provide for consideration of the bill (HR 1699) that would modify federal regulations regarding high-cost mortgages as they apply to manufactured housing. Motion agreed to 229-189 : R 229-0; D 0-189. Nov. 30, 2017.

645. H RES 635, HR 1699, HR 4182. FEDERAL WORKFORCE PROBATION AND HOME LENDING REGULATION/RULE. Adoption of the rule (H Res 635) that would provide for House floor consideration of the bill (HR 4182) that would change the probationary period for certain federal employees in new or promoted positions and provide for consideration of the bill (HR 1699) that would modify federal regulations regarding high-cost mortgages as they apply to manufactured housing. Adopted 226-186 : R 226-0; D 0-186. Nov. 30, 2017.

	639	640	641	642	643	644	645
ALABAMA							
1 **Byrne**	Y	Y	Y	N	Y	Y	Y
2 **Roby**	Y	Y	Y	N	Y	Y	Y
3 **Rogers**	Y	Y	Y	N	Y	Y	Y
4 **Aderholt**	Y	Y	Y	N	Y	Y	Y
5 **Brooks**	Y	Y	Y	N	Y	Y	Y
6 **Palmer**	Y	Y	Y	N	Y	Y	Y
7 Sewell	–	N	N	Y	N	N	N
ALASKA							
AL **Young**	Y	Y	Y	N	Y	Y	Y
ARIZONA							
1 O'Halleran	Y	N	N	Y	N	N	N
2 **McSally**	Y	Y	Y	N	Y	Y	Y
3 Grijalva	N	N	N	Y	N	N	N
4 **Gosar**	Y	Y	Y	N	Y	Y	Y
5 **Biggs**	Y	Y	Y	N	Y	Y	Y
6 **Schweikert**	Y	Y	Y	N	Y	Y	Y
7 Gallego	N	N	N	Y	N	N	N
8 **Franks**	Y	Y	Y	N	Y	Y	Y
9 Sinema	Y	N	N	N	N	N	N
ARKANSAS							
1 **Crawford**	Y	Y	Y	N	Y	Y	Y
2 **Hill**	Y	Y	Y	N	Y	Y	Y
3 **Womack**	Y	Y	Y	N	Y	Y	Y
4 **Westerman**	Y	Y	Y	N	Y	Y	Y
CALIFORNIA							
1 **LaMalfa**	Y	Y	Y	N	Y	Y	Y
2 Huffman	Y	N	N	Y	N	N	N
3 Garamendi	N	N	N	Y	N	N	N
4 **McClintock**	Y	Y	Y	N	Y	Y	Y
5 Thompson	Y	N	N	Y	N	N	N
6 Matsui	Y	N	N	Y	N	N	N
7 Bera	Y	N	N	Y	N	N	N
8 **Cook**	Y	Y	Y	N	Y	Y	Y
9 McNerney	N	N	N	Y	N	N	N
10 **Denham**	Y	Y	Y	N	Y	Y	Y
11 DeSaulnier	N	N	N	Y	N	N	N
12 Pelosi	Y	N	N	Y	N	N	N
13 Lee	N	N	N	Y	N	N	N
14 Speier	Y	N	N	Y	N	N	N
15 Swalwell	N	N	N	Y	N	N	N
16 Costa	Y	N	N	Y	Y	N	N
17 Khanna	N	N	N	?	N	N	N
18 Eshoo	N	N	N	Y	N	N	N
19 Lofgren	N	N	N	Y	N	N	N
20 Panetta	Y	N	N	Y	N	N	N
21 **Valadao**	Y	Y	Y	N	Y	Y	Y
22 **Nunes**	Y	Y	Y	N	Y	Y	Y
23 **McCarthy**	Y	Y	Y	N	Y	Y	Y
24 Carbajal	Y	N	N	Y	N	N	N
25 **Knight**	Y	Y	Y	N	Y	Y	Y
26 Brownley	N	N	N	Y	N	N	N
27 Chu	N	N	N	Y	N	N	N
28 Schiff	Y	N	N	Y	N	N	N
29 Cardenas	Y	N	N	Y	N	N	N
30 Sherman	Y	N	N	Y	N	N	N
31 Aguilar	Y	N	N	Y	N	N	N
32 Napolitano	N	N	N	Y	N	N	N
33 Lieu	N	N	N	Y	N	N	N
34 Gomez	N	N	N	Y	N	N	N
35 Torres	N	N	N	Y	N	N	N
36 Ruiz	N	N	N	Y	N	N	N
37 Bass	N	N	N	Y	N	N	N
38 Sánchez, Linda	Y	N	N	Y	N	N	N
39 **Royce**	Y	Y	Y	N	Y	Y	Y
40 Roybal-Allard	N	N	N	Y	N	N	N
41 Takano	N	N	N	Y	N	N	N
42 **Calvert**	Y	Y	Y	N	Y	Y	Y
43 Waters	Y	N	N	Y	N	N	N
44 Barragan	N	N	N	Y	N	N	N
45 **Walters**	Y	Y	Y	N	Y	Y	Y
46 Correa	Y	N	N	Y	N	N	N
47 Lowenthal	Y	N	N	Y	N	N	N
48 **Rohrabacher**	?	Y	Y	N	Y	Y	Y
49 **Issa**	Y	Y	Y	N	Y	Y	Y
50 **Hunter**	Y	Y	Y	N	Y	Y	Y
51 Vargas	Y	N	N	Y	N	N	N
52 Peters	Y	N	N	Y	N	N	N
53 Davis	N	N	N	Y	N	N	N

	639	640	641	642	643	644	645
COLORADO							
1 DeGette	Y	N	N	Y	N	N	N
2 Polis	N	N	N	Y	N	N	N
3 **Tipton**	Y	Y	Y	N	Y	Y	Y
4 **Buck**	Y	Y	Y	N	Y	Y	Y
5 **Lamborn**	Y	Y	Y	N	Y	Y	Y
6 **Coffman**	Y	Y	Y	N	Y	Y	Y
7 Perlmutter	Y	N	N	Y	N	N	N
CONNECTICUT							
1 Larson	N	?	N	N	N	N	N
2 Courtney	N	N	N	Y	N	N	–
3 DeLauro	N	N	N	Y	N	N	N
4 Himes	N	N	N	Y	N	N	N
5 Esty	N	N	N	Y	N	N	N
DELAWARE							
AL Blunt Rochester	Y	N	N	Y	N	N	N
FLORIDA							
1 **Gaetz**	Y	Y	Y	N	Y	Y	Y
2 **Dunn**	Y	Y	Y	N	Y	Y	Y
3 **Yoho**	Y	Y	Y	N	Y	Y	Y
4 **Rutherford**	Y	Y	Y	N	Y	Y	Y
5 Lawson	Y	N	N	N	N	N	N
6 **DeSantis**	?	Y	Y	N	Y	Y	Y
7 Murphy	N	N	N	Y	N	N	N
8 **Posey**	?	?	?	?	?	?	?
9 Soto	Y	N	N	Y	N	N	N
10 Demings	N	N	N	Y	N	N	N
11 **Webster**	Y	Y	Y	–	+	+	+
12 **Bilirakis**	Y	Y	Y	N	Y	Y	?
13 Crist	N	N	N	Y	N	N	N
14 Castor	?	N	N	Y	N	N	N
15 **Ross**	Y	Y	Y	N	Y	Y	Y
16 **Buchanan**	Y	Y	Y	N	Y	?	?
17 **Rooney, T.**	Y	Y	Y	N	Y	?	?
18 **Mast**	Y	Y	Y	N	Y	Y	Y
19 **Rooney, F.**	?	Y	Y	N	Y	Y	Y
20 Hastings	Y	N	N	Y	N	N	–
21 Frankel	N	N	N	Y	N	N	N
22 Deutch	N	N	N	Y	N	N	N
23 Wasserman Schultz	N	N	N	Y	N	N	N
24 Wilson	N	N	N	Y	N	N	N
25 **Diaz-Balart**	Y	Y	Y	N	Y	Y	Y
26 **Curbelo**	Y	Y	Y	N	Y	Y	Y
27 **Ros-Lehtinen**	Y	Y	Y	N	Y	Y	Y
GEORGIA							
1 **Carter**	Y	Y	Y	N	Y	Y	Y
2 Bishop	Y	N	N	Y	N	N	N
3 **Ferguson**	Y	Y	Y	N	Y	Y	Y
4 Johnson	N	N	N	Y	N	N	N
5 Lewis	N	N	?	Y	N	N	N
6 **Handel**	Y	Y	Y	N	Y	Y	Y
7 **Woodall**	Y	Y	Y	N	Y	Y	Y
8 **Scott, A.**	Y	Y	Y	N	Y	Y	Y
9 **Collins**	Y	Y	Y	–	+	+	+
10 **Hice**	Y	Y	Y	N	Y	Y	Y
11 **Loudermilk**	Y	Y	Y	N	Y	Y	Y
12 **Allen**	Y	Y	Y	N	Y	Y	Y
13 Scott, D.	N	N	N	Y	N	N	N
14 **Graves**	Y	Y	Y	N	Y	Y	Y
HAWAII							
1 Hanabusa	Y	N	N	Y	N	N	N
2 Gabbard	N	N	N	Y	N	N	N
IDAHO							
1 **Labrador**	?	Y	Y	N	Y	Y	Y
2 **Simpson**	Y	Y	Y	N	Y	Y	Y
ILLINOIS							
1 Rush	?	N	N	Y	N	N	N
2 Kelly	N	N	N	Y	N	N	N
3 Lipinski	Y	N	N	Y	N	N	N
4 Gutierrez	–	N	N	+	N	N	N
5 Quigley	N	N	N	Y	N	N	N
6 **Roskam**	Y	Y	Y	N	Y	Y	Y
7 Davis, D.	N	N	N	Y	N	N	N
8 Krishnamoorthi	N	N	N	Y	N	N	N
9 Schakowsky	N	N	N	Y	N	N	N
10 Schneider	N	N	N	Y	N	N	N
11 Foster	N	N	N	Y	N	N	N
12 **Bost**	Y	Y	Y	N	Y	Y	Y
13 **Davis, R.**	Y	Y	Y	N	Y	Y	Y
14 **Hultgren**	Y	Y	Y	N	Y	Y	Y
15 **Shimkus**	?	Y	Y	N	Y	Y	Y

	639	640	641	642	643	644	645
16 **Kinzinger**	Y	Y	Y	N	Y	Y	Y
17 Bustos	Y	N	N	Y	N	N	N
18 **LaHood**	Y	Y	Y	N	Y	Y	Y
INDIANA							
1 Visclosky	Y	N	N	Y	N	N	N
2 **Walorski**	Y	Y	Y	N	Y	Y	Y
3 **Banks**	Y	Y	Y	N	Y	Y	Y
4 **Rokita**	Y	Y	Y	N	Y	Y	Y
5 **Brooks**	Y	Y	Y	N	Y	Y	Y
6 **Messer**	?	Y	Y	N	Y	Y	Y
7 Carson	N	N	N	Y	N	N	N
8 **Bucshon**	Y	Y	Y	N	Y	Y	Y
9 **Hollingsworth**	Y	Y	Y	N	Y	Y	Y
IOWA							
1 **Blum**	Y	Y	Y	N	Y	Y	Y
2 Loebsack	Y	N	N	Y	N	N	N
3 **Young**	Y	Y	Y	N	Y	Y	Y
4 **King**	Y	Y	Y	N	Y	Y	Y
KANSAS							
1 **Marshall**	Y	Y	Y	N	Y	Y	Y
2 **Jenkins**	Y	Y	Y	N	Y	Y	Y
3 **Yoder**	Y	Y	Y	N	Y	Y	Y
4 **Estes**	Y	Y	Y	N	Y	Y	Y
KENTUCKY							
1 **Comer**	Y	Y	Y	N	Y	Y	Y
2 **Guthrie**	Y	Y	Y	N	Y	Y	Y
3 Yarmuth	Y	N	N	Y	N	N	N
4 **Massie**	N	Y	Y	N	Y	Y	Y
5 **Rogers**	Y	Y	Y	N	Y	Y	Y
6 **Barr**	Y	Y	Y	N	Y	Y	Y
LOUISIANA							
1 **Scalise**	Y	Y	Y	N	Y	+	+
2 Richmond	N	N	N	N	N	N	N
3 **Higgins**	Y	Y	Y	N	Y	Y	Y
4 **Johnson**	Y	Y	Y	N	Y	Y	Y
5 **Abraham**	Y	Y	Y	N	Y	Y	Y
6 **Graves**	Y	Y	Y	N	Y	Y	Y
MAINE							
1 Pingree	N	N	N	Y	N	N	N
2 **Poliquin**	Y	Y	Y	N	Y	Y	Y
MARYLAND							
1 **Harris**	Y	Y	Y	N	Y	Y	Y
2 Ruppersberger	Y	N	N	Y	N	N	N
3 Sarbanes	N	N	N	Y	N	N	N
4 Brown	Y	N	N	Y	N	N	N
5 Hoyer	Y	N	N	Y	N	N	N
6 Delaney	+	N	N	Y	N	N	N
7 Cummings	N	N	N	Y	N	N	N
8 Raskin	N	N	N	Y	N	N	N
MASSACHUSETTS							
1 Neal	Y	N	N	Y	N	N	N
2 McGovern	N	N	N	Y	N	N	N
3 Tsongas	?	N	N	Y	N	N	N
4 Kennedy	?	?	?	?	?	?	?
5 Clark	N	N	N	Y	N	N	N
6 Moulton	N	N	N	Y	N	N	N
7 Capuano	N	N	N	Y	N	N	N
8 Lynch	Y	N	N	Y	N	N	N
9 Keating	Y	N	N	Y	N	N	N
MICHIGAN							
1 **Bergman**	Y	Y	Y	N	Y	Y	Y
2 **Huizenga**	Y	Y	Y	N	Y	Y	Y
3 **Amash**	N	Y	Y	N	N	Y	Y
4 **Moolenaar**	Y	Y	Y	N	Y	Y	Y
5 Kildee	Y	N	N	Y	N	?	N
6 **Upton**	Y	Y	Y	N	N	Y	Y
7 **Walberg**	Y	Y	Y	N	Y	Y	Y
8 **Bishop**	Y	Y	Y	N	Y	Y	Y
9 Levin	Y	N	N	Y	N	N	N
10 **Mitchell**	Y	Y	Y	N	Y	Y	Y
11 **Trott**	Y	Y	Y	N	Y	Y	Y
12 Dingell	N	N	N	Y	N	N	N
13 Conyers	?	?	?	?	?	?	?
14 Lawrence	N	N	N	Y	N	N	N
MINNESOTA							
1 Walz	Y	N	N	N	N	N	N
2 **Lewis**	Y	Y	Y	N	Y	Y	Y
3 **Paulsen**	Y	Y	Y	N	N	Y	Y
4 McCollum	N	N	N	Y	N	N	N

	639	640	641	642	643	644	645
5 Ellison	N	N	N	Y	N	N	N
6 **Emmer**	Y	Y	Y	N	Y	Y	Y
7 Peterson	Y	N	N	N	Y	N	N
8 Nolan	Y	N	N	N	Y	N	?
MISSISSIPPI							
1 **Kelly**	Y	Y	Y	N	Y	Y	Y
2 Thompson	Y	N	N	Y	N	N	N
3 **Harper**	Y	Y	Y	?	?	?	?
4 **Palazzo**	Y	Y	Y	N	Y	Y	Y
MISSOURI							
1 Clay	N	N	N	Y	N	N	N
2 **Wagner**	Y	?	?	N	Y	Y	Y
3 **Luetkemeyer**	Y	?	?	N	Y	Y	Y
4 **Hartzler**	Y	+	+	N	Y	Y	Y
5 Cleaver	Y	N	N	Y	N	N	N
6 **Graves**	Y	+	+	N	Y	Y	Y
7 **Long**	Y	+	+	N	Y	Y	Y
8 **Smith**	Y	?	?	N	Y	Y	Y
MONTANA							
AL **Gianforte**	Y	Y	Y	N	Y	Y	Y
NEBRASKA							
1 **Fortenberry**	Y	Y	Y	N	N	Y	Y
2 **Bacon**	Y	Y	Y	N	Y	Y	Y
3 **Smith**	Y	Y	Y	N	Y	Y	Y
NEVADA							
1 Titus	N	N	N	Y	N	N	N
2 **Amodei**	Y	Y	Y	N	Y	Y	Y
3 Rosen	Y	N	N	Y	N	N	N
4 Kihuen	Y	N	N	Y	N	N	N
NEW HAMPSHIRE							
1 Shea-Porter	N	N	N	Y	N	N	N
2 Kuster	N	N	N	Y	N	N	N
NEW JERSEY							
1 Norcross	Y	N	N	Y	Y	N	N
2 **LoBiondo**	Y	Y	Y	N	N	Y	Y
3 **MacArthur**	Y	Y	Y	N	N	Y	Y
4 **Smith**	Y	Y	Y	N	N	Y	Y
5 Gottheimer	Y	N	N	Y	N	N	?
6 Pallone	N	N	N	Y	N	N	N
7 **Lance**	Y	Y	Y	N	N	Y	Y
8 Sires	Y	N	N	Y	N	N	N
9 Pascrell	Y	N	N	Y	Y	N	N
10 Payne	N	N	N	Y	N	N	N
11 **Frelinghuysen**	Y	Y	Y	N	Y	Y	Y
12 Watson Coleman	N	N	N	Y	N	N	N
NEW MEXICO							
1 Lujan Grisham	N	N	N	Y	N	N	N
2 **Pearce**	Y	Y	Y	N	Y	Y	Y
3 Luján	N	N	N	Y	N	N	N
NEW YORK							
1 **Zeldin**	Y	Y	Y	N	Y	Y	Y
2 **King**	Y	Y	Y	N	Y	Y	Y
3 Suozzi	Y	N	?	Y	N	N	N
4 Rice	Y	N	N	Y	N	N	N
5 Meeks	Y	N	N	Y	N	N	N
6 Meng	N	N	N	Y	N	N	N
7 Velázquez	N	N	N	Y	N	N	N
8 Jeffries	Y	N	N	Y	N	N	N
9 Clarke	N	N	N	Y	N	N	N
10 Nadler	N	N	?	Y	N	N	N
11 **Donovan**	Y	Y	Y	N	Y	Y	Y
12 Maloney, C.	N	N	N	Y	N	N	N
13 Espaillat	N	N	N	Y	N	N	N
14 Crowley	N	N	N	Y	N	N	N
15 Serrano	N	N	N	Y	N	N	N
16 Engel	N	N	N	Y	N	N	N
17 Lowey	N	N	N	Y	N	N	N
18 Maloney, S.P.	N	N	N	Y	N	N	N
19 **Faso**	Y	Y	Y	N	Y	Y	Y
20 Tonko	N	N	N	Y	N	N	N
21 **Stefanik**	Y	Y	Y	N	N	Y	Y
22 **Tenney**	Y	Y	Y	N	Y	Y	Y
23 **Reed**	Y	Y	Y	N	N	Y	Y
24 **Katko**	Y	Y	Y	N	N	Y	Y
25 Slaughter	N	N	N	Y	N	N	N
26 Higgins	N	N	N	Y	N	N	N
27 **Collins**	Y	Y	Y	N	Y	Y	Y
NORTH CAROLINA							
1 Butterfield	?	?	?	Y	N	N	N
2 **Holding**	Y	Y	Y	N	Y	Y	Y
3 **Jones**	Y	N	Y	Y	N	Y	Y
4 Price	Y	N	N	Y	N	N	N

	639	640	641	642	643	644	645
5 **Foxx**	Y	Y	Y	N	Y	Y	Y
6 **Walker**	Y	Y	Y	N	Y	Y	Y
7 **Rouzer**	Y	Y	Y	N	Y	Y	Y
8 **Hudson**	Y	Y	Y	N	Y	Y	Y
9 **Pittenger**	+	Y	Y	N	Y	Y	Y
10 **McHenry**	Y	Y	Y	N	Y	Y	Y
11 **Meadows**	Y	Y	Y	N	Y	Y	Y
12 Adams	N	N	N	Y	N	N	N
13 **Budd**	Y	Y	Y	N	Y	Y	Y
NORTH DAKOTA							
AL **Cramer**	Y	Y	Y	N	Y	Y	Y
OHIO							
1 **Chabot**	Y	Y	Y	N	?	Y	Y
2 **Wenstrup**	Y	Y	Y	N	Y	Y	Y
3 Beatty	Y	N	N	Y	N	N	N
4 **Jordan**	Y	Y	Y	N	Y	Y	Y
5 **Latta**	Y	Y	Y	N	Y	Y	Y
6 **Johnson**	Y	Y	Y	N	Y	Y	Y
7 **Gibbs**	Y	Y	Y	N	Y	Y	Y
8 **Davidson**	Y	Y	Y	N	Y	Y	Y
9 Kaptur	Y	N	N	Y	N	N	N
10 **Turner**	Y	Y	Y	N	Y	Y	Y
11 Fudge	Y	N	N	Y	N	N	N
12 **Tiberi**	Y	Y	Y	N	Y	Y	Y
13 Ryan	Y	N	N	Y	N	N	N
14 **Joyce**	Y	Y	Y	N	Y	Y	Y
15 **Stivers**	?	?	?	?	?	?	?
16 **Renacci**	–	Y	Y	?	?	?	?
OKLAHOMA							
1 **Bridenstine**	?	?	?	?	?	?	?
2 **Mullin**	Y	Y	Y	N	Y	Y	Y
3 **Lucas**	?	?	?	N	Y	Y	Y
4 **Cole**	N	Y	Y	N	Y	Y	Y
5 **Russell**	Y	Y	Y	N	Y	Y	Y
OREGON							
1 Bonamici	N	N	N	Y	N	N	N
2 **Walden**	Y	Y	Y	N	Y	Y	Y
3 Blumenauer	N	N	N	Y	N	N	N
4 DeFazio	Y	N	N	N	N	N	N
5 Schrader	Y	N	N	Y	N	N	N
PENNSYLVANIA							
1 Brady	Y	N	N	Y	Y	N	N
2 Evans	Y	N	N	Y	N	N	N
3 **Kelly**	Y	Y	Y	N	Y	Y	Y
4 **Perry**	?	Y	Y	N	Y	Y	Y
5 **Thompson**	Y	Y	Y	N	Y	Y	Y
6 **Costello**	Y	Y	Y	N	N	Y	Y
7 **Meehan**	Y	Y	Y	N	N	Y	Y
8 **Fitzpatrick**	Y	Y	Y	N	N	Y	Y
9 **Shuster**	Y	Y	Y	N	Y	Y	Y
10 **Marino**	Y	Y	Y	N	Y	Y	Y
11 **Barletta**	Y	Y	Y	N	Y	Y	Y
12 **Rothfus**	Y	Y	Y	N	Y	Y	Y
13 Boyle	Y	N	N	Y	N	N	N
14 Doyle	Y	N	N	Y	N	N	N
15 **Dent**	Y	Y	Y	N	Y	Y	Y
16 **Smucker**	Y	Y	Y	N	Y	Y	Y
17 Cartwright	N	N	N	Y	N	N	N
RHODE ISLAND							
1 Cicilline	N	N	N	Y	N	N	N
2 Langevin	N	N	N	Y	N	N	N
SOUTH CAROLINA							
1 **Sanford**	Y	Y	Y	N	N	Y	Y
2 **Wilson**	Y	Y	Y	N	Y	Y	Y
3 **Duncan**	Y	Y	Y	N	Y	Y	Y
4 **Gowdy**	Y	Y	Y	N	Y	Y	Y
5 **Norman**	Y	Y	Y	N	Y	Y	Y
6 Clyburn	Y	N	N	Y	N	N	N
7 **Rice**	Y	Y	Y	N	N	Y	Y
SOUTH DAKOTA							
AL **Noem**	Y	Y	Y	N	Y	Y	Y
TENNESSEE							
1 **Roe**	Y	Y	Y	N	Y	Y	Y
2 **Duncan**	Y	Y	Y	N	Y	Y	Y
3 **Fleischmann**	Y	Y	Y	N	Y	Y	Y
4 **DesJarlais**	Y	Y	Y	N	Y	Y	Y
5 Cooper	Y	N	N	Y	N	N	N
6 **Black**	?	Y	Y	N	Y	Y	Y
7 **Blackburn**	Y	Y	Y	N	Y	Y	Y
8 **Kustoff**	Y	Y	Y	N	Y	Y	Y
9 Cohen	N	N	N	Y	N	N	N

	639	640	641	642	643	644	645
TEXAS							
1 **Gohmert**	Y	Y	Y	N	Y	Y	Y
2 **Poe**	Y	Y	Y	N	Y	Y	Y
3 **Johnson, S.**	Y	Y	Y	N	Y	Y	Y
4 **Ratcliffe**	Y	Y	Y	N	Y	Y	Y
5 **Hensarling**	Y	Y	Y	N	Y	Y	Y
6 **Barton**	Y	Y	Y	N	Y	Y	Y
7 **Culberson**	Y	Y	Y	N	Y	Y	Y
8 **Brady**	Y	Y	Y	N	Y	Y	Y
9 Green, A.	N	N	N	Y	N	N	N
10 **McCaul**	Y	Y	Y	N	Y	Y	Y
11 **Conaway**	Y	Y	Y	N	Y	Y	Y
12 **Granger**	Y	Y	Y	N	Y	Y	Y
13 **Thornberry**	Y	Y	Y	N	Y	Y	Y
14 **Weber**	Y	Y	Y	N	Y	Y	Y
15 Gonzalez	Y	N	N	Y	N	N	N
16 O'Rourke	Y	N	N	Y	N	N	N
17 **Flores**	Y	Y	Y	N	Y	Y	Y
18 Jackson Lee	Y	N	N	Y	N	N	N
19 **Arrington**	Y	Y	Y	N	Y	Y	Y
20 Castro	N	N	N	Y	N	N	N
21 **Smith**	Y	Y	Y	N	Y	Y	Y
22 **Olson**	Y	Y	Y	N	Y	Y	Y
23 **Hurd**	Y	Y	Y	N	Y	Y	Y
24 **Marchant**	Y	Y	Y	N	Y	Y	Y
25 **Williams**	Y	Y	Y	N	Y	Y	Y
26 **Burgess**	Y	Y	Y	N	Y	Y	Y
27 **Farenthold**	Y	Y	Y	N	Y	Y	Y
28 Cuellar	Y	N	N	Y	Y	N	N
29 Green, G.	Y	N	N	Y	Y	N	N
30 Johnson, E.B.	Y	N	N	Y	N	N	N
31 **Carter**	Y	Y	Y	N	Y	Y	Y
32 **Sessions**	Y	Y	Y	N	Y	Y	Y
33 Veasey	Y	N	N	Y	N	N	N
34 Vela	Y	N	N	Y	N	N	N
35 Doggett	N	N	N	Y	N	N	N
36 **Babin**	Y	Y	Y	N	Y	Y	Y
UTAH							
1 **Bishop**	Y	Y	Y	N	Y	Y	Y
2 **Stewart**	Y	Y	Y	N	Y	Y	Y
3 **Curtis**	Y	Y	Y	N	Y	Y	Y
4 **Love**	Y	Y	Y	N	Y	Y	Y
VERMONT							
AL Welch	Y	N	N	Y	N	N	N
VIRGINIA							
1 **Wittman**	Y	Y	Y	N	Y	Y	Y
2 **Taylor**	Y	Y	Y	–	+	+	+
3 Scott	Y	N	N	Y	N	N	N
4 McEachin	N	N	N	Y	N	N	N
5 **Garrett**	Y	Y	Y	N	Y	Y	Y
6 **Goodlatte**	Y	Y	Y	N	Y	Y	Y
7 **Brat**	Y	Y	Y	N	Y	Y	?
8 Beyer	N	N	N	Y	N	N	N
9 **Griffith**	N	Y	Y	N	Y	Y	Y
10 **Comstock**	Y	Y	Y	N	Y	Y	Y
11 Connolly	N	N	N	Y	N	N	N
WASHINGTON							
1 DelBene	N	N	N	Y	N	N	N
2 Larsen	Y	N	N	Y	N	N	N
3 **Herrera Beutler**	+	+	+	N	Y	Y	Y
4 **Newhouse**	Y	Y	Y	N	Y	Y	Y
5 **McMorris Rodgers**	Y	Y	Y	N	Y	Y	Y
6 Kilmer	N	N	N	Y	N	N	N
7 Jayapal	N	–	–	+	–	–	–
8 **Reichert**	Y	Y	Y	N	N	Y	Y
9 Smith	N	N	N	Y	N	N	N
10 Heck	N	N	N	Y	N	N	N
WEST VIRGINIA							
1 **McKinley**	Y	Y	Y	N	Y	Y	Y
2 **Mooney**	Y	Y	Y	N	Y	Y	Y
3 **Jenkins**	Y	Y	Y	N	Y	Y	Y
WISCONSIN							
1 **Ryan**							
2 Pocan	–	–	–	+	–	–	–
3 Kind	Y	N	N	Y	N	N	N
4 Moore	Y	N	N	Y	N	N	N
5 **Sensenbrenner**	Y	Y	Y	N	Y	Y	Y
6 **Grothman**	Y	Y	Y	N	Y	Y	Y
7 **Duffy**	Y	Y	Y	N	Y	Y	Y
8 **Gallagher**	Y	Y	Y	N	Y	Y	Y
WYOMING							
AL **Cheney**	Y	Y	Y	N	Y	Y	Y

VOTE NUMBER

646. HR 4182. FEDERAL WORKFORCE PROBATIONARY PERIOD EXTENSION/EXPERIENCE-BASED EXEMPTION. Hastings, D-Fla., amendment that would exempt an individual who has completed a term of service for a program under the Corporation for National and Community Service, such as PeaceCorps and AmeriCorps, from the bill's required increase in probationary period length. Rejected in Committee of the Whole 195-221: R 6-221; D 189-0. Nov. 30, 2017.

647. HR 4182. FEDEARAL WORKFORCE PROBATIONARY PERIOD EXTENSION/PROBATIONARY PERIOD EXTENSION STUDY. Connolly, D-Va., amendment that would strike the provisions of the bill and require that a study be conducted on the effects of an increase in employment probationary periods within federal agencies. Rejected in Committee of the Whole 193-223 : R 5-223; D 188-0. Nov. 30, 2017.

648. HR 4182. FEDERAL WORKFORCE PROBATIONARY PERIOD EXTENSION/PASSAGE. Passage of the bill that would increase to two years the probationary period for newly hired federal employees, for any individuals promoted to a supervisory or managerial role, and for any individual appointed to the Senior Executive Service. It would also establish a system in which supervisors would be notified near the end of an employee's probationary period. Passed 213-204 : R 211-18; D 2-186. Nov. 30, 2017.

649. HR 3017. EPA BROWNFIELDS PROGRAM REAUTHORIZATION/PASSAGE. Passage of the bill that would authorize $250 million annually, through fiscal 2022, for assistance with environmental assessment, cleanup and job training activities at the EPA's brownfields program sites, and would increase, to $500,000 per site, the amount available for remediation grants for brownfield sites. Passed 409-8 : R 220-8; D 189-0. Nov. 30, 2017.

650. HR 1699. MANUFACTURED HOUSING LENDING REGULATION/RECOMMIT. Waters, D-Calif., motion to recommit the bill to the House Financial Services Committee with instructions to report it back immediately with an amendment that would prohibit companies and lenders that have been convicted of fraud, or shown to have engaged in deceptive, unfair or abusive lending practices, from utilizing the provisions of the bill. Motion rejected 193-227 : R 3-227; D 190-0. Dec. 1, 2017.

651. HR 1699. MANUFACTURED HOUSING LENDING REGULATION/PASSAGE. Passage of the bill that would change the definitions of "mortgage originator" and "loan originator" to exempt companies that manufacture homes and sell manufactured homes from various mortgage-related regulatory requirements. It would increase the maximum allowable rates and fees that may be applied to a manufactured home loan before the loan is classified as a high-cost mortgage. Passed 256-163 : R 229-1; D 27-162. Dec. 1, 2017.

652. PROCEDURAL MOTION/APPROVAL OF HOUSE JOURNAL. Approved 209-169 : R 129-78; D 80-91. Dec. 1, 2017.

	646	647	648	649	650	651	652
ALABAMA							
1 Byrne	N	N	Y	Y	N	Y	Y
2 Roby	N	N	Y	Y	N	Y	Y
3 Rogers	N	N	Y	Y	N	Y	N
4 Aderholt	N	N	Y	Y	N	Y	Y
5 Brooks	N	N	Y	Y	N	Y	Y
6 Palmer	N	N	Y	Y	N	Y	Y
7 Sewell	Y	Y	N	Y	Y	Y	N
ALASKA							
AL Young	N	N	Y	Y	N	Y	N
ARIZONA							
1 O'Halleran	Y	Y	N	Y	Y	Y	N
2 McSally	N	N	Y	Y	N	Y	N
3 Grijalva	Y	Y	?	Y	Y	N	N
4 Gosar	N	N	Y	N	Y	Y	Y
5 Biggs	N	N	Y	N	N	Y	?
6 Schweikert	N	N	Y	Y	N	Y	Y
7 Gallego	Y	Y	N	Y	Y	N	N
8 Franks	N	N	Y	Y	N	Y	Y
9 Sinema	Y	Y	N	Y	Y	Y	N
ARKANSAS							
1 Crawford	N	N	Y	Y	N	Y	?
2 Hill	N	N	Y	Y	N	Y	N
3 Womack	N	N	Y	Y	N	Y	Y
4 Westerman	N	N	Y	Y	N	Y	Y
CALIFORNIA							
1 LaMalfa	N	N	Y	Y	N	Y	Y
2 Huffman	Y	Y	N	Y	Y	Y	N
3 Garamendi	Y	Y	N	Y	Y	N	?
4 McClintock	N	N	Y	Y	N	Y	Y
5 Thompson	Y	Y	N	Y	Y	N	N
6 Matsui	Y	Y	N	Y	Y	N	N
7 Bera	Y	Y	N	Y	Y	N	N
8 Cook	N	N	N	Y	N	Y	Y
9 McNerney	Y	Y	N	Y	Y	N	Y
10 Denham	N	N	N	Y	N	Y	N
11 DeSaulnier	Y	Y	N	Y	Y	N	N
12 Pelosi	Y	Y	N	Y	Y	N	?
13 Lee	Y	Y	N	Y	Y	N	N
14 Speier	Y	Y	N	Y	Y	N	Y
15 Swalwell	Y	Y	N	Y	Y	N	N
16 Costa	Y	Y	N	Y	Y	N	N
17 Khanna	Y	Y	N	Y	Y	N	N
18 Eshoo	Y	Y	N	Y	Y	N	N
19 Lofgren	Y	Y	N	Y	Y	N	Y
20 Panetta	Y	Y	N	Y	Y	Y	Y
21 Valadao	N	N	Y	Y	N	Y	N
22 Nunes	N	N	Y	Y	N	Y	Y
23 McCarthy	N	N	Y	Y	N	Y	Y
24 Carbajal	Y	Y	N	Y	Y	N	N
25 Knight	N	N	Y	Y	N	Y	N
26 Brownley	Y	Y	N	Y	Y	N	N
27 Chu	Y	Y	N	Y	Y	N	Y
28 Schiff	Y	Y	N	Y	Y	N	Y
29 Cardenas	Y	Y	N	Y	Y	N	N
30 Sherman	Y	Y	N	Y	Y	Y	Y
31 Aguilar	Y	Y	N	Y	Y	N	N
32 Napolitano	Y	Y	N	Y	Y	N	Y
33 Lieu	Y	Y	N	Y	Y	N	N
34 Gomez	Y	Y	N	Y	Y	N	N
35 Torres	Y	Y	N	Y	Y	N	N
36 Ruiz	Y	Y	N	Y	Y	N	N
37 Bass	Y	Y	N	Y	Y	N	N
38 Sánchez, Linda	Y	Y	N	Y	Y	N	N
39 Royce	N	N	Y	Y	N	Y	Y
40 Roybal-Allard	Y	Y	N	Y	Y	N	N
41 Takano	Y	Y	N	Y	Y	N	?
42 Calvert	N	N	Y	Y	N	Y	Y
43 Waters	Y	Y	N	Y	Y	N	Y
44 Barragan	Y	Y	N	Y	Y	N	N
45 Walters	N	N	Y	Y	N	Y	?
46 Correa	Y	Y	N	Y	Y	Y	N
47 Lowenthal	Y	Y	N	Y	Y	N	Y
48 Rohrabacher	N	N	Y	Y	N	Y	?
49 Issa	N	N	Y	Y	N	Y	N
50 Hunter	N	N	Y	Y	N	Y	Y
51 Vargas	Y	Y	N	Y	Y	N	Y
52 Peters	Y	Y	N	Y	Y	N	N
53 Davis	Y	Y	N	Y	Y	N	?

	646	647	648	649	650	651	652
COLORADO							
1 DeGette	Y	Y	N	Y	Y	N	Y
2 Polis	Y	Y	N	Y	Y	Y	Y
3 Tipton	N	N	Y	Y	N	Y	N
4 Buck	N	N	Y	Y	N	Y	N
5 Lamborn	N	N	Y	Y	N	Y	Y
6 Coffman	N	N	Y	Y	N	Y	N
7 Perlmutter	Y	Y	N	Y	Y	N	Y
CONNECTICUT							
1 Larson	Y	Y	N	Y	Y	N	Y
2 Courtney	Y	Y	N	Y	Y	N	Y
3 DeLauro	Y	Y	N	Y	Y	N	Y
4 Himes	Y	Y	N	Y	Y	N	?
5 Esty	Y	Y	N	Y	Y	N	N
DELAWARE							
AL Blunt Rochester	Y	Y	N	Y	Y	N	N
FLORIDA							
1 Gaetz	N	N	Y	N	N	Y	N
2 Dunn	N	N	Y	Y	N	Y	Y
3 Yoho	N	N	Y	N	N	Y	Y
4 Rutherford	N	–	Y	Y	N	Y	Y
5 Lawson	Y	Y	N	Y	Y	N	Y
6 DeSantis	N	N	Y	Y	N	Y	N
7 Murphy	Y	Y	N	Y	Y	Y	Y
8 Posey	?	?	?	?	?	?	?
9 Soto	Y	Y	N	Y	Y	N	N
10 Demings	Y	Y	N	Y	Y	N	Y
11 Webster	–	–	+	+	–	+	?
12 Bilirakis	N	N	Y	N	Y	N	Y
13 Crist	Y	Y	N	Y	Y	N	N
14 Castor	Y	Y	N	Y	Y	N	N
15 Ross	N	N	Y	Y	N	Y	?
16 Buchanan	N	N	Y	Y	N	Y	Y
17 Rooney, T.	N	N	Y	Y	N	Y	Y
18 Mast	N	N	Y	Y	N	Y	Y
19 Rooney, F.	N	N	Y	Y	N	Y	Y
20 Hastings	Y	Y	N	Y	Y	N	N
21 Frankel	Y	Y	N	Y	Y	–	?
22 Deutch	Y	Y	N	Y	Y	N	N
23 Wasserman Schultz	Y	Y	N	Y	Y	N	Y
24 Wilson	Y	Y	N	Y	Y	N	?
25 Diaz-Balart	N	N	Y	Y	N	Y	N
26 Curbelo	N	N	Y	Y	N	Y	N
27 Ros-Lehtinen	Y	Y	N	Y	Y	N	N
GEORGIA							
1 Carter	N	N	Y	Y	N	Y	N
2 Bishop	Y	Y	N	Y	Y	Y	N
3 Ferguson	N	N	Y	Y	N	Y	Y
4 Johnson	Y	Y	N	Y	Y	N	Y
5 Lewis	Y	Y	N	Y	Y	N	N
6 Handel	N	N	Y	Y	N	Y	N
7 Woodall	N	N	Y	Y	N	Y	Y
8 Scott, A.	N	N	Y	Y	N	Y	?
9 Collins	–	–	+	+	N	Y	N
10 Hice	N	N	Y	Y	N	Y	?
11 Loudermilk	N	N	Y	Y	N	Y	Y
12 Allen	N	N	Y	Y	N	Y	Y
13 Scott, D.	Y	Y	N	Y	Y	Y	Y
14 Graves	N	N	Y	Y	N	Y	N
HAWAII							
1 Hanabusa	Y	Y	N	Y	Y	N	Y
2 Gabbard	Y	Y	N	Y	Y	N	Y
IDAHO							
1 Labrador	N	N	Y	N	?	?	?
2 Simpson	N	N	N	Y	N	Y	Y
ILLINOIS							
1 Rush	Y	Y	N	Y	Y	N	Y
2 Kelly	Y	Y	N	Y	Y	N	N
3 Lipinski	Y	Y	N	Y	Y	N	N
4 Gutierrez	Y	Y	N	Y	Y	N	N
5 Quigley	Y	Y	N	Y	?	?	?
6 Roskam	N	N	Y	Y	N	Y	Y
7 Davis, D.	Y	Y	N	Y	Y	N	Y
8 Krishnamoorthi	Y	Y	N	Y	Y	N	Y
9 Schakowsky	Y	Y	N	Y	Y	N	N
10 Schneider	Y	Y	N	Y	Y	Y	Y
11 Foster	Y	Y	N	Y	Y	N	Y
12 Bost	N	N	Y	Y	N	Y	N
13 Davis, R.	N	N	Y	Y	N	Y	?
14 Hultgren	N	N	Y	Y	N	Y	Y
15 Shimkus	N	N	Y	Y	N	Y	Y

KEY	Republicans	Democrats	Independents
Y Voted for (yea)	X Paired against	C Voted "present" to avoid possible conflict of interest
# Paired for	– Announced against	
+ Announced for	P Voted "present"	? Did not vote or otherwise make a position known
N Voted against (nay)		

	646	647	648	649	650	651	652
16 **Kinzinger**	N	N	Y	Y	N	Y	N
17 Bustos	Y	Y	N	Y	Y	N	Y
18 **LaHood**	N	N	Y	Y	N	Y	N
INDIANA							
1 Visclosky	Y	Y	N	Y	Y	N	N
2 **Walorski**	N	N	Y	Y	N	Y	Y
3 **Banks**	N	N	Y	Y	N	Y	Y
4 **Rokita**	N	N	Y	Y	N	Y	N
5 **Brooks**	N	N	Y	Y	N	Y	Y
6 **Messer**	N	N	Y	Y	N	Y	Y
7 Carson	Y	Y	N	Y	Y	N	N
8 **Bucshon**	N	N	Y	Y	N	Y	Y
9 **Hollingsworth**	N	N	Y	Y	N	Y	Y
IOWA							
1 **Blum**	N	N	Y	Y	Y	Y	N
2 Loebsack	Y	Y	N	Y	Y	N	N
3 **Young**	N	N	Y	Y	N	Y	Y
4 **King**	N	N	Y	Y	N	Y	Y
KANSAS							
1 **Marshall**	N	N	Y	Y	N	Y	N
2 **Jenkins**	N	N	Y	Y	N	Y	N
3 **Yoder**	N	N	Y	Y	N	Y	N
4 **Estes**	N	N	Y	Y	N	Y	Y
KENTUCKY							
1 **Comer**	N	N	Y	Y	N	Y	Y
2 **Guthrie**	N	N	Y	Y	N	Y	Y
3 Yarmuth	Y	Y	N	Y	Y	N	Y
4 **Massie**	N	N	Y	N	N	Y	Y
5 **Rogers**	N	N	Y	Y	N	Y	Y
6 **Barr**	N	N	Y	Y	N	Y	Y
LOUISIANA							
1 **Scalise**	–	–	+	+	N	Y	Y
2 Richmond	Y	Y	N	Y	Y	N	N
3 **Higgins**	N	N	Y	Y	N	Y	Y
4 **Johnson**	N	N	Y	Y	N	Y	Y
5 **Abraham**	N	N	Y	Y	N	Y	Y
6 **Graves**	N	N	Y	Y	N	Y	N
MAINE							
1 Pingree	Y	Y	N	Y	Y	N	?
2 **Poliquin**	N	N	Y	Y	N	Y	N
MARYLAND							
1 **Harris**	N	N	Y	Y	N	Y	Y
2 Ruppersberger	Y	?	N	Y	Y	Y	Y
3 Sarbanes	Y	Y	N	Y	Y	N	N
4 Brown	Y	Y	N	Y	Y	N	Y
5 Hoyer	Y	Y	N	Y	Y	N	N
6 Delaney	+	+	–	+	Y	Y	N
7 Cummings	Y	Y	N	Y	Y	N	Y
8 Raskin	Y	Y	N	Y	Y	N	N
MASSACHUSETTS							
1 Neal	Y	Y	N	Y	Y	N	N
2 McGovern	Y	Y	N	Y	Y	N	N
3 Tsongas	Y	Y	N	Y	Y	N	Y
4 Kennedy	?	?	?	?	?	?	?
5 Clark	Y	Y	N	Y	Y	N	N
6 Moulton	Y	Y	N	Y	Y	Y	Y
7 Capuano	Y	Y	N	Y	Y	N	N
8 Lynch	Y	Y	N	Y	Y	N	?
9 Keating	Y	Y	N	Y	Y	N	?
MICHIGAN							
1 **Bergman**	N	N	Y	Y	N	Y	N
2 **Huizenga**	N	N	Y	Y	N	Y	N
3 **Amash**	N	N	Y	N	N	Y	N
4 **Moolenaar**	N	N	Y	Y	N	Y	Y
5 Kildee	Y	Y	N	Y	Y	N	Y
6 **Upton**	N	N	N	Y	N	Y	N
7 **Walberg**	N	N	Y	Y	N	Y	N
8 **Bishop**	N	N	Y	Y	N	Y	N
9 Levin	Y	Y	N	Y	Y	N	N
10 **Mitchell**	N	N	Y	Y	N	Y	N
11 **Trott**	N	N	Y	Y	N	Y	Y
12 Dingell	Y	Y	N	Y	Y	N	N
13 Conyers	?	?	?	?	?	?	?
14 Lawrence	Y	Y	N	Y	Y	N	Y
MINNESOTA							
1 Walz	Y	Y	N	Y	Y	N	Y
2 **Lewis**	N	N	Y	Y	N	Y	Y
3 **Paulsen**	N	N	Y	Y	N	Y	N
4 McCollum	Y	Y	N	Y	Y	N	Y

	646	647	648	649	650	651	652
5 Ellison	Y	Y	N	Y	Y	N	Y
6 **Emmer**	N	N	Y	Y	N	Y	Y
7 Peterson	Y	Y	N	Y	Y	Y	?
8 Nolan	Y	Y	N	Y	Y	N	N
MISSISSIPPI							
1 **Kelly**	N	N	Y	Y	N	Y	Y
2 Thompson	Y	Y	N	Y	Y	N	N
3 **Harper**	?	?	?	?	N	Y	Y
4 **Palazzo**	N	N	Y	Y	N	Y	N
MISSOURI							
1 Clay	Y	Y	N	Y	Y	N	Y
2 **Wagner**	N	N	Y	Y	N	Y	?
3 **Luetkemeyer**	N	N	Y	Y	N	Y	Y
4 **Hartzler**	N	N	Y	Y	N	Y	Y
5 Cleaver	Y	Y	N	Y	Y	N	Y
6 **Graves**	N	N	Y	Y	N	Y	N
7 **Long**	N	N	Y	Y	N	Y	Y
8 **Smith**	N	N	Y	Y	N	Y	N
MONTANA							
AL **Gianforte**	N	N	Y	Y	N	Y	Y
NEBRASKA							
1 **Fortenberry**	N	N	Y	Y	N	Y	?
2 **Bacon**	Y	N	Y	Y	N	Y	Y
3 **Smith**	N	N	Y	Y	N	Y	Y
NEVADA							
1 Titus	Y	Y	N	Y	Y	N	Y
2 **Amodei**	N	N	Y	Y	Y	Y	Y
3 Rosen	Y	Y	N	Y	Y	Y	Y
4 Kihuen	Y	Y	N	Y	Y	N	N
NEW HAMPSHIRE							
1 Shea-Porter	Y	Y	N	Y	Y	N	Y
2 Kuster	Y	Y	N	Y	Y	N	Y
NEW JERSEY							
1 Norcross	Y	Y	N	Y	Y	N	N
2 **LoBiondo**	N	N	N	Y	N	Y	N
3 **MacArthur**	N	N	Y	Y	?	?	?
4 **Smith**	N	N	N	Y	N	Y	Y
5 Gottheimer	Y	Y	N	Y	Y	Y	N
6 Pallone	Y	Y	N	Y	Y	N	N
7 **Lance**	N	N	Y	Y	N	Y	N
8 Sires	Y	Y	N	Y	Y	N	?
9 Pascrell	Y	Y	N	Y	Y	N	?
10 Payne	Y	Y	N	Y	Y	N	N
11 **Frelinghuysen**	N	N	Y	Y	N	Y	Y
12 Watson Coleman	Y	Y	N	Y	Y	N	N
NEW MEXICO							
1 Lujan Grisham	Y	Y	N	Y	Y	N	Y
2 **Pearce**	N	N	Y	?	N	Y	N
3 Luján	Y	Y	N	Y	Y	N	Y
NEW YORK							
1 **Zeldin**	N	N	Y	Y	N	Y	N
2 **King**	N	N	N	Y	N	Y	Y
3 Suozzi	Y	Y	N	Y	Y	Y	N
4 Rice	Y	Y	N	Y	Y	Y	N
5 Meeks	Y	Y	N	Y	Y	Y	N
6 Meng	Y	Y	N	Y	Y	N	Y
7 Velázquez	Y	Y	N	Y	Y	N	N
8 Jeffries	Y	Y	N	Y	Y	N	Y
9 Clarke	Y	Y	N	Y	Y	N	N
10 Nadler	Y	Y	N	Y	Y	N	Y
11 **Donovan**	N	N	N	Y	N	Y	Y
12 Maloney, C.	Y	Y	N	Y	Y	N	Y
13 Espaillat	Y	Y	N	Y	Y	N	N
14 Crowley	Y	Y	N	Y	Y	N	N
15 Serrano	Y	Y	N	Y	Y	N	N
16 Engel	Y	Y	N	Y	Y	N	Y
17 Lowey	Y	Y	N	Y	Y	N	Y
18 Maloney, S.P.	Y	Y	N	Y	Y	N	N
19 **Faso**	N	N	Y	Y	N	Y	N
20 Tonko	Y	Y	N	Y	Y	N	P
21 **Stefanik**	N	N	Y	Y	N	Y	Y
22 **Tenney**	N	N	Y	Y	N	Y	N
23 **Reed**	N	N	Y	Y	N	Y	N
24 **Katko**	N	N	N	Y	N	Y	?
25 Slaughter	Y	Y	N	Y	Y	N	N
26 Higgins	Y	Y	N	Y	Y	N	?
27 **Collins**	N	N	Y	Y	N	Y	Y
NORTH CAROLINA							
1 Butterfield	Y	Y	N	Y	Y	N	?
2 **Holding**	N	N	Y	Y	N	Y	N
3 **Jones**	Y	Y	N	Y	Y	N	?
4 Price	Y	Y	N	Y	Y	N	N

	646	647	648	649	650	651	652
5 **Foxx**	N	N	Y	Y	N	Y	N
6 **Walker**	N	N	Y	Y	N	Y	Y
7 **Rouzer**	N	N	Y	Y	N	Y	N
8 **Hudson**	N	N	Y	Y	N	Y	N
9 **Pittenger**	N	N	Y	Y	N	Y	?
10 **McHenry**	N	N	Y	Y	N	Y	Y
11 **Meadows**	N	N	Y	Y	N	Y	Y
12 Adams	Y	Y	N	Y	Y	N	N
13 **Budd**	N	N	Y	N	N	Y	N
NORTH DAKOTA							
AL **Cramer**	N	N	Y	Y	N	Y	?
OHIO							
1 **Chabot**	N	N	Y	Y	N	Y	Y
2 **Wenstrup**	N	N	Y	Y	N	Y	Y
3 Beatty	Y	Y	N	Y	Y	N	N
4 **Jordan**	N	N	Y	Y	N	Y	N
5 **Latta**	N	N	Y	Y	N	Y	Y
6 **Johnson**	N	N	Y	Y	N	Y	N
7 **Gibbs**	N	N	Y	Y	N	Y	?
8 **Davidson**	N	N	Y	Y	N	Y	Y
9 Kaptur	Y	Y	N	Y	Y	N	Y
10 **Turner**	N	N	Y	Y	N	Y	N
11 Fudge	Y	Y	N	Y	Y	N	N
12 **Tiberi**	N	N	N	Y	N	Y	?
13 Ryan	Y	Y	N	Y	Y	N	N
14 **Joyce**	N	N	Y	Y	N	Y	?
15 **Stivers**	?	?	?	?	N	Y	N
16 **Renacci**	?	?	?	?	–	+	–
OKLAHOMA							
1 **Bridenstine**	?	?	?	?	?	?	?
2 **Mullin**	N	N	Y	Y	N	Y	Y
3 **Lucas**	N	N	Y	Y	N	Y	Y
4 **Cole**	Y	Y	N	Y	N	Y	Y
5 **Russell**	N	N	Y	Y	N	Y	Y
OREGON							
1 Bonamici	Y	Y	N	Y	Y	N	Y
2 **Walden**	N	N	Y	Y	N	Y	Y
3 Blumenauer	Y	Y	N	Y	Y	N	Y
4 DeFazio	Y	Y	N	Y	Y	Y	N
5 Schrader	Y	Y	N	Y	Y	N	N
PENNSYLVANIA							
1 Brady	Y	Y	N	Y	Y	N	N
2 Evans	Y	Y	N	Y	Y	N	Y
3 **Kelly**	N	N	Y	Y	N	Y	Y
4 **Perry**	N	N	Y	Y	N	Y	N
5 **Thompson**	N	N	Y	Y	N	Y	N
6 **Costello**	N	N	N	Y	N	Y	N
7 **Meehan**	N	N	Y	Y	N	Y	N
8 **Fitzpatrick**	Y	N	N	Y	N	Y	N
9 **Shuster**	N	N	Y	Y	N	Y	Y
10 **Marino**	N	N	Y	Y	N	Y	Y
11 **Barletta**	?	N	Y	Y	N	Y	Y
12 **Rothfus**	N	N	Y	Y	N	Y	Y
13 Boyle	Y	Y	N	Y	Y	N	N
14 Doyle	Y	Y	N	Y	Y	N	?
15 **Dent**	Y	N	Y	Y	N	Y	Y
16 **Smucker**	N	N	Y	Y	N	Y	N
17 Cartwright	Y	Y	N	Y	Y	N	Y
RHODE ISLAND							
1 Cicilline	Y	Y	N	Y	Y	N	Y
2 Langevin	Y	Y	N	Y	Y	N	Y
SOUTH CAROLINA							
1 **Sanford**	N	N	Y	N	N	Y	Y
2 **Wilson**	N	N	Y	Y	N	Y	Y
3 **Duncan**	N	N	Y	Y	N	Y	Y
4 **Gowdy**	N	N	Y	Y	N	Y	Y
5 **Norman**	?	?	?	?	N	Y	Y
6 Clyburn	Y	Y	N	Y	Y	N	N
7 **Rice**	N	N	Y	Y	N	Y	P
SOUTH DAKOTA							
AL **Noem**	N	N	Y	Y	N	Y	Y
TENNESSEE							
1 **Roe**	N	N	Y	Y	N	Y	Y
2 **Duncan**	N	N	Y	Y	N	Y	Y
3 **Fleischmann**	N	N	Y	Y	N	Y	Y
4 **DesJarlais**	N	N	Y	Y	N	Y	?
5 Cooper	Y	Y	Y	Y	Y	N	Y
6 **Black**	N	N	Y	Y	N	Y	Y
7 **Blackburn**	N	N	Y	Y	N	Y	?
8 **Kustoff**	N	N	Y	Y	N	Y	Y
9 Cohen	Y	Y	N	Y	Y	N	N

	646	647	648	649	650	651	652
TEXAS							
1 **Gohmert**	?	N	Y	Y	N	Y	?
2 **Poe**	N	N	Y	Y	N	Y	N
3 **Johnson, S.**	N	N	Y	Y	N	Y	Y
4 **Ratcliffe**	N	N	Y	Y	N	Y	?
5 **Hensarling**	N	N	Y	Y	N	Y	Y
6 **Barton**	N	N	Y	Y	N	Y	N
7 **Culberson**	N	N	Y	Y	N	Y	Y
8 **Brady**	N	N	Y	Y	N	Y	Y
9 Green, A.	Y	Y	N	Y	Y	N	N
10 **McCaul**	N	N	Y	Y	N	Y	Y
11 **Conaway**	N	N	Y	Y	N	Y	N
12 **Granger**	N	N	Y	Y	N	Y	Y
13 **Thornberry**	N	N	Y	Y	N	Y	Y
14 **Weber**	N	N	Y	Y	N	Y	N
15 Gonzalez	Y	Y	N	Y	Y	Y	?
16 O'Rourke	Y	Y	N	Y	Y	N	Y
17 **Flores**	N	N	Y	Y	?	?	?
18 Jackson Lee	Y	Y	N	Y	Y	N	N
19 **Arrington**	N	N	Y	Y	N	Y	Y
20 Castro	Y	Y	N	Y	Y	N	Y
21 **Smith**	N	N	Y	Y	N	Y	Y
22 **Olson**	N	N	Y	Y	N	Y	Y
23 **Hurd**	N	N	Y	Y	N	Y	Y
24 **Marchant**	N	N	Y	Y	?	?	?
25 **Williams**	N	N	Y	Y	N	Y	Y
26 **Burgess**	N	N	Y	Y	N	Y	N
27 **Farenthold**	N	N	Y	Y	N	Y	Y
28 Cuellar	Y	Y	Y	Y	Y	Y	N
29 Green, G.	Y	Y	N	Y	Y	N	N
30 Johnson, E.B.	Y	Y	N	Y	Y	N	Y
31 **Carter**	N	N	Y	Y	N	Y	Y
32 **Sessions**	N	N	Y	Y	N	Y	Y
33 Veasey	Y	Y	N	Y	Y	N	N
34 Vela	Y	Y	N	Y	Y	N	N
35 Doggett	Y	Y	N	Y	Y	N	Y
36 **Babin**	N	N	Y	Y	N	Y	N
UTAH							
1 **Bishop**	N	N	Y	Y	N	Y	Y
2 **Stewart**	N	N	Y	Y	N	Y	Y
3 **Curtis**	N	N	Y	Y	N	Y	Y
4 **Love**	N	N	Y	Y	N	Y	Y
VERMONT							
AL Welch	Y	Y	N	Y	Y	N	Y
VIRGINIA							
1 **Wittman**	N	N	Y	Y	N	Y	N
2 **Taylor**	–	–	+	+	–	+	–
3 Scott	Y	Y	N	Y	Y	N	Y
4 McEachin	Y	Y	N	Y	Y	N	Y
5 **Garrett**	N	N	Y	N	N	Y	Y
6 **Goodlatte**	N	N	Y	Y	N	Y	Y
7 **Brat**	N	N	Y	Y	N	Y	Y
8 Beyer	Y	Y	N	Y	Y	N	N
9 **Griffith**	N	N	Y	Y	N	Y	Y
10 **Comstock**	N	N	Y	Y	N	Y	Y
11 Connolly	Y	Y	N	Y	Y	N	N
WASHINGTON							
1 DelBene	Y	Y	N	Y	Y	N	Y
2 Larsen	Y	Y	N	Y	Y	N	Y
3 **Herrera Beutler**	N	N	Y	Y	N	Y	N
4 **Newhouse**	N	N	Y	Y	N	Y	Y
5 **McMorris Rodgers**	N	N	Y	Y	N	Y	Y
6 Kilmer	Y	Y	N	Y	Y	N	N
7 Jayapal	+	+	+	+	Y	N	N
8 **Reichert**	N	N	Y	Y	N	Y	Y
9 Smith	Y	Y	N	Y	Y	N	Y
10 Heck	Y	Y	N	Y	Y	N	Y
WEST VIRGINIA							
1 **McKinley**	N	Y	N	Y	N	Y	N
2 **Mooney**	N	N	Y	Y	N	Y	Y
3 **Jenkins**	N	N	Y	Y	N	Y	N
WISCONSIN							
1 **Ryan**							
2 Pocan	+	+	–	+	+	–	+
3 Kind	Y	Y	N	Y	Y	Y	?
4 Moore	Y	Y	N	Y	Y	N	N
5 **Sensenbrenner**	N	N	Y	Y	N	Y	Y
6 **Grothman**	N	N	Y	Y	N	Y	N
7 **Duffy**	N	N	Y	Y	N	Y	N
8 **Gallagher**	N	N	Y	Y	N	Y	N
WYOMING							
AL **Cheney**	N	N	Y	Y	N	Y	N

III HOUSE VOTES

VOTE NUMBER

653. HR 1. TAX OVERHAUL/MOTION TO REQUEST CONFERENCE. Brady, R-Texas, motion that the House disagree with the Senate amendment and request a conference with the Senate on the bill that would revise the federal income tax system by lowering individual and corporate tax rates, repealing various deductions through 2025. Motion agreed to 222-192 : R 222-7; D 0-185. Dec. 4, 2017.

654. HR 1. TAX OVERHAUL/MOTION TO INSTRUCT CONFEREES. Neal, D-Mass., motion to instruct conferees to disagree with the Senate amendment that would repeal the individual health insurance mandate, and to recede from the section House bill that would eliminate the deduction for state and local income taxes through 2025. Motion rejected 186-233 : R 0-233; D 186-0. Dec. 4, 2017.

655. HR 3731. SECRET SERVICE SALARY CAP EXTENSION/PASSAGE. Rutherford, R-Fla., motion to suspend the rules and pass the bill that would extend, through calendar year 2018, an increase of the salary cap for the U.S. Secret Service, which would allow Secret Service personnel to collect overtime pay. The salary cap authority set forth in the bill would be retroactively effective to Dec. 31, 2016. Motion agreed to 407-4 : R 229-4; D 178-0. Dec. 5, 2017.

656. HR 3317. GENITAL MUTILATION MAXIMUM SENTENCE/PASSAGE. Rutherford, R-Fla., motion to suspend the rules and pass the bill that would increase from five to 15 years the maximum federal sentence for female genital mutilation of a minor. Motion agreed to 409-0 : R 228-0; D 181-0. Dec. 5, 2017.

657. PROCEDURAL MOTION/APPROVAL OF HOUSE JOURNAL. Approved 224-183 : R 136-91; D 88-92. Dec. 5, 2017.

658. H RES 646. ARTICLES OF IMPEACHMENT/MOTION TO TABLE. McCarthy, R-Calif., motion to table (kill) the resolution that would impeach President Donald Trump for high misdemeanors, and would provide that the resolution's articles of impeachment be exhibited to the Senate. Motion agreed to 364-58 : R 238-0; D 126-58. Dec. 6, 2017.

659. HR 38, H RES 645. CONCEALED CARRY RECIPROCITY BETWEEN STATES/PREVIOUS QUESTION. Collins, R-Ga., motion to order the previous question (thus ending debate and the possibility of amendment) on the rule (H Res 645) providing for House floor consideration of the bill (HR 38) that would permit any individual authorized by their home state to carry a concealed handgun to also carry that concealed weapon in any other state that permits the carrying of concealed weapons. Motion agreed to 236-189 : R 234-4; D 2-185. Dec. 6, 2017.

	653	654	655	656	657	658	659
ALABAMA							
1 Byrne	Y	N	Y	Y	Y	Y	Y
2 Roby	Y	N	Y	Y	Y	Y	Y
3 Rogers	Y	N	Y	Y	N	Y	Y
4 Aderholt	Y	N	Y	Y	Y	Y	Y
5 Brooks	Y	N	Y	Y	Y	Y	Y
6 Palmer	Y	N	Y	Y	N	Y	Y
7 Sewell	N	Y	Y	Y	N	P	N
ALASKA							
AL Young	Y	N	Y	Y	N	Y	Y
ARIZONA							
1 O'Halleran	N	Y	Y	Y	N	Y	N
2 McSally	Y	N	Y	Y	N	Y	Y
3 Grijalva	N	Y	Y	Y	?	N	N
4 Gosar	Y	N	Y	N	Y	N	Y
5 Biggs	Y	N	Y	Y	N	Y	N
6 Schweikert	Y	N	Y	Y	Y	Y	Y
7 Gallego	N	Y	Y	Y	N	Y	N
8 Franks	Y	N	Y	Y	Y	Y	Y
9 Sinema	N	Y	Y	Y	N	Y	N
ARKANSAS							
1 Crawford	Y	N	Y	Y	Y	Y	Y
2 Hill	Y	N	Y	Y	N	Y	Y
3 Womack	Y	N	Y	Y	Y	Y	Y
4 Westerman	Y	N	Y	Y	N	Y	Y
CALIFORNIA							
1 LaMalfa	Y	N	Y	N	Y	Y	Y
2 Huffman	N	Y	Y	Y	Y	N	N
3 Garamendi	N	Y	Y	Y	N	Y	N
4 McClintock	Y	N	Y	Y	Y	Y	Y
5 Thompson	N	Y	Y	Y	N	Y	N
6 Matsui	N	Y	Y	Y	N	Y	N
7 Bera	N	Y	Y	Y	N	Y	N
8 Cook	Y	N	Y	Y	Y	Y	Y
9 McNerney	N	Y	Y	Y	N	N	N
10 Denham	Y	N	Y	N	Y	Y	Y
11 DeSaulnier	N	Y	Y	Y	N	N	N
12 Pelosi	N	Y	?	?	?	Y	N
13 Lee	N	Y	Y	Y	N	N	N
14 Speier	N	Y	Y	Y	Y	N	N
15 Swalwell	N	Y	Y	Y	N	N	N
16 Costa	N	Y	Y	Y	N	Y	N
17 Khanna	N	Y	Y	Y	N	Y	N
18 Eshoo	N	Y	Y	Y	N	Y	N
19 Lofgren	N	Y	Y	Y	N	Y	N
20 Panetta	N	Y	Y	Y	N	Y	N
21 Valadao	Y	N	Y	N	Y	Y	Y
22 Nunes	Y	N	Y	Y	Y	Y	Y
23 McCarthy	Y	N	Y	Y	Y	Y	Y
24 Carbajal	N	Y	Y	Y	N	Y	N
25 Knight	Y	N	Y	N	Y	N	Y
26 Brownley	N	Y	?	?	?	?	?
27 Chu	N	Y	Y	Y	Y	Y	?
28 Schiff	N	Y	Y	Y	Y	Y	N
29 Cardenas	N	Y	Y	?	N	Y	N
30 Sherman	N	Y	Y	Y	N	N	N
31 Aguilar	N	Y	Y	Y	N	Y	N
32 Napolitano	N	Y	Y	Y	Y	N	N
33 Lieu	N	Y	Y	N	N	N	N
34 Gomez	N	Y	Y	Y	Y	N	N
35 Torres	N	Y	Y	Y	Y	N	N
36 Ruiz	N	Y	Y	Y	Y	Y	N
37 Bass	N	Y	Y	Y	Y	N	N
38 Sánchez, Linda	N	Y	Y	Y	N	Y	N
39 Royce	Y	N	Y	Y	Y	Y	Y
40 Roybal-Allard	N	Y	Y	Y	N	Y	N
41 Takano	N	Y	Y	Y	N	Y	N
42 Calvert	Y	N	Y	Y	Y	Y	Y
43 Waters	N	Y	?	Y	Y	N	N
44 Barragan	N	Y	Y	Y	N	N	N
45 Walters	Y	N	Y	Y	Y	Y	Y
46 Correa	N	Y	Y	Y	N	Y	N
47 Lowenthal	N	Y	Y	Y	N	Y	N
48 Rohrabacher	Y	N	Y	Y	Y	Y	Y
49 Issa	Y	N	Y	Y	N	Y	Y
50 Hunter	Y	N	Y	Y	N	Y	Y
51 Vargas	N	Y	Y	Y	N	N	N
52 Peters	N	Y	Y	Y	N	Y	N
53 Davis	N	Y	Y	Y	Y	Y	N
COLORADO							
1 DeGette	N	Y	Y	Y	Y	Y	N
2 Polis	N	Y	Y	Y	Y	N	N
3 Tipton	Y	N	Y	Y	N	Y	Y
4 Buck	Y	N	Y	N	Y	Y	Y
5 Lamborn	Y	N	Y	Y	N	Y	Y
6 Coffman	Y	N	Y	Y	N	Y	Y
7 Perlmutter	N	Y	Y	Y	N	Y	N
CONNECTICUT							
1 Larson	N	Y	Y	Y	N	Y	N
2 Courtney	N	Y	Y	Y	Y	Y	N
3 DeLauro	N	Y	Y	Y	Y	Y	N
4 Himes	N	Y	Y	Y	Y	Y	N
5 Esty	N	Y	Y	Y	N	Y	N
DELAWARE							
AL Blunt Rochester	N	Y	Y	Y	Y	Y	N
FLORIDA							
1 Gaetz	Y	N	Y	Y	?	Y	Y
2 Dunn	Y	N	Y	Y	Y	Y	Y
3 Yoho	Y	N	Y	Y	N	Y	Y
4 Rutherford	Y	N	Y	Y	N	Y	Y
5 Lawson	N	Y	Y	Y	N	Y	N
6 DeSantis	Y	?	Y	Y	N	Y	Y
7 Murphy	N	Y	Y	Y	Y	Y	N
8 Posey	Y	N	Y	Y	N	Y	Y
9 Soto	N	Y	Y	Y	N	Y	N
10 Demings	N	Y	Y	Y	Y	Y	N
11 Webster	Y	N	Y	?	Y	Y	Y
12 Bilirakis	Y	N	Y	Y	Y	Y	Y
13 Crist	N	Y	Y	Y	N	Y	N
14 Castor	N	Y	Y	Y	Y	Y	N
15 Ross	Y	N	Y	Y	Y	Y	Y
16 Buchanan	?	N	Y	?	Y	Y	Y
17 Rooney, T.	Y	N	Y	Y	Y	Y	Y
18 Mast	Y	N	Y	Y	N	Y	Y
19 Rooney, F.	Y	N	Y	?	Y	Y	Y
20 Hastings	N	Y	Y	Y	N	N	N
21 Frankel	N	Y	Y	Y	Y	N	N
22 Deutch	N	Y	Y	Y	Y	N	N
23 Wasserman Schultz	N	Y	Y	Y	Y	Y	N
24 Wilson	N	Y	Y	Y	N	N	N
25 Diaz-Balart	Y	N	Y	Y	N	Y	Y
26 Curbelo	Y	N	?	?	?	Y	Y
27 Ros-Lehtinen	Y	N	Y	N	Y	Y	Y
GEORGIA							
1 Carter	Y	N	Y	Y	N	Y	Y
2 Bishop	N	Y	Y	Y	N	Y	N
3 Ferguson	Y	N	Y	Y	Y	Y	Y
4 Johnson	N	Y	Y	Y	Y	Y	N
5 Lewis	N	Y	Y	Y	N	N	N
6 Handel	Y	N	Y	Y	Y	Y	Y
7 Woodall	Y	N	Y	Y	Y	Y	Y
8 Scott, A.	Y	?	?	?	?	Y	Y
9 Collins	Y	N	Y	N	Y	Y	Y
10 Hice	Y	N	Y	N	Y	Y	Y
11 Loudermilk	Y	N	Y	Y	N	Y	Y
12 Allen	Y	N	Y	Y	Y	Y	Y
13 Scott, D.	N	Y	Y	Y	Y	Y	N
14 Graves	Y	N	Y	N	Y	Y	Y
HAWAII							
1 Hanabusa	N	Y	Y	Y	Y	Y	N
2 Gabbard	N	Y	Y	Y	Y	Y	N
IDAHO							
1 Labrador	Y	N	Y	Y	Y	Y	Y
2 Simpson	Y	N	+	+	+	Y	Y
ILLINOIS							
1 Rush	N	Y	Y	Y	N	N	N
2 Kelly	N	Y	Y	Y	N	N	N
3 Lipinski	N	Y	Y	Y	Y	Y	N
4 Gutierrez	-	+	+	+	-	-	-
5 Quigley	?	?	?	?	?	Y	N
6 Roskam	Y	N	Y	N	Y	Y	Y
7 Davis, D.	N	Y	Y	Y	N	N	N
8 Krishnamoorthi	N	Y	Y	Y	Y	Y	N
9 Schakowsky	N	Y	Y	Y	N	N	N
10 Schneider	N	Y	Y	Y	Y	Y	N
11 Foster	N	Y	Y	Y	Y	Y	N
12 Bost	Y	N	Y	N	Y	N	Y
13 Davis, R.	Y	N	Y	N	Y	N	Y
14 Hultgren	Y	N	Y	Y	Y	Y	Y
15 Shimkus	Y	N	Y	Y	Y	Y	Y

KEY	Republicans	Democrats	Independents
Y Voted for (yea)		X Paired against	C Voted "present" to avoid possible conflict of interest
# Paired for		– Announced against	
+ Announced for		P Voted "present"	? Did not vote or otherwise make a position known
N Voted against (nay)			

	653	654	655	656	657	658	659
16 **Kinzinger**	Y	N	Y	Y	N	Y	Y
17 Bustos	N	Y	Y	Y	Y	Y	N
18 **LaHood**	Y	N	Y	Y	N	Y	Y
INDIANA							
1 Visclosky	N	Y	Y	Y	N	Y	N
2 **Walorski**	Y	N	Y	Y	Y	Y	Y
3 **Banks**	Y	N	Y	Y	Y	Y	Y
4 **Rokita**	?	N	Y	Y	N	Y	Y
5 **Brooks**	Y	N	Y	Y	Y	Y	Y
6 **Messer**	Y	N	Y	Y	N	Y	Y
7 Carson	N	Y	Y	Y	Y	Y	N
8 **Bucshon**	Y	N	Y	Y	Y	Y	Y
9 **Hollingsworth**	Y	N	Y	Y	Y	Y	Y
IOWA							
1 **Blum**	Y	N	Y	Y	N	Y	Y
2 Loebsack	?	Y	Y	Y	N	Y	N
3 **Young**	Y	N	Y	Y	Y	Y	Y
4 **King**	Y	N	Y	Y	Y	Y	Y
KANSAS							
1 **Marshall**	Y	N	Y	Y	N	Y	Y
2 **Jenkins**	Y	N	Y	Y	N	Y	Y
3 **Yoder**	Y	N	Y	Y	N	Y	Y
4 **Estes**	Y	N	Y	Y	Y	Y	Y
KENTUCKY							
1 **Comer**	Y	N	Y	Y	Y	Y	Y
2 **Guthrie**	Y	N	Y	Y	Y	Y	Y
3 Yarmuth	N	Y	Y	Y	Y	Y	N
4 **Massie**	Y	N	Y	Y	Y	Y	N
5 **Rogers**	Y	N	Y	Y	Y	Y	Y
6 **Barr**	Y	N	Y	Y	N	Y	Y
LOUISIANA							
1 **Scalise**	+	N	Y	Y	Y	Y	Y
2 Richmond	N	Y	Y	Y	N	N	N
3 **Higgins**	Y	N	Y	Y	Y	Y	Y
4 **Johnson**	Y	N	Y	Y	Y	Y	Y
5 **Abraham**	Y	N	Y	Y	Y	Y	Y
6 **Graves**	Y	N	Y	Y	?	Y	Y
MAINE							
1 Pingree	N	Y	Y	Y	Y	N	N
2 **Poliquin**	Y	N	Y	Y	N	Y	Y
MARYLAND							
1 **Harris**	Y	N	Y	Y	Y	Y	Y
2 Ruppersberger	N	?	Y	Y	Y	Y	N
3 Sarbanes	N	Y	Y	Y	N	Y	N
4 Brown	N	Y	Y	Y	Y	Y	N
5 Hoyer	N	Y	Y	Y	N	Y	N
6 Delaney	N	Y	Y	Y	N	Y	N
7 Cummings	N	Y	Y	Y	Y	Y	N
8 Raskin	N	Y	Y	Y	N	N	N
MASSACHUSETTS							
1 Neal	N	Y	?	?	?	Y	N
2 McGovern	N	Y	Y	Y	N	N	N
3 Tsongas	N	Y	Y	Y	Y	Y	N
4 Kennedy	?	?	?	?	?	?	?
5 Clark	N	Y	?	?	?	N	N
6 Moulton	N	Y	Y	Y	Y	N	N
7 Capuano	N	Y	Y	Y	N	N	N
8 Lynch	N	Y	Y	Y	N	Y	N
9 Keating	N	Y	Y	Y	N	Y	N
MICHIGAN							
1 **Bergman**	Y	N	Y	Y	N	Y	Y
2 **Huizenga**	Y	N	Y	Y	N	Y	Y
3 **Amash**	N	N	N	Y	N	Y	Y
4 **Moolenaar**	Y	N	Y	Y	Y	Y	Y
5 Kildee	N	Y	Y	Y	Y	Y	N
6 **Upton**	Y	N	Y	Y	Y	Y	Y
7 **Walberg**	Y	N	Y	Y	N	Y	Y
8 **Bishop**	Y	N	Y	Y	Y	Y	Y
9 Levin	N	Y	Y	Y	N	Y	N
10 **Mitchell**	Y	N	Y	Y	Y	Y	Y
11 **Trott**	Y	N	Y	Y	Y	Y	Y
12 Dingell	N	Y	Y	Y	Y	Y	N
14 Lawrence	N	Y	Y	Y	N	N	N
MINNESOTA							
1 Walz	–	+	+	+	?	N	N
2 **Lewis**	Y	N	Y	Y	Y	Y	Y
3 **Paulsen**	Y	N	Y	Y	N	Y	Y
4 McCollum	N	Y	Y	Y	Y	N	N

	653	654	655	656	657	658	659
5 Ellison	N	Y	Y	Y	Y	N	N
6 **Emmer**	Y	N	Y	Y	N	Y	Y
7 Peterson	N	Y	Y	Y	N	Y	Y
8 Nolan	N	Y	Y	Y	N	Y	N
MISSISSIPPI							
1 **Kelly**	Y	N	Y	Y	Y	Y	Y
2 Thompson	N	Y	Y	Y	N	N	N
3 **Harper**	Y	N	Y	Y	Y	Y	Y
4 **Palazzo**	Y	N	Y	Y	N	Y	Y
MISSOURI							
1 Clay	N	Y	Y	Y	Y	N	N
2 **Wagner**	Y	N	Y	+	Y	Y	Y
3 **Luetkemeyer**	Y	N	Y	Y	Y	Y	Y
4 **Hartzler**	Y	N	Y	Y	Y	Y	Y
5 Cleaver	N	Y	?	Y	N	Y	N
6 **Graves**	Y	N	Y	Y	N	Y	Y
7 **Long**	Y	N	Y	Y	Y	Y	Y
8 **Smith**	Y	N	Y	Y	N	Y	Y
MONTANA							
AL **Gianforte**	Y	N	Y	Y	Y	Y	Y
NEBRASKA							
1 **Fortenberry**	Y	N	Y	Y	Y	Y	Y
2 **Bacon**	Y	N	Y	Y	Y	Y	Y
3 **Smith**	Y	N	Y	Y	Y	Y	Y
NEVADA							
1 Titus	N	Y	Y	Y	Y	N	N
2 **Amodei**	Y	N	Y	?	?	Y	Y
3 Rosen	N	Y	Y	Y	Y	Y	N
4 Kihuen	?	Y	?	Y	N	Y	N
NEW HAMPSHIRE							
1 Shea-Porter	N	Y	Y	Y	Y	P	N
2 Kuster	N	Y	Y	Y	Y	Y	N
NEW JERSEY							
1 Norcross	N	Y	Y	Y	N	N	N
2 **LoBiondo**	N	N	Y	Y	N	Y	Y
3 **MacArthur**	Y	N	Y	Y	N	Y	Y
4 **Smith**	N	N	Y	Y	Y	Y	Y
5 Gottheimer	N	Y	Y	Y	Y	Y	N
6 Pallone	N	Y	Y	Y	N	N	N
7 **Lance**	Y	N	Y	Y	N	Y	Y
8 Sires	N	Y	Y	Y	N	Y	N
9 Pascrell	N	Y	Y	Y	Y	N	N
10 Payne	N	Y	?	?	?	?	?
11 **Frelinghuysen**	Y	N	Y	Y	Y	Y	Y
12 Watson Coleman	N	Y	Y	Y	N	N	N
NEW MEXICO							
1 Lujan Grisham	N	Y	Y	Y	Y	Y	N
2 **Pearce**	Y	N	Y	Y	N	Y	Y
3 Luján	N	Y	Y	Y	Y	Y	N
NEW YORK							
1 **Zeldin**	N	N	Y	Y	N	Y	Y
2 **King**	N	N	Y	Y	Y	Y	Y
3 Suozzi	N	Y	Y	Y	Y	Y	N
4 Rice	N	Y	Y	Y	N	Y	N
5 Meeks	N	Y	?	?	?	Y	N
6 Meng	N	Y	Y	Y	Y	Y	N
7 Velázquez	N	Y	Y	Y	N	Y	N
8 Jeffries	N	Y	Y	Y	Y	Y	N
9 Clarke	N	Y	Y	Y	N	N	N
10 Nadler	N	Y	Y	Y	Y	Y	N
11 **Donovan**	N	N	Y	Y	Y	Y	Y
12 Maloney, C.	N	Y	Y	Y	Y	Y	N
13 Espaillat	N	Y	Y	Y	N	N	N
14 Crowley	N	Y	Y	Y	N	Y	N
15 Serrano	N	Y	Y	Y	N	Y	N
16 Engel	N	Y	Y	Y	Y	N	N
17 Lowey	N	Y	Y	Y	Y	Y	N
18 Maloney, S.P.	N	Y	Y	Y	N	Y	N
19 **Faso**	Y	N	Y	Y	N	Y	Y
20 Tonko	N	Y	Y	Y	P	Y	N
21 **Stefanik**	Y	N	Y	Y	Y	Y	Y
22 **Tenney**	Y	N	Y	Y	N	Y	Y
23 **Reed**	Y	N	Y	Y	N	Y	Y
24 **Katko**	Y	N	Y	Y	N	Y	Y
25 Slaughter	N	Y	Y	Y	N	N	N
26 Higgins	N	Y	Y	Y	Y	N	N
27 **Collins**	Y	N	Y	Y	Y	Y	Y
NORTH CAROLINA							
1 Butterfield	N	Y	Y	Y	Y	Y	N
2 **Holding**	Y	N	Y	Y	N	Y	Y
3 **Jones**	N	N	Y	Y	N	Y	Y
4 Price	N	Y	Y	Y	N	Y	N

	653	654	655	656	657	658	659
5 **Foxx**	Y	N	Y	Y	N	Y	Y
6 **Walker**	Y	N	Y	Y	Y	Y	Y
7 **Rouzer**	Y	N	Y	Y	N	Y	Y
8 **Hudson**	Y	N	Y	Y	N	Y	Y
9 **Pittenger**	Y	N	Y	Y	N	Y	Y
10 **McHenry**	Y	N	Y	Y	Y	Y	Y
11 **Meadows**	Y	N	Y	Y	Y	Y	Y
12 Adams	N	Y	Y	Y	Y	N	N
13 **Budd**	Y	N	Y	Y	N	Y	Y
NORTH DAKOTA							
AL **Cramer**	Y	N	Y	Y	Y	Y	Y
OHIO							
1 **Chabot**	Y	N	Y	Y	Y	Y	Y
2 **Wenstrup**	Y	N	Y	Y	Y	Y	Y
3 Beatty	–	+	Y	Y	Y	N	N
4 **Jordan**	Y	N	Y	Y	N	Y	Y
5 **Latta**	Y	N	Y	Y	Y	Y	Y
6 **Johnson**	Y	N	Y	Y	N	Y	Y
7 **Gibbs**	Y	N	Y	Y	Y	Y	Y
8 **Davidson**	Y	N	N	Y	Y	Y	Y
9 Kaptur	N	Y	Y	Y	Y	Y	N
10 **Turner**	Y	N	Y	Y	Y	Y	Y
11 Fudge	N	Y	Y	Y	N	N	N
12 **Tiberi**	Y	N	Y	Y	Y	Y	Y
13 Ryan	N	Y	Y	Y	N	Y	N
14 **Joyce**	Y	N	Y	Y	N	Y	Y
15 **Stivers**	Y	N	Y	Y	Y	Y	Y
16 **Renacci**	?	?	Y	Y	N	Y	Y
OKLAHOMA							
1 **Bridenstine**	?	?	?	?	?	?	?
2 **Mullin**	Y	N	Y	Y	Y	Y	Y
3 **Lucas**	Y	N	Y	Y	Y	Y	Y
4 **Cole**	Y	N	Y	Y	Y	Y	Y
5 **Russell**	Y	N	Y	Y	Y	Y	Y
OREGON							
1 Bonamici	N	Y	Y	Y	Y	Y	N
2 **Walden**	Y	N	Y	Y	Y	Y	Y
3 Blumenauer	N	Y	Y	Y	Y	Y	N
4 DeFazio	N	Y	Y	Y	N	Y	N
5 Schrader	N	Y	Y	Y	N	Y	N
PENNSYLVANIA							
1 Brady	N	Y	Y	Y	N	N	N
2 Evans	N	Y	Y	Y	N	N	N
3 **Kelly**	Y	N	Y	Y	Y	Y	Y
4 **Perry**	Y	N	Y	Y	N	Y	Y
5 **Thompson**	Y	N	Y	Y	N	Y	Y
6 **Costello**	Y	N	Y	Y	N	Y	Y
7 **Meehan**	Y	N	Y	Y	N	Y	Y
8 **Fitzpatrick**	Y	N	Y	Y	N	Y	Y
9 **Shuster**	Y	N	Y	Y	Y	Y	Y
10 **Marino**	Y	N	Y	Y	Y	Y	Y
11 **Barletta**	Y	N	Y	Y	Y	Y	Y
12 **Rothfus**	Y	N	Y	Y	Y	Y	Y
13 Boyle	N	Y	Y	Y	N	Y	N
14 Doyle	N	Y	Y	Y	Y	Y	N
15 **Dent**	Y	N	?	?	?	Y	Y
16 **Smucker**	Y	N	Y	Y	N	Y	Y
17 Cartwright	N	Y	Y	Y	Y	Y	N
RHODE ISLAND							
1 Cicilline	N	Y	Y	Y	Y	Y	N
2 Langevin	N	Y	Y	Y	N	Y	N
SOUTH CAROLINA							
1 **Sanford**	Y	N	N	Y	N	Y	Y
2 **Wilson**	Y	N	Y	Y	Y	Y	Y
3 **Duncan**	Y	N	Y	Y	Y	Y	Y
4 **Gowdy**	Y	N	Y	Y	Y	Y	Y
5 **Norman**	Y	N	Y	Y	Y	Y	Y
6 Clyburn	N	Y	Y	Y	N	N	N
7 **Rice**	Y	N	Y	Y	Y	Y	Y
SOUTH DAKOTA							
AL **Noem**	Y	N	Y	Y	Y	Y	Y
TENNESSEE							
1 **Roe**	Y	N	Y	Y	Y	Y	Y
2 **Duncan**	Y	N	Y	Y	Y	Y	Y
3 **Fleischmann**	Y	N	Y	Y	Y	Y	Y
4 **DesJarlais**	Y	N	Y	Y	Y	Y	Y
5 Cooper	N	Y	Y	Y	Y	Y	N
6 **Black**	Y	N	Y	Y	Y	Y	Y
7 **Blackburn**	Y	N	Y	Y	Y	Y	Y
8 **Kustoff**	Y	N	Y	Y	Y	Y	Y
9 Cohen	N	Y	Y	Y	N	N	N

	653	654	655	656	657	658	659
TEXAS							
1 **Gohmert**	Y	N	Y	Y	?	Y	N
2 **Poe**	Y	N	Y	Y	N	Y	Y
3 **Johnson, S.**	Y	N	Y	Y	Y	Y	Y
4 **Ratcliffe**	Y	N	Y	Y	Y	Y	Y
5 **Hensarling**	Y	N	Y	Y	Y	Y	Y
6 **Barton**	Y	?	Y	Y	Y	Y	Y
7 **Culberson**	Y	N	Y	Y	Y	Y	Y
8 **Brady**	Y	N	Y	Y	Y	Y	Y
9 Green, A.	N	Y	Y	Y	N	N	N
10 **McCaul**	Y	N	Y	Y	Y	Y	Y
11 **Conaway**	Y	N	Y	Y	N	Y	Y
12 **Granger**	Y	N	Y	Y	Y	Y	Y
13 **Thornberry**	Y	N	Y	Y	Y	Y	Y
14 **Weber**	Y	N	Y	Y	N	Y	Y
15 Gonzalez	N	Y	Y	Y	Y	Y	N
16 O'Rourke	N	Y	Y	Y	Y	Y	N
17 **Flores**	+	?	Y	Y	N	Y	Y
18 Jackson Lee	N	Y	Y	Y	N	N	N
19 **Arrington**	Y	N	Y	Y	Y	Y	Y
20 Castro	N	Y	Y	Y	N	P	N
21 **Smith**	Y	N	Y	Y	Y	Y	Y
22 **Olson**	Y	N	Y	Y	Y	Y	Y
23 **Hurd**	Y	N	Y	Y	N	Y	Y
24 **Marchant**	Y	N	Y	Y	N	Y	Y
25 **Williams**	Y	N	Y	Y	Y	Y	Y
26 **Burgess**	Y	N	Y	Y	N	Y	Y
27 **Farenthold**	Y	N	Y	Y	N	Y	Y
28 Cuellar	N	Y	Y	Y	N	Y	Y
29 Green, G.	N	Y	Y	Y	N	Y	N
30 Johnson, E.B.	N	Y	Y	Y	Y	Y	N
31 **Carter**	Y	N	Y	Y	Y	Y	Y
32 **Sessions**	Y	N	Y	Y	Y	Y	Y
33 Veasey	N	Y	Y	Y	N	P	N
34 Vela	N	Y	?	Y	Y	N	N
35 Doggett	N	Y	Y	Y	Y	N	N
36 **Babin**	Y	N	Y	Y	N	Y	Y
UTAH							
1 **Bishop**	?	N	Y	Y	Y	Y	Y
2 **Stewart**	?	N	Y	Y	?	Y	Y
3 **Curtis**	?	N	Y	Y	Y	Y	Y
4 **Love**	?	N	Y	Y	Y	Y	Y
VERMONT							
AL Welch	N	Y	Y	Y	Y	Y	N
VIRGINIA							
1 **Wittman**	Y	N	Y	Y	Y	Y	Y
2 **Taylor**	Y	N	Y	Y	Y	Y	Y
3 Scott	N	Y	Y	Y	Y	Y	N
4 McEachin	N	Y	Y	Y	Y	Y	N
5 **Garrett**	Y	N	Y	Y	N	Y	Y
6 **Goodlatte**	Y	N	Y	Y	Y	Y	Y
7 **Brat**	Y	N	Y	Y	Y	Y	Y
8 Beyer	N	Y	Y	Y	N	Y	N
9 **Griffith**	Y	N	+	+	?	Y	Y
10 **Comstock**	Y	N	Y	Y	Y	Y	Y
11 Connolly	N	Y	Y	Y	N	Y	N
WASHINGTON							
1 DelBene	N	Y	Y	Y	Y	Y	N
2 Larsen	N	Y	Y	Y	Y	Y	N
3 **Herrera Beutler**	Y	N	Y	Y	N	Y	Y
4 **Newhouse**	Y	N	Y	Y	Y	Y	Y
5 **McMorris Rodgers**	Y	N	Y	Y	Y	Y	Y
6 Kilmer	N	Y	Y	Y	N	Y	N
7 Jayapal	N	Y	Y	Y	N	N	N
8 **Reichert**	Y	N	Y	Y	N	Y	Y
9 Smith	N	Y	Y	Y	Y	Y	N
10 Heck	N	Y	Y	Y	Y	Y	N
WEST VIRGINIA							
1 **McKinley**	Y	N	Y	Y	N	Y	Y
2 **Mooney**	Y	N	Y	Y	Y	Y	Y
3 **Jenkins**	Y	N	Y	Y	N	Y	Y
WISCONSIN							
1 **Ryan**							
2 Pocan	–	+	+	+	+	–	–
3 Kind	N	Y	Y	Y	N	Y	N
4 Moore	N	Y	Y	Y	N	N	N
5 **Sensenbrenner**	Y	N	Y	Y	Y	Y	Y
6 **Grothman**	Y	N	N	Y	Y	Y	Y
7 **Duffy**	Y	N	Y	Y	N	Y	Y
8 **Gallagher**	Y	N	Y	Y	N	Y	Y
WYOMING							
AL **Cheney**	Y	N	Y	Y	Y	Y	Y

⫿ HOUSE VOTES

VOTE NUMBER

660. HR 38, H RES 645. CONCEALED CARRY RECIPROCITY BETWEEN STATES/RULE. Adoption of the rule (H Res 645) that would provide for House floor consideration of the bill (HR 38) that would permit any individual authorized by their home state to carry a concealed handgun to also carry that concealed weapon in any other state that permits the carrying of concealed weapons. Adopted 232-194 : R 228-10; D 4-184. Dec. 6, 2017.

661. S 1266. VA HEALTH FACILITY INDEPENDENT REVIEW/PASSAGE. Roe, R-Tenn., motion to suspend the rules and pass the bill that would permit the secretary of Veterans Affairs to delegate to directors of VA medical facilities and Veterans Integrated Service Network directors the authority to establish contracts with independent accreditation and health care evaluation entities for the purpose of investigating, assessing and reporting on VA facilities and any deficiencies found therein. Motion agreed to 423-0 : R 237-0; D 186-0. Dec. 6, 2017.

662. HR 38. CONCEALED CARRY RECIPROCITY BETWEEN STATES/RECOMMIT. Thompson, D-Calif., motion to recommit the bill to the House Judiciary Committee with instructions to report it back immediately with an amendment that would prohibit a person who has been convicted of a violent crime within the preceding three years from possessing or carrying a concealed handgun in a state where that conviction would otherwise prohibit that individual from doing so. Motion rejected 190-236 : R 2-235; D 188-1. Dec. 6, 2017.

663. HR 38. CONCEALED CARRY RECIPROCITY BETWEEN STATES/PASSAGE. Passage of the bill that would permit any individual authorized by their home state to carry a concealed handgun to also carry that concealed weapon in any other state that permits the carrying of concealed weapons. The bill would require a twice-annual certification by all federal agencies, federal courts and state governments, in coordination with the Department of Justice, to verify that all relevant data has been reported and uploaded to the National Instant Criminal Background Check System regarding individuals who are not eligible to purchase firearms. Passed 231-198 : R 225-14; D 6-184. Dec. 6, 2017.

664. H CON RES 90. BURMESE ROHINGYA GENOCIDE CONDEMNATION/ADOPTION. Royce, R-Calif., motion to suspend the rules and adopt the concurrent resolution that would condemn the attacks against civilians by Burma's military and would call on the Burmese Commander-in-Chief, Min Aung Hlaing, to immediately end attacks against civilians in the state of Rakhine in Burma. Motion agreed to 423-3 : R 235-3; D 188-0. Dec. 6, 2017.

665. HR 3971, HR 477, H RES 647, H J RES 123. SMALL BUSINESS MERGERS, MORTGAGE RELIEF, CHILDREN'S HEALTH INSURANCE PROGRAM AND FISCAL 2018 CONTINUING APPROPRIATIONS/PREVIOUS QUESTION. Woodall, R-Ga., motion to order the previous question (thus limiting debate and the possibility of amendment) on the rule (H Res 647) that would provide for House floor consideration of the bill (HR 477) that would exempt certain mergers and acquisitions brokers from Securities and Exchange Commission registration requirements; of the bill (HR 3971) that would exempt certain companies from home mortgage escrow requirements; and of the joint resolution (H J Res 123) that would fund government operations at current levels through Dec. 22, 2017 and allow state Children's Health and Insurance Programs to receive extra redistribution funds beyond what is currently allowed. Motion agreed to 236-190 : R 236-1; D 0-189. Dec. 7, 2017.

	660	661	662	663	664	665
ALABAMA						
1 **Byrne**	Y	Y	N	Y	Y	Y
2 **Roby**	Y	Y	N	Y	Y	Y
3 **Rogers**	Y	Y	N	Y	Y	Y
4 **Aderholt**	Y	Y	N	Y	Y	Y
5 **Brooks**	Y	Y	N	Y	Y	Y
6 **Palmer**	Y	Y	N	Y	Y	Y
7 Sewell	N	Y	Y	N	Y	N
ALASKA						
AL **Young**	Y	Y	N	Y	Y	Y
ARIZONA						
1 O'Halleran	N	Y	Y	N	Y	N
2 **McSally**	Y	Y	N	Y	Y	Y
3 Grijalva	N	Y	Y	N	Y	N
4 **Gosar**	N	Y	N	Y	Y	Y
5 **Biggs**	N	N	N	Y	N	Y
6 **Schweikert**	Y	Y	N	Y	Y	Y
7 Gallego	N	Y	Y	N	Y	N
8 **Franks**	Y	Y	N	Y	Y	?
9 Sinema	N	Y	Y	N	Y	N
ARKANSAS						
1 **Crawford**	Y	Y	N	Y	Y	Y
2 **Hill**	Y	Y	N	Y	Y	Y
3 **Womack**	Y	Y	N	Y	Y	Y
4 **Westerman**	Y	Y	N	Y	Y	Y
CALIFORNIA						
1 **LaMalfa**	Y	Y	N	Y	Y	Y
2 Huffman	N	Y	Y	N	Y	N
3 Garamendi	N	Y	Y	N	Y	N
4 **McClintock**	Y	Y	N	Y	Y	Y
5 Thompson	N	Y	Y	N	Y	N
6 Matsui	N	Y	Y	N	Y	N
7 Bera	N	Y	Y	N	Y	N
8 **Cook**	Y	Y	N	Y	Y	Y
9 McNerney	N	Y	Y	N	Y	N
10 **Denham**	Y	Y	N	Y	Y	Y
11 DeSaulnier	N	Y	Y	N	Y	N
12 Pelosi	N	Y	Y	N	Y	N
13 Lee	N	Y	Y	N	Y	N
14 Speier	N	Y	Y	N	Y	N
15 Swalwell	N	Y	Y	N	Y	N
16 Costa	N	Y	Y	N	Y	N
17 Khanna	N	Y	Y	N	Y	N
18 Eshoo	N	Y	Y	N	Y	N
19 Lofgren	N	Y	Y	N	Y	N
20 Panetta	N	Y	Y	N	Y	N
21 **Valadao**	Y	Y	N	Y	Y	Y
22 **Nunes**	Y	Y	N	Y	Y	Y
23 **McCarthy**	Y	Y	N	Y	Y	Y
24 Carbajal	N	Y	Y	N	Y	N
25 **Knight**	Y	Y	N	Y	Y	Y
26 Brownley	?	?	?	?	?	?
27 Chu	?	?	Y	N	Y	N
28 Schiff	N	Y	Y	N	Y	N
29 Cardenas	N	Y	Y	N	Y	N
30 Sherman	N	Y	Y	N	Y	N
31 Aguilar	N	Y	Y	N	?	N
32 Napolitano	N	Y	Y	N	Y	N
33 Lieu	N	Y	Y	N	Y	N
34 Gomez	N	Y	Y	N	Y	N
35 Torres	N	Y	Y	N	Y	N
36 Ruiz	N	Y	Y	N	Y	N
37 Bass	N	Y	Y	N	Y	N
38 Sánchez, Linda	N	Y	Y	N	Y	N
39 **Royce**	Y	Y	N	Y	Y	Y
40 Roybal-Allard	N	Y	Y	N	Y	N
41 Takano	N	Y	Y	N	Y	N
42 **Calvert**	Y	Y	N	Y	Y	Y
43 Waters	N	Y	Y	N	Y	N
44 Barragan	N	Y	Y	N	Y	N
45 **Walters**	Y	Y	N	Y	Y	Y
46 Correa	N	Y	Y	N	Y	N
47 Lowenthal	N	Y	Y	N	Y	N
48 **Rohrabacher**	Y	Y	N	Y	Y	Y
49 **Issa**	Y	Y	N	Y	Y	Y
50 **Hunter**	Y	Y	N	Y	Y	Y
51 Vargas	N	Y	Y	N	Y	N
52 Peters	N	Y	Y	N	Y	N
53 Davis	N	Y	Y	N	Y	N
COLORADO						
1 DeGette	N	?	Y	N	Y	N
2 Polis	N	Y	Y	N	Y	N
3 **Tipton**	Y	Y	N	Y	Y	Y
4 **Buck**	Y	Y	N	N	Y	Y
5 **Lamborn**	Y	Y	N	Y	Y	Y
6 **Coffman**	Y	Y	N	Y	Y	Y
7 Perlmutter	N	Y	Y	N	Y	N
CONNECTICUT						
1 Larson	N	Y	Y	N	Y	N
2 Courtney	N	Y	Y	N	Y	N
3 DeLauro	N	Y	Y	N	Y	N
4 Himes	N	Y	Y	N	Y	N
5 Esty	N	Y	Y	N	Y	N
DELAWARE						
AL Blunt Rochester	N	Y	Y	N	Y	N
FLORIDA						
1 **Gaetz**	Y	Y	N	Y	Y	Y
2 **Dunn**	Y	Y	N	Y	Y	Y
3 **Yoho**	Y	Y	N	Y	Y	Y
4 **Rutherford**	Y	Y	N	Y	Y	Y
5 Lawson	N	Y	Y	N	Y	N
6 **DeSantis**	Y	Y	N	Y	Y	Y
7 Murphy	N	Y	Y	N	Y	N
8 **Posey**	Y	Y	N	Y	Y	Y
9 Soto	N	Y	Y	N	Y	N
10 Demings	N	Y	Y	N	Y	N
11 **Webster**	Y	Y	N	Y	Y	Y
12 **Bilirakis**	Y	Y	N	Y	Y	Y
13 Crist	N	Y	Y	N	Y	N
14 Castor	N	Y	Y	N	Y	N
15 **Ross**	Y	Y	N	Y	Y	Y
16 **Buchanan**	Y	Y	N	Y	Y	Y
17 **Rooney, T.**	Y	Y	N	Y	Y	Y
18 **Mast**	Y	Y	N	Y	Y	Y
19 **Rooney, F.**	Y	Y	N	Y	Y	Y
20 Hastings	N	Y	Y	N	Y	N
21 Frankel	N	Y	Y	N	Y	N
22 Deutch	N	Y	Y	N	Y	N
23 Wasserman Schultz	N	Y	Y	N	Y	N
24 Wilson	N	Y	Y	N	Y	N
25 **Diaz-Balart**	Y	Y	N	Y	Y	Y
26 **Curbelo**	Y	Y	N	N	Y	Y
27 **Ros-Lehtinen**	Y	Y	N	N	Y	Y
GEORGIA						
1 **Carter**	Y	Y	N	Y	Y	Y
2 Bishop	Y	Y	Y	Y	Y	N
3 **Ferguson**	Y	Y	N	Y	Y	Y
4 Johnson	N	Y	Y	N	Y	N
5 Lewis	N	Y	Y	N	Y	N
6 **Handel**	Y	Y	N	Y	Y	Y
7 **Woodall**	Y	Y	N	Y	Y	Y
8 **Scott, A.**	Y	Y	N	Y	Y	Y
9 **Collins**	Y	Y	N	Y	Y	Y
10 **Hice**	Y	Y	N	Y	Y	Y
11 **Loudermilk**	Y	Y	N	Y	Y	Y
12 **Allen**	Y	Y	N	Y	Y	Y
13 Scott, D.	N	Y	Y	N	Y	N
14 **Graves**	Y	Y	N	Y	Y	Y
HAWAII						
1 Hanabusa	N	Y	Y	N	Y	N
2 Gabbard	N	Y	Y	N	Y	N
IDAHO						
1 **Labrador**	Y	Y	N	Y	Y	Y
2 **Simpson**	Y	Y	N	Y	Y	Y
ILLINOIS						
1 Rush	N	Y	Y	N	Y	N
2 Kelly	N	Y	Y	N	Y	N
3 Lipinski	N	Y	Y	N	Y	N
4 Gutierrez	-	+	Y	N	Y	N
5 Quigley	N	Y	Y	N	Y	N
6 **Roskam**	Y	Y	N	Y	Y	Y
7 Davis, D.	N	Y	Y	N	Y	N
8 Krishnamoorthi	N	Y	Y	N	Y	N
9 Schakowsky	N	Y	Y	N	Y	N
10 Schneider	N	Y	Y	N	Y	N
11 Foster	N	Y	Y	N	Y	N
12 **Bost**	Y	Y	N	Y	Y	Y
13 **Davis, R.**	Y	Y	N	Y	Y	Y
14 **Hultgren**	Y	Y	N	Y	Y	Y
15 **Shimkus**	Y	Y	N	Y	Y	Y

KEY	**Republicans**		Democrats		*Independents*	
Y	Voted for (yea)		X	Paired against	C	Voted "present" to avoid possible conflict of interest
#	Paired for		-	Announced against		
+	Announced for		P	Voted "present"	?	Did not vote or otherwise make a position known
N	Voted against (nay)					

	660	661	662	663	664	665
16 **Kinzinger**	Y	Y	N	Y	Y	Y
17 Bustos	N	Y	Y	N	Y	N
18 **LaHood**	Y	Y	N	Y	Y	Y
INDIANA						
1 Visclosky	N	Y	Y	N	Y	N
2 **Walorski**	Y	Y	N	Y	Y	Y
3 **Banks**	Y	Y	N	Y	Y	Y
4 **Rokita**	Y	Y	N	Y	Y	Y
5 **Brooks**	Y	Y	N	Y	Y	Y
6 **Messer**	Y	Y	N	Y	Y	Y
7 Carson	N	Y	Y	N	Y	N
8 **Bucshon**	Y	Y	N	Y	Y	Y
9 **Hollingsworth**	Y	Y	N	Y	Y	Y
IOWA						
1 **Blum**	Y	?	Y	Y	Y	Y
2 Loebsack	N	Y	Y	N	Y	N
3 **Young**	Y	Y	N	Y	Y	Y
4 **King**	N	Y	N	Y	Y	Y
KANSAS						
1 **Marshall**	Y	Y	N	Y	Y	Y
2 **Jenkins**	Y	Y	N	Y	Y	Y
3 **Yoder**	Y	Y	N	Y	Y	Y
4 **Estes**	Y	Y	N	Y	Y	Y
KENTUCKY						
1 **Comer**	Y	Y	N	Y	Y	Y
2 **Guthrie**	Y	Y	N	Y	Y	Y
3 Yarmuth	N	Y	Y	N	Y	N
4 **Massie**	N	Y	N	N	N	Y
5 **Rogers**	Y	Y	N	Y	Y	Y
6 **Barr**	Y	Y	N	Y	Y	Y
LOUISIANA						
1 **Scalise**	Y	Y	N	Y	Y	Y
2 Richmond	N	Y	Y	N	Y	N
3 **Higgins**	Y	Y	N	Y	Y	Y
4 **Johnson**	Y	Y	N	Y	Y	Y
5 **Abraham**	Y	Y	N	Y	Y	Y
6 **Graves**	Y	Y	N	Y	Y	Y
MAINE						
1 Pingree	N	Y	Y	N	Y	N
2 **Poliquin**	Y	Y	N	Y	Y	Y
MARYLAND						
1 **Harris**	Y	Y	N	Y	Y	Y
2 Ruppersberger	N	Y	Y	N	Y	N
3 Sarbanes	N	Y	Y	N	Y	N
4 Brown	N	Y	Y	N	Y	N
5 Hoyer	N	Y	Y	N	Y	N
6 Delaney	N	Y	Y	N	Y	N
7 Cummings	N	Y	Y	N	Y	N
8 Raskin	N	Y	Y	N	Y	N
MASSACHUSETTS						
1 Neal	N	Y	Y	N	Y	N
2 McGovern	N	Y	Y	N	Y	N
3 Tsongas	N	Y	Y	N	Y	N
4 Kennedy	?	?	?	?	?	?
5 Clark	N	Y	Y	N	Y	N
6 Moulton	N	Y	Y	N	Y	N
7 Capuano	N	Y	Y	N	Y	N
8 Lynch	N	Y	Y	N	Y	N
9 Keating	N	Y	Y	N	Y	N
MICHIGAN						
1 **Bergman**	Y	Y	N	Y	Y	Y
2 **Huizenga**	Y	Y	N	Y	Y	Y
3 **Amash**	N	Y	N	N	Y	Y
4 **Moolenaar**	Y	Y	N	Y	Y	Y
5 Kildee	N	Y	Y	N	Y	N
6 **Upton**	Y	Y	N	Y	Y	Y
7 **Walberg**	Y	Y	N	Y	Y	Y
8 **Bishop**	Y	Y	N	Y	Y	Y
9 Levin	N	Y	Y	N	Y	N
10 **Mitchell**	Y	Y	N	Y	Y	Y
11 **Trott**	Y	Y	N	Y	Y	Y
12 Dingell	N	Y	Y	N	Y	N
13 Vacant						
14 Lawrence	N	Y	Y	N	Y	N
MINNESOTA						
1 Walz	N	Y	Y	N	Y	N
2 **Lewis**	Y	Y	N	Y	Y	Y
3 **Paulsen**	Y	Y	N	Y	Y	Y
4 McCollum	N	Y	Y	N	Y	N

	660	661	662	663	664	665
5 Ellison	N	Y	Y	N	Y	N
6 **Emmer**	Y	Y	N	Y	Y	Y
7 Peterson	Y	Y	N	Y	Y	N
8 Nolan	N	Y	Y	N	Y	N
MISSISSIPPI						
1 **Kelly**	Y	Y	N	Y	Y	Y
2 Thompson	N	Y	Y	N	Y	N
3 **Harper**	Y	Y	N	Y	Y	Y
4 **Palazzo**	Y	Y	N	Y	Y	Y
MISSOURI						
1 Clay	N	Y	Y	N	Y	N
2 **Wagner**	Y	Y	N	Y	Y	Y
3 **Luetkemeyer**	Y	Y	N	Y	Y	Y
4 **Hartzler**	Y	Y	N	Y	Y	Y
5 Cleaver	N	Y	Y	N	Y	N
6 **Graves**	Y	Y	N	Y	Y	Y
7 **Long**	Y	Y	N	Y	Y	Y
8 **Smith**	Y	Y	N	Y	Y	Y
MONTANA						
AL **Gianforte**	Y	Y	N	Y	Y	Y
NEBRASKA						
1 **Fortenberry**	Y	Y	N	Y	Y	Y
2 **Bacon**	Y	Y	N	Y	Y	Y
3 **Smith**	Y	Y	N	Y	Y	Y
NEVADA						
1 Titus	N	Y	Y	N	Y	N
2 **Amodei**	Y	Y	N	Y	Y	Y
3 Rosen	N	Y	Y	N	Y	N
4 Kihuen	N	Y	Y	N	Y	N
NEW HAMPSHIRE						
1 Shea-Porter	N	Y	Y	N	Y	N
2 Kuster	N	Y	Y	N	Y	N
NEW JERSEY						
1 Norcross	N	Y	Y	N	Y	N
2 **LoBiondo**	Y	Y	N	Y	Y	Y
3 **MacArthur**	Y	Y	N	Y	Y	Y
4 **Smith**	Y	Y	N	N	Y	Y
5 Gottheimer	N	Y	Y	N	Y	N
6 Pallone	N	Y	Y	N	Y	N
7 **Lance**	Y	Y	N	N	Y	Y
8 Sires	N	Y	Y	N	Y	N
9 Pascrell	N	Y	Y	N	Y	N
10 Payne	N	Y	Y	N	Y	N
11 **Frelinghuysen**	Y	Y	N	Y	Y	Y
12 Watson Coleman	N	Y	Y	N	Y	N
NEW MEXICO						
1 Lujan Grisham	N	Y	Y	N	Y	N
2 **Pearce**	Y	Y	N	Y	Y	Y
3 Luján	N	Y	Y	N	Y	N
NEW YORK						
1 **Zeldin**	Y	Y	N	Y	Y	Y
2 **King**	Y	Y	N	N	Y	Y
3 Suozzi	N	Y	?	N	Y	N
4 Rice	N	Y	Y	N	Y	N
5 Meeks	N	Y	Y	N	Y	N
6 Meng	N	Y	Y	N	Y	N
7 Velázquez	N	Y	Y	N	Y	N
8 Jeffries	N	Y	Y	N	Y	N
9 Clarke	N	Y	Y	N	Y	N
10 Nadler	N	Y	Y	N	Y	N
11 **Donovan**	Y	Y	N	N	Y	Y
12 Maloney, C.	N	Y	Y	N	Y	N
13 Espaillat	N	Y	Y	N	Y	N
14 Crowley	N	Y	Y	N	Y	N
15 Serrano	N	Y	Y	N	Y	N
16 Engel	N	Y	Y	N	Y	N
17 Lowey	N	Y	Y	N	Y	N
18 Maloney, S.P.	N	Y	Y	N	Y	N
19 **Faso**	Y	Y	N	Y	Y	Y
20 Tonko	N	Y	Y	N	Y	N
21 **Stefanik**	Y	Y	N	Y	Y	Y
22 **Tenney**	Y	Y	N	Y	Y	Y
23 **Reed**	Y	Y	N	Y	Y	Y
24 **Katko**	Y	Y	N	Y	Y	Y
25 Slaughter	N	Y	Y	N	Y	N
26 Higgins	N	Y	Y	N	Y	N
27 **Collins**	Y	Y	N	Y	Y	Y
NORTH CAROLINA						
1 Butterfield	N	Y	Y	N	Y	N
2 **Holding**	Y	Y	N	Y	Y	Y
3 **Jones**	N	Y	Y	Y	N	N
4 Price	N	Y	Y	N	Y	N

	660	661	662	663	664	665
5 **Foxx**	Y	Y	N	Y	Y	Y
6 **Walker**	Y	Y	N	Y	Y	Y
7 **Rouzer**	Y	Y	N	Y	Y	Y
8 **Hudson**	Y	Y	N	Y	Y	Y
9 **Pittenger**	Y	Y	N	Y	Y	Y
10 **McHenry**	Y	Y	N	Y	Y	Y
11 **Meadows**	Y	Y	N	Y	Y	Y
12 Adams	N	Y	Y	N	Y	N
13 **Budd**	Y	Y	N	Y	Y	Y
NORTH DAKOTA						
AL **Cramer**	Y	Y	N	Y	Y	Y
OHIO						
1 **Chabot**	Y	Y	N	Y	Y	Y
2 **Wenstrup**	Y	Y	N	Y	Y	Y
3 Beatty	N	Y	Y	N	Y	N
4 **Jordan**	N	Y	N	Y	Y	Y
5 **Latta**	Y	Y	N	Y	Y	Y
6 **Johnson**	Y	Y	N	Y	Y	Y
7 **Gibbs**	Y	Y	N	Y	Y	Y
8 **Davidson**	Y	Y	N	Y	Y	Y
9 Kaptur	N	Y	Y	N	Y	N
10 **Turner**	Y	Y	N	Y	Y	Y
11 Fudge	N	Y	Y	N	Y	N
12 **Tiberi**	Y	Y	N	Y	Y	Y
13 Ryan	N	Y	Y	N	Y	?
14 **Joyce**	Y	Y	N	Y	Y	Y
15 **Stivers**	Y	Y	N	Y	Y	Y
16 **Renacci**	Y	Y	N	Y	Y	Y
OKLAHOMA						
1 **Bridenstine**	?	?	?	?	?	?
2 **Mullin**	Y	Y	N	Y	Y	Y
3 **Lucas**	Y	Y	N	Y	Y	Y
4 **Cole**	Y	Y	N	Y	Y	Y
5 **Russell**	Y	Y	N	Y	Y	Y
OREGON						
1 Bonamici	N	Y	Y	N	Y	N
2 **Walden**	Y	Y	N	Y	Y	Y
3 Blumenauer	N	Y	Y	N	Y	N
4 DeFazio	N	Y	Y	N	Y	N
5 Schrader	N	Y	Y	Y	Y	N
PENNSYLVANIA						
1 Brady	N	Y	Y	N	Y	N
2 Evans	N	Y	Y	N	Y	N
3 **Kelly**	Y	Y	N	Y	Y	Y
4 **Perry**	N	Y	N	Y	Y	Y
5 **Thompson**	Y	Y	N	Y	Y	Y
6 **Costello**	Y	Y	N	N	Y	Y
7 **Meehan**	Y	Y	N	N	Y	Y
8 **Fitzpatrick**	Y	Y	N	N	Y	Y
9 **Shuster**	Y	Y	N	Y	Y	Y
10 **Marino**	Y	Y	N	Y	Y	Y
11 **Barletta**	Y	Y	N	Y	Y	Y
12 **Rothfus**	Y	Y	N	Y	Y	Y
13 Boyle	N	Y	Y	N	Y	N
14 Doyle	N	Y	Y	N	Y	N
15 **Dent**	Y	Y	N	Y	Y	Y
16 **Smucker**	Y	Y	N	Y	Y	Y
17 Cartwright	N	Y	Y	N	Y	N
RHODE ISLAND						
1 Cicilline	N	Y	Y	N	Y	N
2 Langevin	N	Y	Y	N	Y	N
SOUTH CAROLINA						
1 **Sanford**	Y	Y	N	Y	Y	Y
2 **Wilson**	Y	Y	N	Y	Y	Y
3 **Duncan**	Y	Y	N	Y	Y	Y
4 **Gowdy**	Y	Y	N	Y	Y	Y
5 **Norman**	Y	Y	N	Y	Y	Y
6 Clyburn	N	Y	Y	N	Y	N
7 **Rice**	Y	Y	?	Y	Y	Y
SOUTH DAKOTA						
AL **Noem**	Y	Y	N	Y	Y	Y
TENNESSEE						
1 **Roe**	Y	Y	N	Y	Y	Y
2 **Duncan**	N	Y	N	Y	Y	Y
3 **Fleischmann**	Y	Y	N	Y	Y	Y
4 **DesJarlais**	Y	Y	N	Y	Y	Y
5 Cooper	N	Y	Y	N	Y	N
6 **Black**	Y	Y	N	Y	Y	Y
7 **Blackburn**	Y	Y	N	Y	Y	Y
8 **Kustoff**	Y	Y	N	Y	Y	Y
9 Cohen	N	Y	Y	N	Y	N

	660	661	662	663	664	665
TEXAS						
1 **Gohmert**	N	Y	N	N	Y	Y
2 **Poe**	Y	Y	N	Y	Y	Y
3 **Johnson, S.**	Y	Y	N	Y	Y	Y
4 **Ratcliffe**	Y	Y	N	Y	Y	Y
5 **Hensarling**	Y	Y	N	Y	Y	Y
6 **Barton**	Y	Y	N	Y	Y	Y
7 **Culberson**	Y	Y	N	Y	Y	Y
8 **Brady**	Y	Y	N	Y	Y	Y
9 Green, A.	N	Y	Y	N	Y	N
10 **McCaul**	Y	Y	N	Y	Y	Y
11 **Conaway**	Y	Y	N	Y	Y	Y
12 **Granger**	Y	Y	N	Y	Y	Y
13 **Thornberry**	Y	Y	N	Y	Y	Y
14 **Weber**	Y	Y	N	Y	Y	Y
15 Gonzalez	Y	Y	Y	Y	Y	N
16 O'Rourke	N	Y	Y	N	Y	N
17 **Flores**	Y	Y	N	Y	Y	Y
18 Jackson Lee	N	Y	Y	N	Y	N
19 **Arrington**	Y	Y	N	Y	Y	Y
20 Castro	N	Y	Y	N	Y	N
21 **Smith**	Y	Y	N	Y	Y	Y
22 **Olson**	Y	Y	N	Y	Y	Y
23 **Hurd**	Y	Y	N	Y	Y	Y
24 **Marchant**	Y	Y	N	Y	Y	Y
25 **Williams**	Y	Y	N	Y	Y	Y
26 **Burgess**	Y	Y	N	Y	Y	Y
27 **Farenthold**	Y	Y	N	Y	Y	Y
28 Cuellar	Y	Y	Y	Y	Y	N
29 Green, G.	N	Y	Y	N	Y	N
30 Johnson, E.B.	N	Y	Y	N	Y	N
31 **Carter**	Y	Y	N	Y	Y	Y
32 **Sessions**	Y	Y	N	Y	Y	Y
33 Veasey	N	Y	Y	N	Y	N
34 Vela	N	Y	Y	N	Y	N
35 Doggett	N	Y	Y	N	Y	N
36 **Babin**	Y	Y	N	Y	Y	Y
UTAH						
1 **Bishop**	Y	Y	N	Y	Y	Y
2 **Stewart**	Y	Y	N	Y	Y	Y
3 **Curtis**	Y	Y	N	Y	Y	Y
4 **Love**	Y	Y	N	Y	Y	Y
VERMONT						
AL Welch	N	Y	Y	N	Y	N
VIRGINIA						
1 **Wittman**	Y	Y	N	Y	Y	Y
2 **Taylor**	Y	Y	N	Y	Y	Y
3 Scott	N	Y	Y	N	Y	N
4 McEachin	N	Y	Y	N	Y	N
5 **Garrett**	Y	Y	N	Y	Y	Y
6 **Goodlatte**	Y	Y	N	Y	Y	Y
7 **Brat**	Y	Y	N	Y	Y	Y
8 Beyer	N	Y	Y	N	Y	N
9 **Griffith**	Y	Y	N	Y	Y	Y
10 **Comstock**	Y	Y	N	Y	Y	Y
11 Connolly	N	Y	Y	N	Y	N
WASHINGTON						
1 DelBene	N	Y	Y	N	Y	N
2 Larsen	N	Y	Y	N	?	N
3 **Herrera Beutler**	Y	Y	N	Y	Y	Y
4 **Newhouse**	Y	Y	N	Y	Y	Y
5 **McMorris Rodgers**	Y	Y	N	Y	Y	Y
6 Kilmer	N	Y	Y	N	Y	N
7 Jayapal	N	?	Y	N	Y	N
8 **Reichert**	Y	Y	N	Y	Y	Y
9 Smith	N	Y	Y	N	Y	N
10 Heck	N	Y	Y	N	Y	N
WEST VIRGINIA						
1 **McKinley**	Y	Y	N	Y	Y	Y
2 **Mooney**	Y	Y	N	Y	Y	Y
3 **Jenkins**	Y	Y	N	Y	Y	Y
WISCONSIN						
1 **Ryan**				Y		
2 Pocan	–	+	+	–	+	–
3 Kind	N	Y	Y	Y	Y	N
4 Moore	N	Y	Y	N	Y	N
5 **Sensenbrenner**	Y	Y	N	Y	Y	Y
6 **Grothman**	Y	Y	N	Y	Y	Y
7 **Duffy**	Y	Y	N	Y	Y	Y
8 **Gallagher**	Y	Y	N	Y	Y	Y
WYOMING						
AL **Cheney**	Y	Y	N	Y	Y	Y

VOTE NUMBER

666. HR 3971, HR 477, H RES 647, H J RES 123. SMALL BUSINESS MERGERS, MORTGAGE RELIEF, CHILDREN'S HEALTH INSURANCE PROGRAM AND FISCAL 2018 CONTINUING APPROPRIATIONS/RULE. Adoption of the rule (H Res 647) that would provide for House floor consideration of the bill (HR 477) that would exempt certain mergers and acquisitions brokers from Securities and Exchange Commission registration requirements; of the bill (HR 3971) that would exempt certain companies from home mortgage escrow requirements; and of the joint resolution (H J Res 123) that would fund government operations at current levels through Dec. 22, 2017 and allow state Children's Health and Insurance Programs to receive extra redistribution funds beyond what is currently allowed. Adopted 238-188 : R 237-1; D 1-187. Dec. 7, 2017.

667. H RES 259. PROMOTION OF VENEZUELAN DEMOCRATIC ELECTIONS AND HUMAN RIGHTS/ADOPTION. Royce, R-Calif., motion to suspend the rules and adopt the resolution that would urge the government of Venezuela to hold free and open elections, release all political prisoners, respect the constitutional rights of the National Assembly and open a channel for international humanitarian assistance. The resolution would also recognize the strong leadership of the Organization of American States Secretary General Luis Almagro in supporting democracy and human rights for the Venezuelan people. Motion agreed to 419-8 : R 229-8; D 190-0. Dec. 7, 2017.

668. PROCEDURAL MOTION/APPROVAL OF HOUSE JOURNAL. Approved 212-205 : R 137-98; D 75-107. Dec. 7, 2017.

669. HR 477. SMALL BUSINESS MERGERS REGULATORY EXEMPTION/ PASSAGE. Passage of the bill that would exempt brokers handling mergers and acquisitions from Securities and Exchange Commission registration requirements in cases in which the company being sold does not have any class of securities required to be registered with the SEC and in the prior fiscal year, the company's earnings, before interest or taxes, are less than $25 million or gross revenue is less than $250 million. Passed 426-0 : R 238-0; D 188-0. Dec. 7, 2017.

670. H J RES 123. SHORT-TERM FISCAL 2018 CONTINUING APPROPRIATIONS/PASSAGE. Passage of the joint resolution that would provide funding for federal government operations and services at current levels through Dec. 22, 2017, at an annualized rate of $1.23 trillion for federal departments and agencies covered by the 12 unfinished fiscal 2018 spending bills, of which an annualized rate of $621.5 billion would be designated for defense and an annualized rate of $511 billion for nondefense discretionary spending. The bill would allow state Children's Health and Insurance Programs to receive extra redistribution funds beyond what is currently allowed, supporting the program's operations through the end of December. Passed 235-193 : R 221-18; D 14-175. Dec. 7, 2017.

671. HR 2658. VENEZUELAN SANCTIONS AND NGO HUMANITARIAN RESPONSE/PASSAGE. Royce, R-Calif., motion to suspend the rules and pass the bill that would require the State Department to develop a plan to provide humanitarian aid to Venezuela through non-governmental organizations. The bill would extend sanctions on people and entities responsible for violence and human rights abuses in Venezuela. Motion agreed to 388-29 : R 206-29; D 182-0. Dec. 7, 2017.

672. HR 2706. FINANCIAL INSTITUTION ACCOUNT TERMINATION CAUSE REQUIREMENT/PASSAGE. Luetkemeyer, R-Mo., motion to suspend the rules and pass the bill that would prohibit the Federal Deposit Insurance Corporation, the National Credit Union Administration, the Office of the Comptroller of the Currency and the Federal Reserve from requesting that a financial institution terminate an account with a specific customer or group of customers unless the agency has a valid reason for doing so that is not solely based on reputational risk. Motion agreed to 395-2 : R 222-0; D 173-2. Dec. 11, 2017.

	666	667	668	669	670	671	672
ALABAMA							
1 Byrne	Y	Y	Y	Y	Y	Y	Y
2 Roby	Y	Y	Y	Y	Y	Y	Y
3 Rogers	Y	Y	N	Y	Y	Y	Y
4 Aderholt	Y	Y	Y	Y	Y	Y	Y
5 Brooks	Y	N	N	Y	N	N	Y
6 Palmer	Y	Y	N	Y	Y	Y	Y
7 Sewell	N	Y	?	Y	N	Y	Y
ALASKA							
AL Young	Y	Y	N	Y	Y	Y	Y
ARIZONA							
1 O'Halleran	N	Y	N	Y	Y	Y	Y
2 McSally	Y	Y	N	Y	Y	Y	Y
3 Grijalva	N	Y	N	Y	N	Y	Y
4 Gosar	Y	N	N	Y	N	N	Y
5 Biggs	Y	N	N	Y	N	N	Y
6 Schweikert	Y	Y	Y	Y	Y	Y	Y
7 Gallego	N	Y	N	Y	N	Y	Y
9 Sinema	N	Y	N	Y	Y	Y	Y
ARKANSAS							
1 Crawford	Y	Y	Y	Y	Y	Y	Y
2 Hill	Y	Y	N	Y	Y	Y	Y
3 Womack	Y	Y	Y	Y	Y	Y	Y
4 Westerman	Y	Y	Y	Y	Y	Y	Y
CALIFORNIA							
1 LaMalfa	Y	Y	Y	Y	Y	Y	Y
2 Huffman	N	Y	N	Y	N	Y	?
3 Garamendi	N	N	N	Y	N	Y	Y
4 McClintock	Y	Y	Y	Y	Y	Y	Y
5 Thompson	N	Y	N	Y	N	Y	Y
6 Matsui	N	Y	N	Y	N	Y	Y
7 Bera	N	Y	N	Y	N	Y	Y
8 Cook	Y	Y	Y	Y	Y	Y	Y
9 McNerney	N	Y	N	Y	N	Y	Y
10 Denham	Y	Y	N	Y	Y	Y	Y
11 DeSaulnier	N	Y	?	Y	N	Y	Y
12 Pelosi	N	Y	N	Y	N	Y	Y
13 Lee	N	Y	N	Y	N	Y	Y
14 Speier	N	Y	N	Y	Y	Y	Y
15 Swalwell	N	Y	N	Y	N	Y	Y
16 Costa	N	Y	N	Y	N	Y	Y
17 Khanna	N	Y	N	Y	N	Y	Y
18 Eshoo	N	Y	?	Y	N	Y	Y
19 Lofgren	N	Y	N	Y	N	Y	Y
20 Panetta	N	Y	N	Y	N	Y	Y
21 Valadao	Y	Y	N	Y	Y	Y	Y
22 Nunes	Y	Y	Y	Y	Y	Y	Y
23 McCarthy	Y	Y	Y	Y	Y	Y	Y
24 Carbajal	N	Y	N	Y	N	Y	Y
25 Knight	Y	Y	N	Y	Y	Y	Y
26 Brownley	?	?	?	?	?	?	Y
27 Chu	N	Y	N	Y	N	Y	Y
28 Schiff	N	Y	N	Y	N	Y	Y
29 Cardenas	N	Y	N	Y	N	Y	Y
30 Sherman	N	Y	N	Y	Y	Y	Y
31 Aguilar	N	Y	N	Y	N	Y	Y
32 Napolitano	N	Y	N	Y	N	Y	N
33 Lieu	N	Y	N	Y	N	Y	Y
34 Gomez	N	Y	N	Y	N	Y	Y
35 Torres	N	Y	N	Y	N	?	Y
36 Ruiz	N	Y	N	Y	Y	Y	Y
37 Bass	N	Y	N	Y	N	Y	?
38 Sánchez, Linda	N	Y	N	Y	N	Y	Y
39 Royce	Y	Y	Y	Y	Y	Y	Y
40 Roybal-Allard	N	Y	N	Y	N	Y	Y
41 Takano	N	Y	N	Y	N	Y	Y
42 Calvert	Y	Y	Y	Y	Y	Y	Y
43 Waters	N	Y	N	Y	N	?	Y
44 Barragan	N	Y	N	Y	N	Y	Y
45 Walters	Y	Y	Y	Y	Y	Y	Y
46 Correa	N	Y	N	Y	N	Y	Y
47 Lowenthal	N	Y	?	Y	N	Y	Y
48 Rohrabacher	Y	Y	Y	Y	Y	Y	?
49 Issa	Y	Y	N	Y	Y	Y	Y
50 Hunter	Y	Y	Y	Y	Y	?	Y
51 Vargas	N	Y	?	Y	N	Y	Y
52 Peters	N	Y	N	Y	Y	Y	Y
53 Davis	N	Y	N	Y	N	Y	Y

	666	667	668	669	670	671	672
COLORADO							
1 DeGette	N	Y	Y	Y	N	Y	Y
2 Polis	N	Y	Y	N	Y	N	Y
3 Tipton	Y	Y	N	Y	Y	Y	Y
4 Buck	Y	Y	N	Y	Y	Y	Y
5 Lamborn	Y	Y	Y	Y	Y	Y	Y
6 Coffman	Y	Y	N	Y	Y	Y	Y
7 Perlmutter	N	Y	Y	Y	N	Y	Y
CONNECTICUT							
1 Larson	N	Y	N	Y	N	+	Y
2 Courtney	N	Y	Y	Y	N	Y	Y
3 DeLauro	N	Y	Y	Y	N	Y	Y
4 Himes	N	Y	Y	Y	N	Y	Y
5 Esty	N	Y	N	Y	N	Y	Y
DELAWARE							
AL Blunt Rochester	N	Y	Y	Y	N	Y	Y
FLORIDA							
1 Gaetz	Y	Y	N	Y	N	N	Y
2 Dunn	Y	Y	Y	Y	Y	Y	Y
3 Yoho	Y	Y	Y	Y	Y	Y	Y
4 Rutherford	Y	Y	N	Y	Y	Y	Y
5 Lawson	N	Y	N	?	?	?	Y
6 DeSantis	Y	Y	N	Y	Y	Y	Y
7 Murphy	N	Y	N	Y	N	Y	Y
8 Posey	Y	Y	Y	Y	Y	Y	Y
9 Soto	N	Y	N	Y	N	Y	Y
10 Demings	N	Y	N	Y	N	Y	Y
11 Webster	Y	Y	Y	Y	Y	Y	Y
12 Bilirakis	Y	Y	N	Y	Y	Y	Y
13 Crist	N	Y	N	Y	N	Y	Y
14 Castor	N	Y	N	Y	N	Y	Y
15 Ross	Y	Y	Y	Y	Y	Y	Y
16 Buchanan	Y	Y	Y	Y	Y	Y	?
17 Rooney, T.	Y	Y	?	Y	Y	Y	Y
18 Mast	Y	Y	N	Y	Y	Y	Y
19 Rooney, F.	Y	Y	N	Y	Y	Y	Y
20 Hastings	N	Y	N	Y	N	Y	Y
21 Frankel	N	Y	N	Y	N	Y	?
22 Deutch	N	Y	Y	Y	N	Y	Y
23 Wasserman Schultz	N	Y	Y	Y	N	Y	Y
24 Wilson	N	Y	N	Y	N	Y	Y
25 Diaz-Balart	Y	Y	N	Y	Y	Y	Y
26 Curbelo	Y	Y	N	Y	Y	Y	Y
27 Ros-Lehtinen	Y	Y	N	Y	Y	Y	Y
GEORGIA							
1 Carter	Y	Y	N	Y	Y	Y	Y
2 Bishop	N	Y	N	Y	N	Y	Y
3 Ferguson	Y	Y	Y	Y	Y	Y	Y
4 Johnson	N	Y	N	Y	N	Y	Y
5 Lewis	N	Y	N	Y	N	Y	Y
6 Handel	Y	Y	N	Y	Y	Y	Y
7 Woodall	Y	Y	N	Y	Y	N	Y
8 Scott, A.	Y	Y	Y	Y	Y	Y	Y
9 Collins	Y	Y	N	Y	Y	Y	Y
10 Hice	Y	Y	N	Y	Y	N	Y
11 Loudermilk	Y	Y	Y	Y	Y	Y	Y
12 Allen	Y	Y	N	Y	Y	N	Y
13 Scott, D.	?	Y	Y	Y	Y	?	Y
14 Graves	Y	Y	N	Y	Y	Y	Y
HAWAII							
1 Hanabusa	N	Y	Y	Y	N	Y	Y
2 Gabbard	N	Y	Y	Y	N	Y	Y
IDAHO							
1 Labrador	Y	Y	Y	Y	N	N	Y
2 Simpson	Y	Y	Y	Y	Y	Y	?
ILLINOIS							
1 Rush	N	Y	N	Y	N	Y	Y
2 Kelly	N	Y	Y	Y	N	Y	Y
3 Lipinski	N	Y	Y	Y	N	Y	Y
4 Gutierrez	N	Y	N	Y	N	Y	+
5 Quigley	N	Y	?	Y	N	Y	Y
6 Roskam	Y	Y	N	Y	Y	Y	Y
7 Davis, D.	N	Y	Y	Y	N	Y	?
8 Krishnamoorthi	N	Y	Y	Y	N	Y	Y
9 Schakowsky	N	Y	N	Y	N	Y	Y
10 Schneider	N	Y	Y	Y	Y	Y	Y
11 Foster	N	Y	N	Y	N	Y	Y
12 Bost	Y	Y	N	Y	Y	Y	Y
13 Davis, R.	Y	Y	N	Y	Y	Y	Y
14 Hultgren	Y	Y	Y	Y	Y	Y	Y
15 Shimkus	Y	Y	Y	Y	Y	Y	Y

	666	667	668	669	670	671	672
16 **Kinzinger**	Y	Y	N	Y	Y	Y	Y
17 Bustos	N	Y	Y	Y	Y	Y	Y
18 **LaHood**	Y	Y	N	Y	Y	Y	Y
INDIANA							
1 Visclosky	N	Y	N	Y	N	Y	Y
2 **Walorski**	Y	Y	Y	Y	Y	Y	Y
3 **Banks**	Y	Y	Y	Y	Y	Y	Y
4 **Rokita**	Y	Y	N	Y	Y	Y	Y
5 **Brooks**	Y	Y	Y	Y	Y	Y	Y
6 **Messer**	Y	Y	Y	Y	Y	Y	?
7 Carson	N	Y	N	Y	N	Y	Y
8 **Bucshon**	Y	Y	Y	Y	Y	Y	Y
9 **Hollingsworth**	Y	Y	Y	Y	N	Y	Y
IOWA							
1 **Blum**	Y	Y	N	Y	Y	N	Y
2 Loebsack	N	Y	N	Y	N	Y	Y
3 **Young**	Y	Y	Y	Y	Y	Y	Y
4 **King**	Y	Y	Y	Y	Y	Y	Y
KANSAS							
1 **Marshall**	Y	Y	Y	Y	Y	Y	Y
2 **Jenkins**	Y	Y	N	Y	Y	Y	Y
3 **Yoder**	Y	Y	N	Y	Y	Y	Y
4 **Estes**	Y	Y	Y	Y	Y	Y	Y
KENTUCKY							
1 **Comer**	Y	Y	N	Y	Y	Y	Y
2 **Guthrie**	Y	Y	Y	Y	Y	Y	Y
3 Yarmuth	N	Y	Y	Y	N	Y	Y
4 **Massie**	Y	N	Y	Y	N	N	Y
5 **Rogers**	Y	Y	Y	Y	Y	Y	Y
6 **Barr**	Y	Y	Y	Y	Y	Y	Y
LOUISIANA							
1 **Scalise**	Y	Y	Y	Y	Y	Y	Y
2 Richmond	N	Y	N	Y	N	Y	?
3 **Higgins**	Y	Y	Y	Y	Y	Y	Y
4 **Johnson**	Y	Y	Y	Y	Y	Y	Y
5 **Abraham**	Y	Y	Y	Y	Y	Y	Y
6 **Graves**	Y	Y	N	Y	Y	Y	Y
MAINE							
1 Pingree	N	Y	Y	Y	N	Y	Y
2 **Poliquin**	Y	Y	N	Y	Y	Y	Y
MARYLAND							
1 **Harris**	Y	Y	Y	Y	N	Y	Y
2 Ruppersberger	N	Y	Y	Y	N	Y	Y
3 Sarbanes	N	Y	N	Y	N	Y	Y
4 Brown	N	Y	Y	Y	N	Y	Y
5 Hoyer	N	Y	N	Y	N	Y	Y
6 Delaney	N	Y	N	Y	N	Y	Y
7 Cummings	N	Y	N	Y	N	Y	Y
8 Raskin	N	Y	N	Y	N	Y	Y
MASSACHUSETTS							
1 Neal	N	Y	N	Y	N	Y	Y
2 McGovern	N	Y	N	Y	N	Y	Y
3 Tsongas	N	Y	Y	Y	N	Y	?
4 Kennedy	?	?	?	?	?	?	?
5 Clark	N	Y	N	Y	N	Y	Y
6 Moulton	N	Y	Y	Y	N	Y	Y
7 Capuano	N	Y	N	Y	N	Y	Y
8 Lynch	N	Y	N	Y	N	?	Y
9 Keating	N	Y	N	Y	N	Y	Y
MICHIGAN							
1 **Bergman**	Y	Y	N	Y	Y	Y	Y
2 **Huizenga**	Y	Y	Y	Y	Y	Y	Y
3 **Amash**	Y	N	N	Y	N	N	Y
4 **Moolenaar**	Y	Y	Y	Y	Y	Y	Y
5 Kildee	N	Y	Y	Y	N	Y	Y
6 **Upton**	Y	Y	N	Y	Y	Y	Y
7 **Walberg**	Y	Y	N	Y	Y	Y	Y
8 **Bishop**	Y	Y	Y	Y	Y	Y	Y
9 Levin	N	Y	N	Y	N	Y	Y
10 **Mitchell**	Y	Y	N	Y	Y	Y	Y
11 **Trott**	Y	Y	Y	Y	Y	Y	Y
12 Dingell	N	Y	N	Y	N	Y	Y
13 Vacant							
14 Lawrence	N	Y	N	Y	N	Y	Y
MINNESOTA							
1 Walz	N	Y	Y	Y	Y	Y	?
2 **Lewis**	Y	Y	Y	Y	Y	Y	Y
3 **Paulsen**	Y	Y	N	Y	Y	Y	Y
4 McCollum	N	Y	Y	Y	N	Y	Y

	666	667	668	669	670	671	672
5 Ellison	N	Y	N	Y	N	Y	N
6 **Emmer**	Y	Y	N	Y	Y	Y	Y
7 Peterson	Y	Y	N	Y	Y	Y	Y
8 Nolan	N	Y	N	Y	N	Y	Y
MISSISSIPPI							
1 **Kelly**	Y	Y	Y	Y	Y	Y	Y
2 Thompson	N	Y	N	Y	N	Y	Y
3 **Harper**	Y	Y	Y	Y	Y	Y	?
4 **Palazzo**	Y	Y	N	Y	Y	Y	Y
MISSOURI							
1 Clay	N	Y	Y	Y	N	Y	?
2 **Wagner**	Y	Y	Y	Y	Y	Y	+
3 **Luetkemeyer**	Y	Y	Y	Y	Y	Y	Y
4 **Hartzler**	Y	Y	N	Y	Y	Y	Y
5 Cleaver	N	Y	N	Y	N	Y	?
6 **Graves**	Y	Y	N	Y	Y	Y	Y
7 **Long**	Y	Y	Y	Y	Y	Y	Y
8 **Smith**	Y	Y	N	Y	Y	Y	Y
MONTANA							
AL **Gianforte**	Y	Y	Y	Y	Y	Y	Y
NEBRASKA							
1 **Fortenberry**	Y	Y	Y	Y	Y	Y	Y
2 **Bacon**	Y	Y	Y	Y	Y	N	Y
3 **Smith**	Y	Y	Y	Y	Y	Y	Y
NEVADA							
1 Titus	N	Y	Y	Y	N	Y	Y
2 **Amodei**	Y	Y	Y	Y	Y	Y	Y
3 Rosen	N	Y	N	Y	Y	Y	Y
4 Kihuen	N	Y	N	Y	N	Y	Y
NEW HAMPSHIRE							
1 Shea-Porter	N	Y	Y	Y	N	Y	Y
2 Kuster	N	Y	Y	Y	N	Y	Y
NEW JERSEY							
1 Norcross	N	Y	N	Y	N	Y	Y
2 **LoBiondo**	Y	Y	N	Y	Y	Y	Y
3 **MacArthur**	Y	Y	N	Y	Y	Y	Y
4 **Smith**	Y	Y	Y	Y	Y	Y	Y
5 Gottheimer	N	Y	Y	Y	Y	Y	Y
6 Pallone	N	Y	N	Y	N	Y	Y
7 **Lance**	Y	Y	N	Y	Y	Y	Y
8 Sires	N	Y	N	Y	N	Y	?
9 Pascrell	N	Y	Y	Y	N	Y	Y
10 Payne	N	Y	N	Y	N	Y	Y
11 **Frelinghuysen**	Y	Y	Y	Y	Y	Y	Y
12 Watson Coleman	N	Y	N	Y	N	Y	Y
NEW MEXICO							
1 Lujan Grisham	N	Y	Y	Y	N	Y	Y
2 **Pearce**	Y	Y	N	Y	Y	Y	Y
3 Luján	N	Y	N	Y	N	Y	Y
NEW YORK							
1 **Zeldin**	Y	Y	N	Y	N	Y	Y
2 **King**	Y	Y	Y	Y	Y	Y	Y
3 Suozzi	N	Y	Y	Y	N	Y	Y
4 Rice	N	Y	?	Y	N	Y	?
5 Meeks	N	Y	Y	Y	N	?	Y
6 Meng	N	Y	Y	Y	N	Y	Y
7 Velázquez	N	Y	N	Y	N	Y	Y
8 Jeffries	N	Y	Y	Y	N	Y	Y
9 Clarke	N	Y	N	Y	N	Y	?
10 Nadler	N	Y	Y	Y	N	Y	Y
11 **Donovan**	Y	Y	Y	Y	Y	Y	Y
12 Maloney, C.	N	Y	N	Y	N	Y	Y
13 Espaillat	N	Y	N	Y	N	Y	Y
14 Crowley	N	Y	N	Y	N	Y	Y
15 Serrano	N	Y	N	Y	N	Y	Y
16 Engel	N	Y	Y	Y	N	Y	Y
17 Lowey	N	Y	N	Y	N	Y	Y
18 Maloney, S.P.	N	Y	N	Y	N	Y	Y
19 **Faso**	Y	Y	N	Y	Y	Y	Y
20 Tonko	N	Y	P	Y	N	Y	Y
21 **Stefanik**	Y	Y	Y	Y	Y	Y	Y
22 **Tenney**	Y	Y	N	Y	Y	Y	Y
23 **Reed**	Y	Y	N	Y	Y	Y	Y
24 **Katko**	Y	Y	N	Y	Y	Y	Y
25 Slaughter	N	Y	N	Y	N	Y	Y
26 Higgins	N	Y	N	Y	N	Y	Y
27 **Collins**	Y	Y	Y	Y	Y	Y	Y
NORTH CAROLINA							
1 Butterfield	N	Y	Y	Y	N	Y	?
2 **Holding**	Y	Y	N	Y	Y	Y	Y
3 **Jones**	N	N	N	Y	N	N	Y
4 Price	N	Y	N	Y	N	Y	Y

	666	667	668	669	670	671	672
5 **Foxx**	Y	Y	N	Y	Y	Y	Y
6 **Walker**	Y	Y	Y	Y	Y	Y	Y
7 **Rouzer**	Y	Y	N	Y	Y	Y	Y
8 **Hudson**	Y	Y	N	Y	Y	Y	Y
9 **Pittenger**	Y	Y	N	Y	Y	Y	Y
10 **McHenry**	Y	Y	Y	Y	Y	Y	Y
11 **Meadows**	Y	Y	Y	Y	Y	Y	Y
12 Adams	N	Y	N	Y	N	Y	Y
13 **Budd**	Y	Y	N	Y	Y	Y	Y
NORTH DAKOTA							
AL **Cramer**	Y	Y	?	Y	Y	Y	Y
OHIO							
1 **Chabot**	Y	Y	Y	Y	Y	Y	Y
2 **Wenstrup**	Y	Y	N	Y	Y	Y	Y
3 Beatty	N	Y	Y	Y	N	Y	Y
4 **Jordan**	Y	Y	N	Y	Y	N	Y
5 **Latta**	Y	Y	N	Y	Y	Y	Y
6 **Johnson**	Y	Y	N	Y	Y	Y	Y
7 **Gibbs**	Y	Y	Y	Y	Y	Y	Y
8 **Davidson**	Y	Y	Y	Y	Y	N	Y
9 Kaptur	N	Y	N	Y	N	Y	Y
10 **Turner**	Y	Y	N	Y	Y	Y	Y
11 Fudge	N	Y	N	Y	N	Y	Y
12 **Tiberi**	Y	Y	Y	Y	Y	?	?
13 Ryan	N	Y	N	Y	N	Y	Y
14 **Joyce**	Y	Y	N	Y	Y	Y	Y
15 **Stivers**	Y	Y	N	Y	Y	Y	Y
16 **Renacci**	Y	Y	N	Y	Y	Y	?
OKLAHOMA							
1 **Bridenstine**	?	?	?	?	?	?	?
2 **Mullin**	Y	Y	Y	Y	Y	Y	Y
3 **Lucas**	Y	Y	Y	Y	Y	Y	Y
4 **Cole**	Y	Y	Y	Y	Y	Y	Y
5 **Russell**	Y	Y	Y	Y	Y	Y	Y
OREGON							
1 Bonamici	N	Y	Y	Y	N	Y	Y
2 **Walden**	Y	Y	N	Y	Y	Y	Y
3 Blumenauer	N	Y	Y	Y	N	Y	Y
4 DeFazio	N	Y	N	Y	N	Y	Y
5 Schrader	N	Y	N	Y	N	Y	Y
PENNSYLVANIA							
1 Brady	N	Y	N	Y	N	Y	Y
2 Evans	N	Y	N	Y	N	Y	Y
3 **Kelly**	Y	Y	Y	Y	Y	Y	Y
4 **Perry**	Y	Y	N	Y	N	N	Y
5 **Thompson**	Y	Y	N	Y	Y	Y	Y
6 **Costello**	Y	Y	N	Y	Y	Y	Y
7 **Meehan**	Y	Y	N	Y	Y	Y	Y
8 **Fitzpatrick**	Y	Y	N	Y	Y	Y	Y
9 **Shuster**	Y	Y	Y	Y	Y	Y	Y
10 **Marino**	Y	Y	Y	Y	Y	Y	Y
11 **Barletta**	Y	Y	Y	Y	Y	Y	?
12 **Rothfus**	Y	Y	Y	Y	Y	Y	Y
13 Boyle	N	Y	N	Y	N	Y	Y
14 Doyle	N	Y	N	Y	N	Y	Y
15 **Dent**	Y	Y	Y	Y	Y	Y	Y
16 **Smucker**	Y	Y	N	Y	Y	Y	Y
17 Cartwright	N	Y	Y	Y	N	Y	Y
RHODE ISLAND							
1 Cicilline	N	Y	Y	Y	N	Y	Y
2 Langevin	N	Y	N	Y	N	Y	Y
SOUTH CAROLINA							
1 **Sanford**	Y	Y	Y	Y	Y	N	+
2 **Wilson**	Y	Y	Y	Y	Y	Y	Y
3 **Duncan**	Y	Y	Y	Y	Y	Y	Y
4 **Gowdy**	Y	Y	Y	Y	Y	Y	?
5 **Norman**	Y	Y	Y	Y	Y	Y	Y
6 Clyburn	N	Y	Y	Y	N	Y	Y
7 **Rice**	Y	Y	Y	Y	Y	N	Y
SOUTH DAKOTA							
AL **Noem**	Y	Y	Y	Y	Y	Y	Y
TENNESSEE							
1 **Roe**	Y	Y	Y	Y	Y	N	Y
2 **Duncan**	Y	N	Y	Y	Y	N	Y
3 **Fleischmann**	Y	Y	Y	Y	Y	Y	Y
4 **DesJarlais**	Y	Y	Y	Y	Y	N	?
5 Cooper	N	Y	Y	Y	N	Y	Y
6 **Black**	Y	Y	Y	Y	Y	N	Y
7 **Blackburn**	Y	Y	N	Y	Y	N	?
8 **Kustoff**	Y	Y	Y	Y	Y	Y	Y
9 Cohen	N	Y	N	Y	N	Y	Y

	666	667	668	669	670	671	672
TEXAS							
1 **Gohmert**	Y	Y	P	Y	N	N	?
2 **Poe**	Y	Y	N	Y	Y	Y	Y
3 **Johnson, S.**	Y	Y	Y	Y	Y	Y	Y
4 **Ratcliffe**	Y	Y	Y	Y	N	Y	Y
5 **Hensarling**	Y	Y	Y	Y	Y	Y	Y
6 **Barton**	Y	?	Y	Y	Y	Y	Y
7 **Culberson**	Y	Y	Y	Y	Y	Y	Y
8 **Brady**	Y	Y	Y	Y	Y	Y	Y
9 Green, A.	N	Y	Y	Y	N	Y	Y
10 **McCaul**	Y	Y	Y	Y	Y	Y	Y
11 **Conaway**	Y	Y	N	Y	Y	Y	Y
12 **Granger**	Y	Y	Y	Y	Y	Y	Y
13 **Thornberry**	Y	Y	Y	Y	Y	Y	Y
14 **Weber**	Y	Y	N	Y	Y	Y	Y
15 Gonzalez	N	Y	Y	Y	N	Y	Y
16 O'Rourke	N	Y	Y	Y	N	Y	Y
17 **Flores**	Y	Y	N	Y	Y	Y	Y
18 Jackson Lee	N	Y	N	Y	N	Y	?
19 **Arrington**	Y	Y	Y	Y	Y	Y	Y
20 Castro	N	Y	Y	Y	N	Y	Y
21 **Smith**	Y	Y	Y	Y	Y	Y	Y
22 **Olson**	Y	Y	Y	Y	Y	Y	Y
23 **Hurd**	Y	Y	N	Y	Y	Y	Y
24 **Marchant**	Y	Y	N	Y	Y	N	Y
25 **Williams**	Y	Y	Y	Y	Y	Y	Y
26 **Burgess**	Y	Y	N	Y	Y	Y	Y
27 **Farenthold**	Y	Y	Y	Y	Y	Y	Y
28 Cuellar	N	Y	Y	Y	N	Y	Y
29 Green, G.	N	Y	N	?	N	Y	Y
30 Johnson, E.B.	N	Y	N	Y	N	Y	Y
31 **Carter**	Y	Y	Y	Y	Y	Y	Y
32 **Sessions**	Y	Y	Y	Y	Y	Y	Y
33 Veasey	N	Y	N	Y	N	Y	Y
34 Vela	N	Y	N	Y	N	Y	Y
35 Doggett	?	Y	N	Y	N	Y	Y
36 **Babin**	Y	Y	N	Y	Y	Y	Y
UTAH							
1 **Bishop**	Y	Y	Y	Y	Y	Y	Y
2 **Stewart**	Y	Y	Y	Y	Y	Y	Y
3 **Curtis**	Y	Y	Y	Y	Y	Y	Y
4 **Love**	Y	Y	Y	Y	Y	Y	Y
VERMONT							
AL Welch	N	Y	Y	Y	N	Y	Y
VIRGINIA							
1 **Wittman**	Y	Y	N	Y	N	Y	Y
2 **Taylor**	Y	Y	Y	Y	Y	Y	Y
3 Scott	N	Y	Y	Y	N	Y	?
4 McEachin	N	Y	Y	Y	N	Y	Y
5 **Garrett**	Y	Y	Y	Y	N	Y	Y
6 **Goodlatte**	Y	Y	Y	Y	Y	N	Y
7 **Brat**	Y	Y	Y	Y	Y	N	Y
8 Beyer	N	Y	N	Y	N	Y	Y
9 **Griffith**	Y	N	Y	Y	N	N	Y
10 **Comstock**	Y	Y	Y	Y	Y	Y	Y
11 Connolly	N	Y	N	Y	N	Y	Y
WASHINGTON							
1 DelBene	N	Y	Y	Y	N	Y	Y
2 Larsen	N	Y	N	Y	N	Y	Y
3 **Herrera Beutler**	Y	Y	N	Y	Y	Y	Y
4 **Newhouse**	Y	Y	N	Y	Y	Y	Y
5 **McMorris Rodgers**	Y	Y	Y	Y	Y	Y	Y
6 Kilmer	N	Y	N	Y	N	Y	Y
7 Jayapal	N	Y	N	Y	N	Y	Y
8 **Reichert**	Y	Y	Y	Y	Y	Y	Y
9 Smith	N	Y	Y	Y	N	Y	Y
10 Heck	N	Y	Y	Y	N	Y	Y
WEST VIRGINIA							
1 **McKinley**	Y	Y	N	Y	Y	Y	Y
2 **Mooney**	Y	Y	Y	Y	N	N	Y
3 **Jenkins**	Y	Y	N	Y	Y	Y	Y
WISCONSIN							
1 **Ryan**				Y			
2 Pocan	–	+	+	+	–	+	+
3 Kind	N	Y	N	Y	N	Y	Y
4 Moore	N	Y	Y	Y	N	?	Y
5 **Sensenbrenner**	Y	Y	Y	Y	Y	Y	Y
6 **Grothman**	Y	Y	N	Y	Y	Y	Y
7 **Duffy**	Y	Y	N	Y	Y	Y	Y
8 **Gallagher**	Y	Y	N	Y	Y	Y	Y
WYOMING							
AL **Cheney**	Y	Y	Y	Y	Y	Y	Y

VOTE NUMBER

673. HR 1730. RELIGIOUS CENTERS/PASSAGE. Goodlatte, R-Va., motion to suspend the rules and pass the bill that would set a additional penalties for destruction of religious real property by intentional fire or explosives, establishing a fine and imprisonment for up to three years. The bill would amend existing provisions on destruction of religious real property to include destruction that results from intentional fire or explosives. It would amend the definition of religious real property to include property owned or leased by a religiously affiliated non-profit organization. Motion agreed to 402-2 : R 222-2; D 180-0. Dec. 11, 2017.

674. HR 3971. MORTGAGE LENDER ESCROW REQUIREMENT EXEMPTION/ RECOMMIT. Titus, D-Nev., motion to recommit the bill to the House Financial Services Committee with instructions to report it back immediately with an amendment that would prohibit any creditor or servicer from qualifying for the exemptions provided for in the bill if the creditor or servicer has been engaged in any unfair, deceptive or abusive actions, or has been convicted of residential mortgage fraud. Motion rejected 190-233 : R 2-233; D 188-0. Dec. 12, 2017.

675. HR 3971. MORTGAGE LENDER ESCROW REQUIREMENT EXEMPTION/ PASSAGE. Passage of the bill that would exempt lenders with assets of $10 billion or less from the 2010 financial regulatory overhaul requirement that such lenders establish escrow accounts for the first five years of so-called "high-priced" mortgage loans, if the lenders hold the loan on its own balance sheet for three years after the loan is made, and it would exempt companies that service up to 20,000 mortgage loans from current loan servicing and escrow account administration requirements. Passed 294-129 : R 234-1; D 60-128. Dec. 12, 2017.

676. HR 4324, HR 1638, H RES 658. IRANIAN FINANCIAL ASSETS AND AIRCRAFT PURCHASE TRANSACTIONS/PREVIOUS QUESTION. Buck, R-Colo., motion to order the previous question (thus ending debate and the possibility of amendment) on the rule (H Res 658) that would provide for House floor consideration of the bill (HR 1638) that would require the Treasury Department to compile and submit to Congress a report concerning Iranian assets held in U.S and foreign institutions, and would provide for consideration of the bill (HR 4324) that would require the Treasury secretary to submit reports to Congress on transactions of financial institutions associated with the purchase and export of aircraft on behalf of Iran. Motion agreed to 229-189 : R 229-0; D 0-189. Dec. 13, 2017.

677. HR 4324, HR 1638, H RES 658. IRANIAN FINANCIAL ASSETS AND AIRCRAFT PURCHASE TRANSACTIONS/RULE. Adoption of the rule (H Res 658) that would provide for House floor consideration of the bill (HR 1638) that would require the Treasury Department to compile and submit to Congress a report concerning Iranian assets held in U.S and foreign institutions, and would provide for consideration of the bill (HR 4324) that would require the Treasury secretary to submit reports to Congress on transactions of financial institutions associated with the purchase and export of aircraft on behalf of Iran. Adopted 238-182 : R 232-0; D 6-182. Dec. 13, 2017.

678. H RES 657, HR 4015, HR 2396. PRIVACY NOTICE REQUIREMENT EXEMPTION AND PROXY ADVISORY FIRM REGISTRATION/PREVIOUS QUESTION. Woodall, R-Ga., motion to order the previous question (thus ending debate and the possibility of amendment) on the rule (H Res 657) that would provide for House floor consideration of the bill (HR 2396) that would exempt financial service companies from a requirement that they send customers annual written privacy notices, and would provide for consideration of the bill (HR 4015) that would require proxy financial advisory firms to register with the Securities and Exchange Commission. Motion agreed to 236-187 : R 236-0; D 0-187. Dec. 13, 2017.

	673	674	675	676	677	678
ALABAMA						
1 Byrne	Y	N	Y	Y	Y	Y
2 Roby	Y	N	Y	Y	Y	Y
3 Rogers	Y	N	Y	Y	Y	Y
4 Aderholt	Y	N	Y	Y	Y	Y
5 Brooks	Y	N	Y	Y	Y	Y
6 Palmer	Y	N	Y	Y	Y	Y
7 Sewell	Y	+	–	N	N	N
ALASKA						
AL Young	Y	N	Y	?	Y	Y
ARIZONA						
1 O'Halleran	Y	Y	Y	N	Y	N
2 McSally	Y	N	Y	Y	Y	Y
3 Grijalva	Y	Y	N	N	N	N
4 Gosar	Y	N	Y	Y	Y	Y
5 Biggs	Y	N	Y	Y	Y	Y
6 Schweikert	Y	N	Y	Y	Y	Y
7 Gallego	Y	Y	N	N	N	N
9 Sinema	Y	Y	Y	N	Y	N
ARKANSAS						
1 Crawford	Y	N	Y	Y	Y	Y
2 Hill	Y	N	Y	Y	Y	Y
3 Womack	Y	N	Y	Y	Y	Y
4 Westerman	Y	N	Y	Y	Y	Y
CALIFORNIA						
1 LaMalfa	Y	N	Y	Y	Y	Y
2 Huffman	Y	Y	N	N	N	N
3 Garamendi	Y	Y	N	N	N	N
4 McClintock	Y	N	Y	Y	Y	Y
5 Thompson	Y	Y	N	N	N	N
6 Matsui	Y	Y	N	N	N	N
7 Bera	Y	Y	Y	N	N	N
8 Cook	Y	N	Y	Y	Y	Y
9 McNerney	Y	Y	N	N	N	N
10 Denham	Y	N	Y	Y	Y	Y
11 DeSaulnier	Y	Y	N	N	N	N
12 Pelosi	Y	Y	N	N	N	N
13 Lee	Y	Y	N	N	N	N
14 Speier	Y	Y	N	N	N	N
15 Swalwell	Y	Y	N	N	N	N
16 Costa	Y	Y	Y	N	N	N
17 Khanna	Y	Y	N	N	N	N
18 Eshoo	Y	Y	N	N	N	N
19 Lofgren	Y	Y	N	N	N	N
20 Panetta	Y	Y	N	N	N	N
21 Valadao	Y	N	Y	Y	Y	Y
22 Nunes	Y	N	Y	Y	Y	Y
23 McCarthy	Y	N	Y	Y	Y	Y
24 Carbajal	Y	Y	N	N	N	N
25 Knight	Y	N	Y	Y	Y	Y
26 Brownley	Y	Y	N	N	N	N
27 Chu	Y	Y	N	N	N	N
28 Schiff	Y	Y	N	N	N	N
29 Cardenas	Y	Y	N	N	N	N
30 Sherman	Y	Y	Y	N	N	N
31 Aguilar	Y	Y	N	N	N	N
32 Napolitano	Y	Y	N	N	N	N
33 Lieu	Y	Y	N	N	N	N
34 Gomez	Y	Y	N	N	N	N
35 Torres	Y	Y	N	N	N	N
36 Ruiz	Y	Y	N	N	N	N
37 Bass	?	Y	N	N	N	N
38 Sánchez, Linda	Y	Y	N	N	N	N
39 Royce	Y	N	Y	Y	Y	Y
40 Roybal-Allard	Y	Y	N	N	N	N
41 Takano	Y	Y	N	N	N	N
42 Calvert	Y	N	Y	Y	Y	Y
43 Waters	Y	Y	N	N	N	N
44 Barragan	Y	Y	Y	N	N	N
45 Walters	Y	N	Y	Y	Y	Y
46 Correa	Y	Y	Y	N	N	N
47 Lowenthal	Y	Y	N	N	N	N
48 Rohrabacher	?	N	Y	Y	Y	Y
49 Issa	Y	N	Y	Y	Y	Y
50 Hunter	Y	N	Y	Y	Y	Y
51 Vargas	Y	Y	Y	N	N	N
52 Peters	Y	Y	Y	N	N	N
53 Davis	Y	Y	Y	N	N	N

	673	674	675	676	677	678
COLORADO						
1 DeGette	Y	Y	N	N	N	N
2 Polis	Y	Y	N	N	N	N
3 Tipton	Y	N	Y	Y	Y	Y
4 Buck	Y	N	Y	Y	Y	Y
5 Lamborn	Y	N	Y	Y	Y	Y
6 Coffman	Y	N	Y	Y	Y	Y
7 Perlmutter	Y	Y	Y	N	N	N
CONNECTICUT						
1 Larson	Y	Y	N	N	N	N
2 Courtney	Y	Y	N	N	N	N
3 DeLauro	Y	Y	N	N	N	N
4 Himes	Y	Y	N	N	N	N
5 Esty	Y	Y	N	N	N	N
DELAWARE						
AL Blunt Rochester	Y	Y	N	N	N	N
FLORIDA						
1 Gaetz	Y	N	Y	Y	Y	Y
2 Dunn	Y	N	Y	Y	Y	Y
3 Yoho	Y	N	Y	Y	Y	Y
4 Rutherford	Y	N	Y	Y	Y	Y
5 Lawson	Y	Y	N	N	N	N
6 DeSantis	Y	N	Y	Y	Y	Y
7 Murphy	Y	Y	Y	N	Y	N
8 Posey	Y	N	Y	Y	Y	Y
9 Soto	Y	Y	N	N	N	N
10 Demings	Y	Y	N	N	N	N
11 Webster	Y	N	Y	Y	Y	Y
12 Bilirakis	Y	N	Y	Y	Y	Y
13 Crist	Y	Y	N	N	N	N
14 Castor	Y	Y	N	N	N	N
15 Ross	Y	N	Y	Y	Y	Y
16 Buchanan	?	N	Y	Y	Y	Y
17 Rooney, T.	Y	N	Y	Y	Y	Y
18 Mast	Y	N	Y	Y	Y	Y
19 Rooney, F.	Y	N	Y	Y	Y	Y
20 Hastings	Y	Y	N	N	?	N
21 Frankel	Y	Y	N	N	N	N
22 Deutch	Y	Y	N	N	N	N
23 Wasserman Schultz	Y	Y	N	N	N	N
24 Wilson	Y	Y	N	N	N	N
25 Diaz-Balart	Y	N	Y	Y	Y	Y
26 Curbelo	Y	N	Y	Y	Y	Y
27 Ros-Lehtinen	Y	N	Y	Y	Y	Y
GEORGIA						
1 Carter	Y	N	Y	Y	Y	Y
2 Bishop	Y	Y	N	N	N	N
3 Ferguson	Y	N	Y	Y	Y	Y
4 Johnson	Y	Y	N	N	N	N
5 Lewis	Y	Y	N	N	N	N
6 Handel	Y	N	Y	Y	Y	Y
7 Woodall	Y	N	Y	Y	Y	Y
8 Scott, A.	Y	N	Y	Y	Y	Y
9 Collins	Y	N	Y	Y	Y	Y
10 Hice	Y	N	Y	Y	Y	Y
11 Loudermilk	Y	N	Y	Y	Y	Y
12 Allen	Y	N	Y	Y	Y	Y
13 Scott, D.	Y	Y	N	N	N	N
14 Graves	Y	N	Y	Y	Y	Y
HAWAII						
1 Hanabusa	Y	Y	N	N	N	N
2 Gabbard	Y	Y	N	N	N	N
IDAHO						
1 Labrador	Y	N	Y	Y	Y	Y
2 Simpson	?	N	Y	Y	Y	Y
ILLINOIS						
1 Rush	Y	Y	N	N	N	N
2 Kelly	Y	Y	N	N	N	N
3 Lipinski	Y	Y	N	N	N	N
4 Gutierrez	+	+	–	N	N	N
5 Quigley	Y	Y	N	N	N	N
6 Roskam	Y	N	Y	Y	Y	Y
7 Davis, D.	?	Y	N	N	N	N
8 Krishnamoorthi	Y	Y	Y	N	N	N
9 Schakowsky	Y	Y	N	N	N	N
10 Schneider	Y	Y	Y	N	N	N
11 Foster	Y	Y	Y	N	N	N
12 Bost	Y	N	Y	Y	Y	Y
13 Davis, R.	Y	N	Y	Y	Y	Y
14 Hultgren	Y	N	Y	Y	Y	Y
15 Shimkus	Y	N	Y	Y	Y	Y

	673	674	675	676	677	678
16 **Kinzinger**	Y	N	Y	Y	Y	Y
17 Bustos	Y	Y	Y	N	N	N
18 **LaHood**	Y	N	Y	Y	Y	Y
INDIANA						
1 Visclosky	Y	Y	N	-	-	-
2 **Walorski**	Y	N	Y	Y	Y	Y
3 **Banks**	Y	N	Y	Y	Y	Y
4 **Rokita**	Y	N	Y	Y	Y	Y
5 **Brooks**	Y	N	Y	Y	Y	Y
6 **Messer**	?	N	Y	Y	Y	Y
7 Carson	Y	Y	N	N	N	N
8 **Bucshon**	Y	N	Y	Y	Y	Y
9 **Hollingsworth**	Y	N	Y	Y	Y	Y
IOWA						
1 **Blum**	Y	Y	Y	Y	Y	Y
2 Loebsack	Y	Y	Y	N	N	N
3 **Young**	Y	N	Y	Y	Y	Y
4 **King**	Y	N	Y	Y	Y	Y
KANSAS						
1 **Marshall**	Y	N	Y	Y	Y	Y
2 **Jenkins**	Y	N	Y	Y	Y	Y
3 **Yoder**	Y	N	Y	Y	Y	Y
4 **Estes**	Y	N	Y	Y	Y	Y
KENTUCKY						
1 **Comer**	Y	N	Y	Y	Y	Y
2 **Guthrie**	Y	N	Y	Y	Y	Y
3 Yarmuth	Y	Y	N	N	N	N
4 **Massie**	N	N	Y	Y	Y	Y
5 **Rogers**	Y	N	Y	Y	Y	Y
6 **Barr**	Y	N	Y	Y	Y	Y
LOUISIANA						
1 **Scalise**	Y	-	+	Y	Y	Y
2 Richmond	?	Y	N	N	N	N
3 **Higgins**	Y	N	Y	Y	Y	Y
4 **Johnson**	Y	N	Y	Y	Y	Y
5 **Abraham**	Y	N	Y	Y	Y	Y
6 **Graves**	Y	N	Y	Y	Y	Y
MAINE						
1 Pingree	Y	Y	N	N	N	N
2 **Poliquin**	Y	N	Y	Y	Y	Y
MARYLAND						
1 **Harris**	Y	N	Y	?	?	Y
2 Ruppersberger	Y	Y	Y	N	N	N
3 Sarbanes	Y	Y	N	N	N	N
4 Brown	Y	Y	N	N	N	N
5 Hoyer	Y	Y	N	N	N	N
6 Delaney	Y	Y	Y	N	N	N
7 Cummings	Y	Y	N	N	N	N
8 Raskin	Y	Y	N	N	N	N
MASSACHUSETTS						
1 Neal	Y	Y	N	N	N	N
2 McGovern	Y	Y	N	N	N	N
3 Tsongas	?	Y	N	N	N	N
4 Kennedy	?	?	?	?	?	?
5 Clark	Y	Y	N	N	N	N
6 Moulton	Y	Y	Y	N	N	N
7 Capuano	Y	Y	N	N	N	N
8 Lynch	Y	Y	N	N	N	N
9 Keating	Y	Y	Y	N	N	N
MICHIGAN						
1 **Bergman**	Y	N	Y	Y	Y	Y
2 **Huizenga**	Y	N	Y	Y	Y	Y
3 **Amash**	N	N	Y	Y	Y	Y
4 **Moolenaar**	Y	N	Y	Y	Y	Y
5 Kildee	Y	Y	N	N	N	N
6 **Upton**	Y	N	Y	Y	Y	Y
7 **Walberg**	Y	N	Y	Y	Y	Y
8 **Bishop**	Y	N	Y	Y	Y	Y
9 Levin	Y	Y	N	N	N	N
10 **Mitchell**	Y	N	Y	Y	Y	Y
11 **Trott**	Y	N	Y	Y	Y	Y
12 Dingell	Y	Y	N	N	N	N
13 Vacant						
14 Lawrence	Y	Y	N	N	N	N
MINNESOTA						
1 Walz	+	?	?	?	?	?
2 **Lewis**	Y	N	Y	Y	Y	Y
3 **Paulsen**	Y	N	Y	Y	Y	Y
4 McCollum	Y	Y	N	N	N	?
5 Ellison	Y	Y	N	N	N	N
6 **Emmer**	Y	N	Y	Y	Y	Y
7 Peterson	Y	Y	Y	N	N	N
8 Nolan	Y	Y	N	N	N	?
MISSISSIPPI						
1 **Kelly**	Y	N	Y	Y	Y	Y
2 Thompson	Y	Y	N	N	N	N
3 **Harper**	?	N	Y	Y	Y	Y
4 **Palazzo**	Y	N	Y	Y	Y	Y
MISSOURI						
1 Clay	?	Y	N	N	N	N
2 **Wagner**	Y	N	Y	Y	Y	Y
3 **Luetkemeyer**	Y	N	Y	Y	Y	Y
4 **Hartzler**	Y	N	Y	Y	Y	Y
5 Cleaver	Y	Y	N	N	N	N
6 **Graves**	Y	N	Y	Y	Y	Y
7 **Long**	Y	N	Y	Y	Y	Y
8 **Smith**	Y	N	Y	Y	Y	Y
MONTANA						
AL **Gianforte**	Y	N	Y	Y	Y	Y
NEBRASKA						
1 **Fortenberry**	Y	N	Y	Y	Y	Y
2 **Bacon**	Y	N	Y	Y	Y	Y
3 **Smith**	Y	N	Y	Y	Y	Y
NEVADA						
1 Titus	Y	Y	N	N	N	N
2 **Amodei**	Y	N	Y	Y	Y	Y
3 Rosen	Y	Y	N	N	N	N
4 Kihuen	Y	Y	N	N	N	N
NEW HAMPSHIRE						
1 Shea-Porter	Y	Y	N	N	N	N
2 Kuster	Y	Y	Y	N	N	N
NEW JERSEY						
1 Norcross	Y	Y	N	N	N	N
2 **LoBiondo**	Y	N	Y	Y	Y	Y
3 **MacArthur**	Y	N	Y	Y	Y	Y
4 **Smith**	Y	N	Y	Y	Y	Y
5 Gottheimer	Y	Y	Y	N	Y	N
6 Pallone	Y	Y	N	N	N	N
7 **Lance**	Y	N	Y	Y	Y	Y
8 Sires	?	Y	N	N	N	N
9 Pascrell	Y	Y	N	N	N	N
10 Payne	Y	Y	N	N	N	N
11 **Frelinghuysen**	Y	N	Y	Y	Y	Y
12 Watson Coleman	Y	Y	N	N	N	N
NEW MEXICO						
1 Lujan Grisham	Y	Y	Y	N	N	N
2 **Pearce**	Y	N	Y	Y	Y	Y
3 Luján	Y	Y	N	N	N	N
NEW YORK						
1 **Zeldin**	Y	N	Y	Y	Y	Y
2 **King**	Y	N	Y	Y	Y	Y
3 Suozzi	Y	Y	Y	N	Y	N
4 Rice	?	Y	Y	N	N	N
5 Meeks	Y	Y	Y	N	N	N
6 Meng	Y	Y	N	N	N	N
7 Velázquez	Y	Y	N	N	N	N
8 Jeffries	Y	Y	N	N	N	N
9 Clarke	Y	Y	N	N	N	N
10 Nadler	Y	Y	N	N	N	N
11 **Donovan**	Y	N	Y	Y	Y	Y
12 Maloney, C.	Y	Y	N	N	N	N
13 Espaillat	Y	Y	N	N	N	N
14 Crowley	Y	Y	N	N	N	N
15 Serrano	Y	Y	N	N	N	N
16 Engel	Y	Y	N	N	N	N
17 Lowey	Y	Y	N	N	N	N
18 Maloney, S.P.	Y	Y	Y	N	N	N
19 **Faso**	Y	N	Y	Y	Y	Y
20 Tonko	Y	Y	N	N	N	N
21 **Stefanik**	Y	N	Y	+	Y	Y
22 **Tenney**	Y	N	Y	Y	Y	Y
23 **Reed**	Y	N	Y	Y	Y	Y
24 **Katko**	Y	N	Y	Y	Y	Y
25 Slaughter	Y	Y	N	N	N	N
26 Higgins	Y	Y	N	N	N	N
27 **Collins**	Y	N	Y	Y	Y	Y
NORTH CAROLINA						
1 Butterfield	?	Y	N	N	N	N
2 **Holding**	Y	N	Y	Y	Y	Y
3 **Jones**	Y	Y	N	Y	Y	Y
4 Price	Y	Y	N	N	N	N
5 **Foxx**	Y	N	Y	Y	Y	Y
6 **Walker**	Y	N	Y	Y	Y	Y
7 **Rouzer**	Y	N	Y	Y	Y	Y
8 **Hudson**	Y	N	Y	Y	Y	Y
9 **Pittenger**	Y	N	Y	Y	Y	Y
10 **McHenry**	Y	N	Y	Y	Y	Y
11 **Meadows**	Y	N	Y	Y	Y	Y
12 Adams	Y	Y	N	N	N	N
13 **Budd**	Y	N	Y	Y	Y	Y
NORTH DAKOTA						
AL **Cramer**	Y	N	Y	Y	Y	Y
OHIO						
1 **Chabot**	Y	N	Y	Y	Y	Y
2 **Wenstrup**	Y	N	Y	Y	Y	Y
3 Beatty	Y	Y	Y	N	N	N
4 **Jordan**	Y	N	Y	Y	Y	Y
5 **Latta**	Y	N	Y	Y	Y	Y
6 **Johnson**	Y	N	Y	?	?	Y
7 **Gibbs**	Y	N	Y	Y	Y	Y
8 **Davidson**	Y	N	Y	Y	Y	Y
9 Kaptur	Y	Y	N	N	N	N
10 **Turner**	Y	N	Y	Y	Y	Y
11 Fudge	Y	Y	N	N	N	N
12 **Tiberi**	?	N	Y	Y	Y	Y
13 Ryan	Y	Y	N	N	N	N
14 **Joyce**	Y	N	Y	Y	Y	Y
15 **Stivers**	Y	N	Y	Y	Y	Y
16 **Renacci**	?	N	Y	Y	Y	Y
OKLAHOMA						
1 **Bridenstine**	?	?	?	?	?	?
2 **Mullin**	Y	N	Y	Y	Y	Y
3 **Lucas**	Y	N	Y	Y	Y	Y
4 **Cole**	Y	N	Y	Y	Y	Y
5 **Russell**	Y	N	Y	Y	Y	Y
OREGON						
1 Bonamici	Y	Y	N	N	N	N
2 **Walden**	Y	N	Y	Y	Y	Y
3 Blumenauer	Y	Y	N	N	N	N
4 DeFazio	Y	Y	N	N	N	N
5 Schrader	Y	Y	Y	N	N	N
PENNSYLVANIA						
1 Brady	Y	Y	N	N	N	N
2 Evans	Y	Y	N	N	N	N
3 **Kelly**	Y	N	Y	Y	Y	Y
4 **Perry**	Y	N	Y	Y	Y	Y
5 **Thompson**	Y	N	Y	Y	Y	Y
6 **Costello**	Y	N	Y	Y	Y	Y
7 **Meehan**	Y	N	Y	Y	Y	Y
8 **Fitzpatrick**	Y	N	Y	Y	Y	Y
9 **Shuster**	Y	N	Y	Y	Y	Y
10 **Marino**	Y	N	Y	Y	Y	Y
11 **Barletta**	?	N	Y	Y	Y	Y
12 **Rothfus**	Y	N	Y	Y	Y	Y
13 Boyle	Y	Y	Y	N	N	N
14 Doyle	Y	Y	N	N	N	N
15 **Dent**	Y	N	Y	Y	Y	Y
16 **Smucker**	Y	N	Y	Y	Y	Y
17 Cartwright	Y	Y	Y	N	N	N
RHODE ISLAND						
1 Cicilline	Y	Y	N	N	N	N
2 Langevin	Y	Y	N	N	N	N
SOUTH CAROLINA						
1 **Sanford**	+	N	Y	Y	Y	Y
2 **Wilson**	Y	N	Y	Y	Y	Y
3 **Duncan**	Y	N	Y	Y	Y	Y
4 **Gowdy**	?	N	Y	Y	Y	Y
5 **Norman**	Y	N	Y	Y	Y	Y
6 Clyburn	Y	Y	N	N	N	N
7 **Rice**	Y	N	Y	Y	?	Y
SOUTH DAKOTA						
AL **Noem**	Y	N	Y	?	Y	Y
TENNESSEE						
1 **Roe**	Y	N	Y	Y	Y	Y
2 **Duncan**	Y	N	Y	Y	Y	Y
3 **Fleischmann**	Y	N	Y	Y	Y	Y
4 **DesJarlais**	?	?	?	Y	Y	Y
5 Cooper	Y	Y	Y	N	N	N
6 **Black**	Y	N	Y	?	Y	Y
7 **Blackburn**	?	N	Y	Y	Y	Y
8 **Kustoff**	Y	N	Y	Y	Y	Y
9 Cohen	Y	Y	N	N	N	N
TEXAS						
1 **Gohmert**	?	N	Y	Y	Y	Y
2 **Poe**	Y	N	Y	Y	Y	Y
3 **Johnson, S.**	Y	N	Y	Y	Y	Y
4 **Ratcliffe**	Y	N	Y	Y	Y	Y
5 **Hensarling**	Y	N	Y	Y	Y	Y
6 **Barton**	Y	N	Y	Y	Y	Y
7 **Culberson**	Y	N	Y	Y	Y	Y
8 **Brady**	Y	N	Y	+	Y	Y
9 Green, A.	Y	Y	N	N	N	N
10 **McCaul**	Y	N	Y	Y	Y	Y
11 **Conaway**	Y	N	Y	Y	Y	Y
12 **Granger**	Y	N	Y	Y	Y	Y
13 **Thornberry**	Y	N	Y	Y	Y	Y
14 **Weber**	Y	N	Y	Y	Y	Y
15 Gonzalez	Y	Y	Y	N	N	N
16 O'Rourke	Y	Y	N	N	N	N
17 **Flores**	Y	N	Y	Y	Y	Y
18 Jackson Lee	?	Y	N	N	N	N
19 **Arrington**	Y	N	Y	Y	Y	Y
20 Castro	Y	Y	N	N	N	N
21 **Smith**	Y	N	Y	Y	Y	Y
22 **Olson**	Y	N	Y	Y	Y	Y
23 **Hurd**	Y	N	Y	Y	Y	Y
24 **Marchant**	Y	N	Y	Y	Y	Y
25 **Williams**	Y	N	Y	Y	Y	Y
26 **Burgess**	Y	N	Y	Y	Y	Y
27 **Farenthold**	Y	N	Y	Y	?	Y
28 Cuellar	Y	Y	Y	N	N	N
29 Green, G.	Y	Y	N	N	N	N
30 Johnson, E.B.	Y	Y	N	N	N	N
31 **Carter**	Y	N	Y	Y	Y	Y
32 **Sessions**	Y	N	Y	Y	Y	Y
33 Veasey	Y	Y	N	N	N	N
34 Vela	Y	Y	Y	N	N	N
35 Doggett	Y	Y	N	N	N	N
36 **Babin**	Y	N	Y	Y	Y	Y
UTAH						
1 **Bishop**	Y	N	Y	Y	Y	Y
2 **Stewart**	Y	N	Y	Y	Y	Y
3 **Curtis**	Y	N	Y	Y	Y	Y
4 **Love**	Y	N	Y	Y	Y	Y
VERMONT						
AL Welch	Y	Y	N	N	N	N
VIRGINIA						
1 **Wittman**	Y	N	Y	Y	Y	Y
2 **Taylor**	Y	N	Y	Y	Y	Y
3 Scott	Y	Y	N	N	N	N
4 McEachin	Y	Y	N	N	N	N
5 **Garrett**	Y	N	Y	Y	Y	Y
6 **Goodlatte**	Y	N	Y	Y	Y	Y
7 **Brat**	Y	N	Y	Y	Y	Y
8 Beyer	Y	Y	Y	N	N	N
9 **Griffith**	Y	N	Y	Y	Y	Y
10 **Comstock**	Y	N	Y	Y	Y	Y
11 Connolly	Y	Y	Y	N	N	N
WASHINGTON						
1 DelBene	Y	Y	Y	N	N	N
2 Larsen	Y	Y	Y	N	N	N
3 **Herrera Beutler**	Y	N	Y	Y	Y	Y
4 **Newhouse**	Y	N	Y	Y	Y	Y
5 **McMorris Rodgers**	Y	N	Y	Y	Y	Y
6 Kilmer	Y	Y	Y	N	N	N
7 Jayapal	Y	Y	N	N	N	N
8 **Reichert**	Y	N	Y	Y	Y	Y
9 Smith	Y	Y	N	N	N	N
10 Heck	Y	Y	Y	N	N	N
WEST VIRGINIA						
1 **McKinley**	Y	N	Y	Y	Y	Y
2 **Mooney**	Y	N	Y	Y	Y	Y
3 **Jenkins**	Y	N	Y	Y	Y	Y
WISCONSIN						
1 **Ryan**						
2 Pocan	+	+	-	-	-	-
3 Kind	Y	Y	Y	N	N	N
4 Moore	Y	Y	N	N	N	N
5 **Sensenbrenner**	Y	N	Y	+	+	+
6 **Grothman**	Y	N	Y	Y	Y	Y
7 **Duffy**	Y	N	Y	Y	Y	Y
8 **Gallagher**	Y	N	Y	Y	Y	Y
WYOMING						
AL **Cheney**	Y	N	Y	Y	Y	Y

VOTE NUMBER

679. H RES 657, HR 4015, HR 2396. PRIVACY NOTICE REQUIREMENT EXEMPTION AND PROXY ADVISORY FIRM REGISTRATION/RULE. Adoption of the rule (H Res 657) that would provide for House floor consideration of the bill (HR 2396) that would exempt financial service companies from a requirement that they send customers annual written privacy notices, and would provide for consideration of the bill (HR 4015) that would require proxy financial advisory firms to register with the Securities and Exchange Commission. Adopted 240-184 : R 236-0; D 4-184. Dec. 13, 2017.

680. HR 1638. IRANIAN ASSET REPORT REQUIREMENT/PASSAGE. Passage of the bill that would require the Department of the Treasury to report to Congress on assets held in U.S. and foreign financial institutions that are under direct or indirect control certain high ranking Iranian officials, and how sanctions may be used to prevent the funds from being used to contribute to the continued development of ballistic missile technology by Iran. The bill requires that such a report be submitted to Congress within 270 days of enactment, and that it be updated by the department annually for at least two years thereafter. Passed 289-135 : R 233-3; D 56-132. Dec. 13, 2017.

681. HR 2396. PRIVACY NOTICE REQUIREMENT EXEMPTION/RECOMMIT. Waters, D-Calif., motion to recommit the bill to the House Financial Services Committee with instructions to report it back immediately with an amendment that would prohibit the exemptions in the bill from being applied to a vehicle financial company that is engaging in or has engaged in a pattern of unsafe banking practices, or has committed any other violations related to consumer harm. Motion rejected 185-235 : R 0-233; D 185-2. Dec. 14, 2017.

682. HR 2396. PRIVACY NOTICE REQUIREMENT EXEMPTION/PASSAGE. Passage of the bill that would exempt vehicle financial companies that have not changed their privacy policies, including companies that share or sell information on consumers to unaffiliated third parties, from the requirement that such companies provide annual written privacy notices to consumers. In order to qualify for the exemption, the company's privacy notice must be available online, and the consumer must be notified of the availability of online privacy notices by other means. Passed 275-146 : R 231-2; D 44-144. Dec. 14, 2017.

683. HR 4324. IRANIAN AIRCRAFT PURCHASE TRANSACTIONS/RECOMMIT. Swalwell, D-Calif., motion to recommit the bill to the House Financial Services Committee with instructions to report it back immediately with an amendment that would require the secretary of the Treasury to certify that no financial institution participating in a transaction involving the sale of an aircraft to Iran has engaged in business with a foreign entity that has been found to have engaged in or authorized cyber-attacks targeting any election held in the United States. Motion rejected 188-233 : R 0-233; D 188-0. Dec. 14, 2017.

684. HR 4324. IRANIAN AIRCRAFT PURCHASE TRANSACTIONS/PASSAGE. Passage of the bill that would require the secretary of the Treasury to report to Congress on any U.S. or foreign financial institutions that are involved in financing the purchase or export of aircraft on behalf of Iran, and to certify that such transactions pose no money-laundering or terrorism-financing risk. Passed 252-167 : R 229-4; D 23-163. Dec. 14, 2017.

685. PROCEDURAL MOTION/CHANGE HOUSE CONVENING TIME. Motion agreed to 216-169 : R 216-1; D 0-168. Dec. 18, 2017.

	679	680	681	682	683	684	685
ALABAMA							
1 Byrne	Y	Y	N	Y	N	Y	Y
2 Roby	Y	Y	N	Y	N	Y	Y
3 Rogers	Y	Y	N	Y	N	Y	Y
4 Aderholt	Y	Y	N	Y	N	Y	Y
5 Brooks	Y	Y	N	Y	N	Y	?
6 Palmer	Y	Y	N	Y	N	Y	Y
7 Sewell	N	N	Y	N	Y	N	–
ALASKA							
AL Young	Y	Y	N	Y	N	Y	Y
ARIZONA							
1 O'Halleran	N	Y	Y	N	Y	Y	N
2 McSally	Y	Y	N	Y	N	Y	Y
3 Grijalva	N	N	Y	N	Y	N	N
4 Gosar	Y	Y	N	Y	N	Y	Y
5 Biggs	Y	Y	N	Y	N	Y	Y
6 Schweikert	Y	Y	N	Y	N	Y	Y
7 Gallego	N	N	Y	N	Y	N	N
9 Sinema	Y	Y	Y	Y	Y	Y	–
ARKANSAS							
1 Crawford	Y	Y	N	Y	N	Y	?
2 Hill	Y	Y	N	Y	N	Y	Y
3 Womack	Y	Y	N	Y	N	Y	Y
4 Westerman	Y	Y	N	Y	N	Y	Y
CALIFORNIA							
1 LaMalfa	Y	Y	N	Y	N	Y	Y
2 Huffman	N	N	Y	N	Y	N	N
3 Garamendi	N	N	Y	N	Y	N	N
4 McClintock	Y	Y	N	Y	N	Y	Y
5 Thompson	N	N	Y	N	Y	N	N
6 Matsui	N	N	Y	N	Y	N	N
7 Bera	N	Y	Y	Y	Y	Y	N
8 Cook	Y	Y	N	Y	N	Y	Y
9 McNerney	N	N	Y	N	Y	N	N
10 Denham	Y	Y	N	Y	N	Y	Y
11 DeSaulnier	N	N	Y	N	Y	N	N
12 Pelosi	N	N	Y	N	Y	N	N
13 Lee	N	N	Y	N	Y	N	N
14 Speier	N	N	Y	N	Y	N	?
15 Swalwell	N	N	Y	N	Y	N	N
16 Costa	N	Y	Y	Y	Y	Y	N
17 Khanna	N	N	Y	N	Y	N	N
18 Eshoo	N	N	Y	N	Y	N	N
19 Lofgren	N	N	Y	N	Y	N	N
20 Panetta	N	Y	Y	N	Y	Y	N
21 Valadao	Y	Y	N	Y	N	Y	Y
22 Nunes	Y	Y	N	Y	N	Y	Y
23 McCarthy	Y	Y	N	Y	N	Y	Y
24 Carbajal	N	Y	Y	Y	Y	N	N
25 Knight	Y	Y	?	Y	N	Y	Y
26 Brownley	N	Y	Y	Y	Y	N	N
27 Chu	N	N	Y	N	Y	N	N
28 Schiff	N	N	Y	N	Y	N	N
29 Cardenas	N	Y	Y	N	Y	N	N
30 Sherman	N	Y	Y	Y	Y	Y	N
31 Aguilar	N	Y	Y	N	Y	Y	N
32 Napolitano	N	N	Y	N	Y	N	–
33 Lieu	N	Y	Y	N	Y	N	N
34 Gomez	N	Y	Y	N	Y	N	N
35 Torres	N	?	Y	Y	Y	N	N
36 Ruiz	N	N	Y	N	Y	N	N
37 Bass	N	N	Y	N	Y	N	N
38 Sánchez, Linda	N	N	Y	N	Y	N	–
39 Royce	Y	Y	N	Y	N	Y	Y
40 Roybal-Allard	N	N	Y	N	Y	N	N
41 Takano	N	N	Y	N	Y	N	N
42 Calvert	Y	Y	N	Y	N	Y	Y
43 Waters	N	N	Y	N	Y	N	N
44 Barragan	N	Y	Y	Y	Y	N	N
45 Walters	Y	Y	N	Y	N	Y	Y
46 Correa	N	Y	Y	Y	Y	N	N
47 Lowenthal	N	N	Y	N	Y	N	N
48 Rohrabacher	Y	Y	N	Y	N	Y	?
49 Issa	Y	Y	N	Y	N	Y	Y
50 Hunter	Y	Y	N	Y	N	Y	Y
51 Vargas	N	Y	Y	N	Y	N	N
52 Peters	N	Y	Y	N	Y	N	N
53 Davis	N	N	Y	N	Y	N	N

	679	680	681	682	683	684	685
COLORADO							
1 DeGette	N	N	Y	N	Y	N	N
2 Polis	N	N	Y	N	Y	N	N
3 Tipton	Y	Y	N	Y	N	Y	Y
4 Buck	Y	Y	N	Y	N	Y	Y
5 Lamborn	Y	Y	N	Y	N	Y	Y
6 Coffman	Y	Y	N	Y	N	Y	Y
7 Perlmutter	N	N	Y	Y	Y	N	N
CONNECTICUT							
1 Larson	N	Y	Y	N	Y	N	–
2 Courtney	N	N	Y	N	Y	N	N
3 DeLauro	N	N	Y	N	Y	N	N
4 Himes	N	N	Y	N	Y	N	N
5 Esty	N	N	Y	N	Y	N	N
DELAWARE							
AL Blunt Rochester	N	N	Y	N	Y	N	N
FLORIDA							
1 Gaetz	Y	Y	N	Y	N	Y	Y
2 Dunn	Y	Y	N	Y	N	Y	Y
3 Yoho	Y	Y	N	Y	N	Y	Y
4 Rutherford	Y	Y	N	Y	N	Y	Y
5 Lawson	N	Y	Y	N	Y	N	N
6 DeSantis	Y	Y	N	Y	N	Y	?
7 Murphy	N	Y	Y	Y	Y	Y	?
8 Posey	Y	Y	N	Y	N	Y	Y
9 Soto	N	Y	Y	N	Y	N	N
10 Demings	N	N	Y	N	Y	N	N
11 Webster	Y	Y	N	Y	N	Y	?
12 Bilirakis	Y	Y	N	Y	N	Y	Y
13 Crist	N	Y	Y	N	Y	?	N
14 Castor	N	N	Y	N	Y	N	N
15 Ross	Y	Y	N	Y	N	Y	Y
16 Buchanan	Y	Y	N	Y	N	Y	Y
17 Rooney, T.	Y	Y	N	Y	N	Y	Y
18 Mast	Y	Y	N	Y	N	Y	Y
19 Rooney, F.	Y	Y	N	Y	N	Y	?
20 Hastings	N	Y	Y	N	Y	N	N
21 Frankel	N	Y	Y	N	Y	Y	N
22 Deutch	N	Y	Y	N	Y	Y	?
23 Wasserman Schultz	N	Y	Y	N	Y	Y	N
24 Wilson	N	N	Y	N	Y	N	N
25 Diaz-Balart	Y	Y	N	Y	N	Y	Y
26 Curbelo	Y	Y	N	Y	N	Y	Y
27 Ros-Lehtinen	Y	Y	N	Y	N	Y	Y
GEORGIA							
1 Carter	Y	Y	N	Y	N	Y	Y
2 Bishop	N	N	Y	Y	Y	N	N
3 Ferguson	Y	Y	N	Y	N	Y	Y
4 Johnson	N	N	Y	Y	Y	N	N
5 Lewis	N	N	Y	N	Y	N	N
6 Handel	Y	Y	N	Y	N	Y	Y
7 Woodall	Y	Y	N	Y	N	Y	Y
8 Scott, A.	Y	Y	N	Y	N	Y	Y
9 Collins	Y	Y	N	Y	N	Y	Y
10 Hice	Y	Y	N	Y	N	Y	Y
11 Loudermilk	Y	Y	N	Y	N	Y	?
12 Allen	Y	Y	N	Y	N	Y	Y
13 Scott, D.	N	Y	Y	Y	Y	N	N
14 Graves	Y	Y	N	Y	N	Y	Y
HAWAII							
1 Hanabusa	N	N	Y	Y	Y	N	N
2 Gabbard	N	N	Y	N	Y	N	N
IDAHO							
1 Labrador	Y	Y	N	Y	N	Y	?
2 Simpson	Y	Y	N	Y	N	Y	Y
ILLINOIS							
1 Rush	N	N	Y	N	Y	N	?
2 Kelly	N	N	Y	N	Y	N	N
3 Lipinski	N	Y	Y	Y	Y	Y	N
4 Gutierrez	N	N	Y	N	Y	N	–
5 Quigley	N	Y	Y	N	Y	N	N
6 Roskam	Y	Y	N	Y	N	Y	N
7 Davis, D.	N	N	Y	N	Y	N	N
8 Krishnamoorthi	N	N	Y	Y	Y	N	N
9 Schakowsky	N	N	Y	N	Y	N	N
10 Schneider	Y	Y	Y	Y	Y	Y	N
11 Foster	N	N	Y	N	Y	N	N
12 Bost	Y	Y	N	Y	N	Y	Y
13 Davis, R.	Y	Y	N	Y	N	Y	Y
14 Hultgren	Y	Y	N	Y	N	Y	Y
15 Shimkus	Y	Y	N	Y	N	Y	Y

	679	680	681	682	683	684	685
16 **Kinzinger**	Y	Y	N	Y	N	Y	Y
17 Bustos	N	N	Y	Y	Y	N	N
18 **LaHood**	Y	Y	N	Y	N	Y	Y
INDIANA							
1 Visclosky	–	–	+	–	+	–	N
2 **Walorski**	Y	Y	N	Y	N	Y	Y
3 **Banks**	Y	Y	N	Y	N	Y	Y
4 **Rokita**	Y	Y	N	Y	N	Y	Y
5 **Brooks**	Y	Y	N	Y	N	Y	Y
6 **Messer**	Y	Y	N	Y	N	Y	Y
7 Carson	N	N	Y	Y	Y	N	N
8 **Bucshon**	Y	Y	N	Y	N	Y	Y
9 **Hollingsworth**	Y	Y	N	Y	N	Y	Y
IOWA							
1 **Blum**	Y	Y	N	Y	N	Y	Y
2 Loebsack	N	N	Y	Y	Y	N	N
3 **Young**	Y	Y	N	Y	N	Y	Y
4 **King**	Y	Y	N	Y	N	Y	Y
KANSAS							
1 **Marshall**	Y	Y	N	Y	N	Y	Y
2 **Jenkins**	Y	Y	N	Y	N	Y	Y
3 **Yoder**	Y	Y	N	Y	N	Y	Y
4 **Estes**	Y	Y	N	Y	N	Y	Y
KENTUCKY							
1 **Comer**	Y	Y	N	Y	N	Y	Y
2 **Guthrie**	Y	Y	N	Y	N	Y	Y
3 Yarmuth	N	N	Y	N	Y	N	N
4 **Massie**	Y	N	N	Y	N	N	Y
5 **Rogers**	Y	Y	N	Y	N	Y	Y
6 **Barr**	Y	Y	N	Y	N	Y	Y
LOUISIANA							
1 **Scalise**	Y	Y	N	Y	N	Y	Y
2 Richmond	N	N	Y	N	Y	N	N
3 **Higgins**	Y	Y	N	Y	N	Y	?
4 **Johnson**	Y	Y	N	Y	N	Y	Y
5 **Abraham**	Y	Y	N	Y	N	Y	Y
6 **Graves**	Y	Y	N	Y	N	Y	Y
MAINE							
1 Pingree	N	N	Y	N	Y	N	N
2 **Poliquin**	Y	Y	N	Y	N	Y	Y
MARYLAND							
1 **Harris**	Y	Y	N	Y	N	Y	Y
2 Ruppersberger	N	Y	Y	N	Y	N	N
3 Sarbanes	N	N	Y	N	Y	N	N
4 Brown	N	Y	Y	N	Y	N	N
5 Hoyer	N	Y	Y	N	Y	N	N
6 Delaney	N	Y	Y	Y	Y	N	N
7 Cummings	N	N	Y	N	Y	N	N
8 Raskin	N	N	Y	N	Y	N	N
MASSACHUSETTS							
1 Neal	N	N	Y	N	Y	N	N
2 McGovern	N	N	Y	N	Y	N	N
3 Tsongas	N	N	Y	N	Y	N	N
4 Kennedy	?	?	?	?	?	?	?
5 Clark	N	N	Y	N	Y	N	N
6 Moulton	N	N	Y	N	Y	N	N
7 Capuano	N	N	Y	N	Y	N	–
8 Lynch	N	Y	Y	N	Y	N	N
9 Keating	N	N	Y	Y	Y	N	N
MICHIGAN							
1 **Bergman**	Y	Y	N	Y	N	Y	Y
2 **Huizenga**	Y	Y	N	Y	N	Y	Y
3 **Amash**	Y	Y	N	N	N	N	N
4 **Moolenaar**	Y	Y	N	Y	N	Y	Y
5 Kildee	N	N	Y	Y	Y	N	N
6 **Upton**	Y	Y	N	Y	N	Y	Y
7 **Walberg**	Y	Y	N	Y	N	Y	Y
8 **Bishop**	Y	Y	N	Y	N	Y	Y
9 Levin	N	N	Y	N	Y	N	N
10 **Mitchell**	Y	Y	N	Y	N	Y	Y
11 **Trott**	Y	Y	N	?	N	Y	Y
12 Dingell	N	N	Y	N	Y	N	N
13 Vacant							
14 Lawrence	N	N	Y	Y	Y	N	–
MINNESOTA							
1 Walz	?	?	?	?	?	?	?
2 **Lewis**	Y	Y	N	Y	N	Y	Y
3 **Paulsen**	Y	Y	N	Y	N	Y	Y
4 McCollum	N	N	Y	N	Y	N	?
5 Ellison	N	N	Y	N	Y	N	N
6 **Emmer**	Y	Y	N	Y	N	Y	Y
7 Peterson	N	Y	N	Y	Y	Y	N
8 Nolan	N	N	Y	N	Y	N	–
MISSISSIPPI							
1 **Kelly**	Y	Y	N	Y	N	Y	+
2 Thompson	N	N	Y	N	Y	N	N
3 **Harper**	Y	Y	N	Y	N	Y	Y
4 **Palazzo**	Y	Y	N	Y	N	Y	Y
MISSOURI							
1 Clay	Y	N	N	Y	Y	N	N
2 **Wagner**	Y	Y	N	Y	N	Y	?
3 **Luetkemeyer**	Y	Y	N	Y	N	Y	Y
4 **Hartzler**	Y	Y	N	Y	N	Y	Y
5 Cleaver	N	N	Y	Y	Y	N	N
6 **Graves**	Y	Y	N	Y	N	Y	Y
7 **Long**	Y	Y	N	Y	N	Y	Y
8 **Smith**	Y	Y	N	Y	N	Y	Y
MONTANA							
AL **Gianforte**	Y	Y	N	Y	N	Y	Y
NEBRASKA							
1 **Fortenberry**	Y	Y	N	Y	N	Y	Y
2 **Bacon**	Y	Y	N	Y	N	Y	Y
3 **Smith**	Y	Y	N	Y	N	?	Y
NEVADA							
1 Titus	N	Y	Y	N	Y	N	N
2 **Amodei**	Y	Y	N	Y	N	Y	Y
3 Rosen	N	Y	Y	Y	Y	Y	–
4 Kihuen	N	Y	Y	N	Y	N	N
NEW HAMPSHIRE							
1 Shea-Porter	N	N	Y	N	Y	N	?
2 Kuster	N	N	Y	N	Y	N	N
NEW JERSEY							
1 Norcross	N	Y	Y	N	Y	Y	N
2 **LoBiondo**	Y	Y	N	Y	N	Y	Y
3 **MacArthur**	Y	Y	N	Y	N	Y	Y
4 **Smith**	Y	Y	N	Y	N	Y	Y
5 Gottheimer	N	Y	Y	N	Y	Y	N
6 Pallone	N	Y	Y	N	Y	N	N
7 **Lance**	Y	Y	N	Y	N	Y	Y
8 Sires	N	Y	Y	N	Y	N	N
9 Pascrell	N	N	Y	N	Y	N	–
10 Payne	N	N	Y	N	Y	N	N
11 **Frelinghuysen**	Y	Y	N	Y	N	Y	Y
12 Watson Coleman	N	N	Y	N	Y	N	N
NEW MEXICO							
1 Lujan Grisham	N	N	Y	N	Y	N	N
2 **Pearce**	Y	Y	N	Y	N	Y	Y
3 Luján	N	N	Y	N	Y	N	N
NEW YORK							
1 **Zeldin**	Y	Y	N	Y	N	Y	Y
2 **King**	Y	Y	N	Y	N	Y	Y
3 Suozzi	Y	Y	Y	Y	Y	Y	N
4 Rice	N	Y	Y	N	Y	N	N
5 Meeks	N	N	Y	Y	Y	N	N
6 Meng	N	Y	Y	N	Y	Y	N
7 Velázquez	N	N	Y	N	Y	N	N
8 Jeffries	N	N	Y	N	Y	N	N
9 Clarke	N	N	Y	N	Y	N	?
10 Nadler	N	N	Y	N	Y	N	N
11 **Donovan**	Y	Y	N	Y	N	Y	Y
12 Maloney, C.	N	N	Y	N	Y	N	N
13 Espaillat	N	Y	Y	N	Y	N	N
14 Crowley	N	N	Y	N	Y	N	N
15 Serrano	N	N	Y	N	Y	N	N
16 Engel	N	Y	Y	N	Y	N	N
17 Lowey	N	Y	Y	N	Y	N	N
18 Maloney, S.P.	N	Y	Y	Y	Y	Y	N
19 **Faso**	Y	Y	N	Y	N	Y	Y
20 Tonko	N	N	Y	N	Y	N	N
21 **Stefanik**	Y	Y	N	Y	N	Y	Y
22 **Tenney**	Y	Y	N	Y	N	Y	Y
23 **Reed**	Y	Y	N	Y	N	Y	Y
24 **Katko**	Y	Y	–	+	+	+	?
25 Slaughter	N	N	Y	N	Y	N	N
26 Higgins	N	N	Y	N	Y	N	N
27 **Collins**	Y	Y	N	Y	N	Y	?
NORTH CAROLINA							
1 Butterfield	N	N	Y	Y	Y	N	N
2 **Holding**	Y	Y	N	Y	N	Y	Y
3 **Jones**	Y	N	N	N	N	N	Y
4 Price	N	N	Y	N	Y	N	N
5 **Foxx**	Y	Y	N	Y	N	Y	Y
6 **Walker**	Y	Y	N	Y	N	Y	Y
7 **Rouzer**	Y	Y	N	Y	N	Y	Y
8 **Hudson**	Y	Y	N	Y	N	Y	?
9 **Pittenger**	Y	Y	N	Y	N	Y	Y
10 **McHenry**	Y	Y	N	Y	N	Y	Y
11 **Meadows**	Y	Y	N	Y	N	Y	Y
12 Adams	N	N	Y	N	Y	N	N
13 **Budd**	Y	Y	N	Y	N	Y	Y
NORTH DAKOTA							
AL **Cramer**	Y	Y	N	Y	N	Y	Y
OHIO							
1 **Chabot**	Y	Y	N	Y	N	Y	Y
2 **Wenstrup**	Y	Y	N	Y	N	Y	Y
3 Beatty	N	N	Y	Y	Y	N	N
4 **Jordan**	Y	Y	N	Y	N	Y	Y
5 **Latta**	Y	Y	N	Y	N	Y	Y
6 **Johnson**	Y	Y	N	Y	N	Y	Y
7 **Gibbs**	Y	Y	N	Y	N	Y	Y
8 **Davidson**	Y	Y	N	Y	N	Y	Y
9 Kaptur	?	N	Y	N	Y	N	N
10 **Turner**	Y	Y	N	Y	N	Y	Y
11 Fudge	N	N	Y	N	Y	N	N
12 **Tiberi**	Y	Y	N	Y	N	Y	?
13 Ryan	N	N	Y	N	Y	N	N
14 **Joyce**	Y	Y	N	Y	N	Y	Y
15 **Stivers**	Y	Y	N	Y	N	Y	Y
16 **Renacci**	Y	Y	N	Y	N	Y	Y
OKLAHOMA							
1 **Bridenstine**	?	?	?	?	?	?	?
2 **Mullin**	Y	Y	N	Y	N	Y	Y
3 **Lucas**	Y	Y	N	Y	N	Y	Y
4 **Cole**	Y	Y	N	Y	N	Y	Y
5 **Russell**	Y	Y	N	Y	N	Y	Y
OREGON							
1 Bonamici	N	N	Y	N	Y	N	N
2 **Walden**	Y	Y	N	Y	N	Y	Y
3 Blumenauer	N	N	+	–	+	–	N
4 DeFazio	N	N	Y	N	Y	N	N
5 Schrader	N	Y	Y	Y	Y	Y	N
PENNSYLVANIA							
1 Brady	N	N	Y	N	Y	N	N
2 Evans	N	N	Y	N	Y	N	N
3 **Kelly**	Y	Y	N	Y	N	Y	Y
4 **Perry**	Y	Y	N	Y	N	Y	Y
5 **Thompson**	Y	Y	N	Y	N	Y	Y
6 **Costello**	Y	Y	N	Y	N	Y	Y
7 **Meehan**	Y	Y	N	Y	N	Y	Y
8 **Fitzpatrick**	Y	Y	N	Y	N	Y	Y
9 **Shuster**	Y	Y	N	Y	N	Y	Y
10 **Marino**	Y	Y	N	Y	N	Y	Y
11 **Barletta**	Y	Y	?	?	?	?	Y
12 **Rothfus**	Y	Y	N	Y	N	Y	Y
13 Boyle	N	Y	Y	N	Y	Y	–
14 Doyle	N	N	Y	N	Y	N	N
15 **Dent**	Y	Y	N	Y	N	Y	Y
16 **Smucker**	Y	Y	N	Y	N	Y	Y
17 Cartwright	N	N	Y	Y	Y	N	N
RHODE ISLAND							
1 Cicilline	N	N	Y	N	Y	N	N
2 Langevin	N	N	Y	N	Y	N	N
SOUTH CAROLINA							
1 **Sanford**	Y	Y	N	Y	N	Y	Y
2 **Wilson**	Y	Y	N	Y	N	Y	Y
3 **Duncan**	Y	Y	N	Y	N	Y	?
4 **Gowdy**	Y	Y	N	Y	N	Y	Y
5 **Norman**	Y	Y	N	Y	N	Y	Y
6 Clyburn	N	N	Y	N	Y	N	N
7 **Rice**	Y	Y	N	Y	N	Y	Y
SOUTH DAKOTA							
AL **Noem**	Y	Y	N	Y	N	Y	Y
TENNESSEE							
1 **Roe**	Y	Y	N	Y	N	Y	Y
2 **Duncan**	Y	N	N	Y	N	N	Y
3 **Fleischmann**	Y	Y	N	Y	N	Y	Y
4 **DesJarlais**	Y	Y	N	Y	N	Y	Y
5 Cooper	N	N	Y	Y	Y	N	N
6 **Black**	Y	Y	N	Y	N	Y	Y
7 **Blackburn**	Y	Y	N	Y	N	Y	Y
8 **Kustoff**	Y	Y	N	Y	N	Y	Y
9 Cohen	N	N	Y	N	Y	N	N
TEXAS							
1 **Gohmert**	Y	Y	N	Y	N	Y	Y
2 **Poe**	Y	Y	N	Y	N	Y	Y
3 **Johnson, S.**	Y	Y	N	Y	N	Y	Y
4 **Ratcliffe**	Y	Y	N	Y	N	Y	Y
5 **Hensarling**	Y	Y	N	Y	N	Y	Y
6 **Barton**	Y	Y	N	Y	N	Y	Y
7 **Culberson**	Y	Y	N	Y	N	Y	Y
8 **Brady**	Y	Y	N	Y	N	Y	Y
9 Green, A.	N	N	Y	N	Y	N	–
10 **McCaul**	Y	Y	N	Y	N	Y	Y
11 **Conaway**	Y	Y	N	Y	N	Y	Y
12 **Granger**	Y	Y	N	Y	N	Y	Y
13 **Thornberry**	Y	Y	N	Y	N	Y	Y
14 **Weber**	Y	Y	N	Y	N	Y	Y
15 Gonzalez	N	N	Y	N	Y	Y	?
16 O'Rourke	N	N	Y	Y	Y	N	–
17 **Flores**	Y	Y	N	Y	N	Y	Y
18 Jackson Lee	N	N	Y	N	Y	N	N
19 **Arrington**	Y	Y	N	Y	N	Y	Y
20 Castro	N	N	Y	N	Y	N	N
21 **Smith**	Y	Y	N	Y	N	Y	?
22 **Olson**	Y	Y	N	Y	N	Y	Y
23 **Hurd**	Y	Y	N	Y	N	Y	Y
24 **Marchant**	Y	Y	?	?	?	?	Y
25 **Williams**	Y	Y	N	Y	N	Y	Y
26 **Burgess**	Y	Y	N	Y	N	Y	Y
27 **Farenthold**	Y	Y	N	Y	N	Y	Y
28 Cuellar	N	Y	Y	Y	Y	Y	N
29 Green, G.	N	Y	Y	N	Y	Y	N
30 Johnson, E.B.	N	N	Y	Y	Y	N	N
31 **Carter**	Y	Y	N	Y	N	Y	?
32 **Sessions**	Y	Y	N	Y	N	Y	Y
33 Veasey	N	N	Y	Y	Y	N	N
34 Vela	N	Y	Y	N	Y	N	N
35 Doggett	N	N	Y	N	Y	N	N
36 **Babin**	Y	Y	N	Y	N	Y	Y
UTAH							
1 **Bishop**	Y	Y	N	Y	N	Y	Y
2 **Stewart**	Y	Y	N	Y	N	Y	Y
3 **Curtis**	Y	Y	N	Y	N	Y	Y
4 **Love**	Y	Y	N	Y	N	Y	Y
VERMONT							
AL Welch	N	N	Y	N	Y	N	N
VIRGINIA							
1 **Wittman**	Y	Y	N	Y	?	Y	Y
2 **Taylor**	Y	Y	N	Y	N	Y	Y
3 Scott	N	N	Y	N	Y	N	N
4 McEachin	N	N	Y	N	Y	N	N
5 **Garrett**	Y	Y	N	Y	N	Y	Y
6 **Goodlatte**	Y	Y	N	Y	N	Y	Y
7 **Brat**	Y	Y	N	Y	N	Y	Y
8 Beyer	N	N	Y	N	Y	N	N
9 **Griffith**	Y	Y	N	Y	N	Y	Y
10 **Comstock**	Y	Y	N	Y	N	Y	Y
11 Connolly	N	N	Y	N	Y	N	N
WASHINGTON							
1 DelBene	N	N	Y	N	Y	N	N
2 Larsen	N	N	Y	N	Y	N	N
3 **Herrera Beutler**	Y	Y	N	Y	N	Y	Y
4 **Newhouse**	Y	Y	N	Y	N	Y	Y
5 **McMorris Rodgers**	Y	Y	N	Y	N	Y	Y
6 Kilmer	N	N	Y	N	Y	N	N
7 Jayapal	N	N	Y	N	Y	N	N
8 **Reichert**	Y	Y	N	Y	N	Y	Y
9 Smith	N	N	Y	N	Y	N	N
10 Heck	N	N	Y	N	Y	N	N
WEST VIRGINIA							
1 **McKinley**	Y	Y	N	Y	N	Y	Y
2 **Mooney**	Y	Y	N	Y	N	Y	?
3 **Jenkins**	Y	Y	N	Y	N	Y	Y
WISCONSIN							
1 **Ryan**							
2 Pocan	–	–	+	–	+	–	–
3 Kind	N	Y	Y	Y	Y	N	N
4 Moore	N	N	?	N	Y	?	N
5 **Sensenbrenner**	+	+	N	Y	N	Y	Y
6 **Grothman**	Y	Y	N	Y	N	Y	Y
7 **Duffy**	Y	Y	N	Y	N	Y	+
8 **Gallagher**	Y	Y	N	Y	N	Y	Y
WYOMING							
AL **Cheney**	Y	Y	N	Y	N	Y	Y

III HOUSE VOTES

VOTE NUMBER

686. HR 4375. STEM MINORITY RESEARCH AND EDUCATION EFFECTIVENESS/PASSAGE. Comstock, R-Va., motion to suspend the rules and pass the bill that would require the National Science Foundation to report to Congress on the effectiveness of all the foundation's research and education programs that work to broaden the participation of women and other historically underrepresented individuals in STEM studies and careers. It would require any science agency with a research and development budget over $100 million in fiscal 2017 to report to Congress annually on applications submitted for merit-reviewed research and development grants. Motion agreed to 376-9 : R 208-9; D 168-0. Dec. 18, 2017.

687. HR 3979. WILDLIFE REFUGE VOLUNTEER PROGRAMS/PASSAGE. Wittman, R-Va, motion to suspend the rules and pass the bill that would extend, through fiscal 2022, U.S. Fish and Wildlife Service's national wildlife refuge volunteer and community partnership programs. The programs would be authorized at current funding level, or $2 million per year. Motion agreed to 371-14 : R 202-14; D 169-0. Dec. 18, 2017.

688. HR 3312, H RES 667, HR 1. ENHANCED SUPERVISION ELIMINATION AND TAX OVERHAUL CONFERENCE REPORT/RULE. Adoption of the rule (H Res 667) that would provide for House floor consideration of the bill (HR 3312) that would modify the enhanced supervision requirement for certain bank holding companies, and provide for consideration of the conference report to accompany the Tax Cuts and Jobs Act (HR 1). Adopted 233-193 : R 233-3; D 0-190. Dec. 19, 2017.

689. HR 3312, H RES 667, HR 1. ENHANCED SUPERVISION ELIMINATION AND TAX OVERHAUL CONFERENCE REPORT/PREVIOUS QUESTION. Session, R-Texas, motion to order the previous question (thus ending debate and the possibility of amendment) on the rule (H Res 667) that would provide House floor consideration of the bill (HR 3312) that would eliminate the enhanced supervision requirement for certain bank holding companies, and provide for consideration of the conference report to accompany the Tax Cuts and Jobs Act (HR 1). Motion agreed to 233-187 : R 233-0; D 0-187. Dec. 19, 2017.

690. HR 4254. WOMEN AND MINORITY STEM CAREERS/PASSAGE. Knight, R-Calif., motion to suspend the rules and pass the bill that would require, starting Oct. 1, 2018, the National Science Foundation to prioritize placement for female fellows with research experience at national labs and NASA Centers through the NSF Noyce Teacher Scholarship Program. It requires NASA to institute a process to prioritize the recruitment of qualified candidates who are women or underrepresented minorities in the fields of science, technology, engineering and mathematics and computer science for internships and fellowships at NASA. Motion agreed to 409-17 : R 220-16; D 189-1. Dec. 19, 2017.

691. HR 1. TAX OVERHAUL/RECOMMIT. Neal, D-Mass., motion to recommit the bill to the Committee of Conference with instructions to the managers on the part of the House that they disagree with provisions related to state and local tax deductions, and related to the bill's language that would effectively repeal the individual health care mandate established by the 2010 health care overhaul. Motion rejected 191-236 : R 0-236; D 191-0. Dec. 19, 2017.

692. HR 1. TAX OVERHAUL/CONFERENCE REPORT. Adoption of the conference report on the bill that would revise the federal income tax system by lowering the corporate tax rate from 35 percent to 21 percent; lowering individual tax rates through 2025; limiting state and local deductions to $10,000 through 2025; decreasing the limit on deductible mortgage debt through 2025; and creating a new system of taxing U.S. corporations with foreign subsidiaries. Specifically, it would repeal personal exemptions and would roughly double the standard deduction through 2025. It would raise the child tax credit to $2,000 through 2025, would repeal the alternative minimum tax for corporations and provide for broader exemptions to the tax for individuals through 2025. It would double individual exemptions to the estate tax and gift tax through 2025, and would establish a new top tax rate for "pass-through" business income through 2025. Adopted (thus sent to the Senate) 227-203 : R 227-12; D 0-191. Dec. 19, 2017.

Member	686	687	688	689	690	691	692
ALABAMA							
1 Byrne	Y	Y	Y	Y	Y	N	Y
2 Roby	Y	Y	Y	Y	Y	N	Y
3 Rogers	Y	Y	Y	Y	Y	N	Y
4 Aderholt	Y	Y	Y	Y	Y	N	Y
5 Brooks	?	?	Y	Y	Y	N	Y
6 Palmer	Y	Y	Y	Y	Y	N	Y
7 Sewell	+	+	N	N	Y	Y	N
ALASKA							
AL Young	Y	Y	Y	Y	Y	N	Y
ARIZONA							
1 O'Halleran	Y	Y	N	N	Y	Y	N
2 McSally	Y	Y	Y	Y	Y	N	Y
3 Grijalva	Y	Y	N	N	Y	Y	N
4 Gosar	N	Y	Y	Y	N	N	Y
5 Biggs	N	N	Y	Y	N	N	Y
6 Schweikert	Y	Y	Y	Y	Y	N	Y
7 Gallego	Y	Y	N	N	Y	Y	N
9 Sinema	+	+	N	N	Y	Y	N
ARKANSAS							
1 Crawford	?	?	Y	Y	Y	N	Y
2 Hill	Y	Y	Y	Y	Y	N	Y
3 Womack	Y	Y	Y	Y	Y	N	Y
4 Westerman	Y	Y	Y	Y	Y	N	Y
CALIFORNIA							
1 LaMalfa	Y	Y	Y	Y	Y	N	Y
2 Huffman	Y	Y	N	N	Y	Y	N
3 Garamendi	Y	Y	N	N	Y	Y	N
4 McClintock	Y	Y	Y	Y	Y	N	Y
5 Thompson	Y	Y	N	N	Y	Y	N
6 Matsui	Y	Y	N	N	Y	Y	N
7 Bera	Y	Y	N	N	Y	Y	N
8 Cook	Y	Y	Y	Y	Y	N	Y
9 McNerney	Y	Y	N	N	Y	Y	N
10 Denham	Y	Y	Y	Y	Y	N	Y
11 DeSaulnier	Y	Y	N	N	Y	Y	N
12 Pelosi	Y	Y	N	N	Y	Y	N
13 Lee	Y	Y	N	N	Y	Y	N
14 Speier	?	?	N	N	Y	Y	N
15 Swalwell	Y	Y	N	N	Y	Y	N
16 Costa	Y	Y	N	N	Y	Y	N
17 Khanna	Y	Y	N	N	Y	Y	N
18 Eshoo	Y	Y	N	N	Y	Y	N
19 Lofgren	Y	Y	N	N	Y	Y	N
20 Panetta	Y	Y	N	N	Y	Y	N
21 Valadao	Y	Y	Y	Y	Y	N	Y
22 Nunes	Y	Y	Y	Y	Y	N	Y
23 McCarthy	Y	Y	Y	Y	Y	N	Y
24 Carbajal	Y	Y	N	N	Y	Y	N
25 Knight	Y	Y	Y	Y	Y	N	Y
26 Brownley	Y	Y	N	N	Y	Y	N
27 Chu	Y	Y	N	N	Y	Y	N
28 Schiff	Y	Y	N	N	Y	Y	N
29 Cardenas	Y	Y	N	N	Y	Y	N
30 Sherman	Y	Y	N	N	Y	Y	N
31 Aguilar	Y	Y	N	N	Y	Y	N
32 Napolitano	+	+	N	N	Y	Y	N
33 Lieu	Y	Y	N	N	Y	Y	N
34 Gomez	Y	Y	N	N	Y	Y	N
35 Torres	Y	Y	N	N	Y	Y	N
36 Ruiz	Y	Y	N	N	Y	Y	N
37 Bass	Y	Y	N	N	Y	Y	N
38 Sánchez, Linda	+	+	N	N	Y	Y	N
39 Royce	Y	Y	Y	Y	Y	N	Y
40 Roybal-Allard	Y	Y	N	N	Y	Y	N
41 Takano	Y	Y	N	N	Y	Y	N
42 Calvert	Y	Y	Y	Y	Y	N	Y
43 Waters	Y	Y	N	N	Y	Y	N
44 Barragan	Y	Y	N	N	Y	Y	N
45 Walters	Y	Y	Y	Y	Y	N	Y
46 Correa	Y	Y	N	N	Y	Y	N
47 Lowenthal	Y	Y	N	N	Y	Y	N
48 Rohrabacher	?	?	Y	Y	Y	N	N
49 Issa	Y	Y	Y	Y	Y	N	N
50 Hunter	Y	N	Y	Y	Y	N	Y
51 Vargas	Y	Y	N	N	Y	Y	N
52 Peters	Y	Y	N	N	Y	Y	N
53 Davis	Y	Y	N	N	Y	Y	N
COLORADO							
1 DeGette	Y	Y	N	N	Y	Y	N
2 Polis	Y	Y	N	N	Y	Y	N
3 Tipton	Y	Y	Y	Y	Y	N	Y
4 Buck	Y	N	Y	N	N	Y	N
5 Lamborn	Y	Y	Y	Y	Y	N	Y
6 Coffman	Y	Y	Y	Y	Y	N	Y
7 Perlmutter	Y	Y	N	N	Y	Y	N
CONNECTICUT							
1 Larson	+	+	N	N	Y	Y	N
2 Courtney	Y	Y	N	N	Y	Y	N
3 DeLauro	Y	Y	N	N	Y	Y	N
4 Himes	Y	Y	N	N	Y	Y	N
5 Esty	Y	Y	N	N	Y	Y	N
DELAWARE							
AL Blunt Rochester	Y	Y	N	N	Y	Y	N
FLORIDA							
1 Gaetz	N	N	Y	Y	N	N	Y
2 Dunn	Y	Y	Y	Y	Y	N	Y
3 Yoho	Y	N	Y	Y	N	N	Y
4 Rutherford	Y	Y	Y	Y	Y	N	Y
5 Lawson	Y	N	N	N	Y	Y	N
6 DeSantis	?	?	Y	Y	Y	N	Y
7 Murphy	?	?	N	N	Y	Y	N
8 Posey	Y	Y	Y	Y	Y	N	Y
9 Soto	Y	Y	N	N	Y	Y	N
10 Demings	Y	Y	N	N	Y	Y	N
11 Webster	?	?	Y	Y	Y	N	Y
12 Bilirakis	Y	Y	Y	Y	Y	N	Y
13 Crist	Y	Y	N	N	Y	Y	N
14 Castor	Y	Y	N	N	Y	Y	N
15 Ross	Y	Y	Y	Y	Y	N	Y
16 Buchanan	Y	Y	?	Y	Y	N	Y
17 Rooney, T.	Y	Y	Y	Y	Y	N	Y
18 Mast	Y	Y	Y	Y	Y	N	Y
19 Rooney, F.	?	?	Y	Y	Y	N	Y
20 Hastings	Y	Y	N	N	Y	Y	N
21 Frankel	Y	Y	N	N	Y	Y	N
22 Deutch	?	?	N	N	Y	Y	N
23 Wasserman Schultz	Y	Y	N	N	Y	Y	N
24 Wilson	Y	Y	N	N	Y	Y	N
25 Diaz-Balart	Y	Y	Y	Y	Y	N	Y
26 Curbelo	Y	Y	Y	Y	Y	N	Y
27 Ros-Lehtinen	Y	Y	Y	Y	Y	N	Y
GEORGIA							
1 Carter	Y	Y	Y	Y	Y	N	Y
2 Bishop	Y	Y	N	N	Y	Y	N
3 Ferguson	Y	Y	N	N	Y	Y	N
4 Johnson	Y	Y	N	N	Y	Y	N
5 Lewis	Y	Y	N	N	Y	Y	N
6 Handel	Y	Y	Y	Y	Y	N	Y
7 Woodall	Y	Y	Y	Y	Y	N	Y
8 Scott, A.	Y	Y	Y	Y	Y	N	Y
9 Collins	Y	Y	Y	Y	Y	N	Y
10 Hice	Y	Y	Y	Y	Y	N	Y
11 Loudermilk	?	?	Y	Y	Y	N	Y
12 Allen	Y	Y	Y	Y	Y	N	Y
13 Scott, D.	Y	Y	N	N	Y	Y	N
14 Graves	Y	Y	Y	Y	Y	N	Y
HAWAII							
1 Hanabusa	Y	Y	N	N	Y	Y	N
2 Gabbard	Y	Y	N	N	Y	Y	N
IDAHO							
1 Labrador	?	?	Y	Y	N	N	Y
2 Simpson	Y	Y	Y	Y	Y	N	Y
ILLINOIS							
1 Rush	?	?	N	N	Y	Y	N
2 Kelly	Y	Y	N	N	Y	Y	N
3 Lipinski	Y	Y	N	N	Y	Y	N
4 Gutierrez	+	+	N	N	Y	Y	N
5 Quigley	Y	Y	N	N	Y	Y	N
6 Roskam	Y	Y	Y	Y	Y	N	Y
7 Davis, D.	Y	Y	?	N	Y	Y	N
8 Krishnamoorthi	Y	Y	N	N	Y	Y	N
9 Schakowsky	Y	Y	N	N	Y	Y	N
10 Schneider	Y	Y	N	N	Y	Y	N
11 Foster	Y	Y	N	N	Y	Y	N
12 Bost	Y	Y	Y	Y	Y	N	Y
13 Davis, R.	Y	Y	Y	Y	Y	N	Y
14 Hultgren	Y	Y	Y	Y	Y	N	Y
15 Shimkus	Y	Y	Y	Y	Y	N	Y

KEY	Republicans	Democrats	Independents
Y Voted for (yea)	**X** Paired against	**C** Voted "present" to avoid possible conflict of interest
# Paired for	**–** Announced against	
+ Announced for	**P** Voted "present"	**?** Did not vote or otherwise make a position known
N Voted against (nay)		

	686	687	688	689	690	691	692
16 **Kinzinger**	Y	Y	Y	Y	Y	N	Y
17 Bustos	Y	Y	N	N	Y	Y	N
18 **LaHood**	Y	Y	Y	Y	Y	N	Y
INDIANA							
1 Visclosky	Y	Y	N	N	Y	Y	N
2 **Walorski**	Y	Y	Y	Y	Y	N	Y
3 **Banks**	Y	Y	Y	Y	Y	N	Y
4 **Rokita**	Y	Y	Y	Y	Y	N	Y
5 **Brooks**	Y	Y	Y	Y	Y	N	Y
6 **Messer**	Y	Y	Y	Y	Y	N	Y
7 Carson	Y	Y	N	N	Y	Y	N
8 **Bucshon**	Y	?	Y	Y	Y	N	Y
9 **Hollingsworth**	Y	Y	Y	Y	Y	N	Y
IOWA							
1 **Blum**	Y	Y	Y	Y	Y	N	Y
2 Loebsack	Y	Y	N	N	Y	Y	N
3 **Young**	Y	Y	Y	Y	Y	N	Y
4 **King**	Y	Y	Y	Y	N	N	Y
KANSAS							
1 **Marshall**	Y	Y	Y	Y	Y	N	Y
2 **Jenkins**	Y	Y	Y	Y	Y	N	Y
3 **Yoder**	Y	Y	Y	Y	Y	N	Y
4 **Estes**	Y	Y	Y	Y	Y	N	Y
KENTUCKY							
1 **Comer**	Y	Y	Y	Y	Y	N	Y
2 **Guthrie**	Y	Y	Y	Y	Y	N	Y
3 Yarmuth	Y	Y	N	N	Y	Y	N
4 **Massie**	N	N	Y	N	N	N	Y
5 **Rogers**	Y	Y	Y	Y	Y	N	Y
6 **Barr**	Y	Y	Y	Y	Y	N	Y
LOUISIANA							
1 **Scalise**	Y	+	Y	Y	Y	N	Y
2 Richmond	Y	Y	?	N	Y	Y	N
3 **Higgins**	?	?	Y	Y	Y	N	Y
4 **Johnson**	Y	Y	Y	Y	Y	N	Y
5 **Abraham**	Y	Y	Y	Y	Y	N	Y
6 **Graves**	Y	Y	Y	Y	Y	N	Y
MAINE							
1 Pingree	Y	Y	N	N	Y	Y	N
2 **Poliquin**	Y	Y	Y	Y	Y	N	Y
MARYLAND							
1 **Harris**	N	Y	Y	Y	N	N	Y
2 Ruppersberger	Y	Y	N	N	Y	Y	N
3 Sarbanes	Y	Y	N	N	Y	Y	N
4 Brown	Y	Y	N	N	Y	Y	N
5 Hoyer	Y	Y	N	N	Y	Y	N
6 Delaney	Y	Y	N	N	Y	Y	N
7 Cummings	Y	Y	N	N	Y	Y	N
8 Raskin	Y	Y	N	N	Y	Y	N
MASSACHUSETTS							
1 Neal	Y	Y	N	N	Y	Y	N
2 McGovern	Y	Y	N	N	Y	Y	N
3 Tsongas	Y	Y	N	N	Y	Y	N
4 Kennedy	?	?	?	?	?	?	?
5 Clark	Y	Y	N	N	Y	Y	N
6 Moulton	Y	Y	N	N	Y	Y	N
7 Capuano	+	+	N	N	Y	Y	N
8 Lynch	Y	Y	N	N	Y	Y	N
9 Keating	Y	Y	N	N	Y	Y	N
MICHIGAN							
1 **Bergman**	Y	Y	Y	Y	Y	N	Y
2 **Huizenga**	Y	Y	Y	Y	Y	N	Y
3 **Amash**	N	N	Y	N	N	N	Y
4 **Moolenaar**	Y	Y	Y	Y	Y	N	Y
5 Kildee	Y	Y	N	N	Y	Y	N
6 **Upton**	Y	Y	Y	Y	Y	N	Y
7 **Walberg**	Y	Y	Y	Y	Y	N	Y
8 **Bishop**	Y	Y	Y	Y	Y	N	Y
9 Levin	Y	Y	N	N	Y	Y	N
10 **Mitchell**	Y	Y	Y	Y	Y	N	Y
11 **Trott**	Y	Y	Y	Y	Y	N	Y
12 Dingell	Y	Y	N	N	Y	Y	N
13 Vacant							
14 Lawrence	+	+	N	N	Y	Y	N
MINNESOTA							
1 Walz	?	?	N	N	Y	Y	N
2 **Lewis**	Y	Y	Y	Y	Y	N	Y
3 **Paulsen**	Y	Y	Y	Y	Y	N	Y
4 McCollum	+	+	N	N	Y	Y	N

	686	687	688	689	690	691	692
5 Ellison	Y	Y	N	N	Y	Y	N
6 **Emmer**	Y	Y	Y	Y	Y	N	Y
7 Peterson	Y	Y	N	N	Y	Y	N
8 Nolan	+	+	N	N	Y	Y	N
MISSISSIPPI							
1 **Kelly**	+	Y	Y	Y	Y	N	Y
2 Thompson	Y	Y	N	N	Y	Y	N
3 **Harper**	Y	Y	Y	Y	Y	N	Y
4 **Palazzo**	Y	Y	Y	Y	Y	N	Y
MISSOURI							
1 Clay	Y	Y	N	N	Y	Y	N
2 **Wagner**	?	?	Y	Y	Y	N	Y
3 **Luetkemeyer**	Y	Y	Y	Y	Y	N	Y
4 **Hartzler**	Y	Y	Y	Y	Y	N	Y
5 Cleaver	Y	Y	N	N	Y	Y	N
6 **Graves**	Y	Y	Y	Y	Y	N	Y
7 **Long**	Y	Y	Y	Y	Y	N	Y
8 **Smith**	Y	Y	Y	Y	Y	N	Y
MONTANA							
AL **Gianforte**	Y	Y	Y	Y	Y	N	Y
NEBRASKA							
1 **Fortenberry**	Y	Y	Y	Y	Y	N	Y
2 **Bacon**	Y	Y	Y	Y	Y	N	Y
3 **Smith**	Y	Y	Y	Y	Y	N	Y
NEVADA							
1 Titus	Y	Y	N	N	Y	Y	N
2 **Amodei**	Y	Y	Y	Y	Y	N	Y
3 Rosen	+	+	N	N	Y	Y	N
4 Kihuen	Y	Y	N	N	Y	Y	N
NEW HAMPSHIRE							
1 Shea-Porter	?	?	N	N	Y	Y	N
2 Kuster	Y	Y	N	N	Y	Y	N
NEW JERSEY							
1 Norcross	Y	Y	N	N	Y	Y	N
2 **LoBiondo**	Y	Y	Y	Y	Y	N	N
3 **MacArthur**	Y	Y	Y	Y	Y	N	Y
4 **Smith**	Y	Y	Y	Y	Y	N	N
5 Gottheimer	Y	Y	N	N	Y	Y	N
6 Pallone	Y	Y	N	N	Y	Y	N
7 **Lance**	Y	Y	Y	Y	Y	N	N
8 Sires	Y	Y	N	N	Y	Y	N
9 Pascrell	+	+	N	N	Y	Y	N
10 Payne	Y	Y	N	N	Y	Y	N
11 **Frelinghuysen**	Y	Y	Y	Y	Y	N	N
12 Watson Coleman	Y	Y	N	N	Y	Y	N
NEW MEXICO							
1 Lujan Grisham	Y	Y	N	N	Y	Y	N
2 **Pearce**	Y	Y	Y	Y	Y	N	Y
3 Luján	Y	Y	N	N	Y	Y	N
NEW YORK							
1 **Zeldin**	Y	Y	Y	Y	Y	N	N
2 **King**	Y	Y	Y	Y	Y	N	N
3 Suozzi	Y	Y	N	N	Y	Y	N
4 Rice	Y	Y	N	N	Y	Y	N
5 Meeks	Y	Y	N	N	Y	Y	N
6 Meng	Y	Y	N	N	Y	Y	N
7 Velázquez	Y	Y	N	N	Y	Y	N
8 Jeffries	Y	Y	N	N	Y	Y	N
9 Clarke	?	?	?	?	?	Y	N
10 Nadler	Y	Y	N	N	Y	Y	N
11 **Donovan**	Y	Y	Y	Y	Y	N	N
12 Maloney, C.	Y	Y	N	N	Y	Y	N
13 Espaillat	Y	Y	N	N	Y	Y	N
14 Crowley	Y	Y	N	N	Y	Y	N
15 Serrano	Y	Y	N	N	Y	Y	N
16 Engel	Y	Y	N	N	Y	Y	N
17 Lowey	Y	Y	N	N	Y	Y	N
18 Maloney, S.P.	Y	Y	N	N	Y	Y	N
19 **Faso**	Y	Y	Y	Y	Y	N	N
20 Tonko	Y	Y	N	N	Y	Y	N
21 **Stefanik**	Y	Y	Y	Y	Y	N	N
22 **Tenney**	Y	Y	Y	Y	Y	N	Y
23 **Reed**	Y	Y	Y	Y	Y	N	Y
24 **Katko**	?	?	Y	Y	Y	N	Y
25 Slaughter	Y	Y	N	N	Y	Y	N
26 Higgins	Y	Y	N	N	Y	Y	N
27 **Collins**	?	?	Y	Y	Y	N	Y
NORTH CAROLINA							
1 Butterfield	Y	Y	N	N	Y	Y	N
2 **Holding**	Y	Y	Y	Y	Y	N	Y
3 **Jones**	Y	Y	Y	N	Y	N	N
4 Price	Y	Y	N	N	Y	Y	N

	686	687	688	689	690	691	692
5 **Foxx**	Y	Y	Y	Y	Y	N	Y
6 **Walker**	Y	Y	Y	Y	Y	N	Y
7 **Rouzer**	Y	Y	Y	Y	Y	N	Y
8 **Hudson**	+	+	?	?	+	N	Y
9 **Pittenger**	Y	Y	Y	Y	Y	N	Y
10 **McHenry**	Y	Y	Y	Y	Y	N	Y
11 **Meadows**	Y	Y	Y	Y	Y	N	Y
12 Adams	Y	Y	N	N	Y	Y	N
13 **Budd**	Y	Y	Y	Y	Y	N	Y
NORTH DAKOTA							
AL **Cramer**	Y	Y	Y	Y	Y	N	Y
OHIO							
1 **Chabot**	Y	Y	Y	Y	Y	N	Y
2 **Wenstrup**	Y	Y	Y	Y	Y	N	Y
3 Beatty	Y	Y	N	N	Y	Y	N
4 **Jordan**	Y	Y	Y	Y	Y	N	Y
5 **Latta**	Y	Y	Y	Y	Y	N	Y
6 **Johnson**	Y	Y	Y	Y	Y	N	Y
7 **Gibbs**	Y	Y	Y	Y	Y	N	Y
8 **Davidson**	Y	Y	?	Y	N	N	Y
9 Kaptur	Y	Y	N	N	Y	Y	N
10 **Turner**	Y	Y	Y	Y	Y	N	Y
11 Fudge	Y	Y	N	N	Y	Y	N
12 **Tiberi**	?	?	Y	Y	Y	N	Y
13 Ryan	Y	Y	N	N	Y	Y	N
14 **Joyce**	Y	Y	Y	Y	Y	N	Y
15 **Stivers**	Y	Y	Y	Y	Y	N	Y
16 **Renacci**	Y	Y	Y	Y	Y	N	Y
OKLAHOMA							
1 **Bridenstine**	?	?	?	?	?	?	Y
2 **Mullin**	Y	Y	Y	Y	Y	N	Y
3 **Lucas**	Y	Y	Y	Y	Y	N	Y
4 **Cole**	Y	Y	Y	Y	Y	N	Y
5 **Russell**	Y	Y	Y	Y	Y	N	Y
OREGON							
1 Bonamici	Y	Y	N	N	Y	Y	N
2 **Walden**	Y	Y	Y	Y	Y	N	Y
3 Blumenauer	Y	Y	N	N	Y	Y	N
4 DeFazio	Y	Y	N	N	Y	Y	N
5 Schrader	Y	Y	N	N	Y	Y	N
PENNSYLVANIA							
1 Brady	Y	Y	N	N	Y	Y	N
2 Evans	Y	Y	N	N	Y	Y	N
3 **Kelly**	Y	Y	Y	Y	Y	N	Y
4 **Perry**	Y	N	Y	Y	N	N	Y
5 **Thompson**	Y	Y	Y	Y	Y	N	Y
6 **Costello**	Y	Y	Y	Y	Y	N	Y
7 **Meehan**	Y	Y	Y	Y	Y	N	Y
8 **Fitzpatrick**	Y	Y	Y	Y	Y	N	Y
9 **Shuster**	Y	Y	Y	Y	Y	N	Y
10 **Marino**	Y	Y	Y	Y	Y	N	Y
11 **Barletta**	Y	Y	Y	Y	Y	N	Y
12 **Rothfus**	Y	Y	Y	Y	Y	N	Y
13 Boyle	+	+	N	N	Y	Y	N
14 Doyle	Y	Y	N	N	Y	Y	N
15 **Dent**	Y	Y	Y	Y	Y	N	Y
16 **Smucker**	Y	Y	Y	Y	Y	N	Y
17 Cartwright	Y	Y	N	N	Y	Y	N
RHODE ISLAND							
1 Cicilline	Y	Y	N	N	Y	Y	N
2 Langevin	Y	Y	N	N	Y	Y	N
SOUTH CAROLINA							
1 **Sanford**	Y	N	Y	Y	N	N	Y
2 **Wilson**	Y	Y	Y	Y	Y	N	Y
3 **Duncan**	?	?	Y	Y	Y	N	Y
4 **Gowdy**	Y	Y	Y	Y	Y	N	Y
5 **Norman**	Y	Y	Y	Y	Y	N	Y
6 Clyburn	Y	Y	N	N	Y	Y	N
7 **Rice**	Y	Y	Y	Y	Y	N	Y
SOUTH DAKOTA							
AL **Noem**	Y	Y	Y	Y	Y	N	Y
TENNESSEE							
1 **Roe**	Y	Y	Y	Y	Y	N	Y
2 **Duncan**	N	Y	Y	Y	N	N	Y
3 **Fleischmann**	Y	Y	Y	Y	Y	N	Y
4 **DesJarlais**	Y	Y	Y	Y	Y	N	Y
5 Cooper	Y	Y	N	N	Y	Y	N
6 **Black**	Y	Y	Y	Y	Y	N	Y
7 **Blackburn**	Y	Y	Y	Y	Y	N	Y
8 **Kustoff**	Y	Y	Y	Y	Y	N	Y
9 Cohen	Y	Y	N	N	Y	Y	N

	686	687	688	689	690	691	692
TEXAS							
1 **Gohmert**	N	N	Y	Y	N	N	Y
2 **Poe**	Y	Y	Y	Y	Y	N	Y
3 **Johnson, S.**	Y	Y	Y	Y	Y	N	Y
4 **Ratcliffe**	Y	Y	Y	Y	Y	N	Y
5 **Hensarling**	Y	Y	Y	Y	Y	N	Y
6 **Barton**	Y	Y	Y	Y	Y	N	Y
7 **Culberson**	Y	Y	Y	Y	Y	N	Y
8 **Brady**	Y	Y	Y	Y	Y	N	Y
9 Green, A.	+	Y	N	N	Y	Y	N
10 **McCaul**	Y	Y	Y	Y	Y	N	Y
11 **Conaway**	Y	Y	Y	Y	Y	N	Y
12 **Granger**	Y	Y	Y	Y	Y	N	Y
13 **Thornberry**	Y	Y	Y	Y	Y	N	Y
14 **Weber**	Y	N	Y	Y	Y	N	Y
15 Gonzalez	?	?	N	N	N	Y	N
16 O'Rourke	+	+	N	N	Y	Y	N
17 **Flores**	Y	Y	Y	Y	Y	N	Y
18 Jackson Lee	Y	Y	N	N	Y	Y	N
19 **Arrington**	Y	Y	Y	Y	Y	N	Y
20 Castro	Y	Y	N	N	Y	Y	N
21 **Smith**	?	?	?	Y	Y	N	Y
22 **Olson**	Y	Y	Y	Y	Y	N	Y
23 **Hurd**	Y	Y	Y	Y	Y	N	Y
24 **Marchant**	Y	Y	Y	Y	Y	N	Y
25 **Williams**	Y	N	Y	Y	Y	N	Y
26 **Burgess**	Y	Y	Y	Y	Y	N	Y
27 **Farenthold**	Y	Y	Y	Y	Y	N	Y
28 Cuellar	Y	Y	N	N	Y	Y	N
29 Green, G.	Y	Y	N	N	Y	Y	N
30 Johnson, E.B.	Y	Y	N	N	Y	Y	N
31 **Carter**	?	?	Y	Y	Y	N	Y
32 **Sessions**	Y	Y	Y	Y	Y	N	Y
33 Veasey	Y	Y	N	N	Y	Y	N
34 Vela	Y	Y	N	N	Y	Y	N
35 Doggett	Y	Y	N	N	Y	Y	N
36 **Babin**	Y	N	Y	Y	Y	N	Y
UTAH							
1 **Bishop**	Y	Y	Y	Y	Y	N	Y
2 **Stewart**	Y	Y	Y	Y	Y	N	Y
3 **Curtis**	Y	Y	Y	Y	Y	N	Y
4 **Love**	Y	Y	Y	Y	Y	N	Y
VERMONT							
AL Welch	Y	Y	N	N	Y	Y	N
VIRGINIA							
1 **Wittman**	Y	Y	Y	Y	Y	N	Y
2 **Taylor**	Y	Y	Y	Y	Y	N	Y
3 Scott	Y	Y	?	N	Y	Y	N
4 McEachin	Y	Y	N	N	Y	Y	N
5 **Garrett**	Y	Y	Y	Y	N	N	Y
6 **Goodlatte**	Y	Y	Y	Y	Y	N	Y
7 **Brat**	Y	Y	Y	Y	Y	?	Y
8 Beyer	Y	Y	N	N	Y	Y	N
9 **Griffith**	Y	Y	Y	Y	Y	N	Y
10 **Comstock**	Y	Y	Y	Y	Y	N	Y
11 Connolly	Y	Y	N	N	Y	Y	N
WASHINGTON							
1 DelBene	Y	Y	N	N	Y	Y	N
2 Larsen	Y	Y	N	N	Y	Y	N
3 **Herrera Beutler**	Y	Y	Y	Y	Y	N	Y
4 **Newhouse**	Y	Y	Y	Y	Y	N	Y
5 **McMorris Rodgers**	Y	Y	Y	Y	Y	N	Y
6 Kilmer	Y	Y	N	N	Y	Y	N
7 Jayapal	Y	Y	N	N	Y	Y	N
8 **Reichert**	Y	Y	Y	Y	Y	N	Y
9 Smith	Y	Y	N	N	Y	Y	N
10 Heck	Y	Y	N	N	Y	Y	N
WEST VIRGINIA							
1 **McKinley**	Y	Y	Y	Y	Y	N	Y
2 **Mooney**	?	?	Y	Y	Y	N	Y
3 **Jenkins**	Y	Y	Y	Y	Y	N	Y
WISCONSIN							
1 **Ryan**							Y
2 Pocan	+	+	–	–	+	+	–
3 Kind	Y	Y	N	N	Y	Y	N
4 Moore	Y	Y	N	N	Y	Y	N
5 **Sensenbrenner**	Y	Y	Y	Y	Y	N	Y
6 **Grothman**	N	N	Y	Y	N	N	Y
7 **Duffy**	+	+	Y	Y	Y	N	Y
8 **Gallagher**	Y	Y	Y	Y	Y	N	Y
WYOMING							
AL **Cheney**	Y	Y	Y	Y	Y	N	Y

VOTE NUMBER

693. HR 4323. VETERANS STEM CAREERS/PASSAGE. Dunn, R-Fla., motion to suspend the rules and pass the bill that would require the National Science Foundation to develop a plan for veterans' outreach that would be required to include a report on existing outreach activities, identify the best way to support veterans in STEM careers and studies, and identify a method to track veteran participation in research and education programs. The bill would make veterans eligible for grants under the NSF Noyce Teacher Scholarship Program, which recruits and trains math and science teachers. Motion agreed to 420-1 : R 232-1; D 188-0. Dec. 19, 2017.

694. HR 3312. ENHANCED SUPERVISION ELIMINATION/PASSAGE. Passage of the bill that would modify the 2010 financial regulatory overhaul by eliminating the requirement for automatic enhanced supervision of bank holding companies with assets totaling more than $50 billion in value, and would require that the Federal Reserve make such designations for enhanced supervision based on factors including the bank's activities and relationships. Passed 288-130 : R 229-2; D 59-128. Dec. 19, 2017.

695. S 1536. DEPT. OF TRANSPORTATION HUMAN TRAFFICKING PREVENTION/PASSAGE. Graves, R-Mo., motion to suspend the rules and pass the bill that would require the Department of Transportation to designate a department official to coordinate with other federal agencies on human trafficking prevention efforts. The bill establishes an advisory committee on human trafficking. Motion agreed to 418-1 : R 230-1; D 188-0. Dec. 19, 2017.

696. PROCEDURAL MOTION/APPROVAL OF HOUSE JOURNAL. Approved 227-180 : R 143-84; D 84-96. Dec. 19, 2017.

697. H RES 668, HR 1. TAX OVERHAUL/RULE. Adoption of the rule (H Res 668) that would provide for House floor consideration of the Senate amendment to the tax overhaul (HR 1) that would provide for reconciliation pursuant to titles II and V of the concurrent resolution on the budget for fiscal year 2018. The Senate amendment to the tax overhaul bill would remove three provisions that violate the Congressional Budget Act. Adopted 232-190 : R 232-1; D 0-189. Dec. 20, 2017.

698. H RES 668, HR 1. TAX OVERHAUL/PREVIOUS QUESTION. Sessions, R-Texas, motion to order the previous question (thus ending debate and the possibility of amendment) on the rule (H Res 668) that would provide House floor consideration of the Senate amendment to the tax overhaul (HR 1) that would provide for reconciliation pursuant to titles II and V of the concurrent resolution on the budget for fiscal year 2018. The Senate amendment to the tax overhaul bill would remove three provisions that violate the Congressional Budget Act. Motion agreed to 234-188 : R 234-0; D 0-188. Dec. 20, 2017.

699. HR 1. TAX OVERHAUL/MOTION TO CONCUR. Brady, R-Texas, motion to concur in the Senate amendment to the tax overhaul that would revise the federal income tax system by: lowering the corporate tax rate from 35 percent to 21 percent; lowering individual tax rates through 2025; limiting state and local deductions to $10,000 through 2025; decreasing the limit on deductible mortgage debt through 2025; and creating a new system of taxing U.S. corporations with foreign subsidiaries. Specifically, it would repeal personal exemptions and would roughly double the standard deduction through 2025. It would raise the child tax credit to $2,000 through 2025, would repeal the alternative minimum tax for corporations and provide for broader exemptions to the tax for individuals through 2025. It would double individual exemptions to the estate tax and gift tax through 2025, and would establish a new top tax rate for "pass-through" business income through 2025. It would effectively eliminate the penalty for not purchasing health insurance under the 2010 health care overhaul law in 2019. It would also open portions of the Arctic National Wildlife Refuge to oil and gas drilling. Motion agreed to 224-201 : R 224-12; D 0-189. Dec. 20, 2017.

	693	694	695	696	697	698	699
ALABAMA							
1 Byrne	Y	Y	Y	N	Y	Y	Y
2 Roby	Y	Y	Y	Y	Y	Y	Y
3 Rogers	Y	Y	Y	N	Y	Y	Y
4 Aderholt	Y	Y	Y	Y	Y	Y	Y
5 Brooks	Y	?	?	?	?	?	?
6 Palmer	Y	Y	Y	N	Y	Y	Y
7 Sewell	Y	Y	Y	N	–	N	N
ALASKA							
AL Young	Y	Y	Y	Y	Y	Y	Y
ARIZONA							
1 O'Halleran	Y	Y	Y	N	N	N	N
2 McSally	Y	Y	Y	N	Y	Y	Y
3 Grijalva	Y	N	N	N	N	N	N
4 Gosar	Y	Y	Y	Y	Y	Y	Y
5 Biggs	Y	Y	Y	N	Y	Y	Y
6 Schweikert	Y	Y	Y	Y	Y	Y	Y
7 Gallego	Y	N	Y	N	N	N	N
9 Sinema	Y	Y	Y	N	N	N	N
ARKANSAS							
1 Crawford	Y	Y	Y	N	Y	Y	Y
2 Hill	Y	Y	Y	N	Y	Y	Y
3 Womack	Y	Y	Y	Y	Y	Y	Y
4 Westerman	Y	Y	Y	Y	Y	Y	Y
CALIFORNIA							
1 LaMalfa	Y	Y	Y	Y	Y	Y	Y
2 Huffman	Y	N	Y	N	N	N	N
3 Garamendi	Y	N	Y	?	N	N	N
4 McClintock	Y	Y	Y	Y	Y	Y	Y
5 Thompson	Y	N	Y	N	N	N	N
6 Matsui	Y	N	Y	N	N	N	N
7 Bera	Y	Y	Y	N	N	N	N
8 Cook	Y	Y	Y	Y	Y	Y	Y
9 McNerney	Y	N	Y	N	N	N	N
10 Denham	Y	Y	Y	N	Y	Y	Y
11 DeSaulnier	Y	N	Y	N	N	N	N
12 Pelosi	Y	N	Y	N	N	N	N
13 Lee	Y	N	Y	N	N	N	N
14 Speier	Y	N	Y	N	N	N	N
15 Swalwell	Y	N	Y	N	N	N	N
16 Costa	Y	Y	Y	N	N	N	N
17 Khanna	Y	N	Y	N	N	N	N
18 Eshoo	Y	N	Y	N	N	N	N
19 Lofgren	Y	N	Y	N	N	N	N
20 Panetta	Y	N	Y	N	N	N	N
21 Valadao	Y	Y	Y	N	Y	Y	Y
22 Nunes	Y	Y	Y	Y	Y	Y	Y
23 McCarthy	Y	Y	Y	Y	Y	Y	Y
24 Carbajal	Y	N	Y	N	N	N	N
25 Knight	Y	Y	Y	N	Y	Y	Y
26 Brownley	Y	Y	Y	N	N	N	N
27 Chu	Y	N	Y	N	N	N	N
28 Schiff	Y	N	Y	N	N	N	N
29 Cardenas	Y	Y	Y	N	N	N	N
30 Sherman	Y	Y	Y	N	N	N	N
31 Aguilar	Y	N	Y	N	N	N	N
32 Napolitano	Y	–	+	?	–	–	–
33 Lieu	Y	N	Y	?	N	N	N
34 Gomez	Y	N	Y	N	N	N	N
35 Torres	Y	Y	Y	N	N	N	N
36 Ruiz	Y	Y	Y	N	N	N	N
37 Bass	Y	N	Y	N	N	N	N
38 Sánchez, Linda	Y	N	Y	?	N	N	N
39 Royce	Y	Y	Y	Y	Y	Y	Y
40 Roybal-Allard	Y	N	Y	N	N	N	N
41 Takano	Y	N	Y	N	N	N	N
42 Calvert	Y	Y	Y	Y	Y	Y	Y
43 Waters	Y	N	Y	N	N	N	N
44 Barragan	Y	N	Y	N	N	N	N
45 Walters	Y	Y	Y	Y	Y	Y	Y
46 Correa	Y	Y	Y	?	N	N	N
47 Lowenthal	Y	N	Y	N	N	N	N
48 Rohrabacher	Y	Y	Y	N	Y	Y	N
49 Issa	Y	Y	Y	Y	Y	Y	Y
50 Hunter	Y	Y	Y	Y	Y	Y	Y
51 Vargas	Y	N	Y	N	N	N	N
52 Peters	Y	Y	Y	N	N	N	N
53 Davis	Y	N	Y	Y	N	N	N

	693	694	695	696	697	698	699
COLORADO							
1 DeGette	Y	N	Y	Y	N	N	N
2 Polis	Y	N	Y	N	N	N	N
3 Tipton	Y	Y	Y	N	Y	Y	Y
4 Buck	Y	Y	Y	N	Y	Y	Y
5 Lamborn	Y	Y	Y	Y	Y	Y	Y
6 Coffman	Y	Y	Y	Y	Y	Y	Y
7 Perlmutter	Y	N	Y	Y	N	N	N
CONNECTICUT							
1 Larson	Y	N	Y	N	N	N	N
2 Courtney	Y	Y	Y	N	N	N	N
3 DeLauro	Y	N	Y	N	N	N	N
4 Himes	Y	Y	Y	N	N	N	N
5 Esty	Y	Y	Y	N	N	N	N
DELAWARE							
AL Blunt Rochester	Y	Y	Y	N	N	N	N
FLORIDA							
1 Gaetz	?	Y	N	N	Y	Y	Y
2 Dunn	Y	Y	Y	Y	Y	Y	Y
3 Yoho	Y	Y	Y	Y	Y	Y	Y
4 Rutherford	Y	Y	Y	Y	Y	Y	Y
5 Lawson	Y	Y	Y	N	N	N	N
6 DeSantis	Y	Y	Y	N	Y	Y	Y
7 Murphy	Y	Y	Y	N	N	N	N
8 Posey	Y	Y	Y	Y	Y	Y	Y
9 Soto	Y	Y	Y	N	N	N	N
10 Demings	Y	Y	Y	N	N	N	N
11 Webster	Y	Y	Y	Y	Y	Y	Y
12 Bilirakis	Y	Y	Y	Y	Y	Y	Y
13 Crist	Y	Y	Y	N	N	N	N
14 Castor	Y	N	Y	N	N	N	N
15 Ross	Y	Y	Y	Y	Y	Y	Y
16 Buchanan	Y	Y	Y	Y	Y	Y	Y
17 Rooney, T.	Y	Y	Y	N	Y	Y	Y
18 Mast	Y	Y	Y	N	Y	Y	Y
19 Rooney, F.	Y	Y	Y	Y	Y	Y	Y
20 Hastings	Y	N	Y	N	N	N	N
21 Frankel	Y	N	Y	N	N	N	N
22 Deutch	Y	N	Y	N	N	N	N
23 Wasserman Schultz	Y	N	Y	N	N	N	N
24 Wilson	Y	N	Y	N	N	N	N
25 Diaz-Balart	Y	Y	Y	N	Y	Y	Y
26 Curbelo	Y	Y	Y	N	Y	Y	Y
27 Ros-Lehtinen	Y	Y	Y	N	Y	Y	Y
GEORGIA							
1 Carter	Y	Y	Y	N	Y	Y	Y
2 Bishop	Y	Y	Y	N	N	N	N
3 Ferguson	Y	Y	Y	Y	Y	Y	Y
4 Johnson	Y	N	Y	N	N	N	N
5 Lewis	?	N	Y	N	N	N	N
6 Handel	Y	Y	Y	Y	Y	Y	Y
7 Woodall	Y	Y	Y	Y	Y	Y	Y
8 Scott, A.	Y	Y	Y	N	Y	Y	Y
9 Collins	Y	Y	Y	Y	Y	Y	Y
10 Hice	Y	Y	Y	Y	Y	Y	Y
11 Loudermilk	?	?	?	?	Y	Y	Y
12 Allen	Y	Y	Y	Y	Y	Y	Y
13 Scott, D.	Y	Y	Y	N	N	N	N
14 Graves	Y	Y	Y	N	Y	Y	Y
HAWAII							
1 Hanabusa	Y	N	Y	N	N	N	N
2 Gabbard	Y	N	Y	N	N	N	N
IDAHO							
1 Labrador	Y	Y	Y	Y	Y	Y	Y
2 Simpson	Y	Y	Y	?	Y	Y	Y
ILLINOIS							
1 Rush	Y	N	Y	?	N	N	N
2 Kelly	Y	Y	Y	N	N	N	N
3 Lipinski	Y	Y	Y	N	N	N	N
4 Gutierrez	Y	N	Y	N	N	N	N
5 Quigley	Y	N	Y	N	N	N	N
6 Roskam	Y	Y	Y	N	Y	Y	Y
7 Davis, D.	Y	N	Y	N	N	N	N
8 Krishnamoorthi	Y	Y	Y	N	N	N	N
9 Schakowsky	Y	N	Y	N	N	N	N
10 Schneider	Y	Y	Y	N	N	N	N
11 Foster	Y	Y	Y	N	N	N	N
12 Bost	Y	Y	Y	N	Y	Y	Y
13 Davis, R.	Y	Y	Y	N	Y	Y	Y
14 Hultgren	Y	Y	Y	Y	Y	Y	Y
15 Shimkus	Y	Y	Y	Y	Y	Y	Y

KEY	Republicans	Democrats	Independents
Y Voted for (yea)		X Paired against	C Voted "present" to avoid possible conflict of interest
# Paired for		– Announced against	
+ Announced for		P Voted "present"	? Did not vote or otherwise make a position known
N Voted against (nay)			

	693	694	695	696	697	698	699
16 **Kinzinger**	Y	Y	Y	N	Y	Y	Y
17 Bustos	Y	N	Y	Y	N	N	N
18 **LaHood**	Y	Y	Y	N	Y	Y	Y
INDIANA							
1 Visclosky	Y	N	Y	N	N	N	N
2 **Walorski**	Y	Y	Y	Y	Y	Y	Y
3 **Banks**	Y	Y	Y	Y	Y	Y	Y
4 **Rokita**	Y	Y	Y	N	Y	Y	Y
5 **Brooks**	Y	Y	Y	Y	Y	Y	Y
6 **Messer**	Y	?	?	?	Y	Y	Y
7 Carson	Y	N	Y	N	N	N	N
8 **Bucshon**	Y	Y	Y	N	Y	Y	Y
9 **Hollingsworth**	Y	Y	Y	Y	Y	Y	Y
IOWA							
1 **Blum**	Y	Y	Y	Y	Y	Y	Y
2 Loebsack	Y	Y	Y	N	N	N	N
3 **Young**	Y	Y	Y	Y	Y	Y	Y
4 **King**	Y	Y	Y	Y	Y	Y	Y
KANSAS							
1 **Marshall**	Y	Y	Y	Y	Y	Y	Y
2 **Jenkins**	Y	Y	Y	N	Y	Y	Y
3 **Yoder**	Y	Y	Y	N	Y	Y	Y
4 **Estes**	Y	Y	Y	Y	Y	Y	Y
KENTUCKY							
1 **Comer**	Y	Y	Y	N	Y	Y	Y
2 **Guthrie**	Y	Y	Y	Y	Y	Y	Y
3 Yarmuth	Y	N	Y	Y	N	N	N
4 **Massie**	Y	Y	Y	Y	Y	Y	Y
5 **Rogers**	Y	Y	Y	Y	Y	Y	Y
6 **Barr**	Y	Y	Y	Y	Y	Y	Y
LOUISIANA							
1 **Scalise**	Y	+	+	+	Y	Y	Y
2 Richmond	Y	Y	Y	N	N	N	N
3 **Higgins**	Y	Y	Y	Y	Y	Y	Y
4 **Johnson**	Y	Y	Y	Y	Y	Y	Y
5 **Abraham**	Y	Y	Y	Y	Y	Y	Y
6 **Graves**	Y	Y	Y	N	Y	Y	Y
MAINE							
1 Pingree	Y	N	Y	Y	N	N	N
2 **Poliquin**	Y	Y	Y	N	Y	Y	Y
MARYLAND							
1 **Harris**	Y	Y	Y	Y	Y	Y	Y
2 Ruppersberger	Y	N	Y	Y	N	N	N
3 Sarbanes	Y	N	Y	N	N	N	N
4 Brown	Y	Y	Y	N	N	N	N
5 Hoyer	Y	N	Y	N	N	N	N
6 Delaney	Y	Y	Y	N	N	N	N
7 Cummings	Y	?	?	?	N	N	N
8 Raskin	Y	N	Y	N	N	N	N
MASSACHUSETTS							
1 Neal	Y	N	Y	N	N	N	N
2 McGovern	Y	N	Y	N	N	N	N
3 Tsongas	Y	N	Y	N	N	N	N
4 Kennedy	?	?	?	?	?	?	?
5 Clark	Y	N	Y	N	N	N	N
6 Moulton	Y	N	Y	Y	N	N	N
7 Capuano	Y	N	Y	N	N	N	N
8 Lynch	Y	–	Y	N	N	N	N
9 Keating	?	N	Y	N	N	N	N
MICHIGAN							
1 **Bergman**	Y	Y	Y	Y	Y	Y	Y
2 **Huizenga**	Y	Y	Y	Y	Y	Y	Y
3 **Amash**	N	Y	Y	N	Y	Y	Y
4 **Moolenaar**	Y	Y	Y	Y	Y	Y	Y
5 Kildee	Y	N	Y	Y	N	N	N
6 **Upton**	Y	Y	Y	N	Y	Y	Y
7 **Walberg**	Y	Y	Y	N	Y	Y	Y
8 **Bishop**	?	Y	Y	Y	Y	Y	Y
9 Levin	Y	N	Y	N	N	N	N
10 **Mitchell**	Y	Y	Y	Y	Y	Y	Y
11 **Trott**	Y	Y	Y	Y	Y	Y	Y
12 Dingell	Y	N	Y	Y	N	N	N
13 Vacant							
14 Lawrence	Y	N	Y	Y	N	N	N
MINNESOTA							
1 Walz	Y	N	Y	Y	N	N	N
2 **Lewis**	Y	Y	Y	Y	Y	Y	Y
3 **Paulsen**	Y	Y	Y	N	Y	Y	Y
4 McCollum	Y	N	Y	Y	N	N	N

	693	694	695	696	697	698	699
5 Ellison	Y	N	Y	Y	N	N	N
6 **Emmer**	Y	Y	Y	N	Y	Y	Y
7 Peterson	Y	Y	Y	N	N	N	N
8 Nolan	Y	N	Y	N	N	N	N
MISSISSIPPI							
1 **Kelly**	Y	Y	Y	Y	Y	Y	Y
2 Thompson	Y	N	?	?	?	?	?
3 **Harper**	Y	Y	Y	Y	Y	Y	Y
4 **Palazzo**	Y	Y	Y	N	Y	Y	Y
MISSOURI							
1 Clay	Y	Y	Y	Y	N	N	N
2 **Wagner**	Y	Y	Y	Y	Y	Y	Y
3 **Luetkemeyer**	Y	Y	Y	Y	Y	Y	Y
4 **Hartzler**	Y	Y	Y	Y	Y	Y	Y
5 Cleaver	Y	N	Y	N	N	N	N
6 **Graves**	Y	Y	Y	N	Y	Y	Y
7 **Long**	Y	Y	Y	Y	Y	Y	Y
8 **Smith**	Y	Y	Y	Y	Y	Y	Y
MONTANA							
AL **Gianforte**	Y	Y	Y	Y	Y	Y	Y
NEBRASKA							
1 **Fortenberry**	Y	Y	Y	Y	Y	Y	Y
2 **Bacon**	Y	Y	Y	Y	Y	Y	Y
3 **Smith**	Y	Y	Y	Y	Y	Y	Y
NEVADA							
1 Titus	Y	N	Y	Y	N	N	N
2 **Amodei**	Y	Y	Y	Y	Y	Y	Y
3 Rosen	Y	Y	Y	N	N	N	N
4 Kihuen	Y	Y	Y	N	N	N	N
NEW HAMPSHIRE							
1 Shea-Porter	Y	N	Y	Y	N	N	N
2 Kuster	Y	N	Y	Y	N	N	N
NEW JERSEY							
1 Norcross	Y	N	Y	N	N	N	N
2 **LoBiondo**	Y	Y	Y	N	Y	Y	N
3 **MacArthur**	Y	Y	Y	N	Y	Y	Y
4 **Smith**	Y	Y	Y	Y	Y	Y	N
5 Gottheimer	Y	Y	Y	N	N	N	N
6 Pallone	Y	N	Y	N	N	N	N
7 **Lance**	Y	Y	Y	N	Y	Y	N
8 Sires	Y	N	Y	N	N	N	N
9 Pascrell	Y	N	Y	N	N	N	N
10 Payne	Y	N	Y	N	N	N	N
11 **Frelinghuysen**	Y	Y	Y	Y	Y	Y	N
12 Watson Coleman	Y	N	Y	N	N	N	N
NEW MEXICO							
1 Lujan Grisham	Y	N	Y	Y	N	N	N
2 **Pearce**	Y	Y	Y	N	Y	Y	Y
3 Luján	Y	N	Y	N	N	N	N
NEW YORK							
1 **Zeldin**	Y	Y	Y	N	Y	Y	N
2 **King**	Y	Y	Y	N	Y	Y	N
3 Suozzi	Y	Y	Y	Y	N	N	N
4 Rice	Y	Y	Y	N	N	N	N
5 Meeks	Y	Y	Y	Y	N	N	N
6 Meng	Y	N	Y	Y	N	N	N
7 Velázquez	Y	N	Y	N	N	N	N
8 Jeffries	Y	?	Y	Y	N	N	N
9 Clarke	Y	N	Y	N	N	N	N
10 Nadler	Y	N	Y	Y	N	N	N
11 **Donovan**	Y	Y	Y	Y	Y	Y	N
12 Maloney, C.	Y	N	Y	N	N	N	N
13 Espaillat	Y	N	Y	N	N	N	N
14 Crowley	Y	N	Y	N	N	N	N
15 Serrano	?	N	Y	N	N	N	N
16 Engel	Y	N	Y	Y	N	N	N
17 Lowey	Y	N	Y	N	N	N	N
18 Maloney, S.P.	Y	Y	Y	N	N	N	N
19 **Faso**	Y	Y	Y	N	Y	Y	N
20 Tonko	Y	N	Y	P	N	N	N
21 **Stefanik**	Y	Y	Y	Y	Y	Y	N
22 **Tenney**	Y	Y	Y	N	Y	Y	Y
23 **Reed**	Y	Y	Y	N	Y	Y	Y
24 **Katko**	Y	Y	Y	N	Y	Y	Y
25 Slaughter	Y	N	Y	N	N	N	N
26 Higgins	Y	Y	Y	Y	N	N	N
27 **Collins**	Y	Y	Y	Y	Y	Y	Y
NORTH CAROLINA							
1 Butterfield	Y	N	Y	Y	N	N	N
2 **Holding**	Y	Y	Y	N	Y	Y	Y
3 **Jones**	Y	N	Y	N	Y	N	N
4 Price	Y	N	Y	N	N	N	N

	693	694	695	696	697	698	699
5 **Foxx**	Y	Y	Y	N	Y	Y	Y
6 **Walker**	Y	Y	Y	Y	Y	Y	Y
7 **Rouzer**	Y	Y	Y	N	Y	Y	Y
8 **Hudson**	Y	Y	Y	N	Y	Y	Y
9 **Pittenger**	Y	Y	Y	N	Y	Y	Y
10 **McHenry**	Y	Y	Y	Y	Y	Y	Y
11 **Meadows**	Y	Y	Y	Y	Y	Y	Y
12 Adams	Y	N	Y	N	N	N	N
13 **Budd**	Y	Y	Y	Y	Y	Y	Y
NORTH DAKOTA							
AL **Cramer**	Y	Y	Y	Y	Y	Y	Y
OHIO							
1 **Chabot**	Y	Y	Y	Y	Y	Y	Y
2 **Wenstrup**	Y	Y	Y	Y	Y	Y	Y
3 Beatty	Y	Y	Y	Y	N	N	N
4 **Jordan**	Y	Y	Y	N	Y	Y	Y
5 **Latta**	Y	Y	Y	Y	Y	Y	Y
6 **Johnson**	Y	Y	Y	N	Y	Y	Y
7 **Gibbs**	Y	Y	Y	Y	Y	Y	Y
8 **Davidson**	Y	Y	Y	Y	Y	Y	Y
9 Kaptur	Y	N	Y	Y	N	N	N
10 **Turner**	Y	Y	Y	N	Y	Y	Y
11 Fudge	Y	N	Y	N	N	N	N
12 **Tiberi**	Y	Y	Y	Y	Y	Y	Y
13 Ryan	Y	N	Y	N	N	N	N
14 **Joyce**	Y	Y	Y	N	Y	Y	Y
15 **Stivers**	Y	Y	Y	N	Y	Y	Y
16 **Renacci**	Y	+	+	+	+	+	+
OKLAHOMA							
1 **Bridenstine**	?	?	?	?	?	?	Y
2 **Mullin**	Y	Y	Y	Y	Y	Y	Y
3 **Lucas**	Y	Y	Y	Y	Y	Y	Y
4 **Cole**	Y	Y	Y	Y	Y	Y	Y
5 **Russell**	Y	Y	Y	Y	Y	Y	Y
OREGON							
1 Bonamici	Y	N	Y	N	N	N	N
2 **Walden**	Y	Y	Y	Y	Y	Y	Y
3 Blumenauer	Y	N	Y	Y	N	N	N
4 DeFazio	Y	N	Y	N	N	N	N
5 Schrader	Y	Y	Y	N	N	N	N
PENNSYLVANIA							
1 Brady	Y	N	Y	N	N	N	N
2 Evans	Y	N	Y	Y	N	N	N
3 **Kelly**	Y	Y	Y	Y	Y	Y	Y
4 **Perry**	Y	Y	Y	N	Y	Y	Y
5 **Thompson**	Y	Y	Y	N	Y	Y	Y
6 **Costello**	Y	Y	Y	Y	Y	Y	Y
7 **Meehan**	Y	Y	Y	N	Y	Y	Y
8 **Fitzpatrick**	Y	Y	Y	N	Y	Y	Y
9 **Shuster**	Y	Y	Y	Y	Y	Y	Y
10 **Marino**	Y	Y	Y	Y	Y	Y	Y
11 **Barletta**	Y	Y	Y	Y	Y	Y	Y
12 **Rothfus**	Y	Y	Y	Y	Y	Y	Y
13 Boyle	Y	N	Y	N	N	N	N
14 Doyle	Y	N	Y	N	N	N	N
15 **Dent**	Y	Y	Y	Y	Y	Y	Y
16 **Smucker**	Y	Y	Y	N	Y	Y	Y
17 Cartwright	Y	N	Y	Y	N	N	N
RHODE ISLAND							
1 Cicilline	Y	N	Y	Y	N	N	N
2 Langevin	Y	N	Y	N	N	N	N
SOUTH CAROLINA							
1 **Sanford**	Y	Y	Y	Y	Y	Y	Y
2 **Wilson**	Y	Y	Y	Y	Y	Y	Y
3 **Duncan**	Y	Y	Y	Y	Y	Y	Y
4 **Gowdy**	Y	Y	Y	Y	Y	Y	Y
5 **Norman**	Y	Y	Y	Y	Y	Y	Y
6 Clyburn	Y	N	Y	N	N	N	N
7 **Rice**	Y	Y	Y	Y	Y	Y	Y
SOUTH DAKOTA							
AL **Noem**	Y	Y	Y	Y	Y	Y	Y
TENNESSEE							
1 **Roe**	Y	Y	Y	Y	Y	Y	Y
2 **Duncan**	Y	N	Y	Y	Y	Y	Y
3 **Fleischmann**	Y	Y	Y	Y	Y	Y	Y
4 **DesJarlais**	Y	Y	Y	Y	Y	Y	Y
5 Cooper	Y	Y	Y	Y	N	N	N
6 **Black**	Y	Y	Y	Y	Y	Y	Y
7 **Blackburn**	Y	Y	Y	N	Y	Y	Y
8 **Kustoff**	Y	Y	Y	Y	Y	Y	Y
9 Cohen	Y	N	Y	N	N	N	N

	693	694	695	696	697	698	699
TEXAS							
1 **Gohmert**	Y	Y	Y	?	Y	Y	Y
2 **Poe**	Y	Y	Y	N	Y	Y	Y
3 **Johnson, S.**	Y	Y	Y	Y	Y	Y	Y
4 **Ratcliffe**	Y	Y	Y	N	Y	Y	Y
5 **Hensarling**	Y	Y	Y	Y	Y	Y	Y
6 **Barton**	Y	Y	Y	N	Y	Y	Y
7 **Culberson**	Y	Y	Y	Y	Y	Y	Y
8 **Brady**	Y	Y	Y	Y	Y	Y	Y
9 Green, A.	Y	N	Y	Y	N	N	N
10 **McCaul**	Y	Y	Y	?	Y	Y	Y
11 **Conaway**	Y	Y	Y	N	Y	Y	Y
12 **Granger**	Y	Y	Y	Y	Y	Y	Y
13 **Thornberry**	Y	Y	Y	Y	Y	Y	Y
14 **Weber**	Y	Y	Y	Y	Y	Y	Y
15 Gonzalez	Y	Y	Y	N	N	N	N
16 O'Rourke	Y	N	Y	Y	N	N	N
17 **Flores**	Y	Y	Y	N	Y	Y	Y
18 Jackson Lee	Y	N	Y	N	N	N	N
19 **Arrington**	?	Y	Y	Y	Y	Y	Y
20 Castro	Y	N	Y	Y	N	N	N
21 **Smith**	Y	?	?	?	?	?	?
22 **Olson**	Y	Y	Y	Y	Y	Y	Y
23 **Hurd**	Y	Y	Y	Y	Y	Y	Y
24 **Marchant**	Y	Y	Y	Y	Y	Y	Y
25 **Williams**	Y	Y	Y	Y	Y	Y	Y
26 **Burgess**	Y	Y	Y	N	Y	Y	Y
27 **Farenthold**	Y	Y	Y	?	Y	Y	Y
28 Cuellar	Y	Y	Y	Y	N	N	N
29 Green, G.	Y	Y	Y	N	N	N	N
30 Johnson, E.B.	Y	Y	Y	Y	N	N	N
31 **Carter**	Y	Y	Y	Y	Y	Y	Y
32 **Sessions**	Y	Y	Y	Y	Y	Y	Y
33 Veasey	Y	Y	Y	N	N	N	N
34 Vela	Y	Y	Y	?	N	N	N
35 Doggett	Y	N	Y	Y	N	N	N
36 **Babin**	Y	Y	Y	Y	Y	Y	Y
UTAH							
1 **Bishop**	Y	Y	Y	Y	Y	?	Y
2 **Stewart**	Y	Y	Y	Y	Y	Y	Y
3 **Curtis**	Y	Y	Y	Y	Y	Y	Y
4 **Love**	Y	Y	Y	Y	Y	Y	Y
VERMONT							
AL Welch	Y	N	Y	Y	N	N	N
VIRGINIA							
1 **Wittman**	Y	Y	Y	N	Y	Y	Y
2 **Taylor**	Y	Y	Y	Y	Y	Y	Y
3 Scott	Y	N	Y	Y	N	N	N
4 McEachin	Y	Y	Y	Y	N	N	N
5 **Garrett**	Y	Y	Y	N	Y	Y	Y
6 **Goodlatte**	Y	Y	Y	Y	Y	Y	Y
7 **Brat**	Y	Y	Y	Y	Y	Y	Y
8 Beyer	Y	Y	Y	?	N	N	N
9 **Griffith**	Y	Y	Y	Y	Y	Y	Y
10 **Comstock**	Y	Y	Y	Y	Y	Y	Y
11 Connolly	Y	Y	Y	N	N	N	N
WASHINGTON							
1 DelBene	Y	N	Y	N	N	N	N
2 Larsen	Y	Y	Y	Y	N	N	N
3 **Herrera Beutler**	Y	Y	Y	N	Y	Y	Y
4 **Newhouse**	Y	Y	Y	Y	Y	Y	Y
5 **McMorris Rodgers**	Y	Y	Y	Y	Y	Y	Y
6 Kilmer	Y	Y	Y	N	N	N	N
7 Jayapal	Y	N	Y	N	N	N	N
8 **Reichert**	Y	Y	Y	N	Y	Y	Y
9 Smith	Y	N	Y	Y	N	N	N
10 Heck	Y	Y	Y	Y	N	N	N
WEST VIRGINIA							
1 **McKinley**	Y	Y	Y	N	Y	Y	Y
2 **Mooney**	Y	Y	Y	Y	Y	Y	Y
3 **Jenkins**	Y	Y	Y	N	Y	Y	Y
WISCONSIN							
1 **Ryan**							Y
2 Pocan	+	–	+	?	–	–	–
3 Kind	Y	Y	Y	N	N	N	N
4 Moore	Y	N	Y	N	N	N	N
5 **Sensenbrenner**	Y	Y	Y	N	Y	Y	Y
6 **Grothman**	Y	Y	Y	Y	Y	Y	Y
7 **Duffy**	Y	Y	Y	Y	Y	Y	Y
8 **Gallagher**	Y	Y	Y	N	Y	Y	Y
WYOMING							
AL **Cheney**	Y	Y	Y	N	Y	Y	Y

VOTE NUMBER

700. HR 1159. U.S.-ISRAEL SPACE AGENCY COOPERATION/PASSAGE.
Dunn, R-Fla., motion to suspend the rules and pass the bill that would require the NASA administrator to work with the Israel Space Agency to identify and cooperatively pursue peaceful space exploration and science initiatives in areas of mutual interest. Motion agreed to 411-0 : R 227-0; D 184-0. Dec. 20, 2017.

701. HR 4015. PROXY ADVISORY FIRM REGISTRATION REQUIREMENT/ RECOMMIT. Sarbanes, D-Md., motion to recommit the bill to the House Financial Services Committee with instructions to report it back immediately with an amendment that would prohibit draft recommendations, as defined in the bill, from including "proxy voting recommendations on shareholder proposals related to political campaign contributions of a company." Motion rejected 189-231 : R 1-231; D 188-0. Dec. 20, 2017.

702. HR 4015. PROXY ADVISORY FIRM REGISTRATION REQUIREMENT/ PASSAGE. Passage of the bill that would require proxy advisory firms to register with the Securities and Exchange Commission. The bill would require such firms to disclose potential conflicts of interest, disclose whether they have a code of ethics, and make publicly available their methodologies for formulating proxy recommendations and analyses. Passed 238-182 : R 226-6; D 12-176. Dec. 20, 2017.

703. PROCEDURAL MOTION/APPROVAL OF HOUSE JOURNAL. Approved 217-194 : R 143-85; D 74-109. Dec. 20, 2017.

704. HR 1370, HR 4667, H RES 670. SHORT-TERM FISCAL 2018 CONTINU- ING APPROPRIATIONS AND SUPPLEMENTAL DISASTER APPROPRIA- TIONS/PREVIOUS QUESTION. Woodall, R-Ga., motion to order the previous question (thus ending debate and the possibility of amendment) on the rule (H Res 670) that would provide for House floor consideration of the Sen- ate amendment to the Department of Homeland Security Blue Campaign Authorization Act (HR 1370) that would fund government operations and certain programs through Jan. 19, 2018, and the disaster supplemental ap- propriations for fiscal 2018 (HR 4667) that would make further supplemental appropriations for disaster assistance for Hurricane Harvey, Irma, and Maria and calendar year 2017 wildfires. Motion agreed to 232-188 : R 232-0; D 0-188. Dec. 21, 2017.

705. HR 1370, HR 4667, H RES 670. SHORT-TERM FISCAL 2018 CONTINUING APPROPRIATIONS AND SUPPLEMENTAL DISASTER APPROPRIATIONS/RULE. Adoption of the rule (H Res 670) that would pro- vide for House floor consideration of the Senate amendment to the Depart- ment of Homeland Security Blue Campaign Authorization Act (HR 1370) that would fund government operations and certain programs through Jan. 19, 2018, and the disaster supplemental appropriations for fiscal 2018 (HR 4667) that would make further supplemental appropriations for disaster assistance for Hurricane Harvey, Irma, and Maria and calendar year 2017 wildfires. Ad- opted 228-188 : R 228-2; D 0-186. Dec. 21, 2017.

706. S 1393. VETERAN COMMERCIAL DRIVERS LICENSE/PASSAGE.
Graves, R-Mo., motion to suspend the rules and pass the bill (S 1393) that would expand the list of qualified medical professionals the Department of Veterans Affairs would allow to conduct medical examinations necessary for a commercial driver's license. The bill would exempt current members of the armed services and reservists from certain testing requirements if they had qualifying experiences while serving in the military. Motion agreed to 418-0 : R 231-0; D 187-0. Dec. 21, 2017.

	700	701	702	703	704	705	706
ALABAMA							
1 **Byrne**	Y	N	Y	N	Y	Y	Y
2 **Roby**	Y	N	Y	Y	Y	Y	Y
3 **Rogers**	Y	N	Y	N	Y	Y	Y
4 **Aderholt**	Y	N	Y	Y	Y	Y	Y
5 **Brooks**	?	?	?	?	?	?	?
6 **Palmer**	Y	N	Y	N	Y	?	Y
7 Sewell	Y	Y	N	N	N	N	Y
ALASKA							
AL **Young**	?	N	Y	N	Y	Y	Y
ARIZONA							
1 O'Halleran	Y	Y	N	N	N	N	Y
2 **McSally**	Y	N	Y	N	Y	Y	Y
3 Grijalva	Y	Y	N	N	N	N	Y
4 **Gosar**	Y	N	Y	N	Y	?	?
5 **Biggs**	Y	N	N	N	Y	Y	Y
6 **Schweikert**	Y	N	Y	Y	Y	Y	Y
7 Gallego	Y	Y	N	N	N	N	Y
9 Sinema	Y	Y	Y	N	N	N	Y
ARKANSAS							
1 **Crawford**	Y	N	Y	N	Y	Y	Y
2 **Hill**	Y	N	Y	Y	Y	Y	Y
3 **Womack**	Y	N	Y	Y	Y	Y	Y
4 **Westerman**	Y	N	Y	Y	Y	Y	Y
CALIFORNIA							
1 **LaMalfa**	?	N	Y	Y	Y	Y	Y
2 Huffman	Y	Y	N	Y	N	N	Y
3 Garamendi	Y	Y	N	Y	N	?	?
4 **McClintock**	Y	N	N	Y	Y	Y	Y
5 Thompson	Y	Y	N	N	N	N	Y
6 Matsui	Y	Y	N	N	N	N	Y
7 Bera	Y	Y	N	N	N	N	Y
8 **Cook**	Y	N	Y	Y	Y	Y	Y
9 McNerney	Y	Y	N	N	N	N	Y
10 **Denham**	Y	N	Y	N	Y	Y	Y
11 DeSaulnier	Y	Y	N	N	N	N	Y
12 Pelosi	Y	Y	N	N	N	N	Y
13 Lee	Y	Y	N	N	N	N	Y
14 Speier	Y	Y	N	N	N	N	Y
15 Swalwell	Y	Y	N	N	N	N	Y
16 Costa	Y	Y	N	N	N	N	Y
17 Khanna	Y	Y	N	N	N	N	Y
18 Eshoo	Y	Y	N	N	N	N	Y
19 Lofgren	Y	Y	N	N	N	N	Y
20 Panetta	Y	Y	N	N	N	N	Y
21 **Valadao**	Y	N	Y	N	Y	Y	Y
22 **Nunes**	Y	N	Y	Y	Y	Y	Y
23 **McCarthy**	Y	N	Y	Y	Y	Y	Y
24 Carbajal	Y	Y	N	N	N	N	Y
25 **Knight**	Y	N	Y	N	Y	Y	Y
26 Brownley	Y	Y	N	N	N	N	Y
27 Chu	Y	Y	N	N	N	N	Y
28 Schiff	Y	Y	N	N	N	N	Y
29 Cardenas	Y	Y	N	N	N	N	Y
30 Sherman	Y	Y	N	N	N	N	Y
31 Aguilar	Y	Y	N	N	N	N	Y
32 Napolitano	+	+	–	–	–	–	–
33 Lieu	Y	Y	N	?	N	N	Y
34 Gomez	Y	Y	N	N	N	N	Y
35 Torres	?	Y	N	N	N	N	Y
36 Ruiz	Y	Y	N	N	N	N	Y
37 Bass	Y	Y	N	N	N	N	Y
38 Sánchez, Linda	Y	Y	N	N	N	N	Y
39 **Royce**	Y	N	Y	Y	Y	Y	Y
40 Roybal-Allard	Y	Y	N	N	N	N	Y
41 Takano	Y	Y	N	N	N	N	Y
42 **Calvert**	Y	N	Y	Y	Y	Y	Y
43 Waters	Y	Y	N	N	N	N	Y
44 Barragan	Y	Y	N	N	N	N	Y
45 **Walters**	Y	N	Y	Y	Y	Y	Y
46 Correa	Y	Y	N	N	N	N	Y
47 Lowenthal	Y	Y	N	N	N	N	Y
48 **Rohrabacher**	Y	N	N	N	Y	Y	Y
49 **Issa**	Y	N	Y	Y	Y	Y	Y
50 **Hunter**	Y	N	Y	Y	Y	Y	Y
51 Vargas	Y	Y	N	N	N	N	Y
52 Peters	Y	Y	Y	Y	N	N	Y
53 Davis	Y	Y	N	Y	N	N	Y

	700	701	702	703	704	705	706
COLORADO							
1 DeGette	Y	Y	N	Y	N	N	Y
2 Polis	Y	Y	N	N	N	N	Y
3 **Tipton**	Y	N	Y	N	Y	Y	Y
4 **Buck**	Y	N	Y	N	Y	Y	Y
5 **Lamborn**	Y	N	Y	Y	Y	Y	Y
6 **Coffman**	Y	N	Y	N	Y	Y	Y
7 Perlmutter	Y	Y	N	Y	N	N	Y
CONNECTICUT							
1 Larson	Y	Y	N	N	N	N	Y
2 Courtney	Y	Y	N	N	N	N	Y
3 DeLauro	Y	Y	N	N	N	N	Y
4 Himes	Y	Y	Y	N	N	N	Y
5 Esty	Y	Y	N	N	N	N	Y
DELAWARE							
AL Blunt Rochester	Y	Y	N	N	N	N	Y
FLORIDA							
1 **Gaetz**	Y	N	Y	?	Y	Y	Y
2 **Dunn**	Y	N	Y	Y	Y	Y	Y
3 **Yoho**	Y	N	Y	Y	Y	Y	Y
4 **Rutherford**	Y	N	Y	Y	Y	Y	Y
5 Lawson	Y	Y	N	N	N	N	Y
6 **DeSantis**	Y	N	Y	Y	Y	Y	Y
7 Murphy	Y	Y	N	N	N	N	Y
8 **Posey**	Y	N	Y	Y	Y	Y	Y
9 Soto	Y	Y	N	N	N	N	Y
10 Demings	Y	Y	N	N	N	N	Y
11 **Webster**	Y	N	Y	Y	Y	Y	Y
12 **Bilirakis**	Y	N	Y	Y	Y	Y	Y
13 Crist	Y	Y	N	Y	N	N	Y
14 Castor	Y	Y	N	?	N	N	Y
15 **Ross**	Y	N	Y	Y	Y	Y	Y
16 **Buchanan**	?	N	Y	Y	Y	Y	Y
17 **Rooney, T.**	Y	N	Y	Y	Y	Y	Y
18 **Mast**	Y	N	Y	N	Y	Y	Y
19 **Rooney, F.**	Y	N	Y	Y	Y	Y	Y
20 Hastings	Y	Y	N	N	N	N	Y
21 Frankel	Y	Y	N	Y	N	N	Y
22 Deutch	Y	Y	N	Y	N	N	Y
23 Wasserman Schultz	Y	Y	N	N	N	N	Y
24 Wilson	Y	?	?	?	N	N	Y
25 **Diaz-Balart**	Y	N	Y	N	Y	Y	Y
26 **Curbelo**	Y	N	Y	N	Y	Y	Y
27 **Ros-Lehtinen**	Y	N	Y	N	Y	Y	Y
GEORGIA							
1 **Carter**	Y	N	Y	N	Y	Y	Y
2 Bishop	?	Y	N	N	N	N	Y
3 **Ferguson**	Y	N	Y	Y	Y	Y	Y
4 Johnson	Y	Y	N	N	N	N	Y
5 Lewis	Y	Y	N	N	N	N	Y
6 **Handel**	Y	N	Y	Y	Y	Y	Y
7 **Woodall**	Y	N	Y	Y	Y	Y	Y
8 **Scott, A.**	Y	N	Y	N	Y	Y	Y
9 **Collins**	Y	N	Y	Y	Y	Y	Y
10 **Hice**	Y	N	Y	Y	Y	Y	Y
11 **Loudermilk**	Y	N	Y	Y	Y	Y	Y
12 **Allen**	Y	N	Y	Y	Y	Y	Y
13 Scott, D.	Y	Y	N	Y	N	N	Y
14 **Graves**	Y	N	Y	Y	Y	Y	Y
HAWAII							
1 Hanabusa	Y	Y	N	N	N	N	Y
2 Gabbard	Y	Y	N	N	N	N	Y
IDAHO							
1 **Labrador**	Y	N	Y	Y	Y	Y	Y
2 **Simpson**	Y	?	?	?	Y	Y	Y
ILLINOIS							
1 Rush	Y	Y	N	N	N	N	Y
2 Kelly	Y	Y	N	N	N	N	Y
3 Lipinski	Y	Y	N	N	N	N	Y
4 Gutierrez	Y	Y	N	N	N	N	Y
5 Quigley	Y	Y	N	Y	N	N	Y
6 **Roskam**	Y	N	Y	N	Y	Y	Y
7 Davis, D.	Y	Y	N	N	N	N	Y
8 Krishnamoorthi	Y	Y	N	N	N	N	Y
9 Schakowsky	Y	Y	N	N	N	N	Y
10 Schneider	Y	Y	N	Y	N	N	Y
11 Foster	Y	Y	Y	Y	?	?	Y
12 **Bost**	Y	N	Y	Y	Y	Y	Y
13 **Davis, R.**	Y	N	Y	Y	Y	Y	Y
14 **Hultgren**	Y	N	Y	Y	Y	Y	Y
15 **Shimkus**	Y	N	Y	Y	Y	Y	Y

	700	701	702	703	704	705	706
16 **Kinzinger**	Y	N	Y	N	Y	Y	Y
17 Bustos	Y	Y	N	Y	N	N	Y
18 **LaHood**	Y	N	Y	N	Y	Y	Y
INDIANA							
1 Visclosky	Y	Y	N	N	N	N	Y
2 **Walorski**	Y	N	Y	Y	Y	Y	Y
3 **Banks**	Y	N	Y	Y	Y	Y	Y
4 **Rokita**	Y	N	Y	N	Y	Y	Y
5 **Brooks**	Y	N	Y	Y	Y	Y	Y
6 **Messer**	Y	N	Y	Y	Y	Y	Y
7 Carson	Y	Y	N	Y	N	N	Y
8 **Bucshon**	Y	N	Y	N	Y	Y	Y
9 **Hollingsworth**	Y	N	Y	Y	Y	Y	Y
IOWA							
1 **Blum**	Y	N	Y	N	Y	Y	Y
2 Loebsack	Y	Y	N	N	N	N	Y
3 **Young**	Y	N	Y	Y	Y	Y	Y
4 **King**	Y	N	Y	Y	Y	Y	Y
KANSAS							
1 **Marshall**	Y	N	Y	N	Y	Y	Y
2 **Jenkins**	Y	N	Y	N	Y	Y	Y
3 **Yoder**	Y	N	Y	N	Y	Y	Y
4 **Estes**	Y	N	Y	Y	Y	Y	Y
KENTUCKY							
1 **Comer**	Y	N	Y	N	Y	Y	Y
2 **Guthrie**	Y	N	Y	Y	Y	Y	Y
3 Yarmuth	Y	Y	N	Y	N	N	Y
4 **Massie**	Y	N	N	Y	Y	N	Y
5 **Rogers**	Y	N	Y	Y	Y	Y	Y
6 **Barr**	Y	N	Y	Y	Y	Y	Y
LOUISIANA							
1 **Scalise**	Y	N	Y	Y	Y	Y	Y
2 Richmond	Y	Y	N	N	N	N	Y
3 **Higgins**	Y	N	Y	Y	Y	Y	Y
4 **Johnson**	Y	N	Y	Y	Y	Y	Y
5 **Abraham**	Y	N	Y	Y	Y	Y	Y
6 **Graves**	Y	N	Y	?	Y	Y	Y
MAINE							
1 Pingree	Y	Y	N	Y	N	N	Y
2 **Poliquin**	Y	N	Y	N	Y	Y	Y
MARYLAND							
1 **Harris**	Y	N	Y	Y	Y	Y	Y
2 Ruppersberger	Y	Y	N	Y	N	N	Y
3 Sarbanes	Y	Y	N	N	N	N	Y
4 Brown	Y	Y	N	Y	N	N	Y
5 Hoyer	Y	Y	N	N	N	N	Y
6 Delaney	Y	Y	Y	N	N	N	Y
7 Cummings	Y	Y	N	N	N	N	Y
8 Raskin	?	Y	N	N	N	N	Y
MASSACHUSETTS							
1 Neal	Y	Y	N	N	N	N	Y
2 McGovern	Y	Y	N	N	N	N	Y
3 Tsongas	Y	Y	N	Y	N	N	Y
4 Kennedy	?	?	?	?	?	?	?
5 Clark	Y	Y	N	Y	N	N	Y
6 Moulton	Y	Y	N	Y	N	N	Y
7 Capuano	Y	Y	N	N	N	N	Y
8 Lynch	Y	Y	N	N	N	N	Y
9 Keating	Y	Y	N	N	N	N	Y
MICHIGAN							
1 **Bergman**	Y	N	Y	Y	Y	Y	Y
2 **Huizenga**	Y	N	Y	Y	Y	Y	Y
3 **Amash**	Y	N	N	N	Y	N	Y
4 **Moolenaar**	Y	N	Y	Y	Y	Y	Y
5 Kildee	Y	Y	N	Y	N	N	Y
6 **Upton**	Y	N	Y	N	Y	Y	Y
7 **Walberg**	Y	N	Y	N	Y	Y	Y
8 **Bishop**	Y	N	Y	N	Y	Y	Y
9 Levin	Y	Y	N	N	N	N	Y
10 **Mitchell**	Y	N	Y	Y	Y	Y	Y
11 **Trott**	Y	N	Y	Y	Y	Y	Y
12 Dingell	Y	Y	N	Y	N	N	Y
13 Vacant							
14 Lawrence	Y	Y	N	N	N	N	Y
MINNESOTA							
1 Walz	Y	Y	N	Y	N	N	Y
2 **Lewis**	Y	N	Y	Y	Y	Y	Y
3 **Paulsen**	Y	N	Y	N	Y	Y	Y
4 McCollum	Y	Y	N	Y	N	N	Y

	700	701	702	703	704	705	706
5 Ellison	Y	Y	N	Y	N	N	Y
6 **Emmer**	Y	N	Y	N	Y	Y	Y
7 Peterson	Y	Y	Y	N	N	N	Y
8 Nolan	Y	Y	N	N	N	N	Y
MISSISSIPPI							
1 **Kelly**	Y	N	Y	Y	Y	Y	Y
2 Thompson	?	?	?	?	N	N	Y
3 **Harper**	Y	N	Y	Y	Y	Y	Y
4 **Palazzo**	Y	N	Y	N	Y	Y	Y
MISSOURI							
1 Clay	Y	Y	N	Y	N	N	Y
2 **Wagner**	Y	N	Y	Y	Y	Y	Y
3 **Luetkemeyer**	Y	N	Y	Y	Y	Y	Y
4 **Hartzler**	?	N	Y	Y	Y	Y	Y
5 Cleaver	Y	Y	N	N	N	N	Y
6 **Graves**	Y	N	Y	N	Y	Y	Y
7 **Long**	Y	N	Y	Y	Y	Y	Y
8 **Smith**	Y	N	Y	Y	Y	Y	Y
MONTANA							
AL **Gianforte**	Y	N	Y	Y	Y	Y	Y
NEBRASKA							
1 **Fortenberry**	Y	N	Y	Y	Y	Y	Y
2 **Bacon**	Y	N	Y	Y	Y	Y	Y
3 **Smith**	Y	N	Y	Y	Y	Y	Y
NEVADA							
1 Titus	Y	Y	N	Y	N	N	Y
2 **Amodei**	Y	N	Y	Y	Y	Y	Y
3 Rosen	Y	Y	Y	N	N	N	Y
4 Kihuen	Y	Y	N	N	N	N	Y
NEW HAMPSHIRE							
1 Shea-Porter	Y	Y	N	Y	N	N	Y
2 Kuster	Y	Y	N	Y	N	N	Y
NEW JERSEY							
1 Norcross	Y	Y	N	N	N	N	Y
2 **LoBiondo**	Y	N	Y	N	Y	Y	Y
3 **MacArthur**	Y	N	Y	N	Y	Y	Y
4 **Smith**	Y	N	Y	Y	Y	Y	Y
5 Gottheimer	Y	Y	Y	N	N	N	Y
6 Pallone	Y	Y	N	N	N	N	Y
7 **Lance**	Y	N	Y	N	Y	Y	Y
8 Sires	Y	Y	N	N	N	N	Y
9 Pascrell	Y	Y	N	Y	N	?	Y
10 Payne	Y	Y	N	N	N	N	Y
11 **Frelinghuysen**	Y	N	Y	Y	Y	Y	Y
12 Watson Coleman	Y	Y	N	N	N	N	Y
NEW MEXICO							
1 Lujan Grisham	Y	Y	N	Y	N	N	Y
2 **Pearce**	Y	N	Y	N	Y	Y	Y
3 Luján	Y	Y	N	N	N	N	Y
NEW YORK							
1 **Zeldin**	Y	N	Y	N	Y	Y	Y
2 **King**	Y	N	Y	Y	Y	Y	Y
3 Suozzi	Y	Y	Y	Y	–	–	+
4 Rice	Y	Y	N	N	N	N	Y
5 Meeks	?	Y	Y	Y	N	N	Y
6 Meng	Y	Y	N	Y	N	N	Y
7 Velázquez	Y	Y	N	Y	N	N	Y
8 Jeffries	Y	Y	N	N	N	N	Y
9 Clarke	Y	Y	N	N	N	N	Y
10 Nadler	Y	Y	N	Y	N	N	Y
11 **Donovan**	Y	N	Y	Y	Y	Y	Y
12 Maloney, C.	Y	Y	N	N	N	N	Y
13 Espaillat	Y	Y	N	N	N	N	Y
14 Crowley	Y	Y	N	?	N	N	Y
15 Serrano	Y	Y	N	N	N	N	Y
16 Engel	Y	Y	N	N	N	N	Y
17 Lowey	Y	Y	N	N	N	N	Y
18 Maloney, S.P.	Y	Y	N	N	N	N	Y
19 **Faso**	Y	N	Y	Y	Y	Y	Y
20 Tonko	Y	Y	N	P	N	N	Y
21 **Stefanik**	Y	N	Y	Y	Y	Y	Y
22 **Tenney**	Y	N	Y	N	Y	Y	Y
23 **Reed**	Y	N	Y	N	Y	Y	Y
24 **Katko**	Y	N	Y	N	Y	Y	Y
25 Slaughter	Y	Y	N	N	N	N	Y
26 Higgins	Y	Y	N	N	N	N	Y
27 **Collins**	Y	N	Y	Y	Y	Y	Y
NORTH CAROLINA							
1 Butterfield	Y	Y	N	Y	N	N	Y
2 **Holding**	Y	N	Y	N	Y	Y	Y
3 **Jones**	Y	Y	N	Y	?	?	?
4 Price	Y	Y	N	N	N	N	Y

	700	701	702	703	704	705	
5 **Foxx**	Y	N	Y	N	Y	Y	Y
6 **Walker**	Y	N	Y	Y	Y	Y	Y
7 **Rouzer**	Y	N	Y	Y	Y	Y	Y
8 **Hudson**	Y	N	Y	N	Y	Y	Y
9 **Pittenger**	Y	N	Y	N	Y	Y	Y
10 **McHenry**	Y	N	Y	Y	Y	Y	Y
11 **Meadows**	Y	N	Y	Y	Y	Y	Y
12 Adams	Y	Y	N	N	N	N	Y
13 **Budd**	Y	N	Y	Y	Y	Y	Y
NORTH DAKOTA							
AL **Cramer**	Y	N	Y	Y	Y	Y	Y
OHIO							
1 **Chabot**	Y	N	Y	Y	Y	Y	Y
2 **Wenstrup**	Y	N	Y	N	Y	Y	Y
3 Beatty	Y	Y	N	?	N	N	Y
4 **Jordan**	Y	N	Y	N	Y	Y	Y
5 **Latta**	Y	N	Y	Y	Y	Y	Y
6 **Johnson**	Y	N	Y	N	Y	Y	Y
7 **Gibbs**	Y	N	Y	Y	Y	Y	Y
8 **Davidson**	Y	N	Y	Y	Y	Y	Y
9 Kaptur	Y	Y	N	Y	N	N	Y
10 **Turner**	Y	N	Y	N	Y	Y	Y
11 Fudge	Y	Y	N	N	N	N	Y
12 **Tiberi**	Y	N	Y	N	Y	Y	Y
13 Ryan	Y	Y	N	N	N	N	Y
14 **Joyce**	Y	N	Y	Y	Y	Y	Y
15 **Stivers**	Y	N	Y	N	Y	Y	Y
16 **Renacci**	+	–	+	–	?	?	?
OKLAHOMA							
1 **Bridenstine**	?	?	?	?	?	?	?
2 **Mullin**	Y	?	?	?	Y	Y	Y
3 **Lucas**	Y	N	Y	Y	Y	Y	Y
4 **Cole**	Y	N	Y	Y	Y	Y	Y
5 **Russell**	Y	N	Y	Y	Y	Y	Y
OREGON							
1 Bonamici	Y	Y	N	N	N	N	Y
2 **Walden**	Y	N	Y	Y	Y	Y	Y
3 Blumenauer	Y	Y	N	Y	N	N	Y
4 DeFazio	Y	Y	N	N	N	N	Y
5 Schrader	Y	Y	N	N	N	N	Y
PENNSYLVANIA							
1 Brady	Y	Y	N	N	N	N	Y
2 Evans	Y	Y	N	Y	N	N	Y
3 **Kelly**	Y	N	Y	Y	Y	Y	Y
4 **Perry**	Y	N	Y	N	Y	Y	Y
5 **Thompson**	Y	N	Y	N	Y	Y	Y
6 **Costello**	Y	N	Y	Y	Y	Y	Y
7 **Meehan**	Y	N	Y	N	Y	Y	Y
8 **Fitzpatrick**	Y	N	Y	N	Y	Y	Y
9 **Shuster**	Y	N	Y	Y	Y	Y	Y
10 **Marino**	Y	N	Y	Y	Y	Y	Y
11 **Barletta**	Y	N	Y	Y	Y	Y	Y
12 **Rothfus**	Y	N	Y	Y	Y	Y	Y
13 Boyle	Y	Y	N	N	N	N	Y
14 Doyle	Y	Y	N	N	N	N	Y
15 **Dent**	Y	N	Y	Y	Y	Y	Y
16 **Smucker**	Y	N	Y	Y	Y	Y	Y
17 Cartwright	Y	Y	N	Y	N	N	Y
RHODE ISLAND							
1 Cicilline	Y	Y	N	Y	N	N	Y
2 Langevin	Y	Y	N	N	N	N	Y
SOUTH CAROLINA							
1 **Sanford**	Y	N	Y	Y	Y	Y	Y
2 **Wilson**	Y	N	Y	Y	Y	Y	Y
3 **Duncan**	Y	N	Y	Y	Y	Y	Y
4 **Gowdy**	Y	N	Y	Y	Y	Y	Y
5 **Norman**	Y	N	Y	N	Y	Y	Y
6 Clyburn	Y	Y	N	N	N	N	Y
7 **Rice**	Y	N	Y	P	Y	Y	Y
SOUTH DAKOTA							
AL **Noem**	Y	N	Y	Y	Y	Y	Y
TENNESSEE							
1 **Roe**	Y	N	Y	Y	Y	Y	Y
2 **Duncan**	Y	N	Y	Y	Y	Y	Y
3 **Fleischmann**	Y	N	Y	Y	Y	Y	Y
4 **DesJarlais**	Y	N	Y	N	Y	Y	Y
5 Cooper	Y	Y	Y	Y	N	N	Y
6 **Black**	Y	N	Y	Y	Y	Y	Y
7 **Blackburn**	Y	N	Y	N	Y	Y	Y
8 **Kustoff**	Y	N	Y	Y	Y	Y	Y
9 Cohen	Y	Y	N	N	N	N	Y

	700	701	702	703	704	705	706
TEXAS							
1 **Gohmert**	Y	N	Y	?	Y	Y	Y
2 **Poe**	Y	N	Y	N	Y	Y	Y
3 **Johnson, S.**	Y	N	Y	Y	Y	Y	Y
4 **Ratcliffe**	Y	N	Y	N	Y	Y	Y
5 **Hensarling**	Y	N	Y	Y	Y	Y	Y
6 **Barton**	Y	N	Y	Y	Y	Y	Y
7 **Culberson**	Y	N	Y	Y	Y	Y	Y
8 **Brady**	Y	N	Y	Y	Y	Y	Y
9 Green, A.	Y	Y	N	N	N	N	Y
10 **McCaul**	Y	N	Y	Y	Y	Y	Y
11 **Conaway**	Y	N	Y	N	Y	Y	Y
12 **Granger**	Y	N	Y	Y	?	?	?
13 **Thornberry**	Y	N	Y	Y	Y	Y	Y
14 **Weber**	Y	N	Y	N	Y	Y	Y
15 Gonzalez	Y	Y	N	N	N	N	Y
16 O'Rourke	Y	Y	N	Y	N	N	Y
17 **Flores**	Y	N	Y	N	Y	Y	Y
18 Jackson Lee	Y	Y	N	N	N	N	Y
19 **Arrington**	Y	N	Y	Y	Y	Y	Y
20 Castro	Y	Y	N	Y	N	N	Y
21 **Smith**	?	?	?	?	?	?	?
22 **Olson**	Y	N	Y	Y	Y	Y	Y
23 **Hurd**	Y	N	Y	N	Y	Y	Y
24 **Marchant**	Y	N	Y	N	Y	Y	Y
25 **Williams**	Y	N	Y	Y	Y	Y	Y
26 **Burgess**	Y	N	Y	N	Y	Y	Y
27 **Farenthold**	Y	N	Y	N	Y	Y	Y
28 Cuellar	Y	Y	Y	Y	N	N	Y
29 Green, G.	Y	Y	N	N	N	N	Y
30 Johnson, E.B.	Y	Y	N	N	N	N	Y
31 **Carter**	?	N	Y	Y	Y	Y	Y
32 **Sessions**	Y	N	Y	Y	Y	Y	Y
33 Veasey	Y	Y	N	N	N	N	Y
34 Vela	Y	Y	N	N	N	N	Y
35 Doggett	Y	Y	N	Y	N	N	Y
36 **Babin**	Y	N	Y	Y	Y	Y	Y
UTAH							
1 **Bishop**	Y	N	Y	Y	Y	Y	Y
2 **Stewart**	Y	N	Y	Y	Y	Y	Y
3 **Curtis**	Y	N	Y	Y	Y	Y	Y
4 **Love**	Y	N	Y	N	Y	Y	Y
VERMONT							
AL Welch	Y	Y	N	Y	N	N	Y
VIRGINIA							
1 **Wittman**	Y	N	Y	Y	Y	Y	Y
2 **Taylor**	Y	N	Y	Y	Y	Y	Y
3 Scott	?	Y	N	Y	N	N	Y
4 McEachin	Y	Y	N	Y	N	N	Y
5 **Garrett**	Y	N	Y	N	Y	Y	Y
6 **Goodlatte**	Y	N	Y	Y	Y	Y	Y
7 **Brat**	Y	N	Y	Y	Y	Y	Y
8 Beyer	Y	Y	N	N	N	N	Y
9 **Griffith**	Y	N	Y	Y	Y	Y	Y
10 **Comstock**	?	N	Y	Y	Y	Y	Y
11 Connolly	Y	Y	N	N	N	N	Y
WASHINGTON							
1 DelBene	Y	Y	N	N	N	N	Y
2 Larsen	Y	Y	N	N	N	N	Y
3 **Herrera Beutler**	Y	N	Y	N	Y	Y	Y
4 **Newhouse**	Y	N	Y	Y	Y	Y	Y
5 **McMorris Rodgers**	Y	N	Y	Y	Y	Y	Y
6 Kilmer	Y	Y	N	N	N	N	Y
7 Jayapal	Y	Y	N	N	N	N	Y
8 **Reichert**	Y	N	Y	Y	Y	Y	Y
9 Smith	Y	Y	N	Y	N	N	Y
10 Heck	Y	Y	N	N	N	N	Y
WEST VIRGINIA							
1 **McKinley**	Y	N	Y	N	Y	Y	Y
2 **Mooney**	Y	N	Y	Y	Y	Y	Y
3 **Jenkins**	Y	N	Y	N	Y	Y	Y
WISCONSIN							
1 **Ryan**							
2 Pocan	+	+	–	+	–	–	+
3 Kind	Y	Y	N	N	N	N	Y
4 Moore	Y	Y	N	N	N	N	Y
5 **Sensenbrenner**	Y	N	Y	Y	Y	Y	Y
6 **Grothman**	?	N	Y	Y	Y	Y	Y
7 **Duffy**	Y	N	Y	Y	Y	Y	Y
8 **Gallagher**	Y	N	Y	N	Y	Y	Y
WYOMING							
AL **Cheney**	Y	N	Y	Y	Y	Y	Y

VOTE NUMBER

707. PROCEDURAL MOTION/APPROVAL OF HOUSE JOURNAL. Approved 225-187 : R 159-66; D 66-121. Dec. 21, 2017.

708. HR 1370. SHORT-TERM FISCAL 2018 CONTINUING APPROPRIATIONS/ MOTION TO CONCUR. Frelinghuysen, R-N.J., motion to concur in the Senate amendment to the bill with a further House amendment that would provide funding for federal government operations and services at current levels through Jan. 19, 2018. The bill, as amended, would authorize $2.1 billion for the Veterans Choice Program, $2.9 billion in mandatory funding for the Children's Health Insurance Program and $550 million in funding to Community Health Centers through Mar. 31. The bill would exempt funding provided to the Children's Health Insurance Fund and other health programs, as well as the tax overhaul package, from statutory pay-as-you-go requirements. It would provide $4.7 billion in emergency supplemental funds for missile defense and Navy ship repairs. It would also extend authorities under the Foreign Intelligence Surveillance Act through Jan. 19, including FISA Section 702, which allows U.S. intelligence agencies to obtain data from electronic service providers or non-U.S. persons who reside outside the U.S. Motion agreed to 231-188 : R 217-16; D 14-172. Dec. 21, 2017.

709. HR 4667. SUPPLEMENTAL DISASTER APPROPRIATIONS/PASSAGE. Passage of the bill that would make further supplemental appropriations for fiscal 2018 for disaster assistance for Hurricanes Harvey, Irma, and Maria and wildfires that occurred in calendar year 2017. The bill would authorizes $81 billion in aid for ongoing response and recovery from 2017 hurricanes and wildfires, and would authorize Puerto Rico to use surplus toll credits to cover the local share of federal highway emergency relief. The bill would remove a cap on federal highway assistance to U.S. territories for fiscal 2018 and 2019. Passed 251-169 : R 182-51; D 69-118. Dec. 21, 2017.

710. S 1532. HUMAN TRAFFICKING FELON COMMERCIAL VEHICLE USE PROHIBITION/PASSAGE. Graves, R-Mo., motion to suspend the rules and pass the bill that would require the Transportation Department to disqualify individuals who have committed a felony involving human trafficking from operating a commercial motor vehicle in the U.S. for their lifetime. Motion agreed to 393-0 : R 221-0; D 172-0. Dec. 21, 2017.

	707	708	709	710
ALABAMA				
1 **Byrne**	N	Y	Y	Y
2 **Roby**	Y	Y	Y	Y
3 **Rogers**	N	Y	Y	Y
4 **Aderholt**	Y	Y	Y	Y
5 **Brooks**	?	?	?	?
6 **Palmer**	N	Y	N	Y
7 Sewell	N	Y	Y	Y
ALASKA				
AL **Young**	N	Y	Y	Y
ARIZONA				
1 O'Halleran	N	Y	Y	Y
2 **McSally**	Y	Y	N	Y
3 Grijalva	N	N	N	Y
4 **Gosar**	?	N	N	Y
5 **Biggs**	N	N	N	Y
6 **Schweikert**	Y	Y	N	Y
7 Gallego	N	N	N	Y
9 Sinema	N	Y	Y	Y
ARKANSAS				
1 **Crawford**	Y	Y	Y	Y
2 **Hill**	Y	Y	Y	Y
3 **Womack**	Y	Y	Y	Y
4 **Westerman**	Y	Y	Y	Y
CALIFORNIA				
1 **LaMalfa**	Y	Y	Y	Y
2 Huffman	Y	N	Y	Y
3 Garamendi	N	N	Y	Y
4 **McClintock**	Y	Y	N	Y
5 Thompson	N	N	Y	Y
6 Matsui	N	N	Y	Y
7 Bera	N	N	Y	Y
8 **Cook**	Y	Y	Y	Y
9 McNerney	Y	N	Y	Y
10 **Denham**	N	Y	Y	Y
11 DeSaulnier	Y	N	Y	Y
12 Pelosi	Y	N	N	Y
13 Lee	N	N	N	Y
14 Speier	Y	N	N	Y
15 Swalwell	N	N	N	Y
16 Costa	N	Y	Y	?
17 Khanna	N	N	N	Y
18 Eshoo	Y	N	N	Y
19 Lofgren	N	N	N	?
20 Panetta	N	N	Y	Y
21 **Valadao**	N	Y	Y	Y
22 **Nunes**	Y	Y	Y	?
23 **McCarthy**	Y	Y	Y	Y
24 Carbajal	N	N	Y	Y
25 **Knight**	N	Y	Y	Y
26 Brownley	N	N	Y	Y
27 Chu	Y	N	N	Y
28 Schiff	N	N	Y	Y
29 Cardenas	N	N	N	Y
30 Sherman	Y	N	Y	Y
31 Aguilar	N	N	Y	Y
32 Napolitano	+	–	–	+
33 Lieu	N	N	Y	Y
34 Gomez	N	N	N	Y
35 Torres	N	N	N	Y
36 Ruiz	N	Y	Y	Y
37 Bass	N	N	N	?
38 Sánchez, Linda	N	N	N	Y
39 **Royce**	Y	Y	Y	Y
40 Roybal-Allard	N	N	N	Y
41 Takano	Y	N	Y	Y
42 **Calvert**	?	Y	Y	Y
43 Waters	Y	N	Y	?
44 Barragan	N	N	N	Y
45 **Walters**	Y	Y	Y	Y
46 Correa	N	N	N	Y
47 Lowenthal	N	N	Y	Y
48 **Rohrabacher**	Y	Y	Y	Y
49 **Issa**	Y	Y	Y	Y
50 **Hunter**	Y	N	Y	Y
51 Vargas	N	N	Y	Y
52 Peters	Y	N	Y	Y
53 Davis	Y	N	Y	Y

	707	708	709	710
COLORADO				
1 DeGette	N	N	N	Y
2 Polis	N	N	N	Y
3 **Tipton**	N	Y	Y	Y
4 **Buck**	N	Y	N	Y
5 **Lamborn**	Y	Y	N	Y
6 **Coffman**	N	Y	Y	Y
7 Perlmutter	Y	N	N	Y
CONNECTICUT				
1 Larson	N	N	N	+
2 Courtney	N	N	N	?
3 DeLauro	Y	N	N	Y
4 Himes	Y	N	Y	Y
5 Esty	N	N	N	Y
DELAWARE				
AL Blunt Rochester	Y	N	N	Y
FLORIDA				
1 **Gaetz**	Y	N	Y	Y
2 **Dunn**	Y	Y	Y	Y
3 **Yoho**	N	Y	Y	Y
4 **Rutherford**	Y	Y	Y	Y
5 Lawson	N	Y	Y	Y
6 **DeSantis**	N	Y	Y	Y
7 Murphy	Y	N	Y	Y
8 **Posey**	Y	Y	Y	Y
9 Soto	N	N	Y	Y
10 Demings	Y	N	Y	Y
11 **Webster**	Y	Y	Y	Y
12 **Bilirakis**	Y	Y	Y	Y
13 Crist	Y	Y	Y	Y
14 Castor	N	N	Y	Y
15 **Ross**	Y	N	Y	Y
16 **Buchanan**	Y	Y	Y	?
17 **Rooney, T.**	?	N	Y	Y
18 **Mast**	N	Y	Y	Y
19 **Rooney, F.**	Y	Y	Y	Y
20 Hastings	N	N	Y	Y
21 Frankel	Y	–	Y	Y
22 Deutch	N	N	Y	Y
23 Wasserman Schultz	Y	N	Y	Y
24 Wilson	N	N	Y	Y
25 **Diaz-Balart**	N	Y	Y	Y
26 **Curbelo**	Y	N	Y	Y
27 **Ros-Lehtinen**	Y	N	Y	Y
GEORGIA				
1 **Carter**	N	Y	Y	Y
2 Bishop	N	Y	Y	Y
3 **Ferguson**	Y	Y	Y	Y
4 Johnson	Y	N	N	?
5 Lewis	N	N	N	Y
6 **Handel**	Y	Y	Y	Y
7 **Woodall**	N	Y	N	Y
8 **Scott, A.**	N	Y	Y	Y
9 **Collins**	Y	Y	Y	Y
10 **Hice**	Y	Y	N	Y
11 **Loudermilk**	Y	Y	N	Y
12 **Allen**	Y	Y	Y	Y
13 Scott, D.	Y	N	Y	Y
14 **Graves**	N	Y	N	Y
HAWAII				
1 Hanabusa	N	N	N	Y
2 Gabbard	Y	N	Y	?
IDAHO				
1 **Labrador**	Y	N	N	?
2 **Simpson**	Y	Y	Y	Y
ILLINOIS				
1 Rush	N	N	N	Y
2 Kelly	N	N	N	Y
3 Lipinski	Y	N	Y	Y
4 Gutierrez	N	N	N	Y
5 Quigley	Y	N	N	?
6 **Roskam**	N	Y	Y	Y
7 Davis, D.	Y	N	N	Y
8 Krishnamoorthi	Y	N	Y	Y
9 Schakowsky	N	N	N	Y
10 Schneider	Y	Y	Y	Y
11 Foster	?	?	?	?
12 **Bost**	N	Y	Y	Y
13 **Davis, R.**	Y	Y	Y	Y
14 **Hultgren**	Y	Y	N	Y
15 **Shimkus**	Y	Y	Y	?

	707	708	709	710
16 Kinzinger	N	Y	Y	Y
17 Bustos	Y	Y	Y	Y
18 LaHood	N	Y	Y	Y
INDIANA				
1 Visclosky	N	N	Y	Y
2 Walorski	Y	Y	Y	Y
3 Banks	Y	Y	N	Y
4 Rokita	Y	Y	N	Y
5 Brooks	Y	Y	Y	Y
6 Messer	Y	Y	N	Y
7 Carson	N	N	N	Y
8 Bucshon	Y	Y	Y	Y
9 Hollingsworth	Y	N	N	Y
IOWA				
1 Blum	N	Y	Y	Y
2 Loebsack	N	Y	Y	Y
3 Young	Y	Y	N	Y
4 King	Y	Y	Y	Y
KANSAS				
1 Marshall	Y	Y	Y	Y
2 Jenkins	N	Y	Y	Y
3 Yoder	N	Y	Y	Y
4 Estes	Y	Y	Y	Y
KENTUCKY				
1 Comer	N	Y	N	Y
2 Guthrie	Y	Y	Y	Y
3 Yarmuth	Y	N	N	Y
4 Massie	Y	N	N	Y
5 Rogers	Y	Y	Y	Y
6 Barr	Y	Y	Y	Y
LOUISIANA				
1 Scalise	Y	Y	Y	Y
2 Richmond	N	N	N	Y
3 Higgins	Y	Y	Y	Y
4 Johnson	Y	Y	Y	Y
5 Abraham	Y	Y	Y	Y
6 Graves	Y	Y	Y	Y
MAINE				
1 Pingree	Y	N	N	Y
2 Poliquin	N	Y	Y	Y
MARYLAND				
1 Harris	Y	Y	N	Y
2 Ruppersberger	Y	N	Y	Y
3 Sarbanes	N	N	N	Y
4 Brown	N	N	N	Y
5 Hoyer	N	N	N	Y
6 Delaney	N	Y	Y	Y
7 Cummings	Y	N	N	Y
8 Raskin	N	N	N	Y
MASSACHUSETTS				
1 Neal	N	N	N	?
2 McGovern	N	N	N	Y
3 Tsongas	Y	N	N	Y
4 Kennedy	?	?	?	?
5 Clark	N	N	N	Y
6 Moulton	N	N	N	Y
7 Capuano	N	N	N	Y
8 Lynch	N	N	N	?
9 Keating	N	N	N	?
MICHIGAN				
1 Bergman	Y	Y	Y	Y
2 Huizenga	Y	Y	Y	?
3 Amash	N	N	N	N
4 Moolenaar	Y	Y	Y	Y
5 Kildee	Y	N	N	Y
6 Upton	N	Y	Y	Y
7 Walberg	Y	Y	Y	Y
8 Bishop	N	Y	Y	Y
9 Levin	N	N	N	Y
10 Mitchell	Y	Y	Y	Y
11 Trott	Y	Y	Y	Y
12 Dingell	Y	N	Y	Y
13 Vacant				
14 Lawrence	N	N	N	Y
MINNESOTA				
1 Walz	Y	N	N	Y
2 Lewis	Y	Y	Y	Y
3 Paulsen	N	Y	Y	Y
4 McCollum	Y	N	N	Y
5 Ellison	Y	N	N	Y
6 Emmer	N	Y	Y	Y
7 Peterson	N	N	N	Y
8 Nolan	N	N	Y	Y
MISSISSIPPI				
1 Kelly	N	Y	Y	Y
2 Thompson	N	N	N	Y
3 Harper	Y	Y	Y	Y
4 Palazzo	Y	Y	Y	Y
MISSOURI				
1 Clay	Y	N	N	Y
2 Wagner	Y	Y	Y	Y
3 Luetkemeyer	Y	Y	Y	Y
4 Hartzler	Y	Y	Y	Y
5 Cleaver	N	N	N	Y
6 Graves	N	Y	Y	Y
7 Long	Y	Y	Y	Y
8 Smith	Y	Y	N	Y
MONTANA				
AL Gianforte	Y	Y	Y	Y
NEBRASKA				
1 Fortenberry	Y	Y	Y	Y
2 Bacon	?	Y	Y	Y
3 Smith	Y	Y	Y	Y
NEVADA				
1 Titus	N	N	N	Y
2 Amodei	Y	Y	Y	Y
3 Rosen	N	N	Y	Y
4 Kihuen	N	N	N	?
NEW HAMPSHIRE				
1 Shea-Porter	N	N	N	Y
2 Kuster	Y	N	Y	Y
NEW JERSEY				
1 Norcross	N	N	N	Y
2 LoBiondo	N	Y	Y	Y
3 MacArthur	N	Y	Y	Y
4 Smith	Y	Y	Y	Y
5 Gottheimer	N	Y	Y	Y
6 Pallone	N	N	N	Y
7 Lance	N	Y	Y	Y
8 Sires	N	N	N	Y
9 Pascrell	Y	N	N	Y
10 Payne	N	N	N	Y
11 Frelinghuysen	Y	Y	Y	Y
12 Watson Coleman	N	N	N	Y
NEW MEXICO				
1 Lujan Grisham	Y	N	N	Y
2 Pearce	N	Y	Y	Y
3 Luján	N	N	N	Y
NEW YORK				
1 Zeldin	Y	Y	Y	Y
2 King	Y	Y	Y	Y
3 Suozzi	+	-	+	+
4 Rice	N	N	N	Y
5 Meeks	Y	N	N	Y
6 Meng	Y	N	N	Y
7 Velázquez	N	N	N	Y
8 Jeffries	N	N	N	Y
9 Clarke	N	N	N	Y
10 Nadler	Y	N	N	Y
11 Donovan	Y	Y	Y	Y
12 Maloney, C.	N	N	N	Y
13 Espaillat	N	N	N	Y
14 Crowley	N	N	N	Y
15 Serrano	Y	N	N	Y
16 Engel	Y	N	N	Y
17 Lowey	Y	N	N	Y
18 Maloney, S.P.	N	N	N	Y
19 Faso	Y	Y	Y	Y
20 Tonko	P	N	N	Y
21 Stefanik	Y	Y	Y	?
22 Tenney	Y	Y	Y	Y
23 Reed	Y	Y	Y	Y
24 Katko	N	Y	Y	Y
25 Slaughter	N	N	N	Y
26 Higgins	N	N	N	Y
27 Collins	Y	Y	Y	Y
NORTH CAROLINA				
1 Butterfield	Y	N	N	Y
2 Holding	N	Y	N	Y
3 Jones	?	?	?	?
4 Price	N	N	N	Y
5 Foxx	N	Y	N	Y
6 Walker	N	Y	N	Y
7 Rouzer	N	Y	N	Y
8 Hudson	N	Y	N	Y
9 Pittenger	N	Y	Y	Y
10 McHenry	Y	Y	Y	Y
11 Meadows	Y	Y	Y	Y
12 Adams	N	N	N	Y
13 Budd	Y	Y	N	Y
NORTH DAKOTA				
AL Cramer	Y	Y	Y	Y
OHIO				
1 Chabot	Y	Y	N	Y
2 Wenstrup	Y	Y	Y	Y
3 Beatty	N	N	N	Y
4 Jordan	N	N	N	Y
5 Latta	Y	Y	Y	Y
6 Johnson	N	Y	Y	Y
7 Gibbs	Y	Y	Y	Y
8 Davidson	Y	Y	N	Y
9 Kaptur	Y	N	Y	Y
10 Turner	Y	Y	Y	Y
11 Fudge	N	N	N	Y
12 Tiberi	Y	Y	Y	Y
13 Ryan	N	N	N	?
14 Joyce	Y	Y	Y	?
15 Stivers	N	Y	Y	Y
16 Renacci	?	?	?	?
OKLAHOMA				
1 Bridenstine	?	?	?	?
2 Mullin	Y	Y	Y	Y
3 Lucas	Y	Y	Y	Y
4 Cole	Y	Y	Y	Y
5 Russell	Y	Y	Y	Y
OREGON				
1 Bonamici	N	N	N	Y
2 Walden	Y	Y	Y	Y
3 Blumenauer	Y	N	N	Y
4 DeFazio	N	N	N	Y
5 Schrader	N	N	N	Y
PENNSYLVANIA				
1 Brady	N	N	N	Y
2 Evans	N	N	N	Y
3 Kelly	Y	Y	Y	Y
4 Perry	Y	N	N	Y
5 Thompson	N	Y	Y	Y
6 Costello	N	Y	Y	Y
7 Meehan	N	Y	Y	Y
8 Fitzpatrick	N	Y	Y	Y
9 Shuster	Y	Y	Y	Y
10 Marino	Y	Y	Y	Y
11 Barletta	Y	Y	Y	Y
12 Rothfus	Y	Y	Y	Y
13 Boyle	N	N	N	Y
14 Doyle	N	N	N	Y
15 Dent	Y	Y	Y	Y
16 Smucker	N	Y	Y	Y
17 Cartwright	Y	N	N	Y
RHODE ISLAND				
1 Cicilline	N	N	N	Y
2 Langevin	N	N	N	Y
SOUTH CAROLINA				
1 Sanford	Y	Y	N	Y
2 Wilson	Y	Y	Y	Y
3 Duncan	Y	Y	N	Y
4 Gowdy	Y	Y	Y	Y
5 Norman	Y	Y	Y	Y
6 Clyburn	N	N	N	Y
7 Rice	Y	Y	Y	Y
SOUTH DAKOTA				
AL Noem	Y	Y	N	Y
TENNESSEE				
1 Roe	Y	Y	N	Y
2 Duncan	Y	Y	N	Y
3 Fleischmann	Y	Y	N	Y
4 DesJarlais	Y	Y	N	Y
5 Cooper	Y	N	Y	Y
6 Black	Y	Y	Y	Y
7 Blackburn	Y	Y	Y	Y
8 Kustoff	Y	Y	Y	Y
9 Cohen	N	N	N	Y
TEXAS				
1 Gohmert	?	Y	Y	Y
2 Poe	Y	Y	Y	Y
3 Johnson, S.	Y	Y	Y	Y
4 Ratcliffe	N	Y	Y	Y
5 Hensarling	Y	Y	N	Y
6 Barton	N	Y	Y	Y
7 Culberson	Y	Y	Y	Y
8 Brady	Y	Y	Y	Y
9 Green, A.	N	N	Y	Y
10 McCaul	Y	Y	Y	Y
11 Conaway	N	Y	Y	Y
12 Granger	?	?	?	?
13 Thornberry	Y	Y	Y	Y
14 Weber	Y	Y	Y	Y
15 Gonzalez	N	N	Y	Y
16 O'Rourke	N	Y	Y	Y
17 Flores	N	Y	Y	Y
18 Jackson Lee	N	N	Y	Y
19 Arrington	Y	Y	Y	?
20 Castro	Y	N	Y	Y
21 Smith	?	?	?	?
22 Olson	?	Y	Y	Y
23 Hurd	Y	Y	Y	Y
24 Marchant	Y	Y	Y	Y
25 Williams	Y	Y	Y	Y
26 Burgess	Y	Y	Y	Y
27 Farenthold	Y	Y	Y	Y
28 Cuellar	Y	N	Y	Y
29 Green, G.	N	-	+	+
30 Johnson, E.B.	N	N	Y	?
31 Carter	Y	Y	Y	Y
32 Sessions	N	Y	Y	Y
33 Veasey	N	N	Y	Y
34 Vela	N	N	Y	Y
35 Doggett	Y	N	N	Y
36 Babin	Y	Y	Y	Y
UTAH				
1 Bishop	Y	Y	Y	Y
2 Stewart	Y	Y	Y	Y
3 Curtis	Y	Y	Y	Y
4 Love	N	Y	Y	?
VERMONT				
AL Welch	Y	N	N	Y
VIRGINIA				
1 Wittman	?	N	N	Y
2 Taylor	Y	Y	Y	Y
3 Scott	Y	N	N	Y
4 McEachin	Y	N	N	Y
5 Garrett	Y	Y	N	Y
6 Goodlatte	Y	Y	Y	Y
7 Brat	Y	Y	N	Y
8 Beyer	Y	N	N	Y
9 Griffith	Y	Y	N	Y
10 Comstock	Y	Y	Y	Y
11 Connolly	N	N	Y	Y
WASHINGTON				
1 DelBene	N	N	Y	Y
2 Larsen	N	N	Y	Y
3 Herrera Beutler	N	Y	Y	Y
4 Newhouse	Y	Y	Y	Y
5 McMorris Rodgers	Y	Y	Y	?
6 Kilmer	N	N	Y	Y
7 Jayapal	N	N	N	Y
8 Reichert	Y	Y	Y	Y
9 Smith	Y	N	Y	Y
10 Heck	Y	N	N	Y
WEST VIRGINIA				
1 McKinley	N	Y	Y	Y
2 Mooney	Y	N	N	Y
3 Jenkins	N	Y	Y	Y
WISCONSIN				
1 Ryan			Y	Y
2 Pocan	+	?	?	?
3 Kind	N	N	N	Y
4 Moore	N	N	N	Y
5 Sensenbrenner	Y	Y	N	Y
6 Grothman	Y	Y	N	Y
7 Duffy	Y	Y	Y	?
8 Gallagher	N	Y	Y	Y
WYOMING				
AL Cheney	Y	Y	Y	Y

Appendix S

Senate Roll Call Votes

VOTES WITH PRESIDENTIAL POSITIONS ARE LISTED ON PAGE B-5

Senate Roll Call Index by Subject

Senate Roll Call Index by Bill Number

HOUSE BILLS

H Con Res 71m S-37, S-38, S-39, S-40, S-41
H J Res 36, S-23
H J Res 37, S-17
H J Res 38, S-11, S-12
H J Res 40, S-15
H J Res 41, S-13
H J Res 42, S-18
H J Res 43, S-20
H J Res 44, S-17
H J Res 57, S-17
H J Res 58, S-17
H J Res 66, S-22, S-23
H J Res 67, S-20

H J Res 69, S-19
H J Res 83, S-19
H J Res 111, S-41
H J Res 123, S-50
HR 1, S-46, S-47, S-48, S-49, S-50, S-52
HR 72, S-9
HR 244, S-23
HR 601, S-33
HR 1370, S-52
HR 1628, S-29, S-30, S-31
HR 2266, S-41
HR 2430, S-32
HR 2810, S-33, S-34
HR 3364, S-31

SENATE BILLS

S 84, S-9
S 89, S-20
S 722, S-25, S-26
S Con Res 3, S-6, S-7, S-8, S-9
S J Res 34, S-19
S J Res 42, S-26
S Res 176, S-25

‖ SENATE VOTES

VOTE NUMBER

1. S CON RES 3. FISCAL 2017 BUDGET/MOTION TO PROCEED. McConnell, R-Ky., motion to proceed to the concurrent resolution that would set broad spending and revenue targets over the next 10 years. It would set budget authority at $3.3 trillion for fiscal 2017, increasing it to $4.1 trillion by fiscal 2022 and $4.9 trillion by fiscal 2026. The concurrent resolution would also include reconciliation instructions for the House Energy and Commerce and Ways and Means Committees as well as the Senate Finance and Health, Education, Labor and Pensions Committees to come up with at least $1 billion each in deficit reduction over a 10-year period by January 27, 2017, which is expected to be used to repeal certain provisions of the 2010 health care overhaul. Motion agreed to 51-48: R 51-1; D 0-45; I 0-2. Jan. 4, 2017.

2. S CON RES 3. FISCAL 2017 BUDGET RESOLUTION/MOTION TO WAIVE. Kaine, D-Va., motion to waive section 305(b) of the Congressional Budget Act with respect to the Enzi, R-Wyo., point of order against the Kaine amendment no. 8 that would ban the consideration of legislation that the Congressional Budget Office determines would reduce the number of Americans enrolled in health insurance coverage, increase health insurance premiums, or reduce the scope and scale of health care benefits when compared to the 2010 health care overhaul (P L 111-148). The ban could be waived by a three-fifths majority of the Senate. Motion rejected 48-52: R 0-52; D 46-0; I 2-0. Jan. 5, 2017.

3. S CON RES 3. FISCAL 2017 BUDGET/SUBSTITUTE AMENDMENT. Paul, R-Ky., amendment no. 1, that would gradually reduce the authorized level of the budget deficit until a budget surplus is required in Fiscal 2024. The substitute amendment would maintain the underlying bill's reconciliation instructions, which are expected to be used to repeal portions of the 2010 health care overhaul (P L 111-148, 111-152). Rejected 14-83: R 14-35; D 0-46; I 0-2. Jan. 9, 2017.

4. S CON RES 3. FISCAL 2017 BUDGET/MEDICARE AND MEDICAID POINT OF ORDER. Hirono, D-Hawaii, motion to waive section 305(b) of the Budget Act and applicable budget resolutions with respect to the Enzi, R-Wyo., point of order against the Sanders, I-Vt., for Hirono amendment no. 20 that would ban legislation from being considered in the Senate that would privatize or raise the eligibility age of Medicare, or that would block grant, impose per capita spending caps, or decrease coverage of Medicaid. The ban would be waived by a three-fifths vote of the Senate. Motion rejected 49-47: R 2-47; D 45-0; I 2-0. Jan. 9, 2017.

5. S CON RES 3. FISCAL 2017 BUDGET/MOTION TO WAIVE. Flake, R-Ariz., motion to waive section 305(b) of the Budget Act and applicable budget resolutions with respect to the Sanders, I-Vt., point of order against the Flake amendment no. 52 that would create a reserve fund relating to protections for the elderly, which could include "strengthening" Social Security and Medicare, "improving" Medicaid and housing, and returning regulation of health insurance markets to states, so long as the legislation would not increase the deficit over a 10 year period. Motion rejected 31-67: R 31-19; D 0-46; I 0-2. Jan. 10, 2017.

6. S CON RES 3. FISCAL 2017 BUDGET/MOTION TO WAIVE. Sanders, I-Vt., motion to waive applicable sections of the Budget Act and applicable budget resolutions with respect to the Enzi, R-Wyo., point of order against the Sanders amendment no. 19 that would result in a reduction of guaranteed benefits under Social Security, increase the retirement age, privatize Social Security, or that would reduce benefits of Medicare or Medicaid. The ban would be waived by a three-fifths vote of the Senate. Motion rejected 49-49: R 1-49; D 46-0; I 2-0. Jan. 10, 2017.

7. S CON RES 3. FISCAL 2017 BUDGET/MOTION TO WAIVE. Sanders, I-Vt., motion to waive section 305(b) of the Budget Act and applicable budget resolutions with respect to the Enzi, R-Wyo., point of order against the Nelson, D-Fla. amendment no. 13 that would ban the Senate from considering legislation that repeals the closing of the gap in coverage in the Medicare prescription drug program under part D of title XVIII of the Social Security Act, unless three-fifths of Senators vote to waive the point of order. Motion rejected 47-51: R 0-51; D 45-0; I 2-0. Jan. 11, 2017.

	1	2	3	4	5	6	7
ALABAMA							
Shelby	Y	N	N	N	N	N	N
Sessions	Y	N	N	N	?	?	?
ALASKA							
Murkowski	Y	N	N	Y	N	N	N
Sullivan	Y	N	N	N	Y	N	N
ARIZONA							
McCain	Y	N	N	N	Y	N	N
Flake	Y	N	Y	N	Y	N	N
ARKANSAS							
Boozman	Y	N	N	N	N	N	N
Cotton	Y	N	N	N	Y	N	N
CALIFORNIA							
Feinstein	?	Y	N	Y	N	Y	?
COLORADO							
Bennet	N	Y	N	Y	N	Y	Y
Gardner	Y	N	N	N	Y	N	N
CONNECTICUT							
Blumenthal	N	Y	N	Y	N	Y	Y
Murphy	N	Y	N	Y	N	Y	Y
DELAWARE							
Carper	N	Y	N	?	N	Y	Y
Coons	N	Y	N	Y	N	Y	Y
FLORIDA							
Nelson	N	Y	N	Y	N	Y	Y
Rubio	Y	N	Y	N	Y	N	N
GEORGIA							
Isakson	Y	N	N	N	N	N	N
Perdue	Y	N	N	N	N	N	N
HAWAII							
Schatz	N	Y	N	Y	N	Y	Y
Hirono	N	Y	N	Y	N	Y	Y
IDAHO							
Crapo	Y	N	Y	N	Y	N	N
Risch	Y	N	Y	N	Y	N	N
ILLINOIS							
Durbin	N	Y	N	Y	N	Y	Y
INDIANA							
Donnelly	N	Y	N	Y	N	Y	Y
IOWA							
Grassley	Y	N	N	N	N	N	N
Ernst	Y	N	N	N	Y	N	N
KANSAS							
Roberts	Y	N	N	N	N	N	N
Moran	Y	N	Y	N	Y	N	N
KENTUCKY							
McConnell	Y	N	N	N	N	N	N
Paul	N	N	Y	N	N	N	N
LOUISIANA							
Cassidy	Y	N	N	N	Y	N	N
MAINE							
Collins	Y	N	N	Y	Y	Y	N
King	N	Y	N	Y	N	Y	Y
MARYLAND							
Cardin	N	Y	N	Y	N	Y	Y
MASSACHUSETTS							
Warren	N	Y	N	Y	N	Y	Y
Markey	N	Y	N	Y	N	Y	Y
MICHIGAN							
Stabenow	N	Y	N	Y	N	Y	Y
Peters	N	Y	N	Y	N	Y	Y
MINNESOTA							
Klobuchar	N	Y	N	Y	N	Y	Y
Franken	N	Y	N	Y	N	Y	Y
MISSISSIPPI							
Cochran	Y	N	N	N	N	N	N
Wicker	Y	N	N	N	N	N	N
MISSOURI							
McCaskill	N	Y	N	Y	N	Y	Y
Blunt	Y	N	?	?	N	N	N
MONTANA							
Tester	N	Y	N	Y	N	Y	Y
Daines	Y	N	Y	N	Y	N	N

	1	2	3	4	5	6	7
NEBRASKA							
Fischer	Y	N	N	N	Y	N	N
Sasse	Y	N	Y	N	Y	N	N
NEVADA							
Heller	Y	N	N	Y	Y	N	N
NEW HAMPSHIRE							
Shaheen	N	Y	N	Y	N	Y	Y
NEW JERSEY							
Menendez	N	Y	N	Y	N	Y	Y
Booker	N	Y	N	Y	N	Y	Y
NEW MEXICO							
Udall	N	Y	N	Y	N	Y	Y
Heinrich	N	Y	N	Y	N	Y	Y
NEW YORK							
Schumer	N	Y	N	Y	N	Y	Y
Gillibrand	N	Y	N	Y	N	Y	Y
NORTH CAROLINA							
Burr	Y	N	N	N	Y	N	N
Tillis	Y	N	?	?	?	?	N
NORTH DAKOTA							
Hoeven	Y	N	N	N	Y	N	N
Heitkamp	N	Y	N	Y	N	Y	Y
OHIO							
Brown	N	Y	N	Y	N	Y	Y
Portman	Y	N	N	N	Y	N	N
OKLAHOMA							
Inhofe	Y	N	N	Y	N	N	N
Lankford	Y	N	N	Y	N	N	N
OREGON							
Wyden	N	Y	N	Y	N	Y	Y
Merkley	N	Y	N	Y	N	Y	Y
PENNSYLVANIA							
Casey	N	Y	N	Y	N	Y	Y
Toomey	Y	N	Y	N	Y	N	N
RHODE ISLAND							
Reed	N	Y	N	Y	N	Y	Y
Whitehouse	N	Y	N	Y	N	Y	Y
SOUTH CAROLINA							
Graham	Y	N	?	?	Y	N	N
Scott	Y	N	Y	N	Y	N	N
SOUTH DAKOTA							
Thune	Y	N	N	Y	N	N	N
Rounds	Y	N	N	N	N	N	N
TENNESSEE							
Alexander	Y	N	N	N	Y	N	N
Corker	Y	N	N	N	Y	N	N
TEXAS							
Cornyn	Y	N	N	N	N	N	N
Cruz	Y	N	Y	N	Y	N	N
UTAH							
Hatch	Y	N	N	N	N	N	N
Lee	Y	N	Y	N	Y	N	N
VERMONT							
Leahy	N	Y	N	Y	N	Y	Y
Sanders	N	Y	N	Y	N	Y	Y
VIRGINIA							
Warner	N	Y	N	Y	N	Y	Y
Kaine	N	Y	N	Y	N	Y	Y
WASHINGTON							
Murray	N	Y	N	Y	N	Y	Y
Cantwell	N	Y	N	Y	N	Y	Y
WEST VIRGINIA							
Manchin	N	Y	N	Y	N	Y	Y
Capito	Y	N	N	N	N	N	N
WISCONSIN							
Johnson	Y	N	N	N	Y	N	N
Baldwin	N	Y	N	Y	N	Y	Y
WYOMING							
Enzi	Y	N	N	N	N	N	N
Barrasso	Y	N	N	N	N	N	N

KEY	**Republicans**	Democrats	*Independents*	
Y Voted for (yea)		X Paired against		C Voted "present" to avoid possible conflict of interest
# Paired for		− Announced against		? Did not vote or otherwise make a position known
+ Announced for		P Voted "present"		
N Voted against (nay)				

VOTE NUMBER

8. S CON RES 3. FISCAL 2017 BUDGET/MOTION TO WAIVE. King, I-Maine, motion to waive section 904 of the Budget Act and applicable budget resolutions with respect to the Enzi, R-Wyo., point of order against the King amendment no. 60 that would ban legislation from being considered in the Senate that would reduce health insurance access to individuals based on their occupations, unless legislation provides comparable benefits. The ban would be waived by a three-fifths vote of the Senate. Motion rejected 48-50: R 1-50; D 45-0; I 2-0. Jan. 11, 2017.

9. S CON RES 3. FISCAL 2017 BUDGET/MOTION TO WAIVE. Barrasso, R-Wyo., motion to waive all applicable sections of the Budget Act and applicable budget resolutions with respect to the Manchin, D-W.Va., point of order against the Barrasso amendment no. 173. Motion rejected 51-47: R 51-0; D 0-45; I 0-2. Jan. 11, 2017.

10. S CON RES 3. FISCAL 2017 BUDGET/MOTION TO WAIVE. Manchin, D-W.Va., motion to waive section 305(b) of the Budget Act and applicable budget resolutions with respect to the Enzi, R-Wyo., point of order against the Manchin amendment no. 64 that would ban legislation from being considered in the Senate that the Congressional Budget Office determines would cause an increase in the rate of uninsured individuals in rural communities in an amount great enough to financially weaken rural hospitals or clinics, or that would reduce federal funds for rural hospitals. The ban would be waived by a three-fifths vote of the Senate. Motion rejected 51-47: R 4-47; D 45-0; I 2-0. Jan. 11, 2017.

11. S CON RES 3. FISCAL 2017 BUDGET/MOTION TO WAIVE. Heller, R-Nev., motion to waive section 305(b) of the Budget Act and applicable budget resolutions with respect to the Sanders, I-Vt., point of order against the Heller amendment no. 167 that is related to Social Security. Motion rejected 51-47: R 51-0; D 0-45; I 0-2. Jan. 11, 2017.

12. S CON RES 3. FISCAL 2017 BUDGET/MOTION TO WAIVE. Baldwin, D-Wis., motion to waive section 305(b) of the Budget Act and applicable budget resolutions with respect to the Enzi, R-Wyo., point of order against the Baldwin amendment no. 81 that would ban legislation from being considered in the Senate that would reduce the number of young Americans enrolled in health insurance, alter the provision of the 2010 health care overhaul that allows children to stay on their parent's health plan until age 26, or increases premiums for young Americans with private insurance. The ban would be waived by a three-fifths vote of the Senate. Motion rejected 48-50: R 1-50; D 45-0; I 2-0. Jan. 11, 2017.

13. S CON RES 3. FISCAL 2017 BUDGET/MOTION TO WAIVE. Flake, R-Ariz., motion to waive applicable sections of the Budget Act and applicable budget resolutions with respect to the Sanders, I-Vt., point of order against the Flake amendment no. 176 related to veteran housing. Motion rejected 50-48: R 50-1; D 0-45; I 0-2. Jan. 11, 2017.

14. S CON RES 3. FISCAL 2017 BUDGET/MOTION TO WAIVE. Tester, D-Mont., motion to waive section 305(b) of the Budget Act and applicable budget resolutions with respect to the Enzi, R-Wyo., point of order against the Tester amendment no. 104 that would authorize funding for the privatizing of Veterans Affairs health care. There would be no process for waiving the point of order that would be created in the amendment. Motion rejected 48-50: R 1-50; D 45-0; I 2-0. Jan. 11, 2017.

State / Senator	8	9	10	11	12	13	14
ALABAMA							
Shelby	N	Y	N	Y	N	Y	N
Sessions	?	?	?	?	?	?	?
ALASKA							
Murkowski	N	Y	N	Y	N	Y	N
Sullivan	N	Y	N	Y	N	Y	N
ARIZONA							
McCain	N	Y	N	Y	N	Y	N
Flake	N	Y	N	Y	N	Y	N
ARKANSAS							
Boozman	N	Y	N	Y	N	Y	N
Cotton	N	Y	N	Y	N	Y	N
CALIFORNIA							
Feinstein	?	?	?	?	?	?	?
Harris	Y	N	Y	N	Y	N	Y
COLORADO							
Bennet	Y	N	Y	N	Y	N	Y
Gardner	N	Y	N	Y	N	Y	N
CONNECTICUT							
Blumenthal	Y	N	Y	N	Y	N	Y
Murphy	Y	N	Y	N	Y	N	Y
DELAWARE							
Carper	Y	N	Y	N	Y	N	Y
Coons	Y	N	Y	N	Y	N	Y
FLORIDA							
Nelson	Y	N	Y	N	Y	N	Y
Rubio	N	Y	N	Y	N	Y	N
GEORGIA							
Isakson	N	Y	N	Y	N	Y	N
Perdue	N	Y	N	Y	N	Y	N
HAWAII							
Schatz	Y	N	Y	N	Y	N	Y
Hirono	Y	N	Y	N	Y	N	Y
IDAHO							
Crapo	N	Y	N	Y	N	Y	N
Risch	N	Y	N	Y	N	Y	N
ILLINOIS							
Durbin	Y	N	Y	N	Y	N	Y
Duckworth	Y	N	Y	N	Y	N	Y
INDIANA							
Donnelly	Y	N	Y	N	Y	N	Y
Young	N	Y	N	Y	N	Y	N
IOWA							
Grassley	N	Y	N	Y	N	Y	N
Ernst	N	Y	N	Y	N	Y	N
KANSAS							
Roberts	N	Y	N	Y	N	Y	N
Moran	N	Y	N	Y	N	Y	N
KENTUCKY							
McConnell	N	Y	N	Y	N	Y	N
Paul	N	Y	N	Y	N	Y	N
LOUISIANA							
Cassidy	N	Y	N	Y	N	Y	N
Kennedy	N	Y	N	Y	N	Y	N
MAINE							
Collins	Y	Y	Y	Y	Y	Y	N
King	Y	N	Y	N	Y	N	Y
MARYLAND							
Cardin	Y	N	Y	N	Y	N	Y
Van Hollen	Y	N	Y	N	Y	N	Y
MASSACHUSETTS							
Warren	Y	N	Y	N	Y	N	Y
Markey	Y	N	Y	N	Y	N	Y
MICHIGAN							
Stabenow	Y	N	Y	N	Y	N	Y
Peters	Y	N	Y	N	Y	N	Y
MINNESOTA							
Klobuchar	Y	N	Y	N	Y	N	Y
Franken	Y	N	Y	N	Y	N	Y
MISSISSIPPI							
Cochran	N	Y	N	Y	N	Y	N
Wicker	N	Y	N	Y	N	Y	N
MISSOURI							
McCaskill	Y	N	Y	N	Y	N	Y
Blunt	N	Y	N	Y	N	Y	N%
MONTANA							
Tester	Y	N	Y	N	Y	N	Y
Daines	N	Y	N	Y	N	Y	N
NEBRASKA							
Fischer	N	Y	N	Y	N	Y	N
Sasse	N	Y	N	Y	N	Y	N
NEVADA							
Heller	N	Y	Y	Y	N	Y	Y
Cortez Masto	Y	N	Y	N	Y	N	Y
NEW HAMPSHIRE							
Shaheen	Y	N	Y	N	Y	N	Y
Hassan	Y	N	Y	N	Y	N	Y
NEW JERSEY							
Menendez	Y	N	Y	N	Y	N	Y
Booker	Y	N	Y	N	Y	N	Y
NEW MEXICO							
Udall	Y	N	Y	N	Y	N	Y
Heinrich	Y	N	Y	N	Y	N	Y
NEW YORK							
Schumer	Y	N	Y	N	Y	N	Y
Gillibrand	Y	N	Y	N	Y	N	Y
NORTH CAROLINA							
Burr	N	Y	N	Y	N	Y	N
Tillis	N	Y	N	Y	N	Y	N
NORTH DAKOTA							
Hoeven	N	Y	N	Y	N	Y	N
Heitkamp	Y	N	Y	N	Y	N	Y
OHIO							
Brown	Y	N	Y	N	Y	N	Y
Portman	N	Y	Y	Y	N	N	N
OKLAHOMA							
Inhofe	N	Y	N	Y	N	Y	N
Lankford	N	Y	N	Y	N	Y	N
OREGON							
Wyden	Y	N	Y	N	Y	N	Y
Merkley	Y	N	Y	N	Y	N	Y
PENNSYLVANIA							
Casey	Y	N	Y	N	Y	N	Y
Toomey	N	Y	N	Y	N	Y	N
RHODE ISLAND							
Reed	Y	N	Y	N	Y	N	Y
Whitehouse	Y	N	Y	N	Y	N	Y
SOUTH CAROLINA							
Graham	N	Y	N	Y	N	Y	N
Scott	N	Y	N	Y	N	Y	N
SOUTH DAKOTA							
Thune	N	Y	N	Y	N	Y	N
Rounds	N	Y	N	Y	N	Y	N
TENNESSEE							
Alexander	N	Y	N	Y	N	Y	N
Corker	N	Y	N	Y	N	Y	N
TEXAS							
Cornyn	N	Y	N	Y	N	Y	N
Cruz	N	Y	N	Y	N	Y	N
UTAH							
Hatch	N	Y	N	Y	N	Y	N
Lee	N	Y	N	Y	N	Y	N
VERMONT							
Leahy	Y	N	Y	N	Y	N	Y
Sanders	Y	N	Y	N	Y	N	Y
VIRGINIA							
Warner	Y	N	Y	N	Y	N	Y
Kaine	Y	N	Y	N	Y	N	Y
WASHINGTON							
Murray	Y	N	Y	N	Y	N	Y
Cantwell	Y	N	Y	N	Y	N	Y
WEST VIRGINIA							
Manchin	Y	N	Y	N	Y	N	Y
Capito	N	Y	Y	Y	N	Y	N
WISCONSIN							
Johnson	N	Y	N	Y	N	Y	N
Baldwin	Y	N	Y	N	Y	N	Y
WYOMING							
Enzi	N	Y	N	Y	N	Y	N
Barrasso	N	Y	N	Y	N	Y	N

KEY Republicans Democrats *Independents*

Y	Voted for (yea)	X	Paired against	C	Voted "present" to avoid possible conflict of interest
#	Paired for	–	Announced against	?	Did not vote or otherwise make a position known
+	Announced for	P	Voted "present"		
N	Voted against (nay)				

VOTE NUMBER

15. S CON RES 3. FISCAL 2017 BUDGET/MOTION TO WAIVE. Casey, D-Pa., motion to waive section 305(b) of the Budget Act and applicable budget resolutions with respect to the Enzi, R-Wyo., point of order against the Casey amendment no. 61 that would ban legislation from being considered in the Senate that would limit, reduce, or eliminate access to care for anyone with a pre-existing condition, place a lifetime or annual cap on health insurance coverage for someone with a disability or chronic condition, or that would allow a health plan to discriminate based on health. The ban would be waived by a three-fifths vote of the Senate. Motion rejected 49-49: R 2-49; D 45-0; I 2-0. Jan. 11, 2017.

16. S CON RES 3. FISCAL 2017 BUDGET/MOTION TO WAIVE. Barrasso, R-Wyo., motion to waive applicable sections of the Budget Act and applicable budget resolutions with respect to the Sanders, I-Vt., point of order against the Barrasso amendment no. 181 that is a side-by-side to the Casey, D-Pa., amendment no. 61. Motion rejected 47-51: R 47-4; D 0-45; I 0-2. Jan. 11, 2017.

17. S CON RES 3. FISCAL 2017 BUDGET/MOTION TO WAIVE. Hatch, R-Utah, motion to waive applicable sections of the Budget Act and applicable budget resolutions with respect to the Menendez, D-N.J, point of order against the Hatch amendment no. 179 that is related to Medicaid and housing. Motion rejected 51-47: R 51-0; D 0-45; I 0-2. Jan. 11, 2017.

18. S CON RES 3. FISCAL 2017 BUDGET/MOTION TO WAIVE. Sanders, I-Vt., motion to waive applicable sections of the Budget Act and applicable budget resolutions with respect to the Enzi, R-Wyo., point of order against the Menendez, D-N.J., amendment no. 81 that would ban legislation from being considered in the Senate that the Congressional Budget Office certifies would increase the number of uninsured Americans, decrease Medicaid enrollment in states that expanded Medicaid, or increase the required state share of Medicaid spending. The ban would be waived by a three-fifths vote of the Senate. Motion rejected 48-50: R 1-50; D 45-0; I 2-0. Jan. 11, 2017.

19. S CON RES 3. FISCAL 2017 BUDGET/MOTION TO WAIVE. Alexander, R-Tenn., motion to waive applicable sections of the Budget Act and applicable budget resolutions with respect to the Sanders, I-Vt., point of order against the Alexander amendment no. 174 that is related to Social Security and Medicare. Motion rejected 49-49: R 49-2; D 0-45; I 0-2. Jan. 11, 2017.

20. S CON RES 3. FISCAL 2017 BUDGET/IMPORTING PRESCRIPTION DRUGS. Klobuchar, D-Minn., amendment no. 178, which is related to importing prescription drugs from Canada. Rejected 46-52: R 12-39; D 32-13; I 2-0. Jan. 11, 2017.

21. S CON RES 3. FISCAL 2017 BUDGET/MOTION TO WAIVE. Wyden, D-Ore., motion to waive section 305(b) of the Budget Act and applicable budget resolutions with respect to the Enzi, R-Wyo., point of order against the Wyden amendment no. 188 that is related to drug prices. Motion rejected 47-51: R 0-51; D 45-0; I 2-0. Jan. 11, 2017.

	15	16	17	18	19	20	21
ALABAMA							
Shelby	N	Y	Y	N	Y	N	N
Sessions	?	?	?	?	?	?	?
ALASKA							
Murkowski	N	Y	Y	N	Y	Y	N
Sullivan	N	Y	Y	N	Y	N	N
ARIZONA							
McCain	N	Y	Y	N	Y	Y	N
Flake	N	Y	Y	N	Y	Y	N
ARKANSAS							
Boozman	N	Y	Y	N	Y	Y	N
Cotton	N	Y	Y	N	Y	N	N
CALIFORNIA							
Feinstein	?	?	?	?	?	?	?
Harris	Y	N	N	Y	N	Y	Y
COLORADO							
Bennet	Y	N	N	Y	N	N	Y
Gardner	N	Y	N	Y	N	N	N
CONNECTICUT							
Blumenthal	Y	N	N	Y	N	Y	Y
Murphy	Y	N	N	Y	N	Y	Y
DELAWARE							
Carper	Y	N	N	Y	N	N	Y
Coons	Y	N	N	Y	N	N	Y
FLORIDA							
Nelson	Y	N	N	Y	N	Y	Y
Rubio	N	Y	Y	N	Y	N	N
GEORGIA							
Isakson	N	Y	Y	N	Y	N	N
Perdue	N	Y	Y	N	Y	N	N
HAWAII							
Schatz	Y	N	N	Y	N	Y	Y
Hirono	Y	N	N	Y	N	Y	Y
IDAHO							
Crapo	N	Y	Y	N	Y	N	N
Risch	N	Y	Y	N	Y	N	N
ILLINOIS							
Durbin	Y	N	N	Y	N	Y	Y
Duckworth	Y	N	N	Y	N	Y	Y
INDIANA							
Donnelly	Y	N	N	Y	N	N	Y
Young	N	Y	Y	N	Y	N	N
IOWA							
Grassley	N	Y	Y	N	N	Y	N
Ernst	N	Y	Y	N	Y	N	N
KANSAS							
Roberts	N	Y	Y	N	Y	N	N
Moran	N	Y	Y	N	Y	N	N
KENTUCKY							
McConnell	N	Y	Y	N	Y	N	N
Paul	N	N	Y	N	Y	Y	N
LOUISIANA							
Cassidy	N	Y	Y	N	Y	N	N
Kennedy	N	Y	Y	N	Y	Y	N
MAINE							
Collins	Y	Y	Y	N	Y	Y	N
King	Y	N	N	Y	N	Y	Y
MARYLAND							
Cardin	Y	N	N	Y	N	Y	Y
Van Hollen	Y	N	N	Y	N	Y	Y
MASSACHUSETTS							
Warren	Y	N	N	Y	N	Y	Y
Markey	Y	N	N	Y	N	Y	Y
MICHIGAN							
Stabenow	Y	N	N	Y	N	Y	Y
Peters	Y	N	N	Y	N	Y	Y
MINNESOTA							
Klobuchar	Y	N	N	Y	N	Y	Y
Franken	Y	N	N	Y	N	Y	Y
MISSISSIPPI							
Cochran	N	Y	Y	N	Y	N	N
Wicker	N	Y	Y	N	Y	N	N
MISSOURI							
McCaskill	Y	N	N	Y	N	Y	Y
Blunt	N	Y	Y	N	Y	N	N

	15	16	17	18	19	20	21
MONTANA							
Tester	Y	N	N	Y	N	N	Y
Daines	N	Y	Y	N	Y	N	N
NEBRASKA							
Fischer	N	Y	Y	N	Y	N	N
Sasse	N	N	Y	N	Y	N	N
NEVADA							
Heller	Y	Y	Y	Y	Y	Y	N
Cortez Masto	Y	N	N	Y	N	Y	Y
NEW HAMPSHIRE							
Shaheen	Y	N	N	Y	N	Y	Y
Hassan	Y	N	N	Y	N	Y	Y
NEW JERSEY							
Menendez	Y	N	N	Y	N	N	Y
Booker	Y	N	N	Y	N	N	Y
NEW MEXICO							
Udall	Y	N	N	Y	N	Y	Y
Heinrich	Y	N	N	Y	N	N	Y
NEW YORK							
Schumer	Y	N	N	Y	N	Y	Y
Gillibrand	Y	N	N	Y	N	Y	Y
NORTH CAROLINA							
Burr	N	Y	Y	N	Y	N	N
Tillis	N	Y	Y	N	Y	N	N
NORTH DAKOTA							
Hoeven	N	Y	Y	N	Y	N	N
Heitkamp	Y	N	N	Y	N	N	Y
OHIO							
Brown	Y	N	N	Y	N	Y	Y
Portman	N	Y	Y	N	Y	N	N
OKLAHOMA							
Inhofe	N	Y	Y	N	Y	N	N
Lankford	N	Y	Y	N	Y	N	N
OREGON							
Wyden	Y	N	N	Y	N	Y	Y
Merkley	Y	N	N	Y	N	Y	Y
PENNSYLVANIA							
Casey	Y	N	N	Y	N	N	Y
Toomey	N	Y	Y	N	Y	N	N
RHODE ISLAND							
Reed	Y	N	N	Y	N	Y	Y
Whitehouse	Y	N	N	Y	N	Y	Y
SOUTH CAROLINA							
Graham	N	Y	Y	N	Y	N	N
Scott	N	Y	Y	N	Y	N	N
SOUTH DAKOTA							
Thune	N	Y	Y	N	Y	N	N
Rounds	N	Y	Y	N	Y	N	N
TENNESSEE							
Alexander	N	Y	Y	N	Y	N	N
Corker	N	Y	Y	N	Y	N	N
TEXAS							
Cornyn	N	Y	Y	N	Y	N	N
Cruz	N	N	Y	N	Y	Y	N
UTAH							
Hatch	N	Y	Y	N	N	N	N
Lee	N	N	Y	N	Y	Y	N
VERMONT							
Leahy	Y	N	N	Y	N	Y	Y
Sanders	Y	N	N	Y	N	Y	Y
VIRGINIA							
Warner	Y	N	N	Y	N	N	Y
Kaine	Y	N	N	Y	N	Y	Y
WASHINGTON							
Murray	Y	N	N	Y	N	N	Y
Cantwell	Y	N	N	Y	N	N	Y
WEST VIRGINIA							
Manchin	Y	N	N	Y	N	Y	Y
Capito	N	Y	Y	N	Y	N	N
WISCONSIN							
Johnson	N	Y	Y	N	Y	N	N
Baldwin	Y	N	N	Y	N	Y	Y
WYOMING							
Enzi	N	Y	Y	N	Y	N	N
Barrasso	N	Y	Y	N	Y	N	N

KEY	Republicans	Democrats	*Independents*
Y Voted for (yea)		X Paired against	C Voted "present" to avoid possible conflict of interest
# Paired for		– Announced against	
+ Announced for		P Voted "present"	? Did not vote or otherwise make a position known
N Voted against (nay)			

VOTE NUMBER

22. S CON RES 3. FISCAL 2017 BUDGET/MOTION TO WAIVE. Fischer, R-Neb., motion to waive section 305(b) of the Budget Act and applicable budget resolutions with respect to the Gillibrand, D-N.Y., point of order against the Fischer, R-Neb., amendment no. 184. Motion rejected 52-46: R 51-0; D 1-44; I 0-2. Jan. 12, 2017.

23. S CON RES 3. FISCAL 2017 BUDGET/MOTION TO WAIVE. Gillibrand, motion to waive section 305(b) of the Budget Act and applicable budget resolutions with respect to the Enzi, R-Wyo., point of order against the Gillibrand, D-N.Y., amendment no. 82 that would reduce access to women's health care, including reproductive health services and birth control through repealing provisions of the 2010 health care overhaul. The ban would be waived by a three-fifths vote of the Senate. Motion rejected 49-49: R 2-49; D 45-0; I 2-0. Jan. 12, 2017.

24. S CON RES 3. FISCAL 2017 BUDGET/MOTION TO WAIVE. Hatch, R-Utah, motion to waive section 305(b) of the Budget Act and applicable budget resolutions with respect to the Brown, D-Ohio, point of order against the Hatch amendment no. 180 that is related to Social Security and is a side-by-side to Brown, D-Ohio, amendment no. 86. Motion rejected 51-47: R 51-0; D 0-45; I 0-2. Jan. 12, 2017.

25. S CON RES 3. FISCAL 2017 BUDGET/MOTION TO WAIVE. Brown, D-Ohio, motion to waive section 305(b) of the Budget Act and applicable budget resolutions with respect to the Enzi, R-Wyo., point of order against the Brown amendment no. 86 that would ban legislation from being considered in the Senate that would make changes to Medicaid, the Children's Health Insurance Program, or federal requirements for private health insurance unless the Congressional Budget Office deems such changes would not reduce benefits or affordability for children's health insurance. The ban would be waived by a three-fifths vote of the Senate. Motion rejected 49-49: R 2-49; D 45-0; I 2-0. Jan. 12, 2017.

26. S CON RES 3. FISCAL 2017 BUDGET RESOLUTION/ADOPTION. Adoption of the concurrent resolution that would set broad spending and revenue targets over the next 10 years. It would set budget authority at $3.3 trillion for fiscal 2017, increasing it to $4.1 trillion by fiscal 2022 and $4.9 trillion by fiscal 2026. The concurrent resolution would also include reconciliation instructions for the House Energy and Commerce and Ways and Means Committees as well as the Senate Finance and Health, Education, Labor and Pensions Committees to come up with at least $1 billion each in deficit reduction over a 10-year period by January 27, 2017, which is expected to be used to repeal certain provisions of the 2010 health care overhaul. Adopted 51-48: R 51-1; D 0-45; I 0-2. Jan. 12, 2017.

27. S 84. DEFENSE SECRETARY WAIVER/PASSAGE. Passage of the bill that would allow the first person to be confirmed secretary of Defense after the bill's enactment to serve in the position, even if the individual has not been retired from the military for seven years, so long as the person has been retired for at least three years. The bill would thus provide an exemption for President-elect Donald Trump's pick for the position, retired Marine Corps Gen. James Mattis, from a requirement for a seven-year waiting period before former servicemembers can be appointed to Defense secretary. Passed 81-17: R 50-0; D 30-16; I 1-1. Jan. 12, 2017.

28. HR 72. GAO ACCESSING AGENCY INFORMATION/PASSAGE. Passage of the bill that would grant the Governmental Accountability Office access to certain information from federal agencies in order to perform the GAO's duties, including audits, evaluations, and investigations. The GAO would be authorized to bring civil action against agencies in order to obtain such records. Additionally, agencies would be required to report to Congress and the GAO with actions taken in response to GAO recommendations. Passed (thus cleared for the president) 99-0: R 51-0; D 46-0; I 2-0. Jan. 17, 2017.

	22	23	24	25	26	27	28
ALABAMA							
Shelby	Y	N	Y	N	Y	Y	Y
Sessions	?	?	?	?	Y	Y	?
ALASKA							
Murkowski	Y	N	Y	N	Y	Y	Y
Sullivan	Y	N	Y	N	Y	Y	Y
ARIZONA							
McCain	Y	N	Y	N	Y	Y	Y
Flake	Y	N	Y	N	Y	Y	Y
ARKANSAS							
Boozman	Y	N	Y	N	Y	Y	Y
Cotton	Y	N	Y	N	Y	Y	Y
CALIFORNIA							
Feinstein	?	?	?	?	?	Y	Y
Harris	N	Y	N	Y	N	Y	Y
COLORADO							
Bennet	N	Y	N	Y	N	Y	Y
Gardner	Y	N	Y	N	Y	Y	Y
CONNECTICUT							
Blumenthal	N	Y	N	Y	N	N	Y
Murphy	N	Y	N	Y	N	N	Y
DELAWARE							
Carper	N	Y	N	Y	N	Y	Y
Coons	N	Y	N	Y	N	Y	Y
FLORIDA							
Nelson	N	Y	N	Y	N	Y	Y
Rubio	Y	N	Y	N	Y	Y	Y
GEORGIA							
Isakson	Y	N	Y	N	Y	Y	Y
Perdue	Y	N	Y	N	Y	Y	Y
HAWAII							
Schatz	N	Y	N	Y	N	Y	Y
Hirono	N	Y	N	Y	N	Y	Y
IDAHO							
Crapo	Y	N	Y	N	Y	Y	Y
Risch	Y	N	Y	N	Y	Y	Y
ILLINOIS							
Durbin	N	Y	N	Y	N	N	Y
Duckworth	N	Y	N	Y	N	N	Y
INDIANA							
Donnelly	N	Y	N	Y	N	Y	Y
Young	Y	N	Y	N	Y	Y	Y
IOWA							
Grassley	Y	N	Y	N	Y	Y	Y
Ernst	Y	N	Y	N	Y	Y	Y
KANSAS							
Roberts	Y	N	Y	N	Y	Y	Y
Moran	Y	N	Y	N	Y	?	Y
KENTUCKY							
McConnell	Y	N	Y	N	Y	Y	Y
Paul	Y	N	Y	N	N	Y	Y
LOUISIANA							
Cassidy	Y	N	Y	N	Y	Y	Y
Kennedy	Y	N	Y	N	Y	Y	Y
MAINE							
Collins	Y	Y	Y	Y	Y	Y	Y
King	N	Y	N	Y	N	Y	Y
MARYLAND							
Cardin	N	Y	N	Y	N	Y	Y
Van Hollen	N	Y	N	Y	N	N	Y
MASSACHUSETTS							
Warren	N	Y	N	Y	N	N	Y
Markey	N	Y	N	Y	N	N	Y
MICHIGAN							
Stabenow	N	Y	N	Y	N	Y	Y
Peters	N	Y	N	Y	N	Y	Y
MINNESOTA							
Klobuchar	N	Y	N	Y	N	Y	Y
Franken	N	Y	N	Y	N	Y	Y
MISSISSIPPI							
Cochran	Y	N	Y	N	Y	Y	Y
Wicker	Y	N	Y	N	Y	Y	Y
MISSOURI							
McCaskill	N	Y	N	Y	N	Y	Y
Blunt	Y	N	Y	N	Y	Y	Y

	22	23	24	25	26	27	28
MONTANA							
Tester	N	Y	N	Y	N	N	Y
Daines	Y	N	Y	N	Y	Y	Y
NEBRASKA							
Fischer	Y	N	Y	N	Y	Y	Y
Sasse	Y	N	Y	N	Y	Y	Y
NEVADA							
Heller	Y	Y	Y	Y	Y	Y	Y
Cortez Masto	N	Y	N	Y	N	Y	Y
NEW HAMPSHIRE							
Shaheen	N	Y	N	Y	N	Y	Y
Hassan	N	Y	N	Y	N	Y	Y
NEW JERSEY							
Menendez	N	Y	N	Y	N	Y	Y
Booker	N	Y	N	Y	N	N	Y
NEW MEXICO							
Udall	N	Y	N	Y	N	N	Y
Heinrich	N	Y	N	Y	N	Y	Y
NEW YORK							
Schumer	N	Y	N	Y	N	Y	Y
Gillibrand	N	Y	N	Y	N	N	Y
NORTH CAROLINA							
Burr	Y	N	Y	N	Y	Y	Y
Tillis	Y	N	Y	N	Y	Y	Y
NORTH DAKOTA							
Hoeven	Y	N	Y	N	Y	Y	Y
Heitkamp	N	Y	N	Y	N	Y	Y
OHIO							
Brown	N	Y	N	Y	N	Y	Y
Portman	Y	N	Y	N	Y	Y	Y
OKLAHOMA							
Inhofe	Y	N	Y	N	Y	Y	Y
Lankford	Y	N	Y	N	Y	Y	Y
OREGON							
Wyden	N	Y	N	Y	N	N	Y
Merkley	N	Y	N	Y	N	N	Y
PENNSYLVANIA							
Casey	N	Y	N	Y	N	Y	Y
Toomey	Y	N	Y	N	Y	Y	Y
RHODE ISLAND							
Reed	N	Y	N	Y	N	Y	Y
Whitehouse	N	Y	N	Y	N	Y	Y
SOUTH CAROLINA							
Graham	Y	N	Y	N	Y	Y	Y
Scott	Y	N	Y	N	Y	Y	Y
SOUTH DAKOTA							
Thune	Y	N	Y	N	Y	Y	Y
Rounds	Y	N	Y	N	Y	Y	Y
TENNESSEE							
Alexander	Y	N	Y	N	Y	+	Y
Corker	Y	N	Y	N	Y	Y	Y
TEXAS							
Cornyn	Y	N	Y	N	Y	Y	Y
Cruz	Y	N	Y	N	Y	Y	Y
UTAH							
Hatch	Y	N	Y	N	Y	Y	Y
Lee	Y	N	Y	N	Y	Y	Y
VERMONT							
Leahy	N	Y	N	Y	N	N	Y
Sanders	N	Y	N	Y	N	N	Y
VIRGINIA							
Warner	N	Y	N	Y	N	Y	Y
Kaine	N	Y	N	Y	N	Y	Y
WASHINGTON							
Murray	N	Y	N	Y	N	Y	Y
Cantwell	N	Y	N	Y	N	Y	Y
WEST VIRGINIA							
Manchin	Y	Y	N	Y	N	Y	Y
Capito	Y	N	Y	N	Y	Y	Y
WISCONSIN							
Johnson	Y	N	Y	N	Y	Y	Y
Baldwin	N	Y	N	Y	N	N	Y
WYOMING							
Enzi	Y	N	Y	N	Y	Y	Y
Barrasso	Y	N	Y	N	Y	Y	Y

KEY	**Republicans**	Democrats	*Independents*
Y	Voted for (yea)	X Paired against	C Voted "present" to avoid possible conflict of interest
#	Paired for	– Announced against	
+	Announced for	P Voted "present"	? Did not vote or otherwise make a position known
N	Voted against (nay)		

VOTE NUMBER

29. MATTIS NOMINATION/CONFIRMATION. Confirmation of President Donald Trump's nomination of James Mattis of Washington to be secretary of Defense. Confirmed 98-1: R 51-0; D 45-1; I 2-0. Jan. 20, 2017.

30. KELLY NOMINATION/CONFIRMATION. Confirmation of President Donald Trump's nomination of John Kelly of Virginia to be secretary of Homeland Security. Confirmed 88-11: R 51-0; D 35-11; I 2-0. Jan. 20, 2017.

31. POMPEO NOMINATION/EXECUTIVE SESSION. McConnell, R-Ky., motion to proceed to executive session to consider President Donald Trump's nomination of Mike Pompeo, R-Kan., to be director of the Central Intelligence Agency. Motion agreed to 89-8: R 50-0; D 38-7; I 1-1. Jan. 20, 2017.

32. POMPEO NOMINATION/CONFIRMATION. Confirmation of President Donald Trump's nomination of Mike Pompeo of Kansas to be director of the Central Intelligence Agency. Confirmed 66-32: R 51-1; D 14-30; I 1-1. Jan. 23, 2017.

33. HALEY NOMINATION/CONFIRMATION. Confirmation of President Donald J. Trump's nomination of Nikki R. Haley of South Carolina to be United Nations ambassador and representative to the United Nations Security Council; and representative to the session of the General Assembly of the United Nations, en bloc. Confirmed 96-4: R 52-0; D 43-3; I 1-1. Jan. 24, 2017.

34. TILLERSON NOMINATION/CLOTURE. Motion to invoke cloture (thus limiting debate) on President Donald J. Trump's nomination of Rex W. Tillerson of Texas to be secretary of State. Motion agreed to 56-43: R 52-0; D 3-42; I 1-1. Jan. 30, 2017.

35. CHAO NOMINATION/CONFIRMATION. Confirmation of President Donald J. Trump's nomination of Elaine L. Chao of Kentucky to be secretary of Transportation. Confirmed 93-6: R 51-0; D 41-5; I 1-1. Jan. 31, 2017.

State / Senator	29	30	31	32	33	34	35
ALABAMA							
Shelby	Y	Y	Y	Y	Y	Y	Y
Sessions	?	?	?	Y	Y	Y	Y
ALASKA							
Murkowski	Y	Y	Y	Y	Y	Y	Y
Sullivan	Y	Y	Y	Y	Y	Y	Y
ARIZONA							
McCain	Y	Y	Y	Y	Y	Y	Y
Flake	Y	Y	Y	Y	Y	Y	Y
ARKANSAS							
Boozman	Y	Y	Y	Y	Y	Y	Y
Cotton	Y	Y	Y	Y	Y	Y	Y
CALIFORNIA							
Feinstein	Y	Y	Y	Y	Y	N	Y
Harris	Y	N	Y	N	Y	N	Y
COLORADO							
Bennet	Y	Y	Y	N	Y	N	Y
Gardner	Y	Y	Y	Y	Y	Y	Y
CONNECTICUT							
Blumenthal	Y	N	N	?	Y	N	Y
Murphy	Y	Y	Y	?	Y	N	Y
DELAWARE							
Carper	Y	Y	Y	N	Y	N	Y
Coons	Y	Y	Y	N	N	N	Y
FLORIDA							
Nelson	Y	Y	Y	N	Y	N	Y
Rubio	Y	Y	Y	Y	Y	Y	Y
GEORGIA							
Isakson	Y	Y	?	Y	Y	Y	Y
Perdue	Y	Y	Y	Y	Y	Y	Y
HAWAII							
Schatz	Y	Y	Y	Y	Y	N	Y
Hirono	Y	Y	Y	N	Y	N	Y
IDAHO							
Crapo	Y	Y	Y	Y	Y	Y	Y
Risch	Y	Y	Y	Y	Y	Y	Y
ILLINOIS							
Durbin	Y	Y	Y	N	Y	N	Y
Duckworth	Y	Y	Y	N	Y	N	Y
INDIANA							
Donnelly	Y	Y	Y	Y	Y	N	Y
Young	Y	Y	Y	Y	Y	Y	Y
IOWA							
Grassley	Y	Y	Y	Y	Y	Y	Y
Ernst	Y	Y	Y	Y	Y	Y	Y
KANSAS							
Roberts	Y	Y	Y	Y	Y	Y	Y
Moran	Y	Y	Y	Y	Y	Y	Y
KENTUCKY							
McConnell	Y	Y	Y	Y	Y	Y	P
Paul	Y	Y	Y	N	Y	Y	Y
LOUISIANA							
Cassidy	Y	Y	Y	Y	Y	Y	Y
Kennedy	Y	Y	Y	Y	Y	Y	Y
MAINE							
Collins	Y	Y	Y	Y	Y	Y	Y
King	Y	Y	Y	Y	Y	Y	Y
MARYLAND							
Cardin	Y	Y	Y	N	Y	N	Y
Van Hollen	Y	N	Y	N	Y	N	Y
MASSACHUSETTS							
Warren	Y	N	N	N	Y	N	N
Markey	Y	Y	Y	N	Y	N	Y
MICHIGAN							
Stabenow	Y	Y	Y	N	Y	N	Y
Peters	Y	Y	Y	N	Y	N	Y
MINNESOTA							
Klobuchar	Y	Y	Y	Y	Y	N	Y
Franken	Y	Y	Y	N	Y	N	Y
MISSISSIPPI							
Cochran	Y	Y	Y	Y	Y	Y	Y
Wicker	Y	Y	Y	Y	Y	Y	Y
MISSOURI							
McCaskill	Y	Y	Y	Y	Y	N	Y
Blunt	Y	Y	Y	Y	Y	Y	Y

State / Senator	29	30	31	32	33	34	35
MONTANA							
Tester	Y	Y	Y	N	Y	N	Y
Daines	Y	Y	Y	Y	Y	Y	Y
NEBRASKA							
Fischer	Y	Y	Y	Y	Y	Y	Y
Sasse	Y	Y	Y	Y	Y	Y	Y
NEVADA							
Heller	Y	Y	Y	Y	Y	Y	Y
Cortez Masto	Y	N	Y	N	Y	N	Y
NEW HAMPSHIRE							
Shaheen	Y	Y	Y	Y	Y	N	Y
Hassan	Y	Y	Y	Y	Y	N	Y
NEW JERSEY							
Menendez	Y	Y	Y	N	Y	N	Y
Booker	Y	N	N	N	Y	N	N
NEW MEXICO							
Udall	Y	N	N	N	N	N	Y
Heinrich	Y	N	Y	N	N	–	Y
NEW YORK							
Schumer	Y	Y	Y	Y	Y	N	N
Gillibrand	N	N	N	N	Y	N	N
NORTH CAROLINA							
Burr	Y	Y	Y	Y	Y	Y	Y
Tillis	Y	Y	Y	Y	Y	Y	Y
NORTH DAKOTA							
Hoeven	Y	Y	Y	Y	Y	Y	Y
Heitkamp	Y	Y	Y	Y	Y	Y	Y
OHIO							
Brown	Y	Y	Y	N	Y	N	Y
Portman	Y	Y	Y	Y	Y	Y	Y
OKLAHOMA							
Inhofe	Y	Y	Y	Y	Y	Y	Y
Lankford	Y	Y	Y	Y	Y	Y	Y
OREGON							
Wyden	Y	N	N	N	Y	N	Y
Merkley	Y	N	N	N	Y	N	N
PENNSYLVANIA							
Casey	Y	Y	Y	N	Y	N	Y
Toomey	Y	Y	Y	Y	Y	Y	Y
RHODE ISLAND							
Reed	Y	Y	Y	Y	Y	N	Y
Whitehouse	Y	Y	Y	Y	Y	N	Y
SOUTH CAROLINA							
Graham	Y	Y	Y	Y	Y	Y	Y
Scott	Y	Y	Y	Y	Y	Y	Y
SOUTH DAKOTA							
Thune	Y	Y	Y	Y	Y	Y	Y
Rounds	Y	Y	Y	Y	Y	Y	Y
TENNESSEE							
Alexander	Y	Y	Y	Y	Y	Y	Y
Corker	Y	Y	Y	Y	Y	Y	Y
TEXAS							
Cornyn	Y	Y	Y	Y	Y	Y	Y
Cruz	Y	Y	Y	Y	Y	Y	Y
UTAH							
Hatch	Y	Y	Y	Y	Y	Y	Y
Lee	Y	Y	Y	Y	Y	Y	Y
VERMONT							
Leahy	Y	Y	Y	N	Y	N	Y
Sanders	Y	N	N	N	N	N	N
VIRGINIA							
Warner	Y	Y	Y	Y	Y	Y	Y
Kaine	Y	Y	?	Y	Y	N	Y
WASHINGTON							
Murray	Y	Y	Y	N	Y	N	Y
Cantwell	Y	Y	Y	N	Y	N	Y
WEST VIRGINIA							
Manchin	Y	Y	Y	Y	Y	N	Y
Capito	Y	Y	Y	Y	Y	Y	Y
WISCONSIN							
Johnson	Y	Y	Y	Y	Y	Y	Y
Baldwin	Y	Y	Y	N	Y	N	Y
WYOMING							
Enzi	Y	Y	Y	Y	Y	Y	Y
Barrasso	Y	Y	Y	Y	Y	Y	Y

KEY   **Republicans**   Democrats   *Independents*

Y Voted for (yea)	X Paired against	C Voted "present" to avoid possible conflict of interest
# Paired for	– Announced against	
+ Announced for	P Voted "present"	? Did not vote or otherwise make a position known
N Voted against (nay)		

VOTE NUMBER

36. TILLERSON NOMINATION/CONFIRMATION. Confirmation of President Donald J. Trump's nomination of Rex W. Tillerson of Texas to be secretary of State. Confirmed 56-43: R 52-0; D 3-42; I 1-1. Feb. 1, 2017.

37. TILLERSON NOMINATION/MOTION TO TABLE. McConnell, R-Ky., motion to table (kill) the McConnell motion to reconsider the vote in which Rex W. Tillerson was confirmed as the secretary of State. Motion agreed to 55-43: R 51-0; D 3-42; I 1-1. Feb. 1, 2017.

38. LEGISLATIVE SESSION/MOTION TO PROCEED. McConnell, R-Ky., motion to proceed to legislative session. Motion agreed to 53-44: R 50-0; D 2-43; I 1-1. Feb. 1, 2017.

39. PROCEDURAL MOTION/JOURNAL. McConnell, R-Ky., motion to approve the Journal to date. Motion agreed to 54-44: R 51-0; D 2-43; I 1-1. Feb. 1, 2017.

40. DEVOS NOMINATION/EXECUTIVE SESSION. McConnell, R-Ky., motion to proceed to executive session to consider President Donald Trump's nomination of Betsy DeVos of Michigan to be secretary of Education. Motion agreed to 52-47: R 52-0; D 0-45; I 0-2. Feb. 1, 2017.

41. LEGISLATIVE SESSION/MOTION TO PROCEED. McConnell, R-Ky., motion to proceed to legislative session. Motion agreed to 55-42: R 51-0; D 4-40; I 0-2. Feb. 1, 2017.

42. H J RES 38. STREAM PROTECTION RULE DISAPPROVAL/MOTION TO PROCEED. McConnell, R-Ky., motion to proceed to the joint resolution that would nullify and disapprove of an Interior Department rule that requires surface coal mining operations, to the extent possible, to avoid disturbing streams and land within 100 feet of the streams. Motion agreed to 56-42: R 52-0; D 4-40; I 0-2. Feb. 1, 2017.

	36	37	38	39	40	41	42
ALABAMA							
Shelby	Y	Y	Y	Y	Y	Y	Y
Sessions	Y	?	?	?	Y	?	Y
ALASKA							
Murkowski	Y	Y	Y	Y	Y	Y	Y
Sullivan	Y	Y	Y	Y	Y	Y	Y
ARIZONA							
McCain	Y	Y	Y	Y	Y	Y	Y
Flake	Y	Y	Y	Y	Y	Y	Y
ARKANSAS							
Boozman	Y	Y	Y	Y	Y	Y	Y
Cotton	Y	Y	Y	Y	Y	Y	Y
CALIFORNIA							
Feinstein	N	N	N	N	N	N	N
Harris	N	N	N	N	N	N	N
COLORADO							
Bennet	N	N	N	N	N	N	N
Gardner	Y	Y	Y	Y	Y	Y	Y
CONNECTICUT							
Blumenthal	N	N	N	N	N	N	N
Murphy	N	N	N	N	N	N	N
DELAWARE							
Carper	N	N	N	N	N	N	N
Coons	?	?	?	?	?	?	?
FLORIDA							
Nelson	N	N	N	N	N	N	N
Rubio	Y	Y	Y	Y	Y	Y	Y
GEORGIA							
Isakson	Y	Y	Y	Y	Y	Y	Y
Perdue	Y	Y	Y	Y	Y	Y	Y
HAWAII							
Schatz	N	N	N	N	N	N	N
Hirono	N	N	N	N	N	N	N
IDAHO							
Crapo	Y	Y	Y	Y	Y	Y	Y
Risch	Y	Y	Y	Y	Y	Y	Y
ILLINOIS							
Durbin	N	N	N	Y	N	–	–
Duckworth	N	N	N	N	N	N	N
INDIANA							
Donnelly	N	N	N	N	N	Y	Y
Young	Y	Y	Y	Y	Y	Y	Y
IOWA							
Grassley	Y	Y	Y	Y	Y	Y	Y
Ernst	Y	Y	Y	Y	Y	Y	Y
KANSAS							
Roberts	Y	Y	Y	Y	Y	Y	Y
Moran	Y	Y	Y	Y	Y	Y	Y
KENTUCKY							
McConnell	Y	Y	Y	Y	Y	Y	Y
Paul	Y	Y	Y	Y	Y	Y	Y
LOUISIANA							
Cassidy	Y	Y	Y	Y	Y	Y	Y
Kennedy	Y	Y	Y	Y	Y	Y	Y
MAINE							
Collins	Y	Y	Y	Y	Y	Y	Y
King	Y	Y	Y	N	N	N	N
MARYLAND							
Cardin	N	N	N	N	N	N	N
Van Hollen	N	N	N	N	N	N	N
MASSACHUSETTS							
Warren	N	N	N	N	N	N	N
Markey	N	N	N	N	N	N	N
MICHIGAN							
Stabenow	N	N	N	N	N	N	N
Peters	N	N	N	N	N	N	N
MINNESOTA							
Klobuchar	N	N	N	N	N	N	N
Franken	N	N	N	N	N	N	N
MISSISSIPPI							
Cochran	Y	Y	Y	Y	Y	Y	Y
Wicker	Y	Y	Y	Y	Y	Y	Y
MISSOURI							
McCaskill	N	N	N	N	N	Y	Y
Blunt	Y	Y	Y	Y	Y	Y	Y
MONTANA							
Tester	N	N	N	N	N	N	N
Daines	Y	Y	Y	Y	Y	Y	Y
NEBRASKA							
Fischer	Y	Y	Y	Y	Y	Y	Y
Sasse	Y	Y	Y	Y	Y	Y	Y
NEVADA							
Heller	Y	Y	Y	Y	Y	Y	Y
Cortez Masto	N	N	N	N	N	N	N
NEW HAMPSHIRE							
Shaheen	N	N	N	N	N	N	N
Hassan	N	N	N	N	N	N	N
NEW JERSEY							
Menendez	N	N	Y	N	N	N	N
Booker	N	N	N	N	N	N	N
NEW MEXICO							
Udall	N	N	N	N	N	N	N
Heinrich	N	N	N	N	N	N	N
NEW YORK							
Schumer	N	N	N	N	N	N	N
Gillibrand	N	N	N	N	N	N	N
NORTH CAROLINA							
Burr	Y	Y	Y	Y	Y	Y	Y
Tillis	Y	Y	?	Y	Y	Y	Y
NORTH DAKOTA							
Hoeven	Y	Y	Y	Y	Y	Y	Y
Heitkamp	Y	Y	Y	Y	N	Y	Y
OHIO							
Brown	N	N	N	N	N	N	N
Portman	Y	Y	Y	Y	Y	Y	Y
OKLAHOMA							
Inhofe	Y	Y	Y	Y	Y	Y	Y
Lankford	Y	Y	Y	Y	Y	Y	Y
OREGON							
Wyden	N	N	N	N	N	N	N
Merkley	N	N	N	N	N	N	N
PENNSYLVANIA							
Casey	N	N	N	N	N	N	N
Toomey	Y	Y	Y	Y	Y	Y	Y
RHODE ISLAND							
Reed	N	N	N	N	N	N	N
Whitehouse	N	N	N	N	N	N	N
SOUTH CAROLINA							
Graham	Y	Y	Y	Y	Y	Y	Y
Scott	Y	Y	Y	Y	Y	Y	Y
SOUTH DAKOTA							
Thune	Y	Y	Y	Y	Y	Y	Y
Rounds	Y	Y	Y	Y	Y	Y	Y
TENNESSEE							
Alexander	Y	Y	Y	Y	Y	Y	Y
Corker	Y	Y	Y	Y	Y	Y	Y
TEXAS							
Cornyn	Y	Y	Y	Y	Y	Y	Y
Cruz	Y	Y	Y	Y	Y	Y	Y
UTAH							
Hatch	Y	Y	Y	Y	Y	Y	Y
Lee	Y	Y	Y	Y	Y	Y	Y
VERMONT							
Leahy	N	N	N	N	N	N	N
Sanders	N	N	N	N	N	N	N
VIRGINIA							
Warner	Y	Y	N	N	N	N	N
Kaine	N	N	N	N	N	N	N
WASHINGTON							
Murray	N	N	N	N	N	N	N
Cantwell	N	N	N	N	N	N	N
WEST VIRGINIA							
Manchin	Y	Y	N	N	N	Y	Y
Capito	Y	Y	Y	Y	Y	Y	Y
WISCONSIN							
Johnson	Y	Y	Y	Y	Y	Y	Y
Baldwin	N	N	N	N	N	N	N
WYOMING							
Enzi	Y	Y	Y	Y	Y	Y	Y
Barrasso	Y	Y	Y	Y	Y	Y	Y

KEY	**Republicans**	Democrats	*Independents*

Y Voted for (yea)	X Paired against	C Voted "present" to avoid possible conflict of interest
# Paired for	– Announced against	
+ Announced for	P Voted "present"	? Did not vote or otherwise make a position known
N Voted against (nay)		

||| SENATE VOTES

VOTE NUMBER

43. H J RES 38. STREAM PROTECTION RULE DISAPPROVAL/PASSAGE. Passage of the joint resolution that would nullify and disapprove of an Office of Surface Mining Reclamation and Enforcement rule that requires surface coal mining operations, to the extent possible, to avoid disturbing streams and land within 100 feet of the streams. The rule also includes provisions related to data collection and restoration and requires native trees and plants to be used to replant reclaimed mine sites. Passed (thus cleared for the president) 54-45: R 50-1; D 4-42; I 0-2. Feb. 2, 2017.

44. SESSIONS NOMINATION/MOTION TO PROCEED. McConnell, R-Ky., motion to proceed to executive session to consider the nomination of Sen. Jeff Sessions, R-Ala., to be attorney general. Motion agreed to 53-45: R 51-0; D 2-43; I 0-2. Feb. 2, 2017.

45. LEGISLATIVE SESSION/MOTION TO PROCEED. McConnell, R-Ky., motion to proceed to legislative session. Motion agreed to 51-47: R 50-0; D 0-46; I 1-1. Feb. 2, 2017.

46. PRICE NOMINATION/MOTION TO PROCEED. McConnell, R-Ky., motion to proceed to executive session to consider the nomination of Rep. Tom Price, R-Ga., to be secretary of Health and Human Services. Motion agreed to 51-48: R 51-0; D 0-46; I 0-2. Feb. 2, 2017.

47. LEGISLATIVE SESSION/MOTION TO PROCEED. McConnell, R-Ky., motion to proceed to legislative session. Motion agreed to 52-47: R 51-0; D 0-46; I 1-1. Feb. 2, 2017.

48. MNUCHIN NOMINATION/MOTION TO PROCEED. McConnell, R-Ky., motion to proceed to executive session to consider the nomination of Steven Mnuchin of California, to be secretary of Treasury. Motion agreed to 51-48: R 51-0; D 0-46; I 0-2. Feb. 2, 2017.

49. LEGISLATIVE SESSION/MOTION TO PROCEED. McConnell, R-Ky., motion to proceed to legislative session. Motion agreed to 52-48: R 52-0; D 0-46; I 0-2. Feb. 2, 2017.

	43	44	45	46	47	48	49
ALABAMA							
Shelby	Y	Y	Y	Y	Y	Y	Y
Sessions	?	?	?	?	?	?	Y
ALASKA							
Murkowski	Y	Y	Y	Y	Y	Y	Y
Sullivan	Y	Y	Y	Y	Y	Y	Y
ARIZONA							
McCain	Y	Y	Y	Y	Y	Y	Y
Flake	Y	Y	Y	Y	Y	Y	Y
ARKANSAS							
Boozman	Y	Y	Y	Y	Y	Y	Y
Cotton	Y	Y	Y	Y	Y	Y	Y
CALIFORNIA							
Feinstein	N	N	N	N	N	N	N
Harris	N	N	N	N	N	N	N
COLORADO							
Bennet	N	N	N	N	N	N	N
Gardner	Y	Y	Y	Y	Y	Y	Y
CONNECTICUT							
Blumenthal	N	N	N	N	N	N	N
Murphy	N	N	N	N	N	N	N
DELAWARE							
Carper	N	?	N	N	N	N	N
Coons	N	N	N	N	N	N	N
FLORIDA							
Nelson	N	N	N	N	N	N	N
Rubio	Y	Y	Y	Y	Y	Y	Y
GEORGIA							
Isakson	Y	Y	Y	Y	Y	Y	Y
Perdue	Y	Y	Y	Y	Y	Y	Y
HAWAII							
Schatz	N	N	N	N	N	N	N
Hirono	N	N	N	N	N	N	N
IDAHO							
Crapo	Y	Y	Y	Y	Y	Y	Y
Risch	Y	Y	Y	Y	Y	Y	Y
ILLINOIS							
Durbin	N	N	N	N	N	N	N
Duckworth	N	N	N	N	N	N	N
INDIANA							
Donnelly	Y	Y	N	N	N	N	N
Young	Y	Y	Y	Y	Y	Y	Y
IOWA							
Grassley	Y	Y	Y	Y	Y	Y	Y
Ernst	Y	Y	Y	Y	Y	Y	Y
KANSAS							
Roberts	Y	Y	Y	Y	Y	Y	Y
Moran	Y	Y	Y	Y	Y	Y	Y
KENTUCKY							
McConnell	Y	Y	Y	Y	Y	Y	Y
Paul	Y	Y	Y	Y	Y	Y	Y
LOUISIANA							
Cassidy	Y	Y	Y	Y	Y	Y	Y
Kennedy	Y	Y	Y	Y	Y	Y	Y
MAINE							
Collins	N	Y	Y	Y	Y	Y	Y
King	N	N	Y	N	Y	N	N
MARYLAND							
Cardin	N	N	N	N	N	N	N
Van Hollen	N	N	N	N	N	N	N
MASSACHUSETTS							
Warren	N	N	N	N	N	N	N
Markey	N	N	N	N	N	N	N
MICHIGAN							
Stabenow	N	N	N	N	N	N	N
Peters	N	N	N	N	N	N	N
MINNESOTA							
Klobuchar	N	N	N	N	N	N	N
Franken	N	N	N	N	N	N	N
MISSISSIPPI							
Cochran	Y	Y	Y	Y	Y	Y	Y
Wicker	Y	Y	Y	Y	Y	Y	Y
MISSOURI							
McCaskill	Y	N	N	N	N	N	N
Blunt	Y	Y	Y	Y	Y	Y	Y
MONTANA							
Tester	N	N	N	N	N	N	N
Daines	Y	Y	Y	Y	Y	Y	Y
NEBRASKA							
Fischer	Y	Y	Y	Y	Y	Y	Y
Sasse	Y	Y	Y	Y	Y	Y	Y
NEVADA							
Heller	Y	Y	Y	Y	Y	Y	Y
Cortez Masto	N	N	N	N	N	N	N
NEW HAMPSHIRE							
Shaheen	N	N	N	N	N	N	N
Hassan	N	N	N	N	N	N	N
NEW JERSEY							
Menendez	N	N	N	N	N	N	N
Booker	N	N	N	N	N	N	N
NEW MEXICO							
Udall	N	N	N	N	N	N	N
Heinrich	N	N	N	N	N	N	N
NEW YORK							
Schumer	N	N	N	N	N	N	N
Gillibrand	N	N	N	N	N	N	N
NORTH CAROLINA							
Burr	Y	Y	Y	Y	Y	Y	Y
Tillis	Y	Y	Y	Y	Y	Y	Y
NORTH DAKOTA							
Hoeven	Y	Y	Y	Y	Y	Y	Y
Heitkamp	Y	N	N	N	N	N	N
OHIO							
Brown	N	N	N	N	N	N	N
Portman	Y	Y	Y	Y	Y	Y	Y
OKLAHOMA							
Inhofe	Y	Y	Y	Y	Y	Y	Y
Lankford	Y	Y	Y	Y	Y	Y	Y
OREGON							
Wyden	N	N	N	N	N	N	N
Merkley	N	N	N	N	N	N	N
PENNSYLVANIA							
Casey	N	N	N	N	N	N	N
Toomey	Y	Y	Y	Y	Y	Y	Y
RHODE ISLAND							
Reed	N	N	N	N	N	N	N
Whitehouse	N	N	N	N	N	N	N
SOUTH CAROLINA							
Graham	Y	Y	?	Y	Y	Y	Y
Scott	Y	Y	Y	Y	Y	Y	Y
SOUTH DAKOTA							
Thune	Y	Y	Y	Y	Y	Y	Y
Rounds	Y	Y	Y	Y	Y	Y	Y
TENNESSEE							
Alexander	Y	Y	Y	Y	Y	Y	Y
Corker	Y	Y	Y	Y	Y	Y	Y
TEXAS							
Cornyn	Y	Y	Y	Y	Y	Y	Y
Cruz	Y	Y	Y	Y	Y	Y	Y
UTAH							
Hatch	Y	Y	Y	Y	Y	Y	Y
Lee	Y	Y	Y	Y	Y	Y	Y
VERMONT							
Leahy	N	N	N	N	N	N	N
Sanders	N	N	N	N	N	N	N
VIRGINIA							
Warner	N	N	N	N	N	N	N
Kaine	N	N	N	N	N	N	N
WASHINGTON							
Murray	N	N	N	N	N	N	N
Cantwell	N	N	N	N	N	N	N
WEST VIRGINIA							
Manchin	Y	Y	N	N	N	N	N
Capito	Y	Y	Y	Y	Y	Y	Y
WISCONSIN							
Johnson	Y	Y	Y	Y	Y	Y	Y
Baldwin	N	N	N	N	N	N	N
WYOMING							
Enzi	Y	Y	Y	Y	Y	Y	Y
Barrasso	Y	Y	Y	Y	Y	Y	Y

KEY	**Republicans**	Democrats	*Independents*

Y Voted for (yea)	X Paired against	C Voted "present" to avoid possible conflict of interest
# Paired for	– Announced against	
+ Announced for	P Voted "present"	? Did not vote or otherwise make a position known
N Voted against (nay)		

VOTE NUMBER

50. H J RES 41. FOREIGN ENERGY DEVELOPMENT DISCLOSURE DISAP-PROVAL/MOTION TO PROCEED. McConnell, R-Ky., motion to proceed to a joint resolution that would disapprove and void a rule submitted by the Securities and Exchange Commission that requires companies to disclose payments made to foreign governments for rights to develop oil, natural gas and mineral products. Motion agreed to 52-48: R 52-0; D 0-46; I 0-2. Feb. 2, 2017.

51. H J RES 41. FOREIGN ENERGY DEVELOPMENT DISCLOSURE DISAP-PROVAL/PASSAGE. Passage of the joint resolution that would nullify and disapprove of a Securities and Exchange Commission rule that requires companies that develop oil, natural gas or minerals to publicly report in detail payments to foreign governments or to the U.S. government totaling at least $100,000 annually per project for extraction, exploration or export of these resources. Passed (thus cleared for the president) 52-47: R 52-0; D 0-45; I 0-2. Feb. 3, 2017.

52. DEVOS NOMINATION/CLOTURE. Motion to invoke cloture (thus limiting debate) on the nomination of Betsy DeVos of Michigan to be secretary of Education. Motion agreed to 52-48: R 52-0; D 0-46; I 0-2. Feb. 3, 2017.

53. PROCEDURAL MOTION/REQUIRE ATTENDANCE. McConnell, R-Ky., motion to instruct the sergeant at arms to request the attendance of absent senators. Motion agreed to 91-4: R 44-4; D 45-0; I 2-0. Feb. 6, 2017.

54. DEVOS NOMINATION/CONFIRMATION. Confirmation of President Donald Trump's nomination of Betsy DeVos of Michigan to be secretary of Education. Confirmed, with Vice President Pence casting a "yea" vote to break the tie, 50-50: R 50-2; D 0-46; I 0-2. Feb. 7, 2017.

55. SESSIONS NOMINATION/CLOTURE. Motion to invoke cloture (thus limiting debate) on President Donald Trump's nomination of Jeff Sessions of Alabama to be attorney general. Motion agreed to 52-47: R 51-0; D 1-45; I 0-2. Feb. 7, 2017.

56. PROCEDURAL MOTION/REQUIRE ATTENDANCE. McConnell, R-Ky., motion to instruct the sergeant at arms to request the attendance of absent senators. Motion agreed to 88-3: R 46-3; D 41-0; I 1-0. Feb. 7, 2017.

	50	51	52	53	54	55	56
ALABAMA							
Shelby	Y	Y	Y	Y	Y	Y	Y
Sessions	Y	Y	Y	Y	Y	P	?
ALASKA							
Murkowski	Y	Y	Y	?	N	Y	Y
Sullivan	Y	Y	Y	Y	Y	Y	Y
ARIZONA							
McCain	Y	Y	Y	Y	Y	Y	Y
Flake	Y	Y	Y	?	Y	Y	Y
ARKANSAS							
Boozman	Y	Y	Y	Y	Y	Y	Y
Cotton	Y	Y	Y	Y	Y	Y	Y
CALIFORNIA							
Feinstein	N	N	N	Y	N	N	?
Harris	N	N	N	Y	N	N	Y
COLORADO							
Bennet	N	N	N	Y	N	N	Y
Gardner	Y	Y	Y	Y	Y	Y	Y
CONNECTICUT							
Blumenthal	N	N	N	Y	N	N	Y
Murphy	N	N	N	Y	N	N	?
DELAWARE							
Carper	N	N	N	Y	N	N	?
Coons	N	N	N	Y	N	N	?
FLORIDA							
Nelson	N	N	N	Y	N	N	Y
Rubio	Y	Y	Y	N	Y	Y	N
GEORGIA							
Isakson	Y	Y	Y	Y	Y	Y	?
Perdue	Y	Y	Y	Y	Y	Y	Y
HAWAII							
Schatz	N	N	N	Y	N	N	Y
Hirono	N	N	N	Y	N	N	Y
IDAHO							
Crapo	Y	Y	Y	Y	Y	Y	Y
Risch	Y	Y	Y	Y	Y	Y	Y
ILLINOIS							
Durbin	N	N	N	Y	N	N	Y
Duckworth	N	N	N	Y	N	N	Y
INDIANA							
Donnelly	N	N	N	Y	N	N	Y
Young	Y	Y	Y	Y	Y	Y	Y
IOWA							
Grassley	Y	Y	Y	Y	Y	Y	Y
Ernst	Y	Y	Y	Y	Y	Y	Y
KANSAS							
Roberts	Y	Y	Y	Y	Y	Y	Y
Moran	Y	Y	Y	Y	Y	Y	Y
KENTUCKY							
McConnell	Y	Y	Y	Y	Y	Y	Y
Paul	Y	Y	Y	Y	Y	Y	Y
LOUISIANA							
Cassidy	Y	Y	Y	Y	Y	Y	Y
Kennedy	Y	Y	Y	Y	Y	Y	Y
MAINE							
Collins	Y	Y	Y	N	N	Y	Y
King	N	N	N	Y	N	N	Y
MARYLAND							
Cardin	N	N	N	Y	N	N	Y
Van Hollen	N	N	N	Y	N	N	Y
MASSACHUSETTS							
Warren	N	N	N	Y	N	N	Y
Markey	N	?	N	Y	N	N	Y
MICHIGAN							
Stabenow	N	N	N	Y	N	N	Y
Peters	N	N	N	Y	N	N	Y
MINNESOTA							
Klobuchar	N	N	N	Y	N	N	Y
Franken	N	N	N	Y	N	N	Y
MISSISSIPPI							
Cochran	Y	Y	Y	Y	Y	Y	Y
Wicker	Y	Y	Y	N	Y	Y	N
MISSOURI							
McCaskill	N	N	N	Y	N	N	Y
Blunt	Y	Y	Y	Y	Y	Y	Y

	50	51	52	53	54	55	56
MONTANA							
Tester	N	N	N	Y	N	N	Y
Daines	Y	Y	Y	Y	Y	Y	Y
NEBRASKA							
Fischer	Y	Y	Y	Y	Y	Y	Y
Sasse	Y	Y	Y	?	Y	Y	Y
NEVADA							
Heller	Y	Y	Y	N	Y	Y	Y
Cortez Masto	N	N	N	Y	N	N	Y
NEW HAMPSHIRE							
Shaheen	N	N	N	Y	N	N	Y
Hassan	N	N	N	Y	N	N	Y
NEW JERSEY							
Menendez	N	N	N	Y	N	N	Y
Booker	N	N	N	Y	N	N	Y
NEW MEXICO							
Udall	N	N	N	?	N	N	Y
Heinrich	N	N	N	Y	N	N	Y
NEW YORK							
Schumer	N	N	N	Y	N	N	Y
Gillibrand	N	N	N	Y	N	N	Y
NORTH CAROLINA							
Burr	Y	Y	Y	Y	Y	Y	Y
Tillis	Y	Y	Y	Y	Y	Y	Y
NORTH DAKOTA							
Hoeven	Y	Y	Y	Y	Y	Y	Y
Heitkamp	N	N	N	Y	N	N	Y
OHIO							
Brown	N	N	N	Y	N	N	Y
Portman	Y	Y	Y	Y	Y	Y	Y
OKLAHOMA							
Inhofe	Y	Y	Y	Y	Y	Y	Y
Lankford	Y	Y	Y	Y	Y	Y	Y
OREGON							
Wyden	N	N	N	Y	N	N	Y
Merkley	N	N	N	Y	N	N	Y
PENNSYLVANIA							
Casey	N	N	N	Y	N	N	Y
Toomey	Y	Y	Y	?	Y	Y	N
RHODE ISLAND							
Reed	N	N	N	Y	N	N	Y
Whitehouse	N	N	N	Y	N	N	Y
SOUTH CAROLINA							
Graham	Y	Y	Y	Y	Y	Y	Y
Scott	Y	Y	Y	Y	Y	Y	Y
SOUTH DAKOTA							
Thune	Y	Y	Y	Y	Y	Y	Y
Rounds	Y	Y	Y	Y	Y	Y	Y
TENNESSEE							
Alexander	Y	Y	Y	Y	Y	Y	Y
Corker	Y	Y	Y	Y	Y	Y	Y
TEXAS							
Cornyn	Y	Y	Y	Y	Y	Y	Y
Cruz	Y	Y	Y	Y	Y	Y	?
UTAH							
Hatch	Y	Y	Y	Y	Y	Y	Y
Lee	Y	Y	Y	Y	Y	Y	Y
VERMONT							
Leahy	N	N	N	Y	N	N	Y
Sanders	N	N	N	Y	N	N	?
VIRGINIA							
Warner	N	N	N	Y	N	N	?
Kaine	N	N	N	Y	N	N	Y
WASHINGTON							
Murray	N	N	N	Y	N	N	Y
Cantwell	N	N	N	Y	N	N	Y
WEST VIRGINIA							
Manchin	N	N	N	Y	N	Y	Y
Capito	Y	Y	Y	Y	Y	Y	Y
WISCONSIN							
Johnson	Y	Y	Y	Y	Y	Y	Y
Baldwin	N	N	N	Y	N	N	Y
WYOMING							
Enzi	Y	Y	Y	Y	Y	Y	Y
Barrasso	Y	Y	Y	Y	Y	Y	Y

KEY	**Republicans**	Democrats	*Independents*
Y	Voted for (yea)	X	Paired against	C	Voted "present" to avoid possible conflict of interest
#	Paired for	–	Announced against		
+	Announced for	P	Voted "present"	?	Did not vote or otherwise make a position known
N	Voted against (nay)				

VOTE NUMBER

57. SESSIONS NOMINATION/RULING OF THE CHAIR. Judgment of the Senate to affirm the ruling of the chair regarding the Warren, D-Mass., motion to appeal the ruling of the chair that she had broken a rule forbidding the impugning the motives of a senator. Ruling of the chair sustained 49-43: R 49-0; D 0-42; I 0-1. Feb. 7, 2017.

58. SESSIONS NOMINATION/MOTION TO PROCEED IN ORDER. Harris, D-Calif., motion that Sen. Elizabeth Warren, D-Mass., be permitted to proceed in order. Motion rejected 43-50: R 0-50; D 42-0; I 1-0. Feb. 7, 2017.

59. SESSIONS NOMINATION/CONFIRMATION. Confirmation of President Donald Trump's nomination of Jeff Sessions of Alabama to be attorney general. Confirmed 52-47: R 51-0; D 1-45; I 0-2. Feb. 8, 2017.

60. PRICE NOMINATION/CLOTURE. Motion to invoke cloture (thus limiting debate) on President Donald Trump's nomination of Tom Price of Georgia to be secretary of Health and Human Services. Motion agreed to 51-48: R 51-0; D 0-46; I 0-2. Feb. 8, 2017.

61. PRICE NOMINATION/CONFIRMATION. Confirmation of President Donald Trump's nomination of Thomas Price of Georgia to be secretary of Health and Human Services. Confirmed 52-47: R 52-0; D 0-45; I 0-2. Feb. 10, 2017.

62. MNUCHIN NOMINATION/CLOTURE. Motion to invoke cloture (thus limiting debate) on President Donald Trump's nomination of Steven Mnuchin of California to be secretary of Treasury. Motion agreed to 53-46: R 52-0; D 1-44; I 0-2. Feb. 10, 2017.

63. MNUCHIN NOMINATION/CONFIRMATION. Confirmation of President Donald Trump's nomination of Steven T. Mnuchin of California to be secretary of the Treasury. Confirmed 53-47: R 52-0; D 1-45; I 0-2. Feb. 13, 2017.

	57	58	59	60	61	62	63
ALABAMA							
Shelby	Y	N	Y	Y	Y	Y	Y
ALASKA							
Murkowski	Y	N	Y	Y	Y	Y	Y
Sullivan	Y	N	Y	Y	Y	Y	Y
ARIZONA							
McCain	Y	N	Y	Y	Y	Y	Y
Flake	Y	N	Y	Y	Y	Y	Y
ARKANSAS							
Boozman	Y	N	Y	Y	Y	Y	Y
Cotton	Y	N	Y	Y	Y	Y	Y
CALIFORNIA							
Feinstein	?	?	N	N	N	N	N
Harris	N	Y	N	N	N	N	N
COLORADO							
Bennet	N	Y	N	N	N	N	N
Gardner	Y	N	Y	Y	Y	Y	Y
CONNECTICUT							
Blumenthal	N	Y	N	N	N	N	N
Murphy	N	Y	N	N	N	N	N
DELAWARE							
Carper	?	?	N	N	N	N	N
Coons	?	?	N	N	N	N	N
FLORIDA							
Nelson	N	Y	N	N	N	N	N
Rubio	Y	N	Y	Y	Y	Y	Y
GEORGIA							
Isakson	?	N	Y	Y	Y	Y	Y
Perdue	Y	N	Y	Y	Y	Y	Y
HAWAII							
Schatz	N	Y	N	N	N	N	N
Hirono	N	Y	N	N	N	N	N
IDAHO							
Crapo	Y	N	Y	Y	Y	Y	Y
Risch	Y	N	Y	Y	Y	Y	Y
ILLINOIS							
Durbin	N	Y	N	N	N	N	N
Duckworth	N	Y	N	N	N	N	N
INDIANA							
Donnelly	N	Y	N	N	N	N	N
Young	Y	N	Y	Y	Y	Y	Y
IOWA							
Grassley	Y	N	Y	Y	Y	Y	Y
Ernst	Y	N	Y	Y	Y	Y	Y
KANSAS							
Roberts	Y	N	Y	Y	Y	Y	Y
Moran	Y	N	Y	Y	Y	Y	Y
KENTUCKY							
McConnell	Y	N	Y	Y	Y	Y	Y
Paul	Y	N	Y	Y	Y	Y	Y
LOUISIANA							
Cassidy	Y	N	Y	Y	Y	Y	Y
Kennedy	Y	N	Y	Y	Y	Y	Y
MAINE							
Collins	Y	N	Y	Y	Y	Y	Y
King	N	Y	N	N	N	N	N
MARYLAND							
Cardin	N	Y	N	N	N	N	N
Van Hollen	N	Y	N	N	N	N	N
MASSACHUSETTS							
Warren	N	Y	N	N	N	N	N
Markey	N	Y	N	N	N	N	N
MICHIGAN							
Stabenow	N	Y	N	N	N	N	N
Peters	N	Y	N	N	N	N	N
MINNESOTA							
Klobuchar	N	Y	N	N	N	N	N
Franken	N	Y	N	N	N	N	N
MISSISSIPPI							
Cochran	Y	N	Y	Y	Y	Y	Y
Wicker	Y	N	Y	Y	Y	Y	Y
MISSOURI							
McCaskill	N	Y	N	N	–	–	N
Blunt	Y	N	Y	Y	Y	Y	Y

	57	58	59	60	61	62	63
MONTANA							
Tester	N	Y	N	N	N	N	N
Daines	Y	N	Y	Y	Y	Y	Y
NEBRASKA							
Fischer	Y	N	Y	Y	Y	Y	Y
Sasse	Y	N	Y	Y	Y	Y	Y
NEVADA							
Heller	Y	N	Y	Y	Y	Y	Y
Cortez Masto	N	Y	N	N	N	N	N
NEW HAMPSHIRE							
Shaheen	N	Y	N	N	N	N	N
Hassan	N	Y	N	N	N	N	N
NEW JERSEY							
Menendez	N	Y	N	N	N	N	N
Booker	N	Y	N	N	N	N	N
NEW MEXICO							
Udall	N	Y	N	N	N	N	N
Heinrich	N	Y	N	N	N	N	N
NEW YORK							
Schumer	N	Y	N	N	N	N	N
Gillibrand	N	Y	N	N	N	N	N
NORTH CAROLINA							
Burr	Y	N	Y	Y	Y	Y	Y
Tillis	Y	N	Y	Y	Y	Y	Y
NORTH DAKOTA							
Hoeven	Y	N	Y	Y	Y	Y	Y
Heitkamp	N	Y	N	N	N	N	N
OHIO							
Brown	N	Y	N	N	N	N	N
Portman	Y	N	Y	Y	Y	Y	Y
OKLAHOMA							
Inhofe	Y	N	Y	Y	Y	Y	Y
Lankford	Y	N	Y	Y	Y	Y	Y
OREGON							
Wyden	N	Y	N	N	N	N	N
Merkley	N	Y	N	N	N	N	N
PENNSYLVANIA							
Casey	N	Y	N	N	N	N	N
Toomey	Y	N	Y	Y	Y	Y	Y
RHODE ISLAND							
Reed	N	Y	N	N	N	N	N
Whitehouse	N	Y	N	N	N	N	N
SOUTH CAROLINA							
Graham	Y	N	Y	Y	Y	Y	Y
Scott	Y	N	Y	Y	Y	Y	Y
SOUTH DAKOTA							
Thune	Y	N	Y	Y	Y	Y	Y
Rounds	Y	N	Y	Y	Y	Y	Y
TENNESSEE							
Alexander	Y	N	Y	Y	Y	Y	Y
Corker	Y	N	Y	Y	Y	Y	Y
TEXAS							
Cornyn	Y	N	Y	Y	Y	Y	Y
Cruz	?	?	Y	Y	Y	Y	Y
UTAH							
Hatch	Y	N	Y	Y	Y	Y	Y
Lee	Y	N	Y	Y	Y	Y	Y
VERMONT							
Leahy	N	Y	N	N	N	N	N
Sanders	?	?	N	N	N	N	N
VIRGINIA							
Warner	?	?	N	N	N	N	N
Kaine	N	Y	N	N	N	N	N
WASHINGTON							
Murray	N	Y	N	N	N	N	N
Cantwell	N	Y	N	N	N	N	N
WEST VIRGINIA							
Manchin	N	Y	Y	N	N	Y	Y
Capito	Y	N	Y	Y	Y	Y	Y
WISCONSIN							
Johnson	Y	N	Y	Y	Y	Y	Y
Baldwin	N	Y	N	N	N	N	N
WYOMING							
Enzi	Y	N	Y	Y	Y	Y	Y
Barrasso	Y	N	Y	Y	Y	Y	Y

KEY	Republicans	Democrats	*Independents*

Y Voted for (yea)	X Paired against	C Voted "present" to avoid possible conflict of interest
# Paired for	– Announced against	? Did not vote or otherwise make a position known
+ Announced for	P Voted "present"	
N Voted against (nay)		

VOTE NUMBER

64. SHULKIN NOMINATION/CONFIRMATION. Confirmation of President Donald Trump's nomination of David J. Shulkin of Pennsylvania to be secretary of Veterans Affairs. Confirmed 100-0: R 52-0; D 46-0; I 2-0. Feb. 13, 2017.

65. MCMAHON NOMINATION/CONFIRMATION. Confirmation of President Donald Trump's nomination of Linda E. McMahon of Connecticut to be administrator of the Small Business Administration. Confirmed 81-19: R 52-0; D 28-18; I 1-1. Feb. 14, 2017.

66. H J RES 40. FIREARMS PURCHASE PROHIBITION DISAPPROVAL/ PASSAGE. Passage of the joint resolution that would disapprove of and nullify a Social Security Administration rule that outlines reporting of information by the agency on certain non-elderly individuals who receive disability insurance or Supplemental Security Income benefits for inclusion in the National Instant Criminal Background Check System for gun purchases if they receive benefits based on a finding of mental impairment and use a "representative payee" because they cannot manage their benefit payments. Passed (thus cleared for the president) 57-43: R 52-0; D 4-42; I 1-1. Feb. 15, 2017.

67. MULVANEY NOMINATION/CLOTURE. Motion to invoke cloture (thus limiting debate) on President Donald Trump's nomination of Mick Mulvaney of South Carolina to be director of the Office of Management and Budget. Motion agreed to 52-48: R 52-0; D 0-46; I 0-2. Feb. 15, 2017.

68. MULVANEY NOMINATION/CONFIRMATION. Confirmation of President Donald Trump's nomination of Mick Mulvaney of South Carolina to be director of the Office of Management and Budget. Confirmed 51-49: R 51-1; D 0-46; I 0-2. Feb. 16, 2017.

69. PRUITT NOMINATION/CLOTURE. Motion to invoke cloture (thus limiting debate) on President Donald Trump's nomination of Scott Pruitt of Oklahoma to be EPA administrator. Motion agreed to 54-46: R 52-0; D 2-44; I 0-2. Feb. 16, 2017.

70. PRUITT NOMINATION/MOTION TO EXTEND DEBATE. Merkley, D-Ore., motion to extend post-cloture debate time on the nomination of Scott Pruitt of Oklahoma to be EPA administrator by 248 hours. Motion rejected 47-51: R 0-51; D 45-0; I 2-0. Feb. 17, 2017.

	64	65	66	67	68	69	70
ALABAMA							
Shelby	Y	Y	Y	Y	Y	Y	N
Strange	Y	Y	Y	Y	Y	Y	N
ALASKA							
Murkowski	Y	Y	Y	Y	Y	Y	N
Sullivan	Y	Y	Y	Y	Y	Y	N
ARIZONA							
McCain	Y	Y	Y	Y	N	Y	?
Flake	Y	Y	Y	Y	Y	Y	N
ARKANSAS							
Boozman	Y	Y	Y	Y	Y	Y	N
Cotton	Y	Y	Y	Y	Y	Y	N
CALIFORNIA							
Feinstein	Y	Y	N	N	N	N	Y
Harris	Y	N	N	N	N	N	Y
COLORADO							
Bennet	Y	Y	N	N	N	N	Y
Gardner	Y	Y	Y	Y	Y	Y	N
CONNECTICUT							
Blumenthal	Y	Y	N	N	N	N	Y
Murphy	Y	Y	N	N	N	N	Y
DELAWARE							
Carper	Y	Y	N	N	N	N	Y
Coons	Y	Y	N	N	N	N	Y
FLORIDA							
Nelson	Y	Y	N	N	N	N	Y
Rubio	Y	Y	Y	Y	Y	Y	N
GEORGIA							
Isakson	Y	Y	Y	Y	Y	Y	N
Perdue	Y	Y	Y	Y	Y	Y	N
HAWAII							
Schatz	Y	N	N	N	N	N	Y
Hirono	Y	Y	N	N	N	N	Y
IDAHO							
Crapo	Y	Y	Y	Y	Y	Y	N
Risch	Y	Y	Y	Y	Y	Y	N
ILLINOIS							
Durbin	Y	N	N	N	N	N	Y
Duckworth	Y	Y	N	N	N	N	Y
INDIANA							
Donnelly	Y	Y	Y	N	N	N	?
Young	Y	Y	Y	Y	Y	Y	N
IOWA							
Grassley	Y	Y	Y	Y	Y	Y	N
Ernst	Y	Y	Y	Y	Y	Y	N
KANSAS							
Roberts	Y	Y	Y	Y	Y	Y	N
Moran	Y	Y	Y	Y	Y	Y	N
KENTUCKY							
McConnell	Y	Y	Y	Y	Y	Y	N
Paul	Y	Y	Y	Y	Y	Y	N
LOUISIANA							
Cassidy	Y	Y	Y	Y	Y	Y	N
Kennedy	Y	Y	Y	Y	Y	Y	N
MAINE							
Collins	Y	Y	Y	Y	Y	Y	N
King	Y	Y	Y	N	N	N	Y
MARYLAND							
Cardin	Y	Y	N	N	N	N	Y
Van Hollen	Y	N	N	N	N	N	Y
MASSACHUSETTS							
Warren	Y	N	N	N	N	N	Y
Markey	Y	N	N	N	N	N	Y
MICHIGAN							
Stabenow	Y	Y	N	N	N	N	Y
Peters	Y	Y	N	N	N	N	Y
MINNESOTA							
Klobuchar	Y	Y	N	N	N	N	Y
Franken	Y	Y	N	N	N	N	Y
MISSISSIPPI							
Cochran	Y	Y	Y	Y	Y	Y	N
Wicker	Y	Y	Y	Y	Y	Y	N
MISSOURI							
McCaskill	Y	Y	N	N	N	N	Y
Blunt	Y	Y	Y	Y	Y	Y	N

	64	65	66	67	68	69	70
MONTANA							
Tester	Y	Y	Y	N	N	N	Y
Daines	Y	Y	Y	Y	Y	Y	N
NEBRASKA							
Fischer	Y	Y	Y	Y	Y	Y	N
Sasse	Y	Y	Y	Y	Y	Y	N
NEVADA							
Heller	Y	Y	Y	Y	Y	Y	N
Cortez Masto	Y	Y	N	N	N	N	Y
NEW HAMPSHIRE							
Shaheen	Y	Y	N	N	N	N	Y
Hassan	Y	Y	N	N	N	N	Y
NEW JERSEY							
Menendez	Y	Y	N	N	N	N	Y
Booker	Y	N	N	N	N	N	Y
NEW MEXICO							
Udall	Y	N	N	N	N	N	Y
Heinrich	Y	N	N	N	N	N	Y
NEW YORK							
Schumer	Y	N	N	N	N	N	Y
Gillibrand	Y	N	N	N	N	N	Y
NORTH CAROLINA							
Burr	Y	Y	Y	Y	Y	Y	N
Tillis	Y	Y	Y	Y	Y	Y	N
NORTH DAKOTA							
Hoeven	Y	Y	Y	Y	Y	Y	N
Heitkamp	Y	Y	Y	N	N	Y	Y
OHIO							
Brown	Y	N	N	N	N	N	Y
Portman	Y	Y	Y	Y	Y	Y	N
OKLAHOMA							
Inhofe	Y	Y	Y	Y	Y	Y	N
Lankford	Y	Y	Y	Y	Y	Y	N
OREGON							
Wyden	Y	N	N	N	N	N	Y
Merkley	Y	N	N	N	N	N	Y
PENNSYLVANIA							
Casey	Y	Y	N	N	N	N	Y
Toomey	Y	Y	Y	Y	Y	Y	N
RHODE ISLAND							
Reed	Y	N	N	N	N	N	Y
Whitehouse	Y	N	N	N	N	N	Y
SOUTH CAROLINA							
Graham	Y	Y	Y	Y	Y	Y	N
Scott	Y	Y	Y	Y	Y	Y	N
SOUTH DAKOTA							
Thune	Y	Y	Y	Y	Y	Y	N
Rounds	Y	Y	Y	Y	Y	Y	N
TENNESSEE							
Alexander	Y	Y	Y	Y	Y	Y	N
Corker	Y	Y	Y	Y	Y	Y	N
TEXAS							
Cornyn	Y	Y	Y	Y	Y	Y	N
Cruz	Y	Y	Y	Y	Y	Y	N
UTAH							
Hatch	Y	Y	Y	Y	Y	Y	N
Lee	Y	Y	Y	Y	Y	Y	N
VERMONT							
Leahy	Y	Y	N	N	N	N	Y
Sanders	Y	N	N	N	N	N	Y
VIRGINIA							
Warner	Y	Y	N	N	N	N	Y
Kaine	Y	Y	N	N	N	N	Y
WASHINGTON							
Murray	Y	N	N	N	N	N	Y
Cantwell	Y	Y	N	N	N	N	Y
WEST VIRGINIA							
Manchin	Y	Y	Y	N	N	Y	Y
Capito	Y	Y	Y	Y	Y	Y	N
WISCONSIN							
Johnson	Y	Y	Y	Y	Y	Y	N
Baldwin	Y	N	N	N	N	N	Y
WYOMING							
Enzi	Y	Y	Y	Y	Y	Y	N
Barrasso	Y	Y	Y	Y	Y	Y	N

KEY	**Republicans**	Democrats	*Independents*
Y Voted for (yea)		X Paired against	C Voted "present" to avoid possible conflict of interest
# Paired for		– Announced against	
+ Announced for		P Voted "present"	? Did not vote or otherwise make a position known
N Voted against (nay)			

VOTE NUMBER

71. PRUITT NOMINATION/CONFIRMATION. Confirmation of President Donald Trump's nomination of Scott Pruitt of Oklahoma to be EPA administrator. Confirmed 52-46: R 50-1; D 2-43; I 0-2. Feb. 17, 2017.

72. ROSS NOMINATION/CLOTURE. Motion to invoke cloture (thus limiting debate) on President Donald Trump's nomination of Wilbur L. Ross Jr. of Florida to be secretary of Commerce. Motion agreed to 66-31: R 50-0; D 15-30; I 1-1. Feb. 17, 2017.

73. ROSS NOMINATION/CONFIRMATION. Confirmation of President Donald Trump's nomination of Wilbur L. Ross Jr. of Florida to be secretary of Commerce. Confirmed 72-27: R 51-0; D 20-26; I 1-1. Feb. 27, 2017.

74. ZINKE NOMINATION/CLOTURE. Motion to invoke cloture (thus limiting debate) on President Donald Trump's nomination of Ryan Zinke of Montana to be secretary of Interior. Motion agreed to 67-31: R 51-0; D 15-30; I 1-1. Feb. 27, 2017.

75. ZINKE NOMINATION/CONFIRMATION. Confirmation of President Donald Trump's nomination of Ryan Zinke of Montana to be secretary of Interior. Confirmed 68-31: R 51-0; D 16-30; I 1-1. March 1, 2017.

76. CARSON NOMINATION/CLOTURE. Motion to invoke cloture (thus limiting debate) on President Donald Trump's nomination of Benjamin S. Carson Sr. of Florida to be secretary of Housing and Urban Development. Motion agreed to 62-37: R 51-0; D 10-36; I 1-1. March 1, 2017.

77. CARSON NOMINATION/CONFIRMATION. Confirmation of President Donald Trump's nomination of Benjamin S. Carson Sr. of Florida to be secretary of Housing and Urban Development. Confirmed 58-41: R 51-0; D 6-40; I 1-1. March 2, 2017.

	71	72	73	74	75	76	77
ALABAMA							
Shelby	Y	Y	Y	Y	Y	Y	Y
Strange	Y	Y	Y	Y	Y	Y	Y
ALASKA							
Murkowski	Y	Y	Y	Y	Y	Y	Y
Sullivan	Y	Y	Y	Y	Y	Y	Y
ARIZONA							
McCain	?	?	Y	Y	Y	Y	Y
Flake	Y	Y	Y	Y	Y	Y	Y
ARKANSAS							
Boozman	Y	Y	Y	Y	Y	Y	Y
Cotton	Y	Y	Y	Y	Y	Y	Y
CALIFORNIA							
Feinstein	N	Y	Y	Y	N	N	N
Harris	N	N	N	N	N	N	N
COLORADO							
Bennet	N	Y	Y	Y	Y	N	N
Gardner	Y	Y	Y	Y	Y	Y	Y
CONNECTICUT							
Blumenthal	N	N	N	N	N	N	N
Murphy	N	N	N	Y	Y	N	N
DELAWARE							
Carper	N	Y	Y	N	N	Y	N
Coons	N	Y	Y	Y	Y	N	N
FLORIDA							
Nelson	N	Y	Y	Y	Y	N	N
Rubio	Y	Y	Y	Y	Y	Y	Y
GEORGIA							
Isakson	Y	Y	?	?	?	?	?
Perdue	Y	Y	Y	Y	Y	Y	Y
HAWAII							
Schatz	N	Y	Y	N	N	N	N
Hirono	N	N	N	N	N	N	N
IDAHO							
Crapo	Y	Y	Y	Y	Y	Y	Y
Risch	Y	Y	Y	Y	Y	Y	Y
ILLINOIS							
Durbin	N	N	N	N	N	N	N
Duckworth	N	Y	Y	N	N	N	N
INDIANA							
Donnelly	?	?	Y	Y	Y	Y	Y
Young	Y	Y	Y	Y	Y	Y	Y
IOWA							
Grassley	Y	Y	Y	Y	Y	Y	Y
Ernst	Y	Y	Y	Y	Y	Y	Y
KANSAS							
Roberts	Y	Y	Y	Y	Y	Y	Y
Moran	Y	Y	Y	Y	Y	Y	Y
KENTUCKY							
McConnell	Y	Y	Y	Y	Y	Y	Y
Paul	Y	Y	Y	Y	Y	Y	Y
LOUISIANA							
Cassidy	Y	?	Y	Y	Y	Y	Y
Kennedy	Y	Y	Y	Y	Y	Y	Y
MAINE							
Collins	N	Y	Y	Y	Y	Y	Y
King	N	Y	Y	Y	Y	Y	Y
MARYLAND							
Cardin	N	N	N	N	N	Y	N
Van Hollen	N	N	N	N	N	N	N
MASSACHUSETTS							
Warren	N	N	N	N	N	N	N
Markey	N	N	N	N	N	N	N
MICHIGAN							
Stabenow	N	N	N	N	N	N	N
Peters	N	N	Y	N	N	N	N
MINNESOTA							
Klobuchar	N	Y	Y	N	N	N	N
Franken	N	N	N	N	N	N	N
MISSISSIPPI							
Cochran	Y	Y	Y	Y	Y	Y	Y
Wicker	Y	Y	Y	Y	Y	Y	Y
MISSOURI							
McCaskill	N	N	Y	N	N	N	N
Blunt	Y	Y	Y	Y	Y	Y	Y
MONTANA							
Tester	N	Y	Y	Y	Y	Y	Y
Daines	Y	Y	Y	Y	Y	Y	Y
NEBRASKA							
Fischer	Y	Y	Y	Y	Y	Y	Y
Sasse	Y	Y	Y	Y	Y	Y	Y
NEVADA							
Heller	Y	Y	Y	Y	Y	Y	Y
Cortez Masto	N	Y	Y	Y	Y	N	N
NEW HAMPSHIRE							
Shaheen	N	Y	Y	N	N	N	N
Hassan	N	Y	Y	N	N	N	N
NEW JERSEY							
Menendez	N	N	N	N	N	Y	N
Booker	N	N	N	N	N	N	N
NEW MEXICO							
Udall	N	N	N	Y	N	N	N
Heinrich	N	N	N	Y	Y	N	N
NEW YORK							
Schumer	N	N	N	N	N	N	N
Gillibrand	N	N	N	N	N	N	N
NORTH CAROLINA							
Burr	Y	Y	Y	Y	Y	Y	Y
Tillis	Y	Y	Y	Y	Y	Y	Y
NORTH DAKOTA							
Hoeven	Y	Y	Y	Y	Y	Y	Y
Heitkamp	Y	Y	Y	Y	Y	Y	Y
OHIO							
Brown	N	N	Y	N	Y	Y	Y
Portman	Y	Y	Y	Y	Y	Y	Y
OKLAHOMA							
Inhofe	Y	Y	Y	Y	Y	Y	Y
Lankford	Y	Y	Y	Y	Y	Y	Y
OREGON							
Wyden	N	N	N	P	Y	N	N
Merkley	N	N	N	N	N	N	N
PENNSYLVANIA							
Casey	N	N	Y	N	N	N	N
Toomey	Y	Y	Y	Y	Y	Y	Y
RHODE ISLAND							
Reed	N	N	N	N	N	Y	N
Whitehouse	N	N	N	N	N	N	N
SOUTH CAROLINA							
Graham	Y	Y	Y	Y	Y	Y	Y
Scott	Y	Y	Y	Y	Y	Y	Y
SOUTH DAKOTA							
Thune	Y	Y	Y	Y	Y	Y	Y
Rounds	Y	Y	Y	Y	Y	Y	Y
TENNESSEE							
Alexander	Y	Y	Y	Y	Y	Y	Y
Corker	Y	Y	Y	Y	Y	Y	Y
TEXAS							
Cornyn	Y	Y	Y	Y	Y	Y	Y
Cruz	Y	Y	Y	Y	Y	Y	Y
UTAH							
Hatch	Y	Y	Y	Y	Y	Y	Y
Lee	Y	Y	Y	Y	Y	Y	Y
VERMONT							
Leahy	N	N	N	N	N	N	N
Sanders	N	N	N	N	N	N	N
VIRGINIA							
Warner	N	Y	Y	Y	Y	Y	Y
Kaine	N	Y	Y	Y	Y	N	N
WASHINGTON							
Murray	N	N	N	N	N	N	N
Cantwell	N	N	N	N	N	N	N
WEST VIRGINIA							
Manchin	Y	N	N	Y	Y	Y	Y
Capito	Y	Y	Y	Y	Y	Y	Y
WISCONSIN							
Johnson	Y	Y	Y	Y	Y	Y	Y
Baldwin	N	N	N	N	N	N	N
WYOMING							
Enzi	Y	Y	Y	Y	Y	Y	Y
Barrasso	Y	Y	Y	Y	Y	Y	Y

KEY   Republicans   Democrats   *Independents*

Y Voted for (yea)	X Paired against	C Voted "present" to avoid possible conflict of interest
# Paired for	– Announced against	
+ Announced for	P Voted "present"	? Did not vote or otherwise make a position known
N Voted against (nay)		

VOTE NUMBER

78. PERRY NOMINATION/CLOTURE. Motion to invoke cloture (thus limiting debate) on President Donald Trump's nomination of James Richard Perry of Texas to be secretary of Energy. Motion agreed to 62-37: R 51-0; D 10-36; I 1-1. March 2, 2017.

79. PERRY NOMINATION/CONFIRMATION. Confirmation of President Donald Trump's nomination of James Richard Perry of Texas to be secretary of Energy. Confirmed 62-37: R 51-0; D 10-36; I 1-1. March 2, 2017.

80. H J RES 37. LABOR LAW VIOLATION DISCLOSURE DISAPPROVAL/ MOTION TO PROCEED. McConnell, R-Ky., motion to proceed to the joint resolution that would disapprove and nullify a Defense Department, General Services Administration and NASA rule that requires companies that bid for federal contracts of more than $500,000 to disclose whether they have been determined in the previous three years to have violated certain federal labor laws and equivalent state laws. Motion agreed to 51-46: R 51-0; D 0-44; I 0-2. March 2, 2017.

81. H J RES 37. LABOR LAW VIOLATION DISCLOSURE DISAPPROVAL/ PASSAGE. Passage of the joint resolution that would nullify and disapprove a Defense Department, General Services Administration and NASA rule that requires companies that bid for federal contracts of more than $500,000 to disclose whether they have been determined in the previous three years to have violated certain federal labor laws and equivalent state laws. Passed (thus cleared for the president) 49-48: R 49-0; D 0-46; I 0-2. March 6, 2017.

82. H J RES 44. PUBLIC LAND MANAGEMENT PLANS DISAPPROVAL/ PASSAGE. Passage of the joint resolution that would nullify and disapprove of a Bureau of Land Management rule that amends the agency's procedures for the development of resource management plans for public lands. The rule directs BLM to design management plans that address resource issues in a number of programs related to wildfire prevention, wildlife habitat protection and demands for renewable and nonrenewable energy. The rule also provides additional opportunities for the public to submit information and comments on a plan revision or amendment. Passed (thus cleared for the president) 51-48: R 51-0; D 0-46; I 0-2. March 7, 2017.

83. H J RES 58. TEACHING PROGRAM EVALUATION DISAPPROVAL/ PASSAGE. Passage of the joint resolution that would nullify and disapprove of an Education Department rule that requires states, in evaluating teacher preparation programs at higher education institutions, to annually report on certain factors including placement and retention rates of graduates, student learning outcomes and feedback from graduates and employers on program effectiveness. Under the rule, federal grants for students who commit to teaching at low-income schools for at least four years are to be limited to students in programs rated by states as effective for at least two of the previous three years. Passed (thus cleared for the president) 59-40: R 51-0; D 7-39; I 1-1.

84. H J RES 57. SCHOOL PERFORMANCE ASSESSMENT DISAPPROVAL/PASSAGE. Passage of the joint resolution that would nullify and disapprove of an Education Department rule that requires states to define, subsequently monitor and intervene with schools deemed to be low-performing schools. Under the department's rule, states are required to measure academic achievement through factors such as graduation rates and English proficiency rates. Passed (thus cleared for the president) 50-49: R 50-1; D 0-46; I 0-2. March 9, 2017.

	78	79	80	81	82	83	84
ALABAMA							
Shelby	Y	Y	Y	Y	Y	Y	Y
Strange	Y	Y	Y	Y	Y	Y	Y
ALASKA							
Murkowski	Y	Y	Y	Y	Y	Y	Y
Sullivan	Y	Y	Y	?	Y	Y	Y
ARIZONA							
McCain	Y	Y	Y	Y	Y	Y	Y
Flake	Y	Y	Y	?	Y	Y	Y
ARKANSAS							
Boozman	Y	Y	Y	Y	Y	Y	Y
Cotton	Y	Y	Y	Y	Y	Y	Y
CALIFORNIA							
Feinstein	N	N	N	N	N	N	N
Harris	N	N	N	N	N	N	N
COLORADO							
Bennet	N	N	N	N	N	N	N
Gardner	Y	Y	Y	Y	Y	Y	Y
CONNECTICUT							
Blumenthal	N	N	N	N	N	N	N
Murphy	N	N	N	N	N	N	N
DELAWARE							
Carper	N	Y	N	N	N	N	N
Coons	N	N	N	N	N	N	N
FLORIDA							
Nelson	N	N	N	N	N	Y	N
Rubio	Y	Y	Y	Y	Y	Y	Y
GEORGIA							
Isakson	?	?	?	?	?	?	?
Perdue	Y	Y	Y	Y	Y	Y	Y
HAWAII							
Schatz	N	N	?	N	N	N	N
Hirono	N	N	N	N	N	N	N
IDAHO							
Crapo	Y	Y	Y	Y	Y	Y	Y
Risch	Y	Y	Y	Y	Y	Y	Y
ILLINOIS							
Durbin	N	N	N	N	N	N	N
Duckworth	N	N	N	N	N	N	N
INDIANA							
Donnelly	Y	Y	N	N	N	Y	Y
Young	Y	Y	Y	Y	Y	Y	Y
IOWA							
Grassley	Y	Y	Y	Y	Y	Y	Y
Ernst	Y	Y	Y	Y	Y	Y	Y
KANSAS							
Roberts	Y	Y	Y	Y	Y	Y	Y
Moran	Y	Y	Y	Y	Y	Y	Y
KENTUCKY							
McConnell	Y	Y	Y	Y	Y	Y	Y
Paul	Y	Y	Y	Y	Y	Y	Y
LOUISIANA							
Cassidy	Y	Y	Y	Y	Y	Y	Y
Kennedy	Y	Y	Y	Y	Y	Y	Y
MAINE							
Collins	Y	Y	Y	Y	Y	Y	Y
King	Y	Y	N	N	N	Y	N
MARYLAND							
Cardin	Y	N	N	N	N	N	N
Van Hollen	N	N	N	N	N	N	N
MASSACHUSETTS							
Warren	N	N	N	N	N	N	N
Markey	N	N	N	N	N	N	N
MICHIGAN							
Stabenow	Y	Y	N	N	N	N	N
Peters	N	N	N	N	N	N	N
MINNESOTA							
Klobuchar	N	N	N	N	N	N	N
Franken	N	N	N	N	N	N	N
MISSISSIPPI							
Cochran	Y	Y	Y	Y	Y	Y	Y
Wicker	Y	Y	Y	Y	Y	Y	Y
MISSOURI							
McCaskill	Y	Y	N	N	N	Y	N
Blunt	Y	Y	Y	Y	Y	Y	Y
MONTANA							
Tester	Y	Y	N	N	N	Y	N
Daines	Y	Y	Y	Y	Y	Y	Y
NEBRASKA							
Fischer	Y	Y	Y	Y	Y	Y	Y
Sasse	Y	Y	Y	Y	Y	Y	Y
NEVADA							
Heller	Y	Y	Y	Y	Y	Y	Y
Cortez Masto	Y	Y	N	N	N	Y	N
NEW HAMPSHIRE							
Shaheen	N	N	N	N	N	N	N
Hassan	N	N	N	N	N	N	N
NEW JERSEY							
Menendez	N	N	N	N	N	N	N
Booker	N	N	N	N	N	N	N
NEW MEXICO							
Udall	Y	Y	N	N	N	N	N
Heinrich	N	N	N	N	N	N	N
NEW YORK							
Schumer	N	N	N	N	N	N	N
Gillibrand	N	N	N	N	N	N	N
NORTH CAROLINA							
Burr	Y	Y	Y	Y	Y	Y	Y
Tillis	Y	Y	Y	Y	Y	Y	Y
NORTH DAKOTA							
Hoeven	Y	Y	Y	Y	Y	Y	Y
Heitkamp	Y	Y	N	N	N	Y	N
OHIO							
Brown	N	N	N	N	N	N	N
Portman	Y	Y	Y	Y	Y	Y	N
OKLAHOMA							
Inhofe	Y	Y	Y	Y	Y	Y	Y
Lankford	Y	Y	Y	Y	Y	Y	Y
OREGON							
Wyden	N	N	N	N	N	N	N
Merkley	N	N	N	N	N	N	N
PENNSYLVANIA							
Casey	N	N	N	N	N	N	N
Toomey	Y	Y	Y	Y	Y	Y	Y
RHODE ISLAND							
Reed	N	N	N	N	N	N	N
Whitehouse	N	N	N	N	N	N	N
SOUTH CAROLINA							
Graham	Y	Y	Y	Y	Y	Y	Y
Scott	Y	Y	Y	Y	Y	Y	Y
SOUTH DAKOTA							
Thune	Y	Y	Y	Y	Y	Y	Y
Rounds	Y	Y	Y	Y	Y	Y	Y
TENNESSEE							
Alexander	Y	Y	Y	Y	Y	Y	Y
Corker	Y	Y	Y	Y	Y	Y	Y
TEXAS							
Cornyn	Y	Y	Y	Y	Y	Y	Y
Cruz	Y	Y	Y	Y	Y	Y	Y
UTAH							
Hatch	Y	Y	Y	Y	Y	Y	Y
Lee	Y	Y	Y	Y	Y	Y	Y
VERMONT							
Leahy	N	N	?	N	N	N	N
Sanders	N	N	N	N	N	N	N
VIRGINIA							
Warner	Y	Y	N	N	N	N	N
Kaine	N	N	N	N	N	N	N
WASHINGTON							
Murray	N	N	N	N	N	N	N
Cantwell	N	N	N	N	N	N	N
WEST VIRGINIA							
Manchin	Y	Y	N	N	N	Y	N
Capito	Y	Y	Y	Y	Y	Y	Y
WISCONSIN							
Johnson	Y	Y	Y	Y	Y	Y	Y
Baldwin	N	N	N	N	N	N	N
WYOMING							
Enzi	Y	Y	Y	Y	Y	Y	Y
Barrasso	Y	Y	Y	Y	Y	Y	Y

KEY	**Republicans**	Democrats	*Independents*

Y	Voted for (yea)	X	Paired against	C	Voted "present" to avoid possible conflict of interest
#	Paired for	–	Announced against		
+	Announced for	P	Voted "present"	?	Did not vote or otherwise make a position known
N	Voted against (nay)				

VOTE NUMBER

85. VERMA NOMINATION/CLOTURE. Motion to invoke cloture (thus limiting debate) on President Donald Trump's nomination of Seema Verma of Indiana to be administrator of the Centers for Medicare and Medicaid Services. Motion agreed to 54-44: R 50-0; D 3-43; I 1-1. March 9, 2017.

86. VERMA NOMINATION/CONFIRMATION. Confirmation of President Donald Trump's nomination of Seema Verma of Indiana to be administrator of the Centers for Medicare and Medicaid Services. Confirmed 55-43: R 51-0; D 3-42; I 1-1. March 13, 2017.

87. H J RES 42. UNEMPLOYMENT DRUG TESTING DISAPPROVAL/ PASSAGE. Passage of the joint resolution that would nullify and disapprove of a Labor Department rule that limits the occupations for which states can require drug tests for individuals applying for unemployment benefits. Under the rule, an individual can be required to be tested for drugs if an individual's typical employment is an occupation for which state or federal laws require an employee to be tested for controlled substances. Passed (thus cleared for the president) 51-48: R 51-0; D 0-46; I 0-2. March 14, 2017.

88. COATS NOMINATION/CLOTURE. Motion to invoke cloture (thus limiting debate) on President Donald Trump's nomination of Dan Coats of Indiana to be director of national intelligence. Motion agreed to 88-11: R 50-1; D 37-9; I 1-1. March 15, 2017.

89. COATS NOMINATION/CONFIRMATION. Confirmation of President Donald Trump's nomination of Dan Coats of Indiana to be director of national intelligence. Confirmed 85-12: R 48-1; D 36-10; I 1-1. March 15, 2017.

90. MCMASTER NOMINATION/CONFIRMATION. Confirmation of President Donald Trump's nomination of Lt. Gen. Herbert R. McMaster Jr. for reappointment to the rank of lieutenant general in the Army. Confirmed 86-10: R 48-0; D 37-9; I 1-1. March 15, 2017.

91. BREYER AND REEVES NOMINATIONS/CONFIRMATION. Confirmation, en bloc, of President Donald Trump's nominations of Charles R. Breyer of California and Danny C. Reeves of Kentucky to be members of the U.S. Sentencing Commission. Confirmed 98-0: R 50-0; D 46-0; I 2-0. March 21, 2017.

	85	86	87	88	89	90	91
ALABAMA							
Shelby	Y	Y	Y	Y	Y	Y	Y
Strange	Y	Y	Y	Y	Y	Y	Y
ALASKA							
Murkowski	Y	Y	Y	Y	Y	Y	Y
Sullivan	Y	Y	Y	Y	Y	Y	Y
ARIZONA							
McCain	Y	Y	Y	Y	Y	Y	Y
Flake	Y	Y	Y	Y	Y	Y	Y
ARKANSAS							
Boozman	Y	Y	Y	Y	Y	Y	Y
Cotton	Y	Y	Y	Y	Y	Y	Y
CALIFORNIA							
Feinstein	N	N	N	Y	Y	Y	Y
Harris	N	N	N	N	N	N	Y
COLORADO							
Bennet	N	N	N	Y	Y	Y	Y
Gardner	Y	Y	Y	Y	Y	Y	Y
CONNECTICUT							
Blumenthal	N	N	N	Y	Y	Y	Y
Murphy	N	N	N	Y	Y	Y	Y
DELAWARE							
Carper	N	N	N	Y	Y	Y	Y
Coons	N	N	N	Y	Y	Y	Y
FLORIDA							
Nelson	N	N	N	Y	Y	Y	Y
Rubio	+	Y	Y	Y	Y	Y	Y
GEORGIA							
Isakson	?	?	?	?	?	?	?
Perdue	Y	Y	Y	Y	Y	Y	Y
HAWAII							
Schatz	N	N	N	Y	Y	Y	Y
Hirono	N	N	N	Y	Y	N	Y
IDAHO							
Crapo	Y	Y	Y	Y	Y	Y	Y
Risch	Y	Y	Y	Y	Y	Y	Y
ILLINOIS							
Durbin	N	N	N	Y	Y	Y	Y
Duckworth	N	N	N	N	N	Y	Y
INDIANA							
Donnelly	Y	Y	N	Y	Y	Y	Y
Young	Y	Y	Y	Y	Y	Y	Y
IOWA							
Grassley	Y	Y	Y	Y	Y	Y	Y
Ernst	Y	Y	Y	Y	Y	Y	Y
KANSAS							
Roberts	Y	Y	Y	Y	Y	Y	Y
Moran	Y	Y	Y	Y	Y	Y	Y
KENTUCKY							
McConnell	Y	Y	Y	Y	Y	Y	Y
Paul	Y	Y	Y	N	N	Y	Y
LOUISIANA							
Cassidy	Y	Y	Y	Y	Y	Y	Y
Kennedy	Y	Y	Y	Y	Y	Y	Y
MAINE							
Collins	Y	Y	Y	Y	Y	Y	Y
King	Y	Y	N	Y	Y	Y	Y
MARYLAND							
Cardin	N	N	N	Y	Y	Y	Y
Van Hollen	N	N	N	Y	Y	Y	Y
MASSACHUSETTS							
Warren	N	N	N	N	N	N	Y
Markey	N	N	N	N	N	N	Y
MICHIGAN							
Stabenow	N	N	N	Y	Y	Y	Y
Peters	N	–	N	Y	Y	Y	Y
MINNESOTA							
Klobuchar	N	N	N	Y	Y	Y	Y
Franken	N	N	N	Y	Y	Y	Y
MISSISSIPPI							
Cochran	Y	Y	Y	Y	Y	Y	Y
Wicker	Y	Y	Y	Y	Y	Y	Y
MISSOURI							
McCaskill	N	N	N	Y	N	N	Y
Blunt	Y	Y	Y	Y	Y	Y	Y
MONTANA							
Tester	N	N	N	Y	Y	Y	Y
Daines	Y	Y	Y	Y	Y	Y	Y
NEBRASKA							
Fischer	Y	Y	Y	Y	Y	Y	Y
Sasse	Y	Y	Y	Y	Y	Y	Y
NEVADA							
Heller	Y	Y	Y	Y	Y	Y	Y
Cortez Masto	N	N	N	Y	Y	Y	Y
NEW HAMPSHIRE							
Shaheen	N	N	N	Y	Y	Y	Y
Hassan	N	N	N	Y	Y	Y	Y
NEW JERSEY							
Menendez	N	N	N	Y	Y	Y	Y
Booker	N	N	N	N	N	N	Y
NEW MEXICO							
Udall	N	N	N	Y	N	Y	Y
Heinrich	N	N	N	Y	Y	Y	Y
NEW YORK							
Schumer	N	N	N	Y	N	Y	Y
Gillibrand	N	N	N	N	N	N	Y
NORTH CAROLINA							
Burr	Y	Y	Y	Y	Y	Y	Y
Tillis	Y	Y	Y	Y	Y	Y	Y
NORTH DAKOTA							
Hoeven	Y	Y	Y	Y	Y	Y	Y
Heitkamp	Y	Y	N	Y	Y	Y	Y
OHIO							
Brown	N	N	N	Y	Y	Y	Y
Portman	Y	Y	Y	Y	Y	Y	Y
OKLAHOMA							
Inhofe	Y	Y	Y	Y	Y	Y	?
Lankford	Y	Y	Y	Y	Y	Y	Y
OREGON							
Wyden	N	N	N	N	N	Y	Y
Merkley	N	N	N	N	N	N	Y
PENNSYLVANIA							
Casey	N	N	N	Y	Y	Y	Y
Toomey	Y	Y	Y	Y	Y	Y	Y
RHODE ISLAND							
Reed	N	N	N	Y	Y	Y	Y
Whitehouse	N	N	N	Y	Y	Y	Y
SOUTH CAROLINA							
Graham	Y	Y	Y	Y	Y	Y	Y
Scott	Y	Y	Y	Y	Y	Y	Y
SOUTH DAKOTA							
Thune	Y	Y	Y	Y	Y	Y	Y
Rounds	Y	Y	Y	Y	Y	Y	Y
TENNESSEE							
Alexander	Y	Y	Y	Y	+	+	Y
Corker	Y	Y	Y	Y	+	+	Y
TEXAS							
Cornyn	Y	Y	Y	Y	Y	Y	Y
Cruz	Y	Y	Y	Y	Y	Y	Y
UTAH							
Hatch	Y	Y	Y	Y	Y	Y	Y
Lee	Y	Y	Y	Y	Y	Y	Y
VERMONT							
Leahy	N	N	N	Y	Y	Y	Y
Sanders	N	N	N	N	N	N	Y
VIRGINIA							
Warner	N	N	N	Y	Y	Y	Y
Kaine	N	N	N	Y	Y	Y	Y
WASHINGTON							
Murray	N	N	N	Y	Y	Y	Y
Cantwell	N	N	N	Y	Y	Y	Y
WEST VIRGINIA							
Manchin	Y	Y	N	Y	Y	Y	Y
Capito	Y	Y	Y	Y	Y	Y	Y
WISCONSIN							
Johnson	Y	Y	Y	Y	Y	Y	Y
Baldwin	N	N	N	N	N	Y	Y
WYOMING							
Enzi	Y	Y	Y	Y	Y	Y	Y
Barrasso	Y	Y	Y	Y	Y	+	Y

KEY **Republicans** Democrats *Independents*

Y	Voted for (yea)	X Paired against	C Voted "present" to avoid possible conflict of interest
#	Paired for	– Announced against	
+	Announced for	P Voted "present"	? Did not vote or otherwise make a position known
N	Voted against (nay)		

VOTE NUMBER

92. H J RES 69. ALASKA PREDATOR HUNTING DISAPPROVAL/PASSAGE. Passage of the joint resolution that would nullify and disapprove of an Interior Department rule that prohibits certain predator control methods on federal lands in Alaska. The rule prevents Alaska, which typically has the authority to manage hunting and trapping practices on federal lands within the state, from allowing certain non-subsistence hunting practices on national wildlife refuges. Under the rule, prohibited practices include using traps to hunt bears and the taking of wolves and coyotes during denning season. Passed (thus cleared for the president) 52-47: R 51-0; D 0-46; I 1-1. March 21, 2017.

93. H J RES 83. OSHA CITATION DISAPPROVAL/PASSAGE. Passage of a joint resolution that would nullify and disapprove of an Occupational Safety and Health Administration rule that extends, from six months to five years, the period in which OSHA can issue citations to employers who do not maintain workplace injury or illness records. Passed (thus cleared for the president) 50-48: R 50-0; D 0-46; I 0-2. March 22, 2017.

94. S J RES 34. BROADBAND PRIVACY DISAPPROVAL/PASSAGE. Passage of the joint resolution that would disapprove and nullify a Federal Communications Commission rule that requires broadband internet service providers to obtain affirmative permission from customers to use or share their sensitive information, such as web browsing history, geolocation information, content of communications and Social Security numbers; to take reasonable measures to secure customer information; and to notify customers, the commission and law enforcement when a data breach occurs that could result in harm. Passed 50-48: R 50-0; D 0-46; I 0-2. March 23, 2017.

95. FRIEDMAN NOMINATION/CLOTURE. Motion to invoke cloture (thus limiting debate) on President Donald Trump's nomination of David Friedman of New York to be U.S. ambassador to Israel. Motion agreed to 52-46: R 50-0; D 2-44; I 0-2. March 23, 2017.

96. FRIEDMAN NOMINATION/CONFIRMATION. Confirmation of President Donald Trump's nomination of David Friedman of New York to be U.S. ambassador to Israel. Confirmed 52-46: R 50-0; D 2-44; I 0-2. March 23, 2017.

97. TREATY DOC 114-12. MONTENEGRO NATO MEMBERSHIP TREATY/CLOTURE. Motion to invoke cloture (thus limiting debate) on the Protocol to the North Atlantic Treaty of 1949 on the Accession of Montenegro (Treaty Doc. 114-12) which would allow the admission of Montenegro into the North Atlantic Treaty Organization. Motion agreed to 97-2: R 49-2; D 46-0; I 2-0. March 27, 2017.

98. TREATY DOC 114-12. MONTENEGRO NATO MEMBERSHIP TREATY/ADOPTION. Adoption of the resolution of ratification of the Protocol to the North Atlantic Treaty of 1949 on the Accession of Montenegro (Treaty Doc. 114-12) which would allow the admission of Montenegro into the North Atlantic Treaty Organization. Adopted (thus consenting to ratification) 97-2: R 49-2; D 46-0; I 2-0. March 28, 2017.

	92	93	94	95	96	97	98
ALABAMA							
Shelby	Y	Y	Y	Y	Y	Y	Y
Strange	Y	Y	Y	Y	Y	Y	Y
ALASKA							
Murkowski	Y	Y	Y	Y	Y	Y	Y
Sullivan	Y	Y	Y	Y	Y	Y	Y
ARIZONA							
McCain	Y	Y	Y	Y	Y	Y	Y
Flake	Y	Y	Y	Y	Y	Y	Y
ARKANSAS							
Boozman	Y	Y	Y	Y	Y	Y	Y
Cotton	Y	Y	Y	Y	Y	Y	Y
CALIFORNIA							
Feinstein	N	N	N	N	N	Y	Y
Harris	N	N	N	N	N	Y	Y
COLORADO							
Bennet	N	N	N	N	N	Y	Y
Gardner	Y	Y	Y	Y	Y	Y	Y
CONNECTICUT							
Blumenthal	N	N	N	N	N	Y	Y
Murphy	N	N	N	N	N	Y	Y
DELAWARE							
Carper	N	N	N	N	N	Y	Y
Coons	N	N	N	N	N	Y	Y
FLORIDA							
Nelson	N	N	N	N	N	Y	Y
Rubio	Y	Y	Y	Y	Y	Y	Y
GEORGIA							
Isakson	?	?	?	?	?	Y	?
Perdue	Y	Y	Y	Y	Y	Y	Y
HAWAII							
Schatz	N	N	N	N	N	Y	Y
Hirono	N	N	N	N	N	Y	Y
IDAHO							
Crapo	Y	Y	Y	Y	Y	Y	Y
Risch	Y	Y	Y	Y	Y	Y	Y
ILLINOIS							
Durbin	N	N	N	N	N	Y	Y
Duckworth	N	N	N	N	N	Y	Y
INDIANA							
Donnelly	N	N	N	N	N	Y	Y
Young	Y	Y	Y	Y	Y	Y	Y
IOWA							
Grassley	Y	Y	Y	Y	Y	Y	Y
Ernst	Y	Y	Y	Y	Y	Y	Y
KANSAS							
Roberts	Y	Y	Y	Y	Y	Y	Y
Moran	Y	Y	Y	Y	Y	Y	Y
KENTUCKY							
McConnell	Y	Y	Y	Y	Y	Y	Y
Paul	Y	?	?	?	?	N	N
LOUISIANA							
Cassidy	Y	Y	Y	Y	Y	Y	Y
Kennedy	Y	Y	Y	Y	Y	Y	Y
MAINE							
Collins	Y	Y	Y	Y	Y	Y	Y
King	Y	N	N	N	N	Y	Y
MARYLAND							
Cardin	N	N	N	N	N	Y	Y
Van Hollen	N	N	N	N	N	Y	Y
MASSACHUSETTS							
Warren	N	N	N	N	N	Y	Y
Markey	N	N	N	N	N	Y	Y
MICHIGAN							
Stabenow	N	N	N	N	N	Y	Y
Peters	N	N	N	N	N	Y	Y
MINNESOTA							
Klobuchar	N	N	N	N	N	Y	Y
Franken	N	N	N	N	N	Y	Y
MISSISSIPPI							
Cochran	Y	Y	Y	Y	Y	Y	Y
Wicker	Y	Y	Y	Y	Y	Y	Y
MISSOURI							
McCaskill	N	N	N	N	N	Y	Y
Blunt	Y	Y	Y	Y	Y	Y	Y

	92	93	94	95	96	97	98
MONTANA							
Tester	N	N	N	N	N	Y	Y
Daines	Y	Y	Y	Y	Y	Y	Y
NEBRASKA							
Fischer	Y	Y	Y	Y	Y	Y	Y
Sasse	Y	Y	Y	Y	Y	Y	Y
NEVADA							
Heller	Y	Y	Y	Y	Y	Y	Y
Cortez Masto	N	N	N	N	N	Y	Y
NEW HAMPSHIRE							
Shaheen	N	N	N	N	N	Y	Y
Hassan	N	N	N	N	N	Y	Y
NEW JERSEY							
Menendez	N	N	N	Y	Y	Y	Y
Booker	N	N	N	N	N	Y	Y
NEW MEXICO							
Udall	N	N	N	N	N	Y	Y
Heinrich	N	N	N	N	N	Y	Y
NEW YORK							
Schumer	N	N	N	N	N	Y	Y
Gillibrand	N	N	N	N	N	Y	Y
NORTH CAROLINA							
Burr	Y	Y	Y	Y	Y	Y	Y
Tillis	Y	Y	Y	Y	Y	Y	Y
NORTH DAKOTA							
Hoeven	Y	Y	Y	Y	Y	Y	Y
Heitkamp	N	N	N	N	N	Y	Y
OHIO							
Brown	N	N	N	N	N	Y	Y
Portman	Y	Y	Y	Y	Y	Y	Y
OKLAHOMA							
Inhofe	Y	Y	Y	Y	Y	Y	Y
Lankford	Y	Y	Y	Y	Y	Y	Y
OREGON							
Wyden	N	N	N	N	N	Y	Y
Merkley	N	N	N	N	N	Y	Y
PENNSYLVANIA							
Casey	N	N	N	N	N	Y	Y
Toomey	Y	Y	Y	Y	Y	Y	Y
RHODE ISLAND							
Reed	N	N	N	N	N	Y	Y
Whitehouse	N	N	N	N	N	Y	Y
SOUTH CAROLINA							
Graham	Y	Y	Y	Y	Y	Y	Y
Scott	Y	Y	Y	Y	Y	Y	Y
SOUTH DAKOTA							
Thune	Y	Y	Y	Y	Y	Y	Y
Rounds	Y	Y	Y	Y	Y	Y	Y
TENNESSEE							
Alexander	Y	Y	Y	Y	Y	Y	Y
Corker	Y	Y	Y	Y	Y	Y	Y
TEXAS							
Cornyn	Y	Y	Y	Y	Y	Y	Y
Cruz	Y	Y	Y	Y	Y	Y	Y
UTAH							
Hatch	Y	Y	Y	Y	Y	Y	Y
Lee	Y	Y	Y	Y	Y	N	N
VERMONT							
Leahy	N	N	N	N	N	Y	Y
Sanders	N	N	N	N	N	Y	Y
VIRGINIA							
Warner	N	N	N	N	N	Y	Y
Kaine	N	N	N	N	N	Y	Y
WASHINGTON							
Murray	N	N	N	N	N	Y	Y
Cantwell	N	N	N	N	N	Y	Y
WEST VIRGINIA							
Manchin	N	N	N	Y	Y	Y	Y
Capito	Y	Y	Y	Y	Y	Y	Y
WISCONSIN							
Johnson	Y	Y	Y	Y	Y	Y	Y
Baldwin	N	N	N	N	N	Y	Y
WYOMING							
Enzi	Y	Y	Y	Y	Y	?	Y
Barrasso	Y	Y	Y	Y	Y	Y	Y

KEY	**Republicans**	Democrats	*Independents*

Y Voted for (yea)	X Paired against	C Voted "present" to avoid possible conflict of interest
# Paired for	– Announced against	? Did not vote or otherwise make a position known
+ Announced for	P Voted "present"	
N Voted against (nay)		

VOTE NUMBER

99. H J RES 67. LOCAL GOVERNMENT RETIREMENT PLANS DISAPPROVAL/PASSAGE. Passage of the joint resolution that would nullify and disapprove of a Labor Department rule that exempts certain local government-administered retirement savings plans for non-government employees from select federal regulations governing pension plans. Under the rule, a city or county must have a population at least as large as the least populated state in the nation, and must administer a retirement plan for its own employees for the program to qualify for the exemption. Passed (thus cleared for the president) 50-49: R 50-1; D 0-46; I 0-2. March 30, 2017.

100. H J RES 43. FAMILY PLANNING FUNDING DISAPPROVAL/MOTION TO PROCEED. McConnell, R-Ky., motion to proceed to the joint resolution that would disapprove and nullify a Health and Human Services Department rule that prevents states that distribute federal family funding from prohibiting participation and receipt of funds by health care providers, such as Planned Parenthood, for any reason other than their ability to provide family planning services. Motion agreed to, with Vice President Pence casting a "yea" vote to break the tie, 50-50: R 50-2; D 0-46; I 0-2. March 30, 2017.

101. H J RES 43. FAMILY PLANNING FUNDING DISAPPROVAL/PASSAGE. Passage of the joint resolution that would nullify and disapprove of a Health and Human Services Department rule that prevents states from restricting federal family planning funding to a health provider, such as denying funds to a center that provides abortions, for any basis other than its ability to provide health services. Under the rule, HHS can withhold family planning grants to any state that restricts the participation of a health provider in the family planning services grant program. Passed (thus cleared for the president), with Vice President Pence casting a "yea" vote to break the tie, 50-50: R 50-2; D 0-46; I 0-2. March 30, 2017.

102. S 89. BOAT FIRE-RETARDANT EXEMPTION/PASSAGE. Passage of the bill that would extend an exemption for boats that have been in operation since before 1968 from fire-retardant materials requirements. To qualify for the exemption, the boat must yearly alter at least 10 percent of the vessel to meet the fire requirements. Prior to the sale of a ticket, the boat operator must inform prospective passengers that the vessel does not meet fire safety standards. Passed 85-12: R 48-2; D 35-10; I 2-0. April 3, 2017.

103. DUKE NOMINATION/CONFIRMATION. Confirmation of President Donald Trump's nomination of Elaine C. Duke of Virginia to be deputy secretary of Homeland Security. Confirmed 85-14: R 51-0; D 33-13; I 1-1. April 4, 2017.

104. GORSUCH NOMINATION/MOTION TO PROCEED. McConnell, R-Ky., motion to proceed to executive session to consider the nomination of Neil Gorsuch of Colorado to be an associate justice of the Supreme Court of the United States. Motion agreed to 55-44: R 51-0; D 4-42; I 0-2. April 4, 2017.

105. GORSUCH NOMINATION/CLOTURE. Motion to invoke cloture (thus limiting debate) on the nomination of Judge Neil Gorsuch of Colorado to be an associate justice of the United States Supreme Court. Motion rejected 55-45: R 51-1; D 4-42; I 0-2. April 6, 2017.

	99	100	101	102	103	104	105
ALABAMA							
Shelby	Y	Y	Y	Y	Y	Y	Y
Strange	Y	Y	Y	Y	Y	Y	Y
ALASKA							
Murkowski	Y	N	N	N	Y	Y	Y
Sullivan	Y	Y	Y	Y	Y	Y	Y
ARIZONA							
McCain	Y	Y	Y	Y	Y	Y	Y
Flake	Y	Y	Y	Y	Y	Y	Y
ARKANSAS							
Boozman	Y	Y	Y	Y	Y	Y	Y
Cotton	Y	Y	Y	Y	Y	Y	Y
CALIFORNIA							
Feinstein	N	N	N	Y	Y	N	N
Harris	N	N	N	Y	N	N	N
COLORADO							
Bennet	N	N	N	Y	Y	Y	Y
Gardner	Y	Y	Y	Y	Y	Y	Y
CONNECTICUT							
Blumenthal	N	N	N	N	N	N	N
Murphy	N	N	N	N	N	N	N
DELAWARE							
Carper	N	N	N	Y	Y	N	N
Coons	N	N	N	Y	Y	N	N
FLORIDA							
Nelson	N	N	N	Y	Y	N	N
Rubio	Y	Y	Y	Y	Y	Y	Y
GEORGIA							
Isakson	?	Y	Y	?	?	?	Y
Perdue	Y	Y	Y	Y	Y	Y	Y
HAWAII							
Schatz	N	N	N	Y	Y	N	N
Hirono	N	N	N	Y	Y	N	N
IDAHO							
Crapo	Y	Y	Y	Y	Y	Y	Y
Risch	Y	Y	Y	Y	Y	Y	Y
ILLINOIS							
Durbin	N	N	N	N	Y	N	N
Duckworth	N	N	N	Y	N	N	N
INDIANA							
Donnelly	N	N	N	Y	Y	Y	Y
Young	Y	Y	Y	Y	Y	Y	Y
IOWA							
Grassley	Y	Y	Y	Y	Y	Y	Y
Ernst	Y	Y	Y	Y	Y	Y	Y
KANSAS							
Roberts	Y	Y	Y	Y	Y	Y	Y
Moran	Y	Y	Y	Y	Y	Y	Y
KENTUCKY							
McConnell	Y	Y	Y	Y	Y	Y	N
Paul	Y	Y	Y	Y	Y	Y	Y
LOUISIANA							
Cassidy	Y	Y	Y	Y	Y	Y	Y
Kennedy	Y	Y	Y	Y	Y	Y	Y
MAINE							
Collins	Y	N	N	N	Y	Y	Y
King	N	N	N	Y	Y	N	N
MARYLAND							
Cardin	N	N	N	Y	N	N	N
Van Hollen	N	N	N	Y	N	N	N
MASSACHUSETTS							
Warren	N	N	N	Y	N	N	N
Markey	N	N	N	Y	N	N	N
MICHIGAN							
Stabenow	N	N	N	Y	Y	N	N
Peters	N	N	N	Y	Y	N	N
MINNESOTA							
Klobuchar	N	N	N	Y	Y	N	N
Franken	N	N	N	Y	Y	N	N
MISSISSIPPI							
Cochran	Y	Y	Y	Y	Y	Y	Y
Wicker	Y	Y	Y	Y	Y	Y	Y
MISSOURI							
McCaskill	N	N	N	Y	Y	N	N
Blunt	Y	Y	Y	Y	Y	Y	Y
MONTANA							
Tester	N	N	N	Y	Y	N	N
Daines	Y	Y	Y	Y	Y	Y	Y
NEBRASKA							
Fischer	Y	Y	Y	Y	Y	Y	Y
Sasse	Y	Y	Y	Y	Y	Y	Y
NEVADA							
Heller	Y	Y	Y	Y	Y	Y	Y
Cortez Masto	N	N	N	Y	N	N	N
NEW HAMPSHIRE							
Shaheen	N	N	N	Y	Y	N	N
Hassan	N	N	N	Y	Y	N	N
NEW JERSEY							
Menendez	N	N	N	N	N	N	N
Booker	N	N	N	Y	N	N	N
NEW MEXICO							
Udall	N	N	N	Y	N	N	N
Heinrich	N	N	N	Y	N	N	N
NEW YORK							
Schumer	N	N	N	Y	Y	N	N
Gillibrand	N	N	N	N	N	N	N
NORTH CAROLINA							
Burr	Y	Y	Y	Y	Y	Y	Y
Tillis	Y	Y	Y	Y	Y	Y	Y
NORTH DAKOTA							
Hoeven	Y	Y	Y	Y	Y	Y	Y
Heitkamp	N	N	N	Y	Y	Y	Y
OHIO							
Brown	N	N	N	Y	Y	N	N
Portman	Y	Y	Y	Y	Y	Y	Y
OKLAHOMA							
Inhofe	Y	Y	Y	Y	Y	Y	Y
Lankford	Y	Y	Y	Y	Y	Y	Y
OREGON							
Wyden	N	N	N	Y	N	N	N
Merkley	N	N	N	Y	N	N	N
PENNSYLVANIA							
Casey	N	N	N	Y	Y	N	N
Toomey	Y	Y	Y	?	Y	Y	Y
RHODE ISLAND							
Reed	N	N	N	Y	N	N	N
Whitehouse	N	N	N	Y	N	N	N
SOUTH CAROLINA							
Graham	Y	Y	Y	Y	Y	Y	Y
Scott	Y	Y	Y	Y	Y	Y	Y
SOUTH DAKOTA							
Thune	Y	Y	Y	Y	Y	Y	Y
Rounds	Y	Y	Y	Y	Y	Y	Y
TENNESSEE							
Alexander	Y	Y	Y	Y	Y	Y	Y
Corker	N	Y	Y	Y	Y	Y	Y
TEXAS							
Cornyn	Y	Y	Y	Y	Y	Y	Y
Cruz	Y	Y	Y	Y	Y	Y	Y
UTAH							
Hatch	Y	Y	Y	Y	Y	Y	Y
Lee	Y	Y	Y	Y	Y	Y	Y
VERMONT							
Leahy	N	N	N	Y	N	N	N
Sanders	N	N	N	Y	N	N	N
VIRGINIA							
Warner	N	N	N	Y	Y	N	N
Kaine	N	N	N	Y	Y	N	N
WASHINGTON							
Murray	N	N	N	Y	N	N	N
Cantwell	N	N	N	?	Y	N	N
WEST VIRGINIA							
Manchin	N	N	N	Y	Y	Y	Y
Capito	Y	Y	Y	Y	Y	Y	Y
WISCONSIN							
Johnson	Y	Y	Y	Y	Y	Y	Y
Baldwin	N	N	N	Y	Y	N	N
WYOMING							
Enzi	Y	Y	Y	Y	Y	Y	Y
Barrasso	Y	Y	Y	Y	Y	Y	Y

KEY   **Republicans**   Democrats   *Independents*

Y Voted for (yea)	X Paired against	C Voted "present" to avoid possible conflict of interest
# Paired for	– Announced against	
+ Announced for	P Voted "present"	? Did not vote or otherwise make a position known
N Voted against (nay)		

VOTE NUMBER

106. GORSUCH NOMINATION/MOTION TO RECONSIDER. McConnell, R-Ky., motion to reconsider the vote in which cloture was not invoked on the nomination of Judge Neil Gorsuch of Colorado to be an associate justice of the United States Supreme Court. Motion agreed to 55-45: R 52-0; D 3-43; I 0-2. April 6, 2017.

107. GORSUCH NOMINATION/MOTION TO POSTPONE. Schumer, D-N.Y., motion to postpone the nomination until 3 p.m. on Monday, April 24, 2017. Motion rejected 48-52: R 0-52; D 46-0; I 2-0. April 6, 2017.

108. GORSUCH NOMINATION/MOTION TO ADJOURN. Schumer, D-N.Y., motion to adjourn until 5 p.m. Motion rejected 48-52: R 0-52; D 46-0; I 2-0. April 6, 2017.

109. GORSUCH NOMINATION/RULING OF THE CHAIR. Judgment of the Senate to affirm the ruling of the chair regarding the McConnell, R-Ky., point of order that the precedent set on November 21, 2013 (that a simple majority is required to invoke cloture on nominations excluding the Supreme Court), applies to cloture votes on all nominations. Ruling of the chair rejected 48-52: R 0-52; D 46-0; I 2-0. April 6, 2017.

110. GORSUCH NOMINATION/CLOTURE. Motion to invoke cloture (thus limiting debate), upon reconsideration, on the nomination of Judge Neil Gorsuch of Colorado to be an associate justice of the United States Supreme Court. Motion agreed to 55-45: R 52-0; D 3-43; I 0-2. April 6, 2017.

111. GORSUCH NOMINATION/CONFIRMATION. Confirmation of President Donald Trump's nomination of Judge Neil Gorsuch of Colorado to be an associate justice of the United States Supreme Court. Confirmed 54-45: R 51-0; D 3-43; I 0-2. April 7, 2017.

112. PERDUE NOMINATION/CONFIRMATION. Confirmation of President Donald Trump's nomination of Sonny Perdue of Georgia to be secretary of Agriculture. Confirmed 87-11: R 50-0; D 36-10; I 1-1. April 24, 2017.

	106	107	108	109	110	111	112
ALABAMA							
Shelby	Y	N	N	N	Y	Y	Y
Strange	Y	N	N	N	Y	Y	Y
ALASKA							
Murkowski	Y	N	N	N	Y	Y	Y
Sullivan	Y	N	N	N	Y	Y	Y
ARIZONA							
McCain	Y	N	N	N	Y	Y	Y
Flake	Y	N	N	N	Y	Y	?
ARKANSAS							
Boozman	Y	N	N	N	Y	Y	Y
Cotton	Y	N	N	N	Y	Y	Y
CALIFORNIA							
Feinstein	N	Y	Y	Y	N	N	Y
Harris	N	Y	Y	Y	N	N	N
COLORADO							
Bennet	N	Y	Y	Y	N	N	Y
Gardner	Y	N	N	N	Y	Y	Y
CONNECTICUT							
Blumenthal	N	Y	Y	Y	N	N	N
Murphy	N	Y	Y	Y	N	N	Y
DELAWARE							
Carper	N	Y	Y	Y	N	N	Y
Coons	N	Y	Y	Y	N	N	Y
FLORIDA							
Nelson	N	Y	Y	Y	N	N	Y
Rubio	Y	N	N	N	Y	Y	Y
GEORGIA							
Isakson	Y	N	N	N	Y	+	Y
Perdue	Y	N	N	N	Y	Y	P
HAWAII							
Schatz	N	Y	Y	Y	N	N	Y
Hirono	N	Y	Y	Y	N	N	Y
IDAHO							
Crapo	Y	N	N	N	Y	Y	Y
Risch	Y	N	N	N	Y	Y	Y
ILLINOIS							
Durbin	N	Y	Y	Y	N	N	Y
Duckworth	N	Y	Y	Y	N	N	Y
INDIANA							
Donnelly	Y	Y	Y	Y	Y	Y	Y
Young	Y	N	N	N	Y	Y	Y
IOWA							
Grassley	Y	N	N	N	Y	Y	Y
Ernst	Y	N	N	N	Y	Y	Y
KANSAS							
Roberts	Y	N	N	N	Y	Y	Y
Moran	Y	N	N	N	Y	Y	Y
KENTUCKY							
McConnell	Y	N	N	N	Y	Y	Y
Paul	Y	N	N	N	Y	Y	Y
LOUISIANA							
Cassidy	Y	N	N	N	Y	Y	Y
Kennedy	Y	N	N	N	Y	Y	Y
MAINE							
Collins	Y	N	N	N	Y	Y	Y
King	N	Y	Y	Y	N	N	Y
MARYLAND							
Cardin	N	Y	Y	Y	N	N	Y
Van Hollen	N	Y	Y	Y	N	N	Y
MASSACHUSETTS							
Warren	N	Y	Y	Y	N	N	N
Markey	N	Y	Y	Y	N	N	N
MICHIGAN							
Stabenow	N	Y	Y	Y	N	N	Y
Peters	N	Y	Y	Y	N	N	Y
MINNESOTA							
Klobuchar	N	Y	Y	Y	N	N	Y
Franken	N	Y	Y	Y	N	N	Y
MISSISSIPPI							
Cochran	Y	N	N	N	Y	Y	Y
Wicker	Y	N	N	N	Y	Y	Y
MISSOURI							
McCaskill	N	Y	Y	Y	N	N	Y
Blunt	Y	N	N	N	Y	Y	Y
MONTANA							
Tester	N	Y	Y	Y	N	N	Y
Daines	Y	N	N	N	Y	Y	Y
NEBRASKA							
Fischer	Y	N	N	N	Y	Y	Y
Sasse	Y	N	N	N	Y	Y	Y
NEVADA							
Heller	Y	N	N	N	Y	Y	Y
Cortez Masto	N	Y	Y	Y	N	N	Y
NEW HAMPSHIRE							
Shaheen	N	Y	Y	Y	N	N	Y
Hassan	N	Y	Y	Y	N	N	Y
NEW JERSEY							
Menendez	N	Y	Y	Y	N	N	N
Booker	N	Y	Y	Y	N	N	N
NEW MEXICO							
Udall	N	Y	Y	Y	N	N	Y
Heinrich	N	Y	Y	Y	N	N	Y
NEW YORK							
Schumer	N	Y	Y	Y	N	N	Y
Gillibrand	N	Y	Y	Y	N	N	N
NORTH CAROLINA							
Burr	Y	N	N	N	Y	Y	Y
Tillis	Y	N	N	N	Y	Y	Y
NORTH DAKOTA							
Hoeven	Y	N	N	N	Y	Y	Y
Heitkamp	Y	Y	Y	Y	Y	Y	Y
OHIO							
Brown	N	Y	Y	Y	N	N	Y
Portman	Y	N	N	N	Y	Y	Y
OKLAHOMA							
Inhofe	Y	N	N	N	Y	Y	Y
Lankford	Y	N	N	N	Y	Y	Y
OREGON							
Wyden	N	Y	Y	Y	N	N	N
Merkley	N	Y	Y	Y	N	N	Y
PENNSYLVANIA							
Casey	N	Y	Y	Y	N	N	Y
Toomey	Y	N	N	N	Y	Y	Y
RHODE ISLAND							
Reed	N	Y	Y	Y	N	N	N
Whitehouse	N	Y	Y	Y	N	N	N
SOUTH CAROLINA							
Graham	Y	N	N	N	Y	Y	Y
Scott	Y	N	N	N	Y	Y	Y
SOUTH DAKOTA							
Thune	Y	N	N	N	Y	Y	Y
Rounds	Y	N	N	N	Y	Y	Y
TENNESSEE							
Alexander	Y	N	N	N	Y	Y	Y
Corker	Y	N	N	N	Y	Y	Y
TEXAS							
Cornyn	Y	N	N	N	Y	Y	Y
Cruz	Y	N	N	N	Y	Y	Y
UTAH							
Hatch	Y	N	N	N	Y	Y	Y
Lee	Y	N	N	N	Y	Y	Y
VERMONT							
Leahy	N	Y	Y	Y	N	N	Y
Sanders	N	Y	Y	Y	N	N	N
VIRGINIA							
Warner	N	Y	Y	Y	N	N	Y
Kaine	N	Y	Y	Y	N	N	Y
WASHINGTON							
Murray	N	Y	Y	Y	N	N	Y
Cantwell	N	Y	Y	Y	N	N	Y
WEST VIRGINIA							
Manchin	Y	Y	Y	Y	Y	Y	Y
Capito	Y	N	N	N	Y	Y	Y
WISCONSIN							
Johnson	Y	N	N	N	Y	Y	Y
Baldwin	N	Y	Y	Y	N	N	Y
WYOMING							
Enzi	Y	N	N	N	Y	Y	Y
Barrasso	Y	N	N	N	Y	Y	Y

KEY	**Republicans**	Democrats	*Independents*
Y Voted for (yea)	X Paired against		C Voted "present" to avoid possible conflict of interest
# Paired for	– Announced against		
+ Announced for	P Voted "present"		? Did not vote or otherwise make a position known
N Voted against (nay)			

VOTE NUMBER

113. ROSENSTEIN NOMINATION/CLOTURE. Motion to invoke cloture (thus limiting debate) on the nomination of Rod J. Rosenstein of Maryland to be deputy attorney general. Motion agreed to 92-6: R 50-0; D 40-6; I 2-0. April 24, 2017.

114. ROSENSTEIN NOMINATION/CONFIRMATION. Confirmation of President Donald Trump's nomination of Rod J. Rosenstein of Maryland to be deputy attorney general. Confirmed 94-6: R 52-0; D 40-6; I 2-0. April 25, 2017.

115. ACOSTA NOMINATION/CLOTURE. Motion to invoke cloture (thus limiting debate) on the nomination of R. Alexander Acosta of Florida to be secretary of Labor. Motion agreed to 61-39: R 52-0; D 8-38; I 1-1. April 26, 2017.

116. ACOSTA NOMINATION/CONFIRMATION. Confirmation of President Donald Trump's nomination of R. Alexander Acosta of Florida to be secretary of Labor. Confirmed 60-38: R 51-0; D 8-37; I 1-1. April 27, 2017.

117. CLAYTON NOMINATION/CLOTURE. Motion to invoke cloture (thus limiting debate) on the nomination of Jay Clayton of New York to be a member of the Securities and Exchange Commission. Motion agreed to 60-36: R 49-0; D 10-35; I 1-1. May 1, 2017.

118. CLAYTON NOMINATION/CONFIRMATION. Confirmation of President Donald Trump's nomination of Jay Clayton of New York to be a member of the Securities and Exchange Commission. Confirmed 61-37: R 51-0; D 9-36; I 1-1. May 2, 2017.

119. H J RES 66. STATE RETIREMENT PLAN DISAPPROVAL/MOTION TO PROCEED. McConnell, R-Ky., motion to proceed to the joint resolution that would nullify and disapprove of a Labor Department rule that exempts certain state-administered retirement savings plans from select federal regulations governing pension plans if the state programs meet certain standards. Under the rule, the savings program must be established and administered by the state, and the savings plans must be voluntary for the employee for the program to qualify for the exemption. Motion agreed to 51-48: R 51-1; D 0-45; I 0-2. May 3, 2017.

	113	114	115	116	117	118	119
ALABAMA							
Shelby	+	Y	Y	Y	Y	Y	Y
Strange	Y	Y	Y	Y	Y	Y	Y
ALASKA							
Murkowski	Y	Y	Y	Y	Y	Y	Y
Sullivan	Y	Y	Y	Y	Y	Y	Y
ARIZONA							
McCain	Y	Y	Y	Y	Y	Y	Y
Flake	?	Y	Y	Y	?	Y	Y
ARKANSAS							
Boozman	Y	Y	Y	Y	Y	Y	Y
Cotton	Y	Y	Y	Y	Y	Y	Y
CALIFORNIA							
Feinstein	Y	Y	N	N	N	N	N
Harris	N	N	N	N	N	N	N
COLORADO							
Bennet	Y	Y	N	N	Y	Y	N
Gardner	Y	Y	Y	Y	Y	Y	Y
CONNECTICUT							
Blumenthal	N	N	N	N	N	N	N
Murphy	Y	Y	N	N	N	N	N
DELAWARE							
Carper	Y	Y	N	N	Y	Y	N
Coons	Y	Y	N	N	N	N	N
FLORIDA							
Nelson	Y	Y	Y	Y	Y	Y	N
Rubio	Y	Y	Y	Y	Y	Y	Y
GEORGIA							
Isakson	Y	Y	Y	Y	?	?	Y
Perdue	Y	Y	Y	Y	Y	Y	Y
HAWAII							
Schatz	Y	Y	N	N	N	N	N
Hirono	Y	Y	N	N	N	N	N
IDAHO							
Crapo	Y	Y	Y	Y	Y	Y	Y
Risch	Y	Y	Y	Y	Y	Y	Y
ILLINOIS							
Durbin	Y	Y	N	N	-	-	-
Duckworth	Y	Y	N	N	N	N	N
INDIANA							
Donnelly	Y	Y	N	N	N	N	N
Young	Y	Y	Y	Y	Y	Y	N
IOWA							
Grassley	Y	Y	Y	Y	Y	Y	Y
Ernst	Y	Y	Y	Y	Y	Y	Y
KANSAS							
Roberts	Y	Y	Y	Y	Y	Y	Y
Moran	Y	Y	Y	Y	Y	Y	Y
KENTUCKY							
McConnell	Y	Y	Y	Y	Y	Y	Y
Paul	Y	Y	Y	Y	Y	Y	Y
LOUISIANA							
Cassidy	Y	Y	Y	Y	Y	Y	Y
Kennedy	Y	Y	Y	Y	Y	Y	Y
MAINE							
Collins	Y	Y	Y	Y	Y	Y	Y
King	Y	Y	Y	Y	Y	Y	N
MARYLAND							
Cardin	Y	Y	N	N	N	N	N
Van Hollen	Y	Y	N	N	N	N	N
MASSACHUSETTS							
Warren	N	N	N	N	N	N	N
Markey	Y	Y	N	N	N	N	N
MICHIGAN							
Stabenow	Y	Y	N	N	N	N	N
Peters	Y	Y	N	-	N	N	N
MINNESOTA							
Klobuchar	Y	Y	N	N	N	N	N
Franken	Y	Y	N	N	N	N	N
MISSISSIPPI							
Cochran	Y	Y	Y	Y	Y	Y	Y
Wicker	Y	Y	Y	Y	Y	Y	Y
MISSOURI							
McCaskill	Y	Y	Y	Y	Y	Y	Y
Blunt	Y	Y	Y	Y	Y	Y	Y

	113	114	115	116	117	118	119
MONTANA							
Tester	Y	Y	Y	Y	Y	Y	N
Daines	Y	Y	Y	Y	Y	Y	Y
NEBRASKA							
Fischer	Y	Y	Y	Y	Y	Y	Y
Sasse	Y	Y	Y	Y	Y	Y	Y
NEVADA							
Heller	Y	Y	Y	Y	?	Y	Y
Cortez Masto	N	N	Y	Y	N	N	N
NEW HAMPSHIRE							
Shaheen	Y	Y	N	N	Y	N	Y
Hassan	Y	Y	N	N	N	N	N
NEW JERSEY							
Menendez	Y	Y	Y	Y	N	N	N
Booker	N	N	N	N	N	N	N
NEW MEXICO							
Udall	Y	Y	N	N	N	N	N
Heinrich	Y	Y	N	N	N	N	N
NEW YORK							
Schumer	Y	Y	N	N	N	N	N
Gillibrand	N	N	N	N	N	N	N
NORTH CAROLINA							
Burr	Y	Y	Y	Y	Y	Y	Y
Tillis	Y	Y	Y	Y	Y	Y	Y
NORTH DAKOTA							
Hoeven	Y	Y	Y	Y	Y	Y	Y
Heitkamp	Y	Y	Y	Y	Y	Y	N
OHIO							
Brown	Y	Y	N	N	N	N	N
Portman	Y	Y	Y	Y	Y	Y	Y
OKLAHOMA							
Inhofe	Y	Y	Y	Y	Y	Y	Y
Lankford	Y	Y	Y	Y	Y	Y	Y
OREGON							
Wyden	Y	Y	N	N	N	N	N
Merkley	Y	Y	N	N	N	N	N
PENNSYLVANIA							
Casey	Y	Y	N	N	N	N	N
Toomey	Y	Y	Y	?	Y	Y	Y
RHODE ISLAND							
Reed	Y	Y	N	N	N	N	N
Whitehouse	Y	Y	N	N	N	N	N
SOUTH CAROLINA							
Graham	Y	Y	Y	Y	Y	Y	Y
Scott	Y	Y	Y	Y	Y	Y	Y
SOUTH DAKOTA							
Thune	Y	Y	Y	Y	Y	Y	Y
Rounds	Y	Y	Y	Y	Y	Y	Y
TENNESSEE							
Alexander	Y	Y	Y	Y	Y	Y	Y
Corker	Y	Y	Y	Y	Y	Y	Y
TEXAS							
Cornyn	Y	Y	Y	Y	Y	Y	Y
Cruz	Y	Y	Y	Y	Y	Y	Y
UTAH							
Hatch	Y	Y	Y	Y	Y	Y	Y
Lee	Y	Y	Y	Y	Y	Y	Y
VERMONT							
Leahy	Y	Y	N	N	N	N	N
Sanders	Y	Y	N	N	N	N	N
VIRGINIA							
Warner	Y	Y	Y	Y	Y	Y	N
Kaine	Y	Y	N	N	N	N	N
WASHINGTON							
Murray	Y	Y	N	N	N	N	N
Cantwell	Y	Y	N	N	N	N	N
WEST VIRGINIA							
Manchin	Y	Y	Y	Y	Y	Y	N
Capito	Y	Y	Y	Y	Y	Y	Y
WISCONSIN							
Johnson	Y	Y	Y	Y	Y	Y	Y
Baldwin	Y	Y	N	N	N	N	N
WYOMING							
Enzi	Y	Y	Y	Y	Y	Y	Y
Barrasso	Y	Y	Y	Y	Y	Y	Y

KEY	**Republicans**	Democrats	*Independents*

Y Voted for (yea)	**X** Paired against	**C** Voted "present" to avoid possible conflict of interest
# Paired for	**–** Announced against	
+ Announced for	**P** Voted "present"	**?** Did not vote or otherwise make a position known
N Voted against (nay)		

VOTE NUMBER

120. H J RES 66. STATE RETIREMENT PLAN DISAPPROVAL/PASSAGE. Passage of the joint resolution that would nullify and disapprove of a Labor Department rule that exempts certain state-administered retirement savings plans from select federal regulations governing pension plans if the state programs meet certain standards. Under the rule, the savings program must be established and administered by the state, and the savings plans must be voluntary for the employee for the program to qualify for the exemption. Passed (thus cleared for the president) 50-49: R 50-2; D 0-45; I 0-2. May 3, 2017.

121. HR 244. FISCAL 2017 OMNIBUS APPROPRIATIONS/MOTION TO CONCUR. McConnell, R-Ky., motion to concur in the House amendment to the Senate amendments to the bill that would provide $1.16 trillion in discretionary appropriations through Sept. 30, 2017 for federal departments and agencies covered by the remaining 11 fiscal 2017 spending bills. Included in that total is: $20.9 billion for Agriculture, $56.6 billion for Commerce-Justice-Science, $593 billion for Defense, $37.8 billion for Energy-Water, $21.5 billion for Financial Services, $42.4 billion for Homeland Security (including $772 million for improvements and maintenance to existing Customs and Border Protection infrastructure and technology), $32.2 billion for Interior-Environment, $161 billion for Labor-HHS-Education, $4.4 billion for Legislative, $53.1 billion for State-Foreign Operations, and $57.7 billion for Transportation-HUD. The measure would authorize classified amounts of funding for fiscal 2017 for 16 U.S. intelligence agencies and intelligence-related activities of the U.S. government. The measure would also provide $608 million for health benefits for retired coal miners, $296 million for Medicaid payments to Puerto Rico, and $341 million to replace 40 miles of existing fencing along the southwestern border, though the designs of the fencing must have been "previously deployed". Motion agreed to, (thus cleared for the president), 79-18: R 32-18; D 45-0; I 2-0. May 4, 2017.

122. WILSON NOMINATION/CONFIRMATION. Confirmation of President Donald Trump's nomination of Heather Wilson of South Dakota to be secretary of the Air Force. Confirmed 76-22: R 51-0; D 24-22; I 1-0. May 8, 2017.

123. GOTTLIEB NOMINATION/CLOTURE. Motion to invoke cloture (thus limiting debate) on the nomination of Scott Gottlieb of Connecticut to be commissioner of the Food and Drug Administration. Motion rejected 57-41: R 51-0; D 5-41; I 1-0. May 8, 2017.

124. GOTTLIEB NOMINATION/CONFIRMATION. Confirmation of President Donald Trump's nomination of Scott Gottlieb of Connecticut to be commissioner of the Food and Drug Administration. Confirmed 57-42: R 51-0; D 5-41; I 1-1. May 9, 2017.

125. H J RES 36. METHANE RELEASE LIMITATION DISAPPROVAL/MOTION TO PROCEED. McConnell, R-Ky., motion to proceed to the joint resolution that would nullify a Bureau of Land Management rule that requires oil and gas operators on public lands to take measures that decrease waste of natural gas. The rule requires these operators to reduce the practice of burning gas by adopting current technologies, to replace outdated equipment to minimize release of gas into the air and to periodically inspect their operations for leaks. Motion rejected 49-51: R 49-3; D 0-46; I 0-2. May 10, 2017.

126. LIGHTHIZER NOMINATION/CLOTURE. Motion to invoke cloture (thus limiting debate) on President Donald Trump's nomination of Robert Lighthizer of Florida to be United States trade representative. Motion agreed to 81-15: R 47-2; D 33-12; I 1-1. May 11, 2017.

	120	121	122	123	124	125	126
ALABAMA							
Shelby	Y	Y	Y	Y	Y	Y	Y
Strange	Y	N	Y	Y	Y	Y	Y
ALASKA							
Murkowski	Y	Y	Y	Y	Y	Y	+
Sullivan	Y	Y	Y	Y	Y	Y	?
ARIZONA							
McCain	Y	Y	Y	Y	Y	N	N
Flake	Y	N	Y	Y	Y	Y	Y
ARKANSAS							
Boozman	Y	Y	Y	Y	Y	Y	Y
Cotton	Y	N	Y	Y	Y	Y	Y
CALIFORNIA							
Feinstein	N	Y	N	N	N	N	Y
Harris	N	Y	N	N	N	N	N
COLORADO							
Bennet	N	Y	Y	Y	Y	N	Y
Gardner	Y	Y	Y	Y	Y	Y	Y
CONNECTICUT							
Blumenthal	N	Y	N	N	N	N	N
Murphy	N	Y	Y	N	N	N	Y
DELAWARE							
Carper	N	Y	Y	Y	N	Y	N
Coons	N	Y	Y	Y	Y	N	Y
FLORIDA							
Nelson	N	Y	Y	Y	Y	N	Y
Rubio	Y	Y	Y	Y	Y	Y	Y
GEORGIA							
Isakson	Y	+	?	?	+	Y	Y
Perdue	Y	Y	Y	Y	Y	Y	Y
HAWAII							
Schatz	N	Y	Y	N	N	N	N
Hirono	N	Y	N	N	N	N	Y
IDAHO							
Crapo	Y	N	Y	Y	Y	Y	Y
Risch	Y	N	Y	Y	Y	Y	Y
ILLINOIS							
Durbin	-	+	Y	N	N	N	Y
Duckworth	N	Y	N	N	N	N	Y
INDIANA							
Donnelly	N	Y	Y	N	N	N	Y
Young	N	Y	Y	Y	Y	Y	Y
IOWA							
Grassley	Y	N	Y	Y	Y	Y	Y
Ernst	Y	N	Y	Y	Y	Y	Y
KANSAS							
Roberts	Y	Y	Y	Y	Y	Y	Y
Moran	Y	Y	Y	Y	Y	Y	Y
KENTUCKY							
McConnell	Y	Y	Y	Y	Y	Y	Y
Paul	Y	N	Y	Y	Y	Y	Y
LOUISIANA							
Cassidy	Y	Y	Y	Y	Y	Y	Y
Kennedy	Y	N	Y	Y	Y	Y	Y
MAINE							
Collins	Y	Y	Y	Y	Y	N	Y
King	N	Y	Y	Y	Y	N	Y
MARYLAND							
Cardin	N	Y	N	N	N	N	Y
Van Hollen	N	Y	N	N	N	N	Y
MASSACHUSETTS							
Warren	N	Y	N	N	N	N	N
Markey	N	Y	N	N	N	N	N
MICHIGAN							
Stabenow	N	Y	Y	N	N	N	Y
Peters	N	Y	Y	N	N	N	Y
MINNESOTA							
Klobuchar	N	Y	Y	N	N	N	Y
Franken	N	Y	N	N	N	N	Y
MISSISSIPPI							
Cochran	Y	Y	Y	Y	Y	Y	Y
Wicker	Y	Y	Y	Y	Y	Y	Y
MISSOURI							
McCaskill	N	Y	Y	N	N	N	+
Blunt	Y	Y	Y	Y	Y	Y	Y

	120	121	122	123	124	125	126
MONTANA							
Tester	N	Y	Y	N	N	N	Y
Daines	Y	N	Y	Y	Y	Y	Y
NEBRASKA							
Fischer	Y	N	Y	Y	Y	Y	Y
Sasse	Y	-	Y	Y	Y	Y	N
NEVADA							
Heller	Y	N	Y	Y	Y	Y	Y
Cortez Masto	N	Y	N	N	N	N	Y
NEW HAMPSHIRE							
Shaheen	N	Y	N	N	N	N	Y
Hassan	N	Y	N	N	N	N	Y
NEW JERSEY							
Menendez	N	Y	N	N	N	N	Y
Booker	N	Y	N	N	N	N	Y
NEW MEXICO							
Udall	N	Y	Y	N	N	N	N
Heinrich	N	Y	Y	N	N	N	N
NEW YORK							
Schumer	N	Y	N	N	N	N	Y
Gillibrand	N	Y	N	N	N	N	N
NORTH CAROLINA							
Burr	Y	Y	Y	Y	Y	Y	Y
Tillis	Y	Y	Y	Y	Y	Y	Y
NORTH DAKOTA							
Hoeven	Y	Y	Y	Y	Y	Y	Y
Heitkamp	N	Y	Y	Y	Y	N	Y
OHIO							
Brown	N	Y	N	N	N	N	Y
Portman	Y	Y	Y	Y	Y	Y	Y
OKLAHOMA							
Inhofe	Y	Y	Y	Y	Y	Y	Y
Lankford	Y	Y	Y	Y	Y	Y	Y
OREGON							
Wyden	N	Y	N	N	N	N	Y
Merkley	N	Y	N	N	N	N	N
PENNSYLVANIA							
Casey	N	Y	Y	N	N	N	Y
Toomey	Y	N	Y	Y	Y	Y	Y
RHODE ISLAND							
Reed	N	Y	N	N	N	N	N
Whitehouse	N	Y	N	N	N	N	N
SOUTH CAROLINA							
Graham	Y	N	Y	Y	Y	N	Y
Scott	Y	N	Y	Y	Y	Y	Y
SOUTH DAKOTA							
Thune	Y	Y	Y	Y	Y	Y	Y
Rounds	Y	Y	Y	Y	Y	Y	Y
TENNESSEE							
Alexander	Y	Y	Y	Y	Y	Y	Y
Corker	N	N	Y	Y	Y	Y	Y
TEXAS							
Cornyn	Y	Y	Y	Y	Y	Y	Y
Cruz	Y	N	Y	Y	Y	Y	Y
UTAH							
Hatch	Y	Y	Y	Y	Y	Y	Y
Lee	Y	N	Y	Y	Y	Y	Y
VERMONT							
Leahy	N	Y	N	N	N	N	Y
Sanders	N	Y	?	?	N	N	N
VIRGINIA							
Warner	N	Y	N	N	N	N	Y
Kaine	N	Y	Y	N	N	N	Y
WASHINGTON							
Murray	N	Y	N	N	N	N	Y
Cantwell	N	Y	N	N	N	N	Y
WEST VIRGINIA							
Manchin	N	Y	Y	N	N	N	Y
Capito	Y	Y	Y	Y	Y	Y	+
WISCONSIN							
Johnson	Y	Y	Y	Y	Y	Y	Y
Baldwin	N	Y	N	N	N	N	Y
WYOMING							
Enzi	Y	Y	Y	Y	Y	Y	Y
Barrasso	Y	Y	Y	Y	Y	Y	Y

KEY	**Republicans**	Democrats	*Independents*

Y Voted for (yea)	X Paired against	C Voted "present" to avoid possible conflict of interest
# Paired for	- Announced against	
+ Announced for	P Voted "present"	? Did not vote or otherwise make a position known
N Voted against (nay)		

VOTE NUMBER

127. LIGHTHIZER NOMINATION/CONFIRMATION. Confirmation of President Donald Trump's nomination of Robert Lighthizer of Florida to be United States trade representative. Confirmed 82-14: R 45-3; D 36-10; I 1-1. May 11, 2017.

128. ROSEN NOMINATION/CLOTURE. Motion to invoke cloture (thus limiting debate) on President Donald Trump's nomination of Jeffrey A. Rosen of Virginia to be deputy secretary of Transportation. Motion agreed to 52-42: R 46-0; D 6-40; I 0-2. May 15, 2017.

129. ROSEN NOMINATION/CONFIRMATION. Confirmation of President Donald Trump's nomination of Jeffrey A. Rosen of Virginia to be deputy secretary of Transportation. Confirmed 56-42: R 50-0; D 6-40; I 0-2. May 16, 2017.

130. BRAND NOMINATION/CLOTURE. Motion to invoke cloture (thus limiting debate) on President Donald Trump's nomination of Rachel L. Brand of Iowa to be associate attorney general. Motion agreed to 51-47: R 51-0; D 0-45; I 0-2. May 17, 2017.

131. BRAND NOMINATION/CONFIRMATION. Confirmation of President Donald Trump's nomination of Rachel L. Brand of Iowa to be associate attorney general. Confirmed 52-46: R 52-0; D 0-44; I 0-2. May 18, 2017.

132. BRANSTAD NOMINATION/CLOTURE. Motion to invoke cloture (thus limiting debate) on President Donald Trump's nomination of Terry Branstad of Iowa to be to be U.S. ambassador to China. Motion agreed to 86-12: R 52-0; D 33-11; I 1-1. May 18, 2017.

133. BRANSTAD NOMINATION/CONFIRMATION. Confirmation of President Donald Trump's nomination of Terry Branstad of Iowa to be to be U.S. ambassador to China. Confirmed 82-13: R 48-0; D 33-12; I 1-1. May 22, 2017.

	127	128	129	130	131	132	133
ALABAMA							
Shelby	Y	Y	Y	Y	Y	Y	Y
Strange	Y	Y	Y	Y	Y	Y	Y
ALASKA							
Murkowski	?	?	Y	Y	Y	Y	+
Sullivan	?	Y	Y	Y	Y	Y	Y
ARIZONA							
McCain	N	Y	Y	Y	Y	Y	Y
Flake	Y	?	Y	Y	Y	Y	Y
ARKANSAS							
Boozman	Y	Y	Y	Y	Y	Y	Y
Cotton	Y	Y	Y	Y	Y	Y	Y
CALIFORNIA							
Feinstein	Y	N	N	N	N	Y	Y
Harris	N	N	N	N	N	N	-
COLORADO							
Bennet	Y	N	N	N	N	Y	Y
Gardner	N	Y	Y	Y	Y	Y	Y
CONNECTICUT							
Blumenthal	N	N	N	N	N	N	N
Murphy	Y	N	N	N	N	Y	Y
DELAWARE							
Carper	Y	N	N	N	N	Y	Y
Coons	Y	N	N	N	N	Y	Y
FLORIDA							
Nelson	Y	N	N	N	N	Y	Y
Rubio	Y	Y	Y	Y	Y	Y	Y
GEORGIA							
Isakson	?	?	?	Y	Y	Y	+
Perdue	Y	Y	Y	Y	Y	Y	Y
HAWAII							
Schatz	N	N	N	N	N	Y	Y
Hirono	Y	N	N	?	?	?	N
IDAHO							
Crapo	Y	Y	Y	Y	Y	Y	Y
Risch	Y	Y	Y	Y	Y	Y	Y
ILLINOIS							
Durbin	Y	N	N	N	N	Y	Y
Duckworth	Y	N	N	N	N	N	N
INDIANA							
Donnelly	Y	Y	Y	N	N	Y	Y
Young	Y	Y	Y	Y	Y	Y	Y
IOWA							
Grassley	Y	Y	Y	Y	Y	Y	Y
Ernst	Y	Y	Y	Y	Y	Y	Y
KANSAS							
Roberts	Y	Y	Y	Y	Y	Y	Y
Moran	Y	+	?	Y	Y	Y	Y
KENTUCKY							
McConnell	Y	Y	Y	Y	Y	Y	Y
Paul	Y	Y	Y	Y	Y	Y	Y
LOUISIANA							
Cassidy	Y	Y	Y	Y	Y	Y	Y
Kennedy	Y	Y	Y	Y	Y	Y	Y
MAINE							
Collins	Y	Y	Y	Y	Y	Y	Y
King	Y	N	N	N	N	Y	Y
MARYLAND							
Cardin	Y	N	N	N	N	Y	Y
Van Hollen	Y	N	N	N	N	Y	Y
MASSACHUSETTS							
Warren	N	N	N	N	N	N	N
Markey	N	N	N	N	N	Y	N
MICHIGAN							
Stabenow	Y	N	N	N	N	N	N
Peters	Y	Y	N	N	N	N	N
MINNESOTA							
Klobuchar	Y	N	N	N	N	Y	Y
Franken	Y	N	N	N	N	Y	Y
MISSISSIPPI							
Cochran	Y	Y	Y	Y	Y	Y	Y
Wicker	Y	Y	Y	Y	Y	Y	Y
MISSOURI							
McCaskill	Y	N	N	N	N	Y	Y
Blunt	Y	Y	Y	Y	Y	Y	Y

	127	128	129	130	131	132	133
MONTANA							
Tester	Y	N	N	N	N	Y	Y
Daines	Y	Y	Y	Y	Y	Y	Y
NEBRASKA							
Fischer	Y	Y	Y	Y	Y	Y	Y
Sasse	N	?	Y	Y	Y	Y	Y
NEVADA							
Heller	Y	Y	Y	Y	Y	Y	Y
Cortez Masto	Y	N	N	N	N	Y	Y
NEW HAMPSHIRE							
Shaheen	Y	N	N	N	N	Y	Y
Hassan	Y	N	N	N	N	Y	Y
NEW JERSEY							
Menendez	Y	N	N	N	N	Y	Y
Booker	Y	N	N	N	N	N	N
NEW MEXICO							
Udall	Y	N	N	N	N	Y	Y
Heinrich	Y	N	N	N	N	Y	Y
NEW YORK							
Schumer	N	N	N	N	N	N	N
Gillibrand	N	N	N	N	N	N	N
NORTH CAROLINA							
Burr	Y	Y	Y	Y	Y	Y	Y
Tillis	Y	Y	Y	?	Y	Y	Y
NORTH DAKOTA							
Hoeven	Y	Y	Y	Y	Y	Y	Y
Heitkamp	Y	Y	Y	N	N	Y	Y
OHIO							
Brown	Y	N	N	N	N	N	N
Portman	Y	Y	Y	Y	Y	Y	Y
OKLAHOMA							
Inhofe	Y	Y	Y	Y	Y	Y	Y
Lankford	Y	Y	Y	Y	Y	Y	Y
OREGON							
Wyden	Y	N	N	N	N	Y	Y
Merkley	N	N	N	N	N	Y	Y
PENNSYLVANIA							
Casey	Y	N	N	N	N	Y	Y
Toomey	Y	?	Y	Y	Y	Y	Y
RHODE ISLAND							
Reed	N	N	N	N	N	Y	Y
Whitehouse	N	N	N	N	N	Y	Y
SOUTH CAROLINA							
Graham	Y	Y	Y	Y	Y	Y	Y
Scott	Y	Y	Y	Y	Y	Y	Y
SOUTH DAKOTA							
Thune	Y	Y	Y	Y	Y	Y	Y
Rounds	Y	Y	Y	Y	Y	Y	Y
TENNESSEE							
Alexander	Y	Y	Y	Y	Y	Y	+
Corker	Y	Y	Y	Y	Y	Y	Y
TEXAS							
Cornyn	Y	Y	Y	Y	Y	Y	Y
Cruz	Y	Y	Y	Y	Y	Y	Y
UTAH							
Hatch	Y	Y	Y	Y	Y	Y	Y
Lee	Y	Y	Y	Y	Y	Y	?
VERMONT							
Leahy	Y	N	N	N	N	Y	Y
Sanders	N	N	N	N	N	N	N
VIRGINIA							
Warner	Y	Y	Y	N	N	Y	Y
Kaine	Y	Y	Y	N	-	+	Y
WASHINGTON							
Murray	Y	N	N	N	N	Y	Y
Cantwell	Y	N	N	N	N	Y	Y
WEST VIRGINIA							
Manchin	Y	Y	Y	N	N	Y	Y
Capito	+	Y	Y	Y	Y	Y	Y
WISCONSIN							
Johnson	Y	Y	Y	Y	Y	Y	Y
Baldwin	Y	N	N	N	N	N	N
WYOMING							
Enzi	Y	Y	Y	Y	Y	Y	Y
Barrasso	Y	Y	Y	Y	Y	Y	Y

KEY	**Republicans**	Democrats	*Independents*
Y Voted for (yea)		X Paired against	C Voted "present" to avoid possible conflict of interest
# Paired for		- Announced against	
+ Announced for		P Voted "present"	? Did not vote or otherwise make a position known
N Voted against (nay)			

VOTE NUMBER

134. SULLIVAN NOMINATION/CLOTURE. Motion to invoke cloture (thus limiting debate) on President Donald Trump's nomination of John J. Sullivan of Maryland to be to be deputy secretary of State. Motion agreed to 93-6: R 51-0; D 41-5; I 1-1. May 23, 2017.

135. SULLIVAN NOMINATION/CONFIRMATION. Confirmation of President Donald Trump's nomination of John J. Sullivan of Maryland to be to be deputy secretary of State. Confirmed 94-6: R 52-0; D 41-5; I 1-1. May 24, 2017.

136. THAPAR NOMINATION/CLOTURE. Motion to invoke cloture (thus limiting debate) on President Donald Trump's nomination of Amul R. Thapar of Kentucky to be a judge for the 6th U.S. Circuit Court of Appeals. Motion agreed to 52-48: R 52-0; D 0-46; I 0-2. May 24, 2017.

137. THAPAR NOMINATION/CONFIRMATION. Confirmation of President Donald Trump's nomination of Amul R. Thapar of Kentucky to be a judge for the 6th U.S. Circuit Court of Appeals. Confirmed 52-44: R 52-0; D 0-42; I 0-2. May 25, 2017.

138. S RES 176. JERUSALEM REUNIFICATION ANNIVERSARY/ADOPTION. Adoption of the resolution that would recognize the 50th anniversary of the reunification of Jerusalem. The resolution would support Israel's commitment to religious freedom, support the American-Israeli relationship, commend Egypt and Jordan for embracing peace with Israel, and reaffirm that American policy on the status of Jerusalem is a matter that will be decided through the actors involved in negotiations of a two-state solution. The resolution would also reaffirm the Jerusalem Embassy Act, which would move the American Embassy in Israel to Jerusalem. Adopted 90-0: R 47-0; D 41-0; I 2-0. June 5, 2017.

139. ELWOOD NOMINATION/CONFIRMATION. Confirmation of President Donald Trump's nomination of Courtney Elwood of Virginia to be general counsel of the Central Intelligence Agency. Confirmed 67-33: R 50-2; D 16-30; I 1-1. June 5, 2017.

140. S 722. IRAN SANCTIONS/CLOTURE. Motion to invoke cloture (thus limiting debate) on the McConnell, R-Ky., motion to proceed to the bill that would impose certain sanctions on Iran. Specifically, the president would be required to block the transactions of any person deemed to knowingly engage in activity contributing to an Iran ballistic missile or mass destruction program, that is related to the Iranian Revolutionary Guard Corps, that is responsible for human rights abuses, or that contributes to the arming of Iran. The bill would also require the departments of Defense and Treasury and the National Intelligence Agency to develop a strategy for deterring Iran from activities or threats against the United States and its allies every two years. Motion agreed to 91-8: R 50-1; D 40-6; I 1-1. June 7, 2017.

	134	135	136	137	138	139	140
ALABAMA							
Shelby	Y	Y	Y	Y	Y	Y	Y
Strange	Y	Y	Y	Y	Y	Y	Y
ALASKA							
Murkowski	Y	Y	Y	Y	?	Y	Y
Sullivan	Y	Y	Y	Y	?	Y	Y
ARIZONA							
McCain	Y	Y	Y	Y	Y	Y	Y
Flake	Y	Y	Y	Y	?	Y	Y
ARKANSAS							
Boozman	Y	Y	Y	Y	Y	Y	Y
Cotton	Y	Y	Y	Y	Y	Y	Y
CALIFORNIA							
Feinstein	Y	Y	N	N	Y	Y	N
Harris	N	N	N	N	Y	Y	Y
COLORADO							
Bennet	Y	Y	N	N	+	Y	Y
Gardner	Y	Y	Y	Y	Y	Y	Y
CONNECTICUT							
Blumenthal	Y	Y	N	N	Y	N	Y
Murphy	Y	Y	N	N	Y	Y	Y
DELAWARE							
Carper	Y	Y	N	N	Y	Y	N
Coons	Y	Y	N	N	Y	N	Y
FLORIDA							
Nelson	Y	Y	N	N	Y	Y	Y
Rubio	Y	Y	Y	Y	Y	Y	Y
GEORGIA							
Isakson	?	Y	Y	Y	Y	Y	Y
Perdue	Y	Y	Y	Y	Y	Y	Y
HAWAII							
Schatz	Y	Y	N	?	Y	N	Y
Hirono	Y	Y	N	?	Y	N	Y
IDAHO							
Crapo	Y	Y	Y	Y	Y	Y	Y
Risch	Y	Y	Y	Y	Y	Y	Y
ILLINOIS							
Durbin	Y	Y	N	N	Y	N	N
Duckworth	N	N	N	N	?	Y	Y
INDIANA							
Donnelly	Y	Y	N	N	Y	Y	Y
Young	Y	Y	Y	Y	Y	Y	Y
IOWA							
Grassley	Y	Y	Y	Y	Y	Y	Y
Ernst	Y	Y	Y	Y	Y	Y	Y
KANSAS							
Roberts	Y	Y	Y	Y	Y	Y	Y
Moran	Y	Y	Y	Y	Y	Y	Y
KENTUCKY							
McConnell	Y	Y	Y	Y	Y	Y	Y
Paul	Y	Y	Y	Y	Y	N	N
LOUISIANA							
Cassidy	Y	Y	Y	Y	Y	Y	Y
Kennedy	Y	Y	Y	Y	Y	Y	Y
MAINE							
Collins	Y	Y	Y	Y	Y	Y	Y
King	Y	Y	N	N	Y	Y	Y
MARYLAND							
Cardin	Y	Y	N	N	Y	N	Y
Van Hollen	Y	Y	N	N	Y	N	Y
MASSACHUSETTS							
Warren	N	N	N	N	Y	N	Y
Markey	Y	Y	N	N	Y	N	Y
MICHIGAN							
Stabenow	Y	Y	N	N	Y	N	Y
Peters	Y	Y	N	N	Y	N	Y
MINNESOTA							
Klobuchar	Y	Y	N	N	Y	Y	Y
Franken	Y	Y	N	N	Y	N	Y
MISSISSIPPI							
Cochran	Y	Y	Y	Y	Y	Y	Y
Wicker	Y	Y	Y	Y	Y	Y	Y
MISSOURI							
McCaskill	Y	Y	N	N	Y	Y	Y
Blunt	Y	Y	Y	Y	Y	Y	Y

	134	135	136	137	138	139	140
MONTANA							
Tester	Y	Y	N	N	Y	N	Y
Daines	Y	Y	Y	Y	Y	Y	Y
NEBRASKA							
Fischer	Y	Y	Y	Y	Y	Y	Y
Sasse	Y	Y	Y	Y	Y	Y	Y
NEVADA							
Heller	Y	Y	Y	Y	Y	Y	Y
Cortez Masto	Y	Y	N	N	Y	N	Y
NEW HAMPSHIRE							
Shaheen	Y	Y	N	N	Y	N	Y
Hassan	Y	Y	N	N	Y	N	Y
NEW JERSEY							
Menendez	Y	Y	N	N	+	N	Y
Booker	N	N	N	N	?	N	Y
NEW MEXICO							
Udall	Y	Y	N	?	Y	N	N
Heinrich	Y	Y	N	N	Y	N	Y
NEW YORK							
Schumer	Y	Y	N	N	Y	N	Y
Gillibrand	N	N	N	N	Y	N	N
NORTH CAROLINA							
Burr	Y	Y	Y	Y	Y	Y	Y
Tillis	Y	Y	Y	?	Y	Y	Y
NORTH DAKOTA							
Hoeven	Y	Y	Y	Y	Y	Y	Y
Heitkamp	Y	Y	N	N	Y	Y	Y
OHIO							
Brown	Y	Y	N	N	Y	N	Y
Portman	Y	Y	Y	Y	Y	Y	Y
OKLAHOMA							
Inhofe	Y	Y	Y	Y	Y	Y	Y
Lankford	Y	Y	Y	Y	Y	Y	Y
OREGON							
Wyden	Y	Y	N	N	Y	N	Y
Merkley	Y	Y	N	N	?	N	N
PENNSYLVANIA							
Casey	Y	Y	N	N	Y	Y	Y
Toomey	Y	Y	Y	?	Y	Y	Y
RHODE ISLAND							
Reed	Y	Y	N	N	Y	N	Y
Whitehouse	Y	Y	N	N	Y	N	Y
SOUTH CAROLINA							
Graham	Y	Y	Y	Y	Y	Y	Y
Scott	Y	Y	Y	Y	Y	Y	Y
SOUTH DAKOTA							
Thune	Y	Y	Y	Y	Y	Y	Y
Rounds	Y	Y	Y	Y	Y	Y	Y
TENNESSEE							
Alexander	Y	Y	Y	Y	Y	Y	Y
Corker	Y	Y	Y	Y	Y	Y	Y
TEXAS							
Cornyn	Y	Y	Y	Y	Y	Y	Y
Cruz	Y	Y	Y	Y	Y	Y	?
UTAH							
Hatch	Y	Y	Y	Y	Y	Y	Y
Lee	Y	Y	Y	Y	Y	Y	Y
VERMONT							
Leahy	Y	Y	N	N	Y	N	Y
Sanders	N	N	N	N	Y	N	N
VIRGINIA							
Warner	Y	Y	N	N	Y	Y	Y
Kaine	Y	Y	N	N	Y	Y	Y
WASHINGTON							
Murray	Y	Y	N	N	Y	N	Y
Cantwell	Y	Y	N	?	Y	N	Y
WEST VIRGINIA							
Manchin	Y	Y	N	N	Y	Y	Y
Capito	Y	Y	Y	Y	Y	Y	Y
WISCONSIN							
Johnson	Y	Y	Y	Y	Y	Y	Y
Baldwin	Y	Y	N	N	Y	N	Y
WYOMING							
Enzi	Y	Y	Y	Y	Y	Y	Y
Barrasso	Y	Y	Y	Y	Y	Y	Y

KEY   **Republicans**   Democrats   *Independents*

Y Voted for (yea)	X Paired against	C Voted "present" to avoid possible conflict of interest
# Paired for	– Announced against	
+ Announced for	P Voted "present"	? Did not vote or otherwise make a position known
N Voted against (nay)		

VOTE NUMBER

141. BROWN NOMINATION/CONFIRMATION. Confirmation of President Donald Trump's nomination of Scott P. Brown of New Hampshire to be U.S. ambassador to New Zealand and the Independent State of Samoa. Confirmed 94-4: R 51-0; D 41-4; I 2-0. June 8, 2017.

142. RAPUANO NOMINATION/CONFIRMATION. Confirmation of President Donald Trump's nomination of Kenneth P. Rapuano of Virginia to be an assistant secretary of Defense. Confirmed 95-1: R 49-0; D 45-0; I 1-1. June 12, 2017.

143. S J RES 42. SAUDI ARMS SALE DISAPPROVAL/MOTION TO DISCHARGE. Paul, R-Ky., motion to discharge the Senate Foreign Relations Committee from further consideration of a joint resolution that would prohibit the proposed sale of laser-guided weapons systems, fighter aircraft, warhead fuze systems, and other weaponry and defense services to Saudi Arabia. The proposed sale was submitted to Congress on May 19, 2017. Motion rejected 47-53: R 4-48; D 41-5; I 2-0. June 13, 2017.

144. S 722. IRANIAN AND RUSSIAN SANCTIONS/RUSSIAN SANCTIONS. McConnell, R-Ky., for Crapo, R-Idaho, amendment no. 232, as modified, that would allow for Congressional review of any changes to Russian sanctions and would codify U.S. sanctions against Russia. The amendment would authorize new sanctions on individuals, including on those who engage in undermining the cybersecurity of a person, democratic institution or government on behalf of Russia. It would impose sanctions on individuals that transfer arms to Syria, and would authorize $250 million over fiscal years 2018 and 2019 for the Countering Russian Influence Fund. Additionally, it would require the president to develop a national strategy for combating the financing of terrorism and would add the secretary of the Treasury to the National Security Council. Adopted 97-2: R 50-2; D 45-0; I 2-0. June 14, 2017.

145. S 722. IRANIAN AND RUSSIAN SANCTIONS/NASA EXEMPTION. Gardner, R-Colo., amendment no. 250, as modified, that would exempt NASA and persons involved in any space launch conducted for NASA or any other non-Department of Defense customer from the bill's provisions. Adopted 94-6: R 47-5; D 45-1; I 2-0. June 15, 2017.

146. 722. IRANIAN AND RUSSIAN SANCTIONS/NATO ARTICLE 5 IMPORTANCE. Corker, R-Ky., for Graham, R-S.C., amendment no. 240, that would express the sense of the Senate that Article 5 of NATO, which states that an armed attack against one or more NATO member is considered an attack against all members, is of vital importance. It would also condemn threats to the sovereignty, territorial integrity, freedom, or democracy of any NATO country. Adopted 100-0: R 52-0; D 46-0; I 2-0. June 15, 2017.

147. S 722. IRANIAN AND RUSSIAN SANCTIONS/PASSAGE. Passage of the bill that would impose new sanctions on Iran. Specifically, the president would be required to block the transactions of any person deemed to knowingly engage in activities contributing to an Iranian ballistic missile or weapons of mass destruction program, who is involved in the Iranian Revolutionary Guard Corps, who is responsible for human rights violations, or who contributes to the arming of Iran. As amended, the bill would allow for Congressional review of any changes to Russian sanctions and would codify U.S. sanctions against Russia. It would authorize new sanctions on individuals, including on those who engage in undermining the cybersecurity of a person, democratic institution or government on behalf of Russia. It would impose sanctions on individuals that transfer arms to Syria, and would authorize $250 million over fiscal years 2018 and 2019 for the Countering Russian Influence Fund. Additionally, it would require the president to develop a national strategy for combating the financing of terrorism and would add the secretary of the Treasury to the National Security Council. Passed 98-2: R 51-1; D 46-0; I 1-1. June 15, 2017.

	141	142	143	144	145	146	147
ALABAMA							
Shelby	Y	Y	N	Y	Y	Y	Y
Strange	Y	Y	N	Y	Y	Y	Y
ALASKA							
Murkowski	Y	Y	N	Y	Y	Y	Y
Sullivan	Y	Y	N	Y	N	Y	Y
ARIZONA							
McCain	Y	Y	N	Y	N	Y	Y
Flake	Y	Y	N	Y	Y	Y	Y
ARKANSAS							
Boozman	Y	Y	N	Y	Y	Y	Y
Cotton	Y	Y	N	Y	Y	Y	Y
CALIFORNIA							
Feinstein	Y	Y	Y	Y	Y	Y	Y
Harris	N	Y	Y	Y	Y	Y	Y
COLORADO							
Bennet	Y	Y	Y	Y	Y	Y	Y
Gardner	Y	Y	N	Y	Y	Y	Y
CONNECTICUT							
Blumenthal	Y	Y	Y	Y	N	Y	Y
Murphy	Y	Y	Y	Y	Y	Y	Y
DELAWARE							
Carper	Y	Y	Y	Y	Y	Y	Y
Coons	Y	Y	Y	Y	Y	Y	Y
FLORIDA							
Nelson	Y	Y	Y	Y	Y	Y	Y
Rubio	Y	Y	N	Y	Y	Y	Y
GEORGIA							
Isakson	Y	Y	N	Y	Y	Y	Y
Perdue	Y	?	N	Y	Y	Y	Y
HAWAII							
Schatz	N	Y	Y	Y	Y	Y	Y
Hirono	Y	Y	Y	Y	Y	Y	Y
IDAHO							
Crapo	Y	Y	N	Y	Y	Y	Y
Risch	Y	?	N	Y	Y	Y	Y
ILLINOIS							
Durbin	Y	Y	Y	Y	Y	Y	Y
Duckworth	Y	Y	Y	Y	Y	Y	Y
INDIANA							
Donnelly	Y	Y	Y	Y	Y	Y	Y
Young	Y	Y	N	Y	Y	Y	Y
IOWA							
Grassley	Y	Y	N	Y	Y	Y	Y
Ernst	Y	Y	N	Y	N	Y	Y
KANSAS							
Roberts	Y	Y	N	Y	Y	Y	Y
Moran	Y	Y	N	Y	Y	Y	Y
KENTUCKY							
McConnell	Y	Y	N	Y	Y	Y	Y
Paul	Y	Y	Y	N	Y	Y	N
LOUISIANA							
Cassidy	Y	Y	N	Y	Y	Y	Y
Kennedy	Y	Y	N	Y	Y	Y	Y
MAINE							
Collins	Y	Y	N	Y	Y	Y	Y
King	Y	Y	Y	Y	Y	Y	Y
MARYLAND							
Cardin	Y	Y	Y	Y	Y	Y	Y
Van Hollen	Y	Y	Y	+	Y	Y	Y
MASSACHUSETTS							
Warren	Y	Y	Y	Y	Y	Y	Y
Markey	Y	Y	Y	Y	Y	Y	Y
MICHIGAN							
Stabenow	Y	+	Y	Y	Y	Y	Y
Peters	Y	Y	Y	Y	Y	Y	Y
MINNESOTA							
Klobuchar	Y	Y	Y	Y	Y	Y	Y
Franken	Y	Y	Y	Y	Y	Y	Y
MISSISSIPPI							
Cochran	Y	Y	N	Y	Y	Y	Y
Wicker	Y	Y	N	Y	Y	Y	Y
MISSOURI							
McCaskill	Y	Y	N	Y	Y	Y	Y
Blunt	Y	Y	N	Y	Y	Y	Y

	141	142	143	144	145	146	147
MONTANA							
Tester	Y	Y	Y	Y	Y	Y	Y
Daines	Y	Y	N	Y	Y	Y	Y
NEBRASKA							
Fischer	Y	Y	N	Y	Y	Y	Y
Sasse	Y	Y	N	Y	N	Y	Y
NEVADA							
Heller	Y	Y	Y	Y	Y	Y	Y
Cortez Masto	Y	Y	Y	Y	Y	Y	Y
NEW HAMPSHIRE							
Shaheen	Y	Y	Y	Y	Y	Y	Y
Hassan	Y	Y	Y	Y	Y	Y	Y
NEW JERSEY							
Menendez	+	Y	Y	Y	Y	Y	Y
Booker	N	Y	Y	Y	Y	Y	Y
NEW MEXICO							
Udall	Y	Y	Y	Y	Y	Y	Y
Heinrich	Y	Y	Y	Y	Y	Y	Y
NEW YORK							
Schumer	Y	Y	Y	Y	Y	Y	Y
Gillibrand	N	Y	Y	Y	Y	Y	Y
NORTH CAROLINA							
Burr	Y	?	N	Y	Y	Y	Y
Tillis	Y	Y	N	Y	Y	Y	Y
NORTH DAKOTA							
Hoeven	Y	Y	N	Y	Y	Y	Y
Heitkamp	Y	Y	Y	Y	Y	Y	Y
OHIO							
Brown	Y	Y	Y	Y	Y	Y	Y
Portman	Y	Y	N	Y	Y	Y	Y
OKLAHOMA							
Inhofe	Y	Y	N	Y	Y	Y	Y
Lankford	Y	Y	N	Y	Y	Y	Y
OREGON							
Wyden	Y	Y	Y	Y	Y	Y	Y
Merkley	Y	Y	Y	Y	Y	Y	Y
PENNSYLVANIA							
Casey	Y	Y	Y	Y	Y	Y	Y
Toomey	Y	Y	N	Y	Y	Y	Y
RHODE ISLAND							
Reed	Y	Y	Y	Y	Y	Y	Y
Whitehouse	Y	Y	Y	Y	Y	Y	Y
SOUTH CAROLINA							
Graham	Y	Y	N	Y	N	Y	Y
Scott	Y	Y	N	Y	Y	Y	Y
SOUTH DAKOTA							
Thune	Y	Y	N	Y	Y	Y	Y
Rounds	Y	Y	N	Y	Y	Y	Y
TENNESSEE							
Alexander	+	Y	N	Y	Y	Y	Y
Corker	Y	Y	N	Y	Y	Y	Y
TEXAS							
Cornyn	Y	Y	N	Y	Y	Y	Y
Cruz	Y	Y	N	Y	Y	Y	Y
UTAH							
Hatch	Y	Y	N	Y	Y	Y	Y
Lee	Y	Y	Y	N	Y	Y	Y
VERMONT							
Leahy	Y	Y	Y	Y	Y	Y	Y
Sanders	Y	N	Y	Y	Y	N	N
VIRGINIA							
Warner	Y	Y	Y	Y	Y	Y	Y
Kaine	Y	Y	Y	Y	Y	Y	Y
WASHINGTON							
Murray	Y	Y	Y	Y	Y	Y	Y
Cantwell	Y	Y	Y	Y	Y	Y	Y
WEST VIRGINIA							
Manchin	Y	Y	N	Y	Y	Y	Y
Capito	Y	Y	N	Y	Y	Y	Y
WISCONSIN							
Johnson	Y	Y	N	Y	Y	Y	Y
Baldwin	Y	Y	Y	Y	Y	Y	Y
WYOMING							
Enzi	Y	Y	N	Y	Y	Y	Y
Barrasso	Y	Y	N	Y	Y	Y	Y

KEY	**Republicans**	Democrats	*Independents*	
Y	Voted for (yea)	X Paired against	C	Voted "present" to avoid possible conflict of interest
#	Paired for	– Announced against		
+	Announced for	P Voted "present"	?	Did not vote or otherwise make a position known
N	Voted against (nay)			

VOTE NUMBER

148. LONG NOMINATION/CONFIRMATION. Confirmation of President Donald Trump's nomination of Brock Long of North Carolina to be administrator of the Federal Emergency Management Agency, Department of Homeland Security. Confirmed 95-4: R 51-0; D 42-4; I 2-0. June 20, 2017.

149. MANDELKER NOMINATION/CLOTURE. Motion to invoke cloture (thus limiting debate) on President Donald Trump's nomination of Sigal Mandelker of New York to be to be undersecretary of the Treasury for terrorism and financial crimes. Motion agreed to 94-5: R 51-0; D 42-4; I 1-1. June 20, 2017.

150. MANDELKER NOMINATION/CONFIRMATION. Confirmation of President Donald Trump's nomination of Sigal Mandelker of New York to be undersecretary of the Treasury for terrorism and financial crimes. Confirmed 96-4: R 52-0; D 42-4; I 2-0. June 21, 2017.

151. BILLINGSLEA NOMINATION/CLOTURE. Motion to invoke cloture (thus limiting debate) on President Donald Trump's nomination of Marshall Billingslea of Virginia to be to be assistant secretary for terrorist financing, Department of the Treasury. Motion agreed to 65-34: R 51-1; D 13-32; I 1-1. June 21, 2017.

152. BILLINGSLEA NOMINATION/CONFIRMATION. Confirmation of President Donald Trump's nomination of Marshall Billingslea of Virginia to be assistant secretary for terrorist financing, Department of the Treasury. Confirmed 65-35: R 52-0; D 12-34; I 1-1. June 22, 2017.

153. SVINICKI NOMINATION/CLOTURE. Motion to invoke cloture (thus limiting debate) on President Donald Trump's nomination of Kristine L. Svinicki of Virginia to be a member of the Nuclear Regulatory Commission. Motion agreed to 89-10: R 50-1; D 38-8; I 1-1. June 22, 2017.

154. SVINICKI NOMINATION/CONFIRMATION. Confirmation of President Donald Trump's nomination of Kristine L. Svinicki of Virginia to be a member of the Nuclear Regulatory Commission. Confirmed 88-9: R 48-1; D 39-7; I 1-1. June 26, 2017.

	148	149	150	151	152	153	154
ALABAMA							
Shelby	Y	Y	Y	Y	Y	Y	Y
Strange	Y	Y	Y	Y	Y	Y	?
ALASKA							
Murkowski	Y	Y	Y	Y	Y	Y	Y
Sullivan	Y	Y	Y	Y	Y	Y	Y
ARIZONA							
McCain	Y	Y	Y	N	Y	Y	Y
Flake	Y	Y	Y	Y	Y	Y	?
ARKANSAS							
Boozman	Y	Y	Y	Y	Y	Y	Y
Cotton	Y	Y	Y	Y	Y	Y	Y
CALIFORNIA							
Feinstein	Y	Y	Y	N	N	Y	Y
Harris	Y	N	N	N	N	N	N
COLORADO							
Bennet	Y	Y	Y	Y	Y	Y	Y
Gardner	Y	Y	Y	Y	Y	Y	Y
CONNECTICUT							
Blumenthal	Y	Y	Y	N	N	Y	Y
Murphy	Y	Y	Y	N	N	Y	Y
DELAWARE							
Carper	Y	Y	Y	N	N	Y	Y
Coons	Y	Y	Y	Y	Y	Y	Y
FLORIDA							
Nelson	Y	Y	Y	Y	Y	Y	Y
Rubio	Y	Y	Y	Y	Y	Y	Y
GEORGIA							
Isakson	Y	Y	Y	Y	Y	Y	?
Perdue	Y	Y	Y	Y	Y	Y	Y
HAWAII							
Schatz	N	Y	Y	N	N	Y	Y
Hirono	Y	Y	Y	N	N	Y	Y
IDAHO							
Crapo	Y	Y	Y	Y	Y	Y	Y
Risch	Y	Y	Y	Y	Y	Y	Y
ILLINOIS							
Durbin	Y	Y	Y	N	N	Y	Y
Duckworth	Y	Y	Y	Y	Y	Y	Y
INDIANA							
Donnelly	Y	Y	Y	Y	Y	Y	Y
Young	Y	Y	Y	Y	Y	Y	Y
IOWA							
Grassley	Y	Y	Y	Y	Y	Y	Y
Ernst	Y	Y	Y	Y	Y	Y	Y
KANSAS							
Roberts	Y	Y	Y	Y	Y	Y	Y
Moran	Y	Y	Y	Y	Y	Y	Y
KENTUCKY							
McConnell	Y	Y	Y	Y	Y	Y	Y
Paul	Y	Y	Y	Y	Y	Y	Y
LOUISIANA							
Cassidy	Y	Y	Y	Y	Y	Y	Y
Kennedy	Y	Y	Y	Y	Y	Y	Y
MAINE							
Collins	Y	Y	Y	Y	Y	Y	Y
King	Y	Y	Y	Y	Y	Y	Y
MARYLAND							
Cardin	Y	Y	Y	Y	N	Y	Y
Van Hollen	Y	Y	Y	N	N	Y	Y
MASSACHUSETTS							
Warren	N	N	N	N	N	N	N
Markey	Y	Y	Y	N	N	N	N
MICHIGAN							
Stabenow	Y	Y	Y	N	N	Y	Y
Peters	Y	Y	Y	N	N	Y	Y
MINNESOTA							
Klobuchar	Y	Y	Y	N	N	Y	Y
Franken	Y	Y	Y	N	N	Y	Y
MISSISSIPPI							
Cochran	Y	Y	Y	Y	Y	Y	Y
Wicker	Y	Y	Y	Y	Y	Y	Y
MISSOURI							
McCaskill	Y	Y	Y	Y	Y	Y	Y
Blunt	Y	Y	Y	Y	Y	Y	Y

	148	149	150	151	152	153	154
MONTANA							
Tester	Y	Y	Y	Y	Y	Y	Y
Daines	Y	Y	Y	Y	Y	Y	Y
NEBRASKA							
Fischer	Y	Y	Y	Y	Y	Y	Y
Sasse	Y	Y	Y	Y	Y	Y	Y
NEVADA							
Heller	Y	Y	Y	Y	Y	N	N
Cortez Masto	Y	Y	Y	N	N	N	N
NEW HAMPSHIRE							
Shaheen	Y	Y	Y	N	N	Y	Y
Hassan	Y	Y	Y	N	N	Y	Y
NEW JERSEY							
Menendez	Y	Y	Y	N	N	Y	Y
Booker	N	N	N	N	N	N	N
NEW MEXICO							
Udall	Y	Y	Y	N	N	Y	Y
Heinrich	Y	Y	Y	N	N	Y	Y
NEW YORK							
Schumer	Y	Y	Y	N	N	Y	Y
Gillibrand	N	N	N	N	N	N	N
NORTH CAROLINA							
Burr	Y	Y	Y	Y	Y	Y	Y
Tillis	Y	Y	Y	Y	Y	Y	Y
NORTH DAKOTA							
Hoeven	Y	Y	Y	Y	Y	Y	Y
Heitkamp	Y	Y	Y	Y	Y	Y	Y
OHIO							
Brown	Y	Y	Y	N	N	Y	Y
Portman	Y	Y	Y	Y	Y	Y	Y
OKLAHOMA							
Inhofe	Y	Y	Y	Y	Y	Y	Y
Lankford	Y	Y	Y	Y	Y	Y	Y
OREGON							
Wyden	Y	Y	Y	N	N	N	Y
Merkley	Y	Y	Y	N	N	N	N
PENNSYLVANIA							
Casey	Y	Y	Y	N	N	Y	Y
Toomey	Y	Y	Y	Y	Y	Y	Y
RHODE ISLAND							
Reed	Y	Y	Y	N	N	Y	Y
Whitehouse	Y	Y	Y	N	N	Y	Y
SOUTH CAROLINA							
Graham	?	?	Y	Y	Y	Y	Y
Scott	Y	Y	Y	Y	Y	Y	Y
SOUTH DAKOTA							
Thune	Y	Y	Y	Y	Y	Y	Y
Rounds	Y	Y	Y	Y	Y	Y	Y
TENNESSEE							
Alexander	Y	Y	Y	Y	Y	+	Y
Corker	Y	Y	Y	Y	Y	Y	Y
TEXAS							
Cornyn	Y	Y	Y	Y	Y	Y	Y
Cruz	Y	Y	Y	Y	Y	Y	Y
UTAH							
Hatch	Y	Y	Y	Y	Y	Y	Y
Lee	Y	Y	Y	Y	Y	Y	Y
VERMONT							
Leahy	Y	Y	Y	?	N	Y	Y
Sanders	Y	N	Y	N	N	N	N
VIRGINIA							
Warner	Y	Y	Y	Y	Y	Y	Y
Kaine	Y	Y	Y	Y	Y	Y	Y
WASHINGTON							
Murray	Y	Y	Y	N	N	Y	Y
Cantwell	Y	Y	Y	N	N	Y	Y
WEST VIRGINIA							
Manchin	Y	Y	Y	Y	Y	Y	Y
Capito	Y	Y	Y	Y	Y	Y	Y
WISCONSIN							
Johnson	Y	Y	Y	Y	Y	Y	Y
Baldwin	Y	Y	Y	Y	Y	Y	Y
WYOMING							
Enzi	Y	Y	Y	Y	Y	Y	Y
Barrasso	Y	Y	Y	Y	Y	Y	Y

KEY	**Republicans**	Democrats	*Independents*

Y Voted for (yea)	X Paired against	C Voted "present" to avoid possible conflict of interest
# Paired for	− Announced against	? Did not vote or otherwise make a position known
+ Announced for	P Voted "present"	
N Voted against (nay)		

||| SENATE VOTES

VOTE NUMBER

155. RAO NOMINATION/CLOTURE. Motion to invoke cloture (thus limiting debate) on President Donald Trump's nomination of Neomi Rao of the District of Columbia to be administrator of the Office of Information and Regulatory Affairs, Office of Management and Budget. Motion agreed to 59-36: R 52-0; D 6-36; I 1-0. June 29, 2017.

156. RAO NOMINATION/CONFIRMATION. Confirmation of President Donald Trump's nomination of Neomi Rao of the District of Columbia to be administrator of the Office of Information and Regulatory Affairs, Office of Management and Budget. Confirmed 54-41: R 48-0; D 5-40; I 1-1. July 10, 2017.

157. NYE NOMINATION/CLOTURE. Motion to invoke cloture (thus limiting debate) on President Donald Trump's nomination of David C. Nye of Idaho to be a judge for the U.S. District Court for the District of Idaho. Motion agreed to 97-0: R 49-0; D 46-0; I 2-0. July 10, 2017.

158. NYE NOMINATION/CONFIRMATION. Confirmation of President Donald Trump's nomination of David C. Nye of Idaho to be a judge for the U.S. District Court for the District of Idaho. Confirmed 100-0: R 52-0; D 46-0; I 2-0. July 12, 2017.

159. HAGERTY NOMINATION/CLOTURE. Motion to invoke cloture (thus limiting debate) on President Donald Trump's nomination of William Francis Hagerty IV of Tennessee to be U.S. ambassador to Japan. Motion agreed to 89-11: R 52-0; D 36-10; I 1-1. July 12, 2017.

160. HAGERTY NOMINATION/CONFIRMATION. Confirmation of President Donald Trump's nomination of William Francis Hagerty IV of Tennessee to be U.S. ambassador to Japan. Confirmed 86-12: R 51-0; D 34-11; I 1-1. July 13, 2017.

161. SHANAHAN NOMINATION/CLOTURE. Motion to invoke cloture (thus limiting debate) on President Donald Trump's nomination of Patrick M. Shanahan of Washington to be deputy secretary of Defense. Motion agreed to 88-6: R 47-0; D 40-5; I 1-1. July 17, 2017.

	155	156	157	158	159	160	161
ALABAMA							
Shelby	Y	Y	Y	Y	Y	Y	Y
Strange	Y	Y	Y	Y	Y	Y	Y
ALASKA							
Murkowski	Y	+	+	Y	Y	Y	Y
Sullivan	Y	?	?	Y	Y	Y	Y
ARIZONA							
McCain	Y	Y	Y	Y	Y	Y	?
Flake	Y	Y	Y	Y	Y	Y	?
ARKANSAS							
Boozman	Y	Y	Y	Y	Y	Y	Y
Cotton	Y	Y	Y	Y	Y	Y	Y
CALIFORNIA							
Feinstein	N	N	Y	Y	Y	Y	Y
Harris	N	N	Y	Y	N	N	N
COLORADO							
Bennet	N	N	Y	Y	Y	Y	Y
Gardner	Y	Y	Y	Y	Y	Y	Y
CONNECTICUT							
Blumenthal	N	N	Y	Y	Y	Y	Y
Murphy	N	N	Y	Y	Y	Y	Y
DELAWARE							
Carper	Y	Y	Y	Y	Y	Y	Y
Coons	N	N	Y	Y	Y	Y	Y
FLORIDA							
Nelson	Y	N	Y	Y	Y	Y	Y
Rubio	Y	Y	Y	Y	Y	Y	Y
GEORGIA							
Isakson	Y	Y	Y	Y	Y	Y	Y
Perdue	Y	Y	Y	Y	Y	Y	Y
HAWAII							
Schatz	N	N	Y	Y	Y	Y	Y
Hirono	?	N	Y	N	N	N	Y
IDAHO							
Crapo	Y	Y	Y	Y	Y	Y	Y
Risch	Y	Y	Y	Y	Y	Y	Y
ILLINOIS							
Durbin	-	N	Y	Y	Y	Y	Y
Duckworth	N	N	Y	Y	Y	Y	?
INDIANA							
Donnelly	Y	Y	Y	Y	Y	Y	Y
Young	Y	Y	Y	Y	Y	Y	Y
IOWA							
Grassley	Y	Y	Y	Y	Y	Y	Y
Ernst	Y	Y	Y	Y	Y	Y	+
KANSAS							
Roberts	Y	Y	Y	Y	Y	Y	Y
Moran	Y	Y	Y	Y	Y	+	Y
KENTUCKY							
McConnell	Y	Y	Y	Y	Y	Y	Y
Paul	Y	Y	Y	Y	Y	Y	Y
LOUISIANA							
Cassidy	Y	Y	Y	Y	Y	Y	Y
Kennedy	Y	Y	Y	Y	Y	Y	Y
MAINE							
Collins	Y	Y	Y	Y	Y	Y	Y
King	Y	Y	Y	Y	Y	Y	Y
MARYLAND							
Cardin	N	N	Y	Y	Y	Y	Y
Van Hollen	N	N	Y	Y	Y	Y	Y
MASSACHUSETTS							
Warren	N	N	Y	N	N	N	N
Markey	N	N	Y	Y	Y	N	N
MICHIGAN							
Stabenow	N	N	Y	Y	N	N	Y
Peters	N	N	Y	Y	N	N	Y
MINNESOTA							
Klobuchar	N	N	Y	Y	Y	Y	Y
Franken	N	N	Y	Y	Y	Y	Y
MISSISSIPPI							
Cochran	Y	Y	Y	Y	Y	Y	Y
Wicker	Y	Y	Y	Y	Y	Y	+
MISSOURI							
McCaskill	Y	Y	Y	Y	Y	+	Y
Blunt	Y	Y	Y	Y	Y	Y	Y
MONTANA							
Tester	N	N	Y	Y	Y	Y	Y
Daines	Y	Y	Y	Y	Y	Y	Y
NEBRASKA							
Fischer	Y	Y	Y	Y	Y	Y	Y
Sasse	Y	Y	Y	Y	Y	Y	Y
NEVADA							
Heller	Y	Y	Y	Y	Y	Y	?
Cortez Masto	N	N	Y	Y	Y	Y	Y
NEW HAMPSHIRE							
Shaheen	N	N	Y	Y	Y	Y	Y
Hassan	N	N	Y	Y	Y	Y	Y
NEW JERSEY							
Menendez	N	N	Y	Y	Y	Y	Y
Booker	N	N	Y	Y	N	N	N
NEW MEXICO							
Udall	?	?	Y	Y	N	N	Y
Heinrich	N	N	Y	Y	N	N	Y
NEW YORK							
Schumer	N	N	Y	Y	Y	Y	Y
Gillibrand	N	N	Y	Y	N	N	N
NORTH CAROLINA							
Burr	Y	Y	Y	Y	Y	Y	Y
Tillis	Y	+	Y	Y	Y	Y	Y
NORTH DAKOTA							
Hoeven	Y	Y	Y	Y	Y	Y	Y
Heitkamp	Y	Y	Y	Y	Y	Y	Y
OHIO							
Brown	N	N	Y	Y	Y	N	Y
Portman	Y	?	?	Y	Y	Y	Y
OKLAHOMA							
Inhofe	Y	Y	Y	Y	Y	Y	Y
Lankford	Y	Y	Y	Y	Y	Y	Y
OREGON							
Wyden	N	N	Y	Y	Y	Y	Y
Merkley	N	N	Y	Y	N	N	Y
PENNSYLVANIA							
Casey	N	N	Y	Y	Y	Y	Y
Toomey	Y	Y	Y	Y	Y	Y	Y
RHODE ISLAND							
Reed	N	N	Y	Y	Y	Y	Y
Whitehouse	N	N	Y	Y	Y	Y	Y
SOUTH CAROLINA							
Graham	Y	Y	Y	Y	Y	Y	Y
Scott	Y	Y	Y	Y	Y	Y	Y
SOUTH DAKOTA							
Thune	Y	Y	Y	Y	Y	Y	Y
Rounds	Y	Y	Y	Y	Y	Y	Y
TENNESSEE							
Alexander	Y	Y	Y	Y	Y	Y	Y
Corker	Y	Y	Y	Y	Y	Y	Y
TEXAS							
Cornyn	Y	Y	Y	Y	Y	Y	Y
Cruz	Y	Y	Y	Y	Y	Y	Y
UTAH							
Hatch	Y	Y	Y	Y	Y	Y	Y
Lee	Y	Y	Y	Y	Y	Y	Y
VERMONT							
Leahy	N	N	Y	Y	Y	Y	Y
Sanders	?	N	Y	N	N	N	N
VIRGINIA							
Warner	?	N	Y	Y	Y	Y	Y
Kaine	N	N	Y	Y	Y	Y	Y
WASHINGTON							
Murray	N	N	Y	Y	Y	Y	Y
Cantwell	N	N	Y	Y	Y	Y	Y
WEST VIRGINIA							
Manchin	Y	Y	Y	Y	Y	Y	Y
Capito	Y	Y	Y	Y	Y	Y	Y
WISCONSIN							
Johnson	Y	Y	Y	Y	Y	Y	Y
Baldwin	N	N	Y	Y	Y	Y	Y
WYOMING							
Enzi	Y	Y	Y	Y	Y	Y	Y
Barrasso	Y	Y	Y	Y	Y	Y	Y

KEY	**Republicans**	Democrats	*Independents*

Y Voted for (yea)	X Paired against	C Voted "present" to avoid possible conflict of interest
# Paired for	- Announced against	? Did not vote or otherwise make a position known
+ Announced for	P Voted "present"	
N Voted against (nay)		

VOTE NUMBER

162. SHANAHAN NOMINATION/CONFIRMATION. Confirmation of President Donald Trump's nomination of Patrick M. Shanahan of Washington to be deputy secretary of Defense. Confirmed 92-7: R 51-0; D 40-6; I 1-1. July 18, 2017.

163. BUSH NOMINATION/CLOTURE. Motion to invoke cloture (thus limiting debate) on President Donald Trump's nomination of John Kenneth Bush of Kentucky to be judge for the 6th U.S. Circuit Court of Appeals. Motion agreed to 51-48: R 51-0; D 0-46; I 0-2. July 19, 2017.

164. BUSH NOMINATION/CONFIRMATION. Confirmation of President Donald Trump's nomination of John Kenneth Bush of Kentucky to be judge for the 6th U.S. Circuit Court of Appeals. Confirmed 51-47: R 51-0; D 0-45; I 0-2. July 20, 2017.

165. BERNHARDT NOMINATION/CLOTURE. Motion to invoke cloture (thus limiting debate) on President Donald Trump's nomination of David Bernhardt of Virginia to be deputy secretary of the Interior. Motion agreed to 56-39: R 49-0; D 6-38; I 1-1. July 20, 2017.

166. BERNHARDT NOMINATION/CONFIRMATION. Confirmation of President Donald Trump's nomination of David Bernhardt of Virginia to be deputy secretary of the Interior. Confirmed 53-43: R 48-0; D 4-42; I 1-1. July 24, 2017.

167. HR 1628. HEALTH CARE MARKETPLACE OVERHAUL/MOTION TO PROCEED. McConnell, R-Ky., motion to proceed to the bill that would make extensive changes to the 2010 health care overhaul law, by effectively repealing the individual and employer mandates as well as most of the taxes that finance the current system and by making extensive changes to Medicaid. Motion agreed to, with Vice President Pence casting a "yea" vote to break the tie, 50-50: R 50-2; D 0-46; I 0-2. July 25, 2017.

168. HR 1628. HEALTH CARE MARKETPLACE OVERHAUL/MOTION TO WAIVE. Cruz, R-Texas, motion to waive applicable sections of the Congressional Budget Act with respect to the Murray, D-Wash., point of order that McConnell, R-Ky., amendment no. 270, to the McConnell substitute amendment no. 267, violates Section 311(a)(2)(b) of the Congressional Budget Act. The McConnell amendment would repeal extensive provisions of the 2010 health care overhaul, including: the individual and employer mandates, the optional Medicaid expansion, subsidies given to individuals buying health insurance and some of the taxes that fund the law. It would create a health care tax credit based on income and age, and would authorize money to stabilize the health care market and for high-risk individuals. Motion rejected 43-57: R 43-9; D 0-46; I 0-2. July 25, 2017.

	162	163	164	165	166	167	168
ALABAMA							
Shelby	Y	Y	Y	Y	Y	Y	Y
Strange	Y	Y	Y	Y	Y	Y	Y
ALASKA							
Murkowski	Y	Y	Y	Y	Y	N	N
Sullivan	Y	Y	Y	Y	Y	Y	Y
ARIZONA							
McCain	+	?	?	?	?	Y	Y
Flake	Y	Y	Y	Y	Y	Y	Y
ARKANSAS							
Boozman	Y	Y	Y	Y	Y	Y	Y
Cotton	Y	Y	Y	Y	Y	Y	N
CALIFORNIA							
Feinstein	Y	N	N	N	N	N	N
Harris	N	N	N	N	N	N	N
COLORADO							
Bennet	Y	N	N	Y	N	Y	N
Gardner	Y	Y	Y	Y	Y	Y	Y
CONNECTICUT							
Blumenthal	Y	N	N	N	N	N	N
Murphy	Y	N	N	N	N	N	N
DELAWARE							
Carper	Y	N	N	N	N	N	N
Coons	Y	N	N	N	N	N	N
FLORIDA							
Nelson	Y	N	N	N	N	N	N
Rubio	Y	Y	Y	Y	Y	Y	Y
GEORGIA							
Isakson	Y	Y	Y	Y	Y	Y	Y
Perdue	Y	Y	Y	Y	Y	Y	Y
HAWAII							
Schatz	Y	N	N	Y	N	N	N
Hirono	Y	N	N	N	N	N	N
IDAHO							
Crapo	Y	Y	Y	Y	Y	Y	Y
Risch	Y	Y	Y	Y	Y	Y	Y
ILLINOIS							
Durbin	Y	N	N	N	N	N	N
Duckworth	N	N	N	N	N	N	N
INDIANA							
Donnelly	Y	N	N	Y	N	Y	N
Young	Y	Y	Y	Y	Y	Y	Y
IOWA							
Grassley	Y	Y	Y	Y	Y	Y	Y
Ernst	Y	Y	Y	Y	Y	Y	Y
KANSAS							
Roberts	Y	Y	Y	Y	Y	Y	Y
Moran	Y	Y	Y	?	Y	Y	N
KENTUCKY							
McConnell	Y	Y	Y	Y	Y	Y	Y
Paul	Y	Y	Y	Y	Y	Y	N
LOUISIANA							
Cassidy	Y	Y	Y	Y	Y	Y	Y
Kennedy	Y	Y	Y	Y	Y	Y	Y
MAINE							
Collins	Y	Y	Y	Y	Y	N	N
King	Y	N	N	Y	Y	N	N
MARYLAND							
Cardin	Y	N	N	N	N	N	N
Van Hollen	Y	N	N	N	N	N	N
MASSACHUSETTS							
Warren	N	N	N	N	N	N	N
Markey	N	N	N	N	N	N	N
MICHIGAN							
Stabenow	Y	N	–	–	N	N	N
Peters	Y	N	N	N	N	N	N
MINNESOTA							
Klobuchar	Y	N	N	N	N	N	N
Franken	Y	N	N	N	N	N	N
MISSISSIPPI							
Cochran	Y	Y	Y	Y	Y	Y	Y
Wicker	Y	Y	Y	Y	Y	Y	Y
MISSOURI							
McCaskill	Y	N	N	N	N	N	N
Blunt	Y	Y	Y	Y	Y	Y	Y

	162	163	164	165	166	167	168
MONTANA							
Tester	Y	N	N	N	N	N	N
Daines	Y	Y	Y	Y	Y	Y	Y
NEBRASKA							
Fischer	Y	Y	Y	Y	Y	Y	Y
Sasse	Y	Y	Y	?	Y	Y	Y
NEVADA							
Heller	Y	Y	Y	Y	Y	Y	N
Cortez Masto	Y	N	N	N	N	N	N
NEW HAMPSHIRE							
Shaheen	Y	N	N	N	N	N	N
Hassan	Y	N	N	N	N	N	N
NEW JERSEY							
Menendez	Y	N	N	N	N	N	N
Booker	N	N	N	N	N	N	N
NEW MEXICO							
Udall	Y	N	N	N	N	N	N
Heinrich	Y	N	N	Y	N	N	N
NEW YORK							
Schumer	Y	N	N	N	N	N	N
Gillibrand	N	N	N	N	N	N	N
NORTH CAROLINA							
Burr	Y	Y	Y	Y	Y	Y	Y
Tillis	Y	Y	Y	Y	Y	Y	Y
NORTH DAKOTA							
Hoeven	Y	Y	Y	Y	Y	Y	Y
Heitkamp	Y	N	N	Y	N	N	N
OHIO							
Brown	Y	N	N	N	N	N	N
Portman	Y	Y	Y	Y	Y	Y	Y
OKLAHOMA							
Inhofe	Y	Y	Y	Y	Y	Y	Y
Lankford	Y	Y	Y	Y	Y	Y	Y
OREGON							
Wyden	Y	N	N	N	N	N	N
Merkley	Y	N	N	N	N	N	N
PENNSYLVANIA							
Casey	Y	N	N	N	N	N	N
Toomey	Y	Y	Y	Y	?	Y	Y
RHODE ISLAND							
Reed	Y	N	N	N	N	N	N
Whitehouse	Y	N	N	N	N	N	N
SOUTH CAROLINA							
Graham	Y	Y	Y	Y	Y	Y	N
Scott	Y	Y	Y	Y	Y	Y	Y
SOUTH DAKOTA							
Thune	Y	Y	Y	Y	Y	Y	Y
Rounds	Y	Y	Y	Y	Y	Y	Y
TENNESSEE							
Alexander	Y	Y	Y	+	Y	Y	Y
Corker	Y	Y	Y	Y	Y	Y	N
TEXAS							
Cornyn	Y	Y	Y	Y	Y	Y	Y
Cruz	Y	Y	Y	Y	Y	Y	Y
UTAH							
Hatch	Y	Y	Y	Y	Y	Y	Y
Lee	Y	Y	Y	Y	Y	Y	N
VERMONT							
Leahy	Y	N	N	?	N	N	N
Sanders	N	N	N	N	N	N	N
VIRGINIA							
Warner	Y	N	N	N	N	N	N
Kaine	Y	N	N	N	N	N	N
WASHINGTON							
Murray	Y	N	N	N	N	N	N
Cantwell	Y	N	N	N	N	N	N
WEST VIRGINIA							
Manchin	Y	N	N	Y	N	N	N
Capito	Y	Y	Y	Y	?	Y	Y
WISCONSIN							
Johnson	Y	Y	Y	Y	Y	Y	Y
Baldwin	Y	N	N	N	N	N	N
WYOMING							
Enzi	Y	Y	Y	Y	Y	Y	Y
Barrasso	Y	Y	Y	Y	Y	Y	Y

KEY	**Republicans**	Democrats	*Independents*

Y Voted for (yea)	X Paired against	C Voted "present" to avoid possible conflict of interest
# Paired for	– Announced against	? Did not vote or otherwise make a position known
+ Announced for	P Voted "present"	
N Voted against (nay)		

VOTE NUMBER

169. HR 1628. HEALTH CARE MARKETPLACE OVERHAUL/REPEAL OF THE 2010 HEALTH CARE OVERHAUL. Enzi, R-Wyo., for Paul, R-Ky., amendment no. 271, to the McConnell, R-Ky., substitute amendment no. 267, that would sunset Medicaid expansion and certain taxes created under the 2010 health care overhaul, repeal the individual and employer mandates, would exclude health plans that cover abortion from certain tax credits and would ban federal funding for abortion providers that receive at least $1 million in federal funding annually. Rejected 45-55: R 45-7; D 0-46; I 0-2. July 26, 2017.

170. HR 1628. HEALTH CARE MARKETPLACE OVERHAUL/COMMIT. Donnelly, D-Ind., motion to commit the bill to the Senate Finance Committee with instructions to report back to the Senate within three days with an amendment that would strike provisions of the bill that would reduce or eliminate Medicaid coverage for eligible individuals, discourage a state from expanding Medicaid, or that would shift health care costs to the states. Motion rejected 48-52: R 0-52; D 46-0; I 2-0. July 26, 2017.

171. HR 1628. HEALTH CARE MARKETPLACE OVERHAUL/COMMIT. Casey, D-Pa., motion to commit the bill to the Senate Finance Committee with instructions to report back to the Senate within three days with an amendment that would strike provisions of the bill that would reduce access to health care for individuals with disabilities or would reduce such individuals' coverage under Medicaid or in the private insurance market. Motion rejected 48-51: R 0-51; D 46-0; I 2-0.

172. HR 1628. HEALTH CARE MARKETPLACE OVERHAUL/MOTION TO WAIVE. Heller, R-Nev., motion to waive applicable sections of the Congressional Budget Act with respect to the Sanders, I-Vt., point of order that Heller amendment no. 288, to McConnell substitute amendment no. 267, violates section 313(b)(1)(a) of the Congressional Budget Act. The Heller amendment would express the sense of the Senate that: Medicaid expansion should be reviewed by the proper committee, the Senate should consider legislation incentivizing states to prioritize Medicaid for individuals with the greatest medical need and the Senate should not consider legislation preventing or discouraging Medicaid expansion or that shifts Medicaid costs to states. Additionally, it would express the sense of the Senate that the 2010 health care overhaul should be repealed and replaced with "patient-centered" legislation. Motion rejected 10-90: R 10-42; D 0-46; I 0-2. July 26, 2017.

173. HR 1628. HEALTH CARE MARKETPLACE OVERHAUL/MEDICARE-FOR-ALL. McConnell, R-Ky., for Daines, R-Mont., amendment no. 340, as modified, to McConnell substitute amendment no. 267, that would establish a universal Medicare program that would cover all people living in the United States. The amendment would require that the program to offer various health and dental benefits and would provide mandatory funding to the program through multiple new taxes. Rejected 0-57: R 0-52; D 0-4; I 0-1. July 27, 2017.

174. HR 1628. HEALTH CARE MARKETPLACE OVERHAUL/MOTION TO WAIVE. Strange, R-Ala., motion to waive applicable sections of the Congressional Budget Act with respect to the Schatz, D-Hawaii, point of order that Strange amendment no. 389, violates section 302(f) of the Congressional Budget Act. The Strange amendment would authorize and appropriate $15 billion in 2018 and 2019 and $10 billion for 2020 and 2021 for states to provide to health insurance issuers for coverage and access disruptions and urgent health needs. The amendment would require insurance providers to certify that they are using the funds accordingly and would require that 1 percent of the funding would go towards states (like Alaska) where the cost of insurance premiums are at least 75 percent higher than the national average. Motion rejected 50-50: R 50-2; D 0-46; I 0-2. July 27, 2017.

	169	170	171	172	173	174
ALABAMA						
Shelby	Y	N	N	N	N	Y
Strange	Y	N	N	N	N	Y
ALASKA						
Murkowski	N	N	N	Y	N	N
Sullivan	Y	N	N	Y	N	Y
ARIZONA						
McCain	N	N	N	Y	N	Y
Flake	Y	N	N	N	N	Y
ARKANSAS						
Boozman	Y	N	N	N	N	Y
Cotton	Y	N	N	N	N	Y
CALIFORNIA						
Feinstein	N	Y	Y	N	P	N
Harris	N	Y	Y	N	P	N
COLORADO						
Bennet	N	Y	Y	N	P	N
Gardner	Y	N	N	Y	N	Y
CONNECTICUT						
Blumenthal	N	Y	Y	N	P	N
Murphy	N	Y	Y	N	P	N
DELAWARE						
Carper	N	Y	Y	N	P	N
Coons	N	Y	Y	N	P	N
FLORIDA						
Nelson	N	Y	Y	N	P	N
Rubio	Y	N	N	N	N	Y
GEORGIA						
Isakson	Y	N	N	N	N	Y
Perdue	Y	N	N	N	N	Y
HAWAII						
Schatz	N	Y	Y	N	P	N
Hirono	N	Y	Y	N	P	N
IDAHO						
Crapo	Y	N	N	N	N	Y
Risch	Y	N	N	N	N	Y
ILLINOIS						
Durbin	N	Y	Y	N	P	N
Duckworth	N	Y	Y	N	P	N
INDIANA						
Donnelly	N	Y	Y	N	P	N
Young	Y	N	N	N	N	Y
IOWA						
Grassley	Y	N	N	N	N	Y
Ernst	Y	N	N	N	N	Y
KANSAS						
Roberts	Y	N	N	N	N	Y
Moran	Y	N	N	N	N	Y
KENTUCKY						
McConnell	Y	N	N	N	N	Y
Paul	Y	N	N	N	N	Y
LOUISIANA						
Cassidy	Y	N	N	Y	N	Y
Kennedy	Y	N	N	N	N	Y
MAINE						
Collins	N	N	N	Y	N	N
King	N	Y	Y	N	N	N
MARYLAND						
Cardin	N	Y	Y	N	P	N
Van Hollen	N	Y	Y	N	P	N
MASSACHUSETTS						
Warren	N	Y	Y	N	P	N
Markey	N	Y	Y	N	P	N
MICHIGAN						
Stabenow	N	Y	Y	N	P	N
Peters	N	Y	Y	N	P	N
MINNESOTA						
Klobuchar	N	Y	Y	N	P	N
Franken	N	Y	Y	N	P	N
MISSISSIPPI						
Cochran	Y	N	N	N	N	Y
Wicker	Y	N	N	N	N	Y
MISSOURI						
McCaskill	N	Y	Y	N	P	N
Blunt	Y	N	N	N	N	Y
MONTANA						
Tester	N	Y	Y	N	N	N
Daines	Y	N	N	N	N	Y
NEBRASKA						
Fischer	Y	N	N	N	N	Y
Sasse	Y	N	N	N	N	Y
NEVADA						
Heller	N	N	N	Y	N	N
Cortez Masto	N	Y	Y	N	P	N
NEW HAMPSHIRE						
Shaheen	N	Y	Y	N	P	N
Hassan	N	Y	Y	N	P	N
NEW JERSEY						
Menendez	N	Y	Y	N	P	N
Booker	N	Y	Y	N	P	N
NEW MEXICO						
Udall	N	Y	Y	N	P	N
Heinrich	N	Y	Y	N	P	N
NEW YORK						
Schumer	N	Y	Y	N	P	N
Gillibrand	N	Y	Y	N	P	N
NORTH CAROLINA						
Burr	Y	N	N	N	N	Y
Tillis	Y	N	N	N	N	Y
NORTH DAKOTA						
Hoeven	Y	N	N	N	N	Y
Heitkamp	N	Y	Y	N	N	N
OHIO						
Brown	N	Y	Y	N	P	N
Portman	N	N	N	Y	N	Y
OKLAHOMA						
Inhofe	Y	N	N	N	N	Y
Lankford	Y	N	N	N	N	Y
OREGON						
Wyden	N	Y	Y	N	P	N
Merkley	N	Y	Y	N	P	N
PENNSYLVANIA						
Casey	N	Y	Y	N	P	N
Toomey	Y	N	N	N	N	Y
RHODE ISLAND						
Reed	N	Y	Y	N	P	N
Whitehouse	N	Y	Y	N	P	N
SOUTH CAROLINA						
Graham	Y	N	N	N	N	Y
Scott	Y	N	N	N	N	Y
SOUTH DAKOTA						
Thune	Y	N	N	N	N	Y
Rounds	Y	N	N	N	N	Y
TENNESSEE						
Alexander	N	N	N	N	N	Y
Corker	Y	N	N	N	N	Y
TEXAS						
Cornyn	Y	N	N	N	N	Y
Cruz	Y	N	N	N	N	Y
UTAH						
Hatch	Y	N	N	N	N	Y
Lee	Y	N	N	N	N	Y
VERMONT						
Leahy	N	Y	Y	N	P	N
Sanders	N	Y	Y	N	P	N
VIRGINIA						
Warner	N	Y	Y	N	P	N
Kaine	N	Y	Y	N	P	N
WASHINGTON						
Murray	N	Y	Y	N	P	N
Cantwell	N	Y	Y	N	P	N
WEST VIRGINIA						
Manchin	N	Y	Y	N	N	N
Capito	N	N	N	Y	N	Y
WISCONSIN						
Johnson	Y	N	?	N	N	Y
Baldwin	N	Y	Y	N	P	N
WYOMING						
Enzi	Y	N	N	Y	N	Y
Barrasso	Y	N	N	N	N	Y

KEY	**Republicans**	Democrats	*Independents*
Y Voted for (yea)	X Paired against	C Voted "present" to avoid possible conflict of interest
# Paired for	– Announced against	
+ Announced for	P Voted "present"	? Did not vote or otherwise make a position known
N Voted against (nay)		

VOTE NUMBER

175. HR 3364. SANCTIONS ON RUSSIA, IRAN AND NORTH KOREA/PASSAGE. Passage of the bill that would codify certain existing sanctions on Russia, including various sanctions tied to Russia's aggression in Ukraine, Moscow's annexation of Crimea, and malicious cyber activities relating to the 2016 U.S. elections. The bill would establish multiple new sanctions on Russia, including sanctions on entities conducting malicious cyber activity on behalf of the Russian government and entities which conduct business with the Russian intelligence and defense sectors. The bill would impose various new or expanded sanctions against Iran, including sanctions on persons that engage in or pose a risk of materially contributing to Iran's ballistic missile program and sanctions on officials, agents or affiliates of Iran's Islamic Revolutionary Guard Corps. The bill would also impose multiple new or expanded sanctions on North Korea, including sanctions against entities that purchase certain metals or minerals from North Korea, and would require the secretary of State to make a determination as to whether North Korea constitutes a "state sponsor of terrorism.". Passed (thus cleared for the president) 98-2: R 51-1; D 46-0; I 1-1. July 27, 2017.

176. HR 1628. HEALTH CARE MARKETPLACE OVERHAUL/COMMIT. Schumer, D-N.Y., motion to commit the bill to the Senate Finance Committee with instructions to report back to the Senate within three days with an amendment that would strike the effective date on the repeal of the tax on high cost employer-sponsored health insurance plans. Motion rejected 43-57: R 0-52; D 41-5; I 2-0. July 27, 2017.

177. HR 1628. HEALTH CARE MARKETPLACE OVERHAUL/EMPLOYER HEALTH INSURANCE TAX. Enzi, R-Wyo., for Heller, R-Nev., amendment no. 502, to the McConnell, R-Ky., substitute amendment no. 267, that would strike language sunsetting the tax on high cost employer-sponsored health insurance plans, which would allow for a permanent repeal of the tax. Adopted 52-48: R 50-2; D 2-44; I 0-2. July 27, 2017.

178. HR 1628. HEALTH CARE MARKETPLACE OVERHAUL/COMMIT. Murray, D-Wash., motion to commit the bill to the Senate Health, Education, Labor, and Pensions Committee for up to three days with instructions to report back to the Senate with an amendment. Motion rejected 48-52: R 0-52; D 46-0; I 2-0. July 28, 2017.

179. HR 1628. HEALTH CARE MARKETPLACE OVERHAUL/2010 HEALTH CARE OVERHAUL REPEAL. McConnell, R-Ky., amendment no. 667, to the McConnell substitute amendment no. 267, that would repeal the individual mandate, repeal the employer mandate through 2024, delay the implementation of the medical device tax through 2020, and block, for one year, federal funding from going to certain medical providers that provide abortions. The amendment would ease the waiver process for states to opt out of the requirement that their health insurance providers include certain benefits on their health care plans. Additionally, the amendment would increase the maximum allowable contribution to health savings accounts and would defund the Prevention and Public Health Fund starting in 2019. Rejected 49-51: R 49-3; D 0-46; I 0-2. July 28, 2017.

180. NEWSOM NOMINATION/CLOTURE. Motion to invoke cloture (thus limiting debate) on President Donald Trump's nomination of Kevin Christopher Newsom of Alabama to be judge for the 11th U.S. Circuit Court of Appeals. Motion agreed to 68-26: R 49-0; D 19-24; I 0-2. July 31, 2017.

181. WRAY NOMINATION/CONFIRMATION. Confirmation of President Donald Trump's nomination of Christopher A. Wray of Georgia to be director of the Federal Bureau of Investigation. Confirmed 92-5: R 50-0; D 40-5; I 2-0. Aug. 1, 2017.

Senator	175	176	177	178	179	180	181
ALABAMA							
Shelby	Y	N	Y	N	Y	Y	Y
Strange	Y	N	Y	N	Y	Y	Y
ALASKA							
Murkowski	Y	N	Y	N	N	Y	Y
Sullivan	Y	N	Y	N	Y	Y	Y
ARIZONA							
McCain	Y	N	Y	N	N	?	?
Flake	Y	N	Y	N	Y	Y	Y
ARKANSAS							
Boozman	Y	N	Y	N	Y	Y	Y
Cotton	Y	N	Y	N	Y	Y	Y
CALIFORNIA							
Feinstein	Y	Y	N	Y	N	Y	Y
Harris	Y	Y	N	Y	N	N	Y
COLORADO							
Bennet	Y	Y	N	Y	N	N	Y
Gardner	Y	N	Y	N	Y	Y	Y
CONNECTICUT							
Blumenthal	Y	Y	N	Y	N	Y	Y
Murphy	Y	N	N	Y	N	Y	Y
DELAWARE							
Carper	Y	Y	N	Y	N	N	Y
Coons	Y	Y	N	Y	N	N	Y
FLORIDA							
Nelson	Y	Y	N	Y	N	Y	Y
Rubio	Y	N	Y	N	Y	Y	Y
GEORGIA							
Isakson	Y	N	Y	N	Y	Y	Y
Perdue	Y	N	Y	N	Y	Y	Y
HAWAII							
Schatz	Y	Y	N	Y	N	N	Y
Hirono	Y	Y	N	Y	N	Y	Y
IDAHO							
Crapo	Y	N	Y	N	Y	Y	Y
Risch	Y	N	Y	N	Y	Y	Y
ILLINOIS							
Durbin	Y	N	N	Y	N	Y	Y
Duckworth	Y	Y	N	Y	N	Y	Y
INDIANA							
Donnelly	Y	Y	N	Y	N	Y	Y
Young	Y	N	Y	N	Y	Y	Y
IOWA							
Grassley	Y	N	Y	N	Y	Y	Y
Ernst	Y	N	Y	N	Y	Y	Y
KANSAS							
Roberts	Y	N	Y	N	Y	Y	Y
Moran	Y	N	Y	N	Y	Y	Y
KENTUCKY							
McConnell	Y	N	Y	N	Y	Y	Y
Paul	N	N	Y	N	Y	Y	Y
LOUISIANA							
Cassidy	Y	N	Y	N	Y	Y	Y
Kennedy	Y	N	Y	N	Y	Y	Y
MAINE							
Collins	Y	N	Y	N	N	Y	Y
King	Y	Y	N	Y	N	N	Y
MARYLAND							
Cardin	Y	Y	N	Y	N	N	Y
Van Hollen	Y	Y	N	Y	N	N	Y
MASSACHUSETTS							
Warren	Y	Y	N	Y	N	N	N
Markey	Y	Y	N	Y	N	N	N
MICHIGAN							
Stabenow	Y	Y	N	Y	N	Y	Y
Peters	Y	Y	N	Y	N	?	Y
MINNESOTA							
Klobuchar	Y	Y	N	Y	N	Y	Y
Franken	Y	Y	N	Y	N	N	?
MISSISSIPPI							
Cochran	Y	N	Y	N	Y	Y	Y
Wicker	Y	N	Y	N	Y	Y	Y
MISSOURI							
McCaskill	Y	Y	N	Y	N	Y	Y
Blunt	Y	N	Y	N	Y	Y	Y
MONTANA							
Tester	Y	Y	N	Y	N	Y	Y
Daines	Y	N	Y	N	Y	Y	Y
NEBRASKA							
Fischer	Y	N	Y	N	Y	Y	Y
Sasse	Y	N	N	N	Y	Y	Y
NEVADA							
Heller	Y	N	Y	N	Y	Y	Y
Cortez Masto	Y	Y	Y	Y	N	N	Y
NEW HAMPSHIRE							
Shaheen	Y	Y	N	Y	N	Y	Y
Hassan	Y	Y	N	Y	N	Y	Y
NEW JERSEY							
Menendez	Y	Y	N	Y	N	?	Y
Booker	Y	Y	N	Y	N	N	Y
NEW MEXICO							
Udall	Y	Y	N	Y	N	N	Y
Heinrich	Y	Y	Y	Y	N	N	Y
NEW YORK							
Schumer	Y	Y	N	Y	N	N	Y
Gillibrand	Y	N	N	Y	N	N	N
NORTH CAROLINA							
Burr	Y	N	Y	N	Y	?	?
Tillis	Y	N	Y	N	Y	Y	Y
NORTH DAKOTA							
Hoeven	Y	N	Y	N	Y	Y	Y
Heitkamp	Y	Y	N	Y	N	Y	Y
OHIO							
Brown	Y	Y	N	Y	N	N	Y
Portman	Y	N	Y	N	Y	Y	Y
OKLAHOMA							
Inhofe	Y	N	Y	N	Y	Y	Y
Lankford	Y	N	Y	N	Y	Y	Y
OREGON							
Wyden	Y	Y	N	Y	N	N	N
Merkley	Y	Y	N	Y	N	?	N
PENNSYLVANIA							
Casey	Y	Y	N	Y	N	Y	Y
Toomey	Y	N	Y	N	Y	Y	Y
RHODE ISLAND							
Reed	Y	Y	N	Y	N	N	Y
Whitehouse	Y	Y	N	Y	N	N	Y
SOUTH CAROLINA							
Graham	Y	N	Y	N	Y	?	Y
Scott	Y	N	Y	N	Y	Y	Y
SOUTH DAKOTA							
Thune	Y	N	Y	N	Y	Y	Y
Rounds	Y	N	Y	N	Y	Y	Y
TENNESSEE							
Alexander	Y	N	Y	N	Y	Y	Y
Corker	Y	N	N	N	Y	Y	Y
TEXAS							
Cornyn	Y	N	Y	N	Y	Y	Y
Cruz	Y	N	Y	N	Y	Y	Y
UTAH							
Hatch	Y	N	Y	N	Y	Y	Y
Lee	Y	N	Y	N	Y	Y	Y
VERMONT							
Leahy	Y	Y	N	Y	N	Y	Y
Sanders	N	Y	N	Y	N	N	Y
VIRGINIA							
Warner	Y	N	N	Y	N	Y	Y
Kaine	Y	N	N	Y	N	N	Y
WASHINGTON							
Murray	Y	Y	N	Y	N	Y	Y
Cantwell	Y	Y	N	Y	N	N	Y
WEST VIRGINIA							
Manchin	Y	Y	N	Y	N	N	Y
Capito	Y	N	Y	N	Y	Y	Y
WISCONSIN							
Johnson	Y	N	Y	N	Y	Y	Y
Baldwin	Y	Y	N	Y	N	N	Y
WYOMING							
Enzi	Y	N	Y	N	Y	Y	Y
Barrasso	Y	N	Y	N	Y	Y	Y

KEY   **Republicans**   Democrats   *Independents*

Y Voted for (yea)	X Paired against	C Voted "present" to avoid possible conflict of interest
# Paired for	− Announced against	
+ Announced for	P Voted "present"	? Did not vote or otherwise make a position known
N Voted against (nay)		

VOTE NUMBER

182. NEWSOM NOMINATION/CONFIRMATION. Confirmation of President Donald Trump's nomination of Kevin Christopher Newsom of Alabama to be judge for the 11th U.S. Circuit Court of Appeals. Confirmed 66-31: R 50-0; D 16-29; I 0-2. Aug. 1, 2017.

183. KAPLAN NOMINATION/CLOTURE. Motion to invoke cloture (thus limiting debate) on President Donald Trump's nomination of Marvin Kaplan of Kansas to be a member of the National Labor Relations Board. Motion agreed to 50-48: R 50-0; D 0-46; I 0-2. Aug. 2, 2017.

184. KAPLAN NOMINATION/CONFIRMATION. Confirmation of President Donald Trump's nomination of Marvin Kaplan of Kansas to be a member of the National Labor Relations Board. Confirmed 50-48: R 50-0; D 0-46; I 0-2. Aug. 2, 2017.

185. HR 2430. FDA REAUTHORIZATION/CLOTURE. Motion to invoke cloture (thus limiting debate) on the McConnell, R-Ky., motion to proceed to the bill that would reauthorize the Food and Drug Administration's ability to collect user fees from the prescription drug and medical devices industries through fiscal 2022, and would update the base fee amounts that could be collected from each industry by the agency. The bill would authorize $25 million in funding for fiscal years 2018 through 2022 to the National Institutes of Health to conduct pediatric trials not being conducted by drug sponsors and would allow the agency to require certain adult cancer drugs receive additional testing on children if such a drug has a molecular target relevant to the growth or progression of a pediatric cancer. Motion agreed to 96-1: R 49-0; D 46-0; I 1-1.

186. BROUILLETTE NOMINATION/CONFIRMATION. Confirmation of President Donald Trump's nomination of Dan R. Brouillette of Texas to be deputy secretary of Energy. Confirmed 79-17: R 47-1; D 31-15; I 1-1. Aug. 3, 2017.

187. HR 2430. FDA REAUTHORIZATION/PASSAGE. Passage of the bill that would reauthorize the Food and Drug Administration's ability to collect user fees from the prescription drug and medical devices industries through fiscal year 2022, and would update the base fee amounts that could be collected from each industry by the agency. The bill would authorize $25 million in funding for fiscal years 2018 through 2022 to the National Institutes of Health to conduct pediatric trials not being conducted by drug sponsors and would allow the agency to require certain adult cancer drugs receive additional testing on children if such a drug has a molecular target relevant to the growth or progression of a pediatric cancer. Passed (thus cleared for the president) 94-1: R 47-0; D 46-0; I 1-1.

188. KELLY NOMINATION/CONFIRMATION. Confirmation of President Donald Trump's nomination of Timothy Kelly of the District of Columbia to be a U.S. district judge for the District of Columbia. Confirmed 94-2: R 50-0; D 42-2; I 2-0. Sept. 5, 2017.

	182	183	184	185	186	187	188
ALABAMA							
Shelby	Y	Y	Y	Y	Y	Y	Y
Strange	Y	Y	Y	Y	Y	Y	Y
ALASKA							
Murkowski	Y	Y	Y	Y	Y	Y	Y
Sullivan	Y	Y	Y	Y	Y	Y	Y
ARIZONA							
McCain	?	?	?	?	?	?	Y
Flake	Y	Y	Y	Y	Y	Y	Y
ARKANSAS							
Boozman	Y	Y	Y	Y	Y	Y	Y
Cotton	Y	Y	Y	Y	Y	Y	Y
CALIFORNIA							
Feinstein	Y	N	N	Y	N	Y	Y
Harris	N	N	N	Y	N	Y	Y
COLORADO							
Bennet	N	N	N	Y	Y	Y	Y
Gardner	Y	Y	Y	Y	Y	Y	Y
CONNECTICUT							
Blumenthal	Y	N	N	Y	Y	Y	Y
Murphy	Y	N	N	Y	Y	Y	Y
DELAWARE							
Carper	N	N	N	Y	Y	Y	Y
Coons	N	N	N	Y	Y	Y	Y
FLORIDA							
Nelson	Y	N	N	Y	Y	Y	Y
Rubio	Y	Y	Y	Y	Y	Y	Y
GEORGIA							
Isakson	Y	Y	Y	Y	Y	+	Y
Perdue	Y	Y	Y	Y	Y	Y	Y
HAWAII							
Schatz	N	N	N	Y	N	Y	Y
Hirono	N	N	N	Y	N	Y	Y
IDAHO							
Crapo	Y	Y	Y	Y	Y	Y	Y
Risch	Y	Y	Y	Y	Y	Y	Y
ILLINOIS							
Durbin	N	N	N	Y	Y	Y	Y
Duckworth	N	N	N	Y	N	Y	Y
INDIANA							
Donnelly	Y	N	N	Y	Y	Y	Y
Young	Y	Y	Y	Y	Y	Y	Y
IOWA							
Grassley	Y	Y	Y	Y	Y	Y	Y
Ernst	Y	Y	Y	Y	Y	Y	Y
KANSAS							
Roberts	Y	Y	Y	Y	Y	Y	Y
Moran	Y	Y	Y	Y	Y	Y	?
KENTUCKY							
McConnell	Y	Y	Y	Y	Y	Y	Y
Paul	Y	Y	Y	Y	Y	Y	Y
LOUISIANA							
Cassidy	Y	Y	Y	Y	Y	Y	Y
Kennedy	Y	Y	Y	Y	Y	Y	Y
MAINE							
Collins	Y	Y	Y	Y	Y	Y	Y
King	N	N	N	Y	Y	Y	Y
MARYLAND							
Cardin	N	N	N	Y	Y	Y	Y
Van Hollen	N	N	N	Y	N	Y	Y
MASSACHUSETTS							
Warren	N	N	N	Y	N	Y	N
Markey	N	N	N	Y	N	Y	Y
MICHIGAN							
Stabenow	Y	N	N	Y	Y	Y	Y
Peters	Y	N	N	Y	Y	Y	Y
MINNESOTA							
Klobuchar	Y	N	N	Y	Y	Y	Y
Franken	?	N	N	Y	N	Y	Y
MISSISSIPPI							
Cochran	Y	Y	Y	Y	Y	Y	?
Wicker	Y	Y	Y	Y	Y	Y	Y
MISSOURI							
McCaskill	Y	N	N	Y	Y	Y	Y
Blunt	Y	Y	Y	Y	Y	Y	Y

	182	183	184	185	186	187	188
MONTANA							
Tester	Y	N	N	Y	Y	Y	Y
Daines	Y	Y	Y	Y	Y	Y	Y
NEBRASKA							
Fischer	Y	Y	Y	Y	Y	Y	Y
Sasse	Y	Y	Y	Y	Y	Y	Y
NEVADA							
Heller	Y	Y	Y	Y	N	Y	Y
Cortez Masto	N	N	N	Y	N	Y	Y
NEW HAMPSHIRE							
Shaheen	Y	N	N	Y	Y	Y	?
Hassan	Y	N	N	Y	Y	Y	Y
NEW JERSEY							
Menendez	N	N	N	Y	N	Y	?
Booker	N	N	N	Y	N	Y	Y
NEW MEXICO							
Udall	N	N	N	Y	Y	Y	Y
Heinrich	N	N	N	Y	Y	Y	Y
NEW YORK							
Schumer	N	N	N	Y	Y	Y	Y
Gillibrand	N	N	N	Y	N	Y	N
NORTH CAROLINA							
Burr	?	?	?	?	?	?	Y
Tillis	Y	Y	Y	Y	Y	Y	Y
NORTH DAKOTA							
Hoeven	Y	Y	Y	Y	?	+	Y
Heitkamp	Y	N	N	Y	Y	Y	Y
OHIO							
Brown	N	N	N	Y	Y	Y	Y
Portman	Y	Y	Y	Y	Y	Y	Y
OKLAHOMA							
Inhofe	Y	Y	Y	?	?	?	Y
Lankford	Y	Y	Y	Y	Y	Y	Y
OREGON							
Wyden	N	N	N	Y	Y	Y	Y
Merkley	N	N	N	Y	N	Y	Y
PENNSYLVANIA							
Casey	Y	N	N	Y	Y	Y	Y
Toomey	Y	Y	Y	Y	Y	Y	Y
RHODE ISLAND							
Reed	N	N	N	Y	N	Y	Y
Whitehouse	N	N	N	Y	N	Y	Y
SOUTH CAROLINA							
Graham	Y	Y	Y	Y	Y	Y	Y
Scott	Y	Y	Y	Y	Y	Y	Y
SOUTH DAKOTA							
Thune	Y	Y	Y	Y	Y	Y	Y
Rounds	Y	Y	Y	Y	Y	Y	Y
TENNESSEE							
Alexander	Y	Y	Y	Y	Y	Y	Y
Corker	Y	Y	Y	Y	Y	Y	Y
TEXAS							
Cornyn	Y	Y	Y	Y	Y	Y	Y
Cruz	Y	Y	Y	Y	Y	Y	Y
UTAH							
Hatch	Y	Y	Y	Y	Y	Y	Y
Lee	Y	Y	Y	Y	Y	Y	Y
VERMONT							
Leahy	Y	N	N	Y	Y	Y	Y
Sanders	N	N	N	N	N	N	Y
VIRGINIA							
Warner	Y	N	N	Y	Y	Y	Y
Kaine	N	N	N	Y	Y	Y	Y
WASHINGTON							
Murray	N	N	N	Y	Y	Y	Y
Cantwell	N	N	N	Y	Y	Y	Y
WEST VIRGINIA							
Manchin	N	N	N	Y	Y	Y	Y
Capito	Y	Y	Y	Y	Y	Y	Y
WISCONSIN							
Johnson	Y	Y	Y	Y	Y	Y	Y
Baldwin	N	N	N	Y	Y	Y	Y
WYOMING							
Enzi	Y	Y	Y	Y	Y	Y	Y
Barrasso	Y	Y	Y	Y	Y	Y	Y

KEY   **Republicans**   Democrats   *Independents*

Y Voted for (yea)	X Paired against	C Voted "present" to avoid possible conflict of interest
# Paired for	– Announced against	
+ Announced for	P Voted "present"	? Did not vote or otherwise make a position known
N Voted against (nay)		

VOTE NUMBER

189. HR 601. FISCAL 2017 DISASTER SUPPLEMENTAL APPROPRIATIONS/MOTION TO TABLE. McConnell, R-Ky., motion to table the McConnell, R-Ky. motion to refer the bill to the Senate Appropriations Committee with instructions to report back immediately with a Paul, R-Ky., amendment no. 816, that would increase by $7.4 billion funding to the Disaster Relief Fund and would require that $15.25 billion in unobligated funds previously made to the United States Agency for International Development be rescinded. Motion agreed to 87-10: R 40-10; D 45-0; I 2-0. Sept. 7, 2017.

190. HR 601. FISCAL 2017 DISASTER SUPPLEMENTAL APPROPRIATIONS/MOTION TO TABLE. McConnell, R-Ky., motion to table the McConnell, R-Ky. motion to refer the bill to the Senate Appropriations Committee with instructions to report back immediately with a Sasse, R-Neb., amendment that would reflect changes that are only within the committee's jurisdiction and would eliminate provisions that are not part of the message originally sent by the House. Motion rejected 72-25: R 25-25; D 45-0; I 2-0. Sept. 7, 2017.

191. HR 601. FISCAL 2017 DISASTER SUPPLEMENTAL APPROPRIATIONS/CLOTURE. McConnell, R-Ky., motion to invoke cloture (thus limiting debate) in the McConnell motion to concur in the House amendment to the bill with a Senate amendment, no. 808, that would make available $15.25 billion in emergency supplemental funding for fiscal 2017 to partially cover the costs of responding to multiple natural disasters, including Hurricane Harvey. The amendment would suspend the public debt limit from the bill's date of enactment until Dec. 8, 2017, and would provide for government operations to be funded at fiscal 2017 levels until Dec. 8. Motion agreed to, Three-fifths of the total Senate (60) is required to invoke cloture., 79-18: R 32-18; D 45-0; I 2-0. Sept. 7, 2017.

192. HR 601. FISCAL 2017 DISASTER SUPPLEMENTAL APPROPRIATIONS/MOTION TO CONCUR. McConnell, R-Ky., motion to concur in the House amendment to the bill with a Senate amendment, no. 808, that would make available $15.25 billion in emergency supplemental funding for fiscal 2017 to partially cover the costs of responding to multiple natural disasters, including Hurricane Harvey. The amendment would suspend the public debt limit from the bill's date of enactment until Dec. 8, 2017, and would provide for government operations to be funded at fiscal 2017 levels until Dec. 8. Motion agreed to 80-17: R 33-17; D 45-0; I 2-0. Sept. 7, 2017.

193. HR 2810. FISCAL 2018 DEFENSE AUTHORIZATION/CLOTURE. Motion to invoke cloture (thus limiting debate) on the McConnell, R-Ky., motion to proceed to the bill that would provide funding for the Defense Department in fiscal 2018. Motion agreed to 89-3: R 45-1; D 43-1; I 1-1. Sept. 11, 2017.

194. HASSETT NOMINATION/CONFIRMATION. Confirmation of President Donald Trump's nomination of Kevin A. Hassett of Massachusetts to be chairman of the Council of Economic Advisers. Confirmed 81-16: R 51-0; D 29-15; I 1-1. Sept. 12, 2017.

195. HR 2810. FISCAL 2018 DEFENSE AUTHORIZATION/MOTION TO TABLE. Corker, R-Tenn., motion to table (kill) the McConnell, R-Ky., for Paul, R-Ky., amendment no. 871 to the McCain, R-Ariz., amendment no. 1003 to the bill. The Paul amendment would sunset, six months after enactment, the 2001 authorization for the use of military force in Afghanistan and the 2002 authorization for the use of military force in Iraq. Motion agreed to 61-36: R 48-3; D 13-31; I 0-2. Sept. 13, 2017.

	189	190	191	192	193	194	195		189	190	191	192	193	194	195
ALABAMA								**MONTANA**							
Shelby	Y	Y	Y	Y	Y	Y	Y	Tester	Y	Y	Y	Y	Y	Y	N
Strange	Y	N	N	Y	?	Y	Y	Daines	Y	N	N	N	Y	Y	Y
ALASKA								**NEBRASKA**							
Murkowski	Y	Y	Y	Y	Y	Y	Y	Fischer	Y	N	N	N	Y	Y	Y
Sullivan	?	?	?	?	Y	Y	Y	Sasse	Y	N	N	N	Y	Y	Y
ARIZONA								**NEVADA**							
McCain	Y	N	N	N	Y	Y	Y	Heller	N	N	Y	Y	Y	Y	N
Flake	N	N	N	N	?	Y	Y	Cortez Masto	Y	Y	Y	Y	Y	N	Y
ARKANSAS								**NEW HAMPSHIRE**							
Boozman	Y	Y	Y	Y	Y	Y	Y	Shaheen	Y	Y	Y	Y	Y	Y	Y
Cotton	Y	Y	Y	Y	Y	Y	Y	Hassan	Y	Y	Y	Y	Y	Y	Y
CALIFORNIA								**NEW JERSEY**							
Feinstein	Y	Y	Y	Y	Y	Y	N	Menendez	?	?	?	?	?	?	?
Harris	Y	Y	Y	Y	N	N	N	Booker	Y	Y	Y	Y	Y	N	N
COLORADO								**NEW MEXICO**							
Bennet	Y	Y	Y	Y	Y	Y	N	Udall	Y	Y	Y	Y	Y	N	N
Gardner	Y	N	Y	Y	Y	Y	Y	Heinrich	Y	Y	Y	Y	Y	N	N
CONNECTICUT								**NEW YORK**							
Blumenthal	Y	Y	Y	Y	N	N	N	Schumer	Y	Y	Y	Y	Y	N	N
Murphy	Y	Y	Y	Y	Y	Y	N	Gillibrand	Y	Y	Y	Y	Y	N	N
DELAWARE								**NORTH CAROLINA**							
Carper	Y	Y	Y	Y	Y	Y	Y	Burr	Y	Y	Y	Y	Y	Y	Y
Coons	Y	Y	Y	Y	Y	Y	N	Tillis	Y	Y	Y	Y	Y	Y	Y
FLORIDA								**NORTH DAKOTA**							
Nelson	Y	Y	Y	Y	?	?	+	Hoeven	Y	Y	Y	Y	Y	Y	Y
Rubio	?	?	?	?	?	?	?	Heitkamp	Y	Y	Y	Y	Y	Y	N
GEORGIA								**OHIO**							
Isakson	Y	Y	Y	Y	?	Y	Y	Brown	Y	Y	Y	Y	Y	Y	N
Perdue	Y	N	Y	Y	Y	Y	Y	Portman	Y	N	Y	Y	Y	Y	Y
HAWAII								**OKLAHOMA**							
Schatz	Y	Y	Y	Y	Y	N	Y	Inhofe	N	N	N	Y	Y	Y	Y
Hirono	Y	Y	Y	Y	Y	N	N	Lankford	N	N	N	N	Y	Y	Y
IDAHO								**OREGON**							
Crapo	Y	Y	Y	Y	Y	Y	Y	Wyden	Y	Y	Y	Y	N	N	N
Risch	N	N	N	N	Y	Y	Y	Merkley	Y	Y	Y	Y	Y	N	N
ILLINOIS								**PENNSYLVANIA**							
Durbin	Y	Y	Y	Y	Y	Y	N	Casey	Y	Y	Y	Y	Y	Y	N
Duckworth	Y	Y	Y	Y	Y	N	N	Toomey	N	N	N	N	Y	Y	Y
INDIANA								**RHODE ISLAND**							
Donnelly	Y	Y	Y	Y	Y	Y	Y	Reed	Y	Y	Y	Y	Y	Y	Y
Young	Y	Y	Y	Y	Y	Y	Y	Whitehouse	Y	Y	Y	Y	Y	Y	Y
IOWA								**SOUTH CAROLINA**							
Grassley	Y	N	N	N	Y	Y	Y	Graham	Y	Y	Y	N	?	Y	Y
Ernst	Y	N	N	N	Y	Y	Y	Scott	N	Y	Y	Y	?	Y	Y
KANSAS								**SOUTH DAKOTA**							
Roberts	Y	Y	Y	Y	Y	Y	Y	Thune	Y	Y	Y	Y	Y	Y	Y
Moran	Y	N	N	N	Y	Y	Y	Rounds	Y	Y	Y	Y	Y	Y	Y
KENTUCKY								**TENNESSEE**							
McConnell	Y	Y	Y	Y	Y	Y	Y	Alexander	Y	Y	Y	Y	Y	Y	Y
Paul	N	N	N	N	N	Y	N	Corker	Y	N	N	N	Y	Y	Y
LOUISIANA								**TEXAS**							
Cassidy	Y	Y	Y	Y	Y	Y	Y	Cornyn	Y	Y	Y	Y	Y	Y	Y
Kennedy	Y	N	N	Y	Y	Y	Y	Cruz	N	Y	Y	Y	Y	Y	Y
MAINE								**UTAH**							
Collins	Y	Y	Y	Y	Y	Y	Y	Hatch	Y	N	Y	Y	Y	Y	Y
King	Y	Y	Y	Y	Y	Y	N	Lee	N	N	N	N	Y	Y	Y
MARYLAND								**VERMONT**							
Cardin	Y	Y	Y	Y	Y	Y	N	Leahy	Y	Y	Y	Y	Y	Y	N
Van Hollen	Y	Y	Y	Y	Y	Y	N	*Sanders*	Y	Y	Y	N	N	N	N
MASSACHUSETTS								**VIRGINIA**							
Warren	Y	Y	Y	Y	Y	N	N	Warner	Y	Y	Y	Y	Y	Y	Y
Markey	Y	Y	Y	Y	Y	N	N	Kaine	Y	Y	Y	Y	Y	Y	N
MICHIGAN								**WASHINGTON**							
Stabenow	Y	Y	Y	Y	Y	Y	Y	Murray	Y	Y	Y	Y	Y	Y	N
Peters	Y	Y	Y	Y	Y	Y	N	Cantwell	Y	Y	Y	Y	Y	Y	N
MINNESOTA								**WEST VIRGINIA**							
Klobuchar	Y	Y	Y	Y	Y	Y	N	Manchin	Y	Y	Y	Y	Y	Y	Y
Franken	Y	Y	Y	Y	Y	Y	N	Capito	Y	Y	Y	Y	Y	Y	Y
MISSISSIPPI								**WISCONSIN**							
Cochran	Y	Y	Y	Y	Y	Y	Y	Johnson	Y	N	N	N	Y	Y	Y
Wicker	Y	Y	Y	Y	Y	Y	Y	Baldwin	Y	Y	Y	Y	Y	Y	N
MISSOURI								**WYOMING**							
McCaskill	Y	Y	Y	Y	Y	Y	Y	Enzi	Y	N	N	N	Y	Y	Y
Blunt	Y	Y	Y	Y	Y	Y	Y	Barrasso	Y	N	Y	Y	Y	Y	Y

KEY	**Republicans**	Democrats	*Independents*

Y	Voted for (yea)	X	Paired against	C	Voted "present" to avoid possible conflict of interest
#	Paired for	–	Announced against		
+	Announced for	P	Voted "present"	?	Did not vote or otherwise make a position known
N	Voted against (nay)				

VOTE NUMBER

196. PATENAUDE NOMINATION/CONFIRMATION. Confirmation of President Donald Trump's nomination of Pamela H. Patenaude of New Hampshire to be deputy secretary of the Housing and Urban Development Department. Confirmed 80-17: R 51-0; D 28-16; I 1-1. Sept. 14, 2017.

197. HR 2810. FISCAL 2018 DEFENSE AUTHORIZATION/CLOTURE. Motion to invoke cloture (thus limiting debate) on the McCain, R-Ariz., substitute amendment no. 1003, as modified, that would authorize $692 billion in discretionary funding for defense programs in fiscal 2018. Motion agreed to 84-9: R 46-2; D 37-6; I 1-1. Sept. 14, 2017.

198. HR 2810. FISCAL 2018 DEFENSE AUTHORIZATION/CLOTURE. Motion to invoke cloture (thus limiting debate) on the bill, as amended, that would authorize $692 billion in discretionary funding for defense programs in fiscal 2018, including $60 billion in Overseas Contingency Operations funding. Motion agreed to 90-7: R 48-2; D 41-4; I 1-1. Sept. 18, 2017.

199. HR 2810. FISCAL 2018 DEFENSE AUTHORIZATION/PASSAGE. Passage of the bill, as amended, that would authorize $692 billion in discretionary funding for defense programs in fiscal 2018, including $60 billion in Overseas Contingency Operations funding. Passed 89-8: R 47-3; D 41-4; I 1-1. Sept. 18, 2017.

200. FRANCISCO NOMINATION/CLOTURE. Motion to invoke cloture (thus limiting debate) on President Donald Trump's nomination of Noel J. Francisco of the District of Columbia to be Solicitor General. Motion agreed to 49-47: R 49-0; D 0-45; I 0-2. Sept. 19, 2017.

201. FRANCISCO NOMINATION/CONFIRMATION. Confirmation of President Donald Trump's nomination of Noel J. Francisco of the District of Columbia to be Solicitor General. Confirmed 50-47: R 50-0; D 0-45; I 0-2. Sept. 19, 2017.

202. EMANUEL NOMINATION/CLOTURE. Motion to invoke cloture (thus limiting debate) on President Donald Trump's nomination of William J. Emanuel of California to be a member of the National Labor Relations Board. Motion agreed to 49-44: R 49-0; D 0-42; I 0-2. Sept. 19, 2017.

	196	197	198	199	200	201	202
ALABAMA							
Shelby	Y	Y	Y	Y	Y	Y	Y
Strange	Y	Y	Y	Y	Y	Y	?
ALASKA							
Murkowski	Y	Y	Y	Y	Y	Y	Y
Sullivan	Y	Y	Y	Y	Y	Y	Y
ARIZONA							
McCain	Y	Y	Y	Y	Y	Y	Y
Flake	Y	Y	Y	Y	Y	Y	Y
ARKANSAS							
Boozman	Y	Y	Y	Y	Y	Y	Y
Cotton	Y	Y	Y	Y	Y	Y	Y
CALIFORNIA							
Feinstein	Y	Y	Y	N	N	N	N
Harris	N	Y	Y	N	N	N	N
COLORADO							
Bennet	Y	Y	Y	N	N	N	N
Gardner	Y	Y	Y	Y	Y	Y	Y
CONNECTICUT							
Blumenthal	N	Y	Y	N	N	N	N
Murphy	Y	Y	Y	N	N	N	N
DELAWARE							
Carper	Y	Y	Y	N	N	N	N
Coons	Y	Y	Y	N	N	N	N
FLORIDA							
Nelson	+	+	Y	N	N	N	-
Rubio	+	+	+	+	Y	Y	Y
GEORGIA							
Isakson	Y	?	Y	Y	Y	Y	Y
Perdue	Y	Y	Y	Y	Y	Y	Y
HAWAII							
Schatz	N	Y	Y	Y	N	N	?
Hirono	N	Y	Y	Y	N	N	?
IDAHO							
Crapo	Y	Y	Y	Y	Y	Y	Y
Risch	Y	Y	Y	Y	Y	Y	Y
ILLINOIS							
Durbin	Y	N	N	N	N	N	N
Duckworth	N	Y	Y	N	N	N	N
INDIANA							
Donnelly	Y	Y	Y	N	N	N	N
Young	Y	Y	Y	Y	Y	Y	Y
IOWA							
Grassley	Y	Y	Y	Y	Y	Y	Y
Ernst	Y	Y	Y	Y	Y	Y	Y
KANSAS							
Roberts	Y	Y	Y	Y	Y	Y	Y
Moran	Y	Y	Y	Y	?	?	?
KENTUCKY							
McConnell	Y	Y	Y	Y	Y	Y	Y
Paul	Y	N	N	N	Y	Y	Y
LOUISIANA							
Cassidy	Y	Y	Y	Y	Y	Y	Y
Kennedy	Y	Y	Y	Y	Y	Y	Y
MAINE							
Collins	Y	Y	Y	Y	Y	Y	Y
King	Y	Y	Y	N	N	N	N
MARYLAND							
Cardin	Y	Y	Y	N	N	N	N
Van Hollen	Y	Y	Y	N	N	N	N
MASSACHUSETTS							
Warren	N	Y	Y	N	N	N	N
Markey	N	N	Y	Y	N	N	N
MICHIGAN							
Stabenow	Y	Y	Y	N	N	N	N
Peters	Y	Y	Y	Y	N	N	N
MINNESOTA							
Klobuchar	Y	Y	Y	N	N	N	N
Franken	Y	Y	Y	N	N	N	N
MISSISSIPPI							
Cochran	Y	Y	Y	Y	?	?	?
Wicker	Y	Y	Y	Y	Y	Y	Y
MISSOURI							
McCaskill	Y	Y	Y	Y	N	N	N
Blunt	Y	Y	Y	Y	Y	Y	Y

	196	197	198	199	200	201	202
MONTANA							
Tester	Y	Y	Y	Y	N	N	N
Daines	Y	Y	Y	Y	Y	Y	Y
NEBRASKA							
Fischer	Y	Y	Y	Y	Y	Y	Y
Sasse	Y	Y	Y	Y	Y	Y	Y
NEVADA							
Heller	Y	Y	Y	Y	Y	Y	Y
Cortez Masto	Y	Y	Y	N	N	N	N
NEW HAMPSHIRE							
Shaheen	Y	Y	Y	N	N	N	N
Hassan	Y	Y	Y	N	N	N	N
NEW JERSEY							
Menendez	?	+	+	+	-	-	-
Booker	N	N	Y	Y	N	N	N
NEW MEXICO							
Udall	N	Y	Y	N	N	N	N
Heinrich	N	Y	Y	N	N	N	N
NEW YORK							
Schumer	N	Y	Y	N	N	N	N
Gillibrand	N	N	N	N	N	N	N
NORTH CAROLINA							
Burr	Y	?	Y	Y	Y	Y	Y
Tillis	Y	Y	Y	Y	Y	Y	Y
NORTH DAKOTA							
Hoeven	Y	Y	Y	Y	Y	Y	Y
Heitkamp	Y	Y	Y	N	N	N	N
OHIO							
Brown	N	Y	Y	N	N	N	N
Portman	Y	Y	Y	Y	Y	Y	Y
OKLAHOMA							
Inhofe	Y	Y	Y	Y	Y	Y	Y
Lankford	Y	Y	Y	Y	Y	Y	Y
OREGON							
Wyden	N	N	N	N	N	N	N
Merkley	N	N	N	N	N	N	N
PENNSYLVANIA							
Casey	Y	Y	Y	N	N	N	N
Toomey	Y	+	Y	Y	Y	Y	Y
RHODE ISLAND							
Reed	Y	Y	Y	N	N	N	N
Whitehouse	N	Y	Y	N	N	N	N
SOUTH CAROLINA							
Graham	Y	Y	?	?	?	Y	Y
Scott	Y	Y	Y	Y	Y	Y	Y
SOUTH DAKOTA							
Thune	Y	Y	Y	Y	Y	Y	Y
Rounds	Y	Y	Y	Y	Y	Y	Y
TENNESSEE							
Alexander	Y	Y	Y	Y	Y	Y	Y
Corker	Y	Y	Y	N	Y	Y	Y
TEXAS							
Cornyn	Y	Y	Y	Y	Y	Y	Y
Cruz	Y	Y	Y	Y	Y	Y	Y
UTAH							
Hatch	Y	Y	Y	Y	Y	Y	Y
Lee	Y	N	N	N	Y	Y	Y
VERMONT							
Leahy	Y	?	Y	N	N	N	N
Sanders	N	N	N	N	N	N	N
VIRGINIA							
Warner	Y	Y	Y	N	N	N	N
Kaine	Y	Y	Y	N	N	N	N
WASHINGTON							
Murray	Y	Y	Y	N	N	N	N
Cantwell	Y	Y	Y	N	N	N	N
WEST VIRGINIA							
Manchin	Y	Y	Y	N	N	N	N
Capito	Y	Y	Y	Y	Y	Y	Y
WISCONSIN							
Johnson	Y	Y	Y	Y	Y	Y	Y
Baldwin	Y	Y	Y	N	N	N	N
WYOMING							
Enzi	Y	Y	Y	Y	Y	Y	Y
Barrasso	Y	Y	Y	Y	Y	Y	Y

KEY   **Republicans**   Democrats   *Independents*

Y Voted for (yea)	X Paired against	C Voted "present" to avoid possible conflict of interest
# Paired for	- Announced against	
+ Announced for	P Voted "present"	? Did not vote or otherwise make a position known
N Voted against (nay)		

VOTE NUMBER

203. EMANUEL NOMINATION/CONFIRMATION. Confirmation of President Donald Trump's nomination of William J. Emanuel of California to be a member of the National Labor Relations Board. Confirmed 49-47: R 49-0; D 0-45; I 0-2. Sept. 25, 2017.

204. TARBET NOMINATION/CONFIRMATION. Confirmation of President Donald Trump's nomination of Heath P. Tarbet of Maryland to be an assistant secretary of the Treasury Department. Confirmed 87-8: R 49-0; D 37-7; I 1-1. Sept. 27, 2017.

205. DELRAHIM NOMINATION/CONFIRMATION. Confirmation of President Donald Trump's nomination of Makan Delrahim of California to be an assistant attorney general. Confirmed 73-21: R 49-0; D 23-20; I 1-1. Sept. 27, 2017.

206. ERICKSON NOMINATION/CLOTURE. Motion to invoke cloture (thus limiting debate) on President Donald Trump's nomination of Ralph R. Erickson of North Dakota to be a U.S. Circuit Judge for the Eighth Circuit. Motion agreed to 95-1: R 50-0; D 43-1; I 2-0. Sept. 28, 2017.

207. ERICKSON NOMINATION/CONFIRMATION. Confirmation of President Donald Trump's nomination of Ralph R. Erickson of North Dakota to be a U.S. Circuit Judge for the Eighth Circuit. Confirmed 95-1: R 49-0; D 44-1; I 2-0. Sept. 28, 2017.

208. PAI NOMINATION/CLOTURE. Motion to invoke cloture (thus limiting debate) on the nomination of Ajit V. Pai of Kansas to be a member of the Federal Communications Commission. Motion agreed to 55-41: R 49-0; D 6-39; I 0-2. Sept. 28, 2017.

209. PAI NOMINATION/CONFIRMATION. Confirmation of President Donald Trump's nomination of Ajit V. Pai of Kansas to be a member of the Federal Communications Commission. Confirmed 52-41: R 48-0; D 4-40; I 0-1. Oct. 2, 2017.

	203	204	205	206	207	208	209
ALABAMA							
Shelby	Y	Y	Y	Y	Y	Y	Y
Strange	?	?	?	?	?	?	Y
ALASKA							
Murkowski	Y	Y	Y	Y	Y	Y	Y
Sullivan	Y	Y	Y	Y	Y	Y	Y
ARIZONA							
McCain	Y	Y	Y	Y	Y	Y	?
Flake	Y	Y	Y	Y	Y	Y	Y
ARKANSAS							
Boozman	Y	Y	Y	Y	Y	Y	Y
Cotton	Y	Y	Y	Y	Y	Y	Y
CALIFORNIA							
Feinstein	N	Y	Y	Y	Y	N	N
Harris	N	N	N	Y	Y	N	N
COLORADO							
Bennet	N	Y	Y	Y	Y	N	N
Gardner	Y	Y	Y	Y	Y	Y	Y
CONNECTICUT							
Blumenthal	N	Y	Y	Y	Y	N	N
Murphy	N	Y	N	Y	Y	N	N
DELAWARE							
Carper	N	Y	Y	Y	Y	Y	N
Coons	N	Y	Y	Y	Y	Y	N
FLORIDA							
Nelson	N	Y	Y	Y	Y	N	N
Rubio	+	Y	Y	Y	Y	Y	Y
GEORGIA							
Isakson	Y	Y	Y	Y	Y	Y	Y
Perdue	Y	Y	Y	Y	Y	Y	Y
HAWAII							
Schatz	N	N	N	Y	Y	N	N
Hirono	N	N	N	Y	Y	N	N
IDAHO							
Crapo	Y	Y	Y	Y	Y	Y	Y
Risch	Y	Y	Y	Y	Y	Y	Y
ILLINOIS							
Durbin	N	Y	Y	Y	Y	N	N
Duckworth	N	Y	N	Y	Y	N	N
INDIANA							
Donnelly	N	+	+	Y	Y	N	N
Young	Y	?	?	Y	Y	Y	Y
IOWA							
Grassley	Y	Y	Y	Y	Y	Y	Y
Ernst	Y	Y	Y	Y	Y	Y	Y
KANSAS							
Roberts	Y	Y	Y	Y	Y	Y	Y
Moran	Y	Y	Y	Y	Y	Y	Y
KENTUCKY							
McConnell	Y	Y	Y	Y	Y	Y	Y
Paul	Y	Y	Y	Y	Y	Y	Y
LOUISIANA							
Cassidy	Y	Y	Y	Y	Y	Y	Y
Kennedy	Y	Y	Y	Y	Y	Y	Y
MAINE							
Collins	Y	Y	Y	Y	Y	Y	Y
King	N	Y	Y	Y	Y	N	N
MARYLAND							
Cardin	N	Y	Y	Y	Y	N	N
Van Hollen	N	Y	?	Y	Y	N	N
MASSACHUSETTS							
Warren	N	N	N	N	N	N	N
Markey	N	N	N	Y	Y	N	N
MICHIGAN							
Stabenow	N	Y	Y	Y	Y	N	N
Peters	N	Y	Y	Y	Y	Y	Y
MINNESOTA							
Klobuchar	N	Y	Y	Y	Y	N	N
Franken	N	Y	Y	?	Y	N	N
MISSISSIPPI							
Cochran	?	?	?	?	?	?	?
Wicker	Y	Y	Y	Y	Y	Y	Y
MISSOURI							
McCaskill	N	Y	Y	Y	Y	Y	Y
Blunt	Y	Y	Y	Y	Y	Y	Y

	203	204	205	206	207	208	209
MONTANA							
Tester	N	Y	Y	Y	Y	Y	Y
Daines	Y	Y	Y	Y	Y	Y	Y
NEBRASKA							
Fischer	Y	Y	Y	Y	Y	Y	Y
Sasse	Y	Y	Y	Y	Y	Y	Y
NEVADA							
Heller	Y	Y	Y	Y	Y	Y	?
Cortez Masto	N	Y	N	Y	Y	N	?
NEW HAMPSHIRE							
Shaheen	N	Y	Y	Y	Y	N	N
Hassan	N	Y	N	Y	Y	N	N
NEW JERSEY							
Menendez	–	–	–	+	+	–	–
Booker	N	Y	N	Y	Y	N	N
NEW MEXICO							
Udall	N	Y	N	Y	Y	N	N
Heinrich	N	Y	N	Y	Y	N	N
NEW YORK							
Schumer	N	Y	N	Y	Y	N	N
Gillibrand	N	N	N	Y	Y	N	N
NORTH CAROLINA							
Burr	Y	Y	Y	Y	Y	Y	Y
Tillis	Y	Y	Y	Y	?	?	Y
NORTH DAKOTA							
Hoeven	Y	Y	Y	Y	Y	Y	Y
Heitkamp	N	Y	Y	Y	Y	N	N
OHIO							
Brown	N	Y	Y	Y	Y	N	N
Portman	Y	Y	Y	Y	Y	Y	Y
OKLAHOMA							
Inhofe	Y	Y	Y	Y	Y	Y	Y
Lankford	Y	Y	Y	Y	Y	Y	Y
OREGON							
Wyden	N	Y	N	Y	Y	N	N
Merkley	N	N	N	Y	Y	N	N
PENNSYLVANIA							
Casey	N	Y	Y	Y	Y	N	N
Toomey	Y	Y	Y	Y	Y	Y	?
RHODE ISLAND							
Reed	N	Y	Y	Y	Y	N	N
Whitehouse	N	Y	N	Y	Y	N	N
SOUTH CAROLINA							
Graham	Y	Y	Y	Y	Y	Y	Y
Scott	Y	Y	Y	Y	Y	Y	Y
SOUTH DAKOTA							
Thune	Y	Y	Y	Y	Y	Y	Y
Rounds	Y	Y	Y	Y	Y	Y	Y
TENNESSEE							
Alexander	Y	Y	Y	Y	Y	Y	Y
Corker	Y	Y	Y	Y	Y	Y	Y
TEXAS							
Cornyn	Y	Y	Y	Y	Y	Y	Y
Cruz	Y	Y	Y	Y	Y	Y	Y
UTAH							
Hatch	Y	Y	Y	Y	Y	Y	Y
Lee	Y	Y	Y	Y	Y	Y	Y
VERMONT							
Leahy	N	Y	Y	Y	Y	N	N
Sanders	N	N	N	Y	Y	N	?
VIRGINIA							
Warner	N	Y	Y	Y	Y	N	N
Kaine	N	Y	N	Y	Y	N	N
WASHINGTON							
Murray	N	Y	N	Y	Y	N	N
Cantwell	N	Y	N	Y	Y	N	N
WEST VIRGINIA							
Manchin	N	Y	Y	Y	Y	Y	Y
Capito	Y	Y	Y	Y	Y	Y	Y
WISCONSIN							
Johnson	Y	Y	Y	Y	Y	Y	Y
Baldwin	N	Y	N	Y	Y	N	N
WYOMING							
Enzi	Y	Y	Y	Y	Y	Y	Y
Barrasso	Y	Y	Y	Y	Y	Y	Y

KEY	**Republicans**	Democrats	*Independents*

Y Voted for (yea)	X Paired against	C Voted "present" to avoid possible conflict of interest
# Paired for	– Announced against	
+ Announced for	P Voted "present"	? Did not vote or otherwise make a position known
N Voted against (nay)		

III SENATE VOTES

VOTE NUMBER

210. HARGAN NOMINATION/CLOTURE. Motion to invoke cloture (thus limiting debate) on President Donald Trump's nomination of Eric D. Hargan of Illinois to be deputy secretary of the Health and Human Services Department. Motion agreed to 57-38: R 49-0; D 7-37; I 1-1. Oct. 4, 2017.

211. HARGAN NOMINATION/CONFIRMATION. Confirmation of President Donald Trump's nomination of Eric D. Hargan of Illinois to be deputy secretary of the Health and Human Services Department. Confirmed 57-38: R 49-0; D 7-37; I 1-1. Oct. 4, 2017.

212. QUARLES NOMINATION/CLOTURE. Motion to invoke cloture (thus limiting debate) on President Donald Trump's nomination of Randal Quarles of Colorado to be a member of the Board of Governors for the Federal Reserve System. Motion agreed to 62-33: R 49-0; D 12-32; I 1-1. Oct. 4, 2017.

213. QUARLES NOMINATION/CONFIRMATION. Confirmation of President Donald Trump's nomination of Randal Quarles of Colorado to be a member of the Board of Governors for the Federal Reserve System. Confirmed 65-32: R 50-0; D 14-31; I 1-1. Oct. 5, 2017.

214. CISSNA NOMINATION/CLOTURE. Motion to invoke cloture (thus limiting debate) on President Donald Trump's nomination of Lee Francis Cissna of Maryland to be director of the United States Citizenship and Immigration Services. Motion agreed to 54-43: R 50-0; D 4-41; I 0-2. Oct. 5, 2017.

215. CISSNA NOMINATION/CONFIRMATION. Confirmation of President Donald Trump's nomination of Lee Francis Cissna of Maryland to be director of the United States Citizenship and Immigration Services. Confirmed 54-43: R 50-0; D 4-41; I 0-2. Oct. 5, 2017.

216. GINGRICH NOMINATION/CLOTURE. Motion to invoke cloture (thus limiting debate) on President Donald Trump's nomination of Callista L. Gingrich of Virginia to be a U.S. ambassador to the Holy See. Motion agreed to 75-20: R 49-0; D 25-19; I 1-1. Oct. 5, 2017.

	210	211	212	213	214	215	216
ALABAMA							
Shelby	Y	Y	Y	Y	Y	Y	Y
Strange	Y	Y	Y	Y	Y	Y	Y
ALASKA							
Murkowski	Y	Y	Y	Y	Y	Y	Y
Sullivan	Y	Y	Y	Y	Y	Y	Y
ARIZONA							
McCain	?	?	?	Y	Y	Y	?
Flake	Y	Y	Y	Y	Y	Y	Y
ARKANSAS							
Boozman	Y	Y	Y	Y	Y	Y	Y
Cotton	Y	Y	Y	Y	Y	Y	Y
CALIFORNIA							
Feinstein	N	N	N	N	N	N	Y
Harris	N	N	N	N	N	N	N
COLORADO							
Bennet	N	N	Y	N	Y	N	Y
Gardner	Y	Y	Y	Y	Y	Y	Y
CONNECTICUT							
Blumenthal	N	N	N	N	N	N	N
Murphy	N	N	N	N	N	N	Y
DELAWARE							
Carper	Y	Y	Y	Y	N	N	Y
Coons	Y	Y	Y	Y	N	N	Y
FLORIDA							
Nelson	N	N	Y	N	Y	N	+
Rubio	Y	Y	Y	Y	Y	Y	Y
GEORGIA							
Isakson	Y	Y	Y	Y	Y	Y	Y
Perdue	Y	Y	Y	Y	Y	Y	Y
HAWAII							
Schatz	N	N	N	N	N	N	N
Hirono	N	N	N	N	N	N	N
IDAHO							
Crapo	Y	Y	Y	Y	Y	Y	Y
Risch	Y	Y	Y	Y	Y	Y	Y
ILLINOIS							
Durbin	Y	Y	N	N	N	N	N
Duckworth	N	N	N	N	N	N	N
INDIANA							
Donnelly	Y	Y	Y	Y	Y	Y	Y
Young	Y	Y	Y	Y	Y	Y	Y
IOWA							
Grassley	Y	Y	Y	Y	Y	Y	Y
Ernst	Y	Y	Y	Y	Y	Y	Y
KANSAS							
Roberts	Y	Y	Y	Y	Y	Y	Y
Moran	Y	Y	Y	Y	Y	Y	Y
KENTUCKY							
McConnell	Y	Y	Y	Y	Y	Y	Y
Paul	Y	Y	Y	Y	Y	Y	Y
LOUISIANA							
Cassidy	Y	Y	Y	Y	Y	Y	Y
Kennedy	Y	Y	Y	Y	Y	Y	Y
MAINE							
Collins	Y	Y	Y	Y	Y	Y	Y
King	Y	Y	Y	Y	N	N	Y
MARYLAND							
Cardin	N	N	N	Y	N	N	Y
Van Hollen	N	N	N	Y	N	N	N
MASSACHUSETTS							
Warren	N	N	N	N	N	N	N
Markey	N	N	N	N	N	N	N
MICHIGAN							
Stabenow	N	N	N	N	N	N	N
Peters	N	N	Y	Y	N	N	N
MINNESOTA							
Klobuchar	N	N	N	N	N	N	Y
Franken	N	N	N	N	N	N	Y
MISSISSIPPI							
Cochran	?	?	?	?	?	?	?
Wicker	Y	Y	Y	Y	Y	Y	Y
MISSOURI							
McCaskill	Y	Y	Y	Y	Y	Y	Y
Blunt	Y	Y	Y	Y	Y	Y	Y

	210	211	212	213	214	215	216
MONTANA							
Tester	N	N	Y	Y	N	N	N
Daines	Y	Y	Y	Y	Y	Y	Y
NEBRASKA							
Fischer	Y	Y	Y	Y	Y	Y	Y
Sasse	Y	Y	Y	Y	Y	Y	Y
NEVADA							
Heller	?	?	?	?	?	?	?
Cortez Masto	?	-	?	-	?	?	+
NEW HAMPSHIRE							
Shaheen	N	N	Y	Y	N	N	Y
Hassan	N	N	N	N	N	N	N
NEW JERSEY							
Menendez	-	-	-	N	N	N	Y
Booker	N	N	N	N	N	N	N
NEW MEXICO							
Udall	N	N	N	N	N	N	N
Heinrich	N	N	N	N	N	N	Y
NEW YORK							
Schumer	N	N	N	N	N	N	Y
Gillibrand	N	N	N	N	N	N	N
NORTH CAROLINA							
Burr	Y	Y	Y	Y	Y	Y	Y
Tillis	Y	Y	Y	Y	Y	Y	Y
NORTH DAKOTA							
Hoeven	Y	Y	Y	Y	Y	Y	Y
Heitkamp	Y	Y	Y	Y	Y	Y	Y
OHIO							
Brown	N	N	N	N	N	N	N
Portman	Y	Y	Y	Y	Y	Y	Y
OKLAHOMA							
Inhofe	Y	Y	Y	Y	Y	Y	Y
Lankford	Y	Y	Y	Y	Y	Y	Y
OREGON							
Wyden	N	N	N	N	N	N	N
Merkley	N	N	N	N	N	N	N
PENNSYLVANIA							
Casey	N	N	N	N	N	N	Y
Toomey	Y	Y	Y	Y	Y	Y	Y
RHODE ISLAND							
Reed	N	N	N	N	N	N	Y
Whitehouse	N	N	N	N	N	N	N
SOUTH CAROLINA							
Graham	Y	Y	Y	Y	Y	Y	Y
Scott	Y	Y	Y	Y	Y	Y	Y
SOUTH DAKOTA							
Thune	Y	Y	Y	Y	Y	Y	Y
Rounds	Y	Y	Y	Y	Y	Y	Y
TENNESSEE							
Alexander	Y	Y	Y	Y	Y	Y	Y
Corker	Y	Y	Y	Y	Y	Y	Y
TEXAS							
Cornyn	Y	Y	Y	Y	Y	Y	Y
Cruz	Y	Y	Y	Y	Y	Y	Y
UTAH							
Hatch	Y	Y	Y	Y	Y	Y	Y
Lee	Y	Y	Y	Y	Y	Y	Y
VERMONT							
Leahy	N	N	N	N	N	N	Y
Sanders	N	N	N	N	N	N	N
VIRGINIA							
Warner	N	N	Y	Y	N	N	Y
Kaine	N	N	N	N	N	N	Y
WASHINGTON							
Murray	N	N	N	N	N	N	N
Cantwell	N	N	N	N	N	N	Y
WEST VIRGINIA							
Manchin	Y	Y	Y	Y	Y	Y	Y
Capito	Y	Y	Y	Y	Y	Y	Y
WISCONSIN							
Johnson	Y	Y	Y	Y	Y	Y	Y
Baldwin	N	N	N	N	N	N	Y
WYOMING							
Enzi	Y	Y	Y	Y	Y	Y	Y
Barrasso	Y	Y	Y	Y	Y	Y	Y

KEY — Republicans Democrats *Independents*

Y Voted for (yea)	X Paired against	C Voted "present" to avoid possible conflict of interest
# Paired for	– Announced against	? Did not vote or otherwise make a position known
+ Announced for	P Voted "present"	
N Voted against (nay)		

VOTE NUMBER

217. GINGRICH NOMINATION/CONFIRMATION. Confirmation of President Donald Trump's nomination of Callista L. Gingrich of Virginia to be a U.S. ambassador to the Holy See. Confirmed 70-23: R 46-0; D 23-22; I 1-1. Oct. 16, 2017.

218. TRACHTENBERG NOMINATION/CONFIRMATION. Confirmation of President Donald Trump's nomination of David Joel Trachtenberg of Virginia to be principal deputy under secretary of the Defense Department. Confirmed 79-17: R 49-0; D 29-16; I 1-1. Oct. 17, 2017.

219. H CON RES 71. FISCAL 2018 BUDGET RESOLUTION/MOTION TO PROCEED. McConnell, R-Ky., motion to proceed to the concurrent resolution that would provide for $3.2 trillion in new budget authority in fiscal 2018, not including off-budget accounts. It would assume $1.22 trillion in discretionary spending in fiscal 2018. It would assume the repeal of the 2010 health care overhaul law. It also would propose reducing spending on mandatory programs such as Medicare and Medicaid and changing programs such as the Supplemental Nutrition Assistance Program (also known as food stamps). It would call for restructuring Medicare into a "premium support" system beginning in 2024. It would also require the House Ways and Means Committee to report out legislation under the budget reconciliation process that would provide for a revenue-neutral, comprehensive overhaul of the U.S. tax code and would include instructions to 11 House committees to trigger the budget reconciliation process to cut mandatory spending. The concurrent resolution would assume that, over 10 years, base (non-Overseas Contingency Operations) discretionary defense spending would be increased by a total of $929 billion over the Budget Control Act caps and non-defense spending be reduced by $1.3 trillion. Motion agreed to 50-47: R 50-0; D 0-45; I 0-2. Oct. 17, 2017.

220. H CON RES 71. FISCAL 2018 BUDGET RESOLUTION/MEDICAID RESERVE FUND. Enzi, R-Wyo., for Hatch, R-Utah, amendment no. 1144, to the Enzi substitute amendment no. 1116, that would authorize the establishment of a reserve fund for legislation related to protecting the Medicaid program, which could include provisions that would improve Medicaid for the "most vulnerable populations," and provisions that would extend the life of the Federal Hospital Insurance Trust Fund. It would require that such legislation could not increase the deficit over the period of fiscal 2018 through 2022 or over the period of fiscal 2018 through 2027. Adopted 89-9: R 50-1; D 38-7; I 1-1. Oct. 18, 2017.

221. H CON RES 71. FISCAL 2018 BUDGET RESOLUTION/MEDICAID AND CHIP INCREASE. Enzi, R-Wyo., for Sanders, I-Vt., amendment no. 1119, to the Enzi amendment no. 1116, that would increase the new budget authority for certain health programs, including Medicaid, the Children's Health Insurance Program and the Federal Employees Health Benefit Program by $20.6 billion for fiscal 2018. Rejected 47-51: R 0-51; D 45-0; I 2-0. Oct. 18, 2017.

222. H CON RES 71. FISCAL 2018 BUDGET RESOLUTION/MEDICARE INCREASE. Enzi, R-Wyo., for Nelson, D-Fla., amendment no. 1150, to the Enzi substitute amendment no. 1116, that would increase the new budget authority for Medicare by $5.9 billion for fiscal 2018. Rejected 47-51: R 0-51; D 45-0; I 2-0. Oct. 18, 2017.

223. H CON RES 71. FISCAL 2018 BUDGET RESOLUTION/LOWER TAXES FOR FAMILIES. Enzi, R-Wyo., for Heller, R-Nev., amendment no. 1146, to the Enzi substitute amendment no. 1116, that would authorize the establishment of a reserve fund for legislation related to changing federal tax laws, which could include provisions that would lower taxes on families with children. It would require that such legislation could not increase the deficit over the period of fiscal 2018 through 2027. Adopted 98-0: R 51-0; D 45-0; I 2-0. Oct. 18, 2017.

	217	218	219	220	221	222	223
ALABAMA							
Shelby	Y	?	?	Y	N	N	Y
Strange	Y	Y	Y	N	N	N	Y
ALASKA							
Murkowski	Y	Y	Y	Y	N	N	Y
Sullivan	Y	Y	Y	Y	N	N	Y
ARIZONA							
McCain	?	Y	Y	Y	N	N	Y
Flake	Y	Y	Y	Y	N	N	Y
ARKANSAS							
Boozman	Y	Y	Y	Y	N	N	Y
Cotton	Y	Y	Y	Y	N	N	Y
CALIFORNIA							
Feinstein	Y	Y	N	Y	Y	Y	Y
Harris	N	N	N	N	Y	Y	Y
COLORADO							
Bennet	Y	Y	N	Y	Y	Y	Y
Gardner	Y	Y	Y	Y	N	N	Y
CONNECTICUT							
Blumenthal	N	Y	N	Y	Y	Y	Y
Murphy	Y	Y	N	Y	Y	Y	Y
DELAWARE							
Carper	Y	Y	N	Y	Y	Y	Y
Coons	Y	Y	N	Y	Y	Y	Y
FLORIDA							
Nelson	N	Y	N	Y	Y	Y	Y
Rubio	Y	Y	Y	Y	N	N	Y
GEORGIA							
Isakson	?	?	Y	Y	N	N	Y
Perdue	Y	Y	Y	Y	N	N	Y
HAWAII							
Schatz	N	N	N	Y	Y	Y	Y
Hirono	N	N	N	N	Y	Y	Y
IDAHO							
Crapo	Y	Y	Y	Y	N	N	Y
Risch	Y	Y	Y	Y	N	N	Y
ILLINOIS							
Durbin	N	N	N	Y	Y	Y	Y
Duckworth	N	Y	N	Y	Y	Y	Y
INDIANA							
Donnelly	Y	Y	N	Y	Y	Y	Y
Young	Y	Y	Y	Y	N	N	Y
IOWA							
Grassley	Y	Y	Y	Y	N	N	Y
Ernst	Y	Y	Y	Y	N	N	Y
KANSAS							
Roberts	Y	Y	Y	Y	N	N	Y
Moran	?	Y	Y	Y	N	N	Y
KENTUCKY							
McConnell	Y	Y	Y	Y	N	N	Y
Paul	Y	Y	Y	Y	N	N	Y
LOUISIANA							
Cassidy	Y	Y	Y	Y	N	N	Y
Kennedy	Y	Y	Y	Y	N	N	Y
MAINE							
Collins	Y	Y	Y	Y	N	N	Y
King	Y	Y	N	Y	Y	Y	Y
MARYLAND							
Cardin	Y	Y	N	Y	Y	Y	Y
Van Hollen	N	N	N	Y	Y	Y	Y
MASSACHUSETTS							
Warren	N	N	N	N	Y	Y	Y
Markey	N	N	N	N	Y	Y	Y
MICHIGAN							
Stabenow	N	Y	N	Y	Y	Y	Y
Peters	N	Y	N	Y	Y	Y	Y
MINNESOTA							
Klobuchar	Y	Y	N	Y	Y	Y	Y
Franken	Y	N	N	Y	Y	Y	Y
MISSISSIPPI							
Cochran	?	?	?	Y	N	N	Y
Wicker	Y	Y	Y	Y	N	N	Y
MISSOURI							
McCaskill	Y	Y	N	Y	Y	Y	Y
Blunt	Y	Y	Y	?	?	?	?

	217	218	219	220	221	222	223
MONTANA							
Tester	N	Y	N	Y	Y	Y	Y
Daines	Y	Y	Y	Y	N	N	Y
NEBRASKA							
Fischer	Y	Y	Y	Y	N	N	Y
Sasse	Y	Y	Y	Y	N	N	Y
NEVADA							
Heller	Y	Y	Y	Y	N	N	Y
Cortez Masto	Y	Y	N	Y	Y	Y	Y
NEW HAMPSHIRE							
Shaheen	Y	Y	N	Y	Y	Y	Y
Hassan	N	Y	N	Y	Y	Y	Y
NEW JERSEY							
Menendez	+	–	–	?	+	+	+
Booker	N	N	N	N	Y	Y	Y
NEW MEXICO							
Udall	N	Y	N	Y	Y	Y	Y
Heinrich	N	Y	N	Y	Y	Y	Y
NEW YORK							
Schumer	Y	Y	N	Y	Y	Y	Y
Gillibrand	N	N	N	N	Y	Y	Y
NORTH CAROLINA							
Burr	Y	Y	Y	Y	N	N	Y
Tillis	Y	Y	Y	Y	N	N	Y
NORTH DAKOTA							
Hoeven	Y	Y	Y	Y	N	N	Y
Heitkamp	Y	Y	N	Y	Y	Y	Y
OHIO							
Brown	N	N	N	Y	Y	Y	Y
Portman	?	Y	Y	Y	N	N	Y
OKLAHOMA							
Inhofe	Y	Y	Y	Y	N	N	Y
Lankford	Y	Y	Y	Y	N	N	Y
OREGON							
Wyden	N	N	N	Y	Y	Y	Y
Merkley	N	N	N	N	Y	Y	Y
PENNSYLVANIA							
Casey	Y	Y	N	Y	Y	Y	Y
Toomey	Y	Y	Y	Y	N	N	Y
RHODE ISLAND							
Reed	Y	Y	N	Y	Y	Y	Y
Whitehouse	Y	Y	N	Y	Y	Y	Y
SOUTH CAROLINA							
Graham	?	Y	Y	Y	N	N	Y
Scott	Y	Y	Y	Y	N	N	Y
SOUTH DAKOTA							
Thune	Y	Y	Y	Y	N	N	Y
Rounds	Y	Y	Y	Y	N	N	Y
TENNESSEE							
Alexander	Y	Y	Y	Y	N	N	Y
Corker	Y	Y	Y	Y	N	N	Y
TEXAS							
Cornyn	Y	Y	Y	Y	N	N	Y
Cruz	Y	Y	Y	Y	N	N	Y
UTAH							
Hatch	Y	Y	Y	Y	N	N	Y
Lee	Y	Y	Y	N	N	N	Y
VERMONT							
Leahy	N	N	N	Y	Y	Y	Y
Sanders	N	N	N	N	Y	Y	Y
VIRGINIA							
Warner	Y	Y	N	Y	Y	Y	Y
Kaine	Y	Y	N	Y	Y	Y	Y
WASHINGTON							
Murray	Y	Y	N	Y	Y	Y	Y
Cantwell	Y	N	N	Y	Y	Y	Y
WEST VIRGINIA							
Manchin	Y	Y	N	Y	Y	Y	Y
Capito	Y	Y	Y	Y	N	N	Y
WISCONSIN							
Johnson	Y	Y	Y	Y	N	N	Y
Baldwin	Y	N	N	Y	Y	Y	Y
WYOMING							
Enzi	Y	Y	Y	Y	N	N	Y
Barrasso	Y	Y	Y	Y	N	N	Y

VOTE NUMBER

224. H CON RES 71. FISCAL 2018 BUDGET RESOLUTION/MOTION TO WAIVE. Sanders, I-Vt., motion to waive applicable sections of the Congressional Budget Act with respect to the Enzi, R-Wyo., point of order that Enzi for Sanders amendment no. 1120 to the Enzi substitute amendment no. 1116 violates section 305(b)(2) of the Congressional Budget Act. The Sanders amendment would create a 60-vote point of order against any reconciliation legislation that would provide a tax cut to the wealthiest one percent of individuals. Motion rejected 46-52: R 0-51; D 44-1; I 2-0. Oct. 18, 2017.

225. H CON RES 71. FISCAL 2018 BUDGET RESOLUTION/ELIMINATE RECONCILIATION INSTRUCTIONS. Wyden, D-Ore., amendment no. 1302, to the Enzi, R-Wyo., substitute amendment no. 1116, that would eliminate the resolution's reconciliation instructions to the Senate Finance Committee and the House Ways and Means Committee. Rejected 47-52: R 0-52; D 45-0; I 2-0. Oct. 19, 2017.

226. H CON RES 71. FISCAL 2018 BUDGET RESOLUTION/FEDERAL DEDUCTIONS. Capito, R-W.Va., amendment no. 1393, to the Enzi, R-Wyo., substitute amendment no. 1116, that would authorize the establishment of a reserve fund for legislation related to reducing federal deductions, such as the state and local tax deduction. It would require that such legislation could not increase the deficit over the period of fiscal 2018 through 2027. Adopted 52-47: R 51-1; D 1-44; I 0-2. Oct. 19, 2017.

227. H CON RES 71. FISCAL 2018 BUDGET RESOLUTION/MOTION TO WAIVE. Cantwell, D-Wash., motion to waive applicable sections of the Congressional Budget Act with respect to the Enzi, R-Wyo., point of order that Cantwell amendment no. 1141 to the Enzi substitute amendment no. 1116 violates section 305(b)(2) of the Congressional Budget Act. The Cantwell amendment would create a 60-vote point of order against any reconciliation legislation that would repeal or limit the state and local tax deduction. Motion rejected 47-52: R 0-52; D 45-0; I 2-0. Oct. 19, 2017.

228. H CON RES 71. FISCAL 2018 BUDGET RESOLUTION/PAY-AS-YOU-GO EXEMPTION. Warner, D-Va., amendment no. 1138 to the Enzi, R-Wyo., substitute amendment no. 1116, that would eliminate the Senate pay-as-you-go exemption for reconciliation legislation related to taxes. It would eliminate the exemption that prevents reconciliation legislation from being subject to a point of order if it would increase in the deficit in excess of $10 billion in any fiscal year without offsets. Rejected 47-51: R 0-51; D 45-0; I 2-0. Oct. 19, 2017.

229. H CON RES 71. FISCAL 2018 BUDGET RESOLUTION/TAX SYSTEM SIMPLIFICATION. Enzi, R-Wyo., for Flake, R-Ariz., amendment no. 1178 to the Enzi substitute amendment no. 1116 that would authorize the establishment of a reserve fund for legislation related to simplifying the tax system. It would require that such legislation could not increase the deficit over the period of fiscal 2018 through 2027. Adopted 98-0: R 51-0; D 45-0; I 2-0. Oct. 19, 2017.

230. H CON RES 71. FISCAL 2018 BUDGET RESOLUTION/DEFICIT INCREASE PROHIBITION. Baldwin, D-Wis., amendment no. 1139 to the Enzi, R-Wyo., substitute amendment no. 1116 that would create a 60-vote point of order against any reconciliation legislation that would increase a deficit or reduce a surplus in either the period of the current fiscal year, the budget year, and the ensuing four fiscal years following the budget year or the period of the current fiscal year, the budget year, and the ensuing nine fiscal years following the budget year. Rejected 47-51: R 0-51; D 45-0; I 2-0. Oct. 19, 2017.

	224	225	226	227	228	229	230
ALABAMA							
Shelby	N	N	Y	N	N	Y	N
Strange	N	N	Y	N	N	Y	N
ALASKA							
Murkowski	N	N	Y	N	N	Y	N
Sullivan	N	N	Y	N	N	Y	N
ARIZONA							
McCain	N	N	Y	N	N	Y	N
Flake	N	N	Y	N	N	Y	N
ARKANSAS							
Boozman	N	N	Y	N	N	Y	N
Cotton	N	N	Y	N	N	Y	N
CALIFORNIA							
Feinstein	Y	Y	N	Y	Y	Y	Y
Harris	Y	Y	N	Y	Y	Y	Y
COLORADO							
Bennet	Y	Y	N	Y	Y	Y	Y
Gardner	N	N	Y	N	N	Y	N
CONNECTICUT							
Blumenthal	Y	Y	N	Y	Y	Y	Y
Murphy	Y	Y	N	Y	Y	Y	Y
DELAWARE							
Carper	Y	Y	N	Y	Y	Y	Y
Coons	Y	Y	N	Y	Y	Y	Y
FLORIDA							
Nelson	Y	Y	N	Y	Y	Y	Y
Rubio	N	N	Y	N	N	Y	N
GEORGIA							
Isakson	N	N	Y	N	N	Y	N
Perdue	N	N	Y	N	N	Y	N
HAWAII							
Schatz	Y	Y	N	Y	Y	Y	Y
Hirono	Y	Y	N	Y	Y	Y	Y
IDAHO							
Crapo	N	N	Y	N	N	Y	N
Risch	N	N	Y	N	N	Y	N
ILLINOIS							
Durbin	Y	Y	N	Y	Y	Y	Y
Duckworth	Y	Y	N	Y	Y	Y	Y
INDIANA							
Donnelly	Y	Y	N	Y	Y	Y	Y
Young	N	N	Y	N	N	Y	N
IOWA							
Grassley	N	N	Y	N	N	Y	N
Ernst	N	N	Y	N	N	Y	N
KANSAS							
Roberts	N	N	Y	N	N	Y	N
Moran	N	N	Y	N	N	Y	N
KENTUCKY							
McConnell	N	N	Y	N	N	Y	N
Paul	N	N	N	N	N	Y	N
LOUISIANA							
Cassidy	N	N	Y	N	N	Y	N
Kennedy	N	N	Y	N	N	Y	N
MAINE							
Collins	N	N	Y	N	N	Y	N
King	Y	Y	N	Y	Y	Y	Y
MARYLAND							
Cardin	Y	Y	N	Y	Y	Y	Y
Van Hollen	Y	Y	N	Y	Y	Y	Y
MASSACHUSETTS							
Warren	Y	Y	N	Y	Y	Y	Y
Markey	Y	Y	N	Y	Y	Y	Y
MICHIGAN							
Stabenow	Y	Y	N	Y	Y	Y	Y
Peters	Y	Y	N	Y	Y	Y	Y
MINNESOTA							
Klobuchar	Y	Y	N	Y	Y	Y	Y
Franken	Y	Y	N	Y	Y	Y	Y
MISSISSIPPI							
Cochran	N	N	Y	N	?	?	?
Wicker	N	N	Y	N	N	Y	N
MISSOURI							
McCaskill	Y	Y	N	Y	Y	Y	Y
Blunt	?	N	Y	N	N	Y	N

	224	225	226	227	228	229	230
MONTANA							
Tester	Y	Y	N	Y	Y	Y	Y
Daines	N	N	Y	N	N	Y	N
NEBRASKA							
Fischer	N	N	Y	N	N	Y	N
Sasse	N	N	Y	N	N	Y	N
NEVADA							
Heller	N	N	Y	N	N	Y	N
Cortez Masto	Y	Y	N	Y	Y	Y	Y
NEW HAMPSHIRE							
Shaheen	Y	Y	N	Y	Y	Y	Y
Hassan	Y	Y	N	Y	Y	Y	Y
NEW JERSEY							
Menendez	+	+	-	+	+	+	+
Booker	Y	Y	N	Y	Y	Y	Y
NEW MEXICO							
Udall	Y	Y	N	Y	Y	Y	Y
Heinrich	Y	Y	N	Y	Y	Y	Y
NEW YORK							
Schumer	Y	Y	N	Y	Y	Y	Y
Gillibrand	Y	Y	N	Y	Y	Y	Y
NORTH CAROLINA							
Burr	N	N	Y	N	N	Y	N
Tillis	N	N	Y	N	N	Y	N
NORTH DAKOTA							
Hoeven	N	N	Y	N	N	Y	N
Heitkamp	N	Y	N	Y	Y	Y	Y
OHIO							
Brown	Y	Y	N	Y	Y	Y	Y
Portman	N	N	Y	N	N	Y	N
OKLAHOMA							
Inhofe	N	N	Y	N	N	Y	N
Lankford	N	N	Y	N	N	Y	N
OREGON							
Wyden	Y	Y	N	Y	Y	Y	Y
Merkley	Y	Y	N	Y	Y	Y	Y
PENNSYLVANIA							
Casey	Y	Y	N	Y	Y	Y	Y
Toomey	N	N	Y	N	N	Y	N
RHODE ISLAND							
Reed	Y	Y	N	Y	Y	Y	Y
Whitehouse	Y	Y	N	Y	Y	Y	Y
SOUTH CAROLINA							
Graham	N	N	Y	N	N	Y	N
Scott	N	N	Y	N	N	Y	N
SOUTH DAKOTA							
Thune	N	N	Y	N	N	Y	N
Rounds	N	N	Y	N	N	Y	N
TENNESSEE							
Alexander	N	N	Y	N	N	Y	N
Corker	N	N	Y	N	N	Y	N
TEXAS							
Cornyn	N	N	Y	N	N	Y	N
Cruz	N	N	Y	N	N	Y	N
UTAH							
Hatch	N	N	Y	N	N	Y	N
Lee	N	N	Y	N	N	Y	N
VERMONT							
Leahy	Y	Y	N	Y	Y	Y	Y
Sanders	Y	Y	N	Y	Y	Y	Y
VIRGINIA							
Warner	Y	Y	N	Y	Y	Y	Y
Kaine	Y	Y	N	Y	Y	Y	Y
WASHINGTON							
Murray	Y	Y	N	Y	Y	Y	Y
Cantwell	Y	Y	N	Y	Y	Y	Y
WEST VIRGINIA							
Manchin	Y	Y	Y	Y	Y	Y	Y
Capito	N	N	Y	N	N	Y	N
WISCONSIN							
Johnson	N	N	Y	N	N	Y	N
Baldwin	Y	Y	N	Y	Y	Y	Y
WYOMING							
Enzi	N	N	Y	N	N	Y	N
Barrasso	N	N	Y	N	N	Y	N

KEY	**Republicans**	Democrats	*Independents*

Y Voted for (yea)	X Paired against	C Voted "present" to avoid possible conflict of interest
# Paired for	- Announced against	
+ Announced for	P Voted "present"	? Did not vote or otherwise make a position known
N Voted against (nay)		

VOTE NUMBER

231. H CON RES 71. FISCAL 2018 BUDGET RESOLUTION/MOTION TO WAIVE. Heitkamp, D-N.D., motion to waive section 305(b)(2) of the Congressional Budget Act with respect to the Enzi, R-Wyo., point of order that Enzi, for Heitkamp, amendment no. 1228 to the Enzi substitute amendment no. 1116 violates section 305(b)(2) of the Congressional Budget Act. The amendment would create a 60-vote point of order against any reconciliation legislation that would raise taxes on taxpayers whose annual income is below $250,000. Motion rejected 47-51: R 0-51; D 45-0; I 2-0. Oct. 19, 2017.

232. H CON RES 71. FISCAL 2018 BUDGET RESOLUTION/TAX BREAKS FOR DOMESTIC COMPANIES. Enzi, R-Wyo., for Brown, R-Ohio, amendment no. 1378 to the Enzi substitute amendment no. 1116 that would authorize the establishment of a reserve fund for legislation related to tax breaks for certain companies that have maintained or expanded their United States workforce and have provided certain benefits to workers. It would require that such legislation could not increase the deficit over the period of fiscal 2018 through 2022 or over the period of fiscal 2018 through 2027. Rejected 47-51: R 0-51; D 45-0; I 2-0. Oct. 19, 2017.

233. H CON RES 71. FISCAL 2018 BUDGET RESOLUTION/DEFICIT REDUCTION. Enzi, R-Wyo., for Paul, R-Ky., amendment no. 1296 to the Enzi substitute amendment no. 1116 that would replace the resolution's reconciliation instructions with new instructions to nine Senate committees to report changes to laws in their respective jurisdictions that would reduce the deficit in fiscal 2018. Rejected 4-94: R 4-47; D 0-45; I 0-2. Oct. 19, 2017.

234. H CON RES 71. FISCAL 2018 BUDGET RESOLUTION/MOTION TO WAIVE. Cardin, D-Md., motion to waive section 305(b)(2) of the Congressional Budget Act with respect to the Enzi, R-Wyo., point of order that Enzi, for Cardin, amendment no. 1375 to the Enzi substitute amendment no. 1116 violates section 305(b)(2) of the Congressional Budget Act. The amendment would create a 60-vote point of order against any reconciliation legislation that would include tax cuts and would increase a deficit or reduce a surplus. Motion rejected 47-52: R 0-52; D 45-0; I 2-0. Oct. 19, 2017.

235. H CON RES 71. FISCAL 2018 BUDGET RESOLUTION/CONGRESSIONAL BUDGET OFFICE ANALYSIS. Enzi, R-Wyo., for Kaine, D-Va., amendment no. 1249 to the Enzi substitute amendment no. 1116 that would eliminate the prohibition in the Senate on consideration of amendments to reconciliation legislation that would cause a net increase in the deficit unless fully offset and would require certain amendments to reconciliation legislation to have an analysis by the Congressional Budget Office posted on the CBO's website no later than 28 hours before a vote on such amendment. Rejected 48-51: R 1-51; D 45-0; I 2-0. Oct. 19, 2017.

236. H CON RES 71. FISCAL 2018 BUDGET RESOLUTION/DISCRETIONARY SPENDING REDUCTION. Enzi, R-Wyo., for Paul, R-Ky., amendment no. 1296 to the Enzi substitute amendment no. 1116 that would cut $43 billion in budget authority in fiscal 2018. Rejected 5-95: R 5-47; D 0-46; I 0-2. Oct. 19, 2017.

237. H CON RES 71. FISCAL 2018 BUDGET RESOLUTION/HEALTH CARE REGULATIONS. Enzi, R-Wyo., for Lee, R-Utah, amendment no. 1430 to the Enzi substitute amendment no. 1116 that would authorize the reserve fund for reconciliation legislation related to repealing or replacing the 2010 health care overhaul law to include such legislation that would nullify certain regulations promulgated by the law. Rejected 32-67: R 32-19; D 0-46; I 0-2. Oct. 19, 2017.

	231	232	233	234	235	236	237
ALABAMA							
Shelby	N	N	N	N	N	N	N
Strange	N	N	N	N	N	N	N
ALASKA							
Murkowski	N	N	N	N	N	N	N
Sullivan	N	N	N	N	N	N	Y
ARIZONA							
McCain	N	N	N	N	N	N	N
Flake	N	N	Y	N	N	Y	Y
ARKANSAS							
Boozman	N	N	N	N	N	N	N
Cotton	N	N	N	N	N	N	Y
CALIFORNIA							
Feinstein	Y	Y	N	Y	Y	N	N
Harris	Y	Y	N	Y	Y	N	N
COLORADO							
Bennet	Y	Y	N	Y	Y	N	N
Gardner	N	N	N	N	N	N	N
CONNECTICUT							
Blumenthal	Y	Y	N	Y	Y	N	N
Murphy	Y	Y	N	Y	Y	N	N
DELAWARE							
Carper	Y	Y	N	Y	Y	N	N
Coons	Y	Y	N	Y	Y	N	N
FLORIDA							
Nelson	Y	Y	N	Y	Y	N	N
Rubio	N	N	N	N	N	N	Y
GEORGIA							
Isakson	N	N	N	N	N	N	N
Perdue	N	N	N	N	N	N	Y
HAWAII							
Schatz	Y	Y	N	Y	Y	N	N
Hirono	Y	Y	N	Y	Y	N	N
IDAHO							
Crapo	N	N	N	N	N	N	Y
Risch	N	N	N	N	N	N	Y
ILLINOIS							
Durbin	Y	Y	N	Y	Y	N	N
Duckworth	Y	Y	N	Y	Y	N	N
INDIANA							
Donnelly	Y	Y	N	Y	Y	N	N
Young	N	N	N	N	N	N	Y
IOWA							
Grassley	N	N	N	N	N	N	N
Ernst	N	N	N	N	N	N	N
KANSAS							
Roberts	N	N	N	N	N	N	Y
Moran	N	N	N	N	N	N	Y
KENTUCKY							
McConnell	N	N	N	N	N	N	Y
Paul	N	N	Y	N	N	Y	Y
LOUISIANA							
Cassidy	N	N	N	N	N	N	N
Kennedy	N	N	N	N	N	N	Y
MAINE							
Collins	N	N	N	Y	N	N	N
King	Y	Y	N	Y	Y	N	N
MARYLAND							
Cardin	Y	Y	N	Y	Y	N	N
Van Hollen	Y	Y	N	Y	Y	N	N
MASSACHUSETTS							
Warren	Y	Y	N	Y	Y	N	N
Markey	Y	Y	N	Y	Y	N	N
MICHIGAN							
Stabenow	Y	Y	N	Y	Y	N	N
Peters	Y	Y	N	Y	Y	N	N
MINNESOTA							
Klobuchar	Y	Y	N	Y	Y	N	N
Franken	Y	Y	N	Y	Y	N	N
MISSISSIPPI							
Cochran	?	?	?	N	N	N	?
Wicker	N	N	N	N	N	N	Y
MISSOURI							
McCaskill	Y	Y	N	Y	Y	N	N
Blunt	N	N	N	N	N	N	N

	231	232	233	234	235	236	237
MONTANA							
Tester	Y	Y	N	Y	Y	N	N
Daines	N	N	N	N	N	Y	Y
NEBRASKA							
Fischer	N	N	N	N	N	N	Y
Sasse	N	N	N	N	N	N	Y
NEVADA							
Heller	N	N	N	N	N	N	Y
Cortez Masto	Y	Y	N	Y	Y	N	N
NEW HAMPSHIRE							
Shaheen	Y	Y	N	Y	Y	N	N
Hassan	Y	Y	N	Y	Y	N	N
NEW JERSEY							
Menendez	+	+	–	+	+	N	N
Booker	Y	Y	N	Y	Y	N	N
NEW MEXICO							
Udall	Y	Y	N	Y	Y	N	N
Heinrich	Y	Y	N	Y	Y	N	N
NEW YORK							
Schumer	Y	Y	N	Y	Y	N	N
Gillibrand	Y	Y	N	Y	Y	N	N
NORTH CAROLINA							
Burr	N	N	N	N	N	N	N
Tillis	N	N	N	N	N	N	N
NORTH DAKOTA							
Hoeven	N	N	N	N	N	N	Y
Heitkamp	Y	Y	N	Y	Y	N	N
OHIO							
Brown	Y	Y	N	Y	Y	N	N
Portman	N	N	N	N	N	N	N
OKLAHOMA							
Inhofe	N	N	N	N	N	N	Y
Lankford	N	N	Y	N	N	Y	Y
OREGON							
Wyden	Y	Y	N	Y	Y	N	N
Merkley	Y	Y	N	Y	Y	N	N
PENNSYLVANIA							
Casey	Y	Y	N	Y	Y	N	N
Toomey	N	N	N	N	N	N	Y
RHODE ISLAND							
Reed	Y	Y	N	Y	Y	N	N
Whitehouse	Y	Y	N	Y	Y	N	N
SOUTH CAROLINA							
Graham	N	N	N	N	N	N	Y
Scott	N	N	N	N	N	N	Y
SOUTH DAKOTA							
Thune	N	N	N	N	N	N	Y
Rounds	N	N	N	N	N	N	N
TENNESSEE							
Alexander	N	N	N	N	N	N	N
Corker	N	N	N	N	N	N	Y
TEXAS							
Cornyn	N	N	N	N	N	N	Y
Cruz	N	N	N	N	N	N	Y
UTAH							
Hatch	N	N	N	N	N	N	Y
Lee	N	N	Y	N	N	Y	Y
VERMONT							
Leahy	Y	Y	N	Y	Y	N	N
Sanders	Y	Y	N	Y	Y	N	N
VIRGINIA							
Warner	Y	Y	N	Y	Y	N	N
Kaine	Y	Y	N	Y	Y	N	N
WASHINGTON							
Murray	Y	Y	N	Y	Y	N	N
Cantwell	Y	Y	N	Y	Y	N	N
WEST VIRGINIA							
Manchin	Y	Y	N	Y	Y	N	N
Capito	N	N	N	N	N	N	N
WISCONSIN							
Johnson	N	N	N	N	N	N	Y
Baldwin	Y	Y	N	Y	Y	N	N
WYOMING							
Enzi	N	N	N	N	N	N	N
Barrasso	N	N	N	N	N	N	Y

KEY	**Republicans**	Democrats	*Independents*

Y Voted for (yea)	X Paired against	C Voted "present" to avoid possible conflict of interest
# Paired for	– Announced against	? Did not vote or otherwise make a position known
+ Announced for	P Voted "present"	
N Voted against (nay)		

238. H CON RES 71. FISCAL 2018 BUDGET RESOLUTION/HEALTH CARE RECONCILIATION. Enzi, R-Wyo., for Paul, R-Ky., amendment no. 1277 to the Enzi substitute amendment no. 1116 that would modify the Senate reconciliation instructions to require the Senate Health, Labor, and Pensions Committee, the Senate Judiciary Committee and the Senate Homeland Security and Governmental Affairs Committee to report legislation within each committee's jurisdiction that would reduce the deficit by no less than $1 million from fiscal 2018 to fiscal 2027. Rejected 33-66: R 33-18; D 0-46; I 0-2. Oct. 19, 2017.

239. H CON RES 71. FISCAL 2018 BUDGET RESOLUTION/PAYMENT IN LIEU OF TAXES PROGRAM. Enzi, R-Wyo., for Udall, D-N.M., amendment no. 1553 to the Enzi substitute amendment no. 1116 that would authorize the establishment of a reserve fund for legislation related to providing full, permanent and mandatory funding for the payment in lieu of taxes program. It would require that such legislation could not increase the deficit over the period of fiscal 2018 through 2022 or over the period of fiscal 2018 through 2027. Adopted 58-41: R 10-41; D 46-0; I 2-0. Oct. 19, 2017.

240. H CON RES 71. FISCAL 2018 BUDGET RESOLUTION/PAYMENT IN LIEU OF TAXES FORMULA. Enzi, R-Wyo., for Lee, R-Utah, amendment no. 1428 to the Enzi substitute amendment no. 1116 that would modify a deficit neutral reserve fund related to public lands and the environment to provide for legislation related to rewriting the formula for the payments in lieu of taxes program. Rejected 50-50: R 49-3; D 1-45; I 0-2. Oct. 19, 2017.

241. H CON RES 71. FISCAL 2018 BUDGET RESOLUTION/DEFICIT INCREASE INSTRUCTIONS. Enzi, R-Wyo., for Paul, R-Ky., amendment no. 1404 to the Enzi substitute amendment no. 1116 that would modify the reconciliation instructions to require the Senate Finance Committee to report changes in laws within its jurisdiction that increase the deficit by not more than $2.5 trillion for the period of fiscal years 2018 through 2027, instead of $1.5 trillion. Rejected 7-93: R 7-45; D 0-46; I 0-2. Oct. 19, 2017.

242. H CON RES 71. FISCAL 2018 BUDGET RESOLUTION/ENDANGERED SPECIES. Enzi, R-Wyo., for Lee, R-Utah, amendment no. 1429 to the Enzi substitute amendment no. 1116 that would authorize the establishment of a reserve fund for legislation related to prohibiting federal regulation of entirely intrastate species under the Endangered Species Act. It would require that such legislation could not increase the deficit over the period of fiscal 2018 through 2022 or over the period of fiscal 2018 through 2027. Rejected 49-51: R 49-3; D 0-46; I 0-2. Oct. 19, 2017.

243. H CON RES 71. FISCAL 2018 BUDGET RESOLUTION/ENERGY AND NATURAL RESOURCES INSTRUCTIONS. Enzi, R-Wyo., for Cantwell, D-Wash., amendment no. 1301 to the Enzi substitute amendment no. 1116 that would eliminate the reconciliation instructions for the Senate Energy and Natural Resources Committee. Rejected 48-52: R 1-51; D 45-1; I 2-0. Oct. 19, 2017.

244. H CON RES 71. FISCAL 2018 BUDGET RESOLUTION/HOUSE OF REPRESENTATIVES INSTRUCTIONS. Enzi, R-Wyo., amendment no. 1561 to the Enzi substitute amendment no. 1116 that would provide for various enforcement provisions related to the House of Representatives. Adopted 52-48: R 52-0; D 0-46; I 0-2. Oct. 19, 2017.

	238	239	240	241	242	243	244
ALABAMA							
Shelby	N	N	Y	N	Y	N	Y
Strange	N	N	Y	N	Y	N	Y
ALASKA							
Murkowski	N	Y	Y	N	Y	N	Y
Sullivan	Y	Y	Y	N	Y	N	Y
ARIZONA							
McCain	N	Y	N	N	Y	N	Y
Flake	Y	N	Y	N	Y	N	Y
ARKANSAS							
Boozman	Y	N	Y	N	Y	N	Y
Cotton	Y	N	Y	N	Y	N	Y
CALIFORNIA							
Feinstein	N	Y	N	N	N	Y	N
Harris	N	Y	N	N	N	Y	N
COLORADO							
Bennet	N	Y	N	N	N	Y	N
Gardner	Y	Y	N	N	Y	N	Y
CONNECTICUT							
Blumenthal	N	Y	N	N	N	Y	N
Murphy	N	Y	N	N	N	Y	N
DELAWARE							
Carper	N	Y	N	N	N	Y	N
Coons	N	Y	N	N	N	Y	N
FLORIDA							
Nelson	N	Y	N	N	N	Y	N
Rubio	Y	N	Y	N	Y	N	Y
GEORGIA							
Isakson	N	N	Y	N	Y	N	Y
Perdue	N	N	Y	Y	Y	N	Y
HAWAII							
Schatz	N	Y	N	N	N	Y	N
Hirono	N	Y	N	N	N	Y	N
IDAHO							
Crapo	Y	Y	Y	N	Y	N	Y
Risch	Y	Y	Y	N	Y	N	Y
ILLINOIS							
Durbin	N	Y	N	N	N	Y	N
Duckworth	N	Y	N	N	N	Y	N
INDIANA							
Donnelly	N	Y	Y	N	N	Y	N
Young	Y	N	Y	N	Y	N	Y
IOWA							
Grassley	Y	N	Y	N	Y	N	Y
Ernst	Y	N	Y	N	Y	N	Y
KANSAS							
Roberts	N	N	Y	Y	Y	N	Y
Moran	N	N	Y	Y	Y	N	Y
KENTUCKY							
McConnell	N	N	Y	N	Y	N	Y
Paul	Y	N	Y	Y	Y	N	Y
LOUISIANA							
Cassidy	N	N	Y	N	Y	N	Y
Kennedy	Y	N	Y	N	Y	N	Y
MAINE							
Collins	N	N	Y	N	N	Y	Y
King	N	Y	N	N	N	Y	N
MARYLAND							
Cardin	N	Y	N	N	N	Y	N
Van Hollen	N	Y	N	N	N	Y	N
MASSACHUSETTS							
Warren	N	Y	N	N	N	Y	N
Markey	N	Y	N	N	N	Y	N
MICHIGAN							
Stabenow	N	Y	N	N	N	Y	N
Peters	N	Y	N	N	N	Y	N
MINNESOTA							
Klobuchar	N	Y	N	N	N	Y	N
Franken	N	Y	N	N	N	Y	N
MISSISSIPPI							
Cochran	?	?	Y	N	Y	N	Y
Wicker	Y	N	Y	N	Y	N	Y
MISSOURI							
McCaskill	N	Y	N	N	N	Y	N
Blunt	N	N	Y	N	Y	N	Y
MONTANA							
Tester	N	Y	N	N	N	Y	N
Daines	Y	Y	N	Y	Y	N	Y
NEBRASKA							
Fischer	Y	N	Y	N	Y	N	Y
Sasse	Y	N	Y	Y	Y	N	Y
NEVADA							
Heller	Y	Y	Y	Y	Y	N	Y
Cortez Masto	N	Y	N	N	N	Y	N
NEW HAMPSHIRE							
Shaheen	N	Y	N	N	N	Y	N
Hassan	N	Y	N	N	N	Y	N
NEW JERSEY							
Menendez	N	Y	N	N	N	Y	N
Booker	N	Y	N	N	N	Y	N
NEW MEXICO							
Udall	N	Y	N	N	N	Y	N
Heinrich	N	Y	N	N	N	Y	N
NEW YORK							
Schumer	N	Y	N	N	N	Y	N
Gillibrand	N	Y	N	N	N	Y	N
NORTH CAROLINA							
Burr	Y	N	Y	N	Y	N	Y
Tillis	Y	N	Y	N	Y	N	Y
NORTH DAKOTA							
Hoeven	Y	N	Y	N	Y	N	Y
Heitkamp	N	Y	N	N	N	Y	N
OHIO							
Brown	N	Y	N	N	N	Y	N
Portman	Y	N	Y	N	Y	N	Y
OKLAHOMA							
Inhofe	Y	N	Y	N	Y	N	Y
Lankford	Y	N	Y	N	Y	N	Y
OREGON							
Wyden	N	Y	N	N	N	Y	N
Merkley	N	Y	N	N	N	Y	N
PENNSYLVANIA							
Casey	N	Y	N	N	N	Y	N
Toomey	N	N	Y	N	Y	N	Y
RHODE ISLAND							
Reed	N	Y	N	N	N	Y	N
Whitehouse	N	Y	N	N	N	Y	N
SOUTH CAROLINA							
Graham	N	N	Y	N	Y	N	Y
Scott	Y	N	Y	N	Y	N	Y
SOUTH DAKOTA							
Thune	Y	N	Y	N	Y	N	Y
Rounds	Y	N	Y	N	Y	N	Y
TENNESSEE							
Alexander	N	N	Y	N	N	N	Y
Corker	N	N	Y	N	N	N	Y
TEXAS							
Cornyn	N	N	Y	N	Y	N	Y
Cruz	Y	N	Y	Y	Y	N	Y
UTAH							
Hatch	Y	Y	Y	N	Y	N	Y
Lee	Y	Y	Y	Y	Y	N	Y
VERMONT							
Leahy	N	Y	N	N	N	Y	N
Sanders	N	Y	N	N	N	Y	N
VIRGINIA							
Warner	N	Y	N	N	N	Y	N
Kaine	N	Y	N	N	N	Y	N
WASHINGTON							
Murray	N	Y	N	N	N	Y	N
Cantwell	N	Y	N	N	N	Y	N
WEST VIRGINIA							
Manchin	N	Y	N	N	N	N	N
Capito	Y	N	Y	N	Y	N	Y
WISCONSIN							
Johnson	Y	N	Y	N	Y	N	Y
Baldwin	N	Y	N	N	N	Y	N
WYOMING							
Enzi	N	N	Y	N	Y	N	Y
Barrasso	Y	N	Y	N	Y	N	Y

KEY Republicans Democrats Independents

Y	Voted for (yea)
#	Paired for
+	Announced for
N	Voted against (nay)
X	Paired against
–	Announced against
P	Voted "present"
C	Voted "present" to avoid possible conflict of interest
?	Did not vote or otherwise make a position known

VOTE NUMBER

245. H CON RES 71. FISCAL 2018 BUDGET RESOLUTION/ADOPTION. Adoption of the concurrent resolution, as amended, that would provide for $3.1 trillion in new budget authority in fiscal 2018, not including off-budget accounts. It would allow the cap on defense spending to be raised to $640 billion for fiscal 2018, without the need for offsets. It would require the Senate Finance Committee to report legislation under the budget reconciliation process that would increase the deficit by no more than $1.5 trillion over the period of fiscal 2018 through fiscal 2027. It would also instruct the Senate Energy and Natural Resources Committee to report legislation under the budget reconciliation process that would reduce the deficit by $1 billion over the period of fiscal 2018 through fiscal 2027. The concurrent resolution would authorize the establishment of various reserve funds, including a deficit-neutral reserve fund related to repealing or replacing the 2010 health care overhaul law, and a revenue-neutral reserve fund related to modifying the federal tax system. Adopted 51-49: R 51-1; D 0-46; I 0-2. Oct. 19, 2017.

246. HR 2266. EMERGENCY HURRICANE AND WILDFIRE DISASTER APPROPRIATIONS LEGISLATIVE VEHICLE/CLOTURE. Motion to invoke cloture (thus limiting debate) on a McConnell, R-Ky., motion to concur in the House amendment to the Senate amendment to the bill that would available $36.5 billion in emergency supplemental funding for fiscal 2018 to partially cover the costs of responding to multiple natural disasters, including hurricanes and wildfires. It would include $18.7 billion for the Federal Emergency Management Agency's Disaster Relief Fund - $4.9 billion of which would be used for disaster relief loans to Puerto Rico and the U.S. Virgin Islands. It would also cancel $16 billion of the Treasury debt incurred by FEMA's National Flood Insurance Program, would release $1.2 billion in contingency reserves from the Supplemental Nutrition Assistance Program for use in Puerto Rico and would provide $577 million in funding to fight wildfires. Motion agreed to 79-16: R 33-16; D 44-0; I 2-0. Oct. 23, 2017.

247. HR 2266. EMERGENCY HURRICANE AND WILDFIRE DISASTER APPROPRIATIONS LEGISLATIVE VEHICLE/MOTION TO WAIVE. Roberts, R-Kan., motion to waive all applicable budgetary points of order under the Congressional Budget Act in relation to a Paul, R-Ky., point of order that the House amendment to the Senate amendment to the bill violates section 314(e) of the Congressional Budget Act. Motion agreed to 80-19: R 33-19; D 45-0; I 2-0. Oct. 24, 2017.

248. HR 2266. EMERGENCY HURRICANE AND WILDLIFE DISASTER APPROPRIATIONS LEGISLATIVE VEHICLE/MOTION TO CONCUR. McConnell, R-Ky., motion to concur in the House amendment to the Senate amendment to the bill that would make available $36.5 billion in emergency supplemental funding for fiscal 2018 to partially cover the costs of responding to multiple natural disasters, including hurricanes and wildfires. It would include $18.7 billion for the Federal Emergency Management Agency's Disaster Relief Fund - $4.9 billion of which would be used for disaster relief loans to Puerto Rico and the U.S. Virgin Islands. It would also cancel $16 billion of the Treasury debt incurred by FEMA's National Flood Insurance Program, would release $1.2 billion in contingency reserves from the Supplemental Nutrition Assistance Program for use in Puerto Rico and would provide $577 million in funding to fight wildfires. Motion agreed to 82-17: R 35-17; D 45-0; I 2-0. Oct. 24, 2017.

249. H J RES 111. CFPB ARBITRATION RULE DISAPPROVAL/PASSAGE. Passage of the joint resolution that would nullify and disapprove of a Consumer Financial Protection Bureau rule that prohibits mandatory arbitration clauses in consumer contracts related to financial services and products. Passed (thus cleared for the president), with Vice President Pence casting a "yea" vote to break the tie, 50-50: R 50-2; D 0-46; I 0-2. Oct. 24, 2017.

250. PALK NOMINATION/CLOTURE. Motion to invoke cloture (thus limiting debate) on President Donald Trump's nomination of Scott L. Palk of Oklahoma to be a U.S. district judge for the Western District of Oklahoma. Motion agreed to 79-18: R 52-0; D 26-17; I 1-1. Oct. 25, 2017.

	245	246	247	248	249	250
ALABAMA						
Shelby	Y	N	N	N	Y	Y
Strange	Y	N	N	N	Y	Y
ALASKA						
Murkowski	Y	Y	Y	Y	Y	Y
Sullivan	Y	?	Y	Y	Y	Y
ARIZONA						
McCain	Y	Y	Y	Y	Y	Y
Flake	Y	N	N	N	Y	Y
ARKANSAS						
Boozman	Y	Y	Y	Y	Y	Y
Cotton	Y	N	N	N	Y	Y
CALIFORNIA						
Feinstein	N	Y	Y	Y	N	N
Harris	N	Y	Y	Y	N	N
COLORADO						
Bennet	N	Y	Y	Y	N	Y
Gardner	Y	Y	Y	Y	Y	Y
CONNECTICUT						
Blumenthal	N	Y	Y	Y	N	N
Murphy	N	Y	Y	Y	N	N
DELAWARE						
Carper	N	Y	Y	Y	N	Y
Coons	N	Y	Y	Y	N	Y
FLORIDA						
Nelson	N	Y	Y	Y	N	Y
Rubio	Y	Y	Y	Y	Y	Y
GEORGIA						
Isakson	Y	Y	Y	Y	Y	Y
Perdue	Y	N	N	N	Y	Y
HAWAII						
Schatz	N	Y	Y	Y	N	N
Hirono	N	Y	Y	Y	N	N
IDAHO						
Crapo	Y	N	N	N	Y	Y
Risch	Y	N	N	N	Y	Y
ILLINOIS						
Durbin	N	Y	Y	Y	N	Y
Duckworth	N	Y	Y	Y	N	N
INDIANA						
Donnelly	N	Y	Y	Y	N	Y
Young	Y	Y	Y	Y	Y	Y
IOWA						
Grassley	Y	Y	Y	Y	Y	Y
Ernst	Y	Y	Y	Y	Y	Y
KANSAS						
Roberts	Y	Y	Y	Y	Y	Y
Moran	Y	?	N	Y	Y	Y
KENTUCKY						
McConnell	Y	Y	Y	Y	Y	Y
Paul	N	N	N	N	Y	Y
LOUISIANA						
Cassidy	Y	Y	Y	Y	Y	Y
Kennedy	Y	Y	Y	Y	N	Y
MAINE						
Collins	Y	Y	Y	Y	Y	Y
King	N	Y	Y	Y	N	Y
MARYLAND						
Cardin	N	Y	Y	Y	N	Y
Van Hollen	N	Y	Y	Y	N	N
MASSACHUSETTS						
Warren	N	Y	Y	Y	N	N
Markey	N	Y	Y	Y	N	N
MICHIGAN						
Stabenow	N	+	Y	Y	N	N
Peters	N	Y	Y	Y	N	Y
MINNESOTA						
Klobuchar	N	Y	Y	Y	N	Y
Franken	N	Y	Y	Y	N	Y
MISSISSIPPI						
Cochran	Y	Y	Y	Y	Y	Y
Wicker	Y	Y	Y	Y	Y	Y
MISSOURI						
McCaskill	N	Y	Y	Y	N	Y
Blunt	Y	Y	Y	Y	Y	Y
MONTANA						
Tester	N	Y	Y	Y	N	Y
Daines	Y	Y	Y	Y	Y	Y
NEBRASKA						
Fischer	Y	Y	Y	Y	Y	Y
Sasse	Y	N	N	N	Y	Y
NEVADA						
Heller	Y	Y	Y	Y	Y	Y
Cortez Masto	N	Y	Y	Y	N	N
NEW HAMPSHIRE						
Shaheen	N	Y	Y	Y	N	Y
Hassan	N	Y	Y	Y	N	Y
NEW JERSEY						
Menendez	N	+	+	+	N	–
Booker	N	Y	Y	Y	N	N
NEW MEXICO						
Udall	N	Y	Y	Y	N	Y
Heinrich	N	Y	Y	Y	N	+
NEW YORK						
Schumer	N	Y	Y	Y	N	Y
Gillibrand	N	Y	Y	Y	N	N
NORTH CAROLINA						
Burr	Y	Y	Y	Y	Y	Y
Tillis	Y	Y	Y	Y	Y	Y
NORTH DAKOTA						
Hoeven	Y	Y	Y	Y	Y	Y
Heitkamp	N	Y	Y	Y	N	Y
OHIO						
Brown	N	Y	Y	Y	N	Y
Portman	Y	Y	Y	Y	Y	Y
OKLAHOMA						
Inhofe	Y	N	N	N	Y	Y
Lankford	Y	N	N	N	Y	Y
OREGON						
Wyden	N	Y	Y	Y	N	N
Merkley	N	Y	Y	Y	N	N
PENNSYLVANIA						
Casey	N	Y	Y	Y	N	Y
Toomey	Y	N	N	N	Y	Y
RHODE ISLAND						
Reed	N	Y	Y	Y	N	Y
Whitehouse	N	Y	Y	Y	N	N
SOUTH CAROLINA						
Graham	Y	?	Y	Y	N	Y
Scott	Y	Y	Y	Y	Y	Y
SOUTH DAKOTA						
Thune	Y	N	N	Y	Y	Y
Rounds	Y	Y	Y	Y	Y	Y
TENNESSEE						
Alexander	Y	Y	Y	Y	Y	Y
Corker	Y	Y	N	N	Y	Y
TEXAS						
Cornyn	Y	Y	Y	Y	Y	Y
Cruz	Y	Y	Y	Y	Y	Y
UTAH						
Hatch	Y	Y	Y	Y	Y	Y
Lee	Y	N	N	N	Y	Y
VERMONT						
Leahy	N	Y	Y	Y	N	?
Sanders	N	Y	Y	Y	N	N
VIRGINIA						
Warner	N	Y	Y	Y	N	Y
Kaine	N	Y	Y	Y	N	Y
WASHINGTON						
Murray	N	Y	Y	Y	N	Y
Cantwell	N	Y	Y	Y	N	Y
WEST VIRGINIA						
Manchin	N	Y	Y	Y	N	Y
Capito	Y	Y	Y	Y	Y	Y
WISCONSIN						
Johnson	Y	N	N	N	Y	Y
Baldwin	N	Y	Y	Y	N	Y
WYOMING						
Enzi	Y	N	N	N	Y	Y
Barrasso	Y	N	N	N	Y	Y

KEY	**Republicans**	Democrats	*Independents*

Y	Voted for (yea)	X	Paired against	C	Voted "present" to avoid possible conflict of interest
#	Paired for	–	Announced against		
+	Announced for	P	Voted "present"	?	Did not vote or otherwise make a position known
N	Voted against (nay)				

||| SENATE VOTES

VOTE NUMBER

251. PALK NOMINATION/CONFIRMATION. Confirmation of President Donald Trump's nomination of Scott L. Palk of Oklahoma to be a U.S. district judge for the Western District of Oklahoma. Confirmed 79-16: R 51-0; D 27-15; I 1-1. Oct. 26, 2017.

252. MCFADDEN NOMINATION/CLOTURE. Motion to invoke cloture (thus limiting debate) on President Donald Trump's nomination of Trevor N. McFadden of Virginia to be U.S. district judge for the District of Columbia. Motion agreed to 85-12: R 52-0; D 32-11; I 1-1. Oct. 26, 2017.

253. MCFADDEN NOMINATION/CONFIRMATION. Confirmation of President Donald Trump's nomination of Trevor N. McFadden of Virginia to be U.S. district judge for the District of Columbia. Confirmed 84-10: R 50-0; D 33-10; I 1-0. Oct. 30, 2017.

254. BARRETT NOMINATION/CLOTURE. Motion to invoke cloture (thus limiting debate) on the nomination of Amy C. Barrett of Indiana to be a U.S. circuit judge for the Seventh Circuit. Motion agreed to 54-42: R 51-0; D 3-41; I 0-1. Oct. 30, 2017.

255. BARRETT NOMINATION/CONFIRMATION. Confirmation of President Donald Trump's nomination of Amy C. Barrett of Indiana to be a U.S. circuit judge for the Seventh Circuit. Confirmed 55-43: R 52-0; D 3-41; I 0-2. Oct. 31, 2017.

256. LARSEN NOMINATION/CLOTURE. Motion to invoke cloture (thus limiting debate) on the nomination of Joan L. Larsen to be a U.S. circuit judge for the Sixth Circuit. Motion agreed to 60-38: R 52-0; D 8-36; I 0-2. Oct. 31, 2017.

257. LARSEN NOMINATION/CONFIRMATION. Confirmation of President Donald Trump's nomination of Joan L. Larsen of Michigan to be a U.S. circuit judge for the Sixth Circuit. Confirmed 60-38: R 52-0; D 8-36; I 0-2. Nov. 1, 2017.

	251	252	253	254	255	256	257
ALABAMA							
Shelby	Y	Y	Y	Y	Y	Y	Y
Strange	Y	Y	Y	Y	Y	Y	Y
ALASKA							
Murkowski	Y	Y	Y	Y	Y	Y	Y
Sullivan	Y	Y	Y	Y	Y	Y	Y
ARIZONA							
McCain	Y	Y	?	?	Y	Y	Y
Flake	Y	Y	Y	Y	Y	Y	Y
ARKANSAS							
Boozman	Y	Y	Y	Y	Y	Y	Y
Cotton	Y	Y	Y	Y	Y	Y	Y
CALIFORNIA							
Feinstein	N	Y	Y	N	N	N	N
Harris	N	N	N	N	N	N	N
COLORADO							
Bennet	Y	Y	Y	N	N	N	N
Gardner	Y	Y	Y	Y	Y	Y	Y
CONNECTICUT							
Blumenthal	N	Y	Y	N	N	N	N
Murphy	N	Y	Y	N	N	N	N
DELAWARE							
Carper	Y	Y	Y	N	N	Y	Y
Coons	Y	Y	Y	N	N	N	N
FLORIDA							
Nelson	Y	Y	Y	N	N	Y	Y
Rubio	Y	Y	Y	Y	Y	Y	Y
GEORGIA							
Isakson	Y	Y	Y	Y	Y	Y	Y
Perdue	Y	Y	Y	Y	Y	Y	Y
HAWAII							
Schatz	N	Y	Y	N	N	N	N
Hirono	N	Y	Y	N	N	N	N
IDAHO							
Crapo	Y	Y	Y	Y	Y	Y	Y
Risch	Y	Y	Y	Y	Y	Y	Y
ILLINOIS							
Durbin	Y	Y	Y	N	N	N	N
Duckworth	N	Y	Y	N	N	N	N
INDIANA							
Donnelly	Y	Y	Y	Y	Y	Y	Y
Young	Y	Y	Y	Y	Y	Y	Y
IOWA							
Grassley	Y	Y	Y	Y	Y	Y	Y
Ernst	Y	Y	Y	Y	Y	Y	Y
KANSAS							
Roberts	Y	Y	Y	Y	Y	Y	Y
Moran	Y	Y	Y	Y	Y	Y	Y
KENTUCKY							
McConnell	Y	Y	Y	Y	Y	Y	Y
Paul	Y	Y	Y	Y	Y	Y	Y
LOUISIANA							
Cassidy	Y	Y	Y	Y	Y	Y	Y
Kennedy	Y	Y	Y	Y	Y	Y	Y
MAINE							
Collins	Y	Y	Y	Y	Y	Y	Y
King	Y	Y	Y	N	N	N	N
MARYLAND							
Cardin	Y	Y	Y	N	N	N	N
Van Hollen	N	Y	Y	N	N	N	N
MASSACHUSETTS							
Warren	N	N	N	N	N	N	N
Markey	N	N	N	N	N	N	N
MICHIGAN							
Stabenow	N	Y	Y	N	N	Y	Y
Peters	Y	N	N	N	N	Y	Y
MINNESOTA							
Klobuchar	Y	Y	Y	N	N	N	N
Franken	Y	Y	Y	N	N	N	N
MISSISSIPPI							
Cochran	Y	Y	Y	Y	Y	Y	Y
Wicker	Y	Y	Y	Y	Y	Y	Y
MISSOURI							
McCaskill	Y	Y	+	–	–	+	+
Blunt	Y	Y	Y	Y	Y	Y	Y

	251	252	253	254	255	256	257
MONTANA							
Tester	Y	Y	Y	N	N	N	N
Daines	Y	Y	Y	Y	Y	Y	Y
NEBRASKA							
Fischer	Y	Y	Y	Y	Y	Y	Y
Sasse	Y	Y	Y	Y	Y	Y	Y
NEVADA							
Heller	Y	Y	Y	Y	Y	Y	Y
Cortez Masto	N	Y	Y	N	N	N	N
NEW HAMPSHIRE							
Shaheen	Y	Y	Y	N	N	N	N
Hassan	Y	Y	Y	N	N	N	N
NEW JERSEY							
Menendez	–	–	+	–	–	–	–
Booker	?	N	N	N	N	N	N
NEW MEXICO							
Udall	Y	Y	Y	N	N	N	N
Heinrich	+	+	Y	N	N	N	N
NEW YORK							
Schumer	Y	Y	Y	N	N	N	N
Gillibrand	N	N	N	N	N	N	N
NORTH CAROLINA							
Burr	Y	Y	Y	Y	Y	Y	Y
Tillis	Y	Y	Y	Y	Y	Y	Y
NORTH DAKOTA							
Hoeven	Y	Y	Y	Y	Y	Y	Y
Heitkamp	Y	Y	Y	N	N	Y	Y
OHIO							
Brown	N	N	N	N	N	N	N
Portman	Y	Y	Y	Y	Y	Y	Y
OKLAHOMA							
Inhofe	Y	Y	Y	Y	Y	Y	Y
Lankford	Y	Y	Y	Y	Y	Y	Y
OREGON							
Wyden	N	N	N	N	N	N	N
Merkley	N	N	?	N	N	N	N
PENNSYLVANIA							
Casey	Y	Y	Y	N	N	N	N
Toomey	Y	Y	Y	Y	Y	Y	Y
RHODE ISLAND							
Reed	Y	Y	Y	N	N	N	N
Whitehouse	?	?	Y	N	N	N	N
SOUTH CAROLINA							
Graham	?	Y	Y	Y	Y	Y	Y
Scott	Y	Y	Y	Y	Y	Y	Y
SOUTH DAKOTA							
Thune	Y	Y	Y	Y	Y	Y	Y
Rounds	Y	Y	Y	Y	Y	Y	Y
TENNESSEE							
Alexander	Y	Y	+	Y	Y	Y	Y
Corker	Y	Y	Y	Y	Y	Y	Y
TEXAS							
Cornyn	Y	Y	Y	Y	Y	Y	Y
Cruz	Y	Y	Y	Y	Y	Y	Y
UTAH							
Hatch	Y	Y	Y	Y	Y	Y	Y
Lee	Y	Y	Y	Y	Y	Y	Y
VERMONT							
Leahy	Y	Y	Y	N	N	N	N
Sanders	N	N	?	?	N	N	N
VIRGINIA							
Warner	Y	Y	Y	N	N	Y	Y
Kaine	Y	Y	Y	Y	N	N	N
WASHINGTON							
Murray	N	N	N	N	N	N	N
Cantwell	N	N	N	N	N	N	N
WEST VIRGINIA							
Manchin	Y	Y	Y	Y	Y	Y	Y
Capito	Y	Y	Y	Y	Y	Y	Y
WISCONSIN							
Johnson	Y	Y	Y	Y	Y	Y	Y
Baldwin	Y	Y	Y	N	N	N	N
WYOMING							
Enzi	Y	Y	Y	Y	Y	Y	Y
Barrasso	Y	Y	Y	Y	Y	Y	Y

KEY   **Republicans**   Democrats   *Independents*

Y Voted for (yea)	X Paired against	C Voted "present" to avoid possible conflict of interest
# Paired for	– Announced against	
+ Announced for	P Voted "present"	? Did not vote or otherwise make a position known
N Voted against (nay)		

VOTE NUMBER

258. EID NOMINATION/CLOTURE. Motion to invoke cloture (thus limiting debate) on the nomination of Allison H. Eid of Colorado to be a U.S. circuit judge for the Tenth Circuit. Motion agreed to 56-42: R 52-0; D 4-40; I 0-2. Nov. 1, 2017.

259. EID NOMINATION/CONFIRMATION. Confirmation of President Donald Trump's nomination of Allison H. Eid of Colorado to be a U.S. circuit judge for the Tenth Circuit. Confirmed 56-41: R 52-0; D 4-39; I 0-2. Nov. 2, 2017.

260. BIBAS NOMINATION/CLOTURE. Motion to invoke cloture (thus limiting debate) on the nomination of Stephanos Bibas of Pennsylvania to be a U.S. circuit judge for the Third Circuit. Motion agreed to 54-43: R 52-0; D 2-41; I 0-2. Nov. 2, 2017.

261. BIBAS NOMINATION/CONFIRMATION. Confirmation of President Donald Trump's nomination of Stephanos Bibas of Pennsylvania to be a U.S. circuit judge for the Third Circuit. Confirmed 53-43: R 52-0; D 1-41; I 0-2. Nov. 2, 2017.

262. GIBSON NOMINATION/CONFIRMATION. Confirmation of President Donald Trump's nomination of John H. Gibson of Texas to be deputy chief management officer of the Defense Department. Confirmed 91-7: R 51-0; D 39-6; I 1-1. Nov. 7, 2017.

263. ENGEL NOMINATION/CLOTURE. Motion to invoke cloture (thus limiting debate) on the nomination of Steven A. Engel of the District of Columbia to be an assistant attorney general. Motion agreed to 51-47: R 50-1; D 1-44; I 0-2. Nov. 7, 2017.

264. ENGEL NOMINATION/CONFIRMATION. Confirmation of President Donald Trump's nomination of Steven A. Engel of the District of Columbia to be an assistant attorney general. Confirmed 51-47: R 50-1; D 1-44; I 0-2. Nov. 7, 2017.

	258	259	260	261	262	263	264
ALABAMA							
Shelby	Y	Y	Y	Y	Y	Y	Y
Strange	Y	Y	Y	Y	Y	Y	Y
ALASKA							
Murkowski	Y	Y	Y	Y	Y	Y	Y
Sullivan	Y	Y	Y	Y	Y	Y	Y
ARIZONA							
McCain	Y	Y	Y	Y	Y	N	N
Flake	Y	Y	Y	Y	Y	Y	Y
ARKANSAS							
Boozman	Y	Y	Y	Y	Y	Y	Y
Cotton	Y	Y	Y	Y	Y	Y	Y
CALIFORNIA							
Feinstein	N	N	N	N	Y	N	N
Harris	N	N	N	N	N	N	N
COLORADO							
Bennet	Y	Y	N	Y	N	N	N
Gardner	Y	Y	Y	Y	Y	Y	Y
CONNECTICUT							
Blumenthal	N	N	N	N	Y	N	N
Murphy	N	N	N	N	Y	N	N
DELAWARE							
Carper	N	N	N	N	Y	N	N
Coons	N	N	N	N	Y	N	N
FLORIDA							
Nelson	N	N	N	?	Y	N	N
Rubio	Y	Y	Y	Y	Y	Y	Y
GEORGIA							
Isakson	Y	Y	Y	Y	Y	Y	Y
Perdue	Y	Y	Y	Y	Y	Y	Y
HAWAII							
Schatz	N	N	N	N	Y	N	N
Hirono	N	N	N	N	Y	N	N
IDAHO							
Crapo	Y	Y	Y	Y	Y	Y	Y
Risch	Y	Y	Y	Y	Y	Y	Y
ILLINOIS							
Durbin	N	N	N	N	Y	N	N
Duckworth	N	N	N	N	Y	N	N
INDIANA							
Donnelly	Y	Y	Y	N	Y	N	N
Young	Y	Y	Y	Y	Y	Y	Y
IOWA							
Grassley	Y	Y	Y	Y	Y	Y	Y
Ernst	Y	Y	Y	Y	Y	Y	Y
KANSAS							
Roberts	Y	Y	Y	Y	Y	Y	Y
Moran	Y	Y	Y	Y	Y	Y	Y
KENTUCKY							
McConnell	Y	Y	Y	Y	Y	Y	Y
Paul	Y	Y	Y	Y	?	?	?
LOUISIANA							
Cassidy	Y	Y	Y	Y	Y	Y	Y
Kennedy	Y	Y	Y	Y	Y	Y	Y
MAINE							
Collins	Y	Y	Y	Y	Y	Y	Y
King	N	N	N	N	Y	N	N
MARYLAND							
Cardin	N	N	N	N	Y	N	N
Van Hollen	N	N	N	N	Y	N	N
MASSACHUSETTS							
Warren	N	N	N	N	N	N	N
Markey	N	N	N	N	N	N	N
MICHIGAN							
Stabenow	N	N	N	N	Y	N	N
Peters	N	N	N	N	Y	N	N
MINNESOTA							
Klobuchar	N	N	N	N	Y	N	N
Franken	N	N	N	N	Y	N	N
MISSISSIPPI							
Cochran	Y	Y	Y	Y	Y	Y	Y
Wicker	Y	Y	Y	Y	Y	Y	Y
MISSOURI							
McCaskill	+	+	–	–	Y	N	N
Blunt	Y	Y	Y	Y	Y	Y	Y
MONTANA							
Tester	N	N	N	N	Y	N	N
Daines	Y	Y	Y	Y	Y	Y	Y
NEBRASKA							
Fischer	Y	Y	Y	Y	Y	Y	Y
Sasse	Y	Y	Y	Y	Y	Y	Y
NEVADA							
Heller	Y	Y	Y	Y	Y	Y	Y
Cortez Masto	N	N	N	N	Y	N	N
NEW HAMPSHIRE							
Shaheen	N	N	N	N	Y	N	N
Hassan	N	N	N	N	Y	N	N
NEW JERSEY							
Menendez	–	–	–	–	+	–	–
Booker	N	N	N	N	N	N	N
NEW MEXICO							
Udall	N	N	N	N	Y	N	N
Heinrich	N	N	N	N	Y	N	N
NEW YORK							
Schumer	N	N	N	N	Y	N	N
Gillibrand	N	N	N	N	N	N	N
NORTH CAROLINA							
Burr	Y	Y	Y	Y	Y	Y	Y
Tillis	Y	Y	Y	Y	Y	Y	Y
NORTH DAKOTA							
Hoeven	Y	Y	Y	Y	Y	Y	Y
Heitkamp	Y	Y	N	N	Y	N	N
OHIO							
Brown	N	N	N	N	Y	N	N
Portman	Y	Y	Y	Y	Y	Y	Y
OKLAHOMA							
Inhofe	Y	Y	Y	Y	Y	Y	Y
Lankford	Y	Y	Y	Y	Y	Y	Y
OREGON							
Wyden	N	N	N	N	Y	N	N
Merkley	N	N	N	N	N	N	N
PENNSYLVANIA							
Casey	N	N	N	N	Y	N	N
Toomey	Y	Y	Y	Y	Y	Y	Y
RHODE ISLAND							
Reed	N	N	N	N	Y	N	N
Whitehouse	N	N	N	N	Y	N	N
SOUTH CAROLINA							
Graham	Y	Y	Y	Y	Y	Y	Y
Scott	Y	Y	Y	Y	Y	Y	Y
SOUTH DAKOTA							
Thune	Y	Y	Y	Y	Y	Y	Y
Rounds	Y	Y	Y	Y	Y	Y	Y
TENNESSEE							
Alexander	Y	Y	Y	Y	Y	Y	Y
Corker	Y	Y	Y	Y	Y	Y	Y
TEXAS							
Cornyn	Y	Y	Y	Y	Y	Y	Y
Cruz	Y	Y	Y	Y	Y	Y	Y
UTAH							
Hatch	Y	Y	Y	Y	Y	Y	Y
Lee	Y	Y	Y	Y	Y	Y	Y
VERMONT							
Leahy	N	N	N	N	Y	N	N
Sanders	N	N	N	N	N	N	N
VIRGINIA							
Warner	N	?	?	?	Y	N	N
Kaine	N	N	N	N	Y	N	N
WASHINGTON							
Murray	N	N	N	N	Y	N	N
Cantwell	N	N	N	N	Y	N	N
WEST VIRGINIA							
Manchin	Y	Y	Y	Y	Y	Y	Y
Capito	Y	Y	Y	Y	Y	Y	Y
WISCONSIN							
Johnson	Y	Y	Y	Y	Y	Y	Y
Baldwin	N	N	N	N	Y	N	N
WYOMING							
Enzi	Y	Y	Y	Y	Y	Y	Y
Barrasso	Y	Y	Y	Y	Y	Y	Y

VOTE NUMBER

265. ROBB NOMINATION/CLOTURE. Motion to invoke cloture (thus limiting debate) on the nomination of Peter B. Robb of Vermont to be general counsel of the National Labor Relations Board. Motion agreed to 51-47: R 51-0; D 0-45; I 0-2. Nov. 7, 2017.

266. ROBB NOMINATION/CONFIRMATION. Confirmation of President Donald Trump's nomination of Peter B. Robb of Vermont to be general counsel of the National Labor Relations Board. Confirmed 49-46: R 49-0; D 0-44; I 0-2. Nov. 8, 2017.

267. WEHRUM NOMINATION/CLOTURE. Motion to invoke cloture (thus limiting debate) on the nomination of William L. Wehrum of Delaware to be an assistant administrator of the Environmental Protection Agency. Motion agreed to 49-46: R 49-0; D 0-44; I 0-2. Nov. 8, 2017.

268. WEHRUM NOMINATION/CONFIRMATION. Confirmation of President Donald Trump's nomination of William L. Wehrum of Delaware to be an assistant administrator of the Environmental Protection Agency. Confirmed 49-47: R 49-1; D 0-44; I 0-2. Nov. 9, 2017.

269. KAN NOMINATION/CLOTURE. Motion to invoke cloture (thus limiting debate) on the nomination of Derek Kan of California to be under secretary of Transportation for policy. Motion agreed to 87-9: R 50-0; D 36-8; I 1-1. Nov. 9, 2017.

270. KAN NOMINATION/CONFIRMATION. Confirmation of President Donald Trump's nomination of Derek Kan of California to be under secretary of Transportation for policy. Confirmed 90-7: R 51-0; D 38-6; I 1-1. Nov. 13, 2017.

271. BRADBURY NOMINATION/CLOTURE. Motion to invoke cloture (thus limiting debate) on the nomination of Steven Bradbury of Virginia to be general counsel of the Department of Transportation. Motion agreed to 50-47: R 49-2; D 1-43; I 0-2. Nov. 13, 2017.

	265	266	267	268	269	270	271
ALABAMA							
Shelby	Y	Y	Y	Y	Y	Y	Y
Strange	Y	Y	Y	Y	Y	Y	Y
ALASKA							
Murkowski	Y	Y	Y	Y	Y	Y	Y
Sullivan	Y	Y	Y	Y	Y	Y	Y
ARIZONA							
McCain	Y	Y	Y	Y	Y	Y	N
Flake	Y	Y	Y	Y	Y	Y	Y
ARKANSAS							
Boozman	Y	Y	Y	Y	Y	Y	Y
Cotton	Y	Y	Y	Y	Y	Y	Y
CALIFORNIA							
Feinstein	N	N	N	N	Y	Y	N
Harris	N	N	N	N	Y	Y	N
COLORADO							
Bennet	N	N	N	N	Y	Y	N
Gardner	Y	Y	Y	Y	Y	Y	Y
CONNECTICUT							
Blumenthal	N	N	N	N	N	Y	N
Murphy	N	N	N	N	Y	Y	N
DELAWARE							
Carper	N	N	N	N	Y	Y	N
Coons	N	N	N	N	Y	Y	N
FLORIDA							
Nelson	N	N	N	N	Y	Y	N
Rubio	Y	Y	Y	Y	Y	Y	Y
GEORGIA							
Isakson	Y	Y	Y	Y	Y	Y	Y
Perdue	Y	Y	Y	Y	Y	Y	Y
HAWAII							
Schatz	N	N	N	N	Y	Y	N
Hirono	N	N	N	N	Y	Y	N
IDAHO							
Crapo	Y	Y	Y	Y	Y	Y	Y
Risch	Y	Y	Y	Y	Y	Y	Y
ILLINOIS							
Durbin	N	N	N	N	Y	Y	N
Duckworth	N	N	N	N	Y	Y	N
INDIANA							
Donnelly	N	N	N	N	Y	Y	N
Young	Y	Y	Y	Y	Y	Y	Y
IOWA							
Grassley	Y	Y	Y	Y	Y	Y	Y
Ernst	Y	Y	Y	Y	Y	Y	Y
KANSAS							
Roberts	Y	+	+	?	?	Y	Y
Moran	Y	Y	Y	Y	Y	Y	Y
KENTUCKY							
McConnell	Y	Y	Y	Y	Y	Y	Y
Paul	?	?	?	?	?	Y	N
LOUISIANA							
Cassidy	Y	Y	Y	Y	Y	Y	Y
Kennedy	Y	Y	Y	Y	Y	Y	Y
MAINE							
Collins	Y	Y	Y	N	Y	Y	Y
King	N	N	N	N	Y	Y	N
MARYLAND							
Cardin	N	N	N	N	Y	Y	N
Van Hollen	N	N	N	N	Y	Y	N
MASSACHUSETTS							
Warren	N	N	N	N	N	N	N
Markey	N	N	N	N	Y	Y	N
MICHIGAN							
Stabenow	N	N	N	N	Y	Y	N
Peters	N	N	N	N	Y	Y	N
MINNESOTA							
Klobuchar	N	N	N	N	Y	Y	N
Franken	N	N	N	N	Y	Y	N
MISSISSIPPI							
Cochran	Y	Y	Y	Y	Y	Y	Y
Wicker	Y	Y	Y	Y	Y	Y	Y
MISSOURI							
McCaskill	N	N	N	N	Y	Y	N
Blunt	Y	Y	Y	Y	Y	Y	Y

	265	266	267	268	269	270	271
MONTANA							
Tester	N	–	–	+	Y	Y	N
Daines	Y	Y	Y	Y	Y	Y	Y
NEBRASKA							
Fischer	Y	Y	Y	Y	Y	Y	Y
Sasse	Y	Y	Y	Y	Y	Y	Y
NEVADA							
Heller	Y	Y	Y	Y	Y	Y	Y
Cortez Masto	N	N	N	N	Y	Y	N
NEW HAMPSHIRE							
Shaheen	N	N	N	N	Y	Y	N
Hassan	N	N	N	N	Y	Y	N
NEW JERSEY							
Menendez	–	–	–	–	–	–	–
Booker	N	N	N	N	N	–	?
NEW MEXICO							
Udall	N	N	N	N	N	N	N
Heinrich	N	N	N	N	Y	Y	N
NEW YORK							
Schumer	N	N	N	N	N	N	N
Gillibrand	N	N	N	N	N	N	N
NORTH CAROLINA							
Burr	Y	Y	Y	Y	Y	Y	Y
Tillis	Y	Y	Y	Y	Y	Y	Y
NORTH DAKOTA							
Hoeven	Y	Y	Y	Y	Y	+	?
Heitkamp	N	N	N	N	Y	Y	N
OHIO							
Brown	N	N	N	N	Y	Y	N
Portman	Y	Y	Y	Y	Y	Y	Y
OKLAHOMA							
Inhofe	Y	Y	Y	Y	Y	Y	Y
Lankford	Y	Y	Y	Y	Y	Y	Y
OREGON							
Wyden	N	N	N	N	N	N	N
Merkley	N	N	N	N	N	N	N
PENNSYLVANIA							
Casey	N	N	N	N	Y	Y	N
Toomey	Y	Y	Y	Y	Y	Y	Y
RHODE ISLAND							
Reed	N	N	N	N	Y	Y	N
Whitehouse	N	N	N	N	Y	Y	N
SOUTH CAROLINA							
Graham	Y	Y	Y	Y	Y	Y	Y
Scott	Y	Y	Y	Y	Y	Y	Y
SOUTH DAKOTA							
Thune	Y	Y	Y	Y	Y	Y	Y
Rounds	Y	Y	Y	Y	Y	Y	Y
TENNESSEE							
Alexander	Y	Y	Y	Y	Y	Y	Y
Corker	Y	Y	Y	Y	Y	Y	Y
TEXAS							
Cornyn	Y	Y	Y	Y	Y	Y	Y
Cruz	Y	?	?	Y	Y	Y	Y
UTAH							
Hatch	Y	Y	Y	Y	Y	Y	Y
Lee	Y	Y	Y	Y	Y	Y	Y
VERMONT							
Leahy	N	N	N	N	Y	Y	N
Sanders	N	N	N	N	N	N	N
VIRGINIA							
Warner	N	N	N	N	Y	Y	N
Kaine	N	N	N	N	Y	Y	N
WASHINGTON							
Murray	N	N	N	N	Y	Y	N
Cantwell	N	N	N	N	Y	Y	N
WEST VIRGINIA							
Manchin	N	N	N	N	Y	Y	N
Capito	Y	Y	Y	Y	Y	Y	Y
WISCONSIN							
Johnson	Y	Y	Y	Y	Y	Y	Y
Baldwin	N	N	N	N	Y	Y	N
WYOMING							
Enzi	Y	Y	Y	Y	Y	Y	Y
Barrasso	Y	Y	Y	Y	Y	Y	Y

KEY — Republicans — Democrats — *Independents*

Y Voted for (yea)	**X** Paired against	**C** Voted "present" to avoid possible conflict of interest
# Paired for	**–** Announced against	**?** Did not vote or otherwise make a position known
+ Announced for	**P** Voted "present"	
N Voted against (nay)		

VOTE NUMBER

272. BRADBURY NOMINATION/CONFIRMATION. Confirmation of the nomination of Steven Bradbury of Virginia to be general counsel of the Department of Transportation. Confirmed 50-47: R 50-2; D 0-43; I 0-2. Nov. 14, 2017.

273. ZATEZALO NOMINATION/CLOTURE. Motion to invoke cloture (thus limiting debate) on the nomination of David G. Zatezalo of West Virginia to be assistant secretary of the Labor Department for mine safety and health. Motion agreed to 52-45: R 52-0; D 0-43; I 0-2. Nov. 14, 2017.

274. ESPER NOMINATION/CONFIRMATION. Confirmation of the nomination of Mark T. Esper of Virginia to be Secretary of the Army. Confirmed 89-6: R 50-0; D 38-5; I 1-1. Nov. 15, 2017.

275. ZATEZALO NOMINATION/CONFIRMATION. Confirmation of President Donald Trump's nomination of David G. Zatezalo of West Virginia to be assistant secretary of the Labor Department for mine safety and health. Confirmed 52-46: R 52-0; D 0-44; I 0-2. Nov. 15, 2017.

276. OTTING NOMINATION/CLOTURE. Motion to invoke cloture (thus limiting debate) on the nomination of Joseph Otting of Nevada to be Comptroller of the Currency. Motion agreed to 54-44: R 52-0; D 2-42; I 0-2. Nov. 15, 2017.

277. OTTING NOMINATION/CONFIRMATION. Confirmation of President Donald Trump's nomination of Joseph Otting of Nevada to be to be Comptroller of the Currency. Confirmed 54-43: R 52-0; D 2-41; I 0-2. Nov. 16, 2017.

278. COGGINS NOMINATION/CLOTURE. Motion to invoke cloture (thus limiting debate) on the nomination of Donald C. Coggins, Jr. of South Carolina to be U.S. district judge for the District of South Carolina. Motion agreed to 96-1: R 52-0; D 42-1; I 2-0. Nov. 16, 2017.

	272	273	274	275	276	277	278
ALABAMA							
Shelby	Y	Y	Y	Y	Y	Y	Y
Strange	Y	Y	Y	Y	Y	Y	Y
ALASKA							
Murkowski	Y	Y	Y	Y	Y	Y	Y
Sullivan	Y	Y	Y	Y	Y	Y	Y
ARIZONA							
McCain	N	Y	Y	Y	Y	Y	Y
Flake	Y	Y	Y	Y	Y	Y	Y
ARKANSAS							
Boozman	Y	Y	Y	Y	Y	Y	Y
Cotton	Y	Y	Y	Y	Y	Y	Y
CALIFORNIA							
Feinstein	N	N	+	N	N	N	Y
Harris	N	N	N	N	N	N	Y
COLORADO							
Bennet	N	N	Y	N	N	N	Y
Gardner	Y	Y	Y	Y	Y	Y	Y
CONNECTICUT							
Blumenthal	N	N	Y	N	N	N	Y
Murphy	N	N	Y	N	N	N	Y
DELAWARE							
Carper	N	N	Y	N	N	N	Y
Coons	N	N	Y	N	N	N	Y
FLORIDA							
Nelson	N	N	Y	N	N	N	Y
Rubio	Y	Y	Y	Y	Y	Y	Y
GEORGIA							
Isakson	Y	Y	Y	Y	Y	Y	Y
Perdue	Y	Y	Y	Y	Y	Y	Y
HAWAII							
Schatz	N	N	Y	N	N	N	Y
Hirono	N	N	Y	N	N	N	N
IDAHO							
Crapo	Y	Y	Y	Y	Y	Y	Y
Risch	Y	Y	Y	Y	Y	Y	Y
ILLINOIS							
Durbin	N	N	Y	N	N	N	Y
Duckworth	N	N	Y	N	N	N	Y
INDIANA							
Donnelly	N	N	Y	N	N	N	Y
Young	Y	Y	Y	Y	Y	Y	Y
IOWA							
Grassley	Y	Y	Y	Y	Y	Y	Y
Ernst	Y	Y	Y	Y	Y	Y	Y
KANSAS							
Roberts	Y	Y	Y	Y	Y	Y	Y
Moran	Y	Y	Y	Y	Y	Y	Y
KENTUCKY							
McConnell	Y	Y	Y	Y	Y	Y	Y
Paul	N	Y	Y	Y	Y	Y	Y
LOUISIANA							
Cassidy	Y	Y	Y	Y	Y	Y	Y
Kennedy	Y	Y	Y	Y	Y	Y	Y
MAINE							
Collins	Y	Y	Y	Y	Y	Y	Y
King	N	N	Y	N	N	N	Y
MARYLAND							
Cardin	N	N	Y	N	N	N	Y
Van Hollen	?	?	Y	N	N	N	Y
MASSACHUSETTS							
Warren	N	N	N	N	N	N	Y
Markey	N	N	N	N	N	N	Y
MICHIGAN							
Stabenow	N	N	Y	N	N	N	Y
Peters	N	N	Y	N	N	N	Y
MINNESOTA							
Klobuchar	N	N	Y	N	N	N	Y
Franken	N	N	Y	N	N	?	?
MISSISSIPPI							
Cochran	Y	Y	Y	Y	Y	Y	Y
Wicker	Y	Y	Y	Y	Y	Y	Y
MISSOURI							
McCaskill	N	N	Y	N	N	N	Y
Blunt	Y	Y	Y	Y	Y	Y	Y

	272	273	274	275	276	277	278
MONTANA							
Tester	N	N	Y	N	N	N	Y
Daines	Y	Y	Y	Y	Y	Y	Y
NEBRASKA							
Fischer	Y	Y	Y	Y	Y	Y	Y
Sasse	Y	Y	Y	Y	Y	Y	Y
NEVADA							
Heller	Y	Y	Y	Y	Y	Y	Y
Cortez Masto	N	N	Y	N	N	N	Y
NEW HAMPSHIRE							
Shaheen	N	N	Y	N	N	N	Y
Hassan	N	N	Y	N	N	N	Y
NEW JERSEY							
Menendez	–	–	+	–	–	–	+
Booker	–	–	–	–	–	–	+
NEW MEXICO							
Udall	N	N	Y	N	N	N	Y
Heinrich	N	N	Y	N	N	N	Y
NEW YORK							
Schumer	N	N	Y	N	N	N	Y
Gillibrand	N	N	N	N	N	N	Y
NORTH CAROLINA							
Burr	Y	Y	Y	Y	Y	Y	Y
Tillis	Y	Y	?	Y	Y	Y	Y
NORTH DAKOTA							
Hoeven	Y	Y	Y	Y	Y	Y	Y
Heitkamp	N	N	Y	N	Y	Y	Y
OHIO							
Brown	N	N	Y	N	N	N	Y
Portman	Y	Y	Y	Y	Y	Y	Y
OKLAHOMA							
Inhofe	Y	Y	Y	Y	Y	Y	Y
Lankford	Y	Y	Y	Y	Y	Y	Y
OREGON							
Wyden	N	N	Y	N	N	N	Y
Merkley	N	N	N	N	N	N	Y
PENNSYLVANIA							
Casey	N	N	Y	N	N	N	Y
Toomey	Y	Y	Y	Y	Y	Y	Y
RHODE ISLAND							
Reed	N	N	Y	N	N	N	Y
Whitehouse	N	N	Y	N	N	N	Y
SOUTH CAROLINA							
Graham	Y	Y	Y	Y	Y	Y	Y
Scott	Y	Y	Y	Y	Y	Y	Y
SOUTH DAKOTA							
Thune	Y	Y	Y	Y	Y	Y	Y
Rounds	Y	Y	Y	Y	Y	Y	Y
TENNESSEE							
Alexander	Y	Y	Y	Y	Y	Y	Y
Corker	Y	Y	Y	Y	Y	Y	Y
TEXAS							
Cornyn	Y	Y	Y	Y	Y	Y	Y
Cruz	Y	Y	+	Y	Y	Y	Y
UTAH							
Hatch	Y	Y	Y	Y	Y	Y	Y
Lee	Y	Y	Y	Y	Y	Y	Y
VERMONT							
Leahy	N	N	Y	N	N	N	Y
Sanders	N	N	N	N	N	N	Y
VIRGINIA							
Warner	N	N	Y	N	N	N	Y
Kaine	N	N	Y	N	N	N	Y
WASHINGTON							
Murray	N	N	Y	N	N	N	Y
Cantwell	N	N	Y	N	N	N	Y
WEST VIRGINIA							
Manchin	N	N	Y	N	Y	Y	Y
Capito	Y	Y	Y	Y	Y	Y	Y
WISCONSIN							
Johnson	Y	Y	Y	Y	Y	Y	Y
Baldwin	N	N	Y	N	N	N	Y
WYOMING							
Enzi	Y	Y	Y	Y	Y	Y	Y
Barrasso	Y	Y	Y	Y	Y	Y	Y

||| SENATE VOTES

VOTE NUMBER

279. FRIEDRICH NOMINATION/CLOTURE. Motion to invoke cloture (thus limiting debate) on the nomination of Dabney L. Friedrich of California to be a U.S. district judge for the District of Columbia. Motion agreed to 93-4: R 51-1; D 40-3; I 2-0. Nov. 16, 2017.

280. COGGINS NOMINATION/CONFIRMATION. Confirmation of President Donald Trump's nomination of Donald C. Coggins, Jr. of South Carolina to be U.S. district judge for the District of South Carolina. Confirmed 96-0: R 51-0; D 43-0; I 2-0. Nov. 16, 2017.

281. FRIEDRICH NOMINATION/CONFIRMATION. Confirmation of President Donald Trump's nomination of Dabney L. Friedrich of California to be a U.S. district judge for the District of Columbia. Confirmed 97-3: R 52-0; D 44-2; I 1-1. Nov. 27, 2017.

282. KATSAS NOMINATION/CLOTURE. Motion to invoke cloture (thus limiting debate) on the nomination of Gregory G. Katsas of Virginia to be a U.S circuit judge for the District of Columbia Circuit. Motion agreed to 52-48: R 51-1; D 1-45; I 0-2. Nov. 27, 2017.

283. KATSAS NOMINATION/CONFIRMATION. Confirmation of President Donald Trump's nomination of Gregory G. Katsas of Virginia to be a U.S circuit judge for the District of Columbia Circuit. Confirmed 50-48: R 49-1; D 1-45; I 0-2. Nov. 28, 2017.

284. HR 1. TAX OVERHAUL/MOTION TO PROCEED. McConnell, R-Ky., motion to proceed to the bill that would revise the federal income tax system by: lowering individual and corporate tax rates; consolidating the current seven tax income rates into four rates; eliminating the deduction for state and local income taxes; limiting certain deductions for property taxes and home mortgages; and creating a new system of taxing U.S. corporations with foreign subsidiaries. Motion agreed to 52-48: R 52-0; D 0-46; I 0-2. Nov. 29, 2017.

285. HR 1. TAX OVERHAUL/COMMIT. Wyden, D-Ore., motion to commit the bill to the Senate Finance Committee with instructions to report it back in three days with changes that would be under the jurisdiction of the committee and would eliminate any provisions "that would raise taxes on millions of middle-class taxpayers." Motion rejected 48-51: R 0-51; D 46-0; I 2-0. Nov. 29, 2017.

	279	280	281	282	283	284	285
ALABAMA							
Shelby	Y	Y	Y	Y	Y	Y	N
Strange	Y	Y	Y	Y	Y	Y	N
ALASKA							
Murkowski	Y	Y	Y	Y	Y	Y	N
Sullivan	Y	Y	Y	Y	Y	Y	N
ARIZONA							
McCain	Y	?	Y	Y	?	Y	?
Flake	Y	Y	Y	Y	Y	Y	N
ARKANSAS							
Boozman	Y	Y	Y	Y	Y	Y	N
Cotton	Y	Y	Y	Y	Y	Y	N
CALIFORNIA							
Feinstein	Y	Y	Y	N	N	N	Y
Harris	Y	Y	Y	N	N	N	Y
COLORADO							
Bennet	Y	Y	Y	N	N	N	Y
Gardner	Y	Y	Y	Y	Y	Y	N
CONNECTICUT							
Blumenthal	Y	Y	Y	N	N	N	Y
Murphy	Y	Y	Y	N	N	N	Y
DELAWARE							
Carper	Y	Y	Y	N	N	N	Y
Coons	Y	Y	Y	N	N	N	Y
FLORIDA							
Nelson	Y	Y	Y	N	N	N	Y
Rubio	Y	Y	Y	Y	Y	Y	N
GEORGIA							
Isakson	Y	Y	Y	Y	Y	Y	N
Perdue	Y	Y	Y	Y	Y	Y	N
HAWAII							
Schatz	Y	Y	Y	N	N	N	Y
Hirono	N	Y	Y	N	N	N	Y
IDAHO							
Crapo	Y	Y	Y	Y	Y	Y	N
Risch	Y	Y	Y	Y	Y	Y	N
ILLINOIS							
Durbin	Y	Y	Y	N	N	N	Y
Duckworth	Y	Y	Y	N	N	N	Y
INDIANA							
Donnelly	Y	Y	Y	N	N	N	Y
Young	Y	Y	Y	Y	Y	Y	N
IOWA							
Grassley	Y	Y	Y	Y	Y	Y	N
Ernst	Y	Y	Y	Y	Y	Y	N
KANSAS							
Roberts	Y	Y	Y	Y	Y	Y	N
Moran	Y	Y	Y	Y	Y	Y	N
KENTUCKY							
McConnell	Y	Y	Y	Y	Y	Y	N
Paul	Y	Y	Y	Y	Y	Y	N
LOUISIANA							
Cassidy	Y	Y	Y	Y	Y	Y	N
Kennedy	N	Y	Y	N	N	N	Y
MAINE							
Collins	Y	Y	Y	Y	Y	Y	N
King	Y	Y	Y	N	N	N	Y
MARYLAND							
Cardin	Y	Y	Y	N	N	N	Y
Van Hollen	Y	Y	Y	N	N	N	Y
MASSACHUSETTS							
Warren	N	Y	N	N	N	N	Y
Markey	Y	Y	N	N	N	N	Y
MICHIGAN							
Stabenow	Y	Y	Y	N	N	N	Y
Peters	Y	Y	Y	N	N	N	Y
MINNESOTA							
Klobuchar	Y	Y	Y	N	N	N	Y
Franken	?	?	Y	N	N	N	Y
MISSISSIPPI							
Cochran	Y	Y	Y	Y	Y	Y	N
Wicker	Y	Y	Y	Y	Y	Y	N
MISSOURI							
McCaskill	Y	Y	Y	N	N	N	Y
Blunt	Y	Y	Y	Y	Y	Y	N

	279	280	281	282	283	284	285
MONTANA							
Tester	Y	Y	Y	N	N	N	Y
Daines	Y	Y	Y	Y	Y	Y	N
NEBRASKA							
Fischer	Y	Y	Y	Y	Y	Y	N
Sasse	Y	Y	Y	Y	Y	Y	N
NEVADA							
Heller	Y	Y	Y	Y	Y	Y	N
Cortez Masto	Y	Y	Y	N	N	N	Y
NEW HAMPSHIRE							
Shaheen	Y	Y	Y	N	N	N	Y
Hassan	Y	Y	Y	N	N	N	Y
NEW JERSEY							
Menendez	+	+	Y	N	N	N	Y
Booker	+	+	Y	N	N	N	Y
NEW MEXICO							
Udall	Y	Y	Y	N	N	N	Y
Heinrich	Y	Y	Y	N	N	N	Y
NEW YORK							
Schumer	Y	Y	Y	N	N	N	Y
Gillibrand	N	Y	N	N	N	N	Y
NORTH CAROLINA							
Burr	Y	Y	Y	Y	Y	Y	N
Tillis	Y	Y	Y	Y	Y	Y	N
NORTH DAKOTA							
Hoeven	Y	Y	Y	Y	Y	Y	N
Heitkamp	Y	Y	Y	N	N	N	Y
OHIO							
Brown	Y	Y	Y	N	N	N	Y
Portman	Y	Y	Y	Y	Y	Y	N
OKLAHOMA							
Inhofe	Y	Y	Y	Y	Y	Y	N
Lankford	Y	Y	Y	Y	Y	Y	N
OREGON							
Wyden	Y	Y	Y	N	N	N	Y
Merkley	Y	Y	Y	N	N	N	Y
PENNSYLVANIA							
Casey	Y	Y	Y	N	N	N	Y
Toomey	Y	Y	Y	Y	Y	Y	N
RHODE ISLAND							
Reed	Y	Y	Y	N	N	N	Y
Whitehouse	Y	Y	Y	N	N	N	Y
SOUTH CAROLINA							
Graham	Y	Y	Y	Y	Y	Y	N
Scott	Y	Y	Y	Y	Y	Y	N
SOUTH DAKOTA							
Thune	Y	Y	Y	Y	Y	Y	N
Rounds	Y	Y	Y	Y	Y	Y	N
TENNESSEE							
Alexander	Y	Y	Y	Y	Y	Y	N
Corker	Y	Y	Y	Y	?	Y	N
TEXAS							
Cornyn	Y	Y	Y	Y	Y	Y	N
Cruz	Y	Y	Y	Y	Y	Y	N
UTAH							
Hatch	Y	Y	Y	Y	Y	Y	N
Lee	Y	Y	Y	Y	Y	Y	N
VERMONT							
Leahy	Y	Y	Y	N	N	N	Y
Sanders	Y	Y	Y	N	N	N	Y
VIRGINIA							
Warner	Y	Y	Y	N	N	N	Y
Kaine	Y	Y	Y	N	N	N	Y
WASHINGTON							
Murray	Y	Y	Y	N	N	N	Y
Cantwell	Y	Y	Y	N	N	N	Y
WEST VIRGINIA							
Manchin	Y	Y	Y	Y	Y	N	Y
Capito	Y	Y	Y	Y	Y	Y	N
WISCONSIN							
Johnson	Y	Y	Y	Y	Y	Y	N
Baldwin	Y	Y	Y	N	N	N	Y
WYOMING							
Enzi	Y	Y	Y	Y	Y	Y	N
Barrasso	Y	Y	Y	Y	Y	Y	N

VOTE NUMBER

286. HR 1. TAX OVERHAUL/COMMIT. Brown, D-Ohio, motion to commit the bill to the Senate Finance Committee. Motion rejected 48-52: R 0-52; D 46-0; I 2-0. Nov. 30, 2017.

287. HR 1. TAX OVERHAUL/COMMIT. Casey, D-Pa., motion to commit the bill to the Senate Finance Committee with instructions to report it back in three days with changes related to employee wages. Motion rejected 48-51: R 0-51; D 46-0; I 2-0. Nov. 30, 2017.

288. HR 1. TAX OVERHAUL/COMMIT. King, I-Maine, motion to commit the bill to the Senate Finance Committee with instructions to report it back to the Senate in three days with changes that are within the jurisdiction of the committee and would ensure that the bill would not increase the deficit for the period of fiscal 2018 through fiscal 2027. Motion rejected 48-52: R 0-52; D 46-0; I 2-0. Nov. 30, 2017.

289. HR 1. TAX OVERHAUL/COMMIT. Stabenow, D-Mich., motion to commit the bill to the Senate Finance Committee with instructions to report it back in three days with changes to the bill that would revert the corporate tax rates to 35 percent in the event that real average household wages do not increase by at least $4,000 by 2020. Motion rejected 45-55: R 0-52; D 43-3; I 2-0. Nov. 30, 2017.

290. HR 1. TAX OVERHAUL/COMMIT. Wyden, D-Ore., for Nelson, D-Fla., motion to commit the bill to the Senate Finance Committee with instructions to report it back to the Senate in three days with changes that would be within the jurisdiction of the committee and and would "provide permanent tax relief for middle-class Americans in a deficit-neutral way.". Motion rejected 48-52: R 0-52; D 46-0; I 2-0. Dec. 1, 2017.

291. HR 1. TAX OVERHAUL/COMMIT. Baldwin, D-Wis., motion to commit the bill to the Senate Finance Committee with instructions to report it back to the Senate in three days with changes that would be within the jurisdiction of the committee and would "support the president's plan to close the carried interest loophole." Motion rejected 48-52: R 0-52; D 46-0; I 2-0. Dec. 1, 2017.

292. HR 1. TAX OVERHAUL/COMMIT. Cardin, D-Md., motion to commit the bill to the Senate Finance Committee with instructions to report it back in three days with changes to the bill that are in the jurisdiction of the committee and would "designate the revenue raised by the deemed repatriation provisions of the bill for infrastructure improvements." Motion rejected 43-57: R 0-52; D 42-4; I 1-1. Dec. 1, 2017.

	286	287	288	289	290	291	292
ALABAMA							
Shelby	N	N	N	N	N	N	N
Strange	N	N	N	N	N	N	N
ALASKA							
Murkowski	N	N	N	N	N	N	N
Sullivan	N	N	N	N	N	N	N
ARIZONA							
McCain	N	?	N	N	N	N	N
Flake	N	N	N	N	N	N	N
ARKANSAS							
Boozman	N	N	N	N	N	N	N
Cotton	N	N	N	N	N	N	N
CALIFORNIA							
Feinstein	Y	Y	Y	Y	Y	Y	Y
Harris	Y	Y	Y	Y	Y	Y	Y
COLORADO							
Bennet	Y	Y	Y	Y	Y	Y	Y
Gardner	N	N	N	N	N	N	N
CONNECTICUT							
Blumenthal	Y	Y	Y	Y	Y	Y	Y
Murphy	Y	Y	Y	Y	Y	Y	Y
DELAWARE							
Carper	Y	Y	Y	Y	Y	Y	Y
Coons	Y	Y	Y	Y	Y	Y	Y
FLORIDA							
Nelson	Y	Y	Y	Y	Y	Y	Y
Rubio	N	N	N	N	N	N	N
GEORGIA							
Isakson	N	N	N	N	N	N	N
Perdue	N	N	N	N	N	N	N
HAWAII							
Schatz	Y	Y	Y	Y	Y	Y	Y
Hirono	Y	Y	Y	Y	Y	Y	Y
IDAHO							
Crapo	N	N	N	N	N	N	N
Risch	N	N	N	N	N	N	N
ILLINOIS							
Durbin	Y	Y	Y	Y	Y	Y	Y
Duckworth	Y	Y	Y	Y	Y	Y	Y
INDIANA							
Donnelly	Y	Y	Y	N	Y	Y	Y
Young	N	N	N	N	N	N	N
IOWA							
Grassley	N	N	N	N	N	N	N
Ernst	N	N	N	N	N	N	N
KANSAS							
Roberts	N	N	N	N	N	N	N
Moran	N	N	N	N	N	N	N
KENTUCKY							
McConnell	N	N	N	N	N	N	N
Paul	N	N	N	N	N	N	N
LOUISIANA							
Cassidy	N	N	N	N	N	N	N
Kennedy	N	N	N	N	N	N	N
MAINE							
Collins	N	N	N	N	N	N	N
King	Y	Y	Y	Y	Y	Y	Y
MARYLAND							
Cardin	Y	Y	Y	Y	Y	Y	Y
Van Hollen	Y	Y	Y	Y	Y	Y	Y
MASSACHUSETTS							
Warren	Y	Y	Y	Y	Y	Y	N
Markey	Y	Y	Y	Y	Y	Y	Y
MICHIGAN							
Stabenow	Y	Y	Y	Y	Y	Y	Y
Peters	Y	Y	Y	Y	Y	Y	Y
MINNESOTA							
Klobuchar	Y	Y	Y	Y	Y	Y	Y
Franken	Y	Y	Y	Y	Y	Y	Y
MISSISSIPPI							
Cochran	N	N	N	N	N	N	N
Wicker	N	N	N	N	N	N	N
MISSOURI							
McCaskill	Y	Y	Y	Y	Y	Y	Y
Blunt	N	N	N	N	N	N	N

	286	287	288	289	290	291	292
MONTANA							
Tester	Y	Y	Y	Y	Y	Y	Y
Daines	N	N	N	N	N	N	N
NEBRASKA							
Fischer	N	N	N	N	N	N	N
Sasse	N	N	N	N	N	N	N
NEVADA							
Heller	N	N	N	N	N	N	N
Cortez Masto	Y	Y	Y	Y	Y	Y	Y
NEW HAMPSHIRE							
Shaheen	Y	Y	Y	Y	Y	Y	Y
Hassan	Y	Y	Y	Y	Y	Y	Y
NEW JERSEY							
Menendez	Y	Y	Y	Y	Y	Y	Y
Booker	Y	Y	Y	Y	Y	Y	N
NEW MEXICO							
Udall	Y	Y	Y	Y	Y	Y	Y
Heinrich	Y	Y	Y	Y	Y	Y	Y
NEW YORK							
Schumer	Y	Y	Y	Y	Y	Y	Y
Gillibrand	Y	Y	Y	Y	Y	Y	N
NORTH CAROLINA							
Burr	N	N	N	N	N	N	N
Tillis	N	N	N	N	N	N	N
NORTH DAKOTA							
Hoeven	N	N	N	N	N	N	N
Heitkamp	Y	Y	Y	N	Y	Y	Y
OHIO							
Brown	Y	Y	Y	Y	Y	Y	Y
Portman	N	N	N	N	N	N	N
OKLAHOMA							
Inhofe	N	N	N	N	N	N	N
Lankford	N	N	N	N	N	N	N
OREGON							
Wyden	Y	Y	Y	Y	Y	Y	Y
Merkley	Y	Y	Y	Y	Y	Y	N
PENNSYLVANIA							
Casey	Y	Y	Y	Y	Y	Y	Y
Toomey	N	N	N	N	N	N	N
RHODE ISLAND							
Reed	Y	Y	Y	Y	Y	Y	Y
Whitehouse	Y	Y	Y	Y	Y	Y	Y
SOUTH CAROLINA							
Graham	N	N	N	N	N	N	N
Scott	N	N	N	N	N	N	N
SOUTH DAKOTA							
Thune	N	N	N	N	N	N	N
Rounds	N	N	N	N	N	N	N
TENNESSEE							
Alexander	N	N	N	N	N	N	N
Corker	N	N	N	N	N	N	N
TEXAS							
Cornyn	N	N	N	N	N	N	N
Cruz	N	N	N	N	N	N	N
UTAH							
Hatch	N	N	N	N	N	N	N
Lee	N	N	N	N	N	N	N
VERMONT							
Leahy	Y	Y	Y	Y	Y	Y	Y
Sanders	Y	Y	Y	Y	Y	Y	N
VIRGINIA							
Warner	Y	Y	Y	Y	Y	Y	Y
Kaine	Y	Y	Y	Y	Y	Y	Y
WASHINGTON							
Murray	Y	Y	Y	Y	Y	Y	Y
Cantwell	Y	Y	Y	Y	Y	Y	Y
WEST VIRGINIA							
Manchin	Y	Y	Y	N	Y	Y	Y
Capito	N	N	N	N	N	N	N
WISCONSIN							
Johnson	N	N	N	N	N	N	N
Baldwin	Y	Y	Y	Y	Y	Y	Y
WYOMING							
Enzi	N	N	N	N	N	N	N
Barrasso	N	N	N	N	N	N	N

KEY	**Republicans**	Democrats	*Independents*

Y Voted for (yea)	**X** Paired against	**C** Voted "present" to avoid possible conflict of interest
# Paired for	**–** Announced against	
+ Announced for	**P** Voted "present"	**?** Did not vote or otherwise make a position known
N Voted against (nay)		

VOTE NUMBER

293. PROCEDURAL MOTION/MOTION TO ADJOURN. Schumer, D-N.Y., motion to adjourn until noon on Monday, Dec. 4, 2017. Motion rejected 48-52: R 0-52; D 46-0; I 2-0. Dec. 1, 2017.

294. HR 1. TAX OVERHAUL/MOTION TO WAIVE. Sanders, I-Vt., motion to waive all applicable sections of the Congressional Budget Act with respect to the Enzi, R-Wyo., point of order that the Sanders amendment no. 1720 to the McConnell, R-Ky., for Hatch, R-Utah, amendment no. 1618 violates section 313(b)(1)(a) of the Congressional Budget Act. The amendment would create a 60-vote point of order against any reconciliation legislation that would result in a reduction in guaranteed Social Security or Medicare benefits, would increase the early or full retirement age for Social Security benefits, would privatize Social Security, or would result in a reduction of Medicare benefits. Motion rejected 46-54: R 1-51; D 43-3; I 2-0. Dec. 1, 2017.

295. HR 1. TAX OVERHAUL/MOTION TO WAIVE. Brown, D-Ohio, motion to waive all applicable sections of the Congressional Budget Act with respect to the Enzi, R-Wyo., point of order that the Brown amendment no. 1854 to the McConnell, R-Ky., for Hatch, R-Utah, substitute amendment no. 1618 violates section 302(f) of the Congressional Budget Act. The amendment would increase the refundable child tax credit to $2,000 for children over the age of six and $2,500 for children under the age of six. Motion rejected 48-52: R 0-52; D 46-0; I 2-0. Dec. 1, 2017.

296. HR 1. TAX OVERHAUL/MOTION TO WAIVE. Rubio, R-Fla., motion to waive all applicable sections of the Congressional Budget Act with respect to the Wyden, D-Ore., point of order that the Rubio amendment no. 1850 to the McConnell R-Ky., for Hatch, R-Utah., substitute amendment no. 1618 violates section 302(f) of the Congressional Budget Act. The amendment would modify the child tax credit and modify the corporate tax rate. Motion rejected 29-71: R 20-32; D 8-38; I 1-1. Dec. 1, 2017.

297. HR 1. TAX OVERHAUL/COMMIT. Menendez, D-N.J., motion to commit the bill to the Senate Finance Committee with instructions to report it back in three days with changes that would be in the jurisdiction of the committee and that would eliminate the bill's repeal of the state and local tax deduction if various services would be reduced or if certain taxes would be increased. Motion rejected 48-52: R 0-52; D 46-0; I 2-0. Dec. 1, 2017.

298. HR 1. TAX OVERHAUL/EDUCATION SAVINGS ACCOUNTS. Cornyn, R-Texas, for Cruz, R-Texas, amendment no. 1852 to the McConnell, R-Ky., for Hatch, R-Utah, substitute amendment no. 1618, that would allow tuition expenses or the cost of school supplies for secondary public, private or religious school to be treated the same as higher education expenses for certain tax purposes. Adopted, with Vice President Pence casting a "yea" vote to break the tie, 50-50: R 50-2; D 0-46; I 0-2. Dec. 1, 2017.

299. HR 1. TAX OVERHAUL/MOTION TO WAIVE. Kaine, D-Va., motion to waive all applicable sections of the Congressional Budget Act and any applicable budget resolutions with respect to the Toomey, R-Pa, point of order that the Cornyn, R-Texas, for Kaine, D-Va., amendment no. 1846 to the McConnell, R-Ky., for Hatch, R-Utah, substitute amendment no. 1618 violates section 4105 of the fiscal 2018 budget resolution. The amendment would permanently adjust certain individual tax rates and would increase the corporate tax rate to 25 percent. Motion rejected 34-65: R 0-52; D 33-12; I 1-1. Dec. 2, 2017.

	293	294	295	296	297	298	299
ALABAMA							
Shelby	N	N	N	N	N	Y	N
Strange	N	N	N	N	N	Y	N
ALASKA							
Murkowski	N	N	N	Y	N	N	N
Sullivan	N	N	N	Y	N	Y	N
ARIZONA							
McCain	N	N	N	N	N	Y	N
Flake	N	N	N	N	N	Y	N
ARKANSAS							
Boozman	N	N	N	N	N	Y	N
Cotton	N	N	N	Y	N	Y	N
CALIFORNIA							
Feinstein	Y	Y	Y	N	Y	N	Y
Harris	Y	Y	Y	N	Y	N	N
COLORADO							
Bennet	Y	Y	Y	N	Y	N	Y
Gardner	N	N	N	Y	N	Y	N
CONNECTICUT							
Blumenthal	Y	Y	Y	N	Y	N	Y
Murphy	Y	Y	Y	N	Y	N	N
DELAWARE							
Carper	Y	N	Y	N	Y	N	Y
Coons	Y	Y	Y	N	Y	N	Y
FLORIDA							
Nelson	Y	Y	Y	Y	Y	N	Y
Rubio	N	N	N	Y	N	Y	N
GEORGIA							
Isakson	N	N	N	N	N	Y	N
Perdue	N	N	N	N	N	Y	N
HAWAII							
Schatz	Y	Y	Y	N	Y	N	Y
Hirono	Y	Y	Y	N	Y	N	N
IDAHO							
Crapo	N	N	N	Y	N	Y	N
Risch	N	N	N	Y	N	Y	N
ILLINOIS							
Durbin	Y	N	Y	N	Y	N	N
Duckworth	Y	Y	Y	N	Y	N	Y
INDIANA							
Donnelly	Y	Y	Y	Y	Y	N	Y
Young	N	N	N	N	N	Y	N
IOWA							
Grassley	N	N	N	N	N	Y	N
Ernst	N	N	N	Y	N	Y	N
KANSAS							
Roberts	N	N	N	N	N	Y	N
Moran	N	N	N	Y	N	Y	N
KENTUCKY							
McConnell	N	N	N	N	N	Y	N
Paul	N	N	N	N	N	Y	N
LOUISIANA							
Cassidy	N	N	N	Y	N	Y	N
Kennedy	N	N	N	Y	N	Y	N
MAINE							
Collins	N	Y	N	N	N	N	N
King	Y	Y	Y	Y	Y	N	Y
MARYLAND							
Cardin	Y	Y	Y	N	Y	N	Y
Van Hollen	Y	Y	Y	N	Y	N	Y
MASSACHUSETTS							
Warren	Y	Y	Y	N	N	N	N
Markey	Y	Y	Y	N	Y	N	N
MICHIGAN							
Stabenow	Y	Y	Y	Y	Y	N	Y
Peters	Y	Y	Y	Y	Y	N	Y
MINNESOTA							
Klobuchar	Y	Y	Y	Y	Y	N	Y
Franken	Y	Y	Y	N	Y	N	Y
MISSISSIPPI							
Cochran	N	N	N	N	N	Y	N
Wicker	N	N	N	N	N	Y	N
MISSOURI							
McCaskill	Y	Y	Y	Y	Y	N	Y
Blunt	N	N	N	Y	N	Y	N

	293	294	295	296	297	298	299
MONTANA							
Tester	Y	Y	Y	N	Y	N	N
Daines	N	N	N	N	N	Y	N
NEBRASKA							
Fischer	N	N	N	Y	N	Y	N
Sasse	N	N	N	Y	N	Y	N
NEVADA							
Heller	N	N	N	Y	N	Y	N
Cortez Masto	Y	Y	Y	N	Y	N	N
NEW HAMPSHIRE							
Shaheen	Y	Y	Y	N	Y	N	Y
Hassan	Y	Y	Y	N	Y	N	Y
NEW JERSEY							
Menendez	Y	Y	Y	N	Y	N	Y
Booker	Y	Y	Y	N	Y	N	N
NEW MEXICO							
Udall	Y	Y	Y	N	Y	N	Y
Heinrich	Y	Y	Y	N	Y	N	Y
NEW YORK							
Schumer	Y	Y	Y	N	Y	N	N
Gillibrand	Y	Y	Y	N	Y	N	N
NORTH CAROLINA							
Burr	N	N	N	N	N	Y	N
Tillis	N	N	N	N	N	Y	N
NORTH DAKOTA							
Hoeven	N	N	N	Y	N	Y	N
Heitkamp	Y	Y	Y	Y	Y	N	?
OHIO							
Brown	Y	Y	Y	N	Y	N	Y
Portman	N	N	N	N	N	Y	N
OKLAHOMA							
Inhofe	N	N	N	N	N	Y	N
Lankford	N	N	N	N	N	Y	N
OREGON							
Wyden	Y	Y	Y	N	Y	N	Y
Merkley	Y	Y	Y	N	Y	N	Y
PENNSYLVANIA							
Casey	Y	Y	Y	N	Y	N	Y
Toomey	N	N	N	N	N	Y	N
RHODE ISLAND							
Reed	Y	Y	Y	N	Y	N	Y
Whitehouse	Y	Y	Y	N	Y	N	Y
SOUTH CAROLINA							
Graham	N	N	N	N	N	Y	N
Scott	N	N	N	N	N	Y	N
SOUTH DAKOTA							
Thune	N	N	N	N	N	Y	N
Rounds	N	N	N	N	N	Y	N
TENNESSEE							
Alexander	N	N	N	N	N	Y	N
Corker	N	N	N	N	N	Y	N
TEXAS							
Cornyn	N	N	N	Y	N	Y	N
Cruz	N	N	N	Y	N	Y	N
UTAH							
Hatch	N	N	N	N	N	Y	N
Lee	N	N	N	Y	N	Y	N
VERMONT							
Leahy	Y	Y	Y	N	Y	N	Y
Sanders	Y	Y	Y	N	Y	N	N
VIRGINIA							
Warner	Y	N	Y	N	Y	N	Y
Kaine	Y	Y	Y	N	Y	N	Y
WASHINGTON							
Murray	Y	Y	Y	N	Y	N	Y
Cantwell	Y	Y	Y	N	Y	N	Y
WEST VIRGINIA							
Manchin	Y	Y	Y	N	Y	N	Y
Capito	N	N	N	Y	N	Y	N
WISCONSIN							
Johnson	N	N	N	N	N	Y	N
Baldwin	Y	Y	Y	N	Y	N	Y
WYOMING							
Enzi	N	N	N	N	N	Y	N
Barrasso	N	N	N	N	N	Y	N

KEY **Republicans** Democrats *Independents*

Y Voted for (yea)	X Paired against	C Voted "present" to avoid possible conflict of interest
# Paired for	– Announced against	
+ Announced for	P Voted "present"	? Did not vote or otherwise make a position known
N Voted against (nay)		

VOTE NUMBER

300. HR 1. TAX OVERHAUL/COMMIT. Manchin, D-W.Va., motion to commit the bill to the Senate Finance Committee with instructions to report it back in three days with changes related to making certain tax cuts permanent. Motion rejected 38-61: R 0-52; D 37-8; I 1-1. Dec. 2, 2017.

301. HR 1. TAX OVERHAUL/MOTION TO WAIVE. Cantwell, D-Wash., motion to waive all applicable sections of the Congressional Budget Act with respect to the Murkowski, R-Alaska, point of order that the Cantwell amendment no. 1717 to the McConnell, R-Ky., for Hatch, R-Utah, substitute amendment no. 1618 violates section 302(f) of the Congressional Budget Act. The amendment would remove the provisions of the bill that would open the Arctic National Wildlife Refuge to oil and gas drilling. Motion rejected 48-52: R 1-51; D 45-1; I 2-0. Dec. 2, 2017.

302. HR 1. TAX OVERHAUL/UNIVERSITY ENDOWMENT TAX. Merkley, D-Ore., amendment no. 1856 to the McConnell, for Hatch, substitute amendment no. 1618 that would remove the provision in the bill that would exempt higher education institutions that opt out of receiving federal funding from a tax on university endowments. Adopted 52-48: R 4-48; D 46-0; I 2-0. Dec. 2, 2017.

303. HR 1. TAX OVERHAUL/PASSAGE. Passage of the bill, as amended, that would revise the federal income tax system by lowering individual and corporate tax rates, repealing various deductions through 2025, specifically by eliminating the deduction for state and local income taxes through 2025, increasing the deduction for pass-through entities and raising the child tax credit through 2025. It would also open parts of the Arctic National Wildlife Refuge to oil and gas drilling. Passed 51-49: R 51-1; D 0-46; I 0-2. Dec. 2, 2017.

304. NIELSEN NOMINATION/CLOTURE. Motion to invoke cloture (thus limiting debate) on the nomination of Kirstjen Nielsen of Virginia to be secretary of Homeland Security. Motion agreed to 59-33: R 48-0; D 10-33; I 1-0. 43073.

305. NIELSEN NOMINATION/CONFIRMATION. Confirmation of President Donald Trump's nomination of Kirstjen Nielsen of Virginia to be secretary of Homeland Security. Confirmed 62-37: R 51-0; D 10-36; I 1-1. 43074.

306. HR 1. TAX OVERHAUL/MOTION TO REQUEST CONFERENCE. McConnell, R-Ky., motion that the Senate insist on its amendment to the bill, agree to the request from the House for a conference, and appoint conferees on the bill that would revise the federal income tax system. Motion agreed to 51-47: R 51-0; D 0-45; I 0-2.

	300	301	302	303	304	305	306
ALABAMA							
Shelby	N	N	N	Y	Y	Y	Y
Strange	N	N	N	Y	Y	Y	Y
ALASKA							
Murkowski	N	N	Y	Y	Y	Y	Y
Sullivan	N	N	N	Y	Y	Y	Y
ARIZONA							
McCain	N	N	N	Y	Y	Y	Y
Flake	N	N	N	Y	Y	Y	Y
ARKANSAS							
Boozman	N	N	N	Y	Y	Y	Y
Cotton	N	N	N	Y	Y	Y	Y
CALIFORNIA							
Feinstein	Y	Y	Y	N	N	N	N
Harris	N	Y	Y	N	N	N	N
COLORADO							
Bennet	Y	Y	Y	N	N	N	N
Gardner	N	N	N	Y	Y	Y	Y
CONNECTICUT							
Blumenthal	Y	Y	Y	N	N	N	N
Murphy	Y	Y	Y	N	N	N	N
DELAWARE							
Carper	Y	Y	Y	N	Y	Y	N
Coons	Y	Y	Y	N	Y	Y	N
FLORIDA							
Nelson	Y	Y	Y	N	Y	Y	N
Rubio	N	N	N	Y	Y	Y	Y
GEORGIA							
Isakson	N	N	N	Y	Y	Y	Y
Perdue	N	N	N	Y	Y	Y	Y
HAWAII							
Schatz	Y	Y	Y	N	N	N	N
Hirono	N	Y	Y	N	N	N	N
IDAHO							
Crapo	N	N	N	Y	Y	Y	Y
Risch	N	N	N	Y	Y	Y	Y
ILLINOIS							
Durbin	N	Y	Y	N	N	N	N
Duckworth	Y	Y	Y	N	N	N	N
INDIANA							
Donnelly	Y	Y	Y	N	Y	Y	N
Young	N	N	N	Y	Y	Y	Y
IOWA							
Grassley	N	N	N	Y	Y	Y	Y
Ernst	N	N	N	Y	Y	Y	Y
KANSAS							
Roberts	N	N	N	Y	Y	Y	Y
Moran	N	N	N	Y	Y	Y	Y
KENTUCKY							
McConnell	N	N	N	Y	Y	Y	Y
Paul	N	N	N	Y	Y	Y	Y
LOUISIANA							
Cassidy	N	N	N	Y	Y	Y	Y
Kennedy	N	N	Y	Y	Y	Y	Y
MAINE							
Collins	N	Y	Y	Y	Y	Y	Y
King	Y	Y	Y	N	Y	Y	N
MARYLAND							
Cardin	Y	Y	Y	N	N	N	N
Van Hollen	Y	Y	Y	N	N	N	N
MASSACHUSETTS							
Warren	N	Y	Y	N	N	N	N
Markey	N	Y	Y	N	N	N	N
MICHIGAN							
Stabenow	Y	Y	Y	N	N	N	N
Peters	Y	Y	Y	N	N	N	N
MINNESOTA							
Klobuchar	Y	Y	Y	N	?	N	N
Franken	Y	Y	Y	N	N	N	?
MISSISSIPPI							
Cochran	N	N	N	Y	Y	Y	Y
Wicker	N	N	N	Y	Y	Y	Y
MISSOURI							
McCaskill	Y	Y	Y	N	Y	Y	N
Blunt	N	N	N	Y	Y	Y	Y

	300	301	302	303	304	305	306
MONTANA							
Tester	Y	Y	Y	N	Y	Y	N
Daines	N	N	N	Y	Y	Y	N
NEBRASKA							
Fischer	N	N	Y	Y	Y	Y	Y
Sasse	N	N	N	Y	Y	Y	Y
NEVADA							
Heller	N	N	N	Y	Y	Y	Y
Cortez Masto	N	Y	Y	N	N	N	N
NEW HAMPSHIRE							
Shaheen	Y	Y	Y	N	N	N	N
Hassan	Y	Y	Y	N	N	N	N
NEW JERSEY							
Menendez	Y	Y	Y	N	N	N	N
Booker	N	Y	Y	N	N	N	N
NEW MEXICO							
Udall	Y	Y	Y	N	N	N	N
Heinrich	Y	Y	Y	N	N	N	N
NEW YORK							
Schumer	Y	Y	Y	N	N	N	N
Gillibrand	N	Y	Y	N	N	N	N
NORTH CAROLINA							
Burr	N	N	N	Y	Y	Y	Y
Tillis	N	N	N	Y	Y	Y	Y
NORTH DAKOTA							
Hoeven	N	N	N	Y	Y	Y	Y
Heitkamp	Y	Y	Y	N	Y	Y	N
OHIO							
Brown	Y	Y	Y	N	N	N	N
Portman	N	N	N	Y	Y	Y	Y
OKLAHOMA							
Inhofe	N	N	N	Y	Y	Y	Y
Lankford	N	N	N	Y	Y	Y	Y
OREGON							
Wyden	Y	Y	Y	N	?	N	N
Merkley	Y	Y	Y	N	?	N	N
PENNSYLVANIA							
Casey	Y	Y	Y	N	N	N	N
Toomey	N	N	N	Y	Y	Y	Y
RHODE ISLAND							
Reed	Y	Y	Y	N	Y	Y	N
Whitehouse	?	Y	Y	N	N	N	N
SOUTH CAROLINA							
Graham	N	N	N	Y	?	Y	Y
Scott	N	N	N	Y	Y	Y	Y
SOUTH DAKOTA							
Thune	N	N	N	Y	Y	Y	Y
Rounds	N	N	N	Y	Y	Y	Y
TENNESSEE							
Alexander	N	N	N	Y	Y	+	+
Corker	N	N	N	N	?	Y	Y
TEXAS							
Cornyn	N	N	N	Y	Y	Y	Y
Cruz	N	N	N	Y	Y	Y	Y
UTAH							
Hatch	N	N	N	Y	?	Y	Y
Lee	N	N	N	Y	?	Y	Y
VERMONT							
Leahy	Y	Y	Y	N	N	N	N
Sanders	N	Y	Y	N	?	N	N
VIRGINIA							
Warner	Y	Y	Y	N	Y	Y	N
Kaine	Y	Y	Y	N	N	N	N
WASHINGTON							
Murray	Y	Y	Y	N	N	N	N
Cantwell	Y	Y	Y	N	N	N	N
WEST VIRGINIA							
Manchin	Y	N	Y	N	Y	Y	N
Capito	N	N	N	Y	Y	Y	Y
WISCONSIN							
Johnson	N	N	N	Y	Y	Y	Y
Baldwin	Y	Y	Y	N	N	N	N
WYOMING							
Enzi	N	N	N	Y	Y	Y	Y
Barrasso	N	N	N	Y	Y	Y	Y

KEY	**Republicans**	Democrats	*Independents*
Y Voted for (yea)		**X** Paired against	**C** Voted "present" to avoid possible conflict of interest
# Paired for		**–** Announced against	
+ Announced for		**P** Voted "present"	**?** Did not vote or otherwise make a position known
N Voted against (nay)			

VOTE NUMBER

307. HR 1. TAX OVERHAUL/MOTION TO INSTRUCT. King, I-Maine, motion to instruct the Senate managers to insist that the final conference report for the bill include language that would ensure that it would not increase the federal budget deficit for the period of fiscal 2018 through fiscal 2027. Motion rejected 48-50: R 1-50; D 45-0; I 2-0. Dec. 6, 2017.

308. HR 1. TAX OVERHAUL/MOTION TO INSTRUCT. Stabenow, D-Mich., motion to instruct the Senate managers to insist that the final conference report for the bill include language related to reverting the corporate tax rates to 35 percent in the event that average household wages do not increase. Motion rejected 44-54: R 0-51; D 42-3; I 2-0. Dec. 6, 2017.

309. HR 1. TAX OVERHAUL/MOTION TO INSTRUCT. Booker, D-N.J., motion to instruct the Senate managers to insist that the final conference report for the bill would not contain any provisions that would increase the number of individuals that do not have health insurance or increase health insurance premiums. Motion rejected 47-51: R 0-51; D 45-0; I 2-0. Dec. 6, 2017.

310. BALASH NOMINATION/CONFIRMATION. Confirmation of President Donald Trump's nomination of Joseph Balash of Alaska to be an assistant secretary of the Interior. Confirmed 61-38: R 52-0; D 8-37; I 1-1. Dec. 7, 2017.

311. H J RES 123. SHORT-TERM FISCAL 2018 CONTINUING APPROPRIATIONS/PASSAGE. Passage of the joint resolution that would provide funding for federal government operations and services at current levels through Dec. 22, 2017, at an annualized rate of $1.23 trillion for federal departments and agencies covered by the 12 unfinished fiscal 2018 spending bills, of which an annualized rate of $621.5 billion would be designated for defense and an annualized rate of $511 billion for nondefense discretionary spending. The bill would allow state Children's Health and Insurance Programs to receive extra redistribution funds beyond what is currently allowed, supporting the program's operations through the end of December. Passed (thus cleared for the president) 81-14: R 42-6; D 38-7; I 1-1. Dec. 7, 2017.

312. GRASZ NOMINATION/CLOTURE. Motion to invoke cloture (thus limiting debate) on the nomination of Leonard S. Grasz of Nebraska to be U.S. circuit judge for the Eighth Circuit. Motion agreed to 48-47: R 48-0; D 0-45; I 0-2. Dec. 11, 2017.

313. GRASZ NOMINATION/CONFIRMATION. Confirmation of President Donald Trump's nomination of Leonard S. Grasz of Nebraska to be U.S. circuit judge for the Eighth Circuit. Confirmed 50-48: R 50-0; D 0-46; I 0-2. Dec. 12, 2017.

	307	308	309	310	311	312	313
ALABAMA							
Shelby	N	N	N	Y	Y	Y	Y
Strange	N	N	N	Y	Y	Y	Y
ALASKA							
Murkowski	N	N	N	Y	Y	Y	Y
Sullivan	N	N	N	Y	Y	Y	Y
ARIZONA							
McCain	N	N	N	Y	N	?	?
Flake	N	N	N	Y	?	Y	Y
ARKANSAS							
Boozman	N	N	N	Y	Y	Y	Y
Cotton	N	N	N	Y	Y	Y	Y
CALIFORNIA							
Feinstein	Y	Y	Y	N	Y	N	N
Harris	Y	Y	Y	N	N	N	N
COLORADO							
Bennet	Y	Y	Y	N	Y	N	N
Gardner	N	N	N	Y	Y	Y	Y
CONNECTICUT							
Blumenthal	Y	Y	Y	N	Y	N	N
Murphy	Y	Y	Y	N	N	N	N
DELAWARE							
Carper	Y	Y	Y	Y	Y	N	N
Coons	Y	Y	Y	Y	Y	N	N
FLORIDA							
Nelson	Y	Y	Y	N	Y	N	N
Rubio	N	N	N	Y	Y	+	Y
GEORGIA							
Isakson	N	N	N	Y	Y	Y	Y
Perdue	N	N	N	Y	Y	Y	Y
HAWAII							
Schatz	Y	Y	Y	Y	Y	?	N
Hirono	Y	Y	Y	N	N	N	N
IDAHO							
Crapo	N	N	N	Y	?	Y	Y
Risch	N	N	N	Y	Y	Y	Y
ILLINOIS							
Durbin	Y	Y	Y	N	Y	N	N
Duckworth	Y	Y	Y	N	Y	N	N
INDIANA							
Donnelly	Y	N	Y	Y	Y	N	N
Young	N	N	N	Y	Y	Y	Y
IOWA							
Grassley	N	N	N	Y	Y	Y	Y
Ernst	N	N	N	Y	N	Y	Y
KANSAS							
Roberts	N	N	N	Y	Y	Y	Y
Moran	N	N	N	Y	Y	Y	Y
KENTUCKY							
McConnell	N	N	N	Y	Y	Y	Y
Paul	N	N	N	Y	?	Y	Y
LOUISIANA							
Cassidy	N	N	N	Y	Y	Y	Y
Kennedy	N	N	N	Y	Y	Y	Y
MAINE							
Collins	N	N	N	Y	Y	Y	Y
King	Y	Y	Y	Y	Y	N	N
MARYLAND							
Cardin	Y	Y	Y	N	Y	N	N
Van Hollen	Y	Y	Y	N	Y	N	N
MASSACHUSETTS							
Warren	Y	Y	Y	N	N	N	N
Markey	Y	Y	Y	N	N	N	N
MICHIGAN							
Stabenow	Y	Y	Y	N	Y	N	N
Peters	Y	Y	Y	N	Y	N	N
MINNESOTA							
Klobuchar	Y	Y	Y	N	Y	N	N
Franken	—	?	?	?	N	N	N
MISSISSIPPI							
Cochran	N	N	N	Y	Y	?	?
Wicker	N	N	N	Y	Y	Y	Y
MISSOURI							
McCaskill	Y	Y	Y	Y	Y	N	N
Blunt	N	N	N	Y	Y	?	Y

	307	308	309	310	311	312	313
MONTANA							
Tester	Y	Y	Y	N	Y	N	N
Daines	N	N	N	Y	Y	Y	Y
NEBRASKA							
Fischer	N	N	N	Y	Y	Y	Y
Sasse	N	N	N	Y	N	Y	Y
NEVADA							
Heller	N	N	N	Y	Y	Y	Y
Cortez Masto	Y	Y	Y	N	Y	N	N
NEW HAMPSHIRE							
Shaheen	Y	Y	Y	N	Y	N	N
Hassan	Y	Y	Y	N	Y	N	N
NEW JERSEY							
Menendez	Y	Y	Y	N	Y	N	N
Booker	Y	Y	Y	N	N	N	N
NEW MEXICO							
Udall	Y	Y	Y	N	Y	N	N
Heinrich	Y	Y	Y	N	Y	N	N
NEW YORK							
Schumer	Y	Y	Y	N	Y	N	N
Gillibrand	Y	Y	Y	N	N	N	N
NORTH CAROLINA							
Burr	N	N	N	Y	Y	Y	Y
Tillis	N	N	N	Y	Y	Y	Y
NORTH DAKOTA							
Hoeven	N	N	N	Y	Y	Y	Y
Heitkamp	Y	N	Y	Y	Y	N	N
OHIO							
Brown	Y	Y	Y	N	Y	N	N
Portman	N	N	N	Y	Y	Y	Y
OKLAHOMA							
Inhofe	N	N	N	Y	Y	Y	Y
Lankford	N	N	N	Y	Y	Y	Y
OREGON							
Wyden	Y	Y	Y	N	Y	N	N
Merkley	Y	Y	Y	N	N	N	N
PENNSYLVANIA							
Casey	Y	Y	Y	N	Y	N	N
Toomey	N	N	N	Y	+	Y	Y
RHODE ISLAND							
Reed	Y	Y	Y	N	Y	N	N
Whitehouse	Y	Y	Y	N	Y	N	N
SOUTH CAROLINA							
Graham	N	N	N	Y	Y	Y	Y
Scott	N	N	N	Y	Y	Y	Y
SOUTH DAKOTA							
Thune	N	N	N	Y	Y	Y	Y
Rounds	N	N	N	Y	N	Y	Y
TENNESSEE							
Alexander	—	—	—	Y	Y	Y	Y
Corker	Y	N	N	Y	Y	Y	Y
TEXAS							
Cornyn	N	N	N	Y	Y	Y	Y
Cruz	N	N	N	Y	N	Y	Y
UTAH							
Hatch	N	N	N	Y	Y	Y	Y
Lee	N	N	N	Y	N	Y	Y
VERMONT							
Leahy	Y	Y	Y	N	Y	N	N
Sanders	Y	Y	Y	N	N	N	N
VIRGINIA							
Warner	Y	Y	Y	Y	Y	N	N
Kaine	Y	Y	Y	N	Y	N	N
WASHINGTON							
Murray	Y	Y	Y	N	Y	N	N
Cantwell	Y	Y	Y	N	Y	N	N
WEST VIRGINIA							
Manchin	Y	N	Y	Y	Y	N	N
Capito	N	N	N	Y	Y	Y	Y
WISCONSIN							
Johnson	N	N	N	Y	Y	Y	Y
Baldwin	Y	Y	Y	N	Y	N	N
WYOMING							
Enzi	N	N	N	Y	Y	Y	Y
Barrasso	N	N	N	Y	Y	Y	Y

KEY	**Republicans**	Democrats	*Independents*
Y Voted for (yea)		X Paired against	C Voted "present" to avoid possible conflict of interest
# Paired for		– Announced against	
+ Announced for		P Voted "present"	? Did not vote or otherwise make a position known
N Voted against (nay)			

VOTE NUMBER

314. WILLETT NOMINATION/CLOTURE. Motion to invoke cloture (thus limiting debate) on the nomination of Don R. Willett of Texas to be a U.S. circuit judge for the Fifth Circuit. Motion agreed to 50-48: R 50-0; D 0-46; I 0-2. Dec. 12, 2017.

315. WILLETT NOMINATION/CONFIRMATION. Confirmation of President Donald Trump's nomination of Don R. Willett of Texas to be a U.S. circuit judge for the Fifth Circuit. Confirmed 50-47: R 50-0; D 0-45; I 0-2. Dec. 13, 2017.

316. HO NOMINATION/CLOTURE. Motion to invoke cloture (thus limiting debate) on the nomination of James C. Ho of Texas to be a U.S. circuit judge for the Fifth Circuit. Motion agreed to 53-44: R 50-0; D 3-42; I 0-2. Dec. 13, 2017.

317. HO NOMINATION/CONFIRMATION. Confirmation of President Donald Trump's nomination of James C. Ho of Texas to be U.S. circuit judge for the Fifth Circuit. Confirmed 53-43: R 50-0; D 3-41; I 0-2. Dec. 14, 2017.

318. COMPTON NOMINATION/CONFIRMATION. Confirmation of President Donald Trump's nomination of J. Paul Compton Jr. of Alabama to be general counsel of the Department of Housing and Urban Development. Confirmed 62-34: R 50-0; D 11-33; I 1-1. Dec. 18, 2017.

319. WEST NOMINATION/CONFIRMATION. Confirmation of President Donald Trump's nomination of Owen West of Connecticut to be an assistant secretary of Defense. Confirmed 74-23: R 51-0; D 22-22; I 1-1. Dec. 18, 2017.

320. NEWSTEAD NOMINATION/CONFIRMATION. Confirmation of President Donald Trump's nomination of Jennifer G. Newstead of New York to be a legal adviser for the State Department. Confirmed 88-11: R 50-1; D 37-9; I 1-1. Dec. 19, 2017.

	314	315	316	317	318	319	320
ALABAMA							
Shelby	Y	Y	Y	Y	Y	Y	Y
Strange	Y	Y	Y	Y	Y	Y	Y
ALASKA							
Murkowski	Y	Y	Y	Y	Y	Y	Y
Sullivan	Y	Y	Y	Y	Y	Y	Y
ARIZONA							
McCain	?	?	?	?	?	?	?
Flake	Y	Y	Y	Y	Y	Y	Y
ARKANSAS							
Boozman	Y	Y	Y	Y	Y	Y	Y
Cotton	Y	Y	Y	Y	Y	Y	Y
CALIFORNIA							
Feinstein	N	N	N	N	N	Y	Y
Harris	N	N	N	N	N	N	N
COLORADO							
Bennet	N	N	N	N	Y	Y	Y
Gardner	Y	Y	Y	Y	Y	Y	Y
CONNECTICUT							
Blumenthal	N	N	N	N	N	Y	Y
Murphy	N	N	N	N	Y	Y	Y
DELAWARE							
Carper	N	N	N	N	Y	Y	Y
Coons	N	N	N	N	Y	Y	Y
FLORIDA							
Nelson	N	N	N	N	Y	Y	Y
Rubio	Y	Y	Y	Y	Y	Y	Y
GEORGIA							
Isakson	Y	Y	Y	Y	Y	Y	Y
Perdue	Y	Y	Y	Y	Y	Y	Y
HAWAII							
Schatz	N	N	N	N	N	N	N
Hirono	N	N	N	N	N	N	Y
IDAHO							
Crapo	Y	Y	Y	Y	Y	Y	Y
Risch	Y	Y	Y	Y	Y	Y	Y
ILLINOIS							
Durbin	N	N	N	N	N	N	Y
Duckworth	N	N	N	N	?	?	Y
INDIANA							
Donnelly	N	N	Y	Y	Y	Y	Y
Young	Y	Y	Y	Y	Y	Y	Y
IOWA							
Grassley	Y	Y	Y	Y	Y	Y	Y
Ernst	Y	Y	Y	Y	Y	Y	Y
KANSAS							
Roberts	Y	Y	Y	Y	Y	Y	Y
Moran	Y	Y	Y	Y	Y	Y	Y
KENTUCKY							
McConnell	Y	Y	Y	Y	Y	Y	Y
Paul	Y	Y	Y	Y	Y	Y	N
LOUISIANA							
Cassidy	Y	Y	Y	Y	Y	Y	Y
Kennedy	Y	Y	Y	Y	Y	Y	Y
MAINE							
Collins	Y	Y	Y	Y	Y	Y	Y
King	N	N	N	N	Y	Y	Y
MARYLAND							
Cardin	N	N	N	N	N	Y	Y
Van Hollen	N	N	N	N	N	N	Y
MASSACHUSETTS							
Warren	N	N	N	N	N	N	N
Markey	N	N	N	N	N	N	N
MICHIGAN							
Stabenow	N	N	N	N	N	N	Y
Peters	N	N	N	N	N	N	Y
MINNESOTA							
Klobuchar	N	N	N	N	N	N	Y
Franken	N	N	N	N	N	N	N
MISSISSIPPI							
Cochran	?	?	?	?	Y	Y	Y
Wicker	Y	Y	Y	Y	Y	Y	Y
MISSOURI							
McCaskill	N	N	Y	Y	Y	Y	Y
Blunt	Y	Y	Y	Y	Y	Y	Y

	314	315	316	317	318	319	320
MONTANA							
Tester	N	N	N	N	Y	Y	Y
Daines	Y	Y	Y	Y	Y	Y	Y
NEBRASKA							
Fischer	Y	Y	Y	Y	Y	Y	Y
Sasse	Y	Y	Y	Y	Y	Y	Y
NEVADA							
Heller	Y	Y	Y	Y	Y	Y	Y
Cortez Masto	N	N	N	N	N	N	Y
NEW HAMPSHIRE							
Shaheen	N	N	N	N	Y	Y	Y
Hassan	N	N	N	N	N	Y	Y
NEW JERSEY							
Menendez	N	N	N	N	N	N	Y
Booker	N	N	N	N	N	N	Y
NEW MEXICO							
Udall	N	N	N	N	Y	Y	Y
Heinrich	N	N	N	N	N	Y	N
NEW YORK							
Schumer	N	N	N	N	N	N	Y
Gillibrand	N	N	N	N	N	N	N
NORTH CAROLINA							
Burr	Y	Y	Y	Y	Y	Y	Y
Tillis	Y	Y	Y	Y	Y	Y	Y
NORTH DAKOTA							
Hoeven	Y	Y	Y	Y	Y	Y	Y
Heitkamp	N	N	Y	Y	Y	Y	Y
OHIO							
Brown	N	N	N	N	N	N	N
Portman	Y	Y	Y	Y	Y	Y	Y
OKLAHOMA							
Inhofe	Y	Y	Y	Y	Y	Y	Y
Lankford	Y	Y	Y	Y	Y	Y	Y
OREGON							
Wyden	N	N	N	N	N	N	N
Merkley	N	N	N	N	N	N	N
PENNSYLVANIA							
Casey	N	N	N	N	N	N	Y
Toomey	Y	Y	Y	Y	Y	Y	Y
RHODE ISLAND							
Reed	N	N	N	N	N	Y	Y
Whitehouse	N	N	N	N	N	Y	Y
SOUTH CAROLINA							
Graham	Y	Y	Y	Y	Y	Y	Y
Scott	Y	Y	Y	Y	Y	Y	Y
SOUTH DAKOTA							
Thune	Y	Y	Y	Y	Y	Y	Y
Rounds	Y	Y	Y	Y	Y	Y	Y
TENNESSEE							
Alexander	Y	Y	Y	Y	Y	Y	Y
Corker	Y	Y	Y	Y	Y	Y	Y
TEXAS							
Cornyn	Y	Y	Y	Y	Y	Y	Y
Cruz	Y	Y	Y	Y	Y	Y	Y
UTAH							
Hatch	Y	Y	Y	Y	Y	Y	Y
Lee	Y	Y	Y	Y	Y	Y	Y
VERMONT							
Leahy	N	N	N	N	N	Y	Y
Sanders	N	N	N	N	N	N	N
VIRGINIA							
Warner	N	N	N	N	N	Y	Y
Kaine	N	N	N	N	N	Y	Y
WASHINGTON							
Murray	N	?	?	?	N	N	Y
Cantwell	N	N	N	N	N	Y	Y
WEST VIRGINIA							
Manchin	N	N	N	?	Y	Y	Y
Capito	Y	Y	Y	Y	?	Y	Y
WISCONSIN							
Johnson	Y	Y	Y	Y	Y	Y	Y
Baldwin	N	N	N	N	?	?	Y
WYOMING							
Enzi	Y	Y	Y	Y	Y	Y	Y
Barrasso	Y	Y	Y	Y	Y	Y	Y

KEY   **Republicans**   Democrats   *Independents*

Y Voted for (yea)	**X** Paired against
# Paired for	**–** Announced against
+ Announced for	**P** Voted "present"
N Voted against (nay)	

C Voted "present" to avoid possible conflict of interest

? Did not vote or otherwise make a position known

VOTE NUMBER

321. HR 1. TAX OVERHAUL/MOTION TO PROCEED. McConnell, R-Ky., motion to proceed to consideration of the conference report to accompany the bill. It would revise the federal income tax system by: lowering the corporate tax rate from 35 percent to 21 percent; lowering individual tax rates through 2025; limiting state and local deductions to $10,000 through 2025; decreasing the limit on deductible mortgage debt through 2025; and creating a new system of taxing U.S. corporations with foreign subsidiaries. Specifically, it would repeal personal exemptions and would roughly double the standard deduction through 2025. The bill would raise the child tax credit to $2,000 through 2025, would repeal the alternative minimum tax for corporations and provide for broader exemptions to the tax for individuals through 2025. It would double individual exemptions to the estate tax and gift tax through 2025, and would establish a new top tax rate for "pass-through" business income through 2025. The bill would effectively eliminate the penalty for not purchasing health insurance under the 2010 health care overhaul law in 2019. It would also open portions of the Arctic National Wildlife Refuge to oil and gas drilling. Motion agreed to 51-48: R 51-0; D 0-46; I 0-2. Dec. 19, 2017.

322. HR 1. TAX OVERHAUL/MOTION TO WAIVE. Enzi, R-Wyo., motion to waive all applicable sections of the Congressional Budget Act of 1974 and any applicable budget resolutions with respect to the following Sanders, I-Vt., points of order regarding the conference report to accompany the bill: that Section 110032(a), from page 75, line 17 to page 76, line 9 of the conference report violates Section 313(b)(1)(D) of the Congressional Budget Act; that Section 11000(a) violates section 313(b)(1)(A) of the Congressional Budget Act; and that the phrase "tuition paying" as it appears on page 309, line 12 and page 309, lines 14-15, both violate Section 313(b)(1)(D) of the Congressional Budget Act. Motion rejected 51-48: R 51-0; D 0-46; I 0-2. Dec. 20, 2017.

323. HR 1. TAX OVERHAUL/MOTION TO RECEDE AND CONCUR. McConnell, R-Ky., motion that the Senate recede from its amendment and concur in the bill with a further amendment. The bill would revise the federal income tax system by lowering the corporate tax rate from 35 percent to 21 percent; lowering individual tax rates through 2025; limiting state and local deductions to $10,000 through 2025; decreasing the limit on deductible mortgage debt through 2025; and creating a new system of taxing U.S. corporations with foreign subsidiaries. Specifically, it would repeal personal exemptions and would roughly double the standard deduction through 2025. It would raise the child tax credit to $2,000 through 2025, would repeal the alternative minimum tax for corporations and provide for broader exemptions to the tax for individuals through 2025. It would double individual exemptions to the estate tax and gift tax through 2025, and would establish a new top tax rate for "pass-through" business income through 2025. Motion agreed to 51-48: R 51-0; D 0-46; I 0-2. Dec. 20, 2017.

324. HR 1370. SHORT-TERM FISCAL 2018 CONTINUING APPROPRIATIONS/MOTION TO WAIVE. Collins, R-Maine, motion to waive all applicable sections of the Congressional Budget Act of 1974 and any applicable budget resolutions with respect to the Paul, R-Ky., point of order that the "pay-as-you-go" waiver provision in the House amendment to the Senate amendment to the bill violates Section 306 of the Congressional Budget Act. Motion agreed to 91-8: R 43-8; D 46-0; I 2-0. Dec. 21, 2017.

325. HR 1370. SHORT-TERM FISCAL 2018 CONTINUING APPROPRIATIONS/MOTION TO CONCUR. McConnell, R-Ky., motion to concur in the House amendment to the Senate amendment to the bill that would provide funding for federal government operations and services at current levels through Jan. 19, 2018. The bill, as amended, would authorize $2.1 billion for the Veterans Choice Program, $2.9 billion in mandatory funding for the Children's Health Insurance Program and $550 million in funding to Community Health Centers through March 31. The bill would exempt funding provided to the Children's Health Insurance Fund and other health programs, as well as the tax overhaul package, from statutory pay-as-you-go requirements. It would provide $4.7 billion in emergency supplemental funds for missile defense and Navy ship repairs. It would also extend authorities under the Foreign Intelligence Surveillance Act through Jan. 19, including FISA Section 702, which allows U.S. intelligence agencies to obtain data from electronic service providers or non-U.S. persons who reside outside the U.S. Motion agreed to 66-32: R 48-2; D 17-29; I 1-1. Dec. 21, 2017.

	321	322	323	324	325		321	322	323	324	325
ALABAMA						**MONTANA**					
Shelby	Y	Y	Y	Y	Y	Tester	N	N	N	Y	Y
Strange	Y	Y	Y	Y	Y	**Daines**	Y	Y	Y	Y	Y
ALASKA						**NEBRASKA**					
Murkowski	Y	Y	Y	Y	Y	**Fischer**	Y	Y	Y	Y	Y
Sullivan	Y	Y	Y	Y	Y	**Sasse**	Y	Y	Y	N	Y
ARIZONA						**NEVADA**					
McCain	?	?	+	?	?	**Heller**	Y	Y	Y	Y	Y
Flake	Y	Y	Y	N	Y	Cortez Masto	N	N	N	Y	N
ARKANSAS						**NEW HAMPSHIRE**					
Boozman	Y	Y	Y	Y	Y	Shaheen	N	N	N	Y	Y
Cotton	Y	Y	Y	Y	Y	Hassan	N	N	N	Y	Y
CALIFORNIA						**NEW JERSEY**					
Feinstein	N	N	N	Y	N	Menendez	N	N	N	Y	N
Harris	N	N	N	Y	N	Booker	N	N	N	Y	N
COLORADO						**NEW MEXICO**					
Bennet	N	N	N	Y	N	Udall	N	N	N	Y	Y
Gardner	Y	Y	Y	Y	Y	Heinrich	N	N	N	Y	Y
CONNECTICUT						**NEW YORK**					
Blumenthal	N	N	N	Y	N	Schumer	N	N	N	Y	N
Murphy	N	N	N	Y	N	Gillibrand	N	N	N	Y	N
DELAWARE						**NORTH CAROLINA**					
Carper	N	N	N	Y	Y	Burr	Y	Y	Y	Y	Y
Coons	N	N	N	Y	Y	**Tillis**	Y	Y	Y	Y	Y
FLORIDA						**NORTH DAKOTA**					
Nelson	N	N	N	Y	Y	Hoeven	Y	Y	Y	Y	Y
Rubio	Y	Y	Y	Y	Y	Heitkamp	N	N	N	Y	Y
GEORGIA						**OHIO**					
Isakson	Y	Y	Y	Y	?	Brown	N	N	N	Y	N
Perdue	Y	Y	Y	Y	Y	Portman	Y	Y	Y	Y	Y
HAWAII						**OKLAHOMA**					
Schatz	N	N	N	Y	N	**Inhofe**	Y	Y	Y	Y	Y
Hirono	N	N	N	Y	N	**Lankford**	Y	Y	Y	Y	Y
IDAHO						**OREGON**					
Crapo	Y	Y	Y	N	Y	Wyden	N	N	N	Y	N
Risch	Y	Y	Y	N	Y	Merkley	N	N	N	Y	N
ILLINOIS						**PENNSYLVANIA**					
Durbin	N	N	N	Y	N	Casey	N	N	N	Y	N
Duckworth	N	N	N	Y	N	**Toomey**	Y	Y	Y	Y	Y
INDIANA						**RHODE ISLAND**					
Donnelly	N	N	N	Y	Y	Reed	N	N	N	Y	N
Young	Y	Y	Y	Y	Y	Whitehouse	N	N	N	Y	N
IOWA						**SOUTH CAROLINA**					
Grassley	Y	Y	Y	Y	Y	**Graham**	Y	Y	Y	Y	Y
Ernst	Y	Y	Y	Y	Y	**Scott**	Y	Y	Y	Y	Y
KANSAS						**SOUTH DAKOTA**					
Roberts	Y	Y	Y	Y	Y	**Thune**	Y	Y	Y	Y	Y
Moran	Y	Y	Y	Y	Y	**Rounds**	Y	Y	Y	Y	Y
KENTUCKY						**TENNESSEE**					
McConnell	Y	Y	Y	Y	Y	**Alexander**	Y	Y	Y	Y	Y
Paul	Y	Y	N	N	N	**Corker**	Y	Y	Y	Y	Y
LOUISIANA						**TEXAS**					
Cassidy	Y	Y	Y	Y	Y	**Cornyn**	Y	Y	Y	Y	Y
Kennedy	Y	Y	Y	N	Y	**Cruz**	Y	Y	Y	N	Y
MAINE						**UTAH**					
Collins	Y	Y	Y	Y	Y	**Hatch**	Y	Y	Y	Y	Y
King	N	N	N	Y	Y	**Lee**	Y	Y	Y	N	N
MARYLAND						**VERMONT**					
Cardin	N	N	N	Y	N	Leahy	N	N	N	Y	Y
Van Hollen	N	N	N	Y	N	*Sanders*	N	N	N	Y	N
MASSACHUSETTS						**VIRGINIA**					
Warren	N	N	N	Y	N	Warner	N	N	N	Y	Y
Markey	N	N	N	Y	N	Kaine	N	N	N	Y	Y
MICHIGAN						**WASHINGTON**					
Stabenow	N	N	N	Y	Y	Murray	N	N	N	Y	N
Peters	N	N	N	Y	Y	Cantwell	N	N	N	Y	N
MINNESOTA						**WEST VIRGINIA**					
Klobuchar	N	N	N	Y	N	Manchin	N	N	N	Y	Y
Franken	N	N	N	Y	N	**Capito**	Y	Y	Y	Y	Y
MISSISSIPPI						**WISCONSIN**					
Cochran	Y	Y	Y	Y	Y	**Johnson**	Y	Y	Y	Y	Y
Wicker	Y	Y	Y	Y	Y	Baldwin	N	N	N	Y	N
MISSOURI						**WYOMING**					
McCaskill	N	N	N	Y	Y	**Enzi**	Y	Y	Y	Y	Y
Blunt	Y	Y	Y	Y	Y	**Barrasso**	Y	Y	Y	Y	Y

KEY	**Republicans**	Democrats	*Independents*
Y Voted for (yea)	X Paired against	C Voted "present" to avoid possible conflict of interest
# Paired for	– Announced against	
+ Announced for	P Voted "present"	? Did not vote or otherwise make a position known
N Voted against (nay)		

Appendix I

GENERAL INDEX

A

A-10 warthog
Authorization, 6–10

Abortion
Late-term, 11–14, C–10
Mexico City policy, 2–42
Regulations, 14–4
Supreme Court cases, 13–6
Unaccompanied illegal immigrant, 13–11

ACLU
Gun restrictions, 13–8
NSA data collection and privacy, 6–17

Acosta, Alexander
Confirmation as Labor secretary, 9–7
Job training, 11–18 to 11–19
Labor-HHS-Education appropriations, 2–37
Wages and salaries, 7–7

Aderholt, Robert B.
Agriculture appropriations, 2–21, 2–22
E-cigarettes, 2–21

Afghanistan
Defense authorization, 6–10

AFL-CIO
Overtime pay, 7–7

Agency for Healthcare Research and Quality
Appropriations, 2–12

Agricultural income and price supports
Appropriations, 2–7, 2–8
Cotton, 2–24

Agricultural Research Service
Appropriations, 2–8, 2–21, 2–23

Agriculture
Appropriations, 2–8
Guest worker visa program, 12–3

Agriculture, Department of
Perdue, Sonny, confirmation as Agriculture Secretary, 9–5

Air pollution
Ozone, 8–8

Airports
Passenger facility charge on airplane tickets, 2–44

Al-Qaida
Authorization for Use of Military Force, 6–11

Alabama
Special election, 5–4 to 5–5

Alaska
ANWR, 4–8, 4–10, 16–6 to 16–7
Hunting and fishing on national wildlife refuges, 14–4
Hunting regulations, 13–7

Alexander, Lamar
Appropriations, 2–6
Education regulations, 11–19
Endangered species, 8–5
Energy research, 2–29
Mixed Oxide Fuel Fabrication Facility, 2–30
NLRB rules, 14–5
Overtime pay, 7–7
Perkins loans, 11–18

Alito, Samuel A.
Free speech, 13–5

Amador, Angelo
Wages and salaries, 7–7

Amash, Justin
Budget resolution, 4–7
Health care law, 11–4
Hurricane Harvey, 2–18
Medical malpractice, 11–17

American Bankers Association
Debt limit, 4–4
Flood insurance, 7–6
Mandatory arbitration clauses in consumer contracts, 3–6

American Bar Association
Grasz, Steve, judicial confirmation, C-6

American Civil Liberties Union. *See* ACLU

American Federation of Government Employees
Federal employees, 7–4

American Gaming Association
Sports betting, 13–7

American Indians and Alaska natives
NLRB rulings, 7–8
Washington Redskins, 13–5

American Legislative Exchange Council
Balanced Budget Amendment, 4–11

American Medical Association
Medical malpractice, 11–17

American Sports Betting Coalition
Sports betting, 13–7

Amodei, Mark
Horse slaughter, 2–23

Animal Plant and Health Inspection Service. *See* APHIS

ANWR
Oil and gas exploration, 4–8, 4–10, 8–3, 8–9, 16–4, 16–6 to 16–7, 16–12

APHIS
Appropriations, 2–22

Appropriations
2018 Minibus, 2–17
2018 Omnibus, 2–17 to 2–20
2017 Omnibus overview, 2–5 to 2–6
2017 Omnibus winners and losers, 2–7
Agriculture
FY 2017, 2–8
FY 2018, 2–21 to 2–24
Commerce-Justice-Science
FY 2017, 2–8 to 2–9
FY 20178, 2–25 to 2–27
Defense
FY 2017, 2–10 to 2–11
FY 2018, 2–17, 2–27 to 2–28
Disaster Supplemental
FY 2017, 2–45, C–6, C–10
Enactment timing history (chart), 2–4
Energy-Water
FY 2017, 2–11
FY 2018, 2–17, 2–29 to 2–30
Financial Services
FY 2017, 2–12
FY 2018, 2–31 to 2–32
FY 2018 Continuing resolutions, 2–18, 2–19
Homeland Security
FY 2017, 2–13
FY 2018, 2–32 to 2–33
Interior-Environment
FY 2017, 2–13

Customs and Border Protection
Appropriations, 2–13

Cybersecurity
Appropriations, 2–13, 2–26
Defense authorization, 6–4
Kaspersky Lab, 6–9
Legislation, 15–4 to 15–6
Sanctions, 10–3

D

DACA
Budget negotiations, 4–5
Effort to end, 1–4, 1–6, 9–4
Legislative history, 12–4
Map, 12–6

Daines, Steve
Medical marijuana, 2–40
Tax overhaul, 16–12

Debt limit
Extension, 2–18
Suspension bill, 4–4 to 4–5

DeFazio, Peter
FAA reauthorization, 17–4, 17–5, 17–6

Defense
Appropriations, 2–7, 2–10 to 2–11
Authorization, 6–3 to 6–11
Authorization for Use of Military Force, 2–27, 6–7, 6–11
Budget negotiations, 4–5
Military readiness, 6–4, 6–14
Spending caps, 4–5

Defense, Department of
Mattis, James, confirmation as Defense Secretary, 9–5

Defense Intelligence Agency
Intelligence reauthorization, 6–18

Defense Science Board
Nuclear disarmament, 6–12

Deferred Action for Childhood Arrivals. *See* DACA

Delaney, John
Artificial intelligence, 15–8

DeLauro, Rosa
Job training, 11–19
Labor-HHS-Education appropriations, 2–35

Denham, Jeff
Health care law, 11–5

Dent, Charlie
Abortion, 11–14
Budget resolution, 4–7
Changes in ethics procedures, 5–14 to 5–15
Health care law, 11–4
Military Construction appropriations, 2–39
Veterans Affairs appropriations, 2–39

DeVos, Betsy
Confirmation as Education secretary, 9–5 to 9–6, C–3
Education regulations, 11–19

Diaz-Balart, Mario
Transportation-HUD appropriations, 2–43 to 2–44
Trump infrastructure plan, 17–4

District of Columbia
Appropriations, 2–12, 2–32

Dodd, Chris
Financial regulation, 3–5

Donnelly, Joe
Coal regulations, 8–4
Gorsuch, Neil, confirmation as Supreme Court justice, 13–4
Methane venting on federal land, 8–7
North Korea, 6–9
Tax cuts, 16–8

Donovan, Shaun
Budget resolution, 4–6

Dubke, Mike
White House tenure, 9–3

Duckworth, Tammy
Urban planning, 14–5

Duffy, Sean P.
Flood insurance, 7–5

Duncan, Jeff
Gun silencers, 13–7

Durbin, Richard J.
Cigars, 2–24
DACA, 12–4
Gorsuch, Neil, confirmation as Supreme Court justice, 13–4

E

E-Trade Financial Corp.
Retirement advice, 3–7

Earmarks
Ban, 5–14 to 5–15

Economic Development Administration
Appropriations, 2–8

Education
Appropriations, 2–36 to 2–37
GI Bill, 6–20
Pell grants, 2–6, 2–14, 2–35, 2–37
Perkins loans, 11–18
Regulations, 11–19
School choice, 2–37
School vouchers, 2–14
Student loans, 2–14
Teacher training evaluation and school performance, 14–3 to 14–4

Education, Department of
Appropriations, 2–14, 2–37
DeVos, Betsy, confirmation as Education secretary, 9–5 to 9–6, C–3

Egypt
Military aid, 2–42

Election Assistance Commission
Appropriations, 2–31

Embassies
U.S.embassy in Israel relocated to Jerusalem, C–5

Employment and unemployment
Career education for unemployed, 2–37
Drug testing for unemployment benefits, 14–4
Job training, 11–18 to 11–19

Endangered species
Appropriations, 2–13.8–3, 8–4 to 8–5
Grey wolf, 13–7

Energy
ANWR oil and gas extraction, 4–8, 8–3, 8–9, 16–4
Appropriations, 2–11, 2–29 to 2–30
ARPA-E program, 2–29
Keystone XL pipeline, 4–8, 8–3, 16–4
Mixed Oxide Fuel Fabrication Facility, 2–30
Russian power plants, 2–11

Appropriations process, 2–17

Authorization for Use of Military Force, 6–12

Coal regulations, 8–4

Debt limit, 4–4

Gorsuch, Neil, confirmation as Supreme Court justice, 13–4

Greenhouse gas emissions from coal, 8–3

Health care for retired miners, 2–9, 2–14

Health care law, 1–3

Health care law repeal, 11–4, 11–6, 16–10

Hurricane Harvey, 2–18

Methane venting on federal land, 8–7

Sessions, Jeff, confirmation as attorney general, 9–7

Supreme Court Senate confirmation rules, 5–13

Tax reform, 16–7

Warren, Elisabeth, ordered to sit down, C–3 to C–4

McGehee, Meredith

Soft money, 13–7

McKinley, David B.

Brownfields, 8–9

Health care for retired miners, 2–9

Miners' retirement and pensions, 7–9

McMaster, H.R.

Authorization for Use of Military Force, 6–12

McMorris Rodgers, Cathy

Energy legislation, 8–5

Meadows, Mark

Appropriations, 2–7

Debt limit, 4–5

Health care law, 11–6

Medicaid

Abortion, 11–14

Health care law, 11–3, 11–4 to 11–5, 11–8 to 11–11

Payments to hospitals, 11–11, 11–12

Puerto Rico, 2–6, 2–7

Support to states, 11–9

U.S. citizenship requirement, 11–13

Work requirements, 11–12

Medicare

Health care law, 11–3

Prescription drugs, 4–7

Meeks, Gregory W.

Financial regulation, 3–4

Members of Congress

Security for members' residences, 2–38

Menendez, Robert

Corruption allegations, 5–13

Flood insurance, 7–5 to 7–6

Haley, Nikki, confirmation as United Nations ambassador, 9–8

Manning, Chelsea, prison sentence commutation, 13–11

State Department restructuring, 10–4

Mental health

Appropriations, 2–36

Merkley, Jeff

Agriculture appropriations, 2–23, 2–24

Asset forfeiture, 13–12

Climate change, 2–42

Defense authorization, 6–9

Gorsuch, Neil, confirmation as Supreme Court justice, 13–4

Mexico

Border adjustment tax, 16–7

Trans-Pacific Partnership, 10–6

Military bases

Defense authorization, 6–4, 6–10

Military personnel issues

Pay raise, 2–7, 2–10, 2–27, 6–4, 6–8, 6–10

Transgender rights, C–9

Tricare authorization, 6–3, 6–8

Troop levels, 2–6, 2–28

Military Reserves

Appropriations, 2–28

Mines and mining

Health care for retired miners, 2–7, 2–9, 2–14, 7–9

Key votes, C–3

Retirement and pensions, 7–9

Missile defense

Appropriations, 2–28

Authorization, 6–3, 6–5, 6–7, 6–10

Mixed Oxide Fuel Fabrication Facility

Appropriations, 2–30

Mnuchin, Steven

Border adjustment tax, 16–5

Confirmation as Treasury secretary, 9–7

Federal financial regulation, 3–3

Tax reform, 16–7

Montana

Balanced Budget Amendment, 4–11

Special elections, 5–7

Moore, Roy

Alabama special election, 5–4 to 5–5

Mortimer, Ed

Trump infrastructure plan, 17–4

Moulton, Seth

Littoral combat ships, 6–7

Mueller, Robert S. III

Russia election interference investigation, 1–4, 1–6, 9–4, 9–10

Mullin, Markwayne

Methane venting on federal land, 8–8

Mulvaney, Mick

Appropriations, 2–6

Appropriations process, 2–17

Border wall, 12–7

CFPB restructuring, 3–8

Confirmation as HHS secretary, 5–3

Confirmation as OMB director, 9–7

Cost of health care law repeal, 4–3

Health care law, 11–4

Skinny budget, 1–4, 9–4

Murkowski, Lisa

ANWR, 8–9, 16–6

DeVos, Betsy, confirmation as Education secretary, 9–6

Energy legislation, 8–5

Genetically-engineered salmon, 2–24

Health care law repeal, 16–10

Horse slaughter, 2–23

Interior appropriations, 2–35

Yucca Mountain, 8–11

Murphy, Christopher S.

Discharged veterans, 2–40

Health care law, 1–4, 11–7

Nuclear first strike, 6–13

State Department restructuring, 10–4

Murphy, Tim

Sexual misconduct allegations, 1–7, 5–3, 5–10

Murray, Patty

DeVos, Betsy, confirmation as Education secretary, 9–6

Education regulations, 11–19

Overtime pay, 7–7

Wild fires, 2–19

Muslim ban
Executive order, 9–3

N

NASA
Appropriations, 2–8 to 2–9, 2–10, 2–25, 2–26
Reauthorization, 15–3

National Airspace System
Appropriations, 2–16

National Defense Restoration Fund
Appropriations, 2–28

National Endowment for the Arts
Appropriations, 2–7, 2–34, 2–35

National Endowment for the Humanities
Appropriations, 2–7, 2–34, 2–35

National flood insurance
Extension, 2–18, 2–45

National Guard
Appropriations, 2–28

National Highway Traffic Safety Administration
Driverless cars, 17–7

National Institute of Family and Life Advocates
Abortion, 13–6

National Institutes of Health. *See* NIH

National Labor Relations Board. *See* NLRB

National Oceanic and Atmospheric Administration. *See* NOAA

National Park Service
Appropriations, 2–13, 2–35
Grand Staircase-Escalante monument, 8–7

National Restaurant Association
Wages and salaries, 7–7

National Rifle Association. *See* NRA

National Science Foundation
Appropriations, 2–26

National Security Council. *See* NSC

National wildlife refuges
Hunting and fishing, 14–4

NATO
Cybersecurity, 6–4

Natural disasters
Hurricane aid, 2–4, 2–45, 4–4, C–6
Wild fires, 2–4, 2–19, 2–35

Neal, Richard E.
Budget resolution, 4–6
Trans-Pacific Partnership, 10–6

Nelson, Bill
FAA reauthorization, 17–5
FEMA, 2–19
Flood insurance, 7–6
Medicare Part D prescription drugs, 4–7, 11–4
NASA reauthorization, 15–3

Nevada
Balanced Budget Amendment, 4–11
Sports betting, 13–7

New Jersey
Sports betting, 13–7

New Mexico
Balanced Budget Amendment, 4–11

New START treaty
Defense authorization, 6–4

New Zealand
Trans-Pacific Partnership, 10–6

Newhouse, Dan
Endangered species, 8–5
H-2A visas, 2–22

Nichols, Rob
Debt limit, 4–4

Nielsen, Kirstjen
Confirmation as Homeland Security secretary, 9–6

NIH
Appropriations, 2–6, 2–14, 2–35

NLRB
Appropriations, 2–37
Joint employer liability, 7–7 to 7–8

NOAA
Appropriations, 2–10, 2–25

Nominations and confirmations
Acosta, Alexander, as Labor secretary, 9–7
Azar, Alex, as HHS secretary, 9–6
Carson, Ben, as HUD secretary, 9–6

Chao, Elaine, as Transportation secretary, 9–7
DeVos, Betsy, as Education secretary, 9–5 to 9–6, C–3
Garland, Merrick, as Supreme Court justice, 13–3
Gorsuch, Neil, as Supreme Court justice, 1–5, 13–3 to 13–4, C–4
Grasz, Steve, as judge, C–6
Haley, Nikki, as United Nations ambassador, 9–8
Kelly, John F., as Homeland Security secretary, 9–6
Lighthizer, Robert E., as U.S.trade representative, 10–5
Mattis, James, as Defense secretary, 9–5
Mnuchin, Steve, as Treasury secretary, 9–7
Mulvaney, Mick, as OMB director, 9–8
Nielsen, Kirsjen., as Homeland Security secretary, 9–6
Otting, Joseph, as Comptroller of the Currency, 3–9
Perdue, Sonny, as Agriculture secretary, 9–5
Perry, Rick, as Energy secretary, 9–5
Pompeo, Mike, as CIA director, 9–8
Powell, Jerome, as Federal Reserve chair, 3–6
Price, Tom, as HHS secretary, 9–6
Pruitt, Scott, as EPA administrator, 9–8
Ross, Wilbur, as Commerce secretary, 9–5
Sessions, Jeff, as attorney general, 9–7
Shulkin, David, as Veterans Affairs secretary, 9–8
Tillerson, Rex, as secretary of State, 9–7
Zinke, Ryan, as Interior secretary, 5–3, 9–6

Norman, Ralph
South Carolina special election, 5–8

North Korea
Defense authorization, 6–3, 6–9
Nuclear disarmament, 6–9, 6–12, 9–4
Nuclear weapons, 9–4
Sanctions, 10–3 to 10–4
Trump position, 1–3 to 1–4

Norton, Eleanor Holmes
School vouchers, 2–14

NRA
Gun restrictions, 13–8

NSA
FISA reauthorization, 6–15

NSC

Nuclear disarmament, 6–12 to 6–13

Treasury Secretary added to council, 10–3

Nuclear weapons

North Korea, 6–9, 6–12, 9–4

Nuclear disarmament, 6–12 to 6–13

Nunes, Devin

Classified information, 5–12

Intelligence reauthorization, 6–18

Russia election interference investigation, 9–10

O

Obama, Barack

Budget negotiations, 4–5

CHIP, 11–15

Debt limit, 4–4

Dodd-Frank financial regulation law, 3–3

Garland, Merrick, nomination as Supreme Court justice, 13–3

Health care law, 11–3

Manning, Chelsea, prison sentence commutation, 13–11

Overtime pay, 7–7

Troop reductions, 2–6

Yucca Mountain, 8–10

Occupational Safety and Health Administration. *See* OSHA

Office of Congressional Ethics

Changes in ethics procedures, 5–14 to 5–15

Office of Fossil Energy

Appropriations, 2–29

Office of Management and Budget. *See* OMB

Office of Renewable Energy and Research

Appropriations, 2–29

Oil and gas industry

Strategic Petroleum Reserve, 16–7

Olson, Pete

Ozone, 8–8

OMB

Defense and border security appropriations offsets, 2–6

Federal employees, 7–3 to 7–4

Mulvaney, Mick, confirmation as OMB director, 9–8

Skinny budget, 9–4

O'Neill, Thomas P. "Tip"

Holman rule, 7–3

Open World Leadership Center

Appropriations, 2–14

Ornstein, Norman J.

Federal employees, 7–3

O'Rourke, Beto

Border wall, 6–6

OSHA

Record maintenance, 14–4

Otting, Joseph

Nomination as Comptroller of the Currency, 3–9

Overseas Contingency Operations

Appropriations, 2–5, 2–6, 2–7, 2–10, 2–27, 2–42

Authorization, 6–7, 6–9

Budget resolution, 4–9

Defense budget negotiations, 4–5

P

Packwood, Bob

Sexual harassment, 5–12

Paddock, Stephen

Gun restrictions, 13–8

Pai, Ajit

FCC reauthorization, 15–7

Rural broadband, 15–5

Palestinian Authority

Economic aid, 2–43

Pallante, Maria

Copyright office, 10–13

Pallone, Frank Jr.

Brownfields, 8–9 to 8–10

Driverless cars, 17–7

FCC reauthorization, 15–7

Papadopoulis, George

Russia interference in U.S. elections, 9–10

Patents and trademarks

Supreme Court cases, 13–5

Paul, Rand

Asset forfeiture, 13–12

Authorization for Use of Military Force, 6–12

Budget resolution, 4–6, 4–7

Defense authorization, 6–9

Health care law, 11–7

Health care law repeal efforts, 1–5, 11–3

Hurricane Harvey, 2–18

Scalise, Steve shooting, 1–6

State Department restructuring, 10–4

Pelosi, Nancy

Changes in ethics procedures, 5–14

DACA, 1–6

Financial regulation, 3–4

Financial Services appropriations, 2–12

FY 2018 Continuing resolutions, 2–19

Health care law, 11–6

Intelligence reauthorization, 6–18

Military Construction-VA appropriations, 2–39

Nuclear first strike, 6–13

Tax reform, 16–8

Pence, Mike

Health care law, 11–6

Mandatory arbitration, 14–4

Mandatory arbitration clauses in consumer contracts, 3–6

Perdue, David

Budget resolution, 4–9

DACA, 12–5

Perdue, Sonny

Agriculture Department reorganization, 2–24

Nomination as Agriculture Secretary, 9–5

Rural issues, 2–23

Perry, Rick

Confirmation as Energy secretary, 9–5

Yucca Mountain, 2–30, 8–10

Perry, Scott

Climate change, 6–7

Personnel issues

Turnover in the Trump administration (chart), 9–9

Peru

Trans-Pacific Partnership, 10–6

Peters, Gary

Driverless cars, 17–6 to 17–7

Peterson, Collin C.

Abortion, 11–14

CFTC reauthorization, 3–9

Endangered species, 8–5

FY 2018 omnibus appropriations, 2–18

Worker protections, 7–8

Phillips, Jack
Gay wedding cakes, 13–6

Pingree, Chellie
Interior appropriations, 2–34

Planned Parenthood
Abortion and immigration, 13–11

Appropriations, 2–5, 2–14, 2–35, 2–37

HHS rule, 14–4

Non-abortion services, 11–8

Poe, Ted
Medical malpractice, 11–17

NSA data collection and privacy, 6–17

Polis, Jared
Worker protections, 7–8

Pompeo, Mike
Confirmation as CIA director, 5–3, 9–8

Health care law, 11–4

Portman, Rob
Education regulations, 11–19

Lighthizer, Robert E., confirmation as USTR, 10–5

Online sex trafficking, 15–7

Poseiden aircraft
Defense authorization, 6–10

Powell, Jerome
Nomination as Federal Reserve chair, 3–6

Prescription drugs
Drugs and medical devices used in defense, 6–3, 6–10

Generic drugs, 13–5

Importation from Canada, 4–7

Medical marijuana, 2–26, 2–40

Medicare, 4–7

Prevention and Public Health Fund
Health bill provisions, 11–9

Price, David E.
ICE agents, 2–33, 11–4

Transportation appropriations, 2–43

Price, Tom
Confirmation as HHS secretary, 5–3, 9–6

Cost of health care law repeal, 4–3

Health care law, 11–4

Priebus, Reince
White House tenure, 9–3

Privacy
FISA reauthorization, 6–15

Internet user data protection, 14–4

Pruitt, Scott
Confirmation as EPA administrator, 9–8

Ozone, 8–8

Waters of the United States, 2–29

Public Citizen
Changes in ethics procedures, 5–14 to 5–15

Public lands
Antiquities Act overhaul, 8–6

Methane venting on federal land, 9–4, 14–4

Puerto Rico
Disaster relief, 2–18, 2–45

Medicaid, 2–6, 2–7

Purdue, Sonny
Agriculture appropriations, 2–8

Q

Quigley, Mike
EPA regional offices, 2–34

GSA appropriations, 2–31

R

Race relations
Trump response to Charlottesville, VA violence, 9–4

Reed, Jack
Authorization for Use of Military Force, 6–12

Transportation-HUD appropriations, 2–44

Regulations
Abortion, 14–4

Bureau of Land Management resource development plans, 14–3

Corporate payments to foreign governments or U.S. government, 14–3

Drug testing for unemployment benefits, 14–4

Education, 11–19

Gun purchases by mentally ill, 14–3

Hunting and fishing on national wildlife refuges in Alaska, 14–4

Internet user data, 14–4

Labor Department, 14–4

Mandatory arbitration, 14–4

Methane venting on federal land, 14–4

REINS Act, 14–5

Stream protection, 14–3

Teacher training evaluation and school performance, 14–3 to 14–4

Urban planning, 14–5

Reichert, Dave
Trans-Pacific Partnership, 10–6

Reid, Harry
Gorsuch, Neil, confirmation as Supreme Court justice, 13–3

Yucca Mountain, 8–10

Republican Study Committee
Earmarks, 4–10

Retirement and pensions
Federal employees, 7–3 to 7–4

Miners, 2–7, 2–9, 2–14, 7–9

Retirement advice, 3–7

Rice, Susan
UAE crown prince meetings, 6–17

Richards, Cecile
Abortion and immigration, 13–11

Roberts, Cecil E.
Miners' retirement and pensions, 7–9

Roberts, John G. Jr.
Gerrymandering, 13–6

Internet use by sex offenders, 13–5

Roberts, Pat
Lighthizer, Robert E., confirmation as USTR, 10–5

Rodriguez, Joanna
DACA, 12–5

Roe, Phil
Independent Payment Advisory Board, 11–16

Medical malpractice, 11–17

Veterans, 6–20

Rogers, Harold
Appropriations process, 2–17

Omnibus appropriations, 2–3

State-Foreign Operations appropriations, 2–41

Rogers, Mike D.
Military readiness, 6–4

Missile defense, 2–7, 2–10, 6–4

Nuclear weapons, 6–13

Space Corps, 6–3, 6–7

Rokita, Todd

NLRB Regulations, 14–5

NLRB rulings, 7–8

Rooney, Tom

Earmarks, 4–10

Ros-Lehtinen, Ileana

Medical malpractice, 11–17

Trump response to Charlottesville, VA racial violence, 9–4

Rosenstein, Rod

Mueller, Robert S. III, appointment as special investigator, 9–4

Russia election interference investigation, 1–4, 1–6, 9–10

Ross, Dennis A.

Payday loans, 3–7

Ross, Elizabeth

Education regulations, 11–19

Ross, Wilbur

Confirmation as Commerce Secretary, 9–5

Rounds, Mike

Health care law, 11–7

Roybal-Allard, Lucille

Homeland Security appropriations, 2–32 to 2–33

Horse slaughter, 2–22, 2–24

Royce, Ed

North Korea sanctions, 10–3

Rubio, Marco

Budget resolution, 4–6

Cigars, 2–24

Flood insurance, 7–6

NASA reauthorization, 15–3

State Department restructuring, 10–4

Tillerson, Rex, confirmation as secretary of State, 9–7

Rural areas

Appropriations, 2–21, 2–24

Broadband, 2–32, 15–5

Rural hospitals, 4–7

Rush, Bobby L.

Energy legislation, 8–5

Russia

Defense authorization, 6–10

Election interference investigation, 1–6, 9–4, 9–10

Kaspersky Lab, 6–9

Sanctions, 10–3 to 10–4, C–5, C–10

Ryan, Paul D.

Appropriations, 2–6

Authorization for Use of Military Force, 6–12

Changes in ethics procedures, 5–14

Earmark ban, 5–14

Earmarks, 4–10

Federal employees, 7–3 to 7–4

FY 2018 omnibus appropriations, 2–18

Health care law, 11–6

Health care law repeal cost, 4–3

Sanctuary cities, 12–4

Scalise, Steve shooting, 5–9

Tax reform, 16–7

Ryan, Tim

Capitol security, 2–38

S

Sanders, Bernie

Defense authorization, 6–9

Health care law repeal efforts, 11–4

Powell, Jerome nomination as Federal Reserve chair, 3–6

Tax cuts, 1–5

Sandoval, Brian

Yucca Mountain, 8–10

Sanford, Mark

Border adjustment tax, 4–9

Overseas Contingency Operations, 4–9

Sarbanes, John

Soft money, 13–7

Sasse, Ben

CFPB restructuring, 3–8

Hurricane Harvey, 2–18

Trans-Pacific Partnership, 10–6

Scalise, Steve

Cost of health care law repeal, 4–3

Shooting, 1–3, 1–6, 5–8 to 5–9, 13–7

Scaramucci, Anthony

Sanctions, 10–3 to 10–4

White House tenure, 9–3

Schatz, Brian

Artificial intelligence, 15–8

Military Construction-VA appropriations, 2–40

Trump response to Charlottesville, VA racial violence, 9–4

Schiff, Adam B.

Intelligence reauthorization, 6–18

Schmidt, Eric

Artificial intelligence, 15–8

Schumer, Charles E.

Budget resolution, 4–6

DACA, 12–4 to 12–5

Disaster aid, 2–45

FY 2018 continuing resolutions, 2–19

Garland, Merrick, confirmation as Supreme Court justice, 5–13, 13–3

Health care law repeal, 16–10

Hurricane Harvey, 2–18

Mnuchin, Steve, confirmation as Treasury secretary, 9–7

Tax cuts, 16–8

Wildfires, 2–18

Scott, Robert C.

Sexual harassment allegations, 5–11

Worker protections, 7–8

SEC

Appropriations, 2–12, 2–32

Campaign finance, 2–10

Corporate payments to foreign governments or U.S. government, 3–3, 14–3

Federal financial regulation, 3–3

Financial regulation, 3–5

Securities and Exchange Commission. *See* SEC

Serrano, Jose E.

Commerce-Justice-Science appropriations, 2–25

Disaster aid, 2–45

Puerto Rico disaster relief, 2–19

Service Employees International Union

Overtime pay, 7–7

Sessions, Jeff

Asset forfeiture, 13–12

Confirmation as attorney general, 5–3, 9–7

DACA, 1–4, 9–4

Russia election interference investigation, 1–6, 9–10

Sessions, Pete
CHIP, 11–15

Earmark ban, 5–14

Earmarks, 4–10

Sex offenders
Internet use by sex offenders, 13–5

Registry, 13–9

Sex trafficking
Online, 15–7

Sexual misconduct
Accusations against members of Congress, 1–7, 5–3, 5–10

Shaheen, Jeanne
Family planning, 2–42

Kaspersky Lab, 6–9

National Science Foundation, 2–26

State Department restructuring, 10–4

Shelby, Richard C.
Asset forfeiture, 13–12

Census, 7–4

Commerce-Justice-Science appropriations, 2–26

Sherman, Brad
Financial regulation, 3–4

Shimkus, John
Brownfields, 8–10

Energy legislation, 8–5

Ozone, 8–8

Ships and ship building
Appropriations, 2–6, 2–11, 2–28

Warships, 6–3, 6–10

Short, Marc
Information requests from members of Congress, 13–12

Shulkin, David
Confirmation as Veterans Affairs secretary, 9–8

VA Choice Program, 6–19 to 6–20

Shumate, Brett
CFPB restructuring, 3–8

Shuster, Bill
FAA reauthorization, 17–4

Trump infrastructure plan, 17–3 to 17–4

Simpson, Mike
Changes in ethics procedures, 5–14 to 5–15

Sinema, Kyrsten
FAA reauthorization, 17–5

Singapore
Trans-Pacific Partnership, 10–6

Small Business Association
Appropriations, 2–32

Smith, Adam
Defense authorization, 6–5

Space Corps, 6–5

Smith, Jason
Regulatory review commission, 14–5

Smith, Tina
Senate appointment, 5–3

SNAP
Appropriations, 2–8, 2–22, 2–23

Snowden, Edward
FISA reauthorization, 6–15 to 6–16

Social Security
Gun rule, C–4, C–7

Society of Human Resource Management
Overtime pay, 7–7

Souder, Mark
Resignation, 5–12

South Carolina
Balanced Budget Amendment, 4–11

Space
Mars mission, 15–3

Space Corps
Defense authorization, 6–3, 6–4 to 6–5, 6–7

Sparks, Phil
Census, 7–4

Special elections
Alabama, 5–4 to 5–5

California, 5–6 to 5–7

Georgia, 5–7

Kansas, 5–6

Montana, 5–7

South Carolina, 5–8

Utah, 5–8

Special Olympics
Appropriations, 2–35

Special Operations Command, U.S.
Authorization, 6–4

Speier, Jackie
Intelligence reauthorization, 6–19

Sexual misconduct, 1–7

Spencer, Richard
Military readiness, 6–14

Spicer, Sean
Border adjustment tax, 16–7

Cost of health care law repeal, 4–3

White House tenure, 9–3

Sports
Sports betting, 13–7

Stabenow, Debbie
Defense authorization, 6–9

State, Department of
Appropriations, 2–15, 2–41

Restructuring, 10–4

Tillerson, Rex, confirmation as secretary of State, 9–7

Stefanik, Elise
Perkins loans, 11–18

Steinle, Kate
Criminal undocumented aliens, 12–4

Stewart, Chris
Authorization for Use of Military Force, 2–27

Grand Staircase-Escalante monument, 8–7

Strange, Luther
Defense authorization, 6–9

Strangio, Chase
Manning, Chelsea, prison sentence commutation, 13–11

Strategic Petroleum Reserve
Release of oil, 16–7, 16–12

Strong, AshLee
House gun control sit-in, 5–15

Substance abuse
Appropriations, 2–36

Supplemental Nutrition Assistance Program. *See* SNAP

Supreme Court
60 percent threshold for nominations, 2–7, C–4

Garland, Merrick, nomination as Supreme Court justice, 13–3

Gorsuch, Neil, confirmation as Supreme Court justice, 13–3 to 13–4, C–4

Supreme Court cases
Abortion, 13–6

Gay wedding cakes, 13–6

Generic drugs, 13–5

Gerrymandering, 13–6

Health care, 11–3

Internet use by sex offenders, 13–5

Labor unions' fees, 13–5

Patents and trademarks, 13–5

Soft money, 13–6 to 13–7

Sports betting, 13–7

Swalwell, Eric
NSA data collection and privacy, 6–17

T

Taliban
Authorization for Use of Military Force, 6–11

Tanning salons
Tax repeal, 11–8

Tax cuts
Budget reconciliation, 4–8, 4–9

Trump policy priorities, 1–4 to 1–5, 9–4

Tax extenders
Budget reconciliation, 4–8

Taxes and taxation
Alternative minimum tax, 16–4, 16–8, 16–12

ANWR oil and gas extraction, 4–8, 16–4

Border adjustment tax, 16–5

Child tax credit, 16–4, 16–12

Corporate tax rate, 16–3, 16–5

Individuals, 16–3 to 16–4

Key votes, C–7, C–11

SALT, 16–8, 16–14

Tax law changes chart, 16–15

Universities and colleges, 16–4

U.S. companies operating overseas, 16–3

Taylor, Scott
Authorization for Use of Military Force, 2–27

Tester, Jon
Veterans, 6–20

Thomas, Clarence
Internet use by sex offenders, 13–5

Thompson, Bennie
Border wall, 12–7

Thompson, Glenn
Job training, 11–18 to 11–19

Thompson, John H.
Resignation as Census Bureau Director, 7–4 to 7–5

Thompson, Mike
Disaster aid, 2–45

Wild fires, 2–19 to 2–20

Thornberry, Mac
Border wall, 6–6

Defense appropriations, 2–27

Defense authorization, 6–3, 6–6, 6–7

Defense budget negotiations, 4–5

Thune, John
Driverless cars, 17–7

FAA reauthorization, 17–5, 17–6

Gun restrictions, 13–8

Health care law repeal, 16–10

Methane venting on federal land, 8–7

Rural broadband, 15–5

Trump infrastructure plan, 17–3

Tillerson, Rex
State Department restructuring, 10–4

Tillis, Thom
Russia interference in U.S. elections, 9–10

Tobacco
Cigars, 2–24

E-cigarettes, 2–7, 2–21, 2–22

Tonko, Paul
Brownfields, 8–9

Ozone, 8–8

Toomey, Patrick J.
Budget reconciliation, 4–9

CHIP, 11–15

North Korea sanctions, 10–3

Trade
Cuba, 2–10

Trans-Pacific Partnership, 10–6

Trade representative, U.S.
Lighthizer, Robert E., confirmation, 10–5

Transportation, Department of
Appropriations, 2–15

Chao, Elaine, confirmation as Transportation secretary, 9–7

Transportation and infrastructure
Appropriations, 2–15 to 216

Urban planning, 14–5

Transportation Investment Generating Economic Recovery program
Appropriations, 2–15, 2–43 to 2–44

Treasury, Department of
Appropriations, 2–32

Mandatory arbitration clauses in consumer contracts, 3–6

Mnuchin, Steve, confirmation as Treasury secretary, 9–7

Terrorist financing, 10–3

Trump, Donald
ANWR, 16–6 to 16–7

Arpaio, Joe, pardon, 9–4

Border wall, 2–6, 4–5, 12–7

Budget process, 4–6

Census, 7–4 to 7–5

Criminal justice reform, 13–9 to 13–10

DACA, 12–4

Debt limit, 4–4

Defense authorization, 6–3

Defense budget, 4–5

Dodd-Frank financial regulation law, 3–3

Environmental agenda, 8–3

Federal employees' wages, 7–3 to 7–4

First year in office, 9–3 to 9–10

Foreign policy, 1–3

Gun restrictions, 13–8

Health care law, 11–5, 11–6

Impeachment resolution, C–10 to C–11

Infrastructure, 17–3 to 17–4

NASA, 15–3

North Korea, 1–3 to 1–4

Nuclear disarmament, 6–12 to 6–13

Omnibus appropriations, 2–3, 2–5

Regulations, 14–3

Relationship with members of Congress, 1–3 to 1–4

Tax overhaul, 16–3, 16–14

Trans-Pacific partnership, 10–6

Turnover in the Trump administration (chart), 9–9

Veterans, 6–19 to 6–20

Trump, Donald Jr.
Russia interference in U.S. elections, 9–10